MANAGERIAL STRATEGY

BEYOND OUR BORDERS

MindTap™

Tap into **engagement**

MindTap empowers you to produce your best work—consistently.

MindTap is designed to help you master the material. Interactive videos, animations, and activities create a learning path designed by your instructor to guide you through the course and focus on what's important.

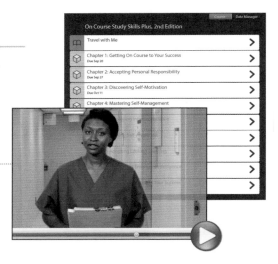

MindTap delivers real-world activities and assignments

that will help you in your academic life as well as your career.

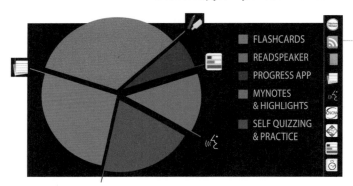

- FLASHCARDS
- READSPEAKER
- PROGRESS APP
- MYNOTES & HIGHLIGHTS
- SELF QUIZZING & PRACTICE

MindTap helps you stay organized and efficient

by giving you the study tools to master the material.

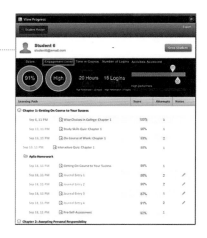

MindTap empowers and motivates

with information that shows where you stand at all times—both individually and compared to the highest performers in class.

"MindTap was very useful—it was easy to follow and everything was right there."
— Student, San Jose State University

"I'm definitely more engaged because of MindTap."
— Student, University of Central Florida

"MindTap puts practice questions in a format that works well for me."
— Student, Franciscan University of Steubenville

Tap into more info at: **www.cengage.com/mindtap**

Engaged with you.
www.cengage.com

CENGAGE Learning®

11th Edition

Business Law Today

STANDARD EDITION TEXT & SUMMARIZED CASES

ROGER LEROY MILLER

Institute for University Studies
Arlington, Texas

CENGAGE
Learning™

Australia • Brazil • Mexico • Singapore • United Kingdom • United States

CENGAGE
Learning™

Business Law Today
Standard Edition
TEXT & SUMMARIZED CASES
11th Edition

Roger LeRoy Miller

Vice President for Social Science and Qualitative Business: *Erin Joyner*

Product Director: *Michael Worls*

Senior Product Manager: *Vicky True-Baker*

Managing Content Developer: *Rebecca von Gillern*

Content Developer: *Leah Wuchnick*

Product Assistant: *Ryan McAndrews*

Marketing Manager: *Katie Jergens*

Marketing Director: *Kristen Hurd*

Marketing Coordinator: *Christopher Walz*

Production Director: *Sharon Smith*

Senior Content Project Manager: *Ann Borman*

Content Digitization Project Manager: *Jennifer Chinn*

Manufacturing Planner: *Kevin Kluck*

Senior Inventory Analyst: *Terina Bradley*

Senior IP Director: *Julie Geagan-Chavez*

IP Analyst: *Jennifer Nonenmacher*

IP Project Manager: *Betsy Hathaway*

Senior Art Director: *Michelle Kunkler*

Interior and Cover Designer: *Liz Harasymczuk*

Cover Images: Gavel and scales: pixhook/iStock.com; Financial graphs: isak55/ShutterStock.com; Financial Systems: isak55/Shutterstock.com; Internet collage: Creativa Images/Shutterstock.com; light on modern buildings: gui jun peng/Shutterstock.com; technology background plus world: watcharakun/Shutterstock.com; abstract digital blue with arrows: winui/Shutterstock.com.

Design Elements: Skyline logo: happydancing, Shutterstock.com; Landmark feature: Yuriy Kulik/Shutterstock.com; Classic Case US Flag: STILLFX/Shutterstock.com; Beyond Our Borders: sebastian-julian/iStock.com; Adapting to Online: everything possible/Shutterstock.com; Spotlight Case: Kamil Krawczyk/iStock.com; Standard Case: Rawpixel/Shutterstock.com; Managerial Strategy 1: Gemenacom/Shutterstock.com and 2: PathDoc/Shutterstock.com; Linking Business Law: bikeriderlondon/Shutterstock.com; Business Application: Konstantin Sutyagin/Shutterstock.com; Featured Case: Bacho/Shutterstock.com; Preventing Legal Disputes: JoemanjiArts/Shutterstock.com; Ethical Issues: Gary Lanfer/Shutterstock.com

Library of Congress Control Number: 2015949178

Student Edition ISBN: 978-1-305-64452-6

Cengage Learning
20 Channel Center Street
Boston, MA 02210
USA

Cengage Learning is a leading provider of customized learning solutions with employees residing in nearly 40 different countries and sales in more than 125 countries around the world. Find your local representative at **www.cengage.com**.

Cengage Learning products are represented in Canada by Nelson Education, Ltd.

To learn more about Cengage Learning Solutions, visit **www.cengage.com**

Purchase any of our products at your local college store or at our preferred online store **www.cengagebrain.com**

Printed in the United States of America
Print Number: 02   Print Year: 2018

Contents in Brief

Contents

iStockPhoto.com/DanBrandenburg

UNIT 2 CONTRACTS AND E-CONTRACTS 243

iStockPhoto.com/Rawpixel

UNIT 3   COMMERCIAL TRANSACTIONS   397

Chapter 18

Performance and Breach of Sales and Lease Contracts   433

Chapter 19

Negotiable Instruments   460

Chapter 20

Banking in the Digital Age   491

iStockPhoto.com/kali9

Chapter 21

Security Interests and Creditors' Rights   514

UNIT 4 AGENCY AND EMPLOYMENT LAW 573

iStockPhoto.com/michaeljung

UNIT 5   BUSINESS ORGANIZATIONS   657

UNIT 6   GOVERNMENT REGULATION   777

iStockPhoto.com/spxChrome

Chapter 33

Liability of Accountants and Other Professionals   830

UNIT 7   PROPERTY AND ITS PROTECTION   855

Chapter 34

Personal Property and Bailments   856

Chapter 35

Real Property and Landlord-Tenant Law   877

APPENDICES

iStockPhoto.com/fstop123

Chapter 36
Insurance, Wills, and Trusts   899

Preface

The study of business and the legal environment has universal applicability. A student entering any field of business must have at least a passing understanding of business law in order to function in the real world. *Business Law Today,* Eleventh Edition, provides the information in an interesting and contemporary way. The Eleventh Edition continues its established tradition of being the most up-to-date text on the market.

Instructors have come to rely on the coverage, accuracy, and applicability of *Business Law Today.* This best-selling text engages your students, solidifies their understanding of legal concepts, and provides the best teaching tools available. I have spent a great deal of effort making this edition more contemporary, exciting, and visually appealing than ever before. Special pedagogical devices within the text focus on legal, ethical, global, and corporate issues, while addressing core curriculum requirements.

The Eleventh Edition incorporates the latest legal developments and United States Supreme Court decisions. It also includes more than fifty new features and seventy new cases, hundreds of new examples and case examples, new exhibits, learning objectives, margin definitions, and case problems.

New Chapter on Internet Law, Social Media, and Privacy

For the Eleventh Edition, I have included an entirely new chapter (Chapter 7) entitled **Internet Law, Social Media, and Privacy.** Social media have entered the mainstream and become a part of everyday life for many businesspersons. Throughout the text, I recognize this trend by incorporating the Internet and social media as they relate to the topics under discussion.

New Features

The Eleventh Edition of *Business Law Today* is filled with exciting new features including the following:

- Twenty-three **Adapting the Law to the Online Environment** features examine cutting-edge cyberlaw issues. Seventeen of these are new and cover topics such as Facebook poker, hacking, patent trolls, paying with smartphones, revenge porn, and social media.
- I have included twenty new **Ethical Issues** that focus on the ethical aspects of a topic being discussed in order to emphasize that ethics is an integral part of a business law course.
- I have also added six new **Beyond Our Borders** features (for a total of twenty-four) that focus on the global legal environment and illustrate how other nations deal with specific legal concepts being discussed.
- For this edition, I have created a new feature entitled **Managerial Strategy** that focuses on the management aspects of business law. There are ten of these new features throughout the text, covering such topics as the commercial use of drones, marriage equality, and the use of company e-mail systems to organize a union.
- Fourteen **Business Application** features and eight **Linking Business Law to [one of the six functional fields of business]** features are included at the end of selected chapters.

The *Business Applications* focus on practical considerations and offer checklists related to the chapter's contents, whereas the *Linking Business Law* features underscore how the law relates to other fields of business.

- Eighteen **Landmark in the Law** features discuss a landmark case, statute, or other legal development that has had a significant effect on business law.

New Cases and Case Problems

The Eleventh Edition of *Business Law Today* has new cases and case problems from 2015 and 2014 in every chapter. The new cases have been carefully selected to illustrate important points of law and be of high interest to students and instructors. I have made it a point to find recent cases that enhance learning and are simple enough for business law students to understand.

Certain cases and case problems have been carefully chosen as good teaching cases and are designated as **Spotlight Cases** and **Spotlight Case Problems.** Some examples include *Spotlight on Apple, Spotlight on Beer Labels, Spotlight on Nike,* and *Spotlight on the Seattle Mariners.* Instructors will find these **Spotlight** decisions useful to illustrate the legal concepts under discussion, and students will enjoy studying these cases because they involve interesting and memorable facts. Other cases have been chosen as **Classic Cases** because they establish a legal precedent in the particular area of law.

Each case concludes with a question, which may be called *Critical Thinking, What If the Facts Were Different?* or *Why Is This Case Important? Classic Cases* conclude with an *Impact of This Case on Today's Law* section that clarifies how the case has affected the legal environment. *Suggested answers to all case-ending questions can be found in the Solutions Manual for this text.*

Many New Highlighted and Numbered Case Examples

Many instructors use cases and examples to illustrate how the law applies to business. For this edition of *Business Law Today,* I have added more than one hundred new highlighted and numbered **Examples,** and more than one hundred new highlighted and consecutively numbered **Case Examples.** *Examples* illustrate how the law applies in a specific situation. *Case Examples* present the facts and issues of an actual case and then describe the court's decision and rationale. The numbered *Examples* and *Case Examples* features are integrated throughout the text to help students better understand how courts apply the principles in the real world.

Critical Thinking and Legal Reasoning Elements

Critical thinking questions conclude most of the features and cases in this text. There is also a **Debate This** question at the end of each chapter that requires students to think critically about the rationale underlying the law on a particular topic.

Answers to all critical thinking questions, as well as to the **Business Scenarios and Case Problems** at the end of every chapter, are presented in the *Solutions Manual* for the text. In addition, the answers to one case problem in each chapter, called the **Business Case Problem with Sample Answer,** appear in *Appendix F.*

The chapter-ending materials also include a separate section of questions that focus on critical thinking and writing. This section always includes a **Business Law Critical Thinking Group Assignment** and may also include the following:

- **Critical Legal Thinking** questions require students to think critically about some aspect of the law discussed in the chapter.
- **Business Law Writing** questions require students to compose a written response to a business-oriented critical-thinking question.
- **Case Analysis Questions** require students to read through a case excerpt in *Appendix G,* brief the case, and then answer a series of questions relating to the case.

Other Pedagogical Devices within Each Chapter

- *Learning Objectives* (questions at the beginning of each chapter and in the margin of the text provide a framework for the student).
- *Preventing Legal Disputes* (integrated text sections offer practical guidance on how businesspersons can avoid legal disputes and litigation in a particular area).
- *Chapter Outline* (an outline of the chapter's first-level headings).
- *Margin definitions.*
- *Highlighted and numbered Examples and Case Examples* (illustrate legal principles).
- *Quotations* and *Know This* (margin features).
- *Exhibits.*
- *Photographs (with critical thinking questions) and cartoons.*

Chapter-Ending Pedagogy

- *Reviewing . . .* **features** (in every chapter).
- *Debate This* (a statement or question at the end of the *Reviewing* feature).
- *Key Terms* (with appropriate page references).
- *Chapter Summary* (in table format).
- *Issue Spotters* (in every chapter with answers in *Appendix D*).
- *Learning Objectives Check* (The *Learning Objectives* questions are presented again to aid students in reviewing the chapter. For this edition, answers to the even-numbered questions for each chapter are provided in *Appendix E*.)
- *Business Scenarios and Case Problems* (Every chapter includes a *Business Case Problem with Sample Answer* answered in *Appendix F*, *A Question of Ethics*, and a *Business Law Critical Thinking Group Assignment*. Selected chapters include a *Spotlight Case Problem*.)

Unit-Ending Pedagogy

Each of the seven units in the Eleventh Edition of *Business Law Today* concludes with the following features (which are answered in the *Solutions Manual*):

- *Business Case Study with Dissenting Opinion*—This feature presents a court case that relates to a topic covered in the unit. It opens with an introductory section, discusses the case background and significance, and then provides excerpts from the court's majority opinion and from a dissenting opinion as well. The case study portion ends with *Questions for Analysis*—a series of questions that prompt the student to think critically about the legal, ethical, economic, international, or general business implications of the case.
- *Business Scenario*—This feature presents a hypothetical business situation and then asks a series of questions about how the law applies to various actions taken by the firm. To answer the questions, the student must apply the laws discussed throughout the unit.
- *Group Project*—The final portion of the unit-ending pedagogy is a *Group Project* that requires students to work together to formulate answers based on materials they learned in the previous chapters.

Supplements

Business Law Today, Eleventh Edition, provides a comprehensive supplements package designed to make the tasks of teaching and learning more enjoyable and efficient. The following supplements are available for instructors.

MindTap Business Law for Business Law Today, Eleventh Edition

MindTap™ is a fully online, highly personalized learning experience built upon authoritative Cengage Learning content. By combining readings, multimedia, activities, and assessments into a singular Learning Path, *MindTap* guides students through their course with ease and engagement. Instructors personalize the Learning Path by customizing Cengage Learning resources and adding their own content via apps that integrate into the *MindTap* framework seamlessly with Learning Management Systems.

The *MindTap Business Law* product provides a four-step Learning Path, Case Repository, Adaptive Test Prep, and an Interactive eBook designed to meet instructors' needs while also allowing instructors to measure skills and outcomes with ease. Each and every item is assignable and gradable. This gives instructors the knowledge of class standings and concepts that may be difficult. Additionally, students gain knowledge about where they stand—both individually and compared to the highest performers in class.

Cengage Learning Testing Powered by Cognero

Cengage Learning Testing Powered by Cognero is a flexible, online system that allows instructors to do the following:

- Author, edit, and manage *Test Bank* content from multiple Cengage Learning solutions.
- Create multiple test versions in an instant.
- Deliver tests from their Learning Management System (LMS), classroom, or wherever they want.

Start Right Away! *Cengage Learning Testing Powered by Cognero* works on any operating system or browser.

- Use your standard browser; no special installs or downloads are needed.
- Create tests from school, home, the coffee shop—anywhere with Internet access.

What Instructors Will Find

- *Simplicity at every step.* A desktop-inspired interface features drop-down menus and familiar, intuitive tools that take instructors through content creation and management with ease.
- *Full-featured test generator.* Create ideal assessments with a choice of fifteen question types—including true/false, multiple choice, opinion scale/Likert, and essay. Multilanguage support, an equation editor, and unlimited metadata help ensure instructor tests are complete and compliant.
- *Cross-compatible capability.* Import and export content into other systems.

Instructor's Companion Web Site

The *Instructor's Companion Web Site* contains the following supplements:

- *Instructor's Manual.* Includes sections entitled *"Additional Cases Addressing This Issue"* at the end of selected case synopses.
- *Solutions Manual.* Provides answers to all questions presented in the text, including the *Learning Objectives,* the questions in each case and feature, the *Issue Spotters,* the *Business Scenarios and Case Problems, Critical Thinking and Writing Assignments,* and the unit-ending features. New for this edition, we also provide a set of *Alternative Case Problems* for every chapter.
- *Test Bank.* A comprehensive test bank contains multiple-choice, true/false, and short essay questions.
- *Case-Problem Cases.*
- *Case Printouts.*
- *PowerPoint Slides.*

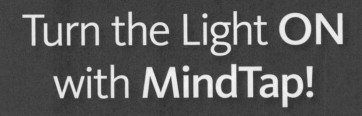

Turn the Light ON with MindTap!

Through personalized paths of dynamic assignments and applications, MindTap is a digital learning solution that turns cookie cutter into cutting edge, apathy into engagement, and memorizers into higher-level thinkers.

With MindTap's carefully curated material, you get the **right content** and groundbreaking tools you need. You can **personalize** every element of your course—from rearranging the Table of Contents to inserting videos, cases, and activities. You'll save time and **improve workflow** by having everything in one place. And, with MindTap's Progress App, you can **monitor student progress in real time**.

⮞ Specifically for this Edition, you'll find:

A pre-built learning path in MindTap that guides students through consistent learning activities to prepare, engage, apply, and analyze business law content.

Worksheets - interactive online "worksheets" PREPARE students for class, ensuring reading and comprehension.

Video Activities - real-world video exercises make business law RELEVANT AND ENGAGING.

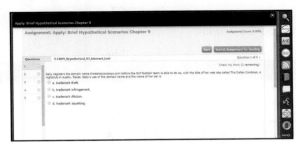

Brief Hypotheticals - these applications help students spot the issue and APPLY the law in the context of a short, factual scenario.

Case Problem Blueprints - promote deeper CRITICAL THINKING and legal reasoning by guiding students step by step through a case problem.

Turn the page to learn more about our exciting NEW **Case Repository**, **Adaptive Test Prep**, and the **Interactive eBook.**

BUSINESS LAW TODAY SERIES

Access Over 900 Cases with our new Case Repository

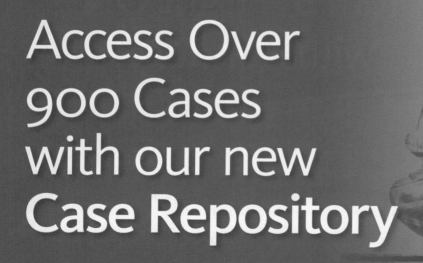

Now, within MindTap, you can search a library of cases from previous editions of your favorite textbooks by relevant criteria and then incorporate those cases in the learning path for your students.

This exciting repository allows you to personalize your course and truly engage students, helping them to reach higher levels of critical thinking.

- Easily search by topic, and then refine your search by subtopic, to find case examples of a specific legal concept.

- Search by court or state to bring a local flavor or interest to your classroom.

- Enjoy over 900 cases at your fingertips. All new edition omitted cases will be added every year, allowing the archive to continually grow.

- Allows you to mix and match cases from different textbooks.

Reduce Exam Anxiety with **Adaptive Test Prep**

MindTap

MindTap's Adaptive Test Prep helps students study for exams with unlimited practice tests, quizzes, and feedback aimed specifically at helping them understand the course concepts.

Students can create an unlimited number of practice tests using similar types of questions seen on exams and test themselves on multiple chapters, by chapter, and by sub-topic levels. All practice test questions are book-specific and students receive immediate feedback with a remediation path, called *My Study Plan*, based on questions they miss.

The feedback provided is available in up to three formats:

- eBook link back to the reading

- written remediation

- video walk-throughs

These resources consist of robust explanations created by some of the best business law educators in the country. *My Study Plan* also provides chapter level resources such as flashcards and chapter summary reviews.

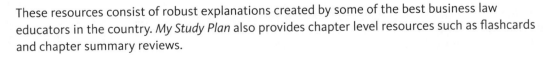

Turn the Light on Engagement with **Interactive eBook Activities**

An eBook environment leads to more interaction with the material and a deeper learning of Business Law concepts. MindTap offers interactive cases, interactive exhibits, and video whiteboard explanations for the business law classroom.

▷ Interactive Cases

Bring cases to life with an interactive environment that pulls students into the material. Instead of reading a boxed case feature, these interactive cases ask questions throughout, provide detailed answers, help guide students to a deeper understanding of the case, and enhance their legal reasoning skills. After reading the case, students are asked application questions to assess their understanding at a broader level.

▷ Interactive Exhibits

Select static exhibits from within the narrative are now interactive. Students can enjoy manipulating figures and exhibits to better solidify their understanding of key concepts in the text. These activities are sure to engage students in the learning process and encourage greater focus and participation.

▷ Video Whiteboard Explanations

Bring key legal concepts to life, literally, with short, entertaining animations. Video whiteboard explanations help students remember and learn key concepts with fun, real-world examples. Each being 3 minutes or less, these videos are an exciting way to help students see how they'd encounter these concepts in their own lives or in the near future when entering the business world.

BUSINESS LAW TODAY SERIES

Acknowledgments for Previous Editions

Since I began this project many years ago, numerous business law professors and users of *Business Law Today* have been kind enough to help me revise the book, including the following:

John J. Balek
Morton College, Illinois

John Jay Ballantine
University of Colorado, Boulder

Lorraine K. Bannai
Western Washington University

Marlene E. Barken
Ithaca College, New York

Laura Barnard
Lakeland Community College, Ohio

Denise A. Bartles, J.D.
Missouri Western State University

Daryl Barton
Eastern Michigan University

Merlin Bauer
Mid State Technical College, Wisconsin

Donna E. Becker
Frederick Community College, Maryland

Richard J. Bennet
Three Rivers Community College, Connecticut

Dr. Anne Berre
Schreiner University, Texas

Robert C. Bird
University of Connecticut

Bonnie S. Bolinger
Ivy Tech Community College,
Wabash Valley Region, Indiana

Brad Botz
Garden City Community College, Kansas

Teresa Brady
Holy Family College, Pennsylvania

Dean Bredeson
University of Texas at Austin

Lee B. Burgunder
California Polytechnic University, San Luis Obispo

Thomas D. Cavenagh
North Central College, Illinois

Bradley D. Childs
Belmont University, Tennessee

Corey Ciocchetti
University of Denver, Colorado

Peter Clapp
St. Mary's College, California

Dale Clark
Corning Community College, New York

Tammy W. Cowart
University of Texas, Tyler

Stanley J. Dabrowski
Hudson County Community College, New Jersey

Sandra J. Defebaugh
Eastern Michigan University

Patricia L. DeFrain
Glendale College, California

Julia G. Derrick
Brevard Community College, Florida

Joe D. Dillsaver
Northeastern State University, Oklahoma

Claude W. Dotson
Northwest College, Wyoming

Larry R. Edwards
Tarrant County Junior College,
South Campus, Texas

Jacolin Eichelberger
Hillsborough Community College, Florida

George E. Eigsti
Kansas City, Kansas, Community College

Florence E. Elliott-Howard
Stephen F. Austin State University, Texas

Tony Enerva
Lakeland Community College, Ohio

Benjamin C. Fassberg
Prince George's Community College, Maryland

Joseph L. Flack
Washtenaw Community College, Michigan

Jerry Furniss
University of Montana

Joan Gabel
Florida State University

Elizabeth J. Guerriero
Northeast Louisiana University

Phil Harmeson
University of South Dakota

Nancy L. Hart
Midland College, Texas

Mo Hassan
Cabrillo College, California

Andy E. Hendrick
Coastal Carolina University, South Carolina

Janine S. Hiller
Virginia Polytechnic Institute & State University

Karen A. Holmes
Hudson Valley Community College, New York

Fred Ittner
College of Alameda, California

Susan S. Jarvis
University of Texas, Pan American

Jack E. Karns
East Carolina University, North Carolina

Sarah Weiner Keidan
Oakland Community College, Michigan

Richard N. Kleeberg
Solano Community College, California

Bradley T. Lutz
Hillsborough Community College, Florida

Diane MacDonald
Pacific Lutheran University, Washington

Darlene Mallick
Anne Arundel Community College, Maryland

John D. Mallonee
Manatee Community College, Florida

Joseph D. Marcus
Prince George's Community College, Maryland

Woodrow J. Maxwell
Hudson Valley Community College, New York

Diane May
Winona State University, Minnesota

Beverly McCormick
Morehead State University, Kentucky

William J. McDevitt
Saint Joseph's University, Pennsylvania

John W. McGee
Aims Community College, Colorado

James K. Miersma
Milwaukee Area Technical Institute, Wisconsin

Susan J. Mitchell
Des Moines Area Community College, Iowa

Jim Lee Morgan
West Los Angeles College, California

Jack K. Morton
University of Montana

Annie Laurie I. Myers
Northampton Community College, Pennsylvania

Solange North
Fox Valley Technical Institute, Wisconsin

Jamie L. O'Brien
South Dakota State University

Ruth R. O'Keefe
Jacksonville University, Florida

Robert H. Orr
Florida Community College at Jacksonville

George Otto
Truman College, Illinois

Thomas L. Palmer
Northern Arizona University

David W. Pan
University of Tulsa, Oklahoma

Victor C. Parker, Jr.
North Georgia College and State University

Donald L. Petote
Genesee Community College, New York

Francis D. Polk
Ocean County College, New Jersey

Gregory Rabb
Jamestown Community College, New York

Brad Reid
Abilene Christian University, Texas

Anne Montgomery Ricketts
University of Findlay, Ohio

Donald A. Roark
University of West Florida

Hugh Rode
Utah Valley State College

Gerald M. Rogers
Front Range Community College, Colorado

Dr. William J. Russell
Northwest Nazarene University, Idaho

William M. Rutledge
Macomb Community College, Michigan

Martha Wright Sartoris
North Hennepin Community College, Minnesota

Anne W. Schacherl
Madison Area Technical College, Wisconsin

Edward F. Shafer
Rochester Community College, Minnesota

Lance Shoemaker, J.D.,
M.C.P., M.A.
West Valley College, California

Lou Ann Simpson
Drake University, Iowa

Denise Smith
Missouri Western State College

Hugh M. Spall
Central Washington University

Catherine A. Stevens
College of Southern Maryland

Maurice Tonissi
Quinsigamond Community College, Massachusetts

James D. Van Tassel
Mission College, California

Russell A. Waldon
College of the Canyons, California

Frederick J. Walsh
Franklin Pierce College, New Hampshire

James E. Walsh, Jr.
Tidewater Community College, Virginia

Randy Waterman
Richland College, Texas

Jerry Wegman
University of Idaho

Edward L. Welsh, Jr.
Phoenix College, Arizona

Clark W. Wheeler
Santa Fe Community College, Florida

Lori Whisenant
University of Houston, Texas

Kay O. Wilburn
The University of Alabama at Birmingham

John G. Williams, J.D.
Northwestern State University, Louisiana

James L. Wittenbach
University of Notre Dame, Indiana

Eric D. Yordy
Northern Arizona University

Joseph Zavaglia, Jr.
Brookdale Community College, New Jersey

In addition, I give my thanks to the staff at Cengage Learning, especially Vicky True-Baker, product manager; Michael Worls, product director; Rebecca von Gillern, managing content developer; Leah Wuchnick, content developer; and Ann Borman, content project manager. I also thank Katie Jergens in marketing; Michelle Kunkler, art director; and Anne Sheroff, photo researcher. I would also like to thank the staff at Lachina, the compositor, for accurately generating pages for this text and making it possible for me to meet my ambitious printing schedule.

I give special thanks to Katherine Marie Silsbee for managing the project and providing exceptional research and editorial skills. I also thank William Eric Hollowell, co-author of the *Solutions Manual* and *Test Bank*, for his excellent research efforts. I am grateful for the copyediting services of Beverly Peavler and proofreading by Sue Bradley. I also thank Vickie Reierson, Roxanna Lee, and Suzanne Jasin for their many efforts on this project and for helping to ensure an error-free text.

Roger LeRoy Miller

Dedication

To John Allen,

The power of rational
analysis never weakens.

R.L.M.

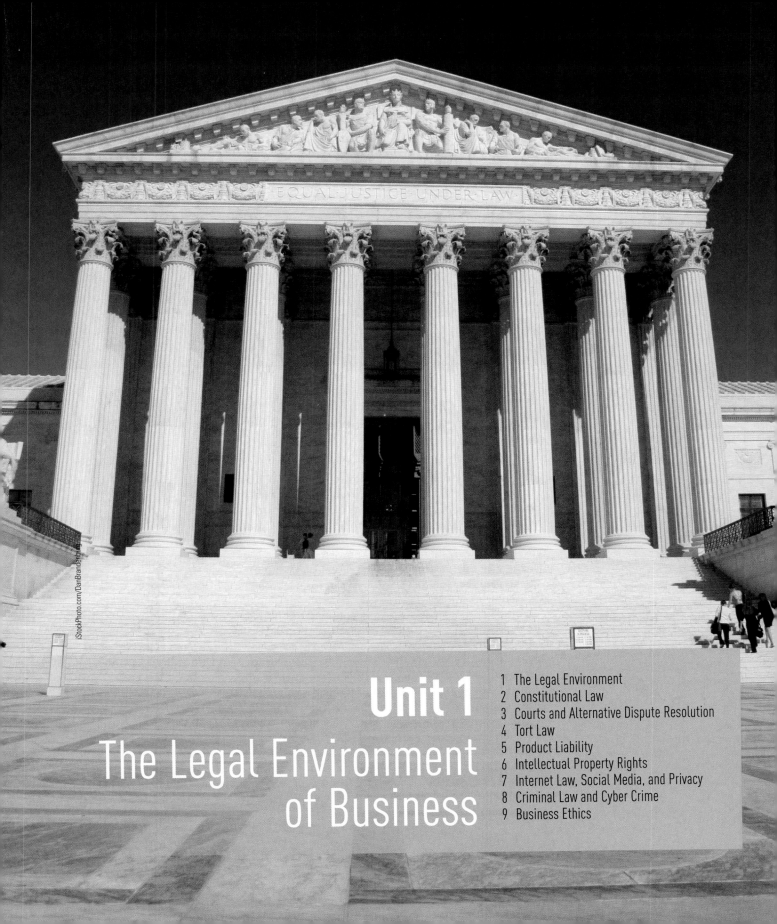

EQUAL JUSTICE UNDER LAW

iStockPhoto.com/DanBrandenburg

Unit 1
The Legal Environment of Business

1

LEARNING OBJECTIVES

The five Learning Objectives *below are designed to help improve your understanding of the chapter. After reading this chapter, you should be able to answer the following questions:*

1. **What are four primary sources of law in the United States?**

2. **What is the common law tradition?**

3. **What is a precedent? When might a court depart from precedent?**

4. **What is the difference between remedies at law and remedies in equity?**

5. **What are some important differences between civil law and criminal law?**

Law A body of enforceable rules governing relationships among individuals and between individuals and their society.

The Legal Environment

In the chapter-opening quotation, Clarence Darrow asserts that law should be created to serve the public. Because you are part of that public, the law is important to you. In particular, those entering the world of business will find themselves subject to numerous laws and government regulations. A basic knowledge of these laws and regulations is beneficial—if not essential—to anyone contemplating a successful career in today's business environment.

"Laws should be like clothes. They should be made to fit the people they are meant to serve."

CLARENCE DARROW
1857–1938
(AMERICAN LAWYER)

Although the law has various definitions, all of them are based on the general observation that **law** consists of *enforceable rules governing relationships among individuals and between individuals and their society*. In some societies, these enforceable rules consist of unwritten principles of behavior. In other societies, they are set forth in ancient or contemporary law codes. In the United States, our rules consist of written laws and court decisions created by modern legislative and judicial bodies. Regardless of how such rules are created, they all have one feature in common: *they establish rights, duties, and privileges that are consistent with the values and beliefs of a society or its ruling group.*

In this introductory chapter, we look first at an important question for any student reading this text: How do business law and the legal environment affect business decision making? Next, we describe the basic sources of American law, the common law tradition, and some schools of legal thought. We conclude the chapter with a discussion of some general classifications of law.

1-1 Business Activities and the Legal Environment

Laws and government regulations affect almost all business activities—from hiring and firing decisions to workplace safety, the manufacturing and marketing of products, business financing, and more. To make good business decisions, businesspersons need to understand the laws and regulations governing these activities.

Realize also that in today's business world, simply being aware of what conduct can lead to legal **liability** is not enough. Businesspersons must develop critical thinking and legal reasoning skills so that they can evaluate how various laws might apply to a given situation and determine the best course of action. Businesspersons are also pressured to make ethical decisions. Thus, the study of business law necessarily involves an ethical dimension.

Liability The state of being legally responsible (liable) for something, such as a debt or obligation.

1-1a Many Different Laws May Affect a Single Business Transaction

As you will note, each chapter in this text covers a specific area of the law and shows how the legal rules in that area affect business activities. Although compartmentalizing the law in this fashion facilitates learning, it does not indicate the extent to which many different laws may apply to just one transaction. Exhibit 1–1 illustrates the various areas of the law that may influence business decision making.

EXAMPLE 1.1 When Mark Zuckerberg started Facebook as a Harvard student, he probably did not imagine all the legal challenges his company would face as a result of his business decisions.

Mark Zuckerberg, founder of Facebook, has faced numerous legal challenges. These include privacy issues and the alleged theft of intellectual property. Can large Internet firms completely avoid such legal problems?

- Shortly after Facebook was launched, others claimed that Zuckerberg had stolen their ideas for a social networking site. Their claims involved alleged theft of intellectual property (see Chapter 6), fraudulent misrepresentation (see Chapter 13), partnership law (see Chapter 27), and securities law (see Chapter 30). Facebook ultimately paid a significant amount ($65 million) to settle those claims out of court.
- By 2015, Facebook had been sued repeatedly for violating users' privacy (such as by disseminating private information to third parties for commercial purposes—see Chapters 4 and 7). In 2012 and 2014, lawsuits were filed against Facebook for violating users' privacy (and federal laws) by tracking their Web site usage and by scanning private messages for purposes of data mining and user profiling. Also in 2014, a suit was filed in Europe against Facebook alleging violations of EU laws governing privacy and data use.
- Facebook's business decisions have come under scrutiny by federal regulators, such as the Federal Trade Commission (FTC) and the Securities and Exchange Commission (SEC). The company settled a complaint filed by the FTC alleging that Facebook failed to keep "friends" lists and other user information private. ■

A key to avoiding business disputes is to think ahead when starting or running a business or entering a contract. Learn what you can about the laws pertaining to that specific enterprise or transaction. Have some idea of the legal ramifications of your business decisions, and seek the advice of a licensed attorney. When you need to choose an attorney, obtain recommendations from friends, relatives, or business associates who have had long-standing relationships with their attorneys.

PREVENTING LEGAL DISPUTES

Exhibit 1–1 Areas of the Law That May Affect Business Decision Making

Contracts

Courts and
Court Procedures

Sales

Professional
Liability

Negotiable
Instruments

Business
Organizations

Business
Decision
Making

Creditors'
Rights

Agency

Intellectual
Property

Torts

E-Commerce

Product
Liability

1–1b Linking Business Law to the Six Functional Fields of Business

In all likelihood, you are taking a business law or legal environment course because you intend to enter the business world, though some of you may plan to become attorneys. Many of you are taking other business school courses and may therefore be familiar with the functional fields of business listed below:

1. Corporate management.
2. Production and transportation.
3. Marketing.
4. Research and development.
5. Accounting and finance.
6. Human resource management.

Why is basic knowledge of business law and the legal environment so important today?

One of our goals in this text is to show how legal concepts can be useful for managers and businesspersons, whether their activities focus on management, marketing, accounting, or some other field. To that end, numerous chapters, including this chapter, conclude with a special feature called *"Linking Business Law to* [one of the six functional fields of business]." The link between business law and accounting is so significant that we discuss it in detail in Chapter 33.

1–1c The Role of the Law in a Small Business

Some of you may end up working in a small business or even owning and running one. The small business owner/operator is the most general of managers. When you seek additional

Exhibit 1–2 Linking Business Law to the Management of a Small Business

Business Organization
What is the most appropriate business organizational form,
and what type of personal liability does it entail?

Taxation
How will the small business be taxed, and are there ways to reduce those taxes?

Intellectual Property
Does the small business have any patents or other intellectual
property that needs to be protected, and if so, what steps should the firm take?

Administrative Law
What types of government regulations apply to the
business, and what must the firm do to comply with them?

Employment
Does the business need an employment manual,
and does management have to explicitly inform employees of their rights?

Contracts, Sales, and Leases
Will the firm be regularly entering into contracts with others,
and if so, should it hire an attorney to review those contracts?

Accounting
Do the financial statements created by an accountant need to be verified for accuracy?

Finance
What are appropriate and legal ways to raise
additional capital so that the business can grow?

financing, you become a finance manager. When you "go over the books" with your book-keeper, you become an accountant. When you decide on a new advertising campaign, you are suddenly the marketing manager. When you hire employees and determine their salaries and benefits, you become a human resources manager.

Just as the functional fields of business are linked to the law, so too are all of the different managerial roles that a small-business owner/operator must perform. Exhibit 1–2 shows some of the legal issues that may arise as part of the management of a small business. Large businesses face most of these issues, too.

1–2 Sources of American Law

There are numerous sources of American law. **Primary sources of law,** or sources that establish the law, include the following:

Primary Source of Law A document that establishes the law on a particular issue, such as a constitution, a statute, an administrative rule, or a court decision.

LEARNING OBJECTIVE 1

What are four primary sources of law in the United States?

- The U.S. Constitution and the constitutions of the various states.
- Statutory law—including laws passed by Congress, state legislatures, and local governing bodies.
- Regulations created by administrative agencies, such as the federal Food and Drug Administration.
- Case law (court decisions).

We describe each of these important primary sources of law in the following pages. (See the appendix at the end of this chapter for a discussion of how to find statutes, regulations, and case law.)

Secondary sources of law are books and articles that summarize and clarify the primary sources of law. Legal encyclopedias, compilations (such as *Restatements of the Law,* which summarize court decisions on a particular topic), official comments to statutes, treatises, articles in law reviews published by law schools, and articles in other legal journals are examples of secondary sources of law. Courts often refer to secondary sources of law for guidance in interpreting and applying the primary sources of law discussed here.

Secondary Source of Law A publication that summarizes or interprets the law, such as a legal encyclopedia, a legal treatise, or an article in a law review.

1–2a Constitutional Law

The federal government and the states have written constitutions that set forth the general organization, powers, and limits of their respective governments. **Constitutional law,** which deals with the fundamental principles by which the government exercises its authority, is the law as expressed in these constitutions.

The U.S. Constitution is the basis of all law in the United States. It provides a framework for statutes and regulations, and thus is the supreme law of the land. A law in violation of the U.S. Constitution, if challenged, will be declared unconstitutional and will not be enforced, no matter what its source. Because of its paramount importance in the American legal system, we discuss the U.S. Constitution at length in Chapter 2 and present its complete text in Appendix B.

The Tenth Amendment to the U.S. Constitution reserves to the states all powers not granted to the federal government. Each state in the union has its own constitution. Unless it conflicts with the U.S. Constitution or a federal law, a state constitution is supreme within that state's borders.

Constitutional Law The body of law derived from the U.S. Constitution and the constitutions of the various states.

1–2b Statutory Law

Laws enacted by legislative bodies at any level of government, such as the statutes passed by Congress or by state legislatures, make up the body of law generally referred to as **statutory law.** When a legislature passes a statute, that statute ultimately is included in the federal code of laws or the relevant state code of laws.

Whenever a particular statute is mentioned in this text, we usually provide a footnote showing its **citation** (a reference to a publication in which a legal authority—such as a statute or a court decision—or other source can be found). In the appendix following this chapter, we explain how you can use these citations to find statutory law.

Statutory law also includes local **ordinances**—regulations passed by municipal or county governing units to deal with matters not covered by federal or state law. Ordinances commonly have to do with city or county land use (zoning ordinances), building and safety codes, and other matters affecting only the local governing unit.

A federal statute, of course, applies to all states. A state statute, in contrast, applies only within the state's borders. State laws thus may vary from state to state. No federal statute may violate the U.S. Constitution, and no state statute or local ordinance may violate the U.S. Constitution or the relevant state constitution.

Statutory Law The body of law enacted by legislative bodies (as opposed to constitutional law, administrative law, or case law).

Citation A reference to a publication in which a legal authority—such as a statute or a court decision—or other source can be found.

Ordinance A regulation enacted by a city or county legislative body that becomes part of that state's statutory law.

Uniform Laws During the 1800s, the differences among state laws frequently created difficulties for businesspersons conducting trade and commerce among the states. To counter these problems, a group of legal scholars and lawyers formed the National Conference of Commissioners on Uniform State Laws (NCCUSL, online at **www.uniformlaws.org**) in 1892 to draft **uniform laws** ("model statutes") for the states to consider adopting. The NCCUSL still exists today and continues to issue uniform laws.

Each state has the option of adopting or rejecting a uniform law. *Only if a state legislature adopts a uniform law does that law become part of the statutory law of that state.* Furthermore, a state legislature may choose to adopt only part of a uniform law or to rewrite the sections that are adopted. Hence, even though many states may have adopted a uniform law, those laws may not be entirely "uniform."

Uniform Law A model law developed by the National Conference of Commissioners on Uniform State Laws for the states to consider enacting into statute.

The Uniform Commercial Code (UCC) One of the most important uniform acts is the Uniform Commercial Code (UCC), which was created through the joint efforts of the NCCUSL and the American Law Institute.[1] The UCC was first issued in 1952 and has been adopted in all fifty states,[2] the District of Columbia, and the Virgin Islands.

The UCC facilitates commerce among the states by providing a uniform, yet flexible, set of rules governing commercial transactions. Because of its importance in the area of commercial law, we cite the UCC frequently in this text. We also present excerpts of the UCC in Appendix C. From time to time, the NCCUSL revises the articles contained in the UCC and submits the revised versions to the states for adoption.

1-2c Administrative Law

Another important source of American law is **administrative law,** which consists of the rules, orders, and decisions of administrative agencies. An **administrative agency** is a federal, state, or local government agency established to perform a specific function.

Rules issued by various administrative agencies affect almost every aspect of a business's operations. Regulations govern a business's capital structure and financing, its hiring and firing procedures, its relations with employees and unions, and the way it manufactures and markets its products. (See the *Linking Business Law to Management* feature at the end of this chapter.)

Administrative Law The body of law created by administrative agencies in order to carry out their duties and responsibilities.

Administrative Agency A federal or state government agency created by the legislature to perform a specific function, such as to make and enforce rules pertaining to the environment.

Federal Agencies At the national level, numerous *executive agencies* exist within the cabinet departments of the executive branch. The Food and Drug Administration, for example, is an agency within the U.S. Department of Health and Human Services. Executive agencies are subject to the authority of the president, who has the power to appoint and remove their officers.

There are also major *independent regulatory agencies* at the federal level, including the Federal Trade Commission, the Securities and Exchange Commission, and the Federal Communications Commission. The president's power is less pronounced in regard to independent agencies, whose officers serve for fixed terms and cannot be removed without just cause.

State and Local Agencies There are administrative agencies at the state and local levels as well. Commonly, a state agency (such as a state pollution-control agency) is created as a parallel to a federal agency (such as the Environmental Protection Agency).

Just as federal statutes take precedence over conflicting state statutes, so do federal agency regulations take precedence over conflicting state regulations. Because the rules of state and local agencies vary widely, we focus here exclusively on federal administrative law.

Agency Creation Because Congress cannot possibly oversee the actual implementation of all the laws it enacts, it delegates such tasks to agencies. Congress creates an administrative

> "Laws and institutions, like clocks, must occasionally be cleaned, wound up, and set to true time."
>
> **HENRY WARD BEECHER**
> 1813–1887
> (AMERICAN CLERGYMAN AND ABOLITIONIST)

---

1. This institute was formed in the 1920s and consists of practicing attorneys, legal scholars, and judges.
2. Louisiana has adopted only Articles 1, 3, 4, 5, 7, 8, and 9.

Which federal agency oversees worker safety?

Enabling Legislation A statute enacted by Congress that authorizes the creation of an administrative agency and specifies the name, composition, purpose, and powers of the agency being created.

Adjudicate To render a judicial decision. Adjudication is the trial-like proceeding in which an administrative law judge hears and resolves disputes involving an administrative agency's regulations.

Administrative Process The procedure used by administrative agencies in administering the law.

Rulemaking The process by which an administrative agency formally adopts a new regulation or amends an old one.

Legislative Rule An administrative agency rule that carries the same weight as a congressionally enacted statute.

Interpretive Rule A nonbinding rule or policy statement issued by an administrative agency that explains how it interprets and intends to apply the statutes it enforces.

agency by enacting **enabling legislation,** which specifies the name, composition, purpose, and powers of the agency being created.

EXAMPLE 1.2 The Federal Trade Commission (FTC) was created in 1914 by the Federal Trade Commission Act.[3] This act prohibits unfair and deceptive trade practices. It also describes the procedures the agency must follow to charge persons or organizations with violations of the act, and it provides for judicial review (review by the courts) of agency orders.

Other portions of the act grant the agency powers to "make rules and regulations for the purpose of carrying out the Act," and to conduct investigations of business practices. In addition, the FTC can obtain reports from interstate corporations concerning their business practices, investigate possible violations of the act, publish findings of its investigations, and recommend new legislation. The act also empowers the FTC to hold trial-like hearings and to **adjudicate** (resolve judicially) certain kinds of disputes involving its regulations. ■

Note that the powers granted to the FTC incorporate functions associated with the legislative branch of government (rulemaking), the executive branch (investigation and enforcement), and the judicial branch (adjudication). Taken together, these functions constitute the **administrative process,** which is the administration of law by administrative agencies. The administrative process involves rulemaking, enforcement, and adjudication.

Rulemaking

A major function of an administrative agency is **rulemaking**—formulating new regulations. When Congress enacts an agency's enabling legislation, it confers the power to make **legislative rules,** or substantive rules, which are legally binding on all businesses.

The Administrative Procedure Act (APA)[4] imposes strict procedural requirements that agencies must follow in legislative rulemaking and other functions. **EXAMPLE 1.3** The Occupational Safety and Health Act authorized the Occupational Safety and Health Administration (OSHA) to develop and issue rules governing safety in the workplace. When OSHA wants to formulate rules regarding safety in the steel industry, it has to follow specific procedures outlined by the APA. ■

Legislative Rules. Legislative rulemaking under the APA typically involves the following three steps (referred to as *notice-and-comment rulemaking*).

1. *Notice of the proposed rulemaking.* The notice must be published in the *Federal Register,* a daily publication of the U.S. government.

2. *A comment period.* The agency must allow ample time for interested parties to comment in writing on the proposed rule. The agency takes these comments into consideration when drafting the final version of the regulation.

3. *The final rule.* Once the agency has drafted the final rule, it is published in the *Federal Register.* (See the appendix at the end of this chapter for an explanation of how to find agency regulations.)

Interpretive Rules. Administrative agencies also issue **interpretive rules** that are not legally binding but simply indicate how an agency plans to interpret and enforce its statutory authority. The APA does not apply to interpretive rulemaking. **EXAMPLE 1.4** The Equal Employment Opportunity Commission periodically issues interpretive rules indicating how it plans to interpret the provisions of certain statutes, such as the Americans with Disabilities Act. These informal rules provide enforcement guidelines for agency officials. ■

Enforcement and Investigation

Agencies often enforce their own rules and have both investigatory and prosecutorial powers. Agencies investigate a wide range of activities, including coal mining, automobile manufacturing, and the industrial discharge of pollutants into the environment.

---

3. 15 U.S.C. Sections 45–58.
4. 5 U.S.C. Sections 551–706.

In an investigation, an agency can request that individuals or organizations hand over specified books, papers, electronic records, or other documents. In addition, agencies may conduct on-site inspections, although a search warrant is normally required for such inspections.[5] Sometimes, a search of a home, an office, or a factory is the only means of obtaining evidence needed to prove a regulatory violation.

After investigating a suspected rule violation, an agency may decide to take action against an individual or a business. Most administrative actions are resolved through negotiated settlement at their initial stages without the need for formal adjudication. If a settlement cannot be reached, though, the agency may issue a formal complaint and proceed to adjudication.

Adjudication Agency adjudication involves a trial-like hearing before an **administrative law judge (ALJ).** Hearing procedures vary widely from agency to agency. After the hearing, the ALJ renders a decision in the case. The ALJ can fine the charged party or prohibit the party from carrying on some specified activity.

Either the agency or the charged party may appeal the ALJ's decision to the commission or board that governs the agency. If the party fails to get relief there, appeal can be made to a federal court. Courts give significant weight (deference) to an agency's judgment and interpretation of its rules, though, and typically uphold the ALJ's decision unless it is unreasonable. If neither side appeals the case, the ALJ's decision becomes final.

Do administrative agencies exercise too much authority? Administrative agencies, such as the Federal Trade Commission, combine in a single governmental entity functions normally divided among the three branches of government. They create rules, conduct investigations, and prosecute and pass judgment on violators. Yet administrative agencies' powers often go unchecked by the other branches. Some businesspersons have suggested that it is unethical for agencies—which are not even mentioned in the U.S. Constitution—to wield so many powers.

Although agency rulemaking must comply with the requirements of the Administrative Procedure Act (APA), the act applies only to legislative, not interpretive, rulemaking. In addition, the APA is largely procedural and aimed at preventing arbitrariness. It does little to ensure that the rules passed by agencies are fair or correct—or even cost effective. On those rare occasions when an agency's ruling is challenged and later reviewed by a court, the court cannot reverse the agency's decision unless the agency exceeded its authority or acted arbitrarily. Courts typically are reluctant to second-guess an agency's rules, interpretations, and decisions. Moreover, once an agency has final regulations in place, it is difficult to revoke or alter them.

Administrative Law Judge (ALJ) One who presides over an administrative agency hearing and has the power to administer oaths, take testimony, rule on questions of evidence, and make determinations of fact.

ETHICAL ISSUE

1–2d Case Law and Common Law Doctrines

The rules of law announced in court decisions constitute another basic source of American law. These rules of law include *interpretations* of constitutional provisions, of statutes enacted by legislatures, and of regulations created by administrative agencies. Today, this body of judge-made law is referred to as **case law.** Case law—the doctrines and principles announced in cases—governs all areas not covered by statutory law or administrative law and is part of our common law tradition. We look at the origins and characteristics of the common law tradition in some detail in the pages that follow.

Case Law The rules of law announced in court decisions. Case law interprets statutes, regulations, constitutional provisions, and other case law.

1–3 Common Law Tradition

Because of our colonial heritage, much American law is based on the English legal system. Knowledge of this tradition is crucial to understanding our legal system today because judges in the United States still apply common law principles when deciding cases.

LEARNING OBJECTIVE 2

What is the common law tradition?

---

5. In some heavily regulated industries, such as the sale of firearms or liquor, agencies can conduct searches without obtaining a warrant.

1–3a **Early English Courts**

After the Normans conquered England in 1066, William the Conqueror and his successors began the process of unifying the country under their rule. One of the means they used to do this was the establishment of the king's courts, or *curiae regis*. Before the Norman Conquest, disputes had been settled according to the local legal customs and traditions in various regions of the country. The king's courts sought to establish a uniform set of rules for the country as a whole. What evolved in these courts was the beginning of the **common law**—a body of general rules that applied throughout the entire English realm. Eventually, the common law tradition became part of the heritage of all nations that were once British colonies, including the United States.

Courts developed the common law rules from the principles underlying judges' decisions in actual legal controversies. Judges attempted to be consistent, and whenever possible, they based their decisions on the principles suggested by earlier cases. They sought to decide similar cases in a similar way and considered new cases with care because they knew that their decisions would make new law. Each interpretation became part of the law on the subject and served as a legal **precedent**—that is, a court decision that furnished an example or authority for deciding subsequent cases involving identical or similar legal principles or facts.

In the early years of the common law, there was no single place or publication where court opinions, or written decisions, could be found. Beginning in the late thirteenth and early fourteenth centuries, however, portions of significant decisions from each year were gathered together and recorded in *Year Books*. The *Year Books* were useful references for lawyers and judges. In the sixteenth century, the *Year Books* were discontinued, and other reports of cases became available. (See the appendix to this chapter for a discussion of how cases are reported, or published, in the United States today.)

1–3b *Stare Decisis*

The practice of deciding new cases with reference to former decisions, or precedents, eventually became a cornerstone of the English and U.S. judicial systems. The practice forms a doctrine called ***stare decisis***[6] ("to stand on decided cases").

The Importance of Precedents in Judicial Decision Making Under the doctrine of *stare decisis*, judges are obligated to follow the precedents established within their jurisdictions. (The term *jurisdiction* refers to a geographic area in which a court or courts have the power to apply the law—see Chapter 3.) Once a court has set forth a principle of law as being applicable to a certain set of facts, that court must apply the principle in future cases involving similar facts. Courts of lower rank (within the same jurisdiction) must do likewise. Thus, *stare decisis* has two aspects:

1. A court should not overturn its own precedents unless there is a strong reason to do so.

2. Decisions made by a higher court are binding on lower courts.

Controlling precedents in a *jurisdiction* are referred to as binding authorities. A **binding authority** is any source of law that a court must follow when deciding a case. Binding authorities include constitutions, statutes, and regulations that govern the issue being decided, as well as court decisions that are controlling precedents within the jurisdiction. United States Supreme Court case decisions, no matter how old, remain controlling until they are overruled by a subsequent decision of the Supreme Court, by a constitutional amendment, or by congressional legislation.

Stare Decisis and Legal Stability The doctrine of *stare decisis* helps the courts to be more efficient because if other courts have carefully reasoned through a similar case, their legal

---

6. Pronounced stahr-ee dih-si-sis.

Common Law The body of law developed from custom or judicial decisions in English and U.S. courts, not attributable to a legislature.

Precedent A court decision that furnishes an example or authority for deciding subsequent cases involving identical or similar facts.

LEARNING OBJECTIVE 3

What is a precedent? When might a court depart from precedent?

Stare Decisis A common law doctrine under which judges are obligated to follow the precedents established in prior decisions.

Binding Authority Any source of law that a court *must* follow when deciding a case.

KNOW THIS

Courts normally must follow the rules set forth by higher courts in deciding cases with similar fact patterns.

reasoning and opinions can serve as guides. *Stare decisis* also makes the law more stable and predictable. If the law on a given subject is well settled, someone bringing a case to court can usually rely on the court to make a decision based on what the law has been.

Departures from Precedent Although courts are obligated to follow precedents, sometimes a court will depart from the rule of precedent. If a court decides that a precedent is simply incorrect or that technological or social changes have rendered the precedent inapplicable, the court may rule contrary to the precedent. Cases that overturn precedent often receive a great deal of publicity.

CASE EXAMPLE 1.5 In *Brown v. Board of Education of Topeka*,[7] the United States Supreme Court expressly overturned precedent when it concluded that separate educational facilities for whites and blacks, which had been upheld as constitutional in numerous previous cases,[8] were inherently unequal. The Supreme Court's departure from precedent in the *Brown* decision received a tremendous amount of publicity as people began to realize the ramifications of this change in the law. ■

Why would this scene not have been likely before 1954?

When There Is No Precedent At times, a case may raise issues that have not been raised before in that jurisdiction, so the court has no precedents on which to base its decision. Technological advances such as the one discussed in this chapter's *Adapting the Law to the Online Environment* feature often raise new legal issues, for example.

When deciding such cases, called "cases of first impression," courts often look at precedents established in other jurisdictions for guidance. Precedents from other jurisdictions, because they are not binding on the court, are referred to as **persuasive authorities.** A court may also consider other factors, including legal principles and policies underlying previous court decisions or existing statutes, fairness, social values and customs, public policy, and data and concepts drawn from the social sciences.

Persuasive Authority Any legal authority or source of law that a court may look to for guidance but need not follow when making its decision.

Remedy The relief given to an innocent party to enforce a right or compensate for the violation of a right.

Plaintiff One who initiates a lawsuit.

1–3c Equitable Remedies and Courts of Equity

A **remedy** is the means given to a party to enforce a right or to compensate for the violation of a right. **EXAMPLE 1.6** Elena is injured because of Rowan's wrongdoing. If Elena files a lawsuit and is successful, a court can order Rowan to compensate Elena for the harm by paying her a certain amount. The compensation is Elena's remedy. ■

The kinds of remedies available in the early king's courts of England were severely restricted. If one person wronged another, the king's courts could award either money or property, including land, as compensation. These courts became known as *courts of law*, and the remedies were called *remedies at law*. Even though this system introduced uniformity in the settling of disputes, when a person wanted a remedy other than economic compensation, the courts of law could do nothing, so "no remedy, no right."

Remedies in Equity *Equity* is a branch of law—founded on notions of justice and fair dealing—that seeks to supply a remedy when no adequate remedy at law is available. When individuals could not obtain an adequate remedy in a court of law, they petitioned the king for relief. Most of these petitions were referred to the *chancellor,* an adviser to the king who had the power to grant new and unique remedies. Eventually, formal chancery courts, or *courts of equity,* were established. The remedies granted by the chancery courts were called *remedies in equity*.

Plaintiffs (those bringing lawsuits) had to specify whether they were bringing an "action at law" or an "action in equity," and they chose their courts accordingly. **EXAMPLE 1.7** A plaintiff

LEARNING OBJECTIVE 4

What is the difference between remedies at law and remedies in equity?

---

7. 347 U.S. 483, 74 S.Ct. 686, 98 L.Ed. 873 (1954).
8. See *Plessy v. Ferguson,* 163 U.S. 537, 16 S.Ct. 1138, 41 L.Ed. 256 (1896).

ADAPTING THE LAW TO THE ONLINE ENVIRONMENT

Can New Laws Prevent People from Wearing Google Glass?

Under what circumstances could a user of Google Glass be violating the right to privacy of others?

Google Glass is a wearable computer. Basically, it's a Bluetooth-enabled, hands-free device that allows wearers to take photos and videos, surf the Internet, and do other things through voice commands. For the most part, Google Glass devices have been sold to consumers. One result has been legal problems, including problems involving privacy issues, safety while driving, and movie pirating.

Invasion of Privacy?

Privacy advocates point out that it is much easier to film or photograph others secretly with wearable video technology than with cameras or even cell phones. The more people use wearable video technology, the greater the problem will become. The so-called sacred precincts of private life will increasingly be violated. This issue came up over a hundred years ago with the creation of low-cost cameras. Initially, there were widespread bans on cameras at beaches.[a] Today, numerous bars and restaurants are banning Google Glass. Corporations are concerned that employees wearing Google Glass can more easily photograph documents that reveal trade secrets.

What about facial recognition software in Google Glass? Such an application could allow anyone to get personal information about another person just by looking at the person through a Google Glass headset. Even Congress has made inquiries about this possibility. In response, Google announced that it would not allow facial recognition applications on Glass.

In any event, the doctrine of a reasonable expectation of privacy is going to be challenged because of Google Glass. If Glass is ubiquitous, can any of us have a reasonable expectation of privacy when we are in public places?

Driving While Watching

When a San Diego policeman pulled over a motorist for speeding, she was also cited for "driving with a monitor visible to driver." California law prohibits in-vehicle video displays that are visible to the vehicles' drivers.[b] The charge was thrown out because of a lack of evidence that the device was in operation at the time of the purported offense.

A number of states have introduced legislation that would restrict the use of Google Glass while driving. All such legislation specifies the prohibited activity as "using" wearable devices, such as Google Glass. William & Mary law professor Adam Gershowitz argues that such driving bans are unenforceable. A police officer has no way of knowing whether a passing driver was *using*, as opposed to simply *wearing*, Google Glass.

The Pirated Movie Problem

Pirated movies offered free on the Internet have greatly affected revenues for movie production companies and movie theaters. Not surprisingly, movie theater owners are on the lookout for camouflaged, hand-held cameras during screenings of movies. When an AMC theater in Columbus, Ohio, noticed a customer wearing a Google Glass device, it contacted the Motion Picture Association of America (MPAA), which then contacted the federal Department of Homeland Security. An hour into the movie, the Glass wearer was removed from the theater by Immigration and Customs Enforcement (ICE) officers. He was released when an officer connected his Glass to a computer, which showed that no video of the movie had been taken.

Both the MPAA and the AMC theater chain stated that wearing "devices with recording capabilities is not appropriate at movie theaters." Note, though, that any restrictions on Google Glass and similar wearable devices will be more difficult to enforce as more individuals use prescription lenses in such devices.

CRITICAL THINKING

■ What benefits could wearers of Google Glass obtain from using facial recognition technology?

---

a. Samuel D. Warren and Louis D. Brandeis, "The Right to Privacy," *Harvard Law Review* 4 (December 15, 1890): 193–220.

b. California Vehicle Code Section 27602.

Defendant One against whom a lawsuit is brought or the accused person in a criminal proceeding.

might ask a court of equity to order the **defendant** (the person against whom a lawsuit is brought) to perform within the terms of a contract. A court of law could not issue such an order because its remedies were limited to the payment of money or property as compensation for damages.

A court of equity, however, could issue a decree for *specific performance*—an order to perform what was promised. A court of equity could also issue an *injunction*, directing a party to do or refrain from doing a particular act. In certain cases, a court of equity could allow for the *rescission* (cancellation) of the contract, thereby returning the parties to the positions that they held prior to the contract's formation. ■ Equitable remedies will be discussed in greater detail in the chapters covering contracts.

The Merging of Law and Equity Today, in most states, the courts of law and equity have merged, and thus the distinction between the two courts has largely disappeared. A plaintiff may now request both legal and equitable remedies in the same action, and the trial court judge may grant either form—or both forms—of relief.

The distinction between legal and equitable remedies remains significant, however, because a court normally will grant an equitable remedy only when the remedy at law (monetary damages) is inadequate. To request the proper remedy, a businessperson (or her or his attorney) must know what remedies are available for the specific kinds of harms suffered. Exhibit 1–3 summarizes the procedural differences (applicable in most states) between an action at law and an action in equity.

Equitable Principles and Maxims Over time, the courts have developed a number of **equitable principles and maxims** that provide guidance in deciding whether plaintiffs should be granted equitable relief. Because of their importance, both historically and in our judicial system today, these principles and maxims are set forth in this chapter's *Landmark in the Law* feature.

1-3d Schools of Legal Thought

How judges apply the law to specific cases, including disputes relating to the business world, depends on their philosophical approaches to law, among other things. The study of law, often referred to as **jurisprudence,** includes learning about different schools of legal thought and discovering how each school's approach to law can affect judicial decision making.

The Natural Law School Those who adhere to the **natural law** theory believe that a higher, or universal, law exists that applies to all human beings and that written laws should imitate these inherent principles. If a written law is unjust, then it is not a true (natural) law and need not be obeyed.

The natural law tradition is one of the oldest and most significant schools of jurisprudence. It dates back to the days of the Greek philosopher Aristotle (384–322 B.C.E.), who distinguished between natural law and the laws governing a particular nation. According to Aristotle, natural law applies universally to all humankind.

The notion that people have "natural rights" stems from the natural law tradition. Those who claim that certain nations, such as China and North Korea, are depriving many of their citizens of their human rights are implicitly appealing to a higher law that has universal applicability.

The question of the universality of basic human rights also comes into play in the context of international business operations. For instance, U.S. companies that have operations abroad

KNOW THIS Even though courts of law and equity have merged, the principles of equity still apply, and courts will not grant an equitable remedy unless the remedy at law is inadequate.

Equitable Principles and Maxims General propositions or principles of law that have to do with fairness (equity).

Jurisprudence The science or philosophy of law.

Natural Law The oldest school of legal thought, based on the belief that the legal system should reflect universal ("higher") moral and ethical principles that are inherent in human nature.

Exhibit 1–3 Procedural Differences between an Action at Law and an Action in Equity

PROCEDURE	ACTION AT LAW	ACTION IN EQUITY
Initiation of lawsuit	By filing a complaint	By filing a petition
Decision	By jury or judge	By judge (no jury)
Result	Judgment	Decree
Remedy	Monetary damages	Injunction, specific performance, or rescission

often hire foreign workers as employees. Should the same laws that protect U.S. employees apply to these foreign employees? This question is rooted implicitly in a concept of universal rights that has its origins in the natural law tradition.

Legal Positivism

Legal Positivism A school of legal thought centered on the assumption that there is no law higher than the laws created by a national government. Laws must be obeyed, even if they are unjust, to prevent anarchy.

In contrast, *positive*, or national, law (the written law of a given society at a particular point in time) applies only to the citizens of that nation or society. Those who adhere to **legal positivism** believe that there can be no higher law than a nation's positive law.

According to the positivist school, there is no such thing as "natural rights." Rather, human rights exist solely because of laws. If the laws are not enforced, anarchy will result. Thus, whether a law is morally "bad" or "good" is irrelevant. The law is the law and must be obeyed until it is changed—in an orderly manner through a legitimate lawmaking process.

A judge with positivist leanings probably would be more inclined to defer to an existing law than would a judge who adheres to the natural law tradition.

The Historical School

Historical School A school of legal thought that looks to the past to determine what the principles of contemporary law should be.

The **historical school** of legal thought emphasizes the evolutionary process of law by concentrating on the origin and history of the legal system. This school looks to the past to discover what the principles of contemporary law should be. The legal doctrines that have withstood the passage of time—those that have worked in the past—are deemed best suited for shaping present laws. Hence, law derives its legitimacy and authority from adhering to the standards that historical development has shown to be workable.

Followers of the historical school are more likely than those of other schools to adhere strictly to decisions made in past cases.

LANDMARK IN THE LAW   Equitable Principles and Maxims

In medieval England, courts of equity were expected to use discretion in supplementing the common law. Even today, when the same court can award both legal and equitable remedies, it must exercise discretion. Students of business law should know that courts often invoke equitable principles and maxims when making their decisions. Here are some of the most significant equitable principles and maxims:

1. *Whoever seeks equity must do equity.* (Anyone who wishes to be treated fairly must treat others fairly.)

2. *Where there is equal equity, the law must prevail.* (The law will determine the outcome of a controversy in which the merits of both sides are equal.)

3. *One seeking the aid of an equity court must come to the court with clean hands.* (Plaintiffs must have acted fairly and honestly.)

4. *Equity will not suffer a wrong to be without a remedy.* (Equitable relief will be awarded when there is a right to relief and there is no adequate remedy at law.)

5. *Equity regards substance rather than form.* (Equity is more concerned with fairness and justice than with legal technicalities.)

6. *Equity aids the vigilant, not those who rest on their rights.* (Equity will not help those who neglect their rights for an unreasonable period of time.)

The last maxim has come to be known as the *equitable doctrine of laches.* The doctrine arose to encourage people to bring lawsuits while the evidence was fresh. If they failed to do so, they would not be allowed to bring a lawsuit. What constitutes a reasonable time, of course, varies according to the circumstances of the case.

Time periods for different types of cases are now usually fixed by *statutes of limitations*—that is, statutes that set the maximum time period during which a certain action can be brought. After the time allowed under a statute of limitations has expired, no action can be brought, no matter how strong the case was originally.

APPLICATION TO TODAY'S WORLD *The equitable maxims listed here underlie many of the legal rules and principles that are commonly applied by the courts today—and that you will read about in this book. For instance, in the contracts materials you will read about the doctrine of promissory estoppel. Under this doctrine, a person who has reasonably and substantially relied on the promise of another may be able to obtain some measure of recovery, even though no enforceable contract exists. The court will estop (bar) the one making the promise from asserting the lack of a valid contract as a defense. The rationale underlying the doctrine of promissory estoppel is similar to that expressed in the fourth and fifth maxims listed.*

Legal Realism   In the 1920s and 1930s, a number of jurists and scholars, known as *legal realists,* rebelled against the historical approach to law. **Legal realism** is based on the idea that law is just one of many institutions in society and that it is shaped by social forces and needs. This school reasons that because the law is a human enterprise, judges should look beyond the law and take social and economic realities into account when deciding cases.

Legal realists also believe that the law can never be applied with total uniformity. Given that judges are human beings with unique experiences, personalities, value systems, and intellects, different judges will obviously bring different reasoning processes to the same case. Female judges, for instance, might be more inclined than male judges to consider whether a decision might have a negative impact on the employment of women or minorities.

Legal Realism   A school of legal thought that holds that the law is only one factor to be considered when deciding cases and that social and economic circumstances should also be taken into account.

1–4   Classifications of Law

The law may be broken down according to several classification systems. One classification system divides law into **substantive law** (all laws that define, describe, regulate, and create legal rights and obligations) and **procedural law** (all laws that establish the methods of enforcing the rights established by substantive law).

EXAMPLE 1.8   A state law that provides employees with the right to workers' compensation benefits for any on-the-job injuries they sustain is a substantive law because it creates legal rights (workers' compensation laws will be discussed in Chapter 24). Procedural laws, in contrast, establish the method by which an employee must notify the employer about an on-the-job injury, prove the injury, and periodically submit additional proof to continue receiving workers' compensation benefits. Note that a law concerning workers' compensation may contain both substantive and procedural provisions. ■

Another classification system divides law into federal law and state law. Still another system distinguishes between private law (dealing with relationships between persons) and public law (addressing the relationship between persons and their governments). Frequently, people use the term **cyberlaw** to refer to the emerging body of law that governs transactions conducted via the Internet, but cyberlaw is not really a classification of law. Rather, it is an informal term used to describe traditional legal principles that have been modified and adapted to fit situations that are unique to the online world. Throughout this book, you will read about how the law is evolving to govern specific legal issues that arise in the online context.

Substantive Law   Law that defines, describes, regulates, and creates legal rights and obligations.

Procedural Law   Law that establishes the methods of enforcing the rights established by substantive law.

Cyberlaw   An informal term used to refer to all laws governing electronic communications and transactions, particularly those conducted via the Internet.

1–4a   Civil Law and Criminal Law

Civil law spells out the rights and duties that exist between persons and between persons and their governments. It also specifies the relief available when a person's rights are violated. Typically, in a civil case, a private party sues another private party to make sure that the other party complies with a duty or pays for the damage caused by the failure to comply with a duty. **EXAMPLE 1.9**   If a seller fails to perform a contract with a buyer, the buyer may bring a lawsuit against the seller. The purpose of the lawsuit will be either to compel the seller to perform as promised or, more commonly, to obtain monetary damages for the seller's failure to perform. ■ The government can also bring civil lawsuits against private parties in many situations.

Much of the law that we discuss in this text—including contract law and tort law—is civil law. Note that *civil law* is not the same as a *civil law system*. As you will read shortly, a **civil law system** is a legal system based on a written code of laws. (See this chapter's *Beyond Our Borders* feature for a discussion of the different legal systems used in other nations.)

Criminal law has to do with wrongs committed against society for which society demands redress. Criminal acts are proscribed by local, state, or federal government statutes. Thus, criminal defendants are prosecuted by public officials, such as a district attorney (D.A.), on behalf of the state, not by their victims or other private parties.

Whereas in a civil case the object is to obtain a remedy (such as monetary damages) to compensate the injured party, in a criminal case the object is to punish the wrongdoer in an

Civil Law   The branch of law dealing with the definition and enforcement of all private or public rights, as opposed to criminal matters.

LEARNING OBJECTIVE 5

What are some important differences between civil law and criminal law?

Civil Law System   A system of law derived from Roman law that is based on codified laws (rather than on case precedents).

Criminal Law   The branch of law that defines and punishes wrongful actions committed against the public.

attempt to deter others from similar actions. Penalties for violations of criminal statutes consist of fines and/or imprisonment—and, in some cases, death.

1–4b National and International Law

Although the focus of this book is U.S. business law, increasingly businesspersons in this country engage in transactions that extend beyond our national borders. In these situations,

BEYOND OUR BORDERS

National Law Systems

Despite their varying cultures and customs, almost all countries have laws governing torts, contracts, employment, and other areas. Two types of legal systems predominate around the globe today. One is the common law system of England and the United States, which we have discussed elsewhere. The other system is based on Roman civil law, or "code law," which relies on the legal principles enacted into law by a legislature or governing body.

Civil Law Systems

Although national law systems share many commonalities, they also have distinct differences. In a *civil law system,* the primary source of law is a statutory code, and case precedents are not judicially binding, as they normally are in a common law system. Although judges in a civil law system commonly refer to previous decisions as sources

of legal guidance, those decisions are not binding precedents (*stare decisis* does not apply).

Common Law and Civil Law Systems Today

Exhibit 1–4 lists some countries that follow either the common law system or the civil law system. Generally, countries that were once colonies of Great Britain have retained their English common law heritage. The civil law system, which is used in most continental European nations, has been retained in the countries that were once colonies of those nations. In the United States, the state of Louisiana, because of its historical ties to France, has in part a civil law system, as do Haiti, Québec, and Scotland.

Islamic Legal Systems

A third, less prevalent legal system is common in Islamic countries, where the law is often influenced by *sharia,* the religious law

of Islam. Islam is both a religion and a way of life. *Sharia* is a comprehensive code of principles that governs the public and private lives of Islamic persons and directs many aspects of their day-to-day lives, including politics, economics, banking, business law, contract law, and social issues.

Although *sharia* affects the legal codes of many Muslim countries, the extent of its impact and its interpretation vary widely. In some Middle Eastern nations, aspects of *sharia* have been codified in modern legal codes and are enforced by national judicial systems.

CRITICAL THINKING

■ Does the civil law system offer any advantages over the common law system, or vice versa? Explain.

Exhibit 1–4 The Legal Systems of Selected Nations

CIVIL LAW		COMMON LAW	
Argentina	Indonesia	Australia	Nigeria
Austria	Iran	Bangladesh	Singapore
Brazil	Italy	Canada	United Kingdom
Chile	Japan	Ghana	United States
China	Mexico	India	Zambia
Egypt	Poland	Israel	
Finland	South Korea	Jamaica	
France	Sweden	Kenya	
Germany	Tunisia	Malaysia	
Greece	Venezuela	New Zealand	

the laws of other nations or the laws governing relationships among nations may come into play. For this reason, those who pursue a career in business today should have an understanding of the global legal environment (discussed further in Chapter 16).

National Law

The law of a particular nation, such as the United States or Sweden, is **national law.** National law, of course, varies from country to country because each country's law reflects the interests, customs, activities, and values that are unique to that nation's culture. Even though the laws and legal systems of various countries differ substantially, broad similarities do exist.

National Law Law that pertains to a particular nation (as opposed to international law).

International Law

In contrast to national law, international law applies to more than one nation. **International law** can be defined as a body of written and unwritten laws observed by independent nations and governing the acts of individuals as well as governments. It is a mixture of rules and constraints derived from a variety of sources, including the laws of individual nations, customs developed among nations, and international treaties and organizations. Each nation is motivated not only by the need to be the final authority over its own affairs, but also by the desire to benefit economically from trade and harmonious relations with other nations. In essence, international law is the result of centuries-old attempts to strike a balance between these competing needs.

International Law The law that governs relations among nations.

The key difference between national law and international law is that government authorities can enforce national law. If a nation violates an international law, however, enforcement is up to other countries or international organizations, which may or may not choose to act. If persuasive tactics fail, the only option is to take coercive actions against the violating nation. Coercive actions range from the severance of diplomatic relations and boycotts to, as a last resort, war. We will examine the laws governing international business transactions in later chapters (including the chapter on international law and the chapters covering contracts for the sale and lease of goods).

Reviewing . . . The Legal Environment

Suppose that the California legislature passes a law that severely restricts carbon dioxide emissions of automobiles in that state. A group of automobile manufacturers files a suit against the state of California to prevent enforcement of the law. The automakers claim that a federal law already sets fuel economy standards nationwide and that these standards are essentially the same as carbon dioxide emission standards. According to the automobile manufacturers, it is unfair to allow California to impose more stringent regulations than those set by the federal law. Using the information presented in the chapter, answer the following questions.

1. Who are the parties (the plaintiffs and the defendant) in this lawsuit?

2. Are the plaintiffs seeking a legal remedy or an equitable remedy? Why?

3. What is the primary source of the law that is at issue here?

4. Read through the appendix that follows this chapter, and then answer the following question: Where would you look to find the relevant California and federal laws?

DEBATE THIS

■ Under the doctrine of *stare decisis,* courts are obligated to follow the precedents established in their jurisdiction unless there is a compelling reason not to do so. Should U.S. courts continue to adhere to this common law principle, given that our government now regulates so many areas by statute?

LINKING BUSINESS LAW TO CORPORATE MANAGEMENT
Dealing with Administrative Law

Whether you work for a large corporation or own a small business, you will be dealing with multiple aspects of administrative law. All federal, state, and local government administrative agencies create rules that have the force of law. As a manager, you probably will need to pay more attention to administrative rules and regulations than to laws passed by local, state, and federal legislatures.

Federal versus State and Local Agency Regulations
The three levels of government create three levels of rules and regulations though their respective administrative agencies. At the federal level, these include the Food and Drug Administration, the Equal Employment Opportunity Commission, and the Occupational Safety and Health Administration. Similar agencies govern business activities at the state level.

As a manager, you will have to learn about agency regulations that pertain to your business activities. It will be up to you, as a manager or small-business owner, to discern which of those regulations are most important and could create the most liability if you violate them.

When Should You Participate in the Rulemaking Process?
All federal agencies and many state agencies invite public comments on proposed rules. Suppose that you manage a large construction company and your state occupational safety agency proposes a new rule requiring every employee on a construction site to wear hearing protection. You believe that the rule will lead to a *less* safe environment because your employees will not be able to communicate easily with one another.

Should you spend time offering comments to the agency? As an efficient manager, you make a trade-off calculation. First, you determine the value of the time that you would spend attempting to prevent or at least alter the proposed rule. Then you compare this implicit cost with your estimate of the potential benefits your company would receive if the rule is *not* put into place.

Be Prepared for Investigations
All administrative agencies have investigatory powers. Agencies' investigators usually have the power to search business premises, although normally they first have to obtain a search warrant. As a manager, you often have the choice of cooperating with agency investigators or providing just the minimum amount of assistance. If your business is routinely investigated, you will often opt for cooperation. In contrast, if your business is rarely investigated, you may decide that the on-site proposed inspection is overreaching. Then you must contact your company's attorney for advice on how to proceed.

If an administrative agency cites you for a regulatory violation, you will probably negotiate a settlement with the agency rather than take your case before an administrative law judge. Again, as a manager, you have to weigh the cost of the negotiated settlement with the potential cost of fighting the enforcement action.

CRITICAL THINKING
- Why are owner/operators of small businesses at a disadvantage relative to large corporations when they attempt to decipher complex regulations that apply to their businesses?

Key Terms

Chapter Summary: The Legal Environment

Sources of American Law	**1.** *Constitutional law*—The law as expressed in the U.S. Constitution and the various state constitutions. The U.S. Constitution is the supreme law of the land. State constitutions are supreme within state borders to the extent that they do not violate the U.S. Constitution or a federal law.
	2. *Statutory law*—Laws or ordinances created by federal, state, and local legislatures and governing bodies. None of these laws can violate the U.S. Constitution or the relevant state constitutions. Uniform laws, when adopted by a state legislature, become statutory law in that state.
	3. *Administrative law*—The rules, orders, and decisions of federal or state government administrative agencies. Federal administrative agencies are created by enabling legislation enacted by the U.S. Congress. Agency functions include rulemaking, investigation and enforcement, and adjudication.
	4. *Case law and common law doctrines*—Judge-made law, including interpretations of constitutional provisions, of statutes enacted by legislatures, and of regulations created by administrative agencies. The common law—the doctrines and principles embodied in case law—governs all areas not covered by statutory law or administrative law.
Common Law Tradition	**1.** *Common law*—Law that originated in medieval England with the creation of the king's courts, or *curiae regis,* and the development of a body of rules that were common to (or applied in) all regions of the country.
	2. *Stare decisis*—A doctrine under which judges "stand on decided cases"—or follow the rule of precedent—in deciding cases. *Stare decisis* is the cornerstone of the common law tradition.
	3. *Remedies*—A remedy is the means by which a court enforces a right or compensates for a violation of a right. Courts typically grant legal remedies (monetary damages) but may also grant equitable remedies (specific performance, injunction, or rescission) when the legal remedy is inadequate or unavailable.
	4. *Schools of legal thought*—Judges' decision making is influenced by their philosophy of law. The following are four important schools of legal thought, or legal philosophies: **a.** Natural law tradition—One of the oldest and most significant schools of legal thought. Those who believe in natural law hold that there is a universal law applicable to all human beings and that this law is of a higher order than positive, or conventional, law. **b.** Legal positivism—A school of legal thought centered on the assumption that there is no law higher than the laws created by the government. Laws must be obeyed, even if they are unjust, to prevent anarchy. **c.** Historical school—A school of legal thought that stresses the evolutionary nature of law and looks to doctrines that have withstood the passage of time for guidance in shaping present laws. **d.** Legal realism—A school of legal thought that generally advocates a less abstract and more realistic approach to the law. This approach takes into account customary practices and the circumstances in which transactions take place.
Classifications of Law	The law may be broken down according to several classification systems, such as substantive or procedural law, federal or state law, and private or public law. Two broad classifications are civil and criminal law, and national and international law. Cyberlaw is not really a classification of law but a term that refers to the growing body of case and statutory law that applies to Internet transactions.

Issue Spotters

1. The First Amendment to the U.S. Constitution provides protection for the free exercise of religion. A state legislature enacts a law that outlaws all religions that do not derive from the Judeo-Christian tradition. Is this law valid within that state? Why or why not? (See *Sources of American Law*.)

2. Apples & Oranges Corporation learns that a federal administrative agency is considering a rule that will have a negative impact on the firm's ability to do business. Does the firm have any opportunity to express its opinion about the pending rule? Explain. (See *Sources of American Law*.)

—**Check your answers to the *Issue Spotters* against the answers provided in Appendix D at the end of this text.**

Learning Objectives Check

1. What are four primary sources of law in the United States?
2. What is the common law tradition?
3. What is a precedent? When might a court depart from precedent?
4. What is the difference between remedies at law and remedies in equity?
5. What are some important differences between civil law and criminal law?

—**Answers to the even-numbered *Learning Objectives Check* questions can be found in Appendix E at the end of this text.**

Business Scenarios and Case Problems

1–1. Binding versus Persuasive Authority. A county court in Illinois is deciding a case involving an issue that has never been addressed before in that state's courts. The Iowa Supreme Court, however, recently decided a case involving a very similar fact pattern. Is the Illinois court obligated to follow the Iowa Supreme Court's decision on the issue? If the United States Supreme Court had decided a similar case, would that decision be binding on the Illinois court? Explain. (See *Common Law Tradition*.)

1–2. Remedies. Arthur Rabe is suing Xavier Sanchez for breaching a contract in which Sanchez promised to sell Rabe a Van Gogh painting for $150,000. (See *Common Law Tradition*.)

1. In this lawsuit, who is the plaintiff, and who is the defendant?
2. If Rabe wants Sanchez to perform the contract as promised, what remedy should Rabe seek?
3. Suppose that Rabe wants to cancel the contract because Sanchez fraudulently misrepresented the painting as an original Van Gogh when in fact it is a copy. In this situation, what remedy should Rabe seek?
4. Will the remedy Rabe seeks in either situation be a remedy at law or a remedy in equity?
5. Suppose that the court finds in Rabe's favor and grants one of these remedies. Sanchez then appeals the decision to a higher court. Read through the subsection entitled "Parties to Lawsuits" in the appendix following this chapter. On appeal, which party in the Rabe-Sanchez case will be the appellant (or petitioner), and which party will be the appellee (or respondent)?

1–3. Philosophy of Law. After World War II ended in 1945, an international tribunal of judges convened at Nuremberg, Germany. The judges convicted several Nazi war criminals of "crimes against humanity." Assuming that the Nazis who were convicted had not disobeyed any law of their country and had merely been following their government's (Hitler's) orders, what law had they violated? Explain. (See *Common Law Tradition*.)

1–4. Spotlight on AOL—Common Law. AOL, LLC, mistakenly made public the personal information of 650,000 of its members. The members filed a suit, alleging violations of

California law. AOL asked the court to dismiss the suit on the basis of a "forum-selection" clause in its member agreement that designates Virginia courts as the place where member disputes will be tried. Under a decision of the United States Supreme Court, a forum-selection clause is unenforceable "if enforcement would contravene a strong public policy of the forum in which suit is brought." California has declared in other cases that the AOL clause contravenes a strong public policy. If the court applies the doctrine of *stare decisis,* will it dismiss the suit? Explain. [*Doe 1 v. AOL, LLC,* 552 F.3d 1077 (9th Cir. 2009)] (See *Common Law Tradition*.)

1–5. Business Case Problem with Sample Answer—Law around the World. Karen Goldberg's husband was killed in a terrorist bombing in Israel. She filed a suit in a U.S. federal court against UBS AG, a Switzerland-based global financial services company. She claimed that UBS aided in her husband's killing because it provided services to the terrorists. UBS argued that the case should be transferred to another country. Like many nations, the United States has a common law system. Other nations have civil law systems. What are the key differences between these systems? [*Goldberg v. UBS AG,* 690 F.Supp.2d 92 (E.D.N.Y. 2010)] (See *Classifications of Law.*)

—**For a sample answer to Problem 1–5, go to Appendix F at the end of this text.**

1–6. Reading Citations. Assume that you want to read the court's entire opinion in the case of *Baker v. Premo,* 268 Or.App. 406, 342 P.3d 142 (2015). Read the section entitled "Finding Case Law" in the appendix that follows this chapter, and then explain specifically where you would find the court's opinion. (See *Finding Case Law.*)

1–7. A Question of Ethics—*Stare Decisis*. On July 5, 1884, Dudley, Stephens, and Brooks—"all able-bodied English seamen"—and a teenage English boy were cast adrift in a lifeboat following a storm at sea. They had no water with them in the boat, and all they had for sustenance were two one-pound tins of turnips. On July 24, Dudley proposed that one of the four in the lifeboat be sacrificed to save the others. Stephens agreed with Dudley, but Brooks refused to consent—and the boy was never asked for his opinion. On July 25, Dudley killed the boy, and the three men then fed on the boy's body and blood. Four days later, the men were rescued by a passing vessel. They were taken to England and tried for the murder of the boy. If the men had not fed on the boy's body, they would probably have died of starvation within the four-day period. The boy, who was in a much weaker condition, would likely have died before the rest. [*Regina v. Dudley and Stephens,* 14 Q.B.D. (Queen's Bench Division, England) 273 (1884)] (See *Common Law Tradition.*)

1. The basic question in this case is whether the survivors should be subject to penalties under English criminal law, given the men's unusual circumstances. You be the judge and decide the issue. Give the reasons for your decision.

2. Should judges ever have the power to look beyond the written "letter of the law" in making their decisions? Why or why not?

Critical Thinking and Writing Assignments

1–8. Business Law Writing. John's company is involved in a lawsuit with a customer, Beth. John argues that for fifty years higher courts in that state have decided cases involving circumstances similar to his case in a way that indicates he can expect a ruling in his company's favor. Write at least one paragraph discussing whether this is a valid argument. Write another paragraph discussing whether the judge in this case must rule as those other judges did, and why. (See *Common Law Tradition.*)

1–9. Business Law Critical Thinking Group Assignment—Court Opinions. Read through the subsection entitled "Decisions and Opinions" in the appendix following this chapter. (See *Reading and Understanding Case Law.*)

1. One group will explain the difference between a concurring opinion and a majority opinion.

2. Another group will outline the difference between a concurring opinion and a dissenting opinion.

3. A third group will explain why judges and justices write concurring and dissenting opinions, given that these opinions will not affect the outcome of the case at hand, which has already been decided by majority vote.

Appendix to Chapter 1

Finding and Analyzing the Law

This text includes numerous references, or *citations,* to primary sources of law—federal and state statutes, the U.S. Constitution and state constitutions, regulations issued by administrative agencies, and court cases. A citation identifies the publication in which a legal authority—such as a statute or court decision—can be found. In this appendix, we explain how you can use citations to find primary sources of law. Note that in addition to being published in sets of books, as described next, most federal and state laws and case decisions are available online.

Finding Statutory and Administrative Law

When Congress passes laws, they are collected in a publication titled *United States Statutes at Large.* When state legislatures pass laws, they are collected in similar state publications. Most frequently, however, laws are referred to in their codified form—that is, the form in which they appear in the federal and state codes. In these codes, laws are compiled by subject.

United States Code

The *United States Code* (U.S.C.) arranges all existing federal laws of a public and permanent nature by subject. Each of the fifty-two subjects into which the U.S.C. arranges the laws is given a title and a title number. For example, laws relating to commerce and trade are collected in "Title 15, Commerce and Trade." Titles are subdivided by sections.

A citation to the U.S.C. includes title and section numbers. Thus, a reference to "15 U.S.C. Section 1" means that the statute can be found in Section 1 of Title 15. ("Section" may be designated by the symbol §, and "Sections" by §§.) In addition to the print publication of the U.S.C., the federal government also provides a searchable online database of the *United States Code* at **www.gpo.gov** (click on "Libraries" and then "Core Documents of Our Democracy" to find the *United States Code*).

Commercial publications of these laws are available and are widely used. For example, Thomson Reuters publishes the *United States Code Annotated* (U.S.C.A.). The U.S.C.A. contains the complete text of laws included in the U.S.C., notes of court decisions that interpret and apply specific sections of the statutes, and the text of presidential proclamations and executive orders. The U.S.C.A. also includes research aids, such as cross-references to related statutes, historical notes, and other references. A citation to the U.S.C.A. is similar to a citation to the U.S.C.: "15 U.S.C.A. Section 1."

State Codes

State codes follow the U.S.C. pattern of arranging laws by subject. The state codes may be called codes, revisions, compilations, consolidations, general statutes, or statutes, depending on the state.

In some codes, subjects are designated by number. In others, they are designated by name. For example, "13 Pennsylvania Consolidated Statutes Section 1101" means that the statute can be found in Title 13, Section 1101, of the Pennsylvania code. "California Commercial Code Section 1101" means the statute can be found in Section 1101 under the subject heading

"Commercial Code" of the California code. Abbreviations may be used. For example, "13 Pennsylvania Consolidated Statutes Section 1101" may be abbreviated "13 Pa. C.S. § 1101," and "California Commercial Code Section 1101" may be abbreviated "Cal. Com. Code § 1101."

Administrative Rules

Rules and regulations adopted by federal administrative agencies are initially published in the *Federal Register,* a daily publication of the U.S. government. Later, they are incorporated into the *Code of Federal Regulations* (C.F.R.).

Like the U.S.C., the C.F.R. is divided into titles. Rules within each title are assigned section numbers. A full citation to the C.F.R. includes title and section numbers. For example, a reference to "17 C.F.R. Section 230.504" means that the rule can be found in Section 230.504 of Title 17.

Finding Case Law

Before discussing the case reporting system, we need to look briefly at the court system. There are two types of courts in the United States: federal courts and state courts.

Both the federal and state court systems consist of several levels, or tiers, of courts. *Trial courts,* in which evidence is presented and testimony is given, are on the bottom tier (which also includes lower courts handling specialized issues). Decisions from a trial court can be appealed to a higher court, which commonly is an intermediate *court of appeals,* or an *appellate court.* Decisions from these intermediate courts of appeals may be appealed to an even higher court, such as a state supreme court or the United States Supreme Court.

State Court Decisions

Most state trial court decisions are not published (except in New York and a few other states, which publish selected trial court opinions). Decisions from state trial courts are typically filed in the office of the clerk of the court, where the decisions are available for public inspection. (Increasingly, they can be found online as well.)

Written decisions of the appellate, or reviewing, courts, however, are published and distributed (in print and online). As you will note, most of the state court cases presented in this book are from state appellate courts. The reported appellate decisions are published in volumes called *reports* or *reporters,* which are numbered consecutively. State appellate court decisions are found in the state reporters of that particular state. Official reports are published by the state, whereas unofficial reports are published by nongovernment entities.

Regional Reporters State court opinions appear in regional units of West's National Reporter System, published by Thomson Reuters. Most lawyers and libraries have these reporters because they report cases more quickly and are distributed more widely than the state-published reports. In fact, many states have eliminated their own reporters in favor of West's National Reporter System.

The National Reporter System divides the states into the following geographic areas: *Atlantic* (A., A.2d, or A.3d), *North Eastern* (N.E. or N.E.2d), *North Western* (N.W. or N.W.2d), *Pacific* (P., P.2d, or P.3d), *South Eastern* (S.E. or S.E.2d), *South Western* (S.W., S.W.2d, or S.W.3d), and *Southern* (So., So.2d, or So.3d). (The *2d* and *3d* in the abbreviations refer to *Second Series* and *Third Series,* respectively.) The states included in each of these regional divisions are indicated in Exhibit 1A–1, which illustrates West's National Reporter System.

Case Citations After appellate decisions have been published, they are normally referred to (cited) by the name of the case and the volume, name, and page number of the reporter(s) in which the opinion can be found. The citation first lists information from the state's official

Exhibit 1A–1 West's National Reporter System—Regional/Federal

Regional Reporters	Coverage Beginning	Coverage
Atlantic Reporter (A., A.2d, or A.3d)	1885	Connecticut, Delaware, District of Columbia, Maine, Maryland, New Hampshire, New Jersey, Pennsylvania, Rhode Island, and Vermont.
North Eastern Reporter (N.E. or N.E.2d)	1885	Illinois, Indiana, Massachusetts, New York, and Ohio.
North Western Reporter (N.W. or N.W.2d)	1879	Iowa, Michigan, Minnesota, Nebraska, North Dakota, South Dakota, and Wisconsin.
Pacific Reporter (P., P.2d, or P.3d)	1883	Alaska, Arizona, California, Colorado, Hawaii, Idaho, Kansas, Montana, Nevada, New Mexico, Oklahoma, Oregon, Utah, Washington, and Wyoming.
South Eastern Reporter (S.E. or S.E.2d)	1887	Georgia, North Carolina, South Carolina, Virginia, and West Virginia.
South Western Reporter (S.W., S.W.2d, or S.W.3d)	1886	Arkansas, Kentucky, Missouri, Tennessee, and Texas.
Southern Reporter (So., So.2d, or So.3d)	1887	Alabama, Florida, Louisiana, and Mississippi.

Federal Reporters		
Federal Reporter (F., F.2d, or F.3d)	1880	U.S. Circuit Courts from 1880 to 1912; U.S. Commerce Court from 1911 to 1913; U.S. District Courts from 1880 to 1932; U.S. Court of Claims (now called U.S. Court of Federal Claims) from 1929 to 1932 and since 1960; U.S. Courts of Appeals since 1891; U.S. Court of Customs and Patent Appeals since 1929; U.S. Emergency Court of Appeals since 1943.
Federal Supplement (F.Supp., F.Supp.2d, or F.Supp.3d)	1932	U.S. Court of Claims from 1932 to 1960; U.S. District Courts since 1932; U.S. Customs Court since 1956.
Federal Rules Decisions (F.R.D.)	1939	U.S. District Courts involving the Federal Rules of Civil Procedure since 1939 and Federal Rules of Criminal Procedure since 1946.
Supreme Court Reporter (S.Ct.)	1882	United States Supreme Court since the October term of 1882.
Bankruptcy Reporter (Bankr.)	1980	Bankruptcy decisions of U.S. Bankruptcy Courts, U.S. District Courts, U.S. Courts of Appeals, and the United States Supreme Court.
Military Justice Reporter (M.J.)	1978	U.S. Court of Military Appeals and Courts of Military Review for the Army, Navy, Air Force, and Coast Guard.

NATIONAL REPORTER SYSTEM MAP

Legend:
- Pacific
- North Western
- South Western
- North Eastern
- Atlantic
- South Eastern
- Southern

reporter (if different from West's National Reporter System), then the *National Reporter,* and then any other selected reporter. (Citing a reporter by volume number, name, and page number, in that order, is common to all citations.) When more than one reporter is cited for the same case, each reference is called a *parallel citation.*

Note that some states have adopted a "public domain citation system" that uses a somewhat different format for the citation. For example, in Ohio, an Ohio court decision might be designated "2015-Ohio-620," meaning that the decision was the 620th decision issued by the Ohio Supreme Court in 2015. Parallel citations to the *Ohio Appellate Court Reporter* and the *North Eastern Reporter* are included after the public domain citation.

Consider the following citation: *Brody v. Brody,* 315 Conn. 300, 105 A.3d 887 (2015). We see that the opinion in this case can be found in Volume 315 of the official *Connecticut Reports,* on page 300. The parallel citation is to Volume 105 of the *Atlantic Reporter, Third Series,* page 877.

When we present opinions in this text (starting in Chapter 2), in addition to the reporter, we give the name of the court hearing the case and the year of the court's decision. Sample citations to state court decisions are listed and explained in Exhibit 1A–2.

Federal Court Decisions

Federal district (trial) court decisions are published unofficially in the *Federal Supplement* (F.Supp., F.Supp.2d, or F.Supp.3d), and opinions from the circuit courts of appeals (federal reviewing courts) are reported unofficially in the *Federal Reporter* (F., F.2d, or F.3d). Cases concerning federal bankruptcy law are published unofficially in West's *Bankruptcy Reporter* (Bankr. or B.R.).

The official edition of United States Supreme Court decisions is the *United States Reports* (U.S.), which is published by the federal government. Unofficial editions of Supreme Court cases include West's *Supreme Court Reporter* (S.Ct.) and the *Lawyers' Edition of the Supreme Court Reports* (L.Ed. or L.Ed.2d). Sample citations for federal court decisions are also listed and explained in Exhibit 1A–2.

Unpublished Opinions

Many court opinions that are not yet published or that are not intended for publication can be accessed through Westlaw® (abbreviated in citations as "WL"), an online legal database. When no citation to a published reporter is available for cases cited in this text, we give the WL citation (such as 2015 WL 687700, which means it was case number 687700 decided in the year 2015).

Sometimes, both in this text and in other legal sources, you will see blanks left in a citation. This occurs when the decision will be published, but the particular volume number or page number is not yet available.

Old Cases

On a few occasions, this text cites opinions from old, classic cases dating to the nineteenth century or earlier. Some of these cases are from the English courts. The citations to these cases may not conform to the descriptions given above.

Reading and Understanding Case Law

The cases in this text have been condensed from the full text of the courts' opinions and paraphrased by the authors. For those wishing to review court cases for future research projects or to gain additional legal information, the following sections will provide useful insights into how to read and understand case law.

Exhibit 1A–2 How to Read Citations

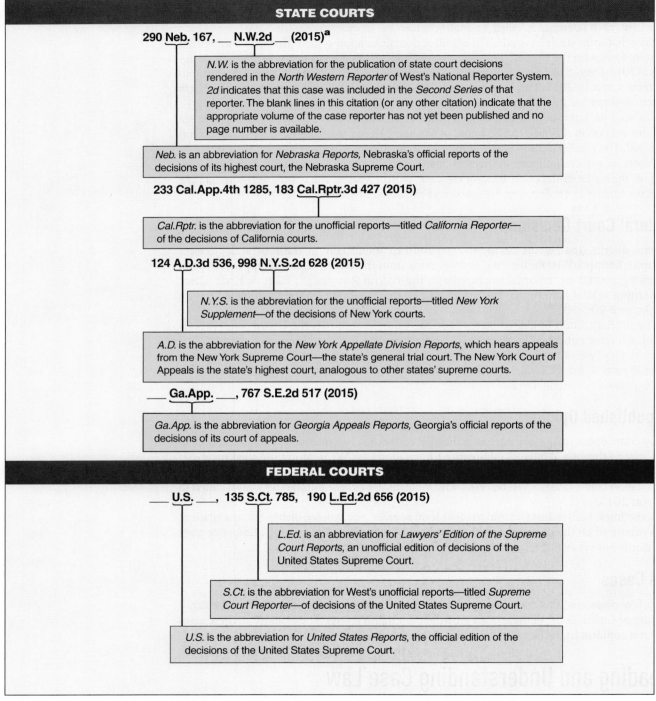

a. The case names have been deleted from these citations to emphasize the publications. It should be kept in mind, however, that the name of a case is as important as the specific page numbers in the volumes in which it is found. If a citation is incorrect, the correct citation may be found in a publication's index of case names. In addition to providing a check on errors in citations, the date of a case is important because the value of a recent case as an authority is likely to be greater than that of older cases from the same court.

Exhibit 1A–2 How to Read Citations

FEDERAL COURTS (Continued)

775 F.3d 1172 (9th Cir. 2015)

9th Cir. is an abbreviation denoting that this case was decided in the U.S. Court of Appeals for the Ninth Circuit.

___ F.Supp.3d ___ 2015 WL 273140 (N.D.Cal. 2015)

N.D.Cal. is an abbreviation indicating that the U.S. District Court for the Northern District of California decided this case.

WESTLAW® CITATIONS[b]

2015 WL 358246

WL is an abbreviation for Westlaw. The number 2015 is the year of the document that can be found with this citation in the Westlaw database. The number 358246 is a number assigned to a specific document. A higher number indicates that a document was added to the Westlaw database later in the year.

STATUTORY AND OTHER CITATIONS

18 U.S.C. Section 1961(1)(A)

U.S.C. denotes *United States Code*, the codification of *United States Statutes at Large.* The number 18 refers to the statute's U.S.C. title number and 1961 to its section number within that title. The number 1 in parentheses refers to a subsection within the section, and the letter A in parentheses to a subsection within the subsection.

UCC 2–206(1)(b)

UCC is an abbreviation for *Uniform Commercial Code.* The first number 2 is a reference to an article of the UCC, and 206 to a section within that article. The number 1 in parentheses refers to a subsection within the section, and the letter b in parentheses to a subsection within the subsection.

***Restatement (Third) of Torts,* Section 6**

Restatement (Third) of Torts refers to the third edition of the American Law Institute's *Restatement of the Law of Torts.* The number 6 refers to a specific section.

17 C.F.R. Section 230.505

C.F.R. is an abbreviation for *Code of Federal Regulations*, a compilation of federal administrative regulations. The number 17 designates the regulation's title number, and 230.505 designates a specific section within that title.

b. Many court decisions that are not yet published or that are not intended for publication can be accessed through Westlaw, an online legal database.

Case Titles and Terminology

The title of a case, such as *Adams v. Jones,* indicates the names of the parties to the lawsuit. The *v.* in the case title stands for *versus,* which means "against." In the trial court, Adams was the plaintiff—the person who filed the suit. Jones was the defendant.

If the case is appealed, however, the appellate court will sometimes place the name of the party appealing the decision first, so the case may be called *Jones v. Adams.* Because some reviewing courts retain the trial court order of names, it is often impossible to distinguish the plaintiff from the defendant in the title of a reported appellate court decision. You must carefully read the facts of each case to identify the parties.

The following terms and phrases are frequently encountered in court opinions and legal publications. Because it is important to understand what these terms and phrases mean, we define and discuss them here.

Parties to Lawsuits
As mentioned, the party initiating a lawsuit is referred to as the *plaintiff or petitioner*, depending on the nature of the action, and the party against whom a lawsuit is brought is the *defendant* or *respondent*. Lawsuits frequently involve more than one plaintiff and/or defendant.

When a case is appealed from the original court or jurisdiction to another court or jurisdiction, the party appealing the case is called the *appellant.* The *appellee* is the party against whom the appeal is taken. (In some appellate courts, the party appealing a case is referred to as the *petitioner,* and the party against whom the suit is brought or appealed is called the *respondent.*)

Judges and Justices
The terms *judge* and *justice* are usually synonymous and are used to refer to the judges in various courts. All members of the United States Supreme Court, for example, are referred to as justices. Justice is the formal title usually given to judges of appellate courts, although this is not always the case. In New York, a justice is a judge of the trial court (which is called the Supreme Court), and a member of the Court of Appeals (the state's highest court) is called a judge. The term *justice* is commonly abbreviated to J., and *justices* to JJ. A Supreme Court case might refer to Justice Sotomayor as Sotomayor, J., or to Chief Justice Roberts as Roberts, C.J.

Decisions and Opinions
Most decisions reached by reviewing, or appellate, courts are explained in written *opinions.* The opinion contains the court's reasons for its decision, the rules of law that apply, and the judgment. You may encounter several types of opinions as you read appellate cases, including the following:

- When all the judges (or justices) agree, a *unanimous opinion* is written for the entire court.
- When there is not unanimous agreement, a **majority opinion** is generally written. It outlines the views of the majority of the judges deciding the case.
- A judge who agrees (concurs) with the majority opinion as to the result but not as to the legal reasoning often writes a **concurring opinion.** In it, the judge sets out the reasoning that he or she considers correct.
- A **dissenting opinion** presents the views of one or more judges who disagree with the majority view. (See the *Business Case Study with Dissenting Opinion* that concludes each unit in this text for an example of a dissenting opinion.)
- Sometimes, no single position is fully supported by a majority of the judges deciding a case. In this situation, we may have a **plurality opinion.** This is the opinion that has the support of the largest number of judges, but the group in agreement is less than a majority.
- Finally, a court occasionally issues a ***per curiam* opinion** (*per curiam* is Latin for "of the court"), which does not indicate which judge wrote the opinion.

Majority Opinion A court opinion that represents the views of the majority (more than half) of the judges or justices deciding the case.

Concurring Opinion A court opinion by one or more judges or justices who agree with the majority but want to make or emphasize a point that was not made or emphasized in the majority's opinion.

Dissenting Opinion A court opinion that presents the views of one or more judges or justices who disagree with the majority's decision.

Plurality Opinion A court opinion that is joined by the largest number of the judges or justices hearing the case, but less than half of the total number.

***Per Curiam* Opinion** A court opinion that does not indicate which judge or justice authored the opinion.

A Sample Court Case

Knowing how to read and analyze a court opinion is an essential step in undertaking accurate legal research. A further step is "briefing," or summarizing, the case. Legal researchers routinely brief cases by reducing the texts of the opinions to their essential elements. Instructions on how to brief a case are given in Appendix A.

The cases within this text have already been analyzed and briefed by the authors, and the essential aspects of each case are presented in a convenient format consisting of four sections: *Facts, Issue, Decision,* and *Reason.* This format is illustrated in the sample court case in Exhibit 1A–3, which has been annotated to explain the kind of information that is contained in each section.

In the remaining chapters of this book, the basic format is often expanded to include special introductory sections. Each case is also followed by a question or section that is designed to enhance your analysis. *Critical Thinking* sections present a question about some issue raised by the case. *Why Is This Case Important?* sections explain the significance of the case. *What If the Facts Were Different?* questions alter the facts slightly and ask you to consider how this would change the outcome. A section entitled *Impact of This Case on Today's Law* concludes each of the *Classic Cases* that appear throughout the text to indicate the significance of the case for today's legal landscape.

The case we present in Exhibit 1A–3 is an actual case that the United States Court of Appeals for the Ninth Circuit decided in 2015. Michael Davis, a former professional football player, and other football players, sued Electronic Arts, Inc., the maker of a video game that replicated the players' physical characteristics. The players alleged a violation of their "right of publicity" (a tort discussed in Chapter 4). One of the issues before the court was whether Electronic Arts' use of the players' likenesses in the video game was protected under the First Amendment to the U.S. Constitution (see Chapter 2).

EXHIBIT 1A–3 A SAMPLE COURT CASE

1

Davis v. Electronic Arts, Inc.

United States Court of Appeals, Ninth Circuit, 775 F.3d 1172 (2015).

2   **3**

FACTS Electronic Arts, Inc. (EA) makes and sells the video game *Madden NFL,* which allows users to play virtual games between National Football League (NFL) teams, both current and "historic." EA's artists create avatars of the players, each of whom is identifiable by position, years in the NFL, height, weight, skin tone, and skill.

4 EA pays a fee to use the likenesses of current players, but not to use the likenesses of former players on the historic teams. Those players filed a suit in a federal district court against EA, alleging a violation of their "right of publicity"—the right to control the use of one's likeness and prevent another from using it for commercial purposes without consent.

EA filed a motion to strike the complaint. The court denied the motion. EA appealed to the U.S. Court of Appeals for the Ninth Circuit, arguing that its use of the likenesses is protected under the First Amendment to the U.S. Constitution as an incidental use.

5 **ISSUE** Are the players likely to prevail against EA's defense of incidental use?

6 **DECISION** Yes. The U.S. Court of Appeals for the Ninth Circuit affirmed the lower court's denial of EA's motion. The appellate

court held that EA's use of the players' likenesses is not incidental "because it is central to EA's main commercial purpose."

7 **REASON** Video games are protected under the First Amendment, because like books and movies, "video games communicate ideas— and even social messages." A number of factors establish an incidental use. These include the uniqueness and significance of the use's contribution to the work's commercial purpose. Here, "the former players' likenesses have unique value and contribute to the commercial value of *Madden NFL*" as indicated by the lengths to which EA goes to achieve realism in representing the players.

Other factors are the relationship of the use to the purpose of the work, and the prominence of, in this case, the likenesses. "The former players' likenesses are featured prominently in a manner that is substantially related to the main purpose and subject of *Madden NFL*—to create an accurate virtual simulation of an NFL game."

8 **CRITICAL THINKING—Political Consideration** *Why is the incidental use of a person's likeness without his or her consent permitted?*

Review of Sample Court Case

1 The name of the case is *Davis v. Electronic Arts, Inc.* The lead plaintiff is Michael Davis, a former professional football player whose physical characteristics were replicated in a video game produced by Electronic Arts, Inc., the defendant.

2 The court deciding this case is the United States Court of Appeals for the Ninth Circuit.

3 The case citation includes a citation to the official *Federal Reporter, Third Series.* The case can be found in Volume 775 of the *Federal Reporter, Third Series,* beginning on page 1172.

4 The *Facts* section identifies the plaintiffs and the defendant, describes the events leading up to this suit, and what the plaintiffs sought to obtain by bringing this action. Because this is a case before an appellate court, the ruling of the lower court is also included here.

5 The *Issue* section presents the central issue (or issues) to be decided by the court. In this case, the court is to determine the likelihood of the success of the plaintiffs' case in light of the defendant's asserted defense. Most cases concern more than one issue, but the author of this textbook has edited each case to focus on just one issue.

6 The *Decision* section, as the term indicates, contains the court's decision on the issue or issues before the court. The decision reflects the opinion of the judge, or the majority of the judges or justices, hearing the case. In this particular case, the court reversed the lower court's judgment. Decisions by appellate courts are frequently phrased in reference to the lower court's decision. That is, the appellate court may "affirm" the lower court's ruling or "reverse" it. In either situation, the appellate court may "remand," or send back, the case for further proceedings.

7 The *Reason* section indicates what relevant laws and judicial principles were applied in forming the particular conclusion arrived at in the case at bar ("before the court"). In this case, the principle concerned a defense under the First Amendment to the U.S. Constitution to a charge that the defendant violated the plaintiffs' right of publicity. The court determined that the defense was not established in the circumstances of this case.

8 The *Critical Thinking—Political Consideration* section raises a question to be considered in relation to the case just presented. Here the question involves a "political" consideration. In other cases presented in this text, the "consideration" may involve a cultural, environmental, ethical, international, legal, social, or technological consideration.

2

CHAPTER OUTLINE

■ The Constitutional
  Powers of Government

■ Business and the Bill of
  Rights

■ Due Process and Equal
  Protection

■ Privacy Rights

Constitutional Law

iStockPhoto.com/larryhw

"The United States
Constitution has
proved itself the most
marvelously elastic
compilation of rules of
government ever written."

FRANKLIN D. ROOSEVELT
1882–1945
(THIRTY-SECOND PRESIDENT OF THE
UNITED STATES, 1933–1945)

The U.S. Constitution is brief. (See Appendix B for the full text of the U.S. Constitution.) It contains only about seven thousand words—less than one-third as many as the average state constitution. Its brevity explains, in part, why the Constitution has proved to be so "marvelously elastic," as Franklin Roosevelt described it in the chapter-opening quotation. Perhaps it also explains why the U.S. Constitution has survived for more than two hundred years—longer than any other written constitution in the world.

Laws that govern business have their origin in the law-making authority granted by the Constitution. Neither Congress nor any state can enact a law that conflicts with the Constitution. Constitutional disputes frequently come before the courts—including disputes involving the Affordable Care Act[1] (Obamacare), gun control, immigration, marijuana, and voter identification.

In this chapter, we first look at some basic constitutional concepts and clauses and their significance for business. Then we examine how certain fundamental freedoms guaranteed by the Constitution affect businesspersons and the workplace. We also examine the constitutional protection of privacy rights.

---

1. *National Federation of Independent Business v. Sebelius,* ___ U.S. ___, 132 S.Ct. 2566, 183 L.Ed.2d 450 (2012).

2–1 The Constitutional Powers of Government

Following the Revolutionary War, the United States created a *confederal* form of government in which the states had the authority to govern themselves and the national government could exercise only limited powers. When problems arose because the nation was facing an economic crisis and state laws interfered with the free flow of commerce, a national convention was called. The delegates drafted the U.S. Constitution. This document, after its ratification by the states in 1789, became the basis for an entirely new form of government.

2–1a A Federal Form of Government

The new government created by the Constitution reflected a series of compromises made by the convention delegates on various issues. Some delegates wanted sovereign power to remain with the states, whereas others wanted the national government alone to exercise sovereign power. The end result was a compromise—a **federal form of government** in which the national government and the states *share* sovereign power.

The Constitution sets forth specific powers that can be exercised by the national government. It also provides that the national government has the implied power to undertake actions necessary to carry out its expressly designated powers. All other powers are "reserved" to the states.

The broad language of the Constitution, though, has left much room for debate over the specific nature and scope of these powers. Generally, it has been the task of the courts to determine where the boundary line between state and national powers should lie—and that line changes over time.

2–1b The Separation of Powers

To make it difficult for the national government to use its power arbitrarily, the Constitution divided the national government's powers among the three branches of government. The legislative branch makes the laws, the executive branch enforces the laws, and the judicial branch interprets the laws. Each branch performs a separate function, and no branch may exercise the authority of another branch.

Additionally, a system of **checks and balances** allows each branch to limit the actions of the other two branches, thus preventing any one branch from exercising too much power. The following are examples of these checks and balances:

1. The legislative branch (Congress) can enact a law, but the executive branch (the president) has the constitutional authority to veto that law.

2. The executive branch is responsible for foreign affairs, but treaties with foreign governments require the advice and consent of the Senate.

3. Congress determines the jurisdiction of the federal courts, and the president appoints federal judges, with the advice and consent of the Senate, but the judicial branch has the power to hold actions of the other two branches unconstitutional.[2]

Federal Form of Government A system of government in which the states form a union and the sovereign power is divided between the central government and the member states.

LEARNING OBJECTIVE 1
What is the basic structure of the U.S. government?

Checks and Balances The principle under which the powers of the national government are divided among three separate branches—the executive, legislative, and judicial branches—each of which exercises a check on the actions of the others.

American Spirit/ShutterStock.com

The U.S. Constitution provides for a system of checks and balances. How does the president check the power of Congress? In what ways can Congress check the power of the president?

---

2. See the *Landmark in the Law* feature in Chapter 3 on the case of *Marbury v. Madison* (1803), in which the doctrine of judicial review was clearly enunciated by Chief Justice John Marshall.

2-1c **The Commerce Clause**

To prevent states from establishing laws and regulations that would interfere with trade and commerce among the states, the Constitution explicitly gave the national government the power to regulate interstate commerce. Article I, Section 8, of the U.S. Constitution expressly permits Congress "[t]o regulate Commerce with foreign Nations, and among the several States, and with the Indian Tribes." This clause, referred to as the **commerce clause,** has had a greater impact on business than any other provision in the Constitution.

Initially, the commerce power was interpreted as being limited to *interstate* commerce (commerce among the states) and not applicable to *intrastate* commerce (commerce within a state). In 1824, however, the United States Supreme Court decided the case of *Gibbons v. Ogden* (see this chapter's *Landmark in the Law* feature). The Court ruled that commerce within a state could also be regulated by the national government as long as the commerce *substantially affected* commerce involving more than one state.

LEARNING OBJECTIVE 2

What constitutional clause gives the federal government the power to regulate commercial activities among the various states?

Commerce Clause The provision in Article I, Section 8, of the U.S. Constitution that gives Congress the power to regulate interstate commerce.

LANDMARK IN THE LAW — *Gibbons v. Ogden* (1824)

The commerce clause of the U.S. Constitution gives Congress the power "[t]o regulate Commerce with foreign Nations, and among the several States, and with the Indian Tribes." Before the commerce clause came into existence, states tended to restrict commerce within and beyond their borders, which made trade more costly and inefficient. The goal of the clause was to unify the states' commerce policies and improve the efficiency of exchanges.

The problem was that although the commerce clause gave Congress some authority to regulate trade among the states, the extent of that power was unclear. What exactly does "to regulate commerce" mean? What does "commerce" entail? These questions came before the United States Supreme Court in 1824 in the case of *Gibbons v. Ogden.*[a]

BACKGROUND In 1803, Robert Fulton, the inventor of the steamboat, and Robert Livingston, who was the ambassador to France, secured a monopoly from the New York legislature on steam navigation on the waters in the state of New York. Their monopoly

extended to interstate waters—waterways between New York and another state. Fulton and Livingston licensed Aaron Ogden, a former governor of New Jersey and a U.S. senator, to operate steam-powered ferryboats between New York and New Jersey.

Thomas Gibbons already operated a ferry service between New Jersey and New York, which had been licensed by Congress under a 1793 act regulating trade along the coast. Although the federal government had licensed Gibbons to operate boats in interstate waters, he did not have the state of New York's permission to compete with Ogden in that area. Ogden sued Gibbons. The New York state courts granted Ogden's request for an injunction—an order prohibiting Gibbons from operating in New York waters. Gibbons appealed the decision to the United States Supreme Court.

MARSHALL'S DECISION The issue before the Court was whether the law regulated commerce that was "among the several states." The chief justice on the Supreme Court was John Marshall, an advocate of a strong national government. Marshall defined the word *commerce* as used in the commerce clause to mean all commercial intercourse—that is, all business dealings that affect more than one state. This broader definition included navigation.

In addition to expanding the definition of commerce, Marshall also validated and increased the power of the national legislature to regulate commerce. Said Marshall, "What is this power? It is the power . . . to prescribe the rule by which commerce is to be governed."

Marshall held that the power to regulate interstate commerce is an exclusive power of the national government. This power includes the power to regulate any intrastate commerce that substantially affects interstate commerce. Accordingly, the Court decided in favor of Gibbons.

APPLICATION TO TODAY'S WORLD *Marshall's broad definition of the commerce power established the foundation for the expansion of national powers in the years to come. Today, the national government continues to rely on the commerce clause for its constitutional authority to regulate business activities.*

Marshall's conclusion that the power to regulate interstate commerce was an exclusive power of the national government has also had significant consequences. By implication, this means that a state cannot regulate activities that extend beyond its borders, such as out-of-state online gambling operations that affect the welfare of in-state citizens. It also means that state regulations over in-state activities normally will be invalidated if the regulations substantially burden interstate commerce.

---

a. 22 U.S. (9 Wheat.) 1, 6 L.Ed. 23 (1824).

The Commerce Clause and the Expansion of National Powers

In *Gibbons v. Ogden*, the commerce clause was expanded to regulate activities that "substantially affect interstate commerce." As the nation grew and faced new kinds of problems, the commerce clause became a vehicle for the additional expansion of the national government's regulatory powers. Even activities that seemed purely local came under the regulatory reach of the national government if those activities were deemed to substantially affect interstate commerce.

CASE EXAMPLE 2.1 In 1942, in *Wickard v. Filburn*,[3] the Supreme Court held that wheat production by an individual farmer intended wholly for consumption on his own farm was subject to federal regulation. The Court reasoned that the home consumption of wheat reduced the market demand for wheat and thus could have a substantial effect on interstate commerce. ■

The following *Classic Case* involved a challenge to the scope of the national government's constitutional authority to regulate local activities.

---

3. 317 U.S. 111, 63 S.Ct. 82, 87 L.Ed. 122 (1942).

★★★ CLASSIC CASE 2.1 ★★★

Heart of Atlanta Motel v. United States

Supreme Court of the United States, 379 U.S. 241, 85 S.Ct. 348, 13 L.Ed.2d 258 (1964).

HISTORICAL AND SOCIAL SETTING *In the first half of the twentieth century, state governments sanctioned segregation on the basis of race. In 1954, the United States Supreme Court held that racially segregated school systems violated the Constitution. In the following decade, the Court ordered an end to racial segregation imposed by the states in other public facilities, such as beaches, golf courses, buses, parks, auditoriums, and courtroom seating. Privately owned facilities that excluded or segregated African Americans and others on the basis of race were not subject to the same constitutional restrictions, however. Congress passed the Civil Rights Act of 1964 to prohibit racial discrimination in "establishments affecting interstate commerce." These facilities included "places of public accommodation."*

FACTS The owner of the Heart of Atlanta Motel, in violation of the Civil Rights Act of 1964, refused to rent rooms to African Americans. The motel owner brought an action in a federal district court to have the Civil Rights Act declared unconstitutional on the ground that Congress had exceeded its constitutional authority to regulate commerce by enacting the statute. The owner argued that his motel was not engaged in interstate commerce but was "of a purely local character." The motel, however, was accessible to state and interstate highways. The owner advertised nationally, maintained billboards throughout the state, and accepted convention trade from outside the state (75 percent of the guests were residents of other states). The district court ruled that the act did not violate the Constitution and enjoined (prohibited) the owner from discriminating on the basis of race. The owner appealed. The case ultimately went to the United States Supreme Court.

ISSUE Did Congress exceed its constitutional power to regulate interstate commerce by enacting the Civil Rights Act of 1964?

President Lyndon Johnson signs the 1964 Civil Rights Act.

LBJ Library photo by Cecil Stoughton

DECISION No. The United States Supreme Court upheld the constitutionality of the act.

REASON The Court noted that the act was passed to correct "the deprivation of personal dignity" accompanying the denial of equal access to "public establishments." Testimony before Congress leading to the passage of the act indicated that African Americans in particular experienced substantial discrimination in attempting to secure lodging while traveling. This discrimination impeded interstate travel and thus impeded interstate commerce.

As for the owner's argument that his motel was "of a purely local character," the Court said that even if this was true, the motel affected interstate commerce. According to the Court, "if it is interstate commerce that feels the pinch, it does not matter how local the operation that applies the squeeze." Therefore, under the commerce clause, "the power of Congress to promote interstate commerce also includes the power to regulate the local incidents thereof, including local activities."

IMPACT OF THIS CASE ON TODAY'S LAW *If the United States Supreme Court had invalidated the Civil Rights Act of 1964, the legal landscape of the United States would be much different today. The act prohibits discrimination based on race, color, national origin, religion, or gender in all "public accommodations," including hotels and restaurants. The act also prohibits discrimination in employment based on these criteria. Although state laws now prohibit many of these forms of discrimination as well, the protections available vary from state to state—and it is not certain whether such laws would have been passed had the outcome in this case been different.*

The Commerce Clause Today Today, at least theoretically, the power over commerce authorizes the national government to regulate almost every commercial enterprise in the United States. The breadth of the commerce clause permits the national government to legislate in areas in which Congress has not explicitly been granted power. Only occasionally has the Supreme Court curbed the national government's regulatory authority under the commerce clause.

Indeed, in one case involving medical marijuana use, the Supreme Court allowed the federal government to regulate noncommercial activities taking place wholly within a state's borders. **CASE EXAMPLE 2.2** A growing number of states, including California, have adopted laws that legalize marijuana for medical purposes (and four states now permit the recreational use of marijuana). Marijuana possession, however, is illegal under the federal Controlled Substances Act (CSA).[4]

After the federal government seized the marijuana that two seriously ill California women were using on the advice of their physicians, the women filed a lawsuit. They argued that it was unconstitutional for the federal statute to prohibit them from using marijuana for medical purposes that were legal within the state. The Supreme Court, though, held that Congress has the authority to prohibit the *intra*state possession and noncommercial cultivation of marijuana as part of a larger regulatory scheme (the CSA).[5] In other words, the federal government may prosecute individuals for possession of marijuana regardless of whether they reside in a state that allows the use of marijuana. ▪

The Regulatory Powers of the States As part of their inherent sovereignty, state governments have the authority to regulate affairs within their borders. This authority stems in part from the Tenth Amendment to the Constitution, which reserves to the states all powers not delegated to the national government.

State regulatory powers are often referred to as **police powers.** The term encompasses not only the enforcement of criminal law but also the right of state governments to regulate private activities in order to protect or promote the public order, health, safety, morals, and general welfare. Fire and building codes, antidiscrimination laws, parking regulations, zoning restrictions, licensing requirements, and thousands of other state statutes have been enacted pursuant to a state's police powers. Local governments, including cities, also exercise police powers.[6]

Although a state may not directly regulate interstate commerce, it may indirectly affect interstate commerce through the reasonable exercise of its police powers. Generally, state laws enacted pursuant to a state's police powers carry a strong presumption of validity.

The "Dormant" Commerce Clause The United States Supreme Court has interpreted the commerce clause to mean that the national government has the *exclusive* authority to regulate commerce that substantially affects trade and commerce among the states. This express grant of authority to the national government, which is often referred to as the "positive" aspect of the commerce clause, implies a negative

Police Powers Powers possessed by the states as part of their inherent sovereignty. These powers may be exercised to protect or promote the public order, health, safety, morals, and general welfare.

iStockPhoto.com/elenaleonova

Because the Constitution reserves to the states all powers not delegated to the national government, the states can and do regulate many types of commercial activities within their borders. So, too, do municipalities. One of these powers is the imposition of building codes. What is the general term that applies to such powers?

---

4. 21 U.S.C. Sections 801 *et seq.*
5. *Gonzales v. Raich*, 545 U.S. 1, 125 S.Ct. 2195, 162 L.Ed.2d 1 (2005).
6. Local governments derive their authority to regulate their communities from the state because they are creatures of the state. In other words, they cannot come into existence unless authorized by the state to do so.

aspect—that the states do *not* have the authority to regulate interstate commerce. This negative aspect of the commerce clause is often referred to as the "dormant" (implied) commerce clause.

The dormant commerce clause comes into play when state regulations affect interstate commerce. In this situation, the courts normally weigh the state's interest in regulating a certain matter against the burden that the state's regulation places on interstate commerce. Because courts balance the interests involved, predicting the outcome in a particular case can be extremely difficult.

CASE EXAMPLE 2.3 Tri-M Group, LLC, a Pennsylvania electrical contractor, was hired to work on a veterans' home in Delaware that was partially state funded. Delaware's regulations allowed contractors on state-funded projects to pay a lower wage rate to apprentices if the contractors had registered their apprenticeship programs in the state. Out-of-state contractors, however, were not eligible to pay the lower rate unless they maintained a permanent office in Delaware.

Tri-M filed a suit in federal court claiming that Delaware's regulations discriminated against out-of-state contractors in violation of the dormant commerce clause. The state argued that the regulations were justified because it had a legitimate interest in safeguarding the welfare of all apprentices by requiring a permanent place of business in Delaware. But the court held that the state had not overcome the presumption of invalidity that applies to discriminatory regulations and that nondiscriminatory alternatives existed for ensuring the welfare of apprentices. Therefore, the regulations violated the dormant commerce clause.[7] ■

2–1d The Supremacy Clause

LEARNING OBJECTIVE 3

What constitutional clause allows laws enacted by the federal government to take priority over conflicting state laws?

Article VI of the Constitution provides that the Constitution, laws, and treaties of the United States are "the supreme Law of the Land." This article, commonly referred to as the **supremacy clause,** is important in the ordering of state and federal relationships.

Supremacy Clause The provision in Article VI of the U.S. Constitution that the Constitution, laws, and treaties of the United States are "the supreme Law of the Land."

Preemption Under the supremacy clause, when there is a direct conflict between a federal law and a state law, the state law is rendered invalid. Because some powers are *concurrent* (shared by the federal government and the states), however, it is necessary to determine which law governs in a particular circumstance.

Preemption occurs when Congress chooses to act exclusively in a concurrent area. In this circumstance, a valid federal statute or regulation will take precedence over a conflicting state or local law or regulation on the same general subject.

Preemption A doctrine under which certain federal laws preempt, or take precedence over, conflicting state or local laws.

Congressional Intent Often, it is not clear whether Congress, in passing a law, intended to preempt an entire subject area against state regulation. In these situations, the courts determine whether Congress intended to exercise exclusive power.

Generally, congressional intent to preempt will be found if a federal law regulating an activity is so pervasive, comprehensive, or detailed that the states have little or no room to regulate in that area. Also, when a federal statute creates an agency—such as the National Labor Relations Board—to enforce the law, the agency's decisions in matters that come within its jurisdiction will likely preempt state laws.

CASE EXAMPLE 2.4 The United States Supreme Court ruled on a case involving a man who alleged that he had been injured by a faulty medical device (a balloon catheter that had been inserted into his artery following a heart attack). The Court noted that the Medical Device Amendments, a federal law, had included a preemption provision. The medical device had passed the U.S. Food and Drug Administration's rigorous premarket approval process.

---

7. *Tri-M Group, LLC v. Sharp*, 638 F.3d 406 (3d Cir. 2011). Sharp was the name of the secretary of the Delaware Department of Labor.

Therefore, the Court ruled that the federal regulation of medical devices preempted the man's state law claims for negligence, strict liability, and implied warranty.[8] ▪

2-2 Business and the Bill of Rights

LEARNING OBJECTIVE 4
What is the Bill of Rights? What freedoms does the First Amendment guarantee?

The importance of having a written declaration of the rights of individuals eventually caused the first Congress of the United States to enact twelve amendments to the Constitution and submit them to the states for approval. The first ten of these amendments, commonly known as the **Bill of Rights,** were adopted in 1791.

The Bill of Rights embodies a series of protections for the individual against various types of conduct by the federal government.[9] Some constitutional protections apply to business entities as well. For example, corporations exist as separate legal entities, or legal persons, and enjoy many of the same rights and privileges as natural persons do.

Bill of Rights The first ten amendments to the U.S. Constitution.

Summarized here are the protections guaranteed by the first ten amendments (see the Constitution in Appendix B for the complete text of each amendment):

1. The First Amendment guarantees the freedoms of religion, speech, and the press and the rights to assemble peaceably and to petition the government.

2. The Second Amendment guarantees the right to keep and bear arms.

3. The Third Amendment prohibits, in peacetime, the lodging of soldiers in any house without the owner's consent.

4. The Fourth Amendment prohibits unreasonable searches and seizures of persons or property.

5. The Fifth Amendment guarantees the rights to *indictment* (formal accusation) by a grand jury, to due process of law, and to fair payment when private property is taken for public use. The Fifth Amendment also prohibits compulsory self-incrimination and double jeopardy (trial for the same crime twice).

6. The Sixth Amendment guarantees the accused in a criminal case the right to a speedy and public trial by an impartial jury and with counsel. The accused has the right to cross-examine witnesses against him or her and to solicit testimony from witnesses in his or her favor.

7. The Seventh Amendment guarantees the right to a trial by jury in a civil (noncriminal) case involving at least twenty dollars.[10]

8. The Eighth Amendment prohibits excessive bail and fines, as well as cruel and unusual punishment.

9. The Ninth Amendment establishes that the people have rights in addition to those specified in the Constitution.

10. The Tenth Amendment establishes that those powers neither delegated to the federal government nor denied to the states are reserved for the states.

Ed Fisher/The New Yorker Collection/Cartoon Bank

---

8. *Riegel v. Medtronic, Inc.*, 552 U.S. 312, 128 S.Ct. 999, 169 L.Ed.2d 892 (2008).

9. One of the proposed amendments was ratified more than two hundred years later (in 1992) and became the Twenty-seventh Amendment to the Constitution. See Appendix B.

10. Twenty dollars was forty days' pay for the average person when the Bill of Rights was written.

We will look closely at several of these amendments in Chapter 8, in the context of criminal law and procedures. In this chapter, we examine two important guarantees of the First Amendment—freedom of speech and freedom of religion. First, though, we look at how the Bill of Rights puts certain limits on government.

2–2a Limits on Federal and State Governmental Actions

As originally intended, the Bill of Rights limited only the powers of the national government. Over time, however, the United States Supreme Court "incorporated" most of these rights into the protections against state actions afforded by the Fourteenth Amendment to the Constitution. That amendment, passed in 1868 after the Civil War, provides, in part, that "[n]o State shall . . . deprive any person of life, liberty, or property, without due process of law."

Starting in 1925, the Supreme Court began to define various rights and liberties guaranteed in the national Constitution as constituting "due process of law," which was required of state governments under the Fourteenth Amendment. Today, most of the rights and liberties set forth in the Bill of Rights apply to state governments as well as to the national government.

Which amendment states that people have the right to keep and bear arms? Does this mean that anyone has the right to buy an assault-type weapon?

The rights secured by the Bill of Rights are not absolute. Many of the rights guaranteed by the first ten amendments are described in very general terms. For instance, the Second Amendment states that people have a right to keep and bear arms, but it does not explain the extent of this right. As the Supreme Court has noted, the right does not extend so far that people can "keep and carry any weapon whatsoever in any manner whatsoever and for whatever purpose."[11] Legislatures can prohibit the carrying of concealed weapons or certain types of weapons, such as machine guns. Ultimately, the Supreme Court, as the final interpreter of the Constitution, gives meaning to constitutional rights and determines their boundaries. (For a discussion of how the Supreme Court may consider other nations' laws when determining the appropriate balance of individual rights, see this chapter's *Beyond Our Borders* feature.)

2–2b The First Amendment—Freedom of Speech

A democratic form of government cannot survive unless people can freely voice their political opinions and criticize government actions or policies. Freedom of speech, particularly political speech, is thus a prized right, and traditionally the courts have protected this right to the fullest extent possible.

Symbolic Speech Nonverbal expressions of beliefs. Symbolic speech, which includes gestures, movements, and articles of clothing, is given substantial protection by the courts.

Symbolic speech—gestures, movements, articles of clothing, and other forms of expressive conduct—is also given substantial protection by the courts. The Supreme Court held that the burning of the American flag to protest government policies is a constitutionally protected form of expression.[12] Similarly, wearing a T-shirt with a photo of a presidential candidate would be a constitutionally protected form of expression.

The test is whether a reasonable person would interpret the conduct as conveying some sort of message. **EXAMPLE 2.5** As a form of expression, Eric has gang signs tattooed on his torso, arms, neck, and legs. If a reasonable person would interpret this conduct as conveying a message, then it might be a protected form of symbolic speech. ■

---

11. *District of Columbia v. Heller*, 554 U.S. 570, 128 S.Ct. 2783, 171 L.Ed.2d 637 (2008).
12. See *Texas v. Johnson*, 491 U.S. 397, 109 S.Ct. 2533, 105 L.Ed.2d 342 (1989).

Reasonable Restrictions Expression—oral, written, or symbolized by conduct—is subject to reasonable restrictions. A balance must be struck between a government's obligation to protect its citizens and those citizens' exercise of their rights. Reasonableness is analyzed on a case-by-case basis.

Content-Neutral Laws. Laws that regulate the time, manner, and place, but not the content, of speech receive less scrutiny by the courts than do laws that restrict the content of expression. If a restriction imposed by the government is content neutral, then a court may allow it. To be content neutral, the restriction must be aimed at combating some secondary societal problem, such as crime, and not be aimed at suppressing the expressive conduct or its message.

Courts have often protected nude dancing as a form of symbolic expression. Nevertheless, the courts typically allow content-neutral laws that ban *all* public nudity. **CASE EXAMPLE 2.6** Rita Ora was charged with dancing nude at an annual "anti-Christmas" protest in Harvard Square in Cambridge, Massachusetts. Ora argued that the statute was overly broad and unconstitutional, and a trial court agreed. On appeal, a state appellate court reversed. The court found that the statute was constitutional because it banned public displays of open and gross lewdness in situations in which there was an unsuspecting or unwilling audience.[13]

Laws That Restrict the Content of Speech. If a law regulates the content of the expression, it must serve a compelling state interest and must be narrowly written to achieve that interest. Under the **compelling government interest** test, the government's interest is balanced against the individual's constitutional right to be free of government interference. For the statute to be valid, there must be a compelling governmental interest that can be furthered only by the law in question.

The United States Supreme Court has held that schools may restrict students' speech at school events. **CASE EXAMPLE 2.7** Some high school students held up a banner saying "Bong

Compelling Government Interest A test of constitutionality that requires the government to have convincing reasons for passing any law that restricts fundamental rights, such as free speech, or distinguishes between people based on a suspect trait.

---

13. *Commonwealth v. Ora*, 451 Mass. 125, 883 N.E.2d 1217 (2008).

BEYOND OUR BORDERS

The Impact of Foreign Law on the United States Supreme Court

The United States Supreme Court interprets the rights provided in the U.S. Constitution. Changing public views on controversial topics, such as privacy in an era of terrorist threats or the rights of gay men and lesbians, may affect the way the Supreme Court decides a case. But should the Court also consider other nations' laws and world opinion when balancing individual rights in the United States?

Justices on the Supreme Court have increasingly considered foreign law when deciding issues of national importance. This trend started in 2003 when, for the first time ever, foreign law was cited in a majority

opinion of the Supreme Court. The case was a controversial one in which the Court struck down laws that prohibited oral and anal sex between consenting adults of the same gender. In the majority opinion, Justice Anthony Kennedy mentioned that the European Court of Human Rights and other foreign courts have consistently acknowledged that homosexuals have a right "to engage in intimate, consensual conduct."[a]

The practice of looking at foreign law has many critics, including Justice Antonin Scalia and other conservative members of the Supreme Court, who believe that foreign

views are irrelevant to rulings on U.S. law. Other Supreme Court justices, however, including Justice Stephen Breyer and Justice Ruth Bader Ginsburg, have publicly stated that in our increasingly global community we should not ignore the opinions of courts in the rest of the world.

CRITICAL THINKING

- Should U.S. courts, and particularly the United States Supreme Court, look to other nations' laws for guidance when deciding important issues—including those involving rights granted by the Constitution? If so, what impact might this have on their decisions? Explain.

---

a. *Lawrence v. Texas*, 539 U.S. 558, 123 S.Ct. 2472, 156 L.Ed.2d 508 (2003).

Hits 4 Jesus" at an off-campus but school-sanctioned event. The majority of the Court ruled that school officials did not violate the students' free speech rights when they confiscated the banner and suspended the students for ten days. Because the banner could reasonably be interpreted as promoting drugs, the Court concluded that the school's actions were justified. Several justices disagreed, however, noting that the majority's holding creates a special exception that will allow schools to censor any student speech that mentions drugs.[14] ▪

ETHICAL ISSUE

Can a high school suspend teenagers from extracurricular activities because they posted suggestive photos of themselves online at social networking sites? T.V. and M.K. were students at a public high school. During summer sleepovers, the girls took photos of each other pretending to suck penis-shaped, rainbow-colored lollipops and holding them in various suggestive positions. They later posted the photos on Facebook, MySpace, and Photo Bucket to be seen by persons granted "friend" status or given a password. When a parent complained to the school about the provocative online display, school officials suspended both girls from the high school volleyball team. M.K. was also suspended from the cheerleading squad and the show choir. Through their parents, the girls filed a lawsuit claiming that the school had violated their First Amendment rights.

A federal judge in Indiana ruled that a high school did not have the right to punish students for posting suggestive photos of themselves on the Internet. Expressive conduct is entitled to First Amendment protection if it is intended to convey a particular message and is likely to be understood by those viewing it as expressing a message. Here, both girls testified that they were just trying to be funny when they took the photos and posted them online for their friends to see. The court reasoned that the conduct depicted in the photos was intended to be humorous and would be understood as such by their teenage audience. Therefore, the photos were entitled to First Amendment protection as symbolic speech.[15]

Corporate Political Speech

Political speech by corporations also falls within the protection of the First Amendment. Many years ago, the United States Supreme Court reviewed a Massachusetts statute that prohibited corporations from making political contributions or expenditures that individuals were permitted to make. The Court ruled that the Massachusetts law

The U.S. Supreme Court decision *Citizens United* allows corporations to spend to elect or defeat candidates for president and Congress. Why did this decision upset some people?

was unconstitutional because it violated the right of corporations to freedom of speech.[16] The Court has also held that a law prohibiting a corporation from using bill inserts to express its views on controversial issues violated the First Amendment.[17]

Corporate political speech continues to be given significant protection under the First Amendment. **CASE EXAMPLE 2.8** In *Citizens United v. Federal Election Commission*,[18] the Supreme Court overturned a twenty-year-old precedent on campaign financing. The case involved Citizens United, a nonprofit corporation that has a *political action committee* (an organization that registers with the government and campaigns for or against political candidates).

Citizens United had produced a film called *Hillary: The Movie* that was critical of Hillary Clinton, who was seeking the Democratic nomination for presidential candidate. Campaign-finance law restricted Citizens United from broadcasting the movie, however. The Court ruled that the restrictions were

---

14. *Morse v. Frederick,* 551 U.S. 393, 127 S.Ct. 2618, 168 L.Ed.2d 290 (2007).
15. *T.V. ex rel. B.V. v. Smith-Green Community School Corp.,* 807 F.Supp.2d 767 (N.D.Ind. 2011).
16. *First National Bank of Boston v. Bellotti,* 435 U.S. 765, 98 S.Ct. 1407, 55 L.Ed.2d 707 (1978).
17. *Consolidated Edison Co. v. Public Service Commission,* 447 U.S. 530, 100 S.Ct. 2326, 65 L.Ed.2d 319 (1980).
18. *Citizens United v. Federal Election Commission,* 558 U.S. 310, 130 S.Ct. 876, 175 L.Ed.2d 753 (2010).

unconstitutional and that the First Amendment prevents limits from being placed on independent political expenditures by corporations. ■

Commercial Speech The courts also give substantial protection to *commercial speech,* which consists of communications—primarily advertising and marketing—made by business firms that involve only their commercial interests. The protection given to commercial speech under the First Amendment is not as extensive as that afforded to noncommercial speech, however. A state may restrict certain kinds of advertising, for instance, in the interest of protecting consumers from being misled.

States also have a legitimate interest in the beautification of roadsides, and this interest allows states to place restraints on billboard advertising. **CASE EXAMPLE 2.9** Café Erotica, a nude dancing establishment, sued the state after being denied a permit to erect a billboard along an interstate highway in Florida. The state appellate court decided that because the law directly advanced a substantial government interest in highway beautification and safety, it was not an unconstitutional restraint on commercial speech.[19] ■

Generally, a restriction on commercial speech will be considered valid as long as it (1) seeks to implement a substantial government interest, (2) directly advances that interest, and (3) goes no further than necessary to accomplish its objective. A substantial government interest is a significant or important connection or concern of the government with respect to a particular matter (such as highway beautification and safety, mentioned in *Case Example 2.9*). This substantial-interest requirement limits the power of the government to regulate commercial speech.

At issue in the following *Spotlight Case* was whether a government agency had unconstitutionally restricted commercial speech when it prohibited the use of a certain illustration on beer labels.

> "If the freedom of speech is taken away, then dumb and silent we may be led like sheep to the slaughter."
>
> **GEORGE WASHINGTON**
> 1732–1799
> (FIRST PRESIDENT OF THE UNITED STATES, 1789–1797)

---

19. *Café Erotica v. Florida Department of Transportation,* 830 So.2d 181 (Fla.App. 1 Dist. 2002); review denied, *Café Erotica/We Dare to Bare v. Florida Department of Transportation,* 845 So.2d 888 (Fla. 2003).

SPOTLIGHT ON BEER LABELS: CASE 2.2

Bad Frog Brewery, Inc. v. New York State Liquor Authority

United States Court of Appeals, Second Circuit, 134 F.3d 87 (1998).

FACTS Bad Frog Brewery, Inc., makes and sells alcoholic beverages. Some of the beverages feature labels with a drawing of a frog making the gesture generally known as "giving the finger." Renaissance Beer Company was Bad Frog's authorized New York distributor. Renaissance applied to the New York State Liquor Authority (NYSLA) for brand label approval, as required by state law before the beer could be sold in New York. The NYSLA denied the application, in part, because "the label could appear in grocery and convenience stores, with obvious exposure on the shelf to children of tender age." Bad Frog filed a suit in a federal district court against the NYSLA, asking for, among other things, an injunction against the denial of the application. The court granted summary judgment in favor of the NYSLA. Bad Frog appealed to the U.S. Court of Appeals for the Second Circuit.

ISSUE Was the NYSLA's ban of Bad Frog's beer labels a reasonable restriction on commercial speech?

Can a label be too offensive?

Eric Isselee/ShutterStock.com

DECISION No. The U.S. Court of Appeals for the Second Circuit reversed the judgment of the district court and remanded the case for judgment to be entered in favor of Bad Frog.

REASON The appellate court held that the NYSLA's denial of Bad Frog's application violated the First Amendment. The ban on the use of the labels lacked a "reasonable fit" with the state's interest in shielding minors from vulgarity. In addition, the NYSLA did not adequately consider alternatives to the ban. The court acknowledged that the NYSLA's interest "in protecting children from vulgar and profane advertising" was "substantial." The question was whether banning Bad Frog's labels "directly advanced" that interest. "In view of the wide currency of vulgar displays throughout contemporary society, including comic books targeted directly at children, barring such displays from labels for alcoholic beverages cannot realistically be expected to reduce children's exposure to such displays to any significant degree."

Continues

The court concluded that a commercial speech limitation must be "part of a substantial effort to advance a valid state interest, not merely the removal of a few grains of offensive sand from a beach of vulgarity." Finally, as to whether the ban on the labels was more extensive than necessary to serve this interest, the court pointed out that there were "numerous less intrusive alternatives." For example, the NYSLA could have placed restrictions on the permissible locations where the appellant's products could be displayed in stores.

WHAT IF THE FACTS WERE DIFFERENT? *If Bad Frog had sought to use the label to market toys instead of beer, would the court's ruling likely have been the same? Explain your answer.*

Unprotected Speech The United States Supreme Court has made it clear that certain types of speech will not be given any protection under the First Amendment. Speech that harms the good reputation of another, or defamatory speech (defamation is discussed in the torts chapter), will not be protected.

Speech that violates criminal laws (such as threatening speech) is not constitutionally protected. (See this chapter's *Adapting the Law to the Online Environment* for a discussion of when threats made on social media become unprotected speech.) Other unprotected speech includes "fighting words," or words that are likely to incite others to respond violently.

Obscenity. The First Amendment, as interpreted by the Supreme Court, also does not protect obscene speech. Numerous state and federal statutes make it a crime to disseminate and possess obscene materials, including child pornography. Objectively defining obscene speech has proved difficult, however. And, obviously, it is difficult to prohibit the dissemination of obscenity and pornography online.

Most of Congress's attempts to pass legislation protecting minors from pornographic materials on the Internet have been struck down on First Amendment grounds when challenged in court. One exception was a law that requires schools public schools and libraries to install **filtering software** on computers to keep children from accessing adult content.[20] Such software is designed to prevent persons from viewing certain Web sites based on a site's Internet address or its **meta tags,** or key words. The Supreme Court held that the act does not unconstitutionally burden free speech because it is flexible and libraries can disable the filters for any patrons who ask.[21]

Virtual Child Pornography. Another exception is a law that makes it a crime to intentionally distribute *virtual child pornography*—which uses computer-generated images, not actual people—without indicating that it is computer-generated.[22] In a case challenging the law's constitutionality, the Supreme Court held that the statute was valid because it does not prohibit a substantial amount of protected speech.[23] Nevertheless, because of the difficulties of policing the Internet, as well as the constitutional complexities of prohibiting online obscenity through legislation, it remains a problem worldwide.

2–2c The First Amendment—Freedom of Religion

The First Amendment states that the government may neither establish any religion nor prohibit the free exercise of religious practices. The first part of this constitutional provision is referred to as the *establishment clause,* and the second part is known as the *free exercise*

Filtering Software A computer program that is designed to block access to certain Web sites, based on their content. The software blocks the retrieval of a site whose URL or key words are on a list within the program.

Meta Tag A key word in a document that can serve as an index reference to the document. On the Web, search engines return results based, in part, on the tags in Web documents.

---

20. Children's Internet Protection Act (CIPA), 17 U.S.C. Sections 1701–1741.
21. *United States v. American Library Association*, 539 U.S. 194, 123 S.Ct. 2297, 156 L.Ed.2d 221 (2003).
22. The Prosecutorial Remedies and Other Tools to End the Exploitation of Children Today Act (Protect Act), 18 U.S.C. Section 2252A(a)(5)(B).
23. *United States v. Williams*, 553 U.S. 285, 128 S.Ct. 1830, 170 L.Ed.2d 650 (2008).

ADAPTING LAW TO THE ONLINE ENVIRONMENT

Should Threats Made on Facebook Be Considered Free Speech?

Many people say things on social media that they do not mean. Often, their statements are full of rage toward another person, a company, or a workplace—especially after a relationship ends or a firing occurs. Are such postings illegal, or are they protected as free speech? That depends on whether the statements constitute a true threat.

Under a federal statute, anyone who "transmits in interstate or foreign commerce any communication containing any threat to kidnap any person or any threat to injure the person of another" has committed a crime.[a] A conviction under this law can result in fines and/or imprisonment for up to five years. Because the Internet is obviously interstate, a person who communicates threats to kidnap or injure another via the Internet can potentially be convicted.

What Is a True Threat?

A true threat is a statement in which the speaker means to communicate a serious intent to commit an unlawful, violent act against a particular person or group. The First Amendment does not protect speech that contains true threats, and thus the government can prohibit them.

Courts have differed on whether the standard for determining whether a statement is a true threat should be objective or subjective. The majority of courts apply

a. 18 U.S.C. Section 875(c).

an objective standard. Under this standard, the speaker must "knowingly and willfully" transmit a communication that a reasonable (or objective) person would find threatening. A subjective standard requires that the speaker must personally (subjectively) intend not only to transmit the communication but also to threaten the victim. Since subjective intent can be difficult to determine, this standard makes it more difficult to prosecute a person for posting threats on the Internet.

Anthony Elonis's Story

Anthony Elonis's wife, Tara, left him in 2010 and took their two young children. Elonis was upset and experienced problems at work. A coworker, Amber Morrissey, filed five sexual harassment reports against him. When Elonis posted a photograph of himself in a Halloween costume holding a knife to Morrissey's neck, he was fired from his job.

Elonis then began posting violent statements on his Facebook page, mostly focusing on his former wife. "There's one way to love you," he wrote, "but a thousand ways to kill you. I'm not going to rest until your body is a mess, soaked in blood and dying from all the little cuts. Hurry up and die, bitch. . . ." Based on statements like these, the court issued a protective order to Tara. But Elonis continued to post statements about killing his wife and eventually was arrested and prosecuted for his online posts.

Were the Facebook Posts Free Speech?

At trial, Elonis claimed the Facebook posts were rap lyrics, inspired by Eminem, which were a "therapeutic" way to deal with his problems. Elonis argued that he did not mean to seriously threaten Tara. (Tara testified, however, that Elonis had not listened to rap music during their marriage.)

Elonis was convicted of violating the statute after a jury trial and ordered to serve four years in prison. He appealed, and a federal appellate court affirmed his conviction.[b] He appealed to the United States Supreme Court, which reversed and remanded the case for further proceedings. The Court ruled that it is not enough that a reasonable person might view the defendant's Facebook posts as threats (which is the negligence standard applied by the lower court). Elonis must have intended to issue threats or known that his statements would be viewed as threats to be convicted of a crime.[c]

CRITICAL THINKING

- When should a statement made on social media be considered a true threat?

b. *United States v. Elonis*, 730 F.3d 321 (3d Cir. 2013); *cert.* granted, 134 S.Ct. 2819 (2014).
c. *Elonis v. United States*, ___ U.S. ___, 135 S.Ct. 2001, ___ L.Ed.2d ___ (2015).

clause. Government action, both federal and state, must be consistent with this constitutional mandate.

The Establishment Clause

The **establishment clause** prohibits the government from establishing a state-sponsored religion, as well as from passing laws that promote (aid or endorse) religion or show a preference for one religion over another. Although the establishment clause involves the separation of church and state, it does not require a complete separation.

Applicable Standard. Establishment clause cases often involve such issues as the legality of allowing or requiring school prayers, using state-issued vouchers to pay tuition at religious schools, and teaching creation theories versus evolution in public schools. Federal or state

Establishment Clause The provision in the First Amendment that prohibits the government from establishing any state-sponsored religion or enacting any law that promotes religion or favors one religion over another.

KNOW THIS

The free exercise clause applies only to the actions of the state and federal governments, not to private employers. Private employers may nonetheless be required to accommodate their employees' religious beliefs.

This large cross on Mount Soledad can be viewed by freeway drivers in San Diego. Because the land on which it sits became public property, should it be removed as a violation of the establishment clause?

Free Exercise Clause The provision in the First Amendment that prohibits the government from interfering with people's religious practices or forms of worship.

laws that do not promote or place a significant burden on religion are constitutional even if they have some impact on religion. For a government law or policy to be constitutional, it must not have the primary effect of promoting or inhibiting religion.

Religious Displays. Religious displays on public property have often been challenged as violating the establishment clause, and the United States Supreme Court has ruled on a number of such cases. Generally, the Court has focused on the proximity of the religious display to nonreligious symbols, such as reindeer and candy canes, or to symbols from different religions, such as a menorah (a nine-branched candelabrum used in celebrating Hanukkah). The Supreme Court eventually took a slightly different approach when it held that public displays having historical, as well as religious, significance do not necessarily violate the establishment clause.[24]

CASE EXAMPLE 2.10 Mount Soledad is a prominent hill near San Diego. There has been a forty-foot cross on top of Mount Soledad since 1913. In the 1990s, a war memorial was constructed next to the cross that included six walls listing the names of veterans. The site was privately owned until 2006, when Congress authorized the property's transfer to the federal government "to preserve a historically significant war memorial."

Steve Trunk and the Jewish War Veterans filed lawsuits claiming that the cross display violated the establishment clause because it endorsed the Christian religion. A federal appellate court agreed, finding that the primary effect of the memorial as a whole sent a strong message of endorsement and exclusion (of non-Christian veterans). The court noted that although not all cross displays at war memorials violate the establishment clause, the cross in this case physically dominated the site. Additionally, the cross was originally dedicated to religious purposes, had a long history of religious use, and was the only portion visible to drivers on the freeway below.[25] ▪

The Free Exercise Clause The **free exercise clause** guarantees that people can hold any religious beliefs they want or can have no religious beliefs. The constitutional guarantee of personal religious freedom restricts only the actions of the government, however, and not those of individuals or private businesses.

Restrictions Must Be Necessary. The government must have a compelling state interest for restricting the free exercise of religion, and the restriction must be the only way to further that interest. **CASE EXAMPLE 2.11** Members of a particular Mennonite church must use horses and buggies for transportation, but they can use tractors to take their agricultural products to market. Their religion requires the tractors to have steel cleats on the tires, and they drove tractors with cleats on county roads for many years. Then the county passed an ordinance that prohibited the use of steel cleats because the cleats tend to damage newly surfaced roads.

When a member of the church received a citation for driving a tractor with cleats, he claimed that the ordinance violated the church's right to freely exercise its religion. Ultimately, the court ruled in his favor. The county had not met its burden of showing that the ordinance served a compelling state interest and was the least restrictive means of attaining that interest. There was no evidence of how much the cleats harmed the roads, other events also harmed the roads, and the county had allowed the cleats to be used for many years. Therefore, the ordinance was not carefully tailored to achieve the stated objective of road preservation.[26] ▪

In the following case, the United States Supreme Court had to decide whether a prison's grooming policy violated an inmate's exercise of his religion.

---

24. See *Van Orden v. Perry*, 545 U.S. 677, 125 S.Ct. 2854, 162 L.Ed.2d 607 (2005). The Court held that a six-foot-tall monument of the Ten Commandments on the Texas state capitol grounds did not violate the establishment clause because the Ten Commandments had historical significance.
25. *Trunk v. City of San Diego*, 629 F.3d 1099 (9th Cir. 2011).
26. *Mitchell County v. Zimmerman*, 810 N.W.2d 1 (Iowa Sup.Ct. 2012).

CASE 2.3

Holt v. Hobbs

United States Supreme Court, __ U.S. __, 135 S.Ct. 853, __ L.Ed.2d __ (2015).

FACTS Gregory Holt, an inmate in an Arkansas state prison, is a devout Muslim who wished to grow a beard in accord with his religious beliefs. The Arkansas Department of Correction prohibited inmates from growing beards (except for medical reasons). Holt asked for an exemption on religious grounds. Prison officials denied his request.

Holt filed a suit in a federal district court against Ray Hobbs, the director of the department, and others. Holt's lawsuit claimed that the restriction was a violation of the Religious Land Use and Institutionalized Persons Act of 2000 (RLUIPA), which governs the exercise of religion by prison inmates. The defendants argued that beards compromise prison safety because they can hide contraband and because an inmate can quickly shave his beard to disguise his identity. The court dismissed the suit. On appeal, the U.S. Court of Appeals for the Eighth Circuit affirmed the dismissal. Hobbs appealed to the United States Supreme Court.

ISSUE Does the department's grooming policy with respect to Holt's beard violate the RLUIPA and his right to freely exercise his religion?

DECISION Yes. The United States Supreme Court reversed the ruling of the lower court and remanded the case for further proceedings. The Supreme Court held that "the Department's grooming

Can prison policy prevent a devout Muslim from keeping a short beard?

iStockPhoto.com/menonsstocks

policy violates RLUIPA insofar as it prevents [Holt] from growing a 1/2-inch beard in accordance with his religious beliefs."

REASON The RLUIPA prohibits a state from taking any action that substantially burdens the religious exercise of an institutionalized person unless the action is the least restrictive means of furthering a compelling governmental interest. In this case, the department's policy substantially burdened Holt's exercise of his religion. The Court doubted that the prohibition against the beard furthered the department's compelling interest in stopping the flow of contraband. "An item of contraband would have to be very small indeed to be concealed by a 1/2-inch beard." And the department did not show that its policy was the least restrictive means of furthering its compelling interest. The department could "satisfy its security concerns by simply searching [Holt's] beard. The Department already searches prisoners' hair and clothing." Finally, the department could solve the identity problem by photographing all inmates periodically to record changes in their appearance.

CRITICAL THINKING—Legal Consideration *Most states and the federal government permit inmates to grow 1/2-inch beards. Would the policies followed at these institutions be relevant in determining the need for a beard restriction in this case? Discuss.*

Public Welfare Exception. When religious *practices* work against public policy and the public welfare, the government can act. For instance, the government can require that a child receive certain types of vaccinations or receive medical treatment when the child's life is in danger—regardless of the child's or parent's religious beliefs.

In other words, when public safety is an issue, an individual's religious beliefs often must give way to the government's interests in protecting the public. **EXAMPLE 2.12** According to the Muslim faith, a woman should not appear in public without a scarf, known as a *hijab*, over her head. Due to public safety concerns, many courts today do not allow the wearing of any headgear (hats or scarves) in courtrooms. ■

2-3 Due Process and Equal Protection

Two other constitutional guarantees of great significance to Americans are mandated by the due process clauses of the Fifth and Fourteenth Amendments and the equal protection clause of the Fourteenth Amendment.

LEARNING OBJECTIVE 5

Where in the Constitution can the due process clause be found?

2-3a **Due Process**

Both the Fifth and the Fourteenth Amendments provide that no person shall be deprived "of life, liberty, or property, without due process of law." The **due process clause** of each of these constitutional amendments has two aspects—procedural and substantive. Note that the due process clause applies to "legal persons," such as corporations, as well as to individuals.

Procedural Due Process   Procedural due process requires that any government decision to take life, liberty, or property must be made fairly. This means that the government must give a person proper notice and an opportunity to be heard. The government must also use fair procedures in determining whether a person will be subjected to punishment or have some burden imposed on him or her.

Fair procedure has been interpreted as requiring that the person have at least an opportunity to object to a proposed action before a fair, neutral decision maker (who need not be a judge). **EXAMPLE 2.13** Doyle Burns, a nursing student in Kansas, poses for a photograph standing next to a placenta used as a lab specimen. Although she quickly deletes the photo from her library, it ends up on Facebook. When the director of nursing sees the photo, Burns is expelled. She sues for reinstatement and wins. The school violated Burns's due process rights by expelling her from the nursing program for taking a photo without giving her an opportunity to present her side to school authorities. ■

PREVENTING LEGAL DISPUTES

Many of the constitutional protections discussed in this chapter have become part of our culture in the United States. Due process, especially procedural due process, has become synonymous with what Americans consider "fair." For this reason, if you wish to avoid legal disputes, consider giving due process to anyone who might object to your business decisions or actions, whether that person is an employee, a partner, an affiliate, or a customer. For instance, provide ample notice of new policies to all affected persons, and give them at least an opportunity to express their opinions on the matter. Providing an opportunity to be heard is often the ideal way to make people feel that they are being treated fairly. People are less likely to sue a businessperson or firm that they believe is fair and listens to both sides of an issue.

Substantive Due Process   Substantive due process focuses on the content of the legislation rather than the fairness of the procedures. Substantive due process limits what the government may do in its legislative and executive capacities. Legislation must be fair and reasonable in content and must further a legitimate governmental objective. Only when official conduct is arbitrary or shocks the conscience, however, will it rise to the level of violating substantive due process.

If a law or other governmental action limits a fundamental right, the courts will hold that it violates substantive due process unless it promotes a compelling or overriding state interest. Fundamental rights include interstate travel, privacy, voting, marriage and family, and all First Amendment rights. Thus, for example, a state must have a substantial reason for taking any action that infringes on a person's free speech rights.

In situations not involving fundamental rights, a law or action does not violate substantive due process if it rationally relates to any legitimate governmental end. It is almost impossible for a law or action to fail the "rationality" test. Under this test, almost any government regulation of business will be upheld as reasonable.

2-3b **Equal Protection**

Under the Fourteenth Amendment, a state may not "deny to any person within its jurisdiction the equal protection of the laws." The United States Supreme Court has used the due process clause of the Fifth Amendment to make the **equal protection clause** applicable to the federal government as well. Equal protection means that the government must treat similarly situated individuals in a similar manner.

Equal protection, like substantive due process, relates to the substance of the law or other governmental action. When a law or action limits the liberty of all persons to do something, it may violate substantive due process. When a law or action limits the liberty of some persons but not others, it may violate the equal protection clause. **EXAMPLE 2.14** If a law prohibits all advertising on the sides of trucks, it raises a substantive due process question. If the law makes an exception to allow truck owners to advertise their own businesses, it raises an equal protection issue. ■

In an equal protection inquiry, when a law or action distinguishes between or among individuals, the basis for the distinction—that is, the classification—is examined. Depending on the classification, the courts apply different levels of scrutiny, or "tests," to determine whether the law or action violates the equal protection clause. The courts use one of three standards: strict scrutiny, intermediate scrutiny, or the "rational basis" test.

Strict Scrutiny If a law or action prohibits or inhibits some persons from exercising a fundamental right, the law or action will be subject to "strict scrutiny" by the courts. A classification based on a *suspect trait*—such as race, national origin, or citizenship status—will also be subject to strict scrutiny. Under this standard, the classification must be necessary to promote a *compelling government interest*.

Compelling state interests include remedying past unconstitutional or illegal discrimination, but do not include correcting the general effects of "society's discrimination." **EXAMPLE 2.15** For a city to give preference to minority applicants in awarding construction contracts, it normally must identify past unconstitutional or illegal discrimination against minority construction firms. Because the policy is based on suspect traits (race and national origin), it will violate the equal protection clause *unless* it is necessary to promote a compelling state interest. ■ Generally, few laws or actions survive strict-scrutiny analysis by the courts.

Equal Protection Clause

The provision in the Fourteenth Amendment that requires state governments to treat similarly situated individuals in a similar manner.

Annette Shaff/ShutterStock.com

Does the equal protection clause protect the homeless? If so, how?

Intermediate Scrutiny Another standard, that of "intermediate scrutiny," is applied in cases involving discrimination based on gender or legitimacy. Laws using these classifications must be substantially related to *important government objectives*. **EXAMPLE 2.16** An important government objective is preventing illegitimate teenage pregnancies. Because males and females are not similarly situated in this regard—only females can become pregnant—a law that punishes men but not women for statutory rape will be upheld even though it treats men and women unequally. ■

The state also has an important objective in establishing time limits (called *statutes of limitation*) for how long after an event a particular type of action can be brought. Nevertheless, the limitation period must be substantially related to the important objective of preventing fraudulent or outdated claims. **EXAMPLE 2.17** A state law requires illegitimate children to bring paternity suits within six years of their births in order to seek support from their fathers. A court will strike down this law if legitimate children are allowed to seek support from their parents at any time. This is because distinguishing between support claims on the basis of legitimacy is not related to the important government objective of preventing fraudulent or outdated claims. ■

The "Rational Basis" Test In matters of economic and social welfare, a classification will be considered valid if there is any conceivable "rational basis" on which the classification might relate to a *legitimate government interest*. It is almost impossible for a law or action to fail the rational basis test.

CASE EXAMPLE 2.18 A Kentucky statute prohibits businesses that sell substantial amounts of staple groceries or gasoline from applying for a license to sell wine and liquor. Maxwell's Pic-Pac (a grocer) filed suit against the state, alleging that the statute and the regulation were unconstitutional under the equal protection clause. The court applied the rational basis test and ruled that the statute and regulation were rationally related to a legitimate government interest in reducing access to products with high alcohol content. The court cited the problems caused by alcohol, including drunk driving, and noted that the state's interest in limiting access to such products extends to the general public. Grocery stores and gas stations pose a greater risk of exposing members of the public to alcohol. For these and other reasons, the state can restrict these places from selling wine and liquor.[27] ■

2-4 Privacy Rights

> "There was, of course, no way of knowing whether you were being watched at any given moment."
>
> **George Orwell**
> 1903–1950
> (English author, from his famous novel *1984*)

The U.S. Constitution does not explicitly mention a general right to privacy. In a 1928 Supreme Court case, *Olmstead v. United States,*[28] Justice Louis Brandeis stated in his dissent that the right to privacy is "the most comprehensive of rights and the right most valued by civilized men." The majority of the justices at that time, however, did not agree with Brandeis.

It was not until the 1960s that a majority on the Supreme Court endorsed the view that the Constitution protects individual privacy rights. In a landmark 1965 case, *Griswold v. Connecticut,*[29] the Supreme Court invalidated a Connecticut law that effectively prohibited the use of contraceptives on the ground that it violated the right to privacy. The Supreme Court held that a constitutional right to privacy was implied by the First, Third, Fourth, Fifth, and Ninth Amendments.

Today, privacy rights receive protection under various federal statutes as well as the U.S. Constitution. State constitutions and statutes also secure individuals' privacy rights, often to a significant degree. In addition, privacy rights are protected to an extent under tort law, consumer law, and employment law. In this section, we touch on some of the most important federal statutes protecting the privacy of individuals, as well as some current topics related to privacy rights. One such topic, the debate over marriage equality laws, is discussed in this chapter's *Managerial Strategy* feature.

2-4a Federal Privacy Legislation

In the last several decades, Congress has enacted a number of statutes that protect the privacy of individuals in various areas of concern. Most of these statutes deal with personal information collected by governments or private businesses.

In the 1960s, Americans were sufficiently alarmed by the accumulation of personal information in government files that they pressured Congress to pass laws permitting individuals to access their files. Congress responded by passing the Freedom of Information Act, which allows any person to request copies of any information on her or him contained in federal government files. Congress later enacted the Privacy Act, which also gives persons the right to access such information.

---

27. *Maxwell's Pic-Pac, Inc. v. Dehner,* 739 F.3d 936 (6th Cir. 2014).
28. 277 U.S. 438, 48 S.Ct. 564, 72 L.Ed. 944 (1928).
29. 381 U.S. 479, 85 S.Ct. 1678, 14 L.Ed.2d 510 (1965).

MANAGERIAL STRATEGY   Marriage Equality and the Constitution

Management Faces a Legal Issue

The debate over same-sex marriage has been raging across the country for years. The legal issues raised by marriage equality involve privacy rights and equal protection. Although marriage equality may not appear at first glance to be business related, it is an important legal issue for managers. Companies like Barilla Pasta, Chick-fil-A, Exxon Mobil, and Target Corporation have lost significant business for supporting anti-gay organizations and legislation.

What the Courts Say

Before 1996, federal law did not define marriage, and the U.S. government recognized any marriage that was recognized by a state. Then Congress passed the Defense of Marriage Act (DOMA), which explicitly defined marriage as a union of one man and one woman. DOMA was later challenged, and a number of federal courts found it to be unconstitutional in the context of bankruptcy, public employee benefits, and estate taxes. In 2013, the United States

Supreme Court struck down part of DOMA as unconstitutional.[a]

Today, once again, no federal law defines marriage, and marriage law is determined at the state level. Thirteen states prohibit same-sex marriages either in their constitutions or through state statutes that define marriage as a union between a man and a woman. Marriage laws that do not permit or recognize same-sex marriage have led to numerous court challenges.

Federal courts have become increasingly likely to invalidate state bans on same-sex marriage. In 2013, a federal district court held that Utah's same-sex marriage ban was unconstitutional.[b] In 2014, federal district courts in Arkansas, Mississippi, and Oklahoma struck down state same-sex marriage bans as unconstitutional.[c] Moreover, public sentiment on the issue has shifted, and more

states are recognizing the rights of same-sex couples. As of 2015, thirty-seven states, as well as the District of Columbia, had legalized same-sex marriage.

In 2015, the United States Supreme Court heard a consolidated appeal and determined that the remaining state-level prohibitions on same-sex marriage were unconstitutional. In a landmark decision, the Court ruled that the Fourteenth Amendment requires individual states to (1) issue marriage licenses to same-sex couples and (2) recognize same-sex marriages performed in other states.[d]

MANAGERIAL IMPLICATIONS

In this era of social networking, a company's policies can become public almost instantly—the boycotts of Target and Barilla were organized largely via Facebook. Consequently, businesspersons must carefully consider their policies toward employees and others who have different sexual orientations. At a minimum, company policies should clearly specify how same-sex partners will be treated in terms of family and medical leave, health insurance coverage, pensions, and other benefits.

---

a. *Windsor v. United States,* ___ U.S. ___, 133 S.Ct. 2675, 186 L.Ed.2d 808 (2013).
b. *Kitchen v. Herbert,* 961 F.Supp.2d 1181 (D.Utah 2013).
c. *Campaign for Southern Equality v. Bryant,* ___ F.Supp.2d ___, 2014 WL 6680570 (S.D. Miss. 2014); *Jernigan v. Crane,* ___ F.Supp.2d ___, 2014 WL 6685391; and *Bishop v. U.S. ex rel. Holder,* 962 F.Supp.2d 1252 (N.D. Okla. 2014).

---

d. *Obergefell v. Hodges,* ___ U.S. ___, ___ S.Ct. ___, ___ L.Ed.2d ___, 2015 WL 2473451 (2015).

In the 1990s, responding to the growing need to protect the privacy of individuals' health records—particularly computerized records—Congress passed the Health Insurance Portability and Accountability Act (HIPAA).[30] This act defines and limits the circumstances in which an individual's "protected health information" may be used or disclosed by health-care providers, health-care plans, and others.

These and other major federal laws protecting privacy rights are listed and briefly described in Exhibit 2–1. (See the *Business Application* at the end of this chapter for a discussion of some laws pertaining to the collection of personal information by businesses.)

2-4b The USA Patriot Act

The USA Patriot Act was passed by Congress in the wake of the terrorist attacks of September 11, 2001, and then reauthorized twice.[31] Unlike laws protecting privacy rights, the act

Most medical records are being put online. What law protects patients' right to privacy with respect to their online medical files?

---

30. HIPAA was enacted as Pub. L. No. 104-191 (1996) and is codified in 29 U.S.C.A. Sections 1181 *et seq.*
31. The Uniting and Strengthening America by Providing Appropriate Tools Required to Intercept and Obstruct Terrorism Act of 2001, also known as the USA Patriot Act, was enacted as Pub. L. No. 107-56 (2001). While the bulk of the Patriot Act is permanent law, the most controversial surveillance provisions must be reauthorized every four years and were reauthorized by Pub. L. No. 109-173 (2006) and Pub. L. No. 112-114 (2011).

Exhibit 2–1 Federal Legislation Relating to Privacy

TITLE OF ACT	PROVISIONS CONCERNING PRIVACY
Freedom of Information Act (1966)	Provides that individuals have a right to obtain access to information about them collected in government files.
Family and Educational Rights and Privacy Act (1974)	Limits access to computer-stored records of education-related evaluations and grades in private and public colleges and universities.
Privacy Act (1974)	Protects the privacy of individuals about whom the federal government has information. Regulates agencies' use and disclosure of data, and gives individuals access to and a means to correct inaccuracies.
Electronic Communications Privacy Act (1986)	Prohibits the interception of information communicated by electronic means.
Driver's Privacy Protection Act (1994)	Prevents states from disclosing or selling a driver's personal information without the driver's consent.
Health Insurance Portability and Accountability Act (1996)	Requires health-care providers and health-care plans to inform patients of their privacy rights and of how their personal medical information may be used. States that medical records may not be used for purposes unrelated to health care or disclosed without permission.
Financial Services Modernization Act (Gramm-Leach-Bliley Act) (1999)	Prohibits the disclosure of nonpublic personal information about a consumer to an unaffiliated third party unless strict disclosure and opt-out requirements are met.

expanded the government's ability to gather information about individuals. The Patriot Act has given government officials increased authority to monitor Internet activities (such as e-mail and Web site visits) and to gain access to personal financial information and student information. Law enforcement officials may now track the telephone and e-mail communications of one party to find out the identity of the other party or parties.

To gain access to these communications, the government must certify that the information likely to be obtained is relevant to an ongoing criminal investigation, but it does not need to provide proof of any wrongdoing. **EXAMPLE 2.19** In 2012, General David Petraeus, who ran the wars in Iraq and Afghanistan, resigned as director of the Central Intelligence Agency after his extramarital affair with Paula Broadwell, his biographer, became public. Apparently, after Petraeus broke off the affair with Broadwell, she sent harassing e-mails to another woman, who reported the harassment. The FBI investigated, accessed Petraeus's e-mail accounts, and discovered that he had communicated with Broadwell via messages left in a draft folder on his e-mail account. Although there was no evidence that Petraeus had done anything illegal, he was urged to resign and did so. ■

Reviewing . . . Constitutional Law

A state legislature enacted a statute that required any motorcycle operator or passenger on the state's highways to wear a protective helmet. Jim Alderman, a licensed motorcycle operator, sued the state to block enforcement of the law. Alderman asserted that the statute violated the equal protection clause because it placed requirements on motorcyclists that were not imposed on other motorists. Using the information presented in the chapter, answer the following questions.

1. Why does this statute raise equal protection issues instead of substantive due process concerns?

2. What are the three levels of scrutiny that the courts use in determining whether a law violates the equal protection clause?

3. Which level of scrutiny or test would apply to this situation? Why?

4. Applying this standard or test, is the helmet statute constitutional? Why or why not?

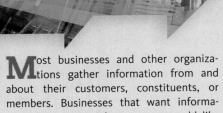

BUSINESS APPLICATION

Is "Pretexting" Illegal?*

Most businesses and other organizations gather information from and about their customers, constituents, or members. Businesses that want information about potential customers would like to obtain names from the mailing lists maintained by these organizations. Unless the owner of a list has a privacy policy that prohibits the sharing of such information without consent, a business may purchase the list and proceed to offer its product or service to all the people on it.

Locating potential customers in this manner may be completely legal, depending on how the information was obtained in the first place. Pretexting is a method of collecting personal information that skirts the boundary between legal and illegal.

What Is "Pretexting"?

A *pretext* is a false motive put forth to hide the real motive, and *pretexting* is the process of obtaining information by false means. The term *pretexting* was first used in the 1990s when scammers obtained Social Security numbers by claiming that they were from the Social Security Administration and that their computer had broken down. Pretexters may try to obtain personal data by claiming that they are taking a survey for a research firm, a political party, or even a charity. Then they ask for information such as the person's insurance or telephone company, where he or she banks, and perhaps the name of his or her broker. Once they obtain the information, the pretexters sell it to a data broker. The broker in turn sells it to someone else, who may be a legitimate businessperson, a private investigator, or an individual intent on identity theft.

Pretexting Legislation

In 1999, Congress passed the Gramm-Leach-Bliley Act, which made pretexting to obtain financial information illegal. Initially, it was not clear whether that law prohibited lying to obtain *nonfinancial* information for purposes other than identity theft.

To clarify the law on pretexting to gain access to phone records, Congress enacted the Telephone Records and Privacy Protection Act. This act makes it a federal crime to pretend to be someone else or to make false representations for the purpose of obtaining another person's confidential phone records. The act also prohibits the buying, selling, transferring, or receiving of such phone records without the phone owner's permission. The Federal Trade Commission investigates and prosecutes violators, who can be fined and sentenced to up to ten years in prison.

CHECKLIST for Providing or Securing Customer Information:

1. Make sure that your company has a privacy policy. If it does not, one should be created.

2. Never provide a third party with information unless your company's privacy policy specifically allows you to do so.

3. If you wish to acquire personal information on potential customers from a third party, make sure the data broker is legitimate, and find out how the information was acquired.

4. Treat all pretexting as illegal.

---

* This *Business Application* is not meant to substitute for the services of an attorney who is licensed to practice law in your state.

Key Terms

Bill of Rights 37
checks and balances 32
commerce clause 33
compelling government interest 39
due process clause 46
equal protection clause 47

establishment clause 43
federal form of government 32
filtering software 42
free exercise clause 44
meta tags 42
police powers 35

preemption 36
supremacy clause 36
symbolic speech 38

Chapter Summary: Constitutional Law

The Constitutional Powers of Government	The U.S. Constitution established a federal form of government, in which government powers are shared by the national government and the state governments. At the national level, government powers are divided among the legislative, executive, and judicial branches.
The Commerce Clause	1. *The expansion of national powers*—The commerce clause expressly permits Congress to regulate commerce. Over time, courts expansively interpreted this clause, thereby enabling the national government to wield extensive powers over the economic life of the nation. 2. *The commerce power today*—Today, the commerce power authorizes the national government, at least theoretically, to regulate almost every commercial enterprise in the United States. 3. *The regulatory powers of the states*—The Tenth Amendment reserves to the states all powers not expressly delegated to the national government. Under their police powers, state governments may regulate private activities in order to protect or promote the public order, health, safety, morals, and general welfare. 4. *The "dormant" commerce clause*—If state regulations substantially interfere with interstate commerce, they will be held to violate the "dormant" commerce clause of the U.S. Constitution. The positive aspect of the commerce clause, which gives the national government the exclusive authority to regulate interstate commerce, implies a "dormant" aspect—that the states do *not* have this power.
The Supremacy Clause	The U.S. Constitution provides that the Constitution, laws, and treaties of the United States are "the supreme Law of the Land." Whenever a state law directly conflicts with a federal law, the state law is rendered invalid.
Business and the Bill of Rights	The Bill of Rights, which consists of the first ten amendments to the U.S. Constitution, embodies a series of protections for individuals—and, in some instances, business entities—against various types of interference by the federal government. Today, most of the protections apply against state governments as well. Freedoms guaranteed by the First Amendment that affect businesses include the following: 1. *Freedom of speech*—Speech, including symbolic speech, is given the fullest possible protection by the courts. Corporate political speech and commercial speech also receive substantial protection under the First Amendment. Certain types of speech, such as defamatory speech and obscene speech, are not protected under the First Amendment. Government attempts to regulate unprotected forms of speech in the online environment have, to date, met with numerous challenges. 2. *Freedom of religion*—Under the First Amendment, the government may neither establish any religion (the establishment clause) nor prohibit the free exercise of religion (the free exercise clause).
Due Process and Equal Protection	1. *Due process*—Both the Fifth and the Fourteenth Amendments provide that no person shall be deprived of "life, liberty, or property, without due process of law." Procedural due process requires that any government decision to take life, liberty, or property must be made fairly, using fair procedures. Substantive due process focuses on the content of legislation. Generally, a law that limits a fundamental right violates substantive due process unless the law promotes a compelling state interest, such as public safety. 2. *Equal protection*—Under the Fourteenth Amendment, a law or action that limits the liberty of some persons but not others may violate the equal protection clause. Such a law may be upheld, however, if there is a rational basis for the discriminatory treatment of a given group or if the law substantially relates to an important government objective.
Privacy Rights	The Constitution does not contain a specific guarantee of a right to privacy, but such a right has been derived from guarantees found in several constitutional amendments. A number of federal statutes protect privacy rights. Privacy rights are also protected by many state constitutions and statutes, as well as under tort law.

Issue Spotters

1. Can a state, in the interest of energy conservation, ban all advertising by power utilities if conservation could be accomplished by less restrictive means? Why or why not? (See *Business and the Bill of Rights*.)

2. Suppose that a state imposes a higher tax on out-of-state companies doing business in the state than it imposes on in-state companies. Is this a violation of equal protection if the only reason for the tax is to protect the local firms from out-of-state competition? Explain. (See *Due Process and Equal Protection*.)

—**Check your answers to the *Issue Spotters* against the answers provided in Appendix D at the end of this text.**

Learning Objectives Check

1. What is the basic structure of the U.S. government?

2. What constitutional clause gives the federal government the power to regulate commercial activities among the various states?

3. What constitutional clause allows laws enacted by the federal government to take priority over conflicting state laws?

4. What is the Bill of Rights? What freedoms does the First Amendment guarantee?

5. Where in the Constitution can the due process clause be found?

—**Answers to the even-numbered *Learning Objectives Check* questions can be found in Appendix E at the end of this text.**

Business Scenarios and Case Problems

2–1. The Free Exercise Clause. Thomas worked in the nonmilitary operations of a large firm that produced both military and nonmilitary goods. When the company discontinued the production of nonmilitary goods, Thomas was transferred to the plant producing military equipment. Thomas left his job, claiming that it violated his religious principles to participate in the manufacture of goods to be used in destroying life. In effect, he argued, the transfer to the military equipment plant forced him to quit his job. He was denied unemployment compensation by the state because he had not been effectively "discharged" by the employer but had voluntarily terminated his employment. Did the state's denial of unemployment benefits to Thomas violate the free exercise clause of the First Amendment? Explain. (See *Business and the Bill of Rights*.)

2–2. Spotlight on Plagiarism—Due Process. The Russ College of Engineering and Technology of Ohio University announced in a press conference that it had found "rampant and flagrant plagiarism" in the theses of mechanical engineering graduate students. Faculty singled out for "ignoring their ethical responsibilities" included Jay Gunasekera, chair of the department. Gunasekera was prohibited from advising students. He filed a suit against Dennis Irwin, the dean of Russ College, for violating his due process rights. What does due process require in these circumstances? Why? [*Gunasekera v. Irwin*, 551 F.3d 461 (6th Cir. 2009)] (See *Due Process and Equal Protection*.)

2–3. Business Case Problem with Sample Answer—Establishment Clause. Judge James DeWeese hung a poster in his courtroom showing the Ten Commandments. The American Civil Liberties Union (ACLU) filed a suit, alleging that the poster violated the establishment clause. DeWeese responded that his purpose was not to promote religion but to express his view about "warring" legal philosophies—moral relativism and moral absolutism. "Our legal system is based on moral absolutes from divine law handed down by God through the Ten Commandments." Does this poster violate the establishment clause? Why or why not? [*American Civil Liberties Union of Ohio Foundation, Inc. v. DeWeese*, 633 F.3d 424 (6th Cir. 2011)] (See *Business and the Bill of Rights*.)

—**For a sample answer to Problem 2–3, go to Appendix F at the end of this text.**

2–4. The Dormant Commerce Clause. In 2001, Puerto Rico enacted a law that requires specific labels on cement sold in Puerto Rico and imposes fines for any violations of these requirements. The law prohibits the sale or distribution of cement manufactured outside Puerto Rico that does not carry a required label warning that the cement may not be used in government-financed construction projects. Antilles Cement Corp., a Puerto Rican firm that imports foreign cement, filed a complaint in federal court, claiming that this law violated the dormant commerce clause. (The dormant commerce clause doctrine applies not only to commerce among the states and U.S. territories, but also to international commerce.) Did the 2001 Puerto Rican law violate the dormant commerce clause? Why or why not? [*Antilles Cement Corp. v. Fortuno*, 670 F.3d 310 (1st Cir. 2012)] (See *The Constitutional Powers of Government*.)

2–5. Freedom of Speech. Mark Wooden sent e-mail to an alderwoman for the city of St. Louis. Attached was a nineteen-minute audio that compared her to the biblical character, Jezebel—she was a "bitch in the Sixth Ward," spending too much time with the rich and powerful and too little time with the poor. In a menacing, maniacal tone, Wooden said that he was "dusting off a sawed-off shotgun," called himself a "domestic terrorist," and referred to the assassination of President John F. Kennedy, the murder of a federal judge, and the shooting of Congresswoman Gabrielle Giffords. Feeling threatened, the alderwoman called the police. Wooden was convicted of harassment under a state criminal statute. Was this conviction unconstitutional under the First Amendment? Discuss. [*State v. Wooden*, 388 S.W.3d 522 (Mo. 2013)] (See *Business and the Bill of Rights*.)

2–6. Equal Protection. Abbott Laboratories licensed SmithKline Beecham Corp. to market an Abbott human immunodeficiency virus (HIV) drug in conjunction with one of SmithKline's drugs. Abbott then increased the price of its drug fourfold, forcing SmithKline to increase its prices and thereby driving business to Abbott's own combination drug. SmithKline filed a suit in a federal district court against Abbott. During jury selection, Abbott struck the only self-identified gay person among the potential jurors. (The pricing of HIV drugs is of considerable concern in the gay community.) Could the equal protection clause be applied to prohibit discrimination based on sexual orientation in jury selection? Discuss. [*SmithKline Beecham Corp. v. Abbott Laboratories*, 740 F.3d 471 (9th Cir. 2014)] (See *Due Process and Equal Protection*.)

2–7. Procedural Due Process. Robert Brown applied for admission to the University of Kansas School of Law. Brown answered "no" to questions on the application asking if he had a criminal history and acknowledged that a false answer constituted "cause for . . . dismissal." In fact, Brown had criminal convictions for domestic battery and driving under the influence. He was accepted for admission to the school. When school officials discovered his history, however, he was notified of their intent to dismiss him and given an opportunity to respond in writing. He demanded a hearing. The officials refused to grant Brown a hearing and then expelled him. Did the school's actions deny Brown due process? Discuss. [*Brown v. University of Kansas*, __ F.3d __, 2015 WL 150271 (10th Cir. 2015)] (See *Due Process and Equal Protection*.)

2–8. A Question of Ethics—Free Speech. Aric Toll owns and manages the Balboa Island Village Inn, a restaurant and bar in Newport Beach, California. Anne Lemen lives across from the Inn. Lemen complained to the authorities about the Inn's customers, whom she called "drunks" and "whores." Lemen told the Inn's bartender Ewa Cook that Cook "worked for Satan." She repeated her statements to potential customers, and the Inn's sales dropped more than 20 percent. The Inn filed a suit against Lemen. [*Balboa Island Village Inn, Inc. v. Lemen*, 40 Cal.4th 1141, 156 P.3d 339 (2007)] (See *Business and the Bill of Rights*.)

1. Are Lemen's statements about the Inn's owners and customers protected by the U.S. Constitution? In whose favor should the court rule? Why?

2. Did Lemen behave unethically in the circumstances of this case? Explain.

Critical Thinking and Writing Assignments

2–9. Business Law Writing. The United States Supreme Court has made it clear that the commerce clause applies not only to interstate commerce, but also to commerce that is purely intrastate. Today, the federal government has the power to regulate almost every commercial enterprise in the United States.

Write a page discussing what expanded federal government power over commerce means for commercial businesses that operate only within the borders of one state. Does it promote or discourage intrastate commerce? (See *The Constitutional Powers of Government*.)

2–10. Business Law Critical Thinking Group Assignment. For many years, New York City has had to deal with the vandalism and defacement of public property caused by unauthorized graffiti. In an effort to stop the damage, the city banned the sale of aerosol spray-paint cans and broad-tipped indelible markers to persons under twenty-one years of age. The new rules also prohibited people from possessing these items on property other than their own. Within a year, five people under age twenty-one were cited for violations of these regulations, and more than eight hundred individuals were arrested for actually making graffiti.

Lindsey Vincenty and other artists wished to create graffiti on legal surfaces, such as canvas, wood, and clothing. Unable to buy supplies in the city or to carry them in the city if they were bought elsewhere, Vincenty and others filed a lawsuit on behalf of themselves and other young artists against Michael Bloomberg, the city's mayor, and others. The plaintiffs claimed that, among other things, the new rules violated their right to freedom of speech. (See *The Constitutional Powers of Government*.)

1. One group will argue in favor of the plaintiffs and provide several reasons why the court should hold that the city's new rules violate the plaintiffs' freedom of speech.

2. Another group will develop a counterargument that outlines the reasons why the new rules do not violate free speech rights.

3. A third group will argue that the city's ban violates the equal protection clause because it applies only to persons under age twenty-one.

3

Courts and Alternative Dispute Resolution

"An eye for an eye will make the whole world blind."

MAHATMA GANDHI
1869–1948
(INDIAN POLITICAL AND SPIRITUAL LEADER)

Every society needs to have an established method for resolving disputes. Without one, as Mahatma Gandhi implied in the chapter-opening quotation, the biblical "eye for an eye" would lead to anarchy. This is particularly true in the business world—almost every businessperson will face a lawsuit at some time in his or her career. For this reason, anyone involved in business needs to have an understanding of court systems in the United States, as well as the various methods of dispute resolution that can be pursued outside the courts.

In this chapter, after examining the judiciary's overall role in the American governmental system, we discuss some basic requirements that must be met before a party may bring a lawsuit before a particular court. We then look at the court systems of the United States in some detail and, to clarify judicial procedures, follow a hypothetical case through a state court system. We also touch upon a current controversy involving the introduction of some Islamic law into certain U.S. courts.

Throughout this chapter, we indicate how court doctrines and procedures are being adapted to the needs of a cyber age. The chapter concludes with an overview of some alternative methods of settling disputes, including online dispute resolution.

LEARNING OBJECTIVES

The five Learning Objectives *below are designed to help improve your understanding of the chapter. After reading this chapter, you should be able to answer the following questions:*

1. What is judicial review? How and when was the power of judicial review established?

2. How are the courts applying traditional jurisdictional concepts to cases involving internet transactions?

3. What is the difference between the focus of a trial court and an appellate court?

4. What is discovery, and how does electronic discovery differ from traditional discovery?

5. What are three alternative methods of resolving disputes?

3-1 The Judiciary's Role in American Government

The body of American law includes the federal and state constitutions, statutes passed by legislative bodies, administrative law, and the case decisions and legal principles that form the common law. These laws would be meaningless, however, without the courts to interpret and apply them. This is the essential role of the judiciary—the courts—in the American governmental system: to interpret and apply the law.

3-1a Judicial Review

Judicial Review The process by which a court decides on the constitutionality of legislative enactments and actions of the executive branch.

As the branch of government entrusted with interpreting the laws, the judiciary can decide, among other things, whether the laws or actions of the other two branches are constitutional. The process for making such a determination is known as **judicial review.**

The power of judicial review enables the judicial branch to act as a check on the other two branches of government, in line with the checks-and-balances system established by the U.S. Constitution. (Today, nearly all nations with constitutional democracies, including Canada, France, and Germany, have some form of judicial review.)

3-1b The Origins of Judicial Review in the United States

The U.S. Constitution does not mention judicial review (although many constitutional scholars believe that the founders intended the judiciary to have this power). How was the doctrine of judicial review established? See this chapter's *Landmark in the Law* feature for the answer.

James Madison (1751–1836) was Thomas Jefferson's secretary of state at the time of the case that established the power of judicial review. What is judicial review?

3-2 Basic Judicial Requirements

Before a court can hear a lawsuit, certain requirements must first be met. These requirements relate to jurisdiction, venue, and standing to sue. We examine each of these important concepts here.

3-2a Jurisdiction

Jurisdiction The authority of a court to hear and decide a specific case.

In Latin, *juris* means "law," and *diction* means "to speak." Thus, "the power to speak the law" is the literal meaning of the term **jurisdiction.** Before any court can hear a case, it must have jurisdiction over the person or company against whom the suit is brought (the defendant) or over the property involved in the suit. The court must also have jurisdiction over the subject matter of the dispute.

Jurisdiction over Persons or Property   Generally, a court with jurisdiction over a particular geographic area can exercise personal jurisdiction (*in personam* jurisdiction) over any person or business that resides in that area. A state trial court, for instance, normally has jurisdictional authority over residents (including businesses) in a particular area of the state, such as a county or district. A state's highest court (often called the state supreme court)[1] has jurisdiction over all residents of that state.

A court can also exercise jurisdiction over property that is located within its boundaries. This kind of jurisdiction is known as *in rem* jurisdiction, or "jurisdiction over the thing." **EXAMPLE 3.1** A dispute arises over the ownership of a boat in dry dock in Fort Lauderdale, Florida. The boat is owned by an Ohio resident, over whom a Florida court normally cannot exercise personal jurisdiction. The other party to the dispute is a resident of Nebraska.

---

1. As will be discussed shortly, a state's highest court is frequently referred to as the state supreme court, but there are exceptions. For example, in New York, the supreme court is a trial court.

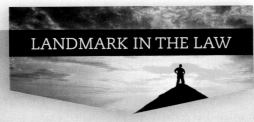

LANDMARK IN THE LAW

Marbury v. Madison (1803)

The power of judicial review was established in the Supreme Court's decision in the case of *Marbury v. Madison.*[a] Although the decision is widely viewed as a cornerstone of constitutional law, the case had its origins in early U.S. politics. When Thomas Jefferson defeated the incumbent president, John Adams, in the presidential elections of 1800, Adams feared the Jeffersonians' antipathy toward business and toward a strong national government. Adams thus rushed to "pack" the judiciary with loyal Federalists (those who believed in a strong national government) by appointing what came to be called "midnight judges" just before he left office. But Adams's secretary of state (John Marshall) was able to deliver only forty-two of the fifty-nine judicial appointment letters by the time Jefferson took over as president. Jefferson refused to order his secretary of state, James Madison, to deliver the remaining commissions.

MARSHALL'S DILEMMA William Marbury and three others to whom the commissions had not been delivered sought a writ of *mandamus* (an order directing a government official to fulfill a duty) from the United States Supreme Court, as authorized by the Judiciary Act in 1789. As fate would have it, John Marshall had just been appointed as chief justice of the Supreme Court. Marshall faced a dilemma: If he ordered the commissions delivered, the new secretary of state (Madison) could simply refuse to deliver them—and the Court had no way to compel him to act. At the same time, if Marshall simply allowed the new administration to do as it wished, the Court's power would be severely eroded.

MARSHALL'S DECISION Marshall masterfully fashioned his decision to enlarge the power of the Supreme Court by affirming the Court's power of judicial review. He stated, "It is emphatically the province and duty of the Judicial Department to say what the law is. . . . If two laws conflict with each other, the Courts must decide on the operation of each. . . . [I]f both [a] law and the Constitution apply to a particular case, . . . the Court must determine which of these conflicting rules governs the case."

Marshall's decision did not require anyone to do anything. He concluded that the highest court did not have the power to issue a writ of *mandamus* in this particular case. Although the Judiciary Act specified that the Supreme Court could issue writs of *mandamus* as part of its original jurisdiction, Article III of the Constitution, which spelled out the Court's original jurisdiction, did not mention such writs. Because Congress did not have the right to expand the Supreme Court's jurisdiction, this section of the Judiciary Act was unconstitutional—and thus void. The *Marbury* decision stands to this day as a judicial and political masterpiece.

APPLICATION TO TODAY'S WORLD *Since the* Marbury v. Madison *decision, the power of judicial review has remained unchallenged and today is exercised by both federal and state courts. If the courts did not have the power of judicial review, the constitutionality of Congress's acts could not be challenged in court—a congressional statute would remain law unless changed by Congress. The courts of other countries that have adopted a constitutional democracy often cite this decision as a justification for judicial review.*

---

a. 5 U.S. (1 Cranch) 137, 2 L.Ed. 60 (1803).

In this situation, a lawsuit concerning the boat could be brought in a Florida state court on the basis of the court's *in rem* jurisdiction. ■

Long Arm Statutes. Under the authority of a state **long arm statute,** a court can exercise personal jurisdiction over certain out-of-state defendants based on activities that took place within the state. Before exercising long arm jurisdiction over a nonresident, however, the court must be convinced that the defendant had sufficient contacts, or *minimum contacts,* with the state to justify the jurisdiction.[2] Generally, this means that the defendant must have enough of a connection to the state for the judge to conclude that it is fair for the state to exercise power over the defendant.

If an out-of-state defendant caused an automobile accident or sold defective goods within the state, for instance, a court will usually find that minimum contacts exist to exercise jurisdiction over that defendant. **CASE EXAMPLE 3.2** After an Xbox game system caught fire in Bonnie Broquet's home in Texas and caused substantial personal injuries, Broquet filed a lawsuit in a Texas court against Ji-Haw Industrial Company, a nonresident company that made

> **Long Arm Statute** A state statute that permits a state to exercise jurisdiction over nonresident defendants.

---

2. The minimum-contacts standard was established in *International Shoe Co. v. State of Washington,* 326 U.S. 310, 66 S.Ct. 154, 90 L.Ed. 95 (1945).

Suppose that a young gamer is injured because Microsoft's Xbox, shown above, released an electrical shock. Whom can the parents sue?

the Xbox components. Broquet alleged that Ji-Haw's components were defective and had caused the fire. Ji-Haw argued that the Texas court lacked jurisdiction over it, but a state appellate court held that the Texas long arm statute authorized the exercise of jurisdiction over the out-of-state defendant.[3] ▪

Similarly, a state may exercise personal jurisdiction over a nonresident defendant who is sued for breaching a contract that was formed within the state. This is true even when that contract was negotiated over the phone or through correspondence.

Corporate Contacts. Because corporations are considered legal persons, courts use the same principles to determine whether it is fair to exercise jurisdiction over a corporation. A corporation normally is subject to personal jurisdiction in the state in which it is incorporated, has its principal office, and is doing business. Courts apply the minimum-contacts test to determine if they can exercise jurisdiction over out-of-state corporations.

The minimum-contacts requirement is usually met if the corporation advertises or sells its products within the state, or places its goods into the "stream of commerce" with the intent that the goods be sold in the state. **EXAMPLE 3.3** A business is incorporated under the laws of Maine but has a branch office and manufacturing plant in Georgia. The corporation also advertises and sells its products in Georgia. These activities would likely constitute sufficient contacts with the state of Georgia to allow a Georgia court to exercise jurisdiction over the corporation. ▪

Some corporations do not sell or advertise products or place any goods in the stream of commerce. Determining what constitutes minimum contacts in these situations can be more difficult. **CASE EXAMPLE 3.4** Independence Plating Corporation is a New Jersey corporation that provides metal-coating services. Its only office and all of its personnel are located in New Jersey, and it does not advertise out of state. Independence had a long-standing business relationship with Southern Prestige Industries, Inc., a North Carolina company. Eventually, Southern Prestige filed suit in North Carolina against Independence for defective workmanship. Independence argued that North Carolina did not have jurisdiction over it, but the court held that Independence had sufficient minimum contacts with the state to justify jurisdiction. The two parties had exchanged thirty-two separate purchase orders in a period of less than twelve months.[4] ▪

Jurisdiction over Subject Matter Jurisdiction over subject matter is a limitation on the types of cases a court can hear. In both the federal and state court systems, there are courts of *general* (unlimited) *jurisdiction* and courts of *limited jurisdiction*. An example of a court of general jurisdiction is a state trial court or a federal district court.

An example of a state court of limited jurisdiction is a probate court. **Probate courts** are state courts that handle only matters relating to the transfer of a person's assets and obligations after that person's death, including matters relating to the custody and guardianship of children. An example of a federal court of limited subject-matter jurisdiction is a bankruptcy court. **Bankruptcy courts** handle only bankruptcy proceedings, which are governed by federal bankruptcy law.

A court's jurisdiction over subject matter is usually defined in the statute or constitution creating the court. In both the federal and state court systems, a court's subject-matter jurisdiction can be limited by any of the following:

Probate Court A state court of limited jurisdiction that conducts proceedings relating to the settlement of a deceased person's estate.

Bankruptcy Court A federal court of limited jurisdiction that handles only bankruptcy proceedings, which are governed by federal bankruptcy law.

---

3. *Ji-Haw Industrial Co. v. Broquet*, 2008 WL 441822 (Tex.App.—San Antonio 2008).
4. *Southern Prestige Industries, Inc. v. Independence Plating Corp.*, 690 S.E.2d 768 (N.C.App. 2010).

1. The subject of the lawsuit.
2. The sum in controversy.
3. Whether the case involves a felony (a more serious type of crime) or a misdemeanor (a less serious type of crime).
4. Whether the proceeding is a trial or an appeal.

Original and Appellate Jurisdiction

The distinction between courts of original jurisdiction and courts of appellate jurisdiction normally lies in whether the case is being heard for the first time. Courts having original jurisdiction are courts of the first instance, or trial courts—that is, courts in which lawsuits begin, trials take place, and evidence is presented. In the federal court system, the *district courts* are trial courts. In the various state court systems, the trial courts are known by various names, as will be discussed shortly.

The key point here is that any court having original jurisdiction is normally known as a trial court. Courts having appellate jurisdiction act as reviewing courts, or appellate courts. In general, cases can be brought before appellate courts only on appeal from an order or a judgment of a trial court or other lower court.

Jurisdiction of the Federal Courts

Because the federal government is a government of limited powers, the jurisdiction of the federal courts is limited. Federal courts have subject-matter jurisdiction in two situations.

Federal Questions. Article III of the U.S. Constitution establishes the boundaries of federal judicial power. Section 2 of Article III states that "[t]he judicial Power shall extend to all Cases, in Law and Equity, arising under this Constitution, the Laws of the United States, and Treaties made, or which shall be made, under their Authority." This clause means that whenever a plaintiff's cause of action is based, at least in part, on the U.S. Constitution, a treaty, or a federal law, then a **federal question** arises, and the federal courts have jurisdiction.

Any lawsuit involving a federal question, such as a person's rights under the U.S. Constitution, can originate in a federal court. Note that in a case based on a federal question, a federal court will apply federal law.

> **Federal Question**
> A question that pertains to the U.S. Constitution, an act of Congress, or a treaty and provides a basis for federal jurisdiction in a case.

Diversity of Citizenship. Federal district courts can also exercise original jurisdiction over cases involving **diversity of citizenship.** The most common type of diversity jurisdiction requires *both* of the following: [5]

1. The plaintiff and defendant must be residents of different states.
2. The dollar amount in controversy must exceed $75,000.

> **Diversity of Citizenship**
> A basis for federal court jurisdiction over a lawsuit between citizens of different states or a lawsuit involving a U.S. citizen and a citizen of a different country.

For purposes of diversity jurisdiction, a corporation is a citizen of both the state in which it is incorporated and the state in which its principal place of business is located. A case involving diversity of citizenship can be filed in the appropriate federal district court. If the case starts in a state court, it can sometimes be transferred, or "removed," to a federal court. A large percentage of the cases filed in federal courts each year are based on diversity of citizenship.

As noted, a federal court will apply federal law in cases involving federal questions. In a case based on diversity of citizenship, in contrast, a federal court will apply the relevant state law (which is often the law of the state in which the court sits).

CASE EXAMPLE 3.5 Kelley Mala, a U.S. citizen of the Virgin Islands, was driving his powerboat near St. Thomas, Virgin Islands. He stopped at Crown Bay Marina to buy gas, and asked a Crown Bay attendant to watch his boat while the pump was running and he paid the cashier. Although the attendant turned off the pump, it malfunctioned. Gas overflowed and spilled

---

5. Diversity jurisdiction also exists in cases between (1) a foreign country and citizens of a state or of different states and (2) citizens of a state and citizens or subjects of a foreign country. These bases for diversity jurisdiction are less commonly used.

If a marina employee commits a negligent act while servicing a boat owned by someone whose legal residence is nearby, can the injured boat owner have the case removed to a federal court?

Concurrent Jurisdiction
Jurisdiction that exists when two different courts have the power to hear a case.

Exclusive Jurisdiction
Jurisdiction that exists when a case can be heard only in a particular court or type of court.

into Mala's boat and the water. Mala cleaned the gas off his boat with soap and water that the attendant provided. When he left the dock, his engine caught fire and exploded, severely burning him and destroying the boat.

Mala sued the marina for negligence in a federal district court in the Virgin Islands. He alleged that the court had diversity jurisdiction and requested a jury trial. (A plaintiff in a maritime case does not have a right to a jury trial unless the court has diversity jurisdiction.) The court found that Crown Bay—like the plaintiff—was a citizen of the Virgin Islands, and therefore, the court did not have diversity jurisdiction. A federal appellate court affirmed this decision. Mala had to sue the marina under admiralty law (law governing transportation on the seas and ocean waters) and did not have a right to a jury trial.[6] ▪

Exclusive versus Concurrent Jurisdiction   When both federal and state courts have the power to hear a case, as is true in lawsuits involving diversity of citizenship, **concurrent jurisdiction** exists. When cases can be tried only in federal courts or only in state courts, **exclusive jurisdiction** exists.

Federal courts have exclusive jurisdiction in cases involving federal crimes, bankruptcy, most patent and copyright claims, suits against the United States, and some areas of admiralty law. State courts also have exclusive jurisdiction over certain subject matter—for instance, divorce and adoption.

When concurrent jurisdiction exists, a party may bring a suit in either a federal court or a state court. A number of factors can affect the decision of whether to litigate in a federal or a state court, such as the availability of different remedies, the distance to the respective courthouses, or the experience or reputation of a particular judge.

A resident of a state other than the one with jurisdiction might also choose a federal court over a state court if he or she is concerned that a state court might be biased against an out-of-state plaintiff. In contrast, a plaintiff might choose to litigate in a state court if it has a reputation for awarding substantial amounts of damages or if the judge is perceived as being pro-plaintiff. The concepts of exclusive and concurrent jurisdiction are illustrated in Exhibit 3–1.

3–2b Jurisdiction in Cyberspace

LEARNING OBJECTIVE 2

How are the courts applying traditional jurisdictional concepts to cases involving Internet transactions?

The Internet's capacity to bypass political and geographic boundaries undercuts the traditional basis on which courts assert personal jurisdiction. As already discussed, for a court to compel a defendant to come before it, there must be at least minimum contacts—the presence of a salesperson within the state, for example. Today, however, courts frequently have to decide what constitutes sufficient minimum contacts when a defendant's only connection to a jurisdiction is through an ad on a Web site.

The "Sliding-Scale" Standard   The courts have developed a standard—called a "sliding-scale" standard—for determining when the exercise of jurisdiction over an out-of-state defendant is proper. The sliding-scale standard identifies three types of Internet business contacts and outlines the following rules for jurisdiction:

---

6. *Mala v. Crown Bay Marina, Inc.,* 704 F.3d 239 (2013).

Exhibit 3–1 **Exclusive and Concurrent Jurisdiction**

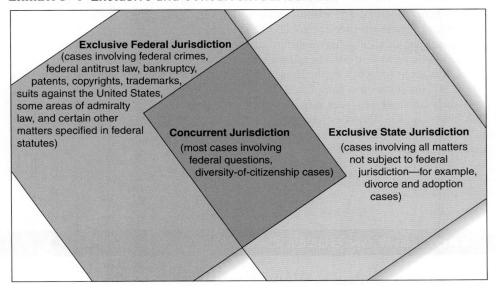

Exclusive Federal Jurisdiction
(cases involving federal crimes, federal antitrust law, bankruptcy, patents, copyrights, trademarks, suits against the United States, some areas of admiralty law, and certain other matters specified in federal statutes)

Concurrent Jurisdiction
(most cases involving federal questions, diversity-of-citizenship cases)

Exclusive State Jurisdiction
(cases involving all matters not subject to federal jurisdiction—for example, divorce and adoption cases)

1. When the defendant conducts *substantial business* over the Internet (such as contracts and sales), jurisdiction is proper. This is true whether the business is conducted with traditional computers, smartphones, or other means of Internet access.

2. When there is *some interactivity* through a Web site, jurisdiction may be proper, depending on the circumstances. Even a single contact can be sufficient to satisfy the minimum-contacts requirement in certain situations.

3. When a defendant merely engages in *passive advertising* on the Web, jurisdiction is never proper.[7]

   CASE EXAMPLE 3.6 A Louisiana resident, Daniel Crummey, purchased a used recreational vehicle (RV) from sellers in Texas after viewing photos of it on eBay. The sellers' statements on eBay claimed that "everything works great on this RV and will provide comfort and dependability for years to come. This RV will go to Alaska and back without problems!"

   Crummey picked up the RV in Texas, but on the drive home, the RV quit working. He filed a suit in Louisiana against the sellers alleging that the vehicle was defective, but the sellers claimed that the Louisiana court lacked jurisdiction. Because the sellers regularly used eBay to market and sell vehicles to remote parties and had sold this RV to a Louisiana buyer, the court found that jurisdiction was proper.[8] ▪

If you purchase a used RV outside your home state through an announcement on eBay, can you bring suit in your own state against the seller who lives in another state? Why or why not?

Those of you with an entrepreneurial spirit may be eager to establish Web sites to promote products and solicit orders. Be aware, however, that you can be sued in states in which you have *never* been physically present if you have had sufficient contacts with residents of those states over the Internet. Before you create a Web site that is the least bit interactive, you need to consult an attorney to find out whether you will be subjecting yourself to jurisdiction in every state. Becoming informed about the extent of your potential exposure to lawsuits in various locations is an important part of preventing litigation.

PREVENTING LEGAL DISPUTES

---

7. For a leading case on this issue, see *Zippo Manufacturing Co. v. Zippo Dot Com, Inc.,* 952 F.Supp. 1119 (W.D.Pa. 1997).

8. *Crummey v. Morgan,* 965 So.2d 497 (La.App.1 Cir. 2007). But note that a single sale on eBay does not necessarily confer jurisdiction. Jurisdiction depends on whether the seller regularly uses eBay as a means for doing business with remote buyers. See *Boschetto v. Hansing,* 539 F.3d 1011 (9th Cir. 2008).

International Jurisdictional Issues Because the Internet is global in scope, it raises international jurisdictional issues. The world's courts seem to be developing a standard that echoes the minimum-contacts requirement applied by U.S. courts.

Most courts are indicating that minimum contacts—doing business within the jurisdiction, for instance—are enough to compel a defendant to appear. The effect of this standard is that a business firm has to comply with the laws in any jurisdiction in which it targets customers for its products. This situation is complicated by the fact that many countries' laws on particular issues—such as free speech—are very different from U.S. laws.

The following case illustrates how federal courts apply a sliding-scale standard to determine if they can exercise jurisdiction over a foreign defendant whose only contact with the United States is through a Web site.

SPOTLIGHT ON GUCCI: CASE 3.1

Gucci America, Inc. v. Wang Huoqing

United States District Court, Northern District of California, 2011 WL 30972 (2011).

COMPANY PROFILE *Gucci America, Inc., a New York corporation headquartered in New York City, is part of Gucci Group, a global fashion firm with offices in China, France, Great Britain, Italy, and Japan. Gucci makes and sells high-quality luxury goods, including footwear, belts, sunglasses, handbags, wallets, jewelry, fragrances, and children's clothing. In connection with its products, Gucci uses twenty-one federally registered trademarks. Gucci also operates a number of boutiques, some of which are located in California.*

Gucci luxury leather products are often counterfeited. Can Gucci sue an Asian company in the United States, nonetheless?

iStockPhoto.com/narvikk

FACTS Wang Huoqing, a resident of the People's Republic of China, operates numerous Web sites. When Gucci discovered that Huoqing's Web sites were selling counterfeit goods—products that carried Gucci's trademarks but were not genuine Gucci articles—it hired a private investigator in San Jose, California, to buy goods from the Web sites. The investigator purchased a wallet that was labeled Gucci but was counterfeit.

Gucci filed a trademark infringement lawsuit against Huoqing in a federal district court in California seeking damages and an injunction to prevent further infringement. Huoqing was notified of the lawsuit via e-mail, but did not appear in court. Gucci asked the court to enter a default judgment—that is, a judgment entered when the defendant fails to appear. The court first had to determine whether it had personal jurisdiction over Huoqing based on the Internet sales.

ISSUE Could a U.S. federal court exercise personal jurisdiction over a resident of China whose only contact with the United States was through an interactive Web site that advertised and sold counterfeit goods?

DECISION Yes. The U.S. District Court for the Northern District of California held that it had personal jurisdiction over the foreign defendant, Huoqing. The court entered a default judgment against Huoqing and granted Gucci an injunction.

REASON The court reasoned that the due process clause allows a federal court to exercise jurisdiction over a defendant who has had sufficient minimum contacts with the court's forum—the place where the court exercises jurisdiction. Specifically, jurisdiction exists when (1) the nonresident defendant engages in some act or transaction with the forum "by which he purposefully avails himself of the privilege of conducting activities in the forum, thereby invoking the benefits and protections of its laws; (2) the claim must be one which arises out of or results from the defendant's forum-related activities; and (3) exercise of jurisdiction must be reasonable."

To determine whether Huoqing had purposefully conducted business activities in California, the court used a sliding-scale analysis. Under this analysis, passive Web sites do not create sufficient contacts for such a finding, but interactive sites may do so. Huoqing's Web sites were fully interactive. In addition, Gucci presented evidence that Huoqing had advertised and sold the counterfeited goods within the court's district, and that he had made one actual sale within the district—the sale to Gucci's private investigator.

WHAT IF THE FACTS WERE DIFFERENT? *Suppose that Gucci had not presented evidence that Huoqing made one actual sale through his Web site to a resident (the private investigator) of the court's district. Would the court still have found that it had personal jurisdiction over Huoqing? Why or why not?*

3–2c Venue

Jurisdiction has to do with whether a court has authority to hear a case involving specific persons, property, or subject matter. **Venue**[9] is concerned with the most appropriate physical location for a trial. Two state courts (or two federal courts) may have the authority to exercise jurisdiction over a case, but it may be more appropriate or convenient to hear the case in one court than in the other.

Basically, the concept of venue reflects the policy that a court trying a suit should be in the geographic neighborhood (usually the county) where the incident leading to the lawsuit occurred or where the parties involved in the lawsuit reside. Venue in a civil case typically is where the defendant resides, whereas venue in a criminal case normally is where the crime occurred. Pretrial publicity or other factors, though, may require a change of venue to another community, especially in criminal cases when the defendant's right to a fair and impartial jury has been impaired.

EXAMPLE 3.7 Police raid a compound of religious polygamists in Texas and remove many children from the ranch. Authorities suspect that some of the children were being sexually and physically abused. The raid receives a great deal of media attention, and the people living in nearby towns are likely influenced by this publicity. In this situation, if the government files criminal charges against a member of the religious sect, that individual may request—and will probably receive—a change of venue to another location. ■

Note that venue has lost some significance in today's world because of the Internet and 24/7 news reporting. Courts now rarely grant requests for a change of venue. Because everyone has instant access to the same information about a purported crime, courts reason that no community is more or less informed about the matter or prejudiced for or against the defendant.

Venue The geographic district in which a legal action is tried and from which the jury is selected.

3–2d Standing to Sue

Before a person can bring a lawsuit before a court, the party must have **standing to sue,** or a sufficient "stake" in the matter to justify seeking relief through the court system. In other words, to have standing, a party must have a legally protected and tangible interest at stake in the litigation.

The party bringing the lawsuit must have suffered a harm, or have been threatened by a harm, as a result of the action about which she or he has complained. At times, a person can have standing to sue on behalf of another person, such as a minor (child) or a mentally incompetent person. Standing to sue also requires that the controversy at issue be a **justiciable**[10] **controversy**—a controversy that is real and substantial, as opposed to hypothetical or academic.

CASE EXAMPLE 3.8 Harold Wagner obtained a loan through M.S.T. Mortgage Group to buy a house in Texas. After the sale, M.S.T. transferred its interest in the loan to another lender, which assigned it to another lender, as is common in the mortgage industry. Eventually, when Wagner failed to make the loan payments, CitiMortgage, Inc., notified him that it was going to foreclose on the property and sell the house. Wagner filed a lawsuit claiming that the lenders had improperly assigned the mortgage loan. In 2014, a federal district court ruled that Wagner lacked standing to contest the assignment. Under Texas law, only the parties directly involved in an assignment can challenge its validity. In this case, the assignment was between two lenders and did not directly involve Wagner.[11] ■

Standing to Sue The legal requirement that an individual must have a sufficient stake in a controversy before he or she can bring a lawsuit.

Justiciable Controversy A controversy that is not hypothetical or academic but real and substantial; a requirement that must be satisfied before a court will hear a case.

---

9. Pronounced *ven-yoo.*
10. Pronounced jus-*tish*-uh-bul.
11. *Wagner v. CitiMortgage, Inc.,* 995 F.Supp.2d 621 (N.D.Tex. 2014).

3–3 The State and Federal Court Systems

As mentioned earlier in this chapter, each state has its own court system. Additionally, there is a system of federal courts. Even though there are fifty-two court systems—one for each of the fifty states, one for the District of Columbia, and a federal system—similarities abound. Exhibit 3–2 illustrates the basic organizational structure characteristic of the court systems in many states. The exhibit also shows how the federal court system is structured.

Keep in mind that the federal courts are not superior to the state courts. They are simply an independent system of courts, which derives its authority from Article III, Sections 1 and 2, of the U.S. Constitution. We turn now to an examination of these court systems, beginning with the state courts.

3–3a The State Court Systems

Typically, a state court system will include several levels, or tiers, of courts. As indicated in Exhibit 3–2, state courts may include (1) trial courts of limited jurisdiction, (2) trial courts of general jurisdiction, (3) appellate courts, and (4) the state's highest court (often called the state supreme court).

Generally, any person who is a party to a lawsuit has the opportunity to plead the case before a trial court and then, if he or she loses, before at least one level of appellate court. If the case involves a federal statute or a federal constitutional issue, the decision of a state supreme court on that issue may be further appealed to the United States Supreme Court. (See this chapter's *Managerial Strategy* feature for a discussion of how state budget cuts are making it more difficult to bring cases in some state courts.)

Trial Courts Trial courts are courts in which trials are held and testimony taken. State trial courts have either general or limited jurisdiction. Trial courts that have general jurisdiction as to subject matter may be called county, district, superior, or circuit courts.[12] The jurisdiction

---

12. The name in Ohio is court of common pleas, and the name in New York is supreme court.

Exhibit 3–2 The State and Federal Court Systems

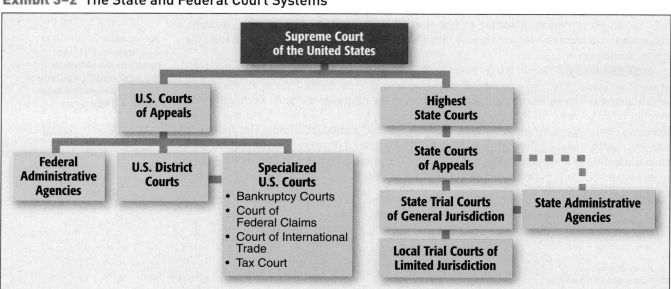

MANAGERIAL STRATEGY

Budget Cuts for State Courts Can Affect Businesses

Management Faces a Legal Issue

In the United States, businesses use the courts far more than anyone else. Most civil court cases involve a business suing another business for breach of contract or fraud, for instance. Additionally, when one company fails to pay another company for products or services, the unpaid company often turns to the court system. If that firm does not have ready access to the courts, its financial stability can be put at risk.

According to the National Center for State Courts, since 2009 forty-one state legislatures have reduced their state court services to the public as a result of budget restrictions. Many state courts have laid off staff members, delayed filling vacancies, and reduced hours of operation. California's courts have experienced the steepest cuts—nearly $1 billion since 2009. Texas has also experienced large cuts in court funding.

What the Courts Say

Today, the value of a company's intellectual property, such as its copyrights and patents, often exceeds the value of its physical property. Not surprisingly, disputes over intellectual property have grown in number and importance. As a result of the court budget cuts, these disputes also take longer to resolve. In California, for example, a typical patent lawsuit used to last twelve months. That same lawsuit now might take three to five years.

If an intellectual property case goes on to an appellate court, three or four more years typically pass before the dispute is resolved. In fact, the United States Supreme Court heard a case in 2014 involving a trademark dispute that had been in the courts for more than sixteen years.[a]

Other types of lawsuits are also taking longer to conclude. Now attorneys must tell businesses to consider not only the cost of bringing a lawsuit, but also the length of time involved. The longer the litigation lasts, the larger the legal bills and the greater the drain on company employees' time. During the years that a lawsuit can take, some businesses find that they cannot expand or hire new employees, and they are reluctant to spend funds on additional marketing and advertising. In fact, it is not unusual for a company to win its case but end up going out of business. As a result of putting its business on hold for years, the company becomes insolvent.

MANAGERIAL IMPLICATIONS

Many investors are reluctant to invest in a company that is the object of a patent or copyright lawsuit because they fear that if the company loses, it may lose the rights to its most valuable asset. Consequently, when litigation drags on for years, investors may abandon a company even though it is otherwise healthy. As a result, the company suffers.

Facing long delays in litigation with potential negative effects on their companies, business managers have become more reluctant to bring lawsuits, even when their cases clearly have merit. In Alabama, for instance, the number of civil cases filed has dropped by more than a third in the last few years. Before bringing a lawsuit, a manager must now take into account the possibility of long delays in resolving the case—delays that must figure into the cost-benefit analysis for undertaking litigation. Managers can no longer stand on principle because they know that they are right and that they will win a lawsuit. They have to look at the bigger picture, which includes substantial court delays.

a. *B&B Hardware Inc. v. Hargis Industries, Inc.,* __ U.S. __, 135 S.Ct. 696, 190 L.Ed.2d 386 (2014).

---

of these courts is often determined by the size of the county in which the court sits. State trial courts of general jurisdiction have jurisdiction over a wide variety of subjects, including both civil disputes and criminal prosecutions. (In some states, trial courts of general jurisdiction may hear appeals from courts of limited jurisdiction.)

Some courts of limited jurisdiction are called special inferior trial courts or minor judiciary courts. **Small claims courts** are inferior trial courts that hear only civil cases involving claims of less than a certain amount, such as $5,000 (the amount varies from state to state). Suits brought in small claims courts are generally conducted informally, and lawyers are not required (in a few states, lawyers are not even allowed). Another example of an inferior trial court is a local municipal court that hears mainly traffic cases. Decisions of small claims courts and municipal courts may sometimes be appealed to a state trial court of general jurisdiction.

Other courts of limited jurisdiction as to subject matter include domestic relations or family courts, which handle primarily divorce actions and child-custody disputes, and probate courts, as mentioned earlier. A few states have even established Islamic law courts, which are

Small Claims Court A special court in which parties can litigate small claims without an attorney.

Can a U.S. court ever use the Qur'an as a basis for reaching a decision?

Question of Fact In a lawsuit, an issue that involves only disputed facts, and not what the law is on a given point.

courts of limited jurisdiction that serve the American Muslim community. (See this chapter's *Beyond Our Borders* feature for a discussion of the rise of Islamic law courts.)

Appellate, or Reviewing, Courts

Every state has at least one court of appeals (appellate court, or reviewing court), which may be an intermediate appellate court or the state's highest court. About three-fourths of the states have intermediate appellate courts. Generally, courts of appeals do not conduct new trials, in which evidence is submitted and witnesses are examined. Rather, an appellate court panel of three or more judges reviews the record of the case on appeal, which includes a transcript of the trial proceedings, and determines whether the trial court committed an error.

Focus on Questions of Law. Appellate courts generally focus on questions of law, not questions of fact. A **question of fact** deals with what really happened in regard to the dispute being tried—such as whether a party

BEYOND OUR BORDERS

Islamic Law Courts Abroad and at Home

Islamic law is one of the world's three most common legal systems, along with civil law and common law systems. In most Islamic countries, the law is based on *sharia*, a system of law derived from the Qur'an and the sayings and doings of Muhammad and his companions. Today, many non-Islamic countries are establishing Islamic courts for their Muslim citizens.

Islamic Law in Britain, Canada, and Belgium

For several years, Great Britain has had councils that arbitrate disputes between British Muslims involving child custody, property, employment, and housing. These councils do not deal with criminal law or with any civil issues that would put *sharia* in direct conflict with British statutory law. Most Islamic law cases involve marriage or divorce. Starting in 2008, Britain officially sanctioned the authority of *sharia* judges to rule on divorce and financial disputes of Muslim couples. Britain now has eighty-five officially recognized *sharia* courts that have the full power

of equivalent courts within the traditional British judicial system.

In Ontario, Canada, a group of Canadian Muslims established a judicial tribunal using *sharia*. To date, this tribunal has resolved only marital disagreements and some other civil disputes. Under Ontario law, the regular judicial system must uphold such agreements as long as they are voluntary and negotiated through an arbitrator. Any agreements that violate Canada's Charter of Rights and Freedoms will not be upheld.

In 2011, Belgium established its first *sharia* court. This court handles primarily family law disputes for Muslim immigrants in Belgium.

Islamic Law Courts in the United States

The use of Islamic courts in the United States has been somewhat controversial. The legality of arbitration clauses that require disputes to be settled in Islamic courts has been upheld by regular state courts in some states, including Minnesota and Texas. In some other states, however, there has been a public backlash against the use of Islamic courts.

For instance, in Detroit, Michigan, which has a large American Muslim population, a controversy erupted over the community's attempt to establish Islamic courts. Legislators in Michigan and many other states started introducing bills to limit consideration of foreign or religious laws in state court decisions. Voters in Oklahoma enacted a referendum banning courts from considering *sharia* law, but the ban was later held to be unconstitutional.[a] Legislation enacted in Arizona, Kansas, Louisiana, North Carolina, Oklahoma, South Dakota, and Tennessee bans judicial consideration of foreign law. (These laws do not explicitly mention Islamic, or *sharia*, law, because that might be ruled unconstitutional.)

CRITICAL THINKING

■ One of the arguments against allowing *sharia* courts in the United States is that we would no longer have a common legal framework within our society. Do you agree or disagree? Why?

---

a. *Awad v. Zirax*, 670 F.3d 1111 (10th Cir. 2012). A lower court later issued a permanent injunction to prevent the ban from being enforced. *Awad v. Zirax*, 966 F.Supp.2d 1198 (2013).

actually burned a flag. A **question of law** concerns the application or interpretation of the law—such as whether flag-burning is a form of speech protected by the First Amendment to the U.S. Constitution. Only a judge, not a jury, can rule on questions of law.

Defer to the Trial Court's Findings of Fact. Appellate courts normally defer (yield or give weight) to a trial court's findings on questions of fact, because the trial court judge and jury were in a better position to evaluate testimony. The trial court could directly observe witnesses' gestures, demeanor, and nonverbal behavior during the trial. At the appellate level, the judges review the written transcript of the trial, which does not include these nonverbal elements.

An appellate court will challenge a trial court's finding of fact only when the finding is clearly erroneous (that is, when it is contrary to the evidence presented at trial or when no evidence was presented to support the finding). **EXAMPLE 3.9** A jury concludes that a manufacturer's product harmed the plaintiff, but no evidence was submitted to the court to support that conclusion. In this situation, the appellate court will hold that the trial court's decision was erroneous. ■ The options exercised by appellate courts will be discussed further later in this chapter.

Highest State Courts The highest appellate court in a state is usually called the supreme court but may be called by some other name. For example, in both New York and Maryland, the highest state court is called the court of appeals. The decisions of each state's highest court are final on all questions of state law. Only when issues of federal law are involved can a decision made by a state's highest court be overruled by the United States Supreme Court.

3–3b The Federal Court System

The federal court system is basically a three-tiered model consisting of (1) U.S. district courts (trial courts of general jurisdiction) and various courts of limited jurisdiction, (2) U.S. courts of appeals (intermediate courts of appeals), and (3) the United States Supreme Court.

Unlike state court judges, who are usually elected, federal court judges—including the justices of the Supreme Court—are appointed by the president of the United States and confirmed by the U.S. Senate. Under Article III, federal judges "hold their offices during Good Behavior." In essence, this means that federal judges receive lifetime appointments.

U.S. District Courts At the federal level, the equivalent of a state trial court of general jurisdiction is the district court. There is at least one federal district court in every state. The number of judicial districts can vary over time, primarily owing to population changes and corresponding caseloads. Today, there are ninety-four federal judicial districts.

U.S. district courts have original jurisdiction in federal matters. Federal cases typically originate in district courts. Federal courts with original, but special (or limited), jurisdiction include the bankruptcy courts and others that were shown in Exhibit 3–2.

U.S. Courts of Appeals In the federal court system, there are thirteen U.S. courts of appeals—also referred to as U.S. circuit courts of appeals. The federal courts of appeals for twelve of the circuits, including the U.S. Court of Appeals for the District of Columbia Circuit, hear appeals from the federal district courts located within their respective judicial circuits.

Question of Law In a lawsuit, an issue involving the application or interpretation of a law.

LEARNING OBJECTIVE 3
What is the difference between the focus of a trial court and an appellate court?

KNOW THIS
The decisions of a state's highest court are final on questions of state law.

Trial decisions are normally determined by juries. Under what types of circumstances might an appellate court reverse a jury's decision?

The Court of Appeals for the Thirteenth Circuit is called the Federal Circuit. It has national appellate jurisdiction over certain types of cases, such as cases involving patent law and cases in which the U.S. government is a defendant.

The decisions of the circuit courts of appeals are final in most cases, but appeal to the United States Supreme Court is possible. Exhibit 3–3 shows the geographic boundaries of the U.S. circuit courts of appeals and the boundaries of the U.S. district courts within each circuit.

The United States Supreme Court The highest level of the three-tiered model of the federal court system is the United States Supreme Court. According to Article III of the U.S. Constitution, there is only one national Supreme Court. All other courts in the federal system are considered "inferior." Congress is empowered to create inferior courts as it deems necessary. The inferior courts that Congress has created include the second tier in our model—the U.S. courts of appeals—as well as the district courts and any other courts of limited, or specialized, jurisdiction.

The United States Supreme Court consists of nine justices. Although the Supreme Court has original, or trial, jurisdiction in rare instances (set forth in Article III, Section 2), most of its work is as an appeals court. The Supreme Court can review any case decided by any of the federal courts of appeals, and it also has appellate authority over some cases decided in the state courts.

Appeals to the Supreme Court. To bring a case before the Supreme Court, a party requests that the Court issue a writ of *certiorari*. A **writ of *certiorari***[13] is an order issued by the Supreme

Writ of *Certiorari* A writ from a higher court asking a lower court for the record of a case.

---

13. Pronounced sur-shee-uh-*rah*-ree.

Exhibit 3–3 Boundaries of the U.S. Courts of Appeals and U.S. District Courts

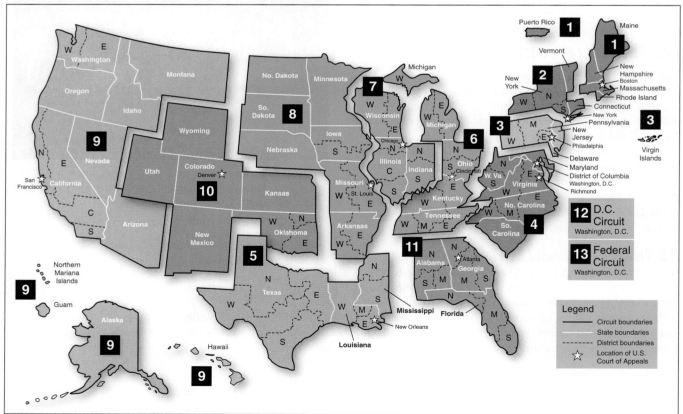

Source: Administrative Office of the United States Courts.

Court to a lower court requiring that court to send the record of the case for review. Under the **rule of four,** the Court will not issue a writ unless at least four of the nine justices approve.

Whether the Court will issue a writ of *certiorari* is entirely within its discretion. The Court is not required to issue one, and most petitions for writs are denied. (Although thousands of cases are filed with the Supreme Court each year, it hears, on average, fewer than one hundred of these cases.)[14] A denial is not a decision on the merits of a case, nor does it indicate agreement with the lower court's opinion. Furthermore, a denial of the writ has no value as a precedent.

Petitions Granted by the Court. Typically, the Court grants petitions when cases raise important constitutional questions or when the lower courts are issuing conflicting decisions on a significant issue. The justices, however, never explain their reasons for hearing certain cases and not others, so it is difficult to predict which type of case the Court might select.

How much weight should Supreme Court justices give to arguments made in *amicus* briefs? Parties not directly involved in a case before the United States Supreme Court are allowed to file friend-of-the-court (*amicus curiae*) briefs. Important, headline-making cases sometimes elicit eighty or more *amicus* briefs. Supreme Court justices often rely on these briefs to buttress their opinions. Law professor Allison Orr Larsen found that over a recent five-term period, the Court's opinions cited factual assertions from *amicus* briefs 124 times.[15]

Critics of the justices' use of *amicus* briefs for factual information, including Larsen, argue that such "information" can be highly unreliable and even outright incorrect. After all, in the age of the Internet, almost anyone can become an "expert." Some recent Supreme Court opinions have cited facts from *amicus* briefs that were backed up only by blog posts or e-mails. Furthermore, some studies presented in *amicus* briefs were paid for by the groups providing the briefs and published only on the Internet. In spite of these problems, Supreme Court justices are increasingly citing *amicus* briefs for statements of fact, rather than citing underlying factual sources and their authority, prompting Justice Antonin Scalia to argue that "Supreme Court briefs are an inappropriate place to develop the key facts in a case."

Library of Congress

3-4 Following a State Court Case

To illustrate the procedures that would be followed in a civil lawsuit brought in a state court, we present a hypothetical case and follow it through the state court system. The case involves an automobile accident in which Kevin Anderson, driving a Lexus, struck Lisa Marconi, driving a Hyundai Genesis. The accident occurred at the intersection of Wilshire Boulevard and Rodeo Drive in Beverly Hills, California. Marconi suffered personal injuries and incurred medical and hospital expenses as a result, as well as lost wages for four months. Anderson and Marconi are unable to agree on a settlement, and Marconi sues Anderson. Marconi is the plaintiff, and Anderson is the defendant. Both are represented by lawyers.

During each phase of the **litigation** (the process of working a lawsuit through the court system), Marconi and Anderson will have to observe strict procedural requirements. A large body of law—procedural law—establishes the rules and standards for determining disputes in courts.

Procedural rules are very complex, and they vary from court to court and from state to state. In addition to the various sets of rules for state courts, the federal courts have their own rules of procedure. Additionally, the applicable procedures will depend on whether the case is

Sidebar (right column)

Rule of Four A rule of the United States Supreme Court under which the Court will not issue a writ of *certiorari* unless at least four justices approve of the decision to issue the writ.

ETHICAL ISSUE

This *amicus* brief was filed on behalf of many well-known recording artists. Are there any rules concerning the quality of the research or facts presented in such briefs?

"Lawsuit: A machine which you go into as a pig and come out of as a sausage."

AMBROSE BIERCE
1842–1914
(AMERICAN JOURNALIST)

Litigation The process of resolving a dispute through the court system.

---

14. From the mid-1950s through the early 1990s, the United States Supreme Court reviewed more cases per year than it has in the last few years. In the Court's 1982–1983 term, for example, the Court issued opinions in 151 cases. In contrast, in its 2014–2015 term, the Court issued opinions in only 76 cases.
15. Allison Orr Larsen, "The Trouble with *Amicus* Facts," *Virginia Law Review* 100 (December 2014).

a civil or criminal proceeding. Generally, the Marconi-Anderson civil lawsuit will involve the procedures discussed in the following subsections. Keep in mind that attempts to settle the case may be ongoing throughout the trial.

3–4a The Pleadings

Pleadings Statements by the plaintiff and the defendant that detail the facts, charges, and defenses of a case.

The complaint and answer (and the counterclaim and reply)—all of which are discussed here—taken together are called the **pleadings.** The pleadings inform each party of the other's claims and specify the issues (disputed questions) involved in the case. The style and form of the pleadings may be quite different in different states.

The Plaintiff's Complaint

Complaint The pleading made by a plaintiff alleging wrongdoing on the part of the defendant. When filed with a court, the complaint initiates a lawsuit.

Marconi's suit against Anderson commences when her lawyer files a **complaint** with the appropriate court. The complaint contains statements alleging:

1. The facts necessary for the court to take *jurisdiction*.

2. A brief summary of the *facts* necessary to show that the plaintiff is entitled to relief (a remedy).[16]

3. A statement of the *remedy* the plaintiff is seeking.

Complaints may be lengthy or brief, depending on the complexity of the case and the rules of the jurisdiction.

Service of Process

Service of Process The delivery of the complaint and summons to a defendant.

Summons A document informing a defendant that a legal action has been commenced against her or him and that the defendant must appear in court on a certain date to answer the plaintiff's complaint.

Default Judgment A judgment entered by a court against a defendant who has failed to appear in court to answer or defend against the plaintiff's claim.

Before the court can exercise personal jurisdiction over the defendant (Anderson)—in effect, before the lawsuit can begin—the court must have proof that the defendant was notified of the lawsuit. Formally notifying the defendant of a lawsuit is called **service of process.** The plaintiff must deliver, or serve, a copy of the complaint and a **summons** (a notice requiring the defendant to appear in court and answer the complaint) to the defendant.

The summons notifies Anderson that he must file an answer to the complaint within a specified time period (twenty days in the federal courts) or suffer a default judgment against him. A **default judgment** in Marconi's favor would mean that she would be awarded the damages alleged in her complaint because Anderson failed to respond to the allegations. In our legal system, no case can proceed to trial unless the plaintiff can prove that he or she has properly served the defendant.

How service of process occurs depends on the rules of the court or jurisdiction in which the lawsuit is brought. Usually, the server hands the summons and complaint to the defendant personally or leaves it at the defendant's residence or place of business. In some states, process can be served by mail if the defendant consents (accepts service). When the defendant cannot be reached, special rules provide for alternative means of service, such as publishing a notice in the local newspaper or serving process via e-mail.

The Defendant's Answer

Answer Procedurally, a defendant's response to the plaintiff's complaint.

The defendant's **answer** either admits the statements or allegations set forth in the complaint or denies them and outlines any defenses that the defendant may have. If Anderson admits to all of Marconi's allegations in his answer, the court will enter a judgment for Marconi. If Anderson denies any of Marconi's allegations, the litigation will go forward.

Counterclaim A claim made by a defendant in a civil lawsuit against the plaintiff. In effect, the defendant is suing the plaintiff.

Reply Procedurally, a plaintiff's response to a defendant's answer.

Anderson can deny Marconi's allegations and set forth his own claim that Marconi was negligent and therefore owes him compensation for the damage to his Lexus. This is appropriately called a **counterclaim.** If Anderson files a counterclaim, Marconi will have to answer it with a pleading, normally called a **reply,** which has the same characteristics as an answer.

---

16. The factual allegations in a complaint must be enough to raise a right to relief above the speculative level. They must plausibly suggest that the plaintiff is entitled to a remedy. See *Bell Atlantic Corp. v. Twombly*, 550 U.S. 544, 127 S.Ct. 1955, 167 L.Ed.2d 929 (2007).

Anderson can also admit the truth of Marconi's complaint but raise new facts that may result in dismissal of the action. This is called raising an *affirmative defense*. For example, Anderson could assert that Marconi was driving negligently at the time of the accident and thus was partially responsible for her own injuries. In some states, a plaintiff's contributory negligence operates as a complete defense, whereas in others it simply reduces the amount of damages that Marconi can recover (see Chapter 4).

Motion to Dismiss A *motion* is a procedural request submitted to the court by an attorney on behalf of her or his client. A **motion to dismiss** requests the court to dismiss the case for stated reasons. Grounds for dismissal of a case include improper delivery of the complaint and summons, improper venue, and the plaintiff's failure to state a claim for which a court could grant relief. For instance, suppose that Marconi had suffered no injuries or losses as a result of Anderson's negligence. In that situation, Anderson could move to have the case dismissed because Marconi would not have stated a claim for which relief could be granted.

If the judge grants the motion to dismiss, the plaintiff generally is given time to file an amended complaint. If the judge denies the motion, the suit will go forward, and the defendant must then file an answer. Note that if Marconi wishes to discontinue the suit because, for example, an out-of-court settlement has been reached, she can likewise move for dismissal. The court can also dismiss the case on its own motion.

CASE EXAMPLE 3.10 Espresso Disposition Corporation 1 entered into a contract with Santana Sales & Marketing Group, Inc. The agreement included a mandatory *forum-selection clause*—which was a provision designating that any disputes arising under the contract would be decided by a court in Illinois. When Santana Sales filed a lawsuit against Espresso in a Florida state court, Espresso filed a motion to dismiss based on the agreement's forum selection clause. Santana claimed that the forum-selection clause had been a mistake. The court denied Espresso's motion to dismiss. Espresso appealed. A state intermediate appellate court reversed the trial court's denial of Espresso's motion to dismiss and remanded the case to the lower court for the entry of an order of dismissal.[17] ■

3–4b Pretrial Motions

Either party may attempt to get the case dismissed before trial through the use of various pretrial motions. We have already mentioned the motion to dismiss. Two other important pretrial motions are the motion for judgment on the pleadings and the motion for summary judgment.

At the close of the pleadings, either party may make a **motion for judgment on the pleadings,** or on the merits of the case. The judge will grant the motion only when there is no dispute over the facts of the case and the sole issue to be resolved is a question of law. In deciding on the motion, the judge may consider only the evidence contained in the pleadings.

In contrast, in a **motion for summary judgment,** the court may consider evidence outside the pleadings, such as sworn statements (affidavits) by parties or witnesses, or other documents relating to the case. Either party can make a motion for summary judgment. Like the motion for judgment on the pleadings, a motion for summary judgment will be granted only if there are no genuine questions of fact and the sole question is a question of law.

3–4c Discovery

Before a trial begins, each party can use a number of procedural devices to obtain information and gather evidence about the case from the other party or from third parties. The process of obtaining such information is known as **discovery.** Discovery includes gaining access to witnesses, documents, records, and other types of evidence.

---

17. *Espresso Disposition Corp. 1 v. Santana Sales & Marketing Group, Inc.,* 105 So.3d 592 (Fla.App. 3 Dist. 2013).

Motion to Dismiss A pleading in which a defendant admits the facts as alleged by the plaintiff but asserts that the plaintiff's claim to state a cause of action has no basis in law.

Motion for Judgment on the Pleadings A motion by either party to a lawsuit at the close of the pleadings requesting the court to decide the issue solely on the pleadings without proceeding to trial. The motion will be granted only if no facts are in dispute.

Motion for Summary Judgment A motion requesting the court to enter a judgment without proceeding to trial. The motion can be based on evidence outside the pleadings and will be granted only if no facts are in dispute.

LEARNING OBJECTIVE 4

What is discovery, and how does electronic discovery differ from traditional discovery?

Discovery A method by which the opposing parties obtain information from each other to prepare for trial.

The Federal Rules of Civil Procedure and similar rules in the states set forth the guidelines for discovery. Generally, discovery is allowed regarding any matter that is not privileged and is relevant to the claim or defense of any party. Discovery rules also attempt to protect witnesses and parties from undue harassment and to safeguard privileged or confidential material from being disclosed.

If a discovery request involves privileged or confidential business information, a court can deny the request and can limit the scope of discovery in a number of ways. For instance, a court can require the party to submit the materials to the judge in a sealed envelope so that the judge can decide if they should be disclosed to the opposing party.

Discovery prevents surprises at trial by giving parties access to evidence that might otherwise be hidden. This allows both parties to learn what to expect during a trial before they reach the courtroom. Discovery also serves to narrow the issues so that trial time is spent on the main questions in the case. The following case shows how vital discovery can be to the outcome of litigation.

CASE 3.2

Brothers v. Winstead

Supreme Court of Mississippi, 129 So.3d 906 (2014).

FACTS Phillips Brothers, LP (limited partnership), Harry Simmons, and Ray Winstead were the owners of Kilby Brake Fisheries, LLC (limited liability company), a catfish farm in Mississippi. For nearly eight years, Winstead operated a hatchery for the firm. During this time, the hatchery had only two profitable years. Consequently, Winstead was fired. He filed a suit in a Mississippi state court against Kilby Brake and its other owners, alleging a "freeze-out." (A freeze-out occurs when a majority of the owners of a firm exclude other owners from certain benefits of participating in the firm.)

The defendants filed a counterclaim of theft. To support this claim, the defendants asked the court to allow them to obtain documents from Winstead regarding his finances, particularly income from his Winstead Cattle Company. The court refused this request. A jury awarded Winstead more than $1.7 million, and the defendants appealed.

ISSUE Were the defendants entitled to discovery of information concerning Winstead's finances to seek evidence to support their claims?

DECISION Yes. The Mississippi Supreme Court reversed the lower court's decision to deny discovery of information on Winstead's outside finances and remanded the case for a new trial.

Why was Winstead fired from his catfish hatchery position?

REASON The state supreme court noted several factors in explaining its reasoning. Winstead testified that Winstead Cattle Company did no business—it was "simply his hunting camp." But during discovery, Winstead provided tax returns that showed substantial income from the company.

Other documents showed income from sales of "cattle" to a fish farmer named Scott Kiker, which did not appear on Winstead's tax returns. Kilby Brake contended that this income represented sales of Kilby Brake fish, not cattle. Kiker testified that he received a load of fish from Kilby Brake, sold the fish, and gave Winstead a commission without paying Kilby Brake.

Winstead countered that he often acted as a "middleman" between a farmer in need of fish and another with fish for sale, taking a commission on the deal. Further discovery of information on Winstead's financial dealings could reveal whether he was selling fish from Kilby Brake and disguising these sales on his tax returns.

CRITICAL THINKING—Ethical Consideration *Does Winstead have an ethical duty to comply with the defendants' discovery request? Discuss.*

Depositions and Interrogatories
Discovery can involve the use of depositions, interrogatories, or both. A **deposition** is sworn testimony by a party to the lawsuit or any witness. The person being deposed (the deponent) answers questions asked by the attorneys, and the questions and answers are recorded by an authorized court official and sworn to and signed by the deponent. (Occasionally, written depositions are taken when witnesses are unable to

Deposition The testimony of a party to a lawsuit or a witness taken under oath before a trial.

appear in person.) The answers given to depositions will, of course, help the attorneys prepare for the trial. They can also be used in court to impeach (challenge the credibility of) a party or a witness who changes her or his testimony at the trial. In addition, a witness's deposition can be used as testimony if he or she is not available for the trial.

Interrogatories are written questions for which written answers are prepared and then signed under oath. The main difference between interrogatories and written depositions is that interrogatories are directed to a party to the lawsuit (the plaintiff or the defendant), not to a witness, and the party can prepare answers with the aid of an attorney. In addition, the scope of interrogatories is broader because parties are obligated to answer the questions, even if that means disclosing information from their records and files.

Note that, as with discovery requests, a court can impose sanctions on a party who fails to answer interrogatories. **CASE EXAMPLE 3.11** Computer Task Group, Inc. (CTG), sued a former employee, William Brotby, for violating the terms of his employment agreement. During discovery, Brotby refused to respond fully to CTG's interrogatories. He gave contradictory answers, made frivolous objections, filed baseless motions, and never disclosed all the information that CTG sought. The court ordered Brotby to comply with discovery requests five times. Nevertheless, Brotby continued to make excuses and changed his story repeatedly, making it impossible for CTG to establish basic facts with any certainty. Eventually, CTG requested and the court granted a default judgment against Brotby based on his failure to cooperate.[18] ■

Requests for Other Information

A party can serve a written request on the other party for an admission of the truth on matters relating to the trial. Any matter admitted under such a request is conclusively established for the trial. For instance, Marconi can ask Anderson to admit that he was driving at a speed of forty-five miles an hour. A request for admission saves time at trial because the parties will not have to spend time proving facts on which they already agree.

A party can also gain access to documents and other items not in her or his possession in order to inspect and examine them. Likewise, a party can gain "entry upon land" to inspect the premises. Anderson's attorney, for instance, normally can gain permission to inspect and photocopy Marconi's car repair bills.

When the physical or mental condition of one party is in question, the opposing party can ask the court to order a physical or mental examination, but the court will do so only if the need for the information outweighs the right to privacy of the person to be examined. If the court issues the order, the opposing party can obtain the results of the examination.

Electronic Discovery

Any relevant material, including information stored electronically, can be the object of a discovery request. The federal rules and most state rules now specifically allow all parties to obtain electronic "data compilations." Electronic evidence, or **e-evidence,** includes all types of computer-generated or electronically recorded information. This might include e-mail, voice mail, tweets, blogs, social media posts, and spreadsheets, as well as documents and other data stored on computers.

E-evidence can reveal significant facts that are not discoverable by other means. Computers, smartphones, cameras, and other devices automatically record certain information about files—such as who created a file and when, and who accessed, modified, or transmitted it—on their hard drives. This information is called **metadata,** which can be thought of as "data about data." Metadata can be obtained only from the file in its electronic format—not from printed-out versions.

EXAMPLE 3.12 In 2012, John McAfee, the programmer responsible for creating McAfee antivirus software, was wanted for questioning in the murder of his neighbor in Belize. McAfee

Interrogatories A series of written questions for which written answers are prepared by a party to a lawsuit, usually with the assistance of the party's attorney, and then signed under oath.

E-Evidence A type of evidence that consists of computer-generated or electronically recorded information.

Metadata Data that are automatically recorded by electronic devices and provide information about who created a file and when, and who accessed, modified, or transmitted the file on their hard drives. Can be described as data about data.

---

18. *Computer Task Group, Inc. v. Brotby*, 364 F.3d 1112 (9th Cir. 2004).

left Belize and was on the run from police, but he allowed a journalist to come with him and photograph him. When the journalist posted photos of McAfee online, some metadata were attached to a photo. The police used the metadata to pinpoint the latitude and longitude of the image and subsequently arrested McAfee in Guatemala. ■

E-Discovery Procedures. The Federal Rules of Civil Procedure deal specifically with the preservation, retrieval, and production of electronic data. Although parties may still use traditional means, such as interrogatories and depositions, to find out about the e-evidence, they must usually hire an expert to retrieve evidence in its electronic format. The expert uses software to reconstruct e-mail exchanges and establish who knew what and when they knew it. The expert can even recover files that the user thought had been deleted from a computer.

Advantages and Disadvantages. E-discovery has significant advantages over paper discovery. Back-up copies of documents and e-mail can provide useful—and often quite damaging— information about how a particular matter progressed over several weeks or months. E-discovery can uncover the proverbial smoking gun that will win the lawsuit, but it is also time consuming and expensive, especially when lawsuits involve large firms with multiple offices. Many companies have found it challenging to fulfill their duty to preserve electronic evidence from a vast number of sources. Failure to do so, however, can lead to sanctions and even force companies to agree to settlements that are not in their best interests.[19]

3–4d Pretrial Conference

Either party or the court can request a pretrial conference, or hearing. Usually, the hearing consists of an informal discussion between the judge and the opposing attorneys after discovery has taken place. The purpose of the hearing is to explore the possibility of a settlement without trial and, if this is not possible, to identify the matters that are in dispute and to plan the course of the trial.

3–4e Jury Selection

A trial can be held with or without a jury. The Seventh Amendment to the U.S. Constitution guarantees the right to a jury trial for cases in *federal* courts when the amount in controversy exceeds $20, but this guarantee does not apply to state courts. Most states have similar guarantees in their own constitutions (although the threshold dollar amount is higher than $20). The right to a trial by jury does not have to be exercised, and many cases are tried without a jury. In most states and in federal courts, one of the parties must request a jury in a civil case, or the judge presumes that the parties waive the right.

Before a jury trial commences, a jury must be selected. The jury selection process is known as **voir dire**.[20] During *voir dire* in most jurisdictions, attorneys for the plaintiff and the defendant ask prospective jurors oral questions to determine whether a potential jury member is biased or has any connection with a party to the action or with a prospective witness. In some jurisdictions, the judge may do all or part of the questioning based on written questions submitted by counsel for the parties.

During *voir dire*, a party may challenge a prospective juror *peremptorily*—that is, ask that an individual not be sworn in as a juror without providing any reason. Alternatively, a party may challenge a prospective juror *for cause*—that is, provide a reason why an individual should not be sworn in as a juror. If the judge grants the challenge, the individual is asked to step down. A prospective juror may not be excluded from the jury by the use of discriminatory challenges, however, such as those based on racial criteria or gender.

"The judicial system is the most expensive machine ever invented for finding out what happened and what to do about it."

IRVING R. KAUFMAN
1910–1992
(AMERICAN JURIST)

KNOW THIS
Picking the "right" jury is often an important aspect of litigation strategy, and a number of firms now specialize in jury-selection consulting services.

Voir Dire An important part of the jury selection process in which the attorneys question prospective jurors about their backgrounds, attitudes, and biases to ascertain whether they can be impartial jurors.

---

19. See, for example, *E. I. Du Pont de Nemours & Co. v. Kolon Industries, Inc.*, 803 F.Supp.2d 469 (E.D.Va. 2011); and *In re Intel Corp. Microprocessor Antitrust Litigation*, 2008 WL 2310288 (D.Del. 2008).
20. Pronounced vwahr *deehr*.

3-4f At the Trial

Once the trial begins, it follows the specific procedures discussed next.

Opening Arguments and Examination of Witnesses
At the beginning of the trial, the attorneys present their opening arguments, setting forth the facts that they expect to prove during the trial. Then the plaintiff's case is presented. In our hypothetical case, Marconi's lawyer would introduce evidence (relevant documents, exhibits, and the testimony of witnesses) to support Marconi's position. The defendant has the opportunity to challenge any evidence introduced and to cross-examine any of the plaintiff's witnesses.

At the end of the plaintiff's case, the defendant's attorney has the opportunity to ask the judge to direct a verdict for the defendant on the ground that the plaintiff has presented no evidence that would justify the granting of the plaintiff's remedy. This is called a **motion for a directed verdict** (known in federal courts as a *motion for judgment as a matter of law*).

If the motion is not granted (it seldom is granted), the defendant's attorney then presents the evidence and witnesses for the defendant's case. At the conclusion of the defendant's case, the defendant's attorney has another opportunity to make a motion for a directed verdict. The plaintiff's attorney can challenge any evidence introduced and cross-examine the defendant's witnesses.

Motion for a Directed Verdict A motion for the judge to take the decision out of the hands of the jury and to direct a verdict for the party making the motion on the ground that the other party has not produced sufficient evidence to support her or his claim.

Closing Arguments and Awards
After the defense concludes its presentation, the attorneys present their closing arguments, each urging a verdict in favor of her or his client. The judge instructs the jury in the law that applies to the case (these instructions are often called *charges*), and the jury retires to the jury room to deliberate a verdict. Typically, jurors are instructed that they must decide the case based only on the information that they learned during the trial. But today, jurors may be tempted to conduct their own investigation of the case using wireless devices—as discussed in this chapter's *Adapting the Law to the Online Environment* feature.

In the Marconi-Anderson case, the jury will not only decide for the plaintiff or for the defendant but, if it finds for the plaintiff, will also decide on the amount of the **award** (the compensation to be paid to her).

Award The monetary compensation given to a party at the end of a trial or other proceeding.

3-4g Posttrial Motions

After the jury has rendered its verdict, either party may make a posttrial motion. If Marconi wins and Anderson's attorney has previously moved for a directed verdict, Anderson's attorney may make a **motion for judgment n.o.v.** (from the Latin *non obstante veredicto,* which means "notwithstanding the verdict"—called a *motion for judgment as a matter of law* in the federal courts). Such a motion will be granted only if the jury's verdict was unreasonable and erroneous. If the judge grants the motion, the jury's verdict will be set aside, and a judgment will be entered in favor of the opposite party (Anderson).

Alternatively, Anderson could make a **motion for a new trial,** asking the judge to set aside the adverse verdict and to hold a new trial. The motion will be granted if, after looking at all the evidence, the judge is convinced that the jury was in error but does not feel that it is appropriate to grant judgment for the other side. A judge can also grant a new trial on the basis of newly discovered evidence, misconduct by the participants or the jury during the trial, or error by the judge.

Motion for Judgment n.o.v. A motion requesting the court to grant judgment in favor of the party making the motion on the ground that the jury's verdict against him or her was unreasonable and erroneous.

Motion for a New Trial A motion asserting that the trial was so fundamentally flawed (because of error, newly discovered evidence, prejudice, or another reason) that a new trial is necessary to prevent a miscarriage of justice.

3-4h The Appeal

Assume here that any posttrial motion is denied and that Anderson appeals the case. (If Marconi wins but receives a smaller monetary award than she sought, she can appeal also.) Keep in mind, though, that a party cannot appeal a trial court's decision simply because he or she is dissatisfied with the outcome of the trial.

ADAPTING THE LAW TO THE ONLINE ENVIRONMENT
Jurors' Use of Wireless Devices and the Internet

One former juror, fresh from trial, complained that the members of the courtroom work group had not provided the jury with enough information to render a fair verdict. "We felt deeply frustrated at our inability to fill those gaps in our knowledge," he added. Until recently, frustrated jury members lacked the means to carry out their own investigations in court. Today, however, jurors with smartphones and tablets can easily access news stories and online research tools. With these wireless devices, they can look up legal terms, blog and tweet about their experiences, and sometimes even try to contact other participants in the trial through "friend" requests on social media Web sites such as Facebook.

What Jurors Are Not Supposed to Learn Outside the Courtroom

Jurors are generally not supposed to obtain background information about the parties to a case or about case events. And certainly, they are prohibited from obtaining outside information about the attorneys, judges, and witnesses they encounter in the courtroom.

In one case, the judge explicitly instructed the jurors that they were not to "use any electronic device or media, such as a telephone, cellphone, smartphone, iPhone, BlackBerry, computer; the Internet, any Internet service, or any text or instant messaging service; or Internet chat room, blog, or Web site, such as Facebook, MySpace, YouTube, or Twitter

How easy is it for judges to prevent Web information searches by jurors during a trial?

iStockPhoto.com/hocus-focus

to communicate to anyone any information in this case or to conduct any research about this case" until after the verdict. When a juror did do Internet research, and that fact came to light during an appeal of the verdict, the appellate court required a new trial.[a]

In another case, a juror used the Internet to access information about the defendant's past criminal history. Again, the verdict was appealed, and the appellate court stated, "Because there is a reasonable possibility that the extrinsic information acquired by the juror influenced the verdict, we reverse and remand for a new trial."[b]

---

a. *Baird v. Owczarek,* 93 A.3d 1222, Del.Supr. (2014).
b. *State v. Johnson,* 177 Wash.App. 1035, 2013 WL 6092149 (2013).

Legislators Are Reacting

In response to widespread mistrials stemming from jurors' use of wireless devices and the Internet, some states have passed legislation to address the problem. California amended its Code of Civil Procedure to require that all trial courts admonish jurors "that the prohibition on research, dissemination of information, and conversation applies to all forms of electronic and wireless communication." Any juror may be found guilty of a misdemeanor for "willful disobedience . . . of a court admonishment related to the prohibition on any form of communication or research about the case, including all forms of electronic or wireless communication or research."[c]

- The Sixth Amendment guarantees the accused a right of trial by an "impartial jury." How does the use of wireless devices in the courtroom or research on the Internet threaten this right?

---

c. California Statutes 2011, Chapter 181, as cited in *Steiner v. Superior Court,* 220 Cal.App.4th 1479, 164 Cal.Rptr. 3d 155, Cal.App. 2 Dist. (2013). This law amended the California Code of Civil Procedure, Section 166, to make it contempt of court for a juror to disobey the judge and use wireless devices to perform research about a case.

A party must have legitimate grounds to file an appeal. In other words, he or she must be able to claim that the lower court committed an error. If Anderson has grounds to appeal the case, a notice of appeal must be filed with the clerk of the trial court within a prescribed time. Anderson now becomes the appellant, or petitioner, and Marconi becomes the appellee, or respondent.

Filing the Appeal   Anderson's attorney files the record on appeal with the appellate court. The record includes the pleadings, the trial transcript, the judge's rulings on motions made by the parties, and other trial-related documents. Anderson's attorney will also provide the reviewing court with a condensation of the record, known as an *abstract,* and a brief. The **brief** is a formal legal document outlining the facts and issues of the case, the judge's rulings or jury's findings that should be reversed or modified, the applicable law, and arguments on Anderson's behalf (citing applicable statutes and relevant cases as precedents).

Brief A written summary or statement prepared by one side in a lawsuit to explain its case to the judge.

Marconi's attorney will file an answering brief. Anderson's attorney can file a reply to Marconi's brief, although it is not required. The reviewing court then considers the case.

Appellate Review
As explained earlier, a court of appeals does not hear evidence. Instead, the court reviews the record for errors of law. Its decision concerning a case is based on the record on appeal, the abstracts, and the attorneys' briefs. The attorneys can present oral arguments, after which the case is taken under advisement.

After reviewing a case, an appellate court has the following options:

1. The court can *affirm* the trial court's decision.

2. The court can *reverse* the trial court's judgment if it concludes that the trial court erred or that the jury did not receive proper instructions.

3. The appellate court can *remand* (send back) the case to the trial court for further proceedings consistent with its opinion on the matter.

4. The court might also affirm or reverse a decision *in part.* For instance, the court might affirm the jury's finding that Anderson was negligent but remand the case for further proceedings on another issue (such as the extent of Marconi's damages).

5. An appellate court can also *modify* a lower court's decision. If the appellate court decides that the jury awarded an excessive amount in damages, for instance, the court might reduce the award to a more appropriate, or fairer, amount.

Do parties to a trial decision always have a right to appeal that decision?

Appeal to a Higher Appellate Court
If the reviewing court is an intermediate appellate court, the losing party may decide to appeal to the state supreme court (the highest state court). Such a petition corresponds to a petition for a writ of *certiorari* from the United States Supreme Court. Although the losing party has a right to ask (petition) a higher court to review the case, the party does not have a right to have the case heard by the higher appellate court.

Appellate courts normally have discretionary power and can accept or reject an appeal. Like the United States Supreme Court, state supreme courts generally deny most appeals. If the appeal is granted, new briefs must be filed before the state supreme court, and the attorneys may be allowed or requested to present oral arguments. Like the intermediate appellate court, the supreme court may reverse or affirm the appellate court's decision or remand the case. At this point, the case typically has reached its end (unless a federal question is at issue and one of the parties has legitimate grounds to seek review by a federal appellate court).

3-4i Enforcing the Judgment

The uncertainties of the litigation process are compounded by the lack of guarantees that any judgment will be enforceable. Even if a plaintiff wins an award of damages in court, the defendant may not have sufficient assets or insurance to cover that amount. Usually, one of the factors considered before a lawsuit is initiated is whether the defendant will be able to pay the damages sought, should the plaintiff win the case.

3-5 Courts Online

Most courts today have sites on the Web. Of course, each court decides what to make available at its site. Some courts display only the names of court personnel and office phone numbers. Others add court rules and forms. Many appellate court sites include judicial decisions, although the decisions may remain online for only a limited time. In addition, in some states, including California and Florida, court clerks offer information about the court's **docket** (its schedule of cases to be heard) and other searchable databases online.

Docket The list of cases entered on a court's calendar and thus scheduled to be heard by the court.

Appellate court decisions are often posted online immediately after they are rendered. Recent decisions of the U.S. courts of appeals, for instance, are available online at their Web sites. The United States Supreme Court also has an official Web site and publishes its opinions there immediately after they are announced to the public. In fact, even decisions that are designated as "unpublished" opinions by the appellate courts are usually published (posted) online.

3-5a Electronic Filing

A number of state and federal courts now allow parties to file litigation-related documents with the courts via the Internet or other electronic means. In fact, the federal court system has implemented its electronic filing system, Case Management/Electronic Case Files (CM/ECF), in nearly all federal courts. The system is available in federal district, appellate, and bankruptcy courts, as well as the U.S. Court of International Trade and the U.S. Court of Federal Claims. More than 33 million cases are on the CM/ECF system. Access to the electronic documents filed on CM/ECF is available through a system called PACER (Public Access to Court Electronic Records), which is a service of the U.S. courts.

A majority of the states have some form of electronic filing, although often it is not yet available in state appellate courts. Some states, including Arizona, California, Colorado, Delaware, Mississippi, New Jersey, New York, and Nevada, offer statewide e-filing systems. Generally, when electronic filing is made available, it is optional. Nonetheless, some state courts have now made e-filing mandatory in certain types of disputes, such as complex civil litigation.

3-5b Cyber Courts and Proceedings

Eventually, litigants may be able to use cyber courts, in which judicial proceedings take place only on the Internet. The parties to a case could meet online to make their arguments and present their evidence. Cyber proceedings might use e-mail submissions, video cameras, designated chat rooms, closed sites, or other Internet and social media facilities. The promise of these virtual proceedings is greater efficiency and lower costs.

Electronic courtroom projects have already been developed in some federal and state courts. The state of Michigan has cyber courts that hear cases involving technology issues and high-tech businesses. Other states that have introduced cyber courts include California, Delaware, Louisiana, and North Carolina. Wisconsin has a rule authorizing the use of video-conferencing in both civil and criminal trials, at the discretion of the trial court.[21] The Federal Rules of Civil Procedure also authorizes video conferencing, and some federal bankruptcy courts offer online chatting at their Web sites.

3-6 Alternative Dispute Resolution

Litigation is expensive. It is also time consuming. Because of the backlog of cases pending in many courts, several years may pass before a case is actually tried. For these and other

---

21. Wisconsin Statute Section 751.12.

reasons, more and more businesspersons are turning to **alternative dispute resolution (ADR)** as a means of settling their disputes.

The great advantage of ADR is its flexibility. Methods of ADR range from the parties sitting down together and attempting to work out their differences to multinational corporations agreeing to resolve a dispute through a formal hearing before a panel of experts. Normally, the parties themselves can control how they will attempt to settle their dispute, what procedures will be used, whether a neutral third party will be present or make a decision, and whether that decision will be legally binding or nonbinding.

Today, more than 90 percent of cases are settled before trial through some form of ADR. Indeed, most states either require or encourage parties to undertake ADR prior to trial. Many federal courts have instituted ADR programs as well. In the following pages, we examine the basic forms of ADR. Keep in mind, though, that new methods of ADR—and new combinations of existing methods—are constantly being devised and employed.

3-6a Negotiation

The simplest form of ADR is **negotiation,** in which the parties attempt to settle their dispute informally, with or without attorneys to represent them. Attorneys frequently advise their clients to negotiate a settlement voluntarily before they proceed to trial. Parties may even try to negotiate a settlement during a trial or after the trial but before an appeal. Negotiation traditionally involves just the parties themselves and (typically) their attorneys. The attorneys, though, are advocates—they are obligated to put their clients' interests first.

3-6b Mediation

In **mediation,** a neutral third party acts as a mediator and works with both sides in the dispute to facilitate a resolution. The mediator talks with the parties separately as well as jointly and emphasizes their points of agreement in an attempt to help them evaluate their options. Although the mediator may propose a solution (called a *mediator's proposal*), he or she does not make a decision resolving the matter. States that require parties to undergo ADR before trial often offer mediation as one of the ADR options or (as in Florida) the only option.

One of the biggest advantages of mediation is that it is not as adversarial as litigation. In a trial, the parties "do battle" with each other in the courtroom, trying to prove each other wrong, while the judge is usually a passive observer. In mediation, the mediator takes an active role and attempts to bring the parties together so that they can come to a mutually satisfactory resolution. The mediation process tends to reduce the hostility between the disputants, allowing them to resume their former relationship without bad feelings. For this reason, mediation is often the preferred form of ADR for disputes involving business partners, employers and employees, or other parties involved in long-term relationships.

EXAMPLE 3.13 Two business partners, Mark Shalen and Charles Rowe, have a dispute over how the profits of their firm should be distributed. If the dispute is litigated, Shalen and Rowe will be adversaries, and their respective attorneys will emphasize how the parties' positions differ, not what they have in common. In contrast, if the dispute is mediated, the mediator will emphasize the common ground shared by Shalen and Rowe and help them work toward agreement. The two men can work out the distribution of profits without damaging their continuing relationship as partners. ■

3-6c Arbitration

In **arbitration,** a more formal method of ADR, an arbitrator (a neutral third party or a panel of experts) hears a dispute and imposes a resolution on the parties. Arbitration differs from other forms of ADR in that the third party hearing the dispute makes a decision for the parties. Exhibit 3–4 outlines the basic differences among the three traditional forms of ADR.

Alternative Dispute Resolution (ADR) The resolution of disputes in ways other than those involved in the traditional judicial process, such as negotiation, mediation, and arbitration.

LEARNING OBJECTIVE 5
What are three alternative methods of resolving disputes?

Negotiation A process in which parties attempt to settle their dispute informally, with or without attorneys to represent them.

Mediation A method of settling disputes outside the courts by using the services of a neutral third party, who acts as a communicating agent between the parties and assists them in negotiating a settlement.

Arbitration The settling of a dispute by submitting it to a disinterested third party (other than a court), who renders a decision.

Exhibit 3-4 Basic Differences in the Traditional Forms of Alternative Dispute Resolution

TYPE OF ADR	DESCRIPTION	NEUTRAL THIRD PARTY PRESENT?	WHO DECIDES THE RESOLUTION?
Negotiation	The parties meet informally with or without their attorneys and attempt to agree on a resolution.	No	The parties themselves reach a resolution.
Mediation	A neutral third party meets with the parties and emphasizes points of agreement to help them resolve their dispute.	Yes	The parties decide the resolution, but the mediator may suggest or propose a resolution.
Arbitration	The parties present their arguments and evidence before an arbitrator at a hearing, and the arbitrator renders a decision resolving the parties' dispute.	Yes	The arbitrator imposes a resolution on the parties that may be either binding or nonbinding.

What are the steps in a typical arbitration proceeding?

Usually, the parties in arbitration agree that the third party's decision will be *legally binding,* although the parties can also agree to *nonbinding* arbitration. (Arbitration that is mandated by the courts often is nonbinding.) In nonbinding arbitration, the parties can go forward with a lawsuit if they do not agree with the arbitrator's decision.

In some respects, formal arbitration resembles a trial, although usually the procedural rules are much less restrictive than those governing litigation. In the typical arbitration, the parties present opening arguments and ask for specific remedies. Both sides present evidence and may call and examine witnesses. The arbitrator then renders a decision.

The Arbitrator's Decision The arbitrator's decision is called an *award.* It is usually the final word on the matter. Although the parties may appeal an arbitrator's decision, a court's review of the decision will be much more restricted in scope than an appellate court's review of a trial court's decision. The general view is that because the parties were free to frame the issues and set the powers of the arbitrator at the outset, they cannot complain about the results. A court will set aside an award only in the event of one of the following:

1. The arbitrator's conduct or "bad faith" substantially prejudiced the rights of one of the parties.

2. The award violates an established public policy.

3. The arbitrator exceeded her or his powers—that is, arbitrated issues that the parties did not agree to submit to arbitration.

Arbitration Clauses Just about any commercial matter can be submitted to arbitration. Parties can agree to arbitrate a dispute after it arises. Frequently, though, parties include an **arbitration clause** in a contract. The clause provides that any dispute that arises under the contract will be resolved through arbitration rather than through the court system.

Arbitration Statutes Most states have statutes (often based in part on the Uniform Arbitration Act) under which arbitration clauses will be enforced. Some state statutes compel arbitration of certain types of disputes, such as those involving public employees. At the federal level, the Federal Arbitration Act (FAA) enforces arbitration clauses in contracts involving maritime activity and interstate commerce (though its applicability to employment contracts has been controversial, as discussed later). Because of the breadth of the commerce clause, arbitration agreements involving transactions only slightly connected to the flow of interstate commerce may fall under the FAA.

Arbitration Clause A clause in a contract that provides that, in the event of a dispute, the parties will submit the dispute to arbitration rather than litigate the dispute in court.

CASE EXAMPLE 3.14 Buckeye Check Cashing, Inc., cashes personal checks for consumers in Florida. Buckeye would agree to delay submitting a consumer's check for payment if the consumer paid a "finance charge." For each transaction, the consumer signed an agreement that included an arbitration clause. A group of consumers filed a lawsuit claiming that Buckeye was charging an illegally high rate of interest in violation of state law. Buckeye filed a motion to compel arbitration, which the trial court denied, and the case was appealed.

The plaintiffs argued that the entire contract—including the arbitration clause—was illegal and therefore arbitration was not required. The United States Supreme Court found that the arbitration provision was *severable,* or capable of being separated, from the rest of the contract. The Court held that when the challenge is to the validity of a contract as a whole, and not specifically to an arbitration clause within the contract, an arbitrator must resolve the dispute. Even if the contract itself later proves to be unenforceable, arbitration will still be required because the FAA established a national policy favoring arbitration and that policy extends to both federal and state courts.[22] ▪

The Issue of Arbitrability
The terms of an arbitration agreement can limit the types of disputes that the parties agree to arbitrate. Disputes can arise, however, when the parties do not specify limits or when the parties disagree on whether a particular matter is covered by their arbitration agreement.

When one party files a lawsuit to compel arbitration, it is up to the court to resolve the issue of *arbitrability.* That is, the court must decide whether the matter is one that must be resolved through arbitration. If the court finds that the subject matter in controversy is covered by the agreement to arbitrate, then it may compel arbitration. Usually, a court will allow the claim to be arbitrated if the court finds that the relevant statute (the state arbitration statute or the FAA) does not exclude such claims.

No party, however, will be ordered to submit a particular dispute to arbitration unless the court is convinced that the party has consented to do so. Additionally, the courts will not compel arbitration if it is clear that the arbitration rules and procedures are inherently unfair to one of the parties.

Mandatory Arbitration in the Employment Context
A significant question for businesspersons has concerned mandatory arbitration clauses in employment contracts. Many employees claim they are at a disadvantage when they are forced, as a condition of being hired, to agree to arbitrate all disputes and thus waive their rights under statutes designed to protect employees. The United States Supreme Court, however, has held that mandatory arbitration clauses in employment contracts are generally enforceable.

CASE EXAMPLE 3.15 In a landmark decision, *Gilmer v. Interstate/Johnson Lane Corp.,*[23] the Supreme Court held that a claim brought under a federal statute prohibiting age discrimination could be subject to arbitration. The Court concluded that the employee had waived his right to sue when he agreed, as part of a required registration application to be a securities representative with the New York Stock Exchange, to arbitrate "any dispute, claim, or controversy" relating to his employment. ▪

Since the *Gilmer* decision, some courts have refused to enforce one-sided arbitration clauses. Employment-related agreements often require the parties to split the costs of arbitration, but some courts have overturned those provisions when an individual worker lacked the ability to pay.[24]

In the following case, the court considered the effect of an arbitration clause included in an employment application.

---

22. *Buckeye Check Cashing, Inc. v. Cardegna,* 546 U.S. 440, 126 S.Ct. 1204, 163 L.Ed.2d 1038 (2006).
23. 500 U.S. 20, 111 S.Ct. 1647, 114 L.Ed.2d 26 (1991).
24. See, for example, *Macias v. Excel Building Services, LLC,* 767 F.Supp.2d 1002 (N.D.Cal. 2011), citing *Davis v. O'Melveny & Myers, LLC,* 485 F.3d 1066 (9th Cir. 2007), and *Nagrampa v. MailCoups, Inc.,* 469 F.3d 1257 (9th Cir. 2006).

CASE 3.3

Cruise v. Kroger Co.

Court of Appeal of California, Second District, Division 3, 233 Cal.App.4th 390, 183 Cal.Rptr.3d 17 (2015).

FACTS Stephanie Cruise applied for a job with Kroger Co.'s Compton Creamery & Deli Kitchen. The application contained a clause requiring arbitration of "employment-related disputes" and referred to the company's arbitration policy. Cruise was hired. Four years later, she was fired. Cruise filed a suit in a California state court against Kroger, alleging employment discrimination—retaliation, sexual harassment, sexual and racial discrimination, and failure to investigate and prevent harassment and retaliation—as well as wrongful termination in violation of public policy, intentional infliction of emotional distress, and defamation. Kroger filed a motion to compel arbitration and provided the court with an undated four-page arbitration policy. Because the company could not prove that the policy was in effect when Cruise signed the employment application, the court held that there was no proof of a written agreement to arbitrate and denied the motion. Kroger appealed.

ISSUE Is an arbitration clause in an employment agreement sufficient to establish an agreement to arbitrate?

DECISION Yes. The state intermediate appellate court reversed the lower court's denial of Kroger's motion to compel arbitration with directions to grant the motion.

When does an employee have to submit to arbitration for employment-related disputes?

REASON The appellate court concluded that the arbitration clause in the employment application established that the parties had agreed to arbitrate their "employment-related disputes." The employment application was signed by Cruise. The arbitration clause, which was initialed by Cruise separately, stated that "any Employee who wishes to initiate or participate in formal proceedings to resolve any Covered Disputes must submit the claims or disputes to final and binding arbitration in accordance with the Policy." The court reasoned that this "language eliminates any argument the parties did not agree to arbitrate their employment-related disputes." Kroger's inability to prove the precise terms of the arbitration policy did not disprove the existence of the arbitration agreement. The court also concluded that all of Cruise's claims were employment-related disputes that fell within the meaning of the arbitration agreement.

CRITICAL THINKING—Legal Consideration *In the circumstances of this case, what procedures should govern the arbitration? Discuss.*

3–6d Other Types of ADR

The three forms of ADR just discussed are the oldest and traditionally the most commonly used. In addition, a variety of newer types of ADR have emerged, including those described here.

1. In *early neutral case evaluation*, the parties select a neutral third party (generally an expert in the subject matter of the dispute) and then explain their respective positions to that person. The case evaluator assesses the strengths and weaknesses of each party's claims.

2. In a *mini-trial*, each party's attorney briefly argues the party's case before the other party and a panel of representatives from each side who have the authority to settle the dispute. Typically, a neutral third party (usually an expert in the area being disputed) acts as an adviser. If the parties fail to reach an agreement, the adviser renders an opinion as to how a court would likely decide the issue.

3. Numerous federal courts now hold **summary jury trials,** in which the parties present their arguments and evidence and the jury renders a verdict. The jury's verdict is not binding, but it does act as a guide to both sides in reaching an agreement during the mandatory negotiations that immediately follow the trial.

Summary Jury Trial (SJT)
A method of settling disputes by holding a trial in which the jury's verdict is not binding but instead guides the parties toward reaching an agreement during the mandatory negotiations that immediately follow.

3–6e Providers of ADR Services

ADR services are provided by both government agencies and private organizations. A major provider of ADR services is the American Arbitration Association (AAA), which handles more than 200,000 claims a year in its numerous offices worldwide. Most of the largest U.S. law firms are members of this nonprofit association. Cases brought before the AAA are heard by an expert or a panel of experts in the area relating to the dispute and are usually settled quickly. The AAA has a special team devoted to resolving large, complex disputes across a wide range of industries.

Hundreds of for-profit firms around the country also provide various dispute-resolution services. Typically, these firms hire retired judges to conduct arbitration hearings or otherwise assist parties in settling their disputes. The judges follow procedures similar to those of the federal courts and use similar rules. Usually, each party to the dispute pays a filing fee and a designated fee for a hearing session or conference.

3–6f Online Dispute Resolution

An increasing number of companies and organizations offer dispute-resolution services using the Internet. The settlement of disputes in these online forums is known as **online dispute resolution (ODR).** The disputes have most commonly involved disagreements over the rights to domain names or over the quality of goods sold via the Internet, including goods sold through Internet auction sites.

Rules being developed in online forums may ultimately become a code of conduct for everyone who does business in cyberspace. Most online forums do not automatically apply the law of any specific jurisdiction. Instead, results are often based on general, universal legal principles. As with most offline methods of dispute resolution, any party may appeal to a court at any time.

ODR may be best suited for resolving small- to medium-sized business liability claims, which may not be worth the expense of litigation or traditional ADR. In addition, some local governments are using ODR to resolve claims. **EXAMPLE 3.16** New York City has used Cybersettle.com to resolve auto accident, sidewalk, and other personal-injury claims made against the city. Parties with complaints submit their demands, and the city submits its offers confidentially online. If an offer exceeds a demand, the claimant keeps half the difference as a bonus. ∎

Online Dispute Resolution (ODR) The resolution of disputes with the assistance of organizations that offer dispute-resolution services via the Internet.

Reviewing . . . Courts and Alternative Dispute Resolution

Stan Garner resides in Illinois and promotes boxing matches for SuperSports, Inc., an Illinois corporation. Garner created the promotional concept of the "Ages" fights—a series of three boxing matches pitting an older fighter (George Foreman) against a younger fighter, such as John Ruiz or Riddick Bowe. The concept included titles for each of the three fights ("Challenge of the Ages," "Battle of the Ages," and "Fight of the Ages"), as well as promotional epithets to characterize the two fighters ("the Foreman Factor").

Garner contacted George Foreman and his manager, who both reside in Texas, to sell the idea, and they arranged a meeting at Caesar's Palace in Las Vegas, Nevada. At some point in the negotiations, Foreman's manager signed a nondisclosure agreement prohibiting him from disclosing Garner's promotional concepts unless they signed a contract. Nevertheless, after negotiations between Garner and Foreman fell through, Foreman used Garner's "Battle of the Ages" concept to promote a subsequent fight. Garner filed a lawsuit against Foreman and his manager in a federal district court in Illinois, alleging breach of contract. Using the information presented in the chapter, answer the following questions.

Continues

1. On what basis might the federal district court in Illinois exercise jurisdiction in this case?

2. Does the federal district court have original or appellate jurisdiction?

3. Suppose that Garner had filed his action in an Illinois state court. Could an Illinois state court have exercised personal jurisdiction over Foreman or his manager? Why or why not?

4. What if Garner had filed his action in a Nevada state court? Would that court have had personal jurisdiction over Foreman or his manager? Explain.

DEBATE THIS

■ In this age of the Internet, when people communicate via e-mail, tweets, social media, and Skype, is the concept of jurisdiction losing its meaning?

Key Terms

alternative dispute resolution (ADR) 79
answer 70
arbitration 79
arbitration clause 80
award 75
bankruptcy court 58
brief 77
complaint 70
concurrent jurisdiction 60
counterclaim 70
default judgment 70
deposition 72
discovery 71
diversity of citizenship 59
docket 78
e-evidence 73
exclusive jurisdiction 60

federal question 59
interrogatories 73
judicial review 56
jurisdiction 56
justiciable controversy 63
litigation 69
long arm statute 57
mediation 79
metadata 73
motion for a directed verdict 75
motion for a new trial 75
motion for judgment *n.o.v.* 75
motion for judgment on the
    pleadings 71
motion for summary judgment 71
motion to dismiss 71
negotiation 79

online dispute resolution (ODR) 83
pleadings 70
probate court 58
question of fact 66
question of law 67
reply 70
rule of four 69
service of process 70
small claims court 65
standing to sue 63
summary jury trial (SJT) 82
summons 70
venue 63
voir dire 74
writ of *certiorari* 68

Chapter Summary: Courts and Alternative Dispute Resolution

The Judiciary's Role in American Government	The role of the judiciary—the courts—in the American governmental system is to interpret and apply the law. Through the process of judicial review—determining the constitutionality of laws—the judicial branch acts as a check on the executive and legislative branches of government.

Basic Judicial Requirements	1. *Jurisdiction*—Before a court can hear a case, it must have jurisdiction over the person against whom the suit is brought or the property involved in the suit, as well as jurisdiction over the subject matter.
	  a. Limited versus general jurisdiction—Limited jurisdiction exists when a court is limited to a specific subject matter, such as probate or divorce. General jurisdiction exists when a court can hear any kind of case.
	  b. Original versus appellate jurisdiction—Original jurisdiction exists when courts have authority to hear a case for the first time (trial courts). Appellate jurisdiction is exercised by courts of appeals, or reviewing courts, which generally do not have original jurisdiction.
	  c. Federal jurisdiction—Arises (1) when a federal question is involved (when the plaintiff's cause of action is based, at least in part, on the U.S. Constitution, a treaty, or a federal law) or (2) when a case involves diversity of citizenship (citizens of different states, for example) and the amount in controversy exceeds $75,000.
	  d. Concurrent versus exclusive jurisdiction—Concurrent jurisdiction exists when two different courts have authority to hear the same case. Exclusive jurisdiction exists when only state courts or only federal courts have authority to hear a case.
	2. *Jurisdiction in cyberspace*—Because the Internet does not have physical boundaries, traditional jurisdictional concepts have been difficult to apply in cases involving activities conducted via the Web. Gradually, the courts are developing standards to use in determining when jurisdiction over a Web site owner or operator located in another state is proper.
	3. *Venue*—Venue has to do with the most appropriate location for a trial, which is usually the geographic area where the event leading to the dispute took place or where the parties reside.
	4. *Standing to sue*—A requirement that a party must have a legally protected and tangible interest at stake sufficient to justify seeking relief through the court system. The controversy at issue must also be a justiciable controversy—one that is real and substantial, as opposed to hypothetical or academic.

The State and Federal Court Systems	1. *Trial courts*—Courts of original jurisdiction, in which legal actions are initiated.
	  a. State—Courts of general jurisdiction can hear any case. Courts of limited jurisdiction include domestic relations courts, probate courts, traffic courts, and small claims courts.
	  b. Federal—The federal district court is the equivalent of the state trial court. Federal courts of limited jurisdiction include the U.S. Tax Court, the U.S. Bankruptcy Court, and the U.S. Court of Federal Claims.
	2. *Intermediate appellate courts*—Courts of appeals, or reviewing courts, which generally do not have original jurisdiction. Many states have intermediate appellate courts. In the federal court system, the U.S. circuit courts of appeals are the intermediate appellate courts.
	3. *Supreme (highest) courts*—Each state has a supreme court, although it may be called by some other name. Appeal from the state supreme court to the United States Supreme Court is possible only if the case involves a federal question. The United States Supreme Court is the highest court in the federal court system and the final arbiter of the U.S. Constitution and federal law.

Following a State Court Case	Rules of procedure prescribe the way in which disputes are handled in the courts. Rules differ from court to court, and separate sets of rules exist for federal and state courts, as well as for criminal and civil cases. A civil court case in a state court would involve the following procedures:
	1. *The pleadings*—
	  a. Complaint—Filed by the plaintiff with the court to initiate the lawsuit. The complaint is served with a summons on the defendant.
	  b. Answer—A response to the complaint in which the defendant admits or denies the allegations made by the plaintiff. The answer may assert a counterclaim or an affirmative defense.
	  c. Motion to dismiss—A request to the court to dismiss the case for stated reasons, such as the plaintiff's failure to state a claim for which relief can be granted.
	2. *Pretrial motions (in addition to the motion to dismiss)*—
	  a. Motion for judgment on the pleadings—May be made by either party. It will be granted if the parties agree on the facts and the only question is how the law applies to the facts. The judge bases the decision solely on the pleadings.
	  b. Motion for summary judgment—May be made by either party. It will be granted if the parties agree on the facts and the sole question is a question of law. The judge can consider evidence outside the pleadings when evaluating the motion.

Continues

Following a State Court Case (Continued)	**3.** *Discovery*—The process of gathering evidence concerning the case. Discovery involves depositions (sworn testimony by a party to the lawsuit or any witness), interrogatories (written questions and answers to these questions made by parties to the action with the aid of their attorneys), and various requests (for admissions, documents, and medical examinations, for example). Discovery may also involve electronically recorded information, such as e-mail, voice mail, word-processing documents, and other data compilations. Although electronic discovery has significant advantages over paper discovery, it is also more time consuming and expensive and often requires the parties to hire experts.
	4. *Pretrial conference*—Either party or the court can request a pretrial conference to identify the matters in dispute after discovery has taken place and to plan the course of the trial.
	5. *Trial*—Following jury selection (*voir dire*), the trial begins with opening statements from both parties' attorneys. The following events then occur:
	a. The plaintiff's introduction of evidence (including the testimony of witnesses) supporting the plaintiff's position. The defendant's attorney can challenge evidence and cross-examine witnesses.
	b. The defendant's introduction of evidence (including the testimony of witnesses) supporting the defendant's position. The plaintiff's attorney can challenge evidence and cross-examine witnesses.
	c. Closing arguments by the attorneys in favor of their respective clients, the judge's instructions to the jury, and the jury's verdict.
	6. *Posttrial motions*—
	a. Motion for judgment *n.o.v.* ("notwithstanding the verdict")—Will be granted if the judge is convinced that the jury was in error.
	b. Motion for a new trial—Will be granted if the judge is convinced that the jury was in error. The motion can also be granted on the grounds of newly discovered evidence, misconduct by the participants during the trial, or error by the judge.
	7. *Appeal*—Either party can appeal the trial court's judgment to an appropriate court of appeals. After reviewing the record on appeal, the abstracts, and the attorneys' briefs, the appellate court holds a hearing and renders its opinion.
Courts Online	A number of state and federal courts now allow parties to file litigation-related documents with the courts via the Internet or other electronic means. Nearly all of the federal appellate courts and bankruptcy courts and a majority of the federal district courts have implemented electronic filing systems. Almost every court now has a Web page offering information about the court and its procedures, and increasingly courts are publishing their opinions online. In the future, we may see cyber courts, in which all trial proceedings are conducted online.
Alternative Dispute Resolution	**1.** *Negotiation*—The parties come together, with or without attorneys to represent them, and try to reach a settlement without the involvement of a third party.
	2. *Mediation*—The parties themselves reach an agreement with the help of a neutral third party, called a mediator. The mediator may propose a solution but does not make a decision resolving the matter.
	3. *Arbitration*—The parties submit their dispute to a neutral third party, the arbitrator, who renders a decision. The decision may or may not be legally binding, depending on the circumstances.
	4. *Other types of ADR*—These include assisted negotiation, early neutral case evaluation, mini-trials, and summary jury trials (SJTs).
	5. *Providers of ADR services*—The leading nonprofit provider of ADR services is the American Arbitration Association. Hundreds of for-profit firms also provide ADR services.
	6. *Online dispute resolution*—A number of organizations and firms are now offering negotiation, mediation, and arbitration services through online forums. These forums have been a practical alternative for the resolution of domain name disputes and e-commerce disputes in which the amount in controversy is relatively small.

Issue Spotters

1. At the trial, after Sue calls her witnesses, offers her evidence, and otherwise presents her side of the case, Tom has at least two choices between courses of action. Tom can call his first witness. What else might he do? (See *Following a State Court Case*.)

2. Sue contracts with Tom to deliver a quantity of computers to Sue's Computer Store. They disagree over the amount, the delivery date, the price, and the quality. Sue files a suit against Tom in a state court. Their state requires that their dispute be submitted to mediation or nonbinding arbitration. If the dispute is not resolved, or if either party disagrees with the decision of the mediator or arbitrator, will a court hear the case? Explain. (See *Alternative Dispute Resolution*.)

—**Check your answers to the *Issue Spotters* against the answers provided in Appendix D at the end of this text.**

Learning Objectives Check

1. What is judicial review? How and when was the power of judicial review established?
2. How are the courts applying traditional jurisdictional concepts to cases involving Internet transactions?
3. What is the difference between the focus of a trial court and an appellate court?
4. What is discovery, and how does electronic discovery differ from traditional discovery?
5. What are three alternative methods of resolving disputes?

—Answers to the even-numbered *Learning Objectives Check* questions can be found in Appendix E at the end of this text.

Business Scenarios and Case Problems

3–1. Standing to Sue. Jack and Maggie Turton bought a house in Jefferson County, Idaho, located directly across the street from a gravel pit. A few years later, the county converted the pit to a landfill. The landfill accepted many kinds of trash that cause harm to the environment, including major appliances, animal carcasses, containers with hazardous content warnings, leaking car batteries, and waste oil. The Turtons complained to the county, but the county did nothing. The Turtons then filed a lawsuit against the county alleging violations of federal environmental laws pertaining to groundwater contamination and other pollution. Do the Turtons have standing to sue? Why or why not? (See *Basic Judicial Requirements*.)

3–2. Discovery. Advance Technology Consultants, Inc. (ATC), contracted with RoadTrac, LLC, to provide software and client software systems for products using global positioning satellite (GPS) technology being developed by RoadTrac. RoadTrac agreed to provide ATC with hardware with which ATC's software would interface. Problems soon arose, however, and RoadTrac filed a lawsuit against ATC alleging breach of contract. During discovery, RoadTrac requested ATC's customer lists and marketing procedures. ATC objected to providing this information because RoadTrac and ATC had become competitors in the GPS industry. Should a party to a lawsuit have to hand over its confidential business secrets as part of a discovery request? Why or why not? What limitations might a court consider imposing before requiring ATC to produce this material? (See *Following a State Court Case*.)

3–3. Spotlight on the National Football League—Arbitration. Bruce Matthews played football for the Tennessee Titans. As part of his contract, he agreed to submit any dispute to arbitration. He also agreed that Tennessee law would determine all matters related to workers' compensation. After Matthews retired, he filed a workers' compensation claim in California. The arbitrator ruled that Matthews could pursue his claim in California but only under Tennessee law. Should the arbitrator's award be set aside? Explain. [*National Football League Players Association v. National Football League*

Management Council, 2011 WL 1137334 (S.D.Cal. 2011)] (See *Alternative Dispute Resolution*.)

3–4. Minimum Contacts. Seal Polymer Industries sold two freight containers of latex gloves to Med-Express, Inc., a company based in North Carolina. When Med-Express failed to pay the $104,000 owed for the gloves, Seal Polymer sued in an Illinois court and obtained a judgment against Med-Express. Med-Express argued that it did not have minimum contacts with Illinois and therefore the Illinois judgment based on personal jurisdiction was invalid. Med-Express stated that it was incorporated under North Carolina law, had its principal place of business in North Carolina, and therefore had no minimum contacts with Illinois. Was this statement alone sufficient to prevent the Illinois judgment from being collected against Med-Express in North Carolina? Why or why not? [*Seal Polymer Industries v. Med-Express, Inc.*, 725 S.E.2d 5 (N.C.App. 2012)] (See *Basic Judicial Requirements*.)

3–5. Arbitration. Horton Automatics and the Industrial Division of the Communications Workers of America—the union that represented Horton's workers—negotiated a collective bargaining agreement. If an employee's discharge for a workplace-rule violation was submitted to arbitration, the agreement limited the arbitrator to determining whether the rule was reasonable and whether the employee had violated it. When Horton discharged its employee Ruben de la Garza, the union appealed to arbitration. The arbitrator found that de la Garza had violated a reasonable safety rule, but "was not totally convinced" that Horton should have treated the violation more seriously than other rule violations. The arbitrator ordered de la Garza reinstated to his job. Can a court set aside this order from the arbitrator? Explain. [*Horton Automatics v. The Industrial Division of the Communications Workers of America, AFL-CIO,* __ F.3d __, 2013 WL 59204 (5th Cir. 2013)] (See *Alternative Dispute Resolution*.)

3–6. Business Case Problem with Sample Answer—Discovery. Jessica Lester died from injuries suffered in an auto accident caused by the driver of a truck owned by Allied Concrete Co. Jessica's widower, Isaiah, filed a suit against Allied for damages. The defendant requested copies of all of Isaiah's Facebook photos and other postings. Before responding, Isaiah "cleaned up" his Facebook page. Allied suspected that some of the items had been deleted, including a photo of Isaiah holding a beer can while wearing a T-shirt that declared "I [heart] hotmoms." Can this material be recovered? If so, how? What effect might Isaiah's "misconduct" have on the result in this case? Discuss. [*Allied Concrete Co. v. Lester*, 736 S.E.2d 699 (Va. 2013)] (See *Following a State Court Case*.)

> **—For a sample answer to Problem 3–6, go to Appendix F at the end of this text.**

3–7. Electronic Filing. Betsy Faden worked for the U.S. Department of Veterans Affairs. Faden was removed from her position in April 2012 and was given until May 29 to appeal the removal decision. She submitted an appeal through the Merit Systems Protection Board's e-filing system seven days after the deadline. Ordered to show good cause for the delay, Faden testified that she had attempted to e-file the appeal while the board's system was down. The board acknowledged that its system had not been functioning on May 27, 28, and 29. Was Faden sufficiently diligent in ensuring a timely filing? Discuss. [*Faden v. Merit Systems Protection Board*, __ F.3d __, 2014 WL 163394 (Fed. Cir. 2014)] (See *Courts Online*.)

3–8. Corporate Contacts. LG Electronics, Inc., and nineteen other foreign companies participated in the global market for cathode ray tube (CRT) products, which were integrated as components in consumer goods, including television sets.

These goods were sold for many years in high volume in the United States, including the state of Washington. Later, the state filed a suit in a Washington state court against LG and the others, alleging a conspiracy to raise prices and set production levels in the market for CRTs in violation of a state consumer protection statute. The defendants filed a motion to dismiss the suit for lack of personal jurisdiction. Should this motion be granted? Explain. [*State of Washington v. LG Electronics, Inc.*, 341 P.3d 346 (Wash. App., Div. 1 2015)] (See *Basic Judicial Requirements*.)

3–9. A Question of Ethics—Agreement to Arbitrate. Nellie Lumpkin, who suffered from dementia, was admitted to the Picayune Convalescent Center, a nursing home. Because of her mental condition, her daughter, Beverly McDaniel, signed the admissions agreement. It included a clause requiring the parties to submit any dispute to arbitration. After Lumpkin left the center two years later, she filed a suit against Picayune to recover damages for mistreatment and malpractice. [*Covenant Health & Rehabilitation of Picayune, LP v. Lumpkin*, 23 So.3d 1092 (Miss. App. 2009)] (See *Alternative Dispute Resolution*.)

1. Is it ethical for this dispute—involving negligent medical care, not a breach of a commercial contract—to be forced into arbitration? Why or why not? Discuss whether medical facilities should be able to impose arbitration when there is generally no bargaining over such terms.

2. Should a person with limited mental capacity be held to the arbitration clause agreed to by her next of kin, who signed on her behalf? Why or why not?

Critical Thinking and Writing Assignments

3–10. Business Law Critical Thinking Group Assignment. Bento Cuisine is a lunch-cart business. It occupies a street corner in Texarkana, a city that straddles the border of Arkansas and Texas. Across the street—and across the state line, which runs down the middle of the street—is Rico's Tacos. The two businesses compete for customers. Recently, Bento has begun to suspect that Rico's is engaging in competitive behavior that is illegal. Bento's manager overheard several of Rico's employees discussing these competitive tactics while on a break at a nearby Starbucks. Bento files a lawsuit against

Rico's in a federal court based on diversity jurisdiction. (See *Basic Judicial Requirements* and *Following a State Court Case*.)

1. One group will determine whether Rico's could file a motion claiming that the federal court lacks jurisdiction over this dispute.

2. Another group will assume that the case goes to trial. Bento believes that it has both the law and the facts on its side. Nevertheless, at the end of the trial, the jury decides against Bento, and the judge issues a ruling in favor of Rico's. If Bento is unwilling to accept this result, what are its options?

corgarashu/ShutterStock.com

Tort Law

"Two wrongs do not make a right."

ENGLISH PROVERB

Most of us agree with the chapter-opening quotation—two wrongs do not make a right. In this chapter, we consider a particular type of wrongful actions called **torts** (the word *tort* is French for "wrong"). As you will see, torts form the basis for many lawsuits.

As noted in earlier chapters, part of doing business today is the risk of being involved in a lawsuit. The list of circumstances in which businesspersons can be sued is long and varied. A customer who is injured by a security guard at a business establishment, for instance, may sue the business owner. A person who slips and falls at a retail store may sue the company for negligence. Any time one party's allegedly wrongful conduct causes injury to another, an action may arise under the law of torts. Through tort law, society compensates those who have suffered injuries as a result of the wrongful conduct of others.

Many of the lawsuits brought by or against business firms are based on the tort theories discussed in this chapter and the next chapter, which covers product liability. In addition, Chapter 7 discusses how tort law applies to wrongful actions in the online environment.

4-1 The Basis of Tort Law

Two notions serve as the basis of all torts: wrongs and compensation. Tort law is designed to compensate those who have suffered a loss or injury due to another person's wrongful act. In a tort action, one person or group brings a personal suit against another person or group to obtain compensation (monetary damages) or other relief for the harm suffered.

LEARNING OBJECTIVES

The five Learning Objectives *below are designed to help improve your understanding of the chapter. After reading this chapter, you should be able to answer the following questions:*

1. What is the purpose of tort law? What types of damages are available in tort lawsuits?

2. What are two basic categories of torts?

3. What is defamation? Name two types of defamation.

4. Identify the four elements of negligence.

5. What is meant by strict liability? In what circumstances is strict liability applied?

Tort A wrongful act (other than a breach of contract) that results in harm or injury to another and leads to civil liability.

LEARNING OBJECTIVE 1

What is the purpose of tort law? What types of damages are available in tort lawsuits?

Damages A monetary award sought as a remedy for a breach of contract or a tortious action.

Compensatory Damages A monetary award equivalent to the actual value of injuries or damage sustained by the aggrieved party.

Special Damages In a tort case, an amount awarded to compensate the plaintiff for quantifiable monetary losses, such as medical expenses, property damage, and lost wages and benefits (now and in the future).

General Damages In a tort case, an amount awarded to compensate individuals for the nonmonetary aspects of the harm suffered, such as pain and suffering. Not available to companies.

Punitive Damages Monetary damages that may be awarded to a plaintiff to punish the defendant and deter similar conduct in the future.

Do tort lawsuits end up in civil or criminal courts?

4-1a The Purpose of Tort Law

Generally, the purpose of tort law is to provide remedies for the invasion of various *protected interests.* Society recognizes an interest in personal physical safety, and tort law provides remedies for acts that cause physical injury or interfere with physical security and freedom. Society also recognizes an interest in protecting property, and tort law provides remedies for acts that cause destruction of or damage to property.

Note that in legal usage, the singular *damage* is used to refer to harm or injury to persons or property. The plural **damages** is used to refer to monetary compensation for such harm or injury.

4-1b Damages Available in Tort Actions

Because the purpose of tort law is to compensate the injured party for the damage suffered, it is important to have a basic understanding of the types of damages that plaintiffs seek in tort actions.

Compensatory Damages   Plaintiffs are awarded **compensatory damages** to compensate or reimburse them for actual losses. Thus, the goal is to make the plaintiffs whole and put them in the same position that they would have been in had the tort not occurred. Compensatory damages awards are often broken down into *special damages* and *general damages.*

Special damages compensate plaintiffs for quantifiable monetary losses, such as medical expenses, lost wages and benefits (now and in the future), extra costs, the loss of irreplaceable items, and the costs of repairing or replacing damaged property. **CASE EXAMPLE 4.1** Seaway Marine Transport operates the *Enterprise,* a large cargo ship with twenty-two hatches for storing coal. When the *Enterprise* moved into position to receive a load of coal on the shores of Lake Erie in Ohio, it struck a land-based coal-loading machine operated by Bessemer & Lake Erie Railroad Company. A federal court found Seaway liable for negligence and awarded $522,000 in special damages to compensate Bessemer for the cost of repairing the damage to the loading machine.[1] ■

General damages compensate individuals (not companies) for the nonmonetary aspects of the harm suffered, such as pain and suffering. A court might award general damages for physical or emotional pain and suffering, loss of companionship, loss of consortium (losing the emotional and physical benefits of a spousal relationship), disfigurement, loss of reputation, or loss or impairment of mental or physical capacity.

Punitive Damages   Occasionally, the courts also award **punitive damages** in tort cases to punish the wrongdoers and deter others from similar wrongdoing. Punitive damages are appropriate only when the defendant's conduct was particularly egregious (flagrant) or reprehensible (blameworthy).

Thus, punitive damages are normally available mainly in intentional tort actions and only rarely in negligence lawsuits (*intentional torts* and *negligence* will be explained later in the chapter). They may be awarded, however, in suits involving *gross negligence,* which can be defined as an intentional failure to perform a manifest duty in reckless disregard of the effect on the life or property of another. (See this chapter's *Business Application* feature for steps businesses can take to avoid tort liability and the large damages awards that may go with it.)

Courts exercise great restraint in granting punitive damages to plaintiffs in tort actions because punitive damages are subject to the limitations imposed by the due process clause of the U.S. Constitution. The United States Supreme Court

---

1. *Bessemer & Lake Erie Railroad Co. v. Seaway Marine Transport,* 596 F.3d 357 (6th Cir. 2010).

has held that, when an award of punitive damages is grossly excessive, it furthers no legitimate purpose and violates due process requirements.[2] Consequently, an appellate court will sometimes reduce the amount of punitive damages awarded to a plaintiff because the amount was excessive and thereby violates the due process clause.

4-1c Tort Reform

Tort law performs a valuable function by enabling injured parties to obtain compensation. Nevertheless, critics contend that certain aspects of today's tort law encourage too many trivial and unfounded lawsuits, which clog the courts and add unnecessary costs. They say that damages awards are often excessive and bear little relationship to the actual damage suffered, which inspires more plaintiffs to file lawsuits. The result, in the critics' view, is a system that disproportionately rewards a few plaintiffs while imposing a "tort tax" on business and society as a whole. Among other consequences, physicians and hospitals order more tests than necessary in an effort to avoid medical malpractice suits, thereby adding to the nation's health-care costs.

"Do you have any picture books that could help a child understand tort reform?"

Types of Reform The federal government and a number of states have begun to take some steps toward tort reform. Measures to reduce the number of tort cases include the following:

1. Limiting the amount of both punitive damages and general damages that can be awarded.

2. Capping the amount that attorneys can collect in *contingency fees* (attorneys' fees that are based on a percentage of the damages awarded to the client).

3. Requiring the losing party to pay both the plaintiff's and the defendant's expenses.

Federal Reform At the federal level, the Class Action Fairness Act (CAFA)[3] shifted jurisdiction over large interstate tort and product liability class-action lawsuits from the state courts to the federal courts. (A *class action* is a lawsuit in which a large number of plaintiffs bring suit as a group. *Product liability* suits involve the manufacture, sale, and distribution of allegedly dangerous or defective goods.)

The CAFA prevents plaintiffs' attorneys from *forum shopping*—looking for a court based on whether the court is likely to provide a favorable judgment. Previously, multiple courts often had jurisdiction over class-action claims. Plaintiffs' attorneys naturally chose to bring suit in state courts that were known to be sympathetic to their clients' cause and predisposed to award large damages. Now, under the CAFA, state courts no longer have jurisdiction over class actions.

State Reform At the state level, more than half of the states have placed caps ranging from $250,000 to $750,000 on noneconomic general damages (for example, pain and suffering), especially in medical malpractice suits. More than thirty states have limited punitive damages, with some imposing outright bans.

Note, though, that the highest courts in about half a dozen states have declared their states' damages caps to be unconstitutional. **CASE EXAMPLE 4.2** Naython Watts was born with disabling brain injuries caused by the negligence of physicians at Cox Medical Centers in Missouri. At the age of six, Naython could not walk, talk, or feed himself. He had the

KNOW THIS

Damage refers to harm or injury to persons or property. *Damages* is a legal term that refers to the monetary compensation awarded to a plaintiff who has suffered such harm or injury.

2. *State Farm Mutual Automobile Insurance Co. v. Campbell*, 538 U.S. 408, 123 S.Ct. 1513, 155 L.Ed.2d 585 (2003).
3. 28 U.S.C. Sections 1453, 1711–1715.

mental capacity of a two-year-old, suffered from seizures, and needed around-the-clock care. His mother, Deborah Watts, sued the medical center on his behalf. A jury awarded Watts $1.45 million in noneconomic damages, plus $3.37 million in future medical damages.

The trial court reduced the noneconomic damages award to $350,000—the statutory cap under Missouri's law. Watts appealed. Missouri's highest court struck down the state's damages cap, holding that it violated the state constitution's right to trial by jury. The court reasoned that the amount of damages is a fact for the jury to determine, and the legislature cannot place caps on jury awards independent of the facts of a case.[4] ■

4-1d Classifications of Torts

There are two broad classifications of torts: *intentional torts* and *unintentional torts* (torts involving negligence). Intentional torts result from the intentional violation of person or property (fault with intent). Negligence results from the breach of a duty to act reasonably (fault without intent). The classification of a particular tort depends largely on how the tort occurs (intentionally or negligently) and the surrounding circumstances.

4-1e Defenses

Even if a plaintiff proves all the elements of a tort, the defendant can raise a number of legally recognized **defenses**—reasons why the plaintiff should not obtain damages. The defenses available may vary depending on the specific tort involved.

A common defense to intentional torts against persons, for instance, is *consent*. When a person consents to the act that damages her or him, there is generally no liability. The most widely used defense in negligence actions is *comparative negligence* (discussed later in this chapter). A successful defense releases the defendant from partial or full liability for the tortious act.

Most states also have a *statute of limitations* that establishes the time limit (often two years from the date of discovering the harm) within which a particular type of lawsuit can be filed. After that time period has run, the plaintiff can no longer file a claim.

4-2 Intentional Torts against Persons

An **intentional tort,** as just mentioned, requires *intent*. The **tortfeasor** (the one committing the tort) must intend to commit an act, the consequences of which interfere with the personal or business interests of another in a way not permitted by law. An evil or harmful motive is not required—in fact, the person committing the action may even have a beneficial motive for committing what turns out to be a tortious act.

In tort law, intent means only that the person intended the consequences of his or her act or knew with substantial certainty that certain consequences would result from the act. The law generally assumes that individuals intend the *normal* consequences of their actions. Thus, forcefully pushing another—even if done in jest and without any evil motive—is an intentional tort if injury results, because the object of a strong push can ordinarily be expected to fall down.

Intent can be transferred when a defendant intends to harm one individual, but unintentionally harms a different person. This is called **transferred intent.** EXAMPLE 4.3 Alex swings a bat intending to hit Blake but misses and hits Carson instead. Carson can sue Alex for the tort of battery (discussed shortly) because Alex's intent to harm Blake can be transferred to Carson. ■

LEARNING OBJECTIVE 2

What are two basic categories of torts?

Defense A reason offered by a defendant in an action or lawsuit as to why the plaintiff should not recover or establish what she or he seeks.

Intentional Tort A wrongful act knowingly committed.

Tortfeasor One who commits a tort.

KNOW THIS

In intentional tort actions, the defendant must intend to commit the act, but need not have intended to cause harm to the plaintiff.

Transferred Intent A legal principle under which a person who intends to harm one individual, but unintentionally harms a different individual, can be liable to the second victim for an intentional tort.

---

4. *Watts v. Lester E. Cox Medical Centers*, 376 S.W.3d 633 (Mo. 2012).

In this section, we discuss intentional torts against persons. These torts include assault and battery, false imprisonment, infliction of emotional distress, defamation, invasion of the right to privacy, appropriation, misrepresentation, abusive or frivolous litigation, and wrongful interference.

4-2a Assault and Battery

An **assault** is any intentional and unexcused threat of immediate harmful or offensive contact—words or acts that create in another person a reasonable apprehension of harmful contact. An assault can be completed even if there is no actual contact with the plaintiff, provided the defendant's conduct causes the plaintiff to have a reasonable apprehension of imminent harm. Tort law aims to protect individuals from having to expect harmful or offensive contact.

If the act that created the apprehension is *completed* and results in harm to the plaintiff, it is a **battery,** which is defined as an unexcused and harmful or offensive physical contact *intentionally* performed.   **EXAMPLE 4.4** Ivan threatens Jean with a gun and then shoots her. The pointing of the gun at Jean is an assault. The firing of the gun (if the bullet hits Jean) is a battery. ■

The contact can be harmful, or it can be merely offensive (such as an unwelcome kiss). Physical injury need not occur. The contact can be made by the defendant or by some force set in motion by the defendant, such as a rock thrown by the defendant. Whether the contact is offensive or not is determined by the *reasonable person standard.*[5]

If the plaintiff shows that there was contact, and the jury (or judge, if there is no jury) agrees that the contact was offensive, the plaintiff has a right to compensation. A plaintiff may be compensated for the emotional harm resulting from a battery, as well as for physical harm. The defendant may raise a number of legally recognized defenses to justify his or her conduct, including self-defense and defense of others.

4-2b False Imprisonment

False imprisonment is the intentional confinement or restraint of another person's activities without justification. False imprisonment interferes with the freedom to move without restraint. The confinement can be accomplished through the use of physical barriers, physical restraint, or threats of physical force. Moral pressure or threats of future harm do not constitute false imprisonment. It is essential that the person under restraint does not wish to be restrained.

Businesspersons may face suits for false imprisonment after they have attempted to confine a suspected shoplifter for questioning. Under the "privilege to detain" granted to merchants in most states, a merchant can use *reasonable force* to detain or delay a person suspected of shoplifting the merchant's property. Although the details of the privilege vary from state to state, generally laws require that any detention be conducted in a *reasonable* manner and for only a *reasonable* length of time. Undue force or unreasonable detention can lead to liability for the business.

Cities and counties may also face lawsuits for false imprisonment if they detain individuals without reason. **CASE EXAMPLE 4.5** Police arrested Adetokunbo Shoyoye for an unpaid subway ticket and for a theft that had been committed by someone who had stolen his identity. A court ordered that he be released, but a county employee mistakenly confused Shoyoye's paperwork with that of another person, who was scheduled to be sent to state prison. As a result, instead of being released, Shoyoye was held in county jail for more than two weeks. Shoyoye later sued the county for false imprisonment and won.[6] ■

Assault Any word or action intended to make another person fearful of immediate physical harm—a reasonably believable threat.

Battery Physical contact with another that is unexcused, harmful or offensive, and intentionally performed.

Can cities and counties be sued for false imprisonment?

---

5. The reasonable person standard is an objective test of how a reasonable person would have acted under the same circumstances. See "The Duty of Care and Its Breach" later in this chapter.
6. *Shoyoye v. County of Los Angeles*, 203 Cal.App.4th 947, 137 Cal.Rptr.3d 839 (2012).

4-2c Intentional Infliction of Emotional Distress

The tort of *intentional infliction of emotional distress* can be defined as extreme and outrageous conduct resulting in severe emotional distress to another. To be **actionable** (capable of serving as the ground for a lawsuit), the conduct must be so extreme and outrageous that it exceeds the bounds of decency accepted by society.

Actionable Capable of serving as the basis of a lawsuit. An actionable claim can be pursued in a lawsuit or other court action.

Outrageous Conduct Courts in most jurisdictions are wary of emotional distress claims and confine them to truly outrageous behavior. Generally, repeated annoyances (such as those experienced by a person who is being stalked), coupled with threats, are sufficient to support a claim. Acts that cause indignity or annoyance alone usually are not enough.

EXAMPLE 4.6 A father attacks a man who has had consensual sexual relations with the father's nineteen-year-old daughter. The father handcuffs the man to a steel pole and threatens to kill him unless he leaves town immediately. The father's conduct may be sufficiently extreme and outrageous to be actionable as an intentional infliction of emotional distress. ■

Limited by the First Amendment When the outrageous conduct consists of speech about a public figure, the First Amendment's guarantee of freedom of speech limits emotional distress claims. **CASE EXAMPLE 4.7** *Hustler* magazine once printed a fake advertisement that showed a picture of the Reverend Jerry Falwell and described him as having lost his virginity to his mother in an outhouse while he was drunk. Falwell sued the magazine for intentional infliction of emotional distress and won, but the United States Supreme Court overturned the decision. The Court held that creators of parodies of public figures are protected under the First Amendment from claims of intentional infliction of emotional distress. (The Court applied the same standards that apply to public figures in defamation lawsuits, discussed next.)[7] ■

Is it legal to create a parody of a public figure, such as the Reverend Jerry Falwell?

4-2d Defamation

As discussed in Chapter 2, the freedom of speech guaranteed by the First Amendment to the U.S. Constitution is not absolute. In interpreting the First Amendment, the courts must balance free speech rights against other strong social interests, including society's interest in preventing and redressing attacks on reputation. (Nations with fewer free speech protections have seen an increase in defamation lawsuits targeting U.S. citizens and journalists as defendants. See this chapter's *Beyond Our Borders* feature for a discussion of this trend.)

The tort of **defamation** involves wrongfully hurting a person's good reputation. The law has imposed a general duty on all persons to refrain from making false, defamatory statements of fact about others. Breaching this duty in writing or another permanent form (such as a digital recording) constitutes the tort of **libel.** Breaching the duty orally is the tort of **slander.** The tort of defamation also arises when a false statement of fact is made about a person's product, business, or legal ownership rights to property.

To establish defamation, a plaintiff normally must prove the following:

1. The defendant made a false statement of fact.

2. The statement was understood as being about the plaintiff and tended to harm the plaintiff's reputation.

3. The statement was published to at least one person other than the plaintiff.

4. In addition, if the plaintiff is a public figure, she or he must prove *actual malice.*

LEARNING OBJECTIVE 3
What is defamation? Name two types of defamation.

Defamation Anything published or publicly spoken that causes injury to another's good name, reputation, or character.

Libel Defamation in writing or another permanent form (such as a digital recording).

Slander Defamation in oral form.

7. *Hustler Magazine, Inc. v. Falwell*, 485 U.S. 46, 108 S.Ct. 876, 99 L.Ed.2d 41 (1988). For another example of how the courts protect parody, see *Busch v. Viacom International, Inc.*, 477 F.Supp.2d 764 (N.D.Tex. 2007), involving a fake endorsement of televangelist Pat Robertson's diet shake.

Statement of Fact Requirement Often at issue in defamation lawsuits (including online defamation, discussed in Chapter 7) is whether the defendant made a *statement of fact* or a *statement of opinion*.[8] Statements of opinion normally are not actionable because they are protected under the First Amendment. In other words, making a negative statement about another person is not defamation unless the statement is false and represents something as a fact (for example, "Lane cheats on his taxes") rather than a personal opinion (for example, "Lane is a jerk").

The Publication Requirement The basis of the tort of defamation is the publication of a statement or statements that hold an individual up to contempt, ridicule, or hatred. *Publication* here means that the defamatory statements are communicated to persons other than the defamed party.

> **EXAMPLE 4.8** If Thompson writes Andrews a private letter or text falsely accusing him of embezzling funds, the action does not constitute libel. If Peters falsely states that Gordon is dishonest and incompetent when no one else is around, the action does not constitute slander. In neither instance was the message communicated to a third party. ■

The courts have generally held that even dictating a letter to a secretary constitutes publication, although the publication may be privileged (as discussed shortly). If a third party overhears defamatory statements by chance, the courts usually hold that this also constitutes publication. Defamatory statements made via the Internet (in e-mail or posted on social media)

---

8. See, for example, *Lott v. Levitt*, 469 F.Supp.2d 575 (N.D.III. 2007).

BEYOND OUR BORDERS — "Libel Tourism"

As mentioned earlier, U.S. plaintiffs have sometimes engaged in forum shopping by trying to have their complaints heard by a particular state court that is likely to be sympathetic to their claims. *Libel tourism* is essentially forum shopping on an international scale. Rather than filing a defamation lawsuit in the United States, where the freedoms of speech and press are strongly protected, a plaintiff files it in a foreign jurisdiction where there is a greater chance of winning.

The Threat of Libel Tourism
Libel tourism can have a chilling effect on the speech of U.S. journalists and authors because the fear of liability in other nations may prevent them from freely discussing topics of profound public importance. Libel tourism might even increase the threat to our nation's security if it discourages authors from writing about persons who support or finance terrorism or other dangerous activities.

The threat of libel tourism captured media attention when Khalid bin Mahfouz, a Saudi Arabian businessman, sued U.S. resident Dr. Rachel Ehrenfeld in London, England. Ehrenfeld had written a book on terrorist financing that claimed Mahfouz financed Islamic terrorist groups. Mahfouz filed the case in England because English law assumes that the offending speech is false (libelous), and the author must prove that the speech is true in order to prevail. The English court took jurisdiction because twenty-three copies of the book had been sold online to residents of the United Kingdom.

Ehrenfeld did not go to England to defend herself, and the court entered a judgment of $225,000 against her. She then countersued Mahfouz in a U.S. court in an attempt to show that she was protected under the First Amendment and had not committed libel, but that case was dismissed for lack of jurisdiction.[a]

The U.S. Response
In response to the *Ehrenfeld* case, the New York state legislature enacted the Libel Terrorism Reform Act in 2008.[b] That act enables New York courts to assert jurisdiction over anyone who obtains a foreign libel judgment against a writer or publisher living in New York State. It also prevents courts from enforcing foreign libel judgments unless the foreign country provides free speech protection equal to or greater than that available in New York. In 2010, the federal government passed similar legislation that makes foreign libel judgments unenforceable in U.S. courts unless they are consistent with the First Amendment.[c]

CRITICAL THINKING
■ Why do we need special legislation designed to control foreign libel claims against U.S. citizens? Explain.

---

a. *Ehrenfeld v. Mahfouz*, 518 F.3d 102 (2d Cir. 2008).

b. McKinney's Consolidated Laws of New York, Sections 302 and 5304.

c. Securing the Protection of our Enduring and Established Constitutional Heritage Act, 28 U.S.C. Sections 4101–4105.

are also actionable, as you will read in Chapter 7. Note further that anyone who republishes or repeats defamatory statements is liable even if that person reveals the source of the statements.

Damages for Libel
Once a defendant's liability for libel is established, general damages (defined earlier) are presumed as a matter of law. General damages are designed to compensate the plaintiff for nonspecific harms such as disgrace or dishonor in the eyes of the community, humiliation, injured reputation, and emotional distress—harms that are difficult to measure. In other words, to recover general damages in a libel case, the plaintiff need not prove that she or he was actually harmed in any specific way as a result of the libelous statement.

Damages for Slander
In contrast to cases alleging libel, in a case alleging slander, the plaintiff must prove *special damages* (defined earlier) to establish the defendant's liability. In other words, the plaintiff must show that the slanderous statement caused the plaintiff to suffer actual economic or monetary losses. Unless this initial hurdle of proving special damages is overcome, a plaintiff alleging slander normally cannot go forward with the suit and recover any damages. This requirement is imposed in cases involving slander because slanderous statements have a temporary quality. In contrast, a libelous (written) statement has the quality of permanence, can be circulated widely, especially through social media, and usually results from some degree of deliberation on the part of the author.

Exceptions to the burden of proving special damages in cases alleging slander are made for certain types of slanderous statements. If a false statement constitutes "slander *per se,*" no proof of special damages is required for it to be actionable. The following four types of false utterances are considered to be slander *per se:*

1. A statement that another has a loathsome disease (historically, leprosy and sexually transmitted diseases, but now also including allegations of mental illness).
2. A statement that another has committed improprieties while engaging in a business, profession, or trade.
3. A statement that another has committed or has been imprisoned for a serious crime.
4. A statement that a person (usually only unmarried persons and sometimes only women) is unchaste or has engaged in serious sexual misconduct.

Defenses to Defamation
Truth is normally an absolute defense against a defamation charge. In other words, if the defendant in a defamation suit can prove that his or her allegedly defamatory statements were true, normally no tort has been committed.

Other defenses to defamation may exist if the statement is privileged or concerns a public figure. Note that the majority of defamation actions in the United States are filed in state courts, and the states may differ both in how they define defamation and in the particular defenses they allow, such as privilege (discussed shortly).

> "My initial response was to sue her for defamation of character, but then I realized that I had no character."
>
> **CHARLES BARKLEY**
> 1963–PRESENT
> (NATIONAL BASKETBALL ASSOCIATION PLAYER, 1984–2000)

ETHICAL ISSUE

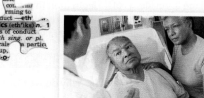

Can a person post online a criticism about a physician's "bedside manner" without being successfully sued for defamation?

When does an online criticism of a physician become defamation? Just as there are online rating sites for college professors, there are rating sites for practicing physicians. A posting at such a site formed the basis for a defamation lawsuit brought by neurologist Dr. David McKee.

McKee went to examine a patient who had been transferred from the intensive care unit (ICU) to a private room. In the room were family members of the patient, including his son. The patient's son later made the following post on a physician-rating Web site: "[Dr. McKee] seemed upset that my father had been moved [into a private room]. Never having met my father or his family, Dr. McKee said 'When you weren't in ICU, I had to spend time finding out if you transferred or died.' When we gaped at him, he said 'Well, 44 percent of hemorrhagic strokes dies within 30 days. I guess this is the better option.'"[9]

McKee filed suit for defamation but lost. The court found that all the statements made by the son were essentially true, and truth is a complete defense to a defamation action. In other words, true statements, however disparaging, are not actionable. Even the presence of minor inaccuracies of expression or detail does not render basically true statements false. As long as the "sting of the libelous charge is justified," defamation has not occurred.

Privileged Communications. In some circumstances, a person will not be liable for defamatory statements because she or he enjoys a **privilege,** or immunity. Privileged communications are of two types: absolute and qualified.[10] Only in judicial proceedings and certain government proceedings is an absolute privilege granted. Thus, statements made in a courtroom by attorneys and judges during a trial are absolutely privileged, as are statements made by government officials during legislative debate.

In other situations, a person will not be liable for defamatory statements because he or she has a *qualified,* or conditional, privilege. An employer's statements in written evaluations of employees are an example of a qualified privilege. Generally, if the statements are made in good faith and the publication is limited to those who have a legitimate interest in the communication, the statements fall within the area of qualified privilege. **EXAMPLE 4.9** Jorge worked at Facebook for five years and was being considered for a management position. His supervisor, Lydia, wrote a memo about Jorge's performance to those evaluating him for the management position. The memo contained certain negative statements. As long as Lydia honestly believed that what she wrote was true and limited her disclosure to company representatives, her statements would likely be protected by a qualified privilege. ■

Public Figures. Politicians, entertainers, professional athletes, and other persons who are in the public eye are considered *public figures.* In general, public figures are considered fair game, and false and defamatory statements about them that appear in the media will not constitute defamation unless the statements are made with **actual malice.**[11] To be made with actual malice, a statement must be made *with either knowledge of its falsity or a reckless disregard of the truth.*

Statements about public figures, especially when made via a public medium, are usually related to matters of general interest. They are made about people who substantially affect all of us. Furthermore, public figures generally have some access to a public medium for answering disparaging (belittling) falsehoods about themselves, whereas private individuals do not. For these reasons, public figures have a greater burden of proof in defamation cases (they must prove actual malice) than do private individuals.

CASE EXAMPLE 4.10 *In Touch* magazine published a story about a former call girl who claimed to have slept with legendary soccer player David Beckham more than once. Beckham sued *In Touch* magazine for libel, seeking $25 million in damages. He said that he had never met the woman, had not cheated on his wife with her, and had not paid her for sex. After months of litigation, a federal district court dismissed the case because Beckham could not show that the magazine had acted with actual malice. Whether or not the statements in the article were accurate, there was no evidence that the defendants had made the statements with knowledge of their falsity or reckless disregard for the truth.[12] ■

Privilege A special right, advantage, or immunity that enables a person or a class of persons to avoid liability for defamation.

Actual Malice The deliberate intent to cause harm that exists when a person makes a statement with either knowledge of its falsity or reckless disregard of the truth. Actual malice is required to establish defamation against public figures.

A publication printed statements by a woman who claimed that she had slept with David Beckham on several occasions. In order for Beckham to prevail in a lawsuit against the publication for defamatory statements, what legal barrier must he overcome?

---

9. *McKee v. Laurion,* Supreme Court of Minnesota, 825 N.W.2d 725 (2013).

10. Note that the term *privileged communication* in this context is *not* the same as privileged communication between a professional, such as an attorney, and his or her client.

11. *New York Times Co. v. Sullivan,* 376 U.S. 254, 84 S.Ct. 710, 11 L.Ed.2d 686 (1964).

12. *Beckham v. Bauer Pub. Co., L.P.,* 2011 WL 977570 (2011).

4–2e Invasion of the Right to Privacy and Appropriation

A person has a right to solitude and freedom from prying public eyes—in other words, to privacy. As discussed in Chapter 2, the Supreme Court has held that a fundamental right to privacy is implied by various amendments to the U.S. Constitution. Some state constitutions also explicitly provide for privacy rights. In addition, a number of federal and state statutes have been enacted to protect individual rights in specific areas.

Tort law also safeguards these rights through the torts of *invasion of privacy* and *appropriation*. Generally, to sue successfully for an invasion of privacy, a person must have a reasonable expectation of privacy, and the invasion must be highly offensive. (See this chapter's *Adapting the Law to the Online Environment* feature for a discussion of how invasion of privacy claims can arise when someone posts pictures or videos taken with digital devices.)

ADAPTING THE LAW TO THE ONLINE ENVIRONMENT
Revenge Porn and Invasion of Privacy

Every digital device today takes photos and videos at virtually no cost. Software allows the recording of conversations via Skype. Many couples immortalize their "private moments" using such digital devices. One partner may take a racy "selfie" and send it as an attachment to a text message to the other partner, for example.

Occasionally, after a couple breaks off their relationship, one of them seeks a type of digital revenge. The result, called revenge porn, has been defined in the Cyber Civil Rights Initiative as "The online distribution of sexually explicit images of a non-consenting individual with the intent to humiliate that person." Until relatively recently, few states had criminal statutes that covered revenge porn. Therefore, victims have sued on the basis of (1) invasion of privacy, (2) public disclosure of private facts, and (3) intentional infliction of emotional distress.

It Is More Than Just Pictures and Videos

The most egregious form of revenge porn occurs when the perpetuator provides detailed information about the victim. Such information may include the victim's name,

Facebook page, address, and phone number, as well as the victim's workplace and children's names. This information, along with the sexually explicit photos and videos, are posted on hosting Web sites. Many such Web sites have been shut down, as was the case with IsAnybodyDown? and Texxxan.com. But others are still active, usually with offshore servers and foreign domain-name owners.

The Injurious Results of Revenge Porn

To be sure, victims of revenge porn suffer extreme embarrassment. They may also have their reputations ruined. Some have lost their jobs. A number of victims have been stalked in the physical world and harassed online and offline. When attempts at having offending photos removed from Web sites have failed, victims have changed their phone numbers and sometimes their names.

A Class Action Lawsuit

Hollie Toups, along with twenty-two other female plaintiffs, sued the domain name registrar and Web hosting company GoDaddy in a Texas court. Although GoDaddy did not create the defamatory and offensive material at issue, GoDaddy knew of the content and did not remove it. The plaintiffs asserted

causes of action "for intentional infliction of emotional distress," among other claims. Additionally, the plaintiffs argued that "by its knowing participation in these unlawful activities, GoDaddy has also committed the intentional Texas tort of invasion of privacy . . . as well as intrusion on Plaintiffs' right to seclusion, the public disclosure of their private facts, [and] the wrongful appropriation of their names and likenesses. . . ." GoDaddy sought to dismiss the case, and an appeals court eventually granted GoDaddy's motion to dismiss.[a]

Another Texas woman had better luck. In a jury trial in early 2014, she won a $500,000 award. The woman's ex-boyfriend had uploaded videos to YouTube and other sites. At the time she made the complaint, revenge porn was not a crime in Texas.

CRITICAL THINKING

- Should domain name hosting companies be liable for revenge porn?

---

a. *GoDaddy.com, LLC. v. Toups*, 429 S.W.3d 752, Tex. App—Beaumont (2014).

Invasion of Privacy Four acts qualify as an invasion of privacy:

1. *Intrusion into an individual's affairs or seclusion.* Invading someone's home or illegally searching someone's briefcase is an invasion of privacy. The tort has been held to extend to eavesdropping by wiretap, the unauthorized scanning of a bank account, compulsory blood testing, and window peeping. **EXAMPLE 4.11** A female sports reporter for ESPN is digitally videoed while naked through the peephole in the door of her hotel room. If she sues, she will likely win a lawsuit against the man who took the video and posted it on the Internet. ■

2. *False light.* Publication of information that places a person in a false light is also an invasion of privacy. For instance, writing a story about a person that attributes ideas and opinions not held by that person is an invasion of privacy. (Publishing such a story could involve the tort of defamation as well.) **EXAMPLE 4.12** An Arkansas newspaper prints an article with the headline "Special Delivery: World's oldest newspaper carrier, 101, quits because she's pregnant!" Next to the article is a picture of a ninety-six-year-old woman who is not the subject of the article (and not pregnant). If she sues the paper for invasion of privacy, she will probably win. ■

3. *Public disclosure of private facts.* This type of invasion of privacy occurs when a person publicly discloses private facts about an individual that an ordinary person would find objectionable or embarrassing. A newspaper account about a private citizen's sex life or financial affairs could be an actionable invasion of privacy, even if the information revealed is true, because it should not be a matter of public concern.

4. *Appropriation of identity.* Under the common law, using a person's name, picture, or other likeness for commercial purposes without permission is a tortious invasion of privacy. An individual's right to privacy normally includes the right to the exclusive use of her or his identity. **EXAMPLE 4.13** An advertising agency asks a singer with a distinctive voice and stage presence to do a marketing campaign for a new automobile. The singer rejects the offer. If the agency then uses someone who imitates the singer's voice and dance moves in the ad, this would be actionable as an appropriation of identity. ■

Appropriation Most states today have codified the common law tort of appropriation of identity in statutes that establish the distinct tort of **appropriation,** or right of publicity. States differ as to the degree of likeness that is required to impose liability for appropriation, however.

Some courts have held that even when an animated character in a video or a video game is made to look like an actual person, there are not enough similarities to constitute appropriation. **CASE EXAMPLE 4.14** The Naked Cowboy, Robert Burck, was a street entertainer in New York City who had achieved some fame performing for tourists. He performed wearing only a white cowboy hat, white cowboy boots, and white underwear and carrying a guitar strategically placed to give the illusion of nudity. Burck sued Mars, Inc., the maker of M&Ms candy, over a video it showed on billboards in Times Square that depicted a blue M&M dressed exactly like The Naked Cowboy. The court, however, held that the use of Burck's signature costume did not amount to appropriation.[13] ■

4–2f Fraudulent Misrepresentation

A misrepresentation leads another to believe in a condition that is different from the condition that actually exists. This is often accomplished through a false or incorrect statement. Although persons sometimes make misrepresentations accidentally because they are unaware of the existing facts, the tort of **fraudulent misrepresentation,** or fraud, involves *intentional* deceit for personal gain. The tort includes several elements:

Appropriation In tort law, the use by one person of another person's name, likeness, or other identifying characteristic without permission and for the benefit of the user.

Under what circumstances, if any, could the use of the image of the Naked Cowboy in an ad constitute appropriation?

Fraudulent Misrepresentation Any misrepresentation, either by misstatement or by omission of a material fact, knowingly made with the intention of deceiving another and on which a reasonable person would and does rely to his or her detriment.

---

13. *Burck v. Mars, Inc.,* 571 F.Supp.2d 446 (S.D.N.Y. 2008). Also see *Kirby v. Sega of America, Inc.,* 144 Cal.App.4th 47, 50 Cal.Rptr.3d 607 (2006).

1. The misrepresentation of facts or conditions with knowledge that they are false or with reckless disregard for the truth.

2. An intent to induce another to rely on the misrepresentation.

3. Justifiable reliance by the deceived party.

4. Damage suffered as a result of the reliance.

5. A causal connection between the misrepresentation and the injury suffered.

Puffery A salesperson's exaggerated claims concerning the quality of property offered for sale. Such claims involve opinions rather than facts and are not legally binding promises or warranties.

For fraud to occur, more than mere **puffery,** or *seller's talk,* must be involved. Fraud exists only when a person represents as a fact something she or he knows is untrue. For example, it is fraud to claim that a roof does not leak when one knows it does. Facts are objectively ascertainable, whereas seller's talk is not. "I am the best accountant in town" is seller's talk because *best* is subjective. In the following case, the court considered each of the elements of fraud.

CASE 4.1

Revell v. Guido

New York Supreme Court, Appellate Division, Third Department, 124 A.D.3d 1006, ___ N.Y.S.2d ___ (2015).

FACTS Joseph Guido bought a parcel of land in Stillwater, New York, that contained nine rental houses. The houses shared a waste disposal system that was defective. Guido had a new septic system installed. When town officials discovered sewage on the property, Guido had the system partially replaced. Prospective buyers, including Danny Revell, were given a property information sheet that stated, "Septic system totally new—each field totally replaced." In response to a questionnaire from the buyers' bank, Guido denied any knowledge of environmental problems. A month after the buyers bought the houses, the septic system failed and required substantial remediation. The lender foreclosed on the property. The buyers filed a suit in a New York state court against Guido and his firm, Real Property Solutions, LLC, alleging fraud. A jury found fraud and awarded damages. The court issued a judgment in the plaintiffs' favor. The defendants appealed.

ISSUE Did the facts of the case and the plaintiffs' proof meet all of the requirements for establishing fraud?

DECISION Yes. The state intermediate appellate court affirmed the lower court's judgment in the plaintiffs' favor.

If a home seller claims that a new septic system was installed when it wasn't, does that constitute fraud?

REASON The court explained that to prove fraud, the plaintiffs had to establish that the defendants, with the intent to deceive, misrepresented a material fact that they knew to be false and on which the plaintiffs justifiably relied, incurring damages. The property's information sheet and Guido's responses to the environmental questionnaire misrepresented the facts. The septic system was not "totally new," and Guido knew that partially treated sewage had been discovered on the property. Guido's intent to deceive was shown by the "cavalier manner" in which he answered the questionnaire and his knowledge of the problems with the septic system. Because a visual inspection of the property did not reveal those problems, "one would assume that the system was working properly." The plaintiffs' reliance on the representation in the property information sheet was thus justified. The evidence of damages included "an abundance of receipts, invoices, billing statements and canceled checks" used by an accountant to calculate the amount.

CRITICAL THINKING—Legal Consideration *Financing for the purchase of the property was conditioned on the bank's review of Guido's answers to the environmental questionnaire. How could the court conclude that the plaintiffs justifiably relied on misrepresentations made to the bank? Explain.*

Statement of Fact versus Opinion Normally, the tort of misrepresentation or fraud occurs only when there is reliance on a *statement of fact.* Sometimes, however, the tort may involve reliance on a *statement of opinion* if the individual making the statement has a superior knowledge of the subject matter. For instance, when a lawyer makes a statement of opinion about the law in a state in which the lawyer is licensed to practice, a court would treat it as a statement of fact.

Negligent Misrepresentation Sometimes, a tort action can arise from misrepresentations that are made negligently rather than intentionally. The key difference between intentional and negligent misrepresentation is whether the person making the misrepresentation had actual knowledge of its falsity. Negligent misrepresentation requires only that the person making the statement or omission did not have a reasonable basis for believing its truthfulness.

Liability for negligent misrepresentation usually arises when the defendant who made the misrepresentation owed a duty of care to the plaintiff to supply correct information. Statements or omissions made by attorneys and accountants to their clients, for instance, can lead to liability for negligent misrepresentation.

4–2g Abusive or Frivolous Litigation

Tort law recognizes that people have a right not to be sued without a legally just and proper reason, and therefore it protects individuals from the misuse of litigation. Torts related to abusive litigation include malicious prosecution and abuse of process.

If a party initiates a lawsuit out of malice and without a legitimate legal reason, and ends up losing the suit, that party can be sued for *malicious prosecution. Abuse of process* can apply to any person using a legal process against another in an improper manner or to accomplish a purpose for which it was not designed.

The key difference between the torts of abuse of process and malicious prosecution is the level of proof required to succeed. Unlike malicious prosecution, abuse of process is not limited to prior litigation and does not require the plaintiff to prove malice. It can be based on the wrongful use of subpoenas, court orders to attach or seize real property, or other types of formal legal process.

4–2h Wrongful Interference

The torts known as **business torts** generally involve wrongful interference with another's business rights. Business torts involving wrongful interference are generally divided into two categories: wrongful interference with a contractual relationship and wrongful interference with a business relationship.

Business Tort Wrongful interference with another's business rights and relationships.

Wrongful Interference with a Contractual Relationship Three elements are necessary for wrongful interference with a contractual relationship to occur:

1. A valid, enforceable contract must exist between two parties.

2. A third party must know that this contract exists.

3. The third party must *intentionally* induce a party to breach the contract.

    CASE EXAMPLE 4.15 A landmark case involved an opera singer, Johanna Wagner, who was under contract to sing for a man named Lumley for a specified period of years. A man named Gye, who knew of this contract, nonetheless "enticed" Wagner to refuse to carry out the agreement, and Wagner began to sing for Gye. Gye's action constituted a tort because it wrongfully interfered with the contractual relationship between Wagner and Lumley.[14] (Of course, Wagner's refusal to carry out the agreement also entitled Lumley to sue Wagner for breach of contract.) ▇

    The body of tort law relating to intentional interference with a contractual relationship has expanded greatly in recent years. In principle, any lawful contract can be the basis for an action of this type. The contract could be between a firm and its employees or a firm and its customers. Sometimes, for instance, a competitor draws away one of a firm's key employees. Only if the original employer can show that the competitor knew of the contract's existence, and intentionally induced the breach, can damages be recovered from the competitor.

GARWOOD & VOIGT Fine & Rare Books Maps & Prints

Opera singer Johanna Jachmann-Wagner is shown here in one of her many roles. She was under contract to sing for one person, but was enticed to break the contract and sing for someone else. Was a tort committed? If so, by whom?

---

14. *Lumley v. Gye,* 118 Eng.Rep. 749 (1853).

Wrongful Interference with a Business Relationship   Businesspersons devise countless schemes to attract customers, but they are prohibited from unreasonably interfering with another's business in their attempts to gain a share of the market. There is a difference between *competitive methods* and *predatory behavior*—actions undertaken with the intention of unlawfully driving competitors completely out of the market. Attempting to attract customers in general is a legitimate business practice, whereas specifically targeting the customers of a competitor is more likely to be predatory.

EXAMPLE 4.16 A shopping mall contains two athletic shoe stores: Joe's and Ultimate Sport. Joe's cannot station an employee at the entrance of Ultimate Sport to divert customers by telling them that Joe's will beat Ultimate Sport's prices. This type of activity constitutes the tort of wrongful interference with a business relationship, which is commonly considered to be an unfair trade practice. If this activity were permitted, Joe's would reap the benefits of Ultimate Sport's advertising. ■

Defenses to Wrongful Interference   A person will not be liable for the tort of wrongful interference with a contractual or business relationship if it can be shown that the interference was justified or permissible. Bona fide competitive behavior is a permissible interference even if it results in the breaking of a contract.

EXAMPLE 4.17 If Antonio's Meats advertises so effectively that it induces Sam's Restaurant to break its contract with Burke's Meat Company, Burke's will be unable to recover against Antonio's Meats on a wrongful interference theory. After all, the public policy that favors free competition in advertising outweighs any possible instability that such competitive activity might cause in contractual relations. ■

4-3 Intentional Torts against Property

Intentional torts against property include trespass to land, trespass to personal property, conversion, and disparagement of property. These torts are wrongful actions that interfere with individuals' legally recognized rights with regard to their land or personal property. The law distinguishes real property from personal property. *Real property* is land and things "permanently" attached to the land. *Personal property* consists of all other items, which are basically movable. Thus, a house and lot are real property, whereas the furniture inside the house is personal property. Cash and stocks and bonds are also personal property.

4-3a Trespass to Land

A **trespass to land** occurs anytime a person, without permission, does any of the following:

1. Enters onto, above, or below the surface of land that is owned by another.

2. Causes anything to enter onto land owned by another.

3. Remains on land owned by another or permits anything to remain on it.

Actual harm to the land is not an essential element of this tort, because the tort is designed to protect the right of an owner to exclusive possession.

Common types of trespass to land include walking or driving on another's land, shooting a gun over the land, and throwing rocks at a building that belongs to someone else. Another common form of trespass involves constructing a building so that part of it is on an adjoining landowner's property.

Establishing Trespass   Before a person can be a trespasser, the real property owner (or other person in actual and exclusive possession of the property) must establish that person as a trespasser. For instance, "posted" trespass signs expressly establish as a trespasser a person

Trespass to Land Entry onto, above, or below the surface of land owned by another without the owner's permission or legal authorization.

who ignores these signs and enters onto the property. Any person who enters onto property to commit an illegal act (such as a thief entering a lumberyard at night to steal lumber) is established impliedly as a trespasser, without posted signs. In contrast, a guest in your home is not a trespasser unless she or he has been asked to leave but refuses.

Damages   At common law, a trespasser is liable for any damage caused to the property and generally cannot hold the owner liable for injuries sustained on the premises. This common law rule is being abandoned in many jurisdictions in favor of a *reasonable duty of care* rule that varies depending on the status of the parties.

For instance, a landowner may have a duty to post a notice that guard dogs patrol the property. Also, if young children are likely to be attracted to the property by some object, such as a swimming pool or a sand pile, and are injured, the landowner may be held liable under the *attractive nuisance doctrine*. An owner can normally use reasonable force to remove a trespasser from the premises—or detain the trespasser for a reasonable time—without liability for damages, however.

Defenses against Trespass to Land   One defense to a claim of trespass to land is to show that the trespass was warranted. This may occur, for instance, when the trespasser entered the property to assist someone in danger.

Another defense is for the trespasser to show that he or she had a license to come onto the land. A *licensee* is one who is invited (or allowed to enter) onto the property of another for the licensee's benefit. A person who enters another's property to read an electric meter, for example, is a licensee. When you purchase a ticket to attend a movie or sporting event, you are licensed to go onto the property of another to view that movie or event.

Note that licenses to enter are *revocable* by the property owner. If a property owner asks a meter reader to leave and the meter reader refuses to do so, the meter reader at that point becomes a trespasser.

4–3b Trespass to Personal Property

Whenever an individual wrongfully takes or harms the personal property of another or otherwise interferes with the lawful owner's possession of personal property, **trespass to personal property** (also called *trespass to chattels* or *trespass to personalty*[15]) occurs. In this context, harm means not only destruction of the property, but also anything that diminishes its value, condition, or quality.

Trespass to personal property involves intentional meddling with a possessory interest (the right to possess), including barring an owner's access to personal property. **EXAMPLE 4.18** Kelly takes Ryan's business law book as a practical joke and hides it so that Ryan is unable to find it for several days before the final examination. Here, Kelly has engaged in a trespass to personal property. (Kelly has also committed the tort of *conversion*—to be discussed next.) ∎

If it can be shown that trespass to personal property was warranted, then a complete defense exists. Most states, for example, allow automobile repair shops to retain a customer's car (under what is called an *artisan's lien*) when the customer refuses to pay for repairs already completed.

4–3c Conversion

Any act that deprives an owner of personal property or of the use of that property without the owner's permission and without just cause can constitute **conversion.** Even the taking of electronic records and data can form the basis of a conversion claim. Often, when conversion occurs, a trespass to personal property also occurs. The original taking of the personal property from the owner was a trespass, and wrongfully retaining the property is conversion.

> **Trespass to Personal Property** Wrongfully taking or harming the personal property of another or otherwise interfering with the lawful owner's possession of personal property.

> **Conversion** Wrongfully taking or retaining possession of an individual's personal property and placing it in the service of another.

---

15. Pronounced *per*-sun-ul-tee.

Conversion is the civil side of crimes related to theft, but it is not limited to theft. Even if the rightful owner consented to the initial taking of the property, so there was no theft or trespass, a failure to return the personal property may still be conversion. **EXAMPLE 4.19** Chen borrows Mark's iPad to use while traveling home from school for the holidays. When Chen returns to school, Mark asks for his iPad back. Chen tells Mark that she gave it to her little brother for Christmas. In this situation, Mark can sue Chen for conversion, and Chen will have to either return the iPad or pay damages equal to its replacement value. ■

Conversion can occur even when a person mistakenly believes that she or he was entitled to the goods. In other words, good intentions are not a defense against conversion. Someone who buys stolen goods, for instance, can be sued for conversion even if he or she did not know that the goods were stolen. If the true owner brings a tort action against the buyer, the buyer must either return the property to the owner or pay the owner the full value of the property (despite having already paid the purchase price to the thief).

In the following case, the court was asked to decide whether the tort of conversion was an appropriate cause of action for the misappropriation and use of a credit card.

CASE 4.2

Welco Electronics, Inc. v. Mora

Court of Appeal of California, Second District, 223 Cal.App.4th 202, 166 Cal.Rptr.3d 877 (2014).

FACTS Darrel Derouis, the president of Welco Electronics, Inc., hired a certified bookkeeper to help him "find where his money went." During the investigation, discrepancies in Welco's credit-card statements were discovered. Statements from the credit-card company contained charges to AQM Supplies—a company established by Nicholas Mora, who worked for Welco as a quality assurance manager. The credit-card charges to AQM, which totaled more than $375,000, did not appear on Welco's copies of the statements. At the time of the transactions, AQM had leased a portable credit-card terminal, and funds paid through the terminal were electronically deposited into Mora's bank account.

Welco filed a suit in a California state court against Mora, alleging conversion. Welco sought the value of the funds allegedly converted, as well as interest, expenses, punitive damages, and other costs. The court ruled in Welco's favor, and Mora appealed.

ISSUE Can the use of a company's credit card by an employee to obtain funds from the company constitute conversion?

DECISION Yes. A state intermediate appellate court affirmed the lower court's judgment.

How can a portable credit card terminal be used for conversion?

©iStock.com/iStockphoto.com

REASON In the words of the court, "The tort of conversion has been adapted to new property rights and modern means of commercial transactions." The court acknowledged that "historically, the tort of conversion was limited to tangible property and did not apply to intangible property," but added that "modern courts . . . have permitted conversion claims against intangible interests." The owner of a checking account, for instance, has an intangible property interest in his or her checks. Other examples of instruments representing intangible property rights include a savings account, an insurance policy, a company's customer list, and a stock certificate.

Credit card, debit card, and PayPal information may also be subject to conversion. The card or account information is similar to the intangible property interest in a check. The court reasoned that when Mora misappropriated Welco's credit card and used it, he took part of Welco's credit balance with the credit-card company. The result was an unauthorized transfer to Mora of Welco's property rights.

CRITICAL THINKING—E-Commerce Consideration *Can the appropriation of an Internet domain name constitute conversion? Explain.*

4–3d Disparagement of Property

Disparagement of Property An economically injurious falsehood about another's product or property.

Disparagement of property occurs when economically injurious falsehoods are made about another's product or property, rather than about another's reputation (as in the tort of defamation). Disparagement of property is a general term for torts specifically referred to as *slander of quality* or *slander of title*.

Publication of false information about another's product, alleging that it is not what its seller claims, constitutes the tort of **slander of quality,** or **trade libel.** To establish trade libel, the plaintiff must prove that the improper publication caused a third party to refrain from dealing with the plaintiff and that the plaintiff sustained economic damages (such as lost profits) as a result. An improper publication may be both a slander of quality and defamation of character. For example, a statement that disparages the quality of a product may also, by implication, disparage the character of the person who would sell such a product.

When a publication denies or casts doubt on another's legal ownership of property, and the property's owner suffers financial loss as a result, the tort of **slander of title** may exist. Usually, this is an intentional tort that occurs when someone knowingly publishes an untrue statement about property with the intent of discouraging a third party from dealing with the property's owner. For instance, a car dealer would have difficulty attracting customers after competitors published a notice that the dealer's stock consisted of stolen automobiles.

> **Slander of Quality (Trade Libel)** The publication of false information about another's product, alleging that it is not what its seller claims.

> **Slander of Title** The publication of a statement that denies or casts doubt on another's legal ownership of property, causing financial loss to that property's owner.

4-4 Unintentional Torts (Negligence)

The tort of **negligence** occurs when someone suffers injury because of another's failure to live up to a required *duty of care*. In contrast to intentional torts, in torts involving negligence, the tortfeasor neither wishes to bring about the consequences of the act nor believes that they will occur. The actor's conduct merely creates a *risk* of such consequences. If no risk is created, there is no negligence. Moreover, the risk must be foreseeable—that is, it must be such that a reasonable person engaging in the same activity would anticipate the risk and guard against it. In determining what is reasonable conduct, courts consider the nature of the possible harm.

Many of the actions giving rise to the intentional torts discussed earlier in the chapter constitute negligence if the element of intent is missing (or cannot be proved). **EXAMPLE 4.20** Juan walks up to Maya and intentionally shoves her. Maya falls and breaks an arm as a result. In this situation, Juan has committed an intentional tort (assault and battery). If Juan carelessly bumps into Maya, however, and she falls and breaks an arm as a result, Juan's action will constitute negligence. In either situation, Juan has committed a tort. ■

To succeed in a negligence action, the plaintiff must prove each of the following:

1. *Duty*. That the defendant owed a duty of care to the plaintiff.
2. *Breach*. That the defendant breached that duty.
3. *Causation*. That the defendant's breach caused the plaintiff's injury.
4. *Damages*. That the plaintiff suffered a legally recognizable injury.

We discuss each of these four elements of negligence next.

> **Negligence** The failure to exercise the standard of care that a reasonable person would exercise in similar circumstances.

> **LEARNING OBJECTIVE 4**
> Identify the four elements of negligence.

4-4a The Duty of Care and Its Breach

Central to the tort of negligence is the concept of a **duty of care.** The basic principle underlying the duty of care is that people in society are free to act as they please so long as their actions do not infringe on the interests of others. When someone fails to comply with the duty to exercise reasonable care, a potentially tortious act may result.

Failure to live up to a standard of care may be an act (setting fire to a building) or an omission (neglecting to put out a campfire). It may be a careless act or a carefully performed but nevertheless dangerous act that results in injury. In determining whether the duty of care has been breached, courts consider several factors:

1. The nature of the act (whether it is outrageous or commonplace).
2. The manner in which the act was performed (cautiously versus heedlessly).
3. The nature of the injury (whether it is serious or slight).

> **Duty of Care** The duty of all persons, as established by tort law, to exercise a reasonable amount of care in their dealings with others. Failure to exercise due care, which is normally determined by the reasonable person standard, constitutes the tort of negligence.

Creating even a very slight risk of a dangerous explosion might be unreasonable, whereas creating a distinct possibility of someone's burning his or her fingers on a stove might be reasonable.

The Reasonable Person Standard

Reasonable Person Standard The standard of behavior expected of a hypothetical "reasonable person." It is the standard against which negligence is measured and that must be observed to avoid liability for negligence.

Tort law measures duty by the **reasonable person standard.** In determining whether a duty of care has been breached, the courts ask how a reasonable person would have acted in the same circumstances. The reasonable person standard is said to be (though in an absolute sense it cannot be) objective. It is not necessarily how a particular person *would* act. It is society's judgment on how people *should* act. If the so-called reasonable person existed, he or she would be careful, conscientious, even tempered, and honest.

The degree of care to be exercised varies, depending on the defendant's occupation or profession, her or his relationship with the plaintiff, and other factors. Generally, whether an action constitutes a breach of the duty of care is determined on a case-by-case basis. The outcome depends on how the judge (or jury, in a jury trial) decides a reasonable person in the position of the defendant would act in the particular circumstances of the case.

Note that the courts frequently use the reasonable person standard in other areas of law as well as in negligence cases. That individuals are required to exercise a reasonable standard of care in their activities is a pervasive concept in business law, and many of the issues discussed in subsequent chapters of this text have to do with this duty.

The Duty of Landowners

> "A little neglect may breed great mischief."
>
> **BENJAMIN FRANKLIN**
> 1706–1790
> (AMERICAN POLITICIAN AND INVENTOR)

Landowners are expected to exercise reasonable care to protect persons coming onto their property from harm. In some jurisdictions, landowners are held to owe a duty to protect even trespassers against certain risks. Landowners who rent or lease premises to tenants are expected to exercise reasonable care to ensure that the tenants and their guests are not harmed in common areas, such as stairways, entryways, and laundry rooms.

Duty to Warn Business Invitees of Risks. Retailers and other firms that explicitly or implicitly invite persons to come onto their premises have a duty to exercise reasonable care to protect these **business invitees.** The duty normally requires storeowners to warn business invitees of foreseeable risks about which the owners knew or *should have known.*

Business Invitee A person, such as a customer or a client, who is invited onto business premises by the owner of those premises for business purposes.

EXAMPLE 4.21 Liz enters a supermarket, slips on a wet floor, and sustains injuries as a result. If there was no sign warning that the floor was wet when Liz slipped, the owner of the supermarket would be liable for damages. A court would hold that the business owner was negligent because the owner failed to exercise a reasonable degree of care in protecting the store's customers against foreseeable risks about which the owner knew or should have known. That a patron might slip on the wet floor and be injured was a foreseeable risk, and the owner should have taken care to avoid this risk or to warn the customer of it (by posting a sign or setting out orange cones, for example). ■

The landowner also has a duty to discover and remove any hidden dangers that might injure a customer or other invitee. Store owners have a duty to protect customers from potentially slipping and injuring themselves on merchandise that has fallen off the shelves, for instance.

Does a "Wet Floor" sign relieve a restaurant owner from being held negligent if a customer slips?

paichoon/ShutterStock.com

Obvious Risks Are an Exception. Some risks, of course, are so obvious that the owner need not warn of them. For instance, a business owner does not need to warn customers to open a door before attempting to walk through it. Other risks, however, may seem obvious to a business owner but may not be so to someone else, such as a child. In addition, even if a risk is obvious, that does not necessarily excuse a business owner from the duty to protect customers from foreseeable harm.

CASE EXAMPLE 4.22 Giorgio's Grill in Hollywood, Florida, is a restaurant that becomes a nightclub after hours. At those times, traditionally—as the manager of Giorgio's knew—the staff and customers throw paper napkins into the air as the music plays. The napkins land on the floor, but no one picks them up. One night, Jane Izquierdo went to Giorgio's. Although she had been to the club on other occasions and knew about the napkin-throwing tradition, she slipped on a napkin and fell, breaking her leg. She sued Giorgio's for negligence but lost at trial because the jury found that the risk of slipping on the napkins was obvious. A state appellate court reversed, however, holding that the obviousness of a risk does not discharge a business owner's duty to its invitees to maintain the premises in a safe condition.[16] ■

PREVENTING LEGAL DISPUTES

It can be difficult to determine whether a risk is obvious. Because you can be held liable if you fail to discover hidden dangers on business premises that could cause injuries to customers, you should post warnings of any conceivable risks on the property. Be vigilant and frequently reassess potential hazards. Train your employees to be on the lookout for possibly dangerous conditions at all times and to notify a supervisor immediately if they notice something. Remember that a finding of liability in a single lawsuit can leave a small enterprise close to bankruptcy. To prevent potential negligence liability, make sure that your business premises are as safe as possible for all persons who might be there, including children, senior citizens, and individuals with disabilities.

The Duty of Professionals Persons who possess superior knowledge, skill, or training are held to a higher standard of care than others. Professionals—such as physicians, dentists, architects, engineers, accountants, and lawyers—are required to have a standard minimum level of special knowledge and ability. In determining what constitutes reasonable care, the law takes their training and expertise into account. Thus, an accountant's conduct is judged not by the reasonable person standard, but by the reasonable accountant standard.

If a professional violates her or his duty of care toward a client, the professional may be sued for **malpractice,** which is essentially professional negligence. For instance, a patient might sue a physician for *medical malpractice*. A client might sue an attorney for *legal malpractice*.

Malpractice Professional misconduct or the lack of the requisite degree of skill as a professional. Negligence on the part of a professional, such as a physician, is commonly referred to as malpractice.

4–4b Causation

Another element necessary in a negligence action is *causation*. If a person breaches a duty of care and someone suffers an injury, the wrongful act must have caused the harm for it to constitute the tort of negligence.

Courts Ask Two Questions In deciding whether there is causation, the court must address two questions:

1. *Is there causation in fact?* Did the injury occur because of the defendant's act, or would it have occurred anyway? If an injury would not have occurred without the defendant's act, then there is **causation in fact.**

   Causation in fact can usually be determined by the use of the *but for* test: "but for" the wrongful act, the injury would not have occurred. Theoretically, causation in fact is limitless. One could claim, for example, that "but for" the creation of the world, a particular injury would not have occurred. Thus, as a practical matter, the law has to establish limits, and it does so through the concept of proximate cause.

Causation in Fact An act or omission without which an event would not have occurred.

2. *Was the act the proximate cause of the injury?* **Proximate cause,** or legal cause, exists when the connection between an act and an injury is strong enough to justify imposing liability. Courts use proximate cause to limit the scope of the defendant's liability to a subset of the

Proximate Cause Legal cause. It exists when the connection between an act and an injury is strong enough to justify imposing liability.

---

16. *Izquierdo v. Gyroscope, Inc.*, 946 So.2d 115 (Fla.App. 2007).

Injuries from car accidents can cause handicaps that last a lifetime. Do such injuries satisfy the injury requirement for a finding of negligence?

total number of potential plaintiffs that might have been harmed by the defendant's actions.

EXAMPLE 4.23 Ackerman carelessly leaves a campfire burning. The fire not only burns down the forest but also sets off an explosion in a nearby chemical plant that spills chemicals into a river, killing all the fish for a hundred miles downstream and ruining the economy of a tourist resort. Should Ackerman be liable to the resort owners? To the tourists whose vacations were ruined? These are questions of proximate cause that a court must decide. ■

Both questions concerning causation must be answered in the affirmative for tort liability to arise. If a defendant's action constitutes causation in fact but a court decides that the action was not the proximate cause of the plaintiff's injury, the causation requirement has not been met—and the defendant normally will not be liable to the plaintiff.

KNOW THIS

Proximate cause can be thought of in terms of social policy. Should the defendant be made to bear the loss instead of the plaintiff?

Foreseeability Questions of proximate cause are linked to the concept of foreseeability. It would be unfair to impose liability on a defendant unless the defendant's actions created a foreseeable risk of injury. Probably the most cited case on proximate cause is the *Palsgraf* case, which is discussed in this chapter's *Landmark in the Law* feature. In determining the issue of proximate cause, the court addressed the following question: Does a defendant's duty of care extend only to those who may be injured as a result of a foreseeable risk, or does it also extend to a person whose injury could not reasonably have been foreseen?

LANDMARK IN THE LAW   *Palsgraf v. Long Island Railroad Co.* (1928)

In 1928, the New York Court of Appeals (that state's highest court) issued its decision in *Palsgraf v. Long Island Railroad Co.,*[a] a case that has become a landmark in negligence law and proximate cause.

THE FACTS OF THE CASE The plaintiff, Helen Palsgraf, was waiting for a train on a station platform. A man carrying a small package wrapped in newspaper was rushing to catch a train that had begun to move away from the platform. As the man attempted to jump aboard the moving train, he seemed unsteady and about to fall. A railroad guard on the train car reached forward to grab him, and another guard on the platform pushed him from behind to help him board the train. In the process, the man's package fell on the railroad tracks and exploded, because it contained fireworks. The repercussions of the

explosion caused scales at the other end of the train platform to fall on Palsgraf, who was injured as a result. She sued the railroad company for damages in a New York state court.

THE QUESTION OF PROXIMATE CAUSE At the trial, the jury found that the railroad guards were negligent in their conduct. On appeal, the question before the New York Court of Appeals was whether the conduct of the railroad guards was the proximate cause of Palsgraf's injuries. In other words, did the guards' duty of care extend to Palsgraf, who was outside the zone of danger and whose injury could not reasonably have been foreseen?

The court stated that the question of whether the guards were negligent *with respect to Palsgraf* depended on whether her injury was *reasonably foreseeable* by the railroad guards. Although the guards may have acted negligently with respect to the man boarding the train, this had no bearing on the question of their negligence with respect to Palsgraf. This was not a situation in which

a person committed an act so potentially harmful (for example, firing a gun at a building) that he or she would be held responsible for any harm that resulted. The court stated that here "there was nothing in the situation to suggest to the most cautious mind that the parcel wrapped in newspaper would spread wreckage through the station." The court thus concluded that the railroad guards were not negligent with respect to Palsgraf, because her injury was not reasonably foreseeable.

APPLICATION TO TODAY'S WORLD *The Palsgraf case established foreseeability as the test for proximate cause. Today, the courts continue to apply this test in determining proximate cause—and thus tort liability for injuries. Generally, if the victim of a harm or the consequences of a harm done are unforeseeable, there is no proximate cause. Note, though, that in the online environment, distinctions based on physical proximity, such as the "zone of danger" cited by the court in this case, are largely inapplicable.*

a. 248 N.Y. 339, 162 N.E. 99 (1928).

4-4c The Injury Requirement and Damages

For a tort to have been committed, the plaintiff must have suffered a *legally recognizable* injury. To recover damages (receive compensation), the plaintiff must have suffered some loss, harm, wrong, or invasion of a protected interest. If no harm or injury results from a given negligent action, there is nothing to compensate—and no tort exists. **EXAMPLE 4.24** If you carelessly bump into a passerby, who stumbles and falls as a result, you may be liable in tort if the passerby is injured in the fall. If the person is unharmed, however, there normally cannot be a suit for damages because no injury was suffered. ■

Essentially, the purpose of tort law is to compensate for legally recognized injuries resulting from wrongful acts. Thus, compensatory damages are the norm in negligence cases. As noted earlier, a court will award punitive damages only if the defendant's conduct was grossly negligent, reflecting an intentional failure to perform a duty with reckless disregard of the consequences to others.

4-4d Defenses to Negligence

Defendants often defend against negligence claims by asserting that the plaintiffs failed to prove the existence of one or more of the required elements for negligence. Additionally, there are three basic *affirmative* defenses in negligence cases (defenses that a defendant can use to avoid liability even if the facts are as the plaintiff states): (1) assumption of risk, (2) superseding cause, and (3) contributory and comparative negligence.

Assumption of Risk A plaintiff who voluntarily enters into a risky situation, knowing the risk involved, will not be allowed to recover. This is the defense of **assumption of risk,** which requires two elements:

1. Knowledge of the risk.
2. Voluntary assumption of the risk.

This defense is frequently asserted when a plaintiff is injured during recreational activities that involve known risk, such as skiing and skydiving. Courts do not apply the assumption of risk doctrine in certain situations, such as those involving emergencies, however.

Assumption of risk can apply not only to participants in sporting events, but to spectators and bystanders who are injured while attending those events. In the following *Spotlight Case,* the issue was whether a spectator at a baseball game voluntarily assumed the risk of being hit by an errant ball thrown while the players were warming up before the game.

Assumption of Risk A defense to negligence that bars a plaintiff from recovering for injuries or damage suffered as a result of risks he or she knew of and voluntarily assumed.

SPOTLIGHT ON THE SEATTLE MARINERS: CASE 4.3

Taylor v. Baseball Club of Seattle, L.P.

Court of Appeals of Washington, 132 Wash.App. 32, 130 P.3d 835 (2006).

FACTS Delinda Middleton Taylor went to a Mariners baseball game at Safeco Field with her boyfriend and two minor sons. Their seats were four rows up from the field along the right field foul line. They arrived more than an hour before the game began so that they could see the players warm up and get their autographs. When she walked in, Taylor saw that Mariners pitcher Freddy Garcia was throwing a ball back

Many fans arrive at baseball games early so they can watch the players warm up.

Alan C. Heison/ShutterStock.com

and forth with José Mesa right in front of their seats. As Taylor stood in front of her seat, she looked away from the field, and a ball thrown by Mesa got past Garcia and struck her in the face, causing serious injuries. Taylor sued the Mariners for the allegedly negligent warm-up throw. The Mariners filed a motion for a summary judgment in which they argued that Taylor, a Mariners fan, was familiar with baseball

Continues

and the inherent risk of balls entering the stands, and therefore assumed the risk of her injury. The trial court granted the motion and dismissed Taylor's case. Taylor appealed.

ISSUE Was the risk of injury from an errant baseball thrown during pregame warm-up foreseeable to a reasonable person with Taylor's familiarity with baseball?

DECISION Yes. The state intermediate appellate court affirmed the lower court's judgment. Taylor, as a spectator in an unprotected area of seats, voluntarily undertook the risk associated with being hit by an errant baseball thrown during warm-ups before the start of the game.

REASON The court observed that there was substantial evidence that Taylor was familiar with the game. She was a seasoned Mariners fan, and both of her sons had played baseball for at least six years. "She attended many of her sons' baseball games, she witnessed balls entering the stands, she had watched Mariners' games both at the

Kingdome [the Mariners' former stadium] and on television, and she knew that there was no screen protecting her seats, which were close to the field. In fact, as she walked to her seat she saw the players warming up and was excited about being in an unscreened area where her party might get autographs from the players and catch balls."

It was not legally relevant that the injury occurred during the pregame warm-up because "it is the normal, every-day practice at all levels of baseball for pitchers to warm up in the manner that led to this incident." The Mariners had satisfied their duty to protect spectators from balls entering the stands by providing a protective screen behind home plate. Taylor chose not to sit in the protected area and thus knowingly put herself at risk.

CRITICAL THINKING—Ethical Consideration *Would the result in this case have been different if Taylor's minor son, rather than Taylor herself, had been struck by the ball? Should courts apply the doctrine of assumption of risk to children? Discuss.*

Superseding Cause An unforeseeable intervening event may break the connection between a wrongful act and an injury to another. If so, the event acts as a *superseding cause*—that is, it relieves a defendant of liability for injuries caused by the intervening event.

EXAMPLE 4.25 While riding his bicycle, Derrick negligently hits Julie, who is walking on the sidewalk. As a result of the impact, Julie falls and fractures her hip. While she is waiting for help to arrive, a small plane crashes nearby and explodes, and some of the fiery debris hits her, causing her to sustain severe burns. Derrick will be liable for Julie's fractured hip because the risk of hitting her with his bicycle was foreseeable. Normally, though, Derrick will not be liable for the burns caused by the plane crash, because the risk of a plane's crashing nearby and injuring Julie was not foreseeable. ■

Contributory Negligence
A rule in tort law, used in only a few states, that completely bars the plaintiff from recovering any damages if the damage suffered is partly the plaintiff's own fault.

Contributory Negligence All individuals are expected to exercise a reasonable degree of care in looking out for themselves. In the past, under the common law doctrine of **contributory negligence,** a plaintiff who was also negligent (who failed to exercise a reasonable degree of care) could not recover anything from the defendant. Under this rule, no matter how insignificant the plaintiff's negligence was relative to the defendant's negligence, the plaintiff was precluded from recovering any damages. Today, only a few jurisdictions still follow this doctrine.

Comparative Negligence
A rule in tort law, used in the majority of states, that reduces the plaintiff's recovery in proportion to the plaintiff's degree of fault, rather than barring recovery completely.

Comparative Negligence In most states, the doctrine of contributory negligence has been replaced by a **comparative negligence** standard. Under this standard, both the plaintiff's and the defendant's negligence are computed, and the liability for damages is distributed accordingly.

Some jurisdictions have adopted a "pure" form of comparative negligence that allows a plaintiff to recover, even if the extent of his or her fault is greater than that of the defendant. For instance, if a plaintiff was 80 percent at fault and the defendant 20 percent at fault, the plaintiff may recover 20 percent of his or her damages.

Many states' comparative negligence statutes, however, contain a "50 percent" rule that prevents a plaintiff from recovering any damages if she or he was more than 50 percent at fault. Under this rule, a plaintiff who is 35 percent at fault could recover 65 percent of his or her damages, but a plaintiff who is 65 percent at fault could recover nothing.

4-4e Special Negligence Doctrines and Statutes

There are a number of special doctrines and statutes relating to negligence. We examine a few of them here.

Res Ipsa Loquitur   Generally, in lawsuits involving negligence, the plaintiff has the burden of proving that the defendant was negligent. In certain situations, however, the courts may infer that negligence has occurred under the doctrine of **res ipsa loquitur**[17] (meaning "the facts speak for themselves"). Then the burden of proof rests on the defendant to prove that she or he was *not* negligent. This doctrine is applied only when the event creating the damage or injury is one that ordinarily would occur only as a result of negligence.

> **CASE EXAMPLE 4.26**   A kidney donor, Darnell Backus, sustained injuries to his cervical spine and to the muscles on the left side of his body as a result of the surgery to harvest his kidney. He sued the hospital and physicians involved in the transplant operation for damages. Backus asserted *res ipsa loquitor* because the injury was of the kind that ordinarily does not occur in the absence of someone's negligence. The burden of proof shifted to the defendants, and because they failed to show that they had *not* been negligent, Backus won.[18] ■

Res Ipsa Loquitur   A doctrine under which negligence may be inferred simply because an event occurred, if it is the type of event that would not occur in the absence of negligence. Literally, the term means "the facts speak for themselves."

Negligence Per Se   Certain conduct, whether it consists of an action or a failure to act, may be treated as **negligence *per se*** (*per se* means "in or of itself"). Negligence *per se* may occur if an individual violates a statute or ordinance and thereby causes the kind of harm that the statute was intended to prevent. The statute must clearly set out what standard of conduct is expected, when and where it is expected, and of whom it is expected. The standard of conduct required by the statute is the duty that the defendant owes to the plaintiff, and a violation of the statute is the breach of that duty.

> **CASE EXAMPLE 4.27**   A Delaware statute states that anyone "who operates a motor vehicle and who fails to give full time and attention to the operation of the vehicle" is guilty of inattentive driving. Michael Moore was cited for inattentive driving after he collided with Debra Wright's car when he backed a truck out of a parking space. Moore paid the ticket, which meant that he pleaded guilty to violating the statute. The day after the accident, Wright began having back pain, which eventually required surgery. She sued Moore for damages, alleging negligence *per se*. The Delaware Supreme Court ruled that the inattentive driving statute set forth a sufficiently specific standard of conduct to warrant application of negligence *per se*.[19] ■

Negligence Per Se   An action or failure to act in violation of a statutory requirement.

"Danger Invites Rescue" Doctrine   Sometimes, a person who is trying to avoid harm—such as an individual who swerves to avoid a head-on collision with a drunk driver—ends up causing harm to another (such as a cyclist riding in the bike lane) as a result. In those situations, the original wrongdoer (the drunk driver in this scenario) is liable to anyone who is injured, even if the injury actually resulted from another person's attempt to escape harm.

The "danger invites rescue" doctrine extends the same protection to a person who is trying to rescue another from harm—the original wrongdoer is liable for injuries to an individual attempting a rescue. The idea is that rescuers should not be held liable for any damages, because they did not cause the danger and because danger invites rescue. Whether rescuers injure themselves, the person rescued, or a passer-by, the original wrongdoer will still be liable.

> **EXAMPLE 4.28**   Ludley drives down a street but fails to see a stop sign because he is trying to quiet his squabbling children in the car's back seat. Salter, who is standing on the curb, realizes that Ludley is about to hit a pedestrian and runs into the street to push the pedestrian out of the way. If Ludley's vehicle hits Salter instead, Ludley will be liable for Salter's injury, as well as for any injuries the other pedestrian sustained. ■

---

17. Pronounced *rehz ihp*-suh *low*-kwuh-tuhr.
18. *Backus v. Kaleida Health*, 91 A.D.3d 1284, 937 N.Y.S.2d 773 (N.Y.A.D. 4 Dept. 2012).
19. *Wright v. Moore*, 931 A.2d 405 (Del.Supr. 2007).

Good Samaritan Statute
A state statute stipulating that persons who provide emergency services to, or rescue, someone in peril cannot be sued for negligence unless they act recklessly and cause further harm.

Dram Shop Act A state statute that imposes liability on the owners of bars and taverns, as well as those who serve alcoholic drinks to the public, for injuries resulting from accidents caused by intoxicated persons when the sellers or servers of alcoholic drinks contributed to the intoxication.

Good Samaritan Statutes Most states have enacted what are called **Good Samaritan statutes.**[20] Under these statutes, someone who is aided voluntarily by another cannot turn around and sue the "Good Samaritan" for negligence. These laws were passed largely to protect physicians and medical personnel who voluntarily render medical services in emergency situations to those in need, such as individuals hurt in car accidents.

Dram Shop Acts Many states have also passed **dram shop acts,**[21] under which a tavern owner or bartender may be held liable for injuries caused by a person who became intoxicated while drinking at the bar or who was already intoxicated when served by the bartender. Some states' statutes also impose liability on *social hosts* (persons hosting parties) for injuries caused by guests who became intoxicated at the hosts' homes. Under these statutes, it is unnecessary to prove that the tavern owner, bartender, or social host was negligent. **EXAMPLE 4.29** Selena hosts a Super Bowl party at which Raul, a minor, sneaks alcoholic drinks. Selena is potentially liable for damages resulting from Raul's drunk driving after the party. ■

4-5 Strict Liability

Another category of torts is called **strict liability,** or *liability without fault.* Intentional torts and torts of negligence involve acts that depart from a reasonable standard of care and cause injuries. Under the doctrine of strict liability, liability for injury is imposed for reasons other than fault.

4-5a Abnormally Dangerous Activities

Strict liability for damages proximately caused by an abnormally dangerous or exceptional activity is one application of this doctrine. Courts apply the doctrine of strict liability in such cases because of the extreme risk of the activity. For instance, even if blasting with dynamite is performed with all reasonable care, there is still a risk of injury. Because of the potential for harm, the person who is engaged in an abnormally dangerous activity—and benefits from it—is responsible for paying for any injuries caused by that activity. Although there is no fault, there is still responsibility because of the dangerous nature of the undertaking.

4-5b Other Applications of Strict Liability

The strict liability principle is also applied in other situations. Persons who keep wild animals, for example, are strictly liable for any harm inflicted by the animals. In addition, an owner of domestic animals may be strictly liable for harm caused by those animals if the owner knew, or should have known, that the animals were dangerous or had a propensity to harm others.

A significant application of strict liability is in the area of *product liability*—liability of manufacturers and sellers for harmful or defective products—discussed in the next chapter. Liability here is a matter of social policy. Manufacturers and sellers can better bear the cost of injuries, and because they profit from making and selling the products, they should be responsible for the injuries the products cause.

Strict Liability Liability regardless of fault, which is imposed on those engaged in abnormally dangerous activities, on persons who keep dangerous animals, and on manufacturers or sellers that introduce into commerce defective and unreasonably dangerous goods.

LEARNING OBJECTIVE 5
What is meant by strict liability? In what circumstances is strict liability applied?

---

20. These laws derive their name from the Good Samaritan story in the Bible. In the story, a traveler who had been robbed and beaten lay along the roadside, ignored by those passing by. Eventually, a man from the country of Samaria (the "Good Samaritan") stopped to render assistance to the injured person.
21. Historically, a *dram* was a small unit of liquid, and spirits were sold in drams. Thus, a dram shop was a place where liquor was sold in drams.

Reviewing . . . Tort Law

Elaine Sweeney went to Ragged Mountain Ski Resort in New Hampshire with a friend. Elaine went snow tubing down a run designed exclusively for snow tubers. No Ragged Mountain employees were present in the snow-tube area to instruct Elaine on the proper use of a snow tube. On her fourth run down the trail, Elaine crossed over the center line between snow-tube lanes, collided with another snow tuber, and was injured. Elaine filed a negligence action against Ragged Mountain seeking compensation for the injuries that she sustained. Two years earlier, the New Hampshire state legislature had enacted a statute that prohibited a person who participates in the sport of skiing from suing a ski-area operator for injuries caused by the risks inherent in skiing. Using the information presented in the chapter, answer the following questions.

1. What defense will Ragged Mountain probably assert?

2. The central question in this case is whether the state statute establishing that skiers assume the risks inherent in the sport applies to Elaine's suit. What would your decision be on this issue? Why?

3. Suppose that the court concludes that the statute applies only to skiing and not to snow tubing. Will Elaine's lawsuit be successful? Explain.

4. Now suppose that the jury concludes that Elaine was partly at fault for the accident. Under what theory might her damages be reduced in proportion to how much her actions contributed to the accident and her resulting injuries?

DEBATE THIS

- Each time a state legislature enacts a law that applies the assumption of risk doctrine to a particular sport, participants in that sport suffer.

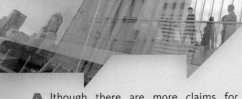

BUSINESS APPLICATION

How Important Is Tort Liability to Business?*

Although there are more claims for breach of contract than for any other category of lawsuits, tort claims are also commonplace for businesses. Furthermore, the dollar amount of damages awarded in tort actions is typically much higher than the awards in contract claims.

Because of the potential for large damages awards for intentional and unintentional acts, businesspersons should take preventive measures to help them avoid tort liability. Remember that, for most torts, injured persons can bring actions against businesses as well as against individuals. In fact, if given a choice, a plaintiff often sues a business rather than an individual because the business is more likely to have "deep pockets" (the ability to pay large damages awards). Moreover, sometimes businesses can be held liable for torts that do not apply to individuals.

The Extent of Business Negligence Liability

A business can be exposed to negligence liability in a wide variety of instances. Liability to business invitees is a clear example. A business that fails to warn invitees that its

---

* This *Business Application* is not meant to substitute for the services of an attorney who is licensed to practice law in your state.

Continues

floor is slippery after a rainstorm, or that its parking lot is icy after a snow, may be liable to an injured customer. Indeed, business owners can be liable for nearly any fall or other injury that occurs on business premises.

Even the hiring of employees can lead to negligence liability. For example, a business can be liable if it fails to do a criminal background check before hiring a person to supervise a child-care center when an investigation would have revealed that the person had previously been convicted of sexual assault. Failure to properly supervise or instruct employees can also lead to liability for a business.

Liability for Torts of Employees and Agents

A business can also be held liable for the negligence or intentional torts of its employees and agents. As you will learn in later chapters, a business is liable for the torts committed by an employee who is acting within the scope of his or her employment or an agent who is acting with the authority of the business. Therefore, if a sales agent commits fraud while acting within the scope of her or his employment, the business will be held liable.

CHECKLIST for Minimizing Business Tort Liability:

1. Constantly inspect the premises and look for areas where customers or employees might trip, slide, or fall. Take corrective action whenever you find a problem.

2. Train employees on the importance of periodic safety inspections and the procedures for reporting unsafe conditions.

3. Routinely maintain all business equipment (including vehicles).

4. Check with your liability insurance company for suggestions on improving the safety of your premises and operations.

5. Make sure that your general liability policy will adequately cover the potential exposure of the business, and reassess your coverage annually.

6. Review the background and qualifications of individuals you are considering hiring as employees or agents.

7. Investigate and review all negligence claims promptly. Most claims can be settled at a lower cost before a lawsuit is filed.

Key Terms

Chapter Summary: Tort Law

Intentional Torts against Persons	1. *Assault and battery*—An assault is an unexcused and intentional act that causes another person to be apprehensive of immediate harm. A battery is an assault that results in physical contact. 2. *False imprisonment*—The intentional confinement or restraint of another person's movement without justification. 3. *Intentional infliction of emotional distress*—An extreme and outrageous act, intentionally committed, that results in severe emotional distress to another. 4. *Defamation (libel or slander)*—A false statement of fact, not made under privilege, that is communicated to a third person and that causes damage to a person's reputation. For public figures, the plaintiff must also prove actual malice. 5. *Invasion of the right to privacy*—Includes four types: wrongful intrusion into a person's private activities; publication of information that places a person in a false light; disclosure of private facts that an ordinary person would find objectionable; and appropriation of identity, which involves the use of a person's name, likeness, or other identifying characteristic, without permission and for a commercial purpose. Most states have enacted statutes establishing appropriation of identity as the tort of *appropriation,* or right of publicity. Courts differ on the degree of likeness required. 6. *Misrepresentation (fraud)*—A false representation made by one party, through misstatement of facts or through conduct, with the intention of deceiving another and on which the other reasonably relies to his or her detriment. Negligent misrepresentation occurs when a person supplies information without having a reasonable basis for believing its truthfulness. 7. *Abusive or frivolous litigation*—A person who initiates a lawsuit out of malice and without probable cause, and loses the suit, can be sued for the tort of *malicious prosecution.* A person who uses a legal process against another improperly or to accomplish a purpose for which it was not designed can be sued for *abuse of process.* 8. *Wrongful interference*—The knowing, intentional interference by a third party with an enforceable contractual relationship or an established business relationship between other parties for the purpose of advancing the economic interests of the third party.
Intentional Torts against Property	1. *Trespass to land*—The invasion of another's real property without consent or privilege. 2. *Trespass to personal property*—Unlawfully damaging or interfering with the owner's right to use, possess, or enjoy her or his personal property. 3. *Conversion*—Wrongfully taking or using the personal property of another without permission. 4. *Disparagement of property*—Any economically injurious falsehood that is made about another's product or property. The term includes the torts of *slander of quality* and *slander of title.*

Unintentional Torts (Negligence)	1. *Negligence*—The careless performance of a legally required duty or the failure to perform a legally required act. A plaintiff must prove that a legal duty of care existed, that the defendant breached that duty, that the breach caused the plaintiff's injury, and that the plaintiff suffered a legally recognizable injury.
	2. *Defenses to negligence*—The basic affirmative defenses in negligence cases are assumption of risk, superseding cause, and contributory or comparative negligence.
	3. *Special negligence doctrines and statutes—*
	  a. *Res ipsa loquitur*—A doctrine under which a plaintiff need not prove negligence on the part of the defendant because "the facts speak for themselves."
	  b. Negligence *per se*—A type of negligence that may occur if a person violates a statute or an ordinance and the violation causes another to suffer the kind of injury that the statute or ordinance was intended to prevent.
	  c. Special negligence statutes—State statutes that prescribe duties and responsibilities in certain circumstances. Violation of these statutes will impose civil liability. Dram shop acts and Good Samaritan statutes are examples.

Strict Liability	Under the doctrine of strict liability, parties may be held liable, regardless of the degree of care exercised, for damages or injuries caused by their products or activities. Strict liability includes liability for harms caused by abnormally dangerous activities, by dangerous animals, and by defective products (product liability).

Issue Spotters

1. Jana leaves her truck's motor running while she enters a Kwik-Pik Store. The truck's transmission engages, and the vehicle crashes into a gas pump, starting a fire that spreads to a warehouse on the next block. The warehouse collapses, causing its billboard to fall and injure Lou, a bystander. Can Lou recover from Jana? Why or why not? (See *Negligence.*)
2. A water pipe bursts, flooding a Metal Fabrication Company utility room and tripping the circuit breakers on a panel in the room. Metal Fabrication contacts Nouri, a licensed electrician with five years' experience, to check the damage and turn the breakers back on. Without testing for short circuits, which Nouri knows that he should do, he tries to switch on a breaker. He is electrocuted, and his wife sues Metal Fabrication for damages, alleging negligence. What might the firm successfully claim in defense? (See *Negligence.*)
—**Check your answers to the *Issue Spotters* against the answers provided in Appendix D at the end of this text.**

Learning Objectives Check

1. What is the purpose of tort law? What types of damages are available in tort lawsuits?
2. What are two basic categories of torts?
3. What is defamation? Name two types of defamation.
4. Identify the four elements of negligence.
5. What is meant by strict liability? In what circumstances is strict liability applied?
   —Answers to the even-numbered *Learning Objectives Check* questions can be found in Appendix E at the end of this text.

Business Scenarios and Case Problems

4–1. Liability to Business Invitees. Kim went to Ling's Market to pick up a few items for dinner. It was a stormy day, and the wind had blown water through the market's door each time it opened. As Kim entered through the door, she slipped and fell in the rainwater that had accumulated on the floor. The manager knew of the weather conditions but had not posted any sign to warn customers of the water hazard. Kim injured her back as a result of the fall and sued Ling's for damages. Can Ling's be held liable for negligence? Discuss. (See *Negligence.*)

4–2. Spotlight on Intentional Torts—Defamation. Sharon Yeagle was an assistant to the vice president of student affairs at Virginia Polytechnic Institute and State University (Virginia Tech). As part of her duties, Yeagle helped students participate in the Governor's Fellows Program. The *Collegiate Times,* Virginia Tech's student newspaper, published an article about the university's success in placing students in the program. The article's text surrounded a block quotation attributed to Yeagle with the phrase "Director of Butt Licking" under her name. Yeagle sued the *Collegiate Times* for defamation. She argued that the phrase implied the commission of sodomy and was therefore actionable. What is *Collegiate Times*'s defense to this claim? [*Yeagle v. Collegiate Times,* 497 S.E.2d 136 (Va. 1998)] (See *Intentional Torts against Persons.*)

4–3. Business Torts. Medtronic, Inc., is a medical technology company that competes for customers with St. Jude Medical S.C., Inc. James Hughes worked for Medtronic as a sales manager. His contract prohibited him from working for a competitor for one year after leaving Medtronic. Hughes sought a position as a sales director for St. Jude. St. Jude told Hughes that his contract with Medtronic was unenforceable and offered him a job. Hughes accepted. Medtronic filed a suit, alleging wrongful interference. Which type of interference was most likely the basis for this suit? Did it occur here? Explain. [*Medtronic, Inc. v. Hughes,* 2011 WL 134973 (Minn.App. 2011)] (See *Intentional Torts against Persons.*)

4–4. Intentional Infliction of Emotional Distress. While living in her home country of Tanzania, Sophia Kiwanuka signed an employment contract with Anne Margareth Bakilana, a Tanzanian living in Washington, D.C. Kiwanuka traveled to the United States to work as a babysitter and maid in Bakilana's house. When Kiwanuka arrived, Bakilana confiscated her passport, held her in isolation, and forced her to work long hours under threat of having her deported. Kiwanuka worked seven days a week without breaks and was subjected to regular verbal and psychological abuse by Bakilana. Kiwanuka filed a complaint against Bakilana for intentional infliction of emotional distress, among other claims. Bakilana argued that Kiwanuka's complaint should be dismissed because the allegations were insufficient to show outrageous intentional conduct that resulted in severe emotional distress. If you were the judge, in whose favor would you rule? Why? [*Kiwanuka v. Bakilana,* 844 F.Supp.2d 107 (D.D.C. 2012)] (See *Intentional Torts against Persons.*)

4–5. Business Case Problem with Sample Answer—Negligence. At the Weatherford Hotel in Flagstaff, Arizona, in Room 59, a balcony extends across thirty inches of the room's only window, leaving a twelve-inch gap with a three-story drop to the concrete below. A sign prohibits smoking in the room but invites guests to "step out onto the balcony" to smoke. Toni Lucario was a guest in Room 59 when she climbed out of the window and fell to her death. Patrick McMurtry, her estate's personal representative, filed a suit against the Weatherford. Did the hotel breach a duty of care to Lucario? What might the Weatherford assert in its defense? Explain. [*McMurtry v. Weatherford Hotel, Inc.,* 293 P.3d 520 (Ariz. App. 2013)] (See *Negligence.*)

—**For a sample answer to Problem 4–5, go to Appendix F at the end of this text.**

4–6. Negligence. Ronald Rawls and Zabian Bailey were in an auto accident in Bridgeport, Connecticut. Bailey rear-ended Rawls at a stoplight. Evidence showed it was more likely than not that Bailey failed to apply his brakes in time to avoid the collision, failed to turn his vehicle to avoid the collision, failed to keep his vehicle under control, and was inattentive to his surroundings. Rawls filed a suit in a Connecticut state court against his insurance company, Progressive Northern Insurance Co., to obtain benefits under an underinsured motorist clause, alleging that Bailey had been negligent. Could Rawls collect? Discuss. [*Rawls v. Progressive Northern Insurance* Co., 310 Conn. 768, 83 A.3d 576 (2014)] (See *Negligence*.)

4–7. Negligence. Charles Robison, an employee of West Star Transportation, Inc., was ordered to cover an unevenly loaded flatbed trailer with a 150-pound tarpaulin. The load included uncrated equipment and pallet crates of different heights, about thirteen feet off the ground at its highest point. While standing on the load, manipulating the tarpaulin without safety equipment or assistance, Robison fell headfirst and sustained a traumatic head injury. He filed a suit against West Star to recover for his injury. Was West Star "negligent in failing to provide a reasonably safe place to work," as Robison claimed? Explain. [*West Star Transportation, Inc. v. Robison*, __ S.W.3d __, 2015 WL 348594 (Tex.App.—Amarillo 2015)] (See *Unintentional Torts (Negligence)*.)

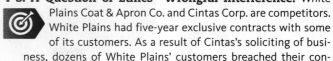

4–8. A Question of Ethics—Wrongful Interference. White Plains Coat & Apron Co. and Cintas Corp. are competitors. White Plains had five-year exclusive contracts with some of its customers. As a result of Cintas's soliciting of business, dozens of White Plains' customers breached their contracts and entered into rental agreements with Cintas. White Plains filed a suit against Cintas, alleging wrongful interference. [*White Plains Coat & Apron Co. v. Cintas Corp.*, 8 N.Y.3d 422, 867 N.E.2d 381 (2007)] (See *Intentional Torts against Persons*.)

1. What are the two policies at odds in wrongful interference cases? When there is an existing contract, which of these interests should be accorded priority? Why?

2. Is a general interest in soliciting business for profit a sufficient defense to a claim of wrongful interference with a contractual relationship? What do you think? Why?

Critical Thinking and Writing Assignments

4–9. Business Law Critical Thinking Group Assignment. Donald and Gloria Bowden hosted a cookout at their home in South Carolina, inviting mostly business acquaintances. Justin Parks, who was nineteen years old, attended the party. Alcoholic beverages were available to all of the guests, even those who, like Parks, were between the ages of eighteen and twenty-one.

Parks consumed alcohol at the party and left with other guests. One of these guests detained Parks at the guest's home to give Parks time to "sober up." Parks then drove himself from this guest's home and was killed in a one-car accident. At the time of death, he had a blood alcohol content of 0.291 percent, which exceeded the state's limit for driving a motor vehicle.

Linda Marcum, Parks's mother, filed a suit in a South Carolina state court against the Bowdens and others, alleging negligence. (See *Negligence*.)

1. The first group will present arguments in favor of holding the social hosts liable in this situation.

2. The second group will formulate arguments against holding the social hosts liable based on principles in this chapter.

3. The states vary widely in assessing liability and imposing sanctions in the circumstances described in this problem. The third group will determine the reasons why courts do not treat social hosts the same as parents who serve alcoholic beverages to their underage children.

iStockPhoto.com/milanklusacek

5

CHAPTER OUTLINE

LEARNING OBJECTIVES

The five Learning Objectives *below are designed to help improve your understanding of the chapter. After reading this chapter, you should be able to answer the following questions:*

1. Can a manufacturer be held liable to any person who suffers an injury proximately caused by the manufacturer's negligently made product?

2. What public policy assumptions underlie strict product liability?

3. What are the elements of a cause of action in strict product liability?

4. What are three types of product defects?

5. What defenses to liability can be raised in a product liability lawsuit?

Product Liability The legal liability of manufacturers, sellers, and lessors of goods for injuries or damage caused by the goods to consumers, users, or bystanders.

Product Liability

An area of tort law of particular importance to businesspersons is product liability. As Warren Buffett implies in the chapter-opening quote, to be successful, a business cannot make too many mistakes. This is especially true for businesses that make or sell products. The manufacturers and sellers of products may incur product liability when product defects cause injury or property damage to consumers, users, or bystanders (people in the vicinity of the product when it fails).

Although multimillion-dollar product liability claims often involve big automakers, pharmaceutical companies, or tobacco companies, many businesses face potential liability. For instance, in the last few years, numerous reports have suggested that energy drinks, such as Monster, Red Bull, Rockstar, and 5-hour Energy, have serious adverse effects—especially on young people. Several individuals have been hospitalized, and some have even died, after consuming large amounts of energy drinks. The federal government has issued a report concerning the adverse effects of these products and is investigating their safety. Meanwhile, the producers of energy drinks are facing a number of product liability actions. For example, the parents of a teenage girl who died after consuming two Monster energy drinks have filed a lawsuit against Monster Beverage Corporation in California.

> "You only have to do a very few things right in your life so long as you don't do too many things wrong."
>
> **WARREN BUFFETT**
> 1930–PRESENT
> (AMERICAN BUSINESSMAN AND THE MOST SUCCESSFUL INVESTOR IN THE TWENTIETH CENTURY)

5-1 Product Liability

Those who make, sell, or lease goods can be held liable for physical harm or property damage caused by those goods to a consumer, user, or bystander. This is called **product liability.**

Product liability claims may be based on the tort theories of negligence, fraudulent misrepresentation, and strict liability. We look here at product liability based on negligence and misrepresentation.

5–1a Negligence

Chapter 4 defined *negligence* as the failure to exercise the degree of care that a reasonable, prudent person would have exercised under the circumstances. If a manufacturer fails to exercise "due care" to make a product safe, a person who is injured by the product may sue the manufacturer for negligence.

Due Care Must Be Exercised The manufacturer must exercise due care in all of the following areas:

1. Designing the product.
2. Selecting the materials.
3. Using the appropriate production process.
4. Assembling and testing the product.
5. Placing adequate warnings on the label to inform the user of dangers of which an ordinary person might not be aware.
6. Inspecting and testing any purchased components used in the final product.

Privity of Contract Not Required A product liability action based on negligence does not require privity of contract between the injured plaintiff and the defendant manufacturer. **Privity of contract** refers to the relationship that exists between the promisor and the promisee of a contract. Privity is the reason that normally only the parties to a contract can enforce that contract.

In the context of product liability law, privity is not required. A person who is injured by a defective product can bring a negligence suit even though he or she was not the one who actually purchased the product—and thus is not in privity. A manufacturer is liable for its failure to exercise due care to *any person* who sustains an injury proximately caused by a negligently made (defective) product.

Relative to the long history of the common law, this exception to the privity requirement is a fairly recent development, dating to the early part of the twentieth century. A leading case in this respect is *MacPherson v. Buick Motor Co.*, which is presented as this chapter's *Landmark in the Law* feature.

5–1b Misrepresentation

When a user or consumer is injured as a result of a manufacturer's or seller's fraudulent misrepresentation, the basis of liability may be the tort of fraud. In this situation, the misrepresentation must have been made knowingly or with reckless disregard for the facts. The intentional mislabeling of packaged cosmetics, for instance, or the intentional concealment of a product's defects constitutes fraudulent misrepresentation.

The misrepresentation must be of a material fact, and the seller must have intended to induce the buyer's reliance on the misrepresentation. Misrepresentation on a label or advertisement is enough to show the intent to induce reliance. Of course, to bring a lawsuit on this ground, the buyer must have relied on the misrepresentation.

iStockPhoto.com/Daniel Loiselle

To what extent are energy drink manufacturers responsible for injuries to those who consume large amounts of their products?

LEARNING OBJECTIVE 1

Can a manufacturer be held liable to any person who suffers an injury proximately caused by the manufacturer's negligently made product?

Privity of Contract The relationship that exists between the promisor and the promisee of a contract.

LANDMARK IN THE LAW   *MacPherson v. Buick Motor Co. (1916)*

In the landmark case of *MacPherson v. Buick Motor Co.,*[a] the New York Court of Appeals—New York's highest court—considered the liability of a manufacturer that had failed to exercise reasonable care in manufacturing a finished product.

CASE BACKGROUND Donald MacPherson suffered injuries while riding in a Buick automobile that suddenly collapsed because one of the wheels was made of defective wood. The spokes crumbled into fragments, throwing MacPherson out of the vehicle and injuring him.

MacPherson had purchased the car from a Buick dealer, but he brought a lawsuit against the manufacturer, Buick Motor Company. Buick itself had not made the wheel but

had bought it from another manufacturer. There was evidence, though, that the defects could have been discovered by a reasonable inspection by Buick and that no such inspection had taken place. MacPherson charged Buick with negligence for putting a human life in imminent danger.

THE ISSUE BEFORE THE COURT AND THE COURT'S RULING The primary issue was whether Buick owed a duty of care to anyone except the immediate purchaser of the car—that is, the Buick dealer. In deciding the issue, Justice Benjamin Cardozo stated that "if the nature of a thing is such that it is reasonably certain to place life and limb in peril when negligently made, it is then a thing of danger. . . . If to the element of danger there is added knowledge that the thing will be used by persons other than the purchaser, and used without new tests, then, irrespective of contract, the manufacturer of this thing of danger is under a duty to make it carefully."

The court concluded that "beyond all question, the nature of an automobile gives warning of probable danger if its construction is defective. This automobile was designed to go 50 miles an hour. Unless its wheels were sound and strong, injury was almost certain." Although Buick itself had not manufactured the wheel, the court held that Buick had a duty to inspect the wheels and that Buick "was responsible for the finished product." Therefore, Buick was liable to MacPherson for the injuries he sustained when he was thrown from the car.

APPLICATION TO TODAY'S WORLD *This landmark decision was a significant step in creating the legal environment of the modern world. As often happens, technological developments necessitated changes in the law. Today, automobile manufacturers are commonly held liable when their negligence causes automobile users to be injured.*

a. 217 N.Y. 382, 111 N.E. 1050 (1916).

5-2 Strict Product Liability

LEARNING OBJECTIVE 2

What public policy assumptions underlie strict product liability?

Under the doctrine of strict liability, people may be liable for the results of their acts regardless of their intentions or their exercise of reasonable care. In addition, liability does not depend on privity of contract. The injured party does not have to be the buyer or a *third party beneficiary* (one for whose benefit a contract is made). In the 1960s, courts applied the doctrine of strict liability in several landmark cases involving manufactured goods, and this doctrine has since become a common method of holding manufacturers liable.

5-2a Strict Product Liability and Public Policy

The law imposes strict product liability as a matter of public policy. This public policy rests on a threefold assumption:

1. Consumers should be protected against unsafe products.

2. Manufacturers and distributors should not escape liability for faulty products simply because they are not in privity of contract with the ultimate user of those products.

3. Manufacturers, sellers, and lessors of products are generally in a better position than consumers to bear the costs associated with injuries caused by their products—costs that they can ultimately pass on to all consumers in the form of higher prices.

Development of the Doctrine California was the first state to impose strict product liability in tort on manufacturers. **CASE EXAMPLE 5.1** William Greenman was injured when his Shopsmith combination power tool threw off a piece of wood that struck him in the head. He sued the manufacturer, claiming that he had followed the product instructions and that the product must be defective.

If a power tool is defective and injures a user, does the user sue under contract law or tort law?

In a landmark decision, *Greenman v. Yuba Power Products, Inc.*,[1] the California Supreme Court set out the reason for applying tort law rather than contract law in cases involving consumers who were injured by defective products. According to the *Greenman* court, the "purpose of such liability is to [e]nsure that the costs of injuries resulting from defective products are borne by the manufacturers . . . rather than by the injured persons who are powerless to protect themselves." ∎ Today, the majority of states recognize strict product liability, although some state courts limit its application to situations involving personal injuries (rather than property damage).

Statement of Public Policy The public policy concerning strict product liability may be expressed in a statute or in the common law. Sometimes, public policy may be revealed in a court's interpretation of a statute, as in the following *Spotlight Case.*

---

1. 59 Cal.2d 57, 377 P.2d 897, 27 Cal.Rptr. 697 (1962).

SPOTLIGHT ON INJURIES FROM VACCINATIONS: CASE 5.1

Bruesewitz v. Wyeth, LLC

Supreme Court of the United States, 562 U.S. 223, 131 S.Ct. 1068, 179 L.Ed.2d 1 (2011).

FACTS When Hannah Bruesewitz was six months old, her pediatrician administered a dose of the diphtheria, tetanus, and pertussis (DTP) vaccine according to the Centers for Disease Control and Prevention's recommended childhood immunization schedule. Within twenty-four hours, Hannah began to experience seizures. She suffered more than one hundred seizures during the next month. Her doctors diagnosed her with "residual seizure disorder" and "developmental delay."

Hannah's parents, Russell and Robalee Bruesewitz, filed a claim for relief in the U.S. Court of Federal Claims under the National Childhood Vaccine Injury Act (NCVIA). The NCVIA set up a no-fault compensation program for persons injured by vaccines. The claim was denied. The Bruesewitzes then filed a suit in a Pennsylvania state court against Wyeth, LLC, the maker of the vaccine, alleging strict product liability. The suit was moved to a federal district court. The court held that the claim was preempted by the NCVIA, which includes provisions protecting manufacturers from liability for "a vaccine's unavoidable, adverse side effects." A federal appellate court affirmed the district court's judgment. The Bruesewitzes appealed to the United States Supreme Court.

ISSUE Was the Bruesewitzes' strict product liability claim against Wyeth for the injuries that their child suffered from vaccination preempted by the National Childhood Vaccine Injury Act?

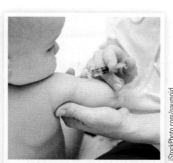

What happens when a vaccine causes adverse side effects?

DECISION Yes. The United States Supreme Court affirmed the lower court's judgment. The NCVIA preempted the Bruesewitzes' claim against Wyeth for injury to their daughter caused by the DTP vaccine's side effects.

REASON The Court reasoned that Congress enacted the NCVIA as a matter of public policy to stabilize the vaccine market and facilitate compensation. In the no-fault compensation program set up by the NCVIA, a person with a vaccine-related claim files a petition with the U.S. Court of Federal Claims. The court may award compensation for legal, medical, rehabilitation, counseling, special education, and vocational training expenses, as well as for diminished earning capacity, pain and suffering, and death. The awards are funded by a tax on the vaccine. In exchange for the "informal, efficient" compensation program, vaccine manufacturers that comply with the regulatory requirements are "immunized" from liability. The statute thus strikes a balance between paying victims harmed by vaccines and protecting the vaccine industry from collapsing under the costs of tort liability.

CRITICAL THINKING—Political Consideration *If the public wants to change the policy outlined in this case, which branch of the government—and at what level—should be lobbied to make the change? Explain.*

5-2b Requirements for Strict Product Liability

After the *Restatement (Second) of Torts* was issued in 1964, Section 402A became a widely accepted statement of how the doctrine of strict liability should be applied to sellers of goods. These sellers include manufacturers, processors, assemblers, packagers, bottlers, wholesalers, distributors, retailers, and lessors.

The bases for an action in strict liability that are set forth in Section 402A can be summarized as the following six requirements. Depending on the jurisdiction, if these requirements are met, a manufacturer's liability to an injured party can be almost unlimited.

1. The product must have been in a *defective condition* when the defendant sold it.
2. The defendant must normally be engaged in the *business of selling* (or otherwise distributing) that product.
3. The product must be *unreasonably dangerous* to the user or consumer because of its defective condition (in most states).
4. The plaintiff must incur *physical harm* to self or property by use or consumption of the product.
5. The defective condition must be the *proximate cause* of the injury or damage.
6. The *goods must not have been substantially changed* from the time the product was sold to the time the injury was sustained.

Does a person injured by a defective air bag have to prove that it was defective when the car was manufactured?

iStockPhoto.com/nikkytok

Proving a Defective Condition Under these requirements, in any action against a manufacturer, seller, or lessor, the plaintiff does not have to show why or how the product became defective. The plaintiff does, however, have to prove that the product was defective at the time it left the seller or lessor and that this defective condition made it "unreasonably dangerous" to the user or consumer. (See this chapter's *Beyond Our Borders* feature for a discussion of how foreign suppliers were held liable for defective goods sold in the United States.)

Unless evidence can be presented that will support the conclusion that the product was defective when it was sold or leased, the plaintiff normally will not succeed. If the product was delivered in a safe condition and subsequent mishandling made it harmful to the user, the seller or lessor usually is not strictly liable.

BEYOND OUR BORDERS

Imposing Product Liability as Far Away as China

U.S. builders began using Chinese drywall in the construction of houses in 2003. By 2007, thousands of homes had been constructed with this product in Alabama, Florida, Louisiana, Mississippi, and a few other states. There was a problem, though—use of the Chinese drywall caused blackening and pitting of electrical wires. Homeowners began to notice an odor similar to rotten eggs in their houses. Air-conditioning units started failing, as did ceiling fans, alarm systems, refrigerators, and other appliances.

Numerous lawsuits were filed against the Chinese drywall manufacturers. The companies initially fought the claims but decided to settle when the number of lawsuits ran into the thousands. The estimated value of the settlement is between $800 million and $1 billion. It includes an uncapped fund to pay for repairs to about 4,500 homes and a separate fund capped at $30 million that will be used to pay for health problems stemming from the defective drywall.

CRITICAL THINKING

- Could U.S. companies that sold Chinese drywall to consumers also be held liable for damages? Why or why not?

Unreasonably Dangerous Products The *Restatement* recognizes that many products cannot possibly be made entirely safe for all uses. Thus, sellers or lessors of these products are held liable only when the products are *unreasonably* dangerous. A court may consider a product so defective as to be an **unreasonably dangerous product** in either of the following situations.

1. The product is dangerous beyond the expectation of the ordinary consumer.

2. A less dangerous alternative was economically feasible for the manufacturer, but the manufacturer failed to produce it.

As will be discussed next, a product may be unreasonably dangerous due to a design or manufacturing flaw or due to an inadequate warning.

If this Chinese-made drywall adversely affects electrical wiring, who has legal liability?

5–2c Product Defects—Restatement (Third) of Torts

The *Restatement (Third) of Torts: Products Liability* defines the three types of product defects that have traditionally been recognized in product liability law—manufacturing defects, design defects, and inadequate warnings.

Manufacturing Defects According to Section 2(a) of the *Restatement (Third) of Torts: Products Liability,* a product "contains a manufacturing defect when the product departs from its intended design even though all possible care was exercised in the preparation and marketing of the product." Basically, a manufacturing defect is a departure from design specifications that results in products that are physically flawed, damaged, or incorrectly assembled. A glass bottle that is made too thin, causing it to explode in a consumer's face, is an example of a product with a manufacturing defect.

Encouraging Higher Standards. Usually, manufacturing defects occur when a manufacturer fails to assemble, test, or check the quality of a product adequately. In fact, the idea behind holding defendants strictly liable for manufacturing defects is to encourage greater investment in product safety and stringent quality control standards.

Note that liability is imposed on a manufacturer (and on the wholesaler and retailer) regardless of whether the manufacturer's quality control efforts were "reasonable." For more information on how effective quality control procedures can help businesses reduce their potential legal liability for defective products, see the *Linking Business Law to Corporate Management* feature at the end of this chapter.

The Role of Expert Testimony. Cases involving allegations of a manufacturing defect are often decided based on the opinions and testimony of experts. **CASE EXAMPLE 5.2** Kevin Schmude purchased an eight-foot stepladder and used it to install radio-frequency shielding in a hospital room. While Schmude was standing on the ladder, it collapsed, and he was seriously injured. He filed a lawsuit against the ladder's maker, Tricam Industries, Inc., based on a manufacturing defect.

Experts testified that when the ladder was assembled during manufacturing, the preexisting holes in the top cap did not properly line up with the holes in the rear right rail and backing plate. As a result of the misalignment, the rear legs of the ladder were not securely fastened in place, causing the ladder to fail. A jury concluded that this manufacturing defect made the ladder unreasonably dangerous and awarded Schmude more than $677,000 in damages.[2] ■

Unreasonably Dangerous Product A product that is so defective that it is dangerous beyond the expectation of an ordinary consumer or a product for which a less dangerous alternative was feasible but the manufacturer failed to produce it.

LEARNING OBJECTIVE 4
What are three types of product defects?

---

2. *Schmude v. Tricam Industries, Inc.*, 550 F.Supp.2d 846 (E.D.Wis. 2008).

Design Defects Unlike a product with a manufacturing defect, a product with a design defect is made in conformity with the manufacturer's design specifications. Nevertheless, it results in injury to the user because the design itself is flawed. The product's design creates an unreasonable risk to the user. A product "is defective in design when the foreseeable risks of harm posed by the product could have been reduced or avoided by the adoption of a reasonable alternative design by the seller or other distributor, or a predecessor in the commercial chain of distribution, and the omission of the alternative design renders the product not reasonably safe."[3]

Test for Design Defects. To successfully assert a design defect, a plaintiff has to show that:

1. A reasonable alternative design was available.

2. As a result of the defendant's failure to adopt the alternative design, the product was not reasonably safe.

In other words, a manufacturer or other defendant is liable only when the harm was reasonably preventable.
CASE EXAMPLE 5.3 After Gillespie cut off several of his fingers while operating a table saw, he filed a lawsuit against the maker of the saw. Gillespie alleged that the blade guards on the saw were defectively designed. At trial, however, an expert testified that the alternative design for blade guards used for table saws could not have been used for the particular cut that Gillespie was performing at the time he was injured. The court found that Gillespie's claim must fail because there was no proof that the "better" design of guard would have prevented his injury.[4] ■

Can a Taser be considered unreasonably dangerous as designed? Taser International, Inc., located in Scottsdale, Arizona, provides nonlethal devices that police personnel can use to "stun" aggressors. When officer Jeremy Baird of the Moberly, Missouri, Police Department used a Taser device after a routine traffic stop, the victim fell to the ground, lost consciousness, and died two hours later. The victim's mother sued the city of Moberly and several police officers. That case was settled for $2.4 million.

The victim's mother then sued Taser International. The claim was that the company did not provide adequate warnings that using the device directly on the chest could lead to cardiac arrest. The lawsuit also argued that the Taser was defectively designed. A federal trial court dismissed the case.

On appeal, the reviewing court pointed out that the plaintiff would have had to prove that additional warnings on the use of the Taser "would have altered the behavior of the officers involved in the incident." But, concluded the court, there was "no dispute on this record that Officer Baird would not have read any additional warning Taser may have added about the cardiac danger" of its device. As to the defective design claim, the court noted that "under strict liability, a manufacturer is not intended to be an ensurer of any and all injuries caused by its products."[5] Just showing a link between the use of the Taser and the victim's injury was insufficient to establish strict liability.

Is showing that a Taser caused the death of a victim sufficient under the doctrine of strict liability?

Factors to Be Considered. According to the Official Comments accompanying the *Restatement (Third) of Torts,* a court can consider a broad range of factors in deciding claims of design defects. These factors include the magnitude and probability of the foreseeable risks, as well

---

3. *Restatement (Third) of Torts: Products Liability,* Section 2(b).
4. *Gillespie v. Sears, Roebuck & Co.,* 386 F.3d 21 (1st Cir. 2004).
5. *Bachtel v. Taser International, Inc.,* 747 F.3d 967 (2014). In contrast, see *Fontenot v. Taser International, Inc.,* 736 F.3d 318 (4th Cir. 2013).

as the relative advantages and disadvantages of the product as it was designed and as it alternatively could have been designed.

CASE EXAMPLE 5.4 Jodie Bullock smoked cigarettes manufactured by Philip Morris for forty-five years. When she was diagnosed with lung cancer, Bullock brought a product liability suit against Philip Morris. She presented evidence that by the late 1950s, scientists had proved that smoking caused lung cancer. Nonetheless, Philip Morris had publicly announced that there was no proof that smoking caused cancer and that "numerous scientists" questioned "the validity of the statistics."

At trial, the judge instructed the jury to consider the gravity of the danger posed by the design, as well as the likelihood that the danger would cause injury. The jury found that there was a defect in the design of the cigarettes and that they had been negligently designed, and awarded Bullock damages. A reviewing court affirmed the jury's verdict on appeal.[6] ■

Risk-Utility Analysis. Most courts engage in a risk-utility analysis, determining whether the risk of harm from the product as designed outweighs its utility to the user and to the public. The court in the following case reviewed whether the plaintiff had satisfied the risk-utility test.

---

6. *Bullock v. Philip Morris USA, Inc.*, 159 Cal.App.4th 655, 71 Cal.Rptr.3d 775 (2008). The California Court of Appeal subsequently upheld a punitive damages award of $13.8 million. See *Bullock v. Philip Morris USA, Inc.*, 198 Cal.App.4th 543, 131 Cal.Rptr.3d 382 (2011).

CASE 5.2

Riley v. Ford Motor Co.

Court of Appeals of South Carolina, 408 S.C. 1, 757 S.E.2d 422 (2014).

FACTS Jasper County Sheriff Benjamin Riley was driving his Ford F-150 pickup truck near Ehrhardt, South Carolina, when it collided with another vehicle. The impact caused Riley's truck to leave the road and roll over. The driver's door of the truck opened in the collision, and Riley was ejected and killed.

Riley's widow, Laura, as the representative of his estate, filed a product liability suit in a South Carolina state court against Ford Motor Company. The plaintiff alleged that the design of the door-latch system of the truck allowed the door to open in the collision. The court awarded the estate $900,000 in damages "because of the stature of Riley and what he's done in life, what he's contributed to his family." Ford appealed, arguing that the plaintiff had not proved the existence of a reasonable alternative design.

ISSUE Did the plaintiff prove the existence of a reasonable alternative design?

DECISION Yes. A state intermediate appellate court affirmed the lower court's ruling. Evidence showed that Ford knew of a reasonable alternative design for the truck's door-latch system. Ford was aware

How can a plaintiff prove that a truck's door latch was defectively designed?

of the safety problems presented by the current system (a rod-linkage system). After conducting a risk-utility analysis of a different system (a cable-linkage system), Ford had concluded that the alternative system was a "feasible, if not superior, alternative."

REASON To meet the risk-utility test, a plaintiff must show a reasonable alternative design for the product at issue. This involves showing that the manufacturer, after weighing costs and benefits, decided to use one design instead of another. In this case, the plaintiff presented evidence of Ford's own design for a cable-linkage door-latch system, which the manufacturer had used in earlier F-150 trucks. According to studies conducted by Ford, cable systems have several advantages over rod systems—"cable systems are easier for assembly plants to handle," "reduce cost and reduce operator dependence," "reduce complexity in service," and "are more robust to crash." The only disadvantage is that cable systems cost more than rod systems.

CRITICAL THINKING—Legal Environment Consideration *By what means did the plaintiff most likely discover the defendant's studies of an alternative design for the door-latch system?*

Consumer-Expectation Test. Instead of the risk-utility test, some courts apply the consumer-expectation test to determine whether a product's design was defective. Under this test, a product is unreasonably dangerous when it fails to perform in the manner that would reasonably be expected by an ordinary consumer.

CASE EXAMPLE 5.5 A representative from Wilson Sporting Goods Company gave Edwin Hickox an umpire's mask that was designed to be safer than other umpire's masks. The mask had a newly designed throat guard that angled forward instead of extending straight down. While Hickox was working as an umpire during a game and wearing the mask, he was was struck by a foul ball and injured. He suffered a concussion and damage to his inner ear, which caused permanent hearing loss. Hickox and his wife sued the manufacturer for product liability based on a defective design and won. A jury awarded $750,000 to Hickox and $25,000 to his wife. Wilson appealed.

The reviewing court affirmed the jury's verdict. The design was defective because "an ordinary consumer would have expected the mask to perform more safely than it did." The evidence presented to the jury had shown that Wilson's mask was more dangerous than comparable masks sold at the time. The new "masks could concentrate energy at the point of impact, rather than distribute energy evenly throughout the padded area of the mask," as an ordinary consumer would have expected a baseball mask to do.[7] ■

Inadequate Warnings A product may also be deemed defective because of inadequate instructions or warnings. A product will be considered defective "when the foreseeable risks of harm posed by the product could have been reduced or avoided by the provision of reasonable instructions or warnings by the seller or other distributor, or a predecessor in the commercial chain of distribution, and the omission of the instructions or warnings renders the product not reasonably safe."[8] Generally, a seller must also warn consumers of the harm that can result from the *foreseeable misuse* of its product.

Content of Warnings. Important factors for a court to consider include the risks of a product, the "content and comprehensibility" and "intensity of expression" of warnings and instructions, and the "characteristics of expected user groups."[9] Courts apply a "reasonableness" test to determine if the warnings adequately alert consumers to the product's risks. For instance, children will likely respond more readily to bright, bold, simple warning labels, while educated adults might need more detailed information. For more on tips on making sure a product's warnings are adequate, see this chapter's *Managerial Strategy* feature.

CASE EXAMPLE 5.6 Jeffrey Johnson was taken to the emergency room for an episode of atrial fibrillation, a heart rhythm disorder. Dr. David Hahn used a defibrillator manufactured by Medtronic, Inc., to deliver electric shocks to Johnson's heart. The defibrillator had synchronous and asynchronous modes, and it reverted to the asynchronous mode after each use. Hahn intended to deliver synchronized shocks, which required him to select the synchronous mode for each shock. Hahn did not read the device's instructions, which Medtronic had provided both in a manual and on the device itself. As a result, he delivered one synchronized shock, followed by twelve asynchronous shocks that endangered Johnson's life.

Johnson and his wife filed a product liability suit against Medtronic asserting that Medtronic had provided inadequate warnings about the defibrillator and that the device had a design defect. A Missouri appellate court held that the Johnsons could not pursue a claim based on the inadequacy of Medtronic's warnings, but they could pursue a claim alleging a design defect. The court reasoned that in some cases, "a manufacturer may be held liable

When is an umpire's mask defectively designed under the consumer-expectation test?

iStockPhoto.com/StushD80

---

7. *Wilson Sporting Goods Co. v. Hickox*, 59 A.3d 1267 (D.C.App. 2013).
8. *Restatement (Third) of Torts: Products Liability*, Section 2(c).
9. *Restatement (Third) of Torts: Products Liability*, Section 2, Comment h.

where it chooses to warn of the danger . . . rather than preclude the danger by design."[10] ■

Obvious Risks. There is no duty to warn about risks that are obvious or commonly known. Warnings about such risks do not add to the safety of a product and could even detract from it by making other warnings seem less significant. As will be discussed later in this chapter, the obviousness of a risk and a user's decision to proceed in the face of that risk may be a defense in a product liability suit based on an inadequate warning.

---

10. *Johnson v. Medtronic, Inc.*, 365 S.W.3d 226 (Mo.App. 2012).

When a physician misuses a defibrillator manufactured by Medtronic without reading its warning label, is Medtronic liable for inadequate warnings?

MANAGERIAL STRATEGY — When Is a Warning Legally Bulletproof?

Management Faces a Legal Issue

A company can develop and sell a perfectly manufactured and designed product, yet still face product liability lawsuits for defective warnings. A product may be defective because of inadequate instructions or warnings when the foreseeable risks of harm posed by the product could have been reduced by reasonable warnings offered by the seller or other distributor. Manufacturers and distributors have a duty to warn users of any hidden dangers of their products. Additionally, they have a duty to instruct users in how to use the product to avoid any dangers. Warnings generally must be clear and specific. They must also be conspicuous.

Not all manufacturers have to provide warnings, as pointed out in the text. People are expected to know that knives can cut fingers, for example, so a seller need not place a bright orange label on each knife sold reminding consumers of this danger. Most household products are generally safe when used as intended.

What the Courts Say

In a 2014 New Jersey case, an appeals court reviewed a product liability case against the manufacturer of a Razor A–type kick scooter. A ten-year-old boy was injured when he fell and struck his face on the scooter's

handlebars. The padded end caps on the handlebars had deteriorated, and the boy's mother had thrown them away, exposing the handlebars' metal ends.

The boy and his mother sued, claiming that the manufacturer was required to provide a warning to prevent injuries of this type. The appellate court noted, however, that the plaintiffs were not able to claim that the Razor A was defective. "Lacking evidence that Razor A's end-cap design was defective, plaintiffs cannot show that Razor A had a duty to warn of such a defect, and therefore cannot make out their failure to warn claim."[a]

In another 2014 case, a woman suffered neurological disorders after taking a generic drug to treat her gastroesophageal reflux disease. Part of her complaint asserted strict liability for failure to warn. The plaintiff claimed that the manufacturer had not updated its label to indicate that usage should not exceed twelve weeks. The reviewing court reasoned that "The adequacy of the instructions . . . made no difference to the outcome . . . because [the plaintiff alleges that her prescribing physician] did not read those materials."[b]

In contrast, in a 2013 Massachusetts case, a family was awarded over $63 million

---

a. *Vann v. Toys R Us*, N.J.Super.A.D., 2014 WL3537937 (N.J.Sup. A.D. 2014).
b. *Brinkley v. Pfizer, Inc.*, 772 F.3d 1133 (8th Cir. 2014).

in a lawsuit against Johnson & Johnson for defective warnings on bottles of children's Motrin. A seven-year-old girl lost 70 percent of her skin, experienced brain damage, and went blind after suffering a reaction to the drug. The drug did have a specific warning label that instructed consumers to stop taking the medication and contact a physician in the event of an allergic reaction. Nonetheless, Johnson & Johnson was found liable for failing to warn about the known risk of severe side effects.

MANAGERIAL IMPLICATIONS

Managers must be aware that whenever a product presents a danger, a warning is required. The seller, though, must know about the danger for the warning to be obligatory. In addition, the danger must not be obvious to a reasonable user. Here is where a manager's task may become difficult, because it is not always clear what would be obvious to a "reasonable user."

When product warnings are supplied, they must be obvious and easy to understand. Here, one issue to be considered is that of warning non-English-speaking users. Some manufacturers publish warnings in foreign languages and also use symbols to indicate dangers. One downside of excessive safety warnings is that so many warnings may be attached to a product that few consumers will bother to read any of them.

How many and what types of warnings against doing back flips on this trampoline must be affixed to eliminate the manufacturer's liability?

CASE EXAMPLE 5.7 Sixteen-year-old Gary Crosswhite failed in an attempt to do a back flip on a trampoline and was paralyzed as a result. The manufacturer had provided nine warning labels affixed to the trampoline, an instruction manual with safety warnings, and a placard to be attached to the entry ladder. Each advised users not to do flips on the trampoline. Crosswhite sued the manufacturer for inadequate warnings. The court found that the warnings were sufficient to make the risks obvious and insulate the manufacturer from liability for Crosswhite's injuries.[11] ▪

Risks that may seem obvious to some users will not be obvious to all users. This is a particular problem when users are likely to be children. A young child may not be able to read or understand warning labels or comprehend the risk of certain activities. To avoid liability, the manufacturer would have to prove that the warnings it provided were adequate to make the risk of injury obvious to a young child.

State Laws and Constitutionality. An action alleging that a product is defective due to an inadequate label can be based on state law, but that law must not violate the U.S. Constitution. **CASE EXAMPLE 5.8** California once enacted a law imposing restrictions and a labeling requirement on the sale or rental of "violent video games" to minors. Although the video game industry had adopted a voluntary rating system for games, the legislators deemed those labels inadequate. The Video Software Dealers Association and the Entertainment Software Association immediately filed a suit in federal court to invalidate the law, and the law was struck down. The court found that the definition of a violent video game in California's law was unconstitutionally vague and violated the First Amendment's guarantee of freedom of speech.[12] ▪

5–2d Market-Share Liability

Generally, in cases involving product liability, a plaintiff must prove that the defective product that caused her or his injury was made by a specific defendant. In a few situations, however, courts have dropped this requirement when a plaintiff cannot prove which of many distributors of a harmful product supplied the particular product that caused the injury. Under a theory of **market-share liability,** a court can hold each manufacturer responsible for a percentage of the plaintiff's damages that is equal to the percentage of its market share.

CASE EXAMPLE 5.9 Suffolk County Water Authority (SWCA) is a municipal water supplier in Suffolk County, New York. SWCA discovered the presence of a toxic chemical, perchloroethylene (PCE), used by dry cleaners and others in its local water. SWCA filed a product liability lawsuit against Dow Chemical Corporation and other companies that manufactured and distributed PCE. Dow filed a motion to dismiss the case for failure to state a claim, since SWCA could not identify each defendant whose allegedly defective product caused the water contamination.

A state trial court refused to dismiss the action, holding that SWCA's allegations were sufficient to invoke market-share liability. Under market-share liability, the burden of identification shifts to defendants if the plaintiff establishes a *prima facie* case on every element of the claim except identification of the specific defendant. (A *prima facie* case is one in which the plaintiff has presented sufficient evidence for the claim to go forward.)[13] ▪

Courts in many jurisdictions do not recognize market-share liability, believing that it deviates too significantly from traditional legal principles. Jurisdictions that do recognize this theory of liability apply it only when it is difficult or impossible to determine which company made a particular product.

Market-Share Liability
A theory under which liability is shared among all firms that manufactured and distributed a particular product during a certain period of time. This form of liability sharing is used only when the specific source of the harmful product is unidentifiable.

---

11. *Crosswhite v. Jumpking, Inc.,* 411 F.Supp.2d 1228 (D.Or. 2006).
12. *Video Software Dealers Association v. Schwarzenegger,* 556 F.3d 950 (9th Cir. 2009); *Brown v. Entertainment Merchants Association,* ___ U.S. ___, 131 S.Ct. 2729, 180 L.Ed.2d 708 (2011).
13. *Suffolk County Water Authority v. Dow Chemical Co.,* 44 Misc.3d 569, 987 N.Y.S.2d 819 (N.Y.Sup. 2014).

5–2e Other Applications of Strict Liability

Almost all courts extend the strict liability of manufacturers and other sellers to injured bystanders. **EXAMPLE 5.10** A forklift that Trent is operating will not go into reverse, and as a result, it runs into a bystander. In this situation, the bystander can sue the manufacturer of the defective forklift under strict liability (and possibly bring a negligence action against the forklift operator as well). ■

Strict liability also applies to suppliers of component parts. **EXAMPLE 5.11** Toyota buys brake pads from a subcontractor and puts them in Corollas without changing their composition. If those pads are defective, both the supplier of the brake pads and Toyota will be held strictly liable for injuries caused by the defects. ■

5–3 Defenses to Product Liability

Defendants in product liability suits can raise a number of defenses. One defense, of course, is to show that there is no basis for the plaintiff's claim. For instance, in a product liability case based on negligence, if a defendant can show that the plaintiff has not met the requirements (such as causation) for an action in negligence, generally the defendant will not be liable. A defendant may also assert that the *statute of limitations* for a product liability claim has lapsed.[14]

In a case involving strict product liability, a defendant can claim that the plaintiff failed to meet one of the requirements. If the defendant establishes that goods were altered after they were sold, for instance, the defendant normally will not be held liable.

In the following case, a product's safety switch had been disabled before the plaintiff used the product.

---

14. Similar state statutes, called *statutes of repose*, place outer time limits on product liability actions.

CASE 5.3

Verost v. Mitsubishi Caterpillar Forklift America, Inc.

New York Supreme Court, Appellate Division, Fourth Department, 124 A.D.3d 1219, 1 N.Y.S.3d 589 (2015).

FACTS Drew Verost was employed at a manufacturing facility in Buffalo, New York, owned by Nuttall Gear, LLC. While operating a forklift at Nuttall's facility, Verost climbed out of the seat and attempted to engage a lever on the vehicle. As he stood on the front of the forklift and reached for the lever with his hand, he inadvertently stepped on the vehicle's gearshift. The activated gears caused part of the forklift to move backward, injuring Verost. He filed a suit in a New York state court against the forklift's maker, Mitsubishi Caterpillar Forklift America, Inc., and others, asserting claims in product liability. The defendants established that the vehicle had been manufactured with a safety switch that would have prevented the accident had it not been disabled after delivery to Nuttall. The court issued a summary judgment in the defendants' favor. Verost appealed.

Under what circumstances can a forklift manufacturer avoid product liability?

iStockPhoto.com/SimplyCreative Photography

ISSUE Is the modification of a product after its sale an effective defense against a claim of product liability?

DECISION Yes. The state intermediate appellate court affirmed the lower court's judgment in the product liability defendants' favor. To succeed in an action based on product liability, the goods at issue must not have been substantially changed from the time the product was sold to the time the injury was sustained.

REASON The forklift was made by Mitsubishi and sold new to Nuttall by Buffalo Lift Trucks, Inc., and Mullen Industrial Handling Corporation. The forklift had been made and delivered to Nuttall with a safety switch to render it inoperable if an operator was not in the driver's seat. At the time of Verost's accident, however, someone—"a third party"—had

Continues

intentionally disabled the safety switch so that the forklift still had power when the operator was not in the driver's seat. Seven of Nuttall's ten forklifts had disabled safety switches. Verost had asserted causes of action in product liability against Mitsubishi, Buffalo Lift, and Mullen. The appellate court concluded that the lower court had properly issued judgment in these defendants' favor. "A manufacturer, who has designed and produced a safe product, will not be liable for injuries resulting from substantial alterations or modifications of the product by a third party which render the product defective or otherwise unsafe."

CRITICAL THINKING—Legal Consideration *Could Verost succeed in an action against Nuttall alleging that the company's failure to maintain the forklift in a safe condition constituted negligence? Discuss.*

5–3a Preemption

LEARNING OBJECTIVE 5

What defenses to liability can be raised in a product liability lawsuit?

A defense that has been successfully raised by defendants in recent years is preemption—that government regulations preempt claims for product liability (see *Spotlight Case 5.1*, for example). An injured party may not be able to sue a manufacturer of defective products that are subject to comprehensive federal regulatory schemes.

Medical devices, for instance, are subject to extensive government regulation and undergo a rigorous premarket approval process. **CASE EXAMPLE 5.12** The United States Supreme Court decided in *Riegel v. Medtronic, Inc.,* that a man who was injured by an approved medical device (a balloon catheter) could not sue its maker for product liability. The Court reasoned that Congress had created a comprehensive scheme of federal safety oversight for medical devices. The U.S. Food and Drug Administration is required to review the design, labeling, and manufacturing of medical devices before they are marketed to make sure that they are safe and effective. Because premarket approval is a "rigorous process," it preempts all common law claims challenging the safety or effectiveness of a medical device that has been approved.[15] ■

Since the *Medtronic* decision, some courts have extended the preemption defense to other product liability actions. Other courts have been unwilling to deny an injured party relief simply because the federal government was supposed to ensure the product's safety.[16] Even the United States Supreme Court refused to extend the preemption defense to preclude a drug maker's liability in one subsequent case.[17]

5–3b Assumption of Risk

Under what circumstances can a tanning salon customer sue for injuries even though she or he signed a release?

Assumption of risk can sometimes be used as a defense in a product liability action. To establish such a defense, the defendant must show that (1) the plaintiff knew and appreciated the risk created by the product defect and (2) the plaintiff voluntarily assumed the risk, even though it was unreasonable to do so. (See Chapter 4 for a more detailed discussion of assumption of risk.)

Although assumption of the risk is a defense in product liability actions, some courts do not allow it to be used as a defense to strict product liability claims. **CASE EXAMPLE 5.13** When Savannah Boles became a customer of Executive Tans, she signed a contract. One clause stated that signers used the company's tanning booths at their own risk. It also released the manufacturer and others from liability for any injuries. Later, Boles's fingers were partially amputated when they came into contact with a tanning booth's fan. Boles sued the manufacturer, claiming strict product liability. The Colorado Supreme Court held that assumption of risk was not applicable because strict product liability is driven by public-policy considerations. The theory focuses on the nature of the product rather than the conduct of either the manufacturer or the person injured.[18] ■

15. *Riegel v. Medtronic, Inc.,* 552 U.S. 312, 128 S.Ct. 999, 169 L.Ed.2d 892 (2008).
16. See, for example, *McGuan v. Endovascular Technologies, Inc.,* 182 Cal.App.4th 974, 106 Cal.Rptr.3d 277 (2010), and *Paduano v. American Honda Motor Co.,* 169 Cal.App.4th 1453, 88 Cal.Rptr.3d 90 (2009).
17. *Wyeth v. Levine,* 555 U.S. 555, 129 S.Ct. 1187, 173 L.Ed.2d 51 (2009).
18. *Boles v. Sun Ergoline, Inc.,* 223 P.3d 724 (Co.Sup.Ct. 2010).

5–3c **Product Misuse**

Similar to the defense of voluntary assumption of risk is that of product misuse, which occurs when a product is used for a purpose for which it was not intended. The courts have severely limited this defense. Today, product misuse is recognized as a defense *only when the particular use was not reasonably foreseeable.* If the misuse is foreseeable, the seller must take measures to guard against it.

CASE EXAMPLE 5.14 David Stults developed "popcorn lung" (bronchiolitis obliterans) from consuming multiple bags of microwave popcorn daily for several years. When he filed suit against the manufacturers of the popcorn and butter flavorings, the defendants asked the court for a summary judgment in their favor. The court denied defendants' motion and found that a manufacturer has a duty to warn of dangers associated with reasonably foreseeable misuses of a product. If it is foreseeable that a person might consume several bags of the popcorn a day, then the manufacturer might have to warn users about the potential health risks associated with doing so.[19] ▪

5–3d **Comparative Negligence (Fault)**

Developments in the area of comparative negligence, or fault (discussed in the torts chapter), have also affected the doctrine of strict liability. Today, courts in many jurisdictions consider the negligent or intentional actions of both the plaintiff and the defendant when apportioning liability and awarding damages. A defendant may be able to limit at least some liability for injuries caused by a defective product if it can show that the plaintiff's misuse of the product contributed to the injuries.

When proved, comparative negligence differs from other defenses in that it does not completely absolve the defendant of liability. It can, however, reduce the amount of damages that will be awarded to the plaintiff. Note that some jurisdictions allow only intentional conduct to affect a plaintiff's recovery, whereas others allow ordinary negligence to be used as a defense to product liability.

CASE EXAMPLE 5.15 Dan Smith, a mechanic, was not wearing a hard hat at work when he was asked to start the diesel engine of an air compressor. Because the compressor was an older model, he had to prop open a door to start it. When the engine started, the door fell from its position and hit Smith's head. The injury caused him to suffer from seizures. Smith sued the manufacturer, claiming that the engine was defectively designed. The manufacturer contended that Smith had been negligent by failing to wear a hard hat and propping open the door in an unsafe manner. Smith argued that ordinary negligence could not be used as a defense in product liability cases. The court ruled that defendants can use the plaintiff's ordinary negligence to reduce their liability proportionately.[20] ▪

5–3e **Commonly Known Dangers**

As mentioned, the dangers associated with certain products (such as sharp knives and guns) are so commonly known that manufacturers need not warn users of those dangers. If a defendant succeeds in convincing the court that a plaintiff's injury resulted from a *commonly known danger,* the defendant normally will not be liable.

CASE EXAMPLE 5.16 In a classic example from 1957, Marguerite Jamieson was injured when an elastic exercise rope slipped off her foot and struck her in the eye, causing a detachment of the retina. Jamieson claimed that the manufacturer should be liable because it had failed to warn users that the exerciser might slip off a foot in such a manner.

---

19. *Stults v. International Flavors and Fragrances, Inc.,* 31 F.Supp.3d 1015 (N.D. Iowa 2014).
20. *Smith v. Ingersoll-Rand Co.,* 14 P.3d 990 (Alaska 2000). See also *Winschel v. Brown,* 171 P.3d 142 (Alaska 2007).

The court stated that to hold the manufacturer liable in these circumstances "would go beyond the reasonable dictates of justice in fixing the liabilities of manufacturers." After all, stated the court, "almost every physical object can be inherently dangerous or potentially dangerous in a sense. . . . A manufacturer cannot manufacture a knife that will not cut or a hammer that will not mash a thumb or a stove that will not burn a finger. The law does not require [manufacturers] to warn of such common dangers."[21] ▪

5–3f Knowledgeable User

A related defense is the *knowledgeable user* defense. If a particular danger (such as electrical shock) is or should be commonly known by particular users of the product (such as electricians), the manufacturer of electrical equipment need not warn these users of the danger.

CASE EXAMPLE 5.17 The parents of a group of teenagers who had become overweight and developed health problems filed a product liability lawsuit against McDonald's. The plaintiffs claimed that the well-known fast-food chain should be held liable for failing to warn customers of the adverse health effects of eating its food products. The court rejected this claim, however, based on the knowledgeable user defense.

According to the court, it is well known that the food at McDonald's contains high levels of cholesterol, fat, salt, and sugar and is therefore unhealthful. The court's opinion, which thwarted numerous future lawsuits against fast-food restaurants, stated: "If consumers know (or reasonably should know) the potential ill health effects of eating at McDonald's, they cannot blame McDonald's if they, nonetheless, choose to satiate [satisfy] their appetite with a surfeit [excess] of supersized McDonald's products."[22] ▪

5–3g Statutes of Limitations and Repose

Tolling Temporary suspension of the running of a prescribed time period, such as a statute of limitations.

Statute of Repose A statute that places outer time limits on product liability actions. Such statutes cut off absolutely the right to bring an action after a specified period of time following some event (often the product's manufacture or purchase) other than the occurrence of an injury.

As mentioned previously, statutes of limitations restrict the time within which an action may be brought. The statute of limitations for product liability cases varies according to state law. Usually, the injured party must bring a product liability claim within two to four years. Often, the running of the prescribed period is **tolled** (that is, suspended) until the party suffering an injury has discovered it or should have discovered it.

To ensure that sellers and manufacturers will not be left vulnerable to lawsuits indefinitely, many states have passed **statutes of repose,** which place outer time limits on product liability actions. For instance, a statute of repose may require that claims be brought within twelve years from the date of sale or manufacture of the defective product. If the plaintiff does not bring an action before the prescribed period expires, the seller cannot be held liable.

---

21. *Jamieson v. Woodward & Lothrop*, 247 F.2d 23, 101 D.C.App. 32 (1957).
22. *Pelman v. McDonald's Corp.*, 237 F.Supp.2d 512 (S.D.N.Y. 2003).

Reviewing . . . Product Liability

Shalene Kolchek bought a Great Lakes Spa from Val Porter, a dealer who was selling spas at the state fair. After Kolchek signed the contract, Porter handed her the manufacturer's paperwork and arranged for the spa to be delivered and installed for her. Three months later, Kolchek left her six-year-old daughter, Litisha, alone in the spa. While exploring the spa's hydromassage jets, Litisha got her index finger stuck in one of the jet holes.

Litisha yanked hard, injuring her finger, and then panicked and screamed for help. Kolchek was unable to remove Litisha's finger, and the local police and rescue team were called to assist. After a three-hour operation that included draining the spa, sawing out a section of the spa's plastic molding, and slicing the jet casing, Litisha's finger was freed. Following this procedure, the spa was no longer functional. Litisha was taken to the local emergency room, where she was told that a bone in her finger was broken in two places. Using the information presented in the chapter, answer the following questions.

1. Under which theories of product liability can Kolchek sue Porter to recover for Litisha's injuries?

2. Would privity of contract be required for Kolchek to succeed in a product liability action against Great Lakes? Explain.

3. For an action in strict product liability against Great Lakes, what six requirements must Kolchek meet?

4. What defenses to product liability might Porter or Great Lakes be able to assert?

DEBATE THIS

■ All liability suits against tobacco companies for causing lung cancer should be thrown out of court now and forever.

LINKING BUSINESS LAW TO CORPORATE MANAGEMENT
Quality Control

In this chapter, you learned that manufacturing and design defects can give rise to liability. Although it is possible to minimize liability through various defenses to product liability claims, all businesspersons know that such defenses do not necessarily fend off expensive lawsuits.

The legal issues surrounding product liability relate directly to quality control. As all of your management courses will emphasize, quality control is a major issue facing managers in every organization. Companies that have cost-effective quality control systems produce products with fewer manufacturing and design defects. As a result, these companies incur fewer potential and actual product liability lawsuits.

Three Types of Quality Control

Most management systems involve three types of quality control—preventive, concurrent, and feedback. They apply at different stages of the manufacturing process: preventive quality control occurs before the process begins, concurrent control takes place during the process, and feedback control occurs after it is finished.

In a typical manufacturing process, for example, preventive quality control might involve inspecting raw materials before they are put into the production process. Once the process begins, measuring and monitoring devices constantly assess quality standards as part of a concurrent quality control system. When the standards are not being met, employees correct the problem.

Once the manufacturing is completed, the products undergo a final quality inspection as part of the feedback quality control system. Of course, there are economic limits to how complete the final inspection will be. A refrigerator can be tested for an hour, a day, or a year. Management faces a trade-off. The less the refrigerator is tested, the sooner it gets to market and the faster the company receives its payment. The shorter the testing period, however, the higher the probability of a defect that will cost the manufacturer.

Total Quality Management (TQM)

Some managers attempt to reduce product liability costs by relying on a concurrent quality control system known as total quality management (TQM). TQM is an organization-wide effort to infuse quality into every activity in a company through continuous improvement.

Quality circles are a popular TQM technique. These are groups of six to twelve employees who volunteer to meet regularly to discuss problems and how to solve them. In a continuous stream manufacturing process, for example, a quality circle might consist of workers from different phases in the production process. Quality circles force changes in the production process that affect workers who are actually on the production line.

Benchmarking is another technique used in TQM. In benchmarking, a company continuously measures its products against those of its toughest competitors or the industry leaders in order to identify areas for improvement. In the automobile industry, benchmarking enabled several Japanese firms to overtake U.S. automakers in terms of quality. Some argue that Toyota gained worldwide market share by effectively using this type of quality control management system.

Continues

Another TQM system is called *Six Sigma*. Motorola introduced the quality principles in this system in the late 1980s, but Six Sigma has now become a generic term for a quality control approach based on a five-step methodology: define, measure, analyze, improve, and control. Six Sigma controls emphasize discipline and a relentless attempt to achieve higher quality (and lower costs). A possible impediment to the institution of a Six Sigma program is that it requires a major commitment from top management because it may involve widespread changes throughout the entire organization.

CRITICAL THINKING

■ Quality control leads to fewer defective products and fewer lawsuits. Consequently, managers know that quality control is important to their company's long-term financial health. At the same time, the more quality control managers impose on their organization, the higher the average cost per unit of whatever is produced and sold. How does a manager decide how much quality control to undertake?

Key Terms

market-share liability 128

product liability 118

privity of contract 119

statute of repose 132

tolled 132

unreasonably dangerous product 123

Chapter Summary: Product Liability

Liability Based on Negligence	**1.** The manufacturer must use due care in designing the product, selecting materials, using the appropriate production process, assembling and testing the product, and placing adequate warnings on the label or product. **2.** Privity of contract is not required. A manufacturer is liable for failure to exercise due care to any person who sustains an injury proximately caused by a negligently made (defective) product. **3.** Fraudulent misrepresentation of a product may result in product liability based on the tort of fraud.
Strict Product Liability—Requirements	**1.** The defendant must have sold the product in a defective condition. **2.** The defendant must normally be engaged in the business of selling that product. **3.** The product must be unreasonably dangerous to the user or consumer because of its defective condition (in most states). **4.** The plaintiff must incur physical harm to self or property by use or consumption of the product. **5.** The defective condition must be the proximate cause of the injury or damage. **6.** The goods must not have been substantially changed from the time the product was sold to the time the injury was sustained.
Strict Product Liability—Product Defects	A product may be defective in three basic ways: **1.** In its manufacture. **2.** In its design. **3.** In the instructions or warnings that come with it.
Market-Share Liability	When plaintiffs cannot prove which of many distributors of a defective product supplied the particular product that caused the plaintiffs' injuries, some courts apply market-share liability. All firms that manufactured and distributed the harmful product during the period in question are then held liable for the plaintiffs' injuries in proportion to the firms' respective share of the market, as directed by the court.
Other Applications of Strict Liability	**1.** Manufacturers and other sellers are liable for harms suffered by bystanders as a result of defective products. **2.** Suppliers of component parts are strictly liable for defective parts that, when incorporated into a product, cause injuries to users.
Defenses to Product Liability	**1.** *Preemption*—An injured party may not be able to sue the manufacturer of a product that is subject to comprehensive federal safety regulations, such as medical devices. **2.** *Assumption of risk*—The user or consumer knew of the risk of harm and voluntarily assumed it. **3.** *Product misuse*—The user or consumer misused the product in a way unforeseeable by the manufacturer. **4.** *Comparative negligence*—Liability may be distributed between the plaintiff and the defendant under the doctrine of comparative negligence if the plaintiff's misuse of the product contributed to the risk of injury. **5.** *Commonly known dangers*—If a defendant succeeds in convincing the court that a plaintiff's injury resulted from a commonly known danger, such as the danger associated with using a sharp knife, the defendant will not be liable. **6.** *Knowledgeable user*—If a particular danger is or should be commonly known by particular users of the product, the manufacturer of the product need not warn these users of the danger.

Issue Spotters

1. Rim Corporation makes tire rims that it sells to Superior Vehicles, Inc., which installs them on cars. One set of rims is defective, which an inspection would reveal. Superior does not inspect the rims. The car with the defective rims is sold to Town Auto Sales, which sells the car to Uri. Soon, the car is in an accident caused by the defective rims, and Uri is injured. Is Superior Vehicles liable? Explain your answer. (See *Product Liability*.)

2. Bensing Company manufactures generic drugs for the treatment of heart disease. A federal law requires generic drug makers to use labels that are identical to the labels on brand-name versions of the drugs. Hunter Rothfus purchased Bensing's generic drugs in Ohio and wants to sue Bensing for defective labeling based on its failure to comply with Ohio state common law (rather than the federal labeling requirements). What defense might Bensing assert to avoid liability under state law? (See *Defenses to Product Liability*.)

—**Check your answers to the *Issue Spotters* against the answers provided in Appendix D at the end of this text.**

Learning Objectives Check

1. Can a manufacturer be held liable to any person who suffers an injury proximately caused by the manufacturer's negligently made product?

2. What public policy assumptions underlie strict product liability?

3. What are the elements of a cause of action in strict product liability?

4. What are three types of product defects?

5. What defenses to liability can be raised in a product liability lawsuit?

—**Answers to the even-numbered *Learning Objectives Check* questions can be found in Appendix E at the end of this text.**

Business Scenarios and Case Problems

5–1. Product Liability. Carmen buys a television set manufactured by AKI Electronics. She is going on vacation, so she takes the set to her mother's house for her mother to use. Because the set is defective, it explodes, causing considerable damage to her mother's house. Carmen's mother sues AKI for the damage to her house. Discuss the theories under which Carmen's mother can recover from AKI. (See *Product Liability*.)

5–2. Product Liability. Jason Clark, an experienced hunter, bought a paintball gun. Clark practiced with the gun and knew how to screw in the carbon dioxide cartridge, pump the gun, and use its safety and trigger. Although Clark was aware that he could purchase protective eyewear, he chose not to. Clark had taken gun safety courses and understood that it was "common sense" not to shoot anyone in the face. Clark's friend, Chris Wright, also owned a paintball gun and was similarly familiar with the gun's use and its risks.

Clark, Wright, and their friends played a game that involved shooting paintballs at cars whose occupants also had the guns. One night, while Clark and Wright were cruising with their guns, Wright shot at Clark's car, but hit Clark in the eye. Clark filed a product liability lawsuit against the manufacturer of Wright's paintball gun to recover for the injury. Clark claimed that the gun was defectively designed. During the trial, Wright testified that his gun "never malfunctioned." In whose favor should the court rule? Why? (See *Product Liability*.)

5–3. Defenses to Product Liability. Brandon Stroud was driving a golf car made by Textron, Inc. The golf car did not have lights, but Textron did not warn against using it on public roads at night. When Stroud attempted to cross a road at 8:30 P.M., his golf car was struck by a vehicle driven by Joseph Thornley. Stroud was killed. His estate filed a suit against Textron, alleging strict product liability and product liability based on negligence. The charge was that the golf car was defective and unreasonably dangerous. What defense might Textron assert? Explain. [*Moore v. Barony House Restaurant*, LLC, 382 S.C. 35, 674 S.E.2d 500 (S.C.App. 2009)] (See *Defenses to Product Liability*.)

5–4. Product Liability. Yun Tung Chow tried to unclog a floor drain in the kitchen of the restaurant where he worked. He used a drain cleaner called Lewis Red Devil Lye that contained crystalline sodium hydroxide. The product label said that users should wear eye protection, put one tablespoon of lye directly into the drain, and keep their faces away from the drain to avoid dangerous backsplash.

Not wearing eye protection, Chow mixed three spoonfuls of lye in a can and poured that mixture down the drain while bending over it. Liquid splashed back into his face, causing injury. He sued for product liability based on inadequate warnings and a design defect. The trial court granted summary judgment to the manufacturer. Chow appealed. An expert for Chow stated that the product was defective because it had a tendency to backsplash. Is that a convincing argument? Why or why not? [*Yun Tung Chow v. Reckitt & Coleman, Inc.,* 17 N.Y.3d 29, 950 N.E.2d 113 (2011)] (See *Product Liability.*)

5–5. Strict Product Liability. David Dobrovolny bought a new Ford F-350 pickup truck. A year later, the truck spontaneously caught fire in Dobrovolny's driveway. The truck was destroyed, but no other property was damaged, and no one was injured. Dobrovolny filed a suit in a Nebraska state court against Ford Motor Co. on a theory of strict product liability to recover the cost of the truck. Nebraska limits the application of strict product liability to situations involving personal injuries. Is Dobrovolny's claim likely to succeed? Why or why not? Is there another basis for liability on which he might recover? Explain. [*Dobrovolny v. Ford Motor Co.,* 281 Neb. 86, 793 N.W.2d 445 (2011)] (See *Strict Product Liability.*)

5–6. Product Misuse. Five-year-old Cheyenne Stark was riding in the backseat of her parents' Ford Taurus. Cheyenne was not sitting in a booster seat. Instead, she was using a seatbelt designed by Ford, but was wearing the shoulder belt behind her back. The car was involved in a collision. As a result, Cheyenne suffered a spinal cord injury and was paralyzed from the waist down. The family filed a suit against Ford Motor Co., alleging that the seatbelt was defectively designed. Could Ford successfully claim that Cheyenne had misused the seatbelt? Why or why not? [*Stark v. Ford Motor Co.,* 365 N.C. 468, 723 S.E.2d 753 (2012)] (See *Defenses to Product Liability.*)

5–7. Business Case Problem with Sample Answer—Product Liability. While driving on Interstate 40 in North Carolina, Carroll Jett became distracted by a texting system in the cab of his tractor-trailer truck. He smashed into several vehicles that were slowed or stopped in front of him, injuring Barbara and Michael Durkee and others. The injured motorists filed a suit in a federal district court against Geologic Solutions, Inc., the maker of the texting system, alleging product liability. Was the accident caused by Jett's inattention or the texting device? Should a manufacturer be required to design a product that is incapable of distracting a driver? Discuss. [*Durkee v. Geologic Solutions, Inc.,* 2013 WL 14717 (4th Cir. 2013)] (See *Product Liability.*)

—For a sample answer to Problem 5–7, go to Appendix F at the end of this text.

5–8. Strict Product Liability. Medicis Pharmaceutical Corp. makes Solodyn, a prescription oral antibiotic. Medicis warns physicians that "autoimmune syndromes, including drug-induced lupus-like syndrome," may be associated with use of the drug. Amanda Watts had chronic acne. Her physician prescribed Solodyn. Information included with the drug did not mention the risk of autoimmune disorders, and Watts was not otherwise advised of it. She was prescribed the drug twice, each time for twenty weeks. Later, she experienced debilitating joint pain and, after being hospitalized, was diagnosed with lupus. On what basis could Watts recover from Medicis in an action grounded in product liability? Explain. [*Watts v. Medicis Pharmaceutical Corp.,* 236 Ariz. 511, 342 P.3d 847 (2015)] (See *Strict Product Liability.*)

5–9. A Question of Ethics—Strict Product Liability. Susan Calles lived with her four daughters, Amanda (age 11), Victoria (age 5), and Jenna and Jillian (age 3). In March 1998, Calles bought an Aim N Flame utility lighter, which she stored on the top shelf of her kitchen cabinet. A trigger can ignite the Aim N Flame after an on/off switch is slid to the "on" position. On the night of March 31, Calles and Victoria left to get videos. Jenna and Jillian were in bed, and Amanda was watching television. Calles returned to find fire trucks and emergency vehicles around her home. Robert Finn, a fire investigator, determined that Jenna had started a fire using the lighter. Jillian suffered smoke inhalation, was hospitalized, and died on April 21. Calles filed a suit in an Illinois state court against Scripto-Tokai Corp., which distributed the Aim N Flame, and others. In her suit, which was grounded, in part, in strict liability claims, Calles alleged that the lighter was an "unreasonably dangerous product." Scripto filed a motion for summary judgment. [*Calles v. Scripto-Tokai Corp.,* 224 Ill.2d 247, 864 N.E.2d 249, 309 Ill.Dec. 383 (2007)] (See *Strict Product Liability.*)

1. A product is "unreasonably dangerous" when it is dangerous beyond the expectation of the ordinary consumer. Whose expectation—Calles's or Jenna's—applies here? Why? Does the lighter pass this test? Explain.

2. A product is also "unreasonably dangerous" when a less dangerous alternative was economically feasible for its maker, and the maker failed to produce it. Scripto contended that because its product was "simple" and the danger was "obvious," it should not be liable under this test. Do you agree? Why or why not?

3. Calles presented evidence as to the likelihood and seriousness of injury from lighters that do not have child-safety devices. Scripto argued that the Aim N Flame is a useful, inexpensive, alternative source of fire and is safer than a match. Calles admitted that she was aware of the dangers presented by lighters in the hands of children. Scripto admitted that it had been a defendant in at least twenty-five suits for injuries that occurred under similar circumstances. With these factors in mind, how should the court rule? Why?

Critical Thinking and Writing Assignments

5–10. Business Law Critical Thinking Group Assignment.
Bret D'Auguste was an experienced skier when he rented equipment to ski at Hunter Mountain Ski Bowl in New York. When D'Auguste entered an extremely difficult trail, he noticed immediately that the surface consisted of ice with almost no snow. He tried to exit the steeply declining trail by making a sharp right turn, but in the attempt, his left ski snapped off. D'Auguste lost his balance, fell, and slid down the mountain, striking his face and head against a fence along the trail. According to a report by a rental shop employee, one of the bindings on D'Auguste's skis had a "cracked heel housing."

D'Auguste filed a lawsuit against the bindings' manufacturer on a theory of strict product liability. The manufacturer filed a motion for summary judgment. (See *Product Liability*.)

1. The first group will take the position of the manufacturer and develop an argument why the court should *grant* the summary judgment motion and dismiss the strict product liability claim.

2. The second group will take the position of D'Auguste and formulate a basis for why the court should *deny* the motion and allow the strict product liability claim.

6

CHAPTER OUTLINE

- Trademarks
- Patents
- Copyrights
- Trade Secrets
- International Protections

LEARNING OBJECTIVES

The five Learning Objectives *below are designed to help improve your understanding of the chapter. After reading this chapter, you should be able to answer the following questions:*

1. What is intellectual property?

2. Why is the protection of trademarks important?

3. How does the law protect patents?

4. What laws protect authors' rights in the works they create?

5. What are trade secrets, and what laws offer protection for this form of intellectual property?

Intellectual Property Property resulting from intellectual and creative processes.

LEARNING OBJECTIVE 1

What is intellectual property?

Intellectual Property Rights

Intellectual property is any property resulting from intellectual, creative processes—the products of an individual's mind, as suggested in the chapter-opening quotation. Although it is an abstract term for an abstract concept, intellectual property is nonetheless familiar to almost everyone. The apps for your iPhone, iPad, or Samsung Galaxy, the movies you see, and the music you listen to are all forms of intellectual property.

More than two hundred years ago, the framers of the U.S. Constitution recognized the importance of protecting creative works in Article I, Section 8 (see Appendix B). Statutory protection of these rights began in the 1940s and continues to evolve to meet the needs of modern society. In today's global economy, however, protecting intellectual property in one country is no longer sufficient. The United States is participating in various international agreements to secure ownership rights in intellectual property in other countries, as you will learn in this chapter.

Whether locally or globally, businesspersons have a vital need to protect their rights in intellectual property, which may be more valuable than their physical property, such as machines and buildings. Consider, for instance, the importance of intellectual property rights to technology companies, such as Apple, Inc., and Samsung Electronics Company. In today's world, intellectual property rights can be a company's most valuable assets, which is why Apple recently sued its rival Samsung. Apple claimed that Samsung's Galaxy line of mobile phones and tablets (those that run Google's Android software) copy the look, design, and user interface of Apple's iPhone and iPad. Although Apple is one of Samsung's biggest customers and buys many of its components from Samsung, Apple also needs to protect its iPhone and iPad revenues from competing Android products. You will read about the verdict in this case later in this chapter.

> "My words and my ideas are my property, and I'll keep and protect them as surely as I do my stable of unicorns."
>
> **JAROD KINTZ**
> 1982–PRESENT
> (AMERICAN AUTHOR)

6-1 Trademarks

A **trademark** is a distinctive word, symbol, sound, or design that identifies the manufacturer as the source of particular goods and distinguishes its products from those made or sold by others. At common law, the person who used a symbol or mark to identify a business or product was protected in the use of that trademark. Clearly, if another company used the trademark, it could lead consumers to believe that its goods were made by the trademark owner. The law seeks to avoid this kind of confusion. (For information on how companies use trademarks and service marks, see the *Linking Business Law to Marketing* feature at the end of this chapter.)

In the following *Classic Case* concerning Coca-Cola, the defendants argued that the Coca-Cola trademark was not entitled to protection under the law because the term did not accurately represent the product.

> **LEARNING OBJECTIVE 2**
>
> Why is the protection of trademarks important?

Trademark A distinctive word, symbol, or design that identifies the manufacturer as the source of particular goods and distinguishes its products from those made or sold by others.

★★★ CLASSIC CASE 6.1 ★★★

Coca-Cola Co. v. Koke Co. of America

Supreme Court of the United States, 254 U.S. 143, 41 S.Ct. 113, 65 L.Ed. 189 (1920).

COMPANY PROFILE *John Pemberton, an Atlanta pharmacist, invented a caramel-colored, carbonated soft drink in 1886. His bookkeeper, Frank Robinson, named the beverage Coca-Cola after two of the ingredients, coca leaves and kola nuts. Asa Candler bought the Coca-Cola Company in 1891 and, within seven years, had made the soft drink available throughout the United States and in parts of Canada and Mexico as well. Candler continued to sell Coke aggressively and to open up new markets, reaching Europe before 1910. In doing so, however, he attracted numerous competitors, some of whom tried to capitalize directly on the Coke name.*

How is Coca-Cola protected?

Rob Wilson/ShutterStock.com

FACTS The Coca-Cola Company brought an action in a federal district court to enjoin (prevent) other beverage companies from using the names Koke and Dope for their products. The defendants contended that the Coca-Cola trademark was a fraudulent representation and that Coca-Cola was therefore not entitled to any help from the courts. By using the Coca-Cola name, the defendants alleged, the Coca-Cola Company represented that the beverage contained cocaine (from coca leaves). The district court granted the injunction, but the federal appellate court reversed. The Coca-Cola Company appealed to the United States Supreme Court.

ISSUE Did the marketing of products called Koke and Dope by the Koke Company of America and other firms constitute an infringement on Coca-Cola's trademark?

DECISION Yes for Koke, but no for Dope. The United States Supreme Court enjoined the competing beverage companies from calling their products Koke but not from calling their products Dope.

REASON The Court noted that before 1900 the Coca-Cola beverage had contained a small amount of cocaine. This ingredient had been deleted from the formula by 1906 at the latest, however, and the Coca-Cola Company had advertised to the public that no cocaine was present in its drink. The court emphasized that Coca-Cola was a widely popular drink "to be had at almost any soda fountain." Because of the public's widespread familiarity with Coca-Cola, the retention of the name (referring to coca leaves and kola nuts) was not misleading: "Coca-Cola probably means to most persons the plaintiff's familiar product to be had everywhere rather than a compound of particular substances." The name Coke was found to be so common a term for the trademarked product Coca-Cola that the defendants' use of the similar-sounding Koke as a name for their beverages was disallowed. The Court could find no reason to restrain the defendants from using the name Dope, however.

WHAT IF THE FACTS WERE DIFFERENT? *Suppose that Coca-Cola had been trying to make the public believe that its product contained cocaine. Would the result in the case likely have been different? Explain your answer.*

IMPACT OF THIS CASE ON TODAY'S LAW *In this early case, the United States Supreme Court made it clear that trademarks and trade names (and nicknames for those marks and names, such as "Coke" for "Coca-Cola") that are in common use receive protection under the common law. This holding is significant historically because it is the predecessor to the federal statute later passed to protect trademark rights (the Lanham Act of 1946, discussed next).*

6–1a Statutory Protection of Trademarks

Statutory protection of trademarks and related property is provided at the federal level by the Lanham Act of 1946.[1] The Lanham Act was enacted in part to protect manufacturers from losing business to rival companies that used confusingly similar trademarks. The Lanham Act incorporates the common law of trademarks and provides remedies for owners of trademarks who wish to enforce their claims in federal court. Many states also have trademark statutes.

Trademark Dilution In 1995, Congress amended the Lanham Act by passing the Federal Trademark Dilution Act,[2] which allowed trademark owners to bring suits in federal court for **trademark dilution.** In 2006, Congress further amended the law on trademark dilution by passing the Trademark Dilution Revision Act (TDRA).[3]

Under the TDRA, to state a claim for trademark dilution, a plaintiff must prove the following:

1. The plaintiff owns a famous mark that is distinctive.

2. The defendant has begun using a mark in commerce that allegedly is diluting the famous mark.

3. The similarity between the defendant's mark and the famous mark gives rise to an *association* between the marks.

4. The association is likely to impair the distinctiveness of the famous mark or harm its reputation.

Trademark dilution laws protect "distinctive" or "famous" trademarks (such as Rolls-Royce, McDonald's, Starbucks, and Apple) from certain unauthorized uses. Such a mark is protected even when the unauthorized use is on noncompeting goods or is unlikely to confuse. More than half of the states have also enacted trademark dilution laws.

The Marks Need Not Be Identical A famous mark may be diluted not only by the use of an *identical* mark but also by the use of a *similar* mark, provided that it reduces the value of the famous mark.[4] A similar mark is more likely to lessen the value of a famous mark when the companies using the marks provide related goods or compete against each other in the same market.

CASE EXAMPLE 6.1 When Samantha Lundberg opened Sambuck's Coffeehouse in Astoria, Oregon, she knew that Starbucks was one of the largest coffee chains in the nation. Starbucks Corporation filed a dilution lawsuit, and a federal court ruled that use of the Sambuck's mark constituted trademark dilution because it created confusion for consumers. Not only was there a "high degree" of similarity between the marks, but also both companies provided coffee-related services through stand-alone retail stores. Therefore, the use of the similar mark (Sambuck's) reduced the value of the famous mark (Starbucks).[5] ■

6–1b Trademark Registration

Trademarks may be registered with the state or with the federal government. To register for protection under federal trademark law, a person must file an application with the U.S. Patent and Trademark Office in Washington, D.C. A mark can be registered (1) if it is currently in commerce or (2) if the applicant intends to put it into commerce within six months.

In special circumstances, the six-month period can be extended by thirty months. Thus, the applicant would have a total of three years from the date of notice of trademark approval

Trademark Dilution The unauthorized use of a distinctive and famous mark in a way that impairs the mark's distinctiveness or harms its reputation.

KNOW THIS
Trademark dilution laws protect the owners of distinctive marks from unauthorized uses even when the defendants' use involves noncompeting goods or is unlikely to cause confusion.

Why can't someone call its coffee shop "Sambuck's"?

iStockPhoto.com/borchee

1. 15 U.S.C. Sections 1051–1128.
2. 15 U.S.C. Section 1125.
3. Pub. L. No. 103-312, 120 Stat. 1730 (2006).
4. See *Moseley v. V Secret Catalogue, Inc.,* 537 U.S. 418, 123 S.Ct. 1115, 155 L.Ed.2d 1 (2003).
5. *Starbucks Corp. v. Lundberg,* 2005 WL 3183858 (D.Or. 2005).

to make use of the mark and to file the required use statement. Registration is postponed until the mark is actually used.

During this waiting period, an applicant can legally protect his or her trademark against a third party who has neither used the mark previously nor filed an application for it. Registration is renewable between the fifth and sixth years after the initial registration and every ten years thereafter (every twenty years for trademarks registered before 1990).

6-1c Trademark Infringement

Registration of a trademark with the U.S. Patent and Trademark Office gives notice on a nationwide basis that the trademark belongs exclusively to the registrant. The registrant is also allowed to use the symbol ® to indicate that the mark has been registered. Whenever that trademark is copied to a substantial degree or used in its entirety by another, intentionally or unintentionally, the trademark has been *infringed* (used without authorization).

When a trademark has been infringed, the owner has a cause of action against the infringer. To succeed in a lawsuit for trademark infringement, the owner must show that the defendant's use of the mark created a likelihood of confusion about the origin of the defendant's goods or services. The owner need not prove that the infringer acted intentionally or that the trademark was registered (although registration does provide proof of the date of inception of the trademark's use).

The most commonly granted remedy for trademark infringement is an *injunction* to prevent further infringement. Under the Lanham Act, a trademark owner that successfully proves infringement can recover actual damages, plus the profits that the infringer wrongfully received from the unauthorized use of the mark. A court can also order the destruction of any goods bearing the unauthorized trademark. In some situations, the trademark owner may also be able to recover attorneys' fees.

KNOW THIS
To prove trademark infringement, the trademark owner must show that the other party's use of the mark has created a likelihood of confusion about the origin of that party's goods or services.

6-1d Distinctiveness of the Mark

A central objective of the Lanham Act is to reduce the likelihood that consumers will be confused by similar marks. For that reason, only those trademarks that are deemed sufficiently distinctive from all competing trademarks will be protected.

Strong Marks Fanciful, arbitrary, or suggestive trademarks are generally considered to be the most distinctive (strongest) trademarks. These marks receive automatic protection because they serve to identify a particular product's source, as opposed to describing the product itself.

Fanciful and Arbitrary Trademarks. Fanciful trademarks use invented words. Examples include *Xerox* for one company's copiers and *Google* for another company's search engine.

Arbitrary trademarks use common words that would not ordinarily be associated with the product, such as *Dutch Boy* as a name for paint. Even a single letter used in a particular style can be an arbitrary trademark. **CASE EXAMPLE 6.2** Sports entertainment company ESPN sued Quiksilver, Inc., a maker of youth-oriented clothing, alleging trademark infringement. ESPN claimed that Quiksilver had used on its clothing the stylized "X" mark that ESPN uses in connection with the "X Games" (competitions in extreme action sports).

Quiksilver filed counterclaims for trademark infringement and dilution, arguing that it had a long history of using the stylized X on its products. ESPN created the X Games in the mid-1990s, and Quiksilver has used the X mark since 1994. ESPN asked the court to dismiss Quiksilver's counterclaims, but the court refused, holding that the X on Quiksilver's clothing was clearly an arbitrary mark. The court found that the two Xs were "similar enough that a consumer might well confuse them." Therefore, Quicksilver could continue its claim for trademark infringement.[6] ▪

---

6. *ESPN, Inc. v. Quiksilver, Inc.,* 586 F.Supp.2d 219 (S.D.N.Y. 2008).

Suggestive Trademarks. Suggestive trademarks indicate something about a product's nature, quality, or characteristics without describing the product directly. For instance, "Blu-ray" is a suggestive mark that is associated with the high-quality, high-definition video contained on a particular optical data storage disc. Although blue-violet lasers are used to read blu-ray discs, the term *blu-ray* does not directly describe the disc.

Secondary Meaning

Descriptive terms, geographic terms, and personal names are not inherently distinctive and do not receive protection under the law until they acquire a secondary meaning. Whether a secondary meaning becomes attached to a term or name usually depends on how extensively the product is advertised, the market for the product, the number of sales, and other factors.

Health maintenance organization insurers exist in many states. If one is called Unity Health and another is called UnityPoint Health, is there a problem?

A secondary meaning may arise when customers begin to associate a specific term or phrase (such as *London Fog*) with specific trademarked items made by a particular company (coats with "London Fog" labels). **CASE EXAMPLE 6.3** Unity Health Plans Insurance Corporation has been a health maintenance organization (HMO) insurer in Wisconsin since 1955. In 2013, another health-care provider, Iowa Health System, began rebranding itself (changing its name and marketing) as UnityPoint Health. When the company expanded into Wisconsin, where Unity Health already had an established presence, Unity Health filed a trademark infringement suit in federal court.

The court found that Unity Health was a descriptive mark, and thus not inherently distinctive. But the court also held that the Unity Health mark had acquired a secondary meaning, largely because it had been used for so long and so exclusively by one health insurer in Wisconsin. It made no difference to the court that only one part of the mark (Unity) was common to both trademarks. To allow Iowa Health Systems to use the mark UnityPoint Health in Wisconsin would likely create confusion for consumers. Therefore, the court issued an injunction and blocked Iowa Health from using the trademark UnityPoint Health.[7] ■

Once a secondary meaning is attached to a term or name, a trademark is considered distinctive and is protected. Even a color can qualify for trademark protection, such as the color schemes used by four state university sports teams, including Ohio State University and Louisiana State University.[8]

Generic Terms

Generic terms that refer to an entire class of products, such as *bicycle* and *computer,* receive no protection, even if they acquire secondary meanings. A particularly thorny problem for a business arises when its trademark acquires generic use. For instance, *aspirin* and *thermos* were originally trademarked products, but today the words are used generically. Other trademarks that have acquired generic use include *escalator, trampoline, raisin bran, dry ice, lanolin, linoleum, nylon,* and *cornflakes.*

A trademark that is commonly used does not automatically become generic, though. **CASE EXAMPLE 6.4** In 2014, David Elliot and Chris Gillespie sought to register numerous domain names, including "googledisney.com" and "googlenewstvs.com." (A **domain name** is part of an Internet address, such as "cengage.com.") They were unable to register the names because all of them used the word *google,* a trademark of Google, Inc.

Elliot and Gillespie brought an action in federal court to have the Google trademark canceled because it had become a generic term. They argued that because most people now use *google* as a verb ("to google") when referring to searching the Internet with any search engine (not just Google), the term should no longer be protected. The court held that even if people do use the word *google* as a verb, it is still a protected trademark if consumers associate the noun with one company. The court concluded that "the primary significance of the word

Domain Name Part of an Internet address, such as "cengage.com."

7. *Unity Health Plans Insurance Co. v. Iowa Health System,* 995 F.Supp.2d 874 (W.D. Wis. 2014).
8. *Board of Supervisors of LA State University v. Smack Apparel Co.,* 438 F.Supp.2d 653 (2006).

google to a majority of the public who utilize Internet search engines is a designation of the Google search engine."[9] ▨

6-1e Service, Certification, and Collective Marks

A **service mark** is essentially a trademark that is used to distinguish the services (rather than the products) of one person or company from those of another. For instance, each airline has a particular mark or symbol associated with its name. Titles and character names used in radio and television are frequently registered as service marks.

Other marks protected by law include certification marks and collective marks. A **certification mark** is used by one or more persons, other than the owner, to certify the region, materials, mode of manufacture, quality, or other characteristic of specific goods or services. Certification marks include such marks as "Good Housekeeping Seal of Approval" and "UL Tested."

When used by members of a cooperative, association, labor union, or other organization, a certification mark is referred to as a **collective mark.** EXAMPLE 6.5 Collective marks appear at the end of a movie's credits to indicate the various associations and organizations that participated in making the movie. The labor union marks found on the tags of certain products are also collective marks. ▨

6-1f Trade Dress

The term **trade dress** refers to the image and overall appearance of a product. Trade dress is a broad concept that can include all or part of the total image or overall impression created by a product or its packaging. EXAMPLE 6.6 The distinctive decor, menu, and style of service of a particular restaurant may be regarded as the restaurant's trade dress. Similarly, trade dress can include the layout and appearance of a mail-order catalogue, the use of a lighthouse as part of a golf hole, the fish shape of a cracker, or the G-shaped design of a Gucci watch. ▨

Basically, trade dress is subject to the same protection as trademarks. In cases involving trade dress infringement, as in trademark infringement cases, a major consideration is whether consumers are likely to be confused by the allegedly infringing use. EXAMPLE 6.7 Converse makes All-Star shoes, which were the first shoes ever endorsed by a famous basketball player, Chuck Taylor. Nike, Inc., which now owns Converse, filed a suit against thirty-one companies, including Ralph Lauren, for manufacturing knock-off versions of these shoes. Nike claims that consumers are likely to be confused because the knock-offs use the same white rubber soles, rubber cap on the toes, canvas tops, and conspicuous stitching as used on All-Stars. In 2015, Ralph Lauren agreed to settle its dispute with Nike by destroying all remaining fake All-Stars and paying Nike an undisclosed sum. ▨

6-1g Counterfeit Goods

Counterfeit goods copy or otherwise imitate trademarked goods but are not genuine. The importation of goods bearing counterfeit trademarks poses a growing problem for U.S. businesses, consumers, and law enforcement. It is estimated that nearly 7 percent of the goods imported into the United States are counterfeit. In addition to having negative financial effects on legitimate businesses, sales of certain counterfeit goods, such as pharmaceuticals and nutritional supplements, can present serious public health risks.

Stop Counterfeiting in Manufactured Goods Act In 2006, Congress enacted the Stop Counterfeiting in Manufactured Goods Act[10] (SCMGA). The act made it a crime to intentionally

Service Mark A trademark that is used to distinguish the services (rather than the products) of one person or company from those of another.

Certification Mark A mark used by one or more persons, other than the owner, to certify the region, materials, mode of manufacture, quality, or other characteristic of specific goods or services.

Collective Mark A mark used by members of a cooperative, association, union, or other organization to certify the region, materials, mode of manufacture, quality, or other characteristic of specific goods or services.

Trade Dress The image and overall appearance of a product.

iStockPhoto.com/ANGELGILD

Can the layout and appearance of a restaurant chain's menu qualify as trade dress?

---

9. *Elliot v. Google Inc.,* ___ F.Supp.3d ___, 2014 WL 4470390 (D.Ariz. 2014).
10. Pub. L. No. 109-181 (2006), which amended 18 U.S.C. Sections 2318–2320.

traffic in, or attempt to traffic in, counterfeit goods or services, or to knowingly use a counterfeit mark on or in connection with goods or services.

Before this act went into effect, the law did not prohibit the creation or shipment of counterfeit labels that were not attached to products. Therefore, counterfeiters would make labels and packaging bearing a counterfeit trademark, ship the labels to another location, and then affix them to inferior products to deceive buyers. The SCMGA closed this loophole by making it a crime to traffic in counterfeit labels, stickers, packaging, and the like, whether or not they are attached to goods.

Penalties for Counterfeiting   Persons found guilty of violating the SCMGA may be fined up to $2 million or imprisoned for up to ten years (or more if they are repeat offenders). If a court finds that the statute was violated, it must order the defendant to forfeit the counterfeit products (which are then destroyed), as well as any property used in the commission of the crime. The defendant must also pay restitution to the trademark holder or victim in an amount equal to the victim's actual loss.

How easy is it to create fake Zig-Zag cigarette rolling papers? Is so doing a civil or criminal wrong?

CASE EXAMPLE 6.7   Wajdi Beydoun pleaded guilty to conspiring to import cigarette-rolling papers from Mexico that were falsely marked as "Zig-Zags" and sell them in the United States. The defendant was sentenced to prison and ordered to pay $566,267 in restitution. On appeal, the court affirmed the prison sentence but ordered the trial court to reduce the amount of restitution because it exceeded the actual loss suffered by the legitimate sellers of Zig-Zag rolling papers.[11] ■

Combating Online Sales of Counterfeit Goods   The United States cannot prosecute foreign counterfeiters under U.S. laws, because our national laws do not apply to them. One effective tool that U.S. officials are using to combat online sales of counterfeit goods is to obtain a court order to close down the domain names of Web sites that sell such goods.

EXAMPLE 6.8   In 2013, U.S. agents shut down 297 domain names on the Monday after Thanksgiving. (This so-called "Cyber Monday" is the online version of "Black Friday," the day after Thanksgiving, when the holiday shopping season begins.) Europol, an international organization, shut down 393 domain names. Of course, some criminal enterprises may continue selling counterfeit products under different domain names. Nevertheless, shutting down the Web sites, particularly on key shopping days, prevents some counterfeit goods from entering the United States. ■

6–1h Trade Names

Trade Name A name that a business uses to identify itself and its brand. A trade name is directly related to a business's reputation and goodwill and is protected under trademark law.

Trademarks apply to *products*. The term **trade name** refers to part or all of a *business's name*, whether the business is a sole proprietorship, a partnership, or a corporation. Generally, a trade name is directly related to a business and its goodwill.

A trade name may be protected as a trademark if the trade name is the same as the company's trademarked product—for instance, Coca-Cola. Unless it is also used as a trademark or service mark, a trade name cannot be registered with the federal government. Trade names are protected under the common law, but only if they are unusual or fancifully used. The word *Safeway,* for example, was sufficiently fanciful to obtain protection as a trade name for a grocery chain.

6–1i Licensing

License An agreement by the owner of intellectual property to permit another to use a trademark, copyright, patent, or trade secret for certain limited purposes.

One way to avoid litigation and still make use of another's trademark or other form of intellectual property is to obtain a license to do so. A **license** in this context is an agreement

---

11. *United States v. Beydoun*, 469 F.3d 102 (5th Cir. 2006).

permitting the use of a trademark, copyright, patent, or trade secret for certain limited purposes. The party that owns the intellectual property rights and issues the license is the *licensor*, and the party obtaining the license is the *licensee*.

A license grants only the rights expressly described in the license agreement. A licensor might, for instance, allow the licensee to use a trademark as part of its company or domain name, but not otherwise use the mark on any products or services. Disputes frequently arise over licensing agreements, particularly when the license involves Internet use.

Typically, license agreements are very detailed and should be carefully drafted. Consult with an attorney before signing any licensing contract to make sure that the wording of the contract is very clear as to what rights are or are not being conveyed. This safeguard can help you to avoid litigation. Moreover, to prevent misunderstandings over the scope of the rights being acquired in intellectual property, determine whether any other parties hold licenses to use the same intellectual property and the extent of those rights.

PREVENTING LEGAL DISPUTES

6-2 Patents

A **patent** is a grant from the government that gives an inventor the exclusive right to make, use, and sell an invention for a period of twenty years. Patents for designs, as opposed to inventions, are given for a fourteen-year period. The applicant must demonstrate to the satisfaction of the U.S. Patent and Trademark Office that the invention, discovery, process, or design is novel, useful, and not obvious in light of current technology.

Until recently, patent law in the United States differed from the laws of many other countries because the first person to invent a product or process obtained the patent rights, rather than the first person to file for a patent. It was often difficult to prove who invented an item first, however, which prompted Congress to change the system in 2011 by passing the America Invents Act.[12] Now, the first person to file an application for a patent on a product or process will receive patent protection. In addition, the law established a nine-month limit for challenging a patent on any ground.

The period of patent protection begins on the date when the patent application is filed, rather than when the patent is issued, which can sometimes be years later. After the patent period ends (either fourteen or twenty years later), the product or process enters the public domain, and anyone can make, sell, or use the invention without paying the patent holder.

Patent A property right granted by the federal government that gives an inventor an exclusive right to make, use, sell, or offer to sell an invention in the United States for a limited time.

LEARNING OBJECTIVE 3

How does the law protect patents?

6-2a Searchable Patent Databases

A significant development relating to patents is the availability online of the world's patent databases. The Web site of the U.S. Patent and Trademark Office (**www .uspto.gov**) provides searchable databases covering U.S. patents granted since 1976. The Web site of the European Patent Office (**www.epo.org**) provides online access to 50 million patent documents in more than seventy nations through a searchable network of databases.

Businesses use these searchable databases in many ways. Companies may conduct patent searches to list or inventory their patents, which are valuable assets. Patent searches also enable companies to study trends and patterns in a specific technology or to gather information about competitors in the industry.

United States Patent and Trademark Office

This is the home page of the U.S. Patent and Trademark Office. Is its database searchable?

---

12. The full title of this law is the Leahy-Smith America Invents Act, Pub. L. No. 112-29 (2011), which amended 35 U.S.C. Sections 1, 41, and 321.

6–2b What Is Patentable?

Under federal law, "[w]hoever invents or discovers any new and useful process, machine, manufacture, or composition of matter, or any new and useful improvement thereof, may obtain a patent therefor, subject to the conditions and requirements of this title."[13] Thus, to be patentable, an invention must be *novel, useful,* and *not obvious* in light of current technology.

Almost anything is patentable, except the laws of nature, natural phenomena, and abstract ideas (including algorithms[14]). Even artistic methods and works of art, certain business processes, and the structures of storylines are patentable, provided that they are novel and not obvious.[15]

Plants that are reproduced asexually (by means other than from seed), such as hybrid or genetically engineered plants, are patentable in the United States, as are genetically engineered (or cloned) microorganisms and animals. **CASE EXAMPLE 6.9** Monsanto, Inc., has sold its patented genetically modified (GM) seeds to farmers to help them achieve higher crop yields using fewer pesticides. Monsanto has required farmers who bought GM seeds to sign agreements promising to plant the seeds for only one crop and to pay a technology fee for each acre planted. To ensure compliance, seventy-five Monsanto employees are assigned to investigate and prosecute farmers who use the GM seeds illegally. Monsanto has filed lawsuits against nearly 150 farmers in the United States and has been awarded more than $15 million in damages (not including out-of-court settlement amounts).[16] ■

A patent application was rejected in the following case as obvious in light of previous patents. The applicant challenged the rejection. The court's decision turned on the meaning of the terms *wireless* and *streaming video.*

---

13. 35 U.S.C. 101.

14. An *algorithm* is a step-by-step procedure, formula, or set of instructions for accomplishing a specific task. An example is the set of rules used by a search engine to rank the listings contained within its index in response to a particular query.

15. For a United States Supreme Court case discussing the obviousness requirement, see *KSR International Co. v. Teleflex, Inc.,* 550 U.S. 398, 127 S.Ct. 1727, 167 L.Ed.2d 705 (2007). For a discussion of business process patents, see *In re Bilski,* 545 F3d 943 (Fed. Cir. 2008).

16. See, for example, *Monsanto Co. v. Bowman,* 657 F.3d 1341 (Fed.Cir. 2011); and *Monsanto Co. v. Scruggs,* 459 F.3d 1328 (2006).

CASE 6.2

In re Imes

United States Court of Appeals, Federal Circuit, 778 F.3d 1250 (2015).

FACTS Kevin Imes filed a patent application for a device that can send digital camera images and videos wirelessly over a network. The U.S. Patent and Trademark Office examiner rejected Imes's device as obvious based on earlier patents—the Schuetzle and Knowles patents. The Schuetzle patent protects a device that can transfer images to a computer via a removable memory card. The examiner concluded that this device was wireless because to transfer images, the card is removed from the camera and inserted into the computer. "In other words, no wire is utilized." The Knowles system allows a user to take multiple consecutive still images and queues them so that they can be serially transmitted as e-mail attachments. The examiner explained that "a continuous process of sending images is the equivalent of streaming video." The Patent Trial and

What constitutes a wireless transfer of data from a digital camera over a network?

iStockPhoto.com/pawel.gaul

Appeal Board affirmed the examiner's rejection of Imes's application. Imes appealed.

ISSUE Did the examiner misconstrue the terms *wireless* and *streaming video?*

DECISION Yes. The U.S. Court of Appeals for the Federal Circuit reversed the Patent Trial and Appeal Board's rejection of Imes's application and remanded the case.

REASON The court concluded that the examiner's construction of the term *wireless* to include communication via the metal contacts of a removable memory card and a computer is "inconsistent with the broadest reasonable interpretation" of the term. Imes's application used wireless "to refer to methods and devices that carry waves through atmospheric space, such as Bluetooth and various cellular protocols." The court found that this was the correct meaning of the term, and this construction did not support the examiner's rejection of Imes's application. As for the examiner's conclusion with respect to the Knowles patent, the court found no substantial evidence to support the examiner's determination that Knowles's system transmits streaming video. "Streaming video is the continuous transmission of video. A series of e-mails with attachments does not meet the definition of 'streaming' and still images do not meet the definition of 'video.'"

CRITICAL THINKING—Legal Consideration *How should an invention be described in a patent application—in broad terms, specific terms, or both? Discuss.*

6-2c Patent Infringement

If a firm makes, uses, or sells another's patented design, product, or process without the patent owner's permission, it commits the tort of patent infringement. Patent infringement may occur even though the patent owner has not put the patented product in commerce. Patent infringement may also occur even though not all features or parts of an invention are copied. (To infringe the patent on a process, however, all steps or their equivalent must be copied.) To read about an important issue in patent infringement today, see this chapter's *Adapting the Law to the Online Environment.*

> "To invent, you need a good imagination and a pile of junk."
>
> **THOMAS EDISON**
> 1847–1931
> (AMERICAN INVENTOR)

Patent Infringement Suits and High-Tech Companies　Obviously, companies that specialize in developing new technology stand to lose significant profits if someone "makes, uses, or sells" devices that incorporate their patented inventions. Because these firms are the holders of numerous patents, they are frequently involved in patent infringement lawsuits (as well as other types of intellectual property disputes).

A complication in many such lawsuits is their global scope. Many companies that make and sell electronics and computer software and hardware are based in foreign nations (for instance, Samsung Electronics Company is a Korean firm). Foreign firms can apply for and obtain U.S. patent protection on items that they sell within the United States, just as U.S. firms can obtain protection in foreign nations where they sell goods.

In the United States, however, the Supreme Court has narrowly construed patent infringement as it applies to exported software. As a general rule, under U.S. law, no patent infringement occurs when a patented product is made and sold in another country. **CASE EXAMPLE 6.10** AT&T Corporation holds a patent on a device used to digitally encode, compress, and process recorded speech. AT&T brought an infringement case against Microsoft Corporation, which admitted that its Windows operating system incorporated software code that infringed on AT&T's patent.

The case reached the United States Supreme Court on the question of whether Microsoft's liability extended to computers made in another country. The Court held that it did not. Microsoft was liable only for infringement in the United States and not for the Windows-based computers produced in foreign locations. The Court reasoned that Microsoft had not "supplied" the software for the computers but had only electronically transmitted a master copy, which the foreign manufacturers then copied and loaded onto the computers.[17] ■

AT&T owns numerous patents, including one for digitally encoding, compressing, and processing recorded speech, which is used in Microsoft's Windows operating system. Is Microsoft liable for infringement of Windows-based computers produced outside the United States?

Apple, Inc. v. Samsung Electronics Company
Apple sued Samsung in federal court alleging that Samsung's Galaxy smartphones and tablets that use Google's HTC Android operating system infringe on Apple's patents. Apple has design patents that cover the devices' graphical user interface, shell, and screen and button design. Apple has also patented the way information is displayed on iPhones and other devices, the way windows pop open, and the way information is scaled and rotated.

---

17. *Microsoft Corp. v. AT&T Corp.*, 550 U.S. 437, 127 S.Ct. 1746, 167 L.Ed.2d 737 (2007).

ADAPTING THE LAW TO THE **ONLINE** ENVIRONMENT
The Problem of Patent Trolls

In recent years, a huge number of patent infringement lawsuits have been filed against software and technology firms. Many patent cases involve companies defending real innovations, but some lawsuits are "shakedowns" by patent trolls.

Patent trolls—more formally called nonpracticing entities (NPEs) or patent assertion entities (PAEs)—are firms that do not make or sell products or services but are in the business of patent litigation. These firms buy patents and then try to enforce them against companies that *do* sell products or services, demanding licensing fees and threatening infringement lawsuits. Patent trolls usually target online businesses.

"I'm Going to Sue You Unless You Pay Me to Go Away"

Patent trolls literally bank on the fact that when threatened with infringement suits, most companies would rather pay to settle than engage in costly litigation, even if they believe they could win. Consider an example. Soverain Software, LLC, sued dozens of online retailers, including Amazon,

Avon, Home Depot, Macy's, Nordstrom, Kohl's, RadioShack, The Gap, and Victoria's Secret. Soverain claimed that it owned patents that covered nearly any use of online shopping-cart technology and that all these retailers had infringed on its patents. Amazon paid millions to settle with Soverain, as did most of the other defendants.

Interestingly, one online retailer, Newegg, Inc., refused to pay Soverain and ultimately won in court. In 2013, a federal appellate court held that the shopping-cart patent claim was invalid on the ground of obviousness because the technology for it already existed before Soverain obtained its patent.[a]

The Role of Software Patents

The patent troll problem is concentrated in software patents, which often include descriptions of what the software does rather than the computer code involved. Many software patents are vaguely worded and overly broad. In the United States, both the patent system and the courts have had

difficulty evaluating and protecting such patents.

As a result, nearly any business that uses basic technology can be a target of patent trolls. In fact, *more than 60 percent of all new patent cases* are filed by patent trolls. The firms most commonly targeted by patent trolls, however, are large technology companies, including AT&T, Google, Apple, Samsung, Amazon, and Verizon. In 2013 alone, "AT&T was sued for patent infringement by so-called patent trolls a startling 54 times—more than once a week."[b]

CRITICAL THINKING

■ Some argue that the best way to stop patent trolls from taking advantage of the system would be to eliminate software patents completely and pass a law that makes software unpatentable. Would this be fair to software and technology companies? Why or why not?

---

a. *Soverain Software, LLC v. Newegg, Inc.*, 728 F.3d 1332 (Fed.Cir. 2013), *cert. denied*, 134 S.Ct. 910 (2014).

b. Roger Parloff, "Taking on the Patent Trolls," *Fortune*, February 27, 2014.

> "The patent system . . . added the fuel to the fire of genius."
>
> **ABRAHAM LINCOLN**
> 1809–1865
> (SIXTEENTH PRESIDENT OF THE UNITED STATES, 1861–1865)

In 2012, a jury issued a verdict in favor of Apple, finding that Samsung had willfully infringed five of Apple's patents. Although the jury awarded more than $1 billion in damages—one of the largest awards ever made in a patent case—a judge later ruled that part of the damages had been incorrectly calculated.[18] The case provided an important precedent for Apple in its legal battles against Android devices made by other companies worldwide. Nevertheless, litigation between Apple and Samsung over the current generation of smartphones and mobile devices has continued.

6–2d Remedies for Patent Infringement

If a patent is infringed, the patent holder may sue for relief in federal court. The patent holder can seek an injunction against the infringer and can also request damages for royalties and lost profits. (A royalty is a payment made to a patent or copyright holder for the privilege of using the patent or the copyrighted work.) In some cases, the court may grant the winning party

---

18. *Apple, Inc. v. Samsung Electronics Co., Ltd.*, 926 F.Supp.2d 1100 (N.D.Cal. 2013); and *Apple, Inc. v. Samsung Electronics Co., Ltd.*, 735 F.3d 1352 (2013).

reimbursement for attorneys' fees and costs. If the court determines that the infringement was willful, the court can triple the amount of damages awarded (treble damages).

In the past, permanent injunctions were routinely granted to prevent future infringement. Today, however, according to the United States Supreme Court, a patent holder must prove that it has suffered irreparable injury and that the public interest would not be *disserved* by a permanent injunction.[19] Thus, courts have the discretion to decide what is equitable in the circumstances and to consider the public interest rather than just the interests of the parties.

CASE EXAMPLE 6.11 Cordance Corporation developed some of the technology and software that automates Internet communications. Cordance sued Amazon.com, Inc., for patent infringement, claiming that Amazon's one-click purchasing interface infringed on one of Cordance's patents. After a jury found Amazon guilty of infringement, Cordance requested the court to issue a permanent injunction against Amazon's infringement or, alternatively, to order Amazon to pay Cordance an ongoing royalty.

The court refused to issue a permanent injunction, because Cordance had not proved that it would otherwise suffer irreparable harm. Cordance and Amazon were not direct competitors in the relevant market. Cordance had never sold or licensed the technology infringed by Amazon's one-click purchasing interface and had presented no market data or evidence to show how the infringement negatively affected Cordance. The court also refused to impose an ongoing royalty on Amazon.[20] ▪

LEARNING OBJECTIVE 4
What laws protect authors' rights in the works they create?

6-3 Copyrights

A **copyright** is an intangible property right granted by federal statute to the author or originator of certain literary or artistic productions. The Copyright Act of 1976,[21] as amended, governs copyrights. Works created after January 1, 1978, are automatically given statutory copyright protection for the life of the author plus 70 years. For copyrights owned by publishing companies, the copyright expires 95 years from the date of publication or 120 years from the date of creation, whichever is first. For works by more than one author, the copyright expires 70 years after the death of the last surviving author.

CASE EXAMPLE 6.12 The popular character Sherlock Holmes originated in stories written by Arthur Conan Doyle and published from 1887 through 1927. Over the years, elements of the characters and stories created by Doyle have appeared in books, movies, and television series, including the recent *Elementary* on CBS and *Sherlock* on BBC. Before 2013, those who wished to use the copyrighted Sherlock material had to pay a licensing fee to Doyle's estate. Then, in 2013, the editors of a book of Holmes-related stories filed a lawsuit in federal court claiming that the basic Sherlock Holmes story elements introduced before 1923 should no longer be protected. The court agreed and ruled that these elements have entered the public domain—that is, the copyright has expired, and they can be used without permission.[22] ▪

Copyrights can be registered with the U.S. Copyright Office (**www.copyright.gov**) in Washington, D.C. Registration is not required, however. A copyright owner need not place a © or *Copr.* or *Copyright* on the work to have the work protected against infringement. Chances are that if somebody created it, somebody owns it.

Generally, copyright owners are protected against the following:

1. Reproduction of the work.

2. Development of derivative works.

3. Distribution of the work.

4. Public display of the work.

Copyright The exclusive right of an author or originator of a literary or artistic production to publish, print, sell, or otherwise use that production for a statutory period of time.

KNOW THIS
A creative work that is not copyrightable may be protected by other intellectual property law.

---

19. *eBay, Inc. v. MercExchange, LLC,* 547 U.S. 388, 126 S.Ct. 1837, 164 L.Ed.2d 641 (2006).
20. *Cordance Corp. v. Amazon.com, Inc.,* 730 F.Supp.2d 333 (D.Del. 2010).
21. 17 U.S.C. Sections 101 *et seq.*
22. *Klinger v. Conan Doyle Estate, Ltd.,* 988 F.Supp.2d 879 (N.D.Ill. 2013).

Artist Shepard Fairey created a poster portrait of Barack Obama. It was clearly based on an Associated Press file photo taken by Manny Garcia. Did Fairey violate copyright law?

6–3a What Is Protected Expression?

Works that are copyrightable include books, records, films, artworks, architectural plans, menus, music videos, product packaging, and computer software. To be protected, a work must be "fixed in a durable medium" from which it can be perceived, reproduced, or communicated. As noted, protection is automatic, and registration is not required.

To obtain protection under the Copyright Act, a work must be original and fall into one of the following categories:

1. Literary works (including newspaper and magazine articles, computer and training manuals, catalogues, brochures, and print advertisements).
2. Musical works and accompanying words (including advertising jingles).
3. Dramatic works and accompanying music.
4. Pantomimes and choreographic works (including ballets and other forms of dance).
5. Pictorial, graphic, and sculptural works (including cartoons, maps, posters, statues, and even stuffed animals).
6. Motion pictures and other audiovisual works (including multimedia works).
7. Sound recordings.
8. Architectural works.

Section 102 Exclusions Generally, anything that is not an original expression will not qualify for copyright protection. Facts widely known to the public are not copyrightable. Page numbers are not copyrightable because they follow a sequence known to everyone. Mathematical calculations are not copyrightable.

In addition, it is not possible to copyright an idea. Section 102 of the Copyright Act specifically excludes copyright protection for any "idea, procedure, process, system, method of operation, concept, principle, or discovery, regardless of the form in which it is described, explained, illustrated, or embodied." Thus, others can freely use the underlying ideas or principles embodied in a work. What is copyrightable is the particular way in which an idea is *expressed*. Whenever an idea and an expression are inseparable, the expression cannot be copyrighted.

An idea and its expression, then, must be separable to be copyrightable. Thus, for the design of a useful item to be copyrightable, the sculptural features—that is, the way it looks—must be separate from its utilitarian (functional) purpose. In the following case, the court was asked to apply this principle.

CASE 6.3

Inhale, Inc. v. Starbuzz Tobacco, Inc.

United States Court of Appeals for the Ninth Circuit, 755 F.3d 1038 (2014).

FACTS A hookah is a device for smoking tobacco by filtering the smoke through water. The water is held in a container at the base of the hookah. Inhale, Inc., claimed to hold a registered copyright on a hookah that covered the shape of the hookah's water container. Inhale filed a suit in a federal district court against Starbuzz Tobacco, Inc., for copyright infringement, alleging that Starbuzz sold hookahs with water containers shaped exactly like the Inhale containers. The court determined that the shape

Is the shape of this hookah's water container copyrightable?

of the water container on Inhale's hookahs was not copyrightable and issued a summary judgment in Starbuzz's favor. Inhale appealed.

ISSUE Was Inhale's registered copyright infringed by Starbuzz's sale of hookahs with water containers identical in shape to Inhale's containers?

DECISION No. The U.S. Court of Appeals for the Ninth Circuit affirmed the lower court's judgment.

REASON The federal appellate court stated, "The shape of a container is not independent of the container's utilitarian function—to hold the contents within its shape—because the shape accomplishes the function." The water container on a hookah is a "useful article." Thus, the shape of the container is copyrightable only if it incorporates sculptural features that can be identified separately from the container's useful aspect. Inhale argued that the shape of its hookah water container was distinctive. In an earlier case involving bottle designs, the U.S. Copyright Office had reasoned that whether an item's shape is distinctive does not affect a determination of whether the item's sculptural features can be separated from the item's utility. With regard to Inhale's water container, "The shape of the alleged artistic features and of the useful article are one and the same." Thus, the shape of the water container on Inhale's hookahs was not copyrightable.

WHAT IF THE FACTS WERE DIFFERENT? *Suppose that Inhale had claimed a copyright in the design of a vodka bottle instead of a hookah. Would the result have been different? Why or why not?*

Compilations of Facts

As mentioned, facts widely known to the public are not copyrightable. *Compilations* of facts, however, may be copyrightable. Under Section 103 of the Copyright Act, a compilation is a work formed by the collection and assembling of preexisting materials or of data that are selected, coordinated, or arranged in such a way that the resulting work as a whole constitutes an original work of authorship.

The key requirement for the copyrightability of a compilation is originality. The White Pages of a telephone directory do not qualify for copyright protection because they simply list names and telephone numbers alphabetically. The Yellow Pages of a directory can be copyrightable, provided that the information is selected, coordinated, or arranged in an original way. Similarly, a court held that a compilation of information about yachts listed for sale may qualify for copyright protection.[23]

6–3b Copyright Infringement

Whenever the form or expression of an idea is copied, an infringement of copyright occurs. The reproduction does not have to be exactly the same as the original, nor does it have to reproduce the original in its entirety. If a substantial part of the original is reproduced, copyright infringement has occurred.

Remedies for Copyright Infringement

Those who infringe copyrights may be liable for damages or criminal penalties. These range from actual damages or statutory damages, imposed at the court's discretion, to criminal proceedings for willful violations. Actual damages are based on the harm caused to the copyright holder by the infringement, while statutory damages, not to exceed $150,000, are provided for under the Copyright Act. In addition, criminal proceedings may result in fines and/or imprisonment. In some instances, a court may grant an injunction against the infringer.

CASE EXAMPLE 6.13 Rusty Carroll operated an online term paper business, R2C2, Inc., that offered up to 300,000 research papers for sale on nine different Web sites. Individuals whose work was posted on these Web sites without their permission filed a lawsuit against Carroll for copyright infringement. Because Carroll repeatedly failed to comply with court orders regarding discovery, the court found that the copyright infringement was likely to continue unless an injunction was issued. The court therefore issued a permanent injunction prohibiting Carroll and R2C2 from selling any term paper without sworn documentary evidence that the paper's author had given permission.[24] ▪

The "Fair Use" Exception

An exception to liability for copyright infringement is made under the "fair use" doctrine. In certain circumstances, a person or organization can reproduce

> "Don't worry about people stealing an idea. If it's original and it's any good, you'll have to ram it down their throats."
>
> **HOWARD AIKEN**
> 1900–1973
> (ENGINEER AND PIONEER IN COMPUTING)

---

23. *BUC International Corp. v. International Yacht Council, Ltd.,* 489 F.3d 1129 (11th Cir. 2007).
24. *Weidner v. Carroll,* 2010 WL 310310 (S.D.Ill. 2010).

copyrighted material without paying royalties. Section 107 of the Copyright Act provides as follows:

> [T]he fair use of a copyrighted work, including such use by reproduction in copies or phonorecords or by any other means specified by [Section 106 of the Copyright Act], for purposes such as criticism, comment, news reporting, teaching (including multiple copies for classroom use), scholarship, or research, is not an infringement of copyright. In determining whether the use made of a work in any particular case is a fair use the factors to be considered shall include—
> (1) the purpose and character of the use, including whether such use is of a commercial nature or is for nonprofit educational purposes;
> (2) the nature of the copyrighted work;
> (3) the amount and substantiality of the portion used in relation to the copyrighted work as a whole; and
> (4) the effect of the use upon the potential market for or value of the copyrighted work.

What Is Fair Use?

Because the fair use guidelines are very broad, the courts determine whether a particular use is fair on a case-by-case basis. Thus, anyone reproducing copyrighted material may be committing a violation. In determining whether a use is fair, courts have often considered the fourth factor to be the most important.

CASE EXAMPLE 6.14 BMG Music Publishing, an owner of copyrighted music, granted a license to Leadsinger, Inc., a manufacturer of karaoke devices. The license gave Leadsinger permission to reproduce the sound recordings, but not to reprint the song lyrics. The lyrics, however, appeared at the bottom of a TV screen when the karaoke device was used.

BMG demanded that Leadsinger pay a "lyric reprint" fee and a "synchronization" fee for this use of the song lyrics. Leadsinger refused, claiming that its use of the lyrics was educational and thus did not constitute copyright infringement under the fair use exception. A federal appellate court disagreed. The court held that Leadsinger's display of the lyrics was not a fair use because it would negatively affect the value of the copyrighted work.[25] ■

Do makers of karaoke machines automatically have the right to reproduce printed lyrics?

ETHICAL ISSUE

Should fair use include the creation of a full-text searchable database of millions of books? Back in 2004, a number of research universities, in partnership with Google, Inc., agreed to digitize books from their libraries and create a repository for them. In 2008, the HathiTrust Digital Library was formed by eighty institutions, including the University of California at Berkeley, Cornell University, and the University of Michigan. As of 2012, the library contained some 10 million digitized works.

Not all authors whose works were represented in the library were happy with what they considered a violation of their intellectual property rights. After all, shouldn't copyright law protect authors (and publishers) from having Google, Inc., electronically scan their books without their permission? Google and the HathiTrust responded that there was no copyright violation. The library's main interest was preservation, and its full-text searchable database of the library's books was an aid to scholarship. It enabled researchers to find terms of interest in the digital volumes—not to read the volumes online. Search results yielded only page numbers where the terms could be found.

In 2011, a group of authors and authors' associations sued the HathiTrust and several associated entities for copyright infringement. The U.S. District Court for the Southern District of New York granted summary judgment in favor of the defendants.[26] On appeal, the reviewing court noted, "A fair use must not excessively damage the market for the original by providing the public with a substitute for that original work." But, the appellate court pointed out, the HathiTrust database "does not allow users to view any portion of the books they are search-

---

25. *Leadsinger, Inc. v. BMG Music Publishing*, 512 F.3d 522 (9th Cir. 2008).
26. *Authors Guild, Inc. v. HathiTrust*, 902 F.Supp.2d 445 (S.D.N.Y. 2012).

ing. Consequently, in providing this service, the [HathiTrust] does not add into circulation any new, human-readable copies of any books." Indeed, the court suggested that full-text searches might add to the value of copyrighted works.[27]

The First Sale Doctrine Section 109(a) of the Copyright Act provides that "the owner of a particular copy or phonorecord lawfully made under [the Copyright Act], or any person authorized by such owner, is entitled, without the authority of the copyright owner, to sell or otherwise dispose of the possession of that copy or phonorecord." This rule is known as the first sale doctrine.

Under this doctrine, once a copyright owner sells or gives away a particular copy of a work, the copyright owner no longer has the right to control the distribution of that copy. **EXAMPLE 6.15** Miranda buys *The Hunger Games* by Suzanne Collins, a copyrighted book. She can legally sell the book to another person. ■

In 2012, the United States Supreme Court heard the appeal of a case involving the resale of textbooks on eBay. To read about the Court's decision in this important case, see this chapter's *Beyond Our Borders* feature.

---

27. *Authors Guild, Inc. v. HathiTrust*, 755 F.3d 87 (2d Cir. 2014).

BEYOND OUR BORDERS

The Resale of Textbooks Purchased Abroad

Students and professors alike complain about the high price of college textbooks. Some enterprising students have found that if they purchase textbooks printed abroad, they may save enough to justify the shipping charges. Textbook prices are lower in other countries because production costs are lower there and average incomes are also lower, so students are unable to pay higher prices.

A University Student Starts a Side Business
Supap Kirtsaeng, a citizen of Thailand, was a graduate student at the University of Southern California. He enlisted friends and family in Thailand to buy copies of textbooks there and ship them to him in the United States. Kirtsaeng resold the textbooks on eBay, where he eventually made about $100,000.

John Wiley & Sons, Inc., had printed eight of those textbooks in Asia. Wiley sued Kirtsaeng in federal district court for copyright

infringement. Kirtsaeng argued that Section 109(a) of the Copyright Act allows the first purchaser-owner of a book to sell it without the copyright owner's permission. But the trial court held in favor of Wiley, and that decision was affirmed on appeal.[a] The lower courts reasoned that the first sale doctrine in the Copyright Act refers specifically to works manufactured in the United States and should not apply to textbooks printed and sold abroad. Kirtsaeng appealed to the United States Supreme Court.

The Supreme Court Weighs In
Can a copy of a book or CD or DVD that was legally produced abroad, acquired abroad, and then imported into the United States be resold in the United States without the copyright owner's permission? That was the issue before the Supreme Court. The answer has implications not only for individuals but

also for discount sellers such as Costco and online businesses such as eBay and Google.

The Supreme Court ruled in Kirtsaeng's favor, reversing the appellate court's decision.[b] The Court held that the first sale doctrine applies even to goods purchased abroad. According to the Court, "the common-law history of the 'first-sale' doctrine . . . favors a non-geographical interpretation." The justices were clearly concerned about what might occur if the Court did not reverse the appellate court's decision. Allowing that decision to stand could have made it possible to "prevent a buyer from domestically selling or even giving away copies of a video game made in Japan."

■ What options do textbook publishers face given this Supreme Court decision?

---

a. *John Wiley & Sons, Inc. v. Kirtsaeng*, 2009 WL 3364037 (S.D.N.Y. 2009); and *John Wiley & Sons, Inc. v. Kirtsaeng*, 654 F.3d 210 (2d Cir. 2011).

b. *Kirtsaeng v. John Wiley & Sons, Inc.*, ___ U.S. ___, 133 S.Ct. 1351, 185 L.Ed.2d 392 (2013).

6-3c Copyright Protection for Software

In 1980, Congress passed the Computer Software Copyright Act, which amended the Copyright Act to include computer programs in the list of creative works protected by federal copyright law. Generally, copyright protection extends to those parts of a computer program that can be read by humans, such as the high-level language of a source code. Protection also extends to the binary-language object code, which is readable only by the computer, and to such elements as the overall structure, sequence, and organization of a program.

Not all aspects of software are protected, however. Courts typically have not extended copyright protection to the "look and feel"—the general appearance, command structure, video images, menus, windows, and other screen displays—of computer programs. **EXAMPLE 6.16** MiTek develops a software program for laying out wood trusses (used in construction). A competing company comes out with a program that has similar elements, including the menu and submenu command structures. MiTek cannot successfully sue for copyright infringement, because the command structure of software is not protected. ■ Note that copying the "look and feel" of another's product may be a violation of trade dress or trademark laws, however.

As will be discussed in Chapter 7, technology has vastly increased the potential for copyright infringement via the Internet.

LEARNING OBJECTIVE 5

What are trade secrets, and what laws offer protection for this form of intellectual property?

Trade Secret A formula, device, idea, process, or other information used in a business that gives the owner a competitive advantage in the marketplace.

6-4   Trade Secrets

The law of trade secrets protects some business processes and information that are not or cannot be protected under patent, copyright, or trademark law. A **trade secret** is basically information of commercial value. A company's customer lists, plans, and research and development are trade secrets. Trade secrets may also include pricing information, marketing techniques, and production methods—anything that makes an individual company unique and that would have value to a competitor.

Unlike copyright and trademark protection, protection of trade secrets extends both to ideas and to their expression. (For this reason, and because there are no registration or filing requirements for trade secrets, trade secret protection may be well suited for software.) Of course, the secret formula, method, or other information must be disclosed to some persons, particularly to key employees. Businesses generally attempt to protect their trade secrets by having all employees who use the process or information agree in their contracts, or in confidentiality agreements, never to divulge it.

6-4a State and Federal Law on Trade Secrets

Under Section 757 of the *Restatement of Torts*, those who disclose or use another's trade secret, without authorization, are liable to that other party if either of the following is true:

1. They discovered the secret by improper means.

2. Their disclosure or use constitutes a breach of a duty owed to the other party.

Stealing of confidential business data by industrial espionage, as when a business taps into a competitor's computer, is a theft of trade secrets without any contractual violation and is actionable in itself.

Although trade secrets have long been protected under the common law, today most states' laws are based on the Uniform Trade Secrets Act, which has been adopted in forty-seven states. Additionally, the Economic Espionage Act made the theft of trade secrets a federal crime, as we will discuss in Chapter 8.

6-4b Trade Secrets in Cyberspace

Today's computer technology undercuts a business firm's ability to protect its confidential information, including trade secrets. For instance, a dishonest employee could e-mail trade secrets in a company's computer to a competitor or a future employer. If e-mail is not an option, the employee might walk out with the information on a flash pen drive.

Misusing a company's social media accounts is yet another way in which employees may appropriate trade secrets. **CASE EXAMPLE 6.17** Noah Kravitz worked for a company called Phone-Dog for four years as a product reviewer and video blogger. PhoneDog provided him with the Twitter account "@PhoneDog_Noah." Kravitz's popularity grew, and he had approximately 17,000 followers by the time he quit in 2010. PhoneDog requested that Kravitz stop using the Twitter account. Although Kravitz changed his handle to "@noahkravitz," he continued to use the account. PhoneDog subsequently sued Kravitz for misappropriation of trade secrets, among other things. Kravitz moved for a dismissal, but the court found that the complaint adequately stated a cause of action for misappropriation of trade secrets and allowed the suit to continue.[28] ■

For a summary of trade secrets and other forms of intellectual property, see Exhibit 6–1.

---

28. *PhoneDog v. Kravitz*, 2011 WL 5415612 (N.D.Cal. 2011).

Exhibit 6–1 Forms of Intellectual Property

	DEFINITION	HOW ACQUIRED	DURATION	REMEDY FOR INFRINGEMENT
Patent	A grant from the government that gives an inventor exclusive rights to an invention.	By filing a patent application with the U.S. Patent and Trademark Office and receiving its approval.	Twenty years from the date of the application; for design patents, fourteen years.	Monetary damages, including royalties and lost profits, plus attorneys' fees. Damages may be tripled for intentional infringement.
Copyright	The right of an author or originator of a literary or artistic work, or other production that falls within a specified category, to have the exclusive use of that work for a given period of time.	Automatic (once the work or creation is put in tangible form). Only the *expression* of an idea (and not the idea itself) can be protected by copyright.	For authors: the life of the author plus 70 years. For publishers: 95 years after the date of publication or 120 years after creation.	Actual damages plus profits received by the party who infringed *or* statutory damages under the Copyright Act, *plus* costs and attorneys' fees in either situation.
Trademark (service mark and trade dress)	Any distinctive word, name, symbol, or device (image or appearance), or combination thereof, that an entity uses to distinguish its goods or services from those of others. The owner has the exclusive right to use that mark or trade dress.	1. At common law, ownership created by use of the mark. 2. Registration with the appropriate federal or state office gives notice and is permitted if the mark is currently in use or will be within the next six months.	Unlimited, as long as it is in use. To continue notice by registration, the owner must renew by filing between the fifth and sixth years, and thereafter, every ten years.	1. Injunction prohibiting the future use of the mark. 2. Actual damages plus profits received by the party who infringed (can be increased under the Lanham Act). 3. Destruction of articles that infringed. 4. *Plus* costs and attorneys' fees.
Trade Secret	Any information that a business possesses and that gives the business an advantage over competitors (including formulas, lists, patterns, plans, processes, and programs).	Through the originality and development of the information and processes that constitute the business secret and are unknown to others.	Unlimited, so long as not revealed to others. Once revealed to others, it is no longer a trade secret.	Monetary damages for misappropriation (the Uniform Trade Secrets Act also permits punitive damages if willful), *plus* costs and attorneys' fees.

6-5 International Protections

For many years, the United States has been a party to various international agreements relating to intellectual property rights. For example, the Paris Convention of 1883, to which about 173 countries are signatory, allows parties in one country to file for patent and trademark protection in any of the other member countries. Other international agreements include the Berne Convention, the Trade-Related Aspects of Intellectual Property Rights (known as the TRIPS agreement), the Madrid Protocol, and the Anti-Counterfeiting Trade Agreement.

6-5a The Berne Convention

Under the Berne Convention of 1886, an international copyright agreement, if a U.S. citizen writes a book, every country that has signed the convention must recognize her or his copyright in the book. Also, if a citizen of a country that has not signed the convention first publishes a book in one of the 168 countries that have signed, all other countries that have signed the convention must recognize that author's copyright. Copyright notice is not needed to gain protection under the Berne Convention for works published after March 1, 1989.

In 2011, the European Union altered its copyright rules under the Berne Convention by agreeing to extend the period of royalty protection for musicians from fifty years to seventy years. This decision aids major record labels as well as performers and musicians. The profits of musicians and record companies have been shrinking in recent years because of the sharp decline in sales of compact discs and the rise in digital downloads (both legal and illegal).

6-5b The TRIPS Agreement

The Berne Convention and other international agreements have given some protection to intellectual property on a worldwide level. None of them, however, has been as significant and far reaching in scope as the TRIPS agreement.

Representatives from more than one hundred nations signed the TRIPS agreement in 1994. The agreement established, for the first time, standards for the international protection of intellectual property rights, including patents, trademarks, and copyrights for movies, computer programs, books, and music. The TRIPS agreement provides that each member country must include in its domestic laws broad intellectual property rights and effective remedies (including civil and criminal penalties) for violations of those rights.

Generally, the TRIPS agreement forbids member nations from discriminating against foreign owners of intellectual property rights in the administration, regulation, or adjudication of such rights. In other words, a member nation cannot give its own nationals (citizens) favorable treatment without offering the same treatment to nationals of all member countries. **EXAMPLE 6.18** A U.S. software manufacturer brings a suit for the infringement of intellectual property rights under Germany's national laws. Because Germany is a member of the TRIPS agreement, the U.S. manufacturer is entitled to receive the same treatment as a German manufacturer. ■

Each member nation must ensure that legal procedures are available for parties who wish to bring actions for infringement of intellectual property rights. Additionally, a related document established a mechanism for settling disputes among member nations.

6-5c The Madrid Protocol

In the past, one of the difficulties in protecting U.S. trademarks internationally was that it was time consuming and expensive to apply for trademark registration in foreign countries. The filing fees and procedures for trademark registration vary significantly among individual countries. The Madrid Protocol, which was signed into law in 2003, may help to resolve these problems.

The Madrid Protocol is an international treaty that has been signed by seventy-three countries. Under its provisions, a U.S. company wishing to register its trademark abroad can submit a single application and designate other member countries in which it would like to register the mark. The treaty was designed to reduce the costs of obtaining international trademark protection by more than 60 percent.

Although the Madrid Protocol may simplify and reduce the cost of trademark registration in foreign nations, it remains to be seen whether it will provide significant benefits to trademark owners. Even with an easier registration process, the question of whether member countries will enforce the law and protect the mark still remains.

6–5d The Anti-Counterfeiting Trade Agreement

In 2011, Australia, Canada, Japan, Korea, Morocco, New Zealand, Singapore, and the United States signed the Anti-Counterfeiting Trade Agreement (ACTA), an international treaty to combat global counterfeiting and piracy. The members of the European Union, Mexico, Switzerland, and other nations that support the ACTA are still developing domestic procedures to comply with its provisions. Once a nation has adopted appropriate procedures, it can ratify the treaty.

Provisions and Goals
The goals of the treaty are to increase international cooperation, facilitate the best law enforcement practices, and provide a legal framework to combat counterfeiting. The treaty will have its own governing body.

The ACTA applies not only to counterfeit physical goods, such as medications, but also to pirated copyrighted works being distributed via the Internet. The idea is to create a new standard of enforcement for intellectual property rights that goes beyond the TRIPS agreement and encourages international cooperation and information sharing among signatory countries.

Border Searches
Under ACTA, member nations are required to establish border measures that allow officials, on their own initiative, to search commercial shipments of imports and exports for counterfeit goods. The treaty neither requires nor prohibits random border searches of electronic devices, such as laptops and iPads, for infringing content.

If border authorities reasonably believe that any goods in transit are counterfeit, the treaty allows them to keep the suspect goods unless the owner proves that the items are authentic and noninfringing. The treaty allows member nations, in accordance with their own laws, to order online service providers to furnish information about (including the identity of) suspected trademark and copyright infringers.

Reviewing . . . Intellectual Property Rights

Two computer science majors, Trent and Xavier, have an idea for a new video game, which they propose to call "Hallowed." They form a business and begin developing their idea. Several months later, Trent and Xavier run into a problem with their design and consult with a friend, Brad, who is an expert in creating computer source codes. After the software is completed but before Hallowed is marketed, a video game called Halo 2 is released for both the Xbox and PlayStation 3 systems. Halo 2 uses source codes similar to those of Hallowed and imitates Hallowed's overall look and feel, although not all the features are alike. Using the information presented in the chapter, answer the following questions.

1. Would the name Hallowed receive protection as a trademark or as trade dress?

2. If Trent and Xavier had obtained a business process patent on Hallowed, would the release of Halo 2 infringe on their patent? Why or why not?

Continues

3. Based only on the facts presented above, could Trent and Xavier sue the makers of Halo 2 for copyright infringement? Why or why not?

4. Suppose that Trent and Xavier discover that Brad took the idea of Hallowed and sold it to the company that produced Halo 2. Which type of intellectual property issue does this raise?

DEBATE THIS

- Congress has amended the Copyright Act several times. Copyright holders now have protection for many decades. Was Congress justified in extending the copyright time periods? Why or why not?

LINKING BUSINESS LAW TO MARKETING
Trademarks and Service Marks

In your marketing courses, you have learned or will learn about the importance of trademarks. If you become a marketing manager, you will likely be involved in creating trademarks or service marks for your firm, protecting the firm's existing marks, and ensuring that the firm does not infringe on anyone else's marks.

The Broad Range of Trademarks and Service Marks
The courts have held that trademarks and service marks consist of much more than well-known brand names, such as Apple and Amazon. As a marketing manager, you will need to be aware that parts of a brand name or other forms of product identification may qualify for trademark protection.

- **Catchy phrases**—Certain brands have established phrases that are associated with the brands, such as Nike's "Just Do It!" Marketing managers for competing product should avoid using similar phrases

in their marketing programs. Note, though, that not all phrases can become part of a trademark or service mark. When a phrase is extremely common, the courts normally will not grant trademark or service mark protection to it.

- **Abbreviations**—The public sometimes abbreviates a well-known trademark. For example, Budweiser beer is known as Bud and Coca-Cola as Coke. Marketing managers should avoid using any name for a product or service that closely resembles a well-known abbreviation, such as Koke for a cola drink.

- **Shapes**—The shape of a brand name, a service mark, or a container can take on exclusivity if the shape clearly aids in product or service identification. For example, just about everyone throughout the world recognizes the shape of a Coca-Cola bottle. Marketing managers would do well to avoid using a similar shape for a new carbonated drink.

- **Ornamental colors**—Sometimes, color combinations can become part of a service mark or trademark. For example,

FedEx established its unique identity with the use of bright orange and purple. The courts have protected this color combination. The same holds for the black-and-copper color combination of Duracell batteries.

- **Ornamental designs**—Symbols and designs associated with a particular mark are normally protected. Marketing managers should not attempt to copy them. Levi's places a small tag on the left side of the rear pocket of its jeans. Cross uses a cutoff black cone on the top of its pens.

- **Sounds**—Sounds can also be protected. For example, the familiar roar of the Metro-Goldwyn-Mayer (MGM) lion is protected.

When to Protect Trademarks and Service Marks
Every business should register its logo as a trademark, and perhaps also its business name and Web site address, to provide the company with the highest level of protection. A trademark will discourage counterfeiting and will give your firm the advantage in the event of future infringement.

Once your company has established a trademark or a service mark, as a manager, you will have to decide how aggressively you wish to protect those marks. If you fail to protect them, your company faces the possibility that they will become generic. Remember that *aspirin, cellophane, thermos, dry ice, shredded wheat,* and many other familiar terms were once legally protected trademarks. Protecting exclusive rights to a mark can be expensive, however, so you will have to determine how much it is worth to your company to protect your rights. If you work in a small company, making major expenditures to protect your trademarks and service marks might not be cost-effective.

Key Terms

certification mark 143
collective mark 143
copyright 149
domain name 142
intellectual property 138

license 144
patent 145
service mark 143
trade dress 143
trade name 144

trade secret 154
trademark 139
trademark dilution 140

Chapter Summary: Intellectual Property Rights

Trademarks	1. A *trademark* is a distinctive word, symbol, or design that identifies the manufacturer as the source of the goods and distinguishes its products from those made or sold by others. 2. The major federal statutes protecting trademarks and related property are the Lanham Act of 1946 and the Federal Trademark Dilution Act of 1995. Generally, to be protected, a trademark must be sufficiently distinctive from all competing trademarks. 3. *Trademark infringement* occurs when one party uses a mark that is the same as, or confusingly similar to, the protected trademark, service mark, trade name, or trade dress of another party without permission when marketing goods or services.
Patents	1. A *patent* is a grant from the government that gives an inventor the exclusive right to make, use, and sell an invention for a period of twenty years (fourteen years for a design patent) from the date when the application for a patent is filed. To be patentable, an invention (or a discovery, process, or design) must be genuine, novel, useful, and not obvious in light of current technology. Computer software may be patented. 2. Almost anything is patentable, except the laws of nature, natural phenomena, and abstract ideas (including algorithms). Even artistic methods and works of art, certain business processes, and the structures of storylines may be patentable. 3. *Patent infringement* occurs when someone uses or sells another's patented design, product, or process without the patent owner's permission. The patent holder can sue the infringer in federal court and request an injunction, but must prove irreparable injury to obtain a permanent injunction against the infringer. The patent holder can also request damages and attorneys' fees. If the infringement was willful, the court can grant treble damages.
Copyrights	1. A *copyright* is an intangible property right granted by federal statute to the author or originator of certain literary or artistic productions. The Copyright Act of 1976, as amended, governs copyrights. 2. *Copyright infringement* occurs whenever the form or expression of an idea is copied without the permission of the copyright holder. An exception applies if the copying is deemed a "fair use." 3. In 1980, Congress passed the Computer Software Copyright Act, which amended the Copyright Act to include computer programs in the list of creative works protected by federal copyright law.
Trade Secrets	*Trade secrets* include customer lists, plans, research and development, and pricing information. Trade secrets are protected under the common law and, in most states, under statutory law against misappropriation by competitors. The Economic Espionage Act made the theft of trade secrets a federal crime.
International Protections	Various international agreements provide international protection for intellectual property. A landmark agreement is the Trade-Related Aspects of Intellectual Property Rights (TRIPS) agreement, which provides for enforcement procedures in all countries signatory to the agreement.

Issue Spotters

1. Roslyn, a food buyer for Organic Cornucopia Food Company, decides to go into business for herself as Roslyn's Kitchen. She contacts Organic's suppliers, offering to buy their entire harvest for the next year. She also contacts Organic's customers, offering to sell her products for less than Organic. Has Roslyn violated any of the intellectual property rights discussed in this chapter? Explain. (See *Trade Secrets*.)

2. Global Products develops, patents, and markets software. World Copies, Inc., sells Global's software without the maker's permission. Is this patent infringement? If so, how might Global save the cost of suing World for infringement and at the same time profit from World's sales? (See *Patents*.)

—**Check your answers to the *Issue Spotters* against the answers provided in Appendix D at the end of this text.**

Learning Objectives Check

1. What is intellectual property?
2. Why is the protection of trademarks important?
3. How does the law protect patents?
4. What laws protect authors' rights in the works they create?
5. What are trade secrets, and what laws offer protection for this form of intellectual property?

—**Answers to the even-numbered *Learning Objectives Check* questions can be found in Appendix E at the end of this text.**

Business Scenarios and Case Problems

6–1. Patent Infringement. John and Andrew Doney invented a hard-bearing device for balancing rotors. Although they obtained a patent for their invention from the U.S. Patent and Trademark Office, it was never used as an automobile wheel balancer. Some time later, Exetron Corp. produced an automobile wheel balancer that used a hard-bearing device similar to the Doneys' device. Given that the Doneys had not used their device for automobile wheel balancing, does Exetron's use of a similar device infringe on the Doneys' patent? (See *Patents*.)

6–2. Fair Use. Professor Wise is teaching a summer seminar in business torts at State University. Several times during the course, he makes copies of relevant sections from business law texts and distributes them to his students. Wise does not realize that the daughter of one of the textbook authors is a member of his seminar. She tells her father about Wise's copying activities, which have taken place without her father's or his publisher's permission. Her father sues Wise for copyright infringement. Wise claims protection under the fair use doctrine. Who will prevail? Explain. (See *Copyrights*.)

6–3. Licensing. Redwin Wilchcombe composed, performed, and recorded a song called *Tha Weedman* at the request of Lil Jon, a member of Lil Jon & the East Side Boyz (LJESB), for LJESB's album *Kings of Crunk*. Wilchcombe was not paid, but was given credit on the album as a producer. After the album had sold two million copies, Wilchcombe filed a suit against LJESB, alleging copyright infringement. The defendants claimed that they had a license to use the song. Do the facts support this claim? Explain. [*Wilchcombe v. TeeVee Toons, Inc.*, 555 F.3d 949 (11th Cir. 2009)] (See *Copyrights*.)

6–4. Spotlight on Macy's—Copyright Infringement. United Fabrics International, Inc., bought a fabric design from an Italian designer and registered a copyright to the design with the U.S. Copyright Office. When Macy's, Inc., began selling garments with a similar design, United filed a copyright infringement suit against Macy's. Macy's argued that United did not own a valid copyright to the design and so could not claim infringement. Does United have to prove that the copyright is valid to establish infringement? Explain. [*United Fabrics International, Inc. v. C & J Wear, Inc.*, 630 F.3d 1255 (9th Cir. 2011)] (See *Copyrights*.)

6–5. Copyright Infringement. SilverEdge Systems Software hired Catherine Conrad to perform a singing telegram. SilverEdge arranged for James Bendewald to record Conrad's performance of her copyrighted song to post on the company's Web site. Conrad agreed to wear a microphone to assist in the recording, told Bendewald what to film, and asked for an additional fee only if SilverEdge used the video for a commercial purpose. Later, the company chose to post a video of a different performer's singing telegram instead. Conrad filed a suit in a federal district court against SilverEdge and Bendewald for copyright infringement. Are the defendants liable? Explain. [*Conrad v. Bendewald*, 2013 WL 310194 (7th Cir. 2013)] (See *Copyrights*.)

6–6. Business Case Problem with Sample Answer—Patents.

The U.S. Patent and Trademark Office (PTO) denied Raymond Gianelli's application for a patent for a "Rowing Machine"—an exercise machine on which a user *pulls* on handles to perform a rowing motion against a selected resistance. The PTO considered the device obvious in light of a previously patented "Chest Press Apparatus for Exercising Regions of the Upper Body"—an exercise machine on which a user *pushes* on handles to overcome a selected resistance. On what ground might this result be reversed on appeal? Discuss. [*In re Gianelli*, 739 F.3d 1375 (Fed. Cir. 2014)] (See *Patents*.)

—For a sample answer to Problem 6–6, go to Appendix F at the end of this text.

6–7. Patents.
Rodney Klassen was employed by the U.S. Department of Agriculture (USDA). Without the USDA's authorization, Klassen gave Jim Ludy, a grape grower, plant material for two unreleased varieties of grapes. For almost two years, most of Ludy's plantings bore no usable fruit, none of the grapes were sold, and no plant material was given to any other person. The plantings were visible from publicly accessible roads, but none of the vines were labeled, and the variety could not be identified by simply viewing the vines. Under patent law, an applicant may not obtain a patent for an invention that is in public use more than one year before the date of the application. Could the USDA successfully apply for patents on the two varieties given to Ludy? Explain. [*Delano Farms Co. v. California Table Grape Commission*, __ F.3d __, 2015 WL 127317 (Fed.Cir. 2015)] (See *Patents*.)

6–8. A Question of Ethics—Copyright Infringement.
Custom Copies, Inc., prepares and sells coursepacks, which contain compilations of readings for college courses. A teacher selects the readings and delivers a syllabus to the copy shop, which obtains the materials from a library, copies them, and binds the copies. Blackwell Publishing, Inc., which owns the copyright to some of the materials, filed a suit, alleging copyright infringement. [*Blackwell Publishing, Inc. v. Custom Copies, Inc.*, 2006 WL 1529503 (N.D.Fla. 2006)] (See *Copyrights*.)

1. Custom Copies argued, in part, that it did not "distribute" the coursepacks. Does a copy shop violate copyright law if it only copies materials for coursepacks? Does the fair use doctrine apply in these circumstances? Discuss.

2. What is the potential impact if copies of a book or journal are created and sold without the permission of, and the payment of royalties or a fee to, the copyright owner? Explain.

Critical Thinking and Writing Assignments

6–9. Case Analysis Question—Copyright Infringement.
Go to Appendix G at the end of this text and examine the excerpt of Case No. 1, *Winstead v. Jackson*. Review and then brief the case, making sure that your brief answers the following questions. (See *Copyrights*.)

1. **Issue:** This case focused on an allegation of copyright infringement involving what parties and which creative works?

2. **Rule of Law:** What is the test for determining whether a creative work infringes the copyright of another work?

3. **Applying the Rule of Law:** How did the court determine whether the claim of copyright infringement was supported in this case?

4. **Conclusion:** Was the defendant liable for copyright infringement? Why or why not?

6–10. Business Law Critical Thinking Group Assignment.
After years of research, your company has developed a product that might revolutionize the green (environmentally conscious) building industry. The product is made from relatively inexpensive and widely available materials combined in a unique way that can substantially lower the heating and cooling costs of residential and commercial buildings. The company has registered the trademark it intends to use for the product and has filed a patent application with the U.S. Patent and Trademark Office. (See *Patents*.)

1. One group should provide three reasons why this product does or does not qualify for patent protection.

2. Another group should develop a four-step plan for how the company can best protect its intellectual property rights (trademark, trade secret, and patent) and prevent domestic and foreign competitors from producing counterfeit goods or cheap knockoffs.

3. Another group should list and explain three ways in which the company can utilize licensing.

7

iStockPhoto.com/temizyurek

CHAPTER OUTLINE

LEARNING OBJECTIVES

The five Learning Objectives *below are designed to help improve your understanding of the chapter. After reading this chapter, you should be able to answer the following questions:*

1. What is cybersquatting, and when is it illegal?

2. What steps have been taken to protect intellectual property rights in the digital age?

3. When does the law protect a person's electronic communications from being intercepted or accessed?

4. What law governs whether Internet service providers are liable for online defamatory statements made by users?

5. How do online retailers track their users' Web browsing activities?

Internet Law, Social Media, and Privacy

The Internet has changed our lives and our laws. Technology has put the world at our fingertips and now allows even the smallest business to reach customers around the globe. Because the Internet allows the world to "pass around notes" so quickly, as Jon Stewart joked in the chapter-opening quotation, it presents a variety of challenges for the law.

Courts are often in uncharted waters when deciding disputes that involve the Internet, social media, and online privacy. There may not be any common law precedents for judges to rely on when resolving cases. Long-standing principles of justice may be inapplicable. New rules are evolving, as we discuss in this chapter, but often not as quickly as technology.

> "The Internet is just the world passing around notes in a classroom."
>
> **JON STEWART**
> 1962–PRESENT
> (AMERICAN COMEDIAN AND FORMER HOST OF *THE DAILY SHOW*)

7-1 Internet Law

A number of laws specifically address issues that arise only on the Internet. These issues include unsolicited e-mail, domain names, cybersquatting, and meta tags, as we discuss here. We also discuss how the law is dealing with problems of trademark infringement and dilution online as well as licensing.

7-1a Spam

Businesses and individuals alike are targets of **spam.**[1] Spam is the unsolicited "junk e-mail" that floods virtual mailboxes with advertisements, solicitations, and similar communications. Considered relatively harmless in the early days of the Internet, spam has become a serious problem. By 2016, it accounted for roughly 75 percent of all e-mails.

Spam Bulk, unsolicited (junk) e-mail.

State Regulation of Spam In an attempt to combat spam, thirty-seven states have enacted laws that prohibit or regulate its use. Many state laws that regulate spam require the senders of e-mail ads to instruct the recipients on how they can "opt out" of further e-mail ads from the same sources. For instance, in some states, an unsolicited e-mail must include a toll-free phone number or return e-mail address that the recipient can use to ask the sender not to send unsolicited e-mails.

The Federal CAN-SPAM Act In 2003, Congress enacted the Controlling the Assault of Non-Solicited Pornography and Marketing (CAN-SPAM) Act.[2] The legislation applies to any "commercial electronic mail messages" that are sent to promote a commercial product or service. Significantly, the statute preempts state antispam laws except those provisions in state laws that prohibit false and deceptive e-mailing practices.

Generally, the act permits the sending of unsolicited commercial e-mail but prohibits certain types of spamming activities. Prohibited activities include the use of a false return address and the use of false, misleading, or deceptive information when sending e-mail. The statute also prohibits the use of "dictionary attacks"—sending messages to randomly generated e-mail addresses—and the "harvesting" of e-mail addresses from Web sites through the use of specialized software.

EXAMPLE 7.1 Federal officials arrested Robert Alan Soloway, considered to be one of the world's most prolific spammers. Soloway, known as the "Spam King," had been using *botnets* (automated spamming networks) to send out hundreds of millions of unwanted e-mails. In 2008, Soloway pleaded guilty to mail fraud, spam, and failure to pay taxes. ■

Arresting prolific spammers, however, has done little to curb spam, which continues to flow at a rate of 70 billion messages per day. In other words, the federal CAN-SPAM act has not successfully reduced the amount of spam.

Feng Yu/ShutterStock.com

Have state and federal laws against spam reduced its use?

The U.S. Safe Web Act The CAN-SPAM Act prohibited false and deceptive e-mails originating in the United States. After that, spamming from servers located in other nations increased. These cross-border spammers generally were able to escape detection and legal sanctions because the Federal Trade Commission (FTC) lacked the authority to investigate foreign spamming.

Congress sought to rectify the situation by enacting the U.S. Safe Web Act (also known as the Undertaking Spam, Spyware, and Fraud Enforcement with Enforcers Beyond Borders Act).[3] The act allows the FTC to cooperate and share information with foreign agencies in investigating and prosecuting those involved in spamming, spyware, and various Internet frauds and deceptions.

---

1. The term *spam* is said to come from the lyrics of a Monty Python song that repeats the word *spam* over and over.
2. 15 U.S.C. Sections 7701 *et seq.*
3. Pub. L. No. 109-455, 120 Stat. 3372 (2006), codified in various sections of 15 U.S.C. and 12 U.S.C. Section 3412.

Internet Service Provider (ISP) A business or organization that offers users access to the Internet and related services.

The Safe Web Act also provides a "safe harbor" for **Internet service providers (ISPs)**—organizations that provide access to the Internet. The safe harbor gives ISPs immunity from liability for supplying information to the FTC concerning possible unfair or deceptive conduct in foreign jurisdictions.

7–1b Domain Names

As e-commerce expanded worldwide, one issue that emerged involved the rights of a trademark owner to use the mark as part of a domain name. A **domain name** is part of an Internet address, such as "cengage.com."

Domain Name The series of letters and symbols used to identify a site operator on the Internet; an Internet "address."

Structure of Domain Names
Every domain name ends with a top-level domain (TLD), which is the part of the name to the right of the period. This part of the name often indicates the type of entity that operates the site. For instance, com is an abbreviation for commercial, and edu is short for education.

Goodwill In the business context, the valuable reputation of a business viewed as an intangible asset.

The second-level domain (SLD)—the part of the name to the left of the period—is chosen by the business entity or individual registering the domain name. Competition for SLDs among firms with similar names and products has led to numerous disputes. By using an identical or similar domain name, one company may attempt to profit from a competitor's **goodwill** (the nontangible value of a business).

> "Almost overnight, the Internet's gone from a technical wonder to a business must."
>
> **BILL SCHRADER**
> 1953–PRESENT
> (INTERNET PIONEER AND CO-FOUNDER OF THE FIRST COMMERCIAL INTERNET SERVICE PROVIDER)

Domain Name Distribution System
The Internet Corporation for Assigned Names and Numbers (ICANN), a nonprofit corporation, oversees the distribution of domain names and operates an online arbitration system. Due to numerous complaints, ICANN recently overhauled the domain name distribution system.

In 2012, ICANN started selling new *generic top-level domain names (gTLDs)* for an initial price of $185,000 plus an annual fee of $25,000. Whereas TLDs were limited to only a few terms (including com, net, and org), gTLDs can take any form. By 2016, many companies and corporations had acquired gTLDs based on their brands, such as aol, bmw, target, and walmart. Some companies have numerous gTLDs. Google's gTLDs, for instance, include android, chrome, gmail, goog, and YouTube.

Because gTLDs have greatly increased the potential number of domain names, domain name registrars have proliferated. Registrar companies charge a fee to businesses and individuals to register new names and to renew annual registrations (often through automated software). Many of these companies also buy and sell expired domain names.

7–1c Cybersquatting

LEARNING OBJECTIVE 1
What is cybersquatting, and when is it illegal?

One of the goals of the new gTLD system was to alleviate the problem of cybersquatting. **Cybersquatting** occurs when a party registers a domain name that is the same as, or confusingly similar to, the trademark of another and then offers to sell the domain name back to the trademark owner.

CASE EXAMPLE 7.2 Apple, Inc., has repeatedly sued cybersquatters that registered domain names similar to the names of its products, such as iphone4s.com and ipods.com. In 2012, Apple won a judgment in litigation at the World Intellectual Property Organization (WIPO) against a company that was squatting on the domain name iPhone5.com.[4] ■

Cybersquatting The act of registering a domain name that is the same as, or confusingly similar to, the trademark of another and then offering to sell that domain name back to the trademark owner.

Anticybersquatting Legislation
Because cybersquatting has led to so much litigation, Congress enacted the Anticybersquatting Consumer Protection Act (ACPA) in 1999.[5] The act amended the Lanham Act—the federal law protecting trademarks. The ACPA makes cybersquatting illegal when both of the following are true:

---

4. WIPO Case No. D2012-0951.
5. 15 U.S.C. Section 1129.

1. The domain name is identical or confusingly similar to the trademark of another.
2. The one registering, trafficking in, or using the domain name has a "bad faith intent" to profit from that trademark.

Despite the ACPA, cybersquatting continues to present a problem for businesses as the Internet continues to evolve.

Cybersquatting and the Domain Name Distribution System

As mentioned, domain name registrars are in the business of registering new domain names and renewing registrations. All registrars are supposed to relay information about these transactions to ICANN and other companies that keep a master list of domain names, but this does not always occur. The speed at which domain names change hands and the difficulty in tracking mass automated registrations have created an environment in which cybersquatting can flourish.

CASE EXAMPLE 7.3 OnNet USA, Inc., owns the English-language rights to 9Dragons, a game with a martial arts theme, and operates a Web site for its promotion. When a party known as "Warv0x" began to operate a pirated version of the game at Play9D.com, OnNet filed an action under the ACPA in a federal court. OnNet was unable to obtain contact information for the owner of Play9D.com through its Australian domain name registrar, however, and thus could not complete service of process. The federal court allowed OnNet to serve the defendant by publishing a notice of the suit in a newspaper in Gold Coast, Australia.[6] ■

Typosquatting

A relatively new form of cybersquatting is **typosquatting,** or registering a name that is a misspelling of a popular brand name, such as googl.com or appple.com. Because many Internet users are not perfect typists, Web pages using these misspelled names may receive a lot of traffic. More traffic generally means increased profit (advertisers often pay Web sites based on the number of unique visits, or hits).

Typosquatters may sometimes fall beyond the reach of the ACPA. If the misspelling that they use is significant, the trademark owner may have difficulty proving that the name is identical or confusingly similar to the trademark of another, as the ACPA requires.

Typosquatting adds costs for businesses seeking to protect their domain name rights. Companies must attempt to register not only legitimate variations of their domain names but also potential misspellings. Large corporations may have to register thousands of domain names across the globe just to protect their basic brands and trademarks.

Applicability and Sanctions of the ACPA

The ACPA applies to all domain name registrations of trademarks. Successful plaintiffs in suits brought under the act can collect actual damages and profits, or they can elect to receive statutory damages ranging from $1,000 to $100,000.

Although some companies have been successful suing under the ACPA, there are roadblocks to pursuing such lawsuits. Some domain name registrars offer privacy services that hide the true owners of Web sites, making it difficult for trademark owners to identify cybersquatters. Thus, before bringing a suit, a trademark owner has to ask the court for a subpoena to discover the identity of the owner of the infringing Web site. Because of the high costs of court proceedings, discovery, and even arbitration, many disputes over cybersquatting are settled out of court.

To facilitate dispute resolution, ICANN now offers the Uniform Rapid Suspension (URS) system. URS allows trademark holders with clear-cut infringement claims to obtain rapid relief. **EXAMPLE 7.4** In the first dispute filed involving gTLDs, IBM filed a complaint with URS against an individual who registered the domain names IBM.guru and IBM.ventures in February 2014. A week later, the URS panel decided in IBM's favor and suspended the two domain names. ■

"National borders aren't even speed bumps on the information superhighway."

TIMOTHY C. MAY
1962–PRESENT
(ENGINEER AND TECHNICAL AND POLITICAL WRITER)

Typosquatting A form of cybersquatting that relies on mistakes, such as typographical errors, made by Internet users when inputting information into a Web browser.

---

6. *OnNet USA, Inc. v. Play9D.com*, 2013 WL 120319 (N.D.Cal. 2013).

7–1d **Meta Tags**

As noted in Chapter 2, *meta tags* are key words that give Internet browsers specific information about a Web page. Meta tags can be used to increase the likelihood that a site will be included in search engine results, even if the site has nothing to do with the key words. Using this technique, one site can appropriate the key words of other sites with more frequent hits so that the appropriating site will appear in the same search engine results as the more popular sites.

Using another's trademark in a meta tag without the owner's permission normally constitutes trademark infringement. Some uses of another's trademark as a meta tag may be permissible, however, if the use is reasonably necessary and does not suggest that the owner authorized or sponsored the use. **CASE EXAMPLE 7.5** Farzad and Lisa Tabari are auto brokers—the personal shoppers of the automotive world. They contact authorized dealers, solicit bids, and arrange for customers to buy from the dealer offering the best combination of location, availability, and price. The Tabaris offered this service at the Web sites buy-a-lexus.com and buyorleaselexus.com.

Toyota Motor Sales U.S.A., Inc., the exclusive distributor of Lexus vehicles and the owner of the Lexus mark, objected to the Tabaris' use of the Lexus trademark. The Tabaris removed Toyota's photographs and logo from their site and added a disclaimer in large type at the top, but they refused to give up their domain names. Toyota sued for infringement. The court forced the Tabaris to stop using any "domain name, service mark, trademark, trade name, meta tag or other commercial indication of origin that includes the mark LEXUS."[7] ■

7–1e **Trademark Dilution in the Online World**

As previously explained, trademark *dilution* occurs when a trademark is used, without authorization, in a way that diminishes the distinctive quality of the mark. Unlike trademark infringement, a claim of dilution does not require proof that consumers are likely to be confused by a connection between the unauthorized use and the mark. For this reason, the products involved need not be similar, as the following *Spotlight Case* illustrates.

---

7. *Toyota Motor Sales, U.S.A., Inc. v. Tabari*, 610 F.3d 1171 (9th Cir. 2010).

SPOTLIGHT ON INTERNET PORN: CASE 7.1

Hasbro, Inc. v. Internet Entertainment Group, Ltd.

United States District Court, Western District of Washington, 1996 WL 84853 (1996).

FACTS Hasbro, Inc., the maker of Candy Land, a children's board game, owns the Candy Land trademark. The defendants, Brian Cartmell and the Internet Entertainment Group, Ltd., used candyland .com as a domain name for a sexually explicit Internet site. Any person who performed an online search for "candyland" was directed to this adult Web site. Hasbro filed a trademark dilution claim in a federal court, seeking a permanent injunction to prevent the defendants from using the CANDYLAND trademark.

Candy Land is a children's board game. Why did its parent company, Hasbro, Inc., sue a Web site?

ISSUE Did the defendants' use of the word *candyland* in connection with a sexually explicit Web site violate Hasbro's trademark rights?

DECISION Yes. The district court granted Hasbro a permanent injunction and ordered the defendants to remove all content from the candyland. com Web site and to stop using the CANDYLAND mark.

REASON The court reasoned that Hasbro had shown that the defendants' use of the CANDYLAND mark and the domain name candyland.com in connection with their Internet site was causing irreparable injury to Hasbro. As required to obtain an injunction, Hasbro had demonstrated a likelihood of prevailing on its claims that the defendants' conduct violated both the federal and the Washington State statutes against trademark dilution. "The probable harm to Hasbro from defendants' conduct outweighs any inconvenience that defendants will experience if they are required to stop using the CANDYLAND name."

WHY IS THIS CASE IMPORTANT? *This was the first case alleging dilution on the Web. The court precluded the use of candyland.com as a URL for an adult site, even though consumers were not likely to confuse an adult Web site with a children's board game.*

7–1f Licensing

Recall that a company may permit another party to use a trademark (or other intellectual property) under a license. A licensor might grant a license allowing its trademark to be used as part of a domain name, for instance.

Another type of license involves the use of a product such as software. This sort of licensing is ubiquitous in the online world. When you download an application on your smartphone, tablet, or other mobile device, for instance, you are typically entering into a license agreement. You are obtaining only a *license* to use the software and not ownership rights in it. Apps published on Google Play, for instance, may use its licensing service to prompt users to agree to a license at the time of installation and use.

Licensing agreements frequently include restrictions that prohibit licensees from sharing the file and using it to create similar software applications. The license may also limit the use of the application to a specific device or give permission to the user for a certain time period.

7–2 Copyrights in Digital Information

Copyright law is probably the most important form of intellectual property protection on the Internet. This is because much of the material on the Internet (including software and database information) is copyrighted, and in order for that material to be transferred online, it must be "copied." Generally, whenever a party downloads software, movies, or music into a computer's random access memory, or RAM, without authorization, a copyright is infringed.

In 1998, Congress passed additional legislation to protect copyright holders—the Digital Millennium Copyright Act (DMCA).[8] Because of its significance in protecting against the piracy of copyrighted materials in the online environment, this act is presented as this chapter's *Landmark in the Law* feature.

LEARNING OBJECTIVE 2
What steps have been taken to protect intellectual property rights in the digital age?

7–2a Copyright Infringement

Technology has vastly increased the potential for copyright infringement. **CASE EXAMPLE 7.6** In one case, a rap song that was included in the sound track of a movie had used a few seconds from the guitar solo of another's copyrighted sound recording without permission. Nevertheless, a federal court held that digitally sampling a copyrighted sound recording of any length constitutes copyright infringement.[9] ■

Federal courts have not consistently found that digital sampling is always illegal. Some courts have allowed the defense of fair use, while others have not. **EXAMPLE 7.7** Hip hop stars

"The Internet is the world's largest library. It's just that all the books are on the floor."

JOHN ALLEN PAULOS
1945–PRESENT
(AMERICAN MATHEMATICS PROFESSOR)

---

8. 17 U.S.C. Sections 512, 1201–1205, 1301–1332; and 28 U.S.C. Section 4001.
9. *Bridgeport Music, Inc. v. Dimension Films*, 410 F.3d 792 (6th Cir. 2005).

LANDMARK IN THE LAW

The Digital Millennium Copyright Act

The United States leads the world in the production of creative products, including books, films, videos, recordings, and software. Exports of U.S. creative products surpass those of every other U.S. industry in value.

Given the importance of intellectual property to the U.S. economy, the United States has actively supported international efforts to protect ownership rights in intellectual property, including copyrights. In 1996, to curb unauthorized copying of copyrighted materials, the member nations of the World Intellectual Property Organization (WIPO) adopted a treaty to upgrade global standards of copyright protection, particularly for the Internet.

IMPLEMENTING THE WIPO TREATY Congress implemented the provisions of the WIPO treaty by enacting a new statute to update U.S. copyright law in 1998. The law—the Digital Millennium Copyright Act (DMCA)—is a landmark step in the protection of copyright owners. Because of the leading position of the United States in the creative industries, the law also serves as a model for other nations. Among other things, the DMCA established civil and criminal penalties for anyone who circumvents (bypasses) encryption software or other technological antipiracy protection. Also prohibited are the manufacture, import, sale, and distribution of devices or services for circumvention.

The act provides for exceptions to fit the needs of libraries, scientists, universities, and others. In general, the law does not restrict the "fair use" of circumvention methods for educational and other noncommercial purposes. For instance, circumvention is allowed to test computer security, conduct encryption research, protect personal privacy, and enable parents to monitor their children's use of the Internet. The exceptions are to be reconsidered every three years.

LIMITING THE LIABILITY OF INTERNET SERVICE PROVIDERS The DMCA also limited the liability of Internet service providers (ISPs). Under the act, an ISP is not liable for any copyright infringement by its customer *unless* the ISP is aware of the subscriber's violation. An ISP may be held liable only if it fails to take action to shut the subscriber down after learning of the violation. A copyright holder has to act promptly, however, by pursuing a claim in court, or the subscriber has the right to be restored to online access.

APPLICATION TO TODAY'S WORLD *Without the DMCA, copyright owners would have a more difficult time obtaining legal redress against those who, without authorization, decrypt or copy copyrighted materials. Nevertheless, problems remain, particularly because of the global nature of the Internet.*

> "We're into a whole new world with the Internet, and whenever we sort of cross another plateau in our development, there are those who seek to take advantage of it. So this is a replay of things that have happened throughout our history."

BILL CLINTON
1946–PRESENT
(FORTY-SECOND PRESIDENT
OF THE UNITED STATES)

Peer-to-Peer (P2P) Networking
The sharing of resources (such as files, hard drives, and processing styles) among multiple computers without the requirement of a central network server.

Jay-Z and Kanye West were sued for digitally sampling music by soul musician Syl Johnson. Given the uncertain outcome of the litigation, they ended up settling the suit in 2012 for an undisclosed amount. ■

Initially, criminal penalties for copyright violations could be imposed only if unauthorized copies were exchanged for financial gain. Yet much piracy of copyrighted materials online was "altruistic" in nature—unauthorized copies were made simply to be shared with others. Then, Congress amended the law and extended criminal liability for the piracy of copyrighted materials to persons who exchange unauthorized copies of copyrighted works without realizing a profit.

What happens if "sharing" involves posting hacked information? See this chapter's *Adapting the Law to the Online Environment* feature to find out what happened when hackers accessed e-mail at Sony Pictures and made damaging information available to the public.

7-2b MP3 and File-Sharing Technology

Soon after the Internet became popular, a few enterprising programmers created software to compress large data files, particularly those associated with music. The best-known compression and decompression system is MP3, which enables music fans to download songs or entire CDs onto their computers or onto portable listening devices, such as smartphones. The MP3 system also made it possible for music fans to access other fans' files by engaging in file-sharing via the Internet.

Methods of File-Sharing File-sharing is accomplished through **peer-to-peer (P2P) networking.** The concept is simple. Rather than going through a central Web server, P2P networking

ADAPTING THE LAW TO THE ONLINE ENVIRONMENT

E-Mail Hacking at Sony Pictures— Can You Put the Cat Back into the Bag?

Sony Pictures was ready to release *The Interview* on Christmas Day, 2014. The comedy described a bogus CIA attempt to assassinate North Korea's dictator, Kim Jong-Un. In late November, hackers entered Sony's internal e-mail system and released 32,000 hacked documents in an apparent attempt to block release of the film.

A Company's Worst Nightmare Comes True

Had the hacked e-mails only concerned corporate decision making, nothing much would have come of the event. Many of the e-mails, though, were quite damaging to Sony's image. In particular, there were spiteful comments from corporate executives about famous stars, such as Angelina Jolie. A high-level executive was revealed to be mocking President Barack Obama. In brief, the hacked e-mails, which were revealed by the press, were embarrassing to Sony management, to say the least.

Sony Reacts, but Perhaps in Vain

Sony went on the offensive against major news organizations. Through its lawyer, it sent letters to the *New York Times* and other publications characterizing the hacked e-mails as "stolen information" and demanding that they be destroyed. Sony warned news media outlets that it did "not consent to [their] possession, review, copying,

When Sony Pictures was about to release a comedy, The Interview, *based on an attempt to assassinate North Korea's leader, that country purportedly hacked into the company's e-mail accounts. Can Sony prohibit news media from publishing those e-mails?*

dissemination, publication, uploading, download, or making any use" of the information.

Can Sony Successfully Sue Those Who Publish Hacked Sony Documents?

There is relatively little precedent concerning the ability to sue news media for publication of readily available hacked e-mails. Two cases have some precedential value, though. One involved copied documents taken from a U.S. senator's office. The copies were sent to investigative reporters, who then published articles based on the documents. The senator sued, claiming invasion of privacy and the use of stolen property (conversion). The D.C. Circuit Court of Appeals rejected the theories.[a]

In another case, a radio commentator replayed an illegally intercepted recording of a private conversation. That case went to the Supreme Court, which rejected the plaintiff's argument that the playing of the recording violated a federal statute that made both the interception and the use of such conversations illegal. The Court argued that playing the illegally intercepted conversation was constitutionally protected because the broadcaster was not involved in the illegal interception and the communication was "a matter of public concern."[b]

If Sony Pictures ultimately sues news media organizations, such as the *New York Times,* for continuing to reveal the contents of hacked e-mails, Sony will probably not prevail. Of the hacked e-mails that were publicly revealed, none disclosed facts about individuals that were highly private. Thus, their publication is not actionable as a tort (the disclosure of private facts).

CRITICAL THINKING

- Sony revealed that the script for a new James Bond movie had been hacked and leaked. Could a news publication legally print or post online that entire script? Why or why not?

---

a. *Pearson v. Dodd,* 410 F.2d 701 (D.C. Cir. 1969).

b. *Bartnicki v. Vopper,* 532 U.S. 514, 121 S.Ct. 1753, 149 L.Ed.2d 787 (2001).

---

uses numerous personal computers (PCs) that are connected to the Internet. Individuals on the same network can access files stored on one another's PCs through a **distributed network.** Parts of the network may be distributed all over the country or the world, which offers an unlimited number of uses. Persons scattered throughout the country or the world can work together on the same project by using file-sharing programs.

A newer method of sharing files via the Internet is **cloud computing,** which is essentially a subscription-based or pay-per-use service that extends a computer's software or storage capabilities. Cloud computing can deliver a single application through a browser to multiple users. Alternatively, cloud computing might be a utility program to pool resources and

Distributed Network
A network that can be used by persons located (distributed) around the country or the globe to share computer files.

Cloud Computing The delivery to users of on-demand services from third-party servers over a network.

As more individuals and companies store their data on "the cloud," what security issues might arise?

provide data storage and virtual servers that can be accessed on demand. Amazon, Facebook, Google, IBM, and Sun Microsystems are using and developing more cloud computing services.

Sharing Stored Music Files   When file-sharing is used to download others' stored music files, copyright issues arise. **CASE EXAMPLE 7.8**   The issue of file-sharing infringement has been the subject of an ongoing debate since the highly publicized cases against two companies (Napster, Inc., and Grokster, Ltd.) that created software used for copyright infringement. In the first case, Napster operated a Web site with free software that enabled users to copy and transfer MP3 files. Firms in the recording industry sued Napster. Ultimately, the court held that Napster was liable for contributory and vicarious (indirect) copyright infringement.

As technology evolved, Grokster, Ltd., and several other companies created and distributed new types of file-sharing software. This software did not maintain a central index of content, but allowed P2P network users to share stored music files. The court held that because the companies distributed file-sharing software "with the object of promoting its use to infringe the copyright," they were liable for the resulting acts of infringement by the software's users.[10] ■

It is not difficult to understand why recording artists and their labels are concerned about file-sharing. They stand to lose large amounts of royalties and revenues if relatively few digital downloads or CDs are purchased and then made available on distributed networks. These concerns have prompted recording companies to pursue not only companies involved in file-sharing but also individuals who have file-shared copyrighted works.

CASE EXAMPLE 7.9   Maverick Recording Company and other recording companies sued Whitney Harper in federal court for copyright infringement. Harper had used a file-sharing program to download a number of copyrighted songs from the Internet and had then shared the audio files with others via a P2P network. The plaintiffs sought $750 per infringed work—the minimum amount of statutory damages available under the Copyright Act.

Harper claimed that she was an "innocent" infringer because she was unaware that her actions constituted copyright infringement. Under the act, innocent infringement can result in a reduced penalty. The court, however, noted that a copyright notice appeared on all the songs that Harper had downloaded. She therefore could not assert the innocent infringer defense, and the court ordered her to pay damages of $750 per infringed work.[11] ■

DVDs and File-Sharing   File-sharing also creates problems for the motion picture industry, which loses significant amounts of revenue annually as a result of pirated DVDs. Numerous Web sites offer software that facilitates the illegal copying of movies. An example is BitTorrent, which enables users to download high-quality files from the Internet.

CASE EXAMPLE 7.10   TorrentSpy, a popular BitTorrent indexing Web site, enabled users to locate and exchange files. The Motion Picture Association of America (MPAA) and Columbia Pictures, Inc., brought a lawsuit against the operators of TorrentSpy for facilitating copyright infringement. The MPAA also claimed that the operators had destroyed evidence that would reveal the identity of individual infringers. The operators had ignored a court order to keep server logs of the Internet addresses of people who had facilitated the trading of files via the site. Because TorrentSpy's operators had willfully destroyed evidence, a federal court found in favor of the MPAA and ordered the defendants to pay a judgment of $111 million.[12] ■

---

10. *A&M Records, Inc. v. Napster, Inc.,* 239 F.3d 1004 (9th Cir. 2001); and *Metro-Goldwyn-Mayer Studios, Inc. v Grokster, Ltd.,* 545 U.S. 913, 125 S.Ct. 2764, 162 L.Ed.2d 781 (2005). Grokster, Ltd., later settled this dispute out of court and stopped distributing its software.
11. *Maverick Recording Co. v. Harper,* 598 F.3d 193 (5th Cir. 2010).
12. *Columbia Pictures, Inc., v. Bunnell,* 2007 WL 4877701 (C.D.Cal. 2007).

7-3 Social Media

Social media provide a means by which people can create, share, and exchange ideas and comments via the Internet. Social networking sites, such as Facebook, Google+, MySpace, LinkedIn, Pinterest, and Tumblr, have become ubiquitous. Studies show that Internet users spend more time on social networks than at any other sites. The amount of time people spend accessing social networks on their smartphones and other mobile devices has increased every year (by nearly 30 percent in 2015 alone).

EXAMPLE 7.11 Facebook, which was launched in 2004, had more than 1.3 billion active users by 2016. Individuals of all ages use Facebook to maintain social contacts, update friends on events, and distribute images to others. Facebook members often share common interests based on their school, location, or recreational affiliation, such as a sports team. ■

7-3a Uses in the Legal Process

The emergence of Facebook and other social networking sites has affected the legal process in various ways. Here, we explain some uses of social media posts in the litigation process, as well as in the investigations that precede prosecutions or other actions. We also discuss what can happen when employees violate their employers' social media policies.

Impact on Litigation Social media posts now are routinely included in discovery in litigation. Such posts can provide damaging information that establishes a person's intent or what she or he knew at a particular time. Like e-mail, posts on social networks can be the smoking gun that leads to liability.

In some cases, social media posts have been used to reduce damages awards. **EXAMPLE 7.12** Omeisha Daniels sued for injuries she sustained in a car accident. She claimed that her injuries made it impossible for her to continue working as a hairstylist. The jury originally awarded her $237,000, but when the jurors saw Daniels's tweets and photographs of her partying in New Orleans and vacationing on the beach, they reduced the damages to $142,000. ■

Impact on Settlement Agreements Social media posts have been used to invalidate settlement agreements that contained confidentiality clauses. **CASE EXAMPLE 7.13** Patrick Snay was the headmaster of Gulliver Preparatory School in Florida. When Gulliver did not renew Snay's employment contract for 2010–2011, Snay sued the school for age discrimination. During mediation, Snay agreed to settle the case for $80,000 and signed a confidentiality clause that required his wife and he not to disclose the "terms and existence" of the agreement. Nevertheless, Snay and his wife told their daughter, Dana, that the dispute had been settled and that they were happy with the results.

Dana, a college student, had recently graduated from Gulliver and, according to Snay, had suffered retaliation at the school. Dana posted a Facebook comment that said, "Mama and Papa Snay won the case against Gulliver. Gulliver is now officially paying for my vacation to Europe this summer. SUCK IT." The comment went out to 1,200 of Dana's Facebook friends, many of whom were Gulliver students, and school officials soon learned of it. The school immediately notified Snay that he had breached the confidentiality clause and refused to pay the settlement amount. Ultimately, a state intermediate appellate court agreed and held that Snay could not enforce the settlement agreement.[13] ■

Criminal Investigations Law enforcement uses social media to detect and prosecute criminals. A surprising number of criminals boast about their illegal activities on social media. **EXAMPLE 7.13** A nineteen-year-old posts a message on Facebook bragging about how

Social Media Forms of communication through which users create and share information, ideas, messages, and other content via the Internet.

"Twitter is just a multiplayer notepad."

BEN MADDOX
(GLOBAL TECHNOLOGY OFFICER AT NEW YORK UNIVERSITY)

---

13. *Gulliver Schools, Inc. v. Snay*, 137 So.3d 1045 (Fla.App. 2014).

drunk he was on New Year's Eve and apologizing to the owner of the parked car that he hit. The next day, police officers arrest him for drunk driving and leaving the scene of an accident. ■ Police may also use social media to help them to locate a particular suspect or to determine the identity of other suspects within a criminal network.

ETHICAL ISSUE

Should police be able to use fake identities on Facebook? As part of Operation Crew Cut, New York Police Department (NYPD) officers routinely pretend to be young women in order to "friend" suspects on Facebook. Using these false identities, officers are able to bypass the social media site's privacy settings and gain valuable information about illegal activities. This practice is hardly limited to the NYPD. Hundreds of federal, state, and local law enforcement agencies encourage their agents to go undercover in this manner, raising not only legal questions but also ethical questions about respect for users' online privacy—or lack thereof.

Certainly, all major police departments have a long tradition of using deceptive practices that are legal. For example, officers often assume false identities to go undercover. But Facebook's statements of rights and responsibilities, or "community standards," include a provision that claiming to be another person violates Facebook terms. Facebook asks users, including law enforcement officials, to use their authentic identities. Facebook's chief security officer, Joe Sullivan, has argued that police officers' creation of fake Facebook identities threatens Facebook's trust-based social ecosystem. Nevertheless, according to at least one court, it is legally acceptable for law enforcement officers to set up a phony social media account to catch a suspect.[14]

Administrative Agencies

Administrative Agencies Federal regulators also use social media posts in their investigations into illegal activities. **EXAMPLE 7.14** Reed Hastings, the top executive of Netflix, stated on Facebook that Netflix subscribers had watched a billion hours of video the previous month. As a result, Netflix's stock price rose, which prompted a federal agency investigation. Under securities laws, such a statement is considered to be material information to investors. Thus, it must be disclosed to all investors, not just a select group, such as those who had access to Hastings's Facebook post.

The agency ultimately concluded that it could not hold Hastings responsible for any wrongdoing because the agency's policy on social media use was not clear. The agency then issued new guidelines that allow companies to disclose material information through social media if investors have been notified in advance. ■

An administrative law judge can base his or her decision on the content of social media posts. **CASE EXAMPLE 7.15** Jennifer O'Brien was a tenured teacher at a public school in New Jersey when she posted two messages on her Facebook page. "I'm not a teacher—I'm a warden for future criminals!" and "They had a scared straight program in school—why couldn't I bring first graders?" Not surprisingly, outraged parents protested. The deputy superintendent of schools filed a complaint against O'Brien with the state's commissioner of education, charging her with conduct unbecoming a teacher.

After a hearing, an administrative law judge (ALJ) ordered that O'Brien be removed from her teaching position. O'Brien appealed to a state court, claiming that her Facebook postings were protected by the First Amendment and could not be used by the school district to discipline or discharge her. The court found that O'Brien had failed to establish that her Facebook postings were protected speech and that the seriousness of O'Brien's conduct warranted removal from her position.[15] ■

Can a public school teacher be fired for making derogatory comments about students on Facebook?

1000 Words/ShutterStock.com

Employers' Social Media Policies

Employers' Social Media Policies Many large corporations have established specific guidelines on using social media in the workplace. Employees who use social media in a way that violates their employer's stated policies may be disciplined or fired from their jobs. Courts and

---

14. *U.S. v. Gatson*, ___ F.Supp.2d ___, 2014 WL 7182275 (D.N.J. 2014).
15. *In re O'Brien*, 2013 WL 132508.

administrative agencies usually uphold an employer's right to terminate a person based on his or her violation of a social media policy.

CASE EXAMPLE 7.16 Virginia Rodriquez worked for Wal-Mart Stores, Inc., for almost twenty years and had been promoted to management. Then she was disciplined for violating the company's policies by having a fellow employee use Rodriquez's password to alter the price of an item that she purchased. Under Wal-Mart's rules, another violation within a year would mean termination.

Nine months later, on Facebook, Rodriquez publicly chastised employees under her supervision for calling in sick to go to a party. The posting violated Wal-Mart's "Social Media Policy," which was "to avoid public comment that adversely affects employees." Wal-Mart terminated Rodriquez. She filed a lawsuit, alleging discrimination, but the court issued a summary judgment in Wal-Mart's favor.[16] ■ Note, though, that some employees' posts on social media may be protected under labor law.

If a Wal-Mart employee posts a comment on Facebook that casts other employees in a negative light, can that employee be fired?

7–3b The Electronic Communications Privacy Act

The Electronic Communications Privacy Act (ECPA)[17] amended federal wiretapping law to cover electronic forms of communications. Although Congress enacted the ECPA many years before social media networks existed, it nevertheless applies to communications through social media.

The ECPA prohibits the intentional interception of any wire, oral, or electronic communication. It also prohibits the intentional disclosure or use of the information obtained by the interception.

LEARNING OBJECTIVE 3
When does the law protect a person's electronic communications from being intercepted or accessed?

Exclusions Excluded from the ECPA's coverage are any electronic communications through devices that an employer provides for its employee to use "in the ordinary course of its business." Consequently, if a company provides the electronic device (cell phone, laptop, tablet) to the employee for ordinary business use, the company is not prohibited from intercepting business communications made on it. This "business-extension exception" to the ECPA permits employers to monitor employees' electronic communications made in the ordinary course of business. It does not permit employers to monitor employees' personal communications. Another exception allows an employer to avoid liability under the act if the employees consent to having the employer monitor their electronic communications.

Stored Communications Part of the ECPA is known as the Stored Communications Act (SCA).[18] The SCA prohibits intentional and unauthorized access to *stored* electronic communications and sets forth criminal and civil sanctions for violators. A person can violate the SCA by intentionally accessing a stored electronic communication. The SCA also prevents "providers" of communication services (such as cell phone companies and social media networks) from divulging private communications to certain entities and individuals.

CASE EXAMPLE 7.17 Two restaurant employees, Brian Pietrylo and Doreen Marino, were fired after their manager uncovered their password-protected MySpace group. The group's communications, stored on MySpace's Web site, contained sexual remarks about customers and management, as well as comments about illegal drug use and violent behavior. One employee said the group's purpose was to "vent about any BS we deal with out of work without any outside eyes spying on us."

---

16. *Rodriquez v. Wal-Mart Stores, Inc.*, 2013 WL 102674 (N.D.Tex. 2013).
17. 18 U.S.C. Sections 2510–2521.
18. 18 U.S.C. Sections 2701–2711.

Suppose that two employees use a private MySpace account to share sometimes offensive remarks about customers. If their employer, without their permission, gains access to that account, can that employer retaliate against the employees for their social media behavior?

"My favorite thing about the Internet is that you get to go into the private world of real creeps without having to smell them."

PENN JILLETTE
1955–PRESENT
(AMERICAN ILLUSIONIST, COMEDIAN, AND AUTHOR)

The restaurant learned about the private MySpace group when a hostess showed it to a manager who requested access. The hostess was not explicitly threatened with termination but feared she would lose her job if she did not comply.

After they were fired, Pietrylo and Marino filed a lawsuit against the restaurant, claiming that their former employer had gained unauthorized access to their MySpace group communications in violation of the SCA. The court allowed the employees' claim, and the jury awarded them $17,003 in compensatory and punitive damages.[19]

7–3c Protection of Social Media Passwords

In recent years, employees and applicants for jobs or colleges have sometimes been asked to divulge their social media passwords. Employers and schools have sometimes looked at an individual's Facebook or other account to see if it included controversial postings such as racially discriminatory remarks or photos of drug parties. Such postings can have a negative effect on a person's prospects even if they were made years earlier or are taken out of context.

By 2016, about half of the states had enacted legislation to protect individuals from having to disclose their social media passwords. These laws vary. Some states, such as Michigan, prohibit employers from taking adverse action against an employee or job applicant based on what the person has posted online. Michigan's law also applies to e-mail and cloud storage accounts. The federal government is considering legislation that would prohibit employers and schools from demanding passwords to social media accounts.

Legislation will not completely prevent employers and others from taking actions against employees or applicants based on their social network postings, however. For example, management and human resources personnel are unlikely to admit that they based a hiring decision on what they saw on someone's Facebook page. They may not even have to admit to looking at the Facebook page if they use private browsing, which enables people to keep their Web browsing activities confidential. How, then, would a rejected job applicant prove that he or she was rejected because the employer accessed social media postings?

7–3d Company-wide Social Media Networks

Many companies, including Dell, Inc., and Nikon Instruments, form their own internal social media networks. Software companies offer a variety of systems, including Salesforce.com's Chatter, Microsoft's Yammer, and Cisco Systems' WebEx Social. Posts on these internal networks, or *intranets,* are quite different from the typical posts on Facebook, LinkedIn, and Twitter. Employees use them to exchange messages about topics related to their work, such as deals that are closing, new products, production flaws, how a team is solving a problem, and the details of customer orders. Thus, the tone is businesslike.

An important advantage to using an internal system for employee communications is that the company can better protect its trade secrets. The company usually decides which employees can see particular intranet files and which employees will belong to each "social group" within the company. Generally, the company will keep the data in its system on its own secure server.

Internal social media systems also offer additional benefits. They provide real-time information about important issues, such as production glitches, along with information about products, customers, and competitors. Another major benefit is a significant reduction in e-mail. Rather than wasting fellow employees' time on mass e-mailings, workers can post messages or collaborate on presentations via the company's social network.

---

19. *Pietrylo v. Hillstone Restaurant Group*, 2009 WL 3128420 (D.N.J. 2009).

7-4 Online Defamation

Cyber torts are torts that arise from online conduct. One of the most prevalent cyber torts is online defamation. Recall that defamation is wrongfully hurting a person's reputation by communicating false statements about that person to others. Because the Internet enables individuals to communicate with large numbers of people simultaneously (via a blog or tweet, for instance), online defamation is a common problem in today's legal environment.

EXAMPLE 7.18 Singer-songwriter Courtney Love was sued for defamation based on remarks she posted about fashion designer Dawn Simorangkir on Twitter. Love claimed that her statements were opinion (rather than statements of fact, as required) and therefore were not actionable as defamation. Nevertheless, Love ended up paying $430,000 to settle the case out of court. ∎

7-4a Identifying the Author of Online Defamation

An initial issue raised by online defamation is simply discovering who is committing it. In the real world, identifying the author of a defamatory remark generally is an easy matter. Suppose, though, that a business firm has discovered that defamatory statements about its policies and products are being posted in an online forum. Such forums allow anyone—customers, employees, or crackpots—to complain about a firm that they dislike while remaining anonymous.

Therefore, a threshold barrier to anyone who seeks to bring an action for online defamation is discovering the identity of the person who posted the defamatory message. An Internet service provider (ISP) can disclose personal information about its customers only when ordered to do so by a court. Consequently, businesses and individuals are increasingly bringing lawsuits against "John Does" (John Doe, Jane Doe, and the like are fictitious names used in lawsuits when the identity of a party is not known or when a party wishes to conceal his or her name for privacy reasons). Then, using the authority of the courts, the plaintiffs can obtain from the ISPs the identity of the persons responsible for the defamatory messages.

Does requiring an ISP to reveal the identities of its anonymous users violate those users' rights under the First Amendment? That was the question before the court in the case that follows.

Cyber Tort A tort committed via the Internet.

> "In cyberspace, the First Amendment is a local ordinance."
>
> **JOHN PERRY BARLOW**
> 1947–PRESENT
> (AMERICAN POET AND ESSAYIST)

CASE 7.2

Yelp, Inc. v. Hadeed Carpet Cleaning, Inc.

Court of Appeals of Virginia, 62 Va.App. 678, 752 S.E.2d 554 (2014).

FACTS Yelp, Inc., operates a social networking Web site that allows users to post and read reviews on local businesses. The site, which has more than 100 million visitors per month, features about 40 million local reviews. Yelp records and stores the Internet protocol address from which each posting is made.

Seven Yelp users posted negative reviews of Hadeed Carpet Cleaning, Inc., of Alexandria, Virginia. Hadeed brought an action in a Virginia state court against the anonymous posters, claiming defamation. Hadeed alleged that the reviewers were not actual customers. Their statements that Hadeed had provided them with shoddy service were therefore false and defamatory. When Yelp failed to comply with a subpoena seeking the users' identities,

Can a business that receives poor reviews on Yelp force Yelp to disclose the reviewers' identities in a lawsuit for online defamation?

the court held the site in contempt. Yelp appealed, arguing that the subpoena violated the users' First Amendment rights.

ISSUE Did requiring Yelp to reveal the identities of some anonymous users who had posted potentially defamatory statements violate those users' First Amendment rights?

DECISION No. A state intermediate appellate court affirmed the lower court's ruling. "The judgment of the [lower] court does not constitute a forbidden intrusion on the field of free expression."

REASON Under the First Amendment, "Congress shall make no law . . . abridging the freedom of speech."

Continues

Internet users do not lose this right "at the log-in screen." Thus, the defendants had a constitutional right to speak—or post— anonymously over the Internet. But their right must be balanced against Hadeed's right to protect its reputation. The First Amendment protects a user's opinion about a business if the user was a customer of the business and the post was based on personal experience. If the user never patronized the business, however, the post is a false statement of fact. "And there is no constitutional value in false statements of fact."

Here, Hadeed was unable to match the anonymous defendants' reviews with the actual customers in its database. Hadeed asked Yelp to identify the defendants, but the site refused. Thus, a subpoena became necessary. "Without the identity of the . . . defendants, Hadeed cannot move forward with its defamation lawsuit. There is no other option."

CRITICAL THINKING—Ethical Consideration *Why would someone post a negative review of a business that he or she had never patronized? Discuss the ethics of this practice.*

PREVENTING LEGAL DISPUTES

In cyberspace, it is relatively common for disgruntled employees, competitors, and others to post negative comments online about business firms. Cyber slurs can obviously damage a firm's reputation and profitability. One way for business owners to deal with online defamation without resorting to costly (and sometimes unsuccessful) litigation is to retain an online reputation management service. Some of these services use automated software to identify negative comments and attempt to get them removed. Owners can often pay a monthly monitoring fee without entering a long-term contract.

7–4b Liability of Internet Service Providers

LEARNING OBJECTIVE 4

What law governs whether Internet service providers are liable for online defamatory statements made by users?

Recall from the discussion of defamation in Chapter 4 that normally those who repeat or otherwise republish a defamatory statement are subject to liability. Thus, newspapers, magazines, and television and radio stations are subject to liability for defamatory content that they publish or broadcast, even though the content was prepared or created by others. Applying this rule to cyberspace, however, raises an important issue: Should ISPs be regarded as publishers and therefore be held liable for defamatory messages that are posted by their users in online forums or other arenas?

General Rule The Communications Decency Act (CDA) states that "[n]o provider or user of an interactive computer service shall be treated as the publisher or speaker of any information provided by another information content provider."[20] Thus, under the CDA, ISPs usually are treated differently from publishers in print and other media and are not liable for publishing defamatory statements that come from a third party.

Exceptions Although the courts generally have construed the CDA as providing a broad shield to protect ISPs from liability for third party content, some courts have started establishing limits to this immunity. **CASE EXAMPLE 7.19** Roommate.com, LLC, operates an online roommate-matching Web site that helps individuals find roommates based on their descriptions of themselves and their roommate preferences. Users respond to a series of online questions, choosing from answers in drop-down and select-a-box menus. Some of the questions asked users to disclose their sex, family status, and sexual orientation—which is not permitted under the federal Fair Housing Act.

When a nonprofit housing organization sued Roommate.com, the company claimed it was immune from liability under the CDA. A federal appellate court disagreed and ordered Roommate.com to pay nearly $500,000. By creating the Web site and the questionnaire and answer

---

20. 47 U.S.C. Section 230.

choices, Roommate.com prompted users to express discriminatory preferences and matched users based on these preferences in violation of federal law.[21] ■

7-5 Privacy

In recent years, Facebook, Google, and Yahoo have all been accused of violating users' privacy rights. The right to privacy is guaranteed by the Bill of Rights and some state constitutions. (See this chapter's *Beyond Our Borders* feature for a discussion of how the European Union now recognizes a "right to be forgotten.") To maintain a suit for the invasion of privacy, though, a person must have a reasonable expectation of privacy in the particular situation.

7-5a Reasonable Expectation of Privacy

People clearly have a reasonable expectation of privacy when they enter their personal banking or credit-card information online. They also have a reasonable expectation that online companies will follow their own privacy policies. But it is probably not reasonable to expect privacy in statements made on Twitter—or photos posted on Twitter, Flickr, or Instagram, for that matter.

> "Science fiction does not remain fiction for long. And certainly not on the Internet."
>
> **VINTON CERF**
> 1943–PRESENT
> (AMERICAN INTERNET PIONEER, COMEDIAN, AND AUTHOR)

---

21. *Fair Housing Council of San Fernando Valley v. Roommate.com, LLC*, 666 F.3d 1216 (9th Cir. 2012).

BEYOND OUR BORDERS
"The Right to Be Forgotten" in the European Union

As the saying goes, the Internet never forgets. If fifteen years ago you had some financial problems and had to sell your house at auction, that information about you remains available forever. A Spanish lawyer, Mario Costeja Gonzàlez, found himself in just that situation. If anyone Googled his name, they discovered that his house had gone into foreclosure when he was a younger man.

Taking Google to Court
Costeja Gonzàlez requested that Google's search engine no longer access those old court records. Google refused. The case ultimately ended up in the European Union Court of Justice. Google lost.[a] The company had to remove the links to publicly available

---

a. *SL, Google Inc. v. Agencia Española de Protección de Datos, Mario Costeja Gonzalez*, Court of Justice for the European Union (Grand Chamber), Case C-131/12, May 13, 2014.

information that Costeja Gonzàlez considered damaging and an invasion of his privacy.

What "The Right to Be Forgotten" Means
The new "right to be forgotten" in the European Union allows individuals to petition Google to remove search result links that are personal in nature and that have become "outdated" or "irrelevant." Does that mean that anyone in Europe can ask that links to old information be removed? Not really. Right now, a European wishing to remove a link to older personal data needs a lawyer to make the request. Moreover, the original "offensive" documents are not removed—only the Google search link to those documents. According to Viviane Reading, vice-president of the European Commission, "It is clear that the right to be forgotten cannot amount to a right of the total erasure of history."

Can the Ruling Be Applied Outside Europe?
As it stands, the Court of Justice's ruling applies only within the twenty-eight countries of the European Union. Nonetheless, in 2015, the head of the French Data Protection Authority, Isabel Falque-Pierrotin, began campaigning to expand the ruling. She argued that if an individual has the right to be delisted from search results, such delisting should happen worldwide.

In 2015, an advisory group sponsored by Google issued a report recommending that the right to be forgotten be limited just to the European Union. According to that report, the same legal framework used in Europe would not work in the U.S. because of the First Amendment.

CRITICAL THINKING

■ How could the "right to be forgotten" affect free speech?

EXAMPLE 7.20 In 2014, Boston Red Sox player David Ortiz used his cell phone to take a "selfie" showing him standing with President Barack Obama. Ortiz tweeted the photo to his followers, who then resent it tens of thousands of times. Eventually, Samsung used the picture in an ad on Twitter (because Ortiz had taken it with a Samsung phone), which prompted an objection from the White House. ■

Sometimes, people mistakenly believe that they are making statements or posting photos in a private forum. **EXAMPLE 7.21** Randi Zuckerberg, the older sister of Mark Zuckerberg (the founder of Facebook), used a mobile app called Poke to post a photo on Facebook of their family gathering during the holidays. Poke allows the sender to decide how long the photo can be seen by others. Facebook allows users to configure their privacy settings to limit access to photos, which Randi thought she had done. Nonetheless, the photo showed up in the Facebook feed of Callie Schweitzer, who then put it on Twitter, where it eventually "went viral." Schweitzer apologized and removed the photo, but it had already gone public for the world to see. ■

In the following case, the court considered whether a Facebook user's expectation of privacy in photos that she posted on the site was reasonable.

CASE 7.3

Nucci v. Target Corp.

District Court of Appeal of Florida, Fourth District, 162 So.3d 146 (2015).

FACTS Maria Nucci filed a suit in a Florida state court against Target Corporation, alleging that she suffered an injury when she slipped and fell on a "foreign substance" on the floor of a Target store. Target filed a motion to compel an inspection of Nucci's Facebook profile, which included 1,249 photos. Target argued that it was entitled to view the profile because Nucci's lawsuit put her physical and mental condition at issue. Nucci responded that her Facebook page's privacy setting prevented the general public from having access to it. She claimed that she had a reasonable expectation of privacy in the profile and that Target's access would invade that privacy right. The court issued an order to compel discovery of certain photos, including some on Nucci's Facebook page, that were relevant to her physical and mental condition before and following the alleged injury. Nucci petitioned a state intermediate appellate court for relief from the order.

ISSUE Did the relevance of the photos on Nucci's Facebook page to her claim outweigh her expectation of privacy?

DECISION Yes. The state intermediate appellate court denied Nucci's petition for relief from the order to compel discovery of her photos. The court concluded that "the photographs sought were reasonably calculated to lead to the discovery of admissible evidence and Nucci's privacy interest in them was minimal."

In a "slip-and-fall" case, can the defendant show example photos from the plaintiff's Facebook account?

iStockPhoto.com/Muhla1

REASON In a personal injury case, the plaintiff's quality of life is subject to examination before and after the event that gave rise to the claim to determine the extent of the alleged loss. The best portrayal of a person's life is in the photos that the person shares through social media. The Florida constitution protects a person's right to privacy, but this protection requires that the person first must have a legitimate expectation of privacy. Generally, the photos posted on a social networking site such as Facebook are not protected by a right of privacy, regardless of the user's privacy settings. Facebook itself does not guarantee privacy. In creating a Facebook account, a user is made aware that her personal information will be shared with others. "Indeed, that is the very nature and purpose of these social networking sites else they would cease to exist." Thus, an expectation that photos posted on the site will be private would not be reasonable.

WHAT IF THE FACTS WERE DIFFERENT? *Suppose that Target had asked for a much broader range of Facebook material that concerned not just Nucci's physical and mental condition at the time of her alleged injury but her personal relationships with her family, romantic partners, and other significant others. Would the result have been the same? Discuss.*

7–5b Data Collection and Cookies

Whenever a consumer purchases items online from a retailer, the retailer collects information about the consumer. **Cookies** are invisible files that computers, smartphones, and other mobile devices create to track a user's Web browsing activities. Cookies provide detailed information to marketers about an individual's behavior and preferences, which is then used to personalize online services.

Over time, a retailer can amass considerable data about a person's shopping habits. Does collecting this information violate the person's right to privacy? Should retailers be able to pass on the data they have collected to their affiliates? Should they be able to use the information to predict what a consumer might want and then create online "coupons" customized to fit the person's buying history?

EXAMPLE 7.22 Facebook, Inc., recently settled a lawsuit over its use of a targeted advertising technique called "Sponsored Stories." An ad would display a Facebook friend's name and profile picture, along with a statement that the friend "likes" the company sponsoring the advertisement. A group of plaintiffs filed suit, claiming that Facebook had used their pictures for advertising without their permission. When a federal court refused to dismiss the case, Facebook agreed to settle. ■

7–5c Internet Companies' Privacy Policies

The Federal Trade Commission (FTC) investigates consumer complaints of privacy violations. The FTC has forced many companies, including Google, Facebook, Twitter, and MySpace, to enter an agreement consenting to give the FTC broad power to review their privacy and data practices. It can then sue companies that violate the terms of the decree.

EXAMPLE 7.23 In 2012, Google settled a suit brought by the FTC alleging that it had misrepresented its use of tracking cookies to users of Apple's Safari Internet browser. Google allegedly had used cookies to trick the Safari browser on Macs, iPhones, and iPads so that Google could monitor users who believed they had blocked such tracking. This violated the consent decree with the FTC. Google agreed to pay $22.5 million to settle the suit without admitting liability. ■

Facebook has faced a number of complaints about its privacy policy and has changed its policy several times to satisfy its critics and ward off potential government investigations. Other companies, including mobile app developers, have also changed their privacy policies to provide more information to consumers. Consequently, it is frequently companies, rather than courts or legislatures, that define the privacy rights of their online users.

7–5d Protecting Consumer Privacy

To protect consumers' personal information, the Obama administration has proposed a consumer privacy bill of rights (see Exhibit 7–1). The goal is to ensure that personal information is safe online.

If this proposed privacy bill of rights becomes law, retailers will have to change some of their procedures. They will have to give customers better choices about what data are collected and how the data are used for marketing. They may also have to take into account consumers' expectations about how their information will be used once it is collected.

Cookie A small file sent from a Web site and stored in a user's Web browser to track the user's Web browsing activities.

Why did Facebook eliminate its advertising program called "Sponsored Stories"?

Exhibit 7–1 Proposed Consumer Privacy Bill of Rights

1. Individual Control—Consumers have a right to exercise control over what personal data organizations collect from them and how they use it.

2. Transparency—Consumers have the right to easily understandable information about privacy and security practices.

3. Respect for Context—Consumers have a right to expect that organizations will collect, use, and disclose personal data in ways that are consistent with the context in which consumers provide the data.

4. Security—Consumers have the right to secure and responsible handling of personal data.

5. Access and Accuracy—Consumers have a right to access and correct personal data in usable formats, in a manner that is appropriate to the sensitivity of the data and the risk of adverse consequences to consumers if the data are inaccurate.

6. Focus Collection—Consumers have a right to reasonable limits on the personal data that companies collect and retain.

7. Accountability—Consumers have a right to have personal data handled by companies with appropriate measures in place to assure that they adhere to the Consumer Privacy Bill of Rights.

Reviewing . . . Internet Law, Social Media, and Privacy

While he was in high school, Joel Gibb downloaded numerous songs to his smartphone from an unlicensed file-sharing service. He used portions of the copyrighted songs when he recorded his own band and posted videos on YouTube and Facebook. He also used BitTorrent to download several movies from the Internet. Now Gibb has applied to Boston University. The admissions office has requested access to his Facebook password, and he has complied. Using the information presented in the chapter, answer the following questions.

1. What laws, if any, did Gibb violate by downloading the music and videos from the Internet?

2. Was Gibb's use of portions of copyrighted songs in his own music illegal? Explain.

3. Can individuals legally post copyrighted content on their Facebook pages? Why or why not?

4. Did Boston University violate any laws when it asked Joel to provide his Facebook password? Explain.

DEBATE THIS

■ Internet service providers should be subject to the same defamation laws as newspapers, magazines, and television and radio stations.

Key Terms

cloud computing 169
cookie 179
cybersquatting 164
cyber tort 175

distributed network 169
domain name 164
goodwill 164
Internet service provider (ISP) 164

peer-to-peer (P2P) networking 168
social media 171
spam 163
typosquatting 165

Chapter Summary: Internet Law, Social Media, and Privacy

Internet Law	**1.** *Spam*—Unsolicited junk e-mail accounts for about three-quarters of all e-mails. Laws to combat spam have been enacted by thirty-seven states and the federal government, but the flow of spam continues.
	   a. The Controlling the Assault of Non-Solicited Pornography and Marketing (CAN-SPAM) Act prohibits false and deceptive e-mails originating in the United States.
	   b. The U.S. Safe Web Act allows U.S. authorities to cooperate and share information with foreign agencies in investigating and prosecuting those involved in spamming, spyware, and various Internet frauds and deceptions. The act includes a safe harbor for Internet service providers.
	2. *Domain names*—Trademark owners often use their mark as part of a domain name (Internet address). The Internet Corporation for Assigned Names and Numbers (ICANN) oversees the distribution of domain names. ICANN recently expanded the available domain names to include new generic top-level domain names (gTLDs).
	3. *Cybersquatting*—Disputes arise when a person registers a domain name that is the same as, or confusingly similar to, the trademark of another and then offers to sell the domain name back to the trademark owner. This is known as cybersquatting, and it is illegal if the one registering, trafficking in, or using the domain name has a "bad faith intent" to profit from that mark. Anticybersquatting legislation is aimed at combatting the problem, but it has had only limited success.
	4. *Meta tags*—Search engines compile their results by looking through a Web site's *meta tags,* or key words. Using another's trademark in a meta tag without the owner's permission normally constitutes trademark infringement.
	5. *Trademark dilution*—When a trademark is used online, without authorization, in a way that diminishes the distinctive quality of the mark, it constitutes trademark dilution. Unlike infringement actions, trademark dilution claims do not require proof that consumers are likely to be confused by a connection between the unauthorized use and the mark.
	6. *Licensing*—Many companies choose to permit others to use their trademarks and other intellectual property online under a license. The purchase of software generally involves a license agreement. Licensing agreements frequently include restrictions that prohibit licensees from sharing the file and using it to create similar software applications.

Copyrights in Digital Information	**1.** *Copyrighted works online*—Much of the material on the Internet (including software and database information) is copyrighted. In order for that material to be transferred online, it must be "copied." Generally, whenever a party downloads software or music without authorization, a copyright is infringed. **2.** *Digital Millennium Copyright Act*—To protect copyrights in digital information, Congress passed the Digital Millennium Copyright Act (DMCA). The DMCA establishes civil and criminal penalties for anyone who bypasses encryption software or other antipiracy technologies, but provides exceptions for certain educational and nonprofit uses. It also limits the liability of Internet service providers for infringement unless the ISP is aware of the user's infringement and fails to take action. **3.** *File-sharing*—When file-sharing is used to download others' stored music files or illegally copy movies, copyright issues arise. Individuals who download the music or movies in violation of copyright laws are liable for infringement. Companies that distribute file-sharing software or provide such services have been held liable for the copyright infringement of their users if the software or technology involved promoted copyright infringement.

Social Media	**1.** *Uses in the legal process*—The emergence of Facebook and other social networking sites has had a number of effects on the legal process. Law enforcement and administrative agencies now routinely use social media to detect illegal activities and conduct investigations, as do many businesses.
	2. The *Electronic Communications Privacy Act* (*ECPA*)—The ECPA prohibits the intentional interception or disclosure of any wire, oral, or electronic communication.
	   a. The ECPA includes a "business-extension exception" that permits employers to monitor employees' electronic communications made in the ordinary course of business (but not personal communications).
	   b. The Stored Communications Act is part of the ECPA and prohibits intentional unauthorized access to *stored* electronic communications (such as backup data stored by an employer).
	3. *Social media passwords*—Private employers and schools have sometimes looked at an individual's Facebook or other social media account to see if it included controversial postings. A number of states have enacted legislation that protects individuals from having to divulge their social media passwords. Such laws may not be completely effective in preventing employers from rejecting applicants or terminating workers based on their social media postings.
	4. *Company-wide social media networks*—Many companies today form their own internal social media networks through which employees can exchange messages about topics related to their work.

Online Defamation	Federal and state statutes apply to certain forms of cyber torts, or torts that occur in cyberspace, such as online defamation. Under the federal Communications Decency Act (CDA), Internet service providers generally are not liable for defamatory messages posted by their subscribers.
Privacy	**1.** *Expectation of privacy*—Numerous Internet companies have been accused of violating users' privacy rights. To sue for invasion of privacy, though, a person must have a reasonable expectation of privacy in the particular situation. It is often difficult to determine how much privacy can reasonably be expected on the Internet. **2.** *Data collection and cookies*—Whenever a consumer purchases items online from a retailer, the retailer collects information about the consumer through "cookies." Consequently, retailers have gathered large amounts of data about individuals' shopping habits. It is not always clear whether collecting such information violates a person's right to privacy. **3.** *Internet companies' privacy policies*—Many companies establish Internet privacy policies, which typically inform users what types of data they are gathering and for what purposes it will be used.

Issue Spotters

1. Karl self-publishes a cookbook titled *Hole Foods,* in which he sets out recipes for donuts, Bundt cakes, tortellini, and other foods with holes. To publicize the book, Karl designs the Web site holefoods.com. Karl appropriates the key words of other cooking and cookbook sites with more frequent hits so that holefoods.com will appear in the same search engine results as the more popular sites. Has Karl done anything wrong? Explain. (See *Internet Law*.)

2. Eagle Corporation began marketing software in 2001 under the mark "Eagle." In 2013, Eagle.com, Inc., a different company selling different products, begins to use *eagle* as part of its URL and registers it as a domain name. Can Eagle Corporation stop this use of *eagle?* If so, what must the company show? (See *Internet Law*.)

—**Check your answers to the *Issue Spotters* against the answers provided in Appendix D at the end of this text.**

Learning Objectives Check

1. What is cybersquatting, and when is it illegal?
2. What steps have been taken to protect intellectual property rights in the digital age?
3. When does the law protect a person's electronic communications from being intercepted or accessed?
4. What law governs whether Internet service providers are liable for online defamatory statements made by users?
5. How do online retailers track their users' Web browsing activities?

—**Answers to the even-numbered *Learning Objectives Check* questions can be found in Appendix E at the end of this text.**

Business Scenarios and Case Problems

7–1. Internet Service Providers. CyberConnect, Inc., is an Internet service provider (ISP). Pepper is a CyberConnect subscriber. Market Reach, Inc., is an online advertising company. Using sophisticated software, Market Reach directs its ads to those users most likely to be interested in a particular product. When Pepper receives one of the ads, she objects to the content. Further, she claims that CyberConnect should pay damages for "publishing" the ad. Is the ISP regarded as a publisher and therefore liable for the content of Market Reach's ad? Why or why not? (See *Online Defamation*.)

7–2. Privacy. SeeYou, Inc., is an online social network. SeeYou's members develop personalized profiles to share information—photos, videos, stories, activity updates, and other items—with other members. Members post the information that they want to share and decide with whom they want to share it. SeeYou launched a program to allow members to share with others what they do elsewhere online. For example, if a member rents a movie through Netflix, SeeYou will broadcast that information to everyone in the member's online network. How can SeeYou avoid complaints that this program violates its members' privacy? (See *Privacy*.)

7–3. Copyrights in Digital Information. When she was in college, Jammie Thomas-Rasset wrote a case study on Napster, the online peer-to-peer (P2P) file-sharing network, and knew that it had been shut down because it was illegal. Later, Capitol Records, Inc., which owns the copyrights to a large number of music recordings, discovered that "tereastarr"—a user name

associated with Thomas-Rasset's Internet protocol address—had made twenty-four songs available for distribution on KaZaA, another P2P network. Capitol notified Thomas-Rasset that she had been identified as engaging in the unauthorized trading of music. She replaced the hard drive on her computer with a new drive that did not contain the songs in dispute. Is Thomas-Rasset liable for copyright infringement? Explain. [*Capitol Records, Inc. v. Thomas-Rasset,* 692 F.3d 899 (8th Cir. 2012)] (See *Copyrights in Digital Information*.)

7–4. Domain Names. Austin Rare Coins, Inc., buys and sells rare coins, bullion, and other precious metals through eight Web sites with different domain names. An unknown individual took control of Austin's servers and transferred the domain names to another registrant without Austin's permission. The new registrant began using the domain names to host malicious content—including hate letters to customers and fraudulent contact information—and to post customers' credit-card numbers and other private information, thereby tarnishing Austin's goodwill. Austin filed a suit in a federal district court against the new registrant under the Anticybersquatting Consumer Protection Act. Is Austin entitled to a transfer of the domain names? Explain. [*Austin Rare Coins, Inc. v. Acoins.com,* 2013 WL 85142 (E.D.Va. 2013)] (See *Internet Law*.)

7–5. Business Case Problem with Sample Answer—Privacy. Using special software, South Dakota law enforcement officers found a person who appeared to possess child pornography at a specific Internet protocol address. The officers subpoenaed Midcontinent Communications, the service that assigned the address, for the personal information of its subscriber. With this information, the officers obtained a search warrant for the residence of John Rolfe, where they found a laptop that contained child pornography. Rolfe argued that the subpoenas violated his "expectation of privacy." Did Rolfe have a privacy interest in the information obtained by the subpoenas issued to Midcontinent? Discuss. [*State of South Dakota v. Rolfe*, 825 N.W.2d 901 (S.Dak. 2013)] (See *Privacy*.)

—For a sample answer to Problem 7–5, go to Appendix F at the end of this text.

7–6. File-Sharing. Dartmouth College professor M. Eric Johnson, in collaboration with Tiversa, Inc., a company that monitors peer-to-peer networks to provide security services, wrote an article titled "Data Hemorrhages in the Health-Care Sector." In preparing the article, Johnson and Tiversa searched the networks for data that could be used to commit medical or financial identity theft. They found a document that contained the Social Security numbers, insurance information, and treatment codes for patients of LabMD, Inc. Tiversa notified LabMD of the find in order to solicit its business. Instead of hiring Tiversa, however, LabMD filed a suit in a federal district court against the company, alleging trespass, conversion, and violations of federal statutes. What do these facts indicate about the security of private information? Explain. How should the court rule? [*LabMD, Inc. v. Tiversa, Inc.*, 2013 WL 425983 (11th Cir. 2013)] (See *Copyrights in Digital Information*.)

7–7. Social Media. Mohammad Omar Aly Hassan and nine others were indicted in a federal district court on charges of conspiring to advance violent jihad (holy war against enemies of Islam) and other offenses related to terrorism. The evidence at Hassan's trial included postings he made on Facebook concerning his adherence to violent jihadist ideology. Convicted, Hassan appealed, contending that the Facebook items had not been properly authenticated (established as his own comments). How might the government show the connection between postings on Facebook and those who post them? Discuss. [*United States v. Hassan*, 742 F.3d 104 (4th Cir. 2014)] (See *Social Media*.)

7–8. Social Media. Kenneth Wheeler was angry at certain police officers in Grand Junction, Colorado, because of a driving-under-the-influence arrest that he viewed as unjust. While in Italy, Wheeler posted a statement to his Facebook page urging his "religious followers" to "kill cops, drown them in the blood of their children, hunt them down and kill their entire bloodlines" and provided names. Later, Wheeler added a post to "commit a massacre in the Stepping Stones Preschool and day care, just walk in and kill everybody." Could a reasonable person conclude that Wheeler's posts were true threats? How might law enforcement officers use Wheeler's posts? Explain. [*United States v. Wheeler*, 776 F.3d 736 (10th Cir. 2015)] (See *Social Media*.)

7–9. A Question of Ethics—Criminal Investigations. After the unauthorized release and posting of classified U.S. government documents to WikiLeaks.org, the U.S. government began a criminal investigation. The government obtained a court order to require Twitter, Inc., to turn over subscriber information and communications to and from the e-mail addresses of Birgitta Jonsdottir and others. The court sealed (restricted from public view) the order and the other documents in the case, reasoning that "there exists no right to public notice of all the types of documents filed in a . . . case." Jonsdottir and the others appealed this decision. [*In re Application of the United States of America for an Order Pursuant to 18 U.S.C. Section 2703(d)*, 707 F3d 283 (4th Cir. 2013)] (See *Social Media*.)

1. Why would the government want to "seal" the documents of an investigation? Why would the individuals under investigation want those documents to be "unsealed"? What factors should be considered in striking a balance between these competing interests?

2. How does law enforcement use social media to detect and prosecute criminals? Is this use of social media an unethical invasion of individuals' privacy? Discuss.

Critical Thinking and Writing Assignments

7–10. Business Law Critical Thinking Group Assignment— File-Sharing. James, Chang, and Sixta are roommates. They are music fans and frequently listen to the same artists and songs. They regularly exchange MP3 music files that contain songs from their favorite artists. (See *Copyrights in Digital Information*.)

1. One group of students will decide whether the fact that the roommates are transferring files among themselves for no monetary benefit protects them from being subject to copyright law.

2. The second group will consider an additional fact. Each roommate regularly buys CDs and copies them to his or her hard drive. Then the roommate gives the CDs to the other roommates to do the same.

iStockPhoto.com/mathieukor

8

LEARNING OBJECTIVES

The five Learning Objectives *below are designed to help improve your understanding of the chapter. After reading this chapter, you should be able to answer the following questions:*

1. What two elements normally must exist before a person can be held liable for a crime?

2. What are five broad categories of crimes? What is white-collar crime?

3. What defenses can be raised to avoid liability for criminal acts?

4. What constitutional safeguards exist to protect persons accused of crimes?

5. How has the Internet expanded opportunities for identity theft?

Criminal Law and Cyber Crime

The "crime problem" is of concern to all Americans, as suggested in the chapter-opening quotation. Not surprisingly, laws dealing with crime are an important part of the legal environment of business.

Society imposes a variety of sanctions to protect businesses from harm so that they can compete and flourish. These sanctions include damages for tortious conduct, damages for breach of contract, and various equitable remedies. Additional sanctions are imposed under criminal law. Many statutes regulating business provide for criminal as well as civil sanctions.

In this chapter, after explaining some essential differences between criminal law and civil law, we look at the elements that must be present for criminal liability to exist. We then examine various categories of crimes, the defenses that can be raised to avoid liability for criminal actions, constitutional safeguards for those accused of crimes, and the rules of criminal procedure.

We conclude with a discussion of crimes that occur in cyberspace, which are often called *cyber crimes*. Cyber attacks are becoming all too common—even e-mail and data of government agencies have been hacked. Many businesses have suffered cyber attacks as well. Smartphones are being infected by malicious software, which puts users' data at risk, as you will read in a feature later in this chapter.

> "The crime problem is getting really serious. The other day, the Statue of Liberty had both hands up."
>
> **JAY LENO**
> 1950–PRESENT
> (AMERICAN COMEDIAN AND FORMER TELEVISION HOST)

8-1 Civil Law and Criminal Law

Remember from Chapter 1 that *civil law* spells out the duties that exist between persons or between persons and their governments. Criminal law, in contrast, has to do with crime.

A **crime** can be defined as a wrong against society proclaimed in a statute and, if committed, punishable by society through fines and/or imprisonment—and, in some cases, death.

Because crimes are *offenses against society* as a whole, they are prosecuted by a public official, such as a district attorney (D.A.) or an attorney general (AG), not by the crime victims. Once a crime has been reported, the D.A.'s office decides whether to file criminal charges and to what extent to pursue the prosecution or carry out additional investigation.

8-1a Key Differences between Civil Law and Criminal Law

Because the state has extensive resources at its disposal when prosecuting criminal cases, and because the sanctions can be so severe, there are numerous procedural safeguards to protect the rights of defendants. We look here at one of these safeguards—the higher burden of proof that applies in a criminal case—and at the sanctions imposed for criminal acts. Exhibit 8–1 summarizes these and other key differences between civil law and criminal law.

Burden of Proof In a civil case, the plaintiff usually must prove his or her case by a *preponderance of the evidence*. Under this standard, the plaintiff must convince the court that, based on the evidence presented by both parties, it is more likely than not that the plaintiff's allegation is true.

In a criminal case, in contrast, the state must prove its case **beyond a reasonable doubt.** If the jury views the evidence in the case as reasonably permitting either a guilty or a not guilty verdict, then the jury's verdict must be *not* guilty. In other words, the prosecutor must prove beyond a reasonable doubt that the defendant has committed every essential element of the offense with which she or he is charged. If the jurors are not convinced of the defendant's guilt beyond a reasonable doubt, they must find the defendant not guilty.

Note also that in a criminal case, the jury's verdict normally must be unanimous—agreed to by all members of the jury—to convict the defendant.[1] In a civil trial by jury, in contrast, typically only three-fourths of the jurors need to agree.

Criminal Sanctions The sanctions imposed on criminal wrongdoers are also harsher than those applied in civil cases. Remember that the purpose of tort law is to allow persons harmed by the wrongful acts of others to obtain compensation from the wrongdoer rather than to punish the wrongdoer.

In contrast, criminal sanctions are designed to punish those who commit crimes and to deter others from committing similar acts in the future. Criminal sanctions include fines as well as the much harsher penalty of the loss of liberty by incarceration in a jail or prison. The harshest criminal sanction is, of course, the death penalty.

Crime A wrong against society proclaimed in a statute and, if committed, punishable by society through fines, imprisonment, or death.

Beyond a Reasonable Doubt The standard of proof used in criminal cases.

---

1. Note that there are exceptions—a few states allow jury verdicts that are not unanimous. Arizona, for example, allows six of eight jurors to reach a verdict in criminal cases. Louisiana and Oregon have also relaxed the requirement of unanimous jury verdicts.

Exhibit 8–1 Key Differences between Civil Law and Criminal Law

ISSUE	CIVIL LAW	CRIMINAL LAW
Party who brings suit	The person who suffered harm.	The state.
Wrongful act	Causing harm to a person or to a person's property.	Violating a statute that prohibits some type of activity.
Burden of proof	Preponderance of the evidence.	Beyond a reasonable doubt.
Verdict	Three-fourths majority (typically).	Unanimous (almost always).
Remedy	Damages to compensate for the harm or a decree to achieve an equitable result.	Punishment (fine, imprisonment, or death).

8–1b Civil Liability for Criminal Acts

Some torts, such as assault and battery, provide a basis for a criminal prosecution as well as a tort action. **EXAMPLE 8.1** Carlos is walking down the street, minding his own business, when suddenly a person attacks him. In the ensuing struggle, the attacker stabs Carlos several times, seriously injuring him. A police officer restrains and arrests the wrongdoer. In this situation, the attacker may be subject both to criminal prosecution by the state and to a tort lawsuit brought by Carlos. ■ Exhibit 8–2 illustrates how the same act can result in both a tort action and a criminal action against the wrongdoer.

8–1c Classification of Crimes

Felony A crime—such as arson, murder, rape, or robbery—that carries the most severe sanctions, ranging from more than one year in a state or federal prison to the death penalty.

Depending on their degree of seriousness, crimes are classified as felonies or misdemeanors. **Felonies** are serious crimes punishable by death or by imprisonment for more than one year.[2] Many states also define several degrees of felony offenses and vary the punishment according to the degree.[3] For instance, most jurisdictions punish a burglary that involves forced entry

2. Federal law and most state laws use this definition, but there is some variation among states as to the length of imprisonment associated with a felony conviction.
3. Although the American Law Institute issued the Model Penal Code in 1962, it is not a uniform code, and each state has developed its own set of laws governing criminal acts. Thus, types of crimes and prescribed punishments may differ from one jurisdiction to another.

Exhibit 8–2 Tort Lawsuit and Criminal Prosecution for the Same Act

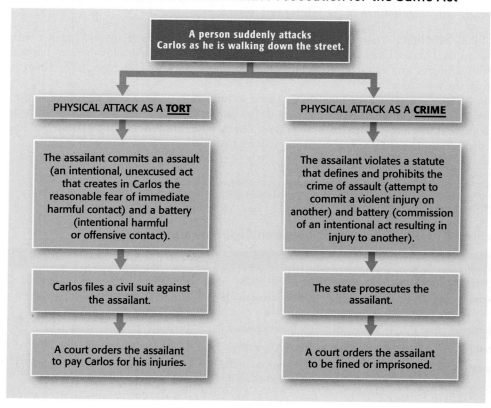

CHAPTER 8: Criminal Law and Cyber Crime

into a home at night more harshly than a burglary that involves breaking into a nonresidential building during the day.

Misdemeanors are less serious crimes, punishable by a fine or by confinement for up to a year. **Petty offenses** are minor violations, such as jaywalking or violations of building codes, considered to be a subset of misdemeanors. Even for petty offenses, however, a guilty party can be put in jail for a few days, fined, or both, depending on state or local law. Whether a crime is a felony or a misdemeanor can determine in which court the case is tried and, in some states, whether the defendant has a right to a jury trial.

Misdemeanor A lesser crime than a felony, punishable by a fine or incarceration in jail for up to one year.

Petty Offense The least serious kind of criminal offense, such as a traffic or building-code violation.

8–2 Criminal Liability

Two elements normally must exist simultaneously for a person to be convicted of a crime: (1) the performance of a prohibited act and (2) a specified state of mind or intent on the part of the actor. Note that to establish criminal liability, there must be a *concurrence* between the act and the intent. In other words, these two elements must occur together.

LEARNING OBJECTIVE 1
What two elements normally must exist before a person can be held liable for a crime?

8–2a The Criminal Act

Every criminal statute prohibits certain behavior. Most crimes require an act of *commission*. That is, a person must *do* something in order to be accused of a crime. In criminal law, a prohibited act is referred to as the **actus reus,**[4] or guilty act. In some situations, an act of *omission* can be a crime, but only when a person has a legal duty to perform the omitted act. For instance, failing to file a tax return is a crime of omission.

The *guilty act* requirement is based on one of the premises of criminal law—that a person is punished for harm done to society. For a crime to exist, the guilty act must cause some harm to a person or to property. Thinking about killing someone or about stealing a car may be wrong, but the thoughts do no harm until they are translated into action. Of course, a person can be punished for *attempting* murder or robbery, but normally only if he or she took substantial steps toward the criminal objective. Additionally, the person must have specifically intended to commit the crime to be convicted of an attempt.

Actus Reus A guilty (prohibited) act; one of the two essential elements required to establish criminal liability.

8–2b State of Mind

A wrongful mental state **(mens rea)**[5] is generally required to establish criminal liability. The required mental state, or intent, is indicated in the applicable statute or law. Theft, for example, involves the guilty act of taking another person's property. The guilty mental state involves both the awareness that the property belongs to another and the intent to deprive the owner of it. A court can also find that the required mental state is present when a defendant's acts are reckless or criminally negligent.

Mens Rea A wrongful mental state ("guilty mind"), or intent; one of the two essential elements required to establish criminal liability.

Recklessness A defendant is *criminally reckless* if he or she consciously disregards a substantial and unjustifiable risk. **EXAMPLE 8.2** A fourteen-year-old New Jersey girl posts a Facebook message saying that she is going to launch a terrorist attack on her high school and asks if anyone wants to help. The police arrest the girl for the crime of making a terrorist threat, which requires the intent to commit an act of violence with "the intent to terrorize" or "in reckless disregard of the risk of causing" terror or inconvenience. Although the girl claims that she does not intend to cause harm, she can be prosecuted under the "reckless disregard" part of the statute. ■

---

4. Pronounced *ak*-tuhs *ray*-uhs.
5. Pronounced *mehns ray*-uh.

Criminal Negligence *Criminal negligence* occurs when the defendant takes an unjustified, substantial, and foreseeable risk that results in harm. A defendant can be negligent even if she or he was not actually aware of the risk but *should have been aware* of it.[6]

A homicide is classified as *involuntary manslaughter* when it results from an act of criminal negligence and there is no intent to kill. **EXAMPLE 8.3** Dr. Conrad Murray, the personal physician of pop star Michael Jackson, was convicted of involuntary manslaughter in 2011 for prescribing the drug that led to Jackson's sudden death in 2009. Murray had given Jackson propofol, a powerful anesthetic normally used in surgery, as a sleep aid on the night of his death, even though Murray knew that Jackson had already taken other sedatives. ■

Strict Liability and Overcriminalization
An increasing number of laws and regulations have imposed criminal sanctions for strict liability crimes—that is, offenses that do not require a wrongful mental state, or malice, to establish criminal liability.

Assume that you do not know that you are on federal lands. What doctrine makes you criminally liable for removing ancient arrowheads even without *mens rea?*

iStockPhoto.com/sleddogtwo

Federal Crimes. The federal criminal code now lists more than four thousand criminal offenses, many of which do not require a specific mental state. In addition, several hundred thousand federal rules can be enforced through criminal sanctions, and many of these rules do not require intent. See this chapter's *Managerial Strategy* feature for a discussion of how these laws and rules affect American businesspersons.

EXAMPLE 8.4 Eddie Leroy Anderson, a retired logger and former science teacher, and his son went digging for arrowheads near a campground in Idaho. They did not realize that they were on federal land and that it is a crime to take artifacts from federal land without a permit. Although the penalty could be as much as two years in prison, the father and son pleaded guilty and were sentenced to probation and a $1,500 fine each. ■

Strict liability crimes are often connected with environmental laws, laws aimed at combating illegal drugs, and other laws related to public health, safety, and welfare. Under federal law, for instance, tenants can be evicted from public housing if one of their relatives or guests used illegal drugs—regardless of whether the tenant knew or should have known about the drug activity.

State Crimes. Many states have also enacted laws that punish behavior as criminal without the need to show criminal intent. **EXAMPLE 8.5** In Arizona, a hunter who shoots an elk outside the area specified by the hunting permit has committed a crime. The hunter can be convicted of the crime regardless of her or his intent or knowledge of the law. ■

8–2c Corporate Criminal Liability

A *corporation* is a legal entity created under the laws of a state. At one time, it was thought that a corporation could not incur criminal liability because, although a corporation is a legal person, it can act only through its agents (corporate directors, officers, and employees). Therefore, the corporate entity itself could not "intend" to commit a crime. Over time, this view has changed. Obviously, corporations cannot be imprisoned, but they can be fined or denied certain legal privileges (such as necessary licenses).

Liability of the Corporate Entity Today, corporations are normally liable for the crimes committed by their agents and employees within the course and scope of their employment.[7] For liability to be imposed, the prosecutor typically must show that the corporation could have prevented the act or that a supervisor within the corporation authorized or had knowledge of

---

6. Model Penal Code Section 2.02(2)(d).
7. See Model Penal Code Section 2.07.

MANAGERIAL STRATEGY The Criminalization of American Business

Management Faces a Legal Issue

What do Bank of America, Citigroup, JPMorgan Chase, and Goldman Sachs have in common? All recently paid hefty fines for purportedly misleading investors about mortgage-backed securities. In fact, these companies paid the government a total of $50 billion in fines. The payments were made in lieu of criminal prosecutions.

Today, several hundred thousand federal rules that apply to businesses carry some form of criminal penalty. That's in addition to more than four thousand federal laws, many of which carry criminal sanctions for their violation. From 2000 to the beginning of 2015, about 2,200 corporations either were convicted or pleaded guilty to violating federal statutes or rules. More than 300 corporations reached so-called non-prosecution agreements, which typically involve multimillion- or multibillion-dollar fines. These numbers do not include fines paid to the Environmental Protection Agency or to the Fish and Wildlife Service.

According to law professors Margaret Lemos and Max Minzner, "Public enforcers often seek large monetary awards for self-interested reasons divorced from the public interest and deterrents. The incentives are strongest when enforcement agencies are permitted to retain all or some of the proceeds of enforcement."[a]

What the Courts Say

The first successful criminal conviction in a federal court against a company—The New York Central and Hudson River Railroad—was upheld by the Supreme Court in 1909 (the violation: cutting prices).[b] Many other successful convictions followed. One landmark case developed the *aggregation test,* now called the Doctrine of Collective Knowledge.[c] This test aggregates the omissions and acts of two or more persons in a corporation, thereby constructing an *actus reus* and a *mens rea* out of the conduct and knowledge of several individuals.

Not all government attempts at applying criminal law to corporations survive. In 2013, for example, Sentinel Offender Services, LLC, prevailed on appeal. There was no actual evidence to show that the company had acted with specific intent to commit theft by deception.[d]

In 2014, the U.S. District Court for the Northern District of California in San Francisco indicted FedEx Corporation for purportedly illegally shipping prescription drugs ordered through Web sites.[e] FedEx has chosen to proceed to court. As suggested earlier, however, many companies choose to reach a settlement agreement with the government rather than fight criminal indictments.

MANAGERIAL IMPLICATIONS

Managers in a large corporation must make sure that the company retains sufficient documents to respond to potential regulatory requests. William Hubbard at the University of Chicago Law School estimates that a typical large company spends more than $40 million annually to do so. Managers also face the question of whether to agree to pay a large fine rather than to be indicted and proceed to trial. Most corporate managers choose the former option because they worry that a criminal indictment will harm their corporation's reputation, its profitability, and ultimately its existence.

---

a. Margaret Lemos and Max Minzner, "For-Profit Public Enforcement," *Harvard Law Review* 127, January 17, 2014.
b. *New York Central and Hudson River Railroad v. United States,* 212 U.S. 481 (1909).
c. *U.S. v. Bank of New England,* 821 F.2d 844 (1987).
d. *McGee v. Sentinel Offender Services, LLC,* 719 F.3d 1236 (2013).

---

e. *United States of America v. FedEx Corporation, FedEx Express, Inc., and FedEx Corporate Services, Inc.,* July 17, 2014.

---

the act. In addition, corporations can be criminally liable for failing to perform specific duties imposed by law (such as duties under environmental laws or securities laws).

CASE EXAMPLE 8.6 A prostitution ring, the Gold Club, was operating out of motels in West Virginia. A motel manager, who was also an officer in the corporation that owned the motels, gave discounted rates to Gold Club prostitutes, and they paid him in cash. The corporation received a portion of the funds generated by the Gold Club's illegal operations. At trial, the jury found that the corporation was criminally liable because a supervisor within the corporation—the motel manager—had knowledge of the prostitution and the corporation had allowed it to continue.[8] ▪

---

8. As a result of the convictions, the motel manager was sentenced to fifteen months in prison, and the corporation was ordered to forfeit the motel property. *United States v. Singh*, 518 F.3d 236 (4th Cir. 2008).

Corporations that operate underground storage tanks are responsible for any leaking gasoline. At what point does the responsible corporate officer doctrine make corporate officers criminally liable for continued leakages?

Liability of Corporate Officers and Directors Corporate directors and officers are personally liable for the crimes they commit, regardless of whether the crimes were committed for their personal benefit or on the corporation's behalf. Additionally, corporate directors and officers may be held liable for the actions of employees under their supervision. Under the *responsible corporate officer doctrine,* a court may impose criminal liability on a corporate officer regardless of whether she or he participated in, directed, or even knew about a given criminal violation.[9]

CASE EXAMPLE 8.7 The Roscoe family owned the Customer Company, which operated an underground storage tank that leaked gasoline. After the leak occurred, an employee, John Johnson, notified the state environmental agency, and the Roscoes hired an environmental services firm to clean up the spill. The clean-up did not occur immediately, however, and the state sent many notices to John Roscoe, a corporate officer, warning him that the company was violating federal and state environmental laws. Roscoe gave the letters to Johnson, who passed them on to the environmental services firm, but the spill was not cleaned up.

The state eventually filed criminal charges against the corporation and the Roscoes individually, and they were convicted. On appeal, the court affirmed the Roscoes' convictions under the responsible corporate officer doctrine. The Roscoes were in positions of responsibility, they had influence over the corporation's actions, and their failure to act constituted a violation of environmental laws.[10]

PREVENTING LEGAL DISPUTES

If you become a corporate officer or director at some point in your career, you will be potentially liable for the crimes of your subordinates. Always be familiar with any criminal statutes relevant to the corporation's industry or trade. Also, make sure that corporate employees are trained in how to comply with the multitude of applicable rules, particularly environmental laws and health and safety regulations, which frequently involve criminal sanctions.

8-3 Types of Crimes

LEARNING OBJECTIVE 2

What are five broad categories of crimes? What is white-collar crime?

Federal, state, and local laws provide for the classification and punishment of hundreds of thousands of different criminal acts. Traditionally, though, crimes have been grouped into five broad categories: violent crime (crimes against persons), property crime, public order crime, white-collar crime, and organized crime. Many crimes may be committed in cyberspace. When crimes occur in the virtual world, we refer to them as cyber crimes, as discussed later in the chapter.

8-3a Violent Crime

Robbery The act of forcefully and unlawfully taking personal property of any value from another.

Certain crimes are called *violent crimes,* or crimes against persons, because they cause others to suffer harm or death. Murder is a violent crime. So, too, is sexual assault, or rape. **Robbery**—defined as the taking of cash, personal property, or any other article of value from a person by means of force or fear—is another violent crime. Typically, states have more severe penalties for *aggravated robbery*—robbery with the use of a deadly weapon.

Assault and battery, which were discussed in Chapter 4 in the context of tort law, are also classified as violent crimes. **EXAMPLE 8.8** Former rap star Flavor Flav (whose real name is William Drayton) was arrested in Las Vegas on assault and battery charges. During an argument with his fiancée, Drayton allegedly threw her to the ground and then grabbed two kitchen knives and chased her son. ■

---

9. For a landmark case in this area, see *United States v. Park*, 421 U.S. 658, 95 S.Ct. 1903, 44 L.Ed.2d 489 (1975).

10. The Roscoes and the corporation were sentenced to pay penalties of $2,493,250. *People v. Roscoe*, 169 Cal.App.4th 829, 87 Cal. Rptr.3d 187 (3 Dist. 2008).

Each of these violent crimes is further classified by degree, depending on the circumstances surrounding the criminal act. These circumstances include the intent of the person committing the crime and whether a weapon was used. For crimes other than murder, the level of pain and suffering experienced by the victim is also a factor.

8–3b Property Crime

The most common type of criminal activity is property crime—crimes in which the goal of the offender is some form of economic gain or the damaging of property. Robbery is a form of property crime, as well as a violent crime, because the offender seeks to gain the property of another. We look here at a number of other crimes that fall within the general category of property crime.

Burglary Traditionally, **burglary** was defined under the common law as breaking and entering the dwelling of another at night with the intent to commit a felony. Originally, the definition was aimed at protecting an individual's home and its occupants. Most state statutes have eliminated some of the requirements found in the common law definition. The time of day at which the breaking and entering occurs, for example, is usually immaterial. State statutes frequently omit the element of breaking, and some states do not require that the building be a dwelling. When a deadly weapon is used in a burglary, the person can be charged with *aggravated burglary* and punished more severely.

The defendant in the following case challenged the sufficiency of the evidence to support his conviction for burglary.

Burglary The unlawful entry or breaking into a building with the intent to commit a felony.

CASE 8.1

State of Minnesota v. Smith

Court of Appeals of Minnesota, 2015 WL 303643 (2015).

FACTS Over a Labor Day weekend in Rochester, Minnesota, two homes and the Rochester Tennis Center, a business, were burglarized. One day later, less than five blocks away, in Albert Smith's room at the Bell Tower Inn, cleaning personnel found a garbage bag containing a passport that belonged to the owner of one of the burglarized homes and documents that belonged to the business. The police arrested Smith. A search of a bag in his possession revealed other stolen items and burglary tools. Smith claimed that he had bought some of the items on Craigslist and had found the documents from the tennis center in a dumpster. Convicted of burglary in a Minnesota state court, Smith appealed.

ISSUE Was the evidence sufficient to support Smith's conviction for burglary?

DECISION Yes. A state intermediate appellate court affirmed Smith's conviction. The appellate court concluded that the circumstances "are consistent with guilt and inconsistent with any rational hypothesis except that of guilt."

REASON The burglarized homes and business were within a few blocks of Smith's hotel. The hotel manager saw Smith carrying a

When a person possesses property that was recently stolen, can a court infer that he or she engaged in burglary?

Sentry safe that had been stolen in one of the burglaries into the hotel. Only a few hours later, Smith was found in possession of property stolen in the burglaries. When arrested, he was carrying a bag that contained other stolen items and the burglary tools. The nature and assortment of the items "suggested that they came directly from the burglaries," illustrating Smith's guilt—the items looked like "the raw loot that a thief quickly grabbed and made off with." The time frame and the short distance between the hotel and the burglary locations were also consistent with a finding that Smith was the thief. The trial court found that Smith's claims as to how he came into possession of the items were not credible. The appellate court considered his claims "improbable" and concluded that "the only rational hypothesis that can be drawn from the proved circumstances is that Smith committed the burglaries."

CRITICAL THINKING—Social Consideration *Who is in the best position to evaluate the credibility of the evidence and the witnesses in a case? Why?*

Larceny The wrongful taking and carrying away of another person's personal property with the intent to permanently deprive the owner of the property.

Larceny　Under the common law, the crime of **larceny** involved the unlawful taking and carrying away of someone else's personal property with the intent to permanently deprive the owner of possession. Put simply, larceny is stealing, or theft. Whereas robbery involves force or fear, larceny does not. Therefore, picking pockets is larceny, not robbery. Similarly, an employee who takes company products and supplies home for personal use without authorization commits larceny.

Most states have expanded the definition of property that is subject to larceny statutes. Stealing computer programs may constitute larceny even though the "property" is not physical (see the discussion of computer crime later in this chapter). So, too, can the theft of natural gas or Internet and television cable service.

Obtaining Goods by False Pretenses

Obtaining goods by means of false pretenses is a form of theft that involves trickery or fraud, such as using someone else's credit-card number without permission to purchase an iPad. Statutes dealing with such illegal activities vary widely from state to state. They often apply not only to property, but also to services and cash.

CASE EXAMPLE 8.9　While Matthew Steffes was incarcerated, he devised a scheme to make free collect calls from prison. (A *collect call* is a telephone call in which the calling party places a call at the called party's expense.) Steffes had his friends and family members set up new phone number accounts by giving false information to AT&T. This information included fictitious business names, as well as personal identifying information stolen from a health-care clinic. Once a new phone number was working, Steffes made unlimited collect calls to it without paying the bill until AT&T eventually shut down the account. For nearly two years, Steffes used sixty fraudulently obtained phone numbers to make hundreds of collect calls. The loss to AT&T was more than $28,000.

Steffes was convicted in a state court of theft by fraud. He appealed, arguing that he had not made false representations to AT&T. The Wisconsin Supreme Court affirmed his conviction. The court held that Steffes had made false representations to AT&T by providing it with fictitious business names and stolen personal identifying information. He made these false representations so that he could make phone calls without paying for them, which deprived the company of its "property"—its electricity.[11]　■

Receiving Stolen Goods

It is a crime to receive goods that a person knows or should have known were stolen or illegally obtained. To be convicted, the recipient of such goods need not know the true identity of the owner or the thief, and need not have paid for the goods. All that is necessary is that the recipient knows or should have known that the goods were stolen, and intended to deprive the true owner of those goods.

Arson The intentional burning of a building.

Arson

The willful and malicious burning of a building (and, in some states, vehicles and other items of personal property) is the crime of **arson.** At common law, arson traditionally applied only to burning down another person's house. The law was designed to protect human life. Today, arson statutes have been extended to cover the destruction of any building, regardless of ownership, by fire or explosion.

Every state has a special statute that covers the act of burning a building for the purpose of collecting insurance. **EXAMPLE 8.10**　Benton owns an insured apartment building that is falling apart. If he sets fire to it or pays someone else to do so, he is guilty not only of arson but also of defrauding the insurer, which is attempted larceny.　■　Of course, the insurer need not pay the claim when insurance fraud is proved.

iStockPhoto.com/Burning building

If this fire was started to obtain insurance money, what type of crime was committed?

---

11. *State of Wisconsin v. Steffes*, 347 Wis.2d 683, 832 N.W.2d 101 (2013).

Forgery The fraudulent making or altering of any writing (including electronic records) in a way that changes the legal rights and liabilities of another is **forgery.** EXAMPLE 8.11 Without authorization, Severson signs Bennett's name to the back of a check made out to Bennett and attempts to cash it. Severson has committed the crime of forgery. ■ Forgery also includes changing trademarks, falsifying public records, counterfeiting, and altering a legal document.

Forgery The fraudulent making or altering of any writing in a way that changes the legal rights and liabilities of another.

8–3c Public Order Crime

Historically, societies have always outlawed activities considered to be contrary to public values and morals. Today, the most common public order crimes include public drunkenness, prostitution, gambling, and illegal drug use. These crimes are sometimes referred to as victimless crimes because they normally harm only the offender. From a broader perspective, however, they are deemed detrimental to society as a whole because they may create an environment that gives rise to property and violent crimes.

EXAMPLE 8.12 A flight attendant observed a man and woman engaging in sex acts while on a flight to Las Vegas in 2013. A criminal complaint was filed, and the two defendants pleaded guilty in federal court to the public order crime of misdemeanor disorderly conduct. ■

8–3d White-Collar Crime

Crimes occurring in the business context are popularly referred to as *white-collar crimes,* although this is not an official legal term. Ordinarily, **white-collar crime** involves an illegal act or series of acts committed by an individual or business entity using some nonviolent means to obtain a personal or business advantage.

Usually, this kind of crime is committed in the course of a legitimate occupation. Corporate crimes fall into this category. In addition, certain property crimes, such as larceny and forgery, may also be white-collar crimes if they occur within the business context.

White-Collar Crime Nonviolent crime committed by individuals or corporations to obtain a personal or business advantage.

Embezzlement The fraudulent appropriation of funds or other property by a person who was entrusted with the funds or property.

Embezzlement When a person who is entrusted with another person's funds or property fraudulently appropriates it, **embezzlement** occurs. Embezzlement is not larceny, because the wrongdoer does not physically take the property from another's possession, and it is not robbery, because force or fear is not used.

Typically, embezzlement is carried out by an employee who steals funds. Banks are particularly prone to this problem, but embezzlement can occur in any firm. In a number of businesses, corporate officers or accountants have fraudulently converted funds for their own benefit and then "fixed" the books to cover up their crime. Embezzlement occurs whether the embezzler takes the funds directly from the victim or from a third person. If the financial officer of a corporation pockets checks from third parties that were given to her to deposit into the corporate account, she is embezzling.

Frequently, an embezzler takes relatively small amounts repeatedly over a long period. This might be done by underreporting income or deposits and embezzling the remaining amount or by creating fictitious persons or accounts and writing checks to them from the corporate account. An employer's failure to remit state withholding taxes that were collected from employee wages can also constitute embezzlement.

The intent to return embezzled property—or its actual return—is not a defense to the crime of embezzlement, as the following *Spotlight Case* illustrates.

iStockPhoto.com/EdStock

Bernard Madoff (center) perpetuated the largest fraudulent investment scheme in modern history.

SPOTLIGHT ON WHITE-COLLAR CRIME: CASE 8.2

People v. Sisuphan
Court of Appeal of California, First District, 181 Cal.App.4th 800, 104 Cal.Rptr.3d 654 (2010).

FACTS Lou Sisuphan was the director of finance at a Toyota dealership. Sisuphan complained repeatedly to management about another employee, Ian McClelland. The general manager, Michael Christian, would not terminate McClelland "because he brought a lot of money into the dealership." To jeopardize McClelland's employment, Sisuphan took and kept an envelope containing a payment of nearly $30,000 from one of McClelland's customers that McClelland had tried to deposit in the company's safe. Later, Sisuphan told the dealership what he had done and returned the money, adding that he had "no intention of stealing the money." Christian fired Sisuphan the next day, and the district attorney later charged Sisuphan with embezzlement. After a jury trial, Sisuphan was found guilty. Sisuphan appealed.

ISSUE Did Sisuphan take the funds with the intent to defraud his employer?

DECISION Yes. The appellate court affirmed Sisuphan's conviction for embezzlement. Sisuphan had the required intent at the time he

A Toyota dealership employee committed embezzlement, but returned the funds. Is this a crime?

took the funds, and the evidence that he repaid the dealership was properly excluded.

REASON The court reasoned that evidence of repayment is admissible only if it shows that a defendant's intent at the time of the taking was not fraudulent. In determining whether Sisuphan's intent was fraudulent at the time of the taking, the main issue was not whether he intended to spend the funds that he had taken, but whether he intended to use the payment "for a purpose other than that for which the dealership entrusted it to him." Sisuphan's stated purpose was to get McClelland fired. Because this purpose was beyond the scope of his responsibility, it was "outside the trust afforded him by the dealership" and indicated fraudulent intent.

CRITICAL THINKING—Legal Consideration *Why was Sisuphan convicted of embezzlement instead of larceny? What is the difference between these two crimes?*

Mail and Wire Fraud
One of the most potent weapons against white-collar criminals are the federal laws that prohibit mail fraud[12] and wire fraud.[13] These laws make it a federal crime to devise any scheme that uses the U.S. mail, commercial carriers (such as FedEx or UPS), or wire (including telegraph, telephone, television, e-mail, or online social media) with the intent to defraud the public. These laws are often applied when persons send advertisements via e-mail or social media with the intent to obtain cash or property by false pretenses.

CASE EXAMPLE 8.13 Cisco Systems, Inc., offers a warranty program to authorized resellers of Cisco parts. Iheanyi Frank Chinasa and Robert Kendrick Chambliss formulated a scheme to use this program to defraud Cisco by obtaining replacement parts to which they were not entitled. The two men sent numerous e-mails and Internet service requests to Cisco to convince the company to ship them new parts via commercial carriers. Ultimately, Chinasa and Chambliss were convicted of mail and wire fraud, as well as conspiracy to commit mail and wire fraud.[14] ■

The maximum penalty under these statutes is substantial. Persons convicted of mail or wire fraud may be imprisoned for up to twenty years and/or fined. If the violation affects a financial institution or involves fraud in connection with emergency disaster-relief funds, the violator may be fined up to $1 million, imprisoned for up to thirty years, or both.

> "It was beautiful and simple as all truly great swindles are."
>
> **O. HENRY**
> 1862–1910
> (AMERICAN WRITER)

---

12. The Mail Fraud Act of 1990, 18 U.S.C. Sections 1341–1342.
13. 18 U.S.C. Section 1343.
14. *United States v. Chinasa*, 789 F.Supp.2d 691 (E.D.Va. 2011).

Bribery   The crime of bribery involves offering something of value to someone in an attempt to influence that person—who is usually, but not always, a public official—to act in a way that serves a private interest. Three types of bribery are considered crimes: bribery of public officials, commercial bribery, and bribery of foreign officials. As an element of the crime of bribery, intent must be present and proved. The bribe itself can be anything the recipient considers to be valuable. Realize that the *crime of bribery occurs when the bribe is offered*—it is not required that the bribe be accepted. *Accepting a bribe* is a separate crime.

Commercial bribery involves corrupt dealings between private persons or businesses. Typically, people make commercial bribes to obtain proprietary information, cover up an inferior product, or secure new business. Industrial espionage sometimes involves commercial bribes. **EXAMPLE 8.14** Kent works at the firm of Jacoby & Meyers. He offers to pay Laurel, an employee in a competing firm, if she will give him her firm's trade secrets and pricing schedules. Kent has committed commercial bribery. ■ So-called kickbacks, or payoffs for special favors or services, are a form of commercial bribery in some situations.

Bankruptcy Fraud   Federal bankruptcy law allows individuals and businesses to be relieved of oppressive debt through bankruptcy proceedings. Numerous white-collar crimes may be committed during the many phases of a bankruptcy proceeding. A creditor may file a false claim against the debtor. Also, a debtor may attempt to protect assets from creditors by fraudulently transferring property to favored parties. For instance, a company-owned automobile may be "sold" at a bargain price to a trusted friend or relative. Closely related to the crime of fraudulently transferring property is the crime of fraudulently concealing property, such as hiding gold coins.

Theft of Trade Secrets   Trade secrets constitute a form of intellectual property that can be extremely valuable for many businesses. The Economic Espionage Act[15] made the theft of trade secrets a federal crime. The act also made it a federal crime to buy or possess trade secrets of another person, knowing that the trade secrets were stolen or otherwise acquired without the owner's authorization.

Violations of the act can result in steep penalties. An individual who violates the act can be imprisoned for up to ten years and fined up to $500,000. A corporation or other organization can be fined up to $5 million. Additionally, any property acquired as a result of the violation, such as airplanes and automobiles, is subject to criminal forfeiture, or seizure by the government. Similarly, any property used in the commission of the violation, such as servers and other electronic devices, is subject to forfeiture. A theft of trade secrets conducted via the Internet, for instance, could result in the forfeiture of every computer or other device used to commit or facilitate the crime.

Insider Trading   An individual who obtains "inside information" about the plans of a publicly listed corporation can often make stock-trading profits by purchasing or selling corporate securities based on the information. **Insider trading** is a violation of securities law and will be discussed more fully later in this text. Generally, the rule is that a person who possesses inside information and has a duty not to disclose it to outsiders may not profit from the purchase or sale of securities based on that information until the information is made available to the public.

Insider Trading The purchase or sale of securities on the basis of information that has not been made available to the public.

8–3e Organized Crime

As mentioned, white-collar crime takes place within the confines of the legitimate business world. *Organized crime,* in contrast, operates *illegitimately* by, among other things, providing illegal goods and services. For organized crime, the traditional markets in the past were

---

15. 18 U.S.C. Sections 1831–1839.

How do criminals launder money?

Money Laundering Engaging in financial transactions to conceal the identity, source, or destination of illegally gained funds.

gambling, prostitution, illegal narcotics, and loan sharking (lending at higher-than-legal interest rates), along with counterfeiting and credit-card scams. Today, organized crime is heavily involved in cyber crime.

Money Laundering Organized crime and other illegal activities generate many billions of dollars in profits each year from illegal drug transactions and, to a lesser extent, from racketeering, prostitution, and gambling. Under federal law, banks and other financial institutions are required to report currency transactions involving more than $10,000. Consequently, those who engage in illegal activities face difficulties when they try to deposit their cash profits from illegal transactions.

As an alternative to simply storing cash from illegal transactions in a safe-deposit box, wrongdoers and racketeers often launder their "dirty" money to make it "clean" by passing it through a legitimate business. **Money laundering** is engaging in financial transactions to conceal the identity, source, or destination of illegally gained funds.

EXAMPLE 8.15 Leo Harris, a successful drug dealer, becomes a partner with a restaurateur. Little by little, the restaurant shows increasing profits. As a partner in the restaurant, Harris is able to report the "profits" of the restaurant as legitimate income on which he pays federal and state taxes. He can then spend those funds without worrying that his lifestyle may exceed the level possible with his reported income. ■

The Racketeer Influenced and Corrupt Organizations Act

To curb the entry of organized crime into the legitimate business world, Congress in 1970 enacted the Racketeer Influenced and Corrupt Organizations Act (RICO).[16] The statute makes it a federal crime to:

1. Use income obtained from racketeering activity to purchase any interest in an enterprise.

2. Acquire or maintain an interest in an enterprise through racketeering activity.

3. Conduct or participate in the affairs of an enterprise through racketeering activity.

4. Conspire to do any of the preceding activities.

Broad Application of RICO. The broad language of RICO has allowed it to be applied in cases that have little or nothing to do with organized crime. RICO incorporates by reference twenty-six separate types of federal crimes and nine types of state felonies.[17] If a person commits two of these offenses, he or she is guilty of "racketeering activity."

Under the criminal provisions of RICO, any individual found guilty is subject to a fine of up to $25,000 per violation, imprisonment for up to twenty years, or both. Additionally, any assets (property or cash) that were acquired as a result of the illegal activity or that were "involved in" or an "instrumentality of" the activity are subject to government forfeiture.

Civil Liability. In the event of a RICO violation, the government can seek not only criminal penalties but also civil penalties, such as the divestiture of a defendant's interest in a business (called forfeiture) or the dissolution of the business. (Divestiture refers to the taking of possession—or forfeiture—of the defendant's interest and its subsequent sale.)

Moreover, in some cases, the statute allows private individuals to sue violators and potentially to recover three times their actual losses (treble damages), plus attorneys' fees, for business injuries caused by a RICO violation. This is perhaps the most controversial aspect of RICO and one that continues to cause debate in the nation's federal courts. The prospect of receiving treble damages in civil RICO lawsuits has given plaintiffs a financial incentive to pursue businesses and employers for violations.

---

16. 18 U.S.C. Sections 1961–1968.
17. See 18 U.S.C. Section 1961(1)(A).

8-4 Defenses to Criminal Liability

Persons charged with crimes may be relieved of criminal liability if they can show that their criminal actions were justified under the circumstances. In certain circumstances, the law may also allow a person to be excused from criminal liability because she or he lacks the required mental state. We look at several of the defenses to criminal liability here.

Note that procedural violations, such as obtaining evidence without a valid search warrant, may also operate as defenses. Evidence obtained in violation of a defendant's constitutional rights normally may not be admitted in court. If the evidence is suppressed, then there may be no basis for prosecuting the defendant.

LEARNING OBJECTIVE 3
What defenses can be raised to avoid liability for criminal acts?

8-4a Justifiable Use of Force

Probably the best-known defense to criminal liability is **self-defense.** Other situations, however, also justify the use of force: the defense of one's dwelling, the defense of other property, and the prevention of a crime. In all of these situations, it is important to distinguish between deadly and nondeadly force. *Deadly force* is likely to result in death or serious bodily harm. *Nondeadly force* is force that reasonably appears necessary to prevent the imminent use of criminal force.

Generally speaking, people can use the amount of nondeadly force that seems necessary to protect themselves, their dwellings, or other property or to prevent the commission of a crime. Deadly force can be used in self-defense if the defender *reasonably believes* that imminent death or grievous bodily harm will otherwise result. In addition, normally the attacker must be using unlawful force, and the defender must not have initiated or provoked the attack.

Many states are expanding the situations in which the use of deadly force can be justified. Florida, for example, allows the use of deadly force to prevent the commission of a "forcible felony," including robbery, carjacking, and sexual battery.

Self-Defense The legally recognized privilege to do what is reasonably necessary to protect oneself, one's property, or someone else against injury by another.

8-4b Necessity

Sometimes, criminal defendants are relieved of liability if they can show that a criminal act was necessary to prevent an even greater harm. **EXAMPLE 8.16** Jake Trevor is a convicted felon and, as such, is legally prohibited from possessing a firearm. While he and his wife are in a convenience store, a man draws a gun, points it at the cashier, and demands all the cash. Afraid that the man will start shooting, Trevor grabs the gun and holds on to it until police arrive. In this situation, if Trevor is charged with possession of a firearm, he can assert the defense of necessity. ■

8-4c Insanity

A person who suffers from a mental illness may be incapable of the state of mind required to commit a crime. Thus, insanity can be a defense to a criminal charge. Note that an insanity defense does not allow a person to avoid imprisonment. It simply means that if the defendant successfully proves insanity, she or he will be placed in a mental institution.

EXAMPLE 8.17 James Holmes opened fire with an automatic weapon in a crowded Colorado movie theater during the screening of *The Dark Knight Rises,* killing twelve people and injuring more than fifty. Holmes had been a graduate student but had increasingly suffered from mental health problems and had left school. Before the incident, he had no criminal history. Holmes's attorneys asserted the defense of insanity in an attempt to avoid

iStockPhoto.com/track5

If a person starts to suffer from mental health problems and opens fire inside a movie theater, can that person use the defense of insanity?

a possible death penalty. If the defense is ultimately successful, Holmes will be confined to a mental institution rather than a prison. ■

The courts have had difficulty deciding what the test for legal insanity should be, and psychiatrists as well as lawyers are critical of the tests used. Almost all federal courts and some states use the relatively liberal substantial-capacity test set forth in the Model Penal Code:

> A person is not responsible for criminal conduct if at the time of such conduct as a result of mental disease or defect he [or she] lacks substantial capacity either to appreciate the wrongfulness of his [or her] conduct or to conform his [or her] conduct to the requirements of the law.

Some states use the *M'Naghten* test.[18] Under this test, a criminal defendant is not responsible if, at the time of the offense, he or she did not know the nature and quality of the act or did not know that the act was wrong. Other states use the irresistible-impulse test. A person operating under an irresistible impulse may know an act is wrong but cannot refrain from doing it.

Under any of these tests, proving insanity is extremely difficult. For this reason, the insanity defense is rarely used and usually is not successful.

8-4d Mistake

Everyone has heard the saying "ignorance of the law is no excuse." Ordinarily, ignorance of the law or a mistaken idea about what the law requires is not a valid defense. A *mistake of fact*, as opposed to a *mistake of law*, can excuse criminal responsibility if it negates the mental state necessary to commit a crime.

EXAMPLE 8.18 If Oliver Wheaton mistakenly walks off with Julie Tyson's briefcase because he thinks it is his, there is no crime. Theft requires knowledge that the property belongs to another. (If Wheaton's act causes Tyson to incur damages, however, she may sue him in a civil action for the tort of trespass to personal property or conversion.) ■

8-4e Duress

Duress Unlawful pressure brought to bear on a person, causing the person to perform an act that she or he would not otherwise perform.

Duress exists when the *wrongful threat* of one person induces another person to perform an act that she or he would not otherwise perform. In such a situation, duress is said to negate the mental state necessary to commit a crime because the defendant was forced or compelled to commit the act.

Duress can be used as a defense to most crimes except murder. The states vary in how duress is defined and what types of crimes it can excuse, however. Generally, to successfully assert duress as a defense, the defendant must reasonably believe that he or she is in immediate danger, and the jury (or judge) must conclude that the defendant's belief was reasonable.

8-4f Entrapment

Entrapment A defense in which a defendant claims that he or she was induced by a public official to commit a crime that he or she would otherwise not have committed.

Entrapment is a defense designed to prevent police officers or other government agents from enticing persons to commit crimes so that they can later be prosecuted for criminal acts. In the typical entrapment case, an undercover agent *suggests* that a crime be committed and pressures or induces an individual to commit it. The agent then arrests the individual for the crime.

For entrapment to succeed as a defense, both the suggestion and the inducement must take place. The defense is not intended to prevent law enforcement agents from ever setting a trap for an unwary criminal. Rather, its purpose is to prevent them from pushing the individual into a criminal act. The crucial issue is whether the person who committed a crime was predisposed to commit the illegal act or did so only because the agent induced it.

---

18. A rule derived from *M'Naghten's* Case, 8 Eng.Rep. 718 (1843).

8-4g Statute of Limitations

With some exceptions, such as for the crime of murder, statutes of limitations apply to crimes just as they do to civil wrongs. In other words, the state must initiate criminal prosecution within a certain number of years. If a criminal action is brought after the statutory time period has expired, the accused person can raise the statute of limitations as a defense.

The running of the time period in a statute of limitations may be *tolled*—that is, suspended or stopped temporarily—if the defendant is a minor or is not in the jurisdiction. When the defendant reaches the age of majority or returns to the jurisdiction, the statutory time period begins to run again.

8-4h Immunity

Accused persons are understandably reluctant to give information if it will be used to prosecute them, and they cannot be forced to do so. The privilege against **self-incrimination** is granted by the Fifth Amendment to the U.S. Constitution. The clause reads "nor shall [any person] be compelled in any criminal case to be a witness against himself."

When the state wishes to obtain information from a person accused of a crime, the state can grant *immunity* from prosecution or agree to prosecute for a less serious offense in exchange for the information. Once immunity is given, the person can no longer refuse to testify on Fifth Amendment grounds because he or she now has an absolute privilege against self-incrimination.

Often, a grant of immunity from prosecution for a serious crime is part of the **plea bargaining** between the defendant and the prosecuting attorney. The defendant may be convicted of a lesser offense, while the state uses the defendant's testimony to prosecute accomplices for serious crimes carrying heavy penalties.

8-5 Constitutional Safeguards and Criminal Procedures

Criminal law brings the power of the state, with all its resources, to bear against the individual. Criminal procedures are designed to protect the constitutional rights of individuals and to prevent the arbitrary use of power by the government.

The U.S. Constitution provides specific safeguards for those accused of crimes. Most of these safeguards protect individuals not only against federal government actions but also, by virtue of the due process clause of the Fourteenth Amendment, against state government actions. These protections are set forth in the Fourth, Fifth, Sixth, and Eighth Amendments.

8-5a Fourth Amendment Protections

The Fourth Amendment protects the "right of the people to be secure in their persons, houses, papers, and effects." Before searching or seizing private property, law enforcement officers must obtain a **search warrant**—an order from a judge or other public official authorizing the search or seizure.

Advances in technology have allowed authorities to track phone calls and vehicle movements with greater ease and precision. The use of such technology can constitute a search within the meaning of the Fourth Amendment. **CASE EXAMPLE 8.19** Antoine Jones owned and operated a nightclub in the District of Columbia. Government agents suspected

Self-Incrimination Giving testimony in a trial or other legal proceeding that could expose the person testifying to criminal prosecution.

Plea Bargaining The process by which a criminal defendant and the prosecutor work out an agreement to dispose of the criminal case, subject to court approval.

LEARNING OBJECTIVE 4

What constitutional safeguards exist to protect persons accused of crimes?

Search Warrant An order granted by a public authority, such as a judge, that authorizes law enforcement personnel to search particular premises or property.

a.katz/ShutterStock.com

Can these officers enter and search a dwelling without first obtaining a search warrant?

that he was also trafficking in narcotics. As part of their investigation, agents obtained a warrant to attach a global positioning system (GPS) to Jones's wife's car, which Jones regularly used. The warrant authorized installation in the District of Columbia and within ten days, but agents installed the device on the eleventh day and in Maryland.

The agents then tracked the vehicle's movement for about a month, eventually arresting Jones for possession and intent to distribute cocaine. Jones was convicted. He appealed, arguing that the government did not have a valid warrant for the GPS tracking. The United States Supreme Court held that the attachment of a GPS tracking device to a suspect's vehicle does constitute a Fourth Amendment search. The Court did not rule on whether the search in this case was unreasonable, however, and allowed Jones's conviction to stand.[19] ■

Probable Cause

Probable Cause Reasonable grounds for believing that a search should be conducted or that a person should be arrested.

To obtain a search warrant, law enforcement officers must convince a judge that they have reasonable grounds, or **probable cause,** to believe a search will reveal a specific illegality. Probable cause requires the officers to have trustworthy evidence that would convince a reasonable person that the proposed search or seizure is more likely justified than not.

Furthermore, the Fourth Amendment prohibits general warrants. It requires a particular description of what is to be searched or seized. General searches through a person's belongings are impermissible. The search cannot extend beyond what is described in the warrant. Although search warrants require specificity, if a search warrant is issued for a person's residence, items in that residence may be searched even if they do not belong to that individual.

Because of the strong governmental interest in protecting the public, a warrant normally is not required for seizures of spoiled or contaminated food. Nor are warrants required for searches of businesses in such highly regulated industries as liquor, guns, and strip mining.

Reasonable Expectation of Privacy

The Fourth Amendment protects only against searches that violate a person's *reasonable expectation of privacy*. A reasonable expectation of privacy exists if (1) the individual actually expects privacy, and (2) the person's expectation is one that society as a whole would think is legitimate.

The issue before the court in the following case was whether a defendant had a reasonable expectation of privacy in cell phone texts stored in the account of another person.

---

19. *United States v. Jones,* __ U.S. __, 132 S.Ct. 945, 181 L.Ed.2d 911 (2012).

State of Oklahoma v. Marcum

Court of Criminal Appeals of Oklahoma, 319 P.3d 681 (2014).

FACTS Angela Marcum, a drug court coordinator associated with a county court in Oklahoma, was romantically involved with James Miller, an assistant district attorney in the same county. When Miller learned that state officials were "in town" investigating suspected embezzlement, he quickly sent Marcum text messages from his personal phone. She sent messages back. The state obtained a search warrant and collected the records of the messages from U.S. Cellular, Miller's phone company. Later, the state charged Marcum

Is there an absolute right to privacy for text messages?

with obstructing the investigation and offered in evidence the messages obtained pursuant to the search warrant. Marcum filed a motion to suppress the records, which the court granted. The state appealed.

ISSUE Does an individual who has exchanged text messages with another person have a reasonable expectation of privacy in those messages when they reside in the other person's account records at the telephone company?

DECISION No. A state intermediate appellate court reversed the ruling of the lower court. The case was reversed and remanded for further proceedings.

REASON According to the court, "Once the messages were both transmitted and received, the expectation of privacy was lost." When Marcum sent texts to Miller's phone, it was similar to mailing a letter—there is no expectation of privacy in the letter once it is delivered. Similarly, a caller cannot claim that a voice mail message, once it has been left and the recipient has played it, is private. In all of these situations, the individual's expectation of privacy in the communication is "defeated" by the decision to transmit a message to an electronic device that could be in anybody's possession. An individual has no reasonable expectation of privacy in the text messages or cell phone account records of another person when the individual does not have a possessory interest in the phone and the warrant is directed to a third party (here, U.S. Cellular).

CRITICAL THINKING—Technological Consideration *If Miller and Marcum had used smartphones and U.S. Cellular had stored its records in the "cloud," would the outcome likely have been different? Explain.*

8–5b Fifth Amendment Protections

The Fifth Amendment offers significant protections for accused persons. One is the guarantee that no one can be deprived of "life, liberty, or property without due process of law." Two other important Fifth Amendment provisions protect persons against double jeopardy and self-incrimination.

Due Process of Law Remember that *due process of law* has both procedural and substantive aspects. Procedural due process requirements underlie criminal procedures. The law must be carried out in a fair and orderly way. In criminal cases, due process means that defendants should have an opportunity to object to the charges against them before a fair, neutral decision maker, such as a judge. Defendants must also be given the opportunity to confront and cross-examine witnesses and accusers and to present their own witnesses.

Double Jeopardy The Fifth Amendment also protects persons from **double jeopardy** (being tried twice for the same criminal offense). The prohibition against double jeopardy means that once a criminal defendant is acquitted (found "not guilty") of a particular crime, the government may not retry him or her for the same crime.

The prohibition against double jeopardy does not preclude the crime victim from bringing a civil suit against that same defendant to recover damages, however. In other words, a person found "not guilty" of assault and battery in a state criminal case can be sued for damages by the victim in a civil tort case.

Additionally, a state's prosecution of a crime will not prevent a separate federal prosecution relating to the same activity (and vice versa), provided the activity can be classified as a different crime. **CASE EXAMPLE 8.20** Professional football player Michael Vick was convicted in federal court for operating a dogfighting ring and sentenced to serve twenty-three months in federal prison. A year later, Virginia, the state where the crime took place, filed its own charges against Vick for dogfighting. He pleaded guilty to those charges and received a *suspended sentence* (meaning that the judge reserved the option of imposing a sentence later if circumstances warranted it).[20] ■

Self-Incrimination As explained earlier, the Fifth Amendment grants a privilege against self-incrimination. Thus, in any criminal proceeding, an accused person cannot be compelled to give testimony that might subject her or him to criminal prosecution.

The Fifth Amendment's guarantee against self-incrimination extends only to natural persons. Because a corporation is a legal entity and not a natural person, the privilege against

> **Double Jeopardy** The Fifth Amendment requirement that prohibits a person from being tried twice for the same criminal offense.

> **KNOW THIS**
> The Fifth Amendment protection against self-incrimination does not cover partnerships or corporations.

---

20. See *United States v. Kizeart*, 2010 WL 3768023 (S.D.Ill. 2010) for a discussion of the Michael Vick dogfighting case.

self-incrimination does not apply to it. Similarly, the business records of a partnership do not receive Fifth Amendment protection. When a partnership is required to produce these records, it must do so even if the information incriminates the persons who constitute the business entity.

ETHICAL ISSUE

Should police be able to force you to unlock your cell phone? Modern cell phones can store countless pages of text, thousands of pictures, and hundreds of videos. Such data can remain on a cell phone for years. Also, since the advent of the "cloud," much of the data viewable on a cell phone is stored on a remote server. Should police nonetheless be able to force you to unlock your phone? Or does this practice violate the Fifth Amendment protection against self-incrimination?

A Virginia circuit court judge ruled that police officers cannot force criminal suspects to divulge cell phone passwords. They can, however, force suspects to use their fingerprints to unlock the phones. The judge argued that biometric information from a fingerprint lies outside the protection of the Fifth Amendment. In the judge's view, giving police a fingerprint is similar to providing a DNA or handwriting sample, which the law permits.[21]

At about the same time, in *Riley v. California*,[22] the United States Supreme Court unanimously held that warrantless search and seizure of digital contents of a cell phone during an arrest is unconstitutional. Chief Justice John Roberts stated, "The fact that technology now allows for an individual to carry [the privacies of life] in his hand does not make the information any less worthy of the protection for which the Founders fought."

8-5c Protections under the Sixth and Eighth Amendments

The Sixth Amendment guarantees several important rights for criminal defendants: the right to a speedy trial, the right to a jury trial, the right to a public trial, the right to confront witnesses, and the right to counsel. The Sixth Amendment right to counsel is one of the rights of which a suspect must be advised when he or she is arrested. In many cases, a statement that a criminal suspect makes in the absence of counsel is not admissible at trial unless the suspect has knowingly and voluntarily waived this right.

The Eighth Amendment prohibits excessive bail and fines, as well as cruel and unusual punishment. Under this amendment, prison officials are required to provide humane conditions of confinement, including adequate food, clothing, shelter, and medical care. If a prisoner has a serious medical problem, for instance, and a correctional officer is deliberately indifferent to it, a court could find that the prisoner's Eighth Amendment rights have been violated. Critics of the death penalty claim that it constitutes cruel and unusual punishment.[23]

8-5d The Exclusionary Rule and the *Miranda* Rule

Two other procedural protections for criminal defendants are the exclusionary rule and the *Miranda* rule.

Exclusionary Rule A rule that prevents evidence that is obtained illegally or without a proper search warrant from being admissible in court.

The Exclusionary Rule Under what is known as the **exclusionary rule,** any evidence obtained in violation of the constitutional rights spelled out in the Fourth, Fifth, and Sixth Amendments generally is not admissible at trial. All evidence derived from the illegally obtained evidence is known as the "fruit of the poisonous tree," and such evidence normally must also be excluded from the trial proceedings. For instance, if a confession is obtained after an illegal arrest, the arrest is the "poisonous tree," and the confession, if "tainted" by the arrest, is the "fruit."

---

21. *Commonwealth of Virginia v. David Charles Baust*, Case No. CR14-1439, 2nd Judicial Circuit, Virginia, October 28, 2014.
22. 573 U.S. ___, 134 S.Ct. 2473, 189 L.Ed.2d 430 (2014).
23. For an example of a case challenging the constitutionality of the death penalty, see *Baze v. Rees*, 553 U.S. 535, 128 S.Ct. 1520, 170 L.Ed.2d 420 (2008).

The purpose of the exclusionary rule is to deter police from conducting warrantless searches and engaging in other misconduct. The rule can sometimes lead to injustice, however. If evidence of a defendant's guilt was obtained improperly (without a valid search warrant, for instance), it normally cannot be used against the defendant in court.

The *Miranda* Rule In *Miranda v. Arizona,* a case decided in 1966, the United States Supreme Court established the rule that individuals who are arrested must be informed of certain constitutional rights. Suspects must be informed of their Fifth Amendment right to remain silent and their Sixth Amendment right to counsel. If the arresting officers fail to inform a criminal suspect of these constitutional rights, any statements the suspect makes normally will not be admissible in court. Because of its importance in criminal procedure, the *Miranda* case is presented as this chapter's *Landmark in the Law* feature.

Exceptions to the *Miranda* Rule Although the Supreme Court's *Miranda* ruling was controversial, the decision has survived attempts by Congress to overrule it. Over time, however, the Supreme Court has made a number of exceptions to the *Miranda* ruling. For instance, the Court has recognized a "public safety" exception that allows certain statements to be admitted even if the defendant was not given *Miranda* warnings. A defendant's statements that reveal the location of a weapon would be admissible under this exception. Additionally, a suspect must unequivocally and assertively ask to exercise her or his right to counsel in order to stop police questioning. Saying, "Maybe I should talk to a lawyer" during an interrogation after being taken into custody is not enough.

KNOW THIS
Once a suspect has been informed of his or her rights, anything that person says can be used as evidence in a trial.

LANDMARK IN THE LAW

Miranda v. Arizona (1966)

The United States Supreme Court's decision in *Miranda v. Arizona*[a] has been cited in more court decisions than any other case in the history of U.S law. Through television shows and other media, the case has also become familiar to most of the adult population in the United States.

The case arose after Ernesto Miranda was arrested in his home on March 13, 1963, for the kidnapping and rape of an eighteen-year-old woman. Miranda was taken to a police station in Phoenix, Arizona, and questioned by two police officers. Two hours later, the officers emerged from the interrogation room with a written confession signed by Miranda.

RULINGS BY THE LOWER COURTS The confession was admitted into evidence at the trial, and Miranda was convicted and sentenced to prison for twenty to thirty years.

a. 384 U.S. 436, 86 S.Ct. 1602, 16 L.Ed.2d 694 (1966).

Miranda appealed his conviction, claiming that he had not been informed of his constitutional rights. He did not assert that he was innocent of the crime or that his confession was false or made under duress. He claimed only that he would not have confessed if he had been advised of his right to remain silent and to have an attorney.

The Supreme Court of Arizona held that Miranda's constitutional rights had not been violated and affirmed his conviction. In its decision, the court emphasized that Miranda had not specifically requested an attorney.

THE SUPREME COURT'S DECISION The *Miranda* case was subsequently consolidated with three other cases involving similar issues and reviewed by the United States Supreme Court. In its decision, the Court stated that whenever an individual is taken into custody, "the following measures are required: He must be warned prior to any questioning that he has the right to remain silent, that anything he says can be used against him in a court of law, that he has the right to the presence of an attorney, and that

if he cannot afford an attorney one will be appointed for him prior to any questioning if he so desires." If the accused waives his or her rights to remain silent and to have counsel present, the government must be able to demonstrate that the waiver was made knowingly, intelligently, and voluntarily.

APPLICATION TO TODAY'S WORLD *Today, both on television and in the real world, police officers routinely advise suspects of their "Miranda rights" on arrest. When Ernesto Miranda himself was later murdered, the suspected murderer was "read his Miranda rights." Interestingly, this decision has also had ramifications for criminal procedure in Great Britain. British police officers are required, when making arrests, to inform suspects, "You do not have to say anything. But if you do not mention now something which you later use in your defense, the court may decide that your failure to mention it now strengthens the case against you. A record will be made of everything you say, and it may be given in evidence if you are brought to trial."*

8-5e Criminal Process

As mentioned, as a result of the effort to safeguard the rights of the individual against the state, a criminal prosecution differs from a civil case in several respects. Exhibit 8–3 summarizes the major procedural steps in processing a criminal case. Here, we discuss three phases of the criminal process—arrest, indictment or information, and trial—in more detail.

Arrest Before a warrant for arrest can be issued, there must be probable cause to believe that the individual in question has committed a crime. As discussed earlier, *probable cause* can be defined as a substantial likelihood that the person has committed or is about to commit a crime. Note that probable cause involves a likelihood, not just a possibility. An arrest can be made without a warrant if there is no time to get one, but the action of the arresting officer is still judged by the standard of probable cause.

Indictment or Information Individuals must be formally charged with having committed specific crimes before they can be brought to trial. If issued by a grand jury, this charge is called an **indictment**.[24] A **grand jury** usually consists of more jurors than the ordinary trial jury. A grand jury does not determine the guilt or innocence of an accused party. Rather, its function is to hear the state's evidence and to determine whether a reasonable basis (probable cause) exists for believing that a crime has been committed and that a trial ought to be held.

Usually, grand juries are used in cases involving serious crimes, such as murder. For lesser crimes, an individual may be formally charged with a crime by what is called an **information,** or criminal complaint. An information will be issued by a government prosecutor if the prosecutor determines that there is sufficient evidence to justify bringing the individual to trial.

Trial At a criminal trial, the accused person does not have to prove anything. The entire burden of proof is on the prosecutor (the state). As mentioned earlier, the prosecution must show that, based on all the evidence presented, the defendant's guilt is established *beyond a reasonable doubt.*

If there is a reasonable doubt as to whether a criminal defendant committed the crime with which she or he has been charged, then the verdict must be "not guilty." A verdict of "not guilty" is not the same as stating that the defendant is innocent. It merely means that not enough evidence was properly presented to the court to prove guilt beyond a reasonable doubt.

Courts have complex rules about what types of evidence may be presented and how the evidence may be brought out in criminal cases. These rules are designed to ensure that evidence in trials is relevant, reliable, and not prejudicial toward the defendant.

8-5f Federal Sentencing Guidelines

The Sentencing Reform Act of 1984 created the U.S. Sentencing Commission to develop standardizing sentences for *federal* crimes. The commission's guidelines established a range of possible penalties for each federal crime. Originally, the guidelines were mandatory. That is, the judge was required to select a sentence from within the set range and was not allowed to deviate from it.

Problems with Constitutionality In 2005, the United States Supreme Court held that certain provisions of the federal sentencing guidelines were unconstitutional. **CASE EXAMPLE 8.21** Freddie Booker was arrested with 92.5 grams of crack cocaine in his possession. Booker admitted to police that he had sold an additional 566 grams of crack cocaine, but he was never charged with, or tried for, possession of this additional quantity. Nevertheless, under the

---

Indictment A formal charge by a grand jury that there is probable cause to believe that a named person has committed a crime.

Grand Jury A group of citizens who decide, after hearing the state's evidence, whether a reasonable basis (probable cause) exists for believing that a crime has been committed and that a trial ought to be held.

Information A formal accusation or complaint (without an indictment) issued in certain types of actions (usually criminal actions involving lesser crimes) by a government prosecutor.

Kevin L. Chesson/ShutterStock.com

How have federal sentencing guidelines for crack cocaine changed?

---

24. Pronounced in-*dyte*-ment.

Exhibit 8–3 Major Procedural Steps in a Criminal Case

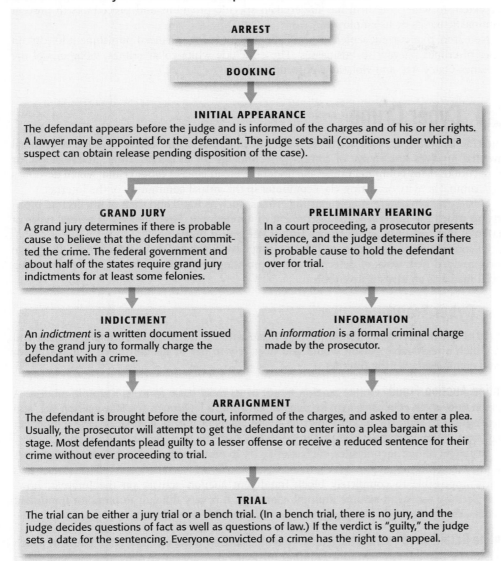

ARREST

BOOKING

INITIAL APPEARANCE
The defendant appears before the judge and is informed of the charges and of his or her rights. A lawyer may be appointed for the defendant. The judge sets bail (conditions under which a suspect can obtain release pending disposition of the case).

GRAND JURY
A grand jury determines if there is probable cause to believe that the defendant committed the crime. The federal government and about half of the states require grand jury indictments for at least some felonies.

PRELIMINARY HEARING
In a court proceeding, a prosecutor presents evidence, and the judge determines if there is probable cause to hold the defendant over for trial.

INDICTMENT
An *indictment* is a written document issued by the grand jury to formally charge the defendant with a crime.

INFORMATION
An *information* is a formal criminal charge made by the prosecutor.

ARRAIGNMENT
The defendant is brought before the court, informed of the charges, and asked to enter a plea. Usually, the prosecutor will attempt to get the defendant to enter into a plea bargain at this stage. Most defendants plead guilty to a lesser offense or receive a reduced sentence for their crime without ever proceeding to trial.

TRIAL
The trial can be either a jury trial or a bench trial. (In a bench trial, there is no jury, and the judge decides questions of fact as well as questions of law.) If the verdict is "guilty," the judge sets a date for the sentencing. Everyone convicted of a crime has the right to an appeal.

federal sentencing guidelines the judge was required to sentence Booker to twenty-two years in prison. The Court ruled that this sentence was unconstitutional because a jury did not find beyond a reasonable doubt that Booker had possessed the additional 566 grams of crack.[25] ▪

Essentially, the Court's ruling changed the federal sentencing guidelines from mandatory to advisory. Depending on the circumstances of the case, a federal trial judge may now depart from the guidelines if she or he believes that it is reasonable to do so.

Factors in Determining the Sentence
The sentencing judge must take into account the various sentencing factors that apply to an individual defendant before concluding that a particular sentence is reasonable. When the defendant is a business firm, these factors include the

> "In school, every period ends with a bell. Every sentence ends with a period. Every crime ends with a sentence."
>
> **STEVEN WRIGHT**
> 1955–PRESENT
> (AMERICAN COMEDIAN)

25. *United States v. Booker*, 543 U.S. 220, 125 S.Ct. 738, 160 L.Ed.2d 621 (2005).

Computer Crime Any violation of criminal law that involves knowledge of computer technology for its perpetration, investigation, or prosecution.

Cyber Crime A crime that occurs in the online environment.

Cyber Fraud Any misrepresentation knowingly made over the Internet with the intention of deceiving another for the purpose of obtaining property or funds.

company's history of past violations, management's cooperation with federal investigators, and the extent to which the firm has undertaken specific programs and procedures to prevent criminal activities by its employees.

Note, too, that current sentencing guidelines provide for enhanced punishment for certain types of crimes relevant to businesses. These include white-collar crimes, violations of the Sarbanes-Oxley Act, and violations of securities laws.[26]

8-6 Cyber Crime

The U.S. Department of Justice broadly defines **computer crime** as any violation of criminal law that involves knowledge of computer technology for its perpetration, investigation, or prosecution. Many computer crimes fall under the broad label of **cyber crime,** which describes any criminal activity occurring via a computer in the virtual community of the Internet.

Most cyber crimes are simply existing crimes, such as fraud and theft of intellectual property, in which the Internet is the instrument of wrongdoing. Here we look at several types of activities that constitute cyber crimes against persons or property.

Of course, just as computers and the Internet have expanded the scope of crime, they have also provided new ways of detecting and combatting crime. For instance, police are using social media as an investigative tool.

8-6a Cyber Fraud

Fraud is any misrepresentation knowingly made with the intention of deceiving another and on which a reasonable person would and does rely to her or his detriment. **Cyber fraud** is fraud committed over the Internet.

Online Auction Fraud
Online auction fraud, in its most basic form, is a simple process. A person puts up an expensive item for auction, on either a legitimate or a fake auction site, and then refuses to send the product after receiving payment. Or, as a variation, the wrongdoer may send the purchaser an item that is worth less than the one offered in the auction.

The larger online auction sites, such as eBay, try to protect consumers against such schemes by providing warnings about deceptive sellers or offering various forms of insurance. It is nearly impossible to completely block fraudulent auction activity on the Internet, however. Because users can assume multiple identities, it is very difficult to pinpoint fraudulent sellers—they will simply change their screen names with each auction.

Online Retail Fraud
Somewhat similar to online auction fraud is online retail fraud, in which consumers pay directly (without bidding) for items that are never delivered. As with other forms of online fraud, it is difficult to determine the actual extent of online sales fraud, but anecdotal evidence suggests that it is a substantial problem.

CASE EXAMPLE 8.22 Jeremy Jaynes grossed more than $750,000 per week selling nonexistent or worthless products such as "penny stock pickers" and "Internet history erasers." By the time he was arrested, he had amassed an estimated $24 million from his various fraudulent schemes.[27] ■

8-6b Cyber Theft

In cyberspace, thieves are not subject to the physical limitations of the "real" world. A thief can steal data stored in a networked computer with Internet access from anywhere on the globe.

---

26. The sentencing guidelines were amended in 2003, as required under the Sarbanes-Oxley Act, to impose stiffer penalties for corporate securities fraud.

27. *Jaynes v. Commonwealth of Virginia,* 276 Va. 443, 666 S.E.2d 303 (2008).

Only the speed of the connection and the thief's computer equipment limit the quantity of data that can be stolen.

Identity Theft   Not surprisingly, there has been a marked increase in identity theft in recent years. **Identity theft** occurs when the wrongdoer steals a form of identification—such as a name, date of birth, or Social Security number—and uses the information to access and steal the victim's financial resources. This crime existed to a certain extent before the widespread use of the Internet. Thieves would rifle through garbage, for example, to find credit-card or bank account numbers and then use those numbers to purchase goods or to withdraw funds from the victims' accounts.

The Internet has provided even easier access to private data. Frequent Web surfers surrender a wealth of information about themselves without knowing it. Most Web sites use "cookies" to collect data on those who visit their sites. Web browsers often store information such as the consumer's name and e-mail address. In addition, every time a purchase is made online, the item is linked to the purchaser's name.

Phishing   In a distinct form of identity theft known as **phishing,** the perpetrators "fish" for financial data and passwords from consumers by posing as a legitimate business such as a bank or credit-card company. The "phisher" sends an e-mail asking the recipient to "update" or "confirm" vital information, often with the threat that an account or some other service will be discontinued if the information is not provided. Once the unsuspecting individual enters the information, the phisher can sell it or use it to masquerade as that person or to drain his or her bank or credit account.

EXAMPLE 8.23 Customers of Wells Fargo Bank receive official-looking e-mails telling them to enter personal information in an online form to complete mandatory installation of a new Internet security certificate. But the Web site is bogus. When the customers complete the forms, their computers are infected and funnel their data to a computer server. The cyber criminals then sell the data. ■

Employment Fraud   Cyber criminals also look for victims at online job-posting sites. Claiming to be an employment officer in a well-known company, the criminal sends bogus e-mails to job seekers. The message asks the unsuspecting job seeker to reveal enough information to allow for identity theft.

EXAMPLE 8.24 The job site Monster.com once asked 4.5 million users to change their passwords. Cyber thieves had broken into its databases and stolen user identities, passwords, and other data in one of Britain's largest cyber theft cases. ■

Credit-Card Numbers   Companies take risks by storing their online customers' credit-card numbers. Although the consumer can make a purchase more quickly without entering a lengthy card number, the electronic warehouses that store the numbers are targets for cyber thieves.

EXAMPLE 8.25 In 2013, a security breach at Target Corporation exposed the personal information of 70 million Target customers. Hackers stole credit- and debit-card numbers and debit-card PINs from the embedded code on the magnetic strips of the cards, as well as customers' names, addresses, and phone numbers. JPMorgan Chase Bank, the world's largest issuer of credit cards, had to replace 2 million credit and debit cards as a result of the breach. ■

Stolen credit-card numbers are much more likely to hurt merchants and credit-card issuers (such as banks) than consumers. In most situations, the legitimate holders of credit cards are not held responsible for the costs of purchases made with a stolen number.

8–6c Hacking

A **hacker** is someone who uses one computer, smartphone, or other device to break into another. The danger posed by hackers has increased significantly because of **botnets,** or

---

Identity Theft The illegal use of someone else's personal information to access the victim's financial resources.

LEARNING OBJECTIVE 5

How has the Internet expanded opportunities for identity theft?

Phishing A form of identity theft in which the perpetrator sends e-mails purporting to be from legitimate businesses to induce recipients to reveal their personal financial data, passwords, or other information.

Hacker A person who uses computers to gain unauthorized access to data.

Botnet A network of compromised computers connected to the Internet that can be used to generate spam, relay viruses, or cause servers to fail.

Not far from Moscow's Red Square, Russian hackers are outside the jurisdiction of U.S. authorities. Why?

Malware Malicious software programs, such as viruses and worms, that are designed to cause harm to a computer, network, or other device.

Worm A software program that automatically replicates itself over a network but does not alter files and is usually invisible to the user until it has consumed system resources.

Virus A software program that can replicate itself over a network and spread from one device to another, altering files and interfering with normal operations.

networks of computers that have been appropriated by hackers without the knowledge of their owners. A hacker may secretly install a program on thousands, if not millions, of personal computer "robots," or "bots." To read about a group of well-known hackers in Russia, see this chapter's *Beyond Our Borders* feature.

EXAMPLE 8.26 When a hacker broke into Sony Corporation's PlayStation 3 video gaming and entertainment networks, the company had to temporarily shut down its online services. This single hacking incident affected more than 100 million online accounts that provide gaming, chat, and music streaming services. ■

Malware Botnets are one form of **malware,** a term that refers to any program that is harmful to a computer or, by extension, its user. A **worm,** for example, is a software program that is capable of reproducing itself as it spreads from one computer to the next.

EXAMPLE 8.27 Within three weeks, the computer worm called Conflicker spread to more than a million personal computers around the world. It was transmitted to some computers through the use of Facebook and Twitter. This worm also infected servers and devices plugged into infected computers via USB ports, such as iPods, iPhones, iPads, and USB flash drives. ■

A **virus,** another form of malware, is also able to reproduce itself, but must be attached to an "infested" host file to travel from one computer network to another. For example, hackers are now capable of corrupting banner ads that use Adobe's Flash Player. When an Internet user clicks on the banner ad, a virus is installed.

Worms and viruses can be programmed to perform a number of functions, such as prompting host computers to continually "crash" and reboot, or to otherwise infect the system. For a discussion of how malware is changing the criminal landscape and even affecting smartphones, see this chapter's *Adapting the Law to the Online Environment* feature.

Service-Based Hacking A recent trend in business computer applications is the use of "software as a service." Instead of buying software to install on a computer, the user connects to

---

BEYOND OUR BORDERS   Hackers Hide in Plain Sight in Russia

According to the security software company Symantec, few Internet users and businesses have completely avoided computer crime. Consumers alone lose about $120 billion a year worldwide to cyber fraud and hacking. In recent years, Russia has become a haven for hackers.

The KoobFace Gang
A group of at least five men who live comfortably in St. Petersburg, Russia, started hacking a few years ago—and are still at it.

Calling themselves KoobFace, they created a system of illegal botnets that includes 800,000 infected personal computers. Via this system, they have succeeded in using the KoobFace worm to infiltrate Facebook accounts. The KoobFace gang continues to make $2 million to $5 million a year from this venture. KoobFace is considered a pioneer in the criminal exploitation of social networks.

Knowing the Perpetrators Does Not Lead to Convictions
Authorities worldwide know the identities of the members of KoobFace, yet so far none of them has been charged with a crime. No

law enforcement agencies have even confirmed that the group is under investigation. Because Western law officials do not have the resources to tackle even well-known hackers, the Russians hackers are free to continue their activities. It is not surprising that Russia has gained a reputation as a "hacker haven."

CRITICAL THINKING

■ Why might it be difficult for U.S. authorities to ever investigate the KoobFace gang?

ADAPTING THE LAW TO THE ONLINE ENVIRONMENT
Malware Is Changing the Criminal Landscape

Recent statistics show that the number of bank robberies occurring annually is on the decline. Criminals have learned that it is easier, less risky, and more profitable to steal via the Internet. Advances in the speed and use of the Internet have fostered the growth of a relatively new criminal industry that uses malware to conduct espionage and profit from crime.

Who Are the Creators of Malware?

While any teenager can buy prepackaged hacking software on the Internet, the malware that businesses and governments are worried about is much more sophisticated. They are concerned about malware that can be used for international diplomatic espionage and industrial espionage. Evidence indicates that this malware is most often developed by so-called cyber mercenaries. According to Steve Sachs of the cyber security firm FireEye, "There are entire little villages dedicated to malware in Russia, villages in China, very sophisticated, very organized, very well-funded."

Flame Malware

Perhaps the most sophisticated global malware has been labeled Flame. Flame was discovered in 2012, although experts believe that it had been lying dormant in thousands of computers worldwide for at least five years. Flame can record screen shots, keyboard strokes, network traffic, and audio. It can also record Skype conversations. It can even turn infected computers into Bluetooth beacons, which can then attempt to download contact information from nearby Bluetooth-enabled devices.

The Malware Can Infect Smartphones

Many smartphone owners are unaware that their phones can be infected with Flame malware or variants of it without their knowledge. The information that is hacked from smartphones can then be sent to a series of command-and-control servers and ultimately to members of international criminal gangs.

Once a computer or smartphone is infected with this malware, all information in the device can be transferred. Additionally, files can be deleted, and files that have been erased can be resurrected. The malware has been responsible for the theft of e-mail databases from Microsoft's e-mail program Outlook and has even captured e-mail from remote servers.[a]

Businesses Are Worried

Until recently, most attacks involved diplomatic espionage, but cyber technicians at large business enterprises are now worried that industrial espionage may be taking place as well. In fact, an extensive hacking operation was uncovered in 2013 that was linked to a Chinese military unit (the "Comment Crew"). The wide-ranging cyber attacks involved the theft of hundreds of terabytes of data and intellectual property of more than 140 corporations in twenty different industries. The goal of the attacks was to help Chinese companies better compete against U.S. and other foreign firms.[b]

CRITICAL THINKING

■ What entities might pay "cyber mercenaries" to create some of the malware described in this feature?

---

a. Mark Stevens, *"CWI Cryptanalyst Discovers New Cryptographic Attack Variant in Flame Spy Malware,"* June 7, 2012, www.cwi.nl/news/2012.

b. David E. Sanger, David Barboza, and Nicole Perlroth, *"Chinese Army Unit Is Seen as Tied to Hacking Against U.S.,"* www.nytimes.com/2013.

Web-based software. The user can then write e-mails, edit spreadsheets, and the like using a Web browser.

Cyber criminals have adapted this method and now offer "crimeware as a service." A would-be thief no longer has to be a computer hacker to create a botnet or steal banking information and credit-card numbers. He or she can rent the online services of cyber criminals to do the work for a small price. The thief can even target individual groups, such as U.S. physicians or British attorneys. (For some tips on protecting a company against hackers, see the *Business Application* at the end of this chapter.)

8–6d Cyberterrorism

Cyberterrorists, as well as hackers, may target businesses. The goals of a hacking operation might include a wholesale theft of data, such as a merchant's customer files, or the monitoring

> "A hacker does for love what others would not do for money."
>
> **LAURA CREIGHTON**
> (COMPUTER PROGRAMMER AND ENTREPRENEUR)

of a computer to discover a business firm's plans and transactions. A cyberterrorist might also want to insert false codes or data into a computer. For instance, the processing control system of a food manufacturer could be changed to alter the levels of ingredients so that consumers of the food would become ill.

A cyberterrorist attack on a major financial institution, such as the New York Stock Exchange or a large bank, could leave securities or money markets in flux and seriously affect the daily lives of millions of citizens. Similarly, any prolonged disruption of computer, cable, satellite, or telecommunications systems due to the actions of expert hackers would have serious repercussions on business operations—and national security—on a global level.

8-6e Prosecution of Cyber Crime

Cyber crime has raised new issues in the investigation of crimes and the prosecution of offenders. Determining the "location" of a cyber crime and identifying a criminal in cyberspace are two significant challenges for law enforcement.

Jurisdiction and Identification Challenges
A threshold issue is, of course, jurisdiction. Jurisdiction is normally based on physical geography, as discussed previously, and each state and nation has jurisdiction over crimes committed within its boundaries. But geographic boundaries simply do not apply in cyberspace. A person who commits an act against a business in California, where the act is a cyber crime, might never have set foot in California but might instead reside in, say, Canada, where the act may not be a crime.

Identifying the wrongdoer can also be difficult. Cyber criminals do not leave physical traces, such as fingerprints or DNA samples, as evidence of their crimes. Even electronic "footprints" (digital evidence) can be hard to find and follow. For instance, e-mail can be sent through a remailer, an online service that guarantees that a message cannot be traced to its source.

For these reasons, laws written to protect physical property are often difficult to apply in cyberspace. Nonetheless, governments at both the state and the federal level have taken significant steps toward controlling cyber crime, both by applying existing criminal statutes and by enacting new laws that specifically address wrongs committed in cyberspace. California, for instance, which has the highest identity theft rate in the nation, has established an eCrime unit to investigate and prosecute cyber crimes. Other states, including Florida, Louisiana, and Texas, also have special law enforcement units that focus solely on Internet crimes.

The Computer Fraud and Abuse Act
Perhaps the most significant federal statute specifically addressing cyber crime is the Counterfeit Access Device and Computer Fraud and Abuse Act.[28] This act is commonly known as the Computer Fraud and Abuse Act, or CFAA.

Among other things, the CFAA provides that a person who accesses a computer online, without authority, to obtain classified, restricted, or protected data (or attempts to do so) is subject to criminal prosecution. Such data could include financial and credit records, medical records, legal files, military and national security files, and other confidential information in government or private computers. The crime has two elements: accessing a computer without authority and taking the data.

This theft is a felony if it is committed for a commercial purpose or for private financial gain, or if the value of the stolen information exceeds $5,000. Penalties include fines and imprisonment for up to twenty years. A victim of computer theft can also bring a civil suit against the violator to obtain damages, an injunction, and other relief.

---

28. 18 U.S.C. Section 1030.

Reviewing . . . Criminal Law and Cyber Crime

Edward Hanousek worked for Pacific & Arctic Railway and Navigation Company (P&A) as a roadmaster of the White Pass & Yukon Railroad in Alaska. As an officer of the corporation, Hanousek was responsible "for every detail of the safe and efficient maintenance and construction of track, structures, and marine facilities of the entire railroad," including special projects. One project was a rock quarry, known as "6-mile," above the Skagway River. Next to the quarry, and just beneath the surface, ran a high-pressure oil pipeline owned by Pacific & Arctic Pipeline, Inc., P&A's sister company. When the quarry's backhoe operator punctured the pipeline, an estimated 1,000 to 5,000 gallons of oil were discharged into the river. Hanousek was charged with negligently discharging a harmful quantity of oil into a navigable water of the United States in violation of the criminal provisions of the Clean Water Act (CWA). Using the information presented in the chapter, answer the following questions.

1. Did Hanousek have the required mental state *(mens rea)* to be convicted of a crime? Why or why not?

2. Which theory discussed in the chapter would enable a court to hold Hanousek criminally liable for violating the statute regardless of whether he participated in, directed, or even knew about the specific violation?

3. Could the quarry's backhoe operator who punctured the pipeline also be charged with a crime in this situation? Explain.

4. Suppose that, at trial, Hanousek argued that he could not be convicted because he was not aware of the requirements of the CWA. Would this defense be successful? Why or why not?

DEBATE THIS

- Because of overcriminalization, particularly by the federal government, Americans may be breaking the law regularly without knowing it. Should Congress rescind many of the more than four thousand federal crimes now on the books?

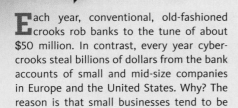

BUSINESS APPLICATION

Protecting Your Company against Hacking of Its Bank Accounts*

Each year, conventional, old-fashioned crooks rob banks to the tune of about $50 million. In contrast, every year cyber-crooks steal billions of dollars from the bank accounts of small and mid-size companies in Europe and the United States. Why? The reason is that small businesses tend to be lax in protecting themselves from hackers. They keep their accounts in community or regional banks, have only rudimentary security measures, and usually fail to hire an on-site cyber security expert.

You May Not Receive Compensation for Your Losses

Many small-business owners believe that if their bank accounts are hacked and disappear, their banks will reimburse them. That is not always the case, however. Just ask Mark Patterson, the owner of Patco Construction in Stanford, Maryland. He lost more than $350,000 to cyberthieves. When People's United Bank would not agree to a settlement, Patterson sued, claiming that the bank should have monitored his account. So far,

---

* This *Business Application* is not meant to substitute for the services of an attorney who is licensed to practice law in your state.

federal judges have agreed with the bank—that its protections were "commercially reasonable," which is the only standard that banks have to follow.

Insurance May Not Be the Answer
Similarly, small-business owners often think that their regular insurance policy will cover cyber losses at their local banks. In reality, unless there is a specific "rider" to a business's insurance policy, its bank accounts are not covered. Thus, even though your insurance company will reimburse you if thieves break

in and steal your machines and network servers, it may not have to reimburse you if cyber-crooks break into your bank account.

CHECKLIST for Preventing Cyberthefts of Your Bank Accounts:

1. Meet with your bank managers and discuss what you can do to protect your company's bank accounts.
2. Have your company sign up for identity-theft-protection services. Many large banks provide these.

3. Change your company's passwords frequently. Always use long, complicated passwords.
4. Instruct your employees never to reply to unknown e-mail requests, particularly if they ask for any information about the company.
5. Have a computer expert test the firewalls safeguarding your internal computer network.

Key Terms

actus reus 187
arson 192
beyond a reasonable doubt 185
botnet 207
burglary 191
computer crime 206
crime 185
cyber crime 206
cyber fraud 206
double jeopardy 201
duress 198
embezzlement 193
entrapment 198

exclusionary rule 202
felony 186
forgery 193
grand jury 204
hacker 207
identity theft 207
indictment 204
information 204
insider trading 195
larceny 192
malware 208
mens rea 187
misdemeanor 187

money laundering 196
petty offense 187
phishing 207
plea bargaining 199
probable cause 200
robbery 190
search warrant 199
self-defense 197
self-incrimination 199
virus 208
white-collar crime 193
worm 208

Chapter Summary: Criminal Law and Cyber Crime

Civil Law and Criminal Law	1. *Civil law*—Spells out the duties that exist between persons or between persons and their governments, excluding the duty not to commit crimes. 2. *Criminal law*—Has to do with crimes, which are wrongs against society proclaimed in statutes and, if committed, punishable by society through fines and/or imprisonment—and, in some cases, death. Because crimes are *offenses against society as a whole,* they are prosecuted by a public official, not by the victims. 3. *Key differences*—An important difference between civil and criminal law is that the standard of proof is higher in criminal cases (see Exhibit 8–1 for other differences between civil and criminal law). 4. *Civil liability for criminal acts*—A criminal act may give rise to both criminal liability and tort liability (see Exhibit 8–2 for an example of criminal and tort liability for the same act). 5. *Classification of crimes*—Crimes may also be classified according to their degree of seriousness. Felonies are serious crimes usually punishable by death or by imprisonment for more than one year. Misdemeanors are less serious crimes punishable by fines or by confinement for up to one year.
Criminal Liability	1. *Guilty act*—In general, some form of harmful act must be committed for a crime to exist. 2. *Intent*—An intent to commit a crime, or a wrongful mental state, is generally required for a crime to exist.

Types of Crimes	1. *Violent crimes*—Violent crimes are those that cause others to suffer harm or death, including murder, assault and battery, sexual assault (rape), and robbery.
	2. *Property crimes*—Property crimes are the most common form of crime. The offender's goal is to obtain some economic gain or to damage property. This category includes burglary, larceny, obtaining goods by false pretenses, receiving stolen property, arson, and forgery.
	3. *Public order crimes*—Public order crimes are acts, such as public drunkenness, prostitution, gambling, and illegal drug use, that a statute has established are contrary to public values and morals.
	4. *White-collar crimes*—White-collar crimes are illegal acts committed by a person or business using nonviolent means to obtain a personal or business advantage. Usually, such crimes are committed in the course of a legitimate occupation. Examples include embezzlement, mail and wire fraud, bribery, bankruptcy fraud, theft of trade secrets, and insider trading.
	5. *Organized crimes*—Organized crime is a form of crime conducted by groups operating illegitimately to satisfy the public's demand for illegal goods and services (such as gambling or illegal narcotics). This category of crime also includes money laundering and racketeering (RICO) violations.
Defenses to Criminal Liability	Defenses to criminal liability include justifiable use of force, necessity, insanity, mistake, duress, entrapment, and the statute of limitations. Also, in some cases defendants may be relieved of criminal liability, at least in part, if they are given immunity.
Criminal Procedures	1. *Fourth Amendment*—Provides protection against unreasonable searches and seizures and requires that probable cause exist before a warrant for a search or an arrest can be issued.
	2. *Fifth Amendment*—Requires due process of law, prohibits double jeopardy, and protects against self-incrimination.
	3. *Sixth Amendment*—Guarantees a speedy trial, a trial by jury, a public trial, the right to confront witnesses, and the right to counsel.
	4. *Eighth Amendment*—Prohibits excessive bail and fines, and cruel and unusual punishment.
	5. *Exclusionary rule*—A criminal procedural rule that prohibits the introduction at trial of all evidence obtained in violation of constitutional rights, as well as any evidence derived from the illegally obtained evidence.
	6. *Miranda rule*—A rule set forth by the Supreme Court in *Miranda v. Arizona* holding that individuals who are arrested must be informed of certain constitutional rights, including their right to counsel.
	7. *Criminal process*—Procedures governing arrest, indictment, and trial for a crime are designed to safeguard the rights of the individual against the government (see Exhibit 8–3).
	8. *Sentencing guidelines*—The federal government has established sentencing laws or guidelines, which are no longer mandatory but provide a range of penalties for each federal crime.
Cyber Crime	1. *Cyber fraud*—Occurs when misrepresentations are knowingly made over the Internet to deceive another. Two widely reported forms are online auction fraud and online retail fraud.
	2. *Cyber theft*—In cyberspace, thieves can steal data from anywhere in the world. Identity theft is made easier by the fact that many e-businesses store information such as consumers' names, e-mail addresses, and credit-card numbers. Phishing and employment fraud are variations of identity theft.
	3. *Hacking*—A hacker is a person who uses one computer to break into another. Malware is any program that is harmful to a computer or, by extension, a computer user. Worms and viruses are examples.
	4. *Cyberterrorism*—Cyberterrorists aim to cause serious problems for computer systems. A cyberterrorist attack on a major U.S. financial institution or telecommunications system could have serious repercussions, including jeopardizing national security.
	5. *Prosecution of cyber crime*—Prosecuting cyber crime is more difficult than prosecuting traditional crime. Identifying the wrongdoer is complicated, and jurisdictional issues may arise. A significant federal statute addressing cyber crime is the computer fraud and abuse act.

Issue Spotters

1. Daisy takes her roommate's credit card, intending to charge expenses that she incurs on a vacation. Her first stop is a gas station, where she uses the card to pay for gas. With respect to the gas station, has she committed a crime? If so, what is it? (See *Types of Crimes*.)

2. Without permission, Ben downloads consumer credit files from a computer belonging to Consumer Credit Agency. He then sells the data to Dawn. Has Ben committed a crime? If so, what is it? (See *Cyber Crime*.)

—**Check your answers to the *Issue Spotters* against the answers provided in Appendix D at the end of this text.**

Learning Objectives Check

1. What two elements normally must exist before a person can be held liable for a crime?
2. What are five broad categories of crimes? What is white-collar crime?
3. What defenses can be raised to avoid liability for criminal acts?
4. What constitutional safeguards exist to protect persons accused of crimes?
5. How has the Internet expanded opportunities for identity theft?

—**Answers to the even-numbered *Learning Objectives Check* questions can be found in Appendix E at the end of this text.**

Business Scenarios and Case Problems

8–1. Types of Cyber Crimes. The following situations are similar, but each represents a variation of a particular crime. Identify the crime and point out the differences in the variations. (See *Cyber Crime.*)

1. Chen, posing fraudulently as Diamond Credit Card Co., sends an e-mail to Emily, stating that the company has observed suspicious activity in her account and has frozen the account. The e-mail asks her to reregister her credit-card number and password to reopen the account.

2. Claiming falsely to be Big Buy Retail Finance Co., Conner sends an e-mail to Dino, asking him to confirm or update his personal security information to prevent his Big Buy account from being discontinued.

3. Felicia posts her résumé on GotWork.com, an online job-posting site, seeking a position in business and managerial finance and accounting. Hayden, who misrepresents himself as an employment officer with International Bank & Commerce Corp., sends her an e-mail asking for more personal information.

8–2. Cyber Scam. Kayla, a student at Learnwell University, owes $20,000 in unpaid tuition. If Kayla does not pay the tuition, Learnwell will not allow her to graduate. To obtain the funds to pay the debt, she sends e-mails to people that she does not know asking them for financial help to send her child, who has a disability, to a special school. In reality, Kayla has no children. Is this a crime? If so, which one? (See *Cyber Crime.*)

8–3. Search. Charles Byrd was in a minimum-security county jail awaiting trial. A team of sheriff's deputies wearing T-shirts and jeans took Byrd and several other inmates into a room for a strip search without any apparent justification. Byrd was ordered to remove all his clothing except his boxer shorts. A female deputy searched Byrd while several male deputies watched. One of the male deputies videotaped the search. Byrd filed a suit against the sheriff's department. Did the search violate Byrd's rights? Discuss. [*Byrd v. Maricopa County Sheriff's Department*, 629 F.3d. 1135 (9th Cir. 2011)] (See *Criminal Procedures.*)

8–4. Credit- and Debit-Card Theft. Jacqueline Barden was shopping for school clothes with her children when her purse and automobile were taken. In Barden's purse were her car keys, credit and debit cards for herself and her children, as well as the children's Social Security cards and birth certificates needed for enrollment at school. Immediately after the purse and car were stolen, Rebecca Mary Turner attempted to use Barden's credit card at a local Exxon gas station, but the card was declined. The gas station attendant recognized Turner because she had previously written bad checks and used credit cards that did not belong to her.

Turner was later arrested while attempting to use one of Barden's checks to pay for merchandise at a Walmart—where the clerk also recognized Turner from prior criminal activity. Turner claimed that she had not stolen Barden's purse or car, and that a friend had told her he had some checks and credit cards and asked her to try using them at Walmart. Turner was convicted at trial. She appealed, claiming that there was insufficient evidence that she committed credit- and debit-card theft. Was the evidence sufficient to uphold her conviction? Why or why not? [*Turner v. State of Arkansas*, 2012 Ark.App. 150 (2012)] (See *Types of Crimes.*)

8–5. Business Case Problem with Sample Answer— Criminal Liability. During the morning rush hour, David Green threw bottles and plates from a twenty-sixth-floor hotel balcony overlooking Seventh Avenue in New York City. A video of the incident also showed him doing cartwheels while holding a beer bottle and sprinting toward the balcony while holding a glass steadily in his hand. When he saw police on the street below and on the roof of the building across the street, he suspended his antics but resumed tossing objects off the balcony after the police left. He later admitted that he could recall what he had done, but claimed to have been intoxicated and said his only purpose was to amuse himself and his friends. Did Green have the mental state required to establish criminal liability? Discuss. [*State of New York v. Green*, 104 A.D.3d 126, 958 N.Y.S.2d 138 (1 Dept. 2013)] (See *Criminal Liability.*)

—**For a sample answer to Problem 8–5, go to Appendix F at the end of this text.**

8–6. White-Collar Crime. Matthew Simpson and others created and operated a series of corporate entities to defraud telecommunications companies, creditors, credit reporting agencies, and others. Through these entities, Simpson and his confederates used routing codes and spoofing services to make long-distance calls appear to be local. They stole other firms' network capacity and diverted payments to themselves. They leased goods and services without paying for them. To hide their association with their corporate entities and with each other, they used false identities, addresses, and credit histories, and issued false bills, invoices, financial statements, and credit references. Did these acts constitute mail and wire fraud? Discuss. [*United States v. Simpson,* 741 F.3d 539 (5th Cir. 2014)] (See *Types of Crimes.*)

8–7. Defenses to Criminal Liability. George Castro told Ambrosio Medrano that a bribe to a certain corrupt Los Angeles County official would buy a contract with the county hospitals. To share in the deal, Medrano recruited Gustavo Buenrostro. In turn, Buenrostro contacted his friend James Barta, the owner of Sav–Rx, which provides prescription benefit management services. Barta was asked to pay a "finder's fee" to Castro. He did not pay, even after frequent e-mails and calls with deadlines and ultimatums delivered over a period of months. Eventually, Barta wrote Castro a Sav–Rx check for $6,500, saying that it was to help his friend Buenrostro. Castro was an FBI agent, and the county official and contract were fictional. Barta was charged with conspiracy to commit bribery. At trial, the government conceded that Barta was not predisposed to commit the crime. Could he be absolved of the charge on a defense of entrapment? Explain. [*United States v. Barta,* __ F.3d __, 2015 WL 350672 (7th Cir. 2015)] (See *Defenses to Criminal Liability.*)

8–8. A Question of Ethics—Criminal Process. Gary Peters fraudulently told an undocumented immigrant that Peters could help him obtain lawful status. Peters said that he knew immigration officials and asked for money to aid the process. The victim paid Peters at least $25,000 in wire transfers and checks. Peters had others call the victim, falsely represent that they were agents with the U.S. Department of Homeland Security, and induce continued payments. He threatened to contact authorities to detain or deport the victim and his wife. Peters was convicted in a federal district court of wire fraud. [*United States v. Peters,* __ F.3d __, 2015 WL 120637 (11th Cir. 2015)] (See *Constitutional Safeguards and Criminal Procedures.*)

1. Peters had previously committed theft and fraud. The court stated, "This is the person he is. He steals from his relatives. He steals from his business partner. He steals from immigrants. He steals from anybody he comes into contact with." What does Peters's conduct indicate about his ethics?

2. Peters's attorney argued that his client's criminal history was partially due to "difficult personal times" caused by divorce, illness, and job loss. Despite this claim, Peters was sentenced to forty-eight months imprisonment, which exceeded the federal sentencing guidelines but was less than the statutory maximum of twenty years. Was this sentence too harsh or too lenient? Discuss.

Critical Thinking and Writing Assignments

8–9. Critical Legal Thinking. Ray steals a purse from an unattended car at a gas station. Because the purse contains money and a handgun, Ray is convicted of grand theft of property (cash) and grand theft of a firearm. On appeal, Ray claims that he is not guilty of grand theft of a firearm because he did not know that the purse contained a gun. Can Ray be convicted of grand theft of a firearm even though he did not know that the gun was in the purse? Explain. (See *Types of Crimes.*)

8–10. Business Law Critical Thinking Group Assignment. Cyber crime costs consumers millions of dollars every year. It costs businesses, including banks and other credit-card issuers, even more. Nonetheless, when cyber criminals are caught and convicted, they are rarely ordered to pay restitution or sentenced to long prison terms. (See *Cyber Crime.*)

1. One group should argue that stiffer sentences would reduce the amount of cyber crime.

2. A second group should determine how businesspersons can best protect themselves from cyber crime and avoid the associated costs.

iStockPhoto.com/vaeenma

9

LEARNING OBJECTIVES

The five Learning Objectives *below are designed to help improve your understanding of the chapter. After reading this chapter, you should be able to answer the following questions:*

1. What is business ethics, and why is it important?

2. How do duty-based ethical standards differ from outcome-based ethical standards?

3. What are five steps that a businessperson can take to evaluate whether his or her actions are ethical?

4. How can business leaders encourage their companies to act ethically?

5. What types of ethical issues might arise in the context of international business transactions?

Ethics Moral principles and values applied to social behavior.

Business Ethics

One of the most complex issues that businesspersons and corporations face is ethics. Ethics is not as clearly defined as the law. To be sure, some ethical scandals arise from illegal conduct, such as when corporate executives trade stock based on inside information (information that has not become public). Others, though, involve activities that are legal but ethically questionable. For instance, in 2014 it was discovered that more than three hundred corporations (many from the United States) had entered into secret agreements that allowed them to funnel cash into Luxembourg to avoid paying billions in taxes. Although there is nothing wrong with minimizing tax liability, dodging taxes completely may have ethical implications.

As the chapter-opening quotation states, "New occasions teach new duties." The ethics scandals of the last several years have taught everyone that business ethics cannot be taken lightly. Ethical behavior, or the lack of it, can have a substantial impact on a firm's finances and reputation. How businesspersons should act and whose interests they should consider—those of the firm, its executives, its employees, its shareholders, and more—are the focus of this chapter on business ethics.

> "New occasions teach new duties."
>
> **JAMES RUSSELL LOWELL**
> 1819–1891
> (AMERICAN EDITOR, POET, AND DIPLOMAT)

9-1 Business Ethics

At the most basic level, the study of **ethics** is the study of what constitutes right or wrong behavior. It is the branch of philosophy that focuses on morality and the way in which moral principles are derived and applied to one's conduct in daily life. Ethics has to do with questions relating to the fairness, justness, rightness, or wrongness of an action.

The study of **business ethics** typically looks at the decisions businesses make and whether those decisions are right or wrong. It has to do with how businesspersons apply moral and ethical principles in making their decisions. Those who study business ethics also evaluate what duties and responsibilities exist or should exist for businesses.

9–1a Why Is Studying Business Ethics Important?

Over the last two hundred years, the public perception of the corporation has changed from an entity that primarily generates revenues for its owners to an entity that participates in society as a corporate citizen. Originally, the only goal or duty of a corporation was to maximize profits. Although many people today may view this idea as greedy or inhumane, the rationale for the profit-maximization theory is still valid.

Profit Maximization as a Goal In theory, if all firms strictly adhere to the goal of profit maximization, resources flow to where they are most highly valued by society. Corporations can focus on their strengths. Other entities that are better suited to deal with social problems and perform charitable acts can specialize in those activities. The government, through taxes and other financial allocations, can shift resources to those other entities to perform public services. Thus, profit maximization can lead to the most efficient allocation of scarce resources.

The Rise of Corporate Citizenship Over the years, many people became dissatisfied with profit-maximization theory. Investors and others began to look beyond profits and dividends and to consider the **triple bottom line**—a corporation's profits, its impact on people, and its impact on the planet. Magazines and Web sites began to rank companies based on their environmental impacts and their ethical decisions (or lack thereof). The corporation came to be viewed as a "citizen" that was expected to participate in bettering communities and society. Even so, many still believe that corporations are fundamentally money-making entities that should have no responsibility other than profit maximization.

9–1b The Importance of Ethics in Making Business Decisions

Whether one believes in profit-maximization theory or corporate citizenship, ethics is important in making business decisions. Corporations should strive to be "good citizens." When making decisions, a business should evaluate each of the following:

1. The legal implications of each decision.
2. The public relations impact.
3. The safety risks for consumers and employees.
4. The financial implications.

This four-part analysis will assist the firm in making decisions that not only maximize profits but also reflect good corporate citizenship.

Short-Run versus Long-Run Profit Maximization In attempting to maximize profits, corporate executives and employees have to distinguish between *short-run* and *long-run* profit maximization. In the short run, a company may increase its profits by continuing to sell a product, even though it knows that the product is defective. In the long run, though, because of lawsuits, large settlements, and bad publicity, such unethical conduct will cause profits to suffer. Thus, business ethics is consistent only with long-run profit maximization. An overemphasis on short-term profit maximization is the most common reason that ethical problems occur in business.

CASE EXAMPLE 9.1 When the powerful narcotic painkiller OxyContin was first marketed, its manufacturer, Purdue Pharma, claimed that it was unlikely to lead to drug addiction or

Business Ethics The application of moral and ethical principles in a business context.

LEARNING OBJECTIVE 1
What is business ethics, and why is it important?

Triple Bottom Line A measure that includes a corporation's profits, its impact on people, and its impact on the planet.

"It's easy to make a buck. It's a lot tougher to make a difference."

TOM BROKAW
1940–PRESENT
(AMERICAN TELEVISION JOURNALIST)

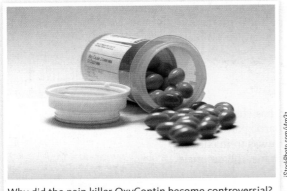

Why did the pain killer OxyContin become controversial?

abuse. Internal company documents later showed that the company's executives knew that OxyContin could be addictive, but kept this risk a secret to boost sales and maximize short-term profits.

Subsequently, Purdue Pharma and three former executives pleaded guilty to criminal charges that they had misled regulators, patients, and physicians about OxyContin's risks of addiction. Purdue Pharma agreed to pay $600 million in fines and other payments. The three former executives agreed to pay $34.5 million in fines and were barred from doing business with federal health programs for fifteen years. Thus, the company's focus on maximizing profits in the short run led to unethical conduct that hurt profits in the long run.[1]

The Internet Can Ruin Reputations   In the past, negative information or opinions about a company might remain hidden. Now, however, cyberspace provides a forum in which disgruntled employees, unhappy consumers, and special interest groups can post derogatory remarks. Thus, the Internet has increased the potential for a major corporation (or other business) to suffer damage to its reputation or loss of profits through negative publicity.

Walmart and Nike have been frequent targets for advocacy groups that believe those corporations exploit their workers. Although these assertions may be unfounded or exaggerated, the courts generally have refused to consider them *defamatory* (defamation was discussed in the torts chapter). Most courts regard online attacks as expressions of opinion, a form of speech protected by the First Amendment. Even so, corporations often incur considerable expense in running marketing campaigns to counteract bad publicity, and they may face legal costs if the allegations lead to litigation.

Image Is Everything   Business ethics relates to the purposes of a business and how that business achieves those purposes. These factors, in turn, involve the business's image and the impacts that the business has on the environment, customers, suppliers, employees, and the global economy. Unethical corporate decision making can negatively affect suppliers, consumers, the community, and society as a whole. It can also harm the reputation of the company and the individuals who run it. Hence, an in-depth understanding of business ethics is important to the long-run viability of any corporation today.

9–1c The Relationship of Law and Ethics

The law does not codify all ethical requirements. Because the law cannot make all our ethical decisions for us, compliance with the law is not always sufficient to determine "right" behavior.

Legal Requirements   Laws have to be general enough to apply in a variety of circumstances. Laws are broad in their purpose and their scope. They prohibit or require certain actions to prevent significant harm to society. When two competing companies secretly agree to set prices on products, for instance, society suffers harm—typically, the companies will charge higher prices than they could if they continued to compete. This harm has negative consequences for the economy, and so

"Have you noticed ethics creeping into some of these deals lately?"

---

1. *United States v. Purdue Frederick Co.*, 495 F.Supp.2d 569 (W.D.Va. 2007).

colluding to set prices is an illegal activity. Similarly, when a company is preparing to issue stock, the law requires certain disclosures to potential investors.

The Moral Minimum Compliance with the law is sometimes called the **moral minimum.** In other words, those who merely comply with the law are acting at the lowest ethical level society will tolerate. The following case illustrates some consequences of a businessperson's failure to meet the moral minimum.

Moral Minimum The minimum level of ethical behavior expected by society, which is usually defined as compliance with the law.

CASE 9.1

Scott v. Carpanzano

United States Court of Appeals, Fifth Circuit, 2014 WL 274493 (2014).

FACTS Rick Scott deposited $2 million in an escrow account maintained by a company owned by Salvatore Carpanzano. Immediately after the deposit was made, in violation of the escrow agreement, the funds were withdrawn. When Scott was unable to recover his money, he filed a suit against Salvatore Carpanzano and others, including Carmela Carpanzano, Salvatore's daughter. In the complaint, Scott made no allegations of acts or knowledge on Carmela's part, and Carmela denied that she was involved in her father's business or the Scott transaction.

Salvatore failed to cooperate with discovery, did not respond to attempts to contact him by certified letters and other means, refused to make an appearance in court, and did not finalize a settlement negotiated between the parties' attorneys. Carmela indicated that she was relying on her father to protect her interests in the lawsuit. The court issued a judgment for more than $6 million in Scott's favor, finding that the defendants had willfully defaulted—that is, intentionally failed to respond to the litigation. The defendants appealed to the U.S. Court of Appeals for the Fifth Circuit.

ISSUE Did the defendants willfully default and thereby justify the judgment against them?

Why is certified mail used?

Corund/ShutterStock.com

DECISION Yes, as to Salvatore. No, as to Carmela. The federal appellate court affirmed the judgment against Salvatore, but reversed the decision against Carmela.

REASON Salvatore failed almost entirely to participate in the litigation in any way. In particular, he did not cooperate with discovery, respond to attempts to communicate with him, appear in court, or finalize his attorneys' negotiated settlement. This intentional failure to respond constituted a willful default. In contrast, Carmela did not willfully default. Rather, she relied on her father to protect her interests in the lawsuit. As for her liability, Scott's complaint made no allegations of acts or knowledge on her part, and she denied that she was involved in her father's business or the Scott transaction. "Even if Scott were able to prove the entirety of the . . . complaint, we fail to see how it would justify a judgment . . . against Ms. Carpanzano."

CRITICAL THINKING—Ethical Consideration *Are Salvatore's actions likely to affect his business's ability to profit in the long run? Discuss.*

Ethical Requirements The study of ethics goes beyond legal requirements to evaluate what is right for society. Businesspersons thus must remember that an action that is legal is not necessarily ethical. For instance, a company's refusal to negotiate liability claims for alleged injuries because of a faulty product is legal. But it may not be ethical if the reason the business refused to negotiate was to increase the injured party's legal costs and force the person to drop a legitimate claim.

Ethics and Private Company Codes of Ethics Most companies attempt to link ethics and law through the creation of internal codes of ethics. (We present the code of ethics of Costco Wholesale Corporation as an example in the appendix following this chapter.) Company codes are not laws. Instead, they are rules that the company sets forth and that it can also enforce (by terminating an employee who does not follow them, for instance). Codes of conduct typically outline the company's policies on particular issues and indicate how employees are expected to act.

> "Never let your sense of morals prevent you from doing what is right."
>
> **ISAAC ASIMOV**
> 1920–1992
> (RUSSIAN-BORN WRITER AND SCIENTIST)

EXAMPLE 9.2 Google's code of conduct starts with the motto "Don't be evil." The code then makes general statements about how Google promotes integrity, mutual respect, and the highest standard of ethical business conduct. Google's code also provides specific rules on a number of issues, such as privacy, drugs and alcohol, conflicts of interest, co-worker relationships, and confidentiality—it even has a dog policy. The company takes a stand against employment discrimination that goes further than the law requires. It prohibits discrimination based on sexual orientation, gender identity or expression, and veteran status. ▪

Numerous industries have also developed codes of ethics. The American Institute of Certified Public Accountants (AICPA) has a comprehensive Code of Professional Conduct for the ethical practicing of accounting. The American Bar Association has model rules of professional conduct for attorneys, and the American Nurses Association has a code of ethics that applies to nurses. These codes can give guidance to decision makers facing ethical questions. Violation of a code may result in discipline of an employee or sanctions against a company from the industry organization. Remember, though, that these internal codes are not laws, so their effectiveness is determined by the commitment of the industry or company leadership to enforcing the codes.

Ethics and "Gray Areas" of the Law Because it is often highly subjective and subject to change over time without any sort of formal process, ethics is less certain than law. But the law can also be uncertain. Numerous "gray areas" in the law make it difficult to predict with certainty how a court will apply a given law to a particular action. In addition, laws frequently change.

Such uncertainty can make decision making difficult, especially when a law requires a court to determine what is "foreseeable" or "reasonable" in a particular situation. Because a business has no way of predicting how a specific court will decide these issues, decision makers need to proceed with caution. In such situations, it is helpful to evaluate an action and its consequences from an ethical perspective. A company that can show it acted ethically, responsibly, and in good faith (honestly) has a better chance of succeeding in a dispute than one that cannot make such a showing.

In the following case, the court considered whether an employer's response to complaints about harassment against one of its employees warranted a large penalty against the employer.

KNOW THIS

When it is not entirely clear how a law applies, a company's best defense to allegations of misconduct is to show that the firm acted honestly and responsibly under the circumstances.

CASE 9.2

May v. Chrysler Group, LLC

United States Court of Appeals, Seventh Circuit, 716 F.3d 963 (2013).

FACTS For three years, Otto May, Jr., a pipefitter at a Chrysler Group, LLC, plant in Illinois, was the target of more than fifty racist, homophobic, and anti-Semitic messages and graffiti. He received death threats, his bike and car tires were punctured, and someone poured sugar into the gas tank of his car. May complained to Chrysler. In response, the employer documented the complaints and began an investigation. Records were checked to determine who was in the building when the incidents occurred, and the graffiti handwriting was examined. The company reminded its workers that employee harassment was not acceptable. The harassers

What other ways can employees be harassed?

Ike Hayden/ShutterStock.com

were never caught, but the incidents became fewer and eventually stopped.

May filed a suit against Chrysler in a federal district court for hostile-work-environment harassment. A jury awarded May $709,000 in compensatory damages and $3.5 million in punitive damages. When the judge overturned the punitive damages award, May appealed.

ISSUE Were the steps Chrysler took to stop and prevent the harassment against May sufficient to protect the company from an assessment of punitive damages?

DECISION Yes. The U.S. Court of Appeals for the Seventh Circuit affirmed the lower court's judgment.

REASON In a case involving charges of hostile-work-environment harassment, an employer must act with malice or reckless indifference to an employee's federally protected rights to support an award of punitive damages. Here, Chrysler did not act with malice or reckless indifference to May's federally protected rights. Instead, the company used several strategies to stop and prevent the harassment. These steps included an increased security presence and anti-harassment training for its employees. Supervisors met with their workers to review Chrysler's anti-harassment policy. A protocol was implemented to document the incidents, take photos, clean up graffiti, and interview witnesses. Management also increased its presence with area walk-throughs. Graffiti handwriting was analyzed.

Ultimately, Chrysler's actions had a positive effect because the harassment gradually decreased in frequency and finally ceased completely. In short, Chrysler could have done more to prevent the harassment against May, but the company did not act with malice or reckless indifference. Thus, the $3.5 million punitive damages award was overturned.

CRITICAL THINKING—Ethical Consideration *Does an organization have an ethical obligation to secure a safe and harassment-free workplace for its employees? Discuss.*

9-2 Business Ethics and Social Media

Although most people may think of social media—Facebook, Instagram, Twitter, Google+, and the like—simply as ways to communicate rapidly, businesses face ethical issues with respect to these same social media platforms.

9-2a Hiring Procedures

In the past, to learn about a prospective employee, an employer would often ask the candidate's former employers for references. Today, employers may also conduct Internet searches to discover what job candidates have posted on their Facebook pages, blogs, and tweets. Many people, however, believe that judging a job candidate based on what she or he does outside the work environment is unethical. Among other things, these critics say that researching candidates' social media posts invades their privacy.

Sometimes, too, the opposite situation occurs, and job candidates are rejected because they *do not* participate in social media. Given that the vast majority of younger people do use social media, some employers have decided that the failure to do so raises a red flag. Some might consider an employer's discriminating against a person for not using social media to be unethical as well.

9-2b Discussion of Work-Related Issues

Americans often discuss work-related issues on social media. Numerous companies have provided strict guidelines to inform their employees about what is appropriate and inappropriate when they make posts on their own or others' social media accounts. A number of companies have fired employees for such activities as criticizing other employees or managers through social media outlets. Until recently, such disciplinary measures were considered ethical and legal. Today, the situation has changed.

The Government Acts A recent ruling by the National Labor Relations Board (NLRB, the federal agency that investigates unfair labor practices) has made some social media guidelines illegal. **EXAMPLE 9.3** Costco's social media policy specified that its employees should not make statements that would damage the company, harm another person's reputation, or violate the company's policies. Employees who violated these rules were subject to discipline and could be fired.

In 2012, the NLRB ruled that Costco's social media policy violated federal labor law, which protects employees' right to engage in "concerted activities." Employees can freely associate

Why did the National Labor Relations Board rule against Costco's social media policy?

with each other and have conversations about common workplace issues without employer interference. This right extends to social media posts. Therefore, Costco cannot broadly prohibit its employees from criticizing the company or co-workers, supervisors, or managers via social media. ■

The Ethical Responsibilities of Employees The discussion in this chapter focuses on business ethics, but employee ethics is also an important issue. Is it ethical for employees to make negative posts in social media about other employees or, more commonly, about managers? After all, disgruntled employees may exaggerate the negative qualities of managers they dislike. These negative comments reflect badly on the managers, who often are reluctant to respond to the criticism via social media.

Some may consider the NLRB decision outlined in *Example 9.3* to be too lenient toward employees and too strict toward management. There is likely to be an ongoing debate about how to balance employees' right to free expression against employers' right to prevent inaccurate, negative statements from being spread across the Internet.

9–3 Approaches to Ethical Reasoning

As Dean Krehmeyer, executive director of the Business Roundtable's Institute for Corporate Ethics, once said, "Evidence strongly suggests being ethical—doing the right thing—pays." Even if ethics "pays," though, instilling ethical business decision making into the fabric of a business organization is no small task. How do business decision makers decide whether a given action is the "right" one for their firms? What ethical standards should be applied?

Broadly speaking, **ethical reasoning**—the application of morals and ethics to a situation—applies to businesses just as it does to individuals. As businesses make decisions, they must analyze the alternatives in a variety of ways, one of which is from an ethical perspective. In analyzing alternatives in this way, businesses may take one of two approaches, which we discuss next.

Generally, the study of ethics is divided into two major categories—duty-based ethics and outcome-based ethics. **Duty-based ethics** is rooted in the idea that every person has certain duties to others, including humans and the planet. Those duties may be derived from religious principles or from other philosophical reasoning. **Outcome-based ethics** focuses on the impacts of a decision on society or on key *stakeholders*.

9–3a Duty-Based Ethics

Duty-based ethics focuses on the obligations of the corporation. It deals with standards for behavior that traditionally were derived from revealed truths, religious authorities, or philosophical reasoning. These standards involve concepts of right and wrong, duties owed, and rights to be protected. Corporations today often describe these values or duties in their mission statements or strategic plans. Some companies base their statements on a nonreligious rationale. Others still derive their values from religious doctrine.

Religious Ethical Principles Nearly every religion has principles or beliefs about how one should treat others. In the Judeo-Christian tradition, which is the dominant religious tradition in the United States, the Ten Commandments of the Old Testament establish these fundamental rules for moral action. The principles of the Muslim faith are set out in the Qur'an, and Hindus find their principles in the four Vedas.

LEARNING OBJECTIVE 2

How do duty-based ethical standards differ from outcome-based ethical standards?

Ethical Reasoning A reasoning process in which an individual links his or her moral convictions or ethical standards to the situation at hand.

Duty-based Ethics An ethical philosophy rooted in the idea that every person has certain duties to others, including both humans and the planet. Those duties may be derived from religious principles or from other philosophical reasoning.

Outcome-based Ethics An ethical philosophy that focuses on the impacts of a decision on society or on key stakeholders.

Religious rules generally are absolute with respect to the behavior of their adherents. For instance, the commandment "Thou shalt not steal" is an absolute mandate for a person who believes that the Ten Commandments reflect revealed truth. Even a benevolent motive for stealing (such as Robin Hood's) cannot justify the act, because the act itself is inherently immoral and thus wrong.

For businesses, religious principles can be a unifying force for employees or a rallying point to increase employee motivation. They can also present problems, however, because different owners, suppliers, employees, and customers may have different religious backgrounds. Taking an action based on religious principles, especially when those principles address socially or politically controversial topics, can lead to negative publicity and even to protests or boycotts.

EXAMPLE 9.4 In 2012, the chief operating officer of the Chick-fil-A restaurant chain made several statements about the company's commitment to supporting traditional marriage. After that, it became public knowledge that Chick-fil-A had made donations to Christian organizations perceived to be opposed to same-sex marriage. Supporters of same-sex marriage held support rallies to gain media attention, and some politicians denounced Chick-fil-A's position and said that they would block expansion of the company in their cities. Eventually, Chick-fil-A issued a statement saying that it had stopped giving donations to any organization that promotes discrimination in any way. Chick-fil-A no longer sponsors charities that discriminate against same-sex couples or persons who identify as gay, lesbian, bisexual, or transgendered. ■

The Principle of Rights

Another view of duty-based ethics focuses on basic rights. The principle that human beings have certain fundamental rights (to life, freedom, and the pursuit of happiness, for example) is deeply embedded in Western culture. As discussed in Chapter 1, the natural law tradition embraces the concept that certain actions (such as killing another person) are morally wrong because they are contrary to nature (the natural desire to continue living).

Those who adhere to the **principle of rights,** or "rights theory," believe that a key factor in determining whether a business decision is ethical is how that decision affects the rights of others. These others include the firm's owners, its employees, the consumers of its products or services, its suppliers, the community in which it does business, and society as a whole.

Conflicting Rights. A potential dilemma for those who support rights theory is that they may disagree on which rights are most important. When considering all those affected by a business decision to downsize a firm, for instance, how much weight should be given to employees relative to shareholders? Which employees should be laid off first—those with the highest salaries or those who have worked for the firm for a shorter time (and have less seniority)? How should the firm weigh the rights of customers relative to the community, or of employees relative to society as a whole?

Resolving Conflicts. In general, rights theorists believe that whichever right is stronger in a particular circumstance takes precedence. **EXAMPLE 9.5** Murray Chemical Corporation has to decide whether to keep a chemical plant in Utah open, thereby saving the jobs of a hundred and fifty workers, or shut it down. Closing the plant will prevent the contamination of a river with pollutants that would endanger the health of tens of thousands of people. In this situation, a rights theorist can easily choose which group to favor because the value of the right to health and well-being is obviously stronger than the basic right to work. (Not all choices are so clear-cut, however.) ■

Kantian Ethical Principles

Duty-based ethical standards may be derived solely from philosophical reasoning. The German philosopher Immanuel Kant (1724–1804) identified some general guiding principles for moral behavior based on what he thought to be the fundamental nature of human beings. Kant believed that human beings are qualitatively different from

"When I do good, I feel good. When I do bad, I feel bad. And that's my religion."

ABRAHAM LINCOLN
1809–1865
(SIXTEENTH PRESIDENT OF THE UNITED STATES, 1861–1865)

Principle of Rights The belief that human beings have certain fundamental rights. Whether an action or decision is ethical depends on how it affects the rights of various groups, such as owners, employees, consumers, suppliers, the community, and society.

other physical objects and are endowed with moral integrity and the capacity to reason and conduct their affairs rationally.

People Are Not a Means to an End. Based on his view of human beings, Kant said that when people are treated merely as a means to an end, they are being treated as the equivalent of objects and are being denied their basic humanity. For instance, a manager who treats subordinates as mere profit-making tools is less likely to retain motivated and loyal employees than a manager who respects his or her subordinates. Management research has shown that employees who feel empowered to share their thoughts, opinions, and solutions to problems are happier and more productive.

The Categorical Imperative. When a business makes unethical decisions, it often rationalizes its action by saying that the company is "just one small part" of the problem or that its decision would have "only a small impact." A central theme in Kantian ethics is that individuals should evaluate their actions in light of the consequences that would follow if everyone in society acted in the same way. This **categorical imperative** can be applied to any action.

Categorical Imperative
An ethical guideline developed by Immanuel Kant under which an action is evaluated in terms of what would happen if everybody else in the same situation, or category, acted the same way.

EXAMPLE 9.6 CHS Fertilizer is deciding whether to invest in expensive equipment that will decrease profits but will also reduce pollution from its factories. If CHS has adopted Kant's categorical imperative, the decision makers will consider the consequences if every company invested in the equipment (or if no company did so). If the result would make the world a better place (less polluted), CHS's decision would be clear. ■

How might a company use Kant's categorical imperative to decide whether to voluntarily reduce pollution?

9–3b Outcome-Based Ethics: Utilitarianism

In contrast to duty-based ethics, outcome-based ethics focuses on the consequences of an action, not on the nature of the action itself or on any set of preestablished moral values or religious beliefs. Outcome-based ethics looks at the impacts of a decision in an attempt to maximize benefits and minimize harms.

The premier philosophical theory for outcome-based decision making is **utilitarianism,** a philosophical theory developed by Jeremy Bentham (1748–1832) and modified by John Stuart Mill (1806–1873)—both British philosophers. "The greatest good for the greatest number" is a paraphrase of the major premise of the utilitarian approach to ethics.

Utilitarianism An approach to ethical reasoning in which an action is evaluated in terms of its consequences for those whom it will affect. A "good" action is one that results in the greatest good for the greatest number of people.

Cost-Benefit Analysis
A decision-making technique that involves weighing the costs of a given action against the benefits of that action.

Cost-Benefit Analysis Under a utilitarian model of ethics, an action is morally correct, or "right," when, among the people it affects, it produces the greatest amount of good for the greatest number (or creates the least amount of harm). When an action affects the majority adversely, it is morally wrong. Applying the utilitarian theory thus requires the following steps:

1. A determination of which individuals will be affected by the action in question.

2. A **cost-benefit analysis,** which involves an assessment of the negative and positive effects of alternative actions on these individuals.

3. A choice among alternative actions that will produce maximum societal utility (the greatest positive net benefits for the greatest number of individuals).

For instance, assume that expanding a factory would provide hundreds of jobs but generate pollution that could endanger the lives of thousands of people. A utilitarian analysis would find that not endangering the lives of thousands creates greater good than providing jobs for hundreds.

Problems with the Utilitarian Approach There are problems with a strict utilitarian analysis. In some situations, an action that produces the greatest good for the most people may not seem to be the most ethical. **EXAMPLE 9.7** Phazim Company is producing a drug that will cure a disease in 95 percent of patients, but the other 5 percent will experience agonizing side effects and a horrible, painful death. A quick utilitarian analysis would suggest that the drug should be produced and marketed because the majority of patients will benefit. Many people, however, have significant concerns about manufacturing a drug that will cause serious harm to anyone. ■

9-3c Corporate Social Responsibility

In pairing duty-based concepts with outcome-based concepts, strategists and theorists developed the idea of the corporate citizen. **Corporate social responsibility (CSR)** combines a commitment to good citizenship with a commitment to making ethical decisions, improving society, and minimizing environmental impact.

CSR is a relatively new concept in the history of business, but a concept that becomes more important every year. CSR is not imposed on corporations by law. Nevertheless, it does involve a commitment to self-regulation that takes into account not only the text of the law, but also the intent of the law, ethical norms, and global standards. A survey of U.S. executives undertaken by the Boston College Center for Corporate Citizenship found that more than 70 percent of those polled agreed that corporate citizenship must be treated as a priority. More than 60 percent said that good corporate citizenship had added to their companies' profits.

CSR can be a highly successful strategy for companies, but corporate decision makers must not lose track of the two descriptors in the title: *corporate* and *social*. The company must link the responsibility of citizenship with the strategy and key principles of the business. Incorporating both the social and the corporate components of CSR and making ethical decisions can help companies grow and prosper.

The Social Aspects of CSR Because business controls so much of the wealth and power in this country, business has a responsibility to use that wealth and power in socially beneficial ways. Thus, the social aspect of CSR requires that corporations demonstrate that they are promoting goals that society deems worthwhile and are moving toward solutions to social problems.

Companies may be judged on how much they donate to social causes, as well as how they conduct their operations with respect to employment discrimination, human rights, environmental concerns, and similar issues. Some corporations publish annual social responsibility reports, which may also be called corporate sustainability (referring to the capacity to endure) or citizenship reports.

EXAMPLE 9.8 The software company Symantec Corporation issues corporate responsibility reports to demonstrate its focus on critical environmental, social, and governance issues. In its 2014 report, Symantec pointed out that 88 percent of facilities it owns or leases on a long-term basis are certified as environmentally friendly by the LEED (Leadership in Energy and Environmental Design) program. Certification requires the achievement of high standards for energy efficiency, material usage in construction, and other environmental qualities. ■

Corporate Social Responsibility (CSR) The idea that corporations can and should act ethically and be accountable to society for their actions.

iStockPhoto.com/EdStock

Bill Gates, co-founder of Microsoft, and his wife run the Bill and Melinda Gates Foundation. How do their actions relate to corporate social responsibility?

The Corporate Aspects of CSR Arguably, any socially responsible activity will benefit a corporation. A corporation may see an increase in goodwill in the local community for creating a park, for instance. Corporations that are viewed as good citizens may see increases in sales.

At times, the benefit may not be immediate. Constructing a new plant that meets the high LEED standards may cost more initially. Nevertheless, over the life of the building, the savings in maintenance and utilities costs may more than make up for the extra cost of construction.

Surveys of college students about to enter the job market confirm that many young people are looking for socially responsible employers. Socially responsible activities may cost a corporation now, but may lead to more impressive, and more committed, employees. Corporations that engage in meaningful social activities retain workers longer, particularly younger ones.

Corporate responsibility is most successful when a company undertakes activities that are significant and related to its business operations. **EXAMPLE 9.9** In an effort to help curb childhood obesity, the Walt Disney Company began issuing strict nutritional standards for all products advertised through its media outlets. In addition to focusing on a major social issue, the initiative was intended to clarify Disney's mission and values, as well as enhance its reputation as a trustworthy, family-friendly company. The initiative was praised by many commentators and politicians and is expected to increase Disney's revenues in the long term. ■

ETHICAL ISSUE

Can outsourcing lead to violations of corporate social responsibility norms? Outsourcing occurs when a domestic company, such as Apple, Nike, or Walmart, has its goods or services produced abroad. Many U.S. companies have manufacturing plants or customer service call centers in other countries, and others outsource information technology tasks.

Companies that are not careful about the social responsibility aspects of outsourcing may find themselves in trouble. Nike provides a classic example. Throughout the 1990s, Nike faced protests accusing it of outsourcing to foreign companies that paid "slave" wages and used other abusive practices—protests that eventually tarnished Nike's reputation. Nike at first attempted to counter complaints about poor working conditions in its outsourced Indonesian plants by creating a factory code of conduct, with little effect.

Then, in 1999, Nike created the Fair Labor Association, a nonprofit group that independently monitors conditions in the factories of Nike and other companies abroad. Over the next several years, the company performed six hundred factory audits. By 2005, Nike had become the first in the industry to publish a complete list of factories that it used for outsourcing. The company now provides audit data as part of its corporate social responsibility reports. These efforts to be socially responsible have helped Nike to rebuild its reputation.

Stakeholders Groups that are affected by corporate decisions. Stakeholders include employees, customers, creditors, suppliers, and the community in which the corporation operates.

Why do companies such as Nike have to worry about outsourcing their manufacturing operations?

Stakeholders One view of CSR stresses that corporations have a duty not just to shareholders, but also to other groups affected by corporate decisions—called **stakeholders.** The rationale for this "stakeholder view" is that, in some circumstances, one or more of these other groups may have a greater stake in company decisions than shareholders do.

Under this approach, a corporation considers the impact of its decisions on its employees, customers, creditors, suppliers, and the community in which it operates. Stakeholders could also include advocacy groups such as environmental groups and animal rights groups. To avoid making a decision that may be perceived as unethical and result in negative publicity or protests, a corporation should consider the impact of its decision on the stakeholders. The most difficult aspect of the stakeholder analysis is determining which group's interests should receive greater weight if the interests conflict.

Stakeholder-sensitive decisions can take many forms. For instance, during the last recession, layoffs numbered in the millions. Nonetheless, some corporations succeeded in reducing labor costs without layoffs. To avoid slashing their workforces, these employers turned to alternatives such as (1) four-day workweeks, (2) unpaid vacations and voluntary furloughs, (3) wage freezes, (4) pension cuts, and (5) flexible work schedules. Some companies asked their workers to accept wage cuts to prevent layoffs, and the workers agreed. Companies finding alternatives to layoffs included Dell (extended unpaid holidays), Cisco Systems (four-day end-of-year shutdowns), Motorola (salary cuts), and Honda (voluntary unpaid vacation time).

9-4 Making Ethical Business Decisions

Even if officers, directors, and others in a company want to make ethical decisions, it is not always clear what is ethical in a given situation. Thinking beyond things that are easily measured, such as profits, can be challenging. It may seem that considering the personal impacts of decisions on employees, shareholders, customers, and even the community requires too much subjectivity. But this subjective component of decision making has a potentially great influence on a company's profits.

Companies once considered leaders in their industry, such as Enron and the worldwide accounting firm Arthur Andersen, were brought down by the unethical behavior of a few. A two-hundred-year-old British investment banking firm, Barings Bank, was destroyed by the actions of one employee and a few of his friends. Clearly, ensuring that all employees get on the ethical business decision-making "bandwagon" is crucial in today's fast-paced world.

Individuals entering the global corporate community, even in entry-level positions, must be prepared to make hard decisions. Sometimes, there is no "good" answer to the questions that arise. Therefore, it is important to have tools to help in the decision-making process and a framework for organizing those tools.

9-4a A Systematic Approach

Organizing ethical concerns and issues and approaching them systematically can help a businessperson eliminate some alternatives and identify the strengths and weaknesses of the remaining alternatives. Ethics consultant Leonard H. Bucklin of Corporate-Ethics.US™ has devised a procedure that he calls Business Process Pragmatism™ to help in this process. It involves five steps:

LEARNING OBJECTIVE 3
What are five steps that a businessperson can take to evaluate whether his or her actions are ethical?

Step 1: Inquiry. First, the decision maker must understand the problem. This step involves identifying the parties involved (the stakeholders) and collecting the relevant facts. Once the ethical problem or problems are clarified, the decision maker lists any relevant legal and ethical principles that will guide the decision.

Step 2: Discussion. In this step, the decision maker lists possible actions. The ultimate goals for the decision are determined, and each option is evaluated using the laws and ethical principles listed in Step 1.

Step 3: Decision. In this step, those participating in the decision making work together to craft a consensus decision or consensus plan of action for the corporation.

Step 4: Justification. In this step, the decision maker articulates the reasons for the proposed action or series of actions. Generally these reasons should come from the analysis done in Step 3. This step essentially results in documentation to be shared with stakeholders explaining why the proposal is an ethical solution to the problem.

Step 5: Evaluation. This final step occurs once the decision has been made and implemented. The solution should be analyzed to determine if it was effective. The results of this evaluation may be used in making future decisions.

9-4b The Importance of Ethical Leadership

Talking about ethical business decision making is meaningless if management does not set standards. Furthermore, managers must apply the same standards to themselves as they do to the company's employees. See this chapter's *Adapting the Law to the Online Environment* feature for a discussion of an ethical dilemma that has arisen from increased demands on employees to stay digitally connected to the workplace after work hours.

ADAPTING THE LAW TO THE ONLINE ENVIRONMENT
Should Employees Have a "Right of Disconnecting"?

Almost all jobs today involve digital technology, whether it be e-mails, Internet access, or smartphone use. Most employees, when interviewed, say that digital technology increases their productivity and flexibility. The downside is what some call an "electronic leash"—employees are constantly connected and therefore end up working when they are not "at work." Over one-third of full-time workers, for example, say that they frequently check e-mails outside normal working hours.

Do Workers Have the Right to Disconnect?
Because the boundaries between being "at work" and being "at leisure" can be so hazy, some labor unions in other countries have attempted to pass rules that allow employees to disconnect from e-mail and other work-related digital communication during nonworking hours. For example, a French labor union representing high-tech workers signed an agreement with a large business association recognizing a "right of disconnecting."

In Germany, Volkswagen and BMW no longer forward e-mail to staff from company servers after the end of the working day. Other German firms have declared that workers are not expected to check e-mail on weekends and holidays. The government

is considering legislating such restrictions nationwide.

The Thorny Issue of Overtime and the Fair Labor Standards Act
Payment for overtime work is strictly regulated under the Fair Labor Standards Act (FLSA). According to the Supreme Court, in this context, *work* is "physical or mental exertion (whether burdensome or not) controlled or required by the employer and pursued necessarily for the benefit of the employer and his business."[a] This definition was extended to off-duty work if such work is an "integral and indispensible part of [employees'] activities."[b]

Today's modern digital connectivity raises issues about the definition of *work*. Employees at several major companies, including Black & Decker, T-Mobile, and Verizon, have sued for unpaid overtime related to smartphone use. In another case, a police sergeant has sued the city of Chicago claiming that he

should have been paid overtime for hours spent using his personal digital assistant (PDA).[c] The police department issues PDAs to officers and requires them to respond to work-related text messages, e-mails, and voice mails not only while on duty, but also while off duty. Off-duty responses are not compensated by the city.

Not All Employees Demand the "Right to Disconnect"
According to a Gallup tracking poll in 2014, 79 percent of full-time employees had either strongly positive or somewhat positive views of using computers, e-mail, tablets, and smartphones to work remotely outside of normal business hours. According to the same poll, 17 percent of them report "better overall lives" because of constant online connectivity with their work. Finally, working remotely after business hours apparently does not necessarily result in additional work-related stress.

CRITICAL THINKING
- From an ethical point of view, is there any difference between calling subordinates during off hours for work-related questions and sending them e-mails or text messages?

a. *Tennessee Coal, Iron & R. Co. v. Muscoda Local No. 123*, 321 U.S. 590, 64 S.Ct. 698, 8 L.Ed. 949 (1944). Although Congress later passed a statute that superseded the holding in this case, the statute gave the courts broad authority to interpret the FLSA's definition of work. 29 U.S.C. Section 251(a). See *Integrity Staffing Solutions, Inc. v. Busk*, __ U.S. __, 135 S.Ct. 513, 190 L.Ed.2d 410 (2014).
b. *Steiner v. Mitchell*, 350 U.S. 247, 76 S.Ct. 330, 100 L.Ed. 267 (1956).

c. *Allen v. City of Chicago*, 2014 WL 5461856 (N.D.Ill 2014).

KNOW THIS
One of the best ways to encourage good business ethics at a workplace is to take immediate corrective action in response to any unethical conduct.

Attitude of Top Management One of the most important ways to create and maintain an ethical workplace is for top management to demonstrate its commitment to ethical decision making. A manager who is not totally committed to an ethical workplace rarely succeeds in creating one. Management's behavior, more than anything else, sets the ethical tone of a firm. Employees take their cues from management. **EXAMPLE 9.10** Devon, a BioTek employee, observes his manager cheating on her expense account. Later, when Devon is promoted to a managerial position, he "pads" his expense account as well, knowing that he is unlikely to face sanctions for doing so. ∎

Managers who set unrealistic production or sales goals increase the probability that employees will act unethically. If a sales quota can be met only through high-pressure, unethical sales tactics, employees will try to act "in the best interest of the company" and will continue to behave unethically.

A manager who looks the other way when she or he knows about an employee's unethical behavior also sets an example—one indicating that ethical transgressions will be accepted. Managers have found that discharging even one employee for ethical reasons has a tremendous impact as a deterrent to unethical behavior in the workplace. This is true even if the company has a written code of ethics. If management does not enforce the company code, the code is essentially nonexistent.

The administration of a university may have had this concept in mind in the following case when it applied the school's professionalism standard to a student who had engaged in serious misconduct.

> "What you do speaks so loudly that I cannot hear what you say."
>
> **RALPH WALDO EMERSON**
> 1803–1882
> (AMERICAN ESSAYIST AND POET)

CASE 9.3

Al-Dabagh v. Case Western Reserve University

United States Court of Appeals, Sixth Circuit, 777 F.3d 355 (2015).

FACTS The curriculum at Case Western Reserve University School of Medicine identifies nine "core competencies." At the top of the list is professionalism, which includes "ethical, honest, responsible and reliable behavior." The university's Committee on Students determines whether a student has met the professionalism requirements. Amir Al-Dabagh enrolled at the school and did well academically. But he sexually harassed fellow students, often asked an instructor not to mark him late for class, received complaints from hospital staff about his demeanor, and was convicted of driving while intoxicated. The Committee on Students unanimously refused to certify him for graduation and dismissed him from the university. He filed a suit in a federal district court against Case Western, alleging a breach of good faith and fair dealing. The court ordered the school to issue a diploma. Case Western appealed.

ISSUE Should a court defer to a university's determination that a student lacks the professionalism required to graduate?

DECISION Yes. The U.S. Court of Appeals for the Sixth Circuit reversed the lower court's order to issue a diploma. The appellate court found nothing to indicate that Case Western had

Under what circumstances can a medical school withhold a diploma from one of its students?

"impermissible motives," acted in bad faith, or dealt unfairly with Al-Dabagh.

REASON The Committee on Students' refusal to approve Al-Dabagh for graduation was an academic judgment. The court explained that it would overturn such a decision only if it substantially departed from accepted academic norms. There was nothing to indicate that such a departure occurred in Al-Dabagh's case. The plaintiff argued that the committee's decision was a "punitive disciplinary measure" unrelated to academics. But Case Western placed a high value on professionalism in the school's *academic* curriculum. Al-Dabagh also argued that the university defined professionalism too broadly and that it should be linked only to test scores and similar academic performance. "That is not how we see it or for that matter how the medical school sees it. . . . Our own standards indicate that professionalism does not end at the courtroom door. Why should hospitals operate any differently?"

WHAT IF THE FACTS WERE DIFFERENT? *Suppose that Case Western had tolerated Al-Dabagh's conduct and awarded him a diploma. What impact might that have had on other students at the school? Why?*

Misbehavior of Owners and Managers Business owners and managers sometimes take more active roles in fostering unethical and illegal conduct. This may indicate to their co-owners, co-managers, employees, and others that unethical business behavior will be tolerated. Business owners' misbehavior can have negative consequences for themselves and their business. Not only can a court sanction the owners and managers, but it can also issue an injunction that prevents them from engaging in similar patterns of conduct in the future.

Ethics Training for Employees For an ethical code to be effective, its provisions must be clearly communicated to employees. Most large companies have implemented ethics training programs, in which managers discuss with employees on a face-to-face basis the firm's policies

LEARNING OBJECTIVE 4

How can business leaders encourage their companies to act ethically?

and the importance of ethical conduct. Smaller firms should also offer some form of ethics training to employees. If a firm is accused of an ethics violation, the court will consider the presence or absence of such training in evaluating the firm's conduct.

Some firms hold periodic ethics seminars during which employees can openly discuss any ethical problems that they may be experiencing and learn how the firm's ethical policies apply to those specific problems. Other companies require their managers to meet individually with employees and grade them on their ethical (or unethical) behavior.

PREVENTING LEGAL DISPUTES

To avoid disputes over ethical violations in your company, you should first create a written ethical code that is expressed in clear and understandable language. The code should establish specific procedures that employees can follow if they have questions or complaints. It should assure employees that their jobs will be secure and that they will not face reprisals if they do file a complaint. A well-written code might also include examples to clarify what the company considers to be acceptable and unacceptable conduct. You should also hold periodic training meetings so that you can explain to employees face to face why ethics is important to the company. If your company does business internationally, you might also communicate the code to firms in your supply chain and make sure they follow your ethics policies.

Companies can comply with the Sarbanes-Oxley Act by using a Web-based system, such as NAVEX Global, that allows employees to report suspected unethical accounting practices.

The Sarbanes-Oxley Act and Web-Based Reporting Systems Congress enacted the Sarbanes-Oxley Act[2] to help reduce corporate fraud and unethical management decisions. The act requires companies to set up confidential systems so that employees and others can "raise red flags" about suspected illegal or unethical auditing and accounting practices.

Some companies have implemented online reporting systems to accomplish this goal. In one such system, employees can click on an icon on their computers that anonymously links them with NAVEX Global, an organization based in Oregon. Through NAVEX Global, employees can report suspicious accounting practices, sexual harassment, and other possibly unethical behavior. NAVEX, in turn, alerts management personnel or the audit committee at the designated company to the possible problem.

9–5 Global Business Ethics

> "If you are uncertain about an issue, it's useful to ask yourself, 'Would I be absolutely comfortable for my actions to be disclosed on the front page of my hometown newspaper?'"
>
> **WARREN E. BUFFETT**
> 1930–PRESENT
> (AMERICAN BUSINESSPERSON AND PHILANTHROPIST)

Given the various cultures and religions throughout the world, it is not surprising that conflicts in ethics frequently arise between foreign and U.S. businesspersons. For instance, in certain countries, the consumption of alcohol is forbidden for religious reasons. Under such circumstances, it would be considered unethical for a U.S. businessperson to start a business that produces alcohol and to employ local workers in alcohol production.

We look here at how laws governing workers in other countries, particularly developing countries, have created some especially difficult ethical problems for U.S. sellers of goods manufactured in foreign countries. We also examine some of the ethical ramifications of laws prohibiting U.S. businesspersons from bribing foreign officials to obtain favorable business contracts.

---

2. 15 U.S.C. Sections 7201 *et seq.*

9-5a Monitoring the Employment Practices of Foreign Suppliers

Many businesses contract with companies in developing nations to produce goods, such as shoes and clothing, because the wage rates in those nations are significantly lower than wages in the United States. Yet what if a foreign company exploits its workers—by hiring women and children at below-minimum-wage rates, for instance, or by requiring its employees to work long hours in a workplace full of health hazards? What if the company's supervisors routinely engage in workplace conduct that is offensive to women? What if plants that are operated abroad routinely violate labor and environmental standards?

Many high-tech companies rely heavily on foreign suppliers for components and assembly. Some of these foreign suppliers engage in unethical practices, which can reflect on the companies that deal with them. **EXAMPLE 9.11** Pegatron Corporation, a company based in China, manufactures and supplies parts to Apple, Inc., for iPads and other Apple products. After an explosion at a Pegatron factory in Shanghai, allegations surfaced that the conditions at the factory violated labor and environmental standards. Similar allegations were made about other Apple suppliers.

Apple started to evaluate practices at companies in its supply chain and to communicate its ethics policies to them. Its audits revealed numerous violations. Apple released a list of its suppliers for the first time and issued a lengthy "Supplier Responsibility Report" detailing supplier practices. Numerous facilities had withheld worker pay as a disciplinary measure. Some had falsified pay records and forced workers to use machines without safeguards. Others had engaged in unsafe environmental practices, such as dumping wastewater on neighboring farms. Apple terminated its relationship with one supplier and turned over its findings to the Fair Labor Association for further inquiry. ■

Given today's global communications network, few companies can assume that their actions in other nations will go unnoticed by "corporate watch" groups that discover and publicize unethical corporate behavior. As a result, U.S. businesses today usually take steps to avoid such adverse publicity—either by refusing to deal with certain suppliers or by arranging to monitor their suppliers' workplaces to make sure that the employees are not being mistreated.

9-5b The Foreign Corrupt Practices Act

Another ethical problem in international business dealings has to do with the legitimacy of certain "side" payments to government officials. In the United States, most contracts are formed within the private sector. In many countries, however, government regulation and control over trade and industry are much more extensive than in the United States, so government officials make the decisions on most major construction and manufacturing contracts. Side payments to government officials in exchange for favorable business contracts are not unusual in such countries where they are not considered to be unethical. In the past, U.S. corporations doing business in these countries largely followed the dictum "When in Rome, do as the Romans do."

In the 1970s, however, large side payments by U.S. corporations to foreign representatives for the purpose of securing advantageous international trade contracts led to a number of scandals. In response, Congress passed the Foreign Corrupt Practices Act[3] (FCPA), which prohibits U.S. businesspersons from bribing foreign officials to secure advantageous contracts. (See this chapter's *Beyond Our Borders* feature for a discussion of Mexico's anticorruption law.)

Prohibition against the Bribery of Foreign Officials The first part of the FCPA applies to all U.S. companies and their directors, officers, shareholders, employees, and agents. This part

LEARNING OBJECTIVE 5
What types of ethical issues might arise in the context of international business transactions?

"Never doubt that a small group of committed citizens can change the world; indeed, it is the only thing that ever has."

MARGARET MEAD
1901–1978
(AMERICAN ANTHROPOLOGIST)

---

3. 15 US.C. Sections 78 dd-1 *et seq.*

BEYOND OUR BORDERS

Bribery and the Foreign Corrupt Practices Act

Many countries have followed in the footsteps of the United States by passing anticorruption laws, some of which are similar to our Foreign Corrupt Practices Act. Nevertheless, some countries are still not diligent in weeding out corruption—of government officials, for instance.

Mexico Faces a Corruption Issue
Recently, Mexico passed an anticorruption law that prevents hospital administrators from approving contracts. Medical device supplier Orthofix International NV, based in Texas, faced a problem after passage of the new law. It wanted to continue providing bone-repair products to Mexico. It therefore bribed regional government officials instead of hospital administrators. Over several years, Orthofix paid more than $300,000 in bribes to Mexican officials to retain government health-care contracts. Employees at Orthofix called these bribes "chocolates." The contracts generated almost $8.7 million in revenues for the company.

The Bribing Process
Before the anticorruption law was enacted, Orthofix's Mexican subsidiary, Promeca, regularly offered cash and gifts, such as vacation packages, televisions, and laptops, to hospital employees in order to secure sales contracts. These employees then submitted falsified receipts for imaginary expenses such as meals and new car tires. When the bribes became too large to hide in this manner, Promeca's employees falsely attributed the payments to promotional and training expenses. After the new law was passed, Mexico formed a special national committee to approve medical contracts. Promeca employees then simply bribed committee members to ensure that the company was awarded the contracts.

No Compliance Policy or Training to Prevent Violations
As it turned out, Orthofix did not provide any training in how to prevent violations of the Foreign Corrupt Practices Act or have a compliance policy in place in Mexico. Orthofix did create a code of ethics and antibribery training materials, but they were distributed only in English. When Orthofix managers found out about Promeca's overbudget expenses, they questioned the amounts, but initially took no further steps.

The U.S. Government Investigates
Sometime after Orthofix learned of the payments, it self-reported them to the U.S. Securities and Exchange Commission (SEC). After negotiations with the SEC, Orthofix agreed to terminate the Promeca executives who had engaged in the bribery and to end Promeca's operations. Orthofix required mandatory training for all employees and strengthened its auditing of company payments. In addition, the company paid more than $7 million in penalties.

CRITICAL THINKING

- Managers are potentially responsible for all actions of their foreign subsidiaries, whether or not they knew of the illegal conduct. Taking that fact into account, what actions should Orthofix's upper management have taken before this corruption scandal came to light?

prohibits the bribery of officials of foreign governments if the purpose of the payment is to induce the officials to act in their official capacity to provide business opportunities.

The FCPA does not prohibit payment of substantial sums to minor officials whose duties are ministerial. A ministerial action is a routine activity, such as the processing of paperwork, that involves little or no discretion. These payments are often referred to as "grease," or facilitating payments. They are meant to accelerate the performance of administrative services that might otherwise be carried out at a slow pace. Thus, for instance, if a firm makes a payment to a minor official to speed up an import licensing process, the firm has not violated the FCPA.

Generally, the act, as amended, permits payments to foreign officials if such payments are lawful within the foreign country. In addition, the act does not prohibit payments to private foreign companies or other third parties unless the U.S. firm knows that the payments will be passed on to a foreign government in violation of the FCPA.

Business firms that violate the FCPA may be fined up to $2 million. Individual officers or directors who violate the act may be fined up to $100,000 (the fine cannot be paid by the company) and may be imprisoned for up to five years.

Accounting Requirements In the past, bribes were often concealed in corporate financial records. Thus, the second part of the FCPA is directed toward accountants. All companies must keep detailed records that "accurately and fairly" reflect the company's financial activities. In addition, all companies must have an accounting system that provides "reasonable assurance" that all transactions entered into by the company are accounted for and legal. These requirements assist in detecting illegal bribes. The FCPA further prohibits any person from making false statements to accountants or false entries in any record or account.

Reviewing . . . Business Ethics

James Stilton is the chief executive officer (CEO) of RightLiving, Inc., a company that buys life insurance policies at a discount from terminally ill persons and sells the policies to investors. RightLiving pays the terminally ill patients a percentage of the future death benefit (usually 65 percent) and then sells the policies to investors for 85 percent of the value of the future benefit. The patients receive the cash to use for medical and other expenses, the investors are "guaranteed" a positive return on their investment, and RightLiving profits on the difference between the purchase and sale prices. Stilton is aware that some sick patients may obtain insurance policies through fraud (by not revealing the illness on the insurance application). An insurance company that discovers such fraud will cancel the policy and refuse to pay. Stilton believes that most of the policies he has purchased are legitimate, but he knows that some probably are not. Using the information presented in this chapter, answer the following questions.

1. Would a person who adheres to the principle of rights consider it ethical for Stilton not to disclose the potential risk of cancellation to investors? Why or why not?

2. Using Immanuel Kant's categorical imperative, are the actions of RightLiving ethical? Why or why not?

3. Under the theory of utilitarianism, are Stilton's actions ethical? Why or why not? Will it make a difference in this analysis if most of the policies are legitimate and valid rather than fraudulently procured and void?

4. Using the Business Process Pragmatism™ steps discussed in this chapter, discuss the decision process Stilton should use in deciding whether to disclose the risk of fraudulent policies to potential investors.

DEBATE THIS

■ Executives in large corporations are ultimately rewarded if their companies do well, particularly as evidenced by rising stock prices. Consequently, shouldn't we just let those who run corporations decide what level of negative side effects is "acceptable" for their companies' products?

LINKING BUSINESS LAW TO ACCOUNTING AND FINANCE
Managing a Company's Reputation

In business school, all of you must take basic accounting courses. Accounting generally is associated with developing balance sheets and profit-and-loss statements, but it can also be used as a support system to provide information that can help managers do their jobs correctly. Enter managerial accounting, which involves the provision of accounting information for a company's internal use. Managerial accounting is used within a company for planning, controlling, and decision making.

Increasingly, managerial accounting is also being used to *manage corporate reputations*. To this end, more than 2,500 multinationals now release to the public large quantities of managerial accounting information.

Continues

Internal Reports Designed for External Scrutiny

Some large companies refer to the managerial accounting information that they release to the public as their corporate sustainability reports. Dow Chemical Company, for example, issues its Global Reporting Initiative Sustainability Report annually. So does Waste Management, Inc., which calls its report "The Color of Our World."

Other corporations call their published documents social responsibility reports. The Hitachi Group releases an Annual Corporate Social Responsibility Report, which outlines its environmental strategy, including its attempts to reduce carbon dioxide emissions (so-called greenhouse gases). The Hitachi Group also has Web pages dedicated to its CSR initiatives and includes reports outlining its environmental strategies, its human rights policies, and its commitment to diversity.

A smaller number of multinationals provide what they call citizenship reports. Citigroup, ExxonMobil, and FedEx release annual Citizenship Reports. General Electric (GE) calls its yearly citizenship report "Sustainable Growth." GE's emphasis is on energy and climate change, demographics, growth markets, and financial markets. The company also has a Web site that provides detailed performance metrics (**www.gesustainability .com**).

Why Use Managerial Accounting to Manage Reputations?

We live in an age of information. Any news about a corporation, whether positive or negative, will be known throughout the world almost immediately given the 24/7 cable and online news networks, social media, and Internet bloggers. Consequently, corporations want to manage their reputations by preparing and releasing the news that the public, their shareholders, and government officials will receive. In a world in which corporations are often blamed for anything bad that happens, corporations are finding that managerial accounting information can provide a useful counterweight. To this end, some corporations have combined their social responsibility reports with their traditional financial accounting information. When a corporation's reputation is on the line, its future is at stake.

CRITICAL THINKING

■ Valuable company resources are used to create and publish corporate social responsibility reports. Under what circumstances can a corporation justify such expenditures?

Key Terms

business ethics 217

categorical imperative 224

corporate social responsibility (CSR) 225

cost-benefit analysis 224

duty-based ethics 222

ethical reasoning 222

ethics 216

moral minimum 219

outcome-based ethics 222

principle of rights 223

stakeholders 226

triple bottom line 217

utilitarianism 224

Chapter Summary: Business Ethics

Business Ethics	1. *Business ethics*—Business ethics focuses on how moral and ethical principles are applied in the business context.
	2. *Short-run versus long-run profit maximization*—One of the most pervasive reasons why ethical breaches occur in the business world is the focus on short-term profit maximization. Only long-run profit maximization is consistent with business ethics.
	3. *The moral minimum and ethics*—Lawful behavior is the moral minimum. The law has its limits, though, and some actions may be legal but not ethical. The study of ethics goes beyond legal requirements to evaluate what is right for society.
	4. *Ethical codes*—Most large firms have internal ethical codes. Many industry associations also have codes of ethics for their members.
	5. *Ethics and "gray areas"*—It may be difficult to predict whether particular actions are legal, given changes in the laws regulating business and "gray areas" in the law. In such cases, a company that can show it acted ethically has a better chance of succeeding in a dispute.
Business Ethics and Social Media	Employers today may conduct Internet searches to see what job candidates have posted on social media. Employers may also look at, but not interfere with, the social media posts of their employees. Many companies have explicit policies regarding the use of social media by workers, but employers must be careful when considering disciplinary action for violations of these policies.

Approaches to Ethical Reasoning	1. *Duty-based ethics*—Ethics based on religious beliefs; philosophical reasoning, such as that of Immanuel Kant; and the basic rights of human beings (the principle of rights). A potential problem for those who support this approach is deciding which rights are more important in a given situation. Management constantly faces ethical conflicts and trade-offs when considering all those affected by a business decision.
	2. *Outcome-based ethics (utilitarianism)*—Ethics based on philosophical reasoning, such as that of Jeremy Bentham and John Stuart Mill. Applying this theory requires a cost-benefit analysis, weighing the negative effects against the positive and deciding which course of action produces the better outcome.
	3. *Corporate social responsibility*—A number of theories based on the idea that corporations can and should act ethically and be accountable to society for their actions. These include the stakeholder approach and corporate citizenship.
Making Ethical Business Decisions	Making ethical business decisions is crucial in today's legal environment. Doing the right thing pays off in the long run, both by increasing profits and by avoiding negative publicity. Management must take the lead in establishing an ethical workplace.
Global Business Ethics	Businesses must take account of the many cultural, religious, and legal differences among nations. Notable differences relate to employment laws governing workplace conditions and the practice of giving side payments to foreign officials to secure favorable contracts.

Issue Spotters

1. Acme Corporation decides to respond to what it sees as a moral obligation to correct for past discrimination by adjusting pay differences among its employees. Does this raise an ethical conflict between Acme and its employees? Between Acme and its shareholders? Explain your answers. (See *Making Ethical Business Decisions*.)

2. Delta Tools, Inc., markets a product that under some circumstances is capable of seriously injuring consumers. Does Delta have an ethical duty to remove this product from the market, even if the injuries result only from misuse? Why or why not? (See *Approaches to Ethical Reasoning*.)

   —**Check your answers to the *Issue Spotters* against the answers provided in Appendix D at the end of this text.**

Learning Objectives Check

1. What is business ethics, and why is it important?
2. How do duty-based ethical standards differ from outcome-based ethical standards?
3. What are five steps that a businessperson can take to evaluate whether his or her actions are ethical?
4. How can business leaders encourage their companies to act ethically?
5. What types of ethical issues might arise in the context of international business transactions?

   —**Answers to the even-numbered *Learning Objectives Check* questions can be found in Appendix E at the end of this text.**

Business Scenarios and Case Problems

9–1. Business Ethics. Jason Trevor owns a commercial bakery in Blakely, Georgia, that produces a variety of goods sold in grocery stores. Trevor is required by law to perform internal tests on food produced at his plant to check for contamination. On three occasions, tests of food products containing peanut butter were positive for salmonella contamination. Trevor was not required to report the results to U.S. Food and Drug Administration officials, however, so he did not. Instead, Trevor instructed his employees to simply repeat the tests until the results were negative. Meanwhile, the products that had originally tested positive for salmonella were eventually shipped out to retailers. Five people who ate Trevor's baked goods that year became seriously ill, and one person died from a salmonella infection.

Even though Trevor's conduct was legal, was it unethical for him to sell goods that had once tested positive for salmonella? Why or why not? (See *Business Ethics*.)

9–2. Ethical Conduct. Internet giant Zoidle, a U.S. company, generated sales of £2.5 billion in the United Kingdom in 2013 (approximately $4 billion in U.S. dollars). Its net profits before taxes on these sales were £200 million, and it paid £6 million in corporate tax, resulting in a tax rate of 3 percent. The corporate tax rate in the United Kingdom is between 20 percent and 24 percent.

The CEO of Zoidle held a press conference stating that he was proud of his company for taking advantage of tax loopholes and for sheltering profits in other nations to avoid paying taxes. He called this practice "capitalism at its finest." He further stated that it would be unethical for Zoidle not to take advantage of loopholes and that it would be verging on illegal to tell shareholders that the company paid more taxes than it had to pay because it felt that it should.

Zoidle receives significant benefits for doing business in the United Kingdom, including tremendous sales tax exemptions and some property tax breaks. The United Kingdom relies on the corporate income tax to provide services to the poor and to help run the agency that regulates corporations. Is it ethical for Zoidle to avoid paying taxes? Why or why not? (See *Business Ethics*.)

9–3. Spotlight on Pfizer—Corporate Social Responsibility.
Methamphetamine (meth) is an addictive drug made chiefly in small toxic labs (STLs) in homes, tents, barns, and hotel rooms. The manufacturing process is dangerous, often resulting in explosions, burns, and toxic fumes. Government entities spend time and resources to find and destroy STLs, imprison meth dealers and users, treat addicts, and provide services for affected families.

Meth cannot be made without ingredients that are also used in cold and allergy medications. Arkansas has one of the highest numbers of STLs in the United States. To recoup the costs of fighting the meth epidemic, twenty counties in Arkansas filed a suit against Pfizer, Inc., which makes cold and allergy medications. What is Pfizer's ethical responsibility here, and to whom is it owed? Why? [*Ashley County, Arkansas v. Pfizer, Inc.*, 552 F.3d 659 (8th Cir. 2009)] (See *Approaches to Ethical Reasoning*.)

9–4. Business Case Problem with Sample Answer—Online
Privacy. Facebook, Inc., launched a program called "Beacon" that automatically updated the profiles of users on Facebook's social networking site when those users had any activity on Beacon "partner" sites. For example, one partner site was Blockbuster.com. When a user rented or purchased a movie through Blockbuster.com, the user's Facebook profile would be updated to share the purchase. The Beacon program was set up as a default setting, so users never consented to the program, but they could opt out. What are the ethical implications of an opt-in program versus an opt-out program in social media? [*Lane v. Facebook, Inc.*, 696 F.3d 811 (9th Cir. 2011)] (See *Business Ethics and Social Media*.)

—**For a sample answer to Problem 9–4, go to Appendix F at the end of this text.**

9–5. Business Ethics. Mark Ramun worked as a manager for Allied Erecting and Dismantling Co., where he had a tense relationship with his father, who was Allied's president. After more than ten years, Mark left Allied, taking 15,000 pages of Allied's documents on DVDs and CDs, which constituted trade secrets. Later, he joined Allied's competitor, Genesis Equipment &

Manufacturing, Inc. Genesis soon developed a piece of equipment that incorporated elements of Allied equipment. How might business ethics have been violated in these circumstances? Discuss. [*Allied Erecting and Dismantling Co. v. Genesis Equipment & Manufacturing, Inc.*, 2013 WL 85907 (6th Cir. 2013)] (See *Making Ethical Business Decisions*.)

9–6. Business Ethics. Stephen Glass made himself infamous as a dishonest journalist by fabricating material for more than forty articles for *The New Republic* magazine and other publications. He also fabricated supporting materials to delude *The New Republic*'s fact checkers. At the time, he was a law student at Georgetown University. Once suspicions were aroused, Glass tried to avoid detection. Later, Glass applied for admission to the California bar. The California Supreme Court denied his application, citing "numerous instances of dishonesty and disingenuousness" during his "rehabilitation" following the exposure of his misdeeds. How do these circumstances underscore the importance of ethics? Discuss. [*In re Glass*, 58 Cal.4th 500, 316 P.3d 1199 (2014)] (See *Business Ethics*.)

9–7. Business Ethics. Operating out of an apartment in Secane, Pennsylvania, Hratch Ilanjian convinced Vicken Setrakian, the president of Kenset Corp., that he was an international businessman who could help Kenset turn around its business in the Middle East. At Ilanjian's insistence, Setrakian provided confidential business documents. Claiming that they had an agreement, Ilanjian demanded full, immediate payment and threatened to disclose the confidential information to a Kenset supplier if payment was not forthcoming. Kenset denied that they had a contract and filed a suit in a federal district court against Ilanjian, seeking return of the documents. During discovery, Ilanjian was uncooperative. Who behaved unethically in these circumstances? Explain. [*Kenset Corp. v. Ilanjian*, __ F.3d __, 2015 WL 344046 (3d Cir. 2015)] (See *Business Ethics*.)

9–8. A Question of Ethics—Consumer Rights. Best Buy, a national electronics retailer, offered a credit card that allowed users to earn "reward points" that could be redeemed for discounts on Best Buy goods. After reading a newspaper advertisement for the card, Gary Davis applied for, and was given, a credit card. As part of the application process, he visited a Web page containing Frequently Asked Questions as well as terms and conditions for the card. He clicked on a button affirming that he understood the terms and conditions. When Davis received his card, it came with seven brochures about the card and the reward point program. As he read the brochures, he discovered that a $59 annual fee would be charged for the card. Davis went back to the Web pages he had visited and found a statement that the card "may" have an annual fee. Davis sued, claiming that the company did not adequately disclose the fee. [*Davis v. HSBC Bank Nevada, N.A.*, 691 F.3d 1152 (9th Cir. 2012)] (See *Business Ethics*.)

1. Online applications frequently have click-on buttons or check boxes for consumers to acknowledge that they have read and understand the terms and conditions of applications or purchases. Often, the terms and conditions go on for so long that they cannot all be seen on one screen, and users must scroll to view the entire document. Is it unethical for companies to put terms and conditions, especially terms that may cost the consumer money, in an electronic document that is too long to read on one screen? Why or why not? Does this differ from having a consumer sign a hard-copy document with terms and conditions printed on it? Why or why not?

2. The Truth-in-Lending Act requires that credit terms be clearly and conspicuously disclosed in application materials. Assuming that the Best Buy credit-card materials had sufficient legal disclosures, discuss the ethical aspects of businesses strictly following the language of the law compared with following the intent of the law.

Critical Thinking and Writing Assignments

9–9. Business Law Writing. Assume that you are a high-level manager for a shoe manufacturer. You know that your firm could increase its profit margin by producing shoes in Indonesia, where you could hire women for $100 a month to assemble them. You also know that human rights advocates recently accused a competing shoe manufacturer of engaging in exploitative labor practices because the manufacturer sold shoes made by Indonesian women for similarly low wages. You personally do not believe that paying $100 a month to Indonesian women is unethical because you know that in their country, $100 a month is a better-than-average wage rate. Write one page explaining whether you would have the shoes manufactured in Indonesia and make higher profits for the company or avoid the risk of negative publicity and its potential adverse consequences for the firm's reputation. Are there other alternatives? Discuss fully. (See *Global Business Ethics*.)

9–10. Business Law Critical Thinking Group Assignment. Pfizer, Inc., developed a new antibiotic called Trovan (trovafloxacinmesylate). Tests showed that in animals Trovan had life-threatening side effects, including joint disease, abnormal cartilage growth, liver damage, and a degenerative bone condition. Several years later, an epidemic of bacterial meningitis swept across Nigeria. Pfizer sent three U.S. physicians to test Trovan on children who were patients in Nigeria's Infectious Disease Hospital. Pfizer did not obtain the patients' consent, alert them to the risks, or tell them that Médecins Sans Frontières (Doctors without Borders) was providing an effective conventional treatment at the same site. Eleven children died in the experiment, and others were left blind, deaf, paralyzed, or brain damaged. Rabi Abdullahi and other Nigerian children filed a suit in a U.S. federal court against Pfizer, alleging a violation of a customary international law norm prohibiting involuntary medical experimentation on humans. (See *Global Business Ethics*.)

1. One group should use the principles of ethical reasoning discussed in this chapter to develop three arguments concerning how Pfizer's conduct was a violation of ethical standards.

2. A second group should take a pro-Pfizer position and argue that the company did not violate any ethical standards (and counter the first group).

3. A third group should come up with proposals for what Pfizer might have done differently to avert the consequences.

Appendix to Chapter 9

COSTCO CODE OF ETHICS

By Jim Sinegal

OBEY THE LAW

The law is irrefutable! Absent a moral imperative to challenge a law, we must conduct our business in total compliance with the laws of every community where we do business.

- Comply with all statutes.
- Cooperate with authorities.
- Respect all public officials and their positions.
- Avoid all conflict of interest issues with public officials.
- Comply with all disclosure and reporting requirements.
- Comply with safety and security standards for all products sold.
- Exceed ecological standards required in every community where we do business.
- Comply with all applicable wage and hour laws.
- Comply with all applicable anti-trust laws.
- Protect "inside information" that has not been released to the general public.

TAKE CARE OF OUR MEMBERS

The member is our key to success. If we don't keep our members happy, little else that we do will make a difference.

- Provide top-quality products at the best prices in the market.
- Provide a safe shopping environment in our warehouses.
- Provide only products that meet applicable safety and health standards.
- Sell only products from manufacturers who comply with "truth in advertising/packaging" standards.
- Provide our members with a 100% satisfaction guaranteed warranty on every product and service we sell, including their membership fee.
- Assure our members that every product we sell is authentic in make and in representation of performance.
- Make our shopping environment a pleasant experience by making our members feel welcome as our guests.
- Provide products to our members that will be ecologically sensitive.

> Our member is our reason for being. If they fail to show up, we cannot survive. Our members have extended a "trust" to Costco by virtue of paying a fee to shop with us. We can't let them down or they will simply go away. We must always operate in the following manner when dealing with our members:
> Rule #1 – The member is always right.
> Rule #2 – In the event the member is ever wrong, refer to rule #1.
>
> There are plenty of shopping alternatives for our members. We will succeed only if we do not violate the trust they have extended to us. We must be committed at every level of our company, with every once of energy and grain of creativity we have, to constantly strive to "bring goods to market at a lower price."

> **If we do these four things throughout our organization, we will realize our ultimate goal, which is to REWARD OUR SHAREHOLDERS.**

TAKE CARE OF OUR EMPLOYEES

To claim "people are our most important asset" is true and an understatement. Each employee has been hired for a very important job. Jobs such as stocking the shelves, ringing members' orders, buying products, and paying our bills are jobs we would all choose to perform because of their importance. The employees hired to perform these jobs are performing as management's "alter egos." Every employee, whether they are in a Costco warehouse, or whether they work in the regional or corporate offices, is a Costco ambassador trained to give our members professional, courteous treatment.

Today we have warehouse managers who were once stockers and callers, and vice presidents who were once in clerical positions for Costco. We believe that Costco's future executive officers are currently working in our warehouses, depots, buying offices, and accounting departments, as well as in our home offices.

To that end, we are committed to these principles:

- Provide a safe work environment.
- Pay a fair wage.
- Make every job challenging, but make it fun!
- Consider the loss of any employee as a failure on the part of the company and a loss to the organization.
- Teach our people how to do their jobs and how to improve personally and professionally.
- Promote from within the company to achieve the goal of a minimum of 80% of management positions being filled by current employees.
- Create an "open door" attitude at all levels of the company that is dedicated to "fairness and listening."

RESPECT OUR VENDORS

Our vendors are our partners in business and for us to prosper as a company, they must prosper with us. It is important that our vendors understand that we will be tough negotiators, but fair in our treatment of them.

- Treat all vendors and their representatives as you would expect to be treated if visiting their places of business.
- Pay all bills within the allocated time frame.
- Honor all commitments.
- Protect all vendor property assigned to Costco as though it were our own.
- Always be thoughtful and candid in negotiations.
- Provide a careful review process with at least two levels of authorization before terminating business with an existing vendor of more than two years.
- Do not accept gratuities of any kind from a vendor.

> These guidelines are exactly that - guidelines, some common sense rules for the conduct of our business. Intended to simplify our jobs, not complicate our lives, these guidelines will not answer every question or solve every problem. At the core of our philosophy as a company must be the implicit understanding that not one of us is required to lie or cheat on behalf of PriceCostco. In fact, dishonest conduct will not be tolerated. To do any less would be unfair to the overwhelming majority of our employees who support and respect Costco's commitment to ethical business conduct.
>
> If you are ever in doubt as to what course of action to take on a business matter that is open to varying ethical interpretations, take the high road and do what is right.
>
> If you want our help, we are always available for advice and counsel. That's our job and we welcome your questions or comments.
>
> Our continued success depends on you. We thank each of you for your contribution to our past success and for the high standards you have insisted upon in our company.

"Truth in advertising/packaging" legal standards are part of the statutes and regulations dealing with consumer law.

Accepting "gratuities" from a vendor might be interpreted as accepting a bribe. This can be a crime. In an international context, a bribe can be a violation of the Foreign Corrupt Practices Act.

If the company did not provide products that comply with safety and health standards, it could be held liable in civil suits on legal grounds that are classified as torts.

If the company fails to honor one of its commitments, it may be sued for breach of contract.

Disclosure of "inside information" that constitutes *trade secrets* could subject an employee to civil liability or criminal prosecution.

Failing to pay bills when they become due could subject the company to the creditors' remedies. The company might even be forced into involuntary bankruptcy.

Antitrust laws apply to illegal restraints of trade—an agreement between competitors to set prices, for example, or an attempt by one company to control an entire market.

Promotions and other benefits of employment cannot be granted or withheld on the basis of discrimination. Employment discrimination is against the law.

Failure to comply with "ecological" standards could be a violation of environmental laws.

Safety standards for the work environment are governed by the Occupational Safety and Health Act and other statutes.

Costco Background

Costco Wholesale Corporation operates a chain of cash-and-carry membership warehouses that sell high-quality, nationally branded, and selected private-label merchandise at low prices. Its target markets include both businesses that buy goods for commercial use or resale and individuals who are employees or members of specific organizations and associations. The company tries to reach high sales volume and fast inventory turnover by offering a limited choice of merchandise in many product groups at competitive prices.

The company takes a strong position on behaving ethically in all transactions and relationships. It expects employees to behave ethically. For example, no one can accept gratuities from vendors. The company also expects employees to behave ethically, according to domestic ethical standards, in any country in which it operates.

Unit One—Business Case Study with Dissenting Opinion

Central Radio Co. v. City of Norfolk, Virginia

In the chapter on constitutional law, we reviewed the meaning and some of the boundaries of the freedom of speech under the First Amendment to the U.S. Constitution. A democratic form of government cannot survive unless people can express their political opinions and criticize government actions. This is an important value in our democracy. Thus, a law that regulates the content of speech is subject to strict scrutiny by the courts. But expression can be subject to reasonable restrictions. A law that regulates the time, place, and manner of speech, rather than its content, and is intended to fulfill a government's obligation to protect its citizens is subject to a lesser standard of review.

In this business case study, we examine *Central Radio Co. v. City of Norfolk, Virginia,*[1] a recent decision focusing on whether a city's sign ordinance was content neutral and whether the ordinance's restrictions and exemptions could survive scrutiny.

Photo courtesy Institute for Justice

This sign protests the taking of Central Radio Company property. Can the city successfully argue that it's too big?

CASE BACKGROUND

In Norfolk, Virginia, the Norfolk Redevelopment and Housing Authority initiated proceedings to take and transfer the property of Central Radio Company to Old Dominion University.

In response, Central Radio hung a 375-square-foot banner on the side of the company's building. The banner depicted an American flag, Central Radio's logo, and a red circle with a slash across the words "Eminent Domain Abuse," and included a message that read "50 YEARS ON THIS STREET/ 78 YEARS IN NORFOLK/ 100 WORKERS/ THREATENED BY/ EMINENT DOMAIN!"

The city cited Central Radio for violating the size restrictions in the city's sign code. Central Radio filed a suit in a federal district court against the city, alleging that the restrictions were unconstitutional. The court ruled in the city's favor. Central Radio appealed this decision to the U.S. Court of Appeals for the Fourth Circuit.

MAJORITY OPINION

BARBARA MILANO KEENAN, Circuit Judge.

* * * *

The core component of the plaintiffs' challenge to the sign code is their argument that the sign code constitutes a content-based restriction on speech, both facially [on its face] and as applied, that cannot survive strict scrutiny.

* * * *

In evaluating the content neutrality of a municipal sign ordinance, *our principal inquiry is whether the government has adopted a regulation of speech because of disagreement with the message it conveys.* * * * A regulation is not a content-based regulation of speech if (1) the regulation is not a regulation of speech, but rather a regulation of the places where some speech may occur; (2) the regulation was not

1. 776 F.3d 229 (4th Cir. 2015).

adopted because of disagreement with the message the speech conveys; or (3) the government's interests in the regulation are unrelated to the content of the affected speech. [Emphasis added.]

* * * *

* * * The City generally allows signs regardless of the message displayed, and simply restricts the time, place, or manner of their location. Exemptions to those restrictions may have an incidental effect on some speakers or messages, but such exemptions do not convert the sign code into a content-based restriction on speech when the exemptions bear a reasonable relationship to the City's asserted interests.

* * * These exemptions do not differentiate between content based on the ideas or views expressed. By exempting the flags or emblems of governmental or religious organizations from reasonable size restrictions, the City has not indicated any preference for a particular governmental or religious speaker or message, and the sign code exerts only an incidental effect on the flags or emblems of other organizations. Also, by exempting works of art that are noncommercial in character, the City has not favored certain artistic messages over others. Given the City's clear content-neutral purpose and the absence of a more specific inquiry in the sign code regarding the content of the regulated signs, we conclude that the sign code is a content-neutral regulation of speech.

* * * *

Because the sign code is content-neutral, we evaluate its constitutionality under intermediate scrutiny. Under this level of deference, a content-neutral regulation is valid if it furthers a substantial government interest, is narrowly tailored to further that interest, and leaves open ample alternative channels of communication. [Emphasis added.]

Initially, we observe that the sign code was enacted to promote the City's physical appearance and to reduce the distractions,

Continues

obstructions and hazards to pedestrian and auto traffic. Such concerns for aesthetics and traffic safety undoubtedly are substantial government interests. Moreover, * * * Central Radio's banner affected those interests * * * . The banner was sufficiently large to be seen from a distance of three city blocks, and * * * passing motorists reacted to the banner by honking their horns, yelling things in support, and waving.

Next, we conclude that the sign code is narrowly tailored because it does not burden substantially more speech than is necessary to further the government's legitimate interests. Instead, the sign code's size and location restrictions demonstrate that the City has carefully calculated the costs and benefits associated with the burden on speech * * * . Such restrictions do no more than eliminate the exact source of the evil [that] the ordinance sought to remedy.

Finally, unlike an outright ban on speech, the sign code leaves open ample alternative channels of communication by generally permitting the display of signs subject only to size and location restrictions.

It is undisputed here that the plaintiffs' 375-square-foot banner would comport with the City's sign code if the banner were reduced to a size of 60 square feet. * * * Such an alternative [is] adequate * * * . Accordingly, because the City's content-neutral sign code satisfies intermediate scrutiny both facially and as applied to the plaintiffs' display, we agree with the district court's holding that the sign code satisfies the constitutional requirements of the First Amendment.

DISSENTING OPINION

GREGORY, Circuit Judge, dissenting:

* * * *

I would apply a content-based test to the City's Sign Code. * * * In a case like this, involving political speech against the heaviest hand of government attempting to seize its citizen's land, we must ensure a reasonable fit between the City's asserted interests in aesthetics and traffic safety, and the Code's exemptions for government and religious emblems and flags.

I disagree that the City has demonstrated this reasonable fit. Why is it that the symbols and text of a government flag do not affect aesthetics or traffic safety and escape regulation, whereas a picture of a flag does negatively affect these interests and must be subjected to size and location restrictions? I see no reason in such a distinction. * * * I find no * * * justification [for the exemptions on the basis of

aesthetics and safety concerns] where the City's regulatory scheme perpetually disadvantages dissidents like Central Radio.

Furthermore, the City has not adequately demonstrated that its adoption of the Code and its exemptions was unrelated to disagreement with a particular message. Although the City maintains this is the case, it references only the Purpose Statement within the Code as support. * * * The mere assertion of a content-neutral purpose is not enough to save a law which, on its face, discriminates based on content. Even if a party need not come forward with voluminous evidence justifying a regulation, surely it must do something more than simply point to a content-neutral justification written into the law's preface. * * * The city [could show] that its legislative interests were unrelated to the ordinance's content distinctions through legislative findings, policy statements, and testimony of [city] officials. I find no such showing in this record.

This case implicates some of the most important values at the heart of our democracy: political speech challenging the government's seizure of private property—exactly the kind of taking that our Fifth Amendment protects against. If a citizen cannot speak out against the king taking her land, I fear we abandon a core protection of our Constitution's First Amendment. Here, Central Radio spoke out against the king * * * . It may be that the Code passes the heightened scrutiny of a content-based inquiry. But to stop short without subjecting the regulation to a more rigorous examination does a disservice to our cherished constitutional right to freedom of speech.

QUESTIONS FOR ANALYSIS

1. *Law.* How did the majority in this case respond to the issue framed at the beginning of this feature? What was the reasoning behind the response?

2. *Law.* Did the dissent agree or disagree with the test that the majority applied to the statute at the center of this case? Why?

3. *Ethics.* Does a party that "speaks out against the king" have an ethical obligation to comply with a law that regulates the time, place, and manner of that speech?

4. *Technological Dimension.* How should the Internet's "ample alternative channels of communication" affect a court's decision about a government's regulation of signs?

5. *Implications for the Business Owner.* What is the significance of the outcome in this case to a business?

iStockPhoto.com/lisafx

Unit One—Business Scenario

CompTac, Inc., which is headquartered in San Francisco, California, is one of the leading software manufacturers in the United States. The company invests millions of dollars to research and develop new software applications and computer games that are sold worldwide. It also has a large service department and takes great pains to offer its customers excellent support services.

1. **Jurisdiction.** CompTac routinely purchases some of the materials necessary to produce its computer games from a New York firm, Electrotex, Inc. A dispute arises between the two firms, and CompTac wants to sue Electrotex for breach of contract. Can CompTac bring the suit in a California state court? Can CompTac bring the suit in a federal court? Explain.

2. **Negligence.** A customer at one of CompTac's retail stores stumbles over a crate in the parking lot and breaks her leg. Just moments earlier, the crate had fallen off a CompTac truck that was delivering goods from a CompTac warehouse to the store. The customer sues CompTac, alleging negligence. Will she succeed in her suit? Why or why not?

3. **Wrongful Interference.** Roban Electronics, a software manufacturer and one of CompTac's major competitors, has been trying to convince one of CompTac's key employees, Jim Baxter, to come to work for Roban. Roban knows that Baxter has a written employment contract with CompTac, which Baxter would breach if he left CompTac before the contract expired. Baxter goes to work for Roban, and the departure of its key employee causes CompTac to suffer substantial losses due to delays in completing new software. Can CompTac sue Roban to recoup some of these losses? If so, on what ground?

4. **Cyber Crime.** One of CompTac's employees in its accounting division, Alan Green, has a gambling problem. To repay a gambling debt of $10,000, Green decides to "borrow" from CompTac to cover the debt. Using his knowledge of CompTac account numbers, Green electronically transfers $10,000 from a CompTac account into his personal checking account. A week later, he is luckier at gambling and uses the same electronic procedures to transfer funds from his personal checking account back to the CompTac account. Has Green committed any crimes? If so, what are they?

5. **Ethical Decision Making.** One of CompTac's best-selling products is a computer game that includes some extremely violent actions. Groups of parents, educators, and consumer activists have bombarded CompTac with letters and e-mail messages calling on the company to stop selling the product. CompTac executives are concerned about the public outcry, but at the same time, they realize that the game is CompTac's major source of profits. If it ceased marketing the game, the company could go bankrupt. If you were a CompTac decision maker, what would your decision be in this situation? How would you justify your decision from an ethical perspective?

6. **Intellectual Property.** CompTac wants to sell one of its best-selling software programs to An Phat Company, a firm located in Ho Chi Minh City, Vietnam. CompTac is concerned, however, that after an initial purchase, An Phat will duplicate the software without permission (and in violation of U.S. copyright laws) and sell the illegal bootleg software to other firms in Vietnam. How can CompTac protect its software from being pirated by An Phat Company?

7. **Social Media.** CompTac seeks to hire fourteen new employees. Its human resources (HR) department asks all candidates during their interview to disclose their social media passwords so that the company can access their social media accounts. Is it legal for employers to ask prospective employees for their social media passwords? Explain. If CompTac does not ask for passwords, can it legally look at a person's online posts when evaluating whether to hire or fire the person?

iStockPhoto.com/Tramino

Unit One—Group Project

Constitutional Law. Assume that your group makes decisions for an automaker that sells cars in every state and that each state has slightly different consumer protection statutes.

1. One group will list two underlying reasons why there is a strong presumption against preemption.

2. One group will evaluate the truth or falsity of the majority's conclusion that "as long as a state's regulation does not require a manufacturer to provide a fuel estimate different from the EPA fuel economy estimate," there is no preemption.

3. Another group will develop the dissent's argument that a presumption against preemption is not triggered when the state regulates in an area where there has been a "history of significant federal presence."

iStockPhoto.com/Rawpixel

Unit 2
Contracts and E-Contracts

iStockPhoto.com/eyescar

10

LEARNING OBJECTIVES

The five Learning Objectives below are designed to help improve your understanding of the chapter. After reading this chapter, you should be able to answer the following questions:

1. What is a contract? What is the objective theory of contracts?

2. What are the four basic elements necessary to the formation of a valid contract?

3. What is the difference between express and implied contracts?

4. How does a void contract differ from a voidable contract? What is an unenforceable contract?

5. What rules guide the courts in interpreting contracts?

Promise A declaration that binds a person who makes it (the promisor) to do or not to do a certain act.

Promisor A person who makes a promise.

Promisee A person to whom a promise is made.

Nature and Classification

As Ralph Waldo Emerson observed in the chapter-opening quotation, people tend to act in their own self-interest, and this influences the terms they seek in their contracts. Contract law must therefore provide rules to determine which contract terms will be enforced.

A contract is based on a **promise**—a declaration by a person (the **promisor**) that binds the person to do or not to do a certain act. As a result, the person to whom the promise is made (the **promisee**) has a right to expect or demand that something either will or will not happen in the future.

Like other types of law, contract law reflects our social values, interests, and expectations at a given point in time. It shows, for example, what kinds of promises our society thinks should be legally binding. It distinguishes between promises that create only moral obligations (such as a promise to take a friend to lunch) and promises that are legally binding (such as a promise to pay for merchandise purchased).

Increasingly, contracts are formed online. While some believe that we need a new body of law to cover e-contracts, others point out that we can apply existing contract law quite easily. Through the following chapters, you will see how contract law can be used to resolve online disputes. For instance, in this chapter you will read about the validity of the *disclaimers* that are often seen on e-mails.

> "All sensible people are selfish, and nature is tugging at every contract to make the terms of it fair."
>
> **RALPH WALDO EMERSON**
> 1803–1882
> (AMERICAN POET)

10-1 An Overview of Contract Law

Before we look at the numerous rules that courts use to determine whether a particular promise will be enforced, it is necessary to understand some fundamental concepts of contract law. In this section, we describe the sources and general function of contract law and introduce the objective theory of contracts.

10–1a Sources of Contract Law

The common law governs all contracts except when it has been modified or replaced by statutory law, such as the Uniform Commercial Code (UCC), or by administrative agency regulations. Contracts relating to services, real estate, employment, and insurance, for example, generally are governed by the common law of contracts.

Contracts for the sale and lease of goods, however, are governed by the UCC—to the extent that the UCC has modified general contract law. The relationship between general contract law and the law governing sales and leases of goods will be explored in detail in the next unit. In the discussion of general contract law that follows, we indicate in footnotes the areas in which the UCC has significantly altered common law contract principles.

House purchases always are completed with explicit contracts. Why?

10–1b The Function of Contracts

No aspect of modern life is entirely free of contractual relationships. You acquire rights and obligations, for instance, when you borrow funds, buy or lease a house, obtain insurance, form a business, or purchase goods or services. Contract law is designed to provide stability and predictability for both buyers and sellers in the marketplace by assuring the parties to these private agreements that the promises they make will be enforceable.

To be sure, when they make an agreement, a promisor and a promisee may decide to honor it for various reasons other than the existence of contract law. Clearly, many promises are kept because the parties involved feel a moral obligation to keep a promise or because keeping a promise is in their mutual self-interest. Nevertheless, in business agreements, the rules of contract law are often followed to avoid potential disputes.

By supplying procedures for enforcing private agreements, contract law provides an essential condition for the existence of a market economy. Without a legal framework of reasonably assured expectations within which to make long-run plans, businesspersons would be able to rely only on the good faith of others. Duty and good faith are usually sufficient to obtain compliance with a promise. When price changes or adverse economic factors make compliance costly, however, these elements may not be enough. Contract law is necessary to ensure compliance with a promise or to entitle the innocent party to some form of relief.

10–1c Definition of a Contract

A **contract** is an agreement that can be enforced in court. It is formed by two or more parties who agree to perform or to refrain from performing some act now or in the future.

Generally, contract disputes arise when there is a promise of future performance. If the contractual promise is not fulfilled, the party who made it is subject to the sanctions of a court. That party may be required to pay damages for failing to perform the contractual promise. In a few instances, the party may be required to perform the promised act.

10–1d The Objective Theory of Contracts

In determining whether a contract has been formed, the element of intent is of prime importance. In contract law, intent is determined by what is referred to as the **objective theory of contracts.** Under this theory, a party's intention to enter into a contract is judged by outward, objective facts as interpreted by a *reasonable person,* rather than by the party's secret, subjective intentions.

LEARNING OBJECTIVE 1

What is a contract? What is the objective theory of contracts?

Contract   A set of promises constituting an agreement between parties, giving each a legal duty to the other and the right to seek a remedy for the breach of the promises or duties.

Objective Theory of Contracts   The view that contracting parties shall only be bound by terms that can be objectively inferred from promises made.

Objective facts include (1) what the party said when entering into the contract, (2) how the party acted or appeared, and (3) the circumstances surrounding the transaction. As will be discussed later in this chapter, in the section on express versus implied contracts, intent to form a contract may be manifested by conduct, as well as by words, oral or written.

A party may have many reasons for entering into an agreement—obtaining real property, goods, or services, for example, and profiting from the deal. Any of these purposes may provide motivation for performing the contract. In the following case, however, one party failed to perform and claimed that he had not intended to enter into the contract when he signed it.

CASE 10.1

Pan Handle Realty, LLC v. Olins

Appellate Court of Connecticut, 140 Conn.App. 556, 59 A.3d 842 (2013).

FACTS Pan Handle Realty, LLC, built a luxury home in Westport, Connecticut. Robert Olins proposed to lease the property. Pan Handle forwarded a draft of a lease to Olins. On January 17, the parties met and negotiated changes to the lease's terms. After the final draft of the lease was signed, Olins gave Pan Handle a check for $138,000, which was the amount of the annual rent. Olins said that he planned to move into the home on January 28. Before that date, according to the lease, Pan Handle was to remove all furnishings from the property.

On January 27, Pan Handle's bank notified the company that Olins had stopped payment on the rental check. Olins then told Pan Handle that he was "unable to pursue any further interest in the property." Pan Handle made substantial efforts to find a new tenant but was unable to do so. Consequently, Pan Handle filed a lawsuit in a Connecticut state court against Olins, alleging that he had breached the lease. The court found in Pan Handle's favor and awarded damages in the amount of $138,000 in unpaid rent, plus $8,000 in utility fees, interest, and attorneys' fees. Olins appealed.

ISSUE Did Olins and Pan Handle intend to be bound by the agreement when they signed the lease?

DECISION Yes. The state intermediate appellate court affirmed the lower court's judgment.

REASON The objective fact—as supported by the evidence—was that the parties intended to be bound by the lease when they signed

Under what circumstances can a property owner prevail when a prospective lessee "backs out" of a lease agreement?

iStockPhoto.com/Franck-Boston

it. Olins contended that because material terms of the lease were still being negotiated there was no "meeting of the minds," which is required to form a contract. As the reviewing court noted, "If there has been a misunderstanding between the parties, or a misapprehension by one or both so that their minds have never met, no contract has been entered into by them and the court will not make for them a contract which they themselves did not make."

Here, though, Olins and a representative of Pan Handle made revisions and signed the final draft of the lease. In addition, Olins tendered a check, on which he noted payment for a one-year lease of the premises. Olins's "apparent unilateral change of heart regarding the lease agreement does not negate the parties' prior meeting of the minds that occurred at the time the lease was executed." Thus, "the lease agreement was a valid and binding contract which the defendant . . . breached."

The court also upheld the lower court's measure of damages, stating that "the unpaid rent . . . may be used by the court in computing the losses suffered" by Pan Handle because of Olins's breach. The company should be placed in the same position it would have been in had the contract been fully performed.

CRITICAL THINKING—Legal Consideration *How did the objective theory of contracts affect the result in this case? Explain.*

10-2 Elements of a Contract

The many topics that will be discussed in the following chapters on contract law require an understanding of the basic elements of a valid contract and the way in which a contract is created. Also important is an understanding of the types of circumstances in which even legally valid contracts will not be enforced.

10-2a Requirements of a Valid Contract

The following list briefly describes the four requirements that must be met for a valid contract to exist.

1. *Agreement.* An agreement to form a contract includes an *offer* and an *acceptance.* One party must offer to enter into a legal agreement, and another party must accept the terms of the offer.
2. *Consideration.* Any promises made by the parties must be supported by legally sufficient and bargained-for consideration (something of value received or promised to convince a person to make a deal).
3. *Contractual capacity.* Both parties entering into the contract must have the contractual capacity to do so. The law must recognize them as possessing characteristics that qualify them as competent parties.
4. *Legality.* The contract's purpose must be to accomplish some goal that is legal and not against public policy.

If any of these elements is lacking, no contract will have been formed. Each item will be explained more fully in subsequent chapters.

LEARNING OBJECTIVE 2
What are the four basic elements necessary to the formation of a valid contract?

10-2b Defenses to the Enforceability of a Contract

Even if all of the requirements listed above are satisfied, a contract may be unenforceable if the following requirements are not met.

1. *Voluntary consent.* The consent of both parties must be voluntary. For instance, if a contract was formed as a result of fraud, mistake, or duress (coercion), the contract may not be enforceable.
2. *Form.* The contract must be in whatever form the law requires. Some contracts must be in writing to be enforceable.

These requirements typically are raised as *defenses* to the enforceability of an otherwise valid contract.

10-3 Types of Contracts

There are many types of contracts. They may be categorized based on legal distinctions as to their *formation, performance,* and *enforceability.*

10-3a Contract Formation

Contracts may be classified based on how and when they are formed. Exhibit 10–1 shows three such classifications, and the following subsections explain them in greater detail.

Bilateral versus Unilateral Contracts Every contract involves at least two parties. The **offeror** is the party making the offer (promising to do or not to do something). The **offeree** is the party to whom the offer is made. A contract is classified as *bilateral* or *unilateral* depending on what the offeree must do to accept the offer and bind the offeror to a contract.

Bilateral Contracts. If the offeree can accept simply by promising to perform, the contract is a **bilateral contract.** Hence, a bilateral contract is a "promise for a promise." An example of a bilateral contract is a contract in which one person agrees to buy another person's automobile for a specified price. No performance, such as the payment of funds or delivery of goods, need take place for a bilateral contract to be formed. The contract comes into existence at the moment the promises are exchanged.

Offeror A person who makes an offer.

Offeree A person to whom an offer is made.

Bilateral Contract A type of contract that arises when a promise is given in exchange for a return promise.

Exhibit 10–1 Classifications Based on Contract Formation

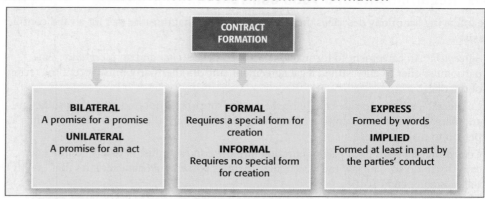

EXAMPLE 10.1 Javier offers to buy Ann's smartphone for $200. Javier tells Ann that he will give her the cash for the phone on the following Friday, when he gets paid. Ann accepts Javier's offer and promises to give him the phone when he pays her on Friday. Javier and Ann have formed a bilateral contract. ■

Unilateral Contracts.   If the offer is phrased so that the offeree can accept only by completing the contract performance, the contract is a **unilateral contract.** Hence, a unilateral contract is a "promise for an act." In other words, the contract is formed not at the moment when promises are exchanged but rather when the contract is *performed*.

EXAMPLE 10.2 Reese says to Kay, "If you drive my car from New York to Los Angeles, I'll give you $1,000." Only on Kay's completion of the act—bringing the car to Los Angeles—does she fully accept Reese's offer to pay $1,000. If she chooses not to accept the offer to drive the car to Los Angeles, there are no legal consequences. ■

Contests, lotteries, and other competitions offering prizes are also examples of offers for unilateral contracts. If a person complies with the rules of the contest—such as by submitting the right lottery number at the right place and time—a unilateral contract is formed. The organization offering the prize is then bound to a contract to perform as promised in the offer. If the person fails to comply with the contest rules, however, no binding contract is formed.

Unilateral Contract A type of contract that results when an offer can be accepted only by the offeree's performance.

ETHICAL
ISSUE

Does a "You break it, you buy it" sign create a unilateral contract? It is not unusual to see posted in retail stores signs that say, "You break it, you buy it." The implication, of course, is that you are legally obligated to buy something if you break it while inspecting it prior to a potential purchase. This "rule" is often known as the "Pottery Barn Rule," even though that retailer has no such rule.

Some argue that posted signs of this nature create unilateral contracts. It is difficult to prove the validity of such contracts, however. After all, for a contract to be formed, the accepting party has to demonstrate acceptance of the terms purposed. Few courts would uphold the notion that every customer agrees to every proposition posted on the walls of retail establishments. Moreover, where is the consideration? That is, what does the retailer give customers in return for their acceptance of a unilateral contract that says, "You break it, you buy it"?

Consider also that every customer in a retail establishment is an *invitee*. Consequently, the retailer accepts the risk that customers may accidentally damage items on display, regardless of posted warnings. Simply stating that once a customer reads a sign and chooses to continue shopping constitutes an acceptance is not only legally problematic, it is ethically bothersome. Merchants cannot transfer the risk of breakage to customers just by posting notices.

Revocation of Offers for Unilateral Contracts. A problem arises in unilateral contracts when the promisor attempts to *revoke* (cancel) the offer after the promisee has begun performance but before the act has been completed. **EXAMPLE 10.3** Seiko offers to buy Jin's sailboat, moored in San Francisco, on delivery of the boat to Seiko's dock in Newport Beach, three hundred miles south of San Francisco. Jin rigs the boat and sets sail. Shortly before his arrival at Newport Beach, Jin receives a message from Seiko withdrawing her offer. Was the offer terminated? ■

In contract law, offers are normally *revocable* (capable of being taken back, or canceled) until accepted. Thus, under the traditional view of unilateral contracts, in *Example 10.3,* Seiko's revocation would terminate the offer. Because Seiko's offer was to form a unilateral contract, only Jin's delivery of the sailboat at her dock would have been an acceptance.

iStockPhoto.com/Wolterk

What is the so-called Pottery Barn Rule?

Because of the harsh effect on the offeree of the revocation of an offer to form a unilateral contract, the modern-day view is different. Today, once performance has been *substantially* undertaken, the offeror cannot revoke the offer. Thus, in *Example 10.3,* even though Jin has not yet accepted the offer by complete performance, Seiko is prohibited from revoking it. Jin can deliver the boat and bind Seiko to the contract.

Formal versus Informal Contracts Another classification system divides contracts into formal contracts and informal contracts. **Formal contracts** are contracts that require a special form or method of creation (formation) to be enforceable.[1] One example is *negotiable instruments,* which include checks, drafts, promissory notes, and certificates of deposit. Negotiable instruments are formal contracts because, under the Uniform Commercial Code, a special form and language are required to create them. *Letters of credit,* which are frequently used in international sales contracts, are another type of formal contract.

Formal Contract An agreement that by law requires a specific form for its validity.

Informal contracts (also called *simple contracts*) include all other contracts. No special form is required (except for certain types of contracts that must be in writing). The contracts are usually based on their substance rather than their form. Typically, though, businesspersons put their contracts in writing to ensure that there is some proof of a contract's existence should problems arise.

Informal Contract A contract that does not require a specific form or method of creation to be valid.

LEARNING OBJECTIVE 3
What is the difference between express and implied contracts?

Express versus Implied Contracts Contracts may also be categorized as express or implied. In an **express contract,** the terms of the agreement are fully and explicitly stated in words, oral or written. A signed lease for an apartment or a house is an express written contract. If a classmate accepts your offer to sell your textbooks from last semester for $100, an express oral contract has been made.

A contract that is implied from the conduct of the parties is called an **implied contract** (or sometimes an *implied-in-fact contract*). This type of contract differs from an express contract in that the *conduct* of the parties, rather than their words, creates and defines at least some of the terms of the contract. For an implied contract to arise, certain requirements must be met.

Express Contract A contract in which the terms of the agreement are stated in words, oral or written.

Implied Contract A contract formed in whole or in part from the conduct of the parties.

Requirements for Implied Contracts. Normally, if the following conditions exist, a court will hold that an implied contract was formed:

1. The plaintiff furnished some service or property.

2. The plaintiff expected to be paid for that service or property, and the defendant knew or should have known that payment was expected.

3. The defendant had a chance to reject the services or property and did not.

---

1. See *Restatement (Second) of Contracts*, Section 6. Remember that *Restatements of the Law* are books that summarize court decisions on a particular topic and that courts often refer to for guidance.

EXAMPLE 10.4 Oleg, a small-business owner, needs an accountant to complete his tax return. He drops by a local accountant's office, explains his situation to the accountant, and learns what fees she charges. The next day, he returns and gives the receptionist all of the necessary documents to complete his tax return. Then he walks out without saying anything further. In this situation, Oleg has entered into an implied contract to pay the accountant the usual fees for her services. The contract is implied because of Oleg's conduct and hers. She expects to be paid for completing the tax return, and by bringing in the records she will need to do the job, Oleg has implied an intent to pay her. ■

Mixed Contracts with Express and Implied Terms.
Note that a contract can be a mixture of an express contract and an implied contract. In other words, a contract may contain some express terms, while others are implied. During the construction of a home, for instance, the homeowner often asks the builder to make changes in the original specifications.

CASE EXAMPLE 10.5 Lamar Hopkins hired Uhrhahn Construction & Design, Inc., for several projects in the construction of his home. For each project, the parties signed a written contract that was based on a cost estimate and specifications and that required changes to the agreement to be in writing. While the work was in progress, however, Hopkins repeatedly asked Uhrhahn to deviate from the contract specifications, which Uhrhahn did. None of these requests was made in writing.

Under what circumstances can an owner be liable for additional costs due to a request for a change in materials even though no written contract modification was created?

One day, Hopkins asked Uhrhahn to use Durisol blocks instead of the cinder blocks specified in the original contract, indicating that the cost would be the same. Uhrhahn used the Durisol blocks but demanded extra payment when it became clear that the Durisol blocks were more complicated to install. Although Hopkins had paid for the other orally requested deviations from the contract, he refused to pay Uhrhahn for the substitution of the Durisol blocks. Uhrhahn sued for breach of contract. The court found that Hopkins, through his conduct, had waived the provision requiring written contract modification and created an implied contract to pay the extra cost of installing the Durisol blocks.[2] ■

Among other implied terms, all contracts include an implied covenant of good faith and fair dealing. This implied term requires the parties to perform in accord with the contract and the parties' reasonable expectations under it. In the following case, the plaintiff claimed that the defendant had breached both the express terms of the parties' contract and the implied covenant of good faith and fair dealing.

---

2. *Uhrhahn Construction & Design, Inc. v. Hopkins*, 179 P.3d 808 (Utah App. 2008).

CASE 10.2

Vukanovich v. Kine

Court of Appeals of Oregon, 342 P.3d 1075 (2015).

FACTS Mark Vukanovich and Larry Kine agreed under a "Letter of Understanding" to work together to buy a certain parcel of real property in Eugene, Oregon, from Umpqua Bank. They expressly agreed to develop the property and to split the cost and profits equally. Vukanovich shared confidential financial information with Kine that he would not otherwise have shared. The bank agreed to accept

Can a "letter of understanding" bind partners to a joint offer for real estate?

$1.6 million for the property, and a closing date was set. Kine then said that he no longer wanted to pursue the deal with Vukanovich or to buy the property. The closing did not occur. A month later, without Vukanovich's knowledge, Kine made a new offer to buy the property. At about the same time, Vukanovich made his own new offer. The bank accepted Kine's offer. Vukanovich filed a suit in an

Oregon state court against Kine, alleging breach of contract. The jury returned a verdict in favor of Vukanovich, awarding him $686,000 on the breach of contract claim and other damages, but the court entered a judgment in favor of Kine. Vukanovich appealed.

ISSUE Was the evidence sufficient to support Vukanovich's claim for breach?

DECISION Yes. A state intermediate appellate court reinstated the jury verdict. "The record contains sufficient evidence permitting the jury to find" that Kine had breached both the express terms of the parties' contract and the implied covenant of good faith and fair dealing.

REASON Vukanovich, Kine, and the bank had agreed on a price for the property and set a closing date, but Kine had refused to close and had then repudiated the agreement with Vukanovich. There was evidence that Kine had lied about his reasons for not closing and that he had subsequently used confidential information given to him by Vukanovich to devise his new offer to buy the property. Kine argued that his separate attempt to buy the property was not a breach of his agreement with Vukanovich because it occurred after that deal had ended. The court explained that it was Kine's "refusal to complete the purchase of the property with plaintiff, his surreptitious use of the information that plaintiff had provided him to devise a more favorable transaction for himself . . . , and his lies to plaintiff about his reasons for not closing the deal" that constituted the breach. These actions had caused the parties' joint effort to fail and damaged Vukanovich by cutting him out of an ownership interest in the property and the profits generated by that property.

CRITICAL THINKING—Economic Consideration *What did the amount of the jury's award of $686,000 in damages represent? Explain.*

10–3b Contract Performance

Contracts are also classified according to their state of performance. A contract that has been fully performed on both sides is called an **executed contract.** A contract that has not been fully performed by the parties is called an **executory contract.** If one party has fully performed but the other has not, the contract is said to be executed on the one side and executory on the other, but the contract is still classified as executory.

> **EXAMPLE 10.6** Jackson, Inc., agreed to buy ten tons of coal from the Northern Coal Company. Northern has delivered the coal to Jackson's steel mill, but Jackson has not yet paid. At this point, the contract is executed on the part of Northern and executory on Jackson's part. After Jackson pays Northern, the contract will be executed on both sides. ■

Executed Contract A contract that has been fully performed by both parties.

Executory Contract A contract that has not yet been fully performed.

10–3c Contract Enforceability

A **valid contract** has the four elements necessary to entitle at least one of the parties to enforce it in court. Those elements, as mentioned earlier, consist of (1) an agreement (offer and acceptance), (2) supported by legally sufficient consideration, (3) made by parties who have the legal capacity to enter into the contract, and (4) for a legal purpose.

As you can see in Exhibit 10–2, valid contracts may be enforceable, voidable, or unenforceable. Additionally, a contract may be referred to as a *void contract.* We look next at the meaning of the terms *voidable, unenforceable,* and *void* in relation to contract enforceability.

Voidable Contracts A **voidable contract** is a valid contract but one that can be avoided at the option of one or both of the parties. The party having the option can elect either to avoid any duty to perform or to *ratify* (make valid) the contract. If the contract is avoided, both parties are released from it. If it is ratified, both parties must fully perform their respective legal obligations.

As a general rule, for instance, contracts made by minors are voidable at the option of the minor (as will be discussed in the chapter covering capacity). Additionally, contracts entered into under fraudulent conditions are voidable at the option of the defrauded party. Contracts entered into under legally defined duress or undue influence are also voidable (as you will learn in the chapter on contract defenses).

LEARNING OBJECTIVE 4

How does a void contract differ from a voidable contract? What is an unenforceable contract?

Valid Contract A contract that results when the elements necessary for contract formation (agreement, consideration, capacity, and legality) are present.

Voidable Contract A contract that may be legally avoided at the option of one or both of the parties.

Exhibit 10–2 Enforceable, Voidable, Unenforceable, and Void Contracts

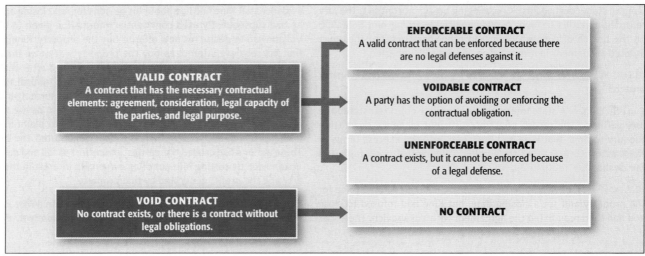

Unenforceable Contract
A valid contract rendered unenforceable by some statute or law.

Unenforceable Contracts An **unenforceable contract** is one that cannot be enforced because of certain legal defenses against it. It is not unenforceable because a party failed to satisfy a legal requirement of the contract. Rather, it is a valid contract rendered unenforceable by some statute or law. For instance, some contracts must be in writing. If they are not, they will not be enforceable except in certain exceptional circumstances.

Void Contract A contract having no legal force or binding effect.

Void Contracts A **void contract** is no contract at all. The terms *void* and *contract* are contradictory. None of the parties has any legal obligations if a contract is void. A contract can be void because one of the parties was previously determined by a court to be mentally incompetent, for instance, or because the purpose of the contract was illegal (such as a contract to burn down a building).

10-4 Quasi Contracts

Quasi Contract An obligation or contract imposed by law (a court), in the absence of an agreement, to prevent the unjust enrichment of one party.

Express contracts and implied contracts are actual or true contracts formed by the words or actions of the parties. **Quasi contracts,** or contracts *implied in law,* are not actual contracts. They are not true contracts because they do not arise from any agreement, express or implied, between the parties themselves. Rather, they are fictional contracts that courts can impose on the parties "as if" the parties had entered into an actual contract. (The word *quasi* is Latin for "as if.")

Quasi contracts are equitable rather than legal contracts. Usually, they are imposed to avoid the *unjust enrichment* of one party at the expense of another. The doctrine of unjust enrichment is based on the theory that individuals should not be allowed to profit or enrich themselves inequitably at the expense of others. **CASE EXAMPLE 10.7** Seawest Services Association operated a water distribution system that served homes inside a housing development (full members) and some homes located outside the subdivision (limited members). Both full and limited members paid water bills and assessments for work performed on the water system when necessary.

The Copenhavers purchased a home outside the housing development. They did not have an express contract with Seawest, but they paid water bills for eight years and paid one $3,950 assessment for water system upgrades. After a dispute arose, the Copenhavers refused to pay their water bills and assessments. Seawest sued. The court found that the Copenhavers had a quasi contract with Seawest and were liable. The Copenhavers had enjoyed the benefits of Seawest's water services and even paid for them prior to their dispute. In addition, "the Copenhavers would be unjustly enriched if they could retain benefits provided by Seawest without paying for them."[3]

When the court imposes a quasi contract, a plaintiff may recover in ***quantum meruit,***[4] a Latin phrase meaning "as much as he or she deserves." *Quantum meruit* essentially describes the extent of compensation owed under a quasi contract.

> ***Quantum Meruit*** A Latin phrase meaning "as much as he or she deserves." The expression describes the extent of compensation owed under a quasi contract.

10-4a Limitations on Quasi-Contractual Recovery

Although quasi contracts exist to prevent unjust enrichment, in some situations, the party who obtains a benefit is not liable for its fair value. Basically, a party who has conferred a benefit on someone else unnecessarily or as a result of misconduct or negligence cannot invoke the doctrine of quasi contract. The enrichment in those situations will not be considered "unjust."

Also, even when it can be shown that a party received some benefit, it is not necessarily sufficient to prove unjust enrichment. **CASE EXAMPLE 10.8** Qwest Wireless, LLC, provided wireless phone services in Arizona and thirteen other states. Qwest marketed and sold handset insurance to its wireless customers, although it did not have a license to sell insurance in Arizona or in any other state. Patrick and Vicki Van Zanen sued Qwest in a federal court for unjust enrichment based on its receipt of sales commissions for the insurance.

The court agreed that Qwest had violated the insurance-licensing statute, but found that the sales commissions did not constitute unjust enrichment because the customers had, in fact, received the handset insurance. Also, Qwest had not retained a benefit (the commissions) without paying for it (providing insurance). Therefore, Qwest had not been unjustly enriched.[5]

10-4b When an Actual Contract Exists

The doctrine of quasi contract generally cannot be used when an actual contract covers the area in controversy. In this situation, a remedy already exists if a party is unjustly enriched because the other fails to perform. The nonbreaching party can sue the breaching party for breach of contract.

EXAMPLE 10.9 Lopez contracts with Cameron to deliver a furnace to a building owned by Grant. Lopez delivers the furnace, but Cameron never pays Lopez. Grant has been unjustly enriched in this situation, to be sure. Nevertheless, Lopez cannot recover from Grant in quasi contract, because Lopez has an actual contract with Cameron. Lopez already has a remedy—he can sue for breach of contract to recover the price of the furnace from Cameron. In this situation, the court does not need to impose a quasi contract to achieve justice.

If you buy smartphone insurance from a company that is not licensed to sell this insurance in your state, has that company obtained unjust enrichment? Why or why not?

10-5 Interpretation of Contracts

Parties may sometimes agree that a contract has been formed but disagree on its meaning or legal effect. One reason that this may happen is the technical legal terminology traditionally used in contracts, sometimes referred to as *legalese*. Today, many contracts are written in

---

3. *Seawest Services Association v. Copenhaver,* 166 Wash.App. 1006 (2012).
4. Pronounced *kwahn*-tuhm *mehr*-oo-wit.
5. *Van Zanen v. Qwest Wireless, LLC,* 522 F.3d 1127 (10th Cir. 2008).

"plain," nontechnical language. Even then, though, a dispute may arise over the meaning of a contract simply because the rights or obligations under the contract are not expressed clearly—no matter how "plain" the language used.

In this section, we look at some common law rules of contract interpretation. These rules provide the courts with guidelines for deciding disputes over how contract terms or provisions should be interpreted. Exhibit 10–3 provides a brief graphic summary of how these rules are applied.

PREVENTING LEGAL DISPUTES

To avoid disputes over contract interpretation, make sure your intentions are clearly expressed in your contracts. Careful drafting of contracts not only helps prevent potential disputes over the meaning of terms but may also be crucial if the firm brings a lawsuit or needs to defend against a lawsuit for breach of contract. By using simple, clear language and avoiding legalese, you can take a major step toward avoiding contract disputes.

10-5a Plain Language Laws

The federal government and a majority of the states have enacted *plain language laws* to regulate legal writing and eliminate legalese. All federal agencies are required to use plain language in most of their forms and written communications. Plain language requirements have been extended to agency rulemaking as well. States frequently have plain language laws that apply to consumer contracts—contracts made primarily for personal, family, or household purposes. The legal profession has also moved toward plain English, and court rules in many jurisdictions require attorneys to use plain language in court documents.

10-5b The Plain Meaning Rule

KNOW THIS
No one can avoid contractual obligations by claiming that she or he did not read the contract. A contract normally is interpreted as if each party had read every word carefully.

When a contract's language is clear and unequivocal, a court will enforce it according to its obvious terms. The meaning of the terms must be determined from *the face of the instrument*—from the written document alone. This is sometimes referred to as the *plain meaning rule*. The words—and their plain, ordinary meanings—determine the intent of the parties at the time they entered into the contract. A court is bound to give effect to the contract according to this intent.

Exhibit 10–3 Rules of Contract Interpretation

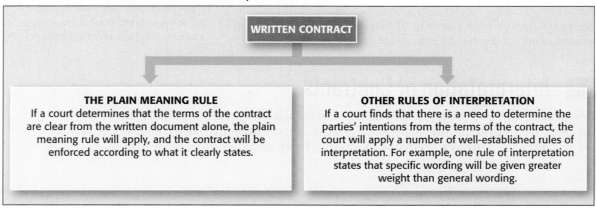

WRITTEN CONTRACT

THE PLAIN MEANING RULE
If a court determines that the terms of the contract are clear from the written document alone, the plain meaning rule will apply, and the contract will be enforced according to what it clearly states.

OTHER RULES OF INTERPRETATION
If a court finds that there is a need to determine the parties' intentions from the terms of the contract, the court will apply a number of well-established rules of interpretation. For example, one rule of interpretation states that specific wording will be given greater weight than general wording.

Ambiguity What if a contract's language is not clear and unequivocal? A court will consider a contract to be unclear, or ambiguous, in the following situations:

1. When the intent of the parties cannot be determined from its language.
2. When it lacks a provision on a disputed issue.
3. When a term is susceptible to more than one interpretation.
4. When there is uncertainty about a provision.

Extrinsic Evidence If a contract term is ambiguous, a court may interpret the ambiguity against the party who drafted the contract term, as discussed shortly. Sometimes, too, a court may consider **extrinsic evidence**—evidence not contained in the document itself—in interpreting ambiguous contract terms. Such evidence may include the testimony of the parties, additional agreements or communications, or other information relevant to determining the parties' intent.

The admissibility of extrinsic evidence can significantly affect the court's interpretation of ambiguous contractual provisions and thus the outcome of litigation. But when the contract is clear and unambiguous, a court normally cannot consider evidence outside the contract. The following *Spotlight Case* illustrates these points.

Extrinsic Evidence
Any evidence not contained in the contract itself, which may include the testimony of the parties, additional agreements or communications, or other information relevant to determining the parties' intent.

SPOTLIGHT ON COLUMBIA PICTURES: CASE 10.3

Wagner v. Columbia Pictures Industries, Inc.

California Court of Appeal, Second District, 146 Cal.App.4th 586, 52 Cal.Rptr.3d 898 (2007).

FACTS Actor Robert Wagner entered into an agreement with Spelling-Goldberg Productions (SGP) "relating to *Charlie's Angels* (herein called the 'series')." The contract entitled Wagner to 50 percent of the net profits that SGP received from broadcasting the series and from all ancillary, music, and subsidiary rights in connection with the series. SGP hired Ivan Goff and Ben Roberts to write the series, under a contract subject to the Writers Guild of America Minimum Basic Agreement (MBA).[a] The MBA stipulated that the writer of a television show retains the right to make and market films based on the material, subject to the producer's right to buy this right if the writer decides to sell it within five years.

Actor Robert Wagner had the rights to the TV series, Charlie's Angels.

Helga Esteb/ShutterStock.com

The first *Charlie's Angels* episode aired in 1976. In 1982, SGP sold its rights to the series to Columbia Pictures Industries, Inc. Thirteen years later, Columbia bought the movie rights to the material from Goff's and Roberts's heirs. In 2000 and 2003, Columbia produced and distributed two *Charlie's Angels* movies. Wagner filed a suit in a California state court against Columbia, claiming a share of the profits from the films. The court granted Columbia's motion for summary judgment. Wagner appealed to a state intermediate appellate court.

ISSUE Did the language of Wagner's contract with SGP entitle Columbia to all of the profits from the two *Charlie's Angels* movies?

DECISION Yes. The state intermediate appellate court affirmed the lower court's judgment.

REASON Wagner offered evidence to show that a previous contract with SGP involving a property titled *Love Song* had been intended to give him half of the net profits that SGP received from the property from all sources without limitation as to source or time. Wagner argued that because the profits provision in the *Charlie's Angels* agreement used identical language, the provision should be interpreted to give him the same share. The court stated that an "agreement is the writing itself." Extrinsic evidence is not admissible "to show intention independent of an unambiguous written instrument." The court reasoned that even if the parties intended Wagner to share in the profits from all sources, "they did not say so in their contract." Under the language of the contract, Wagner was not entitled to share in the profits from the exercise of the movie rights to *Charlie's Angels* if those rights were acquired separately. SGP did not acquire the movie rights to *Charlie's Angels* by exercising this right within the five-year period. Columbia obtained those rights separately more than five years later.

CRITICAL THINKING—Legal Consideration *How might the result in this case have been different if the court had allowed Wagner's extrinsic evidence of the prior contract regarding* Love Song *to be used as evidence in this dispute?*

a. The Writers Guild of America is an association of screen and television writers that negotiates industry-wide agreements with motion picture and television producers to cover the rights of its members.

10-5c Other Rules of Interpretation

Generally, as mentioned, a court will interpret contract language to give effect to the parties' intent *as expressed in the contract*. This is the primary purpose of the rules of interpretation—to determine the parties' intent from the language used in their agreement and to give effect to that intent. A court normally will not make or remake a contract, nor will it normally interpret the language according to what the parties *claim* their intent was when they made the contract.

Rules the Courts Use   The courts use the following rules in interpreting contractual terms:

1. Insofar as possible, a reasonable, lawful, and effective meaning will be given to all of a contract's terms.
2. A contract will be interpreted as a whole. Individual, specific clauses will be considered subordinate to the contract's general intent. All writings that are a part of the same transaction will be interpreted together.
3. Terms that were the subject of separate negotiation will be given greater consideration than standardized terms and terms that were not negotiated separately.
4. A word will be given its ordinary, commonly accepted meaning, and a technical word or term will be given its technical meaning, unless the parties clearly intended something else.
5. Specific and exact wording will be given greater consideration than general language.
6. Written or typewritten terms prevail over preprinted terms.
7. Because a contract should be drafted in clear and unambiguous language, a party that uses ambiguous expressions is held to be responsible for the ambiguities. Thus, when the language has more than one meaning, it will be interpreted *against* the party that drafted the contract.
8. Evidence of *trade usage, prior dealing,* and *course of performance* may be admitted to clarify the meaning of an ambiguously worded contract. (We will define and discuss these terms in the chapter on sales and lease contracts.)

"The difference between the right word and the almost right word is the difference between lightning and a lightning bug."

MARK TWAIN
1835–1910
(AMERICAN AUTHOR AND HUMORIST)

Express Terms Usually Given Most Weight   In situations in which trade usage, prior dealing, and course of performance come into play, the courts observe certain priorities in interpreting contracts. Express terms (terms expressly stated in the contract) are given the greatest weight, followed by course of performance, course of dealing, and custom and usage of trade—in that order. When considering custom and usage, a court will look at the trade customs and usage common to the particular business or industry and to the locale in which the contract was made or is to be performed.

CASE EXAMPLE 10.10   Jessica Robbins bought a house in Tennessee. U.S. Bank financed the purchase, and Tennessee Farmers Mutual Insurance Company issued the homeowner's insurance policy. The policy included a clause that promised payment to the bank for losses unless the loss was due to an "increase in hazard" about which the bank knew but did not tell the insurer. When Robbins fell behind on her mortgage payments, the bank started foreclosure proceedings. No one told the insurer. Robbins filed for bankruptcy, which postponed foreclosure.

Meanwhile, the house was destroyed in a fire. The bank filed a claim under the policy, but the insurer refused to pay on the ground that it had not been told by the bank of an "increase in hazard"—the foreclosure. The bank then filed a lawsuit. The court found that the plain meaning of the words "increase in hazard" in the policy referred to physical conditions on the property that posed a risk, not to events such as foreclosure. Thus, the bank was not required to notify the insurer under the terms of the policy, and the lack of notice did not invalidate the coverage.[6]

---

6. *U.S. Bank, N.A. v. Tennessee Farmers Mutual Insurance Co.*, 277 S.W.3d 381 (Tenn.Sup.Ct. 2009).

Reviewing . . . Nature and Classification

Mitsui Bank hired Ross Duncan as a branch manager in one of its Southern California locations. At that time, Duncan received an employee handbook informing him that Mitsui would review his performance and salary level annually. In 2015, Mitsui decided to create a new lending program to help financially troubled businesses stay afloat. It hired Duncan as the credit development officer (CDO) and gave him a written compensation plan. Duncan's compensation was to be based on the new program's success and involved a bonus and commissions based on new loans and sales volume. The written plan also stated, "This compensation plan will be reviewed and potentially amended after one year and will be subject to such review and amendment annually thereafter."

Duncan's efforts as CDO were successful, and the business-lending program he developed grew to represent 25 percent of Mitsui's business in 2016 and 40 percent by 2017. Nevertheless, Mitsui refused to give Duncan a raise in 2016. Mitsui also amended Duncan's compensation plan to significantly reduce his compensation and to change his performance evaluation schedule to every six months. When he had still not received a raise by 2017, Duncan resigned as CDO and filed a lawsuit claiming breach of contract. Using the information presented in the chapter, answer the following questions.

1. What are the four requirements of a valid contract?

2. Did Duncan have a valid contract with Mitsui for employment as credit development officer? If so, was it a bilateral or a unilateral contract?

3. What are the requirements of an implied contract?

4. Can Duncan establish an implied contract based on the employment manual or the written compensation plan? Why or why not?

DEBATE THIS

■ Companies should be able to make or break employment contracts whenever and however they wish.

Key Terms

bilateral contract 247

contract 245

executed contract 251

executory contract 251

express contract 249

extrinsic evidence 255

formal contract 249

implied contract 249

informal contract 249

objective theory of contracts 245

offeree 247

offeror 247

promise 244

promisee 244

promisor 244

quantum meruit 253

quasi contract 252

unenforceable contract 252

unilateral contract 248

valid contract 251

void contract 252

voidable contract 251

Chapter Summary: Nature and Classification

An Overview of Contract Law	1. *Sources of contract law*—The common law governs all contracts except when it has been modified or replaced by statutory law, such as the Uniform Commercial Code (UCC), or by administrative agency regulations. The UCC governs contracts for the sale or lease of goods.
	2. *The function of contracts*—Contract law establishes what kinds of promises will be legally binding and supplies procedures for enforcing legally binding promises, or agreements.
	3. *Definition of a contract*—A contract is an agreement that can be enforced in court. It is formed by two or more competent parties who agree to perform or to refrain from performing some act now or in the future.
	4. *Objective theory of contracts*—In contract law, intent is determined by objective facts, not by the personal or subjective intent, or belief, of a party.
Elements of a Contract	1. *Requirements of a valid contract*—The four requirements of a valid contract are agreement, consideration, contractual capacity, and legality.
	2. *Defenses to the enforceability of a contract*—Even if the four requirements of a valid contract are met, a contract may be unenforceable if it lacks voluntary consent or is not in the required form.
Types of Contracts	1. *Bilateral*—A promise for a promise.
	2. *Unilateral*—A promise for an act (acceptance is the completed or substantial performance of the contract by the offeree).
	3. *Formal*—Requires a special form for contract formation.
	4. *Informal*—Requires no special form for contract formation.
	5. *Express*—Formed by words (oral, written, or a combination).
	6. *Implied*—Formed at least in part by the conduct of the parties.
	7. *Executed*—A fully performed contract.
	8. *Executory*—A contract not yet fully performed.
	9. *Valid*—A contract that has the four necessary contractual elements of agreement, consideration, capacity, and legality.
	10. *Voidable*—A contract in which a party has the option of avoiding or enforcing the contractual obligation.
	11. *Unenforceable*—A valid contract that cannot be enforced because of a legal defense.
	12. *Void*—No contract exists, or there is a contract without legal obligations.
Quasi Contracts	A quasi contract, or a contract implied in law, is a contract that is imposed by law to prevent unjust enrichment.
Interpretation of Contracts	Increasingly, plain language laws require contracts to be written in plain language so that the terms are clear and understandable to the parties. Under the plain meaning rule, a court will enforce the contract according to its plain terms, the meaning of which must be determined from the written document alone. Other rules applied by the courts when interpreting contracts are set out in Exhibit 10–3.

Issue Spotters

1. Kerin sends a letter to Joli telling her that he has a book to sell at a certain price. Joli signs and returns the letter. When Kerin delivers the book, Joli sends it back, claiming that they do not have a contract. Kerin claims they do. What standard determines whether these parties have a contract? (See *An Overview of Contract Law*.)

2. Dyna tells Ed that she will pay him $1,000 to set fire to her store so that she can collect under a fire insurance policy. Ed sets fire to the store, but Dyna refuses to pay. Can Ed recover? Why or why not? (See *Types of Contracts*.)

—**Check your answers to the *Issue Spotters* against the answers provided in Appendix D at the end of this text.**

Learning Objectives Check

1. What is a contract? What is the objective theory of contracts?

2. What are the four basic elements necessary to the formation of a valid contract?

3. What is the difference between express and implied contracts?

4. How does a void contract differ from a voidable contract? What is an unenforceable contract?

5. What rules guide the courts in interpreting contracts?

—**Answers to the even-numbered *Learning Objectives Check* questions can be found in Appendix E at the end of this text.**

Business Scenarios and Case Problems

10–1. Unilateral Contract. Rocky Mountain Races, Inc., sponsors the "Pioneer Trail Ultramarathon," with an advertised first prize of $10,000. The rules require the competitors to run 100 miles from the floor of Blackwater Canyon to the top of Pinnacle Mountain. The rules also provide that Rocky reserves the right to change the terms of the race at any time. Monica enters the race and is declared the winner. Rocky offers her a prize of $1,000 instead of $10,000. Did Rocky and Monica have a contract? Explain. (See *Types of Contracts.*)

10–2. Implied Contract. Janine was hospitalized with severe abdominal pain and placed in an intensive care unit. Her doctor told hospital personnel to order around-the-clock nursing care for Janine. At the hospital's request, a nursing services firm, Nursing Services Unlimited, provided two weeks of in-hospital care and, after Janine was sent home, two additional weeks of at-home care. During the at-home period of care, Janine was fully aware that she was receiving the benefit of the nursing services. Nursing Services later billed Janine $4,000 for the nursing care, but Janine refused to pay on the ground that she had never contracted for the services, either orally or in writing. In view of the fact that no express contract was ever formed, can Nursing Services recover the $4,000 from Janine? If so, under what legal theory? Discuss. (See *Types of Contracts.*)

10–3. Contract Classification. For employment with the Firestorm Smokejumpers—a crew of elite paratroopers who parachute into dangerous situations to fight fires—applicants must complete a series of tests. The crew chief sends the most qualified applicants a letter stating that they will be admitted to Firestorm's training sessions if they pass a medical exam. Jake Kurzyniec receives the letter and passes the exam, but a new crew chief changes the selection process and rejects him. Is there a contract between Kurzyniec and Firestorm? If there is a contract, what type of contract is it? (See *Types of Contracts.*)

10–4. Spotlight on Taco Bell—Implied Contract. Thomas Rinks and Joseph Shields developed Psycho Chihuahua, a caricature of a Chihuahua dog with a "do-not-back-down" attitude. They promoted and marketed the character through their company, Wrench, LLC. Ed Alfaro and Rudy Pollak, representatives of Taco Bell Corp., learned of Psycho Chihuahua and met with Rinks and Shields to talk about using the character as a Taco Bell "icon." Wrench sent artwork, merchandise, and marketing ideas to Alfaro, who promoted the character within Taco Bell. Alfaro asked Wrench to propose terms for Taco Bell's use of Psycho Chihuahua. Taco Bell did not accept Wrench's terms, but Alfaro continued to promote the character within the company.

Meanwhile, Taco Bell hired a new advertising agency, which proposed an advertising campaign involving a Chihuahua. When Alfaro learned of this proposal, he sent the Psycho Chihuahua materials to the agency. Taco Bell made a Chihuahua the focus of its marketing but paid nothing to Wrench. Wrench filed a suit against Taco Bell in a federal court claiming that it had an implied contract with Taco Bell and that Taco Bell breached that contract. Do these facts satisfy the requirements for an implied contract? Why or why not? [*Wrench, LLC. v. Taco Bell Corp.,* 256 F.3d 446 (6th Cir. 2001), *cert. denied,* 534 U.S. 1114, 122 S.Ct. 921, 151 L.Ed.2d 805 (2002)] (See *Types of Contracts.*)

10–5. Quasi Contract. Kim Panenka asked to borrow $4,750 from her sister, Kris, to make a mortgage payment. Kris deposited a check for that amount into Kim's bank account. Hours later, Kim asked to borrow another $1,100. Kris took a cash advance on her credit card and deposited this amount into Kim's account. When Kim did not repay Kris, the sister filed a suit, arguing that she had "loaned" Kim the money. Can the court impose a contract between the sisters? Explain. [*Panenka v. Panenka,* 331 Wis.2d 731, 795 N.W.2d 493 (2011)] (See *Quasi Contracts.*)

10–6. Business Case Problem with Sample Answer—Quasi Contract. Robert Gutkowski, a sports marketing expert, met with George Steinbrenner, the owner of the New York Yankees, many times to discuss the Yankees Entertainment and Sports Network (YES). Gutkowski was paid as a consultant. Later, he filed a suit, seeking an ownership share in YES. There was no written contract for the share, but he claimed that there were discussions about him being a part owner. Does Gutkowski have a valid claim for payment? Discuss. [*Gutkowski v. Steinbrenner,* 680 F.Supp.2d 602 (S.D.N.Y. 2010)] (See *Quasi Contracts.*)

—For a sample answer to Problem 10–6, go to Appendix F at the end of this text.

10–7. Implied Contracts. Ralph Ramsey insured his car with Allstate Insurance Co. He also owned a house on which he maintained a homeowner's insurance policy with Allstate. Bank of America had a mortgage on the house and paid the insurance premiums on the homeowner's policy from Ralph's account. After Ralph died, Allstate canceled the car insurance. Ralph's son Douglas inherited the house. The bank continued to pay the premiums on the homeowner's policy, but from Douglas's account, and Allstate continued to renew the insurance. When a fire destroyed the house, Allstate denied coverage, however, claiming that the policy was still in Ralph's name. Douglas filed a suit in a federal district court against the insurer. Was Allstate liable under the homeowner's policy? Explain. [*Ramsey* *v. Allstate Insurance Co.,* 2013 WL 467327 (6th Cir. 2013)] (See *Types of Contracts.*)

10–8. Quasi Contracts. Lawrence M. Clarke, Inc., was the general contractor for construction of a portion of a sanitary sewer system in Billings, Michigan. Clarke accepted Kim Draeger's proposal to do the work for a certain price. Draeger arranged with two subcontractors to work on the project. The work provided by Draeger and the subcontractors proved unsatisfactory. All of the work fell under Draeger's contract with Clarke. Clarke filed a suit in a Michigan state court against Draeger, seeking to recover damages on a theory of quasi contract. The court awarded Clarke $900,000 in damages on that theory. A state intermediate appellate court reversed this award. Why? [*Lawrence M. Clarke, Inc. v. Draeger,* __ N.W.2d __, 2015 WL 205182 (Mich.App. 2015)] (See *Quasi Contracts.*)

10–9. A Question of Ethics—Unilateral Contracts. Interna-

tional Business Machines Corp. (IBM) hired Niels Jensen as a software sales representative. According to the brochure on IBM's "Sales Incentive Plan" (SIP), "the more you sell, the more earnings for you." The brochure also stated that "the SIP program does not constitute a promise by IBM. IBM reserves the right to modify the program at any time." Jensen was given a "quota letter" that said he would be paid $75,000 as a base salary and, if he attained his quota, an additional $75,000 as incentive pay. Jensen closed a deal worth more than $24 million to IBM. When IBM paid him less than $500,000 as a commission, Jensen filed a suit. He argued that the SIP was a unilateral offer that became a binding contract when he closed the sale. [*Jensen v. International Business Machines Corp.,* 454 F.3d 382 (4th Cir. 2006)] (See *Types of Contracts.*)

1. Would it be fair to the employer for the court to hold that the SIP brochure and the quota letter created a unilateral contract if IBM did not *intend* to create such a contract? Would it be fair to the employee to hold that *no* contract was created? Explain.

2. The "Sales Incentives" section of IBM's brochure included a clause providing that "management will decide if an adjustment to the payment is appropriate" when an employee closes a large transaction. Does this affect your answers to the above questions? From an ethical perspective, would it be fair to hold that a contract exists despite this statement? Explain.

Critical Thinking and Writing Assignments

10–10. Business Law Critical Thinking Group Assignment. Review the basic requirements for a valid contract listed at the beginning of this chapter. Now consider the relationship entered into when a student enrolls in a college or university. (See *Elements of A Contract.*)

1. One group should analyze and discuss whether a contract has been formed between the student and the college or university.

2. A second group should assume that there is a contract and explain whether it is bilateral or unilateral.

iStockPhoto.com/Dean Mitchell

CHAPTER OUTLINE

- Agreement
- E-Contracts
- The Uniform Electronic Transactions Act

Agreement

"It is necessity that makes laws."

VOLTAIRE
1694–1778
(FRENCH INTELLECTUAL AND WRITER)

Voltaire's statement that it is "necessity that makes laws" is certainly true in regard to contracts. In the last chapter, we pointed out that promises and agreements, and the knowledge that some of those promises and agreements will be legally enforced, are essential to civilized society. The homes we live in, the food we eat, the clothes we wear, and the cars we drive—all of these have been purchased through implicit or explicit contractual agreements. The common law of contracts has developed over time to meet society's need to know with certainty what kinds of promises will be enforced and at what point a valid and binding contract is formed.

For a contract to be valid and enforceable, the requirements listed in the previous chapter must be met. In this chapter, we look closely at the first of these requirements, *agreement*. Agreement is required to form a contract, regardless of whether the contract is formed by exchanging paper documents or by exchanging electronic messages online. We discuss online offers and acceptances and examine some laws that have been created to apply to electronic contracts, or *e-contracts,* in the latter part of the chapter. Can a person's e-mails or instant messages create an enforceable agreement? You will read more on this topic in a feature in this chapter.

11-1 Agreement

An essential element for contract formation is **agreement**—the parties must agree on the terms of the contract. Ordinarily, agreement is evidenced by two events: an *offer* and an *acceptance*. One party offers a certain bargain to another party, who then accepts that bargain.

LEARNING OBJECTIVES

The five Learning Objectives *below are designed to help improve your understanding of the chapter. After reading this chapter, you should be able to answer the following questions:*

1. What elements are necessary for an effective offer? What are some examples of nonoffers?

2. In what circumstances will an offer be irrevocable?

3. What are the elements that are necessary for an effective acceptance?

4. How do shrink-wrap and click-on agreements differ from other contracts? How have traditional laws been applied to these agreements?

5. What is the Uniform Electronic Transactions Act? What are some of the major provisions of this act?

Agreement A mutual understanding or meeting of the minds between two or more individuals regarding the terms of a contract.

Because words often fail to convey the precise meaning intended in such bargaining, the law of contracts generally adheres to the *objective theory of contracts,* as discussed in the preceding chapter. Under this theory, a party's words and conduct are held to mean whatever a reasonable person in the other party's position would think they meant.

11–1a Requirements of the Offer

Offer A promise or commitment to perform or refrain from performing some specified act in the future.

An **offer** is a promise or commitment to perform or refrain from performing some specified act in the future. The party making an offer is called the *offeror,* and the party to whom the offer is made is called the *offeree.*

Three elements are necessary for an offer to be effective:

1. There must be a serious, objective intention by the offeror.

2. The terms of the offer must be reasonably certain, or definite, so that the parties and the court can ascertain the terms of the contract.

3. The offer must be communicated to the offeree.

Once an effective offer has been made, the offeree's acceptance of that offer creates a legally binding contract (providing the other essential elements for a valid and enforceable contract are present).

LEARNING OBJECTIVE 1

What elements are necessary for an effective offer? What are some examples of nonoffers?

Intention The first requirement for an effective offer is serious, objective intent on the part of the offeror. Intent is not determined by the *subjective* intentions, beliefs, or assumptions of the offeror. Rather, it is determined by what a reasonable person in the offeree's position would conclude that the offeror's words and actions meant. Offers made in obvious anger, jest, or undue excitement do not meet the requirement of serious, objective intent. Because these offers are not effective, an offeree's acceptance does not create an agreement.

EXAMPLE 11.1 You ride to school each day with Spencer in his new automobile, which has a market value of $25,000. One cold morning, the car will not start. Spencer yells in anger, "I'll sell this car to anyone for $500!" You drop $500 in his lap. A reasonable person—taking into consideration Spencer's frustration and the obvious difference in value between the car's market price and the purchase price—would realize that Spencer's offer was not made with serious and objective intent. Therefore, no agreement is formed. ∎

The concept of intent can be further clarified through an examination of the types of statements that are *not* offers. We look at these expressions and statements in the subsections that follow. In the *Classic Case* presented next, the court considered whether an offer made "after a few drinks" met the serious-intent requirement.

★★★ CLASSIC CASE 11.1 ★★★

Lucy v. Zehmer

Supreme Court of Appeals of Virginia, 196 Va. 493, 84 S.E.2d 516 (1954).

FACTS W. O. Lucy and A. H. Zehmer had known each other for fifteen to twenty years. For some time, Lucy had wanted to buy Zehmer's farm, but Zehmer had always said that he was not interested in selling. One night, Lucy stopped in to visit with the Zehmers at a restaurant they operated. Lucy said to Zehmer, "I bet you wouldn't take $50,000 for that place." Zehmer replied, "Yes, I would, too; you wouldn't give fifty." Throughout the evening, the conversation

Can an intoxicated person's offer to sell his farm for a specific price meet the serious-intent requirement?

returned to the sale of the farm. All the while, the parties were drinking whiskey.

Eventually, Zehmer wrote up an agreement on the back of a restaurant check for the sale of the farm, and he asked his wife, Ida, to sign it—which she did. When Lucy brought an action in a Virginia state court to enforce the agreement, Zehmer argued that he had been "high as a Georgia pine" at the time and that the offer had been made in jest: "two doggoned drunks bluffing to see who could talk the biggest and say the most." Lucy claimed that he had not been intoxicated and did not think Zehmer had been, either, given the way Zehmer handled the transaction. The trial court ruled in favor of the Zehmers, and Lucy appealed.

ISSUE Did the agreement meet the serious-intent requirement despite the claim of intoxication?

DECISION Yes. The agreement to sell the farm was binding.

REASON The court held that the evidence given about the nature of the conversation, the appearance and completeness of the agreement, and the signing all tended to show that a serious business transaction, not a casual jest, was intended. The court had to look into the objective meaning of the Zehmers' words and acts: "An agreement or mutual assent is of course essential to a valid contract, but the law imputes to a person an intention corresponding to the reasonable meaning of his words and acts. If his words and acts, judged by a reasonable standard, manifest an intention to agree, it is immaterial what may be the real but unexpressed state of mind."

WHAT IF THE FACTS WERE DIFFERENT? *Suppose that after Lucy signed the agreement, he decided he did not want the farm after all, and that Zehmer sued Lucy to perform the contract. Would this change in the facts alter the court's decision that Lucy and Zehmer had created an enforceable contract? Why or why not?*

IMPACT OF THIS CASE ON TODAY'S LAW *This is a classic case in contract law because it so clearly illustrates the objective theory of contracts with respect to determining whether an offer was intended. Today, the courts continue to apply the objective theory of contracts and routinely cite the* Lucy v. Zehmer *decision as a significant precedent in this area.*

Expressions of Opinion. An expression of opinion is not an offer. It does not demonstrate an intention to enter into a binding agreement. **CASE EXAMPLE 11.2** Hawkins took his son to McGee, a physician, and asked McGee to operate on the son's hand. McGee said that the boy would be in the hospital three or four days and that the hand would *probably* heal a few days later. The son's hand did not heal for a month, but nonetheless the father did not win a suit for breach of contract. The court held that McGee did not make an offer to heal the son's hand in three or four days. He merely expressed an opinion as to when the hand would heal.[1] ∎

Statements of Future Intent. A statement of an *intention* to do something in the future is not an offer. **EXAMPLE 11.3** If Samir says, "I *plan* to sell my stock in Novation, Inc., for $150 per share," no contract is created if John "accepts" and gives Samir $150 per share for the stock. Samir has merely expressed his intention to enter into a future contract for the sale of the stock. If John accepts and hands over the $150 per share, no contract is formed, because a reasonable person would conclude that Samir was only *thinking about* selling his stock, not *promising* to sell it. ∎

Preliminary Negotiations. A request or invitation to negotiate is not an offer. It only expresses a willingness to discuss the possibility of entering into a contract. Examples are statements such as "Will you sell Forest Acres?" and "I wouldn't sell my car for less than $8,000." A reasonable person would not conclude that such statements indicated an intention to enter into binding obligations.

A similar situation arises when the government or a private firm invites contractors to submit bids to do construction work. The *invitation* to submit bids is not an offer, and a contractor does not bind the government or private firm by submitting a bid. (The bids that the contractors submit are offers, however, and the government or private firm can bind the contractor by accepting the bid.)

Advertisements, Catalogues, and Circulars. In general, advertisements, catalogues, price lists, and circular letters (meant for the general public) are treated as invitations to negotiate, not as offers to form a contract.[2] This applies whether the publications appear in traditional media or online.

KNOW THIS
An opinion is not an offer and not a contract term. Goods or services can be "perfect" in one party's opinion and "poor" in another's.

---

1. *Hawkins v. McGee*, 84 N.H. 114, 146 A. 641 (1929).
2. *Restatement (Second) of Contracts*, Section 26, Comment b.

When a contractor submits a bid proposal, is that proposal binding on the entity to whom the bid was addressed?

KNOW THIS
Advertisements are not binding, but they cannot be deceptive.

CASE EXAMPLE 11.4 An ad on *Science*NOW's Web site asked for "news tips." Erik Trell, a professor and physician, submitted a manuscript in which he claimed to have solved a famous mathematical problem. When *Science*NOW did not publish his solution, Trell filed a lawsuit for breach of contract. He claimed that *Science*NOW's ad was an offer, which he had accepted by submitting his manuscript. The court dismissed Trell's suit, holding that an ad is only an invitation for offers, and not an offer itself. Hence, responses to an ad are not acceptances—instead, the responses are the offers. Thus, Trell's submission of the manuscript for publication was the offer, which *Science*NOW did not accept.[3] ■

Price lists are another form of invitation to negotiate or trade. A seller's price list is not an offer to sell at that price. It merely invites the buyer to offer to buy at that price. In fact, the seller usually puts "prices subject to change" on the price list. Only in rare circumstances will a price quotation be construed as an offer.

Although most advertisements and the like are treated as invitations to negotiate, an advertisement can occasionally be an offer. In some situations, courts have construed advertisements to be offers because the ads contained definite terms that invited acceptance (such as an ad offering a reward for the return of a lost dog).

Agreements to Agree. In the past, agreements to agree—that is, agreements to agree to the material terms of a contract at some future date—were not considered to be binding contracts. The modern view, however, is that agreements to agree may be enforceable agreements (contracts) if it is clear that the parties intended to be bound by the agreements. In other words, today the emphasis is on the parties' intent rather than on form.

CASE EXAMPLE 11.5 After a customer nearly drowned on a water ride at one of its amusement parks, Six Flags, Inc., filed a lawsuit against the manufacturer that had designed the ride. The manufacturer claimed that the parties did not have a binding contract but had only engaged in preliminary negotiations that were never formalized into a contract to construct the ride.

The court, however, held that a faxed document specifying the details of the ride, along with the parties' subsequent actions (having begun construction and written notes on the faxed document), was sufficient to show an intent to be bound. Because of the court's finding, the manufacturer was required to provide insurance for the water ride at Six Flags, and its insurer was required to defend Six Flags in the personal-injury lawsuit that arose out of the incident.[4] ■

Preliminary Agreements. Increasingly, the courts are holding that a preliminary agreement constitutes a binding contract if the parties have agreed on all essential terms and no disputed issues remain to be resolved.[5] In contrast, if the parties agree on certain major terms but leave other terms open for further negotiation, a preliminary agreement is binding only in the sense that the parties have committed themselves to negotiate the undecided terms in good faith in an effort to reach a final agreement.

In the following *Spotlight Case,* one party claimed that an agreement formed via e-mail was binding, while the other party claimed that it was merely an agreement to agree or to work out the terms of a settlement in the future.

---

3. *Trell v. American Association for the Advancement of Science*, 2007 WL 1500497 (W.D.N.Y. 2007).

4. *Six Flags, Inc. v. Steadfast Insurance Co.*, 474 F.Supp.2d 201 (D.Mass. 2007).

5. See, for example, *Tractebel Energy Marketing, Inc. v. AEP Power Marketing, Inc.*, 487 F.3d 89 (2d Cir. 2007); and *Barrand v. Whataburger, Inc.*, 214 S.W.3d 122 (Tex.App.—Corpus Christi 2006).

SPOTLIGHT ON AMAZON.COM: CASE 11.2

Basis Technology Corp. v. Amazon.com, Inc.

Appeals Court of Massachusetts, 71 Mass.App.Ct. 29, 878 N.E.2d 952 (2008).

FACTS Basis Technology Corporation created software and provided technical services for a Japanese-language Web site operated by Amazon.com, Inc. The agreement between the two companies allowed for separately negotiated contracts for additional services that Basis might provide to Amazon. Later, Basis sued Amazon for various claims, including failure to pay for services not included in the original agreement. During the trial, the two parties appeared to reach an agreement to settle out of court via a series of e-mail exchanges outlining the settlement. When Amazon reneged, Basis served a motion to enforce the proposed settlement. The trial judge entered a judgment against Amazon, which appealed.

ISSUE Did the agreement that Amazon entered into with Basis via e-mail constitute a binding settlement contract?

DECISION Yes. The Appeals Court of Massachusetts affirmed the trial court's finding that Amazon intended to be bound by the terms of the e-mail exchanges.

Can Amazon.com, Inc., be held to an agreement arrived at via e-mail exchanges?

360b/ShutterStock.com

REASON The court examined the evidence consisting of e-mails between the two parties. It pointed out that in open court and on the record, counsel had "reported the result of the settlement without specification of the terms." Amazon claimed that the e-mail terms were incomplete and were not definite enough to form an agreement. The court noted, however, that "provisions are not ambiguous simply because the parties have developed different interpretations of them." In the exchange of e-mails, the essential business terms were indeed resolved. Afterward, the parties were simply proceeding to record the settlement terms, not to create them. The e-mails constituted a complete and unambiguous statement of the parties' desire to be bound by the settlement terms.

WHAT IF THE FACTS WERE DIFFERENT? *Assume that, instead of exchanging e-mails, the attorneys for both sides had had a phone conversation that included all of the terms to which they actually agreed in their e-mail exchanges. Would the court have ruled differently? Why or why not?*

To avoid potential legal disputes, be cautious when drafting a memorandum that outlines a preliminary agreement or understanding with another party. If all the major terms are included, a court might hold that the agreement is binding even though you intended it to be only a tentative agreement. One way to avoid being bound is to include in the writing the points of disagreement, as well as the points on which you and the other party agree. Alternatively, you can add a disclaimer to the memorandum stating that, although you anticipate entering a contract in the future, neither party intends to be legally bound to the terms included in the memorandum. That way, the other party cannot claim that you have already reached an agreement on all essential terms.

PREVENTING LEGAL DISPUTES

Definiteness The second requirement for an effective offer involves the definiteness of its terms. An offer must have reasonably definite terms so that a court can determine if a breach has occurred and give an appropriate remedy.[6] The specific terms required depend, of course, on the type of contract. Generally, a contract must include the following terms, either expressed in the contract or capable of being reasonably inferred from it:

1. The identification of the parties.

2. The identification of the object or subject matter of the contract (also the quantity, when appropriate), including the work to be performed, with specific identification of such items as goods, services, and land.

---

6. *Restatement (Second) of Contracts*, Section 33. The UCC has relaxed the requirements regarding the definiteness of terms in contracts for the sale of goods. See UCC 2–204(3).

3. The consideration to be paid.

4. The time of payment, delivery, or performance.

An offer may invite an acceptance to be worded in such specific terms that the contract is made definite. **EXAMPLE 11.6** Nintendo of America, Inc., contacts your Play 2 Win Games store and offers to sell "from one to twenty-five Nintendo 3DS gaming systems for $75 each. State number desired in acceptance." You agree to buy twenty systems. Because the quantity is specified in the acceptance, the terms are definite, and the contract is enforceable. ■

Communication   A third requirement for an effective offer is communication—the offer must be communicated to the offeree. **EXAMPLE 11.7** Tolson advertises a reward for the return of her lost cat. Dirk, not knowing of the reward, finds the cat and returns it to Tolson. Ordinarily, Dirk cannot recover the reward, because an essential element of a reward contract is that the one who claims the reward must have known it was offered. A few states would allow recovery of the reward, but not on contract principles. Dirk would be allowed to recover on the basis that it would be unfair to deny him the reward just because he did not know about it. ■

11–1b Termination of the Offer

The communication of an effective offer to an offeree gives the offeree the power to transform the offer into a binding, legal obligation (a contract) by an acceptance. This power of acceptance does not continue forever, though. It can be terminated by either the *action of the parties* or by *operation of law*. Termination by the action of the parties can involve a revocation by the offeror or a rejection or counteroffer by the offeree.

Termination by Action of the Offeror   The offeror's act of withdrawing an offer is referred to as **revocation.** Unless an offer is irrevocable, the offeror usually can revoke the offer (even if he or she has promised to keep it open), as long as the revocation is communicated to the offeree before the offeree accepts.

Revocation may be accomplished by an express repudiation of the offer (such as "I withdraw my previous offer of October 17") or by the performance of acts that are inconsistent with the existence of the offer and that are made known to the offeree. **EXAMPLE 11.8** Misha offers to sell some land to Gary. A month passes, and Gary, who has not accepted the offer, learns that Misha has sold the property to Liam. Because Misha's sale of the land to Liam is inconsistent with the continued existence of the offer to Gary, the offer to Gary is effectively revoked. ■

The general rule followed by most states is that a revocation becomes effective when the offeree or the offeree's *agent* (a person acting on behalf of the offeree) actually receives it. Therefore, a statement of revocation sent via FedEx on April 1 and delivered at the offeree's residence or place of business on April 2 becomes effective on April 2.

Termination by Action of the Offeree   If the offeree rejects the offer, either by words or by conduct, the offer is terminated. Any subsequent attempt by the offeree to accept will be construed as a new offer, giving the original offeror (now the offeree) the power of acceptance.

Like a revocation, a rejection is effective only when it is actually received by the offeror or the offeror's agent. **EXAMPLE 11.9** Goldfinch Farms offers to sell specialty Maitake mushrooms to a Japanese buyer, Kinoko Foods. If Kinoko rejects the offer by sending a letter via U.S. mail, the rejection will not be effective (and the offer will not be terminated) until Goldfinch receives the letter. ■

Inquiries about an Offer.   Merely inquiring about an offer does not constitute rejection. **EXAMPLE 11.10** Your friend offers to buy your Inkling digital pen for $100. You respond, "Is that your best offer?" A reasonable person would conclude that you have not rejected the offer but have merely made an inquiry. You could still accept and bind your friend to the $100 price. ■

Counteroffers. A **counteroffer** is a rejection of the original offer and the simultaneous making of a new offer. **EXAMPLE 11.11** Burke offers to sell his home to Lang for $270,000. Lang responds, "Your price is too high. I'll offer to purchase your house for $250,000." Lang's response is a counteroffer because it rejects Burke's offer to sell at $270,000 and creates a new offer by Lang to purchase the home at a price of $250,000. ■

At common law, the **mirror image rule** requires that the offeree's acceptance match the offeror's offer exactly. In other words, the terms of the acceptance must "mirror" those of the offer. If the acceptance materially changes or adds to the terms of the original offer, it will be considered not an acceptance but a counteroffer—which, of course, need not be accepted. The original offeror can, however, accept the terms of the counteroffer and create a valid contract.[7]

Termination by Operation of Law The power of the offeree to transform the offer into a binding, legal obligation can be terminated by operation of law through the occurrence of any of the following events:

1. Lapse of time.

2. Destruction of the specific subject matter of the offer.

3. Death or incompetence of the offeror or the offeree.

4. Supervening illegality of the proposed contract.

Lapse of Time. An offer terminates automatically by law when the period of time *specified in the offer* has passed. If the offer states that it will be left open until a particular date, then the offer will terminate at midnight on that day. If the offer states that it will be left open for a number of days, this time period normally begins to run when the offer is actually *received* by the offeree, not when it is formed or sent.

If the offer does not specify a time for acceptance, the offer terminates at the end of a *reasonable* period of time. A reasonable period of time is determined by the subject matter of the contract, business and market conditions, and other relevant circumstances. An offer to sell farm produce, for instance, will terminate sooner than an offer to sell farm equipment because produce is perishable and subject to greater fluctuations in market value.

Destruction, Death, or Illegality. An offer is automatically terminated if the specific subject matter of the offer (such as a smartphone or a house) is destroyed before the offer is accepted. An offeree's power of acceptance is also terminated when the offeror or offeree dies or becomes legally incapacitated, *unless the offer is irrevocable*. Finally, a statute or court decision that makes an offer illegal automatically terminates the offer.

Irrevocable Offers Although most offers are revocable, some can be made irrevocable. Increasingly, courts refuse to allow an offeror to revoke an offer when the offeree has changed position because of justifiable reliance on the offer (under the doctrine of *promissory estoppel*). In some circumstances, "firm offers" made by merchants may also be considered irrevocable.

Another form of irrevocable offer is an option contract. An **option contract** is created when an offeror promises to hold an offer open for a specified period of time in return for a payment (consideration) given by the offeree. An option contract takes away the offeror's power to revoke an offer for the period of time specified in the option. If no time is specified, then a reasonable period of time is implied.

Option contracts are frequently used in conjunction with the sale of real estate. **EXAMPLE 11.12** Tyrell agrees to lease a house from Jackson, the property owner. The lease contract includes a clause stating that Tyrell is paying an additional $15,000 for an option to purchase the property within a specified period of time. If Tyrell decides not to purchase the house after

---

Counteroffer An offeree's response to an offer in which the offeree rejects the original offer and at the same time makes a new offer.

Mirror Image Rule A common law rule that requires that the terms of the offeree's acceptance adhere exactly to the terms of the offeror's offer for a valid contract to be formed.

KNOW THIS
When an offer is rejected, it is terminated.

LEARNING OBJECTIVE 2
In what circumstances will an offer be irrevocable?

Option Contract A contract under which the offeror cannot revoke the offer for a stipulated time period (because the offeree has given consideration for the offer to remain open).

---

7. The mirror image rule has been greatly modified in regard to sales contracts. Section 2–207 of the UCC provides that a contract is formed if the offeree makes a definite expression of acceptance (such as signing the form in the appropriate location), even though the terms of the acceptance modify or add to the terms of the original offer.

LEARNING OBJECTIVE 3

What are the elements that are necessary for an effective acceptance?

Acceptance The act of voluntarily agreeing, through words or conduct, to the terms of an offer, thereby creating a contract.

the specified period has lapsed, he loses the $15,000, and Jackson is free to sell the property to another buyer. ■

11–1c Acceptance

An **acceptance** is a voluntary act by the offeree that shows assent, or agreement, to the terms of an offer. The offeree's act may consist of words or conduct. The acceptance must be unequivocal and must be communicated to the offeror. Generally, only the person to whom the offer is made or that person's agent can accept the offer and create a binding contract. (See this chapter's *Adapting the Law to the Online Environment* feature for a discussion of how parties can sometimes inadvertently accept a contract via e-mail or instant messages.)

ADAPTING THE LAW TO THE **ONLINE** ENVIRONMENT
Can Your E-Mails or Instant Messages Create a Valid Contract?

Instant messaging and e-mailing are among the most common forms of informal communication. Not surprisingly, parties considering an agreement often exchange offers and counteroffers via e-mail (and, to a lesser extent, instant messaging). The parties may believe that these informal electronic exchanges are for negotiation purposes only. But such communications can lead to the formation of valid contracts.

E-mails and Settlements
After automobile accidents, the parties' attorneys sometimes exchange e-mails as part of the negotiation process. Consider the case of John Forcelli, who claimed that he had been injured in an accident by a vehicle owned by Gelco Corporation. Forcelli commenced litigation. While the litigation was progressing, a representative of Gelco's insurer offered Forcelli's attorneys a $230,000 settlement. The attorneys orally accepted the offer on behalf of Forcelli. The insurance company's representative sent an e-mail message confirming the terms of the settlement, and Forcelli signed a notarized release.

A few days later, however, a New York trial court issued an order granting a motion for summary judgment in favor of Gelco and dismissing Forcelli's claims. Gelco then tried to reject the settlement, claiming that the e-mail message did not constitute a binding written settlement agreement. A New York trial court ruled against Gelco, and an appeal followed.

The reviewing court upheld the trial court's finding. The e-mail contained all the necessary elements of contractual agreement.[a]

"Accidental" Contracts via E-mail
When a series of e-mails signal intent to be bound, a contract may be formed, even though some language in the e-mails may be careless or accidental. Even if a party later claims to have had unstated objections to the terms, the e-mails will prevail. What matters is whether a court determines that it is reasonable for the receiving party to believe that there is an agreement.

Indeed, e-mail contracting has become so common that only unusually strange circumstances will cause a court to reject such contracts.[b] Furthermore, under the Uniform Electronic Transactions Act, a contract "may not be denied legal effect solely because an electronic record was used in its formation." Most states have adopted this act, at least in part, as you will read later in this chapter.

Instant Messaging Can Create Valid Contract Modifications
Like e-mail exchanges, instant messaging conversations between individuals in the process of negotiations can result in the formation (or modification) of a contract. One case involved

an online marketing service, CX Digital Media, Inc., which provides clients with advertising referrals from its network of affiliates.

CX Digital charges a fee for its services based on number of referrals. One of its clients was Smoking Everywhere, Inc., a seller of electronic cigarettes. While the two companies were negotiating a change in contract terms via instant messaging, the issue of the maximum number of referrals per day came up. A CX Digital employee sent an instant message to a Smoking Everywhere executive asking about the maximum number. The executive responded, "NO LIMIT," and CX Digital's employee replied, "awesome!"

After that, CX Digital referred a higher volume of sales leads than previously. Smoking Everywhere refused to pay for these additional referrals, claiming that the instant messaging chat did not constitute an enforceable modification of the initial contract. At trial, CX Digital prevailed. Smoking Everywhere had to pay more than $1 million for the additional sales leads.[c]

CRITICAL THINKING

■ How can a company structure e-mail negotiations to avoid "accidentally" forming a contract?

---

a. *Forcelli v. Gelco Corporation,* 109 A.D.3d 244, 972 N.Y.S.2d 570 (2013).

b. See, for example, *Beastie Boys v. Monster Energy Co.,* 983 F.Supp.2d 338 (S.D.N.Y. 2013).

c. *CX Digital Media, Inc. v. Smoking Everywhere, Inc.,* 2011 WL 1102782 (S.D.Fla. 2011).

Unequivocal Acceptance To exercise the power of acceptance effectively, the offeree must accept unequivocally. This is the mirror image rule previously discussed. If the acceptance is subject to new conditions or if the terms of the acceptance materially change the original offer, the acceptance may be deemed a counteroffer that implicitly rejects the original offer.[8]

Certain terms included in an acceptance will not change the offer sufficiently to constitute rejection. **EXAMPLE 11.13** In response to an art dealer's offer to sell a painting, the offeree, Ashton Gibbs, replies, "I accept. Please send a written contract." Gibbs is requesting a written contract but is not making it a condition for acceptance. Therefore, the acceptance is effective without the written contract. In contrast, if Gibbs replies, "I accept *if* you send a written contract," the acceptance is expressly conditioned on the request for a writing, and the statement is not an acceptance but a counteroffer. (Notice how important each word is!) ■

Whether an offeree's conduct was sufficient to show acceptance of the terms of an offer was the issue at the center of the following case.

An art dealer offers to sell the painting on the front left of this photo. In response, a collector sends an e-mail in which she says "I accept your offer; please send a written contract." Is her acceptance effective?

---

8. As noted in footnote 7, in regard to sales contracts, the UCC provides that an acceptance may still be effective even if some terms are added. The new terms are simply treated as proposals for additions to the contract, unless both parties are merchants. If the parties are merchants, the additional terms (with some exceptions) become part of the contract [UCC 2–207(2)].

CASE 11.3

Brown v. Lagrange Development Corp.

Court of Appeals of Ohio, Sixth District, Lucas County, __ Ohio App.3d __, __ N.E.3d __, 2015 Ohio 133 (2015).

FACTS Lagrange Development Corp. is a non-profit corporation that acquires and rehabilitates real property in Toledo, Ohio. Sonja Brown presented Lagrange with a written offer to buy a house at 52 Rockingham Avenue for $79,900. Lagrange's executive director, Terry Glazer, penciled in modifications to the offer—an increased purchase price of $84,200 and a later date for acceptance. Glazer initialed the changes and signed the document.

Brown initialed the date change but not the price increase, and did not sign the revised document. Brown then applied for and obtained a mortgage, agreed to the closing, and received a deed. Later, Brown filed a suit in an Ohio state court against Lagrange, claiming that she had not agreed to the proposed changes. The court found the modified terms to be a counteroffer, which Brown had accepted by performance. Brown appealed.

ISSUE Was Brown's conduct sufficient to constitute acceptance of Lagrange's counteroffer?

DECISION Yes. A state intermediate appellate court affirmed the judgment of the lower court. Although Brown did not sign the counteroffer, her subsequent conduct showed that she had accepted it.

Under what circumstances are modifications to a real estate contract part of the final bargain?

REASON The appellate court acknowledged that Glazer revised Brown's offer by changing material terms—the price and the closing date. Glazer initialed the changes and signed the document. On receipt of this document, Brown initialed only the date change. This alone was not enough to show acceptance of Lagrange's counteroffer. Brown's subsequent conduct, however, indicated an intent to accept it. She faxed the document with a loan application to obtain a mortgage. Later, she agreed to close the sale on the terms set out in the revised contract and accepted a deed. The court explained that it is not necessary for all of the parties to a contract to sign it for a valid contract to exist. An offeree can accept by performance. "Generally conduct sufficient to show agreement, including performance, constitutes acceptance of an offer." Here, Lagrange's counteroffer did not restrict the manner of acceptance, and Brown accepted its terms by performance.

CRITICAL THINKING—Social Consideration *How should an offeree indicate a definite lack of consent to a counteroffer?*

Silence as Acceptance Ordinarily, silence cannot constitute acceptance, even if the offeror states, "By your silence and inaction, you will be deemed to have accepted this offer." This general rule applies because an offeree should not be put under a burden of liability to act affirmatively in order to reject an offer. No consideration—that is, nothing of value—has passed to the offeree to impose such a liability.

In some instances, however, the offeree does have a duty to speak. If so, his or her silence or inaction will operate as an acceptance. Silence may be an acceptance when an offeree takes the benefit of offered services even though he or she had an opportunity to reject them and knew that they were offered with the expectation of compensation.

EXAMPLE 11.14 Juan earns extra income by washing store windows. Juan taps on the window of a store, catches the attention of the store's manager, and points to the window and raises his cleaner, signaling that he will be washing the window. The manager does nothing to stop him. Here, the store manager's silence constitutes an acceptance, and an implied contract is created. The store is bound to pay a reasonable value for Juan's work. ■

Silence can also operate as an acceptance when the offeree has had prior dealings with the offeror. If a merchant, for instance, routinely receives shipments from a supplier and in the past has always notified the supplier when defective goods were rejected, then silence constitutes acceptance. Also, if a buyer solicits an offer specifying that certain terms and conditions are acceptable, and the seller makes the offer in response to the solicitation, the buyer has a duty to reject—that is, a duty to tell the seller that the offer is not acceptable. Failure to reject (silence) will operate as an acceptance.

Communication of Acceptance Whether the offeror must be notified of the acceptance depends on the nature of the contract. In a unilateral contract, the full performance of some act is called for. Acceptance is usually evident, and notification is therefore unnecessary (unless the law requires it or the offeror asks for it). In a bilateral contract, in contrast, communication of acceptance is necessary, because acceptance is in the form of a promise. The bilateral contract is formed when the promise is made rather than when the act is performed.

CASE EXAMPLE 11.15 Powerhouse Custom Homes, Inc., owed $95,260.42 to 84 Lumber Company under a credit agreement. When Powerhouse failed to pay, 84 Lumber filed a suit to collect. During mediation, the parties agreed to a deadline for objections to whatever agreement they might reach. If there were no objections, the agreement would be binding.

Powerhouse then offered to pay less than the amount owed, but 84 Lumber did not respond. Powerhouse argued that 84 Lumber had accepted the offer by not objecting to it within the deadline. The court ruled in 84 Lumber's favor for the entire amount of the debt. To form a contract, an offer must be accepted unequivocally. Powerhouse made an offer, but 84 Lumber did not communicate acceptance. Therefore, the parties did not reach an agreement on settlement.[9] ■

Mode and Timeliness of Acceptance Acceptance in bilateral contracts must be timely. The general rule is that acceptance in a bilateral contract is timely if it is made before the offer is terminated. Problems may arise, though, when the parties involved are not dealing face to face. In such situations, the offeree should use an authorized mode of communication.

The Mailbox Rule. Acceptance takes effect, and thus completes formation of the contract, at the time the offeree sends or delivers the acceptance via the mode of communication expressly or impliedly authorized by the offeror. This is the so-called **mailbox rule,** also called the *deposited acceptance rule,* which the majority of courts follow. Under this rule, if the authorized mode of communication is the mail, then an acceptance becomes valid when it is dispatched (placed in the control of the U.S. Postal Service)—not when it is received by the offeror. (Note,

---

KNOW THIS

A bilateral contract is a promise for a promise, and a unilateral contract is performance for a promise.

Mailbox Rule A common law rule that acceptance takes effect, and thus completes formation of the contract, at the time the offeree sends or delivers the acceptance via the communication mode expressly or impliedly authorized by the offeror.

---

9. *Powerhouse Custom Homes, Inc. v. 84 Lumber Co.,* 307 Ga.App. 605, 705 S.E.2d 704 (2011).

however, that if the offer stipulates when acceptance will be effective, then the offer will not be effective until the time specified.)

The mailbox rule does not apply to instantaneous forms of communication, such as when the parties are dealing face to face, by phone, by fax, and usually by e-mail. Under the Uniform Electronic Transactions Act (UETA—discussed later in this chapter), e-mail is considered sent when it either leaves the sender's control or is received by the recipient. This rule, which takes the place of the mailbox rule if the parties have agreed to conduct transactions electronically, allows an e-mail acceptance to become effective when sent.

Authorized Means of Communication. A means of communicating acceptance can be expressly authorized by the offeror or impliedly authorized by the facts and circumstances of the situation. An acceptance sent by means not expressly or impliedly authorized normally is not effective until it is received by the offeror.

When an offeror specifies how acceptance should be made, such as by overnight delivery, the contract is not formed unless the offeree uses that mode of acceptance. Both the offeror and the offeree are bound in contract the moment the specified means of acceptance is employed. **EXAMPLE 11.16** Motorola Mobility, Inc., offers to sell 144 Atrix 4G smartphones and 72 Lapdocks to Call Me Plus phone stores. The offer states that Call Me Plus must accept the offer via FedEx overnight delivery. The acceptance is effective (and a binding contract is formed) the moment that Call Me Plus gives the overnight envelope containing the acceptance to the FedEx driver. ■

If the offeror does not expressly authorize a certain mode of acceptance, then acceptance can be made by *any reasonable means.*[10] Courts look at the prevailing business usages and the surrounding circumstances to determine whether the mode of acceptance used was reasonable. Usually, the offeror's choice of a particular means in making the offer implies that the offeree can use the *same or a faster* means for acceptance. **EXAMPLE 11.17** If the offer is made via Priority U.S. mail, it would be reasonable to accept the offer via Priority mail or by a faster method, such as signed scanned documents sent as attachments via e-mail or overnight delivery. ■

Substitute Method of Acceptance. Sometimes, the offeror authorizes a particular method of acceptance, but the offeree accepts by a different means. In that situation, the acceptance may still be effective if the substituted method serves the same purpose as the authorized means. Acceptance by a substitute method is not effective on dispatch, though. No contract will be formed until the acceptance is received by the offeror. **EXAMPLE 11.18** Bennion's offer specifies acceptance via FedEx overnight delivery but the offeree accepts instead by overnight delivery from UPS. The substitute method of acceptance will still be effective, but not until the offeror (Bennion) receives it from UPS. ■

11-2 E-Contracts

Numerous contracts are formed online. Electronic contracts, or **e-contracts,** must meet the same basic requirements (agreement, consideration, contractual capacity, and legality) as paper contracts. Disputes concerning e-contracts, however, tend to center on contract terms and whether the parties voluntarily agreed to those terms.

E-Contract A contract that is formed electronically.

Online contracts may be formed not only for the sale of goods and services but also for *licensing*. The "sale" of software generally involves a license, or a right to use the software, rather than the passage of title (ownership rights) from the seller to the buyer. **EXAMPLE 11.19** Lauren wants to obtain software that will allow her to work on spreadsheets on her smartphone.

---

10. Note that UCC 2–206(1)(a) states specifically that an acceptance of an offer for the sale of goods can be made by any medium that is *reasonable* under the circumstances.

She goes online and purchases GridMagic. During the transaction, she has to click on several on-screen "I agree" boxes to indicate that she understands that she is purchasing only the right to use the software, not ownership rights. After she agrees to these terms (the licensing agreement), she can download the software. ■

As you read through the following subsections, keep in mind that although we typically refer to the offeror and the offeree as a *seller* and a *buyer*, in many online transactions these parties would be more accurately described as a *licensor* and a *licensee*.

11-2a Online Offers

Sellers doing business via the Internet can protect themselves against contract disputes and legal liability by creating offers that clearly spell out the terms that will govern their transactions if the offers are accepted. All important terms should be conspicuous and easy to view.

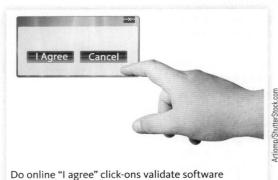

Do online "I agree" click-ons validate software licensing agreements?

Displaying the Offer   The seller's Web site should include a hypertext link to a page containing the full contract so that potential buyers are made aware of the terms to which they are assenting. The contract generally must be displayed online in a readable format such as in a twelve-point typeface. All provisions should be reasonably clear.

EXAMPLE 11.20   Netquip sells a variety of heavy equipment, such as trucks and trailers, online at its Web site. Because Netquip's pricing schedule is very complex, the schedule must be fully provided and explained on the Web site. In addition, the terms of the sale (such as any warranties and the refund policy) must be fully disclosed. ■

Provisions to Include   An important rule to keep in mind is that the offeror (seller) controls the offer and thus the resulting contract. The seller should therefore anticipate the terms she or he wants to include in a contract and provide for them in the offer. In some instances, a standardized contract form may suffice. At a minimum, an online offer should include the following provisions:

1. *Acceptance of terms.* A clause that clearly indicates what constitutes the buyer's agreement to the terms of the offer, such as a box containing the words "I accept" that the buyer can click on to indicate acceptance. (Mechanisms for accepting online offers will be discussed in detail later in this chapter.)

2. *Payment.* A provision specifying how payment for the goods (including any applicable taxes) must be made.

3. *Return policy.* A statement of the seller's refund and return policies.

4. *Disclaimer.* Disclaimers of liability for certain uses of the goods. For example, an online seller of business forms may add a disclaimer that the seller does not accept responsibility for the buyer's reliance on the forms rather than on an attorney's advice.

5. *Limitation on remedies.* A provision specifying the remedies available to the buyer if the goods are found to be defective or if the contract is otherwise breached. Any limitation of remedies should be clearly spelled out.

6. *Privacy policy.* A statement indicating how the seller will use the information gathered about the buyer. (See the *Linking Business Law to Marketing* feature at the end of this chapter for a discussion of how the information may be used.)

7. *Dispute resolution.* Provisions relating to dispute settlement, such as an arbitration clause.

Dispute-Settlement Provisions   Online offers frequently include provisions relating to dispute settlement. For instance, the offer might include an arbitration clause specifying that any dispute arising under the contract will be arbitrated in a designated forum.

"If two men agree on everything, you can be sure one of them is doing the thinking."

LYNDON BAINES JOHNSON
1908–1973
(THIRTY-SIXTH PRESIDENT OF THE UNITED STATES, 1963–1969)

Artiomp/ShutterStock.com

CASE EXAMPLE 11.21 Scott Rosendahl enrolled in an online college, Ashford University. He claimed that the school's adviser had told him that Ashford offered one of the cheapest undergraduate degree programs in the country. In fact, it did not. Rosendahl later sued the school, claiming that it had violated false advertising laws and had engaged in fraud and negligent misrepresentation. The university argued that the enrollment agreement clearly contained a requirement that all disputes be arbitrated. Rosendahl, like other students, had electronically assented to this agreement when he enrolled. Ashford presented the online application forms to the court, and the court dismissed Rosendahl's lawsuit. Rosendahl had agreed to arbitrate any disputes he had with Ashford.[11] ▪

Forum-Selection Clause. Many online contracts also contain a **forum-selection clause** indicating the forum, or location (such as a court or jurisdiction), for the resolution of any dispute arising under the contract. As discussed in the chapter on courts, significant jurisdictional issues may occur when parties are at a great distance, as they often are when they form contracts via the Internet. A forum-selection clause will help to avert future jurisdictional problems and also help to ensure that the seller will not be required to appear in court in a distant state.

CASE EXAMPLE 11.22 Before advertisers can place ads through Google, Inc., they must agree to certain terms that are displayed in an online window. These terms include a forum-selection clause, which provides that any dispute is to be "adjudicated in Santa Clara County, California." Lawrence Feldman, who advertised through Google, complained that he was overcharged and filed a lawsuit against Google in a federal district court in Pennsylvania. The court held that Feldman had agreed to the forum-selection clause in Google's online contract and transferred the case to a court in Santa Clara County.[12] ▪

Choice-of Law Clause. Some online contracts may also include a *choice-of-law clause* specifying that any dispute arising out of the contract will be settled in accordance with the law of a particular jurisdiction, such as a state or country. Choice-of-law clauses are particularly common in international contracts, but they may also appear in e-contracts to specify which state's laws will govern in the United States.

11–2b Online Acceptances

The *Restatement (Second) of Contracts*—a compilation of common law contract principles—states that parties may agree to a contract "by written or spoken words or by other action or by failure to act."[13] The Uniform Commercial Code (UCC), which governs sales contracts, has a similar provision. Section 2–204 of the UCC states that any contract for the sale of goods "may be made in any manner sufficient to show agreement, including conduct by both parties which recognizes the existence of such a contract." The courts have used these provisions in determining what constitutes an online acceptance.

Click-On Agreements The courts have concluded that the act of clicking on a box labeled "I accept" or "I agree" can indicate acceptance of an online offer. The agreement resulting from such an acceptance is often called a **click-on agreement** (sometimes, *click-on license* or *click-wrap agreement*). Exhibit 11–1 shows a portion of a click-on agreement that accompanies a software package.

Generally, the law does not require that the parties have read all of the terms in a contract for it to be effective. Therefore, clicking on a box that states "I agree" to certain terms can be enough to bind a party to these terms. The terms may be contained on a Web site through which the buyer is obtaining goods or services, or they may appear on the screen of

Forum-Selection Clause A provision in a contract designating the court, jurisdiction, or tribunal that will decide any disputes arising under the contract.

Click-On Agreement An agreement that arises when an online buyer clicks on "I agree" or otherwise indicates her or his assent to be bound by the terms of an offer.

---

11. *Rosendahl v. Bridgepoint Education, Inc.*, 2012 WL 667049 (S.D.Cal. 2012).
12. *Feldman v. Google, Inc.*, 513 F.Supp.2d 229 (E.D.Pa. 2007).
13. *Restatement (Second) of Contracts*, Section 19.

Exhibit 11–1 A Click-On Agreement

This exhibit illustrates an online offer to form a contract. To accept the offer, the user simply scrolls down the page and clicks on the "I Accept" button.

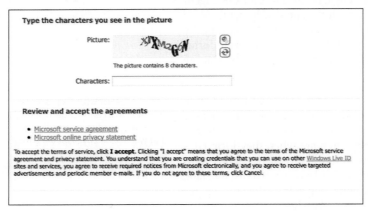

a computer, smartphone, or other device when software is downloaded from the Internet.

CASE EXAMPLE 11.23 The "Terms of Use" that govern Facebook users' accounts include a forum-selection clause that provides for the resolution of all disputes in a court in Santa Clara County. To sign up for a Facebook account, a person must click on a box indicating that he or she has agreed to this term.

Mustafa Fteja was an active user of facebook.com when his account was disabled. He sued Facebook in a federal court in New York, claiming that it had disabled his Facebook page without justification and for discriminatory reasons. Facebook filed a motion to transfer the case to California under the forum-selection clause. The court found that the clause in Facebook's online contract was binding and transferred the case. When Fteja clicked on the button to accept the contract terms, he agreed to resolve all disputes with Facebook in Santa Clara County, California.[14]

LEARNING OBJECTIVE 4

How do shrink-wrap and click-on agreements differ from other contracts? How have traditional laws been applied to these agreements?

Shrink-Wrap Agreement

An agreement whose terms are expressed in a document located inside a box in which goods (usually software) are packaged.

Shrink-Wrap Agreements A **shrink-wrap agreement** (or *shrink-wrap license*) is an agreement whose terms are expressed inside a box in which goods are packaged. (The term *shrink-wrap* refers to the plastic that covers the box.) Usually, the party who opens the box is told that she or he agrees to the terms by keeping the goods. Similarly, when the purchaser opens a software package, he or she agrees to abide by the terms of the limited license agreement.

EXAMPLE 11.24 Arial orders a new iMac from Big Dog Electronics, which ships it to her. Along with the iMac, the box contains an agreement setting forth the terms of the sale, including what remedies are available. The document also states that Arial's retention of the iMac for longer than thirty days will be construed as an acceptance of the terms. ▪

In most instances, a shrink-wrap agreement is not between a retailer and a buyer, but is between the manufacturer of the hardware or software and the ultimate buyer-user of the product. The terms generally concern warranties, remedies, and other issues associated with the use of the product.

Shrink-Wrap Agreements and Enforceable Contract Terms. In some cases, the courts have enforced the terms of shrink-wrap agreements in the same way as the terms of other contracts. These courts have reasoned that by including the terms with the product, the seller proposed a contract that the buyer could accept by using the product after having an opportunity to read the terms. Thus, a buyer's failure to object to terms contained within a shrink-wrapped software package may constitute an acceptance of the terms by conduct.

Shrink-Wrap Terms That May Not Be Enforced. Sometimes, courts have refused to enforce certain terms included in shrink-wrap agreements because the buyer did not expressly consent to them. An important factor is when the parties form their contract.

Suppose that a buyer orders a product over the telephone. If the contract is formed at that time and the seller does not mention terms such as an arbitration clause or a forum-selection clause, clearly the buyer has not expressly agreed to these terms. If the clauses are then included in a shrink-wrap agreement, a court may conclude that those terms were only proposals for additional terms, and not part of the original contract. After all, the buyer did not discover them until *after* the contract was formed.

---

14. *Fteja v. Facebook, Inc.*, 841 F.Supp.2d 829 (S.D.N.Y. 2012).

Is it fair to enforce shrink-wrap and click-wrap terms that buyers were not aware of at the time they agreed to a purchase? Most people realize that if they sign a written contract without reading it, they can be held to its terms. But are most people aware that they can be legally bound by a host of conditions included in the packaging of electronics and software, not to mention the music, movies, and software they download from the Web? Simply by buying and keeping the latest electronic gadgets, we enter into binding contracts with the manufacturers that include rather one-sided terms. The terms may be unfair, but the law says we are bound by them.

For instance, just by installing or downloading certain software, users routinely agree to allow the companies to install tracking software on their computers. Moreover, many software programs—including some that are designed to combat *malware* (harmful programs, as discussed in the criminal law chapter)—automatically delete files from users' hard drives. Consumers and businesspersons are often unaware of these consequences, and yet by buying and installing the software, they have agreed that they will not hold the manufacturer liable.

ETHICAL ISSUE

Browse-Wrap Terms

Browse-Wrap Terms Like the terms of a click-on agreement, **browse-wrap terms** can occur in a transaction conducted over the Internet. Unlike a click-on agreement, however, browse-wrap terms do not require the buyer or user to assent to the terms before, say, downloading or using certain software. In other words, a person can install the software without clicking "I agree" to the terms of a license. Browse-wrap terms are often unenforceable because they do not satisfy the agreement requirement of contract formation.[15]

Browse-Wrap Term A term or condition of use that is presented when an online buyer downloads a product but to which the buyer does not have to agree before installing or using the product.

11–2c Federal Law on E-Signatures and E-Documents

An **e-signature** has been defined as "an electronic sound, symbol, or process attached to or logically associated with a record and executed or adopted by a person with the intent to sign the record."[16] Electronic documents can be signed in a number of ways. Thus, e-signatures include encrypted digital signatures, names (intended as signatures) at the ends of e-mail messages, and "clicks" on a Web page if the clicks include some means of identification.

E-Signature An electronic sound, symbol, or process attached to or logically associated with a record and adopted by a person with the intent to sign the record.

The E-SIGN Act In 2000, Congress enacted the Electronic Signatures in Global and National Commerce Act (E-SIGN Act).[17] The E-SIGN Act provides that no contract, record, or signature may be "denied legal effect" solely because it is in electronic form.

Under the act, an electronic signature is as valid as a signature on paper, and an e-document can be as enforceable as a paper one. For an e-signature to be enforceable, however, the contracting parties must have agreed to use electronic signatures. For an electronic document to be valid, it must be in a form that can be retained and accurately reproduced.

The E-SIGN Act does not apply to all types of documents. Contracts and documents that are exempt include court papers, divorce decrees, evictions, foreclosures, health-insurance terminations, prenuptial agreements, and wills. Also, the only agreements governed by the UCC that fall under this law are those covered by Articles 2 and 2A and UCC 1–107 and 1–206. Despite these limitations, the E-SIGN Act significantly expanded contracting online.

The FACT Act Another federal law, The Fair and Accurate Credit Transactions (FACT) Act,[18] was passed in 2003 to combat identity theft. One provision of the FACT Act involves how credit-card receipts should be handled. In the case of online transactions, these receipts take the form of e-documents. See this chapter's *Managerial Strategy* feature for more details on how the FACT Act's provisions may affect online transactions.

Why are many e-signatures binding today?

---

15. See, for example, *Jesmer v. Retail Magic, Inc.*, 863 N.Y.S.2d 737 (2008).
16. This definition is from the Uniform Electronic Transactions Act.
17. 15 U.S.C. Sections 7001 *et seq.*
18. 15 U.S.C. Section 1681 *et seq.*

MANAGERIAL STRATEGY   E-Mailed Credit Card Receipts

Management Faces a Legal Issue

As more and more sales transactions take place on the Internet, retailers continue to face new issues in online selling. One such issue involves credit-card receipts. Merchants who print out paper receipts must follow strict guidelines. Under the Fair and Accurate Credit Transaction (FACT) Act, merchants may print only the last five digits of a credit or debit card number and may not print the card's expiration date on any receipt provided to the cardholder at the point of sale.

This prohibition, the so-called truncation requirement, applies only to receipts that are "electronically printed." Congress did not indicate exactly what it meant by "electronically printed," however. Internet retailers thus have faced the legal issue of whether online receipts are subject to the FACT Act's truncation requirement.

What the Courts Say

The question, then, is whether a Web screen shot or an e-mailed sale confirmation counts as a receipt under the FACT Act. The courts that have examined this issue have generally concluded that the FACT Act's truncation requirement does not apply to e-mailed credit-card receipts.[a]

One case involved the online sale of contact lenses by a popular telephone and online retailer. The plaintiff was a customer who received an e-mail confirmation that included his credit card's expiration date. He sued the company for violating the FACT Act's truncation requirement. The court ruled in favor of the defendant, noting that the legislative history of the FACT Act clearly shows that Congress intended this law to apply to physical, printed-paper receipts. The court reasoned that the act "makes no use of terms like 'Internet' or 'e-mail' that would signal an intent to reach paperless receipts transmitted to the consumer via e-mail."[b]

MANAGERIAL IMPLICATIONS

Online retailers appear not to be subject to the FACT Act's truncation requirement for credit-card receipts sent via the Internet. Nonetheless, sensible online retailers might wish to conform to the act's provisions simply as a good business practice, to keep customers content and to protect customers' personal information. After all, hackers can sometimes illegally access Web sites and e-mail correspondence.

---

a. See, for example, *Bormes v. U.S.*, 759 F.3d 793 (7th Cir. 2014); and *Simonoff v. Expedia, Inc.*, 643 F.3d 1202 (9th Cir. 2011).

b. *Shlahtichman v. 1-800 Contacts, Inc.*, 615 F.3d 794 (7th Cir. 2010), *cert. denied*, 131 S.Ct. 1007, 178 L.Ed.2d 828 (2011).

11–2d Partnering Agreements

Partnering Agreement An agreement between a seller and a buyer who frequently do business with each other concerning the terms and conditions that will apply to all subsequently formed electronic contracts.

One way that online sellers and buyers can prevent disputes over signatures in their e-contracts, as well as disputes over the terms and conditions of those contracts, is to form partnering agreements. In a **partnering agreement,** a seller and a buyer who frequently do business with each other agree in advance on the terms and conditions that will apply to all transactions subsequently conducted electronically. The partnering agreement can also establish special access and identification codes to be used by the parties when transacting business electronically.

A partnering agreement reduces the likelihood that disputes will arise under the contract because the buyer and the seller have agreed in advance to the terms and conditions that will accompany each sale. Furthermore, if a dispute does arise, a court or arbitration forum will be able to refer to the partnering agreement when determining the parties' intent.

LEARNING OBJECTIVE 5

What is the Uniform Electronic Transactions Act? What are some of the major provisions of this act?

11–3 The Uniform Electronic Transactions Act

Although most states have laws governing e-signatures and other aspects of electronic transactions, these laws vary. To create more uniformity among the states, in 1999 the National Conference of Commissioners on Uniform State Laws and the American Law Institute promulgated the Uniform Electronic Transactions Act (UETA). The UETA has been adopted, at least in part, by forty-eight states.

The primary purpose of the UETA is to remove barriers to e-commerce by giving the same legal effect to electronic records and signatures as is given to paper documents and signatures. The UETA broadly defines an *e-signature* as "an electronic sound, symbol, or process attached to or logically associated with a record and executed or adopted by a person with the intent to sign the record."[19] A **record** is "information that is inscribed on a tangible medium or that is stored in an electronic or other medium and is retrievable in perceivable [visual] form."[20]

Record Information that is either inscribed on a tangible medium or stored in an electronic or other medium and is retrievable.

11-3a The Scope and Applicability of the UETA

The UETA does not create new rules for electronic contracts. Rather, it establishes that records, signatures, and contracts may not be denied enforceability solely due to their electronic form.

The UETA does not apply to all writings and signatures. It covers only electronic records and electronic signatures *relating to a transaction*. A *transaction* is defined as an interaction between two or more parties relating to business, commercial, or governmental activities.[21] The act specifically does not apply to wills or testamentary trusts or to transactions governed by the UCC (other than those covered by Articles 2 and 2A).[22] In addition, the provisions of the UETA allow the states to exclude its application to other areas of law.

11-3b The Federal E-SIGN Act and the UETA

Congress passed the E-SIGN Act in 2000, a year after the UETA was presented to the states for adoption. Thus, a significant issue was to what extent the federal E-SIGN Act preempted the UETA as adopted by the states.

The E-SIGN Act[23] explicitly provides that if a state has enacted the uniform version of the UETA, it is not preempted by the E-SIGN Act. In other words, if the state has enacted the UETA without modification, state law will govern.

The problem is that many states have enacted nonuniform (modified) versions of the UETA, largely for the purpose of excluding other areas of state law from the UETA's terms. The E-SIGN Act specifies that those exclusions will be preempted to the extent that they are inconsistent with the E-SIGN Act's provisions.

The E-SIGN Act explicitly allows the states to enact alternative requirements for the use of electronic records or electronic signatures. Generally, however, the requirements must be consistent with the provisions of the E-SIGN Act, and the state must not give greater legal status or effect to one specific type of technology. Additionally, if a state enacts alternative requirements *after* the E-SIGN Act was adopted, the state law must specifically refer to the E-SIGN Act.

The relationship between the E-SIGN Act and the UETA is illustrated in Exhibit 11–2.

11-3c Highlights of the UETA

The UETA will not apply to a transaction unless the parties have agreed to conduct transactions by electronic means. The agreement may be explicit, or it may be implied by the conduct of the parties and the surrounding circumstances.[24] It may be reasonable, for example, to infer that a person who gives out a business card with an e-mail address on it has consented to transact business electronically.[25] Agreement may also be inferred from a letter or other writing, as well as from verbal communication. Furthermore, a person who has previously agreed

---

19. UETA 102(8).
20. UETA 102(15).
21. UETA 2(12) and 3.
22. UETA 3(b).
23. 15 U.S.C. Section 7002(2)(A)(i).
24. UETA 5(b).
25. UETA 5, Comment 4B.

Exhibit 11–2 The E-SIGN Act and the UETA

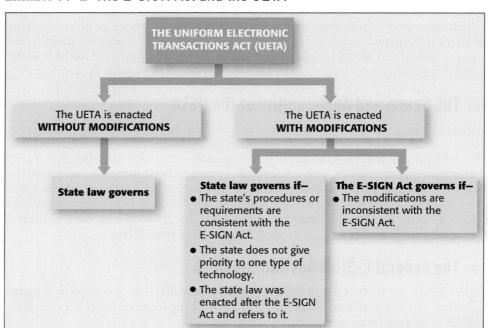

to an electronic transaction can withdraw his or her consent and refuse to conduct further business electronically.

Attribution   Under the UETA, if an electronic record or signature is the act of a particular person, the record or signature may be attributed to that person. If a person types her or his name at the bottom of an e-mail purchase order, for instance, that name will qualify as a "signature" and be attributed to the person whose name appears.

In some contexts, a record may have legal effect even if no one has signed it. **EXAMPLE 11.25** J. P. Darby sends a fax to Corina Scott. The fax contains a letterhead identifying Darby as the sender, but Darby's signature does not appear on the faxed document. Depending on the circumstances, the fax may be attributed to Darby. ■

Authorized Signatures   The UETA contains no express provisions about what constitutes fraud or whether an agent is authorized to enter a contract. Under the UETA, other state laws control if any issues relating to agency, authority, forgery, or contract formation arise. If existing state law requires a document to be notarized, the electronic signature of a notary public or other person authorized to verify signatures satisfies this requirement.

The Effect of Errors   The UETA encourages, but does not require, the use of security procedures (such as encryption) to verify changes to electronic documents and to correct errors. If the parties have agreed to a security procedure and one party does not detect an error because he or she did not follow the procedure, the conforming party can legally avoid the effect of the change or error. To avoid the effect of errors, a party must promptly notify the other party of the error and of her or his intent not to be bound by the error. In addition, the party must take reasonable steps to return any benefit received. Parties cannot avoid a transaction if they have benefited.

If an agreement is sent on letterhead stationery, does it need to be signed to be a valid acceptance?

Timing An electronic record is considered *sent* when it is properly directed to the intended recipient in a form readable by the recipient's computer system. Once the electronic record leaves the control of the sender or comes under the control of the recipient, the UETA deems it to have been sent. An electronic record is considered *received* when it enters the recipient's processing system in a readable form—*even if no individual is aware of its receipt.*

Reviewing . . . Agreement

Ted and Betty Hyatt live in California, a state that has extensive statutory protection for consumers. The Hyatts decided to buy a computer so that they could use e-mail to stay in touch with their grandchildren, who live in another state. Over the phone, they ordered a computer from CompuEdge, Inc. When the box arrived, it was sealed with a brightly colored sticker warning that the terms enclosed within the box would govern the sale unless the recipient returned the computer within thirty days. Among those terms was a clause that required any disputes to be resolved in Tennessee state courts.

The Hyatts then signed up for Internet service through CyberTool, an Internet service provider. They downloaded CyberTool's software and clicked on the "quick install" box, which allowed them to bypass CyberTool's "Terms of Service" page. It was possible to read this page by scrolling to the next screen, but the Hyatts did not realize this. The terms included a clause stating that all disputes were to be submitted to a Virginia state court. As soon as the Hyatts attempted to e-mail their grandchildren, they experienced problems using CyberTool's e-mail service, which continually stated that the network was busy. They also were unable to receive the photos sent by their grandchildren.

Using the information presented in the chapter, answer the following questions.

1. Did the Hyatts accept the list of contract terms included in the computer box? Why or why not? What is this type of e-contract called?

2. What type of agreement did the Hyatts form with CyberTool?

3. Suppose that the Hyatts experienced trouble with the computer's components after they had used the computer for two months. What factors would a court consider in deciding whether to enforce the forum-selection clause? Would a court be likely to enforce the clause in this contract? Why or why not?

4. Are the Hyatts bound by the contract terms specified on CyberTool's "Terms of Service" page, though they did not read these terms? Which of the required elements for contract formation might the Hyatts claim were lacking? How might a court rule on this issue?

DEBATE THIS

■ The terms and conditions in click-on agreements are so long and detailed that no one ever reads the agreements. Therefore, the act of clicking on "Yes, I agree" is not really an acceptance.

LINKING BUSINESS LAW TO MARKETING

Customer Relationship Management

As you learned in this chapter, increasingly the contracting process is moving online. Large and small e-commerce Web sites offer to sell millions of goods and services. The vast amount of data collected from online shoppers has pushed *customer relationship management (CRM)* to the fore. CRM is a marketing strategy that allows companies to acquire information about customers' wants, needs, and behaviors. The companies can then use that information to build customer relationships and loyalty. The focus of CRM is understanding customers as individuals rather than simply as a group of consumers. As Exhibit 11–3 shows, CRM is a closed system that uses feedback from customers to build relationships with those customers.

Two Examples—Netflix and Amazon

If you are a customer of Netflix.com, you choose Blu-ray discs and DVDs that are sent to you by mail or streamed online based on your individual tastes and preferences. Netflix asks you to rate movies that you have rented (or seen in theaters) on a scale of one to five stars. Using a computer algorithm, Netflix then creates an individualized rating system that predicts how you will rate other movies. As you rate more movies, the system's predictions become more accurate. By applying your individual rating system to movies you have not seen, Netflix is able to suggest movies that you might like.

Amazon.com uses similar technology to recommend books and music that you might wish to buy. Amazon sends out numerous "personalized" e-mails to its customers with suggestions based on those customers' individual buying habits.

Thus, CRM allows both Netflix and Amazon to focus their marketing efforts. Such focused efforts are much more effective than the typical shotgun approach used in spam advertising on the Internet.

CRM in Online versus Traditional Companies

For online companies such as Amazon and Netflix, all customer information has some value because the cost of obtaining it, analyzing it, and utilizing it is so small. In contrast, traditional companies often must use a much more costly process to obtain data for CRM. An automobile company, for example, obtains customer information from a variety of sources, including dealers, customer surveys, online inquiries, and the like. Integrating, storing, and managing such information generally makes CRM much more expensive for traditional companies than for online companies.

■ Online companies such as Amazon not only target individual customers but also utilize each customer's buying habits to create generalized marketing campaigns. Might any privacy issues arise as an online company creates a database to be used for generalized marketing campaigns?

Exhibit 11–3 A Customer Relationship Management Cycle

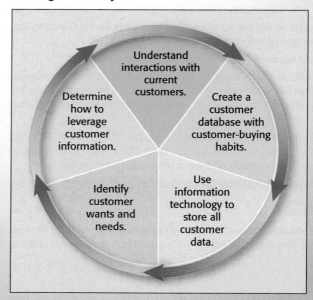

Key Terms

Chapter Summary: Agreement

Requirements of the Offer	**1.** *Intent*—There must be a serious, objective intention by the offeror to become bound by the offer. Nonoffer situations include (a) expressions of opinion; (b) statements of future intent; (c) preliminary negotiations; (d) generally, advertisements, catalogues, price lists, and circulars; and (e) traditionally, agreements to agree in the future. **2.** *Definiteness*—The terms of the offer must be sufficiently definite to be ascertainable by the parties or by a court. **3.** *Communication*—The offer must be communicated to the offeree.

Termination of the Offer	**1.** *By action of the parties*—
	  a. Revocation—Unless the offer is irrevocable, it can be revoked at any time before acceptance without liability. Revocation is not effective until received by the offeree or the offeree's agent. Some offers, such as a merchant's firm offer and option contracts, are irrevocable.
	  b. Rejection—Accomplished by words or actions that demonstrate a clear intent not to accept the offer. A rejection is not effective until it is received by the offeror or the offeror's agent.
	  c. Counteroffer—A rejection of the original offer and the making of a new offer.
	2. *By operation of law*—
	  a. Lapse of time—The offer terminates (1) at the end of the time period specified in the offer or (2) if no time period is stated in the offer, at the end of a reasonable time period.
	  b. Destruction of the specific subject matter of the offer—Automatically terminates the offer.
	  c. Death or incompetence of the offeror or offeree—Terminates the offer unless the offer is irrevocable.
	  d. Illegality—Supervening illegality terminates the offer.

Acceptance	**1.** Can be made only by the offeree or the offeree's agent. **2.** Must be unequivocal. Under the common law (mirror image rule), if new terms or conditions are added to the acceptance, it will be considered a counteroffer. **3.** Acceptance of a unilateral offer is effective on full performance of the requested act. Generally, no communication is necessary. **4.** Except in a few situations, an offeree's silence does not constitute an acceptance. **5.** Acceptance of a bilateral offer can be communicated by the offeree by any authorized mode of communication and is effective on dispatch. If the offeror does not specify the mode of communication, acceptance can be made by any reasonable means. Usually, the same means used by the offeror or a faster means can be used.
Online Offers	The terms of contract offers presented via the Internet should be as inclusive as the terms in an offer made in a written (paper) document. The offer should be displayed in an easily readable format and should include some mechanism, such as an "I agree" or "I accept" box, by which the customer may accept the offer. Because jurisdictional issues frequently arise with online transactions, the offer should include dispute-settlement provisions, as well as a forum-selection clause.

Online Acceptances	**1.** *Click-on agreement*—
	  a. Definition—An agreement created when a buyer, completing an online transaction, is required to indicate her or his assent to be bound by the terms of an offer by clicking on a box that says, for example, "I agree." The terms of the agreement may appear on the Web site through which the buyer is obtaining goods or services, or they may appear on a computer screen when software is downloaded.
	  b. Enforceability—The courts have enforced click-on agreements, holding that by clicking on "I agree," the offeree has indicated acceptance by conduct. In contrast, browse-wrap terms, which do not require any action to indicate agreement, may not be enforced on the ground that the user is not made aware that he or she is entering into a contract.
	2. *Shrink-wrap agreement*—
	  a. Definition—An agreement whose terms are expressed inside a box in which goods are packaged. The party who opens the box is informed that, by keeping the goods, he or she agrees to the terms of the shrink-wrap agreement.
	  b. Enforceability—The courts have often enforced shrink-wrap agreements. A court may deem a shrink-wrap agreement unenforceable, however, if the buyer learns of the shrink-wrap terms after the parties entered into the agreement.

Continues

E-Signatures	1. *Definition*—The Uniform Electronic Transactions Act (UETA) defines an e-signature as "an electronic sound, symbol, or process attached to or logically associated with a record and executed or adopted by a person with the intent to sign the record." E-signatures may include encrypted digital signatures, names at the ends of e-mail messages, and clicks on a Web page. 2. *Federal law on e-signatures and e-documents*—The Electronic Signatures in Global and National Commerce Act (E-SIGN Act) of 2000 gave validity to e-signatures by providing that no contract, record, or signature may be "denied legal effect" solely because it is in an electronic form.
The Uniform Electronic Transactions Act (UETA)	The Uniform Electronic Transactions Act (UETA) has been adopted, at least in part, by most states, to create rules to support the enforcement of e-contracts. Under the UETA, contracts entered into online, as well as other documents, are presumed to be valid. The UETA does not apply to certain transactions governed by the UCC or to wills or testamentary trusts.

Issue Spotters

1. Fidelity Corporation offers to hire Ron to replace Monica, who has given Fidelity a month's notice of her intent to leave the company. Fidelity gives Ron a week to decide whether to accept. Two days later, Monica decides not to leave and signs an employment contract with Fidelity for another year. The next day, Monica tells Ron of the new contract. Ron immediately faxes a formal letter of acceptance to Fidelity. Do Fidelity and Ron have a contract? Why or why not? (See *Agreement*.)

2. Applied Products, Inc., does business with Beltway Distributors, Inc., online. Under the Uniform Electronic Transactions Act, what determines the effect of the electronic documents evidencing the parties' deal? Is a party's "signature" necessary? Explain. (See *The Uniform Electronic Transactions Act*.)

—**Check your answers to the *Issue Spotters* against the answers provided in Appendix D at the end of this text.**

Learning Objectives Check

1. What elements are necessary for an effective offer? What are some examples of nonoffers?
2. In what circumstances will an offer be irrevocable?
3. What are the elements that are necessary for an effective acceptance?
4. How do shrink-wrap and click-on agreements differ from other contracts? How have traditional laws been applied to these agreements?
5. What is the Uniform Electronic Transactions Act? What are some of the major provisions of this act?

—**Answers to the even-numbered *Learning Objectives Check* questions can be found in Appendix E at the end of this text.**

Business Scenarios and Case Problems

11–1. Agreement. Ball writes to Sullivan and inquires how much Sullivan is asking for a specific forty-acre tract of land Sullivan owns. Ball then receives a letter from Sullivan stating, "I will not take less than $60,000 for the forty-acre tract as specified." Ball immediately sends Sullivan a fax stating, "I accept your offer for $60,000 for the forty-acre tract as specified." Discuss whether Ball can hold Sullivan to a contract for sale of the land. (See *Agreement*.)

11–2. Shrink-Wrap Agreements. TracFone Wireless, Inc., sells phones and wireless service. The phones are sold for less than their cost, and TracFone recoups this loss by selling prepaid airtime for their use on its network. Software in the phones prohibits their use on other networks. The phones are sold subject to the condition that the buyer agrees "not to tamper with or

alter the software." This condition is printed on the packaging. Bequator Corp. bought at least 18,616 of the phones, disabled the software so that they could be used on other networks, and resold them. Is Bequator liable for breach of contract? Explain. [*TracFone Wireless, Inc. v. Bequator Corp.*, __ F.Supp.2d __ (S.D.Fla. 2011)] (See *E-Contracts*.)

11–3. Spotlight on Crime Stoppers—Communication. The Baton Rouge Crime Stoppers (BCS) offered a reward for information about the "South Louisiana Serial Killer." The information was to be provided via a hotline. Dianne Alexander had survived an attack by a person suspected of being the killer. She identified a suspect in a police photo lineup and later sought to collect the reward. BCS refused to pay because she had not provided information via the hotline. Did

Alexander comply with the terms of the offer? Explain. [*Alexander v. Lafayette Crime Stoppers, Inc.*, 38 So.3d 282 (La.App. 3 Dist. 2010)] (See *Agreement*.)

11–4. Business Case Problem with Sample Answer—Online Acceptances. Heather Reasonover opted to try Internet service from Clearwire Corp. Clearwire sent her a confirmation e-mail that included a link to its Web site. Clearwire also sent her a modem. In the enclosed written materials, at the bottom of a page, in small type was the Web site URL. When Reasonover plugged in the modem, an "I accept terms" box appeared. Without clicking on the box, Reasonover quit the page. A clause in Clearwire's "Terms of Service," accessible only through its Web site, required its subscribers to submit any dispute to arbitration. Is Reasonover bound to this clause? Why or why not? [*Kwan v. Clearwire Corp.*, 2012 WL 32380 (W.D.Wash. 2012)] (See *E-Contracts*.)

—**For a sample answer to Problem 11–4, go to Appendix F at the end of this text.**

11–5. Acceptance. Judy Olsen, Kristy Johnston, and their mother, Joyce Johnston, owned seventy-eight acres of real property on Eagle Creek in Meagher County, Montana. When Joyce died, she left her interest in the property to Kristy. Kristy wrote to Judy, offering to buy Judy's interest or to sell her own interest to Judy. She requested that Judy "please respond to Bruce Townsend." In a letter to Kristy—not to Bruce—Judy accepted the offer to buy Kristy's interest in the property. By that time, however, Kristy had offered to sell her interest to their brother, Dave, and he had accepted. Did Judy and Kristy have an enforceable binding contract, entitling Judy to specific performance? Or did Kristy's offer so limit its acceptance to one exclusive mode that Judy's reply was not effective? Discuss. [*Olsen v. Johnston*, 368 Mont. 347, 301 P.3d 791 (Mont. 2013)] (See *Agreement*.)

11–6. Agreement. Amy Kemper was seriously injured when her motorcycle was struck by a vehicle driven by Christopher Brown. Kemper's attorney wrote to Statewide Claims Services, the administrator for Brown's insurer, asking for "all the insurance money that Mr. Brown had under his insurance policy." In exchange, the letter indicated that Kemper would sign a "limited release" on Brown's liability, provided that it did not include any language requiring her to reimburse Brown or his insurance company for any of their incurred costs. Statewide then sent a check and release form to Kemper, but the release demanded that Kemper "place money in an escrow account in regards to any and all liens pending." Kemper refused the demand, claiming that Statewide's response was a counteroffer rather than an unequivocal acceptance of the settlement offer. Did Statewide and Kemper have an enforceable agreement? Discuss. [*Kemper v. Brown*, 754 S.E.2d 141 (Ga.App. 2014)] (See *Agreement*.)

11–7. Requirements of the Offer. Technical Consumer Products, Inc. (TCP) makes and distributes energy-efficient lighting products. Emily Bahr was TCP's district sales manager in Minnesota, North Dakota, and South Dakota when the company announced the details of a bonus plan. A district sales manager who achieved 100 percent year-over-year sales growth and a 42 percent gross margin would earn 200 percent of his or her base salary as a bonus. TCP retained absolute discretion to modify the plan. Bahr's base salary was $42,500. Her final sales results for the year showed 113 percent year-over-year sales growth and a 42 percent gross margin. She anticipated a bonus of $85,945, but TCP could not afford to pay the bonuses as planned, and Bahr received only $34,229. In response to Bahr's claim for breach of contract, TCP argued that the bonus plan was too indefinite to be an offer. Is TCP correct? Explain. [*Bahr v. Technical Consumer Products, Inc.*, __ F.3d __, 2015 WL 527468 (6th Cir. 2015)] (See *Agreement*.)

11–8. A Question of Ethics—Dispute-Settlement Provisions. Dewayne Hubbert, Elden Craft, Chris Grout, and Rhonda Byington bought computers from Dell Corp. through its Web site. Before buying, Hubbert and the others configured their own computers. To make a purchase, each buyer completed forms on five Web pages. On each page, Dell's "Terms and Conditions of Sale" were accessible by clicking on a blue hyperlink. A statement on three of the pages read, "All sales are subject to Dell's Term[s] and Conditions of Sale," but a buyer was not required to click an assent to the terms to complete a purchase. The terms were also printed on the backs of the invoices and on separate documents contained in the shipping boxes with the computers. Among those terms was a "Binding Arbitration" clause.

The computers contained Pentium 4 microprocessors, which Dell advertised as the fastest, most powerful Intel Pentium processor available at that time. Hubbert and the others filed a suit in an Illinois state court against Dell, alleging that this marketing was false, misleading, and deceptive. The plaintiffs claimed that the Pentium 4 microprocessor was slower and less powerful, and provided less performance, than either a Pentium III or an AMD Athlon, and at a greater cost. Dell asked the court to compel arbitration. [*Hubbert v. Dell Corp.*, 359 Ill. App.3d 976, 835 N.E.2d 113, 296 Ill.Dec. 258 (5 Dist. 2005)] (See *E-Contracts*.)

1. Should the court enforce the arbitration clause in this case? If you were the judge, how would you rule on this issue?

2. In your opinion, do shrink-wrap, click-on, and browse-wrap terms impose too great a burden on purchasers? Why or why not?

3. An ongoing complaint about shrink-wrap, click-on, and browse-wrap terms is that sellers (often large corporations) draft them and buyers (typically individual consumers) do not read them. Should purchasers be bound in contract by terms that they have not even read? Why or why not?

Critical Thinking and Writing Assignments

11–9. Case Analysis Question. Go to Appendix G at the end of this text and examine the excerpt of Case No. 2, *Gyabaah v. RivLab Transportation Corp.* Review and then brief the case, making sure that your brief answers the following questions. (See *Agreement*.)

1. **Issue:** The dispute between the parties to this case centered on what agreement and asked which question?

2. **Rule of Law:** What rule concerning the existence of a contract did the court apply in this case?

3. **Applying the Rule of Law:** How did the language in the parties' agreement and its context affect the application of the rule of law?

4. **Conclusion:** Why did the court conclude that the parties in this case were not bound by the settlement and release documents signed by Gyabaah?

11–10. Business Law Critical Thinking Group Assignment.
To download a specific app to your smartphone or tablet device, you usually have to check a box indicating that you agree to the company's terms and conditions. Most individuals do so without ever reading those terms and conditions. Print out a specific set of terms and conditions from a downloaded app to use in this assignment. All group members should print out the same set of terms and conditions. (See *E-Contracts*.)

1. One group will determine which of these terms and conditions are favorable to the company.

2. Another group will determine which of these terms and conditions could conceivably be favorable to the individual.

3. A third group will determine which terms and conditions, on net, favor the company too much.

iStockPhoto.com/Neustockimages

Consideration, Capacity, and Legality

"Liberty of contract
is not an absolute
concept. It is relative
to many conditions
of time and place and
circumstance."

BENJAMIN CARDOZO
1870–1938
(ASSOCIATE JUSTICE OF THE UNITED
STATES SUPREME COURT, 1932–1938)

Courts generally want contracts to be enforceable, and
much of the law is devoted to aiding the enforceability of
contracts. Before a court will enforce a contractual promise, however, it must be convinced that there was some
exchange of consideration underlying the bargain.

Furthermore, as indicated in the chapter-opening quotation, "liberty of contract" is not absolute. In other words,
not all people can make legally binding contracts at all
times. Contracts entered into by persons lacking the capacity to do so may be voidable. Similarly, contracts calling for
the performance of an illegal act are illegal and thus void—
they are not contracts at all.

In this chapter, we first examine the requirement of consideration and then look at
contractual capacity and legality. As more commerce is done online, the issues of consideration, capacity, and legality have become the subject of many disputes. In covenants not
to compete, for instance, what constitutes a reasonable time period in the online environment? This is among current topics you will read about in this chapter.

12–1 Consideration

In any legal system, some promises will be enforced, and other promises will not be
enforced. The simple fact that a party has made a promise does not necessarily mean that
the promise is enforceable.

Consideration The value given in return for a promise or performance in a contractual agreement.

Forbearance The act of refraining from an action that one has a legal right to undertake.

When you ask someone to paint your garage, what is the consideration?

"Understanding does not necessarily mean agreement."

HOWARD VERNON
1918–1992
(AMERICAN AUTHOR)

Under the common law, a primary basis for the enforcement of promises is consideration. **Consideration** usually is defined as the value given in return for a promise. Often, consideration is broken down into two parts: (1) something of *legally sufficient value* must be given in exchange for the promise, and (2) there must be a *bargained-for exchange*.

12–1a Legally Sufficient Value

To be legally sufficient, consideration must be something of value in the eyes of the law. The "something of legally sufficient value" may consist of any of the following:

1. A promise to do something that one has no prior legal duty to do (to pay on receipt of certain goods, for example).

2. The performance of an action that one is otherwise not obligated to undertake (such as providing accounting services).

3. The refraining from an action that one has a legal right to undertake (called a **forbearance**).

Consideration in bilateral contracts normally consists of a promise in return for a promise. In a contract for the sale of goods, for instance, the seller promises to ship specific goods to the buyer, and the buyer promises to pay for those goods when they are received. Each of these promises constitutes consideration for the contract.

In contrast, unilateral contracts involve a promise in return for a performance. **EXAMPLE 12.1** Anita says to her neighbor, "If you paint my garage, I will pay you $800." Anita's neighbor paints the garage. The act of painting the garage is the consideration that creates Anita's contractual obligation to pay her neighbor $800. ■

What if, in return for a promise to pay, a person refrains from pursuing harmful habits, such as the use of tobacco and alcohol? Does such forbearance create consideration for the contract? This was the issue in the 1891 case *Hamer v. Sidway*, which we present as this chapter's *Landmark in the Law* feature.

12–1b Bargained-for Exchange

The second element of consideration is that it must provide the basis for the bargain struck between the contracting parties. The item of value must be given or promised by the promisor (offeror) in return for the promisee's promise or performance.

This element of bargained-for exchange distinguishes contracts from gifts. **EXAMPLE 12.2** Sheng-Li says to his son, "In consideration of the fact that you are not as wealthy as your brothers, I will pay you $5,000." The fact that the word *consideration* is used does not, by itself, mean that consideration has been given. Indeed, Sheng-Li's promise is not enforceable, because the son need not do anything to receive the $5,000 promised. Because the son does not need to give Sheng-Li something of legal value in return for his promise, there is no bargained-for exchange. Rather, Sheng-Li has simply stated his motive for giving his son a gift. ■

12–1c Adequacy of Consideration

Adequacy of consideration involves "how much" consideration is given. Essentially, adequacy of consideration concerns the fairness of the bargain.

The General Rule On the surface, when the items exchanged are of unequal value, fairness would appear to be an issue. In general, however, a court will not question the adequacy of consideration based solely on the comparative value of the things exchanged.

Under the doctrine of freedom of contract, courts leave it up to the parties to decide what something is worth, and parties are usually free to bargain as they wish. If people could sue

LANDMARK IN THE LAW   *Hamer v. Sidway* (1891)

In *Hamer v. Sidway*,[a] the issue before the court arose from a contract created in 1869 between William Story, Sr., and his nephew, William Story II. The uncle promised his nephew that if the nephew refrained from drinking alcohol, using tobacco, and playing billiards and cards for money until he reached the age of twenty-one, the uncle would pay him $5,000 (about $75,000 in today's dollars). The nephew, who indulged occasionally in all of these "vices," agreed to refrain from them and did so for the next six years.

Following his twenty-first birthday in 1875, the nephew wrote to his uncle that he had performed his part of the bargain and was thus entitled to the promised $5,000 (plus interest). A few days later, the uncle wrote the nephew a letter stating, "[Y]ou shall have the five thousand dollars, as I promised you." The uncle said that the money was in the bank and that the nephew could "consider this money on interest."

THE ISSUE OF CONSIDERATION The nephew left the money in the care of his uncle, who held it for the next twelve years. When the uncle died in 1887, however, the executor of the uncle's estate refused to pay the $5,000 (plus interest) claim brought by Hamer, a third party to whom the promise had been *assigned*. (The law allows parties to assign, or transfer, rights in contracts to third parties.) The executor, Sidway, contended that the contract was invalid because there was insufficient consideration to support it. The uncle had received nothing, and the nephew had actually benefited by fulfilling the uncle's wishes. Therefore, no contract existed.

THE COURT'S CONCLUSION Although a lower court upheld Sidway's position, the New York Court of Appeals reversed and ruled in favor of the plaintiff, Hamer. "The promisee used tobacco, occasionally drank liquor, and he had a legal right to do so," the court stated. "That right he abandoned for a period of years upon the strength of the promise of the testator [one who makes a will] that for such forbearance he would give him $5,000. We need not speculate on the effort which may have been required to give up the use of those stimulants. It is sufficient that he restricted his lawful freedom of action within certain prescribed limits upon the faith of his uncle's agreement."

APPLICATION TO TODAY'S WORLD *Although this case was decided more than a century ago, the principles enunciated by the court remain applicable to contracts formed today, including online contracts. For a contract to be valid and binding, consideration must be given, and that consideration must be something of legally sufficient value.*

a. 124 N.Y. 538, 27 N.E. 256 (1891).

---

merely because they had entered into an unwise contract, the courts would be overloaded with frivolous suits.

In short, the determination of whether consideration exists does not depend on the values of the things exchanged. Something need not be of direct economic or financial value to be considered legally sufficient consideration. In many situations, the exchange of promises and potential benefits is deemed to be sufficient consideration.

When Voluntary Consent May Be Lacking
Occasionally, an exception may be made to the general rule just discussed. A large disparity in the amount or value of the consideration exchanged may raise a red flag for a court to look more closely at the bargain. Shockingly inadequate consideration can indicate that fraud, duress, or undue influence was involved. Judges are uneasy about enforcing unequal bargains, and it is their task to make certain that there was not some defect in the contract's formation that negated voluntary consent.

12–1d Agreements That Lack Consideration

Sometimes, one or both of the parties to a contract may think that they have exchanged consideration when in fact they have not. Here, we look at some situations in which the parties' promises or actions do not qualify as contractual consideration.

Preexisting Duty
Under most circumstances, a promise to do what one already has a legal duty to do does not constitute legally sufficient consideration. A sheriff, for example, cannot

KNOW THIS
A consumer's signature on a contract does not always guarantee that the contract will be enforced. The contract must also comply with state and federal consumer protection laws.

collect a reward for information leading to the capture of a criminal if the sheriff already has a legal duty to capture the criminal.

Likewise, if a party is already bound by contract to perform a certain duty, that duty cannot serve as consideration for a second contract. **EXAMPLE 12.3** Bauman-Bache, Inc., begins construction on a seven-story office building and after three months demands an extra $75,000 on its contract. If the extra $75,000 is not paid, the firm will stop working. The owner of the land, finding no one else to complete construction, agrees to pay the extra $75,000. The agreement is not enforceable because it is not supported by legally sufficient consideration— Bauman-Bache had a preexisting contractual duty to complete the building. ■

Unforeseen Difficulties. The preexisting duty rule is intended to prevent extortion and the so-called holdup game. Nonetheless, if, during performance of a contract, extraordinary difficulties arise that were totally unforeseen at the time the contract was formed, a court may allow an exception to the rule. The key is whether the court finds that the modification is fair and equitable in view of circumstances not anticipated by the parties when the contract was made.[1]

Are there circumstances under which a contractor, who has performed cement work, can legally demand a payment amount that is greater than what was stated in the contract?

Suppose that in *Example 12.3*, Bauman-Bache asked for the extra $75,000 because it encountered a rock formation that no one knew existed. Suppose, too, that the landowner agreed to pay the extra amount to excavate the rock. In this situation, if the court finds that it is fair to do so, it may enforce the agreement. If rock formations are common in the area, however, the court may determine that the contractor should have known of the risk. In that situation, the court may choose to apply the preexisting duty rule and prevent Bauman-Bache from obtaining the extra $75,000.

Rescission and New Contract. The law recognizes that two parties can mutually agree to rescind, or cancel, their contract, at least to the extent that it is *executory* (still to be carried out). **Rescission**[2] is the unmaking of a contract so as to return the parties to the positions they occupied before the contract was made.

Rescission A remedy whereby a contract is canceled and the parties are returned to the positions they occupied before the contract was made.

Sometimes, parties rescind a contract and make a new contract at the same time. When this occurs, it is often difficult to determine whether there was consideration for the new contract or whether the parties had a preexisting duty under the previous contract. If a court finds there was a preexisting duty, then the new contract will be invalid because there was no consideration.

Past Consideration

Promises made in return for actions or events that have already taken place are unenforceable. These promises lack consideration in that the element of bargained-for exchange is missing. In short, you can bargain for something to take place now or in the future but not for something that has already taken place. Therefore, **past consideration** is no consideration.

Past Consideration An act that takes place before a contract is made and that ordinarily, by itself, cannot later be consideration with respect to that contract.

CASE EXAMPLE 12.4 Jamil Blackmon became friends with Allen Iverson when Iverson was a high school student who showed tremendous promise as an athlete. Blackmon suggested that Iverson use "The Answer" as a nickname in the league tournaments, and said that Iverson would be "The Answer" to the National Basketball Association's declining attendance. Later, Iverson said that he would give Blackmon 25 percent of any proceeds from the merchandising of products that used "The Answer" as a logo or a slogan. Because Iverson's promise was made in return for past consideration (Blackmon's earlier suggestion), it was unenforceable. In effect, Iverson stated his intention to give Blackmon a gift.[3] ■

---

1. *Restatement (Second) of Contracts*, Section 73.
2. Pronounced reh-*sih*-zhen.
3. *Blackmon v. Iverson*, 324 F.Supp.2d 602 (E.D.Pa. 2003).

Illusory Promises If the terms of the contract express such uncertainty of performance that the promisor has not definitely promised to do anything, the promise is said to be *illusory*—without consideration and unenforceable. **EXAMPLE 12.5** The president of Tuscan Corporation says to his employees, "All of you have worked hard, and if profits remain high, a 10 percent bonus at the end of the year will be given—if management thinks it is warranted." This is an *illusory promise,* or no promise at all, because performance depends solely on the discretion of the president (the management). There is no bargained-for consideration. The statement declares merely that management may or may not do something in the future. ■

Option-to-cancel clauses in contracts for specified time periods sometimes present problems because of illusory promises. **EXAMPLE 12.6** Abe contracts to hire Chris for one year at $5,000 per month, reserving the right to cancel the contract at any time. On close examination of these words, you can see that Abe has not actually agreed to hire Chris, as Abe can cancel without liability before Chris starts performance. Abe has not given up the opportunity of hiring someone else. This contract is therefore illusory.

But if, instead, Abe reserves the right to cancel the contract at any time *after* Chris has begun performance by giving Chris *thirty days' notice,* the promise is not illusory. Abe, by saying that he will give Chris thirty days' notice, is relinquishing the opportunity (legal right) to hire someone else instead of Chris for a thirty-day period. If Chris works for one month and Abe then gives him thirty days' notice, Chris has an enforceable claim for two months' salary ($10,000). ■

12–1e Settlement of Claims

Businesspersons and others often enter into contracts to settle legal claims. It is important to understand the nature of the consideration given in these settlement agreements, or contracts. Commonly used settlement agreements include the *accord and satisfaction,* the *release,* and the *covenant not to sue.*

Accord and Satisfaction In an **accord and satisfaction,** a debtor offers to pay, and a creditor accepts, a lesser amount than the creditor originally claimed was owed. The *accord* is the agreement. In the accord, one party undertakes to give or perform, and the other to accept, in satisfaction of a claim, something other than that on which the parties originally agreed. *Satisfaction* is the performance (usually payment) that takes place after the accord is executed.

A basic rule governing such agreements is that there can be no satisfaction unless there is first an accord. In addition, for accord and satisfaction to occur, the amount of the debt *must be in dispute.*

Liquidated Debts. If a debt is *liquidated,* accord and satisfaction cannot take place. A **liquidated debt** is one whose amount has been ascertained, fixed, agreed on, settled, or exactly determined. **EXAMPLE 12.7** Barbara Kwan signs an installment loan contract with her banker. In the contract, Kwan agrees to pay a specified rate of interest on a specified amount of borrowed funds at monthly intervals for two years. Because both parties know the precise amount of the total obligation, it is a liquidated debt. ■

In the majority of states, a creditor's acceptance of a lesser sum than the entire amount of a liquidated debt is not satisfaction, and the balance of the debt is still legally owed. The reason for this rule is that the debtor has given no consideration to satisfy the obligation of paying the balance to the creditor. The debtor has a preexisting legal obligation to pay the entire debt. (Of course, even with liquidated debts, creditors often do negotiate debt settlement agreements with debtors for a lesser amount than was originally owed. Creditors sometimes even forgive or write off a liquidated debt as uncollectable.)

Unliquidated Debts. An **unliquidated debt** is the opposite of a liquidated debt. The amount of the debt is *not* settled, fixed, agreed on, ascertained, or determined, and reasonable persons

Accord and Satisfaction
A common means of settling a disputed claim, whereby a debtor offers to pay a lesser amount than the creditor purports to be owed.

Liquidated Debt A debt whose amount has been ascertained, fixed, agreed on, settled, or exactly determined.

KNOW THIS
Even with liquidated debts, creditors will often enter into settlement agreements that allow debtors to pay a lesser amount than was originally owed.

Unliquidated Debt A debt that is uncertain in amount.

may differ over the amount owed. In these circumstances, acceptance of payment of the lesser sum operates as a satisfaction, or discharge, of the debt because there is valid consideration. The parties give up a legal right to contest the amount in dispute.

Release

Release An agreement in which one party gives up the right to pursue a legal claim against another party.

A **release** is a contract in which one party forfeits the right to pursue a legal claim against the other party. It bars any further recovery beyond the terms stated in the release.

A release will generally be binding if it meets the following requirements:

1. The agreement is made in good faith.

2. The release contract is in a signed writing (required in many states).

3. The contract is accompanied by consideration.[4]

A person involved in an automobile accident may be asked to sign a release. Clearly, the person is better off knowing the extent of his or her injuries or damages before signing. **EXAMPLE 12.8** Kara's car is damaged in an accident caused by Raoul's negligence. Raoul offers to give Kara $3,000 if she will release him from further liability resulting from the accident. Kara agrees and signs the release.

If Kara later discovers that the repairs will cost $4,200, she cannot recover the additional amount from Raoul. Kara is limited to the $3,000 specified in the release because a valid contract was formed. Kara and Raoul both voluntarily agreed to the terms in a signed writing, and sufficient consideration was present. The consideration was the legal right to recover damages that Kara forfeited should her damages be more than $3,000, in exchange for Raoul's promise to give her $3,000. ■

Covenant Not to Sue

Covenant Not to Sue An agreement to substitute a contractual obligation for some other type of legal action based on a valid claim.

Unlike a release, a **covenant not to sue** does not always prevent further recovery. The parties simply substitute a contractual obligation for some other type of legal action based on a valid claim. Suppose in *Example 12.8* that Kara agrees not to sue Raoul for damages in a tort action if he will pay for the damage to her car. If Raoul fails to pay, Kara can bring an action for breach of contract.

As the following *Spotlight Case* illustrates, a covenant not to sue can form the basis for a dismissal of the claims of either party to the covenant.

Is it possible to limit one's liability after a car accident?

---

4. Under the Uniform Commercial Code (UCC), a written, signed waiver by an aggrieved party discharges any further liability for a breach, even without consideration.

SPOTLIGHT ON NIKE: CASE 12.1

Already, LLC v. Nike, Inc.

Supreme Court of the United States, __ U.S. __, 133 S.Ct. 721, 184 L.Ed.2d 553 (2013).

COMPANY PROFILE *Bill Bowerman was a track coach at the University of Oregon, and Phil Knight was an accountant in Portland, Oregon, who had been a track athlete on Bowerman's team. In 1964, the two men shook hands, pledged $500 each, and formed Blue Ribbon Sports to distribute athletic footwear manufactured by a Japanese company. A decade later, Blue Ribbon became Nike, Inc., adopted the familiar "Swoosh" logo, and began marketing shoes of its own design. Today, Nike's markets are global. In 2014, it reported revenue of over $27*

Will a plaintiff's covenant not to sue prevent the defendant from pursuing a counterclaim against the plaintiff?

billion. Nike is the official sponsor of the National Football League in the United States, as well as other athletes and sports teams around the world. Nike continues to design, make, and sell innovative footwear, including a line known as Air Force 1s.

FACTS Nike, Inc., designs, makes, and sells athletic footwear, including a line of shoes known as "Air Force 1." Already, LLC, also designs and markets athletic footwear, including the "Sugar" and "Soulja Boy" lines. Nike filed a suit in a federal district court against Already, alleging that Soulja Boys and Sugars infringed the Air Force 1 trademark. Already filed a counterclaim, contending that the Air Force 1 trademark was invalid.

While the suit was pending, Nike issued a covenant not to sue, promising not to raise any trademark claims against Already based on Already's existing footwear designs or any future Already designs that constituted a "colorable imitation" of Already's current products. Nike then filed a motion to dismiss its own claims and to dismiss Already's counterclaim. Already opposed the dismissal of its counterclaim, but the court granted Nike's motion. The U.S. Court of Appeals for the Second Circuit affirmed. Already appealed to the United States Supreme Court.

ISSUE Did Nike's covenant not to sue Already over the Air Force 1 trademark prevent Already from suing to establish that Nike's trademark was invalid?

DECISION Yes. The United States Supreme Court affirmed the judgment of the lower courts. Under the covenant not to sue, Nike could

not file a trademark infringement claim against Already, and Already could not assert that Nike's trademark was invalid.

REASON The Supreme Court looked at the wording of the covenant not to sue to determine whether Already's counterclaim was *moot*. (A matter is moot if it involves no actual controversy for the court to decide, and federal courts will dismiss moot cases.) Nike had unconditionally and irrevocably promised not to assert any trademark infringement claims against Already relating to the mark used on any of Already's current footwear products and similar future designs. Under the covenant's broad language, the Court noted, "It is hard to imagine a scenario that would potentially infringe Nike's trademark and yet not fall under the covenant." Therefore, further litigation of the trademark dispute was unnecessary, and dismissal was proper.

CRITICAL THINKING—Economic Consideration *Why would any party agree to a covenant not to sue?*

12–2 Promissory Estoppel

Sometimes, individuals rely on promises, and their reliance may form a basis for a court to infer contract rights and duties. Under the doctrine of **promissory estoppel** (also called *detrimental reliance*), a person who has reasonably and substantially relied on the promise of another can obtain some measure of recovery. Promissory estoppel allows a party to recover on a promise even though it was made *without consideration*. Under this doctrine, a court may enforce an otherwise unenforceable promise to avoid an injustice that would otherwise result.

Promissory Estoppel
A doctrine that can be used to enforce a promise when the promisee has justifiably relied on the promise and when justice will be better served by enforcing the promise.

12–2a Requirements to Establish Promissory Estoppel

For the doctrine of promissory estoppel to be applied, the following elements are required:

1. There must be a clear and definite promise.
2. The promisor should have expected that the promisee would rely on the promise.
3. The promisee reasonably relied on the promise by acting or refraining from some act.
4. The promisee's reliance was definite and resulted in substantial detriment.
5. Enforcement of the promise is necessary to avoid injustice.

If these requirements are met, a promise may be enforced even though it is not supported by consideration. In essence, the promisor (the offeror) will be **estopped** (barred or prevented) from asserting lack of consideration as a defense.

Promissory estoppel is similar in some ways to the doctrine of quasi contract that was discussed in a previous chapter. In both situations, a court is acting in the interests of equity and imposes contract obligations on the parties to prevent unfairness even though no actual contract exists. The difference is that with quasi contract, no promise was made at all. In contrast, with promissory estoppel, an otherwise unenforceable promise was made and relied on.

LEARNING OBJECTIVE 2
In what circumstances might a promise be enforced despite a lack of consideration?

Estopped Barred, impeded, or precluded.

12-2b Application of Promissory Estoppel

Promissory estoppel was originally applied to situations involving gifts (I promise to pay you $1,000 a week so that you will not have to work) and donations to charities (I promise to contribute $50,000 a year to the All Saints orphanage). Later, courts began to apply the doctrine in other situations, including business transactions, employment relationships, and disputes among family members.

CASE EXAMPLE 12.9 Jeffrey and Kathryn Dow own 125 acres of land in Corinth, Maine. The Dows regarded the land as their children's heritage, and the subject of the children's living on the land was often discussed within the family.

With the Dows' permission, their daughter Teresa installed a mobile home and built a garage on the land. After Teresa married Jarrod Harvey, the Dows agreed to finance the construction of a house on the land for the couple. When Jarrod died in a motorcycle accident, however, Teresa financed the house with his life insurance proceeds. The construction cost about $200,000.

Teresa then asked her parents for a deed to the property so that she could obtain a mortgage. They refused. Teresa sued her parents based on promissory estoppel. Maine's highest court ruled in Teresa's favor. The court reasoned that the Dows' support and encouragement of their daughter's construction of a house on the land "conclusively demonstrated" their intent to transfer it. For years, they had made general promises to convey the land to their children, including Teresa. Teresa had reasonably relied on their promise in financing construction of the house to her detriment ($200,000). The court concluded that enforcing the promise was the only way to avoid injustice in this situation.[5] ■

When must a property owner transfer a deed to his or her child?

12-3 Contractual Capacity

Contractual Capacity The capacity required by the law for a party who enters into a contract to be bound by that contract.

Contractual capacity is the legal ability to enter into a contractual relationship. Courts generally presume the existence of contractual capacity, but in some situations, capacity is lacking or may be questionable. A person who has been determined by a court to be mentally incompetent, for instance, cannot form a legally binding contract. In other situations, a party may have the capacity to enter into a valid contract but may also have the right to avoid liability under it. For instance, minors—or *infants,* as they are commonly referred to in the law—usually are not legally bound by contracts.

In this section, we look at the effect of youth, intoxication, and mental incompetence on contractual capacity.

12-3a Minors

Age of Majority The age (eighteen in most states) at which a person, formerly a minor, is recognized by law as an adult and is legally responsible for his or her actions.

Emancipation In regard to minors, the act of being freed from parental control.

Today, in almost all states, the **age of majority** (when a person is no longer a minor) for contractual purposes is eighteen years.[6] In addition, some states provide for the termination of minority on marriage.

Minority status may also be terminated by a minor's **emancipation,** which occurs when a child's parent or legal guardian relinquishes the legal right to exercise control over the child. Normally, minors who leave home to support themselves are considered emancipated. Several jurisdictions permit minors to petition a court for emancipation. For business purposes, a minor may petition a court to be treated as an adult.

The general rule is that a minor can enter into any contract that an adult can, provided that the contract is not one prohibited by law for minors (such as a contract involving the sale of alcoholic beverages or tobacco products). A contract entered into by a minor, however, is

---

5. *Harvey v. Dow*, 2011 ME 4, 11 A.3d 303 (2011).
6. The age of majority may still be twenty-one for other purposes, such as the purchase and consumption of alcohol.

voidable at the option of that minor, subject to certain exceptions (to be discussed shortly). To exercise the option to avoid a contract, a minor need only manifest (clearly show) an intention not to be bound by it. The minor "avoids" the contract by disaffirming it.

Disaffirmance   The legal avoidance, or setting aside, of a contractual obligation is referred to as **disaffirmance.** To disaffirm, a minor must express, through words or conduct, his or her intent not to be bound to the contract. The minor must disaffirm the entire contract, not merely a portion of it. For instance, a minor cannot decide to keep part of the goods purchased under a contract and return the remaining goods.

CASE EXAMPLE 12.10 Fifteen-year-old Morgan Kelly was a cadet in her high school's Navy Junior Reserve Officer Training Corps. As part of the program, she visited the U.S. Marine Corps training facility at Camp Lejeune, North Carolina. To enter the camp, she was required to sign a waiver that exempted the Marines from liability for any injuries arising from her visit. While participating in activities on the camp's confidence-building course, Kelly fell from the "Slide for Life" and suffered serious injuries. She filed a suit to recover her medical costs. The Marines asserted that Kelly could not recover because she had signed the waiver of liability. The court ruled in Kelly's favor. Liability waivers are generally enforceable contracts, but a minor can avoid a contract by disaffirming it. In this case, Kelly disaffirmed the waiver when she filed her suit to recover for the cost of her injuries.[7] ■

Note that an adult who enters into a contract with a minor cannot avoid his or her contractual duties on the ground that the minor can do so. Unless the minor exercises the option to disaffirm the contract, the adult party normally is bound by it.

The question in the following case was whether a minor had effectively disaffirmed an agreement to arbitrate with her employer.

---

7. *Kelly v. United States*, 809 F.Supp.2d 429 (E.D.N.C. 2011).

> **LEARNING OBJECTIVE 3**
>
> Does a minor have the capacity to enter into an enforceable contract? What does it mean to disaffirm a contract?

Disaffirmance The legal avoidance, or setting aside, of a contractual obligation.

CASE 12.2

PAK Foods Houston, LLC v. Garcia

Court of Appeals of Texas, Houston (14th District), 433 S.W.3d 171 (2014).

FACTS S.L., a sixteen-year-old minor, worked at a KFC Restaurant operated by PAK Foods Houston, LLC. PAK Foods' policy was to resolve any dispute with an employee through arbitration. At the employer's request, S.L. signed an acknowledgement of this policy. S.L was injured on the job and subsequently terminated her employment. S.L.'s mother, Marissa Garcia, filed a suit on S.L.'s behalf in a Texas state court against PAK Foods to recover the medical expenses for the injury. PAK Foods filed a motion to compel arbitration. The court denied the motion. "To the extent any agreement to arbitrate existed between S.L. and PAK Foods Houston, LLC, S.L. voided such agreement by filing this suit." PAK Foods appealed.

ISSUE Did S.L. disaffirm the agreement to arbitrate?

DECISION Yes. A state intermediate appellate court affirmed the decision of the lower court. A minor may disaffirm a contract at his or her option. S.L. opted to disaffirm the agreement to arbitrate.

REASON In Texas, the age of majority is eighteen years. S.L. was a sixteen-year-old minor when she signed the arbitration agreement,

When minors sign employment agreements with fast-food restaurants, how can they disaffirm those agreements?

and she was a minor throughout the time she was employed by PAK Foods. A contract entered into by a minor may be disaffirmed or ratified after the minor reaches the age of majority at his or her option. PAK Foods argued that S.L. had not signed an employment contract and had not notified PAK Foods that she was disaffirming the arbitration agreement. The appellate court held that "these distinctions do not alter the settled law that a minor may void a contract at her election." In response to PAK Foods's motion to compel arbitration, S.L. and her mother stated that "as S.L.'s disaffirmance of the Arbitration Agreement has manifestly occurred with her termination of employment and election to file suit, she cannot be bound by the terms of the Arbitration Agreement." This response was "a definitive disaffirmance of any agreement to arbitrate."

CRITICAL THINKING—Legal Consideration *Could PAK Foods successfully contend that S.L.'s minority does not bar enforcement of the arbitration agreement because medical expenses are necessaries? Discuss.*

Disaffirmance within a Reasonable Time. A contract can ordinarily be disaffirmed at any time during minority[8] or for a reasonable time after the minor reaches the age of majority. What constitutes a "reasonable" time may vary. If an individual fails to disaffirm an executed contract within a reasonable time after reaching the age of majority, a court will likely hold that the contract has been ratified (*ratification* will be discussed shortly).

A Minor's Obligations on Disaffirmance. All states' laws permit minors to disaffirm contracts (with certain exceptions), including executed contracts. However, state laws differ on the extent of a minor's obligations on disaffirmance.

Courts in most states hold that the minor need only return the goods (or other consideration) subject to the contract, provided the goods are in the minor's possession or control. Even if the minor returns damaged goods, the minor often is entitled to disaffirm the contract and obtain a refund of the purchase price.

A growing number of states place an additional duty on the minor to restore the adult party to the position she or he held before the contract was made. These courts may hold a minor responsible for damage, ordinary wear and tear, and depreciation of goods that the minor used prior to disaffirmance. **EXAMPLE 12.11** Sixteen-year-old Jay Dodd buys a truck for $5,900 from a used-car dealer. The truck develops mechanical problems nine months later, but Dodd continues to drive it until the engine blows up and the truck stops running. Dodd then disaffirms the contract and attempts to return the truck to the dealer for a refund of the full purchase price. In states that hold minors responsible for damage, Dodd can still disaffirm the contract, but he may only recover the depreciated value—not the purchase price—of the truck. ∎

Exceptions to a Minor's Right to Disaffirm

State courts and legislatures have carved out several exceptions to the minor's right to disaffirm. Some contracts, such as marriage contracts and contracts to enlist in the armed services, cannot be avoided. These exceptions are made for reasons of public policy.

In addition, although ordinarily minors can disaffirm contracts even when they have misrepresented their age, a growing number of states have enacted laws to prohibit disaffirmance in such situations. Other states prohibit disaffirmance by minors who misrepresented their age while engaged in business as adults.

Finally, a minor who enters into a contract for necessaries may disaffirm the contract but remains liable for the reasonable value of the goods. **Necessaries** include whatever is reasonably needed to maintain the minor's standard of living. In general, food, clothing, shelter, and medical services are necessaries. What is a necessary for one minor, however, may be a luxury for another, depending on the minors' customary living standard.

Ratification

In contract law, **ratification** is the act of accepting and giving legal force to an obligation that previously was not enforceable. A minor who has reached the age of majority can ratify a contract expressly or impliedly. *Express* ratification occurs when the individual, on reaching the age of majority, states orally or in writing that she or he intends to be bound by the contract. *Implied* ratification takes place when the minor, on reaching the age of majority, behaves in a manner inconsistent with disaffirmance.

EXAMPLE 12.12 Lin enters into a contract to sell her laptop to Andrew, a minor. Andrew does not disaffirm the contract. If, on reaching the age of majority, he writes a letter to Lin stating that he still agrees to buy the laptop, he has expressly ratified the contract. If, instead, Andrew takes possession of the laptop as a minor and continues to use it well after reaching the age of majority, he has impliedly ratified the contract. ∎

If a minor fails to disaffirm a contract within a reasonable time after reaching the age of majority, then a court must determine whether the conduct constitutes implied ratification or

If a minor buys a pickup truck, doesn't maintain it such that the engine explodes, can that minor obtain a full-purchase-price refund?

Necessaries Necessities required for life, such as food, shelter, clothing, and medical attention.

Ratification The acceptance or confirmation of an act or agreement that gives legal force to an obligation that previously was not enforceable.

---

8. In some states, however, a minor who enters into a contract for the sale of land cannot disaffirm the contract until she or he reaches the age of majority.

disaffirmance. Generally, courts presume that executed contracts (fully performed) are ratified and that executor contracts (not yet fully performed by both parties) are disaffirmed.

Parents' Liability   As a general rule, parents are not liable for the contracts made by minor children acting on their own, except contracts for necessaries, which the parents are legally required to provide. This is why businesses ordinarily require parents to cosign any contract made with a minor. The parents then become personally obligated to perform the conditions of the contract, even if their child avoids liability.

12–3b Intoxicated Persons

Intoxication is a condition in which a person's normal capacity to act or think is inhibited by alcohol or some other drug. A contract entered into by an intoxicated person can be either voidable or valid (and thus enforceable). If the person was sufficiently intoxicated to lack mental capacity, then the transaction may be voidable at the option of the intoxicated person, even if the intoxication was purely voluntary. If, despite intoxication, the person understood the legal consequences of the agreement, the contract is enforceable.

Courts look at objective indications of the intoxicated person's condition to determine if he or she possessed or lacked the required capacity. It is difficult to prove that a person's judgment was so severely impaired that he or she could not comprehend the legal consequences of entering into a contract. Therefore, courts rarely permit contracts to be avoided due to intoxication.

12–3c Mentally Incompetent Persons

Contracts made by mentally incompetent persons can be void, voidable, or valid. If a court has previously determined that a person is mentally incompetent and has appointed a guardian to represent the person, any contract made by that person is *void*—no contract exists. Only the guardian can enter into a binding contract on behalf of the mentally incompetent person.

If a court has not previously judged a person to be mentally incompetent but the person was incompetent at the time the contract was formed, the contract is *voidable* in most states. A contract is voidable if the person did not know that he or she was entering into the contract or lacked the mental capacity to comprehend its nature, purpose, and consequences. In such situations, the contract is voidable (or can be ratified) at the option of the mentally incompetent person but not at the option of the other party.

EXAMPLE 12.13 Larry agrees to sell his stock in Google, Inc., to Sergey for substantially less than its market value. At the time of the deal, Larry is confused about the purpose and details of the transaction, but he has not been declared incompetent. Nonetheless, if a court finds that Larry did not understand the nature and consequences of the contract due to a lack of mental capacity, he can avoid the sale. ∎

A contract entered into by a mentally ill person (whom a court has not previously declared incompetent) may also be *valid* if the person had capacity *at the time the contract was formed.* Some people who are incompetent due to age or illness have *lucid intervals*—temporary periods of sufficient intelligence, judgment, and will. During such intervals, they will be considered to have legal capacity to enter into contracts in the majority of states.

12–4 Legality

Legality is the fourth requirement for a valid contract to exist. For a contract to be valid and enforceable, it must be formed for a legal purpose. A contract to do something that is prohibited by federal or state statutory law is illegal and, as such, is void from the outset and thus

KNOW THIS

A minor's station in life (including financial position, social status, and lifestyle) is important in determining whether an item is a necessary or a luxury. For instance, clothing is a necessary, but if a minor from a low-income family contracts to purchase a $2,000 leather coat, a court may deem the coat a luxury. In this situation, the contract would not be for "necessaries."

unenforceable. Additionally, a contract to commit a tortious act (such as engage in fraudulent misrepresentation) or to commit an action that is contrary to public policy is illegal and unenforceable.

12–4a Contracts Contrary to Statute

Statutes often prescribe the terms of contracts. Some statutes set forth rules specifying which terms and clauses may be included in certain contracts and which are prohibited. Others prohibit certain contracts on the basis of their subject matter, the status of the contracting parties, or other factors. Next, we examine several ways in which contracts may be contrary to statute.

Contracts to Commit a Crime Any contract to commit a crime is in violation of a statute. Thus, a contract to sell illegal drugs in violation of criminal laws is unenforceable, as is a contract to hide a corporation's violation of the Dodd-Frank Wall Street Reform and Consumer Protection Act. Similarly, a contract to smuggle undocumented workers from another country into the United States for an employer is illegal, as is a contract to dump hazardous waste in violation of environmental laws.

Sometimes, the object or performance of a contract is rendered illegal by statute *after* the contract has been formed. In that situation, the contract is considered discharged (terminated) by law.

Usury Almost every state has a statute that sets the maximum rate of interest that can be charged for different types of transactions, including ordinary loans. A lender who makes a loan at an interest rate above the lawful maximum commits **usury.**

Usury Charging an illegal rate of interest.

Although usurious contracts are illegal, most states simply limit the interest that the lender may collect on the contract to the lawful maximum interest rate in that state. In a few states, the lender can recover the principal amount of the loan but no interest. In addition, states can make exceptions to facilitate business transactions. For instance, many states exempt corporate loans from the usury laws, and nearly all states allow higher interest rate loans for borrowers who could not otherwise obtain loans.

Gambling Gambling is the creation of risk for the purpose of assuming it. Traditionally, the states have deemed gambling contracts illegal and thus void. Today, many states allow (and regulate) certain forms of gambling, such as horse racing, video poker machines, and charity-sponsored bingo. In addition, nearly all states allow state-operated lotteries and gambling on Native American reservations. Even in states that permit certain types of gambling, though, courts often find that gambling contracts are illegal.

CASE EXAMPLE 12.14 Video poker machines are legal in Louisiana, but their use requires the approval of the state video gaming commission. Gaming Venture, Inc., did not obtain this approval before agreeing with Tastee Restaurant Corporation to install poker machines in some of its restaurants. For this reason, when Tastee allegedly reneged on the deal by refusing to install poker machines, a state court held that their agreement was an illegal gambling contract and therefore void.[9] ■

Licensing Statutes All states require members of certain professions—including physicians, lawyers, real estate brokers, accountants, architects, electricians, and stockbrokers—to have licenses. Some licenses are obtained only after extensive schooling and examinations, which indicate to the public that a special skill has been acquired. Others require only that the person obtaining the license be of good moral character and pay a fee.

Can any video poker vending machine distributor install such machines without a permit?

iStockPhoto.com/spxChrome

---

9. *Gaming Venture, Inc. v. Tastee Restaurant Corp.*, 996 So.2d 515 (La.App. 5 Cir. 2008).

Whether a contract with an unlicensed person is legal and enforceable depends on the purpose of the licensing statute. If the statute's purpose is to protect the public from unauthorized practitioners, then a contract involving an unlicensed practitioner generally is illegal and unenforceable. If the purpose is merely to raise government revenues, however, a contract with an unlicensed person may be enforced (and the unlicensed practitioner fined).

CASE EXAMPLE 12.15 The United Arab Emirates (UAE) held a competition for the design of a new embassy in Washington, D.C. Elena Sturdza—an architect licensed in Maryland but not in the District of Columbia—won. Sturdza and the UAE exchanged proposals, but the UAE stopped communicating with her before the parties had signed a contract. Later, Sturdza learned that the UAE had contracted with a District of Columbia architect to use another design. She filed a suit against the UAE for breach of contract.

Sturdza argued that the licensing statute should not apply to architects who submit plans in international architectural design competitions. The court held, however, that licensing requirements are necessary to ensure the safety of those who work in and visit buildings in the District of Columbia, as well as the safety of neighboring buildings. Because Sturdza was not a licensed architect in the District of Columbia, she could not recover on a contract to perform architectural services there.[10]

12–4b Contracts Contrary to Public Policy

Although contracts involve private parties, some are not enforceable because of the negative impact they would have on society. These contracts are said to be *contrary to public policy*. Examples include a contract to commit an immoral act, such as selling a child, and a contract that prohibits marriage (such as a contract to pay someone not to marry one's daughter). Business contracts that may be contrary to public policy include contracts in restraint of trade and unconscionable contracts or clauses.

Contracts in Restraint of Trade

The United States has a strong public policy favoring competition in the economy. Thus, contracts in restraint of trade (anticompetitive agreements) generally are unenforceable because they are contrary to public policy. Typically, such contracts also violate one or more federal or state antitrust laws.

An exception is recognized when the restraint is reasonable and is an ancillary (secondary, or subordinate) part of the contract. Such restraints often are included in contracts for the sale of an ongoing business and employment contracts.

Covenants Not to Compete and the Sale of an Ongoing Business. Many contracts involve a type of restraint called a **covenant not to compete,** or a restrictive covenant (promise). A covenant not to compete may be created when a merchant who sells a store agrees not to open a new store in a certain geographic area surrounding the old store. Such an agreement enables the seller to sell, and the purchaser to buy, the goodwill and reputation of an ongoing business without having to worry that the seller will open a competing business a block away. Provided the restrictive covenant is reasonable and is an ancillary part of the sale of an ongoing business, it is enforceable.

Covenants Not to Compete in Employment Contracts. Sometimes, agreements not to compete are included in **employment contracts.** People in middle-level and upper-level management positions commonly agree not to work for competitors and not to start a competing business for a specified period of time after terminating employment.

Such agreements are generally legal in most states so long as the specified period of time (of restraint) is not excessive in duration and the geographic restriction is reasonable. To be reasonable, a restriction on competition must protect a legitimate business interest and must

LEARNING OBJECTIVE 4
Under what circumstances will a covenant not to compete be enforced? When will such covenants not be enforced?

Covenant Not to Compete A contractual promise of one party to refrain from conducting business similar to that of another party for a certain period of time and within a specified geographical area.

Employment Contract A contract between an employer and an employee in which the terms and conditions of employment are stated.

---

10. *Sturdza v. United Arab Emirates,* 11 A.3d 251 (D.C.App. 2011).

not be any greater than necessary to protect that interest. What constitutes a reasonable time period may be different in the online environment than in conventional employment contracts. Because the geographical restrictions apply worldwide, the time restrictions may be shorter.

CASE EXAMPLE 12.16 An insurance firm in New York City, Brown & Brown, Inc., hired Theresa Johnson to perform actuarial analysis. On her first day of work, Johnson was asked to sign a nonsolicitation covenant, which prohibited her from soliciting or servicing any of Brown's clients for two years after the termination of her employment. Less than five years later, when Johnson's employment with Brown was terminated, she went to work for Lawley Benefits Group, LLC. Brown sued to enforce the covenant. A state appellate court ruled that the covenant was overly broad and unenforceable because it attempted to restrict Johnson from working for any of Brown's clients, without regard to whether she had had a relationship with those clients.[11] ▪

ETHICAL ISSUE

Are expansive noncompete agreements reducing worker mobility? You would probably expect workers to be asked to sign noncompete agreements that prevented them from, say, taking proprietary software code to a competitor. But would you expect a sandwich chain to require a worker to sign a noncompete agreement related to sandwich making? In the past, such agreements would not have been upheld in court. Today, they increasingly are. James Bessen, a writer for *The Atlantic*, estimates that the number of lawsuits over noncompete agreements and trade secrets has nearly tripled since 2000.

Employees in high-tech firms seem to be the most affected. They often sign noncompete agreements that "freeze" them out of their industry for two years after they leave a high-tech employer, forcing them to seek jobs in other industries where they cannot use key skills and knowledge. The result is that noncompete agreements tend to limit job opportunities for highly skilled workers. In other words, job mobility may be suffering from overly expansive noncompete agreements.

Enforcement Problems. The laws governing the enforceability of covenants not to compete vary significantly from state to state. California prohibits the enforcement of all covenants not to compete. In some states, such as Texas, such a covenant will not be enforced unless the employee has received some benefit in return for signing the noncompete agreement. This is true even if the covenant is reasonable as to time and area. If the employee receives no benefit, the covenant will be deemed void.

Reformation. Occasionally, depending on the jurisdiction, courts will *reform* covenants not to compete. If a covenant is found to be unreasonable in time or geographic area, the court may convert the terms into reasonable ones and then enforce the reformed covenant. This presents a problem, however, in that the judge has implicitly become a party to the contract. Consequently, courts usually resort to contract **reformation** only when necessary to prevent undue burdens or hardships.

Reformation A court-ordered correction of a written contract so that it reflects the true intentions of the parties.

PREVENTING LEGAL DISPUTES

A business clearly has a legitimate interest in having employees sign covenants not to compete and in preventing them from using the valuable skills and training provided by the business for the benefit of a competitor. The problem is that these covenants frequently lead to litigation. Moreover, it is difficult to predict what a court will consider reasonable in a given situation. Therefore, you need to be aware of the difficulties in enforcing noncompete agreements. Seek the advice of counsel in the relevant jurisdiction when drafting covenants not to compete. Avoid overreaching in terms of time and geographic restrictions, particularly if you are the manager of a high-tech or Web-based company. Consider using

---

11. *Brown & Brown, Inc. v. Johnson*, 980 N.Y.S.2d 631 (2014).

noncompete clauses only for key employees and, if necessary, offer them some compensation (consideration) for signing the agreement. If an employee signed a noncompete clause when he or she was hired, be sure to discuss the meaning of that clause and your expectations with the employee at the time of termination.

Unconscionable Contracts or Clauses Ordinarily, a court does not look at the fairness or equity of a contract, or, as discussed earlier, inquire into the adequacy of consideration. Persons are assumed to be reasonably intelligent, and the courts will not come to their aid just because they have made unwise or foolish bargains.

In certain circumstances, however, bargains are so oppressive that the courts relieve innocent parties of part or all of their duties. Such bargains are deemed **unconscionable**[12] because they are so unscrupulous or grossly unfair as to be "void of conscience."

The Uniform Commercial Code (UCC) incorporates the concept of unconscionability in its provisions with regard to the sale and lease of goods.[13] A contract can be unconscionable on either procedural or substantive grounds, as discussed in the following subsections and illustrated graphically in Exhibit 12–1.

Procedural Unconscionability. Procedural unconscionability often involves inconspicuous print, unintelligible language ("legalese"), or the lack of an opportunity to read the contract or ask questions about its meaning. This type of unconscionability typically arises when a party's lack of knowledge or understanding of the contract terms deprive him or her of any meaningful choice.

Procedural unconscionability can also occur when there is such a disparity in bargaining power between the two parties that the weaker party's consent is not voluntary. This type of situation often involves an **adhesion contract,** which is a standard-form contract written

> **Unconscionable (Contract or Clause)** A contract or clause that is void on the basis of public policy because one party was forced to accept terms that are unfairly burdensome and that unfairly benefit the other party.

> **Adhesion Contract** A standard-form contract in which the stronger party dictates the terms.

---

12. Pronounced un-*kon*-shun-uh-bul.
13. See UCC 2–302 and 2–719.

Exhibit 12–1 Unconscionability

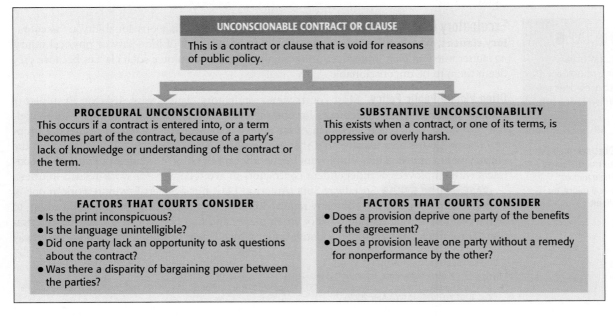

UNCONSCIONABLE CONTRACT OR CLAUSE
This is a contract or clause that is void for reasons of public policy.

PROCEDURAL UNCONSCIONABILITY
This occurs if a contract is entered into, or a term becomes part of the contract, because of a party's lack of knowledge or understanding of the contract or the term.

SUBSTANTIVE UNCONSCIONABILITY
This exists when a contract, or one of its terms, is oppressive or overly harsh.

FACTORS THAT COURTS CONSIDER
- Is the print inconspicuous?
- Is the language unintelligible?
- Did one party lack an opportunity to ask questions about the contract?
- Was there a disparity of bargaining power between the parties?

FACTORS THAT COURTS CONSIDER
- Does a provision deprive one party of the benefits of the agreement?
- Does a provision leave one party without a remedy for nonperformance by the other?

exclusively by one party (the dominant party) and presented to the other (the adhering party) on a take-it-or-leave-it basis. In other words, the adhering party (usually a buyer or borrower) has no opportunity to negotiate the terms of the contract. Not all adhesion contracts are unconscionable, only those that unreasonably favor the drafter.

CASE EXAMPLE 12.17 Roberto Basulto and Raquel Gonzalez responded to an ad they saw on Spanish-language television sponsored by Potamkin Dodge. Because the two men did not speak or read English, which Potamkin's staff knew, the deal was transacted in Spanish. Potamkin's staff explained the English-language purchase contract, but did not explain an accompanying arbitration agreement, which limited the buyers' damages but did not limit the dealer's damages. Basulto and Gonzalez signed the contract to buy a Dodge Caravan but did not fill in all of the blanks on the form.

A dispute arose when Potamkin later filled in a lower trade-in allowance than the parties had agreed to and refused to change it. The buyers returned the van—having driven it a total of seven miles—and asked for a return of their trade-in vehicle, but it had been sold. The buyers sued Potamkin, which sought arbitration. The court refused to enforce the arbitration agreement on the ground that it was unconscionable. The agreement was written in English and was not explained to the buyers in any language. The buyers therefore had not been given a meaningful opportunity to understand the bargain.[14] ■

Substantive Unconscionability. Substantive unconscionability occurs when contracts, or portions of contracts, are oppressive or overly harsh. Courts generally focus on provisions that deprive one party of the benefits of the agreement or leave that party without remedy for nonperformance by the other.

In *Case Example 12.17,* the court held that the contract was substantively, as well as procedurally, unconscionable. The contract was substantively unconscionable because the buyers were limited to seeking damages of $5,000 or less from the dealer, while the dealer could seek a higher amount of damages.

Substantive unconscionability can arise in a wide variety of business contexts. For instance, a contract clause that gives the business entity unrestricted access to the courts but requires the other party to arbitrate any dispute with the firm may be unconscionable. Similarly, contracts drafted by cell phone providers and insurance companies have been struck down as substantively unconscionable when they included provisions that were overly harsh or one sided.[15]

Exculpatory Clauses

Often closely related to the concept of unconscionability are **exculpatory clauses,** which release a party from liability in the event of monetary or physical injury, *no matter who is at fault.* Indeed, courts sometimes refuse to enforce such clauses because they deem them to be unconscionable.

Often Violate Public Policy. Most courts view exculpatory clauses with disfavor. Exculpatory clauses found in rental agreements for commercial property are frequently held to be contrary to public policy, and such clauses are almost always unenforceable in residential property leases. Courts also usually hold that exculpatory clauses are against public policy in the employment context. Thus, employers frequently cannot enforce exculpatory clauses in contracts with employees or independent contractors to avoid liability for work-related injuries.

CASE EXAMPLE 12.18 Speedway SuperAmerica, LLC, hired Sebert Erwin to work in one of its convenience stores. The company required Erwin, who had an eighth-grade education, to sign a contract stating that he was not an employee and had no right to workers' compensation. The contract also included a clause under which Erwin promised not to hold Speedway

LEARNING OBJECTIVE 5

What is an exculpatory clause? In what circumstances might exculpatory clauses be enforced? When will they not be enforced?

Exculpatory Clause A clause that releases a contractual party from liability in the event of monetary or physical injury, no matter who is at fault.

---

14. *Basulto v. Hialeah Automotive,* 141 So.3d 1145 (Fla. 2014).
15. See, for example, *Gatton v. T-Mobile USA, Inc.,* 152 Cal.App.4th 571, 61 Cal.Rptr.3d 344 (2007); and *Aul v. Golden Rule Insurance Co.,* 2007 WL 1695243 (Wis.App. 2007).

liable for anything that happened to him while working for the company. When Erwin was later injured on the job and sued Speedway for damages, the court held that the exculpatory clause was invalid because it was against public policy.[16] ■

When Courts Will Enforce Exculpatory Clauses. Courts do enforce exculpatory clauses if they are reasonable, do not violate public policy, and do not protect parties from liability for intentional misconduct. The language used must not be ambiguous, and the parties must have been in relatively equal bargaining positions. See this chapter's *Managerial Strategy* feature for suggestions on drafting exculpatory clauses that will not be considered unconscionable.

Businesses such as health clubs, racetracks, amusement parks, skiing facilities, horse-rental operations, golf-cart concessions, and skydiving organizations frequently use exculpatory clauses to limit their liability for patrons' injuries. Because these services are not essential, the firms offering them are sometimes considered to have no relative advantage in bargaining strength, and anyone contracting for their services is considered to do so voluntarily. Courts also may enforce reasonable exculpatory clauses in loan documents, real estate contracts, and trust agreements.

In the following case, the court considered whether an exculpatory clause that released "any Event sponsors and their agents and employees" from liability for future negligence was ambiguous.

Can a convenience store company require its employees to sign contracts that state that those employees have no rights to workers' compensation?

---

16. *Speedway SuperAmerica, LLC v. Erwin*, 250 S.W.3d 339 (Ky. 2008).

CASE 12.3

Holmes v. Multimedia KSDK, Inc.
Missouri Court of Appeals, Eastern District, Division 2, 395 S.W.3d 557 (2013).

FACTS Colleen Holmes signed an entry form for the Susan G. Komen Race for the Cure to be held in June 2009 in St. Louis, Missouri. The form included a "RACE WAIVER AND RELEASE" clause under which Holmes agreed to release "any Event sponsors and their agents and employees . . . for any injury or damages" that Holmes might suffer in connection with her participation in the race. Among other causes, the release applied to injury or damages caused by "negligence of the [sponsors]."

Is a waiver of negligence liability that appears on an entry form for a foot race enforceable?

Multimedia KSDK, Inc., was one of the race sponsors and also broadcasted the race. During the event, Holmes was injured when she tripped and fell over a Multimedia audiovisual box. Multimedia employees had placed the box on the ground without barricades or warnings of its presence. Holmes filed a suit in a Missouri state court against Multimedia, alleging negligence. The court entered a judgment in Multimedia's favor, and Holmes appealed.

ISSUE Did the exculpatory clause that Holmes signed clearly release Multimedia from liability for negligence?

DECISION Yes. The state intermediate appellate court affirmed the lower court's judgment in favor of Multimedia.

REASON The appellate court held that the language used in the exculpatory clause clearly released all sponsors and their agents and employees without exclusion from liability for future negligence. The reviewing court was not persuaded by Holmes's argument that the language in the release was ambiguous "because it did not specifically name the individuals and entities released."

Further, "a release that releases claims against 'any and all persons' is unambiguous and enforceable . . . and it is not necessary that the release identify those persons by name or otherwise." The reviewing court noted that while public policy disfavors releases from liability for future negligence, it does not prohibit them. All that is necessary is "there must be no doubt that a reasonable person agreeing to an exculpatory clause actually understands what future claims he or she is waiving." Such was the situation here.

CRICITAL THINKING—Social Consideration *At the time Holmes signed the release, Multimedia had not yet become a sponsor of the event. Should this fact have rendered the clause unenforceable? Explain.*

MANAGERIAL STRATEGY   **Creating Liability Waivers That Are Not Unconscionable**

Management Faces a Legal Issue

Blanket liability waivers that absolve a business from virtually every event, even those caused by the business's own negligence, are usually unenforceable because they are unconscionable. Exculpatory waivers are common, nonetheless. We observe such waivers in gym memberships, on ski lift tickets, on admissions tickets to sporting events, and in simple contracts for the use of campgrounds.

Typically, courts view liability waivers as voluntarily bargained for whether or not they have been read. Thus, a waiver included in the fine print on the back of an admission ticket or on an entry sign to a stadium may be upheld. In general, if such waivers are unambiguous and conspicuous, the assumption is that patrons have had a chance to read them and have accepted their terms.

What the Courts Say

Cases challenging liability waivers have been brought against sky diving operations, skiing operations, bobsledding operations, white-water rafting companies, and health clubs. For example, in *Bergin v. Wild Mountain, Inc.,*[a] an appellate court in Minnesota upheld a ski resort's liability waiver. In that case, the plaintiff hit a snowmaking mound, which was "an inherent risk of skiing." Before the accident, the plaintiff had stated that he knew "that an inherent risk of serious injury in downhill skiing was hitting snowmaking mounds." Furthermore, he had not rejected the season pass that contained the resort's exculpatory clause. Thus, the ski resort prevailed.

While most liability waivers have survived legal challenges, some have not. In *Bagley v. Mt. Bachelor, Inc.,*[b] the Supreme Court of Oregon ruled against a ski resort's "very broad" liability waiver. The case involved an 18-year-old, Myles Bagley, who was paralyzed from the waist down after a snowboarding accident at Mt. Bachelor ski resort. The season pass that Bagley signed included a liability waiver. The waiver stated that the signer agreed not to sue the resort for injury even if "caused by negligence."

Bagley argued that the resort had created a dangerous condition because of the way it had set up a particular ski jump. He sued for $21.5 million and eventually won the right to go forward with his lawsuit. The Oregon Supreme Court found that, for various reasons, enforcement of the release would have been unconscionable. "Because the release is unenforceable, genuine issues of fact exist that preclude summary judgment in defendant's favor."

MANAGERIAL IMPLICATIONS

Whether you manage a campground, a ski resort, a white-water rafting company, or any other enterprise that caters to those engaged in physical activity, you should make sure that any explicit liability waivers are not overly broad. That is, the waivers should not attempt to remove all liability for damages to the signing parties. For instance, waivers should not attempt to cover malicious or intentional acts by the company or its employees.

a. 2014 WL 996788 (Minn.App. 2014).
b. 356 Or. 543, 340 P.3d 27 (Or. Sup.Ct. 2014).

12–5 The Effect of Illegality

In general, an illegal contract is void—that is, the contract is deemed never to have existed, and the courts will not aid either party. In most illegal contracts, both parties are considered to be equally at fault—*in pari delicto.*[17] If the contract is executory (not yet fulfilled), neither party can enforce it. If it has been executed, neither party can recover damages.

The courts usually are not concerned if one wrongdoer in an illegal contract is unjustly enriched at the expense of the other. The main reason for this hands-off attitude is a belief that a plaintiff who has broken the law by entering into an illegal bargain should not be allowed to obtain help from the courts. Another justification is the hoped-for deterrent effect: a plaintiff who suffers a loss because of an illegal bargain will presumably be deterred from entering into similar illegal bargains in the future.

There are exceptions to the general rule that neither party to an illegal bargain can sue for breach and neither party can recover for performance rendered. We look at these exceptions here.

17. Pronounced in-*pah*-ree deh-*lick*-tow.

12-5a Justifiable Ignorance of the Facts

Sometimes, one of the parties to a contract has no reason to know that the contract is illegal and thus is relatively innocent. That party can often recover any benefits conferred in a partially executed contract. The courts will not enforce the contract but will allow the parties to return to their original positions.

A court may sometimes permit an innocent party who has fully performed under a contract to enforce the contract against the guilty party. **EXAMPLE 12.19** A trucking company contracts with Gillespie to carry crates filled with goods to a specific destination for a normal fee of $5,000. The trucker delivers the crates and later finds out that they contained illegal goods. Although the shipment, use, and sale of the goods are illegal under the law, the trucker, being an innocent party, can normally still legally collect the $5,000 from Gillespie. ■

12-5b Members of Protected Classes

When a statute is clearly designed to protect a certain class of people, a member of that class can enforce a contract in violation of the statute even though the other party cannot. **EXAMPLE 12.20** Statutes prohibit certain employees (such as flight attendants or pilots) from working more than a specified number of hours per month. An employee who is required to work more than the maximum can recover for those extra hours of service. ■

Other examples of statutes designed to protect a particular class of people are state statutes that regulate the sale of insurance. If an insurance company violates a statute when selling insurance, the purchaser can still enforce the policy and recover from the insurer.

12-5c Withdrawal from an Illegal Agreement

If the illegal part of a bargain has not yet been performed, the party rendering performance can withdraw from the contract and recover the performance or its value. **EXAMPLE 12.21** Marta and Andy decide to wager (illegally) on the outcome of a boxing match. Each deposits $1,000 with a stakeholder, who agrees to pay the winner of the bet. At this point, each party has performed part of the agreement. Before payment occurs, either party is entitled to withdraw from the agreement by giving notice to the stakeholder of his or her withdrawal. ■

12-5d Severable, or Divisible, Contracts

A contract that is *severable*, or divisible, consists of distinct parts that can be performed separately, with separate consideration provided for each part. With an *indivisible* contract, in contrast, complete performance by each party is essential, even if the contract contains a number of seemingly separate provisions.

When two persons place an illegal bet on the outcome of a boxing match, can either withdraw from the wager?

If a contract is divisible into legal and illegal portions, a court may enforce the legal portion but not the illegal one, so long as the illegal portion does not affect the essence of the bargain. This approach is consistent with the basic policy of enforcing the legal intentions of the contracting parties whenever possible.

EXAMPLE 12.22 Cole signs an employment contract that is valid but includes an overly broad and thus illegal covenant not to compete. In that situation, a court might find the employment contract enforceable but reform the unreasonably broad covenant by converting its terms into reasonable ones. Alternatively, the court could declare the covenant illegal (and thus void) and enforce the remaining employment terms. ■

12-5e Fraud, Duress, or Undue Influence

Often, one party to an illegal contract is more at fault than the other. When one party uses fraud, duress, or undue influence to induce the other party to enter into an agreement, the second party will be allowed to recover for the performance or its value.

Reviewing . . . Consideration, Capacity, and Legality

Renee Beaver started racing go-karts competitively in 2015, when she was fourteen. Many of the races required her to sign an exculpatory clause to participate. She or her parents regularly signed such clauses. In 2017, right before her birthday, Renee participated in the annual Elkhart Grand Prix, a series of races in Elkhart, Indiana. During the event in which she drove, a piece of foam padding used as a course barrier was torn from its base and ended up on the track. A portion of the padding struck Beaver in the head, and another portion was thrown into oncoming traffic, causing a multikart collision during which she sustained severe injuries. Beaver filed an action against the race organizers for negligence. The organizers could not locate the exculpatory clause that Beaver had supposedly signed. Race organizers argued that she must have signed one to enter the race, but even if she had not signed one, her actions showed her intent to be bound by its terms. Using the information presented in the chapter, answer the following questions.

1. Did Beaver have the contractual capacity to enter into a contract with an exculpatory clause? Why or why not?

2. Assuming that Beaver did, in fact, sign the exculpatory clause, did she later disaffirm or ratify the contract? Explain.

3. Now assume that Beaver had stated that she was eighteen years old at the time she signed the exculpatory clause. How might this affect her ability to disaffirm or ratify the contract?

4. Suppose Beaver can prove that she did not actually sign an exculpatory clause and this fact convinces race organizers to pursue a settlement. They offer to pay Beaver one-half of the amount that she is claiming in damages if she now signs a release of all claims. Because Beaver is young and the full effect of her injuries may not yet be clear, what other type of settlement agreement might she prefer? What is the consideration to support any settlement agreement that Beaver enters into with the race organizers?

DEBATE THIS

■ After agreeing to an exculpatory clause or purchasing some item, minors often seek to avoid the contracts. Today's minors are far from naïve and should not be allowed to avoid their contractual obligations.

Key Terms

accord and satisfaction 289

adhesion contract 299

age of majority 292

consideration 286

contractual capacity 292

covenant not to compete 297

covenant not to sue 290

disaffirmance 293

emancipation 292

employment contract 297

estopped 291

exculpatory clause 300

forbearance 286

liquidated debt 289

necessaries 294

past consideration 288

promissory estoppel 291

ratification 294

reformation 298

release 290

rescission 288

unconscionable 299

unliquidated debt 289

usury 296

Chapter Summary: Consideration, Capacity, and Legality

Consideration	**1.** *Elements of consideration*—
	   a. Something of *legally sufficient value* must be given in exchange for a promise.
	   b. There must be a bargained-for exchange.
	 2. *Legal sufficiency and adequacy of consideration*—Legal sufficiency means that something of legal value must be given in exchange for a promise. Adequacy relates to "how much" consideration is given and whether a fair bargain was reached. Courts will inquire into the adequacy of consideration only when fraud, undue influence, duress, or unconscionability may be involved.
	 3. *Contracts that lack consideration*—Consideration is lacking in the following situations:
	   a. Preexisting duty—A promise to do what one already has a legal duty to do is not legally sufficient consideration for a new contract.
	   b. Past consideration—Actions or events that have already taken place do not constitute legally sufficient consideration.
	   c. Illusory promises—When the nature or extent of performance is too uncertain, the promise is rendered illusory (without consideration and unenforceable).
	 4. *Settlement of claims*—Disputes may be settled by the following, which are enforceable provided there is consideration:
	   a. Accord and satisfaction—An *accord* is an agreement in which a debtor offers to pay a lesser amount than the creditor claims is owed. *Satisfaction* takes place when the accord is executed.
	   b. Release—An agreement in which, for consideration, a party forfeits the right to seek further recovery beyond the terms specified in the release.
	   c. Covenant not to sue—An agreement not to sue on a present, valid claim.

Promissory Estoppel	The equitable doctrine of promissory estoppel applies when a promisor should have expected a promise to induce definite and substantial action or forbearance by the promisee, and the promisee does act in reliance on the promise. Such a promise is binding, even though there is no consideration, if injustice can be avoided only by enforcement of the promise. Also known as the doctrine of *detrimental reliance*.

CONTRACTUAL CAPACITY

Minors	**1.** *General rule*—Contracts with minors are voidable at the option of the minor.
	 2. *Disaffirmance*—The legal avoidance of a contractual obligation.
	   a. Disaffirmance can take place (in most states) at any time during minority and within a reasonable time after the minor has reached the age of majority.
	   b. The minor must disaffirm the entire contract, not just part of it.
	   c. When disaffirming executed contracts, the minor has a duty to return the received goods if they are still in the minor's control or (in some states) to pay their reasonable value.
	   d. A minor who has misrepresented her or his age will be denied the right to disaffirm by some courts.
	   e. A minor may disaffirm a contract for necessaries but remains liable for the reasonable value of the goods.
	 3. *Ratification*—The acceptance, or affirmation, of a legal obligation.
	   a. Express ratification—Occurs when the minor, in writing or orally, explicitly assumes the obligations imposed by the contract.
	   b. Implied ratification—Occurs when the conduct of the minor is inconsistent with disaffirmance or when the minor fails to disaffirm an executed contract within a reasonable time after reaching the age of majority.
	 4. *Parents' liability*—Generally, except for contracts for necessaries, parents are not liable for the contracts made by minor children acting on their own.
	 5. *Emancipation*—Occurs when a child's parent or legal guardian relinquishes the legal right to exercise control over the child. Normally, minors who leave home to support themselves are considered emancipated. In some jurisdictions, minors are permitted to petition a court for emancipation.

Intoxicated Persons	**1.** A contract entered into by an intoxicated person is voidable at the option of the intoxicated person if the person was sufficiently intoxicated to lack mental capacity, even if the intoxication was voluntary. **2.** A contract with an intoxicated person is enforceable if, despite being intoxicated, the person understood the legal consequences of entering into the contract.
Mentally Incompetent Persons	**1.** A contract made by a person previously judged by a court to be mentally incompetent is void. **2.** A contract made by a person who is mentally incompetent, but has not been previously declared incompetent by a court, is voidable at the option of that person.

Continues

	LEGALITY
Contracts Contrary to Statute	1. *Usury*—Usury occurs when a lender makes a loan at an interest rate above the lawful maximum, which varies from state to state. 2. *Gambling*—Gambling contracts that violate state statutes are deemed illegal and thus void. 3. *Licensing statutes*—Contracts entered into by persons who do not have a license, when one is required by statute, will not be enforceable unless the underlying purpose of the statute is to raise government revenues (and not to protect the public from unauthorized practitioners).
Contracts Contrary to Public Policy	1. *Contracts in restraint of trade*—Contracts to restrain free competition are illegal and prohibited by statutes. An exception is a *covenant not to compete*. Such covenants usually are enforced by the courts if the terms are secondary to a contract (such as a contract for the sale of a business or an employment contract) and are reasonable as to time and area of restraint. Courts tend to scrutinize covenants not to compete closely and, at times, may reform them if they are overly broad rather than declaring the entire covenant unenforceable. 2. *Unconscionable contracts and clauses*—When a contract or contract clause is so unfair that it is oppressive to one party, it may be deemed unconscionable. As such, it is illegal and cannot be enforced. 3. *Exculpatory clauses*—An exculpatory clause releases a party from liability in the event of monetary or physical injury, no matter who is at fault. In certain situations, exculpatory clauses may be contrary to public policy and thus unenforceable.
	EFFECT OF ILLEGALITY
General Rule	In general, an illegal contract is void, and the courts will not aid either party when both parties are considered to be equally at fault *(in pari delicto)*. If the contract is executory, neither party can enforce it. If the contract is executed, neither party can recover damages.
Exceptions	Several exceptions exist to the general rule that neither party to an illegal bargain will be able to recover. In the following situations, the court may grant recovery: 1. *Justifiable ignorance of the facts*—When one party to the contract is relatively innocent. 2. *Members of protected classes*—When one party to the contract is a member of a group of persons protected by a particular statute. 3. *Withdrawal from an illegal agreement*—When either party seeks to recover consideration given for an illegal contract before the illegal act is performed. 4. *Severable, or divisible, contracts*—When the court can divide the contract into illegal and legal portions and the illegal portion is not essential to the bargain. 5. *Fraud, duress, or undue influence*—When one party was induced to enter into an illegal bargain through fraud, duress, or undue influence.

Issue Spotters

1. In September, Sharyn agrees to work for Totem Productions, Inc., at $500 a week for a year beginning January 1. In October, Sharyn is offered $600 a week for the same work by Umber Shows, Ltd. When Sharyn tells her boss at Totem about the other offer, he tears up their contract and agrees that Sharyn will be paid $575. Is the new contract binding? Explain. (See *Consideration*.)

2. Sun Airlines, Inc., prints on its tickets that it is not liable for any injury to a passenger caused by the airline's negligence. If the cause of an accident is found to be the airline's negligence, can it use the clause as a defense to liability? Why or why not? (See *Legality*.)

—**Check your answers to the *Issue Spotters* against the answers provided in Appendix D at the end of this text.**

Learning Objectives Check

1. What is consideration? What is required for consideration to be legally sufficient?
2. In what circumstances might a promise be enforced despite a lack of consideration?
3. Does a minor have the capacity to enter into an enforceable contract? What does it mean to disaffirm a contract?
4. Under what circumstances will a covenant not to compete be enforced? When will such covenants not be enforced?
5. What is an exculpatory clause? In what circumstances might exculpatory clauses be enforced? When will they not be enforced?

—**Answers to the even-numbered *Learning Objectives Check* questions can be found in Appendix E at the end of this text.**

Business Scenarios and Case Problems

12–1. Contracts by Minors. Kalen is a seventeen-year-old minor who has just graduated from high school. He is attending a university two hundred miles from home and has contracted to rent an apartment near the university for one year at $500 per month. He is working at a convenience store to earn enough income to be self-supporting. After living in the apartment and paying monthly rent for four months, he becomes involved in a dispute with his landlord. Kalen, still a minor, moves out and returns the key to the landlord. The landlord wants to hold Kalen liable for the balance of the payments due under the lease. Discuss fully Kalen's liability in this situation. (See *Contractual Capacity*.)

12–2. Disaffirmance. J.T., a minor, is a motocross competitor. At Monster Mountain MX Park, he signed a waiver of liability to "hold harmless the park for any loss due to negligence." Riding around the Monster Mountain track, J.T. rode over a blind jump, became airborne, and crashed into a tractor that he had not seen until he was in the air. To recover for his injuries, J.T. filed a suit against Monster Mountain, alleging negligence for its failure to remove the tractor from the track. Does the liability waiver bar this claim? Explain. [*J.T. v. Monster Mountain, LLC*, 754 F.Supp.2d 1323 (M.D.Ala. 2010)] (See *Contractual Capacity*.)

12–3. Business Case Problem with Sample Answer— Unconscionable Contracts or Clauses. Geographic Expeditions, Inc. (GeoEx), which guided climbs up Mount Kilimanjaro, required climbers to sign a release to participate in an expedition. The form required any disputes to be submitted to arbitration in San Francisco and limited damages to the cost of the trip. GeoEx told climbers that the terms were nonnegotiable and that other travel firms imposed the same terms. Jason Lhotka died on a GeoEx climb. His mother filed a suit against GeoEx. GeoEx sought arbitration. Was the arbitration clause unconscionable? Why or why not? [*Lhotka v. Geographic Expeditions, Inc.*, 181 Cal.App.4th 816, 104 Cal.Rptr.3d 844 (1 Dist. 2010)] (See *Legality*.)

—**For a sample answer to Problem 12–3, go to Appendix F at the end of this text.**

12–4. Mental Incompetence. Dorothy Drury suffered from dementia and chronic confusion. When she became unable to manage her own affairs, including decisions about medical and financial matters, her son Eddie arranged for her to move to an assisted living facility. During admission, she signed a residency agreement, which included an arbitration clause. After she sustained injuries in a fall at the facility, a suit was filed to recover damages. The facility asked the court to compel arbitration. Was Dorothy bound to the residency agreement? Discuss. [*Drury v. Assisted Living Concepts, Inc.*, 245 Or.App. 217, 262 P.3d 1162 (2011)] (See *Contractual Capacity*.)

12–5. Licensing Statutes. PEMS Co. International, Inc., agreed to find a buyer for Rupp Industries, Inc., for a commission of 2 percent of the purchase price, which was to be paid by the buyer. Using PEMS's services, an investment group bought Rupp for $20 million and changed its name to Temp-Air, Inc. PEMS asked Temp-Air to pay a commission on the sale. Temp-Air refused, arguing that PEMS had acted as a broker in the deal without a license. The applicable statute defines a broker as any person who deals with the sale of a business. If this statute was intended to protect the public, can PEMS collect its commission? Explain. [*PEMS Co. International, Inc. v. Temp-Air, Inc.*, __ N.W.2d __, 2011 WL 69098 (Minn.App. 2011)] (See *Legality*.)

12–6. Spotlight on Kansas City Chiefs—Consideration. On Brenda Sniezek's first day of work for the Kansas City Chiefs Football Club, she signed a document that purported to compel arbitration of any disputes that she might have with the Chiefs. In the document, Sniezek agreed to comply at all times with and be bound by the constitution and bylaws of the National Football League (NFL). She agreed to refer all disputes to the NFL commissioner for a binding decision and to release the Chiefs and others from any related claims. Nowhere in the document did the Chiefs agree to do anything. Was there consideration for the arbitration provision? Explain. [*Sniezek v. Kansas City Chiefs Football Club*, 402 S.W.3d 580 (Mo.App. W.D. 2013)] (See *Consideration*.)

12–7. Minors. D.V.G. (a minor) was injured in a one-car auto accident in Hoover, Alabama. The vehicle was covered by an insurance policy issued by Nationwide Mutual Insurance Co. Stan Brobston, D.V.G.'s attorney, accepted Nationwide's offer of $50,000 on D.V.G.'s behalf. Before the settlement could be submitted to an Alabama state court for approval, D.V.G. died from injuries received in a second, unrelated auto accident. Nationwide argued that it was not bound to the settlement because a minor lacks the capacity to contract and cannot enter into a binding settlement without court approval. Should Nationwide be bound to the settlement? Why or why not? [*Nationwide Mutual Insurance Co. v. Wood*, 121 So.3d 982 (Ala. 2013)] (See *Contractual Capacity*.)

12–8. Consideration. Citynet, LLC, established an employee incentive plan "to enable the Company to attract and retain experienced individuals." The plan provided that a participant who left Citynet's employment was entitled to "cash out" his or her entire vested balance. (When an employee's rights to a particular benefit become *vested*, they belong to that employee and cannot be taken away. The vested balance refers to the part of an account that goes with the employee if he or she leaves the company.) When Citynet employee Ray Toney terminated his employment, he asked to redeem his $87,000.48

vested balance. Citynet refused, citing a provision of the plan that limited redemptions to no more than 20 percent annually. Toney filed a suit in a West Virginia state court against Citynet, alleging breach of contract. Citynet argued that the plan was not a contract but a discretionary bonus over which Citynet had sole discretion. Was the plan a contract? If so, was it bilateral or unilateral, and what was the consideration? [*Citynet, LLC v. Toney,* __ W.Va. __, __ S.E.2d __, 2015 WL 591519 (2015)] (See *Consideration.*)

12–9. A Question of Ethics—Promissory Estoppel. Claudia Aceves borrowed $845,000 from U.S. Bank to buy a home. Less than two years into the loan, she could no longer afford the monthly payments. The bank notified her that it planned to foreclose on her home. (Foreclosure is a process that allows a lender to repossess and sell the property that secures a loan.) The bank offered to modify Aceves's mortgage if she would forgo bankruptcy. In reliance on the bank's promise, she agreed. Once she withdrew the filing, however, the bank foreclosed and began eviction proceedings. Aceves filed a suit against the bank for promissory estoppel. [*Aceves v. U.S. Bank, N.A.,* 192 Cal.App.4th 218, 120 Cal.Rptr.3d 507 (2 Dist. 2011)] (See *Promissory Estoppel.*)

1. Could Aceves succeed in her claim of promissory estoppel? Why or why not?

2. Did Aceves or U.S. Bank behave unethically? Discuss.

Critical Thinking and Writing Assignments

12–10. Business Law Critical Thinking Group Assignment. Melissa Faraj owns a lot and wants to build a house according to a particular set of plans and specifications. She solicits bids from building contractors and receives three bids: one from Carlton for $160,000, one from Feldberg for $158,000, and one from Siegel for $153,000. She accepts Siegel's bid. One month after beginning construction of the house, Siegel contacts Faraj and tells her that because of inflation and a recent price hike for materials, he will not finish the house unless Faraj agrees to pay an extra $13,000. Faraj reluctantly agrees to pay the additional sum. (See *Consideration.*)

1. One group will discuss whether a contractor can ever raise the price of completing construction based on inflation and the rising cost of materials.

2. A second group will assume that after the house is finished, Faraj refuses to pay the extra $13,000. The group will decide whether Faraj is legally required to pay this additional amount.

3. A third group will discuss what types of extraordinary difficulties could arise during construction that would justify a contractor's charging more than the original bid.

13

LEARNING OBJECTIVES

The five Learning Objectives *below are designed to help improve your understanding of the chapter. After reading this chapter, you should be able to answer the following questions:*

1. In what types of situations might voluntary consent to a contract's terms be lacking?

2. What is the difference between a unilateral and a bilateral mistake?

3. What are the elements of fraudulent misrepresentation?

4. What contracts must be in writing to be enforceable?

5. What is parol evidence? When is it admissible to clarify the terms of a written contract?

Defenses to Contract Enforceability

"Understanding is a two-way street."

ELEANOR ROOSEVELT
1884–1962
(FIRST LADY OF THE UNITED STATES, 1933–1945)

An otherwise valid contract may still be unenforceable if the parties have not genuinely agreed to its terms. The lack of voluntary consent is a *defense* to the enforcement of a contract. As Eleanor Roosevelt stated in the chapter-opening quotation, "Understanding is a two-way street." If one party does not voluntarily consent to the terms of a contract, then there is no genuine "meeting of the minds," and the law will not normally enforce the contract, as we discuss in the first part of this chapter.

A contract that is otherwise valid may also be unenforceable if it is not in the proper form. For instance, if a contract is required by law to be in writing and there is no written evidence of the contract, it may not be enforceable. In the second part of this chapter, we examine the kinds of contracts that require a writing under what is called the *Statute of Frauds*. The chapter concludes with a discussion of the parol evidence rule, under which courts determine the admissibility at trial of evidence extraneous (external) to written contracts.

13-1 Voluntary Consent

Voluntary consent (assent) may be lacking because of mistake, fraudulent misrepresentation, undue influence, or duress. Generally, a party who demonstrates that he or she did not genuinely agree to the terms of a contract can choose either to carry out the contract or to rescind (cancel) it and thus avoid the entire transaction. This is one reason why many contracts include definitions of important terms.

LEARNING OBJECTIVE 1

In what types of situations might voluntary consent to a contract's terms be lacking?

13–1a Mistakes

We all make mistakes, so it is not surprising that mistakes are made when contracts are created. In certain circumstances, contract law allows a contract to be avoided on the basis of mistake. It is important to distinguish between *mistakes of fact* and *mistakes of value or quality*. Only a mistake of fact may allow a contract to be avoided.

EXAMPLE 13.1 Paco buys a violin from Beverly for $250. Although the violin is very old, neither party believes that it is valuable. Later, however, an antiques dealer informs the parties that the violin is rare and worth thousands of dollars. Here, both parties were mistaken, but the mistake is a mistake of *value* rather than a mistake of *fact* that warrants contract rescission. Therefore, Beverly cannot rescind the contract. ■

Mistakes of fact occur in two forms—*unilateral* and *bilateral (mutual)*. A unilateral mistake is made by only one of the contracting parties, whereas a mutual mistake is made by both. We look at these two types of mistakes next and illustrate them graphically in Exhibit 13–1.

Unilateral Mistakes A **unilateral mistake** occurs when only one party is mistaken as to a *material fact*—that is, a fact important to the subject matter of the contract. Generally, a unilateral mistake does not give the mistaken party any right to relief from the contract. In other words, the contract normally is enforceable against the mistaken party.

EXAMPLE 13.2 Elena intends to sell her jet ski for $2,500. When she learns that Chin is interested in buying a used jet ski, she sends him an e-mail offering to sell the jet ski to him. When typing the e-mail, however, she mistakenly keys in the price of $1,500. Chin immediately sends Elena an e-mail reply accepting her offer. Even though Elena intended to sell her jet ski for $2,500, she has made a unilateral mistake and is bound by the contract to sell it to Chin for $1,500. ■

This rule has at least two exceptions.[1] The contract may not be enforceable in either of the following situations.

1. The *other* party to the contract knows or should have known that a mistake of fact was made.

2. The error was due to a substantial mathematical mistake in addition, subtraction, division, or multiplication and was made inadvertently and without gross (extreme)

---

1. The *Restatement (Second) of Contracts*, Section 153, liberalizes the general rule to take into account the modern trend of allowing avoidance in some circumstances even though only one party has been mistaken.

Unilateral Mistake A mistake that occurs when one party to a contract is mistaken as to a material fact.

If this jet ski owner wants to sell it for one price, but mistakenly types in a lower price in her e-mail offer, is she bound by the lower price?

iStockPhoto.com/MrPants

Exhibit 13–1 Mistakes of Fact

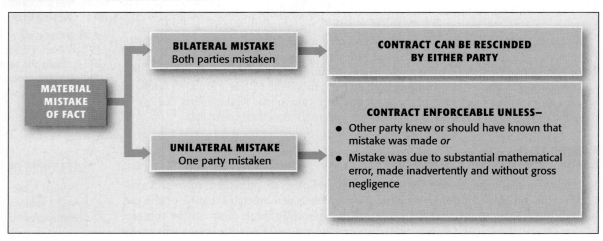

MATERIAL MISTAKE OF FACT

→ **BILATERAL MISTAKE** Both parties mistaken → **CONTRACT CAN BE RESCINDED BY EITHER PARTY**

→ **UNILATERAL MISTAKE** One party mistaken → **CONTRACT ENFORCEABLE UNLESS—**
- Other party knew or should have known that mistake was made *or*
- Mistake was due to substantial mathematical error, made inadvertently and without gross negligence

negligence. If, for instance, a contractor's bid was significantly low because he or she made a mistake in addition when totaling the estimated costs, any contract resulting from the bid normally may be rescinded.

In both situations, the mistake must still involve some material fact.

Bilateral (Mutual) Mistakes

A **bilateral mistake** is a "mutual misunderstanding concerning a basic assumption on which the contract was made."[2] When both parties are mistaken about the same material fact, the contract can be rescinded, or canceled, by either party. Note that, as with unilateral mistakes, the mistake must be about a material fact.

When a bilateral mistake occurs, normally the contract is voidable by the adversely affected party and can be rescinded. **CASE EXAMPLE 13.3** Coleman Holdings LP bought a parcel of real estate subject to setback restrictions imposed by a document entitled "Partial Release of Restrictions" that effectively precluded building a structure on the property. Lance and Joanne Eklund offered to buy the parcel from Coleman, intending to combine it with an adjacent parcel and build a home. Coleman gave the Eklunds a title report that referred to the "Partial Release of Restrictions," but they were not given a copy of the release.

Mistakenly believing that the document released restrictions on the property, the Eklunds did not investigate further. Meanwhile, Coleman mistakenly believed that the setback restrictions had been removed. After buying the property and discovering the restrictions, the Eklunds filed a suit in a Nevada state court against Coleman, seeking rescission of the sale. The court ordered the deal rescinded. The Nevada Supreme Court affirmed the order. "The parties made a mutual mistake in their mutual belief that the parcel had no setback restrictions."[3] ■

A word or term in a contract may be subject to more than one reasonable interpretation. If the parties to the contract attach materially different meanings to the term, their mutual misunderstanding may allow the contract to be rescinded. **CASE EXAMPLE 13.4** L&H Construction Company contracted with Circle Redmont, Inc., to make a cast-iron staircase and a glass flooring system. Redmont's original proposal was to "engineer, fabricate, and install" the staircase and flooring system, but installation was later dropped from the deal as a cost-cutting measure. The final contract stated that payment was due on "Supervision of Installation," although "install" appeared elsewhere in the contract. L&H insisted that installation was included and sued Redmont. The court found that the word *install* in the phrase "engineer, fabricate, and install" was the result of a mutual mistake. Both parties understood that Redmont would only supervise the installation, not perform it.[4] ■

13-1b Fraudulent Misrepresentation

Although fraud is a tort, the presence of fraud also affects the authenticity of the innocent party's consent to a contract. When an innocent party is fraudulently induced to enter into a contract, the contract usually can be avoided because that party has not *voluntarily* consented to the terms.[5] Normally, the innocent party can either rescind the contract and be restored to her or his original position or enforce the contract and seek damages for any harms resulting from the fraud.

Generally, fraudulent misrepresentation refers only to misrepresentation that is consciously false and is intended to mislead another. That is, the person making a fraudulent misrepresentation knows or believes that the assertion is false or knows that she or he does not have a basis (stated or implied) for the assertion.[6]

Bilateral Mistake A mistake that occurs when both parties to a contract are mistaken about the same material fact.

"Mistakes are the inevitable lot of mankind."

SIR GEORGE JESSEL
1824–1883
(ENGLISH JURIST)

When will the use of the word "install" in a contract be considered a mistake?

---

2. *Restatement (Second) of Contracts*, Section 152.
3. *Coleman Holdings Limited Partnership v. Eklund*, 2015 WL 428567 (Nev.Sup.Ct. 2015).
4. *L&H Construction Co. v. Circle Redmont, Inc.*, 55 So.3d 630 (Fla. 2011).
5. *Restatement (Second) of Contracts*, Sections 163 and 164.
6. *Restatement (Second) of Contracts*, Section 162.

LEARNING OBJECTIVE 3
What are the elements of fraudulent misrepresentation?

KNOW THIS
To collect damages in almost any lawsuit, there must be some sort of injury.

"If a man smiles all the time, he's probably selling something that doesn't work."

GEORGE CARLIN
1937–2008
(AMERICAN COMEDIAN)

Typically, fraud involves three elements:

1. A misrepresentation of a material fact must occur.
2. There must be an intent to deceive.
3. The innocent party must justifiably rely on the misrepresentation.

Additionally, to collect damages, a party must have been harmed as a result of the misrepresentation.

Misrepresentation Has Occurred The first element of proving fraud is to show that misrepresentation of a material fact has occurred. This misrepresentation can occur by words or actions. For instance, an art gallery owner's statement "This painting is a Picasso" is a misrepresentation of fact if the painting was done by another artist. Similarly, if a customer asks to see only Jasper Johns paintings and the owner immediately leads the customer over to paintings that were not done by Johns, the owner's actions can be a misrepresentation.

Misrepresentation by Conduct. Misrepresentation also occurs when a party takes specific action to conceal a fact that is material to the contract.[7] Therefore, if a seller, by her or his actions, prevents a buyer from learning of some fact that is material to the contract, the seller's behavior constitutes misrepresentation by conduct. It would also be misrepresentation by conduct for a seller to untruthfully deny knowledge of facts that are material to the contract when a buyer requests such information.

CASE EXAMPLE 13.5 Actor Tom Selleck contracted to purchase a horse named Zorro for his daughter from Dolores Cuenca. Cuenca acted as though Zorro were fit to ride in competitions, when in reality the horse was unfit for this use because of a medical condition. Selleck filed a lawsuit against Cuenca for wrongfully concealing the horse's condition, and a jury awarded Selleck more than $187,000 for Cuenca's misrepresentation by conduct.[8]

Statements of Opinion. Statements of opinion and representations of future facts (predictions) are generally not subject to claims of fraud. Statements such as "This land will be worth twice as much next year" and "This car will last for years and years" are statements of opinion, not fact. Contracting parties should recognize them as opinions and not rely on them. A fact is objective and verifiable, whereas an opinion is usually subject to debate. Therefore, a seller is allowed to use *puffery* to sell her or his goods without being liable for fraud.

Nevertheless, in certain situations, such as when a naïve purchaser relies on an opinion from an expert, the innocent party may be entitled to rescission or reformation. (Recall that reformation is an equitable remedy by which a court alters the terms of a contract to reflect the true intentions of the parties.)

CASE EXAMPLE 13.6 In a classic case, an instructor at an Arthur Murray dance school told Audrey Vokes, a widow without family, that she had the potential to become an accomplished dancer. The instructor sold her 2,302 hours of dancing lessons for a total amount of $31,090.45 (equivalent to $144,000 in 2016). When it became clear to Vokes that she did not, in fact, have the potential to be an excellent dancer, she sued the school for fraudulent misrepresentation. The court held that because the dance school had superior knowledge about a person's dance potential, the instructor's statements could be considered statements of fact rather than opinion.[9]

Misrepresentation of Law. Misrepresentation of law *ordinarily* does not entitle a party to be relieved of a contract. **EXAMPLE 13.7** Cameron has a parcel of property that she is trying to sell to Levi. Cameron knows that a local ordinance prohibits building anything higher than three stories on the property. Nonetheless, she tells Levi, "You can build a condominium one

---

7. *Restatement (Second) of Contracts*, Section 160.
8. *Selleck v. Cuenca*, Case No. GIN056909, North County of San Diego, California, decided September 9, 2009.
9. *Vokes v. Arthur Murray, Inc.*, 212 So.2d 906 (Fla.App. 1968).

hundred stories high if you want to." Levi buys the land and later discovers that Cameron's statement is false. Levi generally cannot avoid the contract, because under the common law, people are assumed to know state and local laws. ■

Exceptions to this rule occur when the misrepresenting party is in a profession known to require greater knowledge of the law than the average citizen possesses. For instance, if Cameron, in *Example 13.7,* had been a lawyer or a real estate broker, her willful misrepresentation of the area's zoning laws probably would have constituted fraud.

Misrepresentation by Silence. Ordinarily, neither party to a contract has a duty to come forward and disclose facts, and a contract normally will not be set aside because certain pertinent information has not been volunteered. **EXAMPLE 13.8** Jude is selling a car that has been in an accident and has been repaired. He does not need to volunteer this information to a potential buyer. If, however, the buyer asks him if the car has had extensive bodywork and he lies, Jude has committed fraudulent misrepresentation. ■

In general, if the seller knows of a serious potential problem that the buyer cannot reasonably be expected to discover, the seller may have a duty to speak. Normally, the seller must disclose only **latent defects**—that is, defects that could not readily be ascertained. Because a buyer of a house could easily discover the presence of termites through an inspection, for instance, termites may not qualify as a latent defect. Also, when the parties are in a *fiduciary relationship*—one of trust, such as partners, physician and patient, or attorney and client—there is a duty to disclose material facts. Failure to do so may constitute fraud.

Latent Defect A defect that is not obvious or cannot readily be ascertained.

Intent to Deceive The second element of fraud is knowledge on the part of the misrepresenting party that facts have been misrepresented. This element, usually called **scienter,**[10] or "guilty knowledge," generally signifies that there was an intent to deceive.

Scienter clearly exists if a party knows that a fact is not as stated. *Scienter* also exists if a party makes a statement that he or she believes not to be true or makes a statement recklessly, without regard to whether it is true or false. Finally, this element is met if a party says or implies that a statement is made on some basis, such as personal knowledge or personal investigation, when it is not.

CASE EXAMPLE 13.9 Robert Sarvis applied for a position as a business law professor two weeks after his release from prison. On his résumé, he said that he had been a corporate president for fourteen years and had taught business law at another college. After he was hired, his probation officer alerted the school to Sarvis's criminal history. The school immediately fired him, and Sarvis sued for breach of his employment contract. The court concluded that by not disclosing his history, Sarvis had clearly exhibited an intent to deceive and that the school had justifiably relied on his misrepresentations. Therefore, the school could rescind Sarvis's employment contract.[11] ■

Scienter Knowledge on the part of a misrepresenting party that material facts have been falsely represented or omitted with an intent to deceive.

If you are selling your car, must you tell every potential buyer about any accidents in which that car was involved?

Innocent Misrepresentation. If a person makes a statement that she or he believes to be true but that actually misrepresents material facts, the person is guilty only of an **innocent misrepresentation,** not of fraud. When an innocent misrepresentation occurs, the aggrieved party can rescind the contract but usually cannot seek damages. **EXAMPLE 13.10** Parris tells Roberta that a tract of land contains 250 acres. Parris is mistaken—the tract contains only 215 acres—but Parris had no knowledge of the mistake. Roberta relies on the statement and contracts to buy the land. Even though the misrepresentation is innocent, Roberta can avoid the contract if the misrepresentation is material. ■

Innocent Misrepresentation
A misrepresentation that occurs when a person makes a false statement of fact that he or she believes is true.

Negligent Misrepresentation. Sometimes, a party will make a misrepresentation through carelessness, believing the statement is true. Such a misrepresentation may constitute **negligent misrepresentation** if the party did not exercise reasonable care in uncovering or disclosing the facts or did not use the skill and competence that her or his business or profession

Negligent Misrepresentation
A misrepresentation that occurs when a person makes a false statement of fact because he or she did not exercise reasonable care or use the skill and competence required by her or his business or profession.

---

10. Pronounced sy-*en*-ter.
11. *Sarvis v. Vermont State Colleges,* 172 Vt. 76, 772 A.2d 494 (2001).

requires. **EXAMPLE 13.11** Dirk, an operator of a weight scale, certifies the weight of Sneed's commodity. If Dirk knows that the scale's accuracy has not been checked for more than three years, his action may constitute negligent misrepresentation. ■

In almost all states, negligent misrepresentation is equal to *scienter*, or knowingly making a misrepresentation. In effect, negligent misrepresentation is treated as fraudulent misrepresentation, even though the misrepresentation was not purposeful. In negligent misrepresentation, culpable ignorance of the truth supplies the intention to mislead, even if the defendant can claim, "I didn't know."

KNOW THIS
A statement of opinion is neither a contract offer, nor a contract term, nor fraud.

Justifiable Reliance on the Misrepresentation The third element of fraud is reasonably justifiable reliance on the misrepresentation of fact. The deceived party must have a justifiable reason for relying on the misrepresentation. Also, the misrepresentation must be an important factor (but not necessarily the sole factor) in inducing the deceived party to enter into the contract.

Reliance is not justified if the innocent party knows the true facts or relies on obviously extravagant statements (such as, "this pickup truck will get fifty miles to the gallon"). The same rule applies to defects in property sold. If the defects would be obvious on inspection, the buyer cannot justifiably rely on the seller's representations. If the defects are hidden or latent, as previously discussed, however, the buyer is justified in relying on the seller's statements.

In the following case, the buyer of a car wash relied on the seller's representations that the property would be "appropriately winterized" to protect it from damage, but it was not. Was the buyer justified in relying on the seller's representations?

CASE 13.1

Cronkelton v. Guaranteed Construction Services, LLC

Court of Appeals of Ohio, Third District, 988 N.E.2d 656, 2013-Ohio-328 (2013).

FACTS A court appointed Patrick Shivley to be the receiver of a foreclosed car wash that was being sold in Bellefontaine, Ohio. (A receiver is an independent, impartial party appointed by a bankruptcy court to manage property in bankruptcy proceedings and dispose of it in an orderly manner for the benefit of the creditors.) The buyer, Clifford Cronkelton, inspected the car wash in November 2009. He knew that some equipment would have to be replaced, but he was concerned that the property needed to be winterized to protect it from damage. In phone calls and e-mails, Shivley assured him that the winterizing would be done.

Shivley contacted Guaranteed Construction Services, which hired Strayer Company to winterize the property. Strayer told Shivley that the only way to avoid problems was to leave the heat on at the car wash, but Shivley knew that the bank had shut off the heat because the property was not generating income. In March 2010, Shivley informed the bank of damage to the property caused by freezing. Shivley did not share this information with Cronkelton, who did not become aware of the damage until after he had bought the car wash in June.

Cronkelton filed a suit in an Ohio state court against Guaranteed and Shivley, asserting fraud. The jury returned a verdict in Cronkelton's favor, and he was awarded more than $140,000 in damages and attorneys' fees. The defendants appealed.

Is it reasonable for the buyer of a car wash to rely on the seller's statements that the property has been properly winterized?

John de la Bastide/ShutterStock.com

ISSUE Did Cronkelton justifiably rely on Shivley's representations that the car wash had been winterized?

DECISION Yes. A state intermediate appellate court affirmed the lower court's judgment in Cronkelton's favor.

REASON The reviewing court found that the jury verdict was supported by "competent, credible evidence" indicating that Cronkelton had reasonably relied on Shivley's representations. No one denied that the damage by freezing was open and obvious upon inspection and that Cronkelton could have inspected the property again before signing the purchase agreement. But Cronkelton testified that Shivley had guaranteed in an e-mail that everything had been taken care of. The jury's finding that Cronkelton had reasonably relied on Shivley's representations appeared justified.

As a receiver, Shivley had a fiduciary duty to take care of the assets under his control. "Under the circumstances of this case, Cronkelton had a reasonable basis to believe that Shivley, who was acting as an arm of the [bankruptcy] court, would take the promised steps to winterize the property."

CRITICAL THINKING—Legal Consideration *Did Shivley's misrepresentations rise to the level of fraud? Explain.*

If you are selling products or services, assume that all clients and customers are naïve and that they rely on your representations. Instruct employees to phrase their comments so that customers understand that any statements that are not factual are the employees' opinion. If someone asks a question that is beyond an employee's knowledge, it is better for the employee to say that he or she does not know than to guess and have the customer rely on a representation that turns out to be false. This can be particularly important when the questions concern topics such as compatibility or speed of electronic and digital goods, software, or related services.

PREVENTING
LEGAL
DISPUTES

Injury to the Innocent Party Most courts do not require a showing of harm in an action to rescind a contract. These courts hold that because rescission returns the parties to the positions they held before the contract was made, a showing of injury to the innocent party is unnecessary.

In contrast, to recover damages caused by fraud, proof of harm is universally required. The measure of damages is ordinarily equal to the property's value had it been delivered as represented, less the actual price paid for the property. (What if someone pretends to be someone else online? Can the victim of the hoax prove injury sufficient to recover for fraudulent misrepresentation? See this chapter's *Adapting the Law to the Online Environment* feature for a discussion of this topic.)

Because fraud actions necessarily involve wrongful conduct, courts may also award *punitive,* or *exemplary, damages,* which compensate a plaintiff over and above the amount of the actual loss. Because of the potential for punitive damages, which normally are not available in contract actions, plaintiffs often include a claim for fraudulent misrepresentation in their contract disputes.

In the following case, a real estate investor claimed that a seller's failure to disclose material facts about the property affected its value. The court had to determine not only if the seller's conduct constituted fraud, but also whether the fraud had caused harm to the property value.

CASE 13.2

Fazio v. Cypress/GR Houston I, LP

Court of Appeals of Texas, First District, 403 S.W.3d 390 (2013).

FACTS Peter Fazio began talks with Cypress/GR Houston I, LP, to buy retail property whose main tenant was a Garden Ridge store. In performing a background investigation, Fazio and his agents became concerned about Garden Ridge's financial health. Nevertheless, after being assured that Garden Ridge had a positive financial outlook, Fazio sent Cypress a letter of intent to buy the property for $7.67 million "[b]ased on the currently reported absolute net income of $805,040.00." Cypress then agreed to provide all information in its possession, but it failed to disclose the following:

1. A consultant for Garden Ridge had recently requested a $240,000 reduction in the annual rent as part of a restructuring of the company's real estate leases.

What does a rent-reduction request from a shopping mall's main tenant indicate?

2. Cypress's bank was so concerned about Garden Ridge's financial health that it had required a personal guaranty of the property's loan.

The parties entered into a purchase agreement, but Garden Ridge went into bankruptcy shortly after the deal closed. Fazio sued Cypress for fraud after he was forced to sell the property three years later for only $3.75 million. A jury found in Fazio's favor. Although the jury agreed that Cypress had failed to disclose a material fact, however, it determined that Fazio was not entitled to any damages. The jury concluded that no damages had been proximately caused by the fraud, because the fraud had not negatively affected the value of the property at the time it was sold to Fazio. The trial court entered a

Continues

judgment notwithstanding the verdict in favor of Cypress, and Fazio appealed.

ISSUE Was Fazio fraudulently induced to enter into the purchase agreement?

DECISION Yes. The appellate court affirmed the jury's verdict. Cypress's failure to disclose these facts constituted fraud. Fazio was not entitled to damages, however, because the misrepresentation had not negatively affected the property's value.

REASON There was sufficient evidence of fraud. Before the parties entered into the purchase agreement, Cypress had agreed to provide all information in its possession. Cypress knew that Fazio had been concerned about Garden Ridge's financial health and that he had based the purchase price on the anticipated income from the property. Moreover, a reasonable person in Fazio's position would have attached significance to Garden Ridge's recent request for a $240,000 rent reduction. The fact that Cypress had been required to provide a personal guaranty of the property's loan was also significant.

There are two measures of direct damages in a fraud case: out-of-pocket damages and benefit-of-the-bargain damages. Out-of-pocket damages measure the difference between the amount the buyer paid and the value of the property the buyer received. Benefit-of-the-bargain damages measure the difference between the value of the property as represented and the actual value of the property. Both measures are determined at the time of the sale, not "at some future time." Here, the jury received a number of instructions on determining the amount of damages and concluded that there were zero damages to Fazio at the time of the purchase agreement.

CRITICAL THINKING—Ethical Consideration *Was Cypress's conduct unethical? Why or why not?*

13–1c Undue Influence

Undue Influence Persuasion that is less than actual force but more than advice and that induces a person to act according to the will or purposes of the dominating party.

Undue influence arises from relationships in which one party can greatly influence another party, thus overcoming that party's free will. A contract entered into under excessive or undue influence lacks voluntary consent and is therefore voidable.[12]

One Party Dominates the Other In various types of relationships, one party may have an opportunity to dominate and unfairly influence another party. Minors and elderly people, for instance, are often under the influence of guardians (persons who are legally responsible for others). If a guardian induces a young or elderly ward (the person whom the guardian looks after) to enter into a contract that benefits the guardian, the guardian may have exerted undue influence. Undue influence can arise from a number of confidential or fiduciary relationships, including attorney-client, physician-patient, guardian-ward, parent-child, husband-wife, and trustee-beneficiary.

The essential feature of undue influence is that the party being taken advantage of does not exercise free will in entering into a contract. It is not enough that a person is elderly or suffers from some mental or physical impairment. There must be clear and convincing evidence that the person did not act out of her or his free will. Similarly, the existence of a fiduciary relationship alone is insufficient to prove undue influence.

A Presumption of Undue Influence in Certain Situations The dominant party in a fiduciary relationship must exercise the utmost good faith in dealing with the other party. When the dominant party benefits from the relationship, a presumption of undue influence may arise. Thus, when a contract enriches the dominant party in a fiduciary relationship, the court will often *presume* that the contract was made under undue influence.

EXAMPLE 13.12 Erik is the guardian for Kinsley, his ward. On her behalf, he enters into a contract from which he benefits financially. If Kinsley challenges the contract, the court will likely presume that the guardian has taken advantage of his ward. To rebut (refute) this presumption, Erik has to show that he made full disclosure to Kinsley and that consideration was present. He must also show that Kinsley received, if available, independent and competent

---

12. *Restatement (Second) of Contracts*, Section 177.

ADAPTING THE LAW TO THE **ONLINE** ENVIRONMENT
"Catfishing": Is That Online "Friend" for Real?

When you are communicating with a person you have met only online, how do you know who that person really is? After all, the person could turn out to be a "catfish."

The term *catfish* comes from a 2010 film of the same name about a fake online persona. According to a story told in the film, when live cod were shipped long distances, they were inactive, and their flesh became mushy. When catfish were added to the tanks, the cod swam around and stayed in good condition. At the end of the film, a character says of the creator of the fake persona, "There are those people who are catfish in life. And they keep you on your toes. They keep you guessing, they keep you thinking, they keep you fresh."

Catfishing Makes National Headlines

Catfishing made headlines when a popular Notre Dame football star supposedly fell victim to it in 2012. Linebacker Manti Te'o said that his girlfriend, Lennay Kekua, a student at Stanford, had died of leukemia after a near-fatal car accident. Although Kekua had Facebook and Twitter accounts and Te'o had communicated with her online and by telephone for several years, reporters could find no evidence of her existence. Te'o later claimed that he had been a victim of a catfishing hoax. Others suggested that his friends had created the persona and her

tragic death to provide an inspirational story that would increase Te'o's chances of winning the Heisman trophy.

Is Online Fraudulent Misrepresentation Actionable?

Some victims of catfishing have turned to the courts, but they have had little success. A few have attempted to sue Internet service providers for allowing fake personas, but the courts have generally dismissed these suits.[a] Laws in some states make it a crime to impersonate someone online, but these laws generally do not apply to those who create totally fictional personas.

Attempts to recover damages for fraudulent misrepresentation have generally failed to meet the requirement that there must be proof of actual injury. For instance, Paula Bonhomme developed an online romantic relationship with a man called Jesse. Jesse was actually a woman named Janna St. James, who also communicated with Bonhomme using her own name and pretending to be a friend of Jesse's.

St. James created a host of fictional characters, including an ex-wife and a son, for Jesse. Bonhomme in turn sent gifts totaling more than $10,000 to Jesse and the other characters. After being told by St. James that

---

a. See, for example, *Beckman v. Match.com*, 2013 WL 2355512 (D.Nev. 2013); and *Robinson v. Match.com, LLC*, 2012 WL 3263992 (N.D.Tex. 2012).

Jesse had attempted suicide, Bonhomme suffered such emotional distress that she incurred more than $5,000 in bills for a therapist. Eventually, she was told that Jesse had died of liver cancer. When Bonhomme finally learned the truth, she suffered additional emotional distress, resulting in more expenses for a therapist and lost earnings due to her "affected mental state."

Although Bonhomme had incurred considerable expenses, the Illinois Supreme Court ruled that she could not bring a suit for fraudulent misrepresentation. The case involved a "purely personal relationship" without any "commercial, transactional, or regulatory component." Bonhomme and St. James "were not engaged in any kind of business dealings or bargaining." The truth of representations "made in the context of purely private personal relationships is simply not something the state regulates or in which the state possesses any kind of valid public policy interest."[b]

CRITICAL THINKING

- So far, victims of catfishing have had little success in the courts. Under what circumstances might a person be able to collect damages for fraudulent misrepresentation involving online impersonation?

---

b. *Bonhomme v. St. James*, 970 N.E.2d 1 (Ill. 2012).

---

advice before completing the transaction. Unless the presumption can be rebutted, the contract will be rescinded. ■

When is assent really assent? Musician Sly Stone, of the group Sly and the Family Stone, had numerous hits in the 1960s and 1970s. Then drug use apparently took its toll on the singer. By the 1980s, Stone was broke.

Along came a group that convinced the former star to sign a series of contracts. Stone became an employee and co-owner of Even St. Productions in 1989. He was to have received a portion of the royalties collected by the new company. Twenty years later, he was homeless. In 2010, Stone sued his business manager, his attorney, and the company for breach of contract.

ETHICAL ISSUE

An additional issue concerned whether he understood all of the complicated contracts that he was asked to sign. In other words, was there unambiguous assent?

In 2015, a Los Angeles Superior Court civil jury found in favor of Stone in his breach of contract lawsuit. The defendants argued that most of the royalties they had collected for him were used to pay off the millions that he owed to the Internal Revenue Service. They are appealing the verdict. Nevertheless, one of Stone's attorney's said, "This was an important verdict for people that are artists, entertainers, and music composers."

13–1d Duress

Agreement to the terms of a contract is not voluntary if one of the parties is *forced* into the agreement. The use of threats to force a party to enter into a contract constitutes *duress*,[13] as does the use of blackmail or extortion to induce consent. Duress is both a defense to the enforcement of a contract and a ground for rescission of a contract.

To establish duress, there must be proof of a threat to do something that the threatening party has no right to do. Generally, for duress to occur, the threatened act must be wrongful or illegal, and it must render the person who receives the threat incapable of exercising free will. A threat to exercise a legal right, such as the right to sue someone, ordinarily does not constitute duress.

13–2 The Writing Requirement

Another defense to the enforceability of a contract is *form*—specifically, some contracts must be in writing. All states require certain types of contracts to be in writing or evidenced by a written memorandum or an electronic record. In addition, the party or parties against whom enforcement is sought must have signed the contract, unless certain exceptions apply (as discussed later in this chapter). In this text, we refer to these state statutes collectively as the **Statute of Frauds.**

The following types of contracts are said to fall "within" or "under" the Statute of Frauds and therefore require a writing:

1. Contracts involving interests in land.

2. Contracts that cannot *by their terms* be performed within one year from the day after the date of formation.

3. Collateral, or secondary, contracts, such as promises to answer for the debt or duty of another.

4. Promises made in consideration of marriage.

5. Under the Uniform Commercial Code, contracts for the sale of goods priced at $500 or more.

The actual name of the Statute of Frauds is misleading because it does not apply to fraud. Rather, in an effort to prevent fraud, the statute denies enforceability to certain contracts that do not comply with its requirements. The name derives from an English act passed in 1677 that was titled "An Act for the Prevention of Frauds and Perjuries."

13–2a Contracts Involving Interests in Land

A contract calling for the sale of land is not enforceable unless it is in writing or evidenced by a written memorandum. Land is *real property* and includes all physical objects that are

LEARNING OBJECTIVE 4
What contracts must be in writing to be enforceable?

Statute of Frauds A state statute that requires certain types of contracts to be in writing to be enforceable.

---

13. *Restatement (Second) of Contracts*, Sections 174 and 175.

permanently attached to the soil, such as buildings, fences, trees, and the soil itself. The Statute of Frauds operates as a defense to the enforcement of an oral contract for the sale of land. **EXAMPLE 13.13** Skylar contracts orally to sell his property in Fair Oaks to Beth. If he later decides not to sell, under most circumstances, Beth cannot enforce the contract. ■

The Statute of Frauds also requires written evidence of contracts for the transfer of other interests in land, such as mortgage agreements and leases. Similarly, an agreement that includes an option to purchase real property must be in writing for the option to be enforced.

13–2b The One-Year Rule

Contracts that cannot, *by their own terms,* be performed within one year *from the day after* the contract is formed must be in writing to be enforceable. The reason for this rule is that the parties' memory of their contract's terms is not likely to be reliable for longer than a year.

Time Period Starts the Day after the Contract Is Formed The one-year period begins to run *the day after the contract is made.* **EXAMPLE 13.14** Superior University forms a contract with Kimi San stating that San will teach three courses in history during the coming academic year (September 15 through June 15). If the contract is formed in March, it must be in writing to be enforceable—because it cannot be performed within one year. If the contract is formed in July, in contrast, it will not have to be in writing to be enforceable—because it can be performed within one year. ■

Must Be Objectively Impossible to Perform within One Year The test for determining whether an oral contract is enforceable under the one-year rule is whether performance is *possible* within one year from the day after the date of contract formation. It does not matter whether the agreement is *likely* to be performed during that period.

When performance of a contract is objectively impossible during the one-year period, the contract must be in writing to be enforceable. **EXAMPLE 13.15** A contract to provide five crops of tomatoes to be grown on a specific farm in Illinois would be objectively impossible to perform within one year. No farmer in Illinois can grow five crops of tomatoes in a single year. ■

If performance is possible within one year under the contract's terms, the contract does not fall under the Statute of Frauds and need not be in writing. **EXAMPLE 13.16** Janine enters into a contract to create a carving of President Barack Obama's face on a mountainside, similar to the carvings of other presidents' faces on Mount Rushmore. It is technically possible—although not very likely—that the contract could be performed within one year. (Mount Rushmore took over fourteen years to complete.) Therefore, Janine's contract need not be in writing to be enforceable. ■ Exhibit 13–2 graphically illustrates the one-year rule.

13–2c Collateral Promises

A **collateral promise,** or secondary promise, is one that is ancillary (subsidiary) to a principal transaction or primary contractual relationship. In other words, a collateral promise is one made by a third party to assume the debts or obligations of a primary party to a contract if that party does not perform. Any collateral promise of this nature falls under the Statute of Frauds and therefore must be in writing to be enforceable.

Primary versus Secondary Obligations A direct party to a contract incurs a *primary obligation* under that contract. A contract in which a party assumes a primary obligation normally does not need to be in writing to be enforceable. **EXAMPLE 13.17** Nigel tells Dr. Lu, an orthodontist, that he will pay for the services provided for Nigel's niece. Because Nigel has assumed direct financial responsibility for his niece's debt, this is a primary obligation and need not be in writing to be enforceable. ■

> "A verbal contract isn't worth the paper it's written on."
>
> **SAMUEL GOLDWYN**
> 1879–1974
> (HOLLYWOOD MOTION PICTURE PRODUCER)

Collateral Promise
A secondary promise to a primary transaction, such as a promise made by one person to pay the debts of another if the latter fails to perform. A collateral promise normally must be in writing to be enforceable.

Exhibit 13–2 The One-Year Rule

Under the Statute of Frauds, contracts that by their terms are impossible to perform within one year from the day after the date of contract formation must be in writing to be enforceable. Put another way, if it is at all possible to perform an oral contract within one year from the day after the contract is made, the contract will fall outside the Statute of Frauds and be enforceable.

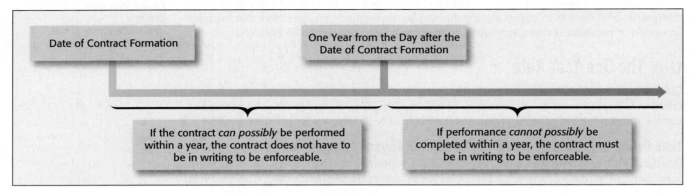

In contrast, a contract in which a party assumes a *secondary obligation* does have to be in writing to be enforceable. **EXAMPLE 13.18** Kareem's mother borrows $10,000 from the Medford Trust Company on a promissory note payable in six months. Kareem promises the bank officer handling the loan that he will pay the $10,000 *if his mother does not pay the loan on time.* Kareem, in this situation, becomes what is known as a *guarantor* on the loan. He is guaranteeing to the bank (the creditor) that he will pay the loan if his mother fails to do so. This kind of collateral promise must be in writing to be enforceable. ∎

An Exception—The "Main Purpose" Rule An oral promise to answer for the debt of another is covered by the Statute of Frauds *unless* the guarantor's purpose in accepting secondary liability is to secure a personal benefit. Under the "main purpose" rule, this type of contract need not be in writing.[14] The assumption is that a court can infer from the circumstances of a case whether a "leading objective" of the promisor was to secure a personal benefit.

EXAMPLE 13.19 Carrie Braswell contracts with Custom Manufacturing Company to have some machines custom made for her factory. She promises Newform Supply, Custom's supplier, that if Newform continues to deliver the materials to Custom for the production of the custom-made machines, she will guarantee payment. This promise need not be in writing, even though the effect may be to pay the debt of another, because Braswell's main purpose is to secure a benefit for herself. ∎

Another typical application of the main purpose doctrine occurs when one creditor guarantees a debtor's debt to another creditor to forestall litigation. The purpose is to allow the debtor to remain in business long enough to generate profits sufficient to pay *both* creditors. In this situation, the guaranty does not need to be in writing to be enforceable.

13–2d Promises Made in Consideration of Marriage

A unilateral promise to make a monetary payment or to give property in consideration of marriage must be in writing. **EXAMPLE 13.20** Evan promises to buy Celeste a house in Maui if she marries him. Celeste would need written evidence of Evan's promise to enforce it. ∎

The same rule applies to **prenuptial agreements**—agreements made before marriage that define each partner's ownership rights in the other partner's property. **EXAMPLE 13.21** Before

Prenuptial Agreement An agreement made before marriage that defines each partner's ownership rights in the other partner's property. Prenuptial agreements must be in writing to be enforceable.

---

14. *Restatement (Second) of Contracts*, Section 116.

marrying country singer Keith Urban, actress Nicole Kidman entered into a prenuptial agreement with him. Kidman agreed that if the couple divorced, she would pay Urban $640,000 for every year they had been married, unless Urban had begun to use drugs again. In that event, he would receive nothing. ∎

13–2e **Contracts for the Sale of Goods**

The Uniform Commercial Code (UCC) includes Statute of Frauds provisions that require written evidence or an electronic record of a contract for the sale of goods priced at $500 or more. (This low threshold amount may be increased in the future.) A writing that will satisfy the UCC requirement need only state the quantity term (6,000 boxes of cotton gauze, for instance). The contract will not be enforceable for any quantity greater than that set forth in the writing.

Other agreed-on terms can be omitted or even stated imprecisely in the writing, as long as they adequately reflect both parties' intentions. The writing normally need not designate the buyer or the seller, the terms of payment, or the price. In addition, a written memorandum or series of communications (including e-mail) evidencing a contract will suffice, provided that the writing is signed by the party against whom enforcement is sought. (See this chapter's *Beyond Our Borders* feature to learn whether other countries have requirements similar to those in the Statute of Frauds.)

"Wallace, have you forgotten our prenuptial contract? No whistling!"

Henry Martin/The New Yorker Collection/ Cartoonbank.com

13–2f **Exceptions to the Statute of Frauds**

Exceptions to the applicability of the Statute of Frauds are made in certain situations. We describe those situations here.

BEYOND OUR BORDERS

The Statute of Frauds and International Sales Contracts

The Convention on Contracts for the International Sale of Goods (CISG) provides rules that govern international sales contracts between citizens of countries that have ratified the convention (agreement). Article 11 of the CISG does not incorporate any Statute of Frauds provisions. Rather, it states that a "contract for sale need not be concluded in or evidenced by writing and is not subject to any other requirements as to form."

Article 11 accords with the legal customs of most nations, which no longer require contracts to meet certain formal or writing requirements to be enforceable. Ironically, even England, the nation that enacted the original Statute of Frauds in 1677, has repealed all of it except the provisions relating to collateral promises and to transfers of interests in land. Many other countries that once had such statutes have also repealed all or parts of them. Civil law countries, such as France, have never required certain types of

contracts to be in writing. Obviously, without a writing requirement, contracts can take on any form.

CRITICAL THINKING

- If a country does not have a Statute of Frauds and a dispute arises over an oral agreement, how can the parties substantiate their positions?

Partial Performance When a contract has been partially performed and the parties cannot be returned to their positions prior to the contract's formation, a court may grant *specific performance*. Specific performance is an equitable remedy that requires that a contract be performed according to its precise terms. The parties still must prove that an oral contract existed, of course.

In cases involving oral contracts for the transfer of interests in land, courts usually look at whether justice is better served by enforcing the oral contract when partial performance has taken place. For instance, if the purchaser has paid part of the price, taken possession, and made valuable improvements to the property, a court may grant specific performance.

In some states, mere reliance on certain types of oral contracts is enough to remove them from the Statute of Frauds. Under the UCC, an oral contract for goods priced at $500 or more is enforceable to the extent that a seller accepts payment or a buyer accepts delivery of the goods.[15]

CASE EXAMPLE 13.22 Pacific Fruit, Inc., exports cargo from Ecuador. NYKCool, based in Sweden, provides maritime transportation. NYKCool and Pacific entered into a written contract with a two-year duration, under which NYKCool agreed to transport weekly shipments of bananas from Ecuador to California and Japan.

At the end of the period, the parties agreed to extend the deal, but a new contract was never signed. The parties continued making weekly shipments for four more years until a dispute arose over unused cargo capacity and unpaid freight charges. An international arbitration panel found that Pacific Fruit was liable to NYKCool for $8.7 million for breach of contract. Pacific Fruit appealed, arguing that there was no contract in place. The court affirmed the award in favor of NYKCool. "The parties' substantial partial performance on the contract weighs strongly in favor of contract formation."[16] ▪

Admissions If a party against whom enforcement of an oral contract is sought "admits" under oath that a contract for sale was made, the contract will be enforceable.[17] The party's admission can occur at any stage of the court proceedings, such as during a deposition or other discovery, pleadings, or testimony.

If a party admits a contract subject to the UCC, the contract is enforceable, but only to the extent of the quantity admitted.[18] **EXAMPLE 13.23** Rachel, the president of Bistro Corporation, admits under oath that an oral agreement was made with Commercial Kitchens, Inc., to buy certain equipment for $10,000. A court will enforce the agreement only to the extent admitted ($10,000), even if Commercial Kitchens claims that the agreement involved $20,000 worth of equipment. ▪

Promissory Estoppel An oral contract that would otherwise be unenforceable under the Statute of Frauds may be enforced under the doctrine of *promissory estoppel*. Section 139 of the *Restatement (Second) of Contracts* provides that an oral promise can be enforceable, notwithstanding the Statute of Frauds, if the promisee has justifiably relied on the promise to his or her detriment. The promisee's reliance must have been foreseeable to the person making the promise, and enforcing the promise must be the only way to avoid injustice.

Note the similarities between promissory estoppel and the doctrine of partial performance discussed previously. Both require reasonable reliance and operate to estop, or prevent, a party from claiming that no contract exists.

Special Exceptions under the UCC Special exceptions to the applicability of the Statute of Frauds exist for sales contracts. Oral contracts for customized goods may be enforced in certain circumstances. Another exception has to do with oral contracts *between merchants* that

If a seller admits under oath that a contract was for only $10,000 of commercial kitchen equipment, does the buyer owe more if additional equipment was installed?

iStockPhoto.com/gerenme

---

15. UCC 2–201(3)(c).

16. *NYKCool A.B. v. Pacific Fruit, Inc.,* 2013 WL 163621 (2d Cir. 2013). The initials *A.B.* stand for *Aktiebolag,* which is the Swedish term for "limited company."

17. *Restatement (Second) of Contracts,* Section 133.

18. UCC 2–201(3)(b).

have been confirmed in a written memorandum. We will examine this exception when we discuss the UCC's Statute of Frauds provisions.

Exhibit 13–3 graphically summarizes the types of contracts that fall under the Statute of Frauds and the various exceptions that apply.

13-3 Sufficiency of the Writing or Electronic Record

A written contract will satisfy the writing requirement of the Statute of Frauds, as will a written memorandum or an electronic record that evidences the agreement and is signed by the party against whom enforcement is sought. The signature need not be placed at the end of the document but can be anywhere in the writing. A signature can consist of a typed name or even just initials rather than the full name.

13-3a What Constitutes a Writing?

A writing can consist of any confirmation, invoice, sales slip, check, fax, or e-mail—or such items in combination. The written contract need not be contained in a single document to constitute an enforceable contract. One document may incorporate another document by expressly referring to it. Several documents may form a single contract if they are physically attached—such as by staple, paper clip, or glue—or even if they are only placed in the same envelope.

EXAMPLE 13.24 Simpson orally agrees to sell some land next to a shopping mall to Terro Properties. Simpson gives Terro an unsigned memo that contains a legal description of the property, and Terro gives Simpson an unsigned first draft of their contract. Simpson sends Terro a signed letter that refers to the memo and to the first and final drafts of the contract. Terro sends Simpson an unsigned copy of the final draft of the contract with a signed check stapled to it. Together, the documents can constitute a writing sufficient to satisfy the Statute of Frauds and bind both parties to the terms of the contract as evidenced by the writings. ■

13-3b What Must Be Contained in the Writing?

A memorandum or note evidencing an oral contract need only contain the essential terms of the contract, not every term. There must, of course, also be some indication that the parties

Exhibit 13–3 Contracts Subject to the Statute of Frauds

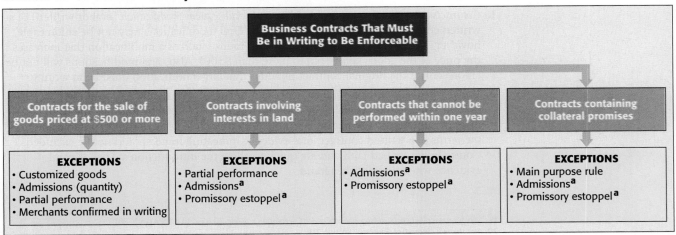

Business Contracts That Must Be in Writing to Be Enforceable

Contracts for the sale of goods priced at $500 or more	Contracts involving interests in land	Contracts that cannot be performed within one year	Contracts containing collateral promises
EXCEPTIONS • Customized goods • Admissions (quantity) • Partial performance • Merchants confirmed in writing	**EXCEPTIONS** • Partial performance • Admissions[a] • Promissory estoppel[a]	**EXCEPTIONS** • Admissions[a] • Promissory estoppel[a]	**EXCEPTIONS** • Main purpose rule • Admissions[a] • Promissory estoppel[a]

a. In some states.

voluntarily agreed to the terms. As mentioned earlier, under the UCC, a writing evidencing a contract for the sale of goods need only state the quantity and be signed by the party against whom enforcement is sought.

Under most state laws, the writing must also name the parties and identify the subject matter, the consideration, and the essential terms with reasonable certainty. In addition, contracts for the sale of land usually must state the price and describe the property with sufficient clarity to allow these terms to be determined without reference to outside sources.[19]

Note that because only the party against whom enforcement is sought must have signed the writing, a contract may be enforceable by one of its parties but not by the other. **EXAMPLE 13.25** Rock orally agrees to buy Betty Devlin's lake house and lot for $350,000. Devlin writes Rock a letter confirming the sale by identifying the parties and the essential terms of the sales contract— price, method of payment, and legal address—and signs the letter. Devlin has made a written memorandum of the oral land contract. Because she signed the letter, she normally can be held to the oral contract by Rock. Devlin cannot enforce the agreement against Rock, however. Because he has not signed or entered into a written contract or memorandum, Rock can plead the Statute of Frauds as a defense. ■

13–4 The Parol Evidence Rule

Parol Evidence Rule A rule of contracts under which a court will not receive into evidence prior or contemporaneous external agreements that contradict the terms of the parties' written contract.

Sometimes, a written contract does not include—or contradicts—an oral understanding reached by the parties before or at the time of contracting. For instance, a landlord might tell a person who agrees to rent an apartment that she or he can have a cat, whereas the lease contract clearly states that no pets are allowed. In determining the outcome of such disputes, the courts look to a common law rule called the **parol evidence rule.**

Under this rule, if a court finds that a written contract represents the complete and final statement of the parties' agreement, then it will not allow either party to present parol evidence. *Parol evidence* is testimony or other evidence of communications between the parties that is not contained in the contract itself. Thus, a party normally cannot present evidence of the parties' "prior or contemporaneous agreements or negotiations" if that evidence contradicts or varies the terms of the parties' written contract.[20]

13–4a Exceptions to the Parol Evidence Rule

Because of the rigidity of the parol evidence rule, courts make several exceptions. These exceptions include the following:

1. *Contracts subsequently modified.* Evidence of a *subsequent modification* (oral or written) of a written contract can be introduced in court. Oral modifications may not be enforceable, however, if they come under the Statute of Frauds (such as a modification that increases the price of the goods being sold to more than $500). Also, oral modifications will not be enforceable if the original contract provides that any modification must be in writing.[21]

2. *Voidable or void contracts.* Oral evidence can be introduced in all cases to show that the contract was voidable or void (for example, induced by mistake, fraud, or misrepresentation). The reason is simple: if deception led one of the parties to agree to the terms of a written contract, oral evidence indicating fraud should not be excluded. Courts frown on bad faith and are quick to allow the introduction at trial of parol evidence when it establishes fraud.

---

19. See, for example, *Beneficial Homeowner Service Corporation v. Steele,* 30 Misc.3d 1208(A) (N.Y. 2011).
20. *Restatement (Second) of Contracts,* Section 213.
21. UCC 2–209(2), (3).

3. *Contracts containing ambiguous terms.* When the terms of a written contract are ambiguous, evidence is admissible to show the meaning of the terms. **CASE EXAMPLE 13.26** Pamela Watkins bought a home from Sandra Schexnider. Their agreement stated that Watkins would make payments on the mortgage until the note was paid in full, when "the house" would become hers. The agreement also stipulated that she would pay for insurance on "the property." The home was destroyed in a hurricane, and the insurance proceeds paid off the mortgage. Watkins claimed that she owned the land, but Schexnider argued that she had sold only the house. The court found that because "the house" term in the contract was ambiguous, parol evidence was admissible. The court concluded that the parties had intended to transfer ownership of both the house and the land, and ordered that title to the property be transferred to Watkins.[22] ■

4. *Incomplete contracts.* Evidence is admissible when the written contract is incomplete in that it lacks one or more of the essential terms. The courts allow evidence to "fill in the gaps" in the contract.

5. *Prior dealing, course of performance, or usage of trade.* Under the UCC, evidence can be introduced to explain or supplement a written contract by showing a prior dealing, course of performance, or usage of trade.[23] This is because when buyers and sellers deal with each other over extended periods of time, certain customary practices develop. These practices are often overlooked in the writing of the contract, so courts allow the introduction of evidence to show how the parties have acted in the past. Usage of trade—practices and customs generally followed in a particular industry—can also shed light on the meaning of certain contract provisions, and thus evidence of trade usage may be admissible.

6. *Contracts subject to an orally agreed-on condition precedent.* Sometimes the parties agree that a condition must be fulfilled before a party is required to perform the contract. This is called a *condition precedent.* If the parties have orally agreed on a condition precedent and the condition does not conflict with the terms of a written agreement, then a court may allow parol evidence to prove the oral condition. The parol evidence rule does not apply here because the existence of the entire written contract is subject to an orally agreed-on condition. Proof of the condition does not alter or modify the written terms but affects the *enforceability* of the written contract.

  EXAMPLE 13.27 A city leases property for an airport from a well-established helicopter business. The lease is renewable every five years. During the second five-year lease, a dispute arises, and the parties go to mediation. They enter into a settlement memorandum under which they agree to amend the lease agreement subject to the approval of the city council. The city amends the lease, but the helicopter business refuses to sign it, contending that the council has not given its approval. In this situation, the council's approval is a condition precedent to the formation of the settlement memorandum contract. Therefore, the parol evidence rule does not apply, and oral evidence is admissible to show that no agreement exists as to the terms of the settlement. ■

7. *Contracts with an obvious or gross clerical (or typographic) error.* When an *obvious* or *gross* clerical (or typographic) error exists that clearly would not represent the agreement of the parties, parol evidence is admissible to correct the error. **EXAMPLE 13.28** Davis agrees to lease office space from Stone Enterprises for $3,000 per month. The signed written lease provides for a monthly lease payment of $300 rather than the $3,000 agreed to by the parties. Because the error is obvious, Stone Enterprises would be allowed to admit parol evidence to correct the mistake. ■

In the following case, an appeals court considered whether the trial court should have admitted parol evidence regarding the terms of an apartment lease.

---

22. *Watkins v. Schexnider,* 31 So.3d 609 (La.App. 3 Cir. 2010).
23. UCC 1–205, 2–202.

KNOW THIS
The parol evidence rule and its exceptions relate to the rules concerning the *interpretation* of contracts.

Assume that a helicopter company agrees to lease property to the city. If a dispute arises, when does the parol evidence rule apply?

CASE 13.3

Frewil, LLC v. Price

Court of Appeals of South Carolina, __ S.C. __, __ S.E.2d __, 2015 WL 446558 (2015).

FACTS Madison Price and Carter Smith were planning to attend the College of Charleston in South Carolina. They contacted Frewil LLC about renting an apartment at the beginning of the fall semester. They asked if the apartment had a washer/dryer and dishwasher, and were told yes. The lease did not expressly state that the unit contained those appliances, but it provided that any overflow from a washing machine or dishwasher was the responsibility of the tenant and that the dishwasher had to be clean for a refund of the security deposit. When Price and Smith arrived to move in, the apartment had no washer/dryer or dishwasher and no connections for them. The students found housing elsewhere. Frewil filed a suit in a South Carolina state court against Price and Smith, claiming breach of contract. The defendants sought to introduce parol evidence to challenge Frewil's claim. The court denied the request and issued a judgment in Frewil's favor. Price and Smith appealed.

ISSUE Was parol evidence admissible to challenge Frewil's claim?

DECISION Yes. A state intermediate appellate court reversed the judgment of the lower court. "The lease was ambiguous thereby permitting the introduction of parol evidence."

If a lease is ambiguous about the existence of a washer and dryer, can parol evidence be introduced in a contract dispute?

<small>iStockPhoto.com/RBOZUK</small>

REASON The appellate court explained that when a contract is ambiguous, parol evidence is admissible to show the contract's "true meaning." A contract is ambiguous when it is subject to more than one reasonable interpretation, "expresses its purpose in an indefinite manner," or does not address a certain situation. In these instances, a court can review the circumstances at the time of contract formation to determine the parties' intent. In this case, the court held that the contract between Frewil and the students was subject to more than one interpretation. The lease did not state that the apartment contained a washer/dryer or a dishwasher, but it did make statements that referred to these appliances. Because the lease was ambiguous on this point, parol evidence was admissible to challenge Frewil's breach of contract claim.

CRITICAL THINKING—Economic Consideration *How does the parol evidence rule save time and money for the parties to a dispute and the court that hears it? Discuss.*

13–4b Integrated Contracts

Integrated Contract A written contract that constitutes the final expression of the parties' agreement. Evidence extraneous to the contract that contradicts or alters the meaning of the contract in any way is inadmissible.

In determining whether to allow parol evidence, courts consider whether the written contract is intended to be a complete and final statement of the terms of the agreement. If it is, the contract is referred to as an **integrated contract,** and extraneous evidence (evidence from outside the contract) is excluded.

EXAMPLE 13.29 TKTS, Inc., offers to sell Gwen season tickets to the Dallas Cowboys football games in Cowboys Stadium. Prices and seat locations are indicated in diagrams in a brochure that accompanies the offer. Gwen responds, listing her seat preference. TKTS sends her the tickets, along with a different diagram showing seat locations. Also enclosed is a document that reads, "This is the entire agreement of the parties," which Gwen signs and returns. When Gwen goes to the first game, she discovers that her seat is not where she expected, based on the brochure. Under the parol evidence rule, however, the brochure is not part of the parties' agreement. The document that Gwen signed was identified as the parties' entire contract. Therefore, she cannot introduce in court any evidence of prior negotiations or agreements that contradict or vary the contract's terms. ■

A contract can be either completely or partially integrated. If it contains all of the terms of the parties' agreement, then it is completely integrated. If it contains only some of the terms and not others, it is partially integrated. If the contract is only partially integrated, evidence of consistent additional terms is admissible to supplement the written agreement.[24] Note that

---

24. *Restatement (Second) of Contracts*, Section 216.

Exhibit 13–4 The Parol Evidence Rule

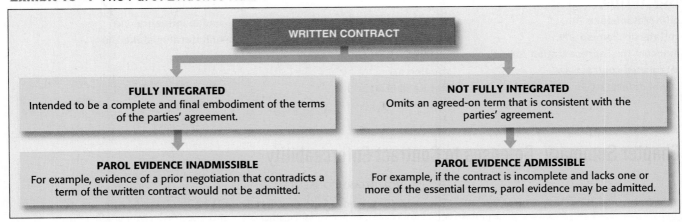

parol evidence is admitted only to add to the terms of a partially integrated contract. For both completely and partially integrated contracts, courts exclude any evidence that *contradicts* the writing.

Exhibit 13–4 illustrates the relationship between integrated contracts and the parol evidence rule.

Reviewing . . . Defenses to Contract Enforceability

Chelene had been a caregiver for Marta's elderly mother, Janis, for nine years. Shortly before Janis passed away, Chelene convinced her to buy Chelene's house for Marta. Janis died before the papers were signed, however. Four months later, Marta used her inheritance to buy Chelene's house without having it inspected. The house was built in the 1950s, and Chelene said it was in "perfect condition." Nevertheless, one year after the purchase, the basement started leaking. Marta had the paneling removed from the basement walls and discovered that the walls were bowed inward and cracked. Marta then had a civil engineer inspect the basement walls, and he found that the cracks had been caulked and painted over before the paneling was installed. He concluded that the "wall failure" had existed "for at least thirty years" and that the basement walls were "structurally unsound." Using the information presented in the chapter, answer the following questions.

1. Can Marta avoid the contract on the ground that both parties made a mistake about the condition of the house? Explain.

2. Can Marta sue Chelene for fraudulent misrepresentation? Why or why not? What element (or elements) might be lacking?

3. Now assume that Chelene knew that the basement walls were cracked and bowed and that she hired someone to install paneling before offering to sell the house. Did she have a duty to disclose this defect to Marta? Could a court find that Chelene's silence in this situation constituted misrepresentation? Explain.

4. Can Marta obtain rescission of the contract based on undue influence? If the sale to Janis had been completed before her death, could Janis have obtained rescission based on undue influence? Explain.

DEBATE THIS

- Many countries have eliminated the Statute of Frauds except for sales of real estate. The United States should do the same.

Key Terms

bilateral mistake 311

collateral promise 319

innocent misrepresentation 313

integrated contract 326

latent defect 313

negligent misrepresentation 313

parol evidence rule 324

prenuptial agreement 320

scienter 313

Statute of Frauds 318

undue influence 316

unilateral mistake 310

Chapter Summary: Defenses to Contract Enforceability

VOLUNTARY CONSENT	
Mistakes	**1.** *Unilateral*—Generally, the mistaken party is bound by the contract *unless* (a) the other party knows or should have known of the mistake or (b) the mistake is an inadvertent mathematical error—such as an error in addition or subtraction—committed without gross negligence. **2.** *Bilateral (mutual)*—When both parties are mistaken about the same material fact, such as identity, either party can avoid the contract.
Fraudulent Misrepresentation	When fraud occurs, usually the innocent party can enforce or avoid the contract. The following elements are necessary to establish fraud: **1.** A misrepresentation of a material fact must occur. **2.** There must be an intent to deceive. **3.** The innocent party must justifiably rely on the misrepresentation.
Undue Influence	Undue influence arises from special relationships, such as fiduciary relationships, in which one party's free will has been overcome by the undue influence exerted by the other party. Usually, the contract is voidable.
Duress	Duress is the tactic of forcing a party to enter a contract under the fear of a threat—for example, the threat of violence or serious economic loss. The party forced to enter the contract can rescind the contract.
FORM	

The Writing Requirement	**1.** *Applicability*—The following types of contracts fall under the Statute of Frauds and must be in writing to be enforceable:
	  a. Contracts involving interests in land, such as sales, leases, or mortgages.
	  b. Contracts that cannot by their terms be fully performed within one year from (the day after) the contract's formation.
	  c. Collateral promises, such as contracts made between a guarantor and a creditor whose terms make the guarantor secondarily liable. *Exception:* the "main purpose" rule.
	  d. Promises made in consideration of marriage, including promises to make a monetary payment or give property in consideration of a promise to marry and prenuptial agreements made in consideration of marriage.
	  e. Contracts for the sale of goods priced at $500 or more under the Statute of Frauds provision in Section 2–201 of the Uniform Commercial Code.
	2. *Exceptions*—Partial performance, admissions, and promissory estoppel.

Sufficiency of the Writing or Electronic Record	To constitute an enforceable contract under the Statute of Frauds, a writing must be signed by the party against whom enforcement is sought, name the parties, identify the subject matter, and state with reasonable certainty the essential terms of the contract. Under the UCC, a contract for a sale of goods is not enforceable beyond the quantity of goods shown in the contract.
The Parol Evidence Rule	The parol evidence rule prohibits the introduction at trial of evidence of the parties' prior or contemporaneous negotiations or agreements if this evidence contradicts or varies the terms of the parties' written contract. The written contract is assumed to be the complete embodiment of the parties' agreement. Because of the rigidity of the parol evidence rule, courts make a number of exceptions. For example, courts may allow parol evidence when a contract is void or voidable, contains ambiguous terms, or is incomplete.

Issue Spotters

1. In selling a house, Matt tells Ann that the wiring, fixtures, and appliances are of a certain quality. Matt knows nothing about the quality, but it is not as specified. Ann buys the house. On learning the true quality, Ann confronts Matt. He says he wasn't trying to fool her, he was only trying to make a sale. Can she rescind the deal? Why or why not? (See *Voluntary Consent*.)

2. My-T Quality Goods, Inc., and Nu! Sales Corporation orally agree to a deal. My-T's president has the essential terms written up on company letterhead stationery, and the memo is filed in My-T's office. If Nu! Sales later refuses to complete the transaction, is this memo a sufficient writing to enforce the contract against it? Explain your answer. (See *Sufficiency of the Writing or Electronic Record*.)

—**Check your answers to the *Issue Spotters* against the answers provided in Appendix D at the end of this text.**

Learning Objectives Check

1. In what types of situations might voluntary consent to a contract's terms be lacking?
2. What is the difference between a unilateral and a bilateral mistake?
3. What are the elements of fraudulent misrepresentation?
4. What contracts must be in writing to be enforceable?
5. What is parol evidence? When is it admissible to clarify the terms of a written contract?

—**Answers to the even-numbered *Learning Objectives Check* questions can be found in Appendix E at the end of this text.**

Business Scenarios and Case Problems

13–1. Voluntary Consent. Jerome is an elderly man who lives with his nephew, Philip. Jerome is totally dependent on Philip's support. Philip tells Jerome that unless Jerome transfers a tract of land he owns to Philip for a price 30 percent below market value, Philip will no longer support and take care of him. Jerome enters into the contract. Discuss fully whether Jerome can set aside this contract. (See *Voluntary Consent*.)

13–2. Statute of Frauds. Gemma promises a local hardware store that she will pay for a lawn mower that her brother is purchasing on credit if the brother fails to pay the debt. Must this promise be in writing to be enforceable? Why or why not? (See *The Writing Requirement*.)

13–3. Misrepresentation. Charter One Bank owned a fifteen-story commercial building. A fire inspector told Charter that the building's drinking-water and fire-suppression systems were linked, which violated building codes. Without disclosing this information, Charter sold the building to Northpoint Properties, Inc. Northpoint spent $280,000 to repair the water and fire-suppression systems and filed a suit against Charter One. Is the seller liable for not disclosing the building's defects? Discuss. [*Northpoint Properties, Inc. v. Charter One Bank,* 2011-Ohio-2512 (Ohio App. 8 Dist. 2011) (See *Voluntary Consent*.)

13–4. Statute of Frauds. Newmark & Co. Real Estate, Inc., contacted 2615 East 17 Street Realty, LLC, to lease certain real property on behalf of a client. Newmark e-mailed the landlord a separate agreement for the payment of Newmark's commission. The landlord e-mailed it back with a separate demand to pay the commission in installments. Newmark revised the agreement and e-mailed a final copy to the landlord. Do the parties have an agreement that qualifies as a writing under the Statute of Frauds? Explain. [*Newmark & Co. Real Estate, Inc. v. 2615 East 17 Street Realty, LLC,* 80 A.D.3d 476, 914 N.Y.S.2d 162 (1 Dept. 2011)] (See *Sufficiency of the Writing or Electronic Record*.)

13–5. The Parol Evidence Rule. Rimma Vaks and her husband, Steven Mangano, executed a written contract with Denise Ryan and Ryan Auction Co. to auction their furnishings. The six-page contract provided a detailed summary of the parties' agreement. It addressed the items to be auctioned, how reserve prices would be determined, and the amount of Ryan's commission. When a dispute arose between the parties, Vaks and Mangano sued Ryan for breach of contract. Vaks and Mangano asserted that, before they executed the contract, Ryan had made various oral representations that were inconsistent with the terms of their written agreement. Assuming that their written contract was valid, can Vaks and Mangano recover for breach of an oral contract? Why or why not? [*Vaks v. Ryan,* 2012 WL 194398 (Mass.App. 2012)] (See *The Parol Evidence Rule*.)

13–6. Promises Made in Consideration of Marriage. After twenty-nine years of marriage, Robert and Mary Lou Tuttle were divorced. They admitted in court that before they were married, they had signed a prenuptial agreement. They agreed that the agreement had stated that each would keep his or her own property and anything derived from that property. Robert came into the marriage owning farmland, while Mary Lou owned no real estate. During the marriage, ten different parcels of land, totaling about six hundred acres, were acquired, and two corporations, Tuttle Grain, Inc., and Tuttle Farms, Inc., were formed. A copy of the prenuptial agreement could not be found. Can the court enforce the agreement without a writing? Why or why not? [*In re Marriage of Tuttle,* 2013 WL 164035 (Ill. App. 5 Dist. 2013)] (See *The Writing Requirement.*)

13–7. Business Case Problem with Sample Answer— Fraudulent Misrepresentation. Joy Pervis and Brenda Pauley worked together as talent agents in Georgia. When Pervis "discovered" actress Dakota Fanning, Pervis sent Fanning's audition tape to Cindy Osbrink, a talent agent in California. Osbrink agreed to represent Fanning in California and to pay 3 percent of Osbrink's commissions to Pervis and Pauley, who agreed to split the payments equally. Six years later, Pervis told Pauley that their agreement with Osbrink had expired and there would be no more payments. Nevertheless, Pervis continued to receive payments from Osbrink. Each time Pauley asked about commissions, however, Pervis replied that she was not receiving any. Do these facts evidence fraud? Explain. [*In re Pervis,* 512 Bankr. 348 (N.D.Ga. 2014)] (See *Voluntary Consent.*)

—**For a sample answer to Problem 13–7, go to Appendix F at the end of this text.**

13–8. Promises Made in Consideration of Marriage. Before their marriage, Linda and Gerald Heiden executed a prenuptial agreement. The agreement provided that "no spouse shall have any right in the property of the other spouse, even in the event of the death of either party." The description of Gerald's separate property included a settlement from a personal injury suit. Twenty-four years later, Linda filed for divorce. The court ruled that the prenuptial agreement applied only in the event of death, not divorce, and entered a judgment that included a property division and spousal support award. The ruling disparately favored Linda, whose monthly income with spousal support would be $4,467, leaving Gerald with only $1,116. Did the court interpret the Heidens' prenuptial agreement correctly? Discuss. [*Heiden v. Heiden,* 2015 WL 849006 (Mich.App. 2015)] (See *The Writing Requirement.*)

13–9. A Question of Ethics—Bilateral Mistake. On behalf of BRJM, LLC, Nicolas Kepple offered Howard Engelsen $210,000 for a parcel of land known as lot five on the north side of Barnes Road in Stonington, Connecticut. Engelsen's company, Output Systems, Inc., owned the land. Engelsen had the lot surveyed and obtained an appraisal. The appraiser valued the property at $277,000, after determining that it was 3 acres in size and thus could not be subdivided because it did not meet the town's minimum legal requirement of 3.7 acres for subdivision. Engelsen responded to Kepple's offer with a counteroffer of $230,000, which Kepple accepted. The parties signed a contract. When Engelsen refused to go through with the deal, BRJM filed a suit against Output, seeking specific performance and other relief. Output asserted the defense of mutual mistake on at least two grounds. [*BRJM, LLC v. Output Systems, Inc.,* 100 Conn.App. 143, 917 A.2d 605 (2007)] (See *Voluntary Consent.*)

1. In the counteroffer, Engelsen asked Kepple to remove from their contract a clause requiring written confirmation of the availability of a "free split," which meant that the property could be subdivided without the town's prior approval. Kepple agreed. After signing the contract, Kepple learned that the property was *not* entitled to a free split. Would this circumstance qualify as a mistake on which the *defendant* could avoid the contract? Why or why not?

2. After signing the contract, Engelsen obtained a second appraisal that established the size of lot five as 3.71 acres, which meant that it could be subdivided, and valued the property at $490,000. Can the defendant avoid the contract on the basis of a mistake in the first appraisal? Explain.

Critical Thinking and Writing Assignments

13–10. Business Law Critical Thinking Group Assignment. Jason Novell, doing business as Novell Associates, hired Barbara Meade as an independent contractor. The parties orally agreed on the terms of employment, including payment of a share of the company's income to Meade, but they did not put anything in writing. Two years later, Meade quit. Novell then told Meade that she was entitled to $9,602— 25 percent of the difference between the accounts receivable and the accounts payable as of Meade's last day of work. Meade disagreed and demanded more than $63,500—25 percent of the revenue from all invoices, less the cost of materials and outside processing, for each of the years that she had worked for Novell. Meade filed a lawsuit against Novell for breach of contract. (See *The Writing Requirement.*)

1. The first group will evaluate whether the parties had an enforceable contract.

2. The second group will decide whether the parties' oral agreement falls within any exception to the Statute of Frauds.

3. The third group will discuss how the lawsuit would be affected if Novell admitted that the parties had an oral contract under which Meade was entitled to 25 percent of the difference between the accounts receivable and payable as of the day Meade quit.

14

Third Party Rights and Discharge

LEARNING OBJECTIVES

The five Learning Objectives *below are designed to help improve your understanding of the chapter. After reading this chapter, you should be able to answer the following questions:*

1. What is an assignment? What is the difference between an assignment and a delegation?

2. In what situations is the delegation of duties prohibited?

3. What factors indicate that a third party beneficiary is an intended beneficiary?

4. How are most contracts discharged?

5. When is a breach considered material, and what effect does that have on the other party's obligation to perform?

"The laws of a state change with the changing times."

AESCHYLUS
525–456 B.C.E.
(GREEK DRAMATIST)

Once it has been determined that a valid and legally enforceable contract exists, attention can turn to the rights and duties of the parties to the contract. A contract is a private agreement between the parties who have entered into it, and traditionally these parties alone have rights and liabilities under the contract. This principle is referred to as **privity of contract,** and it establishes the basic principle that third parties have no rights in contracts to which they are not parties.

You may be convinced by now that for every rule of contract law, there is an exception. As times change, so must the laws, as indicated in the chapter-opening quotation. When justice cannot be served by adherence to a rule of law, exceptions to the rule must be made.

In this chapter, we look at some exceptions to the rule of privity of contract. These exceptions include *assignments, delegations,* and *third party beneficiary contracts.* We also examine how contractual obligations can be *discharged.* Normally, contract discharge is accomplished when both parties perform the acts promised in the contract. In the latter part of the chapter, we look at the degree of performance required to discharge a contractual obligation, as well as at some other ways that contract discharge can occur.

Privity of Contract The relationship that exists between the promisor and the promisee of a contract.

14-1 Assignments

In a bilateral contract, the two parties have corresponding rights and duties. One party has a *right* to require the other to perform some task, and the other has a *duty* to perform it.

331

Assignment The transfer to another of all or part of one's rights arising under a contract.

Sometimes, though, a party will transfer her or his rights under the contract to someone else. The transfer of contract *rights* to a third person is known as an **assignment.** (The transfer of contract duties is a *delegation,* as will be discussed later in this chapter.)

Assignments are important because they are often used in business financing. Lending institutions, such as banks, frequently assign the rights to receive payments under their loan contracts to other firms, which pay for those rights. Lenders that make *mortgage loans* (loans that enable prospective home buyers to purchase real estate), for instance, often assign their rights to collect the mortgage payments to a third party. Following an assignment, the home buyer is notified that future payments must be made to the third party, rather than to the original lender. Billions of dollars change hands daily in the business world in the form of assignments of rights in contracts. If it were not possible to transfer contractual rights, many businesses could not continue to operate.

14–1a Effect of an Assignment

LEARNING OBJECTIVE 1

What is an assignment? What is the difference between an assignment and a delegation?

Assignor A party who transfers (assigns) his or her rights under a contract to another party (the *assignee*).

Assignee A party to whom the rights under a contract are transferred, or assigned.

Obligee One to whom an obligation is owed.

Obligor One who owes an obligation to another.

In an assignment, the party assigning the rights to a third party is known as the **assignor,**[1] and the party receiving the rights is the **assignee.**[2] Other terms traditionally used to describe the parties in assignment relationships are **obligee** (the person to whom a duty, or obligation, is owed) and **obligor** (the person who is obligated to perform the duty). Exhibit 14–1 illustrates assignment relationships.

In general, an assignment can take any form, oral or written, although it is advisable to put all assignments in writing. Of course, assignments covered by the Statute of Frauds—such as an assignment of an interest in land—must be in writing to be enforceable. In addition, most states require contracts for the assignment of wages to be in writing.[3] There are other assignments that must be in writing as well.

---

1. Pronounced uh-*sye*-nore.
2. Pronounced uh-sye-*nee*.
3. See, for example, California Labor Code Section 300.

Exhibit 14–1 Assignment Relationships

In the assignment relationship illustrated here, Alex assigns his *rights* under a contract that he made with Brent to a third party, Carmen. Alex thus becomes the *assignor* and Carmen the *assignee* of the contractual rights. Brent, the *obligor,* now owes performance to Carmen instead of to Alex. Alex's original contract rights are extinguished after the assignment.

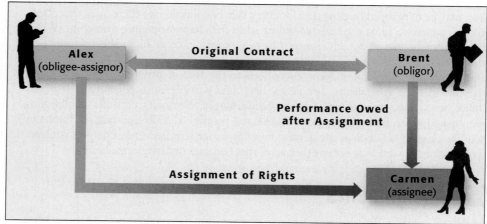

Extinguishes the Rights of the Assignor When rights under a contract are assigned unconditionally, the rights of the assignor are extinguished.[4] The assignee has a right to demand performance from the other original party to the contract, the obligor.

EXAMPLE 14.1 Brent (the obligor) owes Alex $1,000 under a contract in which Brent agreed to buy Alex's MacBook Pro laptop. Alex, the obligee, assigns to Carmen the right to receive the $1,000 (thus, Alex is the assignor). Here, a valid assignment of a debt exists. Carmen, the assignee, can enforce the contract against Brent, the obligor, if he fails to perform (pay the $1,000). ■

Assignee Takes Rights Subject to Defenses The assignee obtains only those rights that the assignor originally had. In addition, the assignee's rights are subject to the defenses that the obligor has against the assignor.

EXAMPLE 14.2 In *Example 14.1,* Brent owes Alex $1,000 under a contract in which Brent agreed to buy Alex's laptop. Alex assigns his right to receive the $1,000 to Carmen. But Brent, in deciding to purchase the laptop, relied on Alex's fraudulent misrepresentation that the computer had sixteen megabytes of memory. When Brent discovers that the computer has only eight megabytes of memory, he tells Alex that he is going to return it and cancel the contract. Even though Alex has assigned his "right" to receive the $1,000 to Carmen, Brent need not pay Carmen the $1,000—Brent can raise the defense of Alex's fraudulent misrepresentation to avoid payment. ■

14–1b Rights That Cannot Be Assigned

As a general rule, all rights can be assigned. Exceptions are made, however, in the following special circumstances.

When a Statute Expressly Prohibits Assignment If a statute expressly prohibits assignment, the right in question cannot be assigned. **EXAMPLE 14.3** Quincy is an employee of Specialty Travel, Inc. Specialty is an employer bound by workers' compensation statutes in this state, and thus Quincy is a covered employee. Quincy is injured on the job and begins to collect monthly workers' compensation checks. In need of a loan, Quincy borrows from Draper, offering to assign to Draper all of her future workers' compensation benefits. A state statute prohibits the assignment of *future* workers' compensation benefits, and thus such rights cannot be assigned. ■

When a Contract Is Personal in Nature When a contract is for personal services, the rights under the contract normally cannot be assigned unless all that remains is a monetary payment.[5] **EXAMPLE 14.4** Anton signs a contract to be a tutor for Marisa's children. Marisa then attempts to assign to Roberto her right to Anton's services. Roberto cannot enforce the contract against Anton. Roberto's children may be more difficult to tutor than Marisa's. Thus, if Marisa could assign her rights to Anton's services to Roberto, it would change the nature of Anton's obligation. Because personal services are unique to the person rendering them, rights to receive personal services are likewise unique and cannot be assigned. ■

When an Assignment Will Significantly Change the Risk or Duties of the Obligor A right cannot be assigned if assignment will significantly alter the risks or the duties of the obligor.[6] **EXAMPLE 14.5** Alex has a hotel, and to insure it, he takes out a policy with Northwest Insurance Company. The policy insures against fire, theft, floods, and vandalism. Alex attempts to assign the insurance policy to Carmen, who also owns a hotel.

Can the rights to receive piano lessons be assigned to another student?

---

4. *Restatement (Second) of Contracts*, Section 317.
5. *Restatement (Second) of Contracts*, Sections 317 and 318.
6. See Section 2–210(2) of the Uniform Commercial Code (UCC).

The assignment is ineffective because it may substantially alter the insurance company's duty of performance and the risk that the company undertakes. An insurance company evaluates the particular risk associated with a specific party and tailors its policy to fit that risk. If the policy were assigned to a third party, the insurance risk would be materially altered. ■

When the Contract Prohibits Assignment

If a contract stipulates that the right cannot be assigned, then *ordinarily* it cannot be assigned. This restraint operates only against the parties themselves. It does not prohibit an assignment by operation of law, such as an assignment pursuant to bankruptcy or death.

Whether an *antiassignment clause* is effective depends, in part, on how it is phrased. A contract that states that *any* assignment is void effectively prohibits any assignment. **EXAMPLE 14.6** Ramirez agrees to build a house for Lee. Their contract states "This contract cannot be assigned by Lee without Ramirez's consent. Any assignment without such consent renders the contract void." This antiassignment clause is effective, and Lee cannot assign her rights without obtaining Ramirez's consent. ■

The rule that a contract can prohibit assignments has several exceptions:

1. A contract cannot prevent an assignment of the right to receive funds. This exception exists to encourage the free flow of funds and credit in modern business settings.

2. The assignment of ownership rights in real estate often cannot be prohibited because such a prohibition is contrary to public policy in most states. Prohibitions of this kind are called restraints against **alienation** (the voluntary transfer of land ownership).

3. The assignment of negotiable instruments (such as checks and promissory notes) cannot be prohibited.

4. In a contract for the sale of goods, the right to receive damages for breach of contract or payment on an account may be assigned even though the sales contract prohibits such an assignment.[7]

The lease and purchase agreement in the following case contained an antiassignment clause. The court had to decide whether the clause was enforceable.

> **Alienation** The transfer of title to real property (which "alienates" the real property from the former owner).

---

7. UCC 2–210(2).

Bass-Fineberg Leasing, Inc. v. Modern Auto Sales, Inc.

Court of Appeals of Ohio, Ninth District, Medina County, __ Ohio App.3d __, __ N.E.3d __, 2015-Ohio-46 (2015).

FACTS Bass-Fineberg Leasing, Inc., leased a tour bus to Modern Auto Sales, Inc., and Michael Cipriani. The lease included an option to buy the bus. The lease prohibited Modern Auto and Cipriani from assigning their rights without Bass-Fineberg's written consent. Later, Cipriani left the bus with Anthony Allie at BVIP Limo Services, Ltd., for repairs. Modern Auto and Cipriani did not pay for the repairs. At the same time, they defaulted on the lease payments to Bass-Fineberg. While BVIP retained possession of the bus, Allie signed an agreement with Cipriani to buy it and to make an initial $5,000 payment to Bass-Fineberg. Bass-Fineberg filed an action in an Ohio

Can the rights to a leased tour bus be assigned?

iStockPhoto.com/mladn61

state court against Modern Auto, Cipriani, BVIP, and Allie to regain possession of the bus. The court ordered the bus returned to Bass-Fineberg and the $5,000 payment refunded to Allie. All of the parties appealed.

ISSUE Was the lease's antiassignment clause enforceable?

DECISION Yes. A state intermediate appellate court affirmed the lower court's order. The bus was to be returned to Bass-Fineberg and the $5,000 was to be refunded to Allie.

REASON An antiassignment clause can be enforceable when it clearly prohibits an assignment. Violation of an enforceable antiassignment provision renders the resulting agreement void. The antiassignment clause in the lease between Bass-Fineberg and Modern Auto and Cipriani was clear—"MODERN AUTO AND CIPRIANI MAY NOT ASSIGN ... [THEIR] RIGHTS ... UNDER THIS LEASE ... WITHOUT BASS-FINEBERG'S PRIOR WRITTEN CONSENT." Bass-Fineberg argued that under this clause, the contract between Cipriani and Allie was void, because Bass-Fineberg had not provided written consent. BVIP contended that if the contract was void, then BVIP should receive a refund of its $5,000 payment. The court agreed with both of these parties. The contract between Cipriani and Allie was void because Cipriani could not assign his rights under the lease without Bass-Fineberg's written consent. Because the contract was void, the parties were to be returned to their precontract status, which included a refund of the $5,000 payment.

CRITICAL THINKING—Economic Consideration *The repairs to the bus cost $1,341.50. Who should pay this amount? Why?*

14-1c Notice of Assignment

Once a valid assignment of rights has been made to a third party, the third party should notify the obligor of the assignment (for example, in Exhibit 14–1, Carmen should notify Brent). Giving notice is not legally necessary to establish the validity of the assignment because an assignment is effective immediately, whether or not notice is given. Two major problems arise, however, when notice of the assignment is *not* given to the obligor.

Priority Issues If the assignor assigns the same right to two different persons, the question arises as to which one has priority—that is, which one has the right to the performance by the obligor. The rule most often observed in the United States is that the first assignment in time is the first in right. Some states, though, follow the English rule, which basically gives priority to the first assignee who gives notice.

EXAMPLE 14.7 Jason owes Alexis $5,000 under a contract. Alexis first assigns the claim to Louisa, who does not give notice to Jason. Then Alexis assigns it to Dorman, who notifies Jason. In most states, Louisa would have priority because the assignment to her was first in time. In some states, however, Dorman would have priority because he gave first notice. ■

Potential for Discharge by Performance to the Wrong Party Until the obligor has notice of an assignment, the obligor can discharge his or her obligation by performance to the assignor, and this performance constitutes a discharge to the assignee. Once the obligor receives proper notice, only performance to the assignee can discharge the obligor's obligations.

EXAMPLE 14.8 Recall that Alexis, the obligee in *Example 14.7*, assigned to Louisa her right to collect $5,000 from Jason, and Louisa did not give notice to Jason. What will happen if Jason later pays Alexis the $5,000? Although the assignment was valid, Jason's payment to Alexis will discharge the debt. Louisa's failure to notify Jason of the assignment will cause her to lose the right to collect the $5,000 from Jason. (Note that Louisa will still have a claim against Alexis for the $5,000.) If Louisa had given Jason notice of the assignment, Jason's payment to Alexis would not have discharged the debt. ■

Providing notice of assignment, though not legally required, is one of the best ways to avoid potential legal disputes over assignments. Whether you are the assignee or the assignor, you should inform the obligor of the assignment. An assignee who does not give notice may lose the right to performance, but failure to notify the obligor may have repercussions for the assignor as well. If no notice is given and the obligor performs the duty for the assignor, the assignee can sue the assignor for breach of contract. Litigation may also ensue if the assignor has assigned a right to two different parties, as may happen when rights that overlap (such as rights to receive various profits from a given enterprise) are assigned.

PREVENTING LEGAL DISPUTES

14-2 Delegations

Delegation of Duties
The transfer to another of a contractual duty.

Delegator A party who transfers (delegates) her or his obligations under a contract to another party (the *delegatee*).

Delegatee A party to whom contractual obligations are transferred, or delegated.

Just as a party can transfer rights to a third party through an assignment, a party can also transfer duties. Duties are not assigned, however. They are *delegated*. Normally, a **delegation of duties** does not relieve the party making the delegation (the **delegator**) of the obligation to perform in the event that the party to whom the duty has been delegated (the **delegatee**) fails to perform.

No special form is required to create a valid delegation of duties. As long as the delegator expresses an intention to make the delegation, it is effective. The delegator need not even use the word *delegate*.

LEARNING OBJECTIVE 2

In what situations is the delegation of duties prohibited?

14-2a Duties That Cannot Be Delegated

As a general rule, any duty can be delegated. This rule has some exceptions, however. Delegation is prohibited in the following circumstances:

1. When performance depends on the personal skill or talents of the obligor.
2. When special trust has been placed in the obligor.
3. When performance by a third party will vary materially from that expected by the obligee.
4. When the contract expressly prohibits delegation.

When the Duties Are Personal in Nature When special trust has been placed in the obligor or when performance depends on the obligor's personal skill or talents, contractual duties cannot be delegated. **EXAMPLE 14.9** O'Brien, who is impressed with Brodie's ability to perform veterinary surgery, contracts with Brodie to have her perform surgery on O'Brien's prize-winning stallion in July. Brodie later decides that she would rather spend the summer at the beach, so she delegates her duties under the contract to Lopez, who is also a competent veterinary surgeon. The delegation is not effective without O'Brien's consent, no matter how competent Lopez is, because the contract is for *personal* performance. ■

In contrast, nonpersonal duties may be delegated. Suppose that, in *Example 14.9*, Brodie contracts with O'Brien to pick up a large horse trailer and deliver it to O'Brien's property. Brodie delegates this duty to Lopez, who owns a towing business. This delegation is effective because the performance required is of a *routine* and *nonpersonal* nature.

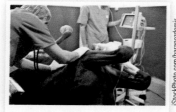

Under what circumstances may a veterinary surgeon delegate her duties to another veterinarian?

When Performance by a Third Party Will Vary Materially from That Expected by the Obligee When performance by a third party will vary materially from that expected by the obligee under the contract, contractual duties cannot be delegated. **EXAMPLE 14.10** Jared, a wealthy investor, established the company Heaven Sent to provide grants of capital to struggling but potentially successful businesses. Jared contracted with Merilyn, whose judgment Jared trusted, to select the recipients of the grants. Later, Merilyn delegated this duty to Donald. Jared did not trust Donald's ability to select worthy recipients. This delegation is not effective because it materially alters Jared's expectations under the contract with Merilyn. ■

When the Contract Prohibits Delegation When the contract expressly prohibits delegation by including an *antidelegation clause,* the duties cannot be delegated. **EXAMPLE 14.11** Dakota Company has contracted with Belisario, a certified public accountant, to perform its audits. Because the contract prohibits delegation, Belisario cannot delegate the duty to perform the audits to another accountant—not even an accountant at the same firm. ■

14-2b Effect of a Delegation

If a delegation of duties is enforceable, the obligee (the one to whom performance is owed) must accept performance from the delegatee (the one to whom the duties are delegated). **EXAMPLE 14.12** Brent has a duty to pick up and deliver heavy construction machinery to Alex's property. Brent delegates his duty to Carmen. In this situation, Alex (the obligee) must accept performance from Carmen (the delegatee) because the delegation is effective. The obligee can legally refuse performance from the delegatee only if the duty is one that cannot be delegated. ■ Exhibit 14–2 graphically illustrates their delegation relationship.

As noted, a valid delegation of duties does not relieve the delegator of obligations under the contract.[8] Although there are many exceptions, the general rule today is that the obligee can sue both the delegatee and the delegator for failure to perform.

EXAMPLE 14.13 In the situation in *Example 14.12,* if Carmen (the delegatee) fails to perform, Brent (the delegator) is still liable to Alex (the obligee). The obligee can also hold the delegatee liable if the delegatee made a promise of performance that will directly benefit the obligee. In this situation, there is an "assumption of duty" on the part of the delegatee, and breach of this duty makes the delegatee liable to the obligee. For instance, if Carmen promised Brent, in a contract, to pick up and deliver the construction equipment to Alex's property but fails to do so, Alex can sue Brent, Carmen, or both. ■

14–2c "Assignment of All Rights"

Sometimes, a contract provides for an "assignment of all rights." This wording may create both an assignment of rights and a delegation of duties.[9] Typically, this situation occurs when general words are used, such as "I assign the contract" or "I assign all my rights under the contract." A court normally will construe such words as implying both an assignment of rights and a delegation of any duties of performance. Thus, the assignor remains liable if the assignee fails to perform the contractual obligations.

---

8. For a classic case on this issue, see *Crane Ice Cream Co. v. Terminal Freezing & Heating Co.*, 147 Md. 588, 128 A. 280 (1925).
9. See UCC 2–210(1), (4); and *Restatement (Second) of Contracts*, Section 328.

KNOW THIS
In an assignment, the assignor's original contract rights are extinguished after the assignment. In a delegation, the delegator remains liable for performance under the contract if the delegatee fails to perform.

Exhibit 14–2 Delegation Relationships

In the delegation relationship illustrated here, Brent delegates his *duties* under a contract that he made with Alex to a third party, Carmen. Brent thus becomes the *delegator* and Carmen the *delegatee* of the contractual duties. Carmen now owes performance of the contractual duties to Alex. Note that a delegation of duties normally does not relieve the delegator (Brent) of liability if the delegatee (Carmen) fails to perform the contractual duties.

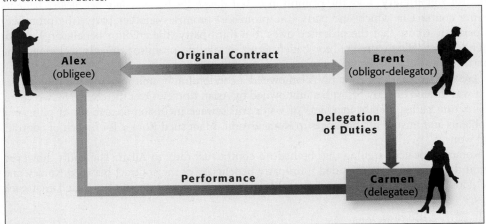

14-3 Third Party Beneficiaries

Third Party Beneficiary
One who is not a party to the contract but who stands to benefit from the contract's performance.

Intended Beneficiary A third party for whose benefit a contract is formed. An intended beneficiary can sue the promisor if the contract is breached.

Another exception to the doctrine of privity of contract may arise when a third party benefits from a contract between two other parties. This **third party beneficiary** may have rights in the contract. Note, though, that the law identifies two types of third party beneficiaries: *intended beneficiaries* and *incidental beneficiaries*. Only intended beneficiaries have legal rights in the contract.

An **intended beneficiary** is one for whose benefit the contract was made. That is, the original parties to the contract agreed when they made the contract that performance should be rendered to or directly benefit a third person. This type of third party beneficiary has legal rights and can sue the promisor directly for breach of the contract.

Who, though, is the promisor? After all, in bilateral contracts, both parties to the contract are promisors because both make promises that can be enforced.

14-3a Who Is the Promisor?

In third party beneficiary contracts, courts determine the identity of the promisor by asking which party made the promise that benefits the third party. That person is the promisor.

In effect, allowing the third party to sue the promisor directly circumvents the "middle person" (the promisee) and thus reduces the burden on the courts. Otherwise, the third party would sue the promisee, who would then sue the promisor. Indeed, at one time, this circuitous route was the rule. The reason was that the third party beneficiary was not a party to the contract and thus, under the doctrine of privity of contract, had no legal rights under the contract.

CASE EXAMPLE 14.14 The classic case that gave third party beneficiaries the right to bring a suit directly against a promisor was decided in 1859. The case involved three parties—Holly, Lawrence, and Fox. Holly had borrowed $300 from Lawrence. Shortly thereafter, Holly loaned $300 to Fox, who in return promised Holly that he would pay Holly's debt to Lawrence on the following day. When Lawrence failed to obtain the $300 from Fox, he sued Fox to recover the funds. The court had to decide whether Lawrence could sue Fox directly (rather than suing Holly). The court held that when "a promise [is] made for the benefit of another, he for whose benefit it is made may bring an action for its breach."[10] ■

14-3b Types of Intended Beneficiaries

Intended beneficiaries can be further classified as *creditor beneficiaries* or *donee beneficiaries*.

Creditor Beneficiary Like the plaintiff in *Case Example 14.14*, a *creditor beneficiary* benefits from a contract in which one party (the promisor) promises another party (the promisee) to perform a duty that the promisee owes to a third party (the creditor beneficiary). As an intended beneficiary, the creditor beneficiary can sue the promisor directly to enforce the contract.

CASE EXAMPLE 14.15 Autumn Allan owned a condominium unit in a Texas complex. Her unit was located directly beneath a unit owned by Aslan Koraev. Over the course of two years, Allan's unit suffered eight incidents of water and sewage incursion as a result of plumbing problems and misuse of appliances in Koraev's unit. Allan sued Koraev for breach of contract and won.

Koraev appealed, arguing that he had no contractual duty to Allan. The court, however, found that Allan was an intended third party beneficiary of the contract between Koraev and the condominium owners' association. Because the governing documents stated that each

---

10. *Lawrence v. Fox*, 20 N.Y. 268 (1859).

owner had to comply strictly with their provisions, failure to comply created grounds for an action by either the condominium association or an aggrieved (wronged) owner. Here, Allan was an aggrieved owner and could sue Koraev directly for his failure to perform his contractual duties to the condominium association.[11] ◼

Donee Beneficiary   When a contract is made for the express purpose of giving a *gift* to a third party, the third party is a *donee beneficiary*. Like a creditor beneficiary, a donee beneficiary can sue the promisor directly to enforce the promise.[12]

The most common donee beneficiary contract is a life insurance contract. **EXAMPLE 14.16** Ang (the promisee) pays premiums to Standard Life, a life insurance company, and Standard Life (the promisor) promises to pay a certain amount on Ang's death to anyone Ang designates as a beneficiary. The designated beneficiary is a donee beneficiary under the life insurance policy and can enforce the promise made by the insurance company to pay her or him on Ang's death. ◼

14–3c When the Rights of an Intended Beneficiary Vest

An intended third party beneficiary cannot enforce a contract against the original parties until the third party's rights have *vested,* meaning that the rights have taken effect and cannot be taken away. Until these rights have vested, the original parties to the contract—the promisor and the promisee—can modify or rescind the contract without the consent of the third party.

When do the rights of third parties vest? Generally, the rights vest when one of the following occurs:

1. When the third party demonstrates express consent to the agreement, such as by sending a letter, a note, or an e-mail acknowledging awareness of, and consent to, a contract formed for her or his benefit.

2. When the third party materially alters his or her position in detrimental reliance on the contract, such as when a donee beneficiary contracts to have a home built in reliance on the receipt of funds promised to him or her in a donee beneficiary contract.

3. When the conditions for vesting are satisfied. For instance, the rights of a beneficiary under a life insurance policy vest when the insured person dies.

14–3d Incidental Beneficiaries

Sometimes, a third person receives a benefit from a contract even though that person's benefit is not the reason the contract was made. Such a person is known as an **incidental beneficiary.** Because the benefit is unintentional, an incidental beneficiary cannot sue to enforce the contract.

CASE EXAMPLE 14.17 Spectators at the infamous boxing match in which Mike Tyson was disqualified for biting his opponent's ear sued Tyson and the fight's promoters for a refund on the basis of breach of contract. The spectators claimed that they were third party beneficiaries of the contract between Tyson and the fight's promoters. The court, however, held that the spectators could not sue, because they were not in contractual privity with the defendants. Any benefits they received from the contract were incidental to the contract. According to the court, the spectators got what they paid for: "the right to view whatever event transpired."[13] ◼

iStockPhoto.com/rognar

When can a condominium owner directly sue another owner in the same building because of water and sewage incursion?

Incidental Beneficiary   A third party who benefits from a contract even though the contract was not formed for that purpose. An incidental beneficiary has no rights in the contract and cannot sue to have it enforced.

---

11. *Allan v. Nersesova*, 307 S.W.3d 564 (Tx.App—Dallas 2010).
12. This principle was first enunciated in *Seaver v. Ransom*, 224 N.Y. 233, 120 N.E. 639 (1918).
13. *Castillo v. Tyson*, 268 A.D.2d 336, 701 N.Y.S.2d 423 (Sup.Ct.App.Div. 2000).

LEARNING OBJECTIVE 3

What factors indicate that a third party beneficiary is an intended beneficiary?

14–3e Identifying Intended versus Incidental Beneficiaries

In determining whether a party is an intended or an incidental beneficiary, the courts focus on the parties' intent, as expressed in the contract language and implied by the surrounding circumstances. Any beneficiary who is not deemed an intended beneficiary is considered incidental. Exhibit 14–3 graphically illustrates the distinction between intended and incidental beneficiaries.

Although no single test can embrace all possible situations, courts often apply the *reasonable person* test: Would a reasonable person in the position of the beneficiary believe that the promisee intended to confer on the beneficiary the right to enforce the contract? In addition, the presence of one or more of the following factors strongly indicates that the third party is an intended beneficiary of the contract:

1. Performance is rendered directly to the third party.

2. The third party has the right to control the details of performance.

3. The third party is expressly designated as a beneficiary in the contract.

CASE EXAMPLE 14.18 Neumann Homes, Inc., contracted to make public improvements for the Village of Antioch, Illinois. Neumann subcontracted the grading work required under the contract to Lake County Grading Company. The subcontractor completed the work but was not paid in full. When Neumann declared bankruptcy, the subcontractor filed a suit against the Village to recover, claiming to be a third party beneficiary of the contract between the Village and Neumann.

The court held in favor of the subcontractor. Under an Illinois statute, the Village was required to obtain a payment bond guaranteeing that a contractor would pay what was owed for the completion of any public works project. The court reasoned that this statute was intended to benefit subcontractors in public works contracts. Thus, it was reasonable for Lake County to believe that it was an intended third party beneficiary. Because the Village had failed to obtain a bond ensuring payment to subcontractors, Lake County could sue for breach of contract.[14]

---

14. *Lake County Grading Co. v. Village of Antioch,* 2014 IL 115805, 19 N.E.3d 615 (Ill. Sup. 2014).

Exhibit 14–3 Third Party Beneficiaries

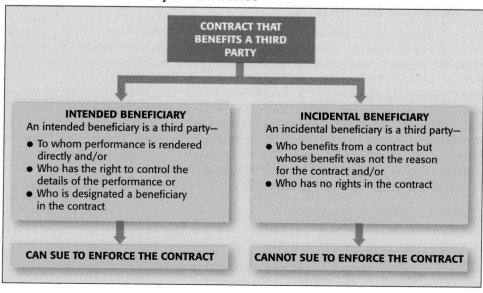

CONTRACT THAT BENEFITS A THIRD PARTY	
INTENDED BENEFICIARY An intended beneficiary is a third party— • To whom performance is rendered directly and/or • Who has the right to control the details of the performance or • Who is designated a beneficiary in the contract	**INCIDENTAL BENEFICIARY** An incidental beneficiary is a third party— • Who benefits from a contract but whose benefit was not the reason for the contract and/or • Who has no rights in the contract
CAN SUE TO ENFORCE THE CONTRACT	**CANNOT SUE TO ENFORCE THE CONTRACT**

14-4 Contract Discharge

The most common way to **discharge,** or terminate, one's contractual duties is by the **performance** of those duties. The duty to perform under a contract may be *conditioned* on the occurrence or nonoccurrence of a certain event, or the duty may be *absolute*. As shown in Exhibit 14–4, in addition to performance, a contract can be discharged in numerous other ways, including discharge by agreement of the parties and discharge by operation of law.

14-4a Conditions of Performance

In most contracts, promises of performance are not expressly conditioned or qualified. Instead, they are *absolute promises*. They must be performed, or the party making the promise will be in breach of contract. **EXAMPLE 14.19** Paloma Enterprises contracts to sell a truckload of organic produce to Tran for $10,000. The parties' promises are unconditional: Paloma will deliver the produce to Tran, and Tran will pay $10,000 to Paloma. The payment does not have to be made if the produce is not delivered. ■

In some situations, however, contractual promises are conditioned. A **condition** is a qualification in a contract based on a possible future event, the occurrence or nonoccurrence of which will trigger the performance of a legal obligation or terminate an existing obligation under a contract. If the condition is not satisfied, the obligations of the parties are discharged.

Three types of conditions can be present in any given contract: *conditions precedent, conditions subsequent,* and *concurrent conditions.*

Conditions Precedent A condition that must be fulfilled before a party's promise becomes absolute is called a **condition precedent.** The condition precedes the absolute duty to perform. Life insurance contracts frequently specify that certain conditions, such as passing a physical examination, must be met before the insurance company will be obligated to perform under the contract.

Many contracts are conditioned on an independent appraisal of value. **EXAMPLE 14.20** Restoration Motors offers to buy Charlie's 1960 Cadillac limousine only if an expert appraiser estimates that it can be restored for less than a certain price. Thus, the parties' obligations are conditioned on the outcome of the appraisal. If the condition is not satisfied—that is, if the appraiser deems the cost to be significantly above that price—their obligations are discharged. ■

Conditions Subsequent When a condition operates to terminate a party's absolute promise to perform, it is called a **condition subsequent.** The condition follows, or is subsequent to, the absolute duty to perform. If the condition occurs, the party need not perform any further. **EXAMPLE 14.21** A law firm hires Julia Darby, a recent law school graduate. Their contract provides that the firm's obligation to continue employing Darby is discharged if she fails to pass the bar exam by her second attempt. This is a condition subsequent because a failure to pass the exam—and thus to obtain a license to practice law—will discharge a duty (employment) that has already arisen. ■

Generally, conditions precedent are common, and conditions subsequent are rare. The *Restatement (Second) of Contracts* omits the terms *condition subsequent* and *condition precedent* and refers to both simply as "conditions."[15]

Concurrent Conditions When each party's absolute duty to perform is conditioned on the other party's absolute duty to perform, **concurrent conditions** are present. These conditions

---

15. *Restatement (Second) of Contracts*, Section 224. Note that a plaintiff must prove a condition precedent, whereas the defendant normally proves a condition subsequent.

Discharge The termination of an obligation, such as occurs when the parties to a contract have fully performed their contractual obligations.

Performance The fulfillment of one's duties under a contract—the normal way of discharging one's contractual obligations.

What is the most common way to discharge a contract for delivery of organic vegetables?

Condition A qualification, provision, or clause in a contractual agreement, the occurrence or nonoccurrence of which creates, suspends, or terminates the obligations of the contracting parties.

Condition Precedent A condition in a contract that must be met before a party's promise becomes absolute.

Condition Subsequent A condition in a contract that, if it occurs, operates to terminate a party's absolute promise to perform.

Concurrent Conditions Conditions that must occur or be performed at the same time—they are mutually dependent. No obligations arise until these conditions are simultaneously performed.

Exhibit 14–4 Contract Discharge

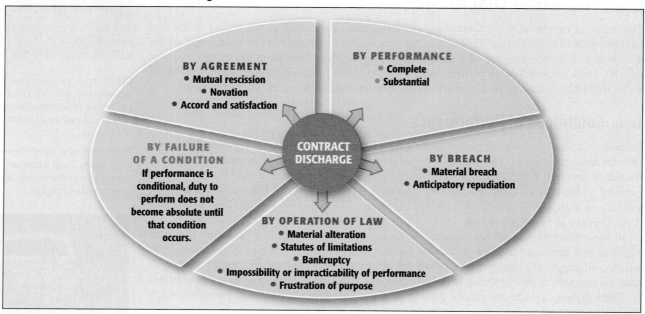

CONTRACT DISCHARGE

BY AGREEMENT
- Mutual rescission
- Novation
- Accord and satisfaction

BY PERFORMANCE
- Complete
- Substantial

BY FAILURE OF A CONDITION
If performance is conditional, duty to perform does not become absolute until that condition occurs.

BY BREACH
- Material breach
- Anticipatory repudiation

BY OPERATION OF LAW
- Material alteration
- Statutes of limitations
- Bankruptcy
- Impossibility or impracticability of performance
- Frustration of purpose

exist only when the parties expressly or impliedly are to perform their respective duties *simultaneously.*

    EXAMPLE 14.22 If Janet Feibush promises to pay for goods when Hewlett-Packard delivers them, the parties' promises to perform are mutually dependent. Feibush's duty to pay for the goods does not become absolute until Hewlett-Packard either delivers or tenders the goods. Likewise, Hewlett-Packard's duty to deliver the goods does not become absolute until Feibush tenders or actually makes payment. Therefore, neither can recover from the other for breach without first tendering performance. ■

14–4b Discharge by Performance

The contract comes to an end when both parties fulfill their respective duties by performing the acts they have promised. Performance can also be accomplished by tender. **Tender** is an unconditional offer to perform by a person who is ready, willing, and able to do so. Therefore, a seller who places goods at the disposal of a buyer has tendered delivery and can demand payment according to the terms of the agreement. A buyer who offers to pay for goods has tendered payment and can demand delivery of the goods.

    Once performance has been tendered, the party making the tender has done everything possible to carry out the terms of the contract. If the other party then refuses to perform, the party making the tender can consider the duty discharged and sue for breach of contract.

If HP agrees to sell and deliver goods to someone who agrees to pay for them, what are the concurrent conditions?

iStockPhoto.com/David McNew

Tender An unconditional offer to perform an obligation by a person who is ready, willing, and able to do so.

Complete Performance When a party performs exactly as agreed, there is no question as to whether the contract has been performed. When a party's performance is perfect, it is said to be complete.

    Normally, conditions expressly stated in the contract must fully occur in all aspects for complete performance (strict performance) of the contract to take place. Any deviation breaches the contract and discharges the other party's obligations to perform.

For instance, most construction contracts require the builder to meet certain specifications. If the specifications are conditions, complete performance is required to avoid material breach. (*Material breach* will be discussed shortly.) If the conditions are met, the other party to the contract must then fulfill her or his obligation to pay the builder.

If the parties to the contract did not expressly make the specifications a condition, however, and the builder fails to meet the specifications, performance is not complete. What effect does that failure have on the other party's obligation to pay? The answer is part of the doctrine of *substantial performance*.

Substantial Performance A party who in good faith performs substantially all of the terms of a contract can enforce the contract against the other party under the doctrine of substantial performance. Note that good faith is required. Intentionally failing to comply with the terms is a breach of the contract.

The basic requirements for performance to qualify as substantial performance are as follows:

1. The party must have performed in good faith. Intentional failure to comply with the contract terms is a breach of the contract.

2. The performance must not vary greatly from the performance promised in the contract. An omission, variance, or defect in performance is considered minor if it can easily be remedied by compensation (monetary damages).

3. The performance must create substantially the same benefits as those promised in the contract.

Courts decide whether performance was substantial on a case-by-case basis, examining all of the facts of the particular situation. **CASE EXAMPLE 14.23** Wisconsin Electric Power Company (WEPCO) contracted with Union Pacific Railroad to transport coal to WEPCO from mines in Colorado. The contract required WEPCO to notify Union Pacific monthly of how many tons of coal (below a certain maximum) it wanted to have shipped the next month. Union Pacific was to make "good faith reasonable efforts" to meet the schedule.

The contract also required WEPCO to supply the railcars. When WEPCO did not supply railcars, Union Pacific used its own railcars and delivered 84 percent of the requested coal. After WEPCO sued for breach of contract, a federal court held that the delivery of 84 percent of the contracted amount constituted substantial performance.[16] ■

Effect on Duty to Perform. If one party's performance is substantial, the other party's duty to perform—for instance, to make payment—remains absolute. (The party can, however, sue for damages due to the minor deviations.) In other words, the parties must continue performing under the contract. If performance is not substantial, there is a *material breach* (to be discussed shortly), and the nonbreaching party is excused from further performance.

Measure of Damages. Because substantial performance is not perfect, the other party is entitled to damages to compensate for the failure to comply with the contract. The measure of the damages is the cost to bring the object of the contract into compliance with its terms, if that cost is reasonable under the circumstances. If the cost is unreasonable, the measure of damages is the difference in value between the performance that was rendered and the performance that would have been rendered if the contract had been performed completely.

Performance to the Satisfaction of Another Contracts often state that completed work must personally satisfy one of the parties or a third person. The question is whether this satisfaction becomes a condition precedent, requiring actual personal satisfaction or approval for discharge, or whether the test of satisfaction is performance that would satisfy a *reasonable person* (substantial performance).

iStockPhoto.com/halbergman

Does Union Pacific Railroad have to deliver 100 percent of promised railcars of coal to an electric power company?

---

16. *Wisconsin Electric Power Co. v. Union Pacific Railroad Co.*, 557 F.3d 504 (7th Cir. 2009).

When the subject matter of the contract is *personal,* a contract to be performed to the satisfaction of one of the parties is conditioned, and performance must actually satisfy that party. For instance, contracts for portraits and works of art are considered personal. Therefore, only the personal satisfaction of the party fulfills the condition (unless a court finds that the party is expressing dissatisfaction to avoid payment or otherwise is not acting in good faith).

Most other contracts need be performed only to the satisfaction of a reasonable person unless they *expressly state otherwise.* When such contracts require performance to the satisfaction of a third party (such as, "to the satisfaction of Robert Ames, the supervising engineer"), the courts are divided. A majority of courts require the work to be satisfactory to a reasonable person. But some courts do require the personal satisfaction of the third party designated in the contract (here, Robert Ames). Again, the personal judgment must be made honestly, or the condition will be excused.

Breach of Contract The failure, without legal excuse, of a promisor to perform the obligations of a contract.

Material Breach of Contract A **breach of contract** is the nonperformance of a contractual duty. A breach is *material* when performance is not at least substantial.[17] If there is a material breach, the nonbreaching party is excused from the performance of contractual duties and can sue for damages caused by the breach.

If the breach is *minor* (not material), the nonbreaching party's duty to perform may sometimes be suspended until the breach is remedied, but the duty is not entirely excused. Once the minor breach is cured (corrected), the nonbreaching party must resume performance of the contractual obligations.

Any breach entitles the nonbreaching party to sue for damages, but only a material breach discharges the nonbreaching party from the contract. The policy underlying these rules is that contracts should go forward when only minor problems occur, but that contracts should be terminated if major problems arise.[18] (Does changing the terms of a service contract on a social networking site constitute a breach of contract? See this chapter's *Adapting the Law to the Online Environment* feature for a look at this issue.)

Both parties in the following case were arguably in breach of their contract. The court had to determine which party's breach was material.

LEARNING OBJECTIVE 5

When is a breach considered material, and what effect does that have on the other party's obligation to perform?

---

17. *Restatement (Second) of Contracts*, Section 241.
18. See UCC 2–612, which deals with installment contracts for the sale of goods.

CASE 14.2

Kohel v. Bergen Auto Enterprises, LLC

Superior Court of New Jersey, Appellate Division, 2013 WL 439970 (2013).

FACTS Marc and Bree Kohel agreed to buy a used 2009 Mazda from Bergen Auto Enterprises, LLC, doing business as Wayne Mazda, Inc. The Kohels were credited $7,000 as a trade-in for their 2005 Nissan Altima. They still owed about $8,000 on the Nissan, which Wayne Mazda agreed to pay. The Kohels took possession of the Mazda with temporary plates.

Sometime later, Wayne Mazda discovered that the Nissan was missing a vehicle identification number (VIN) tag. The dealer therefore refused to make the payment for the Nissan and also refused to give the Kohels permanent plates for the Mazda. The Kohels applied and paid for a replacement VIN tag for the Nissan, but Wayne

When is it considered a material breach for a car dealer to refuse to go through with a sale?

Mazda refused to take their calls on the matter and continued to refuse to supply permanent plates for the Mazda. The Kohels filed a complaint against the dealer in a New Jersey state court, alleging breach of contract. The court ruled in the plaintiffs' favor, and Wayne Mazda appealed.

ISSUE Was it a material breach of the contract for Wayne Mazda to refuse to go through with the sales agreement because the trade-in vehicle was missing a VIN tag?

DECISION Yes. A state intermediate appellate court affirmed the judgment in the Kohel's favor.

REASON While both parties were arguably in breach of their contract, "there is a material distinction in plaintiffs' conduct," which was unintentional, "and defendant's refusal to release the permanent plates for which the plaintiffs had paid." The Kohels had not been aware that their trade-in Nissan lacked a vehicle identification number (VIN) tag. Moreover, "defendant's representatives examined the car twice before accepting it in trade and did not notice the missing VIN tag until they took the car to an auction where they tried to sell it."

The reviewing court found that Wayne Mazda had acted only to maintain "leverage." The Kohels had applied and paid for a replacement VIN tag in an attempt to remedy the problem, but the owner of Wayne Mazda would not even take their calls to discuss the matter. Thus, the court concluded that Wayne Mazda had acted in an unreasonable manner, which was a material breach of the contract.

CRITICAL THINKING—Legal Consideration *What is a material breach of contract? When a material breach occurs, what are the non-breaching party's options?*

ADAPTING THE LAW TO THE ONLINE ENVIRONMENT

When Do Changes in Social Media Terms of Service Constitute a Breach of Contract?

Hundreds of millions of individuals use some form of social media. To do so, they must agree to certain terms of service.

The Terms of Service Are a Contract
Any time you use social media on the Internet or download an app for your mobile device, you must accept the associated terms of service. To be sure, users generally do not read these terms. They just click on "accept" and start using the social media platform or the app. Nonetheless, by clicking the "accept" button, each user is entering into a contract.

An Example: Instagram Changes Its Terms of Service
In 2012, to the consternation of many users, Instagram changed its terms of service to give it the right to transfer and otherwise use user content on the site, apparently without compensation to users. The new terms also limited users' ability to bring class-action lawsuits against Instagram, limited the damages they could recover to $100, and required arbitration of any disputes.

Lucy Funes, an Instagram user in California, filed a class-action lawsuit on behalf of herself and other users, claiming breach of contract and breach of the covenant of good faith and fair dealing that a contract implies.[a] Although Instagram subsequently modified the language that appeared to give it the right to use users' photos without compensation, it retained other controversial terms. They included the mandatory arbitration clause and a provision allowing it to place ads in conjunction with user content.

Instagram Seeks Dismissal of the Lawsuit
While Funes contended that Instagram had breached its contract by changing its terms of service, Instagram argued that Funes could not claim breach of contract. For one thing, she—and other users—had thirty days' notice before the new terms of service took effect. Because Funes continued to use her account after that thirty-day period, Instagram maintained that, in effect, she had agreed to the new terms. The courts ultimately agreed with Instagram and dismissed the lawsuit.

Instagram Changes Its Policies
For several years, Instagram has been using its revised terms of service agreement. As mentioned, it abandoned some of its previous changes and denied any intention to sell user content. In the terms of service, Instagram continues to state that it does "not claim ownership of any content user's post on or through the service."

Nonetheless, the terms state clearly that each user "hereby grants to Instagram a non-exclusive, fully paid and royalty-free, transferable, sublicensable, worldwide license to use content that the user posts." That means that Instagram can reassign the rights or relicense the work to any other party for free or for a fee. The user—anyone who posts on Instagram—need not be compensated or even given notice.

CRITICAL THINKING

■ Instagram's current terms of service state, "We may not always identify paid services, sponsored content, or commercial communications as such." Is it ethical for Instagram to post advertisements without identifying them as advertisements? Discuss.

---

a. *Funes v. Instagram, Inc.,* 3:12-CV06482-WHA (N.D.Cal. 2012). See also *Rodriguez v. Instagram, LLC,* 2013 WL 3732883.

Is it a material breach of contract for a hospital to accept a donation and then refuse to honor part of its commitment? Country singer Garth Brooks was born in Yukon, Oklahoma, and has made generous contributions to charities in that town. When his mother, Colleen Brooks, died, he donated $500,000 to Integris Rural Health, Inc., in that town. Brooks believed that he and the hospital's president had agreed verbally that the donation would be used to build a new women's health center in Yukon, which would be named after his mother. Several years passed, but the health center was not built. Integris claimed that it intended to do something to honor Colleen Brooks but insisted that it had never promised to build a new health center. When Integris refused to return the $500,000, Garth Brooks sued for breach of contract.

Was the hospital's failure to build a women's health center and name it after Brooks's mother a material breach of the verbal contract between Brooks and hospital management? A jury in Rogers County, Oklahoma, thought so and awarded Brooks $500,000 in actual damages for breach of contract. The jury also awarded Brooks another $500,000 because it found the hospital guilty of reckless disregard and intentional malice.

Anticipatory Repudiation of a Contract

Anticipatory Repudiation
An assertion or action by a party indicating that he or she will not perform a contractual obligation.

Before either party to a contract has a duty to perform, one of the parties may refuse to perform her or his contractual obligations. This is called **anticipatory repudiation.**[19]

Repudiation Is a Material Breach. When anticipatory repudiation occurs, it is treated as a material breach of the contract, and the nonbreaching party is permitted to bring an action for damages immediately, even though the scheduled time for performance under the contract may still be in the future. Until the nonbreaching party treats this early repudiation as a breach, however, the breaching party can retract the anticipatory repudiation by proper notice and restore the parties to their original obligations.

An anticipatory repudiation is treated as a present, material breach for two reasons. First, the nonbreaching party should not be required to remain ready and willing to perform when the other party has already repudiated the contract. Second, the nonbreaching party should have the opportunity to seek a similar contract elsewhere. Indeed, that party may have the duty to do so to minimize his or her loss.

KNOW THIS
The risks that prices will fluctuate and values will change are ordinary business risks for which the law does not provide relief.

May Occur When Market Prices Fluctuate. Quite often, an anticipatory repudiation occurs when performance of the contract would be extremely unfavorable to one of the parties because of a sharp fluctuation in market prices.

EXAMPLE 14.24 Mobile X enters into an e-contract to manufacture and sell 100,000 smartphones to Best Com, a global telecommunications company. Delivery is to be made two months from the date of the contract. One month later, three inventory suppliers raise their prices to Mobile X. Because of these higher prices, Mobile X stands to lose $500,000 if it sells the smartphones to Best Com at the contract price. Mobile X immediately sends an e-mail to Best Com, stating that it cannot deliver the 100,000 phones at the contract price. Even though you may sympathize with Mobile X, its e-mail is an anticipatory repudiation of the contract. Best Com can treat the repudiation as a material breach and immediately pursue remedies, even though the contract delivery date is still a month away. ■

14–4c Discharge by Agreement

Any contract can be discharged by agreement of the parties. The agreement can be contained in the original contract, or the parties can form a new contract for the express purpose of discharging the original contract.

---

19. *Restatement (Second) of Contracts,* Section 253; and UCC 2–610.

Discharge by Mutual Rescission As mentioned in previous chapters, rescission occurs when the parties cancel the contract and are returned to the positions they occupied prior to the contract's formation. For *mutual rescission* to take place, the parties must make another agreement that also satisfies the legal requirements for a contract—there must be an *offer,* an *acceptance,* and *consideration.* Ordinarily, if the parties agree to rescind the original contract, their promises not to perform those acts promised in the original contract will be legal consideration for the second contract.

Generally, a rescission agreement may be written or oral. Oral agreements to rescind most executory contracts (that neither party has performed) are enforceable even if the original agreement was in writing. A writing (or electronic record) is required to rescind a contract for the sale of goods under the Uniform Commercial Code when the contract requires a written rescission. Also, agreements to rescind contracts involving transfers of realty must be evidenced by a writing or record.

When one party has fully performed, an agreement to rescind the original contract usually is not enforceable unless additional consideration or restitution is made. Because the performing party has received no consideration for the promise to call off the original bargain, additional consideration is necessary.

Discharge by Novation The process of **novation** substitutes a third party for one of the original parties. Essentially, the parties to the original contract and one or more new parties get together and agree to the substitution. The requirements of a novation are as follows:

Novation The substitution, by agreement, of a new contract for an old one, with the rights under the old one being terminated.

1. A previous valid obligation.

2. An agreement by all of the parties to a new contract.

3. The extinguishing of the old obligation (discharge of the prior party).

4. A new, valid contract.

EXAMPLE 14.25 Union Corporation contracts to sell its pharmaceutical division to British Pharmaceuticals, Ltd. Before the transfer is completed, Union, British Pharmaceuticals, and a third company, Otis Chemicals, execute a new agreement to transfer all of British Pharmaceuticals' rights and duties in the transaction to Otis Chemicals. As long as the new contract is supported by consideration, the novation will discharge the original contract (between Union and British Pharmaceuticals) and replace it with the new contract (between Union and Otis Chemicals). ■

A novation expressly or impliedly revokes and discharges a prior contract. The parties involved may expressly state in the new contract that the old contract is now discharged. If the parties do not expressly discharge the old contract, it will be impliedly discharged if the new contract's terms are inconsistent with the old contract's terms.

Discharge by Accord and Satisfaction As explained in a previous chapter, in an *accord and satisfaction,* the parties agree to accept performance different from the performance originally promised. An *accord* is a contract to perform some act to satisfy an existing contractual duty that has not yet been discharged.[20] A *satisfaction* is the performance of the accord agreement. An accord and its satisfaction discharge the original contractual obligation.

Once the accord has been made, the original obligation is merely suspended until the accord agreement is fully performed. If it is not performed, the party to whom performance is owed can bring an action on the original obligation or for breach of the accord. **EXAMPLE 14.26** Shea obtains a judgment of $8,000 against Marla. Later, both parties agree that the judgment can be satisfied by Marla's transfer of her automobile to Shea. This agreement to accept the auto in lieu of $8,000 in cash is the accord. If Marla transfers her automobile to Shea, the accord agreement is fully performed, and the $8,000 debt is discharged. If Marla refuses to

---

20. *Restatement (Second) of Contracts,* Section 281.

transfer her car, the accord is breached. Because the original obligation is merely suspended, Shea can sue to enforce the judgment for $8,000 in cash or bring an action for breach of the accord. ■

14-4d Discharge by Operation of Law

Under specified circumstances, contractual duties may be discharged by operation of law. These circumstances include material alteration of the contract, the running of the relevant statute of limitations, bankruptcy, and impossibility or impracticability of performance.

Material Alteration To discourage parties from altering written contracts, the law allows an innocent party to be discharged from a contract that has been materially altered. If one party alters a material term of the contract—such as the quantity term or the price term—without the knowledge or consent of the other party, the party who was unaware of the alteration can treat the contract as discharged or terminated.

Statutes of Limitations As mentioned earlier in this text, statutes of limitations limit the period during which a party can sue on a particular cause of action. After the applicable limitations period has passed, a suit can no longer be brought.

The period for bringing lawsuits for breach of oral contracts is usually two to three years, and for written contracts, four to five years. Lawsuits for breach of a contract for the sale of goods must be brought within four years after the cause of action has accrued. In their original contract, the parties can agree to reduce this four-year period to not less than one year. They cannot, however, agree to extend it beyond four years.

Bankruptcy A proceeding in bankruptcy attempts to allocate the debtor's assets to the creditors in a fair and equitable fashion. Once the assets have been allocated, the debtor receives a *discharge in bankruptcy*. A discharge in bankruptcy ordinarily prevents the creditors from enforcing most of the debtor's contracts. Partial payment of a debt *after* discharge in bankruptcy will not revive the debt.

Impossibility of Performance After a contract has been made, supervening events (such as a fire) may make performance impossible in an objective sense. This so-called **impossibility of performance** can discharge the contract.[21] The doctrine of impossibility of performance is applied only when the parties could not have reasonably foreseen, at the time the contract was formed, the event or events that rendered performance impossible.

Objective impossibility ("It cannot be done") must be distinguished from subjective impossibility ("I'm sorry, I personally cannot do it"). An example of subjective impossibility occurs when a party cannot deliver goods on time because of railcar shortages or cannot make payment on time because the bank is closed. In effect, the nonperforming party is saying, "It is impossible for *me* to perform," rather than "It is impossible for *anyone* to perform." Accordingly, such excuses do not discharge a contract, and the nonperforming party is normally held in breach of contract.

When Performance Is Impossible. Three basic types of situations may qualify as grounds for the discharge of contractual obligations based on impossibility of performance:[22]

1. *When a party whose personal performance is essential to the completion of the contract dies or becomes incapacitated prior to performance.* **EXAMPLE 14.27** Fred, a famous dancer, contracts with Ethereal Dancing Guild to play a leading role in its new ballet. Before the ballet can be performed, Fred becomes ill and dies. His personal performance was essential to

Impossibility of Performance
A doctrine under which a party to a contract is relieved of his or her duty to perform when performance becomes objectively impossible or totally impracticable.

---

21. *Restatement (Second) of Contracts*, Section 261.
22. *Restatement (Second) of Contracts*, Sections 262–266; and UCC 2–615.

the completion of the contract. Thus, his death discharges the contract and his estate's liability for his nonperformance. ■

2. *When the specific subject matter of the contract is destroyed.* EXAMPLE 14.28 A-1 Farm Equipment agrees to sell Gunther the green tractor on its lot and promises to have the tractor ready for Gunther to pick up on Saturday. On Friday night, however, a truck veers off the nearby highway and smashes into the tractor, destroying it beyond repair. Because the contract was for this specific tractor, A-1's performance is rendered impossible owing to the accident. ■

3. *When a change in the law renders performance illegal.* EXAMPLE 14.29 Russo contracts with Playlist, Inc., to create a Web site through which users can post and share movies, music, and other forms of digital entertainment. Russo goes to work. Before the site is operational, however, Congress passes the No Online Piracy in Entertainment (NOPE) Act. The NOPE Act makes it illegal to operate a Web site on which copyrighted works are posted without the copyright owners' consent. In this situation, the contract is discharged by operation of law. The purpose of the contract has been rendered illegal, and contract performance is objectively impossible. ■

Can an agreement that prohibits personal contact between two parties affect the performance of contracts between one of these parties and the other party's business? That was the question before the court in the following case.

This dancer has a contract to dance the lead role in a famous ballet that will run for a month of performances. What happens if he breaks a leg before the shows start?

CASE 14.3

Kolodin v. Valenti

New York Supreme Court, Appellate Division, 115 A.D.3d 197, 979 N.Y.S.2d 587 (2014).

FACTS Hilary Kolodin, a jazz singer, was personally involved with John Valenti, the sole shareholder and president of Jayarvee, Inc. Jayarvee manages artists, produces recordings, and owns and operates a jazz club in New York City. Kolodin contracted professionally with Jayarvee for recording and management services. After Kolodin and Valenti's personal relationship deteriorated, Kolodin asked a New York state court to issue a temporary protection order against Valenti, alleging domestic abuse. The parties then agreed under a court-ordered stipulation to have no further contact with one another. The stipulation specified that "no contact shall include no third party contact, excepting counsel." Later, Kolodin filed a suit in a New York state court against Valenti, alleging breach of her Jayarvee contracts and seeking their rescission. The court declared the contracts between Kolodin and Jayarvee terminated. Valenti appealed.

ISSUE Did Kolodin and Valenti's stipulation render the performance of Kolodin's Jayarvee contracts objectively impossible?

DECISION Yes. A state intermediate appellate court affirmed the lower court's ruling. The court concluded that, "In undertaking to perform recording and management contracts, the eventuality that the parties would subsequently stipulate to forbid contact with one another could not have been foreseen or guarded against."

Can severe disagreement within a couple render a personal services contract impossible to perform?

REASON Impossibility excuses a party's performance when the destruction of the means of performance makes performance objectively impossible. But the impossibility must be created by an event that could not have been foreseen at the time of contract formation. In this case, the "no contact" stipulation between Kolodin and Valenti destroyed the means of performing Kolodin's contracts with Jayarvee. The contracts were for personal services and required "substantial and ongoing communication" between Kolodin and Jayarvee. Because Jayarvee is a small organization and Valenti oversees its daily operations, performance of the contracts would have required his input, thereby violating the stipulation. Even if the communication had been carried out only through the company's employees, the stipulation's ban on third party contact would have been violated. Furthermore, it was not foreseeable at the time the Jayarvee contracts were formed that Kolodin and Valenti would agree to have no contact with one another.

CRITICAL THINKING—Legal Environment Consideration *Should Kolodin's role in bringing about the "no contact" stipulation through her request for a protection order have rendered the doctrine of impossibility inapplicable? Explain.*

Temporary Impossibility. An occurrence or event that makes performance temporarily impossible operates to suspend performance until the impossibility ceases. Once the temporary event ends, the parties ordinarily must perform the contract as originally planned.

CASE EXAMPLE 14.30 On August 22, Keefe Hurwitz contracted to sell his home in Louisiana to Wesley and Gwendolyn Payne for $241,500. On August 26—just four days later—Hurricane Katrina made landfall and caused extensive damage to the house. The cost of repairs was estimated at $60,000. Hurwitz refused to pay for the repairs only to sell the property to the Paynes for the previously agreed-on price. The Paynes sued to enforce the contract. Hurwitz claimed that Hurricane Katrina had made it impossible for him to perform and had discharged his duties under the contract. The court ruled that Hurricane Katrina had caused only temporary impossibility. Therefore, Hurwitz had to pay for the necessary repairs and to perform the contract as written. He could not obtain a higher purchase price to offset the cost of the repairs.[23] ■

Sometimes, however, the lapse of time and the change in circumstances surrounding such a contract make it substantially more burdensome for the parties to perform the promised acts. In that situation, the contract may be discharged. **CASE EXAMPLE 14.31** In 1942, actor Gene Autry was drafted into the U.S. Army. Being drafted rendered his contract with a Hollywood movie company temporarily impossible to perform, and it was suspended until the end of World War II in 1945. When Autry got out of the army, the purchasing power of the dollar had declined so much that performance of the contract would have been substantially burdensome to him. Therefore, the contract was discharged.[24] ■

Commercial Impracticability

Courts may also excuse parties from their performance obligations when the performance becomes much more difficult or expensive than the parties originally contemplated. For someone to invoke the doctrine of **commercial impracticability** successfully, however, the anticipated performance must become *extremely difficult or costly*.[25] Furthermore, the added burden of performing *must not have been foreseeable by the parties when the contract was made*.

In one classic case, for instance, a court held that a contract could be discharged because a party would have to pay ten times more than the original estimate to excavate a certain amount of gravel.[26] In another case, a power failure during a wedding reception relieved the owner of a banquet hall from the duty to perform a contract.[27] (See this chapter's *Beyond Our Borders* feature for a discussion of Germany's approach to impracticability and impossibility of performance.)

Frustration of Purpose

Closely allied with the doctrine of commercial impracticability is the doctrine of **frustration of purpose.** In principle, a contract will be discharged if supervening circumstances make it impossible to attain the purpose both parties had in mind when making the contract. As with commercial impracticability, the supervening event must not have been foreseeable at the time of the contracting.[28]

There are some differences between the doctrines, however. Commercial impracticability usually involves an event that increases the cost or difficulty of performance. In contrast, frustration of purpose typically involves an event that decreases the value of what a party receives under the contract.

KNOW THIS
The doctrine of commercial impracticability does not provide relief from such events as ordinary price increases or easily predictable changes in the weather.

Commercial Impracticability
A doctrine that may excuse the duty to perform a contract when performance becomes much more difficult or costly due to forces that neither party could control or foresee at the time the contract was formed.

Frustration of Purpose
A court-created doctrine under which a party to a contract will be relieved of her or his duty to perform when the objective purpose for performance no longer exists due to reasons beyond that party's control.

---

23. *Payne v. Hurwitz*, 978 So.2d 1000 (La.App. 1st Cir. 2008).
24. *Autry v. Republic Productions*, 30 Cal.2d 144, 180 P.2d 888 (1947).
25. *Restatement (Second) of Contracts*, Section 264.
26. *Mineral Park Land Co. v. Howard*, 172 Cal. 289, 156 P. 458 (1916).
27. *Facto v. Panagis*, 390 N.J.Super. 227, 915 A.2d 59 (2007).
28. See, for example, *East Capitol View Community Development Corp. v. Robinson*, 941 A.2d 1036 (D.C.App. 2008).

BEYOND OUR BORDERS

Impossibility or Impracticability of Performance in Germany

In the United States, when a party alleges that contract performance is impossible or impracticable because of circumstances unforeseen at the time the contract was formed, a court will either discharge the party's contractual obligations or hold the party to the contract. In other words, if a court agrees that the contract is impossible or impracticable to perform, the remedy is to rescind (cancel) the contract. Under German law, however, a court may reform (adjust the terms of) a contract in light of economic developments. If an unforeseen event affects the foundation of the agreement, the court can alter the contract's terms to align with the parties' original expectations, thus making the contract fair to the parties.

CRITICAL THINKING

■ When a contract becomes impossible or impracticable to perform, which remedy would a businessperson prefer— rescission or reformation? Why? Explain your answer.

Reviewing . . . Third Party Rights and Discharge

Val's Foods signs a contract to buy 1,500 pounds of basil from Sun Farms, a small organic herb grower, if an independent organization inspects the crop and certifies that it contains no pesticide or herbicide residue. Val's has a contract with several restaurant chains to supply pesto and intends to use Sun Farms' basil in the pesto to fulfill these contracts. When Sun Farms is preparing to harvest the basil, an unexpected hailstorm destroys half the crop. Sun Farms attempts to purchase additional basil from other farms, but it is late in the season, and the price is twice the normal market price. Sun Farms is too small to absorb this cost and immediately notifies Val's that it will not fulfill the contract. Using the information presented in the chapter, answer the following questions.

1. Suppose that Sun Farms supplies the basil that survived the storm but the basil does not pass the chemical-residue inspection. Which concept discussed in the chapter might allow Val's to refuse to perform the contract in this situation?

2. Under which legal theory or theories might Sun Farms claim that its obligation under the contract has been discharged by operation of law? Discuss fully.

3. Suppose that Sun Farms contacts every basil grower in the country and buys the last remaining chemical-free basil anywhere. Nevertheless, Sun Farms is able to ship only 1,475 pounds to Val's. Would this fulfill Sun Farms' obligations to Val's? Why or why not?

4. Now suppose that Sun Farms sells its operations to Happy Valley Farms. As part of the sale, all three parties agree that Happy Valley will provide the basil as stated under the original contract. What is this type of agreement called?

DEBATE THIS

■ The doctrine of commercial impracticability should be abolished.

BUSINESS APPLICATION — Dealing with Third Party Rights*

Assignment of contractual rights and delegation of duties are common in the business world. As you have read in this chapter, third party rights and duties stem from the law on assignments, delegations, and third party beneficiaries. A business may at different times wish to assign or delegate its contractual rights, to prevent a third party from acquiring such rights, or to understand its own third party rights. In any of these situations, some familiarity with the law is essential.

The general rule is that any contractual right or duty can be assigned or delegated unless the assignment or delegation is prohibited by (1) the contract, (2) a statute, or (3) other limitations. Thus, one way to prevent assignment or delegation is to prohibit it when drafting the contract.

For example, a tenant under a long-term lease contract may wish to assign the lease to another party. To avoid such assignments, property owners often prohibit the assignment of the balance of a lease term unless the property owner's consent is obtained.

When a contract calls for the manufacture and sale of goods, the manufacturer may assign or delegate the production of such goods to a third party unless prohibited by the contract. Consequently, most purchase orders (contracts) have a clause that prohibits such assignments or delegations without the buyer's consent.

CHECKLIST for the Businessperson:

1. Determine whether you can assign or delegate your rights or duties under a contract to a third party.

2. If you can assign or delegate your contract rights or performance, attempt to determine your benefits and obligations, such as notice to customers, if you do make the assignment or delegation.

3. If you do not want your contract rights or duties to be assigned or delegated, insert a contract clause that prohibits assignment or delegation without your consent.

4. Whenever you might be a third party beneficiary to a contract, such as a creditor beneficiary, take steps to determine your rights.

* This *Business Application* is not meant to substitute for the services of an attorney who is licensed to practice law in your state.

Key Terms

Chapter Summary: Third Party Rights and Discharge

THIRD PARTY RIGHTS

Assignments	1. An assignment is the transfer of rights under a contract to a third party. The person assigning the rights is the *assignor*, and the party to whom the rights are assigned is the *assignee*. The assignee has a right to demand performance from the other original party to the contract, the *obligor*.
	 2. Generally, all rights can be assigned *unless:*
	   a. A statute expressly prohibits assignment.
	   b. The contract is for personal services.
	   c. The assignment will materially alter the obligor's risk or duties.
	   d. The contract prohibits assignment. (Exception: Contracts cannot generally prohibit assignment of the right to receive funds, of ownership rights in real property, of negotiable instruments, or of certain payments under a sales contract.)
	 3. The assignee should notify the obligor of the assignment. Although not legally required, notification avoids two potential problems:
	   a. If the assignor assigns the same right to two different persons, the first assignment in time is generally the first in right, but in some states the first assignee to give notice takes priority.
	   b. Until the obligor is notified of the assignment, the obligor can tender performance to the assignor. If the assignor accepts the performance, the obligor's duties under the contract are discharged without benefit to the assignee.

Delegations	1. A delegation is the transfer of duties under a contract to a third party (the *delegatee*), who then assumes the obligation of performing the contractual duties previously held by the one making the delegation (the *delegator*).
	 2. As a general rule, any duty can be delegated *unless:*
	   a. Performance depends on the obligor's personal skills or talents, or special trust has been placed in the obligor.
	   b. Performance by a third party will vary materially from that expected by the obligee.
	   c. The contract prohibits delegation.
	 3. A valid delegation of duties does not relieve the delegator of obligations under the contract. If the delegatee fails to perform, the delegator is still liable to the obligee.
	 4. An "assignment of all rights" or an "assignment of the contract" is often construed to mean that both the rights and the duties arising under the contract are transferred to a third party.

Third Party Beneficiaries	A third party beneficiary contract is one made for the purpose of benefiting a third party. 1. *Intended beneficiary*—One for whose benefit a contract is created. When the promisor (the one making the contractual promise that benefits a third party) fails to perform as promised, the third party can sue the promisor directly. Types of third party beneficiaries are creditor and donee beneficiaries. 2. *Incidental beneficiary*—A third party who indirectly (incidentally) benefits from a contract but for whose benefit the contract was not specifically intended. Incidental beneficiaries have no rights to the benefits received and cannot sue to have the contract enforced.

CONTRACT DISCHARGE

Conditions of Performance	Contract obligations may be subject to the following types of conditions: 1. *Condition precedent*—A condition that must be fulfilled before a party's promise becomes absolute. 2. *Condition subsequent*—A condition that, if it occurs, operates to terminate a party's absolute promise to perform. 3. *Concurrent conditions*—Conditions that must be performed simultaneously. Each party's absolute duty to perform is conditioned on the other party's absolute duty to perform.
Discharge by Performance	A contract may be discharged by complete (strict) performance or by substantial performance. In some instances, performance must be to the satisfaction of another. Totally inadequate performance constitutes a material breach of the contract. An anticipatory repudiation of a contract allows the other party to sue immediately for breach of contract.
Discharge by Agreement	Parties may agree to discharge their contractual obligations in several ways: 1. *By rescission*—The parties mutually agree to rescind (cancel) the contract. 2. *By novation*—A new party is substituted for one of the primary parties to a contract. 3. *By accord and satisfaction*—The parties agree to render and accept performance different from that on which they originally agreed.
Discharge by Operation of Law	Parties' obligations under contracts may be discharged by operation of law owing to one of the following: 1. Material alteration. 2. Statutes of limitations. 3. Bankruptcy. 4. Impossibility of performance. 5. Impracticability of performance. 6. Frustration of purpose.

Issue Spotters

1. Eagle Company contracts to build a house for Frank. The contract states that "any assignment of this contract renders the contract void." After Eagle builds the house, but before Frank pays, Eagle assigns its right to payment to Good Credit Company. Can Good Credit enforce the contract against Frank? Why or why not? (See *Assignments*.)

2. Ready Foods contracts to buy two hundred carloads of frozen pizzas from Speedy Distributors. Before Ready or Speedy starts performing, can the parties call off the deal? What if Speedy has already shipped the pizzas? Explain your answers. (See *Contract Discharge*.)

—**Check your answers to the *Issue Spotters* against the answers provided in Appendix D at the end of this text.**

Learning Objectives Check

1. What is an assignment? What is the difference between an assignment and a delegation?
2. In what situations is the delegation of duties prohibited?
3. What factors indicate that a third party beneficiary is an intended beneficiary?
4. How are most contracts discharged?
5. When is a breach considered material, and what effect does that have on the other party's obligation to perform?

—**Answers to the even-numbered *Learning Objectives Check* questions can be found in Appendix E at the end of this text.**

Business Scenarios and Case Problems

14–1. Third Party Beneficiaries. Wilken owes Rivera $2,000. Howie promises Wilken that he will pay Rivera the $2,000 in return for Wilken's promise to give Howie's children guitar lessons. Is Rivera an intended beneficiary of the Howie-Wilken contract? Explain. (See *Third Party Beneficiaries.)*

14–2. Assignment. Aron, a college student, signs a one-year lease agreement that runs from September 1 to August 31. The lease agreement specifies that the lease cannot be assigned without the landlord's consent. In late May, Aron decides not to go to summer school and assigns the balance of the lease (three months) to a close friend, Erica. The landlord objects to the assignment and denies Erica access to the apartment. Aron claims that Erica is financially sound and should be allowed the full rights and privileges of an assignee. Discuss fully whether the landlord or Aron is correct. (See *Assignments.)*

14–3. Spotlight on Drug Testing—Third Party Beneficiaries. Bath Iron Works (BIW) offered a job to Thomas Devine, contingent on Devine's passing a drug test. The testing was conducted by NorDx, a subcontractor of Roche Biomedical Laboratories. When NorDx found that Devine's urinalysis showed the presence of opiates, a result confirmed by Roche, BIW refused to offer Devine permanent employment. Devine sued Roche, claiming that the ingestion of poppy seeds can lead to a positive result and that he had tested positive for opiates only because of his daily consumption of poppy seed muffins. Devine argued that he was a third party beneficiary of the contract between his employer (BIW) and NorDx (Roche). Was Devine an intended third party beneficiary of this contract? Why or why not? Do drug-testing labs have a duty to the employees they test to exercise reasonable care in conducting the tests? Explain. [*Devine v. Roche Biomedical Laboratories,* 659 A.2d 868 (Me. 1995)] (See *Third Party Beneficiaries*.)

14–4. Third Party Beneficiary. David and Sandra Dess contracted with Sirva Relocation, LLC, to assist in selling their home. In their contract, the Desses agreed to disclose all information about the property—information on which Sirva "and other prospective buyers may rely in deciding whether and on what terms to purchase the Property." The Kincaids contracted with Sirva to buy the house. After the closing, they discovered dampness in the walls, defective and rotten windows, mold, and other undisclosed problems. Can the Kincaids bring an action against the Desses for breach of their contract with Sirva? Why or why not? [*Kincaid v. Dess,* 298 P.3d 358 (2013)] (See *Third Party Beneficiaries*.)

14–5. Business Case Problem with Sample Answer—Material Breach. The Northeast Independent School District in Bexar County, Texas, hired STR Constructors, Ltd., to renovate a middle school. STR subcontracted the tile work in the school's kitchen to Newman Tile, Inc. (NTI). The project had already fallen behind schedule. As a result, STR allowed other workers to walk over and damage the newly installed tile before it had cured, forcing NTI to constantly redo its work. Despite NTI's requests for payment, STR remitted only half the amount due under their contract. When the school district refused to accept the kitchen, including the tile work, STR told NTI to quickly make the repairs. A week later, STR terminated their contract. Did STR breach the contract with NTI? Explain. [*STR Constructors, Ltd. v. Newman Tile, Inc.,* 395 S.W.3d 383 (Tex.App.—El Paso 2013)] (See *Contract Discharge.*)

—For a sample answer to Problem 14–5, go to Appendix F at the end of this text.

14–6. Conditions of Performance. Russ Wyant owned Humble Ranch in Perkins County, South Dakota. Edward Humble, whose parents had previously owned the ranch, was Wyant's uncle. Humble held a two-year option to buy the ranch. The option included specific conditions. Once it was exercised, the parties had thirty days to enter into a purchase agreement, and the seller could become the buyer's lender by matching the terms of the proposed financing. After the option was exercised, the parties engaged in lengthy negotiations, but Humble did not respond to Wyant's proposed purchase agreement nor advise him of available financing terms before the option expired. Six months later, Humble filed a suit against Wyant to enforce the option. Is Humble entitled to specific performance? Explain. [*Humble v. Wyant,* 843 N.W.2d 334 (S.Dak. 2014)] (See *Contract Discharge.*)

14–7. Discharge by Operation of Law. Dr. Jake Lambert signed an employment agreement with Baptist Health Services, Inc., to provide cardiothoracic-surgery services to Baptist Memorial Hospital–North Mississippi, Inc., in Oxford, Mississippi. Complaints about Lambert's behavior arose almost immediately. He was evaluated by a team of doctors and psychologists, who diagnosed him as suffering from obsessive-compulsive personality disorder and concluded that he was unfit to practice medicine. Based on this conclusion, the hospital suspended his staff privileges. Citing the suspension, Baptist Health Services claimed that Lambert had breached his employment contract. What is Lambert's best defense to this claim? Explain. [*Baptist Memorial Hospital–North Mississippi, Inc. v. Lambert,* 157 So.3d 109 (Miss.App. 2015)] (See *Contract Discharge.*)

14–8. A Question of Ethics—Assignment and Delegation. Premier Building & Development, Inc., entered a listing agreement giving Sunset Gold Realty, LLC, the exclusive right to find a tenant for some commercial property. The terms of the listing agreement stated that it was binding on both parties and "their * * * assigns." Premier Building did not own the property at the time, but had the option to purchase it. To secure financing for the project, Premier Building established a new company called Cobblestone Associates. Premier Building then bought the property and conveyed it to Cobblestone the same day. Meanwhile, Sunset Gold found a tenant for the property, and Cobblestone became the landlord. Cobblestone acknowledged its obligation to pay Sunset Gold for finding a tenant, but it later refused to pay Sunset Gold's commission. Sunset Gold then sued Premier Building and Cobblestone for breach of the listing agreement. [*Sunset Gold Realty, LLC v. Premier Building & Development, Inc.,* 133 Conn.App. 445, 36 A.3d 243 (2012)] (See *Assignments* and *Delegations.*)

1. Is Premier Building relieved of its contractual duties if it assigned the contract to Cobblestone? Why or why not?

2. Given that Sunset Gold performed its obligations under the listing agreement, did Cobblestone behave unethically in refusing to pay Sunset Gold's commission? Why or why not?

Critical Thinking and Writing Assignments

14–9. Critical Legal Thinking. The concept of substantial performance permits a party to be discharged from a contract even though the party has not fully performed her or his obligations according to the contract's terms. Is this fair? Why or why not? What policy interests are at issue here? (See *Contract Discharge.*)

14–10. Business Law Critical Thinking Group Assignment. ABC Clothiers, Inc., has a contract with John Taylor, owner of Taylor & Sons, a retailer, to deliver one thousand summer suits to Taylor's place of business on or before May 1. On April 1, John receives a letter from ABC informing him that ABC will not be able to make the delivery as scheduled. John is very upset, as he had planned a big ad campaign. (See *Contract Discharge.*)

1. The first group will discuss whether John Taylor can immediately sue ABC for breach of contract (on April 2).

2. Now suppose that John Taylor's son, Tom, tells his father that they cannot file a lawsuit until ABC actually fails to deliver the suits on May 1. The second group will decide who is correct, John or Tom.

3. Assume that Taylor & Sons can either file immediately or wait until ABC fails to deliver the goods. The third group will evaluate which course of action is better, given the circumstances.

15

iStockPhoto.com/BrianAJackson

LEARNING OBJECTIVES

The five Learning Objectives *below are designed to help improve your understanding of the chapter. After reading this chapter, you should be able to answer the following questions:*

1. What is the standard measure of compensatory damages when a contract is breached? How are damages computed differently in construction contracts?

2. What is the difference between compensatory damages and consequential damages? What are nominal damages, and when do courts award nominal damages?

3. Under what circumstances is the remedy of rescission and restitution available?

4. When do courts grant specific performance as a remedy?

5. What is a limitation-of-liability clause, and when will courts enforce it?

Breach and Remedies

Normally, people enter into contracts to secure some advantage. When it is no longer advantageous for a party to fulfill her or his contractual obligations, that party may *breach,* or fail to perform, the contract.[1] Once one party breaches the contract, the other party—the nonbreaching party—can choose one or more of several remedies.

A *remedy* is the relief provided to an innocent party when the other party has breached the contract. It is the means employed to enforce a right or to redress an injury. Although it may be an exaggeration to say there is a remedy for "everything" in life, as Cervantes claimed in in the chapter-opening quotation, there is a remedy available for nearly every contract breach.

The most common remedies available to a nonbreaching party under contract law include damages, rescission and restitution, specific performance, and reformation. Courts distinguish between *remedies at law* and *remedies in equity.* Today, the remedy at law is normally monetary damages. We discuss this remedy in the first part of the chapter. Equitable remedies include rescission and restitution, specific performance, and reformation, all of which we examine later in the chapter. Usually, a court will not award an equitable remedy unless the remedy at law is inadequate.

> "There's a remedy for everything except death."
>
> **MIGUEL DE CERVANTES**
> 1547–1616
> (SPANISH AUTHOR)

15-1 Damages

A breach of contract entitles the nonbreaching party to sue for monetary damages. As you have already learned, tort law damages are designed to compensate a party for harm

---

1. A *breach of contract* occurs when one party fails to perform part or all of the required duties under a contract. *Restatement (Second) of Contracts*, Section 235(2).

suffered as a result of another's wrongful act. In the context of contract law, damages are designed to compensate the nonbreaching party for the loss of the bargain. Often, courts say that innocent parties are to be placed in the position they would have occupied had the contract been fully performed.[2]

15–1a Types of Damages

There are basically four broad categories of damages:

1. Compensatory (to cover direct losses and costs).

2. Consequential (to cover indirect and foreseeable losses).

3. Punitive (to punish and deter wrongdoing).

4. Nominal (to recognize wrongdoing when no monetary loss is shown).

Compensatory and punitive damages were discussed in the context of tort law. Here, we look at these types of damages, as well as consequential and nominal damages, in the context of contract law.

Compensatory Damages Damages that compensate the nonbreaching party for the *loss of the bargain* are known as *compensatory damages.* These damages compensate the injured party only for damages actually sustained and proved to have arisen directly from the loss of the bargain caused by the breach of contract. They simply replace what was lost because of the wrong or damage, and, for this reason, are often said to "make the person whole."

Can an award of damages for a breach of contract elevate the nonbreaching party to a better position than he or she would have been in if the contract not been breached? That was the question in the following case.

---

2. *Restatement (Second) of Contracts*, Section 347.

KNOW THIS
The terms of a contract must be sufficiently definite for a court to determine the amount of damages to award.

CASE 15.1

Hallmark Cards, Inc. v. Murley

United States Court of Appeals, Eighth Circuit, 703 F.3d 456 (2013).

FACTS Janet Murley was the vice president of marketing at Hallmark Cards, Inc., until Hallmark eliminated her position as part of a corporate restructuring. As a vice president, Murley had access to Hallmark's confidential information, including its business plans, market research, and financial statements. In 2002, Murley and the company entered into a separation agreement. Murley agreed not to work in the greeting card or gift industry for a period of eighteen months and not to disclose any confidential information or retain any business records or documents relating to Hallmark. In exchange, Hallmark paid $735,000 to Murley as part of her severance package.

After the expiration of her noncompete agreement, Murley accepted a consulting position with Recycled Paper Greetings (RPG) for $125,000 and disclosed confidential Hallmark information to

When a former Hallmark employee breaches a term in her severance contract, how much can Hallmark recover as damages?

iStockPhoto.com/RiverNorthPhotography

RPG. Hallmark filed a suit in a federal district court against Murley, alleging breach of contract. A jury returned a verdict in Hallmark's favor and awarded $860,000 in compensatory damages (the $735,000 severance payment and $125,000 that Murley received from RPG). Murley appealed.

ISSUE Can Hallmark (the nonbreaching party) obtain compensatory damages in an amount that is more than what it lost ($735,000) as a result of the breach?

DECISION No. The U.S. Court of Appeals for the Eighth District affirmed the judgment in Hallmark's favor but remanded the case to the lower court to reduce the award of damages. Hallmark was entitled to a return of the $735,000 severance it paid Murley, but not the $125,000 she earned from RPG.

Continues

REASON The federal appellate court noted that there was ample evidence that Murley retained and disclosed Hallmark's confidential materials to RPG, a competitor, in violation of the "terms and primary purpose" of the noncompete agreement. "A plaintiff may recover the benefit of his or her bargain as well as damages naturally and proximately caused by the breach and damages that could have been reasonably contemplated by the defendant at the time of the agreement." The court reasoned that by awarding Hallmark more than its $735,000 severance payment, the jury award placed Hallmark in a better position than it would find itself had Murley not breached the agreement. The jury's award of the $125,000 payment by RPG was, therefore, improper.

CRITICAL THINKING—Legal Consideration *What are compensatory damages? What is the standard measure of compensatory damages?*

Standard Measure. The standard measure of compensatory damages is the difference between the value of the breaching party's promised performance under the contract and the value of her or his actual performance. This amount is reduced by any loss that the injured party has avoided.

EXAMPLE 15.1 Randall contracts to perform certain services exclusively for Hernandez during the month of March for $4,000. Hernandez cancels the contract and is in breach. Randall is able to find another job during March but can earn only $3,000. He can sue Hernandez for breach and recover $1,000 as compensatory damages. Randall can also recover from Hernandez the amount that he spent to find the other job. ■ Expenses that are directly incurred because of a breach of contract—such as those incurred to obtain performance from another source—are called **incidental damages.**

Note that the measure of compensatory damages often varies by type of contract. Certain types of contracts deserve special mention.

LEARNING OBJECTIVE 1

What is the standard measure of compensatory damages when a contract is breached? How are damages computed differently in construction contracts?

Incidental Damages Damages that compensate for expenses directly incurred because of a breach of contract, such as those incurred to obtain performance from another source.

Under what circumstances will a court award monetary damages for a breached sale-of-land contract?

Sale of Goods. In a contract for the sale of goods, the usual measure of compensatory damages is the difference between the contract price and the market price.[3] **EXAMPLE 15.2** Medik Laboratories contracts to buy ten model UTS 400 network servers from Cal Industries for $4,000 each, but Cal Industries fails to deliver the servers. The market price of the servers at the time Medik learns of the breach is $4,500. Therefore, Medik's measure of damages is $5,000 (10 × $500), plus any incidental damages (expenses) caused by the breach. ■

Sometimes, the buyer breaches when the seller has not yet produced the goods. In that situation, compensatory damages normally equal the seller's lost profits on the sale, not the difference between the contract price and the market price.

Sale of Land. Ordinarily, because each parcel of land is unique, the remedy for a seller's breach of a contract for a sale of real estate is specific performance. The buyer is awarded the parcel of property for which he or she bargained (specific performance will be discussed more fully later in the chapter). The majority of states follow this rule.

A minority of states apply a different rule when the seller breaches a land-sale contract unintentionally (for instance, when the seller cannot deliver good title to the land for a reason he or she had previously been unaware of). In these states, a prospective buyer is limited to a refund of any down payment made plus any expenses incurred (such as fees for title searches, attorneys, and escrows). Thus, the minority rule effectively returns purchasers to the positions they occupied prior to the sale, rather than to give them the benefit of the bargain.

When the *buyer* is the party in breach, the measure of damages is typically the difference between the contract price and the market price of the land. The same measure is used when

iStockPhoto.com/CHRISsadowski

---

3. This is the difference between the contract price and the market price at the time and place at which the goods were to be delivered or tendered. See Sections 2–708, 2–713, and 2–715(1) of the Uniform Commercial Code (UCC).

specific performance is not available (because the seller has sold the property to someone else, for instance).

Construction Contracts. The measure of damages in a building or construction contract depends on which party breaches and when the breach occurs.

1. *Breach by owner.* The owner may breach at three different stages—before performance has begun, during performance, or after performance has been completed. If the owner breaches *before performance has begun,* the contractor can recover only the profits that would have been made on the contract (that is, the total contract price less the cost of materials and labor). If the owner breaches *during performance,* the contractor can recover the profits plus the costs incurred in partially constructing the building. If the owner breaches *after construction has been completed,* the contractor can recover the entire contract price, plus interest.

2. *Breach by contractor.* When the contractor breaches the contract—either by failing to begin construction or by stopping work partway through the project—the measure of damages is the cost of completion. The cost of completion includes reasonable compensation for any delay in performance. If the contractor finishes late, the measure of damages is the loss of use.

3. *Breach by both owner and contractor.* When the performance of both parties—the construction contractor and the owner—falls short of what their contract required, the courts attempt to strike a fair balance in awarding damages.

CASE EXAMPLE 15.3 Jamison Well Drilling, Inc., contracted to drill a well for Ed Pfeifer for $4,130. Jamison drilled the well and installed a storage tank. The well did not comply with state health department requirements, however, and failed repeated tests for bacteria. The health department ordered the well to be abandoned and sealed. Pfeifer used the storage tank but paid Jamison nothing. Jamison filed a suit to recover. The court held that Jamison was entitled to $970 for the storage tank but was not entitled to the full contract price because the well was not usable.[4] ▪

Exhibit 15–1 summarizes the rules for the measure of damages in breached construction contracts. The *Business Application* feature at the end of this chapter offers some suggestions on what to do if you cannot perform.

Consequential Damages Foreseeable damages that result from a party's breach of contract are called **consequential damages,** or *special damages.* They differ from compensatory damages in that they are caused by special circumstances beyond the contract itself. They flow

> "A long dispute means that both parties are wrong."
>
> **VOLTAIRE**
> 1694–1778
> (FRENCH AUTHOR)

Consequential Damages
Foreseeable damages that result from a party's breach of contract but are caused by special circumstances beyond the contract itself.

When a drilled water well fails bacteria testing, can the buyer of the drilling services keep the storage tank provided without paying for it?

---

4. *Jamison Well Drilling, Inc. v. Pfeifer,* 2011-Ohio-521 (2011).

Exhibit 15–1 Measurement of Damages—Breach of Construction Contracts

PARTY IN BREACH	TIME OF BREACH	MEASUREMENT OF DAMAGES
Owner	Before construction has begun	Profits (contract price less cost of materials and labor)
Owner	During construction	Profits plus costs incurred up to time of breach
Owner	After construction is completed	Full contract price, plus interest
Contractor	Before construction has begun	Cost in excess of contract price to complete work
Contractor	Before construction is completed	Generally, all costs incurred by owner to complete

KNOW THIS
To avoid the risk of consequential damages, a seller can limit the buyer's remedies via contract.

Nominal Damages A small monetary award (often one dollar) granted to a plaintiff when no actual damage was suffered.

Mitigation of Damages The requirement that a plaintiff do whatever is reasonable to minimize the damages caused by the defendant's breach of contract.

from the consequences, or results, of a breach. When a seller fails to deliver goods, knowing that the buyer is planning to use or resell those goods immediately, a court may award consequential damages for the loss of profits from the planned resale.

EXAMPLE 15.4 Mason contracts to buy a certain quantity of Quench, a specialty sports drink, from Nathan. Nathan knows that Mason has contracted with Ruthie to resell and ship the Quench within hours of its receipt. The beverage will then be sold to fans attending the Super Bowl. Nathan fails to deliver the Quench on time. Mason can recover the consequential damages—the loss of profits from the planned resale to Ruthie—caused by the nondelivery. (If Mason purchases Quench from another vendor, he can also recover compensatory damages for the difference between the contract price and the market price.) ■

For the nonbreaching party to recover consequential damages, the breaching party must know (or have reason to know) that special circumstances will cause the nonbreaching party to suffer an additional loss.[5] See this chapter's *Landmark in the Law* feature for a discussion of the nineteenth-century English case that established this rule on consequential damages.

Punitive Damages Punitive, or exemplary, damages, generally are not awarded in an action for breach of contract. Such damages have no legitimate place in contract law because they are, in essence, penalties, and a breach of contract is not unlawful in a criminal sense. A contract is simply a civil relationship between the parties. The law may compensate one party for the loss of the bargain—no more and no less. In a few situations, when a person's actions cause both a breach of contract and a tort, punitive damages may be available. Overall, though, punitive damages are almost never available in contract disputes.

Nominal Damages When no actual damage or financial loss results from a breach of contract and only a technical injury is involved, the court may award **nominal damages** to the innocent party. Nominal damages awards are often small, such as one dollar, but they do establish that the defendant acted wrongfully. Most lawsuits for nominal damages are brought as a matter of principle under the theory that a breach has occurred and some damages must be imposed regardless of actual loss.

EXAMPLE 15.5 Hernandez contracts to buy potatoes from Stanley at fifty cents a pound. Stanley breaches the contract and does not deliver the potatoes. Meanwhile, the price of potatoes falls. Hernandez is able to buy them in the open market at half the price he agreed to pay Stanley. Hernandez is clearly better off because of Stanley's breach. Thus, if Hernandez sues for breach of contract and wins, the court will likely award only nominal damages. ■

15–1b Mitigation of Damages

In most situations, when a breach of contract occurs, the injured party is held to a duty to mitigate, or reduce, the damages that he or she suffers. Under this doctrine of **mitigation of damages,** the required action depends on the nature of the situation.

Employment Contracts In the majority of states, a person whose employment has been wrongfully terminated has a duty to mitigate damages incurred because of the employer's breach of the employment contract. In other words, a wrongfully terminated employee has a duty to take a similar job if one is available.

If the employee fails to do this, the damages received will be equivalent to the person's former salary less the income he or she would have received in a similar job obtained by reasonable means. The employer has the burden of proving that such a job existed and that the employee could have been hired. Normally, a terminated employee is under no duty to take a job that is not of the same type and rank.

---

5. UCC 2–715(2).

LANDMARK IN THE LAW

Hadley v. Baxendale (1854)

The rule that requires a breaching party to have notice of special ("consequential") circumstances that will result in additional loss to the nonbreaching party before consequential damages can be awarded was first enunciated in *Hadley v. Baxendale,*[a] a landmark case decided in 1854.

CASE BACKGROUND The case involved a broken crankshaft used in a flour mill run by the Hadley family in Gloucester, England. The crankshaft attached to the steam engine in the mill broke, and the shaft had to be sent to a foundry in Greenwich so that a new shaft could be made to fit the engine.

The Hadleys hired Baxendale, a common carrier, to transport the shaft from Gloucester to Greenwich. Baxendale received payment in advance and promised to deliver the shaft the following day. It was not delivered for several days, however. The Hadleys had no extra crankshaft on hand to use, so

they had to close the mill during those days. The Hadleys sued Baxendale to recover the profits they lost during that time. Baxendale contended that the loss of profits was "too remote."

In the mid-1800s, it was common knowledge that large mills, such as that run by the Hadleys, normally had more than one crankshaft in case the main one broke and had to be repaired. It is against this background that the parties presented their arguments on whether the damages resulting from the loss of profits while the crankshaft was out for repair were "too remote" to be recoverable.

THE ISSUE BEFORE THE COURT AND THE COURT'S RULING The crucial issue for the court was whether the Hadleys had informed the carrier, Baxendale, of the special circumstances surrounding the crankshaft's repair. Specifically, did Baxendale know at the time of the contract that the mill would have to shut down while the crankshaft was being repaired?

In the court's opinion, the only circumstances communicated by the Hadleys to Baxendale at the time the contract was

made were that the item to be transported was a broken crankshaft of a mill and that the Hadleys were the owners and operators of that mill. The court concluded that these circumstances did not reasonably indicate that the mill would have to stop operations if the delivery of the crankshaft was delayed.

APPLICATION TO TODAY'S WORLD *Today, the rule enunciated by the court in this case still applies. When damages are awarded, compensation is given only for those injuries that the defendant could reasonably have foreseen as a probable result of the usual course of events following a breach. If the alleged injury is outside the usual and foreseeable course of events, the plaintiff must show specifically that the defendant had reason to know the facts and foresee the injury.*

This rule applies to contracts in the online environment as well. For example, suppose that a Web merchant loses business (and profits) due to a computer system's failure. If the failure was caused by malfunctioning software, the merchant normally may recover the lost profits from the software maker if these consequential damages were foreseeable.

a. 9 Exch. 341, 156 Eng.Rep. 145 (1854).

EXAMPLE 15.6 Susan De La Concha works as a librarian at Brigham Young University. When she is fired, she claims that she was terminated in retaliation for filing an employment discrimination claim. Suppose that De La Concha succeeds in her employment discrimination claim but that Brigham Young can show that she has failed to take another librarian position when several comparable positions were available. Brigham Young can assert that she has failed to mitigate damages. In that situation, any compensation she is awarded for wrongful termination will be reduced by the amount she *could have obtained* from other employment. ■

Rental Agreements

Some states require a landlord to use reasonable means to find a new tenant if a tenant abandons the premises and fails to pay rent. If an acceptable tenant becomes available, the landlord is required to lease the premises to this tenant to mitigate the damages recoverable from the former tenant. The former tenant is still liable for the difference between the amount of the rent under the original lease and the rent received from the new tenant. If the landlord has not taken reasonable steps to find a new tenant, a court will likely reduce any award by the amount of rent the landlord could have received had he or she done so.

Assume that a librarian is wrongfully fired for filing an employment discrimination claim. Is she obligated to mitigate damages by taking another librarian position?

15–1c Liquidated Damages versus Penalties

Liquidated Damages
An amount, stipulated in a contract, that the parties to the contract believe to be a reasonable estimation of the damages that will occur in the event of a breach.

Penalty A contract clause that specifies a certain amount to be paid in the event of a default or breach of contract but is unenforceable because it is designed to punish the breaching party rather than to provide a reasonable estimate of damages.

A **liquidated damages** provision in a contract specifies that a certain dollar amount is to be paid in the event of a *future* default or breach of contract. (*Liquidated* means determined, settled, or fixed.)

Liquidated damages differ from penalties. Although a **penalty** also specifies a certain amount to be paid in the event of a default or breach of contract, it is designed to penalize the breaching party, not to make the innocent party whole. Liquidated damages provisions normally are enforceable. In contrast, if a court finds that a provision calls for a penalty, the agreement as to the amount will not be enforced, and recovery will be limited to actual damages.

Enforceability   To determine whether a particular provision is for liquidated damages or a penalty, the court must answer two questions:

1. At the time the contract was formed, was it apparent that damages would be difficult to estimate in the event of a breach?

2. Was the amount set as damages a reasonable estimate and not excessive?[6]

If the answers to both questions are yes, the provision normally will be enforced. If either answer is no, the provision usually will not be enforced.

In the following *Spotlight Case,* the court had to decide whether a clause in a contract was an enforceable liquidated damages provision or an unenforceable penalty.

---

6. *Restatement (Second) of Contracts*, Section 356(1).

SPOTLIGHT ON LIQUIDATED DAMAGES: CASE 15.2

Kent State University v. Ford

Court of Appeals of Ohio, Eleventh District, Portage County, __ Ohio App.3d __, 26 N.E.3d 868, 2015 -Ohio- 41 (2015).

FACTS Gene Ford signed a five-year contract with Kent State University in Ohio to work as the head coach for the men's basketball team. The contract provided that if Ford quit before the end of the term, he would pay to the school liquidated damages in an amount equal to his salary ($300,000), multiplied by the number of years remaining on the contract. Laing Kennedy, Kent State's athletic director, told Ford that the contract would be renegotiated within a few years. Four years before the contract expired, however, Ford left Kent State and began to coach for Bradley University at an annual salary of $700,000. Kent State filed a suit in an Ohio state court against Ford, alleging breach of contract. The court enforced the liquidated damages clause and awarded the university $1.2 million. Ford appealed, arguing that the liquidated damages clause in his employment contract was an unenforceable penalty.

ISSUE Was the liquidated damages clause in Ford's contract enforceable?

DECISION Yes. A state intermediate appellate court affirmed the lower court's award. The clause was not a penalty. "There was justification for seeking liquidated damages to compensate for Kent State's losses" on Ford's breach.

If a college coach quits before the end of his contract, can the university recover liquidated damages?

REASON At the time the contract was entered into, determining the damages that would result from a breach was "difficult, if not impossible." The resignation of a head coach from a university's basketball team may cause a loss in ticket sales and a drop in community and alumni support for the team. The university's ability to recruit players may also be affected. Of course, a search for a new coach and coaching staff will be required. These effects are not easy to measure before they happen, especially considering that such results may be different at different times in a coach's tenure. Kennedy's statement that the contract would be renegotiated indicated that Kent State was interested in the stability of these factors. And in this case, "based on the record, . . . the damages were reasonable." The salary that Bradley was willing to pay Ford showed the cost to Kent State of finding a new coach with his skill and experience. "There was also an asserted decrease in ticket sales, costs associated with the trip for the coaching search, and additional potential sums that may be expended."

CRITICAL THINKING—Cultural Consideration *How does a college basketball team's record of wins and losses, and its ranking in its conference, support the court's decision in this case?*

Common Uses of Liquidated Damages Provisions Liquidated damages provisions are frequently used in construction contracts. For instance, a provision requiring a construction contractor to pay $300 for every day he or she is late in completing the project is a liquidated damages provision.

Such provisions are also common in contracts for the sale of goods.[7] In addition, contracts with entertainers and professional athletes often include liquidated damages provisions. **EXAMPLE 15.7** A television network settled its contract dispute with *Tonight Show* host Conan O'Brien for $33 million. The amount of the settlement was somewhat less than the $40 million O'Brien could have received under a liquidated damages clause in his contract. ■

Why might television personality Conan O'Brien settle a contract dispute for less than that contract's liquidated damages clause?

15–2 Equitable Remedies

Sometimes, damages are an inadequate remedy for a breach of contract. In these situations, the nonbreaching party may ask the court for an equitable remedy. Equitable remedies include rescission and restitution, specific performance, and reformation.

15–2a Rescission and Restitution

As previously discussed, *rescission* is essentially an action to undo, or cancel, a contract—to return nonbreaching parties to the positions that they occupied prior to the transaction.[8] When fraud, mistake, duress, undue influence, lack of capacity, or failure of consideration is present, rescission is available. Rescission may also be available by statute.[9] The failure of one party to perform under a contract entitles the other party to rescind the contract. The rescinding party must give prompt notice to the breaching party.

Restitution To rescind a contract, both parties generally must make **restitution** to each other by returning goods, property, or funds previously conveyed.[10] If the property or goods can be returned, they must be. If the property or goods have been consumed, restitution must be made in an equivalent dollar amount. Essentially, restitution involves the recapture of a benefit conferred on the defendant that has unjustly enriched her or him.

EXAMPLE 15.8 Katie contracts with Mikhail to design a house for her. Katie pays Mikhail $9,000 and agrees to make two more payments of $9,000 (for a total of $27,000) as the design progresses. The next day, Mikhail calls Katie and tells her that he has taken a position with a large architectural firm in another state and cannot design the house. Katie decides to hire another architect that afternoon. Katie can obtain restitution of the $9,000. ■

Restitution Is Not Limited to Rescission Cases Restitution may be required when a contract is rescinded, but the right to restitution is not limited to rescission cases. Because an award of restitution basically returns something to its rightful owner, a party can seek restitution in actions for breach of contract, tort actions, and other types of actions.

For instance, restitution can be obtained when funds or property has been transferred by mistake or because of fraud or incapacity. Similarly, restitution might be available when there has been misconduct by a party with a special relationship with the other party. Even in

LEARNING OBJECTIVE 3
Under what circumstances is the remedy of rescission and restitution available?

Restitution An equitable remedy under which a person is restored to his or her original position prior to loss or injury, or placed in the position he or she would have been in had the breach not occurred.

KNOW THIS
Restitution offers several advantages over traditional damages. First, restitution may be available in situations when damages cannot be proved or are difficult to prove. Second, restitution can be used to recover specific property. Third, restitution sometimes results in a greater overall award.

---

7. Section 2–718(1) of the UCC specifically authorizes the use of liquidated damages provisions.

8. The rescission discussed here refers to *unilateral* rescission, in which only one party wants to undo the contract. In *mutual* rescission, both parties agree to undo the contract. Mutual rescission discharges the contract, whereas unilateral rescission is generally available as a remedy for breach of contract.

9. Many states have laws that allow individuals who enter into "home solicitation contracts" to rescind these contracts within three business days for any reason. See, for example, California Civil Code Section 1689.5.

10. *Restatement (Second) of Contracts*, Section 370.

criminal cases, a court can order restitution of funds or property obtained through embezzlement, conversion, theft, or copyright infringement.

As mentioned, one of the bases that a court may use to order the rescission of a contract is fraud. That was the ground for the order of rescission in the following case.

CASE 15.3

Clara Wonjung Lee, DDS, Ltd. v. Robles

Appellate Court of Illinois, First District, 2014 WL 976776 (2014).

FACTS Clara Lee agreed to buy Rosalina Robles's dental practice and to lease her dental offices in Chicago, Illinois. The price was $267,000, with $133,500 allocated to goodwill—that is, the market value of the business's good reputation. After Lee took over the practice, *Chicago Magazine* and other local media revealed that Gary Kimmel, one of Robles's dentists, had illegally treated underage prostitutes in the practice's offices after hours. The media reported that Kimmel was under investigation by federal officials for this and other activities.

Lee filed a suit in an Illinois state court against Robles, seeking to rescind the contract. Lee alleged that Robles had deliberately withheld the information about Kimmel and that this information "adversely impacted the desirability and economic value of the practice." The court ruled in Lee's favor and awarded rescission and damages, which included the purchase price less Lee's unpaid rent and a portion of her income during her ownership of the practice. Robles appealed.

ISSUE Was Lee entitled to the rescission of her contract with Robles on the basis of fraud?

DECISION Yes. A state intermediate court affirmed the lower court's judgment awarding rescission and damages, finding that the holding

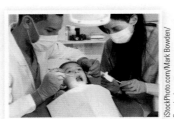

What determines the value of the reputation of a dental office?

iStockPhoto.com/Mark Bowden/ Bowdenimage

"was consistent with the manifest weight of the evidence presented at trial."

REASON The parties' agreement for the sale of the dental practice required Robles to disclose "any material information," including actions by a "governmental agency that materially alters the desirability or economic potential of the assets." The testimony of Lee and a business appraiser at the trial indicated that information about Kimmel's activities "would have been material to a reasonable dentist's decision to purchase the practice." Robles knew about the federal investigation of Kimmel—both the Federal Bureau of Investigation and *Chicago Magazine* had interviewed her about Kimmel's activities. Robles, however, failed to disclose this information to Lee. The evidence showed that Robles's failure was "purposeful and not the result of any mistake or accident." Her "nondisclosure was designed to prevent [Lee] from gaining relevant information that may have caused [her] to not proceed with the sales transaction."

CRITICAL THINKING—Legal Consideration *When rescission is awarded, what is the measure of recovery? What did the recovery include in this case?*

15–2b Specific Performance

Specific Performance
An equitable remedy in which a court orders the parties to perform as promised in the contract. This remedy normally is granted only when the legal remedy (monetary damages) is inadequate.

The equitable remedy of **specific performance** calls for the performance of the act promised in the contract. This remedy is attractive to a nonbreaching party because it provides the exact bargain promised in the contract. It also avoids some of the problems inherent in a suit for monetary damages, such as collecting a judgment and arranging another contract. Moreover, the actual performance may be more valuable (to the promisee) than the monetary damages.

Normally, however, specific performance will not be granted unless the party's legal remedy (monetary damages) is inadequate.[11] For this reason, contracts for the sale of goods rarely qualify for specific performance. Monetary damages ordinarily are adequate in sales contracts because substantially identical goods can be bought or sold in the market. Only if the goods are unique will a court grant specific performance. For instance, paintings, sculptures, and

---

11. *Restatement (Second) of Contracts*, Section 359.

rare books and coins are often unique, and monetary damages will not enable a buyer to obtain substantially identical substitutes in the market.

Sale of Land   A court may grant specific performance to a buyer in an action for a breach of contract involving the sale of land. In this situation, the legal remedy of monetary damages may not compensate the buyer adequately because every parcel of land is unique. The same land in the same location obviously cannot be obtained elsewhere. Only when specific performance is unavailable (such as when the seller has sold the property to someone else) will damages be awarded instead.

CASE EXAMPLE 15.9 Howard Stainbrook entered into a contract to sell Trent Low forty acres of mostly timbered land for $45,000. Low agreed to pay for a survey of the property and other costs in addition to the price. He gave Stainbrook a check for $1,000 to show his intent to fulfill the contract. One month later, Stainbrook died. His son David became the executor of the estate. After he discovered that the timber on the property was worth more than $100,000, David asked Low to withdraw his offer to buy the forty acres. Low refused and filed a suit against David seeking specific performance of the contract. The court found that because Low had substantially performed his obligations under the contract and offered to perform the rest, he was entitled to specific performance.[12] ■

Contracts for Personal Services   Contracts for personal services require one party to work personally for another party. Courts normally refuse to grant specific performance of personal-service contracts. One reason is that ordering a party to perform personal services against his or her will would amount to a type of involuntary servitude.[13]

Moreover, the courts do not want to monitor contracts for personal services, which usually require the exercise of personal judgment or talent. **EXAMPLE 15.10** Nicole contracts with a surgeon to remove a tumor on her brain. If he refuses to perform the surgery, the court will not compel him to perform (nor would Nicole want him to do so). A court cannot ensure meaningful performance in such a situation.[14] ■

If a contract is not deemed personal, the remedy at law of monetary damages may be adequate if a substantially identical service (for instance, lawn mowing) is available from other persons.

15–2c Reformation

Reformation is an equitable remedy used when the parties have *imperfectly* expressed their agreement in writing. Reformation allows a court to rewrite the contract to reflect the parties' true intentions.

Fraud or Mutual Mistake   Courts order reformation most often when fraud or mutual mistake is present. **EXAMPLE 15.11** If Carson contracts to buy a forklift from Yoshie but the written contract refers to a crane, a mutual mistake has occurred. Accordingly, a court could reform the contract so that the writing conforms to the parties' original intention as to which piece of equipment is being sold. ■

Written Contract Incorrectly States the Parties' Oral Agreement   A court will also reform a contract when two parties enter into a binding oral contract but later make an error when they attempt to put the terms into writing. Usually, the court will allow into evidence the correct terms of the oral contract, thereby reforming the written contract.

LEARNING OBJECTIVE **4**
When do courts grant specific performance as a remedy?

What happens when a contract mistakenly specifies a crane instead of a forklift?

---

12. *Stainbrook v. Low*, 842 N.E.2d 386 (Ind.App. 2006).
13. Involuntary servitude, or slavery, is contrary to the public policy expressed in the Thirteenth Amendment to the U.S. Constitution.
14. Similarly, courts often refuse to order specific performance of construction contracts because courts are not set up to operate as construction supervisors or engineers.

Covenants Not to Compete Courts also may reform contracts involving written covenants not to compete, or restrictive covenants. Such covenants, as explained in an earlier chapter, are often included in contracts for the sale of ongoing businesses and in employment contracts. The agreements restrict the area and time in which one party can directly compete with the other party.

If a covenant not to compete is for a valid and legitimate purpose, but the area or time restraints are unreasonable, some courts will reform the restraints by making them reasonable and will then enforce the entire contract as reformed. Other courts will throw out the entire restrictive covenant as illegal. Thus, when businesspersons create restrictive covenants, they must make sure that the restrictions imposed are reasonable.

CASE EXAMPLE 15.12 Cardiac Study Center, Inc., a medical practice group, hired Dr. Robert Emerick. Later, Emerick became a shareholder of Cardiac and signed an agreement that included a covenant not to compete. The covenant stated that a physician who left the group promised not to practice competitively in the surrounding area for a period of five years. After Cardiac began receiving complaints from patients and other physicians about Emerick, it terminated his employment.

Emerick sued Cardiac, claiming that the covenant not to compete that he had signed was unreasonable and should be declared illegal. Ultimately, a state appellate court held that the covenant was both reasonable and enforceable. Cardiac had a legitimate interest in protecting its existing client base and prohibiting Emerick from taking its clients.[15] ■

Exhibit 15–2 graphically presents the remedies, including reformation, that are available to the nonbreaching party.

15–3 Recovery Based on Quasi Contract

In some situations, when no actual contract exists, a court may step in to prevent one party from being unjustly enriched at the expense of another party. As previously discussed, *quasi contract* is a legal theory under which an obligation is imposed in the absence of an agreement. A quasi contract is not a true contract but rather a fictional contract that is imposed on the parties to prevent unjust enrichment.

---

15. *Emerick v. Cardiac Study Center, Inc.,* 166 Wash.App. 1039 (2012).

Exhibit 15–2 Remedies for Breach of Contract

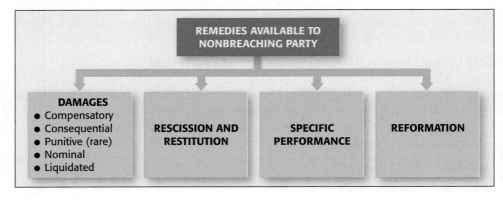

15-3a When Quasi Contract Is Used

Quasi contract allows a court to act as if a contract exists when there is no actual contract or agreement between the parties. Therefore, if the parties have entered into a contract concerning the matter in controversy, a court normally will not impose a quasi contract. A court can also use the doctrine when the parties entered into a contract, but it is unenforceable for some reason.

Quasi-contractual recovery is often granted when one party has partially performed under a contract that is unenforceable. Quasi contracts provide an alternative to suing for damages and allow the party to recover the reasonable value of the partial performance. Depending on the case, the amount of the recovery may be measured either by the benefit received or by the detriment suffered.

EXAMPLE 15.13 Ericson contracts to build two oil derricks for Petro Industries. The derricks are to be built over a period of three years, but the parties do not create a written contract. Therefore, the writing requirement will bar the enforcement of the contract.[16] After Ericson completes one derrick, Petro Industries informs him that it will not pay for the derrick. Ericson can sue Petro Industries under the theory of quasi contract. ■

15-3b The Requirements of Quasi Contract

To recover on a quasi contract theory, the party seeking recovery must show the following:

1. The party conferred a benefit on the other party.
2. The party conferred the benefit with the reasonable expectation of being paid.
3. The party did not act as a volunteer in conferring the benefit.
4. The party receiving the benefit would be unjustly enriched if allowed to retain the benefit without paying for it.

Applying these requirements to *Example 15.13,* Ericson can sue in quasi contract because all of the conditions for quasi-contractual recovery have been fulfilled. Ericson conferred a benefit on Petro Industries by building the oil derrick. Ericson built the derrick with the reasonable expectation of being paid. He did not intend to act as a volunteer. Petro Industries would be unjustly enriched if it was allowed to keep the derrick without paying Ericson for the work. Therefore, Ericson should be able to recover the reasonable value of the oil derrick that was built (under the theory of *quantum meruit*[17]—"as much as he or she deserves"). The reasonable value is ordinarily equal to the fair market value.

KNOW THIS
The function of a quasi contract is to impose a legal obligation on a party who made no actual promise.

Assume that it takes several years to build two oil derricks, but no written contract exists. If one is built, does the purchaser have to pay for it?

15-4 Contract Provisions Limiting Remedies

A contract may include provisions stating that no damages can be recovered for certain types of breaches or that damages will be limited to a maximum amount. A contract may also provide that the only remedy for breach is replacement, repair, or refund of the purchase price. In addition, a contract may provide that one party can seek injunctive relief if the other party breaches the contract. Provisions stating that no damages can be recovered are called *exculpatory clauses.* Provisions that affect the availability of certain remedies are called *limitation-of-liability clauses.*

---

16. Contracts that by their terms cannot be performed within one year from the day after the date of contract formation must be in writing to be enforceable under the Statute of Frauds.
17. Pronounced *kwahn*-tuhm *mehr*-oo-wuht.

ETHICAL ISSUE

Can contracts for mixed martial arts fighters limit a fighter's right to stop fighting? If you are a mixed martial arts champion, the highest-profile league to work for is the Ultimate Fighting Championship, or UFC. But a contract with UFC's parent company, Zuffa, LLC, includes numerous restrictions on your behavior.

The UFC's exclusivity clause, for instance, prevents you from competing in other mixed martial arts leagues. Another clause states that if you refuse a fight—or are injured or disabled—Zuffa can choose to extend the term of your contract. The term may be extended for any period when a fighter is unable or unwilling to compete or train for any reason. Zuffa can even retain the rights to a fighter who wants to retire from mixed martial arts.

You probably also signed an agreement that has a "champions clause." That means that if you become a champion, your contract with the UFC is automatically extended. If you get really famous, you do not even have rights to your likeness. You have signed those away to the UFC. So if a video game is based on your likeness, the UFC obtains the profits, and you do not. Therefore, you will have trouble negotiating with sponsors outside of the UFC, because you really do not own much of yourself to "sell."

A group of current and former mixed martial arts fighters have filed a lawsuit against Zuffa. They claim that these contract limitations are fundamentally unfair. Because the contracts prevent fighters from working with other promoters, profiting from individual marketing deals, and signing with outside sponsors, the suit alleges that the UFC is violating antitrust laws.

15–4a Sales Contracts

The Uniform Commercial Code (UCC) provides that remedies can be limited in a contract for the sale of goods. We will examine the UCC provisions on limitation-of-liability clauses again in the context of the remedies available on the breach of a contract for the sale or lease of goods.[18]

15–4b Enforceability of Limitation-of-Liability Clauses

LEARNING OBJECTIVE 5
What is a limitation-of-liability clause, and when will courts enforce it?

Whether a limitation-of-liability clause in a contract will be enforced depends on the type of breach that is excused by the provision. Clauses that normally will not be enforced include provisions excluding liability for fraudulent or intentional injury or for illegal acts or other violations of law. Clauses excluding liability for negligence may be enforced in certain situations, however. When an exculpatory clause for negligence is contained in a contract made between parties who have roughly equal bargaining positions, the clause usually will be enforced.

CASE EXAMPLE 15.14 Engineering Consulting Services, Ltd. (ECS), contracted with RSN Properties, Inc., a real estate developer, to perform soil studies for $2,200 and render an opinion on the use of septic systems in a residential subdivision being developed. A clause in the contract limited ECS's liability to RSN to the value of the engineering services or the sum of $50,000, whichever was greater.

ECS concluded that most of the lots were suitable for septic systems, so RSN proceeded with development. RSN constructed roads and water lines to the subdivision in reliance on ECS's conclusions, which turned out to be incorrect. RSN sued ECS for breach of contract and argued that the limitation-of-liability clause was against public policy and unenforceable. The court, however, enforced the limitation-of-liability clause as "a reasonable allocation of risks in an arm's-length business transaction."[19] ■

---

18. UCC 2–719.
19. *RSN Properties, Inc. v. Engineering Consulting Services, Ltd.*, 301 Ga.App. 52, 686 S.E.2d 853 (2009).

Reviewing . . . Breach and Remedies

Kyle Bruno enters into a contract with X Entertainment to be a stuntman in a movie. Bruno is widely known as the best motorcycle stuntman in the business, and the movie, *Xtreme Riders,* has numerous scenes involving high-speed freestyle street-bike stunts. Filming is set to begin August 1 and end by December 1 so that the film can be released the following summer. Both parties to the contract have stipulated that the filming must end on time in order to capture the profits from the summer movie market.

The contract states that Bruno will be paid 10 percent of the net proceeds from the movie for his stunts. The contract also includes a liquidated damages provision, which specifies that if Bruno breaches the contract, he will owe X Entertainment $1 million. In addition, the contract includes a limitation-of-liability clause stating that if Bruno is injured during filming, X Entertainment's liability is limited to nominal damages. Using the information presented in the chapter, answer the following questions.

1. One day, while Bruno is preparing for a difficult stunt, he gets into an argument with the director and refuses to perform any stunts. Can X Entertainment seek specific performance of the contract? Why or why not?

2. Suppose that while performing a high-speed wheelie on a motorcycle, Bruno is injured by an intentionally reckless act of an X Entertainment employee. Will a court be likely to enforce the limitation-of-liability clause? Why or why not?

3. What factors would a court consider to determine if the $1 million liquidated damages clause is valid or is a penalty?

4. Suppose that there was no liquidated damages clause (or the court refused to enforce it) and X Entertainment breached the contract. The breach caused the release of the film to be delayed by many months. Could Bruno seek consequential (special) damages for lost profits from the summer movie market in that situation? Explain.

DEBATE THIS

- Courts should always uphold limitation-of-liability clauses, whether or not the two parties to the contract had equal bargaining power.

BUSINESS APPLICATION

What Do You Do When You Cannot Perform?*

Not every contract can be performed. If you are a contractor, you may take on a job that, for one reason or another, you cannot or do not wish to perform. Simply walking away from the job and hoping for the best normally is not the most effective way to avoid litigation—which can be costly, time consuming, and emotionally draining. Instead, you should consider various options that may reduce the likelihood of litigation.

For example, suppose that you are a building contractor and you sign a contract to build a home for the Andersons according to a set of plans that they provided. Performance is to begin on June 15. On June 1, Central Enterprises offers you a position that will pay you two and a half times as much net income as you could earn as an independent builder. To take the job, you have to start on June 15. You cannot be in two places at the same time, so to accept the new position, you must breach the contract with the Andersons.

---

* This *Business Application* is not meant to substitute for the services of an attorney who is licensed to practice law in your state.

Continues

Consider Your Options

What can you do in this situation? One option is to subcontract the work to another builder and oversee the work yourself to make sure it conforms to the contract. Another option is to negotiate with the Andersons for a release. You can offer to find another qualified builder who will build a house of the same quality at the same price. Alternatively, you can offer to pay any additional costs if another builder takes the job and is more expensive. In any event, this additional cost would be one measure of damages that a court would impose on you if the Andersons prevailed in a suit for breach of contract (in addition to any costs the Andersons suffer as a result of the breach, such as costs due to the delay in construction). Thus, by making the offer, you might be able to avoid the expense of litigation—if the Andersons accept your offer.

Offers for Settlement

Often, parties are reluctant to propose compromise settlements because they fear that what they say will be used against them in court if litigation ensues. Generally, however, offers for settlement will not be admitted in court to prove that you are liable for a breach of contract (though they are at times admissible to prove a party breached the duty of good faith).

CHECKLIST for When You Cannot Perform:

1. Consider a compromise.
2. Subcontract out the work and oversee it.
3. Offer to find an alternative contractor to fulfill your obligation.
4. Make a cash offer to "buy" a release from your contract. Work with an attorney in making the offer unless the amount involved is insignificant.

Key Terms

consequential damages 359
incidental damages 358
liquidated damages 362

mitigation of damages 360
nominal damages 360
penalty 362

restitution 363
specific performance 364

Chapter Summary: Breach and Remedies

COMMON REMEDIES AVAILABLE TO NONBREACHING PARTY	

Damages	The legal remedy designed to compensate the nonbreaching party for the loss of the bargain. The nonbreaching party frequently has a duty to *mitigate* (lessen or reduce) the damages suffered. There are four broad categories of damages. In addition, a contract may contain a provision for liquidated damages.
	1. *Compensatory damages*—Damages that compensate the nonbreaching party for injuries actually sustained and proved to have arisen directly from the loss of the bargain resulting from the breach of contract.
	  a. In breached contracts for the sale of goods, the usual measure of compensatory damages is the difference between the contract price and the market price.
	  b. In breached contracts for the sale of land, the measure of damages is ordinarily the same as in contracts for the sale of goods.
	  c. In breached construction contracts, the measure of damages depends on which party breaches and at what stage of construction the breach occurs.
	2. *Consequential damages*—Damages that result from special circumstances beyond the contract itself. The damages flow only from the consequences of a breach. For a party to recover consequential damages, the damages must be the foreseeable result of a breach of contract, and the breaching party must have known at the time the contract was formed that special circumstances existed that would cause the nonbreaching party to incur additional loss on breach of the contract. Also called *special damages*.
	3. *Punitive damages*—Damages awarded to punish the breaching party. Usually not awarded in an action for breach of contract unless a tort is involved.
	4. *Nominal damages*—Damages small in amount (such as one dollar) that are awarded when a breach has occurred but no actual injury has been suffered. Awarded only to establish that the defendant acted wrongfully.
	5. *Liquidated damages*—Damages specified in a contract as the amount to be paid to the nonbreaching party in the event the contract is breached. Clauses providing for liquidated damages are enforced if the damages were difficult to estimate at the time the contract was formed and if the amount stipulated is reasonable. If the amount is construed to be a penalty, the clause will not be enforced.

Rescission and Restitution	1. *Rescission*—A remedy whereby a contract is canceled and the parties are restored to the original positions that they occupied prior to the transaction. Available when fraud, a mistake, duress, or failure of consideration is present. The rescinding party must give prompt notice of the rescission to the breaching party. 2. *Restitution*—When a contract is rescinded, both parties must make restitution to each other by returning the goods, property, or funds previously conveyed. Restitution prevents the unjust enrichment of the parties.
Specific Performance	An equitable remedy calling for the performance of the act promised in the contract. This remedy is available only in special situations—such as those involving contracts for the sale of unique goods or land—when monetary damages would be an inadequate remedy. Specific performance is not available as a remedy for breached contracts for personal services.
Reformation	An equitable remedy allowing a contract to be "reformed," or rewritten, to reflect the parties' true intentions. Available when an agreement is imperfectly expressed in writing.
Recovery Based on Quasi Contract	An equitable theory imposed by the courts to obtain justice and prevent unjust enrichment in a situation in which no enforceable contract exists. The party seeking recovery must show the following: 1. A benefit was conferred on the other party. 2. The party conferring the benefit did so with the expectation of being paid. 3. The benefit was not volunteered. 4. The party receiving the benefit would be unjustly enriched if allowed to retain the benefit without paying for it.
CONTRACT DOCTRINES RELATING TO REMEDIES	
Contract Provisions Limiting Remedies	A contract may provide that no damages (or only a limited amount of damages) can be recovered in the event the contract is breached. Under the Uniform Commercial Code, remedies may be limited in contracts for the sale of goods. Clauses excluding liability for fraudulent or intentional injury or for illegal acts cannot be enforced. Clauses excluding liability for negligence may be enforced if both parties hold roughly equal bargaining power.

Issue Spotters

1. Greg contracts to build a storage shed for Haney. Haney pays Greg in advance, but Greg completes only half the work. Haney pays Ipswich $500 to finish the shed. If Haney sues Greg, what would be the measure of recovery? (See *Damages*.)
2. Lyle contracts to sell his ranch to Marley, who is to take possession on June 1. Lyle delays the transfer until August 1. Marley incurs expenses in providing for cattle that he bought for the ranch. When they made the contract, Lyle had no reason to know of the cattle. Is Lyle liable for Marley's expenses in providing for the cattle? Why or why not? (See *Damages*.)
—**Check your answers to the *Issue Spotters* against the answers provided in Appendix D at the end of this text.**

Learning Objectives Check

1. What is the standard measure of compensatory damages when a contract is breached? How are damages computed differently in construction contracts?
2. What is the difference between compensatory damages and consequential damages? What are nominal damages, and when do courts award nominal damages?
3. Under what circumstances is the remedy of rescission and restitution available?
4. When do courts grant specific performance as a remedy?
5. What is a limitation-of-liability clause, and when will courts enforce it?
—**Answers to the even-numbered *Learning Objectives Check* questions can be found in Appendix E at the end of this text.**

Business Scenarios and Case Problems

15–1. Liquidated Damages. Carnack contracts to sell his house and lot to Willard for $100,000. The terms of the contract call for Willard to make a deposit of 10 percent of the purchase price as a down payment. The terms further stipulate that if the buyer breaches the contract, Carnack will retain the deposit as liquidated damages. Willard makes the deposit, but because her expected financing of the $90,000 balance falls through, she breaches the contract. Two weeks later, Carnack sells the house and lot to Balkova for $105,000. Willard demands her $10,000 back, but Carnack refuses, claiming that Willard's breach and the contract terms entitle him to keep the deposit. Discuss who is correct. (See *Damages*.)

15–2. Mitigation of Damages. Lauren Barton, a single mother with three children, lived in Portland, Oregon. Cynthia VanHorn also lived in Oregon until she moved to New York City to open and operate an art gallery. VanHorn asked Barton to manage the gallery under a one-year contract for an annual salary of $72,000. To begin work, Barton relocated to New York. As part of the move, Barton transferred custody of her children to her husband, who lived in London, England. In accepting the job, Barton also forfeited her husband's alimony and child-support payments, including unpaid amounts of nearly $30,000.

Before Barton started work, VanHorn repudiated the contract. Unable to find employment for more than an annual salary of $25,000, Barton moved to London to be near her children. Barton filed a suit in an Oregon state court against VanHorn, seeking damages for breach of contract. Should the court hold, as VanHorn argued, that Barton did not take reasonable steps to mitigate her damages? Why or why not? (See *Damages*.)

15–3. Quasi Contract. Middleton Motors, Inc., a struggling Ford dealership in Wisconsin, sought managerial and financial assistance from Lindquist Ford, Inc., a successful Ford dealership in Iowa. While the two dealerships negotiated the terms for the services and a cash infusion, Lindquist sent Craig Miller, its general manager, to assume control of Middleton. After a year, the parties had not agreed on the terms, Lindquist had not invested any funds, Middleton had not made a profit, and Miller was fired without being paid. Can Miller recover pay for his time on a quasi-contract theory? Why or why not? Which of the quasi-contractual requirements is most likely to be disputed in this case? Why? [*Lindquist Ford, Inc. v. Middleton Motors, Inc.*, 557 F.3d 469 (7th Cir. 2009)] (See *Recovery Based on Quasi Contract*.)

15–4. Liquidated Damages versus Penalties. Planned Pethood Plus, Inc. (PPP), a veterinary clinic, borrowed $389,000 from KeyBank. The term of the loan was ten years. A "prepayment penalty" clause provided a formula to add an amount to the balance due if PPP offered to repay its loan early. The additional amount depended on the time of the prepayment. Such clauses are common in loan agreements. After one year, PPP offered to pay its loan. KeyBank applied the formula to add $40,525.92 to the balance due. Is this a penalty or liquidated damages? Explain. [*Planned Pethood Plus, Inc. v. KeyCorp, Inc.*, 228 P.3d 262 (Colo.App. 2010)] (See *Damages*.)

15–5. Measure of Damages. Before buying a house, Dean and Donna Testa hired Ground Systems, Inc. (GSI), to inspect the sewage and water disposal system. GSI reported a split system with a watertight septic tank, a wastewater tank, a distribution box, and a leach field. The Testas bought the house. Later, Dean saw that the system was not as GSI described—there was no distribution box or leach field, and there was only one tank, which was not watertight. The Testas arranged for the installation of a new system and sold the house. Assuming that GSI is liable for breach of contract, what is the measure of damages? [*Testa v. Ground Systems, Inc.*, 206 N.J. 330, 20 A.3d 435 (App. Div. 2011)] (See *Damages*.)

15–6. Business Case Problem with Sample Answer—Consequential Damages. After submitting the high bid at a foreclosure sale, David Simard entered into a contract to purchase real property in Maryland for $192,000. Simard defaulted (failed to pay) on the contract, so a state court ordered the property to be resold at Simard's expense, as required by state law. The property was then resold for $163,000, but the second purchaser also defaulted on his contract. The court then ordered a second resale, resulting in a final price of $130,000. Assuming that Simard is liable for consequential damages, what is the extent of his liability? Is he liable for losses and expenses related to the first resale? If so, is he also liable for losses and expenses related to the second resale? Why or why not? [*Burson v. Simard*, 35 A.3d 1154 (Md. 2012)] (See *Damages*.)

—For a sample answer to Problem 15–6, go to Appendix F at the end of this text.

15–7. Liquidated Damages. Cuesport Properties, LLC, sold a condominium in Anne Arundel County, Maryland, to Critical Developments, LLC. As part of the sale, Cuesport agreed to build a wall between Critical Developments' unit and an adjacent unit within thirty days of closing. If Cuesport failed to do so, it was to pay $126 per day until completion. This was an estimate of the amount of rent that Critical Developments would lose until the wall was finished and the unit could be rented. Actual damages were otherwise difficult to estimate at the time of the contract. The wall was built on time, but without a county permit, and it did not comply with the county building code. Critical Developments did not modify the wall to comply with the code until 260 days after the date of the contract deadline for completion of the wall. Does Cuesport have to pay Critical Developments $126 for each of the 260 days? Explain. [*Cuesport Properties, LLC v. Critical Developments, LLC*, 209 Md.App. 607, 61 A.3d 91 (2013)] (See *Damages*.)

15–8. Limitation-of-Liability Clauses. Mia Eriksson was a seventeen-year-old competitor in horseback-riding events. Her riding coach was Kristi Nunnink. Eriksson signed an agreement that released Nunnink from all liability except for damages caused by Nunnink's "direct, willful and wanton negligence." During an event at Galway Downs in Temecula, California, Eriksson's horse struck a hurdle. She fell from the horse and the horse fell on her, causing her death. Her parents, Karan and Stan Eriksson, filed a suit in a California state court against

Nunnink for wrongful death. Is the limitation-of-liability agreement that Eriksson signed likely to be enforced in her parents' case? If so, how would it affect their claim? Explain. [*Eriksson v. Nunnink,* 233 Cal.App.4th 708, 183 Cal.Rptr.3d 234 (4 Dist. 2015)] (See *Contract Provisions Limiting Remedies.*)

15–9. A Question of Ethics—Performance and Damages. On a weekday, Tamara Cohen, a real estate broker, showed a townhouse owned by Ray and Harriet Mayer to Jessica Seinfeld, the wife of comedian Jerry Seinfeld. On the weekend, when Cohen was unavailable because her religious beliefs prevented her from working, the Seinfelds revisited the townhouse on their own and agreed to buy it. The contract stated that the "buyers will pay buyer's real estate broker's fees." [*Cohen v. Seinfeld,* 15 Misc.3d 1118(A), 839 N.Y.S.2d 432 (Sup. 2007)] (See *Damages.*)

1. Is Cohen entitled to payment even though she was not available to show the townhouse to the Seinfelds on the weekend? Explain.

2. What obligation do parties involved in business deals owe to each other with respect to their religious beliefs? How might the situation in this case have been avoided?

Critical Thinking and Writing Assignments

15–10. Critical Legal Thinking. Review the discussion of the doctrine of mitigation of damages in this chapter. What are some of the advantages and disadvantages of this doctrine? (See *Damages.*)

15–11. Business Law Critical Thinking Group Assignment. Frances Morelli agreed to sell Judith Bucklin a house in Rhode Island for $177,000. The sale was supposed to be closed by September 1. The contract included a provision that "if Seller is unable to convey good, clear, insurable, and marketable title, Buyer shall have the option to: (a) accept such title as Seller is able to convey without reduction of the Purchase Price, or (b) cancel this Agreement and receive a return of all Deposits."

An examination of the public records revealed that the house did not have marketable title. Bucklin offered Morelli additional time to resolve the problem, and the closing did not occur as scheduled. Morelli decided that "the deal [was] over" and offered to return the deposit. Bucklin refused and, in mid-October, decided to exercise her option to accept the house without marketable title. She notified Morelli, who did not respond. She then filed a lawsuit against Morelli in a state court. (See *Equitable Remedies.*)

1. One group will discuss whether Morelli has breached the contract and will decide in whose favor the court should rule.

2. A second group will assume that Morelli did breach the contract and will determine what the appropriate remedy is in this situation.

16

iStockPhoto.com/Robert Churchill/Rawpixel

LEARNING OBJECTIVES

The five Learning Objectives *below are designed to help improve your understanding of the chapter. After reading this chapter, you should be able to answer the following questions:*

1. What is the principle of comity, and why do courts deciding disputes involving a foreign law or judicial decree apply this principle?

2. What is the act of state doctrine? In what circumstances is this doctrine applied?

3. Under the Foreign Sovereign Immunities Act, in what situations is a foreign state subject to the jurisdiction of U.S. courts?

4. What are some clauses commonly included in international business contracts?

5. What federal law allows U.S. citizens, as well as citizens of foreign nations, to file civil actions in U.S. courts for torts that were committed overseas?

International Law in a Global Economy

International business transactions are not unique to the modern world. Indeed, commerce has always crossed national borders, as President Thomas Jefferson noted in the chapter-opening quotation. What is new in our day is the dramatic growth in world trade and the emergence of a global business community. Because exchanges of goods, services, and intellectual property on a global level are now routine, students of business law and the legal environment should be familiar with the laws pertaining to international business transactions.

> "The merchant has no country."
>
> **THOMAS JEFFERSON**
> 1743–1826
> (THIRD PRESIDENT OF THE UNITED STATES, 1801–1809)

Laws affecting the international legal environment of business include both international law and national law. *International law* is defined as a body of law—formed as a result of international customs, treaties, and organizations—that governs relations among or between nations. International law may be created when individual nations agree to comply with certain standards (such as by signing a treaty). It may also be created when industries or nations establish international standards for private transactions that cross national borders (such as standards concerning the importation or sale of genetically modified organisms).

National law is the law of a particular nation, such as Brazil, Germany, Japan, or the United States. In some ways, national laws that involve restrictions applied at a nation's borders effectively become international law. (Can officials legally search electronic devices, including laptops and smartphones, of persons who cross national borders? See this chapter's *Beyond Our Borders* feature for the answer.) In this chapter, we examine how both international law and national law frame business operations in the global context.

BEYOND OUR BORDERS

Border Searches of Your Electronic Devices

Every year, tens of millions of travelers arrive at U.S. borders where they are subject to a search. Of these travelers, about 12 million undergo a secondary screening, and approximately five thousand of these screenings involve an electronic device. About three hundred devices—computers, tablets, and smartphones—are sent to the Immigration and Customs Enforcement forensics laboratory in Fairfax, Virginia, for further examination.

The U.S. government has historically had a broad power to search travelers and their property when they enter this country. That power includes the right to inspect papers and other physical documents in the possession of anyone entering the United States, including U.S. citizens. Increasingly, however, instead of being carried in physical form, documents are carried on the hard drives of laptop computers, in tablets, or in smartphones. Indeed, a person might have thousands of photos, e-mails, video clips, and documents on the hard drive of a laptop.

Does the government's power to conduct border searches give it the right to rummage through all of the data on an electronic device? Several recent lawsuits have raised this issue.

A Student Challenges the Extensive Search of His Laptop

When Pascal Abidor, a Ph.D. student who has dual U.S. and French citizenship, traveled by train from Canada to New York, U.S. Customs and Border Control agents pulled him aside and required him to log on to his computer. They then examined much of its contents. Abidor was released after a few hours, but the Department of Homeland Security kept his laptop for eleven days.

Abidor challenged the search. His complaint alleged that the suspicionless search of U.S. citizens' electronic devices at international borders violates their constitutional right to privacy. The lawsuit was dismissed in 2013 when a federal court concluded that Abidor lacked standing to challenge the government's border search policies.[a]

Routine versus Forensic Searches of Electronic Devices

In another case, Ali Saboonchi and his wife were stopped at the border on returning from a day trip to the Canadian side of Niagara Falls. Saboonchi was a dual citizen of the United States and Iran. His name had been flagged in the Homeland Security database because of information from the FBI concerning inquiries he had made about specialized technology with possible medical or military applications. Customs officials performed a secondary search of Saboonchi's vehicle and questioned him and his wife. The officials allowed the couple to reenter the country, but seized two of Saboonchi's smartphones and a flash drive and sent them to Virginia for further testing.

A week later, customs officials returned Saboonchi's electronics. The government then filed criminal charges against Saboonchi in federal court for violating U.S. export restrictions on trade with Iran. The indictment alleged that he had sold specialized equipment to a company in the United Arab Emirates that was linked to a company in Iran. His digital devices had contained contact information about the companies involved, along with other evidence.

Saboonchi argued that the evidence had been illegally seized and that the information obtained from his electronic devices should be excluded from trial. The court recognized a difference between routine border searches and forensic border searches, which involve experts using specialized software. Forensic searches, according to the court, require reasonable suspicion. Nevertheless, the court concluded that the government had reasonable suspicion that Saboonchi was involved in violations of export restrictions.[b]

CRITICAL THINKING

- What are some steps that businesspersons can take to avoid issues at the border with respect to the contents of their electronic devices?

---

a. *Abidor v. Napolitano*, 990 F.Supp.2d 260 (E.D.N.Y. 2013).

b. *U.S. v. Saboonchi*, 990 F.Supp.2d 536 (D.Md. 2014).

16-1 International Law

The major difference between international law and national law is that a nation's government authorities can enforce its national law. What government, however, can enforce international law?

By definition, a *nation* is a sovereign entity—meaning that there is no higher authority to which that nation must submit. If a nation violates an international law and persuasive tactics fail, other countries or international organizations have no recourse except to take coercive actions. Coercive actions may include economic sanctions, severance of diplomatic relations, boycotts, and, as a last resort, war against the violating nation.

EXAMPLE 16.1 In 2014, Russia sent troops into the neighboring nation of Ukraine and supported an election that allowed Crimea (part of Ukraine) to secede from Ukraine. Because Russia's actions violated Ukraine's independent sovereignty, the United States and the European Union imposed economic sanctions on Russia. Nevertheless, Russia continued to support military action in Ukraine as of 2016. ■

In essence, international law is the result of centuries-old attempts to reconcile the need of each country to be the final authority over its own affairs with the desire of nations to benefit economically from trade and harmonious relations with one another. Sovereign nations can, and do, voluntarily agree to be governed in certain respects by international law for the purpose of facilitating international trade and commerce, as well as civilized discourse. As a result, a body of international law has evolved.

When Russia sent troops into Ukraine, what did the U.S. and Western Europe do?

Pavel L Photo and Video/ShutterStock.com

16–1a Sources of International Law

Basically, there are three sources of international law: international customs, treaties and international agreements, and international organizations. We look at each of these sources here.

International Customs One important source of international law consists of the international customs that have evolved among nations in their relations with one another. Article 38(1) of the Statute of the International Court of Justice refers to an international custom as "evidence of a general practice accepted as law." The legal principles and doctrines that you will read about shortly are rooted in international customs and traditions that have evolved over time in the international arena.

Treaties and International Agreements Treaties and other explicit agreements between or among foreign nations provide another important source of international law. A **treaty** is an agreement or contract between two or more nations that must be authorized and ratified by the supreme power of each nation. Under Article II, Section 2, of the U.S. Constitution, the president has the power "by and with the Advice and Consent of the Senate, to make Treaties, provided two-thirds of the Senators present concur."

A *bilateral* agreement, as the term implies, is an agreement formed by two nations to govern their commercial exchanges or other relations with one another. A *multilateral* agreement is formed by several nations. For example, regional trade associations such as the Andean Common Market (ANCOM), the Association of Southeast Asian Nations (ASEAN), and the European Union (EU) are the result of multilateral trade agreements.

Treaty A formal international agreement negotiated between two nations or among several nations.

International Organizations In international law, the term **international organization** generally refers to an organization that is composed mainly of member nations and usually established by treaty. The United States is a member of more than one hundred bilateral and multilateral organizations, including at least twenty through the United Nations.

International Organization An organization composed mainly of member nations and usually established by treaty— for example, the United Nations. More broadly, the term also includes nongovernmental organizations (NGOs) such as the Red Cross.

Adopt Standards. International organizations adopt resolutions, declarations, and other types of standards that often require nations to behave in a particular manner. The General Assembly of the United Nations, for instance, has adopted numerous nonbinding resolutions and declarations that embody principles of international law. Disputes involving these resolutions and declarations may be brought before the International Court of Justice. That court, however, normally has authority to settle legal disputes only when nations voluntarily submit to its jurisdiction.

Create Uniform Rules. International organizations may also create uniform rules. The United Nations Commission on International Trade Law has made considerable progress in establishing uniformity in international law as it relates to trade, for example. One of the commission's most significant creations to date is the 1980 Convention on Contracts for the International Sale of Goods (CISG). The CISG is similar to Article 2 of the Uniform Commercial Code. It is designed to settle disputes between parties to sales contracts if the parties have not agreed otherwise in their contracts. The CISG governs only sales contracts between trading partners in nations that have ratified the CISG, however.

16–1b International Principles and Doctrines

Over time, a number of legal principles and doctrines have evolved and have been employed by the courts of various nations to resolve or reduce conflicts that involve a foreign element. The three important legal principles discussed next are based primarily on courtesy and respect, and are applied in the interests of maintaining harmonious relations among nations.

The Principle of Comity Under the principle of **comity,** one nation will defer to and give effect to the laws and judicial decrees of another country, as long as they are consistent with the law and public policy of the accommodating nation. For instance, a U.S. court ordinarily will recognize and enforce a default judgment from an Australian court because the legal procedures in Australia are compatible with those in the United States. Nearly all nations recognize the validity of marriage decrees (at least, those between a man and a woman) issued in another country.

CASE EXAMPLE 16.2 Karen Goldberg's husband was killed in a terrorist bombing in Israel. She filed a lawsuit in a federal court in New York against UBS AG, a Switzerland-based global financial services company with many offices in the United States. Goldberg claimed that UBS was liable under the U.S. Anti-Terrorism Act for aiding and abetting the murder of her husband because it provided financial services to the terrorist organizations responsible.

UBS argued that the case should be transferred to a court in Israel, which would offer a remedy "substantially the same" as the one available in the United States. The court refused, however. Transferring the case would require an Israeli court to take evidence and judge the emotional damage suffered by Goldberg, "raising distinct concerns of comity and enforceability."[1] ■

In the following case, the defendant wanted the court to give particular weight to the principle of comity.

---

1. *Goldberg v. UBS AG*, 690 F.Supp.2d 92 (E.D.N.Y. 2010).

Comity The principle by which one nation defers to and gives effect to the laws and judicial decrees of another nation. This recognition is based primarily on respect.

iStockPhoto.com/assalve

Can a U.S. citizen sue Swiss-based bank USB for providing financial support to a terrorist organization somewhere else in the world?

CASE 16.1

Linde v. Arab Bank, PLC[a]

United States Court of Appeals, Second Circuit, 706 F.3d 92 (2013).

COMPANY PROFILE *Arab Bank, founded in 1930, is one of the largest financial institutions in the Middle East. Headquartered in Jordan, it serves clients in more than five hundred branches in thirty countries, including branches in Australia, New York, and Switzerland. The bank is a major economic engine in the Middle East and Northern Africa, providing modern banking services and facilitating development and trade throughout the region.*

iStockPhoto.com/Robert Churchill/Rawpixel

What considerations can take precedence over comity?

FACTS Victims of terrorist attacks that were committed in Israel between 1995 and 2004—during a period commonly referred to as the Second Intifada—filed a suit in a federal district court against Arab Bank, seeking damages under the

a. *PLC* stands for "public liability company," which is a publicly traded company in England and Ireland. A PLC is the equivalent to a publicly traded corporation in the United States.

Continues

Anti-Terrorism Act (ATA) and the Alien Tort Claims Act. According to the plaintiffs, Arab Bank provided financial services and support to the terrorists. Over several years, and despite multiple discovery orders, the bank failed to produce certain documents relevant to the case. As a result, the court issued an order imposing sanctions. Arab Bank appealed, arguing that the order was an abuse of discretion.

ISSUE Does the need to impede terrorism through the imposition of tort remedies provided by U.S. law outweigh the interest of other nations in enforcing bank secrecy laws?

DECISION Yes. The U.S. Court of Appeals for the Second Circuit affirmed the lower court's decision and order.

REASON Arab Bank argued that foreign bank secrecy laws covered the documents requested by the plaintiffs. Thus, disclosure of the documents would subject the bank to criminal prosecution in several foreign jurisdictions. The trial court, however, had noted that the documents already obtained through discovery "tended to support the inference that Arab Bank knew that its services benefitted terrorists." The reviewing court therefore reasoned that the lower court had not abused its discretion in concluding that the interest of other nations in enforcing bank secrecy laws is outweighed by the need to impede terrorism.

Arab Bank further argued that the trial court's order to produce the documents should be vacated because it offended "international comity." The reviewing court, however, noted that international comity "requires a particularized analysis of the respective interests of the foreign nation and the requesting nation." In other words, the court must weigh all of the relevant interests of all of the nations affected by its decision. The reviewing court pointed out that the trial court had taken into account the United States' interests in the effective prosecution of civil claims under the ATA and that such an analysis did not "so obviously offend international comity."

CRITICAL THINKING—Ethical Consideration *Is it unethical to give the interest of fighting terrorism precedence over an international legal principle?*

Act of State Doctrine
A doctrine providing that the judicial branch of one country will not examine the validity of public acts committed by a recognized foreign government within its own territory.

The Act of State Doctrine

The **act of state doctrine** provides that the judicial branch of one country will not examine the validity of public acts committed by a recognized foreign government within its own territory.

CASE EXAMPLE 16.3 Spectrum Stores, Inc., a gasoline retailer in the United States, filed a lawsuit in a U.S. court against Citgo Petroleum Corporation, which is owned by the government of Venezuela. Spectrum alleged that Citgo had conspired with other oil companies in Venezuela and Saudi Arabia to limit production of crude oil and thereby fix the prices of petroleum products sold in the United States. Because Citgo is owned by a foreign government, the U.S. court dismissed the case under the act of state doctrine. A government controls the natural resources, such as oil reserves, within its territory. A U.S. court will not rule on the validity of a foreign government's acts within its own territory.[2] ■

LEARNING OBJECTIVE 2
What is the act of state doctrine? In what circumstances is this doctrine applied?

Why might a suit against Citgo, owned by the government of Venezuela, be unsuccessful?

Israel Pabon/ShutterStock.com

When a Foreign Government Takes Private Property. The act of state doctrine can have important consequences for individuals and firms doing business with, and investing in, other countries. This doctrine is frequently employed in situations involving expropriation or confiscation.

Expropriation occurs when a government seizes a privately owned business or privately owned goods for a proper public purpose and awards just compensation. When a government seizes private property for an illegal purpose or without just compensation, the taking is referred to as a **confiscation.** The line between these two forms of taking is sometimes blurred because of differing interpretations of what is illegal and what constitutes just compensation.

Expropriation A government's seizure of a privately owned business or personal property for a proper public purpose and with just compensation.

Confiscation A government's taking of a privately owned business or personal property without a proper public purpose or an award of just compensation.

EXAMPLE 16.4 Flaherty, Inc., a U.S. company, owns a mine in Brazil. The government of Brazil seizes the mine for

---

2. *Spectrum Stores, Inc. v. Citgo Petroleum Corp.*, 632 F.3d 938 (5th Cir. 2011).

public use and claims that the profits that Flaherty realized from the mine in preceding years constitute just compensation. Flaherty disagrees, but the act of state doctrine may prevent the company's recovery in a U.S. court. ■ Note that in a case alleging that a foreign government has wrongfully taken the plaintiff's property, the defendant government has the burden of proving that the taking was an expropriation, not a confiscation.

Doctrine May Immunize a Foreign Government's Actions. When applicable, both the act of state doctrine and the doctrine of *sovereign immunity* (to be discussed next) tend to shield foreign nations from the jurisdiction of U.S. courts. As a result, firms or individuals who own property overseas generally have little legal protection against government actions in the countries in which they operate.

If a U.S. company owns a mine in Brazil that is taken over by that country's government, has the mine been expropriated or confiscated?

The Doctrine of Sovereign Immunity When certain conditions are satisfied, the doctrine of **sovereign immunity** immunizes foreign nations from the jurisdiction of U.S. courts. In 1976, Congress codified this rule in the Foreign Sovereign Immunities Act (FSIA).[3] The FSIA exclusively governs the circumstances in which an action may be brought in the United States against a foreign nation, including attempts to attach a foreign nation's property. Because the law is jurisdictional in nature, a plaintiff has the burden of showing that a defendant is not entitled to sovereign immunity.

Section 1605 of the FSIA sets forth the major exceptions to the jurisdictional immunity of a foreign state. A foreign state is not immune from the jurisdiction of U.S. courts in the following situations:

1. When the foreign state has waived its immunity either explicitly or by implication.

2. When the foreign state has engaged in commercial activity within the United States or in commercial activity outside the United States that has "a direct effect in the United States."

3. When the foreign state has committed a tort in the United States or has violated certain international laws.

In applying the FSIA, questions frequently arise as to whether an entity is a "foreign state" and what constitutes a "commercial activity." Under Section 1603 of the FSIA, a *foreign state* includes both a political subdivision of a foreign state and an instrumentality of a foreign state. Section 1603 broadly defines a *commercial activity* as a regular course of commercial conduct, transaction, or act that is carried out by a foreign state within the United States. Section 1603, however, does not describe the particulars of what constitutes a commercial activity. Thus, the courts are left to decide whether a particular activity is governmental or commercial in nature.

Sovereign Immunity
A doctrine that immunizes foreign nations from the jurisdiction of U.S. courts when certain conditions are satisfied.

LEARNING OBJECTIVE 3

Under the Foreign Sovereign Immunities Act, in what situations is a foreign state subject to the jurisdiction of U.S. courts?

16-2 Doing Business Internationally

A U.S. domestic firm can engage in international business transactions in a number of ways. The simplest way is for U.S. firms to **export** their goods and services to markets abroad. Alternatively, a U.S. firm can establish foreign production facilities so as to be closer to the foreign market or markets in which its products are sold.

Export The sale of goods and services by domestic firms to buyers located in other countries.

16-2a Exporting

Exporting can take two forms: direct and indirect. In *direct exporting,* a U.S. company signs a sales contract with a foreign purchaser that provides for the conditions of shipment and

---

3. 28 U.S.C. Sections 1602–1611.

Distribution Agreement
A contract between a seller and a distributor of the seller's products setting out the terms and conditions of the distributorship.

payment for the goods. If sufficient business develops in a foreign country, a U.S. company may set up a specialized marketing organization in that country. This is called *indirect exporting* and may be accomplished through the use of an agency relationship or a distributorship.

Agency Relationships When a U.S. firm prefers to limit its involvement in an international market, it will typically establish an *agency relationship* with a foreign firm. The foreign firm then acts as the U.S. firm's agent and can enter into contracts in the foreign location on behalf of the principal (the U.S. company).

Distributorships When a foreign country represents a substantial market, a U.S. firm may wish to appoint a distributor located in that country. The U.S. firm and the distributor enter into a **distribution agreement.** This is a contract setting out the terms and conditions of the distributorship, such as price, currency of payment, guarantee of supply availability, and method of payment. Disputes concerning distribution agreements may involve jurisdictional or other issues, as well as contract law, which will be discussed later in this chapter.

16–2b Manufacturing Abroad

An alternative to direct or indirect exporting is the establishment of foreign manufacturing facilities. The advantages of manufacturing abroad may include lower costs, fewer government regulations, and lower taxes and trade barriers.

Typically, U.S. firms establish manufacturing plants abroad if they believe that doing so will reduce their costs—particularly for labor, shipping, and raw materials—and enable them to compete more effectively in foreign markets. Japanese manufacturers, such as Canon, Hitachi, and Toyota, have established U.S. plants to avoid import duties that the U.S. Congress may impose on Japanese products entering this country.

A domestic firm may engage in manufacturing abroad by licensing its technology to an existing foreign company. Alternatively, it may establish overseas subsidiaries or participate in joint ventures.

Licensing A U.S. firm may license a foreign manufacturing company to use its copyrighted, patented, or trademarked intellectual property or trade secrets. A licensing agreement with a foreign-based firm is much the same as any other licensing agreement. Its terms require a payment of royalties on some basis—such as so many cents per unit produced or a certain percentage of profits from units sold in a particular geographic territory. **EXAMPLE 16.5** The Coca-Cola Bottling Company licenses firms worldwide to use (and keep confidential) its secret formula for the syrup used in its soft drink. In return, the foreign firms licensed to make the syrup pay Coca-Cola a percentage of the income earned from the sale of the soft drink. ∎

The firm that receives the license can take advantage of an established reputation for quality. The firm that grants the license receives income from the foreign sales of its products and also establishes a global reputation. Once a firm's trademark is known worldwide, the demand for other products manufactured or sold by that firm may increase. Franchising is a well-known form of licensing.

Subsidiaries A U.S. firm can also expand into a foreign market by establishing a wholly owned subsidiary firm in a foreign country. When a wholly owned subsidiary is established, the parent company, which remains in the United States, retains complete ownership of all the facilities in the foreign country, as well as complete authority and control over all phases of the operation.

Joint Ventures A *joint venture* provides another method that a U.S. firm can use to expand into international markets. In a joint venture, the U.S. company owns only part of the operation. The rest is owned either by local owners in the foreign country or by another foreign entity. All of the firms involved in a joint venture share responsibilities, as well as profits and liabilities.

16-3 Regulation of Specific Business Activities

Doing business abroad can affect the economies, foreign policies, domestic policies, and other national interests of the countries involved. For this reason, nations impose laws to restrict or facilitate international business. Controls may also be imposed by international agreements. Here, we discuss how different types of international activities are regulated.

16-3a Investment Protections

Firms that invest in foreign nations face the risk that the foreign government may take possession of the investment property. Expropriation, as already mentioned, occurs when property is taken and the owner is paid just compensation. Expropriation generally does not violate observed principles of international law.

Confiscation occurs when property is taken without compensation (or without adequate compensation). Unlike expropriation, confiscation normally violates international law. Few remedies are available for confiscation of property by a foreign government, however. Claims are often resolved by lump-sum settlements after negotiations between the United States and the taking nation.

Because the possibility of confiscation may deter potential investors, many countries guarantee that foreign investors will be compensated if their property is taken. A guaranty can take the form of statutory laws or provisions in international treaties. As further protection for foreign investments, some countries provide insurance for their citizens' investments abroad.

16-3b Export Controls

The U.S. Constitution provides in Article I, Section 9, that "No Tax or Duty shall be laid on Articles exported from any State." Thus, Congress cannot impose export taxes. Congress can, however, use a variety of other methods to restrict or encourage exports, including the following:

1. *Export quotas.* Congress sets export quotas on various items, such as grain being sold abroad.
2. *Restrictions on technology exports.* Under the Export Administration Act,[4] the flow of technologically advanced products and technical data can be restricted.
3. *Incentives and subsidies.* Incentives and subsidies are used to stimulate some exports and thereby aid domestic businesses. **EXAMPLE 16.6** The Export Trading Company Act[5] encouraged U.S. banks to invest in export trading companies, which are formed when exporting firms join together to export a line of goods. The Export-Import Bank of the United States has provided financial assistance, primarily in the form of credit guaranties given to commercial banks that, in turn, lend funds to U.S. exporting companies. ■

16-3c Import Controls

Import restrictions include strict prohibitions, quotas, and tariffs. Under the Trading with the Enemy Act,[6] for instance, no goods may be imported from nations that have been designated enemies of the United States. Other laws prohibit the importation of illegal drugs and agricultural products that pose dangers to domestic crops or animals. The import of goods that infringe U.S. patents is also prohibited.

The International Trade Commission investigates allegations that imported goods infringe U.S. patents. The commission imposes penalties if necessary.

KNOW THIS
Countries restrict exports for several reasons, including to protect national security, to further foreign policy objectives, and to conserve resources (or raise their prices).

"The notion dies hard that in some sort of way exports are patriotic but imports are immoral."
LORD HARLECH
1918–1985
(BRITISH WRITER)

---

4. 50 U.S.C. Sections 2401–2420.
5. 15 U.S.C. Sections 4001, 4003.
6. 12 U.S.C. Section 95a.

Quota A set limit on the amount of goods that can be imported.

Quotas   Limits on the amounts of goods that can be imported are known as **quotas.** At one time, the United States had legal quotas on the number of automobiles that could be imported from Japan. Today, Japan "voluntarily" restricts the number of automobiles exported to the United States. (But Japanese automakers build most cars sold in the United States in U.S. factories.)

Tariff A tax on imported goods.

Tariffs   Taxes on imports are called **tariffs.** A tariff usually is a percentage of the value of the import, but it can be a flat rate per unit (for example, per barrel of oil). Tariffs raise the prices of goods. The effect is to cause some consumers to purchase more domestically manufactured goods and fewer imported goods.

Sometimes, countries impose tariffs on goods from a particular nation in retaliation for political acts. **EXAMPLE 16.7** Some years ago, Mexico imposed tariffs of 10 to 20 percent on ninety products exported from the United States in retaliation for the Obama administration's cancellation of a cross-border trucking program. The program had been instituted to comply with a provision in the North American Free Trade Agreement (to be discussed shortly).

U.S. trucking companies opposed the program, however, and consumer protection groups claimed that the Mexican trucks posed safety issues. Because the Mexican tariffs were imposed annually on $2.4 billion of U.S. goods, in 2011 President Barack Obama negotiated a deal that allowed Mexican truckers to enter the United States. In exchange, Mexico agreed to suspend half of the tariffs immediately and the remainder when the first Mexican hauler complied with the new U.S. requirements. ∎

Why might U.S.-based truck drivers be against allowing Mexican-based truckers unimpeded access to U.S. highways?

Dumping The sale of goods in a foreign country at a price below the price charged for the same goods in the domestic market.

Antidumping Duties   The United States has specific laws directed at what it sees as unfair international trade practices. **Dumping,** for instance, is the sale of imported goods at "less than fair value." "Fair value" is usually based on the price of those goods in the exporting country. Foreign firms that engage in dumping in the United States hope to undersell U.S. businesses to obtain a larger share of the U.S. market. To prevent this, an extra tariff—known as an *antidumping duty*—may be assessed on the imports. The duty may be retroactive to cover past dumping.

Two U.S. government agencies are instrumental in imposing antidumping duties: the International Trade Commission (ITC) and the International Trade Administration (ITA). The ITC assesses the effects of dumping on domestic businesses and then makes recommendations to the president concerning temporary import restrictions. The ITA, which is part of the Department of Commerce, decides whether imports were sold at less than fair value. The ITA's determination establishes the amount of antidumping duties, which equal the difference between the price charged in the United States and the price charged in the exporting country.

16–3d Minimizing Trade Barriers

Restrictions on imports are also known as *trade barriers*. The elimination of trade barriers is sometimes seen as essential to the world's economic well-being. The World Trade Organization, as well as various regional trade agreements and associations, work to reduce trade barriers among nations.

The World Trade Organization

Most of the world's leading trading nations are members of the World Trade Organization (WTO), which was established in 1995. To minimize trade barriers among nations, each member country is required to grant **normal trade relations (NTR) status** to other member countries. This means that each member must treat other members at least as well as it treats the country that receives its most favorable treatment with regard to imports or exports.

Normal Trade Relations (NTR) Status A legal trade status granted to member countries of the World Trade Organization.

The European Union (EU)

The European Union (EU) arose out the 1957 Treaty of Rome, which created the Common Market, a free trade zone comprising the nations of Belgium, France, Italy, Luxembourg, the Netherlands, and West Germany. Today, the EU is a single integrated trading unit made up of twenty-eight European nations.

The EU has gone a long way toward creating a new body of law to govern all of the member nations—although some of its efforts to create uniform laws have been confounded by nationalism. The EU's council and commission issue regulations, or directives, that define EU law in various areas, such as environmental law, product liability, anticompetitive practices, and corporations. The directives normally are binding on all member countries.

The North American Free Trade Agreement (NAFTA)   The North American Free Trade Agreement (NAFTA) created a regional trading unit consisting of Canada, Mexico, and the United States. The goal of NAFTA is to eliminate tariffs among these three countries on substantially all goods by reducing the tariffs incrementally over a period of time.

NAFTA gives the three countries a competitive advantage by retaining tariffs on goods imported from countries outside the NAFTA trading unit.

Additionally, NAFTA provides for the elimination of barriers that traditionally have prevented the cross-border movement of services, such as financial and transportation services. NAFTA also attempts to eliminate citizenship requirements for the licensing of accountants, attorneys, physicians, and other professionals.

The Central America–Dominican Republic–United States Free Trade Agreement (CAFTA-DR)   The Central America–Dominican Republic–United States Free Trade Agreement (CAFTA-DR) was formed by Costa Rica, the Dominican Republic, El Salvador, Guatemala, Honduras, Nicaragua, and the United States. Its purpose is to reduce tariffs and improve market access among all of the signatory nations. Legislatures in all seven countries have approved the CAFTA-DR, despite significant opposition in certain nations.

The Republic of Korea–United States Free Trade Agreement (KORUS FTA)   The United States ratified its first free trade agreement with South Korea in 2011. This agreement, called the Republic of Korea–United States Free Trade Agreement (KORUS FTA), will eliminate 95 percent of each nation's tariffs on industrial and consumer exports.

KORUS is the largest free trade agreement the United States has entered into since NAFTA and may boost U.S. exports by more than $10 billion a year. It benefits U.S. automakers, farmers, ranchers, and manufacturers by enabling them to compete in new markets.

Other Free Trade Agreements   Congress has also ratified free trade agreements with Colombia and Panama. The Colombian trade agreement includes a provision requiring an exchange of tax information, and the Panama agreement incorporates labor rights assurances. An agreement still being negotiated is the trans-Pacific trade initiative, aimed at increasing exports to Japan and other Asian nations.

16–4 International Contracts

Like all commercial contracts, an international contract should be in writing. In addition, international contracts often include special provisions aimed at aiding in the resolution of disputes. (For an example of an international sales contract, see the Starbucks Coffee Company contract in the appendix that follows the chapter on forming sales and lease contracts.)

16–4a Contract Clauses

Language and legal differences among nations can create problems for parties to international contracts when disputes arise. To avoid these problems, parties should include provisions that designate the language of the contract, the jurisdiction where any disputes will be resolved, and the substantive law that will be applied in settling any disputes. Parties to an international contract should also indicate in their contract what acts or events will excuse the parties from performance under the contract and whether disputes under the contract will be arbitrated or litigated.

Choice-of-Language Clause
A clause in a contract designating the official language by which the contract will be interpreted in the event of a disagreement over the contract's terms.

Forum-Selection Clause
A provision in a contract designating the court, jurisdiction, or tribunal that will decide any disputes arising under the contract.

Choice-of-Language Clause

A deal struck between a U.S. company and a company in another country normally involves two languages. Typically, many phrases in one language are not readily translatable into the other. Consequently, the complex contractual terms involved may not be understood equally well by both parties. To make sure that no disputes arise out of this language problem, an international sales contract should have a **choice-of-language clause** designating the official language by which the contract will be interpreted in the event of disagreement.

Note also that some nations have mandatory language requirements. In France, for instance, certain legal documents, such as the prospectuses used in securities offerings, must be written in French. In addition, contracts with departmental or local authorities, instruction manuals, and warranties for goods and services must be written in French.

Forum-Selection Clause

When a dispute arises, litigation may be pursued in courts of different nations. There are no universally accepted rules as to which court has jurisdiction over the subject matter or the parties involved in a particular dispute. Consequently, parties to an international transaction should always include in the contract a **forum-selection clause** indicating what court, jurisdiction, or tribunal will decide any disputes arising under the contract.

It is especially important to indicate the specific court that will have jurisdiction. **CASE EXAMPLE 16.8** Intermax Trading Corporation, a New York firm, contracted to act as the North American sales agent for Garware Polyester, Ltd., based in Mumbai, India. The parties executed a series of contracts with provisions stating that the courts of Mumbai, India, would have exclusive jurisdiction over any disputes relating to the agreements.

When Intermax fell behind in its payments to Garware, Garware filed a lawsuit in a U.S. court to collect the balance due. Garware claimed that the forum-selection clause did not apply to sales of goods in a warehouse, but the court sided with Intermax. Because the forum-selection clause was valid and enforceable, Garware had to bring its complaints against Intermax in a court in Mumbai, India.[7] ■ Note that the forum does not necessarily have to be within the geographic boundaries of the home nation of either party.

In the following case, the court considered whether a party that had not signed a forum-selection clause was bound to it.

---

7. *Garware Polyester, Ltd. v. Intermax Trading Corp.*, 2001 WL 1035134 (S.D.N.Y. 2001). See also *Laasko v. Xerox Corp.*, 566 F.Supp.2d 1018 (C.D.Cal. 2008).

CASE 16.2

Carlyle Investment Management LLC v. Moonmouth Company SA

United States Court of Appeals, Third Circuit, 779 F.3d 214 (2015).

FACTS Moonmouth Co. SA (incorporated in the British Virgin Islands) bought stock in Carlyle Capital Corp. Ltd. (CCC), an investment fund (incorporated in Guernsey, a dependency of the United Kingdom), under a subscription agreement. Carlyle Investment Management LLC, which owned CCC, signed the agreement on CCC's behalf. Plaza Management Overseas SA signed it on Moonmouth's behalf. Plaza was Moonmouth's director, and both were owned by Louis Reijtenbagh. The agreement

Will a forum-selection clause in a subscription agreement be enforced?

provided that "the courts of the State of Delaware shall have exclusive jurisdiction over any action . . . with respect to this Subscription Agreement." Later, the global financial crisis depleted CCC's cash reserves, and CCC entered liquidation (the process of liquidating its assets). Plaza then threatened to hold CCC liable for all damages that Moonmouth had sustained in connection with its investment. Carlyle and its owners filed a suit in a Delaware state court against Plaza and its owner to enforce the forum-selection clause. Plaza sought to move the case to a federal district court. That court remanded the case to the state court. Plaza appealed.

ISSUE Was the forum-selection clause enforceable against Plaza?

DECISION Yes. The U.S. Court of Appeals for the Third Circuit affirmed the lower court's remand of the case to state court. Plaza was bound to the forum-selection clause.

REASON The appellate court asked three questions to determine whether Plaza should be bound to the forum-selection clause. Was the clause valid? Was Plaza closely related to the subscription agreement? Did Carlyle's claim arise from Plaza's status in relation to the agreement? In response to the first question, the court stated that a forum-selection clause is valid unless its enforcement would be unreasonable or unjust, or there is evidence of fraud. None of these conditions existed here.

In answering "yes" to the second question, the court considered several factors. Plaza was Moonmouth's director. Plaza and Moonmouth were both owned by Louis Reijtenbagh. All three were involved in negotiating the agreement. Plaza signed the agreement on Moonmouth's behalf, and Plaza's income funded Moonmouth's investment in CCC. As for the third question, the court pointed out that the relationship between the plaintiffs and defendants stemmed from the subscription agreement, and without it, the defendants would not have had a claim.

CRITICAL THINKING—Legal Consideration *Would Plaza have been bound to the forum-selection clause if it had signed the subscription agreement as Moonmouth's director but had no other relation to the agreement? Discuss.*

Choice-of-Law Clause A contractual provision designating the applicable law—such as the law of Germany or the United Kingdom or California—is called a **choice-of-law clause.** Every international contract typically includes a choice-of-law clause.

Various rules apply to how parties choose the law that will govern their contractual relationship. At common law, parties may choose the law that will govern an international agreement provided that the law chosen is the law of a jurisdiction that has a substantial relationship to the parties and to the international business transaction. European civil law systems follow similar rules.

Under Section 1–105 of the Uniform Commercial Code, parties may choose the law that will govern the contract as long as the choice is "reasonable." Article 6 of the United Nations Convention on Contracts for the International Sale of Goods, however, imposes no limitation on the parties' choice. Similarly, the 1986 Hague Convention on the Law Applicable to Contracts for the International Sale of Goods—often referred to as the Choice-of-Law Convention—allows unlimited autonomy in the choice of law. Under that convention, when a contract does not specify a choice of law, the governing law is that of the country in which the seller's place of business is located.

Force Majeure Clause Every contract, particularly those involving international transactions, should have a ***force majeure* clause.** *Force majeure* is a French term meaning "impossible or irresistible force"—sometimes loosely identified as "an act of God." Natural disasters, for instance, are considered "acts of God." In international business contracts, *force majeure* clauses commonly stipulate that in addition to acts of God, a number of other eventualities (such as government orders or embargoes) may excuse a party from liability for nonperformance.

16–4b Civil Dispute Resolution

As noted elsewhere, arbitration has become a popular alternative to litigation for the resolution of civil disputes. International contracts frequently include arbitration clauses. By means of such clauses, the parties agree in advance to be bound by the decision of a specified third party in the event of a dispute.

The United Nations Convention on the Recognition and Enforcement of Foreign Arbitral Awards (often referred to as the *New York Convention*) assists in the enforcement of arbitration

Choice-of-Law Clause
A clause in a contract designating the law (such as the law of a particular state or nation) that will govern the contract.

Force Majeure Clause
A provision in a contract stipulating that certain unforeseen events—such as war, political upheavals, or acts of God—will excuse a party from liability for nonperformance of contractual obligations.

clauses, as do provisions in specific treaties among nations. The New York Convention has been implemented in nearly one hundred countries, including the United States.

Under the New York Convention, a court will compel the parties to arbitrate their dispute if all of the following are true:

1. There is a written (or electronically recorded) agreement to arbitrate the matter.

2. The agreement provides for arbitration in a convention signatory nation.

3. The agreement arises out of a commercial legal relationship.

4. One party to the agreement is not a U.S. citizen. In other words, both parties cannot be U.S. citizens.

If an international contract does not include an arbitration clause, a contract dispute may result in litigation. If the contract contains forum-selection and choice-of-law clauses, the lawsuit will be heard by a court in the specified forum and decided according to that forum's law. If no forum and choice of law have been specified, however, proceedings will be more complex and legally uncertain.

16–5 Payment Methods

Currency differences between nations and the geographic distance between parties to international sales contracts add a degree of complexity to international sales that does not exist in the domestic market. Because international contracts involve greater financial risks, special care should be taken in drafting these contracts to specify both the currency in which payment is to be made and the method of payment.

16–5a Monetary Systems

Foreign Exchange Market A worldwide system in which foreign currencies are bought and sold.

Correspondent Bank A bank that acts on behalf of another bank for the purpose of facilitating fund transfers.

Although our national currency, the U.S. dollar, is one of the primary forms of international currency, any U.S. firm undertaking business transactions abroad must be prepared to deal with other currencies. After all, a Japanese firm may want to be paid in Japanese yen for goods and services sold outside Japan. Both firms therefore must rely on the convertibility of currencies.

Currencies are convertible when they can be freely exchanged one for the other at some specified market rate in a **foreign exchange market.** Foreign exchange markets make up a worldwide system for the buying and selling of foreign currencies. The *foreign exchange rate* is simply the price of a unit of one country's currency in terms of another country's currency.

For instance, if today's exchange rate is eighty Japanese yen for one dollar, that means that anybody with eighty yen can obtain one dollar, and vice versa. Like other prices, the exchange rate is set by the forces of supply and demand.

Frequently, a U.S. company can rely on its domestic bank to take care of all international transfers of funds. Commercial banks often transfer funds internationally through their **correspondent banks** in other countries. **EXAMPLE 16.9** A customer of Citibank wishes to pay a bill in euros to a company in Paris. Citibank can draw a bank check payable in euros on its account in Crédit Agricole, a Paris correspondent bank, and then send the check to the French company to which its customer owes the funds. Alternatively, Citibank's customer can request a wire transfer of the funds to the French company. In this situation, Citibank instructs Crédit Agricole by wire to pay the necessary amount in euros. ■

Ralf Siemieniec/ShutterStock.com

How do businesses pay foreign firms?

16-5b Letters of Credit

Because buyers and sellers engaged in international business transactions are frequently separated by thousands of miles, special precautions are often taken to ensure performance under the contract. Sellers want to avoid delivering goods for which they might not be paid. Buyers desire the assurance that sellers will not be paid until there is evidence that the goods have been shipped. Thus, **letters of credit** are frequently used to facilitate international business transactions. See Exhibit 16–1 for an illustration of a letter-of-credit transaction.

How might a person in the U.S. use the services of this French bank to pay a company in France?

How a Letter of Credit Works

In a simple letter-of-credit transaction, the *issuer* (a bank) agrees to issue a letter of credit and to ascertain whether the *beneficiary* (seller) performs certain acts. In return, the *account party* (buyer) promises to reimburse the issuer for the amount paid to the beneficiary. The transaction may also involve an *advising bank* that transmits information and a *paying bank* that expedites payment under the letter of credit.

Under the letter of credit, the issuer is bound to pay the beneficiary (seller) when the beneficiary has complied with the terms and conditions of the letter of credit. The beneficiary looks to the issuer, not to the account party (buyer), when it presents the documents required by the letter of credit.

Typically, the letter of credit will require that the beneficiary deliver a *bill of lading* to the issuing bank to prove that shipment has been made. A letter of credit assures the beneficiary (seller) of payment and at the same time assures the account party (buyer) that payment will not be made until the beneficiary has complied with the terms and conditions of the letter of credit.

Letter of Credit A written document in which the issuer (usually a bank) promises to honor drafts or other demands for payment by third persons in accordance with the terms of the instrument.

Exhibit 16–1 A Letter-of-Credit Transaction

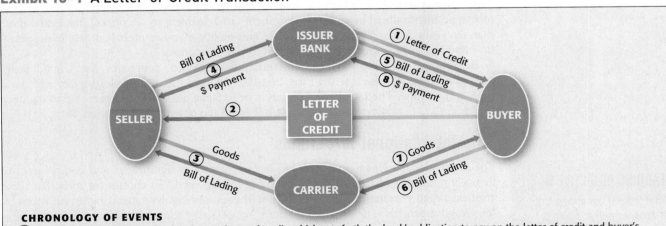

CHRONOLOGY OF EVENTS

1. Buyer contracts with issuer bank to issue a letter of credit, which sets forth the bank's obligation to pay on the letter of credit and buyer's obligation to pay the bank.
2. Letter of credit is sent to seller informing seller that on compliance with the terms of the letter of credit (such as presentment of necessary documents—in this example, a bill of lading), the bank will issue payment for the goods.
3. Seller delivers goods to carrier and receives a bill of lading.
4. Seller delivers the bill of lading to issuer bank and, if the document is proper, receives payment.
5. Issuer bank delivers the bill of lading to buyer.
6. Buyer delivers the bill of lading to carrier.
7. Carrier delivers the goods to the buyer.
8. Buyer settles with issuer bank.

The Value of a Letter of Credit The basic principle behind letters of credit is that payment is made against the documents presented by the beneficiary and not against the facts that the documents purport to reflect. Thus, in a letter-of-credit transaction, the issuer does not police the underlying contract. A letter of credit is independent of the underlying contract between the buyer and the seller. Eliminating the need for banks (issuers) to inquire into whether actual contractual conditions have been satisfied greatly reduces the costs of letters of credit. Moreover, the use of a letter of credit protects both buyers and sellers.

16–6 U.S. Laws in a Global Context

The internationalization of business raises questions about the extraterritorial application of a nation's laws—that is, the effect of the country's laws outside its boundaries. To what extent do U.S. domestic laws apply to other nations' businesses? To what extent do U.S. domestic laws apply to U.S. firms doing business abroad? Here, we discuss the extraterritorial application of certain U.S. laws, including antitrust laws, tort laws, and laws prohibiting employment discrimination.

16–6a U.S. Antitrust Laws

U.S. antitrust laws have a wide application. They may *subject* firms in foreign nations to their provisions, as well as *protect* foreign consumers and competitors from violations committed by U.S. citizens. Section 1 of the Sherman Act—the most important U.S. antitrust law—provides for the extraterritorial effect of the U.S. antitrust laws.

Any conspiracy that has a *substantial effect* on U.S. commerce is within the reach of the Sherman Act. The law applies even if the violation occurs outside the United States, and foreign governments as well as businesses can be sued for violations.

EXAMPLE 16.10 An investigation by the U.S. government revealed that a Tokyo-based auto parts supplier, Furukawa Electric Company, and its executives had conspired with competitors in an international price-fixing agreement (an agreement to set prices) that lasted more than ten years. As a result of the conspiracy, automobile manufacturers had paid noncompetitive and higher prices for parts in cars sold to U.S. consumers.

Because the conspiracy had a substantial effect on U.S. commerce, the United States had jurisdiction to prosecute the case. In 2011, Furukawa agreed to plead guilty and pay a $200 million fine. The Furukawa executives from Japan also agreed to serve up to eighteen months in a U.S. prison and to cooperate fully with the ongoing investigation. ■

16–6b International Tort Claims

The international application of tort liability is growing in significance and controversy. An increasing number of U.S. plaintiffs are suing foreign (or U.S.) entities for torts that these entities allegedly committed overseas. Often, these cases involve human rights violations by foreign governments. The Alien Tort Claims Act (ATCA),[8] adopted in 1789, allows even foreign citizens to bring civil suits in U.S. courts for injuries caused by violations of international law or a treaty of the United States.

Since 1980, plaintiffs have increasingly used the ATCA to bring actions against private companies operating in other countries. Such actions have been brought against companies doing business in Colombia, Ecuador, Egypt, Guatemala, India, Indonesia, Nigeria, and Saudi Arabia, among others. Some of the cases have involved alleged environmental destruction. In addition, mineral companies in Southeast Asia have been sued for collaborating with oppressive government regimes.

8. 28 U.S.C. Section 1350.

In the following *Spotlight Case,* the United States Supreme Court considered the parameters of the ATCA. The question was whether the statute allows U.S. courts to exercise jurisdiction over a cause of action that occurred outside the United States.

SPOTLIGHT ON INTERNATIONAL TORTS: CASE 16.3

Daimler AG v. Bauman

United States Supreme Court, __ U.S. __, 134 S.Ct. 746, 187 L.Ed.2d 624 (2014).

FACTS Barbara Bauman and twenty-one other residents of Argentina filed a suit in a federal district court in California against Daimler AG,[a] a German company. They alleged that Mercedes-Benz (MB) Argentina, a subsidiary of Daimler, had collaborated with state security forces to kidnap, detain, torture, and kill certain MB Argentina workers. These workers included the plaintiffs and some of their relatives. Their claims were asserted under the Alien Tort Claims Act.

Can victims of Argentina's "dirty" wars sue a German company in a U.S. court?

Personal jurisdiction was based on the California contacts of Mercedes-Benz USA (MBUSA), a Daimler subsidiary incorporated in Delaware with its principal place of business in New Jersey. MBUSA distributes Daimler-made vehicles to dealerships throughout the United States, including California. The district court dismissed the suit for lack of jurisdiction. The U.S. Court of Appeals for the Ninth Circuit reversed this ruling. Daimler appealed to the United States Supreme Court.

ISSUE Is there a limit to the authority of a U.S. court to decide a case brought by foreign plaintiffs against a foreign defendant based on events occurring entirely outside of the United States?

DECISION Yes. The United States Supreme Court reversed the decision of the appellate court. The federal district court could not exercise jurisdiction over Daimler given the absence of any California connection to the atrocities, perpetrators, or victims described in the complaint.

REASON The Court explained that only a limited set of connections to a state render a defendant subject to jurisdiction there. For a corporation, the "paradigm forum" for the exercise of jurisdiction is the state in which the corporation is "fairly regarded as at home." A corporation may be regarded as at home in the state in which it incorporated and the state in which it has its principal place of business. Both places are unique and easily located. These bases give plaintiffs at least "one clear and certain forum" in which to sue a corporate defendant.

This does not mean that a corporation is subject to jurisdiction *only* in its state of incorporation or principal place of business. In this case, however, the plaintiffs argued for the exercise of jurisdiction in every state in which a corporation engages in "continuous and systematic" business. That argument went too far, according to the Court. Instead, the appropriate question is whether a corporation's connections with a state are so continuous and systematic as to render it at home there. Here, neither Daimler nor MBUSA was incorporated in California, and neither had its principal place of business there.

CRITICAL THINKING—Legal Consideration *What are the consequences for Daimler of the decision in this case?*

a. The initials *A.G.* stand for "Automotive Group."

16–6c Antidiscrimination Laws

As you probably know, federal laws in the United States prohibit discrimination on the basis of race, color, national origin, religion, gender, age, and disability. These laws, as they affect employment relationships, generally apply extraterritorially.

Thus, U.S. employees working abroad for U.S. employers are protected under the Age Discrimination in Employment Act. Similarly, the Americans with Disabilities Act, which requires employers to accommodate the needs of workers with disabilities, applies to U.S. nationals working abroad for U.S. firms.

In addition, the major law regulating employment discrimination—Title VII of the Civil Rights Act—applies extraterritorially to all U.S. employees working for U.S. employers abroad. U.S. employers must abide by U.S. discrimination laws unless to do so would violate the laws of the country where their workplaces are located. This "foreign laws exception" prevents employers from being subjected to conflicting laws.

Reviewing . . . International Law in a Global Economy

Robco, Inc., was a Florida arms dealer. The armed forces of Honduras contracted to purchase weapons from Robco over a six-year period. After the government was replaced and a democracy installed, the Honduran government sought to reduce the size of its military, and its relationship with Robco deteriorated. Honduras refused to honor the contract by purchasing the inventory of arms, which Robco could sell only at a much lower price. Robco filed a suit in a federal district court in the United States to recover damages for this breach of contract by the government of Honduras. Using the information provided in the chapter, answer the following questions.

1. Should the Foreign Sovereign Immunities Act preclude this lawsuit? Why or why not?

2. Does the act of state doctrine bar Robco from seeking to enforce the contract? Explain.

3. Suppose that before Robco filed its lawsuit, the new government of Honduras had enacted a law making it illegal to purchase weapons from foreign arms dealers. What doctrine might lead a U.S. court to dismiss Robco's case in that situation?

4. Now suppose that the U.S. court hears the case and awards damages to Robco, but the government of Honduras has no assets in the United States that can be used to satisfy the judgment. Under which doctrine might Robco be able to collect the damages by asking another nation's court to enforce the U.S. judgment?

DEBATE THIS

- The U.S. federal courts are accepting too many lawsuits initiated by foreigners that concern matters not relevant to this country.

Key Terms

act of state doctrine 378

choice-of-language clause 384

choice-of-law clause 385

comity 377

confiscation 378

correspondent bank 386

distribution agreement 380

dumping 382

export 379

expropriation 378

force majeure clause 385

foreign exchange market 386

forum-selection clause 384

international organization 376

letter of credit 387

normal trade relations (NTR) status 382

quota 382

sovereign immunity 379

tariff 382

treaty 376

Chapter Summary: International Law in a Global Economy

International Law	1. *Principle of comity*—Under this principle, nations give effect to the laws and judicial decrees of other nations for reasons of courtesy and international harmony. 2. *Act of state doctrine*—Under this doctrine, U.S. courts avoid passing judgment on the validity of public acts committed by a recognized foreign government within its own territory. 3. *Doctrine of sovereign immunity*—When certain conditions are satisfied, foreign nations are immune from U.S. jurisdiction under the Foreign Sovereign Immunities Act of 1976. Exceptions are made when a foreign state (a) has waived its immunity either explicitly or by implication, (b) has engaged in commercial activity within the United States, or (c) has committed a tort within the United States.
Doing Business Internationally	U.S. domestic firms may engage in international business transactions in several ways, including (1) exporting, which may involve foreign agents or distributors, and (2) manufacturing abroad through licensing arrangements, wholly owned subsidiaries, or joint ventures.
Regulation of Specific Business Activities	In the interests of their economies, foreign policies, domestic policies, or other national priorities, nations impose laws that restrict or facilitate international business. Such laws regulate foreign investments, exporting, and importing. The World Trade Organization attempts to minimize trade barriers among nations, as do regional trade agreements and associations, including the European Union and the North American Free Trade Agreement.
International Contracts	International business contracts often include choice-of-language, forum-selection, and choice-of-law clauses to reduce the uncertainties associated with interpreting the language of the agreement and dealing with legal differences. Most domestic and international contracts include *force majeure* clauses. They commonly stipulate that acts of God and certain other events may excuse a party from liability for nonperformance of the contract. Arbitration clauses are also frequently found in international contracts.
Payment Methods	1. *Currency conversion*—Because nations have different monetary systems, payment on international contracts requires currency conversion at a rate specified in a foreign exchange market. 2. *Correspondent banking*—Correspondent banks facilitate the transfer of funds from a buyer in one country to a seller in another. 3. *Letters of credit*—Letters of credit facilitate international transactions by ensuring payment to sellers and assuring buyers that payment will not be made until the sellers have complied with the terms of the letters of credit. Typically, compliance occurs when a bill of lading is delivered to the issuing bank.
U.S. Laws in a Global Context	1. *Antitrust laws*—U.S. antitrust laws may be applied beyond the borders of the United States. Any conspiracy that has a substantial effect on commerce within the United States may be subject to the Sherman Act, even if the violation occurs outside the United States. 2. *Tort laws*—U.S. tort laws may be applied to wrongful acts that take place in foreign jurisdictions under the Alien Tort Claims Act. This act allows even foreign citizens to bring civil suits in U.S. courts for injuries caused by violations of international law or a treaty of the United States. 3. *Antidiscrimination laws*—The major U.S. laws prohibiting employment discrimination, including Title VII of the Civil Rights Act, the Age Discrimination in Employment Act, and the Americans with Disabilities Act, cover U.S. employees working abroad for U.S. firms—*unless* to apply the U.S. laws would violate the laws of the host country.

Issue Spotters

1. Café Rojo, Ltd., an Ecuadoran firm, agrees to sell coffee beans to Dark Roast Coffee Company, a U.S. firm. Dark Roast accepts the beans but refuses to pay. Café Rojo sues Dark Roast in an Ecuadoran court and is awarded damages, but Dark Roast's assets are in the United States. Under what circumstances would a U.S. court enforce the judgment of the Ecuadoran court? (See *International Law.*)

2. Gems International, Ltd., is a foreign firm that has a 12 percent share of the U.S. market for diamonds. To capture a larger share, Gems offers its products at a below-cost discount to U.S. buyers (and inflates the prices in its own country to make up the difference). How can this attempt to undersell U.S. businesses be defeated? (See *Regulation of Specific Business Activities.*)

—**Check your answers to the *Issue Spotters* against the answers provided in Appendix D at the end of this text.**

Learning Objectives Check

1. What is the principle of comity, and why do courts deciding disputes involving a foreign law or judicial decree apply this principle?
2. What is the act of state doctrine? In what circumstances is this doctrine applied?
3. Under the Foreign Sovereign Immunities Act, in what situations is a foreign state subject to the jurisdiction of U.S. courts?
4. What are some clauses commonly included in international business contracts?
5. What federal law allows U.S. citizens, as well as citizens of foreign nations, to file civil actions in U.S. courts for torts that were committed overseas?

—**Answers to the even-numbered** *Learning Objectives Check* **questions can be found in Appendix E at the end of this text.**

Business Scenarios and Case Problems

16–1. Letters of Credit. Antex Industries, a Japanese firm, agreed to purchase 92,000 electronic integrated circuits from Electronic Arrays. The Swiss Credit Bank issued a letter of credit to cover the transaction. The letter of credit specified that the chips would be transported to Tokyo by ship. Electronic Arrays shipped the circuits by air. Payment on the letter of credit was dishonored because the shipment by air did not fulfill the precise terms of the letter of credit. Should a court compel payment? Explain. (See *Payment Methods*.)

16–2. Dumping. U.S. pineapple producers alleged that producers of canned pineapple from the Philippines were selling their canned pineapple in the United States for less than its fair market value (dumping). The Philippine producers also exported other products, such as pineapple juice and juice concentrate, which used separate parts of the same pineapple used for the canned pineapple. All these products shared raw material costs, according to the producers' own financial records. To determine fair value and antidumping duties, the plaintiffs argued that a court should calculate the Philippine producers' cost of production and allocate a portion of the shared fruit costs to the canned fruit. The result of this allocation showed that more than 90 percent of the canned fruit sales were below the cost of production. Is this a reasonable approach to determining the production costs and fair market value of canned pineapple in the United States? Why or why not? (See *Regulation of Specific Business Activities*.)

16–3. International Agreements and Jurisdiction. U.S. citizens who were descendants of victims of the Holocaust (the mass murder of 6 million Jews by the Nazis during World War II) in Europe filed a claim for breach of contract in the United States against an Italian insurance company, Assicurazioni Generali, S.P.A. (Generali). Before the Holocaust, the plaintiffs' ancestors had purchased insurance policies from Generali, but Generali refused to pay benefits under the policies. Due to certain agreements among nations after World War II, such lawsuits could not be filed for many years. In 2000, however, the United States agreed that Germany could establish a foundation—the International Commission on Holocaust-Era Insurance Claims, or ICHEIC—that would compensate victims who had suffered losses at the hands of the Germans during the war. Whenever a German company was sued in a U.S. court based on a Holocaust-era claim, the U.S. government would inform the court that the matter should be referred to the ICHEIC as the exclusive forum and remedy for the resolution. There was no such agreement with Italy, however, so the federal district court dismissed the suit against Generali. The plaintiffs appealed. Did the plaintiffs have to take their claim to the ICHEIC rather than sue in a U.S. court? Why or why not? [*In re Assicurazioni Generali, S.P.A.*, 592 F.3d 113 (2d Cir. 2010)] (See *International Contracts*.)

16–4. Sovereign Immunity. Bell Helicopter Textron, Inc., designs, makes, and sells helicopters with distinctive and famous trade dress that identifies them as Bell aircraft. Bell also owns the helicopters' design patents. Bell's Model 206 Series includes the Jet Ranger. Thirty-six years after Bell developed the Jet Ranger, the Islamic Republic of Iran began to make and sell counterfeit Model 206 Series helicopters and parts. Iran's counterfeit versions—the Shahed 278 and the Shahed 285—used Bell's trade dress. The Shahed aircraft was promoted at an international air show in Iran to aircraft customers. Bell filed a suit in a U.S. district court against Iran, alleging violations of trademark and patent laws. Is Iran—a foreign nation—exempt in these circumstances from the jurisdiction of U.S. courts? Explain. [*Bell Helicopter Textron, Inc. v. Islamic Republic of Iran*, 734 F.3d 1175 (C.A.D.C. 2013)] (See *International Law*.)

16–5. Sovereign Immunity. In 1954, the government of Bolivia began expropriating land from Francisco Loza for public projects, including an international airport. The government directed the payment of compensation in exchange for at least some of his land. But the government never paid the full amount. Decades later, his heirs, Genoveva and Marcel Loza, who were both U.S. citizens, filed a suit in a federal district court in the United States against the government of Bolivia, seeking damages for the taking. Can the court exercise jurisdiction?

Explain. [*Santivanez v. Estado Plurinacional de Bolivia,* 2013 WL 879983 (11th Cir. 2013)] (See *International Law.*)

16–6. Business Case Problem with Sample Answer—Import Controls. The Wind Tower Trade Coalition is an association of domestic manufacturers of utility-scale wind towers. The coalition filed a suit in the U.S. Court of International Trade against the U.S. Department of Commerce, challenging its decision to impose only *prospective* antidumping duties, rather than *retrospective* (retroactive) duties, on imports of utility-scale wind towers from China and Vietnam. The Commerce Department had found that the domestic industry had not suffered any "material injury" or "threat of material injury" from such imports and that it would be protected by a prospective assessment. Can an antidumping duty be assessed retrospectively? If so, should it be assessed here? Discuss. [*Wind Tower Trade Coalition v. United States,* 741 F.3d 89 (Fed. Cir. 2014)] (See *Regulation of Specific Business Activities.*)

— **For a sample answer to Problem 16–6, go to Appendix F at the end of this text.**

16–7. The Principle of Comity. Holocaust survivors and the heirs of Holocaust victims filed a suit in a federal district court in the United States against the Hungarian national railway, the Hungarian national bank, and several private Hungarian banks, alleging that the defendants had participated in expropriating the property of Hungarian Jews who were victims of the Holocaust. The claims arose from events in Hungary seventy years ago. The plaintiffs had not exhausted remedies available through Hungarian courts. Indeed, they had not even attempted to seek remedies in Hungarian courts, and they did not provide a legally compelling reason for their failure to do so. The defendants asked the court to dismiss the suit. Does the principle of comity support the defendants' request? Explain. [*Fischer v. Magyar Államvasutak Zrt.,* 777 F.3d 847 (7th Cir. 2015)] (See *International Law.*)

16–8. A Question of Ethics—Terrorism. On December 21, 1988, Pan Am Flight 103 exploded 31,000 feet in the air over Lockerbie, Scotland, killing all 259 passengers and crew on board and 11 people on the ground. Among those killed was Roger Hurst, a U.S. citizen. An investigation determined that a portable radio–cassette player packed in a brown Samsonite suitcase smuggled onto the plane was the source of the explosion. The explosive device was constructed with a digital timer specially made for, and bought by, Libya. Abdel Basset Ali Al-Megrahi, a Libyan government official and an employee of the Libyan Arab Airline (LAA), was convicted by the Scottish High Court of Justiciary on criminal charges that he had planned and executed the bombing in association with members of the Jamahiriya Security Organization (JSO)—an agency of the former Libyan government that performed security and intelligence functions—or the Libyan military. Members of the victims' families filed a suit in a U.S. federal district court against the JSO, the LAA, Al-Megrahi, and others. The plaintiffs claimed violations of U.S. federal law, including the Anti-Terrorism Act, and state law, including the intentional infliction of emotional distress. [*Hurst v. Socialist People's Libyan Arab Jamahiriya,* 474 F.Supp.2d 19 (D.D.C. 2007)] (See *U.S. Laws in a Global Context.*)

1. Under what doctrine, codified in which federal statute, might the defendants have claimed to be immune from the jurisdiction of a U.S. court? Should this law include an exception for "state-sponsored terrorism"? Why or why not?

2. The defendants agreed to pay $2.7 billion, or $10 million per victim, to settle all claims for "compensatory death damages." The families of eleven victims, including Hurst, were excluded from the settlement because they were "not wrongful death beneficiaries under applicable state law." These plaintiffs continued the suit. The defendants filed a motion to dismiss. Should the motion have been granted on the ground that the settlement barred the plaintiffs' claims? Explain.

Critical Thinking and Writing Assignments

16–9. Business Law Critical Thinking Group Assignment. Assume that you are manufacturing iPad accessories and that your business is becoming more successful. You are now considering expanding operations into another country. (See *Doing Business Internationally.*)

1. One group will explore the costs and benefits of advertising internationally on the Internet.

2. Another group will consider whether to take in a partner from a foreign nation and examine the benefits and risks of doing so.

3. A third group will discuss what problems may arise if you want to manufacture in a foreign location.

Unit Two—Business Case Study with Dissenting Opinion

Braddock v. Braddock[1]

Fraudulent misrepresentation is one of the conditions that may cause a contract to lack voluntary consent. For a misrepresentation to be fraudulent, it must misrepresent a present, material fact. A representation, or prediction, of a future fact does not qualify. The misrepresentation must be consciously false and intended to mislead an innocent party, who must justifiably rely on it. When an innocent party is fraudulently induced to enter into a contract, the party can rescind the contract and be restored to her or his original position or can enforce the contract and seek damages for injuries resulting from the fraud.

In this *Business Case Study with Dissenting Opinion,* we present *Braddock v. Braddock,*[1] a case involving an individual who gave up his career and relocated his home and family based on his cousin's representations about a newly formed entrepreneurial venture. The individual's position in the new enterprise was not what the cousin had told him it would be, however. Were the cousin's statements fraudulent? Or were they simply expressions of expectation—predictions of future possibilities—subject to contingencies that neither party could control?

iStockPhoto.com/kali9

Is it fraudulent to offer a relative a great job, requiring relocation, only to reduce substantially the quality of the promised job?

CASE BACKGROUND

David Braddock wanted to form a company, Broad Oak Energy, Inc. (BOE), to tap oil and gas reserves in Louisiana and Texas. He asked his cousin John, an investment banker in New York, to find an investor to provide BOE with $75 to $150 million and also asked John to come to work for BOE. David assured John that he would be BOE's chief financial officer (CFO) and land manager. He also told John that he would receive half as much stock in the company as would be issued to David, who would serve as the company's chief executive officer. John quit his job, agreed to accept a significantly reduced fee to find an investor for BOE, and moved his family to Texas. As a result of John's efforts, Warburg Pincus, LLC, agreed to provide $150 million in start-up capital.

Two weeks later, David told John that Warburg Pincus insisted that John not be made CFO or land manager. Instead, David offered him a substantially reduced position, that of landman. Surprised, John nevertheless cooperated. He signed "engagement agreements" to accept the lesser position as an "employee at will," subject to discharge for any reason at any time. Stress soon began to take a toll on his health, and he was granted a conditional medical leave of absence. The next month, BOE terminated his employment.

John filed a suit in a New York state court against David, asserting that these circumstances constituted fraud. The court dismissed the complaint. John appealed to a state intermediate appellate court.

MAJORITY OPINION

SAXE, J. [Judge]
* * * *

To plead a claim for [fraud], a plaintiff must assert the misrepresentation of a material fact, which was known by the defendant to be false

1. 60 A.D.3d 84, 871 N.Y.S.2d 68 (1 Dept. 2009).

and intended to be relied on when made, and that there was justifiable reliance and resulting injury. The complaint here sufficiently sets forth these elements. [Emphasis added.]
* * * *

[John's] allegations satisfy the particularity requirement for a fraud claim.
* * * *

* * * Since David and John are cousins, John's reliance on David's good faith may be found to be reasonable even where it might not be reasonable in the context of an arm's length transaction with a stranger. Family members stand in a fiduciary relationship [one of trust] toward one another in a co-owned business venture. * * * Under the circumstances alleged here, John had reason to believe that David would treat him, in their interaction, with good faith and integrity.
* * * *

The situation presented here should be distinguished from cases in which a plaintiff who was involved in a business deal claims that, in the original discussions of the deal, misrepresentations were made as to its terms but the falsity of those representations was revealed by the time the deal was executed. In such cases, the ultimate terms of the deal, if agreed upon, are all that the plaintiff is entitled to, and he will not be permitted to seek damages based upon the original misrepresentations, because he did not rely on them in electing to go through with the deal. Here, in contrast, John's subsequent execution of documents that fundamentally altered the originally promised terms of his position with the company was not merely an election to enter into the deal anyway. First of all, even before he executed * * * the agreements * * *, the deal was essentially under way, at least on his part, in that he had already sacrificed his former life and undertaken tasks to forward the venture, and he was no longer in a position to reject the offered terms or even to negotiate effectively. Indeed, when the allegations are understood in the context of an ongoing attempt by John to salvage something from his dashed expectations, the fact that he subsequently acceded to new and lesser terms should not justify holding * * * that he did not reasonably rely on his cousin's alleged misrepresentations and false assurances, to his own severe detriment.

If all these interactions had been between strangers conducting an arm's length business transaction, strict reliance on the signed written documents, to the exclusion of the parties' words and conduct, would be appropriate. But the expectation of the good faith of a family member in circumstances such as these may justify some reliance on assurances that are not incorporated into written documents drafted and executed later.

* * * *

Here, * * * the issues of material misrepresentation and reasonable reliance are not subject to summary disposition [settlement], and the fiduciary relationship between the parties, with its concomitant [associated] mutual obligation to act in good faith, makes John's reliance on David's assurances all the more reasonable.

* * * *

* * * Defendants' motion to dismiss the complaint for failure to state a cause of action * * * [is] denied * * * so as to reinstate the [plaintiffs' fraud] cause of action.

DISSENTING OPINION

LIPPMAN, P.J. [Presiding Judge], (DISSENTING).

* * * *

* * * It is, in essence, alleged that John's entire course of conduct in providing investment banking services for a discounted fee, giving up his lucrative New York employment as an investment banker and advisor, moving to Texas and agreeing to take the non-executive position with BOE from which he was eventually dismissed * * * was induced by David's * * * assurances.

* * * *

* * * At the time of David's nominal assurances, BOE was but an unfunded shell requiring for its viability an enormous infusion of capital. And, while John was confident of procuring financing for the venture, there had been, at the time, neither a commitment of funds nor even the emergence of a leading candidate to provide such a commitment. Moreover, John, in addition to being an experienced investment banker and financial consultant, was, by reason of his own prior professional involvement in oil and gas ventures and his extensive familial connections to the industry, particularly well aware of the risks such ventures entailed. * * * In these circumstances, * * * no promise of high executive-level employment in the company * * * could reasonably have been viewed as an "assurance" or a "guarantee." * * * What he now terms "assurances" and "guarantees" could have been reasonably understood as only expressions of expectation or intent, the realization of which would depend upon contingencies not within the power of the parties to foreseeably accommodate to their stated objectives.

* * * While he may have had a moral claim to rely upon his cousin even when objective circumstances counseled otherwise, there is no legal right to recovery in fraud that may be vindicated upon such a predicate.

Accordingly, I would affirm the dismissal of plaintiffs' fraud cause of action.

QUESTIONS FOR ANALYSIS

1. *Law.* What did the majority conclude on the issue before the court in this case? What reasoning supported this conclusion?

2. *Law.* On what important point did the dissent disagree with the majority, and why?

3. *Ethics.* How do you view David's statements and John's actions? Did David take unethical advantage of his cousin, luring him in bad faith? Was John too willing to rely on assurances concerning events that he should have known from experience might not occur? Discuss.

4. *Economic Dimensions.* What does this case indicate about employment and employment contracts?

5. *Implications for the Investor.* Why would an investor like Warburg Pincus not want someone like John in an executive role in an enterprise for which the investor was providing significant capital?

iStock/Photo.com/mitza

Unit Two—Business Scenario

Alberto Corelli offers to pay $2,500 to purchase a painting titled *Moonrise* from Tara Shelley, an artist whose works have been causing a stir in the art world. Shelley accepts Corelli's offer. Assuming that the contract has met all of the requirements for a valid contract, answer the following questions.

1. **Minors.** Corelli is a minor when he purchases the painting. Is the contract void? Is it voidable? What is the difference between these two conditions? A month after his eighteenth birthday, Corelli decides that he would rather have the $2,500 than the painting. He informs Shelley that he is disaffirming the contract and requests that Shelley return the $2,500 to him. When she refuses to do so, Corelli brings a court action to recover the $2,500. What will the court likely decide in this situation? Why?

Continues

2. **Statute of Frauds.** Both parties are adults, the contract is oral, and the painting is still in progress. Corelli pays Shelley the $2,500 in return for her promise to deliver the painting to his home when it is finished. A week later, after Shelley finishes the painting, a visitor to her gallery offers her $3,500 for it. Shelley sells the painting to the visitor and sends Corelli a signed letter explaining that she is "canceling" their contract for the sale of the *Moonrise* painting. Corelli sues Shelley to enforce the contract. Is the contract enforceable? Explain.

3. **Capacity.** Both parties are adults, and the contract, which is in writing, states that Corelli will pay Shelley the $2,500 the following day. In the meantime, Shelley allows Corelli to take the painting home with him. The next day, Corelli's son returns the painting to Shelley, stating that he is canceling the contract. He explains that his father has been behaving strangely lately, that he seems to be mentally incompetent at times, and that he clearly was not acting rationally when he bought the painting, which he could not afford. Is the contract enforceable? Discuss fully.

4. **Impossibility of Performance.** Both parties are adults, and the contract is in writing. The contract calls for Shelley to deliver the painting to Corelli's gallery in two weeks. Corelli has already arranged to sell the painting to a third party for $4,000 (a $1,500 profit), but it must be available for the third party in two weeks, or the sale will not go through.

Shelley knows this but does not deliver the painting at the time promised. Corelli sues Shelley for $1,500 in damages. Shelley claims that performance was impossible because her mother fell seriously ill and required Shelley's care. Who will win this lawsuit, and why?

5. **Agreement in E-Contracts.** Both parties are adults. Shelley, on her Web site, offers to sell the painting for $2,500. Corelli accepts the offer by clicking on an "I accept" box on the computer screen displaying the offer. Among other terms, the online offer includes a forum-selection clause stating that any disputes under the contract are to be resolved by a court in California, the state in which Shelley lives. After Corelli receives the painting, he notices a smear of paint across the lower corner that was not visible in the digitized image that appeared on Shelley's Web site. Corelli calls Shelley, tells her about the smear, and says that he wants to cancel the contract and return the painting. When Shelley refuses to cooperate, Corelli sues her in a Texas state court, seeking to rescind the contract. Shelley claims that any suit against her must be filed in a California court in accordance with the forum-selection clause. Corelli maintains that the forum-selection clause is unconscionable and should not be enforced. What factors will the court consider in deciding this case? What will the court likely decide? Would it matter whether Corelli read the terms of the online offer before clicking on "I accept"?

Unit Two—Group Project

RiotGear, LLC, contracts with Standard Transit, Inc., to distribute RiotGear's Occupy Earth/Global Movement line of apparel to retail outlets for a certain price. RiotGear promises to donate a share of the proceeds from the sale of the Occupy Earth/Global Movement line to The Cause, a charitable organization dedicated to supporting those who seek social and economic change through protest. In reliance on the expected donation, The Cause contracts for medical and other supplies. Standard later increases the distribution cost, and RiotGear tells The Cause that there will be no donation.

1. While the goods are in transit, RiotGear receives this tweet from Standard: "Price increase of 99 percent or no delivery." RiotGear agrees and pays, but later sues Standard for the increase over the original price. The first group will identify the rule that a court would apply in this situation and decide whether RiotGear is entitled to the difference in price.

2. The second group will determine whether The Cause can enforce RiotGear's original promise despite the lack of consideration. What doctrine might a court apply in this situation, and what are the requirements to enforce a promise?

iStockPhoto.com/Susan Chiang/kali9

Unit 3
Commercial Transactions

17

iStockPhoto.com/IS_imagesource

The Formation of Sales and Lease Contracts

When we turn to contracts for the sale and lease of goods, we move away from common law principles and into the area of statutory law. State statutory law governing sales and lease transactions is based on the Uniform Commercial Code (UCC), which has been adopted as law by all of the states.[1] (See this chapter's *Landmark in the Law* for more information on the UCC.)

> "I am for free commerce with all nations."
>
> **GEORGE WASHINGTON**
> 1732–1799
> (FIRST PRESIDENT OF THE UNITED STATES, 1789–1797)

The chapter-opening quotation echoes a sentiment that most Americans believe—free commerce will benefit our nation. The Uniform Commercial Code (UCC) seeks to promote commerce. The goal of the UCC is to simplify and to streamline commercial transactions. The UCC allows parties to form sales and lease contracts, including those entered into online, without observing the same degree of formality used in forming other types of contracts. We open this chapter with a discussion of the UCC's Article 2 (on sales) and Article 2A (on leases) as a background to the topic of this chapter, which is the formation of contracts for the sale and lease of goods.

Today, businesses often engage in sales and lease transactions on a global scale. Therefore, we conclude the chapter with an examination of the United Nations Convention on Contracts for the International Sale of Goods (CISG), which governs international sales contracts. The CISG is a model uniform law that applies only when a nation has adopted it, just as the UCC applies only to the extent that it has been adopted by a state.

---

1. Louisiana has not adopted Articles 2 and 2A, however.

The Uniform Commercial Code

Of all the attempts to produce a uniform body of laws relating to commercial transactions in the United States, none has been as successful or comprehensive as the Uniform Commercial Code (UCC).

THE ORIGINS OF THE UCC The UCC was the brainchild of William A. Schnader, president of the National Conference of Commissioners on Uniform State Laws (NCCUSL). The drafting of the UCC began in 1945. The most significant individual involved in the project was its chief editor, Karl N. Llewellyn of the Columbia University Law School. Llewellyn's intellect, continuous efforts, and ability to compromise made the first version of the UCC—completed in 1949—a legal landmark. Over the next several years, the UCC was substantially accepted by almost every state in the nation.

COMPREHENSIVE COVERAGE The UCC attempts to provide a consistent, integrated framework of rules to deal with all phases ordinarily arising in a commercial sales or lease transaction. For example, consider the

following events, all of which may occur during a single transaction:

1. *A contract for the sale or lease of goods is formed and executed.* Article 2 and Article 2A of the UCC provide rules governing all aspects of this transaction.

2. *The transaction may involve a payment—by check, electronic fund transfer, or other means.* Article 3 (on negotiable instruments), Article 4 (on bank deposits and collections), Article 4A (on fund transfers), and Article 5 (on letters of credit) cover this part of the transaction.

3. *The transaction may involve a bill of lading or a warehouse receipt that covers goods when they are shipped or stored.* Article 7 (on documents of title) deals with this subject.

4. *The transaction may involve a demand by the seller or lender for some form of security for the remaining balance owed.* Article 9 (on secured transactions) covers this part of the transaction.

PERIODIC CHANGES AND UPDATES Various articles and sections of the UCC are periodically changed or supplemented to

clarify certain rules or to establish new rules when changes in business customs render the existing UCC provisions inapplicable.

For instance, when leases of goods in the commercial context became important, Article 2A governing leases was added to the UCC. To clarify the rights of parties to commercial fund transfers, particularly electronic fund transfers, Article 4A was issued. Articles 3 and 4, on negotiable instruments and banking relationships, have undergone significant revisions. Because of other changes in business and in the law, the NCCUSL recommended the repeal of Article 6 (on bulk transfers) and offered a revised Article 6 to those states that preferred not to repeal it. The NCCUSL also substantially revised Article 9 on secured transactions, and the revised Article 9 has been adopted by all of the states.

APPLICATION TO TODAY'S WORLD *By periodically revising the UCC's articles, the NCCUSL has been able to adapt its provisions to changing business customs and practices. UCC provisions governing sales and lease contracts have also been extended to contracts formed in the online environment.*

17-1 The Scope of Articles 2 and 2A

Article 2 of the UCC sets forth the requirements for *sales contracts,* as well as the duties and obligations of the parties involved in the sales contract. Article 2A covers similar issues for *lease contracts.* Bear in mind, however, that the parties to sales or lease contracts are free to agree to terms different from those stated in the UCC.

17-1a Article 2—Sales

Article 2 of the UCC governs **sales contracts,** or contracts for the sale of goods. To facilitate commercial transactions, Article 2 modifies some of the common law contract requirements that were discussed in previous chapters.

To the extent that it has not been modified by the UCC, however, the common law of contracts also applies to sales contracts. In other words, the common law requirements for a valid contract—agreement, consideration, capacity, and legality—are also applicable to sales contracts.

In general, the rule is that when a UCC provision addresses a certain issue, the UCC governs, but when the UCC is silent, the common law governs. The relationship between general contract law and the law governing sales of goods is illustrated in Exhibit 17–1.

Sales Contract A contract for the sale of goods.

Exhibit 17–1 The Law Governing Contracts

This exhibit graphically illustrates the relationship between general contract law and statutory law (UCC Articles 2 and 2A) governing contracts for the sale and lease of goods. Sales contracts are not governed exclusively by Article 2 of the UCC but are also governed by general contract law whenever it is relevant and has not been modified by the UCC.

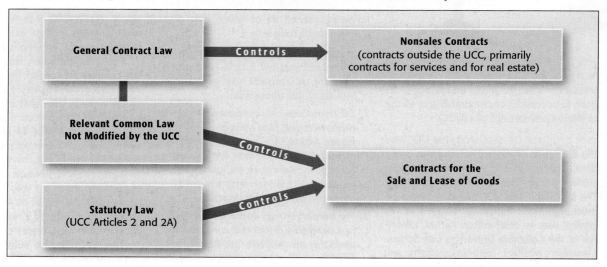

In regard to Article 2, keep two points in mind.

1. Article 2 deals with the sale of *goods*. It does not deal with real property (real estate), services, or intangible property such as stocks and bonds. Thus, if the subject matter of a dispute is goods, the UCC governs. If it is real estate or services, the common law applies.

2. In some situations, the rules can vary depending on whether the buyer or the seller is a *merchant*.

Sale The passing of title to property from the seller to the buyer for a price.

What Is a Sale? The UCC defines a **sale** as "the passing of title [evidence of ownership rights] from the seller to the buyer for a price" [UCC 2–106(1)]. The price may be payable in cash (or its equivalent) or in other goods or services. (For a discussion of whether states can impose taxes on online sales, see this chapter's *Adapting the Law to the Online Environment* feature.)

In the following case, the court was asked to determine who owned the "personal property" damaged in a fire. How did the UCC's definition of a sale affect the answer to that question?

CASE 17.1

Nautilus Insurance Co. v. Cheran Investments LLC

Court of Appeals of Nebraska, 2014 WL 292809 (2014).

FACTS Under a contract with Cheran Investments, LLC, Blasini, Inc., agreed to buy the business assets of the Attic Bar & Grill in Omaha, Nebraska. The contract required Blasini to make a down payment and monthly payments until the price was fully paid. Blasini obtained insurance on the property from Nautilus Insurance Co. Less than three years later, a fire damaged the "personal property" (the business assets, such as furniture and equipment) in the Attic. Because

Who carries the risk of loss and personal property at a bar?

the purchase price had not yet been fully paid, Nautilus filed an action in a Nebraska state court against several defendants, including Cheran, to determine who was entitled to the insurance proceeds for the damage. The court concluded that Blasini had "failed to consummate the purchase agreement" and declared Cheran the owner of the personal property. Blasini appealed, arguing that title to the Attic's assets had passed at the time of the sale.

ISSUE Did the sale of the Attic's assets pass title to those goods to Blasini?

DECISION Yes. A state intermediate appellate court reversed the lower court's ruling. When the contract for the sale of the Attic's assets was formed, title to the assets passed to Blasini, which became the owner. The appellate court remanded the case to the lower court, however, to determine whether Blasini had breached the contract.

REASON The sale of the personal property in the Attic involved "goods," and thus the agreement for their sale was subject to the UCC. All of the items designated in the agreement were movable, and no real estate, intellectual property, or goodwill was transferred under the

agreement. Blasini entered into a contract to buy the assets of the bar and grill and agreed to assume its operation. Under UCC 2–401, title to the goods passed to Blasini at the time the agreement was made. No physical delivery was necessary because Blasini was to assume the operation of the Attic, which is where the goods were located. "Therefore, irrespective of whether Blasini paid the purchase price . . . , Blasini became the owner of the property in the purchase agreement."

WHAT IF THE FACTS WERE DIFFERENT? *Suppose that Blasini had made no payments under the contract for the sale of the Attic's assets. How should that circumstance affect the distribution of the insurance proceeds?*

What Are Goods?

To be characterized as a *good*, the item of property must be *tangible*, and it must be *movable*. **Tangible property** has physical existence—it can be touched or seen. **Intangible property**—such as corporate stocks and bonds, patents and copyrights, and ordinary contract rights—has only conceptual existence and thus does not come under Article 2. A *movable* item can be carried from place to place.

Goods Associated with Real Estate.

Because real estate cannot be carried from place to place, it is excluded from Article 2. Goods *associated* with real estate often fall within the scope of Article 2, however [UCC 2–107]. For instance, a contract for the sale of minerals, oil, or natural gas is a contract for the sale of goods if *severance, or separation, is to be made by the seller*. In contrast, a contract for the sale of growing crops or timber to be cut is a contract for the sale of goods *regardless of who severs them from the land*.

Goods and Services Combined.

When contracts involve a combination of goods and services, courts generally use the **predominant-factor test** to determine whether a contract is primarily for the sale of goods or for the sale of services. If a court decides that a mixed contract is primarily a goods contract, *any* dispute, even a dispute over the services portion, will be decided under the UCC.

CASE EXAMPLE 17.1 Gene and Martha Jannusch agreed to sell Festival Foods, a concessions business, to Lindsey and Louann Naffziger for a price of $150,000. The deal included a truck, a trailer, freezers, roasters, chairs, tables, a fountain service, signs, and lighting. The Naffzigers paid $10,000 down with the balance to come from a bank loan. They took possession of the equipment and began to use it immediately in Festival Foods operations at various events.

After six events, the Naffzigers returned the truck and all the equipment and wanted out of the deal because the business did not generate as much income as they expected. The Jannusches sued the Naffzigers for the balance due on the purchase price, claiming that the Naffzigers could no longer reject the goods under the UCC. The Naffzigers claimed that the UCC did not apply because the deal primarily involved the sale of a business rather than the sale of goods.

The court found that the UCC governed under the predominant-factor test. The primary value of the contract was in the goods, not the value of the business. The parties had agreed on the essential terms of the contract (such as the price). Thus, a contract had been formed, and the Naffzigers had breached it. The Naffzigers had taken possession of the business and had no right to return it.[2] ■

Tangible Property Property that has physical existence and can be distinguished by the senses of touch and sight.

Intangible Property Property that cannot be seen or touched but exists only conceptually, such as corporate stocks. Such property is not governed by Article 2 of the UCC.

LEARNING OBJECTIVE 1

If a contract involves both goods and services, does the UCC apply?

Predominant-Factor Test A test courts use to determine whether a contract is primarily for the sale of goods or for the sale of services.

If a couple buys a concessions business that includes a truck, trailer, and tables and chairs, would this purchase be a sale of goods or services?

---

2. *Jannusch v. Naffziger*, 379 Ill.App.3d 381, 883 N.E.2d 711 (2008).

ADAPTING THE LAW TO THE ONLINE ENVIRONMENT
Taxing Web Purchases

In 1992, the United States Supreme Court ruled that an individual state cannot compel an out-of-state business that lacks a substantial physical presence within that state to collect and remit state taxes.[a] Although Congress has the power to pass legislation requiring out-of-state corporations to collect and remit state sales taxes, it has not yet done so. Thus, only online retailers that also have a physical presence within a state must collect state taxes on any Web sales made to residents of that state. (State residents are supposed to self-report their purchases and pay use taxes to the state, which they rarely do.)

Redefining Physical Presence

Several states have found a way to collect taxes on Internet sales made to state residents by out-of-state corporations. These states have simply redefined *physical presence*. In 2008, New York changed its tax laws in this manner. Now, an online retailer that pays any party within New York to solicit business for its products is considered to have a physical presence in the state and must collect state taxes. Since then, at least seventeen other states have made similar changes in an effort to increase their revenues by collecting sales tax from online retailers.

These new laws are often called "Amazon tax" laws because they are aimed largely at Amazon.com. Nevertheless, they affect all online sellers, especially those that pay affiliates to direct traffic to their Web sites. The laws allow states to tax online commerce even though, to date, Congress has explicitly chosen not to tax Internet sales.

Local Governments Sue Online Travel Companies

Travelocity, Priceline.com, Hotels.com, and Orbitz.com are online travel companies (OTCs) that offer, among other things, hotel booking services. By 2016, more than twenty-five cities, including Atlanta, Charleston, Philadelphia, and San Antonio, had filed suits claiming that the OTCs owed taxes on hotel reservations that they had booked. All of the cities involved in the suits impose a hotel occupancy tax, which is essentially a sales tax.

Initially, some cities won their cases, but more recently, cities have been losing in court.[b] As of 2016, the OTCs had prevailed in eighteen of twenty-five cases nationwide. An exception is a 2014 case in Wyoming in which the state supreme court held that Travelocity, Priceline, Hotwire, Expedia, and Trip Network had to collect and remit sales tax.[c]

The Market Place Fairness Act

By the time you read this, online sales taxes may have become a reality for every online business that has annual revenues of more than $1 million. For several years now, legislation called the Market Place Fairness Act has been under consideration in the U.S. Senate. The act, if passed, would allow states to collect sales taxes from online retailers for in-state transactions.

A significant problem with such legislation is the complexity of collecting taxes for multiple jurisdictions. The current tax system involves 9,600 taxing jurisdictions. Even one zip code may cover multiple taxing entities, such as different cities and counties. Consider that the Dallas–Fort Worth airport includes six separate taxing jurisdictions. Current software enables retailers to collect and remit sales taxes for different jurisdictions, but the software is extremely costly to install and operate. Overstock.com, for example, spent $1.3 million to add just one state to its sales tax collection system.

CRITICAL THINKING

- Some argue that if online retailers are required to collect and pay sales taxes in jurisdictions in which they have no physical presence, they have no democratic way to fight high taxes in those places. Is this an instance of taxation without representation? Discuss.

---

a. *Quill Corp. v. North Dakota,* 504 U.S. 298, 112 S.Ct. 1904, 119 L.Ed.2d 91 (1992).

b. *Travelscape, LLC v. South Carolina Department of Revenue,* 391 S.C. 89, 705 S.E.2d 28 (2011).

c. *Travelocity.com, LP v. Wyoming Dept. of Revenue,* 329 P.3d 131 (2014).

Who Is a Merchant? Article 2 governs the sale of goods in general. It applies to sales transactions between all buyers and sellers. In a limited number of instances, though, the UCC presumes that certain special business standards ought to be imposed because of merchants' relatively high degree of commercial expertise.[3] Such standards do not apply to the casual or inexperienced seller or buyer (consumer).

---

3. The provisions that apply only to merchants deal principally with the Statute of Frauds, firm offers, confirmatory memoranda, warranties, and contract modifications. These special rules reflect expedient business practices commonly known to merchants in the commercial setting. They will be discussed later in this chapter.

Section 2–104 sets out three ways in which merchant status can arise:

1. A merchant is a person who *deals in goods of the kind* involved in the sales contract. Thus, a retailer, a wholesaler, or a manufacturer is a merchant of those goods sold in the business. A merchant for one type of goods is not necessarily a merchant for another type. For instance, a sporting equipment retailer is a merchant when selling tennis rackets but not when selling a used iPad.

2. A merchant is a person who, by occupation, *holds himself or herself out as having special knowledge and skill* related to the practices or goods involved in the transaction. This broad definition may include banks or universities as merchants.

3. A person who *employs a merchant as a broker, agent, or other intermediary* has the status of merchant in that transaction. Hence, if an art collector hires a broker to purchase or sell art for her, the collector is considered a merchant in the transaction.

In summary, a person is a **merchant** when she or he, acting in a mercantile (commercial) capacity, possesses or uses an expertise specifically related to the goods being sold. This basic distinction is not always clear-cut. For instance, state courts appear to be split on whether farmers should be considered merchants.

Merchant Under the UCC, a person who deals in goods of the kind involved in the sales contract or who holds herself or himself out as having skill or knowledge peculiar to the practices or goods being purchased or sold.

Should merchants be allowed to use buying patterns to learn personal information about their customers? Whether you shop on the Internet or in stores, most major retailers compile information about you based on what, when, and how you buy. Sometimes, based on your purchases, you will instantly be given printed coupons at the cash register. These customized coupons reflect your preferences based on past behavior. If you regularly use Amazon .com, for instance, you receive customized offers every time you visit that site.

Target Brands, Inc., uses a very sophisticated data collection process that assigns each shopper a unique guest identification code. Over time, a shopper's habits become the source of predictions for future consumer behavior. For example, Target can accurately predict which female shoppers are pregnant based on their recent purchases of vitamin and mineral supplements. When Target's system detects a buying pattern suggesting that a customer is pregnant, it starts offering coupons for baby-related products and services.

A father in Minneapolis, Minnesota, complained to a Target manager that his daughter was receiving such coupons for no reason. In reality, Target's system had accurately discovered his daughter's pregnancy. The father was even more furious when he learned that his daughter had lied to him. Was Target's action legal? Probably, it was. Target had complied with the relevant federal and state privacy laws. Current laws even allow retailers to share their customer data with affiliate companies.

ETHICAL ISSUE

Is it ethical for Target Brands to data mine information about what its customers have purchased?

17-1b Article 2A—Leases

Leases of personal property (goods such as automobiles and industrial equipment) have become increasingly common. In this context, a **lease** is a transfer of the right to possess and use goods for a period of time in exchange for payment. Article 2A of the UCC was created to fill the need for uniform guidelines in this area.

Article 2A covers any transaction that creates a lease of goods, as well as subleases of goods [UCC 2A–102, 2A–103(1)(k)]. Article 2A is essentially a repetition of Article 2, except that it applies to leases of goods rather than sales of goods and thus varies to reflect differences between sales and lease transactions. (Note that Article 2A does not apply to leases of real property, such as land or buildings.)

Lease Under Article 2A of the UCC, a transfer of the right to possess and use goods for a period of time in exchange for payment.

Lease Agreement An agreement in which one person (the lessor) agrees to transfer the right to the possession and use of property to another person (the lessee) in exchange for rental payments.

Definition of a Lease Agreement

Article 2A defines a **lease agreement** as the bargain between a lessor and a lessee with respect to the lease of goods, as found in their language and

Lessor A person who transfers the right to the possession and use of goods to another in exchange for rental payments.

Lessee A person who acquires the right to the possession and use of another's goods in exchange for rental payments.

as implied by other circumstances, including course of dealing and usage of trade or course of performance [UCC 2A–103(1)(k)]. A **lessor** is one who transfers the right to the possession and use of goods under a lease [UCC 2A–103(1)(p)]. A **lessee** is one who acquires the right to the temporary possession and use of goods under a lease [UCC 2A–103(1)(o)]. In other words, the lessee is the party who is leasing the goods from the lessor.

Article 2A applies to all types of leases of goods, including commercial leases and consumer leases. Special rules apply to certain types of leases, however, including consumer leases.

Consumer Leases Under UCC 2A–103(1)(e), a *consumer lease* involves three elements:

1. A lessor who regularly engages in the business of leasing or selling.

2. A lessee (except an organization) who leases the goods "primarily for a personal, family, or household purpose."

3. Total lease payments that are less than a dollar amount set by state statute.

To ensure special protection for consumers, certain provisions of Article 2A apply only to consumer leases. For instance, one provision states that a consumer may recover attorneys' fees if a court finds that a term in a consumer lease contract is unconscionable [UCC 2A–108(4)(a)].

17–2 The Formation of Sales and Lease Contracts

As mentioned, Article 2 and Article 2A of the UCC modify common law contract rules in several ways. Remember, though, that parties to sales contracts are normally free to establish whatever terms they wish. The UCC comes into play only when the parties have failed to provide in their contract for a contingency that later gives rise to a dispute. The UCC makes this clear time and again by using such phrases as "unless the parties otherwise agree" or "absent a contrary agreement by the parties."

17–2a Offer

In general contract law, the moment a definite offer is met by an unqualified acceptance, a binding contract is formed. In commercial sales transactions, the verbal exchanges, correspondence, and actions of the parties may not reveal exactly when a binding contractual obligation arises. The UCC states that an agreement sufficient to constitute a contract can exist even if the moment of its making is undetermined [UCC 2–204(2), 2A–204(2)].

Open Terms Remember that under the common law of contracts, an offer must be definite enough for the parties (and the courts) to ascertain its essential terms when it is accepted. In contrast, the UCC states that a sales or lease contract will not fail for indefiniteness even if one or more terms are left open as long as *both* of the following are true:

1. The parties intended to make a contract.

2. There is a reasonably certain basis for the court to grant an appropriate remedy [UCC 2–204(3), 2A–204(3)].

KNOW THIS

Under the UCC, it is the actions of the parties that determine whether they intended to form a contract.

The UCC provides numerous *open-term* provisions (discussed next) that can be used to fill the gaps in a contract. Thus, if a dispute occurs, all that is necessary to prove the existence of a contract is an indication (such as a purchase order) that there is a contract. Missing terms can be proved by evidence, or a court can presume that the parties intended whatever is reasonable under the circumstances.

Keep in mind, though, that if too many terms are left open, a court may find that the parties did not intend to form a contract. In addition, the *quantity* of goods involved must be expressly stated in the contract. If the quantity term is left open, the courts will have no basis for determining a remedy.

Open Price Term. If the parties have not agreed on a price, the court will determine a "reasonable price at the time for delivery" [UCC 2–305(1)]. If either the buyer or the seller is to determine the price, the price is to be fixed (set) in good faith [UCC 2–305(2)]. Under the UCC, *good faith* means honesty in fact and the observance of reasonable commercial standards of fair dealing in the trade [UCC 2–103(1)(b)]. The concepts of *good faith* and *commercial reasonableness* permeate the UCC.

Sometimes, the price fails to be fixed through the fault of one of the parties. In that situation, the other party can treat the contract as canceled or fix a reasonable price. **EXAMPLE 17.2** Perez and Merrick enter into a contract for the sale of unfinished doors and agree that Perez will determine the price. Perez refuses to specify the price. Merrick can either treat the contract as canceled or set a reasonable price [UCC 2–305(3)]. ■

Open Payment Term. When parties do not specify payment terms, payment is due at the time and place at which the buyer is to receive the goods [UCC 2–310(a)]. The buyer can tender payment using any commercially normal or acceptable means, such as a check or credit card. If the seller demands payment in cash, the buyer must be given a reasonable time to obtain it [UCC 2–511(2)]. **EXAMPLE 17.3** Max Angel agrees to purchase hay from Wagner's farm. Angel leaves his truck and trailer at the farm for the seller to load the hay. Nothing is said about when payment is due, and the parties are unaware of the UCC's rules. Nevertheless, because the parties did not specify when payment was due, UCC 2–310(a) controls, and payment is due at the time Angel picks up the hay. Therefore, Wagner can refuse to release the hay (or the vehicles on which the hay is loaded) to Angel until he pays for it. ■

Open Delivery Term. When no delivery terms are specified, the buyer normally takes delivery at the seller's place of business [UCC 2–308(a)]. If the seller has no place of business, the seller's residence is used. When goods are located in some other place and both parties know it, delivery is made there. If the time for shipment or delivery is not clearly specified in the sales contract, the court will infer a "reasonable" time for performance [UCC 2–309(1)].

Duration of an Ongoing Contract. A single contract might specify successive performances but not indicate how long the parties are required to deal with each other. In this situation, either party may terminate the ongoing contractual relationship. Principles of good faith and sound commercial practice call for reasonable notification before termination, however, to give the other party time to make substitute arrangements [UCC 2–309(2), (3)].

Options and Cooperation Regarding Performance. When the contract contemplates shipment of the goods but does not specify the shipping arrangements, the *seller* has the right to make these arrangements in good faith, using commercial reasonableness in the situation [UCC 2–311].

When a sales contract omits terms relating to the assortment of goods, the *buyer* can specify the assortment. **EXAMPLE 17.4** Petry Drugs, Inc., enters an e-contract to purchase one thousand toothbrushes from Marconi's Dental Supply. The toothbrushes come in a variety of colors, but the contract does not specify color. Petry, the buyer, has the right to take six hundred blue toothbrushes and four hundred green ones if it wishes. Petry, however, must exercise good faith and commercial reasonableness in making its selection [UCC 2–311]. ■

Open Quantity Terms. Normally, if the parties do not specify a quantity, there is no contract, because a court will have no basis for determining a remedy.

"Business, more than any other occupation, is a continual dealing with the future. It is a continual calculation, an instinctive exercise in foresight."

HENRY R. LUCE
1898–1967
(U.S. EDITOR AND PUBLISHER)

If no time for payment for hay is specified in a sales contract, when is payment due?

There is almost no way for a court to determine objectively what is a reasonable quantity of goods for someone to buy (whereas a court can objectively determine a reasonable price for particular goods by looking at the market). Nevertheless, the UCC recognizes two exceptions involving *requirements* and *output contracts* [UCC 2–306(1)].

Requirements Contract
An agreement in which a buyer agrees to purchase and the seller agrees to sell all or up to a stated amount of what the buyer needs or requires.

1. *Requirements Contracts.* In a **requirements contract,** the buyer agrees to purchase and the seller agrees to sell all or up to a stated amount of what the buyer *needs* or *requires.* **EXAMPLE 17.5** Umpqua Cannery forms a contract with Al Garcia. The cannery agrees to purchase from Garcia, and Garcia agrees to sell to the cannery, all of the green beans that the cannery needs or requires during the following summer. There is implicit consideration in this contract because the buyer (the cannery) gives up the right to buy goods (green beans) from any other seller. This forfeited right creates a legal *detriment—* that is, consideration. ■

Requirements contracts are common in the business world and normally are enforceable. In contrast, if the buyer promises to purchase only if the buyer *wishes* to do so, or if the buyer reserves the right to buy the goods from someone other than the seller, the promise is illusory (without consideration) and unenforceable by either party.

Output Contract An agreement in which a seller agrees to sell and a buyer agrees to buy all or up to a stated amount of what the seller produces.

2. *Output Contracts.* In an **output contract,** the seller agrees to sell and the buyer agrees to buy all or up to a stated amount of what the seller *produces.* **EXAMPLE 17.6** Ruth Sewell has planted two acres of organic tomatoes. Bella Union, a local restaurant, agrees to buy all of the tomatoes that Sewell produces that year to use at the restaurant. ■ Again, because the seller essentially forfeits the right to sell goods to another buyer, there is implicit consideration in an output contract.

The UCC imposes a *good faith limitation* on requirements and output contracts. The quantity under such contracts is the amount of requirements or the amount of output that occurs during a *normal* production year. The actual quantity purchased or sold cannot be unreasonably disproportionate to normal or comparable prior requirements or output [UCC 2–306(1)].

PREVENTING LEGAL DISPUTES

If a business owner leaves certain terms of a sales or lease contract open, the UCC allows a court to supply the missing terms. Although this rule can sometimes be advantageous (to establish that a contract existed, for instance), it can also be a major disadvantage. If a party fails to state a price in the contract offer, for example, a court will impose a reasonable price by looking at the market price of similar goods *at the time of delivery.* Thus, instead of receiving the usual price for the goods, a business will receive what a court considers a reasonable price when the goods are delivered. Therefore, when drafting contracts for the sale or lease of goods, make sure that the contract clearly states any terms that are essential to the bargain, particularly the price. It is generally better to establish the terms of a contract than to leave it up to a court to determine what terms are reasonable after a dispute has arisen.

Merchant's Firm Offer Under regular contract principles, an offer can be revoked at any time before acceptance. The major common law exception is an *option contract,* in which the offeree pays consideration for the offeror's irrevocable promise to keep the offer open for a stated period. The UCC creates a second exception for firm offers made by a merchant to sell, buy, or lease goods.

Firm Offer An offer (by a merchant) that is irrevocable without the necessity of consideration for a stated period of time or, if no definite period is stated, for a reasonable time (neither period to exceed three months).

A **firm offer** arises when a merchant-offeror gives *assurances* in a *signed writing* that the offer will remain open. The offer must be both *written* and *signed* by the offeror.[4] A merchant's firm offer is irrevocable without the necessity of consideration[5] for the stated period or, if no

---

4. *Signed* includes any symbol executed or adopted by a party with a present intention to authenticate a writing [UCC 1–201(39)]. A complete signature is not required. Therefore, initials, a thumbprint, a trade name, or any mark used in lieu of a written signature will suffice, regardless of its location on the document.
5. If the offeree pays consideration, then an option contract (not a merchant's firm offer) is formed.

definite period is stated, a reasonable period (neither period to exceed three months) [UCC 2–205, 2A–205].

EXAMPLE 17.7 Osaka, a used-car dealer, e-mails Saucedo on January 1 stating, "I have a used 2016 Toyota RAV4 on the lot that I'll sell you for $26,000 any time between now and January 31." This e-mail creates a firm offer, and Osaka will be liable for breach if he sells that Toyota RAV4 to someone other than Saucedo before January 31. ■

17–2b Acceptance

Acceptance of an offer to buy, sell, or lease goods generally may be made in any reasonable manner and by any reasonable means. The UCC permits acceptance of an offer to buy goods "either by a prompt *promise* to ship or by the prompt or current shipment of conforming or nonconforming goods" [UCC 2–206(1)(b)]. *Conforming goods* accord with the contract's terms, whereas *nonconforming goods* do not.

Shipment of Nonconforming Goods The prompt shipment of nonconforming goods constitutes both an acceptance, which creates a contract, and a breach of that contract. This rule does not apply if the seller **seasonably** (within a reasonable amount of time) notifies the buyer that the nonconforming shipment is offered only as an *accommodation,* or a favor. The notice of accommodation must clearly indicate to the buyer that the shipment does not constitute an acceptance and that, therefore, no contract has been formed.

EXAMPLE 17.8 McFarrell Pharmacy orders five cases of Johnson & Johnson 3-by-5-inch gauze pads from H.T. Medical Supply, Inc. If H.T. ships five cases of Xeroform 3-by-5-inch gauze pads instead, the shipment acts as both an acceptance of McFarrell's offer and a *breach* of the resulting contract. McFarrell may sue H.T. for any appropriate damages.

If, however, H.T. notifies McFarrell that the Xeroform gauze pads are being shipped *as an accommodation*—because H.T. has only Xeroform pads in stock—the shipment will constitute a counteroffer, not an acceptance. A contract will be formed only if McFarrell accepts the Xeroform gauze pads. ■

Communication of Acceptance Required Under the common law, because a unilateral offer invites acceptance by performance, the offeree need not notify the offeror of performance unless the offeror would not otherwise know about it. In other words, a unilateral offer can be accepted by beginning performance.

The UCC is more stringent than the common law in this regard because it requires notification. Under the UCC, if the offeror is not notified within a reasonable time that the offeree has accepted the contract by beginning performance, then the offeror can treat the offer as having lapsed before acceptance [UCC 2–206(2), 2A–206(2)].

Additional Terms Recall that under the common law, the *mirror image rule* requires that the terms of the acceptance exactly match those of the offer. **EXAMPLE 17.9** Aldrich e-mails an offer to sell twenty Samsung Galaxy Tab S 8.4 tablets to Beale. If Beale accepts the offer but changes it to require Tab S 10.5 tablets, then there is no contract. ■

To avoid these problems, the UCC dispenses with the mirror image rule. Under the UCC, a contract is formed if the offeree's response indicates a *definite* acceptance of the offer, *even if the acceptance includes terms additional to or different from those contained in the offer* [UCC 2–207(1)]. Whether the additional terms become part of the contract depends, in part, on whether the parties are nonmerchants or merchants.

Rules When One Party or Both Parties Are Nonmerchants. If one (or both) of the parties is a *nonmerchant,* the contract is formed according to the terms of the original offer submitted by the original offeror and not according to the additional terms of the acceptance [UCC 2–207(2)].

KNOW THIS
The UCC provides that acceptance can be made by any means that is reasonable under the circumstances—including prompt shipment of the goods.

Seasonably Within a specified time period or, if no period is specified, within a reasonable time.

If a pharmacy orders 3" x 5" gauze pads, but is shipped 2" x 2" pads, is this an acceptance of the pharmacy's order?

LEARNING OBJECTIVE 2

In a sales contract, if an offeree includes additional or different terms in an acceptance, will a contract result? If so, what happens to these terms?

CASE EXAMPLE 17.10 OfficeSupplyStore.com sells office supplies on the Web. Employees of the Kansas City School District in Missouri ordered $17,642.54 worth of office supplies—without the authority or approval of their employer—from the Web site. The invoices accompanying the goods contained a forum-selection clause that required all disputes to be resolved in California.

When the goods were not paid for, Office Supply filed suit in California. The Kansas City School District objected, arguing that the forum-selection clause was not binding. The court held that the forum-selection clause was not part of the parties' contract. The clause was an additional term included in the invoices delivered to a nonmerchant buyer (the school district) with the purchased goods. Therefore, the clause would have become part of the contract only if the buyer expressly agreed, which did not happen in this case.[6] ■

Rules When Both Parties Are Merchants. The drafters of the UCC created a special rule for merchants to avoid the "battle of the forms," which occurs when two merchants exchange separate standard forms containing different contract terms. Under UCC 2–207(2), in contracts *between merchants*, the additional terms *automatically* become part of the contract unless one of the following conditions exists:

1. The original offer expressly limited acceptance to its terms.

2. The new or changed terms materially alter the contract.

3. The offeror objects to the new or changed terms within a reasonable period of time.

When determining whether an alteration is material, courts consider several factors. Generally, if the modification does not involve an unreasonable element of surprise or hardship for the offeror, the court will hold that the modification did not materially alter the contract. As shown in the following case, however, what constitutes a material alteration is frequently a question of fact that only a court can decide.

---

6. *OfficeSupplyStore.com v. Kansas City School Board*, 334S.W.3d 574 (Kan. 2011).

CASE 17.2

C. Mahendra (N.Y.), LLC v. National Gold & Diamond Center, Inc.

New York Supreme Court, Appellate Division, First Department, 125 A.D.3d 454, 3 N.Y.S.3d 27 (2015).

FACTS C. Mahendra (N.Y.), LLC, is a New York wholesaler of loose diamonds. National Gold & Diamond Center, Inc., is a California seller of jewelry. Over a ten-year period, National placed orders, totaling millions of dollars, with Mahendra by phoning and negotiating the terms. Mahendra shipped diamonds "on memorandum" for National to examine. Mahendra then sent invoices for the diamonds that National chose to keep. Both the memoranda and the invoices stated, "You consent to the exclusive jurisdiction of the . . . courts situated in New York County." When two orders totaling $64,000 went unpaid, Mahendra filed a suit in a New York state court against National, alleging breach of contract. National filed a motion to dismiss the complaint for lack of personal jurisdiction, contending that

What happens if one party to an ongoing contract inserts a forum-selection clause without approval?

iStockPhoto.com/rgbdigital

the forum-selection clause was not binding. The court granted the motion. Mahendra appealed.

ISSUE Did the forum-selection clause materially alter the parties' contracts?

DECISION Yes. A state intermediate appellate court agreed that the forum-selection clause was an additional term that materially altered the parties' contracts and was therefore not binding.

REASON The court explained that UCC 2–207 deals with situations in which parties do business through an exchange of forms, such as purchase orders and invoices. In such forms, a merchant often includes terms that were not negotiated with, or even mentioned to, the other party. Under UCC 2–207(2) "the additional terms are to be construed as proposals for addition to the contract. Between merchants such terms become part of the contract unless . . . they materially alter it."

In this case, through phone calls, the parties negotiated the essential terms to form contracts for purchases of diamonds. The memoranda and invoices that Mahendra sent to National were "merely confirmatory." The forum-selection clause in those documents was not a subject of negotiation or discussion, and National did not sign the forms or otherwise consent to the clause. The court thus ruled

that the forum-selection clause was not binding. The court reversed the dismissal of Mahendra's complaint on another ground, however. It found that National's phone calls with Mahendra were sufficient contacts to subject the defendant to personal jurisdiction in New York under the state's long-arm statute.

CRITICAL THINKING—Legal Consideration *What is Mahendra's best argument that the forum-selection clause was, in fact, binding on National? Discuss.*

Prior Dealings Between Merchants. Courts also consider the parties' prior dealings in contracts between merchants. **CASE EXAMPLE 17.11** WPS, Inc., submitted a proposal to manufacture equipment for Expro Americas, LLC, and Surface Production Systems, Inc. (SPS). Expro and SPS then submitted two purchase orders. WPS accepted the first purchase order in part and the second order conditionally. Among other things, WPS's acceptance required that Expro and SPS give their "full release to proceed" and agree to "pay all valid costs associated with any order cancellation." The parties' negotiations continued, and Expro and SPS eventually submitted a third purchase order.

Although the third purchase order did not comply with all of WPS's requirements, it did give WPS full permission to proceed and agreed that Expro and SPS would pay all cancellation costs. With Expro and SPS's knowledge, WPS then began working on that order. Expro and SPS later canceled the order and refused to pay the cancellation costs. When the dispute ended up in court, Expro and SPS claimed that the parties' contract was not enforceable because the additional terms in WPS's acceptance had materially altered the contract. The court found in favor of WPS. Expro and SPS had given a release to proceed that authorized WPS to go forward with manufacturing the equipment. Because "the parties operated as if they had additional time to resolve the outstanding differences," the court reasoned that Expro and SPS were contractually obligated to pay the cancellation costs.[7] ■

Conditioned on Offeror's Assent. Regardless of merchant status, the UCC provides that the offeree's expression cannot be construed as an acceptance if it contains additional or different terms that are explicitly conditioned on the offeror's assent to those terms [UCC 2–207(1)]. **EXAMPLE 17.12** Philips offers to sell Hundert 650 pounds of turkey thighs at a specified price and with specified delivery terms. Hundert responds, "I accept your offer for 650 pounds of turkey thighs *on the condition that you give me ninety days to pay for them.*" Hundert's response will be construed not as an acceptance but as a counteroffer, which Philips may or may not accept. ■

Additional Terms May Be Stricken. The UCC provides yet another option for dealing with conflicting terms in the parties' writings. Section 2–207(3) states that conduct by both parties that recognizes the existence of a contract is sufficient to establish a contract for the sale of goods even though the writings of the parties do not otherwise establish a contract. In this situation, "the terms of the particular contract will consist of those terms on which the writings of the parties agree, together with any supplementary terms incorporated under any other provisions of this Act."

In a dispute over contract terms, this provision allows a court simply to strike from the contract those terms on which the parties do not agree. **EXAMPLE 17.13** SMT Marketing orders

If a supplier offers to sell 100 pounds of turkey thighs at a specific price and delivery date, can the buyer accept on the condition that it pay ninety days after delivery?

7. *WPS, Inc. v. Expro Americas, LLC,* 369 S.W.3d 384 (Tex.App. 2012).

goods over the phone from Brigg Sales, Inc., which ships the goods with an acknowledgment form (confirming the order) to SMT. SMT accepts and pays for the goods. The parties' writings do not establish a contract, but there is no question that a contract exists. If a dispute arises over the terms, such as the extent of any warranties, UCC 2–207(3) provides the governing rule. ■

As noted previously, the fact that a merchant's acceptance frequently contains terms that add to or even conflict with those of the offer is often referred to as the "battle of the forms." Although the UCC tries to eliminate this battle, the problem of differing contract terms still arises in commercial settings, particularly when standard forms for placing and confirming orders are used.

17–2c Consideration

The common law rule that a contract requires consideration also applies to sales and lease contracts. Unlike the common law, however, the UCC does not require a contract modification to be supported by new consideration. An agreement modifying a contract for the sale or lease of goods "needs no consideration to be binding" [UCC 2–209(1), 2A–208(1)]. Of course, a contract modification must be sought in good faith [UCC 1–304].

In some situations, an agreement to modify a sales or lease contract without consideration must be in writing to be enforceable. If the contract itself prohibits any changes to the contract unless they are in a signed writing, for instance, then only those changes agreed to in a signed writing are enforceable.

If a consumer (nonmerchant buyer) is dealing with a merchant and the merchant supplies the form that contains a clause prohibiting oral modification, the consumer must sign a separate acknowledgment of the clause [UCC 2–209(2), 2A–208(2)]. Also, any modification that brings a sales contract under Article 2's Statute of Frauds provision usually must be in writing to be enforceable.

17–2d The Statute of Frauds

The UCC contains Statute of Frauds provisions covering sales and lease contracts. Under these provisions, sales contracts for goods priced at $500 or more and lease contracts requiring payments of $1,000 or more must be in writing to be enforceable [UCC 2–201(1), 2A–201(1)]. (These low threshold amounts may eventually be raised.)

Sufficiency of the Writing A writing, including an e-mail or other electronic record, will be sufficient to satisfy the UCC's Statute of Frauds as long as it meets the following requirements:

1. It indicates that the parties intended to form a contract.

2. It is signed by the party (or agent of the party) against whom enforcement is sought. (Remember that a typed name can qualify as a signature.)

The contract normally will not be enforceable beyond the quantity of goods shown in the writing, however. All other terms can be proved in court by oral testimony. For leases, the writing or record must reasonably identify and describe the goods leased and the lease term.

Special Rules for Contracts between Merchants Once again, the UCC provides a special rule for merchants in sales transactions. (There is no corresponding rule that applies to leases under Article 2A.) Merchants can satisfy the Statute of Frauds if, after the parties have agreed orally, one of the merchants sends a signed written confirmation to the other merchant within a reasonable time.

The communication must indicate the terms of the agreement, and the merchant receiving the confirmation must have reason to know of its contents. Unless the merchant who receives the confirmation gives written notice of objection to its contents within ten days after receipt, the writing or record is sufficient, even though she or he has not signed anything [UCC 2–201(2)].

EXAMPLE 17.14 Alfonso is a merchant-buyer in Cleveland. He contracts over the telephone to purchase $6,000 worth of spare aircraft parts from Goldstein, a merchant-seller in New York City. Two days later, Goldstein e-mails a signed confirmation detailing the terms of the oral contract, and Alfonso receives it. Alfonso does not notify Goldstein in writing of any objection to the contents of the confirmation within ten days of receipt. Therefore, Alfonso cannot raise the Statute of Frauds as a defense against the enforcement of the oral contract. ▪

LEARNING OBJECTIVE 3
What exceptions to the writing requirements of the Statute of Frauds are provided in Article 2 and Article 2A of the UCC?

Exceptions In addition to the special rules for merchants, the UCC defines three exceptions to the writing requirements of the Statute of Frauds. An oral contract for the sale of goods priced at $500 or more—or the lease of goods involving total payments of $1,000 or more—will be enforceable despite the absence of a writing in the circumstances described next [UCC 2–201(3), 2A–201(4)].

Specially Manufactured Goods. An oral contract for the sale or lease of custom-made goods will be enforceable if the following conditions exist:

1. The goods are *specially manufactured* for a particular buyer or specially manufactured or obtained for a particular lessee.

2. The goods are *not suitable for resale or lease* to others in the ordinary course of the seller's or lessor's business.

3. The seller or lessor has *substantially started to manufacture* the goods or has made commitments for the manufacture or procurement of the goods.

Under these conditions, once the seller or lessor has taken action, the buyer or lessee cannot repudiate the agreement claiming the Statute of Frauds as a defense. **EXAMPLE 17.15** Womach orders custom window treatments from Hunter Douglas to use at her day spa business. The contract is oral, and the price is $6,000. When Hunter Douglas manufactures the window coverings and tenders delivery to Womach, she refuses to pay for them, even though the job is completed on time. Womach claims that she is not liable because the contract is oral. If the unique style, size, and color of the window treatments make it improbable that Hunter Douglas can find another buyer, Womach is liable to Hunter Douglas. ▪

Admissions. An oral contract for the sale or lease of goods is enforceable if the party against whom enforcement of the contract is sought admits in pleadings, testimony, or other court proceedings that a contract for sale or lease was made. In this situation, the contract will be enforceable even though it was oral, but enforceability will be limited to the quantity of goods admitted.

CASE EXAMPLE 17.16 Gerald Lindgren, a farmer, agreed by phone to sell his crops to Glacial Plains Cooperative. The parties reached four oral agreements: two for the delivery of soybeans and two for the delivery of corn. Lindgren made the soybean deliveries and part of the first corn delivery, but he sold the rest of his corn to another dealer. Glacial Plains bought corn elsewhere, paying a higher price, and then sued Lindgren for breach of contract. In papers filed with the court, Lindgren acknowledged his oral agreements with Glacial Plains and admitted that he did not fully perform. The court applied the admissions exception and held that the four agreements were enforceable. [8] ▪

Can oral agreements for delivery of corn be enforced if the seller admits that the agreements occurred?

---

8. *Glacial Plains Cooperative v. Lindgren*, 759 N.W.2d 661 (Minn.App. 2009).

Partial Performance. An oral contract for the sale or lease of goods is enforceable if payment has been made and accepted or goods have been received and accepted. This is the "partial performance" exception. The oral contract will be enforced at least to the extent that performance *actually* took place.

EXAMPLE 17.17 Jamal orally contracts to lease to Opus Enterprises a thousand chairs at $2 each to be used during a one-day concert. Before delivery, Opus sends Jamal a check for $1,000, which Jamal cashes. Later, when Jamal attempts to deliver the chairs, Opus refuses delivery, claiming the Statute of Frauds as a defense, and demands the return of its $1,000. Under the UCC's partial performance rule, Jamal can enforce the oral contract by tender of delivery of five hundred chairs for the $1,000 accepted. Similarly, if Opus had made no payment but had accepted the delivery of five hundred chairs from Jamal, the oral contract would have been enforceable against Opus for $1,000, the lease payment due for the five hundred chairs delivered. ■

These exceptions and other ways in which sales law differs from general contract law are summarized in Exhibit 17–2.

17-2e Parol Evidence

Recall that *parol evidence* consists of evidence outside the contract, such as evidence of the parties' prior negotiations, prior agreements, or oral agreements made at the time of contract formation. When a contract completely sets forth all the terms and conditions agreed to by the parties and is intended as a final statement of their agreement, it is considered *fully integrated*. The *parol evidence rule* applies. The terms of a fully integrated contract cannot be contradicted by evidence outside the contract.

If, however, the writing (or record) contains some of the terms the parties agreed on but not others, the contract is *not fully integrated*. In this situation, a court may allow evidence of

Under what conditions will an oral agreement for renting chairs be enforceable?

Exhibit 17–2 Major Differences between Contract Law and Sales Law

TOPIC	CONTRACT LAW	SALES LAW
Contract Terms	Contract must contain all material terms.	Open terms are acceptable, if parties intended to form a contract, but quantity term normally must be specified, and contract is not enforceable beyond quantity term.
Acceptance	Mirror image rule applies. If additional terms are added in acceptance, counteroffer is created.	Additional terms will not negate acceptance unless acceptance is made expressly conditional on assent to the additional terms.
Contract Modification	Modification requires consideration.	Modification does not require consideration.
Irrevocable Offers	Option contracts (with consideration) are irrevocable.	Merchants' firm offers (without consideration) are irrevocable.
Statute of Frauds Requirements	All material terms must be included in the writing.	Writing is required only for the sale of goods priced at $500 or more, but contract is not enforceable beyond quantity specified. Merchants can satisfy the requirement by a confirmatory memorandum evidencing agreement. *Exceptions:* 1. Specially manufactured goods. 2. Admissions by party against whom enforcement is sought. 3. Partial performance.

consistent additional terms to explain or supplement the terms stated in the contract. The court may also allow the parties to submit evidence of *course of dealing, usage of trade,* or *course of performance* [UCC 2–202, 2A–202]. A court will not under any circumstances allow the parties to submit evidence that contradicts the contract's stated terms, however. (This is also the rule under the common law.)

Course of Dealing and Usage of Trade   Under the UCC, the meaning of any agreement, evidenced by the language of the parties and by their actions, must be interpreted in light of commercial practices and other surrounding circumstances. In interpreting a commercial agreement, the court will assume that the course of prior dealing between the parties and the usage of trade were taken into account when the agreement was phrased.

Course of Dealing.   A **course of dealing** is a sequence of actions and communications between the parties to a particular transaction that establishes a common basis for their understanding [UCC 1–303(b)]. A course of dealing is restricted to the sequence of conduct between the parties in their transactions prior to the agreement.

> **Course of Dealing**
> Prior conduct between the parties to a contract that establishes a common basis for their understanding.

Under the UCC, a course of dealing between the parties is relevant in ascertaining the meaning of the parties' agreement. It "may give particular meaning to specific terms of the agreement, and may supplement or qualify the terms of the agreement" [UCC 1–303(d)].

Usage of Trade.   Any practice or method of dealing that is so regularly observed in a place, vocation, or trade as to justify an expectation by the parties that it will be observed in their transaction is a **usage of trade** [UCC 1–303(c)].

> **Usage of Trade**   Any practice or method of dealing that is so regularly observed in a place, vocation, or trade that parties justifiably expect it will be observed in their transaction.

EXAMPLE 17.18   United Loans, Inc., hires Fleet Title Review to search the public records for prior claims on potential borrrowers' assets. Fleet's invoice states, "Liability limited to amount of fee." In the search industry, liability limits are common. After conducting many searches for United, Fleet reports that there are no claims with respect to Main Street Autos. United loans $100,000 to Main, with payment guaranteed by Main's assets.

When Main defaults on the loan, United learns that another lender has priority to Main's assets under a previous claim. If United sues Fleet Title for breach of contract, Fleet's liability will normally be limited to the amount of its fee. The statement in the invoice was part of the contract between United and Title, according to the usage of trade in the industry and the parties' course of dealing. ■

Course of Performance   A **course of performance** is the conduct that occurs under the terms of a particular agreement [UCC 1–303(a)]. Presumably, the parties themselves know best what they meant by their words. Thus, the course of performance actually carried out under their agreement is the best indication of what they meant [UCC 2–208(1), 2A–207(1)].

> **Course of Performance**
> The conduct that occurs under the terms of a particular agreement, which indicates what the parties to that agreement intended the agreement to mean.

EXAMPLE 17.19   Janson's Lumber Company contracts with Lopez to sell Lopez a specified number of two-by-fours. The lumber in fact does not measure exactly 2 inches by 4 inches but rather $1\frac{7}{8}$ inches by $3\frac{3}{4}$ inches. Janson's agrees to deliver the lumber in five deliveries, and Lopez, without objection, accepts the lumber in the first three deliveries. On the fourth delivery, however, Lopez objects that the two-by-fours do not measure 2 inches by 4 inches.

The course of performance in this transaction—that is, Lopez's acceptance of three deliveries without objection under the agreement—is relevant in determining that here the term *two-by-four* actually means "$1\frac{7}{8}$ by $3\frac{3}{4}$." Janson's can also prove that two-by-fours need not be exactly 2 inches by 4 inches by applying course of prior dealing, usage of trade, or both. Janson's can, for example, show that in previous transactions, Lopez took $1\frac{7}{8}$-by-$3\frac{3}{4}$-inch lumber without objection. In addition, Janson's can show that in the lumber trade, two-by-fours are commonly $1\frac{7}{8}$ inches by $3\frac{3}{4}$ inches. ■

Do two-by-fours actually measure 2 inches by 4 inches?

Rules of Construction   The UCC provides *rules of construction* for interpreting contracts. Express terms, course of performance, course of dealing, and usage of trade are to be construed to be consistent with each other whenever reasonable. When such a construction is unreasonable, however, the UCC establishes the following order of priority [UCC 1–303(e), 2–208(2), 2A–207(2)]:

1. Express terms.
2. Course of performance.
3. Course of dealing.
4. Usage of trade.

17–2f Unconscionability

As previously discussed, an unconscionable contract is one that is so unfair and one sided that it would be unreasonable to enforce it. The UCC allows the courts to evaluate unconscionability. If a court deems a contract or a clause in a contract to have been unconscionable at the time it was made, the court can do any of the following [UCC 2–302, 2A–108]:

1. Refuse to enforce the contract.
2. Enforce the remainder of the contract without the unconscionable part.
3. Limit the application of the unconscionable term to avoid an unconscionable result.

The following *Classic Case* illustrates an early application of the UCC's unconscionability provisions.

★★★ CLASSIC CASE 17.3 ★★★

Jones v. Star Credit Corp.

Supreme Court of New York, Nassau County, 59 Misc.2d 189, 298 N.Y.S.2d 264 (1969).

FACTS The Joneses, the plaintiffs, agreed to purchase a freezer for $900 as the result of a salesperson's visit to their home. Tax and financing charges raised the total price to $1,234.80. After making payments totaling $619.88, the plaintiffs brought a suit in a New York state court to have the purchase contract declared unconscionable under the UCC. At trial, the freezer was found to have a maximum retail value of approximately $300.

ISSUE Could this contract be denied enforcement on the ground of unconscionability?

DECISION Yes. The court held that the contract was not enforceable as it stood, and the contract was reformed so that no further payments were required.

REASON The court relied on UCC 2–302(1), which states that if "the court as a matter of law finds the contract or any clause of the contract to have been unconscionable at the time it was made,

Can a retailer sell a freezer at four times its wholesale price?

the court may . . . so limit the application of any unconscionable clause as to avoid any unconscionable result." The court then considered the disparity between the $900 purchase price and the $300 retail value, as well as the fact that the credit charges alone exceeded the retail value. These excessive charges were exacted despite the seller's knowledge of the plaintiffs' limited resources. The court reformed the contract so that the plaintiffs' payments, amounting to more than $600, were regarded as payment in full.

CRITICAL THINKING—Legal Consideration *Why would the seller's knowledge of the buyers' limited resources support a finding of unconscionability?*

IMPACT OF THIS CASE ON TODAY'S LAW *This early case illustrates the approach that many courts today take when deciding whether a sales contract is unconscionable—an approach that focuses on excessive price and unequal bargaining power.*

17-3 Title and Risk of Loss

Before the creation of the UCC, *title*—the right of ownership—was the central concept in sales law and controlled all issues of rights and remedies of the parties to a sales contract. In some situations, title is still relevant under the UCC, and the UCC has special rules for determining who has title. (These rules do not apply to leased goods, obviously, because title remains with the lessor, or owner, of the goods.) In most situations, however, the UCC focuses less on title than on the concepts of *identification, risk of loss,* and *insurable interest.*

> "To win, you have to risk loss."
>
> **JEAN-CLAUDE KILLY**
> 1943–PRESENT
> (FRENCH ALPINE SKIER)

17-3a Identification

Before any interest in specific goods can pass from the seller or lessor to the buyer or lessee, the goods must exist and must be identified as the specific goods designated in the contract. **Identification** takes place when specific goods are designated as the subject matter of a sales or lease contract.

Identification In a sale of goods, the express designation of the goods provided for in the contract.

Identification allows title to pass from the seller to the buyer. (Remember that title to leased goods does not pass to the lessee.) In addition, it allows risk of loss to pass from the seller or lessor to the buyer or lessee. This is important because it gives the buyer or lessee the right to insure the goods and the right to recover from third parties who damage the goods.

For goods already in existence, the parties can agree in their contract on when identification will take place. If the parties do not so specify, the UCC provisions discussed here determine when identification takes place [UCC 2–501(1), 2A–217].

Existing Goods If the contract calls for the sale or lease of specific goods that are already in existence, identification takes place at the time the contract is made. **EXAMPLE 17.20** Litco Company contracts to lease a fleet of five cars designated by their vehicle identification numbers (VINs). Because the cars are identified by their VINs, identification has taken place, and Litco acquires an insurable interest in the cars at the time of contracting. ■

Future Goods Any goods that are not in existence at the time of contracting are known as *future goods.* Various rules apply to identification of future goods, depending on the goods.

- If a sale or lease involves unborn animals to be born within twelve months after contracting, identification takes place when the animals are conceived.
- If a sale involves crops that are to be harvested within twelve months (or the next harvest season occurring after contracting, whichever is longer), identification takes place when the crops are planted. Otherwise, identification takes place when the crops begin to grow.
- In a sale or lease of any other future goods, identification occurs when the goods are shipped, marked, or otherwise designated by the seller or lessor as the goods to which the contract refers.

Can identification take place for automobiles by using vehicle identification numbers?

Centurion Studio/ShutterStock.com

Goods That Are Part of a Larger Mass As a general rule, goods that are part of a larger mass are identified when the goods are marked, shipped, or somehow designated by the seller or lessor as the particular goods that are the subject of the contract. **EXAMPLE 17.21** Carlos orders 10,000 pairs of men's jeans from a lot that contains 90,000 articles of clothing for men, women, and children. Until the seller separates the 10,000 pairs of men's jeans from the other items, title and risk of loss remain with the seller. ■

A common exception to this rule involves fungible goods. **Fungible goods** are goods that are alike naturally, by agreement, or by trade usage. Typical examples include specific grades or types of wheat, petroleum, and cooking oil, which usually are stored in large containers. If

Fungible Goods Goods that are alike by physical nature, agreement, or trade usage.

the owners of these goods hold title as *tenants in common* (owners with undivided shares of the whole), a seller-owner can pass title and risk of loss to the buyer without actually separating the goods. The buyer replaces the seller as an owner in common [UCC 2–105(4)].

17–3b Passage of Title

Once goods are identified, the provisions of UCC 2–401 apply to the passage of title. Parties can expressly agree when and how title will pass. Throughout UCC 2–401, the words "unless otherwise explicitly agreed" appear, meaning that any explicit understanding between the buyer and the seller determines when title passes.

Without an explicit agreement to the contrary, *title passes to the buyer at the time and the place the seller performs by delivering the goods* [UCC 2–401(2)]. For instance, if a person buys cattle at a livestock auction, title will pass to the buyer when the cattle are physically delivered to him or her (unless, of course, the parties agree otherwise).

CASE EXAMPLE 17.22 Timothy Allen contracted with Indy Route 66 Cycles, Inc., to have a motorcycle custom built for him. Indy built the motorcycle and issued a "Certificate of Origin." Two years later, federal law enforcement officers arrested Allen on drug charges and seized his home and other property. The officers also seized the Indy-made motorcycle from the garage of the home of Allen's sister, Tena. Indy filed a claim against the government, arguing that it owned the motorcycle because it still possessed the "Certificate of Origin." The court applied UCC Section 2–401(2) and ruled in favor of the government. Testimony by Indy's former vice president was "inconclusive" but implied that Indy had delivered the motorcycle to Allen. Because Indy had given up possession of the cycle to Allen, this was sufficient to pass title even though Indy had kept a "Certificate of Origin."[9] ■

(In the future, the delivery of goods may sometimes be accomplished by drones. This chapter's *Managerial Strategy* feature discusses the use of drones in commerce.)

Shipment Contract A contract for the sale of goods in which the seller is required or authorized to ship the goods by carrier. The seller assumes liability for any losses or damage to the goods until they are delivered to the carrier.

Shipment and Destination Contracts Unless otherwise agreed, delivery arrangements can determine when title passes from the seller to the buyer. In a **shipment contract,** the seller is required or authorized to ship goods by carrier, such as a trucking company. Under a shipment contract, the seller is required only to deliver conforming goods into the hands of a carrier, and title passes to the buyer at the time and place of shipment [UCC 2–401(2)(a)]. Generally, *all contracts are assumed to be shipment contracts if nothing to the contrary is stated in the contract.*

In a **destination contract,** the seller is required to deliver the goods to a particular destination, usually directly to the buyer, but sometimes to another party designated by the buyer. Title passes to the buyer when the goods are *tendered* at that destination [UCC 2–401(2)(b)]. *Tender of delivery* occurs when the seller places or holds conforming goods at the buyer's disposal (with any necessary notice), enabling the buyer to take possession [UCC 2–503(1)].

When does title pass to the buyer of a motorcycle?

iStockPhoto.com/Hirkophoto

Destination Contract A contract for the sale of goods in which the seller is required or authorized to ship the goods by carrier and tender delivery of the goods at a particular destination. The seller assumes liability for any losses or damage to the goods until they are tendered at the destination specified in the contract.

Document of Title A paper exchanged in the regular course of business that evidences the right to possession of goods (for example, a bill of lading or a warehouse receipt).

Delivery without Movement of the Goods When the sales contract does not call for the seller to ship or deliver the goods (when the buyer is to pick up the goods), the passage of title depends on whether the seller must deliver a **document of title,** such as a bill of lading or a warehouse receipt, to the buyer. A *bill of lading* is a receipt for goods that is signed by a carrier and serves as a contract for the transport of the goods. A *warehouse receipt* is a receipt issued by a warehouser for goods stored in a warehouse.

When a document of title is required, title passes to the buyer *when and where the document is delivered.* Thus, if the goods are stored in a warehouse, title passes to the buyer when the

---

9. *United States v. 2007 Custom Motorcycle,* 2011 WL 232331 (D.Ariz. 2011).

MANAGERIAL STRATEGY — Commercial Use of Drones

Management Faces a Legal Issue

The commercial use of drones—small, pilotless aerial vehicles—has, until recently, been on hold in the United States. Possible commercial uses of drones are numerous—railroad track inspection, oil and gas pipeline review, real estate videos for use by brokers, discovery for land boundary disputes, and many others. In addition, businesses have begun making plans to use drones for delivery of goods. Amazon is developing Amazon Prime Air, a drone-based delivery service. Google Project Wing is another drone-based service that is under development.

The problem has been the Federal Aviation Agency (FAA). The FAA claims authority to regulate *all* unmanned aircraft systems (UASs). In 2012, Congress mandated the FAA "to establish a roadmap for getting UASs integrated into the national air space." Not until 2015, however, did the FAA issue its proposed rules on commercial drone use. The rules require operators to apply for a license

to use drones commercially. Drone flights are expected to be limited to daylight hours, and drones will not be allowed to go above five hundred feet or faster than one hundred miles per hour. The proposed rules also require that licensed drone operators maintain a continuous visual line of sight with the drones during operation.

The proposed FAA rules are now in a public comment period, and it is expected that final rules will be issued in 2016 or 2017. Thus, it is not yet clear how soon your packages from Amazon.com will be delivered by a commercial drone.

What the Courts Say

In the past, the FAA has attempted to fine other-than-recreational users of drones. One case involved Texas EquuSearch, a group that searches for missing persons. The organization requested an emergency injunction after receiving an e-mail from an FAA employee indicating that its drone use was illegal. The U.S. Court of Appeals for the District of Columbia Circuit refused to act on the suit. The court stated that the e-mail from the FAA did not have legal

effect and therefore was not subject to judicial review.[a]

In a case involving an administrative hearing, the FAA assessed a civil penalty against Raphael Pirker for careless and reckless operation of an unmanned aircraft. Pirker flew a drone over the University of Virginia in 2011 while filming a video advertisement for the medical school. Pirker appealed to the National Transportation Safety Board Office of Administrative Law Judges. He prevailed in early 2014.[b] The FAA has appealed the ruling.

MANAGERIAL IMPLICATIONS

In other countries, the commercial drone business is flourishing. In the United States, whether it is worthwhile to create such a business will depend on how strict the final FAA rules on drones are. Delivery by drones via Amazon Prime Air or Google Project Wing may be in jeopardy.

a. *Texas EquuSearch Mounted Search and Recovery Team, RP Search Services, Inc., v. Federal Aviation Administration,* 2014 WL 2860332 (C.A.D.C. 2014).
b. *Huerta v. Pirker,* Decisional Order of National Transportation Safety Board Office of Administrative Judges, Docket CP-217, March 6, 2014.

---

appropriate documents are delivered to the buyer. The goods never move. In fact, the buyer can choose to leave the goods at the same warehouse for a period of time, and the buyer's title to those goods will be unaffected.

When no documents of title are required and delivery is made without moving the goods, title passes at the time and place the sales contract is made, if the goods have already been identified. If the goods have not been identified, title does not pass until identification occurs [UCC 2–401(3)].

EXAMPLE 17.23 Greg sells lumber to Bodan. They agree that Bodan will pick up the lumber at the lumberyard. If the lumber has been identified (segregated, marked, or in any other way distinguished from all other lumber), title passes to Bodan when the contract is signed. If the lumber is still in large storage bins at the lumberyard, title does not pass to Bodan until the particular pieces of lumber to be sold under this contract are identified. ■

Sales or Leases by Nonowners
Problems occur when a person who acquires goods with *imperfect* title attempts to sell or lease them. Sections 2–402 and 2–403 of the UCC deal with the rights of two parties who lay claim to the same goods, sold with imperfect title. Generally, a buyer acquires at least whatever title the seller has to the goods sold.

Void Title. A buyer may unknowingly purchase goods from a seller who is not the owner of the goods. If the seller is a thief, the seller's title is *void*—legally, no title exists. Thus, the buyer

> **LEARNING OBJECTIVE 4**
>
> Risk of loss does not necessarily pass with title. If the parties to a contract do not expressly agree when risk passes and the goods are to be delivered without movement by the seller, when does risk pass?

acquires no title, and the real owner can reclaim the goods from the buyer. If the goods were leased, the same result would occur, because the lessor has no leasehold interest to transfer.

EXAMPLE 17.24 If Saki steals diamonds owned by Bruce, Saki has a *void title* to those diamonds. If Saki sells the diamonds to Shannon, Bruce can reclaim them from Shannon even though Shannon acted in good faith and honestly was not aware that the goods were stolen. ■ Article 2A contains similar provisions for leases.

Voidable Title. A seller has *voidable title* if the goods that she or he is selling were (1) obtained by fraud, (2) paid for with a check that is later *dishonored* (returned for insufficient funds), or (3) purchased on credit when the seller was **insolvent.** Under the UCC, insolvency occurs when a person ceases to pay his or her debts in the ordinary course of business, cannot pay debts as they become due, or is insolvent under federal bankruptcy law [UCC 1–201(23)].

In contrast to a seller with *void title,* a seller with *voidable title* has the power to transfer good title to a good faith purchaser for value. A **good faith purchaser** is one who buys without knowledge of circumstances that would make a person of ordinary prudence inquire about the validity of the seller's title to the goods. One who purchases *for value* gives legally sufficient consideration (value) for the goods purchased. The real, or original, owner cannot recover goods from a good faith purchaser for value [UCC 2–403(1)].[10]

If the buyer of the goods is not a good faith purchaser for value, then the actual owner of the goods can reclaim them from the buyer (or from the seller, if the goods are still in the seller's possession). Exhibit 17–3 illustrates these concepts.

The Entrustment Rule. According to Section 2–403(2), when goods are entrusted to a merchant *who deals in goods of that kind,* the merchant has the power to transfer all rights to *a buyer in the ordinary course of business.* This is known as the **entrustment rule.** Entrusted goods include both goods that are turned over to the merchant and purchased goods left with the

Insolvent A condition in which a person cannot pay his or her debts as they become due or ceases to pay debts in the ordinary course of business.

Good Faith Purchaser A purchaser who buys without notice of any circumstance that would cause a person of ordinary prudence to inquire as to whether the seller has valid title to the goods being sold.

Entrustment Rule The rule that entrusting goods to a merchant who deals in goods of that kind gives that merchant the power to transfer those goods and all rights to them to a buyer in the ordinary course of business.

---

10. The real owner could, of course, sue the person who initially obtained voidable title to the goods.

Exhibit 17–3 Void and Voidable Titles

If goods are transferred from their owner to another by theft, the thief acquires no ownership rights. Because the thief's title is *void,* a later buyer can acquire no title, and the owner can recover the goods. If the transfer occurs by fraud, for instance, the transferee acquires a *voidable* title, as shown in this exhibit. A later good faith purchaser for value can acquire good title, and the original owner cannot recover the goods.

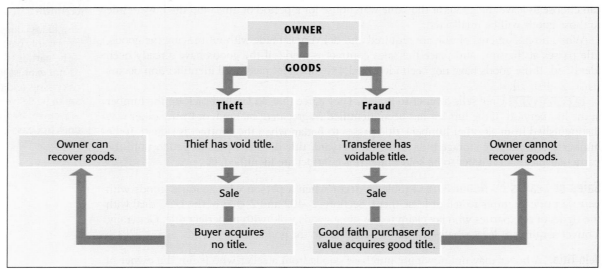

merchant for later delivery or pickup [UCC 2–403(3)]. Article 2A provides a similar rule for leased goods [UCC 2A–305(2)].

Under the UCC, a person is a **buyer in the ordinary course of business** in the following circumstances:

1. She or he buys goods in good faith (honestly).

2. The goods are purchased without knowledge that the sale violates the rights of another person in the goods.

3. The goods are purchased in the ordinary course from a merchant (other than a pawnbroker) in the business of selling goods of that kind.

4. The sale to that person is consistent with the usual or customary practices in the kind of business in which the seller is engaged [UCC 1–201(9)].

The entrustment rule basically allows innocent buyers to obtain legitimate title to goods purchased from merchants even if the merchants do not have good title. **EXAMPLE 17.25** Jan leaves her watch with a jeweler to be repaired. The jeweler sells both new and used watches. The jeweler sells Jan's watch to Kim, a customer, who is unaware that the jeweler has no right to sell it. Kim, as a good faith buyer, gets good title against Jan's claim of ownership.[11] Kim, however, obtains only those rights held by the person entrusting the goods (here, Jan).

Now suppose that Jan stole the watch from Greg and left it with the jeweler to be repaired. The jeweler then sells it to Kim. In this situation, Kim gets good title against Jan, who entrusted the watch to the jeweler, but not against Greg (the real owner), who neither entrusted the watch to Jan nor authorized Jan to entrust it. ■

17–3c Risk of Loss

Under the UCC, risk of loss does not necessarily pass with title. When risk of loss passes from a seller or lessor to a buyer or lessee is generally determined by the contract between the parties. Sometimes, the contract states expressly when the risk of loss passes. At other times, it does not, and a court must interpret the performance and delivery terms of the contract to determine whether the risk has passed.

Like risk of loss, the risk of liability that arises from the goods does not necessarily require the passage of title. In addition, as with risk of loss, when this risk passes from a seller to a buyer is generally determined by the contract between the parties. **CASE EXAMPLE 17.26** Tammy Herring contracted to buy a horse named Toby from Stacy and Gregory Bowman, who owned Summit Stables in Washington. The contract required Herring to make monthly payments until she paid $2,200 in total for Toby. Additionally, Herring agreed to pay Toby's monthly boarding fee at Summit Stables until the purchase price balance was paid. The Bowmans were to provide Toby's registration papers to Herring only when she had paid in full.

One day, another stable boarder, Diana Person, was injured when she was thrown from a buggy drawn by Toby and driven by Herring's daughter. Person sued the Bowmans to recover for her injuries, but the court held that Herring (not the Bowmans) owned Toby at the time of the accident. Herring argued that she did not own the horse because she did not yet have its registration papers, but the court found that the contract clearly showed that Herring owned Toby. Therefore, the Bowmans were not liable for the injuries that Toby caused.[12] ■

Delivery with Movement of the Goods—Carrier Cases
When the contract involves movement of the goods through a common carrier but does not specify when risk of loss passes, the courts first look for specific delivery terms in the contract.

Buyer in the Ordinary Course of Business A buyer who, in good faith and without knowledge that the sale violates the ownership rights or security interest of a third party in the goods, purchases goods in the ordinary course of business from a person in the business of selling goods of that kind.

KNOW THIS
The purpose of holding most goods in inventory is to turn those goods into revenues by selling them. That is one of the reasons for the entrustment rule.

---

11. Jan, of course, can sue the jeweler for the tort of trespass to personalty or conversion for the equivalent cash value of the watch.
12. *Person v. Bowman*, 173 Wash.App. 1024 (2013).

When does the risk of loss pass to the buyer in the sale of a horse?

The terms that have traditionally been used in contracts within the United States are listed and defined in Exhibit 17–4. These terms determine which party will pay the costs of delivering the goods and who bears the risk of loss. If the contract does not include these terms, then the courts must decide whether the contract is a shipment or a destination contract.

Shipment Contracts. In a shipment contract, the seller or lessor is required or authorized to ship goods by carrier, but is not required to deliver them to a particular final destination. The risk of loss in a shipment contract passes to the buyer or lessee when the goods are delivered to the carrier [UCC 2–319(1)(a), 2–509(1)(a), 2A–219(2)(a)].

EXAMPLE 17.27 Pitman, a seller in Texas, sells five hundred cases of grapefruit to a buyer in New York, F.O.B. Houston (free on board in Houston—see Exhibit 17–4). The contract authorizes shipment by carrier. It does not require that the seller tender the grapefruit in New York. Risk passes to the buyer when conforming goods are properly placed in the possession of the carrier in Houston. If the goods are damaged in transit, the loss is the buyer's. (Actually, buyers have recourse against carriers, subject to certain limitations, and buyers usually insure the goods from the time the goods leave the seller.) ■

Destination Contracts. In a destination contract, the risk of loss passes to the buyer or lessee when the goods are tendered to the buyer or lessee at the specified destination [UCC 2–319(1)(b), 2–509(1)(b), 2A–219(2)(b)]. In *Example 17.27*, if the contract had been F.O.B. New York, the risk of loss during transit to New York would have been the seller's. Risk of loss would not have passed to the buyer until the carrier tendered the grapefruit to the buyer in New York.

Delivery without Movement of the Goods The UCC also addresses situations in which the contract does not require the goods to be shipped or moved. Frequently, the buyer or lessee is to pick up the goods from the seller or lessor, or the goods are held by a bailee.

A **bailment** is a temporary delivery of personal property, without passage of title, into the care of another, called a *bailee*. Under the UCC, a *bailee* is a party who, by a bill of lading, warehouse receipt, or other document of title, acknowledges possession of goods and/or contracts to deliver them. For instance, a warehousing company or a trucking company may be a bailee.

Bailment A situation in which the personal property of one person (a bailor) is entrusted to another (a bailee), who is obligated to return the bailed property to the bailor or dispose of it as directed.

Goods Held by the Seller. When the seller keeps the goods for pickup, a document of title usually is not used. If the seller is a merchant, risk of loss to goods held by the seller passes to the buyer when the buyer *actually takes physical possession of the goods* [UCC 2–509(3)]. In

Exhibit 17–4 Contract Terms—Definitions

The contract terms listed and defined in this exhibit help to determine which party will bear the costs of delivery and when risk of loss will pass from the seller to the buyer.

F.O.B. (free on board)—Indicates that the selling price of goods includes transportation costs to the specific F.O.B. place named in the contract. The seller pays the expenses and carries the risk of loss to the F.O.B. place named [UCC 2–319(1)]. If the named place is the place from which the goods are shipped (for example, the seller's city or place of business), the contract is a shipment contract. If the named place is the place to which the goods are to be shipped (for example, the buyer's city or place of business), the contract is a destination contract.

F.A.S. (free alongside ship)—Requires that the seller, at his or her own expense and risk, deliver the goods alongside the carrier before risk passes to the buyer [UCC 2–319(2)]. An F.A.S. contract is essentially an F.O.B. contract for ships.

C.I.F. or **C.&F.** (cost, insurance, and freight, or just cost and freight)—Requires, among other things, that the seller "put the goods in the possession of a carrier" before risk passes to the buyer [UCC 2–320(2)]. (These are basically pricing terms, and the contracts remain shipment contracts, not destination contracts.)

Delivery ex-ship (delivery from the carrying vessel)—Means that risk of loss does not pass to the buyer until the goods are properly unloaded from the ship or other carrier [UCC 2–322].

other words, the merchant bears the risk of loss between the time the contract is formed and the time the buyer picks up the goods.

CASE EXAMPLE 17.28 Henry Ganno purchased a twelve-foot beam at a lumberyard. The lumberyard loaded the beam onto Ganno's truck, but did not tie it down (it was policy not to secure loads for customers). After he drove onto the highway, the beam fell out of Ganno's truck, and he was injured while trying to retrieve it. Ganno sued the lumberyard for negligence, but the court held that Ganno—not the lumberyard—bore the risk of loss and injury after he left the lumberyard's premises. Once the truck was loaded, the risk of loss passed to Ganno under the UCC because he had taken physical possession of the goods.[13] ■

If the seller is not a merchant, the risk of loss to goods held by the seller passes to the buyer on *tender of delivery* [UCC 2–509(3)]. This means that the seller bears the risk of loss until he or she makes the goods available to the buyer and notifies the buyer that the goods are ready to be picked up.

With respect to leases, similar rules apply. The risk of loss passes to the lessee on the lessee's receipt of the goods if the lessor is a merchant. Otherwise, the risk passes to the lessee on tender of delivery [UCC 2A–219(2)(c)].

Goods Held by a Bailee. When a bailee is holding goods for a person who has contracted to sell them and the goods are to be delivered without being moved, the goods are usually represented by a document of title. The title document may be written, such as a bill of lading or a warehouse receipt, or evidenced by an electronic record.

When goods are held by a bailee, risk of loss passes to the buyer when one of the following occurs:

1. The buyer receives a negotiable document of title for the goods.

2. The bailee acknowledges the buyer's right to possess the goods.

3. The buyer receives a nonnegotiable document of title, *and* the buyer has a *reasonable time* to present the document to the bailee and demand the goods. If the bailee refuses to honor the document, the risk of loss remains with the seller [UCC 2–503(4)(b), 2–509(2)].

With respect to leases, if goods held by a bailee are to be delivered without being moved, the risk of loss passes to the lessee on acknowledgment by the bailee of the lessee's right to possession of the goods [UCC 2A–219(2)(b)].

Risk of Loss When the Contract Is Breached
When a sales or lease contract is breached, the transfer of risk operates differently depending on which party breaches. Generally, the party in breach bears the risk of loss.

When the Seller or Lessor Breaches. If the seller or lessor breaches by supplying goods that are so nonconforming that the buyer has the right to reject them, the risk of loss does not pass to the buyer. **EXAMPLE 17.29** A buyer orders ten stainless steel refrigerators from a seller, F.O.B. the seller's plant. The seller ships white refrigerators instead. The white refrigerators (nonconforming goods) are damaged in transit. The risk of loss falls on the seller. Had the seller shipped stainless steel refrigerators (conforming goods) instead, the risk would have fallen on the buyer [UCC 2–510(1)]. ■

With nonconforming goods, the risk of loss does not pass to the buyer until one of the following occurs:

1. The defects are **cured** (that is, the goods are repaired, replaced, or discounted in price by the seller).

2. The buyer accepts the goods in spite of their defects (thus waiving the right to reject).

Cure The right of a party who tenders nonconforming performance to correct his or her performance within the contract period.

---

13. *Ganno v. Lanoga Corp.*, 119 Wash.App. 310, 80 P.3d 180 (2003).

When a seller ships nonconforming refrigerators that are damaged in shipment, who incurs the risk of loss?

If a buyer accepts a shipment of goods and later discovers a defect, acceptance can be revoked. Revocation allows the buyer to pass the risk of loss back to the seller, at least to the extent that the buyer's insurance does not cover the loss [UCC 2–510(2)]. Article 2A provides similar rules for leases.

When the Buyer or Lessee Breaches. The general rule is that when a buyer or lessee breaches a contract, the risk of loss immediately shifts to the buyer or lessee. This rule has three important limitations:

1. The seller or lessor must already have identified the contract goods.

2. The buyer or lessee bears the risk for only a commercially reasonable time after the seller or lessor has learned of the breach.

3. The buyer or lessee is liable only to the extent of any deficiency in the seller's insurance coverage [UCC 2–510(3), 2A–220(2)].

17-3d Insurable Interest

Parties to sales and lease contracts often obtain insurance coverage to protect against damage, loss, or destruction of goods. Any party purchasing insurance must have a sufficient interest in the insured item to obtain a valid policy. Insurance laws—not the UCC—determine sufficiency. The UCC is helpful, however, because it contains certain rules regarding insurable interests in goods.

Insurable Interest of the Buyer or Lessee A buyer or lessee has an **insurable interest** in *identified* goods. The moment the contract goods are identified by the seller or lessor, the buyer or lessee has a property interest in them. That allows the buyer or lessee to obtain necessary insurance coverage for those goods even before the risk of loss has passed [UCC 2–501(1), 2A–218(1)]. When the parties do not explicitly agree on identification in their contract, then the UCC provisions on identification discussed earlier in this chapter apply.

Insurable Interest of the Seller or Lessor A seller has an insurable interest in goods as long as she or he retains title to the goods. Even after title passes to the buyer, a seller who has a *security interest* in the goods (a right to secure payment) still has an insurable interest [UCC 2–501(2)]. Thus, both a buyer and a seller can have an insurable interest in the same goods at the same time. Of course, the buyer or seller must sustain an actual loss to recover from an insurance company. In regard to leases, the lessor retains an insurable interest in leased goods until the lessee exercises an option to buy and the risk of loss has passed to the lessee [UCC 2A–218(3)].

See the *Business Application* feature at the end of this chapter for a discussion of insurance coverage and other measures that buyers and sellers can take to protect against losses.

Insurable Interest A property interest in goods being sold or leased that is sufficiently substantial to permit a party to insure against damage to the goods.

17-4 Contracts for the International Sale of Goods

LEARNING OBJECTIVE 5

What law governs contracts for the international sale of goods?

International sales contracts between firms or individuals located in different countries are governed by the 1980 United Nations Convention on Contracts for the International Sale of Goods (CISG). The CISG governs international contracts only if the countries of the parties to the contract have ratified the CISG and if the parties have not agreed that some other law will govern their contract. As of 2015, the CISG had been adopted by seventy-eight countries, including the United States, Canada, some Central and South American countries, China, most European nations, Japan, and Mexico. That means that the CISG is the uniform international sales law of countries that account for more than two-thirds of all global trade.

17-4a Applicability of the CISG

Essentially, the CISG is to international sales contracts what Article 2 of the UCC is to domestic sales contracts. As discussed earlier, in domestic transactions the UCC applies when the parties to a contract for a sale of goods have failed to specify in writing some important term concerning price, delivery, or the like. Similarly, whenever the parties subject to the CISG have failed to specify in writing the precise terms of a contract for the international sale of goods, the CISG will be applied.

Unlike the UCC, *the CISG does not apply to consumer sales.* Neither the UCC nor the CISG applies to contracts for services.

17–4b A Comparison of CISG and UCC Provisions

The provisions of the CISG, although similar for the most part to those of the UCC, differ from them in certain respects. If the CISG and the UCC conflict, the CISG applies (because it is a treaty of the U.S. national government and therefore takes precedence over state laws under the U.S. Constitution). We look here at some differences with respect to contract formation.

The appendix at the end of this chapter—which shows an actual international sales contract used by Starbucks Coffee Company—illustrates many of the special terms and clauses that are typically contained in international contracts for the sale of goods. Annotations in the appendix explain the meaning and significance of specific contract clauses.

Statute of Frauds Unlike the UCC, the CISG does not include any Statute of Frauds provisions. Under Article 11 of the CISG, an international sales contract does not need to be evidenced by a writing or to be in any particular form.

Offers UCC 2–205 provides that a merchant's firm offer is irrevocable, even without consideration, if the merchant gives assurances in a signed writing or record. In contrast, under the CISG, an offer can become irrevocable without a signed writing or record. Article 16(2) of the CISG provides that an offer will be irrevocable in either of the following circumstances:

1. The offeror states orally that the offer is irrevocable.

2. The offeree reasonably relies on the offer as being irrevocable.

In both of these situations, the offer will be irrevocable without a writing or record and without consideration.

Another difference is that, under the UCC, if the price term is left open, the court will determine "a reasonable price at the time for delivery" [UCC 2–305(1)]. Under the CISG, however, the price term must be specified, or at least provisions for its specification must be included in the agreement. Otherwise, normally no contract will exist.

Acceptances Under the UCC, a definite expression of acceptance that contains additional terms can still result in the formation of a contract, unless the additional terms are conditioned on the assent of the offeror. In other words, the UCC does away with the mirror image rule in domestic sales contracts.

Article 19 of the CISG provides that a contract can be formed even though the acceptance contains additional terms, unless the additional terms materially alter the contract. Under the CISG, however, a "material alteration" includes almost any change in the terms. If an additional term relates to payment, quality, quantity, price, time and place of delivery, extent of one party's liability to the other, or the settlement of disputes, the CISG considers the added term a material alteration. In effect, then, the CISG requires that the terms of the acceptance mirror those of the offer.

Additionally, under the UCC, an acceptance is effective on dispatch, so a contract is created when the acceptance is transmitted. Under the CISG, in contrast, a contract is created not at the time the acceptance is transmitted but only on its *receipt* by the offeror. (The offer becomes *irrevocable,* however, when the acceptance is sent.)

Also, in contrast to the UCC, the CISG provides that acceptance by performance does not require that the offeror be notified of the performance.

Reviewing . . . The Formation of Sales and Lease Contracts

Guy Holcomb owns and operates Oasis Goodtime Emporium, an adult entertainment establishment. Holcomb wanted to create an adult Internet system for Oasis that would offer customers adult theme videos and live chat room programs using performers at the club. On May 10, Holcomb signed a work order authorizing Thomas Consulting Group (TCG) "to deliver a working prototype of a customer chat system, demonstrating the integration of live video and chatting in a Web browser." In exchange for creating the prototype, Holcomb agreed to pay TCG $64,697. On May 20, Holcomb signed an additional work order in the amount of $12,943 for TCG to install a customized firewall system. The work orders stated that Holcomb would make monthly installment payments to TCG, and both parties expected the work would be finished by September.

Due to unforeseen problems largely attributable to system configuration and software incompatibility, the project required more time than anticipated. By the end of the summer, the Web site was still not ready, and Holcomb had fallen behind in the payments to TCG. TCG was threatening to cease work and file suit for breach of contract unless the bill was paid. Rather than make further payments, Holcomb wanted to abandon the Web site project. Using the information presented in the chapter, answer the following questions.

1. Would a court be likely to decide that the transaction between Holcomb and TCG was covered by the Uniform Commercial Code (UCC)? Why or why not?

2. Would a court be likely to consider Holcomb a merchant under the UCC? Why or why not?

3. Did the parties have a valid contract under the UCC? Explain.

4. Suppose that Holcomb and TCG meet in October in an attempt to resolve their problems. At that time, the parties reach an oral agreement that TCG will continue to work without demanding full payment of the past-due amounts and Holcomb will pay CCG $5,000 per week. Assuming that the contract falls under the UCC, is the oral agreement enforceable? Why or why not?

DEBATE THIS

- The UCC should require the same degree of definiteness of terms, especially with respect to price and quantity, as general contract law does.

BUSINESS APPLICATION

Who Bears the Risk of Loss— the Seller or the Buyer?*

The shipment of goods is a major aspect of commercial transactions. Many issues arise when an unforeseen event, such as fire

* This *Business Application* is not meant to substitute for the services of an attorney who is licensed to practice law in your state.

or theft, causes damage to goods in transit. At the time of contract negotiation, both the seller and the buyer should determine the importance of the risk of loss. In some circumstances, risk is relatively unimportant (such as when ten boxes of copier paper are being sold), and the delivery terms should simply reflect costs and price. In other circumstances, risk is extremely important (such as when a fragile piece of pharmaceutical testing equipment is being sold), and the parties will need

an express agreement as to the moment risk is to pass so that they can insure the goods accordingly. Risk should always be considered before a loss occurs, not after.

A major consideration relating to risk is when to insure goods against possible losses. Buyers and sellers should determine the point at which risk passes so that they can obtain insurance coverage to protect themselves against loss when they have an insurable interest in the goods.

Checklist to Determine Risk of Loss

The UCC uses a three-part checklist to determine risk of loss:

1. If the contract includes terms allocating the risk of loss, those terms are binding and must be applied.

2. If the contract is silent as to risk and either party breaches the contract, the breaching party is liable for the risk of loss.

3. If the contract makes no reference to risk and the goods are to be shipped or delivered, the risk of loss is borne by the party having control over the goods (delivery terms) if neither party breaches.

If You Are the Seller

If you are a seller of goods to be shipped, realize that as long as you have control over the goods, you are liable for any loss unless the buyer is in breach or the contract contains an explicit agreement to the contrary. When there is no explicit agreement, the delivery terms in your contract can serve as a basis for determining control. Thus, if goods are shipped "F.O.B. buyer's business," risk of loss does not pass to the buyer until there is a tender of delivery at the destination—the buyer's business. Any loss or damage in transit falls on the seller because the seller has control until proper tender has been made.

If You Are the Buyer

If you are a buyer of goods, it is important to remember that most sellers prefer "F.O.B. seller's business" as a delivery term. Under this term, once the goods are delivered to the carrier, the buyer bears the risk of loss. Thus, if conforming goods are completely destroyed or lost in transit, the buyer not only suffers the loss but is obligated to pay the seller the contract price.

CHECKLIST for the Seller or the Buyer:

1. Before entering into a contract, determine the importance of the risk of loss for a given sale.

2. If risk is extremely important, the contract should expressly state the moment the risk of loss will pass from the seller to the buyer. This clause could even provide that risk will not pass until the goods are "delivered, installed, inspected, and tested (or in running order for a period of time)."

3. If an express clause is not included, delivery terms determine the passage of risk of loss.

4. When appropriate, either party or both parties should consider procuring insurance.

Key Terms

Chapter Summary: The Formation of Sales and Lease Contracts

The Scope of Articles 2 and 2A	1. *The UCC*—The UCC attempts to provide a consistent, uniform, and integrated framework of rules to deal with all phases ordinarily arising in a commercial sales or lease transaction, including contract formation, passage of title and risk of loss, performance, remedies, payment for goods, warehoused goods, and secured transactions. 2. *Article 2 (sales)*—Article 2 governs contracts for the sale of goods (tangible, movable personal property). The common law of contracts also applies to sales contracts to the extent that the common law has not been modified by the UCC. If there is a conflict between a common law rule and the UCC, the UCC controls. 3. *Article 2A (leases)*—Article 2A governs contracts for the lease of goods. Except that it applies to leases, instead of sales, of goods, Article 2A is essentially a repetition of Article 2 and varies only to reflect differences between sales and lease transactions.

Continues

The Formation of Sales and Lease Contracts	1. *Offer*—
	  a. Not all terms have to be included for a contract to be formed (only the subject matter and quantity term must be specified).
	  b. The price does not have to be included for a contract to be formed.
	  c. Particulars of performance can be left open.
	  d. A written and signed offer by a *merchant,* covering a period of three months or less, is irrevocable without payment of consideration.
	2. *Acceptance*—
	  a. Acceptance may be made by any reasonable means of communication. It is effective when dispatched.
	  b. An offer can be accepted by a promise to ship or by prompt shipment of conforming goods, or by prompt shipment of nonconforming goods if not accompanied by a notice of accommodation.
	  c. Acceptance by performance requires notice within a reasonable time. Otherwise, the offer can be treated as lapsed.
	  d. A definite expression of acceptance creates a contract even if the terms of the acceptance differ from those of the offer, unless the additional or different terms in the acceptance are expressly conditioned on the offeror's assent to those terms.
	3. *Consideration*—A modification of a contract for the sale of goods does not require consideration.
	4. *The Statute of Frauds*—
	  a. All contracts for the sale of goods priced at $500 or more must be in writing. A writing is sufficient as long as it indicates a contract between the parties and is signed by the party against whom enforcement is sought. A contract is not enforceable beyond the quantity shown in the writing.
	  b. When written confirmation of an oral contract *between merchants* is not objected to in writing by the receiver within ten days, the contract is enforceable.
	  c. For exceptions to the Statute of Frauds, see Exhibit 17–2.
	5. *Parol evidence rule*—
	  a. The terms of a clear and complete written contract cannot be contradicted by evidence of prior agreements or contemporaneous oral agreements.
	  b. Evidence is admissible to clarify the terms of a writing if the contract terms are ambiguous or if evidence of course of dealing, usage of trade, or course of performance is necessary to learn or to clarify the parties' intentions.
	6. *Unconscionability*—An unconscionable contract is one that is so unfair and one sided that it would be unreasonable to enforce it. If the court deems a sales contract to have been unconscionable at the time it was made, the court can (a) refuse to enforce the contract, (b) refuse to enforce the unconscionable clause, or (c) limit the application of any unconscionable clauses to avoid an unconscionable result.

Title and Risk of Loss	1. *Shipment contract*—In the absence of an agreement, title and risk pass on the seller's or lessor's delivery of conforming goods to the carrier [UCC 2–319(1)(a), 2–401(2)(a), 2–509(1)(a), 2A–219(2)(a)].
	2. *Destination contract*—In the absence of an agreement, title and risk pass on the seller's or lessor's *tender* of delivery of conforming goods to the buyer or lessee at the point of destination [UCC 2–319(1)(b), 2–401(2)(b), 2–509(1)(b), 2A–219(2)(b)].
	3. *Delivery without movement of the goods*—In the absence of an agreement, if the goods are not represented by a document of title, title passes on the formation of the contract, and risk passes on the buyer's or lessee's receipt of the goods if the seller or lessor is a merchant or on the tender of delivery if the seller or lessor is a nonmerchant.
	4. *Sales or leases by nonowners*—Between the owner and a good faith purchaser:
	  a. Void title—Owner prevails [UCC 2–403(1)].
	  b. Voidable title—Buyer prevails [UCC 2–403(1)].
	  c. Entrusted to a merchant—Buyer prevails [UCC 2–403(2), (3); 2A–305(2)].
	5. *Risk of loss when the contract is breached*—
	  a. If the seller or lessor breaches by tendering nonconforming goods that are rejected by the buyer or lessee, the risk of loss does not pass to the buyer or lessee until the defects are cured (unless the buyer or lessee accepts the goods in spite of their defects, thus waiving the right to reject) [UCC 2–510(1), 2A–220(1)].
	  b. If the buyer or lessee breaches the contract, the risk of loss immediately shifts to the buyer or lessee for goods that are identified to the contract. The buyer or lessee bears the risk for only a commercially reasonable time after the seller or lessor has learned of the breach [UCC 2–510(3), 2A–220(2)].

Contracts for the International Sale of Goods	International sales contracts are governed by the United Nations Convention on Contracts for the International Sale of Goods (CISG) if the countries of the parties to the contract have ratified the CISG and if the parties have not agreed that some other law will govern their contract. Essentially, the CISG is to international sales contracts what Article 2 of the UCC is to domestic sales contracts. Whenever parties who are subject to the CISG have failed to specify in writing the precise terms of a contract for the international sale of goods, the CISG will be applied.

Issue Spotters

1. E-Design, Inc., orders 150 computer desks. Fav-O-Rite Supplies, Inc., ships 150 printer stands. Is this an acceptance of the offer or a counteroffer? If it is an acceptance, is it a breach of the contract? What if Fav-O-Rite told E-Design it was sending the printer stands as "an accommodation"? (See *The Formation of Sales and Lease Contracts*.)

2. Truck Parts, Inc. (TPI), often sells supplies to United Fix-It Company (UFC), which services trucks. Over the phone, they negotiate for the sale of eighty-four sets of tires. TPI sends a letter to UFC detailing the terms and two weeks later ships the tires. Is there an enforceable contract between them? Why or why not? (See *The Formation of Sales and Lease Contracts*.)

—**Check your answers to the *Issue Spotters* against the answers provided in Appendix D at the end of this text.**

Learning Objectives Check

1. If a contract involves both goods and services, does the UCC apply?

2. In a sales contract, if an offeree includes additional or different terms in an acceptance, will a contract result? If so, what happens to these terms?

3. What exceptions to the writing requirements of the Statute of Frauds are provided in Article 2 and Article 2A of the UCC?

4. Risk of loss does not necessarily pass with title. If the parties to a contract do not expressly agree when risk passes and the goods are to be delivered without movement by the seller, when does risk pass?

5. What law governs contracts for the international sale of goods?

—**Answers to the even-numbered *Learning Objectives Check* questions can be found in Appendix E at the end of this text.**

Business Scenarios and Case Problems

17–1. Additional Terms. Strike offers to sell Bailey one thousand shirts for a stated price. The offer declares that shipment will be made by Dependable Truck Line. Bailey replies, "I accept your offer for one thousand shirts at the price quoted. Delivery to be by Yellow Express Truck Line." Both Strike and Bailey are merchants. Three weeks later, Strike ships the shirts by Dependable Truck Line, and Bailey refuses to accept delivery. Strike sues for breach of contract. Bailey claims that there never was a contract because his reply, which included a modification of carriers, did not constitute an acceptance. Bailey further claims that even if there had been a contract, Strike would have been in breach because Strike shipped the shirts by Dependable, contrary to the contract terms. Discuss fully Bailey's claims. (See *The Formation of Sales and Lease Contracts*.)

17–2. Spotlight on Goods and Services—The Statute of Frauds. Fallsview Glatt Kosher Caterers ran a business that provided travel packages, including food, entertainment, and lectures on religious subjects, to customers during the Passover holiday at a New York resort. Willie Rosenfeld verbally agreed to pay Fallsview $24,050 for the Passover package for himself and his family. Rosenfeld did not appear at the resort and never paid the money owed. Fallsview sued Rosenfeld for breach of contract. Rosenfeld claimed that the contract was unenforceable because it was not in writing and violated the UCC's Statute of Frauds. Is the contract valid? Explain. [*Fallsview Glatt Kosher Caterers, Inc. v. Rosenfeld*, 794 N.Y.S.2d 790 (N.Y. Super. 2005)] (See *The Formation of Sales and Lease Contracts*.)

17–3. Business Case Problem with Sample Answer— Passage of Title. Kenzie Godfrey was a passenger in a taxi when it collided with a car driven by Dawn Altieri. Altieri had originally leased the car from G.E. Capital Auto Lease, Inc. By the time of the accident, she had bought it, but she had not fully paid for it or completed the transfer-of-title paperwork. Godfrey suffered a brain injury and sought to recover damages from the owner of the car that Altieri was driving. Who had title to the car at the time of the accident? Explain. [*Godfrey v. G.E. Capital Auto Lease, Inc.*, 89 A.D.3d 471, 933 N.Y.S.2d 208 (1 Dept. 2011)] (See *Title and Risk of Loss*.)

—**For a sample answer to Problem 17–3, go to Appendix F at the end of this text.**

17–4. Additional Terms. B.S. International, Ltd. (BSI), makes costume jewelry. JMAM, LLC, is a wholesaler of costume jewelry. JMAM sent BSI a letter with the terms for orders, including the necessary procedure for obtaining credit for items that customers rejected. The letter stated, "By signing below, you agree to the terms." Steven Baracsi, BSI's owner, signed the letter and returned it. For six years, BSI made jewelry for JMAM, which resold it. Items rejected by customers were sent back to JMAM, but were never returned to BSI. BSI filed a suit against JMAM, claiming $41,294.21 for the unreturned items. BSI showed the court a copy of JMAM's terms. Across the bottom had been typed a "PS" requiring the return of rejected merchandise. Was this "PS" part of the contract? Discuss. [*B.S. International, Ltd. v. JMAM, LLC*, 13 A.3d 1057 (R.I. 2011)] (See *Formation of Sales and Lease Contracts*.)

17–5. Goods Held by the Seller or Lessor. Douglas Singletary bought a manufactured home from Andy's Mobile Home and Land Sales. The contract stated that the buyer accepted the home "as is where is." Singletary paid the full price, and his crew began to ready the home to relocate it to his property. The night before the home was to be moved, however, it was destroyed by fire. Who suffered the loss? Explain. [*Singletary, III v. P&A Investments, Inc.,* 712 S.E.2d 681 (N.C.App. 2011)] (See *Title and Risk of Loss.*)

17–6. The Statute of Frauds. Kendall Gardner agreed to buy a specially built shaving mill from B&C Shavings. He planned to use the mill to produce wood shavings for poultry processors. B&C faxed an invoice to Gardner reflecting a purchase price of $86,200, with a 30 percent down payment and the "balance due before shipment." Gardner paid the down payment. B&C finished the mill and wrote Gardner a letter telling him to "pay the balance due or you will lose the down payment." By then, Gardner had lost his customers for the wood shavings, could not pay the balance due, and asked for the return of his down payment. Did these parties have an enforceable contract under the Statute of Frauds? Explain. [*Bowen v. Gardner,* 2013 Ark.App. 52, 425 S.W.3d 875 (2013)] (See *The Formation of Sales and Lease Contracts.*)

17–7. Risk of Loss. Ethicon, Inc., a pharmaceutical company, entered into an agreement with UPS Supply Chain Solutions, Inc., to transport pharmaceuticals. The drivers were provided by International Management Services Co. under a contract with a UPS subsidiary, Worldwide Dedicated Services, Inc. During the transport of a shipment from Ethicon's facility in Texas to buyers "F.O.B. Tennessee," one of the trucks collided with a concrete barrier near Little Rock, Arkansas, and caught fire, damaging the goods. Who was liable for the loss? Why? [*Royal & Sun Alliance Insurance, PLC v. International Management Services Co.,* 703 F.3d 604 (2d Cir. 2013)] (See *Title and Risk of Loss.*)

17–8. Goods and Services Combined. Allied Shelving and Equipment, Inc., sells and installs shelving systems. National Deli, LLC, contracted with Allied to provide and install a parallel rack system (a series of large shelves) in National's warehouse. Both parties were dissatisfied with the result. National filed a suit in a Florida state court against Allied, which filed a counterclaim. Each contended that the other had materially breached the contract. The court applied common law contract principles to rule in National's favor on both claims. Allied appealed, arguing that the court should have applied the UCC. When does a court apply common law principles to a contract that involves both goods and services? In this case, why might an appellate court rule that the UCC should be applied instead? Explain. [*Allied Shelving and Equipment, Inc. v. National Deli, LLC,* 40 Fla. L. Weekly D145, 154 So.3d 482 (Dist.App. 2015)] (See *The Scope of Articles 2 and 2A.*)

17–9. A Question of Ethics—Statute of Frauds. Daniel Fox owned Fox & Lamberth Enterprises, Inc., a kitchen remodeling business. Fox leased a building from Carl Hussong. When Fox planned to close his business, Craftsmen Home Improvement, Inc., expressed an interest in buying his assets. Fox set a price of $50,000. Craftsmen's owners agreed and gave Fox a list of the desired items and a "Bill of Sale" that set the terms for payment. Craftsmen expected to negotiate a new lease with Hussong and modified the premises, including removal of some of the displays. When Hussong and Craftsmen could not agree on new terms, Craftsmen told Fox that the deal was off. [*Fox & Lamberth Enterprises, Inc. v. Craftsmen Home Improvement, Inc.,* __ N.E.2d __ (2 Dist. 2006)]

1. In Fox's suit for breach of contract, Craftsmen raised the Statute of Frauds as a defense. What are the requirements of the Statute of Frauds? Did the deal between Fox and Craftsmen meet these requirements? Did it fall under one of the exceptions? Explain. (See *The Formation and of Sales and Lease Contracts.*)

2. Craftsmen also claimed that the "predominant factor" of its agreement with Fox was a lease for Hussong's building. What is the predominant-factor test? Does it apply here? In any event, is it fair to hold a party to a contract to buy a business's assets when the buyer is unable to negotiate a favorable lease of the premises on which the assets are located? Discuss. (See *The Scope of Articles 2 and 2A.*)

Critical Thinking and Writing Assignments

17–10. Business Law Critical Thinking Group Assignment. Mountain Stream Trout Co. agreed to buy "market size" trout from trout grower Lake Farms, LLC. Their five-year contract did not define *market size.* At the time, in the trade, *market size* referred to fish of one-pound live weight. After three years, Mountain Stream began taking fewer, smaller deliveries of larger fish, claiming that *market size* varied according to whatever its customers demanded and that its customers now demanded larger fish. Lake Farms filed a suit for breach of contract. (See *The Formation of Sales and Lease Contracts.*)

1. The first group will decide whether parol evidence is admissible to explain the terms of this contract. Are there any exceptions that could apply?

2. A second group will determine the impact of course of dealing and usage of trade on the interpretation of contract terms.

3. A third group will discuss how parties to a commercial contract can avoid the possibility that a court will interpret the contract terms in accordance with trade usage.

An Example of a Contract for the International Sale of Coffee

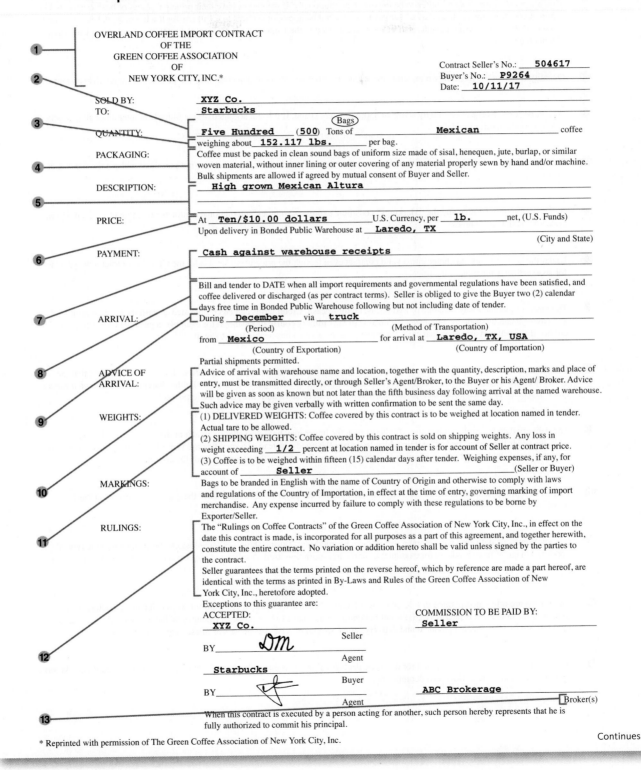

1 OVERLAND COFFEE IMPORT CONTRACT
OF THE
GREEN COFFEE ASSOCIATION
OF
2 NEW YORK CITY, INC.*

Contract Seller's No.: **504617**
Buyer's No.: **P9264**
Date: **10/11/17**

SOLD BY: **XYZ Co.**
TO: **Starbucks**

3 QUANTITY: **Five Hundred** (**500**) Tons of (Bags) **Mexican** coffee
weighing about **152.117 lbs.** per bag.

PACKAGING: Coffee must be packed in clean sound bags of uniform size made of sisal, henequen, jute, burlap, or similar
4 woven material, without inner lining or outer covering of any material properly sewn by hand and/or machine.
Bulk shipments are allowed if agreed by mutual consent of Buyer and Seller.

DESCRIPTION: **High grown Mexican Altura**
5

PRICE: At **Ten/$10.00 dollars** U.S. Currency, per **lb.** net, (U.S. Funds)
Upon delivery in Bonded Public Warehouse at **Laredo, TX**
(City and State)

6 PAYMENT: **Cash against warehouse receipts**

Bill and tender to DATE when all import requirements and governmental regulations have been satisfied, and
coffee delivered or discharged (as per contract terms). Seller is obliged to give the Buyer two (2) calendar
days free time in Bonded Public Warehouse following but not including date of tender.

7 ARRIVAL: During **December** via **truck**
(Period) (Method of Transportation)
from **Mexico** for arrival at **Laredo, TX, USA**
(Country of Exportation) (Country of Importation)
Partial shipments permitted.

8 ADVICE OF Advice of arrival with warehouse name and location, together with the quantity, description, marks and place of
ARRIVAL: entry, must be transmitted directly, or through Seller's Agent/Broker, to the Buyer or his Agent/ Broker. Advice
will be given as soon as known but not later than the fifth business day following arrival at the named warehouse.
Such advice may be given verbally with written confirmation to be sent the same day.

9 WEIGHTS: (1) DELIVERED WEIGHTS: Coffee covered by this contract is to be weighed at location named in tender.
Actual tare to be allowed.
(2) SHIPPING WEIGHTS: Coffee covered by this contract is sold on shipping weights. Any loss in
weight exceeding **1/2** percent at location named in tender is for account of Seller at contract price.
(3) Coffee is to be weighed within fifteen (15) calendar days after tender. Weighing expenses, if any, for
account of **Seller** (Seller or Buyer)

10 MARKINGS: Bags to be branded in English with the name of Country of Origin and otherwise to comply with laws
and regulations of the Country of Importation, in effect at the time of entry, governing marking of import
merchandise. Any expense incurred by failure to comply with these regulations to be borne by
Exporter/Seller.

11 RULINGS: The "Rulings on Coffee Contracts" of the Green Coffee Association of New York City, Inc., in effect on the
date this contract is made, is incorporated for all purposes as a part of this agreement, and together herewith,
constitute the entire contract. No variation or addition hereto shall be valid unless signed by the parties to
the contract.
Seller guarantees that the terms printed on the reverse hereof, which by reference are made a part hereof, are
identical with the terms as printed in By-Laws and Rules of the Green Coffee Association of New
York City, Inc., heretofore adopted.
Exceptions to this guarantee are:
ACCEPTED:
XYZ Co. COMMISSION TO BE PAID BY:
Seller
BY _____ *DM* _____ Seller

Agent
Starbucks
Buyer
12 BY _____ **ABC Brokerage**
Agent Broker(s)

13 When this contract is executed by a person acting for another, such person hereby represents that he is
fully authorized to commit his principal.

Continues

1   This is a contract for a sale of coffee to be *imported* internationally. If the parties have their principal places of business located in different countries, the contract may be subject to the United Nations Convention on Contracts for the International Sale of Goods (CISG). If the parties' principal places of business are located in the United States, the contract may be subject to the Uniform Commercial Code (UCC).

2   Quantity is one of the most important terms to include in a contract. Without it, a court may not be able to enforce the contract.

3   Weight per unit (bag) can be exactly stated or approximately stated. If it is not so stated, usage of trade in international contracts determines standards of weight.

4   Packaging requirements can be conditions for acceptance and payment. Bulk shipments are not permitted without the consent of the buyer.

5   A description of the coffee and the "Markings" constitute express warranties. International contracts rely more heavily on descriptions and models or samples.

6   Under the UCC, parties may enter into a valid contract even though the price is not set. Under the CISG, a contract must provide for an exact determination of the price.

7   The terms of payment may take one of two forms: credit or cash. Credit terms can be complicated. A cash term can be simple, and payment can be made by any means acceptable in the ordinary course of business (for example, a personal check or a letter of credit). If the seller insists on actual cash, the buyer must be given a reasonable time to get it.

8   *Tender* means the seller has placed goods that conform to the contract at the buyer's disposition. This contract requires that the coffee meet all import regulations and that it be ready for pickup by the buyer at a "Bonded Public Warehouse." (A *bonded warehouse* is a place in which goods can be stored without payment of taxes until the goods are removed.)

9   The delivery date is significant because, if it is not met, the buyer may hold the seller in breach of the contract. Under this contract, the seller is given a "period" within which to deliver the goods, instead of a specific day. The seller is also given some time to rectify goods that do not pass inspection (see the "Guarantee" clause on the second page of the contract).

10   As part of a proper tender, the seller (or its agent) must inform the buyer (or its agent) when the goods have arrived at their destination.

11   In some contracts, delivered and shipping weights can be important. During shipping, some loss can be attributed to the type of goods (spoilage of fresh produce, for example) or to the transportation itself. A seller and buyer can agree on the extent to which either of them will bear such losses.

12   Documents are often incorporated in a contract by reference, because including them word for word can make a contract difficult to read. If the document is later revised, the entire contract might have to be reworked. Documents that are typically incorporated by reference include detailed payment and delivery terms, special provisions, and sets of rules, codes, and standards.

13   In international sales transactions, and for domestic deals involving certain products, brokers are used to form the contracts. When so used, the brokers are entitled to a commission.

TERMS AND CONDITIONS

14 — ARBITRATION: All controversies relating to, in connection with, or arising out of this contract, its modification, making or the authority or obligations of the signatories hereto, and whether involving the principals, agents, brokers, or others who actually subscribe hereto, shall be settled by arbitration in accordance with the "Rules of Arbitration" of the Green Coffee Association of New York City, Inc., as they exist at the time of the arbitration (including provisions as to payment of fees and expenses). Arbitration is the sole remedy hereunder, and it shall be held in accordance with the law of New York State, and judgment of any award may be entered in the courts of that State, or in any other court of competent jurisdiction. All notices or judicial service in reference to arbitration or enforcement shall be deemed given if transmitted as required by the aforesaid rules.

15 — GUARANTEE: (a) If all or any of the coffee is refused admission into the country of importation by reason of any violation of governmental laws or acts, which violation existed at the time the coffee arrived at Bonded Public Warehouse, seller is required, as to the amount not admitted and as soon as possible, to deliver replacement coffee in conformity to all terms and conditions of this contract, excepting only the Arrival terms, but not later than thirty (30) days after the date of the violation notice. Any payment made and expenses incurred for any coffee denied entry shall be refunded within ten (10) calendar days of denial of entry, and payment shall be made for the replacement delivery in accordance with the terms of this contract. Consequently, if Buyer removes the coffee from the Bonded Public Warehouse, Seller's responsibility as to such portion hereunder ceases.
(b) Contracts containing the overstamp "No Pass-No Sale" on the face of the contract shall be interpreted to mean: If any or all of the coffee is not admitted into the country of Importation in its original condition by reason of failure to meet requirements of the government's laws or Acts, the contract shall be deemed null and void as to that portion of the coffee which is not admitted in its original condition. Any payment made and expenses incurred for any coffee denied entry shall be refunded within ten (10) calendar days of denial of entry.

16 — CONTINGENCY: This contract is not contingent upon any other contract.

CLAIMS: Coffee shall be considered accepted as to quality unless within *fifteen* (15) calendar days after delivery at Bonded Public Warehouse or within *fifteen* (15) calendar days after all Government clearances have been received, whichever is later, either:
(a) Claims are settled by the parties hereto, or,
(b) Arbitration proceedings have been filed by one of the parties in accordance with the provisions hereof.
17 — (c) If neither (a) nor (b) has been done in the stated period or if any portion of the coffee has been removed from the Bonded Public Warehouse before representative sealed samples have been drawn by the Green Coffee Association of New York City, Inc., in accordance with its rules, Seller's responsibility for quality claims ceases for that portion so removed.
(d) Any question of quality submitted to arbitration shall be a matter of allowance only, unless otherwise provided in the contract.

18 — DELIVERY: (a) No more than three (3) chops may be tendered for each lot of 250 bags.
(b) Each chop of coffee tendered is to be uniform in grade and appearance. All expense necessary to make coffee uniform shall be for account of seller.
(c) Notice of arrival and/or sampling order constitutes a tender, and must be given not later than the fifth business day following arrival at Bonded Public Warehouse stated on the contract.

INSURANCE: Seller is responsible for any loss or damage, or both, until Delivery and Discharge of coffee at the Bonded Public Warehouse in the Country of Importation.

All Insurance Risks, costs and responsibility are for Seller's Account until Delivery and Discharge of coffee at the Bonded Public Warehouse in the Country of Importation.

Buyer's insurance responsibility begins from the day of importation or from the day of tender, whichever is later.

19 — FREIGHT: Seller to provide and pay for all transportation and related expenses to the Bonded Public Warehouse in the Country of Importation.

20 — EXPORT DUTIES/TAXES: Exporter is to pay all Export taxes, duties or other fees or charges, if any, levied because of exportation.

IMPORT DUTIES/TAXES: Any Duty or Tax whatsoever, imposed by the government or any authority of the Country of Importation, shall be borne by the Importer/Buyer.

21 — INSOLVENCY OR FINANCIAL FAILURE OF BUYER OR SELLER: If, at any time before the contract is fully executed, either party hereto shall meet with creditors because of inability generally to make payment of obligations when due, or shall suspend such payments, fail to meet his general trade obligations in the regular course of business, shall file a petition in bankruptcy or, for an arrangement, shall become insolvent, or commit an act of bankruptcy, then the other party may at his option, expressed in writing, declare the aforesaid to constitute a breach and default of this contract, and may, in addition to other remedies, decline to deliver further or make payment or may sell or purchase for the defaulter's account, and may collect damage for any injury or loss, or shall account for the profit, if any, occasioned by such sale or purchase.

This clause is subject to the provisions of (11 USC 365 (e) 1) if invoked.

22 — BREACH OR DEFAULT OF CONTRACT: In the event either party hereto fails to perform, or breaches or repudiates this agreement, the other party shall subject to the specific provisions of this contract be entitled to the remedies and relief provided for by the Uniform Commercial Code of the State of New York. The computation and ascertainment of damages, or the determination of any other dispute as to relief, shall be made by the arbitrators in accordance with the Arbitration Clause herein.

23 — Consequential damages shall not, however, be allowed.

Continues

14   Arbitration is the settling of a dispute by submitting it to a disinterested party (other than a court), which renders a decision. The procedures and costs can be provided for in an arbitration clause or incorporated through other documents. To enforce an award rendered in an arbitration, the winning party can "enter" (submit) the award in a court "of competent jurisdiction."

15   When goods are imported internationally, they must meet certain import requirements before being released to the buyer. Because of this, buyers frequently want a guaranty clause that covers the goods not admitted into the country and that either requires the seller to replace the goods within a stated time or allows the contract for those goods not admitted to be void.

16   In the "Claims" clause, the parties agree that the buyer has a certain time within which to reject the goods. The right to reject is a right by law and does not need to be stated in a contract. If the buyer does not exercise the right within the time specified in the contract, the goods will be considered accepted.

17   Many international contracts include definitions of terms so that the parties understand what they mean. Some terms are used in a particular industry in a specific way. Here, the word *chop* refers to a unit of like-grade coffee beans. The buyer has a right to inspect ("sample") the coffee. If the coffee does not conform to the contract, the seller must correct the nonconformity.

18   The "Delivery," "Insurance," and "Freight" clauses, with the "Arrival" clause on the first page of the contract, indicate that this is a destination contract. The seller has the obligation to deliver the goods to the destination, not simply deliver them into the hands of a carrier. Under this contract, the destination is a "Bonded Public Warehouse" in a specific location. The seller bears the risk of loss until the goods are delivered at their destination. Typically, the seller will have bought insurance to cover the risk.

19   Delivery terms are commonly placed in all sales contracts. Such terms determine who pays freight and other costs and, in the absence of an agreement specifying otherwise, who bears the risk of loss. International contracts may use these delivery terms, or they may use INCOTERMS, which are published by the International Chamber of Commerce. For example, the INCOTERM DDP (delivered duty paid) requires the seller to arrange shipment, obtain and pay for import or export permits, and get the goods through customs to a named destination.

20   Exported and imported goods are subject to duties, taxes, and other charges imposed by the governments of the countries involved. International contracts spell out who is responsible for these charges.

21   This clause protects a party if the other party should become financially unable to fulfill the obligations under the contract. Thus, if the seller cannot afford to deliver, or the buyer cannot afford to pay, for the stated reasons, the other party can consider the contract breached. This right is subject to "11 USC 365(e)(1)," which refers to a specific provision of the U.S. Bankruptcy Code dealing with executory contracts.

22   In the "Breach or Default of Contract" clause, the parties agree that the remedies under this contract are the remedies (except for consequential damages) provided by the UCC, as in effect in the state of New York. The amount and "ascertainment" of damages, as well as other disputes about relief, are to be determined by arbitration.

23   Three clauses frequently included in international contracts are *omitted* here. There is no choice-of-language clause designating the official language to be used in interpreting the contract terms. There is no choice-of-forum clause designating the place in which disputes will be litigated, except for arbitration (law of New York State). Finally, there is no *force majeure* clause relieving the sellers or buyers from nonperformance due to events beyond their control.

pichetw/ShutterStock.com

LEARNING OBJECTIVES

The five Learning Objectives *below are designed to help improve your understanding of the chapter. After reading this chapter, you should be able to answer the following questions:*

1. What are the respective obligations of the parties under a contract for the sale or lease of goods?

2. What is the perfect tender rule? What are some important exceptions to this rule that apply to sales and lease contracts?

3. What options are available to the nonbreaching party when the other party to a sales or lease contract repudiates the contract prior to the time for performance?

4. What remedies are available to a seller or lessor when the buyer or lessee breaches the contract?

5. What implied warranties arise under the UCC?

Performance and Breach of Sales and Lease Contracts

"Gratitude is as the good faith of merchants: it holds commerce together."

FRANÇOIS DE LA ROCHEFOUCAULD
1613–1680
(FRENCH AUTHOR)

The performance required of the parties under a sales or lease contract consists of the duties and obligations each party has under the terms of the contract. The basic obligation of the seller or lessor is to transfer and deliver the goods as stated in the contract, and the basic duty of the buyer or lessee is to accept and pay for the goods.

Keep in mind that "duties and obligations" under the terms of the contract include those specified by the agreement, by custom, and by the Uniform Commercial Code (UCC). Thus, parties to a sales or lease contract may be bound not only by terms they expressly agreed on, but also by terms implied by custom, such as a customary method of weighing or measuring particular goods. Because, as the chapter-opening quotation indicates, good faith "holds commerce together," the UCC also imposes a duty of good faith on the parties involved in commercial contracts. This duty basically requires honesty and fair dealing.

Sometimes, circumstances make it difficult for a person to carry out the promised performance, and the contract is breached. When breach occurs, the aggrieved (wronged) party looks for remedies—which we discuss later in this chapter. We also examine the various types of warranties that arise in sales and lease contracts.

18-1 Performance Obligations

As noted in this chapter's introduction, in the performance of a sales or lease contract, the basic obligation of the seller or lessor is to *transfer and deliver conforming goods.* The basic obligation of the buyer or lessee is to *accept and pay for conforming goods* in accordance with the contract [UCC 2–301, 2A–516(1)].

Overall performance of a sales or lease contract is controlled by the agreement between the parties. When the contract is unclear and disputes arise, the courts look to the UCC and impose standards of good faith and commercial reasonableness.

18-1a The UCC's Good Faith Provision

The obligations of good faith and commercial reasonableness underlie every sales and lease contract. The UCC's good faith provision, which can never be disclaimed, reads as follows: "Every contract or duty within this Act imposes an obligation of good faith in its performance or enforcement" [UCC 1–304].

Good faith means honesty in fact. For a merchant, it means honesty in fact and the observance of reasonable commercial standards of fair dealing in the trade [UCC 2–103(1)(b)]. In other words, merchants are held to a higher standard of performance or duty than are nonmerchants.

The principle of good faith applies to both parties to a sales contract and provides a framework for the entire agreement. If a sales contract leaves open some details of performance, for instance, the parties must exercise good faith and commercial reasonableness when later specifying the details.

Conforming Goods Goods that conform to contract specifications.

Tender of Delivery A seller's or lessor's act of placing conforming goods at the disposal of the buyer or lessee and providing whatever notification is reasonably necessary to enable the buyer or lessee to take delivery.

18-1b Obligations of the Seller or Lessor

The major obligation of the seller or lessor under a sales or lease contract is to deliver or tender delivery of conforming goods to the buyer or lessee. **Conforming goods** are goods that conform to the contract description in every way. **Tender of delivery** occurs when the seller or lessor makes conforming goods available to the buyer or lessee and provides whatever notification is reasonably necessary to enable the buyer or lessee to take delivery [UCC 2–503(1), 2A–508(1)].

Tender must occur at a *reasonable hour* and in a *reasonable manner.* In other words, a seller cannot call the buyer at 2:00 A.M. and say, "The goods are ready. I'll give you twenty minutes to get them." Unless the parties have agreed otherwise, the goods must be tendered for delivery at a reasonable hour and kept available for a reasonable period of time to enable the buyer to take possession of them [UCC 2–503(1)(a)].

Normally, all goods called for by a contract must be tendered in a single delivery, unless the parties have agreed that the goods may be delivered in several lots or *installments* [UCC 2–307, 2–612, 2A–510]. **EXAMPLE 18.1** An order for 1,000 Under Armour men's shirts cannot be delivered two shirts at a time. If, however, the parties agree that the shirts will be delivered in four orders of 250 each as they are produced (for summer, fall, winter, and spring inventory), then tender of delivery may occur in this manner. ■

In the following case, the seller of a log-cabin kit gave the buyers two days' notice to arrange for their final payment on the contract and take delivery. Did this notice comply with UCC 2–503?

iStockPhoto.com/ronen

Why can't a wholesale supplier of men's sweaters deliver 200 of them two at a time?

CASE 18.1

Garziano v. Louisiana Log Home Co.

United States Court of Appeals, Fifth Circuit, __ F.3d __, 569 Fed.Appx. 292 (2014).

FACTS Richard and Nancy Garziano contracted with Louisiana Log Home Co. (LLH) for a log-cabin kit to be delivered to them in Pass Christian, Mississippi. The contract required three installment payments. The final payment, due at delivery, was to include the cost of transportation. Two days before delivery, LLH told the buyers that the final payment would be $7,686.43, plus the transportation cost of $2,625.60. The Garzianos replied that they thought they had paid off the balance for the cabin and that they expected the shipping costs to be lower. They refused to pay more, and LLH did not deliver the kit. The Garzianos filed a claim in a federal district court against LLH, alleging that LLH had breached the contract by failing to inform them of the price of delivery in a timely manner. The court issued a judgment in LLH's favor and allowed the seller to keep the Garzianos' first two installment payments and the log-cabin kit without determining the actual amount of damages suffered. The Garzianos appealed.

Can a purchaser of a log cabin kit refuse to pay because the delivery charges seem excessive?

ISSUE Was LLH's notice in compliance with UCC 2–503?

DECISION Yes. The U.S. Court of Appeals for the Fifth Circuit affirmed the lower court's judgment. Because the lower court had not determined the actual amount of LLH's damages, however, the appellate court remanded the case to the lower court to make that finding and to remit to the Garzianos any funds paid on the contract that were in excess of LLH's actual damages.

REASON UCC 2–503(1) imposes a duty to "hold conforming goods at the buyer's disposition and give the buyer any notification reasonably necessary" to enable the buyer to take delivery. The contract between LLH and the Garzianos provided that "all costs of transportation shall be borne by the purchaser" and that "shipping charges are paid directly to the trucking company at the time of delivery by cash or personal check." The contract also specified an "F.O.B. Factory Price" without shipping costs of $43,656.43 for the log-cabin kit. These terms put the Garzianos on notice that they had not yet paid the full price for the kit and that they were responsible for the shipping costs. When LLH gave two days' notice in an attempt to deliver the goods, the Garzianos breached the contract by refusing to pay the balance due and the shipping costs. "While the Garzianos may have been surprised at the size of the delivery fee, the notice provided to the Garzianos was not so deficient as to prevent them from effectively taking delivery so that their refusal to pay would be excused."

CRITICAL THINKING—Legal Consideration *How might the parties have avoided the dispute in this case?*

Place of Delivery

The UCC provides for the place of delivery under a contract only if the contract does not indicate the place where the buyer or lessee will take possession. If the contract does not indicate where the goods will be delivered, then the place for delivery will be one of the following:

1. The *seller's place of business.*
2. The *seller's residence,* if the seller has no business location [UCC 2–308(a)].
3. The *location of the goods,* if both parties know at the time of contracting that the goods are located somewhere other than the seller's business [UCC 2–308(b)].

   EXAMPLE 18.2 Li Wan and Jo Boyd both live in San Francisco. In San Francisco, Wan contracts to sell Boyd five used trucks, which both parties know are located in a Chicago warehouse. If nothing more is specified in the contract, the place of delivery for the trucks is Chicago. Wan may tender delivery either by giving Boyd a negotiable or nonnegotiable document of title or by obtaining the bailee's (warehouser's) acknowledgment that the buyer is entitled to possession.[1] ■

---

1. If the seller delivers a nonnegotiable document of title or merely instructs the bailee in a writing (or electronic record) to release the goods to the buyer without the bailee's *acknowledgment* of the buyer's rights, this is also a sufficient tender, unless the buyer objects [UCC 2–503(4)]. Risk of loss, however, does not pass until the buyer has a reasonable amount of time in which to present the document or to give the bailee instructions for delivery.

These used trucks are located in Chicago. If nothing is specified in the sales contract, where is their place of delivery?

KNOW THIS

Documents of title include bills of lading, warehouse receipts, and any other documents that, in the regular course of business, entitle a person holding these documents to obtain possession of, and title to, the goods covered.

LEARNING OBJECTIVE 2

What is the perfect tender rule? What are some important exceptions to this rule that apply to sales and lease contracts?

"Resolve to perform what you ought. Perform without fail what you resolve."

BENJAMIN FRANKLIN
1706–1790
(AMERICAN POLITICIAN AND INVENTOR)

Delivery via Carrier In many instances, circumstances or delivery terms in the contract (such as F.O.B. or F.A.S. terms, which were shown in Exhibit 17–4) make it apparent that the parties intended the goods to be moved by a carrier. In carrier contracts, the seller fulfills the obligation to deliver the goods through either a shipment contract or a destination contract.

Shipment Contracts. Recall that a *shipment contract* requires or authorizes the seller to ship goods by a carrier, rather than to deliver them at a particular destination [UCC 2–319, 2–509(1)(a)]. Under a shipment contract, unless otherwise agreed, the seller must do the following:

1. Put the goods into the hands of the carrier.
2. Make a contract for their transportation that is reasonable according to the nature of the goods and their value. (For instance, certain types of goods require refrigeration in transit.)
3. Obtain and promptly deliver or tender to the buyer any documents necessary to enable the buyer to obtain possession of the goods from the carrier.
4. Promptly notify the buyer that shipment has been made [UCC 2–504].

If the seller fails to notify the buyer that shipment has been made or fails to make a proper contract for transportation, the buyer may be able to consider the contract breached and reject the shipment. The buyer can reject the shipment only if a *material loss* of the goods or a *significant delay* results. Of course, the parties can agree in their contract that a lesser amount of loss or delay will be grounds for rejection.

Destination Contracts. In a *destination contract,* the seller agrees to deliver conforming goods to the buyer at a particular destination. The seller must give the buyer appropriate notice about the delivery and hold the goods at the buyer's disposal for a reasonable length of time. The seller must also provide the buyer with any documents of title necessary to enable the buyer to obtain delivery from the carrier [UCC 2–503].

The Perfect Tender Rule As previously noted, the seller or lessor has an obligation to ship or tender *conforming goods,* and the buyer or lessee is required to accept and pay for the goods according to the terms of the contract. Under the common law, the seller was obligated to deliver goods that conformed to the terms of the contract in every detail. This was called the *perfect tender* doctrine.

The UCC preserves the perfect tender doctrine by stating that if the goods or tender of delivery fail *in any respect* to conform to the contract, the buyer or lessee has the right to accept the goods, reject the entire shipment, or accept part and reject part [UCC 2–601, 2A–509].

The corollary to this rule is that if the goods conform in every respect, the buyer or lessee does *not* have a right to reject the goods. **CASE EXAMPLE 18.3** U.S. Golf & Tennis Centers, Inc., agreed to buy 96,000 golf balls from Wilson Sporting Goods Company for a total price of $20,000. Wilson represented that U.S. Golf was receiving its lowest price ($5 per two-dozen unit). Wilson shipped golf balls to U.S. Golf that conformed to the contract in quantity and quality, but it did not receive payment.

U.S. Golf claimed that it had learned that Wilson had sold the product for $2 per unit to another buyer and asked Wilson to reduce the contract price of the balls to $4 per unit (for a total of $16,000). Wilson refused and filed a suit. The court ruled in favor of Wilson. Because it was undisputed that the shipment of golf balls conformed in quantity and quality to the contract specifications, U.S. Golf was obligated to accept the goods and pay the agreed-on price.[2] ∎

---

2. *Wilson Sporting Goods Co. v. U.S. Golf & Tennis Centers, Inc.,* 2012 WL 601804 (Tenn.App. 2012).

Exceptions to the Perfect Tender Rule Because of the rigidity of the perfect tender rule, several exceptions to the rule have been created, some of which are discussed here.

Agreement of the Parties. Exceptions to the perfect tender rule may be established by agreement. If the parties have agreed, for instance, that defective goods or parts will not be rejected if the seller or lessor is able to repair or replace them within a reasonable period of time, the perfect tender rule does not apply.

If the seller ships golf balls that perfectly conform to the sales contract, what must the buyer do?

The Right to Cure. The UCC does not specifically define the term *cure,* but it refers to the right of the seller or lessor to repair, adjust, or replace defective or nonconforming goods [UCC 2–508, 2A–513]. The seller or lessor can attempt to cure a defect when the following are true:

1. A delivery is rejected because the goods were nonconforming.

2. The time for performance has not yet expired.

3. The seller or lessor provides timely notice to the buyer or lessee of the intention to cure.

4. The cure can be made within the contract time for performance.

Even if the contract time for performance has expired, the seller or lessor can still cure if he or she had *reasonable grounds to believe that the nonconforming tender would be acceptable to the buyer or lessee* [UCC 2–508(2), 2A–513(2)]. **EXAMPLE 18.4** In the past, Reddy Electronics has frequently allowed Topps Company to substitute certain goods when the goods that Reddy ordered were not available. Under a new contract for similar goods, Reddy rejects a shipment of substitute goods. In this situation, Topps had reasonable grounds to believe Reddy would accept a substitute. Therefore, Topps can cure within a reasonable time even if conforming delivery will occur after the contract time for performance has ended. ■

A seller or lessor may tender nonconforming goods with a price allowance (discount). This may also serve as "reasonable grounds" for the seller or lessor to believe that the buyer or lessee will accept the nonconforming tender.

The right to cure substantially restricts the right of the buyer or lessee to reject goods. To reject, the buyer or lessee must inform the seller or lessor of the particular defect. If the defect is not disclosed, and if it is one that the seller or lessor could have cured, the buyer or lessee cannot later assert the defect as a defense. Generally, buyers and lessees must act in good faith and state specific reasons for refusing to accept goods [UCC 2–605, 2A–514].

Substitution of Carriers. An agreed-on manner of delivery (such as which carrier will be used to transport the goods) may become impracticable or unavailable through no fault of either party. In that situation, if a commercially reasonable substitute is available, this substitute must be used and will constitute sufficient tender to the buyer [UCC 2–614(1)]. The seller or lessor is required to arrange for the substitute carrier and normally is responsible for any additional shipping costs (unless the contract states otherwise).

EXAMPLE 18.5 A sales contract calls for a large generator to be delivered via Roadway Trucking Corporation on or before June 1. The contract terms clearly state the importance of the delivery date. The employees of Roadway Trucking go on strike. The seller must make a reasonable substitute tender, by another trucking company or perhaps by rail, if it is available. The seller normally will be responsible for any additional shipping costs. ■

KNOW THIS
If goods never arrive, the buyer or seller usually has at least some recourse against the carrier. Also, a buyer normally insures the goods from the time they leave the seller's possession.

Installment Contracts. An **installment contract** is a single contract that requires or authorizes delivery in two or more separate lots to be accepted and paid for separately. With an installment contract, a buyer or lessee can reject an installment *only if the nonconformity substantially impairs the value* of the installment and cannot be cured [UCC 2–307, 2–612(2), 2A–510(1)]. If the buyer or lessee fails to notify the seller or lessor of the rejection, however, and subsequently accepts a nonconforming installment, the contract is reinstated [UCC 2–612(3), 2A–510(2)].

Installment Contract
A contract that requires or authorizes delivery in two or more separate lots to be accepted and paid for separately.

Unless the contract provides otherwise, the entire installment contract is breached only when one or more nonconforming installments *substantially* impair the value of the *whole contract*. **EXAMPLE 18.6** A contract calls for the parts of a machine to be delivered in installments. The first part is necessary for the operation of the machine, but when it is delivered, it is irreparably defective. The failure of this first installment will be a breach of the whole contract because the machine will not operate without the first part.

In contrast, suppose that a contract calls for twenty carloads of plywood and that 6 percent of one carload deviates from the thickness specifications in the contract. It is unlikely that a court will find that a defect in 6 percent of one installment substantially impairs the value of the whole contract. ■

The point to remember is that the UCC significantly alters the right of the buyer or lessee to reject the entire contract if the contract requires delivery to be made in several installments. The UCC strictly limits rejection to cases of *substantial* nonconformity.

Commercial Impracticability. Occurrences unforeseen by either party when a contract was made may make performance commercially impracticable. When this occurs, the rule of perfect tender no longer applies. The seller or lessor must, however, notify the buyer or lessee as soon as practicable that there will be a delay or nondelivery.

EXAMPLE 18.7 Houston Oil Company, which receives its oil from the Middle East, has a contract to supply Northwest Fuels with one hundred thousand barrels of oil. Because of an oil embargo by the Organization of Petroleum Exporting Countries, Houston is unable to secure oil from the Middle East or any other source to meet the terms of the contract. This situation comes fully under the commercial impracticability exception to the perfect tender doctrine because the embargo was unforeseen by either party at the time the contract was made. ■

The doctrine of commercial impracticability does not extend to problems that could have been foreseen, such as an increase in cost resulting from inflation. The nonoccurrence of the contingency must have been a basic assumption on which the contract was made [UCC 2–615, 2A–405].

Commercial Impracticability and Partial Performance. Sometimes, an unforeseen event only *partially* affects the capacity of the seller or lessor to perform. Therefore, the seller or lessor can *partially* fulfill the contract but cannot tender total performance. In this situation, the seller or lessor is required to distribute any remaining goods or deliveries fairly and reasonably among the parties to whom it is contractually obligated to deliver the goods [UCC 2–615(b), 2A–405(b)]. The buyer or lessee must receive notice of the allocation and has the right to accept or reject it [UCC 2–615(c), 2A–405(c)].

EXAMPLE 18.8 A Florida orange grower, Best Citrus, Inc., contracts to sell this season's crop to a number of customers, including Martin's grocery chain. Martin's contracts to purchase two thousand crates of oranges. Best Citrus has sprayed some of its orange groves with a chemical called Karmoxin. When studies show that persons who eat products sprayed with Karmoxin may develop cancer, the Department of Agriculture issues an order prohibiting the sale of these products. Best Citrus picks only those oranges not sprayed with Karmoxin, but there are not enough to meet all the contracted-for deliveries. In this situation, Best Citrus is required to allocate its production. It notifies Martin's that it cannot deliver the full quantity specified in the contract and indicates the amount it will be able to deliver. Martin's can either accept or reject the allocation, but Best Citrus has no further contractual liability. ■

Destruction of Identified Goods. Sometimes, an unexpected event, such as a fire, totally destroys goods through no fault of either party and before risk passes to the buyer or lessee. In such a situation, *if the goods were identified at the time the contract was formed,* the parties are excused from performance [UCC 2–613, 2A–221]. If the goods are only partially destroyed, however,

> "Obstacles are those frightful things you see when you take your eyes off your goal."
>
> **Henry Ford**
> 1863–1947
> (Founder of Ford Motor Company)

If a supplier of imported oil is unable to fulfill a contract for delivery in the U.S. because of an oil embargo, does this situation represent commercial impracticability?

the buyer or lessee can inspect them and either treat the contract as void or accept the goods with a reduction of the contract price.

EXAMPLE 18.9 Atlas Sporting Equipment agrees to lease to River Bicycles sixty bicycles of a particular model that has been discontinued. No other bicycles of that model are available. River specifies that it needs the bicycles to rent to tourists. Before Atlas can deliver the bicycles, they are destroyed by a fire. In this situation, Atlas is not liable to River for failing to deliver the bicycles. The goods were destroyed through no fault of either party, before the risk of loss passed to the lessee. The loss was total, so the contract is avoided. Clearly, Atlas has no obligation to tender the bicycles, and River has no obligation to make the lease payments for them. ■

If a seller of oranges cannot deliver the full quantity as specified in the contract, can the buyer reject this smaller amount?

The Right of Assurance. Another exception to the perfect tender doctrine is the UCC's right of assurance. If one party to a contract has "reasonable grounds" to believe that the other party will not perform as contracted, he or she may "demand adequate assurance of due performance" from the other party. The demand must be made in writing or in an electronic record. Until such assurance is received, he or she may "suspend" further performance (such as payments due under the contract) without liability.

What constitutes "reasonable grounds" is determined by commercial standards. If such assurances are not forthcoming within a reasonable time (not to exceed thirty days), the failure to respond may be treated as a *repudiation* of the contract [UCC 2–609, 2A–401].

CASE EXAMPLE 18.10 Two companies that made road-surfacing materials, Koch Materials Company and Shore Slurry Seal, Inc., entered into a contract. Koch obtained a license to use Novachip, a special material made by Shore, and Shore agreed to buy all of its asphalt from Koch for the next seven years. A few years into the contract term, Shore notified Koch that it was planning to sell its assets to Asphalt Paving Systems, Inc. Koch demanded assurances that Asphalt Paving would continue the deal, but Shore refused to provide assurances. Koch was able to treat Shore's failure to give assurances as a repudiation and immediately sue Shore for breach of contract.[3] ■

Whenever you have doubts about the other party's ability or willingness to perform a sales contract, you should demand adequate assurances. Rather than requiring a party to "wait and see" (and possibly incur significant losses as a result), the UCC allows a party with reasonable suspicions to seek adequate assurance of performance from the other party. If the other party fails to give assurance, you can treat it as an anticipatory repudiation (a breach, as will be discussed shortly) and pursue damages.

Perhaps more important, the other party's failure to give assurance allows you to suspend further performance, which can save your business from sustaining substantial losses that could be recovered only through costly and lengthy litigation. Ultimately, it may be better simply to withdraw from a deal when the other party will not provide assurances of performance than to continue performing under a contract that is likely to be breached anyway.

PREVENTING
LEGAL
DISPUTES

The Duty of Cooperation. Sometimes, the performance of one party depends on the cooperation of the other. The UCC provides an exception to the perfect tender doctrine if one party fails to cooperate. When cooperation is not forthcoming, the other party can suspend her or his own performance without liability and hold the uncooperative party in breach or proceed to perform the contract in any reasonable manner [UCC 2–311(3)].

EXAMPLE 18.11 Aman is required by contract to deliver 1,200 Samsung washing machines to various locations in California on or before October 1. Farrell, the buyer, is to specify the

---

3. *Koch Materials Co. v. Shore Slurry Seal, Inc.,* 205 F.Supp.2d 324 (D.N.J. 2002).

Who is liable for nondelivery of washing machines if the buyer does not provide delivery locations?

locations for delivery. Aman repeatedly requests the delivery locations, but Farrell does not respond. The washing machines are ready for shipment on October 1, but Farrell still refuses to give Aman the delivery locations. If Aman does not ship on October 1, he cannot be held liable. Aman is excused for any resulting delay of performance because of Farrell's failure to cooperate. ■

18-1c Obligations of the Buyer or Lessee

The main obligation of the buyer or lessee under a sales or lease contract is to pay for the goods tendered in accordance with the contract. Once the seller or lessor has adequately tendered delivery, the buyer or lessee is obligated to accept the goods and pay for them according to the terms of the contract.

Payment In the absence of any specific agreement, the buyer or lessee must make payment at the time and place the goods are *received* [UCC 2–310(a), 2A–516(1)]. When a sale is made on credit, the buyer is obligated to pay according to the specified credit terms (for instance, 60, 90, or 120 days), not when the goods are received. The credit period usually begins on the *date of shipment* [UCC 2–310(d)]. Under a lease contract, a lessee must make the lease payment that was specified in the contract [UCC 2A–516(1)].

Payment can be made by any means agreed on by the parties—cash or any other method generally acceptable in the commercial world. If the seller demands cash, the seller must give the buyer reasonable time to obtain it [UCC 2–511].

Right of Inspection Unless the parties otherwise agree, or for C.O.D. (collect on delivery) transactions, the buyer or lessee has an absolute right to inspect the goods before making payment. This right allows the buyer or lessee to verify, before making payment, that the goods tendered or delivered are what were contracted for or ordered. If the goods are *not* what were ordered, the buyer or lessee has no duty to pay. *An opportunity for inspection is therefore a condition precedent to the right of the seller or lessor to enforce payment* [UCC 2–513(1), 2A–515(1)].

Inspection can take place at any reasonable place and time and in any reasonable manner. Generally, what is reasonable is determined by custom of the trade, past practices of the parties, and the like. The buyer bears the costs of inspecting the goods (unless otherwise agreed), but if the goods are rejected because they are not conforming, the buyer can recover the costs of inspection from the seller [UCC 2–513(2)].

Acceptance After having had a reasonable opportunity to inspect the goods, the buyer or lessee can demonstrate acceptance in any of the following ways:

1. The buyer or lessee indicates (by words or conduct) to the seller or lessor that the goods are conforming or that he or she will retain them in spite of their nonconformity [UCC 2–606(1)(a), 2A–515(1)(a)].

2. The buyer or lessee *fails to reject* the goods within a reasonable period of time [UCC 2–602(1), 2–606(1)(b), 2A–515(1)(b)].

3. In sales contracts, the buyer *performs any act inconsistent with the seller's ownership.* For instance, any use or resale of the goods—except for the limited purpose of testing or inspecting the goods—generally constitutes an acceptance [UCC 2–606(1)(c)].

Partial Acceptance If some of the goods delivered do not conform to the contract and the seller or lessor has failed to cure, the buyer or lessee can make a *partial* acceptance [UCC 2–601(c), 2A–509(1)]. The same is true if the nonconformity was not reasonably discoverable before acceptance. (In the latter situation, the buyer or lessee may be able to revoke the acceptance, as will be discussed later in this chapter.)

"Death, they say, acquits us of all obligations."

MICHEL DE MONTAIGNE
1533–1592
(FRENCH WRITER AND PHILOSOPHER)

A buyer or lessee cannot accept less than a single commercial unit, however. The UCC defines a *commercial unit* as a unit of goods that, by commercial usage, is viewed as a "single whole" that cannot be divided without material impairment of the character of the unit, its market value, or its use [UCC 2–105(6), 2A–103(1)(c)]. A commercial unit can be a single article (such as a machine), a set of articles (such as a suite of furniture or an assortment of sizes), a quantity (such as a bale, a gross, or a carload), or any other unit treated in the trade as a single whole for purposes of sale.

18-2 Anticipatory Repudiation

What if, before the time for contract performance, one party clearly communicates to the other the intention not to perform? As discussed earlier in this text, such an action is a breach of the contract by anticipatory repudiation.

18-2a Possible Responses to Repudiation

When anticipatory repudiation occurs, the nonbreaching party has a choice of two responses:

1. Treat the repudiation as a final breach by pursuing a remedy.
2. Wait to see if the repudiating party will decide to honor the contract despite the avowed intention to renege [UCC 2–610, 2A–402].

In either situation, the nonbreaching party may *suspend performance*.

EXAMPLE 18.12 On April 1, Cora Lyn, who owns a small inn, purchases a suite of furniture from Tom Horton, proprietor of Horton's Furniture Warehouse. The contract states that "delivery must be made on or before May 1." On April 10, Horton informs Lyn that he cannot make delivery until May 10 and asks her to consent to the modified delivery date. Lyn has two options. She can either treat Horton's notice of late delivery as a final breach of contract and pursue a remedy or agree to the later delivery date. ■

18-2b A Repudiation May Be Retracted

The UCC permits the breaching party to "retract" his or her repudiation (subject to some limitations). This retraction can be done by any method that clearly indicates the party's intent to perform. Once retraction is made, the rights of the repudiating party under the contract are reinstated. There can be no retraction, however, if since the time of the repudiation the other party has canceled or materially changed position or otherwise indicated that the repudiation is final [UCC 2–611, 2A–403].

EXAMPLE 18.13 Suppose that in *Example 18.12,* Lyn does not respond to Horton's repudiation for two weeks. On April 24, Horton informs Lyn that he will be able to deliver the furniture by May 1 after all. In effect, Horton has retracted his repudiation, reinstating the rights and obligations of the parties under the original contract. Note that if Lyn had told Horton that she was canceling the contract after he repudiated, he would not have been able to retract his repudiation. ■

18-3 Remedies for Breach

When one party fails to carry out the performance promised in a contract, a breach occurs, and the aggrieved party looks for remedies. These remedies range from retaining the goods to requiring the breaching party's performance under the contract. The general purpose of these remedies is to put the aggrieved party "in as good a position as if the other party had fully performed."

> **LEARNING OBJECTIVE 3**
> What options are available to the nonbreaching party when the other party to a sales or lease contract repudiates the contract prior to the time for performance?

Remedies under the UCC are *cumulative,* meaning that an innocent party to a breached sales or lease contract is not limited to one exclusive remedy. Of course, a party still may not recover twice for the same harm.

18–3a Remedies of the Seller or Lessor

When the buyer or lessee is in breach, the remedies available to the seller or lessor depend on the circumstances at the time of the breach. Relevant factors include which party has possession of the goods, whether the goods are in transit, and whether the buyer or lessee has rejected or accepted the goods.

When the Goods Are in the Possession of the Seller or Lessor   If the breach occurs *before the goods have been delivered to the buyer or lessee,* the seller or lessor has the right to pursue a number of remedies, which are listed below and discussed in the following subsections.

1. Cancel (rescind) the contract.

2. Withhold delivery of the goods.

3. Resell or dispose of the goods and sue to recover damages.

4. Sue to recover the purchase price or lease payments due.

5. Sue to recover damages for the buyer's nonacceptance.

The Right to Cancel the Contract.   If the buyer or lessee breaches the contract, the seller or lessor can choose to cancel (rescind) the contract [UCC 2–703(f), 2A–523(1)(a)]. The seller must notify the buyer or lessee of the cancellation, and at that point all remaining obligations of the seller or lessor are discharged. The buyer or lessee is not discharged from all remaining obligations, however. She or he is in breach, and the seller or lessor can pursue remedies available under the UCC for breach.

The Right to Withhold Delivery.   In general, sellers and lessors can withhold or discontinue performance of their obligations under sales or lease contracts when the buyers or lessees are in breach. This is true whether a buyer or lessee has wrongfully rejected or revoked acceptance of contract goods (rejection and revocation of acceptance will be discussed later), failed to make a payment, or repudiated the contract [UCC 2–703(a), 2A–523(1)(c)]. The seller or lessor can also refuse to deliver the goods to a buyer or lessee who is insolvent (unable to pay debts as they become due), unless the buyer or lessee pays in cash [UCC 2–702(1), 2A–525(1)].

The Right to Resell or Dispose of the Goods.   When a buyer or lessee breaches or repudiates the contract while the seller or lessor is still in possession of the goods, the seller or lessor can resell or dispose of the goods. Any resale of the goods must be made in good faith and in a commercially reasonable manner. The seller must give the original buyer reasonable notice of the resale, unless the goods are perishable or will rapidly decline in value [UCC 2–706(2), (3)].

The seller or lessor can retain any profits made as a result of the sale or disposition and can hold the buyer or lessee liable for any loss [UCC 2–703(d), 2–706(1), 2A–523(1)(e), 2A–527(1)]. In sales transactions, the seller can recover any deficiency between the resale price and the contract price, and can also recover *incidental damages,* defined as the costs to the seller resulting from the breach [UCC 2–706(1), 2–710]. In lease transactions, the lessor can lease the goods to another party and recover damages from the original lessee. Damages include any unpaid lease payments up to the time the new lease begins. The lessor can also recover any deficiency between the lease payments due under the original lease and those due under the new lease, along with incidental damages [UCC 2A–527(2)].

When the goods are unfinished at the time of breach, the seller or lessor can do either of the following:

1. Cease manufacturing the goods and resell them for scrap or salvage value.

2. Complete the manufacture, resell or dispose of the goods, and hold the buyer or lessee liable for any difference between the contract price and the sale.

In choosing between these two alternatives, the seller or lessor must exercise reasonable commercial judgment to mitigate the loss and obtain maximum value from the unfinished goods [UCC 2–704(2), 2A–524(2)].

The Right to Sue to Recover the Purchase Price or the Lease Payments Due. Under the UCC, an unpaid seller or lessor can bring an action to recover the purchase price or payments due under the lease contract, plus incidental damages [UCC 2–709(1), 2A–529(1)]. If a seller or lessor is unable to resell or dispose of goods and sues for the contract price or lease payments due, the goods must be held for the buyer or lessee. The seller or lessor can resell or dispose of the goods at any time before collecting the judgment from the buyer or lessee. If the goods are resold, the net proceeds from the sale must be credited to the buyer or lessee because of the duty to mitigate damages.

> **EXAMPLE 18.14** Southern Realty contracts with Gem Point, Inc., to purchase one thousand pens with Southern Realty's name inscribed on them. Gem Point tenders delivery of the pens, but Southern Realty wrongfully refuses to accept them. In this situation, Gem Point can bring an action for the purchase price because it delivered conforming goods, and Southern Realty refused to accept or pay for the goods. Gem Point obviously cannot resell the pens inscribed with the buyer's business name, so this situation falls under UCC 2–709. Gem Point is required to make the pens available for Southern Realty, but can resell them (in the event that it can find a buyer) at any time prior to collecting the judgment from Southern Realty. ■

The Right to Sue to Recover Damages for the Buyer's Nonacceptance. If a buyer or lessee repudiates a contract or wrongfully refuses to accept the goods, a seller or lessor can bring an action to recover the damages sustained. Ordinarily, the amount of damages equals the difference between the contract price or lease payments and the market price or lease payments at the time and place of tender of the goods, plus incidental damages [UCC 2–708(1), 2A–528(1)].

When the ordinary measure of damages is insufficient to put the seller or lessor in the same position as the buyer's or lessee's performance would have, the UCC provides an alternative. In that situation, the proper measure of damages is the lost profits of the seller or lessor, including a reasonable allowance for overhead and other expenses [UCC 2–708(2), 2A–528(2)].

If a buyer wrongfully refuses to accept a shipment of blue pens that she ordered, what is the measure of damages that the seller can recover?

When the Goods Are in Transit
If the seller or lessor has delivered the goods to a carrier or a bailee, but the buyer or lessee has not yet received them, the goods are said to be *in transit.* In limited situations, the seller or lessor can prevent goods in transit from being delivered to the buyer or lessee.

Effect of Insolvency and Breach. If the seller or lessor learns that the buyer or lessee is insolvent, the seller or lessor can stop the carrier or bailee from delivering the goods regardless of the quantity of goods shipped. If the buyer or lessee is in breach but is not insolvent, however, the seller or lessor can stop delivery of goods in transit only if the quantity shipped is at least a carload, a truckload, a planeload, or a larger shipment [UCC 2–705(1), 2A–526(1)].

> **EXAMPLE 18.15** Arturo Ortega orders a truckload of lumber from Timber Products, Inc., to be shipped to Ortega six weeks later. Ortega, who owes payment to Timber Products for a past shipment, promises to pay the debt immediately and to pay for the current shipment as soon as it is received. After the lumber has been shipped, a bankruptcy court judge notifies Timber Products that Ortega has filed a petition in bankruptcy and listed Timber Products as one of his creditors. If the goods are still in transit, Timber Products can stop the carrier from delivering the lumber to Ortega. ■

Requirements for Stopping Delivery. To stop delivery, the seller or lessor must *timely notify* the carrier or other bailee that the goods are to be returned or held for the seller or lessor. If the carrier has sufficient time to stop delivery, it must hold and deliver the goods according to the instructions of the seller or lessor. The seller or lessor is liable to the carrier for any additional costs incurred [UCC 2–705(3), 2A–526(3)].

The seller or lessor has the right to stop delivery of the goods under UCC 2–705(2) and 2A–526(2) until the time when the following occurs:

1. The buyer or lessee obtains possession of the goods.

2. The carrier or the bailee acknowledges the rights of the buyer or lessee in the goods (by reshipping or holding the goods for the buyer or lessee, for example).

3. A negotiable document of title covering the goods has been properly transferred to the buyer (in sales transactions only), giving the buyer ownership rights in the goods [UCC 2–702].

Once the seller or lessor reclaims the goods in transit, she or he can pursue the remedies allowed to sellers and lessors when the goods are in their possession.

When the Goods Are in the Possession of the Buyer or Lessee

When the buyer or lessee breaches the contract while the goods are in his or her possession, the seller or lessor can sue. The seller or lessor can sue to recover the purchase price of the goods or the lease payments due, plus incidental damages [UCC 2–709(1), 2A–529(1)].

In some situations, a seller may also have a right to reclaim the goods from the buyer. For instance, in a sales contract, if the buyer has received the goods on credit and the seller discovers that the buyer is insolvent, the seller can demand return of the goods [UCC 2–702(2)]. Ordinarily, the demand must be made within ten days of the buyer's receipt of the goods.[4] The seller's right to reclaim the goods is subject to the rights of a good faith purchaser or other subsequent buyer in the ordinary course of business who purchases the goods from the buyer before the seller reclaims them.

A lessor may also have a right to reclaim goods. If the lessee is in default (fails to make payments that are due, for example), the lessor may reclaim leased goods that are in the lessee's possession [UCC 2A–525(2)].

18–3b Remedies of the Buyer or Lessee

When the seller or lessor breaches the contract, the buyer or lessee has numerous remedies available under the UCC. Like the remedies available to sellers and lessors, the remedies of buyers and lessees depend on the circumstances existing at the time of the breach. Relevant factors include whether the seller has refused to deliver conforming goods or delivered nonconforming goods.

When the Seller or Lessor Refuses to Deliver the Goods

If the seller or lessor refuses to deliver the goods, or the buyer or lessee has rightfully rejected the goods, the remedies available to the buyer or lessee include the right to:

1. Cancel (rescind) the contract.

2. Obtain goods that have been paid for if the seller or lessor is insolvent.

3. Sue to obtain specific performance if the goods are unique or damages are an inadequate remedy.

4. Buy other goods (obtain *cover*), and obtain damages from the seller.

---

4. The seller can demand and reclaim the goods at any time, though, if the buyer misrepresented his or her solvency in writing within three months prior to the delivery of the goods.

5. Sue to obtain identified goods held by a third party (*replevy* goods).

6. Sue to obtain damages.

The Right to Cancel the Contract. When a seller or lessor fails to make proper delivery or repudiates the contract, the buyer or lessee can cancel, or rescind, the contract. On notice of cancellation, the buyer or lessee is relieved of any further obligations under the contract but retains all rights to other remedies against the seller [UCC 2–711(1), 2A–508(1)(a)]. (The right to cancel the contract is also available to a buyer or lessee who has rightfully rejected goods or revoked acceptance, as will be discussed shortly.)

The Right to Obtain the Goods on Insolvency. If a buyer or lessee has made a partial or full payment for goods that are in the possession of a seller or lessor who is or becomes insolvent, the buyer or lessee has a right to obtain the goods. For this right to be exercised, the goods must be identified to the contract, and the buyer or lessee must pay any remaining balance of the price to the seller or lessor [UCC 2–502, 2A–522].

The Right to Obtain Specific Performance. A buyer or lessee can obtain specific performance when the goods are unique and the remedy at law is inadequate [UCC 2–716(1), 2A–521(1)]. Ordinarily, a successful suit for monetary damages is sufficient to place a buyer or lessee in the position he or she would have occupied if the seller or lessor had fully performed. When the contract is for the purchase of a particular work of art or a similarly unique item, however, monetary damages may not be sufficient. Under these circumstances, equity requires that the seller or lessor perform exactly by delivering the goods identified to the contract (a remedy of specific performance).

   CASE EXAMPLE 18.16 Doreen Houseman and Eric Dare together bought a house and a pedigreed dog. When the couple separated, they agreed that Dare would keep the house (and pay Houseman for her interest in it) and Houseman would keep the dog. Houseman allowed Dare to take the dog for visits. After one such visit, Dare failed to return the dog. Houseman filed a lawsuit seeking specific performance of their agreement. The court found that because pets have special, subjective value to their owners, a dog can be considered a unique good. Thus, an award of specific performance was appropriate.[5] ■

The Right to Obtain Cover. In certain situations, buyers and lessees can protect themselves by obtaining **cover**—that is, by purchasing or leasing other goods to substitute for those due under the contract. This option is available when the seller or lessor repudiates the contract or fails to deliver the goods, or when a buyer or lessee has rightfully rejected goods or revoked acceptance. In purchasing or leasing substitute goods, the buyer or lessee must act in good faith and without unreasonable delay [UCC 2–712, 2A–518].

   After obtaining substitute goods, the buyer or lessee can recover the following from the seller or lessor:

1. The difference between the cost of cover and the contract price (or lease payments).

2. Incidental damages that resulted from the breach.

3. Consequential damages to compensate for indirect losses (such as lost profits) resulting from the breach that were reasonably foreseeable at the time of contract formation.

   Buyers and lessees are not required to cover, and failure to do so will not bar them from using any other remedies available under the UCC. A buyer or lessee who fails to cover, however, may not be able to collect consequential damages that he or she could have avoided by purchasing or leasing substitute goods.

---

5. *Houseman v. Dare*, 405 N.J.Super. 538, 966 A.2d 24 (2009).

Cover A remedy that allows the buyer or lessee, on the seller's or lessor's breach, to obtain substitute goods from another seller or lessor.

iStockPhoto.com/fotojagodka

Can a court order a person to give up ownership of a formerly jointly owned pedigreed dog in favor of the former co-owner of the pet?

Replevin An action that can be used by a buyer or lessee to recover identified goods from a third party, such as a bailee, who is wrongfully withholding them.

KNOW THIS
Consequential damages compensate for a loss (such as lost profits) that is not direct but was reasonably foreseeable at the time of the breach.

The Right to Replevy Goods. Buyers and lessees also have the right to replevy goods. **Replevin**[6] is an action that a buyer or lessee can use to recover specific goods from a third party, such as a bailee, who is wrongfully withholding them. Under the UCC, the buyer or lessee can replevy goods subject to the contract if the seller or lessor has repudiated or breached the contract. To maintain an action to replevy goods, buyers and lessees usually must show that they are unable to cover for the goods after a reasonable effort [UCC 2–716(3), 2A–521(3)].

The Right to Recover Damages. If a seller or lessor repudiates the contract or fails to deliver the goods, the buyer or lessee can sue for damages. For the buyer (or lessee), the measure of recovery is the difference between the contract price (or lease payments) and the market price (or lease payments) at the time the buyer (or lessee) *learned* of the breach. The market price or market lease payments are determined at the place where the seller or lessor was supposed to deliver the goods. The buyer or lessee can also recover incidental and consequential damages, less the expenses that were saved as a result of the breach [UCC 2–713, 2A–519].

CASE EXAMPLE 18.17 Les Entreprises Jacques Defour & Fils, Inc., contracted to buy a 30,000-gallon industrial tank from Dinsick Equipment Corporation for $70,000. Les Entreprises hired Xaak Transport, Inc., to pick up the tank, but when Xaak arrived at the pickup location, there was no tank. Les Entreprises paid Xaak $7,459 for its services and filed a suit against Dinsick. The court awarded compensatory damages of $70,000 for the tank and incidental damages of $7,459 for the transport. Les Entreprises had agreed to buy a tank and had paid the price. Dinsick had failed to tender or deliver the tank, or to refund the price. The shipping costs were a necessary part of performance, so this was a reasonable expense.[7] ■

If a supplier of industrial storage tanks fails to provide a tank when and where specified in the sales contract, can the buyer recover funds paid to a transport company for its shipment?

iStockPhoto.com/Joe_Potato

When the Seller or Lessor Delivers Nonconforming Goods When the seller or lessor delivers nonconforming goods, the buyer or lessee has several remedies available under the UCC. The buyer or lessee may reject the goods, revoke acceptance of the goods, and recover damages for accepted goods.

The Right to Reject the Goods. If either the goods or the tender of the goods by the seller or lessor fails to conform to the contract *in any respect,* the buyer or lessee can reject the goods in whole or in part [UCC 2–601, 2A–509]. If the buyer or lessee rejects the goods, she or he may then obtain cover, cancel the contract, or sue for damages for breach of contract, just as if the seller or lessor had refused to deliver the goods (see the earlier discussion of these remedies).

CASE EXAMPLE 18.18 Jorge Jauregui contracted to buy a new Kawai RX5 piano for $24,282 from Bobb's Piano Sales & Service, Inc. When the piano was delivered with "unacceptable damage," Jauregui rejected it and filed a lawsuit for breach of contract. The court ruled that Bobb's had breached the contract by delivering nonconforming goods. Jauregui was entitled to damages equal to the contract price with interest, plus the sales tax, delivery charge, and attorneys' fees.[8] ■

Rejection of Goods: Timeliness and Identification Required. The buyer or lessee must reject the goods within a reasonable amount of time after delivery and must *seasonably* (timely) notify the seller or lessor [UCC 2–602(1), 2A–509(2)]. If the buyer or lessee fails to reject the goods within a reasonable amount of time, acceptance will be presumed.

When rejecting goods, the buyer or lessee must also designate specific defects that would have been apparent to the seller or lessor on reasonable inspection. Failure to do so precludes the buyer or lessee from using such defects to justify rejection or to establish breach when the seller could have cured the defects if they had been disclosed in a timely fashion [UCC 2–605, 2A–514].

---

6. Pronounced ruh-*pleh*-vun. Note that outside the UCC, the term *replevin* refers to a prejudgment process that permits the seizure of specific personal property in which a party claims a right or an interest.

7. *Les Entreprises Jacques Defour & Fils, Inc. v. Dinsick Equipment Corp.*, 2011 WL 307501 (N.D.Ill. 2011).

8. *Jauregui v. Bobb's Piano Sales & Service, Inc.*, 922 So.2d 303 (Fla.App. 2006).

Rejection of Goods: Duties of Merchant Buyers and Lessees. What happens if a *merchant buyer or lessee* rightfully rejects goods and the seller or lessor has no agent or business at the place of rejection? In that situation, the merchant buyer or lessee has a good faith obligation to follow any reasonable instructions received from the seller or lessor with respect to the goods [UCC 2–603, 2A–511]. The buyer or lessee is entitled to be reimbursed for the care and cost entailed in following the instructions. The same requirements hold if the buyer or lessee rightfully revokes his or her acceptance of the goods at some later time [UCC 2–608(3), 2A–517(5)]. (Revocation of acceptance will be discussed shortly.)

If no instructions are forthcoming and the goods are perishable or threaten to decline in value quickly, the buyer can resell the goods in good faith. The buyer can then take the appropriate reimbursement from the proceeds and a selling commission (not to exceed 10 percent of the gross proceeds) [UCC 2–603(1), (2); 2A–511(1), (2)]. If the goods are not perishable, the buyer or lessee may store them for the seller or lessor or reship them to the seller or lessor [UCC 2–604, 2A–512].

Revocation of Acceptance. Acceptance of the goods precludes the buyer or lessee from exercising the right of rejection, but it does not necessarily prevent the buyer or lessee from pursuing other remedies. In certain circumstances, a buyer or lessee is permitted to *revoke* her or his acceptance of the goods.

Acceptance of a lot or a commercial unit can be revoked if the nonconformity *substantially* impairs the value of the lot or unit *and* if one of the following factors is present:

1. Acceptance was predicated on the reasonable assumption that the nonconformity would be cured, and it was not cured within a reasonable time [UCC 2–608(1)(a), 2A–517(1)(a)].

2. The buyer or lessee did not discover the nonconformity before acceptance, either because it was difficult to discover before acceptance or because assurances made by the seller or lessor that the goods were conforming kept the buyer or lessee from inspecting the goods [UCC 2–608(1)(b), 2A–517(1)(b)].

Revocation of acceptance is not effective until notice is given to the seller or lessor. Notice must occur within a reasonable time after the buyer or lessee either discovers or *should have discovered* the grounds for revocation. Additionally, revocation must occur before the goods have undergone any substantial change (such as spoilage) not caused by their own defects [UCC 2–608(2), 2A–517(4)]. Once acceptance is revoked, the buyer or lessee can pursue remedies just as if the goods had been rejected. (See this chapter's *Beyond Our Borders* feature for a glimpse at how international sales law deals with revocation of acceptance.)

BEYOND OUR BORDERS

The CISG's Approach to Revocation of Acceptance

Under the UCC, a buyer or lessee who has accepted goods may be able to revoke acceptance under the circumstances mentioned in the text above. The United Nations Convention on Contracts for the International Sale of Goods (CISG) also allows buyers to rescind their contracts after they have accepted the goods. The CISG, however, takes a somewhat different—and more direct—approach to the problem.

Under the CISG, the buyer can simply declare that the seller has *fundamentally* breached the contract and proceed to sue the seller for the breach. Article 25 of the CISG states that a "breach of contract committed by one of the parties is fundamental if it results in such detriment to the other party as substantially to deprive him [or her] of what he [or she] is entitled to expect under the contract." For example, to revoke acceptance of a shipment under the CISG, a buyer need not prove that the nonconformity of one shipment substantially impaired the value of the whole lot. The buyer can simply file a lawsuit alleging that the seller is in breach.

CRITICAL THINKING

■ What is the essential difference between revoking acceptance and bringing a suit for breach of contract?

The Right to Recover Damages for Accepted Goods. A buyer or lessee who has accepted noncon-forming goods may also keep the goods and recover damages caused by the breach. To do so, the buyer or lessee must notify the seller or lessor of the breach within a reasonable time after the defect was or should have been discovered. Failure to give notice of the defect (breach) to the seller or lessor bars the buyer or lessee from pursuing any remedy [UCC 2–607(3), 2A–516(3)]. In addition, the parties to a sales or lease contract can insert a provision requiring the buyer or lessee to give notice of any defects in the goods within a set period.

When the goods delivered are not as promised, the measure of damages equals the differ-ence between the value of the goods as accepted and their value if they had been delivered as warranted [UCC 2–714(2), 2A–519(4)]. The buyer or lessee is also entitled to incidental and consequential damages when appropriate [UCC 2–714(3), 2A–519(3)]. The UCC also permits the buyer or lessee, with proper notice to the seller or lessor, to deduct all or any part of the damages from the price or lease payments still due under the contract [UCC 2–717, 2A–516(1)].

Is two years after a sale of goods a reasonable time period in which to discover a defect in the goods and notify the seller of a breach? That was the question in the following *Spotlight Case.*

SPOTLIGHT ON BASEBALL CARDS: CASE 18.2

Fitl v. Strek

Supreme Court of Nebraska, 269 Neb. 51, 690 N.W.2d 605 (2005).

FACTS In 1995, James Fitl attended a sports-card show in San Francisco, California, where he met Mark Strek, doing business as Star Cards of San Francisco, an exhib-itor at the show. Later, on Strek's representation that a certain 1952 Mickey Mantle Topps baseball card was in near-mint condition, Fitl bought the card from Strek for $17,750. Strek delivered the card to Fitl in Omaha, Nebraska, and Fitl placed it in a safe-deposit box.

In May 1997, Fitl sent the card to Professional Sports Authenticators (PSA), a sports-card grading service. PSA told Fitl that the card was ungradable because it had been discolored and doctored. Fitl complained to Strek, who replied that Fitl should have returned the card within "a typical grace period for the unconditional return of a card, . . . 7 days to 1 month" of its receipt. In August, Fitl sent the card to ASA Accu-grade, Inc. (ASA), another grading service, for a sec-ond opinion of the value. ASA also concluded that the card had been refinished and trimmed. Fitl filed a suit in a Nebraska state court against Strek, seeking damages. The court awarded Fitl $17,750, plus his court costs. Strek appealed to the Nebraska Supreme Court.

ISSUE Was two years after the sale of the baseball card a reasonable time to discover a defect and notify the seller of a breach?

DECISION Yes. The state supreme court affirmed the decision of the lower court.

What is a reasonable time period to discover that a baseball card purchased is not authentic?

J.Stone/ShutterStock.com

REASON Section 2–607(3)(a) of the UCC states, "Where a tender has been accepted . . . the buyer must within a reasonable time after he discovers or should have discovered any breach notify the seller of breach or be barred from any remedy." Furthermore, "What is a reasonable time for taking any action depends on the nature, purpose and circumstances of such action" [UCC 1–205(a)]. The state supreme court concluded that the buyer (Fitl) had reasonably relied on the seller's (Strek's) representation that the goods were "authentic," which they were not. Fitl had given timely notice when he discovered the defects.

The court reasoned that "the policies behind the notice requirement, to allow the seller to correct a defect, to prepare for negotiation and litigation, and to protect against stale claims at a time beyond which an investigation can be completed, were not unfairly prejudiced by the lack of an earlier notice to Strek. Any prob-lem Strek may have had with the party from whom he obtained the baseball card was a separate matter from his transaction with Fitl, and an investigation into the source of the altered card would not have minimized Fitl's damages."

WHAT IF THE FACTS WERE DIFFERENT? *Suppose that Fitl and Strek had included in their deal a written clause requiring Fitl to give notice of any defect in the card within "7 days to 1 month" of its receipt. Would the result have been different? Why or why not?*

18-3c Limitation of Remedies

The parties to a sales or lease contract can vary their respective rights and obligations by contractual agreement. For example, a seller and buyer can expressly provide for remedies in addition to those provided in the UCC. They can also provide remedies in lieu of those provided in the UCC, or they can change the measure of damages. Any agreed-on remedy is in addition to those provided in the UCC unless the parties expressly agree that the remedy is exclusive of all others [UCC 2–719(1), 2A–503(1), (2)].

Exclusive Remedies If the parties state that a remedy is exclusive, then it is the sole, or exclusive, remedy. **EXAMPLE 18.19** Standard Tool Company agrees to sell a pipe-cutting machine to United Pipe & Tubing Corporation. The contract limits United's remedy exclusively to repair or replacement of any defective parts. Thus, repair or replacement of defective parts is the buyer's exclusive remedy under this contract. ■

When circumstances cause an exclusive remedy to fail in its essential purpose, however, it is no longer exclusive, and the buyer or lessee may pursue other remedies available under the UCC [UCC 2–719(2), 2A–503(2)]. **EXAMPLE 18.20** In *Example 18.19,* suppose that Standard Tool Company is unable to repair a defective part, and no replacement parts are available. In this situation, because the exclusive remedy failed in its essential purpose, the buyer normally will be entitled to seek other remedies provided by the UCC. ■

Limitations on Consequential Damages As discussed previously, *consequential damages* are special damages that compensate for indirect losses (such as lost profits) resulting from a breach of contract that were reasonably foreseeable. Under the UCC, parties to a contract can limit or exclude consequential damages, provided the limitation is not unconscionable.

When the buyer or lessee is a consumer, any limitation of consequential damages for personal injuries resulting from consumer goods is *prima facie* (presumptively, or on its face) unconscionable. The limitation of consequential damages is not necessarily unconscionable when the loss is commercial in nature—such as lost profits and property damage [UCC 2–719(3), 2A–503(3)].

Statute of Limitations An action for breach of contract under the UCC must be commenced *within four years after the cause of action accrues*—that is, a buyer or lessee must file the lawsuit within four years after the breach occurs [UCC 2–725(1)]. In addition, a buyer or lessee who has accepted nonconforming goods usually must notify the breaching party of the breach within a reasonable time, or the aggrieved party is barred from pursuing any remedy [UCC 2–607(3)(a), 2A–516(3)].

The parties can agree in their contract to reduce this period to not less than one year, but cannot extend it beyond four years [UCC 2–725(1), 2A–506(1)]. A cause of action accrues for breach of warranty (discussed next) when the seller or lessor tenders delivery. This is the rule even if the aggrieved party is unaware that the cause of action has accrued [UCC 2–725(2), 2A–506(2)].

If this pipe-cutting machine has defective parts, can the buyer insist on replacement of the entire machine?

18-4 Warranties

The UCC has numerous rules governing product warranties as they occur in sales and lease contracts. Article 2 and Article 2A designate several types of warranties that can arise in a sales or lease contract, including warranties of title, express warranties, and implied warranties.

18-4a Warranties of Title

Under the UCC, three types of title warranties—*good title, no liens,* and *no infringements*—can automatically arise in sales and lease contracts.

Good Title   In most sales, sellers warrant that they have good and valid title to the goods sold and that transfer of the title is rightful [UCC 2–312(1)(a)]. If the buyer subsequently learns that the seller did not have good title to goods that were purchased, the buyer can sue the seller for breach of this warranty.

   EXAMPLE 18.21 Alexis steals a diamond ring from Calvin and sells it to Emma, who does not know that the ring is stolen. If Calvin discovers that Emma has the ring, then he has the right to reclaim it from Emma. When Alexis sold Emma the ring, Alexis automatically warranted to Emma that the title conveyed was valid and that its transfer was rightful. Because a thief has no title to stolen goods, Alexis breached the warranty of title imposed by the UCC and became liable to Emma for appropriate damages.

   There is no warranty of good title in lease contracts because title to the goods does not pass to the lessee.

No Liens   A second warranty of title shields buyers and lessees who are unaware of any encumbrances, or **liens** (claims, charges, or liabilities), against goods at the time the contract is made [UCC 2–312(1)(b), 2A–211(1)]. This warranty, for instance, protects buyers who unknowingly purchase goods that are subject to a creditor's *security interest* (an interest in the goods that secures payment or performance). If a creditor legally repossesses the goods from a buyer *who had no actual knowledge of the security interest,* the buyer can recover from the seller for breach of warranty.

No Infringements   A third type of title warranty is a warranty against infringement of any patent, trademark, or copyright. When the seller or lessor is a merchant, he or she automatically warrants that the buyer or lessee takes the goods *free of infringements.* In other words, a merchant promises that the goods delivered are free from any copyright, trademark, or patent claims of a third person [UCC 2–312(3), 2A–211(2)].

18–4b Express Warranties

A seller or lessor can create an **express warranty** by making representations concerning the quality, condition, description, or performance potential of the goods. Under UCC 2–313 and 2A–210, express warranties arise when a seller or lessor indicates any of the following:

1. That the goods conform to any *affirmation* (declaration that something is true) or *promise* of fact that the seller or lessor makes to the buyer or lessee about the goods. Such affirmations or promises are usually made during the bargaining process. Statements such as "these drill bits will penetrate stainless steel—and without dulling" are express warranties.

2. That the goods conform to any *description* of them. For example, a label that reads "Crate contains one 150-horsepower diesel engine" or a contract that calls for the delivery of a "wool coat" creates an express warranty.

3. That the goods conform to any *sample* or *model* of the goods shown to the buyer or lessee.

Express warranties can be found in a seller's or lessor's advertisement, e-mail, brochure, or promotional materials, in addition to being made orally or set forth in a provision of a contract.

Basis of the Bargain   To create an express warranty, a seller or lessor does not have to use words such as *warrant* or *guarantee* [UCC 2–313(2), 2A–210(2)]. It is only necessary that a reasonable buyer or lessee would regard the representation of fact as part of the basis of the bargain [UCC 2–313(1), 2A–210(1)]. The UCC does not define *basis of the bargain,* however, and it is a question of fact in each case whether a representation was made at such a time and in such a way that it induced the buyer or lessee to enter into the contract.

Statements of Opinion and Value   Only statements of fact create express warranties. If the seller or lessor makes a statement about the supposed value or worth of the goods, or offers

---

Lien An encumbrance on a property to satisfy a debt or protect a claim for payment of a debt.

Express Warranty A seller's or lessor's promise as to the quality, condition, description, or performance of the goods being sold or leased.

an opinion or recommendation about the goods, the seller or lessor is not creating an express warranty [UCC 2–313(2), 2A–210(2)].

EXAMPLE 18.22 A salesperson claims that "this is the best used car to come along in years. It has four new tires and a 250-horsepower engine just rebuilt this year." The seller has made several affirmations of fact that can create a warranty: the automobile has an engine, the engine has 250 horsepower and was rebuilt this year, and there are four new tires on the automobile. The seller's expressed opinion that the vehicle is "the best used car to come along in years," however, is puffery and creates no warranty. ■

As discussed in an earlier chapter, *puffery*—also known as "seller's talk"—is an expression of opinion by a seller or lessor that is not made as a representation of fact. It is not always easy to determine whether a statement constitutes an express warranty or puffery. The reasonableness of the buyer's or lessee's reliance appears to be the controlling criterion in many cases. For instance, a salesperson's statements that a ladder "will never break" and will "last a lifetime" are so clearly improbable that no reasonable buyer should rely on them.

18-4c Implied Warranties

An express warranty is based on the seller's express promise. In contrast, an **implied warranty** is one that *the law derives* by implication or inference because of the circumstances of a sale. In an action based on breach of implied warranty, it is necessary to show that an implied warranty existed and that the breach of the warranty proximately caused[9] the damage sustained. We look here at some of the implied warranties that arise under the UCC.

Implied Warranty of Merchantability Every sale or lease of goods made *by a merchant who deals in goods of the kind sold or leased* automatically gives rise to an **implied warranty of merchantability** [UCC 2–314, 2A–212]. **EXAMPLE 18.23** Colette, a merchant who is in the business of selling ski equipment, makes an implied warranty of merchantability every time she sells a pair of skis. A neighbor selling his skis at a garage sale does not (because he is not in the business of selling goods of this type). ■

Merchantable Goods. Goods that are *merchantable* are "reasonably fit for the ordinary purposes for which such goods are used." They must be of at least average, fair, or medium-grade quality—quality adequate to pass without objection in the trade or market for goods of the same description. The goods must also be adequately packaged and labeled, and they must conform to the promises or affirmations of fact made on the container or label, if any.

The warranty of merchantability may be breached even though the merchant did not know or could not have discovered that a product was defective (not merchantable). Of course, merchants are not absolute insurers against all accidents occurring in connection with their goods. For instance, a bar of soap is not unmerchantable merely because stepping on it could cause a user to slip and fall.

CASE EXAMPLE 18.24 Darrell Shoop bought a Dodge Dakota truck that had been manufactured by DaimlerChrysler Corporation. Almost immediately, he had problems with the truck. During the first eighteen months, the truck's engine, suspension, steering, transmission, and other components required repairs twelve times, including at least five times for the same defect, which remained uncorrected. Shoop eventually traded in the truck and filed a lawsuit against DaimlerChrysler for breach of the implied warranty of merchantability. The court held that Shoop could maintain an action against DaimlerChrysler and use the fact that the truck had required a significant number of repairs as evidence that it was unmerchantable.[10] ■

Implied Warranty A warranty that arises by law because of the circumstances of a sale and not from the seller's express promise.

Implied Warranty of Merchantability A warranty that goods being sold or leased are reasonably fit for the general purpose for which they are sold or leased, are properly packaged and labeled, and are of proper quality.

LEARNING OBJECTIVE 5
What implied warranties arise under the UCC?

---

9. Proximate, or legal, cause exists when the connection between an act and an injury is strong enough to justify imposing liability.
10. *Shoop v. DaimlerChrysler Corp.*, 371 Ill.App.3d 1058, 864 N.E.2d 785 (2007).

Merchantable Food. The UCC recognizes the serving of food or drink to be consumed on or off the premises as a sale of goods subject to the implied warranty of merchantability [UCC 2–314(1)]. "Merchantable" food means food that is fit to eat.

Courts generally determine whether food is fit to eat on the basis of consumer expectations. The courts assume that consumers should reasonably expect on occasion to find bones in fish fillets, cherry pits in cherry pie, or a nutshell in a package of shelled nuts, for example—because such substances are natural incidents of the food. In contrast, consumers would not reasonably expect to find moth larvae in a can of peas or a piece of glass in a soft drink.

In the following *Classic Case,* the court had to determine whether a diner should reasonably expect to find a fish bone in fish chowder.

★★★ CLASSIC CASE 18.3 ★★★

Webster v. Blue Ship Tea Room, Inc.

Supreme Judicial Court of Massachusetts, 347 Mass. 421, 198 N.E.2d 309 (1964).

HISTORICAL AND CULTURAL SETTING *Chowder, a soup or stew made with fresh fish, originated in fishing villages. Recipes for chowder traditionally did not call for the removal of the fish bones. In fact, many recipes specified that the fish head, tail, and backbone were to be broken in pieces and boiled to create the broth of the soup. By the middle of the twentieth century, there was a considerable body of case law concerning implied warranties and foreign and natural substances in food. It was perhaps inevitable that sooner or later, a consumer injured by a fish bone in chowder would challenge the merchantability of chowder containing fish bones.*

FACTS Blue Ship Tea Room, Inc., was located in Boston in an old building overlooking the ocean. Priscilla Webster, who had been born and raised in New England, went to the restaurant and ordered fish chowder. The chowder was milky in color. After three or four spoonfuls, she felt something lodged in her throat. As a result, she underwent two esophagoscopies (a procedure in which a telescope-like instrument is used to look into the throat). In the second esophagoscopy, a fish bone was found and removed. Webster filed a lawsuit against the restaurant in a Massachusetts state court for breach of the implied warranty of merchantability. The jury rendered a verdict for Webster, and the restaurant appealed to the state's highest court.

ISSUE Does serving fish chowder that contains a bone constitute a breach of an implied warranty of merchantability by the restaurant?

DECISION No. The Supreme Judicial Court of Massachusetts held that Webster could not recover against Blue Ship Tea Room, because no breach of warranty had occurred.

Who is liable for fish bones in seafood chowder?

iStockPhoto.com/hipokrat

REASON The court, citing UCC Section 2–314, stated that "a warranty that goods shall be merchantable is implied in a contract for their sale if the seller is a merchant with respect to goods of that kind. Under this section the serving for value of food or drink to be consumed either on the premises or elsewhere is a sale.... Goods to be merchantable must at least be ... fit for the ordinary purposes for which such goods are used." The question here was whether a fish bone made the chowder unfit for eating. In the judge's opinion, "the joys of life in New England include the ready availability of fresh fish chowder. We should be prepared to cope with the hazards of fish bones, the occasional presence of which in chowders is, it seems to us, to be anticipated, and which, in the light of a hallowed tradition, do not impair their fitness or merchantability."

CRITICAL THINKING—Legal Consideration *If Webster had made the chowder herself from a recipe that she had found on the Internet today, could she have successfully brought an action against its author for a breach of the implied warranty of merchantability? Explain.*

IMPACT OF THIS CASE ON TODAY'S LAW *This classic case, phrased in memorable language, was an early application of the UCC's implied warranty of merchantability to food products. The case established the rule that consumers should expect to occasionally find elements of food products that are natural to the product (such as fish bones in fish chowder). Courts today still apply this rule.*

Implied Warranty of Fitness for a Particular Purpose The **implied warranty of fitness for a particular purpose** arises in the sale or lease of goods when a seller or lessor (merchant or nonmerchant) knows *both* of the following:

1. The particular purpose for which a buyer or lessee will use the goods.
2. That the buyer or lessee is relying on the skill and judgment of the seller or lessor to select suitable goods [UCC 2–315, 2A–213].

A "particular purpose" of the buyer or lessee differs from the "ordinary purpose for which goods are used" (merchantability). Goods can be merchantable but unfit for a particular purpose. **EXAMPLE 18.25** Cheryl needs a gallon of paint to match the color of her living room walls—a light shade of green. She takes a sample to the local hardware store and requests a gallon of paint of that color. Instead, she is given a gallon of bright blue paint. Here, the salesperson has not breached any warranty of implied merchantability—the bright blue paint is of high quality and suitable for interior walls. The salesperson has breached an implied warranty of fitness for a particular purpose, though, because the paint is not the right color for Cheryl's purpose (to match her living room walls). ■

For this implied warranty to arise, the seller or lessor need not have actual knowledge of the buyer's or lessee's particular purpose. It is sufficient if the seller or lessor "has reason to know" the purpose. The buyer or lessee must have relied on the skill or judgment of the seller or lessor in selecting or furnishing suitable goods, however.

Warranties Implied from Prior Dealings or Trade Custom Implied warranties can also arise (or be excluded or modified) as a result of course of dealing or usage of trade [UCC 2–314(3), 2A–212(3)]. In the absence of evidence to the contrary, when both parties to a sales or lease contract have knowledge of a well-recognized trade custom, the courts will infer that both parties intended for that trade custom to apply to their contract. **EXAMPLE 18.26** Industry-wide custom is to lubricate new cars before they are delivered to buyers. If a dealer fails to lubricate a car, the dealer can be held liable to a buyer for damages resulting from the breach of an implied warranty. (This, of course, would also be negligence on the part of the dealer.) ■

18-4d Overlapping Warranties

Sometimes, two or more warranties are made in a single transaction. Thus, an implied warranty of merchantability, an implied warranty of fitness for a particular purpose, or both can exist in addition to an express warranty. **EXAMPLE 18.27** A sales contract for a new car states that "this car engine is warranted to be free from defects for 36,000 miles or thirty-six months, whichever occurs first." This statement creates an express warranty against all defects, as well as an implied warranty that the car will be fit for normal use. ■

The rule under the UCC is that express and implied warranties are construed as *cumulative* if they are consistent with one another [UCC 2–317, 2A–215]. If the warranties are inconsistent, courts apply the following rules to establish which warranty has priority:

1. *Express* warranties displace inconsistent *implied* warranties, except for implied warranties of fitness for a particular purpose.
2. Samples take precedence over inconsistent general descriptions.
3. Exact or technical specifications displace inconsistent samples or general descriptions.

18-4e Warranty Disclaimers

The UCC generally permits warranties to be disclaimed or limited by specific and unambiguous language, provided that the buyer or lessee is protected from surprise. Because each type

Implied Warranty of Fitness for a Particular Purpose
A warranty that goods sold or leased are fit for the particular purpose for which the buyer or lessee will use the goods.

KNOW THIS
Express and implied warranties do not necessarily displace each other. More than one warranty can cover the same goods in the same transaction.

Does the normal new car sales contract create express warranties or implied warranties or both?

of warranty is created in a different way, the manner in which a seller or lessor can disclaim warranties varies with the type of warranty.

Express Warranties   A seller or lessor can disclaim all oral express warranties by including a statement in the written contract. The disclaimer must be in language that is clear and conspicuous, and is called to the buyer's or lessee's attention [UCC 2–316(1), 2A–214(1)]. This allows the seller or lessor to avoid false allegations that oral warranties were made, and it ensures that only representations made by properly authorized individuals are included in the bargain.

Note, however, that a buyer or lessee must be made aware of any warranty disclaimers or modifications *at the time the contract is formed.* In other words, the seller or lessor cannot modify any warranties or disclaimers made during the bargaining process without the consent of the buyer or lessee.

Implied Warranties   Generally, unless circumstances indicate otherwise, the implied warranties of merchantability and fitness are disclaimed by the expressions "as is," "with all faults," or other similar phrases. Both parties must be able to clearly understand from the language used that there are no implied warranties [UCC 2–316(3)(a), 2A–214(3)(a)].

   CASE EXAMPLE 18.28   Mandy Morningstar advertised a "lovely, eleven-year-old mare" with extensive jumping ability for sale. After examining the horse twice, Sue Hallett contracted to buy it. She signed a contract that described the horse as an eleven-year-old mare that was being sold "as is." Shortly after the purchase, a veterinarian determined that the horse was actually sixteen years old and in no condition for jumping. Hallett stopped payment and tried to return the horse. Morningstar sued for breach of contract.

The court held that the statement in the contract describing the horse as eleven years old constituted an express warranty, which Morningstar had breached. The "as is" clause effectively disclaimed any implied warranties of merchantability and fitness for a particular purpose, such as jumping. Nevertheless, the court ruled that the clause did not disclaim the express warranty concerning the horse's age.[11] ■

Note that some states have laws that forbid "as is" sales. Other states do not allow disclaimers of warranties of merchantability for consumer goods.

Disclaimer of the Implied Warranty of Merchantability.   To specifically disclaim an implied warranty of merchantability, a seller or lessor must mention the word *merchantability* [UCC 2–316(2), 2A–214(2)]. The disclaimer need not be written, but if it is, the writing must be conspicuous [UCC 2–316(2), 2A–214(4)].

Under the UCC, a term or clause is conspicuous when it is written or displayed in such a way that a reasonable person would notice it. Words are conspicuous when they are in capital letters or are in a larger font size or a different color than the surrounding text.

Disclaimer of the Implied Warranty of Fitness.   To specifically disclaim an implied warranty of fitness for a particular purpose, the disclaimer must be in a writing and must be conspicuous. The word *fitness* does not have to be mentioned. It is sufficient if, for example, the disclaimer states, "THERE ARE NO WARRANTIES THAT EXTEND BEYOND THE DESCRIPTION ON THE FACE HEREOF."

Buyer's or Lessee's Examination or Refusal to Inspect.   If a buyer or lessee examines the goods (or a sample or model) as fully as desired, *there is no implied warranty with respect to defects that a reasonable examination would reveal or defects that are found on examination* [UCC 2–316(3)(b), 2A–214(2)(b)]. Also, if a buyer or lessee refuses to examine the goods on the seller's or lessor's request that he or she do so, there is no implied warranty with respect to reasonably evident defects.

---

11. *Morningstar v. Hallett,* 858 A.2d 125 (Pa.Super.Ct. 2004).

EXAMPLE 18.29 Janna buys a table at Gershwin's Home Store. No express warranties are made. Gershwin asks Janna to inspect the table before buying it, but she refuses. Had Janna inspected the table, she would have noticed that one of its legs was obviously cracked, which made it unstable. Janna takes the table home and sets a lamp on it. The table later collapses, and the lamp starts a fire that causes significant damage. Janna normally will not be able to hold Gershwin's liable for breach of the warranty of merchantability, because she refused to examine the table as Gershwin requested. Janna therefore assumed the risk that the table was defective. ◼

18–4f Lemon Laws

Purchasers of defective automobiles—called "lemons"—may pursue remedies in addition to those provided by the UCC under state *lemon laws.* Basically, state lemon laws provide remedies to consumers who buy automobiles that repeatedly fail to meet standards of quality and performance because they are "lemons."

Although lemon laws vary by state, typically they apply to automobiles under warranty that are defective in a way that significantly affects their value or use. Lemon laws do not necessarily cover used-car purchases (unless the car is covered by a manufacturer's extended warranty) or vehicles that are leased.

Generally, the seller or manufacturer of the automobile is given a number of opportunities to remedy the defect (usually four). If the seller fails to cure the problem despite a reasonable number of attempts (as specified by state law), the buyer is entitled to a new car, replacement of defective parts, or return of all consideration paid.

Typically, buyers must submit their complaint to the arbitration program specified in the manufacturer's warranty before taking the case to court. Buyers who prevail in a lemon-law dispute may also be entitled to reimbursement of their attorneys' fees.

iStockPhoto.com/piahovak

If a buyer refuses to inspect a new table, and it has an obviously cracked leg, can the buyer later argue that the seller breached the warranty of merchantability?

Reviewing . . . Performance and Breach of Sales and Lease Contracts

GFI, Inc., a Hong Kong company, makes audio decoder chips, one of the essential components used in the manufacture of MP3 players. Egan Electronics contracts with GFI to buy 10,000 chips on an installment contract, with 2,500 chips to be shipped every three months, F.O.B. Hong Kong via Air Express. At the time for the first delivery, GFI delivers only 2,400 chips but explains to Egan that even though the shipment is 4 percent short, the chips are of a higher quality than those specified in the contract and are worth 5 percent more than the contract price. Egan accepts the shipment and pays GFI the contract price. At the time for the second shipment, GFI makes a shipment identical to the first. Egan again accepts and pays for the chips. At the time for the third shipment, GFI ships 2,400 of the same chips, but this time GFI sends them via Hong Kong Air instead of Air Express. While in transit, the chips are destroyed. When it is time for the fourth shipment, GFI again sends 2,400 chips, but this time Egan rejects the chips without explanation. Using the information presented in the chapter, answer the following questions.

1. Did GFI have a legitimate reason to expect that Egan would accept the fourth shipment? Why or why not?

2. Does the substitution of carriers for the third shipment constitute a breach of the contract by GFI? Explain.

3. Suppose that the silicon used for the chips becomes unavailable for a period of time and that GFI cannot manufacture enough chips to fulfill the contract but does ship as many as it can to Egan. Under what doctrine might a court release GFI from further performance of the contract?

4. Under the UCC, does Egan have a right to reject the fourth shipment? Why or why not?

DEBATE THIS

◼ If a contract specifies a particular carrier, then the shipper must use that carrier or be in breach of the contract—no exceptions should ever be allowed.

Key Terms

Chapter Summary: Performance and Breach of Sales and Lease Contracts

	PERFORMANCE OBLIGATIONS
Obligations of the Seller or Lessor	1. The seller or lessor must tender *conforming* goods to the buyer or lessee. Tender must take place at a *reasonable hour* and in a *reasonable manner.* Under the perfect tender doctrine, the seller or lessor must tender goods that conform exactly to the terms of the contract [UCC 2–503(1), 2A–508(1)].
	2. If the seller or lessor tenders nonconforming goods prior to the performance date and the buyer or lessee rejects them, the seller or lessor may *cure* (repair or replace the goods) within the contract time for performance [UCC 2–508(1), 2A–513(1)]. If the seller or lessor had reasonable grounds to believe that the buyer or lessee would accept the tendered goods, on the buyer's or lessee's rejection the seller or lessor has a reasonable time to substitute conforming goods without liability [UCC 2–508(2), 2A–513(2)].
	3. If the agreed-on means of delivery becomes impracticable or unavailable, the seller must substitute an alternative means (such as a different carrier) if one is available [UCC 2–614(1)].
	4. If a seller or lessor tenders nonconforming goods in any one installment under an installment contract, the buyer or lessee may reject the installment only if its value is substantially impaired and cannot be cured. The entire installment contract is breached only when one or more nonconforming installments *substantially* impair the value of the *whole* contract [UCC 2–612, 2A–510].
	5. When performance becomes commercially impracticable owing to circumstances that were not foreseeable when the contract was formed, the perfect tender rule no longer holds [UCC 2–615, 2A–405].
Obligations of the Buyer or Lessee	1. On tender of delivery by the seller or lessor, the buyer or lessee must pay for the goods at the time and place the goods are *received,* unless the sale is made on credit. Payment may be made by any method generally acceptable in the commercial world unless the seller demands cash [UCC 2–310, 2–511]. In lease contracts, the lessee must make lease payments in accordance with the contract [UCC 2A–516(1)].
	2. Unless otherwise agreed, the buyer or lessee has an absolute right to inspect the goods before acceptance [UCC 2–513(1), 2A–515(1)].
	3. The buyer or lessee can manifest acceptance of delivered goods expressly in words or by conduct, or by failing to reject the goods after a reasonable period of time following inspection or after having had a reasonable opportunity to inspect them [UCC 2–606(1), 2A–515(1)]. A buyer will be deemed to have accepted goods if he or she performs any act inconsistent with the seller's ownership [UCC 2–606(1)(c)].
	4. The buyer or lessee can make a partial acceptance if some of the goods do not conform to the contract and the seller or lessor failed to cure [UCC 2–601(c), 2A–509(1)].
Anticipatory Repudiation	If, before the time for performance, one party clearly indicates to the other an intention not to perform, under UCC 2–610 and 2A–402, the aggrieved party may do the following:
	1. Await performance by the repudiating party for a commercially reasonable time.
	2. Resort to any remedy for breach.
	3. In either situation, suspend performance.
	REMEDIES FOR BREACH
Remedies of the Seller or Lessor	1. *When the goods are in the possession of the seller or lessor*—The seller or lessor may do the following:
	a. Cancel the contract [UCC 2–703(f), 2A–523(1)(a)].
	b. Withhold delivery [UCC 2–703(a), 2A–523(1)(c)].
	c. Resell or dispose of the goods [UCC 2–703(d), 2–706(1), 2A–523(1)(e), 2A–527(1)].
	d. Sue to recover the purchase price or lease payments due [UCC 2–709(1), 2A–529(1)].
	e. Sue to recover damages [UCC 2–708, 2A–528].
	2. *When the goods are in transit*—The seller or lessor may stop the carrier or bailee from delivering the goods under certain conditions [UCC 2–705, 2A–526].
	3. *When the goods are in the possession of the buyer or lessee*—The seller or lessor may do the following:
	a. Sue to recover the purchase price or lease payments due [UCC 2–709(1), 2A–529(1)].
	b. Reclaim the goods. A seller may reclaim goods received by an insolvent buyer if the demand is made within ten days of receipt (reclaiming goods excludes all other remedies) [UCC 2–702(2)]. A lessor may repossess goods if the lessee is in default [UCC 2A–525(2)].

Remedies of the Buyer or Lessee	1. *When the seller or lessor refuses to deliver the goods*—The buyer or lessee may do the following:
	    a. Cancel the contract [UCC 2–711(1), 2A–508(1)(a)].
	    b. Recover the goods if the seller or lessor becomes insolvent and the goods are identified to the contract [UCC 2–502, 2A–522].
	    c. Obtain specific performance (when the goods are unique and the remedy at law is inadequate) [UCC 2–716(1), 2A–521(1)].
	    d. Obtain cover [UCC 2–712, 2A–518].
	    e. Replevy the goods (if cover is unavailable) [UCC 2–716(3), 2A–521(3)].
	    f. Sue to recover damages [UCC 2–713, 2A–519].
	2. *When the seller or lessor delivers or tenders delivery of nonconforming goods*—The buyer or lessee may do the following:
	    a. Reject the goods [UCC 2–601, 2A–509].
	    b. Revoke acceptance if the nonconformity *substantially* impairs the value of the unit or lot and if one of the following factors is present:
	        (1) Acceptance was predicated on the reasonable assumption that the nonconformity would be cured, and it was not cured within a reasonable time [UCC 2–608(1)(a), 2A–517(1)(a)].
	        (2) The buyer or lessee did not discover the nonconformity before acceptance, either because it was difficult to discover before acceptance or because the seller's or lessor's assurance that the goods were conforming kept the buyer or lessee from inspecting the goods [UCC 2–608(1)(b), 2A–517(1)(b)].
	    c. Accept the goods and recover damages [UCC 2–607, 2–714, 2–717, 2A–519].

Limitation of Remedies	1. Remedies may be limited in sales or lease contracts by agreement of the parties. If the contract states that a remedy is exclusive, then that is the sole remedy unless the remedy fails in its essential purpose. Sellers and lessors can also limit the rights of buyers and lessees to consequential damages unless the limitation is unconscionable [UCC 2–719, 2A–503]. 2. The UCC has a four-year statute of limitations for actions involving breach of contract. By agreement, the parties to a sales or lease contract can reduce this period to not less than one year, but they cannot extend it beyond four years [UCC 2–725(1), 2A–506(1)].
	WARRANTIES
Warranties of Title	Under the UCC, three types of title warranties can automatically arise in sales and lease contracts. 1. In most sales, sellers warrant that they have good and valid title to the goods sold and that transfer of the title is rightful [UCC 2–312(1)(a)]. 2. The seller or lessor warrants that the goods are free of any encumbrances, or liens, of which the buyer or lessee is unaware [UCC 2–312(1)(b), 2A–211(1)]. 3. When the seller or lessor is a merchant, he or she warrants that the buyer or lessee takes the goods free of infringements [UCC 2–312(3), 2A–211(2)].
Express Warranties	Under the UCC, an express warranty arises under the UCC when a seller or lessor provides, as part of the basis of the bargain, any of the following [UCC 2–313, 2A–210]: 1. An affirmation or promise of fact. 2. A description of the goods. 3. A sample shown as conforming to the contract goods.
Implied Warranty of Merchantability	When a seller or lessor is a merchant who deals in goods of the kind sold or leased, the seller or lessor warrants that the goods sold or leased are properly packaged and labeled, are of proper quality, and are reasonably fit for the ordinary purposes for which such goods are used [UCC 2–314, 2A–212].
Implied Warranty of Fitness for a Particular Purpose	Arises when the buyer's or lessee's purpose or use is expressly or impliedly known by the seller or lessor, and the buyer or lessee purchases or leases the goods in reliance on the seller's or lessor's selection [UCC 2–315, 2A–213].
Warranties Implied from Prior Dealings or Trade Custom	Implied warranties can arise as a result of course of dealing or usage of trade [UCC 2–314(3), 2A–212(3)].
Overlapping Warranties	The UCC construes warranties as cumulative if they are consistent with each other. If warranties are inconsistent, then express warranties take precedence over implied warranties, except for the implied warranty of fitness for a particular purpose. Also, samples take precedence over general descriptions, and exact or technical specifications displace inconsistent samples or general descriptions.
Warranty Disclaimers	1. Express warranties can be disclaimed if the disclaimer is written in clear language, is conspicuous, and is called to the buyer's or lessee's attention at the time the contract is formed. 2. A disclaimer of the implied warranty of merchantability must specifically mention the word *merchantability*. The disclaimer need not be in writing, but if it is written, it must be conspicuous. 3. A disclaimer of the implied warranty of fitness *must* be in writing and must be conspicuous, though it need not mention the word *fitness*.

Issue Spotters

1. Country Fruit Stand orders eighty cases of peaches from Down Home Farms. Without stating a reason, Down Home untimely delivers thirty cases instead of eighty. Does Country have the right to reject the shipment? Explain. (See *Performance Obligations*.)
2. Brite Images, Inc. (BI), agrees to sell Catalog Corporation (CC) five thousand posters of celebrities, to be delivered on May 1. On April 1, BI repudiates the contract. CC informs BI that it expects delivery. Can CC sue BI without waiting until May 1? Why or why not? (See *Anticipatory Repudiation*.)

—**Check your answers to the *Issue Spotters* against the answers provided in Appendix D at the end of this text.**

Learning Objectives Check

1. What are the respective obligations of the parties under a contract for the sale or lease of goods?
2. What is the perfect tender rule? What are some important exceptions to this rule that apply to sales and lease contracts?
3. What options are available to the nonbreaching party when the other party to a sales or lease contract repudiates the contract prior to the time for performance?
4. What remedies are available to a seller or lessor when the buyer or lessee breaches the contract?
5. What implied warranties arise under the UCC?

—**Answers to the even-numbered *Learning Objectives Check* questions can be found in Appendix E at the end of this text.**

Business Scenarios and Case Problems

18–1. Remedies. Genix, Inc., has contracted to sell Larson five hundred washing machines of a certain model at list price. Genix is to ship the goods on or before December 1. Genix produces one thousand washing machines of this model but has not yet prepared Larson's shipment. On November 1, Larson repudiates the contract. Discuss the remedies available to Genix in this situation. (See *Remedies for Breach*.)

18–2. Anticipatory Repudiation. Moore contracted in writing to sell her 2010 Hyundai Santa Fe to Hammer for $16,500. Moore agreed to deliver the car on Wednesday, and Hammer promised to pay the $16,500 on the following Friday. On Tuesday, Hammer informed Moore that he would not be buying the car after all. By Friday, Hammer had changed his mind again and tendered $16,500 to Moore. Although Moore had not sold the car to another party, she refused the tender and refused to deliver. Hammer claimed that Moore had breached their contract. Moore contended that Hammer's repudiation had released her from her duty to perform under the contract. Who is correct, and why? (See *Anticipatory Repudiation*.)

18–3. Right to Recover Damages. Woodridge USA Properties, L.P., bought eighty-seven commercial truck trailers from Southeast Trailer Mart, Inc. (STM). Gerald McCarty, an independent sales agent who arranged the deal, showed Woodridge the documents of title. The documents did not indicate that Woodridge was the buyer. Woodridge then asked McCarty to sell the trailers, and within three months, they were sold. McCarty did not give the proceeds to Woodridge, however. Woodridge—without mentioning the title documents—asked STM to refund the contract price. STM refused. Does Woodridge have a right to recover damages from STM? Explain. [*Woodridge USA Properties, L.P. v. Southeast Trailer Mart, Inc.*, 2011 WL 303204 (11th Cir. 2011)] (See *Remedies for Breach*.)

18–4. Spotlight on Apple—Implied Warranties. Alan Vitt purchased an iBook G4 laptop computer from Apple, Inc. Shortly after the one-year warranty expired, the laptop stopped working due to a weakness in the product manufacture. Vitt sued Apple, arguing that the laptop should have lasted "at least a couple of years," which Vitt believed was a reasonable consumer expectation for a laptop. Vitt claimed that Apple's descriptions of the laptop as "durable," "rugged," "reliable," and "high performance" were affirmative statements concerning the quality and performance of the laptop, which Apple did not meet. How should the court rule? Why? [*Vitt v. Apple Computer, Inc.*, 2012 WL 627702 (9th Cir. 2011)] (See *Warranties*.)

18–5. Business Case Problem with Sample Answer—Nonconforming Goods. Padma Paper Mills, Ltd., converts waste paper into usable paper. In 2007, Padma entered into a contract with Universal Exports, Inc., under which Universal Exports certified that it would ship white envelope cuttings to Padma in exchange for a payment of $131,000. When the shipment arrived, however, Padma discovered that Universal Exports had sent multicolored paper plates and other brightly colored paper products. Padma accepted the goods but notified Universal Exports that they did not conform to the contract. Can Padma recover even though it accepted the goods knowing that they were nonconforming? If so, how? [*Padma Paper Mills, Ltd. v. Universal Exports, Inc.*, 34 Misc.3d 1236(A) (N.Y.Sup. 2012)] (See *Remedies for Breach*.)

—For a sample answer to Problem 18–5, go to Appendix F at the end of this text.

18–6. Implied Warranties. Bariven, S.A., agreed to buy 26,000 metric tons of powdered milk for $123.5 million from Absolute Trading Corp. to be delivered in shipments from China to Venezuela. After the first three shipments, China halted dairy exports due to the presence of melamine in some products. Absolute assured Bariven that its milk was safe, and when China resumed dairy exports, Absolute delivered sixteen more shipments. Tests of samples of the milk revealed that it contained dangerous levels of melamine. Did Absolute breach any implied warranties? Discuss. [*Absolute Trading Corp. v. Bariven S.A.*, 2013 WL 49735 (11th Cir. 2013)] (See *Warranties*.)

18–7. The Right of Rejection. Erb Poultry, Inc., is a distributor of fresh poultry products in Lima, Ohio. CEME, LLC, does business as Bank Shots, a restaurant in Trotwood, Ohio. CEME ordered chicken wings and "dippers" from Erb, which were delivered and for which CEME issued a check in payment. A few days later, CEME stopped payment on the check. When contacted by Erb, CEME alleged that the products were beyond their freshness date, mangled, spoiled, and the wrong sizes. CEME did not provide any evidence to support the claims or arrange to return the products. Is CEME entitled to a full refund of the amount paid for the chicken? Explain. [*Erb Poultry, Inc. v. CEME, LLC*, 20 N.E.3d 1228 (Ohio App. 2 Dist. 2014)] (See *Remedies for Breach*.)

18–8. Remedies for Breach. Reefpoint Brewhouse in Racine, Wisconsin, contracted with Forman Awnings and Construction, LLC, for the fabrication and installation of an awning system over an outdoor seating area. After the system was complete, Reefpoint expressed concerns about the workmanship but did not give Forman a chance to make repairs. The brewhouse used the awning for two months and then had it removed so that siding on the building could be replaced. The parties disagreed about whether cracked and broken welds observed after the removal of the system were due to shoddy workmanship. Reefpoint paid only $400 on the contract price of $8,161. Can Reefpoint rescind the contract and obtain a return of its $400? Is Forman entitled to recover the difference between Reefpoint's payment and the contract price? Discuss. [*Forman Awnings and Construction LLC v. LO Ventures, LLC*, 2015 WL 248034 (2015)] (See *Remedies for Breach*.)

18–9. A Question of Ethics—Lemon Laws. Randal Schweiger bought a 2008 Kia Spectra EX from Kia Motors America, Inc., for his stepdaughter, April Kirichkow. The cost was $17,231, plus sales tax and other charges, and Schweiger financed the entire amount. April soon began having trouble starting the car. The Kia dealership replaced various parts of the motor several times, but was unable to fix the problem. Schweiger sought a refund under the state's lemon law. When Schweiger and Kia could not agree on the amount, Schweiger filed a suit in a Wisconsin state court against Kia. The court ruled in Schweiger's favor, and Kia appealed. [*Schweiger v. Kia Motors America, Inc.*, 347 Wis.2d 550, 830 N.W.2d 723 (Wis.App. 2013)] (See *Warranties*.)

1. Kia offered a refund of $3,306.24. Should this offer bar Schweiger's claim for a refund? Why or why not?

2. Schweiger claimed that Kia's offer did not include the $1,301 cost of a service contract that he purchased with the car. Kia argued that the amount still owed on the purchase, $13,060.16—which Schweiger agreed was the correct amount—"would by definition refund the cost of the service contract." The court found "no logical basis" for this argument. Is it ethical for a party to argue a position for which there is no logical basis? Discuss.

Critical Thinking and Writing Assignments

18–10. Business Law Writing. Suppose that you are a collector of antique cars and you need to purchase spare parts for a 1938 engine. These parts are not made anymore and are scarce. You discover that Beem has the spare parts that you need. You contract with Beem to buy the parts and agree to pay 50 percent of the purchase price in advance. You send the payment on May 1, and Beem receives it on May 2. On May 3, Beem, having found another buyer willing to pay substantially more for the parts, informs you that he will not deliver as contracted. That same day, you learn that Beem is insolvent. Write three paragraphs fully discussing any possible remedies that would enable you to take possession of the parts. (See *Remedies for Breach*.)

18–11. Business Law Critical Thinking Group Assignment. Kodiak agrees to sell one thousand espresso machines to Lin to be delivered on May 1. Due to a strike during the last week of April, there is a temporary shortage of delivery vehicles. Kodiak can deliver the espresso makers two hundred at a time over a period of ten days, with the first delivery on May 1. (See *Performance Obligations*.)

1. The first group will determine if Kodiak has the right to deliver the goods in five lots. What happens if Lin objects to delivery in lots?

2. A second group will analyze whether the doctrine of commercial impracticability applies to this scenario and, if it does, what the result will be.

19

LEARNING OBJECTIVES

The five Learning Objectives *below are designed to help improve your understanding of the chapter. After reading this chapter, you should be able to answer the following questions:*

1. What requirements must an instrument meet to be negotiable?

2. How does the negotiation of order instruments differ from the negotiation of bearer instruments?

3. What are the requirements for attaining the status of a holder in due course (HDC)?

4. What is the difference between signature liability and warranty liability?

5. Name four defenses that can be used against an ordinary holder but are not effective against an HDC.

Negotiable Instrument A signed writing (record) that contains an unconditional promise or order to pay an exact sum on demand or at a specified future time to a specific person or order, or to bearer.

iStockPhoto.com/bluestocking

Negotiable Instruments

Most commercial transactions would be inconceivable without negotiable instruments. A **negotiable instrument** is a signed writing that contains an unconditional promise or order to pay an exact amount, either on demand or at a specified future time. Because negotiable instruments originally were (and often still are) paper documents, they are sometimes referred to as *commercial paper.*

As indicated in the chapter-opening quotation, paper was not fully accepted as a substitute for gold or silver in commerce for "many generations." Today, people are experiencing a similar transition as electronic records substitute more and more for paper documents.

A negotiable instrument can function as a substitute for cash or as an extension of credit. For a negotiable instrument to operate *practically* as either a substitute for cash or a credit device, or both, it is essential that the instrument be *easily transferable without danger of being uncollectible.* Each rule described in this chapter can be examined in light of this essential function of negotiable instruments.

> "It took many generations for people to feel comfortable accepting paper in lieu of gold or silver."
>
> **ALAN GREENSPAN**
> 1926–PRESENT
> (CHAIR OF THE BOARD OF GOVERNORS OF THE FEDERAL RESERVE SYSTEM, 1987–2006)

19-1 Types of Negotiable Instruments

The UCC specifies four types of negotiable instruments: *drafts, checks, promissory notes,* and *certificates of deposit* (CDs). These instruments, which are summarized briefly in Exhibit 19–1, are frequently divided into the two classifications that we will discuss in the following subsections: *orders to pay* (drafts and checks) and *promises to pay* (promissory notes and CDs).

Negotiable instruments may also be classified as either demand instruments or time instruments. A *demand instrument* is payable on demand. In other words, it is payable immediately after it is issued and for a reasonable period of time thereafter. A *time instrument* is payable at a future date.

Note that Section 3–104(b) of the Uniform Commercial Code (UCC) defines *instrument* as a "negotiable instrument."[1] For that reason, whenever the term *instrument* is used in this book, it refers to a negotiable instrument.

19-1a Drafts and Checks (Orders to Pay)

A **draft** is an unconditional written order to pay rather than a promise to pay. Drafts involve three parties. The party creating the draft (the **drawer**) orders another party (the **drawee**) to pay funds, usually to a third party (the **payee**). The most common type of draft is a check, but drafts other than checks may be used in commercial transactions.

Draft Any instrument drawn on a drawee that orders the drawee to pay a certain amount of funds, usually to a third party (the payee), on demand or at a definite future time.

Time Drafts versus Sight Drafts
A *time draft* is payable at a definite future time. A *sight draft* (or demand draft) is payable on sight—that is, when it is presented to the drawee (usually a bank or financial institution) for payment. A draft can be both a time and a sight draft. Such a draft is payable at a stated time after sight (a draft that states it is payable ninety days after sight, for instance).

Exhibit 19–2 shows a typical time draft. For the drawee to be obligated to honor (pay) the order, the drawee must be obligated to the drawer either by agreement or through a debtor-creditor relationship. **EXAMPLE 19.1** On January 16, OurTown Real Estate orders $1,000 worth of office supplies from Eastman Supply Company, with payment due in ninety days. Also on January 16, OurTown sends Eastman a draft drawn on its account with the First National Bank of Whiteacre as payment. In this scenario, the drawer is OurTown, the drawee is OurTown's bank (First National Bank of Whiteacre), and the payee is Eastman Supply Company. ■

Drawer The party that initiates a draft (such as a check), thereby ordering the drawee to pay.

Drawee The party that is ordered to pay a draft or check. With a check, a bank or a financial institution is always the drawee.

Payee A person to whom an instrument is made payable.

Acceptances
A drawee's written promise to pay a draft when it comes due is called an **acceptance.** Usually, the drawee accepts the instrument by writing the word *accepted* on its face, with a signature and a date. A drawee who has accepted an instrument becomes an **acceptor.**

A *trade acceptance* is a type of draft commonly used in the sale of goods. In this draft, the seller is both the drawer and the payee. The buyer to whom credit is extended is the

Acceptance In negotiable instruments law, a drawee's signed agreement to pay a draft when it is presented.

Acceptor A drawee that accepts, or promises to pay, an instrument when it is presented later for payment.

---

1. Note that all of the references to Article 3 of the UCC in this chapter are to the 1990 version of Article 3, which has been adopted by nearly every state.

Exhibit 19–1 Basic Types of Negotiable Instruments

INSTRUMENTS	CHARACTERISTICS	PARTIES
ORDERS TO PAY:		
Draft	An order by one person to another person or to bearer [UCC 3–104(e)].	Drawer—The person who signs or makes the order to pay [UCC 3–103(a)(3)].
Check	A draft drawn on a bank and payable on demand [UCC 3–104(f)]. (With certain types of checks, such as cashier's checks, the bank is both the drawer and the drawee.)	Drawee—The person to whom the order to pay is made [UCC 3–103(a)(2)]. Payee—The person to whom payment is ordered.
PROMISES TO PAY:		
Promissory note	A promise by one party to pay funds to another party or to bearer [UCC 3–104(e)].	Maker—The person who promises to pay [UCC 3–103(a)(5)]. Payee—The person to whom the promise is made.
Certificate of deposit	A note issued by a bank acknowledging a deposit of funds and made payable to the holder of the note [UCC 3–104(j)].	

Exhibit 19–2 A Typical Time Draft

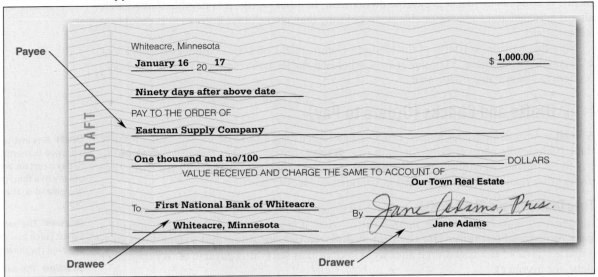

> "The two most beautiful words in the English language are 'check enclosed.'"
>
> **DOROTHY PARKER**
> 1893–1967
> (AMERICAN AUTHOR AND POET)

Check A draft drawn by a drawer ordering the drawee bank or financial institution to pay a certain amount of funds to the payee on demand.

Promissory Note A written promise made by one person (the maker) to pay a fixed amount of funds to another person (the payee or a subsequent holder) on demand or on a specified date.

Maker One who promises to pay a fixed amount of funds to the holder of a promissory note or a certificate of deposit (CD).

drawee. **EXAMPLE 19.2** Jackson Street Bistro buys its restaurant supplies from Osaka Industries. When Jackson requests supplies, Osaka creates a draft ordering Jackson to pay Osaka for the supplies within ninety days. Jackson accepts the draft by signing its face, which obligates it to make the payment. This is a trade acceptance, and Osaka can sell it to a third party at any time before the payment is due. ▇

A *banker's acceptance* is a similar instrument that orders the buyer's bank to pay. Banker's acceptances are often used in international trade.

Checks As mentioned, the most commonly used type of draft is a **check.** The writer of the check is the drawer, the bank on which the check is drawn is the drawee, and the person to whom the check is payable is the payee. Checks are demand instruments because they are payable on demand. Checks will be discussed more fully in the next chapter, but it should be noted here that with certain types of checks, such as *cashier's checks,* the bank is both the drawer and the drawee.

19–1b Promissory Notes (Promises to Pay)

A **promissory note** is a written promise made by one person (the **maker** of the promise to pay) to another (usually a payee). A promissory note, which is often referred to simply as a *note,* can be made payable at a definite time or on demand. It can name a specific payee or merely be payable to bearer (bearer instruments will be discussed later in this chapter). **EXAMPLE 19.3** On April 30, Laurence and Margaret Roberts sign a writing unconditionally promising to pay "to the order of" the First National Bank of Whiteacre $3,000 (with 5 percent interest) on or before June 29. This writing is a promissory note. ▇ A typical promissory note is shown in Exhibit 19–3.

Promissory notes are used in a variety of credit transactions. Often, a promissory note will carry the name of the transaction involved. A note secured by personal property, such as an automobile, is referred to as a *collateral note* because property pledged as security for the satisfaction of a debt is called *collateral.*[2] A note payable in installments, such as installment payments for a large-screen television over a twelve-month period, is called an *installment note.*

---

2. To minimize the risk of loss when making a loan, a creditor often requires the debtor to provide some *collateral,* or security, beyond a promise that the debt will be repaid. When this security takes the form of personal property (such as a motor vehicle), the creditor has an interest in the property known as a *security interest.*

Exhibit 19–3 A Typical Promissory Note

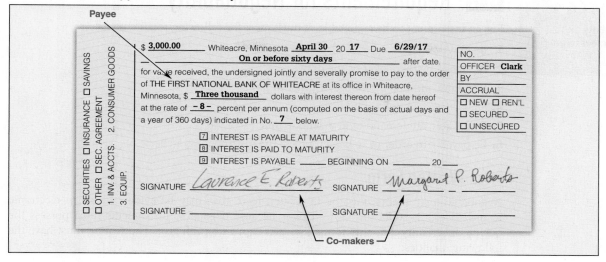

19-1c Certificates of Deposit (Promises to Pay)

A **certificate of deposit (CD)** is a type of note issued when a party deposits funds with a bank that the bank promises to repay, with interest, on a certain date [UCC 3–104(j)]. The bank is the maker of the note, and the depositor is the payee. **EXAMPLE 19.4** On February 15, Sara Levin deposits $5,000 with the First National Bank of Whiteacre. The bank issues a CD, in which it promises to repay the $5,000, plus 1.85 percent annual interest, on August 15. ▪

Because CDs are time deposits, the purchaser-payee typically is not allowed to withdraw the funds before the date of maturity (except in limited circumstances, such as disability or death). If a payee wants to access the funds prior to the maturity date, he or she can sell (negotiate) the CD to a third party. Certificates of deposit in small denominations (for amounts up to $100,000) are often sold by savings and loan associations, savings banks, commercial banks, and credit unions. Exhibit 19–4 shows an example of a small CD.

Certificate of Deposit (CD)
A note issued by a bank in which the bank acknowledges the receipt of funds from a party and promises to repay that amount, with interest, to the party on a certain date.

Exhibit 19–4 A Sample Certificate of Deposit

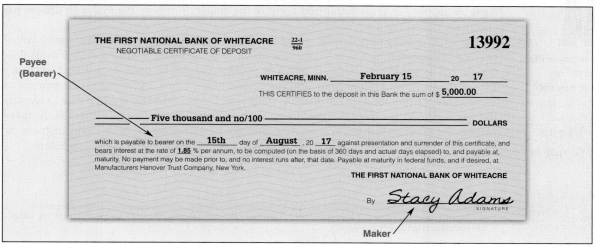

19–2 Requirements for Negotiability

For an instrument to be negotiable, it must meet the following requirements:

1. Be in writing.

2. Be signed by the maker or the drawer.

3. Be an unconditional promise or order to pay.

4. State a fixed amount of money.

5. Be payable on demand or at a definite time.

6. Be payable to order or to bearer, unless the instrument is a check.

19–2a Written Form

Negotiable instruments must be in written form (but may be evidenced by an electronic record) [UCC 3–103(a)(6), (9)].[3] This is because negotiable instruments must possess the quality of certainty that only formal, written expression can give. The writing must have the following qualities:

1. The writing must be on material that lends itself to *permanence*. Instruments carved in blocks of ice or recorded on other impermanent surfaces would not qualify as negotiable instruments. **EXAMPLE 19.5** Suzanne writes in the sand, "I promise to pay $500 to the order of Jack." This cannot be a negotiable instrument, because it lacks permanence. ■

2. The writing must also have *portability*. Although the UCC does not explicitly state this requirement, if an instrument is not movable, it obviously cannot meet the requirement that it be freely transferable. **EXAMPLE 19.6** Charles writes on the side of a cow, "I promise to pay $500 to the order of Jason." Technically, this would meet the requirements of a negotiable instrument—except for portability. A cow cannot easily be transferred in the ordinary course of business. Thus, the "instrument" is nonnegotiable. ■

The UCC nevertheless gives considerable leeway as to what can be a negotiable instrument. Courts have found checks and notes written on napkins, menus, tablecloths, shirts, and a variety of other materials to be negotiable.

19–2b Signatures

For an instrument to be negotiable, it must be signed by (1) the maker, if it is a note or a certificate of deposit, or (2) the drawer, if it is a draft or a check [UCC 3–103(a)(3)]. If a person signs an instrument as an authorized agent of the maker or drawer, the maker or drawer has effectively signed the instrument.

The UCC is quite lenient with regard to what constitutes a signature. Nearly any symbol executed or adopted by a person with the intent to authenticate a written or electronic document can be a signature [UCC 1–201(37)]. A signature can be made by a device, such as a rubber stamp, or by a thumbprint, and can consist of any name, including a trade name, or a word, mark, or symbol [UCC 3–401(b)]. If necessary, parol evidence is admissible to identify the signer. The location of the signature on the document is unimportant, although the usual place is the lower right-hand corner. A *handwritten* statement on the body of the instrument, such as "I, Jerome Garcia, promise to pay Elena Greer," is sufficient to act as a signature.

Would a promise to pay written on the side of this calf be negotiable? Why or why not?

iStockPhoto.com/Karpiyon

"I'm a writer. I write checks. They're not very good."

WENDY LIEBMAN
1961–PRESENT
(AMERICAN COMEDIAN)

---

3. Under the Uniform Electronic Transactions Act (UETA), an electronic record may be sufficient to constitute a negotiable instrument (see UETA Section 16). A small number of states have also adopted amendments to Article 3 that explicitly authorize electronic negotiable instruments.

Although there are almost no limitations on the manner in which a signature can be made, one should be careful about receiving an instrument that has been signed in an unusual way. Oddities on a negotiable instrument can open the door to disputes and lead to litigation. Furthermore, an unusual signature clearly decreases the *marketability* of an instrument because it creates uncertainty.

PREVENTING LEGAL DISPUTES

19-2c Unconditional Promise or Order to Pay

For an instrument to be negotiable, it must contain an express order or promise to pay. The terms of the promise or order must be included in the writing on the face of the instrument. Furthermore, these terms must be unconditional.

Promise The UCC requires that a *promise* be an affirmative (express) undertaking [UCC 3–103(a)(9)]. A mere acknowledgment of a debt, such as an I.O.U., might logically *imply* a promise, but it is *not* sufficient under the UCC. If such words as "to be paid on demand" or "due on demand" are added to an I.O.U., however, the need for an express promise to pay is satisfied.[4]

EXAMPLE 19.7 Kyra executes a promissory note that says "I promise to pay Alvarez $1,000 on demand for the purchase of these goods." These words satisfy the promise-to-pay requirement. ■

Order An *order* is associated with three-party instruments, such as checks, drafts, and trade acceptances. An order directs a third party to pay the instrument as drawn. In the typical check, for instance, the word "pay" (to the order of a payee) is a command to the drawee bank to pay the check when presented—thus, it is an order. "Pay" signifies an order even if it is accompanied by courteous words, as in "Please pay" or "Kindly pay." (In contrast, "I wish you would pay" is not an order.) An order may be addressed to one party or to more than one party, either jointly ("to A *and* B") or alternatively ("to A *or* B") [UCC 3–103(a)(6)].

Unconditionality of Promise or Order Only *unconditional* promises or orders can be negotiable [UCC 3–106(a)]. A promise or order is conditional (and therefore *not* negotiable) if it states *any* of the following:

1. An express condition to payment.

2. That the promise or order is subject to or governed by another writing or record.

3. That the rights or obligations with respect to the promise or order are stated in another writing or record.

A mere reference to another writing, however, does not make the promise or order conditional [UCC 3–106(a)]. For instance, the words "As per contract" or "This debt arises from the sale of goods X and Y" do not render an instrument nonnegotiable. Similarly, a statement in the instrument that payment can be made only out of a particular fund or source will not render the instrument nonnegotiable [UCC 3–106(b)(ii)].

EXAMPLE 19.8 The terms of Biggs's note state that payment will be made out of the proceeds of next year's cotton crop. This does not make the note nonnegotiable. The payee of such a note, however, may find the note commercially unacceptable and refuse to take it. ■

iStockPhoto.com/PeterMuller

If a note indicates that payment will be made out of the proceeds of the following year's cotton crop, is that note still negotiable?

---

4. A certificate of deposit (CD) is an exception in this respect. A CD does not have to contain an express promise, because the bank's acknowledgment of the deposit and the other terms of the instrument clearly indicate a promise by the bank to repay the funds [UCC 3–104(j)].

In the following case, two notes signed to finance the purchase of a pair of alpacas contained references to the underlying contracts. The court had to determine whether the notes qualified as negotiable instruments.

CASE 19.1

Alpacas of America, LLC v. Groome

Court of Appeals of Washington, Division 2, 317 P.3d 1103 (2014).

FACTS Sam and Odalis Groome entered into two contracts with Alpacas of America, LLC (AOA) to buy a pair of alpacas—"Phashion Model" and "Black Thunder's Midnight." To finance the purchases, the buyers signed two notes, one for $18,750 and the other for $20,250. Each note included a reference to a contract, outlined a payment schedule, and contained a security agreement that gave AOA an interest in the alpacas. Within a few months, the Groomes stopped making payments.

More than four years later, AOA filed a suit in a Washington state court against the Groomes to collect the unpaid amounts. The court ruled that the notes were not negotiable instruments but were part of the sales contracts. It thus applied the four-year statute of limitations on contract actions in UCC Article 2 to dismiss the suit. AOA appealed, arguing that the notes were negotiable and thus fell within the six-year limit on actions to collect under UCC Article 3.

ISSUE Were the notes negotiable despite containing references to the underlying contracts?

DECISION Yes. A state intermediate appellate court reversed the ruling of the lower court. The notes contained unconditional promises to pay. Because the notes were negotiable, they were subject to Article 3's six-year limit on actions to collect, and AOA could go forward with its claim.

Is a note for funds to purchase alpacas negotiable?

iStockPhoto.com/terrasprite

REASON The Groomes argued that the notes were not negotiable for three reasons. First, each note stated that its indebtedness arose "pursuant to" one of the contracts. UCC 3–106(a), however, provides that "a reference to another writing does not of itself make the promise or order conditional." The words "pursuant to" were only part of a reference to another writing—they did not condition the promise to pay contained in the notes. Second, each note contained a security agreement that referred to its underlying contract as the source to be consulted to determine the property (collateral) covered by the agreement. But UCC 3–106(b) states that a promise is not made conditional by a "reference to another writing for a statement of rights with respect to collateral." Finally, the note to finance the purchase of Black Thunder's Midnight referred to the underlying contract as the source to be consulted to determine the procedure for giving notice to collect. Again, though, this language did not condition the promise to pay.

WHAT IF THE FACTS WERE DIFFERENT? *If AOA's suit had fallen within the four-year statute of limitations of UCC Article 2, could the seller have filed its claim on either the contracts or the notes? Explain.*

19–2d A Fixed Amount of Money

Negotiable instruments must state with certainty a fixed amount of money to be paid at any time the instrument is payable [UCC 3–104(a)]. This requirement ensures that the value of the instrument can be determined with clarity and certainty.

The term *fixed amount* means an amount that is ascertainable from the face of the instrument. A demand note payable with 8 percent interest meets the requirement of a fixed amount because its amount can be determined at the time it is payable or at any time thereafter [UCC 3–104(a)]. The rate of interest may also be determined from information that is not contained in the instrument itself but described by it, such as a formula or a source [UCC 3–112(b)]. For instance, an instrument that is payable at the *legal rate of interest* (a rate of interest fixed by statute) is negotiable. Mortgage notes tied to a variable rate of interest (a rate that fluctuates as a result of market conditions) are also negotiable.

UCC 3–104(a) provides that a fixed amount is to be *payable in money*. The UCC defines money as "a medium of exchange authorized or adopted by a domestic or foreign government

KNOW THIS

Interest payable on an instrument normally cannot exceed the maximum limit on interest under a state's usury statute.

as a part of its currency" [UCC 1–201(24)]. Gold is not a medium of exchange adopted by the U.S. government, so a note payable in gold is nonnegotiable. An instrument payable in the United States with a face amount stated in a foreign currency is negotiable, however, and can be paid in the foreign currency or in the equivalent amount of U.S. dollars [UCC 3–107].

19–2e Payable on Demand or at a Definite Time

A negotiable instrument must "be payable on demand or at a definite time" [UCC 3–104(a)(2)]. To determine the instrument's value, it is necessary to know when the maker, drawee, or acceptor is required to pay. It is also necessary to know when the obligations of secondary parties, such as *indorsers*,[5] will arise. Furthermore, it is necessary to know when an instrument is due in order to calculate when the statute of limitations may apply [UCC 3–118(a)]. Finally, with an interest-bearing instrument, it is necessary to know the exact interval during which interest will accrue to determine the instrument's present value.

Payable on Demand Instruments that are payable on demand include those that contain the words "Payable at sight" or "Payable upon presentment." **Presentment** is a demand made by or on behalf of a person entitled to enforce an instrument to either pay or accept the instrument [UCC 3–501]. Thus, presentment occurs when a person offers the instrument to the appropriate party for payment or acceptance. Presentment can by made by any commercially reasonable means, including oral, written, or electronic communication.

The very nature of the instrument may indicate that it is payable on demand. For instance, a check, by definition, is payable on demand [UCC 3–104(f)]. If no time for payment is specified and the person responsible for payment must pay on the instrument's presentment, the instrument is payable on demand [UCC 3–108(a)].

CASE EXAMPLE 19.9 National City Bank gave Reger Development, LLC, a line of credit to finance potential development opportunities. Reger signed a promissory note requiring it to "pay this loan in full immediately upon Lender's demand." About a year later, the bank asked Reger to pay down the loan and stated that it would be reducing the amount of cash available through the line of credit. Reger sued, alleging that the bank had breached the terms of the note. The court ruled in the bank's favor. The promissory note was a demand instrument because it explicitly set forth the lender's right to demand payment at any time. Thus, National City had the right to collect payment from Reger at any time on demand.[6] ■

Payable at a Definite Time If an instrument is not payable on demand, to be negotiable it must be payable at a definite time. An instrument is payable at a definite time if it states *any* of the following:

1. That it is payable on a specified date.
2. That it is payable within a definite period of time (such as thirty days) after being presented for payment.
3. That it is payable on a date or time readily ascertainable at the time the promise or order is issued [UCC 3–108(b)].

The maker or drawee in a time draft is under no obligation to pay until the specified time.

When an instrument is payable by the maker or drawer *on or before* a stated date, it is clearly payable at a definite time. The maker or drawer has the *option* of paying before the stated maturity date, but the payee can still rely on payment being made by the maturity date. **EXAMPLE 19.10** Ari gives Ernesto an instrument dated May 1, 2016, that indicates on

Presentment The act of presenting an instrument to the party liable on the instrument in order to collect payment. Presentment also occurs when a person presents an instrument to a drawee for a required acceptance.

---

5. We should note that the UCC uses the spelling *indorse* (*indorsement*, and the like), rather than the more common spelling *endorse* (*endorsement*, and the like). We follow the UCC's spelling here and in other chapters in this text.
6. *Reger Development, LLC v. National City Bank*, 592 F.3d 759 (2010).

its face that it is payable *on or before* May 1, 2017. This instrument satisfies the definite-time requirement.

In contrast, an instrument that is undated and made payable "one month after date" is clearly nonnegotiable. There is no way to determine the maturity date from the face of the instrument. If the date is uncertain, the instrument is not payable at a definite time. **EXAMPLE 19.11** An instrument that states, "One year after the death of my grandfather, Jerome Adams, I promise to pay $5,000 to the order of Lucy Harmon. [Signed] Jacqueline Wells," is nonnegotiable. The date on which the instrument becomes payable is uncertain.

Acceleration Clause

An **acceleration clause** allows a payee or other holder of a time instrument to demand payment of the entire amount due, with interest, if a certain event occurs. (A **holder** is any person in possession of an instrument drawn, issued, or indorsed to him or her, to his or her order, to bearer, or in blank [UCC 1–201(20)].)

EXAMPLE 19.12 Marta lends $1,000 to Ruth, who makes a negotiable note promising to pay $100 per month (plus interest) for ten months. The note contains an acceleration provision that permits Marta or any holder to immediately demand all the payments plus the interest owed to date if Ruth fails to pay an installment. Ruth fails to make the third payment. Marta accelerates the unpaid balance, and the note becomes due and payable in full. Ruth owes Marta the remaining principal plus any unpaid interest to that date.

Instruments that include acceleration clauses are negotiable because the exact value of the instrument can be ascertained. In addition, the instrument will be payable on a specified date if the event allowing acceleration does not occur [UCC 3–108(b)(ii)]. Thus, the specified date is the outside limit used to determine the value and negotiability of the instrument.

Extension Clause

The reverse of an acceleration clause is an **extension clause,** which allows the date of maturity to be extended into the future [UCC 3–108(b)(iii), (iv)]. If the right to extend the time of payment is given to the maker or drawer, the interval of the extension must be specified to keep the instrument negotiable. If, however, the holder can extend the time of payment, the extended maturity date need not be specified for the instrument to be negotiable.

EXAMPLE 19.13 Alek's note reads, "The holder of this note at the date of maturity, January 1, 2017, can extend the time of payment until the following June 1 or later, if the holder so wishes." This note is negotiable. The length of the extension does not have to be specified, because only the holder has the option to extend. After January 1, 2017, the note is, in effect, a demand instrument.

19–2f Payable to Order or to Bearer

Because one of the functions of a negotiable instrument is to serve as a substitute for cash, freedom to transfer is essential. To ensure a proper transfer, the instrument must be "payable to order or to bearer" at the time it is issued or first comes into the possession of the holder [UCC 3–104(a)(1)]. An instrument is not negotiable unless it meets this requirement.

Order Instruments

An **order instrument** is an instrument that is payable (1) "to the order of an identified person" or (2) "to an identified person or order" [UCC 3–109(b)]. An identified person is the person "to whom the instrument is initially payable" as determined by the intent of the maker or drawer [UCC 3–110(a)]. The identified person, in turn, may transfer the instrument to whomever he or she wishes. In this way, the instrument retains its transferability.

Note that in an order instrument, the person specified must be identified with *certainty,* because the transfer of the instrument requires the *indorsement,* or signature, of the payee (indorsements will be discussed later in this chapter). An order instrument made "Payable

Margin Glossary

Acceleration Clause A clause that allows a payee or other holder of a time instrument to demand payment of the entire amount due, with interest, if a certain event occurs, such as a default in the payment of an installment when due.

Holder Any person in possession of an instrument drawn, issued, or indorsed to him or her, to his or her order, to bearer, or in blank.

Extension Clause A clause in a time instrument that allows the instrument's date of maturity to be extended into the future.

Can a note made in exchange for funds contain an acceleration clause and still be negotiable?

evp82/ShutterStock.com

Order Instrument A negotiable instrument that is payable "to the order of an identified person" or "to an identified person or order."

to the order of my nicest cousin," for instance, is not negotiable, because it does not clearly specify the payee.

Bearer Instruments A **bearer instrument** is an instrument that does not designate a specific payee [UCC 3–109(a)]. The term **bearer** refers to a person in possession of an instrument that is payable to bearer or indorsed in blank (with a signature only, as will be discussed shortly) [UCC 1–201(5), 3–109(a), 3–109(c)]. This means that the maker or drawer agrees to pay anyone who presents the instrument for payment.

Any instrument containing terms such as the following is a bearer instrument:

1. "Payable to the order of bearer."

2. "Payable to Simon Reed or bearer."

3. "Payable to bearer."

4. "Pay cash."

5. "Pay to the order of cash."

CASE EXAMPLE 19.14 Amine Nehme applied for credit at the Venetian Resort Hotel Casino in Las Vegas, Nevada, and was granted $500,000 in credit. He signed a marker—that is, a promise to pay a debt—for $500,000. Nehme quickly lost that amount gambling. The Venetian presented the marker for payment to Nehme's bank, Bank of America, which returned it for insufficient funds. The casino's owner, Las Vegas Sands, LLC, filed a suit against Nehme for failure to pay a negotiable instrument.

The court held that the marker fit the UCC's definitions of negotiable instrument and check. It was a means for payment of $500,000 from Bank of America to the order of the Venetian. It did not state a time for payment and thus was payable on demand. It was also unconditional—that is, it stated no promise by Nehme other than the promise to pay a fixed amount of money.[7] ∎

19–2g Factors That Do Not Affect Negotiability

Certain ambiguities or omissions will not affect the negotiability of an instrument. The UCC provides the following rules for clearing up ambiguous terms:

1. Unless the date of an instrument is necessary to determine a definite time for payment, the fact that an instrument is *undated* does not affect its negotiability. A typical example is an undated check, which is still negotiable. If a check is not dated, its date is the date of its issue, meaning the date the maker first delivers the check to another person to give that person rights in the check [UCC 3–113(b)].

2. Antedating or postdating an instrument (using a date before or after the actual current date) does not affect the instrument's negotiability [UCC 3–113(a)]. **EXAMPLE 19.15** Crenshaw draws a check on his account at First Bank, payable to Sirah Imports. He postdates the check by fifteen days. Sirah Imports can immediately negotiate the check, and, unless Crenshaw tells First Bank otherwise, the bank can charge the amount of the check to Crenshaw's account [UCC 4–401(c)]. ∎

3. Handwritten terms outweigh typewritten and printed terms (preprinted terms on forms, for example), and typewritten terms outweigh printed terms [UCC 3–114]. **EXAMPLE 19.16** Most checks are preprinted "Pay to the order of" followed by a blank line, indicating an order instrument. In handwriting, Chad inserts in the blank, "Anita Delgado or bearer." The handwritten terms will outweigh the printed form, and the check will be a bearer instrument. ∎

7. *Las Vegas Sands, LLC v. Nehme,* 632 F.3d 526 (9th Cir. 2011).

Bearer Instrument Any instrument that is not payable to a specific person, including instruments payable to the bearer or to "cash."

Bearer A person in possession of an instrument payable to bearer or indorsed in blank.

Can a gambling marker be a negotiable instrument?

KNOW THIS

An instrument that purports to be payable both to order and to bearer contains a contradiction in terms. Such an instrument is a bearer instrument.

4. Words outweigh figures unless the words are ambiguous [UCC 3–114]. This rule is important when the numerical amount and the written amount on a check differ.

5. When an instrument does not specify a particular interest rate but simply states "with interest," the interest rate is the *judgment rate of interest* (a rate of interest fixed by statute that is applied to court judgments) [UCC 3–112(b)].

6. A check is negotiable even if a notation on it states that it is "nonnegotiable" or "not governed by Article 3." Any other instrument, in contrast, can be made nonnegotiable if the maker or drawer conspicuously notes on it that it is "nonnegotiable" or "not governed by Article 3" [UCC 3–104(d)].

In the following case, the court was asked to compare the words and figures in a note to determine its amount.

CASE 19.2

Charles R. Tips Family Trust v. PB Commercial LLC

Court of Appeals of Texas, Houston, First District, __ S.W.3d __, 2015 WL 730481 (2015).

FACTS The Charles R. Tips Family Trust signed a promissory note in favor of Patriot Bank to obtain a loan to buy a house in Harris County, Texas. The note identified the principal amount of the loan as "ONE MILLION SEVEN THOUSAND AND NO/100 ($1,700,000.00) DOLLARS." The trust made payments totaling only $595,586. PB Commercial, LLC (PBC) acquired the note, sold the residence for $874,125, and pursued litigation in a Texas state court against the borrower, alleging default. The defendant argued that the written words in an instrument control and that the note had been satisfied in full by the amount of the payments and the price on the sale of the house—"in fact, PBC has collected a surplus of $189,111." The court entered a judgment in PBC's favor. The trust appealed, arguing one issue—that the amount of the loan must be determined from the printed words in the note.

ISSUE Was the amount of the note "ONE MILLION SEVEN THOUSAND AND NO/100 * * * DOLLARS?"

DECISION Yes. A state intermediate appellate court reversed the judgment of the lower court. "The words 'one million seven thousand' control over the numerals '$1,700,000' to set the amount."

What happens when the numbers in a promissory note differ from the written amount?

REASON To recover on the note, PBC had to prove the balance that was due. Under UCC 3–114, "if an instrument contains contradictory terms, . . . words prevail over numbers." The principle underlying this rule is that words are more likely to represent the parties' actual intent than numbers. In this case, the meaning of the note's phrase "one million seven thousand and no/100 dollars" is unambiguous—it refers to the sum $1,007,000. This phrase obviously conflicted with the note's numerals, differing by $693,000. The court held that the large size of the discrepancy "does not matter" under Texas Business & Commercial Code Section 3.114 (Texas's version of UCC 3–114) or Texas case law. PBC argued that if the phrase had been "one seven hundred thousand," omitting the word "million," the amount of the note would have been ambiguous, and the court would have had to consider the numerals and other evidence to determine it. "But this hypothetical scenario has no bearing on this case because there is no ambiguity . . . here."

WHAT IF THE FACTS WERE DIFFERENT? *Suppose that the note had described the amount of the loan as "ONE MILLION SEVEN HUNDRED THOUSAND AND NO/100 ($1,007,000.00) DOLLARS." What would have been the result?*

19–3 Transfer of Instruments

Once issued, a negotiable instrument can be transferred by *assignment* or by *negotiation*. The party receiving the instrument obtains the rights of a holder only if the transfer is by negotiation.

19–3a Transfer by Assignment

Recall that an assignment is a transfer of rights under a contract. Under general contract principles, a transfer by assignment gives the assignee only those rights that the assignor possessed. Any defenses that can be raised against an assignor can normally be raised against the assignee. This same principle applies when a negotiable instrument, such as a promissory note, is transferred by assignment. The transferee is an *assignee* rather than a *holder.*

19–3b Transfer by Negotiation

Negotiation is the transfer of an instrument in such a way that the transferee (the person to whom the instrument is transferred) becomes a holder [UCC 3–201(a)]. Under UCC principles, a transfer by negotiation creates a holder who, at the very least, receives the rights of the previous possessor [UCC 3–203(b)].

Unlike an assignment, a transfer by negotiation can make it possible for a holder to receive more rights in the instrument than the prior possessor had [UCC 3–202(b), 3–305, 3–306]. A holder who receives greater rights is known as a *holder in due course,* a concept we will discuss later in this chapter.

There are two methods of negotiating an instrument so that the receiver becomes a holder. The method used depends on whether the instrument is an *order instrument* or a *bearer instrument.*

Negotiating Order Instruments An order instrument contains the name of a payee capable of indorsing it, as in "Pay to the order of Lloyd Sorenson." If the instrument is an order instrument, it is negotiated by delivery with any necessary indorsements.

EXAMPLE 19.17 National Express Corporation issues a payroll check "to the order of Lloyd Sorenson." Sorenson takes the check to the bank, signs his name on the back (an indorsement), gives it to the teller (a delivery), and receives cash. Sorenson has *negotiated* the check to the bank [UCC 3–201(b)]. ■

Negotiating order instruments requires both delivery and indorsement (indorsements will be discussed shortly). If Sorenson had taken the check to the bank and delivered it to the teller without signing it, the transfer would not qualify as a negotiation. In that situation, the transfer would be treated as an assignment, and the bank would become an assignee rather than a holder.

Negotiating Bearer Instruments If an instrument is payable to bearer, it is negotiated by delivery—that is, by transfer into another person's possession. Indorsement is not necessary [UCC 3–201(b)]. The use of bearer instruments thus involves more risk through loss or theft than the use of order instruments.

EXAMPLE 19.18 Richard Kray writes a check "payable to cash" and hands it to Jessie Arnold (a delivery). Kray has issued the check (a bearer instrument) to Arnold. Arnold places the check in her wallet, which is subsequently stolen. The thief has possession of the check. At this point, the thief has no rights to the check. If the thief "delivers" the check to an innocent third person, however, negotiation will be complete. All rights to the check will be passed absolutely to that third person, and Arnold will lose all rights to recover the proceeds of the check from that person [UCC 3–306]. Of course, Arnold can attempt to recover the amount from the thief if the thief can be found. ■

19–3c Indorsements

An indorsement is required whenever an order instrument is negotiated. An **indorsement** is a signature with or without additional words or statements. It is most often written on the back of the instrument itself. If there is no room on the instrument, the indorsement

"Money has little value to its possessor unless it also has value to others."

LELAND STANFORD
1824–1893
(U.S. SENATOR AND FOUNDER OF STANFORD UNIVERSITY)

Negotiation The transfer of an instrument in such form that the transferee (the person to whom the instrument is transferred) becomes a holder.

LEARNING OBJECTIVE 2
How does the negotiation of order instruments differ from the negotiation of bearer instruments?

Is a check made out "payable to cash" a bearer instrument?

Indorsement A signature placed on an instrument for the purpose of transferring ownership rights in the instrument.

can be on a separate piece of paper that is firmly affixed to the instrument, such as with staples [UCC 3–204(a)]. (See this chapter's *Beyond Our Borders* feature for a discussion of the approach to indorsements in France.)

A person who transfers an instrument by signing (indorsing) it and delivering it to another person is an *indorser.* The person to whom the check is indorsed and delivered is the *indorsee.* **EXAMPLE 19.19** Luisa Perez receives a graduation check for $100. She can transfer the check to her mother (or to anyone) by signing it on the back. Luisa is an indorser. If Luisa indorses the check by writing "Pay to Avery Perez," Avery Perez is the indorsee. ■

We examine here the four categories of indorsements: blank, special, qualified, and restrictive. Note that a single indorsement may have characteristics of more than one category.

Blank Indorsement

An indorsement on an instrument that specifies no indorsee. An order instrument that is indorsed in blank becomes a bearer instrument.

Blank Indorsements

A **blank indorsement** does not specify a particular indorsee and can consist of a mere signature [UCC 3–205(b)]. **EXAMPLE 19.20** A check payable "to the order of Alan Luberda" is indorsed in blank if Luberda simply writes his signature on the back of the check, as shown in Exhibit 19–5. ■

An order instrument indorsed in blank becomes a bearer instrument and can be negotiated by delivery alone, as already discussed. In other words, a blank indorsement converts an order instrument to a bearer instrument, which anybody can cash.

Does an instrument that requires an indorsement for negotiation need to contain a handwritten signature? That was the question in the following case.

Exhibit 19–5 A Blank Indorsement

Alan Luberda

CASE 19.3

In re Bass

Supreme Court of North Carolina, 738 S.E.2d 173 (2013).

FACTS Tonya Bass signed a note with Mortgage Lenders Network USA, Inc., to borrow $139,988 to buy a house in Durham County, North Carolina. The note was transferred by rubber-stamp indorsements to Emax Financial Group, LLC, then to Residential Funding Corporation, and finally to U.S. Bank, N.A.

When Bass stopped paying on the note, U.S. Bank filed an action in a North Carolina state court to foreclose. The court issued an order permitting the foreclosure to proceed, and Bass appealed. She argued that the stamp transferring the note from Mortgage Lenders to Emax was invalid because it was not accompanied by a signature. A state intermediate appellate court decided in Bass's favor based on the lack of a "proper indorsement." U.S. Bank appealed.

ISSUE Can an indorsement that does not include a handwritten signature effectively transfer a negotiable instrument?

DECISION Yes. The North Carolina Supreme Court reversed the decision of the lower court, holding that U.S. Bank was the holder of the note.

Can a signature stamp constitute a valid indorsement on a negotiable instrument?

NotarYES/ShutterStock.com

REASON The UCC defines "signature" as "any symbol executed or adopted with present intention to adopt or accept a writing." Under this definition, a handwritten signature is not necessary. A "symbol" can be written, but it may also be printed or stamped. "The question always is whether the symbol was executed or adopted by the party with present intention to adopt or accept the writing." In this case, the stamped indorsement indicates that intent on its face—"Pay to the order of: Emax Financial Group, LLC without recourse By: Mortgage Lenders Network USA, Inc." The stamp's language shows that the indorsement "was executed or adopted by the party with present intention to adopt or accept the writing." Thus, the stamp effectively transferred the note.

CRITICAL THINKING—Economic Consideration *How does presuming that an indorsement is legitimate unless there is evidence to the contrary protect the transferability of a negotiable instrument?*

BEYOND OUR BORDERS

Severe Restrictions on Check Indorsements in France

If you were reading a business law textbook in France, you would find very little on check indorsements. The reason is that checks rarely, if ever, can be indorsed. That means that almost all checks must be deposited in a bank account, rather than transferred to another individual or entity. The French government says that these restrictions on indorsements reduce the risk of loss and theft.

CRITICAL THINKING

■ What would be the cost to individuals and businesses that use checks if a similar rule were passed in this country?

Special Indorsements A **special indorsement** contains the signature of the indorser and identifies the person to whom the instrument is made payable—that is, it names the indorsee [UCC 3–205(a)]. Words such as "Pay to the order of Clay" or "Pay to Clay," followed by the signature of the indorser, create a special indorsement. An instrument indorsed in this way is an order instrument.

To avoid the risk of loss from theft, a holder may convert a blank indorsement to a special indorsement by writing, above the signature of the indorser, words identifying the indorsee [UCC 3–205(c)]. This changes the bearer instrument back to an order instrument.

EXAMPLE 19.21 A check is made payable to Peter Rabe. He indorses the check in blank by signing his name on the back and delivers the check to Anthony Bartomo. Anthony is unable to cash the check immediately and wants to avoid any risk should he lose the check. He therefore prints "Pay to Anthony Bartomo" above Peter's blank indorsement (see Exhibit 19–6). By doing this, Anthony has converted Peter's blank indorsement into a special indorsement. Further negotiation now requires Anthony's indorsement plus delivery. ■

Special Indorsement

An indorsement on an instrument that identifies the specific person to whom the indorser intends to make the instrument payable.

Exhibit 19–6 A Special Indorsement

> Pay to Anthony Bartomo
> Peter Rabe

Qualified Indorsements Generally, an indorser, *merely by indorsing*, impliedly promises to pay the holder or any subsequent indorser the amount of the instrument in the event that the drawer or maker defaults on the payment [UCC 3–415(a)]. Usually, then, indorsements are *unqualified indorsements*, which means that the indorser is guaranteeing payment of the instrument in addition to transferring title to it.

An indorser who does not wish to be liable on an instrument can use a **qualified indorsement** to disclaim this liability [UCC 3–415(b)]. The notation "without recourse" is commonly used to create a qualified indorsement, such as the one shown in Exhibit 19–7. If an instrument with such an indorsement is later dishonored, the holder cannot recover from the qualified indorser unless the indorser has breached one of the transfer warranties discussed later.

Qualified indorsements are often used by persons (agents) acting in a representative capacity. **EXAMPLE 19.22** Insurance agents sometimes receive checks payable to them that are really intended as payment to the insurance company. The agent is merely indorsing the payment through to the insurance company and should not be required to make good on a check if it is later dishonored. The "without recourse" indorsement relieves the agent from any liability on a check. ■

Qualified Indorsement

An indorsement on a negotiable instrument in which the indorser disclaims any contract liability on the instrument. The notation "without recourse" is commonly used to create a qualified indorsement.

Exhibit 19–7 A Qualified Indorsement

> Pay to Elvie Ling, without recourse.
> Bridgett Cage

A qualified indorsement can be accompanied by either a special indorsement or a blank indorsement. In either situation, the instrument can be further negotiated.

- A *special qualified indorsement* includes the name of the indorsee as well as the words *without recourse*. The special indorsement makes the instrument an order instrument requiring an indorsement plus delivery for negotiation.
- A *blank qualified indorsement* ("without recourse, [signed] Jennie Cole") makes the instrument a bearer instrument, and only delivery is required for negotiation.

Restrictive Indorsements

Restrictive Indorsement
An indorsement on a negotiable instrument that requires the indorsee to comply with certain instructions regarding the funds involved.

A **restrictive indorsement** requires the indorsee to comply with certain instructions regarding the funds involved, but it does not generally prohibit further negotiation of the instrument [UCC 3–206(a)]. Although most indorsements are nonrestrictive, many forms of restrictive indorsements do exist, including those discussed here.

Conditional Indorsements. When payment depends on the occurrence of some event specified in the indorsement, the indorsement is conditional. **EXAMPLE 19.23** Ken Barton indorses a check, "Pay to Lars Johansen if he completes the renovation of my kitchen by June 1, 2017 [Signed] Ken Barton." Barton has created a conditional indorsement. ■

Indorsements for Deposit or Collection. A common type of restrictive indorsement is one that makes the indorsee (almost always a bank) a collecting agent of the indorser [UCC 3–206(c)]. **EXAMPLE 19.24** Stephanie Mallak has received a check and wants to deposit it into her checking account at the bank. She can indorse the check "For deposit [or collection] only. [Signed] Stephanie Mallak" (see Exhibit 19–8). She may also wish to write her bank account number on the check. A "For deposit" or "For collection" indorsement prohibits further negotiation except by the bank. Following this indorsement, only the bank can acquire the rights of a holder. ■

Trust Indorsement
An indorsement to a person who is to hold or use funds for the benefit of the indorser or a third person. It is also known as an *agency indorsement*.

Trust (Agency) Indorsements. Indorsements to persons who are to hold or use the funds for the benefit of the indorser or a third party are called **trust indorsements** (also known as *agency indorsements*) [UCC 3–206(d), (e)]. **EXAMPLE 19.25** Robert Emerson asks his accountant, Ada Johnson, to pay some bills for his invalid wife, Sarah, while he is out of the country. He indorses a check as follows: "Pay to Ada Johnson as Agent for Sarah Emerson." This agency indorsement obligates Johnson to use the funds only for the benefit of Sarah Emerson. ■ Exhibit 19–9 shows sample trust (agency) indorsements.

Exhibit 19–8 "For Deposit" and "For Collection" Indorsements

For deposit only
Stephanie Mallak

or

For Collection only
Stephanie Mallak

Exhibit 19–9 Trust (Agency) Indorsements

Pay to Ada Johnson in trust for Sarah Emerson
Robert Emerson

or

Pay to Ada Johnson as Agent for Sarah Emerson
Robert Emerson

Misspelled Names A payee or indorsee whose name is misspelled can indorse with the misspelled name, the correct name, or both [UCC 3–204(d)]. The usual practice is to indorse with the name as it appears on the instrument, followed by the correct name.

Alternative or Joint Payees An instrument payable to two or more persons *in the alternative* (for example, "Pay to the order of Ramirez or Johnson") requires the indorsement of only one of the payees. In contrast, if an instrument is made payable to two or more persons *jointly* (for example, "Pay to the order of Shari and Bob Covington"), all of the payees' indorsements are necessary for negotiation.

If an instrument payable to two or more persons does not clearly indicate whether it is payable in the alternative or jointly ("Pay to the order of John and/or Sara Fitzgerald" or "Pay to the order of J&D Landscaping, Bryson Maintenance"), then the instrument is payable to the persons alternatively [UCC 3–110(d)]. The same principles apply to special indorsements that identify more than one person to whom the indorser intends to make the instrument payable [UCC 3–205(a)].

19–4 Holder in Due Course (HDC)

Often, whether a holder is entitled to obtain payment will depend on whether the holder is a *holder in due course*. An ordinary holder obtains only those rights that the transferor had in the instrument and normally is subject to any defenses that could be asserted against the transferor. In contrast, a **holder in due course (HDC)** takes an instrument *free* of most of the defenses and claims that could be asserted against the transferor. To become an HDC, a holder must meet certain acquisition requirements.

EXAMPLE 19.26 Marcia Cambry signs a $10,000 note payable to Alex Jerrod in payment for some ancient Roman coins. Jerrod negotiates the note to Alicia Larson, who promises to pay Jerrod for it in sixty days. During the next month, Larson learns that Jerrod has breached his contract with Cambry by delivering coins that were not from the Roman era, as promised, and that for this reason Cambry will not honor the $10,000 note.

Whether Larson can hold Cambry liable on the note depends on whether Larson has met the requirements for HDC status. If Larson has met these requirements, she has HDC status and is entitled to payment on the note. If she has not met the requirements, she has the status of an ordinary holder. In that event, Cambry's defense of breach of contract against payment to Jerrod will also be effective against Larson. ■

19–4a Requirements for HDC Status

The basic requirements for attaining HDC status are set forth in UCC 3–302. A holder of a negotiable instrument is an HDC if she or he takes the instrument (1) for value, (2) in good faith, and (3) without notice that it is defective. Next, we examine each of these requirements.

Taking for Value An HDC must have given *value* for the instrument [UCC 3–302(a)(2)(i)]. A person who receives an instrument as a gift or inherits it has not met the requirement of value. In these situations, the person becomes an ordinary holder and does not possess the rights of an HDC.

Under UCC 3–303(a), a holder takes an instrument for value if the holder has done any of the following:

1. Performed the promise for which the instrument was issued or transferred.

2. Acquired a security interest or other lien in the instrument, excluding a lien obtained by a judicial proceeding.

Holder in Due Course (HDC)
A holder who acquires a negotiable instrument for value, in good faith, and without notice that the instrument is defective.

A note is signed for funds to purchase ancient Roman coins. If these coins turn out to be fake, how does that event affect the negotiability of the note?

LEARNING OBJECTIVE 3

What are the requirements for attaining the status of a holder in due course (HDC)?

3. Taken the instrument in payment of, or as security for, a preexisting claim. **EXAMPLE 19.27** Zon owes Dwyer $2,000 on a past-due account. If Zon negotiates a $2,000 note signed by Gordon to Dwyer and Dwyer accepts it to discharge the overdue account balance, Dwyer has given value for the instrument. ■

4. Given a negotiable instrument as payment for the instrument. **EXAMPLE 19.28** Justin issues a six-month, $5,000 negotiable promissory note to Paige. Paige needs cash and does not want to wait for the maturity date to collect. She negotiates the note to her friend Kristen, who pays her $2,000 in cash and writes her a check—a negotiable instrument—for the balance of $3,000. Kristen has given full value for the note. ■

5. Given an irrevocable commitment (such as a letter of credit) as payment for the instrument.

If a person promises to perform or give value in the future, that person is not an HDC. A holder takes an instrument for value *only to the extent that the promise has been performed* [UCC 3–303(a)(1)]. Therefore, in *Example 19.26,* Larson is not an HDC, because she did not take the instrument (Cambry's note) for value—she has not yet paid Jerrod for the note. Thus, Cambry's defense of breach of contract is valid against Larson as well as Jerrod. Exhibit 19–10 illustrates these concepts.

Taking in Good Faith

To qualify as an HDC, a holder must take the instrument in *good faith* [UCC 3–302(a)(2)(ii)]. This means that the holder must have acted honestly and observed reasonable commercial standards of fair dealing in the process of acquiring the instrument [UCC 3–103(a)(4)].

The good faith requirement applies only to the *holder.* It is immaterial whether the transferor acted in good faith. Thus, even a person who takes a negotiable instrument from a thief may become an HDC if the person acquired the instrument in good faith and honestly had no reason to be suspicious of the transaction.

CASE EXAMPLE 19.29 Cassandra Demery worked as a bookkeeper at Freestyle until the owner, Clinton Georg, discovered that she had embezzled more than $200,000. Georg fired Demery and demanded repayment. Demery went to work for her parents' firm, Metro Fixtures, where she had some authority to write checks. Without specific authorization, she wrote a check for $189,000 to Freestyle on Metro's account and deposited it in Freestyle's account. She told Georg that the check was a loan to her from her family.

Exhibit 19–10 Taking for Value

By exchanging defective goods for Cambry's note, Jerrod breached his contract with Cambry. Cambry could assert this defense if Jerrod presented the note to her for payment. Cambry can assert the same defense against Larson if Larson submits the note to Cambry for payment. Because Larson took the note in return for her promise to pay in sixty days, she did not take the note for value and is not a holder in due course. In contrast, if Larson had taken the note for value, Cambry could not assert the defense and would be liable to pay the note.

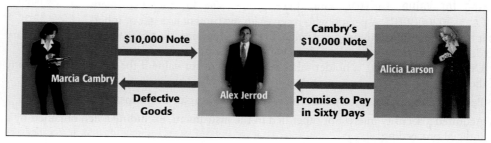

When Metro discovered Demery's theft, it filed a suit against Georg and Freestyle. Freestyle argued that it had taken the check in good faith and was an HDC. The Colorado Supreme Court agreed. Demery was the wrongdoer. She had the authority to issue checks for Metro, and Georg had no reason to know that Demery had lied about this check. Therefore, Freestyle was an HDC, and Metro would bear the loss.[8] ■

Taking without Notice The final requirement for HDC status involves *notice* [UCC 3–302]. A person will not qualify for HDC protection if he or she is *on notice* (knows or has reason to know) that the instrument being acquired is defective in any one of the following ways [UCC 3–302(a)]:

1. It is overdue.

2. It has been dishonored.

3. It is part of a series of which at least one instrument has an uncured (uncorrected) default.

4. It contains an unauthorized signature or has been altered.

5. There is a defense against the instrument or a claim to it.

6. The instrument is so irregular or incomplete as to call its authenticity into question.

Can a recipient of a check become an HDC when the person providing the check has check-writing authority?

What Constitutes Notice? Under UCC 1–201(25), a person is considered to have notice in the following circumstances:

1. The person has actual knowledge of the defect.

2. The person has received a notice or notification concerning the defect (such as a letter from a bank identifying the serial numbers of stolen bearer instruments).

3. The person has reason to know that a defect exists, given all the facts and circumstances known at the time in question.

The holder must also have received notice "at a time and in a manner that gives a reasonable opportunity to act on it" [UCC 3–302(f)]. A purchaser's knowledge of certain facts, such as insolvency proceedings against the maker or drawer of the instrument, does not constitute notice that the instrument is defective [UCC 3–302(b)].

Overdue Instruments. What constitutes notice that an instrument is overdue depends on whether it is a demand instrument or a time instrument.

A purchaser has notice that a *demand instrument* is overdue if she or he either takes the instrument knowing that demand has been made or takes the instrument an unreasonable length of time after its issue. For a check, a "reasonable time" is within ninety days after the date of the check. For all other demand instruments, what will be considered a reasonable time depends on the circumstances [UCC 3–304(a)].

Normally, a *time instrument* is overdue the day after its due date. Anyone who takes a time instrument after the due date is on notice that it is overdue [UCC 3–304(b)(2)]. Thus, if a promissory note due on May 15 is purchased on May 16, the purchaser is an ordinary holder, not an HDC. If an instrument states that it is "Payable in thirty days," counting begins the day after the instrument is dated. Thus, a note dated December 1 that is payable in thirty days is due by midnight on December 31. If the payment date falls on a Sunday or holiday, the instrument is payable on the next business day.

Dishonored Instruments. An instrument is **dishonored** when the party to whom the instrument is presented refuses to pay it. If a holder knows or has reason to know that an instrument has

Dishonor To refuse to pay or to accept a negotiable instrument that has been presented in a timely and proper manner.

---

8. *Georg v. Metro Fixtures Contractors, Inc.,* 178 P.3d 1209 (Colo.Sup.Ct. 2008).

iStockPhoto.com/Szepy

been dishonored, the holder is on notice and cannot claim HDC status [UCC 3–302(a)(2)]. Thus, a person who takes a check clearly stamped "insufficient funds" is put on notice.

Conversely, if a person purchasing an instrument does not know and has no reason to know that it has been dishonored, the person is *not* put on notice and therefore can become an HDC. **EXAMPLE 19.30** Leah Gonzalez holds a demand note dated September 1 issued by Apex, Inc., a local business firm. On September 17, she demands payment, and Apex refuses (that is, dishonors the instrument). On September 22, Gonzalez negotiates the note to Brenner, a purchaser who lives in another state. Brenner does not know, and has no reason to know, that the note has been dishonored. Because Brenner is *not* put on notice, Brenner can become an HDC. ∎

Notice of Claims or Defenses. A holder cannot become an HDC if she or he has notice of any claim to the instrument or any defense against it [UCC 3–302(a)(2)]. Instruments with irregularities and incomplete instruments fall under this rule.

Any *irregularity* on the face of an instrument (such as an obvious forgery or alteration) that calls into question its validity or ownership will bar HDC status. A good forgery of a signature or the careful alteration of an instrument, however, can go undetected by reasonable examination. In that situation, the purchaser can qualify as an HDC.

In addition, a purchaser cannot become an HDC of an instrument so *incomplete* on its face that an element of negotiability is lacking (for instance, the amount is not filled in) [UCC 3–302(a)(1)]. Minor omissions (such as the omission of the date) are permissible, because these do not call into question the validity of the instrument [UCC 3–113(b)].

19–4b Holder through an HDC

A person who does not qualify as an HDC but who derives his or her title through an HDC can acquire the rights and privileges of an HDC. This rule, which is sometimes called the **shelter principle,** is set out in UCC 3–203(b). Under this rule, anyone—no matter how far removed from an HDC—who can ultimately trace his or her title back to an HDC may acquire the rights of an HDC. By extending the benefits of HDC status, the shelter principle promotes the marketability and free transferability of negotiable instruments.

There are some limitations on the shelter principle, though. Certain persons who formerly held instruments cannot improve their positions by later reacquiring the instruments from HDCs [UCC 3–203(b)]. If a holder participated in fraud or illegality affecting the instrument, or had notice of a claim or defense against an instrument, that holder is not allowed to gain the benefits of HDC status by repurchasing the instrument from a later HDC.

19–5   Signature and Warranty Liability

Liability on negotiable instruments can arise either from a person's signature or from the warranties that are implied when the person presents the instrument for negotiation. We discuss signature liability and warranty liability in the subsections that follow.

19–5a Signature Liability

The general rule is that every party, except a qualified indorser,[9] who signs a negotiable instrument is either primarily or secondarily liable for payment of that instrument when it comes due. Signature liability is contractual liability—no person will be held contractually liable for an instrument that he or she has not signed.

---

9. A qualified indorser—one who indorses "without recourse"—undertakes no contractual obligation to pay. A qualified indorser merely assumes warranty liability.

KNOW THIS
A difference between the handwriting in the body of a check and the handwriting in the signature does not affect the validity of the check.

Shelter Principle The principle that the holder of a negotiable instrument who cannot qualify as a holder in due course (HDC), but who derives his or her title through an HDC, acquires the rights of an HDC.

"Most men are admirers of justice—when justice happens to be on their side."
RICHARD WHATELY
1787–1863
(ENGLISH THEOLOGIAN AND LOGICIAN)

Primary Liability A person who is primarily liable on a negotiable instrument is absolutely required to pay the instrument—unless, of course, he or she has a valid defense to payment [UCC 3–305]. Only *makers* and *acceptors* of instruments are primarily liable.

The maker of a promissory note unconditionally promises to pay the note. It is the maker's promise to pay that makes the note a negotiable instrument. If the instrument was incomplete when the maker signed it, the maker is obligated to pay it according to its stated terms or according to terms that were agreed on and later filled in to complete the instrument [UCC 3–115, 3–407(a), 3–412].

EXAMPLE 19.31 Tristan executes a preprinted promissory note to Sharon, without filling in the blank for a due date. If Sharon does not complete the form by adding the date, the note will be payable on demand. If Sharon subsequently fills in a due date that Tristan authorized, the note is payable on the stated due date. In either situation, Tristan (the maker) is obligated to pay the note. ■

As mentioned earlier, an acceptor is a drawee, such as a bank, that promises to pay an instrument when it is presented for payment. Once a drawee accepts a draft, the drawee is obligated to pay the draft when it is presented for payment [UCC 3–409(a)]. Failure to pay an accepted draft when presented leads to primary signature liability.

Secondary Liability *Drawers* and *indorsers* are secondarily liable. On a negotiable instrument, secondary liability is *contingent liability* (similar to that of a guarantor in a contract). In other words, a drawer or an indorser will be liable only if the party that is responsible for paying the instrument dishonors it by refusing to pay.

Parties are secondarily liable on a negotiable instrument *only if* the following events occur:[10]

1. The instrument is properly and timely presented.
2. The instrument is dishonored.
3. Timely notice of dishonor is given to the secondarily liable party.

Proper and Timely Presentment. The holder must present the instrument to the appropriate party in a proper and timely fashion and must give reasonable identification if requested [UCC 3–414(f), 3–415(e), 3–501]. The party to whom the instrument must be presented depends on the type of instrument involved. A note or CD is presented to the maker for payment. A draft is presented to the drawee for acceptance, payment, or both. A check is presented to the drawee for payment [UCC 3–501(a), 3–502(b)].

Presentment can be made by any commercially reasonable means, including oral, written, or electronic communication [UCC 3–501(b)]. Ordinarily, it is effective when received. (If presentment takes place after an established cutoff hour, though, it may be treated as occurring the next business day.)

Timeliness is important for proper presentment [UCC 3–414(f), 3–415(e), 3–501(b)(4)]. Failure to present an instrument on time is the most common reason for improper presentment. If the instrument is payable on demand, the holder should present it for payment or acceptance within a reasonable time. The holder of a domestic check must present that check for payment or collection within thirty days of its *date* to hold the drawer secondarily liable and within thirty days after its indorsement to hold the indorser secondarily liable. The time for proper presentment for various types of instruments is shown in Exhibit 19–11.

Dishonor. As mentioned, an instrument is dishonored when the required acceptance or payment is refused. It is also dishonored when acceptance or payment cannot be obtained within the prescribed time or when the required presentment is excused (as it would be, for instance,

KNOW THIS
A drawee is the party ordered to pay a draft or check, such as a bank or financial institution.

---

10. These requirements are necessary for a secondarily liable party to have signature liability on a negotiable instrument, but they are not necessary for a secondarily liable party to have warranty liability.

Exhibit 19–11 Time for Proper Presentment

TYPE OF INSTRUMENT	FOR ACCEPTANCE	FOR PAYMENT
Time	On or before due date.	On due date.
Demand	Within a reasonable time (after date of issue or after secondary party becomes liable on the instrument).	Within a reasonable time.
Check	Not applicable.	Within thirty days of its date, to hold drawer secondarily liable. Within thirty days of indorsement, to hold indorser secondarily liable.

if the maker had died) and the instrument is not properly accepted or paid [UCC 3–502(e), 3–504].

In certain situations, a delay in payment or a refusal to pay an instrument will not dishonor the instrument.

1. When presentment is made after an established cutoff hour (not earlier than 2:00 P.M.), a bank can postpone payment until the following business day without dishonoring the instrument [UCC 3–501(b)(4)].

2. When the holder refuses to exhibit the instrument, to give reasonable identification, or to sign a receipt for the payment on the instrument, a bank's refusal to pay does not dishonor the instrument [UCC 3–501(b)(2)].

3. When an instrument is returned because it lacks a proper indorsement, the instrument is not dishonored [UCC 3–501(b)(3)(i)].

Proper Notice of Dishonor. Once an instrument has been dishonored, proper notice must be given to secondary parties (drawers and indorsers) for them to be held liable. **EXAMPLE 19.32** Oscar writes a check on his account at People's Bank payable to Bess. Bess indorses the check in blank and cashes it at Midwest Grocery, which transfers it to People's Bank for payment. If People's Bank refuses to pay it, Midwest must timely notify Bess to hold her liable. ■

Notice can be given in any reasonable manner, including an oral, written, or electronic communication, as well as notice written or stamped on the instrument itself. A bank must give any necessary notice before its midnight deadline (midnight of the next banking day after receipt). Notice by any party other than a bank must be given within thirty days following the day of dishonor or the day on which the person who is secondarily liable receives notice of dishonor [UCC 3–503].

Unauthorized Signatures Unauthorized signatures arise in two situations:

1. When a person forges another person's name on a negotiable instrument.

2. When an agent who lacks the authority signs an instrument on behalf of a principal.

The General Rule. The general rule is that an unauthorized signature is wholly inoperative and will not bind the person whose name is signed or forged. **EXAMPLE 19.33** Parker finds Dolby's checkbook lying in the street, writes out a check to himself, and forges Dolby's signature. Banks normally have a duty to determine whether a person's signature on a check is forged. If a bank fails to determine that Dolby's signature is not genuine and cashes the check for Parker, the bank will generally be liable to Dolby for the amount. ■

Who is responsible for validating the signature on a check?

iStockPhoto.com/bluestocking

The general rule also may apply to agents' signatures. If an agent lacks the authority to sign the principal's name or has exceeded the authority given by the principal, the signature does not bind the principal but will bind the "unauthorized signer" [UCC 3–403(a)].

Exceptions to the General Rule. There are two exceptions to the general rule that an unauthorized signature will not bind the person whose name is signed:

1. *Ratification.* When the person whose name is signed ratifies (affirms) the signature, he or she will be bound [UCC 3–403(a)]. For instance, a mother may ratify her daughter's forgery of the mother's signature so that the daughter will not be prosecuted. A person can ratify an unauthorized signature either expressly (by affirming the signature) or impliedly (by other conduct, such as keeping any benefits received in the transaction or failing to repudiate the signature).

2. *Negligence.* When the negligence of the person whose name was forged substantially contributed to the forgery, a court may not allow the person to deny the effectiveness of an unauthorized signature [UCC 3–115, 3–406, 4–401(d)(2)].

Someone finds a checkbook on the sidewalk, writes out a check to himself, and forges the signature of the account holder. Is the bank liable to the true account holder if it cashes the forged check?

Special Rules for Unauthorized Indorsements Generally, when an instrument has a forged or unauthorized indorsement, the burden of loss falls on the first party to take the instrument. The reason for this general rule is that the first party to take an instrument is in the best position to prevent the loss.

EXAMPLE 19.34 Jen Nilson steals a check drawn on Universal Bank that is payable to the order of Inga Leed. Nilson indorses the check "Inga Leed" and presents the check to Universal Bank for payment. The bank, without asking Nilson for identification, pays the check, and Nilson disappears. Leed will not be liable on the check, because her indorsement was forged. The bank will bear the loss, which it might have avoided if it had asked Nilson for identification. ▪

This general rule has two important exceptions that cause the loss to fall on the maker or drawer. These exceptions arise when an indorsement is made by an imposter or by a fictitious payee.

Imposter Rule. An **imposter** is one who, through deception, induces a maker or drawer to issue an instrument in the name of an impersonated payee. If the maker or drawer believes the imposter to be the named payee at the time of issue, the indorsement by the imposter is not treated as unauthorized when the instrument is transferred to an innocent party. This is because the maker or drawer *intended* the imposter to receive the instrument.

In these situations, the unauthorized indorsement of a payee's name can be as effective as if the real payee had signed. The *imposter rule* provides that an imposter's indorsement will be effective—that is, not a forgery—insofar as the drawer or maker is concerned [UCC 3–404(a)].

EXAMPLE 19.35 Carol impersonates Donna and induces Edward to write a check payable to the order of Donna. Carol, continuing to impersonate Donna, negotiates the check to First National Bank as payment on her loan there. As the drawer of the check, Edward is liable for its amount to First National. ▪

Fictitious Payee Rule. When a person causes an instrument to be issued to a payee who will have *no interest* in the instrument, the payee is referred to as a **fictitious payee.** A fictitious payee can be a person or firm that does not exist, or it may be an identifiable party that will not acquire any interest in the instrument. Under the UCC's *fictitious payee rule,* the payee's indorsement is not treated as a forgery, and an innocent holder can hold the maker or drawer liable on the instrument [UCC 3–404(b), 3–405]. Basically, the loss falls on the maker or

Imposter One who induces a maker or drawer to issue a negotiable instrument in the name of an impersonated payee. Indorsements by imposters are treated as authorized indorsements under UCC Article 3.

Fictitious Payee A payee on a negotiable instrument whom the maker or drawer did not intend to have an interest in the instrument. Indorsements by fictitious payees are treated as authorized indorsements under UCC Article 3.

drawer of the instrument rather than on the third party that accepts it or on the bank that cashes it.

Fictitious payees most often arise in two situations:

1. When a dishonest employee deceives the employer into signing an instrument payable to a party with no right to receive payment on the instrument.

2. When a dishonest employee or agent has the authority to issue an instrument on behalf of the employer and issues a check to a party who has no interest in the instrument.

CASE EXAMPLE 19.36 Braden Furniture Company gave its bookkeeper, Bonnie Manning, general authority to create checks. Over the course of seven years, Manning created more than two hundred unauthorized checks, totaling $470,000, which she deposited in her own account at Union State Bank. Braden Furniture was not a customer of the bank. Most of the checks did not identify a payee (the payee line was left blank). Braden Furniture (the drawer) sued Union State Bank for the loss, claiming that the bank had been negligent in accepting and paying the blank checks. The court, however, held that the fictitious payee rule applied. Therefore, under Alabama's version of the UCC, the loss fell on Braden Furniture, not on Union State Bank.[11] ■

19–5b Warranty Liability

Signature liability arises from a transferor's signature. Transferors also make certain implied warranties regarding the instruments that they are negotiating. Warranty liability arises even when a transferor does not sign the instrument [UCC 3–416, 3–417].

Warranty liability is particularly important when a holder cannot hold a party liable on her or his signature, such as when a person delivers a bearer instrument. Unlike secondary signature liability, warranty liability is not subject to the conditions of proper presentment, dishonor, or notice of dishonor.

Warranties fall into two categories: those that arise on the *transfer* of a negotiable instrument and those that arise on *presentment*. Both transfer and presentment warranties attempt to shift liability back to a wrongdoer or to the person who dealt face to face with the wrongdoer and thus was in the best position to prevent the wrongdoing.

Transfer Warranties

Transfer Warranties A person who transfers an instrument *for consideration* makes the following five **transfer warranties** to all subsequent transferees and holders who take the instrument in good faith [UCC 3–416]:[12]

1. The transferor is entitled to enforce the instrument.

2. All signatures are authentic and authorized.

3. The instrument has not been altered.

4. The instrument is not subject to a defense or claim of any party that can be asserted against the transferor.

5. The transferor has no knowledge of any bankruptcy proceedings of the maker, the acceptor, or the drawer of the instrument.

Presentment Warranties

Presentment Warranties A person who presents an instrument for payment or acceptance makes the following **presentment warranties** to anyone who in good faith pays or accepts the instrument [UCC 3–417(a), 3–417(d)]:

---

11. *Braden Furniture Co. v. Union State Bank*, 109 So.3d 625 (Ala. 2012).
12. An amendment to UCC 3–416(a) adds a sixth warranty "with respect to a remotely created consumer item," such as an electronic check, drawn on a consumer account, that is not created by the payor bank and does not contain the drawer's handwritten signature. Under this amendment, which a few states have adopted, a bank that accepts and pays the instrument warrants to the next bank in the collection chain that the consumer authorized the item in that amount.

Sidebar:

"Life is unfair."

MILTON FRIEDMAN
1912–2006
(AMERICAN ECONOMIST)

LEARNING OBJECTIVE 4
What is the difference between signature liability and warranty liability?

Transfer Warranty A person who transfers an instrument for consideration impliedly makes five warranties—relating to good title, authentic signatures, no alterations, defenses, or insolvencies—to all subsequent transferees.

Presentment Warranty A person who presents an instrument for payment or acceptance impliedly makes three warranties relating to good title, no alterations, and no unauthorized signatures.

1. The person obtaining payment or acceptance is entitled to enforce the instrument or is authorized to obtain payment or acceptance on behalf of a person who is entitled to enforce the instrument. (This is, in effect, a warranty that there are no missing or unauthorized indorsements.)

2. The instrument has not been altered.

3. The person obtaining payment or acceptance has no knowledge that the signature of the issuer of the instrument is unauthorized.[13]

The second and third presentment warranties do not apply to makers, acceptors, and drawers when the presenter is an HDC. It is assumed that a drawer or a maker will recognize his or her own signature and that a maker or an acceptor will recognize whether an instrument has been materially altered.

19-6 Defenses, Limitations, and Discharge

Defenses can bar collection from persons who would otherwise be primarily or secondarily liable on a negotiable instrument. There are two general categories of defenses—*universal defenses* and *personal defenses*.

19-6a Universal Defenses

Universal defenses (also called *real defenses*) are valid against *all* holders, including HDCs and holders who take through an HDC. Universal defenses include those described here.

1. *Forgery of a signature on the instrument.* A forged signature will not bind the person whose name is used. Thus, when an instrument is forged, the person whose name is forged normally has no liability to pay any holder the value of the instrument. If the person whose name is forged ratifies the signature, however, he or she may be liable, as discussed earlier.

2. *Fraud in the execution.* If a person is deceived into signing a negotiable instrument, believing that she or he is signing something other than a negotiable instrument (such as a receipt), *fraud in the execution* is committed against the signer [UCC 3–305(a)(1)]. This defense cannot be raised, however, if reasonable inquiry would have revealed the nature and terms of the instrument.
   EXAMPLE 19.37 Connor, a salesperson, asks Javier, a customer, to sign a paper. Connor says that it is a receipt for goods that Javier is picking up from the store. In fact, it is a promissory note, but Javier is unfamiliar with English and does not realize this. Here, even if the note is negotiated to an HDC, Javier has a valid defense against payment. ■

3. *Material alteration.* An alteration is *material* if it changes the obligations of the parties in the instrument *in any way.* Material alterations include completing an incomplete instrument, adding words or numbers, or making any unauthorized changes that affect the obligation of a party [UCC 3–407(a)]. It is not a material alteration, however, to correct the maker's address or to change the figures on a check so that they agree with the written amount.
   Material alteration is a *complete defense* against an ordinary holder, but only a *partial defense* against an HDC. Thus, an ordinary holder can recover nothing on an instrument that has been materially altered. An HDC can enforce the instrument against the maker or drawer according to its original terms but not for the altered amount.

Universal Defense A defense that can be used to avoid payment to all holders of a negotiable instrument, including a holder in due course (HDC) or a holder with the rights of an HDC. Also called a *real defense*.

---

13. Amendments to Article 3 of the UCC provide additional protection for "remotely created" consumer items in the context of presentment also [see Amended UCC 3–417(a)(4)].

4. *Discharge in bankruptcy.* Discharge in bankruptcy is an absolute defense on any instrument, regardless of the status of the holder, because the purpose of bankruptcy is to settle all of the insolvent party's debts [UCC 3–305(a)(1)].

5. *Minority.* Minority, or infancy, is a universal defense only to the extent that state law recognizes it as a defense to a simple contract [UCC 3–305(a)(1)(i)].

6. *Illegality, mental incapacity, or extreme duress.* When the law declares an instrument to be void because it was issued in connection with illegal conduct, illegality is a universal defense. Similarly, if a person who signed the instrument has been declared by a court to be mentally incompetent, or was a under an immediate threat of force or violence, the defense is universal [UCC 3–305(a)(1)(ii)].

19-6b **Personal Defenses**

LEARNING OBJECTIVE 5

Name four defenses that can be used against an ordinary holder but are not effective against an HDC.

Personal Defense A defense that can be used to avoid payment to an ordinary holder of a negotiable instrument but not a holder in due course (HDC) or a holder with the rights of an HDC.

Personal defenses (sometimes called *limited defenses*) are effective against an ordinary holder but not against an HDC or a holder through an HDC. Personal defenses include the following:

1. *Breach of contract or breach of warranty.* When there is a breach of the underlying contract for which the negotiable instrument was issued, the maker of a note can refuse to pay it, or the drawer of a check can stop payment.

2. *Lack or failure of consideration.* The absence of consideration may be a successful personal defense in some instances [UCC 3–303(b), 3–305(a)(2)]. **EXAMPLE 19.38** Tara gives Clem, as a gift, a note that states, "I promise to pay you $100,000." Clem accepts the note. Because there is no consideration for Tara's promise, a court will not enforce the promise. ■

3. *Fraud in the inducement (ordinary fraud).* A person who issues a negotiable instrument based on false statements by the other party will be able to avoid payment on that instrument, unless the holder is an HDC.

4. *Illegality, mental incapacity, or ordinary duress.* If the law declares that an instrument is voidable because of illegality, mental incapacity, or ordinary duress, the defense is personal [UCC 3–305(a)(1)(ii)].

19-6c **Federal Limitations on the Rights of HDCs**

The federal government limits the rights of HDCs in certain circumstances because of the harsh effects that the HDC rules can sometimes have on consumers. Under the HDC doctrine, a consumer who purchased a defective product (such as a defective automobile) would continue to be liable to HDCs even if the consumer returned the defective product to the retailer.

To protect consumers who purchase defective products, the Federal Trade Commission (FTC) adopted Rule 433, which effectively abolished the HDC doctrine in consumer transactions. How does this rule curb the rights of HDCs? See this chapter's *Landmark in the Law* feature to learn more.

19-6d **Discharge from Liability**

If this woman makes a gift by writing out a note that says, "I promise to pay you $1,000," is the note enforceable?

Discharge from liability on an instrument can come from payment, cancellation, or material alteration. The liability of all parties is discharged when the party primarily liable on the instrument pays to the holder the full amount due [UCC 3–602, 3–603]. Payment by any other party (such as an indorser) discharges only the liability of that party and subsequent parties.

Intentional cancellation by the holder of an instrument discharges the liability of all parties [UCC 3–604]. Intentionally writing "Paid" across the face of an instrument cancels it, as does intentionally tearing it up. If a holder intentionally crosses out a party's signature, that party's

LANDMARK IN THE LAW — Federal Trade Commission Rule 433

In 1976, the Federal Trade Commission (FTC) issued Rule 433,[a] which severely limited the rights of HDCs that purchase instruments arising out of *consumer credit* transactions. The rule, entitled "Preservation of Consumers' Claims and Defenses," applies to any seller or lessor of goods or services who takes or receives a consumer credit contract. The rule also applies to a seller or lessor who accepts as full or partial payment for a sale or lease the proceeds of any purchase-money loan[b] made in connection with any consumer credit contract.

Under the rule, these parties must include the following provision in the consumer credit contract:

NOTICE

ANY HOLDER OF THIS CONSUMER CREDIT CONTRACT IS SUBJECT TO ALL CLAIMS AND DEFENSES WHICH THE DEBTOR COULD ASSERT AGAINST THE SELLER OF GOODS OR SERVICES OBTAINED PURSUANT HERETO OR WITH THE PROCEEDS HEREOF. RECOVERY HEREUNDER BY THE DEBTOR SHALL NOT EXCEED AMOUNTS PAID BY THE DEBTOR HEREUNDER.

Thus, a consumer who is a party to a consumer credit transaction can bring any defense she or he has against the seller of a product against a subsequent holder as well. In essence, the FTC rule places an HDC of the negotiable instrument in the position of a contract assignee. The rule makes the buyer's duty to pay conditional on the seller's full performance of the contract. Finally, the rule clearly reduces the degree of transferability of negotiable instruments resulting from consumer credit contracts.

What if the seller does not include the notice in a promissory note and then sells the note to a third party, such as a bank? In this situation, the seller has violated the rule, but the bank has not. Because the FTC rule does not prohibit third parties from purchasing notes or credit contracts that do *not* contain the required provision, the third party does not become subject to the buyer's defenses against the seller. Thus, a few consumers remain unprotected by the FTC rule.

APPLICATION TO TODAY'S WORLD *The FTC rule has been invoked in many cases involving automobiles that turned out to be "lemons," even when the consumer credit contract did not contain the FTC notice. In these and similar actions, when the notice was not included in the contract, the courts have generally inferred its presence as a contract term.*

a. 16 C.F.R. Section 433.2. The rule was enacted pursuant to the FTC's authority under the Federal Trade Commission Act, 15 U.S.C. Sections 41–58.

b. In a *purchase-money loan,* a seller or lessor advances funds to a buyer or lessee, through a credit contract, for the purchase or lease of goods.

liability and the liability of subsequent indorsers who have already indorsed the instrument are discharged.

Materially altering an instrument may discharge the liability of any party affected by the alteration, as previously discussed [UCC 3–407(b)]. An HDC may be able to enforce a materially altered instrument against its maker or drawer according to the instrument's original terms, however.

Discharge of liability can also occur when a holder impairs another party's right of recourse (right to seek reimbursement) on the instrument [UCC 3–605]. This occurs when, for instance, the holder releases, or agrees not to sue, a party against whom the indorser has a right of recourse.

Reviewing . . . Negotiable Instruments

Robert Durbin, a student, borrowed funds from a bank for his education and signed a promissory note for their repayment. The bank loaned the funds under a federal program designed to assist students at postsecondary institutions. Under this program, repayment ordinarily begins nine to twelve months after the student borrower fails to carry at least one-half of the normal full-time course load at his or her school. The federal government guarantees that the note will be fully paid. If the student defaults on the payments, the lender presents the current balance—principal, interest, and costs—to the government. When the government pays the balance, it becomes the lender, and the borrower owes the government directly. After Durbin defaulted on his note, the government paid the lender the balance due and took

Continues

possession of the note. Durbin then refused to pay the government, claiming that the government was not the holder of the note. The government filed a suit in a federal district court against Durbin to collect the amount due. Using the information presented in the chapter, answer the following questions.

1. Was the note that Durbin signed an order to pay or a promise to pay? Explain.

2. Suppose that the note did not state a specific interest rate but instead referred to a statute that established the maximum interest rate for government-guaranteed student loans. Would the note fail to meet the requirements for negotiability in that situation? Why or why not?

3. How does a party who is not named in a negotiable instrument (in this situation, the government) obtain a right to enforce the instrument?

4. Now suppose that the school Durbin attended closed down before he could finish his education. In court, Durbin argues that this resulted in a failure of consideration: he did not get something of value in exchange for his promise to pay. Assuming that the government is a holder of the promissory note, will this argument likely be successful against it? Why or why not?

DEBATE THIS

■ We should eliminate the status of holder in due course for those who possess negotiable instruments.

Key Terms

acceleration clause 468
acceptance 461
acceptor 461
bearer 469
bearer instrument 469
blank indorsement 472
certificate of deposit (CD) 463
check 462
dishonor 477
draft 461
drawee 461
drawer 461

extension clause 468
fictitious payee 481
holder 468
holder in due course (HDC) 475
imposter 481
indorsement 471
maker 462
negotiable instrument 460
negotiation 471
order instrument 468
payee 461
personal defense 484

presentment 467
presentment warranty 482
promissory note 462
qualified indorsement 473
restrictive indorsement 474
shelter principle 478
special indorsement 473
transfer warranty 482
trust indorsement 474
universal defense 483

Chapter Summary: Negotiable Instruments

Types of Instruments	The UCC specifies four types of negotiable instruments: drafts, checks, promissory notes, and certificates of deposit (CDs). These instruments fall into two basic classifications: 1. *Demand instruments versus time instruments*—A demand instrument is payable on demand (when the holder presents it to the maker or drawer). A time instrument is payable at a future date. 2. *Orders to pay versus promises to pay*—Checks and drafts are *orders* to pay. Promissory notes and CDs are *promises* to pay.

Requirements for Negotiability	To be negotiable, an instrument must meet the following requirements.
	1. *Be in writing*—A writing can be on anything that is readily transferable and has a degree of permanence [UCC 3–103(a)(6), (9)].
	2. *Be signed by the maker or drawer*—The signature can be anyplace on the face of the instrument, can be in any form (including a rubber stamp), and can be made in a representative capacity [UCC 3–103(a)(3), 3–401(b)].
	3. *Be an unconditional promise or order to pay*—
	  a. A promise must be more than a mere acknowledgment of a debt [UCC 3–103(a)(6), (9)].
	  b. Such words as "pay on demand" meet this criterion.
	  c. Payment cannot be expressly conditioned on the occurrence of an event and cannot be made subject to or governed by another contract [UCC 3–106].
	4. *State a fixed amount of money*—
	  a. An amount is considered a fixed sum if it is ascertainable from the face of the instrument or (for an interest rate) readily determinable by a formula described in the instrument [UCC –104(a), 3–112(b)].
	  b. Any medium of exchange recognized as the currency of a government is money [UCC 3—201(24)].
	5. *Be payable on demand or at a definite time*—
	  a. Any instrument that is payable on sight, presentation, or issue, or that does not state any time for payment, is a demand instrument [UCC 3—104(a)(2)].
	  b. An instrument is still payable at a definite time, even if it is payable on or before a stated date or within a fixed period after sight or if the drawer or maker has an option to extend the time for a definite period [UCC 3–108(a), (b), (c)].
	  c. Acceleration clauses do not affect the negotiability of the instrument.
	6. *Be payable to order or bearer*—
	  a. An order instrument must identify the payee with certainty.
	  b. An instrument that indicates it is not payable to an identified person is payable to bearer [UCC 3–109(a)(3)].

Factors That Do Not Affect Negotiability	Certain ambiguities (such as differences between the words and figures) or omissions (such as when an instrument is undated, antedated, or postdated) normally will not affect an instrument's negotiability.

Transfer of Instruments	1. *Transfer by assignment*—A transfer by assignment to an assignee gives the assignee only those rights that the assignor possessed. Any defenses against payment that can be raised against an assignor normally can be raised against the assignee.
	2. *Transfer by negotiation*—An order instrument is negotiated by indorsement and delivery. A bearer instrument is negotiated by delivery only.
	3. *Indorsements*—
	  a. Blank indorsements do not specify a particular indorsee and can consist of a mere signature (see Exhibit 19–5).
	  b. Special indorsements contain the signature of the indorser and identify the indorsee (see Exhibit 19–6).
	  c. Qualified indorsements contain language, such as "without recourse," that indicates the indorser is not guaranteeing payment of the instrument (see Exhibit 19–7).
	  d. Restrictive indorsements, such as "For deposit only," require the indorsee to comply with certain instructions regarding the funds involved, but do not prohibit further negotiation of the instrument (see Exhibit 19–8).

Holder in Due Course (HDC)	1. *Holder*—A person in possession of an instrument drawn, issued, or indorsed to him or her, to his or her order, to bearer, or in blank. A holder obtains only those rights that the transferor had in the instrument.
	2. *Holder in due course (HDC)*—A holder who, by meeting certain acquisition requirements, takes an instrument free of most defenses and claims to which the transferor was subject.
	3. *Requirements for HDC status*—To be an HDC, a holder must take the instrument:
	  a. For value—A holder can take an instrument for value in five ways: by performing the promise, acquiring a security interest or lien in the instrument, taking the instrument as payment for a preexisting obligation, giving the instrument as payment, or giving an irrevocable commitment as payment [UCC 3–303].
	  b. In good faith—Good faith is defined as "honesty in fact and the observance of reasonable commercial standards of fair dealing" [UCC 3–103(a)(4)].
	  c. Without notice—To be an HDC, a holder must not be on notice that the instrument is defective because it is overdue, has been dishonored, is part of a series of which at least one instrument has a uncured defect, contains an unauthorized signature or has been altered, or is so irregular or incomplete as to call its authenticity into question.
	4. *Shelter principle*—A holder who cannot qualify as an HDC has the *rights* of an HDC if the holder derives her or his title through an HDC, unless the holder engaged in fraud or illegality affecting the instrument [UCC 3–203(b)].

Continues

Signature and Warranty Liability	Liability on negotiable instruments can arise either from a person's signature or from the warranties that are implied when a person presents the instrument for negotiation.

1. *Signature liability*—Every party (except a qualified indorser) who signs a negotiable instrument is either primarily or secondarily liable for payment of the instrument when it comes due.

   a. Primary liability—Makers and acceptors are primarily liable [UCC 3–115, 3–407, 3–409, 3–412].

   b. Secondary liability—Drawers and indorsers are secondarily liable [UCC 3–412, 3–414, 3–415, 3–501, 3–502, 3–503]. Parties are secondarily liable on an instrument only if (1) presentment is proper and timely, (2) the instrument is dishonored, and (3) they received timely notice of dishonor.

2. *Transfer warranties*—Any person who transfers an instrument for consideration makes five warranties to subsequent transferees and holders [UCC 3–416].

   a. The transferor is entitled to enforce the instrument.

   b. All signatures are authentic and authorized.

   c. The instrument has not been altered.

   d. The instrument is not subject to a defense or claim of any party that can be asserted against the transferor.

   e. The transferor has no knowledge of any bankruptcy proceedings against the maker, the acceptor, or the drawer of the instrument.

3. *Presentment warranties*—Any person who presents an instrument for payment or acceptance makes three warranties to any person who in good faith pays or accepts the instrument [UCC 3–417(a), 3–417(d)].

   a. The person is entitled to enforce the instrument or is authorized to act on behalf of a person who is so entitled.

   b. The instrument has not been altered.

   c. The person has no knowledge that the drawer's signature is unauthorized.

Defenses, Limitations, and Discharge	

1. *Universal (real) defenses*—The following defenses are valid against all holders, including HDCs and holders with the rights of HDCs [UCC 3–305, 3–403, 3–407]:

   a. Forgery.

   b. Fraud in the execution.

   c. Material alteration.

   d. Discharge in bankruptcy.

   e. Minority—if the contract is voidable under state law.

   f. Illegality, mental incapacity, or extreme duress—if the contract is void under state law.

2. *Personal (limited) defenses*—The following defenses are valid against ordinary holders but not against HDCs or holders with the rights of HDCs [UCC 3–303, 3–305]:

   a. Breach of contract or breach of warranty.

   b. Lack or failure of consideration (value).

   c. Fraud in the inducement.

   d. Illegality, mental incapacity, or ordinary duress—if the contract is voidable.

3. *Federal limitations on the rights of HDCs*—Rule 433 of the Federal Trade Commission, issued in 1976, limits the rights of HDCs who purchase instruments arising out of consumer credit transactions. The rule allows a consumer who is a party to such a transaction to bring any defense he or she has against the seller against a subsequent holder as well, even if the subsequent holder is an HDC.

4. *Discharge from liability*—All parties to a negotiable instrument will be discharged when the party primarily liable on it pays to the holder the full amount due. Discharge can also occur in other circumstances (if the instrument has been canceled or materially altered, for example) [UCC 3–602 through 3–605].

Issue Spotters

1. Sabrina owes $600 to Yale, who asks Sabrina to sign an instrument for the debt. If written on the instrument by Sabrina, which of the following would prevent its negotiability: "I.O.U. $600," "I promise to pay $600," or an instruction to the bank stating, "I wish you would pay $600 to Yale"? Why? (See *Requirements for Negotiability*.)

2. Rye signs corporate checks for Suchin Corporation. Rye writes a check payable to U-All Company, even though Suchin does not owe U-All anything. Rye signs the check, forges U-All's indorsement, and cashes the check at Viceroy Bank, the drawee. Does Suchin have any recourse against the bank for the payment? Why or why not? (See *Signature and Warranty Liability*.)

—**Check your answers to the *Issue Spotters* against the answers provided in Appendix D at the end of this text.**

Learning Objectives Check

1. What requirements must an instrument meet to be negotiable?
2. How does the negotiation of order instruments differ from the negotiation of bearer instruments?
3. What are the requirements for attaining the status of a holder in due course (HDC)?
4. What is the difference between signature liability and warranty liability?
5. Name four defenses that can be used against an ordinary holder but are not effective against an HDC.

—Answers to the even-numbered *Learning Objectives Check* questions can be found in Appendix E in at the end of this text.

Business Scenarios and Case Problems

19–1. Negotiable Instruments. Muriel Evans writes the following note on the back of an envelope: "I, Muriel Evans, promise to pay Karen Marvin or bearer $100 on demand." Is this a negotiable instrument? Discuss fully. (See *Requirements for Negotiability*.)

19–2. Material Alteration. Williams purchased a used car from Stein for $1,000. Williams paid for the car with a check (written in pencil) payable to Stein for $1,000. Stein, through careful erasures and alterations, changed the amount on the check to read $10,000 and negotiated the check to Boz. Boz took the check for value, in good faith, and without notice of the alteration and thus met the Uniform Commercial Code's requirements for the status of a holder in due course. Can Williams successfully raise the universal (real) defense of material alteration to avoid payment on the check? Explain. (See *Defenses, Limitations, and Discharge*.)

19–3. Payable on Demand or at a Definite Time. Abby Novel signed a handwritten note that read, "Glen Gallwitz 1-8-2002 loaned me $5,000 at 6 percent interest a total of $10,000.00." The note did not state a time for repayment. Novel used the funds to manufacture and market a patented jewelry display design. More than seven years after Novel signed the note, Gallwitz filed a suit to recover the stated amount. Novel claimed that she did not have to pay because the note was not negotiable—it was incomplete. Is she correct? Explain. [*Gallwitz v. Novel*, 2011 Ohio 297 (5 Dist. 2011)] (See *Requirements for Negotiability*.)

19–4. Defenses. Thomas Klutz obtained a franchise from Kahala Franchise Corp. to operate a Samurai Sam's restaurant. Under their agreement, Klutz could transfer the franchise only if he obtained Kahala's approval and paid a transfer fee. Without telling Kahala, Klutz sold the restaurant to William Thorbecke. Thorbecke signed a note for the price. When Kahala learned of the deal, the franchisor told Thorbecke to stop using the Samurai Sam's name. Thorbecke stopped paying on the note, and Klutz filed a claim for the unpaid amount. In defense, Thorbecke asserted breach of contract and fraud. Are these defenses effective against Klutz? Explain. [*Kahala Franchise Corp. v. Hit Enterprises*, LLC, 159 Wash.App. 1013 (Div. 2 2011)] (See *Defenses, Limitations, and Discharge*.)

19–5. Business Case Problem with Sample Answer— Negotiation. Sandra Ford signed a note and a mortgage on her home in Westwood, New Jersey, to borrow $403,750 from Argent Mortgage Co. Argent transferred the note and mortgage to Wells Fargo Bank, N.A., without indorsement. The following spring, Ford stopped making payments on the note. Wells Fargo filed a suit in a New Jersey state court against Ford to foreclose on the mortgage. Ford asserted that Argent had committed fraud in connection with the note by providing misleading information and charging excessive fees. Ford contended that Wells Fargo was subject to these defenses because the bank was not a holder in due course of the note. Was the transfer of the note from Argent to Wells Fargo a negotiation or an assignment? What difference does it make? If Argent indorsed the note to Wells Fargo later, would the bank's status change? Discuss. [*Wells Fargo Bank, N.A. v. Ford*, 418 N.J.Super. 592, 15 A.3d 327 (App.Div. 2011)] (See *Transfer of Instruments*.)

—For a sample answer to Problem 19–5, go to Appendix F at the end of this text.

19–6. Indorsements. Angela Brock borrowed $544,000 and signed a note payable to Amerifund Mortgage Services, LLC, to buy a house in Silver Spring, Maryland. The note was indorsed in blank and transferred several times "without recourse" before Brock fell behind on the payments. On behalf of Deutsche Bank National Trust Co., BAC Home Loans Servicing LP initiated foreclosure. Brock filed an action in a Maryland state court to block it, arguing that BAC could not foreclose because Deutsche Bank, not BAC, owned the note. Can BAC enforce the note? Explain. [*Deutsche Bank National Trust Co. v. Brock*, 63 A.3d 40 (Md. 2013)] (See *Transfer of Instruments*.)

19–7. Bearer Instruments. Eligio Gaitan borrowed the funds to buy real property in Downers Grove, Illinois, and signed a note payable to Encore Credit Corp. Encore indorsed the note in blank. Later, when Gaitan defaulted on the payments, an action to foreclose on the property was filed in an Illinois state court by U.S. Bank, N.A. The note was in the bank's possession, but there was no evidence that the note had been transferred or negotiated to the bank. Can U.S. Bank enforce payment of the note? Why or why not? [*U.S. Bank National Association v. Gaitan,* 2013 IL App (2d) 120105-U, 2013 WL 160378 (2013)] (See *Requirements for Negotiability.*)

19–8. Transfer by Negotiation. Thao Thi Duong signed a note in the amount of $200,000 in favor of Country Home Loans, Inc., to obtain a loan to buy a house in Marrero, Louisiana. The note was indorsed "PAY TO THE ORDER OF [blank space] WITHOUT RECOURSE COUNTRY HOME LOANS, INC." Almost five years later, Duong defaulted on the payments. The Federal National Mortgage Association (Fannie Mae) had come into possession of the note. Fannie Mae wanted to foreclose on the house and sell it to recover the balance due. Duong argued that the words "to the order of [blank space]" in the indorsement made the note an incomplete order instrument and that Fannie Mae thus could not enforce it. What is Fannie Mae's best response to this argument? [*Federal National Mortgage Association v. Thao Thi Duong,* __ So.3d __, 2015 WL 629284 (La.App. 5 Cir. 2015)] (See *Transfer of Instruments.*)

19–9. A Question of Ethics—Promissory Notes. Clarence Morgan, Jr., owned Easy Way Automotive, a car dealership in D'Lo, Mississippi. Easy Way sold a truck to Loyd Barnard, who signed a note for the amount of the price payable to Trustmark National Bank in six months. Before the note came due, Barnard returned the truck to Easy Way, which sold it to another buyer. Using some of the proceeds from the second sale, Easy Way sent a check to Trustmark to pay Barnard's note. Meanwhile, Barnard obtained another truck from Easy Way, financed through another six-month note payable to Trustmark. After eight of these deals, some of which involved more than one truck, an Easy Way check to Trustmark was dishonored. In a suit in a Mississippi state court, Trustmark sought to recover the amounts of two of the notes from Barnard. Trustmark had not secured titles to two of the trucks covered by the notes, however, and this complicated Barnard's efforts to reclaim the vehicles from the later buyers. [*Trustmark National Bank v. Barnard,* 930 So.2d 1281 (Miss.App. 2006)] (See *Types of Negotiable Instruments.*)

1. On what basis might Barnard be liable on the Trustmark notes? Would he be primarily or secondarily liable? Could this liability be discharged on the theory that Barnard's right of recourse had been impaired when Trustmark did not secure titles to the trucks covered by the notes? Explain.

2. Easy Way's account had been subject to other recent overdrafts, and a week after the check to Trustmark was returned for insufficient funds, Morgan committed suicide. At the same time, Barnard was unable to obtain a mortgage because the unpaid notes affected his credit rating. How do the circumstances of this case underscore the importance of practicing business ethics?

Critical Thinking and Writing Assignments

19–10. Case Analysis Question. Go to Appendix G at the end of this text and examine the excerpt of Case No. 3, *Mills v. Chauvin.* Review and then brief the case, making sure that your brief answers the following questions. (See *Defenses, Limitations, and Discharge.*)

1. **Issue:** What document was at the center of the dispute in this case?
2. **Rule of Law:** What are the elements of consideration? What are the requirements for attaining the status of a holder in due course (HDC)?
3. **Application:** Did the document at the center of the dispute in this case satisfy the elements of consideration? Did the party in possession of the document take it as an HDC? Explain.
4. **Conclusion:** Who did the court determine was liable? Why?

19–11. Business Law Critical Thinking Group Assignment. Peter Gowin was an employee of a granite countertop business owned by Joann Stathis. In November 2016, Gowin signed a promissory note agreeing to pay $12,500 in order to become a co-owner of the business. The note was dated January 15, 2016 (ten months before it was signed), and required him to make installment payments starting in February 2016. Stathis told Gowin not to worry about the note and never requested any payments. Gowin continued to work at the business until 2018, when he quit, claiming that he owned half of the business. Stathis argued that Gowin was not a co-owner because he had never paid the $12,500 into the business. (See *Requirements for Negotiability.*)

1. The first group will argue in favor of Stathis that Gowin did not own any interest in the business.
2. The second group will evaluate the strength of Gowin's argument. Gowin claimed that because compliance with the stated dates was impossible, the note effectively did not state a date for its payment. It therefore was a demand note under UCC 3–108(a). Because no demand for payment had been made, Gowin's obligation to pay had not arisen, and the termination of his ownership interest was improper.

iStockPhoto.com/Spaceliner

20

- Checks
- The Bank-Customer Relationship
- The Bank's Duty to Honor Checks
- The Bank's Duty to Accept Deposits
- Electronic Fund Transfers
- Online Banking and E-Money

Banking in the Digital Age

LEARNING OBJECTIVES

The five Learning Objectives *below are designed to help improve your understanding of the chapter. After reading this chapter, you should be able to answer the following questions:*

"Money is just what we use to keep tally."

HENRY FORD
1863–1947
(AMERICAN AUTOMOBILE MANUFACTURER)

In the chapter-opening quotation, Henry Ford said that "we use money to keep tally." If we do, then checks help us, because checks serve as a substitute for cash. Checks are the most common type of negotiable instruments regulated by the Uniform Commercial Code (UCC). Many people today use debit cards rather than checks for their retail transactions, and payments are increasingly being made via smartphones, iPads, and other mobile devices. Nonetheless, commercial checks remain an integral part of the U.S. economic system.

Articles 3 and 4 of the UCC govern issues relating to checks. Article 4 of the UCC governs bank deposits and collections as well as bank-customer relationships. Article 4 also regulates the relationships of banks with one another as they process checks for payment, and it establishes a framework for deposit and checking agreements between a bank and its customers. A check therefore may fall within the scope of Article 3 as a negotiable instrument and yet be subject to the provisions of Article 4 while in the course of collection. If a conflict between Article 3 and Article 4 arises, Article 4 controls [UCC 4–102(a)].

1. What type of check does a bank agree in advance to accept when the check is presented for payment?

2. When may a bank properly dishonor a customer's check without being liable to the customer?

3. What duties does the Uniform Commercial Code impose on a bank's customers with regard to forged and altered checks? What are the consequences if a customer is negligent in performing those duties?

4. What is electronic check presentment, and how does it differ from the traditional check-clearing process?

5. What are the four most common types of electronic fund transfers?

20-1 Checks

A *check* is a special type of draft that is drawn on a bank, ordering the bank to pay a fixed amount of funds on demand [UCC 3–104(f)]. Article 4 defines a *bank* as "a person engaged in the business of banking, including a savings bank, savings and loan association, credit union or trust company" [UCC 4–105(1)]. If any other institution (such as a brokerage firm) handles a check for payment or for collection, the check is *not* covered by Article 4.

491

A person who writes a check is called the *drawer*. The drawer is a depositor in the bank on which the check is drawn. The person to whom the check is payable is the *payee*. The bank or financial institution on which the check is drawn is the *drawee*. Thus, when Anita Cruzak writes a check from her checking account to pay her college tuition, she is the drawer, her bank is the drawee, and her college is the payee. We now look at some special types of checks.

20–1a Cashier's Checks

Cashier's Check A check drawn by a bank on itself.

Checks usually are three-party instruments, but on certain types of checks, the bank can serve as both the drawer and the drawee. For instance, when a bank draws a check on itself, the check is called a **cashier's check** and is a negotiable instrument at the moment it is issued (see Exhibit 20–1) [UCC 3–104(g)]. Normally, a cashier's check indicates a specific payee. In effect, with a cashier's check, the bank assumes responsibility for paying the check, thus making the check more readily acceptable as a substitute for cash.

EXAMPLE 20.1 Kramer needs to pay a moving company $8,000 for moving his household goods to his new home in another state. The moving company requests payment in the form of a cashier's check. Kramer goes to a bank (he need not have an account at the bank) and purchases a cashier's check, payable to the moving company, in the amount of $8,000. Kramer has to pay the bank the $8,000 for the check, plus a small service fee. He then gives the check to the moving company. ■

Except in very limited circumstances, the issuing bank must honor its cashier's checks when they are presented for payment. If a bank wrongfully dishonors a cashier's check, a holder can recover from the bank all expenses incurred, interest, and consequential damages [UCC 3–411].[1] This same rule applies if a bank wrongfully dishonors a certified check (to be discussed shortly).

---

1. See, for example, *MidAmerica Bank v. Charter One Bank*, 232 Ill.2d 560, 905 N.E.2d 839 (2009).

Exhibit 20–1 A Cashier's Check

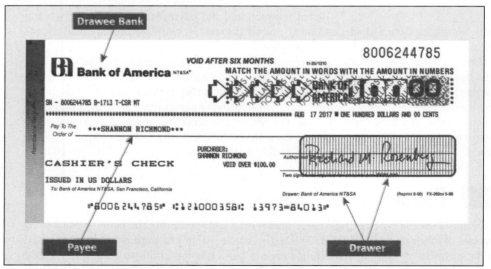

* The abbreviation *NT&SA* stands for National Trust and Savings Association. The Bank of America NT&SA is a subsidiary of Bank of America Corporation, which is engaged in financial services, insurance, investment management, and other businesses.

20-1b Traveler's Checks

A **traveler's check** is an instrument that is payable on demand, drawn on or payable at or through a financial institution (such as a bank), and designated as a traveler's check. The issuing institution is directly obligated to accept and pay its traveler's check according to the check's terms.

Traveler's checks are designed to be a safe substitute for cash for people who are on vacation or traveling. They are issued for fixed amounts, such as $20, $50, or $100. The purchaser is required to sign the check at the time it is bought and again at the time it is used [UCC 3–104(i)]. Most major banks today do not issue their own traveler's checks but, instead, purchase and issue American Express traveler's checks for their customers (see Exhibit 20–2).

20-1c Certified Checks

A **certified check** is a check that has been accepted in writing by the bank on which it is drawn [UCC 3–409(d)]. When a drawee bank certifies a check, it immediately charges the drawer's account with the amount of the check and transfers those funds to its own certified check account. In effect, the bank is agreeing in advance to accept that check when it is presented for payment and to make payment from those funds reserved in its certified check account. Essentially, certification prevents the bank from denying liability. It is a promise that sufficient funds are on deposit *and have been set aside* to cover the check.

To certify a check, the bank writes or stamps the word *certified* on the face of the check and typically writes the amount that it will pay.[2] Once a check is certified, the drawer and any prior indorsers are completely discharged from liability on the check [UCC 3–414(c), 3–415(d)]. Only the certifying bank is required to pay the instrument.

Either the drawer or the holder (payee) of a check can request certification. The drawee bank is not required to certify the check, however, and the bank's refusal to certify a check is not a dishonor of the check [UCC 3–409(d)].

Traveler's Check A check that is payable on demand, drawn on or payable through a financial institution, and designated as a traveler's check.

LEARNING OBJECTIVE 1

What type of check does a bank agree in advance to accept when the check is presented for payment?

Certified Check A check that has been accepted in writing by the bank on which it is drawn. By certifying (accepting) the check, the bank promises to pay the check at the time it is presented.

---

2. If the certification does not state an amount, and the amount is later increased and the instrument negotiated to a holder in due course (HDC), the obligation of the certifying bank is the amount of the instrument when it was taken by the HDC [UCC 3–413(b)].

Exhibit 20–2 A Traveler's Check

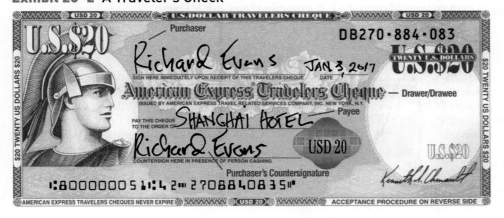

20-2 The Bank-Customer Relationship

The bank-customer relationship begins when the customer opens a checking account and deposits funds that the bank will use to pay for checks written by the customer. Essentially, three types of relationships come into being, as discussed next.

20-2a Creditor-Debtor Relationship

A creditor-debtor relationship is created between a customer and a bank when, for example, the customer makes cash deposits into a checking account. When a customer makes a deposit, the customer becomes a creditor, and the bank a debtor, for the amount deposited.

20-2b Agency Relationship

An agency relationship arises between the customer and the bank when the customer writes a check on his or her account. In effect, the customer is ordering the bank to pay the amount specified on the check to the holder when the holder presents the check to the bank for payment. In this situation, the bank becomes the customer's agent and is obligated to honor the customer's request.

Similarly, if the customer deposits a check into his or her account, the bank, as the customer's agent, is obligated to collect payment on the check from the bank on which the check was drawn. To transfer checking account funds among different banks, each bank acts as the agent of collection for its customer [UCC 4–201(a)].

20-2c Contractual Relationship

When a bank-customer relationship is established, certain contractual rights and duties arise. The contractual rights and duties of the bank and its customer depend on the nature of the transaction. These rights and duties are discussed in detail in the following pages. Another aspect of the bank-customer relationship—deposit insurance—is examined in the *Linking Business Law to Accounting and Finance* feature at the end of this chapter.

The following case arose when a company realized that the balance in its corporate bank account was depleted. In fact, service charges had resulted in a negative balance. Under the parties' account agreement, was the bank liable for the loss of the funds?

CASE 20.1

Royal Arcanum Hospital Association of Kings County, Inc. v. Herrnkind

New York Supreme Court, Appellate Division, Second Department, 113 A.D.3d 672, 978 N.Y.S.2d 355 (2014).

FACTS The board of the Royal Arcanum Hospital Association of Kings County, Inc., passed a resolution to require that all corporate checks be signed by two of three officers—Frank Vassallo, Joseph Rugilio, and William Herrnkind. The three were also named as signatories on the firm's account with Capital One Bank, but the terms of the account did not include the two-signature requirement. After Vassallo and Rugilio died, Herrnkind opened a

Can a customer account require two signatures for any check?

new account in the corporate name that expressly permitted checks to be drawn on it with only one signature. Only Herrnkind's name appeared on the signature card. The account statements were sent to Royal Arcanum "care of William Herrnkind."

Over the next four years, a series of transactions reduced the balance of the account from nearly $200,000 to zero. Royal Arcanum filed a suit in a New York state court against Herrnkind and

Capital One to recover the funds. The court dismissed the complaint against the bank. Royal Arcanum appealed.

ISSUE Was Capital One liable for the payment of unauthorized withdrawals from its customer's corporate accounts?

DECISION No. A state intermediate appellate court affirmed the decision of the lower court to dismiss Royal Arcanum's complaint against Capital One.

REASON The contractual relationship between a bank and its customer includes the understanding that the bank will pay out the customer's funds only as instructed. In this case, although Royal Arcanum's board required two signatures on its corporate checks, the terms of the accounts with Capital Bank did not require two

signatures. Because the terms permitted checks to be drawn with only one signature, the bank did not breach its customer's requirement. Also, "insofar as the Bank's transactions with the plaintiff were concerned, the plaintiff conferred, at the least, apparent authority on Herrnkind to act on its behalf."

Under these circumstances, the bank used "due care and diligence," as there was nothing to "arouse the suspicion of its employees." Thus, the bank was not liable for the payment of unauthorized withdrawals from Royal Arcanum's accounts.

CRITICAL THINKING—Legal Consideration *What circumstances indicated that Herrnkind had Royal Arcanum's authority to act on its behalf?*

20–3 The Bank's Duty to Honor Checks

When a banking institution provides checking services, it agrees to honor the checks written by its customers, with the usual stipulation that the account must have sufficient funds available to pay each check [UCC 4–401(a)]. When a drawee bank *wrongfully* fails to honor a check, it is liable to its customer for damages resulting from its refusal to pay [UCC 4–402(b)]. The customer does not have to prove that the bank breached its contractual commitment or was negligent.

The customer's agreement with the bank includes a general obligation to keep sufficient funds on deposit to cover all checks written. The customer is liable to the payee or to the holder of a check in a civil suit if a check is dishonored for insufficient funds. If intent to defraud can be proved, the customer can also be subject to criminal prosecution for writing a bad check.

When the bank properly dishonors a check for insufficient funds, it has no liability to the customer. The bank may rightfully refuse payment on a customer's check in other circumstances as well. We look here at the rights and duties of both the bank and its customers in specific situations.

Can a bank that issues a refund check to a customer then refuse to cash it for that customer? Rarely does a bank draft a check to a customer, but occasionally it does happen—for instance, when the bank is refunding a deposit or closing a customer's account. If the customer presents the check to the same bank that issued it (and the bank is both drawer and drawee), we would expect that the customer would have no trouble cashing it. Not so for Ama Afiriyie.

When Afiriyie first opened checking and savings accounts with Bank of America (BOA), the bank required her to pay a security deposit of $300 to get a "secured" credit card. A year later, BOA upgraded Afiriyie's credit-card account to unsecured status and issued her a refund check for $300. Afiriyie took the check to a BOA branch inside a grocery store, but the branch manager, Diane Lowe, was suspicious and refused to cash it. Lowe also called the police and reported that Afiriyie was trying to pass a fraudulent or counterfeit check.

Afiriyie was arrested, fingerprinted, and held for several hours until police discovered that the check was legitimate and released her. She filed suit against BOA, alleging wrongful dishonor (among other claims). When a jury found in Afiriyie's favor, BOA appealed. The bank argued that there was no wrongful dishonor, because under UCC 3–503(b)(4), it had until the

ETHICAL ISSUE

day after Afiriyie presented the check to process the payment. The court, however, was not persuaded. "BOA cannot, on the one hand, cause plaintiff to be arrested for attempting to pass a fraudulent check, and, on the other hand, claim that they never dishonored that check." BOA's refusal to cash the check constituted wrongful dishonor.[3]

When you open a checking account, do you establish a contractual relationship?

20-3a Overdrafts

When the bank receives an item properly payable from its customer's checking account but the account contains insufficient funds to cover the amount of the check, the bank has two options. It can dishonor the item, or it can pay the item and charge the customer's account, thus creating an **overdraft**. The bank can subtract the amount of the overdraft (plus a service charge) from the customer's next deposit or other customer funds, because a check carries with it an enforceable implied promise to reimburse the bank.

A bank can expressly agree with a customer to accept overdrafts through what is sometimes called an "overdraft protection agreement." If such an agreement is formed, any failure of the bank to honor a check because it would create an overdraft breaches this agreement and is treated as a wrongful dishonor [UCC 4–402(a)].

20-3b Postdated Checks

A bank may charge a postdated check against a customer's account, unless the customer notifies the bank, in a timely manner, not to pay the check until the stated date. The notice of postdating must be given in time to allow the bank to act on the notice before it pays the check. If the bank fails to act on the customer's notice and charges the customer's account before the date on the postdated check, the bank may be liable for any damages incurred by the customer [UCC 4–401(c)].[4]

20-3c Stale Checks

Commercial banking practice regards a check that is presented for payment more than six months from its date as a **stale check**. A bank is not obligated to pay an uncertified check presented more than six months from its date [UCC 4–404].

When it receives a stale check for payment, the bank has the option of paying or not paying the check. The bank may consult the customer before paying the check. If a bank pays a stale check in good faith without consulting the customer, the bank has the right to charge the customer's account for the amount of the check.

20-3d Stop-Payment Orders

A **stop-payment order** is an order by a customer to his or her bank not to pay or certify a certain check. Only a customer (or a person authorized to draw on the account) can order the bank not to pay the check when it is presented for payment [UCC 4–403(a)].[5] A customer has no right to stop payment on a check that has been certified or accepted by a bank, however. In addition, the customer-drawer must have a *valid legal ground* for issuing such an order, or the holder can sue the customer-drawer for payment.

Overdraft A check that is paid by a bank when the checking account on which the check is written contains insufficient funds to cover the check.

Stale Check A check, other than a certified check, that is presented for payment more than six months after its date.

Stop-Payment Order An order by a bank customer to his or her bank not to pay or certify a certain check.

---

3. *Afiriyie v. Bank of America, N.A.,* 2013 WL 451895 (Sup.Ct. N.J. 2013). The intermediate appellate court also affirmed the trial court's finding that the damages awarded by the jury were too high and that a new trial should be held to determine proper damages.

4. Postdating does not affect the negotiability of a check. A check is usually paid without respect to its date.

5. Any person claiming a legitimate interest in the account of a deceased customer may issue a stop-payment order [UCC 4–405].

Reasonable Time and Manner The customer must issue the stop-payment order within a reasonable time and in a reasonable manner to permit the bank to act on it [UCC 4–403(a)]. Most banks allow stop-payment orders to be submitted electronically via the bank's Web site. A written or electronic stop-payment order is effective for six months, at which time it may be renewed [UCC 4–403(b)]. Although a stop-payment order can be given orally over the phone, it is binding on the bank for only fourteen calendar days unless confirmed in writing (or record).[6]

Bank's Liability for Wrongful Payment If the bank pays the check in spite of a stop-payment order, the bank will be obligated to recredit the customer's account. In addition, if the bank's payment over a stop-payment order causes subsequent checks written on the drawer's account to "bounce," the bank will be liable for the resultant costs the drawer incurs. The bank is liable only for the amount of actual damages suffered by the drawer, however [UCC 4–403(c)].

20-3e Death or Incompetence of a Customer

Neither the death nor the incompetence of a customer revokes a bank's authority to pay an item until the bank is informed of the situation and has had a reasonable amount of time to act on the notice. Without this provision, banks would constantly be required to verify the continued life and competence of their drawers.

Thus, if a bank is unaware that a customer who wrote a check has been declared incompetent or has died, the bank can pay the item without incurring liability [UCC 4–405]. Even when a bank knows of the death of its customer, for ten days after the *date of death,* it can pay or certify checks drawn on or before the date of death. An exception to this rule is made if a person claiming an interest in the account, such as an heir, orders the bank to stop payment.

20-3f Checks with Forged Drawers' Signatures

When a bank pays a check on which the drawer's signature is forged, generally the bank is liable. A bank may be able to recover at least some of the loss from the customer, however, if the customer's negligence contributed to the making of the forgery. A bank may also obtain partial recovery from the forger of the check (if he or she can be found) or from the holder who presented the check for payment (if the holder knew that the signature was forged).

The General Rule A forged signature on a check has no legal effect as the signature of a customer-drawer [UCC 3–403(a)]. For this reason, banks require a signature card from each customer who opens a checking account. Signature cards allow the bank to verify whether the signatures on its customers' checks are genuine. (Banks today normally verify signatures only on checks that exceed a certain threshold, such as $2,500 or some higher amount, because it would be too costly to verify every signature.)

The general rule is that the bank must recredit the customer's account when it pays a check with a forged signature. A bank may contractually shift to the customer the risk of forged checks created electronically or by the use other nonmanual signatures. For instance, the contract might stipulate that the customer is solely responsible for maintaining security over the customer's signature stamp for checks.

Customer Negligence When the customer's negligence substantially contributed to the forgery, the bank normally will not be obligated to recredit the customer's account for the amount of the check [UCC 3–406]. The customer's liability may be reduced, however, by the amount

"Canceled checks will be to future historians and cultural anthropologists what the Dead Sea Scrolls and hieroglyphics are to us."

BRENT STAPLES
1951–PRESENT
(AMERICAN JOURNALIST)

---

6. Some states do not recognize oral stop-payment orders.

of loss caused by negligence on the part of the bank (or other person) paying the instrument or taking it for value if the negligence substantially contributed to the loss [UCC 3–406(b)].

CASE EXAMPLE 20.2 Kenneth Wulf worked for Auto-Owners Insurance Company for ten years. During that time, Wulf opened a checking account at Bank One in the name of "Auto-Owners, Kenneth B. Wulf." Over a period of eight years, he deposited $546,000 worth of checks that he had stolen from Auto-Owners and indorsed with a stamp that read "Auto-Owners Insurance Deposit Only." When the scam was finally discovered, Auto-Owners sued Bank One for negligence.

The insurance company claimed that the bank should not have allowed Wulf to open an account in Auto-Owners' name without proof that he was authorized to do so. The court ruled in favor of the bank, though, finding that Bank One's conduct was not a substantial factor in bringing about the loss. The negligence of Auto-Owners—its lack of oversight of its employee—contributed substantially to its own losses. Therefore, the bank did not have to recredit the customer's account.[7] ■

Timely Examination Required.
Banks typically send or provide online monthly statements that detail the activity in their customers' checking accounts. The statements provide customers with information (check number, amount, and date of payment) that will allow them to reasonably identify the checks that the bank has paid [UCC 4–406(a), (b)]. In the past, banks routinely included the canceled checks themselves (or copies of them) with the statement, but that practice is unusual today. If the bank does retain the canceled checks, it must keep the checks—or legible copies—for seven years [UCC 4–406(b)].

The customer has a duty to promptly examine bank statements (and canceled checks or copies) with reasonable care and to report any alterations or forged signatures [UCC 4–406(c)]. This includes forged signatures of indorsers, if discovered (to be discussed shortly). If the customer fails to fulfill this duty and the bank suffers a loss as a result, the customer will be liable for the loss [UCC 4–406(d)].

Consequences of Failing to Detect Forgeries.
Sometimes, the same wrongdoer has forged a customer's signature on a series of checks. To recover for all the forged items, the customer must discover and report the *first* forged check to the bank within thirty calendar days of the receipt of the bank statement [UCC 4–406(d)(2)]. Failure to notify the bank within this period of time discharges the bank's liability for *all* of the forged checks that it pays prior to notification.

CASE EXAMPLE 20.3 Joseph Montanez, an employee at Espresso Roma Corporation, used stolen software and blank checks to generate company checks on his home computer. The series of forged checks spanned a period of over two years and totaled more than $330,000. When the bank statements containing the forged checks arrived in the mail, Montanez removed the checks so that the forgeries would go undetected.

Eventually, Espresso Roma discovered the forgeries and asked the bank to recredit its account. The bank refused, and litigation ensued. The court held that the bank was not liable for the forged checks because Espresso Roma had failed to report the first forgeries within the UCC's time period of thirty days.[8] ■

When the Bank Is Also Negligent
If a customer who has been negligent can prove that the bank was also negligent, then the bank will also be liable. In this situation, the loss will be allocated between the bank and the customer on the basis of comparative negligence [UCC 4–406(e)]. In other words, even though a customer may have been negligent, the bank may have to recredit the customer's account for a portion of the loss if the bank also failed to exercise

What is the time limit within which a bank customer must report the first in a series of forged checks?

---

7. *Auto-Owners Insurance Co. v. Bank One*, 879 N.E.2d 1086 (Ind.Sup.Ct. 2008).
8. *Espresso Roma Corp. v. Bank of America, N.A.*, 100 Cal.App.4th 525, 124 Cal.Rptr.2d 549 (2002).

ordinary care. (*Ordinary care* means the observance of reasonable banking standards prevailing in the relevant geographical area [UCC 3–103].)

One-Year Time Limit Regardless of the degree of care exercised by the customer or the bank, the UCC places an absolute time limit on the liability of a bank for paying a check with a forged customer signature. A customer who fails to report a forged signature within one year from the date of the bank statement loses the legal right to have the bank recredit his or her account [UCC 4–406(f)]. The parties can also agree in their contract to a lower time limit.

Other Parties from Whom the Bank May Recover As noted earlier, a forged signature on a check has no legal effect as the signature of a drawer. Instead, the person who forged the signature is liable [UCC 3–403(a)]. Therefore, when a bank pays a check on which the drawer's signature is forged, the bank has a right to recover from the party who forged the signature (if he or she can be found).

Forgery of checks by employees and embezzlement of company funds are disturbingly common in today's business world. To avoid significant losses due to forgery or embezzlement, as well as litigation, use care in maintaining business bank accounts. Limit access to your business's bank accounts. Never leave company checkbooks or signature stamps in unsecured areas. Use passwords to limit access to computerized check-writing software. Examine bank statements in a timely fashion, and be on the lookout for suspicious transactions. Remember that if a forgery is not reported within thirty days of the first statement in which the forged item appears, you, as the account holder, normally lose the right to hold the bank liable.

PREVENTING LEGAL DISPUTES

20–3g Checks Bearing Forged Indorsements

A bank that pays a customer's check bearing a forged indorsement must recredit the customer's account or be liable to the customer-drawer for breach of contract. **EXAMPLE 20.4** Simon issues a $500 check "to the order of Antonio." Juan steals the check, forges Antonio's indorsement, and cashes the check. When the check reaches Simon's bank, the bank pays it and debits Simon's account. The bank must recredit the $500 to Simon's account because it failed to carry out Simon's order to pay "to the order of Antonio" [UCC 4–401(a)]. ■

Eventually, *the loss usually falls on the first party to take the instrument bearing the forged indorsement* because a forged indorsement does not transfer title. Thus, whoever takes an instrument with a forged indorsement cannot become a holder. In *Example 20.4*, Simon's bank can recover—for breach of warranty—from the bank that cashed the check when Juan presented it [UCC 4–207(a)(2)].

The customer, in any event, has a duty to report forged indorsements promptly. Failure to report forged indorsements within a three-year period after the forged items have been made available to the customer relieves the bank of liability [UCC 4–111].

In the following case, a bank's contract with its customer altered its statutory duties concerning forged indorsements. The court had to decide whether to follow the UCC or enforce the contract as written.

LEARNING OBJECTIVE 3

What duties does the Uniform Commercial Code impose on a bank's customers with regard to forged and altered checks? What are the consequences if a customer is negligent in performing those duties?

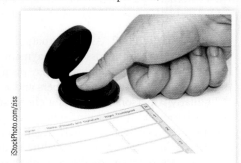

iStockPhoto.com/ziss

Sometimes, when a person attempts to cash a check at a bank, the bank requests a thumbprint on the back of the check. Why?

CASE 20.2

Michigan Basic Property Insurance Association v. Washington

Court of Appeals of Michigan, 2012 WL 205753 (2012).

FACTS The Michigan Basic Property Insurance Association (MBP) issued a check for $69,559.06 from its account with Fifth Third Bank to Joyce Washington, Countrywide Home Loans, and T&C Federal Credit Union as co-payees. Washington indorsed the check herself by signing all three payees' names and did not distribute the proceeds to the co-payees. When the check reached Fifth Third Bank, it notified MBP of the payment through a daily account statement. MBP did not object, so Fifth Third Bank withdrew the funds from MBP's account. Fifth Third Bank also sent information about the check in a monthly account statement. MBP still failed to object, even though the account agreement required it to provide prompt notice of any forgeries. MBP was forced to issue a second check to Countrywide, so it sued Fifth Third Bank and sought to have its account recredited. The trial court found that Fifth Third Bank was liable to MBP, and another party appealed on Fifth Third Bank's behalf.

ISSUE Was Fifth Third Bank liable to MBP for paying a check with forged indorsements?

Checks can be made out to more than one payee.

iStockPhoto.com/bluenemo

DECISION No. The Michigan appellate court reversed the trial court's judgment.

REASON The court noted that, under the Uniform Commercial Code (UCC), the check was not properly payable because it had two forged indorsements. When a bank pays a check bearing a forged indorsement, the UCC ordinarily requires the bank to recredit the customer's account. Nevertheless, the court pointed out that the UCC allows parties to change their duties by contract. In this case, the account agreement obligated MBP to carefully review its checking account statements and to notify Fifth Third Bank of any problems within thirty days. In the absence of such notice, the contract provided that MBP, not Fifth Third Bank, was liable for any forged indorsements. Because MBP did not provide prompt notice of the forgeries, Fifth Third Bank was not required to recredit MBP's account.

CRITICAL THINKING—Legal Consideration *As a practical matter, does it make sense for the customer to bear primary responsibility for discovering instances of fraud? Which party is in a better position to detect any irregularities? Explain.*

20–3h Altered Checks

The customer's instruction to the bank is to pay the exact amount on the face of the check to the holder. The bank has a duty to examine each check before making final payment. If the bank fails to detect an alteration, normally it is liable to its customer for the loss because it did not pay as the customer ordered.

The bank's loss is the difference between the original amount of the check and the amount actually paid [UCC 4–401(d)(1)]. **EXAMPLE 20.5** A check written for $11 is altered to $111. The customer's account will be charged $11 (the amount the customer ordered the bank to pay). The bank normally will be responsible for the $100 difference. ■

Customer Negligence As in a situation involving a forged drawer's signature, a customer's negligence can shift the loss when payment is made on an altered check (unless the bank was also negligent). For instance, this may occur when a person carelessly writes a check leaving large gaps where additional numbers and words can be inserted (see Exhibit 20–3).

Similarly, a person who signs a check and leaves the dollar amount for someone else to fill in is barred from protesting when the bank unknowingly and in good faith pays whatever amount is shown [UCC 4–401(d)(2)]. Finally, if the bank can trace its loss on successive altered checks to the customer's failure to discover the initial alteration, the bank can reduce its liability for reimbursing the customer's account [UCC 4–406].

In every situation involving a forged drawer's signature or an alteration, a bank must observe reasonable commercial standards of care in paying on a customer's checks [UCC 4–406(e)]. The customer's negligence can be used as a defense only if the bank has exercised ordinary care.

Exhibit 20–3 A Poorly Filled-Out Check

```
XYZ CORPORATION                                           2206
10 INDUSTRIAL PARK
ST. PAUL, MINNESOTA  56561
                                    June 8  20 17      22-1
                                                       960
PAY
TO THE     John Duncan                       $ 100.00
ORDER OF
           One hundred and 70/100                    DOLLARS

THE FIRST NATIONAL BANK OF MYTOWN
332 MINNESOTA STREET
MYTOWN, MINNESOTA 55555          Stephanie Roe, President

       ⑈94⑈⑈77577⑈⑈ 0885
```

Other Parties from Whom the Bank May Recover The bank is entitled to recover the amount of loss from the transferor who presented the check for payment. A transferor, by presenting a check for payment, warrants that the check has not been altered.

There are two exceptions to this rule. First, if the bank is also the drawer (as it is on a cashier's check), it cannot recover from the presenting party if the party is a holder in due course (HDC) acting in good faith [UCC 3–417(a)(2), 4–208(a)(2)]. The reason is that an instrument's drawer is in a better position than an HDC to know whether the instrument has been altered.

Second, an HDC who presents a certified check for payment in good faith will not be held liable under warranty principles if the check was altered before the HDC acquired it [UCC 3–417(a)(2), 4–207(a)(2)]. **EXAMPLE 20.6** Jordan draws a check for $500 payable to David. David alters the amount to $5,000. The drawee bank, First National, certifies the check for $5,000. David negotiates the check to Ethan, an HDC. The drawee bank pays Ethan $5,000. On discovering the mistake, the bank cannot recover from Ethan the $4,500 paid by mistake, even though the bank was not in a superior position to detect the alteration. This is in accord with the purpose of certification, which is to obtain the definite obligation of a bank to honor a definite instrument. ■

20–4 The Bank's Duty to Accept Deposits

A bank has a duty to its customer to accept the customer's deposits of cash and checks. When checks are deposited, the bank must make the funds represented by those checks available within certain time frames. A bank also has a duty to collect payment on any checks payable or indorsed to its customers and deposited by them into their accounts. Cash deposits made in U.S. currency are received into customers' accounts without being subject to further collection procedures.

20–4a Availability Schedule for Deposited Checks

The Expedited Funds Availability Act[9] and Regulation CC[10] (the regulation implementing the act) establish when funds from deposited checks must be made available to the customer. The rules are as follows:

---

9. 12 U.S.C. Sections 4001–4010.
10. 12 C.F.R. Sections 229.1–229.42.

If you deposit a check at your bank that is written on another bank, can you withdraw those funds in cash immediately? Why or why not?

1. Any local check (drawn on a bank in the same area) deposited must be available for withdrawal by check or as cash within one business day from the date of deposit.

2. For nonlocal checks, the funds must be available for withdrawal within not more than five business days.

3. Under the Check Clearing in the 21st Century Act[11] (Check 21, which is the subject of this chapter's *Landmark in the Law* feature), a bank must credit a customer's account as soon as the bank receives the funds.

4. For cash deposits, wire transfers, and government checks, funds must be available on the next business day.

5. The first $100 of any deposit must be available for cash withdrawal on the opening of the *next business day* after deposit.

A different availability schedule applies to deposits made at *nonproprietary* automated teller machines (ATMs). These are ATMs that are not owned or operated by the bank receiving the deposits. Basically, a five-day hold is permitted on all deposits, including cash deposits, made at nonproprietary ATMs. Other exceptions also exist. For instance, a banking institution has eight days to make funds available in new accounts (those open less than thirty days).

A bank that places a longer hold on a deposited check than that specified by the rules must notify the customer. A credit union's failure to provide this notice to its customer was at the center of the following case.

---

11. 12 U.S.C. Sections 5001–5018.

CASE 20.3

Shahin v. Delaware Federal Credit Union

United States Court of Appeals, Third Circuit, 2015 WL 509563 (2015).

FACTS Nina Shahin deposited a check in the amount of $2,500 into her checking account at the Delaware Federal Credit Union (DelOne). DelOne placed a two-business-day "local hold" on the check pending verification. Concerned that the drawer's signature did not match the handwriting on the rest of the check, the bank placed it on a fifteen-day "nonverified" hold. Meanwhile, a payment from Shahin's checking account to Bank of America was denied for insufficient funds (NSF), and DelOne transferred funds from her savings account to cover other payments. DelOne then imposed two $30 penalties for NSF, as well as transfer fees totaling $6. Shahin filed a suit in a federal district court against DelOne, alleging that the credit union had failed to give her proper notice of the extended hold. The court issued a summary judgment in Shahin's favor, awarding her the amount of the NSF and transfer fees plus $1,000, the maximum amount of liability for a notice violation under Regulation CC. Shahin appealed, claiming that the amount of damages was insufficient.

ISSUE Did the court award Shahin the proper amount of damages?

DECISION Yes. The U.S Court of Appeals for the Third Circuit affirmed the judgment of the lower court and the amount of the award.

Is the bank liable when it incorrectly returns a check for insufficient funds? If so, what is the proper amount of damages?

REASON Regulation CC sets the requirement for a depositary institution to notify its customer of an extended hold on a deposited check. An institution that fails to comply with this provision is liable to the customer for "any actual damage sustained by that person as a result of the failure" and a penalty of "such additional amount as the court may allow," to a maximum of $1,000. In her motion for summary judgment, Shahin contended that DelOne had imposed $60 in NSF charges and $6 in transfer fees. The lower court found that DelOne was liable to Shahin for these charges and fees—actual damages totaling $66. The court also determined that DelOne was subject to liability to Shahin for a penalty under Regulation CC. The amount of $1,000 was the maximum amount that could be imposed under that provision. On appeal, Shahin claimed that the amount of damages was insufficient. The appellate court pointed out, however, she did not provide evidence to support any other claim for damages.

CRITICAL THINKING—Economic Consideration *Is $1,000 an appropriate penalty for the failure of a depository institution to comply with Regulation CC's notice provision? Why or why not?*

LANDMARK IN THE LAW

Check Clearing in the 21st Century Act (Check 21)

In the traditional collection process, paper checks had to be processed manually and physically transported before they could be cleared. Although the UCC allowed banks to use *electronic presentment*—that is, to transmit check information electronically instead of sending actual paper checks—this method was not widely adopted because it required agreements among individual banks.

PURPOSE OF CHECK 21 To streamline the costly and time-consuming collection process and improve the overall efficiency of the nation's payment system, Congress passed the Check Clearing in the 21st Century Act (Check 21), which went into effect in 2004. Check 21 changed the collection process by creating a new negotiable instrument called a *substitute check*. Although the act did not require banks to change their check-collection practices, the creation of substitute checks has facilitated the use of electronic check processing.

SUBSTITUTE CHECKS A substitute check is a paper reproduction of the front and back of an original check that contains all of the information required for automated processing. A bank creates substitute checks from digital images of original checks. It can then process the check information electronically or deliver substitute checks to banks that wish to continue receiving paper checks. The original check can be destroyed after a substitute check is created, helping to prevent the check from being paid twice and reducing expenses. Nevertheless, at least for a while, not all checks will be converted to substitute checks.

FASTER ACCESS TO FUNDS The Expedited Funds Availability Act requires the Federal Reserve Board to revise the availability schedule for funds from deposited checks to correspond to reductions in check-processing time.[a] Therefore, as the speed of check processing continues to increase under Check 21, the Federal Reserve Board will reduce the maximum time that a bank can hold funds from deposited checks before making them available to the depositors. That means, of course, that account holders will have faster access to their deposited funds. But it also means that they will have less *float time*—the time between when a check is written and when the amount is deducted from the account.

APPLICATION TO TODAY'S WORLD *As more financial institutions transfer digital images of checks, the check-processing system becomes more efficient. Customers are increasingly unable to rely on banking float when they are low on funds, so they should make sure that funds are available to cover checks when they are written. Customers cannot opt out of Check 21. Nor can they refuse to accept a substitute check as proof of payment.*

_____
a. 12 U.S.C. Sections 4001–4010.

20–4b The Traditional Collection Process

Usually, deposited checks involve parties that do business at different banks, but sometimes checks are written between customers of the same bank. Either situation brings into play the bank collection process as it operates within the statutory framework of Article 4 of the UCC. Note that the check-collection process described in the following subsections will be modified as the banking industry continues to implement Check 21.

Designations of Banks The first bank to receive a check for payment is the **depositary bank**.[12] For instance, when a person deposits a tax-refund check into a personal checking account at the local bank, that bank is the depositary bank. The bank on which a check is drawn (the drawee bank) is the **payor bank.** Any bank except the payor bank that handles a check during some phase of the collection process is a **collecting bank.** Any bank except the payor bank or the depositary bank to which an item is transferred in the course of this collection process is an **intermediary bank.**

During the collection process, any bank can take on one or more of the various roles of depositary, payor, collecting, and intermediary bank. **EXAMPLE 20.7** A buyer in New York writes

Depositary Bank The first bank to receive a check for payment.

Payor Bank The bank on which a check is drawn (the drawee bank).

Collecting Bank Any bank handling an item for collection, except the payor bank.

Intermediary Bank Any bank to which an item is transferred in the course of collection, except the depositary or payor bank.

_____
12. All definitions in this section are found in UCC 4–105. The terms *depositary* and *depository* have different meanings in the banking context. A depository bank refers to a *physical place* (a bank or other institution) in which deposits or funds are held or stored.

a check on her New York bank and sends it to a seller in San Francisco. The seller deposits the check in her San Francisco bank account. The seller's bank is both a *depositary bank* and a *collecting bank*. The buyer's bank in New York is the *payor bank*. As the check travels from San Francisco to New York, any collecting bank handling the item in the collection process (other than the depositary bank and the payor bank) is also called an *intermediary bank*. Exhibit 20–4 illustrates how various banks funcion in the collection process in the context of this example. ■

Check Collection between Customers of the Same Bank

An item that is payable by the same bank that receives it (which in this situation is both the depositary bank and the payor bank) is called an "on-us item." Usually, the bank issues a "provisional credit" for on-us items within the same day. If the bank does not dishonor the check by the opening of the second banking day following its receipt, the check is considered paid [UCC 4–215(e)(2)].

EXAMPLE 20.8 Pam Otterley and Jenna Merkowitz have checking accounts at First State Bank. On Monday, Merkowitz deposits into her checking account a $300 check from Otterley. That same day, the bank issues Merkowitz a provisional (temporary) credit for $300. When the bank opens on Wednesday, Otterley's check is considered honored, and Merkowitz's provisional credit becomes a final payment. ■

Check Collection between Customers of Different Banks

Once a depositary bank receives a check payable to another bank, it must arrange to present the check, either directly or through intermediary banks, to the appropriate payor bank. Each bank in the collection chain

Exhibit 20–4 The Check-Collection Process

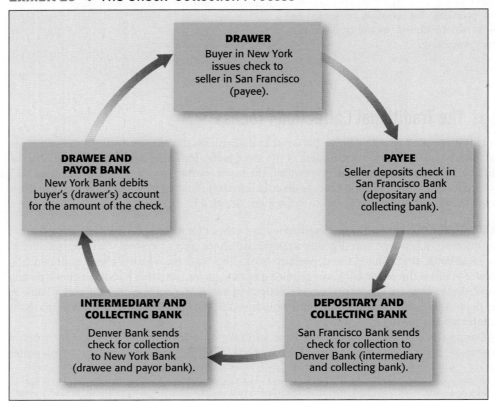

must pass the check on before midnight of the next banking day following its receipt [UCC 4–202(b)].[13] A "banking day" is any part of a day that the bank is open to carry on substantially all of its banking functions. Thus, if only a bank's drive-through facilities are open, a check deposited on Saturday will not trigger the bank's midnight deadline until the following Monday.

The UCC permits what is called *deferred posting*. According to UCC 4–108, "a bank may fix an afternoon hour of 2:00 P.M. or later as a cutoff hour for the handling of money and items and the making of entries on its books." Any checks received after that hour "may be treated as being received at the opening of the next banking day." Thus, if a bank's cutoff hour is 3:00 P.M., a check received by a payor bank at 4:00 P.M. on Monday will be deferred for posting until Tuesday. In this situation, the payor bank's deadline will be midnight Wednesday.

When the check reaches the payor bank, that bank is liable for the face amount of the check, unless the payor bank dishonors the check or returns it by midnight on the next banking day following receipt [UCC 4–302].[14]

How the Federal Reserve System Clears Checks

The **Federal Reserve System** is a network of twelve government banks located around the United States and headed by the Federal Reserve Board of Governors. Most banks in the United States have Federal Reserve accounts. The Federal Reserve System acts as a **clearinghouse**—a system or place where banks exchange checks and drafts drawn on each other and settle daily balances.

EXAMPLE 20.9 Pamela Moy of Philadelphia writes a check to Jeanne Sutton in San Francisco. When Sutton receives the check in the mail, she deposits it in her bank. Her bank then deposits the check in the Federal Reserve Bank of San Francisco, which transfers it to the Federal Reserve Bank of Philadelphia. That Federal Reserve bank then sends the check to Moy's bank, which deducts the amount of the check from Moy's account. ■

Electronic Check Presentment

In the past, as mentioned, most checks were processed manually. Today, most checks are processed electronically, as discussed in the *Landmark in the Law* feature on Check 21. Whereas manual check processing can take days, *electronic check presentment* can be done on the day of deposit. Check information is encoded, transmitted electronically, and processed by other banks' computers. After encoding a check, a bank may retain it and present only its image or description for payment under an electronic presentment agreement [UCC 4–110].[15]

A bank that encodes information for electronic presentment warrants to any subsequent bank or payor that the encoded information is correct [UCC 4–209]. Similarly, a bank that retains a check and presents its image or description for payment warrants that the image or description is accurate.

Regulation CC, which deals with the availability of deposited funds, provides that a returned check must be encoded with the routing number of the depositary bank, the amount of the check, and other information. The regulation further states that a check must still be returned within the deadlines required by the UCC.

> "I saw a bank that said '24-Hour Banking,' but I don't have that much time."
>
> **STEVEN WRIGHT**
> 1955–PRESENT
> (AMERICAN COMEDIAN)

Federal Reserve System
A network of twelve district banks and related branches located around the country and headed by the Federal Reserve Board of Governors. Most banks in the United States have Federal Reserve accounts.

Clearinghouse A system or place where banks exchange checks and drafts drawn on each other and settle daily balances.

LEARNING OBJECTIVE 4

What is electronic check presentment, and how does it differ from the traditional check-clearing process?

iStockPhoto.com/carterdayne

Do bank customers directly deposit checks in the closest Federal Reserve bank?

---

13. A bank may take a "reasonably longer time" in certain circumstances, such as when the bank's computer system is down due to a power failure, but the bank must show that its action is still timely [UCC 4–202(b)].

14. Most checks are cleared by a computerized process, and communication and computer facilities may fail because of electrical outages, equipment malfunction, or other conditions. A bank may be "excused" from liability for failing to meet its midnight deadline if such conditions arise and the bank has exercised "such diligence as the circumstances require" [UCC 4–109(d)].

15. This section of the UCC assumes that no bank will participate in an electronic presentment program without an express agreement (which is no longer true since Check 21 went into effect). See Comment 2 to UCC 4–110.

Electronic Fund Transfer (EFT) A transfer of funds through the use of an electronic terminal, a telephone, a computer, or magnetic tape.

KNOW THIS

The EFTA does not provide for the reversal of an electronic transfer of funds once it has occurred.

LEARNING OBJECTIVE 5

What are the four most common types of electronic fund transfers?

Regulation E A set of rules issued by the Federal Reserve System's Board of Governors to protect users of electronic fund transfer systems.

20-5 Electronic Fund Transfers

An **electronic fund transfer (EFT)** is a transfer of funds through the use of an electronic terminal, smartphone, tablet, computer, or telephone. The law governing EFTs depends on the type of transfer involved. Consumer fund transfers are governed by the Electronic Fund Transfer Act (EFTA).[16] Commercial fund transfers are governed by Article 4A of the UCC.

Transferring funds electronically offers numerous benefits, but it also poses difficulties on occasion. For instance, it is difficult to issue stop-payment orders with electronic banking. Also, fewer records are available to prove or disprove that a transaction took place. The possibilities for tampering with a person's private banking information have also increased.

20-5a Types of EFT Systems

Most banks today offer EFT services. The following are the most common types of EFT systems used by bank customers:

1. *Automated teller machines (ATMs)*—The machines are connected online to the bank's computers. A customer inserts a plastic card (called an ATM or debit card) issued by the bank and keys in a *personal identification number* (PIN) to access her or his accounts and conduct banking transactions.

2. *Point-of-sale systems*—Online terminals allow consumers to transfer funds to merchants to pay for purchases using a debit card.

3. *Direct deposits and withdrawals*—Customers can authorize the bank to allow another party—such as the government or an employer—to make direct deposits into their accounts. Similarly, customers can request the bank to make automatic payments to a third party at regular, recurrent intervals from the customer's funds (insurance premiums or loan payments, for instance).

4. *Online payment systems*—Many financial institutions permit their customers to access the institution's computer system via the Internet and direct a transfer of funds between accounts or pay a particular bill. Payments can be made on a one-time or a recurring basis.

20-5b Consumer Fund Transfers

The Electronic Fund Transfer Act (EFTA) provides a basic framework for the rights, liabilities, and responsibilities of users of EFT systems. Additionally, the act gave the Federal Reserve Board authority to issue rules and regulations to help implement the act's provisions. The Federal Reserve Board's implemental regulation is called **Regulation E.**

The EFTA governs financial institutions that offer electronic fund transfers involving consumer accounts. The types of accounts covered include checking accounts, savings accounts, and any other asset accounts established for personal, family, or household purposes.

Disclosure Requirements The EFTA is essentially a disclosure law benefiting consumers. The act requires financial institutions to inform consumers of their rights and responsibilities, including those listed here, with respect to EFT systems.

1. The bank must provide a monthly statement for every month in which there is an electronic transfer of funds. The statement must show the amount and date of the transfer, the names of the retailers or other third parties involved, the location or identification of the terminal, and the fees.

---

16. 15 U.S.C. Sections 1693–1693r. The EFTA amended Title IX of the Consumer Credit Protection Act.

2. If a customer's debit card is lost or stolen and used without his or her permission, the customer will be required to pay no more than $50 if he or she notifies the bank of the loss or theft within two days of learning about it. Otherwise, the liability increases to $500. The customer may be liable for more than $500 if he or she fails to report the unauthorized use within sixty days after it appears on the customer's statement. (If a customer voluntarily gives her or his debit card to another, who then uses it improperly, the protections just mentioned do not apply.)

3. The customer must discover any error on the monthly statement within sixty days and notify the bank. The bank then has ten days to investigate and must report its conclusions to the customer in writing. If the bank takes longer than ten days, it must return the disputed amount to the customer's account until it finds the error. If there is no error, the customer has to return the disputed funds to the bank.

4. The bank must provide receipts for transactions made through computer terminals, but it is not obligated to do so for telephone transfers.

Violations and Damages   Unauthorized access to an EFT system constitutes a federal felony, and those convicted may be fined up to $10,000 and sentenced to as long as ten years in prison. Banks must strictly comply with the terms of the EFTA and are liable for any failure to adhere to its provisions.

For a bank's violation of the EFTA, a consumer may recover both actual damages (including attorneys' fees and costs) and punitive damages of not less than $100 and not more than $1,000. Even when a customer has sustained no actual damage, the bank may be liable for legal costs and punitive damages if it fails to follow the proper procedures outlined by the EFTA in regard to error resolution.

20–5c **Commercial Fund Transfers**

Another way in which funds are transferred electronically is the transfer of funds "by wire" between commercial parties. In fact, the dollar volume of payments by wire transfer is more than $1 trillion a day—an amount that far exceeds the dollar volume of payments made by other means. The two major wire payment systems are the Federal Reserve's wire transfer network (Fedwire) and the New York Clearing House Interbank Payments Systems (CHIPS).

Commercial wire transfers are governed by Article 4A of the UCC, which has been adopted by most states (and is included in Appendix C at the end of this text). Article 4A uses the term *funds transfer* rather than *wire transfer* to describe the overall payment transaction. **EXAMPLE 20.10** Jellux, Inc., owes $5 million to Perot Corporation. Instead of sending Perot a check or some other instrument that would enable Perot to obtain payment, Jellux instructs its bank, East Bank, to credit $5 million to Perot's account in West Bank. East Bank debits Jellux's East Bank account and wires $5 million to Perot's West Bank account. In more complex transactions, additional banks would be involved. ■

20–6 **Online Banking and E-Money**

Online banking is common in today's world. In a few minutes, anyone with the proper software can access his or her account, transfer funds, write "checks," and pay bills. Also commonplace today is the use of **digital cash,** or **e-money,** which consists of funds stored on microchips in laptops, smartphones, tablets, and other devices. E-money replaces *physical* cash—coins and paper currency—with *virtual* cash in the form of electronic impulses.

How do businesses transfer large sums of funds among themselves?

Digital Cash Prepaid funds stored on microchips in laptops, smartphones, tablets, and other devices.

E-Money Prepaid funds stored on microchips in laptops, smartphones, tablets, and other devices.

20–6a Online Banking

Most customers use three kinds of online banking services: consolidating bills and making payments, transferring funds among accounts, and applying for loans and credit cards.

Withdrawing and depositing funds are two banking functions not yet widely available online. Nevertheless, there are software applications (apps) that enable customers to make deposits into their accounts using electronic devices. **EXAMPLE 20.11** Bobbi, a Chase Bank customer, downloads its free mobile app. The app allows Bobbi to take a photo of both sides of her endorsed check with her smartphone's camera, follow the on-screen instructions, and submit the check for deposit into her account. ■

Mobile payment apps are also becoming popular, as discussed in this chapter's *Adapting the Law to the Online Environment* feature.

20–6b Stored-Value Cards and Smart Cards

Stored-Value Card A card bearing a magnetic strip that holds magnetically encoded data providing access to stored funds.

The simplest kind of e-money system uses **stored-value cards.** These are plastic cards embossed with magnetic strips containing magnetically encoded data. Frequently, a stored-value card can be used only to purchase specific goods and services offered by the card issuer. An example is a gift card that is only redeemable at a particular retail store or restaurant.

ADAPTING THE LAW TO THE ONLINE ENVIRONMENT
Pay with Your Smartphone

A payment revolution is going on right now. Starting in 2009, customers at certain Starbucks locations in New York, San Francisco, and Seattle could use an iPhone app to pay for their lattes. By 2015, some 7,500 Starbucks locations were accepting payments from all types of smartphone-based operating systems. That same year, smartphone point-of-sale payments in the United States reached $4.2 billion. Some experts estimate that the total for 2016 will be $30 billion.

Apple Enters the Mobile Payments Arena
Apple, Inc., provides its own mobile payment and "digital wallet" service, called Apple Pay. Owners of Apple's iPhone 6, iPhone 6 Plus, iPad Air 2, and iPad Mini 3, along with its Apple Watch, have access to the service. Apple Pay enables these devices to communicate wirelessly with special point-of-sale systems using near field communication

(NFC) technology. A person using an iPhone holds it close to the point-of-sale terminal and authenticates the transaction by holding a fingerprint to the phone's Touch ID sensor. Customers' payment information is kept private from the retailer. The system generates a "dynamic security code" for each transaction.

Google and Samsung Provide Competition
Google created the Google Wallet wireless payment system even before Apple Pay was launched. Then, in 2015, Google and the mobile payments company Softcard contracted with AT&T, T-Mobile USA, and Verizon Wireless to preinstall Google Wallet in smartphones sold by those three companies.

Google's Android system is used on most Samsung smartphones. Samsung, a fierce competitor of Apple, announced in 2015 its purchase of LoopPay, a mobile payments startup. Also in 2015, Samsung created a

direct competitor to Apple Pay called Samsung Pay. It was designed to work with existing magnetic-stripe credit-card machines as well as the newer NFC technology.

Linking Digital Wallets to Other Apps on a Smartphone
The ultimate goal in this modern payment system world is a link from a digital wallet to another app within a single smartphone. For example, Google allows its Google Wallet to link to its Google Offers, which is a discount-deal app. Mobile payment systems will eventually be tied to rewards programs and special offers at individual stores.

CRITICAL THINKING

■ Does having a digital wallet in an iPhone, Android-based smartphone, or other smartphone entail more security risks than carrying a physical wallet? Explain.

Smart cards are plastic cards containing tiny microchips that can hold more information than a magnetic strip can. A smart card carries and processes security programming. This capability gives smart cards a technical advantage over stored-value cards. The microprocessors on smart cards can also authenticate the validity of transactions. Retailers can program electronic cash registers to confirm the authenticity of a smart card by examining a unique digital signature stored on its microchip. Common uses for smart cards are as credit cards and ATM cards.

Smart Card A card containing a microprocessor and typically used for financial transactions, personal identification, and other purposes.

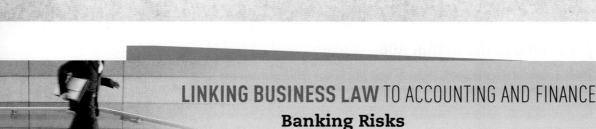

Reviewing . . . Banking in the Digital Age

RPM Pizza, Inc., issued a check for $96,000 to Systems Marketing for an advertising campaign. A few days later, RPM decided not to go through with the deal and placed a written stop-payment order on the check. RPM and Systems had no further contact for many months. Three weeks after the stop-payment order expired, however, Toby Rierson, an employee at Systems, cashed the check. Bank One Cambridge, RPM's bank, paid the check with funds from RPM's account. Because the check was more than six months old, it was stale. Thus, according to standard banking procedures as well as Bank One's own policies, the signature on the check should have been specially verified, but it was not. RPM filed a suit in a federal district court against Bank One to recover the amount of the check. Using the information presented in the chapter, answer the following questions.

1. How long is a written stop-payment order effective? What else could RPM have done to prevent this check from being cashed?

2. What would have happened if RPM had not had a legitimate reason for stopping payment on the check?

3. What are a bank's obligations with respect to stale checks?

4. Would a court be likely to hold the bank liable for the amount of the check because it failed to verify the signature on the check? Why or why not?

DEBATE THIS

- To reduce fraud, checks that utilize mechanical or electronic signature systems should not be honored.

LINKING BUSINESS LAW TO ACCOUNTING AND FINANCE
Banking Risks

In this chapter, you learned about the bank-customer relationship as well as a bank's duty to honor checks and accept deposits. In the macroeconomics courses that your business school offers, the focus on the banking sector is quite different. Among other things, the courses examine banking panics and bank runs and their effects on the economy.

A *bank run* occurs when depositors simultaneously rush to convert their bank deposits into currency because they believe that the assets of their bank are not sufficient to cover its liabilities—the customers' deposits. The largest number of bank runs in modern history occurred during the Great Depression in the 1930s, when nine thousand banks failed.

Federal Deposit Insurance
To prevent bank runs, the federal government set up a system of deposit insurance to assure depositors that their deposits would be safe. The Federal Deposit Insurance

Continues

Corporation (FDIC) and the Federal Savings and Loan Insurance Corporation (FSLIC) were created in the 1930s to insure deposits. In 1971, the National Credit Union Shares Insurance Fund (NCUSIF) was added to insure credit union deposits.

Although the names and form of some of these organizations have changed over the years, the principle remains the same: to insure all accounts in these financial institutions against losses up to a specified limit. In 1933, each account was insured up to $2,500. During the recession that started in December 2007, the federal government wanted to make sure that no banking panics would occur. Therefore, in 2008 the insurance limit was raised to $250,000.

Federal insurance for bank deposits may seem like a good idea. Nevertheless, some problems are associated with it.

Moral Hazard: An Unintended Consequence of Deposit Insurance

In your finance courses, you learn that the riskier a loan is, the higher the interest rate that a lending institution can charge the borrower. Bank managers must weigh the trade-off between risk and return when deciding which loan applicants should receive funds. Loans to poor credit risks offer high profits, assuming that the borrowers actually pay off their debts. Good credit risks are more likely to pay their debts, but can obtain loans at lower rates.

Since the federal deposit insurance limit was increased to $250,000 per account, managers have had a greater incentive to make risky loans. By doing so, in the short run the banks make higher profits, and the managers receive higher salaries and bonuses. If some of these risky loans are not repaid, what is the likely outcome? A bank's losses are limited because the federal government—you, the taxpayer—will cover any shortfall between the bank's assets and its liabilities. Consequently, federal deposit insurance means that banks get to enjoy all of the profits of risk taking without bearing all of the consequences of that risk taking.

In short, an unintended consequence of federal deposit insurance is to encourage *moral hazard*. It creates an incentive for bank managers to take more risks in their lending policies than they would otherwise.

CRITICAL THINKING

- Imagine the United States without federal deposit insurance. What are some of the mechanisms that would arise to "punish" bank managers who acted irresponsibly?

Key Terms

cashier's check 492
certified check 493
clearinghouse 505
collecting bank 503
depositary bank 503
digital cash 507
electronic fund transfer (EFT) 506

e-money 507
Federal Reserve System 505
intermediary bank 503
overdraft 496
payor bank 503
Regulation E 506
smart card 509

stale check 496
stop-payment order 496
stored-value card 508
traveler's check 493

Chapter Summary: Banking in the Digital Age

Checks	1. *Cashier's check*—A check drawn by a bank on itself (the bank is both the drawer and the drawee) and purchased by a customer. In effect, the bank assumes responsibility for paying the check, thus making the check nearly the equivalent of cash.
	2. *Traveler's check*—An instrument on which a financial institution is both the drawer and the drawee. The purchaser is required to sign the check at the time it is bought and again at the time it is used for the check to become a negotiable instrument.
	3. *Certified check*—A check for which the drawee bank certifies in writing that it has set aside funds from the drawer's account to ensure payment of the check on presentation. On certification, the drawer and all prior indorsers are completely discharged from liability on the check.
The Bank-Customer Relationship	1. *Creditor-debtor relationship*—A customer and a bank have a creditor-debtor relationship (the bank is the debtor because it holds the customer's funds on deposit).
	2. *Agency relationship*—Because a bank must act in accordance with the customer's orders in regard to the customer's deposited money, an agency relationship also arises—the bank is the agent for the customer, who is the principal.
	3. *Contractual relationship*—The bank's relationship with its customer is also contractual. Both the bank and the customer assume certain contractual duties when a customer opens a bank account.

The Bank's Duty to Honor Checks	Generally, a bank has a duty to honor its customers' checks, provided that the customers have sufficient funds on deposit to cover the checks [UCC 4–401(a)]. The bank is liable to its customers for actual damages proved to be due to wrongful dishonor [UCC 4–402]. 1. *Overdraft*—The bank has a right to charge a customer's account for any item properly payable, even if the charge results in an overdraft [UCC 4–401]. 2. *Postdated check*—The bank may charge a postdated check against a customer's account, unless the customer notifies the bank, in a timely manner, not to pay the check until the stated date [UCC 4–401]. 3. *Stale check*—The bank is not obligated to pay an uncertified check presented more than six months after its date, but the bank may do so in good faith without liability [UCC 4–404]. 4. *Stop-payment order*—The customer (or a person authorized to draw on the account) must make a stop-payment order in time for the bank to have a reasonable opportunity to act. Oral orders are binding for only fourteen days unless they are confirmed in writing. Written or electronic orders are effective for six months unless renewed in writing [UCC 4–403]. The bank is liable for wrongful payment over a timely stop-payment order to the extent that the customer suffers a loss. 5. *Death or incompetence of a customer*—So long as the bank does not know of the death or incompetence of a customer, the bank can pay an item without liability. Even with knowledge of a customer's death, a bank can honor or certify checks (in the absence of a stop-payment order) for ten days after the date of the customer's death [UCC 4–405]. 6. *Forged signature or alteration*—The customer has a duty to examine account statements with reasonable care on receipt and to notify the bank promptly of any forged signatures or alterations. On a series of forged signatures or alterations by the same wrongdoer, examination and report must be made within thirty calendar days of receipt of the first statement containing a forged or altered item [UCC 4–406]. The customer's failure to comply with these rules releases the bank from liability unless the bank failed to exercise reasonable care, in which case liability may be apportioned according to a comparative negligence standard. Regardless of care or lack of care, the customer is barred from holding the bank liable after one year for forged customer signatures or alterations and after three years for forged indorsements.

The Bank's Duty to Accept Deposits	A bank has a duty to accept deposits made by its customers into their accounts. Funds from deposited checks must be made available to customers according to a schedule mandated by the Expedited Funds Availability Act and Regulation CC. A bank also has a duty to collect payment on any checks deposited by its customers. When checks deposited by customers are drawn on other banks, the check-collection process comes into play.
	
	1. *Definitions of banks*—UCC 4–105 provides the following definitions of banks involved in the collection process:
	  a. Depositary bank—The first bank to accept a check for payment.
	  b. Payor bank—The bank on which a check is drawn.
	  c. Collecting bank—Any bank except the payor bank that handles a check during the collection process.
	  d. Intermediary bank—Any bank except the payor bank or the depositary bank to which an item is transferred in the course of the collection process.
	2. *Check collection between customers of the same bank*—A check payable by the depositary bank that receives it is an "on-us item." If the bank does not dishonor the check by the opening of the second banking day following its receipt, the check is considered paid [UCC 4–215(e)(2)].
	3. *Check collection between customers of different banks*—Each bank in the collection process must pass the check on to the next appropriate bank before midnight of the next banking day following its receipt [UCC 4–108, 4–202(b), 4–302].
	4. *How the Federal Reserve System clears checks*—The Federal Reserve System facilitates the check-clearing process by serving as a clearinghouse for checks.
	5. *Electronic check presentment*—Check information may be encoded, transmitted electronically, and processed by other banks' computers. After encoding a check, a bank may retain it and present only its image or description for payment under an electronic presentment agreement [UCC 4–110].

Electronic Fund Transfers	1. *Types of EFT systems*—
	  a. Automated teller machines (ATMs).
	  b. Point-of-sale systems.
	  c. Direct deposits and withdrawals.
	  d. Online payment systems.
	2. *Consumer fund transfers*—Consumer fund transfers are governed by the Electronic Fund Transfer Act (EFTA). The EFTA is basically a disclosure law that sets forth the rights and duties of the bank and the customer with respect to EFT systems. Banks must comply strictly with EFTA requirements.
	3. *Commercial transfers*—Article 4A of the UCC, which has been adopted by almost all of the states, governs fund transfers not subject to the EFTA or other federal or state statutes.

Online Banking and E-Money	1. *Online banking*—Most customers use three kinds of online banking services:
	  a. Bill consolidation and payment.
	  b. Transferring funds among accounts.
	  c. Applying for loans and credit cards.
	2. *E-money*—Types of e-money include stored-value cards and smart cards.

Issue Spotters

1. Lyn writes a check for $900 to Mac, who indorses the check in blank and transfers it to Jan. She presents the check to Omega Bank, the drawee bank, for payment. Omega does not honor the check. Is Lyn liable to Jan? Could Lyn be subject to criminal prosecution? Why or why not? (See *The Bank's Duty to Honor Checks*.)

2. Roni writes a check for $700 to Sela. Sela indorses the check in blank and transfers it to Titus, who alters the check to read $7,000 and presents it to Union Bank, the drawee, for payment. The bank cashes it. Roni discovers the alteration and sues the bank. How much, if anything, can Roni recover? From whom can the bank recover this amount? (See *The Bank's Duty to Honor Checks*.)

—**Check your answers to the *Issue Spotters* against the answers provided in Appendix D at the end of this text.**

Learning Objectives Check

1. What type of check does a bank agree in advance to accept when the check is presented for payment?
2. When may a bank properly dishonor a customer's check without being liable to the customer?
3. What duties does the Uniform Commercial Code impose on a bank's customers with regard to forged and altered checks? What are the consequences if a customer is negligent in performing those duties?
4. What is electronic check presentment, and how does it differ from the traditional check-clearing process?
5. What are the four most common types of electronic fund transfers?

—**Answers to the even-numbered *Learning Objectives Check* questions can be found in Appendix E at the end of this text.**

Business Scenarios and Case Problems

20–1. Forged Checks. Roy Supply, Inc., and R. M. R. Drywall, Inc., had checking accounts at Wells Fargo Bank. Both accounts required all checks to carry two signatures—that of Edward Roy and that of Twila June Moore, both of whom were executive officers of both companies. Between January 2006 and March 2008, the bank honored hundreds of checks on which Roy's signature was forged by Moore. On January 31, 2009, Roy and the two corporations notified the bank of the forgeries and then filed a suit in a California state court against the bank, alleging negligence. Who is liable for the amounts of the forged checks? Why? (See *The Bank's Duty to Honor Checks*.)

20–2. Customer Negligence. Gary goes grocery shopping and carelessly leaves his checkbook in his shopping cart. His checkbook, with two blank checks remaining, is stolen by Dolores. On May 5, Dolores forges Gary's name on a check for $100 and cashes the check at Gary's bank, Citizens Bank of Middletown. Gary has not reported the loss of his blank checks to his bank. On June 1, Gary receives his monthly bank statement from Citizens Bank that includes the forged check, but he does not notice the item, nor does he examine his bank statement. On June 20, Dolores forges Gary's last check. This check is for $1,000 and is cashed at Eastern City Bank, a bank with which Dolores has previously done business. Eastern City Bank puts the check through the collection process, and Citizens Bank honors it. On July 1, on receipt of his bank statement and canceled checks covering June transactions, Gary discovers both forgeries and immediately notifies Citizens Bank. Dolores cannot be found.

Gary claims that Citizens Bank must recredit his account for both checks, as his signature was forged. Discuss fully Gary's claim. (See *The Bank's Duty to Honor Checks*.)

20–3. Forged Drawers' Signatures. Debbie Brooks and Martha Tingstrom lived together. Tingstrom handled their finances. For five years, Brooks did not look at any statements concerning her accounts. When she finally reviewed the statements, she discovered that Tingstrom had taken $85,500 from Brooks's checking account with Transamerica Financial Advisors. Tingstrom had forged Brooks's name on six checks paid between one and two years earlier. Another year passed before Brooks filed a suit against Transamerica. Who is most likely to suffer the loss for the checks paid with Brooks's forged signature? Why? [*Brooks v. Transamerica Financial Advisors*, 57 So.3d 1153 (La.App. 2 Cir. 2011)] (See *The Bank's Duty to Honor Checks*.)

20–4. Business Case Problem with Sample Answer— Honoring Checks. Adley Abdulwahab (Wahab) opened an account on behalf of W Financial Group, LLC, with Wells Fargo Bank. Wahab was one of three authorized signers on the account. Five months later, Wahab withdrew $1,701,250 from W Financial's account to buy a cashier's check payable to Lubna Lateef. Wahab visited a different Wells Fargo branch and deposited the check into the account of CA Houston Investment Center, LLC. Wahab was the only authorized signer on this account. Lateef never received or indorsed the check. W Financial filed a suit to recover the amount. Applying the rules for payment on a forged indorsement, who is liable? [*Jones v. Wells Fargo Bank*, 666 F.3d 955 (5th Cir. 2012)] (See *The Bank's Duty to Honor Checks*.)

—For a sample answer to Problem 20–4, go to Appendix F at the end of this text.

20–5. Consumer Fund Transfers. Stephen Patterson held an account with Suntrust Bank in Alcoa, Tennessee. Juanita Wehrman—with whom Patterson was briefly involved in a romantic relationship—stole his debit card and used it for sixteen months (well beyond the length of their relationship) to make unauthorized purchases in excess of $30,000. When Patterson learned what was happening, he closed his account. The bank refused to reimburse him more than $677.46—the amount of unauthorized transactions that occurred within sixty days of the transmittal of the bank statement that revealed the first unauthorized transaction. Is the bank's refusal justifiable? Explain. [*Patterson v. Suntrust Bank*, __ S.W.3d __, 2013 WL 139315 (Tenn.App. 2013)] (See *Electronic Fund Transfers*.)

20–6. Forged Drawers' Signatures. Victor Nacim had a checking account at Compass Bank. The "Deposit Agreement" required him to report an unauthorized transaction within thirty days of his receipt of the statement on which it appeared to obtain a recredit. When Nacim moved to a new residence, he asked the bank to update the address on his account. Compass continued to mail his statements to his previous address, however, and Nacim did not receive them. In the meantime, Compass officer David Peterson made an unauthorized withdrawal of $34,000 from Nacim's account. A month later, Peterson told Nacim what he had done. The next month, Nacim asked the bank for a recredit. Compass refused on the ground that he reported the withdrawal more than thirty days after the bank mailed the statement on which it appeared—a statement that Nacim never received. Is Nacim entitled to a recredit? Explain. [*Compass Bank v. Nacim*, __ S.W.3d __, 2015 WL 181721 (Tex. App.—El Paso 2015)] (See *The Bank's Duty to Honor Checks*.)

20–7. A Question of Ethics—Death or Incompetence of a Customer. New York resident Esther Braunstein worked as an usher at Lincoln Center, held an administrative position with Citibank, was a school crossing guard, and assisted disabled persons and others as a volunteer on Roosevelt Island and at the New York Foundling Hospital. Before her death, she drew a $5,000 check payable to each of two of her daughters, Sandra Braunstein and Carol Russo. The checks were drawn on a joint account held in the names of Esther and Sandra. Carol did not cash her check until five months after Esther's death. Sandra filed a suit in a New York state court against Carol to recover the funds. [*Braunstein v. Russo*, 988 N.Y.S.2d 521 (2 Dept. 2014)] (See *The Bank's Duty to Honor Checks*.)

1. Is one sister's attempt to recover funds given to another sister by their mother always unethical? Who is legally entitled to the funds? Discuss.

2. If the check that Carol cashed five months after Esther's death had not been a gift from Esther, but instead had contained a forged drawer's signature, on whom could liability have been imposed? How might that circumstance have affected the ethics of the situation? Explain.

Critical Thinking and Writing Assignments

20–8. Critical Legal Thinking. Since the 1990 revision of Article 4, a bank is no longer required to include the customer's canceled checks when it sends monthly statements to the customer. A bank may simply itemize the checks (by number, date, and amount). It may provide photocopies of the checks as well but is not required to do so. What implications do the revised rules have for bank customers in terms of liability for unauthorized signatures and indorsements? (See *The Bank's Duty to Honor Checks*.)

20–9. Business Law Critical Thinking Group Assignment. On January 5, Brian drafts a check for $3,000 drawn on Southern Marine Bank and payable to his assistant, Shanta. Brian puts last year's date on the check by mistake. On January 7, before Shanta has had a chance to go to the bank, Brian is killed in an automobile accident. Southern Marine Bank is aware of Brian's death. On January 10, Shanta presents the check to the bank, and the bank honors the check by payment to Shanta. Later, Brian's widow, Joyce, claims that because the bank knew of Brian's death and also because the check was by date over one year old, the bank acted wrongfully when it paid Shanta. Joyce, as executor of Brian's estate and sole heir by his will, demands that Southern Marine Bank recredit Brian's estate for the check paid to Shanta. (See *The Bank's Duty to Honor Checks*.)

1. The first group will determine whether the bank acted wrongfully by honoring Brian's check and paying Shanta.

2. The second group will assess whether Joyce has a valid claim against Southern Marine Bank for the amount of the check paid to Shanta.

3. The third group will assume that the check Brian drafted was on his business account rather than on his personal account and that he had two partners in the business. Would a business partner be in a better position to force Southern Marine Bank to recredit Brian's account than his widow? Why or why not?

iStockPhoto.com/zoranm

LEARNING OBJECTIVES

The five Learning Objectives *below are designed to help improve your understanding of the chapter. After reading this chapter, you should be able to answer the following questions:*

1. What is required to create a security interest?

2. How is a purchase-money security interest in consumer goods created?

3. If two parties have perfected security interests in the debtor's collateral, which party has priority on default?

4. How does a mechanic's lien assist creditors?

5. What is a suretyship, and how does it differ from a guaranty?

Secured Transaction Any transaction in which the payment of a debt is guaranteed, or secured, by personal property owned by the debtor or in which the debtor has a legal interest.

Security Interests and Creditors' Rights

When buying or leasing goods, debtors frequently pay some portion of the price now and promise to pay the remainder in the future, as William Shakespeare observed in the chapter-opening quotation. Logically, sellers and lenders do not want to risk nonpayment, so they usually will not sell goods or lend funds unless the payment is somehow guaranteed.

Whenever the payment of a debt is guaranteed, or *secured*, by personal property owned or held by the debtor, the transaction becomes known as a **secured transaction.** The concept of the secured transaction is as basic to modern business practice as the concept of credit. As you will read in this chapter, secured transactions can now take place online.

Article 9 of the Uniform Commercial Code (UCC) governs secured transactions in personal property. Personal property includes accounts, agricultural liens, *chattel paper* (documents or records evidencing a debt secured by personal property), and *fixtures* (certain property that is attached to land). Personal property also includes other types of intangible property, such as negotiable instruments and patents. Article 9 does not cover creditor tools such as liens and garnishments, which are discussed at the conclusion of this chapter.

> "I will pay you some, and, as most debtors do, promise you infinitely."
>
> **WILLIAM SHAKESPEARE**
> 1564–1616
> (ENGLISH DRAMATIST AND POET)

21-1 Terminology of Secured Transactions

In every state, the UCC's terminology is now uniformly used in all documents that involve secured transactions. A brief summary of the UCC's definitions of terms relating to secured transactions follows.

1. A **secured party** is any creditor who has a *security interest* in the *debtor's collateral.* This creditor can be a seller, a lender, a cosigner, or even a buyer of accounts or chattel paper [UCC 9–102(a)(72)].

2. A **debtor** is a person who *owes payment* or other performance of a secured obligation [UCC 9–102(a)(28)].

3. A **security interest** is the *interest* in the collateral (such as personal property or fixtures) that *secures payment or performance of an obligation* [UCC 1–201(37)].

4. A **security agreement** is an *agreement* that *creates* or provides for a *security interest* [UCC 9–102(a)(73)]. In other words, it is the contract in which a debtor agrees to give a creditor the right to take his or her property in the event of default.

5. **Collateral** is the *subject* of the *security interest* [UCC 9–102(a)(12)].

6. A **financing statement**—referred to as the UCC-1 form—is the *instrument normally filed to give public notice to third parties* of the *secured party's security interest* [UCC 9–102(a)(39)].

Together, these basic definitions form the concept under which a debtor-creditor relationship becomes a secured transaction relationship (see Exhibit 21–1).

21-2 Creating and Perfecting a Security Interest

A creditor has two main concerns if the debtor **defaults** (fails to pay the debt as promised): (1) Can the debt be satisfied through the possession and (usually) sale of the collateral? (2) Will the creditor have priority over any other creditors or buyers who may have rights in the same collateral? These two concerns are met through the creation and perfection of a security interest. We begin this section by examining how a security interest is created.

21-2a Requirements to Create a Security Interest

To become a secured party, the creditor must obtain a security interest in the collateral of the debtor. Three requirements must be met for a creditor to have an enforceable security interest:

1. Unless the creditor has possession of the collateral, there must be a written or authenticated security agreement that clearly describes the collateral subject to the security interest and is signed or authenticated by the debtor.

2. The secured party must give something of value to the debtor.

3. The debtor must have "rights" in the collateral.

Secured Party A creditor who has a security interest in the debtor's collateral, including a seller, lender, cosigner, or buyer of accounts or chattel paper.

Debtor Under Article 9 of the UCC, any party who owes payment or performance of a secured obligation.

Security Interest Any interest in personal property or fixtures that secures payment or performance of an obligation.

Security Agreement An agreement that creates or provides for a security interest between the debtor and a secured party.

Collateral Under Article 9 of the UCC, the property subject to a security interest.

Financing Statement A document filed by a secured creditor with the appropriate official to give notice to the public of the creditor's security interest in collateral belonging to the debtor named in the statement.

Default Failure to pay a debt when it is due.

LEARNING OBJECTIVE 1
What is required to create a security interest?

Exhibit 21–1 Secured Transactions—Concept and Terminology

In a security agreement, a debtor and a creditor agree that the creditor will have a security interest in collateral in which the debtor has rights. In essence, the collateral secures the loan and ensures the creditor of payment should the debtor default.

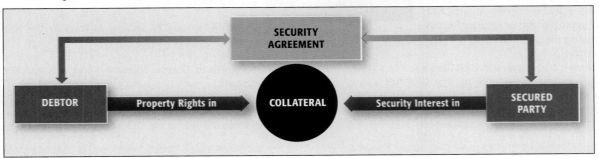

Once these requirements have been met, the creditor's rights are said to attach to the collateral. **Attachment** gives the creditor an enforceable security interest in the collateral [UCC 9–203].[1]

Attachment In a secured transaction, the process by which a secured creditor's interest "attaches" to the collateral and the creditor's security interest becomes enforceable. In the context of judicial liens, a court-ordered seizure of property before a judgment is secured for a past-due debt.

EXAMPLE 21.1 To furnish his new office suite, Bryce applies for a credit card at an office supply store. The application contains a clause stating that the store will retain a security interest in the goods that he buys with the card until he has paid for them in full. This application is a *written security agreement,* which is the first requirement for an enforceable security interest. The goods that Bryce buys with the card are the *something of value* from the secured party (the second requirement). His ownership interest in those goods is the *right* that he has in them (the third requirement). Thus, the requirements for an enforceable security interest are met. When Bryce buys something with the card, the store's rights attach to the purchased goods. ■

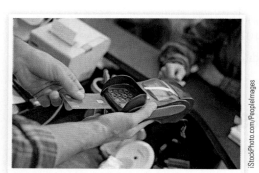

If you use a store-provided credit card at that store, does the store automatically have a security interest in what you purchase?

Written or Authenticated Security Agreement When the collateral is not in the possession of the secured party, the security agreement must be either written or authenticated. It must also describe the collateral.

Here, *authenticate* means to sign, execute, or adopt any symbol on an electronic record that verifies that the person signing has the intent to adopt or accept the record [UCC 9–102(a)(7)(69)]. Authentication provides for electronic filing (the filing process will be discussed later). See this chapter's *Adapting the Law to the Online Environment* feature for a discussion of a type of secured transaction that is performed online.

A security agreement must contain a description of the collateral that reasonably identifies it. Generally, such phrases as "all the debtor's personal property" or "all the debtor's assets" would *not* constitute a sufficient description [UCC 9–108(c)].

If the debtor signs, or otherwise authenticates, a security agreement, does he or she also have to sign an attached list of the collateral to create a valid security interest? That was the question before the court in the following case.

---

1. The term *attachment* has a different meaning in judicial liens, discussed later in this chapter. In that context, it refers to a court-ordered seizure and taking into custody of property before the securing of a court judgment for a past-due debt.

CASE 21.1

Royal Jewelers, Inc. v. Light
Supreme Court of North Dakota, 2015 ND 44, 859 N.W.2d 921 (2015).

FACTS Steven Light bought a $55,050 wedding ring for his wife, Sherri Light, on credit from Royal Jewelers, Inc., a store in Fargo, North Dakota. The receipt granted Royal a security interest in the ring. Later, Royal assigned its interest to GRB Financial Corp. Steven and GRB signed a modification agreement changing the repayment terms. An attached exhibit listed the items pledged as security for the modification, including the ring. Steven did not separately sign the exhibit.

A year later, Steven died. Royal and GRB filed a suit in a North Dakota state court against Sherri, alleging that GRB had a valid security interest in the ring. Sherri cited UCC 9–203, under which there is an enforceable interest only if "the debtor has authenticated a security agreement that provides a description of the

Who retains a security interest in a wedding ring when the buyer dies?

collateral." Sherri argued that the modification agreement did not "properly authenticate" the description of the collateral, including the ring, because Steven had not signed the attached exhibit. The court issued a judgment in GRB's favor. Sherri appealed.

ISSUE Was GRB's security interest in the ring valid and enforceable?

DECISION Yes. The North Dakota Supreme Court affirmed the lower court's judgment.

REASON The court acknowledged that under UCC 9–203, "a security interest is enforceable against the debtor and third parties with respect to the collateral only if . . . the debtor has authenticated a security agreement that provides a description of the collateral." The court explained, however, that under UCC 9–108(2), collateral may be described in a list attached to the security agreement. In fact, several documents may be considered together to comprise a security agreement. Furthermore, "no authority [requires] a debtor to separately sign an exhibit attached to and referenced in a signed security agreement." Here, Steven had granted a valid security interest in the

ring. With Steven's knowledge and consent, Royal had assigned the security interest to GRB. Thus, the lower court "did not err in finding GRB Financial had a valid and enforceable security interest in the ring."

CRITICAL THINKING—Ethical Consideration *Under the circumstances, is it ethical for GRB to enforce its security interest in the ring to recover the unpaid amount of the price? Discuss.*

Secured Party Must Give Value

The secured party must give something of value to the debtor. Some examples of value include a binding commitment to extend credit or consideration to support a simple contract [UCC 1–204]. Normally, the value given by a secured party is in the form of a direct loan or a commitment to sell goods on credit.

Debtor Must Have Rights in the Collateral

The debtor must have rights in the collateral. That means that the debtor must have a current or a future ownership interest in or right to obtain possession of the collateral. For instance, a retail seller-debtor can give a secured party a security interest not only in existing inventory owned by the retailer but also in *future* inventory to be acquired by the retailer. (A common misconception is that the debtor must have title to the collateral to have rights in it, but this is not a requirement.)

ADAPTING THE LAW TO THE ONLINE ENVIRONMENT
Secured Transactions Online

When you buy something online, you typically must use your credit card, make an electronic fund transfer, or send a check before the goods that you bought are sent to you. If you are buying an expensive item, such as a car, you are not likely to send funds without being assured that you will receive the item in the condition promised. Enter the concept of escrow.

Escrow Accounts
Escrow accounts are commonly used in real estate transactions, but they are also useful for smaller transactions, particularly those done on the Internet. An escrow account involves three parties—the buyer, the seller,

and a trusted third party that collects, holds, and disperses funds according to instructions from the buyer and seller. Escrow services are provided by licensed and regulated escrow companies. For example, if you buy a car on the Internet, you and the seller will agree on an escrow company to which you send the funds. When you receive the car and are satisfied with it, the escrow company will release the funds to the seller. This is a type of secured transaction.

Escrow.com
One of the best-known online escrow firms is Escrow.com, which had provided escrow services for more than $2 billion in secured

transactions by 2016. All of its escrow services are offered via its Web site and provided independently by Internet Escrow Services, one of its operating subsidiaries. Escrow .com is particularly useful for transactions that involve an international buyer or seller. It has become the recommended transaction settlement service for AutoTrader, Resale Weekly, Cars.com, eBay Motors, and Flippa .com.

CRITICAL THINKING
- How could online escrow services reduce Internet fraud?

21-2b Perfecting a Security Interest

Perfection The legal process by which secured parties protect themselves against the claims of third parties who may wish to have their debts satisfied out of the same collateral. It is usually accomplished by filing a financing statement with the appropriate government official.

Perfection is the legal process by which secured parties protect themselves against the claims of third parties who may wish to have their debts satisfied out of the same collateral. Whether a secured party's security interest is perfected or unperfected can have serious consequences for the secured party.

What if a debtor has borrowed from two different creditors, for instance, using the same property as collateral for both loans? If the debtor defaults on both loans, which of the two creditors has first rights to the collateral? In this situation, the creditor with a perfected security interest will prevail.

Perfection usually is accomplished by filing a financing statement. In some circumstances, however, a security interest becomes perfected even though no financing statement is filed.

Perfection by Filing The most common means of perfection is by filing a *financing statement* with the office of the appropriate government official. A financing statement gives public notice to third parties of the secured party's security interest. The security agreement itself can also be filed to perfect the security interest. The financing statement must provide the names of the debtor and the secured party, and must identify the collateral covered by the financing statement. A uniform financing statement form is now used in all states [see UCC 9–521].

When a bank finances the purchase of a tractor, how does it perfect its security interest in that tractor?

Communication of the financing statement to the appropriate filing office, together with the correct filing fee, or the acceptance of the financing statement by the filing officer constitutes a filing [UCC 9–516(a)]. The filing can be accomplished electronically [UCC 9–102(a)(18)]. In fact, most states use electronic filing systems. A financing statement may be filed even before a security agreement is made or a security interest attaches [UCC 9–502(d)].

The Debtor's Name. The UCC requires that a financing statement be filed under the name of the debtor [UCC 9–502(a)(1)]. Filings are indexed by the name of the debtor so that they can be located by subsequent searchers. Slight variations in names normally will not be considered misleading if a search of the filing office's records, using a standard computer search engine routinely used by that office, would disclose the filings [UCC 9–506(c)].[2]

UCC 9–503 sets out some detailed rules for determining when the debtor's name as it appears on a financing statement is sufficient.

1. *Corporations.* For corporations, which are organizations that have registered with the state, the debtor's name on the financing statement must be "the name of the debtor indicated on the public record of the debtor's jurisdiction of organization" [UCC 9–503(a)(1)].

2. *Trusts.* If the debtor is a trust or a trustee for property held in trust, the financing statement must disclose this information and provide the trust's name as specified in its official documents [UCC 9–503(a)(3)].

3. *Individuals and organizations.* For all others, the financing statement must disclose "the individual or organizational name of the debtor" [UCC 9–503(a)(4)(A)]. The word *organization* includes unincorporated associations, such as clubs, churches, joint ventures, and general partnerships. If an organizational debtor does not have a group name, the names of the individuals in the group must be listed.

4. *Trade names.* When the debtor's trade name is not the legal name of the business, providing only the trade name in a financing statement is *not* sufficient for perfection [UCC 9–503(c)]. The financing statement must also include the owner-debtor's actual name.

---

2. If the name listed in the financing statement is so inaccurate that a search using the standard search engine will not disclose the debtor's name, then the financing statement is deemed seriously misleading under UCC 9–506. See also UCC 9–507, which governs the effectiveness of financing statements found to be seriously misleading.

If the debtor's name changes, the financing statement remains effective for collateral the debtor acquired before or within four months after the name change. Unless an amendment to the financing statement is filed within this four-month period, collateral acquired by the debtor after the four-month period is unperfected [UCC 9–507(b) and (c)]. A one-page uniform financing statement amendment form is available for filing name changes and for other purposes.

Debtors frequently identify themselves by and change their trade names. This can make it difficult to find out whether an individual debtor's collateral is subject to a prior perfected security interest. For instance, suppose that a business named Bob's Automotive has two owners, Bob and Bill. When Bob decides to leave, Bill changes the trade name to Specialized Auto Repair. Searching the records using Bill's name and the new trade name might not reveal a prior perfected security interest from when the business was jointly owned and operating under a different name. Keep this in mind when making loans or extending credit.

When searching the records, find out if the business has used any other names in the past, and include those former names in your search. Remember that the key to determining if a security interest has been perfected is whether the financing statement adequately notifies other potential creditors that a security interest exists. If a search of the records using the debtor's correct name would disclose the interest, the filing is generally sufficient. To prevent legal problems, make sure that no other creditor has a prior interest in the property being used as collateral, and file the financing statement under the correct name.

Description of the Collateral. Both the security agreement and the financing statement must describe the collateral in which the secured party has a security interest. The security agreement must describe the collateral because no security interest in goods can exist unless the parties agree on which goods are subject to the security interest.

The financing statement must describe the collateral to provide public notice of the fact that certain goods of the debtor are subject to a security interest. Other parties who might later wish to lend funds to the debtor or buy the collateral can thus learn of the security interest by checking with the office in which a financing statement would be filed. For land-related security interests, a legal description of the realty is also required [UCC 9–502(b)].

Sometimes, the descriptions in the two documents vary. The description in the security agreement must be more precise than the description in the financing statement. The UCC permits broad, general descriptions in the financing statement, such as "all assets" or "all personal property," as long as they are accurate [UCC 9–504]. **EXAMPLE 21.2** A security agreement for a commercial loan to a manufacturer may list all of the manufacturer's equipment subject to the loan by serial number. The financing statement for the equipment may simply refer to "all equipment owned or hereafter acquired." ■

Where to File. In most states, a financing statement must be filed centrally in the appropriate state office, such as the office of the secretary of state, in the state where the debtor is located. An exception occurs when the collateral consists of timber to be cut, fixtures, or items to be extracted—such as oil, coal, gas, and minerals [UCC 9–301(3) and (4), 9–502(b)]. In those circumstances, the financing statement is filed in the county where the collateral is located.

Note that the state in which a financing statement should be filed depends on the *debtor's location,* not the location of the collateral [UCC 9–301]. The debtor's location is determined as follows [UCC 9–307]:

1. For *individual debtors,* it is the state of the debtor's principal residence.

2. For an *organization that is registered with the state,* such as a corporation or limited liability company, it is the state in which the organization is registered. Thus, if a debtor is incorporated in Maryland and has its

Tom Cheney The New Yorker Collection/The Cartoon Bank

"O.K., folks, let's move along. I'm sure you've all seen someone qualify for a loan before."

chief executive office in New York, a secured party would file the financing statement in Maryland.

3. For *all other entities,* it is the state in which the business is located or, if the debtor has more than one office, the place from which the debtor manages its business operations and affairs.

Consequences of an Improper Filing. Improper filing renders the security interest unperfected and reduces the secured party's claim in bankruptcy to that of an unsecured creditor. For instance, if the debtor's name on the financing statement is seriously misleading or if the collateral is not sufficiently described in the financing statement, the filing may not be effective.

EXAMPLE 21.3 Arthur Mendez Juarez, a strawberry farmer, leases farmland from Morona Fruits, Inc., and borrows funds from Morona for payroll and production expenses. The sublease and other documents set out Juarez's full name, but Juarez generally goes by the name "Mendez" and signs the sublease "Arthur Mendez." To perfect its interests, Morona files financing statements that identify the debtor as "Arthur Mendez."

Then Juarez contracts to sell strawberries to Frozun Foods, Inc., which also advances him funds secured by a financing statement that identifies the debtor as "Arthur Juarez." By the following year, Juarez is unable to pay his debts and owes Morona more than $200,000 and Frozun nearly $50,000. Both Morona and Frozun file a suit against Juarez claiming to have priority under a perfected security interest. In this situation, a properly filed financing statement would identify the debtor's true name (Arthur Juarez). Because a debtor name search for "Arthur Juarez" would not disclose a financing statement in the name of "Arthur Mendez," Morona's financing statement is seriously misleading. Therefore, Frozun's security interest would have priority because its financing statement was recorded properly. ■

Perfection without Filing

In two types of situations, security interests can be perfected without filing a financing statement. The first situation occurs when the collateral is transferred into the possession of the secured party. The second occurs when the security interest can be perfected on attachment (without a filing and without having to possess the goods) [UCC 9–309].

The phrase *perfected on attachment* means that these security interests are automatically perfected at the time of their creation. Two of the more common security interests that are perfected on attachment are a *purchase-money security interest* in consumer goods (discussed shortly) and an assignment of a beneficial interest in a decedent's estate [UCC 9–309(1), (13)].

Perfection by Possession.
In the past, one of the most common means of obtaining financing was to **pledge** certain collateral as security for the debt and transfer the collateral into the creditor's possession. When the debt was paid, the collateral was returned to the debtor. Article 9 of the UCC retained the common law pledge and the principle that the security agreement need not be in writing to be enforceable if the collateral is transferred to the secured party [UCC 9–310, 9–312(b), 9–313].

Certain items, such as stocks, bonds, negotiable instruments, and jewelry, are commonly transferred into the creditor's possession when they are used as collateral for loans. **EXAMPLE 21.4** Sheila needs cash to pay for a medical procedure. She gets a loan for $4,000 from Trent. As security for the loan, she gives him a promissory note on which she is the payee. Even though the agreement to hold the note as collateral was oral, Trent has a perfected security interest and does not need to file a financing statement. No other creditor of Sheila's can attempt to recover the promissory note from Trent in payment for other debts. ■

For most collateral, however, possession by the secured party is impractical because it denies the debtor the right to use or derive income from the property to pay off the debt. **EXAMPLE 21.5** Jed, a farmer, takes out a loan to finance the purchase of a large corn harvester and uses the equipment as collateral. Clearly, the purpose of the purchase would be defeated if Jed transferred the collateral into the creditor's possession, because he would not be able to use the equipment to harvest his corn. ■

Pledge A security device in which personal property is transferred into the possession of the creditor as security for the payment of a debt and retained by the creditor until the debt is paid.

Perfection by Attachment—The Purchase-Money Security Interest in Consumer Goods. Under the UCC, fourteen types of security interests are perfected automatically at the time they are created [UCC 9–309]. The most common is the **purchase-money security interest (PMSI)** in *consumer goods* (items bought primarily for personal, family, or household purposes). A PMSI in consumer goods is created when a person buys goods on credit. The entity that extends the credit and obtains the PMSI can be either the seller (a store, for example) or a financial institution that lends the buyer the funds with which to purchase the goods [UCC 9–102(a)(2)].

Automatic Perfection. A PMSI in consumer goods is perfected automatically at the time of a credit sale—that is, at the time the PMSI is created. The seller in this situation does not need to do anything more to perfect her or his interest. **EXAMPLE 21.6** Jami purchases an LG washer and dryer from West Coast Appliance for $2,500. Unable to pay the entire amount in cash, Jami signs a purchase agreement to pay $1,000 down and $100 per month until the balance, plus interest, is fully paid. West Coast Appliance is to retain a security interest in the appliances until full payment has been made. Because the security interest was created as part of a purchase agreement with a consumer, it is a PMSI, and West Coast Appliance's security interest is automatically perfected. ▪

Exceptions to the Rule of Automatic Perfection. There are two exceptions to the rule of automatic perfection for PMSIs:

1. Certain types of security interests that are subject to other federal or state laws may require additional steps to be perfected [UCC 9–311]. Many jurisdictions, for instance, have certificate-of-title statutes that establish perfection requirements for security interests in certain goods, including automobiles, trailers, boats, mobile homes, and farm tractors. **EXAMPLE 21.7** Martin Sedek purchases a boat at a Florida dealership. Florida has a certificate-of-title statute. Sedek obtains financing for his purchase through General Credit Corporation. General Credit Corporation will need to file a certificate of title with the appropriate state official to perfect the PMSI. ▪

2. PMSIs in nonconsumer goods, such as a business's inventory or livestock, are not automatically perfected [UCC 9–324]. These types of PMSIs will be discussed later in this chapter in the context of priorities.

Perfection and the Classification of Collateral Where or how to perfect a security interest sometimes depends on the classification or definition of the collateral. Collateral is generally divided into two classifications: *tangible collateral* (collateral that can be seen, felt, and touched) and *intangible collateral* (collateral that consists of or generates rights). Exhibit 21–2 summarizes the various classifications of collateral and the methods of perfecting a security interest in collateral falling within each of those classifications.[3]

Effective Time Duration of Perfection A financing statement is effective for five years from the date of filing [UCC 9–515]. If a **continuation statement** is filed within six months *prior to* the expiration date, the effectiveness of the original statement is continued for another five years, starting with the expiration date of the first five-year period [UCC 9–515(d), (e)]. The effectiveness of the statement can be continued in the same manner indefinitely. Any attempt to file a continuation statement outside the six-month window will render the continuation ineffective, however, and the perfection will lapse at the end of the five-year period.

---

3. There are additional classifications, such as agricultural liens, commercial tort claims, and investment property. For definitions of these types of collateral, see UCC 9–102(a)(5), (a)(13), and (a)(49).

Purchase-Money Security Interest (PMSI) A security interest that arises when a seller or lender extends credit for part or all of the purchase price of goods purchased by a buyer.

LEARNING OBJECTIVE 2

How is a purchase-money security interest in consumer goods created?

If this couple buys a 4K Ultra High Definition television on credit, is a PMSI automatically created?

Continuation Statement A statement that, if filed within six months prior to the expiration date of the original financing statement, continues the perfection of the security interest for another five years.

Exhibit 21–2 Selected Types of Collateral and Their Methods of Perfection

TANGIBLE COLLATERAL		METHOD OF PERFECTION
All things that are movable at the time the security interest attaches or that are attached to land, including timber to be cut and growing crops.		
1. Consumer Goods [UCC 9–301, 9–303, 9–309(1), 9–310(a), 9–313(a)]	Goods used or bought primarily for personal, family, or household purposes—for example, household furniture [UCC 9–102(a)(23)].	For purchase-money security interest, attachment (that is, the creation of a security interest) is sufficient. For boats, motor vehicles, and trailers, filing or compliance with a certificate-of-title statute is required. For other consumer goods, general rules of filing or possession apply.
2. Equipment [UCC 9–301, 9–310(a), 9–313(a)]	Goods bought for or used primarily in business (and not part of inventory or farm products)—for example, a delivery truck [UCC 9–102(a)(33)].	Filing or (rarely) possession by secured party.
3. Farm Products [UCC 9–301, 9–310(a), 9–313(a)]	Crops (including aquatic goods), livestock, or supplies produced in a farming operation—for example, ginned cotton, milk, eggs, and maple syrup [UCC 9–102(a)(34)].	Filing or (rarely) possession by secured party.
4. Inventory [UCC 9–301, 9–310(a), 9–313(a)]	Goods held by a person for sale or under a contract of service or lease; raw materials held for production and work in progress [UCC 9–102(a)(48)].	Filing or (rarely) possession by secured party.
INTANGIBLE COLLATERAL		METHOD OF PERFECTION
Nonphysical property that exists only in connection with something else.		
1. Chattel Paper [UCC 9–301, 9–310(a), 9–312(a), 9–313(a), 9–314(a)]	A writing or electronic record that evidences both a monetary obligation and a security interest in goods and software used in goods—for example, a security agreement [UCC 9–102(a)(11), (a)(31), and (a)(78)].	Filing or possession or control by secured party.
2. Instruments [UCC 9–301, 9–309(4), 9–310(a), 9–312(a) and (e), 9–313(a)]	A negotiable instrument, such as a check, note, certificate of deposit, draft, or other writing that evidences a right to the payment of money and is not a security agreement or lease but rather a type that can ordinarily be transferred (after indorsement, if necessary) by delivery [UCC 9–102(a)(47)].	Normally filing or possession. For the sale of promissory notes, perfection can be by attachment (automatically on the creation of the security interest).
3. Accounts [UCC 9–301, 9–309(2) and (5), 9–310(a)]	Any right to receive payment for property (real or personal), including intellectual licensed property, services, insurance policies, and certain other receivables [UCC 9–102(a)(2) and (a)(46)].	Filing required except for certain assignments that can be perfected by attachment (automatically on the creation of the security interest).
4. Deposit Accounts [UCC 9–104, 9–304, 9–312(b), 9–314(a)]	Any demand, time, savings, passbook, or similar account maintained with a bank [UCC 9–102(a)(29)].	Perfection by control, such as when the secured party is the bank in which the account is maintained or when the parties have agreed that the secured party can direct the disposition of funds in a particular account.

If a financing statement lapses, the security interest that had been perfected by the filing becomes unperfected. A purchaser for value can acquire the collateral as if the security interest had never been perfected [UCC 9–515(c)].

21-3 Scope of a Security Interest

A security interest can cover property in which the debtor has either present or future ownership or possessory rights. Therefore, security agreements can cover not only collateral in the present possession or control of the debtor but also proceeds from the sale of collateral, after-acquired property, and future advances, as discussed next.

21–3a Proceeds

Proceeds are whatever cash or property is received when collateral is sold or disposed of in some other way [UCC 9–102(a)(64)]. A security interest in the collateral gives the secured party a security interest in the proceeds acquired from the sale of that collateral.

EXAMPLE 21.8 People's Bank has a perfected security interest in the inventory of a retail seller of heavy farm machinery. The retailer sells a tractor out of this inventory to Jacob Dunn, a farmer. Dunn agrees, in a security agreement, to make monthly payments to the retailer for a period of twenty-four months. If the retailer goes into default on the loan from the bank, the bank is entitled to the remaining payments Dunn owes to the retailer as proceeds. ■

A security interest in proceeds perfects automatically on the perfection of the secured party's security interest in the original collateral, and it remains perfected for twenty days after the debtor receives the proceeds. The parties can agree to extend the twenty-day automatic perfection period in their original security agreement [UCC 9–315(c), (d)]. This is typically done when the collateral is the type that is likely to be sold, such as a retailer's inventory of tablets or smartphones. The UCC also permits a security interest in identifiable cash proceeds to remain perfected after twenty days [UCC 9–315(d)(2)].

Proceeds Under Article 9 of the UCC, whatever is received when collateral is sold or disposed of in some other way.

21–3b After-Acquired Property

After-acquired property is property that the debtor acquired after the execution of the security agreement. The security agreement may provide for a security interest in after-acquired property, such as a debtor's inventory [UCC 9–204(1)]. Generally, the debtor will purchase new inventory to replace the inventory sold. The secured party wants this newly acquired inventory to be subject to the original security interest. Thus, the after-acquired property clause continues the secured party's claim to any inventory acquired thereafter. (This is not to say that the original security interest will always take priority over the rights of all other creditors with regard to this after-acquired inventory, as will be discussed later.)

EXAMPLE 21.9 Amato buys factory equipment from Bronson on credit, giving as security an interest in all of her equipment—both what she is buying and what she already owns. The security interest with Bronson contains an after-acquired property clause. Six months later, Amato pays cash to another seller of factory equipment for more equipment. Six months after that, Amato goes out of business before she has paid off her debt to Bronson. Bronson has a security interest in all of Amato's equipment, even the equipment bought from the other seller. ■

After-Acquired Property Property that is acquired by the debtor after the execution of a security agreement.

21–3c Future Advances

Often, a debtor will arrange with a bank to have a *continuing line of credit* under which the debtor can borrow funds intermittently. Advances against lines of credit can be subject to a properly perfected security interest in certain collateral. The security agreement may provide that any future advances made against that line of credit are also subject to the security interest in that collateral [UCC 9–204(c)]. Future advances do not have to be of the same type or otherwise related to the original advance to benefit from this type of **cross-collateralization.**[4] Cross-collateralization occurs when an asset that is not the subject of a loan is used to secure that loan.

EXAMPLE 21.10 Stroh is the owner of a small manufacturing plant with equipment valued at $1 million. He has an immediate need for $50,000 of working capital, so he obtains a loan from Midwestern Bank and signs a security agreement, putting up all of his equipment as security. The bank properly perfects its security interest. The security agreement provides that

Cross-Collateralization The use of an asset that is not the subject of a loan to collateralize that loan.

---

4. See official Comment 5 to UCC 9–204.

Can equipment be used as collateral for further advances?

iStockPhoto.com/baranozdemir

Floating Lien A security interest in proceeds, after-acquired property, or collateral subject to future advances by the secured party (or all three). The security interest is retained even when the collateral changes in character, classification, or location.

Stroh can borrow up to $500,000 in the future, using the same equipment as collateral for any future advances. In this situation, Midwestern Bank does not have to execute a new security agreement and perfect a security interest in the collateral each time an advance is made, up to a cumulative total of $500,000. For priority purposes, each advance is perfected as of the date of the *original* perfection. ■

21–3d The Floating-Lien Concept

A security agreement that provides for a security interest in proceeds, in after-acquired property, or in collateral subject to future advances by the secured party (or in all three) is often characterized as a **floating lien.** This type of security interest continues in the collateral or proceeds even if the collateral is sold, exchanged, or disposed of in some other way.

A Floating Lien in Inventory Floating liens commonly arise in the financing of inventories. A creditor is not interested in *specific* pieces of inventory, which are constantly changing, so the lien "floats" from one item to another as the inventory changes.

EXAMPLE 21.11 Cascade Sports, Inc., an Oregon corporation, operates as a cross-country ski dealer and has a line of credit with Portland First Bank to finance its inventory of cross-country skis. Cascade and Portland First enter into a security agreement that provides for coverage of proceeds, after-acquired inventory, present inventory, and future advances. Portland First perfects its security interest in the inventory by filing centrally with the office of the secretary of state in Oregon.

One day, Cascade sells a new pair of the latest cross-country skis and receives a used pair in trade. That same day, Cascade purchases two new pairs of cross-country skis from a local manufacturer for cash. Later that day, to meet its payroll, Cascade borrows $8,000 from Portland First Bank under the security agreement.

Portland First gets a perfected security interest in the used pair of skis under the proceeds clause and a perfected security interest in the two new pairs of skis under the after-acquired property clause. This collateral, as well as other inventory, secures the new funds advanced to Cascade under the future-advances clause. All of this is accomplished under the original perfected security interest. The various items in the inventory have changed, but Portland First still has a perfected security interest in Cascade's inventory. Hence, it has a floating lien in the inventory. ■

A Floating Lien in a Shifting Stock of Goods The concept of the floating lien can also apply to a shifting stock of goods. The lien can start with raw materials, follow them as they become finished goods and inventories, and continue as the goods are sold and are turned into accounts receivable, chattel paper, or cash.

21–4 Priorities, Rights, and Duties

When more than one party claims an interest in the same collateral, which has priority? The UCC sets out detailed rules to answer this question. Although in many situations the party who has a perfected security interest will have priority, there are exceptions. The UCC also provides certain rights and duties to debtors and secured parties.

21–4a General Rules of Priority

The basic rule is that when more than one security interest has been perfected in the same collateral, the first security interest to be perfected (or filed) has priority over any security

KNOW THIS
Secured creditors—perfected or not—have priority over unsecured creditors.

interests that are perfected later. If only one of the conflicting security interests has been perfected, then that security interest has priority. If none of the security interests have been perfected, then the first security interest that attaches has priority.

The UCC's rules of priority can be summarized as follows:

1. *Perfected security interest versus unsecured creditors and unperfected security interests.* When two or more parties have claims to the same collateral, a perfected secured party's interest has priority over the interests of most other parties [UCC 9–322(a)(2)]. This includes priority to the proceeds from a sale of collateral resulting from a bankruptcy (giving the perfected secured party rights superior to that of a bankruptcy trustee).

2. *Conflicting perfected security interests.* When two or more secured parties have perfected security interests in the same collateral, the first to perfect (by filing or taking possession of the collateral) generally has priority [UCC 9–322(a)(1)].

3. *Conflicting unperfected security interests.* When two conflicting security interests are unperfected, the first to attach (be created) has priority [UCC 9–322(a)(3)]. This is sometimes called the "first-in-time" rule.

CASE EXAMPLE 21.12 Ag Venture Financial Services, Inc., made multiple loans to a family-owned dairy farm, Montagne Heifers, Inc. (MHI). Michael Montagne owned the business, and his wife and son were shareholders and employees. In 2005, MHI executed a promissory note and security agreement in favor of Ag Venture, which listed all of MHI's accounts, equipment, farm products, inventory, livestock, and proceeds as collateral. In 2006, Montagne and his wife separated, and he signed a separation agreement that gave her some funds and certain parcels of land.

In 2007, Montagne gave his son a promissory note for $100,000 in exchange for his shares in MHI. The note listed all of MHI's equipment, inventory, livestock, and proceeds as collateral. Also in 2007, Montagne sold a herd of dairy cows for $500,000 and gave his former wife a check for $240,000. In 2008, Montagne filed a petition for bankruptcy, and a dispute arose over which party (Ag Venture, Montagne's son, or Montagne's former wife) was entitled to the proceeds from the 2007 sale of the cows. The court held that because Ag Venture's security interest in the proceeds was the first in time to *attach* (it was created in 2005), Ag Venture had first priority to the proceeds.[5] ■

21–4b Exceptions to the General Priority Rules

Under some circumstances, on the debtor's default, the perfection of a security interest will not protect a secured party against certain other third parties having claims to the collateral. For instance, the UCC provides that in some instances a PMSI, properly perfected,[6] will prevail over another security interest in after-acquired collateral, even though the other was perfected first. We discuss some significant exceptions to the general rules of priority next.

Buyers in the Ordinary Course of Business Under the UCC, a person who buys "in the ordinary course of business" takes the goods free from any security interest created by the seller even if the security interest is perfected and the buyer knows of its existence [UCC 9–320(a)]. A *buyer in the ordinary course of business* is a person who in good faith, and without knowledge that the sale violates the rights of another in the goods, buys goods in the ordinary course from a person in the business of selling goods of that kind [UCC 1–201(9)].[7] The rationale for this rule is obvious. If buyers could not obtain the goods free and clear of any

---

5. *In re Montagne,* 417 Bankr. 214 (D.Vt. 2009).
6. Recall that, with some exceptions (such as motor vehicles), a PMSI in *consumer goods* is automatically perfected—no filing is necessary. A PMSI that is *not* in consumer goods must still be perfected, however.
7. Note that even though a buyer may know about the existence of a perfected security interest, he or she must not know that buying the goods violates the rights of any third party.

security interest the merchant had created—for example, in inventory—the free flow of goods in the marketplace would be hindered.

EXAMPLE 21.13 Dubbs Auto grants a security interest in its inventory to Heartland Bank for a $300,000 line of credit. Heartland perfects its security interest by filing financing statements with the appropriate state offices. Dubbs uses $9,000 of its credit to buy two used trucks and delivers the certificates of title, which designate Dubbs as the owner, to Heartland. Later, Dubbs sells one of the trucks to Shea Murdoch and another to Michael Laxton. National City Bank finances both purchases. New certificates of title designate the buyers as the owners and Heartland as the "first lienholder," but Heartland receives none of the funds from the sales. If Heartland sues National City, claiming that its security interest in the vehicles takes priority, it will lose. Because Murdoch and Laxton are buyers in the ordinary course of business, Heartland's security interest in the motor vehicles was extinguished when the vehicles were sold to them. ◼

Buyers of the Collateral The UCC recognizes that there are certain types of buyers whose interests in purchased goods could conflict with those of a perfected secured party on the debtor's default. These include not only buyers in the ordinary course of business (as just discussed), but also buyers of farm products, chattel paper, instruments, documents, or securities. The UCC sets down special rules of priority for these types of buyers.

21-4c Rights and Duties of Debtors and Creditors

The security agreement itself determines most of the rights and duties of the debtor and the secured party. The UCC, however, imposes some rights and duties that are applicable unless the security agreement states otherwise.

Information Requests At the time of filing, a secured party can furnish a copy of the financing statement and request that the filing officer note the file number, date, and hour of the original filing on the copy [UCC 9–523(a)]. The filing officer must send this copy to the person designated by the secured party.

The filing officer must also give information to a person who is contemplating obtaining a security interest from a prospective debtor [UCC 9–523(c), (d)]. If requested, the filing officer must issue a certificate (for a fee) that provides information on possible perfected financing statements with respect to the named debtor.

Release, Assignment, and Amendment A secured party can release all or part of any collateral described in the financing statement, thereby terminating its security interest in that collateral. The release is recorded by filing a uniform amendment form [UCC 9–512, 9–521(b)]. A secured party can also assign all or part of the security interest to a third party (the assignee). The assignee becomes the secured party of record if the assignment is filed by use of a uniform amendment form [UCC 9–514, 9–521(a)].

If the debtor and the secured party agree, they can amend the filing—to add or substitute new collateral, for example—by filing a uniform amendment form that indicates the file number of the initial financing statement [UCC 9–512(a)]. The amendment does not extend the time period of perfection, but if new collateral is added, the perfection date (for priority purposes) for the new collateral begins on the date the amendment is filed [UCC 9–512(b), (c)].

Confirmation or Accounting Request by Debtor The debtor may believe that the amount of the unpaid debt or the list of collateral subject to the security interest is inaccurate. The debtor has the right to request a confirmation of the unpaid debt or list of collateral [UCC 9–210]. The debtor is entitled to one request without charge every six months.

The secured party must comply with the debtor's confirmation request by authenticating and sending to the debtor an accounting within fourteen days after the request is received.

Otherwise, the secured party will be held liable for any loss suffered by the debtor, plus $500 [UCC 9–210, 9–625(f)].

Termination Statement When the debtor has fully paid the debt, if the secured party perfected the security interest by filing, the debtor is entitled to have a termination statement filed. Such a statement demonstrates to the public that the filed perfected security interest has been terminated [UCC 9–513].

Whenever consumer goods are involved, the secured party *must* file a termination statement (or, alternatively, a release) within one month of the final payment or within twenty days of receiving the debtor's demand, whichever is earlier [UCC 9–513(b)]. When the collateral is not consumer goods, the secured party is not required to file or to send a termination statement unless the debtor demands one [UCC 9–513(c)].

21-5 Default

Article 9 defines the rights, duties, and remedies of the secured party and of the debtor on the debtor's default. If the secured party fails to comply with his or her duties, the debtor is afforded particular rights and remedies under the UCC.

21-5a What Constitutes Default

What constitutes default is not always clear. In fact, Article 9 does not define the term. Consequently, parties are encouraged in practice—and by the UCC—to include in their security agreements the standards under which their rights and duties will be measured [UCC 9–601, 9–603]. In so doing, parties can stipulate the conditions that will constitute a default. Often, these critical terms are shaped by creditors in an attempt to provide themselves with the maximum protection possible. The terms may not, however, run counter to the UCC's provisions regarding good faith and unconscionability.

Any breach of the terms of the security agreement can constitute default. Nevertheless, default occurs most commonly when the debtor fails to meet the scheduled payments or becomes bankrupt.

Execution The implementation of a court's decree or judgment.

Levy The legal process of obtaining funds through the seizure and sale of nonexempt property, usually done after a writ of execution has been issued.

21-5b Basic Remedies

UCC 9–601(a) and (b) set out rights and remedies for secured parties, and these rights and remedies are *cumulative* [UCC 9–601(c)]. Therefore, if a creditor is unsuccessful in enforcing rights by one method, he or she can pursue another method. Generally, a secured party's remedies can be divided into the two basic categories discussed next.

Repossession of the Collateral—The Self-Help Remedy On the debtor's default, a secured party can take peaceful possession of the collateral without the use of judicial process [UCC 9–609(b)]. This provision is often referred to as the "self-help" provision of Article 9.

The UCC does not define *peaceful possession,* however. The general rule is that the collateral has been taken peacefully if the secured party can take possession without committing (1) trespass onto land, (2) assault and/or battery, or (3) breaking and entering.

On taking possession, the secured party may either retain the collateral for satisfaction of the debt [UCC 9–620] or resell the goods and apply the proceeds toward the debt [UCC 9–610].

Judicial Remedies Alternatively, a secured party can relinquish the security interest and use any judicial remedy available, such as obtaining a judgment on the underlying debt, followed by execution and levy. (**Execution** is the implementation of a court's decree or judgment. **Levy**

haveseen/ShutterStock.com

This man is not stealing this car. What might he be doing instead?

is the legal process of obtaining funds through the seizure and sale of nonexempt property, usually done after a writ of execution has been issued.) Execution and levy are rarely undertaken unless the collateral is no longer in existence or has substantially declined in value and the debtor has other assets available that may be legally seized to satisfy the debt [UCC 9–601(a)].[8]

21–5c Disposition of Collateral

Once default has occurred and the secured party has obtained possession of the collateral, the secured party can:

1. Retain the collateral in full or partial satisfaction of the debt (subject to limitations, discussed next).

2. Sell, lease, license, or otherwise dispose of the collateral in any commercially reasonable manner and apply the proceeds toward satisfaction of the debt [UCC 9–602(7), 9–603, 9–610(a), 9–613, 9–620]. Any sale is always subject to procedures established by state law.

Is the sale of collateral at auction a reasonable means of disposing of that collateral?

Retention of Collateral by the Secured Party Parties are sometimes better off if they do not sell the collateral. Therefore, the UCC generally allows secured parties to retain the collateral (except in certain cases involving consumer goods, discussed shortly). The right to retain the collateral is subject to the following conditions:

1. *Notice to debtor.* The secured party must notify the debtor of its proposal to retain the collateral. Notice is required unless the debtor has signed a statement renouncing or modifying her or his rights *after default* [UCC 9–620(a), 9–621].

2. *Notice to other secured parties.* If the collateral is consumer goods, the secured party does not need to give any other notice. In all other situations, the secured party must also send notice to any other secured party (or lienholder) from whom the secured party has received notice of a claim of interest in the collateral in question.

3. *Waiting period for objections.* If, within twenty days after the notice is sent, the secured party receives an objection from the debtor or another party who was notified, the secured party must sell or otherwise dispose of the collateral. If no objection is received, the secured party may retain the collateral in full or partial satisfaction of the debtor's obligation [UCC 9–620(a), 9–621].

Consumer Goods When the collateral is consumer goods and the debtor has paid 60 percent or more of the purchase price on a PMSI or of the loan amount on a non-PMSI, the secured party must sell or otherwise dispose of the repossessed collateral within ninety days [UCC 9–620(e), (f)]. Failure to comply opens the secured party to an action for conversion or other liability under UCC 9–625(b) and (c). A secured party will not be liable, however, if the consumer-debtor signed a written statement *after default* renouncing or modifying the right to demand the sale of the goods [UCC 9–624].

Disposition Procedures A secured party who does not choose to retain the collateral or who is required to sell it must follow the disposition procedures prescribed in the UCC. The secured party may sell, lease, license, or otherwise dispose of any or all of the collateral in its present condition or following any commercially reasonable preparation or processing [UCC 9–610(a)].

KNOW THIS

Conversion is a tort that involves depriving an owner of personal property without the owner's permission.

---

8. Some assets are exempt from creditors' claims.

Notice Requirement. The secured party must notify the debtor and other specified parties in writing ahead of time about the sale or disposition of the collateral. Notification is not required if the collateral is perishable, will decline rapidly in value, or is a type customarily sold on a recognized market [UCC 9–611(b), (c)]. The debtor may waive the right to receive this notice, but only after default [UCC 9–624(a)].

Commercially Reasonable Manner. Every aspect of the disposition's method, manner, time, and place must be *commercially reasonable* [UCC 9–610(b)]. If the secured party does not dispose of the collateral in a commercially reasonable manner, the price paid for the collateral at the sale may be negatively affected. In that situation, a court can reduce the amount of any deficiency that the debtor owes to the secured party [UCC 9–626(a)(3)].

Although the purpose of requiring a commercially reasonable disposition is to obtain a satisfactory price, the courts look at other factors besides price in determining reasonableness. In the following case, the court considered whether a creditor's sale of the debtors' shares of stock was commercially unreasonable.

> "If you think nobody cares if you're alive, try missing a couple of car payments."
>
> **EARL WILSON**
> 1907–1987
> (AMERICAN JOURNALIST)

CASE 21.2

Smith v. Firstbank Corp.
Court of Appeals of Michigan, 2013 WL 951377 (2013).

COMPANY PROFILE *Since its founding in Jackson, Michigan, in 1900, Sparton Corporation has designed, developed, and manufactured electronic and electromechanical devices. From prototype through shipment, Sparton has worked with diverse companies in the aerospace, medical, defense, security, navigation, exploration, and industrial markets. Today, Sparton is headquartered in Schaumberg, Illinois. It has more than 1,300 employees and maintains production facilities in the United States and in Vietnam.*

When can the debtor who pledged stock as collateral successfully claim that its sale was unreasonable?

FACTS Bradley Smith, on his own behalf and on the behalf of the John J. Smith Revocable Living Trust, borrowed funds from Firstbank Corporation secured with pledges of Sparton Corporation stock and other collateral. When the loans were not paid, Firstbank sold the stock in two private transactions, returned the other collateral, and remitted the excess funds collected to Smith and the trust.

Alleging that the sales were commercially unreasonable because a higher price might have been obtained in a different sale, Smith and the trust filed a suit in a Michigan state court against Firstbank. The court granted the defendant's motion for summary judgment, and the plaintiffs appealed.

ISSUE Were Firstbank's sales of the debtors' Sparton stock commercially reasonable?

DECISION Yes. A state intermediate appellate court affirmed the lower court's summary judgment in the bank's favor.

REASON Firstbank had valid reasons for choosing to sell the debtors' stock in private sales and worked to obtain a reasonable price for the shares. Concern about how public sales might have affected the share price supported the bank's decision to seek a private buyer. In previous sales of Sparton stock in the public market, shares had been sold in a series of transactions at declining prices. Firstbank's decision to use private sales avoided this risk.

The manner in which the sales were conducted was also reasonable. Firstbank sought more than one offer for the stock. Because Sparton shares are thinly traded, however, the bank received only one offer, which was at a discount. Firstbank accepted the offer and later was able to sell additional shares in a second transaction for a somewhat higher price. Because of the bank's efforts, Smith and the trust were able to keep "over five million dollars of collateral, as well as a net surplus on the sale of the stock."

CRITICAL THINKING—Economic Consideration *Why does collateral have to be disposed of in a commercially reasonable way? What factors could courts look at to determine reasonableness?*

Distribution of Proceeds from the Disposition Proceeds from the disposition of collateral after default on the underlying debt are distributed in the following order:

1. Reasonable expenses incurred by the secured party in repossessing, storing, and reselling the collateral are paid first.

2. The balance of the debt owed to the secured party is then paid.

3. Other lienholders who have made written or authenticated demands.

4. Unless the collateral consists of accounts, payment intangibles, promissory notes, or chattel paper, any surplus goes to the debtor [UCC 9–608(a); 9–615(a), (e)].

Noncash Proceeds

Noncash Proceeds Sometimes the secured party receives noncash proceeds from the disposition of collateral after default. Whenever that occurs, the secured party must make a value determination and apply this value in a commercially reasonable manner [UCC 9–608(a)(3), 9–615(c)].

Deficiency Judgment

Deficiency Judgment Often, after proper disposition of the collateral, the secured party has not collected all that the debtor still owes. Unless otherwise agreed, the debtor normally is liable for any deficiency, and the creditor can obtain a **deficiency judgment** from a court to collect this amount. Practically speaking, though, debtors who have defaulted on a loan rarely have the cash to pay any deficiency.

Note that if the underlying transaction was a sale of accounts, chattel paper, or promissory notes, the debtor is *not* liable for any deficiency. The debtor normally is entitled to any surplus from the disposition of these types of collateral, however [UCC 9–615(e)].

Deficiency Judgment A judgment against a debtor for the amount of a debt remaining unpaid after the collateral has been repossessed and sold.

ETHICAL ISSUE

How long should a secured party have to seek a deficiency judgment? Because of depreciation, the amount received from the sale of collateral is frequently less than the amount the debtor owes the secured party. As noted, the secured party can file a suit against the debtor in an attempt to collect the balance due. Article 9 does not contain a statute of limitations provision, so it is not clear how long a secured party has after default to file a deficiency suit against a debtor. If the secured party waits until the debtor becomes solvent again, though, the court may not allow the suit. When creditors have sued debtors for deficiencies owed on repossessed cars, for instance, many courts have applied the four-year limitation period in Article 2 because the transaction was a sale of goods, even though a security interest was involved.[9] Is this fair?

Redemption Rights

Redemption Rights The debtor or any other secured party can exercise the right of *redemption* of the collateral. Redemption may occur at any time before the secured party disposes of the collateral, enters into a contract for its disposition, or discharges the debtor's obligation by retaining the collateral. The debtor or other secured party exercises the redemption right by tendering performance of all obligations secured by the collateral and by paying the expenses reasonably incurred by the secured party in retaking and maintaining the collateral [UCC 9–623].

21-6 Other Laws Assisting Creditors

Both the common law and statutory laws other than Article 9 of the Uniform Commercial Code create rights and remedies for creditors. Here we discuss some of these rights and remedies.

21-6a Liens

A *lien* is an encumbrance on (claim against) property to satisfy a debt or protect a claim for the payment of a debt. Creditors' liens may arise under the common law or under statutory law. Statutory liens include *mechanic's liens*, whereas *artisan's liens* were recognized by common

---

9. See, for example, *Credit Acceptance Corp. v. Coates*, 2008 WL 3889424 (2008), and *Price Automotive II, LLC v. Mass Management, LLC*, 2015 WL 300418 (W.D.Va. 2015).

law. *Judicial liens* arise when a creditor attempts to collect on a debt before or after a judgment is entered by a court.

Liens can be useful because a lien creditor generally has priority over an unperfected secured party. In other words, if a creditor obtains a lien *before* another party perfects a security interest in the same property, the lienholder has priority. If the lien is obtained *after* another's security interest in the property is perfected, the perfected security interest has priority. Mechanic's and artisan's liens are exceptions to this rule. They normally take priority *even over perfected security interests,* unless a statute provides otherwise.

Mechanic's Lien Sometimes, a person who has contracted for labor, services, or materials to be furnished for making improvements on real property does not immediately pay for the improvements. When that happens, the creditor can place a **mechanic's lien** on the property. A mechanic's lien creates a special type of debtor-creditor relationship in which the real estate itself becomes security for the debt.

EXAMPLE 21.14 Jeff paints a house for Becky, a homeowner, for an agreed-on price to cover labor and materials. If Becky refuses to pay for the work or pays only a portion of the charges, a mechanic's lien against the property can be created. Jeff is then the lienholder, and the real property is encumbered (burdened) with a mechanic's lien for the amount owed. If Becky does not pay the lien, the property can be sold to satisfy the debt. ■

State law governs the procedures that must be followed to create a mechanic's lien. Generally, the lienholder must file a written notice of lien within a specific time period (usually 60 to 120 days) from the last date that labor or materials were provided. Notice of the foreclosure and sale must be given to the debtor in advance. (*Foreclosure* is the process by which the creditor deprives the debtor of the property.)

Artisan's Lien When a debtor fails to pay for labor and materials furnished for the repair or improvement of personal property, a creditor can recover payment through an **artisan's lien.** In contrast to a mechanic's lien, an artisan's lien is *possessory.* The lienholder ordinarily must have retained possession of the property and have expressly or impliedly agreed to provide the services on a cash, not a credit, basis. The lien remains in existence as long as the lienholder maintains possession of the property, and the lien is terminated once possession is voluntarily surrendered, unless the surrender is only temporary.

EXAMPLE 21.15 MacKenzie takes a sapphire necklace that she inherited to a jewelry store to have it made into a ring and set of earrings. The store's owner agrees to reset the sapphires into custom jewelry for $4,000. MacKenzie comes to pick up the jewelry but refuses to pay the $4,000 she owes. The jeweler can assert an artisan's lien on the jewelry in his possession until MacKenzie pays. If the jeweler gives the jewelry to MacKenzie (without requiring full payment), the lien disappears. ■

Modern statutes permit the holder of an artisan's lien to foreclose and sell the property subject to the lien to satisfy payment of the debt. As with a mechanic's lien, the holder of an artisan's lien must give notice to the owner of the property prior to foreclosure and sale. The sale proceeds are used to pay the debt and the costs of the legal proceedings, and the surplus, if any, is paid to the former owner.

Judicial Liens When a debt is past due, a creditor can bring a legal action against the debtor to collect the debt. If the creditor is successful, the court awards the creditor a judgment against the debtor (usually for the amount of the debt plus any interest and legal costs incurred). Frequently, however, the creditor is unable to collect the awarded amount.

To ensure that a judgment will be collectible, the creditor can request that certain non-exempt property of the debtor be seized to satisfy the debt. (Under state or federal statutes, certain property is exempt from attachment by creditors.) A court's order to seize the debtor's

LEARNING OBJECTIVE 4
How does a mechanic's lien assist creditors?

Mechanic's Lien
A nonpossessory, filed lien on an owner's real estate for labor, services, or materials furnished for making improvements on the realty.

When can a painter place a mechanic's lien on the house?

Artisan's Lien A possessory lien held by a party who has made improvements and added value to the personal property of another party as security for payment for services performed.

property is known as a *writ of attachment* if it is issued before a judgment. If the order is issued after a judgment, it is referred to as a *writ of execution*.

Writ of Attachment.

In the context of judicial liens, *attachment* is a court-ordered seizure of property before a judgment is secured for a past-due debt. Attachment rights are created by state statutes. Because attachment is a *prejudgment* remedy, it occurs either at the time a lawsuit is filed or immediately afterward. The due process clause of the Fourteenth Amendment to the U.S. Constitution requires that the debtor be given notice and an opportunity to be heard before property can be seized.

To use attachment, a creditor must comply with the specific state's statutory restrictions and requirements. The creditor must have an enforceable right to payment of the debt under law and must follow certain procedures. Otherwise, the creditor may be liable for damages for wrongful attachment. The typical procedures for attachment are as follows:

1. The creditor files with the court an *affidavit* (a written statement, made under oath) stating that the debtor has failed to pay and indicating the statutory grounds under which attachment is sought.

2. The creditor must post a bond to cover at least the court costs, the value of the property attached, and the value of the loss of use of that property suffered by the debtor.

3. When the court is satisfied that all the requirements have been met, it issues a **writ of attachment,** which directs the sheriff or other officer to seize the debtor's nonexempt property. If the creditor prevails at trial, the seized property can be sold to satisfy the judgment.

Writ of Execution.

If the creditor wins a judgment against a debtor and the debtor will not or cannot pay the amount due, the creditor can request a **writ of execution.** A writ of execution is an order that directs the sheriff to seize (levy) and sell any of the debtor's nonexempt real or personal property. The writ applies only to property that is within the court's geographic jurisdiction (usually the county in which the courthouse is located).

The proceeds of the sale are used to pay off the judgment, accrued interest, and the costs of the sale. Any excess is paid to the debtor. The debtor can pay the judgment and redeem the nonexempt property any time before the sale takes place. (Because of exemption laws and bankruptcy laws, however, many judgments are uncollectible.)

21–6b Garnishment

Garnishment occurs when a creditor is permitted to collect a debt by seizing property of the debtor (such as wages or funds in a bank account) that is being held by a third party. As a result of a garnishment proceeding, the debtor's employer may be ordered by the court to turn over a portion of the debtor's wages to pay the debt.

CASE EXAMPLE 21.16 Helen Griffin failed to pay a debt she owed to Indiana Surgical Specialists. When Indiana Surgical filed a lawsuit to collect, the court issued a judgment in favor of Indiana Surgical and a garnishment order to withhold the appropriate amount from Griffin's earnings until her debt was paid. At the time, Griffin was working as an independent contractor driving for a courier service. She claimed that her wages could not be garnished because she was not an employee. The court held that payments for the services of an independent contractor fell within the definition of earnings and could be garnished.[10]

Procedures Garnishment can be a prejudgment remedy, requiring a hearing before a court, but it is most often a postjudgment remedy. State law governs garnishment, so the procedure varies. In some states, the creditor needs to obtain only one order of garnishment, which will

Writ of Attachment A court order to seize a debtor's nonexempt property prior to a court's final determination of a creditor's rights to the property.

Writ of Execution A court order directing the sheriff to seize (levy) and sell a debtor's nonexempt real or personal property to satisfy a court's judgment in the creditor's favor.

Garnishment A legal process whereby a creditor collects a debt by seizing property of the debtor that is in the hands of a third party.

---

10. *Indiana Surgical Specialists v. Griffin*, 867 N.E.2d 260 (Ind.App. 2007).

then apply continuously to the debtor's wages until the entire debt is paid. In other states, the judgment creditor must go back to court for a separate order of garnishment for each pay period.

Limitations Both federal and state laws limit the amount that can be taken through garnishment proceedings.[11] Federal law provides a framework to protect debtors from suffering unduly when paying judgment debts by setting limits on how much can be garnished per pay period.[12] State laws also provide dollar exemptions, and these amounts are often larger than those provided by federal law. In addition, under federal law, an employer cannot dismiss an employee because his or her wages are being garnished.

21-6c Creditors' Composition Agreements

Creditors may contract with the debtor for discharge of the debtor's liquidated debts (debts that are definite, or fixed, in amount) on payment of a sum less than that owed. These agreements are called **creditors' composition agreements,** or simply *composition agreements,* and usually are held to be enforceable.

21-6d Suretyship and Guaranty

When a third person promises to pay a debt owed by another in the event that the debtor does not pay, either a *suretyship* or a *guaranty* relationship is created. Exhibit 21–3 illustrates these relationships. The third person's income and assets become the security for the debt owed.

Suretyship and guaranty provide creditors with the right to seek payment from the third party if the primary debtor defaults on her or his obligations. At common law, there were significant differences in the liability of a surety and a guarantor, as discussed in the following subsections. Today, however, the distinctions outlined here have been abolished in some states.

Surety A contract of strict **suretyship** is a promise made by a third person to be responsible for the debtor's obligation. It is an express contract between the **surety** (the third party) and the creditor. The surety in the strictest sense is primarily liable for the debt of the principal. The creditor need not exhaust all legal remedies against the principal debtor before holding

> **Creditors' Composition Agreement** A contract between a debtor and his or her creditors in which the creditors agree to discharge the debts on the debtor's payment of a sum less than the amount actually owed.

> **LEARNING OBJECTIVE 5**
> What is a suretyship, and how does it differ from a guaranty?

> **Suretyship** A promise made by a third party to be responsible for a debtor's obligation.

> **Surety** A third party who promises to be responsible for a debtor's obligation under a suretyship arrangement.

---

11. Some states (for example, Texas) do not permit garnishment of wages by private parties except under a child-support order.
12. For example, the federal Consumer Credit Protection Act of 1968, 15 U.S.C. Sections 1601–1693r, provides that a debtor can retain either 75 percent of disposable earnings per week or a sum equivalent to thirty hours of work paid at federal minimum-wage rates, whichever is greater.

Exhibit 21–3 Suretyship and Guaranty Parties

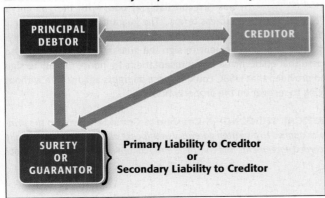

the surety responsible for payment. The creditor can demand payment from the surety from the moment the debt is due.

EXAMPLE 21.17 Roberto Delmar wants to borrow from the bank to buy a used car. Because Roberto is still in college, the bank will not lend him the funds unless his father, José Delmar, who has dealt with the bank before, will cosign the note (add his signature to the note, thereby becoming a surety and thus jointly liable for payment of the debt). When José cosigns the note, he becomes primarily liable to the bank. On the note's due date, the bank can seek payment from either Roberto or José, or both jointly. ■

Guaranty

Guarantor A third party who promises to be responsible for a debtor's obligation under a guaranty arrangement.

With a suretyship arrangement, the surety is *primarily* liable for the debtor's obligation. With a guaranty arrangement, the **guarantor**—the third person making the guaranty—is *secondarily* liable. The guarantor can be required to pay the obligation *only after the principal debtor defaults*, and default usually takes place only after the creditor has made an attempt to collect from the debtor.

EXAMPLE 21.18 BX Enterprises, a small corporation, needs to borrow funds to meet its payroll. The bank is skeptical about the creditworthiness of BX and requires Dawson, who is a wealthy businessperson and the owner of 70 percent of BX Enterprises, to sign an agreement making himself personally liable for payment if BX does not pay off the loan. As a guarantor of the loan, Dawson cannot be held liable until BX Enterprises is in default. ■

The following case concerned a lender's attempt to recover on a loan guaranty.

CASE 21.3

HSBC Realty Credit Corp. (USA) v. O'Neill

United States Court of Appeals, First Circuit, 745 F.3d 564 (2014).

FACTS To finance a development project in Delaware, Brandywine Partners, LLC, borrowed $15.9 million from HSBC Realty Credit Corp. (USA). As part of the deal, Brian O'Neill, principal for Brandywine, signed a guaranty that designated him the "primary obligor" for $8.1 million of the loan. Brandywine defaulted, and HSBC filed a suit in a federal district court against O'Neill to recover on the guaranty. O'Neill filed a counterclaim, alleging fraud.

O'Neill based his fraud claim on two provisions in the loan agreement. The first provision expressed the loan-to-value ratio. O'Neill alleged that this clause valued the property at $26.5 million and that HSBC knew this was not the property's real value. The second provision stated that if Brandywine defaulted, HSBC could recover its loan by selling the property. O'Neill argued that this clause represented that HSBC would try to recover on the property before the guaranty.

The court granted HSBC's motion to dismiss O'Neill's counterclaim and issued a judgment in HSBC's favor. O'Neill appealed, still arguing that HSBC had fraudulently induced him to sign the guaranty.

ISSUE Is a guarantor bound to the clear, unambiguous terms of the guaranty?

When a person signs a personal guaranty to finance his business, can he later get out of paying the debt when his business defaults?

DECISION Yes. The U.S. Court of Appeals for the First Circuit affirmed the lower court's judgment in favor of HSBC. O'Neill's guaranty was enforced according to its express terms.

REASON The court applied the principle that "reliance on supposed misrepresentations that contradict the terms of the parties' agreement is unreasonable as a matter of law and so cannot support a [fraud] claim." O'Neill's claim was "irreconcilably at odds with the guaranty's express terms." The guaranty stated that O'Neill was familiar with the value of the property and that he was not relying on it as an inducement to sign the guaranty. The guaranty also stated that HSBC made no representations to induce O'Neill to sign and provided that HSBC could enforce its rights against him without trying to recover on the property first.

CRITICAL THINKING—E-Commerce Consideration *Do the principles applied to a written guaranty in this case also govern electronically recorded agreements and contracts entered into online? Why or why not?*

Writing or Record Required   Under the Statute of Frauds, a guaranty contract between the guarantor and the creditor normally must be in writing or electronically recorded to be enforceable. A writing or record is required unless the main purpose of the guaranty is to benefit the guarantor. Under common law, a suretyship agreement did not need to be in writing to be enforceable, and oral surety agreements were sufficient. Today, however, some states require a writing or record to enforce a suretyship.

Actions That Release the Surety and Guarantor   Basically, the same actions will release a surety or a guarantor from an obligation. In general, the following rules apply to both sureties and guarantors, but for simplicity, we refer just to sureties:

1. *Material modification.* Making any material modification to the terms of the original contract without the surety's consent will discharge the surety's obligation. The extent to which the surety is discharged depends on whether he or she was compensated and the amount of the loss suffered as a result of the modification. For instance, a father who receives no consideration in return for acting as a surety on his daughter's loan will be completely discharged if the loan contract is modified without his consent.

2. *Surrender of property.* If a creditor surrenders the collateral to the debtor or impairs the collateral without the surety's consent, these acts can reduce the obligation of the surety. If the creditor's actions reduce the value of the property used as collateral, the surety is released to the extent of any loss suffered.

3. *Payment or tender of payment.* Naturally, any payment of the principal obligation by the debtor or by another person on the debtor's behalf will discharge the surety from the obligation. Even if the creditor refused to accept payment of the principal debt when it was tendered, the obligation of the surety can be discharged (if the creditor knew about the suretyship).

Why might a bank refuse to lend funds to a college student to buy a used car? What can the student do?

Defenses of the Surety and the Guarantor   Generally, the surety (or guarantor) can also assert any of the defenses available to the principal debtor to avoid liability on the obligation to the creditor. A few exceptions do exist, however. The surety cannot assert the principal debtor's incapacity or bankruptcy as a defense. Nor can the surety assert the statute of limitations as a defense.

Obviously, a surety (or guarantor) may also have her or his own defenses. For example, the surety can assert her or his own incapacity or bankruptcy as a defense. Furthermore, if the creditor fraudulently induced the surety to guarantee the debt of the debtor, the surety can assert fraud as a defense. In most states, the creditor has a legal duty to inform the surety, before the formation of the suretyship contract, of material facts known by the creditor that would substantially increase the surety's risk. Failure to so inform may constitute fraud and renders the suretyship obligation voidable.

Rights of the Surety and the Guarantor   Usually, when the surety (or guarantor) pays the debt owed to the creditor, the surety (or guarantor) is entitled to certain rights.

The Right of Subrogation.   The surety has the legal **right of subrogation,** which means that any right the creditor had against the debtor now becomes the right of the surety. Included are creditor rights in bankruptcy, rights to collateral possessed by the creditor, and rights to judgments secured by the creditor. In short, the surety stands in the shoes of the creditor and may pursue any remedies that were available to the creditor against the debtor.

CASE EXAMPLE 21.19   Guerrero Brothers, Inc. (GBI), contracted with the Public School System (PSS) to build a high school. Century Insurance Company (CIC) agreed to act as a surety of GBI's performance and to finish the project if GBI defaulted. Four years after construction began, PSS canceled GBI's contract, and CIC fulfilled GBI's obligations by finishing

Right of Subrogation   The right of a party to stand in the place of another, giving the substituted party the same legal rights that the original party had.

construction of the school. Numerous disputes arose, and litigation ensued. Ultimately, PSS agreed to pay GBI $500,000 in contract funds. CIC then filed an action against GBI and PSS to recover $867,000 that it claimed PSS owed it for finishing the school. The court found that CIC, as a performing surety, was entitled to the remaining contract funds through the right of subrogation. It had performed GBI's obligations and therefore stepped into GBI's shoes and had the right to obtain payment from PSS.[13]

Right of Reimbursement
The right of a party to be repaid for costs, expenses, or losses incurred on behalf of another.

The Right of Reimbursement. The surety has a **right of reimbursement** from the debtor. Basically, the surety is entitled to receive from the debtor all outlays made on behalf of the suretyship arrangement. Such outlays can include expenses incurred as well as the actual amount of the debt paid to the creditor.

Co-surety A joint surety; a party who assumes liability jointly with another surety for the payment of a debtor's obligation under a suretyship arrangement.

Right of Contribution The right of a co-surety who pays more than his or her proportionate share on a debtor's default to recover the excess paid from other co-sureties.

The Right of Contribution. Two or more sureties are called **co-sureties.** When one co-surety pays more than her or his proportionate share on a debtor's default, she or he is entitled to recover from the other co-sureties the amount paid above her or his obligation. This is the **right of contribution.** Generally, a co-surety's liability either is determined by agreement between the co-sureties or, in the absence of an agreement, is specified in the suretyship contract itself.

    EXAMPLE 21.20 Two co-sureties—Yasser and Itzhak—are obligated under a suretyship contract to guarantee the debt of Jules. Itzhak's maximum liability is $15,000, and Yasser's is $10,000. Jules owes $10,000 and is in default. Itzhak pays the creditor the entire $10,000. In the absence of an agreement to the contrary, Itzhak can recover $4,000 from Yasser. The amount of the debt that Yasser agreed to cover is divided by the total amount that Itzhak and Yasser together agreed to cover. The result is multiplied by the amount of the default, yielding the amount that Yasser owes: ($10,000 ÷ $25,000) × $10,000 = $4,000. ■

---

13. *Century Insurance Co. v. Guerrero Brothers, Inc.,* 2010 WL 997112 (N.Mariana Islands 2010).

Reviewing . . . Security Interests and Creditors' Rights

Paul Barton owned a small property-management company, doing business as Brighton Homes. In October, Barton went on a spending spree. First, he bought a Bose surround-sound system for his home from KDM Electronics. The next day, he purchased a Wilderness Systems kayak from Outdoor Outfitters, and the day after that he bought a new Toyota 4-Runner financed through Bridgeport Auto. Two weeks later, Barton purchased six new iMac computers for his office, also from KDM Electronics. Barton bought all of these items under installment sales contracts. Six months later, Barton's property-management business was failing. He could not make the payments due on any of these purchases and thus defaulted on the loans. Using the information presented in the chapter, answer the following questions.

1. For which of Barton's purchases (the surround-sound system, the kayak, the 4-Runner, and the six iMacs) would the creditor need to file a financing statement to perfect its security interest?

2. Suppose that Barton's contract for the office computers mentioned only the name *Brighton Homes.* What would be the consequences if KDM Electronics filed a financing statement that listed only Brighton Homes as the debtor's name?

3. Which of these purchases would qualify as a PMSI in consumer goods?

4. Suppose that after KDM Electronics repossesses the surround-sound system, it decides to keep the system rather than sell it. Can KDM do this under Article 9? Why or why not?

DEBATE THIS

■ A financing statement that does not have the debtor's exact name should still be effective because creditors should always be protected when debtors default.

Key Terms

Chapter Summary: Security Interests and Creditors' Rights

Creating a Security Interest	1. Unless the creditor has possession of the collateral, there must be a written or authenticated security agreement that describes the collateral subject to the security interest and is signed or authenticated by the debtor. 2. The secured party must give value to the debtor. 3. The debtor must have rights in the collateral.

Perfecting a Security Interest	1. *Perfection by filing*—The most common method of perfection is by filing a financing statement containing the names of the secured party and the debtor and identifying the collateral covered by the financing statement. The financing statement must be filed under the name of the debtor. Trade names normally are not sufficient.
	2. *Perfection without filing*—
	  a. By possession—The debtor can transfer possession of the collateral to the secured party. A *pledge* is an example of this type of transfer.
	  b. By attachment—Fourteen types of security interests are perfected automatically when they are created. The most common is the purchase-money security interest (PMSI) in consumer goods.
	3. *Classification of collateral*—The classification of collateral determines how and where a security interest is perfected (see Exhibit 21–2).

Scope of a Security Interest	A security agreement can cover the following types of property: 1. *Collateral in the present possession or control of the debtor.* 2. *Proceeds from a sale, exchange, or disposition of secured collateral.* 3. *After-acquired property*—A security agreement may provide that property acquired after execution of the agreement will also be secured by the agreement. This provision is often included in security agreements covering a debtor's inventory. 4. *Future advances*—A security agreement may provide that any future advances made against a line of credit will be subject to the initial security interest in the same collateral.

Priorities	1. *General rules*—
	  a. Perfected security interest versus unsecured creditors and unperfected security interests—A perfected secured party's interest has priority over the interests of most other parties.
	  b. Conflicting perfected security interests—When two or more secured parties have perfected security interests in the same collateral, the first to perfect generally has priority [UCC 9–322(a)(1)].
	  c. Conflicting unperfected security interests—When two conflicting security interests are unperfected, the first to attach (be created) has priority [UCC 9–322(a)(3)].
	2. *Exceptions*—
	  a. In some instances, a PMSI, properly perfected, will prevail over another security interest in after-acquired collateral, even though the other was perfected first.
	  b. A buyer of goods in the ordinary course of the seller's business prevails over a secured party's security interest, even if the security interest is perfected and even if the buyer knows of its existence [UCC 9–320(a)].
	3. Exceptions also exist for buyers of farm products, chattel paper, instruments, documents, or securities.

Continues

Rights and Duties	1. *Information request*—On request by the filing party, the filing officer must send a statement listing the file number, the date, and the hour of the filing of the financing statement to the person making the request.
	2. *Release, assignment, and amendment*—A secured party may (a) release part or all of the collateral described in a filed financing statement, thus ending the creditor's security interest, or (b) assign part or all of the security interest to another party. If the debtor and the secured party agree, they can also amend the filed statement.
	3. *Confirmation or accounting request by debtor*—If the debtor requests a confirmation of the unpaid debt or a list of the collateral, the secured party must send the debtor an authenticated accounting within fourteen days.
	4. *Termination statement*—When a debt is paid, the secured party generally must file a *termination statement*. If the financing statement covers consumer goods, the termination statement must be filed by the secured party within one month after the debt is paid or within twenty days of receiving the debtor's demand, whichever is earlier.
Default	On the debtor's default, the secured party may do either of the following:
	1. Take peaceful possession of the collateral covered by the security agreement and then pursue one of two alternatives:
	a. Retain the collateral (unless the collateral is consumer goods and the debtor has paid 60 percent or more of the purchase price on a PMSI or of the loan amount on a non-PMSI), subject to certain conditions.
	b. Dispose of the collateral in a commercially reasonable manner in accordance with the requirements prescribed in the UCC.
	2. Relinquish the security interest and use any judicial remedy available, such as proceeding to judgment on the underlying debt, followed by execution and levy on the nonexempt assets of the debtor.
Other Laws Assisting Creditors	1. *Mechanic's lien*—A nonpossessory, filed lien on an owner's real estate for labor, services, or materials furnished for making improvements on the realty.
	2. *Artisan's lien*—A possessory lien on an owner's personal property for labor performed or value added.
	3. *Judicial liens*—
	a. Writ of attachment—A court order to seize a debtor's nonexempt property prior to a court's final determination of a creditor's rights to the property. Attachment is available only if the creditor complies with the applicable state statutes.
	b. Writ of execution—A court order directing the sheriff to seize (levy) and sell a debtor's nonexempt real or personal property to satisfy a court's judgment in the creditor's favor.
	4. *Garnishment*—A collection remedy that allows a creditor to collect a debt by seizing property of the debtor that is being held by a third party.
	5. *Creditors' composition agreements*—Contracts between a debtor and his or her creditors in which the creditors agree to discharge the debts on the debtor's payment of a sum less than the amount actually owed.
	6. *Suretyships and guaranty*—Arrangements by which, under contract, a third person agrees to be primarily or secondarily liable for the debt owed by the principal debtor. A creditor can turn to this third person for satisfaction of the debt.

Issue Spotters

1. Liberty Bank loans Michelle $5,000 to buy a car, which is used as collateral to secure the loan. After repaying less than 50 percent of the loan, Michelle defaults. Liberty could repossess and keep the car, but the bank does not want it. What are the alternatives? (See *Priorities, Rights, and Duties*.)

2. Jorge contracts with Midwest Roofing to fix his roof. Jorge pays half of the contract price in advance. Midwest completes the job, but Jorge refuses to pay the rest of the price. What can Midwest do? (See *Other Laws Assisting Creditors*.)

—**Check your answers to the *Issue Spotters* against the answers provided in Appendix D at the end of this text.**

Learning Objectives Check

1. What is required to create a security interest?
2. How is a purchase-money security interest in consumer goods created?
3. If two parties have perfected security interests in the debtor's collateral, which party has priority on default?
4. How does a mechanic's lien assist creditors?
5. What is a suretyship, and how does it differ from a guaranty?

—**Answers to the even-numbered *Learning Objectives Check* questions can be found in Appendix E at the end of this text.**

Business Scenarios and Case Problems

21–1. Priority Disputes. Redford is a seller of electric generators. He purchases a large quantity of generators from a manufacturer, Mallon Corp., by making a down payment and signing an agreement to pay the balance over a period of time. The agreement gives Mallon Corp. a security interest in the generators and the proceeds. Mallon Corp. properly files a financing statement on its security interest. Redford receives the generators and immediately sells one of them to Garfield on an installment contract with payment to be made in twelve equal installments. At the time of the sale, Garfield knows of Mallon's security interest. Two months later, Redford goes into default on his payments to Mallon. Discuss Mallon's rights against purchaser Garfield in this situation. (See *Priorities, Rights, and Duties.*)

21–2. Perfection. Marsh has a prize horse named Arabian Knight. In need of working capital, Marsh borrows $5,000 from Mendez, who takes possession of Arabian Knight as security for the loan. No written agreement is signed. Discuss whether, in the absence of a written agreement, Mendez has a security interest in Arabian Knight. If Mendez does have a security interest, is it a perfected security interest? Explain. (See *Creating and Perfecting a Security Interest.*)

21–3. Disposition of Collateral. PRA Aviation, LLC, borrowed $3 million from Center Capital Corp. to buy a Gates Learjet 55B. Center perfected a security interest in the plane. Later, PRA defaulted on the loan, and Center obtained possession of the jet. Based on a review of the market for similar aircraft, as well as the jet's design and condition, its value was estimated at $1.45 million. The jet was marketed in trade publications, on the Internet, and by direct advertising to select customers for $1.595 million. There were three offers. Center sold the jet to the highest bidder for $1.3 million. Was the sale commercially reasonable? Explain. [*Center Capital Corp. v. PRA Aviation, LLC,* 2011 WL 867516 (E.D.Pa. 2011)] (See *Default.*)

21–4. Business Case Problem with Sample Answer— Perfecting a Security Interest. Thomas Tille owned M.A.T.T. Equipment Co. To operate the business, Tille borrowed funds from Union Bank. For each loan, Union filed a financing statement that included Tille's signature and address, the bank's address, and a description of the collateral. The first loan covered all of Tille's equipment, including "any after-acquired property." The second loan covered a truck crane "whether owned now or acquired later." The third loan covered a "Bobcat mini-excavator." Did these financing statements perfect Union's security interests? Explain. [*Union Bank Co. v. Heban,* 2012 WL 32102 (Ohio App. 2012) (See *Creating and Perfecting a Security Interest.*)

—**For a sample answer to Problem 21–4, go to Appendix F at the end of this text.**

21–5. Guaranty. Timothy Martinez, owner of Koenig & Vits, Inc. (K&V), guaranteed K&V's debt to Community Bank & Trust. The guaranty stated that the bank was not required to seek payment of the debt from any other source before enforcing the guaranty. K&V defaulted. Through a Wisconsin state court, the bank sought payment of $536,739.40, plus interest at the contract rate of 7.5 percent, from Martinez. Martinez argued that the bank could not enforce his guaranty while other funds were available to satisfy K&V's debt. For example, the debt might be paid out of the proceeds of a sale of corporate assets. Is this an effective defense to a guaranty? Why or why not? [*Community Bank & Trust v. Koenig & Vits, Inc.,* 346 Wis.2d 279 (Wis.App. 2013)] (See *Other Laws Assisting Creditors.*)

21–6. Disposition of Collateral. With a loan of 1.4 million euros from Barclays Bank, PLC, Thomas Poynter bought a yacht. The loan agreement gave Barclays multiple options on default. One option required the lender to give ten days' advance notice of a sale. A different option permitted the lender to avoid this requirement. When Poynter did not repay the loan, Barclays repossessed the yacht, notified Poynter that it would be sold— but did not specify a date, time, or place—and sold the yacht two months later. The sale price was less than Poynter owed, and Barclays filed a suit in a federal district court for the deficiency. Is Barclays entitled to collect even though it did not give Poynter ten days' advance notice of the sale? Explain. [*Barclays Bank PLC v. Poynter,* 710 F.3d 16 (1st Cir. 2013)] (See *Default.*)

21–7. Liens. Daniel and Katherine Balk asked Jirak Construction, LLC, to remodel their farmhouse in Lawler, Iowa. Jirak provided the Balks with an initial estimate of $45,975 for the cost. Over the course of the work, the Balks made significant changes to the plan. Jirak agreed to the changes and regularly advised the Balks about the increasing costs. In mid-project, Jirak provided an itemized breakdown at their request. The Balks paid Jirak $67,000, but refused to pay more. Jirak claimed that they still owed $55,000 in labor and materials. Jirak filed a suit in an Iowa state court against the Balks to collect. Which of the liens discussed in this chapter would be most effective to Jirak in its attempt to collect? How does that type of lien work? Is the court likely to enforce it in this case? Explain. [*Jirak Construction, LLC v. Balk,* __ N.W.2d __, 2015 WL 799786 (Iowa App. 2015)] (See *Other Laws Assisting Creditors.*)

21–8. A Question of Ethics—Guaranty Contracts. 73-75 Main Avenue, LLC, agreed to lease commercial property to PP Door Enterprise, Inc., if its principal officers executed personal guaranties and provided credit information. Nan Zhang signed the lease as manager of PP Door. The principals of PP Door signed the lease and guaranty agreements. When PP Door failed to make monthly payments, the lessor sued

PP Door and its owner, Ping Ying Li. Li testified that she was the sole owner of PP Door but denied that Zhang was its manager. She also denied signing the guaranty agreement. She claimed that she had signed the credit authorization form because Zhang had told her he was too young to have good credit. Li claimed to have no knowledge of the lease agreement. She did admit, however, that she had paid the rent because Zhang had been in a car accident and had asked her to help pay his bills,

including the rent. [*73-75 Main Avenue, LLC v. PP Door Enterprise, Inc.*, 120 Conn.App. 150, 991 A.2d 650 (2010)] (See *Other Laws Assisting Creditors*.)

1. Li argued that she was not liable on the lease agreement because Zhang was not authorized to bind her to the lease. Do the facts support Li? Why or why not?

2. Li claimed that the guaranty for rent was not enforceable against her. Why might the court agree?

Critical Thinking and Writing Assignments

21–9. Business Law Writing. Write a few sentences describing the circumstances in which a creditor would resort to each of the following remedies when trying to collect on debt. (See *Other Laws Assisting Creditors*.)

1. Mechanic's lien

2. Artisan's lien

3. Writ of attachment

21–10. Business Law Critical Thinking Group Assignment. Nick Sabol, doing business in the recording industry as Sound Farm Productions, applied to Morton Community Bank for a $58,000 loan to expand his business. Besides the loan application, Sabol signed a promissory note that referred to the bank's rights in "any collateral." Sabol also signed a letter authorizing Morton Community Bank to execute, file, and record all financing statements, amendments,

and other documents required by Article 9 to establish a security interest. Sabol did not sign any other documents, including the financing statement, which contained a description of the collateral. Two years later, without having repaid the loan, Sabol filed for bankruptcy. The bank claimed a security interest in Sabol's sound equipment. (See *Creating and Perfecting a Security Interest*.)

1. The first group will list all the requirements of an enforceable security interest and explain why each of these elements is necessary.

2. The second group will determine if Morton Community Bank had a valid security interest.

3. The third group will discuss whether a bank should be able to execute financing statements on a debtor's behalf without the debtor being present or signing them. Are there are any drawbacks to this practice?

Lane V. Erickson/ShutterStock.com

Bankruptcy

"Capitalism without bankruptcy is like Christianity without hell."

FRANK BORMAN
1928–PRESENT
(U.S. ASTRONAUT AND BUSINESSMAN)

Many people in today's economy are struggling to pay their monthly bills. In the old days, debtors were punished and sometimes sent to jail for failing to pay their debts. Today, the law provides debtors with numerous rights, including the right to have their debts discharged in bankruptcy.

This chapter discusses bankruptcy—a last resort in resolving debtor-creditor problems. As implied by the chapter-opening quotation, bankruptcy may be a necessary evil in our capitalistic society. Hence, every businessperson should have some understanding of the bankruptcy process.

Often, people end up in bankruptcy because they can no longer afford to make the payments on their homes. We therefore begin this chapter with a discussion of mortgages (the loans that borrowers obtain to purchase homes) and the foreclosure process that occurs when people are no longer able to make their mortgage payments. We also look at laws that assist debtors by providing exemptions that protect certain property from the reach of creditors.

LEARNING OBJECTIVES

The five Learning Objectives *below are designed to help improve your understanding of the chapter. After reading this chapter, you should be able to answer the following questions:*

1. What are three ways for a debtor to avoid mortgage foreclosure?

2. In a Chapter 7 bankruptcy, what happens if a court finds that there was "substantial abuse"? How is the means test used?

3. What constitutes a preference in bankruptcy law? When is a trustee able to avoid preferential transfers?

4. In a Chapter 11 reorganization, what is the role of the debtor in possession?

5. How does a Chapter 13 bankruptcy differ from bankruptcy under Chapter 7 and Chapter 11?

22-1 Mortgages

As noted in the preceding chapter, creditors use various means to ensure that they receive payment from debtors. Creditors financing the purchase of real property are no exception.

Down Payment An initial cash payment made when an expensive item, such as a house, is purchased. The payment represents a percentage of the purchase price, and the remainder is financed.

Mortgage A written instrument that gives a creditor an interest in, or lien on, a debtor's real property as security for a debt.

When individuals purchase real property, they typically make a **down payment** in cash and borrow the remaining funds from a financial institution. A **mortgage** is a written instrument that gives this creditor an interest in, or lien on, the debtor's real property as security for the debt. The creditor is the *mortgagee,* and the debtor is the *mortgagor.*

22–1a Fixed-Rate versus Adjustable-Rate Mortgages

Lenders offer various types of mortgages to meet the needs of different borrowers. A basic distinction is whether the interest rate is fixed or variable.

A *fixed-rate mortgage* has a fixed, or unchanging, rate of interest, so the payments remain the same for the duration of the loan. Lenders determine the interest rate for a standard fixed-rate mortgage loan based on a variety of factors, including the borrower's credit history, credit score, income, and debts.

The rate of interest paid by the borrower changes periodically with an *adjustable-rate mortgage (ARM).* Typically, the initial interest rate for an ARM is set at a relatively low fixed rate for a specified period, such as a year or three years. After that time, the interest rate adjusts annually or by some other period, such as biannually or monthly. The adjustment is calculated by adding a certain number of percentage points (called the margin) to an index rate (one of various government interest rates).

ARMs contractually shift the risk that the interest rate will change from the lender to the borrower. Borrowers will have lower initial payments if they are willing to assume the risk that interest rates might rise, resulting in higher payments for the borrowers in the future.

22–1b Mortgage Provisions

Because a mortgage involves a transfer of real property, it must be in writing to comply with the Statute of Frauds. Mortgages normally are lengthy and formal documents containing many provisions, including the following:

1. *The terms of the underlying loan.* These include the loan amount, the interest rate, the period of repayment, and other important financial terms, such as the margin and index rate for an ARM.

Prepayment Penalty Clause A mortgage provision requiring the borrower to pay a penalty if the mortgage is repaid in full within a certain period.

2. *A prepayment penalty clause.* A **prepayment penalty clause** requires the borrower to pay a penalty if the mortgage is repaid in full within a certain period. A prepayment penalty helps to protect the lender should the borrower refinance within a short time after obtaining a mortgage.

3. *Provisions relating to the maintenance of the property.* Because the mortgage conveys an interest in the property to the lender, the lender often requires the borrower to maintain the property to protect the lender's collateral.

4. *A statement obligating the borrower to maintain homeowners' insurance on the property.* **Homeowner's insurance** protects the lender's interest in the event of a loss due to certain hazards, such as fire or storm damage.

Homeowner's Insurance A form of property insurance that protects the holder against damage or loss to the holder's home.

5. *A list of the nonloan financial obligations to be borne by the borrower.* For instance, the borrower typically is required to pay all property taxes, assessments, and other claims against the property.

6. *Creditor protections.* When creditors extend mortgages, they are advancing a significant amount of funds for a number of years. Consequently, creditors usually require debtors to obtain *mortgage insurance* if they do not make a down payment of at least 20 percent of the purchase price. Creditors also record the mortgage with the appropriate office in the county where the property is located, so that the creditors' interest in the house is officially on record.

22-1c **Mortgage Foreclosure**

If a homeowner defaults, or fails to make mortgage payments, the lender has the right to foreclose on the mortgaged property. **Foreclosure** is the legal process by which the lender repossesses and auctions off the property that has secured the loan.

Foreclosure is expensive and time consuming. It generally benefits neither the borrowers, who lose their homes, nor the lenders, which face the prospect of losses on their loans. Therefore, both lenders and borrowers are motivated to avoid foreclosure proceedings if possible.

Ways to Avoid Foreclosure Possible methods of avoiding foreclosure include forbearance, workout agreements, and short sales (see Exhibit 22–1). A **forbearance** is a postponement of part or all of the payments on a loan for a limited time. This option works well when the debtor has short-term financial problems that can likely be solved—for instance, when the debtor has lost a job but is likely to be able to find a new job soon.

A **workout agreement** is a contract that describes the respective rights and responsibilities of the borrower and the lender as they try to resolve the default. Usually, the lender agrees to delay seeking foreclosure in exchange for the borrower's providing additional financial information that might be used to modify the mortgage.

When a borrower is in default, a lender may sometimes agree to a **short sale,** which is a sale of the property for less than the balance due on the mortgage loan. Typically, the borrower

Foreclosure The legal process by which a lender repossesses and disposes of property that has secured a loan.

LEARNING OBJECTIVE **1**
What are three ways for a debtor to avoid mortgage foreclosure?

Forbearance A postponement of part or all of the payments on a loan for a limited time.

Workout Agreement
A contract that describes the respective rights and responsibilities of a borrower and a lender as they try to resolve the borrower's default.

Short Sale A sale of mortgaged property for less than the balance due on the mortgage loan.

Exhibit 22–1 Methods of Avoiding Foreclosure

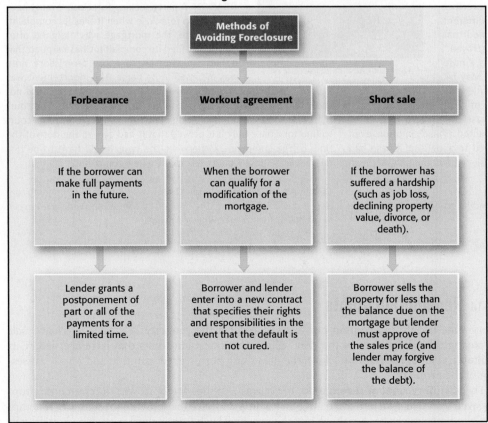

has to show some hardship, such as the loss of job, a decline in the value of the home, a divorce, or a death in the household. The lender often has approval rights in a short sale, so the sale process may take much longer than an ordinary real estate transaction.

Foreclosure Procedure If all efforts to find another solution fail, the lender will proceed to foreclosure. The lender must strictly comply with the state statute governing foreclosures. Many problems arose in the last ten years because lenders, facing a record number of foreclosures during the last recession, had difficulty complying with the required statutory formalities.

To bring a foreclosure action, a bank must have standing to sue. In the following *Spotlight Case,* the court had to decide whether a bank could foreclose a mortgage even though the bank could not prove when it became the owner of the borrower's promissory note.

SPOTLIGHT ON FORECLOSURES: CASE 22.1

McLean v. JPMorgan Chase Bank, N.A.

District Court of Appeal of Florida, 79 So.3d 170 (2012).

FACTS On May 11, 2009, JPMorgan Chase Bank (Chase) filed a foreclosure action against Robert McLean. The complaint alleged that Chase was entitled to enforce the mortgage and promissory note on which McLean had defaulted. Nevertheless, the attached mortgage identified a different mortgagee and lender, and Chase claimed that the note had been "lost, stolen, or destroyed." When McLean filed a motion to dismiss, Chase produced a mortgage assignment dated May 14, 2009, which was three days after it had filed the lawsuit. Eventually, Chase also filed the original note. Although the indorsement to Chase was undated, Chase then filed a motion for summary judgment. The trial court granted Chase's motion even though the accompanying affidavit failed to show that Chase had owned the mortgage or note when it filed the complaint. McLean appealed.

How can Chase Bank foreclose on delinquent mortgages?

ISSUE Did Chase prove that it had standing to bring a foreclosure action against McLean?

DECISION No. The Florida appellate court reversed the trial court's grant of summary judgment to Chase.

REASON A party seeking foreclosure must have standing to foreclose when it files its complaint. In this case, the mortgage was assigned after Chase had filed its complaint. Chase argued that it had standing because the promissory note was indorsed in its name. The indorsement was undated, however, and Chase's affidavit did not show that Chase owned the note when it filed its lawsuit. The court therefore reversed summary judgment and instructed the trial court to find for Chase only if it proved that it had owned the note at the time of the complaint. Otherwise, the case would have to be dismissed, and Chase would need to file a new complaint.

CRITICAL THINKING—Legal Consideration *If Chase cannot prove that it owned the note at the time of its complaint, what will happen next? Will Chase prevail? Why or why not?*

Equitable Right of Redemption The right of a mortgagor who has breached the mortgage agreement to redeem or purchase the mortgaged property prior to foreclosure proceedings.

Statutory Right of Redemption A right provided by statute in some states under which mortgagors can redeem or purchase their property after a judicial foreclosure for a limited time period, such as one year.

22-1d Redemption Rights

Every state allows a defaulting borrower to redeem the property *before the foreclosure sale* by paying the full amount of the debt, plus any interest and costs that have accrued. This **equitable right of redemption** allows the defaulting borrower to gain title and regain possession of the property.

The **statutory right of redemption,** in contrast, entitles the borrower to repurchase property even *after a judicial foreclosure.* In other words, in states that provide for statutory redemption, the homeowner has a right to buy the property back from a third party who bought it at a foreclosure sale. Generally, the borrower may exercise this right for up to one year from the time the house is sold at a foreclosure sale.[1] Some states allow the borrower to retain possession of the property after the foreclosure sale and up until the statutory redemption period ends. If the borrower does not exercise the right of redemption, the new buyer receives title to and possession of the property.

22-2 Laws Assisting Debtors

The preceding chapter emphasized that the law provides many protections for creditors. But the law protects debtors as well. Certain property of the debtor, for instance, is exempt from creditors' actions. Of course, bankruptcy laws are designed specifically to assist debtors, as will be discussed shortly.

In most states, various types of real and personal property are exempt from execution or attachment. State exemption statutes usually include both real and personal property.

22-2a Exempted Real Property

Probably the most familiar real property exemption is the **homestead exemption.** Each state permits the debtor to retain the family home, either in its entirety or up to a specified dollar amount, free from the claims of unsecured creditors or trustees in bankruptcy. The purpose of the homestead exemption is to ensure that the debtor will retain some form of shelter. (As discussed later, federal bankruptcy law limits the amount that debtors can claim under a state's homestead exemption.)

In a few states, statutes allow the homestead exemption only if the judgment debtor has a family. If a judgment debtor does not have a family, a creditor may be entitled to collect the full amount realized from the sale of the debtor's home. In addition, the homestead exemption interacts with other areas of law and can sometimes operate to cancel out a portion of a lien on a debtor's real property.

CASE EXAMPLE 22.1 Antonio Stanley purchased a modular home from Yates Mobile Services Corporation. When Stanley failed to pay the purchase price of the home, Yates obtained a judicial lien against Stanley's property in the amount of $165,138.05. Stanley then filed for bankruptcy and asserted the homestead exemption. The court found that Stanley was entitled to avoid the lien to the extent that it impaired his exemption. Using a bankruptcy law formula, the court determined that the total impairment was $143,639.05 and that Stanley could avoid paying this amount to Yates. Thus, Yates was left with a judicial lien on Stanley's home in the amount of $21,499.[2] ■

Homestead Exemption A law permitting a debtor to retain the family home, either in its entirety or up to a specified dollar amount, free from the claims of unsecured creditors or trustees in bankruptcy.

How does the homestead exemption help debtors who go into bankruptcy?

22-2b Exempted Personal Property

Personal property that is most often exempt under state law includes the following:

1. Household furniture up to a specified dollar amount.

2. Clothing and certain personal possessions, such as family pictures or a religious text.

3. A vehicle (or vehicles) for transportation (at least up to a specified dollar amount).

4. Certain classified animals, usually livestock but including pets.

5. Equipment that the debtor uses in a business or trade, such as tools or professional instruments, up to a specified dollar amount.

---

1. Some states do not allow a borrower to waive the statutory right of redemption. This means that a buyer at auction must wait one year to obtain title to, and possession of, a foreclosed property.

2. *In re Stanley*, 2010 WL 2103441 (M.D.N.C. 2010).

22-3 The Bankruptcy Code

Bankruptcy relief is provided under federal law. Nevertheless, state laws on secured transactions, liens, judgments, and exemptions also play a role in federal bankruptcy proceedings.

Article I, Section 8, of the U.S. Constitution gave Congress the power to establish "uniform laws on the subject of bankruptcies throughout the United States." Federal bankruptcy legislation was first enacted in 1898 and since then has undergone several modifications, most recently in the 2005 Bankruptcy Reform Act.[3] Federal bankruptcy laws are called the Bankruptcy Code or, more simply, the Code.

22-3a Goals of Bankruptcy Law

Bankruptcy law in the United States has two main goals:

1. To protect a debtor by giving him or her a fresh start without creditors' claims.
2. To ensure equitable treatment of creditors who are competing for a debtor's assets.

Thus, the law attempts to balance the rights of the debtor and the creditors.

Although the twin goals of bankruptcy remained the same, the balance between them shifted somewhat after the 2005 reform legislation. Because of its significance for creditors and debtors alike, we present the 2005 Bankruptcy Reform Act as this chapter's *Landmark in the Law* feature.

22-3b Bankruptcy Courts

KNOW THIS

Congress regulates the jurisdiction of the federal courts within the limits set by the U.S. Constitution. Congress can expand or reduce the number of federal courts at any time.

Bankruptcy proceedings are held in federal bankruptcy courts, which are under the authority of U.S. district courts. Rulings by bankruptcy courts can be appealed to the district courts. The bankruptcy court holds proceedings dealing with the procedures required to administer the debtor's estate in bankruptcy (the debtor's assets, as will be discussed shortly).

22-3c Types of Bankruptcy Relief

The Bankruptcy Code is contained in Title 11 of the *United States Code* (U.S.C.) and has eight "chapters." Chapters 1, 3, and 5 of the Code include general definitions and provisions governing case administration and procedures, creditors, the debtor, and the estate. These three chapters of the Code normally apply to all types of bankruptcies.

Four chapters of the Code set forth the most important types of relief that debtors can seek.

1. Chapter 7 provides for *liquidation* proceedings—that is, the selling of all nonexempt assets and the distribution of the proceeds to the debtor's creditors.
2. Chapter 11 governs reorganizations.
3. Chapter 12 (for family farmers and family fishermen) and Chapter 13 (for individuals) provide for adjustment of the debts of parties with regular income.[4]

Note that a debtor (except for a municipality) need not be insolvent[5] to file for bankruptcy relief under the Bankruptcy Code. Anyone obligated to a creditor can declare bankruptcy.

---

3. The full title of the act is the Bankruptcy Abuse Prevention and Consumer Protection Act of 2005, Pub. L. No. 109-8, 119 Stat. 23 (April 20, 2005).
4. There are no Chapters 2, 4, 6, 8, or 10 in Title 11. Such "gaps" are not uncommon in the *United States Code*. They occur because, when a statute is enacted, chapter numbers (or other subdivisional unit numbers) are sometimes reserved for future use. (A gap may also appear if a law has been repealed.)
5. The inability to pay debts as they come due is known as *equitable* insolvency. A *balance-sheet* insolvency, which exists when a debtor's liabilities exceed assets, is not the test. Thus, it is possible for debtors to petition voluntarily for bankruptcy even though their assets far exceed their liabilities. This situation may occur when a debtor's cash-flow problems become severe.

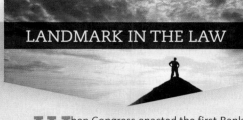

The Bankruptcy Abuse Prevention and Consumer Protection Act

When Congress enacted the first Bankruptcy Reform Act in 1978, many claimed that the law made it too easy for debtors to file for bankruptcy protection. The 2005 Bankruptcy Abuse Prevention and Consumer Protection Act (BAPCPA) was passed, in part, in response to businesses' concerns about the rise in personal bankruptcy filings. From 1978 to 2005, personal bankruptcy filings increased dramatically. Various business groups—including credit-card companies, retailers, and banks—claimed that the bankruptcy process was being abused and that reform was necessary.

MORE REPAYMENT PLANS, FEWER LIQUIDATION BANKRUPTCIES One of the major goals of the BAPCPA is to require consumers to pay as many of their debts as they possibly can instead of having those debts fully discharged in bankruptcy. Before the reforms, the vast majority of bankruptcies

were filed under Chapter 7 of the Bankruptcy Code, which permits debtors, with some exceptions, to have *all* of their debts discharged in bankruptcy. Only about 20 percent of personal bankruptcies were filed under Chapter 13 of the Bankruptcy Code. As you will read later in this chapter, this part of the Bankruptcy Code requires the debtor to establish a repayment plan and pay off as many of his or her debts as possible over a maximum period of five years. Under the BAPCPA, more debtors have to file for bankruptcy under Chapter 13.

OTHER SIGNIFICANT PROVISIONS OF THE ACT BAPCPA also made a number of other changes. One important provision involves the homestead exemption. Before the passage of the act, some states allowed debtors petitioning for bankruptcy to exempt all of the *equity* (the market value minus the outstanding mortgage owed) in their homes during bankruptcy proceedings. The

2005 act leaves these exemptions in place but puts some limits on their use. Another BAPCPA provision gives child-support obligations priority over other debts and allows enforcement agencies to continue efforts to collect child-support payments.

APPLICATION TO TODAY'S WORLD *Under the 2005 bankruptcy reforms, fewer debtors are allowed to have their debts discharged in Chapter 7 liquidation proceedings. At the same time, the act makes it more difficult for debtors to obtain a "fresh start" financially—one of the major goals of bankruptcy law in the United States. Today, more debtors are forced to file under Chapter 13. Additionally, the bankruptcy process has become more time consuming and costly because it requires more extensive documentation and certification. These changes in the law have left many Americans unable to obtain relief from their debts.*

22–3d Special Treatment of Consumer-Debtors

A **consumer-debtor** is a debtor whose debts result primarily from the purchase of goods for personal, family, or household use. The Bankruptcy Code requires that the clerk of the court give all consumer-debtors written notice of the general purpose, benefits, and costs of each chapter of bankruptcy under which they may proceed. In addition, the clerk must provide consumer-debtors with information on the types of services available from credit counseling agencies.

Consumer-Debtor One whose debts result primarily from the purchases of goods for personal, family, or household use.

22–4 Chapter 7—Liquidation

Liquidation under Chapter 7 is the most familiar type of bankruptcy proceeding and is often referred to as an *ordinary*, or *straight, bankruptcy*. Put simply, a debtor in a liquidation bankruptcy turns all assets over to a **bankruptcy trustee,** a person appointed by the court to manage the debtor's funds. The trustee sells the nonexempt assets and distributes the proceeds to creditors. With certain exceptions, the remaining debts are then **discharged** (extinguished), and the debtor is relieved of the obligation to pay the debts.

Any "person"—defined as including individuals, partnerships, and corporations[6]—may be a debtor under Chapter 7. Railroads, insurance companies, banks, savings and loan associations,

Liquidation The sale of the nonexempt assets of a debtor and the distribution of the funds received to creditors.

Bankruptcy Trustee A person appointed by the court to manage the debtor's funds.

Discharge The termination of a bankruptcy debtor's obligation to pay debts.

---

6. The definition of *corporation* includes unincorporated companies and associations. It also covers labor unions.

investment companies licensed by the U.S. Small Business Administration, and credit unions *cannot* be Chapter 7 debtors. Other chapters of the Code or other federal or state statutes apply to them. A husband and wife may file jointly for bankruptcy under a single petition.

A straight bankruptcy may be commenced by the filing of either a voluntary or an involuntary **petition in bankruptcy**—the document that is filed with a bankruptcy court to initiate bankruptcy proceedings. If a debtor files the petition, then it is a *voluntary bankruptcy*. If one or more creditors file a petition to force the debtor into bankruptcy, then it is an *involuntary bankruptcy*. We discuss both voluntary and involuntary bankruptcy proceedings under Chapter 7 in the following subsections.

Petition in Bankruptcy
The document that is filed with a bankruptcy court to initiate bankruptcy proceedings.

22-4a Voluntary Bankruptcy

To bring a voluntary petition in bankruptcy, the debtor files official forms designated for that purpose in the bankruptcy court. Before debtors can file a petition, they must receive credit counseling from an approved nonprofit agency. Debtors filing a Chapter 7 petition must thus include a certificate proving that they have received individual or group counseling from an approved agency within the last 180 days (roughly six months).

A consumer-debtor who is filing a voluntary petition must confirm the accuracy of the petition's contents. The debtor must also state in the petition, at the time of filing, that he or she understands the relief available under other chapters of the Code and has chosen to proceed under Chapter 7.

Attorneys representing consumer-debtors must file an affidavit stating that they have informed the debtors of the relief available under each chapter of the Code. In addition, the attorneys must reasonably attempt to verify the accuracy of the consumer-debtors' petitions and schedules (described next). Failure to do so is considered perjury.

Chapter 7 Schedules The voluntary petition contains the following schedules:

1. A list of both secured and unsecured creditors, their addresses, and the amount of debt owed to each.
2. A statement of the financial affairs of the debtor.
3. A list of all property owned by the debtor, including property claimed by the debtor to be exempt.
4. A list of current income and expenses.
5. A certificate of credit counseling (as mentioned previously).
6. Proof of payments received from employers within sixty days prior to the filing of the petition.
7. A statement of the amount of monthly income, itemized to show how the amount is calculated.
8. A copy of the debtor's federal income tax return for the most recent year ending immediately before the filing of the petition.

The official forms must be completed accurately, sworn to under oath, and signed by the debtor. To conceal assets or knowingly supply false information on these schedules is a crime under the bankruptcy laws.

With the exception of tax returns, failure to file the required schedules within forty-five days after the filing of the petition (unless an extension is granted) will result in an automatic dismissal of the petition. The debtor has up to seven days before the date of the first creditors' meeting to provide a copy of the most recent tax returns to the trustee.

Tax Returns during Bankruptcy A debtor may be required to file a tax return at the end of each tax year while the case is pending and to provide a copy to the court. A request for a copy

of the debtor's tax return may be made by the court, the trustee, or any *party in interest* (a party, such as a creditor, who has a valid interest in the outcome of the proceedings). Debtors may also be required to file tax returns during Chapter 11 and 13 bankruptcies.

Substantial Abuse and the Means Test In the past, a bankruptcy court could dismiss a Chapter 7 petition if the use of Chapter 7 would constitute a "substantial abuse" of bankruptcy law. Today, the law provides a *means test* to determine a debtor's eligibility for Chapter 7.

The purpose of the test is to keep upper-income people from abusing the bankruptcy process by filing for Chapter 7, as was thought to have happened in the past. The test forces more people to file for Chapter 13 bankruptcy rather than have their debts discharged under Chapter 7.

The Basic Formula. A debtor wishing to file for bankruptcy must complete the means test to determine whether she or he qualifies for Chapter 7. The debtor's average monthly income in recent months is compared with the median income in the geographic area in which the person lives. (The U.S. Trustee Program provides these data at its Web site, **justice.gov/ust**.) If the debtor's income is below the median income, the debtor usually is allowed to file for Chapter 7 bankruptcy, as there is no presumption of bankruptcy abuse.

Applying the Means Test to Future Disposable Income. If the debtor's income is above the median income, then further calculations must be made. The goal is to determine whether the person will have sufficient disposable income in the future to repay at least some of his or her unsecured debts. As a basis for the calculations, it is presumed that the debtor's recent monthly income will continue for the next sixty months. *Disposable income* is then calculated by subtracting living expenses and interest payments on secured debt, such as mortgage payments, from monthly income.

Living expenses are the amounts allowed under formulas used by the Internal Revenue Service (IRS). The IRS allowances include modest allocations for food, clothing, housing, utilities, transportation (including car payments), health care, and other necessities. (The U.S. Trustee Program's Web site also provides these amounts.) The allowances do not include expenditures for items such as cell phones and cable television service.

Can the Debtor Afford to Pay Unsecured Debts? Once future disposable income has been estimated, that amount is used to determine whether the debtor will have income that could be applied to unsecured debts. The court may also consider the debtor's bad faith or other circumstances indicating abuse.

CASE EXAMPLE 22.2 Christopher Dean Ng and his wife filed for Chapter 7 bankruptcy, hoping primarily to discharge their mortgage debt of $464,830. At the time the petition was filed, Ng was forty-three years old and worked as an electronic technician, earning a monthly salary of $7,439.47, as well as a military pension of $1,439.88 a month. His wife was not employed. From Ng's monthly salary, he made a voluntary contribution of $520 to an employer 401(k) plan and a $343 payment on a pension loan. In calculating his income, Ng excluded these amounts. He also excluded a $300 payment on prepetition income tax liability.

The U.S. trustee filed a motion to dismiss Ng's petition due to substantial abuse, claiming that the retirement contributions should be disallowed. The court agreed and dismissed the Chapter 7 petition. The Ngs appealed, and the appellate court affirmed. Ng's retirement contributions were not reasonably necessary based on his age, his financial circumstances, and his testimony that he was not planning to retire for at least twenty years. The Ngs could afford to repay some of their debts before they made monthly contributions toward retirement.[7] ∎

---

7. *In re Ng,* 422 Bankr. 118 (9th Cir. 2012).

Additional Grounds for Dismissal   As noted, a debtor's voluntary petition for Chapter 7 relief may be dismissed for substantial abuse or for failing to provide the necessary documents (such as schedules and tax returns) within the specified time. In addition, a motion to dismiss a Chapter 7 filing may be granted in two other situations.

1. If the debtor has been convicted of a violent crime or a drug-trafficking offense, the victim can file a motion to dismiss the voluntary petition.[8]

2. If the debtor fails to pay postpetition domestic-support obligations (which include child and spousal support), the court may dismiss the petition.

Order for Relief   If the voluntary petition for bankruptcy is found to be proper, the filing of the petition will itself constitute an **order for relief.** (An order for relief is the court's grant of assistance to a debtor.) Once a consumer-debtor's voluntary petition has been filed, the clerk of the court (or other appointee) must give the trustee and creditors notice of the order for relief by mail not more than twenty days after the entry of the order.

22–4b Involuntary Bankruptcy

An involuntary bankruptcy occurs when the debtor's creditors force the debtor into bankruptcy proceedings. An involuntary petition should not be used as an everyday debt-collection device. The Code provides penalties for the filing of frivolous (unjustified) petitions against debtors. If the court dismisses an involuntary petition, the petitioning creditors may be required to pay the costs and attorneys' fees incurred by the debtor in defending against the petition. If the petition was filed in bad faith, damages can be awarded for injury to the debtor's reputation. Punitive damages may also be awarded.

Requirements   An involuntary case cannot be filed against a charitable institution or a farmer (an individual or business that receives more than 50 percent of gross income from farming operations). For an involuntary action to be filed against other debtors, the following requirements must be met:

1. If the debtor has twelve or more creditors, three or more of those creditors having unsecured claims totaling at least $15,325 must join in the petition.

2. If a debtor has fewer than twelve creditors, one or more creditors having a claim of $15,325 or more may file.[9]

When the Debtor Challenges the Petition   If the debtor challenges the involuntary petition, a hearing will be held. The debtor's challenge will fail if the bankruptcy court finds either of the following:

1. The debtor generally is not paying debts as they become due.

2. A general receiver, assignee, or custodian took possession of, or was appointed to take charge of, substantially all of the debtor's property within 120 days before the filing of the involuntary petition.

If the court allows the bankruptcy to proceed, the debtor will be required to supply the same information in the bankruptcy schedules as in a voluntary bankruptcy.

Order for Relief A court's grant of assistance to a complainant. In bankruptcy proceedings, the order relieves the debtor of the immediate obligation to pay the debts listed in the bankruptcy petition.

"I hope that after I die, people will say of me: 'That guy sure owed me a lot of money.'"

JACK HANDEY
1949–PRESENT
(AMERICAN HUMORIST)

---

8. Note that the court may not dismiss a case on this ground if the debtor's bankruptcy is necessary to satisfy a claim for a domestic-support obligation.

9. 11 U.S.C. Section 303. The amounts stated in this chapter are in accordance with those computed on April 1, 2013.

22-4c Automatic Stay

The moment a petition, either voluntary or involuntary, is filed, an **automatic stay,** or suspension, of almost all actions by creditors against the debtor or the debtor's property normally goes into effect. Until the bankruptcy proceeding is closed or dismissed, the automatic stay prohibits a creditor from taking any act to collect, assess, or recover a claim against the debtor that arose before the filing of the petition.

If a creditor *knowingly* violates the automatic stay (a willful violation), any injured party, including the debtor, is entitled to recover actual damages, costs, and attorneys' fees and may be entitled to punitive damages as well. **CASE EXAMPLE 22.3** Stefanie Kuehn filed for bankruptcy. When she requested a transcript from the university at which she had obtained her master's degree, the university refused because she owed more than $6,000 in tuition. Kuehn complained to the court. The court ruled that the university had violated the automatic stay when it refused to provide a transcript because it was attempting to collect an unpaid tuition debt.[10] ■

Exceptions to the Automatic Stay The Code provides the following exceptions to the automatic stay:

1. Collection efforts can continue for domestic-support obligations, which include any debt owed to or recoverable by a spouse, a former spouse, a child of the debtor, that child's parent or guardian, or a governmental unit.
2. Proceedings against the debtor related to divorce, child custody or visitation, domestic violence, and support enforcement are not stayed.
3. Investigations by a securities regulatory agency can continue.
4. Certain statutory liens for property taxes are not stayed.

Requests for Relief from the Automatic Stay A secured creditor or other party in interest can petition the bankruptcy court for relief from the automatic stay. If a creditor or other party requests relief from the stay, the stay will automatically terminate sixty days after the request, unless the court grants an extension or the parties agree otherwise.

Secured Property The automatic stay on secured property terminates forty-five days after the creditors' meeting unless the debtor redeems or reaffirms certain debts. (Creditors' meetings and reaffirmation will be discussed later in this chapter.) This means that the debtor cannot keep secured property (such as a financed automobile), even if she or he continues to make payments on it, without reinstating the rights of the secured party to collect on the debt.

Bad Faith If the debtor had two or more bankruptcy petitions dismissed during the prior year, the Code presumes bad faith. In such a situation, the automatic stay does *not* go into effect until the court determines that the petition was filed in good faith.

22-4d Estate in Bankruptcy

On the commencement of a liquidation proceeding under Chapter 7, an **estate in bankruptcy** is created. The estate consists of all the debtor's interests in property currently held, wherever located. The estate in bankruptcy includes all of the following:

1. *Community property* (property jointly owned by a husband and wife in certain states).
2. Property transferred in a transaction voidable by the trustee.
3. Proceeds and profits from the property of the estate.

Automatic Stay In bankruptcy proceedings, the suspension of almost all litigation and other action by creditors against the debtor or the debtor's property. The stay is effective the moment the debtor files a petition in bankruptcy.

Can a university withhold the transcript of a former student who is in bankruptcy?

Estate in Bankruptcy All of the property owned by a person, including real estate and personal property.

---

10. *In re Kuehn,* 563 F.3d 289 (7th Cir. 2009).

Certain after-acquired property—such as gifts, inheritances, property settlements (from divorce), and life insurance death proceeds—to which the debtor becomes entitled *within 180 days after filing* may also become part of the estate. Generally, though, the filing of a bankruptcy petition fixes a dividing line. Property acquired prior to the filing of the petition becomes property of the estate, and property acquired after the filing of the petition, except as just noted, remains the debtor's.

22–4e The Bankruptcy Trustee

Promptly after the order for relief has been entered, a trustee is appointed. The basic duty of the trustee is to collect the debtor's available estate and reduce it to cash for distribution, preserving the interests of both the debtor and the unsecured creditors. This requires that the trustee be accountable for administering the debtor's estate.

To enable the trustee to accomplish this duty, the Code gives the trustee certain powers, stated in both general and specific terms. These powers must be exercised within two years after the order for relief has been entered.

Review for Substantial Abuse The trustee is required to review promptly all materials filed by the debtor to determine if there is substantial abuse. Within ten days after the first meeting of the creditors, the trustee must file a statement as to whether the case is presumed to be an abuse under the means test. The trustee must provide all creditors with a copy of this statement.

When there is a presumption of abuse, the trustee must either file a motion to dismiss the petition (or convert it to a Chapter 13 case) or file a statement explaining why a motion would not be appropriate. If the debtor owes a domestic-support obligation (such as child support), the trustee must provide written notice of the bankruptcy to the claim holder (a former spouse, for instance).

Trustee's Powers The trustee has the power to require persons holding the debtor's property at the time the petition is filed to deliver the property to the trustee.[11] To enable the trustee to implement this power, the Code provides that the trustee has rights *equivalent* to those of certain other parties, such as a creditor who has a judicial lien. This power of a trustee, which is equivalent to that of a lien creditor, is known as the *strong-arm power.*

In addition, the trustee has specific *powers of avoidance.* They enable the trustee to set aside (avoid) a sale or other transfer of the debtor's property and take the property back for the debtor's estate. These powers apply to voidable rights available to the debtor, preferences, and fraudulent transfers by the debtor (as discussed in more detail next).

The debtor shares most of the trustee's avoidance powers. Thus, if the trustee does not take action to enforce one of these rights, the debtor in a liquidation bankruptcy can enforce it.

Voidable Rights A trustee steps into the shoes of the debtor. Thus, any reason that a debtor can use to obtain the return of his or her property can be used by the trustee as well. The grounds for recovery include fraud, duress, incapacity, and mutual mistake.

EXAMPLE 22.4 Ben sells his boat to Inga. Inga gives Ben a check, knowing that she has insufficient funds in her bank account to cover the check. Inga has committed fraud. Ben has the right to avoid that transfer and recover the boat from Inga. If Ben files for Chapter 7 bankruptcy, the trustee can exercise the same right to recover the boat from Inga, and the boat becomes part of the debtor's estate. ■

Preferences A debtor is not permitted to make a property transfer or a payment that favors—or gives a **preference** to—one creditor over others. The trustee is allowed to recover payments made both voluntarily and involuntarily to one creditor in preference over another.

Preference In bankruptcy proceedings, a property transfer or payment made by the debtor that favors one creditor over others.

---

11. Usually, the trustee takes constructive, rather than actual, possession of the debtor's property. For instance, to obtain possession of a business's inventory, a trustee might change the locks on the doors and hire a security guard.

To have made a recoverable preferential payment, an *insolvent* debtor generally must have transferred property for a *preexisting* debt during the *ninety days* before the filing of the petition in bankruptcy. The transfer must have given the creditor more than the creditor would have received as a result of the bankruptcy proceedings. The Code presumes that the debtor is insolvent during the ninety-day period before filing a petition.

If a **preferred creditor** (one who has received a preferential transfer from the debtor) has sold the property to an innocent third party, the trustee cannot recover the property from the innocent party. The trustee can generally force the preferred creditor to pay the value of the property, however.

Preferences to Insiders. Sometimes, a creditor receiving a preference is an *insider*. An insider is any individual, partner, partnership, or officer or director of a corporation (or a relative of one of these) who has a close relationship with the debtor. In this situation, the avoidance power of the trustee is extended to transfers made within *one year* before filing. (If the transfer was fraudulent, as will be discussed shortly, the trustee can avoid transfers made within *two years* before filing.) However, the trustee must prove that the debtor was insolvent at the time the earlier transfer occurred.

Transfers That Do Not Constitute Preferences. Not all transfers are preferences. To be a preference, the transfer must be made in exchange for something other than current consideration. Most courts do not consider a debtor's payment for services rendered within fifteen days prior to the payment to be a preference. If a creditor receives payment in the ordinary course of business, such as payment of last month's cell phone bill, the trustee in bankruptcy cannot recover the payment. In contrast, a transfer for a preexisting debt, such as a year-old landscaping bill, would be a recoverable preference.

In addition, the Code permits a consumer-debtor to transfer any property to a creditor up to a total value of $6,225 without the transfer constituting a preference. Payments of domestic-support debts do not constitute a preference. Neither do payments required under a plan created by an approved credit-counseling agency.

Fraudulent Transfers A trustee can avoid (set aside or cancel) fraudulent transfers or obligations if (1) they were made within two years of the filing of the petition or (2) they were made with actual intent to hinder, delay, or defraud a creditor. **EXAMPLE 22.5** April is planning to petition for bankruptcy, so she sells her gold jewelry, worth $10,000, to a friend for $500. The friend agrees that in the future he will "sell" the jewelry back to April for the same amount. This is a fraudulent transfer that the trustee can undo. ∎

22–4f Exemptions

An individual debtor is entitled to exempt certain property from the bankruptcy under federal or state exemption schemes.

Federal Exemptions The Bankruptcy Code exempts the following property:[12]

1. Up to $22,975 in equity in the debtor's residence and burial plot (the homestead exemption).

2. Interest in a motor vehicle up to $3,675.

---

12. The dollar amounts stated in the Bankruptcy Code are adjusted automatically every three years on April 1 based on changes in the Consumer Price Index. The adjusted amounts are rounded to the nearest $25. The amounts stated in this chapter are in accordance with those computed on April 1, 2013.

LEARNING OBJECTIVE 3
What constitutes a preference in bankruptcy law? When is a trustee able to avoid preferential transfers?

iStockPhoto.com/andreamuscatello

Under what circumstances might a trustee recover the debtor's boat that was sold prior to the bankruptcy?

Preferred Creditor In the context of bankruptcy, a creditor who has received a preferential transfer from a debtor.

KNOW THIS
Usually, when property is recovered as a preference, the trustee sells it and distributes the proceeds to the debtor's creditors.

3. Interest, up to $550 for a particular item, in household goods and furnishings, wearing apparel, appliances, books, animals, crops, and musical instruments (the aggregate total of all items is limited to $12,250).

4. Interest in jewelry up to $1,550.

5. Interest in any other property up to $1,225, plus any unused part of the $22,975 homestead exemption up to $11,500.

6. Interest in any tools of the debtor's trade up to $2,300.

7. A life insurance contract owned by the debtor (other than a credit life insurance contract).

8. Certain interests in accrued dividends and interest under life insurance contracts owned by the debtor, not to exceed $12,250.

9. Professionally prescribed health aids.

10. The right to receive Social Security and certain welfare benefits, alimony and support, certain retirement funds and pensions, and education savings accounts held for specific periods of time.

11. The right to receive certain personal-injury and other awards up to $22,975.

State Exemptions Individual states have the power to pass legislation precluding debtors from using the federal exemptions within the state. A majority of the states have done this. In those states, debtors may use only state, not federal, exemptions. In the rest of the states, an individual debtor (or a husband and wife filing jointly) may choose either the exemptions provided under state law or the federal exemptions.

Limitations on the Homestead Exemption The Bankruptcy Code limits the amount that can be claimed in bankruptcy under the homestead exemption of any state. In general, if the debtor acquired the home within three and one-half years preceding the date of filing, the maximum equity exempted is $155,675, even if state law would permit a higher amount.

In addition, the state homestead exemption is available only if the debtor has lived in the state for two years before filing the petition. A debtor who has violated securities law, been convicted of a felony, or engaged in certain other intentional misconduct may not be permitted to claim the homestead exemption at all.

22-4g Creditors' Meeting and Claims

Within a reasonable time after the order of relief has been granted (not more than forty days), the trustee must call a meeting of the creditors listed in the schedules filed by the debtor. The bankruptcy judge does not attend this meeting, but the debtor must attend and submit to an examination under oath. At the meeting, the trustee ensures that the debtor is aware of the potential consequences of bankruptcy and the possibility of filing under a different chapter of the Code.

To be entitled to receive a portion of the debtor's estate, each creditor normally files a *proof of claim* with the bankruptcy court clerk within ninety days of the creditors' meeting. The proof of claim lists the creditor's name and address, as well as the amount that the creditor asserts is owed to the creditor by the debtor.

When the debtor has no assets—called a "no-asset case"—creditors are notified of the debtor's petition for bankruptcy but are instructed not to file a claim. In no-asset cases, the unsecured creditors will receive no payment, and most, if not all, of these debts will be discharged.

22-4h Distribution of Property

The Code provides specific rules for the distribution of the debtor's property to secured and unsecured creditors. If any amount remains after the priority classes of creditors have been satisfied, it is turned over to the debtor. Exhibit 22–2 illustrates the collection and distribution of property in most voluntary bankruptcies.

Distribution to Secured Creditors Secured creditors have priority. The Code requires that consumer-debtors file a statement of intention with respect to the secured collateral. They can choose to pay off the debt and redeem the collateral, claim that it is exempt, reaffirm the debt and continue making payments, or surrender the property to the secured party.

If the collateral is surrendered to the secured party, the secured creditor can either (1) accept the collateral in full satisfaction of the debt or (2) sell the collateral and use the proceeds to pay off the debt. Thus, the secured party has priority over unsecured parties as to the proceeds from the disposition of the collateral. Should the collateral be insufficient to cover the secured debt owed, the secured creditor becomes an unsecured creditor for the difference.

Distribution to Unsecured Creditors Bankruptcy law establishes an order of priority for classes of debts owed to *unsecured* creditors, and they are paid in the order of their priority. Each class must be fully paid before the next class is entitled to any of the remaining proceeds. If there is any balance remaining after all the creditors are paid, it is returned to the debtor.

In almost all Chapter 7 bankruptcies, the funds will be insufficient to pay all creditors. If there are insufficient proceeds to pay the full amount to all the creditors in a class, the proceeds are distributed *proportionately* to the creditors in that class, and classes lower in priority receive nothing. Claims for domestic-support obligations, such as child support and alimony, have the highest priority among unsecured claims, so these debts must be paid first.

Exhibit 22–2 Collection and Distribution of Property in Most Voluntary Bankruptcies

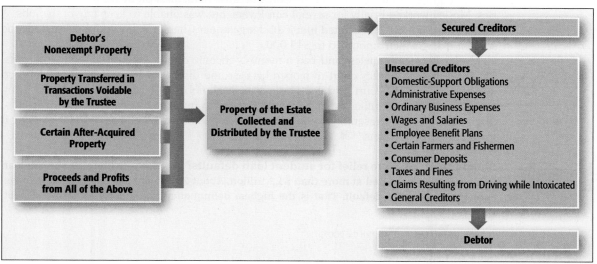

22-4i **Discharge**

From the debtor's point of view, the primary purpose of liquidation is to obtain a fresh start through the discharge of debts. A discharge voids, or sets aside, any judgment on a discharged debt and prevents any action to collect it. Certain debts, however, are not dischargeable in bankruptcy. Also, certain debtors may not qualify to have all debts discharged in bankruptcy. These situations are discussed next.

Exceptions to Discharge   The most important claims that are not dischargeable under Chapter 7 include the following:

1. Claims for back taxes accruing within two years prior to bankruptcy.
2. Claims for amounts borrowed by the debtor to pay federal taxes or any nondischargeable taxes.
3. Claims against property or funds obtained by the debtor under false pretenses or by false misrepresentations.
4. Claims by creditors who were not notified of the bankruptcy. These claims did not appear on the schedules the debtor was required to file.
5. Claims based on fraud or misuse of funds by the debtor or claims involving the debtor's embezzlement or larceny.
6. Domestic-support obligations and property settlements.
7. Claims for amounts due on a retirement loan account.
8. Claims based on willful or malicious conduct by the debtor toward another or toward the property of another.
9. Certain government fines and penalties.
10. Student loans, unless payment of the loans causes an undue hardship for the debtor and the debtor's dependents.
11. Consumer debts of more than $650 for luxury goods or services owed to a single creditor incurred within ninety days of the order for relief.

CASE EXAMPLE 22.6   Keldric Mosley incurred student loans while attending Alcorn State University and then joined the U.S. Army Reserve Officers' Training Corps. He was injured during training and resigned from the Corps because of medical problems related to his injuries. Mosley worked briefly for several employers, but was unable to keep any of the jobs. A federal bankruptcy court granted him a discharge under Chapter 7, but it did not include the student loans, which amounted to $45,000.

Mosley became homeless and had a monthly income of only $210 in disability benefits. He asked the bankruptcy court to reopen his case and discharge his student loans based on undue hardship. The court held that Mosley's medical problems, lack of skills, and "dire living conditions" made it unlikely that he would be able to repay the loans. The court therefore discharged the debt, reasoning that Mosley could not maintain a minimal standard of living if forced to repay the loans.[13] ■

ETHICAL ISSUE

Should there be more relief for student loan defaults?   By 2016, outstanding student loan balances were estimated at more than $1.3 trillion. About 20 percent are ninety or more days' delinquent or are in default. That is the highest delinquency rate among all forms of debt,

---

13. *In re Mosley*, 494 F.3d 1320 (11th Cir. 2007).

including credit cards, automobile loans, and mortgages. The average student loan debt is estimated to be more than $30,000.

Any student borrower who has not made regular payments for nine months is in default. If you are in default on a student loan, the U.S. Department of Education can (1) keep your tax refund if you have one, (2) garnish your paycheck without obtaining a court judgment, and (3) take your federal benefits, such as Social Security retirement payments or disability payments. In addition, in some states any professional license that you have can be revoked. The Department of Education can also bring a lawsuit against you. If it wins, it can collect the judgment from your bank accounts or place a lien on any real property that you own.

Recently, Congress attempted to ease the burden on those who have taken out student loans by reducing the interest rates they can be charged. In addition, President Obama signed an executive order putting into place an income-based repayment plan. This plan caps payments at no more than 10 percent of disposable income. Any balance not paid off after twenty years will be forgiven.

Should the federal government go further? Yes, according to the Obama administration. In 2015, Obama signed a presidential memorandum called the "Student Aid Bill of Rights." The Department of Education must now implement actions to ensure that the debt collection process for defaulted student loans "is fair, transparent, [and] charges reasonable fees to defaulted borrowers." Additionally, many politicians are asking Congress to allow federal student loans to be discharged in most bankruptcy proceedings.

Critics point out that such student loan debt forgiveness could have a cost. They claim that colleges and universities might "hint" to potential students that they need not worry about taking on higher student loans because some portion will be forgiven by the federal government.

Can a reservist who is injured during training succeed in discharging his student loans if he can no longer work?

Objections to Discharge
In addition to the exceptions to discharge previously discussed, a bankruptcy court may deny the discharge based on the debtor's *conduct*. Grounds for denial of discharge of the debtor include the following:

1. The debtor's concealment or destruction of property with the intent to hinder, delay, or defraud a creditor.

2. The debtor's fraudulent concealment or destruction of financial records.

3. The granting of a discharge to the debtor within eight years prior to the filing of the petition.

4. The debtor's failure to complete the required consumer education course (unless such a course was not available).

5. The debtor's involvement in proceedings in which the debtor could be found guilty of a felony. (Basically, a court may not discharge any debt until the completion of the felony proceedings against the debtor.)

When a discharge is denied under any of these circumstances, the debtor's assets are still distributed to the creditors. After the bankruptcy proceeding, however, the debtor remains liable for the unpaid portions of all claims.

A discharge may be revoked (taken back) within one year if it is discovered that the debtor acted fraudulently or dishonestly during the bankruptcy proceeding. If that occurs, a creditor whose claim was not satisfied in the distribution of the debtor's property can proceed with his or her claim against the debtor.

Whether a bankruptcy court properly denied a discharge based on the debtors' conduct was the issue in the following case.

CASE 22.2

In re Cummings

United States Court of Appeals, Ninth Circuit, 595 Fed.Appx. 707 (2015).

FACTS Clarence and Pamela Cummings filed a petition for a Chapter 7 bankruptcy in a federal bankruptcy court. After the debtors filed two amended versions of the required schedules, the trustee asked for additional time to investigate. The court granted the request. The debtors then filed a third amended schedule. In it, they disclosed for the first time the existence of First Beacon Management Company, a corporation that they planned to use as part of their postbankruptcy "fresh start." The trustee then claimed that the Cummingses' failure to disclose their interest in First Beacon as debtor property was a "false oath relating to a material fact made knowingly and fraudulently" in violation of the Bankruptcy Code. The court agreed and denied the debtors a discharge. The Bankruptcy Appellate Panel (BAP) affirmed the court's decision. The Cummingses appealed.

ISSUE Did Clarence and Pamela Cummings commit fraud by not disclosing their interest in First Beacon until they filed their third amended schedule?

DECISION Yes. The U.S. Court of Appeals for the Ninth Circuit affirmed the ruling of the Bankruptcy Appellate Panel. "The sequence of debtors' filings substantiates the presence of fraud."

What constitutes a false oath in Chapter 7 proceedings?

REASON The bankruptcy court rejected the Cummingses' testimony as "not credible" and "beyond not credible," and the BAP found "ample evidence" to support these findings. On appeal, the debtors claimed that the bankruptcy court had failed to consider "voluminous independent and undisputed documentary evidence" that "completely obliterated any suggestion of fraudulent intent." The appellate court found, however, that this evidence did not support the debtors' claim. Instead, it clearly showed their ultimate purpose—"to insulate First Beacon Management Co., . . . the new corporate anchor of their post-petition fresh start, from the stigma of bankruptcy." That they eventually disclosed their interest in First Beacon did not eliminate their fraud. They chose twice to amend their schedules without revealing the corporation and finally admitted to its existence only after the bankruptcy court gave the trustee additional time to investigate.

CRITICAL THINKING—Economic Consideration *Why would a debtor risk the denial of a discharge to conceal assets? Discuss.*

22–4j Reaffirmation of Debt

Reaffirmation Agreement
An agreement between a debtor and a creditor in which the debtor voluntarily agrees to pay a debt dischargeable in bankruptcy.

An agreement to pay a debt dischargeable in bankruptcy is called a **reaffirmation agreement.** A debtor may wish to pay a debt—for instance, a debt owed to a family member, physician, bank, or some other creditor—even though the debt could be discharged in bankruptcy. Also, as noted previously, a debtor cannot retain secured property while continuing to pay without entering into a reaffirmation agreement.

Procedures To be enforceable, reaffirmation agreements must be made before the debtor is granted a discharge. The agreement must be signed and filed with the court (along with disclosure documents, as described next). Court approval is required unless the debtor is represented by an attorney during the negotiation of the reaffirmation agreement and submits the proper documents and certifications. Even when the debtor is represented by an attorney, court approval may be required if it appears that the reaffirmation will result in undue hardship to the debtor.

When court approval is required, a separate hearing will take place. The court will approve the reaffirmation only if it finds that the agreement will not result in undue hardship to the debtor and that the reaffirmation is consistent with the debtor's best interests.

Required Disclosures To discourage creditors from engaging in abusive reaffirmation practices, the law provides specific language for disclosures that must be given to debtors entering reaffirmation agreements. Among other things, these disclosures explain that the debtor is not required to reaffirm any debt, but that liens on secured property, such as mortgages and cars, will remain in effect even if the debt is not reaffirmed.

The reaffirmation agreement must disclose the amount of the debt reaffirmed, the rate of interest, the date payments begin, and the right to rescind. The disclosures also caution the debtor: "Only agree to reaffirm a debt if it is in your best interest. Be sure you can afford the payments you agree to make."

The original disclosure documents must be signed by the debtor, certified by the debtor's attorney, and filed with the court at the same time as the reaffirmation agreement. A reaffirmation agreement that is not accompanied by the original signed disclosures will not be effective.

22-5 Chapter 11—Reorganization

The type of bankruptcy proceeding used most commonly by corporate debtors is the Chapter 11 *reorganization*. In a reorganization, the creditors and the debtor formulate a plan under which the debtor pays a portion of its debts and the rest of the debts are discharged. The debtor is allowed to continue in business. This type of bankruptcy is generally a corporate reorganization. Nonetheless, any debtor (except a stockbroker or commodities broker) who is eligible for Chapter 7 relief is normally eligible for relief under Chapter 11. (Railroads are also eligible.)

Congress has established a "fast-track" Chapter 11 procedure for small-business debtors whose liabilities do not exceed $2.49 million and who do not own or manage real estate. The fast track enables a debtor to avoid the appointment of a creditors' committee and also shortens the filing periods and relaxes certain other requirements. Because the process is shorter and simpler, it is less costly. (See the *Linking Business Law to Corporate Management* feature at the end of this chapter for suggestions on how small businesses can prepare for Chapter 11.)

The same principles that govern the filing of a liquidation (Chapter 7) petition apply to reorganization (Chapter 11) proceedings. The case may be brought either voluntarily or involuntarily. The automatic-stay provision and its exceptions apply in reorganizations as well, as do the provisions regarding substantial abuse and additional grounds for dismissal (or conversion) of bankruptcy petitions.

KNOW THIS
Chapter 11 proceedings are typically prolonged and costly. Whether a firm survives depends on its size and its ability to attract new investors despite its Chapter 11 status.

22-5a Workouts

In some instances, to avoid bankruptcy proceedings, creditors may prefer private, negotiated adjustments of creditor-debtor relations, known as *workouts*. Often, these out-of-court workouts are much more flexible and thus conducive to a speedy settlement. Speed is critical because delay is one of the most costly elements in any bankruptcy proceeding. Another advantage of workouts is that they avoid the various administrative costs of bankruptcy proceedings.

22-5b Reasons for Dismissal

Once a petition for Chapter 11 has been filed, a bankruptcy court, after notice and a hearing, can dismiss or suspend all proceedings in a case at any time if dismissal or suspension would better serve the interests of the creditors. The Bankruptcy Code also allows a court, after notice and a hearing, to dismiss a reorganization case "for cause" when there is no reasonable likelihood of rehabilitation. Similarly, a court can dismiss a Chapter 11 petition when there is an inability to effect a plan or an unreasonable delay by the debtor that may harm the interests of creditors. A debtor whose petition is dismissed for these reasons can file a subsequent Chapter 11 petition in the future.[14]

---

14. See 11 U.S.C. Section 1112(b).

22–5c Debtor in Possession

On entry of the order for relief, the debtor in Chapter 11 generally continues to operate the business as a **debtor in possession (DIP).** The court, however, may appoint a trustee (often referred to as a *receiver*) to operate the debtor's business if gross mismanagement of the business is shown or if appointing a trustee is in the best interests of the estate.

The DIP's role is similar to that of a trustee in a liquidation. The DIP is entitled to avoid preferential payments made to creditors and fraudulent transfers of assets. The DIP can also exercise a trustee's strong-arm powers. The DIP has the power to decide whether to cancel or assume prepetition executory contracts (contracts not yet performed) or unexpired leases.

Debtor in Possession (DIP)
In Chapter 11 bankruptcy proceedings, a debtor who is allowed to continue in possession of the estate in property (the business) and to continue business operations.

Cancellation of executory contracts or unexpired leases can be of substantial benefit to a Chapter 11 debtor. **EXAMPLE 22.7** Five years ago, APT Corporation leased an office building for a twenty-year term. Now, APT can no longer pay the rent due under the lease and has filed for Chapter 11 reorganization. In this situation, the debtor in possession can cancel the lease so that APT will not be required to continue paying the substantial rent due for fifteen more years. ∎

Can a debtor in possession under a Chapter 11 reorganization cancel a long-term lease on an office building?

22–5d Creditors' Committees

As soon as practicable after the entry of the order for relief, a committee of unsecured creditors is appointed.[15] The committee may consult with the trustee or the debtor concerning the administration of the case or the formulation of the plan. Additional creditors' committees may be appointed to represent special interest creditors, and a court may order the trustee to change a committee's membership as needed to ensure adequate representation of the creditors. Generally, no orders affecting the estate will be entered without the consent of the committee or a hearing in which the judge is informed of the position of the committee.

As mentioned earlier, businesses with debts of less than $2.49 million that do not own or manage real estate can avoid creditors' committees. In these fast-track proceedings, orders can be entered without a committee's consent.

22–5e The Reorganization Plan

A reorganization plan is established to conserve and administer the debtor's assets in the hope of an eventual return to successful operation and solvency. The plan must be fair and equitable and must do the following:

1. Designate classes of claims and interests.
2. Specify the treatment to be afforded the classes. (The plan must provide the same treatment for all claims in a particular class.)
3. Provide an adequate means for execution. (Individual debtors must utilize postpetition assets as necessary to execute the plan.)
4. Provide for payment of tax claims over a five-year period.

The plan need not provide for full repayment to unsecured creditors. Instead, creditors receive a percentage of each dollar owed to them by the debtor.

Filing the Plan Only the debtor may file a plan within the first 120 days after the date of the order for relief. This period may be extended, but not beyond eighteen months from the date of the order for relief. If the debtor does not meet the 120-day deadline or obtain an extension,

---

15. If the debtor has filed a plan accepted by the creditors, the trustee may decide not to call a meeting of the creditors.

or if the debtor fails to obtain the required creditor consent (discussed next) within 180 days, any party may propose a plan. If a small-business debtor chooses to avoid a creditors' committee, the time for the debtor's filing is 180 days.

Acceptance and Confirmation of the Plan Once the plan has been developed, it is submitted to each class of creditors for acceptance. For the plan to be adopted, each class must accept it. A class has accepted the plan when a majority of the creditors, representing two-thirds of the amount of the total claim, vote to approve it.

Even when all classes of creditors accept the plan, the court may refuse to confirm it if it is not "in the best interests of the creditors." In addition, confirmation is conditioned on the debtor's certifying that all postpetition domestic-support obligations have been paid in full. For small-business debtors, if the plan meets the listed requirements, the court must confirm the plan within forty-five days (unless this period is extended).

The plan can also be modified upon the request of the debtor, DIP, trustee, U.S. trustee, or holder of an unsecured claim. If an unsecured creditor objects to the plan, specific rules apply to the value of property to be distributed under the plan. Tax claims must be paid over a five-year period.

Even if only one class of creditors has accepted the plan, the court may still confirm the plan under the Code's so-called **cram-down provision.** In other words, the court may confirm the plan over the objections of a class of creditors. Before the court can exercise this right of cram-down confirmation, it must be demonstrated that the plan is fair and equitable.

Cram-Down Provision
A provision of the Bankruptcy Code that allows a court to confirm a debtor's Chapter 11 reorganization plan even though only one class of creditors has accepted it.

Discharge The plan is binding on confirmation. Nevertheless, the law provides that confirmation of a plan does not discharge an individual debtor. *For individual debtors, the plan must be completed before discharge will be granted,* unless the court orders otherwise. For all other debtors, the court may order discharge at any time after the plan is confirmed.

The debtor is given a reorganization discharge from all claims not protected under the plan. This discharge does not apply to any claims that would be denied discharge under liquidation.

22-6 Bankruptcy Relief under Chapter 12 and Chapter 13

In addition to bankruptcy relief through liquidation (Chapter 7) and reorganization (Chapter 11), the Code also provides for family-farmer and family-fisherman debt adjustments (Chapter 12) and individuals' repayment plans (Chapter 13).

22-6a Family Farmers and Fishermen—Chapter 12

To help relieve economic pressure on small farmers, Congress created Chapter 12 of the Bankruptcy Code. In 2005, Congress extended this protection to family fishermen, modified its provisions somewhat, and made it a permanent chapter in the Bankruptcy Code (previously, it had to be periodically renewed by Congress).

For purposes of Chapter 12, a *family farmer* is one whose gross income is at least 50 percent farm dependent and whose debts are at least 50 percent farm related. The total debt must not exceed $4,031,575. A partnership or a close corporation that is at least 50 percent owned by the farm family can also qualify as a family farmer.[16]

A *family fisherman* is one whose gross income is at least 50 percent dependent on commercial fishing operations and whose debts are at least 80 percent related to commercial fishing.

---

16. Note that for a corporation or partnership to qualify under Chapter 12, at least 80 percent of the value of the firm's assets must consist of assets related to the farming operation.

The total debt for a family fisherman must not exceed $1,868,200. As with family farmers, a partnership or close corporation can also qualify.

Filing the Petition   The procedure for filing a family-farmer or family-fisherman bankruptcy plan is similar to the procedure for filing a repayment plan under Chapter 13, which will be discussed in detail shortly. The debtor must file a plan not later than ninety days after the order for relief has been entered. The filing of the petition acts as an automatic stay against creditors' and co-obligors' actions against the estate.

A farmer or fisherman who has already filed a reorganization or repayment plan may convert the plan to a Chapter 12 plan. The debtor may also convert a Chapter 12 plan to a liquidation plan.

Content and Confirmation of the Plan   The content of a plan under Chapter 12 is basically the same as that of a Chapter 13 repayment plan (described next). Generally, the plan must be confirmed or denied within forty-five days of filing.

The plan must provide for payment of secured debts at the value of the collateral. If the secured debt exceeds the value of the collateral, the remaining debt is unsecured.

For unsecured debtors, the plan must be confirmed if either (1) the value of the property to be distributed under the plan equals the amount of the claim or (2) the plan provides that all of the debtor's disposable income to be received in a three-year period (or longer, by court approval) will be applied to making payments. Completion of payments under the plan discharges all debts provided for by the plan.

22-6b Individuals' Repayment Plan—Chapter 13

LEARNING OBJECTIVE 5

How does a Chapter 13 bankruptcy differ from bankruptcy under Chapter 7 and Chapter 11?

Chapter 13 of the bankruptcy code provides for the "adjustment of debts of an individual with regular income." Individuals (not partnerships or corporations) with regular income who owe fixed unsecured debts of less than $383,175 or fixed secured debts of less than $1,149,525 may take advantage of bankruptcy repayment plans.

Among those eligible are salaried employees and sole proprietors, as well as individuals who live on welfare, Social Security, fixed pensions, or investment income. Many small-business debtors have a choice of filing under either Chapter 11 or Chapter 13. Repayment plans offer some advantages because they are typically less expensive and less complicated than reorganization or liquidation proceedings.

Filing the Petition   A Chapter 13 repayment plan case can be initiated only by the debtor's filing of a voluntary petition or by court conversion of a Chapter 7 petition (because of a finding of substantial abuse, for instance). Certain liquidation and reorganization cases may be converted to Chapter 13 with the consent of the debtor.[17]

A trustee, who will make payments under the plan, must be appointed. On the filing of a repayment plan petition, an automatic stay takes effect. Although the stay applies to all or part of the debtor's consumer debt, it does not apply to any business debt incurred by the debtor or to any domestic-support obligations.

Good Faith Requirement   The Bankruptcy Code imposes the requirement of good faith on a debtor in both the filing of the petition and the filing of the plan. The Code does not define good faith, but if the circumstances as a whole indicate bad faith, a court can dismiss a debtor's Chapter 13 petition.

---

17. A Chapter 13 repayment plan may be converted to a Chapter 7 liquidation either at the request of the debtor or, under certain circumstances, "for cause" by a creditor. A Chapter 13 case may be converted to a Chapter 11 case after a hearing.

CASE EXAMPLE 22.8 Roger and Pauline Buis formed an air show business, Otto Airshows, which included a helicopter decorated as "Otto the Clown." After a competitor won a defamation lawsuit against the Buises and Otto Airshows, the Buises stopped doing business as Otto Airshows.

The Buises formed a new firm, Prop and Rotor Aviation, Inc., to which they leased the Otto equipment. Within a month, they filed a bankruptcy petition under Chapter 13. The plan and the schedules did not mention the lawsuit, the equipment lease, and several other items. The court dismissed the Buises' petition due to bad faith. The debtors had not included all of their assets and liabilities on their initial petition, and they had timed its filing to avoid payment on the defamation judgment.[18] ■

In determining whether a Chapter 13 plan was proposed in good faith, should a court consider whether the debtor included his Social Security income in the amount of disposable income available for payment to unsecured creditors? That was the issue in the following case.

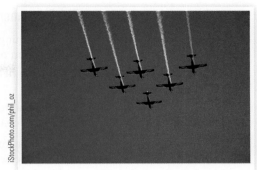

Does the owner of an air show have the right to exclude a pending lawsuit when filing bankruptcy papers?

---

18. *In re Buis*, 337 Bankr. 243 (N.D.Fla. 2006).

CASE 22.3

In re Welsh

United States Court of Appeals, Ninth Circuit, 711 F.3d 1120 (2013).

FACTS David and Sharon Welsh filed a Chapter 13 petition. The bankruptcy trustee objected to their proposed plan on the ground that it was not proposed in good faith. Specifically, the Welshes were making "minuscule" payments on unsecured claims while living in a $400,000 home and paying for various luxury items. In addition, they were failing to commit 100 percent of their disposable income to the plan. As a result, the plan would pay off only about $14,700 of their $180,500 unsecured debt.

Must this couple's Social Security income be included in a Chapter 13 petition?

One issue was the fact that David's Social Security income was excluded from the plan. The reformed Bankruptcy Code excludes Social Security income from the current monthly disposable income calculation, however. For that reason and others, the court ruled in the Welshes' favor. The Bankruptcy Appellate Panel for the Ninth Circuit affirmed the ruling. The trustee appealed to the U.S. Court of Appeals for the Ninth Circuit.

ISSUE Did the Welshes propose their plan in good faith despite their failure to include David's Social Security income in their disposable income?

DECISION Yes. The U.S. Court of Appeals for the Ninth Circuit affirmed the Bankruptcy Appellate Panel's judgment in the Welshes' favor. The federal appellate court concluded that the Bankruptcy

Abuse Prevention and Consumer Protection Act (BAPCPA) "forecloses a court's consideration of a debtor's Social Security income . . . as part of the inquiry into good faith."

REASON Before the BAPCPA, bankruptcy judges had the authority to determine a debtor's ability to pay based on the individual circumstances of each debtor. Congress replaced this discretion with a detailed test that requires debtors with a certain amount of "current monthly income" to calculate their disposable income by subtracting specific expenses. Social Security benefits are expressly excluded from current monthly income.

Thus, for a Social Security recipient such as David Welsh, the result of the disposable income calculation may indicate that there is little disposable income to pay debts. But a court cannot recalculate the amount by substituting its judgment for what Congress stipulated. And a court "cannot conclude . . . that a plan prepared completely in accordance with the very detailed calculations that Congress set forth is not proposed in good faith."

CRITICAL THINKING—Legal Consideration *In evaluating a debtor's petition, what factors should be part of a good faith analysis? Should consideration of disposable income play a role? Why or why not?*

The Repayment Plan

A plan of rehabilitation by repayment must provide for the following:

1. The turning over to the trustee of future earnings or income of the debtor as necessary for execution of the plan.
2. Full payment through deferred cash payments of all claims entitled to priority, such as taxes.[19]
3. Identical treatment of all claims within a particular class. (The Code permits the debtor to list co-debtors, such as guarantors or sureties, as a separate class.)

The repayment plan may provide either for payment of all obligations in full or for payment of a lesser amount. The debtor must begin making payments under the proposed plan within thirty days after the plan has been filed and must continue to make "timely" payments from her or his disposable income. If the debtor fails to make timely payments or does not commence payments within the thirty-day period, the court can convert the case to a liquidation bankruptcy or dismiss the petition.

In putting together a repayment plan, a debtor must apply the means test to identify the amount of disposable income that will be available to repay creditors. The debtor is allowed to deduct certain expenses from monthly income to arrive at this amount. For instance, a debtor can claim a car-ownership deduction if the debtor is making payments on a car. When the debtor owns the car free and clear, however, the debtor cannot claim the car-ownership deduction, according to the United States Supreme Court.[20]

The Length of the Plan. The length of the payment plan can be three or five years, depending on the debtor's family income. If the debtor's family income is less than the median family income in the relevant geographic area under the means test, the term of the proposed plan must be three years.[21] The term may not exceed five years.

Confirmation of the Plan. After the plan is filed, the court holds a confirmation hearing, at which interested parties (such as creditors) may object to the plan. The hearing must be held at least twenty days, but no more than forty-five days, after the meeting of the creditors. The debtor must have filed all prepetition tax returns and paid all postpetition domestic-support obligations before a court will confirm the plan.

The court will confirm a plan with respect to each claim of a secured creditor under any of the following circumstances:

1. If the secured creditors have accepted the plan.
2. If the plan provides that secured creditors retain their liens until there is payment in full or until the debtor receives a discharge.
3. If the debtor surrenders the property securing the claims to the creditors.

In addition, for a motor vehicle purchased within 910 days before the petition is filed, the plan must provide that a creditor with a purchase-money security interest (PMSI) retains its lien until the entire debt is paid. For PMSIs on other personal property, the payment plan must cover debts incurred within a one-year period preceding the filing.

Discharge

After the debtor has completed all payments, the court grants a discharge of all debts provided for by the repayment plan. Generally, all debts are dischargeable except the following:

1. Allowed claims not provided for by the plan.
2. Certain long-term debts provided for by the plan.

---

19. As with a Chapter 11 reorganization plan, full repayment of all claims is not always required.
20. *Ransom v. FIA Card Services, N.A.*, 562 U.S. 61, 131 S.Ct. 716, 178 L.Ed.2d 603 (2011).
21. See 11 U.S.C. Section 1322(d) for details on when a court will find that the Chapter 13 plan should extend to a five-year period.

3. Certain tax claims and payments on retirement accounts.

4. Claims for domestic-support obligations.

5. Debts related to injury or property damage caused while driving under the influence of alcohol or drugs.

An order granting discharge is final as to the debts listed in the repayment plan. **CASE EXAMPLE 22.9** Francisco Espinosa filed a petition for an individual repayment plan under Chapter 13 of the Bankruptcy Code. His plan proposed to pay only the principal on his student loan and to discharge the interest. United Student Aid Funds, Inc. (the creditor), had notice of the plan and did not object. Without finding that payment of the interest would cause undue hardship (as required under the Code), the court confirmed the plan.

Years later, United filed a motion asking the bankruptcy court to rule that its order confirming the plan was void because it was in violation of the rules governing bankruptcy. The court denied United's petition and ordered the creditor to cease its collection efforts. United appealed, and the case ultimately reached the United States Supreme Court. The Court affirmed the decision of the lower court that the bankruptcy court's order was not void. Thus, the student loan debt was discharged.[22] ■

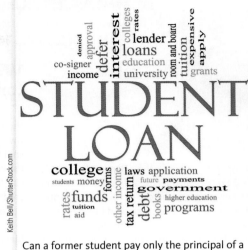

Can a former student pay only the principal of a student loan under Chapter 13?

---

22. *United Student Aid Funds, Inc. v. Espinosa*, 559 U.S. 260, 130 S.Ct. 1367, 176 L.Ed.2d 158 (2010).

Reviewing . . . Bankruptcy

Three months ago, Janet Hart's husband of twenty years died of cancer. Although he had medical insurance, he left Janet with outstanding medical bills of more than $50,000. Janet has worked at the local library for the past ten years, earning $1,500 per month. Since her husband's death, Janet also has received $1,500 in Social Security benefits and $1,100 in life insurance proceeds every month, giving her a monthly income of $4,100. After she pays the mortgage payment of $1,500 and the amounts due on other debts each month, Janet barely has enough left over to buy groceries for her family (she has two teenage daughters at home). She decides to file for Chapter 7 bankruptcy, hoping for a fresh start. Using the information provided in the chapter, answer the following questions.

1. Under the Bankruptcy Code after the reform act, what must Janet do before filing a petition for relief under Chapter 7?

2. How much time does Janet have after filing the bankruptcy petition to submit the required schedules? What happens if Janet does not meet the deadline?

3. Assume that Janet files a petition under Chapter 7. Further assume that the median family income in the state in which Janet lives is $49,300. What steps would a court take to determine whether Janet's petition is presumed to be substantial abuse under the means test?

4. Suppose the court determines that no presumption of substantial abuse applies in Janet's case. Nevertheless, the court finds that Janet does have the ability to pay at least a portion of the medical bills out of her disposable income. What would the court likely order in that situation?

DEBATE THIS

■ Rather than being allowed to file Chapter 7 bankruptcy petitions, individuals and couples should always be forced to make an effort to pay off their debts through Chapter 13.

LINKING BUSINESS LAW TO CORPORATE MANAGEMENT

What Can You Do to Prepare for a Chapter 11 Reorganization?

Chapter 11 of the Bankruptcy Code expresses the broad public policy of encouraging commerce. To this end, Chapter 11 allows a financially troubled business firm to petition for reorganization in bankruptcy while it is still solvent so that the firm's business can continue. Small businesses, however, do not fare very well under Chapter 11. Although some corporations that enter into Chapter 11 emerge as functioning entities, only a small number of companies survive the process.

Plan Ahead

If you ever are a small-business owner contemplating Chapter 11 reorganization, you can improve your chances of being among the survivors by planning ahead. To ensure the greatest possibility of success, you should take action before, not after, entering bankruptcy proceedings. Discuss your financial troubles openly and cooperatively with creditors to see if you can agree on a workout or some other arrangement.

If you appear to have no choice but to file for Chapter 11 protection, try to persuade a lender to loan you funds to see you through the bankruptcy. If your business is a small corporation, you might try to negotiate a favorable deal with a major investor. For example, a small business could offer to transfer ownership of stock to the investor in return for a loan to pay the costs of the bankruptcy proceedings and an option to repurchase the stock when the firm becomes profitable again.

Consult with Creditors

Most important, you should form a Chapter 11 plan before entering bankruptcy proceedings. Consult with creditors in advance to see what kind of plan would be acceptable to them, and prepare your plan accordingly. Having an acceptable plan prepared before you file will expedite the proceedings and thus save substantially on costs.

CRITICAL THINKING

■ Filing for bankruptcy under Chapter 11 may involve a time-consuming process. How might this affect the likelihood that a firm will be able to negotiate a workout agreement with its creditors?

Key Terms

automatic stay 551

bankruptcy trustee 547

consumer-debtor 547

cram-down provision 561

debtor in possession (DIP) 560

discharge 547

down payment 542

estate in bankruptcy 551

equitable right of redemption 544

forbearance 543

foreclosure 543

homeowner's insurance 542

homestead exemption 545

liquidation 547

mortgage 542

order for relief 550

petition in bankruptcy 548

preference 552

preferred creditor 553

prepayment penalty clause 542

reaffirmation agreement 558

short sale 543

statutory right of redemption 544

workout agreement 543

Chapter Summary: Bankruptcy

PROTECTION FOR DEBTORS	
Mortgages	When individuals purchase real estate, they typically make a down payment and take out a mortgage loan for the balance of the purchase price. Loan types include fixed-rate and adjustable-rate mortgages. Several protections, such as mortgage insurance, exist for lenders, but if the borrower defaults, the entire mortgage debt is due and payable, and the lender can foreclose on the mortgaged property.
Laws Assisting Debtors	Certain property of a debtor is exempt from creditors' actions under state laws. Each state permits a debtor to retain the family home, either in its entirety or up to a specified dollar amount, free from the claims of unsecured creditors or trustees in bankruptcy (homestead exemption).

BANKRUPTCY—A COMPARISON OF CHAPTERS 7, 11, 12, AND 13			
Issue	**Chapter 7**	**Chapter 11**	**Chapters 12 and 13**
Who Can Petition	Debtor (voluntary) or creditors (involuntary).	Debtor (voluntary) or creditors (involuntary).	Debtor (voluntary) only.
Who Can Be a Debtor	Any "person" (including partnerships and corporations) except railroads, insurance companies, banks, savings and loan institutions, investment companies licensed by the U.S. Small Business Administration, and credit unions. Farmers and charitable institutions cannot be involuntarily petitioned.	Any debtor eligible for Chapter 7 relief; railroads are also eligible.	*Chapter 12*—Any family farmer (one whose gross income is at least 50 percent farm dependent and whose debts are at least 50 percent farm related) or family fisherman (one whose gross income is at least 50 percent dependent on and whose debts are at least 80 percent related to commercial fishing) or any partnership or close corporation at least 50 percent owned by a family farmer or fisherman, when total debt does not exceed a specified amount. *Chapter 13*—Any individual (not partnerships or corporations) with regular income who owes fixed (liquidated) unsecured debts of less than $383,175 or fixed secured debts of less than $1,149,525.
Procedure Leading to Discharge	Nonexempt property is sold with proceeds to be distributed (in order) to priority groups. Dischargeable debts are terminated.	Plan is submitted. If it is approved and followed, debts are discharged.	Plan is submitted and must be approved if the value of the property to be distributed equals the amount of the claims or if the debtor turns over disposable income for a three-year or five-year period. If the plan is followed, debts are discharged.
Advantages	On liquidation and distribution, most debts are discharged, and the debtor has an opportunity for a fresh start.	Debtor continues in business. Creditors can either accept the plan, or it can be "crammed down" on them. The plan allows for the reorganization and liquidation of debts over the plan period.	Debtor continues in business or possession of assets. If the plan is approved, most debts are discharged after the specified period.

Issue Spotters

1. After graduating from college, Tina works briefly as a salesperson and then files for bankruptcy. As part of her petition, Tina reveals that her only debts are student loans, taxes accruing within the last year, and a claim against her based on her misuse of funds during her employment. Are these debts dischargeable in bankruptcy? Explain. (See *Chapter 7—Liquidation*.)

2. Ogden is a vice president of Plumbing Service, Inc. (PSI). On May 1, Ogden loans PSI $10,000. On June 1, the firm repays the loan. On July 1, PSI files for bankruptcy. Quentin is appointed trustee. Can Quentin recover the $10,000 paid to Ogden on June 1? Why or why not? (See *Chapter 7—Liquidation*.)

—**Check your answers to the *Issue Spotters* against the answers provided in Appendix D at the end of this text.**

Learning Objectives Check

1. What are three ways for a debtor to avoid mortgage foreclosure?
2. In a Chapter 7 bankruptcy, what happens if a court finds that there was "substantial abuse"? How is the means test used?
3. What constitutes a preference in bankruptcy law? When is a trustee able to avoid preferential transfers?
4. In a Chapter 11 reorganization, what is the role of the debtor in possession?
5. How does a Chapter 13 bankruptcy differ from bankruptcy under Chapter 7 and Chapter 11?

Answers to the even-numbered *Learning Objectives Check* questions can be found in Appendix E at the end of this text.

Business Scenarios and Case Problems

22–1. Voluntary versus Involuntary Bankruptcy. Burke has been a rancher all her life, raising cattle and crops. Her ranch is valued at $500,000, almost all of which is exempt under state law. Burke has eight creditors and a total indebtedness of $70,000. Two of her largest creditors are Oman ($30,000 owed) and Sneed ($25,000 owed). The other six creditors have claims of less than $5,000 each. A drought has ruined all of Burke's crops and forced her to sell many of her cattle at a loss. She cannot pay off her creditors. (See *Chapter 7—Liquidation.*)

1. Under the Bankruptcy Code, can Burke, with a $500,000 ranch, voluntarily petition herself into bankruptcy? Explain.
2. Could either Oman or Sneed force Burke into involuntary bankruptcy? Explain.

22–2. Distribution of Property. Montoro petitioned himself into voluntary bankruptcy. There were three major claims against his estate. One was made by Carlton, a friend who held Montoro's negotiable promissory note for $2,500. Another was made by Elmer, Montoro's employee, who claimed that Montoro owed him three months' back wages of $4,500. The last major claim was made by the United Bank of the Rockies on an unsecured loan of $5,000. In addition, Dietrich, an accountant retained by the trustee, was owed $500, and property taxes of $1,000 were owed to Rock County. Montoro's nonexempt property was liquidated, with proceeds of $5,000. Discuss fully what amount each party will receive, and why. (See *Chapter 7—Liquidation.*)

22–3. Protection for Debtors. Bill and Betty Ma owned half of a two-unit residential building. Betty lived in the unit, but Bill did not. To collect a judgment against the Mas, Mei-Fang Zhang obtained a writ of execution directing the sheriff to seize and sell the building. State law allowed a $100,000 homestead exemption if the debtor lived in the home and $175,000 if the debtor was also disabled and "unable to engage in gainful employment." Bill argued that he could not work because of "gout and dizziness." How much of an exemption were the Mas allowed? Why? [*Zhang v. Tse,* 2011 WL 500196 (N.D.Cal. 2011)] (See *Laws Assisting Debtors.*)

22–4. Business Case Problem with Sample Answer— Automatic Stay. Michelle Gholston leased a Chevy Impala from EZ Auto Van Rentals. In November 2011, Gholston filed for bankruptcy. Around November 21, the bankruptcy court notified EZ Auto of Gholston's bankruptcy and the imposition of an automatic stay. Nevertheless, because Gholston had fallen behind on her payments, EZ Auto repossessed the vehicle on November 28. Gholston's attorney then reminded EZ Auto about the automatic stay, but the company failed to return the car. As a result of the car's repossession, Gholston suffered damages that included emotional distress, lost wages, attorneys' fees, and car rental expenses. Can Gholston recover from EZ Auto? Why or why not? [*In re Gholston,* 2012 WL 639288 (M.D.Fla. 2012)] (See *Chapter 7— Liquidation.*)

—**For a sample answer to Problem 22–4, go to Appendix F at the end of this text.**

22–5. Discharge in Bankruptcy. Like many students, Barbara Hann financed her education partially through loans. These loans included three federally insured Stafford Loans of $7,500 each ($22,500 in total). Hann believed that she had repaid the loans, but later, when she filed a Chapter 13 petition, Educational Credit Management Corp. (ECMC) filed an unsecured proof of claim based on the loans. Hann objected. At a hearing at which ECMC failed to appear, Hann submitted correspondence from the lender that indicated the loans had been paid. The court entered an order sustaining Hann's objection. Despite the order, can ECMC resume its effort to collect on Hann's loans? Explain. [*In re Hann,* 711 F.3d 235 (1st Cir. 2013)] (See *Bankruptcy Relief under Chapter 12 and Chapter 13.*)

22–6. Discharge. Michael and Dianne Shankle divorced. An Arkansas state court ordered Michael to pay Dianne alimony and child support, as well as half of the $184,000 in their investment accounts. Instead, Michael withdrew more than half of the investment funds and spent them. Over the next several years, the court repeatedly held Michael in contempt for failing to pay Dianne. Six years later, Michael filed for Chapter 7 bankruptcy, including in the petition's schedule the debt to Dianne of unpaid alimony, child support, and investment funds. Is Michael entitled to a discharge of this debt, or does it qualify as an exception? Explain. [*In re Shankle,* 554 Fed.Appx. 264 (5th Cir. 2014)] (See *Chapter 7—Liquidation.*)

22–7. Discharge under Chapter 13. James Thomas and Jennifer Clark married and had two children. They bought a home in Ironton, Ohio, with a loan secured by a mortgage. Later, they took out a second mortgage. On their divorce, the court gave Clark custody of the children and required Clark to pay the first mortgage. The divorce decree also required Thomas and Clark to make equal payments on the second mortgage and provided that Clark would receive all proceeds on the sale of the home. Thomas failed to make any payments, and Clark sold the home. At that point, she learned that Auto Now had a lien on the home because Thomas had not made payments on his car. Clark used all the sale proceeds to pay off the lien and the mortgages. When Thomas filed a petition for a Chapter 13 bankruptcy in a federal bankruptcy court, Clark filed a proof of claim for the mortgage and lien debts. Clark claimed that Thomas should not be able to discharge these debts because they were part of his domestic-support obligations. Are these debts dischargeable? Explain. [*In re Thomas,* 591 Fed.Appx. 443

(6th Cir. 2015)] (See *Bankruptcy Relief under Chapter 12 and Chapter 13.*)

22–8. A Question of Ethics—Discharge in Bankruptcy. Monica Sexton filed a petition for Chapter 13 reorganization. One of her creditors was Friedman's Jewelers. Her petition misclassified Friedman's claim as $800 of unsecured debt. Within days, Friedman's filed proof of a secured claim for $300 and an unsecured claim for $462. Eventually, Friedman's was sent payments of about $300 by check. None of the checks were cashed. By then, Friedman's had filed its own petition under Chapter 11, Bankruptcy Receivables Management (BRM) had bought Friedman's unpaid accounts, and the checks had not been forwarded. Sexton received a discharge on the completion of her plan. BRM was not notified. BRM wrote to Sexton's attorney to ask about the status of her case, but received no response. BRM demanded that Sexton surrender the collateral on its claim. Sexton asked the court to impose sanctions on BRM for violating the discharge order. [*In re Sexton,* 2011 WL 284180 (E.D.N.C. 2011)] (See *Chapter 7—Liquidation.*)

1. Was Sexton's debt to Friedman's dischargeable? Discuss.
2. Should BRM be sanctioned for willfully violating the discharge order? Why or why not?

Critical Thinking and Writing Assignments

22–9. Business Law Critical Thinking Group Assignment. Cathy Coleman took out loans to complete her college education. After graduation, Coleman was irregularly employed as a teacher. Eventually, she filed a petition in a federal bankruptcy court under Chapter 13. The court confirmed a five-year plan under which Coleman was required to commit all of her disposable income to paying the student loans. Less than a year later, when Coleman was laid off, she still owed more than $100,000 to Educational Credit Management Corp. Coleman asked the court to discharge the debt on the ground that it would be an undue hardship for her to pay it. (See *Bankruptcy Relief under Chapter 12 and Chapter 13.*)

1. The first group will explain when a debtor normally is entitled to a discharge under Chapter 13.
2. The second group will discuss whether student loans are dischargeable and when "undue hardship" is a legitimate ground for an exception.
3. The third group will outline the goals of bankruptcy law and make an argument, based on these facts and principles, in support of Coleman's request.

Unit Three—Business Case Study with Dissenting Opinion

First Bank v. Fischer & Frichtel, Inc.

When a borrower defaults on a mortgage, the lender may recover the remaining debt by foreclosing on the mortgaged property. In a judicial foreclosure—the method used in most states—the property is sold at auction under court supervision. If the proceeds are enough to cover the borrower's debt, the lender gets the proceeds, and the debt is satisfied. But if the proceeds are insufficient to cover the debt, the lender may obtain a deficiency judgment for the difference between the sale price and the amount owed.

In this *Business Case Study with Dissenting Opinion,* we review *First Bank v. Fischer & Frichtel, Inc.*[1] In this case, the lender was the only bidder at a judicial sale and bought the mortgaged property for far less than its fair market value. The Missouri Supreme Court had to determine the amount of the deficiency.

How is the deficiency in a foreclosure sale calculated?

CASE BACKGROUND

Fischer & Frichtel, Inc., is an experienced real estate developer based in Missouri. In June 2000, Fischer & Frichtel borrowed $2.58 million from First Bank in order to buy twenty-one lots of property for a residential development. Over the next five years, Fischer & Frichtel paid First Bank as it sold the lots, which served as collateral for the loan. When the housing market collapsed, however, Fischer & Frichtel was unable to pay First Bank for nine unsold lots.

Through a series of negotiations, First Bank extended the loan's maturity date from July 1, 2003, to September 1, 2008. When the loan matured, Fischer & Frichtel defaulted, still owing $1.13 million. First Bank foreclosed on the unsold lots and was the only bidder at the judicial sale. First Bank's winning bid of $466,000 was based on its estimate of the lots' value, the depressed state of the real estate market, and the fact that it would have to sell the lots in bulk rather than individually.

First Bank filed a suit seeking to recover the unpaid principal and interest on the loan. At trial, Fischer & Frichtel presented expert testimony showing that the lots' fair market value was $918,000. The trial judge instructed the jury that, if it found for First Bank, it "must award . . . the balance due . . . on the date of maturity, less the fair market value of the property at the time of the foreclosure sale, plus interest." Following the judge's instructions, the jury awarded First Bank $215,875. First Bank then moved for a new trial, arguing that it was entitled to the full difference between the sale price and the amount owed. The trial court granted First Bank's motion, and Fischer & Frichtel appealed to the Missouri Supreme Court.

MAJORITY OPINION

Laura Denvir *STITH,* Judge.

* * * *

Missouri and many * * * other states * * * require a debtor to pay as a deficiency the full difference between the debt and the foreclosure sale price. They do not permit a debtor to attack the sufficiency of the foreclosure sale price *as part of the deficiency proceeding* even if the debtor believes that the foreclosure sale price was inadequate.

This does not mean Missouri does not give a debtor a mechanism for attacking an inadequate foreclosure sale price. Rather, a debtor who believes that the foreclosure sale price was inadequate can bring an action to void the *foreclosure sale* itself. If the sale stands, then it has been thought fair to require the debtor to pay any deficiency remaining based on the foreclosure sale price.

* * * *

*Missouri permits the debtor to void a properly noticed and carried out foreclosure sale only by showing that "the inadequacy [of the sale price is] so gross that it shocks the conscience * * * and is in itself evidence of fraud."* * * * Missouri's standard for proving that a foreclosure sale "shocks the conscience" is among the strictest in the country; more than one Missouri case has refused to set aside a sale that was only 20 to 30 percent of the fair market value * * * . [Emphasis added.]

Fischer & Frichtel argues that this standard * * * almost inevitably leads to windfalls for lenders. Fischer & Frichtel suggests that the foreclosure process is unfair in part because cash must be offered for the property by the bidder. This is a problem for the ordinary bidder, particularly a homeowner or small business owner, because the

1. 364 S.W.3d 216 (Mo. 2012).

statutory minimum time period between notice of foreclosure and the actual sale is often less than a month, an insufficient amount of time to allow potential bidders to secure financing.

Fischer & Frichtel notes that the lender does not have this financing problem, as it does not have to pay with cash, but instead simply may deduct the purchase price from the amount of principal the borrower owes. Because realistically the lender often will be the sole bidder, it can buy the foreclosed property for far less than market value, sell the property at a profit and then collect a deficiency from the borrower based on the below-market value it paid for the property.

* * * *

* * * While the foreclosure sale price was barely more than 50 percent of the fair market value later determined by the jury, the lender gave cogent reasons for its lower bid due to the depressed real estate market and the bulk nature of the sale, as of trial the lender had not been able to sell the property, and Fischer & Frichtel has not argued it could not have purchased the property at the foreclosure sale * * *.

This is not a case, therefore, in which to consider a modification of the standard for setting aside a foreclosure sale solely due to inadequacy of price or whether a change should be made in the manner of determining a deficiency where the foreclosure price is less than the fair market value.

* * * *

For the reasons stated, the judgment of the trial court awarding a new trial is affirmed.

DISSENTING OPINION

Richard B. *TEITELMAN*, Chief Justice.

I respectfully dissent. The purpose of a damage award is to make the injured party whole without creating a windfall. Accordingly, in nearly every context in which a party sustains damage to or the loss of a property or business interest, Missouri law measures damages by reference to fair market value. Yet in the foreclosure context, Missouri law ignores the fair market value of the foreclosed property and, instead, measures the lender's damages with reference to the foreclosure sale price. Rather than making the injured party whole, this anomaly in the law of damages, in many cases, will require the defaulting party to subsidize a substantial windfall to the lender. Aside from the fact that this anomaly long has been a part of Missouri law, there is no other compelling reason for continued adherence to a measure of damages that too often enriches one party at the expense of another. Consequently, I would hold that damages in a deficiency action should be measured by reference to the fair market value of the foreclosed property.

* * * *

I would reverse the judgment sustaining First Bank's motion for a new trial and order the trial court to enter judgment consistent with the jury's finding that the fair market value of the foreclosed property was $918,000 and that Fischer & Fritchel therefore owed First Bank a deficiency of $215,875.

QUESTIONS FOR ANALYSIS

1. **Law.** *What was the majority's decision? What were the reasons for its decision?*

2. **Law.** *Why did the dissent disagree with the majority? If the court had adopted the dissent's position, how would this have affected the result?*

3. **Ethics.** *Suppose that First Bank, the only bidder at the judicial sale, had submitted a winning bid of $1,000. Would First Bank's conduct have been ethical? Why or why not?*

4. **Economic Dimensions.** *Are there any reasons why the dissent's position might be more favorable for economic recovery from a recession? Explain your answer.*

5. **Implications for the Businessperson.** *What does the majority's ruling mean for a mortgagee that bids on a foreclosed property at a judicial sale? Explain your answer.*

Unit Three—Business Scenario

Amin Akhavan/ShutterStock.com

Sonja owns a bakery in San Francisco.

1. **Performance of Sales Contracts.** Sonja orders two new model X23 McIntyre ovens from Western Heating Appliances for $16,000. Sonja and Western Heating agree orally, on the telephone, that Western will deliver the ovens within two weeks and that Sonja will pay for the ovens when they are delivered. Two days later, Sonja receives a fax from Western confirming her order. Before delivery, Sonja learns that she can obtain the same ovens from another company at a much lower price. Sonja wants to cancel her order, but Western refuses. Is the contract enforceable against Sonja? Why or why not?

2. **Banking.** To pay a supplier, Sonja issues a check to Milled Grains Co. that is drawn on United First Bank. A Milled Grains employee, with authorization, indorses the check and transfers it to Milled Grains' financial institution, Second Federal Bank. Second Federal puts the check into the regular bank collection process. If United First refuses to honor the check, who will ultimately suffer the loss? Could Sonja be subject to criminal prosecution if United First refuses to honor the check?

Continues

3. **Security Interests.** Sonja wants to borrow $40,000 from Credit National Bank to buy coffee-brewing equipment. If Credit National accepts Sonja's equipment as collateral for the loan, how does it let other potential creditors know of its interest? If Sonja fails to repay the loan, what are Credit National's alternatives with respect to collecting the amount due?

4. **Creditors' Rights.** Sonya borrows $20,000 from Ace Loan Co. to remodel the bakery and gives it to Jones Construction, a contractor, to do the work. The amount covers only half of the cost, but when Jones finishes the work, Sonja fails to pay the rest. Sonja also does not repay Ace for the loan. What can Jones do to collect what it is owed? What can Ace do?

Unit Three—Group Project

iStockPhoto.com/TheAYS

Sara contracted to buy a new Steinway grand piano for $52,400 from InTune Pianos. InTune delivered a piano that had been in storage for a year and had been moved at least six times. Sara considered the piano to be unacceptably damaged.

1. The first group will determine whether Sara can reject the piano.

2. The second group will assume that Sara sued InTune and will decide what would be the proper measure of recovery (what types of damages should be sought and what costs should be covered).

3. A third group will determine what types of warranties were implied in the sale of the piano and consider whether Sara could sue InTune based on breach of warranty.

Unit 4
Agency and Employment Law

23

iStockPhoto.com/sturti

Agency Relationships in Business

LEARNING OBJECTIVES

The five Learning Objectives *below are designed to help improve your understanding of the chapter. After reading this chapter, you should be able to answer the following questions:*

1. What is the difference between an employee and an independent contractor?

2. How do agency relationships arise?

3. What duties do agents and principals owe to each other?

4. When is a principal liable for the agent's actions with respect to third parties? When is the agent liable?

5. What are some of the ways in which an agency relationship can be terminated?

Agency A relationship between two parties in which one party (the agent) agrees to represent or act for the other (the principal).

One of the most common, important, and pervasive legal relationships is that of **agency.** In an agency relationship between two parties, one of the parties, called the *agent,* agrees to represent or act for the other, called the *principal.* The principal has the right to control the agent's conduct in matters entrusted to the agent, and the agent must exercise his or her powers "for the benefit of the principal only," as Justice Joseph Story indicated in the chapter-opening quotation.

Agency relationships are crucial to the business world. Indeed, the only way that some business entities—including corporations and limited liability companies—can function is through their agents. A familiar example of an agent is a corporate officer who serves in a representative capacity for the owners of the corporation. In this capacity, the officer has the authority to bind the principal (the corporation) to a contract.

Using agents provides clear benefits to principals, but agents can also create liability for their principals. Employers, for instance, may be liable for the acts of their employees, because employees generally are their agents. For this reason, businesses sometimes attempt to retain workers as independent contractors or "permalancers" rather than as employees. This strategy may lead to problems with federal and state tax authorities, however, as you will read later in this chapter.

> "[It] is a universal principle in the law of agency, that the powers of the agent are to be exercised for the benefit of the principal only, and not of the agent or of third parties."
>
> **JOSEPH STORY**
> 1779–1845
> (ASSOCIATE JUSTICE OF THE UNITED STATES SUPREME COURT, 1811–1844)

23-1 Agency Relationships

Section 1(1) of the *Restatement (Third) of Agency*[1] defines agency as "the fiduciary relation which results from the manifestation of consent by one person to another that the other shall act in his [or her] behalf and subject to his [or her] control, and consent by the other so to act." In other words, in a principal-agent relationship, the parties have agreed that the agent will act *on behalf and instead of* the principal in negotiating and transacting business with third parties.

The term **fiduciary** is at the heart of agency law. The term can be used both as a noun and as an adjective. When used as a noun, it refers to a person having a duty created by her or his undertaking to act primarily for another's benefit in matters connected with the undertaking. When used as an adjective, as in "fiduciary relationship," it means that the relationship involves trust and confidence.

Agency relationships commonly exist between employers and employees. Agency relationships may sometimes also exist between employers and independent contractors who are hired to perform special tasks or services.

23-1a Employer-Employee Relationships

Normally, all employees who deal with third parties are deemed to be agents. A salesperson in a department store, for instance, is an agent of the store's owner (the principal) and acts on the owner's behalf. Any sale of goods made by the salesperson to a customer is binding on the principal. Similarly, most representations of fact made by the salesperson with respect to the goods sold are binding on the principal.

Because employees who deal with third parties are generally deemed to be agents of their employers, agency law and employment law overlap considerably. Agency relationships, however, can exist outside an employer-employee relationship, so agency law has a broader reach than employment law. Additionally, agency law is based on the common law, whereas much employment law is statutory law.

Note that employment laws (state and federal) apply only to the employer-employee relationship. Statutes governing Social Security, withholding taxes, workers' compensation, unemployment compensation, workplace safety, employment discrimination, and the like are applicable only if employer-employee status exists.

Fiduciary As a noun, a person having a duty created by his or her undertaking to act primarily for another's benefit in matters connected with the undertaking. As an adjective, a relationship founded on trust and confidence.

LEARNING OBJECTIVE 1

What is the difference between an employee and an independent contractor?

iStockPhoto.com/leezsnow

The person on the left works for the owner of this fabric store. Is she an agent of the owner?

23-1b Employer–Independent Contractor Relationships

Independent contractors are not employees because, by definition, those who hire them have no control over the details of their physical performance. Section 2 of the *Restatement (Third) of Agency* defines an **independent contractor** as follows:

> [An independent contractor is] a person who contracts with another to do something for him [or her] but who is not controlled by the other nor subject to the other's right to control with respect to his [or her] physical conduct in the performance of the undertaking. *He [or she] may or may not be an agent.* [Emphasis added.]

Building contractors and subcontractors are independent contractors. A property owner does not control the acts of either of these professionals. Truck drivers who own their equipment and hire themselves out on a per-job basis are independent contractors, whereas truck drivers who drive company trucks on a regular basis are usually employees.

Independent Contractor One who works for, and receives payment from, an employer but whose working conditions and methods are not controlled by the employer. An independent contractor is not an employee but may be an agent.

---

1. The *Restatement (Third) of Agency* is an authoritative summary of the law of agency and is often referred to by judges and other legal professionals.

The relationship between a person or firm and an independent contractor may or may not involve an agency relationship. To illustrate: An owner of real estate who hires a real estate broker to negotiate a sale of the property not only has contracted with an independent contractor (the broker) but also has established an agency relationship for the specific purpose of selling the property. Another example is an insurance agent, who is both an independent contractor and an agent of the insurance company for which she or he sells policies. (Note that an insurance *broker*, in contrast, normally is an agent of the person obtaining insurance and not of the insurance company.)

"I'd like to think of you as a person, David, but it's my job to think of you as personnel."

Dean Vietor/The New Yorker Collection/The Cartoon Bank

23–1c Determining Employee Status

The courts are frequently asked to determine whether a particular worker is an employee or an independent contractor. How a court decides this issue can have a significant effect on the rights and liabilities of the parties. Employers are required to pay certain taxes, such as Social Security and unemployment insurance taxes, for employees but not for independent contractors, for instance.

Criteria Used by the Courts In determining whether a worker has the status of an employee or an independent contractor, the courts often consider the following questions:

1. How much control can the employer exercise over the details of the work? (If an employer can exercise considerable control over the details of the work, this indicates employee status. The employer's degree of control is perhaps the most important factor weighed by the courts in determining employee status.)

2. Is the worker engaged in an occupation or business distinct from that of the employer? (If so, this points to independent-contractor status.)

3. Is the work usually done under the employer's direction or by a specialist without supervision? (If the work is usually done under the employer's direction, this indicates employee status.)

4. Does the employer supply the tools at the place of work? (If so, this indicates employee status.)

5. For how long is the person employed? (If the person is employed for a long, continuous period, this indicates employee status.)

6. What is the method of payment—by time period or at the completion of the job? (Regular payment by time period, such as once a month, indicates employee status.)

7. What degree of skill is required of the worker? (Independent contractors are more likely to be highly skilled or to have unique skills than to be unskilled, so these types of skills may indicate independent-contractor status.)

Disputes Involving Employment Law. Sometimes, workers may benefit from having employee status—for tax purposes and to be protected under certain employment laws, for example. As mentioned earlier, federal statutes governing employment discrimination apply only when an employer-employee relationship exists. Protection under antidiscrimination statutes provides a significant incentive for workers to claim that they are employees rather than independent contractors.

CASE EXAMPLE 23.1 A Puerto Rican television station, WIPR, contracted with a woman to co-host a television show. The woman signed a new contract for each episode and was committed to work for WIPR only during the filming of the episodes. WIPR paid her a lump sum for each contract and did not withhold any taxes.

When the woman became pregnant, WIPR stopped contracting with her. She filed a lawsuit claiming that WIPR was discriminating against her in violation of federal antidiscrimination laws, but the court found in favor of WIPR. Because the parties had structured their relationship through repeated fixed-length contracts and had described the woman as an independent contractor on tax documents, she could not maintain an employment-discrimination suit.[2] ■

Disputes Involving Tort Liability. Whether a worker is an employee or an independent contractor can also affect the employer's liability for the worker's actions. An employer normally is not responsible for the actions of an independent contractor. **CASE EXAMPLE 23.2** AAA North Jersey, Inc., contracted with Five Star Auto Service to perform towing and auto repair services for AAA (formerly the American Automobile Association). One night, Terence Pershad, a Five Star tow-truck driver, responded to an AAA call for assistance by the driver of a car involved in an accident. While at the scene, Pershad got into a fight with Nicholas Coker, a passenger in the disabled car, and assaulted him with a knife.

Coker filed a suit against Pershad, Five Star, and AAA, alleging that AAA was responsible for Pershad's tortious conduct. The court ruled that Pershad was Five Star's employee and that Five Star was an independent contractor, not AAA's employee. An appellate court affirmed the ruling. Because AAA did not control Five Star's work, it was not liable for a tort committed by Five Star's employee.[3] ■

Whether a dump truck operator involved in an accident was an employee or an independent contractor was at issue in the following case.

---

2. *Alberty-Vélez v. Corporación de Puerto Rico para la Difusión Pública*, 361 F.3d 1 (1st Cir. 2004).
3. *Coker v. Pershad*, 2013 WL 1296271 (N.J.App. 2013).

CASE 23.1

Asphalt & Concrete Services, Inc. v. Perry

Court of Special Appeals of Maryland, 221 Md.App. 235, 108 A.3d 558 (2015).

FACTS Asphalt & Concrete Services, Inc. (ACS), was working on a play pad at St. John Regional Catholic School in Frederick, Maryland. ACS project manager Blake Wood contacted William Johnson at Higher Power Trucking, LLC, to arrange for a dump truck to haul stone and asphalt from a quarry to the job site to complete the project.

Johnson had picked up and dropped off one load and was returning to the quarry for a second load when his truck struck and injured Moran Perry, who was crossing an intersection. Perry filed a suit in a Maryland state court against ACS to recover for the injuries. Perry alleged that Johnson's negligence in operating his vehicle was the proximate cause of his injuries and that Johnson was ACS's employee. The defendant claimed that Johnson was an independent contractor. A jury agreed with Perry

When is the owner/driver of a dump truck an independent contractor?

iStockPhoto.com/Bogdanhoda

and awarded him $529,500 in damages. The court issued a judgment in Perry's favor. ACS appealed.

ISSUE Based on the evidence, could the jury find that Johnson was ACS's employee?

DECISION Yes. A state intermediate appellate court affirmed the jury's finding with respect to Johnson's status as ACS's employee. The court disagreed, however, with the lower court's admission of certain evidence that may have influenced the jury's finding of proximate cause. The court reversed the judgment on this ground and remanded the case for a new trial.

REASON Maryland courts consider five factors to determine whether a worker is an employee or an independent contractor.

Continues

These are: (1) the power to hire the worker, (2) the payment of wages, (3) the power to discharge the worker, (4) the power to control the worker's conduct, and (5) whether the work is part of the employer's regular business. The court emphasized that "whether the employer has the right to control and direct the employee in the performance of the work and in the manner in which the work is to be done is the decisive, or controlling, test."

In this case, the evidence showed that ACS told Johnson to pick up certain materials at the quarry and deliver them to the job site.

His time was subject to strict limits—if he was not prompt, ACS could dock his pay, which was hourly, or discharge him. At the job site, ACS told him where to drop the materials, how much to drop, and how many times to return to the quarry. "Based on that evidence, a jury could find that Mr. Johnson was subject to ACS's control."

CRITICAL THINKING—Economic Consideration *Why did ACS contend that Johnson was not its employee? Discuss.*

Criteria Used by the IRS   The Internal Revenue Service (IRS) has established its own criteria for determining whether a worker is an independent contractor or an employee. The most important factor in this determination is the degree of control the business exercises over the worker.

The IRS tends to closely scrutinize a firm's classification of its workers because employers can avoid certain tax liabilities by hiring independent contractors instead of employees. Even when a firm classifies a worker as an independent contractor, the IRS may decide that the worker is actually an employee. In that situation, the employer will be responsible for paying any applicable Social Security, withholding, and unemployment taxes. Microsoft Corporation, for example, was once ordered to pay back payroll taxes for hundreds of workers that the IRS determined had been misclassified as independent contractors.[4] (The *Business Application* feature at the end of this chapter offers suggestions on using independent contractors.)

ETHICAL ISSUE

Should small businesses be allowed to hire "permalancers"? Freelancers, of course, are independent contractors. Small businesses across the country are turning increasingly to freelancers who stay on their payrolls for years—so-called *permalancers*. From an employer's perspective, the advantages are obvious. The cost savings from using freelancers rather than employees can be as much as 30 percent. For one thing, the employer does not have to pay payroll and unemployment taxes or workers' compensation. Additionally, freelancers do not receive health-care and other benefits offered to employees. Finally, during an economic downturn, the employer has more flexibility—it can let freelancers go quickly and usually without cost.

The IRS and state tax authorities, however, view permalancers differently. The IRS has launched an ongoing program examining thousands of companies to make sure that permanent workers have not been misclassified as independent contractors. The IRS has targeted small businesses because they hire a great many freelancers and do not usually have staff attorneys on hand to contest the IRS's classification.

These efforts raise several issues. On the one hand, the tax authorities gain some revenues by pursuing such misclassifications. On the other hand, reducing the flexibility of small businesses involves a cost. If the businesses hire fewer workers as a result, the taxes collected may not be worth the possible increase in unemployment. Another trade-off to consider is between the advantages that a business obtains from hiring permalancers and the disadvantages to those workers of having no employee benefits.

Employee Status and "Works for Hire"   Under the Copyright Act of 1976, any copyrighted work created by an employee within the scope of her or his employment at the request of the employer is a "work for hire," and the *employer* owns the copyright to the work. When an

---

4. See *Vizcaino v. U.S. District Court for the Western District of Washington,* 173 F.3d 713 (9th Cir. 1999).

employer hires an independent contractor—a freelance artist, writer, or computer programmer, for example—the *independent contractor* owns the copyright unless the parties agree in writing that the work is a "work for hire" and the work falls into specified categories, including audiovisual and other works.

CASE EXAMPLE 23.3 Artisan House, Inc., hired a professional photographer, Steven H. Lindner, owner of SHL Imaging, Inc., to take pictures of its products for the creation of color slides to be used by Artisan's sales force. Lindner controlled his own work and carefully chose the lighting and angles used in the photographs. When Artisan published the photographs in a catalogue without Lindner's permission, SHL filed a lawsuit for copyright infringement. Artisan claimed that its publication of the photographs was authorized because they were works for hire. The court, however, held that SHL was an independent contractor and owned the copyrights to the photographs. Because SHL had not given Artisan permission (a license) to reproduce the photographs in other publications, Artisan was liable for copyright infringement.[5] ■

23-2 Formation of an Agency

Agency relationships normally are consensual. They come about by voluntary consent and agreement between the parties. Generally, the agreement need not be in writing,[6] and consideration is not required.

A person must have contractual capacity to be a principal. Those who cannot legally enter into contracts directly should not be allowed to do so indirectly through an agent. Any person can be an agent, though, regardless of whether he or she has the capacity to enter a contract (including minors).

An agency relationship can be created for any legal purpose. An agency relationship that is created for an illegal purpose or that is contrary to public policy is unenforceable. **EXAMPLE 23.4** Sharp (as principal) contracts with McKenzie (as agent) to sell illegal narcotics. The agency relationship here is unenforceable because selling illegal narcotics is a felony and is contrary to public policy. ■ It is also illegal for physicians and other licensed professionals to employ unlicensed agents to perform professional actions.

Generally, an agency relationship can arise in four ways: by agreement of the parties, by ratification, by estoppel, or by operation of law.

23-2a Agency by Agreement

Most agency relationships are based on an express or implied agreement that the agent will act for the principal and that the principal agrees to have the agent so act. An agency agreement can take the form of an express written contract or be created by an oral agreement, such as when a person hires a neighbor to mow his lawn on a regular basis.

An agency agreement can also be implied by conduct. **CASE EXAMPLE 23.5** Gilbert Bishop was admitted to Laurel Creek Health Care Center suffering from various physical ailments. During an examination, Bishop told Laurel Creek staff that he could not use his hands well enough to write or hold a pencil, but he was otherwise found to be mentally competent. Bishop's sister, Rachel Combs, offered to sign the admissions forms, but it was Laurel Creek's policy to have the patient's spouse sign the admissions papers if the patient was unable to do so. Therefore, Gilbert asked Combs to get his wife, Anna, so that she could sign his admissions papers.

LEARNING OBJECTIVE 2
How do agency relationships arise?

---

5. *SHL Imaging, Inc. v. Artisan House, Inc.*, 117 F.Supp.2d 301 (S.D.N.Y. 2000).

6. There are two main exceptions to the statement that agency agreements need not be in writing: (1) When agency authority empowers the agent to enter into a contract that the Statute of Frauds requires to be in writing, the agent's authority from the principal must also be in writing, and (2) a power of attorney given to an agent must be in writing. Both exceptions will be discussed later in the chapter.

ADMITTING

Can a new hospital patient designate someone else to sign all of the "paperwork"?

Ratification A party's act of accepting or giving legal force to a contract or other obligation entered into on his or her behalf by another that previously was not enforceable.

Combs then brought Anna to the hospital, and Anna signed the admissions paperwork, which contained a provision for mandatory arbitration. Later, the Bishops sued the hospital for negligence, and Laurel Creek sought to compel arbitration. The Bishops argued that Anna was not Bishop's agent and had no legal authority to make decisions for him, but the court concluded that an agency relationship between Bishop and his wife, Anna, had been formed by their conduct.[7] ▪

23–2b Agency by Ratification

On occasion, a person who is in fact not an agent (or who is an agent acting outside the scope of her or his authority) may make a contract on behalf of another (a principal). If the principal affirms that contract by word or by action, an agency relationship is created by **ratification.** Ratification involves a question of intent, and intent can be expressed by either words or conduct. The basic requirements for ratification will be discussed later in this chapter.

23–2c Agency by Estoppel

When a principal causes a third person to believe that another person is his or her agent, and the third person deals with the supposed agent, the principal is "estopped to deny" the agency relationship. In such a situation, the principal's actions create the *appearance* of an agency that does not in fact exist.

For an agency by estoppel to be found, the third person must prove that she or he *reasonably* believed that an agency relationship existed. Facts and circumstances must show that an ordinary, prudent person familiar with business practice and custom would have been justified in concluding that the agent had authority.

Note that the acts or declarations of a purported *agent* in and of themselves do not create an agency by estoppel. Rather, it is the deeds or statements of the *principal* that create an agency by estoppel. **CASE EXAMPLE 23.6** Francis Azur was president and chief executive officer of ATM Corporation of America. Michelle Vanek was Azur's personal assistant. Among other duties, she reviewed his credit-card statements. For seven years, Vanek took unauthorized cash advances from Azur's credit-card account with Chase Bank. The charges appeared on at least sixty-five monthly statements.

When Azur discovered Vanek's fraud, he fired her and closed the account. He filed a suit against Chase, arguing that the bank should not have allowed Vanek to take cash advances. The court concluded that Azur (the principal) had given the bank reason to believe that Vanek (the agent) had authority. Therefore, Azur was estopped (prevented) from denying Vanek's authority.[8] ▪

23–2d Agency by Operation of Law

The courts may find an agency relationship in the absence of a formal agreement in other situations as well. This can occur in the family setting. When one spouse purchases certain necessaries and charges them to the other spouse's account, for example, the courts will often rule that the second spouse is liable to pay for the necessaries, either because of a social policy of promoting the general welfare of a spouse or because of a legal duty to supply necessaries to family members.

Agency by operation of law may also occur in emergency situations, when the agent's failure to act outside the scope of his or her authority would cause the principal substantial loss. If the agent is unable to contact the principal, the courts will often grant this emergency power. For instance, a railroad engineer may contract on behalf of her or his employer for medical care for an injured motorist hit by the train.

---

7. *Laurel Creek Health Care Center v. Bishop,* 2010 WL 985299 (Ky.App. 2010).
8. *Azur v. Chase Bank, USA, N.A.,* 601 F.3d 212 (3d Cir. 2010).

23-3 Duties of Agents and Principals

Once the principal-agent relationship has been created, both parties have duties that govern their conduct. Because an agency relationship is *fiduciary* (one of trust), each party owes the other the duty to act with the utmost good faith. In general, for every duty of the principal, the agent has a corresponding right, and vice versa.

23-3a Agent's Duties to the Principal

Generally, the agent owes the principal five duties: (1) performance, (2) notification, (3) loyalty, (4) obedience, and (5) accounting.

Performance An implied condition in every agency contract is the agent's agreement to use reasonable diligence and skill in performing the work. When an agent fails to perform her or his duties, liability for breach of contract may result. The degree of skill or care required of an agent is usually that expected of a reasonable person under similar circumstances. Generally, this is interpreted to mean ordinary care. If an agent has claimed to possess special skill, however, failure to exercise that degree of skill constitutes a breach of the agent's duty.

Not all agency relationships are based on contract. In some situations, an agent acts gratuitously—that is, not for monetary compensation. A gratuitous agent cannot be liable for breach of contract, as there is no contract, but he or she can be subject to tort liability. Once a gratuitous agent has begun to act in an agency capacity, he or she has the duty to continue to perform in that capacity. In addition, a gratuitous agent must perform in an acceptable manner and is subject to the same standards of care and duty to perform as other agents.

EXAMPLE 23.7 Bryan's friend Alice is a real estate broker. Alice offers to sell Bryan's vacation home at no charge. If Alice never attempts to sell the home, Bryan has no legal cause of action to force her to do so. If Alice does attempt to sell the home, but then performs so negligently that the sale falls through, Bryan can sue Alice for negligence. ■

Notification An agent is required to notify the principal of all matters that come to her or his attention concerning the subject matter of the agency. This is the duty of notification, or the duty to inform. **EXAMPLE 23.8** Lang, an artist, is about to negotiate a contract to sell a series of paintings to Barber's Art Gallery for $25,000. Lang's agent learns that Barber is insolvent and will be unable to pay for the paintings. The agent has a duty to inform Lang of this fact because it is relevant to the subject matter of the agency—the sale of Lang's paintings. ■

Generally, the law assumes that the principal knows of any information acquired by the agent that is relevant to the agency—regardless of whether the agent actually passes on this information to the principal. It is a basic tenet of agency law that notice to the agent is notice to the principal.

Loyalty Loyalty is one of the most fundamental duties in a fiduciary relationship. Basically, the agent has the duty to act *solely for the benefit of the principal* and not in the interest of the agent or a third party. For instance, an agent cannot represent two principals in the same transaction unless both know of the dual capacity and consent to it.

The duty of loyalty also means that any information or knowledge acquired through the agency relationship is considered confidential. It would be a breach of loyalty to disclose such information either during the agency relationship or after its termination. Typical examples of confidential information are trade secrets and customer lists compiled by the principal.

In short, the agent's loyalty must be undivided. The agent's actions must be strictly for the benefit of the principal and must not result in any secret profit for the agent. **EXAMPLE 23.9** Don contracts with Leo, a real estate agent, to negotiate the purchase of an office building. Leo discovers that the property owner will sell the building only as a package deal with

If a friend who is a licensed real estate broker agrees to sell your house at no charge, can you sue for nonperformance?

another parcel, so he buys the two properties, intending to resell the building to Don. Leo has breached his fiduciary duty. As a real estate agent, Leo has a duty to communicate all offers to his principal and not to purchase the property secretly and then resell it to his principal. Leo is required to act in Don's best interests and can become the purchaser in this situation only with Don's knowledge and approval. ■

Obedience When acting on behalf of a principal, an agent has a duty to follow all lawful and clearly stated instructions of the principal. Any deviation from such instructions is a violation of this duty. During emergency situations, however, when the principal cannot be consulted, the agent may deviate from the instructions without violating this duty. Whenever instructions are not clearly stated, the agent can fulfill the duty of obedience by acting in good faith and in a manner reasonable under the circumstances.

Accounting Unless an agent and a principal agree otherwise, the agent has the duty to keep and make available to the principal an account of all property and funds received and paid out on behalf of the principal. This includes gifts from third parties in connection with the agency. **EXAMPLE 23.10** Marta is a salesperson for Roadway Supplies. Knife River Construction gives Marta a new tablet as a gift for prompt deliveries of Roadway's paving materials. The tablet belongs to Roadway. ■ The agent has a duty to maintain separate accounts for the principal's funds and for the agent's personal funds, and the agent must not intermingle these accounts.

23–3b Principal's Duties to the Agent

The principal also owes certain duties to the agent. These duties relate to compensation, reimbursement and indemnification, cooperation, and safe working conditions.

Compensation In general, when a principal requests services from an agent, the agent reasonably expects payment. The principal therefore has a duty to pay the agent for services rendered. For instance, when an accountant or an attorney is asked to act as an agent, an agreement to compensate the agent for service is implied. The principal also has a duty to pay that compensation in a timely manner.

Unless the agency is gratuitous and the agent does not act in exchange for payment, the principal must pay the agreed-on value for the agent's services. If no amount has been expressly agreed on, the principal owes the agent the customary compensation for such services. **CASE EXAMPLE 23.11** Keith Miller worked as a sales representative for Paul M. Wolff Company, a subcontractor specializing in concrete finishing services. Sales representatives at Wolff are paid a 15 percent commission on projects that meet a 35 percent gross profit threshold. The commission is paid after the projects are completed. When Miller resigned, he asked for commissions on fourteen projects for which he had secured contracts but which had not yet been completed. Wolff refused, so Miller sued.

The court found that "an agent is entitled to receive commissions on sales that result from the agent's efforts," even after the employment or agency relationship ends. Miller had met the gross profit threshold on ten of the unfinished projects, and therefore he was entitled to more than $21,000 in commissions.[9] ■

PREVENTING LEGAL DISPUTES   **Many disputes arise because the principal and agent did not specify how much the agent would be paid.** To avoid such disputes, always state in writing in advance the amount or rate of compensation that you will pay your agents. Even when dealing with salespersons who customarily are paid a percentage of the value of a sale, such as real estate agents, it is best to explicitly state the rate of compensation.

---

9. *Miller v. Paul M. Wolff Co.*, 178 Wash.App. 957, 316 P.3d 1113 (2014).

Reimbursement and Indemnification Whenever an agent disburses funds at the request of the principal or to pay for necessary expenses in the reasonable performance of his or her agency duties, the principal has the duty to reimburse the agent for these payments. Agents cannot recover for expenses incurred through their own misconduct or negligence, however.

Subject to the terms of the agency agreement, the principal has the duty to compensate, or *indemnify,* an agent for liabilities incurred because of authorized acts and transactions. For instance, if the principal fails to perform a contract formed by the agent with a third party and the third party then sues the agent, the principal must compensate the agent for any costs incurred in defending against the lawsuit.

Additionally, the principal must indemnify the agent for the value of benefits that the agent confers on the principal. The amount of indemnification is usually specified in the agency contract. If it is not, the courts will look to the nature of the benefits and the type of expenses to determine the amount. Note that this rule applies to acts by gratuitous agents as well. Suppose that a person finds a dog that becomes sick, takes the dog to a veterinarian, and pays for the veterinarian's services. The finder is a gratuitous agent and is entitled to be reimbursed by the dog's owner for those costs.

Cooperation A principal has a duty to cooperate with the agent and to assist the agent in performing her or his duties. The principal must do nothing to prevent that performance.

When a principal grants an agent an exclusive territory, for instance, the principal creates an *exclusive agency* and cannot compete with the agent or assign or allow another agent to compete. **EXAMPLE 23.12** Penny (the principal) creates an exclusive agency by granting Andrew (the agent) an exclusive territory within which Andrew may sell Penny's products. If Penny starts to sell the products herself within Andrew's territory—or permits another agent to do so—Penny has failed to cooperate with the agent. Because she has violated the exclusive agency, Penny can be held liable for Andrew's lost sales or profits. ■

Safe Working Conditions A principal is required to provide safe working premises, equipment, and conditions for all agents and employees. The principal has a duty to inspect the working conditions and to warn agents and employees about any hazards. When the agent is an employee, the employer's liability is frequently covered by state workers' compensation insurance, and federal and state statutes often require the employer to meet certain safety standards.

> "Let every eye negotiate for itself and trust no agent."
>
> **WILLIAM SHAKESPEARE**
> 1564–1616
> (ENGLISH POET AND PLAYWRIGHT)

23-4 Agent's Authority

An agent's authority to act can be either *actual* (express or implied) or *apparent*. If an agent contracts outside the scope of his or her authority, the principal may still become liable by ratifying the contract.

23-4a Express Authority

Express authority is authority declared in clear, direct, and definite terms. Express authority can be given orally or in writing.

Equal Dignity Rule In most states, the **equal dignity rule** requires that if the contract being executed is or must be in writing, then the agent's authority must also be in writing. Failure to comply with the equal dignity rule can make a contract voidable *at the option of the principal.* The law regards the contract at that point as a mere offer. If the principal decides to accept the offer, the agent's authority must be ratified, or affirmed, in writing.

EXAMPLE 23.13 Lee (the principal) orally asks Parkinson (the agent) to sell a ranch that Lee owns. Parkinson finds a buyer and signs a sales contract on behalf of Lee to sell the ranch.

Equal Dignity Rule A rule requiring that an agent's authority be in writing if the contract to be made on behalf of the principal must be in writing.

Because a contract for an interest in realty must be in writing, the equal dignity rule applies here. Thus, the buyer cannot enforce the contract unless Lee subsequently ratifies Parkinson's agency status in writing. Once Parkinson's agency status is ratified, either party can enforce rights under the contract. ■

Modern business practice allows exceptions to the equal dignity rule. An executive officer of a corporation normally is not required to obtain written authority from the corporation to conduct *ordinary* business transactions. The equal dignity rule also does not apply when an agent acts in the presence of a principal or when the agent's act of signing is merely perfunctory (routine). Thus, if the principal negotiates a contract but is called out of town the day it is to be signed and orally authorizes his or her agent to sign the contract, the oral authorization is sufficient.

Power of Attorney
Authorization for another to act as one's agent or attorney either in specified circumstances (special) or in all situations (general).

Notary Public A public official authorized to attest to the authenticity of signatures.

Power of Attorney   Giving an agent a **power of attorney** confers express authority on the agent.[10] The power of attorney normally is a written document and is usually notarized. (A document is notarized when a **notary public**—a person authorized by the state to attest to the authenticity of signatures—signs and dates the document and imprints it with his or her seal of authority.) Most states have statutory provisions for creating a power of attorney.

A power of attorney can be special (permitting the agent to do specified acts only), or it can be general (permitting the agent to transact all business for the principal). Because a general power of attorney grants extensive authority to an agent to act on behalf of the principal in many ways, it should be used with great caution. Ordinarily, a power of attorney terminates on the incapacity or death of the person giving the power.[11]

23–4b Implied Authority

An agent has the *implied authority* to do what is reasonably necessary to carry out his or her express authority and accomplish the objectives of the agency. Authority can also be implied by custom or inferred from the position the agent occupies.

EXAMPLE 23.14 Mueller is employed by Al's Supermarket to manage one of its stores. Al's has not expressly stated that Mueller has authority to contract with third persons. In this situation, though, authority to manage a business implies authority to do what is reasonably required (as is customary or can be inferred from a manager's position) to operate the business. It is reasonable to infer that Mueller has the authority to form contracts to hire employees, to buy merchandise and equipment, and to advertise the products sold in the store. ■

Sometimes an employee exceeds his or her implied authority to act on behalf of a principal. If an employee-agent makes unauthorized use of his employer's computer data, has he committed a crime? See this chapter's *Adapting the Law to the Online Environment* feature for a discussion of this issue.

24–4c Apparent Authority

Apparent Authority Authority that is only apparent, not real. An agent's apparent authority arises when the principal causes a third party to believe that the agent has authority, even though she or he does not.

Actual authority (express or implied) arises from what the principal manifests *to the agent*. An agent has **apparent authority** when the principal, by either words or actions, causes a *third party* to reasonably believe that an agent has authority to act, even though the agent has no express or implied authority. If the third party changes his or her position in reliance on the principal's representations, the principal may be estopped (prevented) from denying that the agent had authority.

---

10. An agent who holds the power of attorney is called an *attorney-in-fact* for the principal. The holder does not have to be an attorney-at-law (and often is not).

11. A *durable* power of attorney, however, continues to be effective despite the principal's incapacity. An elderly person, for example, might grant a durable power of attorney to provide for the handling of property and investments or specific health-care needs should she or he become incompetent.

ADAPTING THE LAW TO THE ONLINE ENVIRONMENT

What Happens When an Agent Breaches Company Policy on the Use of Electronic Data?

Suppose that an employee-agent who is authorized to access company trade secrets contained in computer files takes those secrets to a competitor for whom the employee is about to begin working. Clearly, the agent has violated the ethical—and legal—duty of loyalty to the principal. Does this breach of loyalty mean that the employee's act of accessing the trade secrets was unauthorized?

The question has significant implications for both parties. If the act was unauthorized, the employee will be subject to state and federal laws prohibiting unauthorized access to computer information and data, including the Computer Fraud and Abuse Act (CFAA). If the act was authorized, these laws will not apply.

Employees "Exceed Authorized Access" to Their Company's Database

David Nosal worked for Korn/Ferry, an executive recruitment firm, and had access to the company's confidential database. When he left, he encouraged several former colleagues who still worked there to join him in starting a competing firm. He asked them to access Korn/Ferry's database and download source lists, names, and client contact information before they quit. The employees had authority to access the database, but Korn/Ferry's policy forbade disclosure of confidential information.

The government filed charges against Nosal and his colleagues for violating the CFAA, among other things.

A Court Rules That Violating an Employer's Use Restrictions Is Not a Crime

The U.S. Court of Appeals for the Ninth Circuit refused to find that the defendants had violated the CFAA. The court ruled that the phrase "exceed authorized access" in the CFAA refers to restrictions on access, not restrictions on use. The court reasoned that Congress's intent in enacting the CFAA was to prohibit people from hacking into computers without authorization.

The court also stated that the CFAA should not be used to criminally prosecute persons who use data in an unauthorized or unethical way. The court pointed out that "adopting the government's interpretation would turn vast numbers of teens and preteens into juvenile delinquents—and their parents and teachers into delinquency contributors." Furthermore, "the effect this broad construction of the CFAA has on workplace conduct pales by comparison with its effect on everyone else who uses a computer, smart-phone, iPad, Kindle, Nook, X-box, Blu-Ray player or any other Internet-enabled device."[a]

CRITICAL THINKING

- If an employee accesses Facebook at work even though personal use of a workplace computer is against the employer's stated policies, can the employee be criminally prosecuted? Why or why not?

---

a. *United States. v. Nosal*, 676 F.3d 854 (9th Cir. 2012). See also *Facebook, Inc. v. Grunin*, ___ F.Supp.3d ___, 2015 WL 124781 (N.D.Cal. 2015).

Apparent authority usually comes into existence through a principal's pattern of conduct over time. **EXAMPLE 23.15** Bailey is a traveling salesperson. She solicits orders for goods but does not carry them with her. She normally would not have the implied authority to collect payments from customers on behalf of the principal. Suppose that she does accept payments from Corgley Enterprises, however, and submits them to the principal's accounting department for processing. If the principal does nothing to stop Bailey from continuing this practice, a pattern develops over time, and the principal confers apparent authority on Bailey to accept payments from Corgley. ■

At issue in the following *Spotlight Case* was whether the manager of a horse breeding operation had the authority to bind the farm's owner in a contract guaranteeing breeding rights.

This manager's boss never specified to him to what extent he had authority to order fruit and vegetables. Is it reasonable for him to imply this authority nonetheless?

SPOTLIGHT ON APPARENT AUTHORITY OF MANAGERS: CASE 23.2

Lundberg v. Church Farm, Inc.

Court of Appeals of Illinois, 502 N.E.2d 806, 151 Ill.App.3d 452 (1986).

FACTS Gilbert Church owned a horse breeding farm in Illinois managed by Herb Bagley. Advertisements for the breeding rights to one of Church Farm's stallions, Imperial Guard, directed all inquiries to "Herb Bagley, Manager." Vern and Gail Lundberg bred Thoroughbred horses. The Lundbergs contacted Bagley and executed a preprinted contract giving them breeding rights to Imperial Guard "at Imperial Guard's location," subject to approval of the mares by Church. Bagley handwrote a statement on the contract that guaranteed the Lundbergs "six live foals in the first two years." He then signed it "Gilbert G. Church by H. Bagley."

The Lundbergs bred four mares, which resulted in one live foal. Church then moved Imperial Guard from Illinois to Oklahoma. The Lundbergs sued Church for breaching the contract by moving the horse. Church claimed that Bagley was not authorized to sign contracts for Church or to change or add terms, but only to present preprinted contracts to potential buyers. Church testified that although Bagley was his farm manager and the contact person for breeding rights, Bagley had never before modified the preprinted forms or signed Church's name on these contracts. The jury found in favor of the Lundbergs and awarded $147,000 in damages. Church appealed.

Who can guarantee a minimum number of foals during a limited time period?

iStockPhoto.com/Somogyvari

ISSUE Was Bagley authorized to sign and modify contracts on behalf of Church?

DECISION Yes. The state appellate court affirmed the lower court's award of $147,000 to the Lundbergs. Because Church allowed circumstances to lead the Lundbergs to believe Bagley had authority, Church was bound by Bagley's actions.

REASON A principal may be bound by the unauthorized acts of an agent if the principal leads a third party to believe, or allows a third party to believe, that the agent has authority to perform the act. In this case, Church approved the advertisement listing Bagley as Church Farm's manager and point of contact. Bagley generally was the only person available to visitors to the farm. Bagley answered the farm's phone, and the breeding contract had a preprinted signature line for him. Church was not engaged in the actual negotiation or signing of the contracts but left that business for Bagley to complete. Based on Church's actions, a reasonable third party would believe that Bagley had authority to sign and modify contracts.

CRITICAL THINKING—Legal Consideration *What duties to Church might Bagley have violated in this situation?*

23–4d Ratification

Ratification occurs when the principal affirms an agent's *unauthorized* act. When ratification occurs, the principal is bound to the agent's act, and the act is treated as if it had been authorized by the principal *from the outset*. Ratification can be either express or implied.

If the principal does not ratify the contract, the principal is not bound, and the third party's agreement with the agent is viewed as merely an unaccepted offer. Because the third party's agreement is an unaccepted offer, the third party can revoke the offer at any time, without liability, before the principal ratifies the contract.

The requirements for ratification can be summarized as follows:

1. The agent must have acted on behalf of an identified principal who subsequently ratifies the action.

2. The principal must know of all material facts involved in the transaction. If a principal ratifies a contract without knowing all of the facts, the principal can rescind (cancel) the contract.

3. The principal must affirm the agent's act in its entirety.

KNOW THIS

An agent who exceeds his or her authority and enters into a contract that the principal does not ratify may be liable to the third party on the ground of misrepresentation.

4. The principal must have the legal capacity to authorize the transaction at the time the agent engages in the act and at the time the principal ratifies. The third party must also have the legal capacity to engage in the transaction.

5. The principal's affirmation must occur before the third party withdraws from the transaction.

6. The principal must observe the same formalities when approving the act done by the agent as would have been required to authorize it initially.

23–5 Liability in Agency Relationships

Frequently, a question arises as to which party, the principal or the agent, should be held liable for contracts formed by the agent or for torts or crimes committed by the agent. We look here at these aspects of agency law.

23–5a Liability for Contracts

Liability for contracts formed by an agent depends on how the principal is classified and on whether the actions of the agent were authorized or unauthorized. Principals are classified as disclosed, partially disclosed, or undisclosed.[12]

A **disclosed principal** is a principal whose identity is known by the third party at the time the contract is made by the agent. A **partially disclosed principal** is a principal whose identity is not known by the third party, but the third party knows that the agent is or may be acting for a principal at the time the contract is made. **EXAMPLE 23.16** Sarah has contracted with a real estate agent to sell certain property. She wishes to keep her identity a secret, but the agent makes it clear to potential buyers of the property that the agent is acting in an agency capacity. In this situation, Sarah is a partially disclosed principal. ■ An **undisclosed principal** is a principal whose identity is totally unknown by the third party, and the third party has no knowledge that the agent is acting in an agency capacity at the time the contract is made.

Authorized Acts If an agent acts within the scope of her or his authority, normally the principal is obligated to perform the contract regardless of whether the principal was disclosed, partially disclosed, or undisclosed. Whether the agent may also be held liable under the contract, however, depends on the status of the principal.

Disclosed or Partially Disclosed Principal. A disclosed or partially disclosed principal is liable to a third party for a contract made by an agent who is acting within the scope of her or his authority. If the principal is disclosed, an agent has no contractual liability for the nonperformance of the principal or the third party. If the principal is partially disclosed, in most states the agent is also treated as a party to the contract, and the third party can hold the agent liable for contractual nonperformance.[13]

In the following case, the court applied these principles to determine an agent's liability on a contract to install flooring in a commercial building.

LEARNING OBJECTIVE 4
When is a principal liable for the agent's actions with respect to third parties? When is the agent liable?

Disclosed Principal A principal whose identity is known to a third party at the time the agent makes a contract with the third party.

Partially Disclosed Principal A principal whose identity is unknown by a third party, but the third party knows that the agent is or may be acting for a principal at the time the agent and the third party form a contract.

Undisclosed Principal A principal whose identity is unknown by a third party, and that person has no knowledge that the agent is acting for a principal at the time the agent and the third party form a contract.

Can an agent hide the existence or just the name of a principal in the sale of real estate?

---

12. *Restatement (Third) of Agency*, Section 1.04(2).
13. *Restatement (Third) of Agency*, Section 6.02.

CASE 23.3

Stonhard, Inc. v. Blue Ridge Farms, LLC

New York Supreme Court, Appellate Division, Second Department, 114 A.D.3d 757, 980 N.Y.S.2d 507 (2014).

FACTS Stonhard, Inc., makes epoxy and urethane flooring and installs it in industrial and commercial buildings. Marvin Sussman entered into a contract with Stonhard to install flooring at Blue Ridge Farms, LLC, a food-manufacturing facility in Brooklyn, New York. Sussman did not disclose that he was acting as an agent for the facility's owner, Blue Ridge Foods, LLC. When Stonhard was not paid for the work, the flooring contractor filed a suit in a New York state court against the facility, its owner, and Sussman to recover damages for breach of contract. Stonhard filed a motion for summary judgment against the defendants, offering in support of the motion evidence of the contract entered into with Sussman. The court denied Stonhard's motion and dismissed the complaint against Sussman. Stonhard appealed.

ISSUE When an individual who enters into a contract is acting as an agent for a partially disclosed principal, is the agent personally liable on the contract?

DECISION Yes. A state intermediate appellate court reversed the lower court's dismissal of Stonhard's complaint and issued a summary judgment in the plaintiff's favor.

REASON The evidence of the parties' contract indicated that Sussman "at best" was acting as an agent for a partially disclosed

Who is liable when the installer of food plant flooring is not paid?

iStockPhoto.com/IP Galanternik D.U.

principal. In that capacity, Sussman was personally liable on the contract with Stonhard. An agent who contracts on behalf of a disclosed principal is generally not liable for a breach of the contract. But the other party to the contract must have known the principal's identity and must have known that the agent was contracting for the principal. Actual "knowledge of the real principal is the test."

In this case, Stonhard provided "documentary evidence" that it had contracted with Sussman of Blue Ridge Farms to install flooring at the Blue Ridge Farms facility. The evidence also showed that Sussman did not disclose that he was acting as an agent for Blue Ridge Foods. In other words, among these parties, the evidence indicated that the agency relationship was known, but the identity of the principal was undisclosed. Thus, "at best" Sussman acted as an agent for a partially disclosed principal in contracting with Stonhard and was personally liable on the contract.

CRITICAL THINKING—Legal Consideration *The court ruled that Sussman was personally liable on the contract with Stonhard. Is the principal, Blue Ridge Foods, also liable? Explain.*

Undisclosed Principal. Sometimes, neither the fact of agency nor the identity of the principal is disclosed, and the agent is acting within the scope of his or her authority. In this situation, the undisclosed principal is bound to perform just as if the principal had been fully disclosed at the time the contract was made.

The agent is also liable as a party to the contract. When a principal's identity is undisclosed and the agent is forced to pay the third party, however, the agent is entitled to be indemnified (compensated) by the principal. The principal had a duty to perform, even though his or her identity was undisclosed, and failure to do so will make the principal ultimately liable.

Once the undisclosed principal's identity is revealed, the third party generally can elect to hold either the principal or the agent liable on the contract. At the same time, the undisclosed principal can require the third party to fulfill the contract, *except* under any of the following circumstances:

1. The undisclosed principal was expressly excluded as a party in the contract.

2. The contract is a negotiable instrument signed by the agent with no indication of signing in a representative capacity.

3. The performance of the agent is personal to the contract, allowing the third party to refuse the principal's performance.

CASE EXAMPLE 23.17 Bobby Williams bought a car at Sherman Henderson's auto repair business in Monroe, Louisiana, for $3,000. Henderson negotiated and made the sale for the car's owner, Joe Pike, whose name was not disclosed. Three days after the sale, the car erupted in flames. Williams extinguished the blaze and contacted Henderson. The vehicle was soon stolen, which prevented Williams from returning it to Henderson. Williams later filed suits against both Pike and Henderson.

The court noted that the state had issued Pike a permit to sell the car. The car was displayed for sale at Henderson's business, and Henderson actually sold it. This made Pike the principal and Henderson his agent. The fact that their agency relationship was not made clear to Williams made Pike an undisclosed principal. Williams could thus hold both Pike and Henderson liable for the condition of the car.[14] ■

Unauthorized Acts If an agent has no authority but nevertheless contracts with a third party, the principal cannot be held liable on the contract. It does not matter whether the principal was disclosed, partially disclosed, or undisclosed.

In general, the agent is liable on the contract. **EXAMPLE 23.18** Scranton signs a contract for the purchase of a truck, purportedly acting as an agent under authority granted by Johnson. In fact, Johnson has not given Scranton any such authority. Johnson refuses to pay for the truck, claiming that Scranton had no authority to purchase it. The seller of the truck is entitled to hold Scranton liable for payment. ■

If the principal is disclosed or partially disclosed, the agent is liable to the third party only if the third party relied on the agency status. The agent's liability here is based on the breach of an *implied warranty of authority*.[15] If the third party knows at the time the contract is made that the agent does not have authority—or if the agent expresses to the third party *uncertainty* as to the extent of her or his authority—then the agent is not personally liable.

23-5b Liability for Torts and Crimes

Obviously, any person, including an agent, is liable for her or his own torts and crimes. Whether a principal can also be held liable for an agent's torts and crimes depends on several factors. In some situations, a principal may be held liable for the torts of an agent.

Principal's Tortious Conduct A principal conducting an activity through an agent may be liable for harm resulting from the principal's own negligence or recklessness. Thus, a principal may be liable for giving improper instructions, authorizing the use of improper materials or tools, or establishing improper rules that resulted in the agent's committing a tort.

EXAMPLE 23.19 Jack knows that Kate is not qualified to drive large trucks. Jack nevertheless tells Kate to use the company truck to deliver some equipment to a customer. If Kate causes an accident that injures someone, Jack (the principal) will be liable for his own negligence in giving improper instructions to Kate. ■

Principal's Authorization of Agent's Tortious Conduct A principal who authorizes an agent to commit a tort may be liable to persons or property injured thereby, because the act is considered to be the principal's. **EXAMPLE 23.20** Selkow directs his agent, Warren, to cut the corn on specific acreage, which neither of them has the right to do. The harvest is therefore a trespass (a tort), and Selkow is liable to the owner of the corn. ■

Note also that an agent acting at the principal's direction can be liable as a tortfeasor (one who commits a tort), along with the principal, for committing the tortious act even if the agent was unaware of the wrongfulness of the act. Assume in *Example 23.20* that Warren, the agent, was unaware that Selkow had no right to harvest the corn. Warren can nevertheless be held liable to the owner of the field for damages, along with Selkow.

---

14. *Williams v. Pike*, 58 So.3d 525 (La.App. 2011).
15. The agent is not liable on the contract because the agent was never intended personally to be a party to the contract.

Liability for Agent's Misrepresentation

A principal is exposed to tort liability whenever a third person sustains a loss due to the agent's misrepresentation. The principal's liability depends on whether the agent was actually or apparently authorized to make representations and whether the representations were made within the scope of the agency. The principal is always directly responsible for an agent's misrepresentation made within the scope of the agent's authority.

EXAMPLE 23.21 Bassett is a demonstrator for Moore's products. Moore sends Bassett to a home show to demonstrate the products and to answer questions from consumers. Moore has given Bassett authority to make statements about the products. If Bassett makes only true representations, all is fine, but if he makes false claims, Moore will be liable for any injuries or damages sustained by third parties in reliance on Bassett's false representations. ■

Liability for Agent's Negligence

As mentioned, an agent is liable for his or her own torts. A principal may also be liable for harm an agent caused to a third party under the doctrine of ***respondeat superior***,[16] a Latin term meaning "let the master respond."

This doctrine, which is discussed in this chapter's *Landmark in the Law* feature, is similar to the theory of strict liability. It imposes **vicarious liability,** or indirect liability, on the employer—that is, liability without regard to the personal fault of the employer—for torts committed by an employee in the course or scope of employment.

When an agent commits a negligent act, *both* the agent and the principal are liable. **EXAMPLE 23.22** Aegis hires SDI to provide landscaping services for its property. An herbicide sprayed by SDI employee David Hoggatt enters the Aegis building through the air-conditioning system and caused Catherine Warner, an Aegis employee, to suffer a heart attack. If Warner sues, both SDI (principal) and Hoggatt (agent) can be held liable for negligence. An agent is not excused from responsibility for tortious conduct just because he is working for a principal. ■

Determining the Scope of Employment.

The key to determining whether a principal may be liable for an agent's torts under the doctrine of *respondeat superior* is whether the torts are committed within the scope of employment. In determining whether a particular act occurred within the course and scope of employment, the courts consider the following factors:

1. Whether the employee's act was authorized by the employer.
2. The time, place, and purpose of the act.
3. Whether the act was one commonly performed by employees on behalf of their employers.
4. The extent to which the employer's interest was advanced by the act.
5. The extent to which the private interests of the employee were involved.
6. Whether the employer furnished the means or instrumentality (for example, a truck or a machine) by which the injury was inflicted.
7. Whether the employer had reason to know that the employee would do the act in question and whether the employee had ever done it before.
8. Whether the act involved the commission of a serious crime.

The Distinction between a "Detour" and a "Frolic."

A useful insight into the "scope of employment" concept may be gained from the judge's classic distinction between a "detour" and a "frolic" in the case of *Joel v. Morison*.[17] In this case, the English court held that if a servant merely took a detour from his master's business, the master is responsible. If, however, the

Respondeat Superior A doctrine under which a principal or an employer is held liable for the wrongful acts committed by agents or employees while acting within the course and scope of their agency or employment.

Vicarious Liability Indirect liability imposed on a supervisory party (such as an employer) for the actions of a subordinate (such as an employee) because of the relationship between the two parties.

---

16. Pronounced ree-*spahn*-dee-uht soo-*peer*-ee-uhr.
17. 6 Car. & P. 501, 172 Eng.Rep. 1338 (1834).

LANDMARK IN THE LAW

The Doctrine of *Respondeat Superior*

The idea that a master (employer) must respond to third persons for losses negligently caused by the master's servant (employee) first appeared in Lord Holt's opinion in *Jones v. Hart* (1698).[a] By the early nineteenth century, this maxim had been adopted by most courts and was referred to as the doctrine of *respondeat superior*.

THEORIES OF LIABILITY The vicarious (indirect) liability of the master for the acts of the servant has been supported primarily by two theories. The first theory rests on the issue of *control,* or *fault*—the master has control over the acts of the servant and is thus responsible for injuries arising out of such service. The second theory is economic

in nature—the master receives the benefits or profits of the servant's service and therefore should also suffer the losses. Moreover, the master is better able than the servant to absorb such losses.

The control theory is clearly recognized in the *Restatement (Third) of Agency,* which defines a master as "a principal who employs an agent to perform service in his [or her] affairs and who controls, or has the right to control, the physical conduct of the other in the performance of the service." Accordingly, a servant is defined as "an agent employed by a master to perform service in his [or her] affairs whose physical conduct in his [or her] performance of the service is controlled, or is subject to control, by the master."

LIMITATIONS ON THE EMPLOYER'S LIABILITY There are limitations on the master's liability for the acts of the servant. As discussed in the text, an employer (master)

is responsible only for the wrongful conduct of an employee (servant) that occurs in "the scope of employment." Generally, the act must be of a kind that the servant was employed to do, it must have occurred within "authorized time and space limits," and it must have been "activated, at least in part, by a purpose to serve the master."

APPLICATION TO TODAY'S WORLD *The courts have accepted the doctrine of respondeat superior for some two centuries. This theory of vicarious liability has practical implications in all situations in which a principal-agent (master-servant, employer-employee) relationship exists. Today, the small-town grocer with one clerk and the multinational corporation with thousands of employees are equally subject to the doctrine.*

a. K.B. 642, 90 Eng.Rep. 1255 (1698).

---

servant was on a "frolic of his own" and not in any way "on his master's business," the master is not liable.

EXAMPLE 23.23 While driving his employer's vehicle to call on a customer, Mandel decides to stop at the post office—which is one block off his route—to mail a personal letter. Mandel then negligently runs into a parked vehicle owned by Chan. In this situation, because Mandel's detour from the employer's business is not substantial, he is still acting within the scope of employment, and the employer is liable.

But suppose instead that Mandel decides to pick up a few friends for cocktails in another city and in the process negligently runs into Chan's vehicle. In this situation, the departure from the employer's business is substantial—Mandel is on a "frolic" of his own. Thus, the employer normally is not liable to Chan for damages. ■

Employee Travel Time. The time an employee spends going to and from work or to and from meals is usually considered outside the scope of employment. If travel is part of a person's position, however, as it is for a traveling salesperson or a regional representative of a company, then travel time is normally considered within the scope of employment. Thus, for such an employee, the duration of the business trip, including the return trip home, is within the scope of employment unless there is a significant departure from the employer's business.

Notice of Dangerous Conditions. The employer is charged with knowledge of any dangerous conditions discovered by an employee and pertinent to the employment situation. **EXAMPLE 23.24** Brad, a maintenance employee in Martin's apartment building, notices a lead pipe protruding from the ground in

When can an employer be held liable for an employee's negligence while driving?

Is this maintenance employee forced to inform building owners of all safety hazards?

the building's courtyard. Brad neglects either to fix the pipe or to inform Martin of the danger. John trips on the pipe and is injured. The employer is charged with knowledge of the dangerous condition regardless of whether or not Brad actually informed him. That knowledge is imputed to the employer by virtue of the employment relationship. ■

Liability for Agent's Intentional Torts Most intentional torts that employees commit have no relation to their employment. Thus, their employers will not be held liable. Nevertheless, under the doctrine of *respondeat superior,* the employer can be liable for an employee's intentional torts that are committed within the course and scope of employment, just as the employer is liable for negligence. For instance, an employer is liable when an employee (such as a "bouncer" at a nightclub or a security guard at a department store) commits the tort of assault and battery or false imprisonment while acting within the scope of employment.

In addition, an employer who knows or should know that an employee has a propensity for committing tortious acts is liable for the employee's acts even if they ordinarily would not be considered within the scope of employment. For instance, if the employer hires a bouncer knowing that he has a history of arrests for assault and battery, the employer may be liable if the employee viciously attacks a patron in the parking lot after hours.

An employer may also be liable for permitting an employee to engage in reckless actions that can injure others. **EXAMPLE 23.25** The owner of Bates Trucking observes an employee smoking while filling containerized trucks with highly flammable liquids. Failure to stop the employee will cause the employer to be liable for any injuries that result if a truck explodes. ■ (See this chapter's *Beyond Our Borders* feature for a discussion of another approach to an employer's liability for an employee's acts.)

Liability for Independent Contractor's Torts Generally, an employer is not liable for physical harm caused to a third person by the negligent act of an independent contractor in the performance of the contract. This is because the employer does not have the right to control the details of an independent contractor's performance.

Exceptions to this rule are made in certain situations, though, such as when unusually hazardous activities are involved. Typical examples include blasting operations, the transport of highly volatile chemicals, and the use of poisonous gases. In these situations, an employer cannot be shielded from liability merely by using an independent contractor. Strict liability is imposed on the employer-principal as a matter of law. Also, in some states, strict liability may be imposed by statute.

Liability for Agent's Crimes An agent is liable for his or her own crimes. A principal or employer is not liable for an agent's crime even if the crime was committed within the scope of authority or employment, unless the principal participated by conspiracy or other action. In some jurisdictions, under specific statutes, a principal may be liable for an agent's violation in the course and scope of employment. For instance, a principal might be liable when an agent, during work, violates criminal regulations governing sanitation, prices, weights, and the sale of liquor.

KNOW THIS
An agent-employee going to or from work or meals usually is not considered to be within the scope of employment. An agent-employee whose job requires travel, however, is considered to be within the scope of employment for the entire trip, including the return.

23-6 Termination of an Agency

Agency law is similar to contract law in that both an agency and a contract can be terminated *by an act of the parties* or *by operation of law.* Once the relationship between the principal and the agent has ended, the agent no longer has the right (*actual* authority) to bind the principal. For an agent's *apparent* authority to be terminated, third persons may also need to be notified that the agency has been terminated.

BEYOND OUR BORDERS

Islamic Law and *Respondeat Superior*

The doctrine of *respondeat superior* is well established in the legal systems of the United States and most Western countries. As you have already read, under this doctrine employers can be held liable for the acts of their employees. The doctrine of *respondeat superior* is not universal, however. Most Middle Eastern countries, for example, do not follow this doctrine.

Islamic law, as codified in the *sharia*, holds to a strict belief that responsibility for human actions lies with the individual and cannot be vicariously extended to others. This belief and other concepts of Islamic law are based on the writings of Muhammad, the seventh-century prophet whose revelations form the basis of the Islamic religion and, by extension, the *sharia*. Muhammad's prophecies are documented in the Koran (Qur'an), which is the principal source of the *sharia*.

CRITICAL THINKING

■ How would U.S. society be affected if employers could not be held vicariously liable for their employees' torts?

23–6a Termination by Act of the Parties

An agency may be terminated by certain acts of the parties. The acts that will terminate an agency include lapse of time, achievement of the purpose of the agency, occurrence of a specific event, mutual agreement, and the action of one party. Exhibit 23–1 lists and describes the ways in which the parties can terminate an agency.

LEARNING OBJECTIVE 5

What are some of the ways in which an agency relationship can be terminated?

Wrongful Termination Although both parties have the *power* to terminate an agency relationship, they may not always possess the *right* to do so. Wrongful termination can subject the canceling party to a suit for breach of contract. **EXAMPLE 23.26** Rawlins has a one-year employment contract with Munro to act as an agent in return for $65,000. Munro has the *power* to discharge Rawlins before the contract period expires. If he does so, however, he can be sued for breaching the contract because he has no *right* to terminate the agency. ■

Agency Coupled with an Interest A special rule applies to an **agency coupled with an interest,** in which the agent has some legal right (an interest) in the property that is the subject

Agency Coupled with an Interest An agency, created for the benefit of the agent, in which the agent has some legal right (interest) in the property that is the subject of the agency.

Exhibit 23–1 Termination by Act of Parties

METHOD	RULES	ILLUSTRATION
1. Lapse of time.	Agency terminates automatically at the end of the stated time.	Page lists her property for sale with Alex, a real estate agent, for six months. The agency ends in six months.
2. Purpose achieved.	Agency terminates automatically on the completion of the purpose for which it was formed.	Calvin, a cattle rancher, hires Abe as his agent in the purchase of fifty breeding stock. The agency ends when the cattle have been purchased.
3. Occurrence of a specific event.	Agency normally terminates automatically on the event's occurrence.	Meredith appoints Allen to handle her business affairs while she is away. The agency terminates when Meredith returns.
4. Mutual agreement.	Agency terminates when both parties consent to end the agency relationship.	Linda and Greg agree that Greg will no longer be her agent in procuring business equipment.
5. At the option of one party (*revocation,* if by principal; *renunciation,* if by agent).	Either party normally has a right to terminate the agency relationship. Wrongful termination can lead to liability for breach of contract.	When Patrick becomes ill, he informs Alice that he is revoking her authority to be his agent.

of the agency. Because the agent has an additional interest in the property beyond the normal commission for selling it, the agent's position cannot be terminated until the agent's interest ends.

An agency coupled with an interest is not an agency in the usual sense because it is created for the agent's benefit instead of for the principal's benefit. **EXAMPLE 23.27** Sylvia owns Harper Hills. She needs some cash right away, so she enters into an agreement with Rob under which Rob will lend her $10,000. In return, she will grant Rob a one-half interest in Harper Hills and "the exclusive right to sell" it. The loan is to be repaid out of the sale's proceeds. Rob is Silvia's agent, and their relationship is an agency coupled with an interest. The agency was created when the loan agreement was made for the purpose of securing the loan. Therefore, Rob's agency power is irrevocable. ■

An agency coupled with an interest should not be confused with a situation in which the agent merely derives proceeds or profits from the sale of the subject matter. Many agents are paid a commission for their services, but the agency relationship involved does not constitute an agency coupled with an interest. For instance, a real estate agent who merely receives a commission from the sale of real property does not have a beneficial interest in the property itself.

Notice of Termination   No particular form is required for notice of agency termination to be effective. If the agent's authority is written, however, it normally must be revoked in writing. The principal can personally notify the agent, or the agent can learn of the termination through some other means.

When an agency is terminated by act of the parties, it is the principal's duty to inform any third parties who know of the existence of the agency that it has been terminated. If the principal knows that a third party has dealt with the agent, the principal is expected to notify that person *directly*.

Although an agent's actual authority ends when the agency is terminated, an agent's *apparent authority* continues until the third party receives notice (from any source) that such authority has been terminated. **EXAMPLE 23.28** Manning bids on a shipment of steel, and Stone is hired as an agent to arrange transportation of the shipment. When Stone learns that Manning has lost the bid, Stone's authority to make the transportation arrangement terminates. ■

23–6b Termination by Operation of Law

Termination of an agency by operation of law occurs in the circumstances discussed here. Note that when an agency terminates by operation of law, there is no duty to notify third persons.

If the manufacturer of this steel fails to procure an important sales contract for its products, what happens to the prearranged transportation contract?

1. *Death or insanity*. The general rule is that the death or mental incompetence of either the principal or the agent automatically and immediately terminates an ordinary agency relationship. Knowledge of the death is not required. **EXAMPLE 23.29** Gary sends Tyron to China to purchase a rare painting. Before Tyron makes the purchase, Gary dies. Tyron's agent status is terminated at the moment of Gary's death, even though Tyron does not know that Gary has died. ■ (Some states have enacted statutes that change this common law rule to require an agent's knowledge of the principal's death before termination.)

2. *Impossibility*. When the specific subject matter of an agency is destroyed or lost, the agency terminates. **EXAMPLE 23.30** Blake employs Pedro to sell Blake's house, but before any sale takes place, the house is destroyed by fire. In this situation, Pedro's agency and authority to sell Blake's house terminate. ■ Similarly, when it is impossible for the agent to perform the agency lawfully because of a change in the law, the agency terminates.

3. *Changed circumstances.* When an event occurs that has such an unusual effect on the subject matter of the agency that the agent can reasonably infer that the principal will not want the agency to continue, the agency terminates. **EXAMPLE 23.31** Robert hires Miles to sell a tract of land for $20,000. Subsequently, Miles learns that there is oil under the land and that the land is worth $1 million. The agency and Miles's authority to sell the land for $20,000 are terminated. ■

4. *Bankruptcy.* If either the principal or the agent petitions for bankruptcy, the agency is *usually* terminated. In certain circumstances, as when the agent's financial status is irrelevant to the purpose of the agency, the agency relationship may continue. Insolvency (the inability to pay debts when they become due or when liabilities exceed assets), as distinguished from bankruptcy, does not necessarily terminate the relationship.

5. *War.* When the principal's country and the agent's country are at war with each other, the agency is terminated. In this situation, the agency is automatically suspended or terminated because there is no way to enforce the legal rights and obligations of the parties.

Reviewing . . . Agency Relationships in Business

Lynne Meyer, on her way to a business meeting and in a hurry, stopped by a Buy-Mart store for a new car charger for her smartphone. There was a long line at one of the checkout counters, but a cashier, Valerie Watts, opened another counter and began loading the cash drawer. Meyer told Watts that she was in a hurry and asked Watts to work faster. Watts, however, only slowed her pace. At this point, Meyer hit Watts.

It is not clear whether Meyer hit Watts intentionally or, in an attempt to retrieve the car charger, hit her inadvertently. In response, Watts grabbed Meyer by the hair and hit her repeatedly in the back of the head, while Meyer screamed for help. Management personnel separated the two women and questioned them about the incident. Watts was immediately fired for violating the store's no-fighting policy. Meyer subsequently sued Buy-Mart, alleging that the store was liable for the tort (assault and battery) committed by its employee. Using the information presented in the chapter, answer the following questions.

1. Under what doctrine discussed in this chapter might Buy-Mart be held liable for the tort committed by Watts?

2. What is the key factor in determining whether Buy-Mart is liable under this doctrine?

3. How is Buy-Mart's potential liability affected depending on whether Watts's behavior constituted an intentional tort or a tort of negligence?

4. Suppose that when Watts applied for the job at Buy-Mart, she disclosed in her application that she had previously been convicted of felony assault and battery. Nevertheless, Buy-Mart hired Watts as a cashier. How might this fact affect Buy-Mart's liability for Watts's actions?

DEBATE THIS

■ The doctrine of *respondeat superior* should be modified to make agents solely liable for some of their own tortious (wrongful) acts.

BUSINESS APPLICATION

How Can an Employer Use Independent Contractors?*

As an employer, you may at some time consider hiring an independent contractor. Hiring workers as independent contractors instead of as employees may help you reduce both your potential tort liability and your tax liability.

Minimizing Potential Tort Liability

Employers usually are not liable for torts that independent contractors commit against third parties. Nevertheless, there are exceptions. If an employer exercises significant control over the activities of the independent contractor, for example, the contractor may be considered an employee, and the employer can then be liable for the contractor's torts. The employer may also be liable when unusually hazardous activities are involved.

To minimize possible liability, you should check an independent contractor's qualifications and work experience before hiring him or her. How extensively you need to investigate depends on the nature of the work. Hiring an independent contractor to maintain the landscaping should require a relatively limited investigation. A more thorough investigation will be necessary when employing an independent contractor to install the electrical systems that you sell. You will want to make sure that the independent contractor has the necessary skills and experience to perform the installation work. Complete investigations should also be performed anytime the contractor's activities present a potential danger to the public (as in delivering explosives).

Generally, you should have a written contract with the independent contractor in which the contractor assumes liability for harms caused to third parties by the contractor's negligence. You should also require that the independent contractor purchase liability insurance to cover these costs.

Reducing Tax Liability and Other Costs

You do not need to pay or withhold Social Security, income, or unemployment taxes on an independent contractor's behalf. The independent contractor is responsible for paying these taxes. Additionally, an independent contractor is not eligible for any retirement or medical plans you provide to your employees, and this is a cost saving to you. Make sure that your contract with an independent contractor spells out that the contractor is responsible for paying taxes and is not entitled to any employment benefits.

A word of caution, though: simply designating a person as an independent contractor does not make that person an independent contractor. The Internal Revenue Service (IRS) will reclassify individuals as employees if it determines that they are in fact employees, regardless of how you have designated them. Keep proper documentation of such items as the independent contractor's business identification number, business cards, and business letterhead so that you can show the IRS that the contractor works independently.

If you improperly designate an employee as an independent contractor, the penalty may be high. Usually, you will be liable for back Social Security and unemployment taxes, plus interest and penalties. When in doubt, seek professional assistance in such matters.

CHECKLIST for the Employer:

1. Check the qualifications and work experience of any independent contractor you plan to use to reduce the possibility that you might be legally liable for the contractor's negligence.

2. Require in any contract with an independent contractor that the contractor assume liability for harm to a third person caused by the contractor's negligence.

3. Require that independent contractors carry liability insurance. Examine the policy to make sure that it is current, particularly when the contractor will be undertaking actions that are more than normally hazardous to the public.

4. Do not do anything that would lead a third person to believe that an independent contractor is your employee, and do not allow independent contractors to represent themselves as your employees.

5. Regularly inspect the work of the independent contractor to make sure that it is being performed in accordance with contract specifications. Such supervision on your part will not change the worker's status as an independent contractor.

---

* This *Business Application* is not meant to substitute for the services of an attorney who is licensed to practice law in your state.

Key Terms

agency 574
agency coupled with an interest 593
apparent authority 584
disclosed principal 587
equal dignity rule 583

fiduciary 575
independent contractor 575
notary public 584
partially disclosed principal 587
power of attorney 584

ratification 580
respondeat superior 590
undisclosed principal 587
vicarious liability 590

Chapter Summary: Agency Relationships in Business

Agency Relationships	In a *principal-agent* relationship, an agent acts on behalf of and instead of the principal in dealing with third parties. An employee who deals with third parties is normally an agent of the employer. An independent contractor is not an employee, because the employer has no control over the details of the independent contractor's physical performance. An independent contractor may or may not be an agent.
Formation of an Agency	Agency relationships may be formed by the following methods: 1. *Agreement*—The agency relationship is formed through express consent (oral or written) or implied by conduct. 2. *Ratification*—The principal either by act or by agreement ratifies the conduct of a person who is not in fact an agent. 3. *Estoppel*—The principal causes a third person to believe that another person is the principal's agent, and the third person deals with the agent. 4. *Operation of law*—The agency relationship is based on social policy (as in family relationships) or formed in emergency situations when the agent is unable to contact the principal and failure to act outside the scope of the agent's authority would cause the principal substantial loss.

Duties of Agents and Principals	1. *Duties of the agent*—
	  a. Performance—In performing her or his duties, the agent must use reasonable diligence and skill or use the special skills that the agent has claimed to possess.
	  b. Notification—The agent is required to notify the principal of all matters that come to his or her attention concerning the subject matter of the agency.
	  c. Loyalty—The agent has a duty to act solely for the benefit of the principal and not in the interest of the agent or a third party.
	  d. Obedience—The agent must follow all lawful and clearly stated instructions of the principal.
	  e. Accounting—The agent has a duty to make available to the principal records of all property and funds received and paid out on behalf of the principal.
	2. *Duties of the principal*—
	  a. Compensation—Except in a gratuitous agency relationship, the principal must pay the agreed-on value (or reasonable value) for the agent's services.
	  b. Reimbursement and indemnification—The principal must reimburse the agent for all funds disbursed at the request of the principal, as well as for funds disbursed for necessary expenses in the reasonable performance of agency duties.
	  c. Cooperation—A principal must cooperate with and assist an agent in performing her or his duties.
	  d. Safe working conditions—A principal must provide safe working conditions for agents and employees.

Agent's Authority	1. *Express authority*—Can be given orally or in writing. Authorization must be in writing if the agent is to execute a contract that must be in writing. 2. *Implied authority*—Authority deemed necessary for the agent to carry out expressly authorized tasks or authority customarily associated with the agent's position. 3. *Apparent authority*—Exists when the principal, by word or action, causes a third party to reasonably believe that an agent has authority to act, even though the agent has no express or implied authority. 4. *Ratification*—The affirmation by the principal of an agent's unauthorized action or promise. For the ratification to be effective, the principal must be aware of all material facts.

Continues

Liability in Agency Relationships	1. *Liability for contracts*—If the principal's identity is disclosed or partially disclosed at the time the agent forms a contract with a third party, the principal is liable to the third party under the contract if the agent acted within the scope of his or her authority. If the principal's identity is undisclosed at the time of contract formation, the agent is personally liable to the third party, but if the agent acted within the scope of his or her authority, the principal is also bound by the contract.
	2. *Liability for agent's negligence*—Under the doctrine of *respondeat superior,* the principal is liable for any harm caused to another through the agent's torts if the agent was acting within the scope of her or his employment at the time the harmful act occurred.
	3. *Liability for agent's intentional torts*—Usually, employers are not liable for the intentional torts that their agents commit, unless:
	a. The acts are committed within the scope of employment, and thus the doctrine of *respondeat superior* applies.
	b. The employer knows or should know that the employee has a propensity for committing tortious acts.
	c. The employer allowed the employee to engage in reckless acts that caused injury to another.
	4. *Liability for independent contractor's torts*—A principal is not liable for harm caused by an independent contractor's negligence, unless hazardous activities are involved or other exceptions apply.
	5. *Liability for agent's crimes*—An agent is responsible for his or her own crimes, even if the crimes were committed while the agent was acting within the scope of authority or employment. A principal will be liable for an agent's crime only if the principal participated by conspiracy or other action or (in some jurisdictions) if the agent violated certain government regulations in the course of employment.
Termination of an Agency	1. *By act of the parties* (see Exhibit 23–1)—
	a. Lapse of time.
	b. Purpose achieved.
	c. Occurrence of a specific event.
	d. Mutual agreement.
	e. Action of one party.
	Notice to third parties is required when an agency is terminated by act of the parties.
	2. *By operation of law*—
	a. Death or insanity.
	b. Impossibility.
	c. Changed circumstances.
	d. Bankruptcy.
	e. War.

Issue Spotters

1. Dimka Corporation wants to build a new mall on a specific tract of land. Dimka contracts with Nadine to act as its agent in buying the property. When Nadine learns of the difference between the price that Dimka is willing to pay and the price at which the owner is willing to sell, she wants to buy the land and sell it to Dimka herself. Can she do this? Discuss. (See *Duties of Agents and Principals*.)

2. Davis contracts with Estee to buy a certain horse on her behalf. Estee asks Davis not to reveal her identity. Davis makes a deal with Farmland Stables, the owner of the horse, and makes a down payment. Estee does not pay the rest of the price. Farmland Stables sues Davis for breach of contract. Can Davis hold Estee liable for whatever damages he has to pay? Why or why not? (See *Liability in Agency Relationships*.)

—**Check your answers to the *Issue Spotters* against the answers provided in Appendix D at the end of this text.**

Learning Objectives Check

1. What is the difference between an employee and an independent contractor?
2. How do agency relationships arise?
3. What duties do agents and principals owe to each other?
4. When is a principal liable for the agent's actions with respect to third parties? When is the agent liable?
5. What are some of the ways in which an agency relationship can be terminated?

—**Answers to the even-numbered *Learning Objectives Check* questions can be found in Appendix E at the end of this text.**

Business Scenarios and Case Problems

23–1. Ratification by Principal. Springer, who was running for Congress, instructed his campaign staff not to purchase any campaign materials without his explicit authorization. In spite of these instructions, one of his campaign workers contracted with Dubychek Printing Co. to print some promotional materials for Springer's campaign. When the printed materials arrived, Springer did not return them but instead used them during his campaign.

When Springer failed to pay for the materials, Dubychek sued for recovery of the price. Springer contended that he was not liable on the sales contract because he had not authorized his agent to purchase the printing services. Dubychek argued that the campaign worker was Springer's agent and that the worker had authority to make the printing contract. Additionally, Dubychek claimed that even if the purchase was unauthorized, Springer's use of the materials constituted ratification of his agent's unauthorized purchase. Is Dubychek correct? Explain. (See *Formation of an Agency.*)

23–2. Employee versus Independent Contractor. Stephen Hemmerling was a driver for the Happy Cab Co. Hemmerling paid certain fixed expenses and abided by a variety of rules relating to the use of the cab, the hours that could be worked, and the solicitation of fares, among other things. Rates were set by the state. Happy Cab did not withhold taxes from Hemmerling's pay. While driving the cab, Hemmerling was injured in an accident and filed a claim against Happy Cab in a Nebraska state court for workers' compensation benefits. Such benefits are not available to independent contractors. On what basis might the court hold that Hemmerling is an employee? Explain. (See *Agency Relationships.*)

23–3. Spotlight on Taser International—Loyalty. Taser International, Inc., develops and makes video and audio recording devices. Steve Ward was Taser's vice president of marketing when he began to explore the possibility of developing and marketing devices of his own design, including a clip-on camera. Ward talked to patent attorneys and a product development company and completed most of a business plan before he resigned from Taser. He then formed Vievu, LLC, to market the clip-on camera. Did Ward breach the duty of loyalty? Could he have taken any steps toward starting his own firm without breaching this duty? Discuss. [*Taser International, Inc. v. Ward,* 224 Ariz. 389, 231 P.3d 921 (Ariz. App. Div. 1 2010)] (See *Duties of Agents and Principals.*)

23–4. Liability for Contracts. Thomas Huskin and his wife entered into a contract to have their home remodeled by House Medic Handyman Service. Todd Hall signed the contract as an authorized representative of House Medic. It turned out that House Medic was a fictitious name for Hall Hauling, Ltd. The contract did not indicate this, however, and Hall did

not inform the Huskins about Hall Hauling. When a contract dispute later arose, the Huskins sued Todd Hall personally for breach of contract. Can Hall be held personally liable? Why or why not? [*Huskin v. Hall,* 2012 WL 553136 (Ohio Ct.App. 2012)] (See *Liability in Agency Relationships.*)

23–5. Agent's Authority. Basic Research, L.L.C., advertised its products on television networks owned by Rainbow Media Holdings, Inc., through an ad agency, Icebox Advertising, Inc. As Basic's agent, Icebox had the express authority to buy ads from Rainbow on Basic's behalf, but the authority was limited to buying ads with cash in advance. Despite this limit, Rainbow sold ads to Basic through Icebox on credit. Basic paid Icebox for the ads, but Icebox did not pass all of the payments on to Rainbow. Icebox filed for bankruptcy. Can Rainbow recoup the unpaid amounts from Basic? Explain. [*American Movie Classics v. Rainbow Media Holdings,* 2013 WL 323229 (10th Cir. 2013)] (See *Agent's Authority.*)

23–6. Agent's Duties to Principal. William and Maxine Miller, shareholders of Claimsco International, Inc., filed a suit in an Illinois state court against the other shareholders, Michael Harris and Kenneth Hoxie, as well as John Verchota, the accountant who worked for all of them. The Millers alleged that Verchota owed them a duty, which he breached by following Harris's instructions to adjust Claimsco's books to maximize the Millers' financial liabilities, falsely reflect income to them without actually transferring that income, and unfairly disadvantage them compared with the other shareholders. Which duty are the Millers referring to? If the allegations can be proved, did Verchota breach this duty? Explain. [*Miller v. Harris,* 2013 IL App (2d) 120512, 985 N.E. 2d 671 (2013)] (See *Duties of Agents and Principals.*)

23–7. Business Case Problem with Sample Answer—Determining Employee Status. Nelson Ovalles worked as a cable installer for Cox Rhode Island Telecom, LLC, under an agreement with a third party, M&M Communications, Inc. The agreement stated that no employer-employee relationship existed between Cox and M&M's technicians, including Ovalles. Ovalles was required to designate his affiliation with Cox on his work van, clothing, and identification badge, but Cox had minimal contact with him and limited power to control the manner in which he performed his duties. Cox supplied cable wire and similar items, but the equipment was delivered to M&M, not to Ovalles. On a workday, while Ovalles was fulfilling a work order, his van rear-ended a car driven by Barbara Cayer. Is Cox liable to Cayer? Explain. [*Cayer v. Cox Rhode Island Telecom, LLC,* 85 A.3d 1140 (R.I. 2014)] (See *Agency Relationships.*)

—For a sample answer to Problem 23–7, go to Appendix F at the end of this text.

23–8. Agent's Authority. Terry Holden's stepmother, Rosie, was diagnosed with amyotrophic lateral sclerosis (ALS), and Terry's wife, Susan, became Rosie's primary caregiver. Rosie executed a durable power of attorney appointing Susan as her agent. Susan opened a joint bank account with Rosie at Bank of America, depositing $9,643.62 of Rosie's funds. Susan used some of the money to pay for "household expenses to keep us going while we were taking care of her." Rosie died three months later. Terry's father, Charles, as executor of Rosie's estate, filed a petition in a Texas state court against Susan for an accounting. What general duty did Susan owe Rosie as her agent? What does an agent's duty of accounting require? Did Susan breach either of these duties? Explain. [*Holden v. Holden*, __ S.W.3d __, 2015 WL 551121 (Tex.App.—Tyler 2015)] (See *Agent's Authority*.)

23–9. A Question of Ethics—Vicarious Liability. Jamie Paliath worked as a real estate agent for Home Town Realty of Vandalia, LLC (the principal, a real estate broker). Torri Auer, a California resident, relied on Paliath's advice and assistance to buy three rental properties in Ohio. Before the sales, Paliath represented that each property was worth approximately twice as much as what Auer would pay and that there was a waiting list of prospective tenants. Paliath also stated that all of the property needed work and agreed to do the work for a specified price. Nearly a year later, substantial work was still needed, and only a few of the units had been rented. Auer sued Paliath and Home Town Realty for fraudulent misrepresentation. [*Auer v. Paliath*, 140 Ohio St.3d 276, 17 N.E. 3d 561, 2014-Ohio-3632 (2014)] (See *Liability in Agency Relationships*.)

1. Were Paliath's representations to Auer within the scope of her employment? Explain. Will the court hold the principal (Home Town Realty) liable for the misrepresentations of the agent (Paliath)?

2. What is the ethical basis for imposing vicarious liability on a principal for an agent's tort?

Critical Thinking and Writing Assignments

23–10. Critical Legal Thinking. What policy is served by the law that employers do not own the copyrights for works created by independent contractors (unless there is a written "work for hire" agreement)? (See *Agency Relationships*.)

23–11. Business Law Critical Thinking Group Assignment. Dean Brothers Corp. owns and operates a steel-drum manufacturing plant. Lowell Wyden, the plant superintendent, hired Best Security Patrol, Inc. (BSP), a security company, to guard the property and "deter thieves and vandals." Some BSP security guards, as Wyden knew, carried firearms. Pete Sidell, a BSP security guard, was not certified as an armed guard but nevertheless took his gun to work. While working at the Dean plant on October 31, 2014, Sidell fired his gun at Tyrone Gaines, in the belief that Gaines was an intruder. The bullet struck and killed Gaines. Gaines's mother filed a lawsuit claiming that her son's death was the result of BSP's negligence, for which Dean was responsible. (See *Liability in Agency Relationships*.)

1. The first group will determine what the plaintiff's best argument is to establish that Dean is responsible for BSP's actions.

2. The second group will discuss Dean's best defense and formulate arguments in support of it.

24

CHAPTER OUTLINE

- Employment at Will
- Wages, Hours, Layoffs, and Leave
- Health, Safety, and Income Security
- Employee Privacy Rights
- Immigration Law
- Labor Unions

Employment, Immigration, and Labor Law

LEARNING OBJECTIVES

The five Learning Objectives *below are designed to help improve your understanding of the chapter. After reading this chapter, you should be able to answer the following questions:*

1. What is the employment-at-will doctrine?

2. What federal statute governs working hours and wages?

3. Under the Family and Medical Leave Act, in what circumstances may an employee take family or medical leave?

4. What are the two most important federal statutes governing immigration and employment today?

5. What federal statute gave employees the right to organize unions and engage in collective bargaining?

"The employer generally gets the employees he deserves."

SIR WALTER GILBEY
1831–1914
(ENGLISH MERCHANT)

Until the early 1900s, most employer-employee relationships were governed by the common law. Even today, private employers have considerable freedom to hire and fire workers under the common law. (This is one reason that employers generally get the employees they deserve, as the chapter-opening quotation observed.)

Numerous statutes and administrative agency regulations now govern the workplace, however. Thus, to a large extent, statutory law has displaced common law doctrines. In this chapter and the next, we look at the most significant laws regulating employment relationships. We also examine immigration law—a topic of special importance to employers in our diverse society—and labor law.

Note that the distinction made under agency law between employee status and independent-contractor status is important here. The employment laws that will be discussed apply only to the employer-employee relationship. They do not apply to independent contractors.

24-1 Employment at Will

Employment relationships have traditionally been governed by the common law doctrine of **employment at will.** Under this doctrine, either party may terminate the employment

Employment at Will A common law doctrine under which either party may terminate an employment relationship at any time for any reason, unless a contract specifies otherwise.

LEARNING OBJECTIVE **1**
What is the employment-at-will doctrine?

relationship at any time and for any reason, unless doing so would violate an employee's statutory or contractual rights.

Today, the majority of U.S. workers continue to have the legal status of "employees at will." In other words, this common law doctrine is still in widespread use. Only one state (Montana) does not apply it. Nonetheless, federal and state statutes governing employment relationships prevent the doctrine from being applied in a number of circumstances. An employer may not fire an employee if doing so would violate a federal or state statute, such as one prohibiting employment discrimination. The courts have also created several exceptions, discussed next.

24–1a Exceptions to the Employment-at-Will Doctrine

Because of the sometimes harsh effects of the employment-at-will doctrine for employees, the courts have carved out various exceptions to it. These exceptions are based on contract theory, tort theory, and public policy.

Exceptions Based on Contract Theory Some courts have held that an *implied* employment contract exists between an employer and an employee. If an employee is fired outside the terms of the implied contract, he or she may succeed in an action for breach of contract even though no written employment contract exists. **EXAMPLE 24.1** BDI Enterprise's employment manual and personnel bulletin both state that, as a matter of policy, workers will be dismissed only for good cause. If an employee reasonably expects BDI to follow this policy, a court may find that there is an implied contract based on the terms stated in the manual and bulletin. ■ Generally, the employee's reasonable expectations are the key to whether an employment manual creates an implied contractual obligation.

An employer's oral promises to employees regarding discharge policy may also be considered part of an implied contract. If the employer fires a worker in a manner contrary to what was promised, a court may hold that the employer has violated the implied contract and is liable for damages. Most state courts will judge a claim of breach of an implied employment contract by traditional contract standards.

Exceptions Based on Tort Theory In a few situations, the discharge of an employee may give rise to an action for wrongful discharge under tort theories. Abusive discharge procedures may result in a suit for intentional infliction of emotional distress or defamation.

In addition, some courts have permitted workers to sue their employers under the tort theory of fraud. **EXAMPLE 24.2** Goldfinch, Inc., induces Jarvis to leave a lucrative job and move to another state by offering "a long-term job with a thriving business." In fact, Goldfinch not only is having significant financial problems but also is planning a merger that will result in the elimination of the position offered to Jarvis. If Jarvis takes the job in reliance on Goldfinch's representations and is fired shortly thereafter, she may be able to bring an action against the employer for fraud. ■

Exceptions Based on Public Policy The most common exception to the employment-at-will doctrine is made on the basis that the worker was fired for reasons that violate a fundamental public policy of the jurisdiction. Generally, the public policy involved must be expressed clearly in the jurisdiction's statutory law.

KNOW THIS
An implied contract may exist if a party furnishes a service expecting to be paid, and the other party, who knows (or should know) of this expectation, has a chance to reject the service and does not.

The public-policy exception may also apply to an employee who is discharged for **whistleblowing**—that is, telling government authorities, upper-level managers, or the media that her or his employer is engaged in some unsafe or illegal activity. Normally, however, whistleblowers seek protection from retaliatory discharge under federal and state statutory laws, such as the Whistleblower Protection Act of 1989.[1]

CASE EXAMPLE 24.3 Donald Waddell got a job at the Boyce Thompson Institute for Plant Research. Waddell did not have an employment contract for a fixed term, and the institute's

Whistleblowing
An employee's disclosure to government authorities, upper-level managers, or the media that the employer is engaged in unsafe or illegal activities.

---

1. 5 U.S.C. Section 1201.

employee manual said that his job was "terminable at will." Soon after he was hired, the institute implemented a whistleblower policy designed to encourage "the highest standards of financial reporting and lawful and ethical behavior." Waddell repeatedly told his supervisor, Sophia Darling, that she needed to file certain financial documents more promptly. Darling fired Waddell, telling him that he was disrespectful and insubordinate.

Waddell then sued the institute, contending that he should not have been fired because he was acting under the company's whistleblowing policy. A New York appellate court, however, found that Waddell was not protected under the whistleblower policy because it was implemented after his employment. Moreover, Waddell failed to allege that he passed up other job opportunities based on the policy. Because Waddell was employed at will and did not rely on the whistleblower policy, he could be fired.[2] ■

Can an at-will employee who was fired for criticizing his supervisor claim he was protected by a whistleblower policy adopted after he was hired?

24-1b Wrongful Discharge

Whenever an employer discharges an employee in violation of an employment contract or a statute protecting employees, the employee may bring an action for **wrongful discharge.** Even if an employer's actions do not violate any provisions in an employment contract or a statute, the employer may still be subject to liability under a common law doctrine, such as a tort theory or agency.

Note that an employment contract may be established or modified via e-mail exchanges. **CASE EXAMPLE 24.4** Robert Moroni negotiated a deal to provide consulting services for Medco Health Solutions, Inc., a third party administrator of prescription-drug plans. Medco's agent, Brian Griffin, sent Moroni an e-mail setting forth the details of the parties' agreement.

Moroni e-mailed a counteroffer suggesting that he would work on Medco's projects two days a week for thirteen months, in exchange for $17,000 a month plus travel expenses. Medco accepted via e-mail, and Moroni began performing the contract, but Medco refused to pay him. Moroni sued for breach of contract. Medco argued that no enforceable contract existed and that the e-mail showed only an agreement to agree. The court, however, ruled that the e-mail amounted to an agreement to the essential terms of an employment contract.[3] ■

Wrongful Discharge
An employer's termination of an employee's employment in violation of the law or an employment contract.

24-2 Wages, Hours, Layoffs, and Leave

In the 1930s, Congress enacted several laws regulating the wages and working hours of employees.

1. The Davis-Bacon Act[4] requires contractors and subcontractors working on federal government construction projects to pay "prevailing wages" to their employees.

2. The Walsh-Healey Act[5] applies to U.S. government contracts. It requires that a minimum wage, as well as overtime pay at 1.5 times regular pay rates, be paid to employees of manufacturers or suppliers entering into contracts with agencies of the federal government.

3. The Fair Labor Standards Act (FLSA)[6] extended wage-hour requirements to cover all employers engaged in interstate commerce or in producing goods for interstate commerce, plus selected other types of businesses. The FLSA, as amended, provides the most comprehensive federal regulation of wages and hours today.

LEARNING OBJECTIVE 2
What federal statute governs working hours and wages?

KNOW THIS
In today's business world, an employment contract may be established or modified via e-mail exchanges.

---

2. *Waddell v. Boyce Thompson Institute for Plant Research, Inc.,* 940 N.Y.S.2d 331 (2012).
3. *Moroni v. Medco Health Solutions, Inc.,* 2008 WL 3539476 (E.D.Mich. 2008).
4. 40 U.S.C. Sections 276a–276a-5.
5. 41 U.S.C. Sections 35–45.
6. 29 U.S.C. Sections 201–260.

Additional laws were passed in later years. In 1988, Congress passed the Worker Adjustment and Retraining Notification (WARN) Act to give workers advance notice of layoffs. In 1993, Congress passed the Family and Medical Leave Act (FMLA)[7] to give employees a right to take time off work for family or medical reasons.

Should there be special employment laws to cover so-called dependent contractors? Workers in the United States generally fall into two categories: employees and independent contractors. Employees are covered by the full range of employment laws, including minimum wage and antidiscrimination statutes. In contrast, most independent contractors are not covered by the main employment laws. Enter the digital age of on-demand workers who obtain job assignments via apps—for example, cleaning service workers who work through Handy and transportation service providers who work through Uber and Lyft. These companies provide workers on demand to online customers. The service providers who get work through the companies are not employees but independent contractors.

Workers for Lyft, Uber, and Handy choose when and where they will perform their duties. They do not choose how much they will be paid, though. For them, employment is a take-it-or-leave-it proposition. If they want to drive for Lyft, or clean offices for Handy, they electronically accept the platform terms, or they obtain no work assignments. Is this fair?

Not everyone thinks so. Some legal scholars believe that there should be a new category of workers with "dependent-contractor" status who receive some of the protections traditionally given only to employees. Some aspects of current labor law would be attached to the relationships between dependent contractors and their employers, including overtime eligibility under the FLSA and minimum wage laws. In 2015, two judges allowed separate lawsuits to go before juries in San Francisco over the question of whether on-demand drivers should be considered employees rather than independent contractors.[8]

Can children under the age of fourteen legally deliver newspapers?

24–2a Child Labor

The FLSA prohibits oppressive child labor. Children under fourteen years of age are allowed to do certain types of work, such as deliver newspapers, work for their parents, and be employed in entertainment and (with some exceptions) agriculture. Children aged fourteen and fifteen are allowed to work, but not in hazardous occupations. There are also numerous restrictions on how many hours per day and per week children can work.

Working times and hours are not restricted for persons between the ages of sixteen and eighteen, but they cannot be employed in hazardous jobs or in jobs detrimental to their health and well-being. None of these restrictions apply to individuals over the age of eighteen.

24–2b Minimum Wage Requirement

Minimum Wage The lowest wage, either by government regulation or union contract, that an employer may pay an hourly worker.

The FLSA provides that a **minimum wage** (now $7.25 per hour) must be paid to employees in covered industries. Congress periodically revises this minimum wage. Additionally, many states (and some cities) have minimum wages. When the state (or city) minimum wage is greater than the federal minimum wage, the employee is entitled to the higher wage. If an employee who receives tips is also paid at least the federal minimum wage, the FLSA allows employers to take the employee's tips and redistribute them among other employees.

---

7. 29 U.S.C. Sections 2601, 2611–2619, 2651–2654.
8. *Cotter v. Lyft, Inc.,* Case No. 13-CV-04065-VC (N.D.Cal. 2015); *O'Connor v. Uber Technologies, Inc., et al.,* Case No. C-13-3826 EMC (N.D.Cal. 2015).

24–2c Overtime Exemptions

Under the FLSA, employees who work more than forty hours per week normally must be paid 1.5 times their regular pay for all hours over forty. Note that the FLSA overtime provisions apply only after an employee has worked more than forty hours per *week*. Thus, employees who work for ten hours a day, four days per week, are not entitled to overtime pay, because they do not work more than forty hours per week.

Certain employees—usually executive, administrative, and professional employees, as well as outside salespersons and computer programmers—are exempt from the FLSA's overtime provisions. Executive and administrative employees are those whose primary duty is management and who exercise discretion and independent judgment.

Employers are not required to pay overtime wages to exempt employees. Employers can voluntarily pay overtime to ineligible employees but cannot waive or reduce the overtime requirements of the FLSA. (Smartphones and similar technologies have raised new issues concerning overtime wages, as discussed in this chapter's *Beyond Our Borders* feature.)

An employee's underreporting of hours worked can undercut his or her claim for overtime. But can an employee's underreporting *support* such a claim? That question was at the center of the following case.

> "By working faithfully eight hours a day, you may eventually get to be a boss and work twelve hours a day."
>
> **ROBERT FROST**
> 1875–1963
> (AMERICAN POET)

CASE 24.1

Bailey v. TitleMax of Georgia, Inc.

United States Court of Appeals, Eleventh Circuit, 776 F.3d 797 (2015).

FACTS Santonias Bailey was an employee of TitleMax of Georgia, Inc., in Jonesboro, Georgia. Bailey's supervisor told him that TitleMax did not pay overtime, so he regularly worked off the clock. For example, on some Saturdays, he would work from 8:30 A.M. to 5:30 P.M., but—as ordered by his supervisor—would log only seven hours despite having worked nine. His supervisor also edited Bailey's time records to report fewer hours than he actually worked by, for example, subtracting a one-hour lunch break when there had been none.

What might happen if a supervisor changes an employee's time records to avoid paying him overtime?

Bailey resigned from TitleMax and filed a suit in a federal district court against the employer to recover for the unpaid overtime under the Fair Labor Standards Act (FLSA). TitleMax argued that Bailey was responsible for the unpaid time. According to TitleMax, he never complained about his supervisor, and he violated company policy with respect to keeping accurate time records. The court issued a judgment in the defendant's favor. Bailey appealed.

ISSUE Is an employer who knows or has reason to know that its employee underreported his or her hours liable under the FLSA for the unpaid overtime?

DECISION Yes. The U.S. Court of Appeals for the Eleventh Circuit reversed the judgment of the lower court and remanded the case for further proceedings.

REASON If an employee works overtime without pay, he or she can bring an action against the employer for damages. This claim has two elements: the employee worked overtime for which he or she was not paid, and the employer knew or should have known it. Knowledge of the situation can be imputed to an employer when its supervisor is aware of it. In this case, Bailey showed both elements. He worked overtime without pay, and TitleMax knew or should have known it—Bailey's supervisor told him to underreport his hours, and the supervisor edited Bailey's time records. TitleMax contended that it should not be held liable because Bailey did the underreporting himself. But TitleMax could not cite a single case in which a federal appellate court had allowed such a defense in similar circumstances. "The dearth [scarcity] of precedent supporting TitleMax's . . . argument is persuasive, if not conclusive, evidence that its argument is misguided."

CRITICAL THINKING—Legal Consideration *Congress enacted the FLSA in 1938. More than eight thousand FLSA suits are filed in federal district courts each year. How do these facts support the court's reasoning in this case?*

Brazil Requires Employers to Pay Overtime for Use of Smartphones after Work Hours

Workers in the United States are increasingly arguing that they should receive overtime pay for the time they spend staying connected to work through their iPads, smartphones, or other electronic devices. Indeed, many employers require their employees to carry a mobile device to keep in contact.

Checking e-mail, responding to text messages, tweeting, and using LinkedIn or other employment-related apps can be considered work. If employees who are not exempt under the overtime regulations are required to use mobile devices after office hours, the workers may have a valid claim to overtime wages. The FLSA is not clear about what constitutes work, however, so workers have difficulty showing they are entitled to overtime wages.

In Brazil, though, workers who answer work e-mails on their smartphones or other electronic devices after work are entitled to receive overtime wages. Under legislation enacted in 2012 and approved by President Dilma Rousseff, e-mail from an employer is considered the equivalent of orders given directly to an employee, so it constitutes work. A few other nations also require payment to workers for staying connected through smartphones and other devices after hours.

CRITICAL THINKING

■ What are the pros and cons of paying overtime wages to workers who check e-mail and perform other work-related tasks electronically after hours?

24–2d **Layoffs**

During the latest economic recession in the United States, hundreds of thousands of workers lost their jobs as many businesses disappeared. Other companies struggling to keep afloat reduced costs by restructuring their operations and downsizing their workforces, which meant layoffs.

The Worker Adjustment and Retraining Notification Act,[9] or WARN Act, requires large employers to provide sixty days' notice before implementing a mass layoff or closing a plant that employs more than fifty full-time workers. A mass layoff is a layoff of at least one-third of the full-time employees at a particular job site. The act applies to employers with at least one hundred full-time employees.

The WARN Act is intended to give workers advance notice so that they can start looking for new jobs while they are still employed and to alert state agencies so that they can provide training and other resources for displaced workers. Employers thus must provide advance notice of the layoff both to the affected workers (or to their representative, if the workers are members of a labor union) and to state and local government authorities. Even companies that anticipate filing for bankruptcy normally must provide notice under the WARN Act.

Many states also have statutes requiring employers to provide notice before initiating mass layoffs. These laws may have different and even stricter requirements than the WARN Act.

24–2e **Family and Medical Leave**

LEARNING OBJECTIVE 3

Under the Family and Medical Leave Act, in what circumstances may an employee take family or medical leave?

The Family and Medical Leave Act (FMLA)[10] allows employees to take time off from work for family or medical reasons. Additional categories of FMLA leave have been created for military caregivers and for qualifying emergencies that arise due to military service. A majority of the states have similar legislation. In addition, many employers voluntarily offer paid family-leave plans for their workers.

---

9. 29 U.S.C. Sections 2101 *et seq.*
10. 29 U.S.C. Sections 2601, 2611–2619, 2651–2654.

Coverage and Applicability   The FMLA requires employers who have fifty or more employees to provide employees with up to twelve weeks of unpaid family or medical leave during any twelve-month period. The FMLA expressly covers private and public (government) employees who have worked for their employers for at least a year.

An eligible employee may take up to *twelve weeks of leave* within a twelve-month period for any of the following reasons:

1. To care for a newborn baby within one year of birth.

2. To care for an adopted or foster child within one year of the time the child is placed with the employee.

3. To care for the employee's spouse, child, or parent who has a serious health condition.

4. If the employee suffers from a serious health condition and is unable to perform the essential functions of her or his job.

5. For any qualifying exigency (nonmedical emergency) arising out of the fact that the employee's spouse, son, daughter, or parent is a covered military member on active duty.[11] For instance, an employee can take leave to arrange for child care or to deal with financial or legal matters when a spouse is being deployed overseas.

In addition, an employee may take up to *twenty-six weeks of military caregiver leave* within a twelve-month period to care for a family member with a serious injury or illness incurred as a result of military duty.[12]

In the following case, an employee asked for medical leave to care for her mother on a trip to Las Vegas, Nevada.

Under what circumstances can this wife take family leave to care for her sick husband?

---

11. 29 C.F.R. Section 825.126.
12. 29 C.F.R. Section 825.200.

CASE 24.2

Ballard v. Chicago Park District

United States Court of Appeals, Seventh Circuit, 741 F.3d 838 (2014).

FACTS Beverly Ballard worked for the Chicago Park District. She lived with her mother, Sarah, who suffered from end-stage congestive heart failure. Beverly served as Sarah's primary caregiver with support from Horizon Hospice & Palliative Care. The hospice helped Sarah plan and secure funds for an end-of-life goal, a "family trip" to Las Vegas. To accompany Sarah as her caretaker, Beverly asked the Park District for unpaid time off under the Family Medical and Leave Act (FMLA). The employer refused, but Beverly and Sarah took the trip as planned.

Later, the Park District terminated Beverly for "unauthorized absences." She filed a suit in a federal district court against the employer. The court issued a decision in Beverly's favor. The Park District appealed, arguing that Beverly had been absent from work on a "recreational trip."

Under what circumstances does a trip to Las Vegas with an ailing mother qualify for unpaid time off under the FMLA?

ISSUE Does the FMLA protect an employee who takes leave from work to care for a seriously ill family member during a trip?

DECISION Yes. The U.S. Court of Appeals for the Seventh Circuit affirmed the lower court's judgment.

REASON Under the FMLA, an eligible employee is entitled to take leave from work to care for a family member with a serious health condition. The existence of a serious health condition is the only limitation imposed on the care—it is not restricted to a particular place, such as "at home." Sarah's medical, hygienic, and nutritional needs did not change when she was in Las Vegas, and Beverly continued to care for her mother's needs during the trip. The location—Las Vegas,

Continues

as opposed to Chicago—was not relevant to the legitimacy of the request.

The Park District argued that Beverly had requested leave in order to take a "pleasure trip." But the court pointed out that "any worries about opportunistic leave-taking" should be eased by the fact that the request arose out of hospice and palliative (treating symptoms only) care. In addition, for further assurance, the employer could have asked that a health-care provider certify the request.

WHAT IF THE FACTS WERE DIFFERENT? *Suppose that Beverly had requested leave to make arrangements for a change in Sarah's care, such as a transfer to a nursing home. Is it likely that the result would have been different? Explain.*

Benefits and Protections When an employee takes FMLA leave, the employer must continue the worker's health-care coverage on the same terms as if the employee had continued to work. On returning from FMLA leave, most employees must be restored to their original position or to a comparable position (with nearly equivalent pay and benefits, for example). An important exception allows the employer to avoid reinstating a *key employee*—defined as an employee whose pay falls within the top 10 percent of the firm's workforce.

Violations An employer that violates the FMLA can be required to provide various remedies, including the following:

1. Damages to compensate an employee for lost benefits, denied compensation, and actual monetary losses (such as the cost of providing for care of the family member) up to an amount equivalent to the employee's wages for twelve weeks (twenty-six weeks for military caregiver leave).

2. Job reinstatement.

3. Promotion, if a promotion has been denied.

In addition, a successful plaintiff is entitled to court costs and attorneys' fees, and, in cases involving bad faith on the part of the employer, two times the amount of damages awarded by a judge or jury. Supervisors can also be held personally liable, as employers, for violations of the act.

Employers generally are required to notify employees when an absence will be counted against leave authorized under the act. If an employer fails to provide such notice, and the employee consequently suffers an injury because he or she did not receive notice, the employer may be sanctioned.

24-3 Health, Safety, and Income Security

Under the common law, employees who were injured on the job had to file lawsuits against their employers to obtain recovery. Today, numerous state and federal statutes protect employees and their families from the risk of accidental injury, death, or disease resulting from employment. In addition, the government protects employees' income through Social Security, Medicare, unemployment insurance, and the regulation of pensions and health insurance plans.

24-3a The Occupational Safety and Health Act

At the federal level, the primary legislation protecting employees' health and safety is the Occupational Safety and Health Act,[13] which is administered by the Occupational Safety and

---

13. 29 U.S.C. Sections 553, 651–678.

Health Administration (OSHA). The act imposes on employers a general duty to keep workplaces safe.

To this end, OSHA has established specific safety standards for various industries that employers must follow. For instance, OSHA regulations require the use of safety guards on certain mechanical equipment and set maximum levels of exposure to substances in the workplace that may be harmful to a worker's health.

Notices, Records, and Reports The act requires that employers post certain notices in the workplace, perform prescribed record keeping, and submit specific reports. For instance, employers with eleven or more employees are required to keep occupational injury and illness records for each employee. Each record must be made available for inspection when requested by an OSHA compliance officer.

Whenever a work-related injury or disease occurs, employers must report directly to OSHA. If an employee dies or three or more employees are hospitalized because of a work-related incident, the employer must notify OSHA within eight hours. A company that fails to do so will be fined and may also be prosecuted under state law. Following the incident, a complete inspection of the premises is mandatory.

Inspections and Employee Complaints OSHA compliance officers may enter and inspect facilities of any establishment covered by the Occupational Safety and Health Act. Employees may also file complaints of violations and cannot be fired by their employers for doing so. Under the act, an employer cannot discharge an employee who files a complaint or who, in good faith, refuses to work in a high-risk area if bodily harm or death might result.

24-3b State Workers' Compensation Laws

State **workers' compensation laws** establish an administrative procedure for compensating workers injured on the job. Instead of suing, an injured worker files a claim with the administrative agency or board that administers local workers' compensation claims.

Most workers' compensation statutes are similar. No state covers all employees. Typically, domestic workers, agricultural workers, temporary employees, and employees of common carriers (companies that provide transportation services to the public) are excluded, but minors are covered. Usually, the statutes allow employers to purchase insurance from a private insurer or a state fund to pay workers' compensation benefits in the event of a claim. Most states also allow employers to be *self-insured*—that is, employers that show an ability to pay claims do not need to buy insurance.

Requirements for Receiving Workers' Compensation In general, only two requirements must be met for an employee to receive benefits under a state workers' compensation law:

1. The existence of an employment relationship.

2. An *accidental* injury that *occurred on the job or in the course of employment,* regardless of fault. (An injury that occurs while an employee is commuting to or from work usually is not considered to have occurred on the job or in the course of employment and hence is not covered.)

An injured employee must notify her or his employer promptly (usually within thirty days of the accident). Generally, an employee must also file a workers' compensation claim with the appropriate state agency or board within a certain period (sixty days to two years) from the time the injury is first noticed, rather than from the time of the accident.

Workers' Compensation versus Litigation An employee's acceptance of workers' compensation benefits bars the employee from suing for injuries caused by the employer's negligence. By barring lawsuits for negligence, workers' compensation laws also prevent employers from

Workers' Compensation Laws State statutes that establish an administrative process for compensating workers for injuries that arise in the course of their employment, regardless of fault.

raising common law defenses to negligence, such as contributory negligence and assumption of risk. A worker may sue an employer who has *intentionally* injured the worker, however.

24–3c Income Security

Federal and state governments participate in insurance programs designed to protect employees and their families by covering the financial impact of retirement, disability, death, hospitalization, and unemployment. The key federal law on this subject is the Social Security Act.[14]

Social Security The Social Security Act provides for old-age (retirement), survivors', and disability insurance. Hence, the act is often referred to as OASDI. Both employers and employees must "contribute" under the Federal Insurance Contributions Act (FICA)[15] to help pay for Social Security retirement benefits. Retired workers are then eligible to receive monthly payments from the Social Security Administration, which administers the Social Security Act. Social Security benefits are fixed by statute but increase automatically with increases in the cost of living.

What types of information can you find on the Social Security Administration's Web site?

www.ssa.gov

Medicare Medicare is a federal government health-insurance program that is administered by the Social Security Administration for people sixty-five years of age and older and for some under the age of sixty-five who are disabled. Medicare originally had two parts, one pertaining to hospital costs and the other to nonhospital medical costs, such as visits to physicians' offices. It now offers additional coverage options and a prescription-drug plan. People who have Medicare hospital insurance can also obtain additional federal medical insurance by paying small monthly premiums, which increase as the cost of medical care increases.

Tax Contributions As mentioned, under FICA, both employers and employees contribute to Social Security. This is also true for Medicare, although the contributions are determined differently. The employer withholds the employee's FICA contributions from the employee's wages and ordinarily matches the contributions.

For Social Security, the basis for the contributions is the employee's annual wage base—the maximum amount of the employee's wages that is subject to the tax. As of 2015, the maximum amount subject to the tax was $118,500, and the tax rate was 12.4 percent.

The Medicare tax rate is 2.9 percent. Unlike Social Security, Medicare has no cap on the amount of wages subject to the tax. So even if an employee's salary is well above the cap for Social Security, he or she will still owe Medicare tax on the total earned income.

For Social Security and Medicare together, typically the employer and the employee each pay 7.65 percent—6.2 percent (half of 12.4 percent) for Social Security plus 1.45 percent (half of 2.9 percent) for Medicare—up to the maximum wage base. Any earned income above that threshold is taxed at 2.9 percent for Medicare. Self-employed persons pay both the employer's and the employee's portions of the Social Security and Medicare taxes.

Under the Affordable Care Act, starting in 2015, high-income earners have been subject to an additional Medicare tax of 0.9 percent (for a total rate of 3.8 percent). This additional tax applies to wages earned above $200,000 for single earners and wages above $250,000 for married couples.

Private Retirement Plans The major federal act regulating employee retirement plans is the Employee Retirement Income Security Act (ERISA).[16] This act empowers a branch of the U.S.

---

14. 42 U.S.C. Sections 301–1397e.
15. 26 U.S.C. Sections 3101–3125.
16. 29 U.S.C. Sections 1001 *et seq.*

Department of Labor to enforce its provisions governing employers that have private pension funds for their employees. ERISA does not require an employer to establish a pension plan. When a plan exists, however, ERISA specifies standards for its management, including establishing rules on how funds must be invested and records kept.

ERISA created the Pension Benefit Guaranty Corporation (PBGC), an independent federal agency, to provide timely and uninterrupted payment of voluntary private pension benefits. The pension plans pay annual insurance premiums (at set rates adjusted for inflation) to the PBGC, which then pays benefits to participants in the event that a plan is unable to do so.

A key provision of ERISA concerns vesting. **Vesting** gives an employee a legal right to receive pension benefits at some future date when he or she stops working. Before ERISA was enacted, some employees who had worked for companies for as long as thirty years received no pension benefits when their employment terminated because those benefits had not vested. Under ERISA, generally all employee contributions to pension plans vest immediately, and employee rights to employer contributions to a plan vest after five years of employment.

Vesting The creation of an absolute or unconditional right or power.

Unemployment Insurance

The Federal Unemployment Tax Act (FUTA)[17] created a state-administered system that provides unemployment compensation to eligible individuals. Under this system, employers pay into a fund, and the proceeds are paid out to qualified unemployed workers. The FUTA and state laws require employers that fall under the provisions of the act to pay unemployment taxes at regular intervals. The proceeds from these taxes are then paid out to qualified unemployed workers.

To be eligible for unemployment compensation, a worker must be willing and able to work. Workers who have been fired for misconduct or who have voluntarily left their jobs are not eligible for benefits. Normally, workers must be actively seeking employment to continue receiving benefits.

EXAMPLE 24.5 Martha works for Baily Snowboards in Vermont. One day at work, Martha receives a text from her son saying that he has been taken to the hospital. Martha rushes to the hospital and does not return to work for several days. Bailey hires someone else for Martha's position, and Martha files for unemployment benefits. Martha's claim will be denied because she left her job voluntarily and made no effort to maintain contact with her employer. ∎

COBRA

The Consolidated Omnibus Budget Reconciliation Act (COBRA)[18] enables workers to continue, for a limited time, their health-care coverage after they are no longer eligible for their employers' group health-insurance plans. The workers—not the employers—pay the premiums for the continued coverage.

COBRA prohibits an employer from eliminating a worker's medical, optical, or dental insurance when the worker's employment is terminated or when a reduction in the worker's hours would affect coverage. Termination of employment may be voluntary or involuntary. Only workers fired for gross misconduct are excluded from protection.

Employers, with some exceptions, must inform an employee of COBRA's provisions when the employee faces termination or a reduction of hours that would affect his or her eligibility for coverage under the employer's health-insurance plan. An employer that does not comply with COBRA risks substantial penalties, such as a tax of up to 10 percent of the annual cost of the group plan or $500,000, whichever is less.

Employer-Sponsored Group Health Plans

The Health Insurance Portability and Accountability Act (HIPAA)[19] contains provisions that affect employer-sponsored group health plans. HIPAA does not require employers to provide health insurance, but it does establish

KNOW THIS
If an employer does not pay unemployment taxes, a state government can place a lien (claim) on the business's property to secure the debt.

---

17. 26 U.S.C. Sections 3301–3310.
18. 29 U.S.C. Sections 1161–1169.
19. 29 U.S.C.A. Sections 1181 *et seq.*

requirements for those that do. For instance, HIPAA strictly limits an employer's ability to exclude coverage for preexisting conditions.

In addition, HIPAA restricts the manner in which covered employers collect, use, and disclose the health information of employees and their families. Employers must designate privacy officials, distribute privacy notices, and train employees to ensure that employees' health information is not disclosed to unauthorized parties.

Failure to comply with HIPAA regulations can result in civil penalties of up to $100 per person per violation (with a cap of $25,000 per year). The employer is also subject to criminal prosecution for certain types of HIPAA violations and can face up to $250,000 in criminal fines and imprisonment for up to ten years if convicted.

Affordable Care Act   The Affordable Care Act[20] (ACA, commonly referred to as Obamacare) requires most employers with fifty or more full-time employees to offer health-insurance benefits. Under the act, any business offering health benefits to its employees, even if it is not legally required to do so, may be eligible for tax credits of up to 35 percent to offset the costs.

An employer who fails to provide health benefits as required under the statute can be fined up to $2,000 for each employee after the first thirty. (This is known as the 50/30 rule—employers with fifty employees must provide insurance, and those failing to do so will be fined for each employee after the first thirty.) An employer who offers a plan that costs an employee more than 9.5 percent of the employee's income may have to pay a penalty of $3,000 per insured worker.

Employers will be fined for failing to provide benefits only if one of their employees receives a federal subsidy to buy health insurance through a state health-insurance exchange. The act established state exchanges to provide a marketplace for business owners and individuals to compare premiums and purchase policies.

24-4 Employee Privacy Rights

Concerns about the privacy rights of employees have arisen in response to the sometimes invasive tactics used by employers to monitor and screen workers. Perhaps the greatest privacy concern in today's employment arena has to do with electronic monitoring.

24-4a Electronic Monitoring

More than half of employers engage in some form of surveillance of their employees. Many employers review employees' e-mail, as well as their social media posts and other Internet messages. Employers may also make video recordings of their employees at work, monitor their telephone conversations, and listen to their voice mail.

Can employees refuse to be video monitored?

iStockPhoto.com/dlewis33

Employee Privacy Protection   Employees of private (nongovernment) employers have some privacy protection under tort law and state constitutions. In addition, state and federal statutes may limit an employer's conduct in certain respects. For instance, the Electronic Communications Privacy Act prohibits employers from intercepting an employee's personal electronic communications unless they are made on devices and systems furnished by the employer.

Nonetheless, employers do have considerable leeway to monitor employees in the workplace. In addition, private employers generally are free to use filtering software to block access to certain Web sites, such as sites containing sexually explicit images. The First Amendment's

---

20. Pub. L. No. 111-148, 124 Stat. 119, March 23, 2010, codified in various sections of 42 U.S.C.

protection of free speech prevents only *government employers* from restraining speech by blocking Web sites.

Reasonable Expectation of Privacy When determining whether an employer should be held liable for violating an employee's privacy rights, the courts generally weigh the employer's interests against the employee's reasonable expectation of privacy.

Normally, if employees have been informed that their communications are being monitored, they cannot reasonably expect those interactions to be private. Also, if the employer provided the e-mail system or blog that the employee used for communications, a court will typically hold that the employee did not have a reasonable expectation of privacy in those communications. If employees are *not* informed that certain communications are being monitored, however, the employer may be held liable for invading their privacy. (See the *Business Application* feature at the end of this chapter for a discussion of creating workplace policies on the use of Internet and social media.)

Most employers that engage in electronic monitoring notify their employees about the monitoring. Nevertheless, notifying employees of a general policy may not sufficiently protect an employer who monitors forms of communications that the policy fails to mention. For instance, notifying employees that their e-mails and phone calls may be monitored does not necessarily protect an employer who monitors social media posts or blogs.

For a discussion of how some employers are creating their own social media networks, see this chapter's *Adapting the Law to the Online Environment* feature.

> "We are rapidly entering the age of no privacy, where everyone is open to surveillance at all times; where there are no secrets."
>
> **WILLIAM O. DOUGLAS**
> 1898–1980
> (ASSOCIATE JUSTICE OF THE UNITED STATES SUPREME COURT, 1939–1975)

ADAPTING THE LAW TO THE **ONLINE** ENVIRONMENT
Social Media in the Workplace Come of Age

What do corporate giant Dell, Inc., and relatively small Nikon Instruments have in common? They—and many other companies—have created internal social media networks using enterprise social networking software and systems, such as Salesforce.com, Chatter, Yammer, and Socialcast. A glance at the posts on these internal networks reveals that they are quite different from typical posts on Facebook, LinkedIn, and Twitter. Rather than being personal, the tone is businesslike, and the posts deal with workplace concerns such as how a team is solving a problem or how to sell a new product.

Benefits and Pitfalls of Internal Social Media Networks

Internal social media networks offer businesses several advantages. Perhaps the most important is that employees can obtain real-time information about important issues such as production glitches. They can also exchange tips about how to deal with problems, such as difficult customers. News about the company's new products or those of a competitor is available immediately. Furthermore, employees spend much less time sorting through e-mail. Rather than wasting their fellow employees' time by sending mass e-mailings, workers can post messages or collaborate on presentations via the company's internal network.

The downside is that these networks may become polluted with annoying "white noise." If employees start posting comments about what they ate for lunch, for example, the system will lose much of its utility. Companies can prevent this from happening by establishing explicit guidelines on what can be posted.

Keeping the Data Safe

Another concern is how to keep data and corporate secrets safe. When a company sets up a social media network, it usually decides which employees can see which files and which employees will belong to each specific "social" group within the company. Often, the data created through a social media network are kept on the company's own servers in secure "clouds."

CRITICAL THINKING

■ What problems might arise if data from an internal social media system are stored on third party servers?

24-4b Other Types of Monitoring

In addition to monitoring their employees' activities electronically, employers also engage in other types of monitoring. These practices, which have included lie-detector tests and drug tests, have often been subject to challenge as violations of employee privacy rights.

Lie-Detector Tests The Employee Polygraph Protection Act[21] (EPPA) generally prohibits employers from requiring or requesting that employees or job applicants take lie-detector tests. It also prevents employers from asking about the results of a polygraph or taking any negative employment action based on such results.

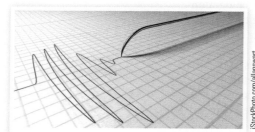

The act applies to most private employers (those with at least two employees and an annual volume of business of $500,000), but not to public employers (federal, state, and local government employers). Also exempt from the EPPA are security services firms and companies that manufacture and distribute controlled substances. Other employers may use lie-detector tests when investigating losses attributable to theft, including embezzlement and the theft of trade secrets.

Does current federal law allow security services firms to use lie-detector tests?

Drug Testing In the interests of public safety, many employers, including government employers, require their employees to submit to drug testing.

Public Employers. Government (public) employers are constrained in drug testing by the Fourth Amendment to the U.S. Constitution, which prohibits unreasonable searches and seizures. Drug testing of public employees is allowed by statute for transportation workers and is normally upheld by the courts when drug use in a particular job may threaten public safety. Also, when there is a reasonable basis for suspecting government employees of using drugs, courts often find that drug testing does not violate the Fourth Amendment.

Private Employers. The Fourth Amendment does not apply to drug testing conducted by private employers. Hence, the privacy rights and drug testing of private-sector employees are governed by state law, which varies widely. Many states have statutes that allow drug testing by private employers but place restrictions on when and how the testing may be performed. A collective bargaining agreement may also provide protection against drug testing (or authorize drug testing under certain conditions).

The permissibility of a private employee's drug test often hinges on whether the employer's testing was reasonable. Random drug tests and even "zero-tolerance" policies (which deny a "second chance" to employees who test positive for drugs) have been held to be reasonable.

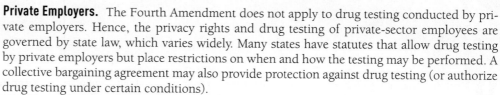

PREVENTING LEGAL DISPUTES

To avoid legal disputes, exercise caution when monitoring employees and make sure that any monitoring is conducted in a reasonable place and manner. With respect to electronic monitoring, for example, establish written policies that include all types of electronic devices used by your employees—even employee-owned devices. Notify employees of how and when they may be monitored on these devices. Consider informing employees of the reasons for the monitoring. Explain what the concern is, what job repercussions could result, and what recourse employees have in the event that a negative action is taken against them. By providing more privacy protection to employees than is legally required, you can both avoid potential privacy complaints and give employees a sense that they retain some degree of privacy in their workplace, which can lead to greater job satisfaction.

---

21. 29 U.S.C. Sections 2001 *et seq.*

24-5 Immigration Law

LEARNING OBJECTIVE **4**
What are the two most important federal statutes governing immigration and employment today?

The United States did not have any laws restricting immigration until the late nineteenth century. Today, the most important laws governing immigration and employment are the Immigration Reform and Control Act[22] (IRCA) of 1986 and the Immigration Act of 1990.[23]

Immigration law has become increasingly important in recent years. An estimated 12 million undocumented immigrants now live in the United States. Many of them came to find jobs. Because U.S. employers face serious penalties if they hire undocumented immigrants, businesspersons need to understand immigration laws.

24-5a Immigration Reform and Control Act (IRCA)

When the IRCA was enacted, it provided amnesty to certain groups of illegal aliens living in the United States at the time. It also established a system that sanctions employers who hire immigrants lacking work authorization. The IRCA makes it illegal to hire, recruit, or refer for a fee someone not authorized to work in this country. Through Immigration and Customs Enforcement officers, the federal government conducts random compliance audits and engages in enforcement actions against employers who hire undocumented immigrants.

I-9 Employment Verification To comply with the IRCA, an employer must perform **I-9 verifications** for new hires, including those hired as "contractors" or "day workers" if they work under the employer's direct supervision. Form I-9, Employment Eligibility Verification, which is available from U.S. Citizenship and Immigration Services,[24] must be completed *within three days* of a worker's commencement of employment. The three-day period is to allow the employer to check the form's accuracy and to review and verify documents establishing the prospective worker's identity and eligibility for employment in the United States.

I-9 Verification The process of verifying the employment eligibility and identity of a new worker. It must be completed within three days after the worker commences employment.

Documentation Requirements The employer must declare, under penalty of perjury, that an employee produced documents establishing his or her identity and legal employability. A U.S. passport establishing the person's citizenship is acceptable documentation, as is a document authorizing a foreign citizen to work in the United States, such as a Permanent Resident Card or an Alien Registration Receipt (discussed shortly).

Most legal actions for violations of I-9 rules are brought against employees who provide false information or documentation. If the employee enters false information on an I-9 form or presents false documentation, the employer can fire the worker, who then may be subject to deportation. Nevertheless, employers must be honest when verifying an employee's documentation. If an employer "should have known" that the worker was unauthorized, the employer has violated the rules.

Enforcement U.S. Immigration and Customs Enforcement (ICE) is the largest investigative arm of the U.S. Department of Homeland Security. ICE has a general inspection program that conducts random compliance audits. Other audits may occur if the agency receives a written complaint alleging an employer's violations. Government inspections include a review of an employer's file of I-9 forms. The government does not need a subpoena or a warrant to conduct such an inspection.

Who is eligible for a permanent residence card?

If an investigation reveals a possible violation, ICE will bring an administrative action and issue a Notice of Intent to Fine, which sets out the charges against the employer. The employer has a right to a hearing on the enforcement action if a request is filed within thirty days. This hearing is conducted before an administrative law judge, and the employer has a right to

---

22. 29 U.S.C. Section 1802.
23. This act amended various provisions of the Immigration and Nationality Act of 1952, 8 U.S.C. Sections 1101 *et seq.*
24. U.S. Citizenship and Immigration Services is a federal agency that is part of the U.S. Department of Homeland Security.

counsel and to discovery. The typical defense in such actions is good faith or substantial compliance with the documentation provisions.

Penalties   An employer who violates the law by hiring an unauthorized alien is subject to substantial penalties. The employer may be fined up to $2,200 for each unauthorized employee for a first offense, $5,000 per employee for a second offense, and up to $11,000 for subsequent offenses.

Employers who have engaged in a "pattern or practice of violations" are subject to criminal penalties, which include additional fines and imprisonment for up to ten years. A company may also be barred from future government contracts for violations. In determining the penalty, ICE considers the seriousness of the violation (such as intentional falsification of documents), the employer's past compliance, and whether the employer cooperated with authorities during the investigation.

24–5b The Immigration Act

Often, U.S. businesses find that they cannot hire enough domestic workers with specialized skills. For this reason, U.S. immigration laws have long made provisions for businesses to hire specially qualified foreign workers.

The Immigration Act placed caps on the number of visas (entry permits) that can be issued to immigrants each year, including employment-based visas. Employment-based visas may be classified as permanent (immigrant) or temporary (nonimmigrant). Employers who wish to hire workers with either type of visa must comply with detailed government regulations.[25]

What are the penalties for employing an unauthorized immigrant?

I-551 Alien Registration Receipts   A company seeking to hire a noncitizen worker on a permanent basis may do so if the worker is self-authorized—that is, if the worker either is a lawful permanent resident or has a valid temporary Employment Authorization Document. A lawful permanent resident can prove his or her status to an employer by presenting an **I-551 Alien Registration Receipt,** known as a "green card," or a properly stamped foreign passport.

Many immigrant workers are not already self-authorized, and an employer that wishes to hire them can attempt to obtain labor certification, or green cards, for them. A limited number of new green cards are issued each year. A green card can be obtained only for a person who is being hired for a permanent, full-time position. (A separate authorization system provides for the temporary entry and hiring of nonimmigrant visa workers.)

To gain authorization for hiring a foreign worker, an employer must show that no U.S. worker is qualified, willing, and able to take the job. The government has detailed regulations governing the advertising of positions as well as the certification process. Any U.S. applicants who meet the stated job qualifications must be interviewed for the position. The employer must also be able to show that the qualifications required for the job are a business necessity.

I-551 Alien Registration Receipt   A document, known as a "green card," that shows that a foreign-born individual can legally work in the United States.

The H-1B Visa Program   The most common and controversial temporary visa program today is the H-1B visa system. To obtain an H-1B visa, the potential employee must be qualified in a "specialty occupation," meaning that the individual has highly specialized knowledge and has attained a bachelor's or higher degree or its equivalent. Individuals with H-1B visas can stay in the United States for three to six years and can work only for the sponsoring employer.

The recipients of these visas include many high-tech workers, such as computer programmers and electronics specialists. A maximum of sixty-five thousand H-1B visas are set aside each year for new immigrants. That limit is typically reached within the first few weeks of the

---

25. The most relevant regulations can be found at 20 C.F.R. Section 655 (for temporary employment) and 20 C.F.R. Section 656 (for permanent employment).

year. Consequently, many businesses continue to lobby Congress to expand the number of H-1B visas available. These companies contend that limits on H-1B visas are keeping some of the world's brightest scientific and engineering minds out of the United States.

An employer who wishes to submit an H-1B application must first file a Labor Certification application on a form known as ETA 9035. The employer must agree to provide a wage level at least equal to the wages offered to other individuals with similar experience and qualifications. The employer must also show that the hiring will not adversely affect other workers similarly employed. The employer is required to inform U.S. workers of the intent to hire a foreign worker by posting the form. The U.S. Department of Labor reviews the applications and may reject them for omissions or inaccuracies.

H-2, O, L, and E Visas Other specialty temporary visas are available for other categories of employees. H-2 visas provide for workers performing agricultural labor of a seasonal nature. O visas provide entry for persons who have "extraordinary ability in the sciences, arts, education, business or athletics which has been demonstrated by sustained national or international acclaim." L visas allow a company's foreign managers or executives to work inside the United States. E visas permit the entry of certain foreign investors and entrepreneurs.

24-5c State Immigration Legislation

Until 2010, immigration and the treatment of illegal immigrants were governed exclusively by federal laws. Then Arizona enacted a law that required Arizona law enforcement officials to identify and charge immigrants in Arizona who were there illegally, potentially leading to the immigrants' deportation. Among other things, that law required immigrants to carry their papers at all times and allowed police to check a person's immigration status during any law enforcement action.

In *Arizona v. United States*,[26] the United States Supreme Court upheld the controversial "show-me-your-papers" provision that requires police to check the immigration status of persons stopped for another violation. All other provisions of Arizona's law were struck down because they were preempted by federal laws. The Supreme Court's decision does not prohibit states from enacting laws related to immigration, but it does set some limits.

24-6 Labor Unions

In the 1930s, in addition to wage-hour laws, the government also enacted the first of several labor laws. These laws protect employees' rights to join labor unions, to bargain with management over the terms and conditions of employment, and to conduct strikes.

24-6a Federal Labor Laws

Federal labor laws governing union-employer relations have developed considerably since the first law was enacted in 1932. Initially, the laws were concerned with protecting the rights and interests of workers. Subsequent legislation placed some restraints on unions and granted rights to employers. We look here at four major federal statutes regulating union-employer relations.

Norris-LaGuardia Act In 1932, Congress protected peaceful strikes, picketing, and boycotts in the Norris-LaGuardia Act.[27] The statute restricted the power of federal courts to issue injunctions against unions engaged in peaceful strikes. In effect, this act established a national policy permitting employees to organize.

> "Immigration is the sincerest form of flattery."
>
> **JACK PAAR**
> 1918–2004
> (AMERICAN ENTERTAINER)

LEARNING OBJECTIVE 5
What federal statute gave employees the right to organize unions and engage in collective bargaining?

---

26. __ U.S. __, 132 S.Ct. 2492, 183 L.Ed.2d 351 (2012).
27. 29 U.S.C. Sections 101–110, 113–115.

When were many labor union laws created?

National Labor Relations Act

One of the foremost statutes regulating labor is the National Labor Relations Act (NLRA), enacted in 1935.[28] This act established the rights of employees to engage in collective bargaining and to strike. The act also specifically defined a number of employer practices as unfair to labor:

1. Interference with the efforts of employees to form, join, or assist labor organizations or to engage in concerted activities for mutual aid or protection.

2. An employer's domination of a labor organization or contribution of financial or other support to it.

3. Discrimination in the hiring of or awarding of tenure to employees based on union affiliation.

4. Discrimination against employees for filing charges under the act or giving testimony under the act.

5. Refusal to bargain collectively with the duly designated representative of the employees.

The National Labor Relations Board (NLRB). The NLRA also created the National Labor Relations Board to oversee union elections and to prevent employers from engaging in unfair and illegal union activities and unfair labor practices.

The NLRB has the authority to investigate employees' charges of unfair labor practices and to file complaints against employers in response to these charges. When violations are found, the NLRB may issue a cease-and-desist order compelling the employer to stop engaging in the unfair practices. Cease-and-desist orders can be enforced by a federal appellate court if necessary. After the NLRB rules on claims of unfair labor practices, its decision may be appealed to a federal court.

CASE EXAMPLE 24.6 Roundy's, Inc., which operates a chain of stores in Wisconsin, became involved in a dispute with a local construction union. When union members started distributing "extremely unflattering" flyers outside the stores, Roundy's ejected them from the property. The NLRB filed a complaint against Roundy's for unfair labor practices. An administrative law judge ruled that Roundy's had violated the law by discriminating against the union, and a federal appellate court affirmed. It is an unfair labor practice for an employer to prohibit union members from distributing flyers outside a store when it allows nonunion members to do so.[29] ■

Good Faith Bargaining. Under the NLRA, employers and unions have a duty to bargain in good faith. Bargaining over certain subjects (such as wages, hours, and benefits) is mandatory, and a party's refusal to bargain over these subjects is an unfair labor practice that can be reported to the NLRB. An employer may be required to bargain with the union over the use of hidden video surveillance cameras, for instance.

Workers Protected by the NLRA. To be protected under the NLRA, an individual must be an *employee,* as that term is defined in the statute. Courts have long held that job applicants fall within the definition (otherwise, the NLRA's ban on discrimination in hiring would mean nothing). Additionally, individuals who are hired by a union to organize a company are to be considered employees of the company for NLRA purposes.

Labor-Management Relations Act

The Labor-Management Relations Act (LMRA), also called the Taft-Hartley Act,[30] was passed in 1947 to proscribe certain unfair union practices, such as the *closed shop.* A **closed shop** requires union membership by its workers as a condition of employment.

Closed Shop A firm that requires union membership by its workers as a condition of employment.

---

28. 20 U.S.C. Section 151.
29. *Roundy's, Inc. v. NLRB,* 674 F.3d 638 (7th Cir. 2012).
30. 29 U.S.C. Sections 141 *et seq.*

Although the act made the closed shop illegal, it preserved the legality of the union shop. A **union shop** does not require membership as a prerequisite for employment but can, and usually does, require that workers join the union after a specified amount of time on the job.

The LMRA also prohibited unions from refusing to bargain with employers, engaging in certain types of picketing, and *featherbedding*—causing employers to hire more employees than necessary. The act also allowed individual states to pass their own **right-to-work laws,** which make it illegal for union membership to be required for *continued* employment in any establishment. Thus, union shops are technically illegal in the twenty-three states that have right-to-work laws.

Labor-Management Reporting and Disclosure Act
In 1959, Congress enacted the Labor-Management Reporting and Disclosure Act (LMRDA).[31] The act established an employee bill of rights and reporting requirements for union activities. The act also outlawed **hot-cargo agreements,** in which employers voluntarily agree with unions not to handle, use, or deal in goods produced by nonunion employees working for other employers.

The LMRDA strictly regulates unions' internal business procedures, including union elections. For example, it requires a union to hold regularly scheduled elections of officers using secret ballots. Ex-convicts are prohibited from holding union office. Moreover, union officials are accountable for union property and funds. Members have the right to attend and to participate in union meetings, to nominate officers, and to vote in most union proceedings.

The LMRDA holds union officers to a high standard of responsibility and ethical conduct in administering the affairs of their union. This standard was at the core of the dispute in the following case.

Union Shop A firm that requires all workers, once employed, to become union members within a specified period of time as a condition of their continued employment.

Right-to-Work Law A state law providing that employees may not be required to join a union as a condition of retaining employment.

Hot-Cargo Agreement An illegal agreement in which employers voluntarily agree with unions not to handle, use, or deal in the nonunion-produced goods of other employers.

---

31. 29 U.S.C. Sections 401 *et seq.*

CASE 24.3

Services Employees International Union v. National Union of Healthcare Workers

United States Court of Appeals, Ninth Circuit, 718 F.3d 1036 (2013).

FACTS The Services Employees International Union (SEIU) consists of 2.2 million members who work in health care, public services, and property services. United Health Workers (UHW) is affiliated with SEIU and represents 150,000 healthcare workers in California. Under its constitution, the SEIU has the authority to realign local unions. The SEIU's constitution also grants it the authority to place a local union into trusteeship "to protect the interests of the membership."

The SEIU proposed moving 150,000 long-term healthcare workers from three separate unions—including 65,000 from the UHW—into a new union chartered by SEIU. The UHW opposed the move. The SEIU placed the UHW into trusteeship. In response, UHW officials blocked access to its buildings to prevent the trustees from entering, removed UHW property from the buildings, and instructed its members not to recognize the trustees' authority.

Meanwhile, the UHW officials, while still on the UHW payroll, created and promoted a new union—the National Union of Healthcare

How can a labor union's officer breach his or her fiduciary duties to members?

Workers (NUHW). The SEIU filed a suit in a federal district court against the NUHW and the UHW officials for breach of *fiduciary duties*—that is, their duty to act primarily for the benefit of the union. The jury returned a verdict against the NUHW and the UHW, on which the court entered a judgment. The defendants appealed.

ISSUE Did the UHW officials violate the standards imposed by the Labor-Management Reporting and Disclosure Act (LMRDA)?

DECISION Yes. The U.S. Court of Appeals for the Ninth Circuit affirmed the lower court's judgment.

REASON Section 501 of the LMRDA creates a fiduciary duty owed by union officials to the union as an organization, not only the union's rank-and-file members. Officials who divert union resources to establish a new competing union breach this duty. The reviewing court

Continues

pointed out that officials of labor unions are required to uphold the highest standards "of responsibility and ethical conduct in administrating the affairs of the union."

The reviewing court was not swayed by the defendants' statement that they believed that their actions assisted those union members by establishing a more democratic union with localized control. In reality, the defendants diverted union resources to weaken their own union and to form a rival union because they did not agree with the constitutionally permissible decision of the international union. "Because no construction of the LMRDA allows such conduct based merely on the defendants' subjective motives, we reject the defendants' argument." The judgment of liability "was properly entered when a correctly instructed jury, on a sufficient factual record, found the defendants in breach of their fiduciary duties."

CRITICAL THINKING—Legal Consideration *If the defendants in this case had only expressed their opinions against the SEIU's imposition of trusteeship and charter of a new union, could they have been held liable for a breach of fiduciary duty? Discuss.*

24–6b Union Organization

Authorization Card A card signed by an employee that gives a union permission to act on his or her behalf in negotiations with management.

Typically, the first step in organizing a union at a particular firm is to have the workers sign authorization cards. An **authorization card** usually states that the worker wishes to have a certain union, such as the United Auto Workers, represent the workforce. If a majority of the workers sign authorization cards, the union organizers (unionizers) present the cards to the employer and ask for formal recognition of the union.

The employer is not required to recognize the union at this point in the process, but it may do so voluntarily on a showing of majority support. (Under pro-labor legislation that has been proposed repeatedly, the employer would be required to recognize the union as soon as a majority of the workers had signed authorization cards—without holding an election, as described next.)[32]

Union Elections

If the employer does not voluntarily recognize the union—or if less than a majority of the workers sign authorization cards—the union organizers present the cards to the NLRB with a petition for an election. For an election to be held, the unionizers must demonstrate that at least 30 percent of the workers to be represented support a union or an election on unionization.

Once the NLRB receives a petition for an organizing election, it determines if an election should be conducted.

Appropriate Bargaining Unit.

The proposed union must represent an *appropriate bargaining unit.* Not every group of workers can form a single union.

One key requirement of an appropriate bargaining unit is a *mutuality of interest* among all the workers to be represented by the union. Factors considered in determining whether there is a mutuality of interest include the similarity of the jobs of all the workers to be unionized and their physical location.

New NLRB Rules Expedite Elections.

New NLRB rules that took effect early in 2015 have significantly reduced the time between the filing of a petition and the ensuing election—from an average of thirty-eight days to as little as ten days. This change favors unions because it gives employers less time to respond to organizing campaigns that unions often spend months preparing.

The NLRB now requires that a company hold a pre-election hearing within eight days after it receives a petition for an organizing election. On the day before the hearing, the company now must also submit a "statement of position" laying out every argument it intends to make against the union. Any argument that the company does not include in its position paper can be excluded from evidence at the hearing. Once the hearing is held, an election can be scheduled right away.

---

32. The proposed legislation is the Employee Free Choice Act.

Voting. If an election is held, the NLRB supervises the election and ensures secret voting and voter eligibility. If the proposed union receives majority support in a fair election, the NLRB certifies the union as the bargaining representative for the employees.

Union Election Campaigns Many disputes between labor and management arise during union election campaigns. Generally, the employer has control over unionizing activities that take place on company property during working hours. Employers may thus limit the campaign activities of union supporters as long as the employer has a legitimate business reason for doing so. The employer may also reasonably limit the times and places that union solicitation occurs so long as the employer is not discriminating against the union. (Can union organizers use company e-mail during campaigns? See this chapter's *Managerial Strategy* feature for a discussion of this topic.)

EXAMPLE 24.7 A union is seeking to organize clerks at a department store owned by Amanti Enterprises. Amanti can prohibit all union solicitation in areas of the store open to the public because that activity could seriously interfere with the store's business. If Amanti allows solicitation for charitable causes in the workplace, however, it may not prohibit union solicitation. ■

An employer may campaign among its workers against the union, but the NLRB carefully monitors and regulates the tactics used by management. Otherwise, management might use

MANAGERIAL STRATEGY — Union Organizing Using Your Company's E-Mail System

Management Faces a Legal Issue

When union organizers start an organizing drive, there are certain restrictions on what they can do, particularly within the workplace. Both employers and employees must comply with Section 7 of the National Labor Relations Act (NLRA). Under Section 7, employees have certain rights to communicate among themselves. Section 7 states, "Employees shall have the right to self-organization, . . . and to engage in other concerted activities for the purpose of collective bargaining or other mutual aid or protection. . . ."

What about communication via e-mail? Can union organizers use a company-operated e-mail system for organizing purposes? Companies typically provide e-mail systems so that employees can communicate with outsiders and among themselves as part of their jobs. Generally, company policies have prohibited the use of company-owned and -operated e-mail systems for other than job-related communications.

Starting in the early 2000s, some union organizers challenged this prohibition.

What the Courts Say

The first major case concerning this issue was decided by the National Labor Relations Board (NLRB) in 2007.[a] The NLRB allowed an employer's written policy that prohibited the use of a company-provided e-mail system for non-job-related solicitations. This decision was affirmed in relevant part by a federal court two years later.[b]

In late 2014, the NLRB reversed its 2007 position. "We decide today that employee use of e-mail for statutorily protected communications on non-working time must presumptively be permitted by employers who have chosen to give employees access to their e-mail systems."[c] The NLRB argued that its 2007 decision had failed to adequately protect "employees' rights under the NLRA."

The board also stated that it had a responsibility "to adapt the Act to the changing patterns of industrial life."

MANAGERIAL IMPLICATIONS

Managers who work for companies that are targets of union-organizing drives must comply with the latest NLRB decision, pending any reversal on appeal. The new rules are clear. Once an organizing election is scheduled, a company must turn over all telephone numbers and home and e-mail addresses of the company's employees within two days. Union organizers can then communicate with employees via the company's e-mail system. Failure to comply with NLRB rules can cause any negative vote on organizing a new union to be rendered null and void.

a. *Register Guard*, 351 NLRB 1110 (2007).
b. *Guard Publishing v. NLRB*, 571 F.3d 53 (D.C. Cir. 2009).
c. *Purple Communications, Inc. and Communication Workers of America, AFL-CIO*, Cases 21-CA-095151, 21-RC-091531, and 21-RC-091584, March 16, 2015.

Can this department store prohibit union solicitation in all areas?

Collective Bargaining
The process by which labor and management negotiate the terms and conditions of employment, including working hours and workplace conditions.

Strike An action undertaken by unionized workers when collective bargaining fails. The workers leave their jobs, refuse to work, and (typically) picket the employer's workplace.

its economic power to coerce the workers into voting against unionization. If an employer issued threats ("If the union wins, you'll all be fired") or engaged in other unfair labor practices, the NLRB could certify the union even though it lost the election. Alternatively, the NLRB could ask a court to order a new election.

24–6c Collective Bargaining

If the NLRB certifies the union, the union becomes the *exclusive bargaining representative* of the workers. The central legal right of a union is to engage in collective bargaining on the members' behalf. **Collective bargaining** is the process by which labor and management negotiate the terms and conditions of employment, including wages, benefits, working conditions, and other matters. Collective bargaining allows union representatives elected by union members to speak on behalf of the members at the bargaining table.

Once an employer and a union sit down at the conference table, they must negotiate in good faith and make a reasonable effort to come to an agreement. They are not obligated to reach an agreement. They must, however, approach the negotiations with the idea that an agreement is possible. Both parties may engage in hard bargaining, but the bargaining process itself must be geared to reaching a compromise—not avoiding a compromise.

Although good faith is a matter of subjective intent, a party's actions can be used to evaluate the party's good or bad faith. Excessive delaying tactics may be proof of bad faith, as is insistence on obviously unreasonable contract terms. If an employer (or a union) refuses to bargain in good faith without justification, it has committed an unfair labor practice. Exhibit 24–1 illustrates some differences between good faith and bad faith bargaining .

24–6d Strikes

Even when labor and management have bargained in good faith, they may be unable to reach a final agreement. When extensive collective bargaining has been conducted and an impasse results, the union may call a strike against the employer to pressure it into making concessions.

In a **strike,** the unionized workers leave their jobs and refuse to work. The workers also typically picket the workplace, standing outside the facility with signs stating their complaints. A strike is an extreme action. Striking workers lose their rights to be paid, and management

Exhibit 24–1 Good Faith versus Bad Faith Bargaining

GOOD FAITH BARGAINING	BAD FAITH BARGAINING
1. Negotiating with the belief that an agreement is possible	1. Excessive delaying tactics
2. Seriously considering the other side's positions	2. Insistence on unreasonable contract terms
3. Making reasonable proposals	3. Rejecting a proposal without offering a counterproposal
4. Being willing to compromise	4. Engaging in a campaign among workers to undermine the union
5. Bargainers who have the authority to enter into agreements for the company	5. Constantly shifting positions on disputed contract terms
	6. Sending bargainers who lack authority to commit the company to a contract

loses production and may lose customers when orders cannot be filled. Labor law regulates the circumstances and conduct of strikes.

Most strikes take the form of "economic strikes," which are initiated because the union wants a better contract. **EXAMPLE 24.8** Teachers in Eagle Point, Oregon, engage in an economic strike after contract negotiations with the school district fail to bring an agreement on pay, working hours, and subcontracting jobs. The unionized teachers picket outside the school building. Classes are canceled for a few weeks until the district can find substitute teachers who will fill in during the strike. ■

The Right to Strike The right to strike is guaranteed by the NLRA, within limits. In addition, certain strike activities, such as picketing, are protected by the free speech guarantee of the First Amendment to the U.S. Constitution. Nonworkers have a right to participate in picketing an employer, and workers have the right to refuse to cross a picket line of fellow workers who are engaged in a lawful strike.

Strikers are not allowed to use (or threaten to use) violence against anyone or to prevent others from entering a facility. Furthermore, a strike may be illegal if it contravenes a no-strike clause that was in the previous collective bargaining agreement between the employer and the union.

After a Strike Ends In a typical strike, the employer has a right to hire permanent replacements during the strike. The employer need not terminate the replacement workers when the economic strikers seek to return to work. In other words, striking workers are not guaranteed the right to return to their jobs after the strike if satisfactory replacement workers have been found.

If the employer has not hired replacement workers to fill the strikers' positions, however, then the employer must rehire the economic strikers to fill any vacancies. Employers may not discriminate against former economic strikers, and those who are rehired retain their seniority rights.

24-6e Lockouts

Lockouts are the employer's counterpart to the worker's right to strike. A **lockout** occurs when the employer shuts down to prevent employees from working.

Lockouts usually are used when the employer believes that a strike is imminent or when the parties have reached a stalemate in collective bargaining.

EXAMPLE 24.9 Owners of the teams in the National Football League (NFL) imposed a lockout on the NFL players' union in 2011 after negotiations on a new collective bargaining agreement broke down. The NFL owners had proposed to reduce players' salaries and extend the season by two games because of decreased profits due to the struggling economy. A settlement was reached before the start of the 2011 football season. The players accepted 3 percent less of the revenue generated (47 percent rather than 50 percent) in exchange for better working conditions and more retirement benefits. The owners agreed to keep the same number of games per season.

The owners of the teams in the National Basketball Association (NBA) also locked out their players in 2011 after the two sides failed to reach a collective bargaining agreement. The dispute involved the division of revenue and a salary cap. During the lockout, the players could not access NBA facilities, trainers, or staff, and the owners could not trade, sign, or contract with players. The lockout lasted 161 days and resulted in the cancellation of all preseason games and several weeks of regular season games. ■

Lockout An action in which an employer shuts down to prevent employees from working, typically because it cannot reach a collective bargaining agreement with the employees' union.

Can football-team owners impose a lockout?

Reviewing . . . Employment, Immigration, and Labor Law

Rick Saldona began working as a traveling salesperson for Aimer Winery in 1994. Sales constituted 90 percent of Saldona's work time. Saldona worked an average of fifty hours per week but received no overtime pay. In June 2017, Saldona's new supervisor, Caesar Braxton, claimed that Saldona had been inflating his reported sales calls and required Saldona to submit to a polygraph test. Saldona reported Braxton to the U.S. Department of Labor, which prohibited Aimer from requiring Saldona to take a polygraph test for this purpose. In August 2017, Saldona's wife, Venita, fell from a ladder and sustained a head injury while employed as a full-time agricultural harvester. Saldona delivered to Aimer's human resources department a letter from his wife's physician indicating that she would need daily care for several months, and Saldona took leave until December 2017. Aimer had sixty-three employees at that time. When Saldona returned to Aimer, he was informed that his position had been eliminated because his sales territory had been combined with an adjacent territory. Using the information presented in the chapter, answer the following questions.

1. Would Saldona have been legally entitled to receive overtime pay at a higher rate? Why or why not?
2. What is the maximum length of time Saldona would have been allowed to take leave to care for his injured spouse?
3. Under what circumstances would Aimer have been allowed to require an employee to take a lie-detector test?
4. Would Aimer likely be able to avoid reinstating Saldona under the *key employee* exception? Why or why not?

DEBATE THIS

- The U.S. labor market is highly competitive, so state and federal laws that require overtime pay are unnecessary and should be abolished.

BUSINESS APPLICATION

How to Develop a Policy on Employee Use of the Internet and Social Media*

Employers that make the Internet, e-mail, smartphones, and social networking sites available to their employees face some obvious risks. The employer could be liable if an employee harasses another employee

* This *Business Application* is not meant to substitute for the services of an attorney who is licensed to practice law in your state.

via e-mail or a social networking site such as Facebook. Similarly, the employer could be liable if an employee uses the Internet to violate copyright or other intellectual property laws. Another risk is that an outside party might intercept confidential information or trade secrets contained in communications transmitted via the Internet. But if the employer monitors employees' use of the Internet and social media in an attempt to avoid these problems, the employer risks being held liable for violating the employees' privacy.

Remember that a small company can be bankrupted by just one successful lawsuit against it. Even if the company wins the suit, it will likely have incurred substantial legal fees. Therefore, if you are an employer and find it necessary to monitor your employees' use of the Internet and social media, you should take care when creating your policy.

Inform Employees of the Monitoring and Obtain Their Consent
First, notify your employees that you will be monitoring their online communications and

specify what will be monitored (e-mail, cell phones, text messages, posts on Facebook and other social media, and the like). Also state clearly whether you will monitor all work-related communications, even those sent via the employees' own devices, or whether you will monitor only communications sent via devices furnished by the company. Second, ask all employees to consent, in writing, to this monitoring.

Spell Out Permissible and Impermissible Uses

To ensure that employees understand what they may and may not do, develop comprehensive guidelines for Internet and social media use. Include specific examples of prohibited activities. The National Labor Relations Board has interpreted federal labor law to mean that employers cannot ban all use of social media by their employees. Therefore,

particularly if your employees are union members, it is a good idea to consult an attorney to ensure that your policy is legal.

Policies for Social Media

Be careful when creating policies on social media use. Employees have free speech and privacy rights, so make sure that you have a legitimate business reason for any restrictions you impose. Do not attempt to interfere with employees' discussions of wages and working conditions on social media sites—these are protected under federal labor law.

An employer can encourage employees to use discretion in posts on social media and can discourage them from making negative comments about co-workers. You probably can prohibit employees from disclosing confidential or personal information about customers, clients, co-workers, and possibly suppliers. You might also be able to restrict

employees from making negative statements about the firm or its products and services.

CHECKLIST for the Employer:

1. Inform employees that their Internet and social media communications will be monitored, and indicate which communications and which devices will be monitored.

2. Obtain employees' written consent to having their electronic communications monitored.

3. Develop a comprehensive policy statement that explains how the Internet and social media should and should not be used.

4. Designate someone in the company to whom employees can go with questions or concerns about the firm's policies on Internet or social media use.

Key Terms

authorization card 620

closed shop 618

collective bargaining 622

employment at will 601

hot-cargo agreement 619

I-551 Alien Registration Receipt 616

I-9 verification 615

lockout 623

minimum wage 604

right-to-work law 619

strike 622

union shop 619

vesting 611

whistleblowing 602

workers' compensation laws 609

wrongful discharge 603

Chapter Summary: Employment, Immigration, and Labor Law

Employment at Will	1. *Employment-at-will doctrine*—Under this common law doctrine, either party may terminate the employment relationship at any time and for any reason ("at will"). 2. *Exceptions to the employment-at-will doctrine*—Courts have made exceptions to the doctrine on the basis of contract theory, tort theory, and public policy. The public policy exception may sometimes apply to whistleblowers. 3. *Wrongful discharge*—Whenever an employer discharges an employee in violation of an employment contract or statutory law protecting employees, the employee may bring a suit for wrongful discharge.
Wages, Hours, Layoffs, and Leave	1. *Davis-Bacon Act*—Requires contractors and subcontractors working on federal government construction projects to pay their employees "prevailing wages." 2. *Walsh-Healey Act*—Requires firms that contract with federal agencies to pay their employees a minimum wage and overtime pay. 3. *Fair Labor Standards Act*—Extended wage and hour requirements to cover all employers whose activities affect interstate commerce plus certain other businesses. The act has specific requirements in regard to child labor, maximum hours, and minimum wages. 4. *The Worker Adjustment and Retraining Notification (WARN) Act*—Applies to employers with at least one hundred full-time employees and requires that sixty days' advance notice of mass layoffs be given to affected employees or their representative (if workers are in a labor union). State layoff notice requirements may be different from and even stricter than the WARN Act's requirements.

Continues

Wages, Hours, Layoffs, and Leave (Continued)	**5.** *The Family and Medical Leave Act (FMLA)*—Requires employers with fifty or more employees to provide employees with up to twelve weeks of unpaid leave (twenty-six weeks for military caregiver leave) during any twelve-month period. **a.** May take family leave to care for a newborn baby, an adopted child, or a foster child. **b.** May take medical leave when the employee or the employee's spouse, child, or parent has a serious health condition requiring care. **c.** May take military caregiver leave to care for a family member with a serious injury or illness incurred as a result of military duty. **d.** May take qualifying exigency leave to handle specified nonmedical emergencies when a spouse, parent, or child is in, or called to, active military duty
Health, Safety, and Income Security	**1.** *Occupational Safety and Health Act*—Requires employers to meet specific safety and health standards that are established and enforced by the Occupational Safety and Health Administration (OSHA). **2.** *State workers' compensation laws*—Establish an administrative procedure for compensating workers who are injured in accidents that occur on the job, regardless of fault. **3.** *Social Security and Medicare*—The Social Security Act provides for old-age (retirement), survivors', and disability insurance. Both employers and employees must make contributions under the Federal Insurance Contributions Act (FICA). The Social Security Administration also administers Medicare, a health-insurance program for older or disabled persons. **4.** *Private retirement plans*—The federal Employee Retirement Income Security Act (ERISA) establishes standards for the management of employer-provided pension plans. **5.** *Unemployment insurance*—The Federal Unemployment Tax Act (FUTA) created a system that provides unemployment compensation to eligible individuals. Employers are taxed to cover the costs. **6.** *COBRA*—The Consolidated Omnibus Budget Reconciliation Act (COBRA) of 1985 requires employers to give employees, on termination of employment, the option of continuing their medical, optical, or dental insurance coverage for a certain period. **7.** *HIPAA*—The Health Insurance Portability and Accountability Act (HIPAA) establishes requirements for employer-sponsored group health plans. The plans must also comply with various safeguards to ensure the privacy of employees' health information.
Employee Privacy Rights	Tort law, state constitutions, and federal and state statutes, as well as the U.S. Constitution, provide some protection for employees' privacy rights. Employer practices that have been challenged by employees as violations of their privacy rights include electronic monitoring, lie-detector tests, and drug testing.
Immigration Law	**1.** *Immigration Reform and Control Act*—Prohibits employers from hiring illegal immigrants. The act is administered by U.S. Citizenship and Immigration Services. Compliance audits and enforcement actions are conducted by U.S. Immigration and Customs Enforcement. **2.** *Immigration Act*—Limits the number of legal immigrants entering the United States by capping the number of visas (entry permits) that are issued each year.
Labor Unions	**1.** *Federal labor laws*— **a.** Norris-LaGuardia Act—Protects peaceful strikes, picketing, and primary boycotts. **b.** National Labor Relations Act—Established the rights of employees to engage in collective bargaining and to strike. It also defined specific employer practices as unfair to labor. The National Labor Relations Board (NLRB) was created to administer and enforce the act. **c.** Labor-Management Relations Act—Proscribes certain unfair union practices, such as the closed shop. **d.** Labor-Management Reporting and Disclosure Act—Established an employee bill of rights and reporting requirements for union activities. **2.** *Union organization*—Union campaign activities and elections must comply with the requirements established by federal labor laws and the NLRB. **3.** *Collective bargaining*—The process by which labor and management negotiate the terms and conditions of employment (such as wages, benefits, and working conditions). The central legal right of a labor union is to engage in collective bargaining on the members' behalf. **4.** *Strikes*—When collective bargaining reaches an impasse, union members may use their ultimate weapon in labor-management struggles—the strike. A strike occurs when unionized workers leave their jobs and refuse to work.

Issue Spotters

1. Erin, an employee of Fine Print Shop, is injured on the job. For Erin to obtain workers' compensation, does her injury have to have been caused by Fine Print's negligence? Does it matter whether the action causing the injury was intentional? Explain. (See *Health, Safety, and Income Security.*)

2. Onyx applies for work with Precision Design Company, which tells her that it requires union membership as a condition of employment. She applies for work with Quality Engineering, Inc., which does not require union membership as a condition of employment but requires employees to join a union after six months on the job. Are these conditions legal? Why or why not? (See *Labor Unions.*)

—Check your answers to the *Issue Spotters* against the answers provided in Appendix D at the end of this text.

Learning Objectives Check

1. What is the employment-at-will doctrine?
2. What federal statute governs working hours and wages?
3. Under the Family and Medical Leave Act, in what circumstances may an employee take family or medical leave?
4. What are the two most important federal statutes governing immigration and employment today?
5. What federal statute gave employees the right to organize unions and engage in collective bargaining?

—Answers to the even-numbered *Learning Objectives Check* questions can be found in Appendix E at the end of this text.

Business Scenarios and Case Problems

24–1. Wages and Hours. Calzoni Boating Co. is an interstate business engaged in manufacturing and selling boats. The company has five hundred nonunion employees. Representatives of these employees are requesting a four-day, ten-hours-per-day workweek, and Calzoni is concerned that this would require paying time and a half after eight hours per day. Which federal act is Calzoni thinking of that might require this? Will the act in fact require paying time and a half for all hours worked over eight hours per day if the employees' proposal is accepted? Explain. (See *Wages, Hours, Layoffs, and Leave.*)

24–2. Wrongful Discharge. Denton and Carlo were employed at an appliance plant. Their job required them to do occasional maintenance work while standing on a wire mesh twenty feet above the plant floor. Other employees had fallen through the mesh, and one was killed by the fall. When Denton and Carlo were asked by their supervisor to do work that would likely require them to walk on the mesh, they refused due to their fear of bodily harm or death. Because of their refusal to do the requested work, the two employees were fired. Was their discharge wrongful? If so, under what federal employment law? To what federal agency or department should they turn for assistance? (*See Health, Safety, and Income Security.*)

24–3. Minimum Wage. Misty Cumbie worked as a waitress in Vita Café in Portland, Oregon. The café was owned and operated by Woody Woo, Inc. Woody Woo paid its servers an hourly wage that was higher than the state's minimum wage, but the servers were required to contribute their tips to a "tip pool." Approximately one-third of the tip-pool funds went to the servers, and the rest was distributed to kitchen staff members, who otherwise rarely received tips for their services. Did this tip-pooling arrangement violate the minimum wage provisions of the Fair Labor Standards Act? Explain. [*Cumbie v. Woody Woo, Inc.,* 596 F.3d 577 (9th Cir. 2010)] (See *Wages, Hours, Layoffs, and Leave.*)

24–4. Workers' Compensation. As a safety measure, Dynea USA, Inc., required an employee, Tony Fairbanks, to wear steel-toed boots. One of the boots caused a sore on Fairbanks's leg. The skin over the sore broke, and within a week, Fairbanks was hospitalized with a methicillin-resistant staphylococcus aureus (MRSA) infection. He filed a workers' compensation claim. Dynea argued that the MRSA bacteria that caused the infection had been on Fairbanks's skin before he came to work. What are the requirements to recover workers' compensation benefits? Does this claim qualify? Explain. [*Dynea USA, Inc. v. Fairbanks,* 241 Or.App. 311, 250 P.3d 389 (2011)] (See *Health, Safety, and Income Security.*)

24–5. Exceptions to the Employment-at-Will Doctrine. Li Li worked for Packard Bioscience, and Mark Schmeizl was her supervisor. In March 2000, Schmeizl told Li Li to call Packard's competitors, pretend to be a potential customer, and request "pricing information and literature." Li Li refused to perform the assignment. She told Schmeizl that she thought the work was illegal and recommended that he contact Packard's legal department. Although a lawyer recommended against the practice, Schmeizl insisted that Li Li perform the calls. Moreover, he later wrote negative performance reviews because she was unable to get the requested information when she called competitors and identified herself as a Packard employee. On June 1, 2000, Li Li was terminated on Schmeizl's recommendation. Can Li Li bring a claim for wrongful discharge? Why or why not? [*Li Li v. Canberra Industries,* 134 Conn.App. 448, 39 A.3d 789 (2012)] (See *Employment at Will.*)

24–6. Collective Bargaining. SDBC Holdings, Inc., acquired Stella D'oro Biscuit Co., a bakery in New York City. At the time, a collective bargaining agreement existed between Stella D'oro and Local 50 of the Bakery, Confectionary, Tobacco Workers and Grain Millers International Union. During negotiations to renew the agreement, Stella D'oro allowed Local 50 to examine and take notes on the company's financial statement but would not give Local 50 a copy of the statement. Did Stella D'oro engage in an unfair labor practice? Discuss. [*SDBC Holdings, Inc. v. National Labor Relations Board,* 711 F.3d 281 (2d Cir. 2013)] (See *Labor Unions.*)

24–7. Business Case Problem with Sample Answer— Unemployment Compensation. Fior Ramirez worked as a housekeeper for Remington Lodging & Hospitality, a hotel in Atlantic Beach, Florida. After her father in the Dominican Republic suffered a stroke, she asked her employer for time off to be with him. Ramirez's manager, Katie Berkowski, refused the request. Two days later, Berkowski received a call from Ramirez to say that she was with her father. He died about a week later, and Ramirez returned to work, but Berkowski told her that she had abandoned her position. Ramirez applied for unemployment compensation. Under the applicable state statute, "an employee is disqualified from receiving benefits if he or she voluntarily left work without good cause." Does Ramirez qualify for benefits? Explain. [*Ramirez v. Reemployment Assistance Appeals Commission*, 135 So.3d 408 (Fla.App. 1 Dist. 2014)] (See *Health, Safety, and Income Security*.)

—**For a sample answer to Problem 24–7, go to Appendix F at the end of this text.**

24–8. Labor Unions. Carol Garcia and Pedro Salgado, bus drivers for Latino Express, Inc., a transportation company, began soliciting signatures from other drivers to certify the Teamsters Local Union No. 777 as the official representative of the employees. Latino Express fired Garcia and Salgado. The two drivers filed a claim with the National Labor Relations Board (NLRB) alleging that the employer had committed an unfair labor practice. Which employer practice defined by the National Labor Relations Act did the plaintiffs most likely charge Latino Express with committing? Is the employer's discharge of Garcia and Salgado likely to be construed as a legitimate act in opposition to union solicitation? If a violation is found, what can the NLRB do? Discuss. [*Ohr v. Latino Express, Inc.*, 776 F.3d 469 (7th Cir. 2015)] (See *Labor Unions*.)

24–9. A Question of Ethics—Workers' Compensation. Beverly Tull had worked for Atchison Leather Products, Inc., for ten years when she began to complain of hand, wrist, and shoulder pain. Atchison recommended that she contact a certain physician. In April 2000, the physician diagnosed the condition as carpal tunnel syndrome "severe enough" for surgery. In August, Tull filed a claim with the state workers' compensation board.

Because Atchison changed workers' compensation insurance companies every year, a dispute arose as to which company should pay Tull's claim. Fearing liability, no insurer would authorize treatment, and Tull was forced to delay surgery until December. The board granted her temporary total disability benefits for the subsequent six weeks that she missed work. On April 23, 2002, Berger Co. bought Atchison. The new employer adjusted Tull's work to be less demanding and stressful, but she continued to suffer pain. In July, a physician diagnosed her condition as permanent. The board granted her permanent partial disability benefits. By May 2005, the bickering over the financial responsibility for Tull's claim involved five insurers—four of which had each covered Atchison for a single year and one of which covered Berger. [*Tull v. Atchison Leather Products, Inc.*, 37 Kan.App.2d 87, 150 P.3d 316 (2007)] (See *Health, Safety, and Income Security*.)

1. When an injured employee files a claim for workers' compensation, there is a proceeding to assess the injury and determine the amount of compensation. Should a dispute between insurers over the payment of the claim be resolved in the same proceeding? Why or why not?

2. The board designated April 23, 2002, as the date of Tull's injury. What is the reason for determining the date of a worker's injury? Should the board in this case have selected this date or a different date? Why?

3. How should the board assess liability for the payment of Tull's medical expenses and disability benefits? Would it be appropriate to impose joint and several liability on the insurers (making them each liable for all of the damages), or should the individual liability of each of them be determined? Explain.

Critical Thinking and Writing Assignments

24–10. Business Law Critical Thinking Group Assignment. Nicole Tipton and Sadik Seferi owned and operated a restaurant in Iowa. Acting on a tip from the local police, agents of Immigration and Customs Enforcement executed search warrants at the restaurant and at an apartment where some restaurant workers lived. The agents discovered six undocumented aliens working at the restaurant and living together. When the I-9 forms for the restaurant's employees were reviewed, none were found for the six aliens. They were paid in cash while other employees were paid by check. Tipton and Seferi were charged with hiring and harboring illegal aliens. (See *Immigration Law*.)

1. The first group will develop an argument that Tipton and Seferi were guilty of hiring and harboring illegal aliens.

2. The second group will assess whether Tipton and Seferi can assert a defense by claiming that they did not know that the workers were unauthorized aliens.

25

Employment Discrimination

LEARNING OBJECTIVES

The five Learning Objectives *below are designed to help improve your understanding of the chapter. After reading this chapter, you should be able to answer the following questions:*

1. What is required to establish a *prima facie* case of disparate-treatment discrimination?

2. What must an employer do to avoid liability for religious discrimination?

3. What is a constructive discharge? To which employment discrimination claims does the theory of constructive discharge apply?

4. What federal act prohibits discrimination based on age?

5. What are three defenses to claims of employment discrimination?

"Equal rights for all, special privileges for none."

THOMAS JEFFERSON
1743–1826
(THIRD PRESIDENT OF THE UNITED STATES, 1801–1809)

Out of the civil rights movement of the 1960s grew a body of law protecting employees against discrimination in the workplace. Legislation, judicial decisions, and administrative agency actions restrict employers from discriminating against workers on the basis of race, color, religion, national origin, gender, age, or disability. A class of persons defined by one or more of these criteria is known as a **protected class.** The laws designed to protect these individuals embody the sentiment expressed by Thomas Jefferson in the chapter-opening quotation.

The federal statutes discussed in this chapter prohibit *employment discrimination* against members of protected classes. Although this chapter focuses on federal statutes, many states have their own laws that protect employees against discrimination, and some provide more protection to employees than federal laws do.

25-1 Title VII of the Civil Rights Act

The most important statute covering employment discrimination is Title VII of the Civil Rights Act.[1] Title VII prohibits discrimination against employees, applicants, and union members on the basis of race, color, national origin, religion, or gender at any stage of employment.

Title VII applies to employers with fifteen or more employees and labor unions with fifteen or more members. Title VII also applies to labor unions that operate hiring halls (to which

Protected Class A group of persons protected by specific laws because of the group's defining characteristics, including race, color, religion, national origin, gender, age, and disability.

---

1. 42 U.S.C. Sections 2000e–2000e-17.

U.S. Attorney General Robert F. Kennedy met with civil rights leaders in the Rose Garden of the White House in 1964. To what employers does Title VII of the Civil Rights Act apply?

members go regularly to be rationed jobs as they become available), employment agencies, and state and local governing units or agencies. A special section of the act prohibits discrimination in most federal government employment.

25–1a The Equal Employment Opportunity Commission

Compliance with Title VII is monitored by the Equal Employment Opportunity Commission (EEOC). A victim of alleged discrimination must file a claim with the EEOC before bringing a suit against the employer. The EEOC may investigate the dispute and attempt to arrange an out-of-court settlement. If a voluntary agreement cannot be reached, the EEOC may file a suit against the employer on the employee's behalf. If the EEOC decides not to investigate the claim, the EEOC issues a "right to sue" that allows the victim to bring her or his own lawsuit against the employer.

The EEOC does not investigate every claim of employment discrimination, regardless of the merits of the claim. Generally, it investigates only "priority cases," such as cases involving retaliatory discharge (firing an employee in retaliation for submitting a claim to the EEOC) and cases involving types of discrimination that are of particular concern to the EEOC.

25–1b Limitations on Class Actions

The United States Supreme Court issued an important decision in 2011 that limits the rights of employees—as a group, or class—to bring discrimination claims against their employer. **CASE EXAMPLE 25.1** A small group of female employees sued Wal-Mart, the nation's largest private employer, alleging that store managers who had discretion over pay and promotions were biased against women and disproportionately favored men. The employees wished to bring a class action—a lawsuit in which a small number of plaintiffs sue on behalf of a larger group. Lower courts ruled that the employees' class-action suit could proceed, and Wal-Mart appealed. The United States Supreme Court ruled in favor of Wal-Mart, effectively blocking the class action. The Court held that the women could not maintain a class action because they had failed to prove a company-wide policy of discrimination that had a common effect on all women covered by the action.[2] ▨

25–1c Intentional and Unintentional Discrimination

Title VII prohibits both intentional and unintentional discrimination.

Intentional Discrimination Intentional discrimination by an employer against an employee is known as **disparate-treatment discrimination.** Because intent can be difficult to prove, courts have established certain procedures for resolving disparate-treatment cases.

A plaintiff who sues on the basis of disparate-treatment discrimination in hiring must first make out a **prima facie case.** *Prima facie* is Latin for "at first sight." Legally, it refers to a fact that is presumed to be true unless contradicted by evidence.

To establish a *prima facie* case of disparate-treatment discrimination in hiring, a plaintiff must show all of the following:

1. The plaintiff is a member of a protected class.
2. The plaintiff applied and was qualified for the job in question.
3. The plaintiff was rejected by the employer.
4. The employer continued to seek applicants for the position or filled the position with a person not in a protected class.

Disparate-Treatment Discrimination A form of employment discrimination that results when an employer intentionally discriminates against employees who are members of protected classes.

***Prima Facie* Case** A case in which the plaintiff has produced sufficient evidence of his or her claim that the case will be decided for the plaintiff unless the defendant produces no evidence to rebut it.

---

2. *Wal-Mart Stores, Inc. v. Dukes,* ___ U.S. ___, 131 S.Ct. 2541, 180 L.Ed.2d 374 (2011).

A plaintiff who can meet these relatively easy requirements has made out a *prima facie* case of illegal discrimination and will win in the absence of a legally acceptable employer defense.

The burden then shifts to the employer-defendant, who must articulate a legal reason for not hiring the plaintiff. If the employer did not have a legal reason for taking the adverse employment action, the plaintiff wins.

If the employer can articulate a legitimate reason for the action, the burden shifts back to the plaintiff. To prevail, the plaintiff must then show that the employer's reason is a *pretext* (not the true reason) and that the employer's decision was actually motivated by discriminatory intent.

Unintentional Discrimination Employers often use interviews and tests to choose from among a large number of applicants for job openings. Minimum educational requirements are also common. These practices and procedures may have an unintended discriminatory impact on a protected class. **Disparate-impact discrimination** occurs when a protected group is adversely affected by an employer's practices, procedures, or tests, even though they do not appear to be discriminatory. (For tips on how human resources managers can prevent these types of discrimination claims, see the *Linking Business Law to Corporate Management* feature at the end of this chapter.)

In a disparate-impact discrimination case, the complaining party must first show statistically that the employer's practices, procedures, or tests are discriminatory in effect. Once the plaintiff has made out a *prima facie* case, the burden of proof shifts to the employer to show that the practices or procedures in question were justified.

There are two ways of proving that disparate-impact discrimination exists, as discussed next.

> **Disparate-Impact Discrimination** Discrimination that results from certain employer practices or procedures that, although not discriminatory on their face, have a discriminatory effect.

Pool of Applicants. A plaintiff can prove a disparate impact by comparing the employer's workforce with the pool of qualified individuals available in the local labor market. The plaintiff must show that (1) as a result of educational or other job requirements or hiring procedures, (2) the percentage of nonwhites, women, or members of other protected classes in the employer's workforce (3) does not reflect the percentage of that group in the pool of qualified applicants. If the plaintiff can show a connection between the practice and the disparity, he or she has made out a *prima facie* case and need not provide evidence of discriminatory intent.

Rate of Hiring. A plaintiff can also prove disparate-impact discrimination by comparing the employer's selection rates of members and nonmembers of a protected class (for instance, whites and nonwhites). When a job requirement or hiring procedure excludes members of a protected class from an employer's workforce at a substantially higher rate than nonmembers, discrimination occurs, regardless of the balance in the employer's workforce.

The EEOC has devised a test, called the "four-fifths rule," to determine whether an employment selection procedure is discriminatory on its face. Under this rule, a selection rate for protected classes that is less than four-fifths, or 80 percent, of the rate for the group with the highest rate will generally be regarded as evidence of disparate impact.

EXAMPLE 25.2 Shady Cove District Fire Department administers an exam to applicants for the position of firefighter. At the exam session, one hundred white applicants take the test, and fifty pass and are hired. At the same exam session, sixty minority applicants take the test, but only twelve pass and are hired. Because twelve is less than four-fifths (80 percent) of fifty, the test will be considered discriminatory under the EEOC guidelines. ■

25-1d Discrimination Based on Race, Color, and National Origin

Title VII prohibits employers from discriminating against employees or job applicants on the basis of race, color, or national origin. If an employer's standards for selecting or promoting employees have a discriminatory effect on job applicants or employees in these protected

How might the "four-fifths rule" apply to the results of a fire department's entrance exam?

classes, then a presumption of illegal discrimination arises. To avoid liability, the employer must then show that its standards have a substantial, demonstrable relationship to realistic qualifications for the job in question.

CASE EXAMPLE 25.3 Jiann Min Chang was an instructor at Alabama Agricultural and Mechanical University (AAMU). When AAMU terminated his employment, Chang filed a lawsuit claiming discrimination based on national origin. Chang established a *prima facie* case because he (1) was a member of a protected class, (2) was qualified for the job, (3) suffered an adverse employment action, and (4) was replaced by someone outside his protected class (a non-Asian instructor).

AAMU, however, showed that Chang had argued with a university vice president and refused to comply with her instructions. The court ruled that the university had not renewed Chang's contract for a legitimate reason—insubordination—and therefore was not liable for unlawful discrimination.[3] ▪

Reverse Discrimination

Note that discrimination based on race can also take the form of *reverse discrimination,* or discrimination against "majority" individuals, such as white males. **EXAMPLE 25.4** An African American woman fires four white men from their management positions at a school district. The men file a lawsuit for reverse discrimination. They argue that the woman was trying to eliminate white males from the district administration in violation of Title VII. The woman claims that the terminations were part of a reorganization plan to cut costs. If the judge (or jury in a jury trial) agrees with the men that they were fired for racially discriminatory reasons, then they will be entitled to damages. If, however, the school district can show that the real reason for the terminations was a legitimate cost-cutting measure, then normally their case will be dismissed. ▪

Potential Section 1981 Claims

Victims of racial or ethnic discrimination may also have a cause of action under 42 U.S.C. Section 1981. This section, which was enacted in 1866 to protect the rights of freed slaves, prohibits discrimination on the basis of race or ethnicity in the formation or enforcement of contracts. Because employment is often a contractual relationship, Section 1981 can provide an alternative basis for a plaintiff's action and is potentially advantageous because it does not place a cap on damages.

25–1e Discrimination Based on Religion

Title VII also prohibits government employers, private employers, and unions from discriminating against persons because of their religion. (This chapter's *Adapting the Law to the Online Environment* feature discusses how employers who examine prospective employees' social media posts, including posts concerning religion, might engage in unlawful discrimination.)

Employers cannot treat their employees more or less favorably based on the employees' religious beliefs or practices and cannot require employees to participate in any religious activity (or forbid them from participating in one). **EXAMPLE 25.5** Jason Sewell, a salesperson for TC Chevy, does not attend the weekly prayer meetings of dealership employees for several months. Then he is discharged by his employer. If he can show that the dealership required its employees to attend prayer gatherings and fired him for not attending, he has a valid claim of religious discrimination. ▪

Reasonable Accommodation

An employer must "reasonably accommodate" the religious practices of its employees, unless to do so would cause undue hardship to the employer's business. Reasonable accommodation is required even if the employee's belief is not based on the doctrines of a traditionally recognized religion, such as Christianity or Judaism, or a

LEARNING OBJECTIVE 2

What must an employer do to avoid liability for religious discrimination?

iStockPhoto.com/Juanmonino

If this salesperson refuses to attend weekly Christian prayer meetings at the company headquarters, what might happen if he is fired as a consequence?

---

3. *Jiann Min Chang v. Alabama Agricultural and Mechanical University*, 2009 WL 3403180 (11th Cir. 2009).

particular denomination, such as Baptist. The only requirement is that the belief be sincerely held by the employee.

Undue Hardship If an employee's religion prohibits him or her from working on a certain day of the week, for instance, the employer must make a reasonable attempt to accommodate this requirement. The employer is not required to permanently give the employee the requested day off, however, if to do so would cause the employer undue hardship.

CASE EXAMPLE 25.6 Miguel Sánchez-Rodríguez sold cell phones in shopping malls for AT&T. After six years, Sánchez informed his supervisors that he had become a Seventh Day

ADAPTING THE LAW TO THE ONLINE ENVIRONMENT
Hiring Discrimination Based on Social Media Posts

Human resource officers in most companies routinely check job candidates' social media posts when deciding whom to hire. Certainly, every young person is warned not to post photos that they might later regret having made available to potential employers. But a more serious issue involves standard reviewing of job candidates' social media information. Specifically, do employers discriminate based on such information?

An Experiment in Hiring Discrimination via Online Social Networks

Two researchers at Carnegie-Mellon University conducted an experiment to determine whether social media information posted by prospective employees influences employers' hiring decisions.[a] The researchers created false résumés and social media profiles. They submitted job applications on behalf of the fictional "candidates" to about four thousand U.S. employers. They then compared employers' responses to different groups—for example, to Muslim candidates versus Christian candidates.

The researchers found that candidates whose public profiles indicated that they were Muslim were less likely to be called for interviews than Christian applicants. The difference was particularly pronounced in parts of the country with more conservative residents. In those locations, Muslims received callbacks only 2 percent of the time, compared with 17 percent for Christian applicants. According to the authors of the study, "Hiring discrimination via online searches of candidates may not be widespread, but online disclosures of personal traits can significantly influence the hiring decisions of a self-selected set of employers."

Job Candidates' Perception of the Hiring Process

In another study, researchers at North Carolina State University looked at how job applicants view prospective employers' use of their social media profiles during the hiring process.[b] Job candidates appear to view the hiring process as unfair when they know that their social media profiles have been used in the selection process. This perception, according to the researchers, makes litigation more likely.

The EEOC Speaks Up

Since 2014, the Equal Employment Opportunity Commission (EEOC) has investigated how prospective employers can use social media to engage in discrimination in the hiring process. Given that the Society for Human Resource Management estimates that more than three-fourths of its members use social media in their employment screening process, the EEOC is interested in regulating this procedure. Social media sites, examined closely, can provide information to a prospective employer on the applicant's race, color, national origin, disability, religion, and other protected characteristics. The EEOC has reminded employers that such information—whether it comes from social media postings or other sources—may not legally be used to make employment decisions on prohibited bases, such as race, gender, and religion.

a. A. Acquisti and C. N. Fong, "An Experiment in Hiring Discrimination Via Online Social Networks," *Social Service Research Network*, October 26, 2014.

b. J. W. Stoughton, L. F. Thompson, and A. W. Meade, "Examining Applicant Reactions to the Use of Social Networking Websites in Pre-Employment Screening," *Journal of Business and Psychology*, November 2013, DOI: 10.1007/s10869-013-9333-6.

Adventist and could no longer work on Saturdays for religious reasons. AT&T responded that his inability to work on Saturdays would cause it hardship.

As a reasonable accommodation, the company suggested that Sánchez swap schedules with others and offered him two other positions that did not require work on Saturdays. Sánchez could not find workers to swap shifts with him, however, and he declined the other jobs because they would result in less income. He began missing work on Saturdays. After a time, AT&T indicated that it would discipline him for any additional Saturdays that he missed. Eventually, he was placed on active disciplinary status. Sánchez resigned and filed a religious discrimination lawsuit against AT&T. The court found in favor of AT&T, and a federal appellate court affirmed. The company had made adequate efforts at accommodation.[4] ■

25–1f Discrimination Based on Gender

Under Title VII, as well as other federal acts, employers are forbidden from discriminating against employees on the basis of gender. Employers are prohibited from classifying jobs as male or female and from advertising positions as male or female unless they can prove that the gender of the applicant is essential to the job. In addition, employers cannot have separate male and female seniority lists and cannot refuse to promote employees based on gender.

Gender Must Be a Determining Factor   Generally, to succeed in a suit for gender discrimination, a plaintiff must demonstrate that gender was a determining factor in the employer's decision to fire or refuse to hire or promote her or him. Typically, this involves looking at all of the surrounding circumstances.

CASE EXAMPLE 25.7 Wanda Collier worked for Turner Industries Group, LLC, in the maintenance department. She complained to her supervisor that Jack Daniell, the head of the department, treated her unfairly. Her supervisor told her that Daniell had a problem with her gender and was harder on women. The supervisor talked to Daniell but did not take any disciplinary action.

A month later, Daniell confronted Collier, pushing her up against a wall and berating her. After this incident, Collier filed a formal complaint and kept a male co-worker with her at all times. A month later, she was fired. She subsequently filed a lawsuit alleging gender discrimination. The court concluded that there was enough evidence that gender was a determining factor in Daniell's conduct to allow Collier's claims to go to a jury.[5] ■

Pregnancy Discrimination   The Pregnancy Discrimination Act[6] expanded Title VII's definition of gender discrimination to include discrimination based on pregnancy. Women affected by pregnancy, childbirth, or related medical conditions must be treated the same as other persons not so affected but similar in ability to work. For instance, an employer cannot discriminate against a pregnant woman by withholding benefits available to others under employee benefit programs.

In the following case, an employer accommodated many of its employees who had lifting restrictions due to disabilities. The employer refused to accommodate a pregnant employee with a similar restriction. Did this refusal constitute a violation of the Pregnancy Discrimination Act?

> "A sign that says 'men only' looks very different on a bathroom door than a courthouse door."
>
> **THURGOOD MARSHALL**
> 1908–1993
> (ASSOCIATE JUSTICE OF THE UNITED STATES SUPREME COURT, 1967–1991)

---

4. *Sánchez-Rodríguez v. AT&T Mobility Puerto Rico, Inc.*, 673 F.3d 1 (1st Cir. 2012).
5. *Collier v. Turner Industries Group, LLC*, 797 F.Supp.2d 1029 (D. Idaho 2011).
6. 42 U.S.C. Section 2000e(k).

CASE 25.1

Young v. United Parcel Service, Inc.

United States Supreme Court, __ U.S. __, 135 S.Ct. 1338, __ L.Ed.2d __ (2015).

FACTS Peggy Young was a driver for United Parcel Service, Inc. (UPS). When she became pregnant, her doctor advised her not to lift more than twenty pounds. UPS required drivers to lift up to seventy pounds and told Young that she could not work under a lifting restriction. She filed a suit in a federal district court against UPS, claiming an unlawful refusal to accommodate her pregnancy-related lifting restriction. She alleged that UPS had multiple light-duty-for-injury categories to accommodate individuals whose non-pregnancy-related disabilities created work restrictions similar to hers. UPS responded that, because Young did not fall into any of those categories, it had not discriminated against her. The court issued a summary judgment in UPS's favor. The U.S. Court of Appeals of the Fourth Circuit affirmed the judgment. Young appealed to the United States Supreme Court.

ISSUE Did Young create a genuine dispute as to whether UPS provided more favorable treatment to employees whose situation could not reasonably be distinguished from hers?

DECISION Yes. The United States Supreme Court vacated the judgment of the U.S. Court of Appeals for the Fourth Circuit and remanded the case for further proceedings. On remand, the court must also determine whether Young created a genuine issue of material fact as

Is UPS required to offer a pregnant employee a less physically demanding job?

to whether UPS's stated reasons for treating Young less favorably were a pretext.

REASON In an action under the Pregnancy Discrimination Act, a plaintiff creates a genuine issue of material fact as to whether an employer's policies impose a significant burden on pregnant employees by providing evidence that the employer accommodates non-pregnant workers while failing to accommodate pregnant workers. In this case, if Young's allegations are true, she can show that UPS accommodates non-pregnant employees with lifting restrictions and does not accommodate pregnant employees with similar limitations. This showing would establish a *prima facie* case of disparate treatment. In response to UPS's defense, Young can point out the fact that the employer has multiple policies to accommodate non-pregnant employees with lifting restrictions. This fact might suggest that UPS's reasons for not accommodating pregnant employees with lifting restrictions are weak—"to the point that a jury could find that its reasons for failing to accommodate pregnant employees give rise to an inference of intentional discrimination."

CRITICAL THINKING—Legal Consideration *Could UPS have succeeded in this case if it had claimed simply that it would be more expensive or less convenient to include pregnant women among those whom it accommodates? Explain.*

Wage Discrimination

The Equal Pay Act of 1963 requires equal pay for male and female employees doing similar work at the same establishment. To determine whether the Equal Pay Act has been violated, a court will look to the primary duties of the two jobs—the job content rather than the job description controls. If the wage differential is due to "any factor other than gender," such as a seniority or merit system, then it does not violate the Equal Pay Act.

In 2009, Congress enacted the Lilly Ledbetter Fair Pay Act,[7] which made discriminatory wages actionable under federal law regardless of when the discrimination began. This act overturned a previous decision by the United States Supreme Court that had limited plaintiffs' time period for filing a wage discrimination complaint to 180 days after the employer's decision.[8] Today, if a plaintiff continues to work for the employer while receiving discriminatory wages, the time period for filing a complaint is basically unlimited.

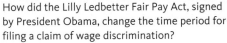

How did the Lilly Ledbetter Fair Pay Act, signed by President Obama, change the time period for filing a claim of wage discrimination?

---

7. Pub. L. No. 111-2, 123 Stat. 5 (January 5, 2009), amending 42 U.S.C. Section 2000e-5[e].
8. *Ledbetter v. Goodyear Tire Co.*, 550 U.S. 618, 127 S.Ct. 2162, 167 L.Ed.2d 982 (2007).

Should corporations be forced to publicize the ratio of CEO-to-worker pay? As part of wide-ranging changes in U.S. financial regulation, the Dodd-Frank Wall Street Reform and Consumer Protection Act[9] set forth new rules intended to hold corporate executives more accountable for their companies' performance. The Securities and Exchange Commission (SEC) was tasked with creating a regulation that forces certain companies not only to disclose how much the chief executive officer (CEO) makes, but also to establish a ratio of that pay to the median pay of the workforce. For example, if the median employee makes $45,790 and the CEO makes $12,260,000, then the pay ratio is 1 to 268. Otherwise stated, the CEO's total compensation is 268 times that of the median annual compensation for all employees.

In announcing this rule, the SEC indicated that it was unsure what potential economic benefits, "if any," would be realized from making this information public. The SEC estimates that the regulation will cost companies, in total, almost 550,000 annual paperwork hours, plus about $75 million per year to hire outside professionals. Supporters of the new regulation, however, argue that it will help investors evaluate the relative value a CEO creates. In other words, pay ratio information is supposed to act as a check against insiders paying themselves "too much."

25–1g Constructive Discharge

The majority of Title VII complaints involve unlawful discrimination in decisions to hire or fire employees. In some situations, however, employees who leave their jobs voluntarily can claim that they were "constructively discharged" by the employer. **Constructive discharge** occurs when the employer causes the employee's working conditions to be so intolerable that a reasonable person in the employee's position would feel compelled to quit.

Constructive Discharge
A termination of employment brought about by making the employee's working conditions so intolerable that the employee reasonably feels compelled to leave.

Proving Constructive Discharge To prove constructive discharge, an employee must present objective proof of intolerable working conditions. The employee must also show that the employer knew or had reason to know about the conditions yet failed to correct them within a reasonable period. In addition, courts generally require the employee to show causation—that the employer's unlawful discrimination caused the working conditions to be intolerable. Put in a different way, the employee's resignation must be a foreseeable result of the employer's discriminatory action.

Although courts weigh the facts on a case-by-case basis, employee demotion is one of the most frequently cited reasons for a finding of constructive discharge, particularly when the employee was subjected to humiliation. **EXAMPLE 25.8** Khalil's employer humiliates him in front of his co-workers by informing him that he is being demoted to an inferior position. Khalil's co-workers continually insult and harass him about his national origin (he is from Iran). The employer is aware of this discriminatory treatment but does nothing to remedy the situation, despite repeated complaints from Khalil. After several months, Khalil quits his job and files a Title VII claim. In this situation, Khalil would likely have sufficient evidence to maintain an action for constructive discharge in violation of Title VII. ■

Applies to All Title VII Discrimination Note that constructive discharge is a theory that plaintiffs can use to establish any type of discrimination claims under Title VII, including race, color, national origin, religion, gender, pregnancy, and sexual harassment. Constructive discharge has also been successfully used in situations involving discrimination based on age or disability, although it is most commonly asserted in sexual harassment cases.

When constructive discharge is claimed, the employee can pursue damages for loss of income, including back pay. These damages ordinarily are not available to an employee who left a job voluntarily.

---

9. Pub. L. No. 111-203, 124 Stat. 1376, 2010 H.R. 4173.

25-1h Sexual Harassment

Title VII also protects employees against **sexual harassment** in the workplace. Sexual harassment can take two forms: *quid pro quo* harassment and hostile-environment harassment.

Quid pro quo is a Latin phrase that is often translated to mean "something in exchange for something else." *Quid pro quo* harassment occurs when sexual favors are demanded in return for job opportunities, promotions, salary increases, and the like.

Hostile-environment harassment occurs when a pattern of sexually offensive conduct permeates the workplace and is sufficiently severe or pervasive to alter the conditions of employment and create an abusive working environment. Some sexual behavior may be acceptable in certain contexts, but unacceptable in others. Therefore, the courts evaluate hostile environment claims on a case-by-case basis.

A court considers a number of factors in assessing the severity and pervasiveness of the alleged sexual harassment. As the following case shows, these factors include the nature and frequency of the conduct and whether it unreasonably interfered with the victim's work performance.

Sexual Harassment
The demanding of sexual favors in return for job promotions or other benefits, or language or conduct that is so sexually offensive that it creates a hostile working environment.

> "Sexual harassment at work: Is it a problem for the self-employed?"
>
> **VICTORIA WOOD**
> 1953–PRESENT
> (ENGLISH COMEDIAN AND ACTOR)

CASE 25.2

Roberts v. Mike's Trucking, Ltd.

Court of Appeals of Ohio, Twelfth District, 9 N.E.3d 483 (2014).

FACTS Teresa Roberts worked for Mike's Trucking, Ltd., in Columbus, Ohio. Her supervisor was the company's owner, Mike Culbertson. According to Roberts, Culbertson called her his "sexretary" and constantly talked about his sex life. He often invited her to sit on "Big Daddy's" lap, rubbed against her, trapped her at the door and asked her for hugs or kisses, and inquired if she needed help in the restroom. Roberts asked him to stop this conduct, but he did not. She became less productive and began to suffer anxiety attacks and high blood pressure. Roberts filed a suit in an Ohio state court against Mike's, alleging a hostile work environment through sexual harassment in violation of Title VII. A jury decided in Roberts's favor, and Mike's appealed.

ISSUE Was Culbertson's conduct sufficiently severe or pervasive to create a hostile work environment through sexual harassment in violation of Title VII?

DECISION Yes. A state intermediate appellate court affirmed the lower court's judgment in Roberts's favor. "There was sufficient and substantial evidence to support the jury's finding that a reasonable person would find Culbertson's conduct created a hostile environment and Roberts found the conduct to be sufficiently severe or pervasive to affect her employment."

Can the constant sexual banter by the owner of a trucking company create a hostile work environment for employees?

REASON To conclude that conduct is severe or pervasive enough to create a hostile or abusive work environment requires a determination that (1) a reasonable person would find the environment objectively hostile and (2) the plaintiff did subjectively find the conduct severe or pervasive.

In this case, the testimony of other company employees and Roberts's fiancé corroborated her account. The witnesses confirmed that Culbertson frequently engaged in conduct ranging from inappropriate discussions to groping women. He talked about his sex life. He asked Roberts and other female employees if they needed help in the restroom. He asked them to sit in "Big Daddy's" lap. The witnesses also confirmed that Culbertson's behavior became worse over time. Additionally, Roberts's testimony that she did not want to go to work anymore, became less productive, and suffered anxiety attacks established that Culbertson's conduct unreasonably interfered with her work performance. Her fiancé confirmed that she had lost confidence in her ability to perform her job.

CRITICAL THINKING—Ethical Consideration *Was Culbertson's conduct at any point unethical? Discuss.*

Tangible Employment Action A significant change in employment status or benefits, such as occurs when an employee is fired, refused a promotion, or reassigned to a lesser position.

Harassment by Supervisors For an employer to be held liable for a supervisor's sexual harassment, the supervisor normally must have taken a *tangible employment action* against the employee. A **tangible employment action** is a significant change in employment status or benefits, such as when an employee is fired, refused a promotion, demoted, or reassigned to a position with significantly different responsibilities. Only a supervisor, or another person acting with the authority of the employer, can cause this sort of injury. A constructive discharge also qualifies as a tangible employment action.

The United States Supreme Court has issued several important rulings in cases alleging sexual harassment by supervisors that established what is known as the "*Ellerth/Faragher* affirmative defense."[10] The defense has two elements:

1. That the employer has taken reasonable care to prevent and promptly correct any sexually harassing behavior (by establishing effective antiharassment policies and complaint procedures, for example).

2. That the plaintiff-employee unreasonably failed to take advantage of any preventive or corrective opportunities provided by the employer to avoid harm.

An employer that can prove both elements will not be liable for a supervisor's harassment.

PREVENTING LEGAL DISPUTES

To avoid sexual-harassment complaints, you should be proactive in preventing sexual harassment in the workplace. Establish written policies, distribute them to employees, and review them annually. Make it clear that the policies prohibiting harassment and discrimination apply to everyone at all levels of your organization. Provide training. Assure employees that no one will be punished for making a complaint. If you receive complaints, always take them seriously and investigate—no matter how trivial they might seem.

Prompt remedial action is key, but normally it must not include any adverse action against the complainant (such as immediate termination). Also, never discourage employees from seeking the assistance of government agencies (such as the EEOC) or threaten or punish them for doing so. It is generally best to obtain the advice of counsel when you receive a sexual-harassment complaint.

Why is a tangible employment action required for a company to be held liable for harassment by supervisors?

Retaliation by Employers

Employers sometimes retaliate against employees who complain about sexual harassment or other Title VII violations. Retaliation can take many forms. An employer might demote or fire the person, or otherwise change the terms, conditions, and benefits of employment. Title VII prohibits retaliation, and employees can sue their employers on that basis.

In a *retaliation claim,* an individual asserts that she or he has suffered a harm as a result of making a charge, testifying, or participating in a Title VII investigation or proceeding. Plaintiffs do not have to prove that the challenged action adversely affected their workplace or employment. Instead, to prove retaliation, plaintiffs must show that the challenged action was one that would likely have dissuaded a reasonable worker from making or supporting a charge of discrimination.

Title VII's retaliation protection has been extended to an employee who spoke out about discrimination during an employer's internal investigation of another employee's complaint.[11] The retaliation provision has also protected an employee who was fired after his fiancée filed a gender discrimination claim against their employer.[12]

---

10. *Burlington Industries, Inc. v. Ellerth,* 524 U.S. 742, 118 S.Ct. 2257, 141 L.Ed.2d 633 (1998); and *Faragher v. City of Boca Raton,* 524 U.S. 775, 118 S.Ct. 2275, 141 L.Ed.2d 662 (1998).
11. See *Crawford v. Metropolitan Government of Nashville and Davidson County, Tennessee,* 555 U.S. 271, 129 S.Ct. 846, 172 L.Ed.2d 650 (2009).
12. See *Thompson v. North American Stainless, LP,* 562 U.S. 170, 131 S.Ct. 863, 178 L.Ed.2d 694 (2011).

In the following case, a female law professor lost her job after she complained about comments made by her dean and colleagues. The court had to decide whether her employer had retaliated against her for engaging in protected conduct.

CASE 25.3

Morales-Cruz v. University of Puerto Rico

United States Court of Appeals, First Circuit, 676 F.3d 220 (2012).

FACTS In 2003, Myrta Morales-Cruz began a tenure-track teaching position at the University of Puerto Rico School of Law. During her five-year probationary period, one of her colleagues in a law school clinic had an affair with one of their students that resulted in a pregnancy. Morales-Cruz did not report the affair, but no university rule required her to do so.

In 2008, Morales-Cruz asked the university's administrative committee to approve a one-year extension for her tenure review. The law school's dean criticized Morales-Cruz for failing to report her colleague's affair. He later recommended granting the extension but called Morales-Cruz "insecure," "immature," and "fragile." Similarly, a law school committee recommended granting the extension, but a dissenting professor commented that Morales-Cruz had shown poor judgment, had "personality flaws," and had trouble with "complex and sensitive" situations.

Morales-Cruz soon learned about the negative comments and complained in writing to the university's chancellor. The dean then recommended denying the one-year extension, and the administrative committee ultimately did so. When her employment was terminated, Morales-Cruz sued the university under Title VII. Among other things, she asserted that the dean had retaliated against her for complaining to the chancellor. A federal district court found that Morales-Cruz had not stated a proper retaliation claim under Title VII, and she appealed.

When a university does not renew an instructor's employment contract after she complains about a supervisor's criticisms of her, can she sue for retaliation?

ISSUE Can Morales-Cruz bring a retaliation claim under Title VII because the law school's dean retaliated against her for complaining to the university's chancellor?

DECISION No. The appellate court affirmed the district court's judgment for the University of Puerto Rico.

REASON Under Title VII, an employer may not retaliate against an employee because he or she has opposed a practice prohibited by Title VII. In this case, Morales-Cruz argued that the dean had recommended not granting the one-year extension because she had complained about "discriminatory" comments. The court found that Morales-Cruz did not allege any facts that could be construed as gender-based discrimination. While the comments were hardly flattering, they were entirely gender-neutral. After all, the dean and the dissenting professor had said only that Morales-Cruz had showed poor judgment, had personality flaws, and was fragile, insecure, and immature. Thus, even if the dean had retaliated against Morales-Cruz, it was not for engaging in conduct protected by Title VII.

CRITICAL THINKING—Ethical Consideration *Could the dean have had legitimate reasons for changing his mind about the one-year extension? If so, what were they?*

Harassment by Co-Workers and Nonemployees When the harassment of co-workers, rather than supervisors, creates a hostile working environment, an employee may still have a cause of action against the employer. Normally, though, the employer will be held liable only if the employer knew, or should have known, about the harassment and failed to take immediate remedial action.

Occasionally, a court may also hold an employer liable for harassment by *nonemployees* if the employer knew about the harassment and failed to take corrective action. **EXAMPLE 25.9** Gordon, who owns and manages a Great Bites restaurant, knows that one of his regular customers, Dean, repeatedly harasses Sharon, a waitress. If Gordon does nothing and permits the harassment to continue, he may be liable under Title VII even though Dean is not an employee of the restaurant. ■

Same-Gender Harassment

In *Oncale v. Sundowner Offshore Services, Inc.*,[13] the United States Supreme Court held that Title VII protection extends to individuals who are sexually harassed by members of the same gender. Proving that the harassment in same-gender cases is "based on sex" can be difficult, though. It is usually easier to establish a case of same-gender harassment when the harasser is homosexual.

Sexual Orientation Harassment

Although federal law (Title VII) does not prohibit discrimination or harassment based on a person's sexual orientation, a growing number of states have enacted laws that prohibit sexual orientation discrimination in private employment. Some states, such as Michigan, explicitly prohibit discrimination based on a person's gender identity or expression. Also, many companies have voluntarily established nondiscrimination policies that include sexual orientation.

Workers in the United States often have more protection against sexual harassment in the workplace than workers in other countries, as this chapter's *Beyond Our Borders* feature explains.

25-1i Online Harassment

Employees' online activities can create a hostile working environment in many ways. Racial jokes, ethnic slurs, or other comments contained in e-mail, text or instant messages, or social media or blog posts can become the basis for a claim of hostile-environment harassment or other forms of discrimination. Similarly, a worker who regularly sees sexually explicit and offensive images on a co-worker's computer screen or tablet device may claim that they create a hostile working environment.

Nevertheless, employers may be able to avoid liability for online harassment if they take prompt remedial action. **EXAMPLE 25.10** While working at TriCom, Shonda Dean receives racially harassing e-mailed jokes from another employee. Shortly afterward, the company issues a warning to the offending employee about the proper use of the e-mail system and holds two meetings to discuss company policy on the use of the system. If Dean sues TriCom

---

13. 523 U.S. 75, 118 S.Ct. 998, 140 L.Ed.2d 207 (1998).

BEYOND OUR BORDERS   Sexual Harassment in Other Nations

The problem of sexual harassment in the workplace is not confined to the United States. Indeed, it is a worldwide problem for female workers.

In Argentina, Brazil, Egypt, Turkey, and many other countries, there is no legal protection against any form of employment discrimination. Even in countries that do have laws prohibiting discriminatory employment practices, including gender-based discrimination, those laws often do not specifically include sexual harassment as a discriminatory practice.

Several countries have attempted to remedy this omission by passing new laws or amending others to specifically prohibit sexual harassment in the workplace. Japan, for example, has amended its Equal Employment Opportunity Law to include a provision making sexual harassment illegal. Thailand has also passed a sexual-harassment law. The European Union has adopted a directive that specifically identifies sexual harassment as a form of discrimination.

Nevertheless, women's groups throughout Europe contend that corporations in European countries tend to view sexual harassment with "quiet tolerance." They contrast this attitude with that of most U.S. corporations, which have implemented specific procedures to deal with harassment claims.

CRITICAL THINKING

■ Why do you think U.S. corporations are more aggressive than European companies in taking steps to prevent sexual harassment in the workplace?

for racial discrimination, a court may find that because the employer took prompt remedial action, TriCom should not be held liable for its employee's racially harassing e-mails. ■

25-1j Remedies under Title VII

Employer liability under Title VII may be extensive. If the plaintiff successfully proves that unlawful discrimination occurred, he or she may be awarded reinstatement, back pay, retroactive promotions, and damages. Compensatory damages are available only in cases of intentional discrimination. Punitive damages may be recovered against a private employer only if the employer acted with malice or reckless indifference to an individual's rights.

The statute limits the total amount of compensatory and punitive damages that the plaintiff can recover from specific employers, depending on the size of the employer. The cap ranges from $50,000 for employers with one hundred or fewer employees to $300,000 for employers with more than five hundred employees.

If this employee receives racially harassing e-mail jokes from another employee, why might she not prevail in a lawsuit for racial discrimination?

25-2 Discrimination Based on Age

LEARNING OBJECTIVE 4
What federal act prohibits discrimination based on age?

Age discrimination is potentially the most widespread form of discrimination, because anyone—regardless of race, color, national origin, or gender—could eventually be a victim. The Age Discrimination in Employment Act (ADEA)[14] prohibits employment discrimination on the basis of age against individuals forty years of age or older. The act also prohibits mandatory retirement for nonmanagerial workers.

For the act to apply, an employer must have twenty or more employees, and the employer's business activities must affect interstate commerce. The EEOC administers the ADEA, but the act also permits private causes of action against employers for age discrimination.

The ADEA includes a provision that extends protections against age discrimination to federal government employees.[15] This provision encompasses not only claims of age discrimination, but also claims of retaliation for complaining about age discrimination, which are not specifically mentioned in the statute.[16] Thus, the ADEA protects federal and private-sector employees from retaliation based on age-related complaints.

25-2a Procedures under the ADEA

The burden-shifting procedure under the ADEA differs from the procedure under Title VII as a result of a United States Supreme Court decision that dramatically changed the burden of proof in age discrimination cases.[17] As explained earlier, if the plaintiff in a Title VII case can show that the employer was motivated, at least in part, by unlawful discrimination, the burden of proof shifts to the employer to articulate a legitimate nondiscriminatory reason. Thus, in cases in which the employer has a "mixed motive" for discharging an employee, the employer has the burden of proving its reason was legitimate.

Under the ADEA, in contrast, a plaintiff must show that the unlawful discrimination was not just a reason but *the* reason for the adverse employment action. In other words, the employee has the burden of establishing "but for" causation—but for the plaintiff's age, the adverse action would not have happened.

---

14. 29 U.S.C. Sections 621–634.
15. See 29 U.S.C. Section 632(a) (2000 ed., Supp. V).
16. *Gomez-Perez v. Potter,* 553 U.S. 474, 128 S.Ct. 1931, 170 L.Ed.2d 887 (2008).
17. *Gross v. FBL Financial Services,* 557 U.S. 167, 129 S.Ct. 2343, 174 L.Ed.2d 119 (2009).

Prima Facie **Age Discrimination Case** To establish a *prima facie* case, the plaintiff must show that he or she was the following:

1. A member of the protected age group.

2. Qualified for the position from which he or she was discharged.

3. Discharged because of age discrimination.

Then the burden shifts to the employer to give a legitimate nondiscriminatory reason for the adverse action.

Pretext If the employer offers a legitimate reason for its action, then the plaintiff must show that the stated reason is only a pretext and that the plaintiff's age was the real reason for the employer's decision.

CASE EXAMPLE 25.11 Josephine Mora, a fund-raiser for Jackson Memorial Foundation, Inc., was sixty-two years old when the foundation's chief executive officer (CEO) fired her. Mora filed an age discrimination suit against the foundation. She asserted that when she was fired, the CEO told her, "I need someone younger I can pay less." A witness heard that statement and also heard the CEO say that Mora was "too old to be working here anyway." The CEO denied making these statements, and the foundation claimed that Mora was terminated for poor job performance.

A district court granted a summary judgment in the foundation's favor, and Mora appealed. A federal appellate court reversed, concluding that the lower court's analysis of causation was incorrect. The court held that a reasonable juror could have accepted that the CEO had made discriminatory remarks and could have found that these remarks were sufficient evidence of a discriminatory motive. If so, that could show that Mora was fired because of her age. The court therefore remanded the case back to the lower court for a trial.[18] ■

25-2b State Employees Not Covered by the ADEA

Generally, the states are immune from lawsuits brought by private individuals in federal court, unless a state consents to the suit. This immunity stems from the United States Supreme Court's interpretation of the Eleventh Amendment (the text of this amendment is included in Appendix B of this text).

State immunity under the Eleventh Amendment is not absolute, however. In some situations, such as when fundamental rights are at stake, Congress has the power to abrogate (revoke) state immunity to private suits through legislation that unequivocally shows Congress's intent to subject states to private suits.[19]

Generally, state employers are immune from private suits brought by employees under the ADEA (for age discrimination), the Americans with Disabilities Act (for disability discrimination), and the Fair Labor Standards Act (which relates to wages and hours). In contrast, states are not immune from the requirements of the Family and Medical Leave Act.

25-3 Discrimination Based on Disability

The Americans with Disabilities Act (ADA)[20] prohibits disability-based discrimination in workplaces with fifteen or more workers (with the exception of state government employers, who are generally immune under the Eleventh Amendment, as just discussed). Basically, the

18. *Mora v. Jackson Memorial Foundation, Inc.,* 597 F.3d 1201 (2010).
19. *Tennessee v. Lane,* 541 U.S. 509, 124 S.Ct. 1978, 158 L.Ed.2d 820 (2004).
20. 42 U.S.C. Sections 12102–12118.

"Growing old is like being increasingly penalized for a crime you have not committed."

ANTHONY POWELL
1905–2000
(ENGLISH NOVELIST)

When is firing an older worker considered age discrimination?

StockLite/ShutterStock.com

ADA requires that employers reasonably accommodate the needs of persons with disabilities unless to do so would cause undue hardship. The ADA Amendments Act broadened the ADA's coverage.[21]

25-3a Procedures under the ADA

To prevail on a claim under the ADA, a plaintiff must show all of the following:

1. The plaintiff has a disability.

2. The plaintiff is otherwise qualified for the employment in question.

3. The plaintiff was excluded from the employment solely because of the disability.

As in Title VII cases, a plaintiff must pursue her or his claim through the EEOC before filing an action in court for a violation of the ADA.

The EEOC may decide to investigate and perhaps even sue the employer on behalf of the employee. If the EEOC decides not to sue, then the employee is entitled to sue in court. The EEOC can bring a suit against an employer for disability-based discrimination even though the employee previously agreed to submit any job-related disputes to arbitration.

Plaintiffs in lawsuits brought under the ADA may obtain many of the same remedies available under Title VII. These include reinstatement, back pay, a limited amount of compensatory and punitive damages (for intentional discrimination), and certain other forms of relief. Repeat violators may be ordered to pay fines of up to $100,000.

25-3b What Is a Disability?

The ADA is broadly drafted to cover persons with a wide range of disabilities. Specifically, the ADA defines *disability* to include any of the following:

1. A physical or mental impairment that substantially limits one or more of an individual's major life activities.

2. A record of such impairment.

3. Being regarded as having such an impairment.

Health conditions that have been considered disabilities under the federal law include alcoholism, acquired immune deficiency syndrome (AIDS), blindness, cancer, cerebral palsy, diabetes, heart disease, muscular dystrophy, and paraplegia. Testing positive for the human immunodeficiency virus (HIV) and morbid obesity (defined as existing when an individual's weight is two times the normal weight for his or her height) have also qualified as disabilities.

Association with Disabled Persons A separate provision in the ADA prevents employers from taking adverse employment actions based on stereotypes or assumptions about individuals who associate with people who have disabilities.[22] **EXAMPLE 25.12** Joan, an employer, refuses to hire Edward, who has a daughter with a physical disability. She bases her decision on the assumption that because of his daughter's disability, Edward will miss work too often or be unreliable. Edward can sue Joan for violating the ADA's provisions. ■

Mitigating Measures At one time, the courts focused on whether a person was disabled *after* the use of corrective devices or medication. Then Congress amended the ADA to strengthen its protections and prohibit employers from considering mitigating measures, such as medications, when determining if an individual has a disability.

> "Jobs are physically easier, but the worker now takes home worries instead of an aching back."
>
> **HOMER BIGART**
> 1907–1991
> (AMERICAN JOURNALIST)

---

21. 42 U.S.C. Sections 12103 and 12205a.
22. 42 U.S.C. Section 12112(b)(4)

Disability is now determined on a case-by-case basis. A condition may fit the definition of disability in one set of circumstances, but not in another. **CASE EXAMPLE 25.13** Larry Rohr, a welding specialist for a power district in Arizona, was diagnosed with type 2 diabetes. If he fails to follow a complex regimen of daily insulin injections and blood tests, as well as a strict diet, his blood sugar will rise to a level that aggravates his disease. Therefore, Rohr's physician forbade him from taking work assignments that involved overnight, out-of-town travel, which were common in his job.

Because of these limitations, the power district asked him to transfer, apply for disability, or take early retirement. Rohr sued for disability discrimination. The lower court granted summary judgment for the employer. Rohr appealed. A federal appellate court reversed. The court held that under the amended ADA, diabetes is a disability if it significantly restricts an individual's eating (a major life activity), as it did for Rohr. Therefore, Rohr was entitled to a trial on his discrimination claim.[23] ▪

This welding specialist suffers from type 2 diabetes and therefore can't travel overnight because of his need for injections, blood tests, and a strict diet. Can his employer force him to take early retirement?

Disclosure of Confidential Medical Information ADA provisions also require employers to keep their employees' medical information confidential.[24] An employee who discovers that an employer has disclosed his or her confidential medical information has a right to sue the employer—even if the employee was not technically disabled.

Employers can expect lawsuits if an employee makes a Facebook post about an injury sustained by someone else in the company. **CASE EXAMPLE 25.14** George Shoun was working at his job at Best Formed Plastics, Inc., when he fell and injured his shoulder. Another Best Formed employee, Jane Stewart, prepared an accident report for the incident and processed Shoun's workers' compensation claim. As a result of the injury, Shoun had to take several months off work and received workers' compensation.

Stewart posted on her Facebook page a statement about how Shoun's shoulder injury "kept him away from work for 11 months and now he is trying to sue us." Shoun sued Best Formed under the ADA for wrongfully disclosing confidential information about his medical condition to other people via Facebook. He claimed the action resulted in loss of employment and impairment of his earning capacity. The court allowed Shoun's claim to go forward to trial.[25] ▪

25–3c Reasonable Accommodation

The ADA does not require that employers accommodate the needs of job applicants or employees with disabilities who are not otherwise qualified for the work. If a job applicant or an employee with a disability can perform essential job functions with a reasonable accommodation, however, the employer must make the accommodation.

Required modifications may include installing ramps for a wheelchair, establishing more flexible working hours, creating or modifying job assignments, and creating or improving training materials and procedures. Generally, employers should give primary consideration to employees' preferences in deciding what accommodations should be made.

Undue Hardship Employers who do not accommodate the needs of persons with disabilities must demonstrate that the accommodations will cause "undue hardship" in terms of being significantly difficult or expensive for the employer. Usually, the courts decide whether an accommodation constitutes an undue hardship on a case-by-case basis by looking at the employer's resources in relation to the specific accommodation.

---

23. *Rohr v. Salt River Project Agricultural Improvement and Power District,* 555 F.3d 850 (9th Cir. 2009).
24. 42 U.S.C. Sections 12112(d)(3)(B), (C), and 12112(d)(4)(C).
25. *Shoun v. Best Formed Plastics, Inc.,* 28 F.Supp.3d 786 (N.D.Ind. 2014).

EXAMPLE 25.15 Bryan Lockhart, who uses a wheelchair, works for a cell phone company that provides parking for its employees. Lockhart informs company supervisors that the parking spaces are so narrow that he is unable to extend the ramp that allows him to get in and out of his van. Lockhart requests that the company reasonably accommodate his needs by paying a monthly fee for him to use a larger parking space in an adjacent lot. In this situation, a court would likely find that it would not be an undue hardship for the employer to pay for additional parking for Lockhart. ■

Job Applications and Preemployment Physical Exams Employers must modify their job-application process so that those with disabilities can compete for jobs with those who do not have disabilities. For instance, a job announcement might be modified to allow job applicants to respond by e-mail or letter, as well as by telephone, so that it does not discriminate against potential applicants with hearing impairments.

Employers are restricted in the kinds of questions they may ask on job-application forms and during preemployment interviews. Furthermore, they cannot require persons with disabilities to submit to preemployment physicals unless such exams are required of all other applicants. Employers can condition an offer of employment on the applicant's successfully passing a medical examination, but can disqualify the applicant only if the medical problems discovered would render the applicant unable to perform the job.

Substance Abuse Drug addiction is a disability under the ADA because drug addiction is a substantially limiting impairment. Those who are actually using illegal drugs are not protected by the act, however. The ADA protects only persons with *former* drug addictions—those who have completed or are now in a supervised drug-rehabilitation program. Individuals who have used drugs casually in the past are not protected under the act. They are not considered addicts and therefore do not have a disability (addiction).

People suffering from alcoholism are protected by the ADA. Employers cannot legally discriminate against employees simply because they are suffering from alcoholism. Of course, employers have the right to prohibit the use of alcohol in the workplace and can require that employees not be under the influence of alcohol while working. Employers can also fire or refuse to hire a person who is an alcoholic if he or she poses a substantial risk of harm either to himself or herself or to others and the risk cannot be reduced by reasonable accommodation.

Exhibit 25–1 illustrates the coverage of the employment discrimination laws discussed in this chapter.

Health-Insurance Plans Workers with disabilities must be given equal access to any health insurance provided to other employees and cannot be excluded from coverage for preexisting

Exhibit 25–1 Coverage of Employment Discrimination Laws

TITLE VII OF THE CIVIL RIGHTS ACT	AGE DISCRIMINATION IN EMPLOYMENT ACT	AMERICANS WITH DISABILITIES ACT (AS AMENDED)
Prohibits discrimination based on race, color, national origin, religion, gender (including wage discrimination), and pregnancy; prohibits sexual harassment.	Prohibits discrimination against persons over 40.	Prohibits discrimination against persons with a mental or physical impairment that substantially limits a major life activity now or in the past, or who are regarded as having such an impairment, or who are associated with a disabled person.
Applies to employers with 15 or more employees.	Applies to employers with 20 or more employees.	Applies to employers with 15 or more employees.

health conditions. An employer can put a limit, or cap, on health-care payments under its group health policy, but such caps must be "applied equally to all insured employees" and must not "discriminate on the basis of disability." Whenever a group health-care plan makes a disability-based distinction in its benefits, the plan violates the ADA (unless the employer can justify its actions under the business necessity defense, discussed shortly).

LEARNING OBJECTIVE 5
What are three defenses to claims of employment discrimination?

25-4 Defenses to Employment Discrimination

The first line of defense for an employer charged with employment discrimination is to assert that the plaintiff has failed to meet his or her initial burden of proving that discrimination occurred. Once a plaintiff succeeds in proving discrimination, the burden shifts to the employer to justify the discriminatory practice.

Possible justifications include that the discrimination was the result of a business necessity, a bona fide occupational qualification, or a seniority system. In addition, as noted earlier, an effective antiharassment policy and prompt remedial action when harassment occurs can sometimes shield employers from liability for sexual harassment under Title VII.

25-4a Business Necessity

Business Necessity A defense to an allegation of employment discrimination in which the employer demonstrates that an employment practice that discriminates against members of a protected class is related to job performance.

An employer may defend against a claim of disparate-impact (unintentional) discrimination by asserting that a practice that has a discriminatory effect is a **business necessity.** EXAMPLE 25.16 EarthFix, Inc., an international consulting agency, requires its applicants to be fluent in at least one foreign language. If requiring a foreign language is shown to have a discriminatory effect, EarthFix can argue that a foreign language is necessary for its workers to perform the job at a required level of competence. If EarthFix can demonstrate a definite connection between foreign language fluency and job performance, it normally will succeed in this business necessity defense. ■

25-4b Bona Fide Occupational Qualification

Bona Fide Occupational Qualification (BFOQ) An identifiable characteristic reasonably necessary to the normal operation of a particular business. Such characteristics can include gender, national origin, and religion, but not race.

Another defense applies when discrimination against a protected class is essential to a job— that is, when a particular trait is a **bona fide occupational qualification (BFOQ).** Race, however, can never be a BFOQ.

Generally, courts have restricted the BFOQ defense to instances in which the employee's gender is essential to the job. For instance, a women's clothing store might legitimately hire only female sales attendants if part of an attendant's job involves assisting clients in the store's dressing rooms. Similarly, the Federal Aviation Administration can legitimately impose age limits for airline pilots—but an airline cannot impose weight limits only on female flight attendants.

25-4c Seniority Systems

Seniority System A system in which those who have worked longest for an employer are first in line for promotions, salary increases, and other benefits, and are last to be laid off if the workforce must be reduced.

An employer with a history of discrimination may have no members of protected classes in upper-level positions. Nevertheless, the employer may have a defense against a discrimination suit if promotions or other job benefits have been distributed according to a fair *seniority system.* In a **seniority system,** workers with more years of service are promoted first or laid off last.

CASE EXAMPLE 25.17 Cathalene Johnson, an African American woman, was a senior service agent for Federal Express Corporation (FedEx) for more than seventeen years. She resigned in 2014 and filed suit against FedEx for discrimination based on race and gender, as well as for violation of the Equal Pay Act. Johnson claimed that FedEx had paid a white male coworker about two dollars more per hour than she received for basically the same position. FedEx argued that the man had seniority. He had worked for FedEx for seven years longer, was the most senior employee at the station where Johnson worked, and had been a courier in addition to being a service agent. The court ruled that FedEx's seniority system was fair and provided a defense to Johnson's claims.[26] ▩

25–4d After-Acquired Evidence of Employee Misconduct

In some situations, employers have attempted to avoid liability for employment discrimination on the basis of *after-acquired evid*ence of an employee's misconduct—that is, evidence that the employer discovered after the employee had filed a lawsuit. **EXAMPLE 25.18** Pratt Legal Services fires Lucy, who then sues Pratt for employment discrimination. During pretrial investigation, Pratt discovers that Lucy made material misrepresentations on her job application. Had Pratt known of these misrepresentations, it would have had grounds to fire Lucy. ▩

After-acquired evidence of wrongdoing cannot shield an employer entirely from liability for discrimination. It may, however, be used to limit the amount of damages for which the employer is liable.

Affirmative Action
Job-hiring policies that give special consideration to members of protected classes in an effort to overcome present effects of past discrimination.

25–5 Affirmative Action

Federal statutes and regulations providing for equal opportunity in the workplace were designed to reduce or eliminate discriminatory practices with respect to hiring, retaining, and promoting employees. **Affirmative action** programs go further and attempt to "make up" for past patterns of discrimination by giving members of protected classes preferential treatment in hiring or promotion. During the 1960s, all federal and state government agencies, private companies that contracted to do business with the federal government, and institutions that received federal funding were required to implement affirmative action policies.

Title VII of the Civil Rights Act neither requires nor prohibits affirmative action. Thus, most private firms have not been required to implement affirmative action policies, though many have voluntarily done so. Affirmative action programs have been controversial, however, particularly when they have resulted in reverse discrimination.

If this job candidate makes material misrepresentations on her application and is hired, can her employer use after-acquired evidence to shield itself from a discrimination lawsuit?

25–5a Equal Protection Issues

Because of their inherently discriminatory nature, affirmative action programs may violate the equal protection clause of the Fourteenth Amendment to the U.S. Constitution. Any federal, state, or local affirmative action program that uses racial or ethnic classifications as the basis for making decisions is subject to strict scrutiny (the highest standard to meet) by the courts.

Today, an affirmative action program normally is constitutional only if it attempts to remedy past discrimination and does not make use of quotas or preferences. Furthermore, once such a program has succeeded in the goal of remedying past discrimination, it must be changed or eliminated.

25–5b State Laws Prohibiting Affirmative Action Programs

Some states, including California, Maryland, Michigan, New Hampshire, Oklahoma, Virginia, and Washington, have enacted laws that prohibit affirmative action programs at public institutions (colleges, universities, and state agencies) within their borders. The United

KNOW THIS
The Fourteenth Amendment prohibits any state from denying any person "the equal protection of the laws." This prohibition applies to the federal government through the due process clause of the Fifth Amendment.

---

26. *Johnson v. Federal Exp. Corp.,* 996 F.Supp.2d 302 (M.D. Pa. 2014).

States Supreme Court recognized that states have the power to enact such bans in 2014. **CASE EXAMPLE 25.19** Michigan voters passed an initiative to amend the state's constitution to prohibit publically funded colleges from granting preferential treatment to any group on the basis of race, sex, color, ethnicity, or national origin. The law also prohibited Michigan from considering race and gender in public hiring and contracting decisions.

A group that supports affirmative action programs in education sued the state's attorney general and others, claiming that the initiative deprived minorities of equal protection and violated the U.S. Constitution. A federal appellate court agreed that the law violated the equal protection clause, but the United States Supreme Court reversed. The Court ruled that a state has the inherent power to ban affirmative action within that state, but it did not rule on the constitutionality of any specific affirmative action program.[27]

---

27. *Schuette v. Coalition to Defend Affirmative Action, Integration and Immigrant Rights*, ___ U.S. ___, 134 S.Ct. 1623, 188 L.Ed.2d 613 (2014).

Reviewing . . . Employment Discrimination

Amaani Lyle, an African American woman, took a job as a scriptwriters' assistant at Warner Brothers Television Productions. She worked for the writers of *Friends*, a popular, adult-oriented television series. One of her essential job duties was to type detailed notes for the scriptwriters during brainstorming sessions in which they discussed jokes, dialogue, and story lines. The writers then combed through Lyle's notes after the meetings for script material.

During the meetings, the three male scriptwriters told lewd and vulgar jokes and made sexually explicit comments and gestures. They often talked about their personal sexual experiences and fantasies, and some of these conversations were later used in episodes of *Friends*. During the meetings, Lyle never complained that she found the writers' conduct offensive.

After four months, Lyle was fired because she could not type fast enough to keep up with the writers' conversations during the meetings. She filed a suit against Warner Brothers alleging sexual harassment and claiming that her termination was based on racial discrimination. Using the information presented in the chapter, answer the following questions.

1. Would Lyle's claim of racial discrimination be for intentional (disparate-treatment) or unintentional (disparate-impact) discrimination? Explain.

2. Can Lyle establish a *prima facie* case of racial discrimination? Why or why not?

3. When she was hired, Lyle was told that typing speed was extremely important to her position. At the time, she maintained that she could type eighty words per minute, so she was not given a typing test. It later turned out that Lyle could type only fifty words per minute. What impact might typing speed have on Lyle's lawsuit?

4. Lyle's sexual-harassment claim is based on the hostile work environment created by the writers' sexually offensive conduct at meetings that she was required to attend. The writers, however, argue that their behavior was essential to the "creative process" of writing *Friends*, a show that routinely contained sexual innuendos and adult humor. Which defense discussed in the chapter might Warner Brothers assert using this argument?

DEBATE THIS

■ Members of minority groups and women have made enough economic progress in the last several decades that they no longer need special legislation to protect them.

LINKING BUSINESS LAW TO CORPORATE MANAGEMENT

Human Resource Management

Your career may lead to running a small business, managing a small part of a larger business, or making decisions for the operations of a big business. In any context, you may be responsible for employment decisions. As this chapter has suggested, an ill-conceived hiring or firing process can lead to a lawsuit. As a manager, you must also ensure that employees do not practice discrimination on the job. Enter the human resource management specialist.

What Is Human Resource Management?

Human resource management (HRM) is concerned with the acquisition, maintenance, and development of an organization's employees. All managers need to be skilled in HRM. Some firms require managers to play an active role in recruiting and selecting personnel, as well as in developing training programs. Anyone engaging in these practices should be aware of the issues outlined in this chapter. That is especially true of those who work in an organization's human resources department.

The Acquisition Phase of HRM

Acquiring talented employees is the first step in an HRM system. All recruitment must be done without violating any of the laws and regulations outlined in this chapter. Obviously, recruitment must be colorblind, as well as indifferent to gender, religion, national origin, and age. Recruitment methods must not have even the slightest hint of discriminatory basis. Recruitment methods must also give an equal chance to people with disabilities. Only the applicant's qualifications can be considered, not his or her disability. If a candidate with a disability is rejected, the employer should make sure to document that the rejection is based solely on the applicant's lack of training or ability.

On-the-Job HRM Issues

In addition, the HRM professional must monitor the working environment. Sexual harassment is a major concern. It may be necessary to work closely with an employment law specialist to develop antiharassment rules and policies. The company must publish these rules and policies and provide training to ensure that all employees are familiar with them. In addition, the company should create and supervise a grievance system so that any harassment can be stopped before it becomes actionable.

HRM Issues Concerning Employee Termination

Even in employment-at-will jurisdictions, lawsuits can arise for improper termination. The company should develop a system to protect itself from lawsuits, such as procedures for documenting an employee's misconduct and the employer's warnings and other disciplinary actions. The company should have an established policy for dealing with improper or incompetent behavior. It should also clearly establish the amount of severance pay that terminated employees will receive. Sometimes, it is better to err on the side of generosity to maintain the goodwill of terminated employees.

CRITICAL THINKING

- What are some types of actions that an HRM professional can take to reduce the probability of harassment lawsuits against her or his company?

Key Terms

affirmative action 647
bona fide occupational qualification
  (BFOQ) 646
business necessity 646
constructive discharge 636

disparate-impact discrimination 631
disparate-treatment
  discrimination 630
prima facie case 630
protected class 629

seniority system 646
sexual harassment 637
tangible employment action 638

Chapter Summary: Employment Discrimination

Title VII of the Civil Rights Act	Title VII prohibits employment discrimination based on race, color, national origin, religion, or gender. 1. *Procedures*—Employees must file a claim with the Equal Employment Opportunity Commission (EEOC). The EEOC may sue the employer on the employee's behalf. If it does not, the employee may sue the employer directly. 2. *Types of discrimination*—Title VII prohibits both intentional (disparate-treatment) and unintentional (disparate-impact) discrimination. Disparate-impact discrimination occurs when an employer's practices or procedures, such as requiring a certain level of education, have the effect of discriminating against a protected class. Title VII extends to discriminatory practices, such as various forms of harassment, in the online environment. 3. *Remedies for discrimination under Title VII*—Remedies include reinstatement, back pay, and retroactive promotions. Damages (both compensatory and punitive) may be awarded for intentional discrimination.
Discrimination Based on Age	The Age Discrimination in Employment Act (ADEA) prohibits employment discrimination on the basis of age against individuals forty years of age or older. Procedures for bringing a case under the ADEA are similar to those for bringing a case under Title VII.
Discrimination Based on Disability	The Americans with Disabilities Act (ADA) prohibits employment discrimination against persons with disabilities who are otherwise qualified to perform the essential functions of the jobs for which they apply. 1. *Procedures and remedies*—To prevail on a claim, the plaintiff must show that she or he has a disability, is otherwise qualified for the employment in question, and was excluded from it solely because of the disability. Procedures and remedies under the ADA are similar to those in Title VII cases. 2. *Definition of disability*—The ADA defines the term *disability* as a physical or mental impairment that substantially limits one or more of an individual's major life activities, a record of such impairment, or being regarded as having such an impairment. 3. *Reasonable accommodation*—Employers are required to reasonably accommodate the needs of qualified persons with disabilities through such measures as modifying the physical work environment and permitting more flexible work schedules.
Defenses to Employment Discrimination	As defenses to claims of employment discrimination, employers may assert that the discrimination was required for reasons of business necessity, to meet a bona fide occupational qualification, or to maintain a legitimate seniority system. Evidence of prior employee misconduct acquired after the employee has been fired is not a defense to discrimination.
Affirmative Action	Affirmative action programs attempt to "make up" for past patterns of discrimination by giving members of protected classes preferential treatment in hiring or promotion. Such programs are subject to strict scrutiny by the courts and are often struck down for violating the Fourteenth Amendment.

Issue Spotters

1. Ruth is a supervisor for a Subs & Suds restaurant. Tim is a Subs & Suds employee. The owner announces that some employees will be discharged. Ruth tells Tim that if he has sex with her, he can keep his job. Is this sexual harassment? Why or why not? (See *Title VII of the Civil Rights Act*.)

2. Koko, a person with a disability, applies for a job at Lively Sales Corporation for which she is well qualified, but she is rejected. Lively continues to seek applicants and eventually fills the position with a person who does not have a disability. Could Koko succeed in a suit against Lively for discrimination? Explain. (See *Discrimination Based on Disability*.)

—**Check your answers to the *Issue Spotters* against the answers provided in Appendix D at the end of this text.**

Learning Objectives Check

1. What is required to establish a *prima facie* case of disparate-treatment discrimination?
2. What must an employer do to avoid liability for religious discrimination?
3. What is a constructive discharge? To which employment discrimination claims does the theory of constructive discharge apply?
4. What federal act prohibits discrimination based on age?
5. What are three defenses to claims of employment discrimination?

—**Answers to the even-numbered *Learning Objectives Check* questions can be found in Appendix E at the end of this text.**

Business Scenarios and Case Problems

25–1. Title VII Violations. Discuss fully whether either of the following actions would constitute a violation of Title VII of the Civil Rights Act.

1. Tennington, Inc., is a consulting firm with ten employees. These employees travel on consulting jobs in seven states. Tennington has an employment record of hiring only white males. (See *Title VII of the Civil Rights Act.*)

2. Novo Films, Inc., is making a film about Africa and needs to employ approximately one hundred extras for this picture. To hire these extras, Novo advertises in all major newspapers in Southern California. The ad states that only African Americans need apply. (See *Defenses to Employment Discrimination.*)

25–2. Religious Discrimination. Gina Gomez, a devout Roman Catholic, worked for Sam's Department Stores, Inc., in Phoenix, Arizona. Sam's considered Gomez a productive employee because her sales exceeded $200,000 per year. The store gave its managers the discretion to grant unpaid leave to employees but prohibited vacations or leave during the holiday season—October through December. Gomez felt that she had a "calling" to go on a "pilgrimage" in October to a location in Bosnia where some persons claimed to have had visions of the Virgin Mary. The Catholic Church had not designated the site an official pilgrimage site, the visions were not expected to be stronger in October, and tours were available at other times. The store managers denied Gomez's request for leave, but she had a nonrefundable ticket and left anyway. Sam's terminated her employment, and she could not find another job. Can Gomez establish a *prima facie* case of religious discrimination? Explain. (See *Title VII of the Civil Rights Act.*)

25–3. Spotlight on Dress Code Policies—Discrimination Based on Gender. Burlington Coat Factory Warehouse, Inc., had a dress code that required male sales clerks to wear business attire consisting of slacks, shirt, and necktie. Female salesclerks, by contrast, were required to wear a smock so that customers could readily identify them. Karen O'Donnell and other female employees refused to wear the smock. Instead they reported to work in business attire and were suspended. After numerous suspensions, the female employees were fired for violating Burlington's dress code policy. All other conditions of employment, including salary, hours, and benefits, were the same for female and male employees. Was the dress code policy discriminatory? Why or why not? [*O'Donnell v. Burlington Coat Factory Warehouse, Inc.,* 656 F.Supp. 263 (S.D. Ohio 1987)] (See *Title VII of the Civil Rights Act.*)

25–4. Sexual Harassment by Co-Worker. Billie Bradford worked for the Kentucky Department of Community Based Services (DCBS). One of Bradford's co-workers, Lisa Stander, routinely engaged in extreme sexual behavior (such as touching herself and making crude comments) in Bradford's presence. Bradford and others regularly complained about Stander's conduct to their supervisor, Angie Taylor. Rather than resolve the problem, Taylor nonchalantly told Stander to stop, encouraged Bradford to talk to Stander, and suggested that Stander was just having fun. Assuming that Bradford was subjected to a hostile-work environment, could DCBS be liable? Why or why not? [*Bradford v. Department of Community Based Services,* 2012 WL 360032 (E.D.Ky. 2012)] (See *Title VII of the Civil Rights Act.*)

25–5. Business Case Problem with Sample Answer—Age Discrimination. Beginning in 1986, Paul Rangel was a sales professional for pharmaceutical company Sanofi-Aventis U.S., LLC (S-A). Rangel had satisfactory performance reviews until 2006, when S-A issued new expectations guidelines with sales call quotas and other standards that he failed to meet. After two years of negative performance reviews, Rangel—who was then more than forty years old—was terminated as part of a nationwide reduction of sales professionals who had not met the expectations guidelines. This sales force reduction also included younger workers. Did S-A engage in age discrimination? Discuss. [*Rangel v. Sanofi Aventis U.S. LLC,* 507 Fed.Appx. 782 (10th Cir. 2013)] (See *Discrimination Based on Age.*)

—For a sample answer to Problem 25–5, go to Appendix F at the end of this text.

25–6. Discrimination Based on Disability. Cynthia Horn worked for Knight Facilities Management–GM, Inc., in Detroit, Michigan, as a janitor. When Horn developed a sensitivity to cleaning products, her physician gave her a "no exposure to cleaning solutions" restriction. Knight discussed possible accommodations with Horn. She suggested that restrooms be eliminated from her cleaning route or that she be provided with a respirator. Knight explained that she would be exposed to cleaning solutions in any situation and concluded that there was no work available within her physician's restriction. Has Knight violated the Americans with Disabilities Act by failing to provide Horn with the requested accommodations? Explain. [*Horn v. Knight Facilities Management–GM, Inc.,* 556 Fed.Appx. 452 (6th Cir. 2014)] (See *Discrimination Based on Disability.*)

25–7. Sexual Harassment. Jamel Blanton, a male employee at a Pizza Hut restaurant operated by Newton Associates, Inc., in San Antonio, Texas, was subjected to sexual and racial harassment by the general manager, who was female. Newton had a clear, straightforward antidiscrimination policy and complaint procedure. The policy provided that in such a situation, an employee should complain to the harasser's supervisor. Blanton alerted a shift leader and an assistant manager about the harassment, but they were subordinate to the general manager and did not report the harassment to higher-level management. When Blanton finally complained to a manager with authority over the general manager, the employer investigated and fired the general manager within four days. Blanton filed a suit in a federal district court against Newton, seeking to impose liability on the employer for the general manager's actions. What is Newton's best defense? Discuss. [*Blanton v. Newton Associates, Inc.*, 593 Fed.Appx. 389 (5th Cir. 2015)] (See *Title VII of the Civil Rights Act.*)

25–8. A Question of Ethics—Retaliation by Employers. Shane Dawson, a male homosexual, worked for Entek International. Some of Dawson's co-workers, including his supervisor, made derogatory comments about his sexual orientation. Dawson's work deteriorated. He filed a complaint with Entek's human resources department. Two days later, he was fired. State law made it unlawful for an employer to discriminate against an individual based on sexual orientation. [*Dawson v. Entek International,* 630 F.3d 928 (9th Cir. 2011)] (See *Title VII of the Civil Rights Act.*)

1. Could Dawson establish a claim for retaliation? Explain.

2. Should homosexuals be a protected class under Title VII of the Civil Rights Act? Discuss the arguments for and against amending federal law to prohibit employment discrimination based on sexual orientation.

Critical Thinking and Writing Assignments

25–9. Critical Legal Thinking. Why has the federal government limited the application of the statutes discussed in this chapter to firms with a specified number of employees, such as fifteen or twenty? Should these laws apply to all employers, regardless of size? Why or why not? (See *Title VII of the Civil Rights Act.*)

25–10. Case Analysis Question. Go to Appendix G at the end of this text and examine the excerpt of Case No. 4, *Dees v. United Rentals North America, Inc.* Review and then brief the case, making sure that your brief answers the following questions. (See *Title VII of the Civil Rights Act.*)

1. **Issue:** What conduct on the part of the plaintiff, and what action on the part of the defendant, were at the center of the dispute in this case?

2. **Rule of Law:** Once a *prima facie* case of employment discrimination has been established, who must prove what as the case moves forward, and who must respond with what evidence?

3. **Applying the Rule of Law:** What was the court's evaluation of the parties' allegations and evidence in this case?

4. **Conclusion:** In whose favor did the court rule? Why?

25–11. Business Law Critical Thinking Group Assignment. Two African American plaintiffs sued the producers of the reality television series *The Bachelor* and *The Bachelorette* for racial discrimination. The plaintiffs claimed that the shows had never featured a person of color in the lead role. Plaintiffs also alleged that the producers had failed to provide people of color who auditioned for lead roles with the same opportunities to compete as white people who auditioned. (See *Title VII of the Civil Rights Act.*)

1. The first group will assess whether the plaintiffs can establish a *prima facie* case of disparate-treatment discrimination.

2. The second group will consider what the plaintiffs would have to show to establish disparate-impact discrimination.

3. The third group will assume that the plaintiffs established a *prima facie* case and that the burden has shifted to the employer to articulate a legal reason for not hiring the plaintiffs. What legitimate reasons might the employer assert for not hiring the plaintiffs in this situation? Should the law require television producers to hire persons of color for lead roles in reality television shows? Explain your answer.

Unit Four—Business Case Study with Dissenting Opinion

EEOC v. Greater Baltimore Medical Center, Inc.

The Americans with Disabilities Act (ADA) prohibits employment discrimination based on disability. Although an employer is often required to reasonably accommodate the needs of an employee with a disability, the ADA does not protect an employee who cannot perform the essential functions of a job even when given a reasonable accommodation.

In this *Business Case Study with Dissenting Opinion,* we review *EEOC v. Greater Baltimore Medical Center, Inc.*[1] In this case, the Equal Employment Opportunity Commission (EEOC) filed an enforcement action on behalf of a disabled employee who was receiving Social Security Disability Income benefits. To receive the benefits, the employee had to state that he was incapable of working. The issue for the court was whether, despite the employee's representations, the EEOC could show that he was capable of performing the job's essential functions.

Can an employee claim protection under the Americans with Disabilities Act while simultaneously receiving Social Security Disability Income benefits?

CASE BACKGROUND

Michael Turner worked as a secretary for Greater Baltimore Medical Center (GBMC). Beginning in January 2005, Turner was hospitalized for five months because of a life-threatening condition called necrotizing fasciitis. Turner returned to work in November 2005 with his doctor's permission, but he soon suffered a stroke and was hospitalized again until late December.

On December 29, 2005, with his mother's help, Turner applied to the Social Security Administration (SSA) for Social Security Disability Income (SSDI) benefits. The application stated, "I became unable to work because of my disabling condition on January 15, 2005. I am still disabled." The application also said that Turner would tell the SSA if his condition improved to the point that he could work. A few days later, Turner's mother also submitted a report stating that Turner could not work because of his disabilities. Turner began receiving SSDI benefits in January 2006.

That same month, Turner told GBMC that he wanted to return to work as a part-time secretary. Turner submitted a form from his physician, but GBMC concluded that his conditions prevented him from performing his old job. As a result, GBMC said that it was not obligated to give Turner a position. By May 2006, Turner's condition had improved, and his doctor found that he could work full-time without any restrictions. But GBMC disagreed, and it terminated Turner in June 2006, when his leave expired. Afterward, Turner did more than 1,100 hours of volunteer work for GBMC. All the while, he continued to receive SSDI benefits.

In February 2007, Turner filed a discrimination charge with the EEOC. In September 2009, the EEOC filed an enforcement action in federal court on Turner's behalf. The district court granted summary judgment for GBMC because it found that, given Turner's SSDI benefits, the EEOC could not show that Turner could perform his old job's essential functions. The EEOC appealed.

MAJORITY OPINION

O'GRADY, District Judge:

* * * *

The ADA prohibits a covered employer from discriminating "against a qualified individual with a disability because of the disability of such individual." *Among other things, EEOC must show that Mr. Turner is a "qualified individual with a disability," that is, "an individual with a disability who, with or without reasonable accommodation, can perform the essential functions of the employment position * * * ."* [Emphasis added.]

Many persons who experience disabling medical problems become eligible for programs like SSDI, at least temporarily, during medical leave. If such a person seeks SSDI benefits and attempts to bring a claim under the ADA, he may assert disability in an application for SSDI benefits while simultaneously asserting that he is a "qualified individual" under the ADA, that is, he is able to work with or without reasonable accommodation. A conflict of this sort may appear to bar the claimant from receiving both disability benefits and ADA coverage.

* * * *

* * * There can be little doubt that the conflict between Mr. Turner's SSDI application and his ability to work with or without reasonable accommodation is genuine. Mr. Turner's SSDI application, submitted on December 29, 2005, states, "I became unable to work because of my disabling condition on January 15, 2005," and, "I am

---

1. 2012 WL 1302604 (4th Cir. 2012).

Continues

still disabled." Moreover, "I [Mr. Turner] agree to notify the Social Security Administration * * * [i]f my medical condition improves so that I would be able to work, even though I have not yet returned to work." The record indicates without contradiction that Mr. Turner was unable to work after he left the hospital on December 27, 2005. Mrs. Turner later submitted a form called a "Function Report" * * * in which she described Mr. Turner's symptoms and impairment. She noted severe disability in his left arm or hand, use of a bedside commode with hand rails, left-sided weakness requiring assistance, leg bracing, inability to drive, inability to lift more than 2–3 pounds, severely limited ability to stand, bend over and back, and walk. * * * Taken together, the SSDI application and documentation reasonably communicated that Mr. Turner was and would continue to be [unable to work].

Consistent with the application, the SSA awarded benefits to Mr. Turner on January 22, 2006. Mr. Turner continued to receive SSDI benefits at the time of the district court's decision. Mr. Turner did not revise his statements to SSDI, and apparently never notified the SSA about a change in his condition.

These reported disabilities conflict with the multiple work releases provided by [Turner's doctor] * * * . They all indicated that Mr. Turner could have returned to work, directly contradicting the assertion in his SSDI application that he was and continued to be unable to work. * * * If Mr. Turner told GBMC in good faith that he could return to work, then he had no reason to believe that his earlier representations of disability were still accurate.

* * * *

* * * We in no way condone GBMC's refusal to reinstate Mr. Turner. Quite the contrary. We are deeply concerned about GBMC's attempts to prevent a partially disabled former employee from returning to work after he was cleared to return without restriction. Our result is nonetheless mandated by the plain language of the ADA and the relevant case law. The district court's judgment is therefore affirmed.

DISSENTING OPINION

GREGORY, Circuit Judge, dissenting:

* * * *

This case * * * involves two different parties' context-related legal representations—Turner's assertion in the proceedings before the

SSA and the *EEOC's* assertion in this action. While it is true that the EEOC is seeking relief on Turner's behalf, it cannot be said that the EEOC made a prior inconsistent statement in Turner's SSDI application. Its action should not be barred through the happenstance of an unemployed victim having applied for and received SSDI benefits. Moreover, the Supreme Court has repeatedly recognized that "the EEOC is not merely a proxy" for the individuals for whom it seeks relief. Rather, the Court has observed, "[w]hen the EEOC acts, albeit at the behest of and for the benefit of specific individuals, it acts also to vindicate the public interest in preventing employment discrimination." [Emphasis in original.]

Barring EEOC enforcement actions based on a charging party's legal assertions of disability in SSA proceedings * * * is also contrary to public policy. The EEOC's enforcement actions typically seek not only victim-specific relief but also injunctive relief such as training, posting of notices, and reporting requirements. As discussed above, these enforcement actions not only benefit the individuals on whose behalf the agency sues, but also benefit the public, which has an interest in the eradication of employment discrimination.

* * * *

QUESTIONS FOR ANALYSIS

1. **Law.** *What was the majority's decision in this case? What were the reasons for its decision?*

2. **Law.** *Why did the dissent disagree with the majority? If the court had adopted the dissent's position, how would this have affected the result?*

3. **Ethics.** *Does the majority express any ethical reservations about its decision? If so, what are they? Do you have any ethical concerns about the majority's decision?*

4. **Economic Dimensions.** *Based on this case, what do you think is the purpose of SSDI benefits? Did Turner need them?*

5. **Implications for the Businessperson.** *What does the majority's ruling mean for employers who have disabled employees? Does the ruling tend to make the repercussions of disability discrimination more or less serious? Explain your answer.*

iStockPhoto.com/KLH49

Unit Four—Business Scenario

Two brothers, Ray and Paul Ashford, start a business—Ashford Brothers, Inc.—manufacturing a new type of battery system for hybrid automobiles. The batteries hit the market at the perfect time and are in great demand.

1. **Agency.** Loren, one of Ashford's salespersons, anxious to make a sale, intentionally quotes a price to a customer that

is $500 lower than Ashford has authorized for the product. The customer purchases the product at the quoted price. When Ashford learns of the deal, it claims that it is not legally bound to the sales contract because it has not authorized Loren to sell the product at that price. Is Ashford bound to the contract? Discuss fully.

2. **Workers' Compensation.** One day, Gina, an Ashford employee, suffered a serious burn when she accidentally spilled some acid on her hand. The accident occurred because another employee, who was suspected of using illegal drugs, carelessly bumped into her. Gina's hand required a series of skin grafts before it healed sufficiently to allow her to return to work. Gina wants to obtain compensation for her lost wages and medical expenses. Can she do that? If so, how?

3. **Drug Testing.** After Gina's injury, Ashford decides to conduct random drug tests on all of its employees. Several employees claim that the testing violates their privacy rights and bring a lawsuit. What factors will the court consider in deciding whether the random drug testing is legally permissible?

4. **COBRA.** Ashford provides health insurance for its two hundred employees, including Dan. For personal medical reasons, Dan takes twelve weeks' leave. During this period, can Dan continue his coverage under Ashford's health-insurance plan? After Dan returns to work, Ashford closes Dan's division and terminates the employees, including Dan. Can Dan continue his coverage under Ashford's health-insurance plan after the termination? Explain.

5. **Sexual Harassment.** Aretha, another employee at Ashford, is disgusted by the sexually offensive behavior of several male employees. She has complained to her supervisor on several occasions about the behavior, but the supervisor merely laughs at her concerns. Aretha decides to bring a legal action against the company for sexual harassment. Does Aretha's complaint concern *quid pro quo* harassment or hostile-environment harassment? What federal statute protects employees from sexual harassment? What remedies are available under that statute? What procedures must Aretha follow in pursuing her legal action?

Unit Four—Group Project

iStockPhoto.com/AndreyPopov

Cerebral palsy limits Eli's use of his legs, but with support, he can get on and off a stool. Eli applied for a cashier position at Mars Market. The job description required "no experience or qualifications." Eli's application was rejected. According to Ravenna, the market's human resources manager, her decision was based on the threat that Eli posed to his safety and the safety of others. Eli claimed that Mars Market had refused to hire him because of his disability.

1. One group will outline the requirements to prove a *prima facie* case of disability discrimination and decide whether Eli can meet these requirements.

2. A second group will decide what reasonable accommodations Mars Market could make in this situation.

3. A third group will discuss whether Eli poses a safety threat to himself and others in the store or whether this reason was just a pretext. It will also determine if Mars Market can establish a defense to employment discrimination.

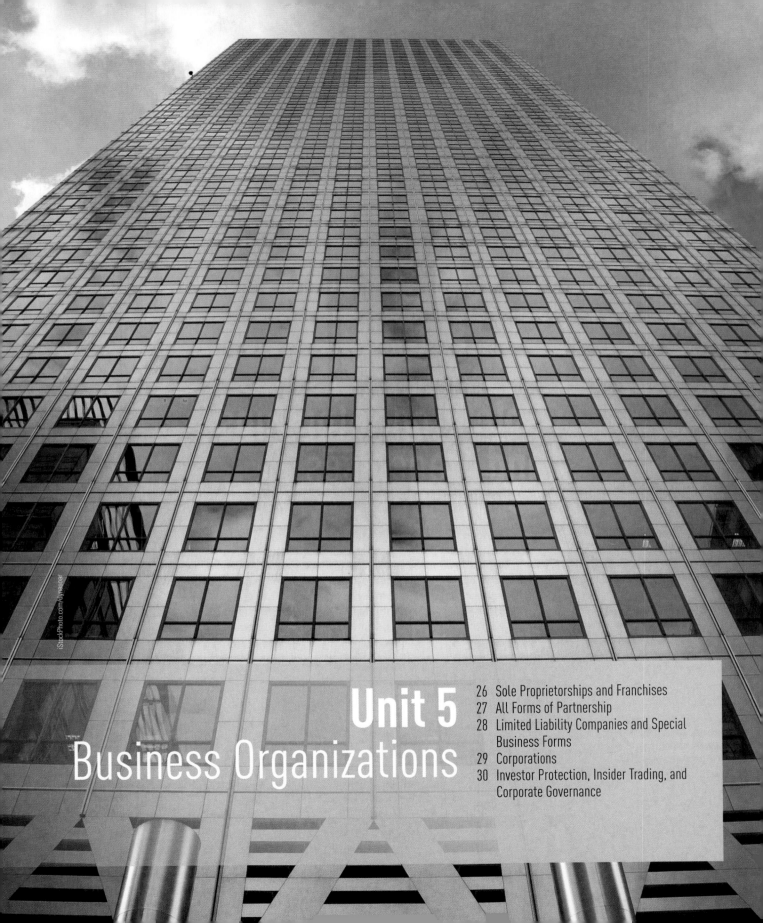

Unit 5
Business Organizations

iStockPhoto.com/dynasoar

iStockPhoto.com/marcnorman

26

LEARNING OBJECTIVES

The four Learning Objectives below are designed to help improve your understanding of the chapter. After reading this chapter, you should be able to answer the following questions:

1. What advantages and disadvantages are associated with the sole proprietorship?

2. What are the most common types of franchises?

3. What are the basic requirements of the Franchise Rule?

4. How are franchises normally terminated? When will a court decide that a franchisor has wrongfully terminated a franchise?

Entrepreneur One who initiates and assumes the financial risk of a new business enterprise and undertakes to provide or control its management.

Sole Proprietorships and Franchises

Many Americans would agree with Frank Scully's comment in the chapter-opening quotation that to succeed in business one must "go out on a limb." Certainly, an entrepreneur's primary motive for "going out on a limb" to begin a business enterprise is to make profits. An **entrepreneur** is one who initiates and assumes the financial risks of a new enterprise and undertakes to provide or control its management.

"Why not go out on a limb? Isn't that where the fruit is?"

FRANK SCULLY
1892–1964
(AMERICAN AUTHOR)

One of the first decisions an entrepreneur must make is which form of business organization will be most appropriate for the new endeavor. In selecting an organizational form, the entrepreneur will consider a number of factors, including (1) ease of creation, (2) the liability of the owners, (3) tax considerations, and (4) the ability to raise capital. Keep these factors in mind as you read this unit and learn about the various forms of business organization. In considering these business forms, remember, too, that the primary motive of an entrepreneur is to make profits.

Traditionally, entrepreneurs have used three major forms to structure their business enterprises—the sole proprietorship, the partnership, and the corporation. In this chapter, we examine sole proprietorships. We also discuss franchises. Although the franchise is not, strictly speaking, a separate business organizational form, it is widely used today by entrepreneurs.

26-1 Sole Proprietorships

The simplest form of business is a **sole proprietorship.** In this form, the owner is the business. Thus, anyone who does business without creating a separate business organization has a sole proprietorship.

More than two-thirds of all U.S. businesses are sole proprietorships. Sole proprietors can own and manage any type of business from an informal, home-office or Web-based undertaking to a large restaurant or construction firm. Most sole proprietorships are small enterprises, however. About 99 percent of the sole proprietorships in the United States have revenues of less than $1 million per year. (For a discussion of the problems small business owners face when targeted by cyber thieves, see this chapter's *Managerial Strategy* feature.)

Sole Proprietorship
The simplest form of business organization, in which the owner is the business. The owner reports business income on his or her personal income tax return and is legally responsible for all debts and obligations incurred by the business.

MANAGERIAL STRATEGY — Cyber Thieves Empty Small-Business Owners' Bank Accounts

Management Faces a Legal Issue
Between 150 and 200 cyber attacks on business organizations occur every day. Cyber thieves in other countries, especially China and Russia, initiate most of these attacks. Thirty percent of the attacks are aimed at small businesses (those with fewer than 250 employees).

If you, as an individual, suffer losses from cybertheft—if cyber thieves take funds from your bank account or put charges on your credit card—your bank is usually responsible for the losses. The laws that protect individuals' bank accounts do not normally extend to small businesses, however.

What the Courts Say
In 2009, an employee at Experi-Metal, Inc., received an e-mail containing a link to a Web page with a Comerica Bank business connect form. Knowing that Comerica was the company's bank, the employee followed a further link and filled in the requested information. Experi-Metal had just been the victim of a *phishing attack*—the most common method used by cyber thieves to obtain the information needed for fraudulent fund transfers. Within minutes, cyber thieves had transferred almost $2 million from Experi-Metal's account to bank accounts in China, Estonia, and Russia.

Experi-Metal sued Comerica, arguing, among other things, that the bank had not observed good faith when it accepted the online command for the wire transfers. Ultimately, the court found that the bank's employees had failed to meet reasonable commercial standards of fair dealing in not questioning the unusual size of the transfers and their destinations.[a]

In another case involving a small business, Pacto Construction Co., cyber thieves installed malware in Pacto's computers. The malware recorded the keystrokes of Pacto's employees. The cyber thieves were then able to answer security questions posed by Pacto's bank for wire transfers. Hundreds of thousands of dollars were transferred from Pacto's bank account to numerous individuals, none of whom had ever done business with Pacto. Pacto sued the bank, and did not prevail in a U.S. district court. On appeal, though, the reviewing court agreed that Pacto's bank had not monitored the transactions effectively and should have notified Pacto before allowing them to be completed.[b]

In a more recent case, the result was less favorable to the small business. This case involved an Internet-based request to make

a wire transfer of $440,000 from an account owned by Choice Escrow and Land Title, LLC. After conducting a successful phishing attack, cyber thieves accessed Choice's online bank account and instructed the bank to wire the funds from Choice's account to a bank account in the Republic of Cyprus. In spite of Choice Escrow's claim that it did not initiate, approve, or authorize the wire transfer, the court granted summary judgment to the bank. The court found that the bank had complied with industry standards.[c]

MANAGERIAL IMPLICATIONS
Small-business owners may have some recourse if cyber thieves steal funds from their bank accounts. Nevertheless, managers should take whatever measures are necessary to secure their companies' computer systems. They should make sure, for example, that secure passwords are used for all company e-mails and that the passwords are changed regularly. When a large wire transfer is being made, a manager should make sure that it is being sent to the intended recipient and that the recipient has received the transfer. Note, too, that payment of invoices with a personal check or credit card may allow for recourse in the event of fraud.

a. *Experi-Metal v. Comerica Bank,* 2011 WL 2433383 (E.D.Mich. 2011).
b. *Pacto Construction Co. v. People's United Bank,* 684 F.3d 197 (1st Cir. 2012).
c. *Choice Escrow & Land Title, LLC v. BancorpSouth Bank,* 754 F.3d 611 (8th Cir. 2014).

LEARNING OBJECTIVE 1

What advantages and
disadvantages are associated
with the sole proprietorship?

26-1a Advantages of the Sole Proprietorship

A major advantage of the sole proprietorship is that the proprietor owns the entire business and has a right to receive all of the profits (because he or she assumes all of the risk). In addition, starting a sole proprietorship is often easier and less costly than starting any other kind of business, as few legal formalities are involved. Generally, no documents need to be filed with the government to start a sole proprietorship.[1]

A sole proprietor pays only personal income taxes (including Social Security and Medicare taxes) on the business's profits, which are reported as personal income on the proprietor's personal income tax return. Sole proprietors are allowed to establish retirement accounts that are tax-exempt until the funds are withdrawn.

A sole proprietorship also offers more flexibility than does a partnership or a corporation. The sole proprietor is free to make any decision she or he wishes concerning the business— including whom to hire, when to take a vacation, and what kind of business to pursue. The sole proprietor can sell or transfer all or part of the business to another party at any time without seeking approval from anyone else. In contrast, approval is typically required from partners in a partnership and from shareholders in a corporation.

ETHICAL ISSUE

Can a small business owner refuse to bake a gay couple's wedding cake? A few years ago, Aaron and Melissa Klein, owners of the Sweet Cakes by Melissa bakery, refused to bake a wedding cake for a same-sex couple's wedding. They claimed that their religious beliefs did not allow them to provide services for same-sex ceremonies. The Oregon State Bureau of Labor and Industries argued that their decision violated the law. In 2015, an administrative law judge ruled against the Kleins' motion to dismiss and ordered them to pay $135,000 in damages. Oregon's law does allow certain exceptions for religious institutions, but "the bakery is not a religious institution."

A similar issue arose with respect to a wedding-photography business in New Mexico. The owners refused to photograph a ceremony held by clients who were gay. They based this refusal on their religious beliefs. New Mexico's highest court ruled against the owners,[2] and the United States Supreme Court declined to hear the case.

Currently, federal law does not provide protection against discrimination based on sexual orientation in the same way that it protects against discrimination based on race, color, and some other "protected" characteristics. Many states, though, do have laws prohibiting discrimination based on sexual orientation, as do many cities.

The intersection of business owners' religious beliefs and the rights of gays and lesbians is certain to be an area in which additional laws will be created.

"Always tell yourself: The difference between running a business and ruining a business is I."

ANONYMOUS

26-1b Disadvantages of the Sole Proprietorship

The major disadvantage of the sole proprietorship is that the proprietor alone bears the burden of any losses or liabilities incurred by the business enterprise. In other words, the sole proprietor has unlimited liability, or legal responsibility, for all obligations incurred in doing business. The personal liability of a sole proprietor was at issue in the following case.

---

1. Sole proprietorships may need to comply with certain zoning requirements, obtain a business license or other appropriate license from the state, and the like.
2. *Elane Photography, LLC. v. Willock*, 2013 –NMSC– 040, 309 P.3d 53 (N.M. 2013).

Quality Car & Truck Leasing, Inc. v. Sark

Court of Appeals of Ohio, Fourth District, 2013 -Ohio- 44, 2013 WL 139359 (2013).

FACTS Michael Sark operated a logging business as a sole proprietorship. To acquire equipment for the business, Sark and his wife, Paula, borrowed funds from Quality Car & Truck Leasing, Inc. When his business encountered financial difficulties, Sark became unable to pay his creditors, including Quality, and filed a bankruptcy petition. The Sarks sold their house (valued at $203,500) to their son, Michael, Jr., for one dollar but continued to live in it. Three months later, Quality obtained a judgment in an Ohio state court against the Sarks for $150,481.85 and then filed a claim to set aside the transfer of the house to Michael, Jr., as a fraudulent conveyance. The trial court ruled in Quality's favor, and the Sarks appealed, arguing that they had not intended to defraud Quality and that they were not actually Quality's debtors.

ISSUE Were the Sarks personally debtors to Quality Leasing?

DECISION Yes. A state intermediate appellate court affirmed the lower court's judgment in Quality's favor.

REASON According to the court, "Reasonable minds can come to only one conclusion, and that conclusion is adverse to the Sarks."

Can a person who owns a logging business as a sole proprietorship avoid liability for the business's debts?

The Sarks "are clearly judgment debtors to Quality Leasing and . . . the judgment has not been satisfied." The reviewing court accepted the trial court's view that "Michael Senior and Paula made a transfer without the exchange of reasonably equivalent value and the debtor was engaged or was about to engage in a business transaction for which the remaining assets of the debtor were unreasonably small in relation to the business or transaction."

Under Ohio law, a creditor need not show that a transfer was made with the intent to defraud in order to prevail. "Thus, the Sarks cannot defeat summary judgment showing that they did not act with fraudulent intent when Michael Senior and Paula transferred the Property to Michael Junior." Further, the Sarks did not challenge the validity of the judgment against them, nor did they show that the judgment had been satisfied. Consequently, there was no "genuine issue of material fact regarding whether Paula and Michael Senior are debtors to Quality Leasing."

CRITICAL THINKING—Economic Consideration *What might the Sarks have done to avoid this dispute, as well as the loss of their home and their business?*

Personal Assets at Risk
Because of the sole proprietor's unlimited liability, creditors can go after his or her personal assets to satisfy any business debts. Although sole proprietors may obtain insurance to protect the business, liability can easily exceed policy limits. This unlimited liability is a major factor to be considered in choosing a business form. (See this chapter's *Adapting the Law to the Online Environment* feature for a discussion of the liability of a sole proprietor who tried to create a Facebook poker-playing application—even after bankruptcy.)

EXAMPLE 26.1 Sheila Fowler operates a golf shop near a world-class golf course as a sole proprietorship. One of Fowler's employees fails to secure a display of golf clubs, and they fall on Dean Maheesh, a professional golfer, and seriously injure him. If Maheesh sues Fowler's shop and wins, Fowler's personal liability could easily exceed the limits of her insurance policy. Fowler could lose not only her business, but also her house, her car, and any other personal assets that can be attached to pay the judgment. ■

Lack of Continuity and Limitations on Funding
The sole proprietorship also has the disadvantage of lacking continuity after the death of the proprietor. When the owner dies, so does the business—it is automatically dissolved. Another disadvantage is that the proprietor's ability to raise capital is limited to personal funds and the funds of those who are willing to make loans.

This sole proprietor enjoys full flexibility about how she runs her business. What are the downsides of this form of business organization?

ADAPTING THE LAW TO THE ONLINE ENVIRONMENT

A Sole Proprietorship, Facebook Poker, and Bankruptcy

One major downside of a sole proprietorship is that it is more difficult for a sole proprietor to obtain funding for startup and expansion. Moreover, if funding is obtained through loans, the sole proprietor is exposed to personal liability.

Personal Liability Exposure for an Online Startup

A case in point went before the United States bankruptcy court in Massachusetts in 2015.[a] Michael Dewhurst, living in Raynham, Massachusetts, sometimes did computer work for Gerald Knappik. Dewhurst decided to start a new business venture—the commercial development of a Facebook poker-playing application. Dewhurst envisioned an application that would enable multiple individuals to play poker together over the Internet through Facebook. Dewhurst informed Knappik of his business plan and predicted

a. *In re Dewhurst*, 2015 WL 1331504 (Bankr. N.D.Mass. 2015).

that his Facebook poker application "was going to be something very big."

Knappik initially loaned $50,000 to Dewhurst for the project. The loan agreement stated, "The sole purpose of this loan agreement is to provide funds on a personal level for the startup of said business project, in conjunction with borrower's personal funds, not limited to startup costs, operating expenses, advertising costs." That was the first of a series of personal loans that ultimately totaled $220,000.

Dewhurst had repaid only $9,000 on the total outstanding debt when he filed for bankruptcy. Ultimately, the bankruptcy court ascertained that at least $120,000 of the loans that were supposed to be used exclusively for the Facebook poker project had been used for other activities. Furthermore, Dewhurst kept "no contemporaneous records of his disbursements and uses of this cash, no cash journal, ledger, or disbursement slips of any kind."

The Lender Objects to a Bankruptcy Discharge of Monies Owed

During bankruptcy proceedings, Knappik requested that the bankruptcy court deny discharge of Dewhurst's debts to him. Upon review, the court stated that "Dewhurst's failure to keep and preserve adequate records makes it impossible to reconstruct an accurate and complete account of financial affairs and business transactions." The bankruptcy judge ultimately denied discharge of $120,000 of the debt owed to Knappik. Thus, a sole proprietor's failed attempt to create an online poker-playing application led to personal liability even after he had filed for bankruptcy.

CRITICAL THINKING

- Sole proprietorships, as well as other businesses, routinely seek funding for online projects. How can the individuals involved avoid personal liability?

26-2 Franchises

| Franchise | Any arrangement in which the owner of a trademark, trade name, or copyright licenses another to use that trademark, trade name, or copyright in the selling of goods or services. |

Instead of setting up a completely independent business, many entrepreneurs opt to purchase a franchise. A **franchise** is an arrangement in which the owner of intellectual property—such as a trademark, a trade name, or a copyright—licenses others to use it in the selling of goods or services. A **franchisee** (a purchaser of a franchise) is generally legally independent of the **franchisor** (the seller of the franchise). At the same time, the franchisee is economically dependent on the franchisor's integrated business system. In other words, a franchisee can operate as an independent businessperson and choose any business form but still obtain the advantages of a regional or national organization.

Franchisee One receiving a license to use another's (the franchisor's) trademark, trade name, or copyright in the sale of goods and services.

Today, franchising companies and their franchisees account for a significant portion of all retail sales in this country. Well-known franchises include McDonald's, 7-Eleven, and Holiday Inn. Franchising has also become a popular way for businesses to expand their operations internationally, as discussed in this chapter's *Beyond Our Borders* feature.

Franchisor One licensing another (the franchisee) to use the owner's trademark, trade name, or copyright in the selling of goods or services.

26-2a Types of Franchises

Many different kinds of businesses now sell franchises, and numerous types of franchises are available. Generally, though, franchises fall into one of three classifications: distributorships, chain-style business operations, or manufacturing or processing-plant arrangements.

BEYOND OUR BORDERS

Franchising in Foreign Nations

In the last twenty-five years, many U.S. companies (particularly fast-food chains and coffeehouses) have successfully expanded through franchising in nations around the globe. Targeted locations include Asia and Central and South America, as well as Canada and Mexico in North America. Franchises offer businesses a way to expand internationally without violating the legal restrictions that many nations impose on foreign ownership of businesses.

Cultural and Legal Differences Are Important

Businesspersons must exercise caution when entering international franchise relationships, however. Differences in language, culture, laws, and business practices can seriously complicate the franchising relationship. If a U.S. franchisor's quality control standards do not mesh with local business practices, for example, how can the franchisor maintain the quality of its product and protect its good reputation? If the law in, say, China does not provide for a high level of intellectual property protection, how can a U.S. franchisor protect its trademark rights or prevent its secret recipe or formula from being copied?

The Need to Assess the Market

Because of the complexities of international franchising, a company seeking to franchise overseas needs to conduct thorough research to determine whether its business will be well received in the target country. It is important to know the political and cultural climate, as well as current economic trends. Marketing surveys to assess the potential success of the franchise location are crucial.

Because compliance with U.S. disclosure laws may not satisfy the legal requirements of other nations, most successful franchisors retain attorneys knowledgeable in the laws of the prospective location. The attorneys can draft dispute-settlement provisions (such as an arbitration clause) for international franchising contracts and advise the franchisor about the tax implications of operating a foreign franchise (such as import taxes and customs duties).

CRITICAL THINKING

■ Should a U.S.-based franchisor be allowed to impose contract terms and quality control standards on franchisees in foreign nations that are different from those imposed on domestic franchisees? Why or why not?

Distributorship   In a *distributorship,* a manufacturer (the franchisor) licenses a dealer (the franchisee) to sell its product. Often, a distributorship covers an exclusive territory. Automobile dealerships and beer distributorships are examples of this type of franchise.

EXAMPLE 26.2 Black Snow Beer Company distributes its beer brands through a network of authorized wholesale distributors, each with an assigned territory. Marik signs a distributorship contract for the area from Gainesville to Ocala, Florida. If the contract states that Marik is the exclusive distributor in that area, then no other franchisee may distribute Black Snow beer in that region. ■

Chain-Style Business Operation   In a *chain-style business operation,* a franchise operates under a franchisor's trade name and is identified as a member of a select group of dealers that engage in the franchisor's business. The franchisee is generally required to follow standardized or prescribed methods of operation. In addition, the franchisee may be required to obtain materials and supplies exclusively from the franchisor.

McDonald's and most other fast-food chains are examples of chain-style franchises. This type of franchise is also common in service-related businesses, including real estate brokerage firms such as Century 21 and tax-preparing services such as H&R Block, Inc.

Manufacturing or Processing-Plant Arrangement   In a *manufacturing or processing-plant arrangement,* the franchisor transmits to the franchisee the essential ingredients or formula to make a particular product. The franchisee then markets the product either at wholesale or at retail in accordance with the franchisor's standards. Examples of this type of franchise are Pepsi-Cola and other soft-drink bottling companies.

LEARNING OBJECTIVE 2

What are the most common types of franchises?

KNOW THIS

Because a franchise involves the licensing of a trademark, a trade name, or a copyright, the law governing intellectual property may apply in some situations.

If these brands of beer are sold through authorized wholesale distributors only, can a potential distributor obtain an exclusive territory?

iStockPhoto.com/alaincouillaud

26–2b Laws Governing Franchising

Because a franchise relationship is primarily a contractual relationship, it is governed by contract law. If the franchise exists primarily for the sale of products manufactured by the franchisor, the law governing sales contracts as expressed in Article 2 of the Uniform Commercial Code applies.

Additionally, the federal government and most states have enacted laws governing certain aspects of franchising. Generally, these laws are designed to protect prospective franchisees from dishonest franchisors and to prohibit franchisors from terminating franchises without good cause.

Federal Regulation of Franchising

The federal government regulates franchising through laws that apply to specific industries and through the Franchise Rule, created by the Federal Trade Commission (FTC).

Industry-Specific Standards. Congress has enacted laws that protect franchisees in certain industries, such as automobile dealerships and service stations. These laws protect the franchisee from unreasonable demands and bad faith terminations of the franchise by the franchisor.

An automobile manufacturer–franchisor cannot make unreasonable demands of dealer-franchisees or set unrealistically high sales quotas, for instance. If an automobile manufacturer–franchisor terminates a franchise because of a dealer-franchisee's failure to comply with unreasonable demands, the manufacturer may be liable for damages.[3]

Similarly, federal law prescribes the conditions under which a franchisor of service stations can terminate a franchise.[4] In addition, federal antitrust laws sometimes apply to prohibit certain types of anticompetitive agreements involving service-station franchises.

The Franchise Rule. The FTC's Franchise Rule requires franchisors to disclose certain material facts that a prospective franchisee needs in order to make an informed decision concerning the purchase of a franchise.[5] Those who violate the Franchise Rule are subject to substantial civil penalties, and the FTC can sue on behalf of injured parties to recover damages.

The rule requires the franchisor to make numerous written disclosures to prospective franchisees (see Exhibit 26–1). All representations made to a prospective franchisee must have a reasonable basis. For instance, if a franchisor provides projected earnings figures, the franchisor must indicate whether the figures are based on actual data or hypothetical examples. If a franchisor makes sales or earnings projections based on actual data for a specific franchise location, the franchisor must disclose the number and percentage of its existing franchises that have achieved this result.

State Regulation of Franchising

State legislation varies but generally is aimed at protecting franchisees from unfair practices and bad faith terminations by franchisors.

State Disclosures. A number of states have laws similar to the federal rules requiring franchisors to provide presale disclosures to prospective franchisees.[6] Many state laws also require that a disclosure document (known as the Franchise Disclosure Document, or FDD) be registered or filed with a state official. A state law may require the disclosure of information such as the actual costs of operation, recurring expenses, and profits earned, along with data substantiating these figures. State deceptive trade practices acts may also apply and may prohibit certain actions on the part of franchisors.

---

3. Automobile Dealers' Franchise Act of 1965, also known as the Automobile Dealers' Day in Court Act, 15 U.S.C. Sections 1221 *et seq.*

4. Petroleum Marketing Practices Act (PMPA) of 1979, 15 U.S.C. Sections 2801 *et seq.*

5. 16 C.F.R. Part 436.

6. These states include California, Florida, Hawaii, Illinois, Indiana, Maryland, Michigan, Minnesota, New York, North Dakota, Oregon, Rhode Island, South Dakota, Texas, Utah, Virginia, Washington, and Wisconsin.

Exhibit 26-1 The FTC's Franchise Rule Requirements

Written (or electronic) disclosures	The franchisor must make numerous disclosures, such as the range of goods and services included and the value and estimated profitability of the franchise. Disclosures can be delivered on paper or electronically. Prospective franchisees must be able to download or save any electronic disclosure documents.
Reasonable basis for any representations	To prevent deception, all representations made to a prospective franchisee must have a reasonable basis at the time they are made.
Projected earnings figures	If a franchisor provides projected earnings figures, the franchisor must indicate whether the figures are based on actual data or hypothetical examples. The Franchise Rule does not require franchisors to provide potential earnings figures, however.
Actual data	If a franchisor makes sales or earnings projections based on actual data for a specific franchise location, the franchisor must disclose the number and percentage of its existing franchises that have achieved this result.
Explanation of terms	Franchisors are required to explain termination, cancellation, and renewal provisions of the franchise contract to potential franchisees before the agreement is signed.

Requirements for Termination. To prevent arbitrary or bad faith terminations, state law may prohibit termination without "good cause" or require that certain procedures be followed in terminating a franchising relationship. **CASE EXAMPLE 26.3** FMS, Inc., entered into a franchise agreement to become an authorized dealership for the sale of Samsung brand construction equipment. Samsung then sold its construction-equipment business to Volvo Construction Equipment North America, Inc., which was to continue selling Samsung brand equipment. Later, Volvo rebranded the construction equipment under its own name and canceled FMS's franchise.

FMS sued, claiming that Volvo had terminated the franchise without good cause in violation of state law. Because Volvo was no longer manufacturing the Samsung brand equipment, however, the court found that Volvo could legally terminate FMS's franchise. If Volvo had continued making the Samsung brand equipment, it could not have terminated the franchise.[7] ■

"You have written more than a book, Ms. McBean— you have written a franchise."

26-3 The Franchise Contract

The franchise relationship is defined by a contract between the franchisor and the franchisee. The franchise contract specifies the terms and conditions of the franchise and spells out the rights and duties of the franchisor and the franchisee. If either party fails to perform the contractual duties, that party may be subject to a lawsuit for breach of contract. Generally, statutes

---

7. *FMS, Inc. v. Volvo Construction Equipment North America, Inc.,* 557 F.3d 758 (7th Cir. 2009).

Can a construction-equipment franchisor cancel the franchise of an authorized dealer because the dealer stopped selling Samsung brand construction equipment?

and case law governing franchising emphasize the importance of good faith and fair dealing in franchise relationships.

Because each type of franchise relationship has its own characteristics, franchise contracts tend to differ. Nonetheless, certain major issues typically are addressed in a franchise contract. We look at some of them next. (The *Business Application* feature at the end of this chapter describes some steps a franchisee can take to avoid problems common in franchise agreements.)

26–3a Payment for the Franchise

The franchisee ordinarily pays an initial fee or lump-sum price for the franchise license (the privilege of being granted a franchise). This fee is separate from the various products that the franchisee purchases from or through the franchisor. The franchise agreement may also require the franchisee to pay a percentage of advertising costs and certain administrative expenses.

In some industries, the franchisor relies heavily on the initial sale of the franchise for realizing a profit. In other industries, the continued dealing between the parties brings profit to both. Generally, the franchisor receives a stated percentage of the annual (or monthly) sales or volume of business done by the franchisee.

26–3b Business Premises

The franchise agreement may specify whether the premises for the business must be leased or purchased outright. Sometimes, a building must be constructed or remodeled to meet the terms of the agreement. The agreement usually specifies whether the franchisor supplies equipment and furnishings for the premises or whether this is the responsibility of the franchisee.

26–3c Location of the Franchise

Typically, the franchisor determines the territory to be served. Some franchise contracts give the franchisee exclusive rights, or "territorial rights," to a certain geographic area. Other franchise contracts, though they define the territory allotted to a particular franchise, either specifically state that the franchise is nonexclusive or are silent on the issue of territorial rights.

Many franchise cases involve disputes over territorial rights, and the implied covenant of good faith and fair dealing often comes into play in this area of franchising. If the franchise contract does not grant exclusive territorial rights to a franchisee and the franchisor allows a competing franchise to be established nearby, the franchisee may suffer a significant loss in profits. In this situation, a court may hold that the franchisor's actions breached an implied covenant of good faith and fair dealing.

26–3d Quality Control by the Franchisor

The day-to-day operation of the franchise business normally is left up to the franchisee. Nonetheless, the franchise agreement may specify that the franchisor will provide some degree of supervision and control so that it can protect the franchise's name and reputation.

Means of Control. When the franchise prepares a product, such as food, or provides a service, such as motel accommodations, the contract often states that the franchisor will establish certain standards for the facility. Typically, the contract will state that the franchisor is permitted to make periodic inspections to ensure that the standards are being maintained.

As a means of controlling quality, franchise agreements also typically limit the franchisee's ability to sell the franchise to another party. **EXAMPLE 26.4** Keller Toyota, an authorized Toyota

> "Business opportunities are like buses, there's always another one coming."
>
> **RICHARD BRANSON**
> 1950–PRESENT
> (BRITISH ENTREPRENEUR)

franchise, contracts to sell its dealership to Wheeler Autos. A Toyota franchise generally cannot be sold without Toyota's permission. Prospective franchisees must meet Toyota's customer satisfaction standards. If Wheeler Autos fails to meet those standards, Toyota can refuse to allow the sale and can terminate the franchise. ■

Degree of Control. As a general rule, the validity of a provision permitting the franchisor to establish and enforce certain quality standards is unquestioned. The franchisor has a legitimate interest in maintaining the quality of the product or service to protect its name and reputation.

If a franchisor exercises too much control over the operations of its franchisees, however, the franchisor risks potential liability. A franchisor may also occasionally be held liable—under the doctrine of *respondeat superior*—for the tortious acts of the franchisees' employees.

EXAMPLE 26.5 In 2014, the National Labor Relations Board (NLRB) ruled that McDonald's USA, LLC, might be held jointly liable along with several of its franchisees for labor and wage violations. The NLRB had received nearly two hundred employee complaints that McDonald's restaurants had engaged in unfair labor practices (such as firing or penalizing workers for participating in protests over wages and working conditions). Investigators found that at least some of the complaints had merit. The NLRB reasoned that McDonald's exerts sufficient control over its franchisees to be found liable for the franchisees' employment law violations. By 2015, the NLRB was reconsidering its ruling. ■

Can a Toyota dealer sell her dealership to another car dealer without the approval of Toyota?

26-3e Pricing Arrangements

Franchises provide the franchisor with an outlet for the firm's goods and services. Depending on the nature of the business, the franchisor may require the franchisee to purchase certain supplies from the franchisor at an established price.[8] A franchisor cannot, however, set the prices at which the franchisee will resell the goods, because such price setting may be a violation of state or federal antitrust laws, or both. A franchisor can suggest retail prices but cannot mandate them.

26-4 Franchise Termination

The duration of the franchise is a matter to be determined between the parties. Sometimes, a franchise will start out for a short period, such as a year, so that the franchisor can determine whether it wants to stay in business with the franchisee. Other times, the duration of the franchise contract correlates with the term of the lease for the business premises, and both are renewable at the end of that period.

26-4a Grounds for Termination

Usually, the franchise agreement specifies that termination must be "for cause" and then defines the grounds for termination. Cause might include, for instance, the death or disability of the franchisee, insolvency of the franchisee, breach of the franchise agreement, or failure to meet specified sales quotas. In the following case, franchise agreements provided that the franchisor could terminate them for good cause.

KNOW THIS
Under the doctrine of *respondeat superior*, an employer may be liable for the torts of employees if they occur within the scope of employment, without regard to the personal fault of the employer.

---

8. Although a franchisor can require franchisees to purchase supplies from it, requiring a franchisee to purchase exclusively from the franchisor may violate federal antitrust laws.

CASE 26.2

Century 21 Real Estate LLC v. All Professional Realty, Inc.

United States Court of Appeals, Ninth Circuit, ___ Fed.Appx. ___, 2015 WL 191502 (2015).

FACTS Carol and Steve Wright owned All Professional Realty, Inc., and All Professional Hawaii Realty, Inc. The Wrights' companies signed four franchise agreements with Century 21 Real Estate, LLC, to operate offices in Sacramento and Folsom, California, and Honolulu, Hawaii, under the name "Century 21 All Professional." The agreements required All Professional to pay royalty and advertising fees. They also permitted Century 21 to terminate the agreements for good cause, including the franchisee's failure to operate at an approved location. All Professional signed a note for $75,000 payable to Century 21 and agreed to make annual payments on the note. Four years later, All Professional stopped remitting the fees and making payments on the note, and it closed the Folsom office. Century 21 terminated the franchise agreements. The Wrights and All Professional filed a suit against Century 21, alleging breach of contract. Century 21 filed a cross-claim for breach. A federal district court issued a summary judgment in the franchisor's favor. All Professional appealed.

ISSUE Did the Wrights' failure to continue paying fees and making note payments, along with their abandonment of the Folsom office, provide Century 21 with legitimate grounds for termination of the franchise agreements?

Under what circumstances can Century 21 terminate a franchise agreement?

iStockPhoto.com/ RiverNorthPhotography

DECISION Yes. The U.S. Court of Appeals for the Sixth Circuit affirmed the lower court's judgment in Century 21's favor. Century 21 did not breach the franchise agreements—All Professional did.

REASON If Century 21 had failed to perform the franchise agreements, this failure might have excused the Wrights' nonperformance. But the Wrights did not show that Century 21 had failed to perform. Under the agreements, Century 21 provided All Professional with access to the Century 21 system. The agreements expressly stated, however, that Century 21 did not thereby guaranty the Wrights' success. Thus, any lack of success on the part of the Wrights was not a breach of the agreements by Century 21. Nor did Century 21 breach the agreements by preventing the Wrights from curing their defaults. The Wrights testified that they did not have the financial resources to cure their defaults. Century 21 did not terminate the agreements in bad faith—it had a legal right to terminate them.

CRITICAL THINKING—Economic Consideration *What is the most likely reason that All Professional stopped paying the franchise fees and the payments on the note, and closed one of its offices? Why is this an insufficient justification for breach of the franchisee's agreements with Century 21?*

Notice Requirements Most franchise contracts provide that notice of termination must be given. If no set time for termination is specified, then a reasonable time, with notice, is implied. A franchisee must be given reasonable time to wind up the business—that is, to do the accounting and return the copyright or trademark or any other property of the franchisor.

Opportunity to Cure a Breach A franchise agreement may state that the franchisee may attempt to cure an ordinary, curable breach within a certain period of time after notice so as to postpone, or even avoid, the termination of the contract. Even when a contract contains a notice-and-cure provision, however, a franchisee's breach of the duty of honesty and fidelity may be enough to allow the franchisor to terminate the franchise.

CASE EXAMPLE 26.6 Pilot Air Freight Corporation is a franchisor that moves freight through its network of operations at airports and other sites. LJL Transportation, Inc., was a franchisee. The franchise agreement required LJL to assign all shipments to the Pilot network. The agreement also provided that "Pilot shall allow Franchisee an opportunity to cure a default within ninety (90) days of receipt of written notice."

After eight years as a Pilot franchisee, LJL began to divert shipments to Northeast Transportation, a competing service owned by LJL's owners. Pilot then terminated the franchise agreement. LJL filed a lawsuit claiming that it should be allowed to cure its breach, but the court ruled in favor of Pilot. A franchise agreement may be terminated immediately when there is a material breach so serious that it goes directly to the heart and essence of the contract.[9] ■

---

9. *LJL Transportation, Inc. v. Pilot Air Freight Corp.*, 599 Pa. 546, 962 A.2d 639 (Pa.Sup.Ct. 2009).

To avoid potential disputes regarding franchise termination, always do preliminary research on a franchisor before agreeing to enter into a franchise contract. Find out whether the franchisor has terminated franchises in the past, how many times, and for what reasons. Contact five to ten franchisees of the franchisor and ask questions about their relationships and any problems they have had. If the franchisor has been honest, reliable, and reasonable with its franchisees in the past, you will have a better chance of avoiding disputes with that franchisor over wrongful termination in the future.

PREVENTING LEGAL DISPUTES

26–4b Wrongful Termination

Because a franchisor's termination of a franchise often has adverse consequences for the franchisee, much franchise litigation involves claims of wrongful termination. Generally, the termination provisions of contracts are more favorable to the franchisor. This means that the franchisee, who normally invests a substantial amount of time and funds to make the franchise operation successful, may receive little or nothing for the business on termination. The franchisor owns the trademark and hence the business.

It is in this area that statutory and case law become important. The federal and state laws discussed earlier attempts, among other things, to protect franchisees from arbitrary or unfair termination of their franchises by the franchisors.

What happens when an air freight franchisee steers much of its business to an unauthorized plane network?

26–4c The Importance of Good Faith and Fair Dealing

Generally, both statutory law and case law emphasize the importance of good faith and fair dealing in terminating a franchise relationship. In determining whether a franchisor has acted in good faith when terminating a franchise agreement, the courts generally try to balance the rights of both parties.

If a court perceives that a franchisor has arbitrarily or unfairly terminated a franchise, the franchisee will be provided with a remedy for wrongful termination. When a franchisor's decision to terminate a franchise was made in the normal course of the franchisor's business operations, however, that weighs in favor of the franchisor. In that situation, a court generally will not consider termination wrongful as long as reasonable notice of termination was given to the franchisee.

The importance of good faith and fair dealing in a franchise relationship is underscored by the consequences of the franchisor's acts in the following case.

LEARNING OBJECTIVE 4

How are franchises normally terminated? When will a court decide that a franchisor has wrongfully terminated a franchise?

SPOTLIGHT ON HOLIDAY INNS: CASE 26.3

Holiday Inn Franchising, Inc. v. Hotel Associates, Inc.

Court of Appeals of Arkansas, 2011 Ark.App. 147, 382 S.W.3d 6 (2011).

FACTS Buddy House was in the construction business. For decades, he collaborated on projects with Holiday Inn Franchising, Inc. Their relationship was characterized by good faith—many projects were undertaken without written contracts. At Holiday Inn's request, House inspected a hotel in Wichita Falls, Texas, to estimate the cost of getting it into shape. Holiday Inn wanted House to renovate the hotel and operate it as a Holiday Inn. House

What actions by franchisors might constitute fraud?

estimated that recovering the cost of renovation would take him more than ten years, so he asked for a franchise term longer than Holiday Inn's usual ten years. Holiday Inn refused, but said that if he ran the hotel "appropriately," the term would be extended at the end of ten years. House bought the hotel, renovated it, and operated it as Hotel Associates, Inc. (HAI), generating substantial profits. He refused offers to sell it for as much as $15 million.

Continues

Before the ten years had passed, Greg Aden, a Holiday Inn executive, developed a plan to license a different local hotel as a Holiday Inn instead of renewing House's franchise license. Aden stood to earn a commission from licensing the other hotel. No one informed House of Aden's plan. When the time came, HAI applied for an extension of its franchise, and Holiday Inn asked for major renovations. HAI spent $3 million to comply with this request. Holiday Inn did not renew the term for HAI, however, and granted a franchise to the other hotel instead. HAI sold its hotel for $5 million and filed a suit against Holiday Inn, asserting fraud. The court awarded HAI compensatory and punitive damages. Holiday Inn appealed.

ISSUE Did Holiday Inn's failure to inform House that it intended to grant the franchise to a different local hotel constitute fraud?

DECISION Yes. A state intermediate appellate court affirmed the lower court's judgment.

REASON The court recognized that a failure to volunteer information normally does not constitute fraud. But silence can amount to fraud when parties are in a relationship of trust and there is an "inequality" of knowledge between them—for example, when one party has information that the other party is justified in assuming does not exist.

In this case, House's relationship with Holiday Inn was characterized by "honesty, trust, and the free flow of pertinent information." With respect to the Wichita Falls hotel, Holiday Inn assured HAI that its franchise would be renewed after ten years if it ran the hotel "appropriately." House was thus justified in assuming that his franchise was not in jeopardy.

Holiday Inn, however, knew of Aden's plan to license a different facility in the same area and did not inform House. In these circumstances, the failure to inform was fraud. Even Holiday Inn personnel, including Aden, admitted that House should have been informed. The appellate court also upheld the lower court's award of compensatory damages and increased the amount of punitive damages, citing Holiday Inn's "degree of reprehensibility."

CRITICAL THINKING—Legal Consideration *Why should House and HAI have been advised of Holiday Inn's plan to grant a franchise to a different hotel in their territory?*

Reviewing . . . Sole Proprietorships and Franchises

Carlos Del Rey decided to open a fast-food Mexican restaurant and signed a franchise contract with a national chain called La Grande Enchilada. Under the franchise agreement, Del Rey purchased the building, and La Grande Enchilada supplied the equipment. The contract required the franchisee to strictly follow the franchisor's operating manual and stated that failure to do so would be grounds for terminating the franchise contract. The manual set forth detailed operating procedures and safety standards, and provided that a La Grande Enchilada representative would inspect the restaurant monthly to ensure compliance.

Nine months after Del Rey began operating his restaurant, a spark from the grill ignited an oily towel in the kitchen. No one was injured, but by the time firefighters put out the fire, the kitchen had sustained extensive damage. The cook told the fire department that the towel was "about two feet from the grill" when it caught fire, which was in compliance with the franchisor's manual that required towels to be at least one foot from the grills. Nevertheless, the next day La Grande Enchilada notified Del Rey that his franchise would terminate in thirty days for failure to follow the prescribed safety procedures. Using the information presented in the chapter, answer the following questions.

1. What type of franchise was Del Rey's La Grande Enchilada restaurant?

2. If Del Rey operates the restaurant as a sole proprietorship, who bears the loss for the damaged kitchen? Explain.

3. Assume that Del Rey files a lawsuit against La Grande Enchilada, claiming that his franchise was wrongfully terminated. What is the main factor a court would consider in determining whether the franchise was wrongfully terminated?

4. Would a court be likely to rule that La Grande Enchilada had good cause to terminate Del Rey's franchise in this situation? Why or why not?

BUSINESS APPLICATION

What Problems Can a Franchisee Anticipate?*

A franchise arrangement appeals to many prospective businesspersons for several reasons. Entrepreneurs who purchase franchises can operate independently and without the risks associated with products that have never before been marketed. Additionally, franchisees can usually rely on the assistance and guidance of a management network that is regional or national in scope and has been in place for some time.

If you ever consider entering into a franchise agreement, however, you should be aware that franchisees do face potential problems. Generally, to avoid possibly significant economic and legal difficulties, it is imperative that you obtain all relevant details about the business and ask an attorney to evaluate the franchise contract for possible pitfalls.

The Franchise Fee

Almost all franchise contracts require a franchise fee payable up front or in installments. This fee often ranges between $10,000 and $50,000. For nationally known franchises, such as McDonald's, the fee may be $500,000 or more. To calculate the true cost of the franchise, however, you must also

---

* This *Business Application* is not meant to substitute for the services of an attorney who is licensed to practice law in your state.

---

include the fees that are paid once the franchise opens for business. For example, as a franchisee, you would probably pay 2 to 8 percent of your gross sales as royalties to the franchisor (for the use of the franchisor's trademark, for example). Another 1 to 2 percent of gross sales might go to the franchisor to cover advertising costs. Although your business would benefit from the advertising, the cost of that advertising might exceed the benefits you would realize.

Electronic Encroachment and Termination Provisions

The franchise contract may give the franchisee exclusive territorial rights. Even when it does, however, many franchisees face problems from so-called electronic encroachment. Encroachment usually occurs when nothing in the franchise agreement prevents the franchisor from selling its products to customers located within the franchisee's territory via the Internet. As a prospective franchisee, you should make sure that your franchise contract covers such contingencies and that its provisions protect you against any losses you might incur from this type of competition.

A major economic consequence, usually of a negative nature, will occur if the franchisor terminates your franchise agreement. Before you sign a franchise contract, make sure that the provisions regarding termination are reasonable, are clearly specified, and provide you with adequate notice and sufficient time to wind up the business.

CHECKLIST for the Franchisee:

1. Find out all you can about the franchisor: How long has the franchisor been in business? How profitable is the business? Is there a growing market for the product?

2. Obtain the most recent financial statement from the franchisor and a complete description of the business.

3. Obtain a clear and complete statement of all fees that you will be required to pay.

4. Determine whether the franchisor will help you find a suitable location, train managers and employees, assist with promotion and advertising, and supply capital or credit.

5. Visit other franchisees in the same business. Ask them about their profitability and their experiences with the product, the market, and the franchisor.

6. Carefully examine the franchise contract provisions relating to termination of the franchise agreement. Find out how many franchises have been terminated in the past several years.

7. Will you have an exclusive geographic territory? If so, for how many years? Does the franchisor have a right to engage in Internet sales to customers within this territory?

8. Finally, the most important way to protect yourself is to have an attorney familiar with franchise law examine the contract before you sign it.

Key Terms

entrepreneur 658

franchise 662

franchisee 662

franchisor 662

sole proprietorship 659

Chapter Summary: Sole Proprietorships and Franchises

Sole Proprietorships	The simplest form of business organization, the sole proprietorship is used by anyone who does business without creating a separate organization. The owner is the business. The owner pays personal income taxes on all profits and is personally liable for all business debts.

Franchises	1. *Types of franchises*—
	   a. Distributorship (for example, automobile dealerships).
	   b. Chain-style operation (for example, fast-food chains).
	   c. Manufacturing/processing-plant arrangement (for example, soft-drink bottling companies, such as Pepsi-Cola).
	2. *Laws governing franchising*—Franchises are governed by contract law. They are also governed by federal and state statutory laws, as well as agency regulations.

The Franchise Contract	The franchise relationship is defined by a contract between the franchisor and the franchisee. The contract normally spells out the following terms: 1. *Payment for the franchise*—Ordinarily, the contract requires the franchisee (purchaser) to pay an initial fee or lump-sum price for the franchise license. 2. *Business premises*—The contract may specify whether the business premises will be leased or purchased by the franchisee and which party will provide the equipment and furnishings. 3. *Location of the franchise*—The franchisor typically specifies the territory to be served by the franchisee. 4. *Quality control*—The franchisor may require the franchisee to abide by certain standards of quality relating to the product or service offered. 5. *Pricing arrangements*—The franchisor may require the franchisee to purchase certain supplies from the franchisor at an established price but cannot set retail resale prices.
Franchise Termination	Usually, the contract provides for the date and/or conditions of termination of the franchise arrangement. Both federal and state statutes attempt to protect franchisees from franchisors who unfairly or arbitrarily terminate franchises.

Issue Spotters

1. Frank plans to open a sporting goods store and to hire Gogi and Hap. Frank will invest only his own funds. He expects that he will not make a profit for at least eighteen months and will make only a small profit in the three years after that. He hopes to expand eventually. Would a sole proprietorship be an appropriate form for Frank's business? Why or why not? (See *Sole Proprietorships*.)

2. Thirsty Bottling Company and U.S. Beverages, Inc. (USB), enter into a franchise agreement that states that the franchise may be terminated at any time "for cause." Thirsty fails to meet USB's specified sales quota. Does this constitute "cause" for termination? Why or why not? (See *Franchise Termination*.)

—**Check your answers to the *Issue Spotters* against the answers provided in Appendix D at the end of this text.**

Learning Objectives Check

1. What advantages and disadvantages are associated with the sole proprietorship?

2. What are the most common types of franchises?

3. What are the basic requirements of the Franchise Rule?

4. How are franchises normally terminated? When will a court find that a franchisor has wrongfully terminated a franchise?

—**Answers to the even-numbered *Learning Objectives Check* questions can be found in Appendix E at the end of this text.**

Business Scenarios and Case Problems

26–1. Franchising. Maria, Pablo, and Vicky are recent college graduates who would like to go into business for themselves. They are considering purchasing a franchise. If they enter into a franchising arrangement, they would have the support of a large company that could answer any questions they might have. Also, a firm that has been in business for many years would be experienced in dealing with some of the problems that novice businesspersons might encounter. These and other attributes of franchises can lessen some of the risks of the marketplace. What other aspects of franchising—positive and negative—should Maria, Pablo, and Vicky consider before committing themselves to a particular franchise? (See *Franchises*.)

26–2. Control of a Franchise. National Foods, Inc., sells franchises to its fast-food restaurants, known as Chicky-D's. Under the franchise agreement, franchisees agree to hire and train employees strictly according to Chicky-D's standards. In addition, Chicky-D's regional supervisors must approve all new hires and policies, which they generally do. Chicky-D's reserves the right to terminate a franchise for violating the franchisor's rules. After several incidents of racist comments and conduct by Tim, a recently hired assistant manager at a Chicky-D's, Sharon, a counterperson at the restaurant, resigns. Sharon files a suit against National. National files a motion for summary judgment, arguing that it is not liable for harassment by franchise employees. Will the court grant National's motion? Why or why not? (See *The Franchise Contract*.)

26–3. Spotlight on McDonald's—Franchise Termination. C.B. Management, Inc., had a franchise agreement with McDonald's Corp. to operate McDonald's restaurants in Cleveland, Ohio. The agreement required C.B. to make monthly payments of certain percentages of the gross sales to McDonald's. If any payment was more than thirty days late, McDonald's had the right to terminate the franchise. The agreement also stated that even if McDonald's accepted a late payment, that would not "constitute a waiver of any subsequent breach." McDonald's sometimes accepted C.B.'s late payments, but when C.B. defaulted on the payments in July 2010, McDonald's gave notice of thirty days to comply or surrender possession of the restaurants. C.B. missed the deadline. McDonald's demanded that C.B. vacate the restaurants, but C.B. refused. McDonald's alleged that C.B. had violated the franchise agreement. C.B. claimed that McDonald's had breached the implied covenant of good faith and fair dealing. Which party should prevail, and why? [*McDonald's Corp. v. C.B. Management Co.*, 13 F.Supp.2d 705 (N.D.Ill. 1998)] (See *Franchise Termination*.)

26–4. The Franchise Contract. Kubota Tractor Corp. makes farm, industrial, and outdoor equipment. Its franchise contracts allow Kubota to enter into dealership agreements with "others at any location." Kejzar Motors, Inc., is a Kubota dealer in Nacogdoches and Jasper, Texas. These two Kejzar stores operate as one dealership with two locations. Kubota granted a dealership to Michael Hammer in Lufkin, Texas, which lies between Kejzar's two store locations. Kejzar filed a suit in a Texas state court against Kubota. Kejzar asked for an injunction to prevent Kubota from locating a dealership in the same market area. Kejzar argued that the new location would cause it to suffer a significant loss of profits. Which party in a franchise relationship typically determines the territory served by a franchisee? Which legal principles come into play in this area? How do these concepts most likely apply in this case? Discuss. [*Kejzar Motors, Inc. v. Kubota Tractor Corp.*, 334 S.W.3d 351 (Tex. App.—Tyler 2011)] (See *The Franchise Contract*.)

26–5. Business Case Problem with Sample Answer—Wrongful Termination of Franchise. George Oshana and GTO Investments, Inc., operated a Mobil gas station franchise in Itasca, Illinois. In 2010, Oshana and GTO became involved in a rental dispute with Buchanan Energy, to which Mobil had assigned the lease for the gas station facility. In November 2011, Buchanan terminated the franchise because Oshana and GTO had failed to pay the rent. Oshana and GTO, however, alleged that they had been "ready, willing, and able to pay the rent" but that Buchanan had failed to accept their electronic funds transfer. Have Oshana and GTO stated a claim for wrongful termination of their franchise? Why or why not? [*Oshana v. Buchanan Energy*, 2012 WL 426921 (N.D.Ill. 2012)] (See *Franchise Termination*.)

—**For a sample answer to Problem 26–5, go to Appendix F at the end of this text.**

26–6. Quality Control. JTH Tax, Inc., doing business as Liberty Tax Service, provides tax preparation and related loan services throughout the United States in more than two thousand company-owned and franchised stores. Liberty's agreement with its franchisees reserved the right to control their ads. In company operations manuals, Liberty provided step-by-step instructions, directions, and limitations to its franchisees regarding their ads. Liberty retained the right to unilaterally modify the steps at any time. The California Attorney General filed a suit in a California state court against Liberty, alleging misleading or deceptive ads by its franchisees regarding refund anticipation loans and e-refund checks. Can Liberty be held liable? Discuss. [*People v. JTH Tax, Inc.*, 212 Cal.App.4th 1219, 151 Cal.Rptr.3d 728 (1 Dist. 2013)] (See *The Franchise Contract*.)

26–7. Quality Control. The franchise agreement of Domino's Pizza, L.L.C., sets out operational standards, including safety requirements, for a franchisee to follow but provides that the franchisee is an independent contractor. Each franchisee is free to use its own means and methods. For example, Domino's does not know whether a franchisee's delivery drivers are complying with vehicle safety requirements. MAC Pizza Management, Inc., operates a Domino's franchise. A vehicle driven by Joshua Balka, a MAC delivery driver, hydroplaned due to a bald tire and wet pavement, and struck the vehicle of Devavaram and Ruth Christopher, killing Ruth and injuring Devavaram. Is Domino's liable for negligence? Explain. [*Domino's Pizza, L.L.C. v. Reddy*, 2015 WL 1247349 (Tex.App.—Beaumont. 2015)] (See *The Franchise Contract.*)

26–8. A Question of Ethics—Sole Proprietorships. In August 2004, Ralph Vilardo contacted Travel Center, Inc., in Cincinnati, Ohio, to buy a trip to Florida in December for his family. Vilardo paid $6,900 to David Sheets, the sole proprietor of Travel Center. Vilardo also paid $195 to Sheets for a separate trip to Florida in February 2005. Sheets assured Vilardo that everything was set, but in fact no arrangements were made. Later, two unauthorized charges for travel services totaling $1,182.35 appeared on Vilardo's credit-card statement. Vilardo filed a suit in an Ohio state court against Sheets and his business, alleging, among other things, fraud and violations of the state consumer protection law. Vilardo served Sheets and Travel Center with copies of the complaint, the summons, a request for admissions, and other documents filed with the court, including a motion for summary judgment. Responses to each of these filings were subject to certain time limits. Sheets responded once on his own behalf with a denial of all of Vilardo's claims. Travel Center did not respond. [*Vilardo v. Sheets*, 2006 –Ohio– 3473 (Ohio App.12 Dist. 2006)] (See *Sole Proprietorships.*)

1. Almost four months after Vilardo filed his complaint, Sheets decided that he was unable to adequately represent himself and retained an attorney who asked the court for more time. Should the court grant this request? Why or why not? Ultimately, what should the court rule in this case?

2. Sheets admitted that "Travel Center" was a sole proprietorship. He also argued that liability might be imposed on his business but not on himself. How would you rule with respect to this argument? Would there be anything unethical about allowing Sheets to avoid liability on this basis? Explain.

Critical Thinking and Writing Assignments

26–9. Business Law Writing. Jordan Mendelson is interested in purchasing a franchise in a meal-preparation business. Customers will come to the business to assemble gourmet dinners and then take the prepared meals to their homes for cooking. The franchisor requires each store to use a specific layout and provides the recipes for various dinners, but the franchisee is not required to purchase the food products from the franchisor. What general factors should Mendelson consider before entering into a contract to buy such a franchise? Is location important? Are there any laws that Mendelson should consider, given that this franchise involves food preparation and sales? Should Mendelson operate this business as a sole proprietorship? Why or why not? (See *The Franchise Contract.*)

26–10. Business Law Critical Thinking Group Assignment. Walid Elkhatib, an Arab American, bought a Dunkin' Donuts franchise in Illinois. Ten years later, Dunkin' Donuts began offering breakfast sandwiches with bacon, ham, or sausage through its franchises. Elkhatib refused to sell these items at his store on the ground that his religion forbade the handling of pork. Elkhatib then opened a second franchise, at which he also refused to sell pork products. The next year, at both locations, Elkhatib began selling meatless sandwiches. He also opened a third franchise. When he proposed to relocate this franchise, Dunkin' Donuts refused to approve the new location and informed him that it would not renew any of his franchise agreements because he did not carry the full sandwich line. Elkhatib filed a lawsuit against Dunkin' Donuts. (See *Franchise Termination.*)

1. The first group will argue on behalf of Elkhatib that Dunkin' Donuts wrongfully terminated his franchises.

2. The second group will take the side of Dunkin' Donuts and justify its decision to terminate the franchises.

3. The third group will assess whether Dunkin' Donuts acted in good faith in its relationship with Elkhatib. It will also consider whether Dunkin' Donuts should be required to accommodate Elkhatib's religious beliefs and allow him not to serve pork in these three locations.

iStockPhoto.com/Pgiam

All Forms of Partnership

Traditionally, the two most common forms of business organization selected by two or more persons going into business together have been the partnership and the corporation. A *partnership* arises from an agreement, express or implied, between two or more persons to carry on a business for profit. Partners are co-owners of a business and have joint control over its operation and the right to share in its profits. As the chapter-opening quotation indicates, all gains are the "fruit of venturing," and partnerships—to the extent that they encourage business ventures—contribute to those gains.

This chapter opens with an examination of ordinary partnerships, or *general partnerships,* and the rights and duties of partners in this traditional business entity. It then examines some special forms of partnerships known as *limited liability partnerships* and *limited partnerships.* Although general partnerships are less common today than in the past, the limited liability forms of partnership are quite prevalent. Accountants, attorneys, and architects frequently organize as limited liability partnerships. DLA Piper, the second-largest U.S. law firm, for instance, is structured as two limited liability partnerships—DLA Piper U.S., LLP, and DLA Piper International, LLP.

27-1 Basic Partnership Concepts

Partnerships are governed both by common law concepts—in particular, those relating to agency—and by statutory law. As in so many other areas of business law, the National Conference of Commissioners on Uniform State Laws has drafted uniform laws for partnerships, and these uniform laws have been widely adopted by the states.

27–1a Agency Concepts and Partnership Law

When two or more persons agree to do business as partners, they enter into a special relationship with one another. To an extent, their relationship is similar to an agency relationship because each partner is deemed to be the agent of the other partners and of the partnership. Thus, the common law agency concepts apply—specifically, the imputation of knowledge of, and responsibility for, acts done within the scope of the partnership relationship. In their relationships with one another, partners, like agents, are bound by fiduciary ties.

In one important way, however, partnership law is distinct from agency law. A partnership is based on a voluntary contract between two or more competent persons who agree to commit financial capital, labor, and skill to a business with the understanding that profits and losses will be shared. In a nonpartnership agency relationship, the agent usually does not have an ownership interest in the business, and he or she is not obliged to bear a portion of the ordinary business losses.

27–1b The Uniform Partnership Act

The Uniform Partnership Act (UPA) has done much to reduce controversies concerning the law relating to partnerships. The UPA governs the operation of partnerships *in the absence of an express agreement*. In other words, the partners are free to establish rules for their partnership that differ from those stated in the UPA.

The majority of the states have adopted the most recent version of the UPA (completed in 1997 and amended in 2011 and 2013 to provide limited liability for partners in a limited liability partnership).[1] We therefore base our discussion of the UPA in this chapter on the 1997 version of the act and refer to older versions of the UPA in footnotes when appropriate.

27–1c Definition of a Partnership

Partnership An agreement by
two or more persons to carry on, as
co-owners, a business for profit.

The UPA defines a **partnership** as "an association of two or more persons to carry on as co-owners a business for profit" [UPA 101(6)]. Note that the UPA's definition of *person* includes corporations, so a corporation can be a partner in a partnership [UPA 101(10)]. The *intent* to associate is a key element of a partnership, and a person cannot join a partnership unless all of the other partners consent [UPA 401(i)].

27–1d Essential Elements of a Partnership

Parties sometimes find themselves in conflict over whether their business enterprise is a legal partnership, especially when there is no formal, written partnership agreement. In determining whether a partnership exists, courts usually look for three essential elements, which are implicit in the UPA's definition of a general partnership:

1. A sharing of profits and losses.

2. A joint ownership of the business.

3. An equal right to be involved in the management of the business.

If the evidence in a particular case is insufficient to establish all three factors, the UPA provides a set of guidelines to be used.

The Sharing of Profits and Losses The sharing of *both profits and losses* from a business creates a presumption (legal inference) that a partnership exists. **EXAMPLE 27.1** Syd and Drake

---

1. More than half of the states, as well as the District of Columbia and the U.S. Virgin Islands, have adopted the 1997 version of the UPA. Excerpts from the latest version of the UPA are presented on the Web site that accompanies this text.

start a business that sells fruit smoothies near a college campus. They open a joint bank account from which they pay for supplies and expenses, and they share the proceeds (and losses) that the smoothie business generates. If a conflict arises as to their business relationship, a court will assume that a partnership exists unless the parties prove otherwise. ■

A court will *not presume* that a partnership exists, however, if shared profits are received as payment of any of the following [UPA 202(c)(3)]:

1. A debt by installments or interest on a loan.

2. Wages of an employee or payment for the services of an independent contractor.

3. Rent to a landlord.

4. An annuity to a surviving spouse or representative of a deceased partner.

5. A sale of the goodwill (valuable reputation) of a business or property.

> **EXAMPLE 27.2** A debtor, Mason Snopel, owes a creditor, Alice Burns, $5,000 on an unsecured debt. They agree that Mason will pay 10 percent of his monthly business profits to Alice until the loan with interest has been paid. Although Mason and Alice are sharing profits from the business, they are not presumed to be partners. ■

Joint Property Ownership Joint ownership of property does not in and of itself create a partnership [UPA 202(c)(1), (2)]. The parties' intentions are key. **EXAMPLE 27.3** Chiang and Burke jointly own farmland and lease it to a farmer for a share of the profits from the farming operation in lieu of fixed rental payments. This arrangement normally would not make Chiang, Burke, and the farmer partners. ■

27–1e Entity versus Aggregate Theory of Partnerships

At common law, a partnership was treated only as an aggregate of individuals and never as a separate legal entity. Thus, at common law a lawsuit could never be brought by or against the firm in its own name. Each individual partner had to sue or be sued.

Today, in contrast, a majority of the states follow the UPA and treat a partnership as an entity for most purposes. For instance, a partnership usually can sue or be sued, collect judgments, and have all accounting procedures in the name of the partnership entity [UPA 201, 307(a)].

As an entity, a partnership may hold the title to real or personal property in its name rather than in the names of the individual partners. Additionally, federal procedural laws permit the partnership to be treated as an entity in lawsuits in federal courts and bankruptcy proceedings.

If the owners of this farmland lease it to a farmer in exchange for a part of his profits, are the owners and the farmer partners?

27–1f Tax Treatment of Partnerships

Modern law does treat a partnership as an aggregate of the individual partners rather than as a separate legal entity in one situation—for federal income tax purposes. The partnership is a pass-through entity and not a taxpaying entity.

A **pass-through entity** is a business entity that has no tax liability—the entity's income is passed through to the owners of the entity, who pay income taxes on it. Thus, the income or losses the partnership incurs are "passed through" the entity framework and attributed to the partners on their individual tax returns. The partnership itself is responsible only for filing an **information return** with the Internal Revenue Service.

A partner's profit from the partnership (whether distributed or not) is taxed as individual income to the individual partner. Similarly, partners can deduct a share of the partnership's losses on their individual tax returns (in proportion to their partnership interests).

Pass-Through Entity A business entity that has no tax liability. The entity's income is passed through to the owners, and they pay taxes on the income.

Information Return A tax return submitted by a partnership that reports the business's income and losses. The partnership itself does not pay taxes on the income, but each partner's share of the profit (whether distributed or not) is taxed as individual income to that partner.

27-2 Formation and Operation

A partnership is a voluntary association of individuals. As such, it is formed by the agreement of the partners.

27-2a The Partnership Agreement

As a general rule, agreements to form a partnership can be *oral, written,* or *implied by conduct.* Some partnership agreements, however, must be in writing to be legally enforceable under the Statute of Frauds. (Recall that a writing may be an electronic record.)

Articles of Partnership
A written agreement that sets forth each partner's rights and obligations with respect to the partnership.

A partnership agreement, called **articles of partnership,** can include any terms that the parties wish, unless the terms are illegal or contrary to public policy or statute [UPA 103]. The terms commonly included in a partnership agreement are listed in Exhibit 27–1. (Creating a partnership agreement in another country may involve additional requirements, as this chapter's *Beyond Our Borders* feature explains.)

The rights and duties of partners are governed largely by the specific terms of their partnership agreement. In the absence of provisions to the contrary in the partnership agreement, the law imposes certain rights and duties, as discussed in the following subsections. The character and nature of the partnership business generally influence the application of these rights and duties.

27-2b Duration of the Partnership

The partnership agreement can specify the duration of the partnership by stating that it will continue until a certain date or the completion of a particular project. A partnership that is specifically limited in duration is called a *partnership for a term.* Generally, withdrawing prematurely (before the expiration date) from a partnership for a term constitutes a breach of the agreement, and the responsible partner can be held liable for any resulting losses [UPA 602(b)(2)].

If no fixed duration is specified, the partnership is a *partnership at will.* A partnership at will can be dissolved at any time without liability.

Exhibit 27–1 Common Terms Included in a Partnership Agreement

TERM	DESCRIPTION
Basic Structure	1. Name of the partnership and names of the partners. 2. Location of the business and the state law under which the partnership is organized. 3. Purpose and duration of the partnership.
Capital Contributions	1. Amount of capital that each partner is contributing. 2. The agreed-on value of any real or personal property that is contributed instead of cash. 3. How losses and gains on contributed capital will be allocated, and whether contributions will earn interest.
Sharing of Profits and Losses	1. Percentage of the profits and losses of the business that each partner will receive. 2. When distributions of profit will be made and how net profit will be calculated.
Management and Control	1. How management responsibilities will be divided among the partners. 2. Name(s) of the managing partner(s) and whether other partners have voting rights.
Dissociation and Dissolution	1. Events that will cause the dissociation of a partner or dissolve the firm, such as the retirement, death, or incapacity of any partner. 2. How partnership property will be valued and apportioned on dissociation and dissolution. 3. Whether an arbitrator will determine the value of partnership property on dissociation and dissolution and whether that determination will be binding.

BEYOND OUR BORDERS   Doing Business with Foreign Partners

U.S. businesspersons who wish to operate a partnership in another country often discover that the country requires local participation. That is, nationals of the host country must own a specific share of the business. In other words, the partnership will have to include one or more partners who live in the host country. Sometimes, U.S. businesspersons are reluctant to establish partnerships in a country that requires local participation. They fear that if the partnership breaks up, the technology and expertise developed by the partnership business may end up in the hands of a future competitor. In that event, the U.S. parties may have little recourse under the host country's laws against their former partners' use of the intellectual property.

CRITICAL THINKING

■ Do local participation rules benefit host countries in the long run? Explain.

27–2c Partnership by Estoppel

When a third person has reasonably and detrimentally relied on a representation that a nonpartner was part of a partnership, a court may conclude that a **partnership by estoppel** exists.

Liability Imposed A partnership by estoppel may arise when a person who is not a partner holds himself or herself out as a partner and makes representations that third parties rely on. In this situation, a court may impose liability—but not partnership rights—on the alleged partner.

Nonpartner as Agent A partnership by estoppel may also be imposed when a partner represents, expressly or impliedly, that a nonpartner is a member of the firm. In this situation, the nonpartner may be regarded as an agent whose acts are binding on the partnership [UPA 308].

   CASE EXAMPLE 27.4 Jackson Paper Manufacturing Company makes paper that is used by Stonewall Packaging, LLC. Jackson and Stonewall have officers and directors in common, and they share employees, property, and equipment. In reliance on Jackson's business reputation, Best Cartage, Inc., agreed to provide transportation services for Stonewall and bought thirty-seven tractor-trailers to use in fulfilling the contract. Best provided the services until Stonewall terminated the agreement.

   Best filed a suit for breach of contract against both Stonewall and Jackson. Best argued that Stonewall and Jackson had a partnership by estoppel. The court agreed, finding that "defendants combined labor, skills, and property to advance their alleged business partnership." Jackson had negotiated the agreement with Best on Stonewall's behalf. Jackson had also bought real estate, equipment, and general supplies for Stonewall with no expectation of payment. These facts were sufficient to prove a partnership by estoppel.[2] ■

Partnership by Estoppel
A partnership imposed by a court when nonpartners have held themselves out to be partners, or have allowed themselves to be held out as partners, and others have detrimentally relied on their misrepresentations.

27–2d Rights of Partners

The rights of partners in a partnership relate to the following areas: management, interest in the partnership, compensation, inspection of books, accounting, and property.

Management Rights In a general partnership, all partners have equal rights in managing the partnership [UPA 401(f)]. Unless the partners agree otherwise, each partner has one vote in management matters *regardless of the proportional size of his or her interest in the firm.* In a large

LEARNING OBJECTIVE 2
What are the rights and duties of partners in an ordinary partnership?

---

2. *Best Cartage, Inc. v. Stonewall Packaging, LLC,* 727 S.E.2d 291 (N.C.App. 2012).

partnership, partners often agree to delegate daily management responsibilities to a management committee made up of one or more of the partners.

The majority rule controls decisions in ordinary matters connected with partnership business, unless otherwise specified in the agreement. Decisions that significantly change the nature of the partnership or its ordinary course of business, however, require the *unanimous* consent of the partners [UPA 301(2), 401(i), (j)]. For instance, unanimous consent is likely required for a partnership to admit new partners, amend the partnership agreement, or enter a new line of business.

Interest in the Partnership
Each partner is entitled to the proportion of business profits and losses designated in the partnership agreement. If the agreement does not apportion profits (indicate how the profits will be shared), the UPA provides that profits will be shared equally. If the agreement does not apportion losses, losses will be shared in the same ratio as profits [UPA 401(b)].

EXAMPLE 27.5 The partnership agreement for Rick and Brent provides for capital contributions of $60,000 from Rick and $40,000 from Brent. If the agreement is silent as to how Rick and Brent will share profits or losses, they will share both profits and losses equally. In contrast, if the agreement provides for profits to be shared in the same ratio as capital contributions, 60 percent of the profits will go to Rick, and 40 percent will go to Brent. Unless the agreement provides otherwise, losses will be shared in the same ratio as profits. ■

Compensation
Devoting time, skill, and energy to partnership business is a partner's duty and generally is not a compensable service. Rather, as mentioned, a partner's income from the partnership takes the form of a distribution of profits according to the partner's share in the business.

Partners can, of course, agree otherwise. For instance, the managing partner of a law firm often receives a salary—in addition to her or his share of profits—for performing special administrative or managerial duties.

Where are partnership books and records normally kept?

Inspection of Books
Partnership books and records must be accessible to all partners. Each partner has the right to receive full and complete information concerning the conduct of all aspects of partnership business [UPA 403]. Partners have a duty to provide the information to the firm, which has a duty to preserve it and keep accurate records.

The partnership's books must be kept at the firm's principal business office (unless partners agree otherwise) and cannot be removed without the consent of all of the partners. Every partner is entitled to inspect all books and records on demand and can make copies of the materials. The personal representative of a deceased partner's estate has the same right of access to partnership books and records that the decedent would have had [UPA 403].

Accounting of Partnership Assets or Profits
An accounting of partnership assets or profits is required to determine the value of each partner's share in the partnership. An accounting can be performed voluntarily, or it can be compelled by court order. Under UPA 405(b), a partner has the right to bring an action for an accounting during the term of the partnership, as well as on the partnership's dissolution.

Property Rights
Property acquired by a partnership is the property of the partnership and not of the partners individually [UPA 203]. Partnership property includes all property that was originally contributed to the partnership and anything later purchased by the partnership or in the partnership's name (except in rare circumstances) [UPA 204]. A partner may use or possess partnership property only on behalf of the partnership [UPA 401(g)]. A partner is *not* a co-owner of partnership property and has no right to sell, mortgage, or transfer it.

> "Forty for you, sixty for me—and equal partners we will be."
>
> **ANONYMOUS**

In other words, partnership property is owned by the partnership as an entity and not by the individual partners. Thus, partnership property cannot be used to satisfy the personal debt of an individual partner. That partner's creditor, however, can petition a court for a **charging order** to attach the partner's *interest* in the partnership (her or his proportionate share of any profits that are distributed) to satisfy the partner's obligation. (A partner can also assign her or his right to a share of the partnership profits to another to satisfy a debt.)

Charging Order In partnership law, an order granted by a court to a judgment creditor that entitles the creditor to attach a partner's interest in the partnership.

27-2e Duties and Liabilities of Partners

The duties and liabilities of partners are basically derived from agency law. Each partner is an agent of every other partner and acts as both a principal and an agent in any business transaction within the scope of the partnership agreement.

Each partner is also a general agent of the partnership in carrying out the usual business of the firm "or business of the kind carried on by the partnership" [UPA 301(1)]. Thus, every act of a partner concerning partnership business, or "business of the kind," and every contract signed in the partnership's name bind the firm.

Fiduciary Duties The fiduciary duties a partner owes to the partnership and to the other partners are the *duty of care* and the *duty of loyalty* [UPA 404(a)]. Under the UPA, a partner's duty of care involves refraining from "grossly negligent or reckless conduct, intentional misconduct, or a knowing violation of law" [UPA 404(c)]. A partner is not liable to the partnership for simple negligence or honest errors in judgment in conducting partnership business.

The duty of loyalty requires a partner to account to the partnership for "any property, profit, or benefit" derived by the partner from the partnership's business or the use of its property [UPA 404(b)]. A partner must also refrain from competing with the partnership in business or dealing with the firm as an adverse party.

The duty of loyalty can be breached by self-dealing, misusing partnership property, disclosing trade secrets, or usurping a partnership business opportunity, as the following *Classic Case* illustrates.

★★★ CLASSIC CASE 27.1 ★★★

Meinhard v. Salmon

Court of Appeals of New York, 249 N.Y. 458, 164 N.E. 545 (1928).

FACTS Walter Salmon negotiated a twenty-year lease for the Hotel Bristol in New York City. To pay for the conversion of the building into shops and offices, Salmon entered into an agreement with Morton Meinhard, who was to assume half of the cost. Salmon and Meinhard agreed to share the profits and losses from the joint venture (a *joint venture* is similar to a partnership but typically is created for a single project, whereas a partnership usually involves an ongoing business). Salmon was to have the sole power to manage the building, however.

Less than four months before the end of the lease term, the building's owner approached Salmon about a project to raze the converted structure and construct a new building. Salmon agreed and signed a

What fiduciary duties does a partner have with respect to renewing a hotel lease?

new lease in the name of his own business, Midpoint Realty Company, without telling Meinhard. When Meinhard learned of the deal, he filed a suit against Salmon. The court ruled in Meinhard's favor, and Salmon appealed.

ISSUE Did Salmon breach his fiduciary duty of loyalty to Meinhard?

DECISION Yes. The Court of Appeals of New York held that Salmon had breached his fiduciary duty by failing to inform Meinhard of the business opportunity and secretly taking advantage of it for himself. The court therefore granted Meinhard an interest "measured by the value of half of the entire lease."

Continues

REASON The court stated, "Joint adventurers, like copartners, owe to one another, while the enterprise continues, the duty of the finest loyalty." Salmon's conduct excluded Meinhard from any chance to compete and from any chance to enjoy the opportunity for benefit. As a partner, Salmon was bound by his "obligation to his copartners in such dealings not to separate his interest from theirs, but, if he acquires any benefit, to communicate it to them." Salmon was also the managing co-adventurer, and thus the court found that "for him and for those like him the rule of undivided loyalty is relentless and supreme."

WHAT IF THE FACTS WERE DIFFERENT? *Suppose that Salmon had disclosed the proposed deal to Meinhard, who had said that he was not interested. Would the result in this case have been different? Explain.*

IMPACT OF THIS CASE ON TODAY'S LAW *This case involved a joint venture, not a partnership. At the time, a member of a joint venture had only the duty to refrain from actively subverting the rights of the other members. The decision in this case imposed the highest standard of loyalty on joint-venture members. The duty is now the same in both joint ventures and partnerships. Courts today frequently quote the eloquent language used in this opinion when describing the standard of loyalty that applies to partnerships.*

Breach and Waiver of Fiduciary Duties A partner's fiduciary duties may not be waived or eliminated in the partnership agreement, and in fulfilling them each partner must act consistently with the obligation of good faith and fair dealing [UPA 103(b), 404(d)]. The agreement can specify acts that the partners agree will violate a fiduciary duty.

Note that a partner may pursue his or her own interests without automatically violating these duties [UPA 404(e)]. The key is whether the partner has disclosed the interest to the other partners. **EXAMPLE 27.6** Jayne Trell, a partner at Jacoby & Meyers, owns a shopping mall. Trell may vote against a partnership proposal to open a competing mall, provided that she has fully disclosed her interest in the existing shopping mall to the other partners at the firm. ■ A partner cannot make secret profits or put self-interest before his or her duty to the interest of the partnership, however.

Authority of Partners The UPA affirms general principles of agency law that pertain to the authority of a partner to bind a partnership in contract. A partner may also subject the partnership to tort liability under agency principles. When a partner is carrying on partnership business with third parties in the usual way, both the partner and the firm share liability.

If a partner acts within the scope of her or his authority, the partnership is legally bound to honor the partner's commitments to third parties. The partnership will not be liable, however, if the third parties *know* that the partner had no authority to commit the partnership.

Limitations on Authority. A partnership may limit the capacity of a partner to act as the firm's agent or transfer property on its behalf by filing a "statement of partnership authority" in a designated state office [UPA 105, 303]. Such limits on a partner's authority normally are effective only with respect to third parties who are notified of the limitations.

Implied Powers. The agency concepts relating to apparent authority, actual authority, and ratification also apply to partnerships. *The extent of implied authority is generally broader for partners than for ordinary agents.*

In an ordinary partnership, the partners can exercise all implied powers reasonably necessary and customary to carry on that particular business. Some customarily implied powers include the authority to make warranties on goods in a retail sales business and the power to enter into contracts consistent with the firm's ordinary course of business.

EXAMPLE 27.7 Jamie Schwab, a partner in a firm that operates a retail tire store, regularly promises that "each tire will be warranted for normal wear for 40,000 miles." Because Schwab has authority to make warranties, the partnership is bound to honor them. Schwab would not, however, have the authority to sell the partnership's office equipment, fixtures, or other property without the consent of all of the other partners. ■

> "Surround yourself with partners who are better than you are."
>
> **DAVID OGILVY**
> 1911–1999
> (SCOTTISH ADVERTISING EXECUTIVE)

Liability of Partners One significant disadvantage associated with a traditional partnership is that partners are *personally* liable for the debts of the partnership. In most states, the liability is essentially unlimited because the acts of one partner in the ordinary course of business subject the other partners to personal liability [UPA 305].

Joint Liability. Each partner in a partnership is jointly liable for the partnership's obligations. **Joint liability** means that a third party must sue all of the partners as a group, but each partner can be held liable for the full amount.[3]

If, for instance, a third party sues one individual partner on a partnership contract, that partner has the right to demand that the other partners be sued with her or him. In fact, if the third party does not name all of the partners in the lawsuit, the assets of the partnership cannot be used to satisfy the judgment. With joint liability, the partnership's assets must be exhausted before creditors can reach the partners' individual assets.

Joint and Several Liability. In the majority of the states, under UPA 306(a), partners are jointly and severally (separately or individually) liable for all partnership obligations, including contracts, torts, and breaches of trust. **Joint and several liability** means that a third party has the option of suing all of the partners together (jointly) or one or more of the partners separately (severally).

All the partners can be held liable regardless of whether a particular partner participated in, knew about, or ratified the conduct that gave rise to the lawsuit. Normally, though, the partnership's assets must be exhausted before a creditor can enforce a judgment against a partner's personal assets [UPA 307(d)]. In addition, a partner who commits a tort may be required to indemnify (reimburse) the partnership for any damages it pays unless the tort was committed in the ordinary course of the partnership's business.

A judgment against one partner severally (separately) does not extinguish the others' liability. (Similarly, a release of one partner does not discharge the partners' several liability.) Those not sued in the first action may be sued subsequently, unless the court in the first action held that the partnership was not liable.

If a plaintiff is successful in a suit against a partner or partners, he or she may collect on the judgment only against the assets of those partners named as defendants. **EXAMPLE 27.8** Brian and Julie are partners. If Tom sues Brian for a debt on a partnership contract and wins, Tom can collect the amount of the judgment against Brian only. If Tom cannot collect enough from Brian, however, Tom can later sue Julie for the difference. ■

Liability of Incoming Partners. A partner newly admitted to an existing partnership is not personally liable for any partnership obligations incurred before the person became a partner [UPA 306(b)]. The new partner's liability to existing creditors of the partnership is limited to her or his capital contribution to the firm.

EXAMPLE 27.9 Smartclub, an existing partnership with four members, admits a new partner, Alex Jaff. He contributes $100,000 to the partnership. Smartclub has debts amounting to $600,000 at the time Jaff joins the firm. Although Jaff's capital contribution of $100,000 can be used to satisfy Smartclub's prior obligations, Jaff is not personally liable for those debts. If, however, Smartclub's managing partner borrows funds from a bank for the partnership after Jaff becomes a partner, Jaff will be personally liable for those amounts, along with all other partners. ■

Joint Liability In partnership law, the partners' shared liability for partnership obligations and debts. A third party must sue all of the partners as a group, but each partner can be held liable for the full amount.

Joint and Several Liability In partnership law, a doctrine under which a plaintiff may sue, and collect a judgment from, all of the partners together (jointly) or one or more of the partners separately (severally, or individually). A partner can be held liable even if she or he did not participate in, ratify, or know about the conduct that gave rise to the lawsuit.

---

3. Under the prior version of the UPA, which is still in effect in a few states, partners were subject to joint liability on partnership debts and contracts, but not on partnership debts arising from torts.

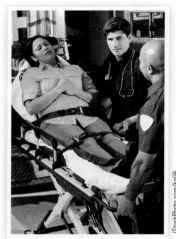

Under what circumstances can a partner be required to reimburse the partnership for damages paid because of that partner's tort while driving the partnership's van?

Dissociation The severance of the relationship between a partner and a partnership.

27–3 Dissociation and Termination

Dissociation occurs when a partner ceases to be associated in the carrying on of the partnership business. Dissociation normally entitles the partner to have his or her interest purchased by the partnership. It also terminates the partner's actual authority to act for the partnership and to participate with the partners in running the business. The partnership normally may continue to do business without the dissociating partner.[4] If the partners no longer wish to (or are unable to) continue the business, the partnership may be terminated (dissolved).

27–3a Events That Cause Dissociation

Under UPA 601, a partner can be dissociated from a partnership in any of the following ways:

1. By the partner's voluntarily giving notice of an "express will to withdraw." (When a partner gives notice of intent to withdraw, the remaining partners must decide whether to continue the partnership business. If they decide not to continue, the voluntary dissociation of a partner will dissolve the firm [UPA 801(1)].)

2. By the occurrence of an event agreed to in the partnership agreement.

3. By a unanimous vote of the other partners under certain circumstances, such as when a partner transfers substantially all of her or his interest in the partnership.

4. By order of a court or arbitrator if the partner has engaged in wrongful conduct that affects the partnership business, breached the partnership agreement, violated a duty owed to the partnership or to the other partners, or engaged in conduct that makes it "not reasonably practicable to carry on the business in partnership with the partner" [UPA 601(5)].

5. By the partner's declaring bankruptcy, assigning his or her interest in the partnership for the benefit of creditors, becoming physically or mentally incapacitated, or by the partner's death.

Wrongful Dissociation A partner always has the *power* to dissociate from the firm, but he or she may not have the *right* to do so. If the partner lacks the right to dissociate, then the dissociation is considered wrongful under the law [UPA 602]. When a partner's dissociation is in breach of the partnership agreement, for instance, it is wrongful.

EXAMPLE 27.10 Jensen & Whalen's partnership agreement states that it is a breach of the agreement for any partner to assign partnership property to a creditor without the consent of the other partners. If Janis, a partner, makes such an assignment, she not only has breached the agreement but also has wrongfully dissociated from the partnership. ■

Similarly, if a partner refuses to perform duties required by the partnership agreement—such as accounting for profits earned from the use of partnership property—this breach can be treated as a wrongful dissociation. A partner who wrongfully dissociates is liable to the partnership and to the other partners for damages caused by the dissociation.

Effects of Dissociation Dissociation (rightful or wrongful) terminates some of the rights of the dissociated partner, requires that the partnership purchase his or her interest, and alters the liability of the parties to third parties.

Rights and Duties. On a partner's dissociation, his or her right to participate in the management and conduct of the partnership business terminates [UPA 603]. The partner's duty of

---

4. Under the previous version of the UPA, when a partner withdrew from a partnership, the partnership was considered dissolved, its business had to be wound up, and the proceeds had to be distributed to creditors and among the partners. The new UPA dramatically changed the law governing partnership breakups and does not require that a partnership be dissolved just because one partner has left the firm.

loyalty also ends. A partner's duty of care continues only with respect to events that occurred before dissociation, unless the partner participates in *winding up* the partnership's business (discussed shortly).

EXAMPLE 27.11 Debbie Pearson, a partner who leaves an accounting firm, Bubb & Ferngold, can immediately compete with that firm for new clients. She must exercise care in completing ongoing client transactions, however, and must account to Bubb & Ferngold for any fees received from the former clients based on those transactions. ▪

Buyouts. After a partner's dissociation, the partnership must purchase his or her partnership interest according to the rules in UPA 701. The **buyout price** is based on the amount that would have been distributed to the partner if the partnership had been wound up on the date of dissociation. Offset against the price are any amounts owed by the partner to the partnership, including any damages to the firm if the dissociation was wrongful.

CASE EXAMPLE 27.12 Wilbur and Dee Warnick and their son, Randall, bought a ranch for $335,000 and formed a partnership to operate it. The partners' initial capital contributions totaled $60,000, of which Randall paid 34 percent. Over the next twenty years, each partner contributed funds to the operation and received cash distributions from the partnership. In 1999, Randall dissociated from the partnership.

When the parties could not agree on a buyout price, Randall filed a lawsuit. The court awarded Randall $115,783.13—the amount of his cash contributions, plus 34 percent of the increase in the value of the partnership's assets above all partners' cash contributions. Randall's parents appealed, arguing that $50,000 should be deducted from the appraised value of the assets for the estimated expenses of selling them. The court affirmed the buyout price, however, because "purely hypothetical costs of sale are not a required deduction in valuing partnership assets" to determine a buyout price.[5] ▪

Buyout Price The amount payable to a partner on his or her dissociation from a partnership, based on the amount distributable to that partner if the firm were wound up on that date, and offset by any damages for wrongful dissociation.

Liability to Third Parties. For two years after a partner dissociates from a continuing partnership, the partnership may be bound by the acts of the dissociated partner based on apparent authority [UPA 702]. In other words, if a third party reasonably believed at the time of a transaction that the dissociated partner was still a partner, the partnership may be liable. In addition, a dissociated partner may be liable for partnership obligations entered into during a two-year period following dissociation [UPA 703].

To avoid this possible liability, a partnership should notify its creditors, customers, and clients of a partner's dissociation. Also, either the partnership or the dissociated partner can file a *statement of dissociation* in the appropriate state office to limit the dissociated partner's authority to ninety days after the filing [UPA 704].

When a partner dissociates from a ranch partnership, how is the buyout price determined?

27-3b Partnership Termination

The same events that cause dissociation can result in the end of the partnership if the remaining partners do not want to (or are unable to) continue the business.

The termination of a partnership is referred to as **dissolution,** which essentially means the commencement of the winding up process. **Winding up** is the actual process of collecting, liquidating, and distributing the partnership assets.

Dissolution Dissolution of a partnership generally can be brought about by acts of the partners, by operation of law, or by judicial decree [UPA 801]. Any partnership (including one for a fixed term) can be dissolved by the partners' agreement. Similarly, if the partnership agreement states that it will dissolve on a certain event, such as a partner's death or bankruptcy, then

Dissolution The formal disbanding of a partnership or a corporation. Partnerships can be dissolved by acts of the partners, by operation of law, or by judicial decree.

Winding Up The second of two stages in the termination of a partnership or corporation, in which the firm's assets are collected, liquidated, and distributed, and liabilities are discharged.

---

5. *Warnick v. Warnick*, 2006 WY 58, 133 P.3d 997 (2006).

the occurrence of that event will dissolve the partnership. A partnership for a fixed term or a particular undertaking is dissolved by operation of law at the expiration of the term or on the completion of the undertaking.

In the following case, one of the three partners in an agricultural partnership died. Despite provisions in the partnership agreement that required its dissolution on a certain date or on a partner's death, whichever came first, the remaining partners did not dissolve the firm and did not liquidate the assets.

CASE 27.2

Estate of Webster v. Thomas

Appellate Court of Illinois, Fifth District, 2013 WL 164041 (2013).

FACTS Clyde Webster, James Theis, and Larry Thomas formed T&T Agri-Partners Company to own and farm 180 acres in Christian County, Illinois. Under the partnership agreement, the firm was to continue until January 31, 2010, unless it was dissolved. The death of any partner would dissolve the partnership.

Webster died in 2002, but Theis and Thomas did not liquidate T&T and distribute its assets. Webster's estate, through its personal representative, Joseph Webster, filed a complaint in an Illinois state circuit court against Theis, Thomas, and the partnership. In December 2009, the court ordered the defendants to dissolve the partnership and liquidate its assets. When this did not happen, the case went to trial. In 2011, after the trial, the court found that the partnership had expired by its own terms on January 31, 2010, and again ordered the partnership dissolved. The court also ordered the defendants to pay the Websters' attorney fees. The defendants appealed.

ISSUE Can a partnership business continue after one partner dies when the partnership agreement specified that the death of one partner would terminate the business?

What happens when a partnership that was supposed to dissolve after one partner's death continues to operate?

DECISION No. A state intermediate appellate court affirmed the lower court's ruling in favor of Webster's estate.

REASON The trial court had properly determined that Theis and Thomas had failed to liquidate and distribute the company's assets in accord with the partnership agreement and the court order. "The partnership agreement clearly provided that upon Clyde's death and the partners' failure to vote to continue the partnership, the partnership dissolved. Pursuant to the plain language of the partnership agreement, the assets upon dissolution were to be liquidated and distributed by paying the partners in proportion to their capital accounts. Yet, the defendants failed to do so." The reviewing court pointed out that despite the agreement's language and despite the circuit court's order, the defendants did nothing. The defendants therefore violated the partnership agreement and were liable for the plaintiff's attorney fees pursuant to the same agreement.

CRITICAL THINKING—Legal Consideration *What lesson might the partners in other partnerships learn from the events of this case and its outcome?*

Illegality or Impracticality. Any event that makes it unlawful for the partnership to continue its business will result in dissolution [UPA 801(4)]. Under the UPA, a court may order dissolution when it becomes obviously impractical for the firm to continue—for instance, if the business can only be operated at a loss [UPA 801(5)]. Even when one partner has brought a court action seeking to dissolve a partnership, the partnership continues to exist until it is legally dissolved by the court or by the parties' agreement.

CASE EXAMPLE 27.13 Members of the Russell family began operating Russell Realty Associates (RRA) as a partnership. Eddie Russell had decision-making authority over the partnership's business, which involved buying, holding, leasing, and selling investment properties. After several years, Eddie and his sister, Nina Russell, became involved in disputes, and Nina began to routinely question Eddie's business decisions. Because of their disagreements, RRA experienced two years of delays before it could sell one piece of property. Although the firm continued to profit, Eddie filed a complaint seeking a judicial dissolution of the partnership, which the court granted. Nina appealed.

The Virginia Supreme Court affirmed the lower court's decision that Russell Realty must be judicially dissolved. The partners' relationship had deteriorated to the point where the partnership was unable to function effectively. As a result, the firm had incurred substantial and unnecessary added costs, which frustrated the partnership's economic purpose and made it impracticable to continue.[6] ■

Good Faith. Each partner must exercise good faith during the dissolution of a partnership. Some state statutes allow partners injured by another partner's bad faith to file a tort claim for wrongful dissolution.

    CASE EXAMPLE 27.14 Attorneys Randall Jordan and Mary Helen Moses formed a two-member partnership for an indefinite term. Jordan ended the partnership three years later and asked the court for declarations concerning the partners' financial obligations. Moses, who had objected to ending the partnership, filed a claim against Jordan for wrongful dissolution and for appropriating $180,000 in fees that should have gone to the partnership.

Ultimately, the court held in favor of Moses. A claim for wrongful dissolution of a partnership may be based on damages arising from the excluded partner's loss of "an existing, or continuing, business opportunity" or of income and material assets. Because Jordan had attempted to appropriate partnership assets through dissolution, Moses could sue for wrongful dissolution.[7] ■

Can a dispute among partners in a real estate agency lead to liability for wrongful dissolution?

Winding Up and Distribution of Assets

After dissolution, the partnership continues for the limited purpose of the winding up process. The partners cannot create new obligations on behalf of the partnership. They have authority only to complete transactions begun but not finished at the time of dissolution and to wind up the partnership's business [UPA 803, 804(1)].

Duties and Compensation. Winding up includes collecting and preserving partnership assets, discharging liabilities (paying debts), and accounting to each partner for the value of her or his interest in the partnership. Partners continue to have fiduciary duties to one another and to the firm during this process. UPA 401(h) provides that a partner is entitled to compensation for services in winding up partnership affairs (and reimbursement for expenses incurred in the process) above and apart from his or her share in the partnership profits.

Creditors' Claims. Both creditors of the partnership and creditors of the individual partners can make claims on the partnership's assets. In general, partnership creditors and the partners' personal creditors share proportionately in the partners' assets, which include their interests in the partnership.

A partnership's assets are distributed according to the following priorities [UPA 807]:

1. Payment of debts, including those owed to partner and nonpartner creditors.

2. Return of capital contributions and distribution of profits to partners.

If the partnership's liabilities are greater than its assets, the partners bear the losses—in the absence of a contrary agreement—in the same proportion in which they shared the profits (rather than, for example, in proportion to their contributions to the partnership's capital).

Before entering a partnership, agree on how the assets will be valued and divided in the event the partnership dissolves. Make express arrangements that will provide for a smooth dissolution. You and your partners can, for example, enter into a buy-sell, or buyout, agreement, which provides that one or more partners will buy out the other or others, should

KNOW THIS

Secured creditors have priority over unsecured creditors to any assets that serve as collateral for a partnership's debts.

PREVENTING LEGAL DISPUTES

---

6. *Russell Realty Associates v. Russell,* 724 S.E.2d 690 (Va.Sup.Ct. 2012).
7. *Jordan v. Moses,* 291 Ga. 39, 727 S.E.2d 460 (2012).

the relationship deteriorate. Agreeing beforehand on who buys what, under which circumstances, and, if possible, at what price may eliminate costly negotiations or litigation later. Alternatively, your agreement can specify that one or more partners will determine the value of the interest being sold and that the other or others will decide whether to buy or sell.

27-4 Limited Liability Partnerships

LEARNING OBJECTIVE 4
What advantages do limited liability partnerships offer to businesspersons that are not offered by general partnerships?

Limited Liability Partnership (LLP) A hybrid form of business organization that is used mainly by professionals who normally do business in a partnership. An LLP is a pass-through entity for tax purposes, but a partner's personal liability for the malpractice of other partners is limited.

The **limited liability partnership (LLP)** is a hybrid form of business designed mostly for professionals who normally do business as partners in a partnership. Almost all of the states have enacted LLP statutes.

The major advantage of the LLP is that it allows a partnership to continue as a pass-through entity for tax purposes but limits the personal liability of the partners. The LLP is especially attractive for professional service firms and family businesses. All of the "Big Four" accounting firms—the four largest international accountancy and professional services firms—are organized as LLPs, including Ernst & Young, LLP, and PricewaterhouseCoopers, LLP.

27-4a Formation of an LLP

LLPs must be formed and operated in compliance with state statutes, which may include provisions of the UPA. The appropriate form must be filed with a central state agency, usually the secretary of state's office, and the business's name must include either "Limited Liability Partnership" or "LLP" [UPA 1001, 1002]. An LLP must file an annual report with the state to remain qualified as an LLP in that state [UPA 1003].

In most states, it is relatively easy to convert a traditional partnership into an LLP because the firm's basic organizational structure remains the same. Additionally, all of the statutory and common law rules governing partnerships still apply (apart from those modified by the LLP statute). Normally, LLP statutes are simply amendments to a state's already existing partnership law.

27-4b Liability in an LLP

An LLP allows professionals, such as attorneys and accountants, to avoid personal liability for the malpractice of other partners. A partner in an LLP is still liable for her or his own wrongful acts, such as negligence, of course. Also liable is the partner who supervised the individual who committed a wrongful act. (This supervisory liability generally applies to all types of partners and partnerships, not just LLPs.)

EXAMPLE 27.15 Five lawyers operate a law firm as a limited liability partnership. One of the attorneys, Dan Kolcher, is sued for malpractice and loses. The firm's malpractice insurance is insufficient to pay the judgment. If the firm had been organized as a general partnership, the personal assets of the other attorneys could be used to satisfy the obligation. Because the firm is organized as an LLP, however, no other partner at the law firm can be held *personally* liable for Kolcher's malpractice, unless she or he acted as Kolcher's supervisor. In the absence of a supervisor, only Kolcher's personal assets can be used to satisfy the judgment. ■

Although LLP statutes vary from state to state, generally each state statute limits the liability of partners in some way. For instance, Delaware law protects each innocent partner from the "debts and obligations of the partnership arising from negligence, wrongful acts, or misconduct." The UPA more broadly exempts partners from personal liability for any partnership obligation, "whether arising in contract, tort, or otherwise" [UPA 306(c)].

Liability outside the State of Formation When an LLP formed in one state wishes to do business in another state, it may be required to register in the second state—for instance, by filing a statement of foreign qualification [UPA 1102]. Because state LLP statutes are not uniform, a question sometimes arises as to which law applies if the LLP statutes in the two states provide different liability protection. Most states apply the law of the state in which the LLP was formed, which is also the rule under UPA 1101.

Sharing Liability among Partners When more than one partner in an LLP is negligent, there is a question as to how liability is to be shared. Is each partner jointly and severally liable for the entire result, as a general partner would be in most states?

What happens when a lawyer in a law firm organized as an LLP is successfully sued for malpractice?

Some states provide instead for proportionate liability—that is, for separate determinations of the negligence of the partners. **EXAMPLE 27.16** Accountants Zach and Lyla are partners in an LLP, with Zach supervising Lyla. Lyla negligently fails to file a tax return for a client, Centaur Tools. Centaur files a suit against Zach and Lyla. Under a proportionate liability statute, Zach will be liable for no more than his portion of the responsibility for the missed tax deadline. In a state that does not allow for proportionate liability, Zach can be held liable for the entire loss. ■

27–5 Limited Partnerships

We now look at a business organizational form that limits the liability of *some* of its owners—the **limited partnership (LP).** Limited partnerships originated in medieval Europe and have been in existence in the United States since the early 1800s. Limited partnerships differ from general partnerships in several ways. Exhibit 27–2 compares characteristics of general and limited partnerships.[8]

Most states and the District of Columbia have adopted the Revised Uniform Limited Partnership Act (RULPA), which we refer to in the following discussion of limited partnerships.

A limited partnership consists of at least one **general partner** and one or more **limited partners.** A general partner assumes management responsibility for the partnership and so has full responsibility for the partnership and for all of its debts. A limited partner contributes cash or other property and owns an interest in the firm but does not undertake any management responsibilities and is not personally liable for partnership debts beyond the amount of his or her investment. A limited partner can forfeit limited liability by taking part in the management of the business.

In the following case, two firms—a corporation and a limited partnership—were involved in the construction of a residential development. One individual served as the president of the corporation and the sole general partner of the partnership, and took charge of the activities at the construction site. How did this individual's status affect his responsibility for those activities?

LEARNING OBJECTIVE 5
What are the key differences between the rights and liabilities of general partners and those of limited partners?

Limited Partnership (LP)
A partnership consisting of one or more general partners and one or more limited partners.

General Partner In a limited partnership, a partner who assumes responsibility for the management of the partnership and has full liability for all partnership debts.

Limited Partner In a limited partnership, a partner who contributes capital to the partnership but has no right to participate in its management and has no liability for partnership debts beyond the amount of her or his investment.

---

8. Under the UPA, a general partnership can be converted into a limited partnership and vice versa [UPA 902, 903]. The UPA also provides for the merger of a general partnership with one or more general or limited partnerships under rules that are similar to those governing corporate mergers [UPA 905].

CASE 27.3

DeWine v. Valley View Enterprises, Inc.

Court of Appeals of Ohio, Eleventh District, Trumbull County, 2015 –Ohio– 1222, __ N.E.2d __ (2015).

FACTS Valley View Enterprises, Inc., built Pine Lakes Golf Club and Estates in Trumbull County, Ohio, in two phases—"Phase I" and "Phase II." Valley View Properties, Ltd., a limited partnership, cut out the roadways and constructed sewer lines, water lines, and storm water lines with water inlets.

Joseph Ferrara was the owner and the president of Valley View Enterprises and the sole general partner of Valley View Properties. Ferrara failed to obtain the proper permits for the development work in a timely manner and failed to comply with their requirements once they had been obtained. On behalf of the state of Ohio, Michael DeWine, the state attorney general, filed a suit in an Ohio state court against the Valley View entities and Ferrara. The suit alleged that the defendants had violated the state water pollution control laws and sought civil penalties. The court entered a judgment in the defendants' favor, holding with respect to Ferrara that "a corporate officer cannot be held liable merely by virtue of his status as a corporate officer." DeWine appealed.

ISSUE Did Ferrara's status as general partner make him responsible for the acts of Valley View Properties?

DECISION Yes. A state intermediate appellate court reversed the lower court's judgment in favor of the defendants. With respect to Valley

Can a general partner be liable for failing to obtain wetlands-fill permits prior to creating roadways for a subdivision?

nata-lunata/ShutterStock.com

View Properties, Ferrara was not "entitled to the insulation from liability of a corporate officer." On remand, the trial court was to determine the number of violations established by the state and issue and apportion penalties among the liable parties.

REASON The state charged three defendants with pollution control violations—Valley View Enterprises, Valley View Properties, and Ferrara. Valley View Enterprises had obtained the Phase I permit. The permit stated, "The permittee must comply with all conditions of this permit, any permit noncompliance constitutes a violation of [state law]." Valley View Properties owned the property on which the development was built and held the Phase II permit.

Ferrara was in charge of both entities and all of the activities performed at the construction site—and he failed to obtain the necessary permits before those activities were undertaken. The lower court's holding that Ferrara was not responsible because "a corporate officer cannot be held liable merely by virtue of his status as a corporate officer" was in error with respect to Valley View Properties. For the limited partnership, Ferrara was not a "corporate officer" but the general partner. In that capacity, he was not entitled to insulation from liability.

CRITICAL THINKING—Legal Consideration *How are the penalties likely to be apportioned among the three defendants? Explain.*

27–5a Formation of an LP

In contrast to the informal, private, and voluntary agreement that usually suffices for a general partnership, the formation of a limited partnership is a public and formal proceeding that must follow statutory requirements. Not only must a limited partnership have at least one general partner and one limited partner, but the partners must also sign a **certificate of limited partnership.**

Certificate of Limited Partnership The document that must be filed with a designated state official to form a limited partnership.

Like *articles of incorporation* (the document needed to form a corporation), this certificate must include certain information, such as the name, mailing address, and capital contribution of each general and limited partner. The certificate must be filed with the designated state official—under the RULPA, the secretary of state. The certificate is usually open to public inspection.

27–5b Liabilities of Partners in an LP

General partners, unlike limited partners, are personally liable to the partnership's creditors. Thus, at least one general partner is necessary in a limited partnership so that someone has personal liability. This policy can be circumvented in states that allow a corporation to be the general partner in a partnership. Because the corporation has limited liability by virtue of

Exhibit 27-2 A Comparison of General Partnerships and Limited Partnerships

CHARACTERISTIC	GENERAL PARTNERSHIP (UPA)	LIMITED PARTNERSHIP (RULPA)
Creation	By agreement of two or more persons to carry on a business as co-owners for profit.	By agreement of two or more persons to carry on a business as co-owners for profit. Must include one or more general partners and one or more limited partners. Filing of a certificate with the secretary of state is required.
Sharing of Profits and Losses	By agreement. In the absence of agreement, profits are shared equally by the partners, and losses are shared in the same ratio as profits.	Profits are shared as required in the certificate agreement, and losses are shared likewise, up to the amount of the limited partners' capital contributions. In the absence of a provision in the certificate agreement, profits and losses are shared on the basis of percentages of capital contributions.
Liability	Unlimited personal liability of all partners.	Unlimited personal liability of all general partners; limited partners liable only to the extent of their capital contributions.
Capital Contribution	No minimum or mandatory amount; set by agreement.	Set by agreement.
Management	By agreement. In the absence of agreement, all partners have an equal voice.	Only the general partner (or the general partners). Limited partners have no voice. Engaging in management activity may subject a limited partner to liability as a general partner (if a third party has reason to believe that the limited partner is a general partner). A limited partner may act as an agent or employee of the partnership and vote on amending the certificate or on selling or dissolving the partnership.
Duration	Terminated by agreement of the partners, but can continue to do business even when a partner dissociates from the partnership.	Terminated by agreement in the certificate or by retirement, death, or mental incompetence of a general partner in the absence of the right of the other general partners to continue the partnership. Death of a limited partner does not terminate the partnership, unless he or she is the only remaining limited partner.
Distribution of Assets on Liquidation—Order of Priorities	1. Payment of debts, including those owed to partner and nonpartner creditors. 2. Return of capital contributions and distribution of profit to partners.	1. Outside creditors and partner creditors. 2. Partners and former partners entitled to distributions of partnership assets. 3. Unless otherwise agreed, return of capital contributions and distribution of profit to partners.

corporate laws, if a corporation is the general partner, no one in the limited partnership has personal liability.

The liability of a limited partner, as mentioned, is limited to the capital that she or he contributes or agrees to contribute to the partnership [RULPA 502]. Limited partners enjoy this limited liability only so long as they do not participate in management [RULPA 303].

A limited partner who participates in management will be just as liable as a general partner to any creditor who transacts business with the limited partnership. Liability arises when the creditor believes, based on the limited partner's conduct, that the limited partner is a general partner [RULPA 303]. The extent of review and advisement a limited partner can engage in before being exposed to liability is not always clear, however.

Should an innocent general partner be jointly liable for fraud? When general partners in a limited partnership jointly engage in fraud, there is usually no question that they are jointly liable. But if one general partner engages in fraud and the other is unaware of the wrongdoing, is it fair to make the innocent partner share in the liability? Many states' limited partnership laws protect innocent general partners from suits for fraud brought by limited partners. The law is less clear, however, in some other situations.

For example, Robert Bisno and James Coxeter formed two limited partnerships to develop property in Berkeley, California. Without Coxeter's knowledge, Bisno took almost $500,000

KNOW THIS
A limited partner is liable only to the extent of any contribution that she or he made to the partnership, but can lose this limited liability by participating in management.

ETHICAL ISSUE

from one of the partnerships to buy a personal home. He also made material misrepresentations to potential investors. One of those investors, George Miske—after purchasing an interest in the limited partnership—discovered the fraud and brought suit. Coxeter argued that Miske was a limited partner, not an innocent third party. Under the state's limited partnership law, that meant Coxeter should be protected from liability.

The court disagreed. The fraud at issue had induced Miske to purchase the limited partnership interest. Therefore, at the time the fraud was perpetrated by Bisno, Miske was an innocent third party. As a result, Coxeter, though innocent of any wrongdoing, was jointly liable.[9]

27-5c Dissociation and Dissolution

A general partner has the power to voluntarily dissociate, or withdraw, from a limited partnership unless the partnership agreement specifies otherwise. A limited partner can withdraw from the partnership by giving six months' notice *unless* the partnership agreement specifies a term, which most do. Also, some states have passed laws prohibiting the withdrawal of limited partners.

Events That Cause Dissociation A limited partnership can be dissolved by court decree [RULPA 802]. In addition, a general partner's voluntary dissociation from the firm normally will lead to dissolution unless all partners agree to continue the business. Similarly, the bankruptcy, retirement, death, or mental incompetence of a general partner will cause the dissociation of that partner and the dissolution of the limited partnership unless the other members agree to continue the firm [RULPA 801].

Bankruptcy of a limited partner, however, does not dissolve the partnership unless it causes the bankruptcy of the firm. Death or an assignment of the interest of a limited partner does not dissolve a limited partnership [RULPA 702, 704, 705].

Distribution of Assets On dissolution, creditors' claims, including those of partners who are creditors, take first priority. After that, partners and former partners receive unpaid distributions of partnership assets and, except as otherwise agreed, amounts representing returns of their capital contributions and proportionate distributions of profits [RULPA 804].

Valuation of Assets Disputes commonly arise about how the partnership's assets should be valued and distributed on dissolution and whether the business should be sold. **CASE EXAMPLE 27.17** Actor Kevin Costner was a limited partner in Midnight Star Enterprises, LP, which runs a casino, bar, and restaurant in South Dakota. There were two other limited partners, Carla and Francis Caneva, who owned a small percentage of the partnership (3.25 units each) and received salaries for managing its operations. Another company owned by Costner, Midnight Star Enterprises, Limited (MSEL), was the general partner. Costner thus controlled a majority of the partnership (93.5 units).

When communications broke down between the partners, MSEL asked a court to dissolve the partnership. MSEL's accountant determined that the firm's fair market value was $3.1 million. The Canevas presented evidence that a competitor would buy the business for $6.2 million. The Canevas wanted the court to force Costner to either buy the business for that price or sell it on the open market to the highest bidder. Ultimately, the state's highest court held in favor of Costner. A partner cannot force the sale of a limited partnership when the other partners want to continue the business. The court also accepted the $3.1 million buyout price of MSEL's accountant and ordered Costner to pay the Canevas the value of their 6.5 partnership units.[10]

> "A friendship founded on business is a good deal better than a business founded on friendship."
>
> **JOHN D. ROCKEFELLER**
> 1839–1937
> (AMERICAN INDUSTRIALIST)

Can a limited partner in actor Kevin Costner's limited partnership force the sale of the entity?

iStockPhoto.com/EdStock

---

9. *Miske v. Bisno*, 204 Cal.App.4th 1249, 139 Cal.Rptr.3d 626 (2012). See also *In re Barlaam*, 2014 WL 3398381 (9th Cir. 2014).
10. *In re Dissolution of Midnight Star Enterprises, LP*, 2006 S.D. 98, 724 N.W.2d 334 (2006).

Buy-Sell Agreements   As mentioned earlier in the *Preventing Legal Disputes* feature, partners can agree ahead of time on how the assets will be valued and divided if the partnership dissolves. This is true for limited partnerships as well as for general partnerships. Buy-sell agreements can help the partners avoid disputes. Nonetheless, buy-sell agreements do not eliminate all potential for litigation, especially if the terms are subject to more than one interpretation.

   CASE EXAMPLE 27.18   Natural Pork Production II, LLP (NPP), an Iowa limited liability partnership, raises hogs. Under a partnership buy-sell agreement, NPP was obligated to buy a dissociating partner's interests but could defer the purchase if it would adversely affect the firm's capital or cash flow. After these "impairment circumstances" changed, NPP was to make the purchase within thirty days. Two of NPP's limited partners, Craton Capital, LP, and Kruse Investment Company, notified NPP of their dissociation. A wave of similar notices from other limited partners followed.

   NPP declared an impairment circumstance and refused to buy out the limited partners. Craton and Kruse filed a suit asking a state court to order NPP to buy their units. NPP claimed that it was not required to buy out the limited partners because of the impairment circumstance. The court ruled in the plaintiffs' favor. The wording of the buyout provision stated the firm "shall" buy out the partners, which meant it was mandatory. The impairment circumstance only deferred the purchase, thus NPP was required to buy out the limited partners.[11] ▨

When does a hog-raising limited partnership have to buy out a dissenting partner?

---

11. *Craton Capital, LP v. Natural Pork Production II, LLP,* 797 N.W.2d 623 (Iowa App. 2011).

Reviewing . . . All Forms of Partnership

Grace Tarnavsky and her sons, Manny and Jason, bought a ranch known as the Cowboy Palace in March 2011. The three orally agreed to share the business for five years. Grace contributed 50 percent of the investment, and each son contributed 25 percent. Manny agreed to handle the livestock, and Jason agreed to do the bookkeeping. The Tarnavskys took out joint loans and opened a joint bank account into which they deposited the ranch's proceeds and from which they made payments for property, cattle, equipment, and supplies.

   In September 2015, Manny severely injured his back while baling hay and became permanently unable to handle livestock. Manny therefore hired additional laborers to tend the livestock, causing the Cowboy Palace to incur significant debt. In September 2016, Al's Feed Barn filed a lawsuit against Jason to collect $12,400 in unpaid debts. Using the information presented in the chapter, answer the following questions.

1. Was this relationship a partnership for a term or a partnership at will?

2. Did Manny have the authority to hire additional laborers to work at the ranch after his injury? Why or why not?

3. Under the UPA, can Al's Feed Barn bring an action against Jason individually for the Cowboy Palace's debt? Why or why not?

4. Suppose that after his back injury in 2015, Manny sent his mother and brother a notice indicating his intent to withdraw from the partnership. Can he still be held liable for the debt to Al's Feed Barn? Why or why not?

DEBATE THIS

■ A partnership should automatically end when one partner dissociates from the firm.

Key Terms

Chapter Summary: All Forms of Partnership

Partnerships	1. A partnership is created by agreement of the parties. 2. A partnership is treated as an entity except for limited purposes. 3. Each partner pays a proportionate share of income taxes on the net profits of the partnership, whether or not they are distributed. The partnership files only an information return with the Internal Revenue Service. 4. Each partner has an equal voice in management unless the partnership agreement provides otherwise. 5. In the absence of an agreement, partners share profits equally and share losses in the same ratio as they share profits. 6. The capital contribution of each partner is determined by agreement. 7. Partners have unlimited liability for partnership debts. 8. A partnership can be terminated by agreement or can be dissolved by action of the partners, operation of law, or court decree.
Limited Liability Partnerships (LLPs)	1. *Formation*—The appropriate form must be filed with a state agency, usually the secretary of state's office. Typically, an LLP is formed by professionals who work together as partners in a partnership. Under most state LLP statutes, it is relatively easy to convert a traditional partnership into an LLP. 2. *Liabilities of partners*—LLP statutes vary, but under the UPA, professionals generally can avoid personal liability for acts committed by other partners. Partners in an LLP continue to be liable for their own wrongful acts and for the wrongful acts of those whom they supervise.
Limited Partnerships (LPs)	1. *Formation*—A certificate of limited partnership must be filed with the secretary of state's office or other designated state official. The certificate must include information about the business, similar to the information included in articles of incorporation. The partnership consists of one or more general partners and one or more limited partners. 2. *Liabilities of partners*—General partners have unlimited liability for partnership obligations. Limited partners are liable only to the extent of their contributions. 3. *Limited partners and management*—Only general partners can participate in management. Limited partners have no voice in management. If they do participate in management, they risk having general-partner liability. 4. *Dissolution*—A general partner's voluntary dissociation, bankruptcy, death, or mental incompetence will cause the partnership's dissolution unless all partners agree to continue the business. The death or assignment of the interest of a limited partner does not dissolve the partnership. Bankruptcy of a limited partner also does not dissolve the partnership unless it causes the bankruptcy of the firm.

Issue Spotters

1. Darnell and Eliana are partners in D&E Designs, an architectural firm. When Darnell dies, his widow claims that as Darnell's heir, she is entitled to take his place as Eliana's partner or to receive a share of the firm's assets. Is she right? Why or why not? (See *Dissociation and Termination.*)

2. Finian and Gloria are partners in F&G Delivery Service. When business is slow, without Gloria's knowledge, Finian leases the delivery vehicles as moving vans. Because the delivery vehicles would otherwise be sitting idle in a parking lot, can Finian keep the income that results from leasing the vehicles? Explain your answer. (See *Formation and Operation.*)

—**Check your answers to the *Issue Spotters* against the answers provided in Appendix D at the end of this text.**

Learning Objectives Check

1. What are the three essential elements of a partnership?
2. What are the rights and duties of partners in an ordinary partnership?
3. What is meant by joint and several liability? Why is this often considered to be a disadvantage of the partnership form of business?
4. What advantages do limited liability partnerships offer to businesspersons that are not offered by general partnerships?
5. What are the key differences between the rights and liabilities of general partners and those of limited partners?

—**Answers to the even-numbered** *Learning Objectives Check* **questions can be found in Appendix E at the end of this text.**

Business Scenarios and Case Problems

27–1. Partnership Formation. Daniel is the owner of a chain of shoe stores. He hires Rubya to be the manager of a new store, which is to open in Grand Rapids, Michigan. Daniel, by written contract, agrees to pay Rubya a monthly salary and 20 percent of the profits. Without Daniel's knowledge, Rubya represents himself to Classen as Daniel's partner, showing Classen the agreement to share profits. Classen extends credit to Rubya. Rubya defaults. Discuss whether Classen can hold Daniel liable as a partner. (See *Formation and Operation.*)

27–2. Limited Partnership. Dorinda, Luis, and Elizabeth form a limited partnership. Dorinda is a general partner, and Luis and Elizabeth are limited partners. Discuss fully whether each of the separate events below constitutes a dissolution of the limited partnership. (See *Limited Partnerships.*)

1. Luis assigns his partnership interest to Ashley.
2. Elizabeth is petitioned into involuntary bankruptcy.
3. Dorinda dies.

27–3. Fiduciary Duties of Partners. Karl Horvath, Hein Rüsen, and Carl Thomas formed a partnership, HRT Enterprises, to buy a manufacturing plant. Rüsen and Thomas leased the plant to their own company, Merkur Steel. Merkur then sublet the premises to other companies owned by Rüsen and Thomas. The rent that these companies paid to Merkur was higher than the rent Merkur paid to HRT. Rüsen and Thomas did not tell Horvath about the subleases. Did Rüsen and Thomas breach their fiduciary duties to HRT and Horvath? Discuss. [*Horvath v. HRT Enterprises*, 489 Mich.App. 992, 800 N.W.2d 595 (2011)] (See *Formation and Operation.*)

27–4. Partnership Formation. Patricia Garcia and Bernardo Lucero were in a romantic relationship. While they were seeing each other, Garcia and Lucero acquired an electronics service center, paying $30,000 each. Two years later, they purchased an apartment complex. The property was deeded to Lucero, but neither Garcia nor Lucero made a down payment. The couple considered both properties to be owned "50/50," and they agreed to share profits, losses, and management rights.

When the couple's romantic relationship ended, Garcia asked a court to declare that she and Lucero had a partnership. In court, Lucero argued that the couple did not have a written partnership agreement and thus did not have a partnership. Did they have a partnership? Why or why not? [*Garcia v. Lucero*, 366 S.W.3d 275 (Tex.App.—El Paso 2012)] (See *Formation and Operation.*)

27–5. Winding Up. Dan and Lori Cole operated a Curves franchise exercise facility in Angola, Indiana, as a partnership. The firm leased commercial space from Flying Cat, LLC, for a renewable three-year term. The Coles renewed the lease for a second three-year term. Two years later, however, the Coles divorced. By the end of the second term, the Coles owed Flying Cat more than $21,000 on the lease. Without telling the landlord about the divorce, Lori signed another extension. More rent went unpaid. Flying Cat obtained a judgment in an Indiana state court against the partnership for almost $50,000. Can Dan be held liable? Why or why not? [*Curves for Women Angola v. Flying Cat, LLC*, 983 N.E.2d 629 (Ind.App. 2013)] (See *Dissociation and Termination.*)

27–6. Business Case Problem with Sample Answer— Partnerships. Karyl Paxton asked Christopher Sacco to work with her interior design business, Pierce Paxton Collections, in New Orleans. At the time, they were in a romantic relationship. Sacco was involved in every aspect of the business—bookkeeping, marketing, and design—but was not paid a salary. He was reimbursed, however, for expenses charged to his personal credit card, which Paxton also used. Sacco took no profits from the firm, saying that he wanted to "grow the business" and "build sweat equity." When Paxton and Sacco's personal relationship soured, she fired him. Sacco objected, claiming that they were partners. Is Sacco entitled to 50 percent of the profits of Pierce Paxton Collections? Explain. [*Sacco v. Paxton*, 133 So.3d 213 (La.App. 2014)] (See *Formation and Operation.*)

—**For a sample answer to Problem 27–6, go to Appendix F at the end of this text.**

27–7. Formation. Leisa Reed and Randell Thurman lived together in Spring City, Tennessee. Randell and his father, Leroy, formed a cattle-raising operation and opened a bank account in the name of L&R Farm. Within a few years, Leroy quit the operation. Leisa and Randell each wrote a personal check for $5,000 to buy his cattle. Leisa picked up supplies, fed and administered medicine to cattle, collected hay, and participated in the book-keeping for L&R. Later, checks drawn on her personal account for $12,000 to buy equipment and $35,000 to buy cattle were deposited into the L&R account. After several years, Leisa decided that she no longer wanted to associate with Randell, but they could not agree on a financial settlement. Was Leisa a partner in L&R? Is she entitled to half of the value of L&R's assets? Explain. [*Reed v. Thurman*, __ S.W.3d __, 2015 WL 1119449 (Tenn.App. 2015)] (See *Formation and Operation*.)

27–8. A Question of Ethics—Dissociation. Elliot Willensky and Beverly Moran formed a partnership to buy, renovate, and sell a house. Moran agreed to finance the effort, which was to cost no more than $60,000. Willensky agreed to oversee the work, which was to be done in six months. Willensky lived in the house during the renovation. As the project progressed, Willensky incurred excessive and unnecessary expenses, misappropriated funds for his personal use, did not pay bills on time, and did not keep Moran informed of the costs. More than a year later, the renovation was still not completed, and Willensky walked off the project. Moran completed the renovation, which ultimately cost $311,222, and sold the house. Moran then sued to dissolve the partnership and recover damages from Willensky for breach of contract and wrongful dissociation. [*Moran v. Willensky*, 339 S.W.3d 651 (Tenn.App. 2010)] (See *Dissociation and Termination*.)

1. Moran alleged that Willensky had wrongfully dissociated from the partnership. When did this dissociation occur? Why was the dissociation wrongful?

2. Which of Willensky's actions breached the partnership agreement? Were any of his acts unethical? If so, which ones?

Critical Thinking and Writing Assignments

27–9. Business Law Writing. Sandra Lerner and Patricia Holmes were friends. One evening, while applying nail polish to Lerner, Holmes layered a raspberry color over black to produce a new color, which Lerner liked. Later, the two created other colors with names like "Bruise," "Smog," and "Oil Slick," and titled their concept "Urban Decay." Lerner and Holmes started a firm to produce and market the polishes but never discussed the sharing of profits and losses. They agreed to build the business and then sell it. Together, they did market research, worked on a logo and advertising, obtained capital, and hired employees. Then Lerner began scheming to edge Holmes out of the firm. (See *Formation and Operation*.)

1. Lerner claimed that there was no partnership agreement because there was no agreement on how to divide profits. Was Lerner right? Why or why not?

2. Suppose that Lerner, but not Holmes, had contributed a significant amount of personal funds to developing and marketing the new nail polish. Would this entitle Lerner to receive more of the profit? Explain.

3. Did Lerner violate her fiduciary duty? Why or why not?

27–10. Business Law Critical Thinking Group Assignment.

At least six months before the Summer Olympic Games in Atlanta, Georgia, a group made up of Stafford Fontenot, Steve Turner, Mike Montelaro, Joe Sokol, and Doug Brinsmade agreed to sell Cajun food at the games and began making preparations. On May 19, the group (calling themselves Prairie Cajun Seafood Catering of Louisiana) applied for a business license with the county health department.

Ted Norris sold members of the group a mobile kitchen in return for an $8,000 check drawn on the "Prairie Cajun Seafood Catering of Louisiana" account and two promissory notes, one for $12,000 and the other for $20,000. The notes, which were dated June 12, listed only Fontenot "d/b/a Prairie Cajun Seafood" as the maker (*d/b/a* is an abbreviation for "doing business as").

On July 31, Fontenot and his friends signed a partnership agreement, which listed specific percentages of profits and losses. They drove the mobile kitchen to Atlanta, but business was disastrous. When the notes were not paid, Norris filed a suit in a Louisiana state court against Fontenot, seeking payment. (See *Formation and Operation*.)

1. The first group will discuss the elements of a partnership and determine whether there was a partnership among Fontenot and the others.

2. The second group will determine who can be held liable on the notes and why.

iStockPhoto.com/MacXever

Limited Liability Companies and Special Business Forms

> "To play it safe is not to play."
>
> **ROBERT ALTMAN**
> 1925–2006
> (AMERICAN FILM DIRECTOR)

Our government allows entrepreneurs to choose from a variety of business organizational forms. Many businesspersons would agree with the chapter-opening quotation that in business "to play it safe is not to play." Because risk is associated with the potential for higher profits, businesspersons are motivated to choose organizational forms that limit their liability while allowing them to take risks that may lead to greater profits.

In this chapter, we focus on a relatively new and increasingly common form of business organization, the *limited liability company (LLC)*. We begin with a *Landmark in the Law* feature examining the origins and evolution of the LLC. Then we look at important characteristics of the LLC, discuss operation and management options in an LLC, and consider how an LLC is dissolved. We conclude with a discussion of several other special business forms, such as joint ventures and cooperatives.

28–1 Limited Liability Companies

As noted in the *Landmark in the Law* feature, a **limited liability company (LLC)** is a hybrid that combines the limited liability aspects of a corporation and the tax advantages of a partnership. The LLC has been available for only a few decades, but it has become the preferred structure for many small businesses.

Limited Liability Company (LLC) A hybrid form of business enterprise that offers the limited liability of a corporation and the tax advantages of a partnership.

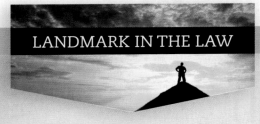

LANDMARK IN THE LAW | Limited Liability Company (LLC) Statutes

A limited liability company (LLC) is a hybrid that combines the limited liability aspects of a corporation and the tax advantages of a partnership. Although LLCs have been used for more than a century in various foreign jurisdictions, including several European and South American nations, they did not emerge in the United States until the late 1970s. Wyoming became the first state to pass legislation authorizing the creation of LLCs in 1977.

TAXATION OF LLCS After Wyoming's adoption of its LLC statute, it still was unclear how the Internal Revenue Service (IRS) would treat LLCs for tax purposes. In 1988, however, the IRS ruled that Wyoming LLCs could be taxed as partnerships instead of corporations, providing that certain requirements were met. This ruling was favorable toward LLCs because it meant that, like a partnership, an LLC could pass through profits to its owners without paying taxes on them. Before the ruling, only one other state—Florida, in 1982—had authorized LLCs. The 1988 ruling encouraged additional states to enact LLC statutes, and in less than a decade, all states had done so.

Other IRS rules also encouraged more widespread use of LLCs in the business world. Under these rules, any unincorporated business with more than one owner is automatically taxed as a partnership unless it indicates otherwise on the tax form or fits into one of the exceptions. The exceptions involve publicly traded companies, companies formed under a state incorporation statute, and certain foreign-owned companies. If a business chooses to be taxed as a corporation, it can indicate this preference by checking a box on the IRS form.

FOREIGN ENTITIES MAY BE LLC MEMBERS Another factor that has encouraged the creation of LLCs in this country is that foreign investors are allowed to become LLC members. In an era increasingly characterized by global business efforts and investments, the LLC often offers U.S. firms and potential investors from other countries greater flexibility and opportunities than are available through partnerships or corporations.

APPLICATION TO TODAY'S WORLD *Once it became clear that LLCs could be taxed as partnerships, the LLC form of business organization was widely adopted. Members could avoid the personal liability associated with the partnership form of business as well as the double taxation of the corporate form of business. Today, LLCs are a common form of business organization.*

KNOW THIS

A uniform law is a "model" law. It does not become the law of any state until the state legislature adopts it, either in part or in its entirety.

Member A person who has an ownership interest in a limited liability company.

LLCs are governed by state LLC statutes, which vary, of course, from state to state. In an attempt to create more uniformity, the National Conference of Commissioners on Uniform State Laws (NCCUSL) issued the Uniform Limited Liability Company Act (ULLCA). Less than twenty states have adopted the act, and so the law governing LLCs remains far from uniform. Some provisions are common to most state statutes, however, and we base our discussion of LLCs on these common elements.

28–1a The Nature of the LLC

LLCs share many characteristics with corporations. Like corporations, LLCs are creatures of the state. In other words, they must be formed and operated in compliance with state law. Like shareholders in a corporation, owners of an LLC, who are called **members,** enjoy limited liability [ULLCA 303].

CASE EXAMPLE 28.1 Penny McFarland was the activities director at a retirement community in Virginia that was owned by an LLC. Her supervisor told her to take the residents outside for a walk on a day when the temperature was 95 degrees. McFarland complained to the state health department and was fired from her job. She sued a number of managers and members of the LLC for wrongful discharge.

The court held that under Virginia law, members, managers, and agents of an LLC are not responsible for its liabilities solely by virtue of their status. The court dismissed the action against all but one defendant, concluding that only those who "have played a key role in contributing to the company's tortious conduct" can be part of a wrongful discharge claim.[1] ■

---

1. *McFarland v. Virginia Retirement Services of Chesterfield, LLC*, 477 F.Supp.2d 727 (D.Va. 2007).

Like corporations, LLCs are legal entities apart from their members. As a legal person, an LLC can sue or be sued, enter into contracts, and hold title to property [ULLCA 201]. The terminology used to describe LLCs formed in other states or nations is also similar to the terminology used in corporate law. For instance, an LLC formed in one state but doing business in another state is referred to in the second state as a *foreign LLC*.

28–1b LLC Formation

LLCs are creatures of statute and thus must follow state statutory requirements. To form an LLC, **articles of organization** must be filed with a central state agency—usually the secretary of state's office [ULLCA 202].[2]

iStockPhoto.com/Nikada

Many hotel chains are franchised as limited liability companies. One of them is Hampton Inn. What is the document required to form an LLC?

Contents of the Articles Typically, the articles must include the name of the business, its principal address, the name and address of a registered agent, the members' names, and information on how the LLC will be managed [ULLCA 203]. The business's name must include the words *Limited Liability Company* or the initials *LLC* [ULLCA 105(a)]. Although a majority of the states permit one-member LLCs, some states require at least two members.

Preformation Contracts Businesspersons sometimes enter into contracts on behalf of a business organization that is not yet formed. For instance, persons forming a corporation may enter into contracts during the process of incorporation but before the corporation becomes a legal entity. These contracts are referred to as preincorporation contracts. Once the corporation is formed and adopts the preincorporation contract (by means of a *novation,* which substitutes a new contract for the old contract), it can then enforce the contract terms.

In dealing with the preorganization contracts of LLCs, courts may apply the well-established principles of corporate law relating to preincorporation contracts. **CASE EXAMPLE 28.2** 607 South Park, LLC, entered into an agreement to sell a hotel to 607 Park View Associates, Ltd., which then assigned the rights to the purchase to another company, 02 Development, LLC. At the time, 02 Development did not yet exist—it was legally created several months later. 607 South Park subsequently refused to sell the hotel to 02 Development, and 02 Development sued for breach of the purchase agreement.

A California appellate court ruled that LLCs should be treated the same as corporations with respect to preorganization contracts. Although 02 Development did not exist when the agreement was executed, once it came into existence, it could enforce any preorganization contract made on its behalf.[3] ■

28–1c Jurisdictional Requirements

One of the significant differences between LLCs and corporations involves federal jurisdictional requirements. Under federal law, a corporation is deemed to be a citizen of the state where it is incorporated and maintains its principal place of business.[4] Federal law does not mention the citizenship of partnerships, LLCs, and other unincorporated associations, but the courts have tended to regard these entities as citizens of every state of which their members are citizens.

The state citizenship of LLCs may come into play when a party sues an LLC based on diversity of citizenship. Remember that when parties to a lawsuit are from different states, a federal court can exercise diversity jurisdiction if the amount in controversy exceeds $75,000. *Total* diversity of citizenship must exist, however.

LEARNING OBJECTIVE 1

How are limited liability companies formed, and who decides how they will be managed and operated?

Articles of Organization
The document filed with a designated state official by which a limited liability company is formed.

"Business is the salt of life."

VOLTAIRE
1694–1778
(FRENCH AUTHOR AND INTELLECTUAL)

---

2. In addition to requiring the filing of articles of organization, a few states require that a notice of the intention to form an LLC be published in a local newspaper.
3. *02 Development, LLC v. 607 South Park, LLC*, 159 Cal.App.4th 609, 71 Cal.Rptr.3d 608 (2008).
4. 28 U.S.C. Section 1332.

LEARNING OBJECTIVE 2

What advantages do limited liability companies offer to businesspersons that are not offered by sole proprietorships or partnerships?

EXAMPLE 28.3 Jen Fong, a citizen of New York, wishes to bring a lawsuit against Skycel, an LLC formed under the laws of Connecticut. One of Skycel's members also lives in New York. Fong will not be able to bring the action against Skycel in federal court on the basis of diversity jurisdiction because the defendant LLC is also considered a citizen of New York. The same would be true if Fong was filing a suit against multiple defendants and one of the defendants lived in New York. ■

28–1d Advantages of the LLC

The LLC offers many advantages to businesspersons, which is why this form of business organization has become increasingly popular. (The *Business Application* feature at the end of this chapter discusses the factors that entrepreneurs need to consider when choosing between LLCs and limited liability partnerships.)

Limited Liability A key advantage of the LLC is that the liability of members is limited to the amount of their investments. Although the LLC as an entity can be held liable for any loss or injury caused by the wrongful acts or omissions of its members, the members themselves generally are not personally liable.

In the following case, a consumer died as a result of using an allegedly defective product made and sold by an LLC. The consumer's children sought to hold the LLC's sole member and manager liable for the actions of the firm.

Can a citizen of New York bring a lawsuit in federal court against an LLC formed in Connecticut if one of the LLC's members lives in New York?

CASE 28.1

Hodge v. Strong Built International, LLC

Court of Appeal of Louisiana, Third Circuit, 159 So.3d 1159 (2015).

FACTS Donald Hodge was hunting in a deer stand when the straps on the stand failed, causing the stand and Hodge to fall to the ground. Hodge was injured in the fall and died as a result. Strong Built International, LLC, a Louisiana limited liability company, was the maker and seller of the deer stand, and Ken Killen was Strong Built International's sole member and manager. Hodge's children, Donald and Rachael Hodge, filed a suit in a Louisiana state court against Strong Built International and Killen. They sought damages on a theory of product liability for the injury and death of their father caused by the allegedly defective deer stand. Killen filed a motion for summary judgment, asserting that he was not personally liable to the plaintiffs. The court granted the motion and issued a summary judgment in Killen's favor. The Hodges appealed.

ISSUE Was Killen personally liable to the Hodges?

DECISION No. A state intermediate appellate court affirmed the judgment in Killen's favor. Under applicable state law, no member or manager of an LLC is liable in that capacity for the liability of the company. There are exceptions, but the plaintiffs failed to show that Killen's actions fell within those exceptions.

Can a member-manager of an LLC that built a defective deer stand be held liable for its collapse?

REASON Under the relevant Louisiana statute, "no member, manager, employee, or agent of a limited liability company is liable in such capacity for a debt, obligation, or liability of the limited liability company." This protection is not unlimited.

A member or manager may be subject to personal liability for a breach of a professional duty or for some other negligent or wrongful act. In this case, Killen asserted that he was "not an engineer, nor a licensed professional in any profession in Louisiana or any other state" and therefore had no professional duty to breach. He also testified that he did not take part in the design, manufacture, or selection of warnings for Strong Built International's deer stand in any capacity but that of member and manager of the LLC. The Hodges offered no evidence to contradict Killen's testimony.

The "other negligent or wrongful act" exception requires that the member or manager owe a duty of care to the plaintiff beyond the duties arising out of the LLC's contract with the plaintiff. The Hodges submitted nothing to show that this exception applied to Killen.

CRITICAL THINKING—Economic Consideration *Why does the law allow—and even encourage—limits to the liability of a business organization's owners and managers for the firm's actions? Discuss.*

Taxation Another advantage is the flexibility of the LLC in regard to taxation. An LLC that has *two or more members* can choose to be taxed either as a partnership or as a corporation. A corporate entity normally must pay income taxes on its profits, and the shareholders then pay personal income taxes on profits distributed as dividends. An LLC that wants to distribute profits to its members may prefer to be taxed as a partnership to avoid the "double taxation" that is characteristic of the corporate entity.

Unless an LLC indicates that it wishes to be taxed as a corporation, the IRS automatically taxes it as a partnership. This means that the LLC as an entity pays no taxes. Rather, as in a partnership, profits are "passed through" the LLC to the members, who then personally pay taxes on the profits.

An LLC's members may want to reinvest the profits in the business, however, rather than distribute the profits to members. In that situation, they may prefer that the LLC be taxed as a corporation. Corporate income tax rates also may be lower than personal tax rates.

An LLC that has only *one member* cannot be taxed as a partnership. For federal income tax purposes, one-member LLCs are automatically taxed as sole proprietorships unless they indicate that they wish to be taxed as corporations. With respect to state taxes, most states follow the IRS rules.

Management and Foreign Investors Still another advantage of the LLC for businesspersons is the flexibility it offers in terms of business operations and management, as will be discussed shortly. Finally, because foreign investors can participate in an LLC, the LLC form of business is attractive as a way to encourage investment. For a discussion of business organizations in other nations that are similar to the LLC, see this chapter's *Beyond Our Borders* feature.

28–1e Disadvantages of the LLC

The main disadvantage of the LLC is that state LLC statutes are not uniform. Therefore, businesses that operate in more than one state may not receive consistent treatment. Generally,

BEYOND OUR BORDERS

Limited Liability Companies in Other Nations

Limited liability companies did not originate in the United States. Many nations have business forms that provide limited liability, although these organizations may differ significantly from our domestic limited liability companies (LLCs).

In Germany, the *GmbH*, or *Gesellschaft mit beschränkter Haftung* (which means "company with limited liability"), is a type of business entity that resembles the LLC. The GmbH is now the most widely used business form in Germany. A GmbH, however, is owned by shareholders and thus resembles a U.S. corporation in certain respects. German

laws also impose numerous restrictions on the operations and business transactions of GmbHs, whereas LLCs in the United States are not even required to have an operating agreement.

Business forms that limit the liability of owners can also be found in various other countries. Limited liability companies known as *limitadas* are common in many Latin American nations. In France, a *société à responsabilité limitée* (SARL, meaning "society with limited liability") is an entity that provides business owners with limited liability.

Although laws in the United Kingdom and Ireland use the term *limited liability partnership*, the entities described by the term

are similar to our domestic LLCs. Japan has created a new type of business organization called the *godo kaisha (GK)*, which is also quite similar to an LLC in the United States.

CRITICAL THINKING

- Clearly, limited liability is an important aspect of doing business globally. Why might a nation limit the number of member-owners in a limited liability entity?

most states apply to a foreign LLC (an LLC formed in another state) the law of the state where the LLC was formed. Difficulties can arise, though, when one state's court must interpret and apply another state's laws.

28-2 LLC Operation and Management

The members of an LLC have considerable flexibility in operating and managing the business. Here, we discuss the operating agreement and general operating procedures of LLCs, management options, and fiduciary duties.

28-2a The LLC Operating Agreement

Operating Agreement
An agreement in which the members of a limited liability company set forth the details of how the business will be managed and operated.

The members of an LLC can decide how to operate the various aspects of the business by forming an **operating agreement** [ULLCA 103(a)]. In many states, an operating agreement is not required for an LLC to exist, and if there is one, it need not be in writing. Generally, though, LLC members should protect their interests by creating a written operating agreement.

Operating agreements typically contain provisions relating to management, profits, transfer of membership interests, dissolution, and other important issues. Exhibit 28–1 lists some common provisions in operating agreements.

If a dispute arises and there is no agreement covering the topic under dispute, the state LLC statute will govern the outcome. For instance, most LLC statutes provide that if the members have not specified how profits will be divided, they will be divided equally among the members. When an issue is not covered by an operating agreement or by an LLC statute, the courts often apply principles of partnership law.

Of course, the members of an LLC are bound by the operating agreement that they make, as the following case illustrates.

CASE 28.2

Mekonen v. Zewdu
Court of Appeals of Washington, 179 Wash.App. 1042 (2014).

FACTS Green Cab Taxi and Disabled Service Association, LLC, is a taxi service company in King County, Washington. The company's operating agreement requires the members to pay weekly fees. Members who do not pay are in default and must return their taxi licenses to the company. In addition, a member in default cannot hold a seat on the board or withdraw from the company without the consent of all of the members.

A disagreement arose among the members concerning the company's management, and several members, including Shumet Mekonen, withdrew from the company without the consent of the other members. Both sides continued to drive under the Green Cab name.

Mekonen's group then filed a suit in a Washington state court against a group of members who had not withdrawn, including Dessie Zewdu. In part, the Mekonen group sought the right to operate as Green Cab. The court held that the plaintiffs could not represent

Can an LLC that operates a cab-company force its members to pay fees or forfeit their taxi licenses?

themselves as Green Cab and ordered them to return their taxi licenses to the company. The plaintiffs appealed the order to return their licenses.

ISSUE Are the members of an LLC bound to the terms of its operating agreement?

DECISION Yes. A state intermediate appellate court upheld the lower court's order to the plaintiffs to return their taxi licenses to Green Cab. Under the provisions of the company's operating agreement, the plaintiffs, as "defaulting members," had no right to retain and use the licenses.

REASON The appellate court pointed out that under Green Cab's operating agreement, the company held all of the rights to the taxi "licenses and permits necessary to operate its vehicles." The LLC's members were allowed to retain and use the licenses as long as they were in "good standing." To maintain this status, members had to pay the required weekly fees, which were used to offset the company's operating expenses. A member who did not pay the fee was considered to be in "default." In addition, members could not withdraw from the firm without the unanimous consent of the other members.

Here, the plaintiffs admitted that they had withdrawn from the firm and had not paid the required fees. "As a result, the Plaintiffs have no legal right to retain the King County taxicab licenses currently in their possession.... Given the relative interests of the

parties and the LLC, the trial court acted well within its discretion to order plaintiffs to return their taxi licenses."

WHAT IF THE FACTS WERE DIFFERENT? *Suppose that Green Cab had maintained a company Web site on which it posted its operating agreement, conducted all internal company business, and offered a forum where members could vent their complaints. How might the result have been different? Why?*

28–2b Management Options

Basically, LLC members have two options for managing the firm, as shown in Exhibit 28–2. It can be either a member-managed LLC or a manager-managed LLC. Most LLC statutes and the ULLCA provide that unless the articles of organization specify otherwise, an LLC is assumed to be member managed [ULLCA 203(a)(6)].

In a *member-managed* LLC, all of the members participate in management, and decisions are made by majority vote [ULLCA 404(a)]. In a *manager-managed* LLC, the members designate a person or group of persons to manage the firm. The management group may consist of only members, both members and nonmembers, or only nonmembers.

However an LLC is managed, its managers need to be aware of the firm's potential liability under employment-discrimination laws. Those laws may sometimes extend to individuals who are not members of a protected class, as discussed in this chapter's *Managerial Strategy* feature.

LEARNING OBJECTIVE 3
What are the two options for managing limited liability companies?

28–2c Fiduciary Duties

Under the ULLCA, managers in a manager-managed LLC owe fiduciary duties (the duty of loyalty and the duty of care) to the LLC and to its members, just as corporate directors and officers owe fiduciary duties to the corporation and to its shareholders [ULLCA 409(a), (h)]. As mentioned, though, not all states have adopted the ULLCA, and some state statutes provide that managers owe fiduciary duties only to the LLC and not to its members.

To whom a fiduciary duty is owed may seem insignificant at first glance, but it can have a dramatic effect on the outcome of litigation. In North Carolina and Virginia, for instance, LLC

Exhibit 28–1 Common Terms in Operating Agreements

1. Who will manage the company and how future managers will be chosen or removed. (Although most LLC statutes are silent on this issue, the ULLCA provides that members may choose and remove managers by majority vote [ULLCA 404(b)(3)].)
2. How profits will be divided.
3. How membership interests may be transferred.
4. Whether the dissociation of a member, such as by death or departure, will trigger dissolution of the LLC.
5. Whether formal members' meetings will be held.
6. How voting rights will be apportioned. (If the agreement does not cover voting, most states' LLC statutes provide that voting rights are apportioned according to each member's capital contributions. A few states provide that, in the absence of an agreement to the contrary, each member has one vote.)
7. How a buyout price will be calculated in the event of a member's dissociation.

Exhibit 28-2 Management of an LLC

```
              ┌─────────────────────┐
              │   LLC Management    │
              │      Options        │
              └─────────────────────┘
                        │
          ┌─────────────┴─────────────┐
          ▼                           ▼
  ┌─────────────────┐        ┌─────────────────┐
  │ Member Managed  │        │ Manager Managed │
  └─────────────────┘        └─────────────────┘
          │                           │
          ▼                           ▼
  ┌─────────────────┐        ┌──────────────────────┐
  │ All members vote│        │ Members designate a  │
  │ on decisions;   │        │ person or group of   │
  │ majority vote   │        │ persons to manage    │
  │ controls        │        │ the LLC, which may   │
  │                 │        │ include nonmembers   │
  └─────────────────┘        └──────────────────────┘
          │                           │
          ▼                           ▼
  ┌─────────────────┐        ┌──────────────────────┐
  │ Most LLC statutes│       │ Members normally     │
  │ assume the firm  │       │ specify that the LLC │
  │ will be member   │       │ is manager managed   │
  │ managed unless   │       │ in the articles      │
  │ the articles     │       │ of organization.     │
  │ state otherwise. │       └──────────────────────┘
  └─────────────────┘
```

statutes do not explicitly state that managers owe fiduciary duties to members.[5] Thus, in those two states, a manager-member owes fiduciary duties only to the LLC and not to its members.[6] In contrast, courts in Idaho and Kentucky have held that a manager-member owes fiduciary duties to the LLC's members and that the members can sue the manager for breaching fiduciary duties.[7]

If a member of an LLC dies, must the LLC be dissolved?

28-3 Dissociation and Dissolution of an LLC

Recall that in the context of partnerships, *dissociation* occurs when a partner ceases to be associated in the carrying on of the business. The same concept applies to LLCs. A member of an LLC has the *power* to dissociate from the LLC at any time, but she or he may not have the *right* to dissociate.

Under the ULLCA, the events that trigger a member's dissociation from an LLC are similar to the events causing a partner to be dissociated under the Uniform Partnership Act (UPA). These include voluntary withdrawal, expulsion by other members or by court order, bankruptcy, incompetence, and death. Generally, if a member dies or otherwise dissociates from an LLC, the other members may continue to carry on the LLC's business, unless the operating agreement provides otherwise.

---

5. North Carolina General Statutes Section 57C-3-22(b); and Virginia Code Section 13.1-1024.1.
6. See, for example, *Atkinson v. Lackey*, 2015 WL 867181 (N.C.Super. 2015).
7. *Bushi v. Sage Health Care, LLC*, 146 Idaho 764, 203 P.3d 694 (2009); Idaho Code Sections 30-6-101 *et seq.*; *Patmon v. Hobbs*, 280 S.W.3d 589 (Ky.App. 2009); and Kentucky Revised Statutes Section 275.170.

MANAGERIAL STRATEGY

Can a Person Who Is Not a Member of a Protected Class Sue for Discrimination?

Management Faces a Legal Issue

Under federal law and the laws of most states, discrimination in employment based on race, color, religion, national origin, gender, age, or disability is prohibited. Persons who are members of these protected classes can sue if they are subjected to discrimination. But can a person subjected to discrimination bring a lawsuit if he is not a member of a protected class, even though managers and other employees believe that he is? This somewhat unusual situation occurred in New Jersey.

What the Courts Say

Myron Cowher worked at Carson & Roberts Site Construction & Engineering, Inc. For more than a year, at least two of his supervisors directed almost daily barrages of anti-Semitic remarks at him. They believed that he was Jewish, although his actual background was German-Irish and Lutheran.

Cowher brought a suit against the supervisors and the construction company, claiming

a hostile work environment. The trial court, however, ruled that he did not have standing to sue under New Jersey law because he was not Jewish and, thus, was not a member of a protected class. Cowher appealed.

The appellate court disagreed with the trial court. The court ruled that if Cowher can prove that the discrimination "would not have occurred but for the perception that he was Jewish," his claim was covered by New Jersey's antidiscrimination law.[a] Thus, in the appellate court's view, the nature of the discriminatory remarks—and not the actual characteristics of the plaintiff—determines whether the remarks are actionable.

Another New Jersey court followed the precedent set by the *Cowher* case to allow Shi-Juan Lin, a Chinese worker whose fiancé and child were black, to recover for racial discrimination. The employer created a hostile

work environment by allowing Lin's supervisor to constantly use the "n" word at work. The employer knew that even though Lin was not black, she was hurt by the supervisor's remarks. Therefore, the court affirmed an administrative law judge's award of damages for pain and suffering, plus attorneys' fees.[b]

MANAGERIAL IMPLICATIONS

The rulings of the New Jersey courts clearly indicate that even misdirected personal slurs in the workplace are unacceptable. Managers of LLCs and other business entities should pay careful attention to employee complaints. They should also strive to create a workplace that promotes tolerance and diversity and discourages discrimination on any basis. Everyone in the firm should know what kind of remarks cross the line and potentially expose the company to liability.

a. *Cowher v. Carson & Roberts Site Construction & Engineering, Inc.*, 425 N.J.Super. 285, 40 A.3d 1171 (2012).

b. *Lin v. Dane Construction Co.*, 2014 WL 8131876 (N.J.Super.A.D. 2015).

After selling real estate to their LLC, can a couple still claim a homestead exemption for the property when filing for bankruptcy? James and Susan Kane deeded their home to their two-member LLC and recorded ownership of the property in the LLC's name. The Kanes subsequently filed for personal bankruptcy. They claimed a homestead exemption for the property on the basis that the LLC had been administratively dissolved and that, since they were its only members, the property had reverted to them.

When one of the couple's debtors objected to the exemption, the court discovered that the LLC still maintained a bank account in its name and had taken out a mortgage on the property. Hence, the court said that the LLC still existed in the *winding up phase* (discussed shortly) and that the property belonged to the LLC because no deed had been executed to transfer the property back to the Kanes. The Kanes' membership interests in the LLC were personal property and thus the property of their bankruptcy estate. Therefore, they could not claim the homestead exemption.[8]

ETHICAL ISSUE

---

8. *In re Kane*, 2011 WL 2119015 (Bankr.D.Mass. 2011). See also *In re Breece*, 487 Bankr. 599 (6th Cir. 2013).

28-3a The Effects of Dissociation

When a member dissociates from an LLC, he or she loses the right to participate in management and the right to act as an agent for the LLC. The member's duty of loyalty to the LLC also terminates, and the duty of care continues only with respect to events that occurred before dissociation.

Generally, the dissociated member also has a right to have his or her interest in the LLC bought out by the other members. The LLC's operating agreement may contain provisions establishing a buyout price, but if it does not, the member's interest is usually purchased at a fair value. In states that have adopted the ULLCA, the LLC must purchase the interest at fair value within 120 days after the dissociation.

If the member's dissociation violates the LLC's operating agreement, it is considered legally wrongful, and the dissociated member can be held liable for damages caused by the dissociation. **EXAMPLE 28.4** Chadwick and Barrel are members of an LLC. Chadwick manages the accounts, and Barrel, who has many connections in the community and is a skilled investor, brings in the business. If Barrel wrongfully dissociates from the LLC, the LLC's business will suffer, and Chadwick can hold Barrel liable for the loss of business resulting from her withdrawal. ■

28-3b Dissolution

Regardless of whether a member's dissociation was wrongful or rightful, normally the dissociated member has no right to force the LLC to dissolve. The remaining members can opt to either continue or dissolve the business.

Members can also stipulate in their operating agreement that certain events will cause dissolution, or they can agree that they have the power to dissolve the LLC by vote. As with partnerships, a court can order an LLC to be dissolved in certain circumstances, such as when the members have engaged in illegal or oppressive conduct, or when it is no longer feasible to carry on the business.

In the following case, three members formed an LLC to develop real estate. The court had to decide whether the LLC could be dissolved because continuing the business was impracticable.

CASE 28.3

Venture Sales, LLC v. Perkins

Supreme Court of Mississippi, 86 So. 3d 910 (2012).

FACTS Walter Perkins, Gary Fordham, and David Thompson formed Venture Sales, LLC, to develop a subdivision in Petal, Mississippi. All three men contributed land and funds to Venture Sales, resulting in total holdings of 466 acres of land and about $158,000 in cash. Perkins, who was an assistant coach for the Cleveland Browns, trusted Fordham and Thompson to develop the property. More than a decade later, however, Fordham and Thompson still had not done so, although they had developed at least two other subdivisions in the area.

What happens when the members fail to develop a subdivision that the LLC was created to develop?

Fordham and Thompson suggested selling the property, but Perkins disagreed with the proposed listing price of $3.5 million. Perkins then sought a judicial dissolution of Venture Sales. Fordham and Thompson told the court that they did not know when they could develop the property and that they had been unable to get the additional funds that they needed to proceed. The trial court ordered the company dissolved. Fordham, Thompson, and Venture Sales appealed.

ISSUE Can Venture Sales be judicially dissolved?

DECISION Yes. The Mississippi Supreme Court affirmed the judgment of the trial court.

REASON Under Mississippi law, an LLC may be judicially dissolved if, among other reasons, "it is not reasonably practicable to carry on the business in conformity with . . . the limited liability company agreement." The statute does not explain when continuing an LLC is "not reasonably practicable." The court therefore followed decisions from other jurisdictions recognizing that dissolution is appropriate when an LLC "is not meeting the economic purpose for which it was established." According to Venture Sales' operating agreement, the company's purpose was "to initially acquire, develop and [sell] commercial and residential properties near Petal, Forrest County, Mississippi."

Nevertheless, more than a decade later, the LLC's property remained undeveloped. Fordham and Thompson pointed to a number of reasons, including poor financial conditions and Hurricane Katrina. But regardless of the reasons, Fordham and Thompson lacked the funds needed to proceed and did not know when they could develop the property as planned. It was immaterial that Perkins did not agree to other business opportunities, such as selling the whole property for $3.5 million. After all, Venture Sales was formed to develop a subdivision. Because the LLC was not meeting that purpose, dissolution was warranted.

CRITICAL THINKING—Legal Consideration *Would dissolution be appropriate if the parties had formed a partnership rather than an LLC? Explain your answer.*

28-3c Winding Up

When an LLC is dissolved, any members who did not wrongfully dissociate may participate in the winding up process. To wind up the business, members must collect, liquidate, and distribute the LLC's assets.

Members may preserve the assets for a reasonable time to optimize their return, and they continue to have the authority to perform reasonable acts in conjunction with winding up. In other words, the LLC will be bound by the reasonable acts of its members during the winding up process.

Once all the LLC's assets have been sold, the proceeds are distributed to pay off debts to creditors first (including debts owed to members who are creditors of the LLC). The members' capital contributions are returned next, and any remaining amounts are then distributed to members in equal shares or according to their operating agreement.

When forming an LLC, carefully draft the operating agreement. Stipulate the events that will cause dissociation and how the fair-value buyout price will be calculated. Set a time limit within which the LLC must compensate the dissociated member (or her or his estate) in the event of withdrawal, disability, or death.

Include provisions that clearly limit the authority of dissociated members to act on behalf of the LLC, and provide a right to seek damages from members who exceed the agreed-on parameters. Identify any third parties who should be notified in the event of a dissociation, and whether a notice of dissociation will be filed with the state. The operating agreement should also specify any events that will automatically cause a dissolution, as well as which members will have a right to participate in—or make decisions about—the winding up process.

PREVENTING LEGAL DISPUTES

28-4 Special Business Forms

Besides the business forms already discussed in this unit, several other forms can be used to organize a business. For the most part, these special business forms are hybrid organizations—that is, they combine features of other organizational forms, such as partnerships and corporations. These forms include joint ventures, syndicates, joint stock companies, business trusts, and cooperatives.

Joint Venture A joint undertaking by two or more persons or business entities to combine their efforts or their property for a single transaction or project or for a related series of transactions or projects. A joint venture is generally treated like a partnership for tax and other legal purposes.

If Intel wants to work with Micron to develop a new storage chip, what type of business organization might the two companies form?

KNOW THIS

A partnership involves a continuing relationship of the partners. A joint venture is often a one-time association.

28–4a Joint Ventures

In a **joint venture,** two or more persons or business entities combine their efforts or their property for a single transaction or project or for a related series of transactions or projects. For instance, when several contractors combine their resources to build and sell houses in a single development, their relationship is a joint venture. Unless otherwise agreed, joint venturers share profits and losses equally.

Joint ventures range in size from very small activities to multimillion-dollar joint actions carried out by some of the world's largest corporations. Large organizations often investigate new markets or new ideas by forming joint ventures with other enterprises. **EXAMPLE 28.5** Intel Corporation and Micron Technology, Inc., formed a joint venture to manufacture NAND flash memory. NAND is a data-storage chip widely used in digital cameras, cell phones, and portable music players. ■

Similarities to Partnerships The joint venture resembles a partnership and is taxed like a partnership. For this reason, most courts apply the same principles to joint ventures as they apply to partnerships. Joint venturers owe each other the same fiduciary duties, including the duty of loyalty, that partners owe each other. Thus, if one of the venturers secretly buys land that was supposed to be acquired by the joint venture, the other joint venturers may be awarded damages for the breach of loyalty.

Liability and Management Rights. A joint venturer can be held personally liable for the venture's debts (because joint venturers share losses as well as profits). Like partners, joint venturers have equal rights to manage the activities of the enterprise, but they can agree to give control of the operation to one of the members.

Authority to Enter Contracts. Joint venturers have authority as agents to enter into contracts for the business that will bind the joint venture. **CASE EXAMPLE 28.6** Murdo Cameron developed components for replicas of vintage P-51 Mustang planes. Cameron and Douglas Anderson agreed in writing to collaborate on the design and manufacture of two P-51s, one for each of them.

Without Cameron's knowledge, Anderson borrowed funds from SPW Associates, LLP, to finance the construction, using the first plane as security for the loan. After Anderson built one plane, he defaulted on the loan. SPW filed a lawsuit to obtain possession of the aircraft.

The court ruled that Anderson and Cameron had entered into a joint venture and that the plane was the venture's property. Under partnership law, partners have the power as agents to bind the partnership. Because this principle applies to joint ventures, Anderson had the authority to grant SPW a security interest in the plane, and SPW was entitled to take possession of the plane.[9] ■

Differences from Partnerships Joint ventures differ from partnerships in several important ways. A joint venture is typically created for a single project or series of transactions, whereas a partnership usually (though not always) involves an ongoing business. Also, unlike most partnerships, a joint venture normally terminates when the project or the transaction for which it was formed has been completed.

Because the activities of a joint venture are more limited than the business of a partnership, the members of a joint venture are presumed to have less power to bind their co-venturers. Accordingly, the members of a joint venture have less implied and apparent authority than the partners in a partnership (each of whom is treated as an agent of the other partners). In *Case Example 28.6,* for instance, if Anderson's contract had not been directly related to the business of building vintage planes, the court might have concluded that Anderson lacked the authority to bind the joint venture.

---

9. *SPW Associates, LLP v. Anderson,* 2006 ND 159, 718 N.W.2d 580 (N.D.Sup.Ct. 2006).

28-4b Syndicates

In a **syndicate,** or *investment group,* several individuals or firms join together to finance a particular project, such as the construction of a shopping center or the purchase of a professional basketball franchise. The form of such groups varies considerably. A syndicate may be organized as a corporation or as a general or limited partnership. In some instances, the members do not have a legally recognized business arrangement but merely purchase and own property jointly.

28-4c Joint Stock Companies

A **joint stock company** is a true hybrid of a partnership and a corporation. It has many characteristics of a corporation in that (1) its ownership is represented by transferable shares of stock, (2) it is usually managed by directors and officers of the company or association, and (3) it can have a perpetual existence.

Most of its other features, however, are more characteristic of a partnership, and it is usually treated like a partnership. Like a partnership, a joint stock company is formed by agreement (not statute). Property is usually held in the names of the members, who are called shareholders, and they have personal liability. In a joint stock company, however, shareholders are not considered to be agents of one another, as they are in a partnership.

28-4d Business Trusts

The **business trust** form of organization was started in Massachusetts in an attempt to obtain the limited liability advantage of a corporation while avoiding restrictions on real property ownership. With a business trust, legal ownership and management of the trust's property stay with one or more of the trustees, and the profits are distributed to the beneficiaries.

A business trust is created by a written trust agreement that sets forth the interests of the beneficiaries and the obligations and powers of the trustees. A business trust resembles a corporation in many respects. Beneficiaries of the trust, for instance, are not personally responsible for the debts or obligations of the trust. In fact, in a number of states, business trusts must pay corporate taxes.

28-4e Cooperatives

A **cooperative** is an association that is organized to provide an economic service to its members (or shareholders). A cooperative may or may not be incorporated. Most cooperatives are organized under state statutes for cooperatives, general business corporations, or LLCs.

Generally, an incorporated cooperative distributes dividends, or profits, to its owners on the basis of their transactions with the cooperative rather than on the basis of the amount of capital they contributed. Members of incorporated cooperatives have limited liability, as do shareholders of corporations and members of LLCs. Cooperatives that are unincorporated are often treated like partnerships, and members have joint liability for the cooperative's acts.

The cooperative form of business is generally adopted by groups of individuals who wish to pool their resources to gain some advantage in the marketplace. *Consumer purchasing co-ops* are formed to obtain lower prices through quantity discounts. *Seller marketing co-ops* are formed to control the market and thereby enable members to sell their goods at higher prices. Co-ops range in size from small, local consumer cooperatives to national businesses such as Ace Hardware and Land O'Lakes, a well-known producer of dairy products.

LEARNING OBJECTIVE 5

What are the essential characteristics of syndicates, joint stock companies, business trusts, and cooperatives?

Syndicate A group of individuals or firms that join together to finance a project. A syndicate is also called an *investment group.*

Joint Stock Company A hybrid form of business organization that combines characteristics of a corporation and a partnership. Usually, a joint stock company is regarded as a partnership for tax and other legal purposes.

Business Trust A form of business organization, created by a written trust agreement, that resembles a corporation. Legal ownership and management of the trust's property stay with the trustees, and the profits are distributed to the beneficiaries, who have limited liability.

Cooperative An association, which may or may not be incorporated, that is organized to provide an economic service to its members. Unincorporated cooperatives are often treated like partnerships for tax and other legal purposes.

Most people believe that cooperatives are small enterprises, but not all are. Ace Hardware is a nationwide "co-op" that was formed over 80 years ago. What is the benefit of forming a co-op?

Reviewing . . . Limited Liability Companies and Special Business Forms

The city of Papagos, Arizona, had a deteriorating bridge in need of repair on a prominent public roadway. The city posted notices seeking proposals for an artistic bridge design and reconstruction. Davidson Masonry, LLC—owned and managed by Carl Davidson and his wife, Marilyn Rowe—decided to submit a bid for a decorative concrete project that incorporated artistic metalwork. They contacted Shana Lafayette, a local sculptor who specialized in large-scale metal creations, to help them design the bridge. The city selected their bridge design and awarded them the contract for a commission of $184,000.

Davidson Masonry and Lafayette then entered into an agreement to work together on the bridge project. Davidson Masonry agreed to install and pay for concrete and structural work, and Lafayette agreed to install the metalwork at her expense. They agreed that overall profits would be split, with 25 percent going to Lafayette and 75 percent going to Davidson Masonry. Lafayette designed numerous metal salmon sculptures that were incorporated into colorful decorative concrete forms designed by Rowe, while Davidson performed the structural engineering. The group worked together successfully until the completion of the project. Using the information presented in the chapter, answer the following questions.

1. Would Davidson Masonry automatically be taxed as a partnership or a corporation? Explain.
2. Is Davidson Masonry member managed or manager managed?
3. When Davidson Masonry and Lafayette entered into an agreement to work together, what kind of special business form was created? Explain.
4. Suppose that during construction, Lafayette entered into an agreement to rent space in a warehouse that was close to the bridge so that she could work on her sculptures near the location where they would be installed. She entered into the contract without the knowledge or consent of Davidson Masonry. In this situation, would a court be likely to hold that Davidson Masonry was bound by the contract? Why or why not?

DEBATE THIS

■ Because LLCs are essentially just partnerships with limited liability for members, all partnership laws should apply.

How Do You Choose between an LLC and an LLP?*

One of the most important decisions that an entrepreneur makes is the selection of the form in which to do business. To make the best decision, a businessperson needs to consider all the legal, tax, licensing, and business consequences.

Newer forms of business organizations, including limited liability partnerships (LLPs) and limited liability companies (LLCs), provide additional options. An initial consideration in choosing between these forms is the number of participants. An LLP must have two or more partners, but in many states, an LLC can have a single member (owner).

Liability Considerations

The members of an LLC are not liable for the obligations of the organization. Members' liability is limited to the amount of their property (investment) interest. The liability of the partners in an LLP varies from state to state. About half of the states exempt the partners from liability for any obligation of the firm. In some states, the partners are individually liable for the contractual obligations of the firm but are not liable for obligations arising from the torts of others. In either situation, a partner who is sued for

malpractice may be on his or her own with respect to liability unless the other partners agree to help.

Distributions from the Firm

As a means of payment, members and partners generally are allowed to withdraw funds from the firm against their share of the profits. In many states, a member of an LLC must repay so-called wrongful distributions even if she or he did not know that the distributions were wrongful (wrongful distributions include those made when the LLC is insolvent). Under most LLP statutes, by contrast, the partners must repay only distributions that were fraudulent.

Taxation

Both LLPs and LLCs can set up whatever management structure the participants desire. For federal income tax purposes, all unincorporated business organizations, including LLPs and LLCs with two or more members, are treated as partnerships. (An LLC can, however, elect to be treated as a corporation instead.[a]) This means that the firms are not taxed at the entity level. Their income is passed through to the partners or members, who report it on their individual

income tax returns. Some states impose additional taxes on LLCs.

Financial and Personal Relationships

Although the legal consequences of choosing a business form are certainly important, they are often secondary to the financial and personal relationships among the participants. Work effort, motivation, ability, and other personal attributes can be significant factors, as may fundamental business concerns such as the expenses and debts of the firm—and the extent of personal liability for these obligations.

Another practical factor to consider is the willingness of others to do business with an LLP or an LLC. A supplier, for example, may not be willing to extend credit to a firm whose partners or members will not accept personal liability for the debt.

CHECKLIST for Choosing a Limited Liability Business Form:

1. Determine the number of participants a state requires, the forms it allows, and the limits on liability the state provides for the participants.

2. Evaluate the tax considerations.

3. Weigh such practical concerns as the financial and personal relationships among the participants and the willingness of others to do business with a particular organizational form.

---

* This *Business Application* is not meant to substitute for the services of an attorney who is licensed to practice law in your state.

a. The chief benefits of electing corporate status for tax purposes are that the members generally are not subject to self-employment taxes and that fringe benefits may be provided to employee-members on a tax-reduced basis. The tax laws are complicated, however, and a professional should be consulted about the details.

Key Terms

articles of organization 699
business trust 709
cooperative 709

joint stock company 709
joint venture 708
limited liability company (LLC) 697

member 698
operating agreement 702
syndicate 709

Chapter Summary: Limited Liability Companies and Special Business Forms

Limited Liability Companies	**1.** *Formation*—Articles of organization must be filed with the appropriate state office—usually the office of the secretary of state—setting forth the name of the business, its principal address, the names of the owners (called *members*), and other relevant information.
	2. *Advantages and disadvantages of the LLC*—Advantages of the LLC include limited liability, the option to be taxed as a partnership or as a corporation, and flexibility in deciding how the business will be managed and operated. The main disadvantage is the absence of uniformity in state LLC statutes.
LLC Operation and Management	**1.** *Operating agreement*—When an LLC is formed, the members decide, in an operating agreement, how the business will be managed and what rules will apply to the organization.
	2. *Management*—An LLC may be managed by members only, by some members and some nonmembers, or by nonmembers only.
Dissociation and Dissolution of an LLC	Members of an LLC have the power to dissociate from the LLC at any time, but they may not have the right to dissociate. Dissociation does not always result in the dissolution of an LLC. The remaining members can choose to continue the business. Dissociated members have a right to have their interest purchased by the other members. If the LLC is dissolved, the business must be wound up and the assets sold. Creditors are paid first, and then members' capital investments are returned. Any remaining proceeds are distributed to members.
Special Business Forms	**1.** *Joint venture*—An organization created by two or more persons in contemplation of a single transaction or project or a related series of transactions or projects. A joint venture is similar to a partnership in many respects.
	2. *Syndicate*—An investment group that undertakes to finance a particular project. A syndicate may be organized as a corporation or as a general or limited partnership.
	3. *Joint stock company*—A business form similar to a corporation in some respects (transferable shares of stock, management by directors and officers, perpetual existence) but otherwise resembling a partnership.
	4. *Business trust*—A business form created by a written trust agreement that sets forth the interests of the beneficiaries and the obligations and powers of the trustees. Beneficiaries are not personally liable for the debts or obligations of the business trust, which is similar to a corporation in many respects.
	5. *Cooperative*—An association organized to provide an economic service, without profit, to its members. A co-op may or may not be incorporated.

Issue Spotters

1. Gabriel, Harry, and Ida are members of Jeweled Watches, LLC. What are their options with respect to the management of their firm? (See *LLC Operation and Management*.)

2. Greener Delivery Company and Hiway Trucking, Inc., form a business trust. Insta Equipment Company and Jiffy Supply Corporation form a joint stock company. Kwik Mart, Inc., and Luscious Produce, Inc., form an incorporated cooperative. What do these forms of business organization have in common? (See *Special Business Forms*.)

—**Check your answers to the *Issue Spotters* against the answers provided in Appendix D at the end of this text.**

Learning Objectives Check

1. How are limited liability companies formed, and who decides how they will be managed and operated?

2. What advantages do limited liability companies offer to businesspersons that are not offered by sole proprietorships or partnerships?

3. What are the two options for managing limited liability companies?

4. What is a joint venture? How is it similar to a partnership? How is it different?

5. What are the essential characteristics of syndicates, joint stock companies, business trusts, and cooperatives?

—**Answers to the even-numbered *Learning Objectives Check* questions can be found in Appendix E at the end of this text.**

Business Scenarios and Case Problems

28–1. Limited Liability Companies. John, Lesa, and Trevor form a limited liability company. John contributes 60 percent of the capital, and Lesa and Trevor each contribute 20 percent. Nothing is decided about how profits will be divided. John assumes that he will be entitled to 60 percent of the profits, in accordance with his contribution. Lesa and Trevor, however, assume that the profits will be divided equally. A dispute over the profits arises, and ultimately a court has to decide the issue. What law will the court apply? In most states, what will result? How could this dispute have been avoided in the first place? Discuss fully. (See *Limited Liability Companies.*)

28–2. Special Business Forms. Faraway Corp. supplies business equipment. Faraway is considering entering into two contracts, one with a joint stock company east of the Mississippi River and the other with a business trust formed by a number of sole proprietors on the West Coast. Both contracts require Faraway to make large capital outlays in order to supply the businesses with restaurant equipment. In both business organizations, at least two shareholders or beneficiaries are personally wealthy, but each organization has limited financial resources. The owner-managers of Faraway are not familiar with either form of business organization. Because each form resembles a corporation, they are concerned about whether they will be able to collect payments from the wealthy members of the business organizations in the event that either organization breaches the contract by failing to make the payments. Discuss fully Faraway's concern. (See *Special Business Forms.*)

28–3. Jurisdiction. Joe, a resident of New Jersey, wants to open a restaurant. He asks his friend Kay, who is an experienced attorney and a New Yorker, for her business and legal advice in exchange for a 20 percent ownership interest in the restaurant. Kay helps Joe negotiate a lease for the restaurant premises and advises Joe to organize the business as a limited liability company (LLC). Joe forms Café Olé, LLC, and, with Kay's help, obtains financing. Then, the night before the restaurant opens, Joe tells Kay that he is "cutting her out of the deal." The restaurant proves to be a success. Kay wants to file a suit in a federal district court against Joe and the LLC. Can a federal court exercise jurisdiction over the parties based on diversity of citizenship? Explain. (See *Limited Liability Companies.*)

28–4. Joint Ventures. Holiday Isle Resort & Marina, Inc., operated four restaurants, five bars, and various food kiosks at its resort in Islamorada, Florida. Holiday entered into a "joint venture agreement" with Rip Tosun to operate a fifth restaurant called Rip's—A Place for Ribs. The agreement gave Tosun authority over the employees and "full authority as to the conduct of the business." It also prohibited Tosun from competing with Rip's without Holiday's approval but did not prevent Holiday from competing. Later, Tosun sold half of his interest in Rip's to Thomas Hallock. Soon, Tosun and Holiday opened the Olde Florida Steakhouse next to Rip's. Holiday stopped serving breakfast at Rip's and diverted employees and equipment from Rip's to the steakhouse, which then started offering breakfast. Hallock filed a suit in a Florida state court against Holiday. Did Holiday breach the joint-venture agreement? Did it breach the duties that joint venturers owe each other? Explain. [*Hallock v. Holiday Isle Resort & Marina, Inc.,* 4 So.3d 17 (Fla.App. 3 Dist. 2009)] (See *Special Business Forms.*)

28–5. LLC Dissolution. Walter Van Houten and John King formed 1545 Ocean Avenue, LLC, with each managing 50 percent of the business. Its purpose was to renovate an existing building and build a new commercial building. Van Houten and King quarreled over many aspects of the work on the properties. As the project neared completion, King demanded that the LLC be dissolved and that Van Houten agree to a buyout. Because the parties could not agree on a buyout, King sued for dissolution. The trial court prevented work on the project from proceeding while the dispute was being settled. As the ground for dissolution, King cited the fights over management decisions. There was no claim of fraud or frustration of purpose. The trial court ordered that the LLC be dissolved. Van Houten appealed. Should either of the owners be forced to dissolve the LLC before completion of its purpose—that is, finishing the building projects? Discuss. [*In re 1545 Ocean Avenue, LLC,* 893 N.Y.S.2d 590 (N.Y.A.D. 2 Dept. 2010)] (See *Dissociation and Dissolution of an LLC.*)

28–6. Business Case Problem with Sample Answer—LLC Operation. James Williford, Patricia Mosser, Marquetta Smith, and Michael Floyd formed Bluewater Logistics, LLC, to bid on construction contracts after Hurricane Katrina struck the Gulf Coast. Under Mississippi law, every member of a member-managed LLC is entitled to participate in managing the business. The operating agreement provided for a "supermajority" 75 percent vote to remove a member who "has either committed a felony or under any other circumstances that would jeopardize the company status" as a contractor. After Bluewater had completed more than $5 million in contracts, Smith told Williford that she, Mosser, and Floyd were exercising their "supermajority" vote to fire him. No reason was provided. Williford sued Bluewater and the other members. Did Smith, Mosser, and Floyd breach the state LLC statute, their fiduciary duties, or the Bluewater operating agreements? Discuss. [*Bluewater Logistics, LLC v. Williford,* 55 So.3d 148 (Miss. 2011)] (See *LLC Operation and Management.*)

—For a sample answer to Problem 28–6, go to Appendix F at the end of this text.

28–7. Jurisdictional Requirements. Fadal Machining Centers, LLC, and MAG Industrial Automation Centers, LLC, sued a New Jersey–based corporation, Mid-Atlantic CNC, Inc., in federal district court. Ten percent of MAG was owned by SP MAG Holdings, a Delaware LLC. SP MAG had six members, including a Delaware limited partnership called Silver Point Capital Fund and a Delaware LLC called SPCP Group III. In turn, Silver Point and SPCP Group had a common member, Robert O'Shea, who was a New Jersey citizen. Assuming that the amount in controversy exceeds $75,000, does the district court have diversity jurisdiction? Why or why not? [*Fadal Machining Centers, LLC v. Mid-Atlantic CNC, Inc.*, 464 Fed.Appx. 672 (9th Cir. 2012)] (See *Limited Liability Companies.*)

28–8. Jurisdictional Requirements. Siloam Springs Hotel, LLC, operates a Hampton Inn in Siloam Springs, Arkansas. Siloam bought insurance from Century Surety Co. to cover the hotel. When guests suffered injuries due to a leak of carbon monoxide from the heating element of an indoor swimming pool, Siloam filed a claim with Century. Century denied coverage. Siloam disputed the denial. Century asked a federal district court to resolve the dispute. In asserting that the federal court had jurisdiction, Century noted that the amount in controversy exceeded $75,000 and that the parties had complete diversity of citizenship: Century is "a corporation organized under the laws of Ohio, with its principal place of business in Michigan," and Siloam is "a corporation organized under the laws of Oklahoma, with its principal place of business in Arkansas." Can the court exercise diversity jurisdiction in this case? Discuss. [*Siloam Springs Hotel, L.L.C. v. Century Surety Co.*, 781 F.3d 1233 (10th Cir. 2015)] (See *Limited Liability Companies.*)

28–9. A Question of Ethics—LLC Operation. Blushing Brides, LLC, a publisher of wedding-planning magazines in Columbus, Ohio, opened an account with Gray Printing Co. in July 2000. On behalf of Blushing Brides, Louis Zacks, the firm's member-manager, signed a credit agreement that identified the firm as the "purchaser" and required payment within thirty days. Despite the agreement, Blushing Brides typically took up to six months to pay the full amount for its orders. Gray printed and shipped 10,000 copies of a fall/winter 2001 issue for *Blushing Brides* but had not been paid when the firm ordered 15,000 copies of a spring/summer 2002 issue. Gray refused to print the new order without an assurance of payment. Zacks signed a promissory note for $14,778, plus interest at 6 percent per year, payable to Gray on June 22. Gray printed the new order but by October had been paid only $7,500. Gray filed a suit in an Ohio state court against Blushing Brides and Zacks to collect the balance. [*Gray Printing Co. v. Blushing Brides, LLC,* 2006 WL 832587 (Ohio App. 2006)] (See *LLC Operation and Management.*)

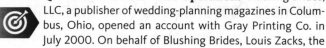

1. Under what circumstances is a member of an LLC liable for the firm's debts? In this case, is Zacks personally liable under the credit agreement for the unpaid amount on Blushing Brides' account? Did Zacks's promissory note affect the parties' liability on the account? Explain.

2. Does a member of an LLC have an ethical responsibility to meet the obligations of the firm? Discuss.

3. Gray shipped only 10,000 copies of the spring/summer 2002 issue of *Blushing Brides* magazine, waiting for the publisher to identify a destination for the other 5,000 copies. The magazine had a retail price of $4.50 per copy. Did Gray have a legal or ethical duty to "mitigate the damages" by attempting to sell or otherwise distribute these copies itself? Why or why not?

Critical Thinking and Writing Assignments

28–10. Business Law Critical Thinking Group Assignment. Newbury Properties Group owns, manages, and develops real property. Jerry Stoker and the Stoker Group, Inc. (the Stokers), also develop real property. Newbury entered into agreements with the Stokers concerning a large tract of property in Georgia. The parties formed Bellemare, LLC, to develop various parcels of the tract for residential purposes. The operating agreement of Bellemare indicated that "no Member shall be accountable to the LLC or to any other Member with respect to any other business or activity even if the business or activity competes with the LLC's business." Later, when the Newbury group contracted with other parties to develop parcels within the tract in competition with Bellemare, LLC, the Stokers sued, alleging breach of fiduciary duty. (See *LLC Operation and Management.*)

1. The first group will discuss and outline the fiduciary duties that the members of an LLC owe to each other.

2. The second group will determine whether the terms of an operating agreement can alter these fiduciary duties.

3. The last group will decide in whose favor the court should rule in this situation.

Corporations

"A corporation is an artificial being, invisible, intangible, and existing only in contemplation of law."

JOHN MARSHALL
1755–1835
(CHIEF JUSTICE OF THE UNITED STATES
SUPREME COURT, 1801–1835)

A **corporation** is a creature of statute—a legal entity created and recognized by state law. As John Marshall indicated in the chapter-opening quotation, a corporation is an artificial being, existing only in law and neither tangible nor visible.

A corporation's existence generally depends on state law. Each state has its own body of corporate law, and these laws are not entirely uniform. Most states have based their laws on one of two model laws—the Model Business Corporation Act (MBCA) or the Revised Model Business Corporation Act (RMBCA). Although the majority of the states used the RMBCA as a guide when drafting their state statutes, differences among state laws still exist.

Corporate directors, officers, and shareholders all play different roles within the corporate entity, as will be discussed in this chapter. One of the key advantages of the corporate form of business is that the shareholders' liability is limited to the amount of their investments.

LEARNING OBJECTIVES

The five Learning Objectives *below are designed to help improve your understanding of the chapter. After reading this chapter, you should be able to answer the following questions:*

1. What is a close corporation?

2. What four steps are involved in bringing a corporation into existence?

3. In what circumstances might a court disregard the corporate entity ("pierce the corporate veil") and hold the shareholders personally liable?

4. What are the duties of corporate directors and officers?

5. What is a voting proxy?

Corporation A legal entity formed in compliance with statutory requirements that is distinct from its shareholder-owners.

29-1 Nature and Classification

A corporation is recognized by law as a "person"—an artificial, legal person—and enjoys many of the same rights and privileges under state and federal law that natural persons enjoy. For instance, corporations possess the same right of access to the courts as natural persons and can sue or be sued. The constitutional guarantees of due process, free speech, and freedom from unreasonable searches and seizures also apply to corporations.

29–1a Corporate Personnel

In a corporation, the responsibility for the overall management of the firm is entrusted to a *board of directors,* whose members are elected by the shareholders. The board of directors hires *corporate officers* and other employees to run the corporation's daily business operations.

When an individual purchases a share of stock (an equity interest) in a corporation, that person becomes a shareholder and thus an owner of the corporation. Unlike the members of a partnership, the body of shareholders can change constantly without affecting the continued existence of the corporation. A shareholder can sue the corporation, the corporation can sue a shareholder, and in certain situations, a shareholder can sue "on behalf of" the corporation.

29–1b The Limited Liability of Shareholders

The major advantage of the corporate form is the limited liability of its owners (shareholders). Corporate shareholders' liability is limited to the amount of their investments. Shareholders usually are not otherwise liable for the debts of the corporation. To enable the firm to obtain credit, however, shareholders in small companies sometimes voluntarily assume personal liability, as guarantors, for corporate obligations.

29–1c Corporate Earnings and Taxation

When a corporation earns profits, it can either pass them on to its shareholders in the form of **dividends** or retain them as profits. These **retained earnings,** if invested properly, will yield higher corporate profits in the future and thus cause the price of the company's stock to rise. Individual shareholders can then reap the benefits of these retained earnings in the capital gains that they receive when they sell their stock.

Whether a corporation retains its profits or passes them on to the shareholders as dividends, those profits are subject to income tax by various levels of government. Failure to pay taxes can lead to severe consequences. The state can suspend the entity's corporate status until the taxes are paid or even dissolve the corporation for failing to pay taxes.

Another important aspect of corporate taxation is that corporate profits can be subject to double taxation. The company pays tax on its profits, and then if the profits are passed on to the shareholders as dividends, the shareholders must also pay income tax on them. The corporation normally does not receive a tax deduction for dividends it distributes to shareholders. This double-taxation feature is one of the major disadvantages of the corporate business form.

29–1d Torts and Criminal Acts

Under modern criminal law, a corporation may be held liable for the criminal acts of its agents and employees. Although corporations cannot be imprisoned, they can be fined. (Of course, corporate directors and officers can be imprisoned, and many have been in recent years.) In addition, under sentencing guidelines for crimes committed by corporate employees (white-collar crimes), corporations can face fines amounting to hundreds of millions of dollars.

A corporation is also liable for the torts committed by its agents or officers within the course and scope of their employment. The doctrine of *respondeat superior* applies to corporations in the same way as it does to other agency relationships.

CASE EXAMPLE 29.1 Mark Bloom was an officer and a director of MB Investment Partners, Inc. (MB), at the time that he formed North Hills, LP, a stock investment fund. Bloom and other MB employees used MB's offices and equipment to administer investments in North Hills. Later, investors in North Hills requested a full redemption of their investments. By that time, however, most of the funds that had been invested were gone. North Hills had, in fact, been a Ponzi scheme that Bloom had used to finance his lavish personal lifestyle, taking at least $20 million from North Hills for his personal use.

Who hires corporate officers?

Dividend A distribution of corporate profits to the corporation's shareholders in proportion to the number of shares held.

Retained Earnings The portion of a corporation's profits that has not been paid out as dividends to shareholders.

Barry Belmont and other North Hills Investors filed a suit in a federal district court against MB, alleging fraud. The court held that MB was liable for Bloom's fraud. MB appealed, and the appellate court affirmed. Tort liability can be attributed to a corporation for the acts of its agent that were committed within the scope of the agent's employment.[1] ▪

29-1e **Classification of Corporations**

Corporations can be classified in several ways. The classification of a corporation normally depends on its location, purpose, and ownership characteristics, as described in the following subsections.

Domestic, Foreign, and Alien Corporations
A corporation is referred to as a **domestic corporation** by its home state (the state in which it incorporates). A corporation formed in one state but doing business in another is referred to in the second state as a **foreign corporation.** A corporation formed in another country (say, Mexico) but doing business in the United States is referred to in the United States as an **alien corporation.**

A corporation does not have an automatic right to do business in a state other than its state of incorporation. In some instances, it must obtain a *certificate of authority* in any state in which it plans to do business. Once the certificate has been issued, the corporation generally can exercise in that state all of the powers conferred on it by its home state. If a foreign corporation does business in a state without obtaining a certificate of authority, the state can impose substantial fines and sanctions on the corporation, and sometimes even on its officers, directors, or agents.

Note that most state statutes specify certain activities, such as soliciting orders via the Internet, that are not considered doing business within the state. Thus, a foreign corporation normally does not need a certificate of authority to sell goods or services via the Internet or by mail.

What constitutes doing business within a state? In the following case, the court answered that question.

When is a corporation liable for the fraud of its officers?

Domestic Corporation

In a given state, a corporation that is organized under the law of that state.

Foreign Corporation

In a given state, a corporation that does business in that state but is not incorporated there.

Alien Corporation

A corporation formed in another country but doing business in the United States.

---

1. *Belmont v. MB Investment Partners, Inc.,* 708 F.3d 470 (3d Cir. 2013).

Drake Manufacturing Co. v. Polyflow, Inc.

Superior Court of Pennsylvania, 2015 PA Super 16, 109 A.3d 250 (2015).

FACTS Drake Manufacturing Company, a Delaware corporation, entered into a contract to sell certain products to Polyflow, Inc., headquartered in Pennsylvania. Drake promised to ship the goods from Drake's plant in Sheffield, Pennsylvania, to Polyflow's place of business in Oaks, Pennsylvania, as well as to addresses in California, Canada, and Holland. When Polyflow withheld payment of about $300,000 for some of the goods, Drake filed a breach of contract suit in a Pennsylvania state court against Polyflow seeking to collect the unpaid amount. But Drake had failed to obtain a certificate of authority to do business in Pennsylvania as a foreign corporation. Polyflow asserted that this failure to register with the state deprived Drake of the capacity to bring an action against Polyflow in the

If a company fails to obtain the required foreign corporation certificate of authority, can it still undertake legal actions?

state's courts. The court issued a judgment in Drake's favor. Polyflow appealed.

ISSUE Did Drake's failure to submit a certificate of authority deprive the company of the capacity to sue in the state's courts?

DECISION Yes. A state intermediate appellate court reversed the judgment that had been in Drake's favor. The trial court should not have allowed Drake to prosecute its action against Polyflow.

REASON A Pennsylvania statute requires a foreign corporation to obtain a certificate of authority before doing

Continues

business in the state. "Doing business" includes maintaining an office to conduct business and entering into contracts relating to business. A foreign corporation that has not obtained a certificate is not permitted to maintain an action in any Pennsylvania state court.

In this case, Drake maintained an office in Pennsylvania to conduct local business and entered into a contract with Polyflow in the state to ship goods to Polyflow's place of business in Pennsylvania. When Polyflow did not pay the full contact price, Drake filed a suit in an attempt to collect the debt. But Drake had failed to obtain and

submit to the trial court the required certificate. This effectively deprived the company of the capacity to sue in the state's courts. Drake also needed the certificate of authority to sue Polyflow in the state for its failure to pay for the out-of-state shipments.

CRITICAL THINKING—Legal Consideration *Why would the appellate court permit Polyflow to get away with not paying for delivered and presumably merchantable goods?*

Is AMTRAK a public or publicly held corporation?

Publicly Held Corporation
A corporation whose shares are publicly traded in securities markets, such as the New York Stock Exchange or the NASDAQ.

KNOW THIS

A private corporation is a voluntary association, but a public corporation is not.

LEARNING OBJECTIVE 1
What is a close corporation?

Close Corporation
A corporation whose shareholders are limited to a small group of persons, often family members.

Public and Private Corporations
A public corporation is one formed by the government to meet some political or governmental purpose. Cities and towns that incorporate are common examples. In addition, many federal government organizations—such as the U.S. Postal Service, the Tennessee Valley Authority, and AMTRAK—are public corporations.

Note that a public corporation is not the same as a *publicly held* corporation (often called a *public company*). A **publicly held corporation** is any corporation whose shares are publicly traded in securities markets, such as the New York Stock Exchange or the NASDAQ. (The NASDAQ is an electronic stock exchange founded by the National Association of Securities Dealers).

Private corporations, in contrast, are created either wholly or in part for private benefit. Most corporations are private. Although they may serve a public purpose, as a public electric or gas utility does, they are owned by private persons rather than by the government.[2] (See this chapter's *Adapting the Law to the Online Environment* for a discussion of a new regulation that applies to private corporations that provide broadband services.)

Nonprofit Corporations
Corporations that are formed without a profit-making purpose are called *nonprofit* or *not-for-profit* corporations. Private hospitals, educational institutions, charities, and religious organizations, for instance, are frequently organized as nonprofit corporations. The nonprofit corporation is a convenient form of organization that allows various groups to own property and to form contracts without exposing the individual members to personal liability.

Close Corporations
Most corporate enterprises in the United States fall into the category of close corporations. A **close corporation** is one whose shares are held by relatively few persons, often members of a family. Close corporations are also referred to as *closely held, family,* or *privately held* corporations.

Usually, the members of the small group constituting a close corporation are personally known to one another. Because the number of shareholders is so small, there is no trading market for the shares. In practice, close corporations often operate somewhat like a partnership because the statutes in many states allow them to depart significantly from certain formalities required by traditional corporation law.[3]

Under the RMBCA, close corporations have considerable flexibility in determining their operating rules [RMBCA 7.32]. If all of a corporation's shareholders agree in writing, the corporation can operate without directors and bylaws. In addition, a close corporation need not

---

2. The United States Supreme Court first recognized the property rights of private corporations and clarified the distinction between public and private corporations in the landmark case *Trustees of Dartmouth College v. Woodward*, 17 U.S. (4 Wheaton) 518, 4 L.Ed. 629 (1819).

3. For example, in some states (such as Maryland), a close corporation need not have a board of directors.

ADAPTING THE LAW TO THE ONLINE ENVIRONMENT
Imposing a 1930s Regulatory Law on Broadband Operators

Since the advent of the Internet, it has remained largely unregulated. President Bill Clinton (1993–2001) said clearly and often that the Internet should remain lightly regulated, at most. During the Obama administration, however, pressure from the president himself applied to the Federal Communications Commission (FCC) started to change that thinking.

An Unsuccessful Attempt to Impose Regulation on Internet Service Providers

In 2010, under the authority of the Telecommunications Act of 1996,[a] the FCC attempted to regulate Internet service providers by enacting the "Open Internet Order." Under this order, the FCC would have required broadband Internet service providers to transfer data files equally, without consideration of the size or source of the files—so-called net

neutrality. The policy prohibited providers from transmitting certain content at slower speeds or higher costs than other types of content. Challenged in court, the order was overturned.[b]

The Advent of "Obamanet"

In early 2015, the FCC voted to regulate Internet service providers as "common carriers" under Title II of the Communications Act of 1934.[c] Normally, a common carrier is a business that transports things from one place to another, such as a trucking company. Under the Communications Act, this definition was widened to include telephone companies. Under the new FCC rules, the Internet would fall under the act as well. The new rules are still under discussion, and legal challenges are expected.

What the New FCC Rules Mean

Here is a summary of the new rules:

- No Internet provider can prevent a user from accessing "legal content, applications, services, or non-harmful devices" on the Internet. The goal to is prevent censorship and discrimination.

- No Internet provider can deliberately reduce the speed of data from particular sites or applications.

- No Internet service provider can charge content providers more to provide them with faster service.

CRITICAL THINKING

- Some observers predict that numerous lawsuits will be filed against the FCC in the immediate future. Why would this be likely?

---

a. 47 U.S.C. § 1302 (a), (b).

b. *Verizon v. Federal Trade Commission,* 740 F.3d 623 (D.C. Cir. 2014).

c. 47 U.S.C. Section 201, *et. seq.*

---

hold annual or special shareholders' or directors' meetings, issue stock certificates, or keep formal records of shareholders' and directors' decisions.[4]

Management of Close Corporations. Management of a close corporation resembles that of a sole proprietorship or a partnership in that a single shareholder or a tightly knit group of shareholders usually hold the positions of directors and officers. As a corporation, however, the firm must meet all specific legal requirements set forth in state statutes.

To prevent a majority shareholder from dominating a close corporation, a close corporation may require that more than a simple majority of the directors approve any action taken by the board. In a larger corporation, such a requirement would typically apply only to extraordinary actions (such as selling all the corporate assets) and not to ordinary business decisions.

Transfer of Shares in Close Corporations. By definition, a close corporation has a small number of shareholders. Thus, the transfer of one shareholder's shares to someone else can cause serious management problems. The other shareholders may find themselves required to share control with someone they do not know or like.

To avoid this situation, the corporation could restrict the transferability of shares to outside persons. Shareholders could be required to offer their shares to the corporation or the other

---

4. Shareholders cannot agree, however, to eliminate certain rights of shareholders, such as the right to inspect corporate books and records and the right to bring lawsuits on behalf of the corporation.

Three sisters own a car wash through a close corporation. Can they prevent one sister from selling her shares to outsiders?

shareholders before selling them to an outside purchaser. In fact, a few states have statutes that prohibit the transfer of close corporation shares unless certain persons—including shareholders, family members, and the corporation—are first given the opportunity to purchase the shares for the same price.

Misappropriation of Close Corporation Funds.

Sometimes, a majority shareholder in a close corporation takes advantage of his or her position and misappropriates company funds. In such situations, the normal remedy for the injured minority shareholders is to have their shares appraised and to be paid the fair market value for them.

CASE EXAMPLE 29.2 John Murray, Stephen Hopkins, and Paul Ryan were officers, directors, employees, and majority shareholders of Olympic Adhesives, Inc. Merek Rubin was a minority shareholder. Murray, Hopkins, and Ryan were paid salaries. Twice a year, they paid themselves additional compensation—between 75 and 98 percent of Olympic's net profits, allocated according to their stock ownership. Rubin filed a suit against the majority shareholders, alleging that their compensation deprived him of his share of Olympic's profits.

The court explained that a salary should reasonably relate to a corporate officer's ability and the quantity and quality of his or her services. The court found that a reasonable amount of compensation would have been 10 percent of Olympic's average annual net sales. Therefore, the additional compensation the majority shareholders paid themselves—based on stock ownership and not on performance—was excessive. The court ordered the defendants to repay Olympic nearly $6 million to be distributed among its shareholders. On appeal, the reviewing court affirmed this decision.[5] ■

S Corporations

A close corporation that meets the qualifying requirements specified in Subchapter S of the Internal Revenue Code can operate as an **S corporation.** (A corporation will automatically be taxed under Subchapter C unless it elects S corporation status.)

S Corporation A close business corporation that has most corporate attributes, including limited liability, but qualifies under the Internal Revenue Code to be taxed as a partnership.

If a corporation has S corporation status, it can avoid the imposition of income taxes at the corporate level while retaining many of the advantages of a corporation, particularly limited liability. Nevertheless, because the limited liability company and the limited liability partnership offer similar advantages and greater flexibility, the S corporation has lost much of its appeal in recent years.

Important Requirements.

Among the numerous requirements for S corporation status, the following are the most important:

1. The corporation must be a domestic corporation.
2. The corporation must not be a member of an affiliated group of corporations.
3. The shareholders must be individuals, estates, or certain trusts. Partnerships and nonqualifying trusts cannot be shareholders. Corporations can be shareholders under certain circumstances.
4. The corporation must have no more than one hundred shareholders.
5. The corporation must have only one class of stock, although all shareholders do not have to have the same voting rights.
6. No shareholder of the corporation may be a nonresident alien.

---

5. *Rubin v Murray*, 79 Mass.App.Ct. 64, 943 N.E.2d 949 (2011).

Tax Effects of the S Election. An S corporation is treated differently from a regular corporation for tax purposes. An S corporation is taxed like a partnership, so the corporate income passes through to the shareholders, who pay personal income tax on it.

This treatment enables the S corporation to avoid the double taxation that is imposed on regular corporations. In addition, the shareholders' tax brackets may be lower than the tax bracket that the corporation would have been in if the tax had been imposed at the corporate level. The resulting tax saving is particularly attractive when the corporation wants to accumulate earnings for some future business purpose. Furthermore, if the corporation has losses, the shareholders can use the losses to offset other taxable income.

Professional Corporations Professionals such as physicians, lawyers, dentists, and accountants can incorporate. Professional corporations typically are identified by the letters *S.C.* (service corporation), *P.C.* (professional corporation), or *P.A.* (professional association). In general, the laws governing the formation and operation of professional corporations are similar to those governing ordinary business corporations. There are some differences in terms of liability, however.

For liability purposes, some courts treat a professional corporation somewhat like a partnership and hold each professional liable for any malpractice committed by others in the firm within the scope of the firm's business. With the exception of malpractice or a breach of duty to clients or patients, a shareholder in a professional corporation generally cannot be held liable for torts committed by other professionals at the firm.

Benefit Corporations A growing number of states have enacted legislation that creates a new corporate form called a *benefit corporation*. A **benefit corporation** is a for-profit corporation that seeks to have a material positive impact on society and the environment. Benefit corporations differ from traditional corporations in the following ways:

1. *Purpose.* Although the corporation is designed to make a profit, its purpose is to benefit the public as a whole (rather than just to provide long-term shareholder value, as in ordinary corporations). The directors of a benefit corporation must, during the decision-making process, consider the impact of their decisions on society and the environment.

2. *Accountability.* Shareholders of a benefit corporation determine whether the company has achieved a material positive impact. Shareholders also have a right of private action, called a *benefit enforcement proceeding,* enabling them to sue the corporation if it fails to pursue or create public benefit.

3. *Transparency.* A benefit corporation must issue an annual benefit report on its overall social and environmental performance that uses a recognized third-party standard to assess its performance. The report must be delivered to the shareholders and posted on a public Web site.

KNOW THIS
The shareholders of professional corporations generally must be licensed professionals.

Benefit Corporation A for-profit corporation that seeks to have a material positive impact on society and the environment. It is available by statute in a number of states.

29-2 Formation and Financing

Many Fortune 500 companies started as sole proprietorships or partnerships and then converted to corporate entities as the businesses grew. Incorporating a business is much simpler today than it was twenty years ago, and many states allow businesses to incorporate via the Internet.

29-2a Promotional Activities

In the past, preliminary steps were taken to organize and promote a business prior to incorporating. Contracts were made with investors and others on behalf of the future corporation.

"A man to carry on a successful business must have imagination. He must see things as in a vision, a dream of the whole thing."

CHARLES M. SCHWAB
1862–1939
(AMERICAN INDUSTRIALIST)

Today, due to the relative ease of forming a corporation in most states, persons incorporating a business rarely, if ever, engage in preliminary promotional activities. Nevertheless, businesspersons need to understand that they are personally liable for any preincorporation contracts made with investors, accountants, or others on behalf of the future corporation. Liability continues until the corporation is formed and explicitly assumes the contract by novation.

29–2b Incorporation Procedures

LEARNING OBJECTIVE 2
What four steps are involved in bringing a corporation into existence?

Each state has its own set of incorporation procedures, which most often are listed on the secretary of state's Web site. Generally, however, all incorporators follow several basic steps, discussed next.

Select the State of Incorporation Because state corporation laws differ, individuals may look for the states that offer the most advantageous tax or other provisions. Many corporations, for instance, have chosen to incorporate in Delaware because it has historically had the least restrictive laws, along with provisions that favor corporate management. For reasons of convenience and cost, though, businesses often choose to incorporate in the state in which the corporation's business will primarily be conducted.

Secure the Corporate Name The choice of a corporate name is subject to state approval to ensure against duplication or deception. Most state statutes require a search to confirm that the chosen corporate name is available. A new corporation's name cannot be the same as, or deceptively similar to, the name of an existing corporation doing business within the state. All states require the corporation name to include the word *Corporation, Incorporated, Company,* or *Limited,* or an abbreviation of one of these terms. If the corporation will have a Web site, a domain name search should be included to ensure the name's availability and avoid trade name infringement.

Articles of Incorporation The document that is filed with the appropriate state official, usually the secretary of state, when a business is incorporated and that contains basic information about the corporation

Prepare the Articles of Incorporation The primary document needed to incorporate a business is the **articles of incorporation.** The articles serve as a primary source of authority for its future organization and business functions.

Basic Information. The articles must include the corporation's name, the number of shares it is authorized to issue, and the name and address of its initial *registered agent* (the person designated to receive legal documents on its behalf). The articles must also include the names and addresses of the *incorporators* (the persons who sign the articles to form the corporation). Other information can be included as well, such as the names and addresses of the initial members of the board of directors and the duration and purpose of the corporation. The articles can also describe the internal structure of the corporation, although this is usually included in the *bylaws,* discussed shortly.

Duration and Purpose. Unless the articles state otherwise, a corporation has perpetual existence. The RMBCA does not require a specific statement of purpose to be included in the articles. A corporation can be formed for any lawful purpose. Some incorporators choose to specify the intended business activities (such as "to engage in the production and sale of agricultural products"). More often, though, the articles include only a general statement of purpose. They may indicate that the corporation is organized for "any legal business." By not mentioning specifics, the corporation avoids the need for future amendments to the corporate articles [RMBCA 2.02(b)(2)(i), 3.01].

File the Articles of Incorporation Once the articles of incorporation have been prepared and signed by the incorporators, they are sent to the appropriate state official. They are most often filed with the secretary of state's office, along with the required filing fee. In most states, the secretary of state then stamps the articles as "Filed" and returns a copy of the articles to the incorporators. Once this occurs, the corporation officially exists.

29-2c First Organizational Meeting to Adopt Bylaws

After incorporation, the first organizational meeting must be held. If the articles of incorporation named the initial board of directors, then the directors, by majority vote, call the meeting. If the articles did not name the directors (as is typical), then the incorporators hold the meeting to elect the directors and complete any other business necessary.

Usually, the most important function of the first organizational meeting is the adoption of the **bylaws,** which are the corporation's internal rules of management. The bylaws cannot conflict with the state corporation statute or the articles of incorporation [RMBCA 2.06].

Under the RMBCA, the shareholders may amend or repeal the bylaws. The board of directors may also amend or repeal the bylaws, unless the articles of incorporation or provisions of the state corporation statute reserve this power to the shareholders exclusively [RMBCA 10.20]. Typical bylaw provisions describe such matters as voting requirements for shareholders, the election and replacement of the board of directors, and the manner and time of holding shareholders' and board meetings.

29-2d Improper Incorporation

The procedures for incorporation are very specific. If they are not followed precisely, others may be able to challenge the existence of the corporation. Errors in the incorporation procedures can become important when, for instance, a third party who is attempting to enforce a contract or bring a suit for a tort injury learns of them.

De Jure Corporations If a corporation has substantially complied with all conditions precedent to incorporation, the corporation is said to have *de jure* (rightful and lawful) existence. In most states and under the RMBCA 2.03(b), the secretary of state's filing of the articles of incorporation is conclusive proof that all mandatory statutory provisions have been met.

Sometimes, the incorporators fail to comply with all statutory mandates. If the defect is minor, such as an incorrect address listed on the articles of incorporation, most courts will overlook the defect and find that a *de jure* corporation exists.

De Facto Corporations If a defect in formation is substantial, such as a corporation's failure to hold an organizational meeting to adopt bylaws, the outcome will vary depending on the court. Some states, including Mississippi, New York, Ohio, and Oklahoma, recognize the common law doctrine of *de facto* corporation.[6] In those states, the courts will treat a corporation as a legal corporation despite the defect in its formation if all three of the following requirements are met:

1. A state statute exists under which the corporation can be validly incorporated.

2. The parties have made a good faith attempt to comply with the statute.

3. The parties have already undertaken to do business as a corporation.

Many states courts, however, have interpreted their states' versions of the RMBCA as abolishing the common law doctrine of *de facto* corporations. These states include Alaska, Arizona, Minnesota, New Mexico, Oregon, South Dakota, Tennessee, Utah, and Washington, as well

What are the routine aspects of forming a corporation?

Bylaws The internal rules of management adopted by a corporation at its first organizational meeting.

KNOW THIS

Unlike the articles of incorporation, bylaws do not need to be filed with a state official.

---

6. See, for example, *In re Hausman*, 13 N.Y.3d 408, 921 N.E.2d 191, 893 N.Y.S.2d 499 (2009); and *Roka LLC v. Lam*, 2014 WL 4312931 (N.Y.Sup.Ct. 2014).

as the District of Columbia. In those states, if there is a substantial defect in complying with the statutory mandates, the corporation does not legally exist, and the incorporators are personally liable.

Corporation by Estoppel Sometimes, a business association holds itself out to others as being a corporation when it has made no attempt to incorporate. In those situations, the firm normally will be estopped (prevented) from denying corporate status in a lawsuit by a third party. The estoppel doctrine most commonly applies when a third party contracts with an entity that claims to be a corporation but has not filed articles of incorporation. It may also be applied when a third party contracts with a person claiming to be an agent of a corporation that does not in fact exist.

When justice requires, the courts treat an alleged corporation as if it were an actual corporation for the purpose of determining the rights and liabilities in a particular circumstance. Recognition of corporate status does not extend beyond the resolution of the problem at hand.

CASE EXAMPLE 29.3 W.P. Media, Inc., and Alabama MBA, Inc., agreed to form a wireless Internet services company. W.P. Media was to create a wireless network, and Alabama MBA was to contribute the capital. Hugh Brown signed the parties' contract on behalf of Alabama MBA as the chair of its board. At the time, however, Alabama MBA's articles of incorporation had not yet been filed. Brown filed the articles of incorporation the following year. Later, Brown and Alabama MBA filed a suit alleging that W.P. Media had breached their contract by not building the wireless network. The Supreme Court of Alabama held that because W.P. Media had treated Alabama MBA as a corporation, W.P. Media was estopped from denying Alabama MBA's corporate existence.[7] ◼

What might be the consequences of a wireless company's failing to timely file incorporation papers?

29–2e Corporate Financing

Part of the process of corporate formation involves financing. Corporations normally are financed by the issuance and sale of corporate securities. **Securities**—stocks and bonds—evidence the right to participate in earnings and the distribution of corporate property or the obligation to pay funds. The ways in which stocks and bonds differ are summarized in Exhibit 29–1.

Securities Generally, stocks, bonds, or other items that represent an ownership interest in a corporation or a promise of repayment of debt by a corporation.

Bond A security that evidences a corporate (or government) debt.

Bonds Bonds (*debentures* or *debt securities*) represent the borrowing of funds. Bonds are issued by business firms and by governments at all levels as evidence of the funds they are borrowing from investors.

Bonds normally have a designated *maturity date*—the date when the principal, or face, amount of the bond is returned to the bondholder. Bondholders also receive fixed-dollar interest payments, usually semiannually, during the period of time before maturity. For that reason, bonds are sometimes referred to as *fixed-income securities*. Because debt financing represents a legal obligation on the part of the corporation, various features and terms of a particular bond issue are specified in a lending agreement.

Of course, not all debt is in the form of debt securities. For instance, some debt is in the form of accounts payable and notes payable, which typically are short-term debts. Bonds are simply a way for the corporation to split up its long-term debt so that it can be more easily marketed.

"Gentlemen prefer bonds."

ANDREW MELLON
1855–1937
(AMERICAN BANKER)

Stock An ownership (equity) interest in a corporation, measured in units of shares.

Stocks Issuing stock is another way that corporations can obtain financing. **Stocks,** or *equity securities,* represent the purchase of ownership in the business firm. Two major types of stock are common stock and preferred stock.

---

7. *Brown v. W.P. Media, Inc.,* 17 So.3d 1167 (Ala. Sup.Ct. 2009).

Exhibit 29–1 How Do Stocks and Bonds Differ?

STOCKS	BONDS
1. Stocks represent ownership.	**1.** Bonds represent debt.
2. Stocks (common) do not have a fixed dividend rate.	**2.** Interest on bonds must always be paid, whether or not any profit is earned.
3. Stockholders can elect the board of directors, which controls the corporation.	**3.** Bondholders usually have no voice in, or control over, management of the corporation.
4. Stocks do not have a maturity date. The corporation usually does not repay the stockholder.	**4.** Bonds have a maturity date, when the corporation is to repay the bondholder the face value of the bond.
5. All corporations issue or offer to sell stocks. This is the usual definition of a corporation.	**5.** Corporations do not necessarily issue bonds.
6. Stockholders have a claim against the property and income of a corporation after all creditors' claims have been met.	**6.** Bondholders have a claim against the property and income of a corporation that must be met *before* the claims of stockholders.

Common Stock. The true ownership of a corporation is represented by **common stock.** Common stock provides a proportionate interest in the corporation with regard to (1) control (voting rights), (2) earnings, and (3) net assets. A shareholder's interest is generally in proportion to the number of shares he or she owns out of the total number of shares issued.

An issuing firm is not obligated to return a principal amount per share to each holder of its common stock, nor does the firm have to guarantee a dividend. Indeed, some corporations never pay dividends. Holders of common stock are investors who assume a *residual* position in the overall financial structure of a business. They benefit when the market price of the stock increases. In terms of receiving payment for their investments, they are last in line.

> **Common Stock** Shares of ownership in a corporation that give the owner a proportionate interest in the corporation with regard to control, earnings, and net assets. Common stock is lowest in priority with respect to payment of dividends and distribution of the corporation's assets on dissolution.

Preferred Stock. **Preferred stock** is stock with *preferences.* Usually, this means that holders of preferred stock have priority over holders of common stock as to dividends and payment on dissolution of the corporation. Holders of preferred stock may or may not have the right to vote.

Holders of preferred stock have a stronger position than common shareholders with respect to dividends and claims on assets, but they will not share in the full prosperity of the firm if it grows successfully over time. Preferred stockholders do receive fixed dividends periodically, however, and they may benefit to some extent from changes in the market price of the shares.

> **Preferred Stock** Stock that has priority over common stock as to payment of dividends and distribution of assets on the corporation's dissolution.

Venture Capital Start-up businesses and high-risk enterprises often obtain venture capital financing. **Venture capital** is capital provided to new business ventures by professional, outside investors (*venture capitalists,* usually groups of wealthy investors and securities firms). Venture capital investments are high risk—the investors must be willing to lose their invested funds—but offer the potential for well-above-average returns at some point in the future.

To obtain venture capital financing, the start-up business typically gives up a share of its ownership to the venture capitalists. In addition to funding, venture capitalists may provide managerial and technical expertise, and they nearly always are given some control over the new company's decisions. Many Internet-based companies, such as Amazon and Google, were initially financed by venture capital.

> **Venture Capital** Financing provided by professional, outside investors (venture capitalists) to new business ventures.

Private Equity Capital Private equity firms pool funds from wealthy investors and use this **private equity capital** to invest in existing corporations. Usually, a private equity firm buys an entire corporation and then reorganizes it. Sometimes, divisions of the purchased company are sold off to pay down debt. Ultimately, the private equity firm may sell shares in the reorganized (and perhaps more profitable) company to the public in an *initial public offering*

> **Private Equity Capital** Funds invested by a private equity firm in an existing corporation, usually to purchase and reorganize it.

(IPO). In this way, the private equity firm can make profits by selling its ownership rights in the company to the public.

Crowdfunding

Start-up businesses can also attempt to obtain financing through *crowdfunding*. **Crowdfunding** is a cooperative activity in which people network and pool funds and other resources via the Internet to assist a cause or invest in a venture. Sometimes, crowdfunding is used to raise funds for charitable purposes, such as disaster relief, but increasingly it is being used to finance budding entrepreneurs. In 2013, the Securities and Exchange Commission removed a decades-old ban on public solicitation for private investments. In essence, this means that companies can advertise investment opportunities to the public, which will encourage more crowdfunding in the future.

Crowdfunding A cooperative activity in which people network and pool funds and other resources via the Internet to assist a cause (such as disaster relief) or invest in a venture (business).

29-2f Termination

Although corporations normally have perpetual existence, they can be dissolved, or terminated, voluntarily by the directors and shareholders. State corporation statutes establish the procedures required to voluntarily dissolve a corporation, but basically, there are two possible methods:

1. By the shareholders' unanimous vote to initiate dissolution proceedings.

2. By a proposal of the board of directors that is submitted to the shareholders at a shareholders' meeting.

The state can also dissolve a corporation in certain circumstances, such as when the controlling shareholders or directors have engaged in fraudulent, illegal, or oppressive conduct.

The termination of a corporation's existence has two phases—dissolution and winding up. *Dissolution* is the legal death of the artificial "person" of the corporation. *Winding up* is the process by which corporate assets are liquidated, or converted into cash and distributed among creditors and shareholders. Usually, the members of the board of directors act are responsible for winding up the affairs of the corporation for the benefit of corporate creditors and shareholders. When the dissolution is involuntary, a court will appoint a **receiver** to wind up the corporate affairs and liquidate corporate assets.

Receiver In a corporate dissolution, a court-appointed person who winds up corporate affairs and liquidates corporate assets.

29-3 Corporate Powers

When a corporation is created, the express and implied powers necessary to achieve its purpose also come into existence. Corporations cannot engage in acts that are beyond their powers, nor can a corporation's owners (shareholders) avoid liability if they misuse the corporate entity for their own personal benefit.

29-3a Express Powers

The express powers of a corporation are found in its articles of incorporation, in the law of the state of incorporation, and in the state and federal constitutions. Corporate bylaws also establish the express powers of the corporation. Because state corporation statutes frequently provide default rules that apply if the company's bylaws are silent on an issue, it is important that the bylaws set forth the specific operating rules of the corporation. In addition, after the bylaws are adopted, the corporation's board of directors will pass resolutions that grant or restrict corporate powers.

29-3b Implied Powers

When a corporation is created, it acquires certain implied powers. Barring express constitutional, statutory, or other prohibitions, the corporation has the implied power to perform all acts reasonably appropriate and necessary to accomplish its corporate purposes. For this reason, a corporation has the implied power to borrow funds within certain limits, to lend funds, and to extend credit to those with whom it has a legal or contractual relationship.

Most often, the president or chief executive officer of the corporation will execute the necessary papers on behalf of the corporation. In so doing, corporate officers have the implied power to bind the corporation in matters directly connected with the *ordinary* business affairs of the enterprise. There is a limit to what a corporate officer can do, though. A corporate officer does not have the authority to bind the corporation to an action that will greatly affect the corporate purpose or undertaking, such as the sale of substantial corporate assets.

29–3c *Ultra Vires* Doctrine

The term *ultra vires* means "beyond the powers." In corporate law, acts of a corporation that are beyond its express and implied powers are **ultra vires acts.**

Nature of *Ultra Vires* Acts
In the past, most cases dealing with *ultra vires* acts involved contracts made for unauthorized purposes. Now, however, most private corporations are organized for "any legal business" and not for a specific purpose, so the *ultra vires* doctrine has declined in importance.

Today, cases that allege *ultra vires* acts usually involve nonprofit corporations or municipal (public) corporations. **CASE EXAMPLE 29.4** Four men formed a nonprofit corporation to create the Armenian Genocide Museum & Memorial (AGM&M). The bylaws appointed them as trustees (similar to corporate directors) for life. One of the trustees, Gerard L. Cafesjian, became the chair and president of AGM&M. Eventually, the relationship among the trustees deteriorated, and Cafesjian resigned.

The corporation then brought a suit claiming that Cafesjian had engaged in *ultra vires* acts, self-dealing, and mismanagement. Although the bylaws required an 80 percent affirmative vote of the trustees to take action, Cafesjian had taken many actions without the board's approval. He had also entered into contracts for real estate transactions in which he had a personal interest. Because Cafesjian had taken actions that exceeded his authority and had failed to follow the rules in the bylaws for board meetings, the court ruled that the corporation could go forward with its suit.[8] ∎

Remedies for *Ultra Vires* Acts
Under Section 3.04 of the RMBCA, shareholders can seek an injunction from a court to prevent (or stop) the corporation from engaging in *ultra vires* acts. The attorney general in the state of incorporation can also bring an action to obtain an injunction against the *ultra vires* transactions or to institute dissolution proceedings against the corporation on the basis of *ultra vires* acts. The corporation or its shareholders (on behalf of the corporation) can seek damages from the officers and directors who were responsible for the *ultra vires* acts.

29–3d Piercing the Corporate Veil

Occasionally, the owners use a corporate entity to perpetrate a fraud, circumvent the law, or in some other way accomplish an illegitimate objective. In these situations, the court will ignore the corporate structure by **piercing the corporate veil** and exposing the shareholders to personal liability.

Generally, courts pierce the veil when the corporate privilege is abused for personal benefit or when the corporate business is treated so carelessly that it is indistinguishable from that of a controlling shareholder. In short, when the facts show that great injustice would result from a shareholder's use of a corporation to avoid individual responsibility, a court will look behind

Ultra Vires Acts Acts of a corporation that are beyond its express and implied powers to undertake (the Latin phrase means "beyond the powers").

How could one of the trustees of a nonprofit corporation created to build a memorial engage in *ultra vires* acts?

Piercing the Corporate Veil The action of a court to disregard the corporate entity and hold the shareholders personally liable for corporate debts and obligations.

---

8. *Armenian Assembly of America, Inc. v. Cafesjian*, 692 F.Supp.2d 20 (D.C. 2010).

LEARNING OBJECTIVE 3

In what circumstances might a court disregard the corporate entity ("pierce the corporate veil") and hold the shareholders personally liable?

Commingle To put funds or goods together into one mass so that they are mixed to such a degree that they no longer have separate identities.

the corporate structure to the individual shareholder. The shareholder/owner is then required to assume personal liability to creditors for the corporation's debts.

Factors That Lead Courts to Pierce the Corporate Veil The following are some of the factors that frequently cause the courts to pierce the corporate veil:

1. A party is tricked or misled into dealing with the corporation rather than the individual.

2. The corporation is set up never to make a profit or always to be insolvent, or it is too thinly capitalized—that is, it has insufficient capital at the time of formation to meet its prospective debts or other potential liabilities.

3. Statutory corporate formalities, such as holding required corporation meetings, are not followed.

4. Personal and corporate interests are **commingled** to such an extent that the corporation has no separate identity.

The court looked for these factors in the circumstances of the following case.

CASE 29.2

Dog House Investments, LLC v. Teal Properties, Inc.

Court of Appeals of Tennessee, 448 S.W.3d 905 (2014).

FACTS Dog House Investments, LLC, operated a dog "camp" in Nashville, Tennessee. Dog House leased the property from Teal Properties, Inc., which was owned by Jerry Teal, its sole shareholder. Under the lease, the landlord promised to repair damage from fire or other causes that rendered the property "untenantable" (unusable). Following a flood, Dog House notified Jerry that the property was untenantable. Jerry assured Dog House that the flood damage was covered by insurance but took no steps to restore the property. The parties then agreed that Dog House would undertake the repairs and be reimbursed by Teal Properties.

Dog House spent $39,000 to repair the damage and submitted invoices for reimbursement. Teal Properties recovered $40,000 from its insurance company but did not pay Dog House. Close to bankruptcy, Dog House filed a suit in a Tennessee state court against Teal Properties and Jerry. The court held Jerry personally liable for the repair costs. Jerry appealed.

ISSUE Should the court pierce the corporate veil of Teal Properties to accomplish justice for Dog House?

DECISION Yes. A state intermediate appellate court affirmed the lower court's decision. Dog House had not been reimbursed for the cost to repair the flood damage, as Jerry promised.

If a leased property for dog kennels floods, what is the landlord's responsibility?

REASON When determining whether piercing a corporate veil is appropriate, the first consideration is whether the corporation has been used to perpetrate a fraud or otherwise commit an injustice. Factors that indicate a corporation is a "sham" or "dummy" corporation include (1) an investment of insufficient capital in the corporation, (2) the sole ownership of its stock by one individual, (3) its use as a conduit for the personal dealings of an individual, and (4) the failure of the owner to maintain an arm's-length relationship with the corporation.

In this case, neither Teal Properties nor Jerry had repaid Dog House for the funds it spent to repair the flood damage to the leased property. Jerry was the sole shareholder of Teal Properties, which had no purpose other than to collect the rent on properties that he owned. Teal Properties itself owned no property or other assets, and the cash it received from rent payments—and, in this case, insurance proceeds—were disbursed immediately to meet Jerry's personal financial obligations. Thus, Jerry "did not maintain an arm's-length relationship with the corporation," and was personally liable to Dog House for the cost of the property repairs.

CRITICAL THINKING—Ethical Consideration *The failure of Teal Properties and Jerry to reimburse the tenant, Dog House, for the repair costs placed Dog House in a dire financial situation. Does this consequence make the landlord's conduct unethical? Discuss.*

A Potential Problem for Close Corporations The potential for corporate assets to be used for personal benefit is especially great in a close corporation. In such a corporation, the separate status of the corporate entity and the shareholders must be carefully preserved. Certain practices invite trouble for a close corporation, such as the commingling of corporate and personal funds or the shareholders' continuous personal use of corporate property (for instance, vehicles).

29-4 Directors and Officers

Corporate directors and officers play different roles in the corporation. In this section, we look first at the role of directors, then at the role of officers, and finally at the duties and liabilities of directors and officers.

29-4a The Role of Directors

The board of directors is the ultimate authority in every corporation. Directors have responsibility for all policymaking decisions necessary to the management of corporate affairs. The board selects and removes the corporate officers, determines the capital structure of the corporation, and declares dividends.

Directors are sometimes inappropriately characterized as *agents* because they act on behalf of the corporation. No *individual* director, however, can act as an agent to bind the corporation. As a group, directors collectively control the corporation in a way that no agent is able to control a principal.

Few qualifications are legally required for directors. Only a handful of states impose minimum age and residency requirements. A director may be a shareholder, but this is not necessary (unless the articles of incorporation or bylaws require it).

Election of Directors Subject to statutory limitations, the number of directors is set forth in the corporation's articles or bylaws. Historically, the minimum number of directors has been three, but today many states permit fewer. Normally, the incorporators appoint the first board of directors at the time the corporation is created. The initial board serves until the first annual shareholders' meeting. Subsequent directors are elected by a majority vote of the shareholders.

Directors usually serve for a term of one year—from annual meeting to annual meeting. Most state statutes permit longer and staggered terms. A common practice is to elect one-third of the board members each year for a three-year term. In this way, there is greater management continuity.

A director can be removed *for cause*—that is, for failing to perform a required duty—either as specified in the articles or bylaws or by shareholder action. When a vacancy occurs or a new position is created through amendment of the articles or bylaws, how the vacancy is filled depends on state law or the provisions of the bylaws. Usually, either the shareholders or the board itself can fill the vacant position by an election. The board cannot attempt to manipulate the election in order to reduce the shareholders' influence, however. If it does, the shareholders can challenge the election in court.

KNOW THIS
The articles of incorporation may provide that a director can be removed only for cause.

Compensation of Directors In the past, corporate directors rarely were compensated. Today, they are often paid at least nominal sums and may receive more substantial compensation in large corporations because of the time, the work, the effort, and especially the risk involved. Most states permit the corporate articles or bylaws to authorize compensation for directors. In fact, the RMBCA states that unless the articles or bylaws provide otherwise, the board of directors itself may set directors' compensation [RMBCA 8.11].

In many corporations, directors are also chief corporate officers (president or chief executive officer, for example) and receive compensation in their managerial positions. A director who is also an officer of the corporation is referred to as an **inside director,** whereas a director who does not hold a management position is an **outside director.** Typically, a corporation's board of directors includes both inside and outside directors.

Inside Director A person on the board of directors who is also an officer of the corporation.

Outside Director A person on the board of directors who does not hold a management position at the corporation.

Board of Directors' Meetings

The board of directors conducts business by holding formal meetings with recorded minutes. The dates of regular meetings are usually established in the articles or bylaws or by board resolution, and ordinarily no further notice is required. Special meetings can be called as well, with notice sent to all directors. Today, most states allow directors to participate in board meetings from remote locations via telephone, Web conferencing, or Skype, provided that all the directors can simultaneously hear each other during the meeting [RMBCA 8.20].

Normally, a majority of the board of directors constitutes a quorum [RMBCA 8.24]. (A **quorum** is the minimum number of members of a body of officials or other group that must be present in order for business to be validly transacted.) Some state statutes specifically allow corporations to set a quorum at less than a majority but not less than one-third of the directors.[9]

Quorum The number of members of a decision-making body that must be present before business may be transacted.

Once a quorum is present, the directors transact business and vote on issues affecting the corporation. Each director present at the meeting has one vote.[10] Ordinary matters generally require a simple majority vote, but certain extraordinary issues may require a greater-than-majority vote.

Committees of the Board of Directors

When a board of directors has a large number of members and must deal with myriad complex business issues, meetings can become unwieldy. Therefore, the boards of large publicly held corporations typically create committees of directors and delegate certain tasks to these committees. Committees focus on individual subjects and increase the efficiency of the board.

Two of the most common types of committees are the *executive committee* and the *audit committee.* An executive committee handles interim management decisions between board meetings. It is limited to making decisions about ordinary business matters and does not have the power to declare dividends, amend the bylaws, or authorize the issuance of stock. The Sarbanes-Oxley Act requires all publicly held corporations to have an audit committee. The audit committee is responsible for the selection, compensation, and oversight of the independent public accountants that audit the firm's financial records.

> "Executive ability is deciding quickly and getting somebody else to do the work."
>
> **J. C. POLLARD**
> 1946–PRESENT
> (BRITISH BUSINESSMAN)

Rights of Directors

A corporate director must have certain rights to function properly in that position and make informed policy decisions for the company. The *right to participation* means that directors are entitled to participate in all board of directors' meetings and to be notified of these meetings. Because the dates of regular board meetings are usually specified in the bylaws, as noted earlier, no notice of these meetings is required. If special meetings are called, however, notice is required unless waived by the director.

A director also has the *right of inspection*, which means that each director can access the corporation's books and records, facilities, and premises. Inspection rights are essential for directors to make informed decisions and to exercise the necessary supervision over corporate officers and employees. This right of inspection is almost absolute and cannot be restricted (by the articles, bylaws, or any act of the board).

hxdbzxy/ShutterStock.com

What are the two most common committees that a board of directors of a large corporation creates?

---

9. See, for example, Delaware Code Annotated Title 8, Section 141(b); and New York Business Corporation Law Section 707.
10. Except in Louisiana, which allows a director to authorize another person to cast a vote in his or her place under certain circumstances.

When a director becomes involved in litigation by virtue of her or his position or actions, the director may also have a *right to indemnification* (reimbursement) for legal costs, fees, and damages incurred. Most states allow corporations to indemnify and purchase liability insurance for corporate directors [RMBCA 8.51].

PREVENTING LEGAL DISPUTES

Whenever businesspersons serve as corporate directors or officers, they may at some point become involved in litigation as a result of their positions. To protect against personal liability, directors or officers should take several steps. First, they should make sure that the corporate bylaws explicitly give them a right to indemnification (reimbursement) for any costs incurred as a result of litigation, as well as for any judgments or settlements. Second, they should have the corporation purchase directors' and officers' liability insurance (D&O insurance). Having D&O insurance enables the corporation to avoid paying the substantial costs involved in defending a particular director or officer. The D&O policies offered by most insurance companies have maximum coverage limits. It is therefore important to make sure that directors and officers will be indemnified in the event that the costs exceed the policy limits.

29–4b The Role of Corporate Officers and Executives

Corporate officers and other executive employees are hired by the board of directors. At a minimum, most corporations have a president, one or more vice presidents, a secretary, and a treasurer. In most states, an individual can hold more than one office, such as president and secretary, and can be both an officer and a director of the corporation. In addition to carrying out the duties articulated in the bylaws, corporate and managerial officers act as agents of the corporation, and the ordinary rules of agency normally apply to their employment.

Corporate officers and other high-level managers are employees of the company, so their rights are defined by employment contracts. The board of directors, though, normally can remove corporate officers at any time with or without cause and regardless of the terms of the employment contracts. The corporation may be liable for breach of contract if an officer's removal violated his or her employment contract, however.

29–4c Duties and Liabilities of Directors and Officers

Directors and officers are deemed fiduciaries of the corporation because their relationship with the corporation and its shareholders is one of trust and confidence. As fiduciaries, directors and officers owe ethical—and legal—duties to the corporation and to the shareholders as a whole. These fiduciary duties include the duty of care and the duty of loyalty.

Duty of Care   Directors and officers must exercise due care in performing their duties. The standard of due care generally requires a director or officer to act in good faith (honestly) and to exercise the care that an ordinarily prudent person would exercise in similar circumstances. In addition, a director or officer is expected to act in what he or she considers to be the best interests of the corporation [RMBCA 8.30]. Directors and officers whose failure to exercise due care results in harm to the corporation or its shareholders can be held liable for negligence (unless the *business judgment rule* applies, as discussed shortly).

Duty to Make Informed and Reasonable Decisions.   Directors and officers are expected to be informed on corporate matters and to conduct a reasonable investigation of the relevant situation before making a decision. They must do what is necessary to keep adequately informed: attend meetings and presentations, ask for information from those who have it, read reports, and review other written materials. They cannot decide on the spur of the moment without adequate research.

KNOW THIS
Shareholders own the corporation, and directors make policy decisions, but the officers who run the corporation's daily business often have significant decision-making power.

LEARNING OBJECTIVE 4
What are the duties of corporate directors and officers?

Business Judgment Rule
A rule under which courts will
not hold corporate officers and
directors liable for honest mistakes
of judgment and bad business
decisions that were made in good
faith.

Although directors and officers are expected to act in accordance with their own knowledge and training, they are also normally entitled to rely on information given to them by certain other persons. Most states and Section 8.30(b) of the RMBCA allow a director to make decisions in reliance on information furnished by competent officers or employees. The director may also rely on information provided by professionals (such as attorneys and accountants) and by committees of the board of directors (on which the director does not serve).

Duty to Exercise Reasonable Supervision. Directors are also expected to exercise a reasonable amount of supervision when they delegate work to corporate officers and employees. **EXAMPLE 29.5** Dale, a corporate bank director, has not attended a board of directors' meetings for five years. In addition, Dale never inspects any of the corporate books or records and generally fails to supervise the efforts of the bank president and the loan committee. Meanwhile, Brennan, the bank president, makes various improper loans and permits large overdrafts. In this situation, Dale can be held liable to the corporation for losses resulting from the unsupervised actions of the bank president and the loan committee. ■

The Business Judgment Rule. Directors and officers are expected to exercise due care and to use their best judgment in guiding corporate management, but they are not insurers of business success. Under the **business judgment rule,** a corporate director or officer will not be liable to the corporation or to its shareholders for honest mistakes of judgment or bad business decisions.

Courts give significant deference to the decisions of corporate directors and officers, and consider the reasonableness of a decision at the time it was made, *without the benefit of hindsight*. Thus, corporate decision makers are not subjected to second-guessing by shareholders or others in the corporation. The business judgment rule will apply as long as the director or officer did the following:

1. Took reasonable steps to become informed about the matter.
2. Had a rational basis for his or her decision.
3. Did not have a conflict of interest between his or her personal interest and that of the corporation.

In fact, if there is a reasonable basis for a business decision, a court is unlikely to interfere with that decision, even if the corporation suffers as a result. The business judgment rule does not apply, however, when a director engages in fraud, dishonesty, or other intentional or reckless misconduct.

CASE EXAMPLE 29.6 The board of directors of the Chugach Alaska Corporation (CAC) voted to remove Sheri Buretta as the chair and install Robert Henrichs. During his term, Henrichs acted without board approval, made decisions with only his supporters present, retaliated against directors who challenged his decisions, and ignored board rules for conducting meetings. Henrichs refused to comply with bylaws that required a special shareholders' meeting in response to a shareholder petition and personally mistreated directors, shareholders, and employees.

After six months, the board voted to reinstall Buretta. CAC filed a suit in an Alaska state court against Henrichs, alleging a breach of fiduciary duty. A jury found Henrichs liable, and the court barred him from serving on CAC's board for five years. The appellate court affirmed. Given the nature and seriousness of Henrichs's misconduct, the business judgment rule did not protect him.[11] ■

Duty of Loyalty *Loyalty* can be defined as faithfulness to one's obligations and duties. In the corporate context, the duty of loyalty requires directors and officers to subordinate their

---

11. *Henrichs v. Chugach Alaska Corp.,* 250 P.3d 531 (Alaska Sup.Ct. 2011).

personal interests to the welfare of the corporation. Directors cannot use corporate funds or confidential corporate information for personal advantage and must refrain from self-dealing. For instance, a director should not personally take advantage of a business opportunity that is offered to the corporation and is in the corporation's best interest.

Cases dealing with the duty of loyalty typically involve one or more of the following:

1. Competing with the corporation.

2. Usurping (taking advantage of) a corporate opportunity.

3. Having an interest that conflicts with the interest of the corporation.

4. Engaging in insider trading (using information that is not public to make a profit trading securities).

5. Authorizing a corporate transaction that is detrimental to minority shareholders.

6. Selling control over the corporation.

The following *Classic Case* illustrates the conflict that can arise between a corporate official's personal interest and his or her duty of loyalty.

★★★ CLASSIC CASE 29.3 ★★★

Guth v. Loft, Inc.
Supreme Court of Delaware, 23 Del.Ch. 255, 5 A.2d 503 (1939).

HISTORICAL SETTING *In the 1920s, Loft Candy Company (Loft, Inc.), based in Long Island City, New York, was a publicly held company with a $13 million candy-and-restaurant chain. The company manufactured its own candies, syrups, and beverages and sold its products in its more than one hundred retail locations throughout the Northeast. In 1930, Charles Guth became Loft's president after a contentious stockholders' meeting. His position there set the stage for the rise of the soft drink Pepsi-Cola.*

Pepsi-Cola got its start when the head of Loft Candy Company usurped a corporate opportunity.

FACTS At the time Charles Guth became Loft's president, Guth and his family owned Grace Company, which made syrups for soft drinks in a plant in Baltimore, Maryland. Coca-Cola Company supplied Loft with cola syrup. Unhappy with what he felt was Coca-Cola's high price, Guth entered into an agreement with Roy Megargel to acquire the trademark and formula for Pepsi-Cola and form Pepsi-Cola Corporation.

Neither Guth nor Megargel could finance the new venture, and Grace Company was insolvent. Without the knowledge of Loft's board of directors, Guth used Loft's capital, credit, facilities, and employees to further the Pepsi enterprise. At Guth's direction, a Loft employee made the concentrate for the syrup, which was sent to Grace Company to add sugar and water. Loft charged Grace Company for the concentrate but allowed forty months' credit. Grace charged Pepsi for the syrup but also granted substantial credit. Grace sold the syrup to Pepsi's customers, including Loft, which paid on delivery or within thirty days. Loft also paid for Pepsi's advertising.

Finally, losing profits at its stores as a result of switching from Coca-Cola, Loft filed a suit in a Delaware state court against Guth, Grace, and Pepsi, seeking their Pepsi stock and an accounting. The court entered a judgment in the plaintiff's favor. The defendants appealed to the Delaware Supreme Court.

ISSUE Did Guth violate his duty of loyalty to Loft, Inc., by acquiring the Pepsi-Cola trademark and formula for himself without the knowledge of Loft's board of directors?

DECISION Yes. The Delaware Supreme Court upheld the judgment of the lower court. The state supreme court was "convinced that the opportunity to acquire the Pepsi-Cola trademark and formula, goodwill and business belonged to [Loft], and that Guth, as its president, had no right to appropriate the opportunity to himself."

REASON The court pointed out that the officers and directors of a corporation stand in a fiduciary relationship to that corporation and to its shareholders. Corporate officers and directors must protect the corporation's interest at all times. They must also "refrain from doing anything that works injury to the corporation." In other words, corporate officers and directors must provide undivided and unselfish loyalty to the corporation, and "there should be no conflict between duty and self-interest." Whenever an opportunity is presented to the corporation, officers and directors with knowledge of that opportunity cannot seize it for themselves. "The corporation may elect to claim all of the benefits of the transaction for itself, and the law will

BrooklynScribe/Shutterstock.com

Continues

impress a trust in favor of the corporation upon the property, interest, and profits required."

Guth clearly created a conflict between his self-interest and his duty to Loft—the corporation of which he was president and director. Guth illegally appropriated the Pepsi-Cola opportunity for himself and thereby placed himself in the position of competing with the company for which he worked.

WHAT IF THE FACTS WERE DIFFERENT? *Suppose that Loft's board of directors had approved Pepsi-Cola's use of its personnel and equipment. Would the court's decision have been different? Discuss.*

IMPACT OF THIS CASE ON TODAY'S LAW *This early Delaware decision was one of the first to set forth a test for determining when a corporate officer or director has breached the duty of loyalty. The test has two basic parts—whether the opportunity was reasonably related to the corporation's line of business, and whether the corporation was financially able to undertake the opportunity. The court also considered whether the corporation had an interest or expectancy in the opportunity and recognized that when the corporation had "no interest or expectancy, the officer or director is entitled to treat the opportunity as his own."*

Disclosure of Conflicts of Interest Corporate directors often have many business affiliations, and a director may sit on the board of more than one corporation. Of course, directors are precluded from entering into or supporting businesses that operate in direct competition with corporations on whose boards they serve. Their fiduciary duty requires them to make a full disclosure of any potential conflicts of interest that might arise in any corporate transaction [RMBCA 8.60].

Sometimes, a corporation enters into a contract or engages in a transaction in which an officer or director has a personal interest. The director or officer must make a *full disclosure* of that interest and must abstain from voting on the proposed transaction.

EXAMPLE 29.7 Southwood Corporation needs office space. Lambert Alden, one of its five directors, owns the building adjoining the corporation's main office building. He negotiates a lease with Southwood for the space, making a full disclosure to Southwood and the other four directors. The lease arrangement is fair and reasonable, and it is unanimously approved by the other four directors. In this situation, Alden has not breached his duty of loyalty to the corporation, and thus the contract is valid. If it were otherwise, directors would be prevented from ever transacting business with the corporations they serve. ■

If a director owns this unrented office space, can she offer it for rent to the corporation for which she is a director?

Liability of Directors and Officers Directors and officers are exposed to liability on many fronts. They are, of course, liable for their own crimes and torts. They also may be held liable for the crimes and torts committed by corporate employees under their supervision. Additionally, if shareholders perceive that the corporate directors are not acting in the best interests of the corporation, they may sue the directors on behalf of the corporation. (This is known as a *shareholder's derivative suit,* which will be discussed later in this chapter.) Directors and officers can also be held personally liable under a number of statutes, such as those enacted to protect consumers or the environment.

29–5 Shareholders

The acquisition of a share of stock makes a person an owner and shareholder in a corporation. Shareholders thus own the corporation, but they generally are not responsible for its daily management. Although they have no legal title to corporate property, such as buildings and equipment, they do have an equitable (ownership) interest in the firm.

KNOW THIS
Shareholders normally are not agents of the corporation.

29–5a Shareholders' Powers

Shareholders must approve fundamental changes affecting the corporation before the changes can be implemented. Hence, shareholders are empowered to amend the articles of incorporation and bylaws, approve a merger or the dissolution of the corporation, and approve the sale of all or substantially all of the corporation's assets. Some of these powers are subject to prior board approval.

Members of the board of directors are elected and removed by a vote of the shareholders. As mentioned earlier, the incorporators choose the first directors, who serve until the first shareholders' meeting. From that time on, the selection and retention of directors are exclusively shareholder functions.

Directors usually serve their full terms. If the shareholders judge them unsatisfactory, they are simply not reelected. Shareholders have the inherent power, however, to remove a director from office for cause (such as for breach of duty or misconduct) by a majority vote. Some state statutes (and some corporate articles) permit removal of directors without cause by the vote of a majority of the holders of outstanding shares entitled to vote.

29-5b Shareholders' Meetings

Shareholders' meetings must occur at least annually. In addition, special meetings can be called to deal with urgent matters. A corporation must notify its shareholders of the date, time, and place of an annual or special shareholders' meeting at least ten days, but not more than sixty days, before the meeting date [RMBCA 7.05].[12] Notice of a special meeting must include a statement of the purpose of the meeting, and business transacted at the meeting is limited to that purpose.

Proxies It is usually not practical for owners of only a few shares of stock of publicly traded corporations to attend shareholders' meetings. Therefore, the law allows stockholders to either vote in person or appoint another person as their agent to vote their shares at the meeting. The agent's formal authorization to vote the shares is called a **proxy** (from the Latin *procurare*, meaning "to manage, take care of"). Proxy materials are sent to all shareholders before shareholders' meetings.

Management often solicits proxies, but any person can solicit proxies to concentrate voting power. Proxies have been used by a group of shareholders as a device for taking over a corporation. Proxies normally are revocable (that is, they can be withdrawn), unless they are specifically designated as irrevocable. Under RMBCA 7.22(c), proxies last for eleven months, unless the proxy agreement provides for a longer period.

Shareholder Proposals When shareholders want to change a company policy, they can put their idea up for a shareholder vote. They can do this by submitting a shareholder proposal to the board of directors and asking the board to include the proposal in the proxy materials that are sent to all shareholders before meetings.

Rules for Proxies and Shareholder Proposals The Securities and Exchange Commission (SEC), which regulates the purchase and sale of securities, has special provisions relating to proxies and shareholder proposals. SEC Rule 14a-8 provides that all shareholders who own stock worth at least $1,000 are eligible to submit proposals for inclusion in corporate proxy materials. The corporation is required to include information on whatever proposals will be considered at the shareholders' meeting along with proxy materials.

Under the SEC's e-proxy rules,[13] all public companies must post their proxy materials on the Internet and notify shareholders how to find that information. Although the law requires proxy materials to be posted online, public companies may still choose among several

> "If it is not in the interest of the public, it is not in the interest of the business."
>
> **JOSEPH H. DEFREES**
> 1812–1885
> (MEMBER OF U.S. CONGRESS)

LEARNING OBJECTIVE 5
What is a voting proxy?

Proxy When a shareholder formally authorizes another to serve as his or her agent and vote his or her shares in a certain manner.

---

12. A shareholder can waive the requirement of written notice by signing a waiver form. In some states, a shareholder who does not receive written notice, but who learns of the meeting and attends without protesting the lack of notice, is said to have waived notice by such conduct. State statutes and corporate bylaws typically set forth the time within which notice must be sent, what methods can be used, and what the notice must contain.
13. 17 C.F.R. Parts 240, 249, and 274.

options—including paper documents and DVDs sent by mail—for delivering the materials to shareholders.

29–5c Shareholder Voting

Shareholders exercise ownership control through the power of their votes. Corporate business matters are presented in the form of *resolutions,* which shareholders vote to approve or disapprove. Each common shareholder is entitled to one vote per share. The articles of incorporation can exclude or limit voting rights, particularly for certain classes of shares. For instance, owners of *preferred stock* usually are denied the right to vote.

How are corporate business matters presented to shareholders?

Quorum Requirements For shareholders to act during a meeting, a quorum must be present. Generally, a quorum exists when shareholders holding more than 50 percent of the outstanding shares are present, but state laws often permit the articles of incorporation to set higher or lower quorum requirements.

CASE EXAMPLE 29.8 Sink & Rise, Inc., had eighty-four shares of voting common stock outstanding. James Case owned twenty shares. In addition, he and his estranged wife, Shirley, jointly owned another sixteen shares. Three different individuals owned sixteen shares each. During a shareholders' meeting, James was the only shareholder present. He elected himself and another shareholder to be directors, replacing Shirley as Sink & Rise's secretary. Shirley sued to set aside the election, claiming the sixteen shares that she owned jointly with James should not have been counted for quorum purposes.

A court, however, held that the shares Shirley owned jointly with James counted for purposes of quorum. The Wyoming Supreme Court affirmed the lower court's judgment. Corporate bylaws required that, in determining a quorum, the shares had to be entitled to vote and represented in person or by proxy. Because the sixteen shares that were jointly held were represented in person by James at the shareholders' meeting, they could be counted for quorum purposes. Consequently, the actions taken at the meeting were accomplished with authority, and Shirley was no longer the company's secretary.[14] ▪

Voting Requirements Once a quorum is present, voting can proceed. If a state statute requires specific voting procedures, the corporation's articles or bylaws must be consistent with the statute.

A majority vote of the shares represented at the meeting usually is required to pass resolutions. At times, more than a simple majority vote is required, either by a state statute or by the corporate articles. Extraordinary corporate matters, such as a merger, consolidation, or dissolution of the corporation, require a higher percentage of all corporate shares entitled to vote [RMBCA 7.27].

Cumulative Voting Most states permit, and some require, shareholders to elect directors by *cumulative voting.* This voting method is designed to allow minority shareholders to be represented on the board of directors.[15]

With cumulative voting, each shareholder is entitled to a total number of votes equal to the number of board members to be elected multiplied by the number of voting shares the shareholder owns. The shareholder can cast all of these votes for one candidate or split them among several candidates. All candidates stand for election at the same time. (When cumulative voting is not required either by statute or under the articles, the entire board can be elected by a simple majority of shares at a shareholders' meeting.)

KNOW THIS

Once a quorum is present, a vote can be taken even if some shareholders leave without casting their votes.

---

14. *Case v. Sink & Rise, Inc.,* 2013 WY 19, 297 P.3d 762 (2013).
15. See, for example, California Corporations Code Section 708. Under RMBCA 7.28, however, no cumulative voting rights exist unless the articles of incorporation provide for them.

EXAMPLE 29.9 Nak corporation has 10,000 shares issued and outstanding. The minority shareholders hold 3,000 shares, and the majority shareholders hold the other 7,000 shares. Three members of the board are to be elected. The majority shareholders' nominees are Acevedo, Barkley, and Craycik. The minority shareholders' nominee is Drake. Can Drake be elected by the minority shareholders?

If cumulative voting is allowed, the answer is yes. Together, the minority shareholders have 9,000 votes (3 directors to be elected times 3,000 shares held by minority shareholders equals 9,000 votes). All of these votes can be cast to elect Drake. The majority shareholders have 21,000 votes (3 times 7,000 equals 21,000), but these votes have to be distributed among their three nominees. No matter how the majority shareholders cast their 21,000 votes, they will not be able to elect all three directors if the minority shareholders cast all of their 9,000 votes for Drake, as illustrated in Exhibit 29–2. ■

Other Voting Techniques Before a shareholders' meeting, a group of shareholders can agree in writing to vote their shares together in a specified manner. Such agreements, called *shareholder voting agreements,* usually are held to be valid and enforceable. As noted earlier, a shareholder can also appoint a voting agent and vote by proxy.

29-5d Rights of Shareholders

Shareholders possess numerous rights in addition to the right to vote their shares, and we examine several here.

Stock Certificates In the past, shareholders had a right to a **stock certificate** that evidenced ownership of a specified number of shares in the corporation. Only a few jurisdictions still require physical stock certificates. Shareholders there have the right to demand that the corporation issue certificates (or replace those that were lost or destroyed). Stock is intangible personal property, however, and the ownership right exists independently of the certificate itself.

In most states today and under RMBCA 6.26, boards of directors may provide that shares of stock will be uncertificated, or "paperless"—that is, no physical stock certificates will be issued. Notice of shareholders' meetings, dividends, and operational and financial reports are distributed according to the ownership lists recorded in the corporation's books.

Preemptive Rights Sometimes, the articles of incorporation grant preemptive rights to shareholders [RMBCA 6.30]. With **preemptive rights,** a shareholder receives a preference over all other purchasers to subscribe to or purchase a prorated share of a new issue of stock. Generally, preemptive rights apply only to additional, newly issued stock and must be exercised within a specified time period (usually thirty days).

A shareholder who is given preemptive rights can purchase a percentage of the new shares being issued that is equal to the percentage of shares she or he already holds in the company. This allows each shareholder to maintain her or his proportionate control, voting power, and financial interest in the

Stock Certificate A certificate issued by a corporation evidencing the ownership of a specified number of shares in the corporation.

Preemptive Rights The right of a shareholder in a corporation to have the first opportunity to purchase a new issue of that corporation's stock in proportion to the amount of stock already owned by the shareholder.

Does the number of shares you hold determine your rights as a shareholder?

Exhibit 29–2 Results of Cumulative Voting

BALLOT	MAJORITY SHAREHOLDERS' VOTES			MINORITY SHAREHOLDERS' VOTES	DIRECTORS ELECTED
	Acevedo	**Barkley**	**Craycik**	**Drake**	
1	10,000	10,000	1,000	9,000	Acevedo/Barkley/Drake
2	9,001	9,000	2,999	9,000	Acevedo/Barkley/Drake
3	6,000	7,000	8,000	9,000	Barkley/Craycik/Drake

corporation. **EXAMPLE 29.10** Alisha, a shareholder who owns 10 percent of a company and who has preemptive rights, can buy 10 percent of any new issue (to maintain her 10 percent position). Thus, if the corporation issues 1,000 more shares, Alisha can buy 100 of the new shares. ■

Preemptive rights are most important in close corporations because each shareholder owns a relatively small number of shares but controls a substantial interest in the corporation. Without preemptive rights, it would be possible for a shareholder to lose his or her proportionate control over the firm.

Dividends

As mentioned, a *dividend* is a distribution of corporate profits or income ordered by the directors and paid to the shareholders in proportion to their shares in the corporation. Dividends can be paid in cash, property, stock of the corporation that is paying the dividends, or stock of other corporations.[16] On one occasion, a distillery declared and paid a "dividend" in bonded whiskey.

State laws vary, but each state determines the general circumstances and legal requirements under which dividends are paid. State laws also control the sources of revenue to be used. All states allow dividends to be paid from the undistributed net profits earned by the corporation, for instance, and a number of states allow dividends to be paid out of any surplus.

Illegal Dividends. Dividends are illegal if they are improperly paid from an unauthorized account, or if their payment causes the corporation to become insolvent (unable to pay its debts as they come due). Whenever dividends are illegal or improper, the board of directors can be held personally liable for the amount of the payment.

Directors' Failure to Declare a Dividend. When directors fail to declare a dividend, shareholders can ask a court to compel the directors to do so. To succeed, the shareholders must show that the directors have acted so unreasonably in withholding the dividend that their conduct is an abuse of their discretion. The mere fact that the firm has sufficient earnings or surplus available to pay a dividend is not enough to compel directors to distribute funds that, in the board's opinion, should not be distributed. There must be a clear abuse of discretion.

Inspection Rights

Shareholders in a corporation enjoy both common law and statutory inspection rights. The RMBCA provides that every shareholder is entitled to examine specified corporate records for a *proper purpose,* provided the request is made in advance. The shareholder can inspect in person, or can have an attorney, accountant, or other authorized agent do so. In some states, a shareholder must have held shares for a minimum period of time immediately preceding the demand to inspect or must hold a minimum number of outstanding shares.

EXAMPLE 29.11 Leah, the majority shareholder of Market Mogul, Inc., sells the firm's assets to herself and sets up another corporation, Nano Research. Leah then tells Market Mogul's minority shareholders that she is dissolving Market Mogul because it is failing financially. Kurt, a minority shareholder, asks to inspect the corporate records so that he can determine Market Mogul's financial condition, the value of its stock, and whether any misconduct has occurred. Kurt has expressed a proper purpose for the inspection and must be allowed to access Market Mogul's records. ■

The power of inspection is fraught with potential abuses, and the corporation is allowed to protect itself from them. For instance, a corporation can properly deny a shareholder access to corporate records to prevent harassment or to protect trade secrets or other confidential corporate information.

---

16. Technically, dividends paid in stock are not dividends. They maintain each shareholder's proportionate interest in the corporation.

Transfer of Shares Corporate stock represents an ownership right in intangible personal property. The law generally recognizes the right to transfer stock to another person unless there are valid restrictions on its transferability, such as frequently occur with close corporation stock. Restrictions must be reasonable and can be set out in the bylaws or in a shareholder agreement.

When shares are transferred, a new entry is made in the corporate stock book to indicate the new owner. Until the corporation is notified and the entry is complete, all rights—including voting rights and the right to dividend distributions—remain with the currently recorded owner.

29-5e The Shareholder's Derivative Suit

When the corporation is harmed by the actions of a third party, the directors can bring a lawsuit in the name of the corporation against that party. If the corporate directors fail to bring a lawsuit, shareholders can do so "derivatively" in what is known as a **shareholder's derivative suit.**

The right of shareholders to bring a derivative action is especially important when the wrong suffered by the corporation results from the actions of corporate directors or officers. This is because the directors and officers would probably be unwilling to take any action against themselves. (Derivative actions are less common in other countries than in the United States, as this chapter's *Beyond Our Borders* feature explains.)

Shareholder's Derivative Suit A suit brought by a shareholder to enforce a corporate cause of action against a third person.

Written Demand Required Before shareholders can bring a derivative suit, they must submit a written demand to the corporation, asking the board of directors to take appropriate action [RMBCA 7.40]. The directors then have ninety days in which to act. Only if they refuse to do so can the derivative suit go forward. In addition, a court will dismiss a derivative suit if the majority of directors or an independent panel determines in good faith that the lawsuit is not in the best interests of the corporation [RMBCA 7.44].

Damages Recovered Go into Corporate Funds When shareholders bring a derivative suit, they are not pursuing rights or benefits for themselves personally but are acting as guardians of the corporate entity. Therefore, if the suit is successful, any damages recovered normally go into the corporation's treasury, not to the shareholders personally.

EXAMPLE 29.12 Zeon Corporation is owned by two shareholders, each holding 50 percent of the corporate shares. One of the shareholders wants to sue the other for misusing corporate assets. In this situation, the plaintiff-shareholder will have to bring a shareholder's derivative suit (not a suit in his or her own name) because the alleged harm was suffered by Zeon, not by

BEYOND OUR BORDERS — Derivative Actions in Other Nations

Today, shareholders' derivative suits account for most of the claims brought against corporate directors and officers in the United States. Other nations, however, put more restrictions on the use of such suits. German law, for example, does not provide for derivative litigation, and a corporation's duty to its employees is just as significant as its duty to its shareholder-owners. The United Kingdom has no statute authorizing derivative actions, which are permitted only to challenge directors' actions that the shareholders could not legally ratify. Japan authorizes derivative actions but also permits a company to sue the plaintiff-shareholder for damages if the action is unsuccessful.

CRITICAL THINKING

- Do corporations benefit from shareholders' derivative suits? If so, how?

the plaintiff personally. Any damages awarded will go to the corporation, not to the plaintiff-shareholder. ■

What type of lawsuit can a shareholder pursue when he or she believes that another shareholder is misusing corporate assets?

29-5f Duties of Majority Shareholders

In some instances, a majority shareholder is regarded as having a fiduciary duty to the corporation and to the minority shareholders. This occurs when a single shareholder (or a few shareholders acting in concert) owns a sufficient number of shares to exercise *de facto* (actual) control over the corporation. In these situations, which commonly involve close corporations, majority shareholders owe a fiduciary duty to the minority shareholders.

When a majority shareholder breaches her or his fiduciary duty to a minority shareholder, the minority shareholder can sue for damages. A breach of fiduciary duties by those who control a close corporation normally constitutes what is known as *oppressive conduct*. A common example of a breach of fiduciary duty occurs when the majority shareholders "freeze out" the minority shareholders and exclude them from certain benefits of participating in the firm.

EXAMPLE 29.13 Brodie, Jordan, and Barbara form a close corporation to operate a machine shop. Brodie and Jordan own 75 percent of the shares in the company, but all three are directors. After disagreements arise, Brodie asks the company to purchase his shares, but his requests are refused. A few years later, Brodie dies, and his wife, Ella, inherits his shares. Jordan and Barbara refuse to perform a valuation of the company, deny Ella access to the corporate information she requests, do not declare any dividends, and refuse to elect Ella as a director. In this situation, the majority shareholders have violated their fiduciary duty to Ella. ■

29-6 Major Business Forms Compared

When deciding which form of business organization would be most appropriate, businesspersons normally take into account several factors, including ease of creation, the liability of the owners, tax considerations, and the need for capital. Each major form of business organization offers distinct advantages and disadvantages with respect to these and other factors. Exhibit 29–3 summarizes the essential advantages and disadvantages of each of the forms of business organization discussed in this unit.

Exhibit 29–3 Major Forms of Business Compared

CHARACTERISTIC	SOLE PROPRIETORSHIP	GENERAL PARTNERSHIP	CORPORATION
Method of Creation	Created at will by owner.	Created by agreement of the parties.	Authorized by the state under the state's corporation law.
Legal Position	Not a separate entity; owner is the business.	A separate legal entity in most states.	Always a legal entity separate and distinct from its owners—a legal fiction for the purposes of owning property and being a party to litigation.
Liability	Unlimited liability.	Unlimited liability.	Limited liability of shareholders—shareholders are not liable for the debts of the corporation.
Duration	Determined by owner; automatically dissolved on owner's death.	Terminated by agreement of the partners, but can continue to do business even when a partner dissociates from the partnership.	Can have perpetual existence.
Transferability of Interest	Interest can be transferred, but individual's proprietorship then ends.	Although partnership interest can be assigned, assignee does not have full rights of a partner.	Shares of stock can be transferred.

CHARACTERISTIC	SOLE PROPRIETORSHIP	GENERAL PARTNERSHIP	CORPORATION
Management	Completely at owner's discretion.	Each partner has a direct and equal voice in management unless expressly agreed otherwise in the partnership agreement.	Shareholders elect directors, who set policy and appoint officers.
Taxation	Owner pays personal taxes on business income.	Each partner pays pro rata share of income taxes on net profits, whether or not they are distributed.	Double taxation—corporation pays income tax on net profits, with no deduction for dividends, and shareholders pay income tax on disbursed dividends they receive.
Organizational Fees, Annual License Fees, and Annual Reports	None or minimal.	None or minimal.	All required.
Transaction of Business in Other States	Generally no limitation.	Generally no limitation.[a]	Normally must qualify to do business and obtain certificate of authority.

CHARACTERISTIC	LIMITED PARTNERSHIP	LIMITED LIABILITY COMPANY	LIMITED LIABILITY PARTNERSHIP
Method of Creation	Created by agreement to carry on a business for profit. At least one party must be a general partner and the other(s) limited partner(s). Certificate of limited partnership is filed. Charter must be issued by the state.	Created by an agreement of the member-owners of the company. Articles of organization are filed. Charter must be issued by the state.	Created by agreement of the partners. A statement of qualification for the limited liability partnership is filed.
Legal Position	Treated as a legal entity.	Treated as a legal entity.	Generally, treated same as a general partnership.
Liability	Unlimited liability of all general partners. Limited partners are liable only to the extent of capital contributions.	Member-owners' liability is limited to the amount of capital contributions or investments.	Varies, but under the Uniform Partnership Act, liability of a partner for acts committed by other partners is limited.
Duration	By agreement in certificate, or by termination of the last general partner or last limited partner.	Unless a single-member LLC, can have perpetual existence (same as a corporation).	Remains in existence until cancellation or revocation.
Transferability of Interest	Interest can be assigned (same as a general partnership), but if assignee becomes a member with consent of other partners, certificate must be amended.	Member interests are freely transferable.	Interest can be assigned the same as in a traditional partnership.
Management	General partners have equal voice, or determined by agreement. Limited partners may not retain limited liability if they actively participate in management.	Member-owners can fully participate in management or can designate a group of persons to manage on behalf of the members.	Same as a traditional partnership.
Taxation	Generally taxed as a partnership.	LLC is not taxed, and members are taxed personally on profits "passed through" the LLC.	Same as a traditional partnership.
Organizational Fees, Annual License Fees, and Annual Reports	Organizational fee required; usually not others.	Organizational fee required. Others vary with states.	Fees are set by each state for filing statements of qualification, statements of foreign qualification, and annual reports.
Transaction of Business in Other States	Generally no limitations.	Generally no limitations, but may vary depending on state.	Must file a statement of foreign qualification before doing business in another state.

a. A few states have enacted statutes requiring that foreign partnerships qualify to do business there.

Reviewing . . . Corporations

William Sharp was the sole shareholder and manager of Chickasaw Club, Inc., an S corporation that operated a popular nightclub of the same name in Columbus, Georgia. Sharp maintained a corporate checking account but paid the club's employees, suppliers, and entertainers in cash out of the club's proceeds. Sharp owned the property on which the club was located. He rented it to the club but made mortgage payments out of the club's proceeds and often paid other personal expenses with Chickasaw corporate funds.

At 12:45 A.M. on July 31, eighteen-year-old Aubrey Lynn Pursley, who was already intoxicated, entered the Chickasaw Club. Chickasaw employees did not check Pursley's identification to verify her age, as required by a city ordinance. Pursley drank more alcohol at Chickasaw and was visibly intoxicated when she left the club at 3:00 A.M. with a beer in her hand. Shortly afterward, Pursley lost control of her car, struck a tree, and was killed. Joseph Dancause, Pursley's stepfather, filed a tort lawsuit against Chickasaw Club and William Sharp. Using the information presented in the chapter, answer the following questions.

1. Under what theory might the court in this case make an exception to the limited liability of shareholders and hold Sharp personally liable for the damages? What factors would be relevant to the court's decision?

2. Suppose that Chickasaw's articles of incorporation failed to describe the corporation's purpose or management structure as required by state law. Would the court be likely to rule that Sharp is personally liable to Dancause on that basis? Why or why not?

3. Suppose that the club extended credit to its regular patrons in an effort to maintain a loyal clientele, although neither the articles of incorporation nor the corporate bylaws authorized this practice. Would the corporation likely have the power to engage in this activity? Explain.

4. How would the court classify Chickasaw Club, Inc.—domestic or foreign, public or private?

DEBATE THIS

- The sole shareholder of an S corporation should not be able to avoid liability for the torts of her or his employees.

Key Terms

alien corporation 717
articles of incorporation 722
benefit corporation 721
bond 724
business judgment rule 732
bylaws 723
close corporation 718
commingle 728
common stock 725
corporation 715
crowdfunding 726

dividend 716
domestic corporation 717
foreign corporation 717
inside director 730
outside director 730
piercing the corporate veil 727
preemptive rights 737
preferred stock 725
private equity capital 725
proxy 735
publicly held corporation 718

quorum 730
receiver 726
retained earnings 716
S corporation 720
securities 724
shareholder's derivative suit 739
stock 724
stock certificate 737
ultra vires acts 727
venture capital 725

Chapter Summary: Corporations

Nature and Classification	A corporation is a legal entity distinct from its owners. Formal statutory requirements, which vary somewhat from state to state, must be followed in forming a corporation. 1. *Corporate personnel*—The shareholders own the corporation. They elect a board of directors to govern the corporation. The board of directors hires corporate officers and other employees to run the firm's daily business. 2. *Corporate taxation*—The corporation pays income tax on net profits, and shareholders pay income tax on the disbursed dividends that they receive from the corporation (double-taxation feature). 3. *Torts and criminal acts*—The corporation is liable for the torts committed by its agents or officers within the course and scope of their employment (under the doctrine of *respondeat superior*). A corporation can be held liable (and be fined) for the criminal acts of its agents and employees. 4. *Domestic, foreign, and alien corporations*—A corporation is referred to as a *domestic corporation* within its home state (the state in which it incorporates), as a *foreign corporation* by any state that is not its home state, and as an *alien corporation* if it originates in another country but does business in the United States. 5. *Public and private corporations*—A public corporation is formed by a government. A private corporation is formed wholly or in part for private benefit. Most corporations are private corporations. 6. *Nonprofit corporations*—Corporations formed without a profit-making purpose. 7. *Close corporations*—Corporations owned by a family or a relatively small number of individuals. Transfer of shares is usually restricted. 8. *S corporations*—Small domestic corporations that, under Subchapter S of the Internal Revenue Code, are taxed like partnerships, thereby allowing shareholders to enjoy limited liability while avoiding double taxation. 9. *Professional corporations*—Corporations formed by professionals (such as physicians and lawyers). For liability purposes, some courts disregard the corporate form and treat the shareholders as partners. 10. *Benefit corporations*—Corporations formed (in some states) to benefit the public as a whole and have a material positive impact on society and the environment.
Formation and Financing	1. *Promotional activities*—A person who enters contracts on behalf of the future corporation is personally liable on all preincorporation contracts until the corporation is formed and assumes the contracts by novation. 2. *Incorporation procedures*—Procedures vary among the states, but the basic steps are as follows: a. Select a state of incorporation. b. Secure the corporate name. c. Prepare the articles of incorporation. The articles must include the corporate name, the number of shares of stock the corporation is authorized to issue, the registered office and agent, and the names and addresses of the incorporators. d. File the articles with the secretary of state. The state's filing of the articles authorizes the corporation to conduct business. 3. *First organizational meeting*—The main function of the meeting is to adopt the bylaws, or internal rules of the corporation, but other business, such as election of the board of directors, may also take place. 4. *Improper incorporation*—A corporation that has complied with the conditions for incorporation has *de jure* status. A minor defect in formation generally does not affect this status. If a defect is substantial, courts in some states may hold that the corporation has *de facto* status and treat it as a corporation despite the defect. 5. *Corporation by estoppel*—If a firm is not incorporated but represents itself to be a corporation and is sued as such by a third party, it may be held to be a corporation by estoppel. 6. *Securities*—Corporations normally are financed by the issuance and sale of securities. *Bonds* are debt securities representing funds borrowed by the firm, and *stocks* are equity securities representing ownership in the firm. 7. *Termination*—Corporations can be dissolved voluntarily by the directors or shareholders and can sometimes be involuntarily terminated by the state.
Corporate Powers	1. *Express and implied powers*—The express powers of a corporation are found in its articles of incorporation, in the law of the state of incorporation, and in the state and federal constitutions. Barring express constitutional, statutory, or other prohibitions, the corporation has the implied power to perform all acts reasonably appropriate and necessary to accomplish its corporate purposes. 2. *Ultra vires doctrine*—Any act of a corporation that is beyond its express or implied powers is an *ultra vires* act and may lead to a lawsuit by the shareholders, corporation, or state attorney general. 3. *Piercing the corporate veil*—To avoid injustice, courts may "pierce the corporate veil" and hold a shareholder or shareholders personally liable. This usually occurs when the corporate privilege is abused for personal benefit or when the corporate business is treated so carelessly that it is indistinguishable from that of a controlling shareholder.

Continues

Directors and Officers	1. *Directors*—Directors are responsible for all policymaking decisions necessary to the management of corporate affairs. Directors are elected by the shareholders and usually serve a one-year term. Compensation is usually specified in the corporate articles or bylaws. The board conducts business by holding formal meetings with recorded minutes. Directors' rights include the rights of participation, inspection, and indemnification. 2. *Corporate officers and executives*—Corporate officers and other executive employees are normally hired by the board of directors and have the rights defined by their employment contracts. 3. *Duty of care*—Directors and officers are obligated to act in good faith, to use prudent business judgment in the conduct of corporate affairs, and to act in the corporation's best interests. If a director fails to exercise this duty of care, she or he can be answerable to the corporation and to the shareholders. 4. *The business judgment rule*—This rule immunizes directors and officers from liability when they acted in good faith, acted in the best interests of the corporation, and exercised due care. For the rule to apply, the directors and officers must have made an informed, reasonable, and loyal decision. 5. *Duty of loyalty*—Directors and officers have a fiduciary duty to subordinate their own interests to those of the corporation in matters relating to the corporation. 6. *Conflicts of interest*—To fulfill their duty of loyalty, directors and officers must make a full disclosure of any potential conflicts between their personal interests and those of the corporation.

Shareholders	1. *Shareholders' powers*—Shareholders' must approve all fundamental changes affecting the corporation and elect the board of directors.
	 2. *Shareholders' meetings*—Shareholders' meetings must occur at least annually. Special meetings can be called when necessary. Notice of the date, time, and place of the meeting (and its purpose, if it is specially called) must be sent to shareholders. Shareholders may vote by proxy and may submit proposals to be included in the proxy materials sent to shareholders before meetings.
	 3. *Shareholder voting*—Shareholder voting requirements and procedures are as follows:
	   a. A minimum number of shareholders (a quorum) must be present at a meeting for business to be conducted. Resolutions are passed (usually) by simple majority vote.
	   b. Cumulative voting may be required or permitted. Cumulative voting gives minority shareholders a better chance to be represented on the board of directors.
	   c. A shareholder voting agreement (an agreement of shareholders to vote their shares together) is usually held to be valid and enforceable.
	 4. *Rights of shareholders*—Shareholders have numerous rights, which may include preemptive rights, the right to dividends, inspection rights, the right to transfer shares, and the right to sue on behalf of the corporation (bring a shareholder's derivative suit).

Issue Spotters

1. Name Brand, Inc., is a small business. Twelve members of a single family own all of its stock. Ordinarily, corporate income is taxed at the corporate and shareholder levels. How can Name Brand avoid this double taxation of income? (See *Nature and Classification*.)

2. Wonder Corporation has an opportunity to buy stock in XL, Inc. The directors decide that instead of Wonder buying the stock, the directors will buy it. Yvon, a Wonder shareholder, learns of the purchase and wants to sue the directors on Wonder's behalf. Can she do it? Explain. (See *Shareholders*.)

—**Check your answers to the *Issue Spotters* against the answers provided in Appendix D at the end of this text.**

Learning Objectives Check

1. What is a close corporation?

2. What four steps are involved in bringing a corporation into existence?

3. In what circumstances might a court disregard the corporate entity ("pierce the corporate veil") and hold the shareholders personally liable?

4. What are the duties of corporate directors and officers?

5. What is a voting proxy?

—**Answers to the even-numbered *Learning Objectives Check* questions can be found in Appendix E at the end of this text.**

Business Scenarios and Case Problems

29–1. Preincorporation. Cummings, Okawa, and Taft are recent college graduates who want to form a corporation to manufacture and sell personal computers. Peterson tells them he will set in motion the formation of their corporation. First, Peterson makes a contract with Owens for the purchase of a piece of land for $20,000. Owens does not know of the prospective corporate formation at the time the contract is signed. Second, Peterson makes a contract with Babcock to build a small plant on the property being purchased. Babcock's contract is conditional on the corporation's formation. Peterson secures all necessary capitalization and files the articles of incorporation. Discuss whether the newly formed corporation, Peterson, or both are liable on the contracts with Owens and Babcock. Is the corporation automatically liable to Babcock on formation? Explain. (See *Formation and Financing*.)

29–2. Conflicts of Interest. Oxy Corp. is negotiating with the Wick Construction Co. for the renovation of the Oxy corporate headquarters. Wick, the owner of the Wick Construction Co., is also one of the five members of Oxy's board of directors. The contract terms are standard for this type of contract. Wick has previously informed two of the other directors of his interest in the construction company. Oxy's board approves the contract by a three-to-two vote, with Wick voting with the majority. Discuss whether this contract is binding on the corporation. (See *Directors and Officers*.)

29–3. Spotlight on Smart Inventions—Piercing the Corporate Veil. Thomas Persson and Jon Nokes founded Smart Inventions, Inc., to market household consumer products. The success of their first product, the Smart Mop, continued with later products, which were sold through infomercials. Persson and Nokes were the firm's officers and equal shareholders, with Persson responsible for product development and Nokes in charge of day-to-day activities. By 1998, they had become dissatisfied with each other's efforts. Nokes represented the firm as financially "dying," "in a grim state, . . . worse than ever," and offered to buy all of Persson's shares for $1.6 million. Persson accepted.

On the day that they signed the agreement to transfer the shares, Smart Inventions began marketing a new product—the Tap Light. It was an instant success, generating millions of dollars in revenues. In negotiating with Persson, Nokes had intentionally kept the Tap Light a secret. Persson sued Smart Inventions, asserting fraud and other claims. Under what principle might Smart Inventions be liable for Nokes's fraud? Is Smart Inventions liable in this case? Explain. [*Persson v. Smart Inventions, Inc.*, 125 Cal.App.4th 1141, 23 Cal.Rptr.3d 335 (2 Dist. 2005)] (See *Corporate Powers*.)

29–4. Close Corporations. Mark Burnett and Kamran Pourgol were the only shareholders in a corporation that built and sold a house. When the buyers discovered that the house exceeded the amount of square footage allowed by the building permit, Pourgol agreed to renovate the house to conform to the permit. No work was done, however, and Burnett filed a suit against Pourgol. Burnett claimed that without his knowledge, Pourgol had submitted incorrect plans to obtain the building permit, misrepresented the extent of the renovation, and failed to fix the house. Was Pourgol guilty of misconduct? If so, how might it have been avoided? Discuss. [*Burnett v. Pourgol*, 83 A.D.3d 756, 921 N.Y.S.2d 280 (2 Dept. 2011)] (See *Nature and Classification*.)

29–5. Rights of Shareholders. Stanka Woods is the sole member of Hair Ventures, LLC. Hair Ventures owns 3 million shares of stock in Biolustré Inc. For several years, Woods and other Biolustré shareholders did not receive notice of shareholders' meetings or financial reports. On learning that Biolustré planned to issue more stock, Woods, through Hair Ventures, demanded to see Biolustré's books and records. Biolustré asserted that the request was not for a proper purpose. Does Woods have a right to inspect Biolustré's books and records? If so, what are the limits? Do any of those limits apply in this case? Explain. [*Biolustré Inc. v. Hair Ventures, LLC*, 2011 WL 540574 (Tex.App.—San Antonio 2011)] (See *Shareholders*.)

29–6. Business Case Problem with Sample Answer—Duty of Loyalty. Kids International Corp. produced children's wear for Walmart and other retailers. Gila Dweck was a Kids director and its chief executive officer. Because she felt that she was not paid enough for the company's success, she started another firm, Success Apparel, to compete with Kids. Success operated out of Kids' premises, used its employees, borrowed on its credit, took advantage of its business opportunities, and capitalized on its customer relationships. As an "administrative fee," Dweck paid Kids 1 percent of Success's total sales. Did Dweck breach any fiduciary duties? Explain. [*Dweck v. Nasser*, 2012 WL 3194069 (Del.Ch. 2012)] (See *Directors and Officers*.)

—**For a sample answer to Problem 29–6, go to Appendix F at the end of this text.**

29–7. Piercing the Corporate Veil. Scott Snapp contracted with Castlebrook Builders, Inc., which was owned by Stephen Kappeler, to remodel a house. Kappeler estimated that the remodeling would cost around $500,000. Eventually, however, Snapp paid Kappeler more than $1.3 million. Snapp filed a suit in an Ohio state court against Castlebrook, alleging breach of contract and fraud, among other things. During the trial, it was revealed that Castlebrook had issued no shares of stock and had commingled personal and corporate funds. The minutes of the corporate meetings all looked exactly the same. In addition, Kappeler could not provide an accounting for the Snapp project. In particular, he could not explain evidence of double and triple billing nor demonstrate that the amount Snapp paid had actually been spent on the remodeling project. Are these sufficient grounds to pierce the corporate veil? Explain. [*Snapp v. Castlebrook Builders, Inc.*, 2014 -Ohio- 163, 7 N.E.3d 574 (2014)] (See *Corporate Powers*.)

29–8. Torts. Jennifer Hoffman took her cell phone to a store owned by R&K Trading, Inc., for repairs. Later, Hoffman filed a suit in a New York state court against R&K, Verizon Wireless, Inc., and others, seeking to recover damages for a variety of torts, including infliction of emotional distress and negligent hiring and supervision. She alleged that an R&K employee, Keith Press, had examined her phone in a back room, accessed private photos of her stored on her phone, and disseminated the photos to the public. Hoffman testified that "after the incident, she learned from another R&K employee that personal information and pictures had been removed from the phones of other customers." Can R&K be held liable for the torts of its employees? Explain. [*Hoffman v. Verizon Wireless, Inc.*, 5 N.Y.S.3d 123, 125 A.D.3d 806 (2015)] (See *Nature and Classification*.)

29–9. A Question of Ethics—Improper Incorporation. Mike Lyons incorporated Lyons Concrete, Inc., in Montana, but did not file its first annual report, so the state involuntarily dissolved the firm in 1996. Unaware of the dissolution, Lyons continued to do business as Lyons Concrete. In 2003, he signed a written contract with William Weimar to form and pour a certain amount of concrete on Weimar's property for $19,810.

Weimar was in a rush to complete the entire project, and he and Lyons orally agreed to additional work on a time-and-materials basis. When scheduling conflicts arose, Weimar had his own employees set some of the forms, which proved deficient. Weimar also directed Lyons to pour concrete in the rain, which undercut its quality. Midproject, Lyons submitted an invoice for $14,389, which Weimar paid. After the work was complete, Lyons billed Weimar for $25,731, but he refused to pay, claiming that the $14,389 covered everything. To recover the unpaid amount, Lyons filed a mechanic's lien as "Mike Lyons d/b/a Lyons Concrete, Inc." against Weimar's property. Weimar filed a suit to strike the lien, and Lyons filed a counterclaim. [*Weimar v. Lyons*, 338 Mont. 242, 164 P.3d 922 (2007)] (See *Formation and Financing*.)

1. Before the trial, Weimar asked for a change of venue on the ground that a sign on the courthouse lawn advertised "Lyons Concrete." How might the sign affect a trial on the parties' dispute? Should the court grant this request?

2. Weimar asked the court to dismiss the counterclaim on the ground that the state had dissolved Lyons Concrete in 1996. Lyons immediately filed new articles of incorporation for "Lyons Concrete, Inc." Under what doctrine might the court rule that Weimar could not deny the existence of Lyons Concrete? What ethical values underlie this doctrine? Should the court make this ruling?

3. At the trial, Weimar argued, in part, that there was no "fixed price" contract between the parties and that even if there was, the poor quality of the work, which required repairs, amounted to a breach, excusing Weimar's further performance. Should the court rule in Weimar's favor on this basis?

Critical Thinking and Writing Assignments

29–10. Business Law Critical Thinking Group Assignment. Milena Weintraub and Larry Griffith were shareholders in Grand Casino, Inc., which operated a casino in South Dakota. Griffith owned 51 percent of the stock and Weintraub 49 percent. Weintraub managed the casino, which Griffith typically visited once a week. At the end of 2012, an accounting audit showed that the cash on hand was less than the amount posted in the casino's books. Later, more shortfalls were discovered. In October 2014, Griffith did a complete audit. Weintraub was unable to account for $200,500 in missing cash. Griffith kept all of the casino's most recent profits, including Weintraub's $90,447.20 share, and, without telling Weintraub, sold the casino for $400,000 and kept all of the proceeds. Weintraub filed a suit against Griffith, asserting a breach of fiduciary duty. Griffith countered with evidence of Weintraub's misappropriation of corporate cash. (See *Shareholders*.)

1. The first group will discuss the duties that these parties owed to each other and determine whether Weintraub or Griffith, or both, breached those duties.

2. The second group will decide how this dispute should be resolved and who should pay what to whom to reconcile the finances.

3. The third group will discuss whether Weintraub or Griffin violated any ethical duties to each other or to the corporation.

Investor Protection, Insider Trading, and Corporate Governance

"You are remembered for the rules you break."

GENERAL DOUGLAS MACARTHUR
1880–1964
(U.S. ARMY GENERAL)

After the stock market crash of 1929, Congress enacted legislation to regulate securities markets. *Securities* generally are defined as any instruments representing corporate ownership (stock) or debts (bonds). The goal of regulation was to provide investors with more information to help them make buying and selling decisions about securities and to prohibit deceptive, unfair, and manipulative practices.

Today, the sale and transfer of securities are heavily regulated by federal and state statutes and by government agencies. Moreover, the Securities and Exchange Commission (SEC) has implemented new regulations since Congress passed the Dodd-Frank Wall Street Reform and Consumer Protection Act in 2010.[1] We discuss the role of the SEC in the regulation of securities laws in this chapter's *Landmark in the Law* feature.

Despite all efforts to regulate the securities markets, people continue to break the rules and are often remembered for it, as observed in the chapter-opening quotation. Consider Keith Seilhan, a former employee of BP. Seilhan was the person in charge of coordinating the company's clean-up efforts after the *Deepwater Horizon* oil spill in the Gulf of Mexico. When Seilhan realized how much oil was flowing into the Gulf—and before that information was released to

---

1. Pub. L. No. 111-203, July 21, 2010, 124 Stat. 1376; 12 U.S.C. Sections 5301 *et seq.*

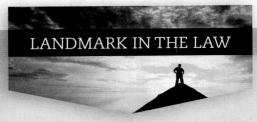

LANDMARK IN THE LAW   The Securities and Exchange Commission

In 1931, in the wake of the stock market crash of 1929, the U.S. Senate passed a resolution calling for an extensive investigation of securities trading. The investigation led, ultimately, to the enactment of the Securities Act of 1933, which is also known as the *truth-in-securities* bill. In the following year, Congress passed the Securities Exchange Act. This 1934 act created the Securities and Exchange Commission (SEC).

MAJOR RESPONSIBILITIES OF THE SEC
The SEC was created as an independent regulatory agency with the function of administering the 1933 and 1934 acts. Its major responsibilities in this respect are as follows:

1. To interpret federal securities laws and investigate securities law violations.

2. To issue new rules and amend existing rules.

3. To oversee the inspection of securities firms, brokers, investment advisers, and ratings agencies.

4. To oversee private regulatory organizations in the securities, accounting, and auditing fields.

5. To coordinate U.S. securities regulation with federal, state, and foreign authorities.

THE SEC'S EXPANDING REGULATORY POWERS Since its creation, the SEC's regulatory functions have gradually been increased by legislation granting it authority in different areas. For instance, the Securities Enforcement Remedies and Penny Stock Reform Act of 1990[a] allowed SEC administrative law judges to hear cases involving more types of alleged securities law violations. In addition, the act gave courts the authority to prevent persons who have engaged in securities fraud from serving as officers and directors of publicly held corporations. The Securities Acts Amendments of 1993[b] authorized the SEC to seek sanctions against those who violate foreign securities laws.

The National Securities Markets Improvement Act of 1996[c] expanded the power of the SEC to exempt persons, securities, and transactions from the requirements of the securities laws. (This act is also known as the

Capital Markets Efficiency Act.) The act also limited the authority of the states to regulate certain securities transactions and investment advisory firms.[d] The Sarbanes-Oxley Act of 2002,[e] which you will read about later in this chapter, further expanded the authority of the SEC by directing it to issue new rules relating to corporate disclosure requirements.

APPLICATION TO TODAY'S WORLD *The SEC is working to make the regulatory process more efficient and more relevant to today's securities trading practices. To this end, the SEC has embraced modern technology and the Internet more completely than many other federal agencies have. For example, the agency now requires companies to file certain information electronically so that it can be posted on the SEC's EDGAR (Electronic Data Gathering, Analysis, and Retrieval) database.*

---

a. 15 U.S.C. Section 77g.
b. 15 U.S.C. Section 78a.
c. 15 U.S.C. Sections 77z-3, 78mm.

---

d. 15 U.S.C. Section 80b-3a.
e. 15 U.S.C. Sections 7201 *et seq.*

---

the public—he sold $1 million of his family's BP securities. By doing so, he avoided significant losses, because when the news came out about the magnitude of the oil spill, BP stock prices dropped by around 48 percent. The SEC charged Seilhan with insider trading in 2014, and he agreed to settle the case and return the ill-gotten gains, plus interest and penalties.

30–1 Securities Act of 1933

LEARNING OBJECTIVE 1

What is meant by the term *securities?*

The Securities Act of 1933[2] governs initial sales of stock by businesses. The act was designed to prohibit various forms of fraud and to stabilize the securities industry by requiring that all essential information concerning the issuance of securities be made available to the investing public. Basically, the purpose of this act is to require disclosure. The act provides that all securities transactions must be registered with the SEC unless they qualify for an exemption.

---

2. 15 U.S.C. Sections 77–77aa.

30-1a What Is a Security?

Section 2(1) of the Securities Act contains a broad definition of securities, which generally include the following:[3]

1. Instruments and interests commonly known as securities, such as preferred and common stocks, treasury stocks, bonds, debentures, and stock warrants.

2. Any interests, such as stock options, puts, calls, or other types of privilege on a security or on the right to purchase a security or a group of securities on a national security exchange.

3. Notes, instruments, or other evidence of indebtedness, including certificates of interest in a profit-sharing agreement and certificates of deposit.

4. Any fractional undivided interest in oil, gas, or other mineral rights.

5. Investment contracts, which include interests in limited partnerships and other investment schemes.

National Archives

During the stock market crash of 1929, hordes of investors crowded Wall Street to find out the latest news. How did the "crash" affect stock trading in the years thereafter?

The Howey Test In interpreting the act, the United States Supreme Court has held that an **investment contract** is any transaction in which a person (1) invests (2) in a common enterprise (3) reasonably expecting profits (4) derived *primarily* or *substantially* from others' managerial or entrepreneurial efforts. Known as the *Howey* test, this definition continues to guide the determination of what types of contracts can be considered securities.[4]

CASE EXAMPLE 30.1 James Nistler and his wife bought undeveloped land in Jackson County, Oregon, and created an LLC to develop it. The property, called Tennessee Acres, was divided into six lots. Nistler obtained investors for the development by telling them that they would earn 12 to 15 percent interest on their investment and be repaid in full within a specified time. The property was never developed, the investors were never paid, and a substantial part of the funds provided by investors were used to pay Nistler and his wife.

Nistler was convicted of securities fraud. He appealed, claiming that the investments at issue did not involve "securities," but a state appellate court affirmed his conviction. The court found that there had been a pooling of funds from a group of investors, whose interests had been secured by the same land. The value of that land had been highly dependent on Nistler's use of the investors' funds to develop the land. In other words, the investors had engaged in a common enterprise from which they reasonably expected to profit, and that profit would be derived from the development efforts of Nistler.[5] ▪

Investment Contract
In securities law, a transaction in which a person invests in a common enterprise reasonably expecting profits that are derived primarily from the efforts of others.

Many Types of Securities For our purposes, it is probably convenient to think of securities in their most common forms—stocks and bonds issued by corporations. Bear in mind, though, that securities can take many forms, including interests in whiskey, cosmetics, worms, beavers, boats, vacuum cleaners, muskrats, and cemetery lots. Almost any stake in the ownership or debt of a company can be considered a security. Investment contracts in condominiums, franchises, limited partnerships in real estate, and oil or gas or other mineral rights have qualified as securities as well.

Securities are not limited to stocks and bonds but can encompass a wide variety of legal claims. The analysis hinges on the nature of the transaction rather than on the particular instrument or rights involved. Because Congress enacted securities laws to regulate

PREVENTING LEGAL DISPUTES

---

3. 15 U.S.C. Section 77b(1). Amendments in 1982 added stock options.
4. *SEC v. W. J. Howey Co.*, 328 U.S. 293, 66 S.Ct. 1100, 90 L.Ed. 1244 (1946).
5. *State v. Nistler*, 286 Or.App. 470, 342 P.3d 1035 (2015).

investments, in whatever form and by whatever name they are called, almost any type of security that might be sold as an investment can be subject to securities laws. When in doubt about whether an investment transaction involves securities, seek the advice of a specialized attorney.

30–1b Registration Statement

Section 5 of the Securities Act of 1933 broadly provides that a security must be *registered* before being offered to the public unless it qualifies for an exemption. The issuing corporation must file a *registration statement* with the SEC and must provide all investors with a *prospectus*.

A **prospectus** is a written disclosure document that describes the security being sold, the financial operations of the issuing corporation, and the investment or risk attaching to the security. The prospectus also serves as a selling tool for the issuing corporation. The SEC now allows an issuer to deliver its prospectus to investors electronically via the Internet.[6]

In principle, the registration statement and the prospectus supply sufficient information to enable unsophisticated investors to evaluate the financial risk involved.

Contents of the Registration Statement

The registration statement must be written in plain English and fully describe the following:

1. The securities being offered for sale, including their relationship to the issuer's other securities.
2. The corporation's properties and business (including a financial statement certified by an independent public accounting firm).
3. The management of the corporation, including managerial compensation, stock options, pensions, and other benefits. Any interests of directors or officers in any material transactions with the corporation must be disclosed.
4. How the corporation intends to use the proceeds of the sale.
5. Any pending lawsuits or special risk factors.

All companies, both domestic and foreign, must file their registration statements electronically so that they can be posted on the SEC's EDGAR (Electronic Data Gathering, Analysis, and Retrieval) database. The EDGAR database includes material on initial public offerings, proxy statements, corporations' annual reports, registration statements, and other documents that have been filed with the SEC. Investors can access the database via the Internet (**www .sec.gov/edgar.shtml**) to obtain information that can be used to make investment decisions.

The Registration Process

The registration statement does not become effective until after it has been reviewed and approved by the SEC (unless it is filed by a *well-known seasoned issuer*, as will be discussed shortly). The process includes several stages, and the 1933 act restricts the types of activities that an issuer can engage in at each stage.

Prefiling Period. During the *prefiling period* (before the registration statement is filed), the issuer normally cannot sell or offer to sell the securities. Once the registration statement has been filed, a waiting period begins while the SEC reviews the registration statement for completeness.[7]

Prospectus A written document required by securities laws when a security is being sold. The prospectus describes the security, the financial operations of the issuing corporation, and the risk attaching to the security.

KNOW THIS

The purpose of the Securities Act of 1933 is disclosure. The SEC does not consider whether a security is worth the investment price.

What act requires securities to be registered?

---

6. Basically, an electronic prospectus must meet the same requirements as a printed prospectus. The SEC has special rules that address situations in which the graphics, images, or audio files in a printed prospectus cannot be reproduced in an electronic form. 17 C.F.R. Section 232.304.
7. The waiting period must last at least twenty days but always extends much longer because the SEC invariably requires numerous changes and additions to the registration statement.

Waiting Period. During the *waiting period,* or *quiet period,* the securities can be offered for sale but cannot legally be sold. Only certain types of offers are allowed during this period.

All issuers can now distribute a *preliminary prospectus,* which contains most of the information that will be included in the final prospectus but often does not include a price. Most issuers can also distribute a *free-writing prospectus.*[8] A **free-writing prospectus** is any type of written, electronic, or graphic offer that describes the issuer or its securities and includes a legend indicating that the investor may obtain the prospectus at the SEC's Web site.

Posteffective Period. Once the SEC has reviewed and approved the registration statement and the waiting period is over, the registration is effective, and the *posteffective period* begins. The issuer can now offer and sell the securities without restrictions. If the company issued a preliminary or free-writing prospectus to investors, it must provide those investors with a final prospectus either before or at the time they purchase the securities. The issuer can force investors to download the final prospectus from a Web site if it notifies them of the appropriate Internet address.

Well-Known Seasoned Issuers

In 2005, the SEC revised the registration process and loosened some of the restrictions on large, experienced issuers.[9] The rules created new categories of issuers depending on their size and presence in the market and provided a simplified registration process for these issuers. The large, well-known firms that issue most securities have the greatest flexibility.

A firm that has issued at least $1 billion in securities in the previous three years or has at least $700 million of value of outstanding stock in the hands of the public is considered a *well-known seasoned issuer* (WKSI). WKSIs can file registration statements the day they announce a new offering and are not required to wait for SEC review and approval. They can also use a free-writing prospectus at any time, even during the prefiling period.

30–1c Exempt Securities and Transactions

Certain types of securities are exempt from the registration requirements of the Securities Act. These securities—which generally can also be resold without being registered—are summarized in Exhibit 30–1 under the "Exempt Securities" heading.[10]

The exhibit also lists and describes certain transactions that are exempt from registration requirements under various SEC regulations. The transaction exemptions are the most important because they are very broad and can enable an issuer to avoid the high cost and complicated procedures associated with registration. Because the coverage of the exemptions overlaps somewhat, an offering may qualify for more than one. Therefore, many sales of securities occur without registration. Even when a transaction is exempt from the registration requirements, the offering is still subject to the antifraud provisions of the 1933 act (as well as those of the 1934 act, to be discussed later in this chapter).

Regulation A Offerings

Securities issued by an issuer that has offered less than $50 million in securities during any twelve-month period are exempt from registration.[11] (The cap was $5 million until 2015, when the SEC approved rule changes to make it easier for small and midsized businesses to raise capital. These changes were made in connection with the Jumpstart Our Business Startups, or JOBS, Act.[12] Expanding the issuers that qualify for exemption under Regulation A will eventually decrease the significance of the other exemptions listed in Exhibit 30–1.)

Free-Writing Prospectus
A written, electronic, or graphic communication associated with the offer to sell a security and used during the waiting period to supplement other information about the security.

KNOW THIS
The issuer of an exempt security does not have to disclose the same information as other issuers.

---

8. See SEC Rules 164 and 433.

9. Securities Offering Reform, codified at 17 C.F.R. Sections 200, 228, 229, 230, 239, 240, 243, 249, and 274.

10. 15 U.S.C. Section 77c.

11. 15 U.S.C. Section 77c(b).

12. Pub. L. No. 112-106 (April 5, 2012).

Exhibit 30–1 Exemptions for Securities Offerings under the 1933 Securities Act

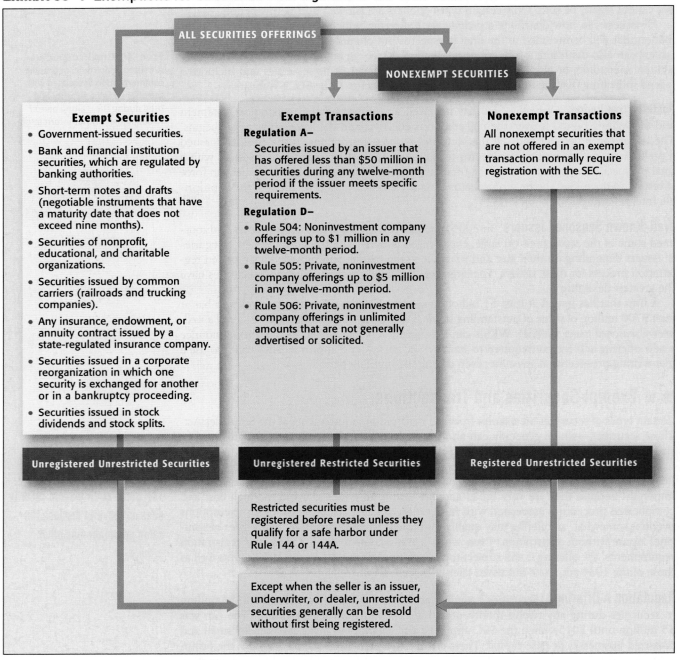

Under Regulation A,[13] the issuer must file with the SEC a notice of the issue and an offering circular, which must also be provided to investors before the sale. Additional review requirements apply to issuers raising between $20 and $50 million. Overall, Regulation A provides a process much simpler and less expensive than full registration.

13. 17 C.F.R. Sections 230.251–230.263.

Companies are allowed to "test the waters" for potential interest before preparing the offering circular. To *test the waters* means to determine potential interest without actually selling any securities or requiring any commitment on the part of those who express interest.

Some companies have sold their securities via the Internet under Regulation A. **EXAMPLE 30.2** The Spring Street Brewing Company became the first company to sell securities via an online initial public offering (IPO). Spring Street raised about $1.6 million—without having to pay any commissions to brokers or underwriters. ■ Such online IPOs are particularly attractive to small companies and start-up ventures that may find it difficult to raise capital from institutional investors or through underwriters.

Small Offerings—Regulation D

The SEC's Regulation D contains several exemptions from registration requirements (Rules 504, 505, and 506) for offers that either involve a small dollar amount or are made in a limited manner.

Rule 504. Rule 504 is the exemption used by most small businesses. It provides that noninvestment company offerings up to $1 million in any twelve-month period are exempt. Noninvestment companies are firms that are not engaged primarily in the business of investing or trading in securities. (In contrast, an **investment company** is a firm that buys a large portfolio of securities and professionally manages it on behalf of many smaller shareholders/owners. A **mutual fund** is a type of investment company.)

EXAMPLE 30.3 Zeta Enterprises is a limited partnership that develops commercial property. Zeta intends to offer $600,000 of its limited partnership interests for sale between June 1 and May 31. According to the definition of a security (discussed earlier in this chapter), this offering would be subject to the registration and prospectus requirements of the 1933 Securities Act.

Under Rule 504, however, the sales of Zeta's interests are exempt from these requirements because Zeta is a noninvestment company making an offering of less than $1 million in a twelve-month period. Therefore, Zeta can sell its limited partnership interests without filing a registration statement with the SEC or issuing a prospectus to any investor. ■

Rule 505. Another exemption is available under Rule 505 for private, noninvestment company offerings up to $5 million in any twelve-month period. The offer may be made to an unlimited number of *accredited investors* and up to thirty-five unaccredited investors. **Accredited investors** include banks, insurance companies, investment companies, employee benefit plans, the issuer's executive officers and directors, and persons whose income or net worth exceeds a certain threshold.

The SEC must be notified of the sales, and precautions must be taken, because these restricted securities may be resold only by registration or in an exempt transaction. No general solicitation or advertising is allowed. The issuer must provide any unaccredited investors with disclosure documents that generally are the same as those used in registered offerings.

Rule 506—Private Placement Exemption. Rule 506 exempts private, noninvestment company offerings in unlimited amounts that are not generally solicited or advertised. This exemption is often referred to as the *private placement* exemption because it exempts "transactions not involving any public offering."[14] To qualify for the exemption, the issuer must believe that each unaccredited investor has sufficient knowledge or experience in financial matters to be capable of evaluating the investment's merits and risks.[15]

The private placement exemption is perhaps most important to firms that want to raise funds through the sale of securities without registering them. **EXAMPLE 30.4** Citco Corporation needs to raise capital to expand its operations. Citco decides to make a private $10 million offering of its common stock directly to two hundred accredited investors and thirty highly

---

14. 15 U.S.C. Section 77d(2).
15. 17 C.F.R. Section 230.506.

Investment Company A company that acts on the behalf of many smaller shareholders-owners by buying a large portfolio of securities and professionally managing that portfolio.

Mutual Fund A specific type of investment company that continually buys or sells to investors shares of ownership in a portfolio.

iStockPhoto.com/g-stockstudio

How did the Spring Street Brewing Company avoid paying commissions to brokers and underwriters when it held its initial public offering (IPO)?

Accredited Investor In the context of securities offerings, sophisticated investors, such as banks, insurance companies, investment companies, the issuer's executive officers and directors, and persons whose income or net worth exceeds certain limits.

KNOW THIS

An investor can be "sophisticated" by virtue of his or her education and experience or by virtue of investing through a knowledgeable, experienced representative.

sophisticated, but unaccredited, investors. Citco provides all of these investors with a prospectus and material information about the firm, including its most recent financial statements.

As long as Citco notifies the SEC of the sale, this offering will likely qualify for the private placement exemption. The offering is nonpublic and not generally advertised. There are fewer than thirty-five unaccredited investors, and each of them possesses sufficient knowledge and experience to evaluate the risks involved. The issuer has provided all purchasers with the necessary material information. Thus, Citco will *not* be required to comply with the registration requirements of the Securities Act of 1933. ■

Resales and Safe Harbor Rules

Most securities can be resold without registration. The Securities Act provides exemptions for resales by most persons other than issuers or underwriters. Thus, the average investor who sells shares of stock does not have to file a registration statement with the SEC.

Resales of restricted securities, however, trigger the registration requirements unless the party selling them complies with Rule 144 or Rule 144A. These rules are sometimes referred to as "safe harbors."

Rule 144. Rule 144 exempts restricted securities from registration on resale if all of the following conditions are met:

1. There is adequate current public information about the issuer. ("Adequate current public information" refers to the reports that certain companies are required to file under the 1934 Securities Exchange Act.)

2. The person selling the securities has owned them for at least six months, if the issuer is subject to the reporting requirements of the 1934 act.[16] If the issuer is not subject to the 1934 act's reporting requirements, the seller must have owned the securities for at least one year.

3. The securities are sold in certain limited amounts in unsolicited brokers' transactions.

4. The SEC is notified of the resale.[17]

Rule 144A. Securities that at the time of issue are not of the same class as securities listed on a national securities exchange or quoted in a U.S. automated interdealer quotation system may be resold under Rule 144A.[18] They may be sold only to a qualified institutional buyer (an institution, such as an insurance company or a bank, that owns and invests at least $100 million in securities). The seller must take reasonable steps to ensure that the buyer knows that the seller is relying on the exemption under Rule 144A.

30–1d Violations of the 1933 Act

It is a violation of the Securities Act to intentionally defraud investors by misrepresenting or omitting facts in a registration statement or prospectus. Liability may also be imposed on those who are negligent with respect to the preparation of these publications. Selling securities before the effective date of the registration statement or under an exemption for which the securities do not qualify also results in liability.

Can the omission of a fact make a statement of opinion misleading to an ordinary investor? That was the question before the United States Supreme Court in the following case.

KNOW THIS
Securities do not have to be held for a specific period (six months) to be exempt from registration on a resale under Rule 144A, as they do under Rule 144.

---

16. Before 2008, when amendments to Rule 144 became effective, the holding period was one year if the issuer was subject to the reporting requirements of the 1934 act. See the revised SEC Rules and Regulations at 72 Federal Rules 71546-01, 2007 WL 4368599, Release No. 33-8869. This reduced holding period allows nonpublic issuers to raise capital electronically from private and overseas sources more quickly.
17. 17 C.F.R. Section 230.144.
18. 17 C.F.R. Section 230.144A.

CASE 30.1

Omnicare, Inc. v. Laborers District Council Construction Industry Pension Fund

Supreme Court of the United States, __ U.S. __, 135 S.Ct. 1318, 191 L.Ed.2d 253 (2015).

FACTS Omnicare, Inc., a pharmacy services company, filed a registration statement in connection with a public offering. The statement expressed the company's opinion that it was in compliance with federal and state laws. Later, the federal government accused Omnicare of receiving kickbacks from pharmaceutical manufacturers. The Laborers District Council Construction Industry Pension Fund and others (the Funds), who had bought the stock, filed a suit in a federal district court against Omnicare.

What requirements does a drug company need to satisfy to file an accurate registration statement?

The plaintiffs alleged that Omnicare's legal-compliance opinion was "untrue" and that Omnicare had, in violation of the Securities Act, "omitted to state [material] facts necessary" to make that opinion not misleading. Omnicare claimed that "no reasonable person, in any context, can understand a pure statement of opinion to convey anything more than the speaker's own mindset." The court dismissed the suit. The U.S. Court of Appeals for the Sixth Circuit reversed the dismissal in part and affirmed in part. The Funds appealed to the United States Supreme Court.

ISSUE If a registration statement omits material facts about the issuer's inquiry into or knowledge concerning a statement of opinion, and those facts conflict with what a reasonable investor would understand from the statement, is the issuer liable under the Securities Act?

DECISION Yes. The Court vacated the lower courts' decision. But because "neither court . . . considered the Funds' omissions theory with the right standard in mind," the Court remanded the case "for

a determination of whether the Funds have stated a viable omissions claim (or, if not, whether they should have a chance to replead)."

REASON Whether a statement is "misleading" depends on the perspective of a reasonable investor. A reasonable investor may, depending on the circumstances, understand a statement of opinion to convey particular facts about the speaker's basis for holding that view. If the real facts are otherwise, and are not provided, the statement will mislead its audience. An opinion statement is not misleading, however, simply because an issuer knows "some fact cutting the other way" and fails to disclose it. A reasonable investor does not expect that every fact known to an issuer supports the issuer's opinion. Moreover, whether an omission of fact makes a statement of opinion misleading depends on the context.

Registration statements are formal documents—a reasonable investor would expect an opinion in such a statement to be more carefully considered than an opinion casually expressed in daily life. In addition, the investor reads the statement "in light of all its surrounding text, including hedges, disclaimers, and apparently conflicting information," as well as the customs and practices of the issuer's business. The Securities Act "creates liability only for the omission of material facts that cannot be squared with such a fair reading."

CRITICAL THINKING—Legal Consideration *Would a reasonable investor have cause to complain if an issuer, without having consulted a lawyer, states, "We believe our conduct is lawful"? Explain.*

Remedies Criminal violations are prosecuted by the U.S. Department of Justice. Violators may be fined up to $10,000, imprisoned for up to five years, or both.

The SEC is authorized to seek civil sanctions against those who willfully violate the 1933 act. It can request an injunction to prevent further sales of the securities involved or ask the court to grant other relief, such as an order to a violator to refund profits. Parties who purchase securities and suffer harm as a result of false or omitted statements may also bring suits in a federal court to recover their losses and other damages.

Defenses There are three basic defenses to charges of violations under the 1933 act. A defendant can avoid liability by proving any of the following:

1. The statement or omission was not material.

2. The plaintiff knew about the misrepresentation at the time of purchasing the stock.

3. The defendant exercised *due diligence* in preparing the registration and reasonably believed at the time that the statements were true and there were no omissions of material facts.

CASE EXAMPLE 30.5 In preparation for an initial public offering (IPO), Blackstone Group, LP, filed a registration statement with the SEC. At the time, Blackstone's corporate private equity investments included FGIC Corporation (which insured investments in subprime mortgages) and Freescale Semiconductor, Inc. Before the IPO, FGIC's customers began to suffer large losses, and Freescale lost an exclusive contract to make wireless 3G chipsets for Motorola, Inc. (its largest customer). The losses suffered by these two companies would affect Blackstone. Nevertheless, Blackstone's registration statement did not mention the impact on its revenues of the investments in FGIC and Freescale.

Martin Litwin and others who invested in Blackstone's IPO filed a suit in a federal district court against Blackstone and its officers, alleging material omissions from the statement. Blackstone argued as a defense that the omissions were not material, and the lower court dismissed the case. The plaintiffs appealed. A federal appellate court ruled in favor of the plaintiffs that the alleged omissions were reasonably likely to be material, and remanded the case. The plaintiffs were entitled to the opportunity to prove at a trial that Blackstone had omitted material information that it was required to disclose.[19] ▪

30–2 Securities Exchange Act of 1934

LEARNING OBJECTIVE 2
What are the two major statutes regulating the securities industry?

Blackstone Group, LP, owned a large interest in Freescale Semiconductor, Inc. Should Blackstone have revealed in its registration statement that Freescale had lost a major 3G chipset order?

SEC Rule 10b-5 A rule of the Securities and Exchange Commission that prohibits the commission of fraud in connection with the purchase or sale of any security.

The 1934 Securities Exchange Act provides for the regulation and registration of securities exchanges, brokers, dealers, and national securities associations, such as the National Association of Securities Dealers (NASD). Unlike the 1933 act, which is a one-time disclosure law, the 1934 act provides for continuous periodic disclosures by publicly held corporations to enable the SEC to regulate subsequent trading.

The Securities Exchange Act applies to companies that have assets in excess of $10 million and five hundred or more shareholders. These corporations are referred to as *Section 12 companies* because they are required to register their securities under Section 12 of the 1934 act. Section 12 companies must file reports with the SEC annually and quarterly, and sometimes even monthly if specified events occur (such as a merger). Other provisions in the 1934 act require all securities brokers and dealers to be registered, to keep detailed records of their activities, and to file annual reports with the SEC.

The act also authorizes the SEC to engage in market surveillance to deter undesirable market practices such as fraud, market manipulation (attempts at illegally influencing stock prices), and misrepresentation. In addition, the act provides for the SEC's regulation of proxy solicitations for voting.

30–2a Section 10(b), SEC Rule 10b-5, and Insider Trading

Section 10(b) is an especially important section of the Securities Exchange Act. This section proscribes the use of any manipulative or deceptive mechanism in violation of SEC rules and regulations. Among the rules that the SEC has promulgated pursuant to Section 10(b) is **SEC Rule 10b-5,** which prohibits the commission of fraud in connection with the purchase or sale of any security.

SEC Rule 10b-5 applies to almost all cases concerning the trading of securities, whether on organized exchanges, in over-the-counter markets, or in private transactions. Generally, the rule covers just about any form of security, and the securities need not be registered under the 1933 act for the 1934 act to apply.

---

19. *Litwin v. Blackstone Group, LP,* 634 F.3d 706 (2d Cir. 2011).

Private parties can sue for securities fraud under the 1934 act and SEC Rule 10b-5. The basic elements of a securities fraud action are as follows:

1. A *material misrepresentation* (or omission) in connection with the purchase and sale of securities.
2. *Scienter* (a wrongful state of mind).
3. *Reliance* by the plaintiff on the material misrepresentation.
4. An *economic loss.*
5. *Causation*, meaning that there is a causal connection between the misrepresentation and the loss.

Insider Trading One of the major goals of Section 10(b) and SEC Rule 10b-5 is to prevent so-called **insider trading,** which occurs when persons buy or sell securities on the basis of information that is not available to the public. Corporate directors, officers, and majority shareholders, for instance, often have advance inside information that can affect the future market value of the corporate stock. Obviously, if they act on this information, their positions give them a trading advantage over the general public and other shareholders.

The 1934 act defines inside information and extends liability to those who take advantage of such information in their personal transactions when they know that the information is unavailable to those with whom they are dealing. Section 10(b) of the 1934 act and SEC Rule 10b-5 apply to anyone who has access to or receives information of a nonpublic nature on which trading is based—not just to corporate "insiders."

Disclosure under SEC Rule 10b-5 Any material omission or misrepresentation of material facts in connection with the purchase or sale of a security may violate not only the Securities Act of 1933 but also the antifraud provisions of Section 10(b) of the 1934 act and SEC Rule 10b-5. The key to liability (which can be civil or criminal) under Section 10(b) and SEC Rule 10b-5 is whether the insider's information is *material.*

The following are some examples of material facts calling for disclosure under SEC Rule 10b-5:

1. Fraudulent trading in the company's stock by a broker-dealer.
2. A dividend change (whether up or down).
3. A contract for the sale of corporate assets.
4. A new discovery, a new process, or a new product.
5. A significant change in the firm's financial condition.
6. Potential litigation against the company.

Note that any one of these facts, by itself, is not *automatically* considered a material fact. Rather, it will be regarded as a material fact if it is significant enough that it would likely affect an investor's decision as to whether to purchase or sell the company's securities.

EXAMPLE 30.6 Sheen, Inc., is the defendant in a class-action product liability suit that its attorney, Paula Frasier, believes that the company will lose. Frasier has advised Sheen's directors, officers, and accountants that the company will likely have to pay a substantial damages award. Sheen plans to make a $5 million offering of newly issued stock before the date when the trial is expected to end. Sheen's potential liability and the financial consequences to the firm are material facts that must be disclosed, because they are significant enough to affect an investor's decision as to whether to purchase the stock. ■

The following is a *Classic Case* interpreting materiality under SEC Rule 10b-5.

★★★ CLASSIC CASE 30.2 ★★★

Securities and Exchange Commission v. Texas Gulf Sulphur Co.

United States Court of Appeals, Second Circuit, 401 F.2d 833 (1968).

HISTORICAL AND ENVIRONMENTAL SETTING *In 1957, the Texas Gulf Sulphur Company began exploring for minerals in eastern Canada. In March 1959, aerial geophysical surveys were conducted over more than fifteen thousand square miles of the area. The operations revealed numerous variations in the conductivity of the rock, which indicated a remarkable concentration of commercially exploitable minerals. One site of such variations was near Timmins, Ontario. On October 29 and 30, 1963, a ground survey of the site near Timmins indicated a need to drill for further evaluation.*

FACTS On November 12, 1963, the Texas Gulf Sulphur Company (TGS) drilled a hole that appeared to yield a core with an exceedingly high mineral content, although further drilling would be necessary to establish whether there was enough ore to be mined commercially. TGS kept secret the results of the core sample.

After learning of the ore discovery, officers and employees of the company made substantial purchases of TGS's stock or accepted stock options (rights to purchase stock). On April 11, 1964, an unauthorized report of the mineral find appeared in the newspapers. On the following day, April 12, TGS issued a press release that played down the discovery and stated that it was too early to tell whether the ore find would be significant.

Later on, TGS announced a strike of at least 25 million tons of ore. The news led to a substantial increase in the price of TGS stock. The Securities and Exchange Commission (SEC) brought a suit in a federal district court against the officers and employees of TGS for violating the insider-trading prohibition of SEC Rule 10b-5. The officers and employees argued that the prohibition did not apply. They reasoned that the information on which they had traded was not material, as the find had not been commercially proved. The trial court held that most of the defendants had not violated SEC Rule 10b-5, and the SEC appealed.

ISSUE Did the officers and employees of TGS violate SEC Rule 10b-5 by buying the stock, even though they did not know the full extent

After sample drilling revealed potential mineral deposits, company executives made large stock purchases. Did they violate insider trading laws?

and profit potential of the ore discovery at the time of their purchases?

DECISION Yes. The U.S. Court of Appeals for the Second Circuit reversed the lower court's decision and remanded the case for further proceedings, holding that the employees and officers had violated SEC Rule 10b-5's prohibition against insider trading.

REASON For SEC Rule 10b-5 purposes, the test of materiality is whether the information would affect the judgment of reasonable investors. Reasonable investors include speculative as well as conservative investors. "A major factor in determining whether the . . . discovery [of the ore] was a material fact is the importance attached to the drilling results by those who knew about it. . . . The timing by those who knew of it of their stock purchases and their purchases of short-term calls [rights to buy shares at a specified price within a specified time period]—purchases in some cases by individuals who had never before purchased calls or even TGS stock—virtually compels the inference that the insiders were influenced by the drilling results. . . . We hold, therefore, that all transactions in TGS stock or calls by individuals apprised of the drilling results . . . were made in violation of Rule 10b-5."

IMPACT OF THIS CASE ON TODAY'S LAW *This landmark case affirmed the principle that the test of whether information is "material," for SEC Rule 10b-5 purposes, is whether it would affect the judgment of reasonable investors. The corporate insiders' purchases of stock and stock options indicated that they were influenced by the results and that the information about the drilling results was material. The courts continue to cite this case when applying SEC Rule 10b-5 to cases of alleged insider trading.*

Outsiders and SEC Rule 10b-5 The traditional insider-trading case involves true insiders—corporate officers, directors, and majority shareholders who have access to (and trade on) inside information. Increasingly, liability under Section 10(b) of the 1934 act and SEC Rule 10b-5 is being extended to certain "outsiders"—persons who trade on inside information acquired indirectly. Two theories have been developed under which outsiders may be held liable for insider trading: the *tipper/tippee theory* and the *misappropriation theory.*

Tipper/Tippee Theory. Anyone who acquires inside information as a result of a corporate insider's breach of his or her fiduciary duty can be liable under SEC Rule 10b-5. This liability extends to **tippees** (those who receive "tips" from insiders) and even remote tippees (tippees of tippees).

Tippee A person who receives inside information.

The key to liability under this theory is that the inside information must be obtained as a result of someone's breach of a fiduciary duty to the corporation whose shares are involved in the trading. The tippee is liable under this theory only if the following requirements are met:

1. There is a breach of a duty not to disclose inside information.
2. The disclosure is in exchange for personal benefit.
3. The tippee knows (or should know) of this breach and benefits from it.

CASE EXAMPLE 30.7 Eric McPhail was a member of the same country club as an executive at American Superconductor. While they were golfing, the executive shared information with McPhail about the company's expected earnings, contracts, and other major developments, trusting that McPhail would keep the information confidential. Instead, McPhail repeatedly tipped six of his other golfing buddies at the country club, and they all used the nonpublic information to their advantage in trading. In this situation, the executive breached his duty not to disclose the information, which McPhail knew. McPhail (the tippee) is liable under SEC Rule 10b-5, and so are his other golfing buddies (remote tippees). All traded on inside information to their benefit.[20] ▪

Misappropriation Theory. Liability for insider trading may also be established under the misappropriation theory. Under this theory, an individual who wrongfully obtains (misappropriates) inside information and trades on it for her or his personal gain should be held liable because, in essence, she or he stole information rightfully belonging to another.

The misappropriation theory has been controversial because it significantly extends the reach of SEC Rule 10b-5 to outsiders who ordinarily would *not* be deemed fiduciaries of the corporations in whose stock they trade. It is not always wrong to disclose material, nonpublic information about a company to another person. Nevertheless, a person who obtains the information and trades securities on it can be liable.[21]

Insider Reporting and Trading—Section 16(b)

Section 16(b) of the 1934 act provides for the recapture by the corporation of all profits realized by an insider on a purchase and sale, or sale and purchase, of the corporation's stock within any six-month period.[22] It is irrelevant whether the insider actually uses inside information—all such **short-swing profits** must be returned to the corporation.

In this context, *insiders* means officers, directors, and large stockholders of Section 12 corporations. (Large stockholders are those owning at least 10 percent of the class of equity securities registered under Section 12 of the 1934 act.) To discourage such insiders from using nonpublic information about their companies for their personal benefit in the stock market, the SEC requires them to file reports concerning their ownership and trading of the corporation's securities.

Section 16(b) applies not only to stock but also to stock warrants, options, and securities convertible into stock. In addition, the courts have fashioned complex rules for determining profits. Note, however, that the SEC exempts a number of transactions under Rule 16b-3.[23]

> "The way to stop financial 'joy-riding' is to arrest the chauffeur, not the automobile."
>
> **WOODROW WILSON**
> 1856–1924
> (TWENTY-EIGHTH PRESIDENT OF THE UNITED STATES, 1913–1921)

A golfer obtains inside information while playing with an executive of a listed company. The golfer then tells his friends about this valuable information. What are the friends called in securities law?

Short-Swing Profits Profits earned by a purchase and sale, or sale and purchase, of the same security within a six-month period.

---

20. Three of the defendants in this case agreed to settle with the SEC and return the trading profits. See SEC press release 2014-134 "SEC Charges Group of Amateur Golfers in Insider Trading Ring."
21. See, for example, *United States v. Gansman,* 657 F.3d 85 (2d Cir. 2011).
22. A person who expects the price of a particular stock to decline can realize profits by "selling short"—selling at a high price and repurchasing later at a lower price to cover the "short sale."
23. 17 C.F.R. Section 240.16b-3.

Exhibit 30–2 Comparison of Coverage, Application, and Liability under SEC Rule 10b-5 and Section 16(b)

AREA OF COMPARISON	SEC RULE 10b-5	SECTION 16(b)
What is the subject matter of the transaction?	Any security (does not have to be registered).	Any security (does not have to be registered).
What transactions are covered?	Purchase or sale.	Short-swing purchase and sale or short-swing sale and purchase.
Who is subject to liability?	Almost anyone with inside information under a duty to disclose—including officers, directors, controlling shareholders, and tippees.	Officers, directors, and shareholders who own 10 percent or more of the relevant class of securities.
Is omission or misrepresentation necessary for liability?	Yes.	No.
Are there any exempt transactions?	No.	Yes, there are a number of exemptions.
Who may bring an action?	A person transacting with an insider, the SEC, or a purchaser or seller damaged by a wrongful act.	A corporation or a shareholder by derivative action.

Exhibit 30–2 compares the effects of SEC Rule 10b-5 and Section 16(b). Because of these and other effects, corporate insiders are wise to seek specialized counsel before trading in the corporation's stock.

The Private Securities Litigation Reform Act

The disclosure requirements of SEC Rule 10b-5 had the unintended effect of deterring the disclosure of forward-looking information. To understand why, consider an example. **EXAMPLE 30.8** BT Company announces that its projected earnings in a future time period will be a certain amount, but the forecast turns out to be wrong. The earnings are in fact much lower, and the price of BT's stock is affected negatively. The shareholders then file suit against BT, claiming that its directors violated SEC Rule 10b-5 by disclosing misleading financial information. ■

To encourage companies to make earnings projections, Congress passed the Private Securities Litigation Reform Act (PSLRA) in 1995.[24] The PSLRA provides a "safe harbor" for publicly held companies that make forward-looking statements, such as financial forecasts. Those who make such statements are protected against liability for securities fraud if they include "meaningful cautionary statements identifying important factors that could cause actual results to differ materially from those in the forward-looking statement."[25]

The PSLRA also affected the level of detail required in securities fraud complaints. Plaintiffs must specify each purportedly misleading statement and say how it led them to a mistaken belief.

Limitations on Class Actions

After the PSLRA was passed, a number of securities class-action suits were filed in state courts to skirt its requirements. In response, Congress passed the Securities Litigation Uniform Standards Act (SLUSA).[26] The act placed stringent limits on the ability of plaintiffs to bring class-action suits in state courts against firms whose securities are traded on national stock exchanges. SLUSA applies to plaintiffs who claim fraud in the purchase or sale of securities and also applies to investors who claim that they were fraudulently induced to hold on to their securities.[27]

---

24. Pub. L. No. 104-67, 109 Stat. 737 (codified in scattered sections of Title 15 of the *United States Code*).
25. 15 U.S.C. Sections 77z-2, 78u-5.
26. Pub. L. No. 105-353. This act amended many sections of Title 15 of the *United States Code*.
27. *Merrill Lynch, Pierce, Fenner & Smith, Inc. v. Dabit*, 547 U.S. 71, 126 S.Ct. 1503, 164 L.Ed.2d 179 (2006).

30-2b Regulation of Proxy Statements

Section 14(a) of the Securities Exchange Act of 1934 regulates the solicitation of proxies (authorization to vote shares) from shareholders of Section 12 companies. The SEC regulates the content of proxy statements. Whoever solicits a proxy must fully and accurately disclose in the proxy statement all of the facts that are pertinent to the matter on which the shareholders are to vote. SEC Rule 14a-9 is similar to the antifraud provisions of SEC Rule 10b-5. Remedies for violations range from injunctions to prevent a vote from being taken to monetary damages.

30-2c Violations of the 1934 Act

As mentioned earlier, violations of Section 10(b) of the Securities Exchange Act and SEC Rule 10b-5, including insider trading, may be subject to criminal or civil liability.

***Scienter* Requirement** For either criminal or civil sanctions to be imposed, *scienter* must exist—that is, the violator must have had an intent to defraud or knowledge of her or his misconduct. *Scienter* can be proved by showing that the defendant made false statements or wrongfully failed to disclose material facts. In some situations, *scienter* can even be proved by showing that the defendant was consciously reckless as to the truth or falsity of his or her statements.

CASE EXAMPLE 30.9 Alvin Gebhart and Jack Archer started a business venture purchasing mobile home parks (MHPs) from owners and converting them to resident ownership. They formed MHP Conversions, LP, to facilitate the conversion process and issue promissory notes that were sold to investors to raise funds for the purchases. Archer ran the MHP program, and Gebhart sold the promissory notes. Gebhart sold nearly $2.4 million in MHP promissory notes to clients, who bought notes based on Gebhart's positive statements about the investment.

During the time Gebhart was selling the notes, however, he never actually looked into the finances of the MHP program. He relied entirely on information that Archer gave him, some of which was not true. When Gebhart was later sued for securities fraud, a federal appellate court concluded that there was sufficient evidence of *scienter*. Gebhart knew that he had no knowledge of the financial affairs of MHP, and he had been consciously reckless as to the truth or falsity of his statements about investing in MHP.[28] ■

***Scienter* Not Required for Section 16(b) Violations** Violations of Section 16(b) include the sale by insiders of stock acquired less than six months before the sale (or less than six months after the sale if selling short). These violations are subject to civil sanctions. Liability under Section 16(b) is strict liability. Neither *scienter* nor negligence is required.

Criminal Penalties For violations of Section 10(b) and Rule 10b-5, an individual may be fined up to $5 million, imprisoned for up to twenty years, or both. A partnership or a corporation may be fined up to $25 million. Section 807 of the Sarbanes-Oxley Act provides that for a *willful* violation of the 1934 act, the violator may be imprisoned for up to twenty-five years in addition to being fined.

For a defendant to be convicted in a criminal prosecution under the securities laws, there can be no reasonable doubt that

Does a man selling promissory notes based on mobile home park conversions have a duty to investigate his statements about the financial soundness of those conversions?

---

28. *Gebhart v. SEC*, 595 F.3d 1034 (9th Cir. 2010).

the defendant knew he or she was acting wrongfully. A jury is not allowed merely to speculate that the defendant may have acted willfully.

CASE EXAMPLE 30.10 Martha Stewart, founder of a well-known media and homemaking empire, was charged with intentionally deceiving investors based on public statements she made. In 2001, Stewart's stockbroker allegedly had informed Stewart that the head of ImClone Systems, Inc., was selling his shares in that company. Stewart then sold her ImClone shares. The next day, ImClone announced that the U.S. Food and Drug Administration had not approved Erbitux, an experimental cancer drug that the company was developing.

After the government began investigating Stewart's ImClone trades, she publicly stated that she had previously instructed her stockbroker to sell her ImClone stock if the price fell to $60 per share. The government prosecutor claimed that this statement was false and that Stewart made it with the intent to deceive investors in her own corporation, Martha Stewart Living Omnimedia, Inc., by offering an explanation for the stock sale. The court, however, acquitted Stewart on this charge because "to find the essential element of criminal intent beyond a reasonable doubt, a rational juror would have to speculate."[29] ■

In the following case, the defendant argued that he should not have been convicted for securities fraud because the government had failed to prove its case.

---

29. *United States v. Stewart*, 305 F.Supp.2d 368 (S.D.N.Y. 2004). Stewart was convicted on other charges relating to her ImClone trading that did not require proof of intent.

CASE 30.3

United States v. Newton
United States Court of Appeals, Eleventh Circuit, 559 Fed.Appx. 902 (2014).

FACTS Douglas Newton was the president and sole director of Real American Brands, Inc. (RLAB), which owned the Billy Martin's USA brand and operated a Billy Martin's retail boutique at the Trump Plaza in New York City. (Billy Martin, the one-time manager of the New York Yankees, co-founded Billy Martin's, a Western wear store.)

Newton agreed to pay kickbacks to Chris Russo, whom he believed to be the manager of a pension fund, to induce the fund to buy shares of RLAB stock. Newton later arranged for his friend Yan Skwara to pay similar kickbacks for the fund's purchase of stock in U.S. Farms, Inc. Skwara was the chief executive officer and president of U.S. Farms. In reality, the pension fund was fictitious, and Newton and Skwara had been dealing with agents of the Federal Bureau of Investigation (FBI). Consequently, Newton and Skwara were charged with securities fraud. Skwara pleaded guilty, and a federal district court jury convicted Newton. Sentenced to thirty months in prison, Newton appealed.

ISSUE Did the government prove beyond a reasonable doubt that Newton knew that the shares of RLAB and U.S. Farms stock were being sold at artificially inflated prices because of the kickbacks?

DECISION Yes. The U.S. Court of Appeals for the Eleventh Circuit affirmed Newton's conviction and sentence for securities fraud.

What does the government have to prove to show that a corporate director intended to defraud a pension fund by paying kickbacks?

REASON The evidence established that in each transaction, the amount of the kickback was added to the price of the stock, which artificially increased the stock price. Because of the kickbacks, the pension fund paid the same price for restricted shares as it would have paid for freely traded shares, although the price of the restricted shares should have been less. The evidence also proved that Newton had engaged in a scheme to defraud the pension fund. The FBI agents had initiated the deal, but Newton had joined the scheme voluntarily and had urged Skwara to participate.

In addition, Newton had tried to conceal the scheme with a false consulting agreement, as shown by e-mail that referred to advice he never actually received. His words and conduct, which were revealed on video at the trial, also showed his intent to defraud the pension fund investors. Thus, the evidence supported the conviction beyond a reasonable doubt. "Accordingly, there was no miscarriage of justice."

CRITICAL THINKING—Ethical Consideration *What is the difference between a sales commission or a transaction fee and a kickback? Why is a kickback unethical? Discuss.*

Civil Sanctions The SEC can also bring suit in a federal district court against anyone violating or aiding in a violation of the 1934 act or SEC rules by purchasing or selling a security while in the possession of material nonpublic information.[30] The violation must occur on or through the facilities of a national securities exchange or through a broker or dealer. A court may assess a penalty for as much as triple the profits gained or the loss avoided by the guilty party.[31] In addition, the 1988 Insider Trading and Securities Fraud Enforcement Act increased the number of persons who may be subject to civil liability for insider trading and gave the SEC authority to pay monetary rewards to informants.[32]

Private parties may also sue violators of Section 10(b) and Rule 10b-5. A private party may obtain rescission (cancellation) of a contract to buy securities or damages to the extent of the violator's illegal profits. Those found liable have a right to seek contribution from those who share responsibility for the violations, including accountants, attorneys, and corporations. For violations of Section 16(b), a corporation can bring an action to recover the short-swing profits.

Martha Stewart is shown here leaving a federal courthouse. On appeal, why did the court affirm her acquittal on the charge that she had engaged in a criminal action?

30-2d Online Securities Fraud

A problem facing the SEC today is how to enforce the antifraud provisions of the securities laws in the online environment. Internet-related forms of securities fraud include many types of investment scams. Spam, online newsletters and bulletin boards, chat rooms, blogs, social media, and tweets can all be used to spread false information and perpetrate fraud. For a relatively small cost, fraudsters can even build sophisticated Web pages to facilitate their investment scams.

Consider investment newsletters as an example. Hundreds of online investment newsletters provide free information on stocks. Legitimate online newsletters can help investors gather valuable information, but some e-newsletters are used for fraud. The law allows companies to pay the people who write these newsletters to tout their securities, but the newsletters are required to disclose who paid for the advertising. Many newsletters do not follow that law, however. Thus, an investor reading an online newsletter may believe that the information is unbiased, when in fact the fraudsters will directly profit by convincing investors to buy or sell particular stocks.

30-3 State Securities Laws

Today, every state has its own corporate securities laws, or "blue sky laws," that regulate the offer and sale of securities within its borders. (The phrase *blue sky laws* dates to a 1917 decision by the United States Supreme Court in which the Court declared that the purpose of such laws was to prevent "speculative schemes which have no more basis than so many feet of 'blue sky.'")[33] Article 8 of the Uniform Commercial Code, which has been adopted by all of the states, also imposes various requirements relating to the purchase and sale of securities.

LEARNING OBJECTIVE 4
What are some of the features of state securities laws?

30-3a Requirements under State Securities Laws

State securities laws apply mainly to intrastate transactions. Typically, state laws have disclosure requirements and antifraud provisions, many of which are patterned after Section 10(b)

---

30. The Insider Trading Sanctions Act of 1984, 15 U.S.C. Section 78u(d).
31. Profit or loss is defined as "the difference between the purchase or sale price of the security and the value of that security as measured by the trading price of the security at a reasonable period of time after public dissemination of the nonpublic information." 15 U.S.C. Section 78u(d)(3)(C).
32. 15 U.S.C. Section 78u-1.
33. *Hall v. Geiger-Jones Co.*, 242 U.S. 539, 37 S.Ct. 217, 61 L.Ed. 480 (1917).

of the Securities Exchange Act and SEC Rule 10b-5. State laws also provide for the registration of securities offered or issued for sale within the state and impose disclosure requirements.

CASE EXAMPLE 30.11 Randall Fincke was the founder, director, and officer of Access Cardiosystems, Inc., a small startup company that sold portable automated external heart defibrillators. Fincke prepared a business plan that stated Access's "patent counsel" had advised the firm "its product does not infringe any patents." This statement was false—patent counsel never offered Access any opinion on the question of infringement.

Fincke gave this plan to potential investors, including Joseph Zimmel who bought $1.5 million in Access shares. When the company later filed for Chapter 11 bankruptcy protection, Zimmel filed a complaint with the federal bankruptcy court, alleging that Fincke had violated the Massachusetts blue sky law. The court awarded Zimmel $1.5 million in damages, and the award was affirmed on appeal. Fincke had solicited investors "by means of" a false statement of material fact, in violation of the fraud provisions in the state's securities laws.[34] ■

Methods of registration, required disclosures, and exemptions from registration vary among states. Unless an exemption from registration is applicable, issuers must register or qualify their stock with the appropriate state official, often called a *corporations commissioner.* Additionally, most state securities laws regulate securities brokers and dealers.

30–3b Concurrent Regulation

Since the adoption of the 1933 and 1934 federal securities acts, the state and federal governments have regulated securities concurrently. Issuers must comply with both federal and state securities laws, and exemptions from federal law are not exemptions from state laws.

The dual federal and state system has not always worked well, particularly during the early 1990s, when the securities markets underwent considerable expansion. Today, most duplicate regulations have been eliminated, and the SEC has exclusive power to regulate most national securities activities. The National Conference of Commissioners on Uniform State Laws also substantially revised the Uniform Securities Act in 2002 to coordinate state and federal securities regulation and enforcement efforts. Seventeen states have adopted the most recent version of the Uniform Securities Act.[35]

30–4 Corporate Governance

Corporate governance can be narrowly defined as the relationship between a corporation and its shareholders. Some argue for a broader definition—that corporate governance specifies the rights and responsibilities among different participants in the corporation, such as the board of directors, managers, shareholders, and other stakeholders, and spells out the rules and procedures for making decisions on corporate affairs. Regardless of the way it is defined, effective corporate governance requires more than just compliance with laws and regulations. (For a discussion of corporate governance in other nations, see this chapter's *Beyond Our Borders* feature.)

Effective corporate governance is essential in large corporations because corporate ownership (by shareholders) is separated from corporate control (by officers and managers). Under these circumstances, officers and managers may attempt to advance their own interests at the expense of the shareholders. The well-publicized corporate scandals in the first decade of the 2000s clearly illustrate the reasons for concern about managerial opportunism.

KNOW THIS
Federal securities laws do not take priority over state securities laws.

Corporate Governance A set of policies specifying the rights and responsibilities of the various participants in a corporation and spelling out the rules and procedures for making corporate decisions.

---

34. *In re Access Cardiosystems, Inc.,* 776 F.3d 30 (1st Cir. 2015).
35. At the time this book went to press, the Uniform Securities Act had been adopted in Georgia, Hawaii, Idaho, Indiana, Iowa, Kansas, Maine, Michigan, Minnesota, Mississippi, Missouri, New Mexico, Oklahoma, South Carolina, South Dakota, Vermont, and Wisconsin, as well as the U.S. Virgin Islands.

BEYOND OUR BORDERS

Corporate Governance in Other Nations

Corporate governance has become an issue of concern not only for U.S. corporations, but also for corporate entities around the world. With the globalization of business, a corporation's bad acts (or lack of control systems) can have far-reaching consequences.

Different models of corporate governance exist in different nations, often depending on the degree of capitalism in the particular nation. In the United States, corporate governance tends to give priority to shareholders' interests. This approach encourages significant innovation, as well as cost and quality competition.

In contrast, the coordinated model of governance that prevails in continental Europe and Japan gives priority to the interests of

so-called stakeholders—employees, managers, suppliers, customers, and the community. The coordinated model still encourages innovation and cost and quality competition, but not to the same extent as the U.S. model.

CRITICAL THINKING

- Why does the presence of a capitalist system affect a nation's perspective on corporate governance?

30-4a Aligning the Interests of Officers and Shareholders

Some corporations have sought to align the financial interests of their officers with those of the company's shareholders by providing the officers with **stock options,** which enable them to purchase shares of the corporation's stock at a set price. When the market price rises above that level, the officers can sell their shares for a profit. Because a stock's market price generally increases as the corporation prospers, the options give the officers a financial stake in the corporation's well-being and supposedly encourage them to work hard for the benefit of the shareholders.

Stock Option A right to buy a given number of shares of stock at a set price, usually within a specified time period.

Problems with Stock Options Options have turned out to be an imperfect device for encouraging effective governance, however. Executives in some companies have been tempted to "cook" the company's books in order to keep share prices higher so that they could sell their stock for a profit. Executives in other corporations have experienced no losses when share prices dropped because their options were "repriced" so that they did not suffer from the share price decline. Thus, although stock options theoretically can motivate officers to protect shareholder interests, stock option plans have sometimes become a way for officers to take advantage of shareholders.

Outside Directors With stock options generally failing to work as planned, there has been an outcry for more outside directors (those with no formal employment affiliation with the company). The theory is that independent directors will more closely monitor the actions of corporate officers. Hence, today we see more boards with outside directors. Note, though, that outside directors may not be truly independent of corporate officers. They may be friends or business associates of the leading officers.

Should shareholders have more control over corporate officers' compensation? Over the last several years, executive compensation has become a hotly debated issue. Many critics argue that the chief executive officers (CEOs) of public companies are paid too much, especially in comparison with the wages earned by the average worker.

The Dodd-Frank Wall Street Reform and Consumer Protection Act includes a "say-on-pay" provision that gives shareholders the right to vote on compensation for senior executives at every public U.S. company. These votes are nonbinding, however—the board of directors does not have to abide by them. Furthermore, more than 90 percent of shareholder votes on

ETHICAL ISSUE

executive pay have been in favor of the proposed compensation plans. Despite the "say on pay" provision, the average compensation for a CEO in 2014 was more than $10.5 million, up 13 percent from the previous year. A typical U.S. employee would have to work about a month to earn what a CEO earns in an hour.

30-4b Promoting Accountability

Effective corporate governance standards are designed to address problems and to motivate officers to make decisions that promote the financial interests of the company's shareholders. Generally, corporate governance entails corporate decision-making structures that monitor employees (particularly officers) to ensure that they are acting for the benefit of the shareholders. Firms that are more accountable to shareholders typically report higher profits, higher sales growth, higher firm value, and other economic advantages. Thus, corporate governance involves, at a minimum:

1. The audited reporting of the corporation's financial progress, so managers can be evaluated.

2. Legal protections for shareholders, so violators of the law who attempt to take advantage of shareholders can be punished for misbehavior and victims may recover damages for any associated losses.

> "Honesty is the single most important factor having a direct bearing on the final success of an individual, corporation, or product."
>
> **Ed McMahon**
> 1923–2009
> (American entertainer)

Governance and Corporation Law
State corporation statutes set up the legal framework for corporate governance. Under the corporate law of Delaware, where most major companies incorporate, all corporations must have certain structures of corporate governance in place. The most important structure, of course, is the board of directors because the board makes the major decisions about the future of the corporation.

The Board of Directors
Under corporate law, a corporation must have a board of directors elected by the shareholders. Directors are responsible for ensuring that the corporation's officers are operating wisely and in the exclusive interest of shareholders. The directors receive reports from the officers and give them managerial direction. In reality, though, corporate directors devote a relatively small amount of time to monitoring officers.

Ideally, shareholders would monitor the directors' supervision of the officers. In practice, however, it can be difficult for shareholders to monitor directors and hold them responsible for corporate failings. Although the directors can be sued for failing to do their jobs effectively, directors are rarely held personally liable.

The Audit Committee.
A crucial committee of the board of directors is the *audit committee*, which oversees the corporation's accounting and financial reporting processes, including both internal and outside auditors. Unless the committee members have sufficient expertise and are willing to spend the time to carefully examine the corporation's bookkeeping methods, however, the audit committee may be ineffective.

The audit committee also oversees the corporation's "internal controls," which are the measures taken to ensure that reported results are accurate. As an example, these controls—carried out largely by the company's internal auditing staff—help to determine whether a corporation's debts are collectible. If the debts are not collectible, it is up to the audit committee to make sure that the corporation's financial officers do not simply pretend that payment will eventually be made.

The Compensation Committee.
Another important committee of the board of directors is the *compensation committee*. This committee monitors and determines the compensation of the company's officers. As part of this process, it is responsible for assessing the officers' performance and for designing a compensation system that will better align the officers' interests with those of the shareholders.

30-4c The Sarbanes-Oxley Act

In 2002, following a series of corporate scandals, Congress passed the Sarbanes-Oxley Act,[36] which addresses certain issues relating to corporate governance. Generally, the act attempts to increase corporate accountability by imposing strict disclosure requirements and harsh penalties for violations of securities laws. The act requires chief corporate executives to take responsibility for the accuracy of financial statements and reports that are filed with the SEC.

Additionally, the act requires that certain financial and stock-transaction reports be filed with the SEC earlier than was required under the previous rules. The act also created a new entity, called the Public Company Accounting Oversight Board, to regulate and oversee public accounting firms. Other provisions of the act established private civil actions and expanded the SEC's remedies in administrative and civil actions.

Because of the importance of this act for corporate leaders and for those dealing with securities transactions, we highlight some of its key provisions relating to corporate accountability in Exhibit 30–3.

---

36. 15 U.S.C. Sections 7201 *et seq.*

Exhibit 30–3 Some Key Provisions of the Sarbanes-Oxley Act Relating to Corporate Accountability

Certification Requirements—Under Section 906 of the Sarbanes-Oxley Act, the chief executive officers (CEOs) and chief financial officers (CFOs) of most major companies listed on public stock exchanges must certify financial statements that are filed with the SEC. CEOs and CFOs must certify that filed financial reports "fully comply" with SEC requirements and that all of the information reported "fairly represents in all material respects, the financial conditions and results of operations of the issuer."

Under Section 302 of the act, CEOs and CFOs of reporting companies are required to certify that a signing officer reviewed each quarterly and annual filing with the SEC and that none contained untrue statements of material fact. Also, the signing officer or officers must certify that they have established an internal control system to identify all material information and that any deficiencies in the system were disclosed to the auditors.

Effectiveness of Internal Controls on Financial Reporting—Under Section 404(a), all public companies are required to assess the effectiveness of their internal control over financial reporting. Section 404(b) requires independent auditors to report on management's assessment of internal controls, but companies with a public float (price times total shares publicly owned) of less than $75 million are exempted from this requirement.

Loans to Directors and Officers—Section 402 prohibits any reporting company, as well as any private company that is filing an initial public offering, from making personal loans to directors and executive officers (with a few limited exceptions, such as for certain consumer and housing loans).

Protection for Whistleblowers—Section 806 protects whistleblowers—employees who report ("blow the whistle" on) securities violations by their employers—from being fired or in any way discriminated against by their employers.

Blackout Periods—Section 306 prohibits certain types of securities transactions during "blackout periods"—periods during which the issuer's ability to purchase, sell, or otherwise transfer funds in individual account plans (such as pension funds) is suspended.

Enhanced Penalties for—
- *Violations of Section 906 Certification Requirements*—A CEO or CFO who certifies a financial report or statement filed with the SEC knowing that the report or statement does not fulfill all of the requirements of Section 906 will be subject to criminal penalties of up to $1 million in fines, ten years in prison, or both. *Willful* violators of the certification requirements may be subject to $5 million in fines, twenty years in prison, or both.
- *Violations of the 1934 Securities Exchange Act*—Penalties for securities fraud under the 1934 act were increased (as discussed earlier in this chapter). Individual violators may be fined up to $5 million, imprisoned for up to twenty years, or both. *Willful* violators may be imprisoned for up to twenty-five years in addition to being fined.
- *Destruction or Alteration of Documents*—Anyone who alters, destroys, or conceals documents or otherwise obstructs any official proceeding will be subject to fines, imprisonment for up to twenty years, or both.
- *Other Forms of White-Collar Crime*—The act stiffened the penalties for certain criminal violations, such as federal mail and wire fraud, and ordered the U.S. Sentencing Commission to revise the sentencing guidelines for white-collar crimes.

Statute of Limitations for Securities Fraud—Section 804 provides that a private right of action for securities fraud may be brought no later than two years after the discovery of the violation or five years after the violation, whichever is earlier.

More Internal Controls and Accountability

The Sarbanes-Oxley Act introduced direct *federal* corporate governance requirements for public companies (companies whose shares are traded in the public securities markets). The law addressed many of the corporate governance procedures discussed here and created new requirements in an attempt to make the system work more effectively. The requirements deal with independent monitoring of company officers by both the board of directors and auditors.

Sections 302 and 404 of Sarbanes-Oxley require high-level managers (the most senior officers) to establish and maintain an effective system of internal controls. The system must include "disclosure controls and procedures" to ensure that company financial reports are accurate and timely and to document financial results prior to reporting.

Senior management must reassess the system's effectiveness annually. Some companies had to take expensive steps to bring their internal controls up to the new federal standard. After the act was passed, hundreds of companies reported that they had identified and corrected shortcomings in their internal control systems.

Exemptions for Smaller Companies

The Sarbanes-Oxley Act initially required all public companies to have an independent auditor file a report with the SEC on management's assessment of internal controls. In 2010, however, Congress enacted an exemption for smaller companies in an effort to reduce compliance costs. Public companies with a market capitalization, or public float (price times total shares publicly owned), of less than $75 million no longer need to have an auditor report on management's assessment of internal controls.

Certification and Monitoring Requirements

Section 906 requires that chief executive officers (CEOs) and chief financial officers (CFOs) certify that the information in the corporate financial statements "fairly represents in all material respects, the financial conditions and results of operations of the issuer." This requirement makes officers directly accountable for the accuracy of their financial reporting and avoids any "ignorance defense" if shortcomings are later discovered.

Sarbanes-Oxley also includes requirements to improve directors' monitoring of officers' activities. All members of the corporate audit committee for public companies must be outside directors. The audit committee must have a written charter that sets out its duties and provides for performance appraisal. At least one "financial expert" must serve on the audit committee, which must hold executive meetings without company officers present. In addition to reviewing the internal controls, the committee also monitors the actions of the outside auditor.

LEARNING OBJECTIVE 5

What certification requirements does the Sarbanes-Oxley Act impose on corporate executives?

Reviewing . . . Investor Protection, Insider Trading, and Corporate Governance

Dale Emerson served as the chief financial officer for Reliant Electric Company, a distributor of electricity serving portions of Montana and North Dakota. Reliant was in the final stages of planning a takeover of Dakota Gasworks, Inc., a natural gas distributor that operated solely within North Dakota. On a weekend fishing trip with his uncle, Ernest Wallace, Emerson mentioned that he had been putting in a lot of extra hours at the office planning a takeover of Dakota Gasworks. When he returned from the fishing trip, Wallace purchased $20,000 worth of Reliant stock. Three weeks later, Reliant made a tender offer to Dakota Gasworks stockholders and purchased 57 percent of Dakota Gasworks stock. Over the next two weeks, the price of Reliant stock rose 72 percent before leveling out. Wallace sold his Reliant stock for a gross profit of $14,400. Using the information presented in the chapter, answer the following questions.

1. Would registration with the SEC be required for Dakota Gasworks securities? Why or why not?
2. Did Emerson violate Section 10(b) of the Securities Exchange Act of 1934 and SEC Rule 10b-5? Why or why not?
3. What theory or theories might a court use to hold Wallace liable for insider trading?
4. Under the Sarbanes-Oxley Act, who would be required to certify the accuracy of financial statements filed with the SEC?

DEBATE THIS

■ Insider trading should be legalized.

Key Terms

accredited investor 753
corporate governance 764
free-writing prospectus 751
insider trading 757

investment company 753
investment contract 749
mutual fund 753
prospectus 750

SEC Rule 10b-5 756
short-swing profits 759
stock option 765
tippee 758

Chapter Summary: Investor Protection, Insider Trading, and Corporate Governance

Securities Act of 1933	Prohibits fraud and stabilizes the securities industry by requiring disclosure of all essential information relating to the issuance of securities to the investing public. 1. *Registration requirements*—Securities, unless exempt, must be registered with the SEC before being offered to the public. The *registration statement* must include detailed financial information about the issuing corporation; the intended use of the proceeds of the securities being issued; and certain disclosures, such as interests of directors or officers and pending lawsuits. 2. *Prospectus*—The issuer must provide investors with a *prospectus* that describes the security being sold, the issuing corporation, and the risk attaching to the security. 3. *Exemptions*—The SEC has exempted certain offerings from the requirements of the Securities Act of 1933. Exemptions may be determined on the basis of the size of the issue, whether the offering is private or public, and whether advertising is involved. Exemptions are summarized in Exhibit 30–1.

Securities Exchange Act of 1934	Provides for the regulation and registration of securities exchanges, brokers, dealers, and national securities associations. Maintains a continuous disclosure system for all corporations with securities on the securities exchanges and for companies that have assets in excess of $10 million and five hundred or more shareholders (Section 12 companies).
	 1. *SEC Rule 10b-5 [under Section 10(b) of the 1934 act]*—
	   a. Applies to almost all trading of securities—a firm's securities do not have to be registered under the 1933 act for the 1934 act to apply.
	   b. Applies to insider trading by corporate officers, directors, majority shareholders, and any persons receiving inside information (information not available to the public) who base their trading on this information.
	   c. Liability for insider trading may be based on the tipper/tippee or the misappropriation theory.
	   d. May be violated by failing to disclose "material facts" that must be disclosed under this rule.
	   e. Liability for violations can be civil or criminal.
	 2. *Insider trading [under Section 16(b) of the 1934 act]*—To prevent corporate insiders from taking advantage of inside information, the 1934 act requires officers, directors, and shareholders owning 10 percent or more of the issued stock of a corporation to turn over to the corporation all short-term profits (called *short-swing profits*) realized from the purchase and sale or sale and purchase of corporate stock within any six-month period.
	 3. *Regulation of proxies*—The SEC regulates the content of proxy statements sent to shareholders of Section 12 companies. Section 14(a) is essentially a disclosure law, with provisions similar to the antifraud provisions of SEC Rule 10b-5.

Continues

State Securities Laws	All states have corporate securities laws (*blue sky laws*) that regulate the offer and sale of securities within state borders. These laws are designed to prevent "speculative schemes which have no more basis than so many feet of 'blue sky.'" States regulate securities concurrently with the federal government. The Uniform Securities Act is designed to promote coordination and reduce duplication between state and federal securities regulation.
Corporate Governance	1. *Definition*—Corporate governance involves a set of policies specifying the rights and responsibilities of the various participants in a corporation and spelling out the rules and procedures for making decisions on corporate affairs. 2. *The need for corporate governance*—Corporate governance is necessary in large corporations because corporate ownership (by the shareholders) is separated from corporate control (by officers and managers). This separation of corporate ownership and control can often result in conflicting interests. Corporate governance standards address such issues. 3. *Sarbanes-Oxley Act*—This act attempts to increase corporate accountability by imposing strict disclosure requirements and harsh penalties for violations of securities laws.

Issue Spotters

1. When a corporation wishes to issue certain securities, it must provide sufficient information for an unsophisticated investor to evaluate the financial risk involved. Specifically, the law imposes liability for making a false statement or omission that is "material." What sort of information would an investor consider material? (See *Securities Exchange Act of 1934*.)

2. Lee is an officer of Magma Oil, Inc. Lee knows that a Magma geologist has just discovered a new deposit of oil. Can Lee take advantage of this information to buy and sell Magma stock? Why or why not? (See *Securities Exchange Act of 1934*.)

—**Check your answers to the *Issue Spotters* against the answers provided in Appendix D at the end of this text.**

Learning Objectives Check

1. What is meant by the term *securities?*
2. What are the two major statutes regulating the securities industry?
3. What is insider trading? Why is it prohibited?
4. What are some of the features of state securities laws?
5. What certification requirements does the Sarbanes-Oxley Act impose on corporate executives?

—**Answers to the even-numbered *Learning Objectives Check* questions can be found in Appendix E at the end of this text.**

Business Scenarios and Case Problems

30–1. Registration Requirements. Langley Brothers, Inc., a corporation incorporated and doing business in Kansas, decides to sell common stock worth $1 million to the public. The stock will be sold only within the state of Kansas. Joseph Langley, the chair of the board, says the offering need not be registered with the Securities and Exchange Commission. His brother, Harry, disagrees. Who is right? Explain. (See *Securities Act of 1933*.)

30–2. Insider Trading. David Gain is the chief executive officer (CEO) of Forest Media Corp., which is interested in acquiring RS Communications, Inc. To initiate negotiations, Gain meets with RS's CEO, Gill Raz, on Friday, July 12. Two days later, Gain phones his brother, Mark, who buys 3,800 shares of RS stock on the following Monday. Mark discusses the deal with their father, Jordan, who buys 20,000 RS shares on Thursday. On July 25, the day before the RS bid is due, Gain phones his parents' home, and Mark buys another 3,200 RS shares. Over the next few days, Gain periodically phones Mark and Jordan, both of whom

continued to buy RS shares. On August 5, RS refuses Forest's bid and announces that it is merging with another company. The price of RS stock rises 30 percent, increasing the value of Mark's and Jordan's shares by nearly $660,000 and $400,000, respectively. Is Gain guilty of insider trading? What is required to impose sanctions for this offense? Could a court hold Gain liable? Why or why not? (See *Securities Exchange Act of 1934*.)

30–3. Business Case Problem with Sample Answer— Violations of the 1934 Act. Matrixx Initiatives, Inc., makes and sells over-the-counter pharmaceutical products. Its core brand is Zicam, which accounts for 70 percent of its sales. Matrixx received reports that some consumers had lost their sense of smell (a condition called *anosmia*) after using Zicam Cold Remedy. Four product liability suits were filed against Matrixx, seeking damages for anosmia. In public statements relating to revenues and product safety, however, Matrixx did not reveal this information.

James Siracusano and other Matrixx investors filed a suit in a federal district court against the company and its executives under Section 10(b) of the Securities Exchange Act of 1934 and SEC Rule 10b-5, claiming that the statements were misleading because they did not disclose the information about the product liability suits. Matrixx argued that to be material, information must consist of a statistically significant number of adverse events that require disclosure. Because Siracusano's claim did not allege that Matrixx knew of a statistically significant number of adverse events, the company contended that the claim should be dismissed. What is the standard for materiality in this context? Should Siracusano's claim be dismissed? Explain. [*Matrixx Initiatives, Inc. v. Siracusano,* __U.S. __, 131 S.Ct. 1309, 179 L.Ed.2d 398 (2011)] (See *Securities Exchange Act of 1934.*)

—For a sample answer to Problem 30–3, go to Appendix F at the end of this text.

30–4. Disclosure under SEC Rule 10b-5. Dodona I, LLC, invested $4 million in two securities offerings from Goldman, Sachs & Co. The investments were in collateralized debt obligations (CDOs). Their value depended on residential mortgage-backed securities (RMBSs), whose value in turn depended on the performance of subprime residential mortgages. Before marketing the CDOs, Goldman had noticed several "red flags" relating to investments in the subprime market, in which it had invested heavily. To limit its risk, Goldman began betting against subprime mortgages, RMBSs, and CDOs, including the CDOs it had sold to Dodona. In an internal e-mail, one Goldman official commented that the company had managed to "make some lemonade from some big old lemons." Nevertheless, Goldman's marketing materials provided only boilerplate statements about the risks of investing in the securities. The CDOs were later downgraded to junk status, and Dodona suffered a major loss while Goldman profited. Assuming that Goldman did not affirmatively misrepresent any facts about the CDOs, can Dodona still recover under SEC Rule 10b-5? If so, how? [*Dodona I, LLC v. Goldman, Sachs & Co.,* 847 F.Supp.2d 624 (S.D.N.Y. 2012)] (See *Securities Exchange Act of 1934.*)

30–5. Violations of the 1933 Act. Three shareholders of iStorage sought to sell their stock through World Trade Financial Corp. The shares were *restricted securities*—that is, securities acquired in an unregistered, private sale. Restricted securities typically bear a "restrictive" legend clearly stating that they cannot be resold in the public marketplace. This legend had been wrongly removed from the iStorage shares, however. Information about the company that was publicly available included the fact that, despite a ten-year life, it had no operating history or earnings. In addition, it had net losses of about $200,000, and its stock was thinly traded. Without investigating the company or the status of its stock, World Trade sold more than 2.3 million shares to the public on behalf of the three customers. Did World Trade violate the Securities Act of 1933? Discuss. [*World*

Trade Financial Corp. v. Securities and Exchange Commission, 739 F.3d 1243 (9th Cir. 2014)] (See *Securities Act of 1933.*)

30–6. Securities Act of 1933. Big Apple Consulting USA, Inc., provided small publicly traded companies with a variety of services, including marketing, business planning, and Web site development and maintenance. CyberKey Corp. sold customizable USB drives. CyberKey falsely informed Big Apple that CyberKey had been awarded a $25 million contract with the Department of Homeland Security (DHS). Big Apple used this information in aggressively promoting CyberKey's stock and was compensated for the effort in the form of CyberKey shares. When the Securities and Exchange Commission (SEC) began to investigate, Big Apple sold its shares for $7.8 million. The SEC filed an action in a federal district court against Big Apple, alleging a violation of the Securities Act of 1933. Can liability be imposed on a seller for a false statement that was made by someone else? Explain. [*U.S. Securities and Exchange Commission v. Big Apple Consulting USA, Inc.,* 783 F.3d 786 (11th Cir. 2015)] (See *Securities Act of 1933.*)

30–7. A Question of Ethics—Violations of the 1934 Act. Melvin Lyttle told John Montana and Paul Knight about a "Trading Program" that purportedly would buy and sell securities in deals that were fully insured, as well as monitored and controlled by the Federal Reserve Board. Without checking the details or even verifying whether the Program existed, Montana and Knight, with Lyttle's help, began to sell interests in the Program to investors.

For a minimum investment of $1 million, the investors were promised extraordinary rates of return—from 10 percent to as much as 100 percent per week—without risk. They were also told that the Program would "utilize banks that can ensure full bank integrity of The Transaction whose undertaking[s] are in complete harmony with international banking rules and protocol and who guarantee maximum security of a Funder's Capital Placement Amount." Nothing was required but the investors' funds and their silence—the Program was to be kept secret. Over a four-month period, Montana raised nearly $23 million from twenty-two investors. The promised gains did not accrue, however. Instead, Montana, Lyttle, and Knight depleted the investors' funds in high-risk trades or spent the funds on themselves. [*SEC v. Montana,* 464 F.Supp.2d 772 (S.D.Ind. 2006)] (See *Securities Exchange Act of 1934.*)

1. The Securities and Exchange Commission (SEC) filed a suit against Montana alleging violations of Section 10(b) and SEC Rule 10b-5. What is required to establish a violation of these laws? Explain how and why the facts in this case meet, or fail to meet, these requirements.

2. Ultimately, about half of the investors recouped the amount they had invested. Should the others be considered at least partly responsible for their own losses? Discuss.

Critical Thinking and Writing Assignments

30–8. Case Analysis Question. Go to Appendix G at the end of this text and examine the excerpt of Case No. 5, *City of Livonia Employees' Retirement System and Local 295/Local 851 v. Boeing Co.* Review and then brief the case, making sure that your brief answers the following questions. (See *Securities Exchange Act of 1934.*)

1. **Issue:** Which pleading was at the center of the dispute in this case? What aspect of this pleading was at issue? Why?

2. **Rule of Law:** What must this pleading state in a suit alleging violations of Section 10(b) and Rule 10b-5?

3. **Applying the Rule of Law:** How did the source of the plaintiffs' allegations and the motive for the defendants' actions influence the result in this case?

4. **Conclusion:** Did the court conclude that the pleading here met the requirement for a suit alleging violations of Section 10(b) and Rule 10b-5?

30–9. Business Law Critical Thinking Group Assignment. Karel Svoboda, a credit officer for Rogue Bank, evaluated and approved his employer's extensions of credit to clients. These responsibilities gave Svoboda access to non-public information about the clients' earnings, performance, acquisitions, and business plans from confidential memos, e-mail, and other sources. Svoboda devised a scheme with Alena Robles, an independent accountant, to use this information to trade securities. Pursuant to their scheme, Robles traded in the securities of more than twenty different companies and profited by more than $2 million. Svoboda also executed trades for his own profit of more than $800,000, despite their agreement that Robles would do all of the trading. Aware that their scheme violated Rogue Bank's policy, they attempted to conduct their trades in such a way as to avoid suspicion. When the bank questioned Svoboda about his actions, he lied, refused to cooperate, and was fired. (See *Securities Exchange Act of 1934.*)

1. The first group will determine whether Svoboda or Robles committed any crimes.

2. The second group will decide whether Svoboda or Robles is subject to civil liability. If so, who could file a suit and on what ground? What are the possible sanctions?

3. A third group will identify any defenses that Svoboda or Robles could raise and determine whether the defenses would be likely to succeed.

Unit Five—Business Case Study with Dissenting Opinion

Notz v. Everett Smith Group, Ltd.

This *Business Case Study with Dissenting Opinion* examines *Notz v. Everett Smith Group, Ltd.*[1] in which a minority shareholder claimed that he had been excluded from some of the benefits of participating in the corporation. The shareholder asserted that the majority shareholder and the board of directors, which was controlled by the majority shareholder, had breached their fiduciary duties to the minority shareholder and to the firm. The court had to answer this question: Could the minority shareholder bring a suit directly to recover personally from the directors, or was he limited to bringing a shareholder's derivative suit on behalf of the corporation?

What does a minority shareholder have to do to show that the majority shareholder and the board of directors breached their fiduciary duties to that shareholder?

CASE BACKGROUND

Albert Trostel & Sons (ATS) began as a tannery in Milwaukee, Wisconsin, in the 1800s. Over the decades, ATS acquired subsidiaries and expanded into the production of rubber and plastics. Everett Smith came to work for ATS in 1938, later became its president, and eventually gained control of the company. Smith formed Everett Smith Group, Ltd., which owned 88.9 percent of ATS by 2003. Edward Notz owned 5.5 percent, and others owned the rest. All of the members of ATS's board of directors were either officers or directors of the Smith Group.

In 2004, ATS had an opportunity to acquire Dickten & Masch, a competing thermoplastics maker. The ATS board chose not to act. Instead, the Smith Group, which had no direct holdings in the plastics field, acquired Dickten & Masch. Within months, the Smith Group's new affiliate bought the assets of ATS's plastics subsidiary, Trostel Specialty Elastomers Group, Inc. (Trostel SEG), from ATS.

Notz filed a suit in a Wisconsin state court against the Smith Group, alleging breach of fiduciary duty for stripping ATS of its most important assets and diverting the corporate opportunity to buy Dickten & Masch. The court dismissed the claim, and a state intermediate appellate court affirmed. Notz appealed to the Wisconsin Supreme Court.

MAJORITY OPINION

N. Patrick *CROOKS*, J. [Judge]
* * * *

Notz's claims of breach of fiduciary duty are primarily based on the series of transactions in which the Smith Group acquired two plastics companies. The allegations are that the Smith Group, as

ATS's majority shareholder, rejected the opportunity ATS had to buy Dickten & Masch; the Smith Group subsequently bought Dickten & Masch itself; and the Smith Group, in its capacity as majority shareholder, orchestrated the sale of ATS's valuable plastics group, Trostel SEG, to its own new acquisition.

The question is whether those allegations support direct claims for breach of fiduciary duty to a minority shareholder. * * * The Smith Group argues that * * * these are derivative claims; Notz argues that * * * these are direct claims.

* * * *Though each shareholder has an individual right to be treated fairly by the board of directors, when the injury from such actions is primarily to the corporation, there can be no direct claim by minority shareholders.* [Emphasis added.]

* * * It is true the fiduciary duty of a director is owed to the individual stockholders as well as to the corporation. Directors in this state may not use their position of trust to further their private interests. Thus, where some individual right of a stockholder is being impaired by the improper acts of a director, the stockholder can bring a direct suit on his own behalf because it is his individual right that is being violated. However, a right of action that belongs to the corporation cannot be pursued as a direct claim by an individual stockholder. * * * *Even where the injury to the corporation results in harm to a shareholder, it won't transform an action from a derivative to a direct one* * * *. That such primary and direct injury to a corporation may have a subsequent impact on the value of the stockholders' shares is clear, but that is not enough to create a right to bring a direct, rather than derivative, action. Where the injury to the corporation is the primary injury, and any injury to stockholders secondary, it is the derivative action alone that can be brought and maintained. That

1. 316 Wis.2d 640, 764 N.W.2d 904 (2009).

Continues

is the general rule, and, if it were to be abandoned, there would be no reason left for the concept of derivative actions for the redress of wrongs to a corporation. [Emphasis added.]

* * * *

Notz alleges self-dealing on the part of the majority shareholder, but * * * a shareholder-director's self-dealing [does not] transform an action that primarily injures the corporation into one that primarily injures a shareholder.

We agree with the Smith Group that breach of fiduciary duty claims, based on the lost opportunity to purchase one company and the sale of a subsidiary with great growth potential, are [derivative claims]. Our analysis * * * centers on a determination of whether the primary injury is to the corporation or to the shareholder. * * * An injury primarily * * * to an individual shareholder [is] one which affects a shareholder's rights in a manner distinct from the effect upon other shareholders. We agree with the court of appeals that the allegations here are essentially that the Smith Group stripped ATS of its most important assets and engaged in various acts of self-dealing, and that those are allegations of injury primarily to ATS. * * * All of the shareholders of ATS were affected equally by the loss of the opportunity to acquire Dickten & Masch and by the sale of Trostel SEG, the plastics division.

* * * *

* * * We agree with the court of appeals that the claims of harm alleged—the loss of a corporate opportunity and the sale of a subsidiary with high growth potential—caused harm primarily to the corporation, and thus we affirm the dismissal of Notz's direct claim of breach of fiduciary duty as to those allegations.

DISSENTING OPINION

Ann Walsh *BRADLEY*, J. [Judge] (* * * DISSENTING * * *).

* * * *

* * * I disagree with the majority * * * that Notz's claim for breach of fiduciary duty arising out of corporate usurpation is a derivative rather than a direct claim and that it thus must be dismissed.

Instead, * * * I conclude that Notz states a direct claim for breach of fiduciary duty arising out of the defendants' usurpation of a corporate opportunity.

* * * *

* * * Officers and directors owe a fiduciary duty to shareholders to act in good faith and to treat each shareholder fairly. The directors and officers of a corporation owe a fiduciary duty to not use their positions for their own personal advantage * * * to the detriment of the interests of the stockholders of the corporation.

That same fiduciary duty is also owed by majority shareholders to minority shareholders.

Officers, directors, and controlling shareholders breach their fiduciary duties when they treat minority shareholders differently, and inequitably, or when they use their position of trust to further their private interests. If through that control a sale of the corporate property is made and the property acquired by the majority, the minority may not be excluded from a fair participation in the fruits of the sale.

* * * *

[The majority's] conclusion is antithetical to the facts. It is true that all shareholders suffered a common injury in that the value of their investment in ATS depreciated. Nonetheless, Notz suffered an additional injury that was unique to the minority shareholders. The Smith Group who planned and executed these transactions received a net gain, but Notz suffered a net loss. * * * Notz's injury was distinct from the injury to the controlling shareholder—unlike the defendants, Notz was denied continued participation in a thriving growth industry.

QUESTIONS FOR ANALYSIS

1. **Law.** *What did the majority rule with respect to the dispute before the court? On what reasoning did the majority base its ruling?*

2. **Law.** *What was the dissent's interpretation of the facts in this case? How would the dissent have applied the law to these facts? Why?*

3. **Ethics.** *From an ethical perspective, should ATS's directors have made different decisions on the choices that came before the board? Discuss.*

4. **Economic Dimensions.** *Could a shareholder in the position of the minority shareholder in this case seek a judicial dissolution? If so, what would be the likely result?*

5. **Implications for the Shareholder.** *Can a shareholder pursue a derivative claim on behalf of a corporation? If so, what steps must the shareholder take? Why might a shareholder be reluctant to take these steps?*

Unit Five—Business Scenario

iStockPhoto.com/Devonyu

John leases an office and buys computer equipment. Initially, to pay for the lease and the equipment, he goes into the business of designing applications for smartphones. He also has an idea for a new software product that he hopes will be more profitable than designing apps. Whenever he has time, he works on the software.

1. **Selecting a Business Organization.** After six months, Mary and Paul come to work in the office to help develop John's idea. John continues to pay the rent and other expenses, including salaries for Mary and Paul. John does not expect to make a profit until the software is developed, which could take months. Even then, there may be very little profit unless the product is marketed successfully. If the software is successful, though, John believes that the firm will be able to follow up with other products. In choosing a form of business organization for this firm, what are the important considerations? What are the advantages and disadvantages of each basic option?

2. **Corporate Nature and Classification.** It is decided that the organizational form for this firm should provide limited liability for the owners. The owners will include John, Mary, Paul, and some members of their respective families. Limited liability is one of the features of the corporate form. Ordinarily, however, corporate income is taxed at both the corporate level and the shareholder level. Which corporate form could the firm use to avoid this double taxation? Which other forms of business organization provide limited liability? What factors, other than liability and taxation, influence a firm's choice among these forms?

3. **Duties of Corporate Directors.** The firm is incorporated as Digital Software, Inc. (DSI). The software is developed and marketed successfully, and DSI prospers. John, Mary, and Paul become directors of DSI. At a board meeting, Paul proposes a marketing strategy for DSI's next product, and John and Mary approve it. Implementing the strategy causes DSI's profits to drop. If the shareholders accuse Paul of breaching his fiduciary duty to DSI, what is Paul's most likely defense? If the shareholders accuse John and Mary of the same breach, what is their best defense? In either case, if the shareholders file a suit, how is a court likely to rule?

4. **Securities Regulation.** Mary and Paul withdraw from DSI to set up their own firm. To obtain operating capital, they solicit investors, who agree to become "general partners." Mary and Paul designate themselves "managing partners." The investors are spread over a wide area geographically and learn about Mary and Paul's business only through contact from Mary and Paul. Are Mary and Paul truly soliciting partners, or are they selling securities? What are the criteria for determining whether an investment is a security? What are the advantages and disadvantages of selling securities versus soliciting partners?

iStockPhoto.com/Avalon_Studio

Unit Five—Group Project

Although a limited liability company (LLC) may be the best organizational form for most businesses, a significant number of firms may be better off as a corporation or some other form of organization.

1. The first group will outline several reasons why a firm might be better off as a corporation than as an LLC.

2. The second group will discuss whether it is preferable for a five-member LLC to be member managed or manager managed and will identify some of the factors that should be taken into consideration.

Unit 6
Government Regulation

31

iStockPhoto.com/jsmith

LEARNING OBJECTIVES

The five Learning Objectives *below are designed to help improve your understanding of the chapter. After reading this chapter, you should be able to answer the following questions:*

1. What is a monopoly? What is market power? How do these concepts relate to each other?

2. What rule do courts apply to price-fixing agreements, and why?

3. What is the main type of activity prohibited by Section 2 of the Sherman Act?

4. What are the four major provisions of the Clayton Act, and what types of activities do these provisions prohibit?

5. What agencies of the federal government enforce the federal antitrust laws?

Antitrust Law and Promoting Competition

The laws regulating economic competition in the United States are referred to as *antitrust laws*. They include the Sherman Antitrust Act of 1890[1] and the Clayton Act[2] and the Federal Trade Commission Act,[3] passed by Congress in 1914 to further curb anticompetitive or unfair business practices. Congress later amended the 1914 acts to broaden and strengthen their coverage. We examine these major federal antitrust statutes in this chapter.

The basis of antitrust legislation is our society's desire to foster competition. As President Herbert Hoover said in the chapter-opening quotation, competition not only protects the consumer, but also provides "the incentive to progress." Consumers and society as a whole benefit when producers strive to develop better products that they can sell at lower prices to beat the competition. Fostering competition remains important in our society today, which is why the government is concerned about the pricing of e-books, as you will read later in this chapter.

> "Competition is not only the basis of protection to the consumer but is the incentive to progress."
>
> **HERBERT HOOVER**
> 1874–1964
> (THIRTY-FIRST PRESIDENT OF THE UNITED STATES, 1929–1933)

---

1. 15 U.S.C. Sections 1–7.
2. 15 U.S.C. Sections 12–27.
3. 15 U.S.C. Sections 41–58.

31-1 The Sherman Antitrust Act

Today's **antitrust laws** are the direct descendants of common law actions intended to limit *restraints of trade* (agreements between or among firms that have the effect of reducing competition in the marketplace). Such actions date to the fifteenth century in England.

After the U.S. Civil War (1861–1865), the American public became increasingly concerned about declining competition in the marketplace. Large corporate enterprises were attempting to reduce or eliminate competition by legally tying themselves together in contracts to create *business trusts* (unincorporated organizations with limited liability). The most powerful of these organizations was the Standard Oil trust.

In 1890, Congress passed "An Act to Protect Trade and Commerce against Unlawful Restraints and Monopolies"—commonly known as the Sherman Antitrust Act or, more simply, as the Sherman Act. The Sherman Act became (and still is) one of the government's most powerful weapons in the effort to maintain a competitive economy. The act and the role of the Standard Oil trust in its passage are examined in this chapter's *Landmark in the Law* feature.

Antitrust Law Laws protecting commerce from unlawful restraints and anticompetitive practices.

31-1a Major Provisions of the Sherman Act

Sections 1 and 2 contain the main provisions of the Sherman Act:

1. Every contract, combination in the form of trust or otherwise, or conspiracy, in restraint of trade or commerce among the several States, or with foreign nations, is hereby declared to be illegal [and is a felony punishable by a fine and/or imprisonment].

LANDMARK IN THE LAW · The Sherman Antitrust Act

The author of the Sherman Antitrust Act, Senator John Sherman, was the brother of the famous Civil War general William Tecumseh Sherman and a recognized financial authority. Sherman had been concerned for years about diminishing competition in U.S. industry and the emergence of monopolies, such as the Standard Oil trust.

THE STANDARD OIL TRUST By 1890, the Standard Oil trust had become the foremost petroleum refining and marketing combination in the United States. Streamlined, integrated, and centrally controlled, Standard Oil maintained an indisputable monopoly over the industry. The trust controlled 90 percent of the U.S. market for refined petroleum products, making it impossible for small producers to compete.

The increasing consolidation in U.S. industry, and particularly the Standard Oil trust, came to the attention of the public in March 1881. Henry Demarest Lloyd, a young journalist from Chicago, published an article in the *Atlantic Monthly* entitled "The Story of a Great Monopoly." The article argued that the U.S. petroleum industry was dominated by one firm—Standard Oil. Lloyd's article was so popular that the issue was reprinted six times. It marked the beginning of the U.S. public's growing concern over monopolies.

THE PASSAGE OF THE SHERMAN ANTITRUST ACT The common law regarding trade regulation was not always consistent. Certainly, it was not very familiar to the members of Congress. The public concern over large business trusts was familiar, however. In 1888, 1889, and again in 1890, Senator Sherman introduced in Congress bills designed to destroy the large combinations of capital that, he felt, were creating imbalance within the nation's economy.

In 1890, the Fifty-First Congress finally enacted the bill into law. Generally, the act prohibits business combinations and conspiracies that restrain trade and commerce, as well as certain monopolistic practices. According to its author, the Sherman Act "does not announce a new principle of law, but applies old and well-recognized principles of the common law."[a]

APPLICATION TO TODAY'S WORLD *The Sherman Antitrust Act remains very relevant to today's world. The U.S. Department of Justice and state attorneys general investigate many complaints and prosecute a number of corporations for Sherman Act violations each year.*

a. 21 *Congressional Record* 2456 (1890).

2. Every person who shall monopolize, or attempt to monopolize, or combine or conspire with any other person or persons, to monopolize any part of the trade or commerce among the several States, or with foreign nations, shall be deemed guilty of a felony [and is similarly punishable].

Monopoly A market in which there is a single seller or a very limited number of sellers.

Monopoly Power The ability of a monopoly to dictate what takes place in a given market.

Market Power The power of a firm to control the market price of its product. A monopoly has the greatest degree of market power.

31–1b Differences between Section 1 and Section 2

The two sections of the Sherman Act are quite different. Violation of Section 1 requires two or more persons, as a person cannot contract or combine or conspire alone. Thus, the essence of the illegal activity is *the act of joining together.* Section 2, though, can apply either to one person or to two or more persons because it refers to "every person." Thus, unilateral conduct can result in a violation of Section 2.

It follows that the cases brought under Section 1 of the Sherman Act differ from those brought under Section 2. Section 1 cases are often concerned with finding an agreement (written or oral) that leads to a restraint of trade. Section 2 cases deal with the structure of a monopoly that already exists in the marketplace. The term **monopoly** generally is used to describe a market in which there is a single seller or a very limited number of sellers. Whereas Section 1 focuses on agreements that are restrictive—that is, agreements that have a wrongful purpose—Section 2 addresses the misuse of **monopoly power** in the marketplace. Monopoly power exists when a firm has an extreme amount of **market power**—the power to affect the market price of its product. Both Section 1 and Section 2 seek to curtail market practices that result in undesired monopoly pricing and output behavior. For a case to be brought under Section 2, however, the "threshold" or "necessary" amount of monopoly power must already exist. We illustrate the different requirements for violating these two sections of the Sherman Act in Exhibit 31–1.

One of Standard Oil's refineries in Richmond, California, around 1900.

Library of Congress Prints and Photographs Division

31–1c Jurisdictional Requirements

The Sherman Act applies only to restraints that have a substantial impact on interstate commerce. Generally, any activity that substantially affects interstate commerce falls within the scope of the Sherman Act. As will be discussed later in this chapter, the Sherman Act also extends to U.S. nationals abroad who are engaged in activities that have an effect on U.S. foreign commerce. Federal courts have exclusive jurisdiction over antitrust cases brought under the Sherman Act. State laws regulate local restraints on competition, and state courts decide claims brought under those laws.

Exhibit 31–1 Required Elements of a Sherman Act Violation

SECTION 1 VIOLATION REQUIREMENTS	SECTION 2 VIOLATION REQUIREMENTS
1. An agreement between two or more parties that **2.** Unreasonably restrains competition and **3.** Affects interstate commerce.	**1.** The possession of monopoly power in the relevant market, and **2.** The willful acquisition or maintenance of that power as distinguished from its growth or development as a consequence of a superior product, business acumen, or historic accident.

31-2 Section 1 of the Sherman Act

The underlying assumption of Section 1 of the Sherman Act is that society's welfare is harmed if rival firms are permitted to join in an agreement that consolidates their market power or otherwise restrains competition. The types of trade restraints that Section 1 of the Sherman Act prohibits generally fall into two broad categories: *horizontal restraints* and *vertical restraints,* both of which will be explained shortly. First, though, we look at the rules that the courts may apply when assessing the anticompetitive impact of alleged restraints on trade.

31-2a *Per Se* Violations versus the Rule of Reason

Some restraints are so blatantly and substantially anticompetitive that they are deemed *per se* violations—illegal *per se* (on their face, or inherently)—under Section 1. Other agreements, however, even though they result in enhanced market power, do not *unreasonably* restrain trade. Using what is called the **rule of reason,** the courts analyze anticompetitive agreements that allegedly violate Section 1 of the Sherman Act to determine whether they actually constitute reasonable restraints on trade.

Why the Rule of Reason Was Developed The need for a rule-of-reason analysis of some agreements in restraint of trade is obvious—if the rule of reason had not been developed, almost any business agreement could conceivably be held to violate the Sherman Act. Justice Louis Brandeis effectively phrased this sentiment in *Chicago Board of Trade v. United States,* a case decided in 1918:

> Every agreement concerning trade, every regulation of trade, restrains. To bind, to restrain, is of their very essence. The true test of legality is whether the restraint imposed is such as merely regulates and perhaps thereby promotes competition or whether it is such as may suppress or even destroy competition.[4]

Factors Courts Consider under the Rule of Reason When analyzing an alleged Section 1 violation under the rule of reason, a court will consider the following factors:

1. The purpose of the agreement.
2. The parties' ability to implement the agreement to achieve that purpose.
3. The effect or potential effect of the agreement on competition.
4. Whether the parties could have relied on less restrictive means to achieve their purpose.

CASE EXAMPLE 31.1 A group of consumers sued NBC Universal, the Walt Disney Company, and other broadcasters, as well as cable and satellite distributors. The consumers claimed that the bundling together of high-demand and low-demand television channels in cable and satellite programming packages violates the Sherman Act. Bundling forces consumers to pay for channels they do not watch to have access to channels they watch regularly.

The consumers argued that the defendants, through their control of high-demand programming, exercised market power that made it impossible for any distributor to offer unbundled programs. A federal appellate court ruled in favor of the defendants and dismissed the case. The court reasoned that the Sherman Act applies to actions that diminish competition and that the bundling of channels does not injure competition.[5] ■

> "I don't know what a monopoly is until somebody tells me."
>
> **STEVE BALLMER**
> 1956–PRESENT
> (CHIEF EXECUTIVE OFFICER OF MICROSOFT CORPORATION, 2000–2014)

Per Se **Violation** A restraint of trade that is so anticompetitive that it is deemed inherently (*per se*) illegal.

Rule of Reason A test used to determine whether an anticompetitive agreement constitutes a reasonable restraint on trade. Courts consider such factors as the purpose of the agreement, its effect on competition, and whether less restrictive means could have been used.

Does forcing consumers to buy bundles of cable and satellite channels constitute an antitrust violation?

---

4. 246 U.S. 231, 38 S.Ct. 242, 62 L.Ed. 683 (1918).
5. *Brantley v. NBC Universal, Inc.,* 675 F.3d 1192 (9th Cir. 2012).

Horizontal Restraint
Any agreement that restrains competition between rival firms competing in the same market.

LEARNING OBJECTIVE 2
What rule do courts apply to price-fixing agreements, and why?

Price-Fixing Agreement
An agreement between competitors to fix the prices of products or services at a certain level.

31–2b Horizontal Restraints

The term **horizontal restraint** is encountered frequently in antitrust law. A horizontal restraint is any agreement that in some way restrains competition between rival firms competing in the same market. Horizontal restraints may include price-fixing, group boycotts, market divisions, and trade associations.

Price Fixing

Any **price-fixing agreement**—an agreement among competitors to fix prices—constitutes a *per se* violation of Section 1. The agreement on price need not be explicit. As long as it restricts output or artificially fixes price, it violates the law.

CASE EXAMPLE 31.2 In a classic price-fixing case, independent oil producers in Texas and Louisiana were caught between falling demand due to the Great Depression of the 1930s and increasing supply from newly discovered oil fields in the region. In response to these conditions, a group of major refining companies agreed to buy "distress" gasoline (excess supplies) from the independents so as to dispose of it in an "orderly manner." Although there was no explicit agreement as to price, it was clear that the purpose of the agreement was to limit the supply of gasoline on the market and thereby raise prices.

There may have been good reasons for the agreement. Nonetheless, the United States Supreme Court recognized the potentially adverse effects that such an agreement could have on open and free competition. The Court held that the reasonableness of a price-fixing agreement is never a defense. Any agreement that restricts output or artificially fixes price is a *per se* violation of Section 1.[6] ∎

Does a price-fixing agreement among manufacturers of flat-screen televisions have to explicitly state a price?

Price-fixing cartels (groups) are still commonplace in today's business world, particularly among global companies. For instance, the Department of Justice has been investigating a global price-fixing scheme in the auto parts industry for several years. The defendants allegedly agreed to set the prices of starter motors, seat belts, radiators, and other auto parts that were sold to automakers in the United States. By 2015, twenty-six firms had pleaded guilty and agreed to pay $2 million in fines, and additional charges had been filed.

International price-fixing conspiracies have been alleged in various industries, such as air freight, computer monitors, digital commerce, and drug manufacturing. This chapter's *Adapting the Law to the Online Environment* feature discusses price-fixing allegations in the e-book industry.

Group Boycott An agreement by two or more sellers to refuse to deal with a particular person or firm.

Group Boycotts

A **group boycott** is an agreement by two or more sellers to refuse to deal with (that is, to boycott) a particular person or firm. Because they involve concerted action, group boycotts have been held to constitute *per se* violations of Section 1 of the Sherman Act.

To prove a violation of Section 1, the plaintiff must demonstrate that the boycott or joint refusal to deal was undertaken with the intention of eliminating competition or preventing entry into a given market. Most boycotts are illegal. A few types of boycotts, such as group boycotts against a supplier for political reasons, may be protected under the First Amendment right to freedom of expression, however.

Horizontal Market Division

It is a *per se* violation of Section 1 of the Sherman Act for competitors to divide up territories or customers. **EXAMPLE 31.3** Axm Electronics Basics, Halprin Servo Supplies, and Aicarus Prime Electronics compete against each other in the states of Kansas, Nebraska, and Oklahoma. The three firms agree that Axm will sell products only in Kansas, Halprin will sell only in Nebraska, and Aicarus will sell only in Oklahoma.

This concerted action reduces marketing costs and allows all three (assuming there is no other competition) to raise the price of the goods sold in their respective states. The same violation would take place if the three firms agreed to divide up their customers by having

---

6. *United States v. Socony-Vacuum Oil Co.*, 310 U.S. 150, 60 S.Ct. 811, 84 L.Ed. 1129 (1940).

ADAPTING THE LAW TO THE ONLINE ENVIRONMENT
The Justice Department Goes After E-Book Pricing

In 2012, the U.S. Justice Department filed a lawsuit against five major book publishers and Apple, Inc., charging that they had conspired to fix the prices of e-books. According to the complaint, publishing executives met "in private rooms for dinner in upscale Manhattan restaurants" to discuss ways to limit e-book price competition. As a result, the Justice Department alleged that consumers paid "tens of millions of dollars more for e-books than they otherwise would have paid."

The E-Book Market Explodes
E-books were only a niche product until Amazon.com released its first Kindle e-book reader. To sell more Kindles, Amazon offered thousands of popular books for downloading at $9.99 per e-book. Amazon kept 50 percent and gave 50 percent to the publishers, who had to agree to Amazon's pricing. Although Amazon lost money on its e-book sales, it made up the losses by selling more Kindles.

Enter Apple's iPad
When the iPad entered the scene, Apple and the book publishers agreed to use Apple's "agency" model, which allowed the publishers to set their own prices while Apple kept 30 percent as a commission. Apple was already using this model for games and apps for its iPhones and iPads.

The agency pricing model has been a standard sales approach in many industries and has been upheld by federal courts for years. Nevertheless, the Justice Department argued that because the publishers involved in the arrangement chose prices that were relatively similar, price fixing was evident and "would not have occurred without the conspiracy among the defendants."

A Federal Court Finds Apple Liable for Conspiring to Fix Prices
Ultimately, a U.S. district court ruled that the agency model is *per se* illegal and held Apple liable for violating the Sherman Act.[a] Apple appealed, arguing that the judge should have applied a rule-of-reason analysis rather than a *per se* analysis, but a federal appellate court affirmed.

The federal appellate court held that Apple's agreement with publishers to raise e-book prices was a *per se* illegal price-fixing conspiracy. As a result, Apple was ordered to pay $400 million to consumers and $50 million in attorneys' fees.[b]

CRITICAL THINKING
■ The publishing business is in dire straits today, with retail bookstores going bankrupt and publishers laying off hundreds of employees. Why do you think the declining book business was worthy of so much attention from the Justice Department?

---

a. *United States v. Apple Inc.*, 952 F.Supp.2d 638 (S.D.N.Y. 2013); see also *In re Electronic Books Antitrust Litigation*, 2014 WL 2535112 (S.D.N.Y. 2014).

b. *United States v. Apple, Inc.*, ___ F.3d ___, 2015 WL 3953243 (2d Cir. 2015). Apple had previously agreed to settle the case for these amounts if its appeal was unsuccessful.

Axm sell only to institutional purchasers (such as governments and schools) in all three states, Halprin only to wholesalers, and Aicarus only to retailers. ■

Trade Associations Businesses in the same general industry or profession frequently organize trade associations to pursue common interests. A trade association may engage in various joint activities, such as exchanging information, representing the members' business interests before governmental bodies, conducting advertising campaigns, and setting regulatory standards to govern the industry or profession.

Generally, the rule of reason is applied to many of these horizontal actions. If a court finds that a trade association practice or agreement that restrains trade is sufficiently beneficial both to the association and to the public, it may deem the restraint reasonable.

In concentrated industries, however, trade associations can be, and have been, used as a means to facilitate anticompetitive actions, such as fixing prices or allocating markets. A **concentrated industry** is one in which either a single firm or a small number of firms control a large percentage of market sales. When trade association agreements have substantially anticompetitive effects, a court will consider them to be in violation of Section 1 of the Sherman Act.

Concentrated Industry An industry in which a single firm or a small number of firms control a large percentage of market sales.

31-2c Vertical Restraints

Vertical Restraint A restraint of trade created by an agreement between firms at different levels in the manufacturing and distribution process.

A **vertical restraint** of trade results from an agreement between firms at different levels in the manufacturing and distribution process. In contrast to horizontal relationships, which occur at the same level of operation, vertical relationships encompass the entire chain of production. The chain of production normally includes the purchase of inventory, basic manufacturing, distribution to wholesalers, and eventual sale of a product at the retail level. When a single firm carries out two or more of the separate functional phases, it is considered to be a **vertically integrated firm.**

Vertically Integrated Firm A firm that carries out two or more functional phases (manufacturing, distribution, and retailing, for example) of the chain of production.

Even though firms operating at different functional levels are not in direct competition with one another, they are in competition with other firms. Thus, agreements between firms standing in a vertical relationship may affect competition. Some vertical restraints are *per se* violations of Section 1. Others are judged under the rule of reason.

Territorial or Customer Restrictions In arranging for the distribution of its products, a manufacturing firm often wishes to insulate dealers from direct competition with other dealers selling the product. To do so, it may institute territorial restrictions or attempt to prohibit wholesalers or retailers from reselling the product to certain classes of buyers, such as competing retailers.

May Have Legitimate Purpose. A firm may have legitimate reasons for imposing such territorial or customer restrictions. For instance, an electronics manufacturer may wish to prevent a dealer from reducing costs and undercutting rivals by offering the manufacturer's products without promotion or customer service. In this situation, the cost-cutting dealer reaps the benefits (sales of the product) paid for by other dealers who undertake promotion and arrange for customer service. By not providing customer service (and relying on a nearby dealer to provide these services), the cost-cutting dealer may also harm the manufacturer's reputation.

Judged under the Rule of Reason. Territorial and customer restrictions were once considered *per se* violations of Section 1, but in 1977, the United States Supreme Court held that they should be judged under the rule of reason. **CASE EXAMPLE 31.4** The Supreme Court case involved GTE Sylvania, Inc., a manufacturer of television sets. Sylvania limited the number of retail franchises that it granted in any given geographic area. It also required each franchise to sell only Sylvania products from that location.

Sylvania retained sole discretion to increase the number of retailers in an area. When the company decided to open a new franchise, it terminated the franchise of Continental T.V., Inc. Continental sued, claiming that Sylvania's vertically restrictive franchise system violated Section 1. The Supreme Court found that "vertical restrictions promote interbrand competition by allowing the manufacturer to achieve certain efficiencies in the distribution of his products." Therefore, Sylvania's vertical system, which was not price restrictive, did not constitute a *per se* violation of Section 1 of the Sherman Act.[7] ▪

The decision in the *Continental* case marked a definite shift from rigid characterization of these kinds of vertical restraints to a more flexible, economic analysis under the rule of reason. A firm may have legitimate reasons for imposing territorial or customer restrictions, and not all such restrictions harm competition.

Resale Price Maintenance Agreements An agreement between a manufacturer and a distributor or retailer in which the manufacturer specifies what the retail prices of its products must be is referred to as a **resale price maintenance agreement.** Such agreements were also once considered to be *per se* violations of the Sherman Act.

Resale Price Maintenance Agreement An agreement between a manufacturer and a retailer in which the manufacturer specifies what the retail prices of its products must be.

---

7. *Continental T.V., Inc. v. GTE Sylvania, Inc.*, 433 U.S. 36, 97 S.Ct. 2549, 53 L.Ed.2d 568 (1977).

Today, however, both *maximum* resale price maintenance agreements and *minimum* resale price maintenance agreements are judged under the rule of reason.[8] The setting of a maximum— or a minimum—price that retailers and distributors can charge for a manufacturer's products may sometimes increase competition and benefit consumers.

31–3 Section 2 of the Sherman Act

Section 1 of the Sherman Act prohibits certain concerted activities that restrain trade. In contrast, Section 2 condemns "every person who shall monopolize, or attempt to monopolize." Thus, two distinct types of behavior are subject to sanction under Section 2: *monopolization* and *attempts to monopolize.*

One tactic that may be involved in either offense is **predatory pricing.** Predatory pricing involves an attempt by one firm to drive its competitors from the market by selling its product at prices substantially *below* the normal costs of production. Once the competitors are eliminated, the firm will presumably attempt to recapture its losses and go on to earn higher profits by driving prices up far above their competitive levels.

31–3a Monopolization

The United States Supreme Court has defined the offense of **monopolization** as involving two elements:

1. The possession of monopoly power in the relevant market.

2. "The willful acquisition or maintenance of [that] power as distinguished from growth or development as a consequence of a superior product, business acumen, or historic accident."[9]

To establish a violation of Section 2, a plaintiff must prove both of these elements—monopoly power and an intent to monopolize.

Defining Monopoly Power The Sherman Act does not define *monopoly.* In economic theory, monopoly refers to control of a single market by a single entity. It is well established in antitrust law, however, that a firm may be deemed a monopolist even though it is not the sole seller in a market.

Additionally, size alone does not determine whether a firm is a monopoly. For instance, a "mom and pop" grocery located in an isolated town is a monopolist if it is the only grocery serving that particular market. Size in relation to the market is what matters, because monopoly involves the power to affect prices.

Proving Monopoly Power Monopoly power may be proved by direct evidence that the firm used its power to control prices and restrict output.[10] Usually, though, there is not enough evidence to show that the firm was intentionally controlling prices, so the plaintiff has to offer indirect, or circumstantial, evidence of monopoly power.

To prove monopoly power indirectly, the plaintiff must show that the firm has a dominant share of the relevant market and that there are significant barriers for new competitors entering that market. **CASE EXAMPLE 31.5** DuPont manufactures and sells para-aramid fiber, a synthetic fiber used to make body armor, fiber-optic cables, and tires, among other things.

LEARNING OBJECTIVE 3
What is the main type of activity prohibited by Section 2 of the Sherman Act?

Predatory Pricing The pricing of a product below cost with the intent to drive competitors out of the market.

Monopolization The possession of monopoly power in the relevant market and the willful acquisition or maintenance of that power, as distinguished from growth or development as a consequence of a superior product, business acumen, or historic accident.

---

8. The United States Supreme Court ruled that maximum resale price agreements should be judged under the rule of reason in *State Oil Co. v. Khan*, 522 U.S. 3, 118 S.Ct. 275, 139 L.Ed.2d 199 (1997). In *Leegin Creative Leather Products, Inc. v. PSKS, Inc.*, 551 U.S. 877, 127 S.Ct. 2705, 168 L.Ed.2d 623 (2007), the Supreme Court found that the rule of reason also applies to minimum resale price agreements.

9. *United States v. Grinnell Corp.*, 384 U.S. 563, 86 S.Ct. 1698, 16 L.Ed.2d 778 (1966).

10. See, for example, *Broadcom Corp. v. Qualcomm, Inc.*, 501 F.3d 297 (3d Cir. 2007).

Although several companies around the world manufacture this fiber, only three sell in the U.S. market—DuPont (based in the United States), Teijin (based in the Netherlands), and Kolon Industries, Inc. (based in Korea). DuPont is the industry leader, and at times has produced 60 percent of all para-aramid fibers purchased in the United States.

After DuPont brought suit against Kolon for theft and misappropriation of trade secrets, Kolon counterclaimed that DuPont had illegally monopolized and attempted to monopolize the U.S. para-aramid market in violation of Section 2. Kolon claimed that, to deter competition, DuPont had illegally used multiyear supply agreements for all of its high-volume para-aramid customers. A federal appellate court, however, found that there was insufficient proof that DuPont possessed monopoly power in the U.S. market during the relevant time period (between 2006 and 2009). Additionally, the court concluded that Kolon had not showed that the supply agreements foreclosed competition. Therefore, the court held in favor of DuPont on the antitrust claims.[11]

ETHICAL ISSUE

Should monopolies in the online world be broken up? Facebook has more than 1.3 billion active members worldwide. Amazon has about 50 percent of the U.S. book market and an even larger share of the market for e-books. Google performs almost 70 percent of online searches in the United States and over 90 percent in Europe. Should these digital monopolies be broken up, as they probably would have been if they were traditional businesses selling physical products?

Critics of Google point out that it favors its own services when it presents search results. Also, because it has such a large trove of data about its users—data valuable to advertisers—it can charge advertisers higher rates than do its competitors. The European Union (EU) has demanded that Google unbundle its search engines from other commercial services. The goal: to ensure a so-called level playing field for European companies. In 2015, the EU formally accused Google of abusing its dominance in Web searches. But in the United States, the Federal Trade Commission considered the same possibility and chose not to act against Google.

Those who do not believe that standard antitrust laws should be applied to digital firms argue that start-ups are, in fact, starting up all the time to take business away from today's digital monopolies. Start-up costs for these new companies are relatively low. Consider that a major social network a few years ago was MySpace, which today is a shadow of its former self. Google spent considerable sums to become the dominant social network—Orkut—in Brazil, but lost out to Facebook. Even today, Facebook is eating away at Google's advertising revenues.

In the end, online consumers have a number of choices among services, and they can make changes at zero cost. Facebook may dominate social media today, for instance, but alternatives exist, including Twitter and Pinterest. Google has a number of competitors, such as Bing and Yahoo. These market realities make it difficult to show that online monopolies truly harm consumers.

Why did Kolon Industries claim DuPont had illegally monopolized?

Relevant Market Before a court can determine whether a firm has a dominant market share, it must define the relevant market. The relevant market consists of two elements: a relevant product market and a relevant geographic market.

Relevant Product Market. The relevant product market includes all products that, although produced by different firms, have identical attributes—for example, tea. It also includes reasonably interchangeable products. Products are considered reasonably interchangeable if consumers treat them as acceptable substitutes (coffee may be substituted for tea, for instance).

Establishing the relevant product market is often a key issue in monopolization cases because the way the market is defined may determine whether a firm

---

11. *Kolon Industries, Inc. v. E.I. DuPont de Nemours & Co.*, 748 F.3d 160 (4th Cir. 2014).

has monopoly power. When the product market is defined narrowly, the degree of a firm's market power appears greater. **EXAMPLE 31.6** White Whale Apps acquires Springleaf Apps, its main competitor in nationwide Android-based mobile phone apps. White Whale maintains that the relevant product market consists of all online retailers of mobile phone apps. The Federal Trade Commission (FTC), however, argues that the relevant product market consists of retailers that sell only apps for Android mobile phones. Under the FTC's narrower definition, White Whale can be seen to have a dominant share of the relevant product market. Thus, the FTC can take appropriate actions against White Whale. ■

In the following case, the FTC alleged that the leading producer of domestic ductile iron pipefittings sought to maintain its alleged monopoly power in violation of antitrust law. The FTC filed this action under Section 5 of the Federal Trade Commission Act. Section 5, like Section 2 of the Sherman Act, requires proof of both the possession of monopoly power in the relevant market and the willful acquisition or maintenance of that power.

CASE 31.1

McWane, Inc. v. Federal Trade Commission

United States Court of Appeals, Eleventh Circuit, 783 F.3d 814 (2015).

FACTS Pipefittings join together pipes and help direct the flow of pressurized water in pipeline systems. Certain municipal, state, and federal laws require waterworks projects to use fittings made in the United States, so specifications for such projects may require the use of "domestic fittings." McWane, Inc., is the dominant producer of domestic ductile iron fittings. When Star Pipe Products entered the market, McWane told its distributors that unless they bought all of their domestic fittings from McWane, they would lose their rebates and be cut off from purchases for twelve weeks. The Federal Trade Commission (FTC) brought an action against McWane. Ultimately, the FTC ordered McWane to stop requiring exclusivity from distributors. McWane appealed.

ISSUE Did McWane's exclusivity policy constitute an illegal attempt to maintain monopoly power?

DECISION Yes. The U.S. Court of Appeals for the Eleventh Circuit affirmed the FTC's order. This conclusion was supported by McWane's market share, the amount of capital needed to enter the market, and McWane's power to control prices in the market.

If an iron pipefitting company forces all customers to buy all fittings from that company, what antitrust law does that violate?

REASON The FTC found that the relevant product market consisted of projects that specified domestically made fittings. When a law or a user's preference required a project to use domestic fittings, imported fittings were not reasonable substitutes. In that market, McWane consistently charged higher prices—20 to 95 percent more than for other projects. As for McWane's monopoly power, the FTC found that the firm's share of the domestic fittings market had been 100 percent until Star Pipes began to compete. But the competitor's share of the market was never more than 10 percent, and its entry into the market had no effect on McWane's ability to control prices. The FTC also found substantial barriers to entry into the market. A "significant" capital investment was required to overcome the existing relationships among manufacturers, distributors, and users, and to develop the necessary pipefitting patterns and moldings. McWane's exclusivity policy posed a further barrier by "shrinking" the number of distributors.

CRITICAL THINKING—Economic Consideration *How did McWane's exclusivity policy harm competition? Explain.*

Relevant Geographic Market. The second component of the relevant market is the market's geographic extent. For products that are sold nationwide, the geographic market encompasses the entire United States. If transportation costs are significant or a producer and its competitors sell in only a limited area (one in which customers have no access to other sources of the product), the geographic market is limited to that area. A national firm may thus compete in several distinct areas and have monopoly power in one area but not in another.

KNOW THIS

Section 2 of the Sherman Act essentially condemns the *act* of monopolizing, not the possession of monopoly power.

Generally, the geographic market is that section of the country within which a firm can increase its price a bit without attracting new sellers or losing many customers to alternative suppliers outside that area. Of course, the Internet and e-commerce are changing the notion of the size and limits of a geographic market. It may become difficult to perceive any geographic market as local, except for products that are not easily transported, such as concrete.

The Intent Requirement   Monopoly power, in and of itself, does not constitute the offense of monopolization under Section 2 of the Sherman Act. The offense also requires an *intent* to monopolize.

A dominant market share may be the result of business acumen or the development of a superior product. It may simply be the result of a historic accident. In these situations, the acquisition of monopoly power is not an antitrust violation. Indeed, it would be contrary to society's interest to condemn every firm that acquired a position of power because it was well managed and efficient and marketed a product desired by consumers.

In contrast, if a firm possesses market power as a result of carrying out some purposeful act to acquire or maintain that power through anticompetitive means, then it is in violation of Section 2. In most monopolization cases, intent may be inferred from evidence that the firm had monopoly power and engaged in anticompetitive behavior.

PREVENTING LEGAL DISPUTES

Because exclusionary conduct can have legitimate efficiency-enhancing effects, it can be difficult to determine when conduct will be viewed as anticompetitive and a violation of Section 2 of the Sherman Act. Thus, a business that possesses monopoly power must be careful that its actions provide no evidence of intent to monopolize. Even a business that does not have a dominant market share will be wise to take precautions.

As a businessperson, make sure that you can articulate clear, legitimate reasons for particular conduct or a particular contract and that you do not provide any direct evidence (damaging e-mails, for example) of an intent to exclude competitors. A court will be less likely to infer the intent to monopolize if the specific conduct was aimed at increasing output and lowering per-unit costs, improving product quality, or protecting a patented technology or innovation.

Unilateral Refusals to Deal   Group boycotts, discussed earlier, are also joint refusals to deal—sellers acting as a group jointly refuse to deal with another business or individual. These group refusals are subject to close scrutiny under Section 1 of the Sherman Act. A single manufacturer acting unilaterally, though, normally is free to deal, or not to deal, with whomever it wishes.[12]

Nevertheless, in limited circumstances, a unilateral refusal to deal will violate antitrust laws. These instances involve offenses proscribed under Section 2 of the Sherman Act. They occur only if (1) the firm refusing to deal has—or is likely to acquire—monopoly power and (2) the refusal is likely to have an anticompetitive effect on a particular market.

EXAMPLE 31.7 Clark Industries, the owner of three of the four major downhill ski areas in Blue Hills, Idaho, refuses to continue participating in a jointly offered six-day "all Blue Hills" lift ticket. Clark's refusal to cooperate with its smaller competitor is a violation of Section 2 of the Sherman Act. Because Clark owns three-fourths of the local ski areas, it has monopoly power. Thus, its unilateral refusal to deal has an anticompetitive effect on the market. ■

31–3b Attempts to Monopolize

Section 2 also prohibits **attempted monopolization** of a market, which requires proof of the following three elements:

Attempted Monopolization
An action by a firm that involves anticompetitive conduct, the intent to gain monopoly power, and a "dangerous probability" of success in achieving monopoly power.

---

12. See, for example, *Pacific Bell Telephone Co. v. Linkline Communications, Inc.*, 555 U.S. 438, 129 S.Ct. 1109, 172 L.Ed.2d 836 (2009).

1. Anticompetitive conduct.

2. The specific intent to exclude competitors and garner monopoly power.

3. A "dangerous" probability of success in achieving monopoly power. The probability cannot be dangerous unless the alleged offender possesses some degree of market power. Only *serious* threats of monopolization are condemned as violations.

As mentioned earlier, predatory pricing is a form of anticompetitive conduct that, in theory, can be used by firms that are attempting to monopolize. (Predatory pricing may also lead to claims of price discrimination, discussed shortly.) Related to predatory pricing is *predatory bidding*. This practice involves the acquisition and use of *monopsony power*, which is market power on the *buy* side of a market. Predatory bidding occurs when a buyer bids up the price of an input too high for its competitors to pay, causing them to leave the market. The predatory bidder then attempts to drive down input prices to reap above-competitive profits and recoup any losses it suffered in bidding up the input prices.

The question in the following *Spotlight Case* was whether a claim of predatory bidding was sufficiently similar to a claim of predatory pricing that the same antitrust test should apply to both.

If the dominant owner of downhill ski facilities refuses to include its smallest competitor in an inclusive all-area lift ticket, why is that a violation of antitrust laws?

SPOTLIGHT ON WEYERHAEUSER: CASE 31.2

Weyerhaeuser Co. v. Ross-Simmons Hardwood Lumber Co.

Supreme Court of the United States, 549 U.S. 312, 127 S.Ct. 1069, 166 L.Ed.2d 911 (2007).

FACTS Weyerhaeuser Company entered the Pacific Northwest's hardwood lumber market in 1980. By 2000, Weyerhaeuser owned six mills processing 65 percent of the red alder logs in the region. Meanwhile, Ross-Simmons Hardwood Lumber Company operated a single competing mill. When the prices of the logs rose and those for the lumber fell, Ross-Simmons suffered heavy losses. Several million dollars in debt, the mill closed in 2001.

Ross-Simmons filed a suit in a federal district court against Weyerhaeuser, alleging attempted monopolization under Section 2 of the Sherman Act. Ross-Simmons claimed that Weyerhaeuser used its dominant position in the market to bid up the prices of logs and prevent its competitors from being profitable. Weyerhaeuser argued that the antitrust test for predatory pricing applies to a claim of predatory bidding and that Ross-Simmons had not met this standard. The district court ruled in favor of the plaintiff, the U.S. Court of Appeals for the Ninth Circuit affirmed, and Weyerhaeuser appealed to the United States Supreme Court.

ISSUE Does the antitrust test that applies to a claim of predatory pricing also apply to a claim of predatory bidding?

Was predatory bidding on the price of alder logs tantamount to predatory pricing and therefore illegal?

DECISION Yes. Because Ross-Simmons conceded that it had not met this standard, the Supreme Court vacated the lower court's judgment and remanded the case.

REASON Both predatory pricing and predatory bidding involve a company's intentional use of pricing for an anticompetitive purpose. Both actions require a company to incur a short-term loss in the expectation of later making a "supra-competitive" profit. Because a "rational" firm is unlikely to "make this sacrifice," both schemes are "rarely tried and even more rarely successful." A failed scheme of either type can benefit consumers.

Under the Supreme Court's predatory-pricing test, a plaintiff must establish two things. First, the plaintiff must show that the competitor's complained-of low prices are below an appropriate measure of the competitor's costs. Second, the plaintiff must show that the competitor has a dangerous probability of recouping the losses incurred by selling below cost.

Because of the similarity of predatory pricing and predatory bidding, the two-part predatory-pricing test should apply to predatory-bidding claims as well. Thus, a plaintiff alleging predatory bidding

Continues

must first prove that the defendant's "bidding on the buy side caused the cost of the relevant output to rise above the revenues generated in the sale of those outputs." The plaintiff must then prove that "the defendant has a dangerous probability of recouping the losses incurred in bidding up input prices through the exercise of monopsony power."

WHY IS THIS CASE IMPORTANT? *Predatory-bidding schemes are rare. Under the standard that the Court imposed in this case, a successful*

claim based on predatory bidding will likely be even more rare. But this may not be a negative development, at least for consumers. A predatory-bidding scheme can actually benefit consumers—a predator's high bidding can cause it to acquire more inputs, which can lead to the manufacture of more outputs, and increases in output generally result in lower prices for consumers.

LEARNING OBJECTIVE 4

What are the four major provisions of the Clayton Act, and what types of activities do these provisions prohibit?

31-4 The Clayton Act

In 1914, Congress attempted to strengthen federal antitrust laws by enacting the Clayton Act. The act was aimed at specific anticompetitive or monopolistic practices that the Sherman Act did not cover. The substantive provisions of the act deal with four distinct forms of business behavior, which are declared illegal but not criminal. In each instance, the act states that the behavior is illegal only if it tends to substantially lessen competition or to create monopoly power.

The major offenses under the Clayton Act are set out in Sections 2, 3, 7, and 8 of the act.

31-4a Section 2—Price Discrimination

Price Discrimination
A seller's act of charging competing buyers different prices for identical products or services.

Section 2 of the Clayton Act prohibits **price discrimination,** which occurs when a seller charges different prices to competing buyers for identical goods or services. Congress strengthened this section by amending it in 1936 with the passage of the Robinson-Patman Act. As amended, Section 2 prohibits price discrimination that cannot be justified by differences in production costs, transportation costs, or cost differences due to other reasons.

Requirements To violate Section 2, the seller must be engaged in interstate commerce, the goods must be of like grade and quality, and goods must have been sold to two or more purchasers. In addition, the effect of the price discrimination must be to substantially lessen competition, tend to create a monopoly, or otherwise injure competition. Without proof of an actual injury resulting from the price discrimination, the plaintiff cannot recover damages.

Price discrimination claims can arise from discounts, offsets, rebates, or allowances given to one buyer over another. Giving favorable credit terms, delivery, or freight charges to only some buyers can also lead to allegations of price discrimination. For instance, in some circumstances, offering goods to different customers at the same price but including free delivery only for some of the customers may violate Section 2.

"Becoming number one is easier than remaining number one."

BILL BRADLEY
1943–PRESENT
(AMERICAN POLITICIAN AND ATHLETE)

Defenses There are several statutory defenses to liability for price discrimination.

1. *Cost justification.* If the seller can justify the price reduction by demonstrating that a particular buyer's purchases saved the seller costs in producing and selling the goods, the seller will not be liable for price discrimination.

2. *Meeting competitor's prices.* If the seller charged the lower price in a good faith attempt to meet an equally low price of a competitor, the seller will not be liable for price discrimination. **EXAMPLE 31.8** Rogue, Inc., is a retail dealer of Mercury Marine outboard motors in Shady Cove, Oregon. Mercury Marine also sells its motors to other dealers in the Shady Cove area. When Rogue discovers that Mercury is selling its outboard motors at a substantial discount to Rogue's largest competitor, it files a price discrimination

lawsuit. Mercury Marine can defend itself by showing that the discounts given to Rogue's competitor were made in good faith to meet the low price charged by another manufacturer of marine motors. ■

3. *Changing market conditions.* A seller may lower its price on an item in response to changing conditions affecting the market for or the marketability of the goods concerned. Thus, if an advance in technology makes a particular product less marketable than it was previously, a seller can lower the product's price.

31-4b Section 3—Exclusionary Practices

Under Section 3 of the Clayton Act, sellers or lessors cannot condition the sale or lease of goods on the buyer's or lessee's promise not to use or deal in the goods of the seller's competitor. In effect, this section prohibits two types of vertical agreements involving exclusionary practices—*exclusive-dealing contracts* and *tying arrangements.*

Exclusive-Dealing Contracts
A contract under which a seller forbids a buyer to purchase products from the seller's competitors is called an **exclusive-dealing contract.** A seller is prohibited from making an exclusive-dealing contract under Section 3 if the effect of the contract is "to substantially lessen competition or tend to create a monopoly."

CASE EXAMPLE 31.9 In a classic case decided by the United States Supreme Court in 1949, Standard Oil Company, the largest gasoline seller in the nation at that time, made exclusive-dealing contracts with independent stations in seven western states. The contracts involved 16 percent of all retail outlets, with sales amounting to approximately 7 percent of all retail sales in that market. The market was substantially concentrated because the seven largest gasoline suppliers all used exclusive-dealing contracts with their independent retailers. Together, these suppliers controlled 65 percent of the market.

The Court looked at market conditions after the arrangements were instituted and found that market shares were extremely stable and entry into the market was apparently restricted. Because competition was "foreclosed in a substantial share" of the relevant market, the Court held that Section 3 of the Clayton Act had been violated.[13] ■ Note that since the Supreme Court's 1949 decision, a number of subsequent decisions have called the holding in this case into doubt.[14]

Today, it is clear that to violate antitrust law, an exclusive-dealing agreement (or a tying arrangement, discussed next) must qualitatively and substantially harm competition. To prevail, a plaintiff must present affirmative evidence that the performance of the agreement will foreclose competition and harm consumers.

Tying Arrangements
When a seller conditions the sale of a product (the tying product) on the buyer's agreement to purchase another product (the tied product) produced or distributed by the same seller, a **tying arrangement** results. The legality of a tying arrangement (or *tie-in sales agreement*) depends on many factors, particularly the purpose of the agreement and its likely effect on competition in the relevant markets (the market for the tying product and the market for the tied product).

EXAMPLE 31.10 Morshigi Precision, Inc., manufactures laptop hardware and provides repair service for the hardware. Morshigi also makes and markets software, but the company will provide support for buyers of the software only if they also buy its hardware service. This is a tying arrangement. Depending on the purpose of the agreement and the effect of the agreement on competition in the market for the two products, the agreement may be illegal. ■

If an outboard motor manufacturer gives discounts to one dealer but not another, is it violating antitrust laws?

Exclusive-Dealing Contract An agreement under which a seller forbids a buyer to purchase products from the seller's competitors.

Tying Arrangement A seller's act of conditioning the sale of a product or service on the buyer's agreement to purchase another product or service from the seller.

---

13. *Standard Oil Co. of California v. United States*, 337 U.S. 293, 69 S.Ct. 1051, 93 L.Ed. 1371 (1949).
14. See, for example, *Illinois Tool Works, Inc. v. Independent Ink, Inc.*, 547 U.S. 28, 126 S.Ct. 1281, 164 L.Ed.2d 26 (2006); and *Stop & Shop Supermarket Co. v. Blue Cross & Blue Shield of Rhode Island*, 373 F.3d 57 (1st Cir. 2004).

A laptop manufacturer also makes software, but will only provide updates for buyers of the software if they bought the hardware. What is this called?

Section 3 of the Clayton Act has been held to apply only to commodities, not to services. Some tying arrangements, however, can also be considered agreements that restrain trade in violation of Section 1 of the Sherman Act. Thus, cases involving tying arrangements of services have been brought under Section 1 of the Sherman Act. Although earlier cases condemned tying arrangements as illegal *per se,* courts now evaluate tying agreements under the rule of reason.

In the following case, a concertgoer claimed that a promoter's inclusion of a parking fee in the price of a ticket was an unlawful tying arrangement.

CASE 31.3

Batson v. Live Nation Entertainment, Inc.

United States Court of Appeals, Seventh Circuit, 746 F.3d 827 (2014).

FACTS James Batson bought a nonrefundable ticket from Live Nation Entertainment, Inc., to attend a rock concert at the Charter One Pavilion in Chicago. The front of the ticket noted that the price included a nine-dollar parking fee. Batson did not have a car to park, however. In fact, he had walked to the concert venue and had bought the ticket just before the performance.

Frustrated at being charged for parking that he did not need, Batson filed a suit in a federal district court against Live Nation. He argued that the bundled parking fee was unfair because consumers were forced to pay it or forego the concert. He asserted that this was a tying arrangement in violation of Section 1 of the Sherman Act. The court dismissed the suit, and Batson appealed.

ISSUE Was bundling a parking fee with the price of a concert ticket a permissible tying arrangement under Section 1 of the Sherman Act?

DECISION Yes. The U.S. Court of Appeals for the Seventh Circuit affirmed the dismissal of Batson's claim.

REASON While the court understood Batson's desire to avoid paying for parking he did not need, it noted, "there is no rule that requires everything to be sold on a fully unbundled basis." A tying arrangement violates Section 1 of the Sherman Act only if a seller

Can Live Nation include a parking fee for all of its tickets?

has sufficient power in the tying product market that forcing the buyer to accept a second product restrains competition in the market for the tied product.

Here, the court was unable to identify a product market in which Live Nation had sufficient power to force consumers who wanted to attend a concert (the tying product) to buy "useless parking rights" (the tied product). The Charter One Pavilion in Chicago or any other "single popular venue is not a stand-alone relevant market." But even if it were, there was no evidence that Live Nation's parking tie-in restrained competition for parking in Chicago. "There are times when consumers are required to accept a package deal in order to get the part of the package they want." For example, a "student may prefer to pay lower tuition and avoid 'free' pizza days. But while some people may find [such] bundles annoying, or even unfair, the tie is not illegal unless the standards [for a violation of antitrust law] have been met."

WHAT IF THE FACTS WERE DIFFERENT? *Suppose that instead of noting on the ticket that the price included a parking fee, Live Nation had simply charged $9 more for the ticket and announced that there was "free" parking for all who needed it. Would the result have been different? Why or why not?*

31-4c Section 7—Mergers

Under Section 7 of the Clayton Act, a person or business organization cannot hold stock or assets in another entity "where the effect . . . may be to substantially lessen competition." Section 7 is the statutory authority for preventing mergers or acquisitions that could result in monopoly power or a substantial lessening of competition in the marketplace.

Market Concentration A crucial consideration in most merger cases is the **market concentration** of a product or business. Determining market concentration involves allocating percentage market shares among the various companies in the relevant market. When a small number of companies control a large share of the market, the market is concentrated.

EXAMPLE 31.11 If the four largest grocery stores in Chicago account for 80 percent of all retail food sales, the market is concentrated in those four firms. If one of these stores absorbs the assets and liabilities of another, so that the other ceases to exist, the result is a merger that further concentrates the market and possibly diminishes competition. ■

Competition is not necessarily diminished solely as a result of market concentration, and courts will consider other factors in determining whether a merger will violate Section 7. One factor of particular importance in evaluating the effects of a merger is whether the merger will make it more difficult for *potential* competitors to enter the relevant market.

Market Concentration The degree to which a small number of firms control a large percentage of a relevant market.

Horizontal Mergers Mergers between firms that compete with each other in the same market are called **horizontal mergers.** If a horizontal merger creates an entity with a significant market share, the merger will be presumed illegal because it increases market concentration.

When analyzing the legality of a horizontal merger, the courts also consider three other factors: the overall concentration of the relevant product market, the relevant market's history of tending toward concentration, and whether the merger is apparently designed to establish market power or to restrict competition.

Horizontal Merger A merger between two firms that are competing in the same market.

Vertical Mergers A **vertical merger** occurs when a company at one stage of production acquires a company at a higher or lower stage of production. An example of a vertical merger is a company merging with one of its suppliers or retailers.

Whether a vertical merger is illegal generally depends on several factors, such as whether the merger would produce a firm controlling an undue proportion of the relevant market. The courts also analyze the concentration of firms in the market, the barriers to entry into the market, and the apparent intent of the merging parties. Mergers that do not prevent competitors of either merging firm from competing in a segment of the market are legal.

Vertical Merger The acquisition by a company at one stage of production of a company at a higher or lower stage of production (such as a company merging with one of its suppliers or retailers).

31-4d Section 8—Interlocking Directorates

Section 8 of the Clayton Act deals with *interlocking directorates*—that is, the practice whereby individuals serve as directors on the boards of two or more competing companies simultaneously. Specifically, no person may be a director in two or more competing corporations at the same time if either of the corporations has capital, surplus, or undivided profits aggregating more than $31,084,000 or competitive sales of $3,108,400 or more. The FTC adjusts the threshold amounts each year. (The amounts given here are those announced by the FTC in 2015.)

The reasoning behind the FTC's prohibition of interlocking directorates is that if two competing businesses share the same officers and directors, the firms are unlikely to compete with one another, or to compete aggressively. If directors or officers do not comply with this prohibition, they may be liable under the Clayton Act.

31-5 Enforcement and Exemptions

The federal agencies that enforce the federal antitrust laws are the U.S. Department of Justice (DOJ) and the Federal Trade Commission (FTC). The FTC was established in 1914 by the Federal Trade Commission Act. Section 5 of that act (mentioned earlier in this chapter) condemns all forms of anticompetitive behavior that are not covered under other federal antitrust laws.

LEARNING OBJECTIVE 5
What agencies of the federal government enforce the federal antitrust laws?

31-5a Enforcement by Federal Agencies

Only the DOJ can prosecute violations of the Sherman Act, which may be either criminal or civil offenses. Violations of the Clayton Act are not crimes, but the act can be enforced by either the DOJ or the FTC through civil proceedings.

Divestiture A company's sale of one or more of its divisions' operating functions under court order as part of the enforcement of the antitrust laws.

The DOJ or the FTC may ask the courts to impose various remedies, including **divestiture** (making a company give up one or more of its operating functions) and dissolution. A meat-packing firm, for instance, might be forced to divest itself of control or ownership of butcher shops. (To find out how you can avoid antitrust problems, see the *Business Application* feature at the end of this chapter.)

The FTC has sole authority to enforce violations of Section 5 of the Federal Trade Commission Act. FTC actions are effected through administrative orders, but if a firm violates an FTC order, the FTC can seek court sanctions for the violation.

31-5b Enforcement by Private Parties

Treble Damages Damages that, by statute, are three times the amount of actual damages suffered.

A private party who has been injured as a result of a violation of the Sherman Act or the Clayton Act can sue for **treble damages** (three times the actual damages suffered) and attorneys' fees. In some instances, private parties may also seek injunctive relief to prevent antitrust violations. A party wishing to sue under the Sherman Act must prove the following:

1. The antitrust violation either caused or was a substantial factor in causing the injury that was suffered.

2. The unlawful actions of the accused party affected business activities of the plaintiff that were protected by the antitrust laws.

KNOW THIS

Section 5 of the Federal Trade Commission Act is broader than the other antitrust laws. It covers nearly all anticompetitive behavior, including conduct that does not violate either the Sherman Act or the Clayton Act.

31-5c Exemptions from Antitrust Laws

There are many legislative and constitutional limitations on antitrust enforcement. Most are statutory or judicially created exemptions applying to the areas listed in Exhibit 31–2. One of the most significant exemptions covers joint efforts by businesspersons to obtain legislative, judicial, or executive action. Under this exemption, for example, Blu-ray producers can jointly lobby Congress to change the copyright laws without being held liable for attempting to restrain trade.

31-6   U.S. Antitrust Laws in the Global Context

U.S. antitrust laws have a broad application. Not only may persons in foreign nations be subject to their provisions, but the laws may also be applied to protect foreign consumers and competitors from violations committed by U.S. business firms. Consequently, *foreign persons*—a term that by definition includes foreign governments—may sue under U.S. antitrust laws in U.S. courts.

31-6a The Extraterritorial Application of U.S. Antitrust Laws

The United States is a major proponent of free competition in the global economy. Accordingly, Section 1 of the Sherman Act provides for the extraterritorial effect of the U.S. antitrust laws. Any conspiracy that has a *substantial effect* on U.S. commerce is within the reach of the Sherman Act. The violation may even occur outside the United States, and foreign persons, including governments, can be sued for violation of U.S. antitrust laws.

Before U.S. courts will exercise jurisdiction and apply antitrust laws, it must be shown that the alleged violation had a substantial effect on U.S. commerce. U.S. jurisdiction is automatically

Exhibit 31–2 Exemptions to Antitrust Enforcement

EXEMPTION	SOURCE AND SCOPE
Labor	Clayton Act—Permits unions to organize and bargain without violating antitrust laws and specifies that strikes and other labor activities normally do not violate any federal law.
Agricultural associations	Clayton Act and Capper-Volstead Act—Allow agricultural cooperatives to set prices.
Fisheries	Fisheries Cooperative Marketing Act—Allows the fishing industry to set prices.
Insurance companies	McCarran-Ferguson Act—Exempts the insurance business in states in which the industry is regulated.
Exporters	Webb-Pomerene Act—Allows U.S. exporters to engage in cooperative activity to compete with similar foreign associations. Export Trading Company Act—Permits the U.S. Department of Justice to exempt certain exporters.
Professional baseball	The United States Supreme Court has held that professional baseball is exempt because it is not "interstate commerce."[a]
Oil marketing	Interstate Oil Compact—Allows states to set quotas on oil to be marketed in interstate commerce.
Defense activities	Defense Production Act—Allows the president to approve, and thereby exempt, certain activities to further the military defense of the United States.
Small businesses' cooperative research	Small Business Administration Act—Allows small firms to undertake cooperative research.
State actions	The United States Supreme Court has held that actions by a state are exempt if the state clearly articulates and actively supervises the policy behind its action.[b]
Regulated industries	Industries (such as airlines) are exempt when a federal administrative agency (such as the Federal Aviation Administration) has primary regulatory authority.
Businesspersons' joint efforts to seek government action	Cooperative efforts by businesspersons to obtain legislative, judicial, or executive action are exempt unless it is clear that an effort is "objectively baseless" and is an attempt to make anticompetitive use of government processes.[c]

a. *Federal Baseball Club of Baltimore, Inc. v. National League of Professional Baseball Clubs,* 259 U.S. 200, 42 S.Ct. 465, 66 L.Ed. 898 (1922). See also *City of San Jose v. Office of the Commissioner of Baseball,* 776 F.3d 686 (9th Cir. 2015).
b. See *Parker v. Brown,* 317 U.S. 341, 63 S.Ct. 307, 87 L.Ed. 315 (1943).
c. *Eastern Railroad Presidents Conference v. Noerr Motor Freight, Inc.,* 365 U.S. 127, 81 S.Ct. 523, 5 L.Ed.2d 464 (1961); and *United Mine Workers of America v. Pennington,* 381 U.S. 657, 89 S.Ct. 1585, 14 L.Ed.2d 626 (1965). These two cases established the exception often referred to as the *Noerr-Pennington* doctrine.

invoked, however, when a *per se* violation occurs. If a domestic firm, for instance, joins a foreign cartel to control the production, price, or distribution of goods, and this cartel has a *substantial effect* on U.S. commerce, a *per se* violation may arise. Hence, both the domestic firm and the foreign cartel could be sued for violation of the U.S. antitrust laws.

Likewise, if a foreign firm doing business in the United States enters into a price-fixing or other anticompetitive agreement to control a portion of U.S. markets, a *per se* violation may exist. **CASE EXAMPLE 31.12** Carrier Corporation is a U.S. firm that manufactures air-conditioning and refrigeration (ACR) equipment. To make these products, Carrier uses ACR copper tubing it buys from Outokumpu Oyj, a Finnish company. Carrier is one of the world's largest purchasers of ACR copper tubing.

After the Commission of the European Communities (EC) found that Outokumpu had conspired with other companies to fix ACR tubing prices in Europe, Carrier filed a suit in a U.S. court. Carrier alleged that the cartel had also conspired to fix prices in the United States by agreeing that only Outokumpu would sell ACR tubing in the U.S. market. The district court dismissed the case for lack of jurisdiction, but a federal appellate court reversed. The appellate court found that the alleged anticompetitive conspiracy had a substantial effect on U.S. commerce. Therefore, the U.S. courts had jurisdiction over the Finnish defendant.[15] ■

---

15. *Carrier Corp. v. Outokumpu Oyj,* 673 F.3d 430 (6th Cir. 2012).

If a price-fixing conspiracy in Europe raises the cost of tubing in domestically produced air conditioners, can U.S. manufacturers sue in our federal courts? Why or why not?

31-6b The Application of Foreign Antitrust Laws

Large U.S. companies increasingly need to worry about the application of foreign antitrust laws as well. The European Union (EU) in particular actively pursues antitrust violators, especially individual companies and cartels that engage in alleged monopolistic conduct. The EU's laws promoting competition are stricter in many respects than those of the United States because they define more conduct as anticompetitive than U.S. laws do. EU investigations of possible antitrust violations often take years, as discussed in this chapter's *Beyond Our Borders* feature.

Many other nations also have laws that promote competition and prohibit trade restraints. Japanese antitrust laws forbid unfair trade practices, monopolization, and restrictions that unreasonably restrain trade. China's antitrust rules restrict monopolization and price fixing (except that the Chinese government can set prices on exported goods). Indonesia, Malaysia, South Korea, and Vietnam all have statutes protecting competition. Argentina, Brazil, Chile, Peru, and several other Latin American countries have adopted modern antitrust laws as well.

Most of these antitrust laws apply extraterritorially, as U.S. antitrust laws do. This means that a U.S. company may be subject to another nation's antitrust laws if the company's conduct has a substantial effect on that nation's commerce. China, for instance, has recently stepped up its enforcement of laws against anticompetitive practices. In 2015, China fined the U.S. chipmaker Qualcomm, Inc., $975 million for violating antitrust laws. China has also targeted Microsoft, Inc., in its antitrust investigations, and has searched Microsoft's company servers in China for evidence of violations.

BEYOND OUR BORDERS   The EU's Lengthy Antitrust Proceedings

Increasingly, major corporations doing business in Europe face investigations into possible antitrust violations. The European Union (EU) has a process to investigate and prosecute antitrust violations. The process often takes years to come to a conclusion.

A Series of Courts Is Involved

All antitrust cases start with the European Commission. This entity acts as the EU executive and antitrust authority. The European Commission usually takes two to three years to reach a decision.

Any challenge to the decision goes to the EU's General Court, the lower chamber of the European Court of Justice. Then a final appeal can be made to the European Court of Justice itself. Once the European Union has started an antitrust investigation, it takes an average of eight years to exhaust all legal appeals.

Amazon.com Could Face Years of Delay

In 2015, the European Commission opened an investigation into whether Internet commerce companies such as Amazon.com are violating the EU's antitrust laws by restricting cross-border trade. According to the European Commissioner in charge of competition policy, "European citizens face too many barriers to accessing goods and services online across borders. Some of these barriers are put in place by companies themselves. [Our] aim is to determine how widespread these barriers are and what effects they have on competition and consumers."[a]

Experts believe that the investigation could eventually lead to cases against Amazon and other individual companies that are suspected of abusing their dominant market position. The predicted time for full resolution is a decade.

CRITICAL THINKING

■ Companies subject to lengthy antitrust investigations and court proceedings in Europe argue that such delays result in "reputational damage." Why might that be so?

a. "Antitrust: Commission Launches e-Commerce Sector Inquiry," European Commission press release, May 6, 2015.

Reviewing . . . Antitrust Law and Promoting Competition

The Internet Corporation for Assigned Names and Numbers (ICANN) is a nonprofit entity that organizes Internet domain names. It is governed by a board of directors elected by various groups with commercial interests in the Internet. One of ICANN's functions is to authorize an entity to serve as a registrar for certain top-level domains (TLDs). ICANN entered into an agreement with VeriSign to provide registry services for the ".com" TLD in accordance with ICANN's specifications. VeriSign complained that ICANN was restricting the services that it could make available as a registrar and was blocking new services, imposing unnecessary conditions on those services, and setting the prices at which the services were offered. VeriSign claimed that ICANN's control of the registry services for domain names violated Section 1 of the Sherman Act. Using the information presented in the chapter, answer the following questions.

1. Should ICANN's actions be judged under the rule of reason or be deemed a *per se* violation of Section 1 of the Sherman Act? Explain.

2. Should ICANN's actions be viewed as a horizontal or a vertical restraint of trade? Explain.

3. Does it matter that ICANN's directors are chosen by groups with a commercial interest in the Internet? Why or why not?

4. If the dispute is judged under the rule of reason, what might be ICANN's defense for having a standardized set of registry services that must be used?

DEBATE THIS

- The Internet and the rise of e-commerce have rendered our antitrust concepts and laws obsolete.

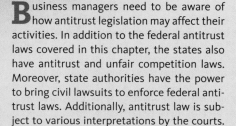

BUSINESS APPLICATION   How Can You Avoid Antitrust Problems?*

Business managers need to be aware of how antitrust legislation may affect their activities. In addition to the federal antitrust laws covered in this chapter, the states also have antitrust and unfair competition laws. Moreover, state authorities have the power to bring civil lawsuits to enforce federal antitrust laws. Additionally, antitrust law is subject to various interpretations by the courts.

---

* This *Business Application* is not meant to substitute for the services of an attorney who is licensed to practice law in your state.

Unless a businessperson exercises caution, a court may decide that his or her actions have violated a federal or state statute.

Pricing Issues

The pricing of a business's goods or services is extremely important not only for its volume of sales, but also for its bottom-line profit. When setting or changing prices, businesses frequently hire a cost accountant to perform an analysis. This is only a start, because a firm must also consider the prices competitors charge for similar or identical products.

Most businesses do not want a "price war" with rapidly declining prices. Thus, it is not uncommon for a business to charge basically the same price as its competitors. A

problem arises when there is an agreement (express or implied) to fix the price. This is a *per se* violation of Section 1 of the Sherman Act and can result in criminal or civil actions (including treble damages).

Knowing the price a competitor charges—and meeting that price—is not a violation in and of itself. Frequently, the legality depends on how the information was obtained. Violations occur when there is a communication (regardless of purpose) between a business owner (or employee) and a direct competitor. If concerned that a communication may cause antitrust pricing problems, businesspersons should consult with an attorney who can explain what is legal when dealing with competitors.

Continues

Implications of Foreign Law

Antitrust issues are not limited to domestic firms doing business in the United States. In today's global economy, many companies conduct business in other nations and with foreign businesses. Antitrust laws in other countries differ from U.S. law and can apply to a U.S. firm that has dealings with businesses located in a foreign nation even though the firm does not have a physical presence there. Always be aware of the antitrust laws of any country in which you are doing business. Generally, any businessperson who is considering doing business overseas should seek counsel from a competent attorney concerning potential antitrust violations.

CHECKLIST for Avoiding Antitrust Problems:

1. Exercise caution when communicating and dealing with competitors.

2. Seek the advice of an attorney specializing in antitrust law to ensure that your business practices and agreements do not violate antitrust laws.

3. If you conduct business in other nations, obtain the advice of an attorney who is familiar with the antitrust laws of those nations.

Key Terms

antitrust law 778
attempted monopolization 788
concentrated industry 783
divestiture 794
exclusive-dealing contract 791
group boycott 782
horizontal merger 793
horizontal restraint 782
market concentration 793
market power 780

monopolization 785
monopoly 780
monopoly power 780
per se violation 781
predatory pricing 785
price discrimination 790
price-fixing agreement 782
resale price maintenance agreement 784
rule of reason 781

treble damages 794
tying arrangement 791
vertically integrated firm 784
vertical merger 793
vertical restraint 784

Chapter Summary: Antitrust Law and Promoting Competition

The Sherman Antitrust Act (1890)	1. *Major provisions*—
	  a. Section 1—Prohibits contracts, combinations, and conspiracies in restraint of trade.
	    (1) Horizontal restraints subject to Section 1 include price-fixing agreements, group boycotts (joint refusals to deal), horizontal market divisions, and trade association agreements.
	    (2) Vertical restraints subject to Section 1 include territorial or customer restrictions, resale price maintenance agreements, and refusals to deal.
	  b. Section 2—Prohibits monopolies and attempts to monopolize.
	2. *Jurisdictional requirements*—The Sherman Act applies only to activities that have a significant impact on interstate commerce.
	3. *Interpretive rules*—
	  a. *Per se* rule—Applied to restraints on trade that are so inherently anticompetitive that they cannot be justified and are deemed illegal as a matter of law.
	  b. Rule of reason—Applied when an anticompetitive agreement may be justified by legitimate benefits. Under the rule of reason, the lawfulness of a trade restraint will be determined by the purpose and effects of the restraint.

The Clayton Act (1914)	The major provisions are as follows:
	 1. *Section 2*—As amended in 1936 by the Robinson-Patman Act, prohibits a seller engaged in interstate commerce from price discrimination that substantially lessens competition.
	 2. *Section 3*—Prohibits exclusionary practices, such as exclusive-dealing contracts and tying arrangements, when the effect may be to substantially lessen competition.
	 3. *Section 7*—Prohibits mergers when the effect may be to substantially lessen competition or to tend to create a monopoly.
	    a. A horizontal merger will be presumed unlawful if the entity created by the merger will have a significant market share.
	    b. A vertical merger will be unlawful if the merger prevents competitors of either merging firm from competing in a segment of the market that otherwise would be open to them, resulting in a substantial lessening of competition.
	 4. *Section 8*—Prohibits interlocking directorates.

Enforcement and Exemptions	1. *Enforcement*—The U.S. Department of Justice and the Federal Trade Commission enforce the federal antitrust laws. Private parties who have been injured as a result of violations of the Sherman Act or Clayton Act may bring civil suits, and, if successful, they may be awarded treble damages and attorneys' fees. 2. *Exemptions*—Numerous exemptions from the antitrust laws have been created. See Exhibit 31–2 for a list of significant exemptions.
U.S. Antitrust Laws in the Global Context	1. *Application of U.S. laws*—U.S. antitrust laws can be applied in foreign nations to protect foreign consumers and competitors. Foreign governments and persons can also bring actions under U.S. antitrust laws. Section 1 of the Sherman Act applies to any conspiracy that has a substantial effect on U.S. commerce. 2. *Application of foreign laws*—Many other nations also have laws that promote competition and prohibit trade restraints, and some are more restrictive than U.S. laws. These foreign antitrust laws are increasingly being applied to U.S. firms.

Issue Spotters

1. Under what circumstances would Pop's Market, a small store in a small, isolated town, be considered a monopolist? If Pop's is a monopolist, is it in violation of Section 2 of the Sherman Act? Why or why not? (See *Section 2 of the Sherman Act.*)

2. Maple Corporation conditions the sale of its syrup on the buyer's agreement to buy Maple's pancake mix. What factors would a court consider to decide whether this arrangement violates the Clayton Act? (See *The Clayton Act.*)

—**Check your answers to the *Issue Spotters* against the answers provided in Appendix D at the end of this text.**

Learning Objectives Check

1. What is a monopoly? What is market power? How do these concepts relate to each other?
2. What rule do courts apply to price-fixing agreements, and why?
3. What is the main type of activity prohibited by Section 2 of the Sherman Act?
4. What are the four major provisions of the Clayton Act, and what types of activities do these provisions prohibit?
5. What agencies of the federal government enforce the federal antitrust laws?

—**Answers to the even-numbered *Learning Objectives Check* questions can be found in Appendix E at the end of this text.**

Business Scenarios and Case Problems

31–1. Sherman Act. An agreement that is blatantly and substantially anticompetitive is deemed a *per se* violation of Section 1 of the Sherman Act. Under what rule is an agreement analyzed if it appears to be anticompetitive but is not a *per se* violation? In making this analysis, what factors will a court consider? (See *Section 1 of the Sherman Act.*)

31–2. Tying Arrangement. John Sheridan owned a Marathon gas station franchise. He sued Marathon Petroleum Co. under Section 1 of the Sherman Act and Section 3 of the Clayton Act, charging it with illegally tying the processing of credit-card sales to the gas station. As a condition of obtaining a Marathon dealership, dealers had to agree to let the franchisor process credit cards. They could not shop around to see if credit-card processing could be obtained at a lower price from another source. The district court dismissed the case for failure to state a claim. Sheridan appealed. Is there a tying arrangement? If so, does it violate the law? [*Sheridan v. Marathon Petroleum Co.*, 530 F.3d 590 (7th Cir. 2008)] (See *The Clayton Act*.)

31–3. Section 2 of the Sherman Act. When Deer Valley Resort Co. (DVRC) was developing its ski resort in the Wasatch Mountains near Park City, Utah, it sold parcels of land in the resort village to third parties. Each sales contract reserved the right of approval over the conduct of certain businesses on the property, including ski rentals. For fifteen years, DVRC permitted Christy Sports, LLC, to rent skis in competition with DVRC's ski rental outlet. When DVRC opened a new midmountain ski rental outlet, it revoked Christy's permission to rent skis. This meant that most skiers who flew into Salt Lake City and shuttled to Deer Valley had few choices: they could carry their ski equipment onto their flights, take a shuttle into Park City and look for cheaper ski rentals there, or rent from DVRC. Christy filed a suit against DVRC. Was DVRC's action an attempt to monopolize in violation of Section 2 of the Sherman Act? Why or why not? [*Christy Sports, LLC v. Deer Valley Resort Co.*, 555 F.3d 1188 (10th Cir. 2009)] (See *Section 2 of the Sherman Act*.)

31–4. Price Fixing. Together, EMI, Sony BMG Music Entertainment, Universal Music Group Recordings, Inc., and Warner Music Group Corp. produced, licensed, and distributed 80 percent of the digital music sold in the United States. The companies formed MusicNet to sell music to online services that sold the songs to consumers. MusicNet required all of the services to sell the songs at the same price and subject to the same restrictions. Digitization of music became cheaper, but MusicNet did not change its prices. Did MusicNet violate the antitrust laws? Explain. [*Starr v. Sony BMG Music Entertainment*, 592 F.3d 314 (2d Cir. 2010)] (See *Section 1 of the Sherman Act*.)

31–5. Business Case Problem with Sample Answer—Price Discrimination. Dayton Superior Corp. sells its products in interstate commerce to several companies, including Spa Steel Products, Inc. The purchasers often compete directly with each other for customers. From 2005 to 2007, one of Spa Steel's customers purchased Dayton Superior's products from two of Spa Steel's competitors. According to the customer, Spa Steel's prices were always 10 to 15 percent higher for the same products. As a result, Spa Steel lost sales to at least that customer and perhaps others. Spa Steel wants to sue Dayton Superior for price discrimination. Which requirements for such a claim under Section 2 of the Clayton Act does Spa Steel

satisfy? What additional facts will it need to prove? [*Dayton Superior Corp. v. Spa Steel Products, Inc.*, 2012 WL 113663 (N.D.N.Y. 2012)] (See *The Clayton Act*.)

— **For a sample answer to Problem 31–5, go to Appendix F at the end of this text.**

31–6. Section 1 of the Sherman Act. The National Collegiate Athletic Association (NCAA) and the National Federation of State High School Associations (NFHS), in an effort to enhance player safety and reduce technology-driven home runs and other big hits, set a standard for non-wood baseball bats to ensure that aluminum and composite bats performed like wood bats. Marucci Sports, LLC, makes non-wood bats. Under the new standard, four of Marucci's eleven products were decertified for use in high school and collegiate games. Marucci filed suit against the NCAA and the NFHS under Section 1 of the Sherman Act. At trial, Marucci's evidence focused on injury to its own business. Did the NCAA and NFHS's standard restrain trade in violation of the Sherman Act? Explain. [*Marucci Sports, L.L.C. v. National Collegiate Athletic Association*, 751 F.3d 368 (5th Cir. 2014)] (See *Section 1 of the Sherman Act*.)

31–7. Mergers. St. Luke's Health Systems, Ltd., operated an emergency clinic in Nampa, Idaho. Saltzer Medical Group, P.A., had thirty-four physicians practicing at its offices in Nampa. Saint Alphonsus Health System, Inc., operated the only hospital in Nampa. St. Luke's acquired Saltzer's assets and entered into a five-year professional service agreement with the Saltzer physicians. This affiliation resulted in a combined share of two-thirds of the Nampa adult primary care provider market. Together, the two entities could impose a significant increase in the prices charged patients and insurers, and correspondence between the parties indicated that they would. Saint Alphonsus filed a suit against St. Luke's to block the merger. Did this affiliation violate antitrust law? Explain. [*Saint Alphonsus Medical Center-Nampa Inc. v. St. Luke's Health System, Ltd.*, 778 F.3d 775 (9th Cir. 2015)] (See *The Clayton Act*.)

31–8. A Question of Ethics—Section 1 of the Sherman Act. In the 1990s, DuCoa, LP, made choline chloride, a B-complex vitamin essential for the growth and development of animals. The U.S. market for choline chloride was divided into thirds among DuCoa, Bioproducts, Inc., and Chinook Group, Ltd. To stabilize the market and keep the price of the vitamin higher than it would otherwise be, the companies agreed to fix the price and allocate market share by deciding which of them would offer the lowest price to each customer. At times, however, the companies disregarded the agreement. During an increase in competitive activity in 1997, Daniel Rose became president of DuCoa and found out about the conspiracy. In 1998, Rose implemented a strategy to persuade DuCoa's competitors to rejoin the conspiracy. By April, the three companies had reallocated their market shares and increased their prices. In June, the U.S. Department of Justice began to investigate allegations of price fixing in the vitamin market. Ultimately, Rose was convicted of conspiracy to violate Section 1 of the Sherman Act. [*United States v. Rose,* 449 F.3d 627 (5th Cir. 2006)] (See *Section 1 of the Sherman Act.*)

1. The court "enhanced" Rose's sentence to thirty months' imprisonment, one year of supervised release, and a $20,000 fine because of his role as "a manager or supervisor" in the conspiracy. Rose appealed this enhancement. Was it fair to increase Rose's sentence on this ground? Why or why not?

2. Was Rose's participation in the conspiracy unethical? If so, how might Rose have behaved ethically instead? Explain.

Critical Thinking and Writing Assignments

31–9. Business Law Writing. Write two paragraphs explaining some ways in which antitrust laws might place too great of a burden on commerce in the global marketplace. (See *Section 2 of the Sherman Act.*)

31–10. Case Analysis Question—Resale Price Maintenance Agreements. Go to Appendix G at the end of this text and examine the excerpt of Case No. 6, *Leegin Creative Leather Products, Inc. v. PSKS, Inc.* Review and then brief the case, making sure that your brief answers the following questions.

1. **Issue:** The dispute in this case was between which parties and turned on what legal issue?

2. **Rule of Law:** In resolving this dispute, what common law rule did the Court overturn, and what rule did the Court create to replace this rejected precedent?

3. **Applying the Rule of Law:** What reasons did the Court give to justify its change in the law, and how did the new rule apply in this case?

4. **Conclusion:** In whose favor did the Court rule and why?

31–11. Business Law Critical Thinking Group Assignment. Residents of the city of Madison, Wisconsin, became concerned about overconsumption of liquor near the campus of the University of Wisconsin (UW). The city initiated a new policy, imposing conditions on area bars to discourage reduced-price "specials" that were believed to encourage high-volume and dangerous drinking. In 2016, the city began to draft an ordinance to ban all drink specials. Bar owners responded by announcing that they had "voluntarily" agreed to discontinue drink specials on Friday and Saturday nights after 8:00 P.M. The city put its ordinance on hold. Several UW students filed a lawsuit against the local bar owners' association alleging violations of antitrust law. (See *Section 1 of the Sherman Act.*)

1. The first group will identify the grounds on which the plaintiffs might base their claim for relief and formulate an argument on behalf of the plaintiffs.

2. The second group will determine whether the defendants are exempt from the antitrust laws.

3. The third group will decide how the court should rule in this dispute and provide reasons for its answer.

iStockPhoto.com/Christophe Testi

32

LEARNING OBJECTIVES

The five Learning Objectives *below are designed to help improve your understanding of the chapter. After reading this chapter, you should be able to answer the following questions:*

1. When will advertising be deemed deceptive?

2. What law protects consumers against contaminated and misbranded foods and drugs?

3. What does Regulation Z require, and how does it relate to the Truth-in-Lending Act?

4. What is contained in an environmental impact statement, and who must file one?

5. What are three main goals of the Clean Water Act?

Consumer and Environmental Law

Congress has enacted a substantial amount of legislation to protect "the good of the people," to borrow Cicero's phrase from the chapter-opening quotation. All statutes, agency rules, and common law judicial decisions that attempt to protect the interests of consumers are classified as *consumer law*.

> "The good of the people is the greatest law."
>
> **MARCUS TULLIUS CICERO**
> 106–43 B.C.E.
> (ROMAN POLITICIAN AND ORATOR)

Sources of consumer protection exist at all levels of government. At the federal level, laws have been passed to define the duties of sellers and the rights of consumers. Exhibit 32–1 indicates some of the areas of consumer law that are regulated by statutes. In recent years, a renewed interest in protecting consumers from credit-card companies, financial institutions, and insurance companies has led to enactment of federal credit-card regulations, financial reforms, and health-care reforms.

In the first part of this chapter, we examine some of the major laws and regulations protecting consumers. We then turn to a discussion of environmental law, which consists of all of the laws and regulations designed to protect and preserve the environment.

32–1 Advertising, Marketing, and Sales

Federal administrative agencies, such as the Federal Trade Commission (FTC), provide an important source of consumer protection. Nearly every agency and department of the federal government has an office of consumer affairs. Most states have one or more such offices, including the offices of state attorneys general, to assist consumers. Many of the complaints received by these offices involve consumers who say they were misled by sellers' advertising, marketing, and sales tactics.

32–1a Deceptive Advertising

One of the most important federal consumer protection laws is the Federal Trade Commission Act.[1] The act created the FTC to carry out the broadly stated goal of preventing unfair and deceptive trade practices, including deceptive advertising.

Generally, **deceptive advertising** involves a claim that would mislead a reasonable consumer. Vague generalities and obvious exaggerations (that a reasonable person would not believe to be true) are permissible. These claims are known as *puffery*. When a claim has the appearance of authenticity, however, it may create problems.

Claims that Appear to Be Based on Factual Evidence Advertising that *appears* to be based on factual evidence but that in fact cannot be scientifically supported will be deemed deceptive. **CASE EXAMPLE 32.1** MedLab, Inc., advertised that its weight-loss supplement ("The New Skinny Pill") would cause users to lose substantial amounts of weight rapidly. The ads claimed that "clinical studies prove" that people who take the pill lose "as much as 15 to 18 pounds per week and as much as 50 percent of all excess weight in just 14 days, without dieting or exercising."

The FTC sued MedLab for deceptive advertising. An expert hired by the FTC to evaluate the claim testified that to lose this much weight, "a 200-pound individual would need to run between 57 and 68 miles every day"—the equivalent of more than two marathons per day. The court concluded that the advertisement was false and misleading, granted the FTC a summary judgment, and issued a permanent injunction to stop MedLab from running the ads.[2] ▪

The following case involved an advertising claim based on limited scientific evidence.

LEARNING OBJECTIVE 1

When will advertising be deemed deceptive?

Deceptive Advertising
Advertising that misleads consumers, either by making unjustified claims about a product's performance or by omitting a material fact concerning the product's composition or performance.

---

1. 15 U.S.C. Sections 41–58.
2. *Federal Trade Commission v. MedLab, Inc*, 615 F.Supp.2d 1068 (N.D.Cal. 2009).

Exhibit 32–1 Selected Areas of Consumer Law Regulated by Statutes

CONSUMER LAW

Advertising
Example—The Federal Trade Commission Act

Labeling and Packaging
Example—The Fair Packaging and Labeling Act

Sales
Example—The FTC Mail-Order Rule

Food and Drugs
Example—The Federal Food, Drug, and Cosmetic Act

Product Safety
Example—The Consumer Product Safety Act

Credit Protection
Example—The Consumer Credit Protection Act

CASE 32.1

POM Wonderful, LLC v. Federal Trade Commission

United States Court of Appeals, District of Columbia Circuit, 777 F.3d 478 (2015).

FACTS POM Wonderful, LLC makes and sells pomegranate-based products. In ads, POM touted medical studies claiming to show that daily consumption of its products could treat, prevent, or reduce the risk of heart disease, prostate cancer, and erectile dysfunction. These ads mischaracterized the scientific evidence.

The Federal Trade Commission (FTC) charged POM with, and held POM liable for, making false, misleading, and unsubstantiated representations in violation of the FTC Act. POM was barred from running future ads asserting that its products treat or prevent any disease unless "randomized, controlled, human clinical trials" (RCTs, for "randomized controlled trials") demonstrated statistically significant results. POM petitioned the U.S. Court of Appeals for the District of Columbia Circuit to review this injunctive order.

ISSUE Can an advertising claim based on limited scientific evidence be deemed deceptive?

DECISION Yes. The U.S. Court of Appeals for the District of Columbia Circuit enforced the FTC's order. "An advertiser who makes express representations about the level of support for a particular claim must possess the level of proof claimed in the ad and must convey that information to consumers in a non-misleading way."

REASON POM's ads conveyed the impression that clinical studies had established the ability of its products to treat, prevent, or reduce

What kinds of health claims about pomegranate juice can its producer make?

the risk of serious disease. To establish such a relationship, however, requires RCTs. The FTC examined the studies that POM cited and concluded that the studies did not qualify as RCTs that would adequately substantiate POM's claims.

Experts in cardiology and urology require "randomized, double-blinded, placebo-controlled clinical trials to substantiate any claim that a product treats, prevents, or reduces the risk of disease." Investigators can use an RCT's control group to distinguish the real effects of a tested product from other changes, such as those due to the act of being treated (the placebo effect). The random assignment of a subject to a treatment or control group increases the likelihood that the groups are similar, so that any difference in the outcome between the groups can be attributed to the treatment. When a study is double-blinded, the participants and the investigators do not know who is in which group, making bias less likely to affect the results.

CRITICAL THINKING—Ethical Consideration *POM argued that it is unethical to require RCTs to substantiate disease-related claims about food products because "doctors cannot . . . ethically deprive a control group of patients of all Vitamin C for a decade to determine whether Vitamin C helps prevent cancer." Is this a valid argument? Why or why not?*

> "Ads are the cave art of the twentieth century."
>
> **MARSHALL MCLUHAN**
> 1911–1980
> (CANADIAN ACADEMIC AND COMMENTATOR)

Bait-and-Switch Advertising Advertising a product at an attractive price and then telling the consumer that the advertised product is not available or is of poor quality and encouraging her or him to purchase a more expensive item.

Claims Based on Half-Truths

Some advertisements contain "half-truths," meaning that the information is true but incomplete and, therefore, leads consumers to a false conclusion. **EXAMPLE 32.2** The maker of Campbell's soups advertised that "most" Campbell's soups were low in fat and cholesterol and thus were helpful in fighting heart disease. What the ad did not say was that Campbell's soups were also high in sodium and that high-sodium diets may increase the risk of heart disease. Hence, the FTC ruled that the company's claims were deceptive. ■ In addition, advertising featuring an endorsement by a celebrity may be deemed deceptive if the celebrity does not actually use the product.

Bait-and-Switch Advertising

The FTC has issued rules that govern specific advertising techniques.[3] Some retailers systematically advertise merchandise at low prices to get customers into their stores and then fail to have that merchandise and encourage customers to purchase a more expensive item instead. This practice, known as **bait-and-switch advertising,** is a form of deceptive advertising.

---

3. 16 C.F.R. Section 288.

The low price is the "bait" to lure the consumer into the store. The salesperson is instructed to "switch" the consumer to a different, more expensive item. According to the FTC, bait-and-switch advertising occurs if the seller refuses to show the advertised item, fails to have reasonable quantities of it available, fails to promise to deliver the advertised item within a reasonable time, or discourages employees from selling the item.

Online Deceptive Advertising

Deceptive advertising occurs in the online environment as well. The FTC actively monitors online advertising and has identified numerous Web sites that have made false or deceptive claims for products and services. Some online ads include fake reviews of products and services—see this chapter's *Adapting the Law to the Online Environment* feature for a discussion of this issue.

The FTC issues guidelines to help online businesses comply with the laws prohibiting deceptive advertising. Current guidelines include the following basic requirements:

1. All advertisements—both online and offline—must be truthful and not misleading.

2. The claims made in an ad must be substantiated—that is, advertisers must have evidence to back up their claims.

3. Ads cannot be unfair, which the FTC defines as "likely to cause substantial consumer injury that consumers could not reasonably avoid and that is not outweighed by the benefit to consumers or competition."

4. Ads must disclose relevant limitations and qualifying information underlying the claims.

5. Required disclosures must be "clear and conspicuous." Because consumers may not read an entire Web page, an online disclosure should be placed as close as possible to the claim being qualified. Generally, hyperlinks to a disclosure are recommended only for lengthy disclosures. If hyperlinks are used, they should be obvious and should be placed as close as possible to the information they qualify.

Federal Trade Commission Actions

The FTC receives complaints from many sources, including competitors of alleged violators, consumers, trade associations, Better Business Bureaus, and government organizations and officials. When the agency receives numerous and widespread complaints about a particular problem, it will investigate.

Formal Complaint. If the FTC concludes that a given advertisement is unfair or deceptive, it sends a formal complaint to the alleged offender. The company may agree to settle the complaint without further proceedings. If not, the FTC can conduct a hearing before an administrative law judge in which the company can present its defense.

FTC Orders and Remedies. If the FTC succeeds in proving that an advertisement is unfair or deceptive, it usually issues a **cease-and-desist order** requiring the company to stop the challenged advertising. In some circumstances, the FTC may also require **counteradvertising,** in which the company advertises anew—in print, on the Internet, on radio, or on television—to inform the public about the earlier misinformation. The FTC sometimes institutes a **multiple product order,** which requires a firm to cease and desist from false advertising in regard to all of its products, not just the product that was the subject of the action.

Damages When Consumers Are Injured. When a company's deceptive ad involves wrongful charges to consumers, the FTC may seek other remedies, including restitution. **CASE EXAMPLE 32.3** The FTC sued Bronson Partners, LLC, for deceptively advertising two products—Chinese Diet Tea and Bio-Slim Patch. Bronson's ads claimed that the diet tea "eliminates 91 percent of absorbed sugars," "prevents 83 percent of fat absorption," and "doubles your metabolic rate to burn calories fast." The Bio-Slim Patch ads promised consumers that "ugly fatty tissue will disappear at a spectacular rate" when they wore the patch and carried on their normal lifestyle.

iStockPhoto.com/LauriPatterson

Can Campbell's advertise that its soups help fight heart disease even if they are high in sodium?

KNOW THIS
Changes in technology often require changes in the law.

Cease-and-Desist Order
An administrative or judicial order prohibiting a person or business firm from conducting activities that an agency or court has deemed illegal.

Counteradvertising New advertising that is undertaken to correct earlier false claims that were made about a product.

Multiple Product Order
An order requiring a firm that has engaged in deceptive advertising to cease and desist from false advertising in regard to all the firm's products.

ADAPTING THE LAW TO THE ONLINE ENVIRONMENT
The FTC's Guideline Regulating Astroturfing

Astroturfing is a term that was first used in politics. Long before the Internet existed, the preferred way of influencing legislation was to "write your congressperson." Groups opposed to or in favor of particular legislation would send out a call for letters to be sent to members of Congress. In that way, it appeared that there was a "grass roots" campaign to initiate, approve, or oppose the legislation. AstroTurf is artificial grass. Hence the term *astroturfing*.

Today, the term also refers to posting fake reviews of products and services online in return for payment. Some have argued that Microsoft is one of hundreds of companies that engage in astroturfing to promote their products.

Astroturfing may take the form of tweets, blog posts, Facebook comments, and Amazon .com reviews, among others. This modern-day version of word-of-mouth advertising is popular because consumers tend to trust reviews written by other consumers. An estimated 60 percent of consumers read online reviews before making a purchase.[a]

Astroturfing Is Everywhere

It has been estimated that from 20 to 40 percent of all online reviews are fake. Indeed, among social media reviews alone, more than 15 percent are undercover promotions, according to the technology research and advisory company Gartner.

A plethora of online reviewing companies pay their reviewers. These reviewers may use a company-written review, which is then posted on several online forums under the writers' own user names or e-mail addresses. It is certainly legal to write such reviews, but failing to disclose the connection between the writer and the employer is illegal.[b]

The FTC Steps In

The act that created the Federal Trade Commission (FTC) states, "Unfair methods of competition and dissemination of false advertisements are illegal."[c] Nonetheless, the FTC did not at first actively pursue online astroturfers. State attorneys general, however, began to sue companies that created fake reviews. One of the first cases occurred in New York in 2009 when that state's attorney general sued Lifestyle Lift, a cosmetic surgery company. Its employees were posting fake consumer reviews online.

Finally, for the first time in over twenty-nine years, the FTC amended its guidelines in an effort to crack down on false reviews posted online. By the time you read this, these guidelines will be in effect. They require full disclosure of all payments to bloggers and consumer reviewers. For instance, anyone who is on a company's payroll must disclose that information when posting online comments, testimonials, or reviews about the company's products or services.

Consumer advocates believe that the new guidelines include blogs by average consumers. If a consumer blogger has received free product samples, the blogger must disclose this fact when reviewing the product. The FTC also can now require proof to support claims about a product. Many companies will have to revise their marketing strategies to ensure compliance with the new FTC rules.

CRITICAL THINKING

■ In the long run, is astroturfing likely to benefit a company that is selling an inferior product? Why or why not?

---

a. Graham Charlton, "e-Commerce Consumer Reviews: Why You Need Them and How to Use Them," *Econsultancy*, March 21, 2012.

b. 16 C.F.R. Section 255.5 (2012).
c. 15 U.S.C. Sections 45, 52 (2012).

Eventually, Bronson conceded that it had engaged in deceptive advertising, and the FTC sought damages. The court awarded the FTC $1,942,325, which was the amount of Bronson's unjust gains and consumer losses from the two products.[4] ■

32–1b False Advertising Claims under the Lanham Act

What remedies can the FTC seek when a company advertises that its tea eliminates almost all absorbed sugars?

The Lanham Act protects trademarks, as discussed earlier in this text. The act also covers false advertising claims. To state a successful claim for false advertising under this act, a business must establish each of the following elements:

1. An injury to a commercial interest in reputation or sales.

2. Direct causation of the injury by false or deceptive advertising.

3. A loss of business from buyers who were deceived by the advertising.

---

4. *Federal Trade Commission v. Bronson Partners, LLC,* 654 F.3d 359 (2d Cir. 2011).

The dispute between the parties in the following case focused initially on a mimicked microchip. When the case reached the United States Supreme Court, the question was whether Static Control Components, Inc., could sue Lexmark International, Inc., for false advertising under the Lanham Act.

CASE 32.2

Lexmark International, Inc. v. Static Control Components, Inc.

United States Supreme Court, __ U.S. __, 134 S.Ct. 1377, 188 L.Ed.2d 392 (2014).

FACTS Lexmark International, Inc., sells the only style of toner cartridges that work with the company's laser printers. Other businesses—known as remanufacturers—acquire and refurbish used Lexmark cartridges to sell in competition with the cartridges sold by Lexmark. To deter remanufacturing, Lexmark introduced a program that gave customers a 20-percent discount on new toner cartridges if they agreed to return the empty cartridges to Lexmark. Static Control Components, Inc., makes and sells components for the remanufactured cartridges, including microchips that mimic the chips in Lexmark's cartridges.

Can a manufacturer's packaging of its toner cartridges lead to false advertising claims?

Lexmark released ads that claimed Static Control's microchips illegally infringed Lexmark's patents. Lexmark then filed a suit in a federal district court against Static Control, alleging violations of intellectual property law. Static Control counterclaimed, alleging that Lexmark engaged in false advertising in violation of the Lanham Act. The court dismissed the counterclaim. On Static Control's appeal, the U.S. Court of Appeals for the Sixth Circuit reversed the dismissal. Lexmark appealed to the United States Supreme Court.

ISSUE Did Static Control adequately plead the elements of a cause of action under the Lanham Act for false advertising?

DECISION Yes. The United States Supreme Court affirmed the lower court's ruling. The Supreme Court's decision clarified that businesses

do not need to be direct competitors to bring an action for false advertising under the act.

REASON A cause of action for false advertising under the Lanham Act extends to plaintiffs whose interests "fall within the zone of interests protected by the law." To establish a claim, a plaintiff must allege an injury to a commercial interest in reputation or sales. The injury must have been proximately caused by a violation of the statute, which can be shown by a loss in business reputation or sales that directly flows from the defendant's false advertising. Under these principles, Static Control fell within the class of plaintiffs who can sue under the Lanham Act.

Static Control alleged injuries consisting of lost sales and damage to its business reputation by Lexmark's advertising. Static Control also alleged that the injuries were proximately caused by the ads. The misrepresentations included Lexmark's assertion that Static Control's business was illegal. And because Static Control's microchips were necessary for, and had no other use than, refurbishing Lexmark's cartridges, any false advertising that reduced the remanufacturers' business also injured Static Control.

WHAT IF THE FACTS WERE DIFFERENT? *Suppose that Lexmark had issued a retraction of its ad claims before this case reached the Supreme Court. Would the outcome have been different? Discuss.*

32–1c Marketing

In addition to regulating advertising practices, Congress has passed several laws to protect consumers against other marketing practices.

Telephone Solicitation The Telephone Consumer Protection Act (TCPA)[5] prohibits telephone solicitation using an automatic telephone dialing system or a prerecorded voice. In addition, most states have statutes regulating telephone solicitation. The TCPA also makes it illegal to transmit ads via fax without first obtaining the recipient's permission.

The Federal Communications Commission (FCC) enforces the TCPA. The FCC imposes substantial fines ($11,000 each day) on companies that violate the junk fax provisions of the

---

5. 47 U.S.C. Sections 227 *et seq.*

act. The TCPA also gives consumers a right to sue and recover either $500 for each violation of the act or the actual monetary losses resulting from a violation, whichever is greater. If a court finds that a defendant willfully or knowingly violated the act, the court has the discretion to treble (triple) the amount of damages awarded.

Fraudulent Telemarketing The Telemarketing and Consumer Fraud and Abuse Prevention Act[6] directed the FTC to establish rules governing telemarketing and to bring actions against fraudulent telemarketers.

The FTC's Telemarketing Sales Rule (TSR)[7] requires a telemarketer to identify the seller's name, describe the product being sold, and disclose all material facts related to the sale (such as the total cost of the goods being sold). The TSR makes it illegal for telemarketers to misrepresent information or facts about their goods or services. A telemarketer must also remove a consumer's name from its list of potential contacts if the customer so requests.

An amendment to the TSR established the national Do Not Call Registry. Telemarketers must refrain from calling consumers who have placed their names on the list. Significantly, the TSR applies to any offer made to consumers in the United States—even if the offer comes from a foreign firm. Thus, the TSR helps to protect consumers from illegal cross-border telemarketing operations.

32–1d Sales

A number of statutes protect consumers by requiring the disclosure of certain terms in sales transactions. The FTC has regulatory authority in this area, as do some other federal agencies.

Many states and the FTC have **"cooling-off" laws** that permit the buyers of goods sold in certain transactions to cancel their contracts within three business days. The FTC rule also requires that consumers be notified in Spanish of this right if the oral negotiations for the sale were in that language.

> **"Cooling-Off" Laws** Laws that allow buyers of goods sold in certain transactions to cancel their contracts within three business days.

The contracts that fall under these cancellation rules include trade show sales contracts, contracts for home equity loans, Internet purchase contracts, and home (door-to-door) sales contracts. In addition, certain states have passed laws allowing consumers to cancel contracts for things like dating services, gym memberships, and weight loss programs.

The FTC's Mail or Telephone Order Merchandise Rule[8] protects consumers who purchase goods via mail, Internet, phone, or fax. Merchants are required to ship orders within the time promised in their advertisements and to notify consumers when orders cannot be shipped on time. If the seller does not give an estimated shipping time, it must ship within thirty days. Merchants must also issue a refund within a specified period of time when a consumer cancels an order.

32–2 Labeling and Packaging

In general, labels must be accurate, and they must use words that are understood by the ordinary consumer. In some instances, labels must specify the raw materials used in the product, such as the percentage of cotton, nylon, or other fibers used in a garment. In other instances, the product must carry a warning, such as those required on cigarette packages and advertising.[9]

---

6. 15 U.S.C. Sections 6101–6108.
7. 16 C.F.R. Sections 310.1–310.8.
8. 16 C.F.R. Sections 435.1–435.2.
9. 15 U.S.C. Sections 1331 *et seq.*

32-2a Automobile Fuel Economy Labels

The Energy Policy and Conservation Act (EPCA)[10] requires automakers to attach an information label to every new car. This label must include the Environmental Protection Agency's fuel economy estimate for the vehicle. **CASE EXAMPLE 32.4** Gaetano Paduano bought a new Honda Civic Hybrid in California. The information label on the car included the fuel economy estimate from the Environmental Protection Agency (EPA). Honda's sales brochure added, "Just drive the Hybrid like you would a conventional car and save on fuel bills."

When Paduano discovered that the car's fuel economy was less than half of the EPA's estimate, he sued Honda for deceptive advertising. The automaker claimed that the federal law (the EPCA) preempted the state's deceptive advertising law, but the court held in Paduano's favor, finding that the federal statute did not preempt a claim for deceptive advertising made under state law.[11] ▪

32-2b Food Labeling

Because the quality and safety of food are so important to consumers, several statutes deal specifically with food labeling. The Fair Packaging and Labeling Act requires that food product labels identify (1) the product, (2) the net quantity of the contents, (3) the manufacturer, and (4) the packager or distributor.[12] The act includes additional requirements concerning descriptions on packages, savings claims, components of nonfood products, and standards for the partial filling of packages.

Can a buyer of a hybrid car sue in state court for deceptive advertising about the car's fuel economy?

Nutritional Content Food products must bear labels detailing the food's nutritional content, including the number of calories and the amounts of various nutrients. The Nutrition Labeling and Education Act requires food labels to provide standard nutrition facts and regulates the use of such terms as *fresh* and *low fat.*

The U.S. Food and Drug Administration (FDA) and the U.S. Department of Agriculture (USDA) are the primary agencies that issue regulations on food labeling. These rules are published in the *Federal Register* and updated annually. For instance, current rules require labels on fresh meats, vegetables, and fruits to indicate where the food originated so that consumers can know if their food was imported.

Caloric Content of Restaurant Foods The health-care reform bill enacted in 2010 (the Affordable Care Act) included provisions aimed at combating the problem of obesity in the United States. All restaurant chains with twenty or more locations are now required to post the caloric content of the foods on their menus so that customers will know how many calories the foods contain.[13] Foods offered through vending machines must also be labeled so that their caloric content is visible to would-be purchasers.

In addition, restaurants must post guidelines on the number of calories that an average person requires daily so that customers can determine what portion of a day's calories a particular food will provide. The hope is that consumers, armed with this information, will consider the number of calories when they make their food choices. The federal law on menu labeling supersedes all state and local laws already in existence.

> "A consumer is a shopper who is sore about something."
>
> **HAROLD COFFIN**
> 1905–1981
> (AMERICAN HUMORIST)

---

10. 49 U.S.C. Section 32908(b)(1).
11. *Paduano v. American Honda Motor Co.*, 169 Cal.App. 4th 1453, 88 Cal.Rptr.3d 90 (2009).
12. 15 U.S.C. Sections 4401–4408.
13. See Section 4205 of the Patient Protection and Affordable Care Act, Pub. L. No.111-148, March 23, 2010, 124 Stat. 119.

32–3 Protection of Health and Safety

Although labeling and packaging laws promote consumer health and safety, there is a significant distinction between regulating the information dispensed about a product and regulating the actual content of the product. The classic example is tobacco products. Producers of tobacco products are required to warn consumers about the hazards associated with the use of their products, but the sale of tobacco products has not been subjected to significant restrictions or banned outright despite the obvious dangers to health. We now examine various laws that regulate the actual products made available to consumers.

32–3a Food and Drugs

The most important legislation regulating food and drugs is the Federal Food, Drug, and Cosmetic Act (FDCA).[14] The act protects consumers against adulterated (contaminated) and misbranded foods and drugs.

The FDCA establishes food standards, specifies safe levels of potentially hazardous food additives, and provides guidelines for advertising and labeling food products. The FDCA also creates a reportable food registry, establishes record-keeping requirements, requires the registration of all food facilities, and provides for inspections. Most of these statutory requirements are monitored and enforced by the FDA. (Some foods considered safe in the United States are prohibited in Europe, as discussed in this chapter's *Beyond Our Borders* feature.)

----

14. 21 U.S.C. Section 301.

BEYOND OUR BORDERS   Europe Bans Foods That Americans Eat

Many Americans believe that the foods sold in our country are some of the safest foods on earth. The Food and Drug Administration (FDA) and other government agencies regulate much of what we eat. Nonetheless, the European Union (EU) and a number of other countries, such as Canada, have banned many common processed foods that the FDA assumes to be safe for human consumption.

Internationally Banned Ingredients
The following ingredients are banned throughout Europe and in some other places.

- Olestra/Olean.
- Brominated vegetable oil.

- Potassium bromate.
- Azodicarbonamide.
- BHA and BHT.

Consequently, any processed foods made in the United States that have these ingredients are banned in the EU and elsewhere. These foods include some soft drinks, such as Mountain Dew, numerous breakfast cereals, and some reconstituted potato chips. Many sports drinks, such as Gatorade, contain brominated vegetable oil. They are therefore banned in the EU. The chemical azodicarbonamide may be found in bagels, bread, and tortillas (as well as flip-flops and yoga mats). Such foods are banned in the EU if they contain this substance.

Banned Colorings
Many countries also ban the use of certain food colorings, such as Blue #1, Blue #2,

Blue #3, Yellow #5, Yellow #6, and Red 40. Therefore, some countries, particularly in Europe, have banned Nutri-Grain bars because they contain Blue #1 food coloring. Austria and Norway have banned Yellow #5. Therefore, you will find no Kraft Macaroni & Cheese in those nations. M&Ms in Europe do not have Blue #2 coloring, as they do in the United States.

CRITICAL THINKING

- One chemist claims that the list of "dangerous" chemicals is an example of "chemophobia." What do you think he meant?

Tainted Foods In the last several years, many people in the United States have contracted food poisoning from eating foods that were contaminated—often with salmonella or *E. coli* bacteria. In response, Congress enacted the Food Safety Modernization Act (FSMA)[15] in 2010, which provides greater government control over the U.S. food safety system.

The goal of the modernization act was to shift the focus of federal regulators from responding to incidents of contamination to preventing them. The act also gives the FDA authority to directly recall any food products that it suspects are tainted, rather than relying on the producers to recall items.

The FSMA requires any party that manufactures, processes, packs, distributes, receives, holds, or imports food products to pay a fee and register with the U.S. Department of Health and Human Services. (There are some exceptions for small farmers.) Owners and operators of such facilities are required to analyze and identify food safety hazards, implement preventive controls, monitor effectiveness, and take corrective actions. The act also places more restrictions on importers of food and requires them to verify that imported foods meet U.S. safety standards.

Drugs and Medical Devices The FDA is also responsible under the FDCA for ensuring that drugs are safe and effective before they are marketed to the public. It is the responsibility of the company seeking to market a drug to test it and submit evidence that it is safe and effective. The FDA has established extensive procedures that drug manufacturers must follow. The FDA also has the authority to regulate medical devices, such as pacemakers, and to withdraw from the market any such device that is mislabeled.[16]

Because the FDA must ensure the safety of new medications, there is always a delay before drugs are available to the public, and this sometimes leads to controversy. **CASE EXAMPLE 32.5** A group of citizens petitioned the FDA to allow everyone access to "Plan B"—the morning-after birth control pill—without a prescription. The FDA denied the petition and continued to require women under the age of seventeen to obtain a prescription. The group appealed to a federal district court, claiming that the prescription requirement can delay access to the pill. The pill should be taken as soon as possible after sexual intercourse, preferably within twenty-four hours. The court ruled in favor of the plaintiffs and ordered the FDA to make the morning-after pill available to people of any age without a prescription.[17] ■

32–3b Consumer Product Safety

The Consumer Product Safety Act[18] created a comprehensive regulatory scheme over consumer safety matters and established the Consumer Product Safety Commission (CPSC).

The CPSC's Authority The CPSC conducts research on the safety of individual products and maintains a clearinghouse on the risks associated with various products. The Consumer Product Safety Act authorizes the CPSC to do the following:

1. Set safety standards for consumer products.

2. Ban the manufacture and sale of any product that the commission believes poses an "unreasonable risk" to consumers. (Products banned by the CPSC have included various types of fireworks, cribs, and toys, as well as many products containing asbestos or vinyl chloride.)

3. Remove from the market any products it believes to be imminently hazardous. The CPSC frequently works with manufacturers to voluntarily recall defective products from

---

15. Pub. L. No. 111-353, 124 Stat. 3885 (January 4, 2011). This statute affected numerous parts of Title 21 of the U.S.C.
16. 21 U.S.C. Sections 352(o), 360(j), 360(k), and 360c–360k.
17. *Tummino v. Hamburg*, 936 F.Supp.2d 162 (E.D.N.Y. 2013).
18. 15 U.S.C. Section 2051.

stores. **EXAMPLE 32.6** In cooperation with the CPSC, the Scandinavian company IKEA recalled three million baby bed canopies and thirty million wall-mounted children's lamps because they posed a strangulation risk to children. ■

4. Require manufacturers to report any products already sold or intended for sale that have proved to be hazardous.

5. Administer other product-safety legislation, including the Child Protection and Toy Safety Act[19] and the Federal Hazardous Substances Act.[20]

Why would IKEA want to cooperate with the Consumer Product Safety Commission?

Notification Requirements The Consumer Product Safety Act imposes notification requirements on distributors of consumer products. Distributors must immediately notify the CPSC when they receive information that a product "contains a defect which . . . creates a substantial risk to the public" or "an unreasonable risk of serious injury or death."

32–3c Health-Care Reforms

The health-care reforms (Obamacare) enacted in 2010 gave Americans new rights and benefits with regard to health care.[21] These laws prohibit certain insurance company practices, such as denial of coverage for preexisting conditions.

Expanded Coverage for Children and Seniors The reforms enabled more children to obtain health-insurance coverage and allowed young adults (under age twenty-six) to remain covered by their parents' health-insurance policies. The legislation also ended lifetime limits and most annual limits on care, and gave patients access to recommended preventive services (such as cancer screenings, vaccinations, and well-baby checks) without cost. Medicare recipients receive a 50 percent discount on name-brand drugs, and a gap that exists in Medicare's prescription drug coverage will be eliminated by 2020.

Controlling Costs of Health Insurance In an attempt to control the rising costs of health insurance, the laws placed restrictions on insurance companies. Insurance companies must spend at least 85 percent of all premium dollars collected from large employers (80 percent of premiums collected from individuals and small employers) on benefits and quality improvement. If insurance companies do not meet these goals, they must provide rebates to consumers. Additionally, states can require insurance companies to justify their premium increases to be eligible to participate in the new health-insurance exchanges mandated by the law.

32–4 Credit Protection

Credit protection is one of the most important aspects of consumer protection legislation. Nearly 80 percent of U.S. consumers have credit cards, and most carry a balance on these cards, which amounts to about $3.4 trillion of debt nationwide. The Consumer Financial Protection Bureau oversees the credit practices of banks, mortgage lenders, and credit-card companies.

19. 15 U.S.C. Section 1262(e).

20. 15 U.S.C. Sections 1261–1273.

21. Patient Protection and Affordable Health Care Act of 2010, Pub. L. No.111-148, March 23, 2010, 124 Stat. 119; and Health Care and Education Reconciliation Act of 2010, Pub. L. No. 111-152, March 30, 2010, 124 Stat. 1029.

32-4a Truth-in-Lending Act

A key statute regulating the credit and credit-card industries is the Truth-in-Lending Act (TILA), the name commonly given to Title 1 of the Consumer Credit Protection Act (CCPA), as amended.[22] The TILA is basically a *disclosure law*. It is administered by the Federal Reserve Board and requires sellers and lenders to disclose credit terms or loan terms (such as the annual percentage rate, or APR, and any finance charges) so that individuals can shop around for the best financing arrangements.

Application   TILA requirements apply only to persons who, in the ordinary course of business, lend funds, sell on credit, or arrange for the extension of credit. Thus, sales or loans made between two consumers do not come under the act. Additionally, this law protects only debtors who are *natural* persons (as opposed to the artificial "person" of a corporation) and does not extend to other legal entities.

Disclosure   The TILA's disclosure requirements are found in **Regulation Z,** issued by the Federal Reserve Board of Governors. If the contracting parties are subject to the TILA, the requirements of Regulation Z apply to any transaction involving an installment sales contract that calls for payment to be made in more than four installments. Transactions subject to Regulation Z typically include installment loans, retail installment sales, car loans, home-improvement loans, and certain real estate loans, if the amount of financing is less than $25,000.

Equal Credit Opportunity   The Equal Credit Opportunity Act (ECOA) amended the TILA. The ECOA prohibits the denial of credit solely on the basis of race, religion, national origin, color, gender, marital status, or age. The act also prohibits credit discrimination on the basis of whether an individual receives certain forms of income, such as public-assistance benefits.

A creditor may not require the signature of an applicant's spouse or a cosigner on a credit instrument if the applicant qualifies under the creditor's standards of creditworthiness for the amount requested. **CASE EXAMPLE 32.7** T.R. Hughes, Inc., and Summit Pointe, LLC, obtained financing from Frontenac Bank to construct two real estate developments near St. Louis, Missouri. The bank also required the builder, Thomas R. Hughes, and his wife, Carolyn Hughes, to sign personal guaranty agreements for the loans.

When the borrowers failed to make the loan payments, the bank sued the two companies and Thomas and Carolyn Hughes personally, and foreclosed on the properties. Carolyn claimed that personal guaranty contracts that she signed were obtained in violation of the ECOA. The court held that because the applicant, Thomas R. Hughes, was creditworthy, the personal guarantees of Carolyn Hughes were obtained in violation of the ECOA and were therefore unenforceable.[23] ■

Credit-Card Rules   The TILA also contains provisions regarding credit cards. One provision limits the liability of a cardholder to $50 per card for unauthorized charges made before the creditor was notified that the card was lost. If a consumer received an *unsolicited* credit card in the mail that was later stolen, the company that issued the card cannot charge the consumer for any unauthorized charges.

Another provision requires credit-card companies to disclose the balance computation method that is used to determine the outstanding balance and to state when finance charges begin to accrue. Other provisions set forth procedures for resolving billing disputes with the credit-card company. These procedures may be used if, for instance, a cardholder wishes to withhold payment for a faulty product purchased with a credit card.

LEARNING OBJECTIVE 3

What does Regulation Z require, and how does it relate to the Truth-in-Lending Act?

Regulation Z A set of rules issued by the Federal Reserve Board of Governors to implement the provisions of the Truth-in-Lending Act.

KNOW THIS

The Federal Reserve Board is part of the Federal Reserve System, which influences the lending and investing activities of commercial banks and the cost and availability of credit.

---

22. 15 U.S.C. Sections 1601–1693r. The TILA was amended in 1980 by the Truth-in-Lending Simplification and Reform Act and again in 2009 by the Credit Card Accountability Responsibility and Disclosure Act.
23. *Frontenac Bank v. T.R. Hughes, Inc.,* 404 S.W.3d 272 (Mo.App. 2012).

Amendments to Credit-Card Rules

Amendments to TILA's credit-card rules added the following protections:

1. A company may not retroactively increase the interest rates on existing card balances unless the account is sixty days delinquent.

2. A company must provide forty-five days' advance notice to consumers before changing its credit-card terms.

3. Monthly bills must be sent to cardholders twenty-one days before the due date.

4. The interest rate charged on a customer's credit-card balance may not be increased except in specific situations, such as when a promotional rate ends.

5. A company may not charge fees for being over the credit card's limit except in specified situations.

6. When the customer has balances at different interest rates, payments in excess of the minimum amount due must be applied first to the balance with the highest rate (for instance, a higher interest rate is commonly charged for cash advances).

7. A company may not compute finance charges based on the previous billing cycle (a practice known as double-cycle billing, which hurts consumers because they are charged interest for the previous cycle even if they have paid the bill in full).

ETHICAL ISSUE

Are arbitration clauses in credit-card and checking-account contracts fair? Currently, clauses in most credit-card and checking-account contracts require consumers to resolve disputes through arbitration. These disputes may involve checking-account fees, for example, or credit-card charges. The arbitration clauses typically prevent individuals from joining group (class-action) litigation concerning such issues.

According to Consumer Financial Protection Bureau (CFPB) director Richard Cordray, the bureau has "found that these arbitration clauses restrict consumer relief in disputes with financial companies by limiting class actions that provide millions of dollars in redress each year." In response, the financial-services industry has argued that the efficiency and lower cost of arbitration provides benefits not only for the industry in general but also for consumers. Notwithstanding the benefits of arbitration, the CFPB is considering barring lenders from requiring consumers to waive their class-action rights when they sign a contract that includes an arbitration clause.

32–4b Fair Credit Reporting Act

The Fair Credit Reporting Act (FCRA)[24] protects consumers against inaccurate credit reporting and requires that lenders and other creditors report correct, relevant, and up-to-date information. The act provides that consumer credit reporting agencies may issue credit reports to users only for specified purposes. Legitimate purposes include the extension of credit, the issuance of insurance policies, and in response to the consumer's request. (See the *Business Application* feature at the end of this chapter for tips on how businesspersons can use credit reporting services.)

Consumer Notification and Inaccurate Information

Any time a consumer is denied credit or insurance on the basis of his or her credit report, the consumer must be notified of that fact. The same notice must be sent to consumers who are charged more than others ordinarily would be for credit or insurance because of their credit reports.

---

24. 15 U.S.C. Sections 1681 *et seq.*

Under the FCRA, consumers can request the source of any information used by the credit agency, as well as the identity of anyone who has received an agency's report. Consumers are also permitted to have access to the information contained about them in a credit reporting agency's files.

If a consumer discovers that the agency's files contain inaccurate information, he or she should report the problem to the agency. On the consumer's written (or electronic) request, the agency must conduct a systematic examination of its records. Any unverifiable or erroneous information must be deleted within a reasonable period of time.

Remedies for Violations A credit reporting agency that fails to comply with the act is liable for actual damages, plus additional damages not to exceed $1,000 and attorneys' fees.[25] Creditors and other companies that use information from credit reporting agencies may also be liable for violations of the FCRA. An insurance company's failure to notify new customers that they are paying higher insurance rates as a result of their credit scores is considered a *willful* violation of the FCRA.[26]

Which law attempts to protect consumers against inaccurate credit information?

CASE EXAMPLE 32.8 Branch Banking & Trust Company of Virginia (BB&T) gave Rex Saunders an auto loan but failed to give him a payment coupon book and rebuffed his attempts to make payments on the loan. Eventually, BB&T discovered its mistake and demanded full payment, plus interest and penalties. When payment was not immediately forthcoming, BB&T declared that Saunders was in default. It then repossessed the car and forwarded adverse credit information about Saunders to credit reporting agencies without noting that Saunders disputed the information. Saunders filed a lawsuit alleging violations of the FCRA and was awarded $80,000 in punitive damages. An appellate court found that the damages award was reasonable, given BB&T's willful violation.[27] ■

32-4c **Fair and Accurate Credit Transactions Act**

Congress passed the Fair and Accurate Credit Transactions (FACT) Act to combat identity theft.[28] The act established a national fraud alert system so that consumers who suspect that they have been or may be victimized by identity theft can place an alert in their credit files. The act also requires the major credit reporting agencies to provide consumers with a free copy of their credit reports every twelve months.

Another provision requires account numbers on credit-card receipts to be truncated (shortened) so that merchants, employees, and others who have access to the receipts cannot obtain a consumer's name and full credit-card number. The act also mandates that financial institutions work with the FTC to identify "red flag" indicators of identity theft and to develop rules for disposing of sensitive credit information.

32-4d **Fair Debt-Collection Practices**

The Fair Debt Collection Practices Act (FDCPA)[29] attempts to curb abuses by collection agencies. The act applies only to specialized debt-collection agencies and attorneys who regularly attempt to collect debts on behalf of someone else, usually for a percentage of the amount owed. Creditors attempting to collect debts are not covered by the act unless, by misrepresenting themselves, they cause the debtors to believe that they are collection agencies.

> "Credit is a system whereby a person who can't pay gets another person who can't pay to guarantee that he can pay."
>
> **CHARLES DICKENS**
> 1812–1870
> (ENGLISH NOVELIST)

---

25. 15 U.S.C. Section 1681n.
26. This was the holding of the United States Supreme Court in *Safeco Insurance Co. of America v. Burr*, 551 U.S. 47, 127 S.Ct. 2201, 167 L.Ed.2d 1045 (2007).
27. *Saunders v. Branch Banking & Trust Co. of Virginia*, 526 F.3d 142 (4th Cir. 2008).
28. Pub. L. No. 108-159, 117 Stat. 1952 (December 4, 2003).
29. 15 U.S.C. Section 1692.

Requirements of the Act   Under the FDCPA, a collection agency may not do any of the following:

1. Contact the debtor at the debtor's place of employment if the debtor's employer objects.
2. Contact the debtor at inconvenient or unusual times (such as three o'clock in the morning), or at any time if the debtor is being represented by an attorney.
3. Contact third parties other than the debtor's parents, spouse, or financial adviser about payment of a debt unless a court authorizes such action.
4. Harass or intimidate the debtor (by using abusive language or threatening violence, for instance) or make false or misleading statements (such as posing as a police officer).
5. Communicate with the debtor at any time after receiving notice that the debtor is refusing to pay the debt, except to advise the debtor of further action to be taken by the collection agency.

The FDCPA also requires a collection agency to include a *validation notice* whenever it initially contacts a debtor for payment of a debt or within five days of that initial contact. The notice must state that the debtor has thirty days in which to dispute the debt and to request a written verification of the debt from the collection agency. The debtor's request for debt validation must be in writing.

Enforcement of the Act   The Federal Trade Commission is primarily responsible for enforcing the FDCPA. A debt collector who fails to comply with the act is liable for actual damages, plus additional damages not to exceed $1,000[30] and attorneys' fees.

Debt collectors who violate the act are exempt from liability if they can show that the violation was not intentional and resulted from a bona fide error. The "bona fide error" defense typically has been applied to mistakes of fact or clerical errors. A few courts have gone further and allowed the defense to be used by collection agencies that had left voice mail messages on a debtor's phone that were later accidentally heard by third parties.[31]

32–5 Protecting the Environment

We now turn to a discussion of the various ways in which businesses are regulated by the government in the interest of attempting to protect the environment. Environmental protection is not without a price. For many businesses, the costs of complying with environmental regulations are high, and for some, they may seem too high.

32–5a Federal Regulation

Congress has enacted a number of statutes to control the impact of human activities on the environment. Some of these laws have been passed in an attempt to improve the quality of air and water. Other laws specifically regulate toxic chemicals, including pesticides, herbicides, and hazardous wastes.

Environmental Regulatory Agencies   The primary agency regulating environmental law is the Environmental Protection Agency (EPA). Other federal agencies with authority to regulate specific environmental matters include the Department of the Interior, the Department of Defense, the Department of Labor, the Food and Drug Administration, and the Nuclear Regulatory Commission.

State and local agencies also play an important role in enforcing federal environmental legislation. In addition, most federal environmental laws provide that private parties can sue to

---

30. According to the U.S. Court of Appeals for the Sixth Circuit, the $1,000 limit on damages applies to each lawsuit, not to each violation. See *Wright v. Finance Service of Norwalk, Inc.*, 22 F.3d 647 (6th Cir. 1994).
31. See, for example, *Zortman v. J.C. Christensen & Associates, Inc.*, 870 F.Supp.2d 694 (D.Minn. 2012); see also *Mbaku v. Bank of America, N.A.*, 2013 WL 425981 (D.Colo. 2013).

enforce environmental regulations if government agencies fail to do so. Typically, a threshold hurdle in such suits is meeting the requirements for standing to sue.

Environmental Impact Statements All agencies of the federal government must take environmental factors into consideration when making significant decisions. The National Environmental Policy Act (NEPA)[32] requires that an **environmental impact statement (EIS)** be prepared for every major federal action that significantly affects the quality of the environment (see Exhibit 32–2). An EIS must analyze the following:

1. The impact that the action will have on the environment.

2. Any adverse effects on the environment and alternative actions that might be taken.

3. Irreversible effects the action might generate.

Note that an EIS must be prepared for every major federal action. An action qualifies as "major" if it involves a substantial commitment of resources (monetary or otherwise). An action is "federal" if a federal agency has the power to control it. **EXAMPLE 32.9** Development of a ski resort by a private developer on federal land may require an EIS. Construction or operation of a nuclear plant, which requires a federal permit, or creation of a dam as part of a federal project requires an EIS. ∎

If an agency decides that an EIS is unnecessary, it must issue a statement supporting this conclusion. Private individuals, consumer interest groups, businesses, and others who believe that a federal agency's actions threaten the environment often use EISs as a means of challenging those actions.

---

32. 42 U.S.C. Sections 4321–4370d.

LEARNING OBJECTIVE 4

What is contained in an environmental impact statement, and who must file one?

Environmental Impact Statement (EIS) A formal analysis required for any major federal action that will significantly affect the quality of the environment to determine the action's impact and explore alternatives.

Exhibit 32–2 Environmental Impact Statements

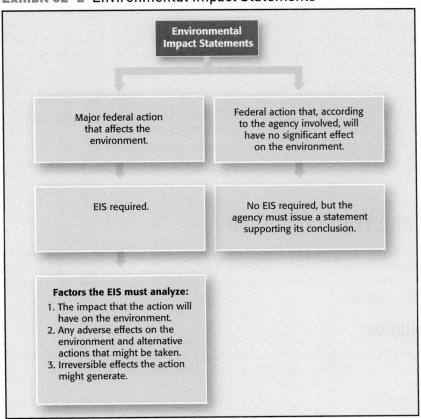

Would any federal agency allow a dam to be built without an environmental impact statement? Why or why not?

Nuisance A common law doctrine under which persons may be held liable for using their property in a manner that unreasonably interferes with others' rights to use or enjoy their own property.

Toxic Tort A civil wrong arising from exposure to a toxic substance, such as asbestos, radiation, or hazardous waste.

32–5b Common Law Actions

Even before there were statutes and regulations explicitly protecting the environment, the common law recognized that individuals have the right not to have their environment contaminated by others. Common law remedies against environmental pollution originated centuries ago in England. Those responsible for operations that created dirt, smoke, noxious odors, noise, or toxic substances were sometimes held liable under common law theories of nuisance or negligence. Today, individuals who have suffered harm from pollution continue to rely on the common law to obtain damages and injunctions against business polluters.

Nuisance Under the common law doctrine of **nuisance,** persons may be held liable if they use their property in a manner that unreasonably interferes with others' rights to use or enjoy their own property. In these situations, the courts commonly balance the harm caused by the pollution against the costs of stopping it.

Courts have often denied injunctive relief on the ground that the hardships that would be imposed on the polluter and on the community are relatively greater than the hardships suffered by the plaintiff. **EXAMPLE 32.10** Hewitt's Factory causes neighboring landowners to suffer from smoke, soot, and vibrations. If the factory is the core of the local economy, a court may leave it in operation and award monetary damages to the injured parties. Damages may include compensation for any decline in the value of their property caused by Hewitt's operation. ■

To obtain relief from pollution under the nuisance doctrine, a property owner may have to identify a distinct harm (a "private" nuisance) separate from that affecting the general public. Under the common law—which is still followed in some states—individuals must establish a private nuisance to have standing to sue. A public authority (such as a state's attorney general), though, can sue to abate a "public" nuisance.

Negligence and Strict Liability An injured party may sue a business polluter under the negligence and strict liability theories discussed in the torts chapter.

A negligence action is based on a business's alleged failure to use reasonable care toward a party whose injury was foreseeable and was caused by the lack of reasonable care. For instance, employees might sue an employer whose failure to use proper pollution controls contaminated the air and caused the employees to suffer respiratory illnesses. Businesses that engage in ultrahazardous activities—such as the transportation of radioactive materials—are strictly liable for any injuries the activities cause. In a strict liability action, the injured party does not need to prove that the business failed to exercise reasonable care.

Lawsuits for personal injuries caused by exposure to a toxic substance, such as asbestos, radiation, or hazardous waste, have given rise to a growing body of tort law known as **toxic torts.** These torts may be based on a theory of negligence or strict liability.

32–6 Air and Water Pollution

The United States has long recognized the need to protect our natural resources. During the industrial revolution, factories began discharging substances into our air and water. Over time, it became clear that many of these substances were harmful to our environment, and the government began regulating.

32–6a Air Pollution

Federal involvement with air pollution goes back to the 1950s and 1960s, when Congress authorized funds for air-pollution research and enacted the Clean Air Act.[33] The Clean Air

---

33. 42 U.S.C. Sections 7401 *et seq.*

Act provides the basis for issuing regulations to control multistate air pollution. It covers both mobile sources of pollution (such as automobiles and other vehicles) and stationary sources of pollution (such as electric utilities and industrial plants).

Mobile Sources of Air Pollution Regulations governing air pollution from automobiles and other mobile sources specify pollution standards and establish time schedules for meeting the standards. The EPA periodically updates the pollution standards to reduce the amount of emissions allowed in light of new developments and data.

The Obama administration announced a long-term goal of reducing emissions of certain pollutants, including those from automobiles, by 80 percent by 2050. The administration also ordered the EPA to develop national standards regulating fuel economy and emissions for medium- and heavy-duty trucks, starting with 2014 models.

Stationary Sources of Air Pollution The Clean Air Act authorizes the EPA to establish air-quality standards for stationary sources (such as manufacturing plants). But the act recognizes that the primary responsibility for preventing and controlling air pollution rests with state and local governments. The standards are aimed at controlling hazardous air pollutants—those likely to cause death or a serious, irreversible, or incapacitating condition, such as cancer or neurological or reproductive damage.

The EPA sets primary and secondary levels of ambient standards—that is, the maximum permissible levels of certain pollutants—and the states formulate plans to achieve those standards. Different standards apply depending on whether the sources of pollution are located in clean areas or polluted areas and whether they are existing sources or major new sources.

Hazardous Air Pollutants. The Clean Air Act requires the EPA to list all regulated hazardous air pollutants on a prioritized schedule. In all, nearly two hundred substances, including asbestos, benzene, beryllium, cadmium, and vinyl chloride, have been classified as hazardous. They are emitted from stationary sources by a variety of business activities, including smelting (melting ore to produce metal), dry cleaning, house painting, and commercial baking.

Maximum Achievable Control Technology. Instead of establishing specific emissions standards for each hazardous air pollutant, the Clean Air Act requires major sources of pollutants to use pollution-control equipment that represents the *maximum achievable control technology,* or MACT, to reduce emissions. The EPA issues guidelines as to what equipment meets this standard.[34]

Greenhouse Gases Although greenhouse gases, such as carbon dioxide (CO_2), are generally thought to contribute to global climate change, the Clean Air Act does not specifically mention CO_2 emissions. Therefore, the EPA did not regulate CO_2 emissions until 2009, after the Supreme Court ruled that it had the authority to do so.

CASE EXAMPLE 32.11 Environmental groups and several states, including Massachusetts, sued the EPA in an effort to force the agency to regulate CO_2 emissions. When the case reached the United States Supreme Court, the EPA argued that the plaintiffs lacked standing. The agency claimed that because climate change has widespread effects, an individual plaintiff cannot show the particularized harm required for standing. The agency also maintained that it did not have authority under the Clean Air Act to address global climate change and regulate CO_2.

The Court, however, ruled that Massachusetts had standing because its coastline, including state-owned lands, faced a threat from the rising sea levels that may result from climate change. The Court also held that the Clean Air Act's broad definition of air pollution gives the EPA authority to regulate CO_2 and requires the EPA to regulate any air pollutants that might "endanger public health or welfare." Accordingly, the Court ordered the EPA to determine

"There's so much pollution in the air now that if it weren't for our lungs, there'd be no place to put it all."

ROBERT ORBEN
1927–PRESENT
(AMERICAN COMEDIAN)

---

34. The EPA has also issued rules to regulate hazardous air pollutants emitted by landfills. See 40 C.F.R. Sections 60.750–60.759.

Does the Environmental Protection Agency have the power to regulate CO_2 emissions from power plants?

whether CO_2 was a pollutant that endangered the public health.[35] ■ The EPA later concluded that greenhouse gases, including CO_2 emissions, do constitute a public danger.

Violations of the Clean Air Act
For violations of emission limits under the Clean Air Act, the EPA can assess civil penalties of up to $25,000 per day. Additional fines of up to $5,000 per day can be assessed for other violations, such as failing to maintain the required records. To penalize those who find it more cost-effective to violate the act than to comply with it, the EPA is authorized to obtain a penalty equal to the violator's economic benefits from noncompliance. Persons who provide information about violators may be paid up to $10,000. Private individuals can also sue violators.

Those who knowingly violate the act may be subject to criminal penalties, including fines of up to $1 million and imprisonment for up to two years (for false statements or failures to report violations). Corporate officers are among those who may be subject to these penalties. The phrase "knowingly violate" was at the center of the dispute in an individual's appeal of his conviction for violations of the Clean Air Act.

---

35. *Massachusetts v. EPA*, 549 U.S. 497, 127 S.Ct. 1438, 167 L.Ed.2d 248 (2007).

CASE 32.3

United States v. O'Malley
United States Court of Appeals, Seventh Circuit, 739 F.3d 1001 (2014).

FACTS Duane O'Malley operated Origin Fire Protection. Michael Pinski hired Origin to remove and dispose of 2,200 feet of insulation from a building Pinski owned in Kankakee, Illinois. The insulation contained asbestos, which Pinski, O'Malley, and O'Malley's employees recognized. O'Malley did not have a license to remove the asbestos, and none of his employees were trained in complying with federal asbestos regulations. Nevertheless, Origin removed the debris and disposed of it at various sites, including a vacant lot where it spilled onto the soil, resulting in clean-up costs of nearly $50,000. In a federal district court, a jury convicted O'Malley of removing, transporting, and dumping asbestos in violation of the Clean Air Act. The court sentenced him to 120 months of imprisonment, three years of supervised release, a $15,000 fine, and $47,085.70 in restitution to the Environmental Protection Agency (EPA). O'Malley appealed.

ISSUE Did O'Malley's knowledge that the insulation around the pipes contained asbestos satisfy the "knowingly violate" requirement of the Clean Air Act?

DECISION Yes. The U.S. Court of Appeals for the Seventh Circuit affirmed the lower court's judgment. "The very fact that O'Malley was knowingly working with asbestos-containing material met the *mens rea* [criminal intent] requirement."

Is a license required for asbestos removal?

REASON O'Malley claimed that the government was required to prove he knew the asbestos was one of the six types regulated by the EPA. The court disagreed. When "dangerous . . . materials are involved, . . . the probability of regulation is so great that anyone who is aware that he is in possession of them or dealing with them must be presumed to be aware of the regulation."

Under the Clean Air Act, the EPA regulates the emission of hazardous air pollutants, including asbestos. The handling of asbestos is subject to an EPA work-practice standard—a prescribed method for dealing with the substance. Any person who "knowingly violates" the work-practice standard commits a crime. The standard applies to six types of asbestos-containing material, which includes friable asbestos material—"any material containing more than 1 percent asbestos . . . that, when dry, can be crumbled, pulverized, or reduced to powder by hand pressure." Here, the insulation clearly met the definition of "friable asbestos material."

WHAT IF THE FACTS WERE DIFFERENT? Suppose that O'Malley had been licensed to remove the asbestos. Would the result have been different? Why or why not?

32–6b Water Pollution

Water pollution stems mostly from industrial, municipal, and agricultural sources. Pollutants entering streams, lakes, and oceans include organic wastes, heated water, sediments from soil runoff, nutrients (including fertilizers and human and animal wastes), and toxic chemicals and other hazardous substances.

Federal regulations governing the pollution of water can be traced back to the 1899 Rivers and Harbors Appropriations Act.[36] These regulations prohibited ships and manufacturers from discharging or depositing refuse in navigable waterways without a permit. In 1948, Congress passed the Federal Water Pollution Control Act (FWPCA),[37] but its regulatory system and enforcement powers proved to be inadequate.

The Clean Water Act In 1972, amendments to the FWPCA—known as the Clean Water Act (CWA)—established the following goals: (1) make waters safe for swimming, (2) protect fish and wildlife, and (3) eliminate the discharge of pollutants into the water. The amendments set specific time schedules, which were extended by amendment and by the Water Quality Act.[38] Under these schedules, the EPA limits the discharge of various types of pollutants based on the technology available for controlling them.

Permit System for Point-Source Emissions. The CWA established a permit system, called the National Pollutant Discharge Elimination System (NPDES), for regulating discharges from "point sources" of pollution. Point sources include industrial facilities, municipal facilities (such as sewer pipes and sewage treatment plants), and agricultural facilities.[39] Under this system, industrial, municipal, and agricultural polluters must apply for permits before discharging wastes into surface waters.

NPDES permits can be issued by the EPA, authorized state agencies, and Indian tribes, but only if the discharge will not violate water-quality standards (either federal or state standards). Special requirements must be met to discharge toxic chemicals and residue from oil spills. NPDES permits must be renewed every five years.

Standards for Equipment. Regulations generally specify that the *best available control technology*, or BACT, be installed. The EPA issues guidelines as to what equipment meets this standard. Essentially, the guidelines require the most effective pollution-control equipment available.

New sources must install BACT equipment before beginning operations. Existing sources are subject to timetables for the installation of BACT equipment and must immediately install equipment that utilizes the *best practical control technology,* or BPCT. The EPA also issues guidelines as to what equipment meets this standard.

Violations of the Clean Water Act Because point-source water pollution control is based on a permit system, the permits are the key to enforcement. States have primary responsibility for enforcing the permit system, subject to EPA monitoring.

Discharging emissions into navigable waters without a permit, or in violation of pollution limits under a permit, violates the CWA. Violators are subject to a variety of civil and criminal penalties. Depending on the violation, civil penalties range from $10,000 to $25,000 per day, but not more than $25,000 per violation.

Criminal penalties, which apply only if a violation was intentional, range from a fine of $2,500 per day and imprisonment for up to one year to a fine of $1 million and fifteen years' imprisonment. Injunctive relief and damages can also be imposed. The polluting party can be required to clean up the pollution or pay for the cost of doing so.

"Among the treasures of our land is water—fast becoming our most valuable, most prized, most critical resource."

DWIGHT D. EISENHOWER
1890–1969
(THIRTY-FOURTH PRESIDENT OF THE UNITED STATES, 1953–1961)

---

36. 33 U.S.C. Sections 401–418.
37. 33 U.S.C. Sections 1251–1387.
38. This act amended 33 U.S.C. Section 1251.
39. 33 U.S.C. Section 1342.

Drinking Water   The Safe Drinking Water Act[40] requires the EPA to set maximum levels for pollutants in public water systems. Public water system operators must come as close as possible to meeting the EPA's standards by using the best available technology that is economically and technologically feasible.

The act, as amended, also requires each supplier of drinking water to send an annual statement describing the source of its water to every household it supplies. The statement must disclose the level of any contaminants in the water and any possible health concerns associated with the contaminants.

Oil Pollution   When more than 10 million gallons of oil leaked into Alaska's Prince William Sound from the *Exxon Valdez* supertanker in 1989, Congress responded by passing the Oil Pollution Act.[41] (At that time, the *Exxon Valdez* disaster was the worst oil spill in U.S. history, but the British Petroleum oil spill in the Gulf of Mexico in 2010 surpassed it.)

Under this act, any onshore or offshore oil facility, oil shipper, vessel owner, or vessel operator that discharges oil into navigable waters or onto an adjoining shore can be liable for clean-up costs and damages. In addition, the polluter can be ordered to pay for damage to natural resources, private property, and the local economy, including the increased cost of providing public services.

32-7 Toxic Chemicals and Hazardous Waste

Originally, most environmental clean-up efforts were directed toward reducing smog and making water safe for fishing and swimming. Today, the control of toxic chemicals used in agriculture and in industry has become increasingly important.

Some industrial, agricultural, and household wastes pose more serious threats than others. If not properly disposed of, these toxic chemicals may present a substantial danger to human health and the environment. If released into the environment, they may contaminate public drinking water resources.

32-7a Pesticides and Herbicides

The Federal Insecticide, Fungicide, and Rodenticide Act (FIFRA)[42] regulates the use of pesticides and herbicides. These substances must be (1) registered before they can be sold, (2) certified and used only for approved applications, and (3) used in limited quantities when applied to food crops. The act gives the EPA authority to oversee the sale and use of these substances and to determine whether, and at what levels, a substance may be harmful.

It is a violation of FIFRA to sell a pesticide or herbicide that is unregistered or has had its registration canceled or suspended. It is also a violation to sell a pesticide or herbicide with a false or misleading label or to destroy or deface any labeling required under the act.

Penalties for commercial dealers include imprisonment for up to one year and a fine of up to $25,000. Farmers and other private users of pesticides or herbicides who violate the act are subject to a $1,000 fine and incarceration for up to thirty days. Note that a state can also regulate the sale and use of federally registered pesticides.

32-7b Toxic Substances

The Toxic Substances Control Act[43] regulates chemicals and chemical compounds that are known to be toxic, such as asbestos and polychlorinated biphenyls (PCBs). The act also

40. 42 U.S.C. Sections 300f to 300j-25.
41. 33 U.S.C. Sections 2701–2761.
42. 7 U.S.C. Sections 135–136y.
43. 15 U.S.C. Sections 2601–2692.

controls the introduction of new chemical compounds by requiring investigation of any possible harmful effects from these substances.

The act authorizes the EPA to require that manufacturers, processors, and other organizations planning to use chemicals first determine their effects on human health and the environment. The EPA can regulate substances that could pose an imminent hazard or an unreasonable risk of injury to health or the environment. The EPA may require special labeling, limit the use of a substance, set production quotas, or prohibit the use of a substance altogether.

32-7c Resource Conservation and Recovery Act

The Resource Conservation and Recovery Act (RCRA)[44] was passed in reaction to concern over the effects of hazardous waste materials on the environment. The RCRA required the EPA to determine which forms of solid waste should be considered hazardous and to establish regulations to monitor and control hazardous waste disposal.

The act authorized the EPA to issue technical requirements for facilities that store and treat hazardous waste. The act also required all producers of hazardous waste materials to label and package properly any hazardous waste to be transported. Amendments to the RCRA decreased the use of land containment in the disposal of hazardous waste and required smaller generators of hazardous waste to comply with the act.

Under the RCRA, a company may be assessed a civil penalty of up to $25,000 for each violation.[45] Penalties are based on the seriousness of the violation, the probability of harm, and the extent to which the violation deviates from RCRA requirements. Criminal penalties include fines of up to $50,000 for each day of violation, imprisonment for up to two years (in most instances), or both.[46] Criminal fines and the period of imprisonment can be doubled for certain repeat offenders.

32-7d Superfund

The Comprehensive Environmental Response, Compensation, and Liability Act (CERCLA),[47] commonly known as Superfund, regulates the clean-up of disposal sites in which hazardous waste is leaking into the environment. CERCLA, as amended, has four primary elements:

1. It established an information-gathering and analysis system that enables the government to identify chemical dump sites and determine the appropriate action.

2. It authorized the EPA to respond to hazardous substance emergencies and to arrange for the clean-up of a leaking site directly if the persons responsible for the problem fail to clean up the site.

3. It created a Hazardous Substance Response Trust Fund (also called Superfund) to pay for the clean-up of hazardous sites using funds obtained through taxes on certain businesses.

4. It allowed the government to recover the cost of clean-up from persons who were (even remotely) responsible for hazardous substance releases.

Potentially Responsible Parties Superfund provides that when a release or a potential release of hazardous chemicals from a site occurs, the following persons may be held responsible for cleaning up the site:

1. The person who generated the wastes disposed of at the site.

2. The person who transported the waste to the site.

---

44. 42 U.S.C. Sections 6901 *et seq.*
45. 42 U.S.C. Section 6928(a).
46. 42 U.S.C. Section 6928(d).
47. 42 U.S.C. Sections 9601–9675.

3. The person who owned or operated the site at the time of the disposal.

4. The current owner or operator of the site.

A person falling within one of these categories is referred to as a **potentially responsible party (PRP).** If the PRPs do not clean up the site, the EPA can clean up the site and recover the clean-up costs from the PRPs.

Potentially Responsible Party (PRP) A party liable for the costs of cleaning up a hazardous waste disposal site under the Comprehensive Environmental Response, Compensation, and Liability Act.

Strict Liability of PRPs
Superfund imposes strict liability on PRPs, and that liability cannot be avoided through transfer of ownership. Thus, selling a site where hazardous wastes were disposed of does not relieve the seller of liability, and the buyer also becomes liable for the clean-up. Liability also extends to businesses that merge with or buy corporations that have violated CERCLA.

Joint and Several Liability
Liability under Superfund is usually joint and several—that is, a person who generated *only a fraction of the hazardous waste* disposed of at the site may nevertheless be liable for *all* of the clean-up costs. CERCLA authorizes a party who has incurred clean-up costs to bring a "contribution action" against any other person who is liable or potentially liable for a percentage of the costs.

PREVENTING LEGAL DISPUTES

One way for a business to minimize its potential liability under Superfund is to conduct environmental compliance audits of its own operations regularly to determine whether any environmental hazards exist. The EPA encourages companies to conduct self-audits and promptly detect, disclose, and correct wrongdoing. Companies that do so are subject to lighter penalties (fines may be reduced as much as 75 percent) for violations of environmental laws.

In addition, under EPA guidelines, the EPA will waive all fines if a small company corrects environmental violations within 180 days after being notified of the violations (or 360 days if pollution-prevention techniques are involved). The policy does not apply to criminal violations of environmental laws or to violations that pose a significant threat to public health, safety, or the environment.

Defenses
There are a few defenses to liability under CERCLA. The most important is the *innocent landowner defense.*[48] Under this defense, an innocent property owner may be able to avoid liability by showing that he or she had no contractual or employment relationship with the person who released the hazardous substance onto the land. If the party who disposed of the substances transferred the property *by contract* to the current owner, the defense normally will not be available.

The current owner may still be able to assert the defense, however, by showing that at the time the property was acquired, she or he had no reason to know that it had been used for hazardous waste disposal. The owner must show that at the time of the purchase, she or he undertook all appropriate investigation into the previous ownership and uses of the property to determine whether there was reason to be concerned about hazardous substances. In effect, this defense protects only property owners who took precautions and investigated the possibility of environmental hazards at the time they bought the property.

---

48. 42 U.S.C. Section 9601(35)(B).

Reviewing . . . Consumer and Environmental Law

Residents of Lake Caliopa, Minnesota, began noticing an unusually high number of lung ailments among the local population. Several concerned citizens pooled their resources and commissioned a study to compare the frequency of these health conditions in Lake Caliopa with national averages. The study concluded that residents of Lake Caliopa experienced four to seven times the rate of frequency of asthma, bronchitis, and emphysema as the population nationwide.

During the study period, citizens began expressing concerns about the large volume of smog emitted by the Cotton Design apparel manufacturing plant on the outskirts of town. The plant had a production facility two miles east of town beside the Tawakoni River and employed seventy workers. Just downstream on the Tawakoni River, the city of Lake Caliopa operated a public waterworks facility, which supplied all city residents with water.

After conducting its own investigation, the Minnesota Pollution Control Agency ordered Cotton Design to install new equipment to control air and water pollution. Later, citizens brought a lawsuit in a Minnesota state court against Cotton Design for various respiratory ailments allegedly caused or compounded by smog from Cotton Design's factory. Using the information presented in the chapter, answer the following questions.

1. Under the common law, what would each plaintiff be required to identify in order to be given relief by the court?

2. What standard for limiting emissions into the air does Cotton Design's pollution-control equipment have to meet?

3. If Cotton Design's emissions violated the Clean Air Act, how much can the EPA assess in fines per day?

4. What information must the city send to every household that it supplies with water?

DEBATE THIS

- Laws against bait-and-switch advertising should be abolished because no consumer is ever forced to buy anything.

BUSINESS APPLICATION

The Proper Approach to Using Credit Reporting Services*

As explained in the chapter, the Fair Credit Reporting Act (FCRA) protects consumers against inaccurate credit reporting. Many credit reporting agencies provide much more than just credit reports, however. Increasingly, they are providing employers with employment history, information on educational attainment, and criminal records for current employees and job applicants.

Disclosure Issues When Making Background Checks

If a company uses credit reporting agencies for background checks, it must disclose this fact to current employees and to applicants. A company that does not conform to the requirements of advance notice, disclosure, and consent may become involved in litigation.

For example, Vitran Express used credit reporting agencies to determine whether prospective employees had criminal records without disclosing this practice to applicants as required by the FCRA. One applicant lost a

* This *Business Application* is not meant to substitute for the services of an attorney who is licensed to practice law in your state.

Continues

job offer because the credit reporting agency forwarded inaccurate information indicating that he had a criminal history when he did not. When he and other job applicants brought a class-action lawsuit against Vitran Express, the company ultimately agreed to pay millions of dollars to settle the case.

Steps That Employers Should Take to Avoid Litigation

To guard against legal problems, all companies must make sure that they comply with federal law when they perform background checks. Employers should certify in writing to each credit reporting agency they hire that they will follow federal rules in this area.

Employers must give advance notice and disclosure and obtain consent to any background check that exceeds a simple credit check. Thus, each employee or applicant should be given a clear disclosure—in a separate document—stating that a background report may be requested from a consumer reporting service. At that time, the employer should obtain the person's written consent.

When a consumer report influences an employer's decision not to hire someone, or to take some other negative employment action, the company should provide the following documents to the individual *before* taking the negative action:

- The Federal Trade Commission document called "A Summary of Your Rights under the Fair Credit Reporting Act."

- A copy of the consumer report on which the company based its negative decision.

CHECKLIST for the Businessperson:

1. You or your in-house counsel should carefully review federal law concerning this matter.

2. Always let employees and job applicants know if you are going to use a consumer reporting service's report in evaluating them.

3. Create a separate document that indicates that you are going to use a consumer reporting service.

Key Terms

bait-and-switch advertising 804
cease-and-desist order 805
"cooling-off" laws 808
counteradvertising 805
deceptive advertising 803

environmental impact
  statement (EIS) 817
multiple product order 805
nuisance 818

potentially responsible
  party (PRP) 824
Regulation Z 813
toxic tort 818

Chapter Summary: Consumer and Environmental Law

	CONSUMER LAW

Advertising, Marketing, and Sales	1. *Deceptive advertising*—Generally, an advertising claim will be deemed deceptive if it would mislead a reasonable consumer.
	 2. *Bait-and-switch advertising*—Advertising a lower-priced product (the bait) to lure consumers into the store and then telling them the product is unavailable and urging them to buy a higher-priced product (the switch) is prohibited by the FTC.
	 3. *Online deceptive advertising*—The FTC has issued guidelines to help online businesses comply with the laws prohibiting deceptive advertising.
	 4. *FTC actions against deceptive advertising*—
	    a. Cease-and-desist orders—Requiring the advertiser to stop the challenged advertising.
	    b. Counteradvertising—Requiring the advertiser to advertise to correct the earlier misinformation.
	 5. *Marketing*—Telemarketers are prohibited from using automatic dialing systems and prerecorded voices and cannot fax ads without the recipient's permission. Telemarketers must identify the seller, describe the product being sold, and disclose all material facts related to the sale.
	 6. *Sales*—"Cooling-off" laws permit buyers of goods sold in certain sales transactions (such as trade shows and door-to-door sales) to cancel their contracts within three business days.

Labeling and Packaging	Manufacturers must comply with the labeling and packaging requirements for their specific products. In general, all labels must be accurate and not misleading.
Protection of Health and Safety	1. *Food and drugs*—The Federal Food, Drug, and Cosmetic Act protects consumers against adulterated and misbranded foods and drugs. The act establishes food standards, specifies safe levels of potentially hazardous food additives, and sets classifications of food and food advertising. 2. *Consumer product safety*—The Consumer Product Safety Act seeks to protect consumers from injury from hazardous products. The Consumer Product Safety Commission has the power to remove products that are deemed imminently hazardous from the market and to ban the manufacture and sale of hazardous products.

Credit Protection	1. *Consumer Credit Protection Act, Title I (Truth-in-Lending Act, or TILA)*—A disclosure law that requires sellers and lenders to disclose credit terms or loan terms in certain transactions, including retail installment sales and loans, car loans, home-improvement loans, and certain real estate loans. Additionally, the TILA provides for the following:
	a. Equal credit opportunity—Creditors are prohibited from discriminating on the basis of race, religion, marital status, gender, national origin, color, or age.
	b. Credit-card protection—Liability of cardholders for unauthorized charges is limited to $50, providing notice requirements are met. Consumers are not liable for unauthorized charges made on unsolicited credit cards. The act also sets out procedures to be used in settling disputes between credit-card companies and their cardholders.
	2. *Fair Credit Reporting Act*—Entitles consumers to request verification of the accuracy of a credit report and to have unverified or false information removed from their files.
	3. *Fair and Accurate Credit Transaction Act*—Combats identity theft by establishing a national fraud alert system. Requires account numbers to be truncated and credit reporting agencies to provide one free credit report per year to consumers.
	4. *Fair Debt Collection Practices Act*—Prohibits debt collectors from using unfair debt-collection practices, such as contacting the debtor at his or her place of employment if the employer objects or at unreasonable times, contacting third parties about the debt, and harassing the debtor.

ENVIRONMENTAL LAW	
Protecting the Environment	1. *Environmental protection agencies*—The primary agency regulating environmental law is the federal Environmental Protection Agency (EPA), which administers most federal environmental policies and statutes.
	2. *Assessing environmental impact*—The National Environmental Policy Act requires the preparation of an environmental impact statement (EIS) for every major federal action. An EIS must analyze the action's impact on the environment, its adverse effects and possible alternatives, and its irreversible effects on environmental quality.
	3. *Nuisance*—A common law doctrine under which persons may be held liable if their use of their property unreasonably interferes with others' rights to use their own property.
	4. *Negligence and strict liability*—Parties may recover damages for injuries sustained as a result of a firm's pollution-causing activities if they can demonstrate that the harm was a foreseeable result of the firm's failure to exercise reasonable care (negligence). Businesses engaging in ultrahazardous activities are liable for whatever injuries the activities cause, regardless of whether the firms exercise reasonable care.
Air and Water Pollution	1. *Air pollution*—Regulated under the authority of the Clean Air Act and its amendments.
	2. *Water pollution*—Regulated under the authority of the Rivers and Harbors Appropriations Act and the Federal Water Pollution Control Act, as amended by the Clean Water Act.
Toxic Chemicals and Hazardous Waste	Pesticides and herbicides, toxic substances, and hazardous waste are regulated under the authority of the Federal Insecticide, Fungicide, and Rodenticide Act; the Toxic Substances Control Act; and the Resource Conservation and Recovery Act, respectively. The Comprehensive Environmental Response, Compensation, and Liability Act (CERCLA), or Superfund, regulates the clean-up of hazardous waste disposal sites.

Issue Spotters

1. United Pharmaceuticals, Inc., has developed a new drug that it believes will be effective in the treatment of patients with AIDS. The drug has had only limited testing, but United wants to make the drug widely available as soon as possible. To market the drug, what must United prove to the U.S. Food and Drug Administration? (See *Protection of Health and Safety*.)

2. ChemCorp generates hazardous wastes from its operations. Disposal Trucking Company transports those wastes to Eliminators, Inc., which owns a site for hazardous waste disposal. Eliminators sells the property on which the disposal site is located to Fluid Properties, Inc. If the Environmental Protection Agency cleans up the site, from whom can it recover the cost? (See *Toxic Chemicals and Hazardous Waste*.)

   —**Check your answers to the *Issue Spotters* against the answers provided in Appendix D at the end of this text.**

Learning Objectives Check

1. When will advertising be deemed deceptive?

2. What law protects consumers against contaminated and misbranded foods and drugs?

3. What does Regulation Z require, and how does it relate to the Truth-in-Lending Act?

4. What is contained in an environmental impact statement, and who must file one?

5. What are three main goals of the Clean Water Act?

   —**Answers to the even-numbered *Learning Objectives Check* questions can be found in Appendix E at the end of this text.**

Business Scenarios and Case Problems

32–1. Environmental Laws. Fruitade, Inc., is a processor of a soft drink called Freshen Up. Fruitade uses returnable bottles, which it cleans with a special acid to allow for further beverage processing. The acid is diluted with water and then allowed to pass into a navigable stream. Fruitade crushes its broken bottles and throws the crushed glass into the stream. Discuss fully any environmental laws that Fruitade may have violated. (See *Air and Water Pollution.*)

32–2. Credit Protection. Maria Ochoa receives two new credit cards on May 1. She has solicited one of them from Midtown Department Store, and the other arrives unsolicited from High-Flying Airlines. During the month of May, Ochoa makes numerous credit-card purchases from Midtown Department Store, but she does not use the High-Flying Airlines card. On May 31, a burglar breaks into Ochoa's home and steals both credit cards, along with other items.

Ochoa notifies Midtown Department Store of the theft on June 2, but she fails to notify High-Flying Airlines. Using the Midtown credit card, the burglar makes a $500 purchase on June 1 and a $200 purchase on June 3. The burglar then charges a vacation flight on the High-Flying Airlines card for $1,000 on June 5. Ochoa receives the bills for these charges and refuses to pay them. Discuss Ochoa's liability in these situations. (See *Credit Protection.*)

32–3. Spotlight on McDonald's—Food Labeling. A McDonald's Happy Meal® consists of an entrée, a small order of French fries, a small drink, and a toy. In the early 1990s, McDonald's Corp. began to aim its Happy Meal marketing at children aged one to three. In 1995, McDonald's began making nutritional information for its food products available in documents known as "McDonald's Nutrition Facts." Each document lists the food items that the restaurant serves and provides a nutritional breakdown, but the Happy Meal is not included.

Marc Cohen filed a suit in an Illinois state court against McDonald's. Cohen alleged, among other things, that McDonald's had violated a state law prohibiting consumer fraud and deceptive business practices by failing to follow the Nutrition Labeling and Education Act (NLEA) of 1990. The NLEA sets out different, less detailed requirements for products specifically intended for children under the age of four. Does it make sense to have different requirements for children of this age? Why or why not? Should a state court impose regulations where the NLEA has not done so? Explain. [*Cohen v. McDonald's Corp.*, 347 Ill.App.3d 627, 808 N.E.2d 1, 283 Ill.Dec. 451 (1 Dist. 2004)] (See *Labeling and Packaging.*)

32–4. Business Case Problem with Sample Answer—Fair Debt-Collection Practices. Bank of America hired Atlantic Resource Management, LLC, to collect a debt from Michael Engler. Atlantic called Engler's employer and asked his supervisor about the company's policy concerning the execution of warrants. The caller then told the supervisor that, to stop process of the warrant, Engler needed to call Atlantic about "Case Number 37291 NY0969" during the first three hours of Engler's next shift. When Engler's supervisor told him about the call, Engler feared that he might be arrested, and he experienced discomfort, embarrassment, and emotional distress at work. Can Engler recover under the Fair Debt Collection Practices Act? Why or why not? [*Engler v. Atlantic Resource Management, LLC,* 2012 WL 464728 (W.D.N.Y. 2012)] (See *Credit Protection.*)

—For a sample answer to Problem 32–4, go to Appendix F at the end of this text.

32–5. Superfund. A by-product of phosphate fertilizer production is pyrite waste, which contains arsenic and lead. From 1884 to 1906, seven phosphate fertilizer plants operated on a forty-three-acre site in Charleston, South Carolina. Planters Fertilizer & Phosphate Co. bought the site in 1906 and continued to make fertilizer. In 1966, Planters sold the site to Columbia Nitrogen Corp. (CNC), which also operated the fertilizer plants. In 1985, CNC sold the site to James Holcombe and J. Henry Fair. Holcombe and Fair subdivided and sold the site to Allwaste Tank Cleaning, Inc., Robin Hood Container Express, the city of Charleston, and Ashley II of Charleston, Inc. Ashley spent almost $200,000 cleaning up the contaminated soil. Who can be held liable for the cost? Why? [*PCS Nitrogen Inc. v. Ashley II of Charleston LLC,* 714 F.3d 161 (4th Cir. 2013)] (See *Toxic Chemicals and Hazardous Waste.*)

32–6. Environmental Impact Statements. The U.S. Forest Service (USFS) proposed a travel management plan (TMP) for the Beartooth Ranger District in the Pryor and Absaroka Mountains in the Custer National Forest of southern Montana. The TMP would convert unauthorized user-created routes within the wilderness to routes authorized for motor vehicle use. It would also permit off-road "dispersed vehicle camping" within 300 feet of the routes, with some seasonal restrictions. The TMP would ban cross-country motorized travel outside the designated routes. Is an environmental impact statement required before the USFS implements the TMP? If so, what aspects of the environment should the USFS consider in preparing it? Discuss. [*Pryors Coalition v. Weldon,* 551 Fed.Appx. 426 (9th Cir. 2014)] (See *Protecting the Environment.*)

32–7. Deceptive Advertising. Innovative Marketing, Inc. (IMI), sold "scareware"—computer security software. IMI's Internet ads redirected consumers to sites where they were told that a scan of their computers had detected dangerous files—viruses, spyware, and "illegal" pornography. In fact, no scans were conducted. Kristy Ross, an IMI cofounder and vice president, reviewed and edited the ads, and was aware of the many complaints that consumers had made about them. An individual can be held liable under the Federal Trade Commission Act's prohibition of deceptive acts or practices if the person (1) participated directly in the deceptive practices or had the authority to control them and (2) had or should have had knowledge of them. Were IMI's ads deceptive? If so, can Ross be held liable? Explain. [*Federal Trade Commission v. Ross,* 743 F.3d 886 (4th Cir. 2014)] (See *Advertising, Marketing, and Sales.*)

32–8. The Clean Water Act. ICG Hazard, LLC, operates the Thunder Ridge surface coal mine in Leslie County, Kentucky, under a National Pollutant Discharge Elimination System permit issued by the Kentucky Division of Water (KDOW). As part of the operation, ICG discharges selenium into the surrounding water. Selenium is a naturally occurring element that endangers aquatic life once it reaches a certain concentration. KDOW knew when it issued the permit that mines in the area could produce selenium but did not specify discharge limits for the element in ICG's permit. Instead, the agency imposed a one-time monitoring requirement, which ICG met. Does ICG's discharge of selenium violate the Clean Water Act? Explain. [*Sierra Club v. ICG Hazard, LLC,* 781 F.3d 281 (6th Cir. 2015)] (See *Air and Water Pollution.*)

32–9. A Question of Ethics—Clean Air Act. In the Clean Air Act, Congress allowed California, which has particular problems with clean air, to adopt its own standard for emissions from cars and trucks. The standard was subject to the approval of the Environmental Protection Agency (EPA), and other states were allowed to adopt the standard after the EPA's approval.

In 2004, in an effort to address climate change, the California Air Resources Board amended the state's standard to attain "the maximum feasible and cost-effective reduction of GHG [greenhouse gas] emissions from motor vehicles." The regulation, which applied to new passenger vehicles and light-duty trucks for 2009 and later, imposed decreasing limits on emissions of carbon dioxide through 2016. While EPA approval was pending, Vermont and other states adopted similar standards. Green Mountain Chrysler Plymouth Dodge Jeep and other auto dealers, automakers, and associations of automakers filed a suit in a federal district court against George Crombie (secretary of the Vermont Agency of Natural Resources) and others, seeking relief from the state regulations. [*Green Mountain Chrysler Plymouth Dodge Jeep v. Crombie,* 508 F.Supp.2d 295 (D.Vt. 2007)] (See *Air and Water Pollution.*)

1. Under the Energy Policy and Conservation Act (EPCA), the National Highway Traffic Safety Administration sets fuel economy standards for new cars. The plaintiffs argued, among other things, that the EPCA, which prohibits states from adopting separate fuel economy standards, preempts Vermont's GHG regulation. Can the GHG rules be treated as equivalent to the fuel economy standards? Discuss.

2. Do Vermont's rules tread on the efforts of the federal government to address climate change internationally? Who should regulate GHG emissions? The federal government? The state governments? Both? Neither? Why?

3. The plaintiffs claimed that they would go bankrupt if they were forced to adhere to the state's GHG standards. Should they be granted relief on this basis? Does history support their claim? Explain.

Critical Thinking and Writing Assignments

32–10. Business Law Critical Thinking Group Assignment.
Many states have enacted laws that go even further than federal laws to protect consumers. These laws vary tremendously from state to state. (See *Advertising, Marketing, and Sales.*)

1. The first group will decide whether having different laws is fair to sellers, who may be prohibited from engaging in a practice in one state that is legal in another.

2. The second group will consider how these different laws might affect a business.

3. A third group will determine whether it is fair that residents of one state have more protection than residents of another.

33

CHAPTER OUTLINE

- Potential Liability to Clients
- Potential Liability to Third Parties
- The Sarbanes-Oxley Act
- Potential Liability of Accountants under Securities Laws
- Potential Criminal Liability
- Confidentiality and Privilege

LEARNING OBJECTIVES

The four Learning Objectives *below are designed to help improve your understanding of the chapter. After reading this chapter, you should be able to answer the following questions:*

1. Under what common law theories may professionals be liable to clients?

2. What are the rules concerning an auditor's liability to third parties?

3. How might an accountant violate federal securities laws?

4. What crimes might an accountant commit under the Internal Revenue Code?

iStockPhoto.com/apolja

Liability of Accountants and Other Professionals

Professionals, such as accountants, attorneys, physicians, and architects, are increasingly faced with the threat of liability. In part, this is because the public has become more aware that professionals are required to deliver competent services and adhere to certain standards of performance within their professions.

The standard of due care to which the members of the American Institute of Certified Public Accountants are expected to adhere is set out in the chapter-opening quotation. Investors rely heavily on the opinions of certified public accountants when making decisions about whether to invest in a company.

The failure of several major companies and leading public accounting firms in the past twenty years has focused attention on the importance of abiding by professional accounting standards. Numerous corporations—from American International Group (AIG, the world's largest insurance company), to HealthSouth, Goldman Sachs, Lehman Brothers, Tyco International, and India-based Satyam Computer Services—have been accused of engaging in accounting fraud. These companies may have reported fictitious revenues, concealed liabilities or debts, or artificially inflated their assets.

Considering the many potential sources of legal liability that they face, accountants, attorneys, and other professionals should be aware of their legal obligations. In this chapter, we look at the potential liability of professionals under both the common law and

> "A member should observe the profession's technical and ethical standards . . . and discharge professional responsibility to the best of the member's ability."
>
> **ARTICLE V, CODE OF PROFESSIONAL CONDUCT, AMERICAN INSTITUTE OF CERTIFIED PUBLIC ACCOUNTANTS**

statutory law. We conclude the chapter with a brief examination of the relationships of professionals, particularly accountants and attorneys, with their clients.

33-1 Potential Liability to Clients

Under the common law, professionals may be liable to clients for breach of contract, negligence, or fraud.

33-1a Liability for Breach of Contract

Accountants and other professionals face liability under the common law for any breach of contract. A professional owes a duty to his or her client to honor the terms of their contract and to perform the contract within the stated time period. If the professional fails to perform as agreed, then he or she has breached the contract, and the client has the right to pursue recovery of damages.

Possible damages include expenses incurred by the client in securing another professional to provide the contracted-for services and any other reasonable and foreseeable losses that arise from the professional's breach. For instance, if the client had to pay penalties for failing to meet deadlines, the court may order the professional to pay an equivalent amount in damages to the client.

33-1b Liability for Negligence

Accountants and other professionals may also be held liable under the common law for negligence in the performance of their services. Recall that the following elements must be proved to establish negligence:

1. A duty of care existed.
2. That duty of care was breached.
3. The plaintiff suffered an injury.
4. The injury was proximately caused by the defendant's breach of the duty of care.

Negligence cases against professionals often focus on the standard of care exercised by the professional. All professionals are subject to standards of conduct established by codes of professional ethics, by state statutes, and by judicial decisions. They are also governed by the contracts they enter into with their clients.

In performing their contracts, professionals must exercise the established standards of care, knowledge, and judgment generally accepted by members of their professional group. Here, we look at the duty of care owed by two groups of professionals that frequently perform services for business firms: accountants and attorneys.

Accountant's Duty of Care Accountants play a major role in a business's financial system. Accountants establish and maintain financial records and design, control, and audit record-keeping systems. They also prepare statements that reflect an individual's or a business's financial status, give tax advice, and prepare tax returns.

Generally, an accountant must possess the skills that an ordinarily prudent accountant would have and must exercise the degree of care that an ordinarily prudent accountant would exercise. The level of skill expected of accountants and the degree of care that they should exercise in performing their services are reflected in the standards discussed next.

GAAP and GAAS. When performing their services, accountants must comply with **generally accepted accounting principles (GAAP)** and **generally accepted auditing standards (GAAS).** The Financial Accounting Standards Board (FASB, usually pronounced "faz-bee") determines

LEARNING OBJECTIVE 1
Under what common law theories may professionals be liable to clients?

Generally Accepted Accounting Principles (GAAP) The conventions, rules, and procedures developed by the Financial Accounting Standards Board to define accepted accounting practices at a particular time.

Generally Accepted Auditing Standards (GAAS) Standards established by the American Institute of Certified Public Accountants to define the professional qualities and judgment that should be exercised by an auditor in performing an audit.

what accounting conventions, rules, and procedures constitute GAAP at a given point in time. GAAS, established by the American Institute of Certified Public Accountants, set forth the professional qualities and judgment that an auditor should exercise in performing an audit. Normally, if an accountant conforms to generally accepted standards and acts in good faith, he or she will not be held liable to the client for incorrect judgment.

A violation of GAAP and GAAS is considered *prima facie* evidence of negligence on the part of the accountant. Compliance with GAAP and GAAS, however, does not *necessarily* relieve an accountant from potential legal liability. An accountant may be held to a higher standard of conduct established by state statute or by judicial decisions.

For a discussion of how global accounting rules are replacing GAAP, see this chapter's *Landmark in the Law* feature.

Defalcation Embezzlement or misappropriation of funds.

International Financial Reporting Standards (IFRS) A set of global accounting standards that are being phased in by companies in the United States.

Discovering Improprieties. An accountant is not required to discover every impropriety, defalcation[1] (embezzlement), or fraud in her or his client's books. If, however, the impropriety, defalcation, or fraud has gone undiscovered because of the accountant's negligence or failure to perform an express or implied duty, the accountant will be liable for any resulting

---

1. This term, pronounced deh-fal-*kay*-shun, is derived from the Latin *de* ("off") and *falx* ("sickle"—a tool from cutting grain or tall grass). As used here, the term refers to the act of an embezzler.

LANDMARK IN THE LAW   The SEC Adopts Global Accounting Rules

At one time, investors and companies considered U.S. accounting rules, known as generally accepted accounting principles (GAAP), to be the gold standard—the best system for reporting earnings and other financial information. Then came the sub-prime mortgage meltdown and a global economic crisis, which caused many to question the effectiveness and superiority of GAAP.

In 2008, the Securities and Exchange Commission (SEC) unanimously approved a plan to require U.S. companies to use a set of global accounting rules known as **International Financial Reporting Standards (IFRS)**. These rules, which are established by the London-based International Accounting Standards Board, are being phased in and will be required for all financial reports filed with the SEC.

WHY SHIFT TO GLOBAL ACCOUNTING STANDARDS? The SEC decided to replace the GAAP with the IFRS for several reasons. GAAP rules are detailed and fill nearly

25,000 pages. The IFRS are simpler and more straightforward, filling only 2,500 pages, and they focus more on general principles than on specific rules. Consequently, companies should eventually find it less difficult to comply with the international rules, and this should lead to cost savings.

Another benefit is that investors will find it easier to make cross-country comparisons between, say, a technology company in Silicon Valley and one in Germany or Japan. Furthermore, having uniform accounting rules that apply to all nations makes sense in a global economy. The European Union and 113 other nations—including nearly all of the United States' trading partners—already use the IFRS.

THE DOWNSIDE TO ADOPTING GLOBAL RULES Despite these benefits, the shift to the global rules has had some drawbacks. Making the change has proven to be both costly and time consuming. Companies have had to upgrade their communications and software systems, study and implement the new rules, and train their employees, accountants, and tax attorneys in the rules'

use. Some smaller U.S. firms have found it difficult to absorb the costs of converting to the IFRS.

Another concern is that although the IFRS are simpler than GAAP, they may not be better. Because the global rules are broader and less detailed, they give companies more leeway in reporting, so less financial information may be disclosed. There are also indications that using the IFRS can lead to wide variances in profit reporting and may tend to boost earnings above what they would have been under GAAP. Finally, the role of the U.S. Financial Accounting Standards Board and the SEC in shaping and overseeing accounting standards will necessarily be reduced because the London-based International Accounting Standards Board sets the IFRS.

APPLICATION TO TODAY'S WORLD *The shift to IFRS received broad bipartisan political support even during the economic recession. Nevertheless, it will take years for the United States to completely implement global accounting rules. Business students should study and understand the IFRS so that they are prepared to use these rules in their future careers.*

losses suffered by the client. Therefore, an accountant who uncovers suspicious financial transactions and fails to investigate the matter fully or to inform the client of the discovery can be held liable to the client for the resulting loss.

Audits. One of the most important tasks that an accountant may perform for a business is an audit. An *audit* is a systematic inspection, by analyses and tests, of a business's financial records. An accountant qualified to perform audits is often called an **auditor.** After performing an audit, the auditor issues an opinion letter stating whether, in his or her opinion, the financial statements fairly present the business's financial position.

The purpose of an audit is to provide the auditor with evidence to support an opinion on the reliability of the business's financial statements. A normal audit is not intended to uncover fraud or other misconduct. Nevertheless, an accountant may be liable for failing to detect misconduct if a normal audit would have revealed it. Also, if the auditor agreed to examine the records for evidence of fraud or other obvious misconduct and then failed to detect it, he or she may be liable.

> **Auditor** An accountant qualified to perform audits (systematic inspections) of a business's financial records.

Qualified Opinions and Disclaimers. In issuing an opinion letter, an auditor may *qualify* the opinion or include a *disclaimer.* In a disclaimer, the auditor basically states that she or he does not have sufficient information to issue an opinion. A qualified opinion or a disclaimer must be specific and must identify the reason for the qualification or disclaimer.
EXAMPLE 33.1 Richard Zehr performs an audit of Lacey Corporation. In the opinion letter, Zehr qualifies his opinion by stating that there is uncertainty about how a lawsuit against the firm will be resolved. In this situation, Zehr will not be liable if the outcome of the suit is unfavorable for the firm. Zehr could still be liable, however, for failing to discover other problems that an audit in compliance with IFRS or GAAS would have revealed. ■

Unaudited Financial Statements. Sometimes, accountants are called on to prepare unaudited financial statements. (A financial statement is considered unaudited if incomplete auditing procedures have been used in its preparation or if insufficient procedures have been used to justify an opinion.) Lesser standards of care are typically required in this situation.

Nevertheless, accountants may be liable for omissions from unaudited statements. Accountants may be subject to liability for failing, in accordance with standard accounting procedures, to designate a balance sheet as "unaudited." An accountant will also be held liable for failure to disclose to a client any facts or circumstances that give reason to believe that misstatements have been made or that a fraud has been committed.

> "Never call an accountant a credit to his profession; a good accountant is a debit to his profession."
>
> **ATTRIBUTED TO CHARLES J. C. LYELL**
> 1943–1996
> (AMERICAN COMMENTATOR)

Defenses to Negligence. If an accountant is found guilty of negligence, the client can collect damages for losses that arose from the accountant's negligence. An accountant facing a claim of negligence, however, has several possible defenses, including the following:

1. The accountant was not negligent.

2. If the accountant was negligent, this negligence was not the proximate cause of the client's losses.

3. The client was also negligent (depending on whether state law allows contributory negligence as a defense).

CASE EXAMPLE 33.2 Coopers & Lybrand, LLP, provided accounting services for Oregon Steel Mills, Inc. (OSM). Coopers advised OSM to report a certain transaction as a $12.3 million gain on its financial statements. Later, when OSM planned to make a public offering of its stock, the Securities and Exchange Commission (SEC) reviewed its financial statements and concluded that the transaction had been treated improperly. OSM then had to correct the statements.

Because of the delay caused by the correction, the public offering did not occur on May 2, when OSM's stock was selling for $16 per share. Instead, it took place on June 13, when, due

Assume that the accounting firm for this steel manufacturer makes an error in a registration statement. If the initial public offering is delayed and the stock price falls in the meantime, is the accounting firm liable for the lower price?

to unrelated factors, the price was $13.50. OSM filed a lawsuit against Coopers, claiming that negligent accounting had resulted in the stock's being sold at a lower price. The court held, however, that although the accounting firm's negligence had delayed the stock offering, the negligence was not the proximate cause of the decline in the stock price. Thus, Coopers could not be held liable for damages based on the price decline.[2] ■

Attorney's Duty of Care The conduct of attorneys is governed by rules established by each state and by the American Bar Association's Code of Professional Responsibility and Model Rules of Professional Conduct. All attorneys owe a duty to provide competent and diligent representation.

Attorneys are required to be familiar with well-settled principles of law applicable to a case and to find relevant law that can be discovered through a reasonable amount of research. They must also investigate and discover facts that could materially affect clients' legal rights.

Normally, an attorney's performance is expected to be that of a reasonably competent general practitioner of ordinary skill, experience, and capacity. An attorney who holds himself or herself out as having expertise in a particular area of law (such as intellectual property) is held to a higher standard of care in that area of the law than attorneys without such expertise.

ETHICAL ISSUE

What are an attorney's responsibilities with respect to protecting data stored in the cloud? To achieve both cost savings and better security, more and more attorneys are storing their data, including confidential client information, on the cloud. Sometimes, professionals assume that once their data have migrated to the cloud, they no longer have to be concerned with keeping the information secure. But cloud computing is simply the virtualization of the computing process. In other words, the professional is still ultimately responsible for the information.

Attorneys' obligations for their clients' information are spelled out in the American Bar Association's Model Rules of Professional Conduct, which serve as the basis for the ethics rules for attorneys adopted by most states. Comment 17 to Model Rule 1.6 states, "The lawyer must take reasonable precautions to prevent the [client's] information from coming into the hands of unintended recipients." Thus, lawyers have an ethical duty to safeguard confidential client information, whether it is stored as documents in a filing cabinet or as electromagnetic impulses on a server that might be located anywhere. (Note that Rule 1.6 does not require an attorney to *guarantee* that a breach of confidentiality will never occur.)

Certainly, it is harder to maintain control over information stored on the cloud. Although the attorney "owns" the data, he or she probably does not even know the location of the computer where the information is stored. Furthermore, a provider of cloud computing services may move data from one server to another. Nevertheless, attorneys should be aware of jurisdictional issues and make sure that their cloud computing service provider is complying with data protection regulations and privacy notification requirements wherever the provider's servers are located.

Misconduct. Typically, a state's rules of professional conduct for attorneys provide that committing a criminal act that reflects adversely on the person's "honesty or trustworthiness, or fitness as a lawyer in other respects" is professional misconduct. The rules often further provide that a lawyer should not engage in conduct involving "dishonesty, fraud, deceit, or misrepresentation." Under these rules, state authorities can discipline attorneys for many types of misconduct.

CASE EXAMPLE 33.3 Michael Inglimo, who was licensed to practice law in Wisconsin, occasionally used marijuana with a person who later became his client in a criminal case. After the trial, the client claimed that Inglimo had been high on drugs during the trial and had not

---

2. *Oregon Steel Mills, Inc. v. Coopers & Lybrand, LLP*, 336 Or. 329, 83 P.3d 322 (2004).

adequately represented him. Two years later, Inglimo was convicted for misdemeanor possession of marijuana. State authorities also discovered that Inglimo had commingled client funds and written several checks for personal expenses out of his client trust account.

The state initiated disciplinary proceedings to have Inglimo's license to practice suspended. Inglimo argued that he should not be suspended, because his misconduct was related to his past use of controlled substances and he no longer used drugs. The court, however, concluded that the suspension was necessary to protect the public in light of Inglimo's "disturbing pattern of disregard" for his professional obligations.[3] ◼

Liability for Malpractice. When an attorney fails to exercise reasonable care and professional judgment, she or he breaches the duty of care and can be held liable for **malpractice** (professional negligence). In malpractice cases—as in all cases involving allegations of negligence— the plaintiff must prove that the attorney's breach of the duty of care actually caused the plaintiff to suffer some injury.

EXAMPLE 33.4 Attorney Lynette Boehmer allows the statute of limitations to lapse on the claim of Karen Anderson, a client. Boehmer can be held liable for malpractice because Anderson can no longer pursue her claim and has lost a potential award of damages. ◼

An attorney has a responsibility to advocate on the behalf of his or her client. In the following case, an attorney was accused of failing to fulfill this responsibility.

---

3. *In re Disciplinary Proceedings against Inglimo*, 2007 WI 126, 305 Wis.2d 71, 740 N.W.2d 125 (2007).

Malpractice Professional negligence, or failure to exercise reasonable care and professional judgment, that results in injury, loss, or damage to those relying on the professional.

When does an attorney's recreational use of illegal drugs rise to the level of disregarding professional obligations?

CASE 33.1

In re B.L.H.

Court of Appeals of North Carolina, 767 S.E.2d 905 (2015).

FACTS The parents of B.L.H. (Barbara) lived in Virginia until their divorce, when primary custody of Barbara was granted to the mother. The mother and Barbara moved to North Carolina. Two years later, the father was convicted of drug-related offenses and incarcerated in a federal prison in Texas. Meanwhile, the mother remarried. Her new spouse sought to adopt Barbara. The mother filed a petition in a North Carolina state court to terminate the father's parental rights.

The summons served on the father notified him that the court had appointed an attorney to represent him in the proceeding. The father responded that he opposed the termination. The response was addressed to the court in care of the attorney. The attorney did not contact the father or present any evidence on his behalf at the hearing. The court terminated the father's parental rights. He appealed the termination, arguing that he had received ineffective assistance of counsel.

ISSUE Did the failure of the father's attorney to make an effort to communicate with the father before the hearing constitute ineffective representation?

DECISION Yes. A state intermediate appellate court vacated the lower court's judgment and ordered a new hearing on the termination of the father's parental rights.

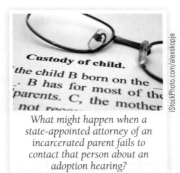

What might happen when a state-appointed attorney of an incarcerated parent fails to contact that person about an adoption hearing?

REASON The appellate court concluded that the failure of the attorney to make an effort to communicate with the father before the hearing deprived the father of a fair procedure. A parent has a "commanding" interest in a decision to terminate his or her parental rights. For this reason, a North Carolina statute provides an indigent parent with a right to counsel in a termination of parental rights proceeding. This includes a right to effective assistance of counsel.

A parent who claims to have received ineffective assistance must show that an attorney's deficient performance deprived the parent of a fair hearing. Here, the father did not have any contact with his attorney—no letter, e-mail, phone call, or conversation. The attorney's only arguable attempt to communicate was to contact the federal prison in which the father was incarcerated to learn about its e-mail system. "A lawyer cannot properly represent a client with whom he has no contact." And, in fact, at the termination hearing, the attorney presented no evidence and declined to make any argument on the father's behalf.

WHAT IF THE FACTS WERE DIFFERENT? *Suppose that the father had failed to cooperate with his attorney or had declined to respond to inquiries from him. Would the result have been different? Explain.*

33-1c Liability for Fraud

Recall that fraud, or fraudulent misrepresentation, involves the following elements:

1. A misrepresentation of a material fact.

2. An intent to deceive.

3. Justifiable reliance by the innocent party on the misrepresentation.

In addition, to obtain damages, the innocent party must have been injured. Both actual and constructive fraud are potential sources of legal liability for an accountant or other professional.

Actual Fraud A professional may be held liable for *actual fraud* when he or she (1) intentionally misstates a material fact to mislead a client and (2) the client is injured as a result of justifiably relying on the misstated fact. A material fact is one that a reasonable person would consider important in deciding whether to act.

Among other penalties, an accountant guilty of fraudulent conduct may suffer penalties imposed by a state board of accountancy. **CASE EXAMPLE 33.5** Michael Walsh, a certified public accountant (CPA), impersonated his brother-in-law, Stephen Teiper, on the phone to obtain financial information from Teiper's insurance company. Teiper wrote a letter reporting Walsh's conduct to the Nebraska Board of Public Accountancy. After a hearing, the board reprimanded Walsh, placed him on probation for three months, and ordered him to attend four hours of ethics training. He also had to pay the costs of the hearing. The Nebraska Supreme Court affirmed the board's decision on appeal.[4] ■

Constructive Fraud Conduct that is treated as fraud under the law even when there is no proof of intent to defraud, usually because of the existence of a special relationship or fiduciary duty.

Constructive Fraud A professional may sometimes be held liable for **constructive fraud** whether or not he or she acted with fraudulent intent. Liability arises because the professional has a duty to the client and violates that duty by making a material misrepresentation. The client must be injured as a result of justifiably relying on the professional's misstatements to obtain damages.

Constructive fraud may be found when an accountant is grossly negligent in performing his or her duties. **EXAMPLE 33.6** Paula, an accountant, is conducting an audit of ComCo, Inc. Paula accepts the explanations of Ron, a ComCo officer, regarding certain financial irregularities, despite evidence that contradicts those explanations and indicates that the irregularities may be illegal. Paula's conduct could be characterized as an intentional failure to perform a duty in reckless disregard of the consequences of such failure. This would constitute gross negligence and could be held to be constructive fraud. ■

33-2 Potential Liability to Third Parties

Traditionally, an accountant or other professional owed a duty only to those with whom she or he had a direct contractual relationship—that is, those with whom she or he was in *privity of contract.* A professional's duty was solely to her or his client. Violations of statutes, fraud, and other intentional or reckless acts of wrongdoing were the only exceptions to this general rule.

Today, numerous third parties—including investors, shareholders, creditors, corporate managers and directors, and regulatory agencies—rely on the opinions of auditors when making decisions. In view of this extensive reliance, many courts have all but abandoned the privity requirement in regard to accountants' liability to third parties.

What sanctions are there for a CPA who impersonates someone else over the phone to obtain financial information?

---

4. *Walsh v. State,* 276 Neb. 1034, 759 N.W.2d 100 (2009).

In this section, we focus primarily on the potential liability of auditors to third parties. The majority of courts now hold that auditors can be held liable to third parties for negligence, but the standard for the imposition of this liability varies.

33–2a The *Ultramares* Rule

The traditional rule regarding an accountant's liability to third parties is based on privity of contract and was enunciated by Chief Judge Benjamin Cardozo in 1931. **CASE EXAMPLE 33.7** Fred Stern & Company hired the public accounting firm of Touche, Niven & Company to review Stern's financial records and prepare a balance sheet for the year ending December 31, 1923.[5] Touche prepared the balance sheet and supplied Stern with thirty-two certified copies. According to the certified balance sheet, Stern had a net worth (assets less liabilities) of $1,070,715.26.

In reality, however, Stern's liabilities exceeded its assets. The company's records had been falsified by insiders at Stern so that assets exceeded liabilities, resulting in a positive net worth. In reliance on the certified balance sheets, Ultramares Corporation loaned substantial amounts to Stern. After Stern was declared bankrupt, Ultramares brought an action against Touche for negligence in an attempt to recover damages.

The New York Court of Appeals (that state's highest court) refused to impose liability on Touche. The court concluded that Touche's accountants owed a duty of care only to those persons for whose "primary benefit" the statements were intended. In this case, the statements were intended only for the primary benefit of Stern. The court held that in the absence of privity or a relationship "so close as to approach that of privity," a party could not recover from an accountant.[6] ▪

To what extent is an accounting firm liable for incorrect balance-sheet information that is distributed to the public?

The Requirement of Privity The requirement of privity has since been referred to as the *Ultramares* rule, or the New York rule. It continues to be used in some states. **CASE EXAMPLE 33.8** Toro Company supplied equipment and credit to Summit Power Equipment Distributors and required Summit to submit audited reports indicating its financial condition. Accountants at Krouse, Kern & Company prepared the reports, which allegedly contained mistakes and omissions regarding Summit's financial condition.

Toro extended large amounts of credit to Summit in reliance on the audited reports. When Summit was unable to repay the loans, Toro brought a negligence action against the accounting firm and proved that accountants at Krouse knew the reports would be used by Summit to induce Toro to extend credit. Nevertheless, under the *Ultramares* rule, the court refused to hold the accounting firm liable because the firm was not in privity with Toro.[7] ▪

"Near Privity" Modification The *Ultramares* rule was modified somewhat in a 1985 New York case, *Credit Alliance Corp. v. Arthur Andersen & Co.*[8] In that case, the court held that if a third party has a sufficiently close relationship or *nexus* (link or connection) with an accountant, then the *Ultramares* privity requirement may be satisfied without the establishment of an accountant-client relationship. The rule enunciated in the *Credit Alliance* case is often referred to as the "near privity" rule. Only a minority of states have adopted this rule.

---

5. Banks, creditors, stockholders, purchasers, or sellers often rely on a balance sheet as a basis for making decisions relating to a company's business.
6. *Ultramares Corp. v. Touche*, 255 N.Y. 170, 174 N.E. 441 (1931).
7. *Toro Co. v. Krouse, Kern & Co.*, 827 F.2d 155 (7th Cir. 1987).
8. 66 N.Y.2d 812, 489 N.E.2d 249, 498 N.Y.S.2d 362 (1985).

33–2b The *Restatement* Rule

The *Ultramares* rule has been severely criticized. Because much of the work performed by auditors is intended for use by persons who are not parties to the contract, many argue that auditors should owe a duty to these third parties. As support for this position has grown, there has been an erosion of the *Ultramares* rule to expose accountants to liability to third parties in some situations.

The majority of courts have adopted the position taken by the *Restatement (Third) of Torts,* which states that accountants are subject to liability for negligence not only to their clients but also to foreseen or *known* users—or classes of users—of their reports or financial statements. Under the *Restatement (Third) of Torts,* an accountant's liability extends to the following:

1. Persons for whose benefit and guidance the accountant "intends to supply the information or knows that the recipient intends to supply it."

2. Persons that the accountant "intends the information to influence or knows that the recipient so intends."

   EXAMPLE 33.9 Steve, an accountant, prepares a financial statement for Tech Software, Inc., a client, knowing that Tech Software will submit the statement when it applies for a loan from First National Bank. If Steve makes negligent misstatements or omissions in the statement, he may be held liable to the bank because he knew that the bank would rely on his work product when deciding whether to make the loan. ■

33–2c The "Reasonably Foreseeable Users" Rule

A small minority of courts hold accountants liable to any users whose reliance on an accountant's statements or reports was *reasonably foreseeable*. This standard has been criticized as extending liability too far and exposing accountants to massive liability.

The majority of courts have concluded that the *Restatement*'s approach is more reasonable because it allows accountants to control their exposure to liability. Liability is "fixed by the accountants' particular knowledge at the moment the audit is published," not by the foreseeability of the harm that might occur to a third party after the report is released. Exhibit 33–1 summarizes the three different views of accountants' liability to third parties.

33–2d Liability of Attorneys to Third Parties

Like accountants, attorneys may be held liable under the common law to third parties who rely on legal opinions to their detriment. Generally, an attorney is not liable to a nonclient

Exhibit 33–1 Three Basic Rules of Accountant's Liability to Third Parties

RULE	DESCRIPTION	APPLICATION
Ultramares **rule**	Liability is imposed only if the accountant is in privity, or near privity, with the third party.	A minority of courts apply this rule.
Restatement **rule**	Liability is imposed only if the third party's reliance is foreseen, or known, or if the third party is among a class of foreseen, or known, users.	The majority of courts have adopted this rule.
"Reasonably foreseeable users" rule	Liability is imposed if the third party's use was reasonably foreseeable.	A small minority of courts use this rule.

unless there is fraud (or malicious conduct) by the attorney. The liability principles stated in the *Restatement (Third) of Torts,* however, may apply to attorneys as well as to accountants.

Should an attorney's duty of care extend to third party beneficiaries whose rights were harmed by the attorney's malpractice? That question was at issue in the following case.

CASE 33.2

Perez[a] v. Stern

Nebraska Supreme Court, 279 Neb. 187, 777 N.W.2d 545 (2010).

FACTS Domingo Martinez and Reyna Guido had two minor children when Martinez was killed in a hit-and-run accident. Guido became the personal representative of Martinez's estate and retained attorney Sandra Stern to file a wrongful death lawsuit. Stern did so, but because the complaint was not served within six months of filing, the case was dismissed.

Several years later, Guido filed a legal malpractice suit against Stern on behalf of herself, the children, and the estate. Stern moved for summary judgment on the ground that the malpractice claim was barred by the Nebraska two-year statute of limitations for professional negligence. The trial court found that the estate's claim against Stern was barred. The court granted summary judgment in favor of Stern and dismissed the case. Guido appealed, claiming that the trial court had erred in granting Stern's motion for summary judgment.

ISSUE Can the minor children of a decedent sue the attorney who failed to properly file a wrongful death claim on their behalf for malpractice?

DECISION Yes. The Nebraska Supreme Court reversed the part of the trial court's ruling that pertained to Martinez's minor children and remanded the case for further proceedings. The court affirmed the lower court's dismissal of Guido's individual claim and the estate's

If a parent is killed in an auto accident, what duty does an attorney have to the children?

claim against Stern on the basis of the two-year statute of limitations.

REASON The question was whether Stern owed an independent duty to the children, who were Martinez's next of kin, to prosecute the underlying wrongful death claim in a timely manner. The reviewing court pointed out that a lawyer's duty does not extend to third parties in most situations. "Courts have repeatedly emphasized that the starting point for analyzing an attorney's duty to a third party is determining whether the third party was a direct and intended beneficiary of the attorney services."

In this situation, Stern did owe a duty to the children to represent their interests competently. "To hold otherwise would deny a legal recourse to the children for whose benefit Stern was hired in the first place." The court concluded that the children had standing to sue Stern for neglecting that duty. The claim was not barred by the statute of limitations because the statutory period did not run while the children were minors.[b]

CRITICAL THINKING—Ethical Consideration *If one of the children had not been a minor at the time of the father's death, the court would have dismissed his or her claims against Stern, even though he or she was an intended beneficiary. Is it fair for the law to treat minors differently than other children with regard to a statute of limitations? Why or why not?*

---

a. Esteban Perez was one of the minor children of Domingo Martinez, the man killed in the accident.

b. In most states, the law allows a person's status as a minor to toll (or stop) the statute of limitations period from running.

33-3 The Sarbanes-Oxley Act

The Sarbanes-Oxley Act of 2002 imposes a number of strict requirements on both domestic and foreign public accounting firms. These requirements apply to firms that provide auditing services to companies ("issuers") whose securities are sold to public investors. The act defines an *issuer* as a company that has securities that are registered under Section 12 of the Securities Exchange Act of 1934, that is required to file reports under Section 15(d) of the 1934 act, or that files—or has filed—a registration statement that has not yet become effective under the Securities Act of 1933.

To the extent that Deloitte & Touche engages in auditing public companies, its procedures are overseen by the Public Company Accounting Oversight Board. What law requires this oversight?

Working Papers
The documents used and developed by an accountant during an audit, such as notes, computations, and memoranda.

33-3a The Public Company Accounting Oversight Board

The Sarbanes-Oxley Act increased government oversight of public accounting practices by creating the Public Company Accounting Oversight Board, which reports to the Securities and Exchange Commission. The board oversees the audit of public companies that are subject to securities laws. The goal is to protect public investors and to ensure that public accounting firms comply with the provisions of the act. The act defines *public accounting firms* as firms "engaged in the practice of public accounting or preparing or issuing audit reports." The key provisions relating to the duties of the oversight board and the requirements relating to public accounting firms are summarized in Exhibit 33–2.

33-3b Requirements for Maintaining Working Papers

Performing an audit for a client involves an accumulation of **working papers**—the documents used and developed during the audit. These include notes, computations, memoranda, copies, and other papers that make up the work product of an accountant's services to a client.

Under the common law, which in this instance has been codified in a number of states, working papers remain the accountant's property. It is important for accountants to retain such records in the event that they need to defend against lawsuits for negligence or other actions in which their competence is challenged. The client also has a right to access an accountant's working papers because they reflect the client's financial situation. On a client's request, an accountant must return to the client any of the client's records or journals, and failure to do so may result in liability.

Section 802(a)(1) of the Sarbanes-Oxley Act required accountants to maintain working papers relating to an audit or review for five years from the end of the fiscal period in which the audit or review was concluded. The requirement was subsequently extended to seven

Exhibit 33–2 Key Provisions of the Sarbanes-Oxley Act Relating to Public Accounting Firms

AUDITOR INDEPENDENCE
To help ensure that auditors remain independent of the firms that they audit, Title II of the Sarbanes-Oxley Act does the following:
1. Makes it unlawful for Registered Public Accounting Firms (RPAFs) to perform both audit and nonaudit services for the same company at the same time. Nonaudit services include the following: • Bookkeeping or other services related to the accounting records or financial statements of the audit client.   • Financial information systems design and implementation.   • Appraisal or valuation services.   • Fairness opinions.   • Management functions.   • Broker or dealer, investment adviser, or investment banking services.
2. Requires preapproval for most auditing services from the issuer's (the corporation's) audit committee.
3. Requires audit partner rotation by prohibiting RPAFs from providing audit services to an issuer if either the lead audit partner or the audit partner responsible for reviewing the audit has provided such services to that corporation in each of the prior five years.
4. Requires RPAFs to make timely reports to the audit committees of the corporations. The report must indicate all critical accounting policies and practices to be used; all alternative treatments of financial information within generally accepted accounting principles that have been discussed with the corporation's management officials, the ramifications of the use of such alternative treatments, and the treatment preferred by the auditor; and other material written communications between the auditor and the corporation's management.
5. Makes it unlawful for an RPAF to provide auditing services to an issuer if the corporation's chief executive officer, chief financial officer, chief accounting officer, or controller was previously employed by the auditor and participated in any capacity in the audit of the corporation during the one-year period preceding the date that the audit began.
DOCUMENT INTEGRITY AND RETENTION
1. The act provides that anyone who destroys, alters, or falsifies records with the intent to obstruct or influence a federal investigation or in relation to bankruptcy proceedings can be criminally prosecuted and sentenced to a fine, imprisonment for up to twenty years, or both.
2. The act requires accountants who audit or review publicly traded companies to retain all working papers related to the audit or review for a period of five years (amended to seven years). Violators can be sentenced to a fine, imprisonment for up to ten years, or both.

years. A knowing violation of this requirement will subject the accountant to a fine, imprisonment for up to ten years, or both.

33-4 Potential Liability of Accountants under Securities Laws

Both civil and criminal liability may be imposed on accountants under the Securities Act of 1933, the Securities Exchange Act of 1934, and the 1995 Private Securities Litigation Reform Act.[9]

33-4a Liability under the Securities Act of 1933

The Securities Act requires issuers to file registration statements with the Securities and Exchange Commission (SEC) prior to an offering of securities.[10] Accountants frequently prepare and certify the financial statements that are included in the issuer's registration statement.

Liability under Section 11 Section 11 of the Securities Act of 1933 imposes civil liability on accountants for misstatements and omissions of material facts in registration statements. Accountants may be liable if a financial statement they prepared for inclusion "contained an untrue statement of a material fact or omitted to state a material fact required to be stated therein or necessary to make the statements therein not misleading."[11]

An accountant's liability for a misstatement or omission of a material fact in a registration statement extends to anyone who acquires a security covered by the registration statement. A purchaser of a security need only demonstrate that she or he has suffered a loss on the security. Proof of reliance on the materially false statement or misleading omission ordinarily is not required. Nor is there a requirement of privity between the accountant and the security purchaser.

The Due Diligence Standard. Section 11 imposes a duty on accountants to use **due diligence** in preparing the financial statements included in registration statements. Thus, after a purchaser has proved a loss on a security, the accountant has the burden of showing that he or she exercised due diligence in preparing the financial statements.

To prove due diligence, an accountant must demonstrate that she or he followed generally accepted standards and did not commit negligence or fraud. Specifically, to avoid liability, the accountant must show that he or she did the following:

1. Conducted a reasonable investigation.

2. Had reasonable grounds to believe and did believe, at the time the registration statement became effective, that the statements therein were true and that there was no omission of a material fact that would be misleading.[12]

In particular, the due diligence standard places a burden on accountants to verify information furnished by a corporation's officers and directors. Merely asking questions is not always sufficient to satisfy the requirement. Accountants have been held liable for failing to detect danger signals in documents that, according to GAAS, require further investigation under the circumstances.[13]

LEARNING OBJECTIVE 3

How might an accountant violate federal securities laws?

"Destroy the old files, but make copies first."

SAMUEL GOLDWYN
1879–1974
(AMERICAN MOTION PICTURE PRODUCER)

Due Diligence A required standard of care that certain professionals, such as accountants, must meet to avoid liability for securities violations.

---

9. Civil and criminal liability may also be imposed on accountants and other professionals under other statutes, including the Racketeer Influenced and Corrupt Organizations Act (RICO), which was discussed in the criminal law chapter.
10. Many securities and transactions are expressly exempted from the 1933 act.
11. 15 U.S.C. Section 77k(a).
12. 15 U.S.C. Section 77k(b)(3).
13. See *In re Cardinal Health, Inc. Securities Litigation*, 426 F.Supp.2d 688 (S.D. Ohio 2006); and *In re WorldCom, Inc. Securities Litigation*, 352 F.Supp.2d 472 (S.D.N.Y. 2005).

When "danger signals" exist, the responsibility to investigate extends beyond accountants. Persons other than accountants, including corporate directors, officers, and managers, can also be liable for failing to perform due diligence. Courts are more likely to impose liability on someone who has ignored warning signs or red flags that suggest accounting errors or misstatements are present. To avoid liability, always investigate the facts underlying financial statements that appear "too good to be true." Compare recent financial statements with earlier ones, read minutes of shareholders' and directors' meetings, and inspect changes in material contracts, bad debts, and newly discovered liabilities. Know what is required to meet due diligence standards in the relevant jurisdiction, and conduct yourself in a manner that is above reproach.

Other Defenses to Liability. Besides proving that he or she has acted with due diligence, an accountant can raise the following defenses to Section 11 liability:

1. There were no misstatements or omissions.

2. The misstatements or omissions were not of material facts.

3. The misstatements or omissions had no causal connection to the plaintiff's loss.

4. The plaintiff-purchaser invested in the securities knowing of the misstatements or omissions.

Liability under Section 12(2)
Section 12(2) of the 1933 Securities Act imposes civil liability for fraud in relation to offerings or sales of securities.[14] Liability arises when an oral statement to an investor or a written prospectus[15] includes an untrue statement or omits a material fact. Some courts have applied Section 12(2) to accountants who aided and abetted (assisted) the seller or the offeror of the securities in violating Section 12(2).

Those who purchase securities and suffer harm as a result of a false or omitted statement, or some other violation, may bring a suit in a federal court to recover their losses and other damages. The U.S. Department of Justice brings criminal actions against those who commit willful violations.

The penalties include fines of up to $10,000, imprisonment for up to five years, or both. The SEC is authorized to seek an injunction against a willful violator to prevent further violations. The SEC can also ask a court to grant other relief, such as an order to a violator to refund profits derived from an illegal transaction.

33–4b Liability under the Securities Exchange Act of 1934

Under Sections 18 and 10(b) of the Securities Exchange Act and SEC Rule 10b-5, an accountant may be found liable for fraud. A plaintiff has a substantially heavier burden of proof under the 1934 act than under the 1933 act because an accountant does not have to prove due diligence to escape liability under the 1934 act.

Liability under Section 18
Section 18 of the 1934 act imposes civil liability on an accountant who makes or causes to be made in any application, report, or document a statement that at the time and in light of the circumstances was false or misleading with respect to any material fact.[16]

Section 18 liability is narrow in that it applies only to applications, reports, documents, and registration statements filed with the SEC. This remedy is further limited in that it applies

---

14. 15 U.S.C. Section 77l.
15. A *prospectus* contains financial disclosures about the corporation for the benefit of potential investors.
16. 15 U.S.C. Section 78r(a).

only to sellers and purchasers. Under Section 18, a seller or purchaser must prove one of the following:

1. That the false or misleading statement affected the price of the security.
2. That the purchaser or seller relied on the false or misleading statement in making the purchase or sale and was not aware of the inaccuracy of the statement.

Good Faith Defense. An accountant will not be liable for violating Section 18 if he or she acted in good faith in preparing the financial statement. To demonstrate good faith, an accountant must show that he or she had no knowledge that the financial statement was false and misleading. In addition, the accountant must have had no intent to deceive, manipulate, defraud, or seek unfair advantage over another party.

Note that "mere" negligence in preparing a financial statement does not lead to liability under the 1934 act. This differs from the 1933 act, under which an accountant is liable for *all* negligent acts.

Other Defenses. In addition to the good faith defense, accountants can escape liability by proving that the buyer or seller of the security in question knew that the financial statement was false and misleading. Also, the statute of limitations may be asserted as a defense to liability under the 1934 act. Sellers and purchasers must bring a cause of action "within one year after the discovery of the facts constituting the cause of action and within three years after such cause of action accrued."[17]

Liability under Section 10(b) and Rule 10b-5
Accountants additionally face potential legal liability under the antifraud provisions contained in the Securities Exchange Act and SEC Rule 10b-5. The scope of these antifraud provisions is very broad and allows private parties to bring civil actions against violators.

Prohibited Conduct. Section 10(b) makes it unlawful for any person, including accountants, to use, in connection with the purchase or sale of any security, any manipulative or deceptive device or contrivance in contravention of SEC rules and regulations.[18] Rule 10b-5 further makes it unlawful for any person, by use of any means or instrumentality of interstate commerce, to do the following:

1. Employ any device, scheme, or artifice (pretense) to defraud.
2. Make any untrue statement of a material fact or omit a material fact necessary to ensure that the statements made were not misleading, in light of the circumstances.
3. Engage in any act, practice, or course of business that operates or would operate as a fraud or deceit on any person, in connection with the purchase or sale of any security.[19]

Extent of Liability. Accountants may be held liable only to sellers or purchasers of securities under Section 10(b) and Rule 10b-5. Privity is not necessary for a recovery.

An accountant may be found liable not only for fraudulent misstatements of material facts in written material filed with the SEC, but also for any fraudulent oral statements or omissions made in connection with the purchase or sale of any security. For a plaintiff to succeed in recovering damages under these antifraud provisions, he or she must prove intent (*scienter*) to commit the fraudulent or deceptive act. Ordinary negligence is not enough.

---

17. 15 U.S.C. Section 17r(c).
18. 15 U.S.C. Section 78j(b)
19. 17 C.F.R. Section 240.10b-5.

Do accountants have a duty to correct misstatements that they discover in *previous* financial statements? What if they know that potential investors are relying on those statements? Those were the questions in the following *Spotlight Case.*

SPOTLIGHT ON AN ACCOUNTANT'S DUTY TO CORRECT MISTAKES: CASE 33.3

Overton v. Todman & Co., CPAs

United States Court of Appeals, Second Circuit, 478 F.3d 479 (2007).

FACTS From 1999 through 2002, Todman & Company, CPAs, audited the financial statements of Direct Brokerage, Inc. (DBI), a broker-dealer in New York registered with the Securities and Exchange Commission (SEC). Each year, Todman issued an unqualified opinion that DBI's financial statements were accurate. DBI filed its statements and Todman's opinions with the SEC.

Despite the certifications of accuracy, Todman made significant errors that concealed DBI's largest liability—its payroll taxes—in the 1999 and 2000 audits. The errors came to light in 2003 when the New York State Division of Taxation subpoenaed DBI's payroll records. It became clear that the company had not filed or paid its payroll taxes for 1999 and 2000. This put DBI in a precarious financial position, owing the state more than $3 million in unpaid taxes, interest, and penalties.

To meet its needs, DBI sought outside investors, including David Overton, who relied on DBI's statements and Todman's opinion for 2002 to invest in DBI. When DBI collapsed under the weight of its liabilities in 2004, Overton and others filed a suit in a federal district court against Todman, asserting, among other things, fraud under Section 10(b) and Rule 10b-5. The court dismissed the complaint. The plaintiffs appealed.

ISSUE Is an accountant liable for securities fraud if the accountant certified a financial statement containing a misstatement and later learned of the misstatement but failed to correct it, even though the accountant knew that investors were relying on the statement?

DECISION Yes. The federal appellate court held that an accountant is liable in these circumstances under Section 10(b) and Rule 10b-5.

Must an accounting firm make public its new knowledge of prior misstatements?

The court vacated the lower court's dismissal and remanded the case for further proceedings.

REASON The court pointed out that any person or entity, including an accountant, "who employs a manipulative device or makes a material misstatement (or omission) on which a purchaser or seller of securities relies may be liable as a primary violator under [Section] 10b-5, assuming all of the requirements for primary liability under Rule 10b-5 are met." One of the requirements is a "duty to speak." Such a duty arises "when one party has information that the other party is entitled to know because of a fiduciary or other similar relation of trust and confidence between them."

When accountants issue a certified opinion, they create the required special relationship with investors. Thus, accountants have a duty to take reasonable steps to correct misstatements that they discover in previous financial statements on which they know the public is relying. Silence in this situation can constitute a false or misleading statement under Section 10(b) and Rule 10b-5. Among other authorities, the court cited Section 10(b), which covers "any person," a United States Supreme Court decision that "labeled a critical element under [Section] 10(b) and Rule 10b-5: reliance by potential investors on the accountant's omission."[a]

WHAT IF THE FACTS WERE DIFFERENT? *If Todman had conducted an audit for DBI but had not issued a certified opinion about DBI's financial statements, would the result have been the same? Explain.*

a. See *Central Bank of Denver v. First Interstate Bank of Denver,* 511 U.S. 164, 114 S.Ct. 1439, 128 L.Ed.2d 119 (1994).

33–4c The Private Securities Litigation Reform Act

The 1995 Private Securities Litigation Reform Act made some changes to the potential liability of accountants and other professionals in securities fraud cases. Among other things, the act imposed a statutory obligation on accountants. An auditor must use adequate procedures in an audit to detect any illegal acts of the company being audited. If something illegal is detected, the auditor must disclose it to the company's board of directors, the audit committee, or the SEC, depending on the circumstances.[20]

---

20. 15 U.S.C. Section 78j-1.

Proportionate Liability The act provides that, in most situations, a party is liable only for the proportion of damages for which he or she is responsible.[21] An accountant who participates in, but is unaware of, illegal conduct may not be liable for the entire loss caused by the illegality.

EXAMPLE 33.10 Nina, an accountant, helps the president and owner of Midstate Trucking company draft financial statements. The statements misrepresent Midstate's financial condition, but Nina is not aware of the fraud. Nina might be held liable, but the amount of her liability could be proportionately less than the entire loss. ■

Aiding and Abetting The act also made it a separate crime to aid and abet a violation of the Securities Exchange Act. Aiding and abetting might include knowingly participating in such an act, assisting in it, or keeping quiet about it. If an accountant knowingly aids and abets a primary violator, the SEC can seek an injunction or monetary damages.

EXAMPLE 33.11 Smith & Jones, an accounting firm, performs an audit for ABC Sales Company that is so inadequate as to constitute gross negligence. ABC uses the materials provided by Smith & Jones as part of a scheme to defraud investors. When the scheme is uncovered, the SEC can bring an action against Smith & Jones for aiding and abetting on the ground that the firm knew or should have known of the material misrepresentations that were in its audit and on which investors were likely to rely. ■

If an accountant is unaware of a company officer's fraud, will she still be held fully liable for any losses caused by the misstatements?

33-5 Potential Criminal Liability

An accountant may be found criminally liable for violations of securities laws and tax laws. In addition, most states make it a crime to (1) knowingly certify false reports, (2) falsify, alter, or destroy books of account, and (3) obtain property or credit through the use of false financial statements.

33-5a Criminal Violations of Securities Laws

Accountants may be subject to criminal penalties for *willful* violations of the 1933 Securities Act and the 1934 Securities Exchange Act. If convicted, they face imprisonment for up to five years and/or a fine of up to $10,000 under the 1933 act, and imprisonment for up to ten years and a fine of $100,000 under the 1934 act. Under the Sarbanes-Oxley Act, if an accountant's false or misleading certified audit statement is used in a securities filing, the accountant may be fined up to $5 million, imprisoned for up to twenty years, or both.

33-5b Criminal Violations of Tax Laws

The Internal Revenue Code makes it a felony to willfully make false statements in a tax return or to willfully aid or assist others in preparing a false tax return. Felony violations are punishable by a fine of $100,000 ($500,000 in the case of a corporation) and imprisonment for up to three years.[22] This provision applies to anyone who prepares tax returns for others for compensation—not just to accountants.[23]

A penalty of $250 per tax return is levied on tax preparers for negligent understatement of the client's tax liability. For willful understatement of tax liability or reckless or intentional disregard of rules or regulations, a penalty of $1,000 is imposed.[24] A tax preparer may also be

LEARNING OBJECTIVE 4
What crimes might an accountant commit under the Internal Revenue Code?

---

21. 15 U.S.C. Section 78u-4(g).
22. 26 U.S.C. Section 7206(2).
23. 26 U.S.C. Section 7701(a)(36).
24. 26 U.S.C. Section 6694.

subject to penalties for failing to furnish the taxpayer with a copy of the return, failing to sign the return, or failing to furnish the appropriate tax identification numbers.

In addition, a tax preparer may be fined $1,000 per document for aiding and abetting another's understatement of tax liability (the penalty is increased to $10,000 in corporate cases).[25] The tax preparer's liability is limited to one penalty per taxpayer per tax year.

33-6 Confidentiality and Privilege

Professionals are restrained by the ethical tenets of their professions to keep all communications with their clients confidential.

33-6a Attorney-Client Relationships

The confidentiality of attorney-client communications is protected by law, which confers a privilege on such communications. This privilege exists because of the client's need to fully disclose the facts of his or her case to the attorney.

To encourage frankness, confidential attorney-client communications relating to representation are normally held in strictest confidence and protected by law. The attorney and her or his employees may not discuss the client's case with anyone—even under court order—without the client's permission. The client holds the privilege, and only the client may waive it—by disclosing privileged information to someone outside the privilege, for instance.

Note, however, that the SEC has implemented rules requiring attorneys who become aware that a client has violated securities laws to report the violation to the SEC. Because reporting a client's misconduct can be a breach of the attorney-client privilege, these rules have created potential conflicts for some attorneys.

33-6b Accountant-Client Relationships

In a few states, accountant-client communications are privileged by state statute. In these states, accountant-client communications may not be revealed even in court or in court-sanctioned proceedings without the client's permission.

The majority of states, however, abide by the common law, which provides that, if a court so orders, an accountant must disclose information about his or her client to the court. Physicians and other professionals may similarly be compelled to disclose in court information given to them in confidence by patients or clients.

Communications between professionals and their clients—other than those between an attorney and her or his client—are not privileged under federal law. In cases involving federal law, state-provided rights to confidentiality of accountant-client communications are not recognized. Thus, in those cases, an accountant must provide all information requested in a court order.

---

25. 26 U.S.C. Section 6701.

Reviewing . . . Liability of Accountants and Other Professionals

Superior Wholesale Corporation planned to purchase Regal Furniture, Inc., and wished to determine Regal's net worth. Superior hired Lynette Shuebke, of the accounting firm Shuebke Delgado, to review an audit that had been prepared by Norman Chase, the accountant for Regal. Shuebke advised Superior that Chase had performed a high-quality audit and that Regal's inventory on the audit dates was stated accurately on the general ledger. As a result of these representations, Superior went forward with its purchase of Regal.

After the purchase, Superior discovered that the audit by Chase had been materially inaccurate and misleading, primarily because the inventory had been grossly overstated on the balance sheet. Later, a former Regal employee who had begun working for Superior exposed an e-mail exchange between Chase and former Regal chief executive officer Buddy Gantry. The exchange revealed that Chase had cooperated in overstating the inventory and understating Regal's tax liability. Using the information presented in the chapter, answer the following questions.

1. If Shuebke's review was conducted in good faith and conformed to generally accepted accounting principles, could Superior hold Shuebke Delgado liable for negligently failing to detect material omissions in Chase's audit? Why or why not?

2. According to the rule adopted by the majority of courts to determine accountants' liability to third parties, could Chase be liable to Superior? Explain.

3. Generally, what requirements must be met before Superior can recover damages under Section 10(b) of the Securities Exchange Act of 1934 and SEC Rule 10b-5? Can Superior meet these requirements?

4. Suppose that a court determined that Chase had aided Regal in willfully understating its tax liability. What is the maximum penalty that could be imposed on Chase?

DEBATE THIS

- Only the largest publicly held companies should be subject to the Sarbanes-Oxley Act.

Key Terms

auditor 833
constructive fraud 836
defalcation 832
due diligence 841

generally accepted accounting
  principles (GAAP) 831
generally accepted auditing standards
  (GAAS) 831

International Financial Reporting
  Standards (IFRS) 832
malpractice 835
working papers 840

Chapter Summary: Liability of Accountants and Other Professionals

COMMON LAW LIABILITY	
Potential Liability to Clients	1. *Breach of contract*—A professional who fails to fulfill contractual obligations can be held liable for breach of contract and resulting damages.
	2. *Negligence*—An accountant, attorney, or other professional, in performing of her or his duties, must use the care, knowledge, and judgment generally used by professionals in the same or similar circumstances. Failure to do so is negligence. An accountant's violation of generally accepted accounting principles and generally accepted auditing standards is *prima facie* evidence of negligence.
	3. *Fraud*—Intentionally misrepresenting a material fact to a client, when the client relies on the misrepresentation, is fraud. Gross negligence in performance of duties is constructive fraud.

Continues

Potential Liability to Third Parties	An accountant may be liable for negligence to any third person the accountant knows or should have known will benefit from the accountant's work. The standard for imposing this liability varies, but generally courts follow one of the following rules (see Exhibit 33–1): 1. *Ultramares rule*—Liability will be imposed only if the accountant is in privity, or near privity, with the third party. 2. *Restatement rule*—Liability will be imposed only if the third party's reliance is foreseen or known, or if the third party is among a class of foreseen or known users. The majority of courts have adopted this rule. 3. *"Reasonably foreseeable users" rule*—Liability will be imposed if the third party's use was reasonably foreseeable.
STATUTORY LIABILITY	
The Sarbanes-Oxley Act	1. *Purpose*—The Sarbanes-Oxley Act imposed requirements on public accounting firms that provide auditing services to companies whose securities are sold to public investors. 2. *Government oversight*—The act created the Public Company Accounting Oversight Board to provide government oversight over public accounting practices. 3. *Working papers*—The act requires accountants to maintain working papers relating to an audit or review for seven years from the end of the fiscal period in which the audit or review was concluded. 4. *Other requirements*—See Exhibit 33–2.
Securities Act of 1933—Section 11	An accountant who makes a false statement or omits a material fact in audited financial statements required for registration of securities under the act may be liable to anyone who acquires securities covered by the registration statement. The accountant's defense is basically the use of due diligence and the reasonable belief that the work was complete and correct. The burden of proof is on the accountant. Willful violations of this act may be subject to criminal penalties.
Securities Act of 1933—Section 12(2)	An accountant may be liable when a prospectus or other communication presented to an investor contained an untrue statement or omitted a material fact.
Securities Exchange Act of 1934—Sections 10(b) and 18	Accountants may be held liable for false and misleading applications, reports, and documents required under the act. The burden is on the plaintiff, and the accountant has numerous defenses, including good faith and lack of knowledge that what was submitted was false.
Potential Criminal Liability	1. Willful violations of the Securities Act of 1933 and the Securities Exchange Act of 1934 may be subject to criminal penalties. 2. Willfully making false statements in or willfully aiding or assisting in the preparation of a false tax return is a felony. Aiding and abetting an individual's understatement of tax liability is a separate crime.

Issue Spotters

1. Dave, an accountant, prepares a financial statement for Excel Company, a client, knowing that Excel will use the statement to obtain a loan from First National Bank. Dave makes negligent omissions in the statement that result in a loss to the bank. Can the bank successfully sue Dave? Why or why not? (See *Potential Liability to Third Parties*.)

2. Nora, an accountant, prepares a financial statement as part of a registration statement that Omega, Inc., files with the Securities and Exchange Commission before making a public offering of securities. The statement contains a misstatement of material fact that is not attributable to Nora's fraud or negligence. Pat relies on the misstatement, buys some of the securities, and suffers a loss. Can Nora be held liable to Pat? Explain. (See *Potential Liability of Accountants under Securities Laws*.)

—**Check your answers to the *Issue Spotters* against the answers provided in Appendix D at the end of this text.**

Learning Objectives Check

1. Under what common law theories may professionals be liable to clients?
2. What are the rules concerning an auditor's liability to third parties?
3. How might an accountant violate federal securities laws?
4. What crimes might an accountant commit under the Internal Revenue Code?

—**Answers to the even-numbered *Learning Objectives Check* questions can be found in Appendix E at the end of this text.**

Business Scenarios and Case Problems

33–1. The *Ultramares* Rule. Larkin, Inc., retains Howard Perkins to manage its books and prepare its financial statements. Perkins, a certified public accountant, lives in Indiana and practices there. After twenty years, Perkins has become a bit bored with generally accepted accounting principles (GAAP) and has adopted more creative accounting methods. Now, though, Perkins has a problem. He is being sued by Molly Tucker, one of Larkin's creditors. Tucker alleges that Perkins either knew or should have known that Larkin's financial statements would be distributed to various individuals. Furthermore, she asserts that these financial statements were negligently prepared and seriously inaccurate. What are the consequences of Perkins's failure to follow GAAP? Under the traditional *Ultramares* rule, can Tucker recover damages from Perkins? Explain. (See *Potential Liability to Third Parties*.)

33–2. The *Restatement* Rule. The accounting firm of Goldman, Walters, Johnson & Co. prepared financial statements for Lucy's Fashions, Inc. After reviewing the financial statements, Happydays State Bank agreed to loan Lucy's Fashions $35,000 for expansion. When Lucy's Fashions declared bankruptcy under Chapter 11 six months later, Happydays State Bank filed an action against Goldman, Walters, Johnson & Co., alleging negligent preparation of financial statements. Assuming that the court has abandoned the *Ultramares* approach, what is the result? What are the policy reasons for holding accountants liable to third parties with whom they are not in privity? (See *Potential Liability to Third Parties*.)

33–3. Accountant's Liability under Rule 10b-5. In early 2016, Bennett, Inc., offered a substantial number of new common shares to the public. Harvey Helms had a long-standing interest in Bennett because his grandfather had once been president of the company. On receiving Bennett's prospectus, Helms was dismayed by the pessimism it embodied, so he decided to delay purchasing stock in the company. Later, Helms asserted that the prospectus prepared by the accountants had been overly pessimistic and had contained materially misleading statements. Discuss fully how successful Helms would be in bringing a suit under Rule 10b-5 against Bennett's accountants. (See *Potential Liability of Accountants under Securities Laws*.)

33–4. Accountant's Liability for Audit. A West Virginia bank ran its asset value from $100 million to $1 billion over seven years by aggressively marketing subprime loans. The Office of the Comptroller of the Currency, a federal regulator, audited the bank and discovered that the books had been falsified for several years and that the bank was insolvent. The Comptroller closed the bank and brought criminal charges against its managers.

The Comptroller fined Grant Thornton, LLP, the bank's accounting firm, $300,000 for recklessly failing to meet generally accepted auditing standards during the years it audited the bank. The Comptroller claimed that Thornton had violated federal law by "participating in . . . unsafe and unsound banking practice." Thornton appealed, contending that its audit function did not qualify as "participating in . . . unsafe and unsound banking practice." What would be the key to determining if the accounting firm could be held liable for the specified violation of federal law? [*Grant Thornton, LLP v. Office of the Comptroller of the Currency,* 514 F.3d 1328 (D.C.Cir. 2008)] (See *Potential Liability of Accountants under Securities Law*.)

33–5. Professional's Liability. Soon after Teresa DeYoung's husband died, her mother-in-law also died, leaving an inheritance of more than $400,000 for DeYoung's children. DeYoung hired John Ruggerio, an attorney, to ensure that her children would receive it. Ruggerio advised her to invest the funds in his real estate business. She declined. A few months later, $300,000 of the inheritance was sent to Ruggerio. Without telling DeYoung, he deposited the $300,000 in his account and began to use the funds in his real estate business. Nine months later, $109,000 of the inheritance was sent to Ruggerio. He paid this to DeYoung. She asked about the remaining amount. Ruggerio lied to hide his theft. Unable to access these funds, DeYoung's children changed their college plans to attend less expensive institutions. Nearly three years later, DeYoung learned the truth. Can she bring a suit against Ruggerio? If so, on what ground? If not, why not? Did Ruggerio violate any standard of professional ethics? Discuss. [*DeYoung v. Ruggerio,* 2009 VT 9, 971 A.2d 627 (2009)] (See *Potential Liability to Clients*.)

33–6. Professional Malpractice. Jeffery Guerrero hired James McDonald, a certified public accountant, to represent him and his business in an appeal to the Internal Revenue Service. The appeal concerned audits that showed Guerrero owed more taxes. When the appeal failed, McDonald assisted in preparing materials for an appeal to the Tax Court, which was not successful. Guerrero then sued McDonald for professional negligence in the preparation of his evidence for the court. Specifically, Guerrero claimed that he would have won the case if McDonald had adequately prepared witnesses and had presented all the arguments that could have been made on his behalf. Guerrero contended that McDonald was liable for all of the additional taxes he was required to pay. Is Guerrero's claim likely to result in liability on McDonald's part? What factors would the court consider? [*Guerrero v. McDonald,* 302 Ga.App. 164, 690 S.E.2d 486 (2010)] (See *Potential Liability to Clients*.)

33–7. Business Case Problem with Sample Answer— Potential Liability to Third Parties. In 2006, twenty-seven parties became limited partners in two hedge funds that had invested with Bernard Madoff and his investment firm. The partners' investment adviser gave them various investment information, including a memorandum indicating that an independent certified public accountant, KPMG, LLP, had audited the hedge funds' annual reports. Since 2004, KPMG had also prepared annual reports addressed to the funds' "partners." Each report stated that KPMG had investigated the funds' financial statements, had followed generally accepted auditing principles, and had concluded that the statements fairly summarized the funds' financial conditions. Moreover, KPMG used the information from its audits to prepare individual tax statements for each fund partner.

In 2008, Madoff was charged with securities fraud for running a massive Ponzi scheme. In a 2009 report, the Securities and Exchange Commission identified numerous "red flags" that should have been discovered by investment advisers and auditors. Unfortunately, they were not, and the hedge funds' partners lost millions of dollars. Is KPMG potentially liable to the funds' partners under the *Restatement (Third) of Torts*? Why or why not? [*Askenazy v. Tremont Group Holdings, Inc.*, 2012 WL 440675 (Mass.Super. 2012)] (See *Potential Liability to Third Parties.*)

—**For a sample answer to Problem 33–7, go to Appendix F at the end of this text.**

33–8. Attorney's Duty of Care. Luis and Maria Rojas contracted to buy a house in Westchester County, New York, from Andrew and Karen Paine. The house was on property designated as "Lot No. 8" on a subdivision map filed in the county clerk's office. The Paines had acquired the property in two parts by the transfer of two separate deeds. At the closing, they delivered a deed stating that it covered "the same property." In fact, however, the legal description attached to the deed covered only the portion of Lot No. 8 described in one of the two previous deeds. Attorney Paul Herrick represented the Rojases in the deal with the Paines. When the Rojases sought to sell the property two years later, the title search revealed that they owned only part of Lot No. 8, and the buyer refused to go through with the sale. Is Herrick liable for malpractice? Explain. [*Rojas v. Paine*, 125 A.D.3d 745, 4 N.Y.S.3d 223 (2 Dept. 2015)] (See *Potential Liability to Clients.*)

33–9. A Question of Ethics—Securities Laws. Portland Shellfish Co. processes live shellfish in Maine. As one of the firm's two owners, Frank Wetmore held 300 voting and 150 nonvoting shares of the stock. Donna Holden held the other 300 voting shares. Donna's husband, Jeff, managed the company's daily operations, including production, procurement, and sales. The board of directors consisted of Frank and Jeff. In 2001, disagreements arose over the company's management. The Holdens invoked the "Shareholders' Agreement," which provided that "in the event of a deadlock, the directors shall hire an accountant at [MacDonald, Page, Schatz, Fletcher & Co., LLC] to determine the value of the outstanding shares. . . . Each shareholder shall have the right to buy out the other shareholder(s)' interest."

MacDonald Page estimated the stock's "fair market value" to be $1.09 million. Donna offered to buy Frank's shares at a price equal to his proportionate share. Frank countered by offering $1.25 million for Donna's shares. Donna rejected Frank's offer and insisted that he sell his shares to her or she would sue. In the face of this threat, Frank sold his shares to Donna for $750,705. Believing the stock to be worth more than twice MacDonald Page's estimate, Frank filed a suit in a federal district court against the accounting firm. [*Wetmore v. MacDonald, Page, Schatz, Fletcher & Co., LLC*, 476 F.3d 1 (1st Cir. 2007)] (See *Potential Liability of Accountants under Securities Law.*)

1. Frank claimed that in valuing the stock, the accounting firm had disregarded "commonly accepted and reliable methods of valuation in favor of less reliable methods." He alleged negligence, among other things. MacDonald Page filed a motion to dismiss the complaint. What are the elements that establish negligence? Which is the most critical element in this case?

2. MacDonald Page evaluated the company's stock by identifying its "fair market value," defined as "[t]he price at which the property would change hands between a willing buyer and a willing seller, neither being under a compulsion to buy or sell and both having reasonable knowledge of relevant facts." The firm knew that the shareholders would use its estimate to determine the price that one would pay to the other. Under these circumstances, was Frank's injury foreseeable? Explain.

3. What factor might have influenced Frank to sell his shares to Donna even if he believed that MacDonald Page's "fair market value" figure was less than half what it should have been? Does this factor represent an unfair, or unethical, advantage? Why or why not?

Critical Thinking and Writing Assignments

33–10. Business Law Critical Thinking Group Assignment.
Napster, Inc., offered a service that allowed its users to browse digital music files on other users' computers and download selections for free. Music industry principals sued Napster for copyright infringement, and the court ordered Napster to remove files that were identified as infringing from its service. When Napster failed to comply, it was shut down.

A few months later, Bertelsmann, a German corporation, loaned Napster $85 million to fund its anticipated transition to a licensed digital music distribution system. The terms allowed Napster to spend the loan on "general, administrative and overhead expenses." In an e-mail, Napster's chief executive officer referred to a "side deal" under which Napster could use up to $10 million of the loan to pay litigation expenses. Napster failed to launch the new system before declaring bankruptcy. The plaintiffs filed a suit against Bertelsmann, alleging that its loan had prolonged Napster's infringement. The plaintiffs asked the court to order the disclosure of all attorney-client communications related to the loan. (See *Confidentiality and Privilege*.)

1. The first group will identify the principle that Bertelsmann could assert to protect these communications and outline the purpose of this protection.

2. The second group will decide whether this principle should protect a client who consults an attorney for advice that will help the client commit fraud.

3. A third group will determine whether the court should grant the plaintiffs' request.

Unit Six—Business Case Study with Dissenting Opinion

Yates v. United States

In this unit, we outlined provisions of the Sarbanes-Oxley Act of 2002 that apply to corporate governance. Congress's passage of this act was prompted by the exposure of Enron Corporation's massive accounting fraud and revelations that the company's outside auditor, Arthur Andersen LLP, had systematically destroyed potentially incriminating documents.

Later, Congress enacted 18 U.S.C. Section 1519 as part of the act. That section provides that a person may be fined or imprisoned for up to twenty years for knowingly destroying, concealing, or covering up "any record, document, or tangible object" to impede a federal investigation. Congress intended to prohibit, in particular, corporate document-shredding to hide evidence of financial wrongdoing.

In this *Business Case Study with Dissenting Opinion,* we focus on *Yates v. United States.*[1] In this decision, the United States Supreme Court considered how broadly to interpret the term "tangible object" as that term is used in Section 1519.

Is the disposal of undersized fish after a government inspection a violation of the Sarbanes-Oxley Act?

CASE BACKGROUND

An inspection of *Miss Katie,* a commercial fishing vessel, in the Gulf of Mexico by John Jones, a deputized agent of the National Marine Fisheries Service, revealed that the ship's catch contained undersized red grouper in violation of federal regulations. Jones told the ship's captain, John Yates, to keep the undersized fish segregated from the rest of the catch until the ship returned to port. Instead, after the officer left, Yates told the crew to throw the fish overboard.

For this offense, Yates was charged with, and convicted of, violating Section 1519. Yates argued that the statute's reference to "tangible object" includes objects used to store information, such as computer hard drives, not fish. The U.S. Court of Appeals for the Eleventh Circuit affirmed the conviction, concluding that the reference includes any object having physical form. Yates appealed to the United States Supreme Court.

MAJORITY OPINION

Justice *GINSBURG* announced the judgment of the Court and delivered an opinion * * * .

* * * *

The ordinary meaning of an "object" that is "tangible," as stated in dictionary definitions, is "a discrete * * * thing" that "possesses physical form."

Whether a statutory term is unambiguous, however, does not turn solely on dictionary definitions of its component words * * * but as well by the specific context in which that language is used, and the broader context of the statute as a whole. * * * In law as in life,

* * * the same words, placed in different contexts, sometimes mean different things.

* * * *

We note first Section 1519's caption: "Destruction, alteration, or falsification of records in Federal investigations and bankruptcy." That heading conveys no suggestion that the section prohibits spoliation [alteration or destruction] of any and all physical evidence, however remote from records. Neither does the title of the section of the Sarbanes-Oxley Act in which Section 1519 was placed, Section 802: "Criminal penalties for altering documents." Furthermore, Section 1520, the only other provision passed as part of Section 802, is titled "Destruction of corporate audit records" and addresses only that specific subset of records and documents. While these headings are not commanding, they supply cues that Congress did not intend "tangible object" in Section 1519 to sweep within its reach physical objects of every kind, including things no one would describe as records, documents, or devices closely associated with them. *If Congress indeed meant to make Section 1519 an all-encompassing ban on the spoliation of evidence, * * * one would have expected a clearer indication of that intent.* [Emphasis added.]

Section 1519's position within * * * Title 18 further signals that Section 1519 was not intended to serve as a cross-the-board ban on the destruction of physical evidence of every kind. Congress placed Section 1519 (and its companion provision Section 1520) * * * following immediately after * * * Section 1516, Section 1517, and Section 1518, each of them prohibiting obstructive acts in specific contexts. See Section 1516 (audits of recipients of federal funds); Section 1517

---

1. 135 S.Ct. 1074, __ U.S. __, 191 L.Ed.2d 64 (2015).

(federal examinations of financial institutions); [and] Section 1518 (criminal investigations of federal health care offenses).

* * * *

The contemporaneous [concurrent] passage of Section 1512(c)(1), which was contained in a section of the Sarbanes-Oxley Act discrete from the section embracing Section 1519 and Section 1520, is also instructive. Section 1512(c)(1) [prohibits a person from "altering, destroying, mutilating, or concealing a record, document, or other object * * * with the intent to impair the object's integrity or availability for use in an official proceeding."]

* * * If Section 1519's reference to "tangible object" already included all physical objects, * * * then Congress had no reason to enact Section 1512(c)(1).

* * * *

The words immediately surrounding "tangible object" in Section 1519—"falsifies, or makes a false entry in any record [or] document"—also cabin [restrain] the contextual meaning of that term. We rely on the principle [that] a word is known by the company it keeps to avoid ascribing to one word a meaning so broad that it is inconsistent with its accompanying words.

* * * "Tangible object" is the last in a list of terms that begins "any record [or] document." The term is therefore appropriately read to refer, not to any tangible object, but specifically to the subset of tangible objects involving records and documents, *i.e.,* objects used to record or preserve information.

This moderate interpretation of "tangible object" accords with the list of actions Section 1519 proscribes. The section applies to anyone who "alters, destroys, mutilates, conceals, covers up, falsifies, or makes a false entry in any record, document, or tangible object" with the requisite obstructive intent. The last two verbs, "falsif[y]" and "mak[e] a false entry in," typically take as grammatical objects records, documents, or things used to record or preserve information, such as logbooks or hard drives.

* * * *

For the reasons stated, * * * we hold that a "tangible object" within Section 1519's compass is one used to record or preserve information. The judgment of the U.S. Court of Appeals for the Eleventh Circuit is therefore reversed, and the case is remanded for further proceedings.

DISSENTING OPINION

Justice *KAGAN*, * * * dissenting.

A criminal law, 18 U.S.C. Section 1519, prohibits tampering with "any record, document, or tangible object" in an attempt to obstruct a federal investigation. This case raises the question whether the term "tangible object" means the same thing in Section 1519 as it means in everyday language—any object capable of being touched.

The answer should be easy: Yes. The term "tangible object" is broad, but clear. Throughout the U.S. Code and many States' laws, it invariably covers physical objects of all kinds. And in Section 1519, context confirms what bare text says: All the words surrounding "tangible object" show that Congress meant the term to have a wide range. That fits with Congress's evident purpose in enacting Section 1519: to punish those who alter or destroy physical evidence—*any* physical evidence—with the intent of thwarting federal law enforcement.

The plurality instead interprets "tangible object" to cover "only objects one can use to record or preserve information." * * * In my view, conventional tools of statutory construction all lead to a more conventional result: A "tangible object" is an object that's tangible. I would apply the statute that Congress enacted and affirm the judgment below.

* * * *

* * * The ordinary meaning of "tangible object" is "a discrete thing that possesses physical form." A fish is, of course, a discrete thing that possesses physical form. So the ordinary meaning of the term "tangible object" in Section 1519 * * * covers fish (including too-small red grouper).

That interpretation accords with endless uses of the term in statute and rule books as construed by courts. Dozens of federal laws and rules of procedure (and hundreds of state enactments) include the term "tangible object" or its first cousin "tangible thing"—some in association with documents, others not. To my knowledge, no court has ever read any such provision to exclude things that don't record or preserve data; rather, all courts have adhered to the statutory language's ordinary * * * meaning. * * * No surprise, then, that—until today—courts have uniformly applied the term "tangible object" in Section 1519 in the same way.

QUESTIONS FOR ANALYSIS

1. *Law.* How did the Court interpret the term "tangible object" in this case? Why?

2. *Law.* Why did the dissent disagree with the Court's interpretation? If the Court had adopted the dissent's position, how would this have affected the result?

3. *Ethics.* Was the ship captain's decision to throw the undersized fish overboard a breach of ethics? Explain.

4. *Political Dimension.* How could a party who disagrees with certain provisions of the Sarbanes-Oxley Act affect a change to those provisions?

5. *Implications for the Business Owner.* How does the Court's interpretation of the term "tangible object" affect businesses' use of computers, servers, and other media on which information is stored?

Unit Six—Business Scenario

Alpha Software, Inc., and Beta Products Corporation—both small firms—are competitors in the business of software research, development, and production.

1. **Antitrust Law.** Alpha and Beta form a joint venture to research, develop, and produce new software for a particular line of computers. Does this business combination violate the antitrust laws? If so, is it a *per se* violation, or is it subject to the rule of reason? Alpha and Beta decide to merge. After the merger, Beta is the surviving firm. What aspect of this firm's presence in the market will be assessed to decide whether this merger is in violation of any antitrust laws?

2. **Consumer Law.** To market its products profitably, Beta considers a number of advertising and labeling proposals. One proposal is that Beta suggest in its advertising that one of its software products has a certain function even though the product does not actually have that capability. Another suggestion is that Beta sell half of a certain program in packaging that misleads the buyer into believing the entire program is included. To obtain the entire program, customers would need to buy a second product. Can Beta implement these suggestions or otherwise market its products in any way it likes? If not, why not?

3. **Environmental Law.** The production part of Beta's operations generates hazardous waste. Gamma Transport Company transports the waste to Omega Waste Corporation, which owns and operates a hazardous waste disposal site. At the site, some containers leak hazardous waste, and the Environmental Protection Agency (EPA) cleans it up. From whom can the EPA recover the cost of the clean-up?

4. **Liability of Accountants.** Beta hires a certified public accountant, Aaron Schleger, to prepare its financial reports and issue opinion letters based on those reports. One year, Beta falls into serious financial trouble, but this is not reflected in Schleger's reports and opinion letters. Relying on Schleger's portrayal of the company's fiscal health, Beta borrows substantial amounts to develop a new product. The bank, in lending funds to Beta, relies on an opinion letter from Schleger, and Schleger is aware of the bank's reliance. Assuming that Schleger was negligent but did not engage in intentional fraud, what is his potential liability in this situation? Discuss fully.

Unit Six—Group Project

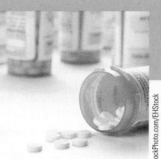

Pharma, Inc., made Cancera, a prescription drug that helped in the treatment of certain forms of cancer. When Cancera's patent was about to expire, Synthetic Chemix Corporation developed a generic version of Cancera and prepared to enter the market. Within weeks of this drug's debut, Pharma offered to pay Synthetic $50 million per year *not* to market the generic version. Synthetic accepted the offer.

1. The first group will determine whether the agreement between Pharma and Synthetic was a violation of antitrust law.

2. The second group will examine the impact of delaying entry of the generic version of Cancera into the market and determine its effect on competition.

3. The third group will decide whether a court, in considering these issues, would apply the *per se* rule or the rule of reason.

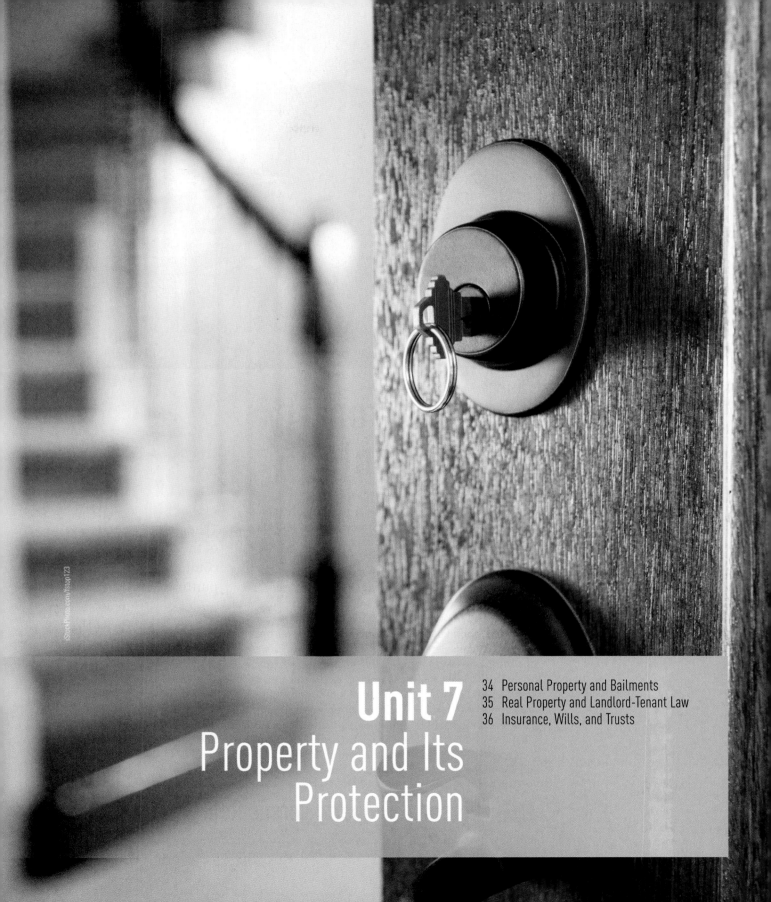

Unit 7
Property and Its
Protection

iStockPhoto.com/fistop123

34

iStockPhoto.com/fergregory

CHAPTER OUTLINE

- Personal Property versus Real Property
- Acquiring Ownership of Personal Property
- Mislaid, Lost, and Abandoned Property
- Bailments

LEARNING OBJECTIVES

The five Learning Objectives *below are designed to help improve your understanding of the chapter. After reading this chapter, you should be able to answer the following questions:*

1. What is real property? What is personal property?

2. What are the three necessary elements for an effective gift?

3. What are the three elements of a bailment?

4. What are the basic duties of a bailee?

5. What standard of care applies to common carriers?

LEARNING OBJECTIVE 1

What is real property? What is personal property?

Real Property Land and everything attached to it, such as trees and buildings.

Personal Property and Bailments

Property consists of the legally protected rights and interests a person has in anything with an ascertainable value that is subject to ownership. For instance, virtual property has become quite valuable in today's world, as you will read later in this chapter. Property would have little value, however, if the law did not define owners' rights to use their property, to sell or dispose of it, and to prevent trespass on it. Indeed, John Locke, as indicated in the chapter-opening quotation, considered the preservation of property to be the primary reason for the establishment of government.

In this chapter, we first examine the differences between personal and real property. We then look at the methods of acquiring ownership of personal property and consider issues relating to mislaid, lost, and abandoned personal property. In the remainder of the chapter, we discuss bailment relationships. A *bailment* is created when personal property is temporarily delivered into the care of another without a transfer of title, such as when a person takes an item of clothing to the dry cleaners.

> "The great . . . end . . . of men united into commonwealths, and putting themselves under government, is the preservation of their property."
>
> **JOHN LOCKE**
> 1632–1704
> (ENGLISH POLITICAL PHILOSOPHER)

34-1 Personal Property versus Real Property

Property is divided into real property and personal property. **Real property** (sometimes called *realty* or *real estate*) consists of land and everything permanently attached to it, including structures and anything permanently attached to the structures. Everything else is **personal property,** or *personalty*. Attorneys sometimes refer to personal property as **chattel,** a term used under the common law to denote all forms of personal property.

Personal property can be tangible or intangible. *Tangible* personal property, such as a home theater, heavy construction equipment, or a car, has physical substance. *Intangible* personal property represents some set of rights and interests but has no physical substance. Stocks and bonds, patents, trademarks, and copyrights—as well as digital and virtual property—are examples of intangible personal property.

Both personal property and real property can be owned by an individual person or by some other entity, such as an organization. When two or more persons own real or personal property together, concurrent ownership exists. (The different types of concurrent ownership will be discussed in the real property chapter.)

In the following case, a concurrent owner of a copyright to an unpublished autobiography contended that she was entitled to an accounting for the use of the work to create a successful theatrical production.

Personal Property Property that is movable. Any property that is not real property.

Chattel Personal property.

CASE 34.1

Corbello v. DeVito

United States Court of Appeals, Ninth Circuit, 777 F.3d 1058 (2015).

FACTS Rex Woodward contracted with Thomas DeVito, one of the original members of the Four Seasons rock band, to ghostwrite DeVito's autobiography. Before it was published, Woodward died, and his interest in the manuscript's copyright passed to his widow, Donna Corbello. Later, DeVito agreed to grant former bandmates Frankie Valli and Bob Gaudio the right to use "aspects of his life related to The Four Seasons including . . . his creative contributions, biographies, events in his life, name and likeness (the Materials)" to develop a musical about the Four Seasons. The result was a Broadway hit called *Jersey Boys*.

Actors and others involved in the show attributed their inspiration in part to DeVito's unpublished autobiography. Corbello filed a suit in a federal district court against DeVito and his bandmates for an accounting of the profit earned from this use of the work. The court issued a judgment in the defendants' favor. Corbello appealed.

ISSUE Is Corbello entitled to an accounting of the profit earned from the use of Woodward's work to create *Jersey Boys?*

DECISION Yes. The U.S. Court of Appeals for the Ninth Circuit reversed the lower court's judgment. As a concurrent owner of the work's copyright, Corbello was entitled to an accounting.

Who retains rights in a biography on which the Broadway musical Jersey Boys *was based?*

REASON A copyright owner has the right to create a work derived from the copyrighted work, and the owner can transfer this right to another party. DeVito agreed to grant to Valli and Gaudio an exclusive right to use "the Materials" in a theatrical production. The agreement defined "Materials" to include "biographies," and Woodward's account of DeVito's life qualifies as a biography.

The theatrical production of *Jersey Boys* is a derivative work. DeVito's granting the right of use constituted a transfer to Valli and Gaudio of DeVito's ownership of the right to create a derivative work from Woodward's work. But a concurrent owner cannot transfer more than he or she holds. Thus, DeVito's grant of his right to Valli and Gaudio did not bind or limit Corbello's rights in the copyright without her consent. "Because copyright co-owners must account to one another for any profits earned by exploiting that copyright, the district court erred in rejecting Corbello's claim for [an] accounting."

CRITICAL THINKING—Legal Consideration *Under what circumstances would Corbello* not *be entitled to an accounting? Why?*

34–1a Why Is the Distinction Important?

The distinction between real and personal property is important for several reasons. How property is taxed and what is required to transfer or acquire the property is determined by whether the property is classified as real or personal.

Taxation   The two types of property are usually subject to different types of taxes. Generally, each state assesses property taxes on real property. Typically, the tax rate is based on the market value of the real property and the various services provided by the city, state, and county in which the property is located. For instance, higher taxes may be imposed on real property located within the city limits to pay for schools, roads, and libraries.

Businesses often also pay taxes on the personal property they own, use, or lease, including office or farm equipment and supplies. Individuals may pay sales tax when purchasing personal property, but generally they are not required to pay annual taxes on personal property that is not used for business.

Acquisition   Another reason for distinguishing between real and personal property has to do with the way the property is acquired or transferred. Personal property can be transferred with a minimum of formality—such as by selling goods on Craigslist or at a garage sale. In contrast, real property transfers generally involve a written sales contract and a *deed* that is recorded with the state.

Similarly, establishing ownership rights is simpler for personal property than for real property. **EXAMPLE 34.1** If Mia gives Shawn an iPad as a gift, Shawn does not need to have any paperwork evidencing title, as he would if she had given him real property. ■ The ways to acquire ownership of personal property will be discussed shortly.

34–1b Conversion of Real Property to Personal Property

Sometimes, real property can be turned into personal property by detaching it from the land. For instance, the trees, bushes, and plants growing on land are considered part of the real property (with the exception of crops that must be planted every year, such as wheat). If the property is sold, all the vegetation growing on the land normally is transferred to the new owner of the real property.

Once the items are severed (removed) from the land, however, they become personal property. If the trees are cut from the land, the timber is personal property. If apples, grapes, or raspberries are picked from trees or vines growing on real property, they become personal property. Similarly, if land contains minerals (including oil) or other natural resources (such as marble), the resources are part of the real property. But once removed, they become personal property.

Conversely, personal property may be converted into real property by permanently attaching it to the real property. Personal property that is affixed to real property in a permanent way, such as tile installed in a house, is known as a *fixture* (we will discuss fixtures in the real property chapter).

34–2 Acquiring Ownership of Personal Property

The most common way of acquiring personal property is by purchasing it. (Today, even virtual property is often purchased—see this chapter's *Adapting the Law to the Online Environment* feature for a discussion.)

We discussed the purchase and sale of goods (which are personal property) in earlier chapters. Often, property is acquired by will or inheritance, as we will discuss in a later chapter. Here, we look at additional ways in which ownership of personal property can be acquired, including acquisition by possession, production, gifts, accession, and confusion.

34–2a Possession

Sometimes, a person can become the owner of personal property merely by possessing it. An example of acquiring ownership by possession is the capture of wild animals. Wild animals belong to no one in their natural state, and the first person to take possession of a wild animal

What is the most common way to acquire ownership rights in personal property?

ADAPTING THE LAW TO THE **ONLINE** ENVIRONMENT
The Exploding World of Digital Property

Jon Jacobs took out a real mortgage on his real house so that he could pay $100,000 in real dollars for a virtual asteroid near the virtual Planet Calypso in the virtual world Entropia Universe. A few years later, he sold Club Neverdie, the virtual space resort he had constructed on the virtual asteroid, for more than $600,000. At the time, Jacobs was making $200,000 per year from players' purchases of virtual goods at the resort.

If the prospect of paying real funds for virtual property seems disconcerting, remember that property does not have to be tangible. Property consists of a bundle of rights in anything that has an ascertainable value and is subject to ownership—a definition that encompasses virtual property, including all the intangible objects used in virtual worlds like Entropia Universe and Second Life.

Digital Goods Have Value, Too

Digital goods include virtual goods, but more important, they include digital books, music libraries, and movie downloads, as well as domain names and expensively created Web sites. This digital property has real value. Some digital music libraries, for example, cost thousands of dollars.

Who Keeps the Digital Goods?

The growing value of digital goods raises some legal questions. For instance, what are the respective rights of the creator/owner of a virtual-world Web site and the players at that site? And what happens when a husband and wife decide to divorce after they have purchased virtual real estate or digital goods with real-world dollars? The couple—or a court—will have to figure out a way to divide the goods. Property and divorce laws will have to adapt to take this changing world into account.

CRITICAL THINKING

- How might a couple who enjoy purchasing digital goods together avoid property division issues in the event of a divorce?

---

normally owns it. A hunter who kills a deer, for instance, has assumed ownership of it (unless he or she acted in violation of the law). Those who find lost or abandoned property can also acquire ownership rights through mere possession of the property, as will be discussed later in this chapter.

34-2b Production

Production—the fruits of labor—is another means of acquiring ownership of personal property. For instance, writers, inventors, and manufacturers produce personal property and thereby acquire title to it. (In some situations, as when a researcher is hired to develop a new product, the researcher-producer may not own what is produced.)

34-2c Gifts

A **gift** is another fairly common means of acquiring and transferring ownership of real and personal property. A gift is essentially a *voluntary* transfer of property ownership for which no consideration is given. The presence of consideration is what distinguishes a contractual obligation from a gift.

For a gift to be effective, the following three elements are required:

1. Donative intent on the part of the *donor* (the one giving the gift).

2. Delivery.

3. Acceptance by the *donee* (the one receiving the gift).

Until these three requirements are met, no effective gift has been made. **EXAMPLE 34.2** Your aunt tells you that she *intends* to give you a new Mercedes-Benz for your next birthday. This is simply a promise to make a gift. It is not considered a gift until the Mercedes-Benz is delivered and accepted. ■

Gift A voluntary transfer of property made without consideration, past or present.

LEARNING OBJECTIVE 2

What are the three necessary elements for an effective gift?

ETHICAL ISSUE

Who owns the engagement ring?   Often, when two people decide to marry, one party (traditionally the man in an opposite-sex relationship) gives the other an engagement ring. What if the engagement is called off? Etiquette authorities routinely counsel that if the woman breaks the engagement, she should return the ring, but if the man calls the wedding off, the woman is entitled to keep the ring. When the party who gave the ring (the donor) sues for its return after a breakup, the courts are split.

Courts in a majority of states, including Kansas, Michigan, New York, and Ohio, hold that an engagement ring is not a real gift. Rather, it is a "conditional gift" that becomes final only if the marriage occurs. If the marriage does not take place, the ring is returned to the donor regardless of who broke the engagement. This position is similar to the law of ancient Rome, which mandated that when an engagement was broken, the woman had to return the ring, as a penalty, regardless of who was at fault. Some judges, however, disagree with the conditional-gift theory and contend that an engagement ring is a gift and, as such, it belongs to the donee, even if the engagement is broken.

If a close relative tells you that she intends to give you a Mercedes-Benz convertible, has she gifted you the car? Why or why not?

Donative Intent   When a gift is challenged in court, the court will determine whether donative intent exists by looking at the language of the donor and the surrounding circumstances. A court may look at the relationship between the parties and the size of the gift in relation to the donor's other assets. When a person has given away a large portion of her or his assets, the court will scrutinize the transaction closely to determine the donor's mental capacity and to look for indications of fraud or duress.

CASE EXAMPLE 34.3 Over a period of three months, Jean Knowles Goodman, who was eighty-five years old, gave Steven Atwood several checks that totaled $56,100. Atwood was a veterinarian who had cared for Goodman's dogs for nearly twenty years, and he and Goodman had become friends. Shortly after writing the last check, Goodman was hospitalized and diagnosed with dementia (loss of brain function) and alcohol dependency.

The guardian who was appointed to represent Goodman filed a lawsuit to invalidate the gifts, claiming that Goodman had lacked mental capacity and donative intent. At trial, a psychiatrist who had examined Goodman testified on behalf of Atwood that while Goodman lacked the capacity to care for herself, she would have understood that she was giving away her funds. Therefore, the court concluded that Goodman had donative intent to make the gifts to Atwood.[1] ■

Delivery   The gift must be delivered to the donee. Delivery may be accomplished by means of a third person who is the agent of either the donor or the donee. Naturally, no delivery is necessary if the gift is already in the hands of the donee. Delivery is obvious in most cases, but some objects cannot be relinquished physically. Then the question of delivery depends on the surrounding circumstances.

Constructive Delivery.   When the object itself cannot be physically delivered, a symbolic, or constructive, delivery will be sufficient. **Constructive delivery** confers the right to take possession of the object in question. EXAMPLE 34.4 Angela wants to make a gift of various rare coins that she has stored in a safe-deposit box. She obviously cannot deliver the box itself to the donee, and she does not want to take the coins out of the bank. Angela can simply deliver the key to the box to the donee and authorize the donee's access to the box and its contents. This action constitutes a constructive delivery of the contents of the box. ■

Constructive Delivery
A symbolic delivery of property that cannot be physically delivered.

---

1. *Goodman v. Atwood,* 78 Mass.App.Ct. 655, 940 N.E.2d 514 (2011).

Constructive delivery is always necessary for gifts of intangible property, such as stocks, bonds, insurance policies, and contracts. What will be delivered are documents that represent rights and are not, in themselves, the true property.

Relinquishing Dominion and Control. An effective delivery also requires giving up complete control and **dominion** (ownership rights) over the subject matter of the gift. The outcome of disputes often turns on whether control has actually been relinquished. The Internal Revenue Service carefully examines transactions between relatives, especially when one claims to have given income-producing property to another who is in a lower marginal tax bracket. Unless complete control over the property has been relinquished, the "donor"—not the family member who received the "gift"—will have to pay taxes on the income from that property.

In the following *Classic Case*, the court focused on the requirement that a donor must relinquish complete control and dominion over property given to the donee before a gift can be effectively delivered.

Dominion Ownership rights in property, including the right to possess and control the property.

★★★ CLASSIC CASE 34.2 ★★★

In re Estate of Piper
Missouri Court of Appeals, 676 S.W.2d 897 (1984).

FACTS Gladys Piper died intestate (without a will) in 1982. At her death, she owned miscellaneous personal property worth $5,000 and had in her purse $200 in cash and two diamond rings. Wanda Brown, Piper's niece, took the contents of the purse, allegedly to preserve the items for the estate. Clara Kaufmann, a friend of Piper's, filed a claim against the estate for $4,800. From October 1974 until Piper's death, Kaufmann had taken Piper to the doctor, beauty shop, and grocery store. Kaufmann had also written Piper's checks to pay her bills and had helped her care for her home.

Kaufmann maintained that Piper had promised to pay her for these services and had given her the diamond rings as a gift. A Missouri state trial court denied her request for payment. The court found that her services had been voluntary. Kaufmann then filed a petition for delivery of personal property—the rings—which was granted by the trial court. Brown, other heirs, and the administrator of Piper's estate appealed.

ISSUE Had Gladys Piper made an effective gift of the rings to Clara Kaufmann?

DECISION No. The state appellate court reversed the judgment of the trial court on the ground that Piper had never delivered the rings to Kaufmann.

REASON Kaufmann claimed that the rings belonged to her by reason of a "consummated gift long prior to the death of Gladys Piper."

How can two diamond rings have been gifted if they remained in the owner's purse after her death?

iStockPhoto.com/poram

Two witnesses testified at the trial that Piper had told them that she was going to wear the rings until she died but that the rings belonged to Kaufmann. The appellate court, however, found "no evidence of any actual delivery." The court pointed out that the essentials of a gift are (1) a present intention to make a gift on the part of the donor, (2) a delivery of the property by the donor to the donee, and (3) an acceptance by the donee. Here, the evidence showed only an intent to make a gift. Because there was no delivery—either actual or constructive—no valid gift was made.

WHAT IF THE FACTS WERE DIFFERENT? *Suppose that Gladys Piper had told Clara Kaufmann that she was giving the rings to Clara but wished to keep them in her possession for a few more days. Would this have affected the court's decision in this case? Explain.*

IMPACT OF THIS CASE ON TODAY'S LAW *This case clearly illustrates the delivery requirement when making a gift. Assuming that Piper did, indeed, intend for Kaufmann to have the rings, it was unfortunate that Kaufmann had no right to receive them after Piper's death. Yet the alternative could lead to perhaps even more unfairness. The policy behind the delivery requirement is to protect property owners and their heirs from fraudulent claims based solely on parol evidence. If not for this policy, a person could easily claim that a gift had been made when, in fact, it had not.*

Acceptance   The final requirement of a valid gift is acceptance by the donee. This rarely presents any problem, as most donees readily accept their gifts. The courts generally assume acceptance unless the circumstances indicate otherwise.

Gifts *Inter Vivos* and Gifts *Causa Mortis*   A gift made during one's lifetime is termed a **gift *inter vivos***. A **gift *causa mortis*** (a so-called *deathbed gift*) is made in contemplation of imminent death. To be effective, a gift *causa mortis* must meet not only the three requirements discussed earlier—donative intent, delivery, and acceptance—but also some additional rules.

Gift *Inter Vivos*   A gift made during one's lifetime and not in contemplation of imminent death, in contrast to a gift *causa mortis*.

Gift *Causa Mortis*   A gift made in contemplation of imminent death. The gift is revoked if the donor does not die as contemplated.

Automatically Revoked if Donor Recovers.   A gift *causa mortis* does not become absolute until the donor dies from the contemplated event, and it is automatically revoked if the donor survives. **EXAMPLE 34.5** Yang, who is about to undergo surgery to remove a cancerous tumor, delivers an envelope to Chao, a close business associate. The envelope contains a letter saying, "I want to give you this check for $1 million in the event of my death from this operation." Chao cashes the check. The surgeon performs the operation and removes the tumor. Yang recovers fully. Several months later, Yang dies from a heart attack that is totally unrelated to the operation.

If the administrator of Yang's estate tries to recover the $1 million, she will normally succeed. The gift *causa mortis* to Chao is automatically revoked if Yang recovers. The *specific event* that was contemplated in making the gift was death from a particular operation. Because Yang's death was not the result of this event, the gift is revoked, and the $1 million passes to Yang's estate. ■

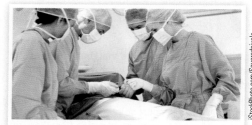

What effect does a patient's survival have on a $1 million check given as a gift to a close friend just before the surgery?

iStockPhoto.com/Squaredpixels

Automatically Revoked if Donee Dies.   A gift *causa mortis* is also revoked if the prospective donee dies before the donor. Therefore, even if Yang in *Example 34.5* had died during the operation, the gift would have been revoked if Chao had died a few minutes earlier. In that event, the $1 million would have passed to Yang's estate, and not to Chao's heirs.

34–2d Accession

Accession means "something added." Accession occurs when someone adds value to an item of personal property by the use of either labor or materials.

Generally, there is no dispute about who owns the property after an accession occurs, especially when the accession is accomplished with the owner's consent. **EXAMPLE 34.6** Harvey buys all the materials necessary to customize his Corvette. He hires Zach, a customizing specialist, to come to his house to perform the work. Harvey pays Zach for the value of the labor, obviously retaining title to the property. ■

Accession   The addition of value to personal property by the use of labor or materials.

If an improvement is made wrongfully—without the permission of the owner—the owner retains title to the property and normally does not have to pay for the improvement. This is true even if the accession increases the value of the property substantially. **EXAMPLE 34.7** Colton steals a truck and puts expensive new tires on it. If the rightful owner later recovers the truck, the owner obviously will not be required to compensate Colton, a thief, for the value of the new tires. ■

34–2e Confusion

Confusion is the commingling (mixing together) of goods to such an extent that one person's personal property cannot be distinguished from another's. Confusion frequently occurs with *fungible goods,* such as grain or oil, which consist of identical units.

Confusion   The mixing together of goods belonging to two or more owners to such an extent that the separately owned goods cannot be identified.

If confusion occurs as a result of agreement, an honest mistake, or the act of some third party, the owners share ownership and will share any loss in proportion to their ownership interests in the property. **EXAMPLE 34.8** Five farmers in a small Iowa community enter into a cooperative arrangement. Each fall, the farmers harvest the same amount of number 2–grade yellow corn and store it in silos that are held by the cooperative. Each farmer thus owns one-fifth of the total corn in the silos. If a fire burns down one of the silos, each farmer will bear one-fifth of the loss. ■ If goods are confused due to an intentional wrongful act, then the innocent party ordinarily acquires title to the whole.

34-3 Mislaid, Lost, and Abandoned Property

As already mentioned, one of the methods of acquiring ownership of property is to possess it. Simply finding something and holding on to it, however, does not necessarily give the finder any legal rights in the property. Different rules apply, depending on whether the property was mislaid, lost, or abandoned. Exhibit 34–1 illustrates the distinctions among these types of property, which are discussed in the following subsections.

34-3a Mislaid Property

Property that has been *voluntarily* placed somewhere by the owner and then inadvertently forgotten is **mislaid property.** A person who finds mislaid property does not obtain title to it. Instead, the owner of the place where the property was mislaid becomes the caretaker of the property because it is highly likely that the true owner will return.[2] **EXAMPLE 34.9** Maya goes to a movie theater. While paying for popcorn at the concessions stand, she sets her iPhone on the counter and then leaves it there. The phone is mislaid property, and the theater owner is entrusted with the duty of reasonably caring for it. ■

34-3b Lost Property

Property that is *involuntarily* left is **lost property.** A finder of the property can claim title to the property against the whole world—*except the true owner.*[3] If the true owner is identified and demands that the lost property be returned, the finder must return it. In contrast, if a third party attempts to take possession of the lost property, the finder will have a better title than the third party.

EXAMPLE 34.10 Kayla works in a large library at night. As she crosses the courtyard on her way home, she finds a gold bracelet set with what seem to be precious stones. She takes the bracelet to a jeweler to have it appraised. While pretending to weigh the bracelet, the jeweler's

If several farmers each keep the same amount of corn mixed together in some silos, how does the destruction of one silo affect each farmer's claim on the remaining stored corn?

Mislaid Property Property that the owner has voluntarily parted with and then has inadvertently forgotten.

Lost Property Property that the owner has involuntarily by the owner.

---

2. The finder of mislaid property is an involuntary bailee.
3. For a classic English case establishing this principle, see *Armory v. Delamirie*, 93 Eng.Rep. 664 (K.B. [King's Bench] 1722).

Exhibit 34-1 Mislaid, Lost, and Abandoned Property

Mislaid Property	Property that is placed somewhere voluntarily by the owner and then inadvertently forgotten. A finder of mislaid property will not acquire title to the goods, and the owner of the place where the property was mislaid becomes a caretaker of the mislaid property.
Lost Property	Property that is involuntarily left by the owner. A finder of lost property can claim title to the property against the whole world except the true owner.
Abandoned Property	Property that has been discarded by the true owner, who has no intention of reclaiming title to the property in the future. A finder of abandoned property can claim title to it against the whole world, including the original owner.

employee removes several of the stones. If Kayla brings an action to recover the stones from the jeweler, she normally will win, because she found lost property and holds title against everyone *except the true owner.* ■

Conversion of Lost Property   When a finder of lost property knows the true owner and fails to return the property to that person, the finder has committed the tort of *conversion* (the wrongful taking of another's property). **EXAMPLE 34.11** In *Example 34.10,* suppose Kayla knows that the gold bracelet she found belongs to Geneva. If Kayla does not return the bracelet, she can be held liable for conversion. ■ Many states require the finder to make a reasonably diligent search to locate the true owner of lost property. (The *Business Application* feature at the end of this chapter discusses the obligations that states often impose on finders of lost property.)

Estray Statute A statute defining finders' rights in property when the true owners are unknown.

Estray Statutes   Many states have **estray statutes,** which encourage and facilitate the return of property to its true owner and reward the finder for honesty if the property remains unclaimed. These laws provide an incentive for finders to report their discoveries by making it possible for them, after a specified period of time, to acquire legal title to the property they have found.

Generally, the item must be lost property, not merely mislaid property, for estray statutes to apply. Estray statutes usually require the finder or the county clerk to advertise the property in an attempt to help the owner recover it.

CASE EXAMPLE 34.12   Drug smugglers often enter the United States illegally from Canada via a frozen river that flows through Van Buren, Maine. When two railroad employees walking near the railroad tracks in Van Buren found a duffel bag that contained $165,580 in cash, they reported their find to U.S. Customs agents, who took custody of the bag and cash. A drug-sniffing dog gave a positive alert on the bag for the scent of drugs. The federal government filed a lawsuit claiming title to the property under criminal forfeiture laws (because the property was involved in illegal drug transactions).

The two employees argued that they were entitled to the $165,580 under Maine's estray statute. That statute required finders to (1) provide written notice to the town clerk within seven days after finding the property, (2) post a public notice in the town, and (3) advertise in the town's newspaper for one month. Because the employees had not fulfilled these requirements, the court ruled that they had not acquired title to the property. Thus, the federal government had a right to seize the cash.[4] ■

34–3c **Abandoned Property**

Abandoned Property Property that has been discarded by the owner, who has no intention of reclaiming it.

Property that has been *discarded* by the true owner, who has *no intention* of reclaiming title to it, is **abandoned property.** Someone who finds abandoned property acquires title to it that is good against the whole world, *including the original owner.* If a person finds abandoned property while trespassing on the property of another, however, the owner of the land, not the finder, will acquire title to the property.

An owner of lost property who eventually gives up any further attempt to find it is frequently held to have abandoned the property. **EXAMPLE 34.13** As Alekis is hiking in the redwoods, her expensive watch falls off. She retraces her route and searches for the watch but cannot find it. She finally gives up her search and returns home some five hundred miles away. When Frye later finds the watch, he acquires title to it that is good even against Alekis. By completely giving up her search, Alekis abandoned the watch just as effectively as if she had intentionally discarded it. ■

---

4. *United States v. One Hundred Sixty-Five Thousand Five Hundred Eighty Dollars ($165,580) in U.S. Currency,* 502 F.Supp.2d 114 (D.Me. 2007).

34-4 Bailments

Many routine personal and business transactions involve bailments. A **bailment** is formed by the delivery of personal property, without transfer of title, by one person, called a **bailor,** to another, called a **bailee.** Usually, a bailment is formed for a particular purpose—for instance, to loan, lease, store, repair, or transport the property. What distinguishes a bailment from a sale or a gift is that there is no passage of title and no intent to transfer title. On completion of the purpose, the bailee is obligated to return the bailed property in the same or better condition to the bailor or a third person or to dispose of it as directed.

Although bailments typically arise by agreement, not all of the elements of a contract must necessarily be present for a bailment to be created. **EXAMPLE 34.14** If Amy lends her bicycle to a friend, a bailment is created, but not by contract, because there is no consideration. Many commercial bailments, such as the delivery of clothing to the cleaners for dry cleaning, are based on contract, though. ∎

The law of bailments applies to many routine personal and business transactions. When a transaction involves a bailment, whether you realize it or not, you are subject to the obligations and duties that arise from the bailment relationship. Consequently, knowing how bailment relationships are created, and what rights, duties, and liabilities flow from ordinary bailments, is critical in avoiding legal disputes. Also important is understanding that bailees can limit the dollar amount of their liability by contract.

Bailment A situation in which the personal property of one person (a bailor) is entrusted to another (a bailee), who is obligated to return the bailed property to the bailor or dispose of it as directed.

Bailor One who entrusts goods to a bailee.

Bailee One to whom goods are entrusted by a bailor.

PREVENTING LEGAL DISPUTES

34-4a Elements of a Bailment

Not all transactions involving the delivery of property from one person to another create a bailment. For such a transfer to become a bailment, the following three elements must be present:

1. Personal property.
2. Delivery of possession without title.
3. Agreement that the property will be returned to the bailor or otherwise disposed of according to its owner's directions.

LEARNING OBJECTIVE 3

What are the three elements of a bailment?

Personal Property Requirement Only personal property, not real property or persons, can be the subject of a bailment. **EXAMPLE 34.15** When you check your bags at the airport, a bailment of your luggage is created because the luggage is personal property. When you board the plane as a passenger, no bailment is created. ∎ Although bailments commonly involve *tangible* items—jewelry, cattle, automobiles, and the like—*intangible* personal property, such as promissory notes and shares of stock, may also be bailed.

Delivery of Possession *Delivery of possession* means the transfer of possession of the property to the bailee. For delivery to occur, the bailee must be given exclusive possession and control over the property, and the bailee must *knowingly* accept the personal property.[5] In other words, the bailee must *intend* to exercise control over it.

If either delivery of possession or knowing acceptance is lacking, there is no bailment relationship. **EXAMPLE 34.16** Sophia goes to a five-star restaurant and checks her coat at the door. She forgets that there is a $20,000 diamond necklace in the coat pocket. In accepting the coat, the bailee does not *knowingly* also accept the necklace. Thus, a bailment of the coat

A friend loaned this bike as a favor. Has a bailment been created?

---

5. The requirements outlined in this sentence apply to *voluntary bailments,* not to *involuntary bailments,* discussed shortly.

exists—because the restaurant has exclusive possession and control over the coat and has knowingly accepted it—but not a bailment of the necklace. ■

Physical versus Constructive Delivery. Either *physical* or *constructive* delivery will result in the bailee's exclusive possession of and control over the property. As discussed earlier, in the context of gifts, constructive delivery is a substitute, or symbolic, delivery. What is delivered to the bailee is not the actual property bailed (such as a car) but something so related to the property (such as the car keys) that the requirement of delivery is satisfied.

Involuntary Bailments. In certain situations, a bailment is found despite the apparent lack of the requisite elements of control and knowledge. One instance occurs when the bailee acquires the property accidentally or by mistake—as in finding someone else's lost or mislaid property. A bailment is created even though the bailor did not voluntarily deliver the property to the bailee. Such bailments are called *constructive* or *involuntary* bailments.

EXAMPLE 34.17 Several corporate managers attend a meeting at the law office of Jacobs & Matheson. One of the corporate officers, Kyle Gustafson, inadvertently leaves his briefcase at the office at the conclusion of the meeting. In this situation, a court may find that an involuntary bailment has been created, even though Gustafson has not voluntarily delivered the briefcase and the law firm has not intentionally accepted it. If an involuntary bailment exists, the firm is responsible for taking care of the briefcase and returning it to Gustafson. ■

Bailment Agreement

A bailment agreement can be express or implied. Although a written contract is not required for bailments of less than one year (that is, the Statute of Frauds does not apply), it is a good idea to have one, especially when valuable property is involved.

The bailment agreement expressly or impliedly provides for the return of the bailed property to the bailor or to a third person, or for the disposal of the property by the bailee. It is assumed that the bailee will return the identical goods originally given by the bailor. In certain types of bailments, such as bailments of fungible goods, however, the property returned need only be equivalent property.

EXAMPLE 34.18 A bailment is created when Holman stores his grain (fungible goods) in Joe's Warehouse. At the end of the storage period, however, the warehouse is not obligated to return to Holman exactly the same grain that he stored. As long as the warehouse returns grain of the same *type, grade,* and *quantity,* the warehouse—the bailee—has performed its obligation. ■

34-4b Ordinary Bailments

Bailments are either *ordinary* or *special (extraordinary)*. There are three types of ordinary bailments. They are distinguished according to *which party receives a benefit from the bailment.* This factor will dictate the rights and liabilities of the parties, and the courts use it to determine the standard of care required of the bailee in possession of the personal property.

The three types of ordinary bailments are as follows:

1. *Bailment for the sole benefit of the bailor.* This is a gratuitous bailment (a bailment that involves no consideration) for the convenience and benefit of the bailor. Basically, the bailee is caring for the bailor's property as a favor. Therefore, the bailee owes only a slight duty of care and will be liable only if she or he is grossly negligent in caring for the property.

   EXAMPLE 34.19 Allen asks his friend Sumi to store his car in her garage while he is away. If Sumi agrees to do so, a gratuitous bailment will be created, because the bailment will be for the sole benefit of the bailor (Allen). If the car is damaged while in Sumi's garage, Sumi will not be responsible for the damage unless it is caused by her gross negligence. ■

2. *Bailment for the sole benefit of the bailee.* This type of bailment typically occurs when one person lends an item to another person (the bailee) solely for the bailee's convenience and benefit. Because the bailee is borrowing the item for her or his own benefit, the bailee owes a duty to exercise the utmost care and will be liable for even slight negligence.

EXAMPLE 34.20 Allen asks to borrow Sumi's boat so that he can go sailing over the weekend. The bailment of the boat is for Allen's (the bailee's) sole benefit. If Allen fails to pay attention and runs the boat aground, damaging its hull, he is liable for the costs of repairing the boat. ◼

3. *Bailment for the mutual benefit of the bailee and the bailor.* This is the most common kind of bailment and involves some form of compensation for storing property or holding property while it is being serviced. It is a contractual bailment and may be referred to as a *bailment for hire* or a *commercial bailment.* In this type of bailment, the bailee owes a duty to exercise a reasonable degree of care.

EXAMPLE 34.21 Allen leaves his car at Quick Lube for an oil change. Because Quick Lube will be paid to change Allen's oil, this is a mutual-benefit bailment. If Quick Lube fails to put the correct amount of oil back into Allen's car and the engine is damaged as a result, Quick Lube will be liable for failure to exercise reasonable care. ◼

What type of bailment is created if this house owner agrees to store a friend's car?

Rights of the Bailee Certain rights are implicit in the bailment agreement. Generally, the bailee has the right to take possession of the property, to utilize the property for accomplishing the purpose of the bailment, to receive some form of compensation, and to limit her or his liability for the bailed goods. These rights of the bailee are present (with some limitations) in varying degrees in all bailment transactions.

Right of Possession. A hallmark of the bailment agreement is that the bailee acquires the *right to control and possess the property temporarily.* The bailee's right of possession permits the bailee to recover damages from any third person for damage or loss of the property. **EXAMPLE 34.22** No-Spot Dry Cleaners sends all suede leather garments to Cleanall Company for special processing. If Cleanall loses or damages any leather goods, No-Spot has the right to recover against Cleanall. ◼ In addition, if the bailed property is stolen, the bailee has a legal right to regain possession of it.

Right to Use Bailed Property. Depending on the type of bailment and the terms of the bailment agreement, a bailee may also have a right to use the bailed property. When no provision is made, the extent of use depends on how necessary it is for the goods to be at the bailee's disposal for the ordinary purpose of the bailment to be carried out.

EXAMPLE 34.23 If Lauren borrows a car to drive Devin to the airport, she, as the bailee, will obviously be expected to use the car. In contrast, if Devin drives his own car to the airport and places it in long-term storage nearby, the storage company, as the bailee, will not be expected to use the car. The ordinary purpose of a storage bailment does not include use of the property. The bailee will, however, be expected to use or move the car if necessary in an emergency (such as a hurricane or flood) to protect it from harm. ◼

Right of Compensation. Except in a gratuitous bailment, a bailee has a right to be compensated as provided for in the bailment agreement. The bailee also has a right to be reimbursed for costs incurred and services rendered in the keeping of the bailed property (even in a gratuitous bailment).

To enforce the right of compensation, the bailee has a right to place a *possessory lien* on the bailed property until he or she has been fully compensated. A lien on bailed property is

Bailee's Lien A possessory (artisan's) lien that a bailee entitled to compensation can place on the bailed property to ensure that he or she will be paid for the services provided.

referred to as a **bailee's lien,** or an *artisan's lien.* If the bailor refuses to pay or cannot pay the charges (compensation), in most states the bailee is entitled to foreclose on the lien and sell the property to recover the amount owed.

EXAMPLE 34.24 Liam leaves his car at Jack's Automotive for repairs. Jack's informs Liam that the car needs a new transmission, and Liam authorizes Jack's to perform the work. When Liam returns to pick up the car, he refuses to pay the amount due for the transmission work. Jack's has a right to keep the car and place a lien on it until Liam pays for the repairs. If Liam continues to refuse payment, Jack's can follow the state statutory process for foreclosing on the lien and selling the car to recover what is owed. ■

Right to Limit Liability. In ordinary bailments, bailees have the right to limit their liability, provided that both of the following are true:

1. *The limitations are called to the attention of the bailor.* It is essential that the bailor be informed of the limitation in some way. **EXAMPLE 34.25** A sign in Nikolai's garage states that Nikolai will not be responsible "for loss due to theft, fire, or vandalism." Whether the sign will constitute notice will depend on the size of the sign, its location, and any other circumstances affecting the likelihood that customers will see it. ■

2. *The limitations are not against public policy.* Even when the bailor knows of the limitation, courts consider certain types of disclaimers of liability to be against public policy and therefore illegal. The courts carefully scrutinize *exculpatory clauses,* which limit a party's liability for the party's own wrongful acts. In bailments, especially mutual-benefit bailments, exculpatory clauses are often held to be illegal. **EXAMPLE 34.26** A receipt from a parking garage expressly disclaims liability for any damage to parked cars, regardless of the cause. Because the bailee (the garage) has attempted to exclude liability for the bailee's own negligence, the clause will likely be deemed unenforceable because it is against public policy. ■

LEARNING OBJECTIVE 4
What are the basic duties of a bailee?

Duties of the Bailee

The bailee's duties are based on a mixture of tort law and contract law and include two basic responsibilities:

1. To take appropriate care of the property.

2. To surrender the property to the bailor or dispose of it in accordance with the bailor's instructions at the end of the bailment.

The Duty of Care. The bailee must exercise reasonable care in preserving the bailed property. What constitutes reasonable care in a bailment situation normally depends on the nature and specific circumstances of the bailment.

The courts determine the appropriate standard of care on the basis of the type of bailment involved. As mentioned earlier, in a bailment for the sole benefit of the bailor, the bailee need exercise only a slight degree of care. In a mutual-benefit bailment, courts normally impose a reasonable standard of care. In a bailment for the sole benefit of the bailee, the bailee must exercise great care. Exhibit 34–2 illustrates these concepts.

Exhibit 34–2 Degree of Care Required of a Bailee

Bailment for the Sole Benefit of the Bailor	Mutual-Benefit Bailment	Bailment for the Sole Benefit of the Bailee
DEGREE OF CARE		
SLIGHT	REASONABLE	GREAT

Determining whether a bailee exercised an appropriate degree of care is usually a question of fact for the jury or (in a nonjury trial) the judge. A bailee's failure to exercise appropriate care in handling the bailor's property results in tort liability.

In the following case, a bailee lost computer data while he was replacing a hard drive. The court had to decide whether the bailee was negligent.

CASE 34.3

Bridge Tower Dental, P.A. v. Meridian Computer Center, Inc.

Supreme Court of Idaho, 152 Idaho 569, 272 P.3d 541 (2012).

FACTS Bridge Tower Dental, P.A., contracted with Meridian Computer Center, Inc., to develop a computer system for its dental practice. Bridge Tower then paid a computer consultant, Al Colson, to install the system and provide maintenance and support. In 2004, Colson noticed that one of the server's two hard drives had stopped working and that the system was backing up data only on the mirrored hard drive. After telling Bridge Tower about the problem, Colson took the server to Meridian Computer to be repaired. The owner of Meridian Computer, Jason Patten, agreed to replace the failing hard drive under the warranty.

In attempting to copy data from the mirrored hard drive, Patten accidentally erased all the data. Following the industry standard, Patten had not backed up the mirrored drive because he had not been asked to do so. As a result, Bridge Tower lost all of its patients' records and contact information. Bridge Tower sued Meridian Computer for negligence, and the jury found for Meridian Computer. Bridge Tower appealed.

ISSUE Did Meridian Computer breach its duty of care?

DECISION Yes. The Idaho Supreme Court reversed the judgment for Meridian Computer and held that Bridge Tower was entitled to recover.

What duty of care is required from a bailee that repairs computer hard drives?

iStockPhoto.com/Lorado

REASON The parties agreed that a bailment existed because Colson acted as Bridge Tower's agent when he entrusted the server to Meridian Computer. The court found that the bailment included both the machine and its contents, including the data that Meridian Computer lost. The court presumed that Meridian Computer was negligent because it damaged the property by erasing all the data on the mirrored hard drive. That presumption was especially appropriate here because Patten admitted that he erased the data by mistake. Meridian Computer argued that it had complied with the industry standard in not backing up the data. The court, however, found that, regardless of the industry standard, Meridian Computer owed "a duty to protect and safeguard bailed property in order to return it in the same condition as it was delivered." Because Meridian Computer could not overcome the presumption of negligence, Bridge Tower was entitled to judgment as a matter of law.

CRITICAL THINKING—Legal Consideration *Based on the facts presented here, what kind of bailment existed? Explain your answer.*

Duty to Return Bailed Property. At the end of the bailment, the bailee normally must hand over the original property to the bailor or to someone the bailor designates, or must otherwise dispose of it as directed. Failure to give up possession at the time the bailment ends is a breach of contract and could result in the tort of conversion or an action based on bailee negligence.

A bailee may be liable for conversion if the goods being held are delivered to the wrong person. Hence, the bailee should verify that the person (other than the bailor) to whom the goods are given is authorized to take possession.

Lost or Damaged Property. If the bailed property has been lost or is returned damaged, a court will presume that the bailee was negligent. The bailee's obligation is excused, however, if the property was destroyed, lost, or stolen through no fault of the bailee (or claimed by a third party with a superior claim). In other words, the bailee can rebut the presumption of negligence by showing that he or she exercised due care.

CASE EXAMPLE 34.27 Michael LaPlace boarded a horse at Pierre Briere's stable, where Charlene Bridgwood also boarded a horse. LaPlace had previously boarded horses at the farm owned by Bridgwood's husband, and Bridgwood had often exercised LaPlace's horses there. One day, Bridgwood helped exercise the horses at Briere's stable. During the exercise, LaPlace's horse suddenly collapsed and died.

LaPlace sued Briere for negligence. The court found that there was a presumption of negligence because the horse died in Briere's care during its bailment. Briere successfully rebutted that presumption, however, by showing that Bridgwood was an experienced handler and exercised the horse in an ordinary manner. Thus, Briere was not liable for the horse's death.[6] ■

Duties of the Bailor

The duties of a bailor are essentially the same as the rights of a bailee. A bailor has a duty to compensate the bailee as agreed and to reimburse the bailee for costs incurred by the bailee in keeping the bailed property. A bailor also has an all-encompassing duty to provide the bailee with goods or chattels that are free from known defects that could cause injury to the bailee.

Is a stable owner liable for negligence any time that a horse dies in its care?

iStockPhoto.com/Somogyvari

Bailor's Duty to Reveal Defects. The bailor's duty to reveal defects to the bailee translates into two rules:

1. In a mutual-benefit bailment, the bailor must notify the bailee of all known defects and any hidden defects that the bailor knows of or could have discovered with reasonable diligence and proper inspection.

2. In a bailment for the sole benefit of the bailee, the bailor must notify the bailee of any known defects.

The bailor's duty to reveal defects is based on a negligence theory of tort law. A bailor who fails to give the appropriate notice is liable to the bailee and to any other person who might reasonably be expected to come into contact with the defective article.

EXAMPLE 34.28 Rentco (the bailor) rents a tractor to Hal Iverson. Unknown to Rentco, the brake mechanism on the tractor is defective at the time the bailment is made. Rentco could have discovered the defect on reasonable inspection. Iverson uses the defective tractor without knowledge of the brake problem and is injured, along with two other field workers, when the tractor rolls downhill out of control after failing to stop. In this situation, Rentco is liable for the injuries sustained by Iverson and the other workers because it negligently failed to discover the defect and notify Iverson. ■

Warranty Liability for Defective Goods. A bailor can also incur *warranty liability* (discussed in an earlier chapter) based on contract law for injuries resulting from the bailment of defective articles. Property that is leased from a bailor must be *fit for the intended purpose of the bailment*. Warranties of fitness arise by law in sales contracts and leases, and courts have held that these warranties apply to bailments "for hire." Article 2A of the Uniform Commercial Code (UCC) extends the implied warranties of merchantability and fitness for a particular purpose to bailments that include rights to use the bailed goods.[7]

34–4c Special Types of Bailments

A business is likely to engage in some special types of bailment transactions in which the bailee's duty of care is *extraordinary* and the bailee's liability for loss or damage to the property is absolute. These situations usually involve common carriers and hotel operators. Warehouse companies have a higher duty of care than ordinary bailees, but are not subject to strict

---

6. *LaPlace v. Briere*, 404 N.J.Super. 585, 962 A.2d 1139 (2009).
7. UCC 2A–212, 2A–213.

liability. Like carriers, warehouse companies are subject to extensive regulation under federal and state laws, including Article 7 of the UCC.

Common Carriers

Common carriers are publicly licensed to transport goods or passengers on regular routes at set rates. They are legally bound to carry all passengers or freight as long as there is enough space, the fee is paid, and there are no reasonable grounds to refuse service.

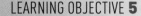

LEARNING OBJECTIVE 5
What standard of care applies to common carriers?

Common carriers differ from private carriers, which operate transportation facilities for only a select clientele. A private carrier is not required to provide service to every person or company making a request.

Strict Liability Applies. The delivery of goods to a common carrier creates a bailment relationship between the shipper (bailor) and the common carrier (bailee). Unlike ordinary bailees, the common carrier is held to a standard of care based on *strict liability,* rather than reasonable care, in protecting the bailed personal property. This means that the common carrier is absolutely liable, regardless of due care, for all loss or damage to goods except when damage was caused by a natural disaster or war.

Limitations on Liability. Common carriers cannot contract away their liability for damaged goods. Subject to government regulations, however, they are permitted to limit their dollar liability to an amount stated on the shipment contract or rate filing.

CASE EXAMPLE 34.29 A jewelry store (Treiber & Straub, Inc.) used UPS to ship a diamond ring worth $105,000. The owner of the jewelry store arranged for the shipment on UPS's Web site, which required him to click on two on-screen boxes to agree to "My UPS Terms and Conditions." In these terms, UPS and its insurer limited their liability and the amount of insurance coverage on packages to $50,000 and refused to ship items worth more than $50,000. Both UPS and its insurer disclaimed liability *entirely* for such items. Nevertheless, the store owner purchased $50,000 in insurance for the package.

When the ring was lost, the jewelry store filed suit against UPS to recover $50,000 under the insurance policy. The court held that UPS's disclaimer of liability was enforceable. It also found that the jewelry store had breached the contract by indicating that the shipment was worth less than $50,000 when the ring was worth much more.[8] ■

Warehouse Companies

Warehousing is the business of storing property for compensation.[9] Like ordinary bailees, warehouse companies are liable for loss or damage to property resulting from negligence. But because a warehouse company is a professional bailee, it is expected to exercise a high degree of care to protect and preserve the goods.

Limitations on Liability. A warehouse company can limit the dollar amount of its liability. Under the UCC, however, it must give the bailor the option of paying a higher storage rate for an increase in the liability limit.[10]

Warehouse Receipts. Warehouse companies often issue *documents of title*—in particular, *warehouse receipts*.[11] A warehouse receipt describes the bailed property and the terms of the bailment contract. It can be negotiable or nonnegotiable, depending on how it is written. It is negotiable if its terms provide

iStockPhoto.com/manley099

If a jewelry storeowner ships this $200,000 diamond ring knowing that the shipper's maximum shipment value is only $50,000, what happens if the ring never arrives at its destination?

---

8. *Treiber & Straub, Inc. v. United Parcel Service, Inc.,* 474 F.3d 379 (7th Cir. 2007).

9. UCC 7–102(h) refers to the person engaged in the storing of goods for hire as a "warehouseman."

10. UCC 7–204(1), (2).

11. A *document of title* is defined in UCC 1–201(15) as any "document which in the regular course of business or financing is treated as adequately evidencing that the person in possession of it is entitled to receive, hold, and dispose of the document and the goods it covers." A *warehouse receipt* is a document of title issued by a person engaged for hire in the business of storing goods for hire.

that the warehouse company will deliver the goods "to the bearer" of the receipt or "to the order of" a person named on the receipt.[12]

The warehouse receipt represents the goods (that is, it indicates title) and hence has value and utility in financing commercial transactions. **EXAMPLE 34.30** Ossip delivers 6,500 cases of canned corn to Chaney, the owner of a warehouse. Chaney issues a negotiable warehouse receipt payable "to bearer" and gives it to Ossip. Ossip sells and delivers the warehouse receipt to Better Foods, Inc. Better Foods is now the owner of the corn and has the right to obtain the cases by simply presenting the warehouse receipt to Chaney. ■

Hotel Operators At common law, hotel owners were strictly liable for the loss of any cash or property that guests brought into their rooms. Today, state statutes continue to apply strict liability to hotel operators for any loss or damage to their guests' personal property. In many states, however, hotel operators can avoid strict liability by providing a safe in which to keep guests' valuables and notifying guests that a safe is available.

In addition, state statutes often limit the liability of hotels with regard to articles that are not kept in the safe and may limit the availability of damages in the absence of negligence. Most statutes require that the hotel post these limitations on the doors of the rooms or otherwise notify guests. The failure of the hotel to follow the state statutory requirements can lead to liability.

EXAMPLE 34.31 A guest at Crown Place hotel is traveling with jewelry valued at $1 million. She puts the jewelry in the safe in her room, but someone comes into the room and removes the jewelry from the safe without the use of force. The woman sues the hotel, which claims that it is not liable under the state statute. If Crown Place did not comply with statutory requirements that it post the legal limitations in the guest rooms, however, it will not be protected from liability. Crown Place will be strictly liable for the loss of the woman's jewelry. ■

---

12. UCC 7–104.

Reviewing . . . Personal Property and Bailments

Vanessa Denai owned forty acres of land in rural Louisiana. On the property were a 1,600-square-foot house and a metal barn. Denai met Lance Finney, who had been seeking a small plot of rural property to rent. After several meetings, Denai invited Finney to live on a corner of her land in exchange for Finney's assistance in cutting wood and tending her property. Denai agreed to store Finney's sailboat in her barn.

With Denai's consent, Finney constructed a concrete and oak foundation on Denai's property and purchased a 190-square-foot dome from Dome Baja for $3,395. The dome was shipped by Doty Express, a transportation company licensed to serve the public. When it arrived, Finney installed the dome frame and fabric exterior so that the dome was detachable from the foundation. A year after Finney installed the dome, Denai wrote Finney a note stating, "I've decided to give you four acres of land surrounding your dome as drawn on this map." This gift violated no local land-use restrictions. Using the information presented in the chapter, answer the following questions.

1. Is the dome real property or personal property? Explain.

2. Is Denai's gift of land to Finney a gift *causa mortis* or a gift *inter vivos?*

3. What type of bailment relationship was created when Denai agreed to store Finney's boat? What degree of care was Denai required to exercise in storing the boat?

4. What standard of care applied to the shipment of the dome by Doty Express?

DEBATE THIS

■ Common carriers should not be able to limit their liability.

What Should You Do with Lost Property?*

If you are walking down a street in New York City and come across a valuable diamond ring lying in the gutter, what should you do? You might be tempted to keep the ring or sell it and enjoy the proceeds, but that would be unethical. It would also be illegal under New York law—and under the laws of many other states as well.

An Example—New York Laws

New York law defines *lost property* to include lost property, mislaid property, and abandoned property, whether it is cash, goods, or some other type of tangible personal property. Generally, the finder of property worth $20 or more must either return it to the rightful owner or report the find to the police

_____

* This *Business Application* is not meant to substitute for the services of an attorney who is licensed to practice law in your state.

and deposit the property at a police station within ten days. Failure to do so is a misdemeanor, subject to a fine and imprisonment for not more than six months. When the finder delivers the property to the authorities, he or she is given a receipt, and the statutory waiting period begins (ranging from three months for property valued at less than $100 to three years for property valued at more than $5,000). The police then attempt to find the rightful owner.

Other States' Lost-Property Laws

Many other states have also enacted lost-property statutes. The statutes differ greatly from state to state, but typically they eliminate the distinctions among lost, mislaid, and abandoned property, as the New York statute does. Many statutes also require the finder to deposit found property with local authorities, although the penalty imposed for failure to do so may not be as severe as under New York's statute. Lost-property statutes also typically require the police to attempt to find the true owner through such measures as calling the owner of the premises where the

property was found. Sometimes, the finder must advertise the property and its discovery through the county court.

Generally, if the true owner cannot be located within a certain period of time, which varies depending on the value of the property and whether the property is perishable, the finder gets the property. In some states, however, the property may be sold and the proceeds disposed of as specified by statute. In California, for instance, the proceeds from such a sale go into a state fund (if the state police had custody of the lost property) or become the property of the city, county, town, or village (if other police had custody).

CHECKLIST for the Finder of Lost Property:

1. To maximize your chances of legally keeping lost property, take the found property to the nearest police station.

2. Make sure you follow the statutory requirements of the jurisdiction, which may require you to advertise the found property.

Key Terms

abandoned property 864
accession 862
bailee 865
bailee's lien 868
bailment 865
bailor 865

chattel 857
confusion 862
constructive delivery 860
dominion 861
estray statute 864
gift 859

gift *causa mortis* 862
gift *inter vivos* 862
lost property 863
mislaid property 863
personal property 857
real property 856

Chapter Summary: Personal Property and Bailments

PERSONAL PROPERTY	
Personal Property versus Real Property	Personal property (personalty or chattel) includes all property not classified as real property (realty). Personal property can be tangible (such as a car) or intangible (such as stocks or bonds). The two types of property are usually subject to different types of taxes. In addition, acquiring or transferring real property requires a greater degree of formality than acquiring or transferring personal property.

Continues

Acquiring Ownership of Personal Property	The most common way of acquiring ownership in personal property is by purchasing it. The following are additional methods of acquiring personal property:
	1. *Possession*—Property may be acquired by possession if no other person has title to the property (for example, capturing wild animals).
	2. *Production*—Any item produced by an individual (with minor exceptions) becomes the property of that individual.
	3. *Gifts*—A gift is effective under the following conditions:
	  a. There is evidence of *intent* to make a gift of the property in question.
	  b. The gift is *delivered* (physically or constructively) to the donee or the donee's agent.
	  c. The gift is *accepted* by the donee.
	4. *Accession*—When value is added to personal property by the use of labor or materials, the owner of the original property generally retains title to the property and benefits from the added value.
	5. *Confusion*—If confusion of fungible goods occurs as a result of agreement, an honest mistake, or the act of some third party, the owners share ownership as tenants in common. If goods are confused due to an intentional wrongful act, the innocent party ordinarily acquires title to the whole.

Mislaid, Lost, and Abandoned Property	The finder of property acquires different rights depending on whether the property was mislaid, lost, or abandoned. 1. *Mislaid property*—Property that is placed somewhere voluntarily by the owner and then inadvertently forgotten. The finder does not acquire title. 2. *Lost property*—Property that is involuntarily left by the owner. The finder can claim title to the property against the whole world except the true owner. 3. *Abandoned property*—Property that is discarded by the owner, who has no intention of reclaiming it in the future. The finder can claim title to the property against the whole world, including the original owner.

BAILMENTS

Elements of a Bailment	1. *Personal property*—Bailments involve only personal property. 2. *Delivery of possession*—For an effective bailment to exist, the bailee (the one receiving the property) must be given exclusive possession and control over the property. In a voluntary bailment, the bailee must knowingly accept the personal property. 3. *The bailment agreement*—Expressly or impliedly provides for the return of the bailed property to the bailor or a third party, or for the disposal of the bailed property by the bailee.

Ordinary Bailments	1. *Types of bailments*—
	  a. Bailment for the sole benefit of the bailor—A gratuitous bailment undertaken for the sole benefit of the bailor (for example, as a favor to the bailor).
	  b. Bailment for the sole benefit of the bailee—A gratuitous loan of an article to a person (the bailee) solely for the bailee's benefit.
	  c. Mutual-benefit (contractual) bailment—The most common kind of bailment. It involves compensation between the bailee and bailor for the service provided.
	2. *Rights of a bailee (duties of a bailor)*—
	  a. The right of possession—Allows a bailee to sue any third persons who damage, lose, or convert the bailed property.
	  b. The right to use the property to the extent it is necessary to carry out the purpose of the bailment.
	  c. The right to be compensated and reimbursed for expenses—In the event of nonpayment, the bailee has the right to place a possessory (bailee's) lien on the bailed property.
	  d. The right to limit liability—An ordinary bailee can limit his or her liability for loss or damage, provided proper notice is given and the limitation is not against public policy. In special bailments, limitations on liability for negligence or on types of losses usually are not allowed, but limitations on the monetary amount of liability are permitted.
	3. *Duties of a bailee (rights of a bailor)*—
	  a. A bailee must exercise appropriate care over property entrusted to her or him. What constitutes appropriate care normally depends on the nature and circumstances of the bailment. See Exhibit 34–2.
	  b. Bailed goods in a bailee's possession must be either returned to the bailor or disposed of according to the bailor's directions. A bailee's failure to return the bailed property creates a presumption of negligence and constitutes a breach of contract or the tort of conversion.

Special Types of Bailments	1. *Common carriers*—Carriers that are publicly licensed to provide transportation services to the general public. A common carrier is held to a standard of care based on strict liability. 2. *Warehouse companies*—Because a warehouse company is a professional bailee, it is expected to exercise a high degree of care to protect and preserve the bailed goods. Warehouse companies often issue documents of title (warehouse receipts) for goods, which may be negotiable. 3. *Hotel operators*—Operators of hotels are subject to strict liability for any loss or damage to their guests' personal property. State statutes may limit liability if the hotel provides a safe and properly notifies its guests.

Issue Spotters

1. While walking to work, Bill finds an expensive ring lying on the curb. Bill gives the ring to his son, Hunter. Two weeks later, Martin Avery, the true owner of the ring, discovers that Bill had found the ring and demands that Hunter return it. Who is entitled to the ring, and why? (See *Mislaid, Lost, and Abandoned Property*.)

2. Rosa de la Mar Corporation ships a load of goods via Southeast Delivery Company. The load of goods is lost in a hurricane in Florida. Who suffers the loss? Explain your answer. (See *Bailments*.)

—**Check your answers to the *Issue Spotters* against the answers provided in Appendix D at the end of this text.**

Learning Objectives Check

1. What is real property? What is personal property?
2. What are the three necessary elements for an effective gift?
3. What are the three elements of a bailment?
4. What are the basic duties of a bailee?
5. What standard of care applies to common carriers?

—**Answers to the even-numbered *Learning Objectives Check* questions can be found in Appendix E at the end of this text.**

Business Scenarios and Case Problems

34–1. Duties of the Bailee. Discuss the standard of care traditionally required of the bailee for the bailed property in each of the following situations, and determine whether the bailee breached that duty. (See *Bailments*.)

1. Ricardo borrows Steve's lawn mower because his own lawn mower needs repair. Ricardo mows his front yard. To mow the backyard, he needs to move some hoses and lawn furniture. He leaves the mower in front of his house while doing so. When he returns to the front yard, he discovers that the mower has been stolen.

2. Alicia owns a valuable speedboat. She is going on vacation and asks her neighbor, Maureen, to store the boat in one stall of Maureen's double garage. Maureen consents, and the boat is moved into the garage. Maureen needs some grocery items for dinner and drives to the store. She leaves the garage door open while she is gone, as is her custom, and the speedboat is stolen during that time.

34–2. Gifts. Jaspal has a severe heart attack and is taken to the hospital. He is aware that he is not expected to live. Because he is a bachelor with no close relatives nearby, Jaspal gives his car keys to his close friend Friedrich, telling Friedrich that he is expected to die and that the car is Friedrich's. Jaspal survives the heart attack, but two months later he dies from pneumonia. Sam, Jaspal's uncle and the executor of his estate, wants Friedrich to return the car. Friedrich refuses, claiming that the car was a gift from Jaspal. Discuss whether Friedrich will be required to return the car to Jaspal's estate. (See *Acquiring Ownership of Personal Property*.)

34–3. Bailments. Curtis is an executive on a business trip to the West Coast. He has driven his car on this trip and checks into the Hotel Ritz. The hotel has a guarded underground parking lot. Curtis gives his car keys to the parking lot attendant but fails to notify the attendant that his wife's $10,000 fur coat is in a box in the trunk. The next day, on checking out, he discovers that his car has been stolen. Curtis wants to hold the hotel liable for both the car and the coat. Discuss the probable success of his claim. (See *Bailments*.)

34–4. Duties of the Bailee. Orlando borrows a rototiller from his neighbor, Max. Max has not used the rototiller for two years. Orlando has never owned a rototiller and is not familiar with using one. Max previously used this rototiller often, and if he had made a reasonable inspection, he would have discovered that a blade was loose. Orlando is injured when the blade becomes detached while he is rototilling his garden. (See *Bailments*.)

1. Can Orlando hold Max liable for his injuries? Why or why not?

2. Would your answer be different if Orlando had rented the rototiller from Max and paid a fee? Explain.

34–5. Gifts. John Wasniewski opened a brokerage account with Quick and Reilly, Inc., in his son James's name. Twelve years later, when the balance was $52,085, the account was closed, and the funds were transferred to a joint account in the names of John and James's brother. James did not learn of the existence of the account in his name until the transfer, when he received a tax form for the account's final year. He filed a suit in a Connecticut state court against Quick and Reilly, alleging breach of contract and seeking to recover the account's principal and interest. What are the elements of a valid gift? Did John's opening of the account with Quick and Reilly constitute a gift to James? What is the likely result in this case, and why? [*Wasniewski v. Quick and Reilly, Inc.,* 292 Conn. 98, 971 A.2d 8 (Conn. 2009)] (See *Acquiring Ownership of Personal Property.*)

34–6. Business Case Problem with Sample Answer—Bailment Obligation. Bob Moreland left his plane at Don Gray's aircraft repair shop to be painted. When Moreland picked up the airplane, he was disappointed in the quality of the work and pointed out numerous defects. Moreland refused to pay Gray and flew the plane to another shop to have the work redone. Gray sued to collect, contending that Moreland had no right to take the plane to another shop without giving Gray a chance to fix any defects. Gray further argued that by taking the plane, Moreland had accepted Gray's work. Moreland counterclaimed for his expenses. Which party should be awarded damages, and why? [*Gray v. Moreland,* 2010 Ark. App. 207 (2010)] (See *Bailments.*)

— **For a sample answer to Problem 34–6, go to Appendix F at the end of this text.**

34–7. Gifts. Jennifer Koerner adopted a dog—called the Stig—from the Anti-Cruelty Society in Chicago, Illinois, for $95. Koerner wrote a poem and presented it to Kent Nielsen, her live-in boyfriend. In the poem, she expressed her intent to give the Stig to him as a gift. While Koerner and Nielsen lived together, they were both involved in the Stig's day-to-day care. They ended their relationship a year later, and Nielsen agreed to leave their shared residence. Can Nielsen take the Stig with him, or is Koerner the Stig's rightful owner? Explain. [*Koerner v. Nielsen,* 8 N.E.3d 161 (Ill.App. 1 Dist. 2014)] (See *Acquiring Ownership of Personal Property.*)

34–8. Lost Property. Sara Simon misplaced her Galaxy cell phone in Manhattan, Kansas. Days later, Shawn Vargo contacted her, claiming to have bought the phone from someone else. He promised to mail it to Simon if she would wire $100 to him through a third party, Mark Lawrence. When Simon spoke to Lawrence about the wire transfer, she referred to the phone as hers and asked, "Are you going to send my phone to me?" Simon

paid, but she did not get the phone. Instead, Lawrence took it to a Best Buy store and traded it in for credit. Charged with the theft of lost property, Lawrence claimed that he did not know Simon was the owner of the phone. Was Simon's phone lost, mislaid, or abandoned? What is the finder's responsibility with respect to this type of property? Can Lawrence successfully argue that he did not know the phone was Simon's? Explain. [*State of Kansas v. Lawrence,* 347 P.3d 240 (Kan.App. 2015)] (See *Mislaid, Lost, and Abandoned Property.*)

34–9. A Question of Ethics—Gifts. Marcella Lashmett was engaged in farming in Illinois. She had two daughters, Christine Montgomery and Cheryl Thomas. Christine was also a farmer. She often borrowed Marcella's farm equipment. More than once, Christine used the equipment as a trade-in on the purchase of new equipment titled in Christine's name alone. After each transaction, Christine paid Marcella an agreed-to amount, and Marcella filed a gift tax return. Marcella died on December 19, 1999. Her heirs included Christine and Cheryl. Marcella's will gave whatever farm equipment remained on her death to Christine. If Christine chose to sell or trade any of the items, however, the proceeds were to be split equally with Cheryl. The will named Christine to handle the disposition of the estate, but she did nothing. Eventually, Cheryl filed a petition with an Illinois state court, which appointed her to administer the will. Cheryl then filed a suit against her sister to discover what assets their mother had owned. [*In re Estate of Lashmett,* 369 Ill.App.3d 1013, 874 N.E.2d 65 (4 Dist. 2007)] (See *Acquiring Ownership of Personal Property.*)

1. Cheryl learned that three months before Marcella's death, Christine had used Marcella's tractor as a trade-in on the purchase of a new tractor. The trade-in credit had been $55,296.28. Marcella had been paid nothing, and no gift tax return had been filed. Christine claimed, among other things, that the old tractor had been a gift. What is a "gift"? What are the elements of a gift? What do the facts suggest on this claim? Discuss.

2. Christine also claimed that she had tried to pay Marcella $20,000 on the trade-in of the tractor but that her mother had refused to accept it. Christine showed a check made out to Marcella for that amount and marked "void." Would you rule in Christine's favor on this claim? Why or why not?

Critical Thinking and Writing Assignments

34–10. Business Law Critical Thinking Group Assignment. On learning that Sébastien planned to travel abroad, Roslyn asked him to deliver $25,000 in cash to her family in Mexico. During a customs inspection at the border, Sébastien told the customs inspector that he carried less than $10,000. The officer discovered the actual amount of cash that Sébastien was carrying, seized it, and arrested Sébastien. Roslyn

asked the government to return what she claimed were her funds, arguing that the arrangement with Sébastien was a bailment and that she still held title to the cash. (See *Bailments.*)

1. The first group will argue that Roslyn is entitled to the cash.

2. The second group will take the position of the government and develop an argument that Roslyn's agreement with Sébastien does not qualify as a bailment.

iStockPhoto.com/-Oxford-

35

Real Property and Landlord-Tenant Law

> "The right of property is the most sacred of all the rights of citizenship."
>
> **JEAN-JACQUES ROUSSEAU**
> 1712–1778
> (FRENCH WRITER AND PHILOSOPHER)

From earliest times, property has provided a means for survival. Primitive peoples lived off the fruits of the land, eating the vegetation and wildlife. Later, as the vegetation was cultivated and the wildlife domesticated, property provided farmland and pasture.

Throughout history, property has continued to be an indicator of family wealth and social position. Indeed, an individual's right to his or her property has become, in the words of Jean-Jacques Rousseau, one of the "most sacred of all the rights of citizenship."

In this chapter, we examine the nature of real property and the ways in which it can be owned and transferred. We even consider whether the buyer of a haunted house can rescind the sale in this chapter's *Spotlight Case*. We also discuss leased property and landlord-tenant relationships.

LEARNING OBJECTIVES

The five Learning Objectives *below are designed to help improve your understanding of the chapter. After reading this chapter, you should be able to answer the following questions:*

1. What is a fixture, and how does it relate to real property rights?
2. What is the difference between a joint tenancy and a tenancy in common?
3. What is an easement? What are three ways in which an easement can be created?
4. What are the requirements for acquiring property by adverse possession?
5. What are the duties of the landlord and the tenant with respect to the use and maintenance of leased property?

35-1 The Nature of Real Property

Real property consists of land and the buildings, plants, and trees that are on it. Real property also includes subsurface and airspace rights, as well as personal property that has become permanently attached to the real property. Whereas personal property is movable, real property—also called *real estate* or *realty*—is immovable.

35-1a Land

Land includes the soil on the surface of the earth and the natural or artificial structures that are attached to it. It further includes all the waters contained on or under the surface and much, but not necessarily all, of the airspace above it. The exterior boundaries of land extend down to the center of the earth and up to the farthest reaches of the atmosphere (subject to certain qualifications).

35-1b Airspace and Subsurface Rights

The owner of real property has rights to the airspace above the land, as well as to the soil and minerals underneath it. Limitations on either airspace rights or subsurface rights normally must be indicated on the document that transfers title at the time of purchase. When no such limitations, or *encumbrances,* are noted, a purchaser generally can expect to have an unlimited right to possession of the property.

Airspace Rights Disputes concerning airspace rights may involve the right of commercial and private planes to fly over property and the right of individuals and governments to seed clouds and produce rain artificially. Flights over private land normally do not violate property rights unless the flights are so low and so frequent that they directly interfere with the owner's enjoyment and use of the land.[1] Leaning walls or buildings and projecting eave spouts or roofs may also violate the airspace rights of an adjoining property owner.

Subsurface Rights In many states, land ownership may be separated, in that the surface of a piece of land and the subsurface may have different owners. Subsurface rights can be extremely valuable, as these rights include the ownership of minerals, oil, and natural gas. Subsurface rights would be of little value, however, if the owner could not use the surface to exercise those rights. Hence, a subsurface owner has a right (called a *profit,* to be discussed later in this chapter) to go onto the surface of the land to, for example, discover and mine minerals.

When ownership is separated into surface and subsurface rights, each owner can pass title to what she or he owns without the consent of the other owner. Of course, conflicts can arise between the surface owner's use of the property and the subsurface owner's need to extract minerals, oil, or natural gas. In that situation, one party's interest may become subservient (secondary) to the other party's interest either by statute or by case law. If the owners of the subsurface rights excavate (dig), they are absolutely liable if their excavation causes the surface to collapse. Many states have statutes that also make the excavators liable for any damage to structures on the land. Typically, these statutes provide precise requirements for excavations of various depths.

Who owns airspace above residential land?

35-1c Plant Life and Vegetation

Plant life, both natural and cultivated, is also considered to be real property. In many instances, the natural vegetation, such as trees, adds greatly to the value of the realty. When a parcel of land is sold and the land has growing crops on it, the sale includes the crops, unless otherwise specified in the sales contract. When crops are sold by themselves, however, they are considered to be personal property, or goods. Consequently, the sale of crops is a sale of goods and thus is governed by the Uniform Commercial Code (UCC) rather than by real property law.[2]

> "The meek shall inherit the earth, but not the mineral rights."
>
> **J. Paul Getty**
> 1892–1976
> (American entrepreneur and industrialist)

---

1. *United States v. Causby,* 328 U.S. 256, 66 S.Ct. 1062, 90 L.Ed. 1206 (1946).
2. See UCC 2–107(2).

35-1d **Fixtures**

Certain personal property can become so closely associated with the real property to which it is attached that the law views it as real property. Such property is known as a **fixture**—an item *affixed* to realty, meaning that it is attached to the real property in a permanent way. The item may be attached, embedded in, or permanently situated on the property by means of cement, plaster, bolts, nails, roots, or screws. The fixture can be physically attached to the real property, be attached to another fixture, or even be without any actual physical attachment to the land (such as a statue). As long as the owner intends the property to be a fixture, normally it will be a fixture.

Fixtures are included in the sale of land if the sales contract does not provide otherwise. The sale of a house includes the land and the house and the garage on the land, as well as the cabinets, plumbing, and windows. Because these are permanently affixed to the property, they are considered to be a part of it. Certain items, such as drapes and window-unit air conditioners, are difficult to classify. Thus, a contract for the sale of a house or commercial realty should indicate which items of this sort are included in the sale.

CASE EXAMPLE 35.1 Sand & Sage Farm had an eight-tower center-pivot irrigation system bolted to a cement slab and connected to an underground well. The bank held a mortgage note on the farm secured by "all buildings, improvements, and fixtures." The farm's owners had also used the property as security for other loans, but the contracts for those loans did not specifically mention fixtures or the irrigation system. Later, when Sand & Sage filed for bankruptcy, a dispute arose between the bank and another creditor over the irrigation system. The court held that the irrigation system was a fixture because it was firmly attached to the land and integral to the operation of the farm. Therefore, the bank's security interest had priority over the other creditor's interest.[3] ▪

When real property is being sold, transferred, or subjected to a security interest, make sure that any contract specifically lists which fixtures are to be included. Without such a list, the parties may have very different ideas as to what is being transferred with the real property (or included as collateral for a loan). It is much simpler and less expensive to itemize fixtures in a contract than to engage in litigation.

Fixture An item of personal property that has become so closely associated with real property that it is legally regarded as part of that real property.

PREVENTING LEGAL DISPUTES

35-2 **Ownership Interests and Leases**

Ownership of real property is abstract and differs from ownership of personal property. No one can actually possess or *hold* a piece of land, the airspace above it, the earth below it, and all the water contained on it. The legal system therefore recognizes certain rights and duties that constitute ownership interests in real property.

Traditionally, ownership interests in real property were referred to as *estates in land*, which include fee simple estates, life estates, and leasehold estates. We examine estates in land, forms of concurrent ownership, and certain other interests in real property in the following subsections.

As you will see, ownership of real property (as well as personal property) can be viewed as a bundle of rights, including the right to possess the property and to dispose of it by sale, gift, lease, or other means. A person can own either the whole bundle of rights (a fee simple) or only a part of the rights. When only some of the rights are transferred, the effect is to limit the ownership rights of both the transferor of the rights and the recipient.

Under what circumstances is an industrial-quality irrigation system considered a fixture?

iStockPhoto.com/Songbird839

---

3. *In re Sand & Sage Farm & Ranch, Inc.*, 266 Bankr. 507 (D.Kans. 2001).

35–2a **Ownership in Fee Simple**

Fee Simple An ownership interest in land in which the owner has the greatest possible aggregation of rights, privileges, and power.

One who possesses the entire bundle of rights is said to hold the property in **fee simple** (usually referring to *fee simple absolute*), which is the most complete form of ownership. An owner in fee simple is entitled to use, possess, or dispose of the property as he or she chooses during his or her lifetime. The owner has the rights of *exclusive* possession and use of the property. The owner can give the property away, sell it, or lease it.

Duration On the fee simple owner's death, the interests in the property descend (pass down) to his or her heirs, even if the owner has not executed a will. Thus, a fee simple is potentially infinite in duration and is assigned forever to a person and her or his heirs without limitation or condition.

Limitations on Use The rights that accompany a fee simple include the right to use the land for whatever purpose the owner sees fit. Of course, other laws, including applicable zoning regulations, noise regulations, and environmental laws, may limit the owner's ability to use the property in certain ways. A fee simple owner cannot build a manufacturing plant on the property if doing so would violate applicable city or county rules and regulations, for instance. Also, a person who uses his or her property in a manner that unreasonably interferes with others' right to use or enjoy their own property can be liable for the tort of *nuisance*.

> "Few . . . men own their property. The property owns them."
>
> **Robert G. Ingersoll**
> 1833–1899
> (American politician and lecturer)

CASE EXAMPLE 35.2 Nancy and James Biglane owned and lived in a building in Natchez, Mississippi. Next door to the Biglanes' property was the Under the Hill Saloon, a popular bar that featured live music. During the summer, the Saloon, which had no air-conditioning, opened its windows and doors, and live music echoed up and down the street.

Although the Biglanes installed extra insulation, thicker windows, and air-conditioning units in their building, the noise from the Saloon kept them awake at night. Eventually, the Biglanes sued the owners of the Saloon for nuisance. The court held that the noise from the bar unreasonably interfered with the Biglanes' right to enjoy their property and prohibited the Saloon from opening its windows and doors while playing music.[4] ■

35–2b **Life Estates**

Life Estate An interest in land that exists only for the duration of the life of a specified individual, usually the holder of the estate.

Conveyance The transfer of title to real property from one person to another by deed or other document.

Waste The use of real property in a manner that damages or destroys its value.

A **life estate** is an estate that lasts for the life of some specified individual. A **conveyance,** or transfer of real property, "to Alex Munson for his life" creates a life estate. In a life estate, the life tenant's ownership rights cease to exist on the life tenant's death.

The life tenant has the right to use the land provided that he or she commits no **waste** (injury to the land). In other words, the life tenant cannot use the land in a manner that would adversely affect its value. **EXAMPLE 35.3** Julian, a life tenant on Blazin Acres, can use the land to harvest crops. If mines and oil wells are already on the land, Julian can extract minerals and oil from it, but he cannot drill new oil wells or excavate mines on the property. ■

The life tenant also has the right to create liens, *easements* (discussed shortly), and leases, but none can extend beyond the life of the tenant. In addition, with a few exceptions, the owner of a life estate has an exclusive right to possession during her or his lifetime.

Along with these rights, the life tenant also has some duties. He or she must keep the property in repair and pay property taxes. In short, the owner of a life estate has the same rights as a fee simple owner, except that the life tenant must maintain the value of the property during her or his tenancy. Also, the life tenant cannot sell the property or leave it to his or her heirs.

In the following case, the life tenant refused to pay the taxes and the premiums for the insurance on the property. Was this waste?

---

4. *Biglane v. Under the Hill Corp.*, 949 So.2d 9 (Miss.Sup.Ct. 2007).

Main Omni Realty Corp. v. Matus

New York Supreme Court, Appellate Division, Second Department, 124 A.D.3d 604, 1 N.Y.S.3d 319 (2015).

FACTS Craig Matus held a life estate in certain residential real property in Huntington, New York. On the termination of the life estate, title to the property was to transfer to Main Omni Realty Corporation, a wholly owned subsidiary of New York Community Bank. For a dozen years, Matus refused to pay premiums for insurance on the property. He also refused to pay the property taxes, resulting in tax liens. To preserve its interest in the property, Main Omni paid the premiums and the liens, which avoided a foreclosure and sale of the property. Main Omni then filed a suit in a New York state court against Matus. The plaintiff sought to recover the amount of the premiums and taxes on the ground of unjust enrichment. In addition, it sought to extinguish (end) the life estate on the ground of waste based on Matus's refusal to pay the taxes. The court denied Main Omni's motion for summary judgment. Main Omni appealed.

ISSUE Did Matus's refusal to pay the taxes and insurance premiums on the property warrant extinguishing his life estate?

DECISION Yes. A state intermediate appellate court reversed the lower court's denial of Main Omni's motion and ordered a summary judgment in the plaintiff's favor. "Equity warrants extinguishing his life estate."

What happens to a life estate when the tenant refuses to pay property taxes?

REASON A life tenant is obligated to pay the taxes and insurance premiums on the property that is the subject of the life estate. An intentional failure to make these payments constitutes waste. In this case, Matus intentionally failed to pay the taxes and insurance on the subject property, and he further expressed an intent not to do so in the future. In this situation, Main Omni's interest in the property would be "in constant danger of forfeiture in a tax lien sale" unless Main Omni paid the taxes and insurance premiums that Matus was otherwise obligated to pay. This circumstance called for extinguishing Matus's life estate in the property. In addition, Main Omni was entitled to restitution for the amounts of the taxes and insurance premiums that it had already paid. It would be "against equity and good conscience to permit the defendant to retain what is sought to be recovered."

CRITICAL THINKING—Economic Consideration *Why would the owner of a life estate refuse to pay the taxes and insurance premiums on the property of the estate? Should any reason have influenced the court's decision in this case?*

35–2c Concurrent Ownership

Persons who share ownership rights simultaneously in particular property (including real property and personal property) are said to have **concurrent ownership.** There are two principal types of concurrent ownership: *tenancy in common* and *joint tenancy.* Concurrent ownership rights can also be held in a *tenancy by the entirety* or as *community property,* but these types of concurrent ownership are less common.

Tenancy in Common   The term **tenancy in common** refers to a form of co-ownership in which each of two or more persons owns an undivided interest in the property. The interest is undivided because each tenant shares rights in the whole property. On the death of a tenant in common, that tenant's interest in the property passes to her or his heirs.

> **EXAMPLE 35.4** Four friends purchase a condominium unit in Hawaii together as tenants in common. This means that each of them has a one-fourth ownership interest in the whole. If one of the four owners dies a year after the purchase, his ownership interest passes to his heirs (his wife and children, for instance) rather than to the other tenants in common. ■

Unless the co-tenants have agreed otherwise, a tenant in common can transfer her or his interest in the property to anyone without the consent of the remaining co-owners. In most states, it is presumed that a co-tenancy is a tenancy in common unless there is specific language indicating the intent to establish a joint tenancy (discussed next).

Concurrent Ownership Joint ownership.

Tenancy in Common Joint ownership of property in which each party owns an undivided interest that passes to his or her heirs at death.

LEARNING OBJECTIVE 2
What is the difference between a joint tenancy and a tenancy in common?

Joint Tenancy Joint ownership of property by two or more co-owners in which each co-owner owns an undivided portion of the property. On the death of one of the joint tenants, his or her interest automatically passes to the surviving joint tenant(s).

Tenancy by the Entirety Joint ownership of property by a married couple in which neither spouse can transfer his or her interest in the property without the consent of the other.

Community Property A form of concurrent property ownership in which each spouse owns an undivided one-half interest in property acquired during the marriage.

Leasehold Estate An interest in real property that gives a tenant a qualified right to possess and/or use the property for a limited time under a lease.

Joint Tenancy In a **joint tenancy,** each of two or more persons owns an undivided interest in the property, but a deceased joint tenant's interest passes to the surviving joint tenant or tenants.

Right of Survivorship. The right of a surviving joint tenant to inherit a deceased joint tenant's ownership interest—referred to as a *right of survivorship*—distinguishes a joint tenancy from a tenancy in common. **EXAMPLE 35.5** Jerrold and Eva are married and purchase a house as joint tenants. The title to the house clearly expresses the intent to create a joint tenancy because it says "to Jerrold and Eva as joint tenants with right of survivorship." Jerrold has three children from a prior marriage. If Jerrold dies, his interest in the house automatically passes to Eva rather than to his children from the prior marriage. ■

Termination of a Joint Tenancy. A joint tenant can transfer her or his rights by sale or gift to another without the consent of the other joint tenants. Doing so terminates the joint tenancy. The person who purchases the property or receives it as a gift becomes a tenant in common, not a joint tenant. **EXAMPLE 35.6** Three brothers, Brody, Saul, and Jacob, own a parcel as joint tenants. Brody is experiencing financial difficulties and sells his interest in the property to Beth. The sale terminates the joint tenancy, and now Beth, Saul, and Jacob hold the property as tenants in common. ■

A joint tenant's interest can also be levied against (seized by court order) to satisfy the tenant's judgment creditors. If this occurs, the joint tenancy terminates, and the remaining owners hold the property as tenants in common. (Judgment creditors can also seize the interests of tenants in a tenancy in common.)

Tenancy by the Entirety A less common form of shared ownership of real property by married persons is a **tenancy by the entirety.** It differs from a joint tenancy in that neither spouse may separately transfer his or her interest during his or her lifetime unless the other spouse consents. In some states in which statutes give the wife the right to convey her property, this form of concurrent ownership has effectively been abolished. A divorce, either spouse's death, or mutual agreement will terminate a tenancy by the entirety.

Community Property A limited number of states[5] allow married couples to own property as **community property.** If property is held as community property, each spouse technically owns an undivided one-half interest in the property. This type of ownership applies to most property acquired by either spouse during the course of the marriage. It generally does *not* apply to property acquired prior to the marriage or to property acquired by gift or inheritance as separate property during the marriage. After a divorce, community property is divided equally in some states and according to the discretion of the court in other states.

35–2d Leasehold Estates

A **leasehold estate** is created when a real property owner or lessor (landlord) agrees to convey the right to possess and use the property to a lessee (tenant) for a certain period of time. The tenant has a *qualified* right to exclusive possession. It is qualified because the landlord has a right to enter onto the premises to ensure that no waste (damage or destruction) is being committed. The *temporary* nature of possession, under a lease, is what distinguishes a tenant from a purchaser, who acquires title to the property. The tenant can use the land—for example, by harvesting crops—but cannot injure it by such activities as cutting down timber for sale or extracting oil.

---

5. These states include Alaska, Arizona, California, Idaho, Louisiana, Nevada, New Mexico, Texas, Washington, and Wisconsin. Puerto Rico allows property to be owned as community property as well.

Fixed-Term Tenancy

A **fixed-term tenancy,** also called a *tenancy for years,* is created by an express contract by which property is leased for a specified period of time. Signing a one-year lease to occupy an apartment, for instance, creates a fixed-term tenancy. Note that the term need not be specified by date and can be conditioned on the occurrence of an event, such as leasing a cabin for the summer or an apartment in New Orleans during Mardi Gras.

At the end of the period specified in the lease, the lease ends (without notice), and possession of the property returns to the lessor. If the tenant dies during the period of the lease, the lease interest passes to the tenant's heirs as personal property. Often, leases include renewal or extension provisions.

Periodic Tenancy

A **periodic tenancy** is created by a lease that does not specify how long it is to last but does specify that rent is to be paid at certain intervals. This type of tenancy is automatically renewed for another rental period unless properly terminated. **EXAMPLE 35.7** Kayla enters into a lease with Capital Properties. The lease states, "Rent is due on the tenth day of every month." This provision creates a periodic tenancy from month to month. ■ This type of tenancy can also extend from week to week or from year to year.

Under the common law, to terminate a periodic tenancy, the landlord or tenant must give at least one period's notice to the other party. If the tenancy extends from month to month, for example, one month's notice must be given prior to the last month's rent payment. Today, however, many states' statutes require a different period for notice of termination in a periodic tenancy.

Tenancy at Will

With a **tenancy at will,** either party can terminate the tenancy without notice. This type of tenancy can arise if a landlord allows a person to live on the premises without paying rent or rents property to a tenant "for as long as both agree." Tenancies at will are rare today because most state statutes require a landlord to provide some period of notice to terminate a tenancy. States may also require a landowner to have sufficient cause to end a residential tenancy.

Tenancy at Sufferance

The mere possession of land without right is called a **tenancy at sufferance.** A tenancy at sufferance is not a true tenancy because it is created when a tenant *wrongfully* retains possession of property. Whenever a tenancy for years or a periodic tenancy ends and the tenant continues to retain possession of the premises without the owner's permission, a tenancy at sufferance is created.

The lease agreement for the apartment in this building states that rent is due on the first of each month. What type of tenancy is created?

35–2e Nonpossessory Interests—Easements, Profits, and Licenses

In contrast to the types of property interests just described, some interests in land do not include any rights to possess the property. These interests are therefore known as **nonpossessory interests.** They include easements, profits, and licenses.

An **easement** is the right of a person to make limited use of another person's real property without taking anything from the property. An easement, for instance, can be the right to walk or drive across another's property. In contrast, a **profit**[6] is the right to go onto land owned by another and take away some part of the land itself or some product of the land.

Fixed-term Tenancy A type of tenancy under which property is leased for a specified period of time, such as a month, a year, or a period of years; also called a *tenancy for years.*

Periodic Tenancy A lease interest in land for an indefinite period involving payment of rent at fixed intervals, such as week to week, month to month, or year to year.

Tenancy at Will A type of tenancy that either the landlord or the tenant can terminate without notice.

Tenancy at Sufferance A tenancy that arises when a tenant wrongfully continues to occupy leased property after the lease has terminated.

Nonpossessory Interest In the context of real property, an interest that involves the right to use land but not the right to possess it.

Easement A nonpossessory right, established by express or implied agreement, to make limited use of another's property without removing anything from the property.

LEARNING OBJECTIVE 3

What is an easement? What are three ways in which an easement can be created?

Profit In real property law, the right to enter onto another's property and remove something of value from that property.

---

6. As used here, the term *profit* does not refer to the profits made by a business firm. Rather, it means a gain or an advantage.

EXAMPLE 35.8 Shawn owns The Dunes. Shawn gives Carmen the right to go there to remove all the sand and gravel that she needs for her cement business. Carmen has a profit. ■

Easements and profits can be classified as either *appurtenant* or *in gross*. Because easements and profits are similar and the same rules apply to both, we discuss them together.

Easement or Profit Appurtenant
An easement or profit *appurtenant* arises when the owner of one piece of land has a right to go onto (or remove something from) an adjacent piece of land owned by another. The land that is benefited by the easement is called the *dominant estate,* and the land that is burdened is called the *servient estate.*

Because easements appurtenant are intended to *benefit the land,* they run (are conveyed) with the land when it is transferred. **EXAMPLE 35.9** Taylor has a right to drive his car across Green's land, which is adjacent to Taylor's land. This right-of-way over Green's property is an easement appurtenant to Acosta's property and can be used only by Taylor. If Taylor sells his land, the easement runs with the land to benefit the new owner. ■

Easement or Profit in Gross
In an easement or profit *in gross,* the right to use or take things from another's land is given to one who does not own an adjacent tract of land. These easements are intended to *benefit a particular person or business,* not a particular piece of land, and cannot be transferred.

EXAMPLE 35.10 Avery owns a parcel of land with a marble quarry. Avery conveys (transfers) to Classic Stone Corporation the right to come onto her land and remove up to five hundred pounds of marble per day. Classic Stone owns a profit in gross and cannot transfer this right to another. ■ Similarly, when a utility company is granted an easement to run its power lines across another's property, it obtains an easement in gross.

Creation of an Easement or Profit
Most easements and profits are created by an express grant in a contract, a deed, or a will. This allows the parties to include terms defining the extent and length of time of use. In some situations, an easement or profit can also be created without an express agreement.

An easement or profit may arise by *implication* when the circumstances surrounding the division of a parcel of property imply its existence. **EXAMPLE 35.11** Mathews owns a parcel of property that has electrical lines running over it. If Mathews divides the parcel of land and conveys some land under the lines to Jarred, the county will have easement by implication, because surrounding circumstances imply the easement's existence. ■

An easement may also be created by *necessity.* An easement by necessity does not require a division of property for its existence. A person who rents an apartment, for instance, has an easement by necessity in the private road leading up to the apartment building.

These electrical lines cross a private individual's property at the time of purchase. What type of easement allows the county to access these lines?

An easement arises by *prescription* when one person exercises an easement, such as a right-of-way, on another person's land without the landowner's consent. The use must be apparent and continue for the length of time required by the applicable statute of limitations. (In much the same way, title to property may be obtained by *adverse possession,* discussed later in this chapter.)

In the following case, an easement had been created by an express grant in a deed. The deed did not specify the easement's precise location, however.

CASE 35.2

Baker v. Walnut Bowls, Inc.

Missouri Court of Appeals, Southern District, Division Two, 423 S.W.3d 293 (2014).

FACTS Junior and Wilma Thompson sold twenty-one of their fifty acres of land in Missouri to Walnut Bowls, Inc. The deed expressly reserved an easement to the Thompsons' remaining twenty-nine acres. The deed did not fix a precise location for the easement, however. James and Linda Baker subsequently bought the remaining acreage of the Thompsons' land.

Decades later—on learning of the easement to the Bakers' property—a potential buyer of Walnut Bowls' property refused to go through with the sale. Walnut Bowls then put steel cables across its driveway entrances, installed a lock and chain on an access gate, and bolted a "No Trespassing" sign facing the Bakers' property. At about the same time, the Bakers filed a suit in a Missouri state court to determine the location of the easement. Citing the lack of an express location, the court held that there was no easement. The Bakers appealed.

ISSUE Did the Bakers have an easement to their property, despite the lack of an express location in the deed?

DECISION Yes. A state intermediate appellate court reversed the decision of the lower court and remanded the case for further proceedings. If a grant or other agreement does not precisely fix an

If an easement's location is not precisely fixed, is it still valid?

easement's location—and it cannot be inferred from past use—the court is obligated to determine the location.

REASON An easement can be created by deed even though its specific location is not identified. When the site of an easement is not specified at its inception, the location can later be fixed by an express agreement between the parties or inferred from the use of a certain part of the property in a particular way. If the easement is not identified in either of these ways, a court must determine the location. In that determination, the easement holder is entitled to "convenient, reasonable and accessible use."

Here, the grant that had created the Bakers' easement had not identified its location. There was no evidence of any later agreement concerning the location, nor was there any way to infer the location from past use. Thus, the Bakers were entitled to have the court determine a route that was convenient, reasonable, and accessible.

WHAT IF THE FACTS WERE DIFFERENT? *Suppose that the original deed had not granted an easement. Further suppose that the Bakers' only route to their property was Walnut Bowls' driveway. Could the Bakers have acquired an easement in this situation? Discuss.*

Termination of an Easement or Profit

An easement or profit can be terminated in several ways. The simplest way is to deed it back to the owner of the land that is burdened by it. Similarly, if the owner of an easement or profit becomes the owner of the property burdened by it, then it is merged into the property.

Another way to terminate an easement or profit is to abandon it and create evidence of intent to relinquish the right to use it. Mere nonuse will not extinguish an easement or profit *unless the nonuse is accompanied by an overt act showing the intent to abandon.*

License

In the context of real property, a **license** is the revocable right to enter onto another person's land. It is a personal privilege that arises from the consent of the owner of the land and can be revoked by the owner. A ticket to attend a movie at a theater or a concert is an example of a license.

In essence, a license grants a person the authority to enter the land of another and perform a specified act or series of acts without obtaining any permanent interest in the land. When a person with a license exceeds the authority granted and undertakes an action that is not permitted, the property owner can sue that person in tort law for trespass.

CASE EXAMPLE 35.12 A Catholic church granted Prince Realty Management, LLC, a three-month license to use a three-foot strip of its property adjacent to Prince's property. The license

License In the context of real property, a revocable right or privilege to enter onto another person's land.

authorized Prince to "put up plywood panels," creating a temporary fence to protect Prince's property during the construction of a new building. During the license's term, Prince installed steel piles and beams on the licensed property. When Prince ignored the church's demands that these structures be removed, the church sued Prince for trespass. The court held that because the license allowed only temporary structures and Prince had exceeded its authority by installing steel piles and beams, the church was entitled to damages.[7] ▆

Exhibit 35–1 illustrates the various interests in property discussed in this chapter.

35–3   Transfer of Ownership

Ownership interests in real property are frequently transferred (conveyed) by sale, and the terms of the transfer are specified in a real estate sales contract.

Real property ownership can also be transferred by gift, by will or inheritance, by possession, or by *eminent domain*. When ownership rights in real property are transferred, the type of interest being transferred and the conditions of the transfer normally are set forth in a *deed* executed by the person who is conveying the property.

35–3a   Real Estate Sales Contracts

In some ways, a sale of real estate is similar to a sale of goods, because it involves a transfer of ownership, often with specific warranties. A sale of real estate, however, is a more complicated transaction that involves certain formalities that are not required in a sale of goods. In part because of these complications, real estate brokers or agents who are licensed by the state generally assist the buyers and sellers during a real estate sales transaction.

Usually, the parties to a sale of real estate enter into a detailed contract setting forth their agreement. A contract for a sale of land includes such terms as the purchase price, the type of deed the buyer will receive, the condition of the premises, and any items that will be included.

Unless the buyer pays cash for the property, he or she must obtain financing through a mortgage loan. Real estate sales contracts are often contingent on the buyer's ability to obtain financing at or below a specified rate of interest. The contract may also be contingent on certain events, such as the completion of a land survey or the property's passing one or more inspections. Normally, the buyer is responsible for having the premises inspected for physical or mechanical defects and for insect infestation.

---

7. *Roman Catholic Church of Our Lady of Sorrows v. Prince Realty Management, LLC*, 47 A.D.3d 909, 850 N.Y.S.2d 569 (2008).

Exhibit 35–1 Interests in Real Property

Ownership Interests	1. *Fee simple*—The most complete form of ownership.
	2. *Life estate*—An estate that lasts for the life of a specified individual.
	3. *Concurrent interests*—When two or more persons hold title to property together, concurrent ownership exists.
	   a. Tenancy in common
	   b. Joint tenancy
	   c. Tenancy by the entirety
	   d. Community property

Leasehold Estates	1. Fixed-term tenancy (tenancy for years) 2. Periodic tenancy 3. Tenancy at will 4. Tenancy at sufferance
Nonpossessory Interests	1. Easements 2. Profits 3. Licenses

Implied Warranties in the Sale of New Homes

Most states recognize a warranty—the **implied warranty of habitability**—in the sale of new homes. Because the warranty is implied, it need not be included in the contract of sale or the deed to be effective.

Under this warranty, the seller of a new home essentially warrants that it is in reasonable working order and is of reasonably sound construction. Thus, the seller is in effect a guarantor of the home's fitness. In some states, the warranty protects not only the first purchaser but any subsequent purchaser as well.

Seller's Duty to Disclose Hidden Defects

In most jurisdictions, courts impose on sellers a duty to disclose any known defect that materially affects the value of the property and that the buyer could not reasonably discover. Failure to disclose such a material defect gives the buyer the right to rescind the contract and to sue for damages based on fraud or misrepresentation. The buyer generally must bring such a suit within a specified time.

CASE EXAMPLE 35.13 Matthew Humphrey partially renovated a house in Louisiana and sold it to Terry and Tabitha Whitehead for $67,000. A few months after the Whiteheads moved in, they discovered rotten wood behind the tile in the bathroom and experienced problems with the fireplace and the plumbing. Two years later, the Whiteheads filed a suit against Humphrey seeking to rescind the sale.

The Whiteheads argued that the plumbing problems were a latent, or hidden, defect that the seller had failed to disclose. Evidence revealed, however, that prior to the sale, the parties had been made aware of issues regarding the sewer system and that corrective actions had been taken. At the time of the sale, the toilets flushed, and neither side realized that the latent defects had not been resolved.

The court ruled that rescission was not warranted, because the Whiteheads had waited too long after their discovery to file a claim against Humphrey. The court did order Humphrey to pay damages for the repairs to the fireplace and for replacing some of the rotten wood, because Humphrey had known about these defects at the time of the sale.[8] ■

In the following *Spotlight Case,* the court had to decide whether the buyer of a "haunted" house had the right to rescind the sales contract.

Implied Warranty of Habitability An implied promise by a seller of a new house that the house is fit for human habitation. Also, the implied promise by a landlord that rented residential premises are habitable.

---

8. *Whitehead v. Humphrey,* 954 So.2d 859 (La.App. 2007).

SPOTLIGHT ON SALES OF HAUNTED HOUSES: CASE 35.3

Stambovsky v. Ackley

Supreme Court, Appellate Division, New York, 572 N.Y.S.2d 672, 169 A.D.2d 254 (1991).

FACTS Jeffrey Stambovsky signed a contract to buy Helen Ackley's house in Nyack, New York. After the contract was signed, Stambovsky discovered that the house was widely reputed to be haunted. The Ackley family claimed to have seen poltergeists on numerous occasions over the previous nine years. The Ackleys had been interviewed about the house in both a national publication (*Reader's Digest*) and the local newspaper. The house was included on a walking tour of Nyack, New York, as "a riverfront Victorian (with ghost)." When Stambovsky learned of the house's reputation, he sued to rescind the contract, alleging that Ackley and her real estate agent had made material

When will a buyer of a house that is allegedly haunted have the right to rescind the deal?

iStockPhoto.com/pixeldigits

misrepresentations when they failed to disclose Ackley's belief that the house was haunted.

ISSUE Was the failure to inform Stambovsky that the house was supposedly haunted a material misrepresentation that would allow him to rescind the contract?

DECISION Yes. The court allowed Stambovsky to rescind the contract.

REASON Ackley and her family had created the house's reputation as haunted and had profited from that reputation over a number of years. That reputation harmed

Continues

the resale value of the home, however. Because the Ackleys had created the impairment and knew that it was not likely to be discovered by a purchaser from out of town, they had an obligation to disclose it. They should have brought the impairment to the attention of all prospective buyers, including Stambovsky. Even though the Ackleys did not actively mislead Stambovsky, they allowed him to sign the contract knowing that he was unaware of the home's haunted reputation. Because they unfairly took advantage of his ignorance, they could not enforce the contract.

CRITICAL THINKING—Ethical Consideration *Assuming that Ackley's behavior was unethical, was it unethical because she failed to tell Stambovsky something about the house that he did not know, or was it unethical because of the nature of the information she omitted? What if Ackley had failed to mention that the roof leaked or that the well was dry—conditions that a buyer would normally investigate? Explain your answer.*

iStockPhoto.com/RuslanDashinsky

If this homeowner discovers numerous defects in her recently purchased house, can she wait years to attempt to rescind the contract?

Deed A document by which title to real property is passed.

KNOW THIS

Gifts of real property are common, and they require deeds even though there is no consideration for the gift.

Warranty Deed A deed that provides the greatest amount of protection for the grantee. The grantor promises that she or he has title to the property conveyed in the deed, that there are no undisclosed encumbrances on the property, and that the grantee will enjoy quiet possession of the property.

35–3b Deeds

Possession and title to land are passed from person to person by means of a **deed**—the instrument of conveyance of real property. Unlike a contract, a deed does not have to be supported by legally sufficient consideration. To be valid, a deed must include the following elements:

1. The names of the grantor (the giver or seller) and the grantee (the donee or buyer).

2. Words evidencing the intent to convey the property (such as, "I hereby bargain, sell, grant, or give"). No specific words are necessary. If the deed does not specify the type of estate being transferred, it is presumed to transfer the property in fee simple absolute.

3. A legally sufficient description of the land. The description must include enough detail to distinguish the property being conveyed from every other parcel of land. The property can be identified by reference to an official survey or recorded plat map, or each boundary can be described by metes and bounds. *Metes and bounds* is a system of measuring boundary lines by the distance between two points, often using physical features of the local geography—for instance, "beginning at the southwesterly intersection of Court and Main Streets, then West 40 feet to the fence, then South 100 feet, then Northeast approximately 120 feet back to the beginning."

4. The grantor's (and usually her or his spouse's) signature.

5. Delivery of the deed.

Different types of deeds provide different degrees of protection against defects of title. A defect of title exists, for example, if an undisclosed third person has an ownership interest in the property.

Warranty Deeds A **warranty deed** contains the greatest number of *covenants,* or promises, of title and thus provides the greatest protection against defects of title. In most states, special language is required to create a general warranty deed. Warranty deeds commonly include the following covenants:

1. A covenant that the grantor has the title to, and the power to convey, the property.

2. A covenant of quiet enjoyment (a warranty that the buyer will not be disturbed in her or his possession of the land).

3. A covenant that transfer of the property is made without knowledge of adverse claims of third parties.

Generally, the warranty deed makes the grantor liable for all defects of title during the time that the property was held by the grantor and previous titleholders. **EXAMPLE 35.14** Mandal sells a two-acre lot and office building by warranty deed to Flash Technologies, LLC. Subsequently, Perkins shows that he has better title to the property than Mandal had and evicts Flash Technologies. Here, Flash Technologies can sue Mandal for breaching the covenant of quiet enjoyment. Flash Technologies can recover the purchase price of the land, plus any other damages incurred as a result. ∎

Special Warranty Deeds A **special warranty deed,** or *limited warranty deed,* in contrast, warrants only that the grantor or seller held good title during his or her ownership of the property. In other words, the grantor does not warrant that there were no defects of title when the property was held by previous owners.

If the special warranty deed discloses all liens and other encumbrances, the seller will not be liable to the buyer if a third person subsequently interferes with the buyer's ownership. If the third person's claim arises out of, or is related to, some act of the seller, though, the seller will be liable to the buyer for damages.

Quitclaim Deeds A **quitclaim deed** offers the least amount of protection against defects of title. Basically, a quitclaim deed conveys to the grantee whatever interest the grantor had. Therefore, if the grantor had no interest, then the grantee receives no interest.

Quitclaim deeds are often used when the seller, or grantor, is uncertain as to the extent of his or her rights in the property. They may also be used to release a party's interest in a particular parcel of property, such as in divorce settlements or business dissolutions when the grantors are dividing up their interests in real property.

Recording Statutes Every state has a **recording statute,** which allows a deed to be recorded for a fee. Deeds are recorded in the county where the property is located. Recording a deed gives notice to the public that a certain person is now the owner of a particular parcel of real estate. By putting everyone on notice as to the true owner, recording a deed prevents the previous owners from fraudulently conveying the land to other purchasers. Thus, prospective buyers can check the public records to see whether there have been earlier transactions creating interests or rights in specific parcels of real property.

35–3c Will or Inheritance

Property that is transferred on an owner's death is passed either by will or by state inheritance laws. If the owner of land dies with a will, the land passes in accordance with the terms of the will. If the owner dies without a will, state inheritance statutes prescribe how and to whom the property will pass.

35–3d Adverse Possession

A person who wrongfully possesses the real property of another (by occupying or using it) may eventually acquire title to it through adverse possession. **Adverse possession** is a means of obtaining title to land without delivery of a deed and without the consent of—or payment to—the true owner. Thus, adverse possession is a method of *involuntarily* transferring title to the property from the true owner to the adverse possessor.

Essentially, when one person possesses the property of another for a certain statutory period, that person acquires title to the land. The statutory period varies from three to thirty years, depending on the state, with ten years being the most common.

Special Warranty Deed
A deed that warrants only that the grantor held good title during his or her ownership of the property and does not warrant that there were no defects of title when the property was held by previous owners.

Quitclaim Deed A deed that conveys only whatever interest the grantor had in the property and therefore offers the least amount of protection against defects of title.

Recording Statute A statute that allow deeds, mortgages, and other real property transactions to be recorded so as to provide notice to future purchasers or creditors of an existing claim on the property.

Adverse Possession
The acquisition of title to real property through open occupation, without the consent of the owner, for a period of time specified by a state statute. The occupation must be actual, exclusive, open, continuous, and in opposition to all others, including the owner.

LEARNING OBJECTIVE 4

What are the requirements for acquiring property by adverse possession?

Requirements for Adverse Possession For property to be held adversely, four elements must be satisfied:

1. *Possession must be actual and exclusive.* The possessor must physically occupy the property. This requirement is clearly met if the possessor lives on the property, but it may also be met if the possessor builds fences, erects structures, plants crops, or even grazes animals on the land.

2. *The possession must be open, visible, and notorious,* not secret or clandestine. The possessor must occupy the land for all the world to see. The obviousness requirement ensures that the true owner is on notice that someone is possessing the owner's property wrongfully.

3. *Possession must be continuous and peaceable for the required period of time.* This requirement means that the possessor must not be interrupted in the occupancy by the true owner or by the courts. *Continuous* does not mean constant. It simply means that the possessor has continuously occupied the property in some fashion for the statutory time. *Peaceable* means that no force was used to possess the land.

4. *Possession must be hostile and adverse.* In other words, the possessor cannot be living on the property with the owner's permission and must claim the property as against the whole world.

    CASE EXAMPLE 35.15 Charles Scarborough and Mildred Rollins were adjoining landowners, sharing one common boundary. Based on Rollins's survey of the property, Rollins believed that she owned a portion of a gravel road located to the south of the apartment buildings she owned. In contrast, Scarborough believed that the gravel road was located totally on his property and that he owned some property north of the gravel road toward Rollins's apartment buildings.

    Scarborough filed a complaint seeking a court order stating that he had title to the property and was its sole owner. The court ruled that Rollins owned a portion of the gravel road by adverse possession. She had used it openly for more than thirty-five years, it was generally thought to be part of her apartment complex, and she had paid taxes on it.[9] ■

Purpose of the Doctrine There are a number of public-policy reasons for the adverse possession doctrine. These include society's interest in resolving boundary disputes, determining title when title to property is in question, and ensuring that real property remains in the stream of commerce. More fundamentally, the doctrine punishes owners who do not take action when they see adverse possession and rewards possessors for putting land to productive use.

35–3e Eminent Domain

No ownership rights in real property can ever really be absolute. Even ownership in fee simple absolute is limited by a superior ownership. The U.S. government has an ultimate ownership right in all land. This right, known as **eminent domain,** is sometimes referred to as the *condemnation power* of government to take land for public use. It gives the government the right to acquire possession of real property in the manner directed by the U.S. Constitution and the laws of the state whenever the public interest requires it. Property normally may be taken only for public use, not for private benefit.

    The power of eminent domain generally is invoked through **condemnation proceedings** that occur before a judge. For instance, when a new public highway is to be built, the government must decide where to build it and how much land it needs. After the government determines that a particular parcel of land is necessary for public use, it will first offer to buy

Eminent Domain The power of a government to take land from private citizens for public use on the payment of just compensation.

Condemnation Proceedings The judicial procedure by which the government exercises its power of eminent domain. It generally involves two phases: a taking and a determination of fair value.

---

9. *Scarborough v. Rollins*, 44 So.3d 381 (2010).

the property. If the owner refuses the offer, the government brings a judicial (*condemnation*) proceeding to obtain title to the land.

Condemnation proceedings usually involve two distinct phases—the first to establish the government's right to take the property, and the second to determine the fair value of the property.

The Taking When the government takes land owned by a private party for public use, it is referred to as a **taking.** Under the *takings clause* of the Fifth Amendment to the U.S. Constitution, the government may take private property for public use with just compensation to the property owner. State constitutions contain similar provisions. In the first phase of condemnation proceedings, the government must prove that it needs to acquire privately owned property for a public use.

EXAMPLE 35.16 Bosque Systems proposes to build a liquefied natural gas pipeline across the property of more than two hundred landowners in Franklin County, Iowa. Some property owners consent to this use and accept Bosque's offer of compensation. Others refuse the firm's offer. A court will likely deem Bosque's pipeline to be a public use. Therefore, the government can exert its eminent domain power to "take" the land, provided that it pays just compensation to the property owners. ■

The Compensation The U.S. Constitution and state constitutions require that the government pay just compensation to the landowner when invoking its condemnation power. Just compensation means fair value. In the second phase of the condemnation proceeding, the court determines the fair value of the land, which usually is approximately equal to its market value.

> **Taking** The taking of private property by the government for public use through the power of eminent domain.

Should eminent domain be used to promote private development? Issues of fairness often arise when the government takes private property for public use. One issue is whether it is fair for a government to take property by eminent domain and then convey it to private developers. For example, suppose a city government decides that it is in the public interest to have a larger parking lot for a local, privately owned sports stadium or to have a manufacturing plant locate in the city to create more jobs. The government may condemn certain tracts of existing housing or business property and then convey the land to the privately owned stadium or manufacturing plant. Such actions may bring in private developers and businesses that provide jobs and increase tax revenues, thus revitalizing communities. But is the land really being taken for "public use," as required by the Fifth Amendment to the U.S. Constitution?

In 2005, the United States Supreme Court ruled that the power of eminent domain may be used to further economic development.[10] At the same time, the Court recognized that individual states have the right to pass laws that prohibit takings for economic development. Since then, the vast majority of the states have passed laws to curb the government's ability to take private property and subsequently give it to private developers. Nevertheless, loopholes in some state legislation would still allow takings for redevelopment of slum areas. Thus, the debate over whether (and when) it is fair for the government to take citizens' property for economic development continues.

ETHICAL ISSUE

35-4 Landlord-Tenant Relationships

A landlord-tenant relationship is established by a lease contract. In most states, statutes require leases for terms exceeding one year to be in writing. The lease should describe the property and indicate the length of the term, the amount of the rent, and how and when it is to be paid.

> **KNOW THIS**
> Sound business practice dictates that a lease for commercial property should be written carefully and should clearly define the parties' rights and obligations.

---

10. See *Kelo v. City of New London, Connecticut,* 545 U.S. 469, 125 S.Ct. 2655, 162 L.Ed.2d 439 (2005).

State or local law often dictates permissible lease terms, particularly in residential leases. For instance, a statute or ordinance might prohibit the leasing of a structure that is not in compliance with local building codes. As in other areas of law, the National Conference of Commissioners on Uniform State Laws has issued a model act to create more uniformity in the laws governing landlord-tenant relationships. Twenty-one states have adopted variations of the Uniform Residential Landlord and Tenant Act (URLTA).

35-4a Rights and Duties

The rights and duties of landlords and tenants generally pertain to four broad areas of concern—the possession, use, and maintenance of the leased property and, of course, rent.

Possession A landlord is obligated to give a tenant possession of the property that the tenant has agreed to lease. After obtaining possession, the tenant retains the property exclusively until the lease expires, unless the lease states otherwise.

Quiet Enjoyment. The covenant of quiet enjoyment mentioned previously also applies to leased premises. Under this covenant, the landlord promises that during the lease term, neither the landlord nor anyone having a superior title to the property will disturb the tenant's use and enjoyment of the property. This covenant forms the essence of the landlord-tenant relationship, and if it is breached, the tenant can terminate the lease and sue for damages.

Eviction. If the landlord deprives the tenant of possession of the leased property or interferes with the tenant's use or enjoyment of it, an **eviction** occurs. **EXAMPLE 35.17** Enrique is the landlord at Sunrise Meadow Apartments. One day, Enrique changes the locks on Emily's apartment door and refuses to give her a new key. Enrique has evicted Emily from her apartment. ■

A **constructive eviction** occurs when the landlord wrongfully performs or fails to perform any of the duties the lease requires, thereby making the tenant's further use and enjoyment of the property exceedingly difficult or impossible. Examples of constructive eviction include a landlord's failure to provide heat in the winter, electricity, or other essential utilities.

Use of the Premises The tenant normally may make any use of the leased property, provided the use is legal and does not injure the landlord's interest. The parties are free to limit by agreement the uses to which the property may be put.

Maintenance of the Premises The tenant is responsible for any damage to the premises that he or she causes, intentionally or negligently, and may be held liable for the cost of returning the property to the physical condition it was in when the lease began. Unless the parties have agreed otherwise, the tenant is not responsible for ordinary wear and tear and the property's consequent depreciation in value.

In some jurisdictions, landlords of residential property are required by statute to maintain the premises in good repair. Landlords must also comply with any applicable state statutes and city ordinances regarding maintenance and repair of buildings.

In addition, the implied warranty of habitability discussed earlier may apply to *residential* leases. The warranty requires a landlord who leases residential property to ensure that the premises are habitable—that is, a safe and suitable place for people to live. Also, the landlord must make repairs to maintain the premises in that condition for the lease's duration.

Generally, this warranty applies to major, or *substantial,* physical defects that the landlord knows or should know about and has had a reasonable time to repair—such as a large hole in the roof or a broken heating system. **EXAMPLE 35.18** Carol and Ken Galprin own a house within the city limits of Redmond. A city regulation states that a residence must be connected to the city sewer system before anyone, including tenants, can live in the residence. The Galprins' house is not connected to the city system. Thus, it is not legally habitable, and they cannot lease it to tenants. ■

LEARNING OBJECTIVE 5
What are the duties of the landlord and the tenant with respect to the use and maintenance of leased property?

Eviction A landlord's act of depriving a tenant of possession of the leased premises.

Constructive Eviction A form of eviction that occurs when a landlord fails to perform adequately any of the duties required by the lease, thereby making the tenant's further use and enjoyment of the property exceedingly difficult or impossible.

KNOW THIS
Options that may be available to a tenant on a landlord's breach of the implied warranty of habitability include repairing the defect and deducting the cost from the rent, canceling the lease, and suing for damages.

Rent *Rent* is the tenant's payment to the landlord for the tenant's occupancy or use of the landlord's real property. Usually, the tenant must pay the rent even if she or he refuses to occupy the property or moves out, as long as the refusal or the move is unjustified and the lease is in force.

EXAMPLE 35.19 Lifetime Insurance Agency enters into a lease with Mallory for a suite of offices in Mallory's building. Lifetime's revenue is less than managers had projected, however, and the rent is now more than they want to pay. Lifetime vacates the offices before the end of the lease. In terms of the landlord-tenant relationship, the move is unjustified, and the lease remains in force. Lifetime must continue to pay the rent. ■

Under the common law, if the leased premises were destroyed by fire or flood, the tenant still had to pay rent. Today, however, if an apartment building is destroyed, most states' laws do not require tenants to continue to pay rent.

In some situations, such as when a landlord breaches the implied warranty of habitability, a tenant may be allowed to withhold rent as a remedy. When rent withholding is authorized under a statute, the tenant must usually put the amount withheld into an *escrow account*. The funds are held in the name of the tenant and are returned to the tenant if the landlord fails to make the premises habitable.

Commercial Lease Terms State statutes often allow tenants and landlords more flexibility in negotiating the terms of a commercial lease. **CASE EXAMPLE 35.20** Lynwood Place, LLC, owned an office building in Newtown, Connecticut. Sandy Hook Hydro, LLC, agreed to lease a part of the building containing a hydroelectric turbine. The lease required Sandy Hook to pay a base annual rent, plus an additional amount of rent equal to 6 percent of any increase in operating expenses incurred by the landlord. "Operating expenses" included all costs of maintenance and repair related to the premises.

When Sandy Hook did not pay the additional rent due under this provision, Lynwood Place filed a suit in a Connecticut state court to take immediate possession of the property. The court issued a judgment in the landlord's favor. The tenant appealed, but the reviewing court affirmed. The court concluded that Sandy Hook had signed the lease, which clearly indicated that the rent was subject to a 6 percent increase for operating expenses. Therefore, even though Sandy Hook occupied only part of the building, the lease gave the landlord the right to increase its rent by that amount.[11] ■

35–4b Transferring Rights to Leased Property

Either the landlord or the tenant may wish to transfer her or his rights to the leased property during the term of the lease. If a landlord transfers complete title to the leased property to another, the tenant becomes the tenant of the new owner. The new owner may collect subsequent rent but must abide by the terms of the existing lease.

If a lessee agrees to rent a part of a building that houses a turbine, what happens when the lessee doesn't pay the agreed-upon annual increase in lease payments?

Assignment The tenant's transfer of his or her entire interest in the leased property to a third person is an *assignment* of the lease. Many leases require the landlord's written consent for an assignment to be valid. The landlord can nullify (avoid) an assignment made without the required consent and evict the assignee. State statutes may specify that the landlord may not unreasonably withhold consent, however. Also, a landlord who knowingly accepts rent from the assignee may be held to have waived the consent requirement.

When an assignment is valid, the assignee acquires all of the tenant's rights under the lease. Nevertheless, an assignment does not release the original tenant (the assignor) from

---

11. *Lynwood Place, LLC v. Sandy Hook Hydro, LLC*, 150 Conn.App. 682, 92 A.3d 996 (2014).

the obligation to pay rent should the assignee default. In addition, if the assignee exercises an option under the original lease to extend the term, the assignor remains liable for the rent during the extension, unless the landlord agrees otherwise.

Subleases   The tenant's transfer of all or part of the premises for a period shorter than the lease term is a **sublease.** Many leases also require the landlord's written consent for a sublease. If the landlord's consent is required, a sublease without such permission is ineffective. Also, like an assignment, a sublease does not release the tenant from her or his obligations under the lease.

> **Sublease**   A tenant's transfer of all or part of the leased premises to a third person for a period shorter than the lease term.

EXAMPLE 35.21 Derek, a student, leases an apartment for a two-year period. Although Derek had planned on attending summer school, he decides to accept a job offer in Europe for the summer months instead. Derek therefore obtains his landlord's consent to sublease the apartment to Ava. Ava is bound by the same terms of the lease as Derek, and the landlord can hold Derek liable if Ava violates the lease terms. ■

35-4c Termination of the Lease

Usually, a lease terminates when its term ends. The tenant surrenders the property to the landlord, who retakes possession. If the lease states the time it will end, the landlord is not required to give the tenant notice. The lease terminates automatically.

A lease can also be terminated in several other ways. If the tenant purchases the leased property from the landlord during the term of the lease, for instance, the lease will be terminated. The parties may also agree to end a tenancy before it would otherwise terminate. In addition, the tenant may *abandon* the premises—move out completely with no intention of returning before the lease term expires.

At common law, a tenant who abandoned leased property was still obligated to pay the rent for the full term of the lease. The landlord could let the property stand vacant and charge the tenant for the remainder of the term. This is still the rule in some states. In most states today, however, the landlord has a duty to *mitigate* his or her damages—that is, to make a reasonable attempt to lease the property to another party. Consequently, the tenant's liability for unpaid rent is restricted to the period of time that the landlord would reasonably need to lease the property to another tenant. Damages may also be allowed for the landlord's costs in leasing the property again.

> "Even in hell the peasant will have to serve the landlord, for, while the landlord is boiling in a cauldron, the peasant will have to put wood under it."
>
> **RUSSIAN PROVERB**

Reviewing . . . Real Property and Landlord-Tenant Law

Vern Shoepke bought a two-story home in Roche, Maine. The warranty deed did not specify what covenants would be included in the conveyance. The property was adjacent to a public park that included a popular Frisbee golf course. (Frisbee golf is a sport similar to golf but using Frisbees.) Wayakichi Creek ran along the north end of the park and along Shoepke's property. The deed allowed Roche citizens the right to walk across a five-foot-wide section of the lot beside Wayakichi Creek as part of a two-mile public trail system. Teenagers regularly threw Frisbee golf discs from the walking path behind Shoepke's property over his yard to the adjacent park. Shoepke habitually shouted and cursed at the teenagers, demanding that they not throw the discs over his yard.

Two months after moving into his Roche home, Shoepke leased the second floor to Lauren Slater for nine months. (The lease agreement did not specify that Shoepke's consent would be required to sublease the second floor.) After three months of tenancy, Slater sublet the second floor to a local artist, Javier Indalecio. Over the remaining six months, Indalecio's use of oil paints damaged the carpeting in Shoepke's home. Using the information presented in the chapter, answer the following questions.

1. What is the term for the right of Roche citizens to walk across Shoepke's land on the trail?

2. What covenants would most courts infer were included in the warranty deed that Shoepke received when he bought his house?

3. Can Shoepke hold Slater financially responsible for the damage to the carpeting caused by Indalecio? Explain.

4. Could the fact that teenagers continually throw Frisbees over Shoepke's yard outside the second-floor windows arguably be a breach of the covenant of quiet enjoyment? Why or why not?

DEBATE THIS

- Under no circumstances should a local government be able to condemn property in order to sell it later to real estate developers for private use.

Key Terms

Chapter Summary: Real Property and Landlord-Tenant Law

The Nature of Real Property	Real property (also called real estate or realty) includes land, subsurface and airspace rights, plant life and vegetation, and fixtures.

Ownership Interests and Leases	1. *Fee simple*—The most complete form of ownership. Owners can use, possess, or dispose of the property as they choose during their lifetimes and pass on the property to their heirs at death.
	2. *Life estate*—An estate that lasts for the life of a specified individual, during which time the individual is entitled to possess, use, and benefit from the estate. The life tenant's ownership rights cease to exist on her or his death.
	3. *Concurrent interests*—When two or more persons hold title to property together, concurrent ownership exists.
	  a. A *tenancy in common* exists when two or more persons own an undivided interest in property. On a tenant's death, that tenant's property interest passes to his or her heirs.
	  b. A *joint tenancy* exists when two or more persons own an undivided interest in property, with a right of survivorship. On the death of a joint tenant, that tenant's property interest transfers to the remaining tenant(s), not to the heirs of the deceased.
	  c. A *tenancy by the entirety* is a form of co-ownership between married persons that is similar to a joint tenancy, except that a spouse cannot separately transfer her or his interest during her or his lifetime.
	  d. *Community property* is a form of co-ownership between married persons in which each spouse technically owns an undivided one-half interest in property acquired during the marriage. This type of ownership exists in only a few states.

Continues

Ownership Interests and Leases (Continued)	**4.** *Leasehold estates*—A leasehold estate is an interest in real property that is held for only a limited period of time, as specified in the lease agreement. Types of tenancies relating to leased property include the following:
	  a. Fixed-term tenancy (tenancy for years)—Tenancy for a period of time stated by express contract.
	  b. Periodic tenancy—Tenancy for a period determined by the frequency of rent payments. It is automatically renewed unless proper notice is given.
	  c. Tenancy at will—Tenancy for as long as both parties agree. No notice of termination is required.
	  d. Tenancy at sufferance—Possession of land without legal right.
	5. *Nonpossessory interest*—An interest that involves the right to use real property but not to possess it. Easements, profits, and licenses are nonpossessory interests.

Transfer of Ownership	**1.** *By deed*—When real property is sold or transferred as a gift, title to the property is conveyed by means of a deed. A deed must meet specific legal requirements. A *warranty deed* provides the most extensive protection against defects of title. A *quitclaim deed* conveys to the grantee only whatever interest the grantor had in the property. A deed may be recorded in the manner prescribed by *recording statutes* in the appropriate jurisdiction to give third parties notice of the owner's interest. **2.** *By will or inheritance*—If the owner dies after having made a valid will, the land passes as specified in the will. If the owner dies without having made a will, the heirs inherit according to state inheritance statutes. **3.** *By adverse possession*—When a person possesses the property of another for a statutory period of time (ten years is the most common), that person acquires title to the property, provided the possession is actual and exclusive, open and visible, continuous and peaceable, and hostile and adverse (without the permission of the owner). **4.** *By eminent domain*—The government can take land for public use, with just compensation, when the public interest requires the taking.

Landlord-Tenant Relationships	**1.** *Lease agreement*—The landlord-tenant relationship is created by a lease agreement. State or local laws may dictate whether the lease must be in writing and what lease terms are permissible.
	2. *Rights and duties*—The rights and duties that arise under a lease agreement generally pertain to the following areas:
	  a. Possession—The tenant has an exclusive right to possess the leased premises. Under the covenant of quiet enjoyment, the landlord promises that during the lease term, neither the landlord nor anyone having superior title to the property will disturb the tenant's use and enjoyment of the property.
	  b. Use of the premises—Unless the parties agree otherwise, the tenant may make any legal use of the property.
	  c. Maintenance of the premises—The tenant is responsible for any damage that he or she causes. The landlord must comply with laws that set specific standards for the maintenance of real property. The implied warranty of habitability requires that the landlord furnish and maintain residential premises in a habitable condition (that is, in a condition safe and suitable for human life).
	  d. Rent—The tenant must pay the rent as long as the lease is in force, unless the tenant justifiably refuses to occupy the property or withholds the rent because of the landlord's failure to maintain the premises properly.
	3. *Transferring rights to leased property*—
	  a. If the landlord transfers complete title to the leased property, the tenant becomes the tenant of the new owner. The new owner may collect the rent but must abide by the existing lease.
	  b. Generally, in the absence of an agreement to the contrary, tenants may assign their rights (but not their duties) under a lease contract to a third person. Tenants may also sublease leased property to a third person, but the original tenant is not relieved of any obligations to the landlord under the lease. In either situation, the landlord's consent may be required, but statutes may prohibit the landlord from unreasonably withholding consent.

Issue Spotters

1. Bernie sells his house to Consuela under a warranty deed. Later, Delmira appears, holding a better title to the house than Consuela has. Delmira wants Consuela off the property. What can Consuela do? (See *Transfer of Ownership*.)

2. Grey owns a commercial building in fee simple. Grey transfers temporary possession of the building to Haven Corporation. Can Haven transfer possession for even less time to Idyll Company? Explain. (See *Landlord-Tenant Relationships*.)

—**Check your answers to the *Issue Spotters* against the answers provided in Appendix D at the end of this text.**

Learning Objectives Check

1. What is a fixture, and how does it relate to real property rights?
2. What is the difference between a joint tenancy and a tenancy in common?
3. What is an easement? What are three ways in which an easement can be created?
4. What are the requirements for acquiring property by adverse possession?
5. What are the duties of the landlord and the tenant with respect to the use and maintenance of leased property?

—Answers to the even-numbered *Learning Objectives Check* questions can be found in Appendix E at the end of this text.

Business Scenarios and Case Problems

35–1. Property Ownership. Twenty-two years ago, Lorenz was a wanderer. At that time, he decided to settle down on an unoccupied, three-acre parcel of land that he did not own. People in the area told him that they had no idea who owned the property. Lorenz built a house on the land, got married, and raised three children while living there. He fenced in the land, installed a gate with a sign above it that read "Lorenz's Homestead," and removed trespassers. Lorenz is now confronted by Joe Reese, who has a deed in his name as owner of the property. Reese, claiming ownership of the land, orders Lorenz and his family off the property. Discuss who has the better "title" to the property. (See *Transfer of Ownership*.)

35–2. Deeds. Wiley and Gemma are neighbors. Wiley's lot is extremely large, and his present and future use of it will not involve the entire area. Gemma wants to build a single-car garage and driveway along the present lot boundary. Because the placement of her existing structures makes it impossible for her to comply with an ordinance requiring buildings to be set back fifteen feet from an adjoining property line, Gemma cannot build the garage. Gemma contracts to purchase ten feet of Wiley's property along their boundary line for $3,000. Wiley is willing to sell but will give Gemma only a quitclaim deed, whereas Gemma wants a warranty deed. Discuss the differences between these deeds as they would affect the rights of the parties if the title to this ten feet of land later proves to be defective. (See *Transfer of Ownership*.)

35–3. Implied Warranty of Habitability. Sarah has rented a house from Frank. The house is only two years old, but the roof leaks every time it rains. The water that has accumulated in the attic has caused stucco to fall off ceilings in the upstairs bedrooms, and one ceiling has started to sag. Sarah has complained to Frank and asked him to have the roof repaired. Frank says that he has caulked the roof, but the roof still leaks. Frank claims that because Sarah has sole control of the leased premises, she has the duty to repair the roof. Sarah insists that repairing the roof is Frank's responsibility. Discuss fully who is responsible for repairing the roof and, if the responsibility belongs to Frank, what remedies are available to Sarah. (See *Landlord-Tenant Relationships*.)

35–4. Commercial Lease Terms. Gi Hwa Park entered into a lease with Landmark HHH, LLC, for retail space in the Plaza at Landmark, a shopping center in Virginia. The lease provided that the landlord would keep the roof "in good repair" and that the tenant would obtain insurance on her inventory and absolve the landlord from any losses to the extent of the insurance proceeds. Park opened a store—The Four Seasons—in the space, specializing in imported men's suits and accessories. Within a month of the store's opening and continuing for nearly eight years, water intermittently leaked through the roof, causing damage. Landmark eventually had a new roof installed, but water continued to leak into The Four Seasons. On a night of record rainfall, the store suffered substantial water damage, and Park was forced to close the store. On what basis might Park seek to recover from Landmark? What might Landmark assert in response? Which party's argument is more likely to succeed, and why? [*Landmark HHH, LLC v. Gi Hwa Park,* 277 Va. 50, 671 S.E.2d 143 (2009)] (See *Landlord-Tenant Relationships*.)

35–5. Business Case Problem with Sample Answer—Adverse Possession. The McKeag family operated a marina on their lakefront property in Bolton, New York. For more than forty years, the McKeags used a section of property belonging to their neighbors, the Finleys, as a beach for the marina's customers. The McKeags also stored a large float on the beach during the winter months, built their own retaining wall, and planted bushes and flowers there. The McKeags prevented others from using the property, including the Finleys. Nevertheless, the families always had a friendly relationship, and one of the Finleys gave the McKeags permission to continue using the beach in 1992. He also reminded them of his ownership several times, to which they said nothing. The McKeags also asked for permission to mow grass on the property and once apologized for leaving a jet ski there. Can the McKeags establish adverse possession over the statutory period of ten years? Why or why not? [*McKeag v. Finley,* 939 N.Y.S.2d 644 (N.Y.App.Div. 2012)] (See *Transfer of Ownership*.)

—For a sample answer to Problem 35–5, go to Appendix F at the end of this text.

35–6. Rent. Flawlace, LLC, leased unfinished commercial real estate in Las Vegas, Nevada, from Francis Lin to operate a beauty salon. The lease required Flawlace to obtain a "certificate of occupancy" from the city to commence business. This required the installation of a fire protection system. The lease did not allocate responsibility for the installation to either party. Lin voluntarily undertook to install the system. After a month of delays, Flawlace moved out. Three months later, the installation was complete, and Lin leased the premises to a new tenant. Did Flawlace owe rent for the three months between the time that it moved out and the time that the new tenant moved in? Explain. [*Tri-Lin Holdings, LLC v. Flawlace, LLC*, 2014 WL 1101577 (Nev.Sup.Ct. 2014)] (See *Landlord-Tenant Relationships*.)

35–7. Landlord-Tenant Relationships. Bhanmattie Kumar was walking on a sidewalk in Flushing, New York, when she tripped over a chipped portion of the sidewalk and fell. The defective sidewalk was in front of a Pretty Girl store—one of a chain of apparel stores headquartered in Brooklyn—on premises leased from PI Associates, LLC. Kumar filed a claim in a New York state court against PI, seeking to recover damages for her injuries.

PI filed a cross-claim against Pretty Girl. On what basis would the court impose liability on PI? In what situation would Pretty Girl be the liable party? Is there any circumstance in which Kumar could be at least partially responsible for her injury? Discuss. [*Bhanmattie Rajkumar Kumar v. PI Associates, LLC,* 125 A.D.3d 609, 3 N.Y.S.3d 372 (2 Dept. 2015)] (See *Landlord-Tenant Relationships*.)

35–8. A Question of Ethics—Adverse Possession. Alana Mansell built a garage on her property that encroached on the property of her neighbor, Betty Hunter, by fourteen feet. Hunter knew of the encroachment and informally agreed to it, but she did not transfer ownership of the property to Mansell. A survey twenty-eight years later confirmed the encroachment, and Hunter sought the removal of the garage. Mansell asked a court to declare that she was the owner of the property by adverse possession. [*Hunter v. Mansell,* 240 P.3d 469 (Colo.App. 2010)] (See *Transfer of Ownership*.)

1. Did Mansell obtain title by adverse possession? Would the open occupation of the property for nearly thirty years be in Mansell's favor? Why or why not?

2. Was Mansell's conduct in any way unethical? Discuss.

Critical Thinking and Writing Assignments

35–9. Case Analysis Question. Go to Appendix G at the end of this text and examine the excerpt of Case No. 7, *Town of Midland v. Morris*. Review and then brief the case, making sure that your brief answers the following questions. (See *Transfer of Ownership*.)

1. **Issue:** On what issue did the parties ask the court to focus?

2. **Rule of Law:** What rule or test did the court apply?

3. **Applying the Rule of Law:** How did the court apply the rule to the facts in this case?

4. **Conclusion:** What did the court conclude? Why?

35–10. Business Law Critical Thinking Group Assignment. The Wallen family owned a cabin on Lummi Island in the state of Washington. A driveway ran from the cabin across their property to South Nugent Road. Floyd Massey bought the adjacent lot and built a cabin on it in 1983. To gain access to his property, Massey used a bulldozer to extend the driveway, without the Wallens' permission but also without their objection. In 2008, the Wallens sold their property to Wright Fish Company. Massey continued to use and maintain the driveway without permission or objection. In 2013, Massey

sold his property to Robert Drake. Drake and his employees continued to use and maintain the driveway without permission or objection, although Drake knew it was located largely on Wright's property. In 2015, Wright sold its lot to Robert Smersh. The next year, Smersh told Drake to stop using the driveway. Drake filed a suit against Smersh, claiming an easement by prescription (which is created by meeting the same requirements as adverse possession). (See *Transfer of Ownership*.)

1. The first group will decide whether Drake's use of the driveway meets all of the requirements for adverse possession (easement by prescription).

2. The second group will determine how the court should rule in this case and why. Does it matter that Drake knew the driveway was located largely on Wright's (and then Smersh's) property? Should it matter?

3. The third group will evaluate the underlying policy and fairness of adverse possession laws. Should the law reward persons who take possession of someone else's land for their own use? Does it make sense to punish owners who allow someone else to use their land without complaint?

iStockPhoto.com/AnthiaCumming

Insurance, Wills, and Trusts

LEARNING OBJECTIVES

The five Learning Objectives *below are designed to help improve your understanding of the chapter. After reading this chapter, you should be able to answer the following questions:*

1. What is an insurable interest? When must an insurable interest exist?

2. How do courts interpret ambiguities in an insurance policy?

3. What are the basic requirements for executing a will?

4. What is the difference between a *per stirpes* distribution and a *per capita* distribution of an estate to the grandchildren of the deceased?

5. What are the four essential elements of a trust?

"Insurance is part charity and part business, but all common sense."

CALVIN COOLIDGE
1872–1933
(THIRTIETH PRESIDENT OF THE
UNITED STATES, 1923–1929)

Most individuals insure their real and personal property (as well as their lives). As Calvin Coolidge asserted in the chapter-opening quotation, insurance is "all common sense"—by insuring our property, we protect ourselves against damage and loss. In the first part of this chapter, we focus on insurance, which is a foremost concern of all property owners.

In the remainder of the chapter, we examine how property is transferred on the death of its owner. Certainly, the laws governing such transfers are a necessary corollary to the concept of private ownership of property. Our laws require that on death, title to the property of the decedent (the one who has died) must be delivered in full somewhere. This can be done through wills, trusts, or state laws prescribing distribution of property among heirs or next of kin.

In today's world, a person's property may include social media. We discuss social media estate planning later in the chapter.

36-1 Insurance

Many precautions may be taken to protect against the hazards of life. For instance, an individual may wear a seat belt to protect against injuries from automobile accidents and install smoke detectors to guard against injury from fire. Of course, no one can predict whether an accident or a fire will ever occur, but individuals and businesses must establish plans to protect their personal and financial interests should some event threaten to undermine their security.

Insurance A contract by which the insurer promises to reimburse the insured or a beneficiary in the event that the insured is injured, dies, or sustains damage to property as a result of particular, stated contingencies.

Risk Management In the context of insurance, the transfer of certain risks from the insured to the insurance company by contractual agreement.

Risk A prediction concerning potential loss based on known and unknown factors.

Insurance is a contract by which the insurance company (the insurer) promises to pay an amount or to give something of value to another (either the insured or the beneficiary) in the event that the insured is injured, dies, or sustains damage to her or his property as a result of particular, stated contingencies. Basically, insurance is an arrangement for *transferring and allocating risk*—that is, for **risk management.** In many instances, **risk** can be described as a prediction concerning potential loss based on known and unknown factors.

Risk management normally involves the transfer of certain risks from the individual to the insurance company by a contractual agreement. The insurance contract and its provisions will be examined shortly. First, however, we look at the different types of insurance that can be obtained, insurance terminology, and the concept of insurable interest.

36–1a Classifications of Insurance

Insurance is classified according to the nature of the risk involved. For instance, fire insurance, casualty insurance, life insurance, and title insurance apply to different types of risk and protect different interests. This is reasonable because the types of losses that are expected and that are foreseeable or unforeseeable vary with the nature of the activity.

Exhibit 36–1 presents a list of selected insurance classifications. For a discussion of insurance policies designed to cover the special kinds of risks faced by online businesses, see the *Business Application* feature at the end of this chapter.

36–1b Insurance Terminology

Policy In insurance law, the contract between the insurer and the insured.

Premium In insurance law, the price paid by the insured for insurance protection for a specified period of time.

Underwriter In insurance law, the insurer, or the one assuming a risk in return for the payment of a premium.

An insurance contract is called a **policy,** the consideration paid to the insurer is called a **premium,** and the insurance company is sometimes called an **underwriter.** The parties to an insurance policy are the *insurer* (the insurance company) and the *insured* (the person covered by its provisions or the holder of the policy).

Insurance contracts are usually obtained through an *agent,* who ordinarily works for the insurance company, or through a *broker,* who is ordinarily an *independent contractor.* When a broker deals with an applicant for insurance, the broker is, in effect, the applicant's agent and not an agent of the insurance company. In contrast, an insurance agent is an agent of the insurance company, not of the applicant. Thus, the agent owes fiduciary duties to the insurance company, but not to the person who is applying for insurance. As a general rule, the insurance company is bound by the acts of its agents when they act within the scope of the agency relationship.

36–1c Insurable Interest

A person can insure anything in which she or he has an **insurable interest.** Without an insurable interest, there is no enforceable insurance contract, and a transaction to purchase insurance coverage would have to be treated as a wager.

LEARNING OBJECTIVE 1
What is an insurable interest? When must an insurable interest exist?

Insurable Interest An interest that exists when a person benefits from the preservation of the health or life of the insured or the property to be insured.

Life Insurance In regard to life insurance, a person must have a reasonable expectation of benefit from the continued life of another in order to have an insurable interest in that person's life. The insurable interest must exist *at the time the policy is obtained.* The benefit may be pecuniary (monetary) or it may be founded on the relationship between the parties (by blood or affinity).

Key-person insurance is a type of life insurance obtained by an organization on the life of a person (such as a talented executive) who is important to that organization. Because the organization expects to experience some financial gain from the continuation of the key person's life or some financial loss from the key person's death, the organization has an insurable interest.

Exhibit 36–1 Selected Insurance Classifications

TYPE OF INSURANCE	COVERAGE
Accident	Covers expenses, losses, and suffering incurred by the insured because of accidents causing physical injury and any consequent disability; sometimes includes a specified payment to heirs of the insured if death results from an accident.
All-risk	Covers all losses that the insured may incur except those that are specifically excluded. Typical exclusions are war, pollution, earthquakes, and floods.
Automobile	May cover damage to automobiles resulting from specified hazards or occurrences (such as fire, vandalism, theft, or collision); normally provides protection against liability for personal injuries and property damage resulting from the operation of the vehicle.
Casualty	Protects against losses incurred by the insured as a result of being held liable for personal injuries or property damage sustained by others.
Disability	Replaces a portion of the insured's monthly income from employment in the event that illness or injury causes a short- or long-term disability. Some states require employers to provide short-term disability insurance. Benefits typically last a set period of time, such as six months for short-term coverage or five years for long-term coverage.
Fire	Covers losses incurred by the insured as a result of fire.
Floater	Covers movable property, as long as the property is within the territorial boundaries specified in the contract.
Homeowners'	Protects homeowners against some or all risks of loss to their residences and the residences' contents or liability arising from the use of the property.
Key-person	Protects a business in the event of the death or disability of a key employee.
Liability	Protects against liability imposed on the insured as a result of injuries to the person or property of another.
Life	Covers the death of the policyholder. On the death of the insured, the insurer pays the amount specified in the policy to the insured's beneficiary.
Major medical	Protects the insured against major hospital, medical, or surgical expenses.
Malpractice	Protects professionals (physicians, lawyers, and others) against malpractice claims brought against them by their patients or clients; a form of liability insurance.
Term life	Provides life insurance for a specified period of time (term) with no cash surrender value; usually renewable.

Property Insurance In regard to real and personal property, an insurable interest exists when the insured derives a pecuniary (monetary) benefit from the preservation and continued existence of the property. Put another way, a person has an insurable interest in property when she or he would sustain a financial loss from its destruction. For property insurance, the insurable interest must exist at the time the loss occurs but need not exist when the policy is purchased.

The existence of an insurable interest is a primary concern in determining liability under an insurance policy. **CASE EXAMPLE 36.1** ABM Industries, Inc., leased office and storage space in the World Trade Center (WTC) in New York City in 2001. ABM also ran the building's heating, ventilation, and air-conditioning systems, and maintained all of the WTC's common areas. At the time, ABM employed more than eight hundred workers at the WTC. Zurich American Insurance Company insured ABM against losses resulting from "business interruption" caused by direct physical loss or damage "to property owned, controlled, used, leased or intended for use" by ABM.

After the World Trade Center was destroyed on September 11, 2001, should the company providing maintenance have been reimbursed by its insurance company for all of its income losses?

After the terrorist attacks on September 11, 2001, ABM filed a claim with Zurich to recover for the loss of all income derived from ABM's WTC operations. Zurich argued that ABM's recovery should be limited to the income lost as a result of the destruction of ABM's office and storage space and supplies. A court, however, ruled that ABM was entitled to compensation for the loss of all of its WTC operations. The court reasoned that the "policy's scope expressly includes real or personal property that the insured 'used,' 'controlled,' or 'intended for use.'" Because ABM's income depended on "the common areas and leased premises in the WTC complex," it had an insurable interest in that property at the time of the loss.[1] ▇

In the following case, the plaintiff sought to retain his insurable interest in a home he no longer owned.

CASE 36.1

Breeden v. Buchanan

Court of Appeals of Mississippi, __ So. 3d __, 2015 WL 433621 (2015).

FACTS Donald Breeden and Willie Buchanan were married in Marion County, Mississippi. They lived in a home in Sandy Hook. Nationwide Property & Casualty Insurance Company insured the home under a policy bought by Breeden that named him as the insured. The policy provided that the spouse of the named insured was covered as an insured. After eight years of marriage, Breeden and Buchanan divorced. Breeden transferred his interest in the home to Buchanan as part of the couple's property settlement. Less than a year later, a fire completely destroyed the home. A claim was filed with Nationwide. Nationwide paid Buchanan. Breeden filed a suit in a Mississippi state court against Buchanan and Nationwide, asserting claims for breach of contract and bad faith, and seeking to recover the proceeds under the policy. The court dismissed the suit. Breeden appealed.

ISSUE Did Breeden's one-time right to the proceeds continue after he transferred his interest in the home to his spouse on their divorce?

DECISION No. A state intermediate appellate court affirmed the lower court's dismissal of Breeden's suit. Buchanan, not Breeden, was entitled to the proceeds of the claim filed with Nationwide.

A year after a couple divorces, fire destroys their house. Who should obtain the insurance proceeds?

REASON Breeden's claims against Nationwide were based on the insurance policy. The policy provided that the spouse of the named insured who resided at the premises was also covered. At the beginning of the policy period, both Breeden and Buchanan had an insurable interest in the home because they were married and lived together in it. Later, Breeden transferred his interest in the insured property to Buchanan as part of a property settlement agreement on their divorce. This occurred several months before the fire that caused the loss of the property. For this reason, the lower court ruled that Breeden did not have an "insurable interest" in the property at the time of the loss and thus had no right to the proceeds of the policy. Because Breeden had no insurable interest in the property, Nationwide did not breach the insurance contract or act in bad faith by failing to pay Breeden the insurance proceeds. Based on these circumstances, "there was simply nothing further that Nationwide owed under the insurance policy."

CRITICAL THINKING—Economic Consideration *Why is an insurable interest required for the enforcement of an insurance contract?*

36-1d The Insurance Contract

An insurance contract is governed by the general principles of contract law, although the insurance industry is heavily regulated by the states.[2] Customarily, a party offers to purchase

---

1. *Zurich American Insurance Co. v. ABM Industries, Inc.*, 397 F.3d 158 (2d Cir. 2005).
2. The states were given authority to regulate the insurance industry by the McCarran-Ferguson Act of 1945, 15 U.S.C. Sections 1011–1015.

insurance by submitting an application to the insurance company. The company can either accept or reject the offer. For the contract to be binding, consideration (in the form of a premium) must be given, and the parties forming the contract must have the required contractual capacity to do so.

Application   The filled-in application form for insurance is usually attached to the policy and made a part of the insurance contract. The person applying for insurance normally is bound by any false statements that appear in the application (subject to certain exceptions). Because the insurance company evaluates the risk factors based on the information included in the insurance application, misstatements or misrepresentations can void a policy. This is particularly true if the insurance company can show that it would not have extended insurance if it had known the true facts.

Effective Date   The effective date of an insurance contract—the date on which the insurance coverage begins—is important. In some situations, the insurance applicant is not protected until a formal written policy is issued. In other situations, the applicant is protected between the time the application is received and the time the insurance company either accepts or rejects it. Four facts should be kept in mind:

1. As stated earlier, a broker is an agent of the applicant, not an agent of the insurance company. Therefore, if a person hires a broker to obtain insurance, and the broker fails to procure a policy, the applicant normally is not insured.

2. A person who seeks insurance from an insurance company's agent is usually protected from the moment the application is made, provided—for life insurance—that some form of premium has been paid. Usually, the agent will write a memorandum, or **binder**, indicating that a policy is pending and stating its essential terms.

3. If the parties agree that the policy will be issued and delivered at a later time, the contract is not effective until the policy is issued and delivered. Thus, any loss sustained between the time of application and the delivery of the policy is not covered.

4. Parties may agree that a life insurance policy will be binding at the time the insured pays the first premium, or the policy may be expressly contingent on the applicant's passing a physical examination. If the applicant pays the premium and passes the examination, then the policy coverage is continuously in effect.

   If the applicant pays the premium but dies before having the physical examination, the policy may still be effective. Then, in order to collect, the applicant's estate normally must show that the applicant *would have passed* the examination had he or she not died.

Coinsurance Clauses   Often, when taking out fire insurance policies, property owners insure their property for less than full value because most fires do not result in a total loss. To encourage owners to insure their property for an amount as close to full value as possible, fire insurance policies commonly include a coinsurance clause.

   Typically, a *coinsurance clause* provides that if the owner insures the property up to a specified percentage—usually 80 percent—of its value, she or he will recover any loss up to the face amount of the policy. If the insurance is for less than the specified percentage, the owner is responsible for a proportionate share of the loss.

   Coinsurance applies only in instances of partial loss. The amount of the recovery is calculated by using the following formula:

$$\text{Loss} \times \left(\frac{\text{Amount of Insurance Coverage}}{\text{Coinsurance Percentage} \times \text{Property Value}} \right) = \text{Amount of Recovery}$$

KNOW THIS
The federal government has the power to regulate the insurance industry under the commerce clause of the U.S. Constitution. Instead of exercising this power itself, Congress allows the states to regulate insurance.

Binder   A written, temporary insurance policy.

EXAMPLE 36.2 Madison, who owns property valued at $200,000, takes out a policy in the amount of $100,000. If Madison then suffers a loss of $80,000, her recovery will be $50,000. Madison will be responsible for (coinsure) the balance of the loss, or $30,000, which is the amount of loss ($80,000) minus the amount of recovery ($50,000).

$$\$80{,}000 \times \left(\frac{\$100{,}000}{0.8 \times \$200{,}000} \right) = \$50{,}000$$

If Madison had taken out a policy in the amount of 80 percent of the value of the property, or $160,000, then according to the same formula, she would have recovered the full amount of the loss (the face amount of the policy). ■

Incontestability Clauses Statutes commonly require that a policy for life or health insurance include an **incontestability clause.** Under this clause, after the policy has been in force for a specified length of time—often two or three years—the insurer cannot contest statements made in the application. Once a policy becomes incontestable, the insurer cannot later avoid a claim on the basis of, for instance, fraud on the part of the insured, unless the clause provides an exception for that circumstance.

Some important provisions and clauses that are frequently included in insurance contracts are described in Exhibit 36–2.

Interpreting the Insurance Contract The courts recognize that most people do not have the special training necessary to understand the intricate terminology used in insurance policies. Therefore, when disputes arise, the courts will interpret the words used in an insurance contract according to their ordinary meanings in light of the nature of the coverage involved.

When there is an ambiguity in the policy, the provision generally is interpreted *against the insurance company.* Also, when it is unclear whether an insurance contract actually exists because the written policy has not been delivered, the uncertainty normally is resolved against the insurance company. The court presumes that the policy is in effect unless the company can show otherwise. Similarly, an insurer must make sure that the insured is adequately notified of any change in coverage under an existing policy.

Incontestability Clause
A clause in a policy for life or health insurance stating that after the policy has been in force for a specified length of time (usually two or three years), the insurer cannot contest statements made in the policyholder's application.

LEARNING OBJECTIVE 2

How do courts interpret ambiguities in an insurance policy?

Exhibit 36–2 Insurance Contract Provisions and Clauses

TYPE OF CLAUSE	DESCRIPTION
Antilapse clause	An antilapse clause provides that the policy will not automatically lapse if no payment is made on the date due. Ordinarily, under such a provision, the insured has a *grace period* of thirty or thirty-one days within which to pay an overdue premium before the policy is canceled.
Appraisal clause	Insurance policies frequently provide that if the parties cannot agree on the amount of a loss covered under the policy or the value of the property lost, an appraisal, or estimate, by an impartial and qualified third party can be demanded.
Arbitration clause	Many insurance policies include clauses that call for arbitration of any disputes that arise between the insurer and the insured concerning the settlement of claims.
Incontestability clause	An incontestability clause provides that after a policy has been in force for a specified length of time—usually two or three years—the insurer cannot contest statements made in the application.
Multiple insurance	Many insurance policies include a clause providing that if the insured has multiple insurance policies that cover the same property and the amount of coverage exceeds the loss, the loss will be shared proportionately by the insurance companies.

Disputes over insurance often focus on the application of an exclusion in the policy, as the following case illustrates.

Valero v. Florida Insurance Guaranty Association, Inc.

District Court of Appeal of Florida, Fourth District, 59 So.3d 1166 (2011).

FACTS Alberto and Karelli Mila were insured under a homeowners' liability policy. "Exclusion k" of the policy stated that coverage did not apply to "bodily injury arising out of sexual molestation, corporal punishment or physical or mental abuse." Verushka Valero, on behalf of her child, filed a suit in a Florida state court against the Milas, charging them with negligent supervision of a perpetrator who had sexually molested Valero's child.

The Milas filed a claim asking their insurer to defend against the charges. The insurer had become insolvent, so the claim was submitted to the Florida Insurance Guaranty Association, Inc. (FIGA). FIGA is a nonprofit corporation created by the Florida legislature to evaluate and resolve claims when insurance companies become insolvent (a similar insurance guaranty association exists in nearly every state). FIGA refused to pay the Milas' claim and asked the court to rule that it had no obligation under the policy to provide such a defense. The court issued a summary judgment in FIGA's favor. Valero and the Milas appealed, arguing that exclusion k was ambiguous.

ISSUE Was the term of the Milas' insurance policy that excluded coverage for "bodily injury arising out of sexual molestation" ambiguous as to whether it covered acts by someone under their supervision?

What acts can be excluded from a homeowner's liability policy?

DECISION No. A state intermediate appellate court affirmed the lower court's judgment. The exclusion applied to preclude coverage in this case.

REASON The Milas pointed out that a different exclusion, exclusion l, used the phrase "by any person," and exclusion k did not. Thus, the Milas contended, it was not clear whether exclusion k applied only to acts of an insured. The court read the entire list of twelve exclusions together and concluded that the phrase in exclusion l was "superfluous." Even if the phrase "by any person" had been used in exclusion k, coverage might still have been denied, as in this case. Valero and the Milas also cited decisions from other jurisdictions to support their argument. The court found these decisions to be "not helpful" because they considered exclusions in isolation, not in the context of other exclusions.

WHAT IF THE FACTS WERE DIFFERENT? *Suppose that exclusion k, instead of exclusion l, had used the phrase "by any person." Would the result have been different? Explain.*

Cancellation
The insured can cancel a policy at any time, and the insurer can cancel under certain circumstances. When an insurance company can cancel its insurance contract, the policy or a state statute usually requires that the insurer give advance written notice of the cancellation to the insured. The same requirement applies when only part of a policy is canceled. Any premium paid in advance may be refundable on the policy's cancellation. The insured may also be entitled to a life insurance policy's cash surrender value.

The insurer may cancel an insurance policy for various reasons, depending on the type of insurance. Following are some examples:

1. Automobile insurance can be canceled for nonpayment of premiums or suspension of the insured's driver's license.

2. Property insurance can be canceled for nonpayment of premiums or for other reasons, including the insured's fraud or misrepresentation, gross negligence, or conviction for a crime that increases the risk assumed by the insurer.

3. Life and health policies can be canceled because of false statements made by the insured in the application, but the cancellation must take place before the effective date of an incontestability clause.

An insurer cannot cancel—or refuse to renew—a policy for discriminatory reasons or other reasons that violate public policy. Also, an insurer cannot cancel a policy because the insured has appeared as a witness in a case brought against the company.

Duties and Obligations of the Parties

Both parties to an insurance contract are responsible for the obligations they assume under the contract. In addition, both the insured and the insurer have an implied duty to act in good faith.

Duties of the Insured. Good faith requires the party who is applying for insurance to reveal everything necessary for the insurer to evaluate the risk. The applicant must disclose all material facts, including all facts that an insurer would consider in determining whether to charge a higher premium or to refuse to issue a policy altogether. Many insurance companies today require that an applicant give the company permission to access other information, such as private medical records and credit ratings, for the purpose of evaluating the risk.

Once the insurance policy is issued, the insured has three basic duties under the contract:

1. To pay the premiums as stated in the contract.

2. To notify the insurer within a reasonable time if an event occurs that gives rise to a claim.

3. To cooperate with the insurer during any investigation or litigation.

Duties of the Insurer. Once the insurer has accepted the risk, and some event occurs that gives rise to a claim, the insurer has a *duty to investigate* to determine the facts. When a policy provides insurance against third party claims, the insurer is obligated to make reasonable efforts to settle such a claim.

If a settlement cannot be reached, then regardless of the claim's merit, the insurer has a *duty to defend* any suit against the insured. Usually, a policy provides that in this situation the insured must cooperate in the defense and attend hearings and trials if necessary. An insurer has a duty to provide or pay an attorney to defend its insured when a complaint alleges facts that could, if proved, impose liability on the insured within the policy's coverage.

CASE EXAMPLE 36.3 Dentist Robert Woo installed implants for one of his employees, Tina Alberts, whose family raised potbellied pigs. As a joke, while Alberts was anesthetized, Woo installed a set of "flippers" (temporary partial bridges) shaped like boar tusks and took photos. A month later, Woo's staff showed the photos to Alberts at a party. Alberts refused to return to work. She filed a suit against Woo for battery.

Woo's insurance company refused to defend him in the suit, and he ended up paying Alberts $250,000 to settle her claim. Woo then sued the insurance company and won. The court held that the insurance company had a duty to defend Woo under the professional liability provision of his policy because Woo's practical joke took place during a routine dental procedure.[3] ▪

Bad Faith Actions. Although insurance law generally follows contract law, most states now recognize a "bad faith" tort action against insurers. Thus, if an insurer in bad faith denies coverage of a claim, the insured may recover in tort in an amount exceeding the policy's coverage limits and may also recover punitive damages. Some courts have held insurers liable for bad faith refusals to settle claims for reasonable amounts within the policy limits.

Defenses against Payment

An insurance company can raise any of the defenses that would be valid in an ordinary action on a contract, as well as some defenses that do not apply in ordinary contract actions.

If a dentist plays a practical joke on a patient for which he is sued, does the dentist's insurance company have to defend him? Why or why not?

---

3. *Woo v. Fireman's Fund Insurance Co.,* 161 Wash.2d 43, 164 P.3d 454 (2007).

1. *Fraud or misrepresentation.* If the insurance company can show that the policy was procured by fraud or misrepresentation, it may have a valid defense for not paying on a claim. (The insurance company may also have the right to disaffirm or rescind the insurance contract.)

2. *Lack of an insurable interest.* An absolute defense exists if the insurer can show that the insured lacked an insurable interest—thus rendering the policy void from the beginning.

3. *Illegal actions of the insured.* Improper actions, such as those that are against public policy or that are otherwise illegal, can also give the insurance company a defense against the payment of a claim or allow it to rescind the contract.

An insurance company can be prevented, or estopped, from asserting some defenses that are usually available. For instance, an insurance company normally cannot escape payment on the death of an insured on the ground that the person's age was stated incorrectly on the application. Also, incontestability clauses prevent the insurer from asserting certain defenses.

36-2 Wills

Not only do the owners of property want to protect it during their lifetime through insurance coverage, but they typically also wish to transfer it to their loved ones at the time of their death. A **will** is the final declaration of how a person desires to have her or his property disposed of after death. It is a formal instrument that must follow exactly the requirements of state law to be effective. A will is referred to as a *testamentary disposition* of property, and one who dies after having made a valid will is said to have died **testate.**

A will can serve other purposes besides the distribution of property. It can appoint a guardian for minor children or incapacitated adults. It can also appoint a personal representative to settle the affairs of the deceased. Exhibit 36–3 presents excerpts from the will of Michael Jackson, the "King of Pop," who died from cardiac arrest at the age of fifty. Jackson held a substantial amount of tangible and intangible property, including the publishing rights to most of the Beatles' music catalogue. The will is a "pour-over" will, meaning that it transfers all of Jackson's property (that is not already held in the name of the trust) into the Michael Jackson Family Trust (trusts are discussed later in this chapter). Jackson's will also appoints his mother, Katherine Jackson, as the guardian of his three minor children.

36-2a Terminology of Wills

A person who makes out a will is known as a **testator** (from the Latin *testari*, "to make a will"). The court responsible for administering any legal problems surrounding a will is called a *probate court.*

When a person dies, a personal representative administers the estate and settles all of the decedent's affairs. An **executor** is a personal representative named in the will, whereas an **administrator** is a personal representative appointed by the court for a decedent who dies without a will. The court will also appoint an administrator if the will does not name an executor or if the named person lacks the capacity to serve as an executor.

A person who dies without having created a valid will is said to have died **intestate.** In this situation, state **intestacy laws** (sometimes referred to as *laws of descent*) prescribe the distribution of the property among heirs or next of kin (relatives). If no heirs or kin can be found, title to the property will be transferred to the state.

A gift of real estate by will is generally called a **devise,** and a gift of personal property by will is called a **bequest,** or **legacy.** The recipient of a gift by will is a **devisee** or a **legatee,** depending on whether the gift was a devise or a legacy.

Will An instrument made by a testator directing what is to be done with her or his property after death.

Testate Having left a will at death.

Testator One who makes and executes a will.

Executor A person appointed by a testator in a will to administer her or his estate.

Administrator One who is appointed by a court to administer a person's estate if the decedent died without a valid will or if the executor named in the will cannot serve.

Intestate As a noun, one who has died without having created a valid will. As an adjective, the state of having died without a will.

Intestacy Laws State statutes that specify how property will be distributed when a person dies intestate (without a valid will).

Devise A gift of real property by will, or the act of giving real property by will.

Bequest A gift of personal property by will (from the verb *to bequeath*).

Legacy A gift of personal property under a will.

Devisee One designated in a will to receive a gift of real property.

Legatee One designated in a will to receive a gift of personal property.

Exhibit 36-3 Excerpts from Michael Jackson's Will

LAST WILL OF MICHAEL JOSEPH JACKSON

I, MICHAEL JOSEPH JACKSON, a resident of the State of California, declare this to be my last Will, and do hereby revoke all former wills and codicils made by me.

I.   I declare that I am not married. My marriage to DEBORAH JEAN ROWE JACKSON has been dissolved. I have three children now living, PRINCE MICHAEL JACKSON, JR., PARIS MICHAEL KATHERINE JACKSON and PRINCE MICHAEL JOSEPH JACKSON, II. I have no other children, living or deceased.

II.   It is my intention by this Will to dispose of all property which I am entitled to dispose of by will. I specifically refrain from exercising all powers of appointment that I may possess at the time of my death.

III.   I give my entire estate to the Trustee or Trustees then acting under that certain Amended and Restated Declaration of Trust executed on March 22, 2002 by me as Trustee and Trustor which is called the MICHAEL JACKSON FAMILY TRUST, giving effect to any amendments thereto made prior to my death. All such assets shall be held, managed and distributed as a part of said Trust according to its terms and not as a separate testamentary trust.

If for any reason this gift is not operative or is invalid, or if the aforesaid Trust fails or has been revoked, I give my residuary estate to the Trustee or Trustees named to act in the MICHAEL JACKSON FAMILY TRUST, as Amended and Restated on March 22, 2002, and I direct said Trustee or Trustees to divide, administer, hold and distribute the trust estate pursuant to the provisions of said Trust * * * .

* * * *

IV.   I direct that all federal estate taxes and state inheritance or succession taxes payable upon or resulting from or by reason of my death (herein "Death Taxes") attributable to property which is part of the trust estate of the MICHAEL JACKSON FAMILY TRUST, including property which passes to said trust from my probate estate shall be paid by the Trustee of said trust in accordance with its terms. Death Taxes attributable to property passing outside this Will, other than property constituting the trust estate of the trust mentioned in the preceding sentence, shall be charged against the taker of said property.

V.   I appoint JOHN BRANCA, JOHN McCLAIN and BARRY SIEGEL as co-Executors of this Will. In the event of any of their deaths, resignations, inability, failure or refusal to serve or continue to serve as a co-Executor, the other shall serve and no replacement need be named. The co-Executors serving at any time after my death may name one or more replacements to serve in the event that none of the three named individuals is willing or able to serve at any time.

The term "my executors" as used in this Will shall include any duly acting personal representative or representatives of my estate. No individual acting as such need past a bond.

I hereby give to my Executors, full power and authority at any time or times to sell, lease, mortgage, pledge, exchange or otherwise dispose of the property, whether real or personal comprising my estate, upon such terms as my Executors shall deem best, to continue any business enterprises, to purchase assets from my estate, to continue in force and pay any insurance policy * * * .

VI.   Except as otherwise provided in this Will or in the Trust referred to in Article III hereof, I have intentionally omitted to provide for my heirs. I have intentionally omitted to provide for my former wife, DEBORAH JEAN ROWE JACKSON.

* * * *

VIII.   If any of my children are minors at the time of my death, I nominate my mother, KATHERINE JACKSON as guardian of the persons and estates of such minor children. If KATHERINE JACKSON fails to survive me, or is unable or unwilling to act as guardian, I nominate DIANA ROSS as guardian of the persons and estates of such minor children.

36-2b Types of Gifts

Gifts by will can be specific, general, or residuary. If a decedent's assets are not sufficient to cover all the gifts identified in the will, an abatement is necessary.

Specific and General Devises

A *specific* devise or bequest (legacy) describes particular property (such as "Eastwood Estate" or "my gold pocket watch") that can be distinguished from all the rest of the testator's property.

A *general* devise or bequest (legacy) does not single out any particular item of property to be transferred by will. For instance, "I devise all my lands" is a general devise. A general bequest may specify the property's value in monetary terms (such as "two diamonds worth $10,000") or simply state a dollar amount (such as "$30,000 to my nephew, Carleton").

Residuary Clause

Sometimes, a will provides that any assets remaining after the estate's debts have been paid and specific gifts have been made are to be distributed in a specific way through a *residuary clause*. Residuary clauses are often used when the exact amount to be distributed cannot be determined until all of the other gifts and payouts have been made. If the testator has not indicated what party or parties should receive the residuary of the estate, the residuary passes according to state laws of intestacy.

> "If you want to see a man's true character, watch him divide an estate."
>
> **BENJAMIN FRANKLIN**
> 1706–1790
> (AMERICAN DIPLOMAT, AUTHOR, AND SCIENTIST)

Abatement   If the assets of an estate are insufficient to pay in full all general bequests provided for in the will, an *abatement* takes place. In an abatement, the legatees receive reduced benefits. **EXAMPLE 36.4** Julie's will leaves $15,000 each to her children, Tamara and Stan. On Julie's death, only $10,000 is available to honor these bequests. By abatement, each child will receive $5,000. ■ If bequests are more complicated, abatement may be more complex. The testator's intent, as expressed in the will, controls.

36–2c Requirements for a Valid Will

A will must comply with statutory formalities designed to ensure that the testator understood his or her actions at the time the will was made. These formalities are intended to help prevent fraud. Unless they are followed, the will is declared void, and the decedent's property is distributed according to the laws of intestacy of that state, as discussed later in this chapter.

Although the required formalities vary among jurisdictions, most states have certain basic requirements for executing a will. The National Conference of Commissioners on Uniform State Laws has issued the Uniform Probate Code (UPC) to govern various aspects of wills, inheritance, and estates. Almost half of the states have enacted some part of the UPC and incorporated it into their own probate codes.

For a valid will, most states require proof of (1) the testator's capacity, (2) testamentary intent, (3) a written document, (4) the testator's signature, and (5) the signatures of persons who witnessed the testator's signing of the will.

LEARNING OBJECTIVE 3
What are the basic requirements for executing a will?

Testamentary Capacity and Intent   To have testamentary capacity, a testator must be of legal age and sound mind *at the time the will is made*. The minimum legal age for executing a will in most states and under the UPC is eighteen years [UPC 2–501]. Thus, the will of a twenty-one-year-old decedent written when the person was sixteen is invalid if, under state law, the legal age for executing a will is eighteen.

The concept of "being of sound mind" refers to the testator's ability to formulate and to comprehend a personal plan for the disposition of property. Persons who have been declared incompetent in a legal proceeding do not meet the sound mind requirement.

Related to the requirement of capacity is the concept of intent. A valid will is one that represents the maker's intention to transfer and distribute her or his property. Generally, a testator must:

If this couple leaves a sum of money to each child, but there are not enough assets to pay the amount specified in the will, what happens?

1. Know the nature of the act (of making a will).
2. Comprehend and remember the people to whom the testator would naturally leave his or her estate (such as family members and friends).
3. Know the nature and extent of her or his property.
4. Understand the distribution of assets called for by the will.

Undue Influence.   When it can be shown that the decedent's plan of distribution was the result of fraud or of undue influence, the will is declared invalid. A court may sometimes infer undue influence when the named beneficiary was in a position to influence the making of the will. If the testator ignored blood relatives and named as a beneficiary a nonrelative who was in constant close contact with the testator, for instance, a court might infer undue influence.

CASE EXAMPLE 36.5 Belton Johnson, whose family owned the famous King Ranch in Texas, was married three times. He had three children from his first marriage and eight grandchildren. While married to his second wife, he executed a will that provided for her during her lifetime and left the remainder of his estate in a trust for his children and grandchildren. When his second wife died, he changed the will to give $1 million to each grandchild and the remainder

KNOW THIS
In most states, the age of majority for contractual purposes is eighteen years.

to five charities. His children were provided for in a separate trust. While married to his third wife, Laura, he executed a will that left $1 million to each grandchild and the rest to Laura. Later, another will left his entire estate in trust to Laura for her life and then to a foundation that she controlled. After Johnson's death, a dispute arose over the validity of the latest will.

The court concluded that Johnson's last will was invalid due to Laura's undue influence. Johnson was an admitted alcoholic with permanent cognitive defects and memory problems that would have caused him to be more susceptible to undue influence. Evidence suggested that Laura had exerted substantial control over many aspects of Johnson's life. Other evidence established that Johnson wanted to provide for his descendants, as well as for the charities named in the earlier will.[4] ■

How would the fact that the rich owner of this ranch was an alcoholic make him more susceptible to undue influence?

Disinheritance. Although a testator must be able to remember the persons who would naturally be heirs to the estate, there is no requirement that testators give their estates to the natural heirs. A testator may decide to disinherit, or leave nothing to, an individual for various reasons. Most states have laws that attempt to prevent accidental disinheritance, however. There are also laws that protect minor children from loss of the family residence. Therefore, the testator's intent to disinherit needs to be clear.

The following case involved a will in the form of a testamentary letter that left the decedent's entire estate to a friend and explicitly disinherited his family. The friend died before the decedent, so the court had to decide whether to follow the state's intestacy laws or enforce the disinheritance clause.

---

4. *In re Estate of Johnson*, 340 S.W.3d 769 (Tex.App.—San Antonio 2011).

CASE 36.3

In re Estate of Melton

Supreme Court of Nevada, 272 P.3d 668 (2012).

FACTS In 1975, William Melton executed a will that, among other things, stated that his daughter, Vicki Palm, was to receive nothing. In 1979, he added a handwritten note to the will, saying that his friend, Alberta Kelleher, was to receive a small portion of his estate. In 1995, Melton sent a signed, handwritten letter to Kelleher. In the letter, Melton said he was returning from his mother's funeral and, because she had died in an automobile accident, he wanted to put "something in writing" leaving Kelleher his "entire estate." Melton also said, "I do not want my brother Larry J. Melton or Vicki Palm or any of my other relatives to have one penny of my estate." When Melton died in 2008, Kelleher had already passed away, and Palm was his only natural heir. The state of Nevada argued that it should receive everything because Palm had been disinherited. Nevertheless, the trial court applied the state's intestacy laws and distributed the entire estate to Palm. The state appealed.

ISSUE Could Melton bypass Nevada's intestacy laws through a will that disinherited his family but failed to dispose of his property?

DECISION Yes. The Nevada Supreme Court reversed the judgment of the lower court. It held that the disinheritance clause was enforceable and that Melton's estate should go to the state of Nevada.

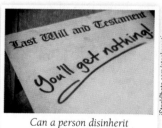

Can a person disinherit his or her daughter?

REASON Under the common law, the courts have developed two rules to determine whether a disinheritance clause should apply to any property that is not distributed by the will. Under the English rule, a disinheritance clause is enforceable only if "at least one . . . heir remain[s] eligible to receive the intestate property." Under the American rule, the testator must "affirmatively dispos[e] of the entire estate through a will." Many courts follow the American rule because disinheritance clauses create complications when they are applied to intestate property. For example, some courts say that such clauses "create an undesirable 'mixing' of the probate and intestacy systems by requiring courts to alter the distribution scheme provided in the intestacy statute." The state of Nevada, however, has rejected the common law rule by defining a will to include a "testamentary instrument that merely . . . excludes or limits the right of an individual or class to succeed to property of the decedent passing by intestate succession." As a result, Melton could disinherit his family without giving his property to someone else. Therefore, the state was entitled to Melton's property.

CRITICAL THINKING—Legal Consideration *Based on the information presented here, did Melton have testamentary intent when he wrote his letter? Why or why not?*

Writing Requirements   Generally, a will must be in writing. The writing itself can be informal as long as it substantially complies with the statutory requirements. In some states, a will can be handwritten in crayon or ink. It can be written on a sheet or scrap of paper, on a paper bag, or on a piece of cloth. A will that is completely in the handwriting of the testator is called a **holographic will** (sometimes referred to as an *olographic will*).

A **nuncupative will** is an oral will made before witnesses. Oral wills are not permitted in most states. Where authorized by statute, such wills are generally valid only if made during the last illness of the testator and are therefore sometimes referred to as *deathbed wills*. Normally, only personal property can be transferred by a nuncupative will. Statutes may also permit members of the military to make nuncupative wills when on active duty.

Holographic Will A will written entirely in the testator's handwriting.

Nuncupative Will An oral will (often called a *deathbed will*) made before witnesses. Usually, such wills are limited to transfers of personal property.

Signature Requirements   A fundamental requirement is that the testator's signature must appear on the will, generally at the end. Each jurisdiction dictates by statute and court decision what constitutes a signature. Initials, an X or other mark, and words such as "Mom" have all been upheld as valid when it was shown that the testators *intended* them to be signatures.

Witness Requirements   A will usually must be attested (sworn to) by two, and sometimes three, witnesses. The number of witnesses, their qualifications, and the manner in which the witnessing must be done are generally set out in a statute. A witness can be required to be disinterested—that is, not a beneficiary under the will. The UPC, however, allows even interested witnesses to attest to a will [UPC 2–505]. There are no age requirements for witnesses, but they must be mentally competent.

The purpose of the witnesses is to verify that the testator actually executed (signed) the will and had the requisite intent and capacity at the time. A witness does not have to read the contents of the will. Usually, the testator and all witnesses sign in the sight or the presence of one another. The UPC does not require all parties to sign in the presence of one another, however, and deems it sufficient if the testator acknowledges her or his signature to the witnesses [UPC 2–502]. The UPC also provides an alternative to traditional witnesses—the signature may be acknowledged by the testator before a notary public.

36–2d Revocation of Wills

The testator can revoke a will at any time during his or her life, either by a physical act or by a subsequent writing. Wills can also be revoked by operation of law. Revocation can be partial or complete, and must follow certain strict formalities.

Revocation by a Physical Act   A testator can revoke a will by *intentionally* burning, tearing, canceling, obliterating, or otherwise destroying it.[5] A testator can also revoke a will by intentionally having someone else destroy it in the testator's presence and at the testator's direction.

In some states, a testator can partially revoke a will by the physical act of crossing out some provisions in the will. Then, those portions that are crossed out are dropped, and the remaining parts of the will are valid. In no circumstances, however, can a provision be crossed out and an additional or substitute provision written in its place. Such altered portions require reexecution (re-signing) and reattestation (rewitnessing).

To revoke a will by physical act, it is necessary to follow the mandates of a state statute exactly. When a state statute prescribes the specific methods for revoking a will by physical act, only those methods can be used to revoke the will.

Revocation by a Subsequent Writing   A will may be wholly or partially revoked by a **codicil,** a written instrument separate from the will that amends or revokes provisions in the will. A codicil eliminates the necessity of redrafting an entire will merely to add to it or amend it. It can also be used to revoke an entire will. The codicil must be executed with the same

Codicil A written supplement or modification to a will. A codicil must be executed with the same formalities as a will.

---

5. The destruction cannot be inadvertent. The testator must have the intent to revoke the will.

Is tearing up a will a legally recognized method of revoking that will?

Petr Malyshev/ShutterStock.com

formalities required for a will, and it must refer expressly to the will. In effect, it updates a will, because the will is "incorporated by reference" into the codicil.

A new will (second will) can be executed that may or may not revoke the first or a prior will, depending on the language used. To revoke a prior will, the second will must use language specifically revoking other wills, such as "This will hereby revokes all prior wills." If the express *declaration of revocation* is missing, then both wills are read together. If there are any discrepancies between the wills, the second will controls.

Revocation by Operation of Law

Revocation by *operation of law* occurs when marriage, divorce or annulment, or the birth of a child takes place after a will has been executed.

Marriage and Divorce. In most states, when a testator marries after executing a will that does not include the new spouse, the spouse can still receive a share of the testator's estate. On the testator's death, the surviving spouse can receive the amount he or she would have taken had the testator died intestate (intestacy laws will be discussed shortly). The rest of the estate is passed under the will [UPC 2–301, 2–508].

If, however, the new spouse is otherwise provided for in the will (or by transfer of property outside the will), he or she will not be given an intestate amount. Also, if the parties had a valid *prenuptial agreement* (a contract made prior to marriage), its provisions dictate what the surviving spouse receives.

Divorce or annulment does not necessarily revoke the entire will. Rather, a divorce or an annulment occurring after a will has been executed revokes those dispositions of property made under the will to the former spouse [UPC 2–508].

Children. If a child is born after a will has been executed, that child may be entitled to a portion of the estate. Most state laws allow a child of the deceased to receive some portion of a parent's estate even if no provision is made in the parent's will. This is true *unless it is clear from the will's terms that the testator intended to disinherit the child* (see Case 36.3 for an example of disinheritance). Under the UPC, the rule is the same.

36-2e **Probate Procedures and Estate Planning**

Probate The process of proving and validating a will and settling all matters pertaining to an estate.

To **probate** a will means to establish its validity and to carry the administration of the estate through a court process. Probate laws vary from state to state. Typically, the procedure depends on the size and complexity of the decedent's estate.

People commonly engage in estate planning in an attempt to avoid formal probate procedures and to maximize the value of their estate by reducing taxes and other expenses. Individuals should also consider formulating a social media estate plan, as discussed in this chapter's *Adapting the Law to the Online Environment* feature.

Informal Probate

For smaller estates, most state statutes provide for the distribution of assets without formal probate proceedings. Faster and less expensive methods are then used. Property can be transferred by *affidavit* (a written statement taken before a person who has authority to affirm it). Problems or questions can be handled during an administrative hearing. Some state statutes allow car titles, savings and checking accounts, and certain other property to be transferred simply by filling out forms.

A majority of states also provide for *family settlement agreements,* which are private agreements among the beneficiaries. Once a will is admitted to probate, the family members can agree among themselves on how to distribute the decedent's assets. Although a family settlement agreement speeds the settlement process, a court order is still needed to protect the estate from future creditors and to clear title to the assets involved.

Formal Probate

For larger estates, formal probate proceedings normally are undertaken, and the probate court supervises every aspect of the process. Additionally, in some situations—such

ADAPTING THE LAW TO THE ONLINE ENVIRONMENT
Social Media Estate Planning

People are generally quite careful about choosing the personal representatives who will deal with their real estate, bank accounts, and investments after they are gone. Today, the same care should be taken in choosing an online executor to deal with a deceased's online identity, particularly in social media.

What an Online Executor Should Do
An online executor is responsible for dealing with a decedent's e-mail addresses, social media profiles, and blogs. E-mail accounts should be closed, but some people do not want their social media profiles to be erased

after they die. They want the profiles to be maintained, at least for some specified time after death, so that family and friends can visit them. Some people ask that their online executors place a memorial profile in their social media accounts.

Why Social Media Estate Planning Is Important
Online estate planning is essential because the deceased can still be a victim of identity theft. Unscrupulous fraudsters often use dead people's online identities to defraud private companies, individuals, and federal and state governments. If all of a person's

e-mail addresses and social media accounts are closed, it is harder for online fraudsters to use them for identity theft.

In addition, closing an e-mail account not only protects family members from being harassed with continuing spam after the person's death but also prevents spammers from hijacking the account. Spammers can use a dead person's e-mail account as the sender of billions of unwanted bulk e-mails.

CRITICAL THINKING

■ Why might an online executor need a copy of the deceased's death certificate?

---

as when a guardian for minor children must be appointed—more formal probate procedures cannot be avoided.

Formal probate proceedings may take several months or several years to complete, depending on the size and complexity of the estate and whether the will is contested. As a result, a sizable portion of the decedent's assets (as much as 10 percent) may go toward payment of court costs and fees charged by attorneys and personal representatives.

Property Transfers outside the Probate Process Often, people can avoid the cost of probate by employing various **will substitutes.** Examples include *living trusts* (discussed later in this chapter), life insurance policies, and individual retirement accounts (IRAs) with named beneficiaries.

One way to transfer property outside the probate process is to make gifts to children or others while one is still living. Another way is to own property in a joint tenancy. As previously discussed, in a joint tenancy, when one joint tenant dies, the other joint tenant or tenants automatically inherit the deceased tenant's share of the property. This is true even if the deceased tenant has provided otherwise in her or his will. Not all alternatives to formal probate administration are suitable to every estate, however.

For most people, estate planning involves not only ensuring that, after they die, their property goes to the intended recipients, but also avoiding probate and maximizing their estates. To this end, many choose to set up living trusts, establish joint tenancies, or use other will substitutes.

If you use will substitutes, though, you should be aware that a court will not apply the same principles in reviewing a transfer outside the probate process as it would apply to a testamentary transfer. Therefore, any such arrangements should be carefully drafted by an attorney and must comply with all legal requirements. To avoid disputes between beneficiaries after your death, make sure that your words and actions in such property transfers are clear and represent the final expression of your intent.

Will Substitutes Various instruments, such as living trusts and life insurance plans, that may be used to avoid the formal probate process.

PREVENTING LEGAL DISPUTES

36–2f Intestacy Laws

As mentioned, each state regulates by statute how property will be distributed when a person dies intestate (without a valid will). Intestacy laws attempt to carry out the likely intent and wishes of the decedent. These laws assume that deceased persons would have intended that their natural heirs (spouses, children, grandchildren, or other family members) inherit their property. Therefore, intestacy statutes set out rules and priorities under which these heirs inherit the property. If no heirs exist, the state will assume ownership of the property. The rules of descent vary widely from state to state.

Surviving Spouse and Children Usually, state statutes provide that the estate must be used to satisfy first the debts of the decedent. Then, the remaining assets pass to the surviving spouse and to the children. A surviving spouse usually receives only a share of the estate—one-half if there is also a surviving child and one-third if there are two or more children. Only if no children or grandchildren survive the decedent will a surviving spouse be entitled to the entire estate.

EXAMPLE 36.6 Allen dies intestate and is survived by his wife, Beth, and his children, Duane and Tara. Allen's property passes according to intestacy laws. After his outstanding debts are paid, Beth will receive the family home (either in fee simple or as a life estate) and ordinarily a one-third interest in all other property. The remaining real and personal property will pass to Duane and Tara in equal portions. ■

Under most state intestacy laws and under the UPC, in-laws do not share in an estate. Thus, if a child dies before his or her parents, the child's spouse will not receive an inheritance on the parents' death. For instance, if Duane died before his father (Allen) in *Example 36.6,* Duane's spouse would not inherit Duane's share of Allen's estate.

When There Is No Surviving Spouse or Child When there is no surviving spouse or child, the order of inheritance is grandchildren, then brothers and sisters, and, in some states, parents of the decedent. These relatives are usually called *lineal descendants.*

If there are no lineal descendants, then *collateral heirs*—nieces, nephews, aunts, and uncles of the decedent—make up the next group to share. If there are no survivors in any of these groups, most statutes provide for the property to be distributed among the next of kin of the collateral heirs.

Stepchildren, Adopted Children, and Illegitimate Children Under intestacy laws, stepchildren are not considered kin. Legally adopted children, however, are recognized as lawful heirs of their adoptive parents (as are children who are in the process of being adopted at the time of the parents' death).

Statutes vary from state to state in regard to the inheritance rights of illegitimate children (children born out of wedlock). In some states, an illegitimate child has the right to inherit only from the mother and her relatives, unless the father's paternity has been established by a legal proceeding. In the majority of states, however, a child born of any union that has the characteristics of a formal marriage relationship (such as unmarried parents who cohabit) is considered to be legitimate. Under the revised UPC, a child is the child of his or her natural (biological) parents, regardless of their marital status, as long as the natural parent has openly treated the child as her or his child [UPC 2–114]. Although illegitimate children may have inheritance rights in most states, their rights are not necessarily identical to those of legitimate children.

Grandchildren Usually, a decedent's will provides for how the estate will be distributed to descendants of deceased children—that is, to the decedent's grandchildren. If a will does not include such a provision—or if a person dies intestate—the question arises as to what share the grandchildren of the decedent will receive. Each state uses one of two methods of distributing the assets of intestate decedents—*per stirpes* or *per capita.*

LEARNING OBJECTIVE 4
What is the difference between a *per stirpes* distribution and a *per capita* distribution of an estate to the grandchildren of the deceased?

Per Stirpes* Distribution.** Under the ***per stirpes[6] method, within a class or group of distributees (such as grandchildren), the children of a descendant take the share that their deceased parent *would have been* entitled to inherit. Thus, a grandchild with no siblings inherits all of his or her parent's share, while grandchildren with siblings divide their parent's share.

    EXAMPLE 36.7 Michael, a widower, has two children, Scott and Jonathan. Scott has two children (Becky and Holly), and Jonathan has one child (Paul). Scott and Jonathan die before their father, and then Michael dies. If Michael's estate is distributed *per stirpes,* Becky and Holly each receive one-fourth of the estate (dividing Scott's one-half share). Paul receives one-half of the estate (taking Jonathan's one-half share). ■ Exhibit 36–4 illustrates the *per stirpes* method of distribution.

Per Capita* Distribution.** An estate may also be distributed on a ***per capita[7] basis, which means that each person in a class or group takes an equal share of the estate. In *Example 36.7,* if Michael's estate is distributed *per capita,* Becky, Holly, and Paul each receive a one-third share. Exhibit 36–5 illustrates the *per capita* method of distribution.

> **Per Stirpes** A method of distributing an intestate's estate so that each heir in a certain class (such as grandchildren) takes the share to which her or his deceased ancestor (such as a mother or father) would have been entitled.

> **Per Capita** A method of distributing an intestate's estate so that each heir in a certain class (such as grandchildren) receives an equal share.

36–3 Trusts

A **trust** is any arrangement through which property is transferred from one person to a trustee to be administered for the transferor's or another party's benefit. It can also be defined as a right of property held by one party for the benefit of another. A trust can be created for any purpose that is not illegal or against public policy, and it can be express or implied.

    The essential elements of a trust are as follows:

1. A designated beneficiary.

2. A designated trustee.

3. A fund sufficiently identified to enable title to pass to the trustee.

4. Actual delivery by the *grantor* (or *settlor,* the person creating the trust) to the trustee with the intention of passing title.

> **Trust** An arrangement in which title to property is held by one person (a trustee) for the benefit of another (a beneficiary).

> **LEARNING OBJECTIVE 5**
> What are the four essential elements of a trust?

---

6. *Per stirpes* is a Latin term meaning "by the roots" or "by stock." When used in estate law, it means proportionally divided among beneficiaries according to their deceased ancestor's share.

7. *Per capita* is a Latin term meaning "per person" or "for each head." When used in estate law, it means equally divided among beneficiaries.

Exhibit 36–4 *Per Stirpes* Distribution

Under this method of distribution, an heir takes the share that his or her deceased parent would have been entitled to inherit had the parent lived. This may mean that a class of distributees—the grandchildren in this example—will not inherit in equal portions. Note that Becky and Holly receive only one-fourth of Michael's estate while Paul inherits one-half.

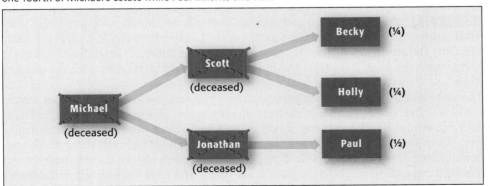

In what two ways will the proceeds from the sale of this property be divided to heirs after the owner's death?

Exhibit 36–5 *Per Capita* Distribution

Under this method of distribution, all heirs in a certain class—in this example, the grandchildren—inherit equally. Note that Becky and Holly in this situation each inherit one-third, as does Paul.

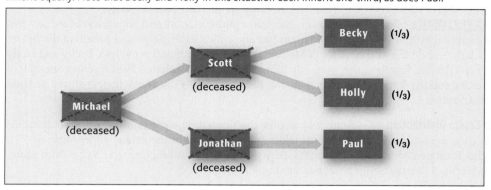

36–3a Express Trusts

An express trust is created or declared in explicit terms, usually in writing. There are many types of express trusts, each with its own special characteristics.

Living (*Inter Vivos*) Trust
A trust created by the grantor (settlor) and effective during his or her lifetime.

Living Trusts A **living (*inter vivos*) trust**—*inter vivos* is Latin for "between or among the living"—is a trust created by a grantor during her or his lifetime. Living trusts have become a popular estate-planning option because at the grantor's death, assets held in a living trust can pass to the heirs without going through probate.

Note, however, that living trusts do not shelter assets from estate taxes. Furthermore, the grantor may have to pay income taxes on trust earnings, depending on whether the trust is revocable or irrevocable.

Revocable Living Trusts. Living trusts can be revocable or irrevocable. In a *revocable* living trust, which is the most common type, the grantor retains control over the trust property. The grantor deeds the property to the trust but retains the power to amend, alter, or revoke the trust during her or his lifetime.

The grantor may also serve as a trustee or co-trustee and can arrange to receive income earned by the trust assets during her or his lifetime. Because the grantor is in control of the funds, she or he is required to pay income taxes on the trust earnings. Unless the trust is revoked, the principal of the trust is transferred to the trust beneficiary or beneficiaries on the grantor's death.

EXAMPLE 36.8 James Cortez owns and operates a large farm. After his wife dies, James contacts his attorney to create a living trust for the benefit of his three children, Alicia, Emma, and Jayden. The attorney prepares the documents creating the trust. James then executes a deed conveying the farm to the trust and transfers the farm's bank accounts into the name of the trust.

The trust designates James as the trustee and names his son, Jayden, as the *successor trustee,* who will take over the management of the trust when James dies or becomes incapacitated. Each of the children (as *income beneficiaries*) will receive income from the trust while James is alive. When James dies, the farm will pass to them without having to go through probate. By holding the property in a revocable living trust, James retains control over the farm during his life (and can make changes to the trust at any time). This trust arrangement is illustrated in Exhibit 36–6. ■

Exhibit 36–6 A Revocable Living Trust Arrangement

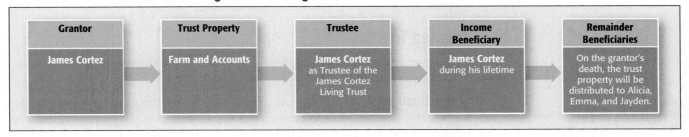

Grantor	Trust Property	Trustee	Income Beneficiary	Remainder Beneficiaries
James Cortez	Farm and Accounts	James Cortez as Trustee of the James Cortez Living Trust	James Cortez during his lifetime	On the grantor's death, the trust property will be distributed to Alicia, Emma, and Jayden.

Irrevocable Living Trusts. In an *irrevocable* living trust, the grantor permanently gives up control over the property to the trustee. The grantor executes a trust deed, and legal title to the trust property passes to the named trustee. The trustee has a duty to administer the property as directed by the grantor for the benefit and in the interest of the beneficiaries.

The trustee must preserve the trust property and make it productive. If required by the terms of the trust agreement, the trustee must pay income to the beneficiaries in accordance with the terms of the trust. Because the grantor has, in effect, given over the property for the benefit of the beneficiaries, he or she is no longer responsible for paying income taxes on the trust earnings.

When a living trust is created, who is normally named as the trustee?

Testamentary Trusts

A **testamentary trust** is created by will and comes into existence on the grantor's death. Although a testamentary trust has a trustee who maintains legal title to the trust property, the trustee's actions are subject to judicial approval. This trustee can be named in the will or be appointed by the court (if not named in the will). The legal responsibilities of the trustee are the same as in a living trust.

If a court finds that the will setting up a testamentary trust is invalid, then the trust will also be invalid. The property that was supposed to be in the trust will then pass according to intestacy laws, not according to the terms of the trust.

Testamentary Trust A trust that is created by will and therefore does not take effect until the death of the testator.

Charitable Trusts

A **charitable trust** is an express trust designed for the benefit of a segment of the public or the public in general. It differs from other types of trusts in that the identities of the beneficiaries are uncertain and it can be established to last indefinitely. Usually, to be deemed a charitable trust, a trust must be created for charitable, educational, religious, or scientific purposes.

Charitable Trust A trust in which the property held by the trustee must be used for a charitable purpose, such as the advancement of health, education, or religion.

Spendthrift Trusts

A **spendthrift trust** is created to provide for the maintenance of a beneficiary by preventing him or her from being careless with the bestowed funds. Unlike the beneficiaries of other trusts, the beneficiary in a spendthrift trust is not permitted to transfer or assign his or her right to the trust's principal or future payments from the trust. Essentially, the beneficiary can withdraw only a certain portion of the total amount to which he or she is entitled at any one time. The majority of states allow spendthrift trust provisions that prohibit creditors from attaching such trusts.

Spendthrift Trust A trust created to protect the beneficiary from spending all the funds to which she or he is entitled. Only a certain portion of the total amount is given to the beneficiary at any one time, and most states prohibit creditors from attaching assets of the trust.

Totten Trusts

A **Totten trust**[8] is created when a grantor deposits funds in her or his own name with instructions that on the grantor's death, whatever is in that account should go to a specific beneficiary. This type of trust is revocable at will until the depositor dies or completes the gift during her or his lifetime (by delivering the funds to the intended beneficiary,

Totten Trust A trust created when a person deposits funds in his or her own name for a specific beneficiary, who will receive the funds on the depositor's death. The trust is revocable at will until the depositor dies or completes the gift.

---

8. This type of trust derives its unusual name from the case *In re Totten*, 179 N.Y. 112, 71 N.E. 748 (1904).

for instance). The beneficiary has no access to the funds until the depositor's death, when the beneficiary obtains property rights to the balance on hand.

36–3b Implied Trusts

Sometimes, a trust will be imposed (implied) by law, even in the absence of an express trust. Implied trusts include resulting trusts and constructive trusts.

Constructive Trusts A **constructive trust** is an equitable trust imposed by a court in the interests of fairness and justice. In a constructive trust, the owner of the property is declared to be a trustee for the parties who are, in fairness, actually entitled to the benefits that flow from the property.

Courts often impose constructive trusts when someone who is in a confidential or fiduciary relationship with another person, such as a guardian to a ward, has breached a duty to that person. A court may also impose a constructive trust when someone wrongfully holds legal title to property—because the property was obtained through fraud or in breach of a legal duty, for instance.

CASE EXAMPLE 36.9 Stella Jankowski added her niece Genevieve Viarengo as a joint owner on bank accounts and other financial assets valued at $500,000. Jankowski also executed a will that divided her estate equally among her ten nieces, nephews, and cousins, and named Viarengo and Richard Golebiewski as coexecutors. She did not tell the attorney who drafted the will about the jointly held accounts.

When Jankowski died, Viarengo emptied her safe, removed her financial records, and claimed that the funds in the accounts were hers. Jankowski's other relatives filed a suit and asked the court to impose a constructive trust. The court found that Viarengo had committed fraud in obtaining the assets that she had held jointly with Jankowski and would be unjustly enriched if she were allowed to retain them. Therefore, the court imposed a constructive trust.[9] ∎

Resulting Trusts A **resulting trust** arises from the conduct of the parties. When circumstances raise an inference that one party holds legal title to the property for the benefit of another, a court may infer a resulting trust.

EXAMPLE 36.10 Gabriela Fuentes wants to put one acre of land she owns on the market for sale. Because she is going out of the country for two years and will not be able to deed the property to a buyer during that period, Fuentes conveys (transfers) the property to her good friend Oswald. Oswald can then attempt to sell the property while Fuentes is gone.

The transaction in which Fuentes conveyed the property to Oswald was intended to be neither a sale nor a gift. Consequently, Oswald will hold the property in a resulting trust for the benefit of Fuentes. When Fuentes returns, Oswald will be required either to deed the property back to her or, if the property has been sold, to turn over the proceeds (held in trust) to her. ∎

36–3c The Trustee

The *trustee* is the person holding the trust property. Anyone legally capable of holding title to, and dealing in, property can be a trustee. If a trust fails to name a trustee, or if a named trustee cannot or will not serve, the trust does not fail—an appropriate court can appoint a trustee.

Trustee's Duties A trustee must act with honesty, good faith, and prudence in administering the trust and must exercise a high degree of loyalty toward the trust beneficiary. The general standard of care is the degree of care a prudent person would exercise in his or her personal affairs.[10] The duty of loyalty requires that the trustee act in the exclusive interest of the beneficiary.

Constructive Trust An equitable trust that is imposed in the interests of fairness and justice when someone wrongfully holds legal title to property.

Resulting Trust An implied trust that arises when one party holds the legal title to another's property only for that other's benefit.

---

9. *Garrigus v. Viarengo*, 112 Conn.App. 655, 963 A.2d 1065 (2009).
10. Revised Uniform Principal and Income Act, Section 2(a)(3); *Restatement (Third) of Trusts (Prudent Investor Rule)*, Section 227. This rule is in force in the majority of states by statute and in a small number of states under the common law.

A trustee's specific duties include the following:

1. Maintain clear and accurate accounts of the trust's administration.
2. Furnish complete and correct information to the beneficiary.
3. Keep trust assets separate from her or his own assets.
4. Pay to an income beneficiary the net income of the trust assets at reasonable intervals.
5. Limit the risk of loss from investments by reasonable diversification and dispose of assets that do not represent prudent investments. (Prudent investment choices might include federal, state, or municipal bonds and some corporate bonds and stocks.)

Trustee's Powers   When a grantor creates a trust, he or she may set forth the trustee's powers and performance. State law governs in the absence of specific terms in the trust, and the states often restrict the trustee's investment of trust funds.

Typically, statutes confine trustees to investments in conservative debt securities such as government, utility, and railroad bonds. Frequently, though, a grantor gives a trustee discretionary investment power. In that circumstance, any statute may be considered only advisory, with the trustee's decisions subject in most states to the prudent person rule.

Of course, a trustee is responsible for carrying out the purposes of the trust. If the trustee fails to comply with the terms of the trust or the controlling statute, he or she is personally liable for any loss.

Allocations between Principal and Income   Often, a grantor will provide one beneficiary with a life estate and another beneficiary with the remainder interest in a trust. A farmer, for instance, may create a testamentary trust providing that the farm's income be paid to the surviving spouse and that on the surviving spouse's death, the farm be given to their children. In this situation, the surviving spouse has a *life estate* in the farm's income, and the children have a *remainder interest* in the farm (the principal).

When a trust is set up in this manner, questions may arise as to how the receipts and expenses for the farm's management and the trust's administration should be allocated between income and principal. When a trust instrument does not provide instructions, a trustee must refer to applicable state law.

The general rule is that ordinary receipts and expenses are chargeable to the income beneficiary, whereas extraordinary receipts and expenses are allocated to the principal beneficiaries.[11] The receipt of rent from trust realty would be ordinary, as would the expense of paying the property's taxes. The cost of long-term improvements and proceeds from the property's sale, however, would be extraordinary.

36–3d Trust Termination

The terms of a trust should expressly state the event on which the grantor wishes it to terminate—for instance, the beneficiary's or the trustee's death. If the trust instrument does not provide for termination on the beneficiary's death, the beneficiary's death will not end the trust. Similarly, without an express provision, a trust will not terminate on the trustee's death.

Typically, a trust instrument specifies a termination date. For instance, a trust created to educate the grantor's child may provide that the trust ends when the beneficiary reaches the age of twenty-five. If the trust's purpose is fulfilled before that date, a court may order the trust's termination. If no date is specified, a trust will terminate when its purpose has been fulfilled. Of course, if a trust's purpose becomes impossible or illegal, the trust will terminate.

"Put not your trust in money, but put your money in trust."

OLIVER WENDELL HOLMES, JR.
1841–1935
(ASSOCIATE JUSTICE OF THE UNITED STATES SUPREME COURT, 1902–1932)

---

11. Revised Uniform Principal and Income Act, Sections 3, 6, 8, and 13; *Restatement (Second) of Trusts*, Section 233.

Reviewing . . . Insurance, Wills, and Trusts

In June 2015, Bernard Ramish set up a $48,000 trust fund through West Plains Credit Union to provide tuition for his nephew, Nathan Covacek, to attend Tri-State Polytechnic Institute. The trust was established under Ramish's control and went into effect that August. In December, Ramish suffered a brain aneurysm that caused frequent, severe headaches but no other symptoms. In August 2016, Ramish developed heat stroke and collapsed on the golf course at La Prima Country Club.

After recuperating at the clubhouse, Ramish quickly wrote his will on the back of a wine list. It stated, "My last will and testament: Upon my death, I give all of my personal property to my friend Bernard Eshom and my home to Lizzie Johansen." He signed the will at the bottom in the presence of five men in the La Prima clubhouse, and all five men signed as witnesses.

A week later, Ramish suffered a second aneurysm and died in his sleep. He was survived by his mother (Dorris Ramish), his nephew (Nathan Covacek), his son-in-law (Bruce Lupin), and his granddaughter (Tori Lupin). Using the information presented in the chapter, answer the following questions.

1. Does Ramish's testament on the back of the wine list meet the requirements for a valid will?

2. Suppose that after Ramish's first aneurysm in 2016, Covacek contacted an insurance company to obtain a life insurance policy on Ramish's life. Would Covacek have had an insurable interest in his uncle's life? Why or why not?

3. What would the order of inheritance have been if Ramish had died intestate?

4. What will most likely happen to the trust fund established for Covacek on Ramish's death?

DEBATE THIS

■ Any changes to existing, fully witnessed wills should also have to be witnessed.

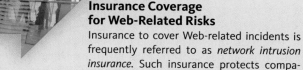

BUSINESS APPLICATION   How Can You Manage Risk in Cyberspace?*

Companies doing business online face many risks that are not covered by traditional types of insurance (listed in Exhibit 36–1). Not surprisingly, a growing number of companies are now offering policies designed to cover Web-related risks.

---

* This *Business Application* is not meant to substitute for the services of an attorney who is licensed to practice law in your state.

Insurance Coverage for Web-Related Risks

Insurance to cover Web-related incidents is frequently referred to as *network intrusion insurance*. Such insurance protects companies from losses stemming from hacking and computer viruses, programming errors, and network and Web site disruptions. It also protects against losses from theft of electronic data and assets, including intellectual property, and losses arising from claims of Web-related defamation, copyright infringement, false advertising, and violations of users' privacy rights.

InsureTrust.com, an insurer affiliated with three leading insurance companies—

American International Group, Lloyd's of London, and Reliance National—is a leading provider of network intrusion insurance. Other insurers, such as Hartford Insurance and the Chubb Group of Insurance Companies, have also added insurance for Web-related perils to their offerings. Clearly, the market for network intrusion insurance is evolving rapidly, and new policies will continue to appear.

Customized Policies

Unlike traditional insurance policies, which are generally drafted by insurance companies and presented to insurance applicants on a take-it-or-leave-it basis, network intrusion insurance policies are usually customized to provide protection against specific risks faced by a particular type of business. For example, an Internet service provider will face different risks than an online merchant, and a banking institution will face different risks than a law firm. The specific business-related risks are taken into consideration when determining the policy premium.

Qualifying Criteria

Many companies that offer network intrusion insurance require applicants to meet high security standards. In other words, to qualify for a policy, a business must have Web-related security measures in place. Several companies assess an applicant's security

system before underwriting a policy. The insurer might, for example, refuse to provide coverage unless the business scores higher than 60 percent in such an assessment. If the business does not score that high, it can contract with the company to improve its Web-related security.

CHECKLIST for the Businessperson:

1. Determine the types of risks that your Web business is exposed to, and try to obtain an insurance policy that protects you against those specific risks.

2. As when procuring any type of insurance, read the policy carefully, including any

exclusions contained in the fine print, before committing to it.

3. Do not be "penny wise and pound foolish" when it comes to insurance protection. Though insurance coverage may seem expensive, it may be much less costly than the loss of intellectual property or the cost of defending against a lawsuit. Opting for a higher deductible can reduce the amount you pay in premiums.

4. Find out what the company's underwriting standards are, and determine whether your Web security measures meet its standards.

Key Terms

administrator 907
bequest 907
binder 903
charitable trust 917
codicil 911
constructive trust 918
devise 907
devisee 907
executor 907
holographic will 911
incontestability clause 904
insurable interest 900

insurance 900
intestacy laws 907
intestate 907
legacy 907
legatee 907
living (*inter vivos*) trust 916
nuncupative will 911
per capita 915
per stirpes 915
policy 900
premium 900
probate 912

resulting trust 918
risk 900
risk management 900
spendthrift trust 917
testamentary trust 917
testate 907
testator 907
Totten trust 917
trust 915
underwriter 900
will 907
will substitutes 913

Chapter Summary: Insurance, Wills, and Trusts

INSURANCE	
Classifications	See Exhibit 36–1 for a list of types of insurance.
Terminology	1. *Policy*—The insurance contract. 2. *Premium*—The consideration paid to the insurer for a policy. 3. *Underwriter*—The insurance company. 4. *Parties*—Include the insurer (the insurance company), the insured (the person covered by insurance), an agent (a representative of the insurance company) or a broker (ordinarily an independent contractor), and a beneficiary (a person to receive proceeds under the policy).
Insurable Interest	An insurable interest exists whenever an individual or entity benefits from the preservation of the health or life of the insured or the property to be insured. For life insurance, an insurable interest must exist at the time the policy is issued. For property insurance, an insurable interest must exist at the time of the loss.

Continues

The Insurance Contract	1. *Laws governing*—The general principles of contract law are applied. The insurance industry is also heavily regulated by the states. 2. *Application*—An insurance applicant is bound by any false statements that appear in the application (subject to certain exceptions), which is part of the insurance contract. Misstatements or misrepresentations may be grounds for voiding the policy. 3. *Effective date*—Coverage on an insurance policy can begin when a *binder* (a written memorandum indicating that a formal policy is pending and stating its essential terms) is written; when the policy is issued; at the time of contract formation; or, depending on the terms of the contract, when certain conditions are met. 4. *Provisions and clauses*—See Exhibit 36–2 for specific provisions. Words will be given their ordinary meanings, and any ambiguity in the policy will be interpreted against the insurance company. When the written policy has not been delivered and it is unclear whether an insurance contract actually exists, the uncertainty will be resolved against the insurance company. The court will presume that the policy is in effect unless the company can show otherwise. 5. *Defenses against payment to the insured*—Defenses include misrepresentation or fraud by the applicant.

	WILLS
Terminology	1. *Intestate*—One who dies without a valid will. 2. *Testator*—A person who makes out a will. 3. *Personal representative*—A person appointed in a will or by a court to settle the affairs of a decedent. A personal representative named in the will is an *executor*. A personal representative appointed by the court for an intestate decedent is an *administrator*. 4. *Devise*—A gift of real estate by will; may be general or specific. The recipient of a devise is a *devisee*. 5. *Bequest, or legacy*—A gift of personal property by will; may be general or specific. The recipient of a bequest (legacy) is a *legatee*.
Requirements for a Valid Will	1. The testator must have testamentary capacity (be of legal age and sound mind at the time the will is made). 2. The testator must have the necessary intent to transfer and distribute his or her property. 3. A will must be in writing (except for nuncupative wills). A holographic will is completely in the handwriting of the testator. 4. A will must be signed by the testator. What constitutes a signature varies from jurisdiction to jurisdiction. 5. A nonholographic will (an attested will) must be witnessed in the manner prescribed by state statute.

Revocation of Wills	1. *By physical act of the maker*—Tearing up, canceling, obliterating, or deliberately destroying part or all of a will.
	2. *By subsequent writing*—
	  a. Codicil—A formal, separate document to amend or revoke an existing will.
	  b. Second will or new will—A new, properly executed will expressly revoking the existing will.
	3. *By operation of law*—
	  a. Marriage—Generally revokes part of a will written before the marriage.
	  b. Divorce or annulment—Revokes dispositions of property made under a will to a former spouse.
	  c. Subsequently born child—Most states allow the child to receive a portion of the estate.

Probate Procedures and Estate Planning	To probate a will means to establish its validity and to carry the administration of the estate through a state court process. Probate procedures may be informal or formal, depending on the size of the estate and other factors, such as whether a guardian for minor children must be appointed.
Intestacy Laws	1. Intestacy laws vary widely from state to state. Usually, the law provides that the surviving spouse and children inherit the property of the decedent (after the decedent's debts are paid). The spouse usually inherits the entire estate if there are no children, one-half of the estate if there is one child, and one-third of the estate if there are two or more children. 2. If there is no surviving spouse or child, then, in order, lineal descendants (grandchildren, brothers and sisters, and—in some states—parents of the decedent) inherit. If there are no lineal descendants, then collateral heirs (nieces, nephews, aunts, and uncles of the decedent) inherit.

	TRUSTS
Definition	A trust is any arrangement through which property is transferred from one person to a trustee to be administered for another party's benefit. The essential elements of a trust are (1) a designated beneficiary, (2) a designated trustee, (3) a fund sufficiently identified to enable title to pass to the trustee, and (4) actual delivery to the trustee with the intention of passing title.
Express Trusts	Express trusts are created by explicit terms, usually in writing, and include the following: 1. *Living (*inter vivos*) trust*—A trust created by a grantor during her or his lifetime. 2. *Testamentary trust*—A trust that is created by will and comes into existence on the death of the grantor. 3. *Charitable trust*—A trust designed for the benefit of a public group or the public in general. 4. *Spendthrift trust*—A trust created to provide for a beneficiary by allowing the beneficiary to withdraw only a certain amount at any one time. 5. *Totten trust*—A trust created when one person deposits funds in his or her own name as a trustee for another.
Implied Trusts	Implied trusts, which are imposed by law in the interests of fairness and justice, include the following: 1. *Constructive trust*—Arises by operation of law when a person wrongfully takes title to property. A court may require the owner to hold the property in trust for those who, in equity, are entitled to enjoy the benefits from the trust. 2. *Resulting trust*—Arises from the conduct of the parties when an apparent intention to create a trust is present.

Issue Spotters

1. Sheila makes out a will, leaving her property in equal thirds to Toby and Uma, her children, and Velda, her niece. Two years later, Sheila is adjudged mentally incompetent, and that same year, she dies. Can Toby and Uma have Sheila's will revoked on the ground that she did not have the capacity to make a will? Why or why not? (See *Wills*.)

2. When Ralph dies, he has not made a will and is survived by many relatives—a spouse, children, adopted children, sisters, brothers, uncles, aunts, cousins, nephews, and nieces. What determines who inherits what? (See *Wills*.)

—**Check your answers to the *Issue Spotters* against the answers provided in Appendix D at the end of this text.**

Learning Objectives Check

1. What is an insurable interest? When must an insurable interest exist?
2. How do courts interpret ambiguities in an insurance policy?
3. What are the basic requirements for executing a will?
4. What is the difference between a *per stirpes* distribution and a *per capita* distribution of an estate to the grandchildren of the deceased?
5. What are the four essential elements of a trust?

—**Answers to the even-numbered *Learning Objectives Check* questions can be found in Appendix E at the end of this text.**

Business Scenarios and Case Problems

36–1. Timing of Insurance Coverage. On October 10, Joleen Vora applied for a $50,000 life insurance policy with Magnum Life Insurance Co. She named her husband, Jay, as the beneficiary. Joleen paid the insurance company the first year's premium on making the application. Two days later, before she had a chance to take the physical examination required by the insurance company and before the policy was issued, Joleen was killed in an automobile accident. Jay submitted a claim to the insurance company for $50,000. Can Jay collect? Explain. (See *Insurance*.)

36–2. Wills and Intestacy Laws. Benjamin is a widower who has two married children, Edward and Patricia. Patricia has two children, Perry and Paul. Edward has no children. Benjamin makes a will leaving all his property equally to Edward and Patricia. The will provides that should a child predecease him, the grandchildren are to take *per stirpes*. The will is witnessed by Patricia and by Benjamin's lawyer and is signed by Benjamin in their presence. Benjamin dies, and Patricia has predeceased him. Edward claims the will is invalid. (See *Wills*.)

1. Discuss whether the will is valid.
2. Discuss the distribution of Benjamin's estate if the will is invalid.
3. Discuss the distribution of Benjamin's estate if the will is valid.

36–3. Intestacy Laws. A Florida statute provides that the right of election of a surviving spouse can be waived by written agreement: "A waiver of 'all rights,' or equivalent language, in the property or estate of a present or prospective spouse . . . is a waiver of all rights to elective share." The day before Mary Ann Taylor married Louis Taylor in Florida, they entered into a prenuptial agreement. The agreement stated that all property belonging to each spouse would "forever remain his or her personal estate," "said property shall remain forever free of claim by the other," and the parties would retain "full rights and authority" over their property as they would have as "if not married." After Louis's death, his only child, Joshua Taylor, filed a petition in a Florida state court for a determination of the beneficiaries of Louis's estate. How much of the estate can Mary Ann elect to receive? Explain. [*Taylor v. Taylor,* 1 So.3d 348 (Fla.App. 1 Dist. 2009)] (See *Wills*.)

36–4. Revocation of a Will. Marion Peterson executed a will that contained a bequest to Vasta Lucas in the form of a trust. On Lucas's death, the trustee was to distribute the assets to four beneficiaries, including Peterson's brother and sister, Arvin and Carolyn. Later, without witnesses, Peterson crossed out the beneficiaries' names, but she left the bequest to Lucas intact. After Peterson's death, Arvin and Carolyn contended that the will had been completely revoked. Were they correct? Explain. [*Peterson v. Harrell,* 286 Ga. 546, 690 S.E.2d 151 (2010)] (See *Wills*.)

36–5. Business Case Problem with Sample Answer—Undue Influence. Susie Walker executed a will that left her entire estate to her grandson. When her grandson died, Susie executed a new will that named her great-grandson as her sole beneficiary and specifically disinherited her son,

Tommy. At the time, Tommy's ex-wife was living with Susie. After Susie died, Tommy filed a suit, claiming that her will was the product of undue influence on the part of his ex-wife. Several witnesses testified that Susie had been mentally competent when she executed her will. Does undue influence appear likely based on these facts? Why or why not? [*In re Estate of Walker*, 80 A.D.3d 865, 914 N.Y.S.2d 379 (3 Dept. 2011)] (See *Wills*.)

—For a sample answer to Problem 36–5, go to Appendix F at the end of this text.

36–6. Insurance Provisions and Clauses. Darling's Rent-a-Car carried property insurance on its cars under a policy issued by Philadelphia Indemnity Insurance Co. The policy listed Darling's as the "insured." Darling's rented a car to Joshuah Farrington. In the rental contract, Farrington agreed to be responsible for any damage to the car and declined the optional insurance. Later, Farrington collided with a moose. Philadelphia paid Darling's for the damage to the car and sought to collect this amount from Farrington. Farrington argued that he was an "insured" under Darling's policy. How should "insured" be interpreted in this case? Why? [*Philadelphia Indemnity Insurance Co. v. Farrington*, 37 A.3d 305 (Me. 2012)] (See *Insurance*.)

36–7. Requirements of a Will. Sherman Hemsley was a well-known actor from the 1970s. Most notably, he played George Jefferson on the television shows *All in the Family* and *The Jeffersons*. He was born to Arsena Chisolm and William Thornton. Thornton was married to another woman, and Hemsley never had a relationship with his father or that side of the family. Hemsley never married and had no children. He lived with Flora Bernal, his business manager. Diagnosed with cancer, Hemsley executed a will naming Bernal the sole beneficiary of his estate. At the signing, Hemsley indicated that he knew he was executing his will and that he had deliberately chosen Bernal, but he did not discuss his relatives or the nature of his property with his attorney or the witnesses. After his death, the Thorntons challenged the will. Was Hemsley of sound mind? Discuss. [*In re Estate of Hemsley*, __ S.W.3d __, 2014 WL 5854220 (Tex.App.—El Paso 2014)] (See *Wills*.)

36–8. Wills. Andrew Walker executed a will giving a certain parcel of real estate in fee simple to his three children from a previous marriage, Mark Walker, Michelle Peters, and Andrea Knox, with a "life use" in the property granted to his current spouse, Nora Walker. A year later, Andrew, who suffered from asbestosis, was discharged from a hospital to spend his last days at home. He told Nora that he wished to execute a new will to change the disposition of the property to devise half of it to her. Nora

recorded his wish and took her notes to the office of attorney Frederick Meagher to have the document drafted. Meagher did not see Nora's notes, he did not talk to Walker, no one from his office was present at the signing of the document, and, when Walker signed it, he did not declare that it was his will, as required by state law. Is the document a valid will? Explain. [*In re Estate of Walker*, 124 A.D.3d 970, 2 N.Y.S.3d 628 (3 Dept. 2015)] (See *Wills*.)

36–9. A Question of Ethics—Will Requirements. Vickie Lynn Smith, an actress and model also known as Anna Nicole Smith, met J. Howard Marshall II in 1991. During their courtship, J. Howard lavished gifts and large sums of money on Anna Nicole, and they married on June 27, 1994. J. Howard died on August 4, 1995. According to Anna Nicole, J. Howard intended to provide for her financial security through a trust, but under the terms of his will, all of his assets were transferred to a trust for the benefit of E. Pierce Marshall, one of J. Howard's sons. While J. Howard's estate was subject to probate proceedings in a Texas state court, Anna Nicole filed for bankruptcy in a federal bankruptcy court. Pierce filed a claim in the bankruptcy proceeding, alleging that Anna Nicole had defamed him when her lawyers told the media that Pierce had engaged in forgery and fraud to gain control of his father's assets. Anna Nicole filed a counterclaim, alleging that Pierce prevented the transfer of his father's assets to a trust for her by, among other things, imprisoning J. Howard against his wishes, surrounding him with security guards to prevent contact with her, and transferring property against his wishes. [*Marshall v. Marshall*, 547 U.S. 293, 126 S.Ct. 1735, 164 L.Ed.2d 480 (2006)] (See *Wills*.)

1. What is the purpose underlying the requirements for a valid will? Which of these requirements might be at issue in this case? How should it apply here? Why?

2. State courts generally have jurisdiction over the probate of a will and the administration of an estate. Does the Texas state court thus have the sole authority to adjudicate all of the claims in this case? Why or why not?

3. How should Pierce's claim against Anna Nicole and her counterclaim be resolved?

4. Anna Nicole executed her will in 2001. The beneficiary—Daniel, her son, who was not J. Howard's child—died in 2006, shortly after Anna Nicole gave birth to a daughter, Dannielynn. In 2007, before executing a new will, Anna Nicole died. What happens if a will's beneficiary dies before the testator? What happens if a child is born after a will is executed?

Critical Thinking and Writing Assignments

36–10. Business Law Critical Thinking Group Assignment.
PAJ, Inc., a jewelry company, had a commercial general liability (CGL) policy from Hanover Insurance Company. The policy required PAJ to notify Hanover of any claim or suit against PAJ "as soon as practicable." Yurman Designs sued PAJ for copyright infringement because of the design of a particular jewelry line. Because PAJ did not realize that the CGL policy had a clause that covered infringement claims, it did not notify Hanover of the suit until four to six months after litigation began. Hanover contended that the policy did not apply to this incident because the late notification had violated its terms.

PAJ sued Hanover, seeking a declaration that it was obligated to defend and indemnify PAJ. (See *Insurance*.)

1. The first group will decide whether Hanover had an obligation to provide PAJ with legal assistance.

2. The second group will determine the effect that PAJ's late notice to the insurance company had on the insurance company's ability to provide assistance and mount a defense. Should the court require the insurance company to indemnify PAJ in this situation? Why or why not?

Unit Seven—Business Case Study with Dissenting Opinion

Kovarik v. Kovarik

When a couple divorces, the division of the marital estate—all of the property that the parties accumulated during their marriage—often leads to disputes. Questions of ownership frequently arise in divorce proceedings: Who owned what property, and how did she or he acquire it? If property was allegedly acquired by gift, did the transfer satisfy the requirements for a valid gift?

Those questions arose in *Kovarik v. Kovarik*,[1] which we examine in this *Business Case Study with Dissenting Opinion*. During a divorce, a dispute arose over whether the couple's marital estate included several certificates of deposit worth about $60,000 in which one spouse allegedly had an interest. The acquisition, division, and transfer of ownership of personal property, as well as other types of property transfers, were covered in this unit.

Are certificates of deposit (CDs) part of the marital estate?

CASE BACKGROUND

Jennifer Stahl and Bradly Kovarik were married in North Dakota in July 2001. A few months later, Bradly's parents, Dennis and Marlene, liquidated their farm business and invested the proceeds in certificates of deposit (CDs). Four of the CDs were in the names of Bradly and his sister, Wanda Morstad, but were retained by their parents.

Jennifer and Bradly separated in August 2007. Jennifer filed for divorce in a North Dakota state court. In a list of their marital property, she included the four CDs. Bradly denied any interest in those items.

At the trial, Bradly testified that he had learned about the CDs from his sister, who had cashed one without giving him any of the proceeds after Jennifer filed for divorce. At their mother's request, his sister had also negotiated the other three CDs before the divorce trial.

The court did not include the CDs in valuing and distributing the Kovariks' marital estate. Jennifer appealed to the North Dakota Supreme Court, arguing that Bradly's interest in the CDs should have been included.

MAJORITY OPINION

SANDSTROM, Justice.

* * * *

A [trial] court's decisions regarding the division of marital property are findings of fact and may be reversed on appeal only if clearly erroneous. A finding of fact is clearly erroneous if it is induced by an erroneous view of the law, if there is no evidence to support it, or if, after reviewing the entirety of the evidence, this Court is left with a definite and firm conviction a mistake has been made. A [trial] court's

findings of fact are presumed correct, and we view the evidence in the light most favorable to its findings.

Division of marital property upon divorce must be equitable. Although the division does not have to be equal, a substantial disparity must be explained. *All of the real and personal property accumulated by the parties, regardless of source, must be included in the marital estate.* [Emphasis added.]

* * * *

A * * * court may consider property to be part of the marital estate, if supported by evidence, even if a party claims it is owned by a nonparty. The principles applicable to *inter vivos* gifts in general apply as well to purported gifts of certificates of deposit. A valid gift made during the donor's lifetime must satisfy certain requirements—donative intent, delivery, actual or constructive, and acceptance by donee. A donor's intent is a question of fact. The actual or constructive delivery must be of a nature sufficient to divest the owner of all dominion [control] over the property and to invest the donee therewith.

Bradly Kovarik's parents testified that after liquidating their farm and equipment * * *, they placed four certificates of deposit in Bradly Kovarik's and his sister's names—"Wanda Morstad or Bradly Kovarik." They also testified they did not intend to give Bradly Kovarik and Morstad any present interest in the certificates. Moreover, Bradly Kovarik's father testified that the certificates, prior to having been cashed out, had been locked in a safe in their home and neither Bradly Kovarik nor his sister could just come and take the certificates.

Bradly Kovarik testified he had no knowledge of the certificates' existence until his sister told him she cashed one out and used some of the proceeds for home repairs. He also testified he did not receive

---

1. 2009 ND 82, 765 N.W.2d 511 (2009).

any of the remaining proceeds. Wanda Morstad testified she did not expect the certificates of deposit to belong to her. When requested, she assisted her parents in cashing out the certificates, which she did with respect to the remaining three certificates.

The [trial] court found Bradly Kovarik's parents did not intend to gift the certificates to him and his sister. The court further found the certificates were never delivered to either Bradly Kovarik or his sister but were retained in their parents' possession. The record does not reflect donative intent or delivery of the certificates to Bradly Kovarik, either actual or constructive. *In the absence of a donative intent and delivery, the [trial] court's finding that there was no valid gift is not clearly erroneous.* [Emphasis added.]

* * * *

We hold the [trial] court's property distribution and property valuation is not clearly erroneous, and affirm.

DISSENTING OPINION

MARING, Justice, dissenting.

I respectfully dissent from * * * the Majority opinion because the [trial] court * * * erred in concluding Bradly Kovarik's parents never gave him the certificates of deposit.

* * * *

First, the [trial] court found Bradly Kovarik's parents did not intend to give the certificates of deposit to Bradly Kovarik or his sister. This finding is not supported by the record. Bradly Kovarik admits that he and his sister were the co-owners of the certificates of deposit. Bradly Kovarik's sister also testified * * * that she was the co-owner of the certificates of deposit with her brother.

* * * *

Dennis Kovarik's testimony establishes that he knew Bradly Kovarik was a joint owner of the certificates of deposit * * *. Marlene Kovarik's testimony establishes that Bradly Kovarik was the joint owner of the certificates of deposit.

These admissions by Bradly Kovarik and his family that he owned the certificates of deposits are supported by the law. The parties do not dispute that Bradly Kovarik's name was on the certificate of deposit together with his sister's name or that neither of his parents' names were on the certificates of deposit. It is presumed that a certificate of deposit belongs to the person whose name appears on the certificate. * * * Bradly Kovarik's parents gave up their exclusive dominion and control over their assets when they placed the money in certificates of deposit in their children's names.

* * * *

The [trial] court found the certificates of deposit were never delivered to Bradly Kovarik or his sister because the parents kept possession of the certificates of deposit. This finding is not supported by the record.

* * * *

* * * Bradly Kovarik's parents divested themselves of the control of the certificates of deposit by first solely placing their children's names on the certificates of deposit and then delivering the certificates of deposit to Wanda Morstad to be cashed.

* * * *

In conclusion, I dissent because the certificates of deposit were completed gifts to Bradly Kovarik and must be included in the marital estate.

QUESTIONS FOR ANALYSIS

1. *Law.* *How does the majority respond to the appellant's argument in this case? What is the majority's reasoning?*

2. *Law.* *How does the dissent analyze the issue before the court?*

3. *Ethics.* *According to Marlene Kovarik, the CDs were obtained in her children's names in an effort to avoid the parents' tax obligations, rather than to give the funds to the children. Is this ethical? Explain.*

4. *Social Dimensions.* *If the Kovariks had invested their funds in real estate in their children's names, instead of CDs, would the result in this case have been the same? Why or why not?*

5. *Implications for the Estate Planner.* *How might Marlene and Dennis Kovarik have avoided the question that Jennifer raised here? Discuss.*

Unit Seven—Business Scenario

iStockPhoto.com/proxyminder

Dave graduates from State University with an engineering degree and goes into business as a self-employed computer programmer.

1. **Ownership of Personal Property.** To advertise his services on the Internet, Dave creates and produces a short digital video. Venture Films, Inc., sees the video and hires Dave to program the special effects for a short sequence in a Venture Films movie. Their contract states that all rights to the sequence

Continues

belong to Venture Films. What belongs to Dave: the digital video, the movie sequence, both, or neither? Explain.

2. **Landlord-Tenant Law.** Dave leases an office in Carl's Riverside Plaza office building for a two-year term. What is Dave's obligation for the rent if he moves out before the end of the term? If Dave dies during the term, who is entitled to possession of the office? What is Dave's obligation for the rent if Carl sells the building to Commercial Investments, Inc., before Dave's lease is up?

3. **Real Property Deeds.** At the end of the lease term, Dave buys the office building from Carl, who gives Dave a warranty deed. Commercial Investments later challenges Dave's ownership of the building and presents its own allegedly valid deed. What will it mean if a court rules that Dave owns the building in fee simple? If Commercial Investments is successful, can Dave recover anything from Carl? Explain.

4. **Insurance.** Dave's programming business expands, and he hires Mary as an employee. Mary becomes invaluable to the business, and Dave obtains a key-person insurance policy on her life. She dies six years later. If the insurance company discovers that Dave understated Mary's age when applying for the policy (which includes an incontestability clause), can the insurer legitimately refuse payment? If Mary had resigned to start her own programming firm one year before she died, could Dave have collected payment under the policy? Why or why not?

5. **Wills and Trusts.** Over time, Dave acquires other commercial property, which eventually becomes the most lucrative part of his business. Dave wants his adult children, Frank and Terry, to get the benefit of this property when he dies. Dave does not think that Frank and Terry can manage the property, however, because they have their own careers and live in other states. How can Dave provide for them to get the benefit of the property under someone else's management? In his will, Dave designates Hal, his attorney, as executor. What does an executor do?

Unit Seven—Group Project

Hobie and Colleen designed and developed a smartphone app called Do It. Do It is a game in which players cooperate rather than compete to complete a task, such as draw a picture, play a tune, or score a point. Documents evidence each party's investment, ownership, and share of profits and losses in the app. In the documents, Hobie and Colleen are referred to as "joint owners" and "tenants."

1. The first group will determine whether the ownership interest of each party is a tenancy in common or a joint tenancy. Is there a presumption that applies? Discuss.

2. The second group will describe the differences between a tenancy in common and a joint tenancy. What happens to Colleen's interest if Hobie dies?

3. The third group will assume that Hobie and Colleen are not married but live together and hold the property as tenants in common. If Hobie has no children and dies without a will, does Colleen inherit his interest in the Do It app? Why or why not? How would most states' intestate succession laws distribute Hobie's property?

How to Brief Cases and Analyze Case Problems

How to Brief Cases

To fully understand the law with respect to business, you need to be able to read and understand court decisions. To make this task easier, you can use a method of case analysis that is called *briefing*. There is a fairly standard procedure that you can follow when you "brief" any court case. You must first read the case opinion carefully. When you feel you understand the case, you can prepare a brief of it.

Although the format of the brief may vary, typically it will present the essentials of the case under headings such as those listed below.

1. **Citation.** Give the full citation for the case, including the name of the case, the date it was decided, and the court that decided it.

2. **Facts.** Briefly indicate (a) the reasons for the lawsuit; (b) the identity and arguments of the plaintiff(s) and defendant(s), respectively; and (c) the lower court's decision—if appropriate.

3. **Issue.** Concisely phrase, in the form of a question, the essential issue before the court. (If more than one issue is involved, you may have two—or even more—questions here.)

4. **Decision.** Indicate here—with a "yes" or "no," if possible—the court's answer to the question (or questions) in the Issue section above.

5. **Reason.** Summarize as briefly as possible the reasons given by the court for its decision (or decisions) and the case or statutory law relied on by the court in arriving at its decision.

For a case-specific example of what should be included under each of the above headings when briefing a case, see the review of the sample court case presented in the appendix to Chapter 1 of this text.

Analyzing Case Problems

In addition to learning how to brief cases, students of business law and the legal environment also find it helpful to know how to analyze case problems. Part of the study of business law and the legal environment usually involves analyzing case problems, such as those included in this text at the end of each chapter.

For each case problem in this book, we provide the relevant background and facts of the lawsuit and the issue before the court.

When you are assigned one of these problems, your job will be to determine how the court should decide the issue, and why. In other words, you will need to engage in legal analysis and reasoning. Here, we offer some suggestions on how to make this task less daunting. We begin by presenting a sample case problem:

> While Janet Lawson, a famous pianist, was shopping in Quality Market, she slipped and fell on a wet floor in one of the aisles. The floor had recently been mopped by one of the store's employees, but there were no signs warning customers that the floor in that area was wet. As a result of the fall, Lawson injured her right arm and was unable to perform piano concerts for the next six months. Had she been able to perform the scheduled concerts, she would have earned approximately $60,000 over that period of time. Lawson sued Quality Market for this amount, plus another $10,000 in medical expenses. She claimed that the store's failure to warn customers of the wet floor constituted negligence and therefore the market was liable for her injuries. Will the court agree with Lawson? Discuss.

Understand the Facts

This may sound obvious, but before you can analyze or apply the relevant law to a specific set of facts, you must clearly understand those facts. In other words, you should read through the case problem carefully—more than once, if necessary—to make sure you understand the identity of the plaintiff(s) and defendant(s) in the case and the progression of events that led to the lawsuit.

In the sample case problem just given, the identity of the parties is fairly obvious. Janet Lawson is the one bringing the suit; therefore, she is the plaintiff. Lawson is bringing the suit against Quality Market, so it is the defendant. Some of the case problems you may work on have multiple plaintiffs or defendants. Often, it is helpful to use abbreviations for the parties. To indicate a reference to a plaintiff, for example, the *pi* symbol—π—is often used, and a defendant is denoted by a *delta*—Δ—a triangle.

The events leading to the lawsuit are also fairly straightforward. Lawson slipped and fell on a wet floor, and she contends that Quality Market should be liable for her injuries because it was negligent in not posting a sign warning customers of the wet floor.

When you are working on case problems, realize that the facts should be accepted as they are given. For instance, in our sample problem, it should be accepted that the floor was wet and that there was no sign. In other words, avoid making conjectures, such as "Maybe the floor wasn't too wet," or "Maybe an employee was getting a sign to put up," or "Maybe someone stole the sign." Questioning the facts as they are presented only adds confusion to your analysis.

Legal Analysis and Reasoning

Once you understand the facts given in the case problem, you can begin to analyze the case. The **IRAC method** is a helpful tool to use in the legal analysis and reasoning process. IRAC is an acronym for **I**ssue, **R**ule, **A**pplication, **C**onclusion. Applying this method to our sample problem would involve the following steps:

1. First, you need to decide what legal **issue** is involved in the case. In our sample case, the basic issue is whether Quality Market's failure to warn customers of the wet floor constituted negligence. Negligence is a *tort*—a civil wrong. In a tort lawsuit, the plaintiff seeks to be compensated for another's wrongful act. A defendant will be deemed negligent if he or she breached a duty of care owed to the plaintiff and the breach of that duty caused the plaintiff to suffer harm.

2. Once you have identified the issue, the next step is to determine what **rule of law** applies to the issue. To make this determination, you will want to carefully review the text discussion relating to the issue involved in the problem. Our sample case problem involves the tort of negligence. The applicable rule of law is the tort law principle that business owners owe a duty to exercise reasonable care to protect their customers (*business invitees*). Reasonable care, in this context, includes either removing—or warning customers of—*foreseeable* risks about which the owner *knew* or *should have known*. Business owners need not warn customers of "open and obvious" risks, however. If a business owner breaches this duty of care (fails to exercise the appropriate degree of care toward customers), and the breach of duty causes a customer to be injured, the business owner will be liable to the customer for the customer's injuries.

3. The next—and usually the most difficult—step in analyzing case problems is the **application** of the relevant rule of law to the specific facts of the case you are studying. In our sample problem, applying the tort law principle just discussed presents few difficulties. An employee of the store had mopped the floor in the aisle where Lawson slipped and fell, but no sign was present indicating that the floor was wet. That a customer might fall on a wet floor is clearly a foreseeable risk. Therefore, the failure to warn customers about the wet floor was a breach of the duty of care owed by the business owner to the store's customers.

4. Once you have completed Step 3 in the IRAC method, you should be ready to draw your **conclusion.** In our sample problem, Quality Market is liable to Lawson for her injuries because the market's breach of its duty of care caused Lawson's injuries.

The fact patterns in the case problems presented in this text are not always as simple as those presented in our sample problem. Often, a case has more than one plaintiff or defendant. A case may also involve more than one issue and have more than one applicable rule of law. Furthermore, in some case problems the facts may indicate that the general rule of law should not apply. Suppose that a store employee told Lawson about the wet floor and advised her not to walk in that aisle, but Lawson decided to walk there anyway. This fact could alter the outcome of the case because the store could then raise the defense of *assumption of risk*. Nonetheless, a careful review of the chapter should always provide you with the knowledge you need to analyze the problem thoroughly and arrive at accurate conclusions.

The Constitution of the United States

Preamble

We the People of the United States, in Order to form a more perfect Union, establish Justice, insure domestic Tranquility, provide for the common defence, promote the general Welfare, and secure the Blessings of Liberty to ourselves and our Posterity, do ordain and establish this Constitution for the United States of America.

Article I

Section 1. All legislative Powers herein granted shall be vested in a Congress of the United States, which shall consist of a Senate and House of Representatives.

Section 2. The House of Representatives shall be composed of Members chosen every second Year by the People of the several States, and the Electors in each State shall have the Qualifications requisite for Electors of the most numerous Branch of the State Legislature.

No Person shall be a Representative who shall not have attained to the Age of twenty five Years, and been seven Years a Citizen of the United States, and who shall not, when elected, be an Inhabitant of that State in which he shall be chosen.

Representatives and direct Taxes shall be apportioned among the several States which may be included within this Union, according to their respective Numbers, which shall be determined by adding to the whole Number of free Persons, including those bound to Service for a Term of Years, and excluding Indians not taxed, three fifths of all other Persons. The actual Enumeration shall be made within three Years after the first Meeting of the Congress of the United States, and within every subsequent Term of ten Years, in such Manner as they shall by Law direct. The Number of Representatives shall not exceed one for every thirty Thousand, but each State shall have at Least one Representative; and until such enumeration shall be made, the State of New Hampshire shall be entitled to chuse three, Massachusetts eight, Rhode Island and Providence Plantations one, Connecticut five, New York six, New Jersey four, Pennsylvania eight, Delaware one, Maryland six, Virginia ten, North Carolina five, South Carolina five, and Georgia three.

When vacancies happen in the Representation from any State, the Executive Authority thereof shall issue Writs of Election to fill such Vacancies.

The House of Representatives shall chuse their Speaker and other Officers; and shall have the sole Power of Impeachment.

Section 3. The Senate of the United States shall be composed of two Senators from each State, chosen by the Legislature thereof, for six Years; and each Senator shall have one Vote.

Immediately after they shall be assembled in Consequence of the first Election, they shall be divided as equally as may be into three Classes. The Seats of the Senators of the first Class shall be vacated at the Expiration of the second Year, of the second Class at the Expiration of the fourth Year, and of the third Class at the Expiration of the sixth Year, so that one third may be chosen every second Year; and if Vacancies happen by Resignation, or otherwise, during the Recess of the Legislature of any State, the Executive thereof may make temporary Appointments until the next Meeting of the Legislature, which shall then fill such Vacancies.

No Person shall be a Senator who shall not have attained to the Age of thirty Years, and been nine Years a Citizen of the United States, and who shall not, when elected, be an Inhabitant of that State for which he shall be chosen.

The Vice President of the United States shall be President of the Senate, but shall have no Vote, unless they be equally divided.

The Senate shall chuse their other Officers, and also a President pro tempore, in the Absence of the Vice President, or when he shall exercise the Office of President of the United States.

The Senate shall have the sole Power to try all Impeachments. When sitting for that Purpose, they shall be on Oath or Affirmation. When the President of the United States is tried, the Chief Justice shall preside: And no Person shall be convicted without the Concurrence of two thirds of the Members present.

Judgment in Cases of Impeachment shall not extend further than to removal from Office, and disqualification to hold and enjoy any Office of honor, Trust, or Profit under the United States: but the Party convicted shall nevertheless be liable and subject to Indictment, Trial, Judgment, and Punishment, according to Law.

Section 4. The Times, Places and Manner of holding Elections for Senators and Representatives, shall be prescribed in each State by the Legislature thereof; but the Congress may at any time by Law make or alter such Regulations, except as to the Places of chusing Senators.

The Congress shall assemble at least once in every Year, and such Meeting shall be on the first Monday in December, unless they shall by Law appoint a different Day.

Section 5. Each House shall be the Judge of the Elections, Returns, and Qualifications of its own Members, and a Majority of each shall constitute a Quorum to do Business; but a smaller Number may adjourn from day to day, and may be authorized to compel the Attendance of absent Members, in such Manner, and under such Penalties as each House may provide.

Each House may determine the Rules of its Proceedings, punish its Members for disorderly Behavior, and, with the Concurrence of two thirds, expel a Member.

Each House shall keep a Journal of its Proceedings, and from time to time publish the same, excepting such Parts as may in their Judgment require Secrecy; and the Yeas and Nays of the Members of either House on any question shall, at the Desire of one fifth of those Present, be entered on the Journal.

Neither House, during the Session of Congress, shall, without the Consent of the other, adjourn for more than three days, nor to any other Place than that in which the two Houses shall be sitting.

Section 6. The Senators and Representatives shall receive a Compensation for their Services, to be ascertained by Law, and paid out of the Treasury of the United States. They shall in all Cases, except Treason, Felony and Breach of the Peace, be privileged from Arrest during their Attendance at the Session of their respective Houses, and in going to and returning from the same; and for any Speech or Debate in either House, they shall not be questioned in any other Place.

No Senator or Representative shall, during the Time for which he was elected, be appointed to any civil Office under the Authority of the United States, which shall have been created, or the Emoluments whereof shall have been increased during such time; and no Person holding any Office under the United States, shall be a Member of either House during his Continuance in Office.

Section 7. All Bills for raising Revenue shall originate in the House of Representatives; but the Senate may propose or concur with Amendments as on other Bills.

Every Bill which shall have passed the House of Representatives and the Senate, shall, before it become a Law, be presented to the President of the United States; If he approve he shall sign it, but if not he shall return it, with his Objections to the House in which it shall have originated, who shall enter the Objections at large on their Journal, and proceed to reconsider it. If after such Reconsideration two thirds of that House shall agree to pass the Bill, it shall be sent together with the Objections, to the other House, by which it shall likewise be reconsidered, and if approved by two thirds of that House, it shall become a Law. But in all such Cases the Votes of both Houses shall be determined by Yeas and Nays, and the Names of the Persons voting for and against the Bill shall be entered on the Journal of each House respectively. If any Bill shall not be returned by the President within ten Days (Sundays excepted) after it shall have been presented to him, the Same shall be a Law, in like Manner as if he had signed it, unless the Congress by their Adjournment prevent its Return in which Case it shall not be a Law.

Every Order, Resolution, or Vote, to which the Concurrence of the Senate and House of Representatives may be necessary (except on a question of Adjournment) shall be presented to the President of the United States; and before the Same shall take Effect, shall be approved by him, or being disapproved by him, shall be repassed by two thirds of the Senate and House of Representatives, according to the Rules and Limitations prescribed in the Case of a Bill.

Section 8. The Congress shall have Power To lay and collect Taxes, Duties, Imposts and Excises, to pay the Debts and provide for the common Defence and general Welfare of the United States; but all Duties, Imposts and Excises shall be uniform throughout the United States;

To borrow Money on the credit of the United States;

To regulate Commerce with foreign Nations, and among the several States, and with the Indian Tribes;

To establish an uniform Rule of Naturalization, and uniform Laws on the subject of Bankruptcies throughout the United States;

To coin Money, regulate the Value thereof, and of foreign Coin, and fix the Standard of Weights and Measures;

To provide for the Punishment of counterfeiting the Securities and current Coin of the United States;

To establish Post Offices and post Roads;

To promote the Progress of Science and useful Arts, by securing for limited Times to Authors and Inventors the exclusive Right to their respective Writings and Discoveries;

To constitute Tribunals inferior to the supreme Court;

To define and punish Piracies and Felonies committed on the high Seas, and Offenses against the Law of Nations;

To declare War, grant Letters of Marque and Reprisal, and make Rules concerning Captures on Land and Water;

To raise and support Armies, but no Appropriation of Money to that Use shall be for a longer Term than two Years;

To provide and maintain a Navy;

To make Rules for the Government and Regulation of the land and naval Forces;

To provide for calling forth the Militia to execute the Laws of the Union, suppress Insurrections and repel Invasions;

To provide for organizing, arming, and disciplining, the Militia, and for governing such Part of them as may be employed in the Service of the United States, reserving to the States respectively, the Appointment of the Officers, and the Authority of training the Militia according to the discipline prescribed by Congress;

To exercise exclusive Legislation in all Cases whatsoever, over such District (not exceeding ten Miles square) as may, by Cession of particular States, and the Acceptance of Congress, become the Seat of the Government of the United States, and to exercise like Authority over all Places purchased by the Consent of the Legislature of the State in which the Same shall be, for the Erection of Forts, Magazines, Arsenals, dock-Yards, and other needful Buildings;—And

To make all Laws which shall be necessary and proper for carrying into Execution the foregoing Powers, and all other Powers vested by this Constitution in the Government of the United States, or in any Department or Officer thereof.

Section 9. The Migration or Importation of such Persons as any of the States now existing shall think proper to admit, shall not be prohibited by the Congress prior to the Year one thousand eight hundred and eight, but a Tax or duty may be imposed on such Importation, not exceeding ten dollars for each Person.

The privilege of the Writ of Habeas Corpus shall not be suspended, unless when in Cases of Rebellion or Invasion the public Safety may require it.

No Bill of Attainder or ex post facto Law shall be passed.

No Capitation, or other direct, Tax shall be laid, unless in Proportion to the Census or Enumeration herein before directed to be taken.

No Tax or Duty shall be laid on Articles exported from any State.

No Preference shall be given by any Regulation of Commerce or Revenue to the Ports of one State over those of another: nor shall Vessels bound to, or from, one State be obliged to enter, clear, or pay Duties in another.

No Money shall be drawn from the Treasury, but in Consequence of Appropriations made by Law; and a regular Statement and Account of the Receipts and Expenditures of all public Money shall be published from time to time.

No Title of Nobility shall be granted by the United States: And no Person holding any Office of Profit or Trust under them, shall, without the Consent of the Congress, accept of any present, Emolument, Office, or Title, of any kind whatever, from any King, Prince, or foreign State.

Section 10. No State shall enter into any Treaty, Alliance, or Confederation; grant Letters of Marque and Reprisal; coin Money; emit Bills of Credit; make any Thing but gold and silver Coin a Tender in Payment of Debts; pass any Bill of Attainder, ex post facto Law, or Law impairing the Obligation of Contracts, or grant any Title of Nobility.

No State shall, without the Consent of the Congress, lay any Imposts or Duties on Imports or Exports, except what may be absolutely necessary for executing its inspection Laws: and the net Produce of all Duties and Imposts, laid by any State on Imports or Exports, shall be for the Use of the Treasury of the United States; and all such Laws shall be subject to the Revision and Controul of the Congress.

No State shall, without the Consent of Congress, lay any Duty of Tonnage, keep Troops, or Ships of War in time of Peace, enter into any Agreement or Compact with another State, or with a foreign Power, or engage in War, unless actually invaded, or in such imminent Danger as will not admit of delay.

Article II

Section 1. The executive Power shall be vested in a President of the United States of America. He shall hold his Office during the Term of four Years, and, together with the Vice President, chosen for the same Term, be elected, as follows:

Each State shall appoint, in such Manner as the Legislature thereof may direct, a Number of Electors, equal to the whole Number of Senators and Representatives to which the State may be entitled in the Congress; but no Senator or Representative, or Person holding an Office of Trust or Profit under the United States, shall be appointed an Elector.

The Electors shall meet in their respective States, and vote by Ballot for two Persons, of whom one at least shall not be an Inhabitant of the same State with themselves. And they shall make a List of all the Persons voted for, and of the Number of Votes for each; which List they shall sign and certify, and transmit sealed to the Seat of the Government of the United States, directed to the President of the Senate. The President of the Senate shall, in the Presence of the Senate and House of Representatives, open all the Certificates, and the Votes shall then be counted. The Person having the greatest Number

of Votes shall be the President, if such Number be a Majority of the whole Number of Electors appointed; and if there be more than one who have such Majority, and have an equal Number of Votes, then the House of Representatives shall immediately chuse by Ballot one of them for President; and if no Person have a Majority, then from the five highest on the List the said House shall in like Manner chuse the President. But in chusing the President, the Votes shall be taken by States, the Representation from each State having one Vote; A quorum for this Purpose shall consist of a Member or Members from two thirds of the States, and a Majority of all the States shall be necessary to a Choice. In every Case, after the Choice of the President, the Person having the greater Number of Votes of the Electors shall be the Vice President. But if there should remain two or more who have equal Votes, the Senate shall chuse from them by Ballot the Vice President.

The Congress may determine the Time of chusing the Electors, and the Day on which they shall give their Votes; which Day shall be the same throughout the United States.

No person except a natural born Citizen, or a Citizen of the United States, at the time of the Adoption of this Constitution, shall be eligible to the Office of President; neither shall any Person be eligible to that Office who shall not have attained to the Age of thirty five Years, and been fourteen Years a Resident within the United States.

In Case of the Removal of the President from Office, or of his Death, Resignation or Inability to discharge the Powers and Duties of the said Office, the same shall devolve on the Vice President, and the Congress may by Law provide for the Case of Removal, Death, Resignation or Inability, both of the President and Vice President, declaring what Officer shall then act as President, and such Officer shall act accordingly, until the Disability be removed, or a President shall be elected.

The President shall, at stated Times, receive for his Services, a Compensation, which shall neither be increased nor diminished during the Period for which he shall have been elected, and he shall not receive within that Period any other Emolument from the United States, or any of them.

Before he enter on the Execution of his Office, he shall take the following Oath or Affirmation: "I do solemnly swear (or affirm) that I will faithfully execute the Office of President of the United States, and will to the best of my Ability, preserve, protect and defend the Constitution of the United States."

Section 2. The President shall be Commander in Chief of the Army and Navy of the United States, and of the Militia of the several States, when called into the actual Service of the United States; he may require the Opinion, in writing, of the principal Officer in each of the executive Departments, upon any Subject relating to the Duties of their respective Offices, and he shall have Power to grant Reprieves and Pardons for Offenses against the United States, except in Cases of Impeachment.

He shall have Power, by and with the Advice and Consent of the Senate to make Treaties, provided two thirds of the Senators present concur; and he shall nominate, and by and with the Advice and Consent of the Senate, shall appoint Ambassadors, other public Ministers and Consuls, Judges of the supreme Court, and all other Officers of the United States, whose Appointments are not herein otherwise provided for, and which shall be established by Law; but the Congress may by Law vest the Appointment of such inferior Officers, as they think proper, in the President alone, in the Courts of Law, or in the Heads of Departments.

The President shall have Power to fill up all Vacancies that may happen during the Recess of the Senate, by granting Commissions which shall expire at the End of their next Session.

Section 3. He shall from time to time give to the Congress Information of the State of the Union, and recommend to their Consideration such Measures as he shall judge necessary and expedient; he may, on extraordinary Occasions, convene both Houses, or either of them, and in Case of Disagreement between them, with Respect to the Time of Adjournment, he may adjourn them to such Time as he shall think proper; he shall receive Ambassadors and other public Ministers; he shall take Care that the Laws be faithfully executed, and shall Commission all the Officers of the United States.

Section 4. The President, Vice President and all civil Officers of the United States, shall be removed from Office on Impeachment for, and Conviction of, Treason, Bribery, or other high Crimes and Misdemeanors.

Article III

Section 1. The judicial Power of the United States, shall be vested in one supreme Court, and in such inferior Courts as the Congress may from time to time ordain and establish. The Judges, both of the supreme and inferior Courts, shall hold their Offices during good Behaviour, and shall, at stated Times, receive for their Services a Compensation, which shall not be diminished during their Continuance in Office.

Section 2. The judicial Power shall extend to all Cases, in Law and Equity, arising under this Constitution, the Laws of the United States, and Treaties made, or which shall be made, under their Authority;—to all Cases affecting Ambassadors, other public Ministers and Consuls;—to all Cases of admiralty and maritime Jurisdiction;—to Controversies to which the United States shall be a Party;—to Controversies between two or more States;—between a State and Citizens of another State;—between Citizens of different States;—between Citizens of the same State claiming Lands under Grants of different States, and between a State, or the Citizens thereof, and foreign States, Citizens or Subjects.

In all Cases affecting Ambassadors, other public Ministers and Consuls, and those in which a State shall be a Party, the supreme Court shall have original Jurisdiction. In all the other Cases before mentioned, the supreme Court shall have appellate Jurisdiction, both as to Law and Fact, with such Exceptions, and under such Regulations as the Congress shall make.

The Trial of all Crimes, except in Cases of Impeachment, shall be by Jury; and such Trial shall be held in the State where the said Crimes shall have been committed; but when not committed within any State, the Trial shall be at such Place or Places as the Congress may by Law have directed.

Section 3. Treason against the United States, shall consist only in levying War against them, or, in adhering to their Enemies, giving them Aid and Comfort. No Person shall be convicted of Treason unless on the Testimony of two Witnesses to the same overt Act, or on Confession in open Court.

The Congress shall have Power to declare the Punishment of Treason, but no Attainder of Treason shall work Corruption of Blood, or Forfeiture except during the Life of the Person attainted.

Article IV

Section 1. Full Faith and Credit shall be given in each State to the public Acts, Records, and judicial Proceedings of every other State. And the Congress may by general Laws prescribe the Manner in which such Acts, Records and Proceedings shall be proved, and the Effect thereof.

Section 2. The Citizens of each State shall be entitled to all Privileges and Immunities of Citizens in the several States.

A Person charged in any State with Treason, Felony, or other Crime, who shall flee from Justice, and be found in another State, shall on Demand of the executive Authority of the State from which he fled, be delivered up, to be removed to the State having Jurisdiction of the Crime.

No Person held to Service or Labour in one State, under the Laws thereof, escaping into another, shall, in Consequence of any Law or Regulation therein, be discharged from such Service or Labour, but shall be delivered up on Claim of the Party to whom such Service or Labour may be due.

Section 3. New States may be admitted by the Congress into this Union; but no new State shall be formed or erected within the Jurisdiction of any other State; nor any State be formed by the Junction of two or more States, or Parts of States, without the Consent of the Legislatures of the States concerned as well as of the Congress.

The Congress shall have Power to dispose of and make all needful Rules and Regulations respecting the Territory or other Property belonging to the United States; and nothing in this Constitution shall be so construed as to Prejudice any Claims of the United States, or of any particular State.

Section 4. The United States shall guarantee to every State in this Union a Republican Form of Government, and shall protect each of them against Invasion; and on Application of the Legislature, or of the Executive (when the Legislature cannot be convened) against domestic Violence.

Article V

The Congress, whenever two thirds of both Houses shall deem it necessary, shall propose Amendments to this Constitution, or, on the Application of the Legislatures of two thirds of the several States, shall call a Convention for proposing Amendments, which, in either Case, shall be valid to all Intents and Purposes, as part of this Constitution, when ratified by the Legislatures of three fourths of the several States, or by Conventions in three fourths thereof, as the one or the other Mode of Ratification may be proposed by the Congress; Provided that no Amendment which may be made prior to the Year One thousand eight hundred and eight shall in any Manner affect the first and fourth Clauses in the Ninth Section of the first Article; and that no State, without its Consent, shall be deprived of its equal Suffrage in the Senate.

Article VI

All Debts contracted and Engagements entered into, before the Adoption of this Constitution shall be as valid against the United States under this Constitution, as under the Confederation.

This Constitution, and the Laws of the United States which shall be made in Pursuance thereof; and all Treaties made, or which shall be made, under the Authority of the United States, shall be the supreme Law of the Land; and the Judges in every State shall be bound thereby, any Thing in the Constitution or Laws of any State to the Contrary notwithstanding.

The Senators and Representatives before mentioned, and the Members of the several State Legislatures, and all executive and judicial Officers, both of the United States and of the several States, shall be bound by Oath or Affirmation, to support this Constitution; but no religious Test shall ever be required as a Qualification to any Office or public Trust under the United States.

Article VII

The Ratification of the Conventions of nine States shall be sufficient for the Establishment of this Constitution between the States so ratifying the Same.

Amendment I [1791]

Congress shall make no law respecting an establishment of religion, or prohibiting the free exercise thereof; or abridging the freedom of speech, or of the press; or the right of the people peaceably to assembly, and to petition the Government for a redress of grievances.

Amendment II [1791]

A well regulated Militia, being necessary to the security of a free State, the right of the people to keep and bear Arms, shall not be infringed.

Amendment III [1791]

No Soldier shall, in time of peace be quartered in any house, without the consent of the Owner, nor in time of war, but in a manner to be prescribed by law.

Amendment IV [1791]

The right of the people to be secure in their persons, houses, papers, and effects, against unreasonable searches and seizures, shall not be violated, and no Warrants shall issue, but upon probable cause, supported by Oath or affirmation, and particularly describing the place to be searched, and the persons or things to be seized.

Amendment V [1791]

No person shall be held to answer for a capital, or otherwise infamous crime, unless on a presentment or indictment of a Grand Jury, except in cases arising in the land or naval forces, or in the Militia, when in actual service in time of War or public danger; nor shall any person be subject for the same offence to be twice put in jeopardy of life or limb; nor shall be compelled in any criminal case to be a witness against himself, nor be deprived of life, liberty, or property, without due process of law; nor shall private property be taken for public use, without just compensation.

Amendment VI [1791]

In all criminal prosecutions, the accused shall enjoy the right to a speedy and public trial, by an impartial jury of the State and district wherein the crime shall have been committed, which district shall have been previously ascertained by law, and to be informed of the nature and cause of the accusation; to be confronted with the witnesses against him; to have compulsory process for obtaining witnesses in his favor, and to have the Assistance of Counsel for his defence.

Amendment VII [1791]

In Suits at common law, where the value in controversy shall exceed twenty dollars, the right of trial by jury shall be preserved, and no fact tried by jury, shall be otherwise re-examined in any Court of the United States, than according to the rules of the common law.

Amendment VIII [1791]

Excessive bail shall not be required, nor excessive fines imposed, nor cruel and unusual punishments inflicted.

Amendment IX [1791]

The enumeration in the Constitution, of certain rights, shall not be construed to deny or disparage others retained by the people.

Amendment X [1791]

The powers not delegated to the United States by the Constitution, nor prohibited by it to the States, are reserved to the States respectively, or to the people.

Amendment XI [1795]

The Judicial power of the United States shall not be construed to extend to any suit in law or equity, commenced or prosecuted against one of the United States by Citizens of another State, or by Citizens or Subjects of any Foreign State.

Amendment XII [1804]

The Electors shall meet in their respective states, and vote by ballot for President and Vice-President, one of whom, at least, shall not be an inhabitant of the same state with themselves; they shall name in their ballots the person voted for as President, and in distinct ballots the person voted for as Vice-President, and they shall make distinct lists of all persons voted for as President, and of all persons voted for as Vice-President, and of the number of votes for each, which lists they shall sign and certify, and transmit sealed to the seat of the government of the United States, directed to the President of the Senate;—The President of the Senate shall, in the presence of the Senate and House of Representatives, open all the certificates and the votes shall then be counted;—The person having the greatest number of votes for President, shall be the President, if such number be a majority of the whole number of Electors appointed; and if no person have such majority, then from the persons having the highest numbers not exceeding three on the list of those voted for as President, the House of Representatives shall choose immediately, by ballot, the President. But in choosing the President, the votes shall be taken by states, the representation from each state having one vote; a quorum for this purpose shall consist of a member or members from two-thirds of the states, and a majority of all states shall be necessary to a choice. And if the House of Representatives shall not choose a President whenever the right of choice shall devolve upon them, before the fourth day of March next following, then the Vice-President shall act as President, as in the case of the death or other constitutional disability of the President.—The person having the greatest number of votes as Vice-President, shall be the Vice-President, if such number be a majority of the whole number of Electors appointed, and if no person have a majority, then from the two highest numbers on the list, the Senate shall choose the Vice-President; a quorum for the purpose shall consist of two-thirds of the whole number of Senators, and a majority of the whole number shall be necessary to a choice. But no person constitutionally ineligible to the office of President shall be eligible to that of Vice-President of the United States.

Amendment XIII [1865]

Section 1. Neither slavery nor involuntary servitude, except as a punishment for crime whereof the party shall have been duly convicted, shall exist within the United States, or any place subject to their jurisdiction.

Section 2. Congress shall have power to enforce this article by appropriate legislation.

Amendment XIV [1868]

Section 1. All persons born or naturalized in the United States, and subject to the jurisdiction thereof, are citizens of the United States and of the State wherein they reside. No State shall make or enforce any law which shall abridge the privileges or immunities of citizens of the United States; nor shall any State deprive any person of life, liberty, or property, without due process of law; nor deny to any person within its jurisdiction the equal protection of the laws.

Section 2. Representatives shall be apportioned among the several States according to their respective numbers, counting the whole number of persons in each State, excluding Indians not taxed. But when the right to vote at any election for the choice of electors for President and Vice President of the United States, Representatives in Congress, the Executive and Judicial officers of a State, or the members of the Legislature thereof, is denied to any of the male inhabitants of such State, being twenty-one years of age, and citizens of the United States, or in any way abridged, except for participation in rebellion, or other crime, the basis of representation therein shall be reduced in the proportion which the number of such male citizens shall bear to the whole number of male citizens twenty-one years of age in such State.

Section 3. No person shall be a Senator or Representative in Congress, or elector of President and Vice President, or hold any office, civil or military, under the United States, or under any State, who having previously taken an oath, as a member of Congress, or as an officer of the United States, or as a member of any State legislature, or as an executive or judicial officer of any State, to support the Constitution of the United States, shall have engaged in insurrection or rebellion against the same, or given aid or comfort to the enemies thereof. But Congress may by a vote of two-thirds of each House, remove such disability.

Section 4. The validity of the public debt of the United States, authorized by law, including debts incurred for payment of pensions and bounties for services in suppressing insurrection or rebellion, shall not be questioned. But neither the United States nor any State shall assume or pay any debt or obligation incurred in aid of insurrection or rebellion against the United States, or any claim for the loss or emancipation of any slave; but all such debts, obligations and claims shall be held illegal and void.

Section 5. The Congress shall have power to enforce, by appropriate legislation, the provisions of this article.

Amendment XV [1870]

Section 1. The right of citizens of the United States to vote shall not be denied or abridged by the United States or by any State on account of race, color, or previous condition of servitude.

Section 2. The Congress shall have power to enforce this article by appropriate legislation.

Amendment XVI [1913]

The Congress shall have power to lay and collect taxes on incomes, from whatever source derived, without apportionment among the several States, and without regard to any census or enumeration.

Amendment XVII [1913]

Section 1. The Senate of the United States shall be composed of two Senators from each State, elected by the people thereof, for six years; and each Senator shall have one vote. The electors in each State shall have the qualifications requisite for electors of the most numerous branch of the State legislatures.

Section 2. When vacancies happen in the representation of any State in the Senate, the executive authority of such State shall issue writs of election to fill such vacancies: *Provided,* That the legislature of any State may empower the executive thereof to make temporary appointments until the people fill the vacancies by election as the legislature may direct.

Section 3. This amendment shall not be so construed as to affect the election or term of any Senator chosen before it becomes valid as part of the Constitution.

Amendment XVIII [1919]

Section 1. After one year from the ratification of this article the manufacture, sale, or transportation of intoxicating liquors within, the importation thereof into, or the exportation thereof from the United States and all territory subject to the jurisdiction thereof for beverage purposes is hereby prohibited.

Section 2. The Congress and the several States shall have concurrent power to enforce this article by appropriate legislation.

Section 3. This article shall be inoperative unless it shall have been ratified as an amendment to the Constitution by the legislatures of the several States, as provided in the Constitution, within seven years from the date of the submission hereof to the States by the Congress.

Amendment XIX [1920]

Section 1. The right of citizens of the United States to vote shall not be denied or abridged by the United States or by any State on account of sex.

Section 2. Congress shall have power to enforce this article by appropriate legislation.

Amendment XX [1933]

Section 1. The terms of the President and Vice President shall end at noon on the 20th day of January, and the terms of Senators and Representatives at noon on the 3d day of January, of the years in which such terms would have ended if this article had not been ratified; and the terms of their successors shall then begin.

Section 2. The Congress shall assemble at least once in every year, and such meeting shall begin at noon on the 3d day of January, unless they shall by law appoint a different day.

Section 3. If, at the time fixed for the beginning of the term of the President, the President elect shall have died, the Vice President elect shall become President. If the President shall not have been chosen before the time fixed for the beginning of his term, or if the President elect shall have failed to qualify, then the Vice President elect shall act as President until a President shall have qualified; and the Congress may by law provide for the case wherein neither a President elect nor a Vice President elect shall have qualified, declaring who shall then act as President, or the manner in which one who is to act shall be selected, and such person shall act accordingly until a President or Vice President shall have qualified.

Section 4. The Congress may by law provide for the case of the death of any of the persons from whom the House of Representatives may choose a President whenever the right of choice shall have devolved upon them, and for the case of the death of any of the persons from whom the Senate may choose a Vice President whenever the right of choice shall have devolved upon them.

Section 5. Sections 1 and 2 shall take effect on the 15th day of October following the ratification of this article.

Section 6. This article shall be inoperative unless it shall have been ratified as an amendment to the Constitution by the legislatures of three-fourths of the several States within seven years from the date of its submission.

Amendment XXI [1933]

Section 1. The eighteenth article of amendment to the Constitution of the United States is hereby repealed.

Section 2. The transportation or importation into any State, Territory, or possession of the United States for delivery or use therein of intoxicating liquors, in violation of the laws thereof, is hereby prohibited.

Section 3. This article shall be inoperative unless it shall have been ratified as an amendment to the Constitution by conventions in the several States, as provided in the Constitution, within seven years from the date of the submission hereof to the States by the Congress.

Amendment XXII [1951]

Section 1. No person shall be elected to the office of the President more than twice, and no person who has held the office of President, or acted as President, for more than two years of a term to which some other person was elected President shall be elected to the office of President more than once. But this Article shall not apply to any person holding the office of President when this Article was proposed by the Congress, and shall not prevent any person who may be holding the office of President, or acting as President, during the term within which this Article becomes operative from holding the office of President or acting as President during the remainder of such term.

Section 2. This article shall be inoperative unless it shall have been ratified as an amendment to the Constitution by the legislatures of three-fourths of the several States within seven years from the date of its submission to the States by the Congress.

Amendment XXIII [1961]

Section 1. The District constituting the seat of Government of the United States shall appoint in such manner as the Congress may direct:

A number of electors of President and Vice President equal to the whole number of Senators and Representatives in Congress to which the District would be entitled if it were a State, but in no event more than the least populous state; they shall be in addition to those appointed by the states, but they shall be considered, for the purposes of the election of President and Vice President, to be electors appointed by a state; and they shall meet in the District and perform such duties as provided by the twelfth article of amendment.

Section 2. The Congress shall have power to enforce this article by appropriate legislation.

Amendment XXIV [1964]

Section 1. The right of citizens of the United States to vote in any primary or other election for President or Vice President, for electors for President or Vice President, or for Senator or Representative in Congress, shall not be denied or abridged by the United States, or any State by reason of failure to pay any poll tax or other tax.

Section 2. The Congress shall have power to enforce this article by appropriate legislation.

Amendment XXV [1967]

Section 1. In case of the removal of the President from office or of his death or resignation, the Vice President shall become President.

Section 2. Whenever there is a vacancy in the office of the Vice President, the President shall nominate a Vice President who shall take office upon confirmation by a majority vote of both Houses of Congress.

Section 3. Whenever the President transmits to the President pro tempore of the Senate and the Speaker of the House of Representatives his written declaration that he is unable to discharge the powers and duties of his office, and until he transmits to them a written declaration to the contrary, such powers and duties shall be discharged by the Vice President as Acting President.

Section 4. Whenever the Vice President and a majority of either the principal officers of the executive departments or of such other body as Congress may by law provide, transmit to the President pro tempore of the Senate and the Speaker of the House of Representatives their written declaration that the President is unable to discharge the powers and duties of his office, the Vice President shall immediately assume the powers and duties of the office as Acting President.

Thereafter, when the President transmits to the President pro tempore of the Senate and the Speaker of the House of Representatives his written declaration that no inability exists, he shall resume the powers and duties of his office unless the Vice President and a majority of either the principal officers of the executive department or of such other body as Congress may by law provide, transmit within four days to the President pro tempore of the Senate and the Speaker of the House of Representatives their written declaration that the President is unable to discharge the powers and duties of his office. Thereupon Congress shall decide the issue, assembling within forty-eight hours for that purpose if not in session. If the Congress, within twenty-one days after receipt of the latter written declaration, or, if Congress is not in session, within twenty-one days after Congress is required to assemble, determines by two-thirds vote of both Houses that the President is unable to discharge the powers and duties of his office, the Vice President shall continue to discharge the same as Acting President; otherwise, the President shall resume the powers and duties of his office.

Amendment XXVI [1971]

Section 1. The right of citizens of the United States, who are eighteen years of age or older, to vote shall not be denied or abridged by the United States or by any State on account of age.

Section 2. The Congress shall have power to enforce this article by appropriate legislation.

Amendment XXVII [1992]

No law, varying the compensation for the services of the Senators and Representatives, shall take effect, until an election of Representatives shall have intervened.

The Uniform Commercial Code (Excerpts)

(Adopted in fifty-two jurisdictions; all fifty States, although Louisiana has adopted only Articles 1, 3, 4, 7, 8, and 9; the District of Columbia; and the Virgin Islands.)

The Uniform Commercial Code consists of the following articles:

Articles:

1. **General Provisions**
2. **Sales**
2A. **Leases**
3. **Negotiable Instruments**
4. **Bank Deposits and Collections**
4A. **Fund Transfers**
5. **Letters of Credit**
6. **Repealer of Article 6—Bulk Transfers and [Revised] Article 6—Bulk Sales**
7. **Warehouse Receipts, Bills of Lading and Other Documents of Title**
8. **Investment Securities**
9. **Secured Transactions**
10. **Effective Date and Repealer**
11. **Effective Date and Transition Provisions**

Article 1
GENERAL PROVISIONS

Part 1   General Provisions

§ 1–101.   Short Titles.

(a) This [Act] may be cited as Uniform Commercial Code.

(b) This article may be cited as Uniform Commercial Code–Uniform Provisions.

§ 1–102.   Scope of Article.

This article applies to a transaction to the extent that it is governed by another article of [the Uniform Commercial Code].

§ 1–103.   Construction of [Uniform Commercial Code] to Promote Its Purpose and Policies; Applicability of Supplemental Principles of Law.

(a) [The Uniform Commercial Code] must be liberally construed and applied to promote its underlying purposes and policies, which are:

(1) to simplify, clarify, and modernize the law governing commercial transactions;

(2) to permit the continued expansion of commercial practices through custom, usage, and agreement of the parties; and

(3) to make uniform the law among the various jurisdictions.

(b) Unless displaced by the particular provisions of [the Uniform Commercial Code], the principles of law and equity, including the law merchant and the law relative to capacity to contract, principal and agent, estoppel, fraud, misrepresentation, duress, coercion, mistake, bankruptcy, and other validating or invalidating cause, supplement its provisions.

§ 1–104.   Construction Against Implicit Repeal.

This Act being a general act intended as a unified coverage of its subject matter, no part of it shall be deemed to be impliedly repealed by subsequent legislation if such construction can reasonably be avoided.

§ 1–105.   Severability.

If any provision or clause of [the Uniform Commercial Code] or its application to any person or circumstance is held invalid, the invalidity does not affect other provisions or applications of [the Uniform Commercial Code] which can be given effect without the invalid provision or application, and to this end the provisions of [the Uniform Commercial Code] are severable.

§ 1–106.   Use of Singular and Plural; Gender.

In [the Uniform Commercial Code], unless the statutory context otherwise requires:

(1) words in the singular number include the plural, and those in the plural include the singular; and

(2) words of any gender also refer to any other gender.

§ 1–107.   Section Captions.

Section captions are part of [the Uniform Commercial Code].

§ 1-108.   Relation to Electronic Signatures in Global and National Commerce Act.

This article modifies, limits, and supersedes the Federal Electronic Signatures in Global and National Commerce Act, 15 U.S.C. Sections 7001 *et seq.*, except that nothing in this article modifies, limits, or supersedes section 7001(c) of that act or authorizes electronic delivery of any of the notices described in section 7003(b) of that Act.

Part 2   General Definitions and Principles of Interpretation

§ 1-201.   General Definitions.

Subject to additional definitions contained in the subsequent Articles of this Act which are applicable to specific Articles or Parts thereof, and unless the context otherwise requires, in this Act:

(1) "Action", in the sense of a judicial proceeding, includes recoupment, counterclaim, set-off, suit in equity, and any other proceedings in which rights are determined.

(2) "Aggrieved party" means a party entitled to resort to a remedy.

(3) "Agreement", as distinguished from "contract", means the bargain of the parties in fact, as found in their language or by implication from other circumstances, including course of performance, course of dealing, or usage of trade as provided in Section 1–303.

(4) "Bank" means a person engaged in the business of banking and includes a savings bank, savings and loan association, credit union, and trust company.

(5) "Bearer" means a person in control of a negotiable electronic document of title or a person in possession of a negotiable instrument, negotiable tangible document of title, or certificated security that is payable to bearer or indorsed in blank.

(6) "Bill of lading" means a document of title evidencing the receipt of goods for shipment issued by a person engaged in the business of directly or indirectly transporting or forwarding goods. The term does not include a warehouse receipt.

(7) "Branch" includes a separately incorporated foreign branch of a bank.

(8) "Burden of establishing" a fact means the burden of persuading the trier of fact that the existence of the fact is more probable than its nonexistence.

(9) "Buyer in ordinary course of business" means a person that buys goods in good faith, without knowledge that the sale violates the rights of another person in the goods, and in the ordinary course from a person, other than a pawnbroker, in the business of selling goods of that kind. A person buys goods in the ordinary course if the sale to the person comports with the usual or customary practices in the kind of business in which the seller is engaged or with the seller's own usual or customary practices. A person that sells oil, gas, or other minerals at the wellhead or minehead is a person in the business of selling goods of that kind. A buyer in ordinary course of business may buy for cash, by exchange of other property, or on secured or unsecured credit, and may acquire goods or documents of title under a pre-existing contract for sale. Only a buyer that takes possession of the goods or has a right to recover the goods from the seller under Article 2 may be a buyer in ordinary course of business. A person that acquires goods in a transfer in bulk or as security for or in total or partial satisfaction of a money debt is not a buyer in ordinary course of business.

(10) "Conspicuous", with reference to a term, means so written, displayed, or presented that a reasonable person against which it is to operate ought to have noticed it. Whether a term is "conspicuous" or not is a decision for the court. Conspicuous terms include the following:

(A) a heading in capitals equal to or greater in size than the surrounding text, or in contrasting type, font, or color to the surrounding text of the same or lesser size; and

(B) language in the body of a record or display in larger type than the surrounding text, or in contrasting type, font, or color to the surrounding text of the same size, or set off from surrounding text of the same size by symbols or other marks that call attention to the language.

(11) "Consumer" means an individual who enters into a transaction primarily for personal, family, or household purposes.

(12) "Contract", as distinguished from "agreement", means the total legal obligation that results from the parties' agreement as determined by [the Uniform Commercial Code] as supplemented by any other laws.

(13) "Creditor" includes a general creditor, a secured creditor, a lien creditor and any representative of creditors, including an assignee for the benefit of creditors, a trustee in bankruptcy, a receiver in equity and an executor or administrator of an insolvent debtor's or assignor's estate.

(14) "Defendant" includes a person in the position of defendant in a counterclaim, cross-action, or third-party claim.

(15) "Delivery" with respect to an electronic document of title means voluntary transfer of control and with respect to an instrument, a tangible document of title, or chattel paper means voluntary transfer of possession.

(16) "Document of title" means a record (i) that in regular course of business or financing is treated as adequately evidencing that the person in possession or control of the record is entitled to receive, control, hold, and dispose of the record and the goods the record covers and (ii) that purports to be issued by or addressed to a bailee and to cover goods in the bailee's possession which are either identified or are fungible portions of an identified mass. The term includes a bill of lading, transport document, dock warrant, dock receipt, warehouse receipt, and order for delivery of goods. An electronic document of title means a document of title evidenced by a record consisting of information stored in an electronic medium. A tangible document of title means a document of title evidenced by a record consisting of information that is inscribed on a tangible medium.

(17) "Fault" means a default, breach, or wrongful act or omission.

(18) "Fungible goods" means:

(A) goods of which any unit, by nature or usage of trade, is the equivalent of any other like unit; or

(B) goods that by agreement are treated as equivalent.

(19) "Genuine" means free of forgery or counterfeiting.

(20) "Good faith," except as otherwise provided in Article 5, means honesty in fact and the observance of reasonable commercial standards of fair dealing.

(21) "Holder" means:

(A) the person in possession of a negotiable instrument that is payable either to bearer or to an identified person that is the person in possession;

(B) the person in possession of a negotiable tangible document of title if the goods are deliverable either to bearer or to the order of the person in possession; or

(C) the person in control of a negotiable electronic document of title.

(22) "Insolvency proceeding" includes an assignment for the benefit of creditors or other proceeding intended to liquidate or rehabilitate the estate of the person involved.

(23) "Insolvent" means:

(A) having generally ceased to pay debts in the ordinary course of business other than as a result of bona fide dispute;

(B) being unable to pay debts as they become due; or

(C) being insolvent within the meaning of federal bankruptcy law.

(24) "Money" means a medium of exchange currently authorized or adopted by a domestic or foreign government. The term includes a monetary unit of account established by an intergovernmental organization or by agreement between two or more countries.

(25) "Organization" means a person other than an individual.

(26) "Party", as distinguished from "third party", means a person that has engaged in a transaction or made an agreement subject to [the Uniform Commercial Code].

(27) "Person" means an individual, corporation, business trust, estate, trust, partnership, limited liability company, association, joint venture, government, governmental subdivision, agency, or instrumentality, public corporation, or any other legal or commercial entity.

(28) "Present value" means the amount as of a date certain of one or more sums payable in the future, discounted to the date certain by use of either an interest rate specified by the parties if that rate is not manifestly unreasonable at the time the transaction is entered into or, if an interest rate is not so specified, a commercially reasonable rate that takes into account the facts and circumstances at the time the transaction is entered into.

(29) "Purchase" means taking by sale, lease, discount, negotiation, mortgage, pledge, lien, security interest, issue or reissue, gift, or any other voluntary transaction creating an interest in property.

(30) "Purchaser" means a person that takes by purchase.

(31) "Record" means information that is inscribed on a tangible medium or that is stored in an electronic or other medium and is retrievable in perceivable form.

(32) "Remedy" means any remedial right to which an aggrieved party is entitled with or without resort to a tribunal.

(33) "Representative" means a person empowered to act for another, including an agent, an officer of a corporation or association, and a trustee, executor, or administrator of an estate.

(34) "Right" includes remedy.

(35) "Security interest" means an interest in personal property or fixtures which secures payment or performance of an obligation. "Security interest" includes any interest of a consignor and a buyer of accounts, chattel paper, a payment intangible, or a promissory note in a transaction that is subject to Article 9. "Security interest" does not include the special property interest of a buyer of goods on identification of those goods to a contract for sale under Section 2–401, but a buyer may also acquire a "security interest" by complying with Article 9. Except as otherwise provided in Section 2–505, the right of a seller or lessor of goods under Article 2 or 2A to retain or acquire possession of the goods is not a "security interest", but a seller or lessor may also acquire a "security interest" by complying with Article 9. The retention or reservation of title by a seller of goods notwithstanding shipment or delivery to the buyer under Section 2–401 is limited in effect to a reservation of a "security interest." Whether a transaction in the form of a lease creates a "security interest" is determined pursuant to Section 1–203.

(36) "Send" in connection with a writing, record, or notice means:

(A) to deposit in the mail or deliver for transmission by any other usual means of communication with postage or cost of transmission provided for and properly addressed and, in the case of an instrument, to an address specified thereon or otherwise agreed, or if there be none to any address reasonable under the circumstances; or

(B) in any other way to cause to be received any record or notice within the time it would have arrived if properly sent.

(37) "Signed" includes using any symbol executed or adopted with present intention to adopt or accept a writing.

(38) "State" means a State of the United States, the District of Columbia, Puerto Rico, the United States Virgin Islands, or any territory or insular possession subject to the jurisdiction of the United States.

(39) "Surety" includes a guarantor or other secondary obligor.

(40) "Term" means a portion of an agreement that relates to a particular matter.

(41) "Unauthorized signature" means a signature made without actual, implied, or apparent authority. The term includes a forgery.

(42) "Warehouse receipt" means a document of title issued by a person engaged in the business of storing goods for hire.

(43) "Writing" includes printing, typewriting, or any other intentional reduction to tangible form. "Written" has a corresponding meaning.

As amended in 2003.

* * * *

§ 1–205.   Reasonable Time; Seasonableness.

(a) Whether a time for taking an action required by [the Uniform Commercial Code] is reasonable depends on the nature, purpose, and circumstances of the action.

(b) An action is taken seasonably if it is taken at or within the time agreed or, if no time is agreed, at or within a reasonable time.

* * * *

Part 3   Territorial Applicability and General Rules

* * * *

§ 1–303.   Course of Performance, Course of Dealing, and Usage of Trade.

(a) A "course of performance" is a sequence of conduct between the parties to a particular transaction that exists if:

(1) the agreement of the parties with respect to the transaction involves repeated occasions for performance by a party; and

(2) the other party, with knowledge of the nature of the performance and opportunity for objection to it, accepts the performance or acquiesces in it without objection.

(b) A "course of dealing" is a sequence of conduct concerning previous transactions between the parties to a particular transaction that is fairly to be regarded as establishing a common basis of understanding for interpreting their expressions and other conduct.

(c) A "usage of trade" is any practice or method of dealing having such regularity of observance in a place, vocation, or trade as to justify an expectation that it will be observed with respect to the transaction in question. The existence and scope of such a usage must be proved as facts. If it is established that such a usage is embodied in a trade code or similar record, the interpretation of the record is a question of law.

(d) A course of performance or course of dealing between the parties or usage of trade in the vocation or trade in which they are engaged or of which they are or should be aware is relevant in ascertaining the meaning of the parties' agreement, may give particular meaning to specific terms of the agreement, and may supplement or qualify the terms of the agreement. A usage of trade applicable in the place in which part of the performance under the agreement is to occur may be so utilized as to that part of the performance.

(e) Except as otherwise provided in subsection (f), the express terms of an agreement and any applicable course of performance, course of dealing, or usage of trade must be construed whenever reasonable as consistent with each other. If such a construction is unreasonable:

(1) express terms prevail over course of performance, course of dealing, and usage of trade;

(2) course of performance prevails over course of dealing and usage of trade; and

(3) course of dealing prevails over usage of trade.

(f) Subject to Section 2–209 and Section 2A–208, a course of performance is relevant to show a waiver or modification of any term inconsistent with the course of performance.

(g) Evidence of a relevant usage of trade offered by one party is not admissible unless that party has given the other party notice that the court finds sufficient to prevent unfair surprise to the other party.

§ 1–304.   Obligation of Good Faith.

Every contract or duty within [the Uniform Commercial Code] imposes an obligation of good faith in its performance and enforcement.

* * * *

§ 1–309.   Option to Accelerate at Will.

A term providing that one party or that party's successor in interest may accelerate payment or performance or require collateral or additional collateral "at will" or when the party "deems itself insecure," or words of similar import, means that the party has power to do so only if that party in good faith believes that the prospect of payment or performance is impaired. The burden of establishing lack of good faith is on the party against which the power has been exercised.

§ 1–310.   Subordinated Obligations.

An obligation may be issued as subordinated to performance of another obligation of the person obligated, or a creditor may subordinate its right to performance of an obligation by agreement with either the person obligated or another creditor of the person obligated. Subordination does not create a security interest as against either the common debtor or a subordinated creditor.

Article 2
SALES

Part 1   Short Title, General Construction and Subject Matter

§ 2–101.   Short Title.

This Article shall be known and may be cited as Uniform Commercial Code—Sales.

§ 2–102.   Scope; Certain Security and Other Transactions Excluded From This Article.

Unless the context otherwise requires, this Article applies to transactions in goods; it does not apply to any transaction which although in the form of an unconditional contract to sell or present sale is intended to operate only as a security transaction nor does this Article impair or repeal any statute regulating sales to consumers, farmers or other specified classes of buyers.

§ 2–103.   Definitions and Index of Definitions.

(1) In this Article unless the context otherwise requires

(a) "Buyer" means a person who buys or contracts to buy goods.

(b) "Good faith" in the case of a merchant means honesty in fact and the observance of reasonable commercial standards of fair dealing in the trade.

(c) "Receipt" of goods means taking physical possession of them.

(d) "Seller" means a person who sells or contracts to sell goods.

(2) Other definitions applying to this Article or to specified Parts thereof, and the sections in which they appear are:

"Acceptance". Section 2–606.

"Banker's credit". Section 2–325.

"Between merchants". Section 2–104.

"Cancellation". Section 2–106(4).

"Commercial unit". Section 2–105.

"Confirmed credit". Section 2–325.

"Conforming to contract". Section 2–106.

"Contract for sale". Section 2–106.

"Cover". Section 2–712.

"Entrusting". Section 2–403.

"Financing agency". Section 2–104.

"Future goods". Section 2–105.

"Goods". Section 2–105.

"Identification". Section 2–501.

"Installment contract". Section 2–612.

"Letter of Credit". Section 2–325.

"Lot". Section 2–105.

"Merchant". Section 2–104.

"Overseas". Section 2–323.

"Person in position of seller". Section 2–707.

"Present sale". Section 2–106.

"Sale". Section 2–106.

"Sale on approval". Section 2–326.

"Sale or return". Section 2–326.

"Termination". Section 2–106.

(3) The following definitions in other Articles apply to this Article:

"Check". Section 3–104.

"Consignee". Section 7–102.

"Consignor". Section 7–102.

"Consumer goods". Section 9–109.

"Dishonor". Section 3–507.

"Draft". Section 3–104.

(4) In addition Article 1 contains general definitions and principles of construction and interpretation applicable throughout this Article.

As amended in 1994 and 1999.

§ 2–104. Definitions: "Merchant"; "Between Merchants"; "Financing Agency".

(1) "Merchant" means a person who deals in goods of the kind or otherwise by his occupation holds himself out as having knowledge or skill peculiar to the practices or goods involved in the transaction or to whom such knowledge or skill may be attributed by his employment of an agent or broker or other intermediary who by his occupation holds himself out as having such knowledge or skill.

(2) "Financing agency" means a bank, finance company or other person who in the ordinary course of business makes advances against goods or documents of title or who by arrangement with either the seller or the buyer intervenes in ordinary course to make or collect payment due or claimed under the contract for sale, as by purchasing or paying the seller's draft or making advances against it or by merely taking it for collection whether or not documents of title accompany the draft. "Financing agency" includes also a bank or other person who similarly intervenes between persons who are in the position of seller and buyer in respect to the goods (Section 2–707).

(3) "Between merchants" means in any transaction with respect to which both parties are chargeable with the knowledge or skill of merchants.

§ 2–105. Definitions: Transferability; "Goods"; "Future" Goods; "Lot"; "Commercial Unit".

(1) "Goods" means all things (including specially manufactured goods) which are movable at the time of identification to the contract for sale other than the money in which the price is to be paid, investment securities (Article 8) and things in action. "Goods" also includes the unborn young of animals and growing crops and other identified things attached to realty as described in the section on goods to be severed from realty (Section 2–107).

(2) Goods must be both existing and identified before any interest in them can pass. Goods which are not both existing and identified are "future" goods. A purported present sale of future goods or of any interest therein operates as a contract to sell.

(3) There may be a sale of a part interest in existing identified goods.

(4) An undivided share in an identified bulk of fungible goods is sufficiently identified to be sold although the quantity of the bulk is not determined. Any agreed proportion of such a bulk or any quantity thereof agreed upon by number, weight or other measure may to the extent of the seller's interest in the bulk be sold to the buyer who then becomes an owner in common.

(5) "Lot" means a parcel or a single article which is the subject matter of a separate sale or delivery, whether or not it is sufficient to perform the contract.

(6) "Commercial unit" means such a unit of goods as by commercial usage is a single whole for purposes of sale and division of which materially impairs its character or value on the market or in use. A commercial unit may be a single article (as a machine) or a set of articles (as a suite of furniture or an assortment of sizes) or a quantity (as a bale, gross, or carload) or any other unit treated in use or in the relevant market as a single whole.

§ 2–106. Definitions: "Contract"; "Agreement"; "Contract for Sale"; "Sale"; "Present Sale"; "Conforming" to Contract; "Termination"; "Cancellation".

(1) In this Article unless the context otherwise requires "contract" and "agreement" are limited to those relating to the present or future sale of goods. "Contract for sale" includes both a present sale of goods and a contract to sell goods at a future time. A "sale" consists in the passing of title from the seller to the buyer for a price (Section 2–401). A "present sale" means a sale which is accomplished by the making of the contract.

(2) Goods or conduct including any part of a performance are "conforming" or conform to the contract when they are in accordance with the obligations under the contract.

(3) "Termination" occurs when either party pursuant to a power created by agreement or law puts an end to the contract otherwise than for its breach. On "termination" all obligations which are still executory on both sides are discharged but any right based on prior breach or performance survives.

(4) "Cancellation" occurs when either party puts an end to the contract for breach by the other and its effect is the same as that of "termination" except that the cancelling party also retains any remedy for breach of the whole contract or any unperformed balance.

§ 2–107.   Goods to Be Severed From Realty: Recording.

(1) A contract for the sale of minerals or the like (including oil and gas) or a structure or its materials to be removed from realty is a contract for the sale of goods within this Article if they are to be severed by the seller but until severance a purported present sale thereof which is not effective as a transfer of an interest in land is effective only as a contract to sell.

(2) A contract for the sale apart from the land of growing crops or other things attached to realty and capable of severance without material harm thereto but not described in subsection (1) or of timber to be cut is a contract for the sale of goods within this Article whether the subject matter is to be severed by the buyer or by the seller even though it forms part of the realty at the time of contracting, and the parties can by identification effect a present sale before severance.

(3) The provisions of this section are subject to any third party rights provided by the law relating to realty records, and the contract for sale may be executed and recorded as a document transferring an interest in land and shall then constitute notice to third parties of the buyer's rights under the contract for sale.

As amended in 1972.

Part 2   Form, Formation and Readjustment of Contract

§ 2–201.   Formal Requirements; Statute of Frauds.

(1) Except as otherwise provided in this section a contract for the sale of goods for the price of $500 or more is not enforceable by way of action or defense unless there is some writing sufficient to indicate that a contract for sale has been made between the parties and signed by the party against whom enforcement is sought or by his authorized agent or broker. A writing is not insufficient because it omits or incorrectly states a term agreed upon but the contract is not enforceable under this paragraph beyond the quantity of goods shown in such writing.

(2) Between merchants if within a reasonable time a writing in confirmation of the contract and sufficient against the sender is received and the party receiving it has reason to know its contents, its satisfies the requirements of subsection (1) against such party unless written notice of objection to its contents is given within ten days after it is received.

(3) A contract which does not satisfy the requirements of subsection (1) but which is valid in other respects is enforceable

(a) if the goods are to be specially manufactured for the buyer and are not suitable for sale to others in the ordinary course of the seller's business and the seller, before notice of repudiation is received and under circumstances which reasonably indicate that the goods are for the buyer, has made either a substantial beginning of their manufacture or commitments for their procurement; or

(b) if the party against whom enforcement is sought admits in his pleading, testimony or otherwise in court that a contract for sale was made, but the contract is not enforceable under this provision beyond the quantity of goods admitted; or

(c) with respect to goods for which payment has been made and accepted or which have been received and accepted (Sec. 2–606).

§ 2–202.   Final Written Expression: Parol or Extrinsic Evidence.

Terms with respect to which the confirmatory memoranda of the parties agree or which are otherwise set forth in a writing intended by the parties as a final expression of their agreement with respect to such terms as are included therein may not be contradicted by evidence of any prior agreement or of a contemporaneous oral agreement but may be explained or supplemented

(a) by course of dealing or usage of trade (Section 1–205) or by course of performance (Section 2–208); and

(b) by evidence of consistent additional terms unless the court finds the writing to have been intended also as a complete and exclusive statement of the terms of the agreement.

§ 2–203.   Seals Inoperative.

The affixing of a seal to a writing evidencing a contract for sale or an offer to buy or sell goods does not constitute the writing a sealed instrument and the law with respect to sealed instruments does not apply to such a contract or offer.

§ 2–204.   Formation in General.

(1) A contract for sale of goods may be made in any manner sufficient to show agreement, including conduct by both parties which recognizes the existence of such a contract.

(2) An agreement sufficient to constitute a contract for sale may be found even though the moment of its making is undetermined.

(3) Even though one or more terms are left open a contract for sale does not fail for indefiniteness if the parties have intended to make a contract and there is a reasonably certain basis for giving an appropriate remedy.

§ 2–205.   Firm Offers.

An offer by a merchant to buy or sell goods in a signed writing which by its terms gives assurance that it will be held open is not revocable, for lack of consideration, during the time stated or if no time is stated for a reasonable time, but in no event may such period of irrevocability exceed three months; but any such term of assurance on a form supplied by the offeree must be separately signed by the offeror.

§ 2–206.   Offer and Acceptance in Formation of Contract.

(1) Unless other unambiguously indicated by the language or circumstances

(a) an offer to make a contract shall be construed as inviting acceptance in any manner and by any medium reasonable in the circumstances;

(b) an order or other offer to buy goods for prompt or current shipment shall be construed as inviting acceptance either by a prompt promise to ship or by the prompt or current shipment of conforming or nonconforming goods, but such a shipment of non-conforming goods does not constitute an acceptance if the seller seasonably notifies the buyer that the shipment is offered only as an accommodation to the buyer.

(2) Where the beginning of a requested performance is a reasonable mode of acceptance an offeror who is not notified of acceptance within a reasonable time may treat the offer as having lapsed before acceptance.

§ 2–207.   Additional Terms in Acceptance or Confirmation.

(1) A definite and seasonable expression of acceptance or a written confirmation which is sent within a reasonable time operates as an acceptance even though it states terms additional to or different from those offered or agreed upon, unless acceptance is expressly made conditional on assent to the additional or different terms.

(2) The additional terms are to be construed as proposals for addition to the contract. Between merchants such terms become part of the contract unless:

(a) the offer expressly limits acceptance to the terms of the offer;

(b) they materially alter it; or

(c) notification of objection to them has already been given or is given within a reasonable time after notice of them is received.

(3) Conduct by both parties which recognizes the existence of a contract is sufficient to establish a contract for sale although the writings of the parties do not otherwise establish a contract. In such case the terms of the particular contract consist of those terms on which the writings of the parties agree, together with any supplementary terms incorporated under any other provisions of this Act.

§ 2–208.   Course of Performance or Practical Construction.

(1) Where the contract for sale involves repeated occasions for performance by either party with knowledge of the nature of the performance and opportunity for objection to it by the other, any course of performance accepted or acquiesced in without objection shall be relevant to determine the meaning of the agreement.

(2) The express terms of the agreement and any such course of performance, as well as any course of dealing and usage of trade, shall be construed whenever reasonable as consistent with each other; but when such construction is unreasonable, express terms shall control course of performance and course of performance shall control both course of dealing and usage of trade (Section 1–205).

(3) Subject to the provisions of the next section on modification and waiver, such course of performance shall be relevant to show a waiver or modification of any term inconsistent with such course of performance.

§ 2–209.   Modification, Rescission and Waiver.

(1) An agreement modifying a contract within this Article needs no consideration to be binding.

(2) A signed agreement which excludes modification or rescission except by a signed writing cannot be otherwise modified or rescinded, but except as between merchants such a requirement on a form supplied by the merchant must be separately signed by the other party.

(3) The requirements of the statute of frauds section of this Article (Section 2–201) must be satisfied if the contract as modified is within its provisions.

(4) Although an attempt at modification or rescission does not satisfy the requirements of subsection (2) or (3) it can operate as a waiver.

(5) A party who has made a waiver affecting an executory portion of the contract may retract the waiver by reasonable notification received by the other party that strict performance will be required of any term waived, unless the retraction would be unjust in view of a material change of position in reliance on the waiver.

§ 2–210.   Delegation of Performance; Assignment of Rights.

(1) A party may perform his duty through a delegate unless otherwise agreed or unless the other party has a substantial interest in having his original promisor perform or control the acts required by the contract. No delegation of performance relieves the party delegating of any duty to perform or any liability for breach.

(2) Except as otherwise provided in Section 9–406, unless otherwise agreed, all rights of either seller or buyer can be assigned except where the assignment would materially change the duty of the other party, or increase materially the burden or risk imposed on him by his contract, or impair materially his chance of obtaining return performance. A right to damages for breach of the whole contract or a right arising out of the assignor's due performance of his entire obligation can be assigned despite agreement otherwise.

(3) The creation, attachment, perfection, or enforcement of a security interest in the seller's interest under a contract is not a transfer that materially changes the duty of or increases materially the burden or risk imposed on the buyer or impairs materially the buyer's chance of obtaining return performance within the purview of subsection (2) unless, and then only to the extent that, enforcement actually results in a delegation of material performance of the seller. Even in that event, the creation, attachment, perfection, and enforcement of the security interest remain effective, but (i) the seller is liable to the buyer for damages caused by the delegation to the extent that the damages could not reasonably by prevented by the buyer, and (ii) a court having jurisdiction may grant other appropriate relief, including cancellation of the contract for sale or an injunction against enforcement of the security interest or consummation of the enforcement.

(4) Unless the circumstances indicate the contrary a prohibition of assignment of "the contract" is to be construed as barring only the delegation to the assignee of the assignor's performance.

(5) An assignment of "the contract" or of "all my rights under the contract" or an assignment in similar general terms is an assignment of rights and unless the language or the circumstances (as in an assignment for security) indicate the contrary, it is a delegation of performance of the duties of the assignor and its acceptance by the assignee constitutes a promise by him to perform those duties. This promise is enforceable by either the assignor or the other party to the original contract.

(6) The other party may treat any assignment which delegates performance as creating reasonable grounds for insecurity and may

without prejudice to his rights against the assignor demand assurances from the assignee (Section 2–609).

As amended in 1999.

Part 3   General Obligation and Construction of Contract

§ 2–301.   General Obligations of Parties.

The obligation of the seller is to transfer and deliver and that of the buyer is to accept and pay in accordance with the contract.

§ 2–302.   Unconscionable Contract or Clause.

(1) If the court as a matter of law finds the contract or any clause of the contract to have been unconscionable at the time it was made the court may refuse to enforce the contract, or it may enforce the remainder of the contract without the unconscionable clause, or it may so limit the application of any unconscionable clause as to avoid any unconscionable result.

(2) When it is claimed or appears to the court that the contract or any clause thereof may be unconscionable the parties shall be afforded a reasonable opportunity to present evidence as to its commercial setting, purpose and effect to aid the court in making the determination.

§ 2–303.   Allocations or Division of Risks.

Where this Article allocates a risk or a burden as between the parties "unless otherwise agreed", the agreement may not only shift the allocation but may also divide the risk or burden.

§ 2–304.   Price Payable in Money, Goods, Realty, or Otherwise.

(1) The price can be made payable in money or otherwise. If it is payable in whole or in part in goods each party is a seller of the goods which he is to transfer.

(2) Even though all or part of the price is payable in an interest in realty the transfer of the goods and the seller's obligations with reference to them are subject to this Article, but not the transfer of the interest in realty or the transferor's obligations in connection therewith.

§ 2–305.   Open Price Term.

(1) The parties if they so intend can conclude a contract for sale even though the price is not settled. In such a case the price is a reasonable price at the time for delivery if

(a) nothing is said as to price; or

(b) the price is left to be agreed by the parties and they fail to agree; or

(c) the price is to be fixed in terms of some agreed market or other standard as set or recorded by a third person or agency and it is not so set or recorded.

(2) A price to be fixed by the seller or by the buyer means a price for him to fix in good faith.

(3) When a price left to be fixed otherwise than by agreement of the parties fails to be fixed through fault of one party the other may at his option treat the contract as cancelled or himself fix a reasonable price.

(4) Where, however, the parties intend not to be bound unless the price be fixed or agreed and it is not fixed or agreed there is no contract. In such a case the buyer must return any goods already received or if unable so to do must pay their reasonable value at the time of delivery and the seller must return any portion of the price paid on account.

§ 2–306.   Output, Requirements and Exclusive Dealings.

(1) A term which measures the quantity by the output of the seller or the requirements of the buyer means such actual output or requirements as may occur in good faith, except that no quantity unreasonably disproportionate to any stated estimate or in the absence of a stated estimate to any normal or otherwise comparable prior output or requirements may be tendered or demanded.

(2) A lawful agreement by either the seller or the buyer for exclusive dealing in the kind of goods concerned imposes unless otherwise agreed an obligation by the seller to use best efforts to supply the goods and by the buyer to use best efforts to promote their sale.

§ 2–307.   Delivery in Single Lot or Several Lots.

Unless otherwise agreed all goods called for by a contract for sale must be tendered in a single delivery and payment is due only on such tender but where the circumstances give either party the right to make or demand delivery in lots the price if it can be apportioned may be demanded for each lot.

§ 2–308.   Absence of Specified Place for Delivery.

Unless otherwise agreed

(a) the place for delivery of goods is the seller's place of business or if he has none his residence; but

(b) in a contract for sale of identified goods which to the knowledge of the parties at the time of contracting are in some other place, that place is the place for their delivery; and

(c) documents of title may be delivered through customary banking channels.

§ 2–309.   Absence of Specific Time Provisions; Notice of Termination.

(1) The time for shipment or delivery or any other action under a contract if not provided in this Article or agreed upon shall be a reasonable time.

(2) Where the contract provides for successive performances but is indefinite in duration it is valid for a reasonable time but unless otherwise agreed may be terminated at any time by either party.

(3) Termination of a contract by one party except on the happening of an agreed event requires that reasonable notification be received by the other party and an agreement dispensing with notification is invalid if its operation would be unconscionable.

§ 2–310.   Open Time for Payment or
Running of Credit; Authority to Ship Under Reservation.

Unless otherwise agreed

(a) payment is due at the time and place at which the buyer is to receive the goods even though the place of shipment is the place of delivery; and

(b) if the seller is authorized to send the goods he may ship them under reservation, and may tender the documents of title, but the buyer may inspect the goods after their arrival before payment is due unless such inspection is inconsistent with the terms of the contract (Section 2–513); and

(c) if delivery is authorized and made by way of documents of title otherwise than by subsection (b) then payment is due at the time and place at which the buyer is to receive the documents regardless of where the goods are to be received; and

(d) where the seller is required or authorized to ship the goods on credit the credit period runs from the time of shipment but post-dating the invoice or delaying its dispatch will correspondingly delay the starting of the credit period.

§ 2–311.   Options and Cooperation Respecting Performance.

(1) An agreement for sale which is otherwise sufficiently definite (subsection (3) of Section 2–204) to be a contract is not made invalid by the fact that it leaves particulars of performance to be specified by one of the parties. Any such specification must be made in good faith and within limits set by commercial reasonableness.

(2) Unless otherwise agreed specifications relating to assortment of the goods are at the buyer's option and except as otherwise provided in subsections (1)(c) and (3) of Section 2–319 specifications or arrangements relating to shipment are at the seller's option.

(3) Where such specification would materially affect the other party's performance but is not seasonably made or where one party's cooperation is necessary to the agreed performance of the other but is not seasonably forthcoming, the other party in addition to all other remedies

(a) is excused for any resulting delay in his own performance; and

(b) may also either proceed to perform in any reasonable manner or after the time for a material part of his own performance treat the failure to specify or to cooperate as a breach by failure to deliver or accept the goods.

§ 2–312.   Warranty of Title and Against Infringement; Buyer's Obligation Against Infringement.

(1) Subject to subsection (2) there is in a contract for sale a warranty by the seller that

(a) the title conveyed shall be good, and its transfer rightful; and

(b) the goods shall be delivered free from any security interest or other lien or encumbrance of which the buyer at the time of contracting has no knowledge.

(2) A warranty under subsection (1) will be excluded or modified only by specific language or by circumstances which give the buyer reason to know that the person selling does not claim title in himself or that he is purporting to sell only such right or title as he or a third person may have.

(3) Unless otherwise agreed a seller who is a merchant regularly dealing in goods of the kind warrants that the goods shall be delivered free of the rightful claim of any third person by way of infringement or the like but a buyer who furnishes specifications to the seller must hold the seller harmless against any such claim which arises out of compliance with the specifications.

§ 2–313.   Express Warranties by Affirmation, Promise, Description, Sample.

(1) Express warranties by the seller are created as follows:

(a) Any affirmation of fact or promise made by the seller to the buyer which relates to the goods and becomes part of the basis of the bargain creates an express warranty that the goods shall conform to the affirmation or promise.

(b) Any description of the goods which is made part of the basis of the bargain creates an express warranty that the goods shall conform to the description.

(c) Any sample or model which is made part of the basis of the bargain creates an express warranty that the whole of the goods shall conform to the sample or model.

(2) It is not necessary to the creation of an express warranty that the seller use formal words such as "warrant" or "guarantee" or that he have a specific intention to make a warranty, but an affirmation merely of the value of the goods or a statement purporting to be merely the seller's opinion or commendation of the goods does not create a warranty.

§ 2–314.   Implied Warranty: Merchantability; Usage of Trade.

(1) Unless excluded or modified (Section 2–316), a warranty that the goods shall be merchantable is implied in a contract for their sale if the seller is a merchant with respect to goods of that kind. Under this section the serving for value of food or drink to be consumed either on the premises or elsewhere is a sale.

(2) Goods to be merchantable must be at least such as

(a) pass without objection in the trade under the contract description; and

(b) in the case of fungible goods, are of fair average quality within the description; and

(c) are fit for the ordinary purposes for which such goods are used; and

(d) run, within the variations permitted by the agreement, of even kind, quality and quantity within each unit and among all units involved; and

(e) are adequately contained, packaged, and labeled as the agreement may require; and

(f) conform to the promises or affirmations of fact made on the container or label if any.

(3) Unless excluded or modified (Section 2–316) other implied warranties may arise from course of dealing or usage of trade.

§ 2–315.   Implied Warranty: Fitness for Particular Purpose.

Where the seller at the time of contracting has reason to know any particular purpose for which the goods are required and that the buyer is relying on the seller's skill or judgment to select or furnish suitable goods, there is unless excluded or modified under the next section an implied warranty that the goods shall be fit for such purpose.

§ 2–316.   Exclusion or Modification of Warranties.

(1) Words or conduct relevant to the creation of an express warranty and words or conduct tending to negate or limit warranty shall be construed wherever reasonable as consistent with each other; but subject to the provisions of this Article on parol or extrinsic evidence (Section 2–202) negation or limitation is inoperative to the extent that such construction is unreasonable.

(2) Subject to subsection (3), to exclude or modify the implied warranty of merchantability or any part of it the language must

mention merchantability and in case of a writing must be conspicuous, and to exclude or modify any implied warranty of fitness the exclusion must be by a writing and conspicuous. Language to exclude all implied warranties of fitness is sufficient if it states, for example, that "There are no warranties which extend beyond the description on the face hereof."

(3) Notwithstanding subsection (2)

(a) unless the circumstances indicate otherwise, all implied warranties are excluded by expressions like "as is", "with all faults" or other language which in common understanding calls the buyer's attention to the exclusion of warranties and makes plain that there is no implied warranty; and

(b) when the buyer before entering into the contract has examined the goods or the sample or model as fully as he desired or has refused to examine the goods there is no implied warranty with regard to defects which an examination ought in the circumstances to have revealed to him; and

(c) an implied warranty can also be excluded or modified by course of dealing or course of performance or usage of trade.

(4) Remedies for breach of warranty can be limited in accordance with the provisions of this Article on liquidation or limitation of damages and on contractual modification of remedy (Sections 2–718 and 2–719).

§ 2–317.   Cumulation and Conflict of Warranties Express or Implied.

Warranties whether express or implied shall be construed as consistent with each other and as cumulative, but if such construction is unreasonable the intention of the parties shall determine which warranty is dominant. In ascertaining that intention the following rules apply:

(a) Exact or technical specifications displace an inconsistent sample or model or general language of description.

(b) A sample from an existing bulk displaces inconsistent general language of description.

(c) Express warranties displace inconsistent implied warranties other than an implied warranty of fitness for a particular purpose.

§ 2–318.   Third Party Beneficiaries of Warranties Express or Implied.

Note: If this Act is introduced in the Congress of the United States this section should be omitted. (States to select one alternative.)

Alternative A

A seller's warranty whether express or implied extends to any natural person who is in the family or household of his buyer or who is a guest in his home if it is reasonable to expect that such person may use, consume or be affected by the goods and who is injured in person by breach of the warranty. A seller may not exclude or limit the operation of this section.

Alternative B

A seller's warranty whether express or implied extends to any natural person who may reasonably be expected to use, consume or be affected by the goods and who is injured in person by breach of the warranty. A seller may not exclude or limit the operation of this section.

Alternative C

A seller's warranty whether express or implied extends to any person who may reasonably be expected to use, consume or be affected by the goods and who is injured by breach of the warranty. A seller may not exclude or limit the operation of this section with respect to injury to the person of an individual to whom the warranty extends.

As amended 1966.

§ 2–319.   F.O.B. and F.A.S. Terms.

(1) Unless otherwise agreed the term F.O.B. (which means "free on board") at a named place, even though used only in connection with the stated price, is a delivery term under which

(a) when the term is F.O.B. the place of shipment, the seller must at that place ship the goods in the manner provided in this Article (Section 2–504) and bear the expense and risk of putting them into the possession of the carrier; or

(b) when the term is F.O.B. the place of destination, the seller must at his own expense and risk transport the goods to that place and there tender delivery of them in the manner provided in this Article (Section 2–503);

(c) when under either (a) or (b) the term is also F.O.B. vessel, car or other vehicle, the seller must in addition at his own expense and risk load the goods on board. If the term is F.O.B. vessel the buyer must name the vessel and in an appropriate case the seller must comply with the provisions of this Article on the form of bill of lading (Section 2–323).

(2) Unless otherwise agreed the term F.A.S. vessel (which means "free alongside") at a named port, even though used only in connection with the stated price, is a delivery term under which the seller must

(a) at his own expense and risk deliver the goods alongside the vessel in the manner usual in that port or on a dock designated and provided by the buyer; and

(b) obtain and tender a receipt for the goods in exchange for which the carrier is under a duty to issue a bill of lading.

(3) Unless otherwise agreed in any case falling within subsection (1)(a) or (c) or subsection (2) the buyer must seasonably give any needed instructions for making delivery, including when the term is F.A.S. or F.O.B. the loading berth of the vessel and in an appropriate case its name and sailing date. The seller may treat the failure of needed instructions as a failure of cooperation under this Article (Section 2–311). He may also at his option move the goods in any reasonable manner preparatory to delivery or shipment.

(4) Under the term F.O.B. vessel or F.A.S. unless otherwise agreed the buyer must make payment against tender of the required documents and the seller may not tender nor the buyer demand delivery of the goods in substitution for the documents.

§ 2–320.   C.I.F. and C. & F. Terms.

(1) The term C.I.F. means that the price includes in a lump sum the cost of the goods and the insurance and freight to the named destination. The term C. & F. or C.F. means that the price so includes cost and freight to the named destination.

(2) Unless otherwise agreed and even though used only in connection with the stated price and destination, the term C.I.F. destination or its equivalent requires the seller at his own expense and risk to

(a) put the goods into the possession of a carrier at the port for shipment and obtain a negotiable bill or bills of lading covering the entire transportation to the named destination; and

(b) load the goods and obtain a receipt from the carrier (which may be contained in the bill of lading) showing that the freight has been paid or provided for; and

(c) obtain a policy or certificate of insurance, including any war risk insurance, of a kind and on terms then current at the port of shipment in the usual amount, in the currency of the contract, shown to cover the same goods covered by the bill of lading and providing for payment of loss to the order of the buyer or for the account of whom it may concern; but the seller may add to the price the amount of the premium for any such war risk insurance; and

(d) prepare an invoice of the goods and procure any other documents required to effect shipment or to comply with the contract; and

(e) forward and tender with commercial promptness all the documents in due form and with any indorsement necessary to perfect the buyer's rights.

(3) Unless otherwise agreed the term C. & F. or its equivalent has the same effect and imposes upon the seller the same obligations and risks as a C.I.F. term except the obligation as to insurance.

(4) Under the term C.I.F. or C. & F. unless otherwise agreed the buyer must make payment against tender of the required documents and the seller may not tender nor the buyer demand delivery of the goods in substitution for the documents.

§ 2–321. C.I.F. or C. & F.: "Net Landed Weights"; "Payment on Arrival"; Warranty of Condition on Arrival.

Under a contract containing a term C.I.F. or C. & F.

(1) Where the price is based on or is to be adjusted according to "net landed weights", "delivered weights", "out turn" quantity or quality or the like, unless otherwise agreed the seller must reasonably estimate the price. The payment due on tender of the documents called for by the contract is the amount so estimated, but after final adjustment of the price a settlement must be made with commercial promptness.

(2) An agreement described in subsection (1) or any warranty of quality or condition of the goods on arrival places upon the seller the risk of ordinary deterioration, shrinkage and the like in transportation but has no effect on the place or time of identification to the contract for sale or delivery or on the passing of the risk of loss.

(3) Unless otherwise agreed where the contract provides for payment on or after arrival of the goods the seller must before payment allow such preliminary inspection as is feasible; but if the goods are lost delivery of the documents and payment are due when the goods should have arrived.

§ 2–322. Delivery "Ex-Ship".

(1) Unless otherwise agreed a term for delivery of goods "ex-ship" (which means from the carrying vessel) or in equivalent language is not restricted to a particular ship and requires delivery from a ship which has reached a place at the named port of destination where goods of the kind are usually discharged.

(2) Under such a term unless otherwise agreed

(a) the seller must discharge all liens arising out of the carriage and furnish the buyer with a direction which puts the carrier under a duty to deliver the goods; and

(b) the risk of loss does not pass to the buyer until the goods leave the ship's tackle or are otherwise properly unloaded.

§ 2–323. Form of Bill of Lading Required in Overseas Shipment; "Overseas".

(1) Where the contract contemplates overseas shipment and contains a term C.I.F. or C. & F. or F.O.B. vessel, the seller unless otherwise agreed must obtain a negotiable bill of lading stating that the goods have been loaded on board or, in the case of a term C.I.F. or C. & F., received for shipment.

(2) Where in a case within subsection (1) a bill of lading has been issued in a set of parts, unless otherwise agreed if the documents are not to be sent from abroad the buyer may demand tender of the full set; otherwise only one part of the bill of lading need be tendered. Even if the agreement expressly requires a full set

(a) due tender of a single part is acceptable within the provisions of this Article on cure of improper delivery (subsection (1) of Section 2–508); and

(b) even though the full set is demanded, if the documents are sent from abroad the person tendering an incomplete set may nevertheless require payment upon furnishing an indemnity which the buyer in good faith deems adequate.

(3) A shipment by water or by air or a contract contemplating such shipment is "overseas" insofar as by usage of trade or agreement it is subject to the commercial, financing or shipping practices characteristic of international deep water commerce.

§ 2–324. "No Arrival, No Sale" Term.

Under a term "no arrival, no sale" or terms of like meaning, unless otherwise agreed,

(a) the seller must properly ship conforming goods and if they arrive by any means he must tender them on arrival but he assumes no obligation that the goods will arrive unless he has caused the non-arrival; and

(b) where without fault of the seller the goods are in part lost or have so deteriorated as no longer to conform to the contract or arrive after the contract time, the buyer may proceed as if there had been casualty to identified goods (Section 2–613).

§ 2–325. "Letter of Credit" Term; "Confirmed Credit".

(1) Failure of the buyer seasonably to furnish an agreed letter of credit is a breach of the contract for sale.

(2) The delivery to seller of a proper letter of credit suspends the buyer's obligation to pay. If the letter of credit is dishonored, the

seller may on seasonable notification to the buyer require payment directly from him.

(3) Unless otherwise agreed the term "letter of credit" or "banker's credit" in a contract for sale means an irrevocable credit issued by a financing agency of good repute and, where the shipment is overseas, of good international repute. The term "confirmed credit" means that the credit must also carry the direct obligation of such an agency which does business in the seller's financial market.

§ 2-326.   Sale on Approval and Sale or Return; Rights of Creditors.

(1) Unless otherwise agreed, if delivered goods may be returned by the buyer even though they conform to the contract, the transaction is

(a) a "sale on approval" if the goods are delivered primarily for use, and

(b) a "sale or return" if the goods are delivered primarily for resale.

(2) Goods held on approval are not subject to the claims of the buyer's creditors until acceptance; goods held on sale or return are subject to such claims while in the buyer's possession.

(3) Any "or return" term of a contract for sale is to be treated as a separate contract for sale within the statute of frauds section of this Article (Section 2-201) and as contradicting the sale aspect of the contract within the provisions of this Article or on parol or extrinsic evidence (Section 2-202).

As amended in 1999.

§ 2-327.   Special Incidents of Sale on Approval and Sale or Return.

(1) Under a sale on approval unless otherwise agreed

(a) although the goods are identified to the contract the risk of loss and the title do not pass to the buyer until acceptance; and

(b) use of the goods consistent with the purpose of trial is not acceptance but failure seasonably to notify the seller of election to return the goods is acceptance, and if the goods conform to the contract acceptance of any part is acceptance of the whole; and

(c) after due notification of election to return, the return is at the seller's risk and expense but a merchant buyer must follow any reasonable instructions.

(2) Under a sale or return unless otherwise agreed

(a) the option to return extends to the whole or any commercial unit of the goods while in substantially their original condition, but must be exercised seasonably; and

(b) the return is at the buyer's risk and expense.

§ 2-328.   Sale by Auction.

(1) In a sale by auction if goods are put up in lots each lot is the subject of a separate sale.

(2) A sale by auction is complete when the auctioneer so announces by the fall of the hammer or in other customary manner. Where a bid is made while the hammer is falling in acceptance of a prior bid the auctioneer may in his discretion reopen the bidding or declare the goods sold under the bid on which the hammer was falling.

(3) Such a sale is with reserve unless the goods are in explicit terms put up without reserve. In an auction with reserve the auctioneer may withdraw the goods at any time until he announces completion of the sale. In an auction without reserve, after the auctioneer calls for bids on an article or lot, that article or lot cannot be withdrawn unless no bid is made within a reasonable time. In either case a bidder may retract his bid until the auctioneer's announcement of completion of the sale, but a bidder's retraction does not revive any previous bid.

(4) If the auctioneer knowingly receives a bid on the seller's behalf or the seller makes or procures such as bid, and notice has not been given that liberty for such bidding is reserved, the buyer may at his option avoid the sale or take the goods at the price of the last good faith bid prior to the completion of the sale. This subsection shall not apply to any bid at a forced sale.

Part 4   Title, Creditors and Good Faith Purchasers

§ 2-401.   Passing of Title; Reservation for Security; Limited Application of This Section.

Each provision of this Article with regard to the rights, obligations and remedies of the seller, the buyer, purchasers or other third parties applies irrespective of title to the goods except where the provision refers to such title. Insofar as situations are not covered by the other provisions of this Article and matters concerning title became material the following rules apply:

(1) Title to goods cannot pass under a contract for sale prior to their identification to the contract (Section 2-501), and unless otherwise explicitly agreed the buyer acquires by their identification a special property as limited by this Act. Any retention or reservation by the seller of the title (property) in goods shipped or delivered to the buyer is limited in effect to a reservation of a security interest. Subject to these provisions and to the provisions of the Article on Secured Transactions (Article 9), title to goods passes from the seller to the buyer in any manner and on any conditions explicitly agreed on by the parties.

(2) Unless otherwise explicitly agreed title passes to the buyer at the time and place at which the seller completes his performance with reference to the physical delivery of the goods, despite any reservation of a security interest and even though a document of title is to be delivered at a different time or place; and in particular and despite any reservation of a security interest by the bill of lading

(a) if the contract requires or authorizes the seller to send the goods to the buyer but does not require him to deliver them at destination, title passes to the buyer at the time and place of shipment; but

(b) if the contract requires delivery at destination, title passes on tender there.

(3) Unless otherwise explicitly agreed where delivery is to be made without moving the goods,

(a) if the seller is to deliver a document of title, title passes at the time when and the place where he delivers such documents; or

(b) if the goods are at the time of contracting already identified and no documents are to be delivered, title passes at the time and place of contracting.

(4) A rejection or other refusal by the buyer to receive or retain the goods, whether or not justified, or a justified revocation of acceptance revests title to the goods in the seller. Such revesting occurs by operation of law and is not a "sale".

§ 2–402. Rights of Seller's Creditors Against Sold Goods.

(1) Except as provided in subsections (2) and (3), rights of unsecured creditors of the seller with respect to goods which have been identified to a contract for sale are subject to the buyer's rights to recover the goods under this Article (Sections 2–502 and 2–716).

(2) A creditor of the seller may treat a sale or an identification of goods to a contract for sale as void if as against him a retention of possession by the seller is fraudulent under any rule of law of the state where the goods are situated, except that retention of possession in good faith and current course of trade by a merchant-seller for a commercially reasonable time after a sale or identification is not fraudulent.

(3) Nothing in this Article shall be deemed to impair the rights of creditors of the seller

(a) under the provisions of the Article on Secured Transactions (Article 9); or

(b) where identification to the contract or delivery is made not in current course of trade but in satisfaction of or as security for a pre-existing claim for money, security or the like and is made under circumstances which under any rule of law of the state where the goods are situated would apart from this Article constitute the transaction a fraudulent transfer or voidable preference.

§ 2–403. Power to Transfer; Good Faith Purchase of Goods; "Entrusting".

(1) A purchaser of goods acquires all title which his transferor had or had power to transfer except that a purchaser of a limited interest acquires rights only to the extent of the interest purchased. A person with voidable title has power to transfer a good title to a good faith purchaser for value. When goods have been delivered under a transaction of purchase the purchaser has such power even though

(a) the transferor was deceived as to the identity of the purchaser, or

(b) the delivery was in exchange for a check which is later dishonored, or

(c) it was agreed that the transaction was to be a "cash sale", or

(d) the delivery was procured through fraud punishable as larcenous under the criminal law.

(2) Any entrusting of possession of goods to a merchant who deals in goods of that kind gives him power to transfer all rights of the entruster to a buyer in ordinary course of business.

(3) "Entrusting" includes any delivery and any acquiescence in retention of possession regardless of any condition expressed between the parties to the delivery or acquiescence and regardless of whether the procurement of the entrusting or the possessor's disposition of the goods have been such as to be larcenous under the criminal law.

(4) The rights of other purchasers of goods and of lien creditors are governed by the Articles on Secured Transactions (Article 9), Bulk Transfers (Article 6) and Documents of Title (Article 7).

As amended in 1988.

Part 5 Performance

§ 2–501. Insurable Interest in Goods; Manner of Identification of Goods.

(1) The buyer obtains a special property and an insurable interest in goods by identification of existing goods as goods to which the contract refers even though the goods so identified are nonconforming and he has an option to return or reject them. Such identification can be made at any time and in any manner explicitly agreed to by the parties. In the absence of explicit agreement identification occurs

(a) when the contract is made if it is for the sale of goods already existing and identified;

(b) if the contract is for the sale of future goods other than those described in paragraph (c), when goods are shipped, marked or otherwise designated by the seller as goods to which the contract refers;

(c) when the crops are planted or otherwise become growing crops or the young are conceived if the contract is for the sale of unborn young to be born within twelve months after contracting or for the sale of crops to be harvested within twelve months or the next normal harvest season after contracting whichever is longer.

(2) The seller retains an insurable interest in goods so long as title to or any security interest in the goods remains in him and where the identification is by the seller alone he may until default or insolvency or notification to the buyer that the identification is final substitute other goods for those identified.

(3) Nothing in this section impairs any insurable interest recognized under any other statute or rule of law.

§ 2–502. Buyer's Right to Goods on Seller's Insolvency.

(1) Subject to subsections (2) and (3) and even though the goods have not been shipped a buyer who has paid a part or all of the price of goods in which he has a special property under the provisions of the immediately preceding section may on making and keeping good a tender of any unpaid portion of their price recover them from the seller if:

(a) in the case of goods bought for personal, family, or household purposes, the seller repudiates or fails to deliver as required by the contract; or

(b) in all cases, the seller becomes insolvent within ten days after receipt of the first installment on their price.

(2) The buyer's right to recover the goods under subsection (1)(a) vests upon acquisition of a special property, even if the seller had not then repudiated or failed to deliver.

(3) If the identification creating his special property has been made by the buyer he acquires the right to recover the goods only if they conform to the contract for sale.

As amended in 1999.

§ 2–503.   Manner of Seller's Tender of Delivery.

(1) Tender of delivery requires that the seller put and hold conforming goods at the buyer's disposition and give the buyer any notification reasonably necessary to enable him to take delivery. The manner, time and place for tender are determined by the agreement and this Article, and in particular

(a) tender must be at a reasonable hour, and if it is of goods they must be kept available for the period reasonably necessary to enable the buyer to take possession; but

(b) unless otherwise agreed the buyer must furnish facilities reasonably suited to the receipt of the goods.

(2) Where the case is within the next section respecting shipment tender requires that the seller comply with its provisions.

(3) Where the seller is required to deliver at a particular destination tender requires that he comply with subsection (1) and also in any appropriate case tender documents as described in subsections (4) and (5) of this section.

(4) Where goods are in the possession of a bailee and are to be delivered without being moved

(a) tender requires that the seller either tender a negotiable document of title covering such goods or procure acknowledgment by the bailee of the buyer's right to possession of the goods; but

(b) tender to the buyer of a non-negotiable document of title or of a written direction to the bailee to deliver is sufficient tender unless the buyer seasonably objects, and receipt by the bailee of notification of the buyer's rights fixes those rights as against the bailee and all third persons; but risk of loss of the goods and of any failure by the bailee to honor the non-negotiable document of title or to obey the direction remains on the seller until the buyer has had a reasonable time to present the document or direction, and a refusal by the bailee to honor the document or to obey the direction defeats the tender.

(5) Where the contract requires the seller to deliver documents

(a) he must tender all such documents in correct form, except as provided in this Article with respect to bills of lading in a set (subsection (2) of Section 2–323); and

(b) tender through customary banking channels is sufficient and dishonor of a draft accompanying the documents constitutes non-acceptance or rejection.

§ 2–504.   Shipment by Seller.

Where the seller is required or authorized to send the goods to the buyer and the contract does not require him to deliver them at a particular destination, then unless otherwise agreed he must

(a) put the goods in the possession of such a carrier and make such a contract for their transportation as may be reasonable having regard to the nature of the goods and other circumstances of the case; and

(b) obtain and promptly deliver or tender in due form any document necessary to enable the buyer to obtain possession of the goods or otherwise required by the agreement or by usage of trade; and

(c) promptly notify the buyer of the shipment.

Failure to notify the buyer under paragraph (c) or to make a proper contract under paragraph (a) is a ground for rejection only if material delay or loss ensues.

§ 2–505.   Seller's Shipment under Reservation.

(1) Where the seller has identified goods to the contract by or before shipment:

(a) his procurement of a negotiable bill of lading to his own order or otherwise reserves in him a security interest in the goods. His procurement of the bill to the order of a financing agency or of the buyer indicates in addition only the seller's expectation of transferring that interest to the person named.

(b) a non-negotiable bill of lading to himself or his nominee reserves possession of the goods as security but except in a case of conditional delivery (subsection (2) of Section 2–507) a non-negotiable bill of lading naming the buyer as consignee reserves no security interest even though the seller retains possession of the bill of lading.

(2) When shipment by the seller with reservation of a security interest is in violation of the contract for sale it constitutes an improper contract for transportation within the preceding section but impairs neither the rights given to the buyer by shipment and identification of the goods to the contract nor the seller's powers as a holder of a negotiable document.

§ 2–506.   Rights of Financing Agency.

(1) A financing agency by paying or purchasing for value a draft which relates to a shipment of goods acquires to the extent of the payment or purchase and in addition to its own rights under the draft and any document of title securing it any rights of the shipper in the goods including the right to stop delivery and the shipper's right to have the draft honored by the buyer.

(2) The right to reimbursement of a financing agency which has in good faith honored or purchased the draft under commitment to or authority from the buyer is not impaired by subsequent discovery of defects with reference to any relevant document which was apparently regular on its face.

§ 2–507.   Effect of Seller's Tender; Delivery on Condition.

(1) Tender of delivery is a condition to the buyer's duty to accept the goods and, unless otherwise agreed, to his duty to pay for them. Tender entitles the seller to acceptance of the goods and to payment according to the contract.

(2) Where payment is due and demanded on the delivery to the buyer of goods or documents of title, his right as against the seller to retain or dispose of them is conditional upon his making the payment due.

§ 2–508.   Cure by Seller of Improper Tender or Delivery; Replacement.

(1) Where any tender or delivery by the seller is rejected because non-conforming and the time for performance has not yet expired,

the seller may seasonally notify the buyer of his intention to cure and may then within the contract time make a conforming delivery.

(2) Where the buyer rejects a non-conforming tender which the seller had reasonable grounds to believe would be acceptable with or without money allowance the seller may if he seasonably notifies the buyer have a further reasonable time to substitute a conforming tender.

§ 2–509. Risk of Loss in the Absence of Breach.

(1) Where the contract requires or authorizes the seller to ship the goods by carrier

(a) if it does not require him to deliver them at a particular destination, the risk of loss passes to the buyer when the goods are duly delivered to the carrier even though the shipment is under reservation (Section 2–505); but

(b) if it does require him to deliver them at a particular destination and the goods are there duly tendered while in the possession of the carrier, the risk of loss passes to the buyer when the goods are there duly so tendered as to enable the buyer to take delivery.

(2) Where the goods are held by a bailee to be delivered without being moved, the risk of loss passes to the buyer

(a) on his receipt of a negotiable document of title covering the goods; or

(b) on acknowledgment by the bailee of the buyer's right to possession of the goods; or

(c) after his receipt of a non-negotiable document of title or other written direction to deliver, as provided in subsection (4)(b) of Section 2–503.

(3) In any case not within subsection (1) or (2), the risk of loss passes to the buyer on his receipt of the goods if the seller is a merchant; otherwise the risk passes to the buyer on tender of delivery.

(4) The provisions of this section are subject to contrary agreement of the parties and to the provisions of this Article on sale on approval (Section 2–327) and on effect of breach on risk of loss (Section 2–510).

§ 2–510. Effect of Breach on Risk of Loss.

(1) Where a tender or delivery of goods so fails to conform to the contract as to give a right of rejection the risk of their loss remains on the seller until cure or acceptance.

(2) Where the buyer rightfully revokes acceptance he may to the extent of any deficiency in his effective insurance coverage treat the risk of loss as having rested on the seller from the beginning.

(3) Where the buyer as to conforming goods already identified to the contract for sale repudiates or is otherwise in breach before risk of their loss has passed to him, the seller may to the extent of any deficiency in his effective insurance coverage treat the risk of loss as resting on the buyer for a commercially reasonable time.

§ 2–511. Tender of Payment by Buyer; Payment by Check.

(1) Unless otherwise agreed tender of payment is a condition to the seller's duty to tender and complete any delivery.

(2) Tender of payment is sufficient when made by any means or in any manner current in the ordinary course of business unless the seller demands payment in legal tender and gives any extension of time reasonably necessary to procure it.

(3) Subject to the provisions of this Act on the effect of an instrument on an obligation (Section 3–310), payment by check is conditional and is defeated as between the parties by dishonor of the check on due presentment.

As amended in 1994.

§ 2–512. Payment by Buyer Before Inspection.

(1) Where the contract requires payment before inspection non-conformity of the goods does not excuse the buyer from so making payment unless

(a) the non-conformity appears without inspection; or

(b) despite tender of the required documents the circumstances would justify injunction against honor under this Act (Section 5–109(b)).

(2) Payment pursuant to subsection (1) does not constitute an acceptance of goods or impair the buyer's right to inspect or any of his remedies.

As amended in 1995.

§ 2–513. Buyer's Right to Inspection of Goods.

(1) Unless otherwise agreed and subject to subsection (3), where goods are tendered or delivered or identified to the contract for sale, the buyer has a right before payment or acceptance to inspect them at any reasonable place and time and in any reasonable manner. When the seller is required or authorized to send the goods to the buyer, the inspection may be after their arrival.

(2) Expenses of inspection must be borne by the buyer but may be recovered from the seller if the goods do not conform and are rejected.

(3) Unless otherwise agreed and subject to the provisions of this Article on C.I.F. contracts (subsection (3) of Section 2–321), the buyer is not entitled to inspect the goods before payment of the price when the contract provides

(a) for delivery "C.O.D." or on other like terms; or

(b) for payment against documents of title, except where such payment is due only after the goods are to become available for inspection.

(4) A place or method of inspection fixed by the parties is presumed to be exclusive but unless otherwise expressly agreed it does not postpone identification or shift the place for delivery or for passing the risk of loss. If compliance becomes impossible, inspection shall be as provided in this section unless the place or method fixed was clearly intended as an indispensable condition failure of which avoids the contract.

§ 2–514. When Documents Deliverable on Acceptance; When on Payment.

Unless otherwise agreed documents against which a draft is drawn are to be delivered to the drawee on acceptance of the draft if it is payable more than three days after presentment; otherwise, only on payment.

§ 2–515. Preserving Evidence of Goods in Dispute.

In furtherance of the adjustment of any claim or dispute

(a) either party on reasonable notification to the other and for the purpose of ascertaining the facts and preserving evidence has the right to inspect, test and sample the goods including such of them as may be in the possession or control of the other; and

(b) the parties may agree to a third party inspection or survey to determine the conformity or condition of the goods and may agree that the findings shall be binding upon them in any subsequent litigation or adjustment.

Part 6   Breach, Repudiation and Excuse

§ 2–601.   Buyer's Rights on Improper Delivery.

Subject to the provisions of this Article on breach in installment contracts (Section 2–612) and unless otherwise agreed under the sections on contractual limitations of remedy (Sections 2–718 and 2–719), if the goods or the tender of delivery fail in any respect to conform to the contract, the buyer may

(a) reject the whole; or

(b) accept the whole; or

(c) accept any commercial unit or units and reject the rest.

§ 2–602.   Manner and Effect of Rightful Rejection.

(1) Rejection of goods must be within a reasonable time after their delivery or tender. It is ineffective unless the buyer seasonably notifies the seller.

(2) Subject to the provisions of the two following sections on rejected goods (Sections 2–603 and 2–604),

(a) after rejection any exercise of ownership by the buyer with respect to any commercial unit is wrongful as against the seller; and

(b) if the buyer has before rejection taken physical possession of goods in which he does not have a security interest under the provisions of this Article (subsection (3) of Section 2–711), he is under a duty after rejection to hold them with reasonable care at the seller's disposition for a time sufficient to permit the seller to remove them; but

(c) the buyer has no further obligations with regard to goods rightfully rejected.

(3) The seller's rights with respect to goods wrongfully rejected are governed by the provisions of this Article on Seller's remedies in general (Section 2–703).

§ 2–603.   Merchant Buyer's Duties as to Rightfully Rejected Goods.

(1) Subject to any security interest in the buyer (subsection (3) of Section 2–711), when the seller has no agent or place of business at the market of rejection a merchant buyer is under a duty after rejection of goods in his possession or control to follow any reasonable instructions received from the seller with respect to the goods and in the absence of such instructions to make reasonable efforts to sell them for the seller's account if they are perishable or threaten to decline in value speedily. Instructions are not reasonable if on demand indemnity for expenses is not forthcoming.

(2) When the buyer sells goods under subsection (1), he is entitled to reimbursement from the seller or out of the proceeds for reasonable expenses of caring for and selling them, and if the expenses include no selling commission then to such commission as is usual

in the trade or if there is none to a reasonable sum not exceeding ten per cent on the gross proceeds.

(3) In complying with this section the buyer is held only to good faith and good faith conduct hereunder is neither acceptance nor conversion nor the basis of an action for damages.

§ 2–604.   Buyer's Options as to Salvage of Rightfully Rejected Goods.

Subject to the provisions of the immediately preceding section on perishables if the seller gives no instructions within a reasonable time after notification of rejection the buyer may store the rejected goods for the seller's account or reship them to him or resell them for the seller's account with reimbursement as provided in the preceding section. Such action is not acceptance or conversion.

§ 2–605.   Waiver of Buyer's Objections by Failure to Particularize.

(1) The buyer's failure to state in connection with rejection a particular defect which is ascertainable by reasonable inspection precludes him from relying on the unstated defect to justify rejection or to establish breach

(a) where the seller could have cured it if stated seasonably; or

(b) between merchants when the seller has after rejection made a request in writing for a full and final written statement of all defects on which the buyer proposes to rely.

(2) Payment against documents made without reservation of rights precludes recovery of the payment for defects apparent on the face of the documents.

§ 2–606.   What Constitutes Acceptance of Goods.

(1) Acceptance of goods occurs when the buyer

(a) after a reasonable opportunity to inspect the goods signifies to the seller that the goods are conforming or that he will take or retain them in spite of their nonconformity; or

(b) fails to make an effective rejection (subsection (1) of Section 2–602), but such acceptance does not occur until the buyer has had a reasonable opportunity to inspect them; or

(c) does any act inconsistent with the seller's ownership; but if such act is wrongful as against the seller it is an acceptance only if ratified by him.

(2) Acceptance of a part of any commercial unit is acceptance of that entire unit.

§ 2–607.   Effect of Acceptance; Notice of Breach; Burden of Establishing Breach After Acceptance; Notice of Claim or Litigation to Person Answerable Over.

(1) The buyer must pay at the contract rate for any goods accepted.

(2) Acceptance of goods by the buyer precludes rejection of the goods accepted and if made with knowledge of a non-conformity cannot be revoked because of it unless the acceptance was on the reasonable assumption that the non-conformity would be seasonably cured but acceptance does not of itself impair any other remedy provided by this Article for non-conformity.

(3) Where a tender has been accepted

(a) the buyer must within a reasonable time after he discovers or should have discovered any breach notify the seller of breach or be barred from any remedy; and

(b) if the claim is one for infringement or the like (subsection (3) of Section 2–312) and the buyer is sued as a result of such a breach he must so notify the seller within a reasonable time after he receives notice of the litigation or be barred from any remedy over for liability established by the litigation.

(4) The burden is on the buyer to establish any breach with respect to the goods accepted.

(5) Where the buyer is sued for breach of a warranty or other obligation for which his seller is answerable over

(a) he may give his seller written notice of the litigation. If the notice states that the seller may come in and defend and that if the seller does not do so he will be bound in any action against him by his buyer by any determination of fact common to the two litigations, then unless the seller after seasonable receipt of the notice does come in and defend he is so bound.

(b) if the claim is one for infringement or the like (subsection (3) of Section 2–312) the original seller may demand in writing that his buyer turn over to him control of the litigation including settlement or else be barred from any remedy over and if he also agrees to bear all expense and to satisfy any adverse judgment, then unless the buyer after seasonable receipt of the demand does turn over control the buyer is so barred.

(6) The provisions of subsections (3), (4) and (5) apply to any obligation of a buyer to hold the seller harmless against infringement or the like (subsection (3) of Section 2–312).

§ 2–608.   Revocation of Acceptance in Whole or in Part.

(1) The buyer may revoke his acceptance of a lot or commercial unit whose non-conformity substantially impairs its value to him if he has accepted it

(a) on the reasonable assumption that its nonconformity would be cured and it has not been seasonably cured; or

(b) without discovery of such non-conformity if his acceptance was reasonably induced either by the difficulty of discovery before acceptance or by the seller's assurances.

(2) Revocation of acceptance must occur within a reasonable time after the buyer discovers or should have discovered the ground for it and before any substantial change in condition of the goods which is not caused by their own defects. It is not effective until the buyer notifies the seller of it.

(3) A buyer who so revokes has the same rights and duties with regard to the goods involved as if he had rejected them.

§ 2–609.   Right to Adequate Assurance of Performance.

(1) A contract for sale imposes an obligation on each party that the other's expectation of receiving due performance will not be impaired. When reasonable grounds for insecurity arise with respect to the performance of either party the other may in writing demand adequate assurance of due performance and until he receives such assurance may if commercially reasonable suspend any performance for which he has not already received the agreed return.

(2) Between merchants the reasonableness of grounds for insecurity and the adequacy of any assurance offered shall be determined according to commercial standards.

(3) Acceptance of any improper delivery or payment does not prejudice the party's right to demand adequate assurance of future performance.

(4) After receipt of a justified demand failure to provide within a reasonable time not exceeding thirty days such assurance of due performance as is adequate under the circumstances of the particular case is a repudiation of the contract.

§ 2–610.   Anticipatory Repudiation.

When either party repudiates the contract with respect to a performance not yet due the loss of which will substantially impair the value of the contract to the other, the aggrieved party may

(a) for a commercially reasonable time await performance by the repudiating party; or

(b) resort to any remedy for breach (Section 2–703 or Section 2–711), even though he has notified the repudiating party that he would await the latter's performance and has urged retraction; and

(c) in either case suspend his own performance or proceed in accordance with the provisions of this Article on the seller's right to identify goods to the contract notwithstanding breach or to salvage unfinished goods (Section 2–704).

§ 2–611.   Retraction of Anticipatory Repudiation.

(1) Until the repudiating party's next performance is due he can retract his repudiation unless the aggrieved party has since the repudiation cancelled or materially changed his position or otherwise indicated that he considers the repudiation final.

(2) Retraction may be by any method which clearly indicates to the aggrieved party that the repudiating party intends to perform, but must include any assurance justifiably demanded under the provisions of this Article (Section 2–609).

(3) Retraction reinstates the repudiating party's rights under the contract with due excuse and allowance to the aggrieved party for any delay occasioned by the repudiation.

§ 2–612.   "Installment Contract"; Breach.

(1) An "installment contract" is one which requires or authorizes the delivery of goods in separate lots to be separately accepted, even though the contract contains a clause "each delivery is a separate contract" or its equivalent.

(2) The buyer may reject any installment which is non-conforming if the non-conformity substantially impairs the value of that installment and cannot be cured or if the non-conformity is a defect in the required documents; but if the non-conformity does not fall within subsection (3) and the seller gives adequate assurance of its cure the buyer must accept that installment.

(3) Whenever non-conformity or default with respect to one or more installments substantially impairs the value of the whole contract there is a breach of the whole. But the aggrieved party reinstates the contract if he accepts a non-conforming installment without seasonably notifying of cancellation or if he brings an action with respect only to past installments or demands performance as to future installments.

§ 2–613.   Casualty to Identified Goods.

Where the contract requires for its performance goods identified when the contract is made, and the goods suffer casualty without fault of either party before the risk of loss passes to the buyer, or in a proper case under a "no arrival, no sale" term (Section 2–324) then

(a) if the loss is total the contract is avoided; and

(b) if the loss is partial or the goods have so deteriorated as no longer to conform to the contract the buyer may nevertheless demand inspection and at his option either treat the contract as voided or accept the goods with due allowance from the contract price for the deterioration or the deficiency in quantity but without further right against the seller.

§ 2–614.   Substituted Performance.

(1) Where without fault of either party the agreed berthing, loading, or unloading facilities fail or an agreed type of carrier becomes unavailable or the agreed manner of delivery otherwise becomes commercially impracticable but a commercially reasonable substitute is available, such substitute performance must be tendered and accepted.

(2) If the agreed means or manner of payment fails because of domestic or foreign governmental regulation, the seller may withhold or stop delivery unless the buyer provides a means or manner of payment which is commercially a substantial equivalent. If delivery has already been taken, payment by the means or in the manner provided by the regulation discharges the buyer's obligation unless the regulation is discriminatory, oppressive or predatory.

§ 2–615.   Excuse by Failure of Presupposed Conditions.

Except so far as a seller may have assumed a greater obligation and subject to the preceding section on substituted performance:

(a) Delay in delivery or non-delivery in whole or in part by a seller who complies with paragraphs (b) and (c) is not a breach of his duty under a contract for sale if performance as agreed has been made impracticable by the occurrence of a contingency the nonoccurrence of which was a basic assumption on which the contract was made or by compliance in good faith with any applicable foreign or domestic governmental regulation or order whether or not it later proves to be invalid.

(b) Where the causes mentioned in paragraph (a) affect only a part of the seller's capacity to perform, he must allocate production and deliveries among his customers but may at his option include regular customers not then under contract as well as his own requirements for further manufacture. He may so allocate in any manner which is fair and reasonable.

(c) The seller must notify the buyer seasonably that there will be delay or non-delivery and, when allocation is required under paragraph (b), of the estimated quota thus made available for the buyer.

§ 2–616.   Procedure on Notice Claiming Excuse.

(1) Where the buyer receives notification of a material or indefinite delay or an allocation justified under the preceding section he may by written notification to the seller as to any delivery concerned, and where the prospective deficiency substantially impairs the value of the whole contract under the provisions of this Article relating to breach of installment contracts (Section 2–612), then also as to the whole,

(a) terminate and thereby discharge any unexecuted portion of the contract; or

(b) modify the contract by agreeing to take his available quota in substitution.

(2) If after receipt of such notification from the seller the buyer fails so to modify the contract within a reasonable time not exceeding thirty days the contract lapses with respect to any deliveries affected.

(3) The provisions of this section may not be negated by agreement except in so far as the seller has assumed a greater obligation under the preceding section.

Part 7   Remedies

§ 2–701.   Remedies for Breach of Collateral Contracts Not Impaired.

Remedies for breach of any obligation or promise collateral or ancillary to a contract for sale are not impaired by the provisions of this Article.

§ 2–702.   Seller's Remedies on Discovery of Buyer's Insolvency.

(1) Where the seller discovers the buyer to be insolvent he may refuse delivery except for cash including payment for all goods theretofore delivered under the contract, and stop delivery under this Article (Section 2–705).

(2) Where the seller discovers that the buyer has received goods on credit while insolvent he may reclaim the goods upon demand made within ten days after the receipt, but if misrepresentation of solvency has been made to the particular seller in writing within three months before delivery the ten day limitation does not apply. Except as provided in this subsection the seller may not base a right to reclaim goods on the buyer's fraudulent or innocent misrepresentation of solvency or of intent to pay.

(3) The seller's right to reclaim under subsection (2) is subject to the rights of a buyer in ordinary course or other good faith purchaser under this Article (Section 2–403). Successful reclamation of goods excludes all other remedies with respect to them.

§ 2–703.   Seller's Remedies in General.

Where the buyer wrongfully rejects or revokes acceptance of goods or fails to make a payment due on or before delivery or repudiates with respect to a part or the whole, then with respect to any goods directly affected and, if the breach is of the whole contract (Section 2–612), then also with respect to the whole undelivered balance, the aggrieved seller may

(a) withhold delivery of such goods;

(b) stop delivery by any bailee as hereafter provided (Section 2–705);

(c) proceed under the next section respecting goods still unidentified to the contract;

(d) resell and recover damages as hereafter provided (Section 2–706);

(e) recover damages for non-acceptance (Section 2–708) or in a proper case the price (Section 2–709);

(f) cancel.

§ 2–704.   Seller's Right to Identify Goods to the Contract Notwithstanding Breach or to Salvage Unfinished Goods.

(1) An aggrieved seller under the preceding section may

(a) identify to the contract conforming goods not already identified if at the time he learned of the breach they are in his possession or control;

(b) treat as the subject of resale goods which have demonstrably been intended for the particular contract even though those goods are unfinished.

(2) Where the goods are unfinished an aggrieved seller may in the exercise of reasonable commercial judgment for the purposes of avoiding loss and of effective realization either complete the manufacture and wholly identify the goods to the contract or cease manufacture and resell for scrap or salvage value or proceed in any other reasonable manner.

§ 2–705.   Seller's Stoppage of Delivery in Transit or Otherwise.

(1) The seller may stop delivery of goods in the possession of a carrier or other bailee when he discovers the buyer to be insolvent (Section 2–702) and may stop delivery of carload, truckload, planeload or larger shipments of express or freight when the buyer repudiates or fails to make a payment due before delivery or if for any other reason the seller has a right to withhold or reclaim the goods.

(2) As against such buyer the seller may stop delivery until

(a) receipt of the goods by the buyer; or

(b) acknowledgment to the buyer by any bailee of the goods except a carrier that the bailee holds the goods for the buyer; or

(c) such acknowledgment to the buyer by a carrier by reshipment or as warehouseman; or

(d) negotiation to the buyer of any negotiable document of title covering the goods.

(3) (a) To stop delivery the seller must so notify as to enable the bailee by reasonable diligence to prevent delivery of the goods.

(b) After such notification the bailee must hold and deliver the goods according to the directions of the seller but the seller is liable to the bailee for any ensuing charges or damages.

(c) If a negotiable document of title has been issued for goods the bailee is not obliged to obey a notification to stop until surrender of the document.

(d) A carrier who has issued a non-negotiable bill of lading is not obliged to obey a notification to stop received from a person other than the consignor.

§ 2–706.   Seller's Resale Including Contract for Resale.

(1) Under the conditions stated in Section 2–703 on seller's remedies, the seller may resell the goods concerned or the undelivered balance thereof. Where the resale is made in good faith and in a commercially reasonable manner the seller may recover the difference between the resale price and the contract price together with any incidental damages allowed under the provisions of this Article (Section 2–710), but less expenses saved in consequence of the buyer's breach.

(2) Except as otherwise provided in subsection (3) or unless otherwise agreed resale may be at public or private sale including sale by way of one or more contracts to sell or of identification to an existing contract of the seller. Sale may be as a unit or in parcels and at any time and place and on any terms but every aspect of the sale including the method, manner, time, place and terms must be commercially reasonable. The resale must be reasonably identified as referring to the broken contract, but it is not necessary that the goods be in existence or that any or all of them have been identified to the contract before the breach.

(3) Where the resale is at private sale the seller must give the buyer reasonable notification of his intention to resell.

(4) Where the resale is at public sale

(a) only identified goods can be sold except where there is a recognized market for a public sale of futures in goods of the kind; and

(b) it must be made at a usual place or market for public sale if one is reasonably available and except in the case of goods which are perishable or threaten to decline in value speedily the seller must give the buyer reasonable notice of the time and place of the resale; and

(c) if the goods are not to be within the view of those attending the sale the notification of sale must state the place where the goods are located and provide for their reasonable inspection by prospective bidders; and

(d) the seller may buy.

(5) A purchaser who buys in good faith at a resale takes the goods free of any rights of the original buyer even though the seller fails to comply with one or more of the requirements of this section.

(6) The seller is not accountable to the buyer for any profit made on any resale. A person in the position of a seller (Section 2–707) or a buyer who has rightfully rejected or justifiably revoked acceptance must account for any excess over the amount of his security interest, as hereinafter defined (subsection (3) of Section 2–711).

§ 2–707.   "Person in the Position of a Seller".

(1) A "person in the position of a seller" includes as against a principal an agent who has paid or become responsible for the price of goods on behalf of his principal or anyone who otherwise holds a security interest or other right in goods similar to that of a seller.

(2) A person in the position of a seller may as provided in this Article withhold or stop delivery (Section 2–705) and resell (Section 2–706) and recover incidental damages (Section 2–710).

§ 2–708.   Seller's Damages for Non-Acceptance or Repudiation.

(1) Subject to subsection (2) and to the provisions of this Article with respect to proof of market price (Section 2–723), the measure of damages for non-acceptance or repudiation by the buyer is the difference between the market price at the time and place for tender and the unpaid contract price together with any incidental damages provided in this Article (Section 2–710), but less expenses saved in consequence of the buyer's breach.

(2) If the measure of damages provided in subsection (1) is inadequate to put the seller in as good a position as performance would have

done then the measure of damages is the profit (including reasonable overhead) which the seller would have made from full performance by the buyer, together with any incidental damages provided in this Article (Section 2–710), due allowance for costs reasonably incurred and due credit for payments or proceeds of resale.

§ 2–709.   Action for the Price.

(1) When the buyer fails to pay the price as it becomes due the seller may recover, together with any incidental damages under the next section, the price

(a) of goods accepted or of conforming goods lost or damaged within a commercially reasonable time after risk of their loss has passed to the buyer; and

(b) of goods identified to the contract if the seller is unable after reasonable effort to resell them at a reasonable price or the circumstances reasonably indicate that such effort will be unavailing.

(2) Where the seller sues for the price he must hold for the buyer any goods which have been identified to the contract and are still in his control except that if resale becomes possible he may resell them at any time prior to the collection of the judgment. The net proceeds of any such resale must be credited to the buyer and payment of the judgment entitles him to any goods not resold.

(3) After the buyer has wrongfully rejected or revoked acceptance of the goods or has failed to make a payment due or has repudiated (Section 2–610), a seller who is held not entitled to the price under this section shall nevertheless be awarded damages for non-acceptance under the preceding section.

§ 2–710.   Seller's Incidental Damages.

Incidental damages to an aggrieved seller include any commercially reasonable charges, expenses or commissions incurred in stopping delivery, in the transportation, care and custody of goods after the buyer's breach, in connection with return or resale of the goods or otherwise resulting from the breach.

§ 2–711.   Buyer's Remedies in General; Buyer's Security Interest in Rejected Goods.

(1) Where the seller fails to make delivery or repudiates or the buyer rightfully rejects or justifiably revokes acceptance then with respect to any goods involved, and with respect to the whole if the breach goes to the whole contract (Section 2–612), the buyer may cancel and whether or not he has done so may in addition to recovering so much of the price as has been paid

(a) "cover" and have damages under the next section as to all the goods affected whether or not they have been identified to the contract; or

(b) recover damages for non-delivery as provided in this Article (Section 2–713).

(2) Where the seller fails to deliver or repudiates the buyer may also

(a) if the goods have been identified recover them as provided in this Article (Section 2–502); or

(b) in a proper case obtain specific performance or replevy the goods as provided in this Article (Section 2–716).

(3) On rightful rejection or justifiable revocation of acceptance a buyer has a security interest in goods in his possession or control

for any payments made on their price and any expenses reasonably incurred in their inspection, receipt, transportation, care and custody and may hold such goods and resell them in like manner as an aggrieved seller (Section 2–706).

§ 2–712.   "Cover"; Buyer's Procurement of Substitute Goods.

(1) After a breach within the preceding section the buyer may "cover" by making in good faith and without unreasonable delay any reasonable purchase of or contract to purchase goods in substitution for those due from the seller.

(2) The buyer may recover from the seller as damages the difference between the cost of cover and the contract price together with any incidental or consequential damages as hereinafter defined (Section 2–715), but less expenses saved in consequence of the seller's breach.

(3) Failure of the buyer to effect cover within this section does not bar him from any other remedy.

§ 2–713.   Buyer's Damages for Non-Delivery or Repudiation.

(1) Subject to the provisions of this Article with respect to proof of market price (Section 2–723), the measure of damages for non-delivery or repudiation by the seller is the difference between the market price at the time when the buyer learned of the breach and the contract price together with any incidental and consequential damages provided in this Article (Section 2–715), but less expenses saved in consequence of the seller's breach.

(2) Market price is to be determined as of the place for tender or, in cases of rejection after arrival or revocation of acceptance, as of the place of arrival.

§ 2–714.   Buyer's Damages for Breach in Regard to Accepted Goods.

(1) Where the buyer has accepted goods and given notification (subsection (3) of Section 2–607) he may recover as damages for any non-conformity of tender the loss resulting in the ordinary course of events from the seller's breach as determined in any manner which is reasonable.

(2) The measure of damages for breach of warranty is the difference at the time and place of acceptance between the value of the goods accepted and the value they would have had if they had been as warranted, unless special circumstances show proximate damages of a different amount.

(3) In a proper case any incidental and consequential damages under the next section may also be recovered.

§ 2–715.   Buyer's Incidental and Consequential Damages.

(1) Incidental damages resulting from the seller's breach include expenses reasonably incurred in inspection, receipt, transportation and care and custody of goods rightfully rejected, any commercially reasonable charges, expenses or commissions in connection with effecting cover and any other reasonable expense incident to the delay or other breach.

(2) Consequential damages resulting from the seller's breach include

(a) any loss resulting from general or particular requirements and needs of which the seller at the time of contracting had reason to know and which could not reasonably be prevented by cover or otherwise; and

(b) injury to person or property proximately resulting from any breach of warranty.

§ 2–716. Buyer's Right to Specific Performance or Replevin.

(1) Specific performance may be decreed where the goods are unique or in other proper circumstances.

(2) The decree for specific performance may include such terms and conditions as to payment of the price, damages, or other relief as the court may deem just.

(3) The buyer has a right of replevin for goods identified to the contract if after reasonable effort he is unable to effect cover for such goods or the circumstances reasonably indicate that such effort will be unavailing or if the goods have been shipped under reservation and satisfaction of the security interest in them has been made or tendered. In the case of goods bought for personal, family, or household purposes, the buyer's right of replevin vests upon acquisition of a special property, even if the seller had not then repudiated or failed to deliver.

As amended in 1999.

§ 2–717. Deduction of Damages From the Price.

The buyer on notifying the seller of his intention to do so may deduct all or any part of the damages resulting from any breach of the contract from any part of the price still due under the same contract.

§ 2–718. Liquidation or Limitation of Damages; Deposits.

(1) Damages for breach by either party may be liquidated in the agreement but only at an amount which is reasonable in the light of the anticipated or actual harm caused by the breach, the difficulties of proof of loss, and the inconvenience or nonfeasibility of otherwise obtaining an adequate remedy. A term fixing unreasonably large liquidated damages is void as a penalty.

(2) Where the seller justifiably withholds delivery of goods because of the buyer's breach, the buyer is entitled to restitution of any amount by which the sum of his payments exceeds

(a) the amount to which the seller is entitled by virtue of terms liquidating the seller's damages in accordance with subsection (1), or

(b) in the absence of such terms, twenty per cent of the value of the total performance for which the buyer is obligated under the contract or $500, whichever is smaller.

(3) The buyer's right to restitution under subsection (2) is subject to offset to the extent that the seller establishes

(a) a right to recover damages under the provisions of this Article other than subsection (1), and

(b) the amount or value of any benefits received by the buyer directly or indirectly by reason of the contract.

(4) Where a seller has received payment in goods their reasonable value or the proceeds of their resale shall be treated as payments for the purposes of subsection (2); but if the seller has notice of the buyer's breach before reselling goods received in part performance, his resale is subject to the conditions laid down in this Article on resale by an aggrieved seller (Section 2–706).

§ 2–719. Contractual Modification or Limitation of Remedy.

(1) Subject to the provisions of subsections (2) and (3) of this section and of the preceding section on liquidation and limitation of damages,

(a) the agreement may provide for remedies in addition to or in substitution for those provided in this Article and may limit or alter the measure of damages recoverable under this Article, as by limiting the buyer's remedies to return of the goods and repayment of the price or to repair and replacement of nonconforming goods or parts; and

(b) resort to a remedy as provided is optional unless the remedy is expressly agreed to be exclusive, in which case it is the sole remedy.

(2) Where circumstances cause an exclusive or limited remedy to fail of its essential purpose, remedy may be had as provided in this Act.

(3) Consequential damages may be limited or excluded unless the limitation or exclusion is unconscionable. Limitation of consequential damages for injury to the person in the case of consumer goods is prima facie unconscionable but limitation of damages where the loss is commercial is not.

§ 2–720. Effect of "Cancellation" or "Rescission" on Claims for Antecedent Breach.

Unless the contrary intention clearly appears, expressions of "cancellation" or "rescission" of the contract or the like shall not be construed as a renunciation or discharge of any claim in damages for an antecedent breach.

§ 2–721. Remedies for Fraud.

Remedies for material misrepresentation or fraud include all remedies available under this Article for non-fraudulent breach. Neither rescission or a claim for rescission of the contract for sale nor rejection or return of the goods shall bar or be deemed inconsistent with a claim for damages or other remedy.

§ 2–722. Who Can Sue Third Parties for Injury to Goods.

Where a third party so deals with goods which have been identified to a contract for sale as to cause actionable injury to a party to that contract

(a) a right of action against the third party is in either party to the contract for sale who has title to or a security interest or a special property or an insurable interest in the goods; and if the goods have been destroyed or converted a right of action is also in the party who either bore the risk of loss under the contract for sale or has since the injury assumed that risk as against the other;

(b) if at the time of the injury the party plaintiff did not bear the risk of loss as against the other party to the contract for sale and there is no arrangement between them for disposition of the recovery, his suit or settlement is, subject to his own interest, as a fiduciary for the other party to the contract;

(c) either party may with the consent of the other sue for the benefit of whom it may concern.

§ 2–723. Proof of Market Price: Time and Place.

(1) If an action based on anticipatory repudiation comes to trial before the time for performance with respect to some or all of the goods, any damages based on market price (Section 2–708 or Section 2–713) shall be determined according to the price of such goods prevailing at the time when the aggrieved party learned of the repudiation.

(2) If evidence of a price prevailing at the times or places described in this Article is not readily available the price prevailing within any reasonable time before or after the time described or at any other

place which in commercial judgment or under usage of trade would serve as a reasonable substitute for the one described may be used, making any proper allowance for the cost of transporting the goods to or from such other place.

(3) Evidence of a relevant price prevailing at a time or place other than the one described in this Article offered by one party is not admissible unless and until he has given the other party such notice as the court finds sufficient to prevent unfair surprise.

§ 2–724.   Admissibility of Market Quotations.

Whenever the prevailing price or value of any goods regularly bought and sold in any established commodity market is in issue, reports in official publications or trade journals or in newspapers or periodicals of general circulation published as the reports of such market shall be admissible in evidence. The circumstances of the preparation of such a report may be shown to affect its weight but not its admissibility.

§ 2–725.   Statute of Limitations in Contracts for Sale.

(1) An action for breach of any contract for sale must be commenced within four years after the cause of action has accrued. By the original agreement the parties may reduce the period of limitation to not less than one year but may not extend it.

(2) A cause of action accrues when the breach occurs, regardless of the aggrieved party's lack of knowledge of the breach. A breach of warranty occurs when tender of delivery is made, except where a warranty explicitly extends to future performance of the goods and discovery of the breach must await the time of such performance the cause of action accrues when the breach is or should have been discovered.

(3) Where an action commenced within the time limited by subsection (1) is so terminated as to leave available a remedy by another action for the same breach such other action may be commenced after the expiration of the time limited and within six months after the termination of the first action unless the termination resulted from voluntary discontinuance or from dismissal for failure or neglect to prosecute.

(4) This section does not alter the law on tolling of the statute of limitations nor does it apply to causes of action which have accrued before this Act becomes effective.

Article 2A
LEASES

Part 1   General Provisions

§ 2A–101.   Short Title.

This Article shall be known and may be cited as the Uniform Commercial Code—Leases.

§ 2A–102.   Scope.

This Article applies to any transaction, regardless of form, that creates a lease.

§ 2A–103.   Definitions and Index of Definitions.

(1) In this Article unless the context otherwise requires:

(a) "Buyer in ordinary course of business" means a person who in good faith and without knowledge that the sale to him [or her] is in violation of the ownership rights or security interest or leasehold interest of a third party in the goods buys in ordinary course from a person in the business of selling goods of that kind but does not include a pawnbroker. "Buying" may be for cash or by exchange of other property or on secured or unsecured credit and includes receiving goods or documents of title under a pre-existing contract for sale but does not include a transfer in bulk or as security for or in total or partial satisfaction of a money debt.

(b) "Cancellation" occurs when either party puts an end to the lease contract for default by the other party.

(c) "Commercial unit" means such a unit of goods as by commercial usage is a single whole for purposes of lease and division of which materially impairs its character or value on the market or in use. A commercial unit may be a single article, as a machine, or a set of articles, as a suite of furniture or a line of machinery, or a quantity, as a gross or carload, or any other unit treated in use or in the relevant market as a single whole.

(d) "Conforming" goods or performance under a lease contract means goods or performance that are in accordance with the obligations under the lease contract.

(e) "Consumer lease" means a lease that a lessor regularly engaged in the business of leasing or selling makes to a lessee who is an individual and who takes under the lease primarily for a personal, family, or household purpose [, if the total payments to be made under the lease contract, excluding payments for options to renew or buy, do not exceed $_____].

(f) "Fault" means wrongful act, omission, breach, or default.

(g) "Finance lease" means a lease with respect to which:

(i) the lessor does not select, manufacture or supply the goods;

(ii) the lessor acquires the goods or the right to possession and use of the goods in connection with the lease; and

(iii) one of the following occurs:

(A) the lessee receives a copy of the contract by which the lessor acquired the goods or the right to possession and use of the goods before signing the lease contract;

(B) the lessee's approval of the contract by which the lessor acquired the goods or the right to possession and use of the goods is a condition to effectiveness of the lease contract;

(C) the lessee, before signing the lease contract, receives an accurate and complete statement designating the promises and warranties, and any disclaimers of warranties, limitations or modifications of remedies, or liquidated damages, including those of a third party, such as the manufacturer of the goods, provided to the lessor by the person supplying the goods in connection with or as part of the contract by which the lessor acquired the goods or the right to possession and use of the goods; or

(D) if the lease is not a consumer lease, the lessor, before the lessee signs the lease contract, informs the lessee in writing (a) of the identity of the person supplying the goods to the lessor, unless the lessee has selected that person and directed the lessor to acquire the goods or the right to possession and use of the goods from that person, (b) that the lessee is entitled under this Article to any promises and warranties, including those of any third party, provided to the lessor by the person supplying the goods in connection with or as part of the contract by which the lessor acquired the goods or the right to possession and use of the goods, and (c) that the lessee may communicate with the person supplying the goods to the lessor and receive an accurate and complete statement of those promises and warranties, including any disclaimers and limitations of them or of remedies.

(h) "Goods" means all things that are movable at the time of identification to the lease contract, or are fixtures (Section 2A–309), but the term does not include money, documents, instruments, accounts, chattel paper, general intangibles, or minerals or the like, including oil and gas, before extraction. The term also includes the unborn young of animals.

(i) "Installment lease contract" means a lease contract that authorizes or requires the delivery of goods in separate lots to be separately accepted, even though the lease contract contains a clause "each delivery is a separate lease" or its equivalent.

(j) "Lease" means a transfer of the right to possession and use of goods for a term in return for consideration, but a sale, including a sale on approval or a sale or return, or retention or creation of a security interest is not a lease. Unless the context clearly indicates otherwise, the term includes a sublease.

(k) "Lease agreement" means the bargain, with respect to the lease, of the lessor and the lessee in fact as found in their language or by implication from other circumstances including course of dealing or usage of trade or course of performance as provided in this Article. Unless the context clearly indicates otherwise, the term includes a sublease agreement.

(l) "Lease contract" means the total legal obligation that results from the lease agreement as affected by this Article and any other applicable rules of law. Unless the context clearly indicates otherwise, the term includes a sublease contract.

(m) "Leasehold interest" means the interest of the lessor or the lessee under a lease contract.

(n) "Lessee" means a person who acquires the right to possession and use of goods under a lease. Unless the context clearly indicates otherwise, the term includes a sublessee.

(o) "Lessee in ordinary course of business" means a person who in good faith and without knowledge that the lease to him [or her] is in violation of the ownership rights or security interest or leasehold interest of a third party in the goods, leases in ordinary course from a person in the business of selling or leasing goods of that kind but does not include a pawnbroker. "Leasing" may be for cash or by exchange of other property or on secured or unsecured credit and includes receiving goods or documents of title under a pre-existing lease contract but does not include a transfer in bulk or as security for or in total or partial satisfaction of a money debt.

(p) "Lessor" means a person who transfers the right to possession and use of goods under a lease. Unless the context clearly indicates otherwise, the term includes a sublessor.

(q) "Lessor's residual interest" means the lessor's interest in the goods after expiration, termination, or cancellation of the lease contract.

(r) "Lien" means a charge against or interest in goods to secure payment of a debt or performance of an obligation, but the term does not include a security interest.

(s) "Lot" means a parcel or a single article that is the subject matter of a separate lease or delivery, whether or not it is sufficient to perform the lease contract.

(t) "Merchant lessee" means a lessee that is a merchant with respect to goods of the kind subject to the lease.

(u) "Present value" means the amount as of a date certain of one or more sums payable in the future, discounted to the date certain. The discount is determined by the interest rate specified by the parties if the rate was not manifestly unreasonable at the time the transaction was entered into; otherwise, the discount is determined by a commercially reasonable rate that takes into account the facts and circumstances of each case at the time the transaction was entered into.

(v) "Purchase" includes taking by sale, lease, mortgage, security interest, pledge, gift, or any other voluntary transaction creating an interest in goods.

(w) "Sublease" means a lease of goods the right to possession and use of which was acquired by the lessor as a lessee under an existing lease.

(x) "Supplier" means a person from whom a lessor buys or leases goods to be leased under a finance lease.

(y) "Supply contract" means a contract under which a lessor buys or leases goods to be leased.

(z) "Termination" occurs when either party pursuant to a power created by agreement or law puts an end to the lease contract otherwise than for default.

(2) Other definitions applying to this Article and the sections in which they appear are:

"Accessions". Section 2A–310(1).

"Construction mortgage". Section 2A–309(1)(d).

"Encumbrance". Section 2A–309(1)(e).

"Fixtures". Section 2A–309(1)(a).

"Fixture filing". Section 2A–309(1)(b).

"Purchase money lease". Section 2A–309(1)(c).

(3) The following definitions in other Articles apply to this Article:

"Accounts". Section 9–106.

"Between merchants". Section 2–104(3).

"Buyer". Section 2–103(1)(a).

"Chattel paper". Section 9–105(1)(b).

"Consumer goods". Section 9–109(1).

"Document". Section 9–105(1)(f).

"Entrusting". Section 2–403(3).

"General intangibles". Section 9–106.

"Good faith". Section 2–103(1)(b).

"Instrument". Section 9–105(1)(i).

"Merchant". Section 2–104(1).

"Mortgage". Section 9–105(1)(j).

"Pursuant to commitment". Section 9–105(1)(k).

"Receipt". Section 2–103(1)(c).

"Sale". Section 2–106(1).

"Sale on approval". Section 2–326.

"Sale or return". Section 2–326.

"Seller". Section 2–103(1)(d).

(4) In addition Article 1 contains general definitions and principles of construction and interpretation applicable throughout this Article.

As amended in 1990 and 1999.

§ 2A–104.   Leases Subject to Other Law.

(1) A lease, although subject to this Article, is also subject to any applicable:

   (a) certificate of title statute of this State: (list any certificate of title statutes covering automobiles, trailers, mobile homes, boats, farm tractors, and the like);

   (b) certificate of title statute of another jurisdiction (Section 2A–105); or

   (c) consumer protection statute of this State, or final consumer protection decision of a court of this State existing on the effective date of this Article.

(2) In case of conflict between this Article, other than Sections 2A–105, 2A–304(3), and 2A–305(3), and a statute or decision referred to in subsection (1), the statute or decision controls.

(3) Failure to comply with an applicable law has only the effect specified therein.

As amended in 1990.

§ 2A–105.   Territorial Application of
Article to Goods Covered by Certificate of Title.

Subject to the provisions of Sections 2A–304(3) and 2A–305(3), with respect to goods covered by a certificate of title issued under a statute of this State or of another jurisdiction, compliance and the effect of compliance or noncompliance with a certificate of title statute are governed by the law (including the conflict of laws rules) of the jurisdiction issuing the certificate until the earlier of

(a) surrender of the certificate, or (b) four months after the goods are removed from that jurisdiction and thereafter until a new certificate of title is issued by another jurisdiction.

§ 2A–106.   Limitation on Power of Parties to
Consumer Lease to Choose Applicable Law and Judicial Forum.

(1) If the law chosen by the parties to a consumer lease is that of a jurisdiction other than a jurisdiction in which the lessee resides at the time the lease agreement becomes enforceable or within 30 days thereafter or in which the goods are to be used, the choice is not enforceable.

(2) If the judicial forum chosen by the parties to a consumer lease is a forum that would not otherwise have jurisdiction over the lessee, the choice is not enforceable.

§ 2A–107.   Waiver or Renunciation of Claim or Right After Default.

Any claim or right arising out of an alleged default or breach of warranty may be discharged in whole or in part without consideration by a written waiver or renunciation signed and delivered by the aggrieved party.

§ 2A–108.   Unconscionability.

(1) If the court as a matter of law finds a lease contract or any clause of a lease contract to have been unconscionable at the time it was made the court may refuse to enforce the lease contract, or it may enforce the remainder of the lease contract without the unconscionable clause, or it may so limit the application of any unconscionable clause as to avoid any unconscionable result.

(2) With respect to a consumer lease, if the court as a matter of law finds that a lease contract or any clause of a lease contract has been induced by unconscionable conduct or that unconscionable conduct has occurred in the collection of a claim arising from a lease contract, the court may grant appropriate relief.

(3) Before making a finding of unconscionability under subsection (1) or (2), the court, on its own motion or that of a party, shall afford the parties a reasonable opportunity to present evidence as to the setting, purpose, and effect of the lease contract or clause thereof, or of the conduct.

(4) In an action in which the lessee claims unconscionability with respect to a consumer lease:

   (a) If the court finds unconscionability under subsection (1) or (2), the court shall award reasonable attorney's fees to the lessee.

   (b) If the court does not find unconscionability and the lessee claiming unconscionability has brought or maintained an action he [or she] knew to be groundless, the court shall award reasonable attorney's fees to the party against whom the claim is made.

   (c) In determining attorney's fees, the amount of the recovery on behalf of the claimant under subsections (1) and (2) is not controlling.

§ 2A–109.   Option to Accelerate at Will.

(1) A term providing that one party or his [or her] successor in interest may accelerate payment or performance or require collateral or additional collateral "at will" or "when he [or she] deems himself [or

herself] insecure" or in words of similar import must be construed to mean that he [or she] has power to do so only if he [or she] in good faith believes that the prospect of payment or performance is impaired.

(2) With respect to a consumer lease, the burden of establishing good faith under subsection (1) is on the party who exercised the power; otherwise the burden of establishing lack of good faith is on the party against whom the power has been exercised.

Part 2   Formation and Construction of Lease Contract

§ 2A–201.   Statute of Frauds.

(1) A lease contract is not enforceable by way of action or defense unless:

(a) the total payments to be made under the lease contract, excluding payments for options to renew or buy, are less than $1,000; or

(b) there is a writing, signed by the party against whom enforcement is sought or by that party's authorized agent, sufficient to indicate that a lease contract has been made between the parties and to describe the goods leased and the lease term.

(2) Any description of leased goods or of the lease term is sufficient and satisfies subsection (1)(b), whether or not it is specific, if it reasonably identifies what is described.

(3) A writing is not insufficient because it omits or incorrectly states a term agreed upon, but the lease contract is not enforceable under subsection (1)(b) beyond the lease term and the quantity of goods shown in the writing.

(4) A lease contract that does not satisfy the requirements of subsection (1), but which is valid in other respects, is enforceable:

(a) if the goods are to be specially manufactured or obtained for the lessee and are not suitable for lease or sale to others in the ordinary course of the lessor's business, and the lessor, before notice of repudiation is received and under circumstances that reasonably indicate that the goods are for the lessee, has made either a substantial beginning of their manufacture or commitments for their procurement;

(b) if the party against whom enforcement is sought admits in that party's pleading, testimony or otherwise in court that a lease contract was made, but the lease contract is not enforceable under this provision beyond the quantity of goods admitted; or

(c) with respect to goods that have been received and accepted by the lessee.

(5) The lease term under a lease contract referred to in subsection (4) is:

(a) if there is a writing signed by the party against whom enforcement is sought or by that party's authorized agent specifying the lease term, the term so specified;

(b) if the party against whom enforcement is sought admits in that party's pleading, testimony, or otherwise in court a lease term, the term so admitted; or

(c) a reasonable lease term.

§ 2A–202.   Final Written Expression: Parol or Extrinsic Evidence.

Terms with respect to which the confirmatory memoranda of the parties agree or which are otherwise set forth in a writing intended by the parties as a final expression of their agreement with respect to such terms as are included therein may not be contradicted by evidence of any prior agreement or of a contemporaneous oral agreement but may be explained or supplemented:

(a) by course of dealing or usage of trade or by course of performance; and

(b) by evidence of consistent additional terms unless the court finds the writing to have been intended also as a complete and exclusive statement of the terms of the agreement.

§ 2A–203.   Seals Inoperative.

The affixing of a seal to a writing evidencing a lease contract or an offer to enter into a lease contract does not render the writing a sealed instrument and the law with respect to sealed instruments does not apply to the lease contract or offer.

§ 2A–204.   Formation in General.

(1) A lease contract may be made in any manner sufficient to show agreement, including conduct by both parties which recognizes the existence of a lease contract.

(2) An agreement sufficient to constitute a lease contract may be found although the moment of its making is undetermined.

(3) Although one or more terms are left open, a lease contract does not fail for indefiniteness if the parties have intended to make a lease contract and there is a reasonably certain basis for giving an appropriate remedy.

§ 2A–205.   Firm Offers.

An offer by a merchant to lease goods to or from another person in a signed writing that by its terms gives assurance it will be held open is not revocable, for lack of consideration, during the time stated or, if no time is stated, for a reasonable time, but in no event may the period of irrevocability exceed 3 months. Any such term of assurance on a form supplied by the offeree must be separately signed by the offeror.

§ 2A–206.   Offer and Acceptance in Formation of Lease Contract.

(1) Unless otherwise unambiguously indicated by the language or circumstances, an offer to make a lease contract must be construed as inviting acceptance in any manner and by any medium reasonable in the circumstances.

(2) If the beginning of a requested performance is a reasonable mode of acceptance, an offeror who is not notified of acceptance within a reasonable time may treat the offer as having lapsed before acceptance.

§ 2A–207.   Course of Performance or Practical Construction.

(1) If a lease contract involves repeated occasions for performance by either party with knowledge of the nature of the performance and opportunity for objection to it by the other, any course of performance accepted or acquiesced in without objection is relevant to determine the meaning of the lease agreement.

(2) The express terms of a lease agreement and any course of performance, as well as any course of dealing and usage of trade, must be construed whenever reasonable as consistent with each other; but if that construction is unreasonable, express terms control course of performance, course of performance controls both course of dealing and usage of trade, and course of dealing controls usage of trade.

(3) Subject to the provisions of Section 2A–208 on modification and waiver, course of performance is relevant to show a waiver or modification of any term inconsistent with the course of performance.

§ 2A–208.   Modification, Rescission and Waiver.

(1) An agreement modifying a lease contract needs no consideration to be binding.

(2) A signed lease agreement that excludes modification or rescission except by a signed writing may not be otherwise modified or rescinded, but, except as between merchants, such a requirement on a form supplied by a merchant must be separately signed by the other party.

(3) Although an attempt at modification or rescission does not satisfy the requirements of subsection (2), it may operate as a waiver.

(4) A party who has made a waiver affecting an executory portion of a lease contract may retract the waiver by reasonable notification received by the other party that strict performance will be required of any term waived, unless the retraction would be unjust in view of a material change of position in reliance on the waiver.

§ 2A–209.   Lessee under Finance Lease as Beneficiary of Supply Contract.

(1) The benefit of the supplier's promises to the lessor under the supply contract and of all warranties, whether express or implied, including those of any third party provided in connection with or as part of the supply contract, extends to the lessee to the extent of the lessee's leasehold interest under a finance lease related to the supply contract, but is subject to the terms warranty and of the supply contract and all defenses or claims arising therefrom.

(2) The extension of the benefit of supplier's promises and of warranties to the lessee (Section 2A–209(1)) does not: (i) modify the rights and obligations of the parties to the supply contract, whether arising therefrom or otherwise, or (ii) impose any duty or liability under the supply contract on the lessee.

(3) Any modification or rescission of the supply contract by the supplier and the lessor is effective between the supplier and the lessee unless, before the modification or rescission, the supplier has received notice that the lessee has entered into a finance lease related to the supply contract. If the modification or rescission is effective between the supplier and the lessee, the lessor is deemed to have assumed, in addition to the obligations of the lessor to the lessee under the lease contract, promises of the supplier to the lessor and warranties that were so modified or rescinded as they existed and were available to the lessee before modification or rescission.

(4) In addition to the extension of the benefit of the supplier's promises and of warranties to the lessee under subsection (1), the lessee retains all rights that the lessee may have against the supplier which arise from an agreement between the lessee and the supplier or under other law.

As amended in 1990.

§ 2A–210.   Express Warranties.

(1) Express warranties by the lessor are created as follows:

(a) Any affirmation of fact or promise made by the lessor to the lessee which relates to the goods and becomes part of the basis of the bargain creates an express warranty that the goods will conform to the affirmation or promise.

(b) Any description of the goods which is made part of the basis of the bargain creates an express warranty that the goods will conform to the description.

(c) Any sample or model that is made part of the basis of the bargain creates an express warranty that the whole of the goods will conform to the sample or model.

(2) It is not necessary to the creation of an express warranty that the lessor use formal words, such as "warrant" or "guarantee," or that the lessor have a specific intention to make a warranty, but an affirmation merely of the value of the goods or a statement purporting to be merely the lessor's opinion or commendation of the goods does not create a warranty.

§ 2A–211.   Warranties Against Interference and Against Infringement; Lessee's Obligation Against Infringement.

(1) There is in a lease contract a warranty that for the lease term no person holds a claim to or interest in the goods that arose from an act or omission of the lessor, other than a claim by way of infringement or the like, which will interfere with the lessee's enjoyment of its leasehold interest.

(2) Except in a finance lease there is in a lease contract by a lessor who is a merchant regularly dealing in goods of the kind a warranty that the goods are delivered free of the rightful claim of any person by way of infringement or the like.

(3) A lessee who furnishes specifications to a lessor or a supplier shall hold the lessor and the supplier harmless against any claim by way of infringement or the like that arises out of compliance with the specifications.

§ 2A–212.   Implied Warranty of Merchantability.

(1) Except in a finance lease, a warranty that the goods will be merchantable is implied in a lease contract if the lessor is a merchant with respect to goods of that kind.

(2) Goods to be merchantable must be at least such as

(a) pass without objection in the trade under the description in the lease agreement;

(b) in the case of fungible goods, are of fair average quality within the description;

(c) are fit for the ordinary purposes for which goods of that type are used;

(d) run, within the variation permitted by the lease agreement, of even kind, quality, and quantity within each unit and among all units involved;

(e) are adequately contained, packaged, and labeled as the lease agreement may require; and

(f) conform to any promises or affirmations of fact made on the container or label.

(3) Other implied warranties may arise from course of dealing or usage of trade.

§ 2A-213.   Implied Warranty of Fitness for Particular Purpose.

Except in a finance of lease, if the lessor at the time the lease contract is made has reason to know of any particular purpose for which the goods are required and that the lessee is relying on the lessor's skill or judgment to select or furnish suitable goods, there is in the lease contract an implied warranty that the goods will be fit for that purpose.

§ 2A-214.   Exclusion or Modification of Warranties.

(1) Words or conduct relevant to the creation of an express warranty and words or conduct tending to negate or limit a warranty must be construed wherever reasonable as consistent with each other; but, subject to the provisions of Section 2A-202 on parol or extrinsic evidence, negation or limitation is inoperative to the extent that the construction is unreasonable.

(2) Subject to subsection (3), to exclude or modify the implied warranty of merchantability or any part of it the language must mention "merchantability", be by a writing, and be conspicuous. Subject to subsection (3), to exclude or modify any implied warranty of fitness the exclusion must be by a writing and be conspicuous. Language to exclude all implied warranties of fitness is sufficient if it is in writing, is conspicuous and states, for example, "There is no warranty that the goods will be fit for a particular purpose".

(3) Notwithstanding subsection (2), but subject to subsection (4),

(a) unless the circumstances indicate otherwise, all implied warranties are excluded by expressions like "as is" or "with all faults" or by other language that in common understanding calls the lessee's attention to the exclusion of warranties and makes plain that there is no implied warranty, if in writing and conspicuous;

(b) if the lessee before entering into the lease contract has examined the goods or the sample or model as fully as desired or has refused to examine the goods, there is no implied warranty with regard to defects that an examination ought in the circumstances to have revealed; and

(c) an implied warranty may also be excluded or modified by course of dealing, course of performance, or usage of trade.

(4) To exclude or modify a warranty against interference or against infringement (Section 2A-211) or any part of it, the language must be specific, be by a writing, and be conspicuous, unless the circumstances, including course of performance, course of dealing, or usage of trade, give the lessee reason to know that the goods are being leased subject to a claim or interest of any person.

§ 2A-215.   Cumulation and Conflict of Warranties Express or Implied.

Warranties, whether express or implied, must be construed as consistent with each other and as cumulative, but if that construction is unreasonable, the intention of the parties determines which warranty is dominant. In ascertaining that intention the following rules apply:

(a) Exact or technical specifications displace an inconsistent sample or model or general language of description.

(b) A sample from an existing bulk displaces inconsistent general language of description.

(c) Express warranties displace inconsistent implied warranties other than an implied warranty of fitness for a particular purpose.

§ 2A-216.   Third-Party Beneficiaries of Express and Implied Warranties.

Alternative A

A warranty to or for the benefit of a lessee under this Article, whether express or implied, extends to any natural person who is in the family or household of the lessee or who is a guest in the lessee's home if it is reasonable to expect that such person may use, consume, or be affected by the goods and who is injured in person by breach of the warranty. This section does not displace principles of law and equity that extend a warranty to or for the benefit of a lessee to other persons. The operation of this section may not be excluded, modified, or limited, but an exclusion, modification, or limitation of the warranty, including any with respect to rights and remedies, effective against the lessee is also effective against any beneficiary designated under this section.

Alternative B

A warranty to or for the benefit of a lessee under this Article, whether express or implied, extends to any natural person who may reasonably be expected to use, consume, or be affected by the goods and who is injured in person by breach of the warranty. This section does not displace principles of law and equity that extend a warranty to or for the benefit of a lessee to other persons. The operation of this section may not be excluded, modified, or limited, but an exclusion, modification, or limitation of the warranty, including any with respect to rights and remedies, effective against the lessee is also effective against the beneficiary designated under this section.

Alternative C

A warranty to or for the benefit of a lessee under this Article, whether express or implied, extends to any person who may reasonably be expected to use, consume, or be affected by the goods and who is injured by breach of the warranty. The operation of this section may not be excluded, modified, or limited with respect to injury to the person of an individual to whom the warranty extends, but an exclusion, modification, or limitation of the warranty, including any with respect to rights and remedies, effective against the lessee is also effective against the beneficiary designated under this section.

§ 2A-217.   Identification.

Identification of goods as goods to which a lease contract refers may be made at any time and in any manner explicitly agreed to by the parties. In the absence of explicit agreement, identification occurs:

(a) when the lease contract is made if the lease contract is for a lease of goods that are existing and identified;

(b) when the goods are shipped, marked, or otherwise designated by the lessor as goods to which the lease contract refers, if the lease contract is for a lease of goods that are not existing and identified; or

(c) when the young are conceived, if the lease contract is for a lease of unborn young of animals.

§ 2A–218.   Insurance and Proceeds.

(1) A lessee obtains an insurable interest when existing goods are identified to the lease contract even though the goods identified are nonconforming and the lessee has an option to reject them.

(2) If a lessee has an insurable interest only by reason of the lessor's identification of the goods, the lessor, until default or insolvency or notification to the lessee that identification is final, may substitute other goods for those identified.

(3) Notwithstanding a lessee's insurable interest under subsections (1) and (2), the lessor retains an insurable interest until an option to buy has been exercised by the lessee and risk of loss has passed to the lessee.

(4) Nothing in this section impairs any insurable interest recognized under any other statute or rule of law.

(5) The parties by agreement may determine that one or more parties have an obligation to obtain and pay for insurance covering the goods and by agreement may determine the beneficiary of the proceeds of the insurance.

§ 2A–219.   Risk of Loss.

(1) Except in the case of a finance lease, risk of loss is retained by the lessor and does not pass to the lessee. In the case of a finance lease, risk of loss passes to the lessee.

(2) Subject to the provisions of this Article on the effect of default on risk of loss (Section 2A–220), if risk of loss is to pass to the lessee and the time of passage is not stated, the following rules apply:

> (a) If the lease contract requires or authorizes the goods to be shipped by carrier
>
> > (i) and it does not require delivery at a particular destination, the risk of loss passes to the lessee when the goods are duly delivered to the carrier; but
> >
> > (ii) if it does require delivery at a particular destination and the goods are there duly tendered while in the possession of the carrier, the risk of loss passes to the lessee when the goods are there duly so tendered as to enable the lessee to take delivery.
>
> (b) If the goods are held by a bailee to be delivered without being moved, the risk of loss passes to the lessee on acknowledgment by the bailee of the lessee's right to possession of the goods.
>
> (c) In any case not within subsection (a) or (b), the risk of loss passes to the lessee on the lessee's receipt of the goods if the lessor, or, in the case of a finance lease, the supplier, is a merchant; otherwise the risk passes to the lessee on tender of delivery.

§ 2A–220.   Effect of Default on Risk of Loss.

(1) Where risk of loss is to pass to the lessee and the time of passage is not stated:

> (a) If a tender or delivery of goods so fails to conform to the lease contract as to give a right of rejection, the risk of their loss remains with the lessor, or, in the case of a finance lease, the supplier, until cure or acceptance.
>
> (b) If the lessee rightfully revokes acceptance, he [or she], to the extent of any deficiency in his [or her] effective insurance coverage, may treat the risk of loss as having remained with the lessor from the beginning.

(2) Whether or not risk of loss is to pass to the lessee, if the lessee as to conforming goods already identified to a lease contract repudiates or is otherwise in default under the lease contract, the lessor, or, in the case of a finance lease, the supplier, to the extent of any deficiency in his [or her] effective insurance coverage may treat the risk of loss as resting on the lessee for a commercially reasonable time.

§ 2A–221.   Casualty to Identified Goods.

If a lease contract requires goods identified when the lease contract is made, and the goods suffer casualty without fault of the lessee, the lessor or the supplier before delivery, or the goods suffer casualty before risk of loss passes to the lessee pursuant to the lease agreement or Section 2A–219, then:

(a) if the loss is total, the lease contract is avoided; and

(b) if the loss is partial or the goods have so deteriorated as to no longer conform to the lease contract, the lessee may nevertheless demand inspection and at his [or her] option either treat the lease contract as avoided or, except in a finance lease that is not a consumer lease, accept the goods with due allowance from the rent payable for the balance of the lease term for the deterioration or the deficiency in quantity but without further right against the lessor.

Part 3   Effect of Lease Contract

§ 2A–301.   Enforceability of Lease Contract.

Except as otherwise provided in this Article, a lease contract is effective and enforceable according to its terms between the parties, against purchasers of the goods and against creditors of the parties.

§ 2A–302.   Title to and Possession of Goods.

Except as otherwise provided in this Article, each provision of this Article applies whether the lessor or a third party has title to the goods, and whether the lessor, the lessee, or a third party has possession of the goods, notwithstanding any statute or rule of law that possession or the absence of possession is fraudulent.

§ 2A–303.   Alienability of Party's Interest Under Lease Contract or of Lessor's Residual Interest in Goods; Delegation of Performance; Transfer of Rights.

(1) As used in this section, "creation of a security interest" includes the sale of a lease contract that is subject to Article 9, Secured Transactions, by reason of Section 9–109(a)(3).

(2) Except as provided in subsections (3) and Section 9–407, a provision in a lease agreement which (i) prohibits the voluntary or involuntary transfer, including a transfer by sale, sublease, creation or enforcement of a security interest, or attachment, levy, or other judicial process, of an interest of a party under the lease contract or of the lessor's residual interest in the goods, or (ii) makes such a transfer an event of default, gives rise to the rights and remedies provided in subsection (4), but a transfer that is prohibited or is an event of default under the lease agreement is otherwise effective.

(3) A provision in a lease agreement which (i) prohibits a transfer of a right to damages for default with respect to the whole lease contract or of a right to payment arising out of the transferor's due performance of the transferor's entire obligation, or (ii) makes such a transfer an event of default, is not enforceable, and such a transfer is not a transfer that materially impairs the propsect of obtaining return performance by, materially changes the duty of, or materially increases the burden or risk imposed on, the other party to the lease contract within the purview of subsection (4).

(4) Subject to subsection (3) and Section 9–407:

(a) if a transfer is made which is made an event of default under a lease agreement, the party to the lease contract not making the transfer, unless that party waives the default or otherwise agrees, has the rights and remedies described in Section 2A–501(2);

(b) if paragraph (a) is not applicable and if a transfer is made that (i) is prohibited under a lease agreement or (ii) materially impairs the prospect of obtaining return performance by, materially changes the duty of, or materially increases the burden or risk imposed on, the other party to the lease contract, unless the party not making the transfer agrees at any time to the transfer in the lease contract or otherwise, then, except as limited by contract, (i) the transferor is liable to the party not making the transfer for damages caused by the transfer to the extent that the damages could not reasonably be prevented by the party not making the transfer and (ii) a court having jurisdiction may grant other appropriate relief, including cancellation of the lease contract or an injunction against the transfer.

(5) A transfer of "the lease" or of "all my rights under the lease", or a transfer in similar general terms, is a transfer of rights and, unless the language or the circumstances, as in a transfer for security, indicate the contrary, the transfer is a delegation of duties by the transferor to the transferee. Acceptance by the transferee constitutes a promise by the transferee to perform those duties. The promise is enforceable by either the transferor or the other party to the lease contract.

(6) Unless otherwise agreed by the lessor and the lessee, a delegation of performance does not relieve the transferor as against the other party of any duty to perform or of any liability for default.

(7) In a consumer lease, to prohibit the transfer of an interest of a party under the lease contract or to make a transfer an event of default, the language must be specific, by a writing, and conspicuous.

As amended in 1990 and 1999.

§ 2A–304.   Subsequent Lease of Goods by Lessor.

(1) Subject to Section 2A–303, a subsequent lessee from a lessor of goods under an existing lease contract obtains, to the extent of the leasehold interest transferred, the leasehold interest in the goods that the lessor had or had power to transfer, and except as provided in subsection (2) and Section 2A–527(4), takes subject to the existing lease contract. A lessor with voidable title has power to transfer a good leasehold interest to a good faith subsequent lessee for value, but only to the extent set forth in the preceding sentence. If goods have been delivered under a transaction of purchase the lessor has that power even though:

(a) the lessor's transferor was deceived as to the identity of the lessor;

(b) the delivery was in exchange for a check which is later dishonored;

(c) it was agreed that the transaction was to be a "cash sale"; or

(d) the delivery was procured through fraud punishable as larcenous under the criminal law.

(2) A subsequent lessee in the ordinary course of business from a lessor who is a merchant dealing in goods of that kind to whom the goods were entrusted by the existing lessee of that lessor before the interest of the subsequent lessee became enforceable against that lessor obtains, to the extent of the leasehold interest transferred, all of that lessor's and the existing lessee's rights to the goods, and takes free of the existing lease contract.

(3) A subsequent lessee from the lessor of goods that are subject to an existing lease contract and are covered by a certificate of title issued under a statute of this State or of another jurisdiction takes no greater rights than those provided both by this section and by the certificate of title statute.

As amended in 1990.

§ 2A–305.   Sale or Sublease of Goods by Lessee.

(1) Subject to the provisions of Section 2A–303, a buyer or sublessee from the lessee of goods under an existing lease contract obtains, to the extent of the interest transferred, the leasehold interest in the goods that the lessee had or had power to transfer, and except as provided in subsection (2) and Section 2A–511(4), takes subject to the existing lease contract. A lessee with a voidable leasehold interest has power to transfer a good leasehold interest to a good faith buyer for value or a good faith sublessee for value, but only to the extent set forth in the preceding sentence. When goods have been delivered under a transaction of lease the lessee has that power even though:

(a) the lessor was deceived as to the identity of the lessee;

(b) the delivery was in exchange for a check which is later dishonored; or

(c) the delivery was procured through fraud punishable as larcenous under the criminal law.

(2) A buyer in the ordinary course of business or a sublessee in the ordinary course of business from a lessee who is a merchant dealing in goods of that kind to whom the goods were entrusted by

the lessor obtains, to the extent of the interest transferred, all of the lessor's and lessee's rights to the goods, and takes free of the existing lease contract.

(3) A buyer or sublessee from the lessee of goods that are subject to an existing lease contract and are covered by a certificate of title issued under a statute of this State or of another jurisdiction takes no greater rights than those provided both by this section and by the certificate of title statute.

§ 2A–306.   Priority of Certain Liens Arising by Operation of Law.

If a person in the ordinary course of his [or her] business furnishes services or materials with respect to goods subject to a lease contract, a lien upon those goods in the possession of that person given by statute or rule of law for those materials or services takes priority over any interest of the lessor or lessee under the lease contract or this Article unless the lien is created by statute and the statute provides otherwise or unless the lien is created by rule of law and the rule of law provides otherwise.

§ 2A–307.   Priority of Liens Arising by Attachment or Levy on, Security Interests in, and Other Claims to Goods.

(1) Except as otherwise provided in Section 2A–306, a creditor of a lessee takes subject to the lease contract.

(2) Except as otherwise provided in subsection (3) and in Sections 2A–306 and 2A–308, a creditor of a lessor takes subject to the lease contract unless the creditor holds a lien that attached to the goods before the lease contract became enforceable.

(3) Except as otherwise provided in Sections 9–317, 9–321, and 9–323, a lessee takes a leasehold interest subject to a security interest held by a creditor of the lessor.

As amended in 1990 and 1999.

§ 2A–308.   Special Rights of Creditors.

(1) A creditor of a lessor in possession of goods subject to a lease contract may treat the lease contract as void if as against the creditor retention of possession by the lessor is fraudulent under any statute or rule of law, but retention of possession in good faith and current course of trade by the lessor for a commercially reasonable time after the lease contract becomes enforceable is not fraudulent.

(2) Nothing in this Article impairs the rights of creditors of a lessor if the lease contract (a) becomes enforceable, not in current course of trade but in satisfaction of or as security for a pre-existing claim for money, security, or the like, and (b) is made under circumstances which under any statute or rule of law apart from this Article would constitute the transaction a fraudulent transfer or voidable preference.

(3) A creditor of a seller may treat a sale or an identification of goods to a contract for sale as void if as against the creditor retention of possession by the seller is fraudulent under any statute or rule of law, but retention of possession of the goods pursuant to a lease contract entered into by the seller as lessee and the buyer as lessor in connection with the sale or identification of the goods is not fraudulent if the buyer bought for value and in good faith.

§ 2A–309.   Lessor's and Lessee's Rights When Goods Become Fixtures.

(1) In this section:

(a) goods are "fixtures" when they become so related to particular real estate that an interest in them arises under real estate law;

(b) a "fixture filing" is the filing, in the office where a mortgage on the real estate would be filed or recorded, of a financing statement covering goods that are or are to become fixtures and conforming to the requirements of Section 9–502(a) and (b);

(c) a lease is a "purchase money lease" unless the lessee has possession or use of the goods or the right to possession or use of the goods before the lease agreement is enforceable;

(d) a mortgage is a "construction mortgage" to the extent it secures an obligation incurred for the construction of an improvement on land including the acquisition cost of the land, if the recorded writing so indicates; and

(e) "encumbrance" includes real estate mortgages and other liens on real estate and all other rights in real estate that are not ownership interests.

(2) Under this Article a lease may be of goods that are fixtures or may continue in goods that become fixtures, but no lease exists under this Article of ordinary building materials incorporated into an improvement on land.

(3) This Article does not prevent creation of a lease of fixtures pursuant to real estate law.

(4) The perfected interest of a lessor of fixtures has priority over a conflicting interest of an encumbrancer or owner of the real estate if:

(a) the lease is a purchase money lease, the conflicting interest of the encumbrancer or owner arises before the goods become fixtures, the interest of the lessor is perfected by a fixture filing before the goods become fixtures or within ten days thereafter, and the lessee has an interest of record in the real estate or is in possession of the real estate; or

(b) the interest of the lessor is perfected by a fixture filing before the interest of the encumbrancer or owner is of record, the lessor's interest has priority over any conflicting interest of a predecessor in title of the encumbrancer or owner, and the lessee has an interest of record in the real estate or is in possession of the real estate.

(5) The interest of a lessor of fixtures, whether or not perfected, has priority over the conflicting interest of an encumbrancer or owner of the real estate if:

(a) the fixtures are readily removable factory or office machines, readily removable equipment that is not primarily used or leased for use in the operation of the real estate, or readily removable replacements of domestic appliances that are goods subject to a consumer lease, and before the goods become fixtures the lease contract is enforceable; or

(b) the conflicting interest is a lien on the real estate obtained by legal or equitable proceedings after the lease contract is enforceable; or

(c) the encumbrancer or owner has consented in writing to the lease or has disclaimed an interest in the goods as fixtures; or

(d) the lessee has a right to remove the goods as against the encumbrancer or owner. If the lessee's right to remove terminates, the priority of the interest of the lessor continues for a reasonable time.

(6) Notwithstanding paragraph (4)(a) but otherwise subject to subsections (4) and (5), the interest of a lessor of fixtures, including the lessor's residual interest, is subordinate to the conflicting interest of an encumbrancer of the real estate under a construction mortgage recorded before the goods become fixtures if the goods become fixtures before the completion of the construction. To the extent given to refinance a construction mortgage, the conflicting interest of an encumbrancer of the real estate under a mortgage has this priority to the same extent as the encumbrancer of the real estate under the construction mortgage.

(7) In cases not within the preceding subsections, priority between the interest of a lessor of fixtures, including the lessor's residual interest, and the conflicting interest of an encumbrancer or owner of the real estate who is not the lessee is determined by the priority rules governing conflicting interests in real estate.

(8) If the interest of a lessor of fixtures, including the lessor's residual interest, has priority over all conflicting interests of all owners and encumbrancers of the real estate, the lessor or the lessee may (i) on default, expiration, termination, or cancellation of the lease agreement but subject to the agreement and this Article, or (ii) if necessary to enforce other rights and remedies of the lessor or lessee under this Article, remove the goods from the real estate, free and clear of all conflicting interests of all owners and encumbrancers of the real estate, but the lessor or lessee must reimburse any encumbrancer or owner of the real estate who is not the lessee and who has not otherwise agreed for the cost of repair of any physical injury, but not for any diminution in value of the real estate caused by the absence of the goods removed or by any necessity of replacing them. A person entitled to reimbursement may refuse permission to remove until the party seeking removal gives adequate security for the performance of this obligation.

(9) Even though the lease agreement does not create a security interest, the interest of a lessor of fixtures, including the lessor's residual interest, is perfected by filing a financing statement as a fixture filing for leased goods that are or are to become fixtures in accordance with the relevant provisions of the Article on Secured Transactions (Article 9).

As amended in 1990 and 1999.

§ 2A-310. Lessor's and Lessee's Rights When Goods Become Accessions.

(1) Goods are "accessions" when they are installed in or affixed to other goods.

(2) The interest of a lessor or a lessee under a lease contract entered into before the goods became accessions is superior to all interests in the whole except as stated in subsection (4).

(3) The interest of a lessor or a lessee under a lease contract entered into at the time or after the goods became accessions is superior to all subsequently acquired interests in the whole except as stated in subsection (4) but is subordinate to interests in the whole existing at the time the lease contract was made unless the holders of such interests in the whole have in writing consented to the lease or disclaimed an interest in the goods as part of the whole.

(4) The interest of a lessor or a lessee under a lease contract described in subsection (2) or (3) is subordinate to the interest of

(a) a buyer in the ordinary course of business or a lessee in the ordinary course of business of any interest in the whole acquired after the goods became accessions; or

(b) a creditor with a security interest in the whole perfected before the lease contract was made to the extent that the creditor makes subsequent advances without knowledge of the lease contract.

(5) When under subsections (2) or (3) and (4) a lessor or a lessee of accessions holds an interest that is superior to all interests in the whole, the lessor or the lessee may (a) on default, expiration, termination, or cancellation of the lease contract by the other party but subject to the provisions of the lease contract and this Article, or (b) if necessary to enforce his [or her] other rights and remedies under this Article, remove the goods from the whole, free and clear of all interests in the whole, but he [or she] must reimburse any holder of an interest in the whole who is not the lessee and who has not otherwise agreed for the cost of repair of any physical injury but not for any diminution in value of the whole caused by the absence of the goods removed or by any necessity for replacing them. A person entitled to reimbursement may refuse permission to remove until the party seeking removal gives adequate security for the performance of this obligation.

§ 2A-311. Priority Subject to Subordination.

Nothing in this Article prevents subordination by agreement by any person entitled to priority.

As added in 1990.

Part 4 Performance of Lease Contract: Repudiated, Substituted and Excused

§ 2A-401. Insecurity: Adequate Assurance of Performance.

(1) A lease contract imposes an obligation on each party that the other's expectation of receiving due performance will not be impaired.

(2) If reasonable grounds for insecurity arise with respect to the performance of either party, the insecure party may demand in writing adequate assurance of due performance. Until the insecure party receives that assurance, if commercially reasonable the insecure party may suspend any performance for which he [or she] has not already received the agreed return.

(3) A repudiation of the lease contract occurs if assurance of due performance adequate under the circumstances of the particular case is not provided to the insecure party within a reasonable time, not to exceed 30 days after receipt of a demand by the other party.

(4) Between merchants, the reasonableness of grounds for insecurity and the adequacy of any assurance offered must be determined according to commercial standards.

(5) Acceptance of any nonconforming delivery or payment does not prejudice the aggrieved party's right to demand adequate assurance of future performance.

§ 2A–402. Anticipatory Repudiation.

If either party repudiates a lease contract with respect to a performance not yet due under the lease contract, the loss of which performance will substantially impair the value of the lease contract to the other, the aggrieved party may:

(a) for a commercially reasonable time, await retraction of repudiation and performance by the repudiating party;

(b) make demand pursuant to Section 2A–401 and await assurance of future performance adequate under the circumstances of the particular case; or

(c) resort to any right or remedy upon default under the lease contract or this Article, even though the aggrieved party has notified the repudiating party that the aggrieved party would await the repudiating party's performance and assurance and has urged retraction. In addition, whether or not the aggrieved party is pursuing one of the foregoing remedies, the aggrieved party may suspend performance or, if the aggrieved party is the lessor, proceed in accordance with the provisions of this Article on the lessor's right to identify goods to the lease contract notwithstanding default or to salvage unfinished goods (Section 2A–524).

§ 2A–403. Retraction of Anticipatory Repudiation.

(1) Until the repudiating party's next performance is due, the repudiating party can retract the repudiation unless, since the repudiation, the aggrieved party has cancelled the lease contract or materially changed the aggrieved party's position or otherwise indicated that the aggrieved party considers the repudiation final.

(2) Retraction may be by any method that clearly indicates to the aggrieved party that the repudiating party intends to perform under the lease contract and includes any assurance demanded under Section 2A–401.

(3) Retraction reinstates a repudiating party's rights under a lease contract with due excuse and allowance to the aggrieved party for any delay occasioned by the repudiation.

§ 2A–404. Substituted Performance.

(1) If without fault of the lessee, the lessor and the supplier, the agreed berthing, loading, or unloading facilities fail or the agreed type of carrier becomes unavailable or the agreed manner of delivery otherwise becomes commercially impracticable, but a commercially reasonable substitute is available, the substitute performance must be tendered and accepted.

(2) If the agreed means or manner of payment fails because of domestic or foreign governmental regulation:

(a) the lessor may withhold or stop delivery or cause the supplier to withhold or stop delivery unless the lessee provides a means or manner of payment that is commercially a substantial equivalent; and

(b) if delivery has already been taken, payment by the means or in the manner provided by the regulation discharges the lessee's obligation unless the regulation is discriminatory, oppressive, or predatory.

§ 2A–405. Excused Performance.

Subject to Section 2A–404 on substituted performance, the following rules apply:

(a) Delay in delivery or nondelivery in whole or in part by a lessor or a supplier who complies with paragraphs (b) and (c) is not a default under the lease contract if performance as agreed has been made impracticable by the occurrence of a contingency the nonoccurrence of which was a basic assumption on which the lease contract was made or by compliance in good faith with any applicable foreign or domestic governmental regulation or order, whether or not the regulation or order later proves to be invalid.

(b) If the causes mentioned in paragraph (a) affect only part of the lessor's or the supplier's capacity to perform, he [or she] shall allocate production and deliveries among his [or her] customers but at his [or her] option may include regular customers not then under contract for sale or lease as well as his [or her] own requirements for further manufacture. He [or she] may so allocate in any manner that is fair and reasonable.

(c) The lessor seasonably shall notify the lessee and in the case of a finance lease the supplier seasonably shall notify the lessor and the lessee, if known, that there will be delay or nondelivery and, if allocation is required under paragraph (b), of the estimated quota thus made available for the lessee.

§ 2A–406. Procedure on Excused Performance.

(1) If the lessee receives notification of a material or indefinite delay or an allocation justified under Section 2A–405, the lessee may by written notification to the lessor as to any goods involved, and with respect to all of the goods if under an installment lease contract the value of the whole lease contract is substantially impaired (Section 2A–510):

(a) terminate the lease contract (Section 2A–505(2)); or

(b) except in a finance lease that is not a consumer lease, modify the lease contract by accepting the available quota in substitution, with due allowance from the rent payable for the balance of the lease term for the deficiency but without further right against the lessor.

(2) If, after receipt of a notification from the lessor under Section 2A–405, the lessee fails so to modify the lease agreement within a reasonable time not exceeding 30 days, the lease contract lapses with respect to any deliveries affected.

§ 2A–407. Irrevocable Promises: Finance Leases.

(1) In the case of a finance lease that is not a consumer lease the lessee's promises under the lease contract become irrevocable and independent upon the lessee's acceptance of the goods.

(2) A promise that has become irrevocable and independent under subsection (1):

(a) is effective and enforceable between the parties, and by or against third parties including assignees of the parties, and

(b) is not subject to cancellation, termination, modification, repudiation, excuse, or substitution without the consent of the party to whom the promise runs.

(3) This section does not affect the validity under any other law of a covenant in any lease contract making the lessee's promises

irrevocable and independent upon the lessee's acceptance of the goods.

As amended in 1990.

Part 5   Default

A. In General

§ 2A-501.   Default: Procedure.

(1) Whether the lessor or the lessee is in default under a lease contract is determined by the lease agreement and this Article.

(2) If the lessor or the lessee is in default under the lease contract, the party seeking enforcement has rights and remedies as provided in this Article and, except as limited by this Article, as provided in the lease agreement.

(3) If the lessor or the lessee is in default under the lease contract, the party seeking enforcement may reduce the party's claim to judgment, or otherwise enforce the lease contract by self-help or any available judicial procedure or nonjudicial procedure, including administrative proceeding, arbitration, or the like, in accordance with this Article.

(4) Except as otherwise provided in Section 1-106(1) or this Article or the lease agreement, the rights and remedies referred to in subsections (2) and (3) are cumulative.

(5) If the lease agreement covers both real property and goods, the party seeking enforcement may proceed under this Part as to the goods, or under other applicable law as to both the real property and the goods in accordance with that party's rights and remedies in respect of the real property, in which case this Part does not apply.

As amended in 1990.

§ 2A-502.   Notice After Default.

Except as otherwise provided in this Article or the lease agreement, the lessor or lessee in default under the lease contract is not entitled to notice of default or notice of enforcement from the other party to the lease agreement.

§ 2A-503.   Modification or Impairment of Rights and Remedies.

(1) Except as otherwise provided in this Article, the lease agreement may include rights and remedies for default in addition to or in substitution for those provided in this Article and may limit or alter the measure of damages recoverable under this Article.

(2) Resort to a remedy provided under this Article or in the lease agreement is optional unless the remedy is expressly agreed to be exclusive. If circumstances cause an exclusive or limited remedy to fail of its essential purpose, or provision for an exclusive remedy is unconscionable, remedy may be had as provided in this Article.

(3) Consequential damages may be liquidated under Section 2A-504, or may otherwise be limited, altered, or excluded unless the limitation, alteration, or exclusion is unconscionable. Limitation, alteration, or exclusion of consequential damages for injury to the person in the case of consumer goods is prima facie unconscionable but limitation, alteration, or exclusion of damages where the loss is commercial is not prima facie unconscionable.

(4) Rights and remedies on default by the lessor or the lessee with respect to any obligation or promise collateral or ancillary to the lease contract are not impaired by this Article.

As amended in 1990.

§ 2A-504.   Liquidation of Damages.

(1) Damages payable by either party for default, or any other act or omission, including indemnity for loss or diminution of anticipated tax benefits or loss or damage to lessor's residual interest, may be liquidated in the lease agreement but only at an amount or by a formula that is reasonable in light of the then anticipated harm caused by the default or other act or omission.

(2) If the lease agreement provides for liquidation of damages, and such provision does not comply with subsection (1), or such provision is an exclusive or limited remedy that circumstances cause to fail of its essential purpose, remedy may be had as provided in this Article.

(3) If the lessor justifiably withholds or stops delivery of goods because of the lessee's default or insolvency (Section 2A-525 or 2A-526), the lessee is entitled to restitution of any amount by which the sum of his [or her] payments exceeds:

(a) the amount to which the lessor is entitled by virtue of terms liquidating the lessor's damages in accordance with subsection (1); or

(b) in the absence of those terms, 20 percent of the then present value of the total rent the lessee was obligated to pay for the balance of the lease term, or, in the case of a consumer lease, the lesser of such amount or $500.

(4) A lessee's right to restitution under subsection (3) is subject to offset to the extent the lessor establishes:

(a) a right to recover damages under the provisions of this Article other than subsection (1); and

(b) the amount or value of any benefits received by the lessee directly or indirectly by reason of the lease contract.

§ 2A-505.   Cancellation and Termination and Effect of Cancellation, Termination, Rescission, or Fraud on Rights and Remedies.

(1) On cancellation of the lease contract, all obligations that are still executory on both sides are discharged, but any right based on prior default or performance survives, and the cancelling party also retains any remedy for default of the whole lease contract or any unperformed balance.

(2) On termination of the lease contract, all obligations that are still executory on both sides are discharged but any right based on prior default or performance survives.

(3) Unless the contrary intention clearly appears, expressions of "cancellation," "rescission," or the like of the lease contract may not be construed as a renunciation or discharge of any claim in damages for an antecedent default.

(4) Rights and remedies for material misrepresentation or fraud include all rights and remedies available under this Article for default.

(5) Neither rescission nor a claim for rescission of the lease contract nor rejection or return of the goods may bar or be deemed inconsistent with a claim for damages or other right or remedy.

§ 2A–506.   Statute of Limitations.

(1) An action for default under a lease contract, including breach of warranty or indemnity, must be commenced within 4 years after the cause of action accrued. By the original lease contract the parties may reduce the period of limitation to not less than one year.

(2) A cause of action for default accrues when the act or omission on which the default or breach of warranty is based is or should have been discovered by the aggrieved party, or when the default occurs, whichever is later. A cause of action for indemnity accrues when the act or omission on which the claim for indemnity is based is or should have been discovered by the indemnified party, whichever is later.

(3) If an action commenced within the time limited by subsection (1) is so terminated as to leave available a remedy by another action for the same default or breach of warranty or indemnity, the other action may be commenced after the expiration of the time limited and within 6 months after the termination of the first action unless the termination resulted from voluntary discontinuance or from dismissal for failure or neglect to prosecute.

(4) This section does not alter the law on tolling of the statute of limitations nor does it apply to causes of action that have accrued before this Article becomes effective.

§ 2A–507.   Proof of Market Rent: Time and Place.

(1) Damages based on market rent (Section 2A–519 or 2A–528) are determined according to the rent for the use of the goods concerned for a lease term identical to the remaining lease term of the original lease agreement and prevailing at the times specified in Sections 2A–519 and 2A–528.

(2) If evidence of rent for the use of the goods concerned for a lease term identical to the remaining lease term of the original lease agreement and prevailing at the times or places described in this Article is not readily available, the rent prevailing within any reasonable time before or after the time described or at any other place or for a different lease term which in commercial judgment or under usage of trade would serve as a reasonable substitute for the one described may be used, making any proper allowance for the difference, including the cost of transporting the goods to or from the other place.

(3) Evidence of a relevant rent prevailing at a time or place or for a lease term other than the one described in this Article offered by one party is not admissible unless and until he [or she] has given the other party notice the court finds sufficient to prevent unfair surprise.

(4) If the prevailing rent or value of any goods regularly leased in any established market is in issue, reports in official publications or trade journals or in newspapers or periodicals of general circulation published as the reports of that market are admissible in evidence. The circumstances of the preparation of the report may be shown to affect its weight but not its admissibility.

As amended in 1990.

B. Default by Lessor

§ 2A–508.   Lessee's Remedies.

(1) If a lessor fails to deliver the goods in conformity to the lease contract (Section 2A–509) or repudiates the lease contract (Section 2A–402), or a lessee rightfully rejects the goods (Section 2A–509) or justifiably revokes acceptance of the goods (Section 2A–517), then with respect to any goods involved, and with respect to all of the goods if under an installment lease contract the value of the whole lease contract is substantially impaired (Section 2A–510), the lessor is in default under the lease contract and the lessee may:

    (a) cancel the lease contract (Section 2A–505(1));

    (b) recover so much of the rent and security as has been paid and is just under the circumstances;

    (c) cover and recover damages as to all goods affected whether or not they have been identified to the lease contract (Sections 2A–518 and 2A–520), or recover damages for nondelivery (Sections 2A–519 and 2A–520);

    (d) exercise any other rights or pursue any other remedies provided in the lease contract.

(2) If a lessor fails to deliver the goods in conformity to the lease contract or repudiates the lease contract, the lessee may also:

    (a) if the goods have been identified, recover them (Section 2A–522); or

    (b) in a proper case, obtain specific performance or replevy the goods (Section 2A–521).

(3) If a lessor is otherwise in default under a lease contract, the lessee may exercise the rights and pursue the remedies provided in the lease contract, which may include a right to cancel the lease, and in Section 2A–519(3).

(4) If a lessor has breached a warranty, whether express or implied, the lessee may recover damages (Section 2A–519(4)).

(5) On rightful rejection or justifiable revocation of acceptance, a lessee has a security interest in goods in the lessee's possession or control for any rent and security that has been paid and any expenses reasonably incurred in their inspection, receipt, transportation, and care and custody and may hold those goods and dispose of them in good faith and in a commercially reasonable manner, subject to Section 2A–527(5).

(6) Subject to the provisions of Section 2A–407, a lessee, on notifying the lessor of the lessee's intention to do so, may deduct all or any part of the damages resulting from any default under the lease contract from any part of the rent still due under the same lease contract.

As amended in 1990.

§ 2A–509.   Lessee's Rights on Improper Delivery; Rightful Rejection.

(1) Subject to the provisions of Section 2A–510 on default in installment lease contracts, if the goods or the tender or delivery fail in any respect to conform to the lease contract, the lessee may reject or accept the goods or accept any commercial unit or units and reject the rest of the goods.

(2) Rejection of goods is ineffective unless it is within a reasonable time after tender or delivery of the goods and the lessee seasonably notifies the lessor.

§ 2A–510.   Installment Lease Contracts: Rejection and Default.

(1) Under an installment lease contract a lessee may reject any delivery that is nonconforming if the nonconformity substantially impairs the value of that delivery and cannot be cured or the nonconformity is a defect in the required documents; but if the

nonconformity does not fall within subsection (2) and the lessor or the supplier gives adequate assurance of its cure, the lessee must accept that delivery.

(2) Whenever nonconformity or default with respect to one or more deliveries substantially impairs the value of the installment lease contract as a whole there is a default with respect to the whole. But, the aggrieved party reinstates the installment lease contract as a whole if the aggrieved party accepts a nonconforming delivery without seasonably notifying of cancellation or brings an action with respect only to past deliveries or demands performance as to future deliveries.

§ 2A–511.   Merchant Lessee's Duties as to Rightfully Rejected Goods.

(1) Subject to any security interest of a lessee (Section 2A–508(5)), if a lessor or a supplier has no agent or place of business at the market of rejection, a merchant lessee, after rejection of goods in his [or her] possession or control, shall follow any reasonable instructions received from the lessor or the supplier with respect to the goods. In the absence of those instructions, a merchant lessee shall make reasonable efforts to sell, lease, or otherwise dispose of the goods for the lessor's account if they threaten to decline in value speedily. Instructions are not reasonable if on demand indemnity for expenses is not forthcoming.

(2) If a merchant lessee (subsection (1)) or any other lessee (Section 2A–512) disposes of goods, he [or she] is entitled to reimbursement either from the lessor or the supplier or out of the proceeds for reasonable expenses of caring for and disposing of the goods and, if the expenses include no disposition commission, to such commission as is usual in the trade, or if there is none, to a reasonable sum not exceeding 10 percent of the gross proceeds.

(3) In complying with this section or Section 2A–512, the lessee is held only to good faith. Good faith conduct hereunder is neither acceptance or conversion nor the basis of an action for damages.

(4) A purchaser who purchases in good faith from a lessee pursuant to this section or Section 2A–512 takes the goods free of any rights of the lessor and the supplier even though the lessee fails to comply with one or more of the requirements of this Article.

§ 2A–512.   Lessee's Duties as to Rightfully Rejected Goods.

(1) Except as otherwise provided with respect to goods that threaten to decline in value speedily (Section 2A–511) and subject to any security interest of a lessee (Section 2A–508(5)):

(a) the lessee, after rejection of goods in the lessee's possession, shall hold them with reasonable care at the lessor's or the supplier's disposition for a reasonable time after the lessee's seasonable notification of rejection;

(b) if the lessor or the supplier gives no instructions within a reasonable time after notification of rejection, the lessee may store the rejected goods for the lessor's or the supplier's account or ship them to the lessor or the supplier or dispose of them for the lessor's or the supplier's account with reimbursement in the manner provided in Section 2A–511; but

(c) the lessee has no further obligations with regard to goods rightfully rejected.

(2) Action by the lessee pursuant to subsection (1) is not acceptance or conversion.

§ 2A–513.   Cure by Lessor of Improper Tender or Delivery; Replacement.

(1) If any tender or delivery by the lessor or the supplier is rejected because nonconforming and the time for performance has not yet expired, the lessor or the supplier may seasonably notify the lessee of the lessor's or the supplier's intention to cure and may then make a conforming delivery within the time provided in the lease contract.

(2) If the lessee rejects a nonconforming tender that the lessor or the supplier had reasonable grounds to believe would be acceptable with or without money allowance, the lessor or the supplier may have a further reasonable time to substitute a conforming tender if he [or she] seasonably notifies the lessee.

§ 2A–514.   Waiver of Lessee's Objections.

(1) In rejecting goods, a lessee's failure to state a particular defect that is ascertainable by reasonable inspection precludes the lessee from relying on the defect to justify rejection or to establish default:

(a) if, stated seasonably, the lessor or the supplier could have cured it (Section 2A–513); or

(b) between merchants if the lessor or the supplier after rejection has made a request in writing for a full and final written statement of all defects on which the lessee proposes to rely.

(2) A lessee's failure to reserve rights when paying rent or other consideration against documents precludes recovery of the payment for defects apparent on the face of the documents.

§ 2A–515.   Acceptance of Goods.

(1) Acceptance of goods occurs after the lessee has had a reasonable opportunity to inspect the goods and

(a) the lessee signifies or acts with respect to the goods in a manner that signifies to the lessor or the supplier that the goods are conforming or that the lessee will take or retain them in spite of their nonconformity; or

(b) the lessee fails to make an effective rejection of the goods (Section 2A–509(2)).

(2) Acceptance of a part of any commercial unit is acceptance of that entire unit.

§ 2A–516.   Effect of Acceptance of Goods; Notice of Default; Burden of Establishing Default after Acceptance; Notice of Claim or Litigation to Person Answerable Over.

(1) A lessee must pay rent for any goods accepted in accordance with the lease contract, with due allowance for goods rightfully rejected or not delivered.

(2) A lessee's acceptance of goods precludes rejection of the goods accepted. In the case of a finance lease, if made with knowledge of a nonconformity, acceptance cannot be revoked because of it. In any other case, if made with knowledge of a nonconformity, acceptance cannot be revoked because of it unless the acceptance was on the reasonable assumption that the nonconformity would be seasonably cured. Acceptance does not of itself impair any other remedy provided by this Article or the lease agreement for nonconformity.

(3) If a tender has been accepted:

(a) within a reasonable time after the lessee discovers or should have discovered any default, the lessee shall notify the lessor and the supplier, if any, or be barred from any remedy against the party notified;

(b) except in the case of a consumer lease, within a reasonable time after the lessee receives notice of litigation for infringement or the like (Section 2A–211) the lessee shall notify the lessor or be barred from any remedy over for liability established by the litigation; and

(c) the burden is on the lessee to establish any default.

(4) If a lessee is sued for breach of a warranty or other obligation for which a lessor or a supplier is answerable over the following apply:

(a) The lessee may give the lessor or the supplier, or both, written notice of the litigation. If the notice states that the person notified may come in and defend and that if the person notified does not do so that person will be bound in any action against that person by the lessee by any determination of fact common to the two litigations, then unless the person notified after seasonable receipt of the notice does come in and defend that person is so bound.

(b) The lessor or the supplier may demand in writing that the lessee turn over control of the litigation including settlement if the claim is one for infringement or the like (Section 2A–211) or else be barred from any remedy over. If the demand states that the lessor or the supplier agrees to bear all expense and to satisfy any adverse judgment, then unless the lessee after seasonable receipt of the demand does turn over control the lessee is so barred.

(5) Subsections (3) and (4) apply to any obligation of a lessee to hold the lessor or the supplier harmless against infringement or the like (Section 2A–211).

As amended in 1990.

§ 2A–517.   Revocation of Acceptance of Goods.

(1) A lessee may revoke acceptance of a lot or commercial unit whose nonconformity substantially impairs its value to the lessee if the lessee has accepted it:

(a) except in the case of a finance lease, on the reasonable assumption that its nonconformity would be cured and it has not been seasonably cured; or

(b) without discovery of the nonconformity if the lessee's acceptance was reasonably induced either by the lessor's assurances or, except in the case of a finance lease, by the difficulty of discovery before acceptance.

(2) Except in the case of a finance lease that is not a consumer lease, a lessee may revoke acceptance of a lot or commercial unit if the lessor defaults under the lease contract and the default substantially impairs the value of that lot or commercial unit to the lessee.

(3) If the lease agreement so provides, the lessee may revoke acceptance of a lot or commercial unit because of other defaults by the lessor.

(4) Revocation of acceptance must occur within a reasonable time after the lessee discovers or should have discovered the ground for it and before any substantial change in condition of the goods which is not caused by the nonconformity. Revocation is not effective until the lessee notifies the lessor.

(5) A lessee who so revokes has the same rights and duties with regard to the goods involved as if the lessee had rejected them.

As amended in 1990.

§ 2A–518.   Cover; Substitute Goods.

(1) After a default by a lessor under the lease contract of the type described in Section 2A–508(1), or, if agreed, after other default by the lessor, the lessee may cover by making any purchase or lease of or contract to purchase or lease goods in substitution for those due from the lessor.

(2) Except as otherwise provided with respect to damages liquidated in the lease agreement (Section 2A–504) or otherwise determined pursuant to agreement of the parties (Sections 1–102(3) and 2A–503), if a lessee's cover is by lease agreement substantially similar to the original lease agreement and the new lease agreement is made in good faith and in a commercially reasonable manner, the lessee may recover from the lessor as damages (i) the present value, as of the date of the commencement of the term of the new lease agreement, of the rent under the new lease agreement applicable to that period of the new lease term which is comparable to the then remaining term of the original lease agreement minus the present value as of the same date of the total rent for the then remaining lease term of the original lease agreement, and (ii) any incidental or consequential damages, less expenses saved in consequence of the lessor's default.

(3) If a lessee's cover is by lease agreement that for any reason does not qualify for treatment under subsection (2), or is by purchase or otherwise, the lessee may recover from the lessor as if the lessee had elected not to cover and Section 2A–519 governs.

As amended in 1990.

§ 2A–519.   Lessee's Damages for Non-Delivery, Repudiation, Default, and Breach of Warranty in Regard to Accepted Goods.

(1) Except as otherwise provided with respect to damages liquidated in the lease agreement (Section 2A–504) or otherwise determined pursuant to agreement of the parties (Sections 1–102(3) and 2A–503), if a lessee elects not to cover or a lessee elects to cover and the cover is by lease agreement that for any reason does not qualify for treatment under Section 2A–518(2), or is by purchase or otherwise, the measure of damages for non-delivery or repudiation by the lessor or for rejection or revocation of acceptance by the lessee is the present value, as of the date of the default, of the then market rent minus the present value as of the same date of the original rent, computed for the remaining lease term of the original lease agreement, together with incidental and consequential damages, less expenses saved in consequence of the lessor's default.

(2) Market rent is to be determined as of the place for tender or, in cases of rejection after arrival or revocation of acceptance, as of the place of arrival.

(3) Except as otherwise agreed, if the lessee has accepted goods and given notification (Section 2A–516(3)), the measure of damages for non-conforming tender or delivery or other default by a lessor is the loss resulting in the ordinary course of events from the lessor's default as determined in any manner that is reasonable together

with incidental and consequential damages, less expenses saved in consequence of the lessor's default.

(4) Except as otherwise agreed, the measure of damages for breach of warranty is the present value at the time and place of acceptance of the difference between the value of the use of the goods accepted and the value if they had been as warranted for the lease term, unless special circumstances show proximate damages of a different amount, together with incidental and consequential damages, less expenses saved in consequence of the lessor's default or breach of warranty.

As amended in 1990.

§ 2A–520.   Lessee's Incidental and Consequential Damages.

(1) Incidental damages resulting from a lessor's default include expenses reasonably incurred in inspection, receipt, transportation, and care and custody of goods rightfully rejected or goods the acceptance of which is justifiably revoked, any commercially reasonable charges, expenses or commissions in connection with effecting cover, and any other reasonable expense incident to the default.

(2) Consequential damages resulting from a lessor's default include:

(a) any loss resulting from general or particular requirements and needs of which the lessor at the time of contracting had reason to know and which could not reasonably be prevented by cover or otherwise; and

(b) injury to person or property proximately resulting from any breach of warranty.

§ 2A–521.   Lessee's Right to Specific Performance or Replevin.

(1) Specific performance may be decreed if the goods are unique or in other proper circumstances.

(2) A decree for specific performance may include any terms and conditions as to payment of the rent, damages, or other relief that the court deems just.

(3) A lessee has a right of replevin, detinue, sequestration, claim and delivery, or the like for goods identified to the lease contract if after reasonable effort the lessee is unable to effect cover for those goods or the circumstances reasonably indicate that the effort will be unavailing.

§ 2A–522.   Lessee's Right to Goods on Lessor's Insolvency.

(1) Subject to subsection (2) and even though the goods have not been shipped, a lessee who has paid a part or all of the rent and security for goods identified to a lease contract (Section 2A–217) on making and keeping good a tender of any unpaid portion of the rent and security due under the lease contract may recover the goods identified from the lessor if the lessor becomes insolvent within 10 days after receipt of the first installment of rent and security.

(2) A lessee acquires the right to recover goods identified to a lease contract only if they conform to the lease contract.

C. Default by Lessee

§ 2A–523.   Lessor's Remedies.

(1) If a lessee wrongfully rejects or revokes acceptance of goods or fails to make a payment when due or repudiates with respect to a part or the whole, then, with respect to any goods involved, and with respect to all of the goods if under an installment lease

contract the value of the whole lease contract is substantially impaired (Section 2A–510), the lessee is in default under the lease contract and the lessor may:

(a) cancel the lease contract (Section 2A–505(1));

(b) proceed respecting goods not identified to the lease contract (Section 2A–524);

(c) withhold delivery of the goods and take possession of goods previously delivered (Section 2A–525);

(d) stop delivery of the goods by any bailee (Section 2A–526);

(e) dispose of the goods and recover damages (Section 2A–527), or retain the goods and recover damages (Section 2A–528), or in a proper case recover rent (Section 2A–529)

(f) exercise any other rights or pursue any other remedies provided in the lease contract.

(2) If a lessor does not fully exercise a right or obtain a remedy to which the lessor is entitled under subsection (1), the lessor may recover the loss resulting in the ordinary course of events from the lessee's default as determined in any reasonable manner, together with incidental damages, less expenses saved in consequence of the lessee's default.

(3) If a lessee is otherwise in default under a lease contract, the lessor may exercise the rights and pursue the remedies provided in the lease contract, which may include a right to cancel the lease. In addition, unless otherwise provided in the lease contract:

(a) if the default substantially impairs the value of the lease contract to the lessor, the lessor may exercise the rights and pursue the remedies provided in subsections (1) or (2); or

(b) if the default does not substantially impair the value of the lease contract to the lessor, the lessor may recover as provided in subsection (2).

As amended in 1990.

§ 2A–524.   Lessor's Right to Identify Goods to Lease Contract.

(1) After default by the lessee under the lease contract of the type described in Section 2A–523(1) or 2A–523(3)(a) or, if agreed, after other default by the lessee, the lessor may:

(a) identify to the lease contract conforming goods not already identified if at the time the lessor learned of the default they were in the lessor's or the supplier's possession or control; and

(b) dispose of goods (Section 2A–527(1)) that demonstrably have been intended for the particular lease contract even though those goods are unfinished.

(2) If the goods are unfinished, in the exercise of reasonable commercial judgment for the purposes of avoiding loss and of effective realization, an aggrieved lessor or the supplier may either complete manufacture and wholly identify the goods to the lease contract or cease manufacture and lease, sell, or otherwise dispose of the goods for scrap or salvage value or proceed in any other reasonable manner.

As amended in 1990.

§ 2A–525.   Lessor's Right to Possession of Goods.

(1) If a lessor discovers the lessee to be insolvent, the lessor may refuse to deliver the goods.

(2) After a default by the lessee under the lease contract of the type described in Section 2A–523(1) or 2A–523(3)(a) or, if agreed, after other default by the lessee, the lessor has the right to take possession of the goods. If the lease contract so provides, the lessor may require the lessee to assemble the goods and make them available to the lessor at a place to be designated by the lessor which is reasonably convenient to both parties. Without removal, the lessor may render unusable any goods employed in trade or business, and may dispose of goods on the lessee's premises (Section 2A–527).

(3) The lessor may proceed under subsection (2) without judicial process if that can be done without breach of the peace or the lessor may proceed by action.

As amended in 1990.

§ 2A–526.   Lessor's Stoppage of Delivery in Transit or Otherwise.

(1) A lessor may stop delivery of goods in the possession of a carrier or other bailee if the lessor discovers the lessee to be insolvent and may stop delivery of carload, truckload, planeload, or larger shipments of express or freight if the lessee repudiates or fails to make a payment due before delivery, whether for rent, security or otherwise under the lease contract, or for any other reason the lessor has a right to withhold or take possession of the goods.

(2) In pursuing its remedies under subsection (1), the lessor may stop delivery until

(a) receipt of the goods by the lessee;

(b) acknowledgment to the lessee by any bailee of the goods, except a carrier, that the bailee holds the goods for the lessee; or

(c) such an acknowledgment to the lessee by a carrier via reshipment or as warehouseman.

(3) (a) To stop delivery, a lessor shall so notify as to enable the bailee by reasonable diligence to prevent delivery of the goods.

(b) After notification, the bailee shall hold and deliver the goods according to the directions of the lessor, but the lessor is liable to the bailee for any ensuing charges or damages.

(c) A carrier who has issued a nonnegotiable bill of lading is not obliged to obey a notification to stop received from a person other than the consignor.

§ 2A–527.   Lessor's Rights to Dispose of Goods.

(1) After a default by a lessee under the lease contract of the type described in Section 2A–523(1) or 2A–523(3)(a) or after the lessor refuses to deliver or takes possession of goods (Section 2A–525 or 2A–526), or, if agreed, after other default by a lessee, the lessor may dispose of the goods concerned or the undelivered balance thereof by lease, sale, or otherwise.

(2) Except as otherwise provided with respect to damages liquidated in the lease agreement (Section 2A–504) or otherwise determined pursuant to agreement of the parties (Sections 1–102(3) and 2A–503), if the disposition is by lease agreement substantially similar to the original lease agreement and the new lease agreement is made in good faith and in a commercially reasonable manner, the lessor may recover from the lessee as damages (i) accrued and

unpaid rent as of the date of the commencement of the term of the new lease agreement, (ii) the present value, as of the same date, of the total rent for the then remaining lease term of the original lease agreement minus the present value, as of the same date, of the rent under the new lease agreement applicable to that period of the new lease term which is comparable to the then remaining term of the original lease agreement, and (iii) any incidental damages allowed under Section 2A–530, less expenses saved in consequence of the lessee's default.

(3) If the lessor's disposition is by lease agreement that for any reason does not qualify for treatment under subsection (2), or is by sale or otherwise, the lessor may recover from the lessee as if the lessor had elected not to dispose of the goods and Section 2A–528 governs.

(4) A subsequent buyer or lessee who buys or leases from the lessor in good faith for value as a result of a disposition under this section takes the goods free of the original lease contract and any rights of the original lessee even though the lessor fails to comply with one or more of the requirements of this Article.

(5) The lessor is not accountable to the lessee for any profit made on any disposition. A lessee who has rightfully rejected or justifiably revoked acceptance shall account to the lessor for any excess over the amount of the lessee's security interest (Section 2A–508(5)).

As amended in 1990.

§ 2A–528.   Lessor's Damages for Non-acceptance, Failure to Pay, Repudiation, or Other Default.

(1) Except as otherwise provided with respect to damages liquidated in the lease agreement (Section 2A–504) or otherwise determined pursuant to agreement of the parties (Section 1–102(3) and 2A–503), if a lessor elects to retain the goods or a lessor elects to dispose of the goods and the disposition is by lease agreement that for any reason does not qualify for treatment under Section 2A–527(2), or is by sale or otherwise, the lessor may recover from the lessee as damages for a default of the type described in Section 2A–523(1) or 2A–523(3)(a), or if agreed, for other default of the lessee, (i) accrued and unpaid rent as of the date of the default if the lessee has never taken possession of the goods, or, if the lessee has taken possession of the goods, as of the date the lessor repossesses the goods or an earlier date on which the lessee makes a tender of the goods to the lessor, (ii) the present value as of the date determined under clause (i) of the total rent for the then remaining lease term of the original lease agreement minus the present value as of the same date of the market rent as the place where the goods are located computed for the same lease term, and (iii) any incidental damages allowed under Section 2A–530, less expenses saved in consequence of the lessee's default.

(2) If the measure of damages provided in subsection (1) is inadequate to put a lessor in as good a position as performance would have, the measure of damages is the present value of the profit, including reasonable overhead, the lessor would have made from full performance by the lessee, together with any incidental damages allowed under Section 2A–530, due allowance for costs reasonably incurred and due credit for payments or proceeds of disposition.

As amended in 1990.

§ 2A–529.   Lessor's Action for the Rent.

(1) After default by the lessee under the lease contract of the type described in Section 2A–523(1) or 2A–523(3)(a) or, if agreed, after other default by the lessee, if the lessor complies with subsection (2), the lessor may recover from the lessee as damages:

(a) for goods accepted by the lessee and not repossessed by or tendered to the lessor, and for conforming goods lost or damaged within a commercially reasonable time after risk of loss passes to the lessee (Section 2A–219), (i) accrued and unpaid rent as of the date of entry of judgment in favor of the lessor (ii) the present value as of the same date of the rent for the then remaining lease term of the lease agreement, and (iii) any incidental damages allowed under Section 2A–530, less expenses saved in consequence of the lessee's default; and

(b) for goods identified to the lease contract if the lessor is unable after reasonable effort to dispose of them at a reasonable price or the circumstances reasonably indicate that effort will be unavailing, (i) accrued and unpaid rent as of the date of entry of judgment in favor of the lessor, (ii) the present value as of the same date of the rent for the then remaining lease term of the lease agreement, and (iii) any incidental damages allowed under Section 2A–530, less expenses saved in consequence of the lessee's default.

(2) Except as provided in subsection (3), the lessor shall hold for the lessee for the remaining lease term of the lease agreement any goods that have been identified to the lease contract and are in the lessor's control.

(3) The lessor may dispose of the goods at any time before collection of the judgment for damages obtained pursuant to subsection (1). If the disposition is before the end of the remaining lease term of the lease agreement, the lessor's recovery against the lessee for damages is governed by Section 2A–527 or Section 2A–528, and the lessor will cause an appropriate credit to be provided against a judgment for damages to the extent that the amount of the judgment exceeds the recovery available pursuant to Section 2A–527 or 2A–528.

(4) Payment of the judgment for damages obtained pursuant to subsection (1) entitles the lessee to the use and possession of the goods not then disposed of for the remaining lease term of and in accordance with the lease agreement.

(5) After default by the lessee under the lease contract of the type described in Section 2A–523(1) or Section 2A–523(3)(a) or, if agreed, after other default by the lessee, a lessor who is held not entitled to rent under this section must nevertheless be awarded damages for non-acceptance under Sections 2A–527 and 2A–528.

As amended in 1990.

§ 2A–530.   Lessor's Incidental Damages.

Incidental damages to an aggrieved lessor include any commercially reasonable charges, expenses, or commissions incurred in stopping delivery, in the transportation, care and custody of goods after the lessee's default, in connection with return or disposition of the goods, or otherwise resulting from the default.

§ 2A–531.   Standing to Sue Third Parties for Injury to Goods.

(1) If a third party so deals with goods that have been identified to a lease contract as to cause actionable injury to a party to the lease contract (a) the lessor has a right of action against the third party, and (b) the lessee also has a right of action against the third party if the lessee:

(i) has a security interest in the goods;

(ii) has an insurable interest in the goods; or

(iii) bears the risk of loss under the lease contract or has since the injury assumed that risk as against the lessor and the goods have been converted or destroyed.

(2) If at the time of the injury the party plaintiff did not bear the risk of loss as against the other party to the lease contract and there is no arrangement between them for disposition of the recovery, his [or her] suit or settlement, subject to his [or her] own interest, is as a fiduciary for the other party to the lease contract.

(3) Either party with the consent of the other may sue for the benefit of whom it may concern.

§ 2A–532.   Lessor's Rights to Residual Interest.

In addition to any other recovery permitted by this Article or other law, the lessor may recover from the lessee an amount that will fully compensate the lessor for any loss of or damage to the lessor's residual interest in the goods caused by the default of the lessee.

As added in 1990.

Revised Article 3
NEGOTIABLE INSTRUMENTS

Part 1   General Provisions and Definitions

§ 3–101.   Short Title.

This Article may be cited as Uniform Commercial Code–Negotiable Instruments.

§ 3–102.   Subject Matter.

(a) This Article applies to negotiable instruments. It does not apply to money, to payment orders governed by Article 4A, or to securities governed by Article 8.

(b) If there is conflict between this Article and Article 4 or 9, Articles 4 and 9 govern.

(c) Regulations of the Board of Governors of the Federal Reserve System and operating circulars of the Federal Reserve Banks supersede any inconsistent provision of this Article to the extent of the inconsistency.

§ 3–103.   Definitions.

(a) In this Article:

(1) "Acceptor" means a drawee who has accepted a draft.

(2) "Drawee" means a person ordered in a draft to make payment.

(3) "Drawer" means a person who signs or is identified in a draft as a person ordering payment.

(4) "Good faith" means honesty in fact and the observance of reasonable commercial standards of fair dealing.

(5) "Maker" means a person who signs or is identified in a note as a person undertaking to pay.

(6) "Order" means a written instruction to pay money signed by the person giving the instruction. The instruction may be addressed to any person, including the person giving the instruction, or to one or more persons jointly or in the alternative but not in succession. An authorization to pay is not an order unless the person authorized to pay is also instructed to pay.

(7) "Ordinary care" in the case of a person engaged in business means observance of reasonable commercial standards, prevailing in the area in which the person is located, with respect to the business in which the person is engaged. In the case of a bank that takes an instrument for processing for collection or payment by automated means, reasonable commercial standards do not require the bank to examine the instrument if the failure to examine does not violate the bank's prescribed procedures and the bank's procedures do not vary unreasonably from general banking usage not disapproved by this Article or Article 4.

(8) "Party" means a party to an instrument.

(9) "Promise" means a written undertaking to pay money signed by the person undertaking to pay. An acknowledgment of an obligation by the obligor is not a promise unless the obligor also undertakes to pay the obligation.

(10) "Prove" with respect to a fact means to meet the burden of establishing the fact (Section 1–201(8)).

(11) "Remitter" means a person who purchases an instrument from its issuer if the instrument is payable to an identified person other than the purchaser.

(b) [Other definitions' section references deleted.]

(c) [Other definitions' section references deleted.]

(d) In addition, Article 1 contains general definitions and principles of construction and interpretation applicable throughout this Article.

§ 3–104. Negotiable Instrument.

(a) Except as provided in subsections (c) and (d), "negotiable instrument" means an unconditional promise or order to pay a fixed amount of money, with or without interest or other charges described in the promise or order, if it:

(1) is payable to bearer or to order at the time it is issued or first comes into possession of a holder;

(2) is payable on demand or at a definite time; and

(3) does not state any other undertaking or instruction by the person promising or ordering payment to do any act in addition to the payment of money, but the promise or order may contain (i) an undertaking or power to give, maintain, or protect collateral to secure payment, (ii) an authorization or power to the holder to confess judgment or realize on or dispose of collateral, or (iii) a waiver of the benefit of any law intended for the advantage or protection of an obligor.

(b) "Instrument" means a negotiable instrument.

(c) An order that meets all of the requirements of subsection (a), except paragraph (1), and otherwise falls within the definition of "check" in subsection (f) is a negotiable instrument and a check.

(d) A promise or order other than a check is not an instrument if, at the time it is issued or first comes into possession of a holder, it contains a conspicuous statement, however expressed, to the effect that the promise or order is not negotiable or is not an instrument governed by this Article.

(e) An instrument is a "note" if it is a promise and is a "draft" if it is an order. If an instrument falls within the definition of both "note" and "draft," a person entitled to enforce the instrument may treat it as either.

(f) "Check" means (i) a draft, other than a documentary draft, payable on demand and drawn on a bank or (ii) a cashier's check or teller's check. An instrument may be a check even though it is described on its face by another term, such as "money order."

(g) "Cashier's check" means a draft with respect to which the drawer and drawee are the same bank or branches of the same bank.

(h) "Teller's check" means a draft drawn by a bank (i) on another bank, or (ii) payable at or through a bank.

(i) "Traveler's check" means an instrument that (i) is payable on demand, (ii) is drawn on or payable at or through a bank, (iii) is designated by the term "traveler's check" or by a substantially similar term, and (iv) requires, as a condition to payment, a countersignature by a person whose specimen signature appears on the instrument.

(j) "Certificate of deposit" means an instrument containing an acknowledgment by a bank that a sum of money has been received by the bank and a promise by the bank to repay the sum of money. A certificate of deposit is a note of the bank.

§ 3–105. Issue of Instrument.

(a) "Issue" means the first delivery of an instrument by the maker or drawer, whether to a holder or nonholder, for the purpose of giving rights on the instrument to any person.

(b) An unissued instrument, or an unissued incomplete instrument that is completed, is binding on the maker or drawer, but nonissuance is a defense. An instrument that is conditionally issued or is issued for a special purpose is binding on the maker or drawer, but failure of the condition or special purpose to be fulfilled is a defense.

(c) "Issuer" applies to issued and unissued instruments and means a maker or drawer of an instrument.

§ 3–106. Unconditional Promise or Order.

(a) Except as provided in this section, for the purposes of Section 3–104(a), a promise or order is unconditional unless it states (i) an express condition to payment, (ii) that the promise or order is subject to or governed by another writing, or (iii) that rights or obligations with respect to the promise or order are stated in another writing. A reference to another writing does not of itself make the promise or order conditional.

(b) A promise or order is not made conditional (i) by a reference to another writing for a statement of rights with respect to collateral, prepayment, or acceleration, or (ii) because payment is limited to resort to a particular fund or source.

(c) If a promise or order requires, as a condition to payment, a countersignature by a person whose specimen signature appears on the promise or order, the condition does not make the promise or order conditional for the purposes of Section 3–104(a). If the person whose specimen signature appears on an instrument fails to countersign the instrument, the failure to countersign is a defense to the obligation of the issuer, but the failure does not prevent a transferee of the instrument from becoming a holder of the instrument.

(d) If a promise or order at the time it is issued or first comes into possession of a holder contains a statement, required by applicable statutory or administrative law, to the effect that the rights of a holder or transferee are subject to claims or defenses that the issuer could assert against the original payee, the promise or order is not thereby made conditional for the purposes of Section 3–104(a); but if the promise or order is an instrument, there cannot be a holder in due course of the instrument.

§ 3-107.   Instrument Payable in Foreign Money.

Unless the instrument otherwise provides, an instrument that states the amount payable in foreign money may be paid in the foreign money or in an equivalent amount in dollars calculated by using the current bank-offered spot rate at the place of payment for the purchase of dollars on the day on which the instrument is paid.

§ 3-108.   Payable on Demand or at Definite Time.

(a) A promise or order is "payable on demand" if it (i) states that it is payable on demand or at sight, or otherwise indicates that it is payable at the will of the holder, or (ii) does not state any time of payment.

(b) A promise or order is "payable at a definite time" if it is payable on elapse of a definite period of time after sight or acceptance or at a fixed date or dates or at a time or times readily ascertainable at the time the promise or order is issued, subject to rights of (i) prepayment, (ii) acceleration, (iii) extension at the option of the holder, or (iv) extension to a further definite time at the option of the maker or acceptor or automatically upon or after a specified act or event.

(c) If an instrument, payable at a fixed date, is also payable upon demand made before the fixed date, the instrument is payable on demand until the fixed date and, if demand for payment is not made before that date, becomes payable at a definite time on the fixed date.

§ 3-109.   Payable to Bearer or to Order.

(a) A promise or order is payable to bearer if it:

  (1) states that it is payable to bearer or to the order of bearer or otherwise indicates that the person in possession of the promise or order is entitled to payment;

  (2) does not state a payee; or

  (3) states that it is payable to or to the order of cash or otherwise indicates that it is not payable to an identified person.

(b) A promise or order that is not payable to bearer is payable to order if it is payable (i) to the order of an identified person or (ii) to an identified person or order. A promise or order that is payable to order is payable to the identified person.

(c) An instrument payable to bearer may become payable to an identified person if it is specially indorsed pursuant to Section 3–205(a). An instrument payable to an identified person may become payable to bearer if it is indorsed in blank pursuant to Section 3–205(b).

§ 3-110.   Identification of Person to Whom Instrument Is Payable.

(a) The person to whom an instrument is initially payable is determined by the intent of the person, whether or not authorized, signing as, or in the name or behalf of, the issuer of the instrument. The instrument is payable to the person intended by the signer even if that person is identified in the instrument by a name or other identification that is not that of the intended person. If more than one person signs in the name or behalf of the issuer of an instrument and all the signers do not intend the same person as payee, the instrument is payable to any person intended by one or more of the signers.

(b) If the signature of the issuer of an instrument is made by automated means, such as a check-writing machine, the payee of the instrument is determined by the intent of the person who supplied the name or identification of the payee, whether or not authorized to do so.

(c) A person to whom an instrument is payable may be identified in any way, including by name, identifying number, office, or account number. For the purpose of determining the holder of an instrument, the following rules apply:

  (1) If an instrument is payable to an account and the account is identified only by number, the instrument is payable to the person to whom the account is payable. If an instrument is payable to an account identified by number and by the name of a person, the instrument is payable to the named person, whether or not that person is the owner of the account identified by number.

  (2) If an instrument is payable to:

    (i) a trust, an estate, or a person described as trustee or representative of a trust or estate, the instrument is payable to the trustee, the representative, or a successor of either, whether or not the beneficiary or estate is also named;

    (ii) a person described as agent or similar representative of a named or identified person, the instrument is payable to the represented person, the representative, or a successor of the representative;

    (iii) a fund or organization that is not a legal entity, the instrument is payable to a representative of the members of the fund or organization; or

    (iv) an office or to a person described as holding an office, the instrument is payable to the named person, the incumbent of the office, or a successor to the incumbent.

(d) If an instrument is payable to two or more persons alternatively, it is payable to any of them and may be negotiated, discharged, or enforced by any or all of them in possession of the instrument. If an instrument is payable to two or more persons not alternatively, it is payable to all of them and may be negotiated, discharged, or enforced only by all of them. If an instrument payable to two or more persons is ambiguous as to whether it is payable to the persons alternatively, the instrument is payable to the persons alternatively.

§ 3–111.   Place of Payment.

Except as otherwise provided for items in Article 4, an instrument is payable at the place of payment stated in the instrument. If no place of payment is stated, an instrument is payable at the address of the drawee or maker stated in the instrument. If no address is stated, the place of payment is the place of business of the drawee or maker. If a drawee or maker has more than one place of business, the place of payment is any place of business of the drawee or maker chosen by the person entitled to enforce the instrument. If the drawee or maker has no place of business, the place of payment is the residence of the drawee or maker.

§ 3–112.   Interest.

(a) Unless otherwise provided in the instrument, (i) an instrument is not payable with interest, and (ii) interest on an interest-bearing instrument is payable from the date of the instrument.

(b) Interest may be stated in an instrument as a fixed or variable amount of money or it may be expressed as a fixed or variable rate or rates. The amount or rate of interest may be stated or described in the instrument in any manner and may require reference to information not contained in the instrument. If an instrument provides for interest, but the amount of interest payable cannot be ascertained from the description, interest is payable at the judgment rate in effect at the place of payment of the instrument and at the time interest first accrues.

§ 3–113.   Date of Instrument.

(a) An instrument may be antedated or postdated. The date stated determines the time of payment if the instrument is payable at a fixed period after date. Except as provided in Section 4–401(c), an instrument payable on demand is not payable before the date of the instrument.

(b) If an instrument is undated, its date is the date of its issue or, in the case of an unissued instrument, the date it first comes into possession of a holder.

§ 3–114.   Contradictory Terms of Instrument.

If an instrument contains contradictory terms, typewritten terms prevail over printed terms, handwritten terms prevail over both, and words prevail over numbers.

§ 3–115.   Incomplete Instrument.

(a) "Incomplete instrument" means a signed writing, whether or not issued by the signer, the contents of which show at the time of signing that it is incomplete but that the signer intended it to be completed by the addition of words or numbers.

(b) Subject to subsection (c), if an incomplete instrument is an instrument under Section 3–104, it may be enforced according to its terms if it is not completed, or according to its terms as augmented by completion. If an incomplete instrument is not an instrument under Section 3–104, but, after completion, the requirements of Section 3–104 are met, the instrument may be enforced according to its terms as augmented by completion.

(c) If words or numbers are added to an incomplete instrument without authority of the signer, there is an alteration of the incomplete instrument under Section 3–407.

(d) The burden of establishing that words or numbers were added to an incomplete instrument without authority of the signer is on the person asserting the lack of authority.

§ 3–116.   Joint and Several Liability; Contribution.

(a) Except as otherwise provided in the instrument, two or more persons who have the same liability on an instrument as makers, drawers, acceptors, indorsers who indorse as joint payees, or anomalous indorsers are jointly and severally liable in the capacity in which they sign.

(b) Except as provided in Section 3–419(e) or by agreement of the affected parties, a party having joint and several liability who pays the instrument is entitled to receive from any party having the same joint and several liability contribution in accordance with applicable law.

(c) Discharge of one party having joint and several liability by a person entitled to enforce the instrument does not affect the right under subsection (b) of a party having the same joint and several liability to receive contribution from the party discharged.

§ 3–117.   Other Agreements Affecting Instrument.

Subject to applicable law regarding exclusion of proof of contemporaneous or previous agreements, the obligation of a party to an instrument to pay the instrument may be modified, supplemented, or nullified by a separate agreement of the obligor and a person entitled to enforce the instrument, if the instrument is issued or the obligation is incurred in reliance on the agreement or as part of the same transaction giving rise to the agreement. To the extent an obligation is modified, supplemented, or nullified by an agreement under this section, the agreement is a defense to the obligation.

§ 3–118.   Statute of Limitations.

(a) Except as provided in subsection (e), an action to enforce the obligation of a party to pay a note payable at a definite time must be commenced within six years after the due date or dates stated in the note or, if a due date is accelerated, within six years after the accelerated due date.

(b) Except as provided in subsection (d) or (e), if demand for payment is made to the maker of a note payable on demand, an action to enforce the obligation of a party to pay the note must be commenced within six years after the demand. If no demand for payment is made to the maker, an action to enforce the note is barred if neither principal nor interest on the note has been paid for a continuous period of 10 years.

(c) Except as provided in subsection (d), an action to enforce the obligation of a party to an unaccepted draft to pay the draft must be commenced within three years after dishonor of the draft or 10 years after the date of the draft, whichever period expires first.

(d) An action to enforce the obligation of the acceptor of a certified check or the issuer of a teller's check, cashier's check, or traveler's check must be commenced within three years after demand for payment is made to the acceptor or issuer, as the case may be.

(e) An action to enforce the obligation of a party to a certificate of deposit to pay the instrument must be commenced within six years after demand for payment is made to the maker, but if the instrument states a due date and the maker is not required to pay before that date, the six-year period begins when a demand for payment is in effect and the due date has passed.

(f) An action to enforce the obligation of a party to pay an accepted draft, other than a certified check, must be commenced (i) within six years after the due date or dates stated in the draft or acceptance if the obligation of the acceptor is payable at a definite time, or (ii) within six years after the date of the acceptance if the obligation of the acceptor is payable on demand.

(g) Unless governed by other law regarding claims for indemnity or contribution, an action (i) for conversion of an instrument, for money had and received, or like action based on conversion, (ii) for breach of warranty, or (iii) to enforce an obligation, duty, or right arising under this Article and not governed by this section must be commenced within three years after the [cause of action] accrues.

§ 3–119.   Notice of Right to Defend Action.

In an action for breach of an obligation for which a third person is answerable over pursuant to this Article or Article 4, the defendant may give the third person written notice of the litigation, and the person notified may then give similar notice to any other person who is answerable over. If the notice states (i) that the person notified may come in and defend and (ii) that failure to do so will bind the person notified in an action later brought by the person giving the notice as to any determination of fact common to the two litigations, the person notified is so bound unless after seasonable receipt of the notice the person notified does come in and defend.

Part 2   Negotiation, Transfer, and Indorsement

§ 3–201.   Negotiation.

(a) "Negotiation" means a transfer of possession, whether voluntary or involuntary, of an instrument by a person other than the issuer to a person who thereby becomes its holder.

(b) Except for negotiation by a remitter, if an instrument is payable to an identified person, negotiation requires transfer of possession of the instrument and its indorsement by the holder. If an instrument is payable to bearer, it may be negotiated by transfer of possession alone.

§ 3–202.   Negotiation Subject to Rescission.

(a) Negotiation is effective even if obtained (i) from an infant, a corporation exceeding its powers, or a person without capacity, (ii) by fraud, duress, or mistake, or (iii) in breach of duty or as part of an illegal transaction.

(b) To the extent permitted by other law, negotiation may be rescinded or may be subject to other remedies, but those remedies may not be asserted against a subsequent holder in due course or a person paying the instrument in good faith and without knowledge of facts that are a basis for rescission or other remedy.

§ 3–203.   Transfer of Instrument; Rights Acquired by Transfer.

(a) An instrument is transferred when it is delivered by a person other than its issuer for the purpose of giving to the person receiving delivery the right to enforce the instrument.

(b) Transfer of an instrument, whether or not the transfer is a negotiation, vests in the transferee any right of the transferor to enforce the instrument, including any right as a holder in due course, but the transferee cannot acquire rights of a holder in due course by a transfer, directly or indirectly, from a holder in due course if the transferee engaged in fraud or illegality affecting the instrument.

(c) Unless otherwise agreed, if an instrument is transferred for value and the transferee does not become a holder because of lack of indorsement by the transferor, the transferee has a specifically enforceable right to the unqualified indorsement of the transferor, but negotiation of the instrument does not occur until the indorsement is made.

(d) If a transferor purports to transfer less than the entire instrument, negotiation of the instrument does not occur. The transferee obtains no rights under this Article and has only the rights of a partial assignee.

§ 3–204.   Indorsement.

(a) "Indorsement" means a signature, other than that of a signer as maker, drawer, or acceptor, that alone or accompanied by other words is made on an instrument for the purpose of (i) negotiating the instrument, (ii) restricting payment of the instrument, or (iii) incurring indorser's liability on the instrument, but regardless of the intent of the signer, a signature and its accompanying words is an indorsement unless the accompanying words, terms of the instrument, place of the signature, or other circumstances unambiguously indicate that the signature was made for a purpose other than indorsement. For the purpose of determining whether a signature is made on an instrument, a paper affixed to the instrument is a part of the instrument.

(b) "Indorser" means a person who makes an indorsement.

(c) For the purpose of determining whether the transferee of an instrument is a holder, an indorsement that transfers a security interest in the instrument is effective as an unqualified indorsement of the instrument.

(d) If an instrument is payable to a holder under a name that is not the name of the holder, indorsement may be made by the holder in the name stated in the instrument or in the holder's name or both, but signature in both names may be required by a person paying or taking the instrument for value or collection.

§ 3–205.   Special Indorsement; Blank Indorsement; Anomalous Indorsement.

(a) If an indorsement is made by the holder of an instrument, whether payable to an identified person or payable to bearer, and the indorsement identifies a person to whom it makes the instrument payable, it is a "special indorsement." When specially indorsed, an instrument becomes payable to the identified person and may be negotiated only by the indorsement of that person. The principles stated in Section 3–110 apply to special indorsements.

(b) If an indorsement is made by the holder of an instrument and it is not a special indorsement, it is a "blank indorsement." When indorsed in blank, an instrument becomes payable to bearer and may be negotiated by transfer of possession alone until specially indorsed.

(c) The holder may convert a blank indorsement that consists only of a signature into a special indorsement by writing, above the signature of the indorser, words identifying the person to whom the instrument is made payable.

(d) "Anomalous indorsement" means an indorsement made by a person who is not the holder of the instrument. An anomalous indorsement does not affect the manner in which the instrument may be negotiated.

§ 3–206.   Restrictive Indorsement.

(a) An indorsement limiting payment to a particular person or otherwise prohibiting further transfer or negotiation of the instrument is not effective to prevent further transfer or negotiation of the instrument.

(b) An indorsement stating a condition to the right of the indorsee to receive payment does not affect the right of the indorsee to enforce the instrument. A person paying the instrument or taking it for value or collection may disregard the condition, and the rights and liabilities of that person are not affected by whether the condition has been fulfilled.

(c) If an instrument bears an indorsement (i) described in Section 4–201(b), or (ii) in blank or to a particular bank using the words "for deposit," "for collection," or other words indicating a purpose of having the instrument collected by a bank for the indorser or for a particular account, the following rules apply:

(1) A person, other than a bank, who purchases the instrument when so indorsed converts the instrument unless the amount paid for the instrument is received by the indorser or applied consistently with the indorsement.

(2) A depositary bank that purchases the instrument or takes it for collection when so indorsed converts the instrument unless the amount paid by the bank with respect to the instrument is received by the indorser or applied consistently with the indorsement.

(3) A payor bank that is also the depositary bank or that takes the instrument for immediate payment over the counter from a person other than a collecting bank converts the instrument unless the proceeds of the instrument are received by the indorser or applied consistently with the indorsement.

(4) Except as otherwise provided in paragraph (3), a payor bank or intermediary bank may disregard the indorsement and is not liable if the proceeds of the instrument are not received by the indorser or applied consistently with the indorsement.

(d) Except for an indorsement covered by subsection (c), if an instrument bears an indorsement using words to the effect that payment is to be made to the indorsee as agent, trustee, or other fiduciary for the benefit of the indorser or another person, the following rules apply:

(1) Unless there is notice of breach of fiduciary duty as provided in Section 3–307, a person who purchases the instrument from the indorsee or takes the instrument from the indorsee for collection or payment may pay the proceeds of payment or the value given for the instrument to the indorsee without regard to whether the indorsee violates a fiduciary duty to the indorser.

(2) A subsequent transferee of the instrument or person who pays the instrument is neither given notice nor otherwise affected by the restriction in the indorsement unless the transferee or payor knows that the fiduciary dealt with the instrument or its proceeds in breach of fiduciary duty.

(e) The presence on an instrument of an indorsement to which this section applies does not prevent a purchaser of the instrument from becoming a holder in due course of the instrument unless the purchaser is a converter under subsection (c) or has notice or knowledge of breach of fiduciary duty as stated in subsection (d).

(f) In an action to enforce the obligation of a party to pay the instrument, the obligor has a defense if payment would violate an indorsement to which this section applies and the payment is not permitted by this section.

§ 3–207.   Reacquisition.

Reacquisition of an instrument occurs if it is transferred to a former holder, by negotiation or otherwise. A former holder who reacquires the instrument may cancel indorsements made after the reacquirer first became a holder of the instrument. If the cancellation causes the instrument to be payable to the reacquirer or to bearer, the reacquirer may negotiate the instrument. An indorser whose indorsement is canceled is discharged, and the discharge is effective against any subsequent holder.

Part 3   Enforcement of Instruments

§ 3–301.   Person Entitled to Enforce Instrument.

"Person entitled to enforce" an instrument means (i) the holder of the instrument, (ii) a nonholder in possession of the instrument who has the rights of a holder, or (iii) a person not in possession of the instrument who is entitled to enforce the instrument pursuant to Section 3–309 or 3–418(d). A person may be a person entitled to enforce the instrument even though the person is not the owner of the instrument or is in wrongful possession of the instrument.

§ 3–302.   Holder in Due Course.

(a) Subject to subsection (c) and Section 3–106(d), "holder in due course" means the holder of an instrument if:

(1) the instrument when issued or negotiated to the holder does not bear such apparent evidence of forgery or alteration or is not otherwise so irregular or incomplete as to call into question its authenticity; and

(2) the holder took the instrument (i) for value, (ii) in good faith, (iii) without notice that the instrument is overdue or has been dishonored or that there is an uncured default with respect to payment of another instrument issued as part of the same series, (iv) without notice that the instrument contains an unauthorized signature or has been altered, (v) without notice of any claim to the instrument described in Section 3–306, and (vi) without notice that any party has a defense or claim in recoupment described in Section 3–305(a).

(b) Notice of discharge of a party, other than discharge in an insolvency proceeding, is not notice of a defense under subsection (a), but discharge is effective against a person who became a holder in due course with notice of the discharge. Public filing or recording of a document does not of itself constitute notice of a defense, claim in recoupment, or claim to the instrument.

(c) Except to the extent a transferor or predecessor in interest has rights as a holder in due course, a person does not acquire rights of a holder in due course of an instrument taken (i) by legal process or by purchase in an execution, bankruptcy, or creditor's sale or similar proceeding, (ii) by purchase as part of a bulk transaction not in ordinary course of business of the transferor, or (iii) as the successor in interest to an estate or other organization.

(d) If, under Section 3–303(a)(1), the promise of performance that is the consideration for an instrument has been partially performed, the holder may assert rights as a holder in due course of the instrument only to the fraction of the amount payable under the instrument equal to the value of the partial performance divided by the value of the promised performance.

(e) If (i) the person entitled to enforce an instrument has only a security interest in the instrument and (ii) the person obliged to pay the instrument has a defense, claim in recoupment, or claim to the instrument that may be asserted against the person who granted the security interest, the person entitled to enforce the instrument may assert rights as a holder in due course only to an amount payable under the instrument which, at the time of enforcement of the instrument, does not exceed the amount of the unpaid obligation secured.

(f) To be effective, notice must be received at a time and in a manner that gives a reasonable opportunity to act on it.

(g) This section is subject to any law limiting status as a holder in due course in particular classes of transactions.

§ 3–303. Value and Consideration.

(a) An instrument is issued or transferred for value if:

(1) the instrument is issued or transferred for a promise of performance, to the extent the promise has been performed;

(2) the transferee acquires a security interest or other lien in the instrument other than a lien obtained by judicial proceeding;

(3) the instrument is issued or transferred as payment of, or as security for, an antecedent claim against any person, whether or not the claim is due;

(4) the instrument is issued or transferred in exchange for a negotiable instrument; or

(5) the instrument is issued or transferred in exchange for the incurring of an irrevocable obligation to a third party by the person taking the instrument.

(b) "Consideration" means any consideration sufficient to support a simple contract. The drawer or maker of an instrument has a defense if the instrument is issued without consideration. If an instrument is issued for a promise of performance, the issuer has a defense to the extent performance of the promise is due and the promise has not been performed. If an instrument is issued for value as stated in subsection (a), the instrument is also issued for consideration.

§ 3–304. Overdue Instrument.

(a) An instrument payable on demand becomes overdue at the earliest of the following times:

(1) on the day after the day demand for payment is duly made;

(2) if the instrument is a check, 90 days after its date; or

(3) if the instrument is not a check, when the instrument has been outstanding for a period of time after its date which is unreasonably long under the circumstances of the particular case in light of the nature of the instrument and usage of the trade.

(b) With respect to an instrument payable at a definite time the following rules apply:

(1) If the principal is payable in installments and a due date has not been accelerated, the instrument becomes overdue upon default under the instrument for nonpayment of an installment, and the instrument remains overdue until the default is cured.

(2) If the principal is not payable in installments and the due date has not been accelerated, the instrument becomes overdue on the day after the due date.

(3) If a due date with respect to principal has been accelerated, the instrument becomes overdue on the day after the accelerated due date.

(c) Unless the due date of principal has been accelerated, an instrument does not become overdue if there is default in payment of interest but no default in payment of principal.

§ 3–305. Defenses and Claims in Recoupment.

(a) Except as stated in subsection (b), the right to enforce the obligation of a party to pay an instrument is subject to the following:

(1) a defense of the obligor based on (i) infancy of the obligor to the extent it is a defense to a simple contract, (ii) duress, lack of legal capacity, or illegality of the transaction which, under other law, nullifies the obligation of the obligor, (iii) fraud that induced the obligor to sign the instrument with neither knowledge nor reasonable opportunity to learn of its character or its essential terms, or (iv) discharge of the obligor in insolvency proceedings;

(2) a defense of the obligor stated in another section of this Article or a defense of the obligor that would be available if the person entitled to enforce the instrument were enforcing a right to payment under a simple contract; and

(3) a claim in recoupment of the obligor against the original payee of the instrument if the claim arose from the transaction that gave rise to the instrument; but the claim of the obligor may be asserted against a transferee of the instrument only to reduce the amount owing on the instrument at the time the action is brought.

(b) The right of a holder in due course to enforce the obligation of a party to pay the instrument is subject to defenses of the obligor stated in subsection (a)(1), but is not subject to defenses of the obligor stated in subsection (a)(2) or claims in recoupment stated in subsection (a)(3) against a person other than the holder.

(c) Except as stated in subsection (d), in an action to enforce the obligation of a party to pay the instrument, the obligor may not assert against the person entitled to enforce the instrument a defense, claim in recoupment, or claim to the instrument (Section 3–306) of another person, but the other person's claim to the instrument may be asserted by the obligor if the other person is joined in the action and personally asserts the claim against the person entitled to enforce the instrument. An obligor is not obliged to pay the instrument if the person seeking enforcement of the instrument does not have rights of a holder in due course and the obligor proves that the instrument is a lost or stolen instrument.

(d) In an action to enforce the obligation of an accommodation party to pay an instrument, the accommodation party may assert against the person entitled to enforce the instrument any defense or claim in recoupment under subsection (a) that the accommodated party could assert against the person entitled to enforce the instrument, except the defenses of discharge in insolvency proceedings, infancy, and lack of legal capacity.

§ 3–306.   Claims to an Instrument.

A person taking an instrument, other than a person having rights of a holder in due course, is subject to a claim of a property or possessory right in the instrument or its proceeds, including a claim to rescind a negotiation and to recover the instrument or its proceeds. A person having rights of a holder in due course takes free of the claim to the instrument.

§ 3–307.   Notice of Breach of Fiduciary Duty.

(a) In this section:

(1) "Fiduciary" means an agent, trustee, partner, corporate officer or director, or other representative owing a fiduciary duty with respect to an instrument.

(2) "Represented person" means the principal, beneficiary, partnership, corporation, or other person to whom the duty stated in paragraph (1) is owed.

(b) If (i) an instrument is taken from a fiduciary for payment or collection or for value, (ii) the taker has knowledge of the fiduciary status of the fiduciary, and (iii) the represented person makes a claim to the instrument or its proceeds on the basis that the transaction of the fiduciary is a breach of fiduciary duty, the following rules apply:

(1) Notice of breach of fiduciary duty by the fiduciary is notice of the claim of the represented person.

(2) In the case of an instrument payable to the represented person or the fiduciary as such, the taker has notice of the breach of fiduciary duty if the instrument is (i) taken in payment of or as security for a debt known by the taker to be the personal debt of the fiduciary, (ii) taken in a transaction known by the taker to be for the personal benefit of the fiduciary, or (iii) deposited to an account other than an account of the fiduciary, as such, or an account of the represented person.

(3) If an instrument is issued by the represented person or the fiduciary as such, and made payable to the fiduciary personally, the taker does not have notice of the breach of fiduciary duty unless the taker knows of the breach of fiduciary duty.

(4) If an instrument is issued by the represented person or the fiduciary as such, to the taker as payee, the taker has notice of the breach of fiduciary duty if the instrument is (i) taken in payment of or as security for a debt known by the taker to be the personal debt of the fiduciary, (ii) taken in a transaction known by the taker to be for the personal benefit of the fiduciary, or (iii) deposited to an account other than an account of the fiduciary, as such, or an account of the represented person.

§ 3–308.   Proof of Signatures and Status as Holder in Due Course.

(a) In an action with respect to an instrument, the authenticity of, and authority to make, each signature on the instrument is admitted unless specifically denied in the pleadings. If the validity of a signature is denied in the pleadings, the burden of establishing validity is on the person claiming validity, but the signature is presumed to be authentic and authorized unless the action is to enforce the liability of the purported signer and the signer is dead or incompetent at the time of trial of the issue of validity of the signature. If an action to enforce the instrument is brought against a person as the undisclosed principal of a person who signed the instrument as a party to the instrument, the plaintiff has the burden of establishing that the defendant is liable on the instrument as a represented person under Section 3–402(a).

(b) If the validity of signatures is admitted or proved and there is compliance with subsection (a), a plaintiff producing the instrument is entitled to payment if the plaintiff proves entitlement to enforce the instrument under Section 3–301, unless the defendant proves a defense or claim in recoupment. If a defense or claim in recoupment is proved, the right to payment of the plaintiff is subject to the defense or claim, except to the extent the plaintiff proves that the plaintiff has rights of a holder in due course which are not subject to the defense or claim.

§ 3–309.   Enforcement of Lost, Destroyed, or Stolen Instrument.

(a) A person not in possession of an instrument is entitled to enforce the instrument if (i) the person was in possession of the instrument and entitled to enforce it when loss of possession occurred, (ii) the loss of possession was not the result of a transfer by the person or a lawful seizure, and (iii) the person cannot reasonably obtain possession of the instrument because the instrument was destroyed, its whereabouts cannot be determined, or it is in the wrongful possession of an unknown person or a person that cannot be found or is not amenable to service of process.

(b) A person seeking enforcement of an instrument under subsection (a) must prove the terms of the instrument and the person's right to enforce the instrument. If that proof is made, Section 3–308 applies to the case as if the person seeking enforcement had produced the instrument. The court may not enter judgment in favor of the person seeking enforcement unless it finds that the person required to pay the instrument is adequately protected against loss that might occur by reason of a claim by another person to enforce the instrument. Adequate protection may be provided by any reasonable means.

§ 3–310.   Effect of Instrument on Obligation for Which Taken.

(a) Unless otherwise agreed, if a certified check, cashier's check, or teller's check is taken for an obligation, the obligation is discharged to the same extent discharge would result if an amount of money equal to the amount of the instrument were taken in payment of the obligation. Discharge of the obligation does not affect any liability that the obligor may have as an indorser of the instrument.

(b) Unless otherwise agreed and except as provided in subsection (a), if a note or an uncertified check is taken for an obligation, the obligation is suspended to the same extent the obligation would be discharged if an amount of money equal to the amount of the instrument were taken, and the following rules apply:

(1) In the case of an uncertified check, suspension of the obligation continues until dishonor of the check or until it is paid or certified. Payment or certification of the check results in discharge of the obligation to the extent of the amount of the check.

(2) In the case of a note, suspension of the obligation continues until dishonor of the note or until it is paid. Payment of the note results in discharge of the obligation to the extent of the payment.

(3) Except as provided in paragraph (4), if the check or note is dishonored and the obligee of the obligation for which the instrument was taken is the person entitled to enforce the instrument, the obligee may enforce either the instrument or the obligation. In the case of an instrument of a third person which is negotiated to the obligee by the obligor, discharge of the obligor on the instrument also discharges the obligation.

(4) If the person entitled to enforce the instrument taken for an obligation is a person other than the obligee, the obligee may not enforce the obligation to the extent the obligation is suspended. If the obligee is the person entitled to enforce the instrument but no longer has possession of it because it was lost, stolen, or destroyed, the obligation may not be enforced to the extent of the amount payable on the instrument, and to that extent the obligee's rights against the obligor are limited to enforcement of the instrument.

(c) If an instrument other than one described in subsection (a) or (b) is taken for an obligation, the effect is (i) that stated in subsection (a) if the instrument is one on which a bank is liable as maker or acceptor, or (ii) that stated in subsection (b) in any other case.

§ 3–311.   Accord and Satisfaction by Use of Instrument.

(a) If a person against whom a claim is asserted proves that (i) that person in good faith tendered an instrument to the claimant as full satisfaction of the claim, (ii) the amount of the claim was unliquidated or subject to a bona fide dispute, and (iii) the claimant obtained payment of the instrument, the following subsections apply.

(b) Unless subsection (c) applies, the claim is discharged if the person against whom the claim is asserted proves that the instrument or an accompanying written communication contained a conspicuous statement to the effect that the instrument was tendered as full satisfaction of the claim.

(c) Subject to subsection (d), a claim is not discharged under subsection (b) if either of the following applies:

(1) The claimant, if an organization, proves that (i) within a reasonable time before the tender, the claimant sent a conspicuous statement to the person against whom the claim is asserted that communications concerning disputed debts, including an instrument tendered as full satisfaction of a debt, are to be sent to a designated person, office, or place, and (ii) the instrument or accompanying communication was not received by that designated person, office, or place.

(2) The claimant, whether or not an organization, proves that within 90 days after payment of the instrument, the claimant tendered repayment of the amount of the instrument to the person against whom the claim is asserted. This paragraph does not apply if the claimant is an organization that sent a statement complying with paragraph (1)(i).

(d) A claim is discharged if the person against whom the claim is asserted proves that within a reasonable time before collection of the instrument was initiated, the claimant, or an agent of the claimant having direct responsibility with respect to the disputed obligation, knew that the instrument was tendered in full satisfaction of the claim.

§ 3–312.   Lost, Destroyed, or Stolen Cashier's Check, Teller's Check, or Certified Check.

(a) In this section:

(1) "Check" means a cashier's check, teller's check, or certified check.

(2) "Claimant" means a person who claims the right to receive the amount of a cashier's check, teller's check, or certified check that was lost, destroyed, or stolen.

(3) "Declaration of loss" means a written statement, made under penalty of perjury, to the effect that (i) the declarer lost possession of a check, (ii) the declarer is the drawer or payee of the check, in the case of a certified check, or the remitter or payee of the check, in the case of a cashier's check or teller's check, (iii) the loss of possession was not the result of a transfer by the declarer or a lawful seizure, and (iv) the declarer cannot reasonably obtain possession of the check because the check was destroyed, its whereabouts cannot be determined, or it is in the wrongful possession of an unknown person or a person that cannot be found or is not amenable to service of process.

(4) "Obligated bank" means the issuer of a cashier's check or teller's check or the acceptor of a certified check.

(b) A claimant may assert a claim to the amount of a check by a communication to the obligated bank describing the check with reasonable certainty and requesting payment of the amount of the check, if (i) the claimant is the drawer or payee of a certified check or the remitter or payee of a cashier's check or teller's check, (ii) the communication contains or is accompanied by a declaration of loss of the claimant with respect to the check, (iii) the communication is received at a time and in a manner affording the bank a reasonable time to act on it before the check is paid, and (iv) the claimant provides reasonable identification if requested by the obligated bank. Delivery of a declaration of loss is a warranty of the truth of the statements made in the declaration. If a claim is asserted in compliance with this subsection, the following rules apply:

(1) The claim becomes enforceable at the later of (i) the time the claim is asserted, or (ii) the 90th day following the date of the check, in the case of a cashier's check or teller's check, or the 90th day following the date of the acceptance, in the case of a certified check.

(2) Until the claim becomes enforceable, it has no legal effect and the obligated bank may pay the check or, in the case of a teller's check, may permit the drawee to pay the check. Payment to a person entitled to enforce the check discharges all liability of the obligated bank with respect to the check.

(3) If the claim becomes enforceable before the check is presented for payment, the obligated bank is not obliged to pay the check.

(4) When the claim becomes enforceable, the obligated bank becomes obliged to pay the amount of the check to the claimant if payment of the check has not been made to a person entitled to enforce the check. Subject to Section 4–302(a)(1), payment to the claimant discharges all liability of the obligated bank with respect to the check.

(c) If the obligated bank pays the amount of a check to a claimant under subsection (b)(4) and the check is presented for payment by a person having rights of a holder in due course, the claimant is obliged to (i) refund the payment to the obligated bank if the check is paid, or (ii) pay the amount of the check to the person having rights of a holder in due course if the check is dishonored.

(d) If a claimant has the right to assert a claim under subsection (b) and is also a person entitled to enforce a cashier's check, teller's check, or certified check which is lost, destroyed, or stolen, the claimant may assert rights with respect to the check either under this section or Section 3–309.

Added in 1991.

Part 4 Liability of Parties

§ 3–401. Signature.

(a) A person is not liable on an instrument unless (i) the person signed the instrument, or (ii) the person is represented by an agent or representative who signed the instrument and the signature is binding on the represented person under Section 3–402.

(b) A signature may be made (i) manually or by means of a device or machine, and (ii) by the use of any name, including a trade or assumed name, or by a word, mark, or symbol executed or adopted by a person with present intention to authenticate a writing.

§ 3–402. Signature by Representative.

(a) If a person acting, or purporting to act, as a representative signs an instrument by signing either the name of the represented person or the name of the signer, the represented person is bound by the signature to the same extent the represented person would be bound if the signature were on a simple contract. If the represented person is bound, the signature of the representative is the "authorized signature of the represented person" and the represented person is liable on the instrument, whether or not identified in the instrument.

(b) If a representative signs the name of the representative to an instrument and the signature is an authorized signature of the represented person, the following rules apply:

(1) If the form of the signature shows unambiguously that the signature is made on behalf of the represented person who is identified in the instrument, the representative is not liable on the instrument.

(2) Subject to subsection (c), if (i) the form of the signature does not show unambiguously that the signature is made in a representative capacity or (ii) the represented person is not identified in the instrument, the representative is liable on the instrument to a holder in due course that took the instrument without notice that the representative was not intended to be liable on the instrument. With respect to any other person, the representative is liable on the instrument unless the representative proves that the original parties did not intend the representative to be liable on the instrument.

(c) If a representative signs the name of the representative as drawer of a check without indication of the representative status and the check is payable from an account of the represented person who is identified on the check, the signer is not liable on the check if the signature is an authorized signature of the represented person.

§ 3–403. Unauthorized Signature.

(a) Unless otherwise provided in this Article or Article 4, an unauthorized signature is ineffective except as the signature of the unauthorized signer in favor of a person who in good faith pays the instrument or takes it for value. An unauthorized signature may be ratified for all purposes of this Article.

(b) If the signature of more than one person is required to constitute the authorized signature of an organization, the signature of the organization is unauthorized if one of the required signatures is lacking.

(c) The civil or criminal liability of a person who makes an unauthorized signature is not affected by any provision of this Article which makes the unauthorized signature effective for the purposes of this Article.

§ 3–404. Impostors; Fictitious Payees.

(a) If an impostor, by use of the mails or otherwise, induces the issuer of an instrument to issue the instrument to the impostor, or to a person acting in concert with the impostor, by impersonating the payee of the instrument or a person authorized to act for the payee, an indorsement of the instrument by any person in the name of the payee is effective as the indorsement of the payee in favor of a person who, in good faith, pays the instrument or takes it for value or for collection.

(b) If (i) a person whose intent determines to whom an instrument is payable (Section 3–110(a) or (b)) does not intend the person identified as payee to have any interest in the instrument, or (ii) the person identified as payee of an instrument is a fictitious person, the following rules apply until the instrument is negotiated by special indorsement:

(1) Any person in possession of the instrument is its holder.

(2) An indorsement by any person in the name of the payee stated in the instrument is effective as the indorsement of the payee in favor of a person who, in good faith, pays the instrument or takes it for value or for collection.

(c) Under subsection (a) or (b), an indorsement is made in the name of a payee if (i) it is made in a name substantially similar to that of the payee or (ii) the instrument, whether or not indorsed, is deposited in a depositary bank to an account in a name substantially similar to that of the payee.

(d) With respect to an instrument to which subsection (a) or (b) applies, if a person paying the instrument or taking it for value or for collection fails to exercise ordinary care in paying or taking the instrument and that failure substantially contributes to loss resulting from payment of the instrument, the person bearing the loss may recover from the person failing to exercise ordinary care to the extent the failure to exercise ordinary care contributed to the loss.

§ 3–405.   Employer's Responsibility for Fraudulent Indorsement by Employee.

(a) In this section:

(1) "Employee" includes an independent contractor and employee of an independent contractor retained by the employer.

(2) "Fraudulent indorsement" means (i) in the case of an instrument payable to the employer, a forged indorsement purporting to be that of the employer, or (ii) in the case of an instrument with respect to which the employer is the issuer, a forged indorsement purporting to be that of the person identified as payee.

(3) "Responsibility" with respect to instruments means authority (i) to sign or indorse instruments on behalf of the employer, (ii) to process instruments received by the employer for bookkeeping purposes, for deposit to an account, or for other disposition, (iii) to prepare or process instruments for issue in the name of the employer, (iv) to supply information determining the names or addresses of payees of instruments to be issued in the name of the employer, (v) to control the disposition of instruments to be issued in the name of the employer, or (vi) to act otherwise with respect to instruments in a responsible capacity. "Responsibility" does not include authority that merely allows an employee to have access to instruments or blank or incomplete instrument forms that are being stored or transported or are part of incoming or outgoing mail, or similar access.

(b) For the purpose of determining the rights and liabilities of a person who, in good faith, pays an instrument or takes it for value or for collection, if an employer entrusted an employee with responsibility with respect to the instrument and the employee or a person acting in concert with the employee makes a fraudulent indorsement of the instrument, the indorsement is effective as the indorsement of the person to whom the instrument is payable if it is made in the name of that person. If the person paying the instrument or taking it for value or for collection fails to exercise ordinary care in paying or taking the instrument and that failure substantially contributes to loss resulting from the fraud, the person bearing the loss may recover from the person failing to exercise ordinary care to the extent the failure to exercise ordinary care contributed to the loss.

(c) Under subsection (b), an indorsement is made in the name of the person to whom an instrument is payable if (i) it is made in a name substantially similar to the name of that person or (ii) the instrument, whether or not indorsed, is deposited in a depositary bank to an account in a name substantially similar to the name of that person.

§ 3–406.   Negligence Contributing to Forged Signature or Alteration of Instrument.

(a) A person whose failure to exercise ordinary care substantially contributes to an alteration of an instrument or to the making of a forged signature on an instrument is precluded from asserting the alteration or the forgery against a person who, in good faith, pays the instrument or takes it for value or for collection.

(b) Under subsection (a), if the person asserting the preclusion fails to exercise ordinary care in paying or taking the instrument and that failure substantially contributes to loss, the loss is allocated between the person precluded and the person asserting the preclusion according to the extent to which the failure of each to exercise ordinary care contributed to the loss.

(c) Under subsection (a), the burden of proving failure to exercise ordinary care is on the person asserting the preclusion. Under subsection (b), the burden of proving failure to exercise ordinary care is on the person precluded.

§ 3–407.   Alteration.

(a) "Alteration" means (i) an unauthorized change in an instrument that purports to modify in any respect the obligation of a party, or (ii) an unauthorized addition of words or numbers or other change to an incomplete instrument relating to the obligation of a party.

(b) Except as provided in subsection (c), an alteration fraudulently made discharges a party whose obligation is affected by the alteration unless that party assents or is precluded from asserting the alteration. No other alteration discharges a party, and the instrument may be enforced according to its original terms.

(c) A payor bank or drawee paying a fraudulently altered instrument or a person taking it for value, in good faith and without notice of the alteration, may enforce rights with respect to the instrument (i) according to its original terms, or (ii) in the case of an incomplete instrument altered by unauthorized completion, according to its terms as completed.

§ 3–408.   Drawee Not Liable on Unaccepted Draft.

A check or other draft does not of itself operate as an assignment of funds in the hands of the drawee available for its payment, and the drawee is not liable on the instrument until the drawee accepts it.

§ 3–409.   Acceptance of Draft; Certified Check.

(a) "Acceptance" means the drawee's signed agreement to pay a draft as presented. It must be written on the draft and may consist of the drawee's signature alone. Acceptance may be made at any time and becomes effective when notification pursuant to instructions is given or the accepted draft is delivered for the purpose of giving rights on the acceptance to any person.

(b) A draft may be accepted although it has not been signed by the drawer, is otherwise incomplete, is overdue, or has been dishonored.

(c) If a draft is payable at a fixed period after sight and the acceptor fails to date the acceptance, the holder may complete the acceptance by supplying a date in good faith.

(d) "Certified check" means a check accepted by the bank on which it is drawn. Acceptance may be made as stated in subsection (a) or by a writing on the check which indicates that the check is certified. The drawee of a check has no obligation to certify the check, and refusal to certify is not dishonor of the check.

§ 3–410.   Acceptance Varying Draft.

(a) If the terms of a drawee's acceptance vary from the terms of the draft as presented, the holder may refuse the acceptance and treat the draft as dishonored. In that case, the drawee may cancel the acceptance.

(b) The terms of a draft are not varied by an acceptance to pay at a particular bank or place in the United States, unless the acceptance states that the draft is to be paid only at that bank or place.

(c) If the holder assents to an acceptance varying the terms of a draft, the obligation of each drawer and indorser that does not expressly assent to the acceptance is discharged.

§ 3–411.   Refusal to Pay Cashier's Checks, Teller's Checks, and Certified Checks.

(a) In this section, "obligated bank" means the acceptor of a certified check or the issuer of a cashier's check or teller's check bought from the issuer.

(b) If the obligated bank wrongfully (i) refuses to pay a cashier's check or certified check, (ii) stops payment of a teller's check, or (iii) refuses to pay a dishonored teller's check, the person asserting the right to enforce the check is entitled to compensation for expenses and loss of interest resulting from the nonpayment and may recover consequential damages if the obligated bank refuses to pay after receiving notice of particular circumstances giving rise to the damages.

(c) Expenses or consequential damages under subsection (b) are not recoverable if the refusal of the obligated bank to pay occurs because (i) the bank suspends payments, (ii) the obligated bank asserts a claim or defense of the bank that it has reasonable grounds to believe is available against the person entitled to enforce the instrument, (iii) the obligated bank has a reasonable doubt whether the person demanding payment is the person entitled to enforce the instrument, or (iv) payment is prohibited by law.

§ 3–412.   Obligation of Issuer of Note or Cashier's Check.

The issuer of a note or cashier's check or other draft drawn on the drawer is obliged to pay the instrument (i) according to its terms at the time it was issued or, if not issued, at the time it first came into possession of a holder, or (ii) if the issuer signed an incomplete instrument, according to its terms when completed, to the extent stated in Sections 3–115 and 3–407. The obligation is owed to a person entitled to enforce the instrument or to an indorser who paid the instrument under Section 3–415.

§ 3–413.   Obligation of Acceptor.

(a) The acceptor of a draft is obliged to pay the draft (i) according to its terms at the time it was accepted, even though the acceptance states that the draft is payable "as originally drawn" or equivalent terms, (ii) if the acceptance varies the terms of the draft, according to the terms of the draft as varied, or (iii) if the acceptance is of a draft that is an incomplete instrument, according to its terms when completed, to the extent stated in Sections 3–115 and 3–407. The obligation is owed to a person entitled to enforce the draft or to the drawer or an indorser who paid the draft under Section 3–414 or 3–415.

(b) If the certification of a check or other acceptance of a draft states the amount certified or accepted, the obligation of the acceptor is that amount. If (i) the certification or acceptance does not state an amount, (ii) the amount of the instrument is subsequently raised, and (iii) the instrument is then negotiated to a holder in due course, the obligation of the acceptor is the amount of the instrument at the time it was taken by the holder in due course.

§ 3–414.   Obligation of Drawer.

(a) This section does not apply to cashier's checks or other drafts drawn on the drawer.

(b) If an unaccepted draft is dishonored, the drawer is obliged to pay the draft (i) according to its terms at the time it was issued or, if not issued, at the time it first came into possession of a holder, or (ii) if the drawer signed an incomplete instrument, according to its terms when completed, to the extent stated in Sections 3–115 and 3–407. The obligation is owed to a person entitled to enforce the draft or to an indorser who paid the draft under Section 3–415.

(c) If a draft is accepted by a bank, the drawer is discharged, regardless of when or by whom acceptance was obtained.

(d) If a draft is accepted and the acceptor is not a bank, the obligation of the drawer to pay the draft if the draft is dishonored by the acceptor is the same as the obligation of an indorser under Section 3–415(a) and (c).

(e) If a draft states that it is drawn "without recourse" or otherwise disclaims liability of the drawer to pay the draft, the drawer is not liable under subsection (b) to pay the draft if the draft is not a check. A disclaimer of the liability stated in subsection (b) is not effective if the draft is a check.

(f) If (i) a check is not presented for payment or given to a depositary bank for collection within 30 days after its date, (ii) the drawee suspends payments after expiration of the 30-day period without paying the check, and (iii) because of the suspension of payments, the drawer is deprived of funds maintained with the drawee to cover payment of the check, the drawer to the extent deprived of funds may discharge its obligation to pay the check by assigning to the person entitled to enforce the check the rights of the drawer against the drawee with respect to the funds.

§ 3–415.   Obligation of Indorser.

(a) Subject to subsections (b), (c), and (d) and to Section 3–419(d), if an instrument is dishonored, an indorser is obliged to pay the amount due on the instrument (i) according to the terms of the instrument at the time it was indorsed, or (ii) if the indorser indorsed an incomplete instrument, according to its terms when completed, to the extent stated in Sections 3–115 and 3–407. The obligation of the indorser is owed to a person entitled to enforce the instrument or to a subsequent indorser who paid the instrument under this section.

(b) If an indorsement states that it is made "without recourse" or otherwise disclaims liability of the indorser, the indorser is not liable under subsection (a) to pay the instrument.

(c) If notice of dishonor of an instrument is required by Section 3–503 and notice of dishonor complying with that section is not given to an indorser, the liability of the indorser under subsection (a) is discharged.

(d) If a draft is accepted by a bank after an indorsement is made, the liability of the indorser under subsection (a) is discharged.

(e) If an indorser of a check is liable under subsection (a) and the check is not presented for payment, or given to a depositary bank for collection, within 30 days after the day the indorsement was made, the liability of the indorser under subsection (a) is discharged.

As amended in 1993.

§ 3–416.   Transfer Warranties.

(a) A person who transfers an instrument for consideration warrants to the transferee and, if the transfer is by indorsement, to any subsequent transferee that:

(1) the warrantor is a person entitled to enforce the instrument;

(2) all signatures on the instrument are authentic and authorized;

(3) the instrument has not been altered;

(4) the instrument is not subject to a defense or claim in recoupment of any party which can be asserted against the warrantor; and

(5) the warrantor has no knowledge of any insolvency proceeding commenced with respect to the maker or acceptor or, in the case of an unaccepted draft, the drawer.

(b) A person to whom the warranties under subsection (a) are made and who took the instrument in good faith may recover from the warrantor as damages for breach of warranty an amount equal to the loss suffered as a result of the breach, but not more than the amount of the instrument plus expenses and loss of interest incurred as a result of the breach.

(c) The warranties stated in subsection (a) cannot be disclaimed with respect to checks. Unless notice of a claim for breach of warranty is given to the warrantor within 30 days after the claimant has reason to know of the breach and the identity of the warrantor, the liability of the warrantor under subsection (b) is discharged to

the extent of any loss caused by the delay in giving notice of the claim.

(d) A [cause of action] for breach of warranty under this section accrues when the claimant has reason to know of the breach.

§ 3–417.   Presentment Warranties.

(a) If an unaccepted draft is presented to the drawee for payment or acceptance and the drawee pays or accepts the draft, (i) the person obtaining payment or acceptance, at the time of presentment, and (ii) a previous transferor of the draft, at the time of transfer, warrant to the drawee making payment or accepting the draft in good faith that:

(1) the warrantor is, or was, at the time the warrantor transferred the draft, a person entitled to enforce the draft or authorized to obtain payment or acceptance of the draft on behalf of a person entitled to enforce the draft;

(2) the draft has not been altered; and

(3) the warrantor has no knowledge that the signature of the drawer of the draft is unauthorized.

(b) A drawee making payment may recover from any warrantor damages for breach of warranty equal to the amount paid by the drawee less the amount the drawee received or is entitled to receive from the drawer because of the payment. In addition, the drawee is entitled to compensation for expenses and loss of interest resulting from the breach. The right of the drawee to recover damages under this subsection is not affected by any failure of the drawee to exercise ordinary care in making payment. If the drawee accepts the draft, breach of warranty is a defense to the obligation of the acceptor. If the acceptor makes payment with respect to the draft, the acceptor is entitled to recover from any warrantor for breach of warranty the amounts stated in this subsection.

(c) If a drawee asserts a claim for breach of warranty under subsection (a) based on an unauthorized indorsement of the draft or an alteration of the draft, the warrantor may defend by proving that the indorsement is effective under Section 3–404 or 3–405 or the drawer is precluded under Section 3–406 or 4–406 from asserting against the drawee the unauthorized indorsement or alteration.

(d) If (i) a dishonored draft is presented for payment to the drawer or an indorser or (ii) any other instrument is presented for payment to a party obliged to pay the instrument, and (iii) payment is received, the following rules apply:

(1) The person obtaining payment and a prior transferor of the instrument warrant to the person making payment in good faith that the warrantor is, or was, at the time the warrantor transferred the instrument, a person entitled to enforce the instrument or authorized to obtain payment on behalf of a person entitled to enforce the instrument.

(2) The person making payment may recover from any warrantor for breach of warranty an amount equal to the amount paid plus expenses and loss of interest resulting from the breach.

(e) The warranties stated in subsections (a) and (d) cannot be disclaimed with respect to checks. Unless notice of a claim for breach of warranty is given to the warrantor within 30 days after the claimant has reason to know of the breach and the identity of the warrantor, the liability of the warrantor under subsection (b) or (d) is discharged to the extent of any loss caused by the delay in giving notice of the claim.

(f) A [cause of action] for breach of warranty under this section accrues when the claimant has reason to know of the breach.

§ 3–418.   Payment or Acceptance by Mistake.

(a) Except as provided in subsection (c), if the drawee of a draft pays or accepts the draft and the drawee acted on the mistaken belief that (i) payment of the draft had not been stopped pursuant to Section 4–403 or (ii) the signature of the drawer of the draft was authorized, the drawee may recover the amount of the draft from the person to whom or for whose benefit payment was made or, in the case of acceptance, may revoke the acceptance. Rights of the drawee under this subsection are not affected by failure of the drawee to exercise ordinary care in paying or accepting the draft.

(b) Except as provided in subsection (c), if an instrument has been paid or accepted by mistake and the case is not covered by subsection (a), the person paying or accepting may, to the extent permitted by the law governing mistake and restitution, (i) recover the payment from the person to whom or for whose benefit payment was made or (ii) in the case of acceptance, may revoke the acceptance.

(c) The remedies provided by subsection (a) or (b) may not be asserted against a person who took the instrument in good faith and for value or who in good faith changed position in reliance on the payment or acceptance. This subsection does not limit remedies provided by Section 3–417 or 4–407.

(d) Notwithstanding Section 4–215, if an instrument is paid or accepted by mistake and the payor or acceptor recovers payment or revokes acceptance under subsection (a) or (b), the instrument is deemed not to have been paid or accepted and is treated as dishonored, and the person from whom payment is recovered has rights as a person entitled to enforce the dishonored instrument.

§ 3–419.   Instruments Signed for Accommodation.

(a) If an instrument is issued for value given for the benefit of a party to the instrument ("accommodated party") and another party to the instrument ("accommodation party") signs the instrument for the purpose of incurring liability on the instrument without being a direct beneficiary of the value given for the instrument, the instrument is signed by the accommodation party "for accommodation."

(b) An accommodation party may sign the instrument as maker, drawer, acceptor, or indorser and, subject to subsection (d), is obliged to pay the instrument in the capacity in which the accommodation party signs. The obligation of an accommodation party may be enforced notwithstanding any statute of frauds and whether or not the accommodation party receives consideration for the accommodation.

(c) A person signing an instrument is presumed to be an accommodation party and there is notice that the instrument is signed for accommodation if the signature is an anomalous indorsement or is accompanied by words indicating that the signer is acting as surety or guarantor with respect to the obligation of another party to the instrument. Except as provided in Section 3–605, the obligation of an accommodation party to pay the instrument is not affected by the fact that the person enforcing the obligation had notice when the instrument was taken by that person that the accommodation party signed the instrument for accommodation.

(d) If the signature of a party to an instrument is accompanied by words indicating unambiguously that the party is guaranteeing collection rather than payment of the obligation of another party to the instrument, the signer is obliged to pay the amount due on the instrument to a person entitled to enforce the instrument only if (i) execution of judgment against the other party has been returned unsatisfied, (ii) the other party is insolvent or in an insolvency proceeding, (iii) the other party cannot be served with process, or (iv) it is otherwise apparent that payment cannot be obtained from the other party.

(e) An accommodation party who pays the instrument is entitled to reimbursement from the accommodated party and is entitled to enforce the instrument against the accommodated party. An accommodated party who pays the instrument has no right of recourse against, and is not entitled to contribution from, an accommodation party.

§ 3–420.   Conversion of Instrument.

(a) The law applicable to conversion of personal property applies to instruments. An instrument is also converted if it is taken by transfer, other than a negotiation, from a person not entitled to enforce the instrument or a bank makes or obtains payment with respect to the instrument for a person not entitled to enforce the instrument or receive payment. An action for conversion of an instrument may not be brought by (i) the issuer or acceptor of the instrument or (ii) a payee or indorsee who did not receive delivery of the instrument either directly or through delivery to an agent or a co-payee.

(b) In an action under subsection (a), the measure of liability is presumed to be the amount payable on the instrument, but recovery may not exceed the amount of the plaintiff's interest in the instrument.

(c) A representative, other than a depositary bank, who has in good faith dealt with an instrument or its proceeds on behalf of one who was not the person entitled to enforce the instrument is not liable in conversion to that person beyond the amount of any proceeds that it has not paid out.

Part 5   Dishonor

§ 3–501.   Presentment.

(a) "Presentment" means a demand made by or on behalf of a person entitled to enforce an instrument (i) to pay the instrument made to the drawee or a party obliged to pay the instrument or, in the case of a note or accepted draft payable at a bank, to the bank, or (ii) to accept a draft made to the drawee.

(b) The following rules are subject to Article 4, agreement of the parties, and clearing-house rules and the like:

(1) Presentment may be made at the place of payment of the instrument and must be made at the place of payment if the

instrument is payable at a bank in the United States; may be made by any commercially reasonable means, including an oral, written, or electronic communication; is effective when the demand for payment or acceptance is received by the person to whom presentment is made; and is effective if made to any one of two or more makers, acceptors, drawees, or other payors.

(2) Upon demand of the person to whom presentment is made, the person making presentment must (i) exhibit the instrument, (ii) give reasonable identification and, if presentment is made on behalf of another person, reasonable evidence of authority to do so, and (. . .) sign a receipt on the instrument for any payment made or surrender the instrument if full payment is made.

(3) Without dishonoring the instrument, the party to whom presentment is made may (i) return the instrument for lack of a necessary indorsement, or (ii) refuse payment or acceptance for failure of the presentment to comply with the terms of the instrument, an agreement of the parties, or other applicable law or rule.

(4) The party to whom presentment is made may treat presentment as occurring on the next business day after the day of presentment if the party to whom presentment is made has established a cut-off hour not earlier than 2 p.m. for the receipt and processing of instruments presented for payment or acceptance and presentment is made after the cut-off hour.

§ 3–502.   Dishonor.

(a) Dishonor of a note is governed by the following rules:

(1) If the note is payable on demand, the note is dishonored if presentment is duly made to the maker and the note is not paid on the day of presentment.

(2) If the note is not payable on demand and is payable at or through a bank or the terms of the note require presentment, the note is dishonored if presentment is duly made and the note is not paid on the day it becomes payable or the day of presentment, whichever is later.

(3) If the note is not payable on demand and paragraph (2) does not apply, the note is dishonored if it is not paid on the day it becomes payable.

(b) Dishonor of an unaccepted draft other than a documentary draft is governed by the following rules:

(1) If a check is duly presented for payment to the payor bank otherwise than for immediate payment over the counter, the check is dishonored if the payor bank makes timely return of the check or sends timely notice of dishonor or nonpayment under Section 4–301 or 4–302, or becomes accountable for the amount of the check under Section 4–302.

(2) If a draft is payable on demand and paragraph (1) does not apply, the draft is dishonored if presentment for payment is duly made to the drawee and the draft is not paid on the day of presentment.

(3) If a draft is payable on a date stated in the draft, the draft is dishonored if (i) presentment for payment is duly made to

the drawee and payment is not made on the day the draft becomes payable or the day of presentment, whichever is later, or (ii) presentment for acceptance is duly made before the day the draft becomes payable and the draft is not accepted on the day of presentment.

(4) If a draft is payable on elapse of a period of time after sight or acceptance, the draft is dishonored if presentment for acceptance is duly made and the draft is not accepted on the day of presentment.

(c) Dishonor of an unaccepted documentary draft occurs according to the rules stated in subsection (b)(2), (3), and (4), except that payment or acceptance may be delayed without dishonor until no later than the close of the third business day of the drawee following the day on which payment or acceptance is required by those paragraphs.

(d) Dishonor of an accepted draft is governed by the following rules:

(1) If the draft is payable on demand, the draft is dishonored if presentment for payment is duly made to the acceptor and the draft is not paid on the day of presentment.

(2) If the draft is not payable on demand, the draft is dishonored if presentment for payment is duly made to the acceptor and payment is not made on the day it becomes payable or the day of presentment, whichever is later.

(e) In any case in which presentment is otherwise required for dishonor under this section and presentment is excused under Section 3–504, dishonor occurs without presentment if the instrument is not duly accepted or paid.

(f) If a draft is dishonored because timely acceptance of the draft was not made and the person entitled to demand acceptance consents to a late acceptance, from the time of acceptance the draft is treated as never having been dishonored.

§ 3–503.   Notice of Dishonor.

(a) The obligation of an indorser stated in Section 3–415(a) and the obligation of a drawer stated in Section 3–414(d) may not be enforced unless (i) the indorser or drawer is given notice of dishonor of the instrument complying with this section or (ii) notice of dishonor is excused under Section 3–504(b).

(b) Notice of dishonor may be given by any person; may be given by any commercially reasonable means, including an oral, written, or electronic communication; and is sufficient if it reasonably identifies the instrument and indicates that the instrument has been dishonored or has not been paid or accepted. Return of an instrument given to a bank for collection is sufficient notice of dishonor.

(c) Subject to Section 3–504(c), with respect to an instrument taken for collection by a collecting bank, notice of dishonor must be given (i) by the bank before midnight of the next banking day following the banking day on which the bank receives notice of dishonor of the instrument, or (ii) by any other person within 30 days following the day on which the person receives notice of dishonor. With respect to any other instrument, notice of dishonor must be given within 30 days following the day on which dishonor occurs.

§ 3–504.   Excused Presentment and Notice of Dishonor.

(a) Presentment for payment or acceptance of an instrument is excused if (i) the person entitled to present the instrument cannot with reasonable diligence make presentment, (ii) the maker or acceptor has repudiated an obligation to pay the instrument or is dead or in insolvency proceedings, (iii) by the terms of the instrument presentment is not necessary to enforce the obligation of indorsers or the drawer, (iv) the drawer or indorser whose obligation is being enforced has waived presentment or otherwise has no reason to expect or right to require that the instrument be paid or accepted, or (v) the drawer instructed the drawee not to pay or accept the draft or the drawee was not obligated to the drawer to pay the draft.

(b) Notice of dishonor is excused if (i) by the terms of the instrument notice of dishonor is not necessary to enforce the obligation of a party to pay the instrument, or (ii) the party whose obligation is being enforced waived notice of dishonor. A waiver of presentment is also a waiver of notice of dishonor.

(c) Delay in giving notice of dishonor is excused if the delay was caused by circumstances beyond the control of the person giving the notice and the person giving the notice exercised reasonable diligence after the cause of the delay ceased to operate.

§ 3–505. Evidence of Dishonor.

(a) The following are admissible as evidence and create a presumption of dishonor and of any notice of dishonor stated:

(1) a document regular in form as provided in subsection (b) which purports to be a protest;

(2) a purported stamp or writing of the drawee, payor bank, or presenting bank on or accompanying the instrument stating that acceptance or payment has been refused unless reasons for the refusal are stated and the reasons are not consistent with dishonor;

(3) a book or record of the drawee, payor bank, or collecting bank, kept in the usual course of business which shows dishonor, even if there is no evidence of who made the entry.

(b) A protest is a certificate of dishonor made by a United States consul or vice consul, or a notary public or other person authorized to administer oaths by the law of the place where dishonor occurs. It may be made upon information satisfactory to that person. The protest must identify the instrument and certify either that presentment has been made or, if not made, the reason why it was not made, and that the instrument has been dishonored by nonacceptance or nonpayment. The protest may also certify that notice of dishonor has been given to some or all parties.

Part 6   Discharge and Payment

§ 3–601. Discharge and Effect of Discharge.

(a) The obligation of a party to pay the instrument is discharged as stated in this Article or by an act or agreement with the party which would discharge an obligation to pay money under a simple contract.

(b) Discharge of the obligation of a party is not effective against a person acquiring rights of a holder in due course of the instrument without notice of the discharge.

§ 3–602. Payment.

(a) Subject to subsection (b), an instrument is paid to the extent payment is made (i) by or on behalf of a party obliged to pay the instrument, and (ii) to a person entitled to enforce the instrument.

To the extent of the payment, the obligation of the party obliged to pay the instrument is discharged even though payment is made with knowledge of a claim to the instrument under Section 3–306 by another person.

(b) The obligation of a party to pay the instrument is not discharged under subsection (a) if:

(1) a claim to the instrument under Section 3–306 is enforceable against the party receiving payment and (i) payment is made with knowledge by the payor that payment is prohibited by injunction or similar process of a court of competent jurisdiction, or (ii) in the case of an instrument other than a cashier's check, teller's check, or certified check, the party making payment accepted, from the person having a claim to the instrument, indemnity against loss resulting from refusal to pay the person entitled to enforce the instrument; or

(2) the person making payment knows that the instrument is a stolen instrument and pays a person it knows is in wrongful possession of the instrument.

§ 3–603. Tender of Payment.

(a) If tender of payment of an obligation to pay an instrument is made to a person entitled to enforce the instrument, the effect of tender is governed by principles of law applicable to tender of payment under a simple contract.

(b) If tender of payment of an obligation to pay an instrument is made to a person entitled to enforce the instrument and the tender is refused, there is discharge, to the extent of the amount of the tender, of the obligation of an indorser or accommodation party having a right of recourse with respect to the obligation to which the tender relates.

(c) If tender of payment of an amount due on an instrument is made to a person entitled to enforce the instrument, the obligation of the obligor to pay interest after the due date on the amount tendered is discharged. If presentment is required with respect to an instrument and the obligor is able and ready to pay on the due date at every place of payment stated in the instrument, the obligor is deemed to have made tender of payment on the due date to the person entitled to enforce the instrument.

§ 3–604. Discharge by Cancellation or Renunciation.

(a) A person entitled to enforce an instrument, with or without consideration, may discharge the obligation of a party to pay the instrument (i) by an intentional voluntary act, such as surrender of the instrument to the party, destruction, mutilation, or cancellation of the instrument, cancellation or striking out of the party's signature, or the addition of words to the instrument indicating discharge, or (ii) by agreeing not to sue or otherwise renouncing rights against the party by a signed writing.

(b) Cancellation or striking out of an indorsement pursuant to subsection (a) does not affect the status and rights of a party derived from the indorsement.

§ 3–605. Discharge of Indorsers and Accommodation Parties.

(a) In this section, the term "indorser" includes a drawer having the obligation described in Section 3–414(d).

(b) Discharge, under Section 3–604, of the obligation of a party to pay an instrument does not discharge the obligation of an indorser or accommodation party having a right of recourse against the discharged party.

(c) If a person entitled to enforce an instrument agrees, with or without consideration, to an extension of the due date of the obligation of a party to pay the instrument, the extension discharges an indorser or accommodation party having a right of recourse against the party whose obligation is extended to the extent the indorser or accommodation party proves that the extension caused loss to the indorser or accommodation party with respect to the right of recourse.

(d) If a person entitled to enforce an instrument agrees, with or without consideration, to a material modification of the obligation of a party other than an extension of the due date, the modification discharges the obligation of an indorser or accommodation party having a right of recourse against the person whose obligation is modified to the extent the modification causes loss to the indorser or accommodation party with respect to the right of recourse. The loss suffered by the indorser or accommodation party as a result of the modification is equal to the amount of the right of recourse unless the person enforcing the instrument proves that no loss was caused by the modification or that the loss caused by the modification was an amount less than the amount of the right of recourse.

(e) If the obligation of a party to pay an instrument is secured by an interest in collateral and a person entitled to enforce the instrument impairs the value of the interest in collateral, the obligation of an indorser or accommodation party having a right of recourse against the obligor is discharged to the extent of the impairment. The value of an interest in collateral is impaired to the extent (i) the value of the interest is reduced to an amount less than the amount of the right of recourse of the party asserting discharge, or (ii) the reduction in value of the interest causes an increase in the amount by which the amount of the right of recourse exceeds the value of the interest. The burden of proving impairment is on the party asserting discharge.

(f) If the obligation of a party is secured by an interest in collateral not provided by an accommodation party and a person entitled to enforce the instrument impairs the value of the interest in collateral, the obligation of any party who is jointly and severally liable with respect to the secured obligation is discharged to the extent the impairment causes the party asserting discharge to pay more than that party would have been obliged to pay, taking into account rights of contribution, if impairment had not occurred. If the party asserting discharge is an accommodation party not entitled to discharge under subsection (e), the party is deemed to have a right to contribution based on joint and several liability rather than a right to reimbursement. The burden of proving impairment is on the party asserting discharge.

(g) Under subsection (e) or (f), impairing value of an interest in collateral includes (i) failure to obtain or maintain perfection or recordation of the interest in collateral, (ii) release of collateral without substitution of collateral of equal value, (iii) failure to perform a duty to preserve the value of collateral owed, under Article 9 or other law, to a debtor or surety or other person secondarily liable, or (iv) failure to comply with applicable law in disposing of collateral.

(h) An accommodation party is not discharged under subsection (c), (d), or (e) unless the person entitled to enforce the instrument knows of the accommodation or has notice under Section 3–419(c) that the instrument was signed for accommodation.

(i) A party is not discharged under this section if (i) the party asserting discharge consents to the event or conduct that is the basis of the discharge, or (ii) the instrument or a separate agreement of the party provides for waiver of discharge under this section either specifically or by general language indicating that parties waive defenses based on suretyship or impairment of collateral.

ADDENDUM TO REVISED ARTICLE 3

Notes to Legislative Counsel

1. If revised Article 3 is adopted in your state, the reference in Section 2–511 to Section 3–802 should be changed to Section 3–310.

2. If revised Article 3 is adopted in your state and the Uniform Fiduciaries Act is also in effect in your state, you may want to consider amending Uniform Fiduciaries Act § 9 to conform to Section 3–307(b)(2)(iii) and (4)(iii). See Official Comment 3 to Section 3–307.

Revised Article 4
BANK DEPOSITS AND COLLECTIONS

Part 1   General Provisions and Definitions

§ 4–101.   Short Title.

This Article may be cited as Uniform Commercial Code—Bank Deposits and Collections.

As amended in 1990.

§ 4–102.   Applicability.

(a) To the extent that items within this Article are also within Articles 3 and 8, they are subject to those Articles. If there is conflict, this Article governs Article 3, but Article 8 governs this Article.

(b) The liability of a bank for action or non-action with respect to an item handled by it for purposes of presentment, payment, or collection is governed by the law of the place where the bank is located. In the case of action or non-action by or at a branch or separate office of a bank, its liability is governed by the law of the place where the branch or separate office is located.

§ 4–103.   Variation by Agreement; Measure of Damages; Action Constituting Ordinary Care.

(a) The effect of the provisions of this Article may be varied by agreement, but the parties to the agreement cannot disclaim a bank's responsibility for its lack of good faith or failure to exercise ordinary care or limit the measure of damages for the lack or failure. However, the parties may determine by agreement the standards by which the bank's responsibility is to be measured if those standards are not manifestly unreasonable.

(b) Federal Reserve regulations and operating circulars, clearing-house rules, and the like have the effect of agreements under subsection (a), whether or not specifically assented to by all parties interested in items handled.

(c) Action or non-action approved by this Article or pursuant to Federal Reserve regulations or operating circulars is the exercise of ordinary care and, in the absence of special instructions, action or non-action consistent with clearing-house rules and the like or with a general banking usage not disapproved by this Article, is prima facie the exercise of ordinary care.

(d) The specification or approval of certain procedures by this Article is not disapproval of other procedures that may be reasonable under the circumstances.

(e) The measure of damages for failure to exercise ordinary care in handling an item is the amount of the item reduced by an amount that could not have been realized by the exercise of ordinary care. If there is also bad faith it includes any other damages the party suffered as a proximate consequence.

As amended in 1990.

§ 4–104.　Definitions and Index of Definitions.

(a) In this Article, unless the context otherwise requires:

(1) "Account" means any deposit or credit account with a bank, including a demand, time, savings, passbook, share draft, or like account, other than an account evidenced by a certificate of deposit;

(2) "Afternoon" means the period of a day between noon and midnight;

(3) "Banking day" means the part of a day on which a bank is open to the public for carrying on substantially all of its banking functions;

(4) "Clearing house" means an association of banks or other payors regularly clearing items;

(5) "Customer" means a person having an account with a bank or for whom a bank has agreed to collect items, including a bank that maintains an account at another bank;

(6) "Documentary draft" means a draft to be presented for acceptance or payment if specified documents, certificated securities (Section 8–102) or instructions for uncertificated securities (Section 8–102), or other certificates, statements, or the like are to be received by the drawee or other payor before acceptance or payment of the draft;

(7) "Draft" means a draft as defined in Section 3–104 or an item, other than an instrument, that is an order;

(8) "Drawee" means a person ordered in a draft to make payment;

(9) "Item" means an instrument or a promise or order to pay money handled by a bank for collection or payment. The term does not include a payment order governed by Article 4A or a credit or debit card slip;

(10) "Midnight deadline" with respect to a bank is midnight on its next banking day following the banking day on which it receives the relevant item or notice or from which the time for taking action commences to run, whichever is later;

(11) "Settle" means to pay in cash, by clearing-house settlement, in a charge or credit or by remittance, or otherwise as agreed. A settlement may be either provisional or final;

(12) "Suspends payments" with respect to a bank means that it has been closed by order of the supervisory authorities, that a public officer has been appointed to take it over, or that it ceases or refuses to make payments in the ordinary course of business.

(b) [Other definitions' section references deleted.]

(c) [Other definitions' section references deleted.]

(d) In addition, Article 1 contains general definitions and principles of construction and interpretation applicable throughout this Article.

§ 4–105.　"Bank"; "Depositary Bank"; "Payor Bank"; "Intermediary Bank"; "Collecting Bank"; "Presenting Bank".

In this Article:

(1) "Bank" means a person engaged in the business of banking, including a savings bank, savings and loan association, credit union, or trust company;

(2) "Depositary bank" means the first bank to take an item even though it is also the payor bank, unless the item is presented for immediate payment over the counter;

(3) "Payor bank" means a bank that is the drawee of a draft;

(4) "Intermediary bank" means a bank to which an item is transferred in course of collection except the depositary or payor bank;

(5) "Collecting bank" means a bank handling an item for collection except the payor bank;

(6) "Presenting bank" means a bank presenting an item except a payor bank.

§ 4–106.　Payable Through or Payable at Bank: Collecting Bank.

(a) If an item states that it is "payable through" a bank identified in the item, (i) the item designates the bank as a collecting bank and does not by itself authorize the bank to pay the item, and (ii) the item may be presented for payment only by or through the bank.

Alternative A

(b) If an item states that it is "payable at" a bank identified in the item, the item is equivalent to a draft drawn on the bank.

Alternative B

(b) If an item states that it is "payable at" a bank identified in the item, (i) the item designates the bank as a collecting bank and does not by itself authorize the bank to pay the item, and (ii) the item may be presented for payment only by or through the bank.

(c) If a draft names a nonbank drawee and it is unclear whether a bank named in the draft is a co-drawee or a collecting bank, the bank is a collecting bank.

As added in 1990.

§ 4–107.　Separate Office of Bank.

A branch or separate office of a bank is a separate bank for the purpose of computing the time within which and determining the place at or to which action may be taken or notices or orders shall be given under this Article and under Article 3.

As amended in 1962 and 1990.

§ 4–108.   Time of Receipt of Items.

(a) For the purpose of allowing time to process items, prove balances, and make the necessary entries on its books to determine its position for the day, a bank may fix an afternoon hour of 2 p.m. or later as a cutoff hour for the handling of money and items and the making of entries on its books.

(b) An item or deposit of money received on any day after a cutoff hour so fixed or after the close of the banking day may be treated as being received at the opening of the next banking day.

As amended in 1990.

§ 4–109.   Delays.

(a) Unless otherwise instructed, a collecting bank in a good faith effort to secure payment of a specific item drawn on a payor other than a bank, and with or without the approval of any person involved, may waive, modify, or extend time limits imposed or permitted by this [act] for a period not exceeding two additional banking days without discharge of drawers or indorsers or liability to its transferor or a prior party.

(b) Delay by a collecting bank or payor bank beyond time limits prescribed or permitted by this [act] or by instructions is excused if (i) the delay is caused by interruption of communication or computer facilities, suspension of payments by another bank, war, emergency conditions, failure of equipment, or other circumstances beyond the control of the bank, and (ii) the bank exercises such diligence as the circumstances require.

§ 4–110.   Electronic Presentment.

(a) "Agreement for electronic presentment" means an agreement, clearing-house rule, or Federal Reserve regulation or operating circular, providing that presentment of an item may be made by transmission of an image of an item or information describing the item ("presentment notice") rather than delivery of the item itself. The agreement may provide for procedures governing retention, presentment, payment, dishonor, and other matters concerning items subject to the agreement.

(b) Presentment of an item pursuant to an agreement for presentment is made when the presentment notice is received.

(c) If presentment is made by presentment notice, a reference to "item" or "check" in this Article means the presentment notice unless the context otherwise indicates.

As added in 1990.

§ 4–111.   Statute of Limitations.

An action to enforce an obligation, duty, or right arising under this Article must be commenced within three years after the [cause of action] accrues.

As added in 1990.

Part 2   Collection of Items:
Depositary and Collecting Banks

§ 4–201.   Status of Collecting Bank as Agent and Provisional
Status of Credits; Applicability of Article; Item Indorsed "Pay Any Bank".

(a) Unless a contrary intent clearly appears and before the time that a settlement given by a collecting bank for an item is or becomes final, the bank, with respect to an item, is an agent or sub-agent of the owner of the item and any settlement given for the item is provisional. This provision applies regardless of the form of indorsement or lack of indorsement and even though credit given for the item is subject to immediate withdrawal as of right or is in fact withdrawn; but the continuance of ownership of an item by its owner and any rights of the owner to proceeds of the item are subject to rights of a collecting bank, such as those resulting from outstanding advances on the item and rights of recoupment or setoff. If an item is handled by banks for purposes of presentment, payment, collection, or return, the relevant provisions of this Article apply even though action of the parties clearly establishes that a particular bank has purchased the item and is the owner of it.

(b) After an item has been indorsed with the words "pay any bank" or the like, only a bank may acquire the rights of a holder until the item has been:

(1) returned to the customer initiating collection; or

(2) specially indorsed by a bank to a person who is not a bank.

As amended in 1990.

§ 4–202.   Responsibility for Collection or Return; When Action Timely.

(a) A collecting bank must exercise ordinary care in:

(1) presenting an item or sending it for presentment;

(2) sending notice of dishonor or nonpayment or returning an item other than a documentary draft to the bank's transferor after learning that the item has not been paid or accepted, as the case may be;

(3) settling for an item when the bank receives final settlement; and

(4) notifying its transferor of any loss or delay in transit within a reasonable time after discovery thereof.

(b) A collecting bank exercises ordinary care under subsection (a) by taking proper action before its midnight deadline following receipt of an item, notice, or settlement. Taking proper action within a reasonably longer time may constitute the exercise of ordinary care, but the bank has the burden of establishing timeliness.

(c) Subject to subsection (a)(1), a bank is not liable for the insolvency, neglect, misconduct, mistake, or default of another bank or person or for loss or destruction of an item in the possession of others or in transit.

As amended in 1990.

§ 4–203.   Effect of Instructions.

Subject to Article 3 concerning conversion of instruments (Section 3–420) and restrictive indorsements (Section 3–206), only a collecting bank's transferor can give instructions that affect the bank or constitute notice to it, and a collecting bank is not liable to prior parties for any action taken pursuant to the instructions or in accordance with any agreement with its transferor.

§ 4–204.   Methods of Sending and Presenting; Sending Directly to Payor Bank.

(a) A collecting bank shall send items by a reasonably prompt method, taking into consideration relevant instructions, the nature of the item, the number of those items on hand, the cost of collection involved, and the method generally used by it or others to present those items.

(b) A collecting bank may send:

(1) an item directly to the payor bank;

(2) an item to a nonbank payor if authorized by its transferor; and

(3) an item other than documentary drafts to a nonbank payor, if authorized by Federal Reserve regulation or operating circular, clearing-house rule, or the like.

(c) Presentment may be made by a presenting bank at a place where the payor bank or other payor has requested that presentment be made.

As amended in 1990.

§ 4–205.   Depository Bank Holder of Unindorsed Item.

If a customer delivers an item to a depositary bank for collection:

(1) the depositary bank becomes a holder of the item at the time it receives the item for collection if the customer at the time of delivery was a holder of the item, whether or not the customer indorses the item, and, if the bank satisfies the other requirements of Section 3–302, it is a holder in due course; and

(2) the depositary bank warrants to collecting banks, the payor bank or other payor, and the drawer that the amount of the item was paid to the customer or deposited to the customer's account.

As amended in 1990.

§ 4–206.   Transfer Between Banks.

Any agreed method that identifies the transferor bank is sufficient for the item's further transfer to another bank.

As amended in 1990.

§ 4–207.   Transfer Warranties.

(a) A customer or collecting bank that transfers an item and receives a settlement or other consideration warrants to the transferee and to any subsequent collecting bank that:

(1) the warrantor is a person entitled to enforce the item;

(2) all signatures on the item are authentic and authorized;

(3) the item has not been altered;

(4) the item is not subject to a defense or claim in recoupment (Section 3–305(a)) of any party that can be asserted against the warrantor; and

(5) the warrantor has no knowledge of any insolvency proceeding commenced with respect to the maker or acceptor or, in the case of an unaccepted draft, the drawer.

(b) If an item is dishonored, a customer or collecting bank transferring the item and receiving settlement or other consideration is obliged to pay the amount due on the item (i) according to the terms of the item at the time it was transferred, or (ii) if the transfer was of an incomplete item, according to its terms when completed as stated in Sections 3–115 and 3–407. The obligation of a transferor is owed to the transferee and to any subsequent collecting bank that takes the item in good faith. A transferor cannot disclaim its obligation under this subsection by an indorsement stating that it is made "without recourse" or otherwise disclaiming liability.

(c) A person to whom the warranties under subsection (a) are made and who took the item in good faith may recover from the warrantor as damages for breach of warranty an amount equal to the loss suffered as a result of the breach, but not more than the amount of the item plus expenses and loss of interest incurred as a result of the breach.

(d) The warranties stated in subsection (a) cannot be disclaimed with respect to checks. Unless notice of a claim for breach of warranty is given to the warrantor within 30 days after the claimant has reason to know of the breach and the identity of the warrantor, the warrantor is discharged to the extent of any loss caused by the delay in giving notice of the claim.

(e) A cause of action for breach of warranty under this section accrues when the claimant has reason to know of the breach.

As amended in 1990.

§ 4–208.   Presentment Warranties.

(a) If an unaccepted draft is presented to the drawee for payment or acceptance and the drawee pays or accepts the draft, (i) the person obtaining payment or acceptance, at the time of presentment, and (ii) a previous transferor of the draft, at the time of transfer, warrant to the drawee that pays or accepts the draft in good faith that:

(1) the warrantor is, or was, at the time the warrantor transferred the draft, a person entitled to enforce the draft or authorized to obtain payment or acceptance of the draft on behalf of a person entitled to enforce the draft;

(2) the draft has not been altered; and

(3) the warrantor has no knowledge that the signature of the purported drawer of the draft is unauthorized.

(b) A drawee making payment may recover from a warrantor damages for breach of warranty equal to the amount paid by the drawee less the amount the drawee received or is entitled to receive from the drawer because of the payment. In addition, the drawee is entitled to compensation for expenses and loss of interest resulting from the breach. The right of the drawee to recover damages under this subsection is not affected by any failure of the drawee to exercise ordinary care in making payment. If the drawee accepts the draft (i) breach of warranty is a defense to the obligation of the acceptor, and (ii) if the acceptor makes payment with respect to the draft, the acceptor is entitled to recover from a warrantor for breach of warranty the amounts stated in this subsection.

(c) If a drawee asserts a claim for breach of warranty under subsection (a) based on an unauthorized indorsement of the draft or an alteration of the draft, the warrantor may defend by proving that the indorsement is effective under Section 3–404 or 3–405 or the drawer is precluded under Section 3–406 or 4–406 from asserting against the drawee the unauthorized indorsement or alteration.

(d) If (i) a dishonored draft is presented for payment to the drawer or an indorser or (ii) any other item is presented for payment to a party obliged to pay the item, and the item is paid, the person obtaining payment and a prior transferor of the item warrant to the person making payment in good faith that the warrantor is, or was, at the time the warrantor transferred the item, a person entitled to enforce the item or authorized to obtain payment on behalf of a person entitled to enforce the item. The person making payment may recover from any warrantor for breach of warranty an amount equal to the amount paid plus expenses and loss of interest resulting from the breach.

(e) The warranties stated in subsections (a) and (d) cannot be disclaimed with respect to checks. Unless notice of a claim for breach of warranty is given to the warrantor within 30 days after the claimant has reason to know of the breach and the identity of the warrantor, the warrantor is discharged to the extent of any loss caused by the delay in giving notice of the claim.

(f) A cause of action for breach of warranty under this section accrues when the claimant has reason to know of the breach.

As amended in 1990.

§ 4–209.   Encoding and Retention Warranties.

(a) A person who encodes information on or with respect to an item after issue warrants to any subsequent collecting bank and to the payor bank or other payor that the information is correctly encoded. If the customer of a depositary bank encodes, that bank also makes the warranty.

(b) A person who undertakes to retain an item pursuant to an agreement for electronic presentment warrants to any subsequent collecting bank and to the payor bank or other payor that retention and presentment of the item comply with the agreement. If a customer of a depositary bank undertakes to retain an item, that bank also makes this warranty.

(c) A person to whom warranties are made under this section and who took the item in good faith may recover from the warrantor as damages for breach of warranty an amount equal to the loss suffered as a result of the breach, plus expenses and loss of interest incurred as a result of the breach.

As added in 1990.

§ 4–210.   Security Interest of Collecting Bank in Items, Accompanying Documents and Proceeds.

(a) A collecting bank has a security interest in an item and any accompanying documents or the proceeds of either:

(1) in case of an item deposited in an account, to the extent to which credit given for the item has been withdrawn or applied;

(2) in case of an item for which it has given credit available for withdrawal as of right, to the extent of the credit given, whether or not the credit is drawn upon or there is a right of charge-back; or

(3) if it makes an advance on or against the item.

(b) If credit given for several items received at one time or pursuant to a single agreement is withdrawn or applied in part, the security interest remains upon all the items, any accompanying documents or the proceeds of either. For the purpose of this section, credits first given are first withdrawn.

(c) Receipt by a collecting bank of a final settlement for an item is a realization on its security interest in the item, accompanying documents, and proceeds. So long as the bank does not receive final settlement for the item or give up possession of the item or accompanying documents for purposes other than collection, the security interest continues to that extent and is subject to Article 9, but:

(1) no security agreement is necessary to make the security interest enforceable (Section 9–203(1)(a));

(2) no filing is required to perfect the security interest; and

(3) the security interest has priority over conflicting perfected security interests in the item, accompanying documents, or proceeds.

As amended in 1990 and 1999.

§ 4–211.   When Bank Gives Value for Purposes of Holder in Due Course.

For purposes of determining its status as a holder in due course, a bank has given value to the extent it has a security interest in an item, if the bank otherwise complies with the requirements of Section 3–302 on what constitutes a holder in due course.

As amended in 1990.

§ 4–212.   Presentment by Notice of Item Not Payable by, Through, or at Bank; Liability of Drawer or Indorser.

(a) Unless otherwise instructed, a collecting bank may present an item not payable by, through, or at a bank by sending to the party to accept or pay a written notice that the bank holds the item for acceptance or payment. The notice must be sent in time to be received on or before the day when presentment is due and the bank must meet any requirement of the party to accept or pay under Section 3–501 by the close of the bank's next banking day after it knows of the requirement.

(b) If presentment is made by notice and payment, acceptance, or request for compliance with a requirement under Section 3–501 is not received by the close of business on the day after maturity or, in the case of demand items, by the close of business on the third banking day after notice was sent, the presenting bank may treat the item as dishonored and charge any drawer or indorser by sending it notice of the facts.

As amended in 1990.

§ 4–213.   Medium and Time of Settlement by Bank.

(a) With respect to settlement by a bank, the medium and time of settlement may be prescribed by Federal Reserve regulations or circulars, clearing-house rules, and the like, or agreement. In the absence of such prescription:

(1) the medium of settlement is cash or credit to an account in a Federal Reserve bank of or specified by the person to receive settlement; and

(2) the time of settlement is:

(i) with respect to tender of settlement by cash, a cashier's check, or teller's check, when the cash or check is sent or delivered;

(ii) with respect to tender of settlement by credit in an account in a Federal Reserve Bank, when the credit is made;

(iii) with respect to tender of settlement by a credit or debit to an account in a bank, when the credit or debit is made or, in the case of tender of settlement by authority to charge an account, when the authority is sent or delivered; or

(iv) with respect to tender of settlement by a funds transfer, when payment is made pursuant to Section 4A–406(a) to the person receiving settlement.

(b) If the tender of settlement is not by a medium authorized by subsection (a) or the time of settlement is not fixed by subsection (a), no settlement occurs until the tender of settlement is accepted by the person receiving settlement.

(c) If settlement for an item is made by cashier's check or teller's check and the person receiving settlement, before its midnight deadline:

(1) presents or forwards the check for collection, settlement is final when the check is finally paid; or

(2) fails to present or forward the check for collection, settlement is final at the midnight deadline of the person receiving settlement.

(d) If settlement for an item is made by giving authority to charge the account of the bank giving settlement in the bank receiving settlement, settlement is final when the charge is made by the bank receiving settlement if there are funds available in the account for the amount of the item.

As amended in 1990.

§ 4–214. Right of Charge-Back or Refund; Liability of Collecting Bank: Return of Item.

(a) If a collecting bank has made provisional settlement with its customer for an item and fails by reason of dishonor, suspension of payments by a bank, or otherwise to receive settlement for the item which is or becomes final, the bank may revoke the settlement given by it, charge back the amount of any credit given for the item to its customer's account, or obtain refund from its customer, whether or not it is able to return the item, if by its midnight deadline or within a longer reasonable time after it learns the facts it returns the item or sends notification of the facts. If the return or notice is delayed beyond the bank's midnight deadline or a longer reasonable time after it learns the facts, the bank may revoke the settlement, charge back the credit, or obtain refund from its customer, but it is liable for any loss resulting from the delay. These rights to revoke, charge back, and obtain refund terminate if and when a settlement for the item received by the bank is or becomes final.

(b) A collecting bank returns an item when it is sent or delivered to the bank's customer or transferor or pursuant to its instructions.

(c) A depositary bank that is also the payor may charge back the amount of an item to its customer's account or obtain refund in accordance with the section governing return of an item received by a payor bank for credit on its books (Section 4–301).

(d) The right to charge back is not affected by:

(1) previous use of a credit given for the item; or

(2) failure by any bank to exercise ordinary care with respect to the item, but a bank so failing remains liable.

(e) A failure to charge back or claim refund does not affect other rights of the bank against the customer or any other party.

(f) If credit is given in dollars as the equivalent of the value of an item payable in foreign money, the dollar amount of any charge-back or refund must be calculated on the basis of the bank-offered spot rate for the foreign money prevailing on the day when the person entitled to the charge-back or refund learns that it will not receive payment in ordinary course.

As amended in 1990.

§ 4–215. Final Payment of Item by Payor Bank; When Provisional Debits and Credits Become Final; When Certain Credits Become Available for Withdrawal.

(a) An item is finally paid by a payor bank when the bank has first done any of the following:

(1) paid the item in cash;

(2) settled for the item without having a right to revoke the settlement under statute, clearing-house rule, or agreement; or

(3) made a provisional settlement for the item and failed to revoke the settlement in the time and manner permitted by statute, clearing-house rule, or agreement.

(b) If provisional settlement for an item does not become final, the item is not finally paid.

(c) If provisional settlement for an item between the presenting and payor banks is made through a clearing house or by debits or credits in an account between them, then to the extent that provisional debits or credits for the item are entered in accounts between the presenting and payor banks or between the presenting and successive prior collecting banks seriatim, they become final upon final payment of the item by the payor bank.

(d) If a collecting bank receives a settlement for an item which is or becomes final, the bank is accountable to its customer for the amount of the item and any provisional credit given for the item in an account with its customer becomes final.

(e) Subject to (i) applicable law stating a time for availability of funds and (ii) any right of the bank to apply the credit to an obligation of the customer, credit given by a bank for an item in a customer's account becomes available for withdrawal as of right:

(1) if the bank has received a provisional settlement for the item, when the settlement becomes final and the bank has had a reasonable time to receive return of the item and the item has not been received within that time;

(2) if the bank is both the depositary bank and the payor bank, and the item is finally paid, at the opening of the bank's second banking day following receipt of the item.

(f) Subject to applicable law stating a time for availability of funds and any right of a bank to apply a deposit to an obligation of the depositor, a deposit of money becomes available for withdrawal as of right at the opening of the bank's next banking day after receipt of the deposit.

As amended in 1990.

§ 4–216. Insolvency and Preference.

(a) If an item is in or comes into the possession of a payor or collecting bank that suspends payment and the item has not been finally paid, the item must be returned by the receiver, trustee, or agent in charge of the closed bank to the presenting bank or the closed bank's customer.

(b) If a payor bank finally pays an item and suspends payments without making a settlement for the item with its customer or the presenting bank which settlement is or becomes final, the owner of the item has a preferred claim against the payor bank.

(c) If a payor bank gives or a collecting bank gives or receives a provisional settlement for an item and thereafter suspends payments, the suspension does not prevent or interfere with the settlement's becoming final if the finality occurs automatically upon the lapse of certain time or the happening of certain events.

(d) If a collecting bank receives from subsequent parties settlement for an item, which settlement is or becomes final and the bank suspends payments without making a settlement for the item with its customer which settlement is or becomes final, the owner of the item has a preferred claim against the collecting bank.

As amended in 1990.

Part 3   Collection of Items: Payor Banks

§ 4–301.   Deferred Posting; Recovery of Payment by Return of Items; Time of Dishonor; Return of Items by Payor Bank.

(a) If a payor bank settles for a demand item other than a documentary draft presented otherwise than for immediate payment over the counter before midnight of the banking day of receipt, the payor bank may revoke the settlement and recover the settlement if, before it has made final payment and before its midnight deadline, it

(1) returns the item; or

(2) sends written notice of dishonor or nonpayment if the item is unavailable for return.

(b) If a demand item is received by a payor bank for credit on its books, it may return the item or send notice of dishonor and may revoke any credit given or recover the amount thereof withdrawn by its customer, if it acts within the time limit and in the manner specified in subsection (a).

(c) Unless previous notice of dishonor has been sent, an item is dishonored at the time when for purposes of dishonor it is returned or notice sent in accordance with this section.

(d) An item is returned:

(1) as to an item presented through a clearing house, when it is delivered to the presenting or last collecting bank or to the clearing house or is sent or delivered in accordance with clearing-house rules; or

(2) in all other cases, when it is sent or delivered to the bank's customer or transferor or pursuant to instructions.

As amended in 1990.

§ 4–302.   Payor Bank's Responsibility for Late Return of Item.

(a) If an item is presented to and received by a payor bank, the bank is accountable for the amount of:

(1) a demand item, other than a documentary draft, whether properly payable or not, if the bank, in any case in which it is not also the depositary bank, retains the item beyond midnight of the banking day of receipt without settling for it or, whether or not it is also the depositary bank, does not pay or return the item or send notice of dishonor until after its midnight deadline; or

(2) any other properly payable item unless, within the time allowed for acceptance or payment of that item, the bank

either accepts or pays the item or returns it and accompanying documents.

(b) The liability of a payor bank to pay an item pursuant to subsection (a) is subject to defenses based on breach of a presentment warranty (Section 4–208) or proof that the person seeking enforcement of the liability presented or transferred the item for the purpose of defrauding the payor bank.

As amended in 1990.

§ 4–303.   When Items Subject to Notice, Stop-Payment Order, Legal Process, or Setoff; Order in Which Items May Be Charged or Certified.

(a) Any knowledge, notice, or stop-payment order received by, legal process served upon, or setoff exercised by a payor bank comes too late to terminate, suspend, or modify the bank's right or duty to pay an item or to charge its customer's account for the item if the knowledge, notice, stop-payment order, or legal process is received or served and a reasonable time for the bank to act thereon expires or the setoff is exercised after the earliest of the following:

(1) the bank accepts or certifies the item;

(2) the bank pays the item in cash;

(3) the bank settles for the item without having a right to revoke the settlement under statute, clearing-house rule, or agreement;

(4) the bank becomes accountable for the amount of the item under Section 4–302 dealing with the payor bank's responsibility for late return of items; or

(5) with respect to checks, a cutoff hour no earlier than one hour after the opening of the next banking day after the banking day on which the bank received the check and no later than the close of that next banking day or, if no cutoff hour is fixed, the close of the next banking day after the banking day on which the bank received the check.

(b) Subject to subsection (a), items may be accepted, paid, certified, or charged to the indicated account of its customer in any order.

As amended in 1990.

Part 4   Relationship Between Payor Bank and Its Customer

§ 4–401.   When Bank May Charge Customer's Account.

(a) A bank may charge against the account of a customer an item that is properly payable from the account even though the charge creates an overdraft. An item is properly payable if it is authorized by the customer and is in accordance with any agreement between the customer and bank.

(b) A customer is not liable for the amount of an overdraft if the customer neither signed the item nor benefited from the proceeds of the item.

(c) A bank may charge against the account of a customer a check that is otherwise properly payable from the account, even though payment was made before the date of the check, unless the customer has given notice to the bank of the postdating describing the check with reasonable certainty. The notice is effective for the period stated in Section 4–403(b) for stop-payment orders, and must be received at such time and in such manner as to afford the bank a reasonable opportunity to act on it before the bank takes any action with respect to the check described in Section 4–303. If a bank charges against the account of a customer a check before the date stated in the notice of postdating, the bank is liable for damages for the loss resulting from its act. The loss may include damages for dishonor of subsequent items under Section 4–402.

(d) A bank that in good faith makes payment to a holder may charge the indicated account of its customer according to:

(1) the original terms of the altered item; or

(2) the terms of the completed item, even though the bank knows the item has been completed unless the bank has notice that the completion was improper.

As amended in 1990.

§ 4–402.   Bank's Liability to Customer for Wrongful Dishonor; Time of Determining Insufficiency of Account.

(a) Except as otherwise provided in this Article, a payor bank wrongfully dishonors an item if it dishonors an item that is properly payable, but a bank may dishonor an item that would create an overdraft unless it has agreed to pay the overdraft.

(b) A payor bank is liable to its customer for damages proximately caused by the wrongful dishonor of an item. Liability is limited to actual damages proved and may include damages for an arrest or prosecution of the customer or other consequential damages. Whether any consequential damages are proximately caused by the wrongful dishonor is a question of fact to be determined in each case.

(c) A payor bank's determination of the customer's account balance on which a decision to dishonor for insufficiency of available funds is based may be made at any time between the time the item is received by the payor bank and the time that the payor bank returns the item or gives notice in lieu of return, and no more than one determination need be made. If, at the election of the payor bank, a subsequent balance determination is made for the purpose of reevaluating the bank's decision to dishonor the item, the account balance at that time is determinative of whether a dishonor for insufficiency of available funds is wrongful.

As amended in 1990.

§ 4–403.   Customer's Right to Stop Payment; Burden of Proof of Loss.

(a) A customer or any person authorized to draw on the account if there is more than one person may stop payment of any item drawn on the customer's account or close the account by an order to the bank describing the item or account with reasonable certainty received at a time and in a manner that affords the bank a reasonable opportunity to act on it before any action by the bank with respect to the item described in Section 4–303. If the signature of more than one person is required to draw on an account, any of these persons may stop payment or close the account.

(b) A stop-payment order is effective for six months, but it lapses after 14 calendar days if the original order was oral and was not confirmed in writing within that period. A stop-payment order may be renewed for additional six-month periods by a writing given to the bank within a period during which the stop-payment order is effective.

(c) The burden of establishing the fact and amount of loss resulting from the payment of an item contrary to a stop-payment order or

order to close an account is on the customer. The loss from payment of an item contrary to a stop-payment order may include damages for dishonor of subsequent items under Section 4–402.

As amended in 1990.

§ 4–404.   Bank Not Obliged to Pay Check More Than Six Months Old.

A bank is under no obligation to a customer having a checking account to pay a check, other than a certified check, which is presented more than six months after its date, but it may charge its customer's account for a payment made thereafter in good faith.

§ 4–405.   Death or Incompetence of Customer.

(a) A payor or collecting bank's authority to accept, pay, or collect an item or to account for proceeds of its collection, if otherwise effective, is not rendered ineffective by incompetence of a customer of either bank existing at the time the item is issued or its collection is undertaken if the bank does not know of an adjudication of incompetence. Neither death nor incompetence of a customer revokes the authority to accept, pay, collect, or account until the bank knows of the fact of death or of an adjudication of incompetence and has reasonable opportunity to act on it.

(b) Even with knowledge, a bank may for 10 days after the date of death pay or certify checks drawn on or before the date unless ordered to stop payment by a person claiming an interest in the account.

As amended in 1990.

§ 4–406.   Customer's Duty to Discover and Report Unauthorized Signature or Alteration.

(a) A bank that sends or makes available to a customer a statement of account showing payment of items for the account shall either return or make available to the customer the items paid or provide information in the statement of account sufficient to allow the customer reasonably to identify the items paid. The statement of account provides sufficient information if the item is described by item number, amount, and date of payment.

(b) If the items are not returned to the customer, the person retaining the items shall either retain the items or, if the items are destroyed, maintain the capacity to furnish legible copies of the items until the expiration of seven years after receipt of the items. A customer may request an item from the bank that paid the item, and that bank must provide in a reasonable time either the item or, if the item has been destroyed or is not otherwise obtainable, a legible copy of the item.

(c) If a bank sends or makes available a statement of account or items pursuant to subsection (a), the customer must exercise reasonable promptness in examining the statement or the items to determine whether any payment was not authorized because of an alteration of an item or because a purported signature by or on behalf of the customer was not authorized. If, based on the statement or items provided, the customer should reasonably have discovered the unauthorized payment, the customer must promptly notify the bank of the relevant facts.

(d) If the bank proves that the customer failed, with respect to an item, to comply with the duties imposed on the customer by subsection (c), the customer is precluded from asserting against the bank:

(1) the customer's unauthorized signature or any alteration on the item, if the bank also proves that it suffered a loss by reason of the failure; and

(2) the customer's unauthorized signature or alteration by the same wrongdoer on any other item paid in good faith by the bank if the payment was made before the bank received notice from the customer of the unauthorized signature or alteration and after the customer had been afforded a reasonable period of time, not exceeding 30 days, in which to examine the item or statement of account and notify the bank.

(e) If subsection (d) applies and the customer proves that the bank failed to exercise ordinary care in paying the item and that the failure substantially contributed to loss, the loss is allocated between the customer precluded and the bank asserting the preclusion according to the extent to which the failure of the customer to comply with subsection (c) and the failure of the bank to exercise ordinary care contributed to the loss. If the customer proves that the bank did not pay the item in good faith, the preclusion under subsection (d) does not apply.

(f) Without regard to care or lack of care of either the customer or the bank, a customer who does not within one year after the statement or items are made available to the customer (subsection (a)) discover and report the customer's unauthorized signature on or any alteration on the item is precluded from asserting against the bank the unauthorized signature or alteration. If there is a preclusion under this subsection, the payor bank may not recover for breach or warranty under Section 4–208 with respect to the unauthorized signature or alteration to which the preclusion applies.

As amended in 1990.

§ 4–407.   Payor Bank's Right to Subrogation on Improper Payment.

If a payor has paid an item over the order of the drawer or maker to stop payment, or after an account has been closed, or otherwise under circumstances giving a basis for objection by the drawer or maker, to prevent unjust enrichment and only to the extent necessary to prevent loss to the bank by reason of its payment of the item, the payor bank is subrogated to the rights

(1) of any holder in due course on the item against the drawer or maker;

(2) of the payee or any other holder of the item against the drawer or maker either on the item or under the transaction out of which the item arose; and

(3) of the drawer or maker against the payee or any other holder of the item with respect to the transaction out of which the item arose.

As amended in 1990.

Part 5   Collection of Documentary Drafts

§ 4–501.   Handling of Documentary Drafts; Duty to Send for Presentment and to Notify Customer of Dishonor.

A bank that takes a documentary draft for collection shall present or send the draft and accompanying documents for presentment and, upon learning that the draft has not been paid or accepted in due course, shall seasonably notify its customer of the fact even though it may have discounted or bought the draft or extended credit available for withdrawal as of right.

As amended in 1990.

§ 4–502.   Presentment of "On Arrival" Drafts.

If a draft or the relevant instructions require presentment "on arrival", "when goods arrive" or the like, the collecting bank need not present until in its judgment a reasonable time for arrival of the goods has expired. Refusal to pay or accept because the goods have not arrived is not dishonor; the bank must notify its transferor of the refusal but need not present the draft again until it is instructed to do so or learns of the arrival of the goods.

§ 4–503.   Responsibility of Presenting Bank for Documents and Goods; Report of Reasons for Dishonor; Referee in Case of Need.

Unless otherwise instructed and except as provided in Article 5, a bank presenting a documentary draft:

(1) must deliver the documents to the drawee on acceptance of the draft if it is payable more than three days after presentment, otherwise, only on payment; and

(2) upon dishonor, either in the case of presentment for acceptance or presentment for payment, may seek and follow instructions from any referee in case of need designated in the draft or, if the presenting bank does not choose to utilize the referee's services, it must use diligence and good faith to ascertain the reason for dishonor, must notify its transferor of the dishonor and of the results of its effort to ascertain the reasons therefor, and must request instructions.

However, the presenting bank is under no obligation with respect to goods represented by the documents except to follow any reasonable instructions seasonably received; it has a right to reimbursement for any expense incurred in following instructions and to prepayment of or indemnity for those expenses.

As amended in 1990.

§ 4–504.   Privilege of Presenting Bank to Deal With Goods; Security Interest for Expenses.

(a) A presenting bank that, following the dishonor of a documentary draft, has seasonably requested instructions but does not receive them within a reasonable time may store, sell, or otherwise deal with the goods in any reasonable manner.

(b) For its reasonable expenses incurred by action under subsection (a) the presenting bank has a lien upon the goods or their proceeds, which may be foreclosed in the same manner as an unpaid seller's lien.

As amended in 1990.

Article 4A
FUNDS TRANSFERS

Part 1   Subject Matter and Definitions

§ 4A–101.   Short Title.

This Article may be cited as Uniform Commercial Code—Funds Transfers.

§ 4A–102.   Subject Matter.

Except as otherwise provided in Section 4A–108, this Article applies to funds transfers defined in Section 4A–104.

§ 4A–103.   Payment Order–Definitions.

(a) In this Article:

(1) "Payment order" means an instruction of a sender to a receiving bank, transmitted orally, electronically, or in writing, to pay, or to cause another bank to pay, a fixed or determinable amount of money to a beneficiary if:

(i) the instruction does not state a condition to payment to the beneficiary other than time of payment,

(ii) the receiving bank is to be reimbursed by debiting an account of, or otherwise receiving payment from, the sender, and

(iii) the instruction is transmitted by the sender directly to the receiving bank or to an agent, funds-transfer system, or communication system for transmittal to the receiving bank.

(2) "Beneficiary" means the person to be paid by the beneficiary's bank.

(3) "Beneficiary's bank" means the bank identified in a payment order in which an account of the beneficiary is to be credited pursuant to the order or which otherwise is to make payment to the beneficiary if the order does not provide for payment to an account.

(4) "Receiving bank" means the bank to which the sender's instruction is addressed.

(5) "Sender" means the person giving the instruction to the receiving bank.

(b) If an instruction complying with subsection (a)(1) is to make more than one payment to a beneficiary, the instruction is a separate payment order with respect to each payment.

(c) A payment order is issued when it is sent to the receiving bank.

§ 4A–104.   Funds Transfer–Definitions.

In this Article:

(a) "Funds transfer" means the series of transactions, beginning with the originator's payment order, made for the purpose of making payment to the beneficiary of the order. The term includes any payment order issued by the originator's bank or an intermediary bank intended to carry out the originator's payment order. A funds transfer is completed by acceptance by the beneficiary's bank of a payment order for the benefit of the beneficiary of the originator's payment order.

(b) "Intermediary bank" means a receiving bank other than the originator's bank or the beneficiary's bank.

(c) "Originator" means the sender of the first payment order in a funds transfer.

(d) "Originator's bank" means (i) the receiving bank to which the payment order of the originator is issued if the originator is not a bank, or (ii) the originator if the originator is a bank.

§ 4A–105.   Other Definitions.

(a) In this Article:

(1) "Authorized account" means a deposit account of a customer in a bank designated by the customer as a source of payment of payment orders issued by the customer to the bank. If a customer does not so designate an account, any account of the customer is an authorized account if payment of a payment order from that account is not inconsistent with a restriction on the use of that account.

(2) "Bank" means a person engaged in the business of banking and includes a savings bank, savings and loan association, credit union, and trust company. A branch or separate office of a bank is a separate bank for purposes of this Article.

(3) "Customer" means a person, including a bank, having an account with a bank or from whom a bank has agreed to receive payment orders.

(4) "Funds-transfer business day" of a receiving bank means the part of a day during which the receiving bank is open for the receipt, processing, and transmittal of payment orders and cancellations and amendments of payment orders.

(5) "Funds-transfer system" means a wire transfer network, automated clearing house, or other communication system of a clearing house or other association of banks through which a payment order by a bank may be transmitted to the bank to which the order is addressed.

(6) "Good faith" means honesty in fact and the observance of reasonable commercial standards of fair dealing.

(7) "Prove" with respect to a fact means to meet the burden of establishing the fact (Section 1–201(8)).

(b) Other definitions applying to this Article and the sections in which they appear are:

"Acceptance"	Section 4A–209
"Beneficiary"	Section 4A–103
"Beneficiary's bank"	Section 4A–103
"Executed"	Section 4A–301
"Execution date"	Section 4A–301
"Funds transfer"	Section 4A–104
"Funds-transfer system rule"	Section 4A–501
"Intermediary bank"	Section 4A–104
"Originator"	Section 4A–104
"Originator's bank"	Section 4A–104
"Payment by beneficiary's bank to beneficiary"	Section 4A–405
"Payment by originator to beneficiary"	Section 4A–406
"Payment by sender to receiving bank"	Section 4A–403
"Payment date"	Section 4A–401
"Payment order"	Section 4A–103
"Receiving bank"	Section 4A–103
"Security procedure"	Section 4A–201
"Sender"	Section 4A–103

(c) The following definitions in Article 4 apply to this Article:

"Clearing house"   Section 4–104

"Item"   Section 4–104

"Suspends payments"   Section 4–104

(d) In addition, Article 1 contains general definitions and principles of construction and interpretation applicable throughout this Article.

§ 4A–106.   Time Payment Order Is Received.

(a) The time of receipt of a payment order or communication cancelling or amending a payment order is determined by the rules applicable to receipt of a notice stated in Section 1–201(27). A receiving bank may fix a cut-off time or times on a funds-transfer business day for the receipt and processing of payment orders and communications cancelling or amending payment orders. Different cut-off times may apply to payment orders, cancellations, or amendments, or to different categories of payment orders, cancellations, or amendments. A cut-off time may apply to senders generally or different cut-off times may apply to different senders or categories of payment orders. If a payment order or communication cancelling or amending a payment order is received after the close of a funds-transfer business day or after the appropriate cut-off time on a funds-transfer business day, the receiving bank may treat the payment order or communication as received at the opening of the next funds-transfer business day.

(b) If this Article refers to an execution date or payment date or states a day on which a receiving bank is required to take action, and the date or day does not fall on a funds-transfer business day, the next day that is a funds-transfer business day is treated as the date or day stated, unless the contrary is stated in this Article.

§ 4A–107.   Federal Reserve Regulations and Operating Circulars.

Regulations of the Board of Governors of the Federal Reserve System and operating circulars of the Federal Reserve Banks supersede any inconsistent provision of this Article to the extent of the inconsistency.

§ 4A–108.   Exclusion of Consumer Transactions Governed by Federal Law.

This Article does not apply to a funds transfer any part of which is governed by the Electronic Fund Transfer Act of 1978 (Title XX, Public Law 95–630, 92 Stat. 3728, 15 U.S.C. § 1693 *et seq.*) as amended from time to time.

Part 2   Issue and Acceptance of Payment Order

§ 4A–201.   Security Procedure.

"Security procedure" means a procedure established by agreement of a customer and a receiving bank for the purpose of (i) verifying that a payment order or communication amending or cancelling a payment order is that of the customer, or (ii) detecting error in the transmission or the content of the payment order or communication. A security procedure may require the use of algorithms or other codes, identifying words or numbers, encryption, callback procedures, or similar security devices. Comparison of a signature on a payment order or communication with an authorized specimen signature of the customer is not by itself a security procedure.

§ 4A–202.   Authorized and Verified Payment Orders.

(a) A payment order received by the receiving bank is the authorized order of the person identified as sender if that person authorized the order or is otherwise bound by it under the law of agency.

(b) If a bank and its customer have agreed that the authenticity of payment orders issued to the bank in the name of the customer as sender will be verified pursuant to a security procedure, a payment order received by the receiving bank is effective as the order of the customer, whether or not authorized, if (i) the security procedure is a commercially reasonable method of providing security against unauthorized payment orders, and (ii) the bank proves that it accepted the payment order in good faith and in compliance with the security procedure and any written agreement or instruction of the customer restricting acceptance of payment orders issued in the name of the customer. The bank is not required to follow an instruction that violates a written agreement with the customer or notice of which is not received at a time and in a manner affording the bank a reasonable opportunity to act on it before the payment order is accepted.

(c) Commercial reasonableness of a security procedure is a question of law to be determined by considering the wishes of the customer expressed to the bank, the circumstances of the customer known to the bank, including the size, type, and frequency of payment orders normally issued by the customer to the bank, alternative security procedures offered to the customer, and security procedures in general use by customers and receiving banks similarly situated. A security procedure is deemed to be commercially reasonable if (i) the security procedure was chosen by the customer after the bank offered, and the customer refused, a security procedure that was commercially reasonable for that customer, and (ii) the customer expressly agreed in writing to be bound by any payment order, whether or not authorized, issued in its name and accepted by the bank in compliance with the security procedure chosen by the customer.

(d) The term "sender" in this Article includes the customer in whose name a payment order is issued if the order is the authorized order of the customer under subsection (a), or it is effective as the order of the customer under subsection (b).

(e) This section applies to amendments and cancellations of payment orders to the same extent it applies to payment orders.

(f) Except as provided in this section and in Section 4A–203(a)(1), rights and obligations arising under this section or Section 4A–203 may not be varied by agreement.

§ 4A–203.   Unenforceability of Certain Verified Payment Orders.

(a) If an accepted payment order is not, under Section 4A–202(a), an authorized order of a customer identified as sender, but is effective as an order of the customer pursuant to Section 4A–202(b), the following rules apply:

   (1) By express written agreement, the receiving bank may limit the extent to which it is entitled to enforce or retain payment of the payment order.

   (2) The receiving bank is not entitled to enforce or retain payment of the payment order if the customer proves that the order was not caused, directly or indirectly, by a person

(i) entrusted at any time with duties to act for the customer with respect to payment orders or the security procedure, or (ii) who obtained access to transmitting facilities of the customer or who obtained, from a source controlled by the customer and without authority of the receiving bank, information facilitating breach of the security procedure, regardless of how the information was obtained or whether the customer was at fault. Information includes any access device, computer software, or the like.

(b) This section applies to amendments of payment orders to the same extent it applies to payment orders.

§ 4A–204.   Refund of Payment and Duty of Customer to Report with Respect to Unauthorized Payment Order.

(a) If a receiving bank accepts a payment order issued in the name of its customer as sender which is (i) not authorized and not effective as the order of the customer under Section 4A–202, or (ii) not enforceable, in whole or in part, against the customer under Section 4A–203, the bank shall refund any payment of the payment order received from the customer to the extent the bank is not entitled to enforce payment and shall pay interest on the refundable amount calculated from the date the bank received payment to the date of the refund. However, the customer is not entitled to interest from the bank on the amount to be refunded if the customer fails to exercise ordinary care to determine that the order was not authorized by the customer and to notify the bank of the relevant facts within a reasonable time not exceeding 90 days after the date the customer received notification from the bank that the order was accepted or that the customer's account was debited with respect to the order. The bank is not entitled to any recovery from the customer on account of a failure by the customer to give notification as stated in this section.

(b) Reasonable time under subsection (a) may be fixed by agreement as stated in Section 1–204(1), but the obligation of a receiving bank to refund payment as stated in subsection (a) may not otherwise be varied by agreement.

§ 4A–205.   Erroneous Payment Orders.

(a) If an accepted payment order was transmitted pursuant to a security procedure for the detection of error and the payment order (i) erroneously instructed payment to a beneficiary not intended by the sender, (ii) erroneously instructed payment in an amount greater than the amount intended by the sender, or (iii) was an erroneously transmitted duplicate of a payment order previously sent by the sender, the following rules apply:

(1) If the sender proves that the sender or a person acting on behalf of the sender pursuant to Section 4A–206 complied with the security procedure and that the error would have been detected if the receiving bank had also complied, the sender is not obliged to pay the order to the extent stated in paragraphs (2) and (3).

(2) If the funds transfer is completed on the basis of an erroneous payment order described in clause (i) or (iii) of subsection (a), the sender is not obliged to pay the order and the receiving bank is entitled to recover from the beneficiary any

amount paid to the beneficiary to the extent allowed by the law governing mistake and restitution.

(3) If the funds transfer is completed on the basis of a payment order described in clause (ii) of subsection (a), the sender is not obliged to pay the order to the extent the amount received by the beneficiary is greater than the amount intended by the sender. In that case, the receiving bank is entitled to recover from the beneficiary the excess amount received to the extent allowed by the law governing mistake and restitution.

(b) If (i) the sender of an erroneous payment order described in subsection (a) is not obliged to pay all or part of the order, and (ii) the sender receives notification from the receiving bank that the order was accepted by the bank or that the sender's account was debited with respect to the order, the sender has a duty to exercise ordinary care, on the basis of information available to the sender, to discover the error with respect to the order and to advise the bank of the relevant facts within a reasonable time, not exceeding 90 days, after the bank's notification was received by the sender. If the bank proves that the sender failed to perform that duty, the sender is liable to the bank for the loss the bank proves it incurred as a result of the failure, but the liability of the sender may not exceed the amount of the sender's order.

(c) This section applies to amendments to payment orders to the same extent it applies to payment orders.

§ 4A–206.   Transmission of Payment Order through Funds-Transfer or Other Communication System.

(a) If a payment order addressed to a receiving bank is transmitted to a funds-transfer system or other third party communication system for transmittal to the bank, the system is deemed to be an agent of the sender for the purpose of transmitting the payment order to the bank. If there is a discrepancy between the terms of the payment order transmitted to the system and the terms of the payment order transmitted by the system to the bank, the terms of the payment order of the sender are those transmitted by the system. This section does not apply to a funds-transfer system of the Federal Reserve Banks.

(b) This section applies to cancellations and amendments to payment orders to the same extent it applies to payment orders.

§ 4A–207.   Misdescription of Beneficiary.

(a) Subject to subsection (b), if, in a payment order received by the beneficiary's bank, the name, bank account number, or other identification of the beneficiary refers to a nonexistent or unidentifiable person or account, no person has rights as a beneficiary of the order and acceptance of the order cannot occur.

(b) If a payment order received by the beneficiary's bank identifies the beneficiary both by name and by an identifying or bank account number and the name and number identify different persons, the following rules apply:

(1) Except as otherwise provided in subsection (c), if the beneficiary's bank does not know that the name and number refer to different persons, it may rely on the number as the proper identification of the beneficiary of the order. The

beneficiary's bank need not determine whether the name and number refer to the same person.

(2) If the beneficiary's bank pays the person identified by name or knows that the name and number identify different persons, no person has rights as beneficiary except the person paid by the beneficiary's bank if that person was entitled to receive payment from the originator of the funds transfer. If no person has rights as beneficiary, acceptance of the order cannot occur.

(c) If (i) a payment order described in subsection (b) is accepted, (ii) the originator's payment order described the beneficiary inconsistently by name and number, and (iii) the beneficiary's bank pays the person identified by number as permitted by subsection (b)(1), the following rules apply:

(1) If the originator is a bank, the originator is obliged to pay its order.

(2) If the originator is not a bank and proves that the person identified by number was not entitled to receive payment from the originator, the originator is not obliged to pay its order unless the originator's bank proves that the originator, before acceptance of the originator's order, had notice that payment of a payment order issued by the originator might be made by the beneficiary's bank on the basis of an identifying or bank account number even if it identifies a person different from the named beneficiary. Proof of notice may be made by any admissible evidence. The originator's bank satisfies the burden of proof if it proves that the originator, before the payment order was accepted, signed a writing stating the information to which the notice relates.

(d) In a case governed by subsection (b)(1), if the beneficiary's bank rightfully pays the person identified by number and that person was not entitled to receive payment from the originator, the amount paid may be recovered from that person to the extent allowed by the law governing mistake and restitution as follows:

(1) If the originator is obliged to pay its payment order as stated in subsection (c), the originator has the right to recover.

(2) If the originator is not a bank and is not obliged to pay its payment order, the originator's bank has the right to recover.

§ 4A-208.   Misdescription of Intermediary Bank or Beneficiary's Bank.

(a) This subsection applies to a payment order identifying an intermediary bank or the beneficiary's bank only by an identifying number.

(1) The receiving bank may rely on the number as the proper identification of the intermediary or beneficiary's bank and need not determine whether the number identifies a bank.

(2) The sender is obliged to compensate the receiving bank for any loss and expenses incurred by the receiving bank as a result of its reliance on the number in executing or attempting to execute the order.

(b) This subsection applies to a payment order identifying an intermediary bank or the beneficiary's bank both by name and an identifying number if the name and number identify different persons.

(1) If the sender is a bank, the receiving bank may rely on the number as the proper identification of the intermediary or beneficiary's bank if the receiving bank, when it executes the sender's order, does not know that the name and number identify different persons. The receiving bank need not determine whether the name and number refer to the same person or whether the number refers to a bank. The sender is obliged to compensate the receiving bank for any loss and expenses incurred by the receiving bank as a result of its reliance on the number in executing or attempting to execute the order.

(2) If the sender is not a bank and the receiving bank proves that the sender, before the payment order was accepted, had notice that the receiving bank might rely on the number as the proper identification of the intermediary or beneficiary's bank even if it identifies a person different from the bank identified by name, the rights and obligations of the sender and the receiving bank are governed by subsection (b)(1), as though the sender were a bank. Proof of notice may be made by any admissible evidence. The receiving bank satisfies the burden of proof if it proves that the sender, before the payment order was accepted, signed a writing stating the information to which the notice relates.

(3) Regardless of whether the sender is a bank, the receiving bank may rely on the name as the proper identification of the intermediary or beneficiary's bank if the receiving bank, at the time it executes the sender's order, does not know that the name and number identify different persons. The receiving bank need not determine whether the name and number refer to the same person.

(4) If the receiving bank knows that the name and number identify different persons, reliance on either the name or the number in executing the sender's payment order is a breach of the obligation stated in Section 4A–302(a)(1).

§ 4A-209.   Acceptance of Payment Order.

(a) Subject to subsection (d), a receiving bank other than the beneficiary's bank accepts a payment order when it executes the order.

(b) Subject to subsections (c) and (d), a beneficiary's bank accepts a payment order at the earliest of the following times:

(1) When the bank (i) pays the beneficiary as stated in Section 4A–405(a) or 4A–405(b), or (ii) notifies the beneficiary of receipt of the order or that the account of the beneficiary has been credited with respect to the order unless the notice indicates that the bank is rejecting the order or that funds with respect to the order may not be withdrawn or used until receipt of payment from the sender of the order;

(2) When the bank receives payment of the entire amount of the sender's order pursuant to Section 4A–403(a)(1) or 4A–403(a)(2); or

(3) The opening of the next funds-transfer business day of the bank following the payment date of the order if, at that time, the amount of the sender's order is fully covered by a withdrawable credit balance in an authorized account of the sender or the bank has otherwise received full payment from

the sender, unless the order was rejected before that time or is rejected within (i) one hour after that time, or (ii) one hour after the opening of the next business day of the sender following the payment date if that time is later. If notice of rejection is received by the sender after the payment date and the authorized account of the sender does not bear interest, the bank is obliged to pay interest to the sender on the amount of the order for the number of days elapsing after the payment date to the day the sender receives notice or learns that the order was not accepted, counting that day as an elapsed day. If the withdrawable credit balance during that period falls below the amount of the order, the amount of interest payable is reduced accordingly.

(c) Acceptance of a payment order cannot occur before the order is received by the receiving bank. Acceptance does not occur under subsection (b)(2) or (b)(3) if the beneficiary of the payment order does not have an account with the receiving bank, the account has been closed, or the receiving bank is not permitted by law to receive credits for the beneficiary's account.

(d) A payment order issued to the originator's bank cannot be accepted until the payment date if the bank is the beneficiary's bank, or the execution date if the bank is not the beneficiary's bank. If the originator's bank executes the originator's payment order before the execution date or pays the beneficiary of the originator's payment order before the payment date and the payment order is subsequently cancelled pursuant to Section 4A–211(b), the bank may recover from the beneficiary any payment received to the extent allowed by the law governing mistake and restitution.

§ 4A–210.   Rejection of Payment Order.

(a) A payment order is rejected by the receiving bank by a notice of rejection transmitted to the sender orally, electronically, or in writing. A notice of rejection need not use any particular words and is sufficient if it indicates that the receiving bank is rejecting the order or will not execute or pay the order. Rejection is effective when the notice is given if transmission is by a means that is reasonable in the circumstances. If notice of rejection is given by a means that is not reasonable, rejection is effective when the notice is received. If an agreement of the sender and receiving bank establishes the means to be used to reject a payment order, (i) any means complying with the agreement is reasonable and (ii) any means not complying is not reasonable unless no significant delay in receipt of the notice resulted from the use of the noncomplying means.

(b) This subsection applies if a receiving bank other than the beneficiary's bank fails to execute a payment order despite the existence on the execution date of a withdrawable credit balance in an authorized account of the sender sufficient to cover the order. If the sender does not receive notice of rejection of the order on the execution date and the authorized account of the sender does not bear interest, the bank is obliged to pay interest to the sender on the amount of the order for the number of days elapsing after the execution date to the earlier of the day the order is cancelled pursuant to Section 4A–211(d) or the day the sender receives notice or learns that the order was not executed, counting the final day of the period as an elapsed day. If the withdrawable credit balance

during that period falls below the amount of the order, the amount of interest is reduced accordingly.

(c) If a receiving bank suspends payments, all unaccepted payment orders issued to it are are deemed rejected at the time the bank suspends payments.

(d) Acceptance of a payment order precludes a later rejection of the order. Rejection of a payment order precludes a later acceptance of the order.

§ 4A–211.   Cancellation and Amendment of Payment Order.

(a) A communication of the sender of a payment order cancelling or amending the order may be transmitted to the receiving bank orally, electronically, or in writing. If a security procedure is in effect between the sender and the receiving bank, the communication is not effective to cancel or amend the order unless the communication is verified pursuant to the security procedure or the bank agrees to the cancellation or amendment.

(b) Subject to subsection (a), a communication by the sender cancelling or amending a payment order is effective to cancel or amend the order if notice of the communication is received at a time and in a manner affording the receiving bank a reasonable opportunity to act on the communication before the bank accepts the payment order.

(c) After a payment order has been accepted, cancellation or amendment of the order is not effective unless the receiving bank agrees or a funds-transfer system rule allows cancellation or amendment without agreement of the bank.

(1) With respect to a payment order accepted by a receiving bank other than the beneficiary's bank, cancellation or amendment is not effective unless a conforming cancellation or amendment of the payment order issued by the receiving bank is also made.

(2) With respect to a payment order accepted by the beneficiary's bank, cancellation or amendment is not effective unless the order was issued in execution of an unauthorized payment order, or because of a mistake by a sender in the funds transfer which resulted in the issuance of a payment order (i) that is a duplicate of a payment order previously issued by the sender, (ii) that orders payment to a beneficiary not entitled to receive payment from the originator, or (iii) that orders payment in an amount greater than the amount the beneficiary was entitled to receive from the originator. If the payment order is cancelled or amended, the beneficiary's bank is entitled to recover from the beneficiary any amount paid to the beneficiary to the extent allowed by the law governing mistake and restitution.

(d) An unaccepted payment order is cancelled by operation of law at the close of the fifth funds-transfer business day of the receiving bank after the execution date or payment date of the order.

(e) A cancelled payment order cannot be accepted. If an accepted payment order is cancelled, the acceptance is nullified and no person has any right or obligation based on the acceptance. Amendment of a payment order is deemed to be cancellation of the original order at the time of amendment and issue of a new payment order in the amended form at the same time.

(f) Unless otherwise provided in an agreement of the parties or in a funds-transfer system rule, if the receiving bank, after accepting a payment order, agrees to cancellation or amendment of the order by the sender or is bound by a funds-transfer system rule allowing cancellation or amendment without the bank's agreement, the sender, whether or not cancellation or amendment is effective, is liable to the bank for any loss and expenses, including reasonable attorney's fees, incurred by the bank as a result of the cancellation or amendment or attempted cancellation or amendment.

(g) A payment order is not revoked by the death or legal incapacity of the sender unless the receiving bank knows of the death or of an adjudication of incapacity by a court of competent jurisdiction and has reasonable opportunity to act before acceptance of the order.

(h) A funds-transfer system rule is not effective to the extent it conflicts with subsection (c)(2).

§ 4A–212.   Liability and Duty of Receiving Bank Regarding Unaccepted Payment Order.

If a receiving bank fails to accept a payment order that it is obliged by express agreement to accept, the bank is liable for breach of the agreement to the extent provided in the agreement or in this Article, but does not otherwise have any duty to accept a payment order or, before acceptance, to take any action, or refrain from taking action, with respect to the order except as provided in this Article or by express agreement. Liability based on acceptance arises only when acceptance occurs as stated in Section 4A–209, and liability is limited to that provided in this Article. A receiving bank is not the agent of the sender or beneficiary of the payment order it accepts, or of any other party to the funds transfer, and the bank owes no duty to any party to the funds transfer except as provided in this Article or by express agreement.

Part 3   Execution of Sender's Payment Order by Receiving Bank

§ 4A–301.   Execution and Execution Date.

(a) A payment order is "executed" by the receiving bank when it issues a payment order intended to carry out the payment order received by the bank. A payment order received by the beneficiary's bank can be accepted but cannot be executed.

(b) "Execution date" of a payment order means the day on which the receiving bank may properly issue a payment order in execution of the sender's order. The execution date may be determined by instruction of the sender but cannot be earlier than the day the order is received and, unless otherwise determined, is the day the order is received. If the sender's instruction states a payment date, the execution date is the payment date or an earlier date on which execution is reasonably necessary to allow payment to the beneficiary on the payment date.

§ 4A–302.   Obligations of Receiving Bank in Execution of Payment Order.

(a) Except as provided in subsections (b) through (d), if the receiving bank accepts a payment order pursuant to Section 4A–209(a), the bank has the following obligations in executing the order:

(1) The receiving bank is obliged to issue, on the execution date, a payment order complying with the sender's order and to follow the sender's instructions concerning (i) any intermediary bank or funds-transfer system to be used in carrying out the funds transfer, or (ii) the means by which payment orders are to be transmitted in the funds transfer. If the originator's bank issues a payment order to an intermediary bank, the originator's bank is obliged to instruct the intermediary bank according to the instruction of the originator. An intermediary bank in the funds transfer is similarly bound by an instruction given to it by the sender of the payment order it accepts.

(2) If the sender's instruction states that the funds transfer is to be carried out telephonically or by wire transfer or otherwise indicates that the funds transfer is to be carried out by the most expeditious means, the receiving bank is obliged to transmit its payment order by the most expeditious available means, and to instruct any intermediary bank accordingly. If a sender's instruction states a payment date, the receiving bank is obliged to transmit its payment order at a time and by means reasonably necessary to allow payment to the beneficiary on the payment date or as soon thereafter as is feasible.

(b) Unless otherwise instructed, a receiving bank executing a payment order may (i) use any funds-transfer system if use of that system is reasonable in the circumstances, and (ii) issue a payment order to the beneficiary's bank or to an intermediary bank through which a payment order conforming to the sender's order can expeditiously be issued to the beneficiary's bank if the receiving bank exercises ordinary care in the selection of the intermediary bank. A receiving bank is not required to follow an instruction of the sender designating a funds-transfer system to be used in carrying out the funds transfer if the receiving bank, in good faith, determines that it is not feasible to follow the instruction or that following the instruction would unduly delay completion of the funds transfer.

(c) Unless subsection (a)(2) applies or the receiving bank is otherwise instructed, the bank may execute a payment order by transmitting its payment order by first class mail or by any means reasonable in the circumstances. If the receiving bank is instructed to execute the sender's order by transmitting its payment order by a particular means, the receiving bank may issue its payment order by the means stated or by any means as expeditious as the means stated.

(d) Unless instructed by the sender, (i) the receiving bank may not obtain payment of its charges for services and expenses in connection with the execution of the sender's order by issuing a payment order in an amount equal to the amount of the sender's order less the amount of the charges, and (ii) may not instruct a subsequent receiving bank to obtain payment of its charges in the same manner.

§ 4A–303.   Erroneous Execution of Payment Order.

(a) A receiving bank that (i) executes the payment order of the sender by issuing a payment order in an amount greater than the amount of the sender's order, or (ii) issues a payment order in execution of the sender's order and then issues a duplicate order, is entitled to payment of the amount of the sender's order under Section 4A–402(c) if that subsection is otherwise satisfied. The bank is entitled to recover from the beneficiary of the erroneous order the excess payment received to the extent allowed by the law governing mistake and restitution.

(b) A receiving bank that executes the payment order of the sender by issuing a payment order in an amount less than the amount of the sender's order is entitled to payment of the amount of the sender's order under Section 4A–402(c) if (i) that subsection is otherwise satisfied and (ii) the bank corrects its mistake by issuing an additional payment order for the benefit of the beneficiary of the sender's order. If the error is not corrected, the issuer of the erroneous order is entitled to receive or retain payment from the sender of the order it accepted only to the extent of the amount of the erroneous order. This subsection does not apply if the receiving bank executes the sender's payment order by issuing a payment order in an amount less than the amount of the sender's order for the purpose of obtaining payment of its charges for services and expenses pursuant to instruction of the sender.

(c) If a receiving bank executes the payment order of the sender by issuing a payment order to a beneficiary different from the beneficiary of the sender's order and the funds transfer is completed on the basis of that error, the sender of the payment order that was erroneously executed and all previous senders in the funds transfer are not obliged to pay the payment orders they issued. The issuer of the erroneous order is entitled to recover from the beneficiary of the order the payment received to the extent allowed by the law governing mistake and restitution.

§ 4A–304.   Duty of Sender to Report Erroneously Executed Payment Order.

If the sender of a payment order that is erroneously executed as stated in Section 4A–303 receives notification from the receiving bank that the order was executed or that the sender's account was debited with respect to the order, the sender has a duty to exercise ordinary care to determine, on the basis of information available to the sender, that the order was erroneously executed and to notify the bank of the relevant facts within a reasonable time not exceeding 90 days after the notification from the bank was received by the sender. If the sender fails to perform that duty, the bank is not obliged to pay interest on any amount refundable to the sender under Section 4A–402(d) for the period before the bank learns of the execution error. The bank is not entitled to any recovery from the sender on account of a failure by the sender to perform the duty stated in this section.

§ 4A–305.   Liability for Late or Improper Execution or Failure to Execute Payment Order.

(a) If a funds transfer is completed but execution of a payment order by the receiving bank in breach of Section 4A–302 results in delay in payment to the beneficiary, the bank is obliged to pay interest to either the originator or the beneficiary of the funds transfer for the period of delay caused by the improper execution. Except as provided in subsection (c), additional damages are not recoverable.

(b) If execution of a payment order by a receiving bank in breach of Section 4A–302 results in (i) noncompletion of the funds transfer,

(ii) failure to use an intermediary bank designated by the originator, or (iii) issuance of a payment order that does not comply with the terms of the payment order of the originator, the bank is liable to the originator for its expenses in the funds transfer and for incidental expenses and interest losses, to the extent not covered by subsection (a), resulting from the improper execution. Except as provided in subsection (c), additional damages are not recoverable.

(c) In addition to the amounts payable under subsections (a) and (b), damages, including consequential damages, are recoverable to the extent provided in an express written agreement of the receiving bank.

(d) If a receiving bank fails to execute a payment order it was obliged by express agreement to execute, the receiving bank is liable to the sender for its expenses in the transaction and for incidental expenses and interest losses resulting from the failure to execute. Additional damages, including consequential damages, are recoverable to the extent provided in an express written agreement of the receiving bank, but are not otherwise recoverable.

(e) Reasonable attorney's fees are recoverable if demand for compensation under subsection (a) or (b) is made and refused before an action is brought on the claim. If a claim is made for breach of an agreement under subsection (d) and the agreement does not provide for damages, reasonable attorney's fees are recoverable if demand for compensation under subsection (d) is made and refused before an action is brought on the claim.

(f) Except as stated in this section, the liability of a receiving bank under subsections (a) and (b) may not be varied by agreement.

Part 4   Payment

§ 4A–401.   Payment Date.

"Payment date" of a payment order means the day on which the amount of the order is payable to the beneficiary by the beneficiary's bank. The payment date may be determined by instruction of the sender but cannot be earlier than the day the order is received by the beneficiary's bank and, unless otherwise determined, is the day the order is received by the beneficiary's bank.

§ 4A–402.   Obligation of Sender to Pay Receiving Bank.

(a) This section is subject to Sections 4A–205 and 4A–207.

(b) With respect to a payment order issued to the beneficiary's bank, acceptance of the order by the bank obliges the sender to pay the bank the amount of the order, but payment is not due until the payment date of the order.

(c) This subsection is subject to subsection (e) and to Section 4A–303. With respect to a payment order issued to a receiving bank other than the beneficiary's bank, acceptance of the order by the receiving bank obliges the sender to pay the bank the amount of the sender's order. Payment by the sender is not due until the execution date of the sender's order. The obligation of that sender to pay its payment order is excused if the funds transfer is not completed by acceptance by the beneficiary's bank of a payment order instructing payment to the beneficiary of that sender's payment order.

(d) If the sender of a payment order pays the order and was not obliged to pay all or part of the amount paid, the bank receiving payment is obliged to refund payment to the extent the sender was not obliged to pay. Except as provided in Sections 4A–204 and 4A–304, interest is payable on the refundable amount from the date of payment.

(e) If a funds transfer is not completed as stated in subsection (c) and an intermediary bank is obliged to refund payment as stated in subsection (d) but is unable to do so because not permitted by applicable law or because the bank suspends payments, a sender in the funds transfer that executed a payment order in compliance with an instruction, as stated in Section 4A–302(a)(1), to route the funds transfer through that intermediary bank is entitled to receive or retain payment from the sender of the payment order that it accepted. The first sender in the funds transfer that issued an instruction requiring routing through that intermediary bank is subrogated to the right of the bank that paid the intermediary bank to refund as stated in subsection (d).

(f) The right of the sender of a payment order to be excused from the obligation to pay the order as stated in subsection (c) or to receive refund under subsection (d) may not be varied by agreement.

§ 4A–403.   Payment by Sender to Receiving Bank.

(a) Payment of the sender's obligation under Section 4A–402 to pay the receiving bank occurs as follows:

  (1) If the sender is a bank, payment occurs when the receiving bank receives final settlement of the obligation through a Federal Reserve Bank or through a funds-transfer system.

  (2) If the sender is a bank and the sender (i) credited an account of the receiving bank with the sender, or (ii) caused an account of the receiving bank in another bank to be credited, payment occurs when the credit is withdrawn or, if not withdrawn, at midnight of the day on which the credit is withdrawable and the receiving bank learns of that fact.

  (3) If the receiving bank debits an account of the sender with the receiving bank, payment occurs when the debit is made to the extent the debit is covered by a withdrawable credit balance in the account.

(b) If the sender and receiving bank are members of a funds-transfer system that nets obligations multilaterally among participants, the receiving bank receives final settlement when settlement is complete in accordance with the rules of the system. The obligation of the sender to pay the amount of a payment order transmitted through the funds-transfer system may be satisfied, to the extent permitted by the rules of the system, by setting off and applying against the sender's obligation the right of the sender to receive payment from the receiving bank of the amount of any other payment order transmitted to the sender by the receiving bank through the funds-transfer system. The aggregate balance of obligations owed by each sender to each receiving bank in the funds-transfer system may be satisfied, to the extent permitted by the rules of the system, by setting off and applying against that balance the aggregate balance of obligations owed to the sender by other members of the system. The aggregate balance is determined after the right of setoff stated in the second sentence of this subsection has been exercised.

(c) If two banks transmit payment orders to each other under an agreement that settlement of the obligations of each bank to the other under Section 4A–402 will be made at the end of the day or other period, the total amount owed with respect to all orders transmitted by one bank shall be set off against the total amount owed with respect to all orders transmitted by the other bank. To the extent of the setoff, each bank has made payment to the other.

(d) In a case not covered by subsection (a), the time when payment of the sender's obligation under Section 4A–402(b) or 4A–402(c) occurs is governed by applicable principles of law that determine when an obligation is satisfied.

§ 4A–404.   Obligation of Beneficiary's Bank to Pay and Give Notice to Beneficiary.

(a) Subject to Sections 4A–211(e), 4A–405(d), and 4A–405(e), if a beneficiary's bank accepts a payment order, the bank is obliged to pay the amount of the order to the beneficiary of the order. Payment is due on the payment date of the order, but if acceptance occurs on the payment date after the close of the funds-transfer business day of the bank, payment is due on the next funds-transfer business day. If the bank refuses to pay after demand by the beneficiary and receipt of notice of particular circumstances that will give rise to consequential damages as a result of nonpayment, the beneficiary may recover damages resulting from the refusal to pay to the extent the bank had notice of the damages, unless the bank proves that it did not pay because of a reasonable doubt concerning the right of the beneficiary to payment.

(b) If a payment order accepted by the beneficiary's bank instructs payment to an account of the beneficiary, the bank is obliged to notify the beneficiary of receipt of the order before midnight of the next funds-transfer business day following the payment date. If the payment order does not instruct payment to an account of the beneficiary, the bank is required to notify the beneficiary only if notice is required by the order. Notice may be given by first class mail or any other means reasonable in the circumstances. If the bank fails to give the required notice, the bank is obliged to pay interest to the beneficiary on the amount of the payment order from the day notice should have been given until the day the beneficiary learned of receipt of the payment order by the bank. No other damages are recoverable. Reasonable attorney's fees are also recoverable if demand for interest is made and refused before an action is brought on the claim.

(c) The right of a beneficiary to receive payment and damages as stated in subsection (a) may not be varied by agreement or a funds-transfer system rule. The right of a beneficiary to be notified as stated in subsection (b) may be varied by agreement of the beneficiary or by a funds-transfer system rule if the beneficiary is notified of the rule before initiation of the funds transfer.

§ 4A–405.   Payment by Beneficiary's Bank to Beneficiary.

(a) If the beneficiary's bank credits an account of the beneficiary of a payment order, payment of the bank's obligation under Section 4A–404(a) occurs when and to the extent (i) the beneficiary is notified of the right to withdraw the credit, (ii) the bank lawfully applies the credit to a debt of the beneficiary, or (iii) funds with respect to the order are otherwise made available to the beneficiary by the bank.

(b) If the beneficiary's bank does not credit an account of the beneficiary of a payment order, the time when payment of the bank's obligation under Section 4A–404(a) occurs is governed by principles of law that determine when an obligation is satisfied.

(c) Except as stated in subsections (d) and (e), if the beneficiary's bank pays the beneficiary of a payment order under a condition to payment or agreement of the beneficiary giving the bank the right to recover payment from the beneficiary if the bank does not receive payment of the order, the condition to payment or agreement is not enforceable.

(d) A funds-transfer system rule may provide that payments made to beneficiaries of funds transfers made through the system are provisional until receipt of payment by the beneficiary's bank of the payment order it accepted. A beneficiary's bank that makes a payment that is provisional under the rule is entitled to refund from the beneficiary if (i) the rule requires that both the beneficiary and the originator be given notice of the provisional nature of the payment before the funds transfer is initiated, (ii) the beneficiary, the beneficiary's bank, and the originator's bank agreed to be bound by the rule, and (iii) the beneficiary's bank did not receive payment of the payment order that it accepted. If the beneficiary is obliged to refund payment to the beneficiary's bank, acceptance of the payment order by the beneficiary's bank is nullified and no payment by the originator of the funds transfer to the beneficiary occurs under Section 4A–406.

(e) This subsection applies to a funds transfer that includes a payment order transmitted over a funds-transfer system that (i) nets obligations multilaterally among participants, and (ii) has in effect a loss-sharing agreement among participants for the purpose of providing funds necessary to complete settlement of the obligations of one or more participants that do not meet their settlement obligations. If the beneficiary's bank in the funds transfer accepts a payment order and the system fails to complete settlement pursuant to its rules with respect to any payment order in the funds transfer, (i) the acceptance by the beneficiary's bank is nullified and no person has any right or obligation based on the acceptance, (ii) the beneficiary's bank is entitled to recover payment from the beneficiary, (iii) no payment by the originator to the beneficiary occurs under Section 4A–406, and (iv) subject to Section 4A–402(e), each sender in the funds transfer is excused from its obligation to pay its payment order under Section 4A–402(c) because the funds transfer has not been completed.

§ 4A–406. Payment by Originator to Beneficiary; Discharge of Underlying Obligation.

(a) Subject to Sections 4A–211(e), 4A–405(d), and 4A–405(e), the originator of a funds transfer pays the beneficiary of the originator's payment order (i) at the time a payment order for the benefit of the beneficiary is accepted by the beneficiary's bank in the funds transfer and (ii) in an amount equal to the amount of the order accepted by the beneficiary's bank, but not more than the amount of the originator's order.

(b) If payment under subsection (a) is made to satisfy an obligation, the obligation is discharged to the same extent discharge would result from payment to the beneficiary of the same amount in money, unless (i) the payment under subsection (a) was made by a means prohibited by the contract of the beneficiary with respect to the obligation, (ii) the beneficiary, within a reasonable time after receiving notice of receipt of the order by the beneficiary's bank, notified the originator of the beneficiary's refusal of the payment, (iii) funds with respect to the order were not withdrawn by the beneficiary or applied to a debt of the beneficiary, and (iv) the beneficiary would suffer a loss that could reasonably have been avoided if payment had been made by a means complying with the contract. If payment by the originator does not result in discharge under this section, the originator is subrogated to the rights of the beneficiary to receive payment from the beneficiary's bank under Section 4A–404(a).

(c) For the purpose of determining whether discharge of an obligation occurs under subsection (b), if the beneficiary's bank accepts a payment order in an amount equal to the amount of the originator's payment order less charges of one or more receiving banks in the funds transfer, payment to the beneficiary is deemed to be in the amount of the originator's order unless upon demand by the beneficiary the originator does not pay the beneficiary the amount of the deducted charges.

(d) Rights of the originator or of the beneficiary of a funds transfer under this section may be varied only by agreement of the originator and the beneficiary.

Part 5   Miscellaneous Provisions

§ 4A–501.   Variation by Agreement and Effect of Funds-Transfer System Rule.

(a) Except as otherwise provided in this Article, the rights and obligations of a party to a funds transfer may be varied by agreement of the affected party.

(b) "Funds-transfer system rule" means a rule of an association of banks (i) governing transmission of payment orders by means of a funds-transfer system of the association or rights and obligations with respect to those orders, or (ii) to the extent the rule governs rights and obligations between banks that are parties to a funds transfer in which a Federal Reserve Bank, acting as an intermediary bank, sends a payment order to the beneficiary's bank. Except as otherwise provided in this Article, a funds-transfer system rule governing rights and obligations between participating banks using the system may be effective even if the rule conflicts with this Article and indirectly affects another party to the funds transfer who does not consent to the rule. A funds-transfer system rule may also govern rights and obligations of parties other than participating banks using the system to the extent stated in Sections 4A–404(c), 4A–405(d), and 4A–507(c).

§ 4A–502.   Creditor Process Served on Receiving Bank; Setoff by Beneficiary's Bank.

(a) As used in this section, "creditor process" means levy, attachment, garnishment, notice of lien, sequestration, or similar process issued by or on behalf of a creditor or other claimant with respect to an account.

(b) This subsection applies to creditor process with respect to an authorized account of the sender of a payment order if the creditor process is served on the receiving bank. For the purpose of determining rights with respect to the creditor process, if the receiving bank accepts the payment order the balance in the authorized account is deemed to be reduced by the amount of the payment order to the extent the bank did not otherwise receive payment of the order, unless the creditor process is served at a time and in a manner affording the bank a reasonable opportunity to act on it before the bank accepts the payment order.

(c) If a beneficiary's bank has received a payment order for payment to the beneficiary's account in the bank, the following rules apply:

(1) The bank may credit the beneficiary's account. The amount credited may be set off against an obligation owed by the beneficiary to the bank or may be applied to satisfy creditor process served on the bank with respect to the account.

(2) The bank may credit the beneficiary's account and allow withdrawal of the amount credited unless creditor process with respect to the account is served at a time and in a manner affording the bank a reasonable opportunity to act to prevent withdrawal.

(3) If creditor process with respect to the beneficiary's account has been served and the bank has had a reasonable opportunity to act on it, the bank may not reject the payment order except for a reason unrelated to the service of process.

(d) Creditor process with respect to a payment by the originator to the beneficiary pursuant to a funds transfer may be served only on the beneficiary's bank with respect to the debt owed by that bank to the beneficiary. Any other bank served with the creditor process is not obliged to act with respect to the process.

§ 4A–503.   Injunction or Restraining Order with Respect to Funds Transfer.

For proper cause and in compliance with applicable law, a court may restrain (i) a person from issuing a payment order to initiate a funds transfer, (ii) an originator's bank from executing the payment order of the originator, or (iii) the beneficiary's bank from releasing funds to the beneficiary or the beneficiary from withdrawing the funds. A court may not otherwise restrain a person from issuing a payment order, paying or receiving payment of a payment order, or otherwise acting with respect to a funds transfer.

§ 4A–504.   Order in Which Items and Payment Orders May Be Charged to Account; Order of Withdrawals from Account.

(a) If a receiving bank has received more than one payment order of the sender or one or more payment orders and other items that are payable from the sender's account, the bank may charge the sender's account with respect to the various orders and items in any sequence.

(b) In determining whether a credit to an account has been withdrawn by the holder of the account or applied to a debt of the holder of the account, credits first made to the account are first withdrawn or applied.

§ 4A–505.   Preclusion of Objection to Debit of Customer's Account.

If a receiving bank has received payment from its customer with respect to a payment order issued in the name of the customer as sender and accepted by the bank, and the customer received notification reasonably identifying the order, the customer is precluded from asserting that the bank is not entitled to retain the payment unless the customer notifies the bank of the customer's objection to the payment within one year after the notification was received by the customer.

§ 4A–506.   Rate of Interest.

(a) If, under this Article, a receiving bank is obliged to pay interest with respect to a payment order issued to the bank, the amount payable may be determined (i) by agreement of the sender and receiving bank, or (ii) by a funds-transfer system rule if the payment order is transmitted through a funds-transfer system.

(b) If the amount of interest is not determined by an agreement or rule as stated in subsection (a), the amount is calculated by multiplying the applicable Federal Funds rate by the amount on which interest is payable, and then multiplying the product by the number of days for which interest is payable. The applicable Federal Funds rate is the average of the Federal Funds rates published by the Federal Reserve Bank of New York for each of the days for which interest is payable divided by 360. The Federal Funds rate for any day on which a published rate is not available is the same as the published rate for the next preceding day for which there is a published rate. If a receiving bank that accepted a payment order is required to refund payment to the sender of the order because the funds transfer was not completed, but the failure to complete was not due to any fault by the bank, the interest payable is reduced by a percentage equal to the reserve requirement on deposits of the receiving bank.

§ 4A–507.   Choice of Law.

(a) The following rules apply unless the affected parties otherwise agree or subsection (c) applies:

(1) The rights and obligations between the sender of a payment order and the receiving bank are governed by the law of the jurisdiction in which the receiving bank is located.

(2) The rights and obligations between the beneficiary's bank and the beneficiary are governed by the law of the jurisdiction in which the beneficiary's bank is located.

(3) The issue of when payment is made pursuant to a funds transfer by the originator to the beneficiary is governed by the law of the jurisdiction in which the beneficiary's bank is located.

(b) If the parties described in each paragraph of subsection (a) have made an agreement selecting the law of a particular jurisdiction to govern rights and obligations between each other, the law of that jurisdiction governs those rights and obligations, whether or not the payment order or the funds transfer bears a reasonable relation to that jurisdiction.

(c) A funds-transfer system rule may select the law of a particular jurisdiction to govern (i) rights and obligations between participating banks with respect to payment orders transmitted or processed through the system, or (ii) the rights and obligations of some or all parties to a funds transfer any part of which is carried out by means of the system. A choice of law made pursuant to clause (i) is binding on participating banks. A choice of law made pursuant to clause (ii) is binding on the originator, other sender, or a receiving bank having notice that the funds-transfer system might be used in the funds transfer and of the choice of law by the system when the originator, other sender, or receiving bank issued or accepted a payment order. The beneficiary of a funds transfer is bound by the choice of law if, when the funds transfer is initiated, the beneficiary has notice that the funds-transfer system might be used in the funds transfer and of the choice of law by the system. The law of a jurisdiction selected pursuant to this subsection may govern, whether or not that law bears a reasonable relation to the matter in issue.

(d) In the event of inconsistency between an agreement under subsection (b) and a choice-of-law rule under subsection (c), the agreement under subsection (b) prevails.

(e) If a funds transfer is made by use of more than one funds-transfer system and there is inconsistency between choice-of-law rules of the systems, the matter in issue is governed by the law of the selected jurisdiction that has the most significant relationship to the matter in issue.

* * * *

Revised Article 9
SECURED TRANSACTIONS

Part 1 General Provisions

[Subpart 1. Short Title, Definitions, and General Concepts]

§ 9–101. Short Title.

This article may be cited as Uniform Commercial Code—Secured Transactions.

§ 9–102. Definitions and Index of Definitions.

(a) In this article:

(1) "Accession" means goods that are physically united with other goods in such a manner that the identity of the original goods is not lost.

(2) "Account", except as used in "account for", means a right to payment of a monetary obligation, whether or not earned by performance, (i) for property that has been or is to be sold, leased, licensed, assigned, or otherwise disposed of, (ii) for services rendered or to be rendered, (iii) for a policy of insurance issued or to be issued, (iv) for a secondary obligation incurred or to be incurred, (v) for energy provided or to be provided, (vi) for the use or hire of a vessel under a charter or other contract, (vii) arising out of the use of a credit or charge card or information contained on or for use with the card, or (viii) as winnings in a lottery or other game of chance operated or sponsored by a State, governmental unit of a State, or person licensed or authorized to operate the game by a State or governmental unit of a State. The term includes health-care insurance receivables. The term does not include (i) rights to payment evidenced by chattel paper or an instrument, (ii) commercial tort claims, (iii) deposit accounts, (iv) investment property, (v) letter-of-credit rights or letters of credit, or (vi) rights to payment for money or funds advanced or sold, other than rights arising out of the use of a credit or charge card or information contained on or for use with the card.

(3) "Account debtor" means a person obligated on an account, chattel paper, or general intangible. The term does not include persons obligated to pay a negotiable instrument, even if the instrument constitutes part of chattel paper.

(4) "Accounting", except as used in "accounting for", means a record:

(A) authenticated by a secured party;

(B) indicating the aggregate unpaid secured obligations as of a date not more than 35 days earlier or 35 days later than the date of the record; and

(C) identifying the components of the obligations in reasonable detail.

(5) "Agricultural lien" means an interest, other than a security interest, in farm products:

(A) which secures payment or performance of an obligation for:

(i) goods or services furnished in connection with a debtor's farming operation; or

(ii) rent on real property leased by a debtor in connection with its farming operation;

(B) which is created by statute in favor of a person that:

(i) in the ordinary course of its business furnished goods or services to a debtor in connection with a debtor's farming operation; or

(ii) leased real property to a debtor in connection with the debtor's farming operation; and

(C) whose effectiveness does not depend on the person's possession of the personal property.

(6) "As-extracted collateral" means:

(A) oil, gas, or other minerals that are subject to a security interest that:

(i) is created by a debtor having an interest in the minerals before extraction; and

(ii) attaches to the minerals as extracted; or

(B) accounts arising out of the sale at the wellhead or minehead of oil, gas, or other minerals in which the debtor had an interest before extraction.

(7) "Authenticate" means:

(A) to sign; or

(B) to execute or otherwise adopt a symbol, or encrypt or similarly process a record in whole or in part, with the present intent of the authenticating person to identify the person and adopt or accept a record.

(8) "Bank" means an organization that is engaged in the business of banking. The term includes savings banks, savings and loan associations, credit unions, and trust companies.

(9) "Cash proceeds" means proceeds that are money, checks, deposit accounts, or the like.

(10) "Certificate of title" means a certificate of title with respect to which a statute provides for the security interest in question to be indicated on the certificate as a condition or result of the security interest's obtaining priority over the rights of a lien creditor with respect to the collateral.

(11) "Chattel paper" means a record or records that evidence both a monetary obligation and a security interest in specific goods, a security interest in specific goods and software used in the goods, a security interest in specific goods and license of software used in the goods, a lease of specific goods, or a lease of specific goods and license of software used in the goods. In this paragraph, "monetary obligation" means a monetary obligation secured by the goods or owed under a lease of the goods and includes a monetary obligation with respect to software used in the goods. The term does not include (i) charters or other contracts involving the use or hire of a vessel or (ii) records that evidence a right to payment arising out of the use of a credit or charge card or information contained on or for use with the card. If a transaction is evidenced by records that include an instrument or series of instruments, the group of records taken together constitutes chattel paper.

(12) "Collateral" means the property subject to a security interest or agricultural lien. The term includes:

(A) proceeds to which a security interest attaches;

(B) accounts, chattel paper, payment intangibles, and promissory notes that have been sold; and

(C) goods that are the subject of a consignment.

(13) "Commercial tort claim" means a claim arising in tort with respect to which:

(A) the claimant is an organization; or

(B) the claimant is an individual and the claim:

(i) arose in the course of the claimant's business or profession; and

(ii) does not include damages arising out of personal injury to or the death of an individual.

(14) "Commodity account" means an account maintained by a commodity intermediary in which a commodity contract is carried for a commodity customer.

(15) "Commodity contract" means a commodity futures contract, an option on a commodity futures contract, a commodity option, or another contract if the contract or option is:

(A) traded on or subject to the rules of a board of trade that has been designated as a contract market for such a contract pursuant to federal commodities laws; or

(B) traded on a foreign commodity board of trade, exchange, or market, and is carried on the books of a commodity intermediary for a commodity customer.

(16) "Commodity customer" means a person for which a commodity intermediary carries a commodity contract on its books.

(17) "Commodity intermediary" means a person that:

(A) is registered as a futures commission merchant under federal commodities law; or

(B) in the ordinary course of its business provides clearance or settlement services for a board of trade that has been designated as a contract market pursuant to federal commodities law.

(18) "Communicate" means:

(A) to send a written or other tangible record;

(B) to transmit a record by any means agreed upon by the persons sending and receiving the record; or

(C) in the case of transmission of a record to or by a filing office, to transmit a record by any means prescribed by filing-office rule.

(19) "Consignee" means a merchant to which goods are delivered in a consignment.

(20) "Consignment" means a transaction, regardless of its form, in which a person delivers goods to a merchant for the purpose of sale and:

(A) the merchant:

(i) deals in goods of that kind under a name other than the name of the person making delivery;

(ii) is not an auctioneer; and

(iii) is not generally known by its creditors to be substantially engaged in selling the goods of others;

(B) with respect to each delivery, the aggregate value of the goods is $1,000 or more at the time of delivery;

(C) the goods are not consumer goods immediately before delivery; and

(D) the transaction does not create a security interest that secures an obligation.

(21) "Consignor" means a person that delivers goods to a consignee in a consignment.

(22) "Consumer debtor" means a debtor in a consumer transaction.

(23) "Consumer goods" means goods that are used or bought for use primarily for personal, family, or household purposes.

(24) "Consumer-goods transaction" means a consumer transaction in which:

(A) an individual incurs an obligation primarily for personal, family, or household purposes; and

(B) a security interest in consumer goods secures the obligation.

(25) "Consumer obligor" means an obligor who is an individual and who incurred the obligation as part of a transaction

entered into primarily for personal, family, or household purposes.

(26) "Consumer transaction" means a transaction in which (i) an individual incurs an obligation primarily for personal, family, or household purposes, (ii) a security interest secures the obligation, and (iii) the collateral is held or acquired primarily for personal, family, or household purposes. The term includes consumer-goods transactions.

(27) "Continuation statement" means an amendment of a financing statement which:

(A) identifies, by its file number, the initial financing statement to which it relates; and

(B) indicates that it is a continuation statement for, or that it is filed to continue the effectiveness of, the identified financing statement.

(28) "Debtor" means:

(A) a person having an interest, other than a security interest or other lien, in the collateral, whether or not the person is an obligor;

(B) a seller of accounts, chattel paper, payment intangibles, or promissory notes; or

(C) a consignee.

(29) "Deposit account" means a demand, time, savings, passbook, or similar account maintained with a bank. The term does not include investment property or accounts evidenced by an instrument.

(30) "Document" means a document of title or a receipt of the type described in Section 7–201(2).

(31) "Electronic chattel paper" means chattel paper evidenced by a record or records consisting of information stored in an electronic medium.

(32) "Encumbrance" means a right, other than an ownership interest, in real property. The term includes mortgages and other liens on real property.

(33) "Equipment" means goods other than inventory, farm products, or consumer goods.

(34) "Farm products" means goods, other than standing timber, with respect to which the debtor is engaged in a farming operation and which are:

(A) crops grown, growing, or to be grown, including:

(i) crops produced on trees, vines, and bushes; and

(ii) aquatic goods produced in aquacultural operations;

(B) livestock, born or unborn, including aquatic goods produced in aquacultural operations;

(C) supplies used or produced in a farming operation; or

(D) products of crops or livestock in their unmanufactured states.

(35) "Farming operation" means raising, cultivating, propagating, fattening, grazing, or any other farming, livestock, or aquacultural operation.

(36) "File number" means the number assigned to an initial financing statement pursuant to Section 9–519(a).

(37) "Filing office" means an office designated in Section 9–501 as the place to file a financing statement.

(38) "Filing-office rule" means a rule adopted pursuant to Section 9–526.

(39) "Financing statement" means a record or records composed of an initial financing statement and any filed record relating to the initial financing statement.

(40) "Fixture filing" means the filing of a financing statement covering goods that are or are to become fixtures and satisfying Section 9–502(a) and (b). The term includes the filing of a financing statement covering goods of a transmitting utility which are or are to become fixtures.

(41) "Fixtures" means goods that have become so related to particular real property that an interest in them arises under real property law.

(42) "General intangible" means any personal property, including things in action, other than accounts, chattel paper, commercial tort claims, deposit accounts, documents, goods, instruments, investment property, letter-of-credit rights, letters of credit, money, and oil, gas, or other minerals before extraction. The term includes payment intangibles and software.

(43) "Good faith" means honesty in fact and the observance of reasonable commercial standards of fair dealing.

(44) "Goods" means all things that are movable when a security interest attaches. The term includes (i) fixtures, (ii) standing timber that is to be cut and removed under a conveyance or contract for sale, (iii) the unborn young of animals, (iv) crops grown, growing, or to be grown, even if the crops are produced on trees, vines, or bushes, and (v) manufactured homes. The term also includes a computer program embedded in goods and any supporting information provided in connection with a transaction relating to the program if (i) the program is associated with the goods in such a manner that it customarily is considered part of the goods, or (ii) by becoming the owner of the goods, a person acquires a right to use the program in connection with the goods. The term does not include a computer program embedded in goods that consist solely of the medium in which the program is embedded. The term also does not include accounts, chattel paper, commercial tort claims, deposit accounts, documents, general intangibles, instruments, investment property, letter-of-credit rights, letters of credit, money, or oil, gas, or other minerals before extraction.

(45) "Governmental unit" means a subdivision, agency, department, county, parish, municipality, or other unit of the government of the United States, a State, or a foreign country. The term includes an organization having a separate corporate existence if the organization is eligible to issue debt on which interest is exempt from income taxation under the laws of the United States.

(46) "Health-care-insurance receivable" means an interest in or claim under a policy of insurance which is a right to payment of a monetary obligation for health-care goods or services provided.

(47) "Instrument" means a negotiable instrument or any other writing that evidences a right to the payment of a monetary obligation, is not itself a security agreement or lease, and is of a type that in ordinary course of business is transferred by delivery with any necessary indorsement or assignment. The term does not include (i) investment property, (ii) letters of credit, or (iii) writings that evidence a right to payment arising out of the use of a credit or charge card or information contained on or for use with the card.

(48) "Inventory" means goods, other than farm products, which:

(A) are leased by a person as lessor;

(B) are held by a person for sale or lease or to be furnished under a contract of service;

(C) are furnished by a person under a contract of service; or

(D) consist of raw materials, work in process, or materials used or consumed in a business.

(49) "Investment property" means a security, whether certificated or uncertificated, security entitlement, securities account, commodity contract, or commodity account.

(50) "Jurisdiction of organization", with respect to a registered organization, means the jurisdiction under whose law the organization is organized.

(51) "Letter-of-credit right" means a right to payment or performance under a letter of credit, whether or not the beneficiary has demanded or is at the time entitled to demand payment or performance. The term does not include the right of a beneficiary to demand payment or performance under a letter of credit.

(52) "Lien creditor" means:

(A) a creditor that has acquired a lien on the property involved by attachment, levy, or the like;

(B) an assignee for benefit of creditors from the time of assignment;

(C) a trustee in bankruptcy from the date of the filing of the petition; or

(D) a receiver in equity from the time of appointment.

(53) "Manufactured home" means a structure, transportable in one or more sections, which, in the traveling mode, is eight body feet or more in width or 40 body feet or more in length, or, when erected on site, is 320 or more square feet, and which is built on a permanent chassis and designed to be used as a dwelling with or without a permanent foundation when connected to the required utilities, and includes the plumbing, heating, air-conditioning, and electrical systems contained therein. The term includes any structure that meets all of the requirements of this paragraph except the size requirements and with respect to which the manufacturer voluntarily files a certification required by the United States Secretary of Housing and Urban Development and complies with the standards established under Title 42 of the United States Code.

(54) "Manufactured-home transaction" means a secured transaction:

(A) that creates a purchase-money security interest in a manufactured home, other than a manufactured home held as inventory; or

(B) in which a manufactured home, other than a manufactured home held as inventory, is the primary collateral.

(55) "Mortgage" means a consensual interest in real property, including fixtures, which secures payment or performance of an obligation.

(56) "New debtor" means a person that becomes bound as debtor under Section 9–203(d) by a security agreement previously entered into by another person.

(57) "New value" means (i) money, (ii) money's worth in property, services, or new credit, or (iii) release by a transferee of an interest in property previously transferred to the transferee. The term does not include an obligation substituted for another obligation.

(58) "Noncash proceeds" means proceeds other than cash proceeds.

(59) "Obligor" means a person that, with respect to an obligation secured by a security interest in or an agricultural lien on the collateral, (i) owes payment or other performance of the obligation, (ii) has provided property other than the collateral to secure payment or other performance of the obligation, or (iii) is otherwise accountable in whole or in part for payment or other performance of the obligation. The term does not include issuers or nominated persons under a letter of credit.

(60) "Original debtor", except as used in Section 9–310(c), means a person that, as debtor, entered into a security agreement to which a new debtor has become bound under Section 9–203(d).

(61) "Payment intangible" means a general intangible under which the account debtor's principal obligation is a monetary obligation.

(62) "Person related to", with respect to an individual, means:

(A) the spouse of the individual;

(B) a brother, brother-in-law, sister, or sister-in-law of the individual;

(C) an ancestor or lineal descendant of the individual or the individual's spouse; or

(D) any other relative, by blood or marriage, of the individual or the individual's spouse who shares the same home with the individual.

(63) "Person related to", with respect to an organization, means:

(A) a person directly or indirectly controlling, controlled by, or under common control with the organization;

(B) an officer or director of, or a person performing similar functions with respect to, the organization;

(C) an officer or director of, or a person performing similar functions with respect to, a person described in subparagraph (A);

(D) the spouse of an individual described in subparagraph (A), (B), or (C); or

(E) an individual who is related by blood or marriage to an individual described in subparagraph (A), (B), (C), or (D) and shares the same home with the individual.

(64) "Proceeds", except as used in Section 9–609(b), means the following property:

(A) whatever is acquired upon the sale, lease, license, exchange, or other disposition of collateral;

(B) whatever is collected on, or distributed on account of, collateral;

(C) rights arising out of collateral;

(D) to the extent of the value of collateral, claims arising out of the loss, nonconformity, or interference with the use of, defects or infringement of rights in, or damage to, the collateral; or

(E) to the extent of the value of collateral and to the extent payable to the debtor or the secured party, insurance payable by reason of the loss or nonconformity of, defects or infringement of rights in, or damage to, the collateral.

(65) "Promissory note" means an instrument that evidences a promise to pay a monetary obligation, does not evidence an order to pay, and does not contain an acknowledgment by a bank that the bank has received for deposit a sum of money or funds.

(66) "Proposal" means a record authenticated by a secured party which includes the terms on which the secured party is willing to accept collateral in full or partial satisfaction of the obligation it secures pursuant to Sections 9–620, 9–621, and 9–622.

(67) "Public-finance transaction" means a secured transaction in connection with which:

(A) debt securities are issued;

(B) all or a portion of the securities issued have an initial stated maturity of at least 20 years; and

(C) the debtor, obligor, secured party, account debtor or other person obligated on collateral, assignor or assignee of a secured obligation, or assignor or assignee of a security interest is a State or a governmental unit of a State.

(68) "Pursuant to commitment", with respect to an advance made or other value given by a secured party, means pursuant to the secured party's obligation, whether or not a subsequent event of default or other event not within the secured party's control has relieved or may relieve the secured party from its obligation.

(69) "Record", except as used in "for record", "of record", "record or legal title", and "record owner", means information that is inscribed on a tangible medium or which is stored in an electronic or other medium and is retrievable in perceivable form.

(70) "Registered organization" means an organization organized solely under the law of a single State or the United

States and as to which the State or the United States must maintain a public record showing the organization to have been organized.

(71) "Secondary obligor" means an obligor to the extent that:

(A) the obligor's obligation is secondary; or

(B) the obligor has a right of recourse with respect to an obligation secured by collateral against the debtor, another obligor, or property of either.

(72) "Secured party" means:

(A) a person in whose favor a security interest is created or provided for under a security agreement, whether or not any obligation to be secured is outstanding;

(B) a person that holds an agricultural lien;

(C) a consignor;

(D) a person to which accounts, chattel paper, payment intangibles, or promissory notes have been sold;

(E) a trustee, indenture trustee, agent, collateral agent, or other representative in whose favor a security interest or agricultural lien is created or provided for; or

(F) a person that holds a security interest arising under Section 2–401, 2–505, 2–711(3), 2A–508(5), 4–210, or 5–118.

(73) "Security agreement" means an agreement that creates or provides for a security interest.

(74) "Send", in connection with a record or notification, means:

(A) to deposit in the mail, deliver for transmission, or transmit by any other usual means of communication, with postage or cost of transmission provided for, addressed to any address reasonable under the circumstances; or

(B) to cause the record or notification to be received within the time that it would have been received if properly sent under subparagraph (A).

(75) "Software" means a computer program and any supporting information provided in connection with a transaction relating to the program. The term does not include a computer program that is included in the definition of goods.

(76) "State" means a State of the United States, the District of Columbia, Puerto Rico, the United States Virgin Islands, or any territory or insular possession subject to the jurisdiction of the United States.

(77) "Supporting obligation" means a letter-of-credit right or secondary obligation that supports the payment or performance of an account, chattel paper, a document, a general intangible, an instrument, or investment property.

(78) "Tangible chattel paper" means chattel paper evidenced by a record or records consisting of information that is inscribed on a tangible medium.

(79) "Termination statement" means an amendment of a financing statement which:

(A) identifies, by its file number, the initial financing statement to which it relates; and

(B) indicates either that it is a termination statement or that the identified financing statement is no longer effective.

(80) "Transmitting utility" means a person primarily engaged in the business of:

(A) operating a railroad, subway, street railway, or trolley bus;

(B) transmitting communications electrically, electromagnetically, or by light;

(C) transmitting goods by pipeline or sewer; or

(D) transmitting or producing and transmitting electricity, steam, gas, or water.

(b) The following definitions in other articles apply to this article:

"Applicant."	Section 5–102
"Beneficiary."	Section 5–102
"Broker."	Section 8–102
"Certificated security."	Section 8–102
"Check."	Section 3–104
"Clearing corporation."	Section 8–102
"Contract for sale."	Section 2–106
"Customer."	Section 4–104
"Entitlement holder."	Section 8–102
"Financial asset."	Section 8–102
"Holder in due course."	Section 3–302
"Issuer" (with respect to a letter of credit or letter-of-credit right).	Section 5–102
"Issuer" (with respect to a security).	Section 8–201
"Lease."	Section 2A–103
"Lease agreement."	Section 2A–103
"Lease contract."	Section 2A–103
"Leasehold interest."	Section 2A–103
"Lessee."	Section 2A–103
"Lessee in ordinary course of business."	Section 2A–103
"Lessor."	Section 2A–103
"Lessor's residual interest."	Section 2A–103
"Letter of credit."	Section 5–102
"Merchant."	Section 2–104
"Negotiable instrument."	Section 3–104
"Nominated person."	Section 5–102
"Note."	Section 3–104
"Proceeds of a letter of credit."	Section 5–114
"Prove."	Section 3–103
"Sale."	Section 2–106
"Securities account."	Section 8–501
"Securities intermediary."	Section 8–102
"Security."	Section 8–102
"Security certificate."	Section 8–102
"Security entitlement."	Section 8–102
"Uncertificated security."	Section 8–102

(c) Article 1 contains general definitions and principles of construction and interpretation applicable throughout this article.
Amended in 1999 and 2000.

§ 9–103.   Purchase-Money Security Interest; Application of Payments; Burden of Establishing.

(a) In this section:

(1) "purchase-money collateral" means goods or software that secures a purchase-money obligation incurred with respect to that collateral; and

(2) "purchase-money obligation" means an obligation of an obligor incurred as all or part of the price of the collateral or for value given to enable the debtor to acquire rights in or the use of the collateral if the value is in fact so used.

(b) A security interest in goods is a purchase-money security interest:

(1) to the extent that the goods are purchase-money collateral with respect to that security interest;

(2) if the security interest is in inventory that is or was purchase-money collateral, also to the extent that the security interest secures a purchase-money obligation incurred with respect to other inventory in which the secured party holds or held a purchase-money security interest; and

(3) also to the extent that the security interest secures a purchase-money obligation incurred with respect to software in which the secured party holds or held a purchase-money security interest.

(c) A security interest in software is a purchase-money security interest to the extent that the security interest also secures a purchase-money obligation incurred with respect to goods in which the secured party holds or held a purchase-money security interest if:

(1) the debtor acquired its interest in the software in an integrated transaction in which it acquired an interest in the goods; and

(2) the debtor acquired its interest in the software for the principal purpose of using the software in the goods.

(d) The security interest of a consignor in goods that are the subject of a consignment is a purchase-money security interest in inventory.

(e) In a transaction other than a consumer-goods transaction, if the extent to which a security interest is a purchase-money security interest depends on the application of a payment to a particular obligation, the payment must be applied:

(1) in accordance with any reasonable method of application to which the parties agree;

(2) in the absence of the parties' agreement to a reasonable method, in accordance with any intention of the obligor manifested at or before the time of payment; or

(3) in the absence of an agreement to a reasonable method and a timely manifestation of the obligor's intention, in the following order:

(A) to obligations that are not secured; and

(B) if more than one obligation is secured, to obligations secured by purchase-money security interests in the order in which those obligations were incurred.

(f) In a transaction other than a consumer-goods transaction, a purchase-money security interest does not lose its status as such, even if:

(1) the purchase-money collateral also secures an obligation that is not a purchase-money obligation;

(2) collateral that is not purchase-money collateral also secures the purchase-money obligation; or

(3) the purchase-money obligation has been renewed, refinanced, consolidated, or restructured.

(g) In a transaction other than a consumer-goods transaction, a secured party claiming a purchase-money security interest has the burden of establishing the extent to which the security interest is a purchase-money security interest.

(h) The limitation of the rules in subsections (e), (f), and (g) to transactions other than consumer-goods transactions is intended to leave to the court the determination of the proper rules in consumer-goods transactions. The court may not infer from that limitation the nature of the proper rule in consumer-goods transactions and may continue to apply established approaches.

§ 9–104.   Control of Deposit Account.

(a) A secured party has control of a deposit account if:

(1) the secured party is the bank with which the deposit account is maintained;

(2) the debtor, secured party, and bank have agreed in an authenticated record that the bank will comply with instructions originated by the secured party directing disposition of the funds in the deposit account without further consent by the debtor; or

(3) the secured party becomes the bank's customer with respect to the deposit account.

(b) A secured party that has satisfied subsection (a) has control, even if the debtor retains the right to direct the disposition of funds from the deposit account.

§ 9–105.   Control of Electronic Chattel Paper.

A secured party has control of electronic chattel paper if the record or records comprising the chattel paper are created, stored, and assigned in such a manner that:

(1) a single authoritative copy of the record or records exists which is unique, identifiable and, except as otherwise provided in paragraphs (4), (5), and (6), unalterable;

(2) the authoritative copy identifies the secured party as the assignee of the record or records;

(3) the authoritative copy is communicated to and maintained by the secured party or its designated custodian;

(4) copies or revisions that add or change an identified assignee of the authoritative copy can be made only with the participation of the secured party;

(5) each copy of the authoritative copy and any copy of a copy is readily identifiable as a copy that is not the authoritative copy; and

(6) any revision of the authoritative copy is readily identifiable as an authorized or unauthorized revision.

§ 9–106.   Control of Investment Property.

(a) A person has control of a certificated security, uncertificated security, or security entitlement as provided in Section 8–106.

(b) A secured party has control of a commodity contract if:

(1) the secured party is the commodity intermediary with which the commodity contract is carried; or

(2) the commodity customer, secured party, and commodity intermediary have agreed that the commodity intermediary will apply any value distributed on account of the commodity contract as directed by the secured party without further consent by the commodity customer.

(c) A secured party having control of all security entitlements or commodity contracts carried in a securities account or commodity account has control over the securities account or commodity account.

§ 9–107.   Control of Letter-of-Credit Right.

A secured party has control of a letter-of-credit right to the extent of any right to payment or performance by the issuer or any nominated person if the issuer or nominated person has consented to an assignment of proceeds of the letter of credit under Section 5–114(c) or otherwise applicable law or practice.

§ 9–108.   Sufficiency of Description.

(a) Except as otherwise provided in subsections (c), (d), and (e), a description of personal or real property is sufficient, whether or not it is specific, if it reasonably identifies what is described.

(b) Except as otherwise provided in subsection (d), a description of collateral reasonably identifies the collateral if it identifies the collateral by:

(1) specific listing;

(2) category;

(3) except as otherwise provided in subsection (e), a type of collateral defined in [the Uniform Commercial Code];

(4) quantity;

(5) computational or allocational formula or procedure; or

(6) except as otherwise provided in subsection (c), any other method, if the identity of the collateral is objectively determinable.

(c) A description of collateral as "all the debtor's assets" or "all the debtor's personal property" or using words of similar import does not reasonably identify the collateral.

(d) Except as otherwise provided in subsection (e), a description of a security entitlement, securities account, or commodity account is sufficient if it describes:

(1) the collateral by those terms or as investment property; or

(2) the underlying financial asset or commodity contract.

(e) A description only by type of collateral defined in [the Uniform Commercial Code] is an insufficient description of:

(1) a commercial tort claim; or

(2) in a consumer transaction, consumer goods, a security entitlement, a securities account, or a commodity account.

[Subpart 2. Applicability of Article]

§ 9–109.   Scope.

(a) Except as otherwise provided in subsections (c) and (d), this article applies to:

(1) a transaction, regardless of its form, that creates a security interest in personal property or fixtures by contract;

(2) an agricultural lien;

(3) a sale of accounts, chattel paper, payment intangibles, or promissory notes;

(4) a consignment;

(5) a security interest arising under Section 2–401, 2–505, 2–711(3), or 2A–508(5), as provided in Section 9–110; and

(6) a security interest arising under Section 4–210 or 5–118.

(b) The application of this article to a security interest in a secured obligation is not affected by the fact that the obligation is itself secured by a transaction or interest to which this article does not apply.

(c) This article does not apply to the extent that:

(1) a statute, regulation, or treaty of the United States preempts this article;

(2) another statute of this State expressly governs the creation, perfection, priority, or enforcement of a security interest created by this State or a governmental unit of this State;

(3) a statute of another State, a foreign country, or a governmental unit of another State or a foreign country, other than a statute generally applicable to security interests, expressly governs creation, perfection, priority, or enforcement of a security interest created by the State, country, or governmental unit; or

(4) the rights of a transferee beneficiary or nominated person under a letter of credit are independent and superior under Section 5–114.

(d) This article does not apply to:

(1) a landlord's lien, other than an agricultural lien;

(2) a lien, other than an agricultural lien, given by statute or other rule of law for services or materials, but Section 9–333 applies with respect to priority of the lien;

(3) an assignment of a claim for wages, salary, or other compensation of an employee;

(4) a sale of accounts, chattel paper, payment intangibles, or promissory notes as part of a sale of the business out of which they arose;

(5) an assignment of accounts, chattel paper, payment intangibles, or promissory notes which is for the purpose of collection only;

(6) an assignment of a right to payment under a contract to an assignee that is also obligated to perform under the contract;

(7) an assignment of a single account, payment intangible, or promissory note to an assignee in full or partial satisfaction of a preexisting indebtedness;

(8) a transfer of an interest in or an assignment of a claim under a policy of insurance, other than an assignment by or to a health-care provider of a health-care-insurance receivable and any subsequent assignment of the right to payment, but Sections 9–315 and 9–322 apply with respect to proceeds and priorities in proceeds;

(9) an assignment of a right represented by a judgment, other than a judgment taken on a right to payment that was collateral;

(10) a right of recoupment or set-off, but:

(A) Section 9–340 applies with respect to the effectiveness of rights of recoupment or set-off against deposit accounts; and

(B) Section 9–404 applies with respect to defenses or claims of an account debtor;

(11) the creation or transfer of an interest in or lien on real property, including a lease or rents thereunder, except to the extent that provision is made for:

(A) liens on real property in Sections 9–203 and 9–308;

(B) fixtures in Section 9–334;

(C) fixture filings in Sections 9–501, 9–502, 9–512, 9–516, and 9–519; and

(D) security agreements covering personal and real property in Section 9–604;

(12) an assignment of a claim arising in tort, other than a commercial tort claim, but Sections 9–315 and 9–322 apply with respect to proceeds and priorities in proceeds; or

(13) an assignment of a deposit account in a consumer transaction, but Sections 9–315 and 9–322 apply with respect to proceeds and priorities in proceeds.

§ 9–110.   Security Interests Arising under Article 2 or 2A.

A security interest arising under Section 2–401, 2–505, 2–711(3), or 2A–508(5) is subject to this article. However, until the debtor obtains possession of the goods:

(1) the security interest is enforceable, even if Section 9–203(b)(3) has not been satisfied;

(2) filing is not required to perfect the security interest;

(3) the rights of the secured party after default by the debtor are governed by Article 2 or 2A; and

(4) the security interest has priority over a conflicting security interest created by the debtor.

Part 2   Effectiveness of Security Agreement; Attachment of Security Interest; Rights of Parties to Security Agreement

[Subpart 1. Effectiveness and Attachment]

§ 9–201.   General Effectiveness of Security Agreement.

(a) Except as otherwise provided in [the Uniform Commercial Code], a security agreement is effective according to its terms between the parties, against purchasers of the collateral, and against creditors.

(b) A transaction subject to this article is subject to any applicable rule of law which establishes a different rule for consumers and [insert reference to (i) any other statute or regulation that regulates the rates, charges, agreements, and practices for loans, credit sales, or other extensions of credit and (ii) any consumer-protection statute or regulation].

(c) In case of conflict between this article and a rule of law, statute, or regulation described in subsection (b), the rule of law, statute, or regulation controls. Failure to comply with a statute or regulation described in subsection (b) has only the effect the statute or regulation specifies.

(d) This article does not:

(1) validate any rate, charge, agreement, or practice that violates a rule of law, statute, or regulation described in subsection (b); or

(2) extend the application of the rule of law, statute, or regulation to a transaction not otherwise subject to it.

§ 9–202.   Title to Collateral Immaterial.

Except as otherwise provided with respect to consignments or sales of accounts, chattel paper, payment intangibles, or promissory notes, the provisions of this article with regard to rights and obligations apply whether title to collateral is in the secured party or the debtor.

§ 9–203.   Attachment and Enforceability of Security Interest; Proceeds; Supporting Obligations; Formal Requisites.

(a) A security interest attaches to collateral when it becomes enforceable against the debtor with respect to the collateral, unless an agreement expressly postpones the time of attachment.

(b) Except as otherwise provided in subsections (c) through (i), a security interest is enforceable against the debtor and third parties with respect to the collateral only if:

(1) value has been given;

(2) the debtor has rights in the collateral or the power to transfer rights in the collateral to a secured party; and

(3) one of the following conditions is met:

(A) the debtor has authenticated a security agreement that provides a description of the collateral and, if the security interest covers timber to be cut, a description of the land concerned;

(B) the collateral is not a certificated security and is in the possession of the secured party under Section 9–313 pursuant to the debtor's security agreement;

(C) the collateral is a certificated security in registered form and the security certificate has been delivered to the secured party under Section 8–301 pursuant to the debtor's security agreement; or

(D) the collateral is deposit accounts, electronic chattel paper, investment property, or letter-of-credit rights, and the secured party has control under Section 9–104, 9–105, 9–106, or 9–107 pursuant to the debtor's security agreement.

(c) Subsection (b) is subject to Section 4–210 on the security interest of a collecting bank, Section 5–118 on the security interest of a letter-of-credit issuer or nominated person, Section 9–110 on a security interest arising under Article 2 or 2A, and Section 9–206 on security interests in investment property.

(d) A person becomes bound as debtor by a security agreement entered into by another person if, by operation of law other than this article or by contract:

(1) the security agreement becomes effective to create a security interest in the person's property; or

(2) the person becomes generally obligated for the obligations of the other person, including the obligation secured under the security agreement, and acquires or succeeds to all or substantially all of the assets of the other person.

(e) If a new debtor becomes bound as debtor by a security agreement entered into by another person:

(1) the agreement satisfies subsection (b)(3) with respect to existing or after-acquired property of the new debtor to the extent the property is described in the agreement; and

(2) another agreement is not necessary to make a security interest in the property enforceable.

(f) The attachment of a security interest in collateral gives the secured party the rights to proceeds provided by Section 9–315 and is also attachment of a security interest in a supporting obligation for the collateral.

(g) The attachment of a security interest in a right to payment or performance secured by a security interest or other lien on personal or real property is also attachment of a security interest in the security interest, mortgage, or other lien.

(h) The attachment of a security interest in a securities account is also attachment of a security interest in the security entitlements carried in the securities account.

(i) The attachment of a security interest in a commodity account is also attachment of a security interest in the commodity contracts carried in the commodity account.

§ 9–204.   After-Acquired Property; Future Advances.

(a) Except as otherwise provided in subsection (b), a security agreement may create or provide for a security interest in after-acquired collateral.

(b) A security interest does not attach under a term constituting an after-acquired property clause to:

(1) consumer goods, other than an accession when given as additional security, unless the debtor acquires rights in them within 10 days after the secured party gives value; or

(2) a commercial tort claim.

(c) A security agreement may provide that collateral secures, or that accounts, chattel paper, payment intangibles, or promissory notes are sold in connection with, future advances or other value, whether or not the advances or value are given pursuant to commitment.

§ 9–205.   Use or Disposition of Collateral Permissible.

(a) A security interest is not invalid or fraudulent against creditors solely because:

(1) the debtor has the right or ability to:

(A) use, commingle, or dispose of all or part of the collateral, including returned or repossessed goods;

(B) collect, compromise, enforce, or otherwise deal with collateral;

(C) accept the return of collateral or make repossessions; or

(D) use, commingle, or dispose of proceeds; or

(2) the secured party fails to require the debtor to account for proceeds or replace collateral.

(b) This section does not relax the requirements of possession if attachment, perfection, or enforcement of a security interest depends upon possession of the collateral by the secured party.

§ 9–206.   Security Interest Arising in Purchase or Delivery of Financial Asset.

(a) A security interest in favor of a securities intermediary attaches to a person's security entitlement if:

(1) the person buys a financial asset through the securities intermediary in a transaction in which the person is obligated to pay the purchase price to the securities intermediary at the time of the purchase; and

(2) the securities intermediary credits the financial asset to the buyer's securities account before the buyer pays the securities intermediary.

(b) The security interest described in subsection (a) secures the person's obligation to pay for the financial asset.

(c) A security interest in favor of a person that delivers a certificated security or other financial asset represented by a writing attaches to the security or other financial asset if:

(1) the security or other financial asset:

(A) in the ordinary course of business is transferred by delivery with any necessary indorsement or assignment; and

(B) is delivered under an agreement between persons in the business of dealing with such securities or financial assets; and

(2) the agreement calls for delivery against payment.

(d) The security interest described in subsection (c) secures the obligation to make payment for the delivery.

[Subpart 2. Rights and Duties]

§ 9–207.   Rights and Duties of Secured Party Having Possession or Control of Collateral.

(a) Except as otherwise provided in subsection (d), a secured party shall use reasonable care in the custody and preservation of collateral in the secured party's possession. In the case of chattel paper or an instrument, reasonable care includes taking necessary steps to preserve rights against prior parties unless otherwise agreed.

(b) Except as otherwise provided in subsection (d), if a secured party has possession of collateral:

(1) reasonable expenses, including the cost of insurance and payment of taxes or other charges, incurred in the custody, preservation, use, or operation of the collateral are chargeable to the debtor and are secured by the collateral;

(2) the risk of accidental loss or damage is on the debtor to the extent of a deficiency in any effective insurance coverage;

(3) the secured party shall keep the collateral identifiable, but fungible collateral may be commingled; and

(4) the secured party may use or operate the collateral:

(A) for the purpose of preserving the collateral or its value;

(B) as permitted by an order of a court having competent jurisdiction; or

(C) except in the case of consumer goods, in the manner and to the extent agreed by the debtor.

(c) Except as otherwise provided in subsection (d), a secured party having possession of collateral or control of collateral under Section 9–104, 9–105, 9–106, or 9–107:

(1) may hold as additional security any proceeds, except money or funds, received from the collateral;

(2) shall apply money or funds received from the collateral to reduce the secured obligation, unless remitted to the debtor; and

(3) may create a security interest in the collateral.

(d) If the secured party is a buyer of accounts, chattel paper, payment intangibles, or promissory notes or a consignor:

(1) subsection (a) does not apply unless the secured party is entitled under an agreement:

(A) to charge back uncollected collateral; or

(B) otherwise to full or limited recourse against the debtor or a secondary obligor based on the nonpayment or other default of an account debtor or other obligor on the collateral; and

(2) subsections (b) and (c) do not apply.

§ 9–208.   Additional Duties of Secured Party Having Control of Collateral.

(a) This section applies to cases in which there is no outstanding secured obligation and the secured party is not committed to make advances, incur obligations, or otherwise give value.

(b) Within 10 days after receiving an authenticated demand by the debtor:

(1) a secured party having control of a deposit account under Section 9–104(a)(2) shall send to the bank with which the deposit account is maintained an authenticated statement that releases the bank from any further obligation to comply with instructions originated by the secured party;

(2) a secured party having control of a deposit account under Section 9–104(a)(3) shall:

(A) pay the debtor the balance on deposit in the deposit account; or

(B) transfer the balance on deposit into a deposit account in the debtor's name;

(3) a secured party, other than a buyer, having control of electronic chattel paper under Section 9–105 shall:

(A) communicate the authoritative copy of the electronic chattel paper to the debtor or its designated custodian;

(B) if the debtor designates a custodian that is the designated custodian with which the authoritative copy of the electronic chattel paper is maintained for the secured party, communicate to the custodian an authenticated record releasing the designated custodian from any further obligation to comply with instructions originated by the secured party and instructing the custodian to comply with instructions originated by the debtor; and

(C) take appropriate action to enable the debtor or its designated custodian to make copies of or revisions to the authoritative copy which add or change an identified assignee of the authoritative copy without the consent of the secured party;

(4) a secured party having control of investment property under Section 8–106(d)(2) or 9–106(b) shall send to the securities intermediary or commodity intermediary with which the security entitlement or commodity contract is maintained an authenticated record that releases the securities intermediary or commodity intermediary from any further obligation to comply with entitlement orders or directions originated by the secured party; and

(5) a secured party having control of a letter-of-credit right under Section 9–107 shall send to each person having an unfulfilled obligation to pay or deliver proceeds of the letter of credit to the secured party an authenticated release from any further obligation to pay or deliver proceeds of the letter of credit to the secured party.

§ 9–209. Duties of Secured Party If Account Debtor Has Been Notified of Assignment.

(a) Except as otherwise provided in subsection (c), this section applies if:

(1) there is no outstanding secured obligation; and

(2) the secured party is not committed to make advances, incur obligations, or otherwise give value.

(b) Within 10 days after receiving an authenticated demand by the debtor, a secured party shall send to an account debtor that has received notification of an assignment to the secured party as assignee under Section 9–406(a) an authenticated record that releases the account debtor from any further obligation to the secured party.

(c) This section does not apply to an assignment constituting the sale of an account, chattel paper, or payment intangible.

§ 9–210. Request for Accounting; Request Regarding List of Collateral or Statement of Account.

(a) In this section:

(1) "Request" means a record of a type described in paragraph (2), (3), or (4).

(2) "Request for an accounting" means a record authenticated by a debtor requesting that the recipient provide an accounting of the unpaid obligations secured by collateral and reasonably identifying the transaction or relationship that is the subject of the request.

(3) "Request regarding a list of collateral" means a record authenticated by a debtor requesting that the recipient approve or correct a list of what the debtor believes to be the collateral securing an obligation and reasonably identifying the transaction or relationship that is the subject of the request.

(4) "Request regarding a statement of account" means a record authenticated by a debtor requesting that the recipient approve or correct a statement indicating what the debtor believes to be the aggregate amount of unpaid obligations secured by collateral as of a specified date and reasonably identifying the transaction or relationship that is the subject of the request.

(b) Subject to subsections (c), (d), (e), and (f), a secured party, other than a buyer of accounts, chattel paper, payment intangibles, or promissory notes or a consignor, shall comply with a request within 14 days after receipt:

(1) in the case of a request for an accounting, by authenticating and sending to the debtor an accounting; and

(2) in the case of a request regarding a list of collateral or a request regarding a statement of account, by authenticating and sending to the debtor an approval or correction.

(c) A secured party that claims a security interest in all of a particular type of collateral owned by the debtor may comply with a request regarding a list of collateral by sending to the debtor an authenticated record including a statement to that effect within 14 days after receipt.

(d) A person that receives a request regarding a list of collateral, claims no interest in the collateral when it receives the request, and claimed an interest in the collateral at an earlier time shall comply with the request within 14 days after receipt by sending to the debtor an authenticated record:

(1) disclaiming any interest in the collateral; and

(2) if known to the recipient, providing the name and mailing address of any assignee of or successor to the recipient's interest in the collateral.

(e) A person that receives a request for an accounting or a request regarding a statement of account, claims no interest in the obligations when it receives the request, and claimed an interest in the obligations at an earlier time shall comply with the request within 14 days after receipt by sending to the debtor an authenticated record:

(1) disclaiming any interest in the obligations; and

(2) if known to the recipient, providing the name and mailing address of any assignee of or successor to the recipient's interest in the obligations.

(f) A debtor is entitled without charge to one response to a request under this section during any six-month period. The secured party may require payment of a charge not exceeding $25 for each additional response.

As amended in 1999.

Part 3   Perfection and Priority

[Subpart 1. Law Governing Perfection and Priority]

§ 9–301.   Law Governing Perfection and Priority of Security Interests.

Except as otherwise provided in Sections 9–303 through 9–306, the following rules determine the law governing perfection, the effect of perfection or nonperfection, and the priority of a security interest in collateral:

(1) Except as otherwise provided in this section, while a debtor is located in a jurisdiction, the local law of that jurisdiction governs perfection, the effect of perfection or nonperfection, and the priority of a security interest in collateral.

(2) While collateral is located in a jurisdiction, the local law of that jurisdiction governs perfection, the effect of perfection or nonperfection, and the priority of a possessory security interest in that collateral.

(3) Except as otherwise provided in paragraph (4), while negotiable documents, goods, instruments, money, or tangible chattel paper is located in a jurisdiction, the local law of that jurisdiction governs:

(A) perfection of a security interest in the goods by filing a fixture filing;

(B) perfection of a security interest in timber to be cut; and

(C) the effect of perfection or nonperfection and the priority of a nonpossessory security interest in the collateral.

(4) The local law of the jurisdiction in which the wellhead or minehead is located governs perfection, the effect of perfection or nonperfection, and the priority of a security interest in as-extracted collateral.

§ 9–302.   Law Governing Perfection and Priority of Agricultural Liens.

While farm products are located in a jurisdiction, the local law of that jurisdiction governs perfection, the effect of perfection or nonperfection, and the priority of an agricultural lien on the farm products.

§ 9–303.   Law Governing Perfection and Priority of Security Interests in Goods Covered by a Certificate of Title.

(a) This section applies to goods covered by a certificate of title, even if there is no other relationship between the jurisdiction under whose certificate of title the goods are covered and the goods or the debtor.

(b) Goods become covered by a certificate of title when a valid application for the certificate of title and the applicable fee are delivered to the appropriate authority. Goods cease to be covered by a certificate of title at the earlier of the time the certificate of title ceases to be effective under the law of the issuing jurisdiction or the time the goods become covered subsequently by a certificate of title issued by another jurisdiction.

(c) The local law of the jurisdiction under whose certificate of title the goods are covered governs perfection, the effect of perfection or nonperfection, and the priority of a security interest in goods covered by a certificate of title from the time the goods become covered by the certificate of title until the goods cease to be covered by the certificate of title.

§ 9–304.   Law Governing Perfection and Priority of Security Interests in Deposit Accounts.

(a) The local law of a bank's jurisdiction governs perfection, the effect of perfection or nonperfection, and the priority of a security interest in a deposit account maintained with that bank.

(b) The following rules determine a bank's jurisdiction for purposes of this part:

(1) If an agreement between the bank and the debtor governing the deposit account expressly provides that a particular jurisdiction is the bank's jurisdiction for purposes of this part, this article, or [the Uniform Commercial Code], that jurisdiction is the bank's jurisdiction.

(2) If paragraph (1) does not apply and an agreement between the bank and its customer governing the deposit account expressly provides that the agreement is governed by the law of a particular jurisdiction, that jurisdiction is the bank's jurisdiction.

(3) If neither paragraph (1) nor paragraph (2) applies and an agreement between the bank and its customer governing the deposit account expressly provides that the deposit account is maintained at an office in a particular jurisdiction, that jurisdiction is the bank's jurisdiction.

(4) If none of the preceding paragraphs applies, the bank's jurisdiction is the jurisdiction in which the office identified in an account statement as the office serving the customer's account is located.

(5) If none of the preceding paragraphs applies, the bank's jurisdiction is the jurisdiction in which the chief executive office of the bank is located.

§ 9–305.   Law Governing Perfection and Priority of Security Interests in Investment Property.

(a) Except as otherwise provided in subsection (c), the following rules apply:

(1) While a security certificate is located in a jurisdiction, the local law of that jurisdiction governs perfection, the effect of perfection or nonperfection, and the priority of a security interest in the certificated security represented thereby.

(2) The local law of the issuer's jurisdiction as specified in Section 8–110(d) governs perfection, the effect of perfection or nonperfection, and the priority of a security interest in an uncertificated security.

(3) The local law of the securities intermediary's jurisdiction as specified in Section 8–110(e) governs perfection, the effect of perfection or nonperfection, and the priority of a security interest in a security entitlement or securities account.

(4) The local law of the commodity intermediary's jurisdiction governs perfection, the effect of perfection or nonperfection, and the priority of a security interest in a commodity contract or commodity account.

(b) The following rules determine a commodity intermediary's jurisdiction for purposes of this part:

(1) If an agreement between the commodity intermediary and commodity customer governing the commodity account expressly provides that a particular jurisdiction is the commodity intermediary's jurisdiction for purposes of this part, this article, or [the Uniform Commercial Code], that jurisdiction is the commodity intermediary's jurisdiction.

(2) If paragraph (1) does not apply and an agreement between the commodity intermediary and commodity customer governing the commodity account expressly provides that the agreement is governed by the law of a particular jurisdiction, that jurisdiction is the commodity intermediary's jurisdiction.

(3) If neither paragraph (1) nor paragraph (2) applies and an agreement between the commodity intermediary and commodity customer governing the commodity account expressly provides that the commodity account is maintained at an office in a particular jurisdiction, that jurisdiction is the commodity intermediary's jurisdiction.

(4) If none of the preceding paragraphs applies, the commodity intermediary's jurisdiction is the jurisdiction in which the office identified in an account statement as the office serving the commodity customer's account is located.

(5) If none of the preceding paragraphs applies, the commodity intermediary's jurisdiction is the jurisdiction in which the chief executive office of the commodity intermediary is located.

(c) The local law of the jurisdiction in which the debtor is located governs:

(1) perfection of a security interest in investment property by filing;

(2) automatic perfection of a security interest in investment property created by a broker or securities intermediary; and

(3) automatic perfection of a security interest in a commodity contract or commodity account created by a commodity intermediary.

§ 9–306.   Law Governing Perfection and Priority of Security Interests in Letter-of-Credit Rights.

(a) Subject to subsection (c), the local law of the issuer's jurisdiction or a nominated person's jurisdiction governs perfection, the effect of perfection or nonperfection, and the priority of a security interest in a letter-of-credit right if the issuer's jurisdiction or nominated person's jurisdiction is a State.

(b) For purposes of this part, an issuer's jurisdiction or nominated person's jurisdiction is the jurisdiction whose law governs the liability of the issuer or nominated person with respect to the letter-of-credit right as provided in Section 5–116.

(c) This section does not apply to a security interest that is perfected only under Section 9–308(d).

§ 9–307.   Location of Debtor.

(a) In this section, "place of business" means a place where a debtor conducts its affairs.

(b) Except as otherwise provided in this section, the following rules determine a debtor's location:

(1) A debtor who is an individual is located at the individual's principal residence.

(2) A debtor that is an organization and has only one place of business is located at its place of business.

(3) A debtor that is an organization and has more than one place of business is located at its chief executive office.

(c) Subsection (b) applies only if a debtor's residence, place of business, or chief executive office, as applicable, is located in a jurisdiction whose law generally requires information concerning the existence of a nonpossessory security interest to be made generally available in a filing, recording, or registration system as a condition or result of the security interest's obtaining priority over the rights of a lien creditor with respect to the collateral. If subsection (b) does not apply, the debtor is located in the District of Columbia.

(d) A person that ceases to exist, have a residence, or have a place of business continues to be located in the jurisdiction specified by subsections (b) and (c).

(e) A registered organization that is organized under the law of a State is located in that State.

(f) Except as otherwise provided in subsection (i), a registered organization that is organized under the law of the United States and a branch or agency of a bank that is not organized under the law of the United States or a State are located:

(1) in the State that the law of the United States designates, if the law designates a State of location;

(2) in the State that the registered organization, branch, or agency designates, if the law of the United States authorizes the registered organization, branch, or agency to designate its State of location; or

(3) in the District of Columbia, if neither paragraph (1) nor paragraph (2) applies.

(g) A registered organization continues to be located in the jurisdiction specified by subsection (e) or (f) notwithstanding:

(1) the suspension, revocation, forfeiture, or lapse of the registered organization's status as such in its jurisdiction of organization; or

(2) the dissolution, winding up, or cancellation of the existence of the registered organization.

(h) The United States is located in the District of Columbia.

(i) A branch or agency of a bank that is not organized under the law of the United States or a State is located in the State in which the branch or agency is licensed, if all branches and agencies of the bank are licensed in only one State.

(j) A foreign air carrier under the Federal Aviation Act of 1958, as amended, is located at the designated office of the agent upon which service of process may be made on behalf of the carrier.

(k) This section applies only for purposes of this part.

[Subpart 2. Perfection]

§ 9–308.   When Security Interest or Agricultural Lien Is Perfected; Continuity of Perfection.

(a) Except as otherwise provided in this section and Section 9–309, a security interest is perfected if it has attached and all of the applicable requirements for perfection in Sections 9–310 through 9–316 have been satisfied. A security interest is perfected when it attaches if the applicable requirements are satisfied before the security interest attaches.

(b) An agricultural lien is perfected if it has become effective and all of the applicable requirements for perfection in Section 9–310 have been satisfied. An agricultural lien is perfected when it becomes effective if the applicable requirements are satisfied before the agricultural lien becomes effective.

(c) A security interest or agricultural lien is perfected continuously if it is originally perfected by one method under this article and is later perfected by another method under this article, without an intermediate period when it was unperfected.

(d) Perfection of a security interest in collateral also perfects a security interest in a supporting obligation for the collateral.

(e) Perfection of a security interest in a right to payment or performance also perfects a security interest in a security interest, mortgage, or other lien on personal or real property securing the right.

(f) Perfection of a security interest in a securities account also perfects a security interest in the security entitlements carried in the securities account.

(g) Perfection of a security interest in a commodity account also perfects a security interest in the commodity contracts carried in the commodity account.

Legislative Note: Any statute conflicting with subsection (e) must be made expressly subject to that subsection.

§ 9–309.   Security Interest Perfected upon Attachment.

The following security interests are perfected when they attach:

(1) a purchase-money security interest in consumer goods, except as otherwise provided in Section 9–311(b) with respect to consumer goods that are subject to a statute or treaty described in Section 9–311(a);

(2) an assignment of accounts or payment intangibles which does not by itself or in conjunction with other assignments to the same assignee transfer a significant part of the assignor's outstanding accounts or payment intangibles;

(3) a sale of a payment intangible;

(4) a sale of a promissory note;

(5) a security interest created by the assignment of a health-care-insurance receivable to the provider of the health-care goods or services;

(6) a security interest arising under Section 2–401, 2–505, 2–711(3), or 2A–508(5), until the debtor obtains possession of the collateral;

(7) a security interest of a collecting bank arising under Section 4–210;

(8) a security interest of an issuer or nominated person arising under Section 5–118;

(9) a security interest arising in the delivery of a financial asset under Section 9–206(c);

(10) a security interest in investment property created by a broker or securities intermediary;

(11) a security interest in a commodity contract or a commodity account created by a commodity intermediary;

(12) an assignment for the benefit of all creditors of the transferor and subsequent transfers by the assignee thereunder; and

(13) a security interest created by an assignment of a beneficial interest in a decedent's estate; and

(14) a sale by an individual of an account that is a right to payment of winnings in a lottery or other game of chance.

§ 9–310.   When Filing Required to Perfect Security Interest or Agricultural Lien; Security Interests and Agricultural Liens to Which Filing Provisions Do Not Apply.

(a) Except as otherwise provided in subsection (b) and Section 9–312(b), a financing statement must be filed to perfect all security interests and agricultural liens.

(b) The filing of a financing statement is not necessary to perfect a security interest:

(1) that is perfected under Section 9–308(d), (e), (f), or (g);

(2) that is perfected under Section 9–309 when it attaches;

(3) in property subject to a statute, regulation, or treaty described in Section 9–311(a);

(4) in goods in possession of a bailee which is perfected under Section 9–312(d)(1) or (2);

(5) in certificated securities, documents, goods, or instruments which is perfected without filing or possession under Section 9–312(e), (f), or (g);

(6) in collateral in the secured party's possession under Section 9–313;

(7) in a certificated security which is perfected by delivery of the security certificate to the secured party under Section 9–313;

(8) in deposit accounts, electronic chattel paper, investment property, or letter-of-credit rights which is perfected by control under Section 9–314;

(9) in proceeds which is perfected under Section 9–315; or

(10) that is perfected under Section 9–316.

(c) If a secured party assigns a perfected security interest or agricultural lien, a filing under this article is not required to continue the perfected status of the security interest against creditors of and transferees from the original debtor.

§ 9–311. Perfection of Security Interests in Property Subject to Certain Statutes, Regulations, and Treaties.

(a) Except as otherwise provided in subsection (d), the filing of a financing statement is not necessary or effective to perfect a security interest in property subject to:

(1) a statute, regulation, or treaty of the United States whose requirements for a security interest's obtaining priority over the rights of a lien creditor with respect to the property preempt Section 9–310(a);

(2) [list any certificate-of-title statute covering automobiles, trailers, mobile homes, boats, farm tractors, or the like, which provides for a security interest to be indicated on the certificate as a condition or result of perfection, and any non-Uniform Commercial Code central filing statute]; or

(3) a certificate-of-title statute of another jurisdiction which provides for a security interest to be indicated on the certificate as a condition or result of the security interest's obtaining priority over the rights of a lien creditor with respect to the property.

(b) Compliance with the requirements of a statute, regulation, or treaty described in subsection (a) for obtaining priority over the rights of a lien creditor is equivalent to the filing of a financing statement under this article. Except as otherwise provided in subsection (d) and Sections 9–313 and 9–316(d) and (e) for goods covered by a certificate of title, a security interest in property subject to a statute, regulation, or treaty described in subsection (a) may be perfected only by compliance with those requirements, and a security interest so perfected remains perfected notwithstanding a change in the use or transfer of possession of the collateral.

(c) Except as otherwise provided in subsection (d) and Section 9–316(d) and (e), duration and renewal of perfection of a security interest perfected by compliance with the requirements prescribed by a statute, regulation, or treaty described in subsection (a) are governed by the statute, regulation, or treaty. In other respects, the security interest is subject to this article.

(d) During any period in which collateral subject to a statute specified in subsection (a)(2) is inventory held for sale or lease by a person or leased by that person as lessor and that person is in the business of selling goods of that kind, this section does not apply to a security interest in that collateral created by that person.

Legislative Note: This Article contemplates that perfection of a security interest in goods covered by a certificate of title occurs upon receipt by appropriate State officials of a properly tendered application for a certificate of title on which the security interest is to be indicated, without a relation back to an earlier time. States whose certificate-of-title statutes provide for perfection at a different time or contain a relation-back provision should amend the statutes accordingly.

§ 9–312. Perfection of Security Interests in Chattel Paper, Deposit Accounts, Documents, Goods Covered by Documents, Instruments, Investment Property, Letter-of-Credit Rights, and Money; Perfection by Permissive Filing; Temporary Perfection without Filing or Transfer of Possession.

(a) A security interest in chattel paper, negotiable documents, instruments, or investment property may be perfected by filing.

(b) Except as otherwise provided in Section 9–315(c) and (d) for proceeds:

(1) a security interest in a deposit account may be perfected only by control under Section 9–314;

(2) and except as otherwise provided in Section 9–308(d), a security interest in a letter-of-credit right may be perfected only by control under Section 9–314; and

(3) a security interest in money may be perfected only by the secured party's taking possession under Section 9–313.

(c) While goods are in the possession of a bailee that has issued a negotiable document covering the goods:

(1) a security interest in the goods may be perfected by perfecting a security interest in the document; and

(2) a security interest perfected in the document has priority over any security interest that becomes perfected in the goods by another method during that time.

(d) While goods are in the possession of a bailee that has issued a nonnegotiable document covering the goods, a security interest in the goods may be perfected by:

(1) issuance of a document in the name of the secured party;

(2) the bailee's receipt of notification of the secured party's interest; or

(3) filing as to the goods.

(e) A security interest in certificated securities, negotiable documents, or instruments is perfected without filing or the taking of possession for a period of 20 days from the time it attaches to the extent that it arises for new value given under an authenticated security agreement.

(f) A perfected security interest in a negotiable document or goods in possession of a bailee, other than one that has issued a negotiable document for the goods, remains perfected for 20 days without filing if the secured party makes available to the debtor the goods or documents representing the goods for the purpose of:

(1) ultimate sale or exchange; or

(2) loading, unloading, storing, shipping, transshipping, manufacturing, processing, or otherwise dealing with them in a manner preliminary to their sale or exchange.

(g) A perfected security interest in a certificated security or instrument remains perfected for 20 days without filing if the secured party delivers the security certificate or instrument to the debtor for the purpose of:

(1) ultimate sale or exchange; or

(2) presentation, collection, enforcement, renewal, or registration of transfer.

(h) After the 20-day period specified in subsection (e), (f), or (g) expires, perfection depends upon compliance with this article.

§ 9–313. When Possession by or Delivery to Secured Party Perfects Security Interest without Filing.

(a) Except as otherwise provided in subsection (b), a secured party may perfect a security interest in negotiable documents, goods, instruments, money, or tangible chattel paper by taking possession of the collateral. A secured party may perfect a security interest in certificated securities by taking delivery of the certificated securities under Section 8–301.

(b) With respect to goods covered by a certificate of title issued by this State, a secured party may perfect a security interest in the goods by taking possession of the goods only in the circumstances described in Section 9–316(d).

(c) With respect to collateral other than certificated securities and goods covered by a document, a secured party takes possession of collateral in the possession of a person other than the debtor, the secured party, or a lessee of the collateral from the debtor in the ordinary course of the debtor's business, when:

> (1) the person in possession authenticates a record acknowledging that it holds possession of the collateral for the secured party's benefit; or

> (2) the person takes possession of the collateral after having authenticated a record acknowledging that it will hold possession of collateral for the secured party's benefit.

(d) If perfection of a security interest depends upon possession of the collateral by a secured party, perfection occurs no earlier than the time the secured party takes possession and continues only while the secured party retains possession.

(e) A security interest in a certificated security in registered form is perfected by delivery when delivery of the certificated security occurs under Section 8–301 and remains perfected by delivery until the debtor obtains possession of the security certificate.

(f) A person in possession of collateral is not required to acknowledge that it holds possession for a secured party's benefit.

(g) If a person acknowledges that it holds possession for the secured party's benefit:

> (1) the acknowledgment is effective under subsection (c) or Section 8–301(a), even if the acknowledgment violates the rights of a debtor; and

> (2) unless the person otherwise agrees or law other than this article otherwise provides, the person does not owe any duty to the secured party and is not required to confirm the acknowledgment to another person.

(h) A secured party having possession of collateral does not relinquish possession by delivering the collateral to a person other than the debtor or a lessee of the collateral from the debtor in the ordinary course of the debtor's business if the person was instructed before the delivery or is instructed contemporaneously with the delivery:

> (1) to hold possession of the collateral for the secured party's benefit; or

> (2) to redeliver the collateral to the secured party.

(i) A secured party does not relinquish possession, even if a delivery under subsection (h) violates the rights of a debtor. A person to which collateral is delivered under subsection (h) does not owe any duty to the secured party and is not required to confirm the delivery to another person unless the person otherwise agrees or law other than this article otherwise provides.

§ 9–314.   Perfection by Control.

(a) A security interest in investment property, deposit accounts, letter-of-credit rights, or electronic chattel paper may be perfected by control of the collateral under Section 9–104, 9–105, 9–106, or 9–107.

(b) A security interest in deposit accounts, electronic chattel paper, or letter-of-credit rights is perfected by control under Section 9–104, 9–105, or 9–107 when the secured party obtains control and remains perfected by control only while the secured party retains control.

(c) A security interest in investment property is perfected by control under Section 9–106 from the time the secured party obtains control and remains perfected by control until:

> (1) the secured party does not have control; and

> (2) one of the following occurs:

>> (A) if the collateral is a certificated security, the debtor has or acquires possession of the security certificate;

>> (B) if the collateral is an uncertificated security, the issuer has registered or registers the debtor as the registered owner; or

>> (C) if the collateral is a security entitlement, the debtor is or becomes the entitlement holder.

§ 9–315.   Secured Party's Rights on Disposition of Collateral and in Proceeds.

(a) Except as otherwise provided in this article and in Section 2–403(2):

> (1) a security interest or agricultural lien continues in collateral notwithstanding sale, lease, license, exchange, or other disposition thereof unless the secured party authorized the disposition free of the security interest or agricultural lien; and

> (2) a security interest attaches to any identifiable proceeds of collateral.

(b) Proceeds that are commingled with other property are identifiable proceeds:

> (1) if the proceeds are goods, to the extent provided by Section 9–336; and

> (2) if the proceeds are not goods, to the extent that the secured party identifies the proceeds by a method of tracing, including application of equitable principles, that is permitted under law other than this article with respect to commingled property of the type involved.

(c) A security interest in proceeds is a perfected security interest if the security interest in the original collateral was perfected.

(d) A perfected security interest in proceeds becomes unperfected on the 21st day after the security interest attaches to the proceeds unless:

> (1) the following conditions are satisfied:

>> (A) a filed financing statement covers the original collateral;

>> (B) the proceeds are collateral in which a security interest may be perfected by filing in the office in which the financing statement has been filed; and

>> (C) the proceeds are not acquired with cash proceeds;

> (2) the proceeds are identifiable cash proceeds; or

> (3) the security interest in the proceeds is perfected other than under subsection (c) when the security interest attaches to the proceeds or within 20 days thereafter.

(e) If a filed financing statement covers the original collateral, a security interest in proceeds which remains perfected under subsection (d)(1) becomes unperfected at the later of:

(1) when the effectiveness of the filed financing statement lapses under Section 9–515 or is terminated under Section 9–513; or

(2) the 21st day after the security interest attaches to the proceeds.

§ 9–316.   Continued Perfection of Security Interest Following Change in Governing Law.

(a) A security interest perfected pursuant to the law of the jurisdiction designated in Section 9–301(1) or 9–305(c) remains perfected until the earliest of:

(1) the time perfection would have ceased under the law of that jurisdiction;

(2) the expiration of four months after a change of the debtor's location to another jurisdiction; or

(3) the expiration of one year after a transfer of collateral to a person that thereby becomes a debtor and is located in another jurisdiction.

(b) If a security interest described in subsection (a) becomes perfected under the law of the other jurisdiction before the earliest time or event described in that subsection, it remains perfected thereafter. If the security interest does not become perfected under the law of the other jurisdiction before the earliest time or event, it becomes unperfected and is deemed never to have been perfected as against a purchaser of the collateral for value.

(c) A possessory security interest in collateral, other than goods covered by a certificate of title and as-extracted collateral consisting of goods, remains continuously perfected if:

(1) the collateral is located in one jurisdiction and subject to a security interest perfected under the law of that jurisdiction;

(2) thereafter the collateral is brought into another jurisdiction; and

(3) upon entry into the other jurisdiction, the security interest is perfected under the law of the other jurisdiction.

(d) Except as otherwise provided in subsection (e), a security interest in goods covered by a certificate of title which is perfected by any method under the law of another jurisdiction when the goods become covered by a certificate of title from this State remains perfected until the security interest would have become unperfected under the law of the other jurisdiction had the goods not become so covered.

(e) A security interest described in subsection (d) becomes unperfected as against a purchaser of the goods for value and is deemed never to have been perfected as against a purchaser of the goods for value if the applicable requirements for perfection under Section 9–311(b) or 9–313 are not satisfied before the earlier of:

(1) the time the security interest would have become unperfected under the law of the other jurisdiction had the goods not become covered by a certificate of title from this State; or

(2) the expiration of four months after the goods had become so covered.

(f) A security interest in deposit accounts, letter-of-credit rights, or investment property which is perfected under the law of the bank's jurisdiction, the issuer's jurisdiction, a nominated person's jurisdiction, the securities intermediary's jurisdiction, or the commodity intermediary's jurisdiction, as applicable, remains perfected until the earlier of:

(1) the time the security interest would have become unperfected under the law of that jurisdiction; or

(2) the expiration of four months after a change of the applicable jurisdiction to another jurisdiction.

(g) If a security interest described in subsection (f) becomes perfected under the law of the other jurisdiction before the earlier of the time or the end of the period described in that subsection, it remains perfected thereafter. If the security interest does not become perfected under the law of the other jurisdiction before the earlier of that time or the end of that period, it becomes unperfected and is deemed never to have been perfected as against a purchaser of the collateral for value.

[Subpart 3. Priority]

§ 9–317.   Interests That Take Priority over or Take Free of Security Interest or Agricultural Lien.

(a) A security interest or agricultural lien is subordinate to the rights of:

(1) a person entitled to priority under Section 9–322; and

(2) except as otherwise provided in subsection (e), a person that becomes a lien creditor before the earlier of the time:

(A) the security interest or agricultural lien is perfected; or

(B) one of the conditions specified in Section 9–203(b)(3) is met and a financing statement covering the collateral is filed.

(b) Except as otherwise provided in subsection (e), a buyer, other than a secured party, of tangible chattel paper, documents, goods, instruments, or a security certificate takes free of a security interest or agricultural lien if the buyer gives value and receives delivery of the collateral without knowledge of the security interest or agricultural lien and before it is perfected.

(c) Except as otherwise provided in subsection (e), a lessee of goods takes free of a security interest or agricultural lien if the lessee gives value and receives delivery of the collateral without knowledge of the security interest or agricultural lien and before it is perfected.

(d) A licensee of a general intangible or a buyer, other than a secured party, of accounts, electronic chattel paper, general intangibles, or investment property other than a certificated security takes free of a security interest if the licensee or buyer gives value without knowledge of the security interest and before it is perfected.

(e) Except as otherwise provided in Sections 9–320 and 9–321, if a person files a financing statement with respect to a purchase-money security interest before or within 20 days after the debtor receives delivery of the collateral, the security interest takes priority over the rights of a buyer, lessee, or lien creditor which arise between the time the security interest attaches and the time of filing.

As amended in 2000.

§ 9–318.   No Interest Retained in Right to Payment That Is Sold; Rights and Title of Seller of Account or Chattel Paper with Respect to Creditors and Purchasers.

(a) A debtor that has sold an account, chattel paper, payment intangible, or promissory note does not retain a legal or equitable interest in the collateral sold.

(b) For purposes of determining the rights of creditors of, and purchasers for value of an account or chattel paper from, a debtor that has sold an account or chattel paper, while the buyer's security interest is unperfected, the debtor is deemed to have rights and title to the account or chattel paper identical to those the debtor sold.

§ 9–319.   Rights and Title of Consignee with Respect to Creditors and Purchasers.

(a) Except as otherwise provided in subsection (b), for purposes of determining the rights of creditors of, and purchasers for value of goods from, a consignee, while the goods are in the possession of the consignee, the consignee is deemed to have rights and title to the goods identical to those the consignor had or had power to transfer.

(b) For purposes of determining the rights of a creditor of a consignee, law other than this article determines the rights and title of a consignee while goods are in the consignee's possession if, under this part, a perfected security interest held by the consignor would have priority over the rights of the creditor.

§ 9–320.   Buyer of Goods.

(a) Except as otherwise provided in subsection (e), a buyer in ordinary course of business, other than a person buying farm products from a person engaged in farming operations, takes free of a security interest created by the buyer's seller, even if the security interest is perfected and the buyer knows of its existence.

(b) Except as otherwise provided in subsection (e), a buyer of goods from a person who used or bought the goods for use primarily for personal, family, or household purposes takes free of a security interest, even if perfected, if the buyer buys:

(1) without knowledge of the security interest;

(2) for value;

(3) primarily for the buyer's personal, family, or household purposes; and

(4) before the filing of a financing statement covering the goods.

(c) To the extent that it affects the priority of a security interest over a buyer of goods under subsection (b), the period of effectiveness of a filing made in the jurisdiction in which the seller is located is governed by Section 9–316(a) and (b).

(d) A buyer in ordinary course of business buying oil, gas, or other minerals at the wellhead or minehead or after extraction takes free of an interest arising out of an encumbrance.

(e) Subsections (a) and (b) do not affect a security interest in goods in the possession of the secured party under Section 9–313.

§ 9–321.   Licensee of General Intangible and Lessee of Goods in Ordinary Course of Business.

(a) In this section, "licensee in ordinary course of business" means a person that becomes a licensee of a general intangible in good faith, without knowledge that the license violates the rights of another person in the general intangible, and in the ordinary course from a person in the business of licensing general intangibles of that kind. A person becomes a licensee in the ordinary course if the license to the person comports with the usual or customary practices in the kind of business in which the licensor is engaged or with the licensor's own usual or customary practices.

(b) A licensee in ordinary course of business takes its rights under a nonexclusive license free of a security interest in the general intangible created by the licensor, even if the security interest is perfected and the licensee knows of its existence.

(c) A lessee in ordinary course of business takes its leasehold interest free of a security interest in the goods created by the lessor, even if the security interest is perfected and the lessee knows of its existence.

§ 9–322.   Priorities among Conflicting Security Interests in and Agricultural Liens on Same Collateral.

(a) Except as otherwise provided in this section, priority among conflicting security interests and agricultural liens in the same collateral is determined according to the following rules:

(1) Conflicting perfected security interests and agricultural liens rank according to priority in time of filing or perfection. Priority dates from the earlier of the time a filing covering the collateral is first made or the security interest or agricultural lien is first perfected, if there is no period thereafter when there is neither filing nor perfection.

(2) A perfected security interest or agricultural lien has priority over a conflicting unperfected security interest or agricultural lien.

(3) The first security interest or agricultural lien to attach or become effective has priority if conflicting security interests and agricultural liens are unperfected.

(b) For the purposes of subsection (a)(1):

(1) the time of filing or perfection as to a security interest in collateral is also the time of filing or perfection as to a security interest in proceeds; and

(2) the time of filing or perfection as to a security interest in collateral supported by a supporting obligation is also the time of filing or perfection as to a security interest in the supporting obligation.

(c) Except as otherwise provided in subsection (f), a security interest in collateral which qualifies for priority over a conflicting security interest under Section 9–327, 9–328, 9–329, 9–330, or 9–331 also has priority over a conflicting security interest in:

(1) any supporting obligation for the collateral; and

(2) proceeds of the collateral if:

(A) the security interest in proceeds is perfected;

(B) the proceeds are cash proceeds or of the same type as the collateral; and

(C) in the case of proceeds that are proceeds of proceeds, all intervening proceeds are cash proceeds, proceeds of the same type as the collateral, or an account relating to the collateral.

(d) Subject to subsection (e) and except as otherwise provided in subsection (f), if a security interest in chattel paper, deposit accounts, negotiable documents, instruments, investment property, or letter-of-credit rights is perfected by a method other than filing, conflicting perfected security interests in proceeds of the collateral rank according to priority in time of filing.

(e) Subsection (d) applies only if the proceeds of the collateral are not cash proceeds, chattel paper, negotiable documents, instruments, investment property, or letter-of-credit rights.

(f) Subsections (a) through (e) are subject to:

(1) subsection (g) and the other provisions of this part;

(2) Section 4–210 with respect to a security interest of a collecting bank;

(3) Section 5–118 with respect to a security interest of an issuer or nominated person; and

(4) Section 9–110 with respect to a security interest arising under Article 2 or 2A.

(g) A perfected agricultural lien on collateral has priority over a conflicting security interest in or agricultural lien on the same collateral if the statute creating the agricultural lien so provides.

§ 9–323. Future Advances.

(a) Except as otherwise provided in subsection (c), for purposes of determining the priority of a perfected security interest under Section 9–322(a)(1), perfection of the security interest dates from the time an advance is made to the extent that the security interest secures an advance that:

(1) is made while the security interest is perfected only:

(A) under Section 9–309 when it attaches; or

(B) temporarily under Section 9–312(e), (f), or (g); and

(2) is not made pursuant to a commitment entered into before or while the security interest is perfected by a method other than under Section 9–309 or 9–312(e), (f), or (g).

(b) Except as otherwise provided in subsection (c), a security interest is subordinate to the rights of a person that becomes a lien creditor to the extent that the security interest secures an advance made more than 45 days after the person becomes a lien creditor unless the advance is made:

(1) without knowledge of the lien; or

(2) pursuant to a commitment entered into without knowledge of the lien.

(c) Subsections (a) and (b) do not apply to a security interest held by a secured party that is a buyer of accounts, chattel paper, payment intangibles, or promissory notes or a consignor.

(d) Except as otherwise provided in subsection (e), a buyer of goods other than a buyer in ordinary course of business takes free of a security interest to the extent that it secures advances made after the earlier of:

(1) the time the secured party acquires knowledge of the buyer's purchase; or

(2) 45 days after the purchase.

(e) Subsection (d) does not apply if the advance is made pursuant to a commitment entered into without knowledge of the buyer's purchase and before the expiration of the 45-day period.

(f) Except as otherwise provided in subsection (g), a lessee of goods, other than a lessee in ordinary course of business, takes the leasehold interest free of a security interest to the extent that it secures advances made after the earlier of:

(1) the time the secured party acquires knowledge of the lease; or

(2) 45 days after the lease contract becomes enforceable.

(g) Subsection (f) does not apply if the advance is made pursuant to a commitment entered into without knowledge of the lease and before the expiration of the 45-day period.

As amended in 1999.

§ 9–324. Priority of Purchase-Money Security Interests.

(a) Except as otherwise provided in subsection (g), a perfected purchase-money security interest in goods other than inventory or livestock has priority over a conflicting security interest in the same goods, and, except as otherwise provided in Section 9–327, a perfected security interest in its identifiable proceeds also has priority, if the purchase-money security interest is perfected when the debtor receives possession of the collateral or within 20 days thereafter.

(b) Subject to subsection (c) and except as otherwise provided in subsection (g), a perfected purchase-money security interest in inventory has priority over a conflicting security interest in the same inventory, has priority over a conflicting security interest in chattel paper or an instrument constituting proceeds of the inventory and in proceeds of the chattel paper, if so provided in Section 9–330, and, except as otherwise provided in Section 9–327, also has priority in identifiable cash proceeds of the inventory to the extent the identifiable cash proceeds are received on or before the delivery of the inventory to a buyer, if:

(1) the purchase-money security interest is perfected when the debtor receives possession of the inventory;

(2) the purchase-money secured party sends an authenticated notification to the holder of the conflicting security interest;

(3) the holder of the conflicting security interest receives the notification within five years before the debtor receives possession of the inventory; and

(4) the notification states that the person sending the notification has or expects to acquire a purchase-money security interest in inventory of the debtor and describes the inventory.

(c) Subsections (b)(2) through (4) apply only if the holder of the conflicting security interest had filed a financing statement covering the same types of inventory:

(1) if the purchase-money security interest is perfected by filing, before the date of the filing; or

(2) if the purchase-money security interest is temporarily perfected without filing or possession under Section 9–312(f), before the beginning of the 20-day period thereunder.

(d) Subject to subsection (e) and except as otherwise provided in subsection (g), a perfected purchase-money security interest in livestock that are farm products has priority over a conflicting security interest in the same livestock, and, except as otherwise provided in Section 9–327, a perfected security interest in their identifiable proceeds and identifiable products in their unmanufactured states also has priority, if:

(1) the purchase-money security interest is perfected when the debtor receives possession of the livestock;

(2) the purchase-money secured party sends an authenticated notification to the holder of the conflicting security interest;

(3) the holder of the conflicting security interest receives the notification within six months before the debtor receives possession of the livestock; and

(4) the notification states that the person sending the notification has or expects to acquire a purchase-money security interest in livestock of the debtor and describes the livestock.

(e) Subsections (d)(2) through (4) apply only if the holder of the conflicting security interest had filed a financing statement covering the same types of livestock:

(1) if the purchase-money security interest is perfected by filing, before the date of the filing; or

(2) if the purchase-money security interest is temporarily perfected without filing or possession under Section 9–312(f), before the beginning of the 20-day period thereunder.

(f) Except as otherwise provided in subsection (g), a perfected purchase-money security interest in software has priority over a conflicting security interest in the same collateral, and, except as otherwise provided in Section 9–327, a perfected security interest in its identifiable proceeds also has priority, to the extent that the purchase-money security interest in the goods in which the software was acquired for use has priority in the goods and proceeds of the goods under this section.

(g) If more than one security interest qualifies for priority in the same collateral under subsection (a), (b), (d), or (f):

(1) a security interest securing an obligation incurred as all or part of the price of the collateral has priority over a security interest securing an obligation incurred for value given to enable the debtor to acquire rights in or the use of collateral; and

(2) in all other cases, Section 9–322(a) applies to the qualifying security interests.

§ 9–325.   Priority of Security Interests in Transferred Collateral.

(a) Except as otherwise provided in subsection (b), a security interest created by a debtor is subordinate to a security interest in the same collateral created by another person if:

(1) the debtor acquired the collateral subject to the security interest created by the other person;

(2) the security interest created by the other person was perfected when the debtor acquired the collateral; and

(3) there is no period thereafter when the security interest is unperfected.

(b) Subsection (a) subordinates a security interest only if the security interest:

(1) otherwise would have priority solely under Section 9–322(a) or 9–324; or

(2) arose solely under Section 2–711(3) or 2A–508(5).

§ 9–326.   Priority of Security Interests Created by New Debtor.

(a) Subject to subsection (b), a security interest created by a new debtor which is perfected by a filed financing statement that is effective solely under Section 9–508 in collateral in which a new debtor has or acquires rights is subordinate to a security interest in the same collateral which is perfected other than by a filed financing statement that is effective solely under Section 9–508.

(b) The other provisions of this part determine the priority among conflicting security interests in the same collateral perfected by filed financing statements that are effective solely under Section 9–508. However, if the security agreements to which a new debtor became bound as debtor were not entered into by the same original debtor, the conflicting security interests rank according to priority in time of the new debtor's having become bound.

§ 9–327.   Priority of Security Interests in Deposit Account.

The following rules govern priority among conflicting security interests in the same deposit account:

(1) A security interest held by a secured party having control of the deposit account under Section 9–104 has priority over a conflicting security interest held by a secured party that does not have control.

(2) Except as otherwise provided in paragraphs (3) and (4), security interests perfected by control under Section 9–314 rank according to priority in time of obtaining control.

(3) Except as otherwise provided in paragraph (4), a security interest held by the bank with which the deposit account is maintained has priority over a conflicting security interest held by another secured party.

(4) A security interest perfected by control under Section 9–104(a)(3) has priority over a security interest held by the bank with which the deposit account is maintained.

§ 9–328.   Priority of Security Interests in Investment Property.

The following rules govern priority among conflicting security interests in the same investment property:

(1) A security interest held by a secured party having control of investment property under Section 9–106 has priority over a

security interest held by a secured party that does not have control of the investment property.

(2) Except as otherwise provided in paragraphs (3) and (4), conflicting security interests held by secured parties each of which has control under Section 9–106 rank according to priority in time of:

(A) if the collateral is a security, obtaining control;

(B) if the collateral is a security entitlement carried in a securities account and:

(i) if the secured party obtained control under Section 8–106(d)(1), the secured party's becoming the person for which the securities account is maintained;

(ii) if the secured party obtained control under Section 8–106(d)(2), the securities intermediary's agreement to comply with the secured party's entitlement orders with respect to security entitlements carried or to be carried in the securities account; or

(iii) if the secured party obtained control through another person under Section 8–106(d)(3), the time on which priority would be based under this paragraph if the other person were the secured party; or

(C) if the collateral is a commodity contract carried with a commodity intermediary, the satisfaction of the requirement for control specified in Section 9–106(b)(2) with respect to commodity contracts carried or to be carried with the commodity intermediary.

(3) A security interest held by a securities intermediary in a security entitlement or a securities account maintained with the securities intermediary has priority over a conflicting security interest held by another secured party.

(4) A security interest held by a commodity intermediary in a commodity contract or a commodity account maintained with the commodity intermediary has priority over a conflicting security interest held by another secured party.

(5) A security interest in a certificated security in registered form which is perfected by taking delivery under Section 9–313(a) and not by control under Section 9–314 has priority over a conflicting security interest perfected by a method other than control.

(6) Conflicting security interests created by a broker, securities intermediary, or commodity intermediary which are perfected without control under Section 9–106 rank equally.

(7) In all other cases, priority among conflicting security interests in investment property is governed by Sections 9–322 and 9–323.

§ 9–329.   Priority of Security Interests in Letter-of-Credit Right.

The following rules govern priority among conflicting security interests in the same letter-of-credit right:

(1) A security interest held by a secured party having control of the letter-of-credit right under Section 9–107 has priority to the extent of its control over a conflicting security interest held by a secured party that does not have control.

(2) Security interests perfected by control under Section 9–314 rank according to priority in time of obtaining control.

§ 9–330.   Priority of Purchaser of Chattel Paper or Instrument.

(a) A purchaser of chattel paper has priority over a security interest in the chattel paper which is claimed merely as proceeds of inventory subject to a security interest if:

(1) in good faith and in the ordinary course of the purchaser's business, the purchaser gives new value and takes possession of the chattel paper or obtains control of the chattel paper under Section 9–105; and

(2) the chattel paper does not indicate that it has been assigned to an identified assignee other than the purchaser.

(b) A purchaser of chattel paper has priority over a security interest in the chattel paper which is claimed other than merely as proceeds of inventory subject to a security interest if the purchaser gives new value and takes possession of the chattel paper or obtains control of the chattel paper under Section 9–105 in good faith, in the ordinary course of the purchaser's business, and without knowledge that the purchase violates the rights of the secured party.

(c) Except as otherwise provided in Section 9–327, a purchaser having priority in chattel paper under subsection (a) or (b) also has priority in proceeds of the chattel paper to the extent that:

(1) Section 9–322 provides for priority in the proceeds; or

(2) the proceeds consist of the specific goods covered by the chattel paper or cash proceeds of the specific goods, even if the purchaser's security interest in the proceeds is unperfected.

(d) Except as otherwise provided in Section 9–331(a), a purchaser of an instrument has priority over a security interest in the instrument perfected by a method other than possession if the purchaser gives value and takes possession of the instrument in good faith and without knowledge that the purchase violates the rights of the secured party.

(e) For purposes of subsections (a) and (b), the holder of a purchase-money security interest in inventory gives new value for chattel paper constituting proceeds of the inventory.

(f) For purposes of subsections (b) and (d), if chattel paper or an instrument indicates that it has been assigned to an identified secured party other than the purchaser, a purchaser of the chattel paper or instrument has knowledge that the purchase violates the rights of the secured party.

§ 9–331.   Priority of Rights of Purchasers of Instruments, Documents, and Securities under Other Articles; Priority of Interests in Financial Assets and Security Entitlements under Article 8.

(a) This article does not limit the rights of a holder in due course of a negotiable instrument, a holder to which a negotiable document of title has been duly negotiated, or a protected purchaser of a security. These holders or purchasers take priority over an earlier security interest, even if perfected, to the extent provided in Articles 3, 7, and 8.

(b) This article does not limit the rights of or impose liability on a person to the extent that the person is protected against the assertion of a claim under Article 8.

(c) Filing under this article does not constitute notice of a claim or defense to the holders, or purchasers, or persons described in subsections (a) and (b).

§ 9–332.   Transfer of Money; Transfer of Funds from Deposit Account.

(a) A transferee of money takes the money free of a security interest unless the transferee acts in collusion with the debtor in violating the rights of the secured party.

(b) A transferee of funds from a deposit account takes the funds free of a security interest in the deposit account unless the transferee acts in collusion with the debtor in violating the rights of the secured party.

§ 9–333.   Priority of Certain Liens Arising by Operation of Law.

(a) In this section, "possessory lien" means an interest, other than a security interest or an agricultural lien:

(1) which secures payment or performance of an obligation for services or materials furnished with respect to goods by a person in the ordinary course of the person's business;

(2) which is created by statute or rule of law in favor of the person; and

(3) whose effectiveness depends on the person's possession of the goods.

(b) A possessory lien on goods has priority over a security interest in the goods unless the lien is created by a statute that expressly provides otherwise.

§ 9–334.   Priority of Security Interests in Fixtures and Crops.

(a) A security interest under this article may be created in goods that are fixtures or may continue in goods that become fixtures. A security interest does not exist under this article in ordinary building materials incorporated into an improvement on land.

(b) This article does not prevent creation of an encumbrance upon fixtures under real property law.

(c) In cases not governed by subsections (d) through (h), a security interest in fixtures is subordinate to a conflicting interest of an encumbrancer or owner of the related real property other than the debtor.

(d) Except as otherwise provided in subsection (h), a perfected security interest in fixtures has priority over a conflicting interest of an encumbrancer or owner of the real property if the debtor has an interest of record in or is in possession of the real property and:

(1) the security interest is a purchase-money security interest;

(2) the interest of the encumbrancer or owner arises before the goods become fixtures; and

(3) the security interest is perfected by a fixture filing before the goods become fixtures or within 20 days thereafter.

(e) A perfected security interest in fixtures has priority over a conflicting interest of an encumbrancer or owner of the real property if:

(1) the debtor has an interest of record in the real property or is in possession of the real property and the security interest:

(A) is perfected by a fixture filing before the interest of the encumbrancer or owner is of record; and

(B) has priority over any conflicting interest of a predecessor in title of the encumbrancer or owner;

(2) before the goods become fixtures, the security interest is perfected by any method permitted by this article and the fixtures are readily removable:

(A) factory or office machines;

(B) equipment that is not primarily used or leased for use in the operation of the real property; or

(C) replacements of domestic appliances that are consumer goods;

(3) the conflicting interest is a lien on the real property obtained by legal or equitable proceedings after the security interest was perfected by any method permitted by this article; or

(4) the security interest is:

(A) created in a manufactured home in a manufactured-home transaction; and

(B) perfected pursuant to a statute described in Section 9–311(a)(2).

(f) A security interest in fixtures, whether or not perfected, has priority over a conflicting interest of an encumbrancer or owner of the real property if:

(1) the encumbrancer or owner has, in an authenticated record, consented to the security interest or disclaimed an interest in the goods as fixtures; or

(2) the debtor has a right to remove the goods as against the encumbrancer or owner.

(g) The priority of the security interest under paragraph (f)(2) continues for a reasonable time if the debtor's right to remove the goods as against the encumbrancer or owner terminates.

(h) A mortgage is a construction mortgage to the extent that it secures an obligation incurred for the construction of an improvement on land, including the acquisition cost of the land, if a recorded record of the mortgage so indicates. Except as otherwise provided in subsections (e) and (f), a security interest in fixtures is subordinate to a construction mortgage if a record of the mortgage is recorded before the goods become fixtures and the goods become fixtures before the completion of the construction. A mortgage has this priority to the same extent as a construction mortgage to the extent that it is given to refinance a construction mortgage.

(i) A perfected security interest in crops growing on real property has priority over a conflicting interest of an encumbrancer or owner of the real property if the debtor has an interest of record in or is in possession of the real property.

(j) Subsection (i) prevails over any inconsistent provisions of the following statutes:

[List here any statutes containing provisions inconsistent with subsection (i).]

Legislative Note: States that amend statutes to remove provisions inconsistent with subsection (i) need not enact subsection (j).

§ 9–335.   Accessions.

(a) A security interest may be created in an accession and continues in collateral that becomes an accession.

(b) If a security interest is perfected when the collateral becomes an accession, the security interest remains perfected in the collateral.

(c) Except as otherwise provided in subsection (d), the other provisions of this part determine the priority of a security interest in an accession.

(d) A security interest in an accession is subordinate to a security interest in the whole which is perfected by compliance with the requirements of a certificate-of-title statute under Section 9–311(b).

(e) After default, subject to Part 6, a secured party may remove an accession from other goods if the security interest in the accession has priority over the claims of every person having an interest in the whole.

(f) A secured party that removes an accession from other goods under subsection (e) shall promptly reimburse any holder of a security interest or other lien on, or owner of, the whole or of the other goods, other than the debtor, for the cost of repair of any physical injury to the whole or the other goods. The secured party need not reimburse the holder or owner for any diminution in value of the whole or the other goods caused by the absence of the accession removed or by any necessity for replacing it. A person entitled to reimbursement may refuse permission to remove until the secured party gives adequate assurance for the performance of the obligation to reimburse.

§ 9–336.   Commingled Goods.

(a) In this section, "commingled goods" means goods that are physically united with other goods in such a manner that their identity is lost in a product or mass.

(b) A security interest does not exist in commingled goods as such. However, a security interest may attach to a product or mass that results when goods become commingled goods.

(c) If collateral becomes commingled goods, a security interest attaches to the product or mass.

(d) If a security interest in collateral is perfected before the collateral becomes commingled goods, the security interest that attaches to the product or mass under subsection (c) is perfected.

(e) Except as otherwise provided in subsection (f), the other provisions of this part determine the priority of a security interest that attaches to the product or mass under subsection (c).

(f) If more than one security interest attaches to the product or mass under subsection (c), the following rules determine priority:

(1) A security interest that is perfected under subsection (d) has priority over a security interest that is unperfected at the time the collateral becomes commingled goods.

(2) If more than one security interest is perfected under subsection (d), the security interests rank equally in proportion to the value of the collateral at the time it became commingled goods.

§ 9–337.   Priority of Security Interests in Goods Covered by Certificate of Title.

If, while a security interest in goods is perfected by any method under the law of another jurisdiction, this State issues a certificate of title that does not show that the goods are subject to the security interest or contain a statement that they may be subject to security interests not shown on the certificate:

(1) a buyer of the goods, other than a person in the business of selling goods of that kind, takes free of the security interest if the buyer gives value and receives delivery of the goods after issuance of the certificate and without knowledge of the security interest; and

(2) the security interest is subordinate to a conflicting security interest in the goods that attaches, and is perfected under Section 9–311(b), after issuance of the certificate and without the conflicting secured party's knowledge of the security interest.

§ 9–338.   Priority of Security Interest or Agricultural Lien Perfected by Filed Financing Statement Providing Certain Incorrect Information.

If a security interest or agricultural lien is perfected by a filed financing statement providing information described in Section 9–516(b)(5) which is incorrect at the time the financing statement is filed:

(1) the security interest or agricultural lien is subordinate to a conflicting perfected security interest in the collateral to the extent that the holder of the conflicting security interest gives value in reasonable reliance upon the incorrect information; and

(2) a purchaser, other than a secured party, of the collateral takes free of the security interest or agricultural lien to the extent that, in reasonable reliance upon the incorrect information, the purchaser gives value and, in the case of chattel paper, documents, goods, instruments, or a security certificate, receives delivery of the collateral.

§ 9–339.   Priority Subject to Subordination.

This article does not preclude subordination by agreement by a person entitled to priority.

[Subpart 4. Rights of Bank]

§ 9–340.   Effectiveness of Right of Recoupment or Set-Off against Deposit Account.

(a) Except as otherwise provided in subsection (c), a bank with which a deposit account is maintained may exercise any right of recoupment or set-off against a secured party that holds a security interest in the deposit account.

(b) Except as otherwise provided in subsection (c), the application of this article to a security interest in a deposit account does not affect a right of recoupment or set-off of the secured party as to a deposit account maintained with the secured party.

(c) The exercise by a bank of a set-off against a deposit account is ineffective against a secured party that holds a security interest in the deposit account which is perfected by control under Section 9–104(a)(3), if the set-off is based on a claim against the debtor.

§ 9–341.   Bank's Rights and Duties with Respect to Deposit Account.

Except as otherwise provided in Section 9–340(c), and unless the bank otherwise agrees in an authenticated record, a bank's rights and duties with respect to a deposit account maintained with the bank are not terminated, suspended, or modified by:

(1) the creation, attachment, or perfection of a security interest in the deposit account;

(2) the bank's knowledge of the security interest; or

(3) the bank's receipt of instructions from the secured party.

§ 9–342.   Bank's Right to Refuse to Enter into or Disclose Existence of Control Agreement.

This article does not require a bank to enter into an agreement of the kind described in Section 9–104(a)(2), even if its customer so requests or directs. A bank that has entered into such an agreement is not required to confirm the existence of the agreement to another person unless requested to do so by its customer.

Part 4   Rights of Third Parties

§ 9–401.   Alienability of Debtor's Rights.

(a) Except as otherwise provided in subsection (b) and Sections 9–406, 9–407, 9–408, and 9–409, whether a debtor's rights in collateral may be voluntarily or involuntarily transferred is governed by law other than this article.

(b) An agreement between the debtor and secured party which prohibits a transfer of the debtor's rights in collateral or makes the transfer a default does not prevent the transfer from taking effect.

§ 9–402.   Secured Party Not Obligated on Contract of Debtor or in Tort.

The existence of a security interest, agricultural lien, or authority given to a debtor to dispose of or use collateral, without more, does not subject a secured party to liability in contract or tort for the debtor's acts or omissions.

§ 9–403.   Agreement Not to Assert Defenses against Assignee.

(a) In this section, "value" has the meaning provided in Section 3–303(a).

(b) Except as otherwise provided in this section, an agreement between an account debtor and an assignor not to assert against an assignee any claim or defense that the account debtor may have against the assignor is enforceable by an assignee that takes an assignment:

(1) for value;

(2) in good faith;

(3) without notice of a claim of a property or possessory right to the property assigned; and

(4) without notice of a defense or claim in recoupment of the type that may be asserted against a person entitled to enforce a negotiable instrument under Section 3–305(a).

(c) Subsection (b) does not apply to defenses of a type that may be asserted against a holder in due course of a negotiable instrument under Section 3–305(b).

(d) In a consumer transaction, if a record evidences the account debtor's obligation, law other than this article requires that the record include a statement to the effect that the rights of an assignee are subject to claims or defenses that the account debtor could assert against the original obligee, and the record does not include such a statement:

(1) the record has the same effect as if the record included such a statement; and

(2) the account debtor may assert against an assignee those claims and defenses that would have been available if the record included such a statement.

(e) This section is subject to law other than this article which establishes a different rule for an account debtor who is an individual and who incurred the obligation primarily for personal, family, or household purposes.

(f) Except as otherwise provided in subsection (d), this section does not displace law other than this article which gives effect to an agreement by an account debtor not to assert a claim or defense against an assignee.

§ 9–404.   Rights Acquired by Assignee; Claims and Defenses against Assignee.

(a) Unless an account debtor has made an enforceable agreement not to assert defenses or claims, and subject to subsections (b) through (e), the rights of an assignee are subject to:

(1) all terms of the agreement between the account debtor and assignor and any defense or claim in recoupment arising from the transaction that gave rise to the contract; and

(2) any other defense or claim of the account debtor against the assignor which accrues before the account debtor receives a notification of the assignment authenticated by the assignor or the assignee.

(b) Subject to subsection (c) and except as otherwise provided in subsection (d), the claim of an account debtor against an assignor may be asserted against an assignee under subsection (a) only to reduce the amount the account debtor owes.

(c) This section is subject to law other than this article which establishes a different rule for an account debtor who is an individual and who incurred the obligation primarily for personal, family, or household purposes.

(d) In a consumer transaction, if a record evidences the account debtor's obligation, law other than this article requires that the record include a statement to the effect that the account debtor's recovery against an assignee with respect to claims and defenses against the assignor may not exceed amounts paid by the account debtor under the record, and the record does not include such a statement, the extent to which a claim of an account debtor against the assignor may be asserted against an assignee is determined as if the record included such a statement.

(e) This section does not apply to an assignment of a health-care-insurance receivable.

§ 9–405.   Modification of Assigned Contract.

(a) A modification of or substitution for an assigned contract is effective against an assignee if made in good faith. The assignee acquires corresponding rights under the modified or substituted contract. The assignment may provide that the modification or substitution is a breach of contract by the assignor. This subsection is subject to subsections (b) through (d).

(b) Subsection (a) applies to the extent that:

(1) the right to payment or a part thereof under an assigned contract has not been fully earned by performance; or

(2) the right to payment or a part thereof has been fully earned by performance and the account debtor has not received notification of the assignment under Section 9–406(a).

(c) This section is subject to law other than this article which establishes a different rule for an account debtor who is an individual and who incurred the obligation primarily for personal, family, or household purposes.

(d) This section does not apply to an assignment of a health-care-insurance receivable.

§ 9–406.   Discharge of Account Debtor; Notification of Assignment; Identification and Proof of Assignment; Restrictions on Assignment of Accounts, Chattel Paper, Payment Intangibles, and Promissory Notes Ineffective.

(a) Subject to subsections (b) through (i), an account debtor on an account, chattel paper, or a payment intangible may discharge its obligation by paying the assignor until, but not after, the account debtor receives a notification, authenticated by the assignor or the assignee, that the amount due or to become due has been assigned and that payment is to be made to the assignee. After receipt of the notification, the account debtor may discharge its obligation by paying the assignee and may not discharge the obligation by paying the assignor.

(b) Subject to subsection (h), notification is ineffective under subsection (a):

(1) if it does not reasonably identify the rights assigned;

(2) to the extent that an agreement between an account debtor and a seller of a payment intangible limits the account debtor's duty to pay a person other than the seller and the limitation is effective under law other than this article; or

(3) at the option of an account debtor, if the notification notifies the account debtor to make less than the full amount of any installment or other periodic payment to the assignee, even if:

(A) only a portion of the account, chattel paper, or payment intangible has been assigned to that assignee;

(B) a portion has been assigned to another assignee; or

(C) the account debtor knows that the assignment to that assignee is limited.

(c) Subject to subsection (h), if requested by the account debtor, an assignee shall seasonably furnish reasonable proof that the assignment has been made. Unless the assignee complies, the account debtor may discharge its obligation by paying the assignor, even if the account debtor has received a notification under subsection (a).

(d) Except as otherwise provided in subsection (e) and Sections 2A–303 and 9–407, and subject to subsection (h), a term in an agreement between an account debtor and an assignor or in a promissory note is ineffective to the extent that it:

(1) prohibits, restricts, or requires the consent of the account debtor or person obligated on the promissory note to the assignment or transfer of, or the creation, attachment, perfection, or enforcement of a security interest in, the account, chattel paper, payment intangible, or promissory note; or

(2) provides that the assignment or transfer or the creation, attachment, perfection, or enforcement of the security interest may give rise to a default, breach, right of recoupment, claim, defense, termination, right of termination, or remedy under the account, chattel paper, payment intangible, or promissory note.

(e) Subsection (d) does not apply to the sale of a payment intangible or promissory note.

(f) Except as otherwise provided in Sections 2A–303 and 9–407 and subject to subsections (h) and (i), a rule of law, statute, or regulation that prohibits, restricts, or requires the consent of a government, governmental body or official, or account debtor to the assignment or transfer of, or creation of a security interest in, an account or chattel paper is ineffective to the extent that the rule of law, statute, or regulation:

(1) prohibits, restricts, or requires the consent of the government, governmental body or official, or account debtor to the assignment or transfer of, or the creation, attachment, perfection, or enforcement of a security interest in the account or chattel paper; or

(2) provides that the assignment or transfer or the creation, attachment, perfection, or enforcement of the security interest may give rise to a default, breach, right of recoupment, claim, defense, termination, right of termination, or remedy under the account or chattel paper.

(g) Subject to subsection (h), an account debtor may not waive or vary its option under subsection (b)(3).

(h) This section is subject to law other than this article which establishes a different rule for an account debtor who is an individual and who incurred the obligation primarily for personal, family, or household purposes.

(i) This section does not apply to an assignment of a health-care-insurance receivable.

(j) This section prevails over any inconsistent provisions of the following statutes, rules, and regulations:

[List here any statutes, rules, and regulations containing provisions inconsistent with this section.]

Legislative Note: States that amend statutes, rules, and regulations to remove provisions inconsistent with this section need not enact subsection (j).

As amended in 1999 and 2000.

§ 9–407.   Restrictions on Creation or Enforcement of Security Interest in Leasehold Interest or in Lessor's Residual Interest.

(a) Except as otherwise provided in subsection (b), a term in a lease agreement is ineffective to the extent that it:

(1) prohibits, restricts, or requires the consent of a party to the lease to the assignment or transfer of, or the creation, attachment, perfection, or enforcement of a security interest

in an interest of a party under the lease contract or in the lessor's residual interest in the goods; or

(2) provides that the assignment or transfer or the creation, attachment, perfection, or enforcement of the security interest may give rise to a default, breach, right of recoupment, claim, defense, termination, right of termination, or remedy under the lease.

(b) Except as otherwise provided in Section 2A–303(7), a term described in subsection (a)(2) is effective to the extent that there is:

(1) a transfer by the lessee of the lessee's right of possession or use of the goods in violation of the term; or

(2) a delegation of a material performance of either party to the lease contract in violation of the term.

(c) The creation, attachment, perfection, or enforcement of a security interest in the lessor's interest under the lease contract or the lessor's residual interest in the goods is not a transfer that materially impairs the lessee's prospect of obtaining return performance or materially changes the duty of or materially increases the burden or risk imposed on the lessee within the purview of Section 2A–303(4) unless, and then only to the extent that, enforcement actually results in a delegation of material performance of the lessor.

As amended in 1999.

§ 9–408.   Restrictions on Assignment of Promissory Notes, Health-Care-Insurance Receivables, and Certain General Intangibles Ineffective.

(a) Except as otherwise provided in subsection (b), a term in a promissory note or in an agreement between an account debtor and a debtor which relates to a health-care-insurance receivable or a general intangible, including a contract, permit, license, or franchise, and which term prohibits, restricts, or requires the consent of the person obligated on the promissory note or the account debtor to, the assignment or transfer of, or creation, attachment, or perfection of a security interest in, the promissory note, health-care-insurance receivable, or general intangible, is ineffective to the extent that the term:

(1) would impair the creation, attachment, or perfection of a security interest; or

(2) provides that the assignment or transfer or the creation, attachment, or perfection of the security interest may give rise to a default, breach, right of recoupment, claim, defense, termination, right of termination, or remedy under the promissory note, health-care-insurance receivable, or general intangible.

(b) Subsection (a) applies to a security interest in a payment intangible or promissory note only if the security interest arises out of a sale of the payment intangible or promissory note.

(c) A rule of law, statute, or regulation that prohibits, restricts, or requires the consent of a government, governmental body or official, person obligated on a promissory note, or account debtor to the assignment or transfer of, or creation of a security interest in, a promissory note, health-care-insurance receivable, or general intangible, including a contract, permit, license, or franchise between an account debtor and a debtor, is ineffective to the extent that the rule of law, statute, or regulation:

(1) would impair the creation, attachment, or perfection of a security interest; or

(2) provides that the assignment or transfer or the creation, attachment, or perfection of the security interest may give rise to a default, breach, right of recoupment, claim, defense, termination, right of termination, or remedy under the promissory note, health-care-insurance receivable, or general intangible.

(d) To the extent that a term in a promissory note or in an agreement between an account debtor and a debtor which relates to a health-care-insurance receivable or general intangible or a rule of law, statute, or regulation described in subsection (c) would be effective under law other than this article but is ineffective under subsection (a) or (c), the creation, attachment, or perfection of a security interest in the promissory note, health-care-insurance receivable, or general intangible:

(1) is not enforceable against the person obligated on the promissory note or the account debtor;

(2) does not impose a duty or obligation on the person obligated on the promissory note or the account debtor;

(3) does not require the person obligated on the promissory note or the account debtor to recognize the security interest, pay or render performance to the secured party, or accept payment or performance from the secured party;

(4) does not entitle the secured party to use or assign the debtor's rights under the promissory note, health-care-insurance receivable, or general intangible, including any related information or materials furnished to the debtor in the transaction giving rise to the promissory note, health-care-insurance receivable, or general intangible;

(5) does not entitle the secured party to use, assign, possess, or have access to any trade secrets or confidential information of the person obligated on the promissory note or the account debtor; and

(6) does not entitle the secured party to enforce the security interest in the promissory note, health-care-insurance receivable, or general intangible.

(e) This section prevails over any inconsistent provisions of the following statutes, rules, and regulations:

[List here any statutes, rules, and regulations containing provisions inconsistent with this section.]

Legislative Note: States that amend statutes, rules, and regulations to remove provisions inconsistent with this section need not enact subsection (e).

As amended in 1999.

§ 9–409.   Restrictions on Assignment of Letter-of-Credit Rights Ineffective.

(a) A term in a letter of credit or a rule of law, statute, regulation, custom, or practice applicable to the letter of credit which prohibits, restricts, or requires the consent of an applicant, issuer, or nominated person to a beneficiary's assignment of or creation of a security interest in a letter-of-credit right is ineffective to the extent that the term or rule of law, statute, regulation, custom, or practice:

(1) would impair the creation, attachment, or perfection of a security interest in the letter-of-credit right; or

(2) provides that the assignment or the creation, attachment, or perfection of the security interest may give rise to a default, breach, right of recoupment, claim, defense, termination, right of termination, or remedy under the letter-of-credit right.

(b) To the extent that a term in a letter of credit is ineffective under subsection (a) but would be effective under law other than this article or a custom or practice applicable to the letter of credit, to the transfer of a right to draw or otherwise demand performance under the letter of credit, or to the assignment of a right to proceeds of the letter of credit, the creation, attachment, or perfection of a security interest in the letter-of-credit right:

(1) is not enforceable against the applicant, issuer, nominated person, or transferee beneficiary;

(2) imposes no duties or obligations on the applicant, issuer, nominated person, or transferee beneficiary; and

(3) does not require the applicant, issuer, nominated person, or transferee beneficiary to recognize the security interest, pay or render performance to the secured party, or accept payment or other performance from the secured party.

As amended in 1999.

Part 5   Filing

[Subpart 1. Filing Office; Contents and Effectiveness of Financing Statement]

§ 9–501.   Filing Office.

(a) Except as otherwise provided in subsection (b), if the local law of this State governs perfection of a security interest or agricultural lien, the office in which to file a financing statement to perfect the security interest or agricultural lien is:

(1) the office designated for the filing or recording of a record of a mortgage on the related real property, if:

(A) the collateral is as-extracted collateral or timber to be cut; or

(B) the financing statement is filed as a fixture filing and the collateral is goods that are or are to become fixtures; or

(2) the office of [ ] [or any office duly authorized by [ ]], in all other cases, including a case in which the collateral is goods that are or are to become fixtures and the financing statement is not filed as a fixture filing.

(b) The office in which to file a financing statement to perfect a security interest in collateral, including fixtures, of a transmitting utility is the office of [ ]. The financing statement also constitutes a fixture filing as to the collateral indicated in the financing statement which is or is to become fixtures.

Legislative Note: The State should designate the filing office where the brackets appear. The filing office may be that of a governmental official (e.g., the Secretary of State) or a private party that maintains the State's filing system.

§ 9–502.   Contents of Financing Statement; Record of Mortgage as Financing Statement; Time of Filing Financing Statement.

(a) Subject to subsection (b), a financing statement is sufficient only if it:

(1) provides the name of the debtor;

(2) provides the name of the secured party or a representative of the secured party; and

(3) indicates the collateral covered by the financing statement.

(b) Except as otherwise provided in Section 9–501(b), to be sufficient, a financing statement that covers as-extracted collateral or timber to be cut, or which is filed as a fixture filing and covers goods that are or are to become fixtures, must satisfy subsection (a) and also:

(1) indicate that it covers this type of collateral;

(2) indicate that it is to be filed [for record] in the real property records;

(3) provide a description of the real property to which the collateral is related [sufficient to give constructive notice of a mortgage under the law of this State if the description were contained in a record of the mortgage of the real property]; and

(4) if the debtor does not have an interest of record in the real property, provide the name of a record owner.

(c) A record of a mortgage is effective, from the date of recording, as a financing statement filed as a fixture filing or as a financing statement covering as-extracted collateral or timber to be cut only if:

(1) the record indicates the goods or accounts that it covers;

(2) the goods are or are to become fixtures related to the real property described in the record or the collateral is related to the real property described in the record and is as-extracted collateral or timber to be cut;

(3) the record satisfies the requirements for a financing statement in this section other than an indication that it is to be filed in the real property records; and

(4) the record is [duly] recorded.

(d) A financing statement may be filed before a security agreement is made or a security interest otherwise attaches.

Legislative Note: Language in brackets is optional. Where the State has any special recording system for real property other than the usual grantor-grantee index (as, for instance, a tract system or a title registration or Torrens system) local adaptations of subsection (b) and Section 9–519(d) and (e) may be necessary. See, e.g., Mass. Gen. Laws Chapter 106, Section 9–410.

§ 9–503.   Name of Debtor and Secured Party.

(a) A financing statement sufficiently provides the name of the debtor:

(1) if the debtor is a registered organization, only if the financing statement provides the name of the debtor indicated on the public record of the debtor's jurisdiction of organization which shows the debtor to have been organized;

(2) if the debtor is a decedent's estate, only if the financing statement provides the name of the decedent and indicates that the debtor is an estate;

(3) if the debtor is a trust or a trustee acting with respect to property held in trust, only if the financing statement:

(A) provides the name specified for the trust in its organic documents or, if no name is specified, provides the name of the settlor and additional information sufficient to distinguish the debtor from other trusts having one or more of the same settlors; and

(B) indicates, in the debtor's name or otherwise, that the debtor is a trust or is a trustee acting with respect to property held in trust; and

(4) in other cases:

(A) if the debtor has a name, only if it provides the individual or organizational name of the debtor; and

(B) if the debtor does not have a name, only if it provides the names of the partners, members, associates, or other persons comprising the debtor.

(b) A financing statement that provides the name of the debtor in accordance with subsection (a) is not rendered ineffective by the absence of:

(1) a trade name or other name of the debtor; or

(2) unless required under subsection (a)(4)(B), names of partners, members, associates, or other persons comprising the debtor.

(c) A financing statement that provides only the debtor's trade name does not sufficiently provide the name of the debtor.

(d) Failure to indicate the representative capacity of a secured party or representative of a secured party does not affect the sufficiency of a financing statement.

(e) A financing statement may provide the name of more than one debtor and the name of more than one secured party.

§ 9–504.   Indication of Collateral.

A financing statement sufficiently indicates the collateral that it covers if the financing statement provides:

(1) a description of the collateral pursuant to Section 9–108; or

(2) an indication that the financing statement covers all assets or all personal property.

As amended in 1999.

§ 9–505.   Filing and Compliance with Other Statutes and Treaties for Consignments, Leases, Other Bailments, and Other Transactions.

(a) A consignor, lessor, or other bailor of goods, a licensor, or a buyer of a payment intangible or promissory note may file a financing statement, or may comply with a statute or treaty described in Section 9–311(a), using the terms "consignor", "consignee", "lessor", "lessee", "bailor", "bailee", "licensor", "licensee", "owner", "registered owner", "buyer", "seller", or words of similar import, instead of the terms "secured party" and "debtor".

(b) This part applies to the filing of a financing statement under subsection (a) and, as appropriate, to compliance that is equivalent to filing a financing statement under Section 9–311(b), but the filing or compliance is not of itself a factor in determining whether the collateral secures an obligation. If it is determined for another reason that the collateral secures an obligation, a security interest held by the consignor, lessor, bailor, licensor, owner, or buyer which attaches to the collateral is perfected by the filing or compliance.

§ 9–506.   Effect of Errors or Omissions.

(a) A financing statement substantially satisfying the requirements of this part is effective, even if it has minor errors or omissions, unless the errors or omissions make the financing statement seriously misleading.

(b) Except as otherwise provided in subsection (c), a financing statement that fails sufficiently to provide the name of the debtor in accordance with Section 9–503(a) is seriously misleading.

(c) If a search of the records of the filing office under the debtor's correct name, using the filing office's standard search logic, if any, would disclose a financing statement that fails sufficiently to provide the name of the debtor in accordance with Section 9–503(a), the name provided does not make the financing statement seriously misleading.

(d) For purposes of Section 9–508(b), the "debtor's correct name" in subsection (c) means the correct name of the new debtor.

§ 9–507.   Effect of Certain Events on Effectiveness of Financing Statement.

(a) A filed financing statement remains effective with respect to collateral that is sold, exchanged, leased, licensed, or otherwise disposed of and in which a security interest or agricultural lien continues, even if the secured party knows of or consents to the disposition.

(b) Except as otherwise provided in subsection (c) and Section 9–508, a financing statement is not rendered ineffective if, after the financing statement is filed, the information provided in the financing statement becomes seriously misleading under Section 9–506.

(c) If a debtor so changes its name that a filed financing statement becomes seriously misleading under Section 9–506:

(1) the financing statement is effective to perfect a security interest in collateral acquired by the debtor before, or within four months after, the change; and

(2) the financing statement is not effective to perfect a security interest in collateral acquired by the debtor more than four months after the change, unless an amendment to the financing statement which renders the financing statement not seriously misleading is filed within four months after the change.

§ 9–508.   Effectiveness of Financing Statement If New Debtor Becomes Bound by Security Agreement.

(a) Except as otherwise provided in this section, a filed financing statement naming an original debtor is effective to perfect a security interest in collateral in which a new debtor has or acquires rights to the extent that the financing statement would have been effective had the original debtor acquired rights in the collateral.

(b) If the difference between the name of the original debtor and that of the new debtor causes a filed financing statement that is effective under subsection (a) to be seriously misleading under Section 9–506:

(1) the financing statement is effective to perfect a security interest in collateral acquired by the new debtor before, and within four months after, the new debtor becomes bound under Section 9B–203(d); and

(2) the financing statement is not effective to perfect a security interest in collateral acquired by the new debtor more than four months after the new debtor becomes bound under Section 9–203(d) unless an initial financing statement providing the name of the new debtor is filed before the expiration of that time.

(c) This section does not apply to collateral as to which a filed financing statement remains effective against the new debtor under Section 9–507(a).

§ 9–509.   Persons Entitled to File a Record.

(a) A person may file an initial financing statement, amendment that adds collateral covered by a financing statement, or amendment that adds a debtor to a financing statement only if:

(1) the debtor authorizes the filing in an authenticated record or pursuant to subsection (b) or (c); or

(2) the person holds an agricultural lien that has become effective at the time of filing and the financing statement covers only collateral in which the person holds an agricultural lien.

(b) By authenticating or becoming bound as debtor by a security agreement, a debtor or new debtor authorizes the filing of an initial financing statement, and an amendment, covering:

(1) the collateral described in the security agreement; and

(2) property that becomes collateral under Section 9–315(a)(2), whether or not the security agreement expressly covers proceeds.

(c) By acquiring collateral in which a security interest or agricultural lien continues under Section 9–315(a)(1), a debtor authorizes the filing of an initial financing statement, and an amendment, covering the collateral and property that becomes collateral under Section 9–315(a)(2).

(d) A person may file an amendment other than an amendment that adds collateral covered by a financing statement or an amendment that adds a debtor to a financing statement only if:

(1) the secured party of record authorizes the filing; or

(2) the amendment is a termination statement for a financing statement as to which the secured party of record has failed to file or send a termination statement as required by Section 9–513(a) or (c), the debtor authorizes the filing, and the termination statement indicates that the debtor authorized it to be filed.

(e) If there is more than one secured party of record for a financing statement, each secured party of record may authorize the filing of an amendment under subsection (d).

As amended in 2000.

§ 9–510.   Effectiveness of Filed Record.

(a) A filed record is effective only to the extent that it was filed by a person that may file it under Section 9–509.

(b) A record authorized by one secured party of record does not affect the financing statement with respect to another secured party of record.

(c) A continuation statement that is not filed within the six-month period prescribed by Section 9–515(d) is ineffective.

§ 9–511.   Secured Party of Record.

(a) A secured party of record with respect to a financing statement is a person whose name is provided as the name of the secured party or a representative of the secured party in an initial financing statement that has been filed. If an initial financing statement is filed under Section 9–514(a), the assignee named in the initial financing statement is the secured party of record with respect to the financing statement.

(b) If an amendment of a financing statement which provides the name of a person as a secured party or a representative of a secured party is filed, the person named in the amendment is a secured party of record. If an amendment is filed under Section 9–514(b), the assignee named in the amendment is a secured party of record.

(c) A person remains a secured party of record until the filing of an amendment of the financing statement which deletes the person.

§ 9–512.   Amendment of Financing Statement.

[Alternative A]

(a) Subject to Section 9–509, a person may add or delete collateral covered by, continue or terminate the effectiveness of, or, subject to subsection (e), otherwise amend the information provided in, a financing statement by filing an amendment that:

(1) identifies, by its file number, the initial financing statement to which the amendment relates; and

(2) if the amendment relates to an initial financing statement filed [or recorded] in a filing office described in Section 9–501(a)(1), provides the information specified in Section 9–502(b).

[Alternative B]

(a) Subject to Section 9–509, a person may add or delete collateral covered by, continue or terminate the effectiveness of, or, subject to subsection (e), otherwise amend the information provided in, a financing statement by filing an amendment that:

(1) identifies, by its file number, the initial financing statement to which the amendment relates; and

(2) if the amendment relates to an initial financing statement filed [or recorded] in a filing office described in Section 9–501(a)(1), provides the date [and time] that the initial financing statement was filed [or recorded] and the information specified in Section 9–502(b).

[End of Alternatives]

(b) Except as otherwise provided in Section 9–515, the filing of an amendment does not extend the period of effectiveness of the financing statement.

(c) A financing statement that is amended by an amendment that adds collateral is effective as to the added collateral only from the date of the filing of the amendment.

(d) A financing statement that is amended by an amendment that adds a debtor is effective as to the added debtor only from the date of the filing of the amendment.

(e) An amendment is ineffective to the extent it:

(1) purports to delete all debtors and fails to provide the name of a debtor to be covered by the financing statement; or

(2) purports to delete all secured parties of record and fails to provide the name of a new secured party of record.

Legislative Note: States whose real-estate filing offices require additional information in amendments and cannot search their records by both the name of the debtor and the file number should enact Alternative B to Sections 9–512(a), 9–518(b), 9–519(f), and 9–522(a).

§ 9–513.   Termination Statement.

(a) A secured party shall cause the secured party of record for a financing statement to file a termination statement for the financing statement if the financing statement covers consumer goods and:

(1) there is no obligation secured by the collateral covered by the financing statement and no commitment to make an advance, incur an obligation, or otherwise give value; or

(2) the debtor did not authorize the filing of the initial financing statement.

(b) To comply with subsection (a), a secured party shall cause the secured party of record to file the termination statement:

(1) within one month after there is no obligation secured by the collateral covered by the financing statement and no commitment to make an advance, incur an obligation, or otherwise give value; or

(2) if earlier, within 20 days after the secured party receives an authenticated demand from a debtor.

(c) In cases not governed by subsection (a), within 20 days after a secured party receives an authenticated demand from a debtor, the secured party shall cause the secured party of record for a financing statement to send to the debtor a termination statement for the financing statement or file the termination statement in the filing office if:

(1) except in the case of a financing statement covering accounts or chattel paper that has been sold or goods that are the subject of a consignment, there is no obligation secured by the collateral covered by the financing statement and no commitment to make an advance, incur an obligation, or otherwise give value;

(2) the financing statement covers accounts or chattel paper that has been sold but as to which the account debtor or other person obligated has discharged its obligation;

(3) the financing statement covers goods that were the subject of a consignment to the debtor but are not in the debtor's possession; or

(4) the debtor did not authorize the filing of the initial financing statement.

(d) Except as otherwise provided in Section 9–510, upon the filing of a termination statement with the filing office, the financing statement to which the termination statement relates ceases to be effective. Except as otherwise provided in Section 9–510, for purposes of Sections 9–519(g), 9–522(a), and 9–523(c), the filing with the filing office of a termination statement relating to a financing statement that indicates that the debtor is a transmitting utility also causes the effectiveness of the financing statement to lapse.

As amended in 2000.

§ 9–514.   Assignment of Powers of Secured Party of Record.

(a) Except as otherwise provided in subsection (c), an initial financing statement may reflect an assignment of all of the secured party's power to authorize an amendment to the financing statement by providing the name and mailing address of the assignee as the name and address of the secured party.

(b) Except as otherwise provided in subsection (c), a secured party of record may assign of record all or part of its power to authorize an amendment to a financing statement by filing in the filing office an amendment of the financing statement which:

(1) identifies, by its file number, the initial financing statement to which it relates;

(2) provides the name of the assignor; and

(3) provides the name and mailing address of the assignee.

(c) An assignment of record of a security interest in a fixture covered by a record of a mortgage which is effective as a financing statement filed as a fixture filing under Section 9–502(c) may be made only by an assignment of record of the mortgage in the manner provided by law of this State other than [the Uniform Commercial Code].

§ 9–515.   Duration and Effectiveness of Financing Statement; Effect of Lapsed Financing Statement.

(a) Except as otherwise provided in subsections (b), (e), (f), and (g), a filed financing statement is effective for a period of five years after the date of filing.

(b) Except as otherwise provided in subsections (e), (f), and (g), an initial financing statement filed in connection with a public-finance transaction or manufactured-home transaction is effective for a period of 30 years after the date of filing if it indicates that it is filed in connection with a public-finance transaction or manufactured-home transaction.

(c) The effectiveness of a filed financing statement lapses on the expiration of the period of its effectiveness unless before the lapse a continuation statement is filed pursuant to subsection (d). Upon lapse, a financing statement ceases to be effective and any security interest or agricultural lien that was perfected by the financing statement becomes unperfected, unless the security interest is perfected otherwise. If the security interest or agricultural lien becomes unperfected upon lapse, it is deemed never to have been perfected as against a purchaser of the collateral for value.

(d) A continuation statement may be filed only within six months before the expiration of the five-year period specified in subsection

(a) or the 30-year period specified in subsection (b), whichever is applicable.

(e) Except as otherwise provided in Section 9–510, upon timely filing of a continuation statement, the effectiveness of the initial financing statement continues for a period of five years commencing on the day on which the financing statement would have become ineffective in the absence of the filing. Upon the expiration of the five-year period, the financing statement lapses in the same manner as provided in subsection (c), unless, before the lapse, another continuation statement is filed pursuant to subsection (d). Succeeding continuation statements may be filed in the same manner to continue the effectiveness of the initial financing statement.

(f) If a debtor is a transmitting utility and a filed financing statement so indicates, the financing statement is effective until a termination statement is filed.

(g) A record of a mortgage that is effective as a financing statement filed as a fixture filing under Section 9–502(c) remains effective as a financing statement filed as a fixture filing until the mortgage is released or satisfied of record or its effectiveness otherwise terminates as to the real property.

§ 9–516.   What Constitutes Filing; Effectiveness of Filing.

(a) Except as otherwise provided in subsection (b), communication of a record to a filing office and tender of the filing fee or acceptance of the record by the filing office constitutes filing.

(b) Filing does not occur with respect to a record that a filing office refuses to accept because:

(1) the record is not communicated by a method or medium of communication authorized by the filing office;

(2) an amount equal to or greater than the applicable filing fee is not tendered;

(3) the filing office is unable to index the record because:

(A) in the case of an initial financing statement, the record does not provide a name for the debtor;

(B) in the case of an amendment or correction statement, the record:

(i) does not identify the initial financing statement as required by Section 9–512 or 9–518, as applicable; or

(ii) identifies an initial financing statement whose effectiveness has lapsed under Section 9–515;

(C) in the case of an initial financing statement that provides the name of a debtor identified as an individual or an amendment that provides a name of a debtor identified as an individual which was not previously provided in the financing statement to which the record relates, the record does not identify the debtor's last name; or

(D) in the case of a record filed [or recorded] in the filing office described in Section 9–501(a)(1), the record does not provide a sufficient description of the real property to which it relates;

(4) in the case of an initial financing statement or an amendment that adds a secured party of record, the record does not provide a name and mailing address for the secured party of record;

(5) in the case of an initial financing statement or an amendment that provides a name of a debtor which was not previously provided in the financing statement to which the amendment relates, the record does not:

(A) provide a mailing address for the debtor;

(B) indicate whether the debtor is an individual or an organization; or

(C) if the financing statement indicates that the debtor is an organization, provide:

(i) a type of organization for the debtor;

(ii) a jurisdiction of organization for the debtor; or

(iii) an organizational identification number for the debtor or indicate that the debtor has none;

(6) in the case of an assignment reflected in an initial financing statement under Section 9–514(a) or an amendment filed under Section 9–514(b), the record does not provide a name and mailing address for the assignee; or

(7) in the case of a continuation statement, the record is not filed within the six-month period prescribed by Section 9–515(d).

(c) For purposes of subsection (b):

(1) a record does not provide information if the filing office is unable to read or decipher the information; and

(2) a record that does not indicate that it is an amendment or identify an initial financing statement to which it relates, as required by Section 9–512, 9–514, or 9–518, is an initial financing statement.

(d) A record that is communicated to the filing office with tender of the filing fee, but which the filing office refuses to accept for a reason other than one set forth in subsection (b), is effective as a filed record except as against a purchaser of the collateral which gives value in reasonable reliance upon the absence of the record from the files.

§ 9–517.   Effect of Indexing Errors.

The failure of the filing office to index a record correctly does not affect the effectiveness of the filed record.

§ 9–518.   Claim Concerning Inaccurate or Wrongfully Filed Record.

(a) A person may file in the filing office a correction statement with respect to a record indexed there under the person's name if the person believes that the record is inaccurate or was wrongfully filed.

[Alternative A]

(b) A correction statement must:

(1) identify the record to which it relates by the file number assigned to the initial financing statement to which the record relates;

(2) indicate that it is a correction statement; and

(3) provide the basis for the person's belief that the record is inaccurate and indicate the manner in which the person believes the record should be amended to cure any inaccuracy or provide the basis for the person's belief that the record was wrongfully filed.

[Alternative B]

(b) A correction statement must:

(1) identify the record to which it relates by:

(A) the file number assigned to the initial financing statement to which the record relates; and

(B) if the correction statement relates to a record filed [or recorded] in a filing office described in Section 9–501(a)(1), the date [and time] that the initial financing statement was filed [or recorded] and the information specified in Section 9–502(b);

(2) indicate that it is a correction statement; and

(3) provide the basis for the person's belief that the record is inaccurate and indicate the manner in which the person believes the record should be amended to cure any inaccuracy or provide the basis for the person's belief that the record was wrongfully filed.

[End of Alternatives]

(c) The filing of a correction statement does not affect the effectiveness of an initial financing statement or other filed record.

Legislative Note: States whose real-estate filing offices require additional information in amendments and cannot search their records by both the name of the debtor and the file number should enact Alternative B to Sections 9–512(a), 9–518(b), 9–519(f), and 9–522(a).

[Subpart 2.   Duties and Operation of Filing Office]

§ 9–519.   Numbering, Maintaining, and Indexing Records; Communicating Information Provided in Records.

(a) For each record filed in a filing office, the filing office shall:

(1) assign a unique number to the filed record;

(2) create a record that bears the number assigned to the filed record and the date and time of filing;

(3) maintain the filed record for public inspection; and

(4) index the filed record in accordance with subsections (c), (d), and (e).

(b) A file number [assigned after January 1, 2002,] must include a digit that:

(1) is mathematically derived from or related to the other digits of the file number; and

(2) aids the filing office in determining whether a number communicated as the file number includes a single-digit or transpositional error.

(c) Except as otherwise provided in subsections (d) and (e), the filing office shall:

(1) index an initial financing statement according to the name of the debtor and index all filed records relating to the initial financing statement in a manner that associates with one another an initial financing statement and all filed records relating to the initial financing statement; and

(2) index a record that provides a name of a debtor which was not previously provided in the financing statement to which the record relates also according to the name that was not previously provided.

(d) If a financing statement is filed as a fixture filing or covers as-extracted collateral or timber to be cut, [it must be filed for record and] the filing office shall index it:

(1) under the names of the debtor and of each owner of record shown on the financing statement as if they were the mortgagors under a mortgage of the real property described; and

(2) to the extent that the law of this State provides for indexing of records of mortgages under the name of the mortgagee, under the name of the secured party as if the secured party were the mortgagee thereunder, or, if indexing is by description, as if the financing statement were a record of a mortgage of the real property described.

(e) If a financing statement is filed as a fixture filing or covers as-extracted collateral or timber to be cut, the filing office shall index an assignment filed under Section 9–514(a) or an amendment filed under Section 9–514(b):

(1) under the name of the assignor as grantor; and

(2) to the extent that the law of this State provides for indexing a record of the assignment of a mortgage under the name of the assignee, under the name of the assignee.

[Alternative A]

(f) The filing office shall maintain a capability:

(1) to retrieve a record by the name of the debtor and by the file number assigned to the initial financing statement to which the record relates; and

(2) to associate and retrieve with one another an initial financing statement and each filed record relating to the initial financing statement.

[Alternative B]

(f) The filing office shall maintain a capability:

(1) to retrieve a record by the name of the debtor and:

(A) if the filing office is described in Section 9–501(a)(1), by the file number assigned to the initial financing statement to which the record relates and the date [and time] that the record was filed [or recorded]; or

(B) if the filing office is described in Section 9–501(a)(2), by the file number assigned to the initial financing statement to which the record relates; and

(2) to associate and retrieve with one another an initial financing statement and each filed record relating to the initial financing statement.

[End of Alternatives]

(g) The filing office may not remove a debtor's name from the index until one year after the effectiveness of a financing statement naming the debtor lapses under Section 9–515 with respect to all secured parties of record.

(h) The filing office shall perform the acts required by subsections (a) through (e) at the time and in the manner prescribed by filing-office rule, but not later than two business days after the filing office receives the record in question.

[(i) Subsection[s] [(b)] [and] [(h)] do[es] not apply to a filing office described in Section 9–501(a)(1).]

Legislative Notes:

1. States whose filing offices currently assign file numbers that include a verification number, commonly known as a "check digit," or can implement this requirement before the effective date of this Article should omit the bracketed language in subsection (b).

2. In States in which writings will not appear in the real property records and indices unless actually recorded the bracketed language in subsection (d) should be used.

3. States whose real-estate filing offices require additional information in amendments and cannot search their records by both the name of the debtor and the file number should enact Alternative B to Sections 9–512(a), 9–518(b), 9–519(f), and 9–522(a).

4. A State that elects not to require real-estate filing offices to comply with either or both of subsections (b) and (h) may adopt an applicable variation of subsection (i) and add "Except as otherwise provided in subsection (i)," to the appropriate subsection or subsections.

§ 9–520. Acceptance and Refusal to Accept Record.

(a) A filing office shall refuse to accept a record for filing for a reason set forth in Section 9–516(b) and may refuse to accept a record for filing only for a reason set forth in Section 9–516(b).

(b) If a filing office refuses to accept a record for filing, it shall communicate to the person that presented the record the fact of and reason for the refusal and the date and time the record would have been filed had the filing office accepted it. The communication must be made at the time and in the manner prescribed by filing-office rule but [, in the case of a filing office described in Section 9–501(a)(2),] in no event more than two business days after the filing office receives the record.

(c) A filed financing statement satisfying Section 9–502(a) and (b) is effective, even if the filing office is required to refuse to accept it for filing under subsection (a). However, Section 9–338 applies to a filed financing statement providing information described in Section 9–516(b)(5) which is incorrect at the time the financing statement is filed.

(d) If a record communicated to a filing office provides information that relates to more than one debtor, this part applies as to each debtor separately.

Legislative Note: A State that elects not to require real-property filing offices to comply with subsection (b) should include the bracketed language.

§ 9–521. Uniform Form of Written Financing Statement and Amendment.

(a) A filing office that accepts written records may not refuse to accept a written initial financing statement in the following form and format except for a reason set forth in Section 9–516(b):

[NATIONAL UCC FINANCING STATEMENT (FORM UCC1) (REV. 7/29/98)]

[NATIONAL UCC FINANCING STATEMENT ADDENDUM (FORM UCC1Ad) (REV. 07/29/98)]

(b) A filing office that accepts written records may not refuse to accept a written record in the following form and format except for a reason set forth in Section 9–516(b):

[NATIONAL UCC FINANCING STATEMENT AMENDMENT (FORM UCC3) (REV. 07/29/98)]

[NATIONAL UCC FINANCING STATEMENT AMENDMENT ADDENDUM (FORM UCC3Ad) (REV. 07/29/98)]

§ 9–522. Maintenance and Destruction of Records.

[Alternative A]

(a) The filing office shall maintain a record of the information provided in a filed financing statement for at least one year after the effectiveness of the financing statement has lapsed under Section 9–515 with respect to all secured parties of record. The record must be retrievable by using the name of the debtor and by using the file number assigned to the initial financing statement to which the record relates.

[Alternative B]

(a) The filing office shall maintain a record of the information provided in a filed financing statement for at least one year after the effectiveness of the financing statement has lapsed under Section 9–515 with respect to all secured parties of record. The record must be retrievable by using the name of the debtor and:

(1) if the record was filed [or recorded] in the filing office described in Section 9–501(a)(1), by using the file number assigned to the initial financing statement to which the record relates and the date [and time] that the record was filed [or recorded]; or

(2) if the record was filed in the filing office described in Section 9–501(a)(2), by using the file number assigned to the initial financing statement to which the record relates.

[End of Alternatives]

(b) Except to the extent that a statute governing disposition of public records provides otherwise, the filing office immediately may destroy any written record evidencing a financing statement. However, if the filing office destroys a written record, it shall maintain another record of the financing statement which complies with subsection (a).

Legislative Note: States whose real-estate filing offices require additional information in amendments and cannot search their records by both the name of the debtor and the file number should enact Alternative B to Sections 9–512(a), 9–518(b), 9–519(f), and 9–522(a).

§ 9–523. Information from Filing Office; Sale or License of Records.

(a) If a person that files a written record requests an acknowledgment of the filing, the filing office shall send to the person an image of the record showing the number assigned to the record pursuant to Section 9–519(a)(1) and the date and time of the filing of the record. However, if the person furnishes a copy of the record to the filing office, the filing office may instead:

(1) note upon the copy the number assigned to the record pursuant to Section 9–519(a)(1) and the date and time of the filing of the record; and

(2) send the copy to the person.

(b) If a person files a record other than a written record, the filing office shall communicate to the person an acknowledgment that provides:

(1) the information in the record;

(2) the number assigned to the record pursuant to Section 9–519(a)(1); and

(3) the date and time of the filing of the record.

(c) The filing office shall communicate or otherwise make available in a record the following information to any person that requests it:

(1) whether there is on file on a date and time specified by the filing office, but not a date earlier than three business days before the filing office receives the request, any financing statement that:

(A) designates a particular debtor [or, if the request so states, designates a particular debtor at the address specified in the request];

(B) has not lapsed under Section 9–515 with respect to all secured parties of record; and

(C) if the request so states, has lapsed under Section 9–515 and a record of which is maintained by the filing office under Section 9–522(a);

(2) the date and time of filing of each financing statement; and

(3) the information provided in each financing statement.

(d) In complying with its duty under subsection (c), the filing office may communicate information in any medium. However, if requested, the filing office shall communicate information by issuing [its written certificate] [a record that can be admitted into evidence in the courts of this State without extrinsic evidence of its authenticity].

(e) The filing office shall perform the acts required by subsections (a) through (d) at the time and in the manner prescribed by filing-office rule, but not later than two business days after the filing office receives the request.

(f) At least weekly, the [insert appropriate official or governmental agency] [filing office] shall offer to sell or license to the public on a nonexclusive basis, in bulk, copies of all records filed in it under this part, in every medium from time to time available to the filing office.

Legislative Notes:

1. States whose filing office does not offer the additional service of responding to search requests limited to a particular address should omit the bracketed language in subsection (c)(1)(A).

2. A State that elects not to require real-estate filing offices to comply with either or both of subsections (e) and (f) should specify in the appropriate subsection(s) only the filing office described in Section 9–501(a)(2).

§ 9–524. Delay by Filing Office.

Delay by the filing office beyond a time limit prescribed by this part is excused if:

(1) the delay is caused by interruption of communication or computer facilities, war, emergency conditions, failure of equipment, or other circumstances beyond control of the filing office; and

(2) the filing office exercises reasonable diligence under the circumstances.

§ 9–525. Fees.

(a) Except as otherwise provided in subsection (e), the fee for filing and indexing a record under this part, other than an initial financing statement of the kind described in subsection (b), is [the amount specified in subsection (c), if applicable, plus]:

(1) $[X] if the record is communicated in writing and consists of one or two pages;

(2) $[2X] if the record is communicated in writing and consists of more than two pages; and

(3) $[½X] if the record is communicated by another medium authorized by filing-office rule.

(b) Except as otherwise provided in subsection (e), the fee for filing and indexing an initial financing statement of the following kind is [the amount specified in subsection (c), if applicable, plus]:

(1) $_____ if the financing statement indicates that it is filed in connection with a public-finance transaction;

(2) $_____ if the financing statement indicates that it is filed in connection with a manufactured-home transaction.

[Alternative A]

(c) The number of names required to be indexed does not affect the amount of the fee in subsections (a) and (b).

[Alternative B]

(c) Except as otherwise provided in subsection (e), if a record is communicated in writing, the fee for each name more than two required to be indexed is $_____.

[End of Alternatives]

(d) The fee for responding to a request for information from the filing office, including for [issuing a certificate showing] [communicating] whether there is on file any financing statement naming a particular debtor, is:

(1) $_____ if the request is communicated in writing; and

(2) $_____ if the request is communicated by another medium authorized by filing-office rule.

(e) This section does not require a fee with respect to a record of a mortgage which is effective as a financing statement filed as a fixture filing or as a financing statement covering as-extracted collateral or timber to be cut under Section 9–502(c). However, the recording and satisfaction fees that otherwise would be applicable to the record of the mortgage apply.

Legislative Notes:

1. To preserve uniformity, a State that places the provisions of this section together with statutes setting fees for other services should do so without modification.

2. A State should enact subsection (c), Alternative A, and omit the bracketed language in subsections (a) and (b) unless its indexing system entails a substantial additional cost when indexing additional names.

As amended in 2000.

§ 9–526. Filing-Office Rules.

(a) The [insert appropriate governmental official or agency] shall adopt and publish rules to implement this article. The filing-office rules must be[:

(1)] consistent with this article[; and

(2) adopted and published in accordance with the [insert any applicable state administrative procedure act]].

(b) To keep the filing-office rules and practices of the filing office in harmony with the rules and practices of filing offices in other jurisdictions that enact substantially this part, and to keep the technology used by the filing office compatible with the technology used by filing offices in other jurisdictions that enact substantially this part, the [insert appropriate governmental official or agency], so far as is consistent with the purposes, policies, and provisions of this article, in adopting, amending, and repealing filing-office rules, shall:

(1) consult with filing offices in other jurisdictions that enact substantially this part; and

(2) consult the most recent version of the Model Rules promulgated by the International Association of Corporate Administrators or any successor organization; and

(3) take into consideration the rules and practices of, and the technology used by, filing offices in other jurisdictions that enact substantially this part.

§ 9–527. Duty to Report.

The [insert appropriate governmental official or agency] shall report [annually on or before _____] to the [Governor and Legislature] on the operation of the filing office. The report must contain a statement of the extent to which:

(1) the filing-office rules are not in harmony with the rules of filing offices in other jurisdictions that enact substantially this part and the reasons for these variations; and

(2) the filing-office rules are not in harmony with the most recent version of the Model Rules promulgated by the International Association of Corporate Administrators, or any successor organization, and the reasons for these variations.

Part 6 Default

[Subpart 1. Default and Enforcement of Security Interest]

§ 9–601. Rights after Default; Judicial Enforcement; Consignor or Buyer of Accounts, Chattel Paper, Payment Intangibles, or Promissory Notes.

(a) After default, a secured party has the rights provided in this part and, except as otherwise provided in Section 9–602, those provided by agreement of the parties. A secured party:

(1) may reduce a claim to judgment, foreclose, or otherwise enforce the claim, security interest, or agricultural lien by any available judicial procedure; and

(2) if the collateral is documents, may proceed either as to the documents or as to the goods they cover.

(b) A secured party in possession of collateral or control of collateral under Section 9–104, 9–105, 9–106, or 9–107 has the rights and duties provided in Section 9–207.

(c) The rights under subsections (a) and (b) are cumulative and may be exercised simultaneously.

(d) Except as otherwise provided in subsection (g) and Section 9–605, after default, a debtor and an obligor have the rights provided in this part and by agreement of the parties.

(e) If a secured party has reduced its claim to judgment, the lien of any levy that may be made upon the collateral by virtue of an execution based upon the judgment relates back to the earliest of:

(1) the date of perfection of the security interest or agricultural lien in the collateral;

(2) the date of filing a financing statement covering the collateral; or

(3) any date specified in a statute under which the agricultural lien was created.

(f) A sale pursuant to an execution is a foreclosure of the security interest or agricultural lien by judicial procedure within the meaning of this section. A secured party may purchase at the sale and thereafter hold the collateral free of any other requirements of this article.

(g) Except as otherwise provided in Section 9–607(c), this part imposes no duties upon a secured party that is a consignor or is a buyer of accounts, chattel paper, payment intangibles, or promissory notes.

§ 9–602. Waiver and Variance of Rights and Duties.

Except as otherwise provided in Section 9–624, to the extent that they give rights to a debtor or obligor and impose duties on a secured party, the debtor or obligor may not waive or vary the rules stated in the following listed sections:

(1) Section 9–207(b)(4)(C), which deals with use and operation of the collateral by the secured party;

(2) Section 9–210, which deals with requests for an accounting and requests concerning a list of collateral and statement of account;

(3) Section 9–607(c), which deals with collection and enforcement of collateral;

(4) Sections 9–608(a) and 9–615(c) to the extent that they deal with application or payment of noncash proceeds of collection, enforcement, or disposition;

(5) Sections 9–608(a) and 9–615(d) to the extent that they require accounting for or payment of surplus proceeds of collateral;

(6) Section 9–609 to the extent that it imposes upon a secured party that takes possession of collateral without judicial process the duty to do so without breach of the peace;

(7) Sections 9–610(b), 9–611, 9–613, and 9–614, which deal with disposition of collateral;

(8) Section 9–615(f), which deals with calculation of a deficiency or surplus when a disposition is made to the secured party, a person related to the secured party, or a secondary obligor;

(9) Section 9–616, which deals with explanation of the calculation of a surplus or deficiency;

(10) Sections 9–620, 9–621, and 9–622, which deal with acceptance of collateral in satisfaction of obligation;

(11) Section 9–623, which deals with redemption of collateral;

(12) Section 9–624, which deals with permissible waivers; and

(13) Sections 9–625 and 9–626, which deal with the secured party's liability for failure to comply with this article.

§ 9–603.   Agreement on Standards Concerning Rights and Duties.

(a) The parties may determine by agreement the standards measuring the fulfillment of the rights of a debtor or obligor and the duties of a secured party under a rule stated in Section 9–602 if the standards are not manifestly unreasonable.

(b) Subsection (a) does not apply to the duty under Section 9–609 to refrain from breaching the peace.

§ 9–604.   Procedure If Security Agreement Covers Real Property or Fixtures.

(a) If a security agreement covers both personal and real property, a secured party may proceed:

(1) under this part as to the personal property without prejudicing any rights with respect to the real property; or

(2) as to both the personal property and the real property in accordance with the rights with respect to the real property, in which case the other provisions of this part do not apply.

(b) Subject to subsection (c), if a security agreement covers goods that are or become fixtures, a secured party may proceed:

(1) under this part; or

(2) in accordance with the rights with respect to real property, in which case the other provisions of this part do not apply.

(c) Subject to the other provisions of this part, if a secured party holding a security interest in fixtures has priority over all owners and encumbrancers of the real property, the secured party, after default, may remove the collateral from the real property.

(d) A secured party that removes collateral shall promptly reimburse any encumbrancer or owner of the real property, other than the debtor, for the cost of repair of any physical injury caused by the removal. The secured party need not reimburse the encumbrancer or owner for any diminution in value of the real property caused by the absence of the goods removed or by any necessity of replacing them. A person entitled to reimbursement may refuse permission to remove until the secured party gives adequate assurance for the performance of the obligation to reimburse.

§ 9–605.   Unknown Debtor or Secondary Obligor.

A secured party does not owe a duty based on its status as secured party:

(1) to a person that is a debtor or obligor, unless the secured party knows:

(A) that the person is a debtor or obligor;

(B) the identity of the person; and

(C) how to communicate with the person; or

(2) to a secured party or lienholder that has filed a financing statement against a person, unless the secured party knows:

(A) that the person is a debtor; and

(B) the identity of the person.

§ 9–606.   Time of Default for Agricultural Lien.

For purposes of this part, a default occurs in connection with an agricultural lien at the time the secured party becomes entitled to enforce the lien in accordance with the statute under which it was created.

§ 9–607.   Collection and Enforcement by Secured Party.

(a) If so agreed, and in any event after default, a secured party:

(1) may notify an account debtor or other person obligated on collateral to make payment or otherwise render performance to or for the benefit of the secured party;

(2) may take any proceeds to which the secured party is entitled under Section 9–315;

(3) may enforce the obligations of an account debtor or other person obligated on collateral and exercise the rights of the debtor with respect to the obligation of the account debtor or other person obligated on collateral to make payment or otherwise render performance to the debtor, and with respect to any property that secures the obligations of the account debtor or other person obligated on the collateral;

(4) if it holds a security interest in a deposit account perfected by control under Section 9–104(a)(1), may apply the balance of the deposit account to the obligation secured by the deposit account; and

(5) if it holds a security interest in a deposit account perfected by control under Section 9–104(a)(2) or (3), may instruct the bank to pay the balance of the deposit account to or for the benefit of the secured party.

(b) If necessary to enable a secured party to exercise under subsection (a)(3) the right of a debtor to enforce a mortgage nonjudicially, the secured party may record in the office in which a record of the mortgage is recorded:

(1) a copy of the security agreement that creates or provides for a security interest in the obligation secured by the mortgage; and

(2) the secured party's sworn affidavit in recordable form stating that:

(A) a default has occurred; and

(B) the secured party is entitled to enforce the mortgage nonjudicially.

(c) A secured party shall proceed in a commercially reasonable manner if the secured party:

(1) undertakes to collect from or enforce an obligation of an account debtor or other person obligated on collateral; and

(2) is entitled to charge back uncollected collateral or otherwise to full or limited recourse against the debtor or a secondary obligor.

(d) A secured party may deduct from the collections made pursuant to subsection (c) reasonable expenses of collection and enforcement, including reasonable attorney's fees and legal expenses incurred by the secured party.

(e) This section does not determine whether an account debtor, bank, or other person obligated on collateral owes a duty to a secured party.

As amended in 2000.

§ 9–608.   Application of Proceeds of Collection or Enforcement; Liability for Deficiency and Right to Surplus.

(a) If a security interest or agricultural lien secures payment or performance of an obligation, the following rules apply:

   (1) A secured party shall apply or pay over for application the cash proceeds of collection or enforcement under Section 9–607 in the following order to:

      (A) the reasonable expenses of collection and enforcement and, to the extent provided for by agreement and not prohibited by law, reasonable attorney's fees and legal expenses incurred by the secured party;

      (B) the satisfaction of obligations secured by the security interest or agricultural lien under which the collection or enforcement is made; and

      (C) the satisfaction of obligations secured by any subordinate security interest in or other lien on the collateral subject to the security interest or agricultural lien under which the collection or enforcement is made if the secured party receives an authenticated demand for proceeds before distribution of the proceeds is completed.

   (2) If requested by a secured party, a holder of a subordinate security interest or other lien shall furnish reasonable proof of the interest or lien within a reasonable time. Unless the holder complies, the secured party need not comply with the holder's demand under paragraph (1)(C).

   (3) A secured party need not apply or pay over for application noncash proceeds of collection and enforcement under Section 9–607 unless the failure to do so would be commercially unreasonable. A secured party that applies or pays over for application noncash proceeds shall do so in a commercially reasonable manner.

   (4) A secured party shall account to and pay a debtor for any surplus, and the obligor is liable for any deficiency.

(b) If the underlying transaction is a sale of accounts, chattel paper, payment intangibles, or promissory notes, the debtor is not entitled to any surplus, and the obligor is not liable for any deficiency.

As amended in 2000.

§ 9–609.   Secured Party's Right to Take Possession after Default.

(a) After default, a secured party:

   (1) may take possession of the collateral; and

   (2) without removal, may render equipment unusable and dispose of collateral on a debtor's premises under Section 9–610.

(b) A secured party may proceed under subsection (a):

   (1) pursuant to judicial process; or

   (2) without judicial process, if it proceeds without breach of the peace.

(c) If so agreed, and in any event after default, a secured party may require the debtor to assemble the collateral and make it available to the secured party at a place to be designated by the secured party which is reasonably convenient to both parties.

§ 9–610.   Disposition of Collateral after Default.

(a) After default, a secured party may sell, lease, license, or otherwise dispose of any or all of the collateral in its present condition or following any commercially reasonable preparation or processing.

(b) Every aspect of a disposition of collateral, including the method, manner, time, place, and other terms, must be commercially reasonable. If commercially reasonable, a secured party may dispose of collateral by public or private proceedings, by one or more contracts, as a unit or in parcels, and at any time and place and on any terms.

(c) A secured party may purchase collateral:

   (1) at a public disposition; or

   (2) at a private disposition only if the collateral is of a kind that is customarily sold on a recognized market or the subject of widely distributed standard price quotations.

(d) A contract for sale, lease, license, or other disposition includes the warranties relating to title, possession, quiet enjoyment, and the like which by operation of law accompany a voluntary disposition of property of the kind subject to the contract.

(e) A secured party may disclaim or modify warranties under subsection (d):

   (1) in a manner that would be effective to disclaim or modify the warranties in a voluntary disposition of property of the kind subject to the contract of disposition; or

   (2) by communicating to the purchaser a record evidencing the contract for disposition and including an express disclaimer or modification of the warranties.

(f) A record is sufficient to disclaim warranties under subsection (e) if it indicates "There is no warranty relating to title, possession, quiet enjoyment, or the like in this disposition" or uses words of similar import.

§ 9–611.   Notification before Disposition of Collateral.

(a) In this section, "notification date" means the earlier of the date on which:

   (1) a secured party sends to the debtor and any secondary obligor an authenticated notification of disposition; or

   (2) the debtor and any secondary obligor waive the right to notification.

(b) Except as otherwise provided in subsection (d), a secured party that disposes of collateral under Section 9–610 shall send to the persons specified in subsection (c) a reasonable authenticated notification of disposition.

(c) To comply with subsection (b), the secured party shall send an authenticated notification of disposition to:

   (1) the debtor;

   (2) any secondary obligor; and

   (3) if the collateral is other than consumer goods:

(A) any other person from which the secured party has received, before the notification date, an authenticated notification of a claim of an interest in the collateral;

(B) any other secured party or lienholder that, 10 days before the notification date, held a security interest in or other lien on the collateral perfected by the filing of a financing statement that:

(i) identified the collateral;

(ii) was indexed under the debtor's name as of that date; and

(iii) was filed in the office in which to file a financing statement against the debtor covering the collateral as of that date; and

(C) any other secured party that, 10 days before the notification date, held a security interest in the collateral perfected by compliance with a statute, regulation, or treaty described in Section 9–311(a).

(d) Subsection (b) does not apply if the collateral is perishable or threatens to decline speedily in value or is of a type customarily sold on a recognized market.

(e) A secured party complies with the requirement for notification prescribed by subsection (c)(3)(B) if:

(1) not later than 20 days or earlier than 30 days before the notification date, the secured party requests, in a commercially reasonable manner, information concerning financing statements indexed under the debtor's name in the office indicated in subsection (c)(3)(B); and

(2) before the notification date, the secured party:

(A) did not receive a response to the request for information; or

(B) received a response to the request for information and sent an authenticated notification of disposition to each secured party or other lienholder named in that response whose financing statement covered the collateral.

§ 9–612.   Timeliness of Notification before Disposition of Collateral.

(a) Except as otherwise provided in subsection (b), whether a notification is sent within a reasonable time is a question of fact.

(b) In a transaction other than a consumer transaction, a notification of disposition sent after default and 10 days or more before the earliest time of disposition set forth in the notification is sent within a reasonable time before the disposition.

§ 9–613.   Contents and Form of Notification before Disposition of Collateral: General.

Except in a consumer-goods transaction, the following rules apply:

(1) The contents of a notification of disposition are sufficient if the notification:

(A) describes the debtor and the secured party;

(B) describes the collateral that is the subject of the intended disposition;

(C) states the method of intended disposition;

(D) states that the debtor is entitled to an accounting of the unpaid indebtedness and states the charge, if any, for an accounting; and

(E) states the time and place of a public disposition or the time after which any other disposition is to be made.

(2) Whether the contents of a notification that lacks any of the information specified in paragraph (1) are nevertheless sufficient is a question of fact.

(3) The contents of a notification providing substantially the information specified in paragraph (1) are sufficient, even if the notification includes:

(A) information not specified by that paragraph; or

(B) minor errors that are not seriously misleading.

(4) A particular phrasing of the notification is not required.

(5) The following form of notification and the form appearing in Section 9–614(3), when completed, each provides sufficient information:

NOTIFICATION OF DISPOSITION OF COLLATERAL

To: [*Name of debtor, obligor, or other person to which the notification is sent*]

From: [*Name, address, and telephone number of secured party*]

Name of Debtor(s): [*Include only if debtor(s) are not an addressee*]

[*For a public disposition:*]

We will sell [or lease or license, *as applicable*] the [*describe collateral*] [to the highest qualified bidder] in public as follows:

Day and Date: _____

Time: _____

Place: _____

[*For a private disposition:*]

We will sell [or lease or license, *as applicable*] the [*describe collateral*] privately sometime after [*day and date*].

You are entitled to an accounting of the unpaid indebtedness secured by the property that we intend to sell [or lease or license, *as applicable*] [for a charge of $_____]. You may request an accounting by calling us at [*telephone number*].

[End of Form]

As amended in 2000.

§ 9–614.   Contents and Form of Notification before Disposition of Collateral: Consumer-Goods Transaction.

In a consumer-goods transaction, the following rules apply:

(1) A notification of disposition must provide the following information:

(A) the information specified in Section 9–613(1);

(B) a description of any liability for a deficiency of the person to which the notification is sent;

(C) a telephone number from which the amount that must be paid to the secured party to redeem the collateral under Section 9–623 is available; and

(D) a telephone number or mailing address from which additional information concerning the disposition and the obligation secured is available.

(2) A particular phrasing of the notification is not required.

(3) The following form of notification, when completed, provides sufficient information:

> [*Name and address of secured party*]
>
> [*Date*]

NOTICE OF OUR PLAN TO SELL PROPERTY

[*Name and address of any obligor who is also a debtor*]

Subject: [*Identification of Transaction*]

We have your [*describe collateral*], because you broke promises in our agreement.

> [*For a public disposition:*]

We will sell [*describe collateral*] at public sale. A sale could include a lease or license. The sale will be held as follows:

> Date: _____
>
> Time: _____
>
> Place: _____

You may attend the sale and bring bidders if you want.

> [*For a private disposition:*]

We will sell [*describe collateral*] at private sale sometime after [*date*]. A sale could include a lease or license.

The money that we get from the sale (after paying our costs) will reduce the amount you owe. If we get less money than you owe, you [*will or will not, as applicable*] still owe us the difference. If we get more money than you owe, you will get the extra money, unless we must pay it to someone else.

You can get the property back at any time before we sell it by paying us the full amount you owe (not just the past due payments), including our expenses. To learn the exact amount you must pay, call us at [*telephone number*].

If you want us to explain to you in writing how we have figured the amount that you owe us, you may call us at [telephone number] [or write us at [*secured party's address*]] and request a written explanation. [We will charge you $_____ for the explanation if we sent you another written explanation of the amount you owe us within the last six months.]

If you need more information about the sale call us at [*telephone number*] [or write us at [secured party's address]].

We are sending this notice to the following other people who have an interest in [*describe collateral*] or who owe money under your agreement:

[*Names of all other debtors and obligors, if any*]

[End of Form]

(4) A notification in the form of paragraph (3) is sufficient, even if additional information appears at the end of the form.

(5) A notification in the form of paragraph (3) is sufficient, even if it includes errors in information not required by paragraph (1), unless the error is misleading with respect to rights arising under this article.

(6) If a notification under this section is not in the form of paragraph (3), law other than this article determines the effect of including information not required by paragraph (1).

§ 9–615.   Application of Proceeds of Disposition; Liability for Deficiency and Right to Surplus.

(a) A secured party shall apply or pay over for application the cash proceeds of disposition under Section 9–610 in the following order to:

> (1) the reasonable expenses of retaking, holding, preparing for disposition, processing, and disposing, and, to the extent provided for by agreement and not prohibited by law, reasonable attorney's fees and legal expenses incurred by the secured party;
>
> (2) the satisfaction of obligations secured by the security interest or agricultural lien under which the disposition is made;
>
> (3) the satisfaction of obligations secured by any subordinate security interest in or other subordinate lien on the collateral if:
>
> > (A) the secured party receives from the holder of the subordinate security interest or other lien an authenticated demand for proceeds before distribution of the proceeds is completed; and
> >
> > (B) in a case in which a consignor has an interest in the collateral, the subordinate security interest or other lien is senior to the interest of the consignor; and
>
> (4) a secured party that is a consignor of the collateral if the secured party receives from the consignor an authenticated demand for proceeds before distribution of the proceeds is completed.

(b) If requested by a secured party, a holder of a subordinate security interest or other lien shall furnish reasonable proof of the interest or lien within a reasonable time. Unless the holder does so, the secured party need not comply with the holder's demand under subsection (a)(3).

(c) A secured party need not apply or pay over for application noncash proceeds of disposition under Section 9–610 unless the failure to do so would be commercially unreasonable. A secured party that applies or pays over for application noncash proceeds shall do so in a commercially reasonable manner.

(d) If the security interest under which a disposition is made secures payment or performance of an obligation, after making the payments and applications required by subsection (a) and permitted by subsection (c):

> (1) unless subsection (a)(4) requires the secured party to apply or pay over cash proceeds to a consignor, the secured party shall account to and pay a debtor for any surplus; and
>
> (2) the obligor is liable for any deficiency.

(e) If the underlying transaction is a sale of accounts, chattel paper, payment intangibles, or promissory notes:

> (1) the debtor is not entitled to any surplus; and
>
> (2) the obligor is not liable for any deficiency.

(f) The surplus or deficiency following a disposition is calculated based on the amount of proceeds that would have been realized in a disposition complying with this part to a transferee other than the secured party, a person related to the secured party, or a secondary obligor if:

(1) the transferee in the disposition is the secured party, a person related to the secured party, or a secondary obligor; and

(2) the amount of proceeds of the disposition is significantly below the range of proceeds that a complying disposition to a person other than the secured party, a person related to the secured party, or a secondary obligor would have brought.

(g) A secured party that receives cash proceeds of a disposition in good faith and without knowledge that the receipt violates the rights of the holder of a security interest or other lien that is not subordinate to the security interest or agricultural lien under which the disposition is made:

(1) takes the cash proceeds free of the security interest or other lien;

(2) is not obligated to apply the proceeds of the disposition to the satisfaction of obligations secured by the security interest or other lien; and

(3) is not obligated to account to or pay the holder of the security interest or other lien for any surplus.

As amended in 2000.

§ 9–616.   Explanation of Calculation of Surplus or Deficiency.

(a) In this section:

(1) "Explanation" means a writing that:

(A) states the amount of the surplus or deficiency;

(B) provides an explanation in accordance with subsection (c) of how the secured party calculated the surplus or deficiency;

(C) states, if applicable, that future debits, credits, charges, including additional credit service charges or interest, rebates, and expenses may affect the amount of the surplus or deficiency; and

(D) provides a telephone number or mailing address from which additional information concerning the transaction is available.

(2) "Request" means a record:

(A) authenticated by a debtor or consumer obligor;

(B) requesting that the recipient provide an explanation; and

(C) sent after disposition of the collateral under Section 9–610.

(b) In a consumer-goods transaction in which the debtor is entitled to a surplus or a consumer obligor is liable for a deficiency under Section 9–615, the secured party shall:

(1) send an explanation to the debtor or consumer obligor, as applicable, after the disposition and:

(A) before or when the secured party accounts to the debtor and pays any surplus or first makes written demand on the consumer obligor after the disposition for payment of the deficiency; and

(B) within 14 days after receipt of a request; or

(2) in the case of a consumer obligor who is liable for a deficiency, within 14 days after receipt of a request, send to the consumer obligor a record waiving the secured party's right to a deficiency.

(c) To comply with subsection (a)(1)(B), a writing must provide the following information in the following order:

(1) the aggregate amount of obligations secured by the security interest under which the disposition was made, and, if the amount reflects a rebate of unearned interest or credit service charge, an indication of that fact, calculated as of a specified date:

(A) if the secured party takes or receives possession of the collateral after default, not more than 35 days before the secured party takes or receives possession; or

(B) if the secured party takes or receives possession of the collateral before default or does not take possession of the collateral, not more than 35 days before the disposition;

(2) the amount of proceeds of the disposition;

(3) the aggregate amount of the obligations after deducting the amount of proceeds;

(4) the amount, in the aggregate or by type, and types of expenses, including expenses of retaking, holding, preparing for disposition, processing, and disposing of the collateral, and attorney's fees secured by the collateral which are known to the secured party and relate to the current disposition;

(5) the amount, in the aggregate or by type, and types of credits, including rebates of interest or credit service charges, to which the obligor is known to be entitled and which are not reflected in the amount in paragraph (1); and

(6) the amount of the surplus or deficiency.

(d) A particular phrasing of the explanation is not required. An explanation complying substantially with the requirements of subsection (a) is sufficient, even if it includes minor errors that are not seriously misleading.

(e) A debtor or consumer obligor is entitled without charge to one response to a request under this section during any six-month period in which the secured party did not send to the debtor or consumer obligor an explanation pursuant to subsection (b)(1). The secured party may require payment of a charge not exceeding $25 for each additional response.

§ 9–617.   Rights of Transferee of Collateral.

(a) A secured party's disposition of collateral after default:

(1) transfers to a transferee for value all of the debtor's rights in the collateral;

(2) discharges the security interest under which the disposition is made; and

(3) discharges any subordinate security interest or other subordinate lien [other than liens created under [cite acts

or statutes providing for liens, if any, that are not to be discharged]].

(b) A transferee that acts in good faith takes free of the rights and interests described in subsection (a), even if the secured party fails to comply with this article or the requirements of any judicial proceeding.

(c) If a transferee does not take free of the rights and interests described in subsection (a), the transferee takes the collateral subject to:

(1) the debtor's rights in the collateral;

(2) the security interest or agricultural lien under which the disposition is made; and

(3) any other security interest or other lien.

§ 9–618.   Rights and Duties of Certain Secondary Obligors.

(a) A secondary obligor acquires the rights and becomes obligated to perform the duties of the secured party after the secondary obligor:

(1) receives an assignment of a secured obligation from the secured party;

(2) receives a transfer of collateral from the secured party and agrees to accept the rights and assume the duties of the secured party; or

(3) is subrogated to the rights of a secured party with respect to collateral.

(b) An assignment, transfer, or subrogation described in subsection (a):

(1) is not a disposition of collateral under Section 9–610; and

(2) relieves the secured party of further duties under this article.

§ 9–619.   Transfer of Record or Legal Title.

(a) In this section, "transfer statement" means a record authenticated by a secured party stating:

(1) that the debtor has defaulted in connection with an obligation secured by specified collateral;

(2) that the secured party has exercised its post-default remedies with respect to the collateral;

(3) that, by reason of the exercise, a transferee has acquired the rights of the debtor in the collateral; and

(4) the name and mailing address of the secured party, debtor, and transferee.

(b) A transfer statement entitles the transferee to the transfer of record of all rights of the debtor in the collateral specified in the statement in any official filing, recording, registration, or certificate-of-title system covering the collateral. If a transfer statement is presented with the applicable fee and request form to the official or office responsible for maintaining the system, the official or office shall:

(1) accept the transfer statement;

(2) promptly amend its records to reflect the transfer; and

(3) if applicable, issue a new appropriate certificate of title in the name of the transferee.

(c) A transfer of the record or legal title to collateral to a secured party under subsection (b) or otherwise is not of itself a disposition of collateral under this article and does not of itself relieve the secured party of its duties under this article.

§ 9–620.   Acceptance of Collateral in Full or Partial Satisfaction of Obligation; Compulsory Disposition of Collateral.

(a) Except as otherwise provided in subsection (g), a secured party may accept collateral in full or partial satisfaction of the obligation it secures only if:

(1) the debtor consents to the acceptance under subsection (c);

(2) the secured party does not receive, within the time set forth in subsection (d), a notification of objection to the proposal authenticated by:

(A) a person to which the secured party was required to send a proposal under Section 9–621; or

(B) any other person, other than the debtor, holding an interest in the collateral subordinate to the security interest that is the subject of the proposal;

(3) if the collateral is consumer goods, the collateral is not in the possession of the debtor when the debtor consents to the acceptance; and

(4) subsection (e) does not require the secured party to dispose of the collateral or the debtor waives the requirement pursuant to Section 9–624.

(b) A purported or apparent acceptance of collateral under this section is ineffective unless:

(1) the secured party consents to the acceptance in an authenticated record or sends a proposal to the debtor; and

(2) the conditions of subsection (a) are met.

(c) For purposes of this section:

(1) a debtor consents to an acceptance of collateral in partial satisfaction of the obligation it secures only if the debtor agrees to the terms of the acceptance in a record authenticated after default; and

(2) a debtor consents to an acceptance of collateral in full satisfaction of the obligation it secures only if the debtor agrees to the terms of the acceptance in a record authenticated after default or the secured party:

(A) sends to the debtor after default a proposal that is unconditional or subject only to a condition that collateral not in the possession of the secured party be preserved or maintained;

(B) in the proposal, proposes to accept collateral in full satisfaction of the obligation it secures; and

(C) does not receive a notification of objection authenticated by the debtor within 20 days after the proposal is sent.

(d) To be effective under subsection (a)(2), a notification of objection must be received by the secured party:

(1) in the case of a person to which the proposal was sent pursuant to Section 9–621, within 20 days after notification was sent to that person; and

(2) in other cases:

(A) within 20 days after the last notification was sent pursuant to Section 9–621; or

(B) if a notification was not sent, before the debtor consents to the acceptance under subsection (c).

(e) A secured party that has taken possession of collateral shall dispose of the collateral pursuant to Section 9–610 within the time specified in subsection (f) if:

(1) 60 percent of the cash price has been paid in the case of a purchase-money security interest in consumer goods; or

(2) 60 percent of the principal amount of the obligation secured has been paid in the case of a non-purchase-money security interest in consumer goods.

(f) To comply with subsection (e), the secured party shall dispose of the collateral:

(1) within 90 days after taking possession; or

(2) within any longer period to which the debtor and all secondary obligors have agreed in an agreement to that effect entered into and authenticated after default.

(g) In a consumer transaction, a secured party may not accept collateral in partial satisfaction of the obligation it secures.

§ 9–621.   Notification of Proposal to Accept Collateral.

(a) A secured party that desires to accept collateral in full or partial satisfaction of the obligation it secures shall send its proposal to:

(1) any person from which the secured party has received, before the debtor consented to the acceptance, an authenticated notification of a claim of an interest in the collateral;

(2) any other secured party or lienholder that, 10 days before the debtor consented to the acceptance, held a security interest in or other lien on the collateral perfected by the filing of a financing statement that:

(A) identified the collateral;

(B) was indexed under the debtor's name as of that date; and

(C) was filed in the office or offices in which to file a financing statement against the debtor covering the collateral as of that date; and

(3) any other secured party that, 10 days before the debtor consented to the acceptance, held a security interest in the collateral perfected by compliance with a statute, regulation, or treaty described in Section 9–311(a).

(b) A secured party that desires to accept collateral in partial satisfaction of the obligation it secures shall send its proposal to any secondary obligor in addition to the persons described in subsection (a).

§ 9–622.   Effect of Acceptance of Collateral.

(a) A secured party's acceptance of collateral in full or partial satisfaction of the obligation it secures:

(1) discharges the obligation to the extent consented to by the debtor;

(2) transfers to the secured party all of a debtor's rights in the collateral;

(3) discharges the security interest or agricultural lien that is the subject of the debtor's consent and any subordinate security interest or other subordinate lien; and

(4) terminates any other subordinate interest.

(b) A subordinate interest is discharged or terminated under subsection (a), even if the secured party fails to comply with this article.

§ 9–623.   Right to Redeem Collateral.

(a) A debtor, any secondary obligor, or any other secured party or lienholder may redeem collateral.

(b) To redeem collateral, a person shall tender:

(1) fulfillment of all obligations secured by the collateral; and

(2) the reasonable expenses and attorney's fees described in Section 9–615(a)(1).

(c) A redemption may occur at any time before a secured party:

(1) has collected collateral under Section 9–607;

(2) has disposed of collateral or entered into a contract for its disposition under Section 9–610; or

(3) has accepted collateral in full or partial satisfaction of the obligation it secures under Section 9–622.

§ 9–624.   Waiver.

(a) A debtor or secondary obligor may waive the right to notification of disposition of collateral under Section 9–611 only by an agreement to that effect entered into and authenticated after default.

(b) A debtor may waive the right to require disposition of collateral under Section 9–620(e) only by an agreement to that effect entered into and authenticated after default.

(c) Except in a consumer-goods transaction, a debtor or secondary obligor may waive the right to redeem collateral under Section 9–623 only by an agreement to that effect entered into and authenticated after default.

[Subpart 2.   Noncompliance with Article]

§ 9–625.   Remedies for Secured Party's Failure to Comply with Article.

(a) If it is established that a secured party is not proceeding in accordance with this article, a court may order or restrain collection, enforcement, or disposition of collateral on appropriate terms and conditions.

(b) Subject to subsections (c), (d), and (f), a person is liable for damages in the amount of any loss caused by a failure to comply with this article. Loss caused by a failure to comply may include loss resulting from the debtor's inability to obtain, or increased costs of, alternative financing.

(c) Except as otherwise provided in Section 9–628:

(1) a person that, at the time of the failure, was a debtor, was an obligor, or held a security interest in or other lien on the collateral may recover damages under subsection (b) for its loss; and

(2) if the collateral is consumer goods, a person that was a debtor or a secondary obligor at the time a secured party failed to comply with this part may recover for that failure in

any event an amount not less than the credit service charge plus 10 percent of the principal amount of the obligation or the time-price differential plus 10 percent of the cash price.

(d) A debtor whose deficiency is eliminated under Section 9–626 may recover damages for the loss of any surplus. However, a debtor or secondary obligor whose deficiency is eliminated or reduced under Section 9–626 may not otherwise recover under subsection (b) for noncompliance with the provisions of this part relating to collection, enforcement, disposition, or acceptance.

(e) In addition to any damages recoverable under subsection (b), the debtor, consumer obligor, or person named as a debtor in a filed record, as applicable, may recover $500 in each case from a person that:

(1) fails to comply with Section 9–208;

(2) fails to comply with Section 9–209;

(3) files a record that the person is not entitled to file under Section 9–509(a);

(4) fails to cause the secured party of record to file or send a termination statement as required by Section 9–513(a) or (c);

(5) fails to comply with Section 9–616(b)(1) and whose failure is part of a pattern, or consistent with a practice, of noncompliance; or

(6) fails to comply with Section 9–616(b)(2).

(f) A debtor or consumer obligor may recover damages under subsection (b) and, in addition, $500 in each case from a person that, without reasonable cause, fails to comply with a request under Section 9–210. A recipient of a request under Section 9–210 which never claimed an interest in the collateral or obligations that are the subject of a request under that section has a reasonable excuse for failure to comply with the request within the meaning of this subsection.

(g) If a secured party fails to comply with a request regarding a list of collateral or a statement of account under Section 9–210, the secured party may claim a security interest only as shown in the list or statement included in the request as against a person that is reasonably misled by the failure.

As amended in 2000.

§ 9–626.   Action in Which Deficiency or Surplus Is in Issue.

(a) In an action arising from a transaction, other than a consumer transaction, in which the amount of a deficiency or surplus is in issue, the following rules apply:

(1) A secured party need not prove compliance with the provisions of this part relating to collection, enforcement, disposition, or acceptance unless the debtor or a secondary obligor places the secured party's compliance in issue.

(2) If the secured party's compliance is placed in issue, the secured party has the burden of establishing that the collection, enforcement, disposition, or acceptance was conducted in accordance with this part.

(3) Except as otherwise provided in Section 9–628, if a secured party fails to prove that the collection, enforcement, disposition, or acceptance was conducted in accordance with the provisions of this part relating to collection, enforcement, disposition, or acceptance, the liability of a debtor or

a secondary obligor for a deficiency is limited to an amount by which the sum of the secured obligation, expenses, and attorney's fees exceeds the greater of:

(A) the proceeds of the collection, enforcement, disposition, or acceptance; or

(B) the amount of proceeds that would have been realized had the noncomplying secured party proceeded in accordance with the provisions of this part relating to collection, enforcement, disposition, or acceptance.

(4) For purposes of paragraph (3)(B), the amount of proceeds that would have been realized is equal to the sum of the secured obligation, expenses, and attorney's fees unless the secured party proves that the amount is less than that sum.

(5) If a deficiency or surplus is calculated under Section 9–615(f), the debtor or obligor has the burden of establishing that the amount of proceeds of the disposition is significantly below the range of prices that a complying disposition to a person other than the secured party, a person related to the secured party, or a secondary obligor would have brought.

(b) The limitation of the rules in subsection (a) to transactions other than consumer transactions is intended to leave to the court the determination of the proper rules in consumer transactions. The court may not infer from that limitation the nature of the proper rule in consumer transactions and may continue to apply established approaches.

§ 9–627.   Determination of Whether Conduct Was Commercially Reasonable.

(a) The fact that a greater amount could have been obtained by a collection, enforcement, disposition, or acceptance at a different time or in a different method from that selected by the secured party is not of itself sufficient to preclude the secured party from establishing that the collection, enforcement, disposition, or acceptance was made in a commercially reasonable manner.

(b) A disposition of collateral is made in a commercially reasonable manner if the disposition is made:

(1) in the usual manner on any recognized market;

(2) at the price current in any recognized market at the time of the disposition; or

(3) otherwise in conformity with reasonable commercial practices among dealers in the type of property that was the subject of the disposition.

(c) A collection, enforcement, disposition, or acceptance is commercially reasonable if it has been approved:

(1) in a judicial proceeding;

(2) by a bona fide creditors' committee;

(3) by a representative of creditors; or

(4) by an assignee for the benefit of creditors.

(d) Approval under subsection (c) need not be obtained, and lack of approval does not mean that the collection, enforcement, disposition, or acceptance is not commercially reasonable.

§ 9–628.   Nonliability and Limitation on Liability of Secured Party; Liability of Secondary Obligor.

(a) Unless a secured party knows that a person is a debtor or obligor, knows the identity of the person, and knows how to communicate with the person:

(1) the secured party is not liable to the person, or to a secured party or lienholder that has filed a financing statement against the person, for failure to comply with this article; and

(2) the secured party's failure to comply with this article does not affect the liability of the person for a deficiency.

(b) A secured party is not liable because of its status as secured party:

(1) to a person that is a debtor or obligor, unless the secured party knows:

(A) that the person is a debtor or obligor;

(B) the identity of the person; and

(C) how to communicate with the person; or

(2) to a secured party or lienholder that has filed a financing statement against a person, unless the secured party knows:

(A) that the person is a debtor; and

(B) the identity of the person.

(c) A secured party is not liable to any person, and a person's liability for a deficiency is not affected, because of any act or omission arising out of the secured party's reasonable belief that a transaction is not a consumer-goods transaction or a consumer transaction or that goods are not consumer goods, if the secured party's belief is based on its reasonable reliance on:

(1) a debtor's representation concerning the purpose for which collateral was to be used, acquired, or held; or

(2) an obligor's representation concerning the purpose for which a secured obligation was incurred.

(d) A secured party is not liable to any person under Section 9–625(c)(2) for its failure to comply with Section 9–616.

(e) A secured party is not liable under Section 9–625(c)(2) more than once with respect to any one secured obligation.

Part 7   Transition

§ 9–701.   Effective Date.

This [Act] takes effect on July 1, 2001.

§ 9–702.   Savings Clause.

(a) Except as otherwise provided in this part, this [Act] applies to a transaction or lien within its scope, even if the transaction or lien was entered into or created before this [Act] takes effect.

(b) Except as otherwise provided in subsection (c) and Sections 9–703 through 9–709:

(1) transactions and liens that were not governed by [former Article 9], were validly entered into or created before this [Act] takes effect, and would be subject to this [Act] if they had been entered into or created after this [Act] takes effect, and the rights, duties, and interests flowing from those transactions and liens remain valid after this [Act] takes effect; and

(2) the transactions and liens may be terminated, completed, consummated, and enforced as required or permitted by this [Act] or by the law that otherwise would apply if this [Act] had not taken effect.

(c) This [Act] does not affect an action, case, or proceeding commenced before this [Act] takes effect.

As amended in 2000.

§ 9–703.   Security Interest Perfected before Effective Date.

(a) A security interest that is enforceable immediately before this [Act] takes effect and would have priority over the rights of a person that becomes a lien creditor at that time is a perfected security interest under this [Act] if, when this [Act] takes effect, the applicable requirements for enforceability and perfection under this [Act] are satisfied without further action.

(b) Except as otherwise provided in Section 9–705, if, immediately before this [Act] takes effect, a security interest is enforceable and would have priority over the rights of a person that becomes a lien creditor at that time, but the applicable requirements for enforceability or perfection under this [Act] are not satisfied when this [Act] takes effect, the security interest:

(1) is a perfected security interest for one year after this [Act] takes effect;

(2) remains enforceable thereafter only if the security interest becomes enforceable under Section 9–203 before the year expires; and

(3) remains perfected thereafter only if the applicable requirements for perfection under this [Act] are satisfied before the year expires.

§ 9–704.   Security Interest Unperfected before Effective Date.

A security interest that is enforceable immediately before this [Act] takes effect but which would be subordinate to the rights of a person that becomes a lien creditor at that time:

(1) remains an enforceable security interest for one year after this [Act] takes effect;

(2) remains enforceable thereafter if the security interest becomes enforceable under Section 9–203 when this [Act] takes effect or within one year thereafter; and

(3) becomes perfected:

(A) without further action, when this [Act] takes effect if the applicable requirements for perfection under this [Act] are satisfied before or at that time; or

(B) when the applicable requirements for perfection are satisfied if the requirements are satisfied after that time.

§ 9–705.   Effectiveness of Action Taken before Effective Date.

(a) If action, other than the filing of a financing statement, is taken before this [Act] takes effect and the action would have resulted in priority of a security interest over the rights of a person that becomes a lien creditor had the security interest become enforceable before this [Act] takes effect, the action is effective to perfect a security interest that attaches under this [Act] within one year after this [Act] takes effect. An attached security interest becomes unperfected one year after this [Act] takes effect unless the security interest becomes a perfected security interest under this [Act] before the expiration of that period.

(b) The filing of a financing statement before this [Act] takes effect is effective to perfect a security interest to the extent the filing would satisfy the applicable requirements for perfection under this [Act].

(c) This [Act] does not render ineffective an effective financing statement that, before this [Act] takes effect, is filed and satisfies the applicable requirements for perfection under the law of the jurisdiction governing perfection as provided in [former Section 9–103]. However, except as otherwise provided in subsections (d) and (e) and Section 9–706, the financing statement ceases to be effective at the earlier of:

(1) the time the financing statement would have ceased to be effective under the law of the jurisdiction in which it is filed; or

(2) June 30, 2006.

(d) The filing of a continuation statement after this [Act] takes effect does not continue the effectiveness of the financing statement filed before this [Act] takes effect. However, upon the timely filing of a continuation statement after this [Act] takes effect and in accordance with the law of the jurisdiction governing perfection as provided in Part 3, the effectiveness of a financing statement filed in the same office in that jurisdiction before this [Act] takes effect continues for the period provided by the law of that jurisdiction.

(e) Subsection (c)(2) applies to a financing statement that, before this [Act] takes effect, is filed against a transmitting utility and satisfies the applicable requirements for perfection under the law of the jurisdiction governing perfection as provided in [former Section 9–103] only to the extent that Part 3 provides that the law of a jurisdiction other than the jurisdiction in which the financing statement is filed governs perfection of a security interest in collateral covered by the financing statement.

(f) A financing statement that includes a financing statement filed before this [Act] takes effect and a continuation statement filed after this [Act] takes effect is effective only to the extent that it satisfies the requirements of Part 5 for an initial financing statement.

§ 9–706. When Initial Financing Statement Suffices to Continue Effectiveness of Financing Statement.

(a) The filing of an initial financing statement in the office specified in Section 9–501 continues the effectiveness of a financing statement filed before this [Act] takes effect if:

(1) the filing of an initial financing statement in that office would be effective to perfect a security interest under this [Act];

(2) the pre-effective-date financing statement was filed in an office in another State or another office in this State; and

(3) the initial financing statement satisfies subsection (c).

(b) The filing of an initial financing statement under subsection (a) continues the effectiveness of the pre-effective-date financing statement:

(1) if the initial financing statement is filed before this [Act] takes effect, for the period provided in [former Section 9–403] with respect to a financing statement; and

(2) if the initial financing statement is filed after this [Act] takes effect, for the period provided in Section 9–515 with respect to an initial financing statement.

(c) To be effective for purposes of subsection (a), an initial financing statement must:

(1) satisfy the requirements of Part 5 for an initial financing statement;

(2) identify the pre-effective-date financing statement by indicating the office in which the financing statement was filed and providing the dates of filing and file numbers, if any, of the financing statement and of the most recent continuation statement filed with respect to the financing statement; and

(3) indicate that the pre-effective-date financing statement remains effective.

§ 9–707. Amendment of Pre-Effective-Date Financing Statement.

(a) In this section, "Pre-effective-date financing statement" means a financing statement filed before this [Act] takes effect.

(b) After this [Act] takes effect, a person may add or delete collateral covered by, continue or terminate the effectiveness of, or otherwise amend the information provided in, a pre-effective-date financing statement only in accordance with the law of the jurisdiction governing perfection as provided in Part 3. However, the effectiveness of a pre-effective-date financing statement also may be terminated in accordance with the law of the jurisdiction in which the financing statement is filed.

(c) Except as otherwise provided in subsection (d), if the law of this State governs perfection of a security interest, the information in a pre-effective-date financing statement may be amended after this [Act] takes effect only if:

(1) the pre-effective-date financing statement and an amendment are filed in the office specified in Section 9–501;

(2) an amendment is filed in the office specified in Section 9–501 concurrently with, or after the filing in that office of, an initial financing statement that satisfies Section 9–706(c); or

(3) an initial financing statement that provides the information as amended and satisfies Section 9–706(c) is filed in the office specified in Section 9–501.

(d) If the law of this State governs perfection of a security interest, the effectiveness of a pre-effective-date financing statement may be continued only under Section 9–705(d) and (f) or 9–706.

(e) Whether or not the law of this State governs perfection of a security interest, the effectiveness of a pre-effective-date financing statement filed in this State may be terminated after this [Act] takes effect by filing a termination statement in the office in which the pre-effective-date financing statement is filed, unless an initial financing statement that satisfies Section 9–706(c) has been filed in the office specified by the law of the jurisdiction governing perfection as provided in Part 3 as the office in which to file a financing statement.

As amended in 2000.

§ 9–708. Persons Entitled to File Initial Financing Statement or Continuation Statement.

A person may file an initial financing statement or a continuation statement under this part if:

(1) the secured party of record authorizes the filing; and

(2) the filing is necessary under this part:

(A) to continue the effectiveness of a financing statement filed before this [Act] takes effect; or

(B) to perfect or continue the perfection of a security interest.

As amended in 2000.

§ 9–709. Priority.

(a) This [Act] determines the priority of conflicting claims to collateral. However, if the relative priorities of the claims were established before this [Act] takes effect, [former Article 9] determines priority.

(b) For purposes of Section 9–322(a), the priority of a security interest that becomes enforceable under Section 9–203 of this [Act] dates from the time this [Act] takes effect if the security interest is perfected under this [Act] by the filing of a financing statement before this [Act] takes effect which would not have been effective to perfect the security interest under [former Article 9]. This subsection does not apply to conflicting security interests each of which is perfected by the filing of such a financing statement.

As amended in 2000.

* * * *

Appendix D

Answers to *Issue Spotters*

Chapter 1

1. No. The U.S. Constitution is the supreme law of the land and applies to all jurisdictions. A law in violation of the Constitution (in this question, the First Amendment to the Constitution) will be declared unconstitutional.

2. Yes. Administrative rulemaking starts with the publication of a notice of the rulemaking in the *Federal Register*. Among other details, this notice states where and when the proceedings, such as a public hearing, will be held. Proponents and opponents can offer their comments and concerns regarding the pending rule. After reviewing all the comments from the proceedings, the agency's decision makers consider what was presented and draft the final rule.

Chapter 2

1. No. Even if commercial speech is not related to illegal activities or misleading, it may be restricted if a state has a substantial government interest that cannot be achieved by less restrictive means. In this case, the interest in energy conservation is substantial, but it could be achieved by less restrictive means. That would be the utilities' defense against the enforcement of this state law.

2. Yes. The tax would limit the liberty of some persons, such as out-of-state businesses, so it is subject to a review under the equal protection clause. Protecting local businesses from out-of-state competition is not a legitimate government objective. Thus, such a tax would violate the equal protection clause.

Chapter 3

1. Tom could file a motion for a directed verdict. This motion asks the judge to direct a verdict for Tom on the ground that Sue presented no evidence that would justify granting her relief. The judge grants the motion if there is insufficient evidence to raise an issue of fact.

2. Yes. Submission of the dispute to mediation or nonbinding arbitration is mandatory, but compliance with the decision of the mediator or arbitrator is voluntary.

Chapter 4

1. Probably. To recover on the basis of negligence, the injured party as a plaintiff must show that the truck's owner owed the plaintiff a duty of care, that the owner breached that duty, that the plaintiff was injured, and that the breach caused the injury. In this problem, the owner's actions breached the duty of reasonable care. The billboard falling on the plaintiff was the direct cause of the injury, not the plaintiff's own negligence. Thus, liability turns on whether the plaintiff can connect the breach of duty to the injury. This involves the test of proximate cause—the question of foreseeability. The consequences to the injured party must have been a foreseeable result of the owner's carelessness.

2. The company might defend against this electrician's claim by asserting that the electrician should have known of the risk and, therefore, the company had no duty to warn. According to the problem, the danger is common knowledge in the electrician's field and should have been apparent to this electrician, given his years of training and experience. In other words, the company most likely had no need to warn the electrician of the risk.

The firm could also raise comparative negligence. Both parties' negligence, if any, could be weighed and the liability distributed proportionally. The defendant could furthermore assert assumption of risk, claiming that the electrician voluntarily entered into a dangerous situation, knowing the risk involved.

Chapter 5

1. Yes. The manufacturer is liable for the injuries to the user of the product. A manufacturer is liable for its failure to exercise due care to any person who sustains an injury proximately caused by a negligently made (defective) product. In this scenario, the failure to inspect is a failure to use due care. Thus, Rim Corporation is liable to the injured buyer, Uri. Of course, the maker of the component part may also be liable.

2. Bensing can assert the defense of preemption. An injured party may not be able to sue the manufacturer of defective products that are subject to comprehensive federal regulatory schemes (such as medical devices and vaccinations). In this situation, it is likely that a court would conclude that the federal regulations pertaining to drug labeling preempt Ohio's common law rules. Therefore, Bensing would not be liable to Rothfus for defective labeling if it complied with federal law.

Chapter 6

1. Yes, Roslyn has committed theft of trade secrets. Lists of suppliers and customers cannot be patented, copyrighted, or trademarked, but the information they contain is protected against appropriation by others as trade secrets. And most likely, Roslyn signed a contract, agreeing not to use this information outside her employment by Organic. But even without this contract, Organic could have made a convincing case against its ex-employee for a theft of trade secrets.

2. This is patent infringement. A software maker in this situation might best protect its product, save litigation costs, and profit from its patent by the use of a license. In the context of this problem, a license would grant permission to sell a patented item. (A license can be limited to certain purposes and to the licensee only.)

Chapter 7

1. Karl may have committed trademark infringement. Search engines compile their results by looking through Web sites' keyword fields. Key words, or meta tags, increase the likelihood that a site will be included in search engine results, even if the words have no connection to the site.

A site that appropriates the key words of other sites with more frequent hits will appear in the same search engine results as the more popular sites. But using another's trademark as a key word without the owner's permission normally constitutes trademark infringement. Of course, some uses of another's trademark as a meta tag may be permissible if the use is reasonably necessary and does not suggest that the owner authorized or sponsored the use.

2. Yes. This may be an instance of trademark dilution. Dilution occurs when a trademark is used, without permission, in a way that diminishes the distinctive quality of the mark. Dilution does not require proof that consumers are likely to be confused by the use of the unauthorized mark. The products involved do not have to be similar. Dilution does require, however, that a mark be famous when the dilution occurs.

Chapter 8

1. Yes. With respect to the gas station, Daisy has obtained goods by false pretenses. She might also be charged with the crimes of larceny and forgery, and most states have special statutes covering illegal use of credit cards.

2. Yes. The Counterfeit Access Device and Computer Fraud and Abuse Act provides that a person who accesses a computer online, without permission, to obtain classified data—such as consumer credit files in a credit agency's database—is subject to criminal prosecution. The crime has two elements: accessing the computer without permission and taking data. It is a felony if done for private financial gain. Penalties include fines and imprisonment for up to twenty years. The victim of the theft can also bring a civil suit against the criminal to obtain damages and other relief.

Chapter 9

1. When a corporation decides to respond to what it sees as a moral obligation to correct for past discrimination by adjusting pay differences among its employees, an ethical conflict is raised between the firm and its employees and between the firm and its shareholders. This dilemma arises directly out of the effect such a decision has on the firm's profits. If satisfying this obligation increases profitability, then the dilemma is easily resolved in favor of "doing the right thing."

2. Maybe. On the one hand, it is not the company's "fault" when a product is misused. Also, keeping the product on the market is not a violation of the law, and stopping sales would hurt profits. On the other hand, suspending sales could reduce suffering and could prevent negative publicity that might occur if sales continued.

Chapter 10

1. Under the objective theory of contracts, if a reasonable person would have thought that Joli had accepted Kerin's offer when she signed and returned the letter, then a contract was made, and Joli is obligated to buy the book. This depends, in part, on what was said in the letter and what was said in response. For instance, did the letter contain a valid offer, and did the response constitute a valid acceptance? Under any circumstances, the issue is not whether either party subjectively believed that they did, or did not, have a contract.

2. No. This contract, although not fully executed, is for an illegal purpose and therefore is void. A void contract gives rise to no legal obligation on the part of any party. A contract that is void is no contract. There is nothing to enforce.

Chapter 11

1. No. Revocation of an offer may be implied by conduct inconsistent with the offer. When Fidelity Corporation rehired Monica, and Ron learned of the hiring, the offer was revoked. His acceptance was too late.

2. First, it might be noted that the Uniform Electronic Transactions Act (UETA) does not apply unless the parties to a contract agree to use e-commerce in their transaction. In this deal, of course, the parties used e-commerce. The UETA removes barriers to e-commerce by giving the same legal effect to e-records and e-signatures as to paper documents and signatures. The UETA itself does not include rules for e-commerce transactions, however.

Chapter 12

1. Yes. The original contract was executory—that is, not yet performed by both parties. The parties rescinded the original contract and agreed to a new contract.

2. No. Generally, an exculpatory clause (a clause attempting to absolve a party of negligence or other wrongs) is not enforced if the party seeking its enforcement is involved in a business that is important to the public as a matter of practical necessity, such as an airline. Because of the essential nature of such services, the party would have an advantage in bargaining strength and could insist that anyone contracting for its services agree not to hold it liable.

Chapter 13

1. Yes. Rescission may be granted on the basis of fraudulent misrepresentation. The elements of fraudulent misrepresentation include intent to deceive, or *scienter*. *Scienter* exists if a party makes a statement recklessly, without regard to whether it is true or false, or if a party says or implies that a statement is made on some basis such as personal knowledge or personal investigation when it is not.

2. No. This memo is not a sufficient writing to enforce the contract against Nu! Sales, because it does not include Nu!'s signature. If My-T had been the party refusing to complete the deal, however, the memo would be considered a sufficient writing to enforce the contract against it. Letterhead stationery can constitute a signature. If the memo names the parties, the subject matter, the consideration, and the quantity involved in the transaction, it may be sufficient to be enforced against the party whose letterhead appears on it.

Chapter 14

1. Yes. Generally, if a contract clearly states that a right is not assignable, no assignment will be effective, but there are exceptions. Assignment of the right to receive monetary payment cannot be prohibited.

2. Contracts that are executory on both sides—contracts on which neither party has performed—can be rescinded solely by agreement. Contracts that are executed on one side—contracts on which one party has performed—can be rescinded only if the party who has performed receives consideration for the promise to call off the deal.

Chapter 15

1. A nonbreaching party is entitled to her or his benefit of the bargain under the contract. Here, the innocent party is entitled to be put in the position she would have been in if the contract had been fully performed. The measure of the benefit is the cost to complete the work ($500). These are compensatory damages.

2. No. To recover damages that flow from the consequences of a breach but that are caused by circumstances beyond the contract

(consequential damages), the breaching party must know, or have reason to know, that special circumstances will cause the nonbreaching party to suffer the additional loss. That was not the circumstance in this problem.

Chapter 16

1. Under the principle of comity, a U.S court would defer and give effect to foreign laws and judicial decrees that are consistent with U.S. law and public policy.

2. The practice described in this problem is known as dumping, which is regarded as an unfair international trade practice. Dumping is the sale of imported goods at "less than fair value." Based on the price of those goods in the exporting country, an extra tariff—known as an antidumping duty—can be imposed on the imports.

Chapter 17

1. A shipment of nonconforming goods constitutes an acceptance and a breach, unless the seller seasonably notifies the buyer that the nonconforming shipment does not constitute an acceptance and is offered only as an accommodation. Thus, since there was no notification in this problem, the shipment was both an acceptance and a breach.

2. Yes. In a transaction between merchants, the requirement of a writing is satisfied if one of them sends to the other a signed written confirmation that indicates the terms of the agreement, and the merchant receiving it has reason to know of its contents. If the merchant who receives the confirmation does not object in writing within ten days after receipt, the writing will be enforceable against him or her even though he or she has not signed anything.

Chapter 18

1. Yes. A seller is obligated to deliver goods in conformity with a contract in every detail. This is the perfect tender rule. The exception of the seller's right to cure does not apply here because the seller delivered too little too late to take advantage of this exception.

2. Yes. When anticipatory repudiation occurs, a buyer (or lessee) can resort to any remedy for breach even if the buyer tells the seller (the repudiating party in this problem) that the buyer will wait for the seller's performance.

Chapter 19

1. A statement that "I.O.U." money (or anything else) or an instruction to a bank stating, "I wish you would pay," would render any instrument nonnegotiable. To be negotiable, an instrument must contain an express promise to pay. An I.O.U. is only an acknowledgment of indebtedness. An order stating, "I wish you would pay," is not sufficiently precise.

2. No. When a drawer's employee provides the drawer with the name of a fictitious payee (a payee whom the drawer does not actually intend to have any interest in an instrument), a forgery of the payee's name is effective to pass good title to subsequent transferees.

Chapter 20

1. Yes, to both questions. In a civil suit, a drawer (Lyn) is liable to a payee (Nan) or to a holder of a check that is not honored. If intent to defraud can be proved, the drawer (Lyn) can also be subject to criminal prosecution for writing a bad check.

2. The drawer is entitled to $6,300—the amount to which the check was altered ($7,000) less the amount that the drawer ordered the bank to pay ($700). The bank may recover this amount from the party who presented the altered check for payment.

Chapter 21

1. When collateral consists of consumer goods, and the debtor has paid less than 60 percent of the debt or the purchase price, the creditor has the option of disposing of the collateral in a commercially reasonable manner. This generally requires notice to the debtor of the place, time, and manner of sale. A debtor can waive the right to notice, but only after default. Before the disposal, a debtor can redeem the collateral by tendering performance of all of the obligations secured by the collateral and by paying the creditor's reasonable expenses in retaking and maintaining the collateral.

2. Each of the parties can place a mechanic's lien on the debtor's property. If the debtor does not pay what is owed, the property can be sold to satisfy the debt. The only requirements are that the lien be filed within a specific time from the time of the work, depending on the state statute, and that notice of the foreclosure and sale be given to the debtor in advance.

Chapter 22

1. No. Besides the claims listed in this problem, the debts that cannot be discharged in bankruptcy include amounts borrowed to pay back taxes, goods obtained by fraud, debts that were not listed in the petition, domestic support obligations, certain cash advances, and others.

2. Yes. A debtor's payment to a creditor made for a preexisting debt, within ninety days (one year in the case of an insider or fraud) of a bankruptcy filing, can be recovered if it gives a creditor more than he or she would have received in the bankruptcy proceedings. A trustee can recover this preference using his or her specific avoidance powers.

Chapter 23

1. No. Nadine, as an agent, is prohibited from taking advantage of the agency relationship to obtain property that the principal

(Dimka Corporation) wants to purchase. This is the *duty of loyalty* that arises with every agency relationship.

2. Yes. A principal has a duty to indemnify (reimburse) an agent for liabilities incurred because of authorized and lawful acts and transactions and for losses suffered because of the principal's failure to perform his or her duties.

Chapter 24

1. Workers' compensation laws establish a procedure for compensating workers who are injured on the job. Instead of suing to collect benefits, an injured worker notifies the employer of the injury and files a claim with the appropriate state agency. The right to recover is normally determined without regard to negligence or fault, but intentionally inflicted injuries are not covered. Unlike the potential for recovery in a lawsuit based on negligence or fault, recovery under a workers' compensation statute is limited to the specific amount designated in the statute for the employee's injury.

2. No. A closed shop (a company that requires union membership as a condition of employment) is illegal. A union shop (a company that does not require union membership as a condition of employment but requires workers to join the union after a certain time on the job) is illegal in a state with a right-to-work law, which makes it illegal to require union membership for continued employment.

Chapter 25

1. Yes. One type of sexual harassment occurs when a request for sexual favors is a condition of employment, and the person making the request is a supervisor or acts with the authority of the employer. A tangible employment action, such as continued employment, may also lead to the employer's liability for the supervisor's conduct. That the injured employee is a male and the supervisor a female, instead of the other way around, would not affect the outcome. Same-gender harassment is also actionable.

2. Yes, Koko could succeed in a discrimination suit if she can show that she was not hired solely because of her disability. The other elements for a discrimination suit based on a disability are that the plaintiff (1) has a disability and (2) is otherwise qualified for the job. Both of these elements appear to be satisfied in this scenario.

Chapter 26

1. When a business is relatively small and is not diversified, employs relatively few people, has modest profits, and is not likely to expand significantly or require extensive financing in the immediate future, the most appropriate form for doing business may be a sole proprietorship.

2. Yes. Failing to meet a specified sales quota can constitute a breach of a franchise agreement. If the franchisor is acting in good faith, "cause" may also include the death or disability of the franchisee, the insolvency of the franchisee, and a breach of another term of the franchise agreement.

Chapter 27

1. No. A widow (or widower) has no right to take a dead partner's place. A partner's death causes dissociation after which the partnership must purchase the dissociated partner's partnership interest. Therefore, the surviving partners must pay the decedent's estate (for his widow) the value of the deceased partner's interest in the partnership.

2. No. Under the partners' fiduciary duty, a partner must account to the partnership for any personal profits or benefits derived without the consent of all the partners in connection with the use of any partnership property. Here, the leasing partner may not keep the funds.

Chapter 28

1. The members of a limited liability company (LLC) may designate a group to run their firm. In that situation, the firm would be a manager-managed LLC. The group may include only members, only nonmembers, or members and nonmembers. If, instead, all members participate in management, the firm would be a member-managed LLC. In fact, unless the members agree otherwise, all members are considered to participate in the management of the firm.

2. Although there are differences, all of these forms of business organizations resemble corporations. A joint stock company, for example, features ownership by shares of stock, it is managed by directors and officers, and it has perpetual existence. A business trust, like a corporation, distributes profits to persons who are not personally responsible for the debts of the organization, and management of the business is in the hands of trustees, just as the management of a corporation is in the hands of directors and officers. An incorporated cooperative, which is subject to state laws covering nonprofit corporations, distributes profits to its owners.

Chapter 29

1. Yes. Small businesses that meet certain requirements can qualify as S corporations, created specifically to permit small businesses to avoid double taxation. The six requirements of an S corporation are (1) the firm must be a domestic corporation; (2) the firm must not be a member of an affiliated group of corporations; (3) the firm must have fewer than a certain number of shareholders; (4) the shareholders must be individuals, estates, or qualified trusts (or corporations in some cases); (5) there can be only one class of stock; and (6) no shareholder can be a nonresident alien.

2. Yes. A shareholder can bring a derivative suit on behalf of a corporation if some wrong is done to the corporation. Normally, any damages recovered go into the corporate treasury.

Chapter 30

1. The average investor is not concerned with minor inaccuracies but with facts that if disclosed would tend to deter him or her from buying the securities. These would include material facts that have an important bearing on the condition of the issuer and its business—such as liabilities, loans to officers and directors, customer delinquencies, and pending lawsuits.

2. No. The Securities Exchange Act of 1934 extends liability to officers and directors in their personal transactions for taking advantage of inside information when they know it is unavailable to the persons with whom they are dealing.

Chapter 31

1. Size alone does not determine whether a firm is a monopoly— size in relation to the market is what matters. A small store in a small, isolated town is a monopolist if it is the only store serving that market. Monopoly involves the power to affect prices and output. If a firm has sufficient market power to control prices and exclude competition, that firm has monopoly power. Monopoly power in itself is not a violation of Section 2 of the Sherman Act. The offense also requires an intent to acquire or maintain that power through anticompetitive means.

2. This agreement is a tying arrangement. The legality of a tying arrangement depends on the purpose of the agreement, the agreement's likely effect on competition in the relevant markets (the market for the tying product and the market for the tied product), and other factors. Tying arrangements for commodities are subject to Section 3 of the Clayton Act. Tying arrangements for services can be agreements in restraint of trade in violation of Section 1 of the Sherman Act.

Chapter 32

1. Under an extensive set of procedures established by the U.S. Food and Drug Administration, which administers the federal Food, Drug, and Cosmetic Act, drugs must be shown to be effective as well as safe before they may be marketed to the public. In general, manufacturers are responsible for ensuring that the drugs they offer for sale are free of any substances that could injure consumers.

2. The Comprehensive Environmental Response, Compensation, and Liability Act (CERCLA) regulates the cleanup of hazardous waste disposal sites. Any potentially responsible party can be charged with the entire cost of cleaning up a site. Potentially responsible parties include the person that generated the waste (ChemCorp), the person that transported the waste to the site (Disposal), the person that owned or operated the site at the time of the disposal (Eliminators), and the current owner or operator of the site (Fluid). A party held responsible for the entire cost may be able to recoup some of it in a lawsuit against other potentially responsible parties.

Chapter 33

1. Yes. In these circumstances, when the accountant knows that the bank will use the statement, the bank is a foreseeable user. A foreseeable user is a third party within the class of parties to whom an accountant may be liable for negligence.

2. No. In the circumstances described, the accountant will not be held liable to a purchaser of the securities. Although an accountant may be liable under securities laws for including untrue statements or omitting material facts from financial statements, due diligence is a defense to liability. Due diligence requires an accountant to conduct a reasonable investigation and have reason to believe that the financial statements were true at the time. The facts say that the misstatement of material fact in Omega's financial statement was not attributable to any fraud or negligence on Nora's part. Therefore, Nora can show that she used due diligence and will not be held liable to Pat.

Chapter 34

1. The ring is classified as lost property because it was discovered under circumstances indicating that the owner had not placed the property there voluntarily. The general rule is that the finder of the lost property has the right to possession (and eventual title) over all others *except* the true owner of the lost property. Therefore, Martin, as the true owner of the ring, is entitled to repossess the ring from Hunter.

2. Rosa de la Mar Corporation, the shipper, suffers the loss. A common carrier is liable for damage caused by the willful acts of third persons or by an accident. Other losses must be borne by the shipper (or the recipient, depending on the terms of their contract). In this situation, this shipment was lost due to an act of God.

Chapter 35

1. This is a breach of the warranty deed's covenant of quiet enjoyment. Consuela can sue Bernie and recover the purchase price of the house, plus any damages.

2. Yes. An owner of a fee simple has the most rights possible—he or she can give the property away, sell it, transfer it by will, use it for almost any purpose, possess it to the exclusion of all the world, or, as in this case, transfer possession for any period of time. The party to whom possession is transferred can also transfer her or his interest (usually only with the owner's permission) for any lesser period of time.

Chapter 36

1. No. To have testamentary capacity, a testator must be of legal age and sound mind *at the time the will is made.* Generally, the testator must (1) know the nature of the act, (2) comprehend and remember the "natural objects of his or her bounty," (3) know the nature and extent of her or his property, and (4) understand the distribution of assets called for by the will. In this situation, Sheila had testamentary capacity at the time she made the will. The fact that she was ruled mentally incompetent two years after making the will does not provide sufficient grounds to revoke it.

2. The estate will pass according to the state's intestacy laws. Intestacy laws set out how property is distributed when a person dies without a will. Their purpose is to carry out the likely intent of the decedent. The laws determine which of the deceased's natural heirs (including, in this order, the surviving spouse, lineal descendants, parents, and collateral heirs) inherit his or her property.

Appendix E

Answers to Even-Numbered *Learning Objectives Check* Questions

Chapter 1

2. What is the common law tradition?

Because of our colonial heritage, much of American law is based on the English legal system. After the Norman Conquest of England in 1066, the king's courts sought to establish a uniform set of rules for the entire country. What evolved in these courts was the common law—a body of general legal principles that applied throughout the entire English realm. Courts developed the common law rules from the principles underlying judges' decisions in actual legal controversies.

4. What is the difference between remedies at law and remedies in equity?

An award of compensation in either money or property, including land, is a remedy at law. Remedies in equity include the following:

1. A decree for specific performance—that is, an order to perform what was promised.

2. An injunction, which is an order directing a party to do or refrain from doing a particular act.

3. A rescission, or cancellation, of a contract and a return of the parties to the positions that they held before the contract's formation.

As a rule, courts will grant an equitable remedy only when the remedy at law (monetary damages) is inadequate. Remedies in equity on the whole are more flexible than remedies at law.

Chapter 2

2. What constitutional clause gives the federal government the power to regulate commercial activities among the various states?

To prevent states from establishing laws and regulations that would interfere with trade and commerce among the states, the Constitution expressly delegated to the national government the power to regulate interstate commerce. The commerce clause—Article I, Section 8, of the U.S. Constitution—expressly permits Congress "to regulate Commerce with foreign Nations, and among the several States, and with the Indian Tribes."

4. What is the Bill of Rights? What freedoms does the First Amendment guarantee?

The Bill of Rights consists of the first ten amendments to the U.S. Constitution. Adopted in 1791, the Bill of Rights embodies protections for individuals against interference by the federal government. Some of the protections also apply to business entities. The First Amendment guarantees the freedoms of religion, speech, and the press, and the rights to assemble peaceably and to petition the government.

Chapter 3

2. How are the courts applying traditional jurisdictional concepts to cases involving Internet transactions?

To hear a case, a court must have jurisdiction over the person against whom the suit is brought or over the property involved in the suit. The court must also have jurisdiction over the subject matter. Generally, courts apply a "sliding-scale" standard to determine when it is proper to exercise jurisdiction over a defendant whose only connection with the jurisdiction is the Internet.

4. What is discovery, and how does electronic discovery differ from traditional discovery?

Discovery is the process of obtaining information and evidence about a case from the other party or third parties. Discovery entails gaining access to witnesses, documents, records, and other types of evidence. Electronic discovery differs in its subject—that is, e-media, such as e-mail or text messages, rather than traditional sources of information, such as paper documents.

Chapter 4

2. What are two basic categories of torts?

Generally, the purpose of tort law is to provide remedies for the invasion of legally recognized and protected interests, such as personal safety, freedom of movement, property, and some intangibles, including privacy and reputation. The two broad categories of torts are intentional and unintentional.

4. Identify the four elements of negligence.

The four elements of negligence are as follows:

1. A duty of care owed by the defendant to the plaintiff.
2. The defendant's breach of that duty.
3. The plaintiff's suffering a legally recognizable injury.
4. The in-fact and proximate cause of that injury by the defendant's breach.

Chapter 5

2. What public policy assumptions underlie strict product liability?

The law imposes strict product liability as a matter of public policy. This public policy rests on the threefold assumption that:

1. Consumers should be protected against unsafe products.

2. Manufacturers and distributors should not escape liability for faulty products simply because they are not in privity of contract with the ultimate user of those products.

3. Manufacturers, sellers, and lessors of products are generally in a better position than consumers to bear the costs associated with injuries caused by their products—costs that they can ultimately pass on to all consumers in the form of higher prices.

4. What are three types of product defects?

The three types of product defects traditionally recognized in product liability law are manufacturing defects, design defects, and defective (inadequate) warnings.

A manufacturing defect is a departure from a product unit's design specifications that results in products that are physically flawed, damaged, or incorrectly assembled.

A product with a design defect is made in conformity with the manufacturer's design specifications, but it nevertheless results in injury to the user because the design itself is flawed.

A product may also be deemed defective because of inadequate instructions or warnings about foreseeable risks. The seller or other distributor must include comprehensible warnings if the product will not be reasonably safe without them. The seller must also warn consumers about foreseeable misuses of the product.

Chapter 6

2. Why is the protection of trademarks important?

Article I, Section 8, of the U.S. Constitution authorizes Congress "to promote the Progress of Science and useful Arts, by securing for limited Times to Authors and Inventors the exclusive Right to their respective Writings and Discoveries." Laws protecting trademarks—and patents and copyrights as well—are designed to protect and reward inventive and artistic creativity.

4. What laws protect authors' rights in the works they create?

Copyright law protects the rights of the authors of certain literary or artistic productions. The Copyright Act of 1976, as amended, covers these rights.

Chapter 7

2. What steps have been taken to protect intellectual property rights in the digital age?

The steps that have been taken to protect intellectual property in today's digital age include the application of traditional and existing law in the cyber context. For example, the passage of such federal laws as the Digital Millennium Copyright Act and the drafting of such state laws as the Uniform Electronic Transactions Act (UETA) are major steps in protecting intellectual property rights. Additionally, the signing of such treaties as the Trade-Related Aspects of Intellectual Property Rights (TRIPS) agreement and the World Intellectual Property Organization (WIPO) Copyright Treaty add protection on a global level.

4. What law governs whether Internet service providers are liable for online defamatory statements made by users?

The Communications Decency Act (CDA) sets out the liability of Internet service providers (ISPs) for online defamatory statements made by users.

Under the CDA, "No provider or user of an interactive computer service shall be treated as the publisher or speaker of any information provided by another information content provider." Thus, an ISP is usually not liable for the publication of a user's defamatory statement. This is a broad shield, and some courts have established some limits. For example, an ISP that prompts its users to make such statements would likely not be permitted to avoid liability for the statements.

Chapter 8

2. What are five broad categories of crimes? What is white-collar crime?

Traditionally, crimes have been grouped into the following categories: violent crime (crimes against persons), property crime, public order crime, white-collar crime, and organized crime.

White-collar crime is an illegal act or series of acts committed by an individual or business entity using some nonviolent means, usually in the course of a legitimate occupation.

4. What constitutional safeguards exist to protect persons accused of crimes?

Under the Fourth Amendment, before searching or seizing private property, law enforcement officers must obtain a search warrant, which requires probable cause.

Under the Fifth Amendment, no one can be deprived of "life, liberty, or property without due process of law." The Fifth Amendment also protects persons against double jeopardy and self-incrimination.

The Sixth Amendment guarantees the right to a speedy trial, the right to a jury trial, the right to a public trial, the right to confront witnesses, and the right to counsel. Individuals who are arrested must be informed of certain constitutional rights, including their Fifth Amendment right to remain silent and their Sixth Amendment right to counsel. All evidence obtained in violation of the Fourth, Fifth, and Sixth Amendments, as well as all evidence derived from the illegally obtained evidence, must be excluded from the trial.

The Eighth Amendment prohibits excessive bail and fines, and cruel and unusual punishment.

Chapter 9

2. How do duty-based ethical standards differ from outcome-based ethical standards?

Duty-based ethical standards are derived from religious precepts or philosophical principles. Outcome-based ethics focus on the consequences of an action, not on the nature of the action or on a set of pre-established moral values or religious beliefs.

4. How can business leaders encourage their companies to act ethically?

Ethical leadership is important to create and maintain an ethical workplace. Managers can set standards and then apply those standards to themselves and their firm's employees.

Chapter 10

2. What are the four basic elements necessary to the formation of a valid contract?

The basic elements for the formation of a valid contract are an agreement, consideration, contractual capacity, and legality.

4. How does a void contract differ from a voidable contract? What is an unenforceable contract?

A void contract is not a valid contract—it is not a contract at all. A voidable contract is a valid contract, but one that can be avoided at the option of one or both of the parties.

An unenforceable contract is one that cannot be enforced because of certain legal defenses against it.

Chapter 11

2. In what circumstances will an offer be irrevocable?

An offeror may not effectively revoke an offer if the offeree has changed position in justifiable reliance on the offer. Also, an option contract takes away the offeror's power to revoke an offer for the period of time specified in the option (or, if unspecified, for a reasonable time).

4. How do shrink-wrap and click-on agreements differ from other contracts? How have traditional laws been applied to these agreements?

With a shrink-wrap agreement, the terms are expressed inside the box in which the goods are packaged. A click-on agreement arises when a buyer, completing a transaction on a computer, is required to indicate assent to the terms by clicking on a button that says, for example, "I agree."

Generally, courts have enforced the terms of these agreements the same as the terms of other contracts, applying the traditional common law of contracts. Article 2 of the Uniform Commercial Code provides that acceptance can be made by conduct. The *Restatement (Second) of Contracts* has a similar provision. Under these provisions, a binding contract can be created by conduct, including conduct accepting the terms in a shrink-wrap or click-on agreement.

Chapter 12

2. In what circumstances might a promise be enforced despite a lack of consideration?

Under the doctrine of promissory estoppel (or detrimental reliance), a promisor (the offeror) is estopped, or prevented, from revoking a promise even in the absence of consideration. There are three required elements:

1. A clear and definite promise.
2. The promisee's justifiable reliance on the promise.
3. Reliance of a substantial and definite character.

4. Under what circumstances will a covenant not to compete be enforced? When will such covenants not be enforced?

A covenant not to compete can be enforced:

1. If it is ancillary (secondary) to an agreement to sell an ongoing business, thus enabling the seller to sell, and the purchaser to buy, the goodwill and reputation of the business.
2. If it is contained in an employment contract and is reasonable in terms of time and geographic area.

A covenant not to compete will be unenforceable if it does not protect a legitimate business interest or is broader than necessary to protect a legitimate interest. This is because such a covenant would unreasonably restrain trade and be contrary to public policy.

Chapter 13

2. What is the difference between a unilateral mistake and a bilateral mistake?

A unilateral mistake occurs when only one party is mistaken as to a material fact underlying the contract. Normally, the contract is enforceable even if one party made a mistake, unless an exception applies. A bilateral, or mutual, mistake occurs when both parties are mistaken about the same material fact. When the mistake is mutual, the contract can be rescinded, or canceled, by either party.

4. What contracts must be in writing to be enforceable?

Contracts that are normally required to be in writing or evidenced by a written memorandum include:

- Contracts involving interests in land.
- Contracts that cannot by their terms be performed within one year from the day after the date of formation.
- Collateral contracts, such as promises to answer for the debt or duty of another.

- Promises made in consideration of marriage.
- Contracts for the sale of goods priced at $500 or more.

Chapter 14

2. In what situations is the delegation of duties prohibited?

Delegation of duties is prohibited in the following situations:

1. When the performance depends on the personal skill or talents of the obligor.
2. When special trust has been placed in the obligor.
3. When performance by a third party will vary materially from that expected by the obligee under the contract.
4. When the contract expressly prohibits delegation.

4. How are most contracts discharged?

The most common way to discharge, or terminate, a contract is by the performance of contractual duties.

Chapter 15

2. What is the difference between compensatory damages and consequential damages? What are nominal damages, and when do courts award nominal damages?

Compensatory damages compensate an injured party for injuries or damages. Foreseeable damages that result from a party's breach of contract are consequential damages. Consequential damages differ from compensatory damages in that they are caused by special circumstances beyond the contract.

Nominal damages are awarded to an innocent party when no actual damage has been suffered. Nominal damages might be awarded as a matter of principle to establish fault or wrongful behavior.

4. When do courts grant specific performance as a remedy?

Specific performance might be granted as a remedy when damages offer an inadequate remedy and the subject matter of the contract is unique.

Chapter 16

2. What is the act of state doctrine? In what circumstances is this doctrine applied?

The act of state doctrine is a judicially created doctrine that provides that the judicial branch of one country will not examine the validity of public acts committed by a recognized foreign government within its own territory. This doctrine is often employed in cases involving expropriation or confiscation.

4. What are some clauses commonly included in international business contracts?

Choice-of-language, forum-selection, choice-of-law, and *force majeure* clauses are commonly used in international business contracts.

Chapter 17

2. In a sales contract, if an offeree includes additional or different terms in an acceptance, will a contract result? If so, what happens to these terms?

Under the Uniform Commercial Code, a contract can be formed even if the offeree's acceptance includes additional or different terms. If one of the parties is a nonmerchant, the contract does not include the additional terms. If both parties are merchants, the additional terms automatically become part of the contract unless one of the following occurs:

1. The original offer expressly limits acceptance to the terms of the offer.
2. The new or changed terms materially alter the contract.
3. The offeror objects to the new or changed terms within a reasonable period of time.

(If the additional terms expressly require the offeror's assent, the offeree's response is not an acceptance, but a counteroffer.) Under some circumstances, a court might strike the additional terms.

4. Risk of loss does not necessarily pass with title. If the parties to a contract do not expressly agree when risk passes and the goods are to be delivered without movement by the seller, when does risk pass?

If the seller holds the goods and is a merchant, the risk of loss passes to the buyer when the buyer takes physical possession of the goods. If the seller holds the goods and is not a merchant, the risk of loss passes to the buyer on tender of delivery. When a bailee is holding the goods, the risk of loss passes to the buyer when (1) the buyer receives a negotiable document of title for the goods, (2) the bailee acknowledges the buyer's right to possess the goods, or (3) the buyer receives a nonnegotiable document of title and has had a reasonable time to present the document to the bailee and demand the goods.

Chapter 18

2. What is the perfect tender rule? What are some important exceptions to this rule that apply to sales and lease contracts?

Under the perfect tender rule, the seller or lessor has an obligation to ship or tender conforming goods. If the goods or tender of delivery fails in any respect, the buyer or lessee has the right to accept the goods, reject the entire shipment, or accept part and reject part. Exceptions to the rule may be established by agreement.

When goods are rejected because they are nonconforming and the time for performance has not expired, the seller or lessor can notify the buyer or lessee promptly of the intention to cure and then do so within the contract time for performance. If the time for performance has expired, the seller or lessor can still cure within a reasonable time if, at the time of delivery, he or she had reasonable grounds to believe that the nonconforming tender would be acceptable. When an agreed-on manner of delivery becomes impracticable or unavailable through no fault of either party, a seller may choose a commercially reasonable substitute.

4. What remedies are available to a seller or lessor when the buyer or lessee breaches the contract?

Depending on the circumstances at the time of a buyer's or lessee's breach, a seller or lessor may have the right to cancel the contract, withhold delivery, or resell or dispose of the goods subject to the contract. In addition, a seller or lessor may have the right to recover the purchase price (or lease payments), recover damages, stop delivery in transit, or reclaim the goods.

Chapter 19

2. What is the advantage of transferring an instrument by negotiation? How does the negotiation of order instruments differ from the negotiation of bearer instruments?

Negotiation is the only way to transfer an instrument that allows the party receiving the instrument to obtain the rights of a holder. Unlike a transfer by assignment, a transfer by negotiation can make it possible for a holder to receive more rights in the instrument than the prior possessor had [UCC 3–202(b), 3–305, 3–306].

Negotiating order instruments requires both delivery and indorsement. In contrast, negotiating bearer instruments is accomplished by delivery alone (without the need for indorsement).

4. What is the difference between signature liability and warranty liability?

The key to liability on a negotiable instrument is a signature. Every party, except a qualified indorser, who signs a negotiable instrument is primarily or secondarily liable for payment of that instrument when it comes due.

Signature liability arises from indorsing an instrument. Warranty liability arises from transferring an instrument, whether or not the transferor also indorses it.

Chapter 20

2. When may a bank properly dishonor a customer's check without being liable to the customer?

A bank may dishonor a customer's check without liability to the customer when the customer's account contains insufficient funds to pay the check, providing the bank did not agree to cover overdrafts. A bank may also properly dishonor a stale check, a timely check subject to a valid stop-payment order, a check drawn after the customer's death, and forged or altered checks.

4. What is electronic check presentment, and how does it differ from the traditional check-clearing process?

With electronic check presentment, items are encoded with information (such as the amount of the check) that is read and processed by other banks' computers. A check may sometimes be retained at its place of deposit, and then only its image or description is presented for payment. A bank that encodes information on an item warrants to any subsequent bank or payor that the encoded information is correct.

This differs from the traditional check-clearing process because employees of each bank in the collection chain no longer have to physically handle each check that passes through the bank for collection or payment. Therefore, obtaining payment is much quicker. Whereas manual check processing can take days, electronic check presentment can be done on the day of deposit.

Chapter 21

2. How is a purchase-money security interest in consumer goods created and perfected?

A purchase-money security interest (PMSI) in consumer goods is created when a person buys goods and the seller or lender agrees to extend credit for part or all of the purchase price of the goods. The entity that extends the credit and obtains the PMSI can be either the seller (a store, for example) or a financial institution that lends the buyer the funds with which to purchase the goods [UCC 9–102(a)(2)].

A PMSI in consumer goods is perfected automatically at the time of a credit sale—that is, at the time the PMSI is created. The seller in this situation does not need to do anything more to perfect her or his interest.

4. How does a mechanic's lien assist creditors?

When a creditor follows the individual state's procedure to create a mechanic's lien, the debtor's real estate becomes security for the debt. If the debtor continues not to pay the underlying debt, the creditor can foreclose on the debtor's real property to collect the amount due.

Chapter 22

2. In a Chapter 7 bankruptcy, what happens if a court finds that there was "substantial abuse"? How is the means test used?

If a court concludes there was substantial abuse, the court can dismiss a petition or convert it from a Chapter 7 to a Chapter 11 or Chapter 13 case. In the means test, the debtor's average monthly income in recent months is compared with the median income in the geographic area in which the person lives. If the debtor's income is below the median income, the debtor usually is allowed to file for Chapter 7 bankruptcy. If the debtor's income is above the median income, then further calculations are necessary to determine if there is substantial abuse. The goal is to determine whether the person will have sufficient disposable income in the future to repay at least some of his or her unsecured debts.

4. In a Chapter 11 reorganization, what is the role of the debtor in possession?

Under Chapter 11, a debtor in possession (DIP) is allowed to continue to operate his or her business while the bankruptcy proceeds. The DIP's role is similar to that of a trustee in a liquidation, or Chapter 7, proceeding. Like a trustee, the DIP has certain powers and can avoid preferential transfers and cancel unperformed contracts and unexpired leases.

Chapter 23

2. How do agency relationships arise?

Agency relationships normally are consensual—that is, they arise by voluntary consent and agreement between the parties.

4. When is a principal liable for the agent's actions with respect to third parties? When is the agent liable?

A disclosed or partially disclosed principal is liable to a third party for a contract made by an agent who was acting within the scope of her or his authority. If the agent exceeds the scope of authority and the principal fails to ratify the contract, the agent may be liable (and the principal may not).

When neither the fact of agency nor the identity of the principal is disclosed, the agent is liable, and if the agent has acted within the scope of his or her authority, the undisclosed principal is also liable. Each party is liable for his or her own torts and crimes. A principal may also be liable for an agent's torts committed within the course or scope of employment. A principal is liable for an agent's crime if the principal participated by conspiracy or other action.

Chapter 24

2. What federal statute governs working hours and wages?

The Fair Labor Standards Act is the most significant federal statute governing working hours and wages.

4. What are the two most important federal statutes governing immigration and employment today?

The most important federal statutes governing immigration and the employment of noncitizens are the Immigration Reform and Control Act (IRCA) and the Immigration Act.

Chapter 25

2. What must an employer do to avoid liability for religious discrimination?

Employers cannot treat their employees more or less favorably based on their religious beliefs or practices. Employers also cannot require employees to participate in any religious activity (or forbid them from participating in one). An employer must reasonably accommodate the religious practices of its employees, unless to do so would cause undue hardship to the employer's business.

4. What federal act prohibits discrimination based on age?

The Age Discrimination in Employment Act prohibits discrimination on the basis of age.

Chapter 26

2. What are the most common types of franchises?

The majority of franchises are distributorships, chain-style business operations, or manufacturing or processing-plant arrangements.

4. How are franchises normally terminated? When will a court decide that a franchisor has wrongfully terminated a franchise?

Franchise agreements are usually terminated through provisions in the franchise contract, which often specify that the termination must be "for cause." Cause might include, for instance, the death or disability of the franchisee, insolvency of the franchisee, breach of the franchise agreement, or failure to meet specified sales quotas.

Usually, notice of the termination must be given to the franchisee. The franchisee may be given a chance to cure a breach of the contract within a specific period of time.

If a franchisor has acted arbitrarily or unfairly terminated a franchise (i.e., not in good faith) a court may decide that the termination was wrongful and provide a remedy to the franchisee. Courts look at the good faith and fair dealing of the parties in the franchise relationship when deciding whether the termination was wrongful.

Chapter 27

2. What are the rights and duties of partners in an ordinary partnership?

The rights and duties of partners may be whatever the partners declare them to be. In the absence of partners' agreements to the contrary, the law imposes certain rights and duties. These include:

- A sharing of profits and losses in equal measure.
- The ability to assign a partnership interest.
- Equal rights in managing the firm (subject to majority rule).
- Access to all of the firm's books and records.
- An accounting of assets and profits.
- A sharing of the firm's property.

The duties include fiduciary duties, being bound to third parties through contracts entered into with other partners, and liability for the firm's debts and liabilities.

4. What advantages do limited liability partnerships offer to businesspersons that are not offered by general partnerships?

An advantage of a limited liability partnership over a general partnership is that, depending on the applicable state statute, the liability of the partners for partnership and partners' debts and torts can be limited to the amount of the partners' investments. Another advantage is that partners in a limited liability partnership generally are not liable for other partners' malpractice.

Chapter 28

2. What advantages do limited liability companies offer to businesspersons that are not offered by sole proprietorships or partnerships?

An important advantage of limited liability companies (LLCs) is that the liability of the members is limited to the amount of their investments. Another advantage of LLCs is the flexibility they offer in regard to taxation and management.

4. What is a joint venture? How is it similar to a partnership? How is it different?

A joint venture is an enterprise in which two or more persons or business entities combine their efforts or their property for a single transaction or project, or a related series of transactions or projects.

Generally, partnership law applies to joint ventures, although joint venturers have less implied and apparent authority than partners because they have less power to bind the members of their organization.

Chapter 29

2. What four steps are involved in bringing a corporation into existence?

The four basic steps to bring a corporation into existence include (1) selecting the state of incorporation, (2) securing the corporate name, (3) preparing the articles of incorporation, and (4) filing those articles with the state.

4. What are the duties of corporate directors and officers?

Directors and officers are fiduciaries of the corporation. The fiduciary duties of the directors and officers include the duty of care and the duty of loyalty.

Chapter 30

2. What are the two major statutes regulating the securities industry?

The major statutes regulating the securities industry are the Securities Act of 1933 and the Securities Exchange Act of 1934, which created the Securities and Exchange Commission.

4. What are some of the features of state securities laws?

Typically, state laws have disclosure requirements and anti-fraud provisions patterned after Section 10(b) of the Securities Exchange Act of 1934 and SEC Rule 10b-5. State laws provide for the registration or qualification of securities offered or issued for sale within the state with the appropriate state official. Also, most state securities laws regulate securities brokers and dealers.

Chapter 31

2. What rule do courts apply to price-fixing agreements, and why?

Courts apply the *per se* rule to price-fixing agreements. Because agreements to fix prices are so blatantly and substantially anticompetitive, they are deemed *per se* illegal. That is, even if the parties had good reasons for entering the agreement, if the agreement restricts output or artificially fixes prices, it violates Section 1 of the Sherman Act.

4. What are the four major provisions of the Clayton Act, and what types of activities do these provisions prohibit?

Section 2 of the Clayton Act prohibits price discrimination. Section 3 prohibits two types of vertical agreements involving exclusionary practices: exclusive-dealing contracts and tying arrangements. Section 7 prohibits mergers or acquisitions that result in monopoly power or a substantial lessening of competition in the marketplace. Section 8 prohibits a person from being a director in two or more competing corporations at the same time if either of the corporations has capital, surplus, or undivided profits aggregating more than a specified amount or competitive sales of a certain amount or more (the dollar limits are changed periodically by Congress).

Chapter 32

2. What law protects consumers against contaminated and misbranded foods and drugs?

The Federal Food, Drug, and Cosmetic Act (FDCA) protects consumers against adulterated and misbranded foods and drugs. The FDCA establishes food standards, specifies safe levels of potentially hazardous food additives, and provides classifications of foods and food advertising.

4. What is contained in an environmental impact statement, and who must file one?

An environmental impact statement (EIS) analyzes the following:

1. The impact on the environment that an action will have.

2. Any adverse effects on the environment and alternative actions that might be taken.

3. Irreversible effects the action might generate.

An EIS must be prepared for every major federal action that significantly affects the quality of the environment. An action is "major" if it involves a substantial commitment of resources (monetary or otherwise). An action is "federal" if a federal agency has the power to control it.

Chapter 33

2. What are the rules concerning an auditor's liability to third parties?

An auditor may be liable to a third party on the ground of negligence, when the auditor knew or should have known that the third party would benefit from the auditor's work. Depending on the jurisdiction, liability may be imposed only if one of the following occurs:

1. The auditor is in privity, or near privity, with the third party.

2. The third party's reliance on the auditor's work was foreseen, or the third party was within a class of known or foreseeable users.

3. The third party's use of the auditor's work was reasonably foreseeable.

4. What crimes might an accountant commit under the Internal Revenue Code?

Crimes under the Internal Revenue Code include the following:

1. Aiding or assisting in the preparation of a false tax return.

2. Aiding or abetting an individual's understatement of tax liability.

3. Negligently or willfully understating a client's tax liability, or recklessly or intentionally disregarding Internal Revenue Code rules or regulations.

4. Failing to provide a taxpayer with a copy of a tax return, failing to sign the return, or failing to furnish the appropriate tax identification numbers.

Chapter 34

2. What are the three necessary elements for an effective gift?

To make an effective gift, the donor must intend to make the gift, the gift must be delivered to the donee, and the donee must accept the gift.

4. What are the basic duties of a bailee?

The bailee has two basic responsibilities: (1) to take appropriate care of the property and (2) to surrender the property at the end of the bailment. The appropriate degree of care required for the bailor's property depends on whether the bailment is for the benefit of the bailor, the benefit of the bailee, or for their mutual benefit.

Chapter 35

2. What is the difference between a joint tenancy and a tenancy in common?

A tenancy in common is a form of co-ownership in which each of two or more persons owns an undivided interest in the whole property. On the death of a tenant in common, that tenant's interest passes to his or her heirs. In a joint tenancy, each of two or more persons owns an undivided interest in the property, and a deceased joint tenant's interest passes to the surviving joint tenant or tenants. This right distinguishes the joint tenancy from the tenancy in common.

4. What are the requirements for acquiring property by adverse possession?

The adverse possessor's possession must be (1) actual and exclusive, (2) open, visible, and notorious, not secret or clandestine, (3) continuous and peaceable for the statutory period of time, and (4) hostile and adverse.

Chapter 36

2. How do courts interpret ambiguities in an insurance policy?

The courts will interpret the words used in an insurance contract according to their ordinary meanings in light of the nature of the coverage involved. When there is an ambiguity in the policy, the provision generally is interpreted *against the insurance company*.

4. What is the difference between a *per stirpes* distribution and a *per capita* distribution of an estate to the grandchildren of the deceased?

Per stirpes distribution dictates that grandchildren share the part of the estate that their deceased parent (and descendant of the deceased grandparent) would have been entitled to inherit.

Per capita distribution dictates that each grandchild takes an equal share of the estate.

Appendix F

Sample Answers for *Business Case Problems with Sample Answer*

1–6. Sample Answer—Law around the World.

The common law system spread throughout medieval England after the Norman Conquest in 1066. Courts developed the common law rules from the principles behind the decisions in actual legal controversies. Judges attempted to be consistent. When possible, they based their decisions on the principles suggested by earlier cases. They sought to decide similar cases in a similar way and considered new cases with care because they knew that their decisions would make new law. Each interpretation became part of the law on the subject and served as a legal precedent. Later cases that involved similar legal principles or facts could be decided with reference to that precedent.

The practice of deciding new cases with reference to former decisions, or precedents, eventually became a cornerstone of the English and American judicial systems. It forms a doctrine called stare decisis. Under this doctrine, judges are obligated to follow the precedents established within their jurisdictions. Generally, those countries that were once colonies of Great Britain retained their English common law heritage after they achieved their independence. Today, common law systems exist in Australia, Canada, India, Ireland, and New Zealand, as well as the United States.

Most of the other European nations base their legal systems on Roman civil law. Civil law is codified law—an ordered grouping of legal principles enacted into law by a legislature or governing body. In a civil law system, the primary source of law is a statutory code, and case precedents are not judicially binding as they are in a common law system. Nonetheless, judges in such systems commonly refer to previous decisions as sources of legal guidance. The difference is that judges in a civil law system are not bound by precedent—in other words, the doctrine of *stare decisis* does not apply.

2–3. Sample Answer—Establishment Clause.

The establishment clause prohibits the government from passing laws or taking actions that promote religion or show a preference for one religion over another. In assessing a government action, the courts look at the predominant purpose for the action and ask whether the action has the effect of endorsing religion.

Although DeWeese claimed to have a nonreligious purpose for displaying the poster of the Ten Commandments in a courtroom, his own statements showed a religious purpose. These statements reflected his views about "warring" legal philosophies and his belief that "our legal system is based on moral absolutes from

divine law handed down by God through the Ten Commandments." This plainly constitutes a religious purpose that violates the establishment clause because it has the effect of endorsing Judaism or Christianity over other religions. In the case on which this problem is based, the court ruled in favor of the American Civil Liberties Union.

3–6. Sample Answer—Discovery.

Yes, the items that were deleted from a Facebook page can be recovered. Normally, a party must hire an expert to recover material in an electronic format, and this can be time consuming and expensive.

Electronic evidence, or e-evidence, consists of all computer-generated or electronically recorded information, such as posts on Facebook and other social media sites. The effect that e-evidence can have in a case depends on its relevance and what it reveals. In the facts presented in this problem, Isaiah should be sanctioned—he should be required to cover Allied's cost to hire the recovery expert and attorney's fees to confront the misconduct. In a jury trial, the court might also instruct the jury to presume that any missing items are harmful to Isaiah's case. If all of the material is retrieved and presented at the trial, any prejudice (disadvantage) to Allied's case might thereby be mitigated (lessened). If not, of course, the court might go so far as to order a new trial.

In the actual case on which this problem is based, Allied hired an expert, who determined that Isaiah had in fact removed some photos and other items from his Facebook page. After the expert testified about the missing material, Isaiah provided Allied with all of it, including the photos that he had deleted. Allied sought a retrial, but the court instead reduced the amount of Isaiah's damages by the amount that it cost Allied to address his "misconduct."

4–5. Sample Answer—Negligence.

Negligence requires proof that (a) the defendant owed a duty of care to the plaintiff, (b) the defendant breached that duty, (c) the defendant's breach caused the plaintiff's injury, and (d) the plaintiff suffered a legally recognizable injury. With respect to the duty of care, a business owner has a duty to use reasonable care to protect business invitees. This duty includes an obligation to discover and correct or warn of unreasonably dangerous conditions that the owner of the premises should reasonably foresee might endanger an invitee. Some risks are so obvious that an owner need not warn of them. But even if a risk is obvious, a business owner may not be excused from the duty to protect the business's customers from foreseeable harm.

Because Lucario was the Weatherford's business invitee, the hotel owed her a duty of reasonable care to make its premises safe for her use. The balcony ran nearly the entire width of the window in Lucario's room. She could have reasonably believed that the window was a means of access to the balcony. The window/balcony configuration was dangerous, however, because the window opened wide enough for an adult to climb out, but the twelve-inch gap between one side of the window and the balcony was unprotected. This unprotected gap opened to a drop of more than three stories to a concrete surface below.

Should the hotel have anticipated the potential harm to a guest opening the window in Room 59 and attempting to access the balcony? The hotel encouraged guests to "step out onto the balcony" to smoke. The dangerous window/balcony configuration could have been remedied at a minimal cost. These circumstances could be perceived as creating an "unreasonably dangerous" condition. And it could be concluded that the hotel created or knew of the condition and failed to take reasonable steps to warn of it or correct it. Of course, the Weatherford might argue that the window/balcony configuration was so obvious that the hotel was not liable for Lucario's fall.

In the actual case on which this problem is based, the court concluded that the Weatherford did not breach its duty of care to Lucario. On McMurtry's appeal, a state intermediate appellate court held that this conclusion was in error, vacated the lower court's judgment in favor of the hotel on this issue, and remanded the case.

5–7. Sample Answer—Product Liability.

The accident in this case was caused by Jett's inattention, not by the texting device in the cab of his truck. In a product-liability case based on a design defect, the plaintiff has to prove that the product was defective at the time it left the hands of the seller or lessor. The plaintiff must also show that this defective condition made it "unreasonably dangerous" to the user or consumer. If the product was delivered in a safe condition and subsequent mishandling made it harmful to the user, the seller or lessor normally is not liable. To successfully assert a design defect, a plaintiff has to show that a reasonable alternative design was available and that the defendant failed to use it.

The plaintiffs could argue that the defendant manufacturer of the texting device owed them a duty of care because injuries to vehicle drivers, passengers, and others on the roads were reasonably foreseeable. They could claim that the product's design (1) required the driver to divert his eyes from the road to view an incoming text, and (2) permitted the receipt of texts while the vehicle was moving.

But manufacturers are not required to design a product incapable of distracting a driver. The duty owed by a manufacturer to the user or consumer of a product does not require guarding against hazards that are commonly known or obvious. Nor does a manufacturer's duty extend to protecting against injuries that result from a user's careless conduct, such as Jett's carelessness in this situation.

6–6. Sample Answer—Patents.

One ground on which the denial of the patent application in this problem could be reversed on appeal is that the design of Raymond Gianelli's "Rowing Machine" is *not obvious* in light of the design of the "Chest Press Apparatus for Exercising Regions of the Upper Body."

To obtain a patent, an applicant must demonstrate to the satisfaction of the U.S. Patent and Trademark Office (PTO) that the invention, discovery, process, or design is novel, useful, and not obvious in light of current technology. In this problem, the PTO denied Gianelli's application for a patent for his "Rowing Machine"— an exercise machine on which a user *pulls* on handles to perform a rowing motion against a selected resistance to strengthen the back muscles. The PTO considered the device obvious in light of a patented "Chest Press Apparatus for Exercising Regions of the Upper Body"—a chest press exercise machine on which a user *pushes* on handles to overcome a selected resistance. But it can be easily argued that it is *not* obvious to modify a machine with handles designed to be *pushed* into one with handles designed to be *pulled*. In fact, anyone who has used exercise machines knows that a way to cause injury is to use a machine in a manner not intended by the manufacturer.

In the actual case on which this problem is based, the U.S. Court of Appeals for the Federal Circuit reversed the PTO's denial of Gianelli's application for a patent, based on the reasoning stated above.

7–5. Sample Answer—Privacy.

No, Rolfe did not have a privacy interest in the information obtained by the subpoenas issued to Midcontinent Communications. The courts have held that the right to privacy is guaranteed by the U.S. Constitution's Bill of Rights, and some state constitutions contain an explicit guarantee of the right. A person must have a reasonable expectation of privacy, though, to maintain a suit or to assert a successful defense for an invasion of privacy.

People clearly have a reasonable expectation of privacy when they enter their personal banking or credit-card information online. They also have a reasonable expectation that online companies will follow their own privacy policies. But people do not have a reasonable expectation of privacy in statements made on Twitter and other data that they publicly disseminate. In other words, there is no violation of a subscriber's right to privacy when a third party Internet service provider receives a subpoena and discloses the subscriber's information.

Here, Rolfe supplied his e-mail address and other personal information, including his Internet protocol address, to Midcontinent. In other words, Rolfe publicly disseminated this information. Law enforcement officers obtained this information from Midcontinent through the subpoenas issued by the South Dakota state court. Rolfe provided his information to Midcontinent—he has no legitimate expectation of privacy in that information.

In the actual case on which this problem is based, Rolfe was charged with, and convicted of, possessing, manufacturing, and distributing child pornography, as well as other crimes. As part of the proceedings, the court found that Rolfe had no expectation of privacy in the information that he made available to Midcontinent. On appeal, the South Dakota Supreme Court upheld the conviction.

8–5. Sample Answer—Criminal Liability.

Yes, Green exhibited the required mental state to establish criminal liability. A wrongful mental state (*mens rea*) is one of the elements typically required to establish criminal liability. The required mental state, or intent, is indicated in an applicable statute or law. For example, for murder, the required mental state is the intent to take another's life. A court can also find that the required mental state is present when a defendant's acts are reckless or criminally negligent. A defendant is criminally reckless if he or she consciously disregards a substantial and unjustifiable risk.

In this problem, Green was clearly aware of the danger to which he was exposing people on the street below, but he did not indicate that he specifically intended to harm anyone. The risk of death created by his conduct, however, was obvious. He must have known what was likely to happen if a bottle or plate thrown from the height of twenty-six stories hit a pedestrian or the windshield of an occupied motor vehicle on the street below. Despite his claim that he was intoxicated, he was sufficiently aware to stop throwing things from the balcony when he saw police in the area, and he later recalled what he had done and what had happened.

In the actual case on which this problem is based, after a jury trial, Green was convicted of reckless endangerment. On appeal, a state intermediate appellate court affirmed the conviction, based in part on the reasoning just stated.

9–4. Sample Answer—Online Privacy.

Facebook created a program that makes decisions for users. Many believe that privacy is an extremely important right that should be fiercely protected. Thus, using duty-based ethics, any program that has a default setting of giving out information is unethical. Facebook should create the program as an opt-in program.

In addition, under the Kantian categorical imperative, if every company used opt-out programs that allowed the disclosure of potentially personal information, privacy might become merely theoretical. If privacy were reduced or eliminated, the world might not be a better place. From a utilitarian or outcome-based approach, an opt-out program might offer the benefits of being easy to created and start, as well as making it easy to recruit partner programs. On the negative side, the program would eliminate users' ability to chose whether to disclose information about themselves. An opt-in program would maintain that user control but might entail higher start-up costs because it would require more marketing to users up front to persuade them to opt in.

10–6. Sample Answer—Quasi Contract.

Gutkowski does not have a valid claim for payment, nor should he recover on the basis of a quasi contract. Quasi contracts are imposed by courts on parties in the interest of fairness and justice. Usually, a quasi contract is imposed to avoid the unjust enrichment of one party at the expense of another. Gutkowski was compensated as a consultant. For him to establish a claim that he is due more compensation based on unjust enrichment, he must have proof. As it is, he has only his claim that there were discussions

about him being a part owner of YES. Discussions and negotiations are not a basis for recovery on a quasi contract.

In the actual case on which this problem is based, the court dismissed Gutkowski's claim for payment.

11–4. Sample Answer—Online Acceptances.

No. A shrink-wrap agreement is an agreement whose terms are expressed inside the box in which the goods are packaged. The party who opens the box may be informed that he or she agrees to the terms by keeping whatever is in the box. In many cases, the courts have enforced the terms of shrink-wrap agreements just as they enforce the terms of other contracts.

But not all of the terms presented in shrink-wrap agreements have been enforced by the courts. One important consideration is whether the buyer had adequate notice of the terms. A click-on agreement is formed when a buyer, completing a transaction on a computer, is required to indicate his or her assent to be bound by the terms of an offer by clicking on a button that says, for example, "I agree."

In Reasonover's situation, the confirmation e-mail sent by Clearwire was not adequate notice of its "Terms of Service" (TOS). The e-mail did not contain a direct link to the terms—accessing them required clicks on further links through the firm's homepage. The written, shrink-wrap materials accompanying the modem did not provide adequate notice of the TOS. There was only a reference to Clearwire's Web site in small print at the bottom of one page.

Similarly, Reasonover's access to an "I accept terms" box did not establish notice of the terms. She did not click on the box but quit the page. Even if any of these references were sufficient notice, Reasonover kept the modem only because Clearwire told her that she could not return it. In the actual case on which this problem is based, the court refused to compel arbitration on the basis of the clause in Clearwire's TOS.

12–3. Sample Answer—Unconscionable Contracts or Clauses.

In this case, the agreement that restricted the buyer's options for resolution of a dispute to arbitration and limited the amount of damages was both procedurally and substantively unconscionable. Procedural unconscionability concerns the manner in which the parties enter into a contract. Substantive unconscionability can occur when a contract leaves one party to the agreement without a remedy for the nonperformance of the other.

Here, GeoEx told customers that the arbitration terms in its release form were nonnegotiable and that climbers would encounter the same requirements with any other travel company. This amounted to procedural unconscionability, underscoring the customers' lack of bargaining power. The imbalance resulted in oppressive terms, with no real negotiation and an absence of meaningful choice. Furthermore, the restriction on forum (San Francisco) and the limitation on damages (the cost of the trip)—with no limitation on GeoEx's damages—amounted to substantive unconscionability.

In the actual case on which this problem is based, the court ruled that the agreement was unconscionable.

13–7. Sample Answer—Fraudulent Misrepresentation.

Yes, the facts in this problem evidence fraud. There are three elements to fraud: (1) the misrepresentation of a material fact, (2) an intent to deceive, and (3) an innocent party's justifiable reliance on the misrepresentation. To collect damages, the innocent party must suffer an injury.

Here, Pervis represented to Pauley that no further commission would be paid by Osbrink. This representation was false—despite Pervis's statement to the contrary, Osbrink continued to send payments to Pervis. Pervis knew the representation was false, as shown by the fact that she made it more than once during the time that she was continuing to receive payments from Osbrink. Each time Pauley asked about commissions, Pervis replied that she was not receiving any. Pauley's reliance on her business associate's statements was justified and reasonable. And for the purpose of recovering damages, Pauley suffered an injury in the amount of her share of the commissions that Pervis received as a result of the fraud.

In the actual case on which this problem is based, Pauley filed a suit in a Georgia state court against Pervis, who filed for bankruptcy in a federal bankruptcy court to stay the state action. The federal court held Pervis liable on the ground of fraud for the amount of the commissions that were not paid to Pauley, and denied Pervis a discharge of the debt.

14–5. Sample Answer—Material Breach.

Yes, STR breached the contract with NTI. A breach of contract is the nonperformance of a contractual duty. A breach is *material* when performance is not at least substantial. On a material breach, the nonbreaching party is excused from performance. If a breach is *minor,* the nonbreaching party's duty to perform can sometimes be suspended until the breach has been remedied, but the duty to perform is not entirely excused. Once a minor breach has been cured, the nonbreaching party must resume performance. Any breach—material or minor—entitles the nonbreaching party to sue for damages.

In this problem, NTI had to redo its work constantly because STR permitted its employees and the employees of other subcontractors to walk over and damage the newly installed tile. Furthermore, despite NTI's requests for payment, STR remitted only half the amount due under their contract. Thus, NTI was deprived of at least half of the money it was owed under the contract. And STR terminated the contract, apparently wrongfully and without cause. The tile work would have been completed satisfactorily if STR had not allowed other workers to trample the newly installed tile before it had cured.

In the actual case on which this problem is based, when STR refused to pay NTI and then terminated their contract, the subcontractor filed a suit in a Texas state court to recover. From a jury verdict in NTI's favor, STR appealed. A state intermediate appellate court affirmed. "The evidence presented was legally sufficient for the jury to conclude that STR materially breached the contract."

15–6. Sample Answer—Consequential Damages.

Simard is liable only for the losses and expenses related to the first resale. Simard could reasonably anticipate that his breach would require another sale and that the sales price might be less than what he agreed to pay. Therefore, he should be liable for the difference between his sales price and the first resale price ($29,000), plus any expenses arising from the first resale.

Simard is not liable, however, for any expenses and losses related to the second resale. After all, Simard did not cause the second purchaser's default, and he could not reasonably foresee that default as a probable result of his breach.

16–6. Sample Answer—Import Controls.

Yes, an antidumping duty can be assessed retrospectively (retroactively). But it does not seem likely that such a duty should be assessed here.

In this problem, the Wind Tower Trade Coalition (an association of domestic manufacturers of utility scale wind towers) filed a suit in the U.S. Court of International Trade against the U.S. Department of Commerce. Wind Tower challenged the Commerce Department's decision to impose only *prospective* antidumping duties on imports of utility scale wind towers from China and Vietnam. The Commerce Department had found that the domestic industry had not suffered any "material injury" or "threat of material injury," and that it would be protected by a prospective assessment. Because there was no previously cognizable injury—and any retrospective duties collected would not be payable to the members of the domestic industry—it does not seem likely that retroactive duties should be imposed.

In the actual case on which this problem is based, the court denied the plaintiff's request for an injunction. On appeal, the U.S. Court of Appeals for the Federal Circuit affirmed the denial, holding that the lower court acted within its discretion in determining that retrospective duties were not appropriate.

17–3. Sample Answer—Passage of Title.

Altieri held title to the car that she was driving at the time of the accident in which Godfrey was injured. Once goods exist and are identified, title can be determined. Under the UCC, any explicit understanding between the buyer and the seller determines when title passes. If there is no such agreement, title passes to the buyer at the time and place that the seller physically delivers the goods.

In lease contracts, title to the goods is retained by the lessor-owner of the goods. The UCC's provisions relating to passage to title do not apply to leased goods. Here, Altieri originally leased the car from G.E. Capital Auto Lease, Inc., but by the time of the accident she had bought it. Even though she had not fully paid for the car or completed the transfer-of-title paperwork, she owned it. Title to the car passed to Altieri when she bought it and took delivery of it. Thus, Altieri, not G.E., was the owner of the car at the time of the accident.

In the actual case on which this problem is based, the court concluded that G.E. was not the owner of the vehicle when Godfrey was injured.

18–5. Sample Answer—Nonconforming Goods.

Padma notified Universal Exports about its breach, so Padma has two ways to recover even though it accepted the goods. Padma's first option is to argue that it revoked its acceptance, giving it the right to reject the goods. To revoke acceptance, Padma would have to show that:

1. The nonconformity substantially impaired the value of the shipment.

2. It predicated its acceptance on a reasonable assumption that Universal Exports would cure the nonconformity.

3. Universal Exports did not cure the nonconformity within a reasonable time.

Padma's second option is to keep the goods and recover for the damages caused by Universal Exports' breach. Under this option, Padma could recover at least the difference between the value of the goods as promised and their value as accepted.

19–5. Sample Answer—Negotiation.

A negotiable instrument can be transferred by assignment or by negotiation. An assignment is a transfer of rights by contract. A transfer by assignment to an assignee gives the assignee only those rights that the assignor possessed. Any defenses that can be raised against the assignor can be raised against the assignee. When an instrument is transferred by negotiation, the transferee becomes a holder. A holder receives at least the rights of the previous possessor.

Unlike an assignment, a transfer by negotiation can make it possible for the holder to receive more rights in the instrument than the prior possessor had. A holder who receives greater rights is a holder in due course (HDC) and takes the instrument free of any claims to it and defenses against its payment. Negotiating order instruments requires delivery and indorsement. If a party to whom a negotiable note is made payable signs it and delivers it to a bank, the transfer is a negotiation, and the bank becomes a holder. If the party does not sign it, however, the transfer would be treated as an assignment, and the bank would become an assignee instead of a holder.

In this problem, Argent was the payee of the note and its holder. Argent transferred the note to Wells Fargo without an indorsement. Thus, the transfer was not a negotiation but an assignment. Wells Fargo did not then become a holder of the note but an assignee. As an assignee, the bank acquired only those rights that the lender possessed before the assignment. And any defenses—including fraud in connection with the note—that Ford could assert against the lender could also be asserted by the borrower against the bank. If Argent indorsed the note to Wells Fargo now, after the defendant's response to the complaint, the bank could become a holder of the note, but it could not become an HDC. One of the requirements for HDC status is that a holder must take an instrument without notice of defenses against payment. The bank could not do this, because it is now aware of the borrower's defenses.

In the actual case on which this problem is based, the court issued a judgment in Wells Fargo's favor, and Ford appealed. A state intermediate appellate court reversed the judgment and remanded the case for trial, finding that the bank had failed to prove that it was a holder, an assignee, or even a transferee of the note.

20–4. Sample Answer—Honoring Checks.

Wells Fargo is liable to W Financial for the amount of the check. A bank that pays a customer's check bearing a forged indorsement must recredit the customer's account or be liable to the customer-drawer for breach of contract. The bank must recredit the account because it failed to carry out the drawer's order to pay to the order of the named party. Eventually, the loss falls on the first party to take the instrument bearing the forged indorsement because a forged indorsement does not transfer title. Thus, whoever takes an instrument with a forged indorsement cannot become a holder.

Under these rules, Wells Fargo is liable to W Financial for the amount of the check. The bank had an obligation to ensure that the check was properly indorsed. The bank did not pay the check to the order of Lateef, the named payee, but accepted the check for deposit into the account of CA Houston without Lateef's indorsement. The bank did not obtain title to the instrument and could not become a holder, nor was it entitled to enforce the instrument on behalf of any other party who was entitled to enforce it.

In the actual case on which this problem is based, the court held the bank liable to pay the amount of the check to W Financial.

21–4. Sample Answer—Perfecting a Security Interest.

Yes, these financing statements were sufficient to perfect the bank's security interests in Tille's equipment. In most situations, perfection is accomplished by filing a financing statement with the appropriate official. To effectively perfect a security interest, a financing statement must contain (1) the debtor's signature, (2) the debtor's and creditor's addresses, and (3) a description of the collateral by type or item.

In this case, all of Union's financing statements were sufficient to perfect security interests. They each provided the name and address of the debtor (Tille), the name and address of the secured party (Union Bank), and a description of the collateral covered by the financing statement. One loan covered all of Tille's equipment, including after-acquired property; another loan covered the truck crane; and the third loan was for a Bobcat mini excavator. These descriptions were clearly sufficient to put a prospective creditor on notice that the collateral was the subject of a security interest.

In the actual case on which this problem is based, the court concluded that all of the statements created perfected security interests.

22–4. Sample Answer—Automatic Stay.

Gholston can recover damages because EZ Auto willfully violated the automatic stay. EZ Auto repossessed the car even though it received notice of the automatic stay from the bankruptcy court. Moreover, EZ Auto retained the car even after it was reminded of the stay by Gholston's attorney. Thus, EZ Auto knew about the automatic stay and violated it intentionally. Because Gholston suffered direct damages as a result, she can recover from EZ Auto.

23–7. Sample Answer—Determining Employee Status.

No, Cox is not liable to Cayer for the injuries or damage that she sustained in the accident with Ovalles. Generally, an employer is not liable for physical harm caused to a third person by the negligent act of an independent contractor in the performance of a contract. This is because the employer does not have the right to control the details of the performance. In determining whether a worker has the status of an independent contractor, how much control the employer can exercise over the details of the work is the most important factor weighed by the courts.

In this problem, Ovalles worked as a cable installer for Cox under an agreement with M&M. The agreement disavowed any employer-employee relationship between Cox and M&M's installers. Ovalles was required to designate his affiliation with Cox on his van, clothing, and an I.D. badge. But Cox had minimal contact with Ovalles and limited power to control the manner in which he performed his work. Cox supplied cable wire and other equipment, but these items were delivered to M&M, not Ovalles. These facts indicate that Ovalles was an independent contractor, not an employee. Thus, Cox was not liable to Cayer for the harm caused to her by Ovalles when his van rear-ended Cayer's car.

In the actual case on which this problem is based, the court issued a judgment in Cox's favor. The Rhode Island Supreme Court affirmed, applying the principles stated above to arrive at the same conclusion.

24–7. Sample Answer—Unemployment Compensation.

Yes, Ramirez qualifies for unemployment compensation. Generally, to be eligible for unemployment compensation, a worker must be willing and able to work. Workers who have been fired for misconduct or who have voluntarily left their jobs are not eligible for benefits. In the facts of this problem, the applicable state statute disqualifies an employee from receiving benefits if he or she voluntarily leaves work without "good cause."

The issue is whether Ramirez left her job for "good cause." When her father in the Dominican Republic had a stroke, she asked her employer for time off to be with him. Her employer refused the request. But Ramirez left to be with her father and called to inform her employer. It seems likely that this family emergency would constitute "good cause," and Ramirez's call and return to work after her father's death indicated that she did not disregard her employer's interests.

In the actual case on which this problem is based, the state of Florida denied Ramirez unemployment compensation. On Ramirez's appeal, a state intermediate appellate court reversed, on the reasoning stated above.

25–7. Sample Answer—Age Discrimination.

No, Sanofi-Aventis U.S. LLC (S-A) does not appear to have engaged in age discrimination. The Age Discrimination in Employment Act (ADEA) prohibits employment discrimination on the basis of age against individuals forty years of age or older. For the act to apply, an employer must have twenty or more employees, and the employer's business activities must affect interstate commerce.

To establish a *prima facie* case, a plaintiff must show that he or she was (1) a member of the protected age group, (2) qualified for the position from which he or she was discharged, and (3) discharged because of age discrimination. If the employer offers a legitimate reason for its action, the plaintiff must show that the stated reason is only a pretext.

In this problem, Rangel was over forty years old. But he also had negative sales performance reviews for more than two years before he was terminated as part of S-A's nationwide reduction in force of all sales professionals who had not met the "Expectations" guidelines, including younger workers. The facts do not indicate that a person younger than Rangel replaced him or that S-A intended to discriminate against him on the basis of age. Based on these facts, Rangel could not establish a *prima facie* case of age discrimination on the part of S-A.

In the actual case on which this problem is based, in Rangel's suit against S-A under the ADEA, alleging age discrimination, a federal district court issued a judgment in S-A's favor. On Rangel's appeal, the U.S. Court of Appeals for the Tenth Circuit affirmed, according to the reasoning stated above.

26–5. Sample Answer—Wrongful Termination of a Franchise.

Oshana and GTO have stated a claim for wrongful termination of their franchise. A franchisor must act in good faith when terminating a franchise agreement. If the termination is arbitrary or unfair, a franchisee may have a claim for wrongful termination.

In this case, Oshana and GTO have alleged that Buchanan acted in bad faith. Their failure to pay rent would ordinarily be a valid basis for termination, but not if it was entirely precipitated by Buchanan. Thus, Oshana and GTO may recover if they can prove that their allegations are true.

27–6. Sample Answer—Partnerships.

Yes, Sacco is entitled to 50 percent of the profits of Pierce Paxton Collections, PPDS, and KPD. The requirements for establishing a partnership are (1) a sharing of profits and losses, (2) a joint ownership of the business, and (3) an equal right to be involved in the management of the business.

The effort and time that Sacco expended in the business constituted a sharing of losses. His proprietary interest in the assets of the partnership consisted of his share of the profits, which he had expressly left in the business to "grow the company" and "build sweat equity" for the future. He was involved in every aspect of the business. Although he was not paid a salary, he was reimbursed for business expenses charged to his personal credit card, which Paxton also used. These facts arguably meet the requirements for establishing a partnership.

In the actual case on which this problem is based, Sacco filed a suit in a Louisiana state court against Paxton, and the court awarded Sacco 50 percent of the profits. A state intermediate appellate court affirmed, based generally on the reasoning stated above.

28–6. Sample Answer—LLC Operation.

No. One Bluewater member could not unilaterally "fire" another member without providing a reason. Part of the attractiveness of an LLC as a form of business enterprise is its flexibility. The members can decide how to operate the business through an operating agreement. For example, the agreement can set forth procedures for choosing or removing members or managers.

Here, the Bluewater operating agreement provided for a "super majority" vote to remove a member under circumstances that would jeopardize the firm's contractor status. Thus, one Bluewater member could not unilaterally "fire" another member without providing a reason. In fact, a majority of the members could not terminate the other's interest in the firm without providing a reason. Moreover, the only acceptable reason would be a circumstance that undercut the firm's status as a contractor.

The flexibility of the LLC business form relates to its framework, not to its members' capacity to violate its operating agreement. In the actual case on which this problem is based, Smith attempted to "fire" Williford without providing a reason. In Williford's suit, the court issued a judgment in his favor.

29–6. Sample Answer—Duty of Loyalty.

Dweck breached the fiduciary duty of loyalty that a director and officer owes to his or her corporation—in this case, Kids. The essence of the duty of loyalty is the subordination of self-interest to the interest of the entity to which the duty is owed. The duty presumes constant loyalty to the corporation on the part of the directors and officers. The duty prohibits directors from using corporate funds or confidential corporate information for their personal advantage.

Here, Dweck breached her duty of loyalty to Kids by establishing a competing company that usurped Kids' business opportunities and converted Kids' resources—employees, office space, credit, and customer relationships—to conduct the competing firm's operations. The "administrative fee" was most likely insufficient compensation. Dweck would be liable to Kids for the damages caused by this breach of duty.

In the actual case on which this problem is based, the court held that Dweck breached her duty of loyalty to Kids and awarded as damages the lost profits that Kids would have generated from the business diverted to Success.

30–3. Sample Answer—Violations of the 1934 Act.

An omission or misrepresentation of a material fact in connection with the purchase or sale of a security may violate Section 10(b) of the Securities Exchange Act of 1934 and SEC Rule 10b-5. The key question is whether the omitted or misrepresented information is material. A fact, by itself, is not automatically material. A fact will be regarded as material only if it is significant enough that it would likely affect an investor's decision as to whether to buy or sell the company's securities. For example, a company's potential liability in a product liability suit and the financial consequences to the firm are material facts that must be disclosed because they are significant enough to affect an investor's decision as to whether to buy stock in the company.

In this case, the plaintiffs' claim should not be dismissed. To prevail on their claim that the defendants made material omissions in violation of Section 10(b) and SEC Rule 10-5, the plaintiffs must prove that the omission was material. Their complaint alleged the omission of information linking Zicam and anosmia (a loss of the sense of smell) and plausibly suggested that reasonable investors would have viewed this information as material. Zicam products account for 70 percent of Matrixx's sales. Matrixx received reports of consumers who suffered anosia after using Zicam Cold Remedy.

In public statements discussing revenues and product safety, Matrixx did not disclose this information. But the information was significant enough to likely affect a consumer's decision to use the product, and this would affect revenue and ultimately the commercial viability of the product. The information was therefore significant enough to likely affect an investor's decision whether to buy or sell Matrixx's stock, and this would affect the stock price.

Thus, the plaintiffs' allegations were sufficient. Contrary to the defendants' assertion, statistical sampling is not required to show materiality—reasonable investors could view reports of adverse events as material even if the reports did not provide statistically significant evidence.

31–5. Sample Answer—Price Discrimination.

Spa Steel satisfies most of the requirements for a price discrimination claim under Section 2 of the Clayton Act. Dayton Superior is engaged in interstate commerce, and it sells goods of like grade and quality to at least three purchasers. Moreover, Spa Steel can show that, because it sells Dayton Superior's products at a higher price, it lost business and thus suffered an injury. To recover, however, Spa Steel will also need to prove that Dayton Superior charged Spa Steel's competitors a lower price for the same product. Spa Steel cannot recover if its prices were higher for reasons related to its own business, such as having higher overhead or seeking a larger profit.

32–4. Sample Answer—Fair Debt Collection Practices.

Engler may recover under the Fair Debt Collection Practices Act (FDCPA). Atlantic is subject to the FDCPA because it is a debt-collection agency and it was attempting to collect a debt on behalf of Bank of America. Atlantic also used offensive tactics to collect from Engler. After all, Atlantic gave Engler's employer the false impression that Engler was a criminal, had a pending case, and was about to be arrested. Finally, Engler suffered harm because he experienced discomfort, embarrassment, and distress as a result of Atlantic's abusive conduct. Engler may recover actual damages, statutory damages, and attorneys' fees from Atlantic.

33–7. Sample Answer—Potential Liability to Third Parties.

KPMG is potentially liable to the hedge funds' partners under the *Restatement (Third) of Torts*. Under Section 552 of the *Restatement,* an auditor owes a duty to "persons for whose benefit and guidance the accountant intends to supply . . . information."

In this case, KPMG prepared annual reports on the hedge funds and addressed them to the funds' "Partners." Additionally, KPMG knew who the partners were because it prepared individual tax forms for them each year. Thus, KPMG's annual reports were for the partners' benefit and guidance. The partners relied on the reports, including their representations that they complied with generally accepted accounting principles.

As a result, they lost millions of dollars, which exposes KPMG to possible liability under Section 552.

34–6. Sample Answer—Bailment Obligation.

Moreland should be awarded damages, and Gray should take nothing. The bailee must exercise reasonable care in preserving the bailed property. What constitutes reasonable care in a bailment situation normally depends on the nature and specific circumstances of the bailment. If the bailed property has been lost or is returned damaged, a court will presume that the bailee was negligent.

In the circumstances of this problem, when the bailor (Moreland, the owner of the aircraft) entrusted the plane to the bailee's (Gray's) repair shop for painting, the work was not properly performed. This violated the bailee's duty to exercise reasonable care and breached the bailment contract. Because the plane was returned damaged, this may also constitute negligence. In the event of a breach, the bailor may sue for damages. The measure of damages is the difference between the value of the bailed property in its present condition and what it would have been worth if the work had been properly performed.

Thus, Gray is liable to Moreland for failing to properly paint the plane. In the actual case on which this problem is based, the court upheld a jury award to Moreland of damages and attorneys' fees.

35–5. Sample Answer—Adverse Possession.

The McKeags satisfied the first three requirements for adverse possession:

1. Their possession was actual and exclusive because they used the beach and prevented others from doing so, including the Finleys.

2. Their possession was open, visible, and notorious because they made improvements to the beach and regularly kept their belongings there.

3. Their possession was continuous and peaceable for the required ten years. They possessed the property for more than four decades, and they even kept a large float there during the winter months.

Nevertheless, the McKeags' possession was *not* hostile and adverse, which is the fourth requirement. The Finleys had substantial evidence that they gave the McKeags permission to use the beach. Rather than reject the Finleys' permission as unnecessary, the McKeags sometimes said nothing and other times seemingly affirmed that the property belonged to the Finleys. Thus, because the McKeags did not satisfy all four requirements, they cannot establish adverse possession.

36–5. Sample Answer—Undue Influence.

No, undue influence does not appear to have occurred in this problem. To invalidate a will on the basis of undue influence, a plaintiff must show that the decedent's plan of distribution was the result of improper pressure brought by another person. Undue influence may be inferred if the testator ignores blood relatives and names as a beneficiary a nonrelative who is in constant close contact and in a position to influence the making of the will.

In this problem, although Tommy's ex-wife lived with Susie Walker and was thus in a position to influence Susie's will, she was not a beneficiary under it, so there is no inference of undue influence. Moreover, neither of the wills that Walker executed left any property to her son, so there was no indication that she had been influenced to change her mind regarding the distribution of her estate. Additionally, she expressly disinherited her son, and several witnesses testified that she was mentally competent at the time she made the will.

In the actual case on which this problem is based, the court presumed that Walker's will was valid.

Appendix G

Case Excerpts for *Case Analysis Questions*

Case No. 1 for Chapter 6

Winstead v. Jackson
United States Court of Appeals, Third Circuit, 2013 WL 139622 (2013).

PER CURIAM. [By the Whole Court]
* * * *

* * * Winstead filed his * * * complaint in the United States District Court for the District of New Jersey, claiming that Jackson's album/CD and film derived their contents from, and infringed the copyright of, his book.
* * * *

* * * The District Court dismissed Winstead's * * * complaint * * * , concluding that Jackson * * * did not improperly copy protected aspects of Winstead's book.
* * * *

Winstead appeals.
* * * *

Here, it is not disputed that Winstead is the owner of the copyrighted property * * *. However, *not all copying is copyright infringement, so even if actual copying is proven, the court must decide, by comparing the allegedly infringing work with the original work, whether the copying was unlawful. Copying may be proved inferentially by showing that the allegedly infringing work is substantially similar to the copyrighted work.* A court compares the allegedly infringing work with the original work, and considers whether a "lay-observer" would believe that the copying was of protectable aspects of the copyrighted work. The inquiry involves distinguishing between the author's expression and the idea or theme that he or she seeks to convey or explore, because the former is protected and the latter is not. The court must determine whether the allegedly infringing work is similar because it appropriates the unique expressions of the original work, or merely because it contains elements that would be expected when two works express the same idea or explore the same theme. [Emphasis added.]

* * * A lay observer would not believe that Jackson's album/CD and film copied protectable aspects of Winstead's book. Jackson's album/CD is comprised of 16 individual songs, which explore drug-dealing, guns and money, vengeance, and other similar clichés of hip hop gangsterism. Jackson's fictional film is the story of a young man who turns to violence when his mother is killed in a drive-by shooting. The young man takes revenge by killing the man who killed his mother, and then gets rich by becoming an "enforcer" for a powerful criminal. He takes up with a woman who eventually betrays him, and is shot to death by her boyfriend, who has just been released from prison. The movie ends with his younger brother vowing to seek vengeance. Winstead's book purports to be autobiographical and tells the story of a young man whose beloved father was a Bishop in the church. The protagonist was angry as a child because his stepmother abused him, but he found acceptance and self-esteem on the streets of Newark because he was physically powerful. He earned money robbing and beating people, went to jail, returned to crime upon his release, and then made even more money. The protagonist discusses his time at Rahway State Prison in great and compelling detail. The story ends when the protagonist learns that his father has passed away; he conveys his belief that this tragedy has led to his redemption, and he hopes that others might learn from his mistakes.

* * * Although Winstead's book and Jackson's works share similar themes and setting, the story of an angry and wronged protagonist who turns to a life of violence and crime has long been a part of the public domain [and is therefore not protected by copyright law]. Winstead argues * * * that a protagonist asking for God's help when his father dies, cutting drugs with mixing agents to maximize profits, and complaining about relatives who are addicts and steal the product, are protectable, but these things are not unique. To the extent that Jackson's works contain these elements, they are to be expected when two works express the same idea about "the streets" or explore the same theme. Winstead argues that not every protagonist whose story concerns guns, drugs, and violence in an urban setting winds up in prison or loses a parent, but this argument only serves to illustrate an important difference between his book and Jackson's film. Jackson's protagonist never spends any time in prison, whereas Winstead's protagonist devotes a considerable part of his story to his incarcerations.

In addition, Winstead's book and Jackson's works are different with respect to character, plot, mood, and sequence of events. Winstead's protagonist embarks on a life of crime at a very young age, but is redeemed by the death of his beloved father. Jackson's protagonist turns to crime when he is much older and only after his mother is murdered. He winds up dead at a young age, unredeemed. Winstead's book is hopeful; Jackson's film is characterized * * * by moral apathy. It is true that both works involve the loss of a parent and the protagonist's recognition of the parent's importance in his life, but nowhere does Jackson appropriate anything unique about Winstead's expression of this generic topic.

Winstead contends that direct phrases from his book appear in Jackson's film. * * * He emphasizes these phrases: "Yo, where is my money at," "I would never have done no shit like that to you," "my father, my strength was gone," "he was everything to me," and "I did not know what to do," but, like the phrases "putting the work in," "get the dope, cut the dope," "let's keep it popping," and "the strong take from the weak but the smart take from everybody," they are either common in general or common with respect to hip hop culture, and do not enjoy copyright protection. *The average person reading or listening to these phrases in the context of an overall story or song would not regard them as unique and protectable.* Moreover, words and short phrases do not enjoy copyright protection. The similarity between Winstead's book and the lyrics to Jackson's songs on the album/CD is even more tenuous. "Stretching the dope" and "bloodshot red eyes" are common phrases that do not enjoy copyright protection. *A side-by-side comparison of Winstead's book and the lyrics from Jackson's album/CD do not support a claim of copyright infringement.* [Emphasis added.]

For the foregoing reasons, we will affirm the order of the District Court dismissing [Winstead's] complaint.

Case No. 2 for Chapter 11

Gyabaah v. Rivlab Transportation Corp.
New York Supreme Court, Appellate Division, First Department, 102 A.D.3d 451, 958 N.Y.S.2d 109 (2013).

TOM, J.P. [Judge Presiding], *ANDRIAS, RENWICK, DEGRASSE, ABDUS-SALAAM,* JJ. [Judges]
* * * *

[Adwoa Gyabaah was hit by a bus owned by Rivlab Transportation Corporation. She retained attorney Jeffrey Aronsky to represent her in negotiations with Rivlab, its insurer National Casualty Company, and their attorneys. Gyabaah agreed to pay Aronsky a contingency fee of one-third of the amount of her recovery. Aronsky] commenced this personal injury action on plaintiff's behalf on August 25, 2010 [against Rivlab]. By letter to Aronsky dated October 1, 2010, defendant's carrier tendered its $1 million policy limits for purposes of settlement. Aronsky explained the proposal to plaintiff who, at that time, chose to accept the settlement. Accordingly, plaintiff executed a general release on October 5, 2010 * * *. Aronsky advised plaintiff that he would hold the release pending receipt of * * * advice from plaintiff as to whether she preferred to have the settlement structured [paid over a period of time rather than in one lump sum].

By December 9, 2010, plaintiff had retained new counsel, Kenneth A. Wilhelm, Esq. [Esquire, or lawyer]. On that date, Wilhelm advised Aronsky that plaintiff did not wish to settle the case or have the release sent to defendant. Aronsky moved the court below for an order enforcing what he contended was a $1 million settlement and setting his firm's contingency fee at one-third of the recovery pursuant to plaintiff's retainer agreement. In making

his motion, Aronsky did not allege that acceptance of the offer was ever communicated to defendant or its carrier. This omission is fatal to Aronsky's claim of a settlement for reasons that follow. Aronsky maintained that "plaintiff's signing of the General Release constituted a binding legal contract." The court denied the motion and vacated the release in what it perceived to be the interest of justice.

* * * The application of contract law * * * required the denial of Aronsky's motion. A general release is governed by principles of contract law. * * * *It is essential in any bilateral contract that the fact of acceptance be communicated to the offeror. Therefore, this action was not settled because the executed release was never forwarded to defendant nor was acceptance of the offer otherwise communicated to defendant or its carrier.* This record does not contain a single affidavit by anyone asserting that either occurred. * * * We do not share the * * * view that an October 6, 2010 letter from defendant's counsel to Aronsky "evidenced" an agreement to settle. Defense counsel's statement in the letter that he was "advised" of a settlement does not suffice as evidence that such a settlement was effected. * * * Because there has been no settlement, the amount of Aronsky's fee should be determined upon the disposition of this action [as a percentage of the fee recovered by the Wilhelm firm based on the *pro rata* share of the work the two attorneys performed in obtaining the recovery]. [Emphasis added.]

* * * We see no need for a hearing to determine whether Aronsky was discharged for cause. The record discloses that plaintiff has not made a *prima facie* showing of any cause for Aronsky's discharge. Plaintiff stated in her affidavit that she signed the release * * * because she felt "pressured" to do so. Plaintiff made no mention of what the pressure consisted of or, more importantly, what professional misconduct, if any, brought it about. To be sure, a hearing was not warranted by plaintiff's untenable [indefensible] argument that Aronsky disobeyed her instructions by making the instant motion albeit [although] after he had already been discharged as her attorney.

[The order of the lower court denying Aronsky's motion insofar as it sought to enforce a purported settlement and set Aronsky's fee accordingly is affirmed.]

Case No. 3 for Chapter 19

Mills v. Chauvin
Supreme Court of New York, Appellate Division, Third Department, 103 A.D.3d 1041, 962 N.Y.S.2d 412 (2013).

PER CURIAM. [By the Whole Court]
* * * *

Plaintiff, Gregory Mills, and defendant, Robert Chauvin, are two experienced attorneys who shared both a friendship and a professional/business relationship. Those longstanding relationships deteriorated and gave rise to this action.
* * * *

* * * The parties formed a partnership and took ownership of a commercial office building located on Crescent Road in the Town of Clifton Park, Saratoga County. * * * After Chauvin decided, for a

variety of reasons, that he no longer wished to maintain his ownership of the Crescent Road property, the parties agreed that Mills would purchase Chauvin's one-half interest in such property and they executed a purchase and sale agreement establishing a purchase price of $261,176.67 and a closing date.

* * * *

Chauvin was an investor in the Amelia Village [real estate development] project [in Virginia]. Over a course of time, Mills made multiple monetary payments to Chauvin—totaling $395,750—which Chauvin claims were investments in the project and Mills claims were loans. Ultimately, Mills requested that Chauvin return the payments he had advanced. In connection therewith, Chauvin executed a promissory note * * * that obligated him to pay Mills $395,750. However, Chauvin later challenged the validity of the promissory note and claimed that Mills was not entitled to a return of his investments.

* * * *

Mills subsequently filed [a] complaint [in a New York state court against Chauvin] to recover the payments Mills had made with respect to the Amelia Village project, based upon claims of breach of contract and unjust enrichment, respectively.

* * * *

The action proceeded to a nonjury trial * * *. At the conclusion thereof, Supreme Court [the trial court] found * * * that the promissory note was valid and enforceable and that Mills was entitled to recover pursuant to its terms. Chauvin now appeals from the judgment entered upon that decision.

* * * *

* * * Initially, we reject Chauvin's claim that Supreme Court erred in concluding that the * * * promissory note was enforceable. Chauvin does not dispute that Mills had previously paid him $395,750 in connection with the Amelia Village project, that he signed the promissory note promising to repay that amount to Mills, or that he tendered the note to Mills for the purpose of providing documentation to Mills' lending institution in support of Mills' application for financing of the purchase of the Crescent Road property. Instead, Chauvin claims that the promissory note was not enforceable because it was not given to secure a debt and, therefore, lacked consideration.

In this regard, Mills testified that * * * the parties * * * agreed that Chauvin would repay Mills all of the money that Mills had contributed to the Amelia Village project and that the promissory note confirmed their agreement. On the other hand, Chauvin claims that the payments that Mills made to the Amelia Village project were investments that could not be returned when Mills withdrew from that project, and that the promissory note was not intended to be a promise of repayment.

* * * *

The record amply supports Supreme Court's finding that the consideration for the promissory note was the $395,750 that Mills had provided to Chauvin in connection with the Amelia Village project and that the promissory note represented security for Chauvin's antecedent obligation to repay such funds. *The note itself—which was drafted by Chauvin, signed by him, notarized and transmitted to Mills clearly states that it was executed in return for a loan received by Chauvin and contained an unconditional promise*

or order to pay a sum certain in money. In addition, Mills took the note as a holder in due course. Based upon our independent evaluation of the evidence and, giving due deference to the trial court's credibility determinations concerning witnesses, we conclude that Supreme Court's determination that Chauvin failed to establish a bona fide defense of lack of consideration is supported by the record. [Emphasis added.]

* * * *

ORDERED that the order and judgments are affirmed, with costs to plaintiff.

Case No. 4 for Chapter 25

Dees v. United Rentals North America, Inc.
United States Court of Appeals, Ninth Circuit, 505 Fed.Appx. 302 (2013).

PER CURIAM:

* * * *

In * * * 2006 [Ellis Dees, an African American, applied] to United Rentals for employment at its Gulfport, Mississippi location, and was offered a service technician position in St. Rose, Louisiana. Branch Manager Mike Sauve made the decision to make the offer, which Dees accepted.

Although the first two years of Dees' employment in St. Rose went smoothly, United Rentals contends that his attitude and work performance deteriorated beginning in 2009. Specifically, it alleges that he began, with increasing frequency, to mark equipment as fit to be rented even though it was not in working order. Dees' managers—Sauve and Lee Vincent—coached him when these incidents occurred, and noted them in his 2009 mid-year and full-year performance reviews. Dees was also given written warnings in August 2009, October 2009, February 2010, and March 2010. Dees was given a "final written warning" on March 4, 2010, advising him that "the next incident will result in immediate termination." Following a further incident six days later, Sauve and Vincent told Dees that he was fired. Dees was sixty-two years old at the time.

Dees filed a charge with the Equal Employment Opportunity Commission, alleging employment discrimination based on his race and age [in violation of Title VII of the Civil Rights Act and the Age Discrimination in Employment Act (ADEA)]. After receiving a "right to sue" notice, he filed suit in [a federal district court]. United Rentals filed a motion for summary judgment, which the district court granted * * *. Dees timely appealed.

* * * *

* * * [Under Title VII or the ADEA] Dees first must make a *prima facie* case of discrimination based on age or race. To establish a *prima facie* case, Dees must show that he: (1) was a member of a protected group; (2) qualified for the position in question; (3) was subjected to an adverse employment action; and (4) received less favorable treatment due to his membership in the protected class than did other similarly situated employees who were not members of the protected class, under nearly identical circumstances.

If Dees makes a prima facie *case, the burden then shifts to United Rentals to articulate a legitimate, non-discriminatory reason for firing him.* If it does so, Dees must, as to his Title VII claim, offer sufficient evidence to create a genuine issue of material fact either (1) that United Rentals' reason is not true, but is instead a pretext for discrimination * * *; or (2) that United Rentals' reason, while true, is only one of the reasons for its conduct, and another motivating factor is Dees' protected characteristic. [Emphasis added.]

* * * *

The district court assumed, without deciding, that Dees established a *prima facie* case of discrimination under Title VII and the ADEA. The district court * * * determined that United Rentals had provided extensive evidence of a legitimate, non-discriminatory reason for Dees' termination—namely, unsatisfactory job performance. * * * The burden shifted back to Dees to produce evidence that United Rentals' reason was a pretext for discrimination. The district court concluded that Dees had only made conclusory [conclusive] allegations that he was discriminated against.

* * * *

His termination notice states that he was terminated for failing to follow United Rentals' policy of ensuring that the batteries in rental equipment were in good working order prior to delivery of the equipment.

* * * Dees has presented nothing to tie United Rentals' final termination decision to a discriminatory motive. * * * Dees himself describes United Rentals as motivated by an "I ain't missing no rents" philosophy that encouraged renting out equipment regardless of its readiness. No evidence shows that United Rentals' philosophy also included discriminating against African Americans or senior workers. Similarly, no evidence demonstrates that United Rentals' decision to discharge Dees was motivated by his race or age. * * * Dees' subjective belief that United Rentals discriminated against him is clearly insufficient to demonstrate pretext.

* * * *

For the reasons set forth above, we AFFIRM the district court's grant of summary judgment in United Rentals' favor.

Case No. 5 for Chapter 30

City of Livonia Employees' Retirement System and Local 295/ Local 851 v. Boeing Co.
United States Court of Appeals, Seventh Circuit, 711 F.3d 754 (2013).

POSNER, Circuit Judge.

* * * *

* * * On April 21 [2009] Boeing [Company] performed a stress test on the wings of its new 787-8 Dreamliner, a plane that had not yet flown. The wings failed the test * * *. Yet Boeing announced on May 3 that "all structural tests required on the static airframe prior to first flight are complete" and that "the initial results of the test are positive" * * *. The implication was that the plane was on track for its "First Flight," which had been scheduled for June 30.

In mid-May, after making some changes in the design * * *, Boeing conducted another test. Although the plane failed that test too, [Boeing's chief executive officer James] McNerney stated publicly that he thought the plane would fly in June. Later [the head of Boeing's commercial aircraft division Scott] Carson told [the media] that the Dreamliner "definitely will fly" this month (June).

* * * Yet on June 23, * * * Boeing announced that the First Flight of the Dreamliner had been canceled because, Carson explained, of an "anomaly" revealed by the * * * tests. He said that Boeing had hoped to be able to solve the problem in time for a First Flight in June, but had been unable to do so. In fact the First Flight did not take place until December 2009.

When Boeing announced the cancellation of the First Flight, it also announced that the cancellation would cause a delay of unspecified length in the delivery of the Dreamliner, which many airlines had already ordered. In the two days after these announcements, Boeing's stock price dropped by more than 10 percent. * * * Persons who bought Boeing stock between the tests and the announcements of the cancellation and of the delay in delivery and who therefore lost money when the price dropped [filed a suit in a federal district court against Boeing and its officers, alleging violations of Section 10(b) and Rule 10b-5].

The district judge dismissed the * * * complaint. [The plaintiffs appealed.]

There is no securities fraud by hindsight. The law does not require public disclosure of mere risks of failure. No prediction—even a prediction that the sun will rise tomorrow—has a 100 percent probability of being correct. The future is shrouded in uncertainty. If a mistaken prediction is deemed a fraud, there will be few predictions, including ones that are well grounded, as no one wants to be held hostage to an unknown future. [Emphasis added.]

Any sophisticated purchaser of a product that is still on the drawing boards knows, moreover, that its market debut may be delayed, or indeed that the project may be abandoned before it yields salable product. The purchasers of the Dreamliner protected themselves against the possibility of delay in delivery by reserving the right to cancel their orders; there are no allegations regarding cancellation penalties, or for that matter penalties imposed on Boeing for delivery delays. And therefore * * * the defendants * * * had, so far as appears, little incentive to delay the announcement of the postponement.

Without a motive to commit securities fraud, businessmen are unlikely to commit it. A more plausible inference than that of fraud is that the defendants, unsure whether they could fix the problem by the end of June, were reluctant to tell the world "we have a problem and maybe it will cause us to delay the First Flight and maybe not, but we're working on the problem and we hope we can fix it in time to prevent any significant delay, but we can't be sure, so stay tuned." There is a difference * * * between a duty of truthfulness and a duty of candor, or between a lie and reticence [uncommunicativeness]. There is no duty of total corporate transparency—no rule that every hitch or glitch, every pratfall [embarrassing mistake], in a company's operations must be disclosed in real time, forming a running commentary, a baring of the corporate innards, day and night. [Emphasis added.]

* * * *

* * * The * * * complaint alleged [that] what McNerney and Carson knew about the likely postponement of the First Flight * * * was confirmed by "internal e-mails" of Boeing. The reference to internal e-mails implied that someone inside Boeing was aiding the plaintiffs. But as no such person was identified, the judge could not determine whether such e-mails * * * existed.

Allegations * * * merely implying unnamed confidential sources of damaging information require a heavy discount. The sources may be ill-informed, may be acting from spite rather than knowledge, may be misrepresented, may even be nonexistent * * *. The district judge therefore rightly refused to give any weight to the "internal e-mails" to which the complaint referred.

* * * *

The judgment dismissing the suit is affirmed.

Case No. 6 for Chapter 31

Leegin Creative Leather Products, Inc. v. PSKS, Inc.
Supreme Court of the United States, 551 U.S. 877, 127 S.Ct. 2705, 168 L.Ed.2d 623 (2007).

Justice *KENNEDY* delivered the opinion of the Court.

* * * *

Petitioner, Leegin Creative Leather Products, Inc. (Leegin), designs, manufactures, and distributes leather goods and accessories. In 1991, Leegin began to sell [products] under the brand name "Brighton."

Respondent, PSKS, Inc. (PSKS), operates Kay's Kloset, a women's apparel store in Lewisville, Texas. * * * It first started purchasing Brighton goods from Leegin in 1995.

* * * *

In December 2002, Leegin discovered Kay's Kloset had been marking down Brighton's entire line by 20 percent. * * * Leegin stopped selling [Brighton products] to the store.

PSKS sued Leegin in the United States District Court for the Eastern District of Texas. It alleged, among other claims, that Leegin had violated the antitrust laws by "enter[ing] into agreements with retailers to charge only those prices fixed by Leegin." * * * [The court] entered judgment against Leegin in the amount of $3,975,000.80.

The [U.S.] Court of Appeals for the Fifth Circuit affirmed. * * * We granted *certiorari* * * *.

* * * *

The rule of reason is the accepted standard for testing whether a practice restrains trade in violation of [Section] 1 [of the Sherman Act].

* * * *

Resort to per se *rules is confined to restraints * * * that would always or almost always tend to restrict competition and decrease output. To justify a* per se *prohibition a restraint must have manifestly anticompetitive effects, and lack * * * any redeeming virtue.* [Emphasis added.]

As a consequence, the *per se* rule is appropriate only after courts have had considerable experience with the type of restraint at issue, and only if courts can predict with confidence that it would be invalidated in all or almost all instances under the rule of reason.

* * * *

The reasoning of the Court's more recent jurisprudence has rejected the rationales on which [the application of the *per se* rule to minimum resale price maintenance agreements] was based. * * * [These rationales were] based on formalistic legal doctrine rather than demonstrable economic effect. * * *

* * * Furthermore [the Court] treated vertical agreements a manufacturer makes with its distributors as analogous to a horizontal combination among competing distributors. * * * Our recent cases formulate antitrust principles in accordance with the appreciated differences in economic effect between vertical and horizontal agreements * * *.

* * * *

The justifications for vertical price restraints are similar to those for other vertical restraints. *Minimum resale price maintenance can stimulate interbrand competition * * * by reducing intrabrand competition * * *.* The promotion of interbrand competition is important because the primary purpose of the antitrust laws is to protect this type of competition. * * * *Resale price maintenance also has the potential to give consumers more options so that they can choose among low-price, low-service brands; high-price, high-service brands; and brands that fall in between.* [Emphasis added.]

* * * *

While vertical agreements setting minimum resale prices can have procompetitive justifications, they may have anticompetitive effects in other cases; and unlawful price fixing, designed solely to obtain monopoly profits, is an ever present temptation.

* * * *

Notwithstanding the risks of unlawful conduct, it cannot be stated with any degree of confidence that resale price maintenance always or almost always tends to restrict competition and decrease output. Vertical agreements establishing minimum resale prices can have either procompetitive or anticompetitive effects, depending upon the circumstances in which they are formed. * * * As the [*per se*] rule would proscribe a significant amount of procompetitive conduct, these agreements appear ill suited for *per se* condemnation.

* * * *

The judgment of the Court of Appeals is reversed, and the case is remanded for proceedings consistent with this opinion.

Case No. 7 for Chapter 35

Town of Midland v. Morris
Court of Appeals of North Carolina, 704 S.E.2d 329 (2011).

STEPHENS, Judge.

The Transcontinental Pipeline transports and distributes natural gas from the Gulf of Mexico to the northeastern United States. In April 2002, the City of Monroe, North Carolina, decided to supply the citizens of Monroe and the surrounding area with natural gas by a direct connection between its natural gas distribution system and the Transcontinental Pipeline. To directly connect to the Transcontinental Pipeline, Monroe needed to acquire the rights to property through which to run a pipeline along the forty-two miles between Monroe and the direct connection on the Transcontinental Pipeline located in Iredell County.

To facilitate the acquisition of land for the construction of the new pipeline ("Pipeline"), Monroe, located in Union County, entered into interlocal agreements with the Town of Mooresville, located in Iredell County, and the Town of Midland, located in Cabarrus County.

The relevant terms of the interlocal agreement between Midland and Monroe * * * provide as follows:

4. Midland shall be responsible for obtaining either by acquisition or by the power of eminent domain and holding in its name for the benefit of the parties and this Interlocal Agreement all easements (both permanent and temporary construction), rights of way, and real property required for the project in Cabarrus County.
* * * *

20. * * * Midland shall retain a perpetual right to locate and install one (1) tap in the pipeline within the corporate limits of Midland from which to operate and supply its own natural gas distribution utility for the benefit of Midland's utility customers in Cabarrus County only. The one tap for Midland's use shall be subject to a right of first refusal granted to a private natural gas provider to serve customers that would otherwise be served by Midland. . . .

* * * *

In 2008 Midland began the process of acquiring the property necessary for the construction of the Pipeline. When negotiations for voluntary acquisitions for the rights of way failed, Midland exercised its eminent domain authority to condemn the needed property.

The present controversy stems from fifteen condemnation actions filed by the Town of Midland in Cabarrus County Superior Court. In those fifteen actions, the opposing parties (hereinafter "Property Owners") filed defenses and counterclaims, challenging Midland's power to condemn the properties in question * * *.

* * * *

Property Owners first argue that because Midland neither currently provides natural gas services to its citizens, nor currently has any plans to provide natural gas to its citizens in the future, the condemnations were undertaken in violation of the statutes governing eminent domain. We disagree.

* * * *

* * * *We find it manifest [obvious] that Midland may acquire property by condemnation to establish a gas transmission and distribution system, even in the absence of a concrete, immediate plan to furnish gas services to its citizens.* [Emphasis added.]

While we acknowledge the existence of the requirement that the public enterprise be established and conducted for the city and its citizens, we conclude that this requirement is satisfied by Midland's placement of a tap on the Pipeline and by Midland's acquisition of the right to low-cost natural gas. Further, * * * *there is nothing in the record to indicate that Midland will never offer natural gas services to its citizens. In fact, Midland's contracted-for right to install a tap on the Pipeline "from which to operate and supply its own natural gas distribution utility for the benefit of Midland's utility customers" indicates just the opposite*: that Midland will, eventually, furnish natural gas services to its citizens. [Emphasis added.]

* * * *

Property Owners further argue that Midland's condemnations violate [the state's statute] because the condemnations are not "for the public use or benefit."
* * * *

It is clear from the statutory language that establishing a gas transmission and distribution system is an appropriate purpose for the condemnation of property under [the relevant provisions].

Despite the disjunctive language of this statutory requirement, our courts have determined the propriety of a condemnation under [the statute] based on the condemnation's satisfaction of both a "public use test" and a "public benefit test."

The first approach—the public use test—asks whether the public has a right to a definite use of the condemned property. The second approach—the public benefit test—asks whether some benefit accrues to the public as a result of the desired condemnation.

Under the public use test, "the principal and dispositive determination is whether the general public has a right to a definite use of the property sought to be condemned." * * * Applying this test to the present case in the appropriate context, there is nothing to indicate that gas services—were they to be provided by Midland—would be available to anything less than the entire population. Accordingly, there can be no doubt that the Midland condemnations would pass the public use test * * *.
* * * *

Under the public benefit test, "*a given condemnor's desired use of the condemned property in question is for 'the public use or benefit' if that use would contribute to the general welfare and prosperity of the public at large.*" In this case, we must take care in defining Midland's "desired use" of the property. Midland is condemning the property to run the Pipeline and to control a tap on the Pipeline, not to immediately provide gas to the citizens of Midland. Accordingly, it is the *availability* of natural gas that must contribute to the general welfare and prosperity of the public at large. [Emphasis added.]

As noted by our Courts, the construction and extension of public utilities, and especially the concomitant commercial and residential growth, provide a clear public benefit to local citizens. * * * Midland's tap on the Pipeline, and its potential to provide natural gas service, likely will spur growth, as well as provide Midland with an advantage in industrial recruitment. These opportunities must be seen as public benefits accruing to the citizens of Midland, such that Midland's condemnations are for the public benefit.
* * * *

Accordingly, we conclude that the Midland condemnations were not undertaken to provide a solely private benefit.
* * * *

We hold that Midland lawfully exercised its eminent domain power.

Glossary

A

Abandoned Property Property that has been discarded by the owner, who has no intention of reclaiming it.

Acceleration Clause A clause that allows a payee or other holder of a time instrument to demand payment of the entire amount due, with interest, if a certain event occurs, such as a default in the payment of an installment when due.

Acceptance The act of voluntarily agreeing, through words or conduct, to the terms of an offer, thereby creating a contract. In negotiable instruments law, a drawee's signed agreement to pay a draft when it is presented.

Acceptor A drawee that accepts, or promises to pay, an instrument when it is presented later for payment.

Accession The addition of value to personal property by the use of labor or materials.

Accord and Satisfaction A common means of settling a disputed claim, whereby a debtor offers to pay a lesser amount than the creditor purports to be owed.

Accredited Investor In the context of securities offerings, sophisticated investors, such as banks, insurance companies, investment companies, the issuer's executive officers and directors, and persons whose income or net worth exceeds certain limits.

Act of State Doctrine A doctrine providing that the judicial branch of one country will not examine the validity of public acts committed by a recognized foreign government within its own territory.

Actionable Capable of serving as the basis of a lawsuit. An actionable claim can be pursued in a lawsuit or other court action.

Actual Malice The deliberate intent to cause harm that exists when a person makes a statement with either knowledge of its falsity or reckless disregard of the truth. Actual malice is required to establish defamation against public figures.

Actus Reus A guilty (prohibited) act; one of the two essential elements required to establish criminal liability.

Adhesion Contract A standard-form contract in which the stronger party dictates the terms.

Adjudicate To render a judicial decision. Adjudication is the trial-like proceeding in which an administrative law judge hears and resolves disputes involving an administrative agency's regulations.

Administrative Agency A federal or state government agency created by the legislature to perform a specific function, such as to make and enforce rules pertaining to the environment.

Administrative Law The body of law created by administrative agencies in order to carry out their duties and responsibilities.

Administrative Law Judge (ALJ) One who presides over an administrative agency hearing and has the power to administer oaths, take testimony, rule on questions of evidence, and make determinations of fact.

Administrative Process The procedure used by administrative agencies in administering the law.

Administrator One who is appointed by a court to administer a person's estate if the decedent died without a valid will or if the executor named in the will cannot serve.

Adverse Possession The acquisition of title to real property through open occupation, without the consent of the owner, for a period of time specified by a state statute. The occupation must be actual, exclusive, open, continuous, and in opposition to all others, including the owner.

Affirmative Action Job-hiring policies that give special consideration to members of protected classes in an effort to overcome present effects of past discrimination.

After-Acquired Property Property that is acquired by the debtor after the execution of a security agreement.

Age of Majority The age (eighteen in most states) at which a person, formerly a minor, is recognized by law as an adult and is legally responsible for his or her actions.

Agency A relationship between two parties in which one party (the agent) agrees to represent or act for the other (the principal).

Agency Coupled with an Interest An agency, created for the benefit of the agent, in which the agent has some legal right (interest) in the property that is the subject of the agency.

Agreement A mutual understanding or meeting of the minds between two or more individuals regarding the terms of a contract.

Alien Corporation A corporation formed in another country but doing business in the United States.

Alienation The transfer of title to real property (which "alienates" the real property from the former owner).

Alternative Dispute Resolution (ADR) The resolution of disputes in ways other than those involved in the traditional judicial process, such as negotiation, mediation, and arbitration.

Answer Procedurally, a defendant's response to the plaintiff's complaint.

Anticipatory Repudiation An assertion or action by a party indicating that he or she will not perform a contractual obligation.

Antitrust Law Laws protecting commerce from unlawful restraints and anticompetitive practices.

Apparent Authority Authority that is only apparent, not real. An agent's apparent authority arises when the principal causes a third party to believe that the agent has authority, even though she or he does not.

Appropriation In tort law, the use by one person of another person's name, likeness, or other identifying characteristic without permission and for the benefit of the user.

Arbitration The settling of a dispute by submitting it to a disinterested third party (other than a court), who renders a decision.

Arbitration Clause A clause in a contract that provides that, in the event of a dispute, the parties will submit the dispute to arbitration rather than litigate the dispute in court.

Arson The intentional burning of a building.

Articles of Incorporation The document that is filed with the appropriate state official, usually the secretary of state, when a business is incorporated and that contains basic information about the corporation

Articles of Organization The document filed with a designated state official by which a limited liability company is formed.

Articles of Partnership A written agreement that sets forth each partner's rights and obligations with respect to the partnership.

Artisan's Lien A possessory lien held by a party who has made improvements and added value to the personal property of another party as security for payment for services performed.

Assault Any word or action intended to make another person fearful of immediate physical harm—a reasonably believable threat.

Assignee A party to whom the rights under a contract are transferred, or assigned.

Assignment The transfer to another of all or part of one's rights arising under a contract.

Assignor A party who transfers (assigns) his or her rights under a contract to another party (the *assignee*).

Assumption of Risk A defense to negligence that bars a plaintiff from recovering for injuries or damage suffered as a result of risks he or she knew of and voluntarily assumed.

Attachment In a secured transaction, the process by which a secured creditor's interest "attaches" to the collateral and the creditor's security interest becomes enforceable. In the context of judicial liens, a court-ordered seizure of property before a judgment is secured for a past-due debt.

Attempted Monopolization An action by a firm that involves anticompetitive conduct, the intent to gain monopoly power, and a "dangerous probability" of success in achieving monopoly power.

Auditor An accountant qualified to perform audits (systematic inspections) of a business's financial records.

Authorization Card A card signed by an employee that gives a union permission to act on his or her behalf in negotiations with management.

Automatic Stay In bankruptcy proceedings, the suspension of almost all litigation and other action by creditors against the debtor or the debtor's property. The stay is effective the moment the debtor files a petition in bankruptcy.

Award The monetary compensation given to a party at the end of a trial or other proceeding.

B

Bailee One to whom goods are entrusted by a bailor.

Bailee's Lien A possessory (artisan's) lien that a bailee entitled to compensation can place on the bailed property to ensure that he or she will be paid for the services provided.

Bailment A situation in which the personal property of one person (a bailor) is entrusted to another (a bailee), who is obligated to return the bailed property to the bailor or dispose of it as directed.

Bailor One who entrusts goods to a bailee.

Bait-and-Switch Advertising Advertising a product at an attractive price and then telling the consumer that the advertised product is not available or is of poor quality and encouraging her or him to purchase a more expensive item.

Bankruptcy Court A federal court of limited jurisdiction that handles only bankruptcy proceedings, which are governed by federal bankruptcy law.

Bankruptcy Trustee A person appointed by the court to manage the debtor's funds.

Battery Physical contact with another that is unexcused, harmful or offensive, and intentionally performed.

Bearer A person in possession of an instrument payable to bearer or indorsed in blank.

Bearer Instrument Any instrument that is not payable to a specific person, including instruments payable to the bearer or to "cash."

Benefit Corporation A for-profit corporation that seeks to have a material positive impact on society and the environment. It is available by statute in a number of states.

Bequest A gift of personal property by will (from the verb *to bequeath*).

Beyond a Reasonable Doubt The standard of proof used in criminal cases.

Bilateral Contract A type of contract that arises when a promise is given in exchange for a return promise.

Bilateral Mistake A mistake that occurs when both parties to a contract are mistaken about the same material fact.

Bill of Rights The first ten amendments to the U.S. Constitution.

Binder A written, temporary insurance policy.

Binding Authority Any source of law that a court *must* follow when deciding a case.

Blank Indorsement An indorsement on an instrument that specifies no indorsee. An order instrument that is indorsed in blank becomes a bearer instrument.

Bona Fide Occupational Qualification (BFOQ) An identifiable characteristic reasonably necessary to the normal operation of a particular business. Such characteristics can include gender, national origin, and religion, but not race.

Bond A security that evidences a corporate (or government) debt.

Botnet A network of compromised computers connected to the Internet that can be used to generate spam, relay viruses, or cause servers to fail.

Breach of Contract The failure, without legal excuse, of a promisor to perform the obligations of a contract.

Brief A written summary or statement prepared by one side in a lawsuit to explain its case to the judge.

Browse-Wrap Term A term or condition of use that is presented when an online buyer downloads a product but to which the buyer does not have to agree before installing or using the product.

Burglary The unlawful entry or breaking into a building with the intent to commit a felony.

Business Ethics The application of moral and ethical principles in a business context.

Business Invitee A person, such as a customer or a client, who is invited onto business premises by the owner of those premises for business purposes.

Business Judgment Rule A rule under which courts will not hold corporate officers and directors liable for honest mistakes of judgment and bad business decisions that were made in good faith.

Business Necessity A defense to an allegation of employment discrimination in which the employer demonstrates that an employment practice that discriminates against members of a protected class is related to job performance.

Business Tort Wrongful interference with another's business rights and relationships.

Business Trust A form of business organization, created by a written trust agreement, that resembles a corporation. Legal ownership and management of the trust's property stay with the trustees, and the profits are distributed to the beneficiaries, who have limited liability.

Buyer in the Ordinary Course of Business A buyer who, in good faith and without knowledge that the sale violates the ownership rights or security interest of a third party in the goods, purchases goods in the ordinary course of business from a person in the business of selling goods of that kind.

Buyout Price The amount payable to a partner on his or her dissociation from a partnership, based on the amount distributable to that partner if the firm were wound up on that date, and offset by any damages for wrongful dissociation.

Bylaws The internal rules of management adopted by a corporation at its first organizational meeting.

C

Case Law The rules of law announced in court decisions. Case law interprets statutes, regulations, constitutional provisions, and other case law.

Cashier's Check A check drawn by a bank on itself.

Categorical Imperative An ethical guideline developed by Immanuel Kant under which an action is evaluated in terms of what would happen if everybody else in the same situation, or category, acted the same way.

Causation in Fact An act or omission without which an event would not have occurred.

Cease-and-Desist Order An administrative or judicial order prohibiting a person or business firm from conducting activities that an agency or court has deemed illegal.

Certificate of Deposit (CD) A note issued by a bank in which the bank acknowledges the receipt of funds from a party and promises to repay that amount, with interest, to the party on a certain date.

Certificate of Limited Partnership The document that must be filed with a designated state official to form a limited partnership.

Certification Mark A mark used by one or more persons, other than the owner, to certify the region, materials, mode of manufacture, quality, or other characteristic of specific goods or services.

Certified Check A check that has been accepted in writing by the bank on which it is drawn. By certifying (accepting) the check, the bank promises to pay the check at the time it is presented.

Charging Order In partnership law, an order granted by a court to a judgment creditor that entitles the creditor to attach a partner's interest in the partnership.

Charitable Trust A trust in which the property held by the trustee must be used for a charitable purpose, such as the advancement of health, education, or religion.

Chattel Personal property.

Check A draft drawn by a drawer ordering the drawee bank or financial institution to pay a certain amount of funds to the payee on demand.

Checks and Balances The principle under which the powers of the national government are divided among three separate branches— the executive, legislative, and judicial branches—each of which exercises a check on the actions of the others.

Choice-of-Language Clause A clause in a contract designating the official language by which the contract will be interpreted in the event of a disagreement over the contract's terms.

Choice-of-Law Clause A clause in a contract designating the law (such as the law of a particular state or nation) that will govern the contract.

Citation A reference to a publication in which a legal authority—such as a statute or a court decision—or other source can be found.

Civil Law The branch of law dealing with the definition and enforcement of all private or public rights, as opposed to criminal matters.

Civil Law System A system of law derived from Roman law that is based on codified laws (rather than on case precedents).

Clearinghouse A system or place where banks exchange checks and drafts drawn on each other and settle daily balances.

Click-On Agreement An agreement that arises when an online buyer clicks on "I agree" or otherwise indicates her or his assent to be bound by the terms of an offer.

Close Corporation A corporation whose shareholders are limited to a small group of persons, often family members.

Closed Shop A firm that requires union membership by its workers as a condition of employment.

Cloud Computing The delivery to users of on-demand services from third-party servers over a network.

Codicil A written supplement or modification to a will. A codicil must be executed with the same formalities as a will.

Collateral Under Article 9 of the UCC, the property subject to a security interest.

Collateral Promise A secondary promise to a primary transaction, such as a promise made by one person to pay the debts of another if the latter fails to perform. A collateral promise normally must be in writing to be enforceable.

Collecting Bank Any bank handling an item for collection, except the payor bank.

Collective Bargaining The process by which labor and management negotiate the terms and conditions of employment, including working hours and workplace conditions.

Collective Mark A mark used by members of a cooperative, association, union, or other organization to certify the region, materials, mode of manufacture, quality, or other characteristic of specific goods or services.

Comity The principle by which one nation defers to and gives effect to the laws and judicial decrees of another nation. This recognition is based primarily on respect.

Commerce Clause The provision in Article I, Section 8, of the U.S. Constitution that gives Congress the power to regulate interstate commerce.

Commercial Impracticability A doctrine that may excuse the duty to perform a contract when performance becomes much more difficult or costly due to forces that neither party could control or foresee at the time the contract was formed.

Commingle To put funds or goods together into one mass so that they are mixed to such

a degree that they no longer have separate identities.

Common Law The body of law developed from custom or judicial decisions in English and U.S. courts, not attributable to a legislature.

Common Stock Shares of ownership in a corporation that give the owner a proportionate interest in the corporation with regard to control, earnings, and net assets. Common stock is lowest in priority with respect to payment of dividends and distribution of the corporation's assets on dissolution.

Community Property A form of concurrent property ownership in which each spouse owns an undivided one-half interest in property acquired during the marriage.

Comparative Negligence A rule in tort law, used in the majority of states, that reduces the plaintiff's recovery in proportion to the plaintiff's degree of fault, rather than barring recovery completely.

Compelling Government Interest A test of constitutionality that requires the government to have convincing reasons for passing any law that restricts fundamental rights, such as free speech, or distinguishes between people based on a suspect trait.

Compensatory Damages A monetary award equivalent to the actual value of injuries or damage sustained by the aggrieved party.

Complaint The pleading made by a plaintiff alleging wrongdoing on the part of the defendant. When filed with a court, the complaint initiates a lawsuit.

Computer Crime Any violation of criminal law that involves knowledge of computer technology for its perpetration, investigation, or prosecution.

Concentrated Industry An industry in which a single firm or a small number of firms control a large percentage of market sales.

Concurrent Conditions Conditions that must occur or be performed at the same time— they are mutually dependent. No obligations arise until these conditions are simultaneously performed.

Concurrent Jurisdiction Jurisdiction that exists when two different courts have the power to hear a case.

Concurrent Ownership Joint ownership.

Concurring Opinion A court opinion by one or more judges or justices who agree with the majority but want to make or emphasize a point that was not made or emphasized in the majority's opinion.

Condemnation Proceedings The judicial procedure by which the government exercises its power of eminent domain. It generally involves two phases: a taking and a determination of fair value.

Condition A qualification, provision, or clause in a contractual agreement, the occurrence or nonoccurrence of which creates, suspends, or terminates the obligations of the contracting parties.

Condition Precedent A condition in a contract that must be met before a party's promise becomes absolute.

Condition Subsequent A condition in a contract that, if it occurs, operates to terminate a party's absolute promise to perform.

Confiscation A government's taking of a privately owned business or personal property without a proper public purpose or an award of just compensation.

Conforming Goods Goods that conform to contract specifications.

Confusion The mixing together of goods belonging to two or more owners to such an extent that the separately owned goods cannot be identified.

Consequential Damages Foreseeable damages that result from a party's breach of contract but are caused by special circumstances beyond the contract itself.

Consideration The value given in return for a promise or performance in a contractual agreement.

Constitutional Law The body of law derived from the U.S. Constitution and the constitutions of the various states.

Constructive Delivery A symbolic delivery of property that cannot be physically delivered.

Constructive Discharge A termination of employment brought about by making the employee's working conditions so intolerable that the employee reasonably feels compelled to leave.

Constructive Eviction A form of eviction that occurs when a landlord fails to perform adequately any of the duties required by the lease, thereby making the tenant's further use and enjoyment of the property exceedingly difficult or impossible.

Constructive Fraud Conduct that is treated as fraud under the law even where there is no proof of intent to defraud, usually because of the existence of a special relationship or fiduciary duty.

Constructive Trust An equitable trust that is imposed in the interests of fairness and justice when someone wrongfully holds legal title to property.

Consumer-Debtor One whose debts result primarily from the purchases of goods for personal, family, or household use.

Continuation Statement A statement that, if filed within six months prior to the expiration date of the original financing statement, continues the perfection of the security interest for another five years.

Contract A set of promises constituting an agreement between parties, giving each a

legal duty to the other and the right to seek a remedy for the breach of the promises or duties.

Contractual Capacity The capacity required by the law for a party who enters into a contract to be bound by that contract.

Contributory Negligence A rule in tort law, used in only a few states, that completely bars the plaintiff from recovering any damages if the damage suffered is partly the plaintiff's own fault.

Conversion Wrongfully taking or retaining possession of an individual's personal property and placing it in the service of another.

Conveyance The transfer of title to real property from one person to another by deed or other document.

Cookie A small file sent from a Web site and stored in a user's Web browser to track the user's Web browsing activities.

"Cooling-Off" Laws Laws that allow buyers of goods sold in certain transactions to cancel their contracts within three business days.

Cooperative An association, which may or may not be incorporated, that is organized to provide an economic service to its members. Unincorporated cooperatives are often treated like partnerships for tax and other legal purposes.

Copyright The exclusive right of an author or originator of a literary or artistic production to publish, print, sell, or otherwise use that production for a statutory period of time.

Corporate Governance A set of policies specifying the rights and responsibilities of the various participants in a corporation and spelling out the rules and procedures for making corporate decisions.

Corporate Social Responsibility (CSR) The idea that corporations can and should act ethically and be accountable to society for their actions.

Corporation A legal entity formed in compliance with statutory requirements that is distinct from its shareholder-owners.

Correspondent Bank A bank that acts on behalf of another bank for the purpose of facilitating fund transfers.

Cost-Benefit Analysis A decision-making technique that involves weighing the costs of a given action against the benefits of that action.

Co-Surety A joint surety; a party who assumes liability jointly with another surety for the payment of a debtor's obligation under a suretyship arrangement.

Counteradvertising New advertising that is undertaken to correct earlier false claims that were made about a product.

Counterclaim A claim made by a defendant in a civil lawsuit against the plaintiff. In effect, the defendant is suing the plaintiff.

Counteroffer An offeree's response to an offer in which the offeree rejects the original offer and at the same time makes a new offer.

Course of Dealing Prior conduct between the parties to a contract that establishes a common basis for their understanding.

Course of Performance The conduct that occurs under the terms of a particular agreement, which indicates what the parties to that agreement intended the agreement to mean.

Covenant Not to Compete A contractual promise of one party to refrain from conducting business similar to that of another party for a certain period of time and within a specified geographical area.

Covenant Not to Sue An agreement to substitute a contractual obligation for some other type of legal action based on a valid claim.

Cover A remedy that allows the buyer or lessee, on the seller's or lessor's breach, to obtain substitute goods from another seller or lessor.

Cram-Down Provision A provision of the Bankruptcy Code that allows a court to confirm a debtor's Chapter 11 reorganization plan even though only one class of creditors has accepted it.

Creditors' Composition Agreement A contract between a debtor and his or her creditors in which the creditors agree to discharge the debts on the debtor's payment of a sum less than the amount actually owed.

Crime A wrong against society proclaimed in a statute and, if committed, punishable by society through fines, imprisonment, or death.

Criminal Law The branch of law that defines and punishes wrongful actions committed against the public.

Cross-Collateralization The use of an asset that is not the subject of a loan to collateralize that loan.

Crowdfunding A cooperative activity in which people network and pool funds and other resources via the Internet to assist a cause (such as disaster relief) or invest in a venture (business).

Cure The right of a party who tenders nonconforming performance to correct his or her performance within the contract period.

Cyber Crime A crime that occurs in the online environment.

Cyber Fraud Any misrepresentation knowingly made over the Internet with the intention of deceiving another for the purpose of obtaining property or funds.

Cyberlaw An informal term used to refer to all laws governing electronic communications and transactions, particularly those conducted via the Internet.

Cybersquatting The act of registering a domain name that is the same as, or confusingly similar to, the trademark of another and then offering to sell that domain name back to the trademark owner.

Cyber Tort A tort committed via the Internet.

D

Damages A monetary award sought as a remedy for a breach of contract or a tortious action.

Debtor Under Article 9 of the UCC, any party who owes payment or performance of a secured obligation.

Debtor in Possession (DIP) In Chapter 11 bankruptcy proceedings, a debtor who is allowed to continue in possession of the estate in property (the business) and to continue business operations.

Deceptive Advertising Advertising that misleads consumers, either by making unjustified claims about a product's performance or by omitting a material fact concerning the product's composition or performance.

Deed A document by which title to real property is passed.

Defalcation Embezzlement or misappropriation of funds.

Defamation Anything published or publicly spoken that causes injury to another's good name, reputation, or character.

Default Failure to pay a debt when it is due.

Default Judgment A judgment entered by a court against a defendant who has failed to appear in court to answer or defend against the plaintiff's claim.

Defendant One against whom a lawsuit is brought or the accused person in a criminal proceeding.

Defense A reason offered by a defendant in an action or lawsuit as to why the plaintiff should not recover or establish what she or he seeks.

Deficiency Judgment A judgment against a debtor for the amount of a debt remaining unpaid after the collateral has been repossessed and sold.

Delegatee A party to whom contractual obligations are transferred, or delegated.

Delegation of Duties The transfer to another of a contractual duty.

Delegator A party who transfers (delegates) her or his obligations under a contract to another party (the *delegatee*).

Depositary Bank The first bank to receive a check for payment.

Deposition The testimony of a party to a lawsuit or a witness taken under oath before a trial.

Destination Contract A contract for the sale of goods in which the seller is required or authorized to ship the goods by carrier and tender delivery of the goods at a particular destination. The seller assumes liability for any losses or damage to the goods until they are tendered at the destination specified in the contract.

Devise A gift of real property by will, or the act of giving real property by will.

Devisee One designated in a will to receive a gift of real property.

Digital Cash Prepaid funds stored on microchips in laptops, smartphones, tablets, and other devices.

Disaffirmance The legal avoidance, or setting aside, of a contractual obligation.

Discharge The termination of an obligation, such as occurs when the parties to a contract have fully performed their contractual obligations. The termination of a bankruptcy debtor's obligation to pay debts.

Disclosed Principal A principal whose identity is known to a third party at the time the agent makes a contract with the third party.

Discovery A method by which the opposing parties obtain information from each other to prepare for trial.

Dishonor To refuse to pay or to accept a negotiable instrument that has been presented in a timely and proper manner.

Disparagement of Property An economically injurious falsehood about another's product or property.

Disparate-Impact Discrimination Discrimination that results from certain employer practices or procedures that, although not discriminatory on their face, have a discriminatory effect.

Disparate-Treatment Discrimination A form of employment discrimination that results when an employer intentionally discriminates against employees who are members of protected classes.

Dissenting Opinion A court opinion that presents the views of one or more judges or justices who disagree with the majority's decision.

Dissociation The severance of the relationship between a partner and a partnership.

Dissolution The formal disbanding of a partnership or a corporation. Partnerships can be dissolved by acts of the partners, by operation of law, or by judicial decree.

Distributed Network A network that can be used by persons located (distributed) around the country or the globe to share computer files.

Distribution Agreement A contract between a seller and a distributor of the seller's products

setting out the terms and conditions of the distributorship.

Diversity of Citizenship A basis for federal court jurisdiction over a lawsuit between citizens of different states or a lawsuit involving a U.S. citizen and a citizen of a different country.

Divestiture A company's sale of one or more of its divisions' operating functions under court order as part of the enforcement of the antitrust laws.

Dividend A distribution of corporate profits to the corporation's shareholders in proportion to the number of shares held.

Docket The list of cases entered on a court's calendar and thus scheduled to be heard by the court.

Document of Title A paper exchanged in the regular course of business that evidences the right to possession of goods (for example, a bill of lading or a warehouse receipt).

Domain Name Part of an Internet address, such as "cengage.com." The series of letters and symbols used to identify a site operator on the Internet; an Internet "address."

Domestic Corporation In a given state, a corporation that is organized under the law of that state.

Dominion Ownership rights in property, including the right to possess and control the property.

Double Jeopardy The Fifth Amendment requirement that prohibits a person from being tried twice for the same criminal offense.

Down Payment An initial cash payment made when an expensive item, such as a house, is purchased. The payment represents a percentage of the purchase price, and the remainder is financed.

Draft Any instrument drawn on a drawee that orders the drawee to pay a certain amount of funds, usually to a third party (the payee), on demand or at a definite future time.

Dram Shop Act A state statute that imposes liability on the owners of bars and taverns, as well as those who serve alcoholic drinks to the public, for injuries resulting from accidents caused by intoxicated persons when the sellers or servers of alcoholic drinks contributed to the intoxication.

Drawee The party that is ordered to pay a draft or check. With a check, a bank or a financial institution is always the drawee.

Drawer The party that initiates a draft (such as a check), thereby ordering the drawee to pay.

Due Diligence A required standard of care that certain professionals, such as accountants, must meet to avoid liability for securities violations.

Due Process Clause The provisions in the Fifth and Fourteenth Amendments that guarantee that no person shall be deprived of life, liberty, or property without due process of law. State constitutions often include similar clauses.

Dumping The sale of goods in a foreign country at a price below the price charged for the same goods in the domestic market.

Duress Unlawful pressure brought to bear on a person, causing the person to perform an act that she or he would not otherwise perform.

Duty-based Ethics An ethical philosophy rooted in the idea that every person has certain duties to others, including both humans and the planet. Those duties may be derived from religious principles or from other philosophical reasoning.

Duty of Care The duty of all persons, as established by tort law, to exercise a reasonable amount of care in their dealings with others. Failure to exercise due care, which is normally determined by the reasonable person standard, constitutes the tort of negligence.

E

Easement A nonpossessory right, established by express or implied agreement, to make limited use of another's property without removing anything from the property.

E-Contract A contract that is formed electronically.

E-Evidence A type of evidence that consists of computer-generated or electronically recorded information.

Electronic Fund Transfer (EFT) A transfer of funds through the use of an electronic terminal, a telephone, a computer, or magnetic tape.

Emancipation In regard to minors, the act of being freed from parental control.

Embezzlement The fraudulent appropriation of funds or other property by a person who was entrusted with the funds or property.

Eminent Domain The power of a government to take land from private citizens for public use on the payment of just compensation.

E-Money Prepaid funds stored on microchips in laptops, smartphones, tablets, and other devices.

Employment at Will A common law doctrine under which either party may terminate an employment relationship at any time for any reason, unless a contract specifies otherwise.

Employment Contract A contract between an employer and an employee in which the terms and conditions of employment are stated.

Enabling Legislation A statute enacted by Congress that authorizes the creation of an administrative agency and specifies the name, composition, purpose, and powers of the agency being created.

Entrapment A defense in which a defendant claims that he or she was induced by a public official to commit a crime that he or she would otherwise not have committed.

Entrepreneur One who initiates and assumes the financial risk of a new business enterprise and undertakes to provide or control its management.

Entrustment Rule The rule that entrusting goods to a merchant who deals in goods of that kind gives that merchant the power to transfer those goods and all rights to them to a buyer in the ordinary course of business.

Environmental Impact Statement (EIS) A formal analysis required for any major federal action that will significantly affect the quality of the environment to determine the action's impact and explore alternatives.

Equal Dignity Rule A rule requiring that an agent's authority be in writing if the contract to be made on behalf of the principal must be in writing.

Equal Protection Clause The provision in the Fourteenth Amendment that requires state governments to treat similarly situated individuals in a similar manner.

Equitable Principles and Maxims General propositions or principles of law that have to do with fairness (equity).

Equitable Right of Redemption The right of a mortgagor who has breached the mortgage agreement to redeem or purchase the mortgaged property prior to foreclosure proceedings.

E-Signature An electronic sound, symbol, or process attached to or logically associated with a record and adopted by a person with the intent to sign the record.

Establishment Clause The provision in the First Amendment that prohibits the government from establishing any state-sponsored religion or enacting any law that promotes religion or favors one religion over another.

Estate in Bankruptcy All of the property owned by a person, including real estate and personal property.

Estopped Barred, impeded, or precluded.

Estray Statute A statute defining finders' rights in property when the true owners are unknown.

Ethical Reasoning A reasoning process in which an individual links his or her moral convictions or ethical standards to the situation at hand.

Ethics Moral principles and values applied to social behavior.

Eviction A landlord's act of depriving a tenant of possession of the leased premises.

Exclusionary Rule A rule that prevents evidence that is obtained illegally or without a proper search warrant from being admissible in court.

Exclusive-Dealing Contract An agreement under which a seller forbids a buyer to purchase products from the seller's competitors.

Exclusive Jurisdiction Jurisdiction that exists when a case can be heard only in a particular court or type of court.

Exculpatory Clause A clause that releases a contractual party from liability in the event of monetary or physical injury, no matter who is at fault.

Executed Contract A contract that has been fully performed by both parties.

Execution The implementation of a court's decree or judgment.

Executor A person appointed by a testator in a will to administer her or his estate.

Executory Contract A contract that has not yet been fully performed.

Export The sale of goods and services by domestic firms to buyers located in other countries.

Express Contract A contract in which the terms of the agreement are stated in words, oral or written.

Express Warranty A seller's or lessor's promise as to the quality, condition, description, or performance of the goods being sold or leased.

Expropriation A government's seizure of a privately owned business or personal property for a proper public purpose and with just compensation.

Extension Clause A clause in a time instrument that allows the instrument's date of maturity to be extended into the future.

Extrinsic Evidence Any evidence not contained in the contract itself, which may include the testimony of the parties, additional agreements or communications, or other information relevant to determining the parties' intent.

F

Federal Form of Government A system of government in which the states form a union and the sovereign power is divided between the central government and the member states.

Federal Question A question that pertains to the U.S. Constitution, an act of Congress, or a treaty and provides a basis for federal jurisdiction in a case.

Federal Reserve System A network of twelve district banks and related branches located around the country and headed by the

Federal Reserve Board of Governors. Most banks in the United States have Federal Reserve accounts.

Fee Simple An ownership interest in land in which the owner has the greatest possible aggregation of rights, privileges, and power.

Felony A crime—such as arson, murder, rape, or robbery—that carries the most severe sanctions, ranging from more than one year in a state or federal prison to the death penalty.

Fictitious Payee A payee on a negotiable instrument whom the maker or drawer did not intend to have an interest in the instrument. Indorsements by fictitious payees are treated as authorized indorsements under UCC Article 3.

Fiduciary As a noun, a person having a duty created by his or her undertaking to act primarily for another's benefit in matters connected with the undertaking. As an adjective, a relationship founded on trust and confidence.

Filtering Software A computer program that is designed to block access to certain Web sites, based on their content. The software blocks the retrieval of a site whose URL or key words are on a list within the program.

Financing Statement A document filed by a secured creditor with the appropriate official to give notice to the public of the creditor's security interest in collateral belonging to the debtor named in the statement.

Firm Offer An offer (by a merchant) that is irrevocable without the necessity of consideration for a stated period of time or, if no definite period is stated, for a reasonable time (neither period to exceed three months).

Fixed-Term Tenancy A type of tenancy under which property is leased for a specified period of time, such as a month, a year, or a period of years; also called a *tenancy for years*.

Fixture An item of personal property that has become so closely associated with real property that it is legally regarded as part of that real property.

Floating Lien A security interest in proceeds, after-acquired property, or collateral subject to future advances by the secured party (or all three). The security interest is retained even when the collateral changes in character, classification, or location.

Forbearance A postponement of part or all of the payments on a loan for a limited time. The act of refraining from an action that one has a legal right to undertake.

Force Majeure Clause A provision in a contract stipulating that certain unforeseen events—such as war, political upheavals, or acts of God—will excuse a party from liability for nonperformance of contractual obligations.

Foreclosure The legal process by which a lender repossesses and disposes of property that has secured a loan.

Foreign Corporation In a given state, a corporation that does business in that state but is not incorporated there.

Foreign Exchange Market A worldwide system in which foreign currencies are bought and sold.

Forgery The fraudulent making or altering of any writing in a way that changes the legal rights and liabilities of another.

Formal Contract An agreement that by law requires a specific form for its validity.

Forum-Selection Clause A provision in a contract designating the court, jurisdiction, or tribunal that will decide any disputes arising under the contract.

Franchise Any arrangement in which the owner of a trademark, trade name, or copyright licenses another to use that trademark, trade name, or copyright in the selling of goods or services.

Franchisee One receiving a license to use another's (the franchisor's) trademark, trade name, or copyright in the sale of goods and services.

Franchisor One licensing another (the franchisee) to use the owner's trademark, trade name, or copyright in the selling of goods or services.

Fraudulent Misrepresentation Any misrepresentation, either by misstatement or by omission of a material fact, knowingly made with the intention of deceiving another and on which a reasonable person would and does rely to his or her detriment.

Free Exercise Clause The provision in the First Amendment that prohibits the government from interfering with people's religious practices or forms of worship.

Free-Writing Prospectus A written, electronic, or graphic communication associated with the offer to sell a security and used during the waiting period to supplement other information about the security.

Frustration of Purpose A court-created doctrine under which a party to a contract will be relieved of her or his duty to perform when the objective purpose for performance no longer exists due to reasons beyond that party's control.

Fungible Goods Goods that are alike by physical nature, agreement, or trade usage.

G

Garnishment A legal process whereby a creditor collects a debt by seizing property of the debtor that is in the hands of a third party.

General Damages In a tort case, an amount awarded to compensate individuals for the nonmonetary aspects of the harm suffered, such as pain and suffering. Not available to companies.

Generally Accepted Accounting Principles (GAAP) The conventions, rules, and procedures developed by the Financial Accounting Standards Board to define accepted accounting practices at a particular time.

Generally Accepted Auditing Standards (GAAS) Standards established by the American Institute of Certified Public Accountants to define the professional qualities and judgment that should be exercised by an auditor in performing an audit.

General Partner In a limited partnership, a partner who assumes responsibility for the management of the partnership and has full liability for all partnership debts.

Gift A voluntary transfer of property made without consideration, past or present.

Gift *Causa Mortis* A gift made in contemplation of imminent death. The gift is revoked if the donor does not die as contemplated.

Gift *Inter Vivos* A gift made during one's lifetime and not in contemplation of imminent death, in contrast to a gift *causa mortis*.

Good Faith Purchaser A purchaser who buys without notice of any circumstance that would cause a person of ordinary prudence to inquire as to whether the seller has valid title to the goods being sold.

Good Samaritan Statute A state statute stipulating that persons who provide emergency services to, or rescue, someone in peril cannot be sued for negligence unless they act recklessly and cause further harm.

Goodwill In the business context, the valuable reputation of a business viewed as an intangible asset.

Grand Jury A group of citizens who decide, after hearing the state's evidence, whether a reasonable basis (probable cause) exists for believing that a crime has been committed and that a trial ought to be held.

Group Boycott An agreement by two or more sellers to refuse to deal with a particular person or firm.

Guarantor A third party who promises to be responsible for a debtor's obligation under a guaranty arrangement.

H

Hacker A person who uses computers to gain unauthorized access to data.

Historical School A school of legal thought that looks to the past to determine what the principles of contemporary law should be.

Holder Any person in possession of an instrument drawn, issued, or indorsed to him or her, to his or her order, to bearer, or in blank.

Holder in Due Course (HDC) A holder who acquires a negotiable instrument for value, in good faith, and without notice that the instrument is defective.

Holographic Will A will written entirely in the testator's handwriting.

Homeowner's Insurance A form of property insurance that protects the holder against damage or loss to the holder's home.

Homestead Exemption A law permitting a debtor to retain the family home, either in its entirety or up to a specified dollar amount, free from the claims of unsecured creditors or trustees in bankruptcy.

Horizontal Merger A merger between two firms that are competing in the same market.

Horizontal Restraint Any agreement that restrains competition between rival firms competing in the same market.

Hot-Cargo Agreement An illegal agreement in which employers voluntarily agree with unions not to handle, use, or deal in the nonunion-produced goods of other employers.

I

I-551 Alien Registration Receipt A document, known as a "green card," that shows that a foreign-born individual can legally work in the United States.

I-9 Verification The process of verifying the employment eligibility and identity of a new worker. It must be completed within three days after the worker commences employment.

Identification In a sale of goods, the express designation of the goods provided for in the contract.

Identity Theft The illegal use of someone else's personal information to access the victim's financial resources.

Implied Contract A contract formed in whole or in part from the conduct of the parties.

Implied Warranty A warranty that arises by law because of the circumstances of a sale and not from the seller's express promise.

Implied Warranty of Fitness for a Particular Purpose A warranty that goods sold or leased are fit for the particular purpose for which the buyer or lessee will use the goods.

Implied Warranty of Habitability An implied promise by a seller of a new house that the house is fit for human habitation. Also, the implied promise by a landlord that rented residential premises are habitable.

Implied Warranty of Merchantability A warranty that goods being sold or leased are reasonably fit for the general purpose for which they are sold or leased, are properly packaged and labeled, and are of proper quality.

Impossibility of Performance A doctrine under which a party to a contract is relieved of his or her duty to perform when performance becomes objectively impossible or totally impracticable.

Imposter One who induces a maker or drawer to issue a negotiable instrument in the name of an impersonated payee. Indorsements by imposters are treated as authorized indorsements under UCC Article 3.

Incidental Beneficiary A third party who benefits from a contract even though the contract was not formed for that purpose. An incidental beneficiary has no rights in the contract and cannot sue to have it enforced.

Incidental Damages Damages that compensate for expenses directly incurred because of a breach of contract, such as those incurred to obtain performance from another source.

Incontestability Clause A clause in a policy for life or health insurance stating that after the policy has been in force for a specified length of time (usually two or three years), the insurer cannot contest statements made in the policyholder's application.

Independent Contractor One who works for, and receives payment from, an employer but whose working conditions and methods are not controlled by the employer. An independent contractor is not an employee but may be an agent.

Indictment A formal charge by a grand jury that there is probable cause to believe that a named person has committed a crime.

Indorsement A signature placed on an instrument for the purpose of transferring ownership rights in the instrument.

Informal Contract A contract that does not require a specific form or method of creation to be valid.

Information A formal accusation or complaint (without an indictment) issued in certain types of actions (usually criminal actions involving lesser crimes) by a government prosecutor.

Information Return A tax return submitted by a partnership that reports the business's income and losses. The partnership itself does not pay taxes on the income, but each partner's share of the profit (whether distributed or not) is taxed as individual income to that partner.

Innocent Misrepresentation A misrepresentation that occurs when a person makes a false statement of fact that he or she believes is true.

Inside Director A person on the board of directors who is also an officer of the corporation.

Insider Trading The purchase or sale of securities on the basis of information that has not been made available to the public.

Insolvent A condition in which a person cannot pay his or her debts as they become due or ceases to pay debts in the ordinary course of business.

Installment Contract A contract that requires or authorizes delivery in two or more separate lots to be accepted and paid for separately.

Insurable Interest A property interest in goods being sold or leased that is sufficiently substantial to permit a party to insure against damage to the goods. An interest that exists when a person benefits from the preservation of the health or life of the insured or the property to be insured.

Insurance A contract by which the insurer promises to reimburse the insured or a beneficiary in the event that the insured is injured, dies, or sustains damage to property as a result of particular, stated contingencies.

Intangible Property Property that cannot be seen or touched but exists only conceptually, such as corporate stocks. Such property is not governed by Article 2 of the UCC.

Integrated Contract A written contract that constitutes the final expression of the parties' agreement. Evidence extraneous to the contract that contradicts or alters the meaning of the contract in any way is inadmissible.

Intellectual Property Property resulting from intellectual and creative processes.

Intended Beneficiary A third party for whose benefit a contract is formed. An intended beneficiary can sue the promisor if the contract is breached.

Intentional Tort A wrongful act knowingly committed.

Intermediary Bank Any bank to which an item is transferred in the course of collection, except the depositary or payor bank.

International Financial Reporting Standards (IFRS) A set of global accounting standards that are being phased in by companies in the United States.

International Law The law that governs relations among nations.

International Organization An organization composed mainly of member nations and usually established by treaty—for example, the United Nations. More broadly, the term also includes nongovernmental organizations (NGOs) such as the Red Cross.

Internet Service Provider (ISP) A business or organization that offers users access to the Internet and related services.

Interpretive Rule A nonbinding rule or policy statement issued by an administrative agency that explains how it interprets and intends to apply the statutes it enforces.

Interrogatories A series of written questions for which written answers are prepared by a party to a lawsuit, usually with the assistance of the party's attorney, and then signed under oath.

Intestacy Laws State statutes that specify how property will be distributed when a person dies intestate (without a valid will).

Intestate As a noun, one who has died without having created a valid will. As an adjective, the state of having died without a will.

Investment Company A company that acts on the behalf of many smaller shareholders-owners by buying a large portfolio of securities and professionally managing that portfolio.

Investment Contract In securities law, a transaction in which a person invests in a common enterprise reasonably expecting profits that are derived primarily from the efforts of others.

J

Joint and Several Liability In partnership law, a doctrine under which a plaintiff may sue, and collect a judgment from, all of the partners together (jointly) or one or more of the partners separately (severally, or individually). A partner can be held liable even if she or he did not participate in, ratify, or know about the conduct that gave rise to the lawsuit.

Joint Liability In partnership law, the partners' shared liability for partnership obligations and debts. A third party must sue all of the partners as a group, but each partner can be held liable for the full amount.

Joint Stock Company A hybrid form of business organization that combines characteristics of a corporation and a partnership. Usually, a joint stock company is regarded as a partnership for tax and other legal purposes.

Joint Tenancy Joint ownership of property by two or more co-owners in which each co-owner owns an undivided portion of the property. On the death of one of the joint tenants, his or her interest automatically passes to the surviving joint tenant(s).

Joint Venture A joint undertaking by two or more persons or business entities to combine their efforts or their property for a single transaction or project or for a related series of transactions or projects. A joint venture is generally treated like a partnership for tax and other legal purposes.

Judicial Review The process by which a court decides on the constitutionality of legislative enactments and actions of the executive branch.

Jurisdiction The authority of a court to hear and decide a specific case.

Jurisprudence The science or philosophy of law.

Justiciable Controversy A controversy that is not hypothetical or academic but real and substantial; a requirement that must be satisfied before a court will hear a case.

L

Larceny The wrongful taking and carrying away of another person's personal property with the intent to permanently deprive the owner of the property.

Latent Defect A defect that is not obvious or cannot readily be ascertained.

Law A body of enforceable rules governing relationships among individuals and between individuals and their society.

Lease Under Article 2A of the UCC, a transfer of the right to possess and use goods for a period of time in exchange for payment.

Lease Agreement An agreement in which one person (the lessor) agrees to transfer the right to the possession and use of property to another person (the lessee) in exchange for rental payments.

Leasehold Estate An interest in real property that gives a tenant a qualified right to possess and/or use the property for a limited time under a lease.

Legacy A gift of personal property under a will.

Legal Positivism A school of legal thought centered on the assumption that there is no law higher than the laws created by a national government. Laws must be obeyed, even if they are unjust, to prevent anarchy.

Legal Realism A school of legal thought that holds that the law is only one factor to be considered when deciding cases and that social and economic circumstances should also be taken into account.

Legatee One designated in a will to receive a gift of personal property.

Legislative Rule An administrative agency rule that carries the same weight as a congressionally enacted statute.

Lessee A person who acquires the right to the possession and use of another's goods in exchange for rental payments.

Lessor A person who transfers the right to the possession and use of goods to another in exchange for rental payments.

Letter of Credit A written document in which the issuer (usually a bank) promises to honor drafts or other demands for payment by third persons in accordance with the terms of the instrument.

Levy The legal process of obtaining funds through the seizure and sale of nonexempt

property, usually done after a writ of execution has been issued.

Liability The state of being legally responsible (liable) for something, such as a debt or obligation.

Libel Defamation in writing or another permanent form (such as a digital recording).

License An agreement by the owner of intellectual property to permit another to use a trademark, copyright, patent, or trade secret for certain limited purposes. In the context of real property, a revocable right or privilege to enter onto another person's land.

Lien An encumbrance on a property to satisfy a debt or protect a claim for payment of a debt.

Life Estate An interest in land that exists only for the duration of the life of a specified individual, usually the holder of the estate.

Limited Liability Company (LLC) A hybrid form of business enterprise that offers the limited liability of a corporation and the tax advantages of a partnership.

Limited Liability Partnership (LLP) A hybrid form of business organization that is used mainly by professionals who normally do business in a partnership. An LLP is a pass-through entity for tax purposes, but a partner's personal liability for the malpractice of other partners is limited.

Limited Partner In a limited partnership, a partner who contributes capital to the partnership but has no right to participate in its management and has no liability for partnership debts beyond the amount of her or his investment.

Limited Partnership (LP) A partnership consisting of one or more general partners and one or more limited partners.

Liquidated Damages An amount, stipulated in a contract, that the parties to the contract believe to be a reasonable estimation of the damages that will occur in the event of a breach.

Liquidated Debt A debt whose amount has been ascertained, fixed, agreed on, settled, or exactly determined.

Liquidation The sale of the nonexempt assets of a debtor and the distribution of the funds received to creditors.

Litigation The process of resolving a dispute through the court system.

Living (*Inter Vivos*) Trust A trust created by the grantor (settlor) and effective during his or her lifetime.

Lockout An action in which an employer shuts down to prevent employees from working, typically because it cannot reach a collective bargaining agreement with the employees' union.

Long Arm Statute A state statute that permits a state to exercise jurisdiction over nonresident defendants.

Lost Property Property that the owner has involuntarily by the owner.

M

Mailbox Rule A common law rule that acceptance takes effect, and thus completes formation of the contract, at the time the offeree sends or delivers the acceptance via the communication mode expressly or impliedly authorized by the offeror.

Majority Opinion A court opinion that represents the views of the majority (more than half) of the judges or justices deciding the case.

Maker One who promises to pay a fixed amount of funds to the holder of a promissory note or a certificate of deposit (CD).

Malpractice Professional misconduct or the lack of the requisite degree of skill as a professional. Professional negligence, or failure to exercise reasonable care and professional judgment, that results in injury, loss, or damage to those relying on the professional.

Malware Malicious software programs, such as viruses and worms, that are designed to cause harm to a computer, network, or other device.

Market Concentration The degree to which a small number of firms control a large percentage of a relevant market.

Market Power The power of a firm to control the market price of its product. A monopoly has the greatest degree of market power.

Market-Share Liability A theory under which liability is shared among all firms that manufactured and distributed a particular product during a certain period of time. This form of liability sharing is used only when the specific source of the harmful product is unidentifiable.

Mechanic's Lien A nonpossessory, filed lien on an owner's real estate for labor, services, or materials furnished for making improvements on the realty.

Mediation A method of settling disputes outside the courts by using the services of a neutral third party, who acts as a communicating agent between the parties and assists them in negotiating a settlement.

Member A person who has an ownership interest in a limited liability company.

Mens Rea A wrongful mental state ("guilty mind"), or intent; one of the two essential elements required to establish criminal liability.

Merchant Under the UCC, a person who deals in goods of the kind involved in the sales contract or who holds herself or himself out as having skill or knowledge peculiar to the practices or goods being purchased or sold.

Metadata Data that are automatically recorded by electronic devices and provide information about who created a file and when, and who accessed, modified, or transmitted the file on their hard drives. Can be described as data about data.

Meta Tag A key word in a document that can serve as an index reference to the document. On the Web, search engines return results based, in part, on the tags in Web documents.

Minimum Wage The lowest wage, either by government regulation or union contract, that an employer may pay an hourly worker.

Mirror Image Rule A common law rule that requires that the terms of the offeree's acceptance adhere exactly to the terms of the offeror's offer for a valid contract to be formed.

Misdemeanor A lesser crime than a felony, punishable by a fine or incarceration in jail for up to one year.

Mislaid Property Property that the owner has voluntarily parted with and then has inadvertently forgotten.

Mitigation of Damages The requirement that a plaintiff do whatever is reasonable to minimize the damages caused by the defendant's breach of contract.

Money Laundering Engaging in financial transactions to conceal the identity, source, or destination of illegally gained funds.

Monopolization The possession of monopoly power in the relevant market and the willful acquisition or maintenance of that power, as distinguished from growth or development as a consequence of a superior product, business acumen, or historic accident.

Monopoly A market in which there is a single seller or a very limited number of sellers.

Monopoly Power The ability of a monopoly to dictate what takes place in a given market.

Moral Minimum The minimum level of ethical behavior expected by society, which is usually defined as compliance with the law.

Mortgage A written instrument that gives a creditor an interest in, or lien on, a debtor's real property as security for a debt.

Motion for a Directed Verdict A motion for the judge to take the decision out of the hands of the jury and to direct a verdict for the party making the motion on the ground that the other party has not produced sufficient evidence to support her or his claim.

Motion for a New Trial A motion asserting that the trial was so fundamentally flawed (because of error, newly discovered evidence, prejudice, or another reason) that a new trial is necessary to prevent a miscarriage of justice.

Motion for Judgment n.o.v. A motion requesting the court to grant judgment in favor of the party making the motion on the ground that the jury's verdict against him or her was unreasonable and erroneous.

Motion for Judgment on the Pleadings A motion by either party to a lawsuit at the close of the pleadings requesting the court to decide the issue solely on the pleadings without proceeding to trial. The motion will be granted only if no facts are in dispute.

Motion for Summary Judgment A motion requesting the court to enter a judgment without proceeding to trial. The motion can be based on evidence outside the pleadings and will be granted only if no facts are in dispute.

Motion to Dismiss A pleading in which a defendant admits the facts as alleged by the plaintiff but asserts that the plaintiff's claim to state a cause of action has no basis in law.

Multiple Product Order An order requiring a firm that has engaged in deceptive advertising to cease and desist from false advertising in regard to all the firm's products.

Mutual Fund A specific type of investment company that continually buys or sells to investors shares of ownership in a portfolio.

N

National Law Law that pertains to a particular nation (as opposed to international law).

Natural Law The oldest school of legal thought, based on the belief that the legal system should reflect universal ("higher") moral and ethical principles that are inherent in human nature.

Necessaries Necessities required for life, such as food, shelter, clothing, and medical attention.

Negligence The failure to exercise the standard of care that a reasonable person would exercise in similar circumstances.

Negligence Per Se An action or failure to act in violation of a statutory requirement.

Negligent Misrepresentation A misrepresentation that occurs when a person makes a false statement of fact because he or she did not exercise reasonable care or use the skill and competence required by her or his business or profession.

Negotiable Instrument A signed writing (record) that contains an unconditional promise or order to pay an exact sum on demand or at a specified future time to a specific person or order, or to bearer.

Negotiation A process in which parties attempt to settle their dispute informally, with or without attorneys to represent them. In the context of negotiable instruments, the transfer of an instrument in such form that the transferee (the person to whom the instrument is transferred) becomes a holder.

Nominal Damages A small monetary award (often one dollar) granted to a plaintiff when no actual damage was suffered.

Nonpossessory Interest In the context of real property, an interest that involves the right to use land but not the right to possess it.

Normal Trade Relations (NTR) Status A legal trade status granted to member countries of the World Trade Organization.

Notary Public A public official authorized to attest to the authenticity of signatures.

Novation The substitution, by agreement, of a new contract for an old one, with the rights under the old one being terminated.

Nuisance A common law doctrine under which persons may be held liable for using their property in a manner that unreasonably interferes with others' rights to use or enjoy their own property.

Nuncupative Will An oral will (often called a *deathbed will*) made before witnesses. Usually, such wills are limited to transfers of personal property.

O

Objective Theory of Contracts The view that contracting parties shall only be bound by terms that can be objectively inferred from promises made.

Obligee One to whom an obligation is owed.

Obligor One who owes an obligation to another.

Offer A promise or commitment to perform or refrain from performing some specified act in the future.

Offeree A person to whom an offer is made.

Offeror A person who makes an offer.

Online Dispute Resolution (ODR) The resolution of disputes with the assistance of organizations that offer dispute-resolution services via the Internet.

Operating Agreement An agreement in which the members of a limited liability company set forth the details of how the business will be managed and operated.

Option Contract A contract under which the offeror cannot revoke the offer for a stipulated time period (because the offeree has given consideration for the offer to remain open).

Order for Relief A court's grant of assistance to a complainant. In bankruptcy proceedings, the order relieves the debtor of the immediate obligation to pay the debts listed in the bankruptcy petition.

Order Instrument A negotiable instrument that is payable "to the order of an identified person" or "to an identified person or order."

Ordinance A regulation enacted by a city or county legislative body that becomes part of that state's statutory law.

Outcome-based Ethics An ethical philosophy that focuses on the impacts of a decision on society or on key stakeholders.

Output Contract An agreement in which a seller agrees to sell and a buyer agrees to buy all or up to a stated amount of what the seller produces.

Outside Director A person on the board of directors who does not hold a management position at the corporation.

Overdraft A check that is paid by a bank when the checking account on which the check is written contains insufficient funds to cover the check.

P

Parol Evidence Rule A rule of contracts under which a court will not receive into evidence prior or contemporaneous external agreements that contradict the terms of the parties' written contract.

Partially Disclosed Principal A principal whose identity is unknown by a third party, but the third party knows that the agent is or may be acting for a principal at the time the agent and the third party form a contract.

Partnering Agreement An agreement between a seller and a buyer who frequently do business with each other concerning the terms and conditions that will apply to all subsequently formed electronic contracts.

Partnership An agreement by two or more persons to carry on, as co-owners, a business for profit.

Partnership by Estoppel A partnership imposed by a court when nonpartners have held themselves out to be partners, or have allowed themselves to be held out as partners, and others have detrimentally relied on their misrepresentations.

Pass-Through Entity A business entity that has no tax liability. The entity's income is passed through to the owners, and they pay taxes on the income.

Past Consideration An act that takes place before a contract is made and that ordinarily, by itself, cannot later be consideration with respect to that contract.

Patent A property right granted by the federal government that gives an inventor an exclusive right to make, use, sell, or offer to sell an invention in the United States for a limited time.

Payee A person to whom an instrument is made payable.

Payor Bank The bank on which a check is drawn (the drawee bank).

Peer-to-Peer (P2P) Networking The sharing of resources (such as files, hard drives, and processing styles) among multiple computers without the requirement of a central network server.

Penalty A contract clause that specifies a certain amount to be paid in the event of a default or breach of contract but is unenforceable because it is designed to punish the breaching party rather than to provide a reasonable estimate of damages.

Per Capita A method of distributing an intestate's estate so that each heir in a certain class (such as grandchildren) receives an equal share.

Per Curiam **Opinion** A court opinion that does not indicate which judge or justice authored the opinion.

Perfection The legal process by which secured parties protect themselves against the claims of third parties who may wish to have their debts satisfied out of the same collateral. It is usually accomplished by filing a financing statement with the appropriate government official.

Performance The fulfillment of one's duties under a contract—the normal way of discharging one's contractual obligations.

Periodic Tenancy A lease interest in land for an indefinite period involving payment of rent at fixed intervals, such as week to week, month to month, or year to year.

Per Se **Violation** A restraint of trade that is so anticompetitive that it is deemed inherently (*per se*) illegal.

Personal Defense A defense that can be used to avoid payment to an ordinary holder of a negotiable instrument but not a holder in due course (HDC) or a holder with the rights of an HDC.

Personal Property Property that is movable. Any property that is not real property.

Per Stirpes A method of distributing an intestate's estate so that each heir in a certain class (such as grandchildren) takes the share to which her or his deceased ancestor (such as a mother or father) would have been entitled.

Persuasive Authority Any legal authority or source of law that a court may look to for guidance but need not follow when making its decision.

Petition in Bankruptcy The document that is filed with a bankruptcy court to initiate bankruptcy proceedings.

Petty Offense The least serious kind of criminal offense, such as a traffic or building-code violation.

Phishing A form of identity theft in which the perpetrator sends e-mails purporting to be from legitimate businesses to induce recipients to reveal their personal financial data, passwords, or other information.

Piercing the Corporate Veil The action of a court to disregard the corporate entity and hold the shareholders personally liable for corporate debts and obligations.

Plaintiff One who initiates a lawsuit.

Plea Bargaining The process by which a criminal defendant and the prosecutor work out an agreement to dispose of the criminal case, subject to court approval.

Pleadings Statements by the plaintiff and the defendant that detail the facts, charges, and defenses of a case.

Pledge A security device in which personal property is transferred into the possession of the creditor as security for the payment of a debt and retained by the creditor until the debt is paid.

Plurality Opinion A court opinion that is joined by the largest number of the judges or justices hearing the case, but less than half of the total number.

Police Powers Powers possessed by the states as part of their inherent sovereignty. These powers may be exercised to protect or promote the public order, health, safety, morals, and general welfare.

Policy In insurance law, the contract between the insurer and the insured.

Potentially Responsible Party (PRP) A party liable for the costs of cleaning up a hazardous waste disposal site under the Comprehensive Environmental Response, Compensation, and Liability Act.

Power of Attorney Authorization for another to act as one's agent or attorney either in specified circumstances (special) or in all situations (general).

Precedent A court decision that furnishes an example or authority for deciding subsequent cases involving identical or similar facts.

Predatory Pricing The pricing of a product below cost with the intent to drive competitors out of the market.

Predominant-Factor Test A test courts use to determine whether a contract is primarily for the sale of goods or for the sale of services.

Preemption A doctrine under which certain federal laws preempt, or take precedence over, conflicting state or local laws.

Preemptive Rights The right of a shareholder in a corporation to have the first opportunity to purchase a new issue of that corporation's stock in proportion to the amount of stock already owned by the shareholder.

Preference In bankruptcy proceedings, a property transfer or payment made by the debtor that favors one creditor over others.

Preferred Creditor In the context of bankruptcy, a creditor who has received a preferential transfer from a debtor.

Preferred Stock Stock that has priority over common stock as to payment of dividends and distribution of assets on the corporation's dissolution.

Premium In insurance law, the price paid by the insured for insurance protection for a specified period of time.

Prenuptial Agreement An agreement made before marriage that defines each partner's ownership rights in the other partner's property. Prenuptial agreements must be in writing to be enforceable.

Prepayment Penalty Clause A mortgage provision requiring the borrower to pay a penalty if the mortgage is repaid in full within a certain period.

Presentment The act of presenting an instrument to the party liable on the instrument in order to collect payment. Presentment also occurs when a person presents an instrument to a drawee for a required acceptance.

Presentment Warranty A person who presents an instrument for payment or acceptance impliedly makes three warranties relating to good title, no alterations, and no unauthorized signatures.

Price Discrimination A seller's act of charging competing buyers different prices for identical products or services.

Price-Fixing Agreement An agreement between competitors to fix the prices of products or services at a certain level.

***Prima Facie* Case** A case in which the plaintiff has produced sufficient evidence of his or her claim that the case will be decided for the plaintiff unless the defendant produces no evidence to rebut it.

Primary Source of Law A document that establishes the law on a particular issue, such as a constitution, a statute, an administrative rule, or a court decision.

Principle of Rights The belief that human beings have certain fundamental rights. Whether an action or decision is ethical depends on how it affects the rights of various groups, such as owners, employees, consumers, suppliers, the community, and society.

Private Equity Capital Funds invested by a private equity firm in an existing corporation, usually to purchase and reorganize it.

Privilege A special right, advantage, or immunity that enables a person or a class of persons to avoid liability for defamation.

Privity of Contract The relationship that exists between the promisor and the promisee of a contract.

Probable Cause Reasonable grounds for believing that a search should be conducted or that a person should be arrested.

Probate The process of proving and validating a will and settling all matters pertaining to an estate.

Probate Court A state court of limited jurisdiction that conducts proceedings relating to the settlement of a deceased person's estate.

Procedural Law Law that establishes the methods of enforcing the rights established by substantive law.

Proceeds Under Article 9 of the UCC, whatever is received when collateral is sold or disposed of in some other way.

Product Liability The legal liability of manufacturers, sellers, and lessors of goods for injuries or damage caused by the goods to consumers, users, or bystanders.

Profit In real property law, the right to enter onto another's property and remove something of value from that property.

Promise A declaration that binds a person who makes it (the promisor) to do or not to do a certain act.

Promisee A person to whom a promise is made.

Promisor A person who makes a promise.

Promissory Estoppel A doctrine that can be used to enforce a promise when the promisee has justifiably relied on the promise and when justice will be better served by enforcing the promise.

Promissory Note A written promise made by one person (the maker) to pay a fixed amount of funds to another person (the payee or a subsequent holder) on demand or on a specified date.

Prospectus A written document required by securities laws when a security is being sold. The prospectus describes the security, the financial operations of the issuing corporation, and the risk attaching to the security.

Protected Class A group of persons protected by specific laws because of the group's defining characteristics, including race, color, religion, national origin, gender, age, and disability.

Proximate Cause Legal cause. It exists when the connection between an act and an injury is strong enough to justify imposing liability.

Proxy When a shareholder formally authorizes another to serve as his or her agent and vote his or her shares in a certain manner.

Publicly Held Corporation A corporation whose shares are publicly traded in securities markets, such as the New York Stock Exchange or the NASDAQ.

Puffery A salesperson's exaggerated claims concerning the quality of property offered for sale. Such claims involve opinions rather than facts and are not legally binding promises or warranties.

Punitive Damages Monetary damages that may be awarded to a plaintiff to punish the defendant and deter similar conduct in the future.

Purchase-Money Security Interest (PMSI) A security interest that arises when a seller or lender extends credit for part or all of the purchase price of goods purchased by a buyer.

Q

Qualified Indorsement An indorsement on a negotiable instrument in which the indorser disclaims any contract liability on the instrument. The notation "without recourse" is commonly used to create a qualified indorsement.

Quantum Meruit A Latin phrase meaning "as much as he or she deserves." The expression describes the extent of compensation owed under a quasi contract.

Quasi Contract An obligation or contract imposed by law (a court), in the absence of an agreement, to prevent the unjust enrichment of one party.

Question of Fact In a lawsuit, an issue that involves only disputed facts, and not what the law is on a given point.

Question of Law In a lawsuit, an issue involving the application or interpretation of a law.

Quitclaim Deed A deed that conveys only whatever interest the grantor had in the property and therefore offers the least amount of protection against defects of title.

Quorum The number of members of a decision-making body that must be present before business may be transacted.

Quota A set limit on the amount of goods that can be imported.

R

Ratification The acceptance or confirmation of an act or agreement that gives legal force to an obligation that previously was not enforceable.

Reaffirmation Agreement An agreement between a debtor and a creditor in which the debtor voluntarily agrees to pay a debt dischargeable in bankruptcy.

Real Property Land and everything attached to it, such as trees and buildings.

Reasonable Person Standard The standard of behavior expected of a hypothetical "reasonable person." It is the standard against which negligence is measured and that must be observed to avoid liability for negligence.

Receiver In a corporate dissolution, a court-appointed person who winds up corporate affairs and liquidates corporate assets.

Record Information that is either inscribed on a tangible medium or stored in an electronic or other medium and is retrievable.

Recording Statute A statute that allow deeds, mortgages, and other real property transactions to be recorded so as to provide notice to future purchasers or creditors of an existing claim on the property.

Reformation A court-ordered correction of a written contract so that it reflects the true intentions of the parties.

Regulation E A set of rules issued by the Federal Reserve System's Board of Governors to protect users of electronic fund transfer systems.

Regulation Z A set of rules issued by the Federal Reserve Board of Governors to implement the provisions of the Truth-in-Lending Act.

Release An agreement in which one party gives up the right to pursue a legal claim against another party.

Remedy The relief given to an innocent party to enforce a right or compensate for the violation of a right.

Replevin An action that can be used by a buyer or lessee to recover identified goods from a third party, such as a bailee, who is wrongfully withholding them.

Reply Procedurally, a plaintiff's response to a defendant's answer.

Requirements Contract An agreement in which a buyer agrees to purchase and the seller agrees to sell all or up to a stated amount of what the buyer needs or requires.

Resale Price Maintenance Agreement An agreement between a manufacturer and a retailer in which the manufacturer specifies what the retail prices of its products must be.

Rescission A remedy whereby a contract is canceled and the parties are returned to the positions they occupied before the contract was made.

Res Ipsa Loquitur A doctrine under which negligence may be inferred simply because an event occurred, if it is the type of event that would not occur in the absence of negligence. Literally, the term means "the facts speak for themselves."

Respondeat Superior A doctrine under which a principal or an employer is held liable for the wrongful acts committed by agents or employees while acting within the course and scope of their agency or employment.

Restitution An equitable remedy under which a person is restored to his or her original position prior to loss or injury, or placed in the position he or she would have been in had the breach not occurred.

Restrictive Indorsement An indorsement on a negotiable instrument that requires the indorsee to comply with certain instructions regarding the funds involved.

Resulting Trust An implied trust that arises when one party holds the legal title to another's property only for that other's benefit.

Retained Earnings The portion of a corporation's profits that has not been paid out as dividends to shareholders.

Revocation The withdrawal of a contract offer by the offeror. Unless an offer is irrevocable, it can be revoked at any time prior to acceptance without liability.

Right of Contribution The right of a co-surety who pays more than his or her proportionate share on a debtor's default to recover the excess paid from other co-sureties.

Right of Reimbursement The right of a party to be repaid for costs, expenses, or losses incurred on behalf of another.

Right of Subrogation The right of a party to stand in the place of another, giving the substituted party the same legal rights that the original party had.

Right-to-Work Law A state law providing that employees may not be required to join a union as a condition of retaining employment.

Risk A prediction concerning potential loss based on known and unknown factors.

Risk Management In the context of insurance, the transfer of certain risks from the insured to the insurance company by contractual agreement.

Robbery The act of forcefully and unlawfully taking personal property of any value from another.

Rulemaking The process by which an administrative agency formally adopts a new regulation or amends an old one.

Rule of Four A rule of the United States Supreme Court under which the Court will not issue a writ of *certiorari* unless at least four justices approve of the decision to issue the writ.

Rule of Reason A test used to determine whether an anticompetitive agreement constitutes a reasonable restraint on trade. Courts consider such factors as the purpose of the agreement, its effect on competition, and whether less restrictive means could have been used.

S

Sale The passing of title to property from the seller to the buyer for a price.

Sales Contract A contract for the sale of goods.

Scienter Knowledge on the part of a misrepresenting party that material facts have been falsely represented or omitted with an intent to deceive.

S Corporation A close business corporation that has most corporate attributes, including limited liability, but qualifies under the Internal Revenue Code to be taxed as a partnership.

Search Warrant An order granted by a public authority, such as a judge, that authorizes law enforcement personnel to search particular premises or property.

Seasonably Within a specified time period or, if no period is specified, within a reasonable time.

Secondary Source of Law A publication that summarizes or interprets the law, such as a legal encyclopedia, a legal treatise, or an article in a law review.

SEC Rule 10b-5 A rule of the Securities and Exchange Commission that prohibits the commission of fraud in connection with the purchase or sale of any security.

Secured Party A creditor who has a security interest in the debtor's collateral, including a seller, lender, cosigner, or buyer of accounts or chattel paper.

Secured Transaction Any transaction in which the payment of a debt is guaranteed, or secured, by personal property owned by the debtor or in which the debtor has a legal interest.

Securities Generally, stocks, bonds, or other items that represent an ownership interest in a corporation or a promise of repayment of debt by a corporation.

Security Agreement An agreement that creates or provides for a security interest between the debtor and a secured party.

Security Interest Any interest in personal property or fixtures that secures payment or performance of an obligation.

Self-Defense The legally recognized privilege to do what is reasonably necessary to protect oneself, one's property, or someone else against injury by another.

Self-Incrimination Giving testimony in a trial or other legal proceeding that could expose the person testifying to criminal prosecution.

Seniority System A system in which those who have worked longest for an employer are first in line for promotions, salary increases, and other benefits, and are last to be laid off if the workforce must be reduced.

Service Mark A trademark that is used to distinguish the services (rather than the products) of one person or company from those of another.

Service of Process The delivery of the complaint and summons to a defendant.

Sexual Harassment The demanding of sexual favors in return for job promotions or other benefits, or language or conduct that is so sexually offensive that it creates a hostile working environment.

Shareholder's Derivative Suit A suit brought by a shareholder to enforce a corporate cause of action against a third person.

Shelter Principle The principle that the holder of a negotiable instrument who cannot qualify as a holder in due course (HDC), but who derives his or her title through an HDC, acquires the rights of an HDC.

Shipment Contract A contract for the sale of goods in which the seller is required or authorized to ship the goods by carrier. The seller assumes liability for any losses or damage to the goods until they are delivered to the carrier.

Short Sale A sale of mortgaged property for less than the balance due on the mortgage loan.

Short-Swing Profits Profits earned by a purchase and sale, or sale and purchase, of the same security within a six-month period.

Shrink-Wrap Agreement An agreement whose terms are expressed in a document located inside a box in which goods (usually software) are packaged.

Slander Defamation in oral form.

Slander of Quality (Trade Libel) The publication of false information about another's product, alleging that it is not what its seller claims.

Slander of Title The publication of a statement that denies or casts doubt on another's legal ownership of property, causing financial loss to that property's owner.

Small Claims Court A special court in which parties can litigate small claims without an attorney.

Smart Card A card containing a microprocessor and typically used for financial transactions, personal identification, and other purposes.

Social Media Forms of communication through which users create and share information, ideas, messages, and other content via the Internet.

Sole Proprietorship The simplest form of business organization, in which the owner is the business. The owner reports business income on his or her personal income tax return and is legally responsible for all debts and obligations incurred by the business.

Sovereign Immunity A doctrine that immunizes foreign nations from the jurisdiction of U.S. courts when certain conditions are satisfied.

Spam Bulk, unsolicited (junk) e-mail.

Special Damages In a tort case, an amount awarded to compensate the plaintiff for quantifiable monetary losses, such as medical expenses, property damage, and lost wages and benefits (now and in the future).

Special Indorsement An indorsement on an instrument that identifies the specific person to whom the indorser intends to make the instrument payable.

Special Warranty Deed A deed that warrants only that the grantor held good title during his or her ownership of the property and does not warrant that there were no defects of title when the property was held by previous owners.

Specific Performance An equitable remedy in which a court orders the parties to perform as promised in the contract. This remedy normally is granted only when the legal remedy (monetary damages) is inadequate.

Spendthrift Trust A trust created to protect the beneficiary from spending all the funds to which she or he is entitled. Only a certain portion of the total amount is given to the beneficiary at any one time, and most states prohibit creditors from attaching assets of the trust.

Stakeholders Groups that are affected by corporate decisions. Stakeholders include employees, customers, creditors, suppliers, and the community in which the corporation operates.

Stale Check A check, other than a certified check, that is presented for payment more than six months after its date.

Standing to Sue The legal requirement that an individual must have a sufficient stake in a controversy before he or she can bring a lawsuit.

Stare Decisis A common law doctrine under which judges are obligated to follow the precedents established in prior decisions.

Statute of Frauds A state statute that requires certain types of contracts to be in writing to be enforceable.

Statute of Repose A statute that places outer time limits on product liability actions. Such statutes cut off absolutely the right to bring an action after a specified period of time following some event (often the product's manufacture or purchase) other than the occurrence of an injury.

Statutory Law The body of law enacted by legislative bodies (as opposed to constitutional law, administrative law, or case law).

Statutory Right of Redemption A right provided by statute in some states under which mortgagors can redeem or purchase their property after a judicial foreclosure for a limited time period, such as one year.

Stock An ownership (equity) interest in a corporation, measured in units of shares.

Stock Certificate A certificate issued by a corporation evidencing the ownership of a specified number of shares in the corporation.

Stock Option A right to buy a given number of shares of stock at a set price, usually within a specified time period.

Stop-Payment Order An order by a bank customer to his or her bank not to pay or certify a certain check.

Stored-Value Card A card bearing a magnetic strip that holds magnetically encoded data providing access to stored funds.

Strict Liability Liability regardless of fault, which is imposed on those engaged in abnormally dangerous activities, on persons who keep dangerous animals, and on manufacturers or sellers that introduce into commerce defective and unreasonably dangerous goods.

Strike An action undertaken by unionized workers when collective bargaining fails. The workers leave their jobs, refuse to work, and (typically) picket the employer's workplace.

Sublease A tenant's transfer of all or part of the leased premises to a third person for a period shorter than the lease term.

Substantive Law Law that defines, describes, regulates, and creates legal rights and obligations.

Summary Jury Trial (SJT) A method of settling disputes by holding a trial in which the jury's verdict is not binding but instead guides the parties toward reaching an agreement during the mandatory negotiations that immediately follow.

Summons A document informing a defendant that a legal action has been commenced against her or him and that the defendant must appear in court on a certain date to answer the plaintiff's complaint.

Supremacy Clause The provision in Article VI of the U.S. Constitution that the Constitution, laws, and treaties of the United States are "the supreme Law of the Land."

Surety A third party who promises to be responsible for a debtor's obligation under a suretyship arrangement.

Suretyship A promise made by a third party to be responsible for a debtor's obligation.

Symbolic Speech Nonverbal expressions of beliefs. Symbolic speech, which includes gestures, movements, and articles of clothing, is given substantial protection by the courts.

Syndicate A group of individuals or firms that join together to finance a project. A syndicate is also called an *investment group*.

T

Taking The taking of private property by the government for public use through the power of eminent domain.

Tangible Employment Action A significant change in employment status or benefits, such as occurs when an employee is fired, refused a promotion, or reassigned to a lesser position.

Tangible Property Property that has physical existence and can be distinguished by the senses of touch and sight.

Tariff A tax on imported goods.

Tenancy at Sufferance A tenancy that arises when a tenant wrongfully continues to occupy leased property after the lease has terminated.

Tenancy at Will A type of tenancy that either the landlord or the tenant can terminate without notice.

Tenancy by the Entirety Joint ownership of property by a married couple in which neither spouse can transfer his or her interest in the property without the consent of the other.

Tenancy in Common Joint ownership of property in which each party owns an undivided interest that passes to his or her heirs at death.

Tender An unconditional offer to perform an obligation by a person who is ready, willing, and able to do so.

Tender of Delivery A seller's or lessor's act of placing conforming goods at the disposal of the buyer or lessee and providing whatever notification is reasonably necessary to enable the buyer or lessee to take delivery.

Testamentary Trust A trust that is created by will and therefore does not take effect until the death of the testator.

Testate Having left a will at death.

Testator One who makes and executes a will.

Third Party Beneficiary One who is not a party to the contract but who stands to benefit from the contract's performance.

Tippee A person who receives inside information.

Tolling Temporary suspension of the running of a prescribed time period, such as a statute of limitations.

Tort A wrongful act (other than a breach of contract) that results in harm or injury to another and leads to civil liability.

Tortfeasor One who commits a tort.

Totten Trust A trust created when a person deposits funds in his or her own name for a specific beneficiary, who will receive the funds on the depositor's death. The trust is revocable at will until the depositor dies or completes the gift.

Toxic Tort A civil wrong arising from exposure to a toxic substance, such as asbestos, radiation, or hazardous waste.

Trade Dress The image and overall appearance of a product.

Trademark A distinctive word, symbol, or design that identifies the manufacturer as the source of particular goods and distinguishes its products from those made or sold by others.

Trademark Dilution The unauthorized use of a distinctive and famous mark in a way that impairs the mark's distinctiveness or harms its reputation.

Trade Name A name that a business uses to identify itself and its brand. A trade name is directly related to a business's reputation and goodwill and is protected under trademark law.

Trade Secret A formula, device, idea, process, or other information used in a business that gives the owner a competitive advantage in the marketplace.

Transferred Intent A legal principle under which a person who intends to harm one individual, but unintentionally harms a different individual, can be liable to the second victim for an intentional tort.

Transfer Warranty A person who transfers an instrument for consideration impliedly makes five warranties—relating to good title, authentic signatures, no alterations, defenses, or insolvencies—to all subsequent transferees.

Traveler's Check A check that is payable on demand, drawn on or payable through a financial institution, and designated as a traveler's check.

Treaty A formal international agreement negotiated between two nations or among several nations.

Treble Damages Damages that, by statute, are three times the amount of actual damages suffered.

Trespass to Land Entry onto, above, or below the surface of land owned by another without the owner's permission or legal authorization.

Trespass to Personal Property Wrongfully taking or harming the personal property of another or otherwise interfering with the lawful owner's possession of personal property.

Triple Bottom Line A measure that includes a corporation's profits, its impact on people, and its impact on the planet.

Trust An arrangement in which title to property is held by one person (a trustee) for the benefit of another (a beneficiary).

Trust Indorsement An indorsement to a person who is to hold or use funds for the benefit of the indorser or a third person. It is also known as an *agency indorsement*.

Tying Arrangement A seller's act of conditioning the sale of a product or service on the buyer's agreement to purchase another product or service from the seller.

Typosquatting A form of cybersquatting that relies on mistakes, such as typographical errors, made by Internet users when inputting information into a Web browser.

U

***Ultra Vires* Acts** Acts of a corporation that are beyond its express and implied powers to undertake (the Latin phrase means "beyond the powers").

Unconscionable (Contract or Clause) A contract or clause that is void on the basis of public policy because one party was forced to accept terms that are unfairly burdensome and that unfairly benefit the other party.

Underwriter In insurance law, the insurer, or the one assuming a risk in return for the payment of a premium.

Undisclosed Principal A principal whose identity is unknown by a third party, and that person has no knowledge that the agent is acting for a principal at the time the agent and the third party form a contract.

Undue Influence Persuasion that is less than actual force but more than advice and that induces a person to act according to the will or purposes of the dominating party.

Unenforceable Contract A valid contract rendered unenforceable by some statute or law.

Uniform Law A model law developed by the National Conference of Commissioners on Uniform State Laws for the states to consider enacting into statute.

Unilateral Contract A type of contract that results when an offer can be accepted only by the offeree's performance.

Unilateral Mistake A mistake that occurs when one party to a contract is mistaken as to a material fact.

Union Shop A firm that requires all workers, once employed, to become union members within a specified period of time as a condition of their continued employment.

Universal Defense A defense that can be used to avoid payment to all holders of a negotiable instrument, including a holder in due course (HDC) or a holder with the rights of an HDC. Also called a *real defense*.

Unliquidated Debt A debt that is uncertain in amount.

Unreasonably Dangerous Product A product that is so defective that it is dangerous beyond the expectation of an ordinary consumer or a product for which a less dangerous alternative was feasible but the manufacturer failed to produce it.

Usage of Trade Any practice or method of dealing that is so regularly observed in a place, vocation, or trade that parties justifiably expect it will be observed in their transaction.

Usury Charging an illegal rate of interest.

Utilitarianism An approach to ethical reasoning in which an action is evaluated in terms of its consequences for those whom it will affect. A "good" action is one that results in the greatest good for the greatest number of people.

V

Valid Contract A contract that results when the elements necessary for contract formation (agreement, consideration, capacity, and legality) are present.

Venture Capital Financing provided by professional, outside investors (venture capitalists) to new business ventures.

Venue The geographic district in which a legal action is tried and from which the jury is selected.

Vertically Integrated Firm A firm that carries out two or more functional phases (manufacturing, distribution, and retailing, for example) of the chain of production.

Vertical Merger The acquisition by a company at one stage of production of a company at a higher or lower stage of production (such as a company merging with one of its suppliers or retailers).

Vertical Restraint A restraint of trade created by an agreement between firms at different levels in the manufacturing and distribution process.

Vesting The creation of an absolute or unconditional right or power.

Vicarious Liability Indirect liability imposed on a supervisory party (such as an employer) for the actions of a subordinate (such as an employee) because of the relationship between the two parties.

Virus A software program that can replicate itself over a network and spread from one device to another, altering files and interfering with normal operations.

Voidable Contract A contract that may be legally avoided at the option of one or both of the parties.

Void Contract A contract having no legal force or binding effect.

Voir Dire An important part of the jury selection process in which the attorneys question prospective jurors about their backgrounds, attitudes, and biases to ascertain whether they can be impartial jurors.

W

Warranty Deed A deed that provides the greatest amount of protection for the grantee. The grantor promises that she or he has title to the property conveyed in the deed, that there are no undisclosed encumbrances on the property, and that the grantee will enjoy quiet possession of the property.

Waste The use of real property in a manner that damages or destroys its value.

Whistleblowing An employee's disclosure to government authorities, upper-level managers, or the media that the employer is engaged in unsafe or illegal activities.

White-Collar Crime Nonviolent crime committed by individuals or corporations to obtain a personal or business advantage.

Will An instrument made by a testator directing what is to be done with her or his property after death.

Will Substitutes Various instruments, such as living trusts and life insurance plans, that may be used to avoid the formal probate process.

Winding Up The second of two stages in the termination of a partnership or corporation, in which the firm's assets are collected, liquidated, and distributed, and liabilities are discharged.

Workers' Compensation Laws State statutes that establish an administrative process for compensating workers for injuries that arise in the course of their employment, regardless of fault.

Working Papers The documents used and developed by an accountant during an audit, such as notes, computations, and memoranda.

Workout Agreement A contract that describes the respective rights and responsibilities of a borrower and a lender as they try to resolve the borrower's default.

Worm A software program that automatically replicates itself over a network but does not alter files and is usually invisible to the user until it has consumed system resources.

Writ of Attachment A court order to seize a debtor's nonexempt property prior to a court's final determination of a creditor's rights to the property.

Writ of *Certiorari* A writ from a higher court asking a lower court for the record of a case.

Writ of Execution A court order directing the sheriff to seize (levy) and sell a debtor's nonexempt real or personal property to satisfy a court's judgment in the creditor's favor.

Wrongful Discharge An employer's termination of an employee's employment in violation of the law or an employment contract.

Table of Cases

For your convenience and reference, here is a list of all the cases mentioned in this text, including those within the footnotes, features, and case problems. The summarized cases in the chapters of this text are given special emphasis by having their titles appear in **boldface**.

Index

Requirements, *continued*
    of HDC status, 475–478
    for security interest, 515–517
    under state securities laws, 763–764
    for stopping delivery, 444
Requirements contract, 406
    good faith in, 406
Resale
    of goods, 442–443
    of securities, 754
Resale price, maintenance agreement,
    784–785
Rescission, 13. *See also* Cancellation
    for breach of contract, 356, 363–364
    of contract, 13, 288, 763
    discharge by, 347
Residuary clause, 908
Res ipsa loquitur, 111
Resolutions, corporate, 736
Resource Conservation and Recovery Act
    (RCRA, 1976), 823
Respondeat superior, 590, 591, 592, 593
    corporations and, 716
Respondent, 28
Restatement (Second) of Contracts
    on conditions, 341
    on online acceptances, 273
    on oral promise, 322
    on promissory estoppel, 322
Restatement (Second) of Torts, strict product
    liability requirements and, 122
Restatement (Third) of Torts
    accountant's liability, 838, 839
    attorney's liability and, 838, 839
    Product Liability, 123, 124–125
Restatements of the Law, 6
Restaurants, menu labeling and, 809
Restitution, for breach of contract, 356,
    363–364
Restraint of trade
    contracts in, 297–298
    limitations on, 779
Restrictive covenant, 366
Restrictive indorsement, 474
Resulting trust, 918
Retail fraud, online, 206
Retained earnings, 716
Retaliation, by employers, 638–639, 641
Retirement accounts, for sole
    proprietor, 660
Retirement insurance. *See* Social Security
Retirement plans, 610–611
Retraction, of repudiation, 441
Return, of goods purchased online, 272
Reversal, of trial court decision, 77
Reverse discrimination, 632
Review, appellate, 77
Reviewing courts. *See* Federal court system,
    appellate courts of; State court system,
    appellate courts of
Revised Model Business Corporation Act
    (RMBCA), 715, 718
Revised Uniform Limited Partnership Act
    (RULPA), 689
Revocable licenses, 103

Revocable living trust, 916, 917
Revocable offers, 249
Revocation. *See also* Cancellation
    of acceptance, 422, 447
    of agency relationship, 593
    defined, 266
    of gift, 862
    of offer, 249, 266
        for unilateral contracts, 249
    of will, 911–912
RICO (Racketeer Influenced and Corrupt
    Organizations Act, 1970), 196
Right(s). *See also* Bill of Rights
    of assignment, 331–335
    assignment of all, 337
    of assurance, 439
    of bailee, 867–868
    to cancel contract, 442, 445
    cannot be assigned, 333–334
    conflicting, 223
    of contribution, 536
    of cover, 445
    of creditors, 516, 526–527, 530–536
    to cure, 437
    of debtors, 515, 517, 526–527
    of directors, 730–731
    dissociation and, 684–685, 704
    to indemnification, 731
    of inspection, 440, 730
    intellectual property, 138–159
    of landlords and tenants, 892–893
    natural, 13
    to obtain goods upon insolvency, 445
    to obtain specific performance, 445
    to participation, 730
    of parties to contract, 331
    of partners, 679–681
    principle of, 223–224
    privacy, 612–614
    to recover
        damages for accepted goods, 443, 448
        purchase price or lease payments
            due, 443
    of redemption, 544–545
    of reimbursement, 536
    of rejection, 446
    to resell or dispose of goods, 442–443
    of shareholders, 737–739
    of strike, 623
    of subrogation, 535–536
    of surety and guarantor, 535–536
    of survivorship, 882
    to withhold delivery, 442
"Right of disconnecting," for employees, 228
"Right to be forgotten," in EU, 177
Right-to-work laws, 619
Risk
    assignment and, 333–334
    assumption of, 109, 130
    defined, 900
    insurance classification by, 900
    landowner's duty to warn, 106
    of loss (*See* Risk of loss)
    obvious, 106–107, 127
Risk management, 900

Risk of loss, 419–422, 424–425
    UCC checklist to determine, 425
    when sales or lease contract breached,
        421–422
Risk-utility analysis, 125
Rivers and Harbors Appropriations Act
    (1899), 821
RMBCA. *See* Revised Model Business
    Corporation Act
Robbery, 190
Royalties, franchisor, 671
Rule(s)
    administrative, 23
    of construction, from UCC, 413–414
    of contract interpretation, 254
    credit-card, 813
    entrustment, 418–419
    equal dignity, 583–584
    final, 8
    of interpretation, 8, 253–256
    interpretive, 8
    uniform international, 376–377
Rule 10b-5 (SEC), 756–759, 760
    compared with Section 16(b), 760
Rule 14a-9 (SEC), 761
Rule 144 (SEC), 754
Rule 144A (SEC), 754
Rule 433 (FTC), 484, 485
Rule 504 (SEC), 753
Rule 505 (SEC), 753
Rule 506 (SEC), 753–754
Rulemaking, 8, 18
Rule of four, 69
Rule of reason, *per se* antitrust violations vs.,
    781, 784–785

S

Safe harbor
    for publicly held companies making
        forward-looking statements, 760
    resales of securities and, 754
Safety
    consumer protection and, 120, 811–812
    drug, 810, 811
    employee, 583, 608–609 (*See also* Workplace)
    food, 810–811
Sale(s)
    advertising, marketing, and, 802–808
    of collateral in default, 528
    consumer protection in, 808
    of counterfeit goods, 144
    credit, 521
    defined, 400
    of goods, 321, 358, 403, 422–423
    of land, compensatory damages for, 358
    by nonowners, 417–419
    online, 402
    small business and, 5
    warranties and (*See* Warranty)
Sales contracts, 399. *See also* Damages;
    International contract; Performance;
    Statute of Frauds
    breach of contract, 368, 421–422, 441–449

LANDMARK IN THE LAW

LINKING BUSINESS LAW TO...